CONSTITUTIONAL LAW
CASES, HISTORY, AND DIALOGUES

ANDERSON'S

Law School Publications

ADMINISTRATIVE LAW ANTHOLOGY
by Thomas O. Sargentich

ADMINISTRATIVE LAW: CASES AND MATERIALS
by Daniel J. Gifford

ALTERNATIVE DISPUTE RESOLUTON: STRATEGIES FOR LAW AND BUSINESS
by E. Wendy Trachte-Huber and Stephen K. Huber

AN ADMIRALTY LAW ANTHOLOGY
by Robert M. Jarvis

ANALYTIC JURISPRUDENCE ANTHOLOGY
by Anthony D'Amato

AN ANTITRUST ANTHOLOGY
by Andrew I. Gavil

APPELLATE ADVOCACY: PRINCIPLES AND PRACTICE (Second Edition)
Cases and Materials
by Ursula Bentele and Eve Cary

A CAPITAL PUNISHMENT ANTHOLOGY (and Electronic Caselaw Appendix)
by Victor L. Streib

CASES AND PROBLEMS IN CRIMINAL LAW (Third Edition)
by Myron Moskovitz

THE CITATION WORKBOOK
by Maria L. Ciampi, Rivka Widerman, and Vicki Lutz

CIVIL PROCEDURE: CASES, MATERIALS, AND QUESTIONS
by Richard D. Freer and Wendy C. Perdue

COMMERCIAL TRANSACTIONS: PROBLEMS AND MATERIALS
Vol. 1: Secured Transactions Under the UCC
Vol. 2: Sales Under the UCC and the CISG
Vol. 3: Negotiable Instruments Under the UCC and the CIBN
by Louis F. Del Duca, Egon Guttman, and Alphonse M. Squillante

COMMUNICATIONS LAW: MEDIA, ENTERTAINMENT, AND REGULATION
by Donald E. Lively, Allen S. Hammond, Blake D. Morant, and Russell L. Weaver

A CONSTITUTIONAL LAW ANTHOLOGY
by Michael J. Glennon

CONSTITUTIONAL LAW: CASES, HISTORY, AND DIALOGUES
by Donald E. Lively, Phoebe A. Haddon, Dorothy E. Roberts, and Russell L. Weaver

THE CONSTITUTIONAL LAW OF THE EUROPEAN UNION
by James D. Dinnage and John F. Murphy

CONSTITUTIONAL TORTS
by Sheldon H. Nahmod, Michael L. Wells, and Thomas A. Eaton

CONTRACTS
Contemporary Cases, Comments, and Problems
by Michael L. Closen, Richard M. Perlmutter, and Jeffrey D. Wittenberg

A CONTRACTS ANTHOLOGY (Second Edition)
by Peter Linzer

CORPORATE AND WHITE COLLAR CRIME: AN ANTHOLOGY
by Leonard Orland

A CRIMINAL LAW ANTHOLOGY
by Arnold H. Loewy

CRIMINAL LAW: CASES AND MATERIALS
by Arnold H. Loewy

A CRIMINAL PROCEDURE ANTHOLOGY
by Silas J. Wasserstrom and Christie L. Snyder

CRIMINAL PROCEDURE: ARREST AND INVESTIGATION
by Arnold H. Loewy and Arthur B. LaFrance

CRIMINAL PROCEDURE: TRIAL AND SENTENCING
by Arthur B. LaFrance and Arnold H. Loewy

ECONOMIC REGULATION: CASES AND MATERIALS
by Richard J. Pierce, Jr.

ELEMENTS OF LAW
by Eva H. Hanks, Michael E. Herz, and Steven S. Nemerson

ENDING IT: DISPUTE RESOLUTION IN AMERICA
Descriptions, Examples, Cases and Questions
by Susan M. Leeson and Bryan M. Johnston

ENVIRONMENTAL LAW (Second Edition)
Vol. 1: Environmental Decisionmaking: NEPA and the Endangered Species Act
Vol. 2: Water Pollution
Vol. 3: Air Pollution
Vol. 4: Hazardous Wastes
by Jackson B. Battle, Robert L. Fischman, Maxine I. Lipeles, and Mark S. Squillace

AN ENVIRONMENTAL LAW ANTHOLOGY
by Robert L. Fischman, Maxine I. Lipeles, and Mark S. Squillace

ENVIRONMENTAL PROTECTION AND JUSTICE
Readings and Commentary on Environmental Law and Practice
by Kenneth A. Manaster

AN EVIDENCE ANTHOLOGY
by Edward J. Imwinkelried and Glen Weissenberger

FEDERAL EVIDENCE COURTROOM MANUAL
by Glen Weissenberger

FEDERAL RULES OF EVIDENCE (Second Edition)
Rules, Legislative History, Commentary and Authority
by Glen Weissenberger

FEDERAL RULES OF EVIDENCE FOR UNITED STATES COURTS AND MAGISTRATES
by Publisher's Staff

FIRST AMENDMENT ANTHOLOGY
by Donald E. Lively, Dorothy E. Roberts, and Russell L. Weaver

INTERNATIONAL ENVIRONMENTAL LAW ANTHOLOGY
by Anthony D'Amato and Kirsten Engel

INTERNATIONAL HUMAN RIGHTS: LAW, POLICY AND PROCESS
Problems and Materials
by Frank C. Newman and David Weissbrodt

INTERNATIONAL INTELLECTUAL PROPERTY ANTHOLOGY
by Anthony D'Amato and Doris Estelle Long

INTERNATIONAL LAW ANTHOLOGY
by Anthony D'Amato

INTERNATIONAL LAW COURSEBOOK
by Anthony D'Amato

INTRODUCTION TO THE STUDY OF LAW: CASES AND MATERIALS
by John Makdisi

JUDICIAL EXTERNSHIPS: THE CLINIC INSIDE THE COURTHOUSE
by Rebecca A. Cochran

JUSTICE AND THE LEGAL SYSTEM
A Coursebook
by Anthony D'Amato and Arthur J. Jacobson

THE LAW OF DISABILITY DISCRIMINATION
by Ruth Colker

Continued

THE LAW OF MODERN PAYMENT SYSTEMS AND NOTES
by Fred H. Miller and Alvin C. Harrell

LAWYERS AND FUNDAMENTAL MORAL RESPONSIBILITY
by Daniel R. Coquillette

MICROECONOMIC PREDICATES TO LAW AND ECONOMICS
by Mark Seidenfeld

PATIENTS, PSYCHIATRISTS AND LAWYERS
Law and the Mental Health System
by Raymond L. Spring, Roy B. Lacoursiere, M.D., and Glen Weissenberger

PROBLEMS AND SIMULATIONS IN EVIDENCE (Second Edition)
by Thomas F. Guernsey

A PRODUCTS LIABILITY ANTHOLOGY
by Anita Bernstein

PROFESSIONAL RESPONSIBILITY ANTHOLOGY
by Thomas B. Metzloff

A PROPERTY ANTHOLOGY
by Richard H. Chused

THE REGULATION OF BANKING
Cases and Materials on Depository Institutions and Their Regulators
by Michael P. Malloy

A SECTION 1983 CIVIL RIGHTS ANTHOLOGY
by Sheldon H. Nahmod

SPORTS LAW: CASES AND MATERIALS (Second Edition)
by Raymond L. Yasser, James R. McCurdy, and C. Peter Goplerud

A TORTS ANTHOLOGY
by Lawrence C. Levine, Julie A. Davies, and Edward J. Kionka

TRIAL PRACTICE
by Lawrence A. Dubin and Thomas F. Guernsey

TRIAL PRACTICE AND CASE FILES
by Edward R. Stein and Lawrence A. Dubin

TRIAL PRACTICE AND CASE FILES with *Video* Presentation
by Edward R. Stein and Lawrence A. Dubin

FORTHCOMING PUBLICATIONS

BASIC ACCOUNTING PRINCIPLES FOR LAWYERS:
With Present Value and Expected Value
by C. Steven Bradford and Gary A. Ames

CONSTITUTIONAL CONFLICTS
by Derrick A. Bell, Jr.

A CONSTITUTIONAL LAW ANTHOLOGY (Second Edition)
by Donald E. Lively, Michael J. Glennon, Phoebe A. Haddon, Dorothy E. Roberts and Russell L. Weaver

A JUVENILE LAW ANTHOLOGY
by Victor L. Streib and Lynn Sametz

EUROPEAN COMMUNITY LAW ANTHOLOGY
by Anthony D'Amato and Karen V. Kole

INTERNATIONAL HUMAN RIGHTS: LAW POLICY, AND PROCESS (Second Edition)
by Frank C. Newman and David Weissbrodt

PRINCIPLES OF EVIDENCE (Third Edition)
by Irving Younger, Michael Goldsmith, and David A. Sonenshein

UNINCORPORATED BUSINESS ENTITIES
by Larry E. Ribstein

CONSTITUTIONAL LAW
CASES, HISTORY, AND DIALOGUES

DONALD E. LIVELY

Dean and Professor of Law
Florida Coastal School of Law

PHOEBE A. HADDON

Professor of Law
Temple University School of Law

DOROTHY E. ROBERTS

Professor of Law
Rutgers, The State University of New Jersey

RUSSELL L. WEAVER

Professor of Law
University of Louisville

ANDERSON PUBLISHING CO.
CINCINNATI

LIVELY, HADDON, ROBERTS & WEAVER, CONSTITUTIONAL LAW: CASES, HISTORY, AND DIALOGUES

© 1996 by Anderson Publishing Co.
2035 Reading Road / Cincinnati, Ohio 45202
800 582-7295 / E-mail: andpubco@aol.com / Fax: 513 562-5430

Library of Congress Cataloging-in-Publication Data

Constitutional law : cases, history, and dialogues / Donald E. Lively
    . . . [et al.].
          p.   cm.
      Includes index.
      ISBN 0-87084-125-4 (alk. paper)
      1. United States--Constitutional law--Cases. I. Lively, Donald
E., 1947-   .
342.73--dc20
[347.302]
                                                      96-981
                                                       CIP

CONTENTS

PART II: THE DISTRIBUTION OF NATIONAL POWERS

PART III: POWER TO REGULATE OR AFFECT THE ECONOMY

PART IV: EQUALITY CONCEPTS

PART V: THE FIRST AMENDMENT

TABLE OF CASES

PREFACE

The effort to author the ideal constitutional law casebook increasingly seems to parody the aim of writing the great American novel. Common to both enterprises is the reality that the objective has been and probably always will be elusive. In an increasingly crowded field, this book is calculated to establish a niche among teachers and students of constitutional law who are not entirely satisfied with the editorial methodologies of existing casebooks. It reflects the authors' sense that the craft generally has not adapted well to the massive growth and development of constitutional law or to pluralistic realities. Despite the numerous entries in the field, the choice too often is reduced to either of two models—one that prioritizes exhaustive coverage of cases and commentary and thus overwhelms with detail and another that in an effort to be more reader friendly sacrifices perspective.

An especially unfortunate casualty in the response to constitutional law's enormous rate of growth has been historical context and appreciation. Even among books that are touted for their devotion to detail, for instance, it is rare to find meaningful attention to the profoundly instructive and relevant case of *Dred Scott v. Sandford*.[1] Scarcer still is attention to the Constitution's accommodation of slavery, which in Madison's own words was the most divisive issue in Philadelphia over the summer of 1787.[2] Missing altogether or heavily discounted is coverage of racially significant law in the North or South that preceded Reconstruction or helped beget the separate but equal doctrine. Disconnected from its antecedents, the defining case of an era (*Brown v. Board of Education*[3]) suffers from invariable distortion.

This book has been inspired by and constructed pursuant to the authors' collective sense that context, especially historical circumstance, is imperative to understanding and enjoying constitutional law. The authoring of text and editing of cases, especially those that on their face might appear dated or idiosyncratic, reflect a diligent effort to incorporate meaningful background and perspective into presentation of each subject. In the process, the authors have rediscovered and retrieved much of the richness and texture of cases that over the years have been pared down to cold and uninspiring forms. Instead of relying heavily upon excerpts from numerous commentators and other note materials, that either disrupt the reader's attention or are lightly skimmed if read at all, the authors whenever possible also have allowed competing perspectives and values to radiate from the opinions themselves. Primary cases thus have been selected and sparingly edited in deference to their capacity to inform and stimulate reflection, comparative analysis, and independent thinking. The incorporation controversy and debate over the legitimacy of fundamental rights, for instance, are delineated less by snippets from multiple sources than by extensive playback of opinions by juridical architects such as Justices Black and Harlan.

Apart from its attention to context, the book has two other distinguishing characteristics that may be striking and even startling to those familiar with the form and substance of the subject matter. First, although the chapter on judicial review com-

---

[1] 60 U.S. 393 (1857).

[2] MAX FARRANO, THE RECORDS OF THE FEDERAL CONVENTION, 1787, 486 (1937).

[3] 347 U.S. 483 (1954).

mences from the traditional starting point of *Marbury v. Madison*,[4] it progresses well beyond the usual ending point. Included in the section are substantive due process cases that typically are covered in a separate and independent chapter. The logic of the structure is that once the judiciary's power "to say what the law is"[5] has been established, it makes sense to move from there to the abiding debate over permissible reference points for constitutional definition. The interpretivist-noninterpretivist debate, initiated in *Calder v. Bull*[6] several years before *Marbury,* thus is allowed its natural evolution to the present by riding the vehicle that most effectively negotiates the territory—judicial review pursuant to the due process clauses of the Fifth and Fourteenth Amendments.

A second distinctive feature of this book are frequent dialogues among the authors. These discussions are calculated to serve multiple purposes. They provide competing perspectives, disclose the ideologies that the authors bring to their work, factor in viewpoints that otherwise might be consigned to citations haphazardly noted by the reader and initiate discussion that teachers and students may pick up with in class.

The authors are grateful for the support and assistance they have received in producing this book. Donald E. Lively singles out Fran Molnar at The University of Toledo College of Law for tireless processing efforts on a very tiring project. He also appreciates the research contributions of Karla Perkins and Tom Adams.

Phoebe Haddon thanks her research assistants, Michael Daly and Cathy Washington, for their substantial support; and for the patience and insights of her husband, Frank McClellan, she is, as always, grateful. Dorothy Roberts is grateful to Christine Bacon and Margaret Hall for their excellent research assistance and to Bobbie Leach for his diligent secretarial support. Russell Weaver dedicates this book to Mary Kay, Karen, and Annie. He is also grateful to his research assistant, Vicki Miller.

Each of the authors welcomes feedback from teachers and students.

D. E. L.
P. A. H.
D. E. R.
R. L. W.

---

[4] 5 U.S. 137 (1803).

[5] *Id.* at 177.

[6] 3 U.S. 386 (1798).

PART I

JUDICIAL POWER

A. The Power "To Say What the Law Is"

Unlike the powers of the executive and legislative branches, the authority of the federal judiciary is not delineated by the Constitution. Article III vests "[t]he judicial Power of the United States . . . in one supreme Court, and in such inferior Courts as the Congress may from time to time ordain and establish." Although identifying the power, Article III amplifies neither its scope or nature. Rather, the balance of Article III focuses upon other concerns, including the tenure and compensation of judges, jurisdiction, jury trials for criminal cases and grounds for treason.

Not surprisingly, in a politically competitive environment, the function of the judiciary became an early post-ratification issue. The final years of the eighteenth century were characterized by intense rivalry between Federalists who controlled the executive and legislative branches and Jeffersonians who eventually prevailed in the 1800 elections. Having lost at the polls, the Federalists during their final days in office worked to preserve influence over the nation's governance. Central to their strategy was a plan to reconstruct the federal courts and pack them with judges sympathetic to Federalist ideology. The outgoing Federalist Congress not only reduced the size of the Supreme Court, thereby making it more difficult for a successor administration to make appointments, but expanded the number of inferior courts and created new justice of the peace positions in the District of Columbia.

A primary figure in the Federalist scheme was John Marshall. As President Adams' Secretary of State, Marshall was responsible for executing and delivering commissions to the newly appointed jurists. While serving in the executive branch, Marshall was nominated and confirmed as Chief Justice of the Supreme Court. Given the predictable hostility of the Jeffersonians to the court packing plan, time was of the essence in confirming and commissioning the new Federalist judges. Despite his new position as Chief Justice, Marshall carried on as Secretary of State to oversee the process.

Best efforts of the Federalists notwithstanding, some judicial appointees had not received their commissions by the time Jefferson took office as the nation's third president. When Jefferson refused to deliver the outstanding commissions, several frustrated justice of the peace appointees attempted to force the president's hand. In an original action to the Supreme Court, they sought a writ of mandamus that would compel Secretary of State James Madison to deliver the commissions. When the Court ordered Madison "to show cause why a mandamus should not issue," the scene was set for a constitutional showdown of immense magnitude and consequence.

The case of *Marbury v. Madison* presented Chief Justice Marshall with an opportunity to resolve a controversy that he had helped create. To characterize Marshall as an interested party is not an understatement. His appointment as chief justice was attributable to his Federalist stripes, which he continued to earn over the course of 34 years of service in that capacity. History credits Marshall with administrative skills that vastly enhanced the high court's prestige and focus. Prior to his appointment as chief justice, service on the Court was characterized by poor working conditions—including long and tiresome circuit-riding—that complicated the task of attracting strong legal talent. In refusing reappointment as the nation's first chief justice, John Jay complained that the Court had no real authority or stature. The Court's output also tended to be cumbersome and confusing, given the practice of writing seriatim opinions. As chief justice, Marshall developed the format of opinions by the Court and, much to the lament of Jefferson and his successors, successfully discouraged dissent. Marshall's organizational efforts laid significant groundwork for an identity of an institutional rather than Babel-like nature.

None of the impressive Marshall legacy, including his elevation of the Court's status and constitutional interpretations that promoted a strong central government and nationalist economic policy, would have been possible without an adroit disposition of the *Marbury* case. At a time when the power of the judiciary at best was unclear, and the president himself had asserted that he would not be bound by a court order to deliver the commissions, the Court's position was delicate and precarious. The challenge for the Marshall Court, as it reviewed the *Marbury* case, was to establish the judiciary's authority without igniting an interbranch controversy bound to undo the Court. Because the judiciary relies upon the executive branch for enforcement of its orders, a decree that the president simply ignored would have relegated the Court's status to that of a windbag. The challenge to Marshall thus was to assert the power of judicial review but avoid exercising it in a way that would ruin that authority.

Marbury v. Madison
5 U.S. 137 (1803)

. . .

Mr. Chief Justice Marshall delivered the opinion or the Court.

. . .

In the order in which the court has viewed this subject, the following questions have been considered and decided.

1s. Has the applicant a right to the commission he demands?

2dly. If he has a right, and that right has been violated, do the laws of his country afford him a remedy?

3dly. If they do afford him a remedy, is it a mandamus issuing from this court?

The first object of enquiry is,

1st. Has the applicant a right to the commission he demands?

His right originates in an act of congress passed in February 1801, concerning the district of Columbia.

After dividing the district into two counties, the 11th section of this law enacts, "that there shall be appointed in and for each or the said counties, such number of discreet persons to be justices of the peace as the president of the United States shall, from time to time, think expedient, to continue in office for five years."

It appears, from the affidavits, that in compliance with this law, a commission for William Marbury as a justice of peace for the county of Washington, was signed by John Adams, then president of the United States; after which the seal of the United States was affixed to it; but the commission has never reached the person for whom it was made out.

In order to determine whether he is entitled to this commission, it becomes necessary to enquire whether he has been appointed to the office. For if he has been appointed, the law continues him in office for five years, and he is entitled to the possession of those evidences of office which, being completed, became his property.

The 2d section of the 2d article of the constitution, declares, that, "the president shall nominate, and, by and with the advice and consent of the senate, shall appoint ambassadors, other public ministers and consuls, and all other officers of the United States, whose appointments are not otherwise provided for."

The third section declares, that "he shall commission all the officers of the United States." . . .

It is therefore decidedly the opinion of the court, that when a commission has been signed by the President, the appointment is made; and that the commission is complete, when the seal of the United States has been affixed to it by the secretary of state. . . .

To withhold his commission, therefore, is an act deemed by the court not warranted by law, but violative of a vested legal right.

This brings us to the second enquiry; which is.

2dly. If he has a right, and that right has

been violated, do the laws of his country afford him a remedy?

The very essence of civil liberty certainly consists in the right of every individual to claim the protection of the laws, whenever he receives an injury. One of the first duties of Government is to afford that protection.

. . .

The government of the United States has been emphatically termed a government of laws, and not of men. It will certainly cease to deserve this high appellation, if the laws furnish no remedy for the violation of a vested legal right.

. . .

It follows then that the question, whether the legality of an act of the head of a department be examinable in a court of justice or not, must always depend on the nature of that act. . . .

By the constitution of the United States, the President is invested with certain important political powers, in the exercise of which he is to use his own discretion, and is accountable only to his country in his political character, and to his own conscience. To aid him in the performance of these duties, he is authorized to appoint certain officers, who act by his authority and in conformity with his orders.

In such cases, their acts are his acts; and whatever opinion may be entertained of the manner in which executive discretion may be used, still there exists, and can exist, no power to control that discretion. The subjects are political. They respect the nation, not individual rights, and being entrusted to the executive, the decision of the executive is conclusive. The application of this remark will be perceived by adverting to the act of congress for establishing the department of foreign affairs. This officer, as his duties were prescribed by that act, is to conform precisely to the will of the President. He is the mere organ by whom that will is communicated. The acts of such an officer, as an officer, can never be examinable by the courts.

But when the legislature proceeds to impose on that officer other duties; when he is directed peremptorily to perform certain acts; when the rights of individuals are dependent on the performance of those acts; he is so far the Officer of the law; is amenable to the laws for his conduct; and cannot at his discretion sport away the vested rights of others.

The conclusion from this reasoning is, that where the heads of departments are the political or confidential agents of the executive, merely to execute the will of the President, or rather to act in cases in which the executive possesses a constitutional or legal discretion nothing can be more perfectly clear than that their acts are only politically examinable. But where a specific duty is assigned by law, and individual rights depend upon the performance

of that duty, it seems equally clear that the individual who where a specific duty is assigned by law, and individual rights depend upon considers himself injured, has a right to resort to the laws of his country for a remedy. . . .

It remains to be enquired whether,

3dly. He is entitled to the remedy for which he applies. This depends on,

1st. The nature of the writ applied for, and,

2dly. The power of this court. . . .

This original and supreme will organizes the government, and assigns, to different departments, their respective powers. It may either stop here; or establish certain limits not to be transcended by those departments.

The government of the United States is of the latter description. The powers of the legislature are defined, and limited; and that those limits may not be mistaken, or forgotten, the constitution is written. To what purpose are powers limited. and to what purpose is that limitation committed to writing, if these limits may, at any time, be passed by those intended to be restrained? The distinction, between a government with limited and unlimited powers, is abolished, if those limits do not confine the persons on whom they are imposed, and if acts prohibited and acts allowed, are of equal obligation. It is a proposition too plain to be contested, that the constitution controls any legislative act not repugnant to it; or, that the legislature may alter the constitution in an ordinary act.

Between the alternatives there is no middle ground. The constitution is either a superior, paramount law, unchangeable by ordinary means, or it is on a level with ordinary legislative acts, and like other acts, is alterable when the legislature shall please to alter it.

If the former part of the alternative be true, then a legislative act contrary to the constitution is not law: if the latter part be true, then written constitutions are absurd attempts, on the part of the people, to limit a power, in its own nature illimitable.

Certainly all those who have framed written constitutions contemplate them as forming the fundamental and paramount law of the nation, and consequently the theory of every such government must be, that an act of the legislature, repugnant to the constitution, is void.

This theory is essentially attached to a written constitution, and is consequently to be considered, by this court, as one of the fundamental principles of our society. It is not therefore to be lost sight of in the further consideration of this subject.

If an act of the legislature, repugnant to the constitution, is void, does it, notwithstanding its invalidity, bind the courts, and oblige them to give it effect? Or, in other words, though it be not law, does it constitute a rule as operative as if it was a law? This would be to overthrow in fact what was established in theory; and would seem, at first view an absurdity too gross to be insisted on. It shall, however, receive a more attentive consideration.

It is emphatically the province and duty of the judicial department to say what the law is. Those who apply the rule to particular cases, must of necessity expound and interpret that rule. If two laws conflict with each other, the courts must decide on the operation of each.

So if a law be in opposition to the constitution; if both the law and the constitution apply to a particular case, so that the court must either decide that case conformably to the law disregarding the constitution, or conformably to the constitution disregarding the law; the court must determine which of these conflicting rules governs the case. This is of the very essence of judicial duty.

If then the courts are to regard the constitution, and the constitution is superior to any ordinary act of the legislature, the constitution, and not such ordinary act, must govern the case to which they both apply.

Those then who controvert the principle that the constitution is to be considered, in court, as a paramount law, are reduced to the necessity of maintaining that courts must close their eyes on the constitution, and see only the law.

This doctrine would subvert the very foundation of all written constitutions. It would declare that an act, which, according to the principles and theory of our government, is entirely void, is yet, in practice, completely obligatory. It would declare, that if the legislature shall do what is expressly forbidden, such act, notwithstanding the express prohibition, is in reality effectual. It would be giving to the legislature a practical and real omnipotence, with the same breath which professes to restrict their powers within narrow limits. It is prescribing limits, and "daring that those limits may be passed at pleasure.

That it thus reduces to nothing what we have deemed the greatest improvement on political institutions—a written constitution—would of itself be sufficient, in America, where written constitutions have been viewed with so much reverence, for rejecting the construction. But the peculiar expressions of the constitution of the United States furnish additional arguments in favor of its rejection.

The judicial power of the United States is extended to all cases arising under the constitution.

Could it be the intention of those who gave this power, to say that, in using it, the constitution should not be looked into? That a case arising under the constitution should be decided without examining the instrument under which it arises?

This is too extravagant to be maintained.

In some cases then, the constitution must be looked into by the judges. And if they can open it at all, what part of it are they forbidden to read, or to obey?

There are many other parts of the constitution which serve to illustrate this subject.

It is declared that "no tax or duty shall be laid on articles exported from any state." Suppose a duty on the export of cotton, of tobacco or of flour; and a suit instituted to recover it. Ought judgment to be rendered in such a case? ought the judges to close their eyes on the constitution, and only see the law?

The constitution declares that "no bill of attainder or ex post facto law shall be passed."

If, however such a bill should be passed and a person should be prosecuted under it; must the court condemn to death those victims whom the constitution endeavors to preserve?

"No person," says the constitution, "shall be convicted of treason unless on the testimony of two witnesses to the same overt act, or on confession in open court."

Here the language of the constitution is addressed especially to the courts. It prescribes, directly for them, a rule of evidence not to be departed from. If the legislature should change that rule, and declare one witness, or a confession out of court, sufficient for conviction, must the constitutional principle yield to the legislative act?

From these, and many other selections which might be made, it is apparent, that the framers of the constitution contemplated that instrument, as a rule for the government of courts, as well as of the legislature.

Why otherwise does it direct the judges to take an oath to support it? This oath certainly applies, in an especial manner, to their conduct in their official character. How immoral to impose it on them, if they were to be used as the instruments, and the knowing instruments, for violating what they swear to support.

The oath of office, too, imposed by the legislature, is completely demonstrative of the legislative opinion on this subject. It is in these words, "I do solemnly swear, that I will administer justice without respect to persons, and do equal right to the poor and to the rich; and that I will faithfully and impartially discharge all the duties incumbent on me as _____ according to the best of my abilities and understanding, agreeably to the constitution, and laws of the United States."

Why does a judge swear to discharge his duties agreeably to the constitution of the United States, if that constitution forms no rule for his govern*ment? if* it is closed upon him, and cannot be inspected by him?

If such be the real state of things, this is worse than solemn mockery. To prescribe, or to take this oath, becomes equally a crime.

It is also not entirely unworthy of observation, that in declaring what shall be the supreme law of the land, the constitution itself is first mentioned; and not the laws of the United States generally, but those only which shall be made in pursuance of the constitution, have that rank.

Thus, the particular phraseology of the constitution of the United States confirms and strengthens the principle, supposed to be essential to all written constitutions, that a law repugnant to the constitution is void; and that courts, as well as other departments, are bound by that instrument.

The rule must be discharged.

The genius of Marshall's opinion was identifying a right to the commissions that had vested in the judicial appointees but concluding that legislative conferral of original jurisdiction was at odds with the Constitution. By technically resolving the immediate political controversy in Jefferson's favor, Marshall defused opposition to the underlying and enduring principle of the decision. The logic of *Marbury* was extended several years later, when the Court determined that state sovereignty did not foreclose its power to review the constitutionality of state court decisions. *Martin v. Hunter's Lessee* concerned the Virginia Court of Appeals' refusal to obey the Supreme Court's mandate in a previous case. The Supreme Court had determined that a state law taking land owned by British subjects conflicted with anti-confiscation provisions of federal treaties with Great Britain. Responding to arguments that "appellate jurisdiction over state courts is inconsistent with the genius of our governments, and the spirit of the Constitution," the Court determined otherwise.

Martin v. Hunter's Lessee
14 U. S. 304 (1816)

STORY, J., delivered the opinion of the Court.

This is a writ of error from the Court of Appeals of Virginia, founded upon the refusal of that court to obey the mandate of this court, requiring the judgment rendered in this very cause . . . to be carried into due execution. . . .

The government . . . can claim no powers which are not granted to it by the constitution, and the powers actually granted, must be such as are expressly given, or given by necessary implication. On the other hand, this instrument, like every other grant, is to have a reasonable construction, according to the import of its terms; and where a power is expressly given in general terms, it is not to be restrained to particular cases, unless that construction grows out of the context expressly, or by necessary implication. The words are to be taken in their natural and obvious sense, and not in a sense unreasonably restricted or enlarged. . . .

But, even admitting that the language of the constitution is not mandatory, and that Congress may constitutionally omit to vest the judicial power in courts of the United States, it cannot be denied that when it is vested it may be exercised to the utmost constitutional extent.

. . .

It is a mistake that the constitution was not designed to operate upon states, in their corporate capacities. It is crowded with provisions which restrain or annul the sovereignty of the states in some of the highest branches of their prerogatives. The tenth section of the first article contains a long list of disabilities and prohibitions imposed upon the states. Surely, when such essential portions of state sovereignty are taken away, or prohibited to be exercised, it cannot be correctly asserted that the constitution does not act upon the states. The language of the constitution is also imperative upon the states as to the performance of many duties. It is imperative upon the state legislatures to make laws prescribing the time, places, and manner of holding elections for senators and representatives, and for electors of President and Vice-President. And in these, as well as some other cases, Congress have a right to revise, amend, or supersede the laws which may be passed by state legislatures. When, therefore, the states are stripped of some of the highest attributes of sovereignty, and the same are given to the United States; when the legislatures of the states are, in some respects, under the control of Congress, and in every case are, under the constitution, bound by the paramount authority of the United States; it is certainly difficult to support the argument that the appellate power over the decisions of state courts is contrary to the genius of our institutions. The courts of the United States can, without question, revise the proceedings of the executive and legislative authorities of the states, and if they are found to be contrary to the constitution, may declare them to be of no legal validity. Surely the exercise of the same right over judicial tribunals is not a higher or more dangerous act of sovereign power.

. . .

. . . From the very nature of things, the absolute right of decision, in the last resort, must rest somewhere—wherever it may be vested it is susceptible of abuse. In all questions of jurisdiction the inferior, or appellate court, must pronounce the final judgment; and common sense, as well as legal reasoning, has conferred it upon the latter. . . .

This is not all. A motive of another kind, perfectly compatible with the most sincere respect for state tribunals, might induce the grant of appellate power over their decisions. That motive is the importance, and even necessity of uniformity of decisions throughout the whole United States, upon all subjects within the purview of the constitution. Judges of equal learning and integrity, in different states, might differently interpret a statute, or a treaty of the United States, or even the constitution itself. If there were no revising authority to control these jarring and discordant judgments, and harmonize them into uniformity, the laws, the treaties and the constitution of the United States would be different in different states, and might, perhaps, never have precisely the same construction, obligation, or efficacy, in any two states. The public mischiefs that would attend such a state of things would be truly deplorable; and it cannot be believed that they could have escaped the enlightened convention which formed the constitution. What, indeed, might then have been only prophecy, has now become fact; and the appellate jurisdiction must continue to be the only adequate remedy for such evils. . . .

On the whole, the court are of the opinion that the appellate power of the United States does extend to cases pending in the state courts; and that the 25th section of the judiciary act, which authorizes the exercise of this jurisdiction in the specified cases, by a writ of error, is supported by the letter and spirit of the constitution. We find no clause in that instrument which limits this power; and we dare not interpose a limitation where the people have not been disposed to create one. . . .

Because he had participated in a prior legislated settlement regarding the property, and had an ownership interest in some of the land at issue, Chief Justice Marshall had recused himself from the case. Justice Story's opinion nonetheless was consistent with Marshall's Federalist vision. A contrary result would have enabled each state to interpret the federal constitution pursuant to its own understanding and resulted in a body of constitutional law at war with itself.

Declaration of the Court's power "to say what the law is" represented nothing less than an arrogation of authority. One and a half centuries later, Justice Frankfurter observed that the *Marbury* principle "has been deemed by great English speaking Courts an indispensable, implied characteristic of a written Constitution."[1] As noted previously, however, the Constitution itself is bereft of any terminology indicating what function the judiciary was to perform. The Jeffersonian position, to the effect that each branch of government has power within its own sphere to interpret the Constitution, suggests that the role of the judiciary as final arbiter of the document's meaning was not even implicitly ordained. Much intellectual energy has been expended in attempting to prove that the power of judicial review was or was not anticipated by the framers. The results have been equivocal to the point that one commentator was moved to observe that "(t)he people who say the framers intended [judicial supremacy] are talking nonsense, and the people who say they did not intend it are talking nonsense."[2]

---

[1] Felix Frankfurter, *John Marshall and the Judicial Function*, 69 HARV. L. REV. 217, 219 (1955).

[2] LEONARD LEVY, JUDICIAL REVIEW AND THE SUPREME COURT 4 (1967) (quoting Edward Corwin, Reorganization of the Federal Judiciary: Hearings on S. 1392 Before the Senate Committee on the Judiciary pt. 2, 75th Cong., 1st Sess. 176 (1937).

Even if not announced by the Constitution itself, or indisputably discernible from its drafting history, the power of the judiciary "to say what the law is" has hardened into constitutional reality. Over the course of nearly two centuries, the judiciary's authority has not gone unchallenged. Response to the Court's determination half a century later in *Dred Scott v. Sandford*, that the federal government could not regulate slavery and persons of African descent could not be citizens of the union, included widespread defiance in the North. Many members of the emerging Republican Party took the Jeffersonian position that the political branches were not bound by the Court's decision. In the 1860 presidential campaign, Abraham Lincoln argued that the Court's judgment controlled the disposition of the actual case but did not bind the government or become general law until "fully settled."[3] Even before ratification of the Thirteenth Amendment, the *Dred Scott* decision was nullified for practical purposes by the Lincoln administration's purposeful neglect of it.

Subsequent challenges to judicial authority have included President Roosevelt's Court-packing plan which, as discussed in Chapter 3, was begotten by presidential frustration with persistent invalidation of New Deal legislation. The Court's determination that racially segregated education was "inherently unequal" and must be remedied by desegregation inspired direct attacks upon the judiciary's power to bind states with its constitutional interpretations. In *Cooper v. Aaron*, the Court referenced *Marbury* in rejecting arguments that its constitutional interpretations could be ignored by a state.

---

[3] DON E. FEHRENBACHER, THE DRED SCOTT CASE 442 (1978).

Cooper v. Aaron
358 U.S. 1 (1958)

Opinion of the Court by THE CHIEF JUSTICE, MR. JUSTICE BLACK, MR. JUSTICE FRANKFURTER, MR. JUSTICE DOUGLAS, MR. JUSTICE BURTON, MR. JUSTICE CLARK, MR. JUSTICE HARLAN, MR. JUSTICE BRENNAN, and MR. JUSTICE WHITTAKER.

As this case reaches us it raises questions of the highest importance to the maintenance of our federal system of government. It necessarily involves a claim by the Governor and Legislature of a State that there is no duty on state officials to obey federal court orders resting on this Court's considered interpretation of the United States Constitution. Specifically it involves actions by the governor and Legislature of Arkansas upon the premise that they are not bound by our holding in *Brown v. Board of Education*, 347 U.S. 483. That holding was that the Fourteenth Amendment forbids States to use their governmental powers to bar children on racial grounds from attending schools where there is state participation through any arrangement, management, funds or property. We are urged to uphold a suspension of the Little Rock School Board's plan to do away with segregated public schools in Little Rock until state laws and efforts to upset and nullify our hold in *Brown v. Board of Education* have been further challenged and tested in the courts. We reject these contentions.

. . .

The constitutional rights of respondents are not to be sacrificed or yielded to the violence and disorder which have followed upon the actions of the Governor and Legislature. As this Court said some 41 years ago in a unanimous opinion in a case involving another aspect of racial segregation: "It is urged that this proposed segregation will promote the public peace by preventing race conflicts. Desirable as this is, and important as is the preservation of the public peace, this aim cannot be accomplished by laws or ordinances which deny rights created or protected by the Federal Constitution." *Buchanan v. Warley*, 245 U.S. 60, 81. Thus law and order are not here to be preserved by depriving the Negro children of their constitutional rights. The record before us clearly establishes that the growth of the Board's difficulties to a magnitude beyond its unaided power to control is the product of state action. Those difficulties, as counsel for the Board forthrightly conceded on the oral argument in this Court, can also be brought under control.

. . .

What has been said, in the light of the facts developed, is enough to dispose of the case. However, we should answer the premise of the actions of the Governor and Legislature that they are not bound by our holding in the *Brown* case. It is necessary only to recall some basic constitutional propositions which are settled doctrine.

Article VI of the Constitution makes the Constitution the "supreme Law of the Land." In 1803, Chief Justice Marshall, speaking for a unanimous Court, referring to the Constitution as "the fundamental and paramount law of the nation," declared in the notable case of *Marbury v. Madison*, 1 Cranch 137, 177, that "It is emphatically the province and duty of the judicial department to say what the law is." This decision declared the basic principle that the federal judiciary is supreme in the exposition of the law of the Constitution, and that principle has ever since been respected by this Court and the Country as a permanent and indispensable feature of our constitutional system. It follows that the interpretation of the Fourteenth Amendment enunciated by this Court in the *Brown* case is the supreme law of the land, and Art. VI of the Constitution makes it of binding effect on the States "any Thing in the Constitution or Laws of any State to the Contrary notwithstanding." Every state legislator and executive and judicial officer is solemnly committed by oath taken pursuant to Art. VI, cl. 3, "to support this Constitution." Chief Justice Taney, speaking for a unanimous Court in 1859, said that this requirement reflected the framers' "anxiety to preserve it [the Constitution] in full force, in all its powers, and to guard against resistance to or evasion of its authority, on the part of a State. . . . "

No state legislator or executive or judicial officer can war against the Constitution without violating his undertaking to support it. Chief Justice Marshall spoke for a unanimous Court in saying that: "If the legislatures of the several states may, at will, annul the judgments of the courts of the United States, and destroy the rights acquired under those judgments, the constitution itself becomes a solemn mockery. . . . " . . . A Governor who asserts a power to nullify a federal court order is similarly restrained. If he had such power, said Chief Justice Hughes, in 1932, also for a unanimous Court, "it is manifest that the fiat of a state Governor, and the Constitution of the United States, would be the supreme law of the land; that the restrictions of the Federal Constitution upon the exercise of state power would be but impotent phrases. . . .

. . .

. . . Since the first *Brown* opinion three new Justices have come to the Court. They are at one with the Justices still on the Court who participated in that basic decision as to its correctness, and that decision is now unanimously reaffirmed. The principles announced in that decision and the obedience of the States to them, according to the command of the Constitution, are indispensable for the protection of the freedoms guaranteed by our fundamental charter for all of us. Our Constitutional ideal of equal justice under law is thus made a living truth.

The state argument in *Cooper* was reminiscent of a common northern response to the *Dred Scott* decision a century earlier, at least to the extent that resistance was based upon the premise that the Court's decision was not binding. The immediate aftermath of upholding slavery, as would be the case after ordering desegregation, included the Court restating the nature and effect of judicial power in response to state arguments challenging its legitimacy.[4] Recent volleys across the judiciary's bow have included challenges reminiscent of what the Court repudiated in *Cooper*. The Reagan Administration Justice Department, for instance, urged distinguishing between "the constitution which is the law, . . . [and] the decisions of the Court."[5]

Given a two century legacy of judicial review, and notwithstanding periodic challenges to the exercise of that power, it is doubtful that institutional authority will revert to anything less than what Chief Justice Marshall depicted in 1803. Dramatic illustration of that condition was provided when the Court in 1974 ruled that executive privilege did not shield President Nixon from having to disclose tapes and documents

---

[4] *E.g.*, Ableman v. Booth, 62 U.S. 506 (1859).
[5] Edwin Meese III, *The Law of the Constitution*, 61 Tul. L. Rev. 979, 983 (1987).

sought by a special prosecutor in the Watergate investigation. Unlike President Jefferson, who promised to ignore any order to deliver judicial commissions, Nixon complied and effectively reaffirmed the judiciary's power "to say what the law is."

B. The Persisting Controversy over the Judiciary's Function

Unresolved and as intensely debated now as it was even before *Marbury* is how and when the judiciary should exercise its power. Because federal judges and justices are unelected and appointed for life, and judicial review may trump exercises of power by representative branches of government, concern historically has existed with the anti-democratic potential of the judiciary. Criticism of the judiciary is especially intense when it strikes down legislation on grounds that it conflicts with a right or liberty not actually enumerated by the Constitution. Dissenting from the Court's articulation of a right of privacy, for instance, Justice Black alleged that the judiciary was simply trading in natural law.[6] Repudiating what he perceived as a superlegislative function, Black warned against being "ruled by a bevy of Platonic guardians."[7] As the right of privacy was expanded to protect a woman's liberty to elect an abortion,[8] further criticism hailed down on the Court for "creating rights out of whole cloth that are not in the Constitution."[9]

Debate over the reference points that the judiciary may use in reviewing the output of representative governance is rich, extensive and sometimes self-serving. The historical controversy has evolved into a virtual cottage industry among legal scholars who are divided generally between interpretivists and noninterpretivists. The interpretivist position comprehends theories of review grounded in literalism, originalism and neutrality of principle. Noninterpretivists endorse a judiciary that develops rights and liberties, even if not enumerated by the Constitution, and thus assumes the risk of trading in natural law. Contemporary arguments are the progeny of a debate aired by the Court within a decade of the Constitution's ratification. The positions of Justice Iredell and Chase, who respectively urged a more restrained and more activist judicial function, staked out the terms of a debate that persists no less vigorously two centuries later.

---

[6] Griswold v. Connecticut, 381 U.S. 479, 508 (1965) (Black, J., dissenting).

[7] *Id.*

[8] Roe v. Wade, 410 U.S. 113 (1973).

[9] Ronald Brownstein, *With or Without Supreme Court Changes, Reagan Will Reshape the Federal Bench*, 49 Nat. J. 2338, 2341 (1984).

Calder v. Bull
3 U.S. 386 (1798)

Iredell, J.,

It is true, that some speculative jurists have held, that a legislative act against natural justice must, in itself, be void; but I cannot think that, under such a government any court of justice would possess a power to declare it so. . . .

In order, therefore, to guard against so great an evil, it has been the policy of all the American states, which have, individually, framed their state constitutions, since the revolution, and of the people of the United States,

when they framed the federal constitution, to define with precision the objects of the legislative power, and to restrain its exercise within marked and settled boundaries. If any act of congress, or of the legislature of a state, violates those constitutional provisions, it is unquestionably void; though, I admit, that as the authority to declare it void is of a delicate and awful nature, the court will never resort to that authority, but in a clear and urgent case. If, on the other hand, the legislature of the Union, or the legislature of any member of the Union, shall pass a law, within the general scope of their constitutional power, the court cannot pronounce it to be void, merely because it is, in their judgment, contrary to the principles of natural justice. The ideas of natural justice are regulated by no fixed standard: the ablest and the purest men have differed upon the subject; and all that the court could properly say, in such an event, would be, that the legislature (possessed of an equal right of opinion) had passed an act which, in the opinion of the judges, was inconsistent with the abstract principles of natural justice. There are then but two lights, in which the subject can be viewed: 1st. If the legislature pursue the authority delegated to them, their acts are valid. 2d. If they transgress the boundaries of that authority, their acts are invalid. In the former case, they exercise the discretion vested in them by the people, to whom alone they are responsible for the faithful discharge of their trust.

. . .

CHASE, J.,

I cannot subscribe to the omnipotence of a state legislature, or that it is absolute and without control; although its authority should not be expressly restrained by the constitution, or fundamental law of the state. The people of the United States erected their constitutions or forms of government, to establish justice, to promote the general welfare, to secure the blessings of liberty, and to protect their persons and property from violence. The purposes for which men enter into society will determine the nature and terms of the social compact, and as they are the foundation of the legislative power, they will decide what are the proper objects of it. The nature, and ends of legislative power will limit the exercise of it. This fundamental principle flows from the very nature of our free republican governments, that no man should be compelled to do what the laws do not require; nor to refrain from acts which the laws permit. There are acts which the federal, or state legislature cannot do, without exceeding their authority. There are certain vital principles in our free republican governments, which will determine and overrule an apparent and flagrant abuse of legislative power; as to authorize manifest injustice by positive law; or to take away that security, for personal liberty, or private property, for the protection whereof the government was established. An act of the legislature (for I cannot call it a law), contrary to the great first principles of the social compact, cannot be considered a rightful exercise of legislative authority. The obligation of a law, in governments established on express compact, and on republican principles, must be determined by the nature of the power on which it is founded. . . .

The legislature may enjoin, permit, forbid and punish; they may declare new crimes; and establish rules of conduct for all its citizens in future cases; they may command what is right, and prohibit what is wrong; but they cannot change innocence into guilt; or punish innocence as a crime; or violate the right of an antecedent lawful private contract; or the right of private property. To maintain that our federal, or state legislature possesses such powers, if they had not been expressly restrained; would, in my opinion, be a political heresy, altogether inadmissible in our free republican governments.

The debate between Iredell and Chase remains largely unresolved. Even as courts generally profess a preference for the Iredell position, their legacy includes much that conforms with Chase's perspective. Factoring of natural law was not uncommon in courts of the early nineteenth century. The Supreme Court itself flirted with principles of natural justice, in *Fletcher v. Peck*, when it declared revocation of a state land grant invalid "either by general principles which are common to our free institutions, or by the particular provisions of the constitution [i.e., the contracts clause]."[10] In a concurring opinion Justice Johnson was more blunt in referencing natural law. As he put it, "I do not hesitate to declare, that a state does not possess the power of revoking its own grants. But I do it, on a general principle, on the reason and nature of things; a principle which will impose laws even on the Deity."[11] Shades of natural law have been evidenced, for instance, in the Court's identification of a fundamental right to own slaves prior to the Civil War,[12] economic liberty during the late nineteenth and early

---

[10] Fletcher v. Peck, 10 U.S. 87, 139 (1810).
[11] *Id.* at 143.
[12] Dred Scott v. Sandford, 60 U.S. 393, 450–52 (1857).

twentieth centuries[13] and a right of privacy that has evolved since the middle of this century.[14] Official segregation, in the late nineteenth century, was described by the Court as "in the nature of things."[15]

1. Interpretivism and Noninterpretivism

The tension between judicial word and deed is reflected in the vigorous debate that persists between interpretivists and noninterpretivists. It is a central tenet of representative governance that power may not be ratified without the consent of the governed. Amplifying essentially the arguments presented by Iredell and Chase, modern interpretivists and noninterpretivists respectively challenge and defend a judicial function that includes the identification of rights and liberties not enumerated by constitutional text or evidenced by original intent. An entirely satisfactory theory of review, or even one that is consensually subscribed to, remains elusive and perhaps an illusion.

---

[13] *E.g.*, Lochner v. New York, 198 U.S. 45 (1905); Allgeyer v. Louisiana, 165 U.S. 575, 592–93 (1897).

[14] *E.g.*, Griswold v. Connecticut 381 U.S. 479 (1965).

[15] Plessy v. Ferguson, 163 U.S. 537, 544 (1896).

Donald E. Lively
Constitutional Turf Wars:
Competing for the Consent of the Governed
42 HASTINGS LAW JOURNAL 1527, 1531–45 (1991)*

1. The Sirens of Jurisprudential Apoliticism

A fundamental miscalculation of any constitutional theorist is to expect a perfect theory of judicial review. Positive law is not akin to physical or other types of law that are susceptible to empirical testing and proof. Legal theories are evaluated not merely on the basis of predictability and reliability, but also for efficiency, integrity, and ideology. The one certain impact of any propounded theory of review is arousal of critical and adverse reaction. Susceptibility to reproval, owing to disparate visions of and expectations from the judiciary, counsels that any general theory should be a function of modest rather than great expectations.

A. Literalism

The literalist (or strict constructionist) school instructs that documental text is the departure, and whenever possible the termination, point for constitutional review. "Lay[ing] the article of the Constitution . . . beside the statute, however, offers more imagery utility. Literalism affords no guidance when documental termination is unclear or its meaning is dis-

puted. Strict constructionism thus makes sense only when terms or conditions are irrefutably clear and not susceptible to dispute and litigation anyway. Because the Constitution does not always speak for itself, strict constructionism is unserviceable when it is most needed.

Although the powers of the federal government are documentally prescribed, delineation of authority is imprecise. Congress' power to regulate interstate commerce, for example, is a primary source of comprehensive and extensive federal regulation of activity ranging from purely economic matters to civil rights and criminal conduct. Despite its prolific use, the interstate commerce power has been subject to divergent perceptions of what constitutes interstate transactions and commerce itself. The documental charge for Congress to enact "necessary and proper" laws, although facilitating the exercise of enumerated powers, has raised more questions than it has answered.

The poverty of literalism is even more profound when examined in the context of individual rights. Though a literal focus may be apt if, for instance, the issue is whether a twenty-five-year-old Jamaican can run for president, litigation and the need for judicial review are improbable when answers are manifest. The Constitution enumerates basic rights in such inexact terms as: "freedom of speech, or of the press," "the free exercise" of religion; "[t]he right . . . to be secure . . . against unreasonable searches and seizures"; "the right to a speedy and public trial"; the right to "an impartial jury"; the right to "assistance of counsel"; the right to be free from "[e]xcessive bail" and the guarantee against "cruel and unusual punishment"; the right to unabridged "privileges [or] immunities"; the right to "due process of law"; and the right to "equal protection of the laws." Terms such as unreasonable, speedy, impartial, excessive, cruel, unusual, due, and equal are noteworthy for their imprecision, and so present points of analytical commencement rather than pretermission.

Notwithstanding its patently limited utility, strict constructionism has not been without prominent advocates. Justice Black urged a seemingly unqualified version of freedom of speech and of the press that was essentially literalist. For Black, the framers had performed all balancing permissible between first amendment interests and competing concerns. Ultimately, even Black himself disclosed the limited utility of strict constructionism. His distinction between speech and conduct, and his support for a diminished constitutional status for new media, evinced participation in precisely the value-driven first amendment differentiation that he purportedly condemned.

Literalism may be most notable as a source of political mischief and demagoguery. Richard Nixon's 1968 campaign promise to appoint strict constructionists effectively tapped into public concern over the Warren Court with respect to desegregation. Despite professed opposition to judicially crafted law, Ronald Reagan pledged to appoint judges who would "respect traditional family values and the sanctity of innocent human life." George Bush promised to appoint judges who would interpret the Constitution as it was written. In each instance, the promise of nonpoliticism was pitched toward manifestly political ends. Strict constructionism thus has proved serviceable as a means of advancing rather than minimizing politicism.

B. Originalism

Few if any jurists or legal scholars regard literalism as an exclusive analytical methodology. When strict constructionism fails, as it invariably does, exponents of restraint suggest originalism as the apt jurisprudential alternative. Inquiry into official purpose, however, too often constitutes an exercise in delusion rather than discovery. Searching for original intent, like any other effort to glean the purpose of a decision or policy making body comprised of diverse individuals, is destined to founder upon discernment of competing and compromised aims and agendas. Justice Scalia, in the estab-

lishment clause context, effectively depicted the unserviceability of motive-based inquiry in noting that:

> [t]he number of possible motivations, to begin with, is not binary, or indeed even finite. . . . [A] particular legislator need not have voted for [a law] either because he wanted to foster religion or because he wanted to improve education. He may have thought the bill would provide jobs for his district, or may have wanted to make amends with a faction of his party he had alienated on another vote, or he may have been a close friend of the bill's sponsor, or he may have been repaying a favor he owed the majority leader, or he may have hoped the Governor would appreciate his vote and make a fundraising appearance for him, or he may have been pressured to vote for a bill he disliked by a wealthy contributor or by a flood of constituent mail, or he may have been seeking favorable publicity, or he may have been reluctant to hurt the feelings of a loyal staff member who worked on the bill, or he may have been settling an old score with a legislator who opposed the bill, or he may have been mad at his wife who opposed the bill, or he may been intoxicated and utterly unmotivated when the vote was called, or he may have accidentally voted 'yes' instead of 'no' or, of course, he may have had (and very likely did have) a combination of some of the above and many other motivations. To look for *the sole purpose* of even a single legislator is probably to look for something that does not exist.

Despite effective criticisms and even general repudiation of motive-based inquiry, the Court continues to invest in it for purposes of equal protection review. Since formulating the discriminatory intent standard as a prerequisite for establishing constitutionally significant racial discrimination, equal protection has been substantially devitalized as a guarantee for minorities. Because criteria consequently are attuned to discerning overtly race-dependent policies, the guarantee now operates mainly to preclude or destabilize affirmative action initiatives.

Subscription to motive-based inquiry is problematic not only because of its selectiveness but also because of its notorious lack of productivity. Framers may have supported the document or a particular provision for diverse reasons. Ratifiers had at least as many mixed motives in approving it. What awaits any inquiry into the past, therefore, are competing and uncertain motives. The obstacle to original understanding is not mitigated by the notion that what the framers and ratifiers meant "must be taken to be what the public of that time would have understood the words to mean." Discerning "what the public understood" would be as confounding an inquiry and, given the even greater permutations of opinion and sentiments, many times more vain.

Modern champions of judicial restraint, who propound originalism as a viable interpretive methodology, themselves appear to engage in review at variance with apoliticism. First amendment jurisprudence, for instance, has evolved a classification process that essentially ranks variants of speech for constitutional purposes. While obscenity and fighting words have been excluded from the first amendment's protective ambit, defamatory, privacy breaching, and commercial speech have been afforded qualified protection. Political speech is identified, especially by judicial conservatives, as the most constitutionally revered and protected form of expression.

The reservation of maximum first amendment concern for speech relating to informed self-government is incongruous with events contemporaneous to the Constitution's introduction. Rivalry between Federalists and Republicans, relating back to the chartering process, defined the political culture in the years immediately after ratification. In 1798, President Adams and a Federalist Congress, endeavoring to neuter their Republican competition, enacted the Sedition Act which among other things criminalized speech critical of the government. The first amendment, by its literal and original terms, guarantees against abridgment of "freedom of speech, or of the press" by Congress. Introduction of a draconian scheme to suppress expression, within several years of ratification and by some of the Constitution's own fabricators, suggests that advertence to original intent may furnish some unsettling advice. Given a document that is the work of multiple aims rather than any singular purpose, inquiry into original intent affords an opportunity for selecting principles that are convenient rather than consensual. Originalism thus may be useful for precisely the political purposes that its advocates deplore.

C. Neutrality

Beyond literalism and originalism, neutrality has been advanced as a methodology for ensuring that the judiciary does not operate in an antidemocratic fashion. The crux of neutrality is that courts, having derived a principle from text or original understanding, must apply that precept in all cases to which it reasonably relates. The selection and operation of a principle supposedly will not be influenced by consideration of its political meaning or impact.

As a methodology of review, neutrality neither offers comprehensive guidance nor precludes politically inspired decisions. Once a principle is neutrally derived, its ambit or level of generality must be ascertained. The equal protection guarantee, for instance, affords options of black equality, racial equality, or general equality. Original understanding of the fourteenth amendment, as revealed by legislative history and initial jurisprudence, intimates primary attention to a discrete racial class. History also discloses a qualified constitutional concern with equal opportunity for black material self-development and parity before the law, but a tolerance of "[m]ere discriminations."

Neutral principles tied to original understanding, if rigorously observed, would continue to graft a doctrinal formula for official segregation onto the fourteenth amendment. Emergence of the desegregation mandate creates a dilemma for neutralists, insofar as original intent manifestly did not contemplate desegregation and pointedly accommodated racial separation. Proponents of neutrality have endeavored to square the desegregation principle with apolitical demands by suggesting that the challenge to official discrimination required the Court either to invest in a methodology disfavored by the fourteenth amendment's framers or deactivate equal protection altogether. The notion that a proper choice in *Brown v. Board of Education* was between two extreme alternatives, each of which was at odds with original understandings, represents a procrustean effort to reconcile a political but constitutionally apt decision with principles of restraint. Attempted harmonization of the desegregation mandate with neutrality succeeds only in straining doctrinal reality. An explanation and accounting aimed at establishing critical respectability is itself reducible to political imperative resulting in self-inflicted damage to credibility. The devolution of *Brown* pursuant to limiting principles, such as the discriminatory intent standard, has revealed a third option which is closer to original aims than the either-or choice identified by professed neutralists. Distinctions between *de jure and de facto* segregations and the consequent constriction of the duty to desegregate, compounded by reversion of review from strict scrutiny to mere rationality when discriminatory purpose is not established, reveal a jurisprudential development consonant in spirit with original qualified equalization concerns.

Even assuming no political motivation, the neutrality model also may be problematic in explaining variations in pitch or degree of principle. The issue of race-conscious remediation, for instance, has engendered arguments for and against the notion that all racial classifications should be constitutionally suspect. The idea that the Constitution is absolutely colorblind transcends original vision and is associated with a sense of the fourteenth amendment as a guarantee of comprehensive racial equality. Contentions that historically disadvantaged racial groups should be excluded from that general proposition are consonant with an intuitive sense that equal protection has special meaning for them. Insofar as the neutrality model does not yield obvious choices, opportunity for politically-motivated judgment is not foreclosed. Like originalism, neutrality actually may obscure ideological inspiration.

At worst, neutrality may be a disguise rather than a cure for result-oriented jurisprudence. Even if not facilitating blind adherence to precedent, insistence upon constancy and congruity discounts inevitable disagreement over which facts and issues are comparable. Neutrality also disregards the multiplicity and relativity of principles that should be factored into a given decision. Since a particular jurisprudential result may be attributable to more than one reason, subsequent outcomes may differ because of honest but nonetheless disputed perceptual variances over what is significant. Introduction of principle, moreover, does not preclude amplification, compounding, or mutation of political judgment. As a check upon the purported evil of anti-democratic jurisprudence, neutrality is more illusory than real.

D. Structuralism

Some theorists have suggested that, when constitutional specifics and original indications fail, documental structure may inform prudential understanding. Appurtenant to the promptings of structural awareness and appreciation is the proposition that jurists should understand that the Constitution intended a "workable government." Attention to documental structure of and consequences for governance is redolent of Chief Justice Marshall's sense that it was necessary to understand the "great objects" for which the Constitution and system of government were created. A focus on structure, however, may create more opportunities for political judgment than it denies.

Reference to structure has contributed to the Court's development of a fundamental right to travel. State regulations, conditioning the enjoyment of certain benefits on duration of residency, thus have been invalidated as breaching a basic, albeit unenumerated, guarantee. The etching of constitutional lines between allowable and impermissible residency periods, however, has less linkage to what is structurally implicit than to disputable perceptions of what constitutes a reasonable waiting period and how significant a service or benefit is.

The notion that the first amendment occupies a preferred position in the constitutional order also is the result of a structural inference. Freedom of expression may be critical to effectuating other fundamental liberties. It is at least as debatable as it is unprovable, however, that the first amendment's prominent placement has special significance. Insofar as some amendment had to be first it is unsafe to draw inferences merely from the fact of being at the front of the line. General context and circumstance are at least as significant and more discernible for purposes of acquiring understanding. The Bill Rights, for instance, was a supplement tacked on to the original document to facilitate ratification. Because economic disarray was the primary motivation for convening a constitutional convention, it is arguable that structure implies priority for economic rather than expressive concerns and for commercial rather than political speech.

As a principle for depoliticizing the judiciary, structuralism suggests that detailed documental attention to Congress implies the legislative branch's primacy. Extensive accounting for legislative powers, however, conversely may be attributed to a dominant concern that congressional authority should be limited. Thus, a contrary message arguably would radiate from the less detailed charting of the judicial function. A fundamental deficiency of structuralism is an assumption akin to the premise that the Constitution speaks for itself. If structure conveys any information, the message is mixed, debatable, susceptible to, rather than immune from, ideological filtration. Principles attributed to structural implication, in reality, may be the result of subjective inference.

E. Noninterpretivism

The counterpoint to literalism, originalism, neutrality, and structuralism is noninterpretivism. The basic premise of the concept is that constitutional meaning may be glossed by reference to extra-documental values. Insofar as noninterpretivism concedes the validity of constitutional decisions as political choices, it probably reflects a logical implication of constitutional litigation. Constitutional advocacy often is an extension of competing political agendas and at least implicitly acknowledges the Court as a political institution. Arguments that segregation diminished the nation's global image and efficacy, for instance, had no more relationship to constitutional interpretation than the competing sentiment that racial separation was dictated by tradition and custom and facilitated public peace and order.

Modern jurisprudence, to the extent it fashions fundamental rights not documentally explicated, engages in noninterpretivist work. Although not confined by the four corners of the Constitution, the Court, responding to concern with an impartial function, has developed principles that ostensibly limit its political potential. It thus has tied recognition of fundamental rights to their being implicit in the concept of ordered liberty or embedded in the nation's traditions and conscience. Fathoming what liberty implies or what is rooted in the nation's ideals, however, invites rather than preempts subjectivism. How an issue is perceived may be especially determinative of its resolution. In *Bowers v. Hardwick*, for instance, the Court considered whether a state antisodomy law was at odds with the fourteenth amendment. The majority characterized the issue as whether a right to engage in homosexual sodomy was grounded in the nation's ideals. Dissenting justices depicted the question in terms of whether the right of personal autonomy comprehended such activity. The rival denominations of the issue, reflecting extensions of moral perceptions, preordained the disparate conclusions that followed.

Discernment of the values and priorities reposed in society's conscience, although a process abhorrent to exponents of restraint, actually may translate effectively into the respect for popular will that apoliticists demand. Linkage of legal principle to dominant cultural ideals would support liberty to elect an abortion only insofar as that result were consistent with a pervasive popular preference for personal choice. Honest advertence to societal traditions and moral development also would have required endorsement of segregation, which was deeply embedded in the North as well as the South, and slavery, which was constitutionally accommodated from the republic's inception.

Noninterpretivism that merely rubber-stamps dominant impulses may be problematic insofar as doctrinal results are considered morally unacceptable. The problem for noninterpretivists, in establishing credibility and securing popular consent, is demonstrating that their methodology is not exotic or elitist. Diverse theories have suggested that value-inspired jurisprudence is legitimate to the extent it: is referenced to an unwritten higher law embracing deeply held ideals; "enforces the requirement of a greatest equal liberty" rather than majoritarianism as the paramount moral imperative; reflects "evolving standards of decency"; or factors in aspirational as well as original meanings. No matter how elegantly framed, the analytical options are reducible to

moral relativity. The resultant doctrine becomes the extension of competing values and thus an exercise in natural justice. Noninterpretivism often reflects impatience with the output of democratic institutions in accounting for imperatives of autonomy, diversity, and equality. By refusing to be bound by apolitical constraints, noninterpretivists assume the essentially political risk of constitutional results inspired by competing moralities or ideologies.

F. Voidism

Textual or historical uncertainty, for noninterpretivists, invites reference to extra-documental principle. To voidists, it mandates judicial retreat. If the meaning of the Constitution cannot be deciphered pursuant to approved interpretive principles of apoliticism, voidism requires that "judges . . . stand aside and let current democratic majorities rule, because there is no law superior to theirs. The essence of voidism is that if the Constitution does not speak clearly, it does not speak at all.

The privileges and immunities clause has been offered as an example of a constitutional mystery that, according to voidist imperatives, merits jurisprudential disregard. The problem with the premise is discerning when evidence of meaning or significance is nonexistent as opposed to denied. For instance, a historically supportable argument exists that the privileges and immunities clause, although judicially eviscerated in its infancy, incorporated substantive liberties into the fourteenth amendment. Devitalization of the provision resulted not from incomprehensibility but from judicial disagreement over its significance, aptness, and desirability.

Voidism has the potential of minimizing the judiciary's function to the point that constitutional guarantees themselves become only marginally relevant. Traditionally, the establishment clause has been construed as creating a "wall of separation between church and state." Such understanding has been challenged on grounds that the first amendment proscribes only a national religion and, possibility, sectarian discrimination. Because both sides cite James Madison as support for their respective positions, a logical conclusion is that actual meaning is indeterminate. Voidism would solve the problem by negating the establishment clause altogether. Such a possibility discloses the potential for review which operates in the guise of restraint while actually functioning in a profoundly activist fashion that may realign, redistribute, redefine, or replace transcendent rights or duties. Like all other theories of judicial review, voidism immunizes against political or ideological inspiration more as a matter of imagery than reality.

DEL: Competing theories of review are a logical consequence of the relative dearth of constitutional direction defining the judiciary's function. To the extent a power vacuum exists, when competing agendas exist and diverse interests are at stake, it is predictable that vying concepts will rush to fill it. Much of the debate over interpretivism and noninterpretivism, however, seems hyperinflated and more an exercise in academic exhibitionism than responsive to the real world of judicial review. Justice Robert Jackson observed that "(e)very justice has been accused of legislating and every one has joined in that accusation of others."[16] Put another way, principles of restraint have been honored more in the breach than in the observance.[17]

A classic example of such performance is provided by Chief Justice Rehnquist, whose reputation has been built upon a reputation for deference to the political process. Rehnquist's appointment to the Supreme Court fulfilled a campaign promise by Richard Nixon in 1968 to nominate "strict constructionists" to the Supreme Court. It is reasonable to assume strict constructionism was used as a political term of art, rather than in its precise sense, to denote a judicial philosophy that would be resistant to development of fundamental rights not enumerated by constitutional text. Among the most prominent aspects of Rehnquist's jurisprudential output has been his persistent excoriation of the Court for functioning as a superlegislature. He thus characterized the Court's development of a right to privacy, to comprehend a women's freedom to elect an abortion, as "closely attuned to . . . the majority opinion in *Lochner* and other cases" that generated the largely discredited body of case law establishing economic liberty as fundamental.[18] In like fashion, Rehnquist has criticized extension of the right of privacy to account for marital interests, family relationships and the right to travel.[19] Yet, it was he who authored the Court's opinion recognizing "a constitutionally protected liberty interest in refusing unwanted medical treatment."[20] In the words of perhaps a "stricter constructionist," Justice Scalia, "the Constitution says nothing about the matter."[21]

The Rehnquist experience is not unique. Justice Holmes, another ardent exponent of restraint and deference to the political process, could not resist signing on with the Court in identifying parental liberty in rearing and educating their children as a fundamental right.[22] Justice Black, among the most noted critics of a superlegislative function, himself acknowledged a right of association that expanded and developed a distinction between speech and conduct that limited the First Amendment's scope.[23] For all the debate over whether the judiciary has overreached and functioned anti-democratically, and the formalistic regimes that have been engendered, the problem is probably less profound than all the posturing would indicate. With few exceptions, the judiciary has been reluctant to venture far beyond the bounds of political tolerance—a pattern consistent with the understanding that the Court relies upon the coordinate branches of government to respect

---

[16] Robert Jackson, The Supreme Court in the American System of Government 80 (1955).

[17] Thomas Powell, Vagaries and Varieties in Constitutional Interpretation 42–43 (1956).

[18] Roe v. Wade, 410 U.S. 113, 174 (1973) (Rehnquist, J., dissenting). The era of Lochnerism which established and developed economic liberty as a constitutional imperative of the Fourteenth Amendment, emblemized by Lochner v. New York, 198 U.S. 45 (1905), is discussed at pages 39–63.

[19] Zablocki v. Redhail, 434 U.S. 374, 407 (1978) (Rehnquist, J., dissenting) (criticizing right to marry); Moore v. City of East Cleveland, 431 U.S. 494, 537 (1977) (Stewart, J. and Rehnquist, J., dissenting) (criticizing protection of extended family relationship); Vlandis v. Kline, 412 U.S. 441, 467–68 (1978) (Rehnquist, J., dissenting) (criticizing right to travel).

[20] Cruzan v. Director, Missouri Department of Health, 497 U.S. 261, 277 (1990).

[21] *Id.* at 293 (Scalia, J., concurring).

[22] Pierce v. Society of Sisters, 268 U.S. 510 (1925).

[23] NAACP v. Button, 371 U.S. 415 (1958) (right to associate); Tinker v. Des Moines Independent Community School Board, 393 U.S. 503 (1969) (distinguishing between speech and conduct).

and enforce its will. To the extent that it has strained against the margins of popular acceptance, the Court has risked its legitimacy and influence. Such was the consequence of the *Dred Scott* decision, when the Lincoln Administration and Congress simply ignored it and enacted legislation at odds with the Court's mandate. Desegregation begot widespread evasion, resistance and delay, and the Court eventually curtailed its operation. Similarly, persistent criticism of the judicially crafted liberty to elect an abortion has resulted in case law largely in line with popular thinking. Judicial commitment to economic liberty, during the first third of this century, probably represents the primary example of intransigence and impedance of popular will. Even that dedication gave way eventually, as a new generation of justices rejected that body of jurisprudence. The bottom line is that, notwithstanding the theoretical potential of anti-democratic performance, reality is that the judiciary seldom is adventurous and when it is the liberty or equality interest or right established is likely to be ephemeral.

PAH: Clearly the construction of a theory of judicial review which responds both to the "countermajoritarian difficulty" and to the need for protection against majority excess has preoccupied scholars, particularly in the four decades following the desegregation decision of *Brown v. Board of Education.* I confess that, as a student of *Brown,* I became intellectually attracted to the notion, perhaps best spelled out by Owen Fiss[24], of the court as articulator of public values. The idea is that judges by training and experience possess the competency and functional qualities which enable them to give meaning to our constitutional values. Through the resolution of social disputes in the adjudicative process—including dialogue through the opinions of judges over time and as a case wends its way through the courts—judges clarify the meaning of liberty, equality and the other values which stand abstract and ambiguous in the constitution. Professor Fiss challenges us to question the preference for legislative or majoritarian decision making, constructing a theory of adjudication as a social process of exchange of ideas, regulated by disciplined, insulated professionals. Under this model, courts can be viewed not as antithetical but as part of democratic decision making. Professor Fiss seeks to construct this model of adjudication through an account of the Court's effort to translate the rule of *Brown v. Board of Education* into practice. Unfortunately for me, later lessons of *Brown* ultimately suggest not only that judicial elitism which promotes insensitivity to minority interests limits the institutional capacity to resolve social disputes, but also that courts by nature are political.

The fact that the judges who we authorize to displace legislative policies are *unelected* is not as much of concern as the fact that they have not clearly shown themselves able to resist an inclination to serve majoritarian interests and popular preferences. Thus, although the assumption has been that the courts provide an alternative arena where minorities who cannot expect to get a fair shake in the political process can be heard, the unfortunate reality is that "rather than protecting minority interests from majority abrogation, as envisioned by the traditional model of judicial review, the Supreme Court appears actually to serve the function of advancing majority interests at minority expense, while operating behind the veil of countermajoritarian adjudication."[25]

---

[24] *See, e.g.,* Owen Fiss, The Supreme Court 1978 Term—Foreword: The Forms of Justice, 93 Harv. L. Rev. 33 (1979). *See also* Frank Michelman, Foreword: Traces of Self-government, 100 Harv. L. Rev. 63 (1986).

[25] Girardeau A. Spann, *Pure Politics,* 88 Mich. L. Rev. 1971 (1990).

2. The Fundamental Rights Debate

a. Economic Liberty Prior to 1937

The identification and development of fundamental rights and liberties, not specifically itemized by constitutional text, primarily are phenomena of the past century.

Prior to the Civil War, the notion of constitutional rights not enumerated by the Constitution was a matter of theory. One strain of abolitionist sentiment, for instance, regarded the due process clause of the Fifth Amendment and the privileges and immunities clause of Article IV, Section 2 as reference points for the premise that slavery was unconstitutional. The argument competed against a document that by its terms and interpretation at least accommodated slavery. Given that reality, such constitutional utopianism has been characterized as another exercise in natural law.[26]

The Supreme Court's first reference to a specific constitutional right, not literally related by the Constitution itself, was made in the context of its effort to resolve the slavery controversy. With the political process largely paralyzed by sectional antagonism, judicial review offered the possibility of a final resolution of the slavery controversy as a function of constitutional imperative. In addition to determining that persons of African descent could not be citizens of the United States and that Congress could not prohibit slavery in the territories, Chief Justice Taney asserted that "a right of property in a slave is distinctly and expressly affirmed in the Constitution."[27] Although the Constitution at least accommodated slavery by prohibiting interference with international trading in slaves until 1808, accounting for fugitive slaves, and counting slaves as three-fifths of a person for representational and taxation purposes, Taney's identification of a right to own slaves turned the document and historical understanding on their ear. As discussed in Chapter 4, slavery was allowed or prohibited as a matter of self-determination by the individual states.

Taney's rhetoric previewed an analytical methodology that would gain currency even as slavery itself was abolished. Notwithstanding its Reconstruction origins, the Fourteenth Amendment soon became an attraction for those urging the identification and development of textually unenumerated rights and liberties. The privileges and immunities clause became the immediate focal point of attention for arguments that the Court must account for fundamental rights and liberties even when they are not specified by the Constitution.

> The precursor to the Fourteenth Amendment was the Civil Rights Act of 1866, which provided that: there shall be no discrimination in civil rights or immunities . . . on account of race . . . but the inhabitants of every race . . . shall have the same rights to make and enforce contracts, to sue, be parties, and give evidence, to inherit, purchase, lease, sell, hold and convey real and personal property, and to full and equal benefit of all laws and proceedings for the security of persons and property, and shall be subject to like punishment.[28]

The civil rights legislation was grounded in a relatively new concept of federal citizenship and itemized some of its basic incidents. It tracked in large part Justice Washington's inquiry four decades earlier, in *Corfield v. Coryell,* into the "privileges and immunities of citizens in the several states[.]"[29]

---

[26] ROBERT COVER, JUSTICE ACCUSED 156 (1975).

[27] Dred Scott v. Sandford, 60 U.S. 393, 451 (1857).

[28] Cong. Globe, 39th Cong., 1st Sess. 474 (1866).

[29] Corfield v. Coryell, 6 F. Cas. 546, 551–52 (C.C.D. Pa. 1823).

Corfield v. Coryell
6 Fed. Cas. 546, 551–52 (C.C.D. Pa. 1823)

We feel no hesitation in confining these expressions to those privileges and immunities which are, in their nature, fundamental; which belong, of right, to the citizens of all free governments; and which have, at all times, been enjoyed by the citizens of the several states which compose this Union, from the time of their becoming free, independent and sovereign. What these fundamental principles are, it would perhaps be more tedious than difficult to enumerate. They may, however, be all comprehended under the following general heads. Protection by the government; the enjoyment of life and liberty, with the right to acquire and possess property of every kind, and to pursue and obtain happiness and safety; . . . [t]he right of a citizen of one state to pass through, or to reside in any other state, for purposes of trade, agriculture, professional pursuits, or otherwise; to claim the benefit of the writ of habeas corpus; to institute and maintain actions of any kind in the courts of the state; to take, hold and dispose of property, either real or personal; and an exemption from higher taxes than are paid by other citizens of the state; . . . [and] the elective franchise, as regulated and established by the law or constitution of the state in which it is to be exercised.

A significant dimension of the Civil Rights Act of 1866 was its delineation of fundamental incidents of citizenship as a federal interest. Recognition that the legislation might be imperiled by eventual return of southern states to the union fold contributed to eventual adoption of the Fourteenth Amendment. Constitutionalization of the civil rights enactment, as described by one of its supporters, was intended to secure the incidents of federal citizenship "beyond normal politics . . . [and] fix [them] in the serene sky, in the eternal firmament of the Constitution, where no storm of passion can shake . . . and no cloud can obscure."[30] Even supporters of a broader constitutional accounting acknowledged that "[v]irtually every speaker in the debates on the Fourteenth Amendment . . . said or agreed that [it] was designed to embody or incorporate the Civil Rights Act."[31]

Post-ratification debate over the Fourteenth Amendment renewed some of the same disagreements that emerged in the framing process. It was not long until the dispute was aired in a litigative context. In its initial review of the Fourteenth Amendment, the Supreme Court assessed the nature and significance of privileges and immunities incidental to federal citizenship and offered some passing observations on the meaning of the due process clause and equal protection guarantee. Although the majority in the *Slaughter-House Cases* took a restrictive view of each, the dissent offered a theory of judicially crafted fundamental rights and liberties that eventually would define Fourteenth Amendment jurisprudence. The *Slaughter-House Cases* concerned a challenge to a state-granted monopoly on slaughter houses in New Orleans. The regulation was adopted as a health measure and designed to relocate from heavily populated areas "the noxious slaughterhouses and large and offensive collections of animals."[32]

A circuit court decision authored by Justice Bradley accepted the argument that the monopoly violated the Fourteenth Amendment. As Bradley saw it, the privileges and immunities clause protected freedom "to adopt and follow such lawful industrial pursuit" and "the possession and enjoyment of property."[33] A Supreme Court majority rejected that constitutional vision.

---

[30] Cong. Globe, 39th Cong., 1st Sess. 2462 (Rep. Garfield).

[31] HOWARD GRAHAM, EVERYMAN'S CONSTITUTION 291 n.73 (1968).

[32] Slaughter-House Cases, 83 U.S. 36, 64 (1873).

[33] Live-Stock Dealers & Butchers Association v. Crescent City Live-Stock Landing & Slaughterhouse Co., 15 Fed. Cas. 649, 652 (C.C.D. 1870).

Slaughter-House Cases
83 U.S. 36 (1873)

MR. JUSTICE MILLER . . . delivered the opinion of the Court.

. . .

This statute is denounced not only as creating a monopoly and conferring odious and exclusive privileges upon a small number of persons at the expense of the great body of the community of New Orleans, but it is asserted that it deprives a large and meritorious class of citizens—the whole of the butchers of the city—of the right to exercise their trade, the business to which they have been trained and on which they depend for the support of themselves and their families; and that the unrestricted exercise of the business of butchering is necessary to the daily subsistence of the population of the city.

. . .

We repeat, then, in the light of this recapitulation of events, almost too recent to be called history, but which are familiar to us all; and on the most casual examination of the language of these amendments, no once can fail to be impressed with the one pervading purpose found in them all, lying at the foundation of each, and without which none of them would have been even suggested; we mean the freedom of the slave race, the security and firm establishment of that freedom, and the protection of the newly-made freemen and citizen from the opressions of those who had formerly exercised unlimited dominion over him. . . .

We do not say that no one else but the Negro can share in this protection. . . .

. . . But what we do say, and what we wish to be understood is, that in any fair and just construction of any section or phrase of these amendments, it is necessary to look to the purpose which we have said was the pervading spirit of them all, the evil which they were designed to remedy, and the process of continued addition to the Constitution, until that purpose was supposed to be accomplished, as far as constitutional law can accomplish it.

The first section of the fourteenth article, to which our attention is more specially invited, opens with a definition of citizenship—not only citizenship of the United States, but citizenship of the States. No such definition was previously found in the Constitution, nor had any attempt been made to define it by act of Congress. . . .

To remove this difficulty primarily, and to establish a clear and comprehensive definition of citizenship which should declare what should constitute citizenship of the United States, and also citizenship of a State, the first clause of the first section was framed.

"All persons born or naturalized in the United States, and subject to the jurisdiction thereof, are citizens of the United States and the State wherein they reside."

The first observation we have to make on this clause is, that it puts at rest both the questions which we stated to have been the subject of differences of opinion. It declares that persons may be citizens of the United States without regard to their citizenship of a particular State, and it overturns the Dred Scott decision by making *all persons* born within the United States and subject to its jurisdiction citizens of the United States. That its main purpose was to establish the citizenship of the Negro can admit of no doubt. . . .

The next observation is more important in view of the arguments of counsel in the present case. It is, that the distinction between citizenship of the United States and citizenship of a State is clearly recognized and established. Not only may a man be a citizen of a State, but an important element is necessary to convert the former into the latter. He must reside within the State to make him a citizen of it, but it is only necessary that he should be born or naturalized in the United States to be a citizen of the Union.

It is quite clear, then, that there is a citizenship of the United States, and a citizenship of a State, which are distinct from each other, and which depend upon different characteristics or circumstances in the individual.

We think this distinction and its explicit recognition in this amendment of great weight in this argument, because the next paragraph of this same section, which is the one mainly relied on by the plaintiffs in error, speaks only of privileges and immunities of citizens of the United States, and does not speak of those of citizens of the several States. The argument, however, in favor of the plaintiffs rests wholly on the assumption that the citizenship is the same, and the privileges and immunities guaranteed by the clause are the same.

The language is, "No State shall make or enforce any law which shall abridge the privileges or immunities of citizens of *the United States*." It is a little remarkable, if this clause was intended as a protection to the citizen of a State against the legislative power of his own State, that the word citizen of the State should be left out when it is so carefully used, and used in contradistinction to citizens of the United States, in the very sentence which precedes it. It is too clear for argument that the change in phraseology was adopted understandingly and with a purpose.

Of the privileges and immunities of the citizen of the United States, and of the privileges and immunities of the citizen of the State, and what they respectively are, we will presently consider; but we wish to state here that it is only the former which are placed by this clause under the protection of the Federal Constitution, and that the latter, whatever they may be, are not intended to have any additional protection by this paragraph of the amendment.

If, then, there is a difference between the privileges and immunities belonging to a citizen of the United States as such, and those belonging to the citizen of the State as such, the latter must rest for their security and protection where they have heretofore rested; for they are not embraced by this paragraph of the amendment.

The first occurrence of the words "privileges and immunities" in our constitutional history, is to be found in the fourth of the articles of the old Confederation.

It declares "that the better to secure and perpetuate mutual friendship and intercourse among the people of the different States in this Union, the free inhabitants of each of these States, paupers, vagabonds, and fugitives from justice excepted, shall be entitled to all the privileges and immunities of free citizens in the several States; and the people of each State shall have free ingress and regress to and from any other State, and shall enjoy therein all the privileges of trade and commerce, subject to the same duties, impositions, and restrictions as the inhabitants thereof respectively."

In the Constitution of the United States, which superseded the Articles of Confederation, the corresponding provision is found in section two of the fourth article, in the following words: "The citizens of each State shall be entitled to all the privileges and immunities of citizens of the several States."

There can be but little question that the purpose of both these provisions is the same, and that the privileges and immunities intended are the same in each. In the article of the Confederation we have some of these specifically mentioned, and enough perhaps to give some general idea of the class of civil rights meant by the phrase.

Fortunately we are not without judicial construction of this clause of the Constitution. The first and the leading case on the subject is that of *Corfield v. Coryell*, decided by Mr. Justice Washington in the Circuit Court for the District of Pennsylvania in 1823.

"The inquiry," he says, "is, what are the privileges and immunities of citizens of the several States? We feel no hesitation in confining these expression to those privileges and immunities which are *fundamental*; which belong of right to the citizens of all free governments, and which have at all times been enjoyed by citizens of the several States which compose this Union, from the time of their becoming free, independent, and sovereign. What these fundamental principles are, it would be more tedious than difficult to enumerate. They may all, however, be comprehended under the following general heads: protection by the government, with the right to acquire and possess property of every kind, and to pursue and obtain happiness and safety, subject, nevertheless, to such restraints as the government may prescribe for the general good of the whole."

. . .

It would be the vainest show of learning to attempt to prove by citations of authority, that up to the adoption of the recent amendments, no claim or pretense was set up that those rights depended on the Federal government for their existence or protection, beyond the very few express limitations which the Federal Constitution imposed upon the States—such, for instance, as the prohibition against ex post facto laws, bills of attainder, and laws impairing the obligation of contracts. But with the exception of these and a few other restrictions, the entire domain of the privileges and immunities of citizens of the States, as above defined, lay within the constitutional and legislative power of the States, and without that of the Federal government. Was it the purpose of the fourteenth amendment, by the simple declaration that no State should make or enforce any law which shall abridge the privileges and immunities of *citizens of the United States*, to transfer the security and protection of all the civil rights which we have mentioned, from the States to the Federal government? And where it is declared that Congress shall have the power to enforce that article, was it intended to bring within the power of Congress the entire domain of civil rights heretofore belonging exclusively to the States?

All this and more must follow, if the proposition of the plaintiffs in error be sound. For not only are these rights subject to the control of Congress whenever in its discretion any of them are supposed to be abridged by State legislation, but that body may also pass laws in advance, limiting and restricting the exercise of legislative power by the States, in their most ordinary and usual functions, as in its judgment it may think proper on all such subjects. And still further, such a construction followed by the reversal of the judgments of the Supreme Court of Louisiana in these cases, would constitute this court a perpetual censor upon all legislation of the States, on the civil rights of their own citizens, with authority to nullify such as it did not approve as consistent with those rights, as they existed at the time of the adoption of this amendment. The argument we admit is not always the most conclusive which is drawn from the consequences urged against the adoption of a particular construction of an instrument. But when, as in the case before us, these consequences are so serious, so far-reaching and pervading, so great a departure form the structure and spirit of our institutions; when the effect is to fetter and degrade the State governments by subjecting them to the control of Congress, in the exercise of powers heretofore universally conceded to them of the most ordinary and fundamental character; when in fact it radically changes the whole theory of the relations of the State and Federal governments to each other and of both these governments to the people; the argument has a force that is irresistible, in the absence of language which expresses such a purpose too clearly to admit of doubt.

We are convinced that no such results were intended by the Congress which proposed these amendments, nor by the legislatures of the States which ratified them.

Having shown that the privileges and immunities relied on in the argument are those which belong to the citizens of the States as such, and that they are left to the State governments for security and protection, and not by this article placed under the special care of the Federal government, we may hold ourselves excused from defining the privileges and immunities of citizens of the United States which no State can abridge, until some case involving those privileges may make it necessary to do so.

But lest it should be said that no such privileges and immunities are to be found if those we have been considering are excluded, we venture to suggest some which owe their existence to the Federal government, its National character, its Constitution, or its laws. [They include] the right of the citizen of this great country, protected by implied guarantees of its Constitution, "to come to the seat of government to assert any claim he may have upon that government, to transact any business he may have with it, to seek its protection, to share its offices, to engage in administering its functions. He has the right of free access to its seaports, through which all operations of a foreign commerce are conducted, to the subtreasuries, land offices, and courts of justice in the several States." And quoting from the language of Chief Justice Taney in another case, it is said "that *for all the great purposes for which the Federal government* was established, we are one people, with one common country, *we are all citizens of the United States;*" and it is, as such citizens that their rights are supported in this court in *Crandall v. Nevada.*

Another privilege of a citizen of the United States is to demand the care and protection of the Federal government over his life, liberty, and property when on the high seas or within the jurisdiction of a foreign government. Of this there can be no doubt, nor that the right depends upon his character as a citizen of the United States. The right to peaceably assemble and petition for redress of grievances, the privilege of the writ of *habeas corpus*, are rights of the citizen guaranteed by the Federal Constitution. The right to use the navigable waters of the United States, however they may penetrate the territory of the several States, all rights secured to our citizens by treaties with foreign nations, are dependent upon citizenship of the United States, and not citizenship of a State. One of these privileges is conferred by the very article under consideration. It is that a citizen of the United States can, of his own volition, become a citizen of any State of the Union by a *bonâ fide* residence therein, with the same rights as other citizens of that State. To these may be added the rights secured by the thirteenth and fifteenth articles of amendment, and by the other clause of the fourteenth, . . .

But it is useless to pursue this branch of the inquiry, since we are of opinion that the rights claimed by these plaintiffs in error, if they have any existence, are not privileges and immunities of citizens of the United States within the meaning of the clause of the fourteenth amendment under consideration.

. . .

FIELD, J. dissenting.

. . . The question presented is, therefore, one of the gravest importance, not merely to the parties here, but to the whole country. It is nothing less than the question whether the recent amendments to the Federal Constitution protect the citizens of the United States against the deprivation of their common rights by State legislation. In my judgement the fourteenth amendment does afford such protection, and was so intended by the Congress which framed and the States which adopted it. . . .

The amendment does not attempt to confer any new privileges or immunities upon citizens, or to enumerate or define those already existing. It assumes that there are such privileges and immunities which belong of right to citizens as such, and ordains that they shall not be abridged by State legislation. If this inhibition has no reference to privileges and immunities of this character, but only refers, as held by the majority of the court in their opinion, to such privileges and immunities as were before its adoption specially designated in the Constitution or necessarily implied as belonging to citizens of the United States, it was a vain and idle enactment, which accomplished nothing, and most unnecessarily excited Congress and the people on its passage. With privileges and immunities thus designated or implied no State could ever have interfered by its laws, and no new constitutional provision was required to inhibit such interference. The supremacy of the Constitution and the laws of the United States always controlled any State legislation of that character. But if the amendment refers to the natural and inalienable rights which belong to all citizens, the inhibition has a profound significance and consequence.

. . .

What, then, are the privileges and immunities which are secured against abridgment by State legislation?

In the first section of the Civil Rights Act Congress has given its interpretation to these terms, or at least has stated some of the rights which, in its judgment, these terms include; it has there declared that they include the right "to make and enforce contracts, to sue, be parties and give evidence, to inherit, purchase, lease, sell, hold, and convey real and personal property, and to full and equal benefit of all laws and proceedings for the security of person and property." That act, it is true, was passed before the fourteenth amendment, but the amendment was adopted, as I have already said, to obviate objections to the act, or, speaking more accurately, I should say, to obviate objections to legislation of a similar character, extending the protection of the National government over the common rights of all citizens of the United States. Accordingly, after its ratification, Congress reenacted the act under the belief that whatever doubts may have previously existed of its validity, they were removed by the amendment.

The terms "privileges and immunities" are not new in the amendment; they were in the Constitution before the amendment was adopted. They are found in the second section of the fourth article, which declares that "the citizens of each State shall be entitled to all privileges and immunities of citizens of the several States," and they have been the subject of frequent consideration in judicial decisions. In *Corfield v. Coryell*, Mr. Justice Washington said he had "no hesitation in confining these expressions to those privileges and immunities which were, in their nature, fundamental; which belong of right to citizens of all free governments, and compose the Union, from the time of their becoming free, independent, and sovereign"; and, in considering what those fundamental privileges were, he said that perhaps it would be more tedious than difficult to enumerate them, but that they might be "all comprehended under the following general heads: protection by the government; the enjoyment of life and liberty, with the right to acquire and possess property of every kind, and to pursue and obtain happiness and safety, subject, nevertheless, to such restraints as the govern-

ment may justly prescribe for the general good of the whole." This appears to me to be a sound construction of the clause in question. The privileges and immunities designated are those *which of right belong to the citizens of all free governments.* Clearly among these must be placed the right to pursue a lawful employment in a lawful manner, without other restraint than such as equally affects all persons. . . .

The privileges and immunities designated in the second section of the fourth article of the Constitution are, then, according to the decision cited, those which of right belong to the citizens of all free governments, and they can be enjoyed under that clause by the citizens of each State in the several States upon the same terms and conditions as they are enjoyed by the citizens of the latter States. No discrimination can be made by one State against the citizens of other States in enjoyment, nor can any greater imposition be levied than such as is laid upon its own citizens. It is a clause which insures equality in the enjoyment of these rights between citizens of the several States whilst in the same State. . . .

Now, what the clause in question does for the protection of one State against the creation of monopolies in favor of citizens of other States, the fourteenth amendment does for the protection of every citizen of the United States against the creation of any monopoly whatever. The privileges and immunities of citizens of the United States, of every one of them, is secured against abridgment in any form by any State. The fourteenth amendment places them under the guardianship of the National authority.

. . .

BRADLEY, J., dissenting.

. . .

The right of a State to regulate the conduct of its citizens is undoubtedly a very broad and extensive one, and not to be lightly restricted. But there are certain fundamental rights which this right of regulation cannot infringe. It may prescribe the manner of their exercise, but it cannot subvert the rights themselves. I speak now of the rights of citizens of any free government. Granting for the present that the citizens of one government cannot claim the privileges of citizens in another government; that prior to the union of our North American States the citizens of one State could not claim the privileges of citizens in another State; or, that after the union was formed the citizens of the United States, as such, could not claim the privileges of citizens in any particular State; yet the citizens of each of the States and the citizens of the United States would be entitled to certain privileges and immunities as citizens, at the hands of their own government—privileges and immunities which their own governments respectively would be bound to respect and maintain. In this free country, the people of which inherited certain traditional rights and privileges from their ancestors, citizenship means something. It has certain privileges and immunities attached to it which the government, whether restricted by express or implied limitations, cannot take away or impair. It may do so temporarily by force, but it cannot do so by right. And these privileges and immunities attach as well to citizenship of the United States as to citizenship of the states.

. . .

But we are bound to resort to implication, or to the constitutional history of England, to find an authoritative declaration of some of the most important privileges and immunities of citizens of the United States. It is in the Constitution itself. The Constitution, it is true, as it stood prior to the recent amendments, specifies, in terms, only a few of the personal privileges and immunities of citizens, but they are very comprehensive in their character. The States were merely prohibited from passing bills of attainder, *ex post facto* laws, laws impairing the obligation of contracts, and perhaps one or two more, but others of the greatest consequence were enumerated, although they were only secured, in express terms, from invasion by the Federal government; such as the right of *habeas corpus*, the right of trial by jury, of free exercise of religious worship, the right of free speech and a free press, the right peaceably to assemble for the discussion of public measures, the right to be secure against unreasonable searches and seizures, and above all, and including almost all the rest, the right of *not being deprived of life, liberty, or property, without due process of law*. These, and still others are specified in the original Constitution, or in the early amendments of it, as among the privileges and immunities of citizens of the United States, or, what is still stronger for the force of argument, the rights of all persons, whether citizens or not.

. . .

But even if the Constitution were silent, the fundamental privileges and immunities of citizens, as such, would be no less real and no less inviolable than they now are. It was not necessary to say in words that the citizens of the United States should have and exercise all the privileges of citizens; the privilege of buying, selling, and enjoying property; the privilege of engaging in any lawful employment for a livelihood; the privilege of resorting to the laws for redress of injuries, and the like. Their very citizenship conferred these privileges, if they did not possess them before. And these privileges they would enjoy whether they were citizens of any State or not. Inhabitants of Federal territories and new citizens, made such by annexation of territory or naturalization, though without any status as citizens of a State, could, nevertheless, as citizens of the United States, lay claim to every one of the privileges and immunities which have been enumerated; and among these none is more essential and fundamental than the right to follow such profession or employment as each one may choose, subject only to uniform regulations equally applicable to all.

. . .

It is futile to argue that none but persons of the African race are intended to be benefitted by this amendment. They may have been the primary cause of the amendment, but its language is general, embracing all citizens, and I think it was purposely so expressed.

The mischief to be remedied was not merely slavery and its incidents and consequences; but that spirit of insubordination and disloyalty to the National government which had troubled the country for so many years in some of the States, and that intolerance of free speech and free discussion which often rendered life and property insecure, and led to much unequal legislation. The amendment was an attempt to give voice to the strong National yearning for that time and that condition of things, in which American citizenship should be a sure guaranty of safety, and in which every citizen of the United States might stand erect on every portion of its soil, in the full enjoyment of every right and privilege belonging to a freeman, without fear of violence or molestation.

But great fears are expressed that this construction of the amendment will lead to enactments by Congress interfering with the internal affairs of the States, and establishing therein civil and criminal codes of law for the government of the citizens, and thus abolishing the State governments in everything but name; or else, that it will lead the Federal courts to draw to their cognizance the supervision of State tribunals on every subject of judicial inquiry, on the plea of ascertaining whether the privileges and immunities of citizens have not been abridged.

In my judgment no such practical inconveniences would arise. Very little, if any, legislation on the part of Congress would be required to carry the amendment into effect. Like the prohibition against passing a law impairing the obligation of a contract, it would execute itself. The point would be regularly raised, in a suit at law, and settled by final reference to the Federal court. As the privileges and immunities protected are only those fundamental ones which belong to every citizen, they would soon become so far defined as to cause but a slight accumulation of business in the Federal courts. Besides, the recognized existence of the law would prevent its frequent violation. But even if the business of the National courts should be increased, Congress could easily supply the remedy by increasing their number and efficiency. The great question is, What is the true construction of the amendment? When once we find that, we shall find the means of giving it effect. The argument from inconvenience ought not to have a very controlling influence in questions of this sort. The National will and National interest are of far greater importance.

. . .

The *Slaughter-House* decision discounted the significance of the privileges and immunities clause to the point that it persists as a largely vestigial provision. Only once since the *Slaughter-House* ruling has the Court referenced the privileges and immunities clause to strike down a state law.[34] Even that exception to the analytical norm has become a historical curiosity, insofar as the decision was overruled several years later.[35]

---

[34] Colgate v. Harvey, 296 U.S. 404 (1935).
[35] Madden v. Kentucky, 309 U.S. 83 (1940).

DEL: It is instructive that notwithstanding the Court's emphasis upon the "one pervading purpose" of the Fourteenth Amendment, which was to account for the "freedom of the slave race,"[36] initial review was drawn toward a general rather than racially significant concern. The decision thus previewed the Fourteenth Amendment's capture by political and economic interests that were hardly relevant to the reason for or process of reconstructing the union. Nevertheless, as subsequent interpretations would demonstrate, the Fourteenth Amendment would have much more value to the interests of the established economic order before its mandate for racially specific social change was taken seriously. The narrow understanding of the privileges and immunities of federal citizenship disclosed a sense on the part of the Court that Reconstruction was a discrete rather than comprehensive exercise in redistributing interests in citizenship and its incidents from state to federal authority. Prior to its ratification, state citizenship had primary value and civil and political rights emanated from and were protected by the states. A new national identity and the primacy of national citizenship were forged by the union's civil war experience. The Fourteenth Amendment inverted prior understanding, reflected in the *Dred Scott* decision, that national citizenship derived from state citizenship. It redistributed from the states to the nation an interest in establishing and accounting for incidents of citizenship, most especially the responsibility of protecting civil rights. The *Slaughter-House* majority's response to the revised blueprint of governance was "that the existence of the States with powers for domestic and local government, including the regulation of civil rights—the rights of person and of property—was essential to the perfect working of our complex form of government."[37] The *Slaughter-House* Court's interpretation of the meaning and implications of national citizenship, and its subsequent judicial performance with respect to racially significant Fourteenth Amendment claims, translated the Reconstruction process itself into a relatively discrete social engineering exercise. As economic rights doctrine soon achieved through the due process clause what the *Slaughter-House* Court had precluded through the privileges and immunities clause, the Fourteenth Amendment increasingly became a primary context within which the judiciary's function in identifying and developing textually unenumerated rights would be debated.

PAH: It is intriguing to think of visions of the privileges and immunities of national citizenship alternative to the cribbed reading of *Slaughter-House*. What rights are fundamental to exis-

---

[36] Slaughter-House Cases, 83 U.S. 36, 80–81 (1873).
[37] *Id.* at 82

tence? Scholars like Daniel Farber and Suzanna Sherry[38] have pointed out that the natural law tradition influenced the Republicans who drafted the Fourteenth Amendment, and, as Senator Trumball said of the Civil Rights Act of 1866 (which the Fourteenth Amendment was meant to constitutionalize[39]), "the right of American citizenship means something."[40]

Apparently concerned about the effect on our federalism and the power of states to define important rights, the majority in *Slaughter-House*, over dissent, virtually rendered the privileges and immunities meaningless. But a different reading by a reconstituted court need not necessarily have been wholly desirable. Notably, Justice Bradley the dissenter in *Slaughter-House*, who supported the recognition of rights, wrote a concurring decision in *Bradwell v. Illinois*,[41] denying Myra Bradwell her claim to a license to practice law. Agreeing with the state, he posited that "in the nature of things" and under "the law of the creator" such a privilege need not be among the fundamental rights and privileges accorded women. Thus consistent with a rights-focused reading of the privileges and immunities clause, the state could properly deny her a license.

Even though an equality-centered reading of the Fourteenth Amendment has emerged it may be worth considering whether a substantive rights focus would be preferable today. It bears noting that in recent years some feminists have questioned the value of rights, at least as we have come to understand rights as highly individualistic in our liberal framework.[42] A richer understanding of affirmative rights—such as the right to minimum shelter and sustenance—may better serve the interests of marginalized citizens but such rights have often been characterized as contrary to our political traditions.[43]

---

[38] *See* DANIEL FARBER & SUZANNA SHERRY, A HISTORY OF THE CONSTITUTION ch.9 (1990).

[39] *Id.* at 302.

[40] CONG. GLOBE, 39th CONG., 1st Sess. 1757 (1866), quoted in FARBER & SHERRY, *supra* note 38, at 304.

[41] 83 U.S. (16 Wall.) 130 (1873).

[42] MARTHA MINOW, JUSTICE AND THE POLITIC OF DIFFERENCE (1990); Robin West, *The Supreme Court, 1989 Term—Foreword: Taking Freedom Seriously*, 104 HARV. L. REV. 43 (1990). A contrasting approach is taken by Professor Patricia Williams who argues that the interests of people of color continue to be served by the recognition of rights. Patricia Williams, *Alchemical Notes: Reconstructing Ideals from Deconstructed Rights*, 22 Harv. C.R.-C.L. . Rev. 401 (1987).

[43] *See, e.g,* JOHN HART ELY, DEMOCRACY AND DISTRUST (1980).

b. The Rise of Substantive Due Process Review

Despite the *Slaughter-House* majority's refusal to regard the privileges and immunities clause as a storehouse of fundamental rights, incidental to federal citizenship, the dissenters' views have had profound long-term constitutional significance. What was impossible to achieve through the privileges and immunities clause soon became attainable through the due process clause. Until the late nineteenth century, the concept of due process was concerned only with procedural fairness. As Alexander Hamilton had noted, due process was "only applicable to the process and proceedings of the courts of justice; [it] can never be referred to an act of the legislature."[44] Notwithstanding Chief Justice Taney's references to due process as a basis for slave owner rights in *Dred Scott*, case law until the final few decades of the nineteenth century largely rejected the notion of substantive due process. The *Slaughter-House* majority's cursory attention to the due process challenge, following its analysis of the privileges and immunities clause, evidenced no inclination to diverge from the Hamiltonian vision. As the Court observed

---

[44] RAOUL BERGER, GOVERNMENT BY JUDICIARY 196 n.11 (1977) (quoting Alexander Hamilton).

The argument has not been much pressed in these cases that the defendant's charter deprives the plaintiffs of their property without due process of law. . . [which] has been in the Constitution since the adoption of the Fifth Amendment, as a restraint upon the federal power. It is also to be found in some form of expression in the constitutions of nearly all the states, as a restraint upon the power of the States.

Under no construction of that provision that we have ever seen, or any that we deem admissible, can the restraint imposed by the state of Louisiana upon the exercise of their trade by the butchers of New Orleans be held to be a deprivation of property within the meaning of that provision.[45]

As Reconstruction coursed into its final stages, and the nation turned its attention to industrial development and economic growth, regulatory energies shifted toward governance of economic activity and social consequences. New regulatory schemes, governing manufacturing, transportation and communications, begot an interest in protection from legislative power. Influential legal scholars such as Thomas Cooley propounded a theory of due process as a check on legislative power. Despite the Court's rejection of economic rights arguments in the *Slaughter-House Cases*, the Fourteenth Amendment soon yielded results more akin to the dissenters' perspective.

Previewing the emergence of substantive due process review, Justice Miller—who spoke for the Court in the *Slaughter-House Cases*—authored an opinion striking down a local law giving relocating businesses a preferential tax rate. In *Loan Association v. City of Topeka,* Miller wrote that the tax had no "public character, but was purely in aid of private or personal objects beyond the legislative power and an authorized invasion of private right."[46] The law was struck down on grounds that it violated rights, not that were specified, but that were implied by the Constitution. As Miller put it

The theory of our governments, State and National, is opposed to the deposit of unlimited power anywhere. The executive, the legislative, and the judicial branches of these governments are all of limited and defined powers. There are limitations on such power which grow out of the essential nature of all free governments, implied reservations of individual rights, without which the social compact could not exist, and which are respected by all governments entitled to the name. No court, for instance, would hesitate to declare void a statute which enacted that A, and B, who were husband and wife to each other should be so no longer, but that A, should thereafter be the husband of C, and B, the wife of D. Or which should enact that the homestead now owned by A, should no longer be his, but should henceforth be the property of B.

Even assuming limitations upon governmental power attributable to the "essential nature of all free governments," debate has persisted over whether the judiciary should account for those interests to the extent they are not identified by constitutional text. As Justice Black put it nearly a century later, the due process clause did not vest the judiciary with the power "to measure constitutionality by our belief that legislation is arbitrary, capricious or unreasonable, or accomplishes no justifiable purpose, or is offensive to our own notions of 'civilized standards of conduct.'"[47] By striking down legislation without identifying a specific constitutional right or liberty that had been invaded, nonetheless, the Court abandoned the restraint of its *Slaughter-House* reasoning and engaged in analysis that eventually would typify substantive due process review.

The evolution of economic rights doctrine was advanced further by the Court's

---

[45] Slaughter-House Cases, 83 U.S. 36, 80–81 (1873).

[46] Loan Association v. City of Topeka, 87 U.S. 655, 663 (1874).

[47] Griswold v. Connecticut, 381 U.S. 479, 513–14 (1965) (Black, J., dissenting).

decision in *Munn v. Illinois*, as the Court indicated that the due process clause might function as a check on the exercise of state legislative power. Typifying due process analysis is independent inquiry by the judiciary into whether regulation is reasonable or justified. In *Munn*, the Court declined to consider the reasonableness of grain elevator rate regulation because the activity concerned "a public interest."[48] It noted, however, that "in mere private contacts, relating to matters in which the public has no interest, what is reasonable must be judicially ascertained."[49] The Court thus laid additional analytical groundwork for closer review of regulation affecting economic interests.

In the *Railroad Commission Cases*, the Court upheld state railroad rate regulation but reiterated its interest in scrutinizing the wisdom of legislative policy. It pointed out, moreover, that a state could not regulate rates in a way that represented "a taking of private property without just compensation, or without due process of law."[50]

Again without actually striking down regulation, the Court was more specific about its willingness to entertain due process challenges. In *Mugler v. Kansas*, the Court upheld a state ban on liquor sales. Although recognizing legislative power to control activity that "will injuriously affect the public," it observed that "[t]here are, of necessity, limits beyond which state police powers cannot rightfully go."[51] It further identified its own

> solemn duty—to look at the substance of things, whenever they enter upon the inquiry whether the legislature has transcended the limits of its authority. If, therefore, a statute purporting to have been enacted to protect the public health, the public morals, or the public safety, has no real or substantial relation to those objects, or is a palpable invasion of rights secured by the fundamental law, it is the duty of the courts to so adjudge, and thereby give effect to the Constitution.

With such an analytical regimen in place, it was only a matter of time before social and economic enactments regularly would be undone by an understanding of the due process clause as a check on legislative power.

From the late nineteenth century through the first third of the twentieth century, concepts of economic liberty in the form especially of contractual freedom and property rights became central to the Court's understanding of due process. Political output at the time reflected trends in many states toward regulating conditions of employment. Persistently challenged, usually successfully, were laws establishing maximum hours of and minimum wages for work, allowing collective bargaining and interfering with the use or transfer of property.

In *Allgeyer v. Louisiana*, the Court achieved through the due process clause what it had refused to allow by means of the privileges and immunities clause a quarter century before. At issue in *Allgeyer* was a law prohibiting insurance contracts written by out-of-state companies that had not been certified by Louisiana. In striking down the regulation on jurisdiction grounds, the Court amplified its understanding of due process as a check on legislative power. It accordingly observed that

> [t]he statute which forbids such act does not become due process of law, because it is inconsistent with the provisions of the Constitution of the Union. The liberty mentioned in that amendment means not only the right of the citizen

---

[48] Munn v. Illinois, 94 U.S. 113 (1876).

[49] *Id.* at 134.

[50] Railroad Commission Case, 116 U.S. 307, 331 (1886).

[51] Mugler v. Kansas, 123 U.S. 623, 661 (1887).

to be free from the mere physical restraint of his person, as by incarceration, but the term is deemed to embrace the right of the citizen to be free in the enjoyment of all his faculties; to be free to use them in all lawful ways; to live and work where he will; to earn his livelihood by any lawful calling; to pursue any livelihood or avocation, and for that purpose to enter into all contracts which may be proper, necessary and essential to his carrying out to a successful conclusion the purposes above mentioned. . . . [52]

The *Allgeyer* decision identified the Court's readiness to strike down laws interfering with a laissez-faire economic system. When put in a broader Fourteenth Amendment context, the departure from the *Slaughter-House* decision was even more profound. In the *Slaughter-House Cases*, the Court rejected economic rights doctrine and stressed the central purpose of the Fourteenth Amendment as a means of ensuring "the freedom of the slave race, the security of and firm establishment of that freedom, and the protection of the newly-made free man and citizen from the oppressions of those who had formerly exercised unlimited dominion over him."[53] The *Allgeyer* Court's investment in previously repudiated economic rights theory followed one year after it had deferred to prescriptive segregation as reasonable exercises of state police power.[54] What initially had been peripheral to the Fourteenth Amendment thus had become central, and what once was at its core had become marginal.

Fourteenth Amendment rhetoric finally became formal reality in *Lochner v. New York*, when the Court held that wage and hour regulation of the baking industry violated liberty of contract and thus violated the due process clause of the Fourteenth Amendment.[55]

---

[52] Allgeyer v. Louisiana, 165 U.S. 578, 592–93 (1897).
[53] Slaughter-House Cases, 83 U.S. 36, 71 (1873).
[54] Plessy v. Ferguson, 163 U.S. 537, 550 (1896).
[55] Lochner v. New York, 198 U.S. 45 (1905).

Lochner v. New York
198 U.S. 45 (1905)

. . .
MR. JUSTICE PECKHAM . . . delivered the opinion of the Court.

The indictment, it will be seen, charges that the plaintiff in error violated . . . labor law of the State of New York, in that he wrongfully and unlawfully required and permitted an employè working for him to work more than sixty hours in one week. . . .

The mandate of the statute that "no employè shall be required or permitted to work," is the substantial equivalent of an enactment that "no employè shall contract or agree to work" more than ten hours per day, and as there is no provision for special emergencies the statue is mandatory in all cases. It is not an act merely fixing the number of hours which shall constitute a legal day's work, but an absolute prohibition upon the employer, permitting, under any circumstances, more than ten hours work to be done in his establishment.

The employè may desire to earn the extra money, which would arise from his working more than the prescribed time, but this statute forbids the employer from permitting the employè to earn it. The statute necessarily interferes with the right of contract between the employer and employès, concerning the number of hours in which the latter may labor in the bakery of the employer. The general right to make a contract in relation to his business is part of the liberty of the individual protected by the Fourteenth Amendment of the Federal Constitution. *Allgeyer v. Louisiana.* Under that provision no State can deprive any person of life, liberty or property without due process of law. . . .

This is not a question of substituting the judgment of the court for that of the legislature. If the act be within the power of the State it is valid, although the judgment of the court might be totally opposed to the enactment of such a law. But the question would still remain: Is it within the police power of the State? and that question must be answered by the court.

The question whether this act is valid as a labor law, pure and simple, may be dismissed in a few words. There is no reasonable ground for interfering with the liberty of person or the right of free contract, by determining the hours of labor, in the occupation of a baker. There is no contention that bakers as a class are not equal in intelligence and capacity to men of other trades or manual occupations, or that they are not able to assert their rights and care for themselves without the protecting arm of the State, interfering with their independence of judgment and of action. They are in no sense wards of the State. Viewed in the light of a purely labor law, with no reference whatever to the question of health, we think that a law like the one before us involves neither the safety, the morals nor the welfare of the public, and that the interest of the public is not in the slightest degree affected by such an act. The law must be upheld, if at all, as a law pertaining to the health of the individual engaged in the occupation of a baker. It does not affect any other portion of the public than those who are engaged in that occupation. Clean and wholesome bread does not depend upon whether the baker works but ten hours per day or only sixty hours a week. The limitation of the hours of labor does not come within the police power on that ground.

It is a question of which of two powers or rights shall prevail—the power of the State to legislate or the right of the individual to liberty of person and freedom of contract. There mere assertion that the subject relates though but in a remote degree to the public health does not necessarily render the enactment valid. The act must have a more direct relation, as a means to an end, and the end itself must be appropriate and legitimate, before an act can be held to be valid which interferes with the general right of an individual to be free in his person and in his power to contract in relation to his own labor.

. . .

We think the limit of the police power has been reached and passed in this case. There is,

in our judgment, no reasonable foundation for holding this to be necessary or appropriate as a health law to safeguard to public health or the health of the individuals who are following the trade of a baker. If this statute be valid, and if, therefore, a proper case is made out in which to deny the right of an individual, *sui juris,* as employer or employè, to make contracts for the labor of the latter under the protection of the provisions of the Federal Constitution, there would seem to be no length to which legislation of this nature might not go. . . .

It is impossible for us to shut our eyes to the fact that many of the laws of this character, while passed under what is claimed to be the police power for the purpose of protecting the public health or welfare, are, in reality, passed for other motives. We are justified in saying so when, from the character of the law and the subject upon which it legislates, it is apparent that the public health or welfare bears but the most remote relation to the law. The purpose of a statute must be determined from the nature and legal effect of the language employed; and whether it is or is not repugnant to the Constitution of the United States must be determined from the natural effect of such statutes when put into operation, and not from their proclaimed purpose. The court looks beyond the mere letter of the law in such cases.

It is manifest to us that the limitation of the hours of labor as provided for this section of the statute under which the indictment was found, and the plaintiff in error convicted, has no such direct relation to and no such substantial effect upon the health of the employè, as to justify us in regarding the section as really a health law. It seems to us that the real object and purpose were simply to regulate the hours of labor between the master and his employès (all being men, *sui juris*), in a private business, not dangerous in any degree to morals or in any real and substantial degree, to the health of the employès. Under such circumstances the freedom of master and employè to contract with each other in relation to their employment, and in defining the same, cannot be prohibited or interfered with, without violating the Federal Constitution.

. . .

Lochnerism over the course of time has become a short-hand term of derision used by critics of substantive due process review. The *Lochner* decision was followed by three decades of jurisprudence elevating contractual liberty and property rights to a level of constitutional significance capable of thwarting a panoply of social and economic legislation. Although denying that its ruling represented "substituting the judgment of the court for that of the legislature," the Court at a later juncture in its opinion concluded that "[w]e do not believe in the soundness of the views which uphold this law."[56] The net result was a standard of review by which the Court independently assessed the premises and merits of legislation and struck down what it considered an unreasonable intrusion upon economic freedom.

For social and economic regulation to survive such review, two requirements had to be satisfied. First, it was essential to establish that a state's exercise of its police power responded to health and safety concerns. The Court's sense that "the trade of a baker . . . is not an unhealthy one" had facilitated its determination in *Lochner*, that the regulation was "purely [a] labor law."[57] Second, even if a legitimate health or safety purpose was established, it was necessary to demonstrate that the regulation was reasonable. Legislative policy thus competed against the judiciary's sense of economic and social imperative.

The logical response to such standards of review was presentation of detailed evidence establishing health and safety concerns prompting regulation and arguments demonstrating why such governance was essential. A classic example of such litigative technique was provided by Louis Brandeis in *Muller v. Oregon*. Arguing in defense of a state law that limited working hours for women, he filed what became known as a "Brandeis brief"—a memorandum heavily laden with social science data establishing a link between regulatory means and ends and demonstrating the wisdom of legislative action. The Court in *Muller* upheld the law in significant part because of perceptions regarding the special needs and conditions of women.[58]

---

[56] *Id.* at 57, 61.

[57] *Id.* at 59.

[58] Muller v. Oregon, 208 U.S. 412, 421 (1908).

Muller v. Oregon
208 U.S. 412 (1908)

MR. JUSTICE BREWER delivered the opinion of the court:

[T]he legislature of the state of Oregon passed an act . . . the first section of which is in these words:

"[N]o female [shall] be employed in any mechanical establishment, or factory, or laundry in this state more than ten hours during any one day. The hours of work may be so arranged as to permit the employment of females "at any time so that they shall not work more than ten hours during the twenty-four hours of any one day."

. . .

It is undoubtedly true, as more than once declared by this court, that the general right to contract in relation to one's business is part of the liberty of the individual, protected by the 14th Amendment to the Federal Constitution; yet it is equally well settled that this liberty is not absolute and extending to all contracts, and that a state may, without conflicting with the provisions of the 14th Amendment, restrict in many respects the individual's power of contract. . . .

That woman's physical structure and the performance of maternal functions place her at a disadvantage in the struggle for subsistence is obvious. This is especially true when the burdens of motherhood are upon her. Even when they are not, by abundant testimony of the medical fraternity continuance for a long time on her feet at work, repeating this from day to day, tends to injurious effects upon the body, and, as healthy mothers are essential to vigorous offspring, the physical well-being of woman becomes an object of public interest and care in order to preserve the strength and vigor of the race.

Still again, history discloses the fact that woman has always been dependent upon man. He established his control at the outset by superior physical strength, and this control in various forms, with diminishing intensity, has continued to the present. As minors [sic], though not to the same extent, she has been looked upon in the courts as needing especial care that her rights may be preserved. Education was long denied her, and while now the doors of the schoolroom are opened and her opportunities for acquiring knowledge are great, yet even with that and the "consequent increase of capacity for business affairs it is still true that in the struggle for subsistence she is not an equal competitor with her brother. Though limitations upon personal and contractual rights may be removed by legislation, there is that in her disposition and habits of life which will operate against a full assertion of those rights. She will still be where some legislation to protect her seems necessary to secure a real equality of right. Doubtless there are individual exceptions, and there are many respects in which she has an advantage over him; but looking at it from the viewpoint of the effort to maintain an independent position in life, she is not upon an equality. Differentiated by these matters from the other sex, she is properly placed in a class by herself, and legislation designed for her protection may be sustained, even when like legislation is not necessary for men, and could not be sustained. It is impossible to close one's eyes to the fact that she still looks to her brother and depends upon him. Even though all restrictions on political, personal, and contractual rights were taken away, and she stood, so far as statutes are concerned, upon an absolutely equal plane with him, it would still be true that she is so constituted that she will rest upon and look to him for protection; that her physical structure and a proper discharge of her maternal functions—having in view not merely her own health, but the well-being of the race—justify legislation to protect her from the greed as well as the passion of man. The limitations which this statute places upon her contractual powers, upon her right to agree with her employer as to the time she shall labor, are not imposed solely for her benefit, but also largely for the benefit of all. Many words cannot make this plainer. The two sexes differ in structure of body, in the functions to be performed by each, in the amount of physical strength, in the capacity for long-continued labor, particularly when done standing, the influence of vigorous health upon the future well-being of the race, the self-reliance which enables one to assert full rights, and in the capacity to maintain the struggle for subsistence. This difference justifies a difference in legislation, and upholds that which is designed to compensate for some of the burdens which rest upon her.

We have not referred in this discussion to the denial of the elective franchise in the state of Oregon, for while that may disclose a lack of political equality in all things with her brother, that is not of itself decisive. The reason runs deeper, and rests in the inherent difference between the two sexes, and in the different functions in life which they perform.

For these reasons, and without questioning in any respect the decision in *Lochner v. New York,* we are of the opinion that it cannot be adjudged that the act in question is in conflict with the Federal Constitution, so far as it respects the work of a female in a laundry, and the judgment of the Supreme Court of Oregon is affirmed.

A similar fact-based argument convinced the Court, a decade later in *Bunting v. Oregon*, to uphold a law setting maximum hours for male employees in manufacturing plants.[59] Although *Lochner* itself was overruled by the *Bunting* decision, the *Lochner* legacy soon reasserted itself. The Court thus struck down federal and state law establishing minimum wages[60] and state rate and price regulation.[61] For the first few decades of the twentieth century, it consistently blunted organized labor's achievements through the political process. Toward that end, laws prohibiting discharge of employees for union activity and employment contracts conditioning employment upon refraining from union association were upheld.[62]

Constitutionally unenumerated liberties, found nonetheless to be fundamental freedoms protected by the due process clause, did not evolve without significant objec-

---

[59] Bunting v. Oregon, 243 U.S. 426 (1917).

[60] Murphy v. Sardell, 269 U.S. 530 (1925) (state minimum wage law violates Fourteenth Amendment due process guarantee); Adkins v. Children's Hospital, 261 U.S. 525 (1923) (federal minimum wage law violates Fifth Amendment due process guarantee).

[61] Williams v. Standard Oil Co., 278 U.S. 235 (1929) (gasoline price regulation); Tyson & Bros. v. Banton, 273 U.S. 418 (1927) (theater ticket price regulation),

[62] Coppage v. Kansas, 236 U.S. 1 (1915) (state labor law violated Fourteenth Amendment due process guarantee); Adair v. United States, 208 U.S. 161 (1908) (federal labor law violated Fifth Amendment due process guarantee).

tion. As noted previously, a majority of the Court in the *Slaughter-House Cases* resisted such analysis. Jurisprudential investment in fundamental rights development, as a function of the Fourteenth Amendment, prompted two significant dissenting perspectives in *Lochner v. New York*. Justice Harlan asserted among other things, that the majority had overextended the Fourteenth Amendment and itself.

Lochner v. New York
198 U.S. 45 (1905)

MR. JUSTICE HARLAN (with whom MR. JUSTICE WHITE and MR. JUSTICE DAY concurred) dissenting.

. . .

I take it to be firmly established that what is called the liberty of contract may, within certain limits, be subjected to regulations designed and calculated to promote the general welfare, or to guard the public health, the public morals, or the public safety. . . .

Granting, then, that there is a liberty of contract which cannot be violated even under the sanction of direct legislative enactment, but assuming, as according to settled law we may assume, that such liberty of contract is subject to such regulations as the state may reasonably prescribe for the common good and the well being of society, what are the conditions under which the judiciary may declare such regulations to be in excess of legislative authority and void? Upon this point there is no room for dispute; for the rule is universal that a legislative enactment, Federal or state, is never to be disregarded or held invalid unless it be, beyond question, plain and palpably in excess of legislative power. . . . If there be doubt as to the validity of the statute, that doubt must therefore be resolved in favor of its validity, and the courts must keep their hands off, leaving the legislature to meet the responsibility for unwise legislation. If the end which the legislature seeks to accomplish be one to which its power extends, and if the means employed to that end, although not the wisest or best, are yet not plainly and palpably unauthorized by law, then the court cannot interfere. In other words, when the validity of a statute is questioned, the burden of proof, so to speak, is upon those who assert it to be unconstitutional.

. . .

It is plain that this statute was enacted in order to protect the physical well-being of those who work in bakery and confectionery establishments. . . .

. . .

. . . Whether or not this be wise legislation it is not the province of the court to inquire. Under our systems of government the courts are not concerned with the wisdom or policy of legislation. So that, in determining the question of power to interfere with liberty of contract, the court may inquire whether the means devised by the state are germane to an end which may be lawfully accomplished and have a real or substantial relation to the protection of health, as involved in the daily work of the persons, male and female, engaged in bakery and confectionery establishments. But when this inquiry is entered upon I find it impossible, in view of common experience, to say that there is here no real or substantial relation between the means employed by the state and the end sought to be accomplished by its legislation. . . . Nor can I say that the statute has no appropriate or direct connection with that protection to health which each state owes to her citizens. . . .

. . .

I do not stop to consider whether any particular view of this economic question presents the sounder theory. What the precise facts are it may be difficult to say. It is enough for the determination of this case, and it is enough for this court to know, that the question is one about which there is room for debate and for an honest difference of opinion. There are many reasons of a weighty, substantial character, based upon the experience of mankind, in support of the theory that, all things considered, more than ten hours' steady work each day, from week to week, in a bakery or confectionery establishment, may endanger the health and shorten the lives of the workmen, thereby diminishing their physical and mental capacity to serve the state and to provide for those dependent upon them.

If such reasons exist that ought to be the end of this case, for the state is not amenable to the judiciary, in respect of its legislative enactments, unless such enactments are plainly, palpably, beyond all question, inconsistent with the Constitution of the United States. We are not to presume that the state of New York has acted in bad faith. Nor can we assume that its legislature acted without due deliberation, or that it did not determine this question upon the fullest attainable information and for the common good. We cannot say that the state has acted without reason, nor ought we to proceed upon the theory that its action is a mere sham. Our duty, I submit, is to sustain the statute as not being in conflict with the Federal Constitution, for the reason—and such is an all-sufficient reason—it is not shown to be plainly and palpably inconsistent with that instrument. Let the state alone in the management of its purely domestic affairs, so long as it does not appear beyond all question that it has violated the Federal Constitution. This view necessarily results from the principle that the health and safety of the people of a state are primarily for the state to guard and protect.

I take leave to say that the New York statute, in the particulars here involved, cannot be held to be in conflict with the 14th Amendment, without enlarging the scope of the amendment far beyond its original purpose, and without bringing under the supervision of this court matters which have been supposed to belong exclusively to the legislative departments of the several states when exerting their conceded power to guard the health and safety of their citizens by such regulations as they in their wisdom deem best. . . .

For all of Harlan's rhetoric, to the effect that the wisdom of policy is beyond the judiciary's purview, his dissent included a scouring of the evidentiary record to demonstrate the health interest and substantiality of the relationship between regulatory means and ends. Arguably, the difference between the majority and Harlan was not over the level of proof required to establish a health interest and, disclaimers notwithstanding, the adequacy of relationship between regulatory methods and objectives. Justice Holmes refused to indulge any assessment of legislative goals or means. As he saw it, substantive due process review had emerged as a means for the Court to second-guess legislative judgment and substitute its own pet social and economic theories.

Lochner v. New York
198 U.S. 45 (1905)

MR. JUSTICE HOLMES dissenting.

I regret sincerely that I am unable to agree with the judgment in this case, and that I think it my duty to express my dissent.

This case is decided upon an economic theory which a large part of the country does not entertain. If it were a question whether I agreed with that theory, I should desire to study it further and long before making up my mind. But I do not conceive that to be my duty, because I strongly believe that my agreement or disagreement has nothing to do with the right of a majority to embody their opinions in law. It is settled by various decision of this court that state constitutions and state laws may regulate life in many ways which we as legislators might think as injudicious or if you like as tyrannical as this, and which equally with this interfere with the liberty to contract. Sunday laws and usury laws are ancient examples. A more modern one is the prohibition of lotteries. The liberty of the citizen to do as he likes so long as he does not interfere with the liberty of others to do the same, which has been a shibboleth for some well-known writers, is interfered with by school laws, by the Post Office, by every state or municipal institution which takes his money for purposes thought desirable, whether he likes it or not. The Fourteenth Amendment does not enact Mr. Herbert Spencer's Social Statics. . . .

As the *Lochner* era progressed, Harlan and Holmes diverged in their positions. In *Adair v. United States*, Harlan authored a majority opinion referenced to the contractual liberty principles of *Lochner* in upholding an unlimited right of employers to discharge employees.[63] Over the nearly three decades he served on the Court after *Lochner*, Holmes consistently and vigorously challenged the logic of and authority for trading

---

[63] Adair v. United States, 208 U.S. 161 (1908).

in substantive due process review. As he put it in *Truax v. Carrigan*, nearly two decades after *Lochner*, "[t]here is nothing I more deprecate than the use of the Fourteenth Amendment beyond the absolute compulsion of its words to prevent the making of social experiments that an important part of the community desires."[64] Shortly before stepping down from the Court, Holmes reiterated his disdain for interpreting the due process guarantee as a restriction on legislative power.

---

[64] Truax v. Corrigan, 257 U.S. 312, 344 (1921).

Baldwin v. Missouri
281 U.S. 586 (1930)

HOLMES, J., dissenting.

I have not yet adequately expressed the more than anxiety that I feel at the ever increasing scope given to the Fourteenth Amendment in cutting down what I believe to be the constitutional rights of the States. As the decisions now stand, I see hardly any limit but the sky to the invalidating of those rights if they happen to strike a majority of this Court as for any reason undesirable. I cannot believe that the Amendment was intended to give us *carte blanche* to embody our economic or moral beliefs in its prohibitions. Yet I can think of no narrower reason that seems to me to justify the present and the earlier decisions to which I have referred. Of course the words "due process of law," if taken in their literal meaning, have no application to this case; and while it is too late to deny that they have been given a much more extended and artificial signification, still we ought to remember the great caution shown by the Constitution in limiting the power of the States, and should be slow to construe the clause in the Fourteenth Amendment as committing to the Court, with no guide but the Court's own discretion, the validity of whatever laws the States may pass.

The Great Depression of the 1930s spurred new initiatives for official management of the economy that conflicted with Fourteenth Amendment precepts of marketplace liberty. At the federal level, laws regulating industry, mining, labor and prices were defeasible on grounds they exceeded Congress' power to regulate interstate commerce and violated the due process clause of the Fifth Amendment.[65] State laws were subject to challenge on grounds they exceeded the police power or were unreasonable.

Notwithstanding Holmes' resignation from the Court in 1932, the long-term influence of his arguments began to manifest itself a couple of years later when a closely divided Court upheld state milk price controls against a due process challenge.[66]

---

[65] Commerce Clause analysis is discussed in Chapter 3.
[66] Nebbia v. New York, 291 U.S. 502 (1934).

Nebbia v. New York
291 U.S. 502 (1934)

MR. JUSTICE ROBERTS delivered the opinion of the Court.

. . .

. . . The argument runs that the public control of rates or prices is per se unreasonable and unconstitutional save as applied to businesses affected with a public interest; that a business so affected is one in which property is devoted to an enterprise of a sort which the public itself might appropriately undertake, or one whose owner relies on a public grant or franchise for the right to conduct the business, or in which he is bound to serve all who apply; in short, such as is commonly called a public utility; or a business in its nature a monopoly. The milk industry, it is said, possesses none of these characteristics, and therefore, not being affected with a public interest, its charges may not be controlled by the state. . . .

It is clear that there is no closed class or category of businesses affected with a public interest and the function of courts in the application of the Fifth and Fourteenth Amendments is to determine in each case whether circumstances vindicate the challenged regulation as a reasonable exertion of governmental authority or condemn it as arbitrary or discriminatory. . . . The phrase "affected with a public interest" can in the nature of things, mean no more than that an industry, for adequate reason, is subject to control for the public good. In several of the decisions of this court wherein the expressions "affected with a public interest," and "clothed with a public use," have been brought forward as the criteria of the validity of price control, it has been admitted that they are not susceptible of definition and form an unsatisfactory test of the constitutionality of legislation directed at business practices or prices. These decisions must rest, finally, upon the basis that the requirements of due process were not met because the laws were found arbitrary, in their operation and effect. But there can be no doubt that upon proper occasion and by appropriate measures the state may regulate a business in any of its aspects, including the prices to be charged for the products or commodities it sells.

So far as the requirement of due process is concerned, and in the absence of other constitutional restriction, a state is free to adopt whatever economic policy may reasonably be deemed to promote public welfare, and to enforce that policy by legislation adopted to its purpose. The courts are without authority either to declare such policy, or, when it is declared by the legislature, to override it. If the laws passed are seen to have a reasonable relation to a proper legislative purpose, and are neither arbitrary nor discriminatory, the requirements of due process are satisfied, and judicial determination to that effect renders a court functus officio. . . . With the wisdom of the policy adopted, with the adequacy or practicability of the law enacted to forward it, the courts are both incompetent and unauthorized to deal. The course of decision in this court exhibits a firm adherence to these principles. Times without number we have said that the Legislature is primarily the judge of the necessity of such an enactment, that every possible presumption is in favor of its validity, and that though the court may hold views inconsistent with the wisdom of the law, it may not be annulled unless palpably in excess of legislative power. . . . Price control, like any other form of regulation, is unconstitutional only if arbitrary, discriminatory, or demonstrably irrelevant to the policy the Legislature is free to adopt, and hence an unnecessary and unwarranted interference with individual liberty.

The *Nebbia* decision was significant not only because it employed a relaxed standard of review but because it also repudiated one of the jurisprudential building blocks in the late nineteenth century evolution toward substantive due process review. It thus rejected as artificial the distinction between industries clothed and those not affected with a public interest—a differentiation that in *Munn v. Illinois* had represented significant progress in the development of due process analysis. Although hinting at what was to come, the *Nebbia* decision did not represent a final break with independent review of economic regulation. Two years later, in *Morehead v. New York ex rel. Tipaldo,* the Court struck down a state minimum wage law on grounds it invaded contractual liberty.[67]

c. Economic Liberty Since 1937

In *Lochner v. New York,* both the majority and Holmes had advocated a standard of review referenced to notions of "reasonableness." The term, however, had different implications for each. For the majority, it became a basis for close review. For Holmes, "reasonableness" was a code word for deference. A year after *Morehead,* evolution toward more deferential standards of review became more certain.

---

[67] Morehead v. New York ex rel. Tipaldo, 298 U.S. 587 (1936)

West Coast Hotel Co. v. Parrish
300 U.S. 379 (1937)

MR. CHIEF JUSTICE HUGHES delivered the opinion of the Court.

This case presents the question of the constitutional validity of the minimum wage law of the State of Washington.

The Act, entitled "Minimum Wages for Women," authorizes the fixing of minimum wages for women and minors. . . .

. . .

The appellant conducts a hotel. The appellee Elsie Parrish was employed as a chambermaid and (with her husband) brought this suit to recover the difference between the wages paid her and the minimum wage fixed pursuant to the state law. The minimum wage was $14.50 per week of 48 hours. The appellant challenged the act as repugnant to the due process cause of the Fourteenth Amendment of the Constitution of the United States. The Supreme Court of the State, reversing the trial court, sustained the statute and directed judgment for the plaintiffs. . . .

The appellant relies upon the decision of this Court in *Adkins v. Children's Hospital,* . . . which held invalid the District of Columbia Minimum Wage Act, which was attacked under the due process clause of the Fifth Amendment. . . .

. . .

The principle which must control our decision is not in doubt. The constitutional provision invoked is the due process clause of the Fourteenth Amendment governing the States, as the due process clause invoked in the *Adkins* case governed Congress. In each case the violation alleged by those attacking minimum wage regulation for women is deprivation of freedom of contract. What is this freedom? The Constitution does not speak of freedom of contract. It speaks of liberty and prohibits the deprivation of liberty without due process of law. In prohibiting that deprivation the Constitution does not recognize an absolute and uncontrollable liberty. Liberty in each of its phases has its history and connotation. But the liberty safeguarded is liberty in a social organization which requires the protection of law against the evils which menace the health, safety, morals and welfare of the people. Liberty under the Constitution is thus necessarily subject to the restraints of due process, and regulation which is reasonable in relation to its subject, and is adopted in the interests of the community is due process.

This essential limitation of liberty in general governs freedom of contract in particular. More than twenty-five years ago we set forth the applicable principle in these words, after referring to the cases where the liberty guaranteed by the Fourteenth Amendment had been broadly described:

"But it was recognized in the cases cited, as in many others, that freedom of contract is a qualified and not an absolute right. There is no absolute freedom to do as one wills or to contract as one chooses. The guaranty of liberty does not withdraw from legislative supervision that wide department of activity which consists of the making of contracts, or deny to government the power to provide restrictive safeguards. Liberty implies the absence of arbitrary restraint, not immunity from reasonable regulation and prohibitions imposed in the interests of the community."

. . .

The point that has been strongly stressed that adult employees should be deemed competent to make their own contracts was decisively met nearly forty years ago in *Holden v. Hardy, supra,* where we pointed out the inequality in the footing of the parties. We said ". . . their interests are, to a certain extent conflicting. The former naturally desire to obtain as much labor as possible from their employees, while the latter are often induced by the fear of discharge to conform to regulations which their judgment, fairly exercised, would pronounce to be detrimental to their health or strength. In other words, the proprietors lay down the rules and the labors are practically constrained to obey them. In such cases self interest is often an unsafe guide, and the legislature may properly interpose its authority."

And we added that the fact "that both parties are of full age to contract does not necessarily deprive the State of the power to interfere where the parties do not stand upon an equality, or where the public health demands that one party to the contract shall be protected against himself." "The State still retains an interest in his welfare, however reckless he may be. The whole is no greater than the sum of all the parts, and when the individual health, safety and welfare are sacrificed or neglected, the State must suffer."

It is manifest that this established principle is peculiarly applicable in relation to the employment of women in whose protection the State has a special interest. That phase of the subject received elaborate consideration in *Muller v. Oregon,* where the constitutional authority of the State to limit the working hours of women was sustained. . . .

. . .

The minimum wage to be paid under the Washington statute is fixed after full consideration by representatives of employers, employees and the public. It may be assumed that the minimum wage is fixed in consideration of the services that are performed in the particular occupations under normal conditions. Provision is made for special licenses at less wages in the case of women who are incapable of full service. The statement of Mr. Justice Holmes in the *Adkins* case is pertinent: "This statute does not compel anybody to pay anything. It simply forbids employment at rates below those fixed as the minimum requirement of health and right living. It is safe to assume that women will not be employed at even the lowest wages allowed unless they earn them, or unless the employers' business can sustain the burden. In short the law in its character and operation is like hundreds of so-called police laws that have been upheld." And Chief Justice Taft forcibly pointed out the consideration which is basic in a statute of this character: "Legislatures which adopt a requirement of maximum hours or minimum wages may be presumed to believe that when sweating employers are prevented from paying unduly low wages by positive law they will continue their business, abating that part of their profits, which were wrung from the necessities of their employees, and will concede the better terms required by the law; and that while in individual cases hardship may result, the restriction will enure to the benefit of the general class of employees in whose interest the law is passed and so to that of the community at large."

We think that the views thus expressed are sound and that the decision in the *Adkins* case was a departure from the true application of the principles governing the regulation by the State of the relation of employer and employed. . . .

. . . What can be closer to the public interest than the health of women and their protection from unscrupulous and overreaching employers? And if the protection of women is a legitimate end of the exercise of state power, how can it be said that the requirement of the payment of a minimum wage fairly fixed in order to meet the very necessities of existence is not an admissible means to that end? The legislature of the State was clearly entitled to consider the situation of women in employment, the fact that they are in the class receiving the least pay, that their bargaining power is relatively weak, and that they are the ready victims of those who would take advantage of their necessitous circumstances. The legislature was entitled to adopt measures to reduce the evils of the "sweating system," the exploiting of workers at wages so low as to be insuffi-

cient to meet the bare cost of living, thus making their very helplessness the occasion of a most injurious competition. The legislature had the right to consider that its minimum wage requirements would be an important aid in carrying out its policy of protection. The adoption of similar requirements by many States evidences a deep-seated conviction both as to the presence of the evil and as to the means adapted to check it. Legislative response to that conviction cannot be regarded as arbitrary or capricious, and that is all we have to decide. Even if the wisdom of the policy be regarded as debatable and its effects uncertain, still the legislature is entitled to its judgment.

There is an additional and compelling consideration which recent economic experience has brought into a strong light. The exploitation of a class of workers who are in an unequal position with respect to bargaining power and are thus relatively defenseless against the denial of a living wage is not only detrimental to their health and well being but casts a direct burden for their support upon the community. What these workers lose in wages the taxpayers are called upon to pay. The bare cost of living must be met. We may take judicial notice of the unparalled demands for relief which arose during the recent period of depression and still continue to an alarming extent despite the degree of economic recovery which has been achieved. It is unnecessary to cite official statistics to establish what is of common knowledge through the length and breadth of the land. While in the instant case no factual brief has been presented, there is no reason to doubt that the State of Washington has encountered the same social problem that is present elsewhere. The community is not bound to provide what is in effect a subsidy for unconscionable employers. The community may direct its lawmaking power to correct the abuse which springs from their selfish disregard of the public interest. The argument that the legislation in question constitutes all arbitrary discrimination, because it does not extend to men, is unavailing. This Court has frequently held that the legislative authority, acting within its proper field, is not bound to extend its regulation to all cases which it might possibly reach. The legislature "is free to recognize degrees of harm and it may confine its restrictions to those classes of cases where the need is deemed to be clearest." If "the law presumably hits the evil where it is most felt, it is not to be overthrown because there are other instances to which it might have been applied." . . .

Our conclusion is that the case of *Adkins* v. *Children's Hospital,* supra, should be, and it is, overruled. The judgment of the Supreme Court of the State of Washington is affirmed.

The *Parrish* case represented a virtual last stand for economic rights under the Fourteenth Amendment. Four dissenting justices thus made a final pitch for economic rights doctrine as a function of substantive due process review.

West Coast Hotel Co. v. Parrish
300 U.S. 379 (1937)

MR. JUSTICE SUTHERLAND, dissenting:

MR. JUSTICE VAN DEVANTER, MR. JUSTICE McREYNOLDS, MR. JUSTICE BUTLER and I think the judgment of the court below should be reversed.

. . .

Under our form of government, where the written Constitution, by its own terms, is the supreme law, some agency, of necessity, must have the power to say the final word as to the validity of a statute assailed as unconstitutional. The Constitution makes it clear that the power has been intrusted to this court when the question arises in a controversy within its jurisdiction; and so long as the power remains there, its exercise cannot be avoided without betrayal of the trust.

It has been pointed out many times, as in the *Adkins* case, that this judicial duty is one of gravity and delicacy; and that rational doubts must be resolved in favor of the constitutionality of the statute. But whose doubts, and by whom resolved? Undoubtedly it is the duty of a member of the court, in the process of reaching a right conclusion, to give weight to the opposing views of his associates; but in the end, the question which he must answer is not whether such views seem sound to those who entertain them, but whether they convince him that the statute is constitutional or engender in his mind a rational doubt upon that issue. The oath which he takes as a judge is not a composite oath, but an individual one. And in passing upon the validity of a statute, he discharges a duty imposed upon *him* which cannot be consummated justly by all automatic acceptance of the views of others which have neither convinced, nor created a reasonable doubt in, his mind. If upon a question so important he thus surrender his deliberate judgment, he stands forsworn. He cannot subordinate his convictions to that extent and keep faith with his oath or retain his judicial and moral independence.

The suggestion that the only check upon the exercise of the judicial power, when properly invoked, to declare a constitutional right superior to an unconstitutional statute is the judges' own faculty of self-restraint, is both ill considered and mischievous. Self-restraint belongs in the domain of will and not of judgment. The check upon the judge is that imposed by his oath of office, by the Constitution and by his own conscientious and informed convictions; and since he has the duty to make up his own mind and adjudge accordingly, it is hard to see how there could be any other restraint. This court acts as a unit. It cannot act in any other way; and the majority (whether a bare majority or a majority of all but one of its members), therefore, establishes the controlling rule as the decision of the court, binding, so long as it remains unchanged, equally upon those who disagree and upon those who subscribe to it. Otherwise, orderly administration of justice would cease. But it is the right of those in the minority to disagree, and sometimes, in matters of grave importance, their imperative duty to voice their disagreement at such length as the occasion demands—always, of course, in terms which, however forceful, do not offend the proprieties or impugn the good faith of those who think otherwise.

It is urged that the question involved should now receive fresh consideration, among other reasons, because of "the economic conditions which have supervened"; but the meaning of the Constitution does not change with the ebb and flow of economic events. We frequently are told in more general words that the Constitution must be construed in the light of the present. If by that it is meant that the Constitution is made up of living words that apply to *every* new condition which they include, the statement is quite true. But to say, if that be intended, that the words of the Constitution mean today what they did not mean when written—that is, that they do not apply to a situation now to which they would have applied then—is to rob that instrument of the essential element which continues it in force as the people have made it until they, and not their official agents, have made it otherwise.

. . .

The judicial function is that of interpretation; it does not include the power of amendment under the guise of interpretation. To miss the point of difference between the two is to miss all that the phrase "supreme law of the land" stands for and to convert what was intended as inescapable and enduring mandates into mere moral reflections.

If the Constitution, intelligently and reasonably construed in the light of these principles, stands in the way of desirable legislation, the blame must rest upon that instrument, and not upon the court for enforcing it according to its terms. The remedy in that situation—and the only true remedy—is to amend the Constitution. Judge Cooley, in the first volume of his Constitutional Limitations, very clearly pointed out that much of the benefit expected from written constitutions would be lost if their provisions were to be bent to circumstances or modified by public opinion. He pointed out that the common law, unlike a constitution, was subject to modification by public sentiment and action which the courts might recognize; but that "a court or legislature which should allow a change in public sentiment to influence it in giving to a written constitution a construction not warranted by the intention of its founders, would be justly chargeable with reckless disregard of official oath and public duty; and if its course could become a precedent, these instruments would be of little avail. . . . What a court is to do, therefore, is *to declare the law as* written, leaving it to the people themselves to make such changes as new circumstances may require. The meaning of the constitution is fixed when it is adopted, and it is not different at any subsequent time when a court has occasion to pass upon it."

The *Adkins* case dealt with an act of Congress which had passed the scrutiny both of the legislative and executive branches of the government. We recognized that thereby these departments had affirmed the validity of the statute, and properly declared that their determination must be given great weight, but we then concluded, after thorough consideration, that their view could not be sustained. We think it not inappropriate now to add a word on that subject before coming to the question immediately under review.

The people by their Constitution created three separate, distinct, independent, and coequal departments of government. The governmental structure rests, and was intended to rest, not upon any one or upon any two, but upon all three of these fundamental pillars. It seems unnecessary to repeat, what so often has been said, that the powers of these departments are different and are to be exercised independently. The differences clearly and definitely appear in the Constitution. Each of the departments is an agent of its creator for what it does, and not to another agent. Each is answerable to its creator for what it does, and not to another agent. The view, therefore, of the Executive and of Congress that an act is consti-

tutional is persuasive in a high degree; but it is not controlling.

Coming, then, to a consideration of the Washington statute, it first is to be observed that it is in every substantial respect identical with the statute involved in the *Adkins* case. Such vices as existed in the latter are present in the former. And if the *Adkins* case was properly decided, as we who join in this opinion think it was, it necessarily follows that the Washington statute is invalid.

In support of minimum-wage legislation it has been urged, on the one hand, that great benefits will result in favor of underpaid labor, and, on the other hand, that the danger of such legislation is that the minimum will tend to become the maximum and thus bring down the earnings of the more efficient toward the level of the less-efficient employees. But with these speculations we have nothing to do. We are concerned only with the question of constitutionality.

That the clause of the Fourteenth Amendment which forbids a state to deprive any person of life, liberty or property without due process of law includes freedom of contract is so well settled as to be no longer open to question. Nor reasonably can it be disputed that contracts of employment of labor are included in the rule.

. . .

Neither the statute involved in the *Adkins* case nor the Washington statute, so far as it is involved here, has the slightest relation to the capacity or earning power of the employee, to the number of hours which constitute the day's work, the character of the place where the work is to be done, or the circumstances or surroundings of the employment. The sole basis upon which the question of validity rests is the assumption that the employee is entitled to receive a sum of money sufficient to provide a living for her, keep her in health and preserve her morale. And as we pointed out at some length in that case . . . the question thus presented for the determination of the board can not be solved by any general formula prescribed by a statutory bureau, since it is not a composite but an individual question to be answered for each individual, considered by herself. What we said further in that case . . . is equally applicable here:

> "The law takes account of the necessities of only one party to the contract. It ignores the necessities of the employer by compelling him to pay not less than a certain sum, not only whether the employee is capable of earning it, but irrespective of the ability of his business to sustain the burden, generously leaving him, of course, the privilege of abandoning his business is

all alternative for going on at a loss. Within the limits of the minimum sum, he is precluded, under penalty of fine and imprisonment, from adjusting compensation to the differing merits of his employees. It compels him to pay at least the sum fixed in any event, because the employee needs it, but requires no service of equivalent value from the employee. It therefore undertakes to solve but one-half of the problem. . . .

. . . In principle, there can be no difference between the case of selling labor and the case of selling goods. If one goes to the butcher, the baker or grocer to buy food, he is morally entitled to obtain the worth of his money but he is not entitled to more. If what he gets is worth what he pays he is not justified in demanding more simply because he needs more; and the shopkeeper, having dealt fairly and honestly in that transaction, is not concerned in any peculiar sense with the question of his customer's necessities. Should a statute undertake to vest in a commission power to determine the quantity of food necessary for individual support and require the shopkeeper, if he sell to the individual at all, to furnish that quantity at not more than a fixed maximum, it would undoubtedly fall below the constitutional test. The fallacy of any argument in support of the validity of such a statute would be quickly exposed. The argument in support of that now being considered is equally fallacious, though the weakness of it may not be so plain. A statute requiring all employers, to pay in money, to pay at prescribed and regular intervals, to pay the value of the services rendered, even to pay with fair relation to the extent of the benefit obtained from the service, would be understandable. But a statute which prescribes payment without regard to any of these things and solely with relation to circumstances apart from the contract of employment, the business affected by it and the work done under it, is so clearly the product of a naked, arbitrary exercise of power that it cannot be allowed to stand under the Constitution of the United States."

. . .

The Washington statute, like the one for the District of Columbia, fixes minimum wages for adult women. Adult men and their employers are left free to bargain as they please; and it is a significant and an important fact that all state statutes to which our attention has been called are of like character. The common-law rules restricting the power of women to make contracts have, under our systems long since practically disappeared. Women today stand upon a legal and political equality with men. There is no longer any reason why they should be put in different classes in respect of their legal right to make contracts; nor should they be denied, in effect, the right to compete with men for work paying lower wages which men may be willing to accept. And it is an arbitrary exercise of the legislative power to do so. . . .

. . .

An appeal to the principle that the legislature is free to recognize degrees of harm and confine its restrictions accordingly, is but to beg the question, which is—since the contractual rights of men and women are the same, does the legislation here involved, by restricting only the rights of women to make contracts as to wages, create an arbitrary discrimination? We think it does. Difference of sex affords no reasonable ground for making a restriction applicable to the wage contracts of all working women from which like contracts of all working men are left free. Certainly a suggestion that the bargaining ability of the average woman is not equal to that of the average man would lack substance. The ability to make a fair bargain, as everyone knows, does not depend upon sex.

. . .

Finally, it may be said that a statute absolutely fixing wages in the various industries at definite sums and forbidding employers and employees from contracting for any other than those designated, would probably not be thought to be constitutional. It is hard to see why the power to fix minimum wages does not connote a like power in respect of maximum wages. And yet, if both powers be exercised in such a way that the minimum and the maximum so nearly approach each other as to become substantially the same, the right to make any contract in respect of wages will have been completely abrogated.

. . .

From 1937 to 1940, death or resignation of personnel resulted in the turnover of seven seats on the Supreme Court. New appointees were distinguished in significant part by their commitment to deference toward legislature judgment on economic policy. The case for economic rights, as a function of substantive due process review, soon was depleted. For more than half a century now, the Court persistently has refused to account for economic freedom through the due process clause. Rather, the Court has evinced an interest in distancing itself from any meaningful scrutiny of economic policy and discrediting that era of review. A year after its *Parrish* decision, the Court more formally disassociated itself from economic rights analysis as a function of due process review.

United States v. Carolene Products Co.
304 U.S. 144 (1938)

MR. JUSTICE STONE delivered the opinion of the Court.

The question for decision is whether the "Filled Milk Act" of Congress . . . which prohibits the shipment in interstate commerce of skimmed milk compounded with any fat or oil other than milk fat, so as to resemble milk or cream; transcends the power of Congress to regulate interstate commerce or infringes the Fifth Amendment.

. . .

. . . We may assume for present purposes that no pronouncement of a legislature can forestall attack upon the constitutionality of the prohibition which it enacts by applying opprobrious epithets to the prohibited act, and that a statute would deny due process which precluded the disproof in judicial proceedings of all facts which would show or tend to show that a statute depriving the suitor of life, liberty or property had a rational basis.

But such we think is not the purpose or construction of the statutory characterization of filled milk as injurious to health and as a fraud upon the public. There is no need to consider it here as more than a declaration of the legislative findings deemed to support and justify the action taken as a constitutional exertion of the legislative power, aiding informed judicial review, as do the reports of legislative committees, by revealing the rationale of the legislation. Even in the absence of such aids the existence of facts supporting the legislative judgment is to be presumed, for regulatory legislation affecting ordinary commercial transactions is not to be pronounced unconstitutional unless in the light of the facts made known or generally assumed it is of such a character as to preclude the assumption that it rests upon some rational basis within the knowledge and experience of the legislators. . . .

. . .

There may be narrower scope for operation of the presumption of constitutionality when legislation appears on its face to be within a specific prohibition of the Constitution, such as those of the first ten amendments, which are deemed equally specific when held to be embraced within the Fourteenth.

It is unnecessary to consider whether legislation which restricts those political processes which can ordinarily be expected to bring about repeal of undesirable legislation, is to be subjected to more exacting judicial scrutiny under the general prohibitions of the Fourteenth Amendment than are most other types of legislation. . . .

Nor need we inquire whether similar considerations enter into the review of statutes directed at particular religious, or national, or racial minorities, whether prejudice against discrete and insular minorities may be a special condition, which tends seriously to curtail the operation of those political processes ordinarily to be relied upon to protect minorities, and which may call for a correspondingly more searching judicial inquiry.

A similarly deferential inclination was manifested two years later when the Court amplified its disinterest in the wisdom of legislative policy.

Olsen v. Nebraska
313 U.S. 236 (1941)

MR. JUSTICE DOUGLAS delivered the opinion of the Court.

. . .

. . . [T]he Supreme Court of Nebraska held . . . that a statute of that state fixing the maximum compensation which a private employment agency might collect from an applicant for employment was unconstitutional under the due process clause of the Fourteenth Amendment. . . .

We disagree with the Supreme Court of Nebraska. The statutory provisions in question do not violate the due process clause of the Fourteenth Amendment.

. . .

[R]espondents maintain that the statute here in question is invalid for other reasons. They insist that special circumstances must be shown to support the validity of such drastic legislation as price-fixing, that the executive, technical and professional workers which respondents serve have not been shown to be in need of special protection from exploitation, that legislative limitation of maximum fees for employment agencies is certain to react unfavorably upon those members of the community for whom it is most difficult to obtain jobs, that the increasing competition of public employment agencies and of charitable, labor union and employer association employment agencies have curbed excessive fees by private agencies, and that there is nothing in this record to overcome the presumption as to the result of the operation of such competitive, economic forces. And in the latter connection respondents urge that, since no circumstances are shown which curb competition between the private agencies and the other types of agencies, there are no conditions which the legislature might reasonable believe would redound to the public injury unless corrected by such legislation.

We are not concerned, however, with the wisdom, need, or appropriateness of the legislation. Differences of opinion on that score suggest a choice which "should be left where . . . it was left by the Constitution—to the States and to Congress." There is no necessity for the state to demonstrate before us that evils persist despite the competition which attends the bargaining in this field. In final analysis, the only constitutional prohibitions or restraints which respondents have suggested for the invalidation of this legislation are those notions of public policy embedded in earlier decisions of this Court but which, as Mr. Justice Holmes long admonished, should not be read into the Constitution. Since they do not find expression in the Constitution, we cannot give them continuing vitality as standards by which the constitutionality of the economic and social programs of the states is to be determined.

. . .

Among the more poignant repudiations of the *Lochner* era was *Ferguson v. Skrupa*, decided 25 years after *Carolene Products*. In his *Lochner* dissent, Justice Holmes had stressed that the Fourteenth Amendment did not enshrine "Mr. Herbert Spencer's Social Statics theories."[68] Justice Black, writing for the Court in *Ferguson*, observed that whether "the legislature takes for its textbook Adam Smith, Herbert Spencer, Lord Keynes or some other is no concern of ours."[69]

Nearly a century later, the *Lochner* decision remains a common reference point for those concerned with an anti-democratic judicial function. The Court itself, even as it resurrected substantive due process to establish and account for a right of privacy, attempted to distinguish such jurisprudence from *Lochner* and its progeny.[70] At least to the extent general social and economic policy is at stake, the Court continues to distance itself from its Lochnerist past. Upholding a law requiring pharmacists to transmit the identity of all persons obtaining prescription drugs, the Court in *Whalen v. Roe* stressed its disinterest in independently assessing the enactment's wisdom.

[68] Lochner v. New York, 198 U.S. at 75 (Holmes, J., dissenting).

[69] Ferguson v. Skrupa, 372 U.S. 726, 732 (1963).

[70] *E.g.*, Griswold v. Connecticut, 381 U.S. 479, 482 (1965) ("some arguments suggest that *Lochner* should be our guide. . . [b]ut we decline that invitation").

Whalen v. Roe
429 U.S. 589 (1977)

MR. JUSTICE STEVENS delivered the opinion of the Court.

The constitutional question presented is whether the State of New York may record, in a centralized computer file, the names and addresses of all persons who have obtained, pursuant to a doctor's prescription, certain drugs for which there is both a lawful and unlawful market.

. . .

The District Court found that the State had been unable to demonstrate the necessity for the patient-identification requirement on the basis of its experience during the first 20 months of administration of the new statute. There was a time when that alone would have provided a basis for invalidating the statute. *Lochner v. New York* involved legislation making it a crime for a baker to permit his employees to work more than 60 hours in a week. In an opinion no longer regarded as authoritative, the Court held the statute unconstitutional as "an unreasonable, unnecessary interference with the right of the individual to his personal liberty. . . ."

The holding in *Lochner* has been implicitly rejected many times. State legislation which has some effect on individual liberty or privacy may not be held unconstitutional simply because a court finds it unnecessary, in whole or in part. For we have frequently recognized that individual States have broad latitude in experimenting with possible solutions to problems of vital local concern.

The New York statute challenged in this case represents a considered attempt to deal with such a problem. It is manifestly the product of an orderly and rational legislative decision. It was recommended by a specially appointed commission which held extensive hearings on the proposed legislation, and drew on experience with similar programs in other States. There surely was nothing unreasonable in the assumption that the patient-identification requirement might aid in the enforcement of laws designed to minimize the use of dangerous drugs. . . .

DEL: The extreme deference toward legislative judgment on social and economic policy over the past half century may represent an exercise in overreaction and deceit. Reality is that for all of its disclamation of *Lochnerism*, the Court selectively has continued to utilize substantive due process to undo social legislation. Admittedly the reference point has changed from economic liberty to privacy rights, but the analytical process is not entirely different. Nor is linkage to the *Lochner* era itself unbroken in case law itself. Modern notions of constitutional privacy are rooted, as the Court itself has acknowledged, in some of the expansive liberty notions developed in pre-*Carolene Products* decisions such as *Meyer v. Nebraska* and *Pierce v. Society of Sisters*.

A more accurate depiction of what the judiciary has learned from the *Lochner* era was provided by Justice Brennan, who observed "that the constitution . . . can actively intrude into . . . economic and policy matters only if . . . prepared to bear enormous institutional and social costs."[71] Reality is, given the Court's development of privacy rights to defeat various social policies, that wholesale abandonment of substantive due process has been confined to economic legislation. In the equal protection context, where standards of review over the past several decades largely have tracked those of due process, Justice Powell warned that significant interests may be compromised if legislative judgment is subject to no real review.[72] Although not arguing for a reversion to the intense scrutiny of methods and goals characteristic of the *Lochner* era, Justice Stevens has urged a level of review that at least is higher than "tautological recognition of the fact that [the legislature] did what it intended to do."[73]

---

[71] United States Trust Co. v. New Jersey, 431 U.S. 1, 62 (1978) (Brennan, J., dissenting).

[72] Schweiker v. Wilson, 450 U.S. 221, 247 (1981) (Powell, J., dissenting).

[73] United States Railroad Retirement Board v. Fritz, 449 U.S. 166, 180 (1980) (Stevens, J., concurring).

Arguments that the Court has overreacted to the *Lochner* experience might be referenced to case law of the *Carolene Products* era. In *Day-Brite Lighting v. Missouri*, for instance, the Court reviewed a state law requiring employers to give employees half the day off with pay on election day. The law was justified on grounds that it ensured workers an opportunity to vote. A meaningful level of review would have inquired into whether the regulatory means actually achieved their ends and whether less restrictive methods of attaining legislative goals were available. Even if the half day off did facilitate the law's purpose, it is likely that provisions for voting hours extending beyond the workday would have been adequate to achieve the state's aim without compromising the employer's economic interest. Even if a rational basis test is understood as requiring only a conceivable or arguable reason for enactment, deference under such circumstances seems indistinguishable from abdication. As Justice Jackson noted in dissent

> The constitutional issue in this case, if not very vital in its present application, surely is a debatable one. Two courts of last resort, the only ones to consider similar legislation have held it unconstitutional. Only unreviewed decisions of intermediate courts can be cited in support of the Court's holding.
>
> Appellant employed one Grotemeyer, under a Union contract, on an hourly basis at $1.60 per hour for each hour worked. He demanded a four-hour leave of absence, with full pay, on election day to do campaigning and to get out the vote. It is stipulated that his residence was 200 feet from the polling place and that it actually took him about five minutes to vote. Appellant closed the day's work for all employees one and one-half hours earlier than usual, which gave them the statutory four hours before the polls closed. For failure to pay something less than $3 for this hour and a half which Grotemeyer did not work and for which his contract did not provide that he should be paid, the employer is convicted of crime under the statute set forth in the Court's opinion.
>
> To sustain this statute by resort to the analogy of minimum wage laws seems so farfetched and unconvincing as to demonstrate its weakness rather than strength. Because a State may require payment of a minimum wage for hours that are worked it does not follow that it may compel payment for time that is not worked. To overlook a distinction so fundamental is to confuse the point in issue.
>
> The Court, by speaking of the statute as though it applies only to industry, sinister and big, further obscures the real principle involved. The statute plainly requires farmers, small service enterprises, professional offices, housewives with domestic help, and all other employers, not only to allow their employees time to vote, but to pay them for time to do so. It does not, however, require the employee to use any part of such time for that purpose. Such legislation stands in a class by itself and should not be uncritically commended as a mere regulation of practices in the business-labor field."
>
> Obtaining a full and free expression from all qualified voters at the polls is so fundamental to a successful representative government that a State rightly concerns itself with the removal of every obstruction to the right and opportunity to vote freely. Courts should go far to sustain legislation designed to relieve employees from obligations to private employers which would stand in the way of their duty as citizens.
>
> But there must be some limit to the power to shift the whole voting burden from the voter to someone else who happens to stand in some economic relationship to him. Getting out the vote is not the business of employers; indeed, I have regarded it as a political abuse when employers concerned themselves with their employees' voting. It is either the voter's own business or the State's business. I do not question that the incentive which this statute offers will help swell the vote; to

require that employees be paid time-and-a-half would swell it still more, and double-time would even better. But does the success of an enticement to vote justify putting its cost on some other citizen?

The discriminatory character of this statute is flagrant. It is obvious that not everybody will be for voting and the "rational basis" on which the State has ordered some be paid while others are not eludes me. If there is a need for a subsidy to get out the vote, no reason is apparent to me why it should go to one who lives 200 feet from his polling place but not to a self-employed farmer who may have to lay down his work and let his equipment idle for several hours while he travels several miles over bad roads to do his duty as a citizen. If he has a hired man, he must also lose his hand's time and his pay. Perhaps some plan will be forthcoming to pay the farmer by requiring his mortgagee to rebate some proportion of the interest on the mortgage if he will vote. It would not differ in principle. But no way occurs to me by which the doctor can charge some patient or the lawyer some client for the call he did not receive while he was voting.

. . .

It undoubtedly is the right of every union negotiating with an employer to bargain for voting without loss of pay. It is equally the right of any individual employee to make that part of his hire. I have no reason to doubt that a large number of voters already have voluntary arrangements which make their absence for voting without cost. But a constitutional philosophy which sanctions intervention by the State to fix terms of pay without work may be available tomorrow to give constitutional sanction to state-imposed terms of employment less benevolent.

Still the Court, sensitive to the lessons of its past, rejected liberty of contract overtures and reiterated that "[o]ur recent decisions make plain that we do not sit as a super-legislature to weigh the wisdom of legislation nor to decide whether the policy it expresses offends the public welfare."[74] Despite a good case for the proposition that not even an arguable basis existed for the enactment, the Court concluded that "if our recent cases mean anything, they leave debatable issues as respects business, economic and social affairs to legislative decisions."[75]

For all of its discrediting, the *Lochner* legacy is widely misunderstood. Even critics differ as to whether the judiciary's function was perverted by the Court's trading in natural law, by its selection of the wrong values to inspire fundamental rights or by its long-term resistance to social change. A not insignificant body of scholarship to this day, in fact, vigorously maintains that the *Lochner* Court's accounting for economic liberty was on the right track.[76] If constitutional emanations or penumbras truly exist, as the Court suggested in *Griswold v. Connecticut*,[77] it may be easier to infer an interest in economic liberty than one in general privacy. The Constitutional Convention was begotten by an overarching imperative of creating a more viable economic union. Liberty of contract itself has an arguable connection to constitutional text insofar as the contracts clause established a check on the exercise of state power and actually functioned as the primary restraint on economic regulation until the rise of substantive due process.

What many critics of the *Lochner* era tend to overlook is its seminal contributions to an expanded understanding of constitutional rights and liberties. It was after *Lochner* but before *Carolene Products*, for instance, that freedom of speech and of the press and

---

[74] Day-Brite Lighting v. Missouri, 342 U.S. 421, 423 (1952).
[75] *Id.*
[76] *E.g.*, RICHARD EPSTEIN, TAKINGS (1985).
[77] 381 U.S. 479, 484 (1965) ("specific guarantees in the Bill of Rights have penumbras, formed by emanations from those guarantees that help give them life and substance").

the right to counsel in criminal trials were applied to the states through a broadened understanding of what the liberty component of the Fourteenth Amendment's due process clause required.[78] To the extent that definition of the Court's function has been framed in absolute terms, so that any factoring of textually or historically unsupported values represent anti-democratic performance, the debate is etched in the relatively parochial terms of academic insularity. The *Lochner* legacy, which for many is distinguishable from *Dred Scott* before it and *Roe v. Wade* later, discloses a peril to representative governance when the judiciary resists the will of the people as expressed by their agents. Except for some doctrinal purists, however, few would be comfortable with the consequence if the Court failed to stop the political process from draconian policy such as the poorly conceived wholesale sterilizations upheld in *Buck v. Bell*.[79] For Justice Black and those convinced that "the Court has no power to add to or subtract from the procedures set forth by the Founders" for constitutional change,[80] the challenge for them is whether they would stand idly by in *Buck*-like circumstances. More adventurous methods of constitutional development must reckon with profound challenges of their own, insofar as principled stopping points must be identified for transcending text and history and decision-making may have to be sold to the political branches and public. To the extent that its marketing efforts are successful, consent of the governed may be inferred from an aftermath of ratification rather than resistance.

PAH: Our understanding of the court's contribution to constitutional development and assessment of its "threat" to democratic decision making should take account of dissent and other opportunities for judges to engage in dialogue. Two competing characterizations come to mind. Frank Michelman has argued that as the Supreme Court struggles over important social concerns in separate opinions it often sets forth questions which "correspond to a parallel set of problems troubling other normative disciplines and thus confirm law's contemporanity within a broader world of values and ideas."[81] He suggests that in the give and take of decision making the court is practicing self-government in the republican tradition, a practice which we should celebrate and not discourage by constrained deference to "political" branches. In contrast with majoritarian politics, the court's opportunity to explore, persuade, explain and examine doubts in the context of a case, giving reasons for the conclusions reached, seems consistent with the republican representative tradition and promotes freedom. Robin West, in contrast, offers a more pragmatically political image of dissents capable of responding to the failures of judicial decision making, particularly the court's refusal to take responsibility for substantive choices it makes when other alternative exist.[82] She also recognizes the dissent's ability to expose the experiences of those who are affected by the court's decision making and thereby challenge dominant ideological assumptions of society.[83]

Any intimation that the judiciary has jettisoned all constitutional means of accounting

---

[78] Powell v. Alabama, 287 U.S. 45 (1932) (right to counsel); Near v. Minnesota, 283 U.S. 697 (1931) (freedom of the press); Gitlow v. New York, 268 U.S. 652 (1925) (freedom of speech).

[79] 274 U.S. 200 (1927). Involuntary sterilization of persons that the state determined to be "mentally defective" elicited from the Court, in an opinion authored by Justice Holmes, the observation that "three generations of imbeciles is enough." Id. at 208. Despite the law's gross overreaching, it operated minus identification of a fundamental right that would have provided the basis for searching review.

[80] In re Winship, 397 U.S. 358, 377 (1970) (Black, J. dissenting).

[81] Frank Michelman, *The Supreme Court 1985 Term—Foreword: Traces of Self-government*, 100 HARV. L. REV. 13 (1986).

[82] Robin West, *The Supreme Court 1989 Term—Foreword: Taking Freedom Seriously*, 104 HARV. L. REV. 43, 105 (1990).

[83] *Id.* at 106.

for economic rights, or that it no longer utilizes them, would be misleading. Two specific provisions, the contract clause[84] and the taking clause,[85] have significant legacies as constitutional grounds for curbing state economic regulation.

---

[84] U.S. Const., art. I, § 10(1) ("[n]o State shall . . . pass any . . . Law impairing the Obligation of Contracts").

[85] *Id.*, amend. V ("private property [shall not] be taken for public use, without just compensation").

C. Accounting for Economic Rights—Beyond the Fourteenth Amendment

1. The Contract Clause

Prior to the rise of substantive due process review, the contract clause was the primary check upon state economic regulation. Seminal contract clause analysis represented another aspect of the Marshall Court's development of constitutional principles facilitating Federalist ideology. In *Dartmouth College v. Woodward*, the Court reviewed a state law revoking a private college's charter and making the institution a public entity. Acknowledging that the contracts clause probably was concerned with private agreements, Marshall nonetheless interpreted it as a check on state action.

Dartmouth College v. Woodward

17 U.S. 518 (1819)

The opinion of the court was delivered by Marshall, Ch. J.:

This is an action of trover, brought by the trustees of Dartmouth College against William H. Woodward in the State Court of New Hampshire, for the book of records, corporate seal, and other corporate property, to which the plaintiffs allege themselves to be entitled.

. . .

This is plainly a contract to which the donors, the trustees, and the crown (to whose rights and obligations New Hampshire succeeds), were the original parties. It is a contract made on a valuable consideration. It is a contract for the security and disposition of property. It is a contract, on the faith of which real and personal estate has been conveyed to the corporation. It is then a contract within the letter of the constitution . . .

It is more than possible that the preservation of rights of this description was not particularly in the view of the framers of the constitution when the clause under consideration was introduced into that instrument. It is probable that interferences of more frequent recurrence, to which the temptation was stronger, and of which the mischief was more extensive, constituted the great motive for imposing this restriction of the state legislatures. But although

a particular and a rare case may not, in itself, be of sufficient magnitude to induce a rule, yet it must be governed by the rule, when established unless some plain and strong reason for excluding it can be given. It is not enough to say that this particular case was not in the mind of the convention when the article was framed, nor of the American people when it was adopted. It is necessary to go farther, and to say that, had this particular case been suggested, the language would have been so varied, as to exclude it, or it would have been made a special exception. The case being within the words of the rule, must be within its operation likewise, unless there be something in the literal construction so obviously absurd, or mischievous, or repugnant to the general spirit of the instrument, as to justify those who expound the constitution in making it an exception.

On what safe and intelligible ground can this exception stand. There is no exception in the constitution, no sentiment delivered by its contemporaneous expounders, which would justify us in making it. In the absence of all authority of this kind, is there, in the nature and reason of the case itself, that which would sustain a construction of the constitution, not warranted by its words? Are contracts of this description of a character to excite so little interest that we must exclude them from the provisions of the constitution, as being unworthy of the attention of those who framed the instrument? Or does public policy so imperiously demand their remaining exposed to legislative alteration, as to compel us, or rather permit us to say that these words, which were introduced to give stability to contracts, and which in their plain import comprehend this contract, must yet be so construed as to exclude it?

. . .

If the insignificance of the object does not require that we should exclude contracts respecting it from the protection of the constitution, neither, as we conceive, is the policy of leaving them subject to legislative alteration so apparent as to require a forced construction of that instrument in order to effect it. These eleemosynary institutions do not fill the place, which would otherwise be occupied by government, but that which would otherwise remain vacant. They are complete acquisitions to literature. They are donations to education; donations which any government must be disposed rather to encourage than to discountenance. It requires no very critical examination of the human mind to enable us to determine that one great inducement to these gifts is the conviction felt by the giver, that the disposition he makes of them is immutable. It is probable that no man ever was, and that no man ever will be, the founder of a college, believing at the time that an act of incorporation constitutes no security for the institution; believing that it is immediately to be deemed a public institution, whose funds are to be governed and applied, not by the will of the donor, but by the will of the legislature. All such gifts are made in the pleasing, perhaps delusive hope, that the charity will flow forever in the channel which the givers have marked out for it. If every man

finds in his own bosom strong evidence of the universality of this sentiment, that there can be but little reason to the framers of our constitution who were strangers to it, and that, feeling the necessity and policy of giving permanence and security to contracts, of withdrawing them from the influence of legislative bodies, whose fluctuating policy, and repeated interferences, produced the most perplexing and injurious embarrassments, they still deemed it necessary to leave these contracts subject to those interferences. The motives for such an exception must be very powerful, to justify the construction which makes it.

. . .

The opinion of the court, after mature deliberation, is, that this is a contract, the obligation of which cannot be impaired without violating the constitution of the United States. This opinion appears to us to be equally supported by reason, and by the former decisions of this court. . . .

From the review of this charter, which has been taken, it appears that the whole power of governing the college, of appointing and removing tutors, of fixing their salaries, of directing the course of study to be pursued by the students and of filling up vacancies created in their own body, was vested in the trustees. On the part of the crown it was expressly stipulated that this corporation, thus constituted, should continue forever; and the number of trustees should forever consist of twelve, and no more. By this contract the crown was bound, and could have made no violent alteration in its essential terms, impairing its obligation.

. . .

It results from this opinion, that the acts of the legislature of New Hampshire, which are stated in the special verdict found in this cause, are repugnant to the constitution of the United States. . . .

The *Dartmouth College* decision contributed to a constitutional framework within which emerging corporations, evolving processes of production and distribution, could rely upon the charters enabling them to exist and operate. For private enterprise, the decision accounted for interests of security and stability. As due process concepts emerged as the primary basis of accounting for economic liberty during the late nineteenth and early twentieth century, the utility of the contract clause diminished. With the abandonment of economic liberty as a function of due process, the contract clause has emerged as an object of renewed interest.

Considerations taken into account for determining whether the contract clause has been violated include those referenced by Justice Blackmun in *Energy Reserves Group, Inc. v. Kansas Power & Light Co.*

"Although the language of the Contract Clause is facially absolute, its prohibition must be accommodated to the inherent police power of the State "to safeguard the vital interests of its people." . . .

The threshold inquiry is "whether the state law has, in fact, operated as a substantial impairment of a contractual relationship." The severity of the impairment is said to increase the level of scrutiny to which the legislation will be subjected. Total destruction of contractual expectations is not necessary for a finding of substantial impairment. On the other hand, state regulation that restricts a party to gains it reasonably expected from the contract does not necessarily constitute a substantial impairment. In determining the extent of the impairment, we are to consider whether the industry the complaining party has entered has been regulated in the past. The Court long ago observed: "One whose rights, such as they are, are subject to state restriction, cannot remove them from the power of the State by making a contract about them."

"If the state regulation constitutes a substantial impairment, the State, in justification, must have a significant and legitimate public purpose behind the regulation, such as the remedying broad and general social or economic problem. Furthermore, since *Blaisdell,* the Court has indicated that the public purpose need not be addressed to an emergency or temporary situation. One legitimate state interest is the elimination of unforeseen windfall profits. The requirement of a legitimate public purpose guarantees that the State is exercising its police power, rather than providing a benefit to special interests."

Once a legitimate public purpose has been identified, the next inquiry is whether the adjustment of "the rights and responsibilities of contracting parties [is based] upon reasonable conditions and [is] of a character appropriate to the public purpose justifying [the legislation's] adoption." Unless the State itself is a contracting party, "[a]s is customary in reviewing economic and social regulation, . . . courts properly defer to legislative judgment as to the necessity and reasonableness of a particular measure."[86]

Modern case law indicates that contract clause analysis is not toothless. In *Allied Structural Steel Co. v. Spannaus*, the Court identified a constitutional violation pursuant to a state's imposition of pension obligations exceeding those of the plan a company had established for its employees. The law required companies ceasing operations in the state to furnish full pensions to all employees with ten or more years of service, notwithstanding a vesting provision requiring a longer employment relationship.

---

[86] Energy Reserves Group, Inc. v. Kansas Power & Light Co., 459 U.S. 400, 410–13 (1983).

Allied Structural Steel Co. v. Spannaus
438 U.S. 234 (1978)

Mr. Justice Stewart delivered the opinion of the Court.

. . .

There can be no question of the impact of the Minnesota Private Pension Benefits Protection Act upon the company's contractual relationships with its employees. The Act substantially altered those relationships by superimposing pension obligations upon the company conspicuously beyond those that it had voluntarily agreed to undertake. But it does not inexorably follow that the Act, as applied to the company, violates the Contract Clause of the Constitution.

The language of the Contract Clause appears unambiguously absolute: "No State shall . . . pass any . . . Law impairing the Obligation of Contracts." U.S. Const. Art. I. § 10. The Clause is not, however, the draconian provision that its words might seem to imply. As the Court has recognized, "literalism in the construction of the contract clause . . . would make it destructive of the public interest by depriving the State of its prerogative of self-protection."

Although it was perhaps the strongest single constitutional check on state legislation during our early years as a Nation, the Contract Clause receded into comparative desuetude with the adoption of the Fourteenth Amendment, and particularly with the development of the large body of jurisprudence under the Due Process Clause of that Amendment in modern constitutional history. Nonetheless, the Contract Clause remains part of the Constitution. It is not a dead letter. . . .

First of all, . . . the Contract Clause does not operate to obliterate the police power of the States. "It is the settled law of this court that the interdiction of statutes impairing the obligation of contracts does not prevent the State from exercising such powers as are vested in it for the promotion of the common weal, or are necessary for the general good of the public, though contracts previously entered into between individuals may thereby be affected. This power, which in its various ramifications is known as the police power, is an exercise of the sovereign right of the Government to protect the lives, health, morals, comfort and general welfare of the people, and is paramount to any rights under contracts between individuals." As Mr. Justice Holmes succinctly put the matter . . . "One whose rights, such as they are, are subject to state restriction, cannot remove them from the power of the State by making a contract about them. The contract will carry with it the infirmity of the subject matter."

If the Contract Clause is to retain any meaning at all, however, it must be understood to impose some limits upon the power of a State to abridge existing contractual relationships, even in the exercise of its otherwise legitimate police power. The existence and nature of those limits were clearly indicated in a series of cases in this Court arising from the efforts of the States to deal with the unprecedented emergencies brought on by the severe economic depression of the early 1930's.

. . .

In *Home Building & Loan Assn. v. Blaisdell,* . . . the Court upheld against a Contract Clause attack a mortgage moratorium law that Minnesota had enacted to provide relief for homeowners threatened with foreclosure. Although the legislation conflicted directly with lenders' contractual foreclosure rights, the Court there acknowledged that, despite the Contract Clause, the States retain residual authority to enact laws "to safeguard " the Vital interests of [their] people." . . . In upholding the state mortgage moratorium law, the Court found five factors significant. First, the state legislature had declared in the Act itself that an emergency need for the protection of homeowners existed. . . . Second, the state law was enacted to protect a basic societal interest, not a favored group. . . . Third, the relief was appropriately tailored to the emergency that it was designed to meet. . . . Fourth, the imposed conditions were reasonable. . . . And, finally, the legislation was limited to the duration of the emergency. . . .

The Blaisdell opinion thus clearly implied that if the Minnesota moratorium legislation had not possessed the characteristics attributed to it by the Court, it would have been invalid under the Contract Clause of the Constitution. These implications were given concrete force in three cases that followed closely in *Blaisdell's* wake.

In *W. B. Worthen Co. v. Thomas,* the Court dealt with an Arkansas law that exempted the proceeds of a life insurance policy from collection by the beneficiary's judgment creditors. Stressing the retroactive effect of the state law, the Court held that it was invalid under the Contract Clause, since it was not precisely and reasonably designed to meet a grave, temporary emergency in the interest of the general welfare. In *W. B. Worthen Co. v. Kavanaugh,* 295 U.S. 56, the Court was confronted with another Arkansas law that diluted the rights and remedies of mortgage bondholders. The Court held the law invalid under the Contract Clause. "Even when the public welfare is invoked as an excuse," Mr. Justice Cardozo wrote for the Court, the security of a mortgage cannot be cut down "without moderation or reason or in a spirit of oppression." . . . And finally, in *Treigle v. Acme Homestead Assn.,* 297 U.S. 189, the Court held invalid under the Contract Clause a Louisiana law that modified the existing withdrawal rights of the members of a building and loan association. "Such an interference with the right of contract," said the Court, "cannot be justified by saying that in the public interest the operations of building associations may be controlled and regulated, or that in the same interest their charters may be amended."

. . .

In applying these principles to the present case, the first inquiry must be whether the state law has, in fact, operated as a substantial impairment of a contractual relationship. The severity of the impairment measures the height of the hurdle the state legislation must clear. Minimal alteration of contractual obligations may end the inquiry at its first stage. Severe impairment, on the other hand, will push the inquiry to a careful examination of the nature and purpose of the state legislation.

The severity of an impairment of contractual obligations can be measured by the factors that reflect the high value the Framers placed on the protection of private contracts. Contracts enable individuals to order their personal and business affairs according to their particular needs and interests. Once arranged, those rights and obligations are binding under the law, and parties are entitled to rely on them.

Here, the company's contracts of employment with its employees included as a fringe benefit or additional form of compensation, the pension plan. The company's maximum obligation was to set aside each year an amount based on the plan's requirements for vesting. The plan satisfied the current federal income tax code and was subject to no other legislative requirements. And, of course, the company was free to amend or terminate the pension plan at any time. The company thus had no reason to anticipate that its employees' pension rights could become vested except in accordance with the *terms* of the plan. It relied heavily, and reasonably, on this legitimate contractual expectation in calculating its annual contributions to the pension fund.

The effect of Minnesota's Private Pension Benefits Protection Act on this contractual obligation was severe. The company was required in 1974 to have made its contributions throughout the pre-1974 life of its plan as if employees' pension rights had vested after 10 years, instead of vesting in accord with the terms of the plan. Thus a basic term of the pension contract—one on which the company had relied for 10 years—was substantially modified. The result was that although the company's past contributions were adequate when made, they were not adequate when computed under the 10-year statutory vesting requirement. The Act thus forced a current recalculation of the past 10 years, contributions based on the new, unanticipated 10-year vesting requirement.

Not only did the state law thus retroactively modify the compensation that the company had agreed to pay its employees from 1963 to 1974, but it did so by changing the company's obligations in an area where the element of reliance was vital—the funding of a pension plan. . . .

Moreover, the retroactive state-imposed vesting requirement was applied only to those employers who terminated their pension plans or who, like the company, closed their Minnesota offices. The company was thus forced to make all the retroactive changes in its contractual obligations at one time. By simply proceeding to close its office in Minnesota, a move that had been planned before the passage of the Act, the company was assessed an immediate pension funding charge of approximately $185,000.

Thus, the statute in question here nullifies express terms of the company's contractual obligations and imposes a completely unexpected liability in potentially disabling amounts. There is not even any provision for gradual applicability or grace periods. Compare the Employee Retirement Income Security Act, 29 U.S.C. §§ 1061(b)(2), 1086(b), and 1144. . . . Yet there is no showing in the record before us that this severe disruption of contractual expectations was necessary to meet an important general social problem. The presumption favoring "legislative judgment as to the necessity and reasonableness of a particular measure," . . . simply cannot stand in this case.

. . .

The judgment of the District Court is reversed.

. . .

MR. JUSTICE BLACKMUN took no part in the consideration or decision of this case.

MR. JUSTICE BRENNAN, with whom MR. JUSTICE WHITE and MR. JUSTICE MARSHALL join, dissenting.

. . .

Today's decision greatly expands the reach of the [Contract] Clause. The Minnesota Private Pension Benefits Protection Act (Act) does not abrogate or dilute any obligation due a party to a private contract; rather, like all positive social legislation, the Act imposes new, additional obligations on a particular class of persons. In *my* view, any constitutional infirmity in the law must therefore derive, not from the Contract Clause, but from the Due Process Clause of the Fourteenth Amendment. I perceive nothing in the Act that works a denial of Due Process and therefore I dissent.

. . .

The primary question in this case is whether the Contract Clause is violated by state legislation enacted to protect employees covered by a pension plan by requiring an employer to make outlays—which, although not in this case, will largely be offset against future savings—to provide terminated employees with the equivalent of benefits reasonably to be expected under the plan. The Act does not relieve either the employer or his employees of any existing contract obligation. Rather, the Act simply creates an additional, supplemental duty of the employer, no different in kind from myriad duties created by a wide variety of legislative measures which defeat settled expectations but which have nonetheless been sustained by this Court.

. . . For this reason, the Minnesota Act, in my view, does not implicate the Contract Clause in any way. The basic fallacy *of* today's decision is its mistaken view that the Contract Clause protects all contract based expectations, including that of an employer that his obligations to his employees will not be legislatively enlarged beyond those explicitly provided in his pension plan.

. . .

More fundamentally, the Court's distortion of the meaning of the Contract Clause creates anomalies of its own and threatens to undermine the jurisprudence of property rights developed over the last 40 years. The Contract Clause, of course, is but one of several clauses in the Constitution that protect existing economic values from governmental interference. The Fifth Amendment's command that "private property [shall not] be taken for public use, without just compensation" is such a clause. A second is the Due Process Clause, which during the heyday of substantive due process . . . largely supplanted the Contract Clause in importance and operated as a potent limitation on Government's ability to interfere with economic expectations. . . . Decisions over the past 50 years have developed a coherent, unified interpretation of all the constitutional provisions that may protect economic expectations and these decisions have recognized a broad latitude in States to effect even severe interference with existing economic values when reasonably necessary to promote the general welfare. See *Penn Central Transp. Co. v. New York City*, 438 U.S. 104. . . . At the same time the prohibition of the Contract Clause, consistently with its wording and historic purposes, has been limited in application to state laws that diluted, with utter indifference to the legitimate interests of the beneficiary of a contract duty, the existing contract obligation. . . .

Today's conversion of the Contract Clause

into a limitation on the power of States to enact laws that impose duties additional to obligations assumed under private contracts must inevitably produce results difficult to square with any rational conception of a constitutional order. Under the Court's opinion, any law that may be characterized as "superimposing" new obligations on those provided for by contract is to be regarded as creating sudden, substantial, and unanticipated burdens" and then to be subjected to the most exacting scrutiny. The validity of such a law will turn upon whether judges see it as a law that deals with a generalized social problem, whether it is temporary (as few will be) or permanent, whether it operates in an area previously subject to regulation, and, finally, whether its duties apply to a broad class of persons. . . . The necessary consequence of the extreme malleability of these rather vague criteria is to vest judges with broad subjective discretion to protect property interests that happen to appeal to them.

. . .

Modern debate over the contract clause has included attention to whether it applies to a state's action altering its own contractual obligations. In *United States Trust Co. of New York v. New Jersey*, the Court referenced the contract clause in undoing the repeal of state laws that had dedicated government bonds to a specific purpose.

United States Trust Co. of New York v. New Jersey
431 U.S. 1 (1977)

MR. JUSTICE BLACKMUN delivered the opinion of the Court.

. . .

At the time the Constitution was adopted, and for nearly a century thereafter, the Contract Clause was one of the few express limitations on state power. The many decisions of this Court involving the Contract Clause are evidence of its important place in our constitutional jurisprudence. Over the century, however, the Fourteenth Amendment has assumed a far larger place in constitutional adjudication concerning the States. We feel that the present role of the Contract Clause is largely illuminated by two of this Court's decisions. In each, legislation was sustained despite a claim that it had impaired the obligations of contracts.

Home Building & Loan Assn. v. Blaisdell, 290 U.S. 398 (1934), is regarded as the leading case in the modern era of Contract Clause interpretation. At issue was the Minnesota Mortgage Moratorium Law, enacted in 1933, during the depth of the Depression and when that state was under severe economic stress, and appeared to have no effective alternative. The

statute was a temporary measure that allowed judicial extension of the time for redemption; a mortgagor who remained in possession during the extension period was required to pay a reasonable income or rental value to the mortgagee. A closely divided Court, in an opinion by Mr. Chief Justice Hughes, observed that "emergency may furnish the occasion for the exercise of power" and that the "Constitutional question presented in the light of an emergency is whether the power possessed embraces the particular exercise of it in response to particular conditions." It noted that the debates in the Constitutional Convention were of little aid in the construction of the Contract Clause, but that the general purpose of the Clause was clear: to encourage trade and credit by promoting confidence in the stability of contractual obligations. Nevertheless, a State "continues to possess authority to safeguard the vital interests of its people. This principle of harmonizing the constitutional prohibition "with the necessary residuum of state power has had progressive recognition in the decisions of this Court." The great clauses of the Constitution are to be considered in the light of our whole experience, and not merely as they would be interpreted by its Framers in the conditions and with the outlook of their time.

This Court's most recent Contract Clause decision is *El Paso v. Simmons.* That case concerned a 1941 Texas statute that limited to a 5-year period the reinstatement rights of an interest-defaulting purchaser of land from the State. For many years prior to the enactment of that statute, such a defaulting purchaser, under Texas law, could have reinstated his claim to the land upon written request and payment of delinquent interest, unless rights of third parties had intervened. This Court held that "it is not every modification of a contractual promise that impairs the obligation of contract under federal law." It observed that the State "has the 'sovereign right . . . to protect the . . . general welfare of the people'" and "'we must respect the "wide discretion on the part of the legislature in determining what is and what is not necessary."'" The Court recognized that "the power of a State to modify or affect the obligation of contract is not without limit," but held that "the objects of the Texas statute make abundantly clear that it impairs no protected right under the Contract Clause."

Both of these cases eschewed a rigid application of the Contract Clause to invalidate state legislation. Yet neither indicated that the Contract Clause was without meaning in modern constitutional jurisprudence, or that its limitation on state power was illusory. Whether or not the protection or contract rights comports with current views of wise public policy, the Contract Clause remains a part of our written Constitution. We therefore must attempt to apply that constitutional provision to the instant case with due respect for its purpose and the prior decisions of this Court.

We first examine appellant's general claim that repeal of the 1962 covenant impaired the obligation of the States' contract with the bondholders. It long has been established that the Contract Clause limits the power of the States to modify their own contracts as well as to regulate those between private parties. Yet the Contract Clause does not prohibit the States from repealing or amending statutes generally, or from enacting legislation with retroactive effects. . . .

Although the Contract Clause appears literally to proscribe "any" impairment, this Court observed in *Blaisdell* that "the prohibition is not an absolute one and is not to be read with literal exactness like a mathematical formula." Thus, a finding that there has been a technical impairment is merely a preliminary step in resolving the more difficult question whether that impairment is permitted under the Constitution. In the instant case, as in

Blaisdell, we must attempt to reconcile the strictures of the Contract Clause with the "essential attributes of sovereign power," necessarily reserved by the States to safeguard the welfare or their citizens.

The trial court concluded that repeal of the 1962 covenant was a valid exercise of New Jersey's police power because repeal served important public interests in mass transportation, energy conservation, and environmental protection. Yet the Contract Clause limits otherwise legitimate exercises of state legislative authority, and the existence of an important public interest is not always sufficient to overcome that limitation. "Undoubtedly, whatever is reserved of state power must be consistent with the fair intent of the constitutional limitation of that power." Moreover, the scope of the State's reserved power depends on the nature or the contractual relationship with which the challenged law conflicts.

The States must possess broad power to adopt general regulatory measures without being concerned that private contracts will be impaired, or even destroyed, as a result. Otherwise, one would be able to obtain immunity from the state regulation by making private contractual arrangements. This principle is summarized in Mr. Justice Holmes' well-known dictum: "One whose rights, such as they are, are subject to state restriction, cannot remove them from the power of the State by making a contract about them."

Yet private contracts are not subject to unlimited modification under the police power. The Court in *Blaisdell* recognized that laws intended to regulate existing contractual relationships must serve a legitimate public purpose. A State could not "adopt as its policy the repudiation of debts or the destruction of contracts or the denial of means to enforce them." Legislation adjusting the rights and responsibilities of contracting parties must be upon reasonable conditions and of a character appropriate to the public purpose justifying its adoption. As is customary in reviewing economic and social regulation, however, courts properly defer to legislative judgment as to the necessity and reasonableness of a particular measure.

. . .

When a State impairs the obligation of its own contract, the reserved powers doctrine has a different basis. The initial inquiry concerns the ability of the State to enter into an agreement that limits its power to act in the future. As early as *Fletcher v. Peck,* the Court considered the argument that one legislature cannot abridge the powers of a succeeding legislature." It is often stated that "the legislature cannot bargain away the police power of a State." *Stone v. Mississippi.* This doctrine requires a determination of the State's power to create irrevocable contract rights in the first place, rather than an inquiry into the purpose or reasonableness of the subsequent impairment. In short, the Contract Clause does not require a State to adhere to a contract that surrenders an essential attribute of its sovereignty.

In deciding whether a State's contract was invalid *ab initio* under the reserved powers doctrine, earlier decisions relied on distinctions among the various powers of the State. Thus, the police power and the power of eminent domain were among those that could not be "contracted away," but the State could bind itself in the future exercise of the taxing and spending powers. Such formalistic distinctions perhaps cannot be dispositive, but they contain an important element of truth. Whatever the propriety of a State's binding itself to a future course of conduct in other contexts, the power to enter into effective financial contracts cannot be questioned. Any financial obligation could be regarded in theory as a relinquishment of the State's spending power, since money spent to repay debts is not available for other purposes. Similarly, the taxing power may have to be exercised if debts are to be repaid. Notwithstanding these effects, the Court has regularly held that the States are bound by their debt contracts.

The instant case involves a financial obligation and thus as a threshold matter may not be said automatically to fall within the reserved powers that cannot be contracted away. Not every security provision, however, is necessarily financial. For example, a revenue bond might be secured by the State's promise to continue operating the facility in question; yet such a promise surely could not validly be construed to bind the State never to close the facility for health or safety reasons. The security provision at issue here, however, is different: the States promised that revenues and reserves securing the bonds would not be depleted by the Port Authority's operation of deficit-producing passenger railroads beyond the level of "permitted deficits." Such a promise is purely financial and thus not necessary a compromise of the State's reserved powers.

Of course, to say that the financial restrictions of the 1962 covenant were valid when adopted does not finally resolve this case. The Contract Clause is not an absolute bar to subsequent modification of a State's own financial obligations. As with laws impairing the obligations of private contracts, an impairment may be constitutional if it is reasonable and necessary to serve an important public purpose. In applying this standard, however, complete deference to a legislative assessment of reasonableness and necessity is not appropriate because the State's self-interest is at stake. A

governmental entity can always find a use for extra money, especially when taxes do not have to be raised. If a State could reduce its financial obligations whenever it wanted to spend the money for what it regarded as an important public purpose, the Contract Clause would provide no protection at all.

The trial court recognized to an extent the special status of a State's financial obligations when it held that *total* repudiation, presumably for even a worthwhile public purpose, would be unconstitutional. But the trial court regarded the protection of the Contract Clause as available only in such an extreme case: "The states' inherent power to protect the public welfare may be validly exercised under the Contract Clause even if it impairs a contractual obligation so long as it does not destroy it."

. . . The extent of impairment is certainly a relevant factor in determining its reasonableness. But we cannot sustain the repeal of the 1962 covenant simply because the bondholders' rights were not totally destroyed.

Mass transportation, energy conservation, and environmental protection are goals that are important and of legitimate public concern. Appellees contend that these goals are so important that any harm to bondholders from repeal of the 1962 covenant is greatly outweighed by the public benefit. We do not accept this invitation to engage in a utilitarian comparison of public benefit and private loss. Contrary to Mr. Justice Black's fear expressed on sole dissent in *El Paso v. Simmons*, the Court has not "balanced away" the limitation on state action imposed by the Contract Clause. Thus a State cannot refuse to meet its legitimate financial obligations simply because it would prefer to spend the money to promote the public good rather than the private welfare of its creditors. We can only sustain the repeal of the 1962 covenant if that impairment was both reasonable and necessary to serve the admittedly important purposes claimed by the State.

The more specific justification offered for the repeal of the 1962 covenant was the States' plan for encouraging users of private automobiles to shift to public transportation. The States intended to discourage private automobile use by raising bridge and tunnel tolls and to use the extra revenue from those tolls to subsidize improved commuter railroad service. Appellees contend that repeal of the 1962 covenant was necessary to implement this plan because the new mass transit facilities could not possibly be self-supporting and the covenant's "permitted deficits" level had already been exceeded. We reject this justification because the repeal was neither necessary to achievement of the plan nor reasonable in light of the circumstances.

The determination of necessity can be considered on two levels. First, it cannot be said that total repeal of the covenant was essential; a less drastic modification would have permitted the contemplated plan without entirely removing the covenant's limitations on the use of Port Authority revenues and reserves to subsidize commuter railroads. Second, without modifying the covenant at all, the States could have adopted alternative means of achieving their twin goals of discouraging automobile use and improving mass transit. Appellees contend, however, that choosing among these alternatives is a matter for legislative discretion. But a State is not completely free to consider impairing the obligations of its own contracts on a par with other policy alternatives. Similarly, a State is not free to impose a drastic impairment when an evident and more moderate course would serve its purposes equally well. In *El Paso v. Simmons,* the . . . Court held that adoption of a statute of limitation was a reasonable means to "restrict a party to those gains reasonably to be expected from the contract" when it was adopted.

By contrast, in the instant case the need for mass transportation in the New York metropolitan area was not a new development, and the likelihood that publicly owned commuter railroads would produce substantial deficits was well known. As early as 1922, over a half century ago, there were pressures to involve the Port Authority in mass transit. It was with full knowledge of these concerts that the 1962 covenant was adopted. Indeed, the covenant was specifically intended to protect the pledged revenues and reserved against the possibility that such concerns would lead the Port Authority into greater involvement in deficit mass transit.

During the 12-year period between adoption of the covenant and its repeal, public perception of the importance of mass transit undoubtedly grew because of increased public concern with environmental protection and energy conservation. But these concerns were not unknown in 1962, and the subsequent changes were of degree and not of kind. We cannot say that these changes caused the covenant to have a substantially different impact in 1974 than when it was adopted in 1962. And we cannot conclude that the repeal was reasonable in the light of changed circumstances.

We therefore hold that the Contract Clause of the United States Constitution prohibits the retroactive repeal of the 1962 covenant. The judgment of the Supreme Court of New Jersey is reversed.

. . .

MR. JUSTICE STEWART took no part in the decision of this case.

MR. JUSTICE POWELL took no part in the consideration or decision of this case.

MR. CHIEF JUSTICE BURGER concurring.

. . .

MR. JUSTICE BRENNAN, with whom MR. JUSTICE WHITE and MR. JUSTICE MARSHALL join, dissenting.

Decisions of this Court for at least a century have construed the Contract Clause largely to be powerless in binding a State to contracts limiting the authority of successor legislatures to enact laws in furtherance of the health, safety, and similar collective interests of the polity. In short, those decisions established the principle that lawful exercises of a State's police powers stand paramount to private rights held under contract. Today's decision, in invalidating the New Jersey Legislature's 1974 repeal of its predecessor's 1962 covenant, rejects this previous understanding and remolds the determinations of the state legislature. At the same time, by creating a constitutional safe haven for property rights embodied in a contract, the decision substantially distorts modern constitutional jurisprudence governing regulation of private economic interests. I might understand, though I could not accept this revival of the Contract Clause were it in accordance with some coherent and constructive view of public policy. But elevation of the clause to the status of regulator of the municipal bond market at the heavy price of frustration of sound legislative policy making is as demonstrably unwise as it is unnecessary. The justification for today's decision, therefore, remains a mystery to me, and I respectfully dissent.

. . .

. . . Given that this is the first case in some 40 years in which this Court has seen fit to invalidate purely economic and social legislation on the strength of the Contract Clause, one may only hope that it will prove a rare phenomenon, turning on the Court's particularized appraisal or the facts before it. But there also is reason for broader concern. It is worth remembering that there is nothing sacrosanct about a contract. All property rights, no less than a contract, are rooted in certain "expectations" about the sanctity of one's right of ownership. . . . And other constitutional doctrines are akin to the Contract Clause in directing their protections to the property interests of private parties. Hence the command of the Fifth Amendment that "private property [shall not] be taken for public use, without just compensation" also "remains a part of our written Constitution." And during the heyday of economic due process associated with *Lochner v. New York,* and similar cases long since discarded, . . . the Court treated "the liberty of contract" under the Due Process Clause as virtually indistinguishable from the Contract Clause. . . . In more recent times, however, the Court wisely has come to embrace a coherent, unified interpretation of all such constitutional provisions, and has granted wide latitude to "a valid exercise of [the States'] police powers," *Goldblatt v. Hempstead*, 369 U.S. 590, 592 (1962) even if it results in severe violations of property rights. . . . If today's case signals a return to substantive constitutional review of States' policies, and a new resolve to protect property owners whose interest or circumstances may happen to appeal to Members of this Court, then more than the citizens of New Jersey and New York will be the losers.

I would not want to be read as suggesting that the States should blithely proceed down the path of repudiating their obligations, financial or otherwise. Their credibility in the credit market obviously is highly dependent on exercising their vast lawmaking powers with self-restraint and discipline, and I, for one, have little doubt that few, if any, jurisdictions would choose to use their authority "so foolish[ly] as to kill a goose that lays golden eggs for them." But in the final analysis, there is no reason to doubt that appellant's financial welfare is being adequately policed by the political processes and the bond marketplace itself. The role to be played by the Constitution is at most a limited one. For this Court should have learned long ago that the Constitution—be it through the Contract or Due Process Clause—can actively intrude into such economic and policy matters only if my Brethren are prepared to bear enormous institutional and social costs. Because I consider the potential dangers of such judicial interference to be intolerable, I dissent.

Several years after *Spannaus*, the Court in *Exxon Corp. v. Eagerton* concluded that a state law prohibiting oil and gas producers from passing the costs of a severance tax increase on to consumers did not violate the contract clause even though the law superseded existing contracts. Crucial considerations were what the Court perceived as the law's general applicability and incidental effect.

Exxon Corp. v. Eagerton
462 U.S. 176 (1983)

. . .

MARSHALL, J., delivered the opinion of the Court.

These cases concern an Alabama statute which increased the severance tax on oil and gas extracted from Alabama wells, exempted royalty owners from the tax increase, and prohibited producers from passing on the increase to their purchasers. Appellants challenge the pass-through prohibition and the royalty-owner exemption under the Supremacy Clause, the Contract Clause, and the Equal Protection Clause.

. . .

[T]he pass-through prohibition did restrict contractual obligations of which appellants were the beneficiaries. Appellants were parties to sale contracts that permitted them to include in their prices any increase in the severance taxes that they were required to pay on the oil or gas being sold. The contracts were entered into before the pass-through prohibition was enacted and their terms extended through the period during which the prohibition was in effect. By barring appellants from passing the tax increase through to their purchasers, the pass-through prohibition nullified *pro tanto* the purchasers' contractual obligations to reimburse appellants for any severance taxes.

While the pass-through prohibition thus affects contractual obligations of which appellants were the beneficiaries, it does not follow that the prohibition constituted a "Law impairing the Obligations of Contracts" within the meaning of the Contract Clause. "Although the language of the Contract Clause is facially absolute, its prohibition must be accommodated to the inherent police power of the State 'to safeguard the vital interests of its people.'" This Court has long recognized that a statute does not violate the Contract Clause simply because it has the effect of restricting, or even barring altogether, the performance of duties created by contracts entered into prior to its enactment. If the law were otherwise, "one would be able to obtain immunity from state regulation by making private contractual arrangements."

The Contract Clause does not deprive the States of their "broad power to adopt general regulatory measures without being concerned that private contracts will be impaired, or even destroyed, as a result." As Justice Holmes put it: "One whose rights, such as they are, are subject to state restriction, cannot remove them from the power of the State by making a contract about them. The contract will carry with it the infirmity of the subject matter." Thus, a state prohibition law may be applied to contracts for the sale of beer that were valid when entered into, a law barring lotteries may be applied to lottery tickets that were valid when issued, and a workmen's compensation law may be applied to employers and employees operating under pre-existing contracts of employment that made no provision for work-related injuries.

Like the laws upheld in these cases, the pass-through prohibition did not prescribe a rule limited in effect to contractual obligations or remedies, but instead imposed a generally applicable rule of conduct designed to advance "a broad societal interest," protecting consumers from excessive prices. The prohibition applied to all oil and gas producers, regardless of whether they happened to be parties to sale contracts that contained a provision permitting them to pass tax increases through to their purchasers. The effect of the pass-through prohibition on existing contracts that did not contain such a provision was incidental to its main effect of shielding consumers from the burden of the tax increase.

Because the pass-through prohibition imposed a generally applicable rule of conduct, it is sharply distinguishable from the measures struck down in *United States Trust Co. v. New Jersey, supra,* and *Allied Structural Steel Co. v. Spannaus, supra. United States Trust Co.* involved New York and New Jersey statutes whose sole effect was to repeal a covenant that the two States had entered into with the holders of bonds issued by The Port Authority of New York and New Jersey. Similarly, the statute at issue in *Allied Structural Steel Co.* directly " 'adjust[ed] the rights and responsibilities of contracting parties,'" quoting *United States Trust Co. v. New Jersey.* The statute required a private employer that had contracted with its employees to provide pension benefits to pay additional benefits, beyond those it had

agreed to provide, if it terminated the pension plan or closed a Minnesota office. Since the statute applied only to employers that had entered into pension agreements, its sole effect was to alter contractual duties.

Producers Transportation Co. v. Railroad Comm'n of California, 251 U.S. 228 (1920), is particularly instructive for present purposes. In that case the Court upheld an order issued by a state commission under a newly enacted statute empowering the commission to set the rates that could be charged by individuals or corporations offering to transport oil by pipeline. The Court rejected the contention of a pipeline owner that the statute could not override preexisting contracts:

> "That some of the contracts . . . were entered into before the statute was adopted or the order made is not material. A common carrier cannot by making contracts for future transportation or by mortgaging its property or pledging its income prevent or postpone the exertion by the State of the power to regulate the carrier's rates and practices. Nor does the contract clause of the Constitution interpose any obstacle to the exertion of that power."

There is no material difference between *Producers Transportation Co.* and the cases before us. If a party that has entered into a contract to transport oil is not immune from subsequently enacted state regulation of the rates that may be charged for such transportation, parties that have entered into contracts to sell oil and gas likewise are not immune from state regulation of the prices that may be charged for those commodities. And if the Contract Clause does not prevent a State from dictating the price that sellers may charge their customers, plainly it does not prevent a State from requiring that sellers absorb a tax increase themselves rather than pass it through to their customers. If one form of state regulation is permissible under the Contract Clause notwithstanding its incidental effect on pre-existing contracts, the other form of regulation must be permissible as well.

2. The Taking Clause

Taking clause analysis, at least on its face, may appear incongruous insofar as notable exponents of judicial restraint have extended the concept of government taking of private property and narrowed grounds for permissible state regulation. Justice Holmes, whose legacy includes unrelenting resistance to substantive due process review, wrote for the Court in determining that land use control could be the functional

---

[87] Pennsylvania Coal Co. v. Mahon, 260 U.S. 393 (1922).

equivalent of a physical taking.[87] Several decades later, Justice Scalia (perhaps the foremost advocate of judicial restraint on the modern Court) authored an opinion to the effect that, when a state deprives an owner of all economically beneficial use of land, it can avoid a taking only when the regulation conforms with restrictions inherent in title to the property.[88]

Criticism of nondeferential standards of review and consequent displacement of legislative judgment in the taking area has emanated, among other sources, from justices whose record is characterized by trade in substantive due process review.[89] Arguments for a harder look at legislation, when taking is alleged, distinguish the enumerated nature of the interest under the Fifth Amendment from the natural law aspects of substantive due process.[90] Detractors, who suggest a revival of *Lochnerist* agendas, maintain that relevant history indicates no intention to limit a state's power to regulate harmful land use even to the extent a property's value is destroyed.[91] Included were objections from justices whose analysis of the taking clause have prompted some to observe that, in Justice Brennan's words, the Court is reinvesting in analysis "that has been discredited for the better part of this century."[92]

Responding to criticism of a neo-*Lochnerist* function, the Court has maintained that it traditionally has required that regulation "substantially advance" rather than reasonably relate to a "legitimate state interest."[93] As Justice Scalia has put it

> there is no reason to believe (and the language of our cases gives some reason to believe) that so long as the regulation of property is at issue, the standards for taking challenges, due process challenges, and equal protection challenges are identical; any more than there is any reason to believe that so long as the regulation of speech is at issue the standards for due process challenges, equal protection challenges, and First Amendment challenges are identical."[94]

Although the taking clause may be less amorphous than the due process concept of liberty, it nonetheless has begotten significant debate over the meaning of its terms. Primary sources of litigation have been the "public use" provision, setting forth a basic requirement for a constitutional taking, and land use regulation.

Contrasted with standards for what amounts to a taking, criteria for what constitutes a public use are relatively deferential. The Court has noted that its role in reviewing legislative judgment of what constitutes a public use is "extremely narrow."

---

[88] Lucas v. South Carolina Coastal Council, 112 S.Ct. 2886, 2899-2900 (1992).

[89] Nollan v. California Coastal Commission, 483 U.S. 825, 842 (1987) (Brennan and Marshall, J.J., dissenting).

[90] *Id.* at 834 n.3 (majority opinion).

[91] *Lucas*, 112 S.Ct. at 2914–17 (Blackmun, J., dissenting).

[92] Nollan, 483 U.S. at 842 (1987) (Brennan, J., dissenting).

[93] *Id.* at 834 n.3 (majority opinion).

[94] *Id.*

Hawaii Housing Authority v. Midkiff
467 U.S. 229 (1984)

Justice O'Connor delivered the opinion of the Court.

The Fifth Amendment of the United States Constitution provides, in pertinent part, that "private property [shall not] be taken for public use, without just compensation." These cases present the question whether the Public Use Clause of that Amendment, made applicable to the States through the Fourteenth Amendment, prohibits the State of Hawaii from taking, with just compensation, title in real property from lessors and transferring it to lessees in order to reduce the concentration of ownership of fees simple in the State. We conclude that it does not.

The Hawaiian Islands were originally settled by Polynesian immigrants from the western Pacific. These settlers developed an economy around a feudal land tenure system in which one island high chief, the ali'i nui, controlled the land and assigned it for development to certain subchiefs. The subchiefs would then reassign the land to other lower ranking chiefs, who would administer the land and govern the farmers and other tenants working it. All land was held at the will of the ali'i nui and eventually had to be returned to his trust. There was no private ownership of land.

Beginning in the early 1800's, Hawaiian leaders and American settlers repeatedly attempted to divide the lands of the kingdom among the crown, the chiefs, and the common people. These efforts proved largely unsuccessful, however, and the land remained in the hands of a few. In the mid 1960's, after extensive hearings, the Hawaii Legislature discovered that, while the State and Federal Governments owned almost 49% of the State's land, another 47% was in the hands of only 72 private landowners.

The legislature further found that 18 landholders, with tracts of 21,000 acres or more, owned more than 40% of this land and that on Oahu, the most urbanized of the islands, 22 landowners owned 72.5% of the fees simple. The legislature concluded that concentrated land ownership was responsible for skewing the State's residential fee simple market, inflating land prices, and injuring the public tranquility and welfare.

To redress these problems, the legislature decided to compel the large landowners to break up their estates. The legislature considered requiring large landowners to sell lands which they were leasing to homeowners. However, the owners strongly resisted this scheme, pointing out the significant federal tax liabilities they would incur. Indeed, the landowners claimed that the federal tax laws were the primary reason they previously had chosen to lease, and not sell, their lands. Therefore, to accommodate the needs of both lessors and lessees, the Hawaii Legislature enacted the Land Reform Act of 1967, which created a mechanism for condemning residential tracts and for transferring ownership of the condemned fees simple to existing lessees. By condemning the land in question, the Hawaii Legislature intended to make the land sales involuntary, thereby making the federal tax consequences

less severe while still facilitating the redistribution of fees simple. . . .

. . .

The starting point for our analysis of the Act's constitutionality is the Court's decision in *Berman v. Parker,* 348 U.S. 26 (1954). In *Berman,* the Court held constitutional the District of Columbia Redevelopment Act of 1945. That Act provided both for the comprehensive use of the eminent domain power to redevelop slum areas and for the possible sale or lease of the condemned lands to private interests. In discussing whether the takings authorized by that Act were for "public use," id., at 31, the Court stated:

> "We deal, in other words, with what traditionally has been known as the police power. An attempt to define its reach or trace its outer limits is fruitless, for each case must turn on its own facts. The definition is essentially the product of legislative determinations addressed to the purposes of government, purposes neither abstractly nor historically capable of complete definition. Subject to specific constitutional limitations, when the legislature has spoken, the public interest has been declared in terms well-nigh conclusive. In such cases the legislature, not the judiciary, is the main guardian of the public needs to be served by social legislation, whether it be Congress legislating concerning the District of Columbia . . . or the States legislating concerning local affairs. . . . This principle admits of no exception merely because the power of eminent domain is involved. . . . "

The Court explicitly recognized the breadth of the principle it was announcing, noting:

> "Once the object is within the authority of Congress, the right to realize it through the exercise of eminent domain is clear. For the power of eminent domain is merely the means to the end. . . . Once the object is within the authority of Congress, the means by which it will be attained is also for Congress to determine. Here one of the means chosen is the use of private enterprise for redevelopment of the area. Appellants argue that this makes the project a taking from one businessman for the benefit of another businessman. But the means of executing the project are for Congress and Congress alone to determine, once the public purpose has been established."

The "public use' requirement is thus coterminous with the scope of a sovereign's police powers.

There is, of course, a role for courts to play in reviewing a legislature's judgment of what constitutes a public use, even when the eminent domain power is equated with the police power. But [that role] . . . is "an extremely narrow" one. In short, the Court has made clear that it will not substitute its judgment for a legislature's judgment as to what constitutes a public use "unless the use be palpably without reasonable foundation." *United States v. Gettysburg Electric R. Co.*, 160 U.S. 668, 680 (1896).

. . . [W]here the exercise of the eminent domain power is rationally related to a conceivable public purpose, the Court has never held a compensated taking to be proscribed by the Public Use Clause.

On this basis, we have no trouble concluding that the Hawaii Act is constitutional. The people of Hawaii have attempted, much as the settlers of the original 13 Colonies did, to reduce the perceived social and economic evils of a land oligopoly traceable to their monarchs. The land oligopoly has, according to the Hawaii Legislature, created artificial deterrents to the normal functioning of the State's residential land market and forced thousands of individual homeowners to lease, rather than buy, the land underneath their homes. Regulating oligopoly and the evils associated with it is a classic exercise of a State's police powers. We cannot disapprove of Hawaii's exercise of this power.

Nor can we condemn as irrational the Act's approach to correcting the land oligopoly problem. The Act presumes that when a sufficiently large number of persons declare that they are willing but unable to buy lots at fair prices the land market is malfunctioning. When such a malfunction is signalled, the Act authorizes HHA to condemn lots in the relevant tract. The Act limits the number of lots any one tenant can purchase and authorizes HHA to use public funds to ensure that the market dilution goals will be achieved. This is a comprehensive and rational approach to identifying and correcting market failure.

Of course, this Act, like any other, may not be successful in achieving its intended goals. . . . When the legislature's purpose is legitimate and its means are not irrational, our cases make clear that empirical debates over the wisdom of taking—no less than debates over the wisdom of other kinds of socioeconomic legislation—are not to be carried out in the federal courts. Redistribution of fees simple to correct deficiencies in the market determined by the state legislature to be attributable to land oligopoly is a rational exercise of the eminent domain power. Therefore, the Hawaii statute must pass the scrutiny of the Public Use Clause.

Until this century, the concept of a taking for constitutional purposes comprehended only a "direct appropriation" of property.[95] An expanded understanding of taking emerged when, in *Pennsylvania Coal Co. v. Mahon,* the Court determined that land use restrictions effectively rendering property valueless also constituted a taking.[96] In *Mahon*, the Court struck down a state law prohibiting with few exceptions coal mining that would cause the subsidence of nearby houses. To the extent the regulation made commercial coal mining impracticable, and functionally equated with total destruction of mining rights, the Court found a taking without just compensation. Justice Holmes' opinion for the majority elicited from Justice Brandeis a dissenting perspective to the effect that restriction on harmful use is not inappropriate even when "it deprives the owner of the only use to which the property can then be profitably put."[97] As the discussion below discloses, the debate between Holmes and Brandeis has carried over into modern case law. More than half a century after *Mahon*, the Court reviewed another Pennsylvania law barring coal mining that caused damage to buildings, water supplies and the environment, requiring half of the coal in protected zones to be left in the ground. The Court, in *Keystone Bituminous Coal Assn. v. DeBenedictis*, distinguished *Mahon* on grounds the "petitioners ha[d] not come close to satisfying their burden of proving that they have been denied the economically viable use of th[eir] property."[98] Chief Justice Rehnquist, joined by Justices O'Connor and Scalia, dissented and argued that the Court had failed to view the coal as a separate property interest rendered

---

[95] Legal Tender Cases, 79 U.S. 457, 551 (1871).

[96] Pennsylvania Coal Co. v. Mahon, 260 U.S. 393, 414–16 (1922).

[97] *Id.* at 418 (Brandeis, J., dissenting).

[98] Keystone Bituminous Coal Assn. v. DeBenedictis, 480 U.S. 470, 499 (1987).

entirely valueless.[99] The majority's distinction based upon the totality versus partiality of impairment nonetheless reflected the influence of *Penn Central Transportation Co. v. New York City*, in which the Court a decade before had rejected arguments that a landmark preservation law constituted a taking.

---

[99] *Id.* at 514–18 (Rehnquist, C.J., dissenting).

Penn Central Transportation Co. v. New York City
438 U.S. 104 (1978)

Mr. Justice Brennan delivered the opinion of the Court.

The question presented is whether a city may, as part of a comprehensive program to preserve historic landmarks and historic districts, place restrictions on the development of individual historic landmarks—in addition to those imposed by applicable zoning ordinances—without affecting a "taking" requiring the payment of "just compensation." Specifically, we must decide whether the application of New York City's Landmarks Preservation Law to the parcel of land occupied by Grand Central Terminal has "taken" its owners' property in violation of the Fifth and Fourteenth Amendments.

. . .

The New York City law is typical of many urban landmark laws in that its primary method of achieving its goals is not by acquisitions of historic properties, but rather by involving public entities in land-use decisions affecting these properties and providing services, standards, controls, and incentives that will encourage preservation by private owners and users. While the law does place special restrictions on landmark properties as a necessary feature to the attainment of its larger objectives, the major theme of the law is to ensure the owners of any such properties both a "reasonable return" on their investments and maximum latitude to use their parcels for purposes not inconsistent with the preservation goals.

. . .

The issues presented by appellants are (1) whether the restrictions imposed by New York City's law upon appellants' exploitation of the Terminal site effect a "taking" of appellants' property for a public use within the meaning of the Fifth Amendment, which of course is made applicable to the States through the Fourteenth Amendment, and, (2), if so, whether the transferable development rights afforded appellants constitute "just compensation" within the meaning of the Fifth Amendment. We need only address the question whether a "taking" has occurred.

Before considering appellants' specific contentions, it will be useful to review the factors that have shaped the jurisprudence of the Fifth Amendment injunction "nor shall private property be taken for public use, without just compensation." The question of what constitutes a "taking" for purposes of the Fifth Amendment has proved to be a problem of considerable difficulty. While this Court has recognized that the "Fifth Amendment's guarantee . . . [is] designed to bar Government from forcing some people alone to bear public burdens which, in all fairness and justice, should be borne by the public as a whole," *Armstrong v. United States,* 364 U.S. 40, 49 (1960), this Court, quite simply, has been unable to develop any "set formula" for determining when "justice and fairness" require that economic injuries caused by public action be compensated by the government, rather than remain disproportionately concentrated on a few persons. Indeed, we have frequently observed that whether a particular restriction will be invalid by the government's failure to pay for any losses proximately caused by it depends largely "upon the particular circumstances [in that] case."

In engaging in these essentially ad hoc, factual inquiries, the Court's decisions have identified several factors that have particular significance. The economic impact of the regulation on the claimant and, particularly, the extent to which the regulation has interfered with distinct investment-backed expectations are of course, relevant considerations. So, too, is the character of the governmental action. A "taking" may more readily be found when the interference with property can be characterized as a physical invasion by government, than when interference arises from some public program adjusting the benefits and burdens of economic life to promote the common good.

"Government hardly could go on if to some extent values incident to property could not be diminished without paying for every such change in the general law," *Pennsylvania Coal Co. v. Mahon,* and this Court has accordingly recognized, in a wide variety of contexts, that government may execute laws or programs that adversely affect recognized economic values. Exercises of the taxing power are one obvious example. . . .

More importantly for the present case, in instances in which a state tribunal reasonably concluded that "the health, safety, morals, or general welfare" would be promoted by prohibiting particular contemplated uses of land, this Court has upheld land-use regulations that destroyed or adversely affected recognized real property interests. Zoning laws are, of course, the classic example, which have been viewed as permissible governmental action even when prohibiting the most beneficial use of the property.

Zoning laws generally do not affect existing uses of real property, but "taking" challenges have also been held to be without merit in a wide variety of situations when the challenged governmental actions prohibited a beneficial use to which individual parcels had previously been devoted and thus caused substantial individualized harm.

. . .

Pennsylvania Coal Co. v. Mahon is the leading case for the proposition that a state statute that substantially furthers important public policies may so frustrate distinct investment-backed expectations as to amount to a "taking." There the claimant had sold the surface rights to particular parcels of property, but expressly reserved the right to remove the coal thereunder. A Pennsylvania statute, enacted after the transactions, forbade any mining of coal that caused the subsidence of any house, unless the house was the property of the owner of the underlying coal and was more than 150 feet from the improved property of another. Because the statute made it commercially impracticable to mine the coal, and thus had nearly the same effect as the complete destruction of rights claimant had reserved from the owners of the surface land, the Court held that the statute was invalid as effecting a "taking" without just compensation.

Finally, government actions that may be characterized as acquisitions of resources to permit or facilitate uniquely public functions have often been held to constitute "taking." *United States v. Causby* is illustrative. In, holding that direct overflights above the claimant's land, that destroyed the present use of the land as a chicken farm, constituted a "taking," *Causby* emphasized that Government had not "merely destroyed property [but was] using a part of it for the flight of its planes."

In contending that the New York City law has "taken" their property in violation of the Fifth and Fourteenth Amendments, appellants make a series of arguments, which, while tailored to the facts of this case, essentially urge that any substantial restriction imposed pursuant to a landmark law must be accompanied by just compensation if it is to be constitutional. . . . [A]ppellants do not contest that New York City's objective of preserving structures and areas with special historic, architectural, or cultural significance is an entirely permissible governmental goal. They also do not dispute that the restrictions imposed on its parcel are appropriate means of securing the purposes of the New York City law. Finally, appellants do not challenge any of the specific factual premises of the decision below. They accept for present purposes both that the parcel of land occupied by Grand Central Terminal must, in its present state, be regarded as capable of earning a reasonable return, and that the transferable development rights afforded appellants by virtue of the Terminal's designation as a landmark are valuable, even if not as valuable as the right to construct above the Terminal. In appellants' view none of these factors derogate from their claim that New York City's law has affected a "taking."

They first observe that the airspace above the Terminal is a valuable property interest, citing *United States v. Causby, supra.* They urge that the Landmarks Law has deprived them of any gainful use of their "air rights" above the Terminal and that, irrespective of the value of the remainder of their parcel, the city has "taken" their right to this superjacent airspace. thus entitling them to "just compensation" measured by the fair market value of these air rights. Apart from our own disagreement with appellant's characterization of the effect of the New York City law, . . . the submission that appellants may establish a "taking" simply by showing that they have been denied the ability to exploit a property interest that they heretofore had believed was available for development is quite simply untenable. . . .

. . . "Taking" jurisprudence does not divide a single parcel into discrete segments and attempt to determine whether rights in a particular segment have been entirely abrogated. In deciding whether a particular governmental action has effected a taking, this Court focuses rather both on the character of the action and on the nature and extent of the interference with rights in the parcel as a whole—here, the city tax block designated as the "landmark site."

Secondly, appellants, focusing on the character and impact of the New York City law, argue that it effects a "taking" because its operation has significantly diminished the value of the Terminal site. Appellants concede that the decisions sustaining other land-use regulations, which, like the New York City law, are reasonably related to the promotion of the general welfare, uniformly reject the proposition that diminution in property value, standing alone, can establish a "taking," and that the "taking" issue in these contexts is resolved focusing on the uses the regulations permit. Appellants, moreover, also do not dispute that a showing of diminution in property value would not establish a "taking" if the restriction had been imposed as a result of historic-district legislation, but appellants argue that New York City's regulation of individual landmarks is fundamentally different from zoning or from historic-district legislation because the controls imposed by New York City's law apply only to individuals who own selected properties.

Stated baldly, appellants' position appears to be that the only means of ensuring that selected owners are not singled out to endure financial hardship for no reason is to hold that any restriction imposed on individual landmarks pursuant to the New York City scheme is a "taking" requiring the payment of "just compensation." Agreement with this argument would, of course, invalidate not just New York City's law, but all comparable landmark legislation in the Nation. We find no merit in it.

It is true, as appellants emphasize, that both historic-district legislation and zoning laws regulate all properties within given physical communities whereas landmark laws apply only to selected parcels. But, contrary to appellants' suggestions, landmark laws are not like discriminatory, or "reverse spot," zoning: that is, a land-use decision which arbitrarily singles out a particular parcel for different, less favorable treatment than the neighboring ones. In contrast to discriminatory zoning, which is the antithesis of land-use control as part of some comprehensive plan, the New York City law embodies a comprehensive plan to preserve structures of historic or aesthetic interest wherever they might be found in the city, and as noted, over 400 landmarks and 31 historic districts have been designated pursuant to this plan.

. . .

Rejection of appellants' broad arguments is not, however, the end of our inquiry, for all we thus far have established is that the New York City law is not rendered invalid by its failure to provide "just compensation" whenever a landmark owner is restricted in the exploitation of property interests, such as air rights, to a greater extent than provided for under applicable zoning laws. We now must consider whether the interference with appellants' property is of such a magnitude that "there must be an exercise of eminent domain and compensation to sustain [it]." *Pennsylvania Coal Co. v. Mahon.* That inquiry may be narrowed to the question of the severity of the impact of the law on appellants' parcel, and its resolution in turn requires a careful assessment of the impact of the regulation on the Terminal site.

Unlike the governmental acts [challenged in prior cases], the New York City law does not interfere in any way with the present uses of the Terminal. Its designation as a landmark not only permits but contemplates that appellants may continue to use the property precisely as it has been used for the past 65 years: as a railroad terminal containing office space and concessions. So the law does not interfere with what must be regarded as Penn Central's primary expectation concerning the use of the parcel. More importantly, on this record, we must regard the New York City law as permitting Penn Central not only to profit from the Terminal but also to obtain a "reasonable return" on its investment.

. . .

On this record, we conclude that the application of New York City's Landmarks Law has not effected a "taking" of appellants' property. The restrictions imposed are substantially related to the promotion of the general welfare and not only permit reasonable beneficial use of the landmark site but also afford appellants opportunities further to enhance not only the Terminal site proper but also other properties.

Affirmed.

MR. JUSTICE REHNQUIST, with whom THE CHIEF JUSTICE and MR. JUSTICE STEVENS join, dissenting.

Of the over one million buildings and structures in the city of New York, appellees have singled out 400 for designation as official landmarks. The owner of a building might initially be pleased that his property has been chosen by a distinguished committee of architects, historians, and city planners for such a singular distinction. But he may well discover, as appellant Penn Central Transportation Co. did here, that the landmark designation imposes upon him a substantial cost, with little or no offsetting benefit except for the honor of the designation. The question in this case is whether the cost associated with the city of New York's desire to preserve a limited number of "landmarks" within its borders must be borne by all of its taxpayers or whether it can instead be imposed entirely on the owners of the individual properties.

Only in the most superficial sense of the word can this case be said to involve "zoning." Typical zoning restrictions may, it is true, so limit the prospective uses of a piece of property as to diminish the value of that property in the abstract because it may not be used for forbidden purposes. But any such abstract decrease in value will more than likely be offset by the value which flows from similar restrictions as to use on neighboring properties. All property owners in a designated area are placed under the same restrictions, not only for the benefit of the municipality as a whole but also for the common benefit of one another. . . .

Where a relatively few individual buildings, all separated from one another, are singled out and treated differently from surrounding buildings, no such reciprocity exists.... Under the historic-landmark preservation scheme adopted by New York, the property owner is under an affirmative duty to preserve his property as a landmark at his own expense. To suggest that because traditional zoning results in some limitation of use of the property zoned, the New York City landmark preservation scheme should likewise be upheld, represents the ultimate in treating as alike things which are different. The rubric of "zoning" has not yet sufficed to avoid the well-established proposition that the Fifth Amendment bars the "Government from forcing some people alone to bear public burdens which, should be borne by the public as a whole."

. . .

Appellees have thus destroyed—in a literal sense, "taken"—substantial property rights of Penn Central. While the term "taken" might have been narrowly interpreted to include only physical seizures of property rights, "the construction of the phrase has not been so narrow. The courts have held that the deprivation of the former owner rather than the accretion of a right or interest to the sovereign constitutes the taking." ... Because "not every destruction or injury to property by governmental action has been held to be a 'taking' in the constitutional sense," however, this does not end our inquiry. But all examination of the two exceptions where the destruction of property does not constitute a taking demonstrates that a compensable taking has occurred here.

As early as 1887, the Court recognized that the government can prevent a property owner from using his property to injure others without having to compensate the owner for the value of the forbidden use....

Appellees are not prohibiting a nuisance. The record is clear that the proposed addition to the Grand Central Terminal would be in full compliance with zoning, height limitations, and other health and safety requirements. Instead, appellees are seeking to preserve what they believe to be an outstanding example of beaux arts architecture. Penn Central is prevented from further developing its property basically because *too good* a job was done in designing the building. The city of New York, because of its unadorned admiration for the design, has decided that the owners of the build-

ing must preserve it unchanged for the benefit of sightseeing New Yorkers and tourists.

. . .

Even where the government prohibits a noninjurious use, the Court has ruled that a taking does not take place if the prohibition applies over a broad cross section of land and thereby "secure[s] an average reciprocity of advantage." *Pennsylvania Coal Co. v. Mahon.* It is for this reason that zoning does not constitute a "taking." While zoning at times reduces *individual* property values, the burden is shared relatively evenly and it is reasonable to conclude that on the whole an individual who is harmed by one aspect of the zoning will be benefited by another.

Here, however, a multimillion dollar loss has been imposed on appellants; it is uniquely felt and is not offset by any benefits flowing from the preservation of some 400 other "landmarks" in New York City. Appellees have imposed a substantial cost on less than one one-tenth of one percent of the buildings in New York City for the general benefit of all its people. It is exactly this imposition of general costs on a few individuals at which the "taking" protection is directed....

As Mr. Justice Holmes pointed out in *Pennsylvania Coal Co. v. Mahon,* "the question at bottom" in an eminent domain case "is upon whom the loss of the changes desired should fall." The benefits that appellees believe will flow from preservation of Grand Central Terminal will accrue to all the citizens of New York City. There is no reason to believe that appellants will enjoy a substantially greater share of these benefits. If the cost of preserving Grand Central Terminal were spread evenly across the entire population of the city of New York, the burden per person would be in cents per year—a minor cost appellees would surely concede for the benefit accrued. Instead, however, appellees would impose the entire cost of several million dollars per year on Penn Central. But it is precisely this sort of discrimination that the Fifth Amendment prohibits."...

A taking does not become a noncompensable exercise of police power simply because the government in its grace allows the owner to make some "reasonable" use of his property. "[I]t is the character of the invasion, not the amount of damage resulting from it, so long as the damage is substantial, that determines the question whether it is a taking."

In recent years, the Court has invigorated the taking clause to protect landowners from governmental conditions on land development. In *Nollan v. California Coastal Commission*, the Court determined that a building permit for a beachfront house expansion—conditioned upon granting an eight foot public easement along the beach—constituted a taking without just compensation.[100] The Court conceded that the state could have banned construction altogether as a means of preserving the public's view of the ocean,[101] or even required a public viewing spot on the property.[102] As the majority saw it, however, the oceanfront easement did not substantially achieve the objective of protecting the view, facilitating public access to the beach or minimizing congestion thereof.[103] The Court thus concluded that "unless [a] permit condition serves the same governmental purpose as [a] development ban, the building restriction is not a valid regulation of land use but 'an out-and-out plan of extortion.'"[104] A similar result was reached when a landowner challenged a state law prohibiting construction of any habitable structure on beachfront property in South Carolina.

---

[100] Nollan v. California Coastal Commission, 483 U.S. 825 (1987).

[101] *Id.* at 836.

[102] *Id.* at 838–40.

[103] *Id.* at 835–36 (1987).

[104] *Id.* at 837.

Lucas v. South Carolina Coastal Council Commission
112 S. Ct. 2886 (1992)

JUSTICE SCALIA delivered the opinion of the Court.

In 1986, petitioner David H. Lucas paid $975,000 for two residential lots on the Isle of Palms in Charleston County, South Carolina, on which he intended to build single-family homes. In 1988, however, the South Carolina Legislature enacted the Beachfront Management Act, which had the direct effect of barring petitioner from erecting any permanent habitable structures on his two parcels. A state trial court found that this prohibition rendered Lucas's parcels "valueless." This case requires us to decide whether the Act's dramatic effect on the economic value of Lucas's lots accomplished a taking of private property under the Fifth and Fourteenth Amendments requiring the payment of "just compensation."

. . .

Prior to Justice Holmes' exposition in *Pennsylvania Coal Co. v Mahon*, it was generally thought that the Takings Clause reached only a "direct appropriation" of property, or the functional equivalent of a "practical ouster of [the owner's] possession." Justice Holmes recognized in *Mahon*, however, that if the protection against physical appropriations of private property was to be meaningfully enforced, the government's power to redefine the range of interests included in the ownership of property was necessarily constrained by constitutional limits. If, instead, the uses of private property were subject to unbridled, uncompensated qualification under the police power, "the natural tendency of human nature [would be] to extend the qualification more and more until at

last private property disappear[ed]." These considerations gave birth in that case to the oft-cited maxim that, "while property may be regulated to a certain extent, if regulation goes too far it will be recognized as a taking."

Nevertheless, our decision in *Mahon* offered little insight into when, and under what circumstances, a given regulation would be seen as going "too far" for purposes of the Fifth Amendment. In 70-odd years of succeeding "regulatory taking" jurisprudence, we have generally eschewed any "set formula" for determining how far is too far, preferring to "engag[e] in . . . essentially ad hoc, factual inquiries." We have, however, described at least two discrete categories of regulatory action as compensable without case-specific inquiry into the public interest advanced, in support of the restraint. The first encompasses regulations that compel the property owner to suffer a physical "invasion" of his property. In general (at least with regard to permanent invasions), no matter how minute the intrusion and no matter how weighty the public purpose behind it, we have required compensation. We determined that New York's law requiring landlords to allow television cable companies to emplace cable facilities in their apartment buildings constituted a taking, even though the facilities occupied at most only 1½ cubic feet of the landlords' property. . . .

The second situation in which we have found categorical treatment appropriate is where regulation denies all economically beneficial or productive use of land. As we have said on numerous occasions, the Fifth Amendment is violated when land use regulation "does not substantially advance legitimate state interests *or denies an owner economically viable use of his land.*"

We have never set forth the justification for this rule. Perhaps it is simply, as Justice Brennan suggested, that total deprivation of beneficial use is, from the landowner's point of view, the equivalent of a physical appropriation. "[F]or what is the land but the profits thereof[?]" Surely, at least, in the extraordinary circumstance when *no* productive or economically beneficial use of land is permitted, it is less realistic to indulge our usual assumption that the legislature is simply "adjusting the benefits and burdens of economic life," in a manner that secures an "average reciprocity of advantage," to everyone concerned. And the *functional* basis for permitting the government, by regulation, to affect property values without compensation—that "Government hardly could go on if to some extent values incident to property could not be diminished without paying for every such change in the general law"—does not apply to the relatively rare situations where the government has deprived a landowner of all economically beneficial uses.

On the other side of the balance, affirmatively supporting a compensation requirement, is the fact that regulations that leave the owner of land without economically beneficial or productive options for its use—typically, as here, by requiring land to be left substantially in its natural state—carry with them a heightened risk that private property is being pressed into some form of public service under the guise of mitigating serious public harm. . . .

We think, in short, that there are good reasons for our frequently expressed belief that when the owner of real property has been called upon to sacrifice *all* economically beneficial uses in the name of the common good, that is, to leave his property economically idle, he has suffered a taking.

. . .

It is correct that many of our prior opinions have suggested that "harmful or noxious uses" of property may be proscribed by government regulation without the requirement of compensation. For a number of reasons, however, we think the South Carolina Supreme Court was too quick to conclude that principle decides the present case. The "harmful or noxious uses" principle was the Court's early attempt to describe in theoretical terms why government may, consistent with the Takings Clause, affect property values by regulation without incurring an obligation to compensate—a reality we nowadays acknowledge explicitly with respect to the full scope of the State's police power. . . . "Harmful or noxious use" analysis

was, in other words, simply the progenitor of our more contemporary statements that "land-use regulation does not effect a taking if it 'substantially advance[s] legitimate state interests. . . .'"

The transition from our early focus on control of "noxious" uses to our contemporary understanding of the broad realm within which government may regulate without compensation was an easy one, since the distinction between "harm-preventing" and "benefit-conferring" regulation is often in the eye of the beholder. It is quite possible, for example, to describe in *either* fashion the ecological, economic, and aesthetic concerns that inspired the South Carolina legislature in the present case. One could say that imposing a servitude on Lucas's land is necessary in order to prevent his use of it from "harming" South Carolina's ecological resources; or, instead, in order to achieve the "benefits" of ecological preserve. . . . Whether one or the other of the competing characterizations will come to one's lips in a particular case depends primarily upon one's evaluation of the worth of competing uses of real estate. . . . A given restraint will be seen as mitigating "harm" to the adjacent parcels or securing a "benefit" for them, depending upon the importance of the use that the restraint favors. . . . Whether Lucas's construction of single-family residences on his parcels should be described as bringing "harm" to South Carolina's adjacent ecological resources thus depends principally upon whether the describer believes that the State's use interest in nurturing those resources is so important that any competing adjacent use must yield.

When it is understood that "prevention of harmful use" was merely our early formulation of the police power justification necessary to sustain (without compensation) any regulatory diminution in value; and that the distinction between regulation that "prevents harmful use" and that which "confers benefits" is difficult, if not impossible, to discern on an objective, value-free basis; it becomes self-evident that noxious-use logic cannot serve as a touchstone to distinguish regulatory "takings"—which require compensation—from regulatory deprivations that do not require compensation. A fortiori the legislature's recitation of a noxious-use justification cannot be the basis for departing from our categorical rule that total regulatory taking must be compensated. If it were, departure would virtually always be allowed. The South Carolina Supreme Court's approach would essentially nullify *Mahon*'s affirmation of limits to the noncompensable exercise of the police power. Our cases provide no support for this: None of them that employed the logic of "harmful use" prevention to sustain a regulation involved an allegation that the regulation wholly eliminated the value of the claimant's land.

Where the State seeks to sustain regulation that deprives land of all economically beneficial use, we think it may resist compensation only if the logically antecedent inquiry into the nature of the owner's estate shows that the proscribed use interests were not part of his title to begin with. This accords, we think, with our "taking" jurisprudence, which has traditionally been guided by the understandings of our citizens regarding the content of, and the State's power over, the "bundle of rights" that they acquire when they obtain title to property. It seems to us that the property owner necessarily expects the uses of his property to be restricted, from time to time, by various measures newly enacted by the State in legitimate exercise of its police powers; "[a]s long recognized, some values are enjoyed under an implied limitation and must yield to the police power." And in the case of personal property, by reason of the State's traditionally high degree of control over commercial dealings, he ought to be aware of the possibility that new regulation might even render his property economically worthless, at least if the property's only economically productive use is sale or manufacture for sale. In the case of land, however, we think the notion pressed by the Council that title is somehow held subject to the "implied limitation" that the State may subsequently eliminate all economically valuable use is inconsistent with the historical compact recorded in the Takings Clause that has become part of our constitutional culture.

Where "permanent physical occupation" of land is concerned, we have refused to allow the government to decree it anew (without compensation), no matter how weighty the asserted "public interests" involved, though we, assuredly would permit the government to assert a permanent easement that was a preexisting limitation upon the landowner's title. We believe similar treatment must be accorded confiscatory regulations, i.e., regulations that prohibit all economically beneficial use of land. Any limitation so severe cannot be newly legislated or decreed (without compensation), but must inhere in the title itself, in the restrictions that background principles of the State's law of property and nuisance already place upon land ownership. A law or decree with such an effect must, in other words, do more than duplicate the result that could have been achieved in the courts—by adjacent landowners (or other uniquely affected persons) under the State's law of private nuisance, or by the State under its complementary power to abate nuisances that affect the public generally, or otherwise.

On this analysis, the owner of a lake bed, for example, would not be entitled to compensation when he is denied the requisite permit to engage in a landfilling operation that would have the effect of flooding others' land. Nor would the corporate owner of a nuclear generating plant, when it is directed to remove all improvements from its land upon discovery that the plant sits astride an earthquake fault. Such regulatory action may well have the effect of eliminating the land's only economically productive use, but it does not proscribe a productive use that was previously permissible under relevant property and nuisance principles. The use of these properties for what are now expressly prohibited purposes was always unlawful, and (subject to other constitutional limitations) it was open to the State at any point to make the implication of those background principles of nuisance and property law explicit. In light of our traditional resort to "existing rules or understandings that stem from an independent source such as state law" to define the range of interests that qualify for protection as "property" under the Fifth (and Fourteenth) Amendments, this recognition that the Takings Clause does not require compensation when an owner is barred from putting land to a use that is proscribed by those "existing rules or understandings" is surely unexceptional. When, however, a regulation that declares "off-limits" all economically productive or beneficial uses of land goes beyond what the relevant background principles would dictate, compensation must be paid to sustain it.

The "total taking" inquiry we require today will ordinarily entail (as the application of state nuisance law ordinarily entails) analysis of, among other things, the degree of harm to public lands and resources, or adjacent private property, posed by the claimant's proposed activities, the social value of the claimant's activities and their suitability to the locality in question, and the relative ease with which the alleged harm can be avoided through measures taken by the claimant and the government (or adjacent private landowners) alike. The fact that a particular use has long been engaged in by similarly situated owners ordinarily imports a lack of any common-law prohibition though changed circumstances or new knowledge may make what was previously permissible no longer so. So also does the fact that other landowners, similarly situated, are permitted to continue the use denied to the claimant.

It seems unlikely that common-law principles would have prevented the erection of any habitable or productive improvements on petitioner's land; they rarely support prohibition of the "essential use" of land. The question, however, is one of state law to be dealt with on remand. We emphasize that to win its case

South Carolina must do more than proffer the legislature's declaration that the uses Lucas desires are inconsistent with the public interest, or the conclusory assertion that they violate a common-law maxim such as sic utere tuo ut alienum non laedas. As we have said, a "State, by ipse dixit, may not transform private property into public property without compensation. . . . " Instead, as it would be required to do if it sought to restrain Lucas in a common-law action for public nuisance, South Carolina must identify background principles of nuisance and property law that prohibit the uses he now intends in the circumstances in which the property is presently found. Only on this showing can the State fairly claim that, in proscribing all such beneficial uses, the Beachfront Management Act is taking nothing.

JUSTICE KENNEDY, concurring in the judgment.

. . .

. . . The Takings Clause, while conferring substantial protection on property owners, does not eliminate the police power of the State to enact limitations on the use of their property. The rights conferred by the Takings Clause and the police power of the State may coexist without conflict. Property is bought and sold, investments are made, subject to the State's power to regulate. Where a taking is alleged from regulations which deprive the property of all value, the test must be whether the deprivation is contrary to reasonable investment-backed expectations.

There is an inherent tendency towards circularity in this synthesis, of course; for if the owner's reasonable expectations are shaped by what courts allow as a proper exercise of governmental authority, property tends to become what courts say it is. Some circularity must be tolerated in these matters, however, as it is in other spheres. The definition, moreover, is not circular in its entirety. The expectations protected by the Constitution are based on objective rules and customs that can be understood as reasonable by all parties involved.

In my view, reasonable expectations must be understood in light of the whole of our legal tradition. The common law of nuisance is too narrow a confine for the exercise of regulatory power in a complex and interdependent society. The State should not be prevented from enacting new regulatory initiatives in response to changing conditions, and courts must consider all reasonable expectations whatever their source. The Taking Clause does not require a static body of state property law; it protects private expectations to ensure private investment. I agree with the Court that nuisance prevention accords with the most common expectations of property owners who face regulation, but I do not believe this can be the sole source of state authority to impose severe restrictions. Coastal property may present such unique concerns for a fragile land system that the State can go further in regulating its development and use than the common law of nuisance might otherwise permit.

The Supreme Court of South Carolina erred, in my view, by reciting the general purposes for which the state regulations were enacted without a determination that they were in accord with the owner's reasonable expectations and therefore sufficient to support a severe restriction on specific parcels of property. The promotion of tourism, for instance, ought not to suffice to deprive specific property of all value without a corresponding duty to compensate. Furthermore, the means as well as the ends of regulation must accord with the owner's reasonable expectations. Here, the State did not act until after the property had been zoned for individual lot development and most other parcels had been improved, throwing the whole burden of the regulation on the remaining lots. This too must be measured in the balance.

With these observations, I concur in the judgment of the Court.

JUSTICE BLACKMUN, dissenting.

Today the Court launches a missile to kill a mouse.

The State of South Carolina prohibited petitioner Lucas from building a permanent structure on his property from 1988 to 1990. Relying on an unreviewed (and implausible) state trial court finding that this restriction left Lucas' property valueless, this Court granted review to determine whether compensation must be paid in cases where the State prohibits all economic use of real estate. According to the Court, such an occasion never has arisen in any of our prior cases, and the Court imagines, that it will arise "relatively rarely" or only in "extraordinary circumstances." Almost certainly it did not happen in this case.

Nonetheless, the Court presses on to decide the issue, and as it does, it ignores its jurisdictional limits, remakes its traditional rules of review, and creates simultaneously a new categorical rule and an exception (neither of which is rooted in our prior case law, common law, or common sense). I protest not only the Court's decision, but each step taken to reach it. More fundamentally, I question the Court's wisdom in issuing sweeping new rules to decide such a narrow case. Surely, as Justice Kennedy demonstrates, the Court could have reached the result it wanted without inflicting this damage upon our Taking Clause jurisprudence.

My fear is that the Court's new policies will spread beyond the narrow confines of the present case. For that reason, I, like the Court, will give far greater attention to this case than its narrow scope suggests—not because I can intercept the Court's missile, or save the targeted mouse, but because I hope perhaps to limit the collateral damage.

. . .

The South Carolina Supreme Court found that the Beach Management Act did not take petitioner's property without compensation. The decision rested on two premises that until today were unassailable—that the State has the power to prevent any use of property it finds to be harmful to its citizens, and that a state statute is entitled to a presumption of constitutionality.

. . .

Petitioner never challenged the legislature's findings that a building ban was necessary to protect property and life. Nor did he contend that the threatened harm was not sufficiently serious to make building a house in a particular location a "harmful" use, that the legislature had not made sufficient findings, or that the legislature was motivated by anything other than a desire to minimize damage to coastal areas. Indeed, petitioner objected at trial that evidence as to the purpose of the setback requirement was irrelevant. . . .

Nothing in the record undermines the General Assembly's assessment that prohibitions on building in front of the setback line are necessary to protect people and property from storms, high tides, and beach erosion. Because that legislative determination cannot be disregarded in the absence of such evidence, and because its determination of harm to life and property from building is sufficient to prohibit that use under this Court's cases, the South Supreme Court correctly found no taking.

. . .

. . . The Court creates its new taking jurisprudence based on the trial court's finding that the property had lost all economic value. This finding is almost certainly erroneous. Petitioner still can enjoy other attributes of ownership, such as the right to exclude others, "one of the most essential sticks in the bundle of rights that are commonly characterized as property." Petitioner can picnic, swim, camp in a tent, or live on the property in a movable trailer. State courts frequently have recognized that land has economic value where the only residual economic uses are recreation or camping. Petitioner also retains the right to alienate the land, which would have value for neighbors and for those prepared to enjoy proximity to the ocean without a house.

Yet the trial court, apparently believing that "less value" and "valueless" could be used interchangeably, found the property "valueless." The court accepted no evidence from the State on the property's value without a home,

and petitioner's appraiser testified that he never had considered what the value would be absent a residence. The appraiser's value was based on the fact that the "highest and best use of these lots [is] luxury single family detached dwellings." The trial court appeared to believe that the property could be considered "valueless" if it was not available for its most profitable use. Absent that erroneous assumption, I find no evidence in the record supporting the trial court's conclusions that the damage to the lots by virtue of the restrictions was "total."

. . .

The threshold inquiry for imposition of the Court's new rule, "deprivation of all economically valuable use," itself cannot be determined objectively. "As the Court admits, whether the owner has been deprived of all economic value of his property will depend on how "property" is defined. The "composition of the denominator in our, 'deprivation' fraction," is the" dispositive inquiry. Yet there is no "objective" way to define what that denominator should be. "We have long understood that any land-use regulation can be characterized as the 'total' deprivation of an aptly defined entitlement. . . . Alternatively, the same regulation can always be characterized as a mere partial withdrawal from full, unencumbered ownership of the landholding affected by the regulation. . . . "

Even more perplexing, however, is the Court's reliance on common-law principles of nuisance in its quest for a value-free taking jurisprudence. In determining what is a nuisance at common law, state courts make exactly the decision that the Court finds so troubling when made by the South Carolina General Assembly today: they determine whether the use is harmful. Common-law public and private nuisance is simply a determination whether a particular use causes harm. . . . There is nothing magical in the reasoning of judges long dead. They determined a harm in the same way as state judges and legislatures do today. If judges in the 18th and 19th centuries can distinguish a harm from a benefit, why not judges in the 20th century, and if judges can, why not legislators? There simply is no reason to believe that new interpretations of the hoary common law nuisance doctrine will be particularly "objective" or "value-free." Once one abandons the level of generality of *sic utere tuo ut alienum non laedas*, one searches in vain, I think, for anything resembling a principle in the common law of nuisance.

Finally, the Court justifies its new rule that the legislature may not deprive a property owner of the only economically valuable use of his land, even if the legislature finds it to be a harmful use, because such action is not part of the "long recognized" "understandings, of our citizens." These "understandings" permit such regulation only if the use is a nuisance under the common law. Any other course is "inconsistent with the historical compact recorded in the Takings Clause." It is not clear from the Court's opinion where our "historical compact" or "citizens' understanding" comes from, but it does not appear to be history.

The principle that the State should compensate individuals for property taken for public use was not widely established in America at the time of the Revolution.

. . .

Even into the 19th century, state governments often felt free to take property for roads and other public projects without paying compensation to the owners. As one court declared in 1802, citizens "were bound to contribute as much of [land], as by the laws of the country, were deemed necessary for the public convenience." There was an obvious movement toward establishing the just compensation principle during the 20th century, but "there continued to be a strong current in American legal thought that regarded compensation simply as a 'bounty given . . . by the State' out of 'kindness' and not out of justice."

Although, prior to the adoption of the Bill of Rights, America was replete with land use regulations describing which activities were considered noxious and forbidden, the Fifth Amendment's Taking Clause originally did not extend to regulations of property, whatever the effect. Most courts agreed with this narrow interpretation of a taking. "Until the end of the nineteenth century . . . jurists held that the constitution protected possession only, and not value."

. . .

Nor does history indicate any common-law on the State's power to regulate harmful uses even to the point of destroying all economic value. Nothing in the discussions in Congress concerning the Taking Clause indicates that the Clause was limited by the common-law nuisance doctrine. Common law courts themselves rejected such an understanding. They regularly recognized that it is "for the legislature to interpose, and by positive enactment to prohibit a use of property which would be injurious to the public." . . .

In short, I find no clear and accepted "historical compact" or "understanding of our citizens" justifying the Court's new taking doctrine. Instead, the Court seems to treat history as a grab-bag of principles, to be adopted where they support the Court's theory, and ignored where they do not. If the Court decided that the early common law provides the background principles for interpreting the Taking Clause, then regulation, as opposed to physical confiscation would not be compensable. If the Court decided that the law of a later period provides the background principles, then regulation

might be compensable, but the Court would have to confront the fact that legislatures regularly determined which uses were prohibited, independent of the common law, and dependent of whether the uses were lawful when the owner purchased. What makes the Court's analysis unworkable is its attempt to package the law of two incompatible eras and peddle it as historical fact.

The Court makes sweeping and, in my view, misguided and unsupported changes in our taking doctrine. While it limits these changes to the most narrow subset of government regulation—those that eliminate all economic value from land—these changes go far beyond what is necessary to secure petitioner Lucas' private benefit. One hopes they do not go beyond the narrow confines the Court assigns them to today.

I dissent.

Justice Stevens, dissenting.

. . .

In its analysis of the merits, the Court starts from the premise that this Court has adopted a "categorical rule that total regulatory taking must be compensated," and then sets itself to the task of identifying the exceptional cases in which a State may be relieved of this categorical obligation. The test the Court announces is that the regulation must do no more than duplicate the result that could have been achieved under a State's nuisance law. Under this test the categorical rule will apply unless the regulation merely makes explicit what was otherwise an implicit limitation on the owner's property rights.

In my opinion, the Court is doubly in error. The categorical rule the Court establishes is an unsound and unwise addition to the law and the Court's formulation of the exception to that rule is too right and too narrow.

. . .

In addition to lacking support in past decisions, the Court's new rule is wholly arbitrary. A landowner whose property is diminished in value 95% recovers nothing, while an owner whose property is diminished 100% recovers the land's full value. . . .

Finally, the Court's justification for its new categorical rule is remarkably thin. The Court mentions in passing three arguments in support of its rule; none is convincing. First, the Court suggests that "total deprivation of feasible use is, from the landowner's point of view, the equivalent of a physical appropriation." This argument proves too much. From the "landowner's point of view," a regulation that diminishes a lot's value by 50% is as well "the equivalent" of the condemnation of half of the lot. Yet, it is well established that a 50% diminution in value does not by itself constitute a taking. Thus, the landowner's perception of the regulation cannot justify the Court's new rule.

Second, the Court emphasizes that because total takings are "relatively rare" its new rule will not adversely affect the government's ability to "go on." This argument proves too little. Certainly it is true that defining a small class of regulations that are per se taking will not greatly hinder important governmental functions—but this is true of any small class of regulations. The Court's suggestion only begs the question of why regulations of this particular class should always be found to effect taking.

Finally, the Court suggests that "regulations that leave the owner . . . without economically beneficial use . . . carry with them a heightened risk that private property is being pressed into some form of public service." I agree that the risks of such singling out are of central concern in taking law. However, such risks do not justify a per se rule for total regulatory taking. There is no necessary correlation between "singling out" and total taking: a regulation may single out a property owner without depriving him of all of his property, and it may deprive him of all of his property without singling him out. What matters in such cases is not the degree of diminution of value, but rather the specificity of the expropriating act. For this reason, the Court's third justification for its new rule also fails.

In short, the Court's new rule is unsupported by prior decisions, arbitrary and unsound in practice, and theoretically unjustified. In my opinion, a categorical rule as important as the one established by the Court today should be supported by more history or more reason than has yet been provided.

. . .

The Court's categorical approach rules will, I fear, greatly hamper the efforts of local officials and planners who must deal with increasingly complex problems in land-use and environmental regulation. As this case—in which the claims of an individual property owner exceed $1 million—well demonstrates, these officials face both substantial uncertainty because of the ad hoc nature of taking law and unacceptable penalties if they guess incorrectly about that law.

Viewed more broadly, the Court's new rule and exception conflict with the very character of our taking jurisprudence. We have frequently and consistently recognized that the definition of a taking cannot be reduced to a "set formula" and that determining whether a regulation is a taking is "essentially [an] ad hoc, factual inquir[y]." This is unavoidable, for the determination whether a law effects a taking is ultimately a matter of "fairness and justice," and "necessarily requires a weighing of private and public interests." The rigid rules fixed by the Court today clash with this enterprise: "fairness and justice" are often disserviced by categorical rules.

It is well established that a taking case "entails inquiry into [several factors:] the character of the governmental action, its economic impact, and its interference with reasonable investment-backed expectations. The Court's analysis today focuses on the last two of these three factors: the categorical rule addresses a regulation's "economic impact," while the nuisance exception recognizes that ownership brings with it only certain "expectations." Neglected by the Court today is the first, and in some ways, the most important factor in taking analysis: the character of the regulatory action.

The Just Compensation Clause was designed to bar Government from forcing some people alone to bear public burdens which, in all fairness and justice, should be borne by the public as a whole." Accordingly, one of the central concerns of our taking, jurisprudence is "prevent[ing] the public from loading upon one individual more than his just share of the burdens of government." We have, therefore, in our taking law frequently looked to the *generality* of a regulation of property. . . .

The presumption that a permanent physical occupation, no matter how slight, effects a taking is wholly consistent with this principle. A physical taking entails a "certain amount of "singling out." Consistent with this principle, physical occupations by third parties are more likely to effect taking than other physical occupations. Thus, a regulation requiring the installation of a junction box owned by a third party, is more troubling than a regulation requiring the installation of sprinklers or smoke detectors; just as an order granting third parties access to a marina, is more troubling than an order requiring the placement of safety buoys in the marina.

In analyzing taking claims, courts have long recognized the difference between a regulation that targets one or two parcels of land and a regulation that enforces a state-wide policy. . . .

In considering Lucas' claim, the generality of the Beachfront Management Act is significant. The Act does not target particular landowners, but rather regulates the use of the coastline of the entire State. Indeed, South Carolina's Act is best understood as part of a national effort to protect the coastline, one initiated by the Federal Coastal Zone Management Act of 1972. Pursuant to the Federal Act, every coastal State has implemented coastline regulations. Moreover, the Act did not single out owners of undeveloped land. The Act also prohibited owners of developed land from rebuilding if their structures were destroyed, and what is equally significant, from repairing erosion control devices, such as seawalls. In addition, in some situations, owners of developed land were required to "renouris[h] the beach . . . on a yearly basis with an amount . . . of sand . . . not . . . less than one and one-half times the yearly volume of sand lost due to erosion. In short, the South Carolina Act imposed substantial burdens on owners of developed and undeveloped land alike. This generality indicates that the Act is not an effort to expropriate owners of undeveloped land.

Admittedly, the economic impact of this regulation is dramatic and petitioner's investment-backed expectations are substantial. Yet, if anything, the costs to and expectations of the owners of developed land are even greater: I doubt, however that the cost to owners: of developed land of renourishing the beach and allowing their seawalls to deteriorate effects a taking. The costs imposed on the owners of undeveloped land, such as petitioner, differ from these costs only in degree, not in kind.

The impact of the ban on developmental uses must also be viewed in light of the purposes of the Act. The legislature stated the purposes of the Act as "protect[ing], preserv[ing], restor[ing] and enhanc[ing] the beach/dune system" of the State not only for recreational and ecological purposes, but also to protec[t] life and property." The State, with much science on its side, believes that the "beach/dune system [acts] as a buffer from high tides, storm surge, [and] hurricanes." This is a traditional and important exercise of the State's police power, as demonstrated by Hurricane Hugo, which in 1989, caused 29 deaths and more than $6 billion in property damage in South Carolina alone. In view of all of these factors, even assuming that petitioner's property was rendered valueless, the risk inherent in investments of the sort made by petitioner, the generality of the Act, and the compelling purpose motivating the South Carolina Legislature persuade me that the Act did not effect a taking of petitioner's property.

Accordingly, I respectful dissent.

Given the Court's sense that the state had denied "all economically beneficial use" of the land, it was unclear whether a similar standard of review and result would follow in the event of a less dramatic regulatory impact. In *Dolan v. City of Tigard*, however, the Court employed heightened scrutiny to a land use control plan conditioning a building permit upon dedication of part of the property to open space and bicycle pathways. The "rough proportionality" between regulatory means and objectives.

Dolan v. Tigard
114 S. Ct. 2309 (1994)

CHIEF JUSTICE REHNQUIST delivered the opinion of the Court.

Petitioner challenges the decision of the Oregon Supreme Court which held that the city of Tigard could condition the approval of her building permit on the dedication of a portion of her property for flood control and traffic improvements. We granted certiorari to resolve a question left open by our decision in *Nollan v. California Coastal Comm'n* of what is the required degree of connection between the exactions imposed by the city and the projected impacts of the proposed development.

[T]he city of Tigard, a community of some 30,000 residents on the southwest edge of Portland, developed a comprehensive plan and codified it in its Community Development Code (CDC). The CDC requires property owners in the area zoned Central Business District to comply with a 15% open space and landscaping requirement, which limits total site coverage,

including all structures and paved parking, to 85% of the parcel. After the completion of a transportation study that identified congestion in the Central Business District as a particular problem, the city adopted a plan for a pedestrian/bicycle pathway intended to encourage alternatives to automobile transportation for short trips. The CDC requires that new development facilitate this plan by dedicating land for pedestrian pathways where provided for in the pedestrian/bicycle pathway plan.

The city also adopted a Master Drainage Plan (Drainage Plan). The Drainage Plan noted that flooding occurred in several areas along Fanno Creek, including areas near petitioner's property. The Drainage Plan also established that the increase in impervious surfaces associated with continued urbanization would exacerbate these flooding problems. To combat these risks, the Drainage Plan suggested a series of improvements to the Fanno

Creek Basin, including channel excavation in the area next to petitioner's property. Other recommendations included ensuring that the floodplain remains free of structures and that it be preserved as greenways to minimize flood damage to structures. The Drainage Plan concluded that the cost of these improvements should be shared based on both direct and indirect benefits, with property owners along the waterways paying more due to the direct benefit that they would receive. . . .

Petitioner applied to the city for a permit to redevelop the site. Her proposed plans called for nearly doubling the size of the store to 17,600 square feet, and paving a 39-space parking lot. The existing store, located on the opposite side of the parcel, would be razed in sections as construction progressed on the new building. In the second phase of the project, petitioner proposed to build an additional structure on the northeast side of the site for complementary businesses, and to provide more parking. The proposed expansion and intensified use are consistent with the city's zoning scheme in the Central Business District. § 18.66.030.

The City Planning Commission granted petitioner's permit application subject to conditions imposed by the city's CDC. The CDC establishes the following standard for site development review approval:

> "Where landfill and/or development is allowed within and adjacent to the 100-year floodplain, the city shall require the dedication of sufficient open land area for greenway adjoining and within the floodplain. This area shall include portions at a suitable elevation for the construction of a pedestrian/bicycle pathway within the floodplain in accordance with the adopted pedestrian/bicycle plan."

Thus, the Commission required that petitioner dedicate the portion of her property lying within the 100-year floodplain for improvement of a storm drainage system along Fanno Creek and that she dedicate an additional 15-foot strip of land adjacent to the floodplain as a pedestrian/bicycle pathway. The dedication required by that condition encompasses approximately 7,000 square feet, or roughly 10% of the property. In accordance with city practice, petitioner could rely on the dedicated property to meet the 15% open space and landscaping requirement mandated by the city's zoning scheme. The city would bear the cost of maintaining a landscaped buffer between the dedicated area and the new store.

Petitioner requested variances from the CDC standards. Variances are granted only where it can be shown that, owing to special circumstances related to a specific piece of the land, the literal interpretation of the applicable zoning provisions would cause "an undue or unnecessary hardship" unless the variance is granted. Rather than posing alternative mitigating measures to offset the expected impacts of her proposed development, as allowed under the CDC, petitioner simply argued that her proposed development would not conflict with the policies of the comprehensive plan. The Commission denied the request.

The Commission made a series of findings concerning the relationship between the dedicated conditions and the projected impacts of petitioner's project. First, the commission noted that "[i]t is reasonable to assume that customers and employees of the future uses of this site could utilize a pedestrian/bicycle pathway adjacent to this development for their transportation and recreation needs." The Commission noted that the site plan has provided for bicycle parking in a rack in front of the proposed building and "[i]t is reasonable to expect that some of the users of the bicycle parking provided for by the site plan will use the pathway adjacent to Fanno Creek if it is constructed." In addition, the Commission found that creation of a convenient, safe pedestrian/bicycle pathway system as an alternative means of transportation "could offset some of the traffic demand on [nearby] streets and lessen the increase in traffic congestion."

The Commission went on to note that the required floodplain dedication would be reasonably related to petitioner's request to intensify the use of the site given the increase in the impervious surface. The Commission stated that the "anticipated increased storm water flow from the subject property to an already strained creek and drainage basin can only add to the public need to manage the stream channel and floodplain for drainage purposes." Based on this anticipated increased storm water flow, the Commission concluded that "the requirement of dedication of the floodplain area on the site is related to the applicant's plan to intensify development on the site." The Tigard City Council approved the Commission's final order. . . .

Petitioner appealed to the Land Use Board of Appeals (LUBA) on the ground that the city's dedication requirements were not related to the proposed development, and, therefore, those requirements constituted an uncompensated taking of their property under the Fifth Amendment. . . . Given the undisputed fact that the proposed larger building and paved parking area would increase the amount of impervious surfaces and the runoff into Fanno Creek, LUBA concluded that "there is a 'reasonable relationship' between the proposed development and the requirement to dedicate land along Fanno Creek for a greenway." With respect to the pedestrian/bicycle pathway, LUBA noted the Commission's finding that a significantly larger retail sales building and parking lot would attract larger numbers of customers and employees and their vehicles. It again found a "reasonable relationship" between alleviating the impacts of increased traffic from the development and facilitating the provision of a pedestrian/bicycle pathway as an alternative means of transportation.

The Oregon Court of Appeals affirmed, rejecting petitioner's contention that in *Nollan*, we had abandoned the "reasonable relationship" test in favor of a stricter "essential nexus" test. The Oregon Supreme Court affirmed. The court also disagreed with petitioner's contention that the *Nollan* Court abandoned the "reasonably related" test. Instead, the court read *Nollan* to mean that an "exaction is reasonably related to an impact if the exaction serves the same purpose that a denial of the permit would serve." The court decided that both the pedestrian/bicycle pathway condition and the storm drainage dedication had an essential nexus to the development of the proposed site. Therefore, the court found the conditions to be reasonably related to the impact of the expansion of petitioner's business. . . .

The Takings Clause of the Fifth Amendment of the United States Constitution, made applicable to the States through the Fourteenth Amendment, *Chicago, B.&Q. R. Co. v. Chicago*, 166 U.S. 226, 239 (1897), provides: "[N]or shall private property be taken for public use, without just compensation." One of the principal purposes of the Takings Clause is "to bar Government from forcing some people alone to bear public burdens which, in all fairness and justice, should be borne by the public as a whole." *Armstrong v. United States*, 364 U.S. 40, 49 (1960). Without question, had the city simply required petitioner to dedicate a strip of land along Fanno Creek for public use, rather than conditioning the grant of her permit to redevelop her property on such a dedication, a taking would have occurred. Such public access would deprive petitioner of the right to exclude others, "one of the most essential sticks in the bundle of rights that are commonly characterized as property." *Kaiser Aetna v. United States*, 444 U.S. 164, 176 (1979).

On the other side of the ledger, the authority of state and local governments to engage in land use planning has been sustained against constitutional challenge as long ago as our decision in *Euclid v. Ambler Realty Co.*, 272 U.S. 365 (1926). "Government hardly could go on if to some extent values incident to property could not be diminished without paying for every such change in the general law." *Pennsylvania Coal Co. v. Mahon*, 260 U.S. 393, 413 (1922). A land use regulation does not effect a taking if it "substantially advance[s] legitimate state interests" and does not "den[y] an owner economically viable use of his land." *Agins v. Tiburon*, 447 U.S. 255, 260 (1980).

The sort of land use regulations discussed in the cases just cited, however, differ in two relevant particulars from the present case. First, they involved essentially legislative determinations classifying entire areas of the city, whereas here the city made an adjudicative decision to condition petitioner's application for a building permit on an individual parcel. Second, the conditions imposed were not simply a limitation the use petitioner might make of her own parcel, but a requirement that she deed portions of the property to the city. In *Nollan*, we held that governmental authority to extact such a condition was circumscribed by the Fifth and Fourteenth Amendments. Under the well-settled doctrine of "unconstitutional conditions," the government may not require a person to give up a constitutional right—here the right to receive just compensation when property is taken for a public use—in exchange for a discretionary benefit conferred by the government where the property sought has little or no relationship to the benefit.

Petitioner contends that the city has forced her to choose between the building permit and her right under the Fifth Amendment to just compensation for the public easements. Petitioner does not quarrel with the city's authority to exact some form of dedication as a condition for the grant of a building permit, but challenges the showing made by the city to justify these exactions. She argues that the city has identified "no special benefits" conferred on her, and has not identified any "special quantifiable burdens" created by her new store that would justify the particular dedications required from her which are not required from the public at large.

In evaluating petitioner's claim, we must first determine whether the "essential nexus" exists between the "legitimate state interest" and the permit condition exacted by the city. If we find that a nexus exists, we must then decide the required degree of connection between the exactions and the projected impact of the proposed development. We were not required to reach this question in *Nollan*, because we concluded that the connection did not meet even the loosest standard. Here, however, we must decide this question.

We addressed the essential nexus question in *Nollan*. The California Coastal Commission demanded a lateral public easement across the Nollans' beachfront lot in exchange for a permit to demolish an existing bungalow and replace it with a three-bedroom house. The public easement was designed to connect two public beaches that were separated by the Nollans' property. The Coastal Commission had asserted that the public easement condition was imposed to promote the legitimate state interest of diminishing the "blockage of the view of the ocean" caused by construction of the larger house.

. . .

. . . How enhancing the public's ability to "traverse to and along the shorefront" served the same governmental purpose of "visual access to the ocean" from the roadway was beyond our ability to countenance. The absence of a nexus left the Coastal Commission in the position of simply trying to obtain an easement through gimmickry, which converted a valid regulation of land use into "an out-and-out plan of extortion."

No such gimmicks are associated with the permit conditions imposed by the city in this case. Undoubtedly, the prevention of flooding along Fanno Creek and the reduction of traffic congestion in the Central Business District qualify as the type of legitimate public purposes we have upheld. It seems equally obvious that a nexus exists between preventing flooding along Fanno Creek and limiting development within the creek's 100-year floodplain. Petitioner proposes to double the size of her retail store and to pave her now-gravel parking lot, thereby expanding the impervious surface on the property and increasing the amount of stormwater run-off into Fanno Creek.

The same may be said for the city's attempt to reduce traffic congestion by providing for alternative means of transportation. In theory, a pedestrian/bicycle pathway provides a useful alternative means of transportation for workers and shoppers: "Pedestrians and bicyclists occupying dedicated spaces for walking and/or bicycling . . . remove potential vehicles from streets, resulting in an overall improvement in total transportation system flow."

The second part of our analysis requires us to determine whether the degree of the exactions demanded by the city's permit conditions bear the required relationship to the projected impact of petitioner's proposed development. . . .

The city required that petitioner dedicate "to the city as Greenway all portions of the site that fall within the existing 100-year floodplain [of Fanno Creek] . . . and all property 15 feet above [the floodplain] boundary." In addition, the city demanded that the retail store be designed so as not to intrude into the greenway area. The city relies on the Commission's rather tentative findings that increased stormwater flow from petitioner's property "can only add to the public need to manage the [floodplain] for drainage purposes" to support its conclusion that the "requirement of dedication of the floodplain area on the site is related

to the applicant's plan to intensify development on the site."

The city made the following specific findings relevant to the pedestrian/bicycle pathway:

"In addition, the proposed expanded use of this site is anticipated to generate additional vehicular traffic thereby increasing congestion on nearby collector and arterial streets. Creation of a convenient, safe pedestrian/bicycle pathway system as an alternative means of transportation could offset some of the traffic demand on these nearby streets and lessen the increase in traffic congestion."

The question for us is whether these findings are constitutionally sufficient to justify the conditions imposed by the city on petitioner's building permit. Since state courts have been dealing with this question a good deal longer than we have, we turn to representative decisions made by them.

In some States, very generalized statements as to the necessary connection between the required dedication and the proposed development seem to suffice. . . .

Other state courts require a very exacting correspondence described as the "specif[c] and uniquely attributable" test. . . .

A number of state courts have taken an intermediate position, requiring the municipality to show a "reasonable relationship" between the required dedication and the impact of the proposed development. . . .

We think the "reasonable relationship" test adopted by a majority of the state courts is closer to the federal constitutional norm than either of those previously discussed. But we do not adopt it as such, partly because the term "reasonably relationship" seems confusingly similar to the term "rational basis" which describes the minimal level of scrutiny under the Equal Protection Clause of the Fourteenth Amendment. We think a term such as "rough proportionality" best encapsulates what we hold to be the requirement of the Fifth Amendment. No precise mathematical calculations are required, but the city must make some sort of individualized determination that the required dedication is related both in nature and extent to the impact of the proposed development.

JUSTICE STEVENS' dissent relies upon a law review article for the proposition that the city's conditional demands for part of petitioner's property are "a species of business regulation that heretofore warranted a strong presumption of constitutional validity." But simply denominating a governmental measure as a "business regulation" does not immunize it from constitutional challenge on the grounds that it violates a provision of the Bill of Rights.

In *Marshall v. Barlow's, Inc.*, 436 U.S. 307 (1978), we held that a statute authorizing a warrantless search of business premises in order to detect OSHA violations violated the Fourth Amendment. And in *Central Hudson Gas & Electric Corp. v. Public Service Comm'n of N.Y.*, 447 U.S. 557 (1980), we held that an order of the New York Public Service Commission, designed to cut down the use of electricity because of a fuel shortage, violated the First Amendment insofar as it prohibited advertising by a utility company to promote the use of electricity. We see no reason why the Takings Clause of the Fifth Amendment, as much a part of the Bill of Rights as the First Amendment or Fourth Amendment, should be relegated to the status of a poor relation in these comparable circumstances. We turn now to analysis of whether the findings relied upon the city here, first with respect to the floodplain easement, and second with respect to the pedestrian/bicycle path, satisfied these requirements.

It is axiomatic that increasing the amount of impervious surface will increase the quantity and rate of stormwater flow from petitioner's property. Therefore, keeping the floodplain open and free from development would likely confine the pressures on Fanno Creek created by petitioner's development. In fact, because petitioner's property lies within the Central Business District, the Community Development Code already required that petitioner leave 15% of it as open space and the undeveloped floodplain would have nearly satisfied that requirement. But the city demanded more—it not only wanted petitioner not to build in the floodplain, but it also wanted petitioner's property along Fanno Creek for its Greenway system. The city has never said why a public greenway, as opposed to a private one, was required in the interest of flood control.

The difference to petitioner, of course, is the loss of her ability to exclude others. As we have noted, this right to exclude others is "one of the most essential sticks in the bundle of rights that are commonly characterized as property." It is difficult to see why recreational visitors trampling along petitioner's floodplain easement are sufficiently related to the city's legitimate interest in reducing flooding problems along Fanno Creek, and the city has not attempted to make any individualized determination to support this part of its request.

The city contends that recreational easement along the Greenway is only ancillary to the city's chief purpose in controlling flood hazards. If further asserts that unlike the residential property at issue in *Nollan*, petitioner's property is commercial in character and therefore, her right to exclude others is compromised. The city maintains that "[t]here is nothing to suggest that preventing [petitioner] from

prohibiting [the easements] will unreasonably impair the value of [her] property as a [retail store]."

Admittedly, petitioner wants to build a bigger store to attract members of the public to her property. She also wants, however, to be able to control the time and manner in which they enter. The recreational easement on the Greenway is different in character from the exercise of state-protected rights of free expression and petition that we permitted in *PruneYard*. In *PruneYard*, we held that a major private shopping center that attracted more than 25,000 daily patrons had to provide access to persons exercising their state constitutional rights to distribute pamphlets and ask passersby to sign their petitions. We based our decision, in part, on the fact that the shopping center "may restrict expressive activity by adopting time, place, and manner regulations that will minimize any interference with its commercial functions." By contrast, the city wants to impose a permanent recreational easement upon petitioner's property that borders Fanno Creek. Petitioner would lose all rights to regulate the time in which the public entered onto the Greenway, regardless of any interference it might pose with her retail store. Her right to exclude would not be regulated, it would be eviscerated.

... We conclude that the findings upon which the city relies do not show the required reasonable relationship between the floodplain easement and the petitioner's proposed new building.

With respect to the pedestrian/bicycle pathway, we have no doubt that the city was correct in finding that the larger retail sales facility proposed by petitioner will increase traffic on the streets of the Central Business District. The city estimates that the proposed development would generate roughly 435 additional trips per day. Dedications for streets, sidewalks, and other public ways are generally reasonable exactions to avoid excessive congestion from a proposed property use. But on the record before us, the city has not met its burden of demonstrating that the additional number of vehicle and bicycle trips generated by the petitioner's development reasonably relate to the city's requirement for a dedication of the pedestrian/bicycle pathway easement. The city simply found that the creation of the pathway "could offset some of the traffic demand . . . and lessen the increase in traffic congestion."

As Justice Peterson of the Supreme Court of Oregon explained in his dissenting opinion, however, "[t]he findings of fact that the bicycle pathway system '*could* offset some of the traffic demand' is a far cry from a finding that the bicycle pathway system *will*, or is *likely to*, offset some of the traffic demand." No precise mathematical calculation is required, but the city must make some effort to quantify its findings in support of the dedication for the pedestrian/bicycle pathway beyond the conclusory statement that it could offset some of the traffic demand generated.

Cities have long engaged in the commendable task of land use planning, made necessary by increasing urbanization particularly in metropolitan areas such as Portland. The city's goals of reducing flooding hazards and traffic congestion, and providing for public greenways, are laudable, but there are outer limits to how this may be done. "A strong public desire to improve the public condition [will not] warrant achieving the desire by a shorter cut than the constitutional way of paying for the change." *Pennsylvania Coal*, 260 U.S., at 416.

The judgment of the Supreme Court of Oregon is reversed, and the case is remanded for further proceedings consistent with this opinion.

It is so ordered.

Justice Stevens, with whom Justice Blackmun and Justice Ginsburg join, dissenting.

The record does not tell us the dollar value of petitioner Florence Dolan's interest in excluding the public from the greenway adjacent to her hardware business. The mountain of briefs that the case has generated nevertheless makes it obvious that the pecuniary value of her victory is far less important than the rule of law that this case has been used to establish. It is unquestionably an important case.

Certain propositions are not in dispute. The enlargement of the Tigard unit in Dolan's chain of hardware stores will have an adverse impact on the city's legitimate and substantial interests in controlling drainage in Fanno Creek and minimizing traffic congestion in Tigard's business district. That impact is sufficient to justify an outright denial of her application for approval of the expansion. The city has nevertheless agreed to grant Dolan's application if she will comply with two conditions, each of which admittedly will mitigate the adverse effects of her proposed development. The disputed question is whether the city has violated the Fourteenth Amendment to the Federal Constitution by refusing to allow Dolan's planned construction to proceed unless those conditions are met.

The Court is correct in concluding that the city may not attach arbitrary conditions to a building permit or to a variance even when it can rightfully deny the application outright. I also agree that state court decisions dealing with ordinances that govern municipal development plans provide useful guidance in a case of this kind. Yet the Court's description of the doctrinal underpinnings of its decision, the

phrasing of its fledgling test of "rough proportionality," and the application of that test to this case, run contrary to the traditional treatment of these cases and break considerable and unpropitious new ground.

Candidly acknowledging the lack of federal precedent for its exercise in rulemaking, the Court purports to find guidance in 12 "representative" state court decisions. To do so is certainly appropriate. The state cases the Court consults, however, either fail to support or decidedly undermine the Court's conclusions in key respects.

First, although discussion of the state cases permeates the Court's analysis of the appropriate test to apply in this case, the test on which the Court settles is not naturally derived from those courts' decisions. The Court recognizes as an initial matter that the city's conditions satisfy the "essential nexus" requirement announced in *Nollan*, because they serve the legitimate interest in minimizing floods and traffic congestions. The Court goes on, however, to erect a new constitutional hurdle in the path of these conditions. In addition to showing a rational nexus to a public purpose that would justify an outright denial of the permit, the city must also demonstrate "rough proportionality" between the harm caused by the new land use and the benefit obtained by the condition. The Court also decides for the first time that the city has the burden of establishing the constitutionality of its conditions by making an "individualized determination" that the condition in question satisfies the proportionality requirement.

Not one of the state cases cited by the Court announces anything akin to a "rough proportionality" requirement. For the most part, moreover, those cases that invalidated municipal ordinances did so on state law or unspecified grounds roughly equivalent to *Nollan's* "essential nexus" requirement. . . .

In addition, the Court ignores the state court's willingness to consider what the property owner gains from the exchange in question. . . .

The state court decisions also are enlightening in the extent to which they required that the *entire parcel* be given controlling importance. All but one of the cases involve challenges to provisions in municipal ordinances requiring developers to dedicate either a percentage of the entire parcel (usually 7 or 10 percent of the platted subdivision) or an equivalent value in cash (usually a certain dollar amount per lot) to help finance the construction of roads, utilities, schools, parks and playgrounds. In assessing the legality of the conditions, the courts gave no indication that the transfer of an interest in realty was any more objectionable than a cash payment. None of the decisions identified the surrender of the fee owner's "power to exclude" as having any special significance. Instead, the courts uniformly examined the character of the entire economic transaction.

In *Penn Central Transportation Co. v. New York City,* 438 U.S. 104 (1978), we stated that takings jurisprudence "does not divide a single parcel into discrete segments and attempt to determine whether rights in a particular segment have been entirely abrogated." Instead, this Court focuses "both on the character of the action and on the nature and extent of the interference with rights in the parcel as a whole." *Andrus v. Allard,* 444 U.S. 51 (1979), reaffirmed the nondivisibility principle outlined in *Penn Central,* stating that "[a]t least where an owner possesses a full 'bundle' of property rights, the destruction of one 'strand' of the bundle is not taking, because the aggregate must be viewed in its entirety." As recently as last Term, we approved the principle again. See *Concrete Pipe & Products, Inc. v. Construction Laborers Pension Trust,* 508 U.S. ___, _____ (1993) (explaining that "a claimant's parcel of property [cannot] first be divided into what was taken and what was left" to demonstrate a compensable taking). Although limitation of the right to exclude others undoubtedly constitutes a significant infringement upon property ownership, restrictions on that right do not alone constitute a taking, and do not do so in any event unless they "unreasonably impair the value or use" of the property. *PruneYard Shopping Center v. Robbins,* 447 U.S. 74, 82–84 (1980).

The Court's narrow focus on one strand in the property owner's bundle of rights is particularly misguided in a case involving the development of commercial property. As Professor Johnston has noted:

> "The subdivider is a manufacturer, processor, and marketer of a product; land is but one of his raw materials. In subdivision control disputes, the developer is not defending hearth and home against the king's intrusion, but simply attempting to maximize his profits from the sale of a finished product. As applied to him, subdivision control excavations are actually business regulations." Johnston, Constitutionality of Subdivision Control Exactions: The Quest for a Rationale, 52 Cornell L.Q. 871, 923 (1967).

The exactions associated with the development of a retail business are likewise a species of business regulation that heretofore warranted a strong presumption of constitutional validity.

In Johnston's view, "if the municipality can demonstrate that its assessment of financial burdens against subdividers is rational, impartial, and conducive to fulfillment of authorized planning objectives, its action need be invalidated only in those extreme and presumably rare cases where the burden of compliance is sufficiently great to deter the owner from proceeding with his planned development." The city of Tigard has demonstrated that its plan is rational and impartial and that the conditions at issue are "conducive to fulfillment of authorized planning objectives." Dolan, on the other hand, has offered no evidence that her burden of compliance has any impact at all on the value or profitability of her planned development. Following the teaching of the cases on which it purports to rely, the Court should not isolate the burden associated with the loss of the power to exclude from an evaluation of the benefit to be derived from the permit to enlarge the store and the parking lot.

The Court's assurances that its "rough proportionality" test leaves ample room for cities to pursue the "commendable task of land use planning,"—even twice avowing that "[n]o precise mathematical calculation is required,"—are wanting given the result that test compels here. Under the Court's approach, a city must not only "quantify its findings," and make "individualized determination" with respect to the nature *and* the extent of the relationship between the conditions and the impact, but also demonstrate "proportionality." The correct inquiry should instead concentrate on whether the required nexus is present and venture beyond considerations of a condition's nature or germaneness only if the developer establishes that a concededly germane condition is so grossly disproportionate to the proposed development's adverse effects that it manifests motives other than land use regulation on the part of the city. The heightened requirement the Court imposes on cities is even more unjustified when all the tools needed to resolve the questions presented by this case can be garnered from our existing case law.

Applying its new standard, the Court finds two defects in the city's case. First, while the record would adequately support a requirement that Dolan maintain the portion of the floodplain on her property as undeveloped open space, it does not support the additional requirement that the floodplain be dedicated to the city. Second, while the city adequately established the traffic increase that the proposed development would generate, it failed to quantify the offsetting decrease in automobile traffic that the bike path will produce. Even under the Court's new rule, both defects are, at most, nothing more than harmless error.

In her objections to the floodplain condition, Dolan made no effort to demonstrate that the dedication of that portion of her property would be any more onerous than a simple prohibition against any development on that portion of her property. Given the commercial character of both the existing and the proposed use of the property as a retail store, it seems likely that potential customers "trampling along petitioner's floodplain," are more valuable than a useless parcel of land. Moreover, the duty to pay taxes and the responsibility for potential tort liability may well make ownership of the fee interest in useless land a liability rather than an asset. . . .

The Court's rejection of the bike path condition amounts to nothing more than a play on words. Everyone agrees that the bike path "could" offset some of the increased traffic flow that the larger store will generate, but the findings do not unequivocally state that it *will* do so, or tell us just how many cyclists will replace motorists. Predictions on such matters are inherently nothing more than estimates. Certainly the assumption that there will be an offsetting benefit here is entirely reasonable and should suffice whether it amounts to 100 percent, 35 percent, or only 5 percent of the increase in automobile traffic that would otherwise occur. If the Court proposes to have the federal judiciary micromanage state decisions of this kind, it is indeed extending its welcome mat to a significant new class of litigants. Although there is no reason to believe that state courts have failed to rise to task, property owners have surely found a new friend today.

The Court has made a serious error by abandoning the traditional presumption of constitutionality and imposing a novel burden of proof on a city implementing an admittedly valid comprehensive land use plan. Even more consequential than its incorrect disposition of this case, however, is the Court's resurrection of a species of substantive due process analysis that it firmly rejected decades ago.

The Court begins its constitutional analysis by citing *Chicago, B.&Q. R. Co. v. Chicago*, 166 U.S. 266, 239 (1897), for the proposition that the Takings Clause of the Fifth Amendment is "applicable to the States through the Fourteenth Amendment." That opinion, however, contains no mention of either the Takings Clause or the Fifth Amendment; it held that the protection afforded by the Due Process Clause of the Fourteenth Amendment extends to matters of substance as well as procedure, and that the substance of "the due process of law enjoined by the Fourteenth Amendment requires compensation to be made or adequately secured to the owner of private property taken for public use under the authority of a State." *Chicago, B.&Q.R. Co.* It applied the same kind of substantive due process of analysis more frequently identified with a better known case that accorded similar substantive protection to a baker's liberty interest in working 60 hours a week and 10 hours a day. See *Lochner v. New York*, 198 U.S. 45 (1905).

Later cases have interpreted the Fourteenth Amendment's substantive protection against uncompensated deprivations of private property by the States as though it incorporated the text of the Fifth Amendment's Takings Clause. See, *e.g.*, *Keystone Bituminous Coal Assn. v. DeBenedictis*, 480 U.S. 470, 481 n.10 (1987). There was nothing problematic about that interpretation in cases enforcing the Fourteenth Amendment against state action that involved the actual physical invasion of private property. See *Loretto v. Teleprompter Manhattan CATV Corp.*, 458 U.S. 419, 427–433 (1982); *Kaiser Aetna v. United States*, 444 U.S. 164, 178–180 (1979). Justice Holmes charted a significant new course, however, when he opined that a state law making it "commercially impracticable to mine certain coal" had "very nearly the same effect for constitutional purposes as appropriating or destroying it." *Pennsylvania Coal Co. v. Mahon.* The so-called "regulatory takings" doctrine that the Holmes dictum kindled has an obvious kinship with the line of substantive process cases that *Lochner* exemplified. Besides having similar ancestry, both doctrines are potentially open-ended sources of judicial power to invalidate state economic regulations that Members of this Court view as unwise or unfair.

This case inaugurates an even more recent judicial innovation than the regulatory takings doctrine: the application of the "unconstitutional conditions" label to a mutually beneficial transaction between a property owner and a city. The court tells us that the city's refusal to grant Dolan a discretionary benefit infringes her right to receive just compensation for the property interests that she has refused to dedicate to the city "where the property sought has little or no relationship to the benefit." Although it is well settled that a government cannot deny a benefit on a basis that infringes constitutionally protected interests—"especially [one's] interest in freedom of speech,"—the "unconstitutional conditions" doctrine provides an inadequate framework in which to analyze this case.

Dolan has no right to be compensated for a taking unless the city acquires the property interests that she has refused to surrender. Since no taking has yet occurred, there has not been any infringement of her constitutional right to compensation.

Even if Dolan should accept the city's conditions in exchange for the benefit that she seeks, it would not necessarily follow that she had been denied "just compensation." Particularly in the absence of any evidence on the point, we should not presume that the discretionary benefit that the city has offered is less valuable than the property interests that Dolan can retain or surrender at her option. But even if that discretionary benefit were so trifling that it could not be considered just compensation when it has "little or no relationship" to the property, the Court fails to explain why the same value would suffice when the required nexus is present. In this respect, the Court's reliance on the "unconstitutional conditions" doctrine is assuredly novel, and arguably incoherent. The city's conditions are by no means immune from constitutional scrutiny. The level of scrutiny, however, does not approximate the kind of review that would apply if the city had insisted on a surrender of Dolan's First Amendment rights in exchange for a building permit. One can only hope that the Court's reliance today on First Amendment cases, and its candid disavowal of the term "rational basis" to describe its new standard of review, do not signify a reassertion of the kind of superlegislative power the Court exercised during the *Lochner* era.

The Court has decided to apply its heightened scrutiny to a single strand—the power to exclude—in the bundle of rights that enables a commercial enterprise to flourish in an urban environment. That intangible interest is undoubtedly worthy of constitutional protection—much like the grandmother's interest in deciding which of her relatives may share her home in *Moore v. East Cleveland*, 431 U.S. 494 (1977). Both interests are protected from arbitrary state action by the Due Process Clause of the Fourteenth Amendment. It is, however, a curious irony that Members of the majority in this case would impose an almost insurmountable burden of proof on the property owner in *Moore* case while saddling the city with a heightened burden in this case.

In its application of what is essentially the doctrine of substantive due process, the Court confuses the past with the present. On November 13, 1992, the village of Euclid, Ohio, adopted a zoning ordinance that effectively confiscated 75 percent of the value of property owned by the Ambler Realty Company. Despite its recognition that such an ordinance "would have been rejected as arbitrary and oppressive" at an earlier date, the Court (over the dissent of Justices Van Devanter, McReynolds and Butler) upheld the ordinance. Today's majority should heed the words of Justice Sutherland:

> "Such regulations are sustained, under the complex conditions of our day, for reasons analogous to those which justify traffic regulations, which, before the advent of automobiles and rapid transit street railways, would have been condemned as fatally arbitrary and unreasonable. And in this there is no inconsistency, for while the meaning of constitutional guaranties never varies, the scope of their application must expand or contract to meet the new and different conditions which are constantly coming within the field of their op-

eration. In a changing world, it is impossible that it should be otherwise." *Euclid v. Ambler Co.,* 272 U.S. 365, 387 (1926).

In our changing world one thing is certain: uncertainty will characterize predictions about the impact of new urban developments on the risks of floods, earthquakes, traffic congestion, or environmental harms. When there is doubt concerning the magnitude of those impacts, the public interest in averting them must outweigh the private interest of the commercial entrepreneur. If the government can demonstrate that the conditions it has imposed in a land-use permit are rational, impartial and conducive to fulfilling the aims of a valid land-use plan, a strong presumption of validity should attach to those conditions. The burden of demonstrating that those conditions have unreasonably impaired the economic value of the proposed improvement belongs squarely on the shoulders of the party challenging the state action's constitutionality. That allocation of burdens has served us well in the past. The Court has stumbled badly today by reversing it.

I respectfully dissent.

JUSTICE SOUTER, dissenting.

... The Court treats this case as raising ... questions, ... about the degree, of connection required between such an exaction and the adverse effects of development. The Court's opinion announces a test to address this question, but as I read the opinion, the Court does not apply that test to these facts, which do not raise the question the Court addresses.

... [T]he city of Tigard never sought to justify the public access portion of the dedication as related to flood control. It merely argued that whatever recreational uses were made of the bicycle path and the one foot edge on either side, were incidental to the permit condition requiring dedication of the 15-foot easement for an 8-foot-wide bicycle path and for flood control, including open space requirements and relocation of the bank of the river by some five feet. It seems to me such incidental recreational use can stand or fall with the bicycle path, which the city justified by reference to traffic congestion. As to the relationship the Court examines, between the recreational easement and a purpose never put forth as a justification by the city, the Court unsurprisingly finds a recreation area to be unrelated to flood control.

Second, as to the bicycle path, the Court again acknowledges the "theor[etically]" reasonable relationship between "the city's attempt to reduce traffic congestion by providing [a bicycle path] for alternative means of transportation," and the "correct" finding of the city that "the larger retail sales facility proposed by petitioner will increase traffic on the streets of the Central Business District." The Court only faults the city for saying that the bicycle path "could" rather than "would" offset the increased traffic from the store. That again, as far as I can tell, is an application of *Nollan*, for the Court holds that the stated connection ("could offset") between traffic congestion and bicycle paths is too tenuous; only if the bicycle path "would" offset the increased traffic by some amount, could the bicycle path be said to be related to the city's legitimate interest in reducing traffic congestion.

I cannot agree that the application of *Nollan* is a sound one here, since it appears that the Court has placed the burden of producing evidence of relationship on the city, despite the usual rule in cases involving the police power that the government is presumed to have acted constitutionally. Having thus assigned the burden, the Court concludes that the City loses based on one word ("could" instead of "would"), and despite the fact that this record shows the connection the Court looks for. Dolan has put forward no evidence that the burden of granting a dedication for the bicycle path is unrelated in kind to the anticipated increase in traffic congestion, nor, if there exists a requirement that the relationship be related in degree, has Dolan shown that the addition fails any

such test. The city, by contrast, calculated the increased traffic flow that would result from Dolan's proposed development to be 435 trips per day, and its Comprehensive Plan, applied here, relied on studies showing the link between alternative modes of transportation, including bicycle paths, and reduced street traffic congestion. *Nollan*, therefore, is satisfied, and on that assumption the city's conditions should not be held to fail a further rough proportionality test or any other that might be devised to give meaning to the constitutional limits. As Members of this Court have said before, "the common zoning regulations requiring subdividers to . . . dedicate certain areas to public streets, are in accord with our constitutional traditions because the proposed property use would otherwise be the cause of excessive congestion." The bicycle path permit condition is fundamentally no different from these.

In any event, on my reading, the Court's conclusions about the city's vulnerability carry the Court no further than *Nollan* has gone already, and I do not view this case as a suitable vehicle for taking the law beyond that point. The right case for the enunciation of takings doctrine seems hard to spot. . . .

The *Tigard* Court predicated a takings claim upon a showing of rough proportionality between regulatory requirements and impact upon land use. Lower court response to *Tigard*, however, indicates that significant questions remain unanswered. Some courts have distinguished from the rule of *Tigard*, for instance, alleged takings that result from legislative acts.[105] To the extent that such a distinction has been made, review is characterized by a less stringent standard focusing upon whether an ordinance "advances legitimate governmental interests and leaves the plaintiffs with an economically viable use of their property.[106] The Court's refusal to consider the constitutionality of an Atlanta ordinance, requiring surface parking lots to landscape at least 10% of paved areas and provide one tree for every eight parking spaces, elicited a significant dissent by Justice Thomas that was joined by Justice O'Connor. After noting conflict among lower courts over *Tigard*'s applicability to alleged takings through legislative acts, Thomas observed that

> [i]t is not clear why the existence of a taking should turn on the type of governmental entity responsible for the taking. A city council can take property just as well as a planning commission can. Moreover, the general applicability of the ordinance should not be relevant in a takings analysis. If Atlanta had seized several hundred homes in order to build a freeway, there would be no doubt that Atlanta had taken property. The distinction between sweeping legislative takings and particularized administrative takings appears to be a distinction without a constitutional difference.[107]

---

[105] *E.g.*, Harris v. Wichita, 862 F. Supp. 287 (D. Kan. 1994).
[106] *Id.* at 294 (quoting Agins v. Tiburon, 447 U.S. 255 (1980)).
[107] Parking Assn. of Georgia, Inc. v. Atlanta, 115 S. Ct. 2268 (1995) (Thomas, J., dissenting).

DEL: Heightened attention to the taking clause, especially the concept of regulatory takings, in recent years has indicated that economic rights doctrine in the post-*Lochner* era has been reconfigured rather than buried. Decisions such as *Nollan, Lucas* and *Tigard* challenge a common understanding that the *Lochner* era's central lesson is "that the Constitution . . . can actively intrude into . . . economic and policy matters only if . . . prepared to bear enormous institutional and social costs."[108] Critics of an invigorated takings jurisprudence sometimes assert the false distinction between personal and property rights and tend to discount the centrality of economic rights to the republic's founding and reconstruction. However, if takings clause analysis is merely a front for a favored ideology subscribed to by those who rail against modern substantive due process review, *Lochner-ism* has reinvented itself at a higher level of specificity than has been achieved by *Griswold* and its progeny. To the extent driven primarily by dogma, a takings clause revitalization also would reaffirm the proposition "that . . . judicial professions of automatism are most insistent when it is most obvious that they are being honored in the breach rather than in the observance."[109]

---

[108] United States Trust Co. v. New Jersey, 431 U.S. 1, 62 (1978) (Brennan, J., dissenting).
[109] Thomas R. Powell, Vagaries and Varieties in Constitutional Interpretation 43 (1956).

3. The Incorporation Controversy

As originally conceived, the Bill of Rights represented a constitutional afterthought. A recitation of basic rights and liberties initially was inimical to the Federalist position, which anticipated protection of basic freedoms by representative government and warned that itemization might imply exclusivity. A bill of rights eventually was agreed to for tactical reasons, at least, as it satisfied enough antifederalist concern to achieve ratification of the Constitution itself.

The Bill of Rights, as initially conceived and ratified, checked only the exercise of federal power. Such attention was consistent with the perception that liberty was most imperiled by the creation of a new national government. To the extent rights and liberties limited the exercise of state power, they did so as a function of state constitutional provisions or understandings of natural law. Interest in making the Bill of Rights applicable to the states manifested itself within the first few decades of the republic's existence. Writing for the Court, Chief Justice Marshall rejected such an expanded purview for the Bill of Rights.

Barron v. Mayor and City Council of Baltimore
32 U.S. 242 (1833)

. . .
. . . This case was instituted by the plaintiff in error, against the city of Baltimore, under its corporate title of "The Mayor and City Council of Baltimore" to recover damages for injuries to the wharf property of the plaintiff arising from the acts of the corporation. . . .

MARSHALL, CH. J., delivered the opinion of the Court.

. . . The plaintiff in error contends, that it comes within the fifth amendment to the constitution, which inhibits the taking of private property for public use, without just compensation. He insists, that this amendment being in favor of the liberty of the citizen, ought to be so construed as to restrain the legislative power of a state, as well as that of the United States. If this proposition be untrue, the court can take no jurisdiction of the cause.

The question thus presented is, we think, of great importance, but not of much difficulty. The constitution was ordained and established by the people of the United States for themselves, for their own government, and not for the government of the individual states. Each state established a constitution for itself, and in that constitution, provided such limitations and restrictions on the powers of its particular government, as its judgment dictated. The people of the United States framed such a government for the United States as they supposed best adapted to their situation and best calculated to promote their interests. The powers they conferred on this government were to be exercised by itself; and the limitations on power, if expressed in general terms, are naturally, and, we think, necessarily, applicable to the government created by the instrument. They are limitations of power granted in the instrument itself; not of distinct governments, framed by different persons and for different purposes.

If these propositions be correct, the fifth amendment must be understood as restraining the power of the general government, not as applicable to the states. In their several consti-

tutions, they have imposed such restrictions on their respective governments, as their own wisdom suggested; such as they deemed most proper for themselves. It is a subject on which they judge exclusively, and with which others interfere no further than they are supposed to have a common interest.

. . .

We are of opinion, that the provision in the fifth amendment to the constitution, declaring that private property shall not be taken for public use, without just compensation, is intended solely as a limitation on the exercise of power by the government of the United States, and is not applicable to the legislation of the states. We are, therefore, of opinion, that there is no repugnancy between the several acts of the general assembly of Maryland, given in evidence by the defendants at the trial of this case, in the court of that state, and the constitution of the United States. This court, therefore, has no jurisdiction of the cause, and it is dismissed.

Constitutional reckoning with the aftermath of slavery generated new interest in applying the Bill of Rights to the states. Supporters of the Fourteenth Amendment were divided over the rights and freedoms accounted for under the provision. Although some viewed it narrowly as constitutionalizing the Civil Rights Act of 1866—which concerned itself essentially with incidents of economic liberty, freedom to travel and equal standing before the law—others touted an incorporation of rights and liberties set forth by the Declaration of Independence and the Bill of Rights. Despite the *Slaughter-House* Court's narrow understanding of the privileges and immunities of federal citizenship, a significant dissenting perspective favored the broader incorporation theory initially rejected by the Court. After reciting some of the more significant aspects of the Bill of Rights, which he considered newly protected by the Fourteenth Amendment from state interference, Justice Bradley observed that "[t]hese, and still others are specified in the original Constitution, or in the early amendments of it, as among the privileges and immunities of citizens of the United States."[110]

With the rise of substantive due process, many aspects of the Bill of Rights were accounted for against the states by an expanded understanding of liberty under the Fourteenth Amendment. States' actions that interfered with religion[111] or constituted a taking,[112] for instance, were reckoned with not by applying respectively the First Amendment and Fifth Amendment but by finding a violation of the Fourteenth Amendment due process guarantee. As the *Lochner* era of substantive due process review wound down, the Court in *Carolene Products* stressed that it would reserve a higher level of scrutiny "when legislation appears on its face to be within a specific provision of the Constitution, such as the first ten amendments, which are deemed equally specific when held to be embraced within the Fourteenth."[113] By the process of incorporation, over the course of a few decades, most of the Bill of Rights were made applicable to the states. The incorporation debate eventually evolved into a controversy over

---

[110] Slaughter-House Cases, 83 U.S. 36, 118–19 (1873) (Bradley, J., dissenting).
[111] Pierce v. Society of Sisters, 269 U.S. 510 (1925).
[112] Chicago, B. & Q. R.R. Co. v. City of Chicago, 166 U.S. 225 (1897).
[113] United States v. Carolene Products, 304 U.S. 144, 154 n.4 (1938).

whether the entire Bill of Rights was to operate through the Fourteenth Amendment, or whether specific guarantees were to apply selectively. Finding that the double jeopardy clause should of the Fifth Amendment should not be incorporated through the Fourteenth Amendment, Justice Cardozo set forth the groundwork for theory of selective incorporation that largely has been subscribed to since.

Palko v. Connecticut
302 U.S. 319 (1937)

MR. JUSTICE CARDOZO delivered the opinion of the Court.

A statute of Connecticut permitting appeals in criminal cases to be taken by the state is challenged by appellant as an infringement of the Fourteenth Amendment of the Constitution of the United States. Whether the challenge should be upheld is now to be determined.

Appellant was indicted in Fairfield County, Conn., for the crime of murder in the first degree. A jury found him guilty of murder in the second degree and he was sentenced to confinement in the state prison for life. Thereafter the State of Connecticut, with the permission of the judge presiding at the trial, gave notice of appeal to the Supreme Court of Errors. This it did pursuant to an act adopted in 1886.

. . .

Pursuant to the mandate of the Supreme Court of Errors, defendant was brought to trial again. Before a jury was impaneled, and also at later stages of the case, he made the objection that the effect of the new trial was to place him twice in jeopardy for the same offense, and in so doing to violate the Fourteenth Amendment of the Constitution of the United States. . . .

1. The execution of the sentence will not deprive appellant of his life without the process of law assured to him by the Fourteenth Amendment of the Federal Constitution.

The argument for appellant is that whatever is forbidden by the Fifth Amendment is forbidden by the Fourteenth also. The Fifth Amendment, which is not directed to the States, but solely to the federal government, creates immunity from double jeopardy. No person shall be "subject for the same offense to be twice put in jeopardy of life or limb." The Fourteenth Amendment ordains, "nor shall any State deprive any person of life, liberty, or property, without due process of law." To retry a defendant, though under one indictment and only one, subjects him, it is said, to double jeopardy in violation of the Fifth Amendment, if

the prosecution is one on behalf of the United States. From this the consequence is said to follow that there is a denial of life or liberty without due process of law if the prosecution is one on behalf of the people of a state. . . .

We have said that in appellant's view the Fourteenth Amendment is to be taken as embodying the prohibitions of the Fifth. His thesis is even broader. Whatever would be a violation of the original bill of rights (Amendments 1 to 8) if done by the federal government is now equally unlawful by force of the Fourteenth Amendment if done by a state. There is no such general rule.

The Fifth Amendment provides, among other things, that no person shall be held to answer for a capital or otherwise infamous crime unless on presentment or indictment of a grand-jury. This court has held that, in prosecutions by a state, presentment or indictment by a grand jury may give way to information at the instance of a public officer.

The Fifth Amendment provides also that no person shall be compelled in any criminal case to be a witness against himself. This court has said that, in prosecutions by a state the exemption will fail if the state elects to end it. The Sixth Amendment calls for a jury trial in criminal cases and the Seventh for a jury trial in civil cases at common law where the value in controversy shall exceed $20. This court has ruled that consistently with those amendments trial by jury may be modified by a state or abolished altogether.

On the other hand, the due process clause of the Fourteenth Amendment may make it unlawful for a state to abridge by its statutes the freedom of speech which the First Amendment safeguards against encroachment by the Congress . . . or the like freedom of the press, . . . or the free exercise of religion, . . . or the right of peaceable assembly, without which speech would be unduly trammeled, . . . or the right of one accused of crime to the benefit of counsel. In these and other situations immunities that are valid as against the federal government by force of the specific pledges of particular amendments have been found to be implicit in the concept of ordered liberty, and thus, through the Fourteenth Amendment become valid as against the states.

...

The line of division may seem to be wavering and broken if there is a hasty catalogue of the cases on the one side and the other. Reflection and analysis will induce a different view. There emerges the perception of a rationalizing principle which gives to discrete instances a proper order and coherence. The right to trial by jury and the immunity from prosecution except as the result of an indictment may have value and importance. Even so, they are not of the very essence of a scheme of ordered liberty. To abolish them is not to violate a "principle of justice so rooted in the traditions and conscience of our people as to be ranked as fundamental." Few would be so narrow or provincial as to maintain that a fair and enlightened system of justice would be impossible without them. What is true of jury trials and indictments is true also, as the cases show, of the immunity from compulsory self-incrimination. This too might be lost, and justice still be done. Indeed, today as in the past there are students of our penal system who look upon the immunity as a mischief rather than a benefit, and who would limit its scope, or destroy it altogether. No doubt there would remain the need to give protection against torture, physical or mental. Justice, however, would not perish if the accused were subject to a duty to respond to orderly inquiry. The exclusion of these immunities and privileges from the privileges and immunities protected against the action of the States has not been arbitrary or casual. It has been dictated by a study and appreciation of the meaning, the essential implications, of liberty itself.

We reach a different plane of social and moral values when we pass to the privileges and immunities that have been taken over from the earlier articles of the Federal Bill of Rights and brought within the Fourteenth Amendment by a process of absorption. These in their origin were effective against the federal government alone. If the Fourteenth Amendment has absorbed them, the process of absorption has had its source in the belief that neither liberty nor justice would exist if they were sacrificed.... This is true, for illustration, of freedom of thought and speech. Of that freedom one *may* say that it is the matrix, the indispensable condition, of nearly every other form of freedom. With rare aberrations a pervasive recognition of that truth can be traced in our history, political and legal. So it has come about that the domain of liberty, withdrawn by the Fourteenth Amendment from encroachment by the states, has been enlarged by latter-day judgments to include liberty of the mind as well as liberty of action. The extension became indeed, a logical imperative when once it was recognized, as long ago it was, that liberty is something more than exemption from physical restraint, and that even in the field of substantive rights and duties the legislative judgment, if oppressive and arbitrary, may be overridden by the courts. ...

...

Our survey of the cases serves, we think, to justify the statement that the dividing line between them, if not unfaltering throughout its course, has been true for the most part to a unifying principle. On which side of the line the case made out by the appellant has appropriate location must be the next inquiry and the final one. Is that kind of double jeopardy to which the statute has subjected him a hardship so acute and shocking that our policy will not endure it? Does it violate those "fundamental principles of liberty and justice which lie at the base of all our civil and political institutions? The answer surely must be "no." What the answer would have to be if the state were permitted after a trial free from error to try the accused over again or to bring another case against him, we have no occasion to consider. We deal with the statute before us and no other. The state is not attempting to wear the accused out by a multitude of cases with accumulated trials. It asks no more than this, that the case against him shall go on until there shall be a trial free from the corrosion of substantial legal error.... This is not cruelty at all, nor even vexation in any immoderate degree. If the trial had been infected with error adverse to the accused, there might have been review at his instance, and as often as necessary to purge the vicious taint. A reciprocal privilege, subject at all times to the discretion of the presiding judge ... has now been granted to the state. ...

Competing against the selective incorporation theory were Justice Frankfurter's understanding that liberty was to be defined independently by the Court and not necessarily coextensively with the Bill of Rights, the notion of total incorporation expounded most notably by Justice Black and the view that not only all textually ordained rights but implied fundamental liberties applied to the states.

Adamson v. California
332 U.S. 46 (1947)

MR. JUSTICE REED delivered the opinion of the Court.

. . .

[A]pellant urges that the provision of the Fifth Amendment that no person "shall be compelled in any criminal case to be a witness against himself" is a fundamental national privilege or immunity protected against state abridgment by the Fourteenth Amendment or a privilege or immunity secured, through the Fourteenth Amendment, against deprivation by state action because it is a personal right, enumerated in the federal Bill of Rights.

. . .

The reasoning that leads to those conclusions starts with the unquestioned premise that the Bill of Rights, when adopted, was for the protection of the individual against the federal government and its provisions were inapplicable to similar actions done by the states. With the adoption of the Fourteenth Amendment, it was suggested that the dual citizenship recognized by its first sentence secured for citizens federal protection for their elemental privileges and immunities of state citizenship. The *Slaughter-House Cases* decided, contrary to the suggestion, that these rights, as privileges and immunities of state citizenship, remain under the sole protection of the state governments. . . .

. . .

Appellant . . . contends that . . . the privilege against self-incrimination . . . to its full scope under the Fifth Amendment, inheres in the right to a fair trial. A right to a fair trial is a right admittedly protected by the due process clause of the Fourteenth Amendment. Therefore, appellant argues, the due process clause of the Fourteenth Amendment protects his privilege against self-incrimination. The due process clause of the Fourteenth Amendment, however, does not draw all the rights of the federal Bill of Rights under its protection. That contention was made and rejected in *Palko v. Connecticut*. It was rejected with citation of the cases excluding several of the rights, protected by the Bill of Rights, against infringement by the National Government. Nothing has been called to our attention that either the framers of the Fourteenth Amendment or the states adopted intended its due process clause to draw within its scope the earlier amendments to the Constitution. *Palko* held that such provisions of the Bill of Rights as were "implicit in the concept of ordered liberty" became secure from state interference by the clause. But it held nothing more.

. . .

MR. JUSTICE FRANKFURTER, concurring.

. . .

Between the incorporation of the Fourteenth Amendment into the Constitution and the beginning of the present membership of the Court—a period of seventy years—the scope of that Amendment was passed upon by forty-three judges. Of all these judges, only one, who may respectfully be called an eccentric exception, ever indicated the belief that the Fourteenth Amendment was a shorthand summary of the first eight Amendments theretofore limiting only the Federal Government, and that due process incorporated those eight Amendments as restrictions upon the powers of the States. Among these judges were not only those who would have to be included among the greatest in the history of the Court, but—it is especially relevant to note—they included those whose services in the cause of human rights and the spirit of freedom are the most conspicuous in our history. It is not invidious to single out Miller, Davis, Bradley, Waite, Matthews, Gray, Fuller, Holmes, Brandeis, Stone and Cardozo (to speak only of the dead) as judges who were alert in safeguarding and promoting the interest of liberty and human dignity through law. But they were also judges mindful of the relation of our federal system to a progressively democratic society and therefore duly regardful of the scope of authority that was left to the States even after the Civil War. And so they did not find that the Fourteenth Amendment, concerned as it was with matters fundamental to the pursuit of justice, fastened upon the States procedural arrangements which, in the language of Mr. Justice Cardozo, only those who are "narrow or provincial" would deem essential to "a fair and enlightened system of justice." To suggest that it is inconsistent with a truly free society to begin prosecutions without an indictment, to try petty civil cases without the paraphernalia of a common law jury, to take into consideration that one who has full opportunity to make a defense remains silent is, in de Tocqueville's phrase, to confound the familiar with the necessary.

The short answer to the suggestion that the provision of the Fourteenth Amendment, which ordains "nor shall any State deprive any person of life, liberty, or property, without due process of law," was a way of saying that every State must thereafter initiate prosecutions through indictment by a grand jury, must have a trial by a jury of twelve in criminal cases, and must have trial by such a jury in common law suits where the amount in controversy exceeds twenty dollars, is that it is a strange way of saying it. It would be extraordinarily strange for a Constitution to convey such specific commands in such a round-about and inexplicit way. After all, an amendment to the Constitution should be read in a " 'sense most obvious to the common understanding at the time of its adoption.' . . . for it was for public adoption that it was proposed." Those reading the English language with the meaning which it ordinarily conveys, those conversant with the political and legal history of the concept of due process, those sensitive to the relations of the States to the central government as well as the relation of some of the provisions of the Bill of Rights to the process of justice, would hardly recognize the Fourteenth Amendment as a cover for the various explicit provisions of the first eight Amendments. Some of these are enduring reflections of experience with human nature, while some express the restricted views of Eighteenth-Century England regarding the best methods for the ascertainment of facts. The notion that the Fourteenth Amendment was a covert way of imposing upon the States all the rules which it seemed important to Eighteenth Century statesmen to write into the Federal Amendments, was rejected by judges who were themselves witnesses of the process by which the Fourteenth Amendment became part of the Constitution. Arguments that may now be adduced to prove that the first eight Amendments were concealed within the historic phrasing of the Fourteenth Amendment were not unknown at the time of its adoption. A surer estimate of their bearing was possible for judges at the time than distorting distance is likely to vouchsafe. Any evidence of design or purpose not contemporaneously known could hardly have influenced those who ratified the Amendment. Remarks of a particular proponent of the Amendment, no matter how influential, are not to be deemed part of the Amendment. What was submitted for ratification was his proposal, not his speech. Thus, at the time of the ratification of the Fourteenth Amendment the constitutions of nearly half of the ratifying States did not have the rigorous requirements of the Fifth Amendment for instituting criminal proceedings through a grand jury. It could hardly have occurred to these States that by ratifying the Amendment they uprooted their established methods for prosecuting crime and fastened upon themselves a new prosecutorial system.

Indeed, the suggestion that the Fourteenth Amendment incorporates the first eight Amendments as such is not unambiguously urged. Even the boldest innovator would shrink from suggesting to more than half the States that they may no longer initiate prosecutions without indictment by grand jury, or

that thereafter all the States of the Union must furnish a jury of twelve for every case involving a claim above twenty dollars. There is suggested merely a selective incorporation of the first eight Amendments into the Fourteenth Amendment. Some are in and some are out, but we are left in the dark as to which are in and which are out. Nor are we given the calculus for determining which go in and which stay out. If the basis of selection is merely that those provisions of the first eight Amendments are incorporated which commend themselves to individual justices as indispensable to the dignity and happiness of a free man, we are thrown back to a merely subjective test. The protection against unreasonable search and seizure might have primacy for one judge while trial by a jury of twelve for every claim above twenty dollars might appear to another as an ultimate need in a free society. In the history of thought "natural law" has a much longer and much better founded meaning and justification than such subjective selection of the first eight Amendments for incorporation into the Fourteenth. If all that is meant is that due process contains within itself certain minimal standards which are "of the very essence of a scheme of ordered liberty," *Palko v. Connecticut,* putting upon this Court the duty of applying these standards from time to time, then we have merely arrived at the insight which our predecessors long ago expressed. We are called upon to apply to the difficult issues of our own day the wisdom afforded by the great opinions in this field. This guidance bids us to be duly mindful of the heritage of the past, with its great lessons of how liberties are won and how they are lost. As judges charged with the delicate task of subjecting the government of a continent to the Rule of Law we must be particularly mindful that it is "a *constitution* we are expounding," so that it should not be imprisoned in what are merely legal forms even though they have the sanction of the Eighteenth Century.

. . .

A construction which gives to due process no independent function but turns it into a summary of the specific provisions of the Bill of Rights would, as has been noted, tear up by the roots much of the fabric of law in the several States, and would deprive the States of opportunity for reforms in legal process designed for extending the area of freedom. It would assume that no other abuses would reveal themselves in the course of time than those which had become manifest in 1791. Such a view not only disregards the historic meaning of "due process." It leads inevitably to a warped construction of specific provisions of the Bill of Rights to bring within their scope conduct clearly condemned by due process but not easily fitting into the pigeon-holes of the specific provisions. It seems pretty late in the day to suggest that a phrase so laden with historic meaning should be given an improvised content consisting of some but not all of the provisions of the first eight Amendments, selected on an undefined basis, with improvisation of content for the provisions so selected.

And so, when, as in a case like the present, a conviction in a State court is here for review under a claim that a right protected by the Due Process Clause of the Fourteenth Amendment had been denied, the issue is not whether an infraction of one of the specific provisions of the first eight Amendments is disclosed by the record. The relevant question is whether the criminal proceedings which resulted in conviction deprived the accused of the due process of law to which the United States Constitution entitled him. Judicial review of that guaranty of the Fourteenth Amendment inescapably imposes upon this Court an exercise of judgment upon the whole course of the proceedings in order to ascertain whether they offend those canons of decency and fairness which express the notions of justice of English-speaking peoples even toward those charged with the most heinous offenses. These standards of justice are not authoritatively formulated anywhere as though they were prescriptions in a pharmacopoeia. But neither does the application of the Due Process Clause imply that judges are wholly at large. The judicial judgment in applying the Due Process Clause must move within the limits of accepted notions of justice and is not to be based upon the idiosyncrasies of a merely personal judgment. The fact that judges among themselves may differ whether in a particular case a trial offends accepted notions of justice is not disproof that general rather than idiosyncratic standards are supplied. An important safeguard against such merely individual judgment is an alert deference to the judgment of the State court under review.

MR. JUSTICE BLACK, dissenting.

. . .

This decision reasserts a constitutional theory spelled out in *Twining v. New Jersey,* that this Court is endowed by the Constitution with boundless power under "natural law" periodically to expand and contract constitutional standards to conform to the Court's conception of what at a particular time constitutes "civilized decency" and "fundamental liberty and justice." Invoking this *Twining* rule, the Court concludes that although comment upon testimony in a federal court would violate the Fifth Amendment, identical comment in a state court does not violate today's fashion in civilized decency and fundamentals and is therefore not prohibited by the Federal Constitution as amended.

The *Twining* case was the first, as it is the only, decision of this Court which has squarely held that states were free, notwithstanding the Fifth and Fourteenth Amendments, to extort evidence from one accused of crime. I agree that if *Twining* be reaffirmed, the result reached might appropriately follow. But I would not reaffirm the *Twining* decision. I think that decision and the "natural law" theory of the Constitution upon which it relies degrade the constitutional safeguards of the Bill of Rights and simultaneously appropriate for this Court a broad power which we are not authorized by the Constitution to exercise. . . .

The first ten amendments were proposed and adopted largely because of fear that government might unduly interfere with prized individual liberties. The people wanted and demanded a Bill of Rights written into their Constitution. The amendments embodying the Bill of Rights were intended to curb all branches of the Federal Government in the Fields touched by the amendments—Legislative, Executive, and Judicial. The Fifth, Sixth, and Eighth Amendments were pointedly aimed at confining exercise of power by courts and judges within precise boundaries, particularly in the procedure used for the trial of criminal cases. Past history provided strong reasons for the apprehensions which brought these procedural amendments into being and attest the wisdom of their adoption. For the fears of arbitrary court action sprang largely from the past use of courts in the imposition of criminal punishments to suppress speech, press, and religion. Hence the constitutional limitations of courts' power were, in the view of the Founders, essential supplements to the First Amendment, which was itself designed to protect the widest scope for all people to believe and to express the most divergent political, religious, and other views.

But these limitations were not expressly imposed upon state court action. In 1833, *Barron v. Baltimore,* was decided by this Court. It specifically held inapplicable to the states that provision of the Fifth Amendment which declares: "nor shall private property be taken for public use, without just compensation." In deciding the particular point raised, the Court there said that it could not hold that the first eight Amendments applied to the states. This was the controlling constitutional rule when the Fourteenth Amendment was proposed in 1866.

My study of the historical events that culminated in the Fourteenth Amendment, and the expressions of those who sponsored and favored, as well as those who opposed its submission and passage, persuades me that one of the chief objects that the provisions of the Amendments's first section, separately, and as a whole, were intended to accomplish was to make the Bill of Rights applicable to the states. With full knowledge of the import of the *Barron* decision, the framers and backers of the Fourteenth Amendment proclaimed its purpose to be to overturn the constitutional rule that case had announced. This historical purpose has never received full consideration or exposition in any opinion of this Court interpreting the Amendment.

In construing other constitutional provisions, this Court has almost uniformly followed the precept that "It is never to be forgotten that, in the construction of the language of the Constitution . . . , as indeed in all other instances where construction becomes necessary, we are to place ourselves as nearly as possible in the condition of the men who framed that instrument."

Investigation of the cases relied upon in *Twining v. New Jersey* to support the conclusion there reached that neither the Fifth Amendment's prohibition of compelled testimony, nor any of the Bill of Rights, applies to the States, reveals an unexplained departure from this salutary practice. . . .

In the *Twining* case itself, the Court was cited to a then recent book, Guthrie, Fourteenth Amendment to the Constitution (1898). A few pages of that work recited some of the legislative background of the Amendment, emphasizing the speech of Senator Howard. But Guthrie did not emphasize the speeches of Congressman Bingham, or the part he played in the framing and adoption of the first section of the Fourteenth Amendment. Yet Congressman Bingham may, without extravagance, be called the Madison of the first section of the Fourteenth Amendment. In the *Twining* opinion, the Court explicitly declined to give weight to the historical demonstration that the first section of the Amendment was intended to apply to the states the several protections of the Bill of Rights. It held that that question was "no longer open" because of previous decisions of this Court which, however, had not appraised the historical evidence on that subject. The Court admitted that its action had resulted in giving "much less effect to the Fourteenth Amendment than some of the public men active in framing it" had intended it to have. With particular reference to the guarantee against compelled testimony, the Court stated that "Much might be said in favor of the view that the privilege was guaranteed against state impairment as a privilege and immunity of National citizenship, but, as has been shown, the decisions of this court have foreclosed that view." Thus the Court declined, and again today declines, to appraise the relevant historical evidence of the intended scope of the first

section of the Amendment. Instead it relied upon previous cases, none of which had analyzed the evidence showing that one purpose of those who framed, advocated, and adopted the Amendment had been to make the Bill of Rights applicable to the States. None of the cases relied upon by the Court today made such an analysis.

For this reason, I am attaching to this dissent an appendix which contains a resumé, by no means complete, of the Amendment's history. In my judgment that history conclusively demonstrates that the language of the first section of the Fourteenth Amendment, taken as a whole, was thought by those responsible for its submission to the people, and by those who opposed its submission, sufficiently explicit to guarantee that thereafter no state could deprive its citizens of the privileges and protections of the Bill of Rights. Whether this Court ever will, or whether it now should, in the light of past decisions, give full effect to what the Amendment was intended to accomplish is not necessarily essential to a decision here. However that may be, our prior decisions, including *Twining,* do not prevent our carrying out that purpose, at least to the extent of making applicable to the states, not a mere part, as the Court has, but the full protection of the Fifth Amendment's provision against compelling evidence from an accused to convict him of crime. And I further contend that the "natural law" formula which the Court uses to reach its conclusion in this case should be abandoned as an incongruous excrescence on our Constitution. I believe that formula to be itself a violation of our Constitution, in that it subtly conveys to courts, at the expense of legislatures, ultimate power over public policies in fields where no specific provision of the Constitution limits legislative power. And my belief seems to be in accord with the views expressed by this Court, at least for the first two decades after the Fourteenth Amendment was adopted.

In 1872, four years after the Amendment was adopted, the *Slaughter-House* cases came to this Court. The Court was not presented in that case with the evidence which showed that the special sponsors of the Amendment in the House and Senate had expressly explained one of its principal purposes to be to change the Constitution as construed in *Barron v. Baltimore,* and make the Bill of Rights applicable to the states. Nor was there reason to do so. . . . In effect, the *Slaughter-House* cases rejected the very natural justice formula the Court today embraces. The court did not meet the question of whether the safeguards of the Bill of Rights were protected against state invasion by the Fourteenth Amendment. And it specifically did not say as the Court now does, that particular provisions of the Bill of Rights could be breached by states in part, but not breached in other respects, according to this Court's notions of "civilized standards," "canons of decency," and "fundamental justice."

Thus, up to and for some years after 1873, when *Munn v. Illinois* was decided, this Court steadfastly declined to invalidate states' legislative regulation of property rights or business practices under the Fourteenth Amendment unless there were racial discrimination involved in the state law challenged. The first significant breach in this policy came in 1889, in *Chicago, M.&ST.P.R. Co. v. Minnesota.* A state's railroad rate regulatory statute was there stricken as violative of the due process clause of the Fourteenth Amendment. This was accomplished by reference to a due process formula which did not necessarily operate so as to protect the Bill of Rights' personal liberty safeguards, but which gave a new and hitherto undiscovered scope for the Court's use of the due process clause to protect property rights under natural law concepts. And in 1896, in *Chicago, B.& Q. R. Co. v. Chicago,* this Court, in effect, overruled *Davidson v. New Orleans,* by holding, under the new due process-natural law formula, that the Fourteenth Amendment forbade a state from taking private property for public use without payment of just compensation.

The foregoing constitutional doctrine, judicially created and adopted by expanding the previously accepted meaning of "due process," marked a complete departure from the *Slaughter-House* interpretation and represented a failure to carry out the avowed purpose of the Amendment's sponsors. . . .

The *Twining* decision, rejecting the compelled testimony clause of the Fifth Amendment, and indeed rejecting all the Bill of Rights, is the end product of one phase of this philosophy. At the same time, that decision consolidated the power of the court assumed in past cases by laying broader foundations for the Court to invalidate state and even federal regulatory legislation. For the *Twining* decision, giving separate consideration to "due process" and "privileges or immunities," went all the way to say that the "privileges or immunities" clause of the Fourteenth Amendment "did not forbid the States to abridge the personal rights enumerated in the first eight Amendments. . . ." *Twining v. New Jersey.* And in order to be certain, so far as possible, to leave this Court wholly free to reject all the Bill of Rights as specific restraints upon state action, the decision declared that even if this Court should decide that the due process clause forbids the states to infringe personal liberties guaranteed by the Bill of Rights, it

would do so, not "because those rights are enumerated in the first eight Amendments, but because they are of such a nature that they are included in the conception of due process of law."

At the same time that the *Twining* decision held that the states need not conform to the specific provisions of the Bill of Rights, it consolidated the power that the Court assumed under the due process clause by laying even broader foundations for the Court to invalidate state and even federal regulatory legislation. For under the *Twining* formula, which includes non-regard for the first eight Amendments, what are "fundamental rights" and in accord with "canons of decency," as the Court said in *Twining,* and today reaffirms, is to be independently "ascertained from time to time by judicial action" [and] "what is due process of law depends on circumstances." Thus the power of legislatures became what this Court would declare it to be at a particular time independently of the specific guarantees of the Bill of Rights such as the right to freedom of speech, religion and assembly, the right to just compensation for property taken for a public purpose, the right to jury trial or the right to be secure against unreasonable searches and seizures. Neither the contraction of the Bill of Rights safeguards nor the invalidating of regulatory laws by this Court's appraisal of "circumstances" would readily be classified as the most satisfactory contribution of this Court to the nation. . . .

Later decisions of this Court have completely undermined that phase of the *Twining* doctrine which broadly precluded reliance on the Bill of Rights to determine what is and what is not a "fundamental" right. Later cases have also made the *Hurtado* case an inadequate support for this phase of the *Twining* formula. . . . [T]his Court has now held that the Fourteenth Amendment protects from state invasion [several] "fundamental" rights safeguarded by the Bill of Rights. . . .

In *Palko v. Connecticut,* a case which involved former jeopardy only, this Court re-examined the path it had traveled in interpreting the Fourteenth Amendment since the *Twining* opinion was written. In *Twining* the Court had declared that none of the rights enumerated in the first eight Amendments were protected against state invasion because they were incorporated in the Bill of Rights. But the Court in *Palko* answered a contention that all eight applied with the more guarded statement, similar to that the Court had used in *Maxwell v. Dow,* that "there is no such general rule." Implicit in this statement, and in the cases decided in the interim between *Twining* and *Palko* and since, is the understanding that some of the eight Amendments do apply by their very terms. Thus the Court said in the *Palko* case that the Fourteenth Amendment may make it unlawful for a state to abridge by its statutes the "freedom of speech which the First Amendment safeguards against encroachment by the Congress . . . or the like freedom of the press . . . or the free exercise of religion . . . , or the right of peaceable assembly . . . or the right of one accused of crime to the benefit of counsel. . . . In these and other situations immunities that are valid as against the federal government by force of the specific pledges of particular amendments have been found to be implicit in the concept of ordered liberty, and thus, through the Fourteenth Amendment, become valid as against the states." The Court went on to describe the Amendments made applicable to the States as "the privileges and immunities that have been taken over from the earlier articles of the federal bill of rights and brought within the Fourteenth Amendment by a process of absorption." In the *Twining* case fundamental liberties were things apart from the Bill of Rights. Now it appears that at least some of the provisions of the Bill of Rights in their very terms satisfy the Court as sound and meaningful expressions of fundamental liberty. If the Fifth Amendment's protection against self-incrimination be such an expersion of fundamental liberty, I ask, and have not found a satisfactory answer, why the Court today should consider that it should be "absorbed" in part but not in full? Nothing in the *Palko* opinion requires that when the Court decides that a Bill of Rights' provision is to be applied to the States, it is to be applied piecemeal. Nothing in the *Palko* opinion recommends that the Court apply part of an amendment's established meaning and discard that part which does not suit the current style of fundamentals.

   . . .

I cannot consider the Bill of Rights to be an outworn 18th Century "strait jacket" as the *Twining* opinion did. Its provisions may be thought outdated abstractions by some. And it is true that they were designed to meet ancient evils. But they are the same kind of human evils that have emerged from century to century wherever excessive power is sought by the few at the expense of the many. In my judgment the people of no nation can lose their liberty so long as a Bill of Rights like ours survives and its basic purposes are conscientiously interpreted, enforced and respected so as to afford continuous protection against old, as well as new, devices and practices which might thwart those purposes. I fear to see the conse-

quences of the Court's practice of substituting its own concepts of decency and fundamental justice for the language of the Bill of Rights as its point of departure in interpreting and enforcing that Bill of Rights. If the choice must be between the selective process of the *Palko* decision applying some of the Bill of Rights to the States, or the *Twining* rule applying none of them, I would choose the *Palko* selective process. But rather than accept either of these choices, I would follow what I believe was the original purpose of the Fourteenth Amendment—to extend to all the people of the nation the complete protection of the Bill of Rights. To hold that this Court can determine what, if any, provisions of the Bill of Rights will be enforced, and if so to what degree, is to frustrate the great design of a written Constitution.

Since *Marbury v. Madison* was decided, the practice has been firmly established, for better or worse, that courts can strike down legislative enactments which violate the Constitution. This process, of course, involves interpretation, and since words can have many meanings, interpretation, obviously may result in contraction or extension of the original purpose of a constitutional provision, thereby affecting policy. But to pass upon the constitutionality of statutes by looking to the particular standards enumerated in the Bill of Rights and other parts of the Constitution is one thing; to invalidate statutes because of application of "natural law" deemed to be above and undefined by the Constitution is another. "In the one instance, courts proceeding within clearly marked constitutional boundaries seek to execute polices written into the Constitution; in the other, they roam at will in the limitless area of their own beliefs as to reasonableness and actually select policies, a responsibility which the Constitution entrusts to the legislative representatives of the people."

   . . .

MR. JUSTICE MURPHY, with whom MR. JUSTICE RUTLEDGE concurs, dissenting.

While in substantial agreement with the views of MR. JUSTICE BLACK, I have one reservation and one addition to make.

I agree that the specific guarantees of the Bill of Rights should be carried over intact into the first section of the Fourteenth Amendment. But I am not prepared to say that the latter is entirely and necessarily limited by the Bill of Rights. Occasions may arise where a proceeding falls so far short of conforming to fundamental condemnations in terms of a lack of due process despite the absence of a specific provisions in the Bill of Rights.

   . . .

The original selective incorporation formula enunciated in *Palko* considered whether a particular amendment was so fundamental as to be "implicit in the concept of ordered liberty" or "so rooted in the traditions and conscience of our people as to be fundamental."[114] Three decades later, the Court amended its incorporation criteria to consider whether an enumerated right of liberty was "fundamental to the American scheme of justice."[115]

---

[114] Palko v. Connecticut, 302 U.S. 319, 325 (1937).
[115] Duncan v. Louisiana, 391 U.S. 145, 148–49 (1968).

Duncan v. Louisiana
391 U.S. 145 (1968)

MR. JUSTICE WHITE delivered the opinion of the Court.

Appellant, Gary Duncan, was convicted of simple battery[,] a misdemeanor, punishable by two years' imprisonment and a $300 fine. Appellant sought trial by jury, but because the Louisiana Constitution grants jury trials only in cases in which capital punishment or imprisonment at hard labor may be imposed, the trial judge denied the request. Appellant was convicted and sentenced to serve 60 days in the parish prison and pay a fine of $150. Appellant sought review in the Supreme Court of Louisiana, asserting that the denial of jury trial violated rights guaranteed to him by the United States Constitution. The Supreme Court, finding "no error of law in the ruling complained of," denied appellant a writ of certiorari. [A]ppellant sought review in this Court, alleging that the Sixth and Fourteenth Amendments to the United States Constitution secure the right to jury trial in state criminal prosecutions where a sentence as long as two-years may be imposed. We noted probable jurisdiction. . . .

The Fourteenth Amendment denies the States the power to "deprive *any* person of life, liberty, or property, without due process of law." In resolving conflicting claims concerning the meaning of this spacious language, the Court has looked increasingly to the Bill of Rights for guidance; many of the rights guaranteed by the first eight Amendments to the Constitution have been held to be protected against state action by the Due Process Clause of the Fourteenth Amendment. That clause now protects the right to compensation for property taken by the State; the rights of speech, press, and religion covered by the First Amendment; the Fourth Amendment rights to be free from unreasonable searches and seizures and to have excluded from criminal trials any evidence illegally seized; the right guaranteed by the Fifth Amendment to be free of compelled self-incrimination; and the Sixth Amendment

rights to counsel, to a speedy and public trial, to confrontation of opposing witnesses, and to compulsory process for obtaining witnesses.

The test for determining whether a right extended by the Fifth and Sixth Amendments with respect to federal criminal proceedings is also protected against state action by the Fourteenth Amendment has been phrased in a variety of ways in the opinions of this Court. The question has been asked whether a right is among those " 'fundamental principles of liberty and justice which lie at the base of all our civil and political institutions,' " and whether it is "basic in our system of jurisprudence," and whether it is "a fundamental right, essential to a fair trial." The claim before us is that the right to trial by jury guaranteed by the Sixth Amendment meets these tests. The position of Louisiana, on the other hand, is that the Constitution imposes upon the States no duty to give a jury trial in any criminal case, regardless of the seriousness of the crime or the size of the punishment which may be imposed. Because we believe that trial by jury in criminal cases is fundamental to the American scheme of justice, we hold that the Fourteenth Amendment guarantees a right of jury trial in all criminal cases which—were they to be tried in a federal court—would come within the Sixth Amendment's guarantee." Since we consider the appeal before us to be such a case, we hold that the Constitution was violated when appellant's demand for jury trial was refused.

. . .

The guarantees of jury trial in the Federal and State Constitutions reflect a profound judgment about the way in which law should be enforced and justice administered. A right to jury trial is granted to criminal defendants in order to prevent oppression by the Government. . . . The deep commitment of the Nation to the right of jury trial in serious criminal cases as a defense against arbitrary law enforcement qualifies for protection under the

Due Process Clause of the Fourteenth Amendment, and must therefore be respected by the States.

. . .

. . . Plainly, this is not the import of our holding. Our conclusion is that in the American States, as in the federal judicial system, a general grant of jury trial for serious offenses is a fundamental right, essential for preventing miscarriages of justice and for assuring that fair trials are provided for all defendants. We would not assert, however, that every criminal trial—or any particular trial—held before a judge alone is unfair or that a defendant may never be as fairly treated by a judge as he would be by a jury. Thus we hold no constitutional doubts about the practices, common in both federal and state courts, of accepting waivers of jury trial and prosecuting petty crimes without extending a right to jury trial. However, the fact is that in most places more trials for serious crimes are to juries than to a court alone; a great many defendants prefer the judgment of a jury to that of a court. Even where defendants are satisfied with bench trials, the right to a jury trial very likely serves its intended purpose of making judicial or prosecutorial unfairness less likely.

. . .

The judgment below is reversed and the case is remanded for proceedings not inconsistent with this opinion.

MR. JUSTICE BLACK, with whom MR. JUSTICE DOUGLAS joins, concurring.
. . . The dissent in this case . . . makes a spirited and forceful defense of [the] now discredited [*Twining*] doctrine. I do not believe that it is necessary for me to repeat the historical and logical reasons for my challenge to the *Twining* holding contained in my *Adamson* dissent and Appendix to it. My Brother Harlan's objections to my *Adamson* dissent history, like that of most or the objectors, relies most heavily on a criticism written by Professor Charles Fairman[,] . . . [, which] in my view . . . has completely failed to refute the inferences and arguments that I suggested in my *Adamson* dissent. Professor Fairman's "history" relies very heavily on what was not said in the state legislatures that passed on the Fourteenth Amendment. Instead of relying on this kind of negative pregnant, my legislative experience has convinced me that it is far wiser to rely on what *was* said, and most importantly, said by the men who actually sponsored the Amendment in the Congress. . . . [B]oth its sponsors and those who opposed it believed the Fourteenth Amendment made the first eight Amendments of the Constitution (The Bill of Rights) applicable to the States.

. . .

Finally . . . I am not bothered by the argument that applying the Bill of Rights to the States, "according to the same standards that protect those rights against federal encroachment," interferes with our concept of federalism in that it may prevent States from trying novel social and economic experiments. I have never believed that under the guise of federalism the States should be able to experiment with the protections afforded our citizens through the Bill of Rights. . . . It seems to me totally inconsistent to advocate, on the one hand, the power of this Court to strike down any state law or practice which it finds "unreasonable" or "unfair," and on the other hand urge that the States be given maximum power to develop their own laws and procedures. Yet the due process approach of my Brothers Harlan and Fortas . . . does just that since in effect it restricts the States to practices which a majority of this Court is willing to approve on a case-by-case basis. No one is more concerned than I that the States be allowed to use the full scope of their powers as their citizens see fit. And that is why I have continually fought against the expansion of this Court's authority over the States through the use of a broad, general interpretation of due process that permits judges to strike down state laws they do not like.

. . . I believe as strongly as ever that the Fourteenth Amendment was intended to make the Bill of Rights applicable to the States. I have been willing to support the selective incorporation doctrine, however, as an alternative, although perhaps less historically supportable than complete incorporation. The selective incorporation process, if used properly, does limit the Supreme Court in the Fourteenth Amendment field to specific Bill of Rights' protections only and keeps judges from roaming at will in their own notions of what policies outside the Bill of Rights are desirable and what are not. And, most importantly for me, the selective incorporation process has the virtue of having already worked to make most of the Bill of Rights' protections applicable to the States.

MR. JUSTICE FORTAS, concurring.
I join the judgments and opinions of the Court in these cases because I agree that the Due Process Clause of the Fourteenth Amendment requires that the States accord the right to jury trial in prosecutions for offenses that are not petty. . . .

. . .

MR. JUSTICE HARLAN, whom MR. JUSTICE STEWART joins, dissenting.
Every American jurisdiction provides for trial by jury in criminal cases. The question before us is not whether jury trial is an ancient institution, which it is; nor whether it plays a significant role in the administration of crimi-

nal justice, which it does; nor whether it will endure, which it shall. The question in this case is whether the State of Louisiana, which provides trial by jury for all felonies, is prohibited by the Constitution from trying charges of simple battery to the court alone. In my view, the answer to that question, mandated alike by our constitutional history and by the longer history of trial by jury, is clearly "no."

. . .

I believe I am correct in saying that every member of the Court for at least the last 135 years has agreed that our Founders did not consider the requirements of the Bill of Rights so fundamental that they should operate directly against the States. They were wont to believe rather that the security of liberty in America rested primarily upon the dispersion of governmental power across a federal system. . . .

. . . The overwhelming historical evidence marshalled by Profession Fairman demonstrates, to me conclusively, that the Congressmen and state legislators who wrote, debated, and ratified the Fourteenth Amendment did not think they were "incorporating" the Bill of Rights[9] and the very breath and generality of

the Amendment's provisions suggests that its authors did not suppose that the Nation would always be limited to mid-19th century conceptions, of "liberty" and "due process of law" ... [N]either history, nor sense, supports using the Fourteenth Amendment to put the States in a constitutional straitjacket with respect to their own development in the administration of criminal or civil law.

. . .

Apart from the ... absolute incorporationists, I can see only one method of analysis that has any internal logic. That is to start with the words "liberty" and "due process of law" and attempt to define them in a way that accords with American traditions and our system of government. This approach, involving a much more discriminating process of adjudication than does "incorporation," is, albeit difficult, the one that was followed throughout the Nineteenth and most of the present century. It entails a "gradual process of judicial inclusion and exclusion," seeking, with due recognition of constitutional tolerance for state experimentation and disparity, to ascertain those "immutable principles of free government which no member of the Union may disregard." ...

---

[9] Fairman, Does the Fourteenth Amendment Incorporate the Bill of Rights? The Original Understanding, 2 *Stan. L Rev.* 5 (1949). Professor Fairman was not content to rest upon the overwhelming fact that the great words of the four clauses or first section of the Fourteenth Amendment would have been an exceedingly peculiar way to say that "The rights heretofore guaranteed against federal intrusion by the first eight Amendments are henceforth guaranteed against state intrusion as well." He therefore sifted the mountain of material comprising the debates and committee reports relating to the Amendment in both Houses of Congress and in the state legislatures, that passed upon it. He found that in the immense corpus of comments on the purpose and effects of the proposed amendment, and on its virtues and defects, there is almost no evidence whatever for "incorporation." The first eight amendments are so much mentioned by only two members of Congress, one of *whom* effectively demonstrated (a) that he did

not understand Barron v. Baltimore, Pet. 243, and therefore did not understand the question of incorporation, and (b) that he was not himself understood by his colleagues. One state legislative committee report, rejected by the legislature as a whole, found § I of the Fourteenth Amendment superfluous because it duplicated the Bill of Rights: the committee obviously did not understand Barron v. Baltimore either. That is all Professor Fairman could find, in hundreds of pages of legislative discussion prior to passage of the Amendment, that even suggests incorporation.

To this negative evidence the judicial history of the Amendment could be added. For example, it proved possible for a court whose members had lived through Reconstruction to reiterate the doctrine of Barron v. Baltimore, that the Bill of Rights did not apply to the States, without so much as questioning whether the Fourteenth Amendment had any effect on the continued validity of that principle.

Selective incorporation has achieved much of what would have been attained pursuant to the total incorporation theory. Only the grand jury clause of the Fifth Amendment[116] and Seventh Amendment guarantee of a jury trial in a civil case[117] remain specifically rejected as applicable to the states. Despite achievement of virtually total incorporation as a consequence of the selective incorporation process, some have argued that federal rights and liberties should not operate "jot for jot" and "case for case" against the states.

---

[116] Hurtado v. California, 110 U.S. 516 (1884).

[117] Minneapolis & St. Louis R.R. Co. v. Bombolis, 241 U.S. 211 (1916).

Malloy v. Hogan
378 U.S. 1 (1964)

MR. JUSTICE HARLAN, whom MR. JUSTICE CLARK joins dissenting.

. . .

I can only read the Court's opinion as accepting in fact what it rejects in theory: the application to the States, via the fourteenth Amendment, of the forms of federal criminal procedure embodied within the first eight Amendments to the Constitution. While it is true that the Court deals today with only one aspect of state criminal procedure, and rejects the wholesale "incorporation" of such federal constitutional requirements, the logical gap between the Court's premises and its novel constitutional conclusion can, I submit, be bridged only by the additional premise that the Due Process Clause of the Fourteenth Amendment is a shorthand directly to this court to pick and choose among the provisions of the first eight Amendments and apply those chosen, freighted with their entire accompanying body of federal doctrine, to law enforcement in the States.

I accept and agree with the proposition that continuing reexamination of the constitutional conception of Fourteenth Amendment "due process" of law is required, and that development of the community's sense of justice may in time lead to expansion of the protection which, due process affords. . . . I do not understand, however, how this process of re-examination, which must refer always to the guiding standard of due process of law, including, of course, reference to the particular guarantees of the Bill of Rights, can be short-circuited by the simple device of incorporating into due process, without critical examination, the whole body of law which surrounds a specific prohibition directed against the Federal Government. The consequence of such an approach to due process as it pertains to the States is inevitably disregard of all relevant differences which may exist between state and federal criminal law and its enforcement. The ultimate result is compelled uniformity, which is inconsistent with the purpose of our federal system and which is achieved either by encroachment on the States' sovereign powers or by dilution in federal law enforcement of specific protections found in the Bill of Rights.

. . .

. . . Approaching the question more broadly, it is equally plain that the line of cases exemplified by *Palko v. Connecticut,* in which this Court has reconsidered the requirements which the Due Process Clause imposes on the States in the light of current standards, furnishes no general theoretical framework for what the Court does today.

The view of the Due Process Clause of the Fourteenth Amendment which this court has consistently accepted and which has "thus far prevailed," is that its requirements are as "old as a principle of civilized government," the specific applications of which must be ascertained "by the gradual process of judicial inclusion and exclusion. . . . " Due process requires "observance of those general rules established in our system of jurisprudence for the security of private rights."

"This court has never attempted to define with precision the words 'due process of law'. . . . It is sufficient to say that there are certain immutable principles of justice which inhere in the very idea of free government which no member of the Union may disregard." *Holden v. Hardy.*

It followed from this recognition that due process encompassed the fundamental safeguards of the individual against the abusive exercise of governmental power that some of the restraints on the Federal Government which were specifically enumerated in the Bill of Rights applied also against the States. But, while inclusion of a particular provision in the Bill of Rights might provide historical evidence that the right involved was traditionally regarded as fundamental, inclusion of the right in due process was otherwise entirely independent of the first eight Amendments:

" . . . [I]t is that some of the personal rights safeguarded by the first eight Amendments against National action may also be safeguarded against state action, because a denial of them would be a denial of due process of law. . . . *If this is so, it is not because those rights are enumerated in the first eight Amendments, but because they are of such a nature that they are included in the conception of due process of law."* *Twining.*

. . .

Relying heavily on *Twining,* Mr. Justice Cardozo provided what may be regarded as a classic expression of this approach in *Palko v. Connecticut, supra.* After considering a number of individual rights (including the right to incriminate oneself) which were "not of the very essence of a scheme of ordered liberty," he said:

"We reach a different plane of social and moral values when we pass to the privileges and immunities that have been taken over from the earlier articles of the federal bill of rights and brought within the Fourteenth Amendment by a process of absorption. These in their origin were effective against the federal government alone. If the Fourteenth Amendment has absorbed them, the process of absorption has had its source in the belief that neither liberty nor justice would exist if they were sacrificed."

Further on, Mr. Justice Cardozo made the independence of the Due Process Clause from the provisions of the first eight Amendments explicit:

"Fundamental . . . in the concept of due process, and so in that of liberty, is the thought that condemnation shall be rendered only after trial. The hearing, moreover, must be a real one, not a sham or a pretense. For that reason, ignorant defendants in a capital case were held to have been condemned unlawfully when in truth, though not in form, they were refused the aid of counsel. The decision did not turn upon the fact that the benefit of counsel would have been guaranteed to the defendants by the provisions of the Sixth Amendment if they had been prosecuted in federal court. The decision turned upon the fact that in the particular situation laid before us in the evidence the benefit of counsel was essential to the substance of a hearing."

It is apparent that Mr. Justice Cardozo's metaphor of "absorption" was *not* intended to suggest the transplantation of case law surrounding the specifics of the first eight Amendments to the very different soil of the Fourteenth Amendment's Due Process Clause. For, as he made perfectly plain, what the Fourteenth Amendment requires of the States does not basically depend on what the first eight Amendments require of the Federal Government.

Seen in proper perspective, therefore, the fact that First Amendment protections have generally been given equal scope in the federal and state domains or that in some areas of criminal procedure the Due Process Clause demands as much of the States as the Bill of Rights demands of the Federal Government, is only tangentially relevant to the question now before us. It is toying with constitutional principles to assert that the Court has "rejected the notion that the Fourteenth Amendment applies to the states only a 'watered-down, subjective version of the individual guarantees of the Bill of Rights.'" What the Court has with [a] single exception . . . consistently rejected is the notion that the Bill of Rights, as such, applies to the States in any aspect at all.

If one attends to those areas to which the Court points, in which the prohibitions against

the state and federal governments have moved in parallel tracks, the cases in fact reveal again that the Court's usual approach has been to ground the prohibitions against state action squarely on due process, without intermediate reliance on any of the first eight Amendments. Although more recently the Court has referred to the First Amendment to describe the protection of free expression against state infringement, earlier cases leave no doubt that such references are "shorthand" for doctrines developed by another route. . . .

. . .

The Court's approach in the present case is in fact nothing more or less than "incorporation" in snatches. If, however, the Due Process Clause *is* something more than a reference to the Bill of Rights and protects only those rights which derive from fundamental principles, as the majority purports to believe, it is just as contrary to precedent and just as illogical to incorporate the provisions of the Bill of Rights one at a time as it is to incorporate them all at once.

The Court's undiscriminating approach to the Due Process Clause carries serious implications for the sound working of our federal system in the field of criminal law.

The Court concludes, almost without discussion that "the same standards must determine whether an accused's silence in either a federal or state proceeding is justified." About all that the Court offers in explanation of this conclusion is the observation that it would be "incongruous" if different standards governed the assertion of a privilege to remain silent in state and federal tribunals. Such "incongruity," however, is at the heart of our federal system. The powers and responsibilities of the state and federal governments are not congruent; under our Constitution, they are not intended to be. Why should it be thought, as an *a priori* matter, that limitations on the investigative power of the States are in all respects identical with limitations on the investigative power of the Federal Government? This certainly does not follow from the fact that we deal here with constitutional requirements; for the provisions of the Constitution which are construed are different.

As the Court pointed out in *Abbate v. United States,* "the States under our federal system have the principal responsibility for defining and prosecuting crimes." The Court endangers this allocation of responsibility for the prevention of crime when it applies to the States doctrines developed in the context of federal law enforcement, without any attention to the special problems which the States as a group or particular States may face. If the power of the States to deal with local crime is unduly restricted, the likely consequence is a shift of responsibility in this area to the Fed-

eral Government, with its vastly greater resources. Such a shift, if it occurs, may in the
end serve to weaken the very liberties which
the Fourteenth Amendment safeguards by
bringing us closer to the monolithic society
which our federalism rejects. Equally dangerous to our liberties is the alternative of watering down protections against the Federal Government embodied in the Bill of Rights so as
not unduly to restrict the powers of the
States. . . .

Rather than insisting, almost by rote, that
the Connecticut court, in considering the petitioner's claim of privilege, was required to
apply the "federal standard," the Court should
have fulfilled its responsibility under the Due
Process Clause by inquiring whether the proceedings below met the demands of fundamental fairness which due process embodies. Such
an approach may not satisfy those who see in
the Fourteenth Amendment a set of easily applied "absolutes" which can afford a haven from
unsettling doubt. It is, however, truer to the
spirit which requires this Court constantly to
re-examine fundamental principles and at the
same time enjoins it from reading its own preferences into the Constitution.

. . .

Responding to Harlan's perspective, Justice Brennan on behalf of the Court referenced decisions to the effect that previously incorporated rights and liberties were

> enforced against the States under the Fourteenth Amendment according to the
> same standards that protect those personal rights against federal encroach-
> ment. . . . The Court thus has rejected the notion that the Fourteenth Amend-
> ment applies to the States only a 'watered-down, subjective version of the indi-
> vidual guarantees of the Bill of Rights.'[118]

Despite maintaining that not only the textual bag but its interpretative baggage
applies to the states, review of the right to a jury trial allowed different methodologies
in the federal and state systems. In the early 1970s, the Court upheld state provisions
for six-person juries and conviction pursuant to a nonunanimous verdict. Validation
of six-person juries, in *Williams v. Florida*, reflected the majority's sense that the traditional twelve person panel was a historical accident and thus not even required by the
Sixth Amendment.[119] In a concurring opinion, Justice Harlan worried that the Court
was attempting both to maintain its "jot for jot and case by case" incorporative model
and give states breathing room for diverse methods—an exercise that he considered
treacherous insofar as it resulted in diluting constitutional guarantees at the federal
level.[120] The Court, in *Apodaca v. Oregon*, affirmed that dimensions of the right to a
jury trial are identical at the federal and state level but divided evenly on whether
the Sixth Amendment required unanimity.[121] In a separate opinion, that resolved the
particular controversy in favor of a nonunanimous verdict, Justice Powell adopted the
Harlan view and concluded that the aspect of the federal right in question was not
"fundamental to the essentials of jury trial."[122]

4. Modern Substantive Due Process

a. Precursors to the Right of Privacy

Although the Court abandoned its zealous protection of economic due process, it has
pursued another version of substantive due process in more recent decisions involving
personal and family liberty. The modern concept of constitutional privacy can trace its

---

[118] Malloy v. Hogan, 378 U.S. 1, 10–11 (1964) (incorporating self-incrimination provision of
Fifth Amendment).

[119] Williams v. Florida, 399 U.S. 78, 86–103 (1970).

[120] *Id.* at 129–38 (Harlan, J., concurring).

[121] Apodaca v. Oregon, 406 U.S. 404, 410–11 (1972).

[122] *Id.* at 369–77 (Powell, J., concurring).

origins to the expansive liberty notions developed in pre-*Carolene Products* decisions. The first of these cases from the *Lochner* era, *Meyer v. Nebraska*, considered the conviction of a parochial school teacher for violating a statute that prohibited teaching in any language other than English in the elementary grades of public or private school. Nebraska was among thirty-one states that enacted laws banning foreign language instruction in the wake of anti-German sentiment and a broader Progressive movement to assimilate immigrants into American life. It was also a time when the eugenics movement preached the dangers of genetic degeneracy due to the influx of undesirable immigrants from Eastern and Southern Europe. (A year later, Congress passed the National Origins Act of 1924, severely restricting the number of immigrants from these regions who could enter the country.)

Meyer reflected the clash between immigrants' desire to preserve their cultural identity and the legislature's determination that a common language was essential to American citizenship. The Court held that the liberty guaranteed by the Fourteenth Amendment encompassed the teacher's right to teach German and the parents' right to engage him to instruct their children.

Meyer v. State of Nebraska
262 U.S. 390 (1923)

MR. JUSTICE McREYNOLDS delivered the opinion of the Court.

. . .

The problem for our determination is whether the statute as construed and applied unreasonably infringes the liberty guaranteed to the plaintiff in error by the Fourteenth Amendment.

While this court has not attempted to define with exactness the liberty thus guaranteed, the term has received much consideration and some of the included things have been definitely stated. Without doubt, it denotes not merely freedom from bodily restraint but also the right of the individual to contract, to engage in any of the common occupations of life, to acquire useful knowledge, to marry, establish a home and bring up children, to worship God according to the dictates of his own conscience, and generally to enjoy those privileges long recognized at common law as essential to the orderly pursuit of happiness by free men. *Slaughter-House Cases; Lochner v. New York; Twining v. New Jersey*. The established doctrine is that this liberty may not be interfered with, under the guise of protecting the public interest, by legislative action which is arbitrary or without reasonable relation to some purpose within the competency of the state to effect. Determination by the Legislature of what constitutes proper exercise of police power is not final or conclusive but is subject to supervision by the courts.

. . .

Corresponding to the right of control, it is

the natural duty of the parent to give his children education suitable to their station in life; and nearly all the states, including Nebraska, enforce this obligation by compulsory laws.

Practically, education of the young is only possible in schools conducted by especially qualified persons who devote themselves thereto. The calling always has been regarded as useful and honorable, essential, indeed, to the public welfare. Mere knowledge of the German languages cannot reasonably be regarded as harmful. Heretofore it has been commonly looked upon as helpful and desirable. Plaintiff in error taught this language in school as part of his occupation. His right thus to teach and the right of parents to engage him so to instruct their children, we think, are within the liberty of the amendment.

. . .

It is said the purpose of the legislation was to promote civic development by inhibiting training and education of the immature in foreign tongues and ideals before they could learn English and acquire American ideals, and "that the English language should be and become the mother tongue of all children reared in this state." It is also affirmed that the foreign born population is very large, that certain communities commonly use foreign words, follow foreign leaders, move in a foreign atmosphere, and that the children are thereby hindered from becoming citizens of the most useful type and the public safety is imperiled.

. . .

For the welfare of his Ideal Commonwealth, Plato suggested a law which should provide: "That the wives of our guardians are to be common, and their children are to be common, and no parent is to know his own child, nor any child his parent. . . . The proper officers will take the offspring of the good parents to the pen or fold, and there they will deposit them with certain nurses who dwell in a separate quarter; but the offspring of the inferior, or of the better when they chance to be deformed, will be put away in some mysterious, unknown place, as they should be." In order to submerge the individual and develop ideal citizens, Sparta assembled the males at seven into barracks and intrusted their subsequent education and training to official guardians. Although such measures have been deliberately approved by men of great genius their ideas touching the relation between individual and state were wholly different from those upon which our institutions rest; and it hardly will be affirmed that any Legislature could impose such restrictions upon the people of a state without doing violence to both letter and spirit of the Constitution.

The desire of the Legislature to foster a homogeneous people with American ideals prepared readily to understand current discussions of civic matters is easy to appreciate. Unfortunate experiences during the late war and aversion toward every character of truculent adversaries were certainly enough to quicken that aspiration. But the means adopted, we think, exceed the limitations upon the power of the state and conflict with rights assured to plaintiff in error. The interference is plain enough and no adequate reason therefor in time of peace and domestic tranquility has been shown.

. . .

Justice Oliver Wendell Holmes, joined by Justice Sutherland, dissented on the ground that Nebraska's regulation of teachers' livelihood was not unreasonable. Holmes interpreted the issue in terms familiar to the *Lochner* Court: "The only question is whether the means adopted [to promote a common language] deprive teachers of the liberty secured to them by the Fourteenth Amendment . . . I think I appreciate the objection to the law but it appears to me to present a question upon which men reasonably might differ and therefore I am unable to say that the Constitution of the United States prevents the experiment being tried." While the conservative Justice McReynolds took an activist stance in reviewing social and economic legislation, Holmes believed in judicial deference to legislative judgments about social welfare.

Two years later, in *Pierce v. Society of Sisters*, the Court followed its reasoning in *Meyer* to strike down an Oregon statute requiring parents to send their children to public school: "[W]e think it entirely plain that the [statute] unreasonably interferes with the liberty of parents and guardians to direct the upbringing and education of children under their control."[123] The political battle that generated *Pierce* had been waged between advocates of universal common schooling and supporters of private education since the turn of the century. Elaborating his rejection in *Meyer* of the Platonic and Spartan methods of educating citizens, Justice McReynolds stressed that the "fundamental theory of liberty . . . excludes any general power of the state to standardize its children by forcing them to accept instruction from public teachers only. The child is not the mere creature of the state; those who nurture him and direct his destiny have the right, coupled with the high duty, to recognize and prepare him for additional obligations."

Meyer and *Pierce* extended the concept of liberty beyond economic due process to the area of personal and family autonomy, laying the foundation for the modern right of privacy decisions. Yet they also preserved a traditional view of the family by safeguarding parental authority over children from democratic efforts to achieve social reform. Indeed, it has been argued that these decisions were animated by "a conservative attachment to the patriarchal family, to a class-stratified society, and to a parent's

---

[123] Pierce v. Society of Sisters, 268 U.S. 510 (1925).

private property rights to his children."[124] We shall see that this reference to traditional notions of the family continues to govern many of the Court's substantive due process decisions. One way to interpret the *Meyer* and *Pierce* decisions is to see them as a logical extension of, rather than a radical departure from, their economic due process counterparts of the *Lochner* era. Just as the Fourteenth Amendment protected individuals' freedom to contract and right to their own property from economic regulation, it protected parents' freedom to control their children from social regulation.

Felix Frankfurter, an opponent of economic due process, observed shortly after the *Meyer* and *Pierce* decisions that the same doctrine of liberty that prevailed against socially intolerant legislation was also used to thwart economically progressive legislation. "In rejoicing over the Nebraska and Oregon cases," Frankfurter cautioned, "we must not forget that a heavy price has to be paid for these occasional services to liberalism. The New York bakeshop case, the invalidation of trade union laws, the sanctification of the injunction in labor cases, the veto of minimum wage legislation, are not wiped out by the Oregon decision."[125] Frankfurter's prediction proved correct for a time: the *Lochner* era Court cited *Meyer* in a number of subsequent cases to support its invalidation of economic regulation under economic due process.[126] *Meyer's* doctrine of personal liberty protected by substantive due process survived the demise of economic due process, re-emerging decades later as precedent for the Court's landmark right of privacy decision, *Roe v. Wade*.

b. Contraception and the Right of Privacy

In the late nineteenth century, many states enacted statutes prohibiting contraceptives, as well as the distribution of information about them. The Comstock Law, passed by Congress in 1873, classified information about contraceptives as obscene and made its circulation through the mail a crime. By 1960, however, a movement for increased access to birth control had succeeded in obtaining the repeal of these laws or a more permissive approach to contraceptives in most states. Connecticut was an exception. The Connecticut birth control law, the most restrictive in the country, was originally passed in 1879, as part of a broader obscenity statute. It imposed an absolute ban on the use of contraceptives; a separate accessory statute allowed prosecutors to charge physicians, clinic personnel, and others who aided and counseled the use of birth control.

The United States Supreme Court declined the opportunity to consider the constitutionality of the Connecticut statute in two cases—*Tileston v. Ullman*[127] and *Poe v. Ullman*.[128] In *Tileston*, the Court unanimously dismissed the appeal on the ground that the physician who brought the declaratory judgment action lacked standing; in *Poe*, a four-member plurality of the justices found that the lawsuit (this time brought by several anonymous patients as well as a physician) raised no immediate controversy since the statute was no longer enforced. In fact, the Connecticut birth control prohibi-

---

[124] Barbara Bennett Woodhouse, *Who Owns the Child?: Meyer and Pierce and the Child as Property*, 33 Wm. & Mary L. Rev. 995, 997 (1992).

[125] Felix Frankfurter, *Can the Supreme Court Guarantee Toleration?*, reprinted in Felix Frankfurter on the Supreme Court: Extrajudicial Essays on the Court and the Constitution 174, 176 (Philip B. Kurland ed., 1970).

[126] *See, e.g.*, Weaver v. Palmer Bros. Co., 270 U.S. 402 (1926) (invalidating a Pennsylvania statute prohibiting the use of shoddy in bedding); Chas. Wolff Packing Co. v. Court of Industrial Relations, 262 U.S. 522 (1923) (invalidating a Kansas statute authorizing an administrative board to fix hours of labor in food, clothing and fuel industries during labor disputes).

[127] 318 U.S. 44 (1943) (per curiam).

[128] 367 U.S. 497 (1961).

tion had been enforced against the personnel of birth control clinics, resulting in the closure of these clinics for twenty-five years. Although birth control was generally available to middle-class and wealthy patients, who could obtain prescriptions from private physicians, it was denied to the poor who depended on public health services.[129]

Justice Harlan wrote an influential dissent in *Poe v. Ullman* which defended an independent guarantee of liberty found in the Fourteenth Amendment:

> Were due process merely a procedural safeguard it would fail to reach those situations where deprivation of life, liberty or property was accomplished by legislation which by operating in the future could, given even the fairest possible procedure in application to individuals, nevertheless destroy the enjoyment of all three. . . .
>
> . . . Again and again this Court has resisted the notion that the Fourteenth Amendment is no more than a shorthand reference to what is explicitly set out elsewhere in the Bill of Rights. Indeed the fact that an identical provision limiting federal action is found among the first eight Amendments, applying to the Federal Government, suggests that due process is a discrete concept which subsists as an independent guaranty of liberty and procedural fairness, more general and inclusive than the specific prohibitions.
>
> Due process has not been reduced to any formula; its content cannot be determined by reference to any code. The best that can be said is that through the course of this Court's decisions it has represented the balance which our Nation, built upon postulates of respect for the liberty of the individual, has struck between that liberty and the demands of organized society. If the supplying of content to this Constitutional concept has of necessity been a rational process, it certainly has not been one where judges have felt free to roam where unguided speculation might take them. The balance of which I speak is the balance struck by this country, having regard to what history teaches are the traditions from which it developed as well as the traditions from which it broke. That tradition is a living thing. A decision of this Court which radically departs from it could not long survive, while a decision which builds on what has survived is likely to be sound. No formula could serve as a substitute, in this area, for judgment and restraint.
>
> . . . [The] full scope of the liberty guaranteed by the Due Process Clause cannot be found in or limited by the precise terms of the specific guarantees elsewhere provided in the Constitution. The "liberty" is not a series of isolated points pricked out in terms of the taking of property; the freedom of speech, press, and religion; the right to keep and bear arms; the freedom from unreasonable searches and seizures; and so on. It is a rational continuum which, broadly speaking, includes a freedom from all substantial arbitrary impositions and purposeless restraints, and which also recognizes, what a reasonable and sensitive judgment must, that certain interests require particularly careful scrutiny of the state needs asserted to justify their abridgement.

The dismissal in *Poe v. Ullman* allowed the Connecticut birth control statute to continue to deter the distribution of contraceptives through birth control clinics. On November 1, 1961, on the heels of *Poe*, The Planned Parenthood League of Connecticut opened a birth control clinic at its headquarters in New Haven, virtually inviting prosecution. Ten days later, after the clinic had served seventy-five women, police arrested

---

[129] Mary L. Dudziak, *Just Say No: Birth Control in the Connecticut Supreme Court Before Griswold v. Connecticut*, 75 IOWA L. REV. 915, 917 (1990); Catherine G. Roraback, *Griswold v. Connecticut: A Brief Case History*, 16 OHIO N.U. L. REV. 395, 396–97 (1989).

the League's executive director, Estelle Griswold, and medical director, Dr. C. Lee Buxton, chairman of the Department of Obstetrics and Gynecology at Yale Medical School. Griswold and Buxton, who was also the physician-plaintiff in *Poe*, were found guilty as accessories to violations of the birth control law, and the Connecticut courts affirmed their convictions.

This time the Supreme Court considered the constitutionality of the Connecticut statute. The justices sharply debated whether they would overstep their constitutional function by enforcing a concept of liberty or by failing to enforce one. Although seven of the justices agreed that the Constitution's protection extends beyond the specific guarantees of the Bill of Rights, they disagreed on that protection's scope and source. In their concurring opinions, Harlan and White relied on the due process clause of the Fourteenth Amendment to invalidate the Connecticut law. Goldberg, on the other hand, wrote a concurrence based on the Ninth Amendment, which provides that "[t]he enumeration in the Constitution, of certain rights, shall not be construed to deny or disparage others retained by the people." The Ninth Amendment, according to Goldberg, authorized federal judges to protect citizens' unenumerated freedoms.

While the concurring justices argued that the Court was required by the Ninth and Fourteenth Amendments to safeguard citizens' liberty from the irrational Connecticut law, Black and Stewart argued in dissent that this judicial action usurped the power to legislate which the Constitution reserved to the states. For example, Black and Stewart interpreted the Ninth Amendment as a reservation of *state* power, rather than a shield of federally enforceable liberties.

Douglas's opinion for the Court, disclaiming a doctrinal connection to the repudiated *Lochner*, notably avoided any reliance on liberty, due process, or the Fourteenth Amendment. Instead, it elaborately pieced together a realm of constitutional protection not explicitly mentioned in the Constitution—the right of privacy. The phrase "right to privacy" was already established as a legal claim as a result of a law review article written by Samuel Warren and (later Justice) Louis Brandeis in 1890 about a different aspect of privacy.[130] Warren and Brandeis advocated that states should give some form of tort relief to citizens whose personal affairs were exploited by others, including the "yellow press." Following the article, most states created a cause of action, either by statute or common law, for wrongful public exposure of private information and other invasions of privacy. Warren and Brandeis described the right to privacy as the right "to be let alone." Douglas's opinion in *Griswold* reconstructed privacy as a constitutional right.

---

[130] Samuel Warren & Louis Brandeis, *The Right to Privacy,* 4 HARV. L. REV. 193 (1890).

Griswold v. Connecticut
381 U.S. 479 (1965)

MR. JUSTICE DOUGLAS delivered the opinion of the Court.

. . .

Coming to the merits, we are met with a wide range of questions that implicate the Due Process Clause of the Fourteenth Amendment. Overtones of some arguments suggest that *Lochner v. State of New York*, should be our guide. But we decline that invitation. . . . We do not sit as a super-legislature to determine the wisdom, need, and propriety of laws that touch economic problems, business affairs, or social conditions. This law, however, operates directly on an intimate relation of husband and wife and their physician's role in one aspect of that relation.

The association of people is not mentioned in the Constitution nor in the Bill of Rights. The right to educate a child in a school of the parents' choice—whether public or private or parochial—is also not mentioned. Nor is the right to study any particular subject or any foreign language. Yet the First Amendment has been construed to include certain of those rights.

. . .

In *NAACP v. State of Alabama*, we protected the "freedom to associate and privacy in one's associations," noting that freedom of association was a peripheral First Amendment right. Disclosure of membership lists of a constitutionally valid association, we held, was invalid, as entailing the likelihood of a substantial restraint upon the exercise by petitioner's members of their right to freedom of association." In other words, the First Amendment has a penumbra where privacy is protected from governmental intrusion. In like context, we have protected forms of "association" that are not political in the customary sense but pertain to the social, legal, and economic benefit of the members. . . .

Those cases involved more than the "right of assembly"—a right that extends to all irrespective of their race or ideology. The right of "association," like the right of belief is more than the right to attend a meeting; it includes the right to express one's attitudes or philosophies by membership in a group or by affiliation with it or by other lawful means. Association in that context is a form of expression of opinion; and while it is not expressly included in the First Amendment its existence is necessary in making the express guarantees fully meaningful.

The foregoing cases suggest that specific guarantees in the Bill of Rights have penumbras formed by emanations from those guarantees that help give them life and substance. See *Poe v. Ullman* (dissenting opinion). Various guarantees create zones of privacy. The right of association contained in the penumbra of the First Amendment is one, as we have seen. The Third Amendment in its prohibition against the quartering of soldiers "in any house" in time of peace without the consent of the owner is another facet of that privacy. The Fourth Amendment explicitly affirms the "right of the people to be secure in their persons, houses, papers, and effects, against unreasonable searches and seizures." The Fifth Amendment in its Self-Incrimination Clause enables the citizen to create a zone of privacy which government may not force him to surrender to his detriment. The Ninth Amendment provides: "The enumeration in the Constitution, of certain rights, shall not be construed to deny or disparage others retained by the people."

The Fourth and Fifth Amendments were described in *Boyd v. United States*, 116 U.S. 616, as protection against all governmental invasions "of the sanctity of a man's home and the privacies of life." We recently referred in *Mapp v. Ohio*, 367 U.S. 643, to the Fourteenth Amendment as creating a "right to privacy, no less important than any other right carefully and particularly reserved to the people."

. . .

The present case, then, concerns a relationship lying within the zone of privacy created by several fundamental constitutional guarantees. And it concerns a law which, in forbidding the *use* of contraceptives rather than regulating their manufacture or sale, seeks to achieve its goals by means having a maximum destructive impact upon that relationship. Such a law cannot stand in light of the familiar principle, so often applied by this Court, that a "governmental purpose to control or prevent activities constitutionally subject to state regulation may not be achieved by means which sweep unnecessarily broadly and thereby invade the area of protected freedoms." *NAACP v. Alabama*. Would we allow the police to search the sacred precincts of marital bedrooms for telltale signs of the use of contraceptives? The very idea is repulsive to the notions of privacy surrounding the marriage relationship.

We deal with a right of privacy older than the Bill of Rights—older than our political parties, older than our school system. Marriage is a coming together for better or for worse, hopefully enduring, and intimate to the degree of being sacred. It is an association that promotes a way of life, not causes; a harmony in living, not political faiths; a bilateral loyalty, not commercial or social projects. Yet it is an association for as noble a purpose as any involved in our prior decisions.

Reversed.

MR. JUSTICE GOLDBERG, whom THE CHIEF JUSTICE [WARREN] and Mr. Justice BRENNAN join, concurring.

I agree with the Court that Connecticut's birth-control law unconstitutionally intrudes upon the right of marital privacy, and I join in its opinion and judgment. Although I have not accepted the view that "due process" as used in the Fourteenth Amendment includes all of the first eight Amendments, . . . I do agree that the concept of liberty protects those personal rights that are fundamental, and is not confined to the specific terms of the Bill of Rights. My conclusion that the concept of liberty is not so restricted and that it embraces the right of marital privacy though that right is not mentioned explicitly in the Constitution is supported both by numerous decisions of this Court, referred to in the Court's opinion, and by the language and history of the Ninth Amendment. In reaching the conclusion that the right of marital privacy is protected, as being within the protected penumbra of specific guarantees of the Bill of Rights, the Court refers to the Ninth Amendment. I add these words to emphasize the relevance of that Amendment to the Court's holding.

The Court stated many years ago that the Due Process Clause protects those liberties that are "so rooted in the traditions and conscience of our people as to be ranked as fundamental." *Snyder v. Com. of Massachusetts*, 291 U.S. 97. . . . This Court, in a series of decisions, has held that the Fourteenth Amendment absorbs and applies to the States those specifics of the first eight amendments which express fundamental personal rights. The language and history of the Ninth Amendment reveal that the Framers of the Constitution believed that there are additional fundamental rights, protected from governmental infringement, which exist alongside those fundamental rights specifically mentioned in the first eight constitutional amendments.

The Ninth Amendment reads, "The enumeration in the Constitution, of certain rights, shall not be construed to deny or disparage others retained by the people." The Amendment is almost entirely the work of James Madison. It was introduced in Congress by him and passed the House and Senate with little or no debate and virtually no change in language. It was proffered to quiet expressed fears that a bill of specifically enumerated rights could not be sufficiently broad to cover all essential rights and that the specific mention of certain rights would be interpreted as a denial that others were protected.[4]

---

[4] Alexander Hamilton was opposed to a bill of rights on the ground that it was unnecessary because the Federal Government was a government of delegated powers and it was not granted the power to intrude upon fundamental personal rights. The Federalist, No. 84 (Cooke ed. 1961). He also argued, "I go further, and affirm that bills of rights, in the sense and in the extent in which they are contended for, are not only unnecessary in the proposed constitution, but would even be dangerous. They would contain various exceptions to powers which are granted; and on this very account, would afford a colourable pretext to claim more than were granted. For why declare that things shall not be done which there is no power to do? Why for instance, should it be said, that the liberty of the press shall not be restrained, when no power is given by which restrictions may be imposed? I will not contend that such a provision would confer a regulating power; but it is evident that it would furnish, to men disposed to usurp, a plausible pretence for claiming that power." The Ninth Amendment and the Tenth Amendment, which provides, "The powers not delegated to the United States by the Constitution, nor prohibited by it to the States, are reserved to the States respectively, or to the people," were apparently also designed in part to meet the above-quoted argument of Hamilton.

In presenting the proposed Amendment, Madison said:

> "It has been objected also against a bill of rights, that, by enumerating particular exceptions to the grant of power, it would disparage those rights which were not placed in that enumeration; and it might follow by implication, that those rights which were not singled out, were intended to be assigned into the hands of the General Government, and were consequently insecure. This is one of the most plausible arguments I have ever heard urged against the admission of a bill of rights into this system; but, I conceive, that it may be guarded against. I have attempted it, as gentlemen may see by turning to the last clause of the fourth resolution [the Ninth Amendment]." I Annals of Congress 439.

. . . These statements of Madison . . . make clear that the Framers did not intend that the first eight amendments be construed to exhaust the basic and fundamental rights which the Constitution guaranteed to the people.

While this Court has had little occasion to interpret the Ninth Amendment, "[i]t cannot be presumed that any clause in the constitution is intended to be without effect." *Marbury v. Madison.* . . . The Ninth Amendment to the Constitution may be regarded by some as a recent discovery but since 1791 it has been a basic part of the Constitution which we are sworn to uphold. To hold that a right so basic and fundamental and so deep-rooted in our society as the right of privacy in marriage may be infringed because that right is not guaranteed in so many words by the first eight amendments to the Constitution is to ignore the Ninth Amendment and to give it no effect whatsoever. Moreover, a judicial construction that this fundamental right is not protected by the Constitution because it is not mentioned in explicit terms by one of the first eight amendments or elsewhere in the Constitution would violate the Ninth Amendment, which specifically states that "[t]he enumeration in the Constitution, of certain rights shall not be *construed* to deny or disparage others retained by the people." (Emphasis added).

A dissenting opinion suggests that my interpretation of the Ninth Amendment somehow "broaden[s] the powers of this Court." With all due respect, I believe that it misses the import of what I am saying. I do not take the position of my Brother Black in his dissent in *Adamson v. People of State of California*, 332 U.S. 45, that the entire Bill of Rights is incorporated in the Fourteenth Amendment, and I do not mean to imply that the Ninth Amendment is applied against the States by the Fourteenth. Nor do I mean to state that the Ninth

Amendment constitutes an independent source of rights protected from infringement by either the States or the Federal Government. Rather, the Ninth Amendment shows a belief of the Constitution's authors that fundamental rights exist that are not expressly enumerated in the first eight amendments and an intent that the list of rights included there not be deemed exhaustive. . . . I do not see how this broadens the authority of the Court; rather it serves to support what this Court has been doing in protecting fundamental rights.

Nor am I turning somersaults with history in arguing that the Ninth Amendment is relevant in a case dealing with a *State's* infringement of a fundamental right. While the Ninth Amendment—and indeed the entire Bill of Rights—originally concerned restrictions upon *federal* power, the subsequently enacted Fourteenth Amendment prohibits the States as well from abridging fundamental personal liberties. And, the Ninth Amendment, in indicating that not all such liberties are specifically mentioned in the first eight amendments, is surely relevant in showing the existence of other fundamental personal rights, now protected from state, as well as federal, infringement. In sum, the Ninth Amendment simply lends strong support to the view that the "liberty" protected by the Fifth and Fourteenth Amendments from infringement by the Federal Government or the States is not restricted to rights specifically mentioned in the first eight amendments.

In determining which rights are fundamental, judges are not left at large to decide cases in light of their personal and private notions. Rather, they must look to the "traditions and [collective] conscience of our people" to determine whether a principle is "so rooted [there] . . . as to be ranked as fundamental." *Snyder v. Com. of Massachusetts.* The inquiry is whether a right involved "is of such a character that it cannot be denied without violating those 'fundamental principles of liberty and justice which lie at the base of all our civil and political institutions'. . . . " *Powell v. State of Alabama*, 287 U.S. 45, "Liberty" also "gains content from the emanations of * * * specific [constitutional] guarantees" and from experience with the requirements of a free society." *Poe v. Ullman* (dissenting opinion of Mr. Justice Douglas).

. . .

The entire fabric of the Constitution and the purposes that clearly underlie its specific guarantees demonstrate that the rights to marital privacy and to marry and raise a family are of similar order and magnitude as the fundamental rights specifically protected.

Although the Constitution does not speak in so many words of the right of privacy in marriage, I cannot believe that it offers these fundamental rights no protection. The fact that no particular provision of the Constitution explicitly forbids the State from disrupting the traditional relation of the family—a relation as old and as fundamental as our entire civilization—surely does not show that the Government was meant to have the power to do so. Rather, as the Ninth Amendment expressly recognizes, there are fundamental personal rights such as this one, which are protected from abridgment by the Government though not specifically mentioned in the Constitution.

. . .

The logic of the dissents would sanction federal or state legislation that seems to me even more plainly unconstitutional than the statute before us. Surely the Government, absent a showing of a compelling subordinating state interest, could not decree that all husbands and wives must be sterilized after two children have been born to them. Yet by their reasoning such an invasion of marital privacy would not be subject to constitutional challenge because, while it might be "silly," no provision of the Constitution specifically prevents the Government from curtailing the marital right to bear children and raise a family. While it may shock some of my Brethren that the Court today holds that the Constitution protects the right of marital privacy, in my view it is far more shocking to believe that the personal liberty guaranteed by the Constitution does not include protection against such totalitarian limitation of family size, which is at complete variance with our constitutional concepts. Yet, if upon a showing of a slender basis of rationality, a law outlawing voluntary birth control by married persons is valid, then, by the same reasoning, a law requiring compulsory birth control also would seem to be valid. In my view, however, both types of law would unjustifiably intrude upon rights of marital privacy which are constitutionally protected.

. . .

Although the Connecticut birth-control law obviously encroaches upon a fundamental personal liberty, the State does not show that the law serves any "sub-ordinating [state] interest which is compelling" or that it is "necessary . . . to the accomplishment of a permissible state policy." The State, at most, argues that . . . preventing the use of birth-control devices by married persons helps prevent the indulgence by some in . . . extra-marital relations. The rationality of this justification is dubious, particularly in light of the admitted widespread availability to all persons in the State of Connecticut, unmarried as well as married, of birth-control devices for the prevention of disease, as distinguished from the prevention of conception. But, in any event, it is clear that the state interest in safe-guarding marital fidelity can be served by a more discriminately tailored statute, which does not, like the present one, sweep unnecessarily broadly, reaching far beyond the evil sought to be dealt with and intruding upon the privacy of all married couples. . . .

. . .

MR. JUSTICE HARLAN, concurring in the judgment.

I fully agree with the judgment of reversal, but find myself unable to join the Court's opinion. The reason is that it seems to me to evince an approach to this case very much like that taken by my Brothers BLACK and STEWART in dissent, namely: the Due Process Clause of the Fourteenth Amendment does not touch this Connecticut statute unless the enactment is found to violate some right assured by the letter or penumbra of the Bill of Rights.

In other words, what I find implicit in the Court's opinion is that the "incorporation" doctrine may be used to *restrict* the reach of Fourteenth Amendment Due Process. For me this is just as unacceptable constitutional doctrine as is the use of the "incorporation" approach to *impose* upon the States all the requirements of the Bill of Rights as found in the provisions of the first eight amendments and in the decisions of this Court interpreting them.

In my view, the proper constitutional inquiry in this case is whether this Connecticut statute infringes the Due Process Clause of the Fourteenth Amendment because the enactment violates basic values "implicit in the concept of ordered liberty." *Palko v. State of Connecticut*, 302 U.S. 319. For reasons stated at length in my dissenting opinion in *Poe v. Ullman*, I believe that it does. While the relevant inquiry may be aided by resort to one or more of the provisions of the Bill of Rights, it is not dependent on them or any of their radiations. The Due Process Clause of the Fourteenth Amendment stands, in my opinion, on its own bottom.

A further observation seems in order respecting the justification of my Brothers BLACK and STEWART for their "incorporation" approach to this case. Their approach does not rest on historical reasons, which are of course wholly lacking, but on the thesis that by limiting the content of the Due Process Clause of the Fourteenth Amendment to the protection of rights which can be found elsewhere in the Constitution, in this instance in the Bill of Rights, judges will thus be confined to "interpretation" of specific constitutional provisions, and will thereby be restrained from introducing their own notions of constitutional right and wrong into the "vague contours of the Due Process Clause."

While I could not more heartily agree that judicial "self restraint" is an indispensable ingredient of sound constitutional adjudication, I do submit that the formula suggested for achieving it is more hollow than real. "Specific" provisions of the Constitution, no less than "due process," lend themselves as readily to "personal" interpretations by judges whose constitutional outlook is simply to keep the Constitution in supposed "tune with the times."

. . .

Judicial self-restraint will not, I suggest, be brought about in the "due process" area by the historically unfounded incorporation formula long advanced by my Brother BLACK, and now in part espoused by my Brother STEWART. It will be achieved in this area, as in other constitutional areas, only by continual insistence upon respect for the teachings of history, solid recognition of the basic values that underlie our society, and wise appreciation of the great roles that the doctrines of federalism and separation of powers have played in establishing and preserving American freedoms. Adherence to these principles will not, of course, obviate all constitutional differences of opinion among judges, nor should it. Their continued recognition will, however, go farther toward keeping most judges from roaming at large in the constitutional field than will the interpolation into the Constitution of an artificial and largely illusory restriction on the content of the Due Process Clause.

MR. JUSTICE WHITE, concurring in the judgment.

In my view this Connecticut law as applied to married couples deprives them of "liberty" without due process of law, as that concept is used in the Fourteenth Amendment. I therefore concur in the judgment of the Court reversing these convictions under Connecticut's aiding and abetting statute.

It would be unduly repetitious, and belaboring the obvious, to expound on the impact of this statute on the liberty guaranteed by the Fourteenth Amendment against arbitrary or capricious denials or on the nature of this liberty. Suffice it to say that this is not the first time this Court has had occasion to articulate that the liberty entitled to protection under the Fourteenth Amendment includes the right "to marry, establish a home and bring up children," *Meyer v. State of Nebraska*, and "the liberty . . . to direct the upbringing and education of children," *Pierce v. Society of Sisters*, and that these are among "the basic civil rights of man." *Skinner v. State of Oklahoma*. These decisions affirm that there is a "realm of family life which the state cannot enter" without substantial justification. *Prince v. Com. of Massachusetts*, 321 U.S. 158. . . .

. . .

As I read the opinions of the Connecticut courts and the argument of Connecticut in this

Court, the State claims but one justification for its anti-use statute. . . . There is no serious contention that Connecticut thinks the use of artificial or external methods of contraception immoral or unwise in itself, or that the anti-use statute is founded upon any policy of promoting population expansion. Rather, the statute is said to serve the State's policy against all forms of promiscuous or illicit sexual relationships, be they premarital or extramarital, concededly a permissible and legitimate legislative goal.

Without taking issue with the premise that the fear of conception operates as a deterrent to such relationships in addition to the criminal proscriptions Connecticut has against such conduct, I wholly fail to see how the ban on the use of contraceptives by married couples in any way reinforces the State's ban on illicit sexual relationships. . . . The only way Connecticut seeks to limit or control the availability of such devices is through its general aiding and abetting statute whose operation in this context has been quite obviously ineffective and whose most serious use has been against birth-control clinics rendering advice to married, rather than unmarried, persons. . . .

. . . It is purely fanciful to believe that the broad proscription on use facilitates discovery of use by persons engaging in a prohibited relationship or for some other reason makes such use more unlikely and thus can be supported by any sort of administrative consideration. . . . A statute limiting its prohibition on use to persons engaging in the prohibited relationship would serve the end posited by Connecticut in the same way, and with the same effectiveness, or ineffectiveness, as the broad anti-use statute under attack in this case. I find nothing in this record justifying the sweeping scope of this statute, with its telling effect on the freedoms of married persons, and therefore conclude that it deprives such persons of liberty without due process of law.

MR. JUSTICE BLACK, with whom Mr. Justice STEWART joins, dissenting.

I agree with my Brother STEWART'S dissenting opinion. And like him I do not to any extent whatever base my view that this Connecticut law is constitutional on a belief that the law is wise or that its policy is a good one. In order that there may be no room at all to doubt why I vote as I do, I feel constrained to add that the law is every bit as offensive to me as it is to my Brethren of the majority and my Brothers HARLAN, WHITE and GOLDBERG who, reciting reasons why it is offensive to them, hold it unconstitutional. There is no single one of the graphic and eloquent strictures and criticisms fired at the policy of this Connecticut law either by the Court's opinion or by those of my concurring Brethren to which I cannot subscribe—except their conclusion that the evil qualities they see in the law make it unconstitutional.

. . .

The Court talks about a constitutional "right of privacy" as though there is some constitutional provision or provisions forbidding any law ever to be passed which might abridge the "privacy" of individuals. But there is not. There are, of course, guarantees in certain specific constitutional provisions which are designed in part to protect privacy at certain times and places with respect to certain activities. Such, for example, is the Fourth Amendment's guarantee against "unreasonable searches and seizures." But I think it belittles that Amendment to talk about it as though it protects nothing but "privacy." To treat it that way is to give it a niggardly interpretation, not the kind of liberal reading I think any Bill of Rights provision should be given. The average man would very likely not have his feelings soothed any more by having his property seized openly than by having it seized privately and by stealth. He simply wants his property left alone. And a person can be just as much, if not more, irritated, annoyed and injured by an unceremonious public arrest by a policeman as he is by a seizure in the privacy of his office or home.

One of the most effective ways of diluting or expanding a constitutionally guaranteed right is to substitute for the crucial word or words of a constitutional guarantee another word or words, more or less flexible and more or less restricted in meaning. This fact is well illustrated by the use of the term "right of privacy" as a comprehensive substitute for the Fourteenth Amendment's guarantee against "unreasonable searches and seizures." "Privacy" is a broad, abstract and ambiguous concept which can easily be shrunken in meaning but which can also, on the other hand, easily be interpreted as a constitutional ban against many things other than searches and seizures. . . . For these reasons I get nowhere in this case by talk about a constitutional "right or privacy" as an emanation from one or more constitutional provisions. I like my privacy as well as the next one, but I am nevertheless compelled to admit that government has a right to invade it unless prohibited by some specific constitutional provision. For these reasons I cannot agree with the Court's judgment and the reasons it gives for holding this Connecticut law unconstitutional.

. . .

The due process argument which my Brothers HARLAN and WHITE adopt here is based, as their opinions indicate, on the premise that this Court is vested with power to invalidate all state laws that it considers to be arbitrary, capricious, unreasonable, or oppressive, or this Court's belief that a particular state law under scrutiny has no "rational or justifying" purpose, or is offensive to a "sense of fairness and justice." If these formulas based on "natural justice," or others which mean the same thing, are to prevail, they require judges to determine what is or is not constitutional on the basis of their own appraisal of what laws are unwise or unnecessary. The power to make such decisions is of course that of a legislative body. Surely it has to be admitted that no provision of the Constitution specifically gives such blanket power to courts to exercise such a supervisory veto over the wisdom and value of legislative policies and to hold unconstitutional those laws which they believe unwise or dangerous. I readily admit that no legislative body, state or national, should pass laws that can justly be given any of the invidious labels invoked as constitutional excuses to strike down state laws. But perhaps it is not too much to say that no legislative body ever does pass laws without believing that they will accomplish a sane, rational, wise and justifiable purpose. While I completely subscribe to the holding of *Marbury v. Madison* and subsequent cases, that our Court has constitutional power to strike down statutes, state or federal, that violate commands of the Federal Constitution, I do not believe that we are granted power by the Due Process Clause or any other constitutional provision or provisions to measure constitutionality by our belief that legislation is arbitrary, capricious or unreasonable, or accomplishes no justifiable purpose, or is offensive to our own notions of "civilized standards of conduct." Such an appraisal of the wisdom of legislation is an attribute of the power to make laws, not of the power to interpret them. The use by federal courts of such a formula or doctrine or whatnot to veto federal or state laws simply takes away from Congress and States the power to make laws based on their own judgment of fairness and wisdom and transfers that power to this Court for ultimate determination—a power which was specifically denied to federal courts by the convention that framed the Constitution.

. . .

My Brother GOLDBERG has adopted the recent discovery that the Ninth Amendment as well as the Due Process Clause can be used by this Court as authority to strike down all state legislation which this Court thinks violates "fundamental principles of liberty and justice," or is contrary to the "traditions and [collective] conscience of our people." He also states, without proof satisfactory to me, that in making decisions on this basis judges will not consider "their personal and private notions." One may ask how they can avoid considering them. Our Court certainly has no machinery with which

to take a Gallup Poll. And the scientific miracles of this age have not yet produced a gadget which the Court can use to determine what traditions are rooted in the "[collective] conscience of our people." Moreover, one would certainly have to look far beyond the language of the Ninth Amendment to find that the Framers vested in this Court any such awesome veto powers over lawmaking, either by the States or by the Congress. Nor does anything in the history of the Amendment offer any support for such a shocking doctrine. The whole history of the adoption of the Constitution and Bill of Rights points the other way, and the very material quoted by my Brother GOLDBERG shows that the Ninth Amendment was intended to protect against the idea that "by enumerating particular exceptions to the grant of power" to the Federal Government, "those rights which were not singled out, were intended to be assigned into the hands of the General Government [the United States], and were consequently insecure." That amendment was passed, not to broaden the powers of this Court or any other department of "the General Government," but, as every student of history knows, to assure the people that the Constitution in all its provisions was intended to limit the Federal Government to the powers granted expressly or by necessary implication. If any broad, unlimited power to hold laws unconstitutional because they offend what this Court conceives to be the "[collective] conscience of our people" is vested in this Court by the Ninth Amendment, the Fourteenth Amendment, or any other provision of the Constitution, it was not given by the Framers, but rather has been bestowed on the Court by the Court. This fact is perhaps responsible for the peculiar phenomenon that for a period of a century and a half no serious suggestion was ever made that the Ninth Amendment, enacted to protect state powers against federal invasion, could be used as a weapon of federal power to prevent state legislatures from passing laws they consider appropriate to govern local affairs. Use of any such broad, unbounded judicial authority would make of this Court's members a day-to-day constitutional convention.

. . .

MR. JUSTICE STEWART, whom MR. JUSTICE BLACK joins, dissenting.
. . . I think this is an uncommonly silly law. As a practical matter, the law is obviously unenforceable, except in the oblique context of the present case. As a philosophical matter, I believe the use of contraceptives in the relationship of marriage should be left to personal and private choice, based upon each individual's moral, ethical, and religious beliefs. As a matter of social policy, I think professional counsel about methods of birth control should

be available to all, so that each individual's choice can be meaningfully made. But we are not asked in this case to say whether we think this law is unwise, or even asinine. We are asked to hold that it violates the United States Constitution. And that I cannot do.

In the course of its opinion the Court refers to no less than six Amendments to the Constitution: the First, the Third, the Fourth, the Fifth, the Ninth, and the Fourteenth. But the Court does not say which of these Amendments, if any, it thinks is infringed by this Connecticut law.

We *are* told that the Due Process Clause of the Fourteenth Amendment is not, as such, the "guide" in this case. With that much I agree. . . . There is no claim that the appellants were denied any of the elements of procedural due process at their trial, so as to make their convictions constitutionally invalid. And, as the Court says, the day has long passed since the Due Process Clause was regarded as a proper instrument for determining "the wisdom, need, and propriety" of state laws. . . .

The Court also quotes the Ninth Amendment, and my Brother GOLDBERG'S concurring opinion relies heavily upon it. But to say that the Ninth Amendment has anything to do with this case is to turn somersaults with history. The Ninth Amendment . . . was framed by James Madison and adopted by the States simply to make clear that the adoption of the Bill of Rights did not alter the plan that the *Federal* Government was to be a government of express and limited powers, and that all rights and powers not delegated to it were retained by the people and the individual States. Until today no member of this Court has ever suggested that the Ninth Amendment meant anything else, and the idea that a federal court could ever use the Ninth Amendment to annul a law passed by the elected representatives of the people of the State of Connecticut would have caused James Madison no little wonder.

What provision of the Constitution, then, does make this state law invalid? The Court says it is the right of privacy "created by several fundamental constitutional guarantees." With all deference, I can find no such general right of privacy in the Bill of Rights, or in any case ever before decided by this Court. . . . It is the essence of judicial duty to subordinate our own personal views, our own ideas of what legislation is wise and what is not. If, as I should surely hope, the law before us does not reflect the standards of the people of Connecticut, the people of Connecticut can freely exercise their true Ninth and Tenth Amendment rights to persuade their elected representatives to repeal it. That is the constitutional way to take this law off the books.

Two subsequent decisions concerning contraception extended the holding in *Griswold* beyond "the marital bedroom." *Eisenstadt v. Baird* struck down a Massachusetts statute that prohibited distribution of contraceptives to single adults, while allowing physicians to prescribe them for married couples.[131] Although the Court decided *Eisenstadt* on equal protection grounds, Justice Brennan's opinion stated in *dicta* a broad interpretation of the right of privacy that included a right of individuals to use contraceptives.

> It is true that in *Griswold* the right of privacy in question inhered in the marital relationship. Yet the marital couple is not an independent entity with a mind and heart of its own, but an association of two individuals each with a separate intellectual and emotional makeup. If the right of privacy means anything, it is the right of the *individual*, married or single, to be free from unwarranted governmental intrusion into matters so fundamentally affecting a person as the decision whether to bear or beget a child.

While *Griswold* protected the privacy of the marital unit, *Eisenstadt* protected the liberty of the autonomous individual. Thus, *Eisenstadt* revived a central theme of the *Lochner*-era decisions that *Griswold* avoided: it protected the individual's freedom from unjustified government restraint. But *Eisenstadt*'s shift in focus from family privacy to individual liberty also reflected a dramatic social change that had occurred since the time of *Lochner*. "For over a century, Americans had assumed that the autonomous

---

[131] Eisenstadt v. Baird, 405 U.S. 438 (1972).

individual existed in the market, but not in the home. *Eisenstadt* is significant for envisioning the autonomous individual at the center of the domestic unit."[132] *Eisenstadt*'s interpretation of the right of privacy as a guarantee of individual autonomy in important decisions about personal and family life soon became the predominant conception of this right.

In *Carey v. Population Services International*, the Court invalidated a New York statute that prohibited the distribution of contraceptives to adults except by a licensed pharmacist and banned altogether their distribution to minors.[133] A majority of the justices relied on *Griswold* and *Eisenstadt* to invalidate the restriction on contraceptive sales to adults, but the justices differed in their reasoning about the statute's infirmity as applied to minors. Brennan's plurality opinion subjected the statute to heightened scrutiny and concluded that it infringed minors' right of privacy. The concurring justices, on the other hand, recognized the state's power to regulate minors' sexual activity, but objected to the unreasonable means New York had chosen to deter it.

c. The Constitutional Right to an Abortion

The Court's next application of the right of privacy following *Griswold* embroiled the Court in one of the most divisive political and jurisprudential battles of our time. *Roe v. Wade* and its companion case, *Doe v. Bolton*,[134] presented constitutional challenges to state criminal abortion legislation. The Texas statutes at issue in *Roe* made it a crime to "procure an abortion" or to attempt one, except with respect to "an abortion procured or attempted by medical advice for the purpose of saving the life of the mother." Similar statutes were in existence in a majority of the States. Jane Roe, a single woman who was pregnant, sought a declaratory judgment that the Texas criminal abortion statutes were unconstitutional on their face, and an injunction restraining Wade, the district attorney of her county, from enforcing the statutes. Roe alleged that "she wished to terminate her pregnancy by an abortion 'performed by a competent, licensed physician, under safe, clinical conditions'; that she was unable to get a 'legal' abortion in Texas because her life did not appear to be threatened by the continuation of her pregnancy; and that she could not afford to travel to another jurisdiction in order to secure a legal abortion under safe conditions." She claimed that the Texas statutes abridged her right of personal privacy, protected by the First, Fourth, Fifth, Ninth, and Fourteenth Amendments.

Before addressing the constitutionality of the Texas abortion law, Justice Blackmun's majority opinion extensively surveyed the history of criminal abortion statutes, as well as the state purposes and interests behind them. That history showed that the laws before the Court were the product of a relatively recent nineteenth century campaign to criminalize abortion.

> It perhaps is not generally appreciated that the restrictive criminal abortion laws in effect in a majority of States today are of relatively recent vintage. Those laws, generally proscribing abortion or its attempt at any time during pregnancy except when necessary to preserve the pregnant woman's life, are not of ancient or even of common-law origin. Instead, they derive from statutory changes effected, for the most part, in the latter half of the 19th century.
>
> . . .
>
> It is undisputed that at common law, abortion performed *before* "quickening"—the first recognizable movement of the fetus in utero, appearing usually

---

[132] Janet L. Dolgin, *The Family in Transition: From Griswold to Eisenstadt and Beyond*, 82 Geo. L.J. 1519, 1555 (1994).

[133] Carey v. Population Services International, 431 U.S. 678 (1977).

[134] 410 U.S. 179 (1973).

from the 16th to the 18th week of pregnancy—was not an indictable offense. The absence of a common-law crime for pre-quickening abortion appears to have developed from a confluence of earlier philosophical, theological, and civil and canon law concepts of when life begins. These disciplines variously approached the question in terms of the point at which the embryo or fetus became "formed" or recognizably human, or in terms of when a "person" came into being, that is, infused with a "soul" or "animated." A loose consensus evolved in early English law that these events occurred at some point between conception and live birth. . . .

Whether abortion of a *quick* fetus was a felony at common law, or even a lesser crime, is still disputed. Bracton, writing early in the 13th century, thought it homicide. But the later and predominant view, following the great common-law scholars, has been that it was, at most, a lesser offense. . . .

. . .

In this country, the law in effect in all but a few States until mid-19th century was the pre-existing English common law. Connecticut, the first State to enact abortion legislation, adopted in 1821 that part of Lord Ellenborough's Act that related to a woman "quick with child." The death penalty was not imposed. Abortion before quickening was made a crime in that State only in 1860. In 1828, New York enacted legislation that, in two respects, was to serve as a model for early anti-abortion statutes. First, while barring destruction of an unquickened fetus as well as a quick fetus, it made the former only a misdemeanor, but the latter second-degree manslaughter. Second, it incorporated a concept of therapeutic abortion by providing that an abortion was excused if it "shall have been necessary to preserve the life of such mother, or shall have been advised by two physicians to be necessary for such purpose." By 1840, when Texas had received the common law, only eight American States had statutes dealing with abortion. It was not until after the War Between the States that legislation began generally to replace the common law. Most of these initial statutes dealt severely with abortion after quickening but were lenient with it before quickening. Most punished attempts equally with completed abortions. While many statutes included the exception for an abortion thought by one or more physicians to be necessary to save the mother's life, that provision soon disappeared and the typical law required that the procedure actually be necessary for that purpose.

Gradually, in the middle and late 19th century the quickening distinction disappeared from the statutory law of most States and the degree of the offense and the penalties were increased. By the end of the 1950's, a large majority of the jurisdictions banned abortion, however and whenever performed, unless done to save or preserve the life of the mother. . . . In the past several years, however, a trend toward liberalization of abortion statutes has resulted in adoption, by about one-third of the States, of less stringent laws. . . .

It is thus apparent that at common law, at the time of the adoption of our Constitution, and throughout the major portion of the 19th century, abortion was viewed with less disfavor than under most American statutes currently in effect. Phrasing it another way, a woman enjoyed a substantially broader right to terminate a pregnancy than she does in most States today. At least with respect to the early stage of pregnancy, and very possibly without such a limitation, the opportunity to make this choice was present in this country well into the 19th century. Even later, the law continued for some time to treat less punitively an abortion procured in early pregnancy.

. . . The anti-abortion mood prevalent in this country in the late 19th century was shared by the medical profession. Indeed, the attitude of the profession may have played a significant role in the enactment of stringent criminal abortion legislation during that period.

. . .

Parties challenging state abortion laws have sharply disputed in some courts the contention that a purpose of these laws, when enacted, was to protect prenatal life. Pointing to the absence of legislative history to support the contention, they claim that most state laws were designed solely to protect the woman. Because medical advances have lessened this concern, at least with respect to abortion in early pregnancy, they argue that with respect to such abortions the laws can no longer be justified by any state interest. There is some scholarly support for this view of original purpose. The few state courts called upon to interpret their laws in the late 19th and early 20th centuries did focus on the State's interest in protecting the woman's health rather than in preserving the embryo and fetus. Proponents of this view point out that in many States, including Texas, by statute or judicial interpretation, the pregnant woman herself could not be prosecuted for self-abortion or for cooperating in an abortion performed upon her by another. They claim that adoption of the 'quickening' distinction through received common law and state statutes tacitly recognizes the greater health hazards inherent in late abortion and impliedly repudiates the theory that life begins at conception.

It is with these interests, and the weight to be attached to them, that this case is concerned.

Although the Court acknowledged that the medical profession influenced the nineteenth century campaign to criminalize abortion, it failed to convey the extent to which doctors led the effort and the social motivations and rhetoric that propelled it. More recent historical accounts of nineteenth century abortion reform demonstrate that "[t]he doctors who advocated criminalizing abortion quite openly argued that regulating women's reproductive conduct was necessary, not merely to protect potential life, but also to ensure women's performance of marital and maternal obligations and to preserve the ethnic character of the nation."[135] The American Medical Association during that period argued for protecting unborn life based on women's marital duty to procreate and the state's need to regulate reproduction for the benefit of the nation.

After reviewing this history, the Court turned to Roe's claim that the Texas abortion law violated her constitutional right to terminate her pregnancy. The Court explicitly acknowledged that the right of privacy articulated in *Griswold* was grounded in the due process clause of the Fourteenth Amendment. Moreover, because this right was "fundamental," the Court required the Texas law to pass strict scrutiny review; the law could be justified only by a compelling state interest. In so doing, the Court's opinion in *Roe* revived not only substantive due process but also the heated debate over "noninterpretivist" judicial review. As John Hart Ely wrote, *Roe* "forced all of us who work in the area to think about which camp we fall into."[136]

---

[135] Reva Siegel, *Reasoning from the Body: A Historical Perspective on Abortion Regulation and Question of Equal Protection*, 44 STAN. L. REV. 261, 279 (1992). Siegel's sources include LINDA GORDON, WOMAN'S BODY, WOMAN'S RIGHT: A SOCIAL HISTORY OF BIRTH CONTROL IN AMERICA (1976); KRISTIN LUKER, ABORTION AND THE POLITICS OF MOTHERHOOD (1984); JAMES C. MOHR, ABORTION IN AMERICA: THE ORIGINS AND EVOLUTION OF NATIONAL POLICY, 1800–1900 (1978); CARROLL SMITH-ROSENBERG, DISORDERLY CONDUCT: VISIONS OF GENDER IN VICTORIAN AMERICA 217–44 (1985).

[136] JOHN HART ELY, DEMOCRACY AND DISTRUST 2–3 (1980).

Roe v. Wade
410 U.S. 113 (1973)

MR. JUSTICE BLACKMUN delivered the opinion of the Court.

. . .

We forthwith acknowledge our awareness of the sensitive and emotional nature of the abortion controversy, of the vigorous opposing views, even among physicians, and of the deep and seemingly absolute convictions that the subject inspires. One's philosophy, one's experiences, one's exposure to the raw edges of human existence, one's religious training, one's attitudes toward life and family and their values, and the moral standards one establishes and seeks to observe, are all likely to influence and to color one's thinking and conclusions about abortion.

In addition, population growth, pollution, poverty, and racial overtones tend to complicate and not to simplify the problem.

Our task, of course, is to resolve the issue by constitutional measurement, free of emotion and of predilection. We seek earnestly to do this, and, because we do, we have inquired into, and in this opinion place some emphasis upon, medical and medical-legal history and what that history reveals about man's attitudes toward the abortion procedure over the centuries. We bear in mind, too, Mr. Justice Holmes' admonition in his now-vindicated dissent in *Lochner v. New York*:

> "[The Constitution] is made for people of fundamentally differing views, and the accident of our finding certain opinions natural and familiar, or novel, and even shocking, ought not to conclude our judgment upon the question whether statutes embodying them conflict with the Constitution of the United States."

. . .

The principal thrust of appellant's attack on the Texas statutes is that they improperly invade a right, said to be possessed by the pregnant woman, to choose to terminate her pregnancy. Appellant would discover this right in the concept of personal 'liberty' embodied in the Fourteenth Amendment's Due Process Clause; or in personal marital, familial, and sexual privacy said to be protected by the Bill of Rights or its penumbras, see *Griswold v. Connecticut*; or among those rights reserved to the people by the Ninth Amendment, *Griswold v. Connecticut* (Goldberg, J., concurring).

. . .

The Constitution does not explicitly mention any right of privacy. In a line of decisions, however, going back perhaps as far as *Union Pacific R. Co. v. Botsford*, 141 U.S. 250, 251 (1891), the Court has recognized that a right of personal privacy, or a guarantee of certain areas or zones of privacy, does exist under the Constitution. In varying contexts, the Court or individual Justices have, indeed, found at least the roots of that right in the First Amendment; in the Fourth and Fifth Amendments; in the penumbras of the Bill of Rights; in the Ninth Amendment; or in the concept of liberty guaranteed by the first section of the Fourteenth Amendment, see *Meyer v. Nebraska*. These decisions make it clear that only personal rights that can be deemed "fundamental" or "implicit in the concept of ordered liberty," *Palko v. Connecticut*, 302 U.S. 319, 325, (1937), are included in this guarantee of personal privacy. They also make it clear that the right has some extension to activities relating to marriage, *Loving v. Virginia*, 388 U.S. 1 (1967); procreation, *Skinner v. Oklahoma*, 316 U.S. 535 (1942); contraception, *Eisenstadt v. Baird*; family relationships, *Prince v. Massachusetts*, 321 U.S. 158 (1944); and child rearing and education, *Pierce v. Society of Sisters*, *Meyer*.

This right of privacy, whether it be founded in the Fourteenth Amendment's concept of personal liberty and restrictions upon state action, as we feel it is, or, as the District Court determined, in the Ninth Amendment's reservation of rights to the people, is broad enough to encompass a woman's decision whether or not to terminate her pregnancy. The detriment that the State would impose upon the pregnant woman by denying this choice altogether is apparent. Specific and direct harm medically diagnosable even in early pregnancy may be involved. Maternity, or additional offspring, may force upon the woman a distressful life and future. Psychological harm may be imminent. Mental and physical health may be taxed by child care. There is also the distress, for all concerned, associated with the unwanted child, and there is the problem of bringing a child into a family already unable, psychologically and otherwise, to care for it. In other cases, as in this one, the additional difficulties and continuing stigma of unwed motherhood may be involved. All these are factors the woman and her responsible physician necessarily will consider in consultation.

On the basis of elements such as these, appellant and some *amici* argue that the woman's right is absolute and that she is entitled to terminate her pregnancy at whatever time, in whatever way, and for whatever reason she alone chooses. With this we do not agree. Appellant's arguments that Texas either has no valid interest at all in regulating the abortion decision, or no interest strong enough to support any limitation upon the woman's sole determination, are unpersuasive. The Court's decisions recognizing a right of privacy also acknowledge that some state regulation in areas protected by that right is appropriate. . . . [A] State may properly assert important interests in safeguarding health, in maintaining medical standards, and in protecting potential life. At some point in pregnancy, these respective interests become sufficiently compelling to sustain regulation of the factors that govern the abortion decision. The privacy right involved, therefore, cannot be said to be absolute. In fact, it is not clear to us that the claim asserted by some amici that one has an unlimited right to do with one's body as one pleases bears a close relationship to the right of privacy previously articulated in the Court's decisions. The Court has refused to recognize an unlimited right of this kind in the past.

We, therefore, conclude that the right of personal privacy includes the abortion decision, but that this right is not unqualified and must be considered against important state interests in regulation.

. . .

Where certain "fundamental rights" are involved, the Court has held that regulation limiting these rights may be justified only by a "compelling state interest," and that legislative enactments must be narrowly drawn to express only the legitimate state interests at stake.

. . .

The District Court held that the appellee failed to meet his burden of demonstrating that the Texas statute's infringement upon Roe's rights was necessary to support a compelling state interest, and that, although the appellee presented "several compelling justifications for state presence in the area of abortions," the statutes outstripped these justifications and swept "far beyond any areas of compelling state interest." Appellant and appellee both contest that holding. Appellant, as has been indicated, claims an absolute right that bars any state imposition of criminal penalties in the area. Appellee argues that the State's determination to recognize and protect prenatal life from and after conception constitutes a compelling state interest. As noted above, we do not agree fully with either formulation.

A. The appellee and certain *amici* argue that the fetus is a "person" within the language and meaning of the Fourteenth Amendment. In support of this, they outline at length and in detail the well-known facts of fetal development. If this suggestion of personhood is established, the appellant's case, of course, collapses, for the fetus' right to life would then be guaranteed specifically by the Amendment.

The appellant conceded as much on reargument. On the other hand, the appellee conceded on reargument that no case could be cited that holds a fetus is a person within the meaning of the Fourteenth Amendment.

The Constitution does not define "person" in so many words. Section 1 of the Fourteenth Amendment contains three references to "person." The first, in defining "citizens," speaks of "persons born or naturalized in the United States." The word also appears both in the Due Process Clause and in the Equal Protection Clause. "Person" is used in other places in the Constitution. . . . But in nearly all these instances, the use of the word is such that it has application only postnatally. None indicates, with any assurance, that it has any possible prenatal application.

All this, together with our observation that throughout the major portion of the 19th century prevailing legal abortion practices were far freer than they are today, persuades us that the word "person," as used in the Fourteenth Amendment, does not include the unborn. . . .

B. The pregnant woman cannot be isolated in her privacy. She carries an embryo and, later, a fetus, if one accepts the medical definitions of the developing young in the human uterus. The situation therefore is inherently different from marital intimacy, or bedroom possession of obscene material, or marriage, or procreation, or education, with which *Eisenstadt* and *Griswold, Stanley, Loving, Skinner* and *Pierce* and *Meyer* were respectively concerned. As we have intimated above, it is reasonable and appropriate for a State to decide that at some point in time another interest, that of health of the mother or that of potential human life, becomes significantly involved. The woman's privacy is no longer sole and any right of privacy she possesses must be measured accordingly.

Texas urges that, apart from the Fourteenth Amendment, life begins at conception and is present throughout pregnancy, and that, therefore, the State has a compelling interest in protecting that life from and after conception. We need not resolve the difficult question of when life begins. When those trained in the respective disciplines of medicine, philosophy, and theology are unable to arrive at any consensus, the judiciary, at this point in the development of man's knowledge, is not in a position to speculate as to the answer.

It should be sufficient to note briefly the wide divergence of thinking on this most sensitive and difficult question. There has always been strong support for the view that life does not begin until live birth. This was the belief of the Stoics. It appears to be the predominant, though not the unanimous, attitude of the Jewish faith. It may be taken to represent also the position of a large segment of the Protestant community, insofar as that can be ascertained; organized groups that have taken a formal position on the abortion issue have generally regarded abortion as a matter for the conscience of the individual and her family. As we have noted, the common law found greater significance in quickening. Physicians and their scientific colleagues have regarded that event with less interest and have tended to focus either upon conception, upon live birth, or upon the interim point at which the fetus becomes "viable," that is, potentially able to live outside the mother's womb, albeit with artificial aid. Viability is usually placed at about seven months (28 weeks) but may occur earlier, even at 24 weeks. The Aristotelian theory of "mediate animation," that held sway throughout the Middle Ages and the Renaissance in Europe, continued to be official Roman Catholic dogma until the 19th century, despite opposition to this "ensoulment" theory from those in the Church who would recognize the existence of life from the moment of conception. The latter is now, of course, the official belief of the Catholic Church. As one brief amicus discloses, this is a view strongly held by many non-Catholics as well, and by many physicians. Substantial problems for precise definition of this view are posed, however, by new embryological data that purport to indicate that conception is a "process" over time, rather than an event, and by new medical techniques such as menstrual extraction, the "morning-after" pill, implantation of embryos, artificial insemination, and even artificial wombs.

. . .

In view of all this, we do not agree that, by adopting one theory of life, Texas may override the rights of the pregnant woman that are at stake. We repeat, however, that the State does have an important and legitimate interest in preserving and protecting the health of the pregnant woman, whether she be a resident of the State or a non-resident who seeks medical consultation and treatment there, and that it has still *another* important and legitimate interest in protecting the potentiality of human life. These interests are separate and distinct. Each grows in substantiality as the woman approaches term and, at a point during pregnancy, each becomes "compelling."

With respect to the State's important and legitimate interest in the health of the mother, the "compelling" point, in the light of present medical knowledge, is at approximately the end of the first trimester. This is so because of the now-established medical fact that until the end of the first trimester mortality in abortion may be less than mortality in normal childbirth. It follows that, from and after this point, a State may regulate the abortion procedure to the extent that the regulation reasonably relates to the preservation and protection of maternal health. Examples of permissible state regulation in this area are requirements as to the qualifications of the person who is to perform the abortion; as to the licensure of that person; as to the facility in which the procedure is to be performed, that is, whether it must be a hospital or may be a clinic or some other place of less-than-hospital status; as to the licensing of the facility; and the like.

This means, on the other hand, that, for the period of pregnancy prior to this "compelling" point, the attending physician, in consultation with his patient, is free to determine, without regulation by the State, that, in his medical judgment, the patient's pregnancy should be terminated. If that decision is reached, the judgment may be effectuated by an abortion free of interference by the State.

With respect to the State's important and legitimate interest in potential life, the "compelling" point is at viability. This is so because the fetus then presumably has the capability of meaningful life outside the mother's womb. State regulation protective of fetal life after viability thus has both logical and biological justifications. If the State is interested in protecting fetal life after viability, it may go so far as to proscribe abortion during that period, except when it is necessary to preserve the life or health of the mother.

Measured against these standards, Art. 1196 of the Texas Penal Code, in restricting legal abortions to those "procured or attempted by medical advice for the purpose of saving the life of the mother," sweeps too broadly. The statute makes no distinction between abortions performed early in pregnancy and those performed later, and it limits to a single reason, "saving" the mother's life, the legal justification for the procedure. The statute, therefore, cannot survive the constitutional attack made upon it here.

. . .

To summarize and to repeat:

A state criminal abortion statute of the current Texas type, that excepts from criminality only a *life-saving* procedure on behalf of the mother, without regard to pregnancy stage and without recognition of the other interests involved, is violative of the Due Process Clause of the Fourteenth Amendment.

(a) For the stage prior to approximately the end of the first trimester, the abortion decision and its effectuation must be left to the medical judgment of the pregnant woman's attending physician.

(b) For the stage subsequent to approximately the end of the first trimester, the State, in promoting its interest in the health of the mother, may, if it chooses, regulate the abortion procedure in ways that are reasonably related to maternal health.

(c) For the stage subsequent to viability, the State in promoting its interest in the potentiality of human life may, if it chooses, regulate, and even proscribe, abortion except where it is necessary, in appropriate medical judgment, for the preservation of the life or health of the mother.

. . .

This holding, we feel, is consistent with the relative weights of the respective interests involved, with the lessons and examples of medical and legal history, with the lenity of the common law, and with the demands of the profound problems of the present day. The decision leaves the State free to place increasing restrictions on abortion as the period of pregnancy lengthens, so long as those restrictions are tailored to the recognized state interests. The decision vindicates the right of the physician to administer medical treatment according to his professional judgment up to the points where important state interests provide compelling justifications for intervention. Up to those points, the abortion decision in all its aspects is inherently, and primarily, a medical decision, and basic responsibility for it must rest with the physician. If an individual practitioner abuses the privilege of exercising proper medical judgment, the usual remedies, judicial and intra-professional, are available.

. . .

MR. JUSTICE STEWART, concurring.

In 1963, this Court, in *Ferguson v. Skrupa*, 372 U.S. 726, purported to sound the death knell for the doctrine of substantive due process, a doctrine under which many state laws had in the past been held to violate the Fourteenth Amendment. As Mr. Justice Black's opinion for the Court in *Skrupa* put it: "We have returned to the original constitutional proposition that courts do not substitute their social and economic beliefs for the judgment of legislative bodies, who are elected to pass laws."

Barely two years later, in *Griswold v. Connecticut*, the Court held a Connecticut birth control law unconstitutional. In view of what had been so recently said in *Skrupa*, the Court's opinion in *Griswold* understandably did its best to avoid reliance on the Due Process Clause of the Fourteenth Amendment as the ground for decision. Yet, the Connecticut law did not violate any provision of the Bill of Rights, nor any other specific provision of the Constitution. So it was clear to me then, and it is equally clear to me now, that the *Griswold* decision can be rationally understood only as a holding that the Connecticut statute substantively invaded the "liberty" that is protected by the Due Process Clause of the Fourteenth Amendment. As so understood,

Griswold stands as one in a long line of pre-*Skrupa* cases decided under the doctrine of substantive due process, and I now accept it as such.

. . .

Several decisions of this Court make clear that freedom of personal choice in matters of marriage and family life is one of the liberties protected by the Due Process Clause of the Fourteenth Amendment. As recently as last Term, in *Eisenstadt v. Baird*, we recognized "the right of the individual, married or single, to be free from unwarranted governmental intrusion into matters so fundamentally affecting a person as the decision whether to bear or beget a child." That right necessarily includes the right of a woman to decide whether or not to terminate her pregnancy. "Certainly the interests of a woman in giving of her physical and emotional self during pregnancy and the interests that will be affected throughout her life by the birth and raising of a child are of a far greater degree of significance and personal intimacy than the right to send a child to private school protected in *Pierce v. Society of Sisters* or the right to teach a foreign language protected in *Meyer v. Nebraska*." *Abele v. Markle*, 351 F.Supp. 224, 227 (Conn. 1972).

Clearly, therefore, the Court today is correct in holding that the right asserted by Jane Roe is embraced within the personal liberty protected by the Due Process Clause of the Fourteenth Amendment.

. . .

MR. CHIEF JUSTICE BURGER, concurring [in both *Roe v. Wade* and *Doe v. Bolton*].

I agree that, under the Fourteenth Amendment to the Constitution, the abortion statutes of Georgia and Texas impermissibly limit the performance of abortion necessary to protect the health of pregnant women, using the term health in its broadest medical context. I am somewhat troubled that the Court has taken notice of various scientific and medical data in reaching its conclusion; however, I do not believe that the Court has exceeded the scope of judicial notice accepted in other contexts.

. . .

I do not read the Court's holdings today as having the sweeping consequences attributed to them by the dissenting Justices; the dissenting views discount the reality that the vast majority of physicians observe the standards of their profession, and act only on the basis of carefully deliberated medical judgments relating to life and health. Plainly, the Court today rejects any claim that the Constitution requires abortions on demand.

MR. JUSTICE DOUGLAS, concurring [in both *Roe v. Wade* and *Doe v. Bolton*].

While I join the opinion of the Court, I add a few words.

I

. . .

The Ninth Amendment obviously does not create federally enforceable rights. It merely says, "The enumeration in the Constitution, of certain rights, shall not be construed to deny or disparage others retained by the people." But a catalogue of these rights includes customary, traditional, and time-honored rights, amenities, privileges, and immunities that come within the sweep of "the Blessings of Liberty" mentioned in the preamble to the Constitution. Many of them, in my view, come within the meaning of the term "liberty" as used in the Fourteenth Amendment.

First is the autonomous control over the development and expression of one's intellect, interests, tastes, and personality.

These are rights protected by the First Amendment and, in my view, they are absolute, permitting of no exceptions. . . .

Second is freedom of choice in the basic decisions of one's life respecting marriage, divorce, procreation, contraception, and the education and upbringing of children.

These rights, unlike those protected by the First Amendment, are subject to some control by the police power. Thus, the Fourth Amendment speaks only of "unreasonable searches and seizures" and of "probable cause." These rights are "fundamental," and we have held that in order to support legislative action the statute must be narrowly and precisely drawn and that a "compelling state interest" must be shown in support of the limitation.

. . .

Third is the freedom to care for one's health and person, freedom from bodily restraint or compulsion, freedom to walk, stroll, or loaf.

These rights, though fundamental, are likewise subject to regulation on a showing of "compelling state interest." . . .

The Georgia statute is at war with the clear message of these cases—that a woman is free to make the basic decision whether to bear an unwanted child. Elaborate argument is hardly necessary to demonstrate that childbirth may deprive a woman of her preferred lifestyle and force upon her a radically different and undesired future. For example, rejected applicants under the Georgia statute are required to endure the discomforts of pregnancy; to incur the pain, higher mortality rate, and aftereffects of childbirth; to abandon educational plans; to sustain loss of income; to forgo the satisfactions of careers; to tax further mental and physical health in providing child care; and, in some cases, to bear the lifelong stigma of unwed motherhood, a badge which may haunt, if not deter, later legitimate family relationships.

II

Such reasoning is, however, only the beginning of the problem. The State has interests to protect. Vaccinations to prevent epidemics are one example, as *Jacobson* [*v. Com. of Massachusetts*, 197 U.S. 11 (1905)] holds. The Court held that compulsory sterilization of imbeciles afflicted with hereditary forms of insanity or imbecility is another. *Buck v. Bell*, 274 U.S. 200. Abortion affects another. While childbirth endangers the lives of some women, voluntary abortion at any time and place regardless of medical standards would impinge on a rightful concern of society. The woman's health is part of that concern; as is the life of the fetus after quickening. These concerns justify the State in treating the procedure as a medical one.

One difficulty is that this statute as construed and applied apparently does not give full sweep to the "psychological as well as physical well-being" of women patients. . . .

The vicissitudes of life produce pregnancies which may be unwanted, or which may impair "health" in the broad . . . sense of the term, or which may imperil the life of the mother, or which in the full setting of the case may create such suffering, dislocations, misery, or tragedy as to make an early abortion the only civilized step to take. These hardships may be properly embraced in the "health" factor of the mother as appraised by a person of insight. Or they may be part of a broader medical judgment based on what is "appropriate" in a given case, though perhaps not "necessary" in a strict sense.

The "liberty" of the mother, though rooted as it is in the Constitution, may be qualified by the State for the reasons we have stated. But where fundamental personal rights and liberties are involved, the corrective legislation must be "narrowly drawn to prevent the supposed evil," and not be dealt with in an "unlimited and indiscriminate" manner. Unless regulatory measures are so confined and are addressed to the specific areas of compelling legislative concern, the police power would become the great leveler of constitutional rights and liberties.

Mr. Justice Rehnquist, dissenting.

. . .

. . . I have difficulty in concluding, as the Court does, that the right of "privacy" is involved in this case. Texas, by the statute here challenged, bars the performance of a medical abortion by a licensed physician on a plaintiff such as Roe. A transaction resulting in an operation such as this is not "private" in the ordinary usage of that word. Nor is the "privacy" that the Court finds here even a distant relative of the freedom from searches and seizures protected by the Fourth Amendment to the Constitution, which the Court has referred to as embodying a right to privacy.

If the Court means by the term "privacy" no more than that the claim of a person to be free from unwanted state regulation of consensual transactions may be a form of "liberty" protected by the Fourteenth Amendment, there is no doubt that similar claims have been upheld in our earlier decisions on the basis of that liberty. I agree with the statement of MR. JUSTICE STEWART in his concurring opinion that the "liberty," against deprivation of which without due process the Fourteenth Amendment protects, embraces more than the rights found in the Bill of Rights. But that liberty is not guaranteed absolutely against deprivation, only against deprivation without due process of law. The test traditionally applied in the area of social and economic legislation is whether or not a law such as that challenged has a rational relation to a valid state objective. *Williamson v. Lee Optical Co.*, 348 U.S. 483, 491 (1955). The Due Process Clause of the Fourteenth Amendment undoubtedly does place a limit, albeit a broad one, on legislative power to enact laws such as this. If the Texas statute were to prohibit an abortion even where the mother's life is in jeopardy, I have little doubt that such a statute would lack a rational relation to a valid state objective under the test stated in *Williamson*. But the Court's sweeping invalidation of any restrictions on abortion during the first trimester is impossible to justify under that standard, and the conscious weighing of competing factors that the Court's opinion apparently substitutes for the established test is far more appropriate to a legislative judgment than to a judicial one.

The Court eschews the history of the Fourteenth Amendment in its reliance on the "compelling state interest" test. But the Court adds a new wrinkle to this test by transposing it from the legal considerations associated with the Equal Protection Clause of the Fourteenth Amendment to this case arising under the Due Process Clause of the Fourteenth Amendment. Unless I misapprehend the consequences of this transplanting of the "compelling state interest test," the Court's opinion will accomplish the seemingly impossible feat of leaving this area of the law more confused than it found it.

While the Court's opinion quotes from the dissent of Mr. Justice Holmes in *Lochner v. New York*, the result it reaches is more closely attuned to the majority opinion of Mr. Justice Peckham in that case. As in *Lochner* and similar cases applying substantive due process standards to economic and social welfare legislation, the adoption of the compelling state interest standard will inevitably require this Court to examine the legislative policies and pass on the wisdom of these policies in the very process of deciding whether a particular state interest put forward may or may not be "compelling." The decision here to break pregnancy into three distinct terms and to outline the permissible restrictions the State may impose in each one, for example, partakes more of judicial legislation than it does of a determination of the intent of the drafters of the Fourteenth Amendment.

The fact that a majority of the States, reflecting after all the majority sentiment in those States, have had restrictions on abortions for at least a century is a strong indication, it seems to me, that the asserted right to an abortion is not "so rooted in the traditions and conscience of our people as to be ranked as fundamental," *Snyder v. Massachusetts*, 291 U.S. 97, 105 (1934). Even today, when society's views on abortion are changing, the very existence of the debate is evidence that the "right" to an abortion is not so universally accepted as the appellant would have us believe.

To reach its result, the Court necessarily has had to find within the scope of the Fourteenth Amendment a right that was apparently completely unknown to the drafters of the Amendment. As early as 1821, the first state law dealing directly with abortion was enacted by the Connecticut Legislature. By the time of the adoption of the Fourteenth Amendment in 1868, there were at least 36 laws enacted by state or territorial legislatures limiting abortion. While many States have amended or updated their laws, 21 of the laws on the books in 1868 remain in effect today. Indeed, the Texas statute struck down today was, as the majority notes, first enacted in 1857 and "has remained substantially unchanged to the present time."

There apparently was no question concerning the validity of this provision or of any of the other state statutes when the Fourteenth Amendment was adopted. The only conclusion possible from this history is that the drafters did not intend to have the Fourteenth Amendment withdraw from the States the power to legislate with respect to this matter.

. . .

MR. JUSTICE WHITE, with whom MR. JUSTICE REHNQUIST joins, dissenting [in both *Roe v. Wade* and *Doe v. Bolton*].

At the heart of the controversy in these cases are those recurring pregnancies that pose no danger whatsoever to the life or health of the mother but are, nevertheless, unwanted for any one or more of a variety of reasons—convenience, family planning, economics, dislike of children, the embarrassment of illegitimacy, etc. The common claim before us is that for any one of such reasons, or for no reason at all, and without asserting or claiming any threat to life or health, any woman is entitled to an abortion at her request if she is able to find a medical advisor willing to undertake the procedure.

The Court for the most part sustains this position: During the period prior to the time the fetus becomes viable, the Constitution of the United States values the convenience, whim, or caprice of the putative mother more than the life or potential life of the fetus; the Constitution, therefore, guarantees the right to an abortion as against any state law or policy seeking to protect the fetus from an abortion not prompted by more compelling reasons of the mother.

With all due respect, I dissent. I find nothing in the language or history of the Constitution to support the Court's judgment. The Court simply fashions and announces a new constitutional right for pregnant mothers and, with scarcely any reason or authority for its action, invests that right with sufficient substance to override most existing state abortion statutes. The upshot is that the people and the legislature of the 50 States are constitutionally disentitled to weigh the relative importance of the continued existence and development of the fetus, on the one hand, against a spectrum of possible impacts on the mother, on the other hand. As an exercise of raw judicial power, the Court perhaps has authority to do what it does today; but in my view its judgment is an improvident and extravagant exercise of the power of judicial review that the Constitution extends to this Court.

The Court apparently values the conveniences of the pregnant mother more than the continued existence and development of the life or potential life that she carries. Whether or not I might agree with that marshaling of values, I can in no event join the Court's judgment because I find no constitutional warrant for imposing such an order of priorities on the people and legislatures of the States. In a sensitive area such as this, involving as it does issues over which reasonable men may easily and heatedly differ, I cannot accept the Court's exercise of its clear power of choice by interposing a constitutional barrier to state efforts to protect human life and by investing mothers and doctors with the constitutionally protected right to exterminate it. This issue, for the most part, should be left with the people and to the political processes the people have devised to govern their affairs.

. . .

DER: The Court in *Roe v. Wade* took a doctrinal step that Justice Douglas tried to avoid in *Griswold*: it stated definitively that the Fourteenth Amendment's concept of liberty provides substantive due process protection against the states. Justice Rehnquist criticized the majority for relying on the individual's *Lochnerean* claim to a fundamental freedom from unwanted state regulation, which Rehnquist thought had been soundly rejected. To this challenge, the majority would undoubtedly respond: "The type of substantive due process sustained in *Roe* is different from the type of substantive due process applied in *Lochner*." The *Lochner* Court decisions protected liberty of contract from economic regulation. *Roe*, on the other hand, protected a more fundamental personal liberty that concerns important family and life-defining decisions. The Court thus distinguished two aspects of substantive due process—one economic and the other personal. If the Constitution protects a realm of personal privacy, then surely the decision whether or not to bear a child falls within that realm. Unwanted pregnancy both deprives a woman of "bodily self-possession" and profoundly affects the course of a woman's life.[137]

But did the Court successfully articulate the reason this distinction between economic and personal rights makes a difference for constitutional doctrine? Why does the Fourteenth Amendment create a fundamental right of personal due process but not economic due process? The Court failed to offer any rationale for this constitutional divide. It simply stated that it exists. The Court must have sensed a moral distinction between state infringement of the ability to contract freely and state infringement of critical aspects of personhood. Yet the opinion lacked a moral vision explaining the contours of privacy and its

---

[137] See Susan Estrich & Kathleen Sullivan, *Abortion Politics: Writing for an Audience of One*, 138 U. Pa. L. Rev. 119 (1989); Jed Rubenfeld, *The Right of Privacy*, 102 Harv. L. Rev. 737, 789–802 (1989).

relation to the constitutional text. Such an explanation would have given women's right to an abortion stronger doctrinal and moral support.

In addition, some feminist scholars have argued that the principle of gender equality provides a better foundation for the right to an abortion than does the Court's privacy rationale.[138] The equality approach contends that laws punishing abortion impose a sex-specific injury and penalize women for their reproductive capacity: "They make women criminals for a medical procedure only women need . . . when much of the need for this procedure as well as barriers to access to it have been created by social conditions of sex inequality. Forced motherhood is sex inequality."[139] Privacy doctrine, on the other hand, has been criticized for its reliance on traditions that have subjugated women, as well as on the false liberal assumption that government nonintervention into the private sphere promotes women's autonomy. The individual woman's legal right of privacy, according to Catharine MacKinnon, functions instead as "a means of subordinating women's collective needs to the imperatives of male supremacy."[140]

Despite these valid criticisms, privacy concepts have benefits for advocating women's reproductive freedom. The right of privacy stresses the important values of personhood and self-determination. The process of defining one's self and declaring one's personhood defies the denial of self-ownership inherent in slavery and other repressive regimes. Subsequent scholarship has attempted to fill the void in *Roe*'s reasoning. One view holds that the right of privacy is a limit on the state's totalitarian power: it prevents the government from taking control over the shape and purposes of citizens' lives.[141] State-compelled pregnancy and childbirth control a woman's body, consciousness, and life plans to a degree drastically different from economic regulations. A more progressive and expansive understanding of privacy addresses the problem of unequal social power that influences the shape of citizens' lives as much as government control. This view of privacy compels the state to reduce the distorting impact of sexual and economic inequality, racism, and homophobia on the institutional contexts of individuals' moral decisionmaking.[142]

RLW: Professor Roberts broadly states the right to have an abortion: "[i]f the Constitution protects a realm of personal privacy, then surely the decision whether or not to bear a child falls within that realm." Many can, and do, disagree with her. Chief Justice Rehnquist dissented in *Roe*, and has continued to press for a reversal of that decision. In recent years, the Court has backed away from *Roe*—in the sense that it no longer treats the right to an abortion as a "fundamental constitutional right." Pro-Life advocates might argue that, in her discussions of feminist theory and gender equality, Professor Roberts gives no weight to the fetus—either as a person (as the pro-Life movement would do) or as the potential for human life (as *Roe* does). The more value one places on the fetus, the less "sure" the woman's right to have an abortion becomes.

---

[138] *See*, for example, Rhonda Copelon, *Unpacking Patriarchy: Reproduction, Sexuality, Originalism, and Constitutional Change*, in A Less Than Perfect Union: Alternative Perspectives on the U.S. Constitution 303, 322–26 (Jules Lobel ed. 1988); Ruth Bader Ginsburg, *Some Thoughts on Autonomy and Equality in Relation to Roe v. Wade*, 63 N.C. L. Rev. 375 (1985); Sylvia A. Law, *Rethinking Sex and the Constitution*, 132 U. Pa. L. Rev. 955, 1016–28 (1984); Catharine MacKinnon, *Reflections on Sex Equality Under Law*, 100 Yale L.J. 1281 (1991); Catharine MacKinnon, *Roe v. Wade: A Study in Male Ideology*, in Abortion: Moral and Legal Perspectives 45 (J. Garfield & P. Hennessey eds. 1984).

[139] MacKinnon, Reflections on Sex Equality Under Law, at 1319.

[140] MacKinnon, Roe v. Wade: A Study in Male Ideology, at 49.

[141] Rubenfeld, *The Right of Privacy*.

[142] *See* Stephen J. Schnably, *Beyond Griswold: Foucauldian and Republican Approaches to Privacy*, 23 Conn. L. Rev. 861, 930–48 (1991); Robin West, *Progressive and Conservative Constitutionalism*, 88 Mich. L. Rev. 641, 707 (1990).

The judiciary must have the authority to articulate new constitutional rights, but the method by which the judiciary does so has always been subject to controversy. Ultimately, *Roe* supports Professor Lively's thesis that political considerations inherently limit and influence the scope of judicial authority. If *Roe's* holding were "sure" or "obvious," the Court's retreat from *Roe* would have been less possible.

DEL: Whether "the Constitution protects a realm of personal privacy" is the big "if" that even the most zealous critics of the *Roe* decision seem disinclined to confront. As the foremost detractor of modern substantive due process review, on grounds the Court "has no authority to inject itself into every field of human activity where irrationality and oppression may theoretically occur,"[143] even Justice Scalia is on record as accepting the right of privacy initially established in *Griswold*.

The basic challenge to *Roe*, as well as to *Griswold*, is presented by Justice Black. Although acknowledging that "I like my privacy as well as the next one," Black was "nevertheless compelled to admit that government has a right to invade it unless prohibited by some specific constitutional provision."[144] Stressing that "judges should not use the due process formula . . . to invalidate legislation offensive to their 'personal preferences,' " Black referenced Learned Hand's observation that "[f]or myself it would be most irksome to be ruled by a bevy of Platonic Guardians, even if I knew how to choose them, which I assuredly do not."[145]

The notion that the Court should weave fundamental law out of pure constitutional cloth, rather than its own moral fabric, is the common thread linking Justice Iredell in *Calder v. Bull* to Justice Black in *Griswold* and Justice Scalia thereafter. Collectively, these jurists and other interpretivists present a significant intellectual challenge to those who approve of *Roe* and its ilk. If the *Lochner* Court is to be faulted for holding the political process hostage to a favored ideology, it is hard to avoid a like analysis of modern substantive due process review. Reality is that distinctions between personal and economic rights are artificial. If penumbras or emanations are to be searched for, moreover, a better basis exists for contractual liberty deriving from the contracts clause and initial concerns of the Fourteenth Amendment's framers than supports the right of privacy. It is hard to see *Roe* as distinguishable from the *Lochner* exercise in moral prioritization that, to this date, the Court strains to distance itself from at least in rhetoric. The decision's transparency is aptly noted in Justice Rehnquist's observation that "a majority of the States . . . hav[ing] had restrictions on abortion for at least a century is a strong indication . . . that the asserted right to an abortion is not 'so rooted in the traditions and conscience of our people as to be ranked as fundamental.' "[146] Honest application of what is "rooted in the traditions and conscience of our people," to determine what values are fundamental, probably does not lead to identification of many interests that the majority already has not accounted for through the political process. To the extent such an inquiry may reveal realities of racism and sexism as deeply rooted, moreover, the analysis hardly preordains challenge to the established order.

For all the concern with principled jurisprudence and avoiding anti-democratic functioning by the judiciary, it is possible that the abandonment of fundamental rights analysis would present an even greater threat to the will of the people. Regardless of what original intentions may have been with respect to the Court's role, the judiciary has established itself as an institution that is expected at times to second-guess the wisdom and even displace the output of the legislative process. Regardless of how the Court did it, few are uncomfortable with a decision such as *Skinner* that invalidates a forced sterilization law. More inexplicable to mass understanding and expectation would likely be the Court's

---

[143] Cruzan v. Director, Missouri Dept. of Health, 497 U.S. 261, 300-01 (1990) (Scalia, J., concurring).

[144] Griswold v. Connecticut, 381 U.S. 479, 510 (1965) (Black, J., dissenting).

[145] *Id.* at 526-27 (quoting LEARNED HAND, THE BILL OF RIGHTS 73 (1958)).

[146] Roe v. Wade, 410 U.S. 113, 174 (Rehnquist, J., dissenting).

decision, in *Buck v. Bell*, to uphold involuntary sterilization of persons with low intelligence. Despite his fulminations about a right of privacy, even Justice Black signed on to the majority opinion in *Skinner*. It is Justice Holmes' conclusion in *Buck*, supported by his observation that "three generations of imbeciles is enough,"[147] that has emerged as an object of scorn and cause of disbelief. Taking Justices Black and Scalia's concerns to their logical end, however, the *Buck* decision is at least academically correct and principled.

Provocative and unsettling to dominant impulses as the Court's decisions have been at times, such instances are infrequent to the point of being rare. Decisions that appear to trump the legislative branch, moreover, tend to be a transit point rather than an ending point for further political processing. Reacting to any fundamental right asserted by the Court, political and litigative processes typically respond in a fashion that in the end achieves results largely consistent with the consent of the governed. The imperial nature of fundamental rights development earlier this century eventually was undone by litigative innovation, evidenced by the emergence of "Brandeis briefs," and the political system's inexorable push for an increased regulatory presence. Similarly, judicial fiat in the form of desegregation imperatives and abortion as a choice has been shaped in subsequent years by clamoring, resistance and litigative challenge that have reworked doctrine to a point that it is largely coextensive with the society's moral development. Whether denominated as a right to own slaves, economic liberty or the right of privacy, fundamental rights and freedoms identified by the Court have been criticized as the product of overreaching. These guarantees, however, have a tendency to mutate and vanish as quickly as they emerged. It thus may be the ephemeral nature of judicially inscribed rights and liberties that helps to accommodate them and in perceiving them as an academic rather than real threat to the process of representative governance.

---

[147] Buck v. Bell, 274 U.S. 200, 208 (1927).

d.   Post-*Roe* Abortion Regulations

After its decision in *Roe*, the Court considered the constitutionality of a series of state and federal statutes that restricted women's access to abortion services. These statutes fell into three categories—state regulations of abortion procedures, requirements that women seeking abortions obtain spousal or parental consent, and laws that denied public funding for abortion. Between 1973 and 1989, the Court generally invalidated state abortion regulations that discouraged women from seeking an abortion or made the procedure more difficult or expensive to obtain. For example, the Court struck down regulations that required that second trimester abortions be performed in a hospital (*Akron v. Akron Center for Reproductive Health*[148]), that physicians inform women of particular medical risks of abortion, that physicians determine the viability of the fetus, and that a second physician be present during an abortion when viability is possible (*Colautti v. Franklin*[149]; *Thornburgh v. American College of Obstetricians and Gynecologists*[150]). In *Planned Parenthood v. Danforth*, the Court held unconstitutional a requirement of spousal consent for married women seeking an abortion and parental consent for unmarried teenagers under age eighteen, unless the abortion was necessary to save the mother's life.[151] The state, the Court reasoned, could not delegate to husbands or parents a veto over the woman's decision.

---

[148] 462 U.S. 416 (1983).
[149] 439 U.S. 379 (1979).
[150] 476 U.S. 747 (1986).
[151] Planned Parenthood v. Danforth, 428 U.S. 52 (1976)

During this period, however, the Court refused to require government to pay for the cost of abortions for poor women. In *Maher v. Roe*, the Court upheld a Connecticut statute that denied public funding of abortions that were not medically necessary, even though the state paid for the expenses incident to childbirth.[152] Recognizing first that "[t]he Constitution imposes no obligation on the States to pay the pregnancy-related medical expenses of indigent women, or indeed to pay any of the medical expenses of indigents," the majority reasoned further that states may make "a value judgment favoring childbirth over abortion and . . . implement that judgment by the allocation of public funds." Three years later, in *Harris v. McRae*, the Court narrowly (5 to 4) upheld the Hyde Amendment, which prohibited federal reimbursement of Medicaid funds even for most therapeutic abortions.[153] The Court again distinguished between the government's affirmative interference with abortions and its failure to pay for them: "although government may not place obstacles in the path of a woman's choice, it need not remove those not of its own creation. . . . Whether the freedom of a woman to choose to terminate her pregnancy for health reasons lies at the core or the periphery of the due process liberty recognized in *Wade*, it simply does not follow that a woman's freedom of choice carries with it a constitutional entitlement to the financial resources to avail herself of the full range of protected choices."

By 1989, support for *Roe* on the Supreme Court had become progressively uncertain. Justices O'Connor, Rehnquist, and White (two of whom had dissented in *Roe*) criticized *Roe* in dissenting opinions in the abortion regulation cases. Justices Scalia and Kennedy replaced two *Roe* supporters, Burger and Powell. When the Supreme Court agreed to consider Missouri's abortion regulation, there was widespread concern that a majority of justices would vote to overturn *Roe*. *Roe* survived *Webster*, but the decision marked a turning point in the Court's abortion jurisprudence. The plurality attacked *Roe*'s trimester framework, weakened the standard of review, and appeared to invite the states to impose greater restrictions on women's access to abortions.

---

[152] Maher v. Roe, 432 U.S. 464 (1977).
[153] Harris v. McRae, 448 U.S. 297 (1980).

Webster v. Reproductive Health Services
492 U.S. 490 (1989)

CHIEF JUSTICE REHNQUIST announced the judgment of the Court and delivered the opinion of the Court with respect to Parts I, II-A, II-B, and II-C, and an opinion with respect to Parts II-D and III, in which JUSTICE WHITE and JUSTICE KENNEDY join.

. . .

I

In June 1986, the Governor of Missouri signed into law Missouri Senate Committee Substitute for House Bill No. 1596 (hereinafter Act or statute), which amended existing state law concerning unborn children and abortions. The Act consisted of 20 provisions, 5 of which are now before the Court. The first provision, or preamble, contains "findings" by the state legislature that "[t]he life of each human being begins at conception," and that "unborn children have protectable interests in life, health, and well-being." The Act further requires that all Missouri laws be interpreted to provide unborn children with the same rights enjoyed by other persons, subject to the Federal Constitution and this Court's precedents. Among its other provisions, the Act requires that, prior to performing an abortion on any woman whom a physician has reason to believe is 20 or more weeks pregnant, the physician ascertain whether the fetus is viable by performing "such medical examinations and tests as are necessary to make a finding of the gestational age, weight, and lung maturity of the unborn child." The Act also prohibits the use of public employees and facilities to perform or assist abortions not necessary to save the mother's life. . . .

[The District Court declared these provisions unconstitutional, and the Court of Appeals for the Eighth Circuit affirmed.]

. . .

II

A

. . .

The State contends that the preamble itself is precatory and imposes no substantive restrictions on abortions, and that appellees therefore do not have standing to challenge it. Appellees, on the other hand, insist that the preamble is an operative part of the Act intended to guide the interpretation of other provisions of the Act. They maintain, for example, that the preamble's definition of life may prevent physicians in public hospitals from dispensing certain forms of contraceptives, such as the intrauterine device.

. . . Certainly the preamble does not by its terms regulate abortion or any other aspect of appellees' medical practice. The Court has emphasized that *Roe v. Wade* "implies no limitation on the authority of a State to make a value judgment favoring childbirth over abortion." *Maher v. Roe*. The preamble can be read simply to express that sort of value judgment.

We think the extent to which the preamble's language might be used to interpret other state statutes or regulations is something that only the courts of Missouri can definitively decide. State law has offered protections to unborn children in tort and probate law, and [the preamble] can be interpreted to do no more than that. . . . It will be time enough for federal courts to address the meaning of the preamble should it be applied to restrict the activities of appellees in some concrete way. Until then, this Court "is not empowered to decide . . . abstract propositions, or to declare, for the government of future cases, principles or rules of law which cannot affect the result as to the thing in issue in the case before it." *Tyler v. Judges of Court of Registration*, 179 U.S. 405, 409 (1900). We therefore need not pass on the constitutionality of the Act's preamble.

B

Section 188.210 provides that "[i]t shall be unlawful for any public employee within the scope of his employment to perform or assist an abortion, not necessary to save the life of the mother," while § 188.215 makes it "unlawful for any public facility to be used for the purpose of performing or assisting an abortion not necessary to save the life of the mother." The Court of Appeals held that these provisions contravened this Court's abortion decisions. We take the contrary view.

As we said earlier this Term in *DeShaney v. Winnebago County Dept. of Social Services*, 489 U.S. 189, 196 (1989): "[O]ur cases have recognized that the Due Process Clauses generally confer no affirmative right to governmental aid, even where such aid may be necessary to secure life, liberty, or property interests of which the government itself may not deprive the individual." [The Court also discussed *Maher v. Roe* and *Harris v.McRae*.]

The Court of Appeals distinguished these cases on the ground that "[t]o prevent access to a public facility does more than demonstrate a political choice in favor of childbirth; it clearly narrows and in some cases forecloses the availability of abortion to women." The court reasoned that the ban on the use of public facilities "could prevent a woman's chosen doctor from performing an abortion because of his unprivileged status at other hospitals or because a private hospital adopted a similar anti-abortion stance." It also thought that "[s]uch a rule could increase the cost of obtaining an abortion and delay the timing of it as well."

We think that this analysis is much like that which we rejected in *Maher* . . . and *McRae*. As in those cases, the State's decision here to use public facilities and staff to encourage childbirth over abortion "places no governmental obstacle in the path of a woman who chooses to terminate her pregnancy." *McRae*. Just as Congress' refusal to fund abortions in McRae left "an indigent woman with at least the same range of choice in deciding whether to obtain a medically necessary abortion as she would have had if Congress had chosen to subsidize no health care costs at all," Missouri's refusal to allow public employees to perform abortions in public hospitals leaves a pregnant woman with the same choices as if the State had chosen not to operate any public hospitals at all. The challenged provisions only restrict a woman's ability to obtain an abortion to the extent that she chooses to use a physician affiliated with a public hospital. This circumstance is more easily remedied, and thus considerably less burdensome, than indigency, which "may make it difficult—and in some cases, perhaps, impossible—for some women to have abortions" without public funding. *Maher*. Having held that the State's refusal to fund abortions does not violate *Roe v. Wade*, it strains logic to reach a contrary result for the use of public facilities and employees. If the State may "make a value judgment favoring childbirth over abortion and . . . implement that judgment by the allocation of public funds," *Maher*, surely it may do so through the allocation of other public resources, such as hospitals and medical staff.

. . .

D

. . .

The viability-testing provision of the Missouri Act is concerned with promoting the State's interest in potential human life rather than in maternal health. Section 188.029 creates what is essentially a presumption of viability at 20 weeks, which the physician must rebut with tests indicating that the fetus is not viable prior to performing an abortion. It also directs the physician's determination as to viability by specifying consideration, if feasible, of gestational age, fetal weight, and lung capacity. The District Court found that "the medical evidence is uncontradicted that a 20-week fetus is *not* viable," and that "23½ to 24 weeks gestation is the earliest point in pregnancy where a reasonable possibility of viability exists." But it also found that there may be a 4-week error in estimating gestational age, which supports testing at 20 weeks.

. . .

In *Colautti v. Franklin*, upon which appellees rely, the Court held that a Pennsylvania statute regulating the standard of care to be used by a physician performing an abortion of a possibly viable fetus was void for vagueness. But in the course of reaching that conclusion, the Court reaffirmed its earlier statement in *Planned Parenthood of Central Mo. v. Danforth*, that "'the determination of whether a particular fetus is viable is, and must be, a matter for the judgment of the responsible attending physician.'" . . . To the extent that § 188.029 regulates the method for determining viability, it undoubtedly does superimpose state regulation on the medical determination whether a particular fetus is viable. The Court of Appeals and the District Court thought it unconstitutional for this reason. To the extent that the viability tests increase the cost of what are in fact second-trimester abortions, their validity may also be questioned under *Akron [v. Akron Center for Reproductive Health]*, where the Court held that a requirement that second-trimester abortions must be performed in hospitals was invalid because it substantially increased the expense of those procedures. We think that the doubt cast upon the Missouri statute by these cases is not so much a flaw in the statute as it is a reflection of the fact that the rigid trimester analysis of the course of a pregnancy enunciated in *Roe* has resulted in subsequent cases like *Colautti* and *Akron* making constitutional law in this area a virtual Procrustean bed. Statutes specifying elements of informed consent to be provided abortion patients, for example, were invalidated if they were thought to "structur[e] . . . the dialogue between the woman and her phy-

sician." *Thornburgh v. American College of Obstetricians and Gynecologists*. As the dissenters in Thornburgh pointed out, such a statute would have been sustained under any traditional standard of judicial review or for any other surgical procedure except abortion.

Stare decisis is a cornerstone of our legal system, but it has less power in constitutional cases, where, save for constitutional amendments, this Court is the only body able to make needed changes. We have not refrained from reconsideration of a prior construction of the Constitution that has proved "unsound in principle and unworkable in practice." We think the *Roe* trimester framework falls into that category.

In the first place, the rigid *Roe* framework is hardly consistent with the notion of a Constitution cast in general terms, as ours is, and usually speaking in general principles, as ours does. The key elements of the *Roe* framework—trimesters and viability—are not found in the text of the Constitution or in any place else one would expect to find a constitutional principle. Since the bounds of the inquiry are essentially indeterminate, the result has been a web of legal rules that have become increasingly intricate, resembling a code of regulations rather than a body of constitutional doctrine. As Justice WHITE has put it, the trimester framework has left this Court to serve as the country's "*ex officio* medical board with powers to approve or disapprove medical and operative practices and standards throughout the United States." *Planned Parenthood of Central Mo. v. Danforth* (opinion concurring in part and dissenting in part).

In the second place, we do not see why the State's interest in protecting potential human life should come into existence only at the point of viability, and that there should therefore be a rigid line allowing state regulation after viability but prohibiting it before viability. The dissenters in *Thornburgh*, writing in the context of the *Roe* trimester analysis, would have recognized this fact by positing against the "fundamental right" recognized in Roe the State's "compelling interest" in protecting potential human life throughout pregnancy. "[T]he State's interest, if compelling after viability, is equally compelling before viability." *Thornburgh* (WHITE, J., dissenting).

The tests that § 188.029 requires the physician to perform are designed to determine viability. The State here has chosen viability as the point at which its interest in potential human life must be safeguarded. It is true that the tests in question increase the expense of abortion, and regulate the discretion of the physician in determining the viability of the fetus. Since the tests will undoubtedly show in many cases that the fetus is not viable, the tests will have been performed for what were in fact second-trimester abortions. But we are satisfied that the requirement of these tests permissibly furthers the State's interest in protecting potential human life, and we therefore believe § 188.029 to be constitutional.

The dissent takes us to task for our failure to join in a "great issues" debate as to whether the Constitution includes an "unenumerated" general right to privacy as recognized in cases such as *Griswold v. Connecticut* and *Roe*. But *Griswold v. Connecticut,* unlike *Roe*, did not purport to adopt a whole framework, complete with detailed rules and distinctions, to govern the cases in which the asserted liberty interest would apply. As such, it was far different from the opinion, if not the holding, of *Roe v. Wade*, which sought to establish a constitutional framework for judging state regulation of abortion during the entire term of pregnancy. That framework sought to deal with areas of medical practice traditionally subject to state regulation, and it sought to balance once and for all by reference only to the calendar the claims of the State to protect the fetus as a form of human life against the claims of a woman to decide for herself whether or not to abort a fetus she was carrying. The experience of the Court in applying *Roe v. Wade* in later cases suggests to us that there is wisdom in not unnecessarily attempting to elaborate the abstract differences between a "fundamental right" to abortion, as the Court described it in *Akron*, a "limited fundamental constitutional right," which Justice BLACKMUN'S today treats *Roe* as having established, or a liberty interest protected by the Due Process Clause, which we believe it to be. The Missouri testing requirement here is reasonably designed to ensure that abortions are not performed where the fetus is viable—an end which all concede is legitimate—and that is sufficient to sustain its constitutionality.

The dissent also accuses us, *inter alia*, of cowardice and illegitimacy in dealing with "the most politically divisive domestic legal issue of our time." There is no doubt that our holding today will allow some governmental regulation of abortion that would have been prohibited under the language of cases such as *Colautti v. Franklin* and *Akron v. Akron Center for Reproductive Health, Inc.* But the goal of constitutional adjudication is surely not to remove inexorably "politically divisive" issues from the ambit of the legislative process, whereby the people through their elected representatives deal with matters of concern to them. The goal of constitutional adjudication is to hold true the balance between that which the Constitution puts beyond the reach of the democratic process and that which it does not. We think we have done that today. The dissent's suggestion

that legislative bodies, in a Nation where more than half of our population is women, will treat our decision today as an invitation to enact abortion regulation reminiscent of the Dark Ages not only misreads our views but does scant justice to those who serve in such bodies and the people who elect them.

III

Both appellants and the United States as *amicus curiae* have urged that we overrule our decision in *Roe v. Wade*. The facts of the present case, however, differ from those at issue in *Roe*. Here, Missouri has determined that viability is the point at which its interest in potential human life must be safeguarded. In *Roe*, on the other hand, the Texas statute criminalized the performance of all abortions, except when the mother's life was at stake. This case therefore affords us no occasion to revisit the holding of *Roe*, which was that the Texas statute unconstitutionally infringed the right to an abortion derived from the Due Process Clause, and we leave it undisturbed. To the extent indicated in our opinion, we would modify and narrow *Roe* and succeeding cases.

Because none of the challenged provisions of the Missouri Act properly before us conflict with the Constitution, the judgment of the Court of Appeals is

Reversed.

JUSTICE O'CONNOR, concurring in part and concurring in the judgment. I concur in Parts I, II-A, II-B, and II-C of the Court's opinion.

. . .

II

Unlike the plurality, I do not understand these viability testing requirements to conflict with any of the Court's past decisions concerning state regulation of abortion. Therefore, there is no necessity to accept the State's invitation to reexamine the constitutional validity of *Roe v. Wade*. Where there is no need to decide a constitutional question, it is a venerable principle of this Court's adjudicatory processes not to do so, for "[t]he Court will not 'anticipate a question of constitutional law in advance of the necessity of deciding it.'" . . . When the constitutional invalidity of a State's abortion statute actually turns on the constitutional validity of *Roe v. Wade*, there will be time enough to reexamine *Roe*. And to do so carefully.

. . .

I do not think the [viability testing requirement], as interpreted by the Court, imposes a degree of state regulation on the medical determination of viability that in any way conflicts with prior decisions of this Court. As the plurality recognizes, the requirement that, where not imprudent, physicians perform examinations and tests useful to making subsidiary findings to determine viability "promot[es] the State's interest in potential human life rather than in maternal health." No decision of this Court has held that the State may not directly promote its interest in potential life when viability is possible. Quite the contrary. . . .

It is clear to me that requiring the performance of examinations and tests useful to determining whether a fetus is viable, when viability is possible, and when it would not be medically imprudent to do so, does not impose an undue burden on a woman's abortion decision. On this ground alone I would reject the suggestion that § 188.029 as interpreted is unconstitutional. The second-trimester hospitalization requirement struck down in *Akron* imposed, in the majority's view, "a heavy, and unnecessary, burden," more than doubling the cost of "women's access to a relatively inexpensive, otherwise accessible, and safe abortion procedure." By contrast, the cost of examinations and tests that could usefully and prudently be performed when a woman is 20–24 weeks pregnant to determine whether the fetus is viable would only marginally, if at all, increase the cost of an abortion. . . .

Moreover, the examinations and tests required by § 188.029 are to be performed when viability is possible. . . . As the Court recognized in *Thornburgh*, the State's compelling interest in potential life post-viability renders its interest in determining the critical point of viability equally compelling. . . .

JUSTICE SCALIA, concurring in part and concurring in the judgment.

I join Parts I, II-A, II-B, and II-C of the opinion of the Court. As to Part II-D, I share Justice BLACKMUN's view, that it effectively would overrule *Roe v. Wade*. I think that should be done, but would do it more explicitly. Since today we contrive to avoid doing it, and indeed to avoid almost any decision of national import, I need not set forth my reasons, some of which have been well recited in dissents of my colleagues in other cases.

The outcome of today's case will doubtless be heralded as a triumph of judicial statesmanship. It is not that, unless it is statesmanlike needlessly to prolong this Court's self-awarded sovereignty over a field where it has little proper business since the answers to most of the cruel questions posed are political and not juridical—a sovereignty which therefore quite properly—but to the great damage of the Court, makes it the object of the sort of organized public pressure that political institutions in a democracy ought to receive.

Justice O'CONNOR's assertion that a "'fundamental rule of judicial restraint'" requires us to avoid reconsidering *Roe* cannot be taken seriously. By finessing *Roe* we do not, as she suggests adhere to the strict and venerable

rule that we should avoid "'decid[ing] questions of a constitutional nature.'" We have not disposed of this case on some statutory or procedural ground, but have decided, and could not avoid deciding, whether the Missouri statute meets the requirements of the United States Constitution. The only choice available is whether, in deciding that constitutional question, we should use *Roe v. Wade* as the benchmark, or something else. What is involved, therefore, is not the rule of avoiding constitutional issues where possible, but the quite separate principle that we will not "'formulate a rule of constitutional law broader than is required by the precise facts to which it is to be applied.'" The latter is a sound general principle, but one often departed from when good reason exists. . . . I have not identified with certainty the first instance of our deciding a case on broader constitutional grounds than absolutely necessary, but it is assuredly no later than *Marbury v. Madison*, where we held that mandamus could constitutionally issue against the Secretary of State, although that was unnecessary given our holding that the law authorizing issuance of the mandamus by this Court was unconstitutional.

. . . It would be wrong, in any decision, to ignore the reality that our policy not to "formulate a rule of constitutional law broader than is required by the precise facts" has a frequently applied good-cause exception. But it seems particularly perverse to convert the policy into an absolute in the present case, in order to place beyond reach the inexpressibly "broader-than-was-required-by-the-precise-facts" structure established by *Roe v. Wade*.

The real question, then, is whether there are valid reasons to go beyond the most stingy possible holding today. It seems to me there are not only valid but compelling ones. Ordinarily, speaking no more broadly than is absolutely required avoids throwing settled law into confusion; doing so today preserves a chaos that is evident to anyone who can read and count. Alone sufficient to justify a broad holding is the fact that our retaining control, through *Roe*, of what I believe to be, and many of our citizens recognize to be, a political issue, continuously distorts the public perception of the role of this Court. We can now look forward to at least another Term with carts full of mail from the public, and streets full of demonstrators, urging us—their unelected and life-tenured judges who have been awarded those extraordinary, undemocratic characteristics precisely in order that we might follow the law despite the popular will—to follow the popular will. Indeed, I expect we can look forward to even more of that than before, given our indecisive decision today. . . . It thus appears that the mansion of constitutionalized abortion law, constructed overnight in *Roe v. Wade*, must be disassembled doorjamb by doorjamb, and never entirely brought down, no matter how wrong it may be.

Of the four courses we might have chosen today—to reaffirm *Roe*, to overrule it explicitly, to overrule it *sub silentio*, or to avoid the question—the last is the least responsible. On the question of the constitutionality of § 188.029, I concur in the judgment of the Court and strongly dissent from the manner in which it has been reached.

JUSTICE BLACKMUN, with whom JUSTICE BRENNAN and JUSTICE MARSHALL join, concurring in part and dissenting in part.

Today, *Roe v. Wade* and the fundamental constitutional right of women to decide whether to terminate a pregnancy, survive but are not secure. Although the Court extricates itself from this case without making a single, even incremental, change in the law of abortion, the plurality and Justice SCALIA would overrule *Roe* (the first silently, the other explicitly) and would return to the States virtually unfettered authority to control the quintessentially intimate, personal, and life-directing decision whether to carry a fetus to term. Although today, no less than yesterday, the Constitution and the decisions of this Court prohibit a State from enacting laws that inhibit women from the meaningful exercise of that right, a plurality of this Court implicitly invites every state legislature to enact more and more restrictive abortion regulations in order to provoke more and more test cases, in the hope that sometime down the line the Court will return the law of procreative freedom to the severe limitations that generally prevailed in this country before January 22, 1973. Never in my memory has a plurality announced a judgment of this Court that so foments disregard for the law and for our standing decisions.

Nor in my memory has a plurality gone about its business in such a deceptive fashion. At every level of its review, from its effort to read the real meaning out of the Missouri statute, to its intended evisceration of precedents and its deafening silence about the constitutional protections that it would jettison, the plurality obscures the portent of its analysis. With feigned restraint, the plurality announces that its analysis leaves *Roe* "undisturbed," albeit "modif[ied] and narrow[ed]." But this disclaimer is totally meaningless. The plurality opinion is filled with winks, and nods, and knowing glances to those who would do away with *Roe* explicitly, but turns a stone face to anyone in search of what the plurality conceives as the scope of a woman's right under the Due Process Clause to terminate a pregnancy free from the coercive and brooding influence of the State. The simple truth is that *Roe* would not survive the plurality's analysis, and that the plurality provides no substitute for *Roe*'s protective umbrella.

I fear for the future. I fear for the liberty and equality of the millions of women who have lived and come of age in the 16 years since Roe was decided. I fear for the integrity of, and public esteem for, this Court.

I dissent.

. . .

1

The plurality opinion is far more remarkable for the arguments that it does not advance than for those that it does. The plurality does not even mention, much less join, the true jurisprudential debate underlying this case: whether the Constitution includes an "unenumerated" general right to privacy as recognized in many of our decisions, most notably *Griswold v. Connecticut*, and *Roe*, and, more specifically, whether, and to what extent, such a right to privacy extends to matters of childbearing and family life, including abortion. These are questions of unsurpassed significance in this Court's interpretation of the Constitution, and mark the battleground upon which this case was fought, by the parties, by the United States as *amicus* on behalf of petitioners, and by an unprecedented number of *amici*. On these grounds, abandoned by the plurality, the Court should decide this case.

But rather than arguing that the text of the Constitution makes no mention of the right to privacy, the plurality complains that the critical elements of the *Roe* framework—trimesters and viability—do not appear in the Constitution and are, therefore, somehow inconsistent with a Constitution cast in general terms. Were this a true concern, we would have to abandon most of our constitutional jurisprudence. As the plurality well knows, or should know, the "critical elements" of countless constitutional doctrines nowhere appear in the Constitution's text. The Constitution makes no mention, for example, of the First Amendment's "actual malice" standard for proving certain libels, see *New York Times Co. v. Sullivan*, or of the standard for determining when speech is obscene. See *Miller v. California*. Similarly, the Constitution makes no mention of the rational-basis test, or the specific verbal formulations of intermediate and strict scrutiny by which this Court evaluates claims under the Equal Protection Clause. The reason is simple. Like the *Roe* framework, these tests or standards are not, and do not purport to be, rights protected by the Constitution. Rather, they are judge-made methods for evaluating and measuring the strength and scope of constitutional rights or for balancing the constitutional rights of individuals against the competing interests of government.

With respect to the *Roe* framework, the general constitutional principle, indeed the fundamental constitutional right, for which it was developed is the right to privacy, see, e.g., *Griswold v. Connecticut*, a species of "liberty" protected by the Due Process Clause, which under our past decisions safeguards the right of women to exercise some control over their own role in procreation.... The trimester framework simply defines and limits that right to privacy in the abortion context to accommodate, not destroy, a State's legitimate interest in protecting the health of pregnant women and in preserving potential human life. Fashioning such accommodations between individual rights and the legitimate interests of government, establishing benchmarks and standards with which to evaluate the competing claims of individuals and government, lies at the very heart of constitutional adjudication. To the extent that the trimester framework is useful in this enterprise, it is not only consistent with constitutional interpretation, but necessary to the wise and just exercise of this Court's paramount authority to define the scope of constitutional rights.

2

The plurality next alleges that the result of the trimester framework has "been a web of legal rules that have become increasingly intricate, resembling a code of regulations rather than a body of constitutional doctrine." Again, if this were a true and genuine concern, we would have to abandon vast areas of our constitutional jurisprudence....

That numerous constitutional doctrines result in narrow differentiations between similar circumstances does not mean that this Court has abandoned adjudication in favor of regulation. Rather, these careful distinctions reflect the process of constitutional adjudication itself, which is often highly fact specific, requiring such determinations as whether state laws are "unduly burdensome" or "reasonable" or bear a "rational" or "necessary" relation to asserted state interests. ... If, in delicate and complicated areas of constitutional law, our legal judgments "have become increasingly intricate," it is not, as the plurality contends, because we have overstepped our judicial role. Quite the opposite: the rules are intricate because we have remained conscientious in our duty to do justice carefully, especially when fundamental rights rise or fall with our decisions.

3

Finally, the plurality asserts that the trimester framework cannot stand because the State's interest in potential life is compelling throughout pregnancy, not merely after viability. The opinion contains not one word of rationale for its view of the State's interest. This "it-is-so-because-we-say-so" jurisprudence constitutes nothing other than an attempted exercise of brute force; reason, much less persuasion, has no place.

. . .

... I remain convinced, as six other Members of this Court 16 years ago were convinced, that the *Roe* framework, and the viability standard in particular, fairly, sensibly, and effectively functions to safeguard the constitutional liberties of pregnant women while recognizing and accommodating the State's interest in potential human life. The viability line reflects the biological facts and truths of fetal development; it marks that threshold moment prior to which a fetus cannot survive separate from the woman and cannot reasonably and objectively be regarded as a subject of rights or interests distinct from, or paramount to, those of the pregnant woman. At the same time, the viability standard takes account of the undeniable fact that as the fetus evolves into its postnatal form, and as it loses its dependence on the uterine environment, the State's interest in the fetus' potential human life, and in fostering a regard for human life in general, becomes compelling. As a practical matter, because viability follows "quickening"—the point at which a woman feels movement in her womb—and because viability occurs no earlier than 23 weeks gestational age, it establishes an easily applicable standard for regulating abortion while providing a pregnant woman ample time to exercise her fundamental right with her responsible physician to terminate her pregnancy. Although I have stated previously for a majority of this Court that "[c]onstitutional rights do not always have easily ascertainable boundaries," to seek and establish those boundaries remains the special responsibility of this Court. *Thornburgh*. In *Roe*, we discharged that responsibility as logic and science compelled. The plurality today advances not one reasonable argument as to why our judgment in that case was wrong and should be abandoned.

C

Having contrived an opportunity to reconsider the *Roe* framework, and then having discarded that framework, the plurality finds the testing provision unobjectionable because it "permissibly furthers the State's interest in protecting potential human life." This newly minted standard is circular and totally meaningless. Whether a challenged abortion regulation "permissibly furthers" a legitimate state interest is the *question* that courts must answer in abortion cases, not the standard for courts to apply. In keeping with the rest of its opinion, the plurality makes no attempt to explain or to justify its new standard, either in the abstract or as applied in this case. Nor could it. The "permissibly furthers" standard has no independent meaning, and consists of nothing other than what a majority of this Court may believe at any given moment in any given case. The plurality's novel test appears to be nothing more than a dressed-up version of rational-basis review, this Court's most lenient level of scrutiny. One thing is clear, however: were the plurality's "permissibly furthers" standard adopted by the Court, for all practical purposes, *Roe* would be overruled.

The "permissibly furthers" standard completely disregards the irreducible minimum of *Roe*: the Court's recognition that a woman has a limited fundamental constitutional right to decide whether to terminate a pregnancy. That right receives no meaningful recognition in the plurality's written opinion. Since, in the plurality's view, the State's interest in potential life is compelling as of the moment of conception, and is therefore served only if abortion is abolished, every hindrance to a woman's ability to obtain an abortion must be "permissible." Indeed, the more severe the hindrance, the more effectively (and permissibly) the State's interest would be furthered. A tax on abortions or a criminal prohibition would both satisfy the plurality's standard. So, for that matter, would a requirement that a pregnant woman memorize and recite today's plurality opinion before seeking an abortion.

. . .

D

Thus, "not with a bang, but a whimper," the plurality discards a landmark case of the last generation, and casts into darkness the hopes and visions of every woman in this country who had come to believe that the Constitution guaranteed her the right to exercise some control over her unique ability to bear children. The plurality does so either oblivious or insensitive to the fact that millions of women, and their families, have ordered their lives around the right to reproductive choice, and that this right has become vital to the full participation of women in the economic and political walks of American life. The plurality would clear the way once again for government to force upon women the physical labor and specific and direct medical and psychological harms that may accompany carrying a fetus to term. The plurality would clear the way again for the State to conscript a woman's body and to force upon her a "distressful life and future." *Roe*.

. . .

Of the aspirations and settled understandings of American women, of the inevitable and brutal consequences of what it is doing, the tough-approach plurality utters not a word. This silence is callous. It is also profoundly destructive of this Court as an institution. To overturn a constitutional decision is a rare and grave undertaking. To overturn a constitutional decision that secured a fundamental personal liberty to millions of persons would be unprecedented in our 200 years of constitutional history.

. . .

. . . Today's decision involves the most politically divisive domestic legal issue of our time. By refusing to explain or to justify its proposed revolutionary revision in the law of abortion, and by refusing to abide not only by our precedents, but also by our canons for reconsidering those precedents, the plurality invites charges of cowardice and illegitimacy to our door. I cannot say that these would be undeserved.

II

For today, at least, the law of abortion stands undisturbed. For today, the women of this Nation still retain the liberty to control their destinies. But the signs are evident and very ominous, and a chill wind blows.

I dissent.

[The opinion of Justice Stevens, concurring in part and dissenting in part, is omitted.]

After *Webster*, the Court decided two important decisions involving minors' abortion rights. In *Ohio v. Akron Center for Reproductive Health*,[154] and *Hodgson v. Minnesota*,[155] the Court upheld parental notification statutes that provided for a judicial bypass procedure allowing minors who could demonstrate sufficient maturity to obtain court approval.

Roe's future became even more precarious when Justices Brennan and Marshall were replaced by Justices Souter and Thomas. The United States Solicitor General filed amicus briefs in six cases, asking the Court to overrule *Roe*. Right-to-life opposition

---

[154] 497 U.S. 502 (1990).
[155] 497 U.S. 417 (1990).

to *Roe* had also become more visible. Although *Roe* sought to avoid the moral issues inherent in the debate over abortion, an alliance of Catholics and Protestant fundamentalists passionately defended their pro-life position in staunchly religious terms. In April 1990, more than 200,000 opponents of the abortion right held a march in Washington, D.C. At abortion clinics, protest sometimes turned into harassment and even physical violence. In the wake of *Webster*'s signal to the states, Pennsylvania amended its Abortion Control Act in 1989 to include several restrictions, including some that the Court had previously struck down as unconstitutional. Prior to oral argument, abortion rights activists organized a march of more than 500,000 people in the capital. As the nation awaited the Court's decision in *Casey*, many predicted Roe's final demise.

Planned Parenthood of South-Eastern Pennsylvania v. Casey
505 U.S.____, 112 S.Ct. 2791 (1992)

JUSTICE O'CONNOR, JUSTICE KENNEDY, and JUSTICE SOUTER announced the judgment of the Court and delivered the opinion of the Court with respect to Parts I, II, III, V-A, V-C, and VI, an opinion with respect to Part V-E, in which JUSTICE STEVENS joins, and an opinion with respect to Parts IV, V-B, and V-D.

I

Liberty finds no refuge in a jurisprudence of doubt. Yet 19 years after our holding that the Constitution protects a woman's right to terminate her pregnancy in its early stages, *Roe v. Wade*, that definition of liberty is still questioned. Joining the respondents as *amicus curiae*, the United States, as it has done in five other cases in the last decade, again asks us to overrule *Roe*.

At issue in these cases are five provisions of the Pennsylvania Abortion Control Act of 1982 as amended in 1988 and 1989. . . . The Act requires that a woman seeking an abortion give her informed consent prior to the abortion procedure, and specifies that she be provided with certain information at least 24 hours before the abortion is performed. For a minor to obtain an abortion, the Act requires the informed consent of one of her parents, but provides for a judicial bypass option if the minor does not wish to or cannot obtain a parent's consent. Another provision of the Act requires that, unless certain exceptions apply, a married woman seeking an abortion must sign a statement indicating that she has notified her husband of her intended abortion. The Act exempts compliance with these three requirements in the event of a "medical emergency." . . . In addition to the above provisions regulating the performance of abortions, the Act imposes certain reporting requirements on facilities that provide abortion services.

. . .

. . . [W]e acknowledge that our decisions after *Roe* cast doubt upon the meaning and reach of its holding. Further, the CHIEF JUSTICE admits that he would overrule the central holding of *Roe* and adopt the rational relationship test as the sole criterion of constitutionality. State and federal courts as well as legislatures throughout the Union must have guidance as they seek to address this subject in conformance with the Constitution. Given these premises, we find it imperative to review once more the principles that define the rights of the woman and the legitimate authority of the state respecting the termination of pregnancies by abortion procedures.

After considering the fundamental constitutional questions resolved by *Roe*, principles of institutional integrity, and the rule of *stare decisis*, we are led to conclude this: the essential holding of *Roe v. Wade* should be retained and once again reaffirmed.

It must be stated at the outset and with clarity that *Roe*'s essential holding, the holding we reaffirm, has three parts. First is a recognition of the right of the woman to choose to have an abortion before viability and to obtain it without undue interference from the State. Before viability, the State's interests are not strong enough to support a prohibition of abortion or the imposition of a substantial obstacle to the woman's effective right to elect the procedure. Second is a confirmation of the State's power to restrict abortions after fetal viability, if the law contains exceptions for pregnancies which endanger a woman's life or health. And third is the principle that the State has legitimate interests from the outset of the pregnancy in protecting the health of the woman and the life of the fetus that may become a child. These principles do not contradict one another; and we adhere to each.

II

Constitutional protection of the woman's decision to terminate her pregnancy derives from the Due Process Clause of the Fourteenth Amendment. . . . Neither the Bill of Rights nor the specific practices of States at the time of the adoption of the Fourteenth Amendment marks the outer limits of the substantive sphere of liberty which the Fourteenth Amendment protects. As the second Justice Harlan recognized:

> "[T]he full scope of the liberty guaranteed by the Due Process Clause cannot be found in or limited by the precise terms of the specific guarantees elsewhere provided in the Constitution. . . . It is a rational continuum which, broadly speaking, includes a freedom from all substantial arbitrary impositions and purposeless restraints, . . . and which also recognizes, what a reasonable and sensitive judgment must, that certain interests require particularly careful scrutiny of the state needs asserted to justify their abridgment." *Poe v. Ullman*, (Harlan, J., dissenting from dismissal on jurisdictional grounds).

. . . It is settled now, as it was when the Court heard arguments in *Roe v. Wade*, that the Constitution places limits on a State's right to interfere with a person's most basic decisions about family and parenthood, see *Carey v. Population Services International*; *Moore v. East Cleveland*; *Eisenstadt v. Baird*; *Loving v. Virginia*; *Griswold v. Connecticut*; *Skinner v. Oklahoma ex rel. Williamson*; *Pierce v. Society of Sisters*; *Meyer v. Nebraska*, as well as bodily integrity.

The inescapable fact is that adjudication of substantive due process claims may call upon the Court in interpreting the Constitution to exercise that same capacity which by tradition courts always have exercised: reasoned judgment. Its boundaries are not susceptible of expression as a simple rule. That does not mean we are free to invalidate state policy choices with which we disagree; yet neither does it permit us to shrink from the duties of our office. . . .

Men and women of good conscience can disagree, and we suppose some always shall disagree, about the profound moral and spiritual implications of terminating a pregnancy, even in its earliest stage. Some of us as individuals find abortion offensive to our most basic principles of morality, but that cannot control our decision. Our obligation is to define the liberty of all, not to mandate our own moral code. The underlying constitutional issue is whether the State can resolve these philosophic questions in such a definitive way that a woman lacks all choice in the matter, except perhaps in those rare circumstances in which the pregnancy is itself a danger to her own life or health, or is the result of rape or incest.

. . .

Our law affords constitutional protection to personal decisions relating to marriage, procreation, contraception, family relationship, child rearing, and education. . . . These matters, involving the most intimate and personal choices a person may make in a lifetime, choices central to personal dignity and autonomy, are central to the liberty protected by the Fourteenth Amendment. At the heart of liberty is the right to define one's own concept of existence, of meaning, of the universe, and of the mystery of human life. Beliefs about these matters could not define the attributes of personhood were they formed under compulsion of the State.

These considerations begin our analysis of the woman's interest in terminating her pregnancy but cannot end it, for this reason: though the abortion decision may originate within the zone of conscience and belief, it is more than a philosophic exercise. Abortion is a unique act. It is an act fraught with consequences for others: for the woman who must live with the implications of her decision; for the persons who perform and assist in the procedure; for the spouse, family, and society which must confront the knowledge that these procedures exist, procedures some deem nothing short of an act of violence against innocent human life; and, depending on one's beliefs, for the life or potential life that is aborted. Though abortion is conduct, it does not follow that the State is entitled to proscribe it in all instances. That is because the liberty of the woman is at stake in a sense unique to the human condition and so unique to the law. The mother who carries a child to full term is subject to anxieties, to physical constraints, to pain that only she must bear. That these sacrifices have from the beginning of the human race been endured by woman with a pride that ennobles her in the eyes of others and give to the infant a bond of love cannot alone be grounds for the State to insist she make the sacrifice. Her suffering is too intimate and personal for the State to insist, without more, upon its own vision of the woman's role, however dominant that vision has been in the course of our history and our culture. The destiny of the woman must be shaped to a large extent on her own conception of her spiritual imperatives and her place in society.

. . .

While we appreciate the weight of the arguments made on behalf of the State in the case before us, arguments which in their ultimate formulation conclude that *Roe* should be overruled, the reservations any of us may have in reaffirming the central holding of *Roe* are outweighed by the explication of individual liberty we have given combined with the force of *stare decisis*. We turn now to that doctrine.

III

A

. . .

. . . [I]n this case we may inquire whether *Roe*'s central rule has been found unworkable; whether the rule's limitation on state power could be removed without serious inequity to those who have relied upon it or significant damage to the stability of the society governed by the rule in question; whether the law's growth in the intervening years has left *Roe*'s central rule a doctrinal anachronism discounted by society; and whether *Roe*'s premises of fact have so far changed in the ensuing two decades as to render its central holding somehow irrelevant or unjustifiable in dealing with the issue it addressed.

1

Although *Roe* has engendered opposition, it has in no sense proven "unworkable," representing as it does a simple limitation beyond which a state law is unenforceable. While *Roe* has, of course, required judicial assessment of state laws affecting the exercise of the choice guaranteed against government infringement, and although the need for such review will remain as a consequence of today's decision, the required determinations fall within judicial competence.

2

The inquiry into reliance counts the cost of a rule's repudiation as it would fall on those who have relied reasonably on the rule's continued application. . . . Abortion is customarily chosen as an unplanned response to the consequence of unplanned activity or to the failure of conventional birth control, and except on the assumption that no intercourse would have occurred but for *Roe*'s holding, such behavior may appear to justify no reliance claim. . . . To eliminate the issue of reliance that easily, however, one would need to limit cognizable reliance to specific instances of sexual activity. But to do this would be simply to refuse to face the fact that for two decades of economic and social developments, people have organized intimate relationships and choices that define their views of themselves and their places in society, in reliance on the availability of abortion in the event that contraception should fail. The ability of women to participate equally in the economic and social life of the Nation has been facilitated by their ability to control their reproductive lives. The Constitution serves human values, and while the effect of reliance on *Roe* cannot be exactly measured, neither can the certain cost of overruling *Roe* for people who have ordered their thinking and living around that case be dismissed.

3

No evolution of legal principle has left *Roe*'s doctrinal footings weaker than they were in 1973. No development of constitutional law since the case was decided has implicitly or explicitly left *Roe* behind as a mere survivor of obsolete constitutional thinking.

It will be recognized, of course, that *Roe* stands at an intersection of two lines of decisions, but in whichever doctrinal category one reads the case, the result for present purposes will be the same. The *Roe* Court itself placed its holding in the succession of cases most prominently exemplified by *Griswold v. Connecticut*. When it is so seen, *Roe* is clearly in no jeopardy, since subsequent constitutional developments have neither disturbed, nor do they threaten to diminish, the scope of recognized protection accorded to the liberty relating to intimate relationships, the family, and decisions about whether or not to beget or bear child.

Roe, however, may be seen not only as an exemplar of *Griswold* liberty but as a rule (whether or not mistaken) of personal autonomy and bodily integrity, with doctrinal affinity to cases recognizing limits on governmental power to mandate medical treatment or to bar its rejection. If so, our cases since *Roe* accord with *Roe*'s view that a State's interest in the protection of life falls short of justifying any plenary override of individual liberty claims. *Cruzan v. Director, Missouri Dept. of Health*.

Finally, one could classify *Roe* as *sui generis*. If the case is so viewed, then there clearly has been no erosion of its central determination. . . . In *Webster v. Reproductive Health Services*, although two of the present authors questioned the trimester framework in a way consistent with our judgment today, a majority of the Court either decided to reaffirm or declined to address the constitutional validity of the central holding of *Roe*.

4

We have seen how time has overtaken some of *Roe*'s factual assumptions: advances in maternal health care allow for abortions safe to the mother later in pregnancy than was true in 1973, and advances in neonatal care have advanced viability to a point somewhat earlier. But these facts go only to the scheme of time limits on the realization of competing interests, and the divergences from the factual premises of 1973 have no bearing on the validity of *Roe*'s central holding, that viability marks the earliest point at which the State's interest in fetal life is constitutionally adequate to justify a legislative ban on nontherapeutic abortions. The soundness or unsoundness of that constitutional judgment in no sense turns on whether viability occurs at approximately 28 weeks, as was usual at the time of *Roe*, at 23 to 24 weeks, as it sometime does today, or at some moment even slightly earlier in pregnancy, as it may if fetal respiratory capacity can somehow be enhanced in the future. Whenever it may occur, the attainment of viability may continue to serve as the critical fact, just as it has done since *Roe* was decided; which is to say that no change in *Roe*'s factual underpinning has left its central holding obsolete, and none supports an argument for overruling it.

. . .

B

In a less significant case, *stare decisis* analysis could, and would, stop at the point we have reached. But the sustained and widespread debate *Roe* has provoked calls for some comparison between that case and others of comparable dimension that have responded to national controversies and taken on the impress of the controversies addressed. Only two such decisional lines from the past century present themselves for examination, and in each instance the result reached by the Court accorded with the principles we apply today.

The first example is that line of cases identified with *Lochner v. New York*, which imposed substantive limitations on legislation limiting economic autonomy in favor of health and welfare regulation, adopting, in Justice Holmes' view, the theory of laissez-faire. The *Lochner* decisions were exemplified by *Adkins v. Children's Hospital of D.C.*, 261 U.S. 525 (1923), in which this Court held it to be an infringement of constitutionally protected liberty of contract to require the employers of adult women to satisfy minimum wage standards. Fourteen years later, *West Coast Hotel Co. v. Parrish*, 300 U.S. 379 (1937), signalled the demise of *Lochner* by overruling *Adkins*. In the meantime, the Depression had come and, with it, the lesson than seemed unmistakable to most people by 1937, that the interpretation of contractual freedom protected in *Adkins* rested on fundamentally false factual assumptions about the capacity of a relatively unregulated market to satisfy minimal levels of human welfare. As Justice Jackson wrote of the constitutional crisis of 1937 shortly before he came on the bench, "The older world of laissez-faire was recognized everywhere outside the Court to be dead." The facts upon which the earlier case had premised a constitutional resolution of social controversy had proved to be untrue, and history's demonstration of their untruth not only justified but required the new choice of

constitutional principle that *West Coast Hotel* announced. . . .

The second comparison that 20th century history invites is with the cases employing the separate-but-equal rule for applying the Fourteenth Amendment's equal protection guarantee. They began with *Plessy v. Ferguson*, holding that legislatively mandated racial segregation in public transportation works no denial of equal protection, rejecting the argument that racial separation enforced by the legal machinery of American society treats the black race as inferior. The *Plessy* Court considered "the underlying fallacy of the plaintiff's argument to consist in the assumption that the enforced separation of the two races stamps the colored race with a badge of inferiority. If this be so, it is not by reason of anything found in the act, but solely because the colored race chooses to put that construction upon it." Whether, as a mater of historical fact, the Justices in the *Plessy* majority believed this or not, this understanding of the implication of segregation was the stated justification for the Court's opinion. But this understanding of the facts and the rule it was stated to justify were repudiated in *Brown v. Board of Education*. . . .

The Court in *Brown* addressed these facts of life by observing that whatever may have been the understanding in *Plessy*'s time of the power of segregation to stigmatize those who were segregated with a "badge of inferiority," it was clear by 1954 that legally sanctioned segregation had just such an effect, to the point that racially separate public educational facilities were deemed inherently unequal. Society's understanding of the facts upon which a constitutional ruling was sought in 1954 was thus fundamentally different from the basis claimed for the decision in 1896. While we think *Plessy* was wrong the day it was decided, we must also recognize that the *Plessy* Court's explanation for its decision was so clearly at odds with the facts apparent to the Court in 1954 that the decision to reexamine *Plessy* was on this ground alone not only justified but required.

West Coast Hotel and *Brown* each rested on facts, or an understanding of facts, changed from those which furnished the claimed justifications for the earlier constitutional resolutions. Each case was comprehensible as the Court's response to facts that the country could understand, or had come to understand already, but which the Court of an earlier day, as its own declarations disclosed, had not been able to perceive. As the decisions were thus comprehensible they were also defensible, not merely as the victories of one doctrinal school over another by dint of numbers (victories though they were), but as applications of constitutional principle to facts as they had not been seen by the Court before. In constitutional adjudication as elsewhere in life, changed circumstances may impose new obligations, and the thoughtful part of the Nation could accept each decision to overrule a prior case as a response to the Court's constitutional duty.

Because the case before us presents no such occasion it could be seen as no such response. Because neither the factual underpinnings of *Roe*'s central holding nor our understanding of it has changed (and because no other indication of weakened precedent has been shown) the Court could not pretend to be reexamining the prior law with any justification beyond a present doctrinal disposition to come out differently from the Court of 1973. . . .

C

The examination of the conditions justifying the repudiation of *Adkins* by *West Coast Hotel* and *Plessy* by *Brown* is enough to suggest the terrible price that would have been paid if the Court had not overruled as it did. In the present case, however, as our analysis to this point makes clear, the terrible price would be paid for overruling. Our analysis would not be complete, however, without explaining why overruling *Roe*'s central holding would not only reach an unjustifiable result under principles of *stare decisis*, but would seriously weaken the Court's capacity to exercise the judicial power and to function as the Supreme Court of a Nation dedicated to the rule of law. To understand why this would be so it is necessary to understand the source of this Court's authority, the conditions necessary for its preservation, and its relationship to the country's understanding of itself as a constitutional Republic.

The root of American governmental power is revealed most clearly in the instance of the power conferred by the Constitution upon the Judiciary of the United States and specifically upon this Court. As Americans of each succeeding generation are rightly told, the Court cannot buy support for its decisions by spending money and, except to a minor degree, it cannot independently coerce obedience to its decrees. The Court's power lies, rather, in its legitimacy, a product of substance and perception that shows itself in the people's acceptance of the Judiciary as fit to determine what the Nation's law means and to declare what it demands.

The Court must take care to speak and act in ways that allow people to accept its decisions on the terms the Court claims for them, as grounded truly in principle, not as compromises with social and political pressures having, as such, no bearing on the principled choices that the Court is obliged to make. Thus, the Court's legitimacy depends on making legally principled decisions under circumstances in which their principled character is sufficiently plausible to be accepted by the Nation.

. . . Where, in the performance of its judicial duties, the Court decides a case in such a way as to resolve the sort of intensely divisive controversy reflected in *Roe* and those rare, comparable cases, its decision has a dimension that the resolution of the normal case does not carry. It is the dimension present whenever the Court's interpretation of the Constitution calls the contending sides of national controversy to end their national division by accepting a common mandate rooted in the Constitution.

The Court is not asked to do this very often, having thus addressed the Nation only twice in our lifetime, in the decisions of *Brown* and *Roe*. But when the Court does act in this way, its decision requires an equally rare precedential force to counter the inevitable efforts to overturn it and to thwart its implementation. Some of those efforts may be mere unprincipled emotional reactions; others may proceed from principles worthy of profound respect. But whatever the premises of opposition may be, only the most convincing justification under accepted standards of precedent could suffice to demonstrate that a later decision overruling the first was anything but a surrender to political pressure, and an unjustified repudiation of the principle on which the Court staked its authority in the first instance. So to overrule under fire in the absence of the most compelling reason to reexamine a watershed decision would subvert the Court's legitimacy beyond any serious question.

. . . Some cost will be paid by anyone who approves or implements a constitutional decision where it is unpopular, or who refuses to work to undermine the decision or to force its reversal. The price may be criticism or ostracism, or it may be violence. An extra price will be paid by those who themselves disapprove of the decision's results when viewed outside of constitutional terms, but who nevertheless struggle to accept it, because they respect the rule of law. To all those who will be so tested by following, the Court implicitly undertakes to remain steadfast, lest in the end a price be paid for nothing. . . .

It is true that diminished legitimacy may be restored, but only slowly. Unlike the political branches, a Court thus weakened could not seek to regain its position with a new mandate from the voters, and even if the Court could somehow go to the polls, the loss of its principled character could not be retrieved by the casting of so many votes. Like the character of an individual, the legitimacy of the Court must be earned over time. So, indeed, must be the character of a Nation of people who aspire to live according to the rule of law. Their belief in themselves as such a people is not readily separable from their understanding of the Court invested with the authority to decide their constitutional cases and speak before all others for their constitutional ideals. If the Court's legitimacy should be undermined, then, so would the country be in its very ability to see itself through its constitutional ideals. The Court's concern with legitimacy is not for the sake of the Court but for the sake of the Nation to which it is responsible.

The Court's duty in the present case is clear. In 1973, it confronted the already-divisive issue of governmental power to limit personal choice to undergo abortion, for which it provided a new resolution based on the due process guaranteed by the Fourteenth Amendment. Whether or not a new social consensus is developing on that issue, its divisiveness is no less today than in 1973, and pressure to overrule the decision, like pressure to retain it, has grown only more intense. A decision to overrule *Roe*'s essential holding under the existing circumstances would address error, if error there was, at the cost of both profound and unnecessary damage to the Court's legitimacy, and to the Nation's commitment to the rule of law. It is therefore imperative to adhere to the essence of *Roe*'s original decision, and we do so today.

IV

From what we have said so far it follows that it is a constitutional liberty of the woman to have some freedom to terminate her pregnancy. We conclude that the basic decision in Roe was based on a constitutional analysis which we cannot now repudiate. The woman's liberty is not so unlimited, however, that from the outset the State cannot show its concern for the life of the unborn, and at a later point in fetal development the State's interest in life has sufficient force so that the right of the woman to terminate the pregnancy can be restricted.

That brings us, of course, to the point where much criticism has been directed at *Roe*, a criticism that always inheres when the Court draws a specific rule from what in the Constitution is but a general standard. We conclude, however, that the urgent claims of the woman to retain the ultimate control over her destiny and her body, claims implicit in the meaning of liberty, require us to perform that function. Liberty must not be extinguished for want of a line that is clear. And it falls to us to give some real substance to the woman's liberty to determine whether to carry her pregnancy to full term.

We conclude the line should be drawn at viability, so that before that time the woman has a right to choose to terminate her pregnancy. . . . The woman's right to terminate her pregnancy before viability is the most central principle of *Roe v. Wade*. It is a rule of law and a component of liberty we cannot renounce.

On the other side of the equation is the interest of the State in the protection of potential life. The *Roe* Court recognized the State's "important and legitimate interest in protecting the potentiality of human life." The weight to be given this state interest, not the strength of the woman's interest, was the difficult question faced in *Roe*. . . .

Yet it must be remembered that *Roe v. Wade* speaks with clarity in establishing not only the woman's liberty but also the State's "important and legitimate interest in potential life." That portion of the decision in *Roe* has been given too little acknowledgment and implementation by the Court in its subsequent cases. Those cases decided that any regulation touching upon the abortion decision must survive strict scrutiny, to be sustained only if drawn in narrow terms to further a compelling state interest. Not all of the cases decided under that formulation can be reconciled with the holding in *Roe* itself that the State has legitimate interests in the health of the woman and in protecting the potential life within her. In resolving this tension, we choose to rely upon *Roe*, as against the later cases.

. . .

We reject the trimester framework, which we do not consider to be part of the essential holding of *Roe*. Measures aimed at ensuring that a woman's choice contemplates the consequences for the fetus do not necessarily interfere with the right recognized in Roe, although those measures have been found to be inconsistent with the rigid trimester framework announced in that case. A logical reading of the central holding in *Roe* itself, and a necessary reconciliation of the liberty of the woman and the interest of the State in promoting prenatal life, require, in our view, that we abandon the trimester framework as a rigid prohibition on all pre-viability regulation aimed at the protection of fetal life. The trimester framework suffers from these basic flaws: in its formulation it misconceives the nature of the pregnant woman's interest; and in practice it undervalues the State's interest in potential life, as recognized in *Roe*.

As our jurisprudence relating to all liberties save perhaps abortion has recognized, not every law which makes a right more difficult to exercise is, *ipso facto*, an infringement of that right. An example clarifies the point. We have held that not every ballot access limitation amounts to an infringement of the right to vote. Rather, the States are granted substantial flexibility in establishing the framework within which voters choose the candidates for whom they wish to vote.

The abortion right is similar. Numerous forms of state regulation might have the incidental effect of increasing the cost or decreasing the availability of medical care, whether for abortion or any other medical procedure. The fact that a law which serves a valid purpose, one not designed to strike at the right itself, has the incidental effect of making it more difficult or more expensive to procure an abortion cannot be enough to invalidate it. Only where state regulation imposes an undue burden on a woman's ability to make this decision does the power of the State reach into the heart of the liberty protected by the Due Process Clause.

. . .

Not all governmental intrusion is of necessity unwarranted; and that brings us to the other basic flaw in the trimester framework: even in *Roe*'s terms, in practice it undervalues the State's interest in the potential life within the woman. *Roe v. Wade* was express in its recognition of the State's "important and legitimate interest(s) in preserving and protecting the health of the pregnant woman [and] in protecting the potentiality of human life." The trimester framework, however, does not fulfill *Roe*'s own promise that the State has an interest in protecting fetal life or potential life. *Roe* began the contradiction by using the trimester framework to forbid any regulation of abortion designed to advance that interest before viability. Before viability, *Roe* and subsequent cases treat all governmental attempts to influence a woman's decision on behalf of the potential life within her as unwarranted. This treatment is, in our judgment, incompatible with the recognition that there is a substantial state interest in potential life throughout pregnancy.

. . .

A finding of an undue burden is a shorthand for the conclusion that a state regulation has the purpose or effect of placing a substantial obstacle in the path of a woman seeking an abortion of a nonviable fetus. A statute with this purpose is invalid because the means chosen by the State to further the interest in potential life must be calculated to inform the woman's free choice, not hinder it. And a statute which, while furthering the interest in potential life or some other valid state interest, has the effect of placing a substantial obstacle in the path of a woman's choice cannot be considered a permissible means of serving its legitimate ends. . . . In our considered judgment, an undue burden is an unconstitutional burden. . . .

Some guiding principles should emerge. What is at stake is the woman's right to make the ultimate decision, not a right to be insulated from all others in doing so. Regulations which do no more than create a structural mechanism by which the State, or the parent or guardian of a minor, may express profound respect for the life of the unborn are permitted,

if they are not a substantial obstacle to the woman's exercise of the right to choose. Unless it has that effect on her right of choice, a state measure designed to persuade her to choose childbirth over abortion will be upheld if reasonably related to that goal. Regulations designed to foster the health of a woman seeking an abortion are valid if they do not constitute an undue burden.

. . . We give this summary:

(a) To protect the central right recognized by *Roe v. Wade* while at the same time accommodating the State's profound interest in potential life, we will employ the undue burden analysis as explained in this opinion. An undue burden exists, and therefore a provision of law is invalid, if its purpose or effect is to place a substantial obstacle in the path of a woman seeking an abortion before the fetus attains viability.

(b) We reject the rigid trimester framework of *Roe v. Wade*. To promote the State's profound interest in potential life, throughout pregnancy the State may take measures to ensure that the woman's choice is informed, and measures designed to advance this interest will not be invalidated as long as their purpose is to persuade the woman to choose childbirth over abortion. These measures must not be an undue burden on the right.

(c) As with any medical procedure, the State may enact regulations to further the health or safety of a woman seeking an abortion. Unnecessary health regulations that have the purpose or effect of presenting a substantial obstacle to a woman seeking an abortion impose an undue burden on the right.

(d) Our adoption of the undue burden analysis does not disturb the central holding of *Roe v. Wade*, and we reaffirm that holding. Regardless of whether exceptions are made for particular circumstances, a State may not prohibit any woman from making the ultimate decision to terminate her pregnancy before viability.

(e) We also reaffirm *Roe*'s holding that "subsequent to viability, the State in promoting its interest in the potentiality of human life may, if it chooses, regulate, and even proscribe, abortion except where it is necessary, in appropriate medical judgment, for the preservation of the life or health of the mother."

. . .

V

. . .

B

. . . Except in a medical emergency, the statute requires that at least 24 hours before performing an abortion a physician inform the woman of the nature of the procedure, the health risks of the abortion and of childbirth, and the "probable gestational age of the unborn child." The physician or a qualified nonphysician must inform the woman of the availability of printed materials published by the State describing the fetus and providing information about medical assistance for childbirth, information about child support from the father, and a list of agencies which provide adoption and other services as alternatives to abortion. An abortion may not be performed unless the woman certifies in writing that she has been informed of the availability of these printed materials and has been provided them if she chooses to view them.

. . .

To the extent *Akron I* and *Thornburgh* find a constitutional violation when the government requires, as it does here, the giving of truthful, nonmisleading information about the nature of the procedure, the attendant health risks and those of childbirth, and the "probable gestational age" of the fetus, those cases go too far, are inconsistent with *Roe*'s acknowledgment of an important interest in potential life, and are overruled. This is clear even on the very terms of *Akron I* and *Thornburgh*. Those decisions, along with *Danforth*, recognize a substantial government interest justifying a requirement that a woman be apprised of the health risks of abortion and childbirth. It cannot be questioned that psychological well-being is a facet of health. Nor can it be doubted that most women considering an abortion would deem the impact on the fetus relevant, if not dispositive, to the decision. In attempting to ensure that a woman apprehend the full consequences of her decision, the State furthers the legitimate purpose of reducing the risk that a woman may elect an abortion, only to discover later, with devastating psychological consequences, that her decision was not fully informed. If the information the State requires to be made available to the woman is truthful and not misleading, the requirement may be permissible.

We also see no reason why the State may not require doctors to inform a woman seeking an abortion of the availability of materials relating to the consequences to the fetus, even when those consequences have no direct relation to her health. An example illustrates the point. We would think it constitutional for the State to require that in order for there to be informed consent to a kidney transplant operation the recipient must be supplied with information about risks to the donor as well as risks to himself or herself. . . .

. . .

Our analysis of Pennsylvania's 24-hour waiting period between the provision of the information deemed necessary to informed consent and the performance of an abortion under the undue burden standard requires us to reconsider the premise behind the decision in *Akron I* invalidating a parallel requirement. In *Akron I* we said: "Nor are we convinced that the State's legitimate concern that the woman's decision be informed is reasonably served by requiring a 24-hour delay as a matter of course." We consider that conclusion to be wrong. The idea that important decisions will be more informed and deliberate if they follow some period of reflection does not strike us as unreasonable, particularly where the statute directs that important information become part of the background of the decision. . . . In theory, at least, the waiting period is a reasonable measure to implement the State's interest in protecting the life of the unborn, a measure that does not amount to an undue burden.

Whether the mandatory 24-hour waiting period is nonetheless invalid because in practice it is a substantial obstacle to a woman's choice to terminate her pregnancy is a closer question. The findings of fact by the District Court indicate that because of the distances many women must travel to reach an abortion provider, the practical effect will often be a delay of much more than a day because the waiting period requires that a woman seeking an abortion make at least two visits to the doctor. The District Court also found that in many instances this will increase the exposure of women seeking abortions to "the harassment and hostility of anti-abortion protestors demonstrating outside a clinic." As a result, the District Court found that for those women who have the fewest financial resources, those who must travel long distances, and those who have difficulty explaining their whereabouts to husbands, employers, or others, the 24-hour waiting period will be "particularly burdensome."

These findings are troubling in some respects, but they do not demonstrate that the waiting period constitutes an undue burden. We do not doubt that, as the District Court held, the waiting period has the effect of "increasing the cost and risk of delay of abortions," but the District Court did not conclude that the increased costs and potential delays amount to substantial obstacles. . . .

We also disagree with the District Court's conclusion that the "particularly burdensome" effects of the waiting period on some women require its invalidation. A particular burden is not of necessity a substantial obstacle. Whether a burden falls on a particular group is a distinct inquiry from whether it is a substantial obstacle even as to the women in that group. And the District Court did not conclude that the waiting period is such an obstacle even for the women who are most burdened by it. Hence, on the record before us, and in the context of this facial challenge, we are not convinced that the 24-hour waiting period constitutes an undue burden.

...

C

Section 3209 of Pennsylvania's abortion law provides, except in cases of medical emergency, that no physician shall perform an abortion on a married woman without receiving a signed statement from the woman that she has notified her spouse that she is about to undergo an abortion. The woman has the option of providing an alternative signed statement certifying that her husband is not the man who impregnated her; that her husband could not be located; that the pregnancy is the result of spousal sexual assault which she has reported; or that the woman believes that notifying her husband will cause him or someone else to inflict bodily injury upon her. A physician who performs an abortion on a married woman without receiving the appropriate signed statement will have his or her license revoked, and is liable to the husband for damages.

[The opinion presented the District Court's findings of fact and various studies documenting the prevalence of domestic violence.]

...

This information and the District Court's findings reinforce what common sense would suggest. In well-functioning marriages, spouses discuss important intimate decisions such as whether to bear a child. But there are millions of women in this country who are the victim of regular physical and psychological abuse at the hands of their husbands. Should these women become pregnant, they may have very good reasons for not wishing to inform their husbands of their decision to obtain an abortion. Many may have justifiable fears of physical abuse, but may be no less fearful of the consequences of reporting prior abuse to the Commonwealth of Pennsylvania. Many may have a reasonable fear that notifying their husbands will provoke further instances of child abuse; these women are not exempt from [the Act's] notification requirement. Many may fear devastating forms of psychological abuse from the husbands, including verbal harassment, threats of future violence, the destruction of possessions, physical confinement to the home, the withdrawal of financial support, or the disclosure of the abortion to family and friends. These methods of psychological abuse may act as even more of a deterrent to notification than the possibility of physical violence, but women who are the victims of the abuse are not exempt from [the Act's] notification requirement. And many women who are pregnant as a result of sexual assaults by their husbands will be unable to avail themselves of the exception for spousal sexual assault because

the exception requires that the woman have notified law enforcement authorities within 90 days of the assault, and her husband will be notified of her report once an investigation begins. If anything in this field is certain, it is that victims of spousal sexual assault are extremely reluctant to report the abuse to the government; hence, a great many spousal rape victims will not be exempt from the notification requirement.

The spousal notification requirement is thus likely to prevent a significant number of women from obtaining an abortion. It does not merely make abortions a little more difficult or expensive to obtain; for many women, it will impose a substantial obstacle. We must not blind ourselves to the fact that the significant number of women who fear for their safety and the safety of their children are likely to be deterred from procuring an abortion as surely as if the Commonwealth had outlawed abortion in all cases.

...

This conclusion is in no way inconsistent with our decision upholding parental notification or consent requirements. Those enactments, and our judgment that they are constitutional, are based on the quite reasonable assumption that minors will benefit from consultation with their parents and that children will often not realize that their parents have their best interests at heart. We cannot adopt a parallel assumption about adult women.

...

In keeping with our rejection of the common-law understanding of a woman's role within the family, the Court held in Danforth that the Constitution does not permit a State to require a married woman to obtain her husband's consent before undergoing an abortion. The principles that guided the Court in Danforth should be our guides today. For the great many women who are victims of abuse inflicted by their husbands, or whose children are the victims of such abuse, a spousal notice require requirement enables the husband to wield an effective veto over his wife's decision. Whether the prospect of notification itself deters such women from seeking abortions, or whether the husband, through physical force or psychological pressure or economic coercion, prevents his wife from obtaining an abortion until it is too late, the notice requirement will often be tantamount to the veto found unconstitutional in Danforth. The women most affected by this law—those who must reasonably fear the consequences of notifying their husbands that they are pregnant—are in the gravest danger.

...

[Parts V-D and V-E of the opinion concluded that the informed parental consent and recordkeeping and reporting requirements (except one pertaining to spousal notification) were constitutional.]

VI

Our Constitution is a covenant running from the first generation of Americans to us and then to future generations. It is a coherent succession. Each generation must learn anew that the Constitution's written terms embody ideas and aspirations that must survive more ages than one. We accept our responsibility not to retreat from interpreting the full meaning of the covenant in light of all of our precedents. We invoke it once again to define the freedom guaranteed by the Constitution's own promise, the promise of liberty.

. . .

Justice STEVENS, concurring in part and dissenting in part.

The portion of the Court's opinion that I have joined are more important than those with which I disagree. I shall therefore first comment on significant areas of agreement, and then explain the limited character of my disagreement.

I

The Court is unquestionably correct in concluding that the doctrine of *stare decisis* has controlling significance in a case of this kind, notwithstanding an individual justice's concerns about the merits. The central holding of *Roe v. Wade* has been a "part of our law" for almost two decades. It was a natural sequel to the protection of individual liberty established in *Griswold v. Connecticut*. The societal costs of overruling *Roe* at this late date would be enormous. *Roe* is an integral part of a correct understanding of both the concept of liberty and the basic equality of men and women.

. . .

II

My disagreement with the joint opinion begins with its understanding of the trimester framework established in *Roe*. Contrary to the suggestion of the joint opinion, it is not a "contradiction" to recognize that the State may have a legitimate interest in potential human life and, at the same time, to conclude that that interest does not justify the regulation of abortion before viability (although other interests, such as maternal health, may). The fact that the State's interest is legitimate does not tell us when, if ever, that interest outweighs the pregnant woman's interest in personal liberty.

. . .

Weighing the State's interest in potential life and the woman's liberty interest, I agree with the joint opinion that the State may "'expres[s] a preference for normal childbirth,'" that the State may take steps to ensure that a

woman's choice "is thoughtful and informed," and that "States are free to enact laws to provide a reasonable framework for a woman to make a decision that has such profound and lasting meaning." Serious questions arise, however, when a State attempts to "persuade the woman to choose childbirth over abortion." Decisional autonomy must limit the State's power to inject into a woman's most personal deliberations its own views of what is best. The State may promote its preferences by funding childbirth, by creating and maintaining alternatives to abortion, and by espousing the virtues of family; but it must respect the individual's freedom to make such judgments.

. . .

Those sections [which] require a physician or counselor to provide the woman with a range of materials clearly designed to persuade her to choose not to undergo the abortion [are unconstitutional]. While the State is free, pursuant to § 3208 of the Pennsylvania law, to produce and disseminate such material, the State may not inject such information into the woman's deliberations just as she is weighing such an important choice.

. . . Those sections[ ] which require the physician to inform a woman of the nature and risks of the abortion procedure and the medical risks of carrying to term, are neutral requirements comparable to those imposed in other medical procedures. Those sections indicate no effort by the State to influence the woman's choice in any way. If anything, such requirements *enhance*, rather than skew, the woman's decisionmaking.

III

The 24-hour waiting period . . . raises even more serious concerns. Such a requirement arguably furthers the State's interests in two ways, neither of which is constitutionally permissible.

First, it may be argued that the 24-hour delay is justified by the mere fact that it is likely to reduce the number of abortions, thus furthering the State's interest in potential life. But such an argument would justify any form of coercion that placed an obstacle in the woman's path. The State cannot further its interests by simply wearing down the ability of the pregnant woman to exercise her constitutional right.

Second, it can more reasonably be argued that the 24-hour delay furthers the State's interest in ensuring that the woman's decision is informed and thoughtful. But there is no evidence that the mandated delay benefits women or that it is necessary to enable the physician to convey any relevant information to the patient. The mandatory delay thus appears to rest on outmoded and unacceptable assumptions about the decisionmaking capacity of women. While there are well-established and consistently maintained reasons for the State to view with skepticism the ability of minors to make decisions, none of those reasons applies to an adult woman's decisionmaking ability. Just as we have left behind the belief that a woman must consult her husband before undertaking serious matters, so we must reject the notion that a woman is less capable of deciding matters of gravity.

In the alternative, the delay requirement may be premised on the belief that the decision to terminate a pregnancy is presumptively wrong. This premise is illegitimate. Those who disagree vehemently about the legality and morality of abortion agree about one thing: The decision to terminate a pregnancy is profound and difficult. No person undertakes such a decision lightly—and States may not presume that a woman has failed to reflect adequately merely because her conclusion differs from the State's preference. A woman who has, in the privacy of her thoughts and conscience, weighed the options and made her decision cannot be forced to reconsider all, simply because the State believes she has come to the wrong conclusion.

Part of the constitutional liberty to choose is the equal dignity to which each of us is entitled. A woman who decides to terminate her pregnancy is entitled to the same respect as a woman who decides to carry the fetus to term. The mandatory waiting period denies women that equal respect.

. . .

Accordingly, while I disagree with Parts IV, V-B, and V-D of the joint opinion, I join the remainder of the Court's opinion.

Justice BLACKMUN, concurring in part, concurring in the judgment in part, and dissenting in part.

I join parts I, II, III, V-A, V-C, and VI of the joint opinion of Justices O'CONNOR, KENNEDY, and SOUTER.

Three years ago, in *Webster v. Reproductive Health Serv.*, four Members of this Court appeared poised to "cas[t] into darkness the hopes and visions of every woman in this country" who had come to believe that the Constitution guaranteed her the right to reproductive choice. (BLACKMUN, J., dissenting). All that remained between the promise of *Roe* and the darkness of the plurality was a single, flickering flame. Decisions since *Webster* gave little reason to hope that this flame would cast much light. But now, just when so many expected the darkness to fall, the flame has grown bright.

I do not underestimate the significance of today's joint opinion. Yet I remain steadfast in my belief that the right to reproductive choice is entitled to the full protection afforded by this Court before *Webster*. And I fear for the darkness as four Justices anxiously await the single vote necessary to extinguish the light.

I

Make no mistake, the joint opinion of Justices O'CONNOR, KENNEDY, and SOUTER is an act of personal courage and constitutional principle. In contrast to previous decisions in which Justices O'CONNOR and KENNEDY postponed reconsideration of *Roe v. Wade*, the authors of the joint opinion today join Justice STEVENS and me in concluding that "the essential holding of *Roe* should be retained and once again reaffirmed." In brief, five Members of this Court today recognize that "the Constitution protects a woman's right to terminate her pregnancy in its early stages."

. . .

II

Today, no less than yesterday, the Constitution and decisions of this Court require that a State's abortion restrictions be subjected to the strictest of judicial scrutiny. Our precedents and the joint opinion's principles require us to subject all non-*de minimis* abortion regulations to strict scrutiny. Under this standard, the Pennsylvania statute's provisions requiring content-based counseling, a 24-hour delay, informed parental consent, and reporting of abortion-related information must be invalidated.

A

The Court today reaffirms the long recognized rights of privacy and bodily integrity.

State restrictions on abortion violate a woman's right of privacy in two ways. First, compelled continuation of a pregnancy infringes upon a woman's right to bodily integrity by imposing substantial physical intrusions and significant risks of physical harm. During pregnancy, women experience dramatic physical changes and a wide range of health consequences. Labor and delivery pose additional health risks and physical demands. In short, restrictive abortion laws force women to endure physical invasions far more substantial than those this Court has held to violate the constitutional principle of bodily integrity in other contexts.

Further, when the State restricts a woman's right to terminate her pregnancy, it deprives a woman of the right to make her own decision about reproduction and family planning—critical life choices that this Court long has deemed central to the right to privacy. The decision to terminate or continue a pregnancy has no less an impact on a woman's life than decisions about contraception or marriage. Because motherhood has a dramatic impact on a woman's educational prospects, employment opportunities, and self-determination, restrictive abortion laws deprive her of basic control over her life. For these reasons, "the decision whether or not to beget or bear a child" lies at "the very heart of this cluster of constitutionally protected choices." *Carey v. Population Services, Int'l.*

A State's restrictions on a woman's right to terminate her pregnancy also implicate constitutional guarantees of gender equality. State restrictions on abortion compel women to continue pregnancies they otherwise might terminate. By restricting the right to terminate pregnancies, the State conscripts women's bodies into its service, forcing women to continue their pregnancies, suffer the pains of childbirth, and in most instances, provide years of maternal care. The State does not compensate women for their services; instead, it assumes that they owe this duty as a matter of course. This assumption—that women can simply be forced to accept the "natural" status and incidents of motherhood—appears to rest upon a conception of women's role that has triggered the protection of the Equal Protection Clause. The joint opinion recognizes that these assumptions about women's place in society "are no longer consistent with our understanding of the family, the individual, or the Constitution."

B

The Court has held that limitations on the right of privacy are permissible only if they survive "strict" constitutional scrutiny—that is, only if the governmental entity imposing the restriction can demonstrate that the limitation is both necessary and narrowly tailored to serve a compelling governmental interest. We have applied this principle specifically in the context of abortion regulations.

. . .

In my view, application of [*Roe's*] analytical framework is no less warranted than when it was approved by seven Members of this Court in *Roe*. Strict scrutiny of state limitations on reproductive choice still offers the most secure protection of the woman's right to make her own reproductive decisions, free from state coercion.

. . .

[W]hile a State has "legitimate interests from the outset of the pregnancy in protecting the health of the woman and the life of the fetus that may become a child," legitimate interests are not enough. To overcome the burden of strict scrutiny, the interests must be compelling. The question then is how best to accommodate the State's interest in potential human life with the constitutional liberties of pregnant women. . . . I stand by the views I expressed in *Webster*.

In sum, *Roe's* requirement of strict scrutiny as implemented through a trimester framework should not be disturbed. No other approach has gained a majority, and no other is more protective of the woman's fundamental right. Lastly, no other approach properly accommodates the woman's constitutional right with the State's legitimate interests.

C

Application of the strict scrutiny standard results in the invalidation of all the challenged provisions. Indeed, as this Court has invalidated virtually identical provisions in prior cases, *stare decisis* requires that we again strike them down.

This Court has upheld informed and written consent requirements only where the State has demonstrated that they genuinely further important health-related state concerns. . . .

Measured against these principles, some aspects of the Pennsylvania informed-consent scheme are unconstitutional. While it is unobjectionable for the Commonwealth to require that the patient be informed of the nature of the procedure, the health risks of the abortion and of childbirth, and the probable gestational age of the unborn child, I remain unconvinced that there is a vital state need for insisting that the information be provided by a physician rather than a counselor.

. . . [T]he Act further requires that the physician or a qualified non-physician inform the woman that printed materials are available from the Commonwealth that describe the fetus and provide information about medical assistance for childbirth, information about child support from the father, and a list of agencies offering . . . adoption and other services as alternatives to abortion. *Thornburgh* invalidated biased patient-counseling requirements virtually identical to the one at issue here. What we said of those requirements fully applies in this case. . . .

The 24-hour waiting period following the provision of the foregoing information is also clearly unconstitutional. . . . In *Akron* this Court invalidated a similarly arbitrary or inflexible waiting period because, as here, it furthered no legitimate state interest.

. . . The requirement that women consider this obvious and slanted information for an additional 24 hours contained in these provisions will only influence the woman's decision in improper ways. The vast majority of women will know this information—of the few that do not, it is less likely that their minds will be changed by this information than it will be either by the realization that the State opposes their choice or the need once again to endure abuse and harassment on return to the clinic.

Except in the case of a medical emergency,

§ 3206 requires a physician to obtain the informed consent of a parent or guardian before performing an abortion on an unemancipated minor or an incompetent woman. . . . The requirement of an in-person visit would carry with it the risk of a delay of several days or possibly weeks, even where the parent is willing to consent. While the State has an interest in encouraging parental involvement in the minor's abortion decision, § 3206 is not narrowly drawn to serve that interest.

[Justice Blackmun also concluded that the Act's recordkeeping and reporting requirements are unconstitutional.]

. . .

III

At long last, THE CHIEF JUSTICE and those who have joined him admit it. Gone are the contentions that the issue need not be (or has not been) considered. There, on the first page, for all to see, is what was expected: "We believe that *Roe* was wrongly decided, and that it can and should be overruled consistently with our traditional approach to *stare decisis* in constitutional cases." If there is much reason to applaud the advances made by the joint opinion today, there is far more to fear from THE CHIEF JUSTICE'S opinion.

THE CHIEF JUSTICE'S criticism of *Roe* follows from his stunted conception of individual liberty. While recognizing that the Due Process Clause protects more than simple physical liberty, he then goes on to construe this Court's personal-liberty cases as establishing only a laundry list of particular rights, rather than a principled account of how these particular rights are grounded in a more general right of privacy. This constricted view is reinforced by THE CHIEF JUSTICE'S exclusive reliance on tradition as a source of fundamental rights. . . .

Even more shocking than THE CHIEF JUSTICE'S cramped notion of individual liberty is his complete omission of any discussion of the effects that compelled childbirth and motherhood have on women's lives. The only expression of concern with women's health is purely instrumental—for THE CHIEF JUSTICE, only women's *psychological* health is a concern, and only to the extent that he assumes that every woman who decides to have an abortion does so without serious consideration of the moral implications of their decision. In short, THE CHIEF JUSTICE'S view of the State's compelling interest in maternal health has less to do with health than it does with compelling women to be maternal.

. . .

THE CHIEF JUSTICE'S narrow conception of individual liberty and *stare decisis* leads him to propose the same standard of review proposed by the plurality in *Webster*. "States may regulate abortion procedures in ways rationally related to a legitimate state interest." THE CHIEF JUSTICE then further weakens the test by providing an insurmountable requirement for facial challenges: petitioners must "'show that no set of circumstances exists under which the [provision] would be valid.'" In short, in his view, petitioners must prove that the statute cannot constitutionally be applied to *anyone.* . . .

. . .

But, we are reassured, there is always the protection of the democratic process. While there is much to be praised about our democracy, our country since its founding has recognized that there are certain fundamental liberties that are not to be left to the whims of an election. A woman's right to reproductive choice is one of those fundamental liberties. Accordingly, that liberty need not seek refuge at the ballot box.

IV

In one sense, the Court's approach is worlds apart from that of THE CHIEF JUSTICE and Justice SCALIA. And yet, in another sense, the distance between the two approaches is short—the distance is but a single vote.

I am 83 years old. I cannot remain on this Court forever, and when I do step down, the confirmation process for my successor well may focus on the issue before us today. That, I regret, may be exactly where the choice between the two worlds will be made.

Chief Justice REHNQUIST, with whom Justice WHITE, Justice SCALIA, and Justice THOMAS join, concurring in the judgment in part and dissenting in part.

The joint opinion, following its newly-minted variation on *stare decisis*, retains the outer shell of *Roe v. Wade* but beats a wholesale retreat from the substance of that case. We believe that *Roe* was wrongly decided, and that it can and should be overruled consistently with our traditional approach to *stare decisis* in constitutional cases. We would adopt the approach of the plurality in *Webster v. Reproductive Health Services*, and uphold the challenged provisions of the Pennsylvania statute in their entirety.

I

We agree with the Court of Appeals that our decision in *Roe* is not directly implicated by the Pennsylvania statute, which does not prohibit, but simply regulates abortion. But, as the Court of Appeals found, the state of our post-*Roe* decisional law dealing with the regulation of abortion is confusing and uncertain, indicating that a reexamination of that line of cases is in order. Unfortunately for those who must apply this Court's decisions, the reexamination undertaken today leaves the Court no less divided than beforehand. Although they reject the trimester framework that formed the underpinning of *Roe*, Justices O'CONNOR, KENNEDY, and SOUTER adopt a revised undue burden standard to analyze the challenged regulations. We conclude, however, that such an outcome is an unjustified constitutional compromise, one which leaves the Court in a position to closely scrutinize all types of abortion regulations despite the fact that it lacks the power to do so under the Constitution.

. . .

In *Roe v. Wade*, the Court recognized a "guarantee of personal privacy" which "is broad enough to encompass a woman's decision whether or not to terminate her pregnancy." We are now of the view that, in terming this right fundamental, the Court in *Roe* read the earlier opinions upon which it based its decision much too broadly. Unlike marriage, procreation and contraception, abortion "involves the purposeful termination of potential life." The abortion decision must therefore "be recognized as *sui generis*, different in kind from the others that the Court has protected under the rubric of personal or family privacy and autonomy." *Thornburgh v. American College of Obstetricians and Gynecologists* (WHITE, J., dissenting). One cannot ignore the fact that a woman is not isolated in her pregnancy, and that the decision to abort necessarily involves the destruction of a fetus.

Nor do the historical traditions of the American people support the view that the right to terminate one's pregnancy is "fundamental." The common law which we inherited from England made abortion after "quickening" an offense. At the time of the adoption of the Fourteenth Amendment, statutory prohibitions or restrictions on abortion were commonplace; in 1868, at least 28 of the then-37 States and 8 Territories had statutes banning or limiting abortion. By the turn of the century virtually every State had a law prohibiting or restricting abortion on its books. By the middle of the present century, a liberalization trend had set in. But 21 of the restrictive abortion laws in effect in 1868 were still in effect in 1973 when *Roe* was decided, and an overwhelming majority of the States prohibited abortion unless necessary to preserve the life or health of the mother. On this record, it can scarcely be said that any deeply rooted tradition of relatively unrestricted abortion in our history supported the classification of the right to abortion as "fundamental" under the Due Process Clause of the Fourteenth Amendment.

We think, therefore, both in view of this history and of our decided cases dealing with substantive liberty under the Due Process Clause, that the Court was mistaken in *Roe* when it classified a woman's decision to terminate her pregnancy as a "fundamental right" that could be abridged only in a manner which withstood "strict scrutiny." . . .

. . .

II

The joint opinion of Justices O'CONNOR, KENNEDY, and SOUTER cannot bring itself to say that *Roe* was correct as an original matter, but the authors are of the view that "the immediate question is not the soundness of *Roe*'s resolution of the issue, but the precedential force that must be accorded to its holding." Instead of claiming that *Roe* was correct as a matter of original constitutional interpretation, the opinion therefore contains an elaborate discussion of *stare decisis*. This discussion of the principle of stare decisis appears to be almost entirely dicta, because the joint opinion does not apply that principle in dealing with *Roe*. *Roe* decided that a woman had a fundamental right to an abortion. The joint opinion rejects that view. *Roe* decided that abortion regulations were to be subjected to "strict scrutiny" and could be justified only in the light of "compelling state interest." The joint opinion rejects that view. *Roe* analyzed abortion regulation under a rigid trimester framework, a framework which has guided this Court's decision-making for 19 years. The joint opinion rejects that framework.

Stare decisis is defined in Black's Law Dictionary as meaning "to abide by, or adhere to, decided cases." Whatever the "central holding" of *Roe* that is left after the joint opinion finishes dissecting it is surely not the result of that principle. While purporting to adhere to precedent, the joint opinion instead revises it. *Roe* continues to exist, but only in the way a storefront on a western movie set exists: a mere facade to give the illusion of reality. . . .

In our view, authentic principles of *stare decisis* do not require that any portion of the reasoning in *Roe* be kept intact. "*Stare decisis* is not . . . a universal, inexorable command," especially in cases involving the interpretation of the Federal Constitution. Erroneous decisions in such constitutional cases are uniquely durable, because correction through legislative action, save for constitutional amendment, is impossible. It is therefore our duty to reconsider constitutional interpretations that "depar[t] from a proper understanding" of the Constitution. Our constitutional watch does not cease merely because we have spoken before on an issue; when it becomes clear that a prior constitutional interpretation is unsound we are obliged to reexamine the question.

. . .

The joint opinion . . . turns to what can only be described as an unconventional—and unconvincing—notion of reliance, a view based on the surmise that the availability of abortion since *Roe* has led to "two decades of economic and social developments" that would be undercut if the error of *Roe* were recognized. The joint opinion's assertion of this fact is undeveloped and totally conclusory. In fact, one can not be sure to what economic and social developments the opinion is referring. Surely it is dubious to suggest that women have reached their "places in society" in reliance upon *Roe*, rather than as a result of their determination to obtain higher education and compete with men in the job market, and of society's increasing recognition of their ability to fill positions that were previously thought to be reserved only for men.

In the end, having failed to put forth any evidence to prove any true reliance, the joint opinion's argument is based solely on generalized assertions about the national psyche, on a belief that the people of this country have grown accustomed to the *Roe* decision over the last 19 years and have "ordered their thinking and living around" it. As an initial matter, one might inquire how the joint opinion can view the "central holding" of *Roe* as so deeply rooted in our constitutional culture, when it so casually uproots and disposes of that same decision's trimester framework. Furthermore, at various points in the past, the same could have been said about this Court's erroneous decisions that the Constitution allowed "separate but equal" treatment of minorities, see *Plessy v. Ferguson*, or that "liberty" under the Due Process Clause protected "freedom of contract." See *Adkins v. Children's Hospital of D.C.*; *Lochner v. New York*. The "separate but equal" doctrine lasted 58 years after *Plessy*, and *Lochner*'s protection of contractual freedom lasted 32 years. However, the simple fact that a generation or more had grown used to these major decisions did not prevent the Court from correcting its errors in those cases, nor should it prevent us from correctly interpreting the Constitution here.

Apparently realizing that conventional *stare decisis* principles do not support its position, the joint opinion advances a belief that retaining a portion of *Roe* is necessary to protect the "legitimacy" of this Court. Because the Court must take care to render decisions "grounded truly in principle," and not simply as political and social compromises, the joint opinion properly declares it to be this Court's duty to ignore the public criticism and protest that may arise as a result of a decision. Few would quarrel with this statement, although it may be doubted that Members of this Court, holding their tenure as they do during constitutional "good behavior," are at all likely to be intimidated by such public protests.

But the joint opinion goes on to state that when the Court "resolve[s] the sort of intensely divisive controversy reflected in *Roe* and those rare, comparable cases," its decision is exempt from reconsideration under established principles of *stare decisis* in constitutional cases. This is so, the joint opinion contends, because in those "intensely divisive" cases the Court has "call[ed] the contending sides of a national controversy to end their national division by accepting a common mandate rooted in the Constitution," and must therefore take special care not to be perceived as "surrender[ing] to political pressure" and continued opposition. This is a truly novel principle, one which is contrary to both the Court's historical practice and to the Court's traditional willingness to tolerate criticism of its opinions. Under this principle, when the Court has ruled on a divisive issue, it is apparently prevented from overruling that decision for the sole reason that it was incorrect, *unless opposition to the original decision has died away.*

. . .

The joint opinion picks out and discusses two prior Court rulings that it believes are of the "intensely divisive" variety, and concludes that they are of comparable dimension to *Roe*. It appears to us very odd indeed that the joint opinion chooses as benchmarks two cases in which the Court chose not to adhere to erroneous constitutional precedent, but instead enhanced its stature by acknowledging and correcting its error, apparently in violation of the joint opinion's "legitimacy" principle. . . . But just as the Court should not respond to that sort of protest by retreating from the decision simply to allay the concerns of the protesters, it should likewise not respond by determining to adhere to the decision at all costs lest it seem to be retreating under fire. Public protests should not alter the normal application of *stare decisis*, lest perfectly lawful protest activity be penalized by the Court itself.

The joint opinion agrees that the Court's stature would have been seriously damaged if in *Brown* and *West Coast Hotel* it had dug in its heels and refused to apply normal principles of *stare decisis* to the earlier decisions. But the opinion contends that the Court was entitled to overrule *Plessy* and *Lochner* in those cases, despite the existence of opposition to the original decisions, only because both the Nation and the Court had learned new lessons in the interim. This is at best a feebly supported, post hoc rationalization for those decisions.

. . .

When the Court finally recognized its error in *West Coast Hotel*, it did not engage in the *post hoc* rationalization that the joint opinion attributes to it today; it did not state that *Lochner* had been based on an economic view that had fallen into disfavor, and that it therefore should be overruled. Chief Justice Hughes in his opinion for the Court simply recognized what Justice Holmes had previously recognized in his *Lochner* dissent, that "[t]he Constitution does not speak of freedom of contract." *West Coast Hotel Co. v. Parrish*; *Lochner v. New York*, (Holmes, J., dissenting). Although the Court did acknowledge in the last paragraph of its opinion the state of affairs during the then-current Depression, the theme of the opinion is that the Court had been mistaken as a matter of constitutional law when it embraced "freedom of contract" 32 years previously.

. . .

[Similarly,] the Court in *Brown* simply recognized, as Justice Harlan had recognized beforehand, that the Fourteenth Amendment does not permit racial segregation. The rule of *Brown* is not tied to popular opinion about the evils of segregation; it is a judgment that the Equal Protection Clause does not permit racial segregation, no matter whether the public might come to believe that it is beneficial. On that ground it stands, and on that ground alone the Court was justified in properly concluding that the *Plessy* Court had erred.

There is also a suggestion in the joint opinion that the propriety of overruling a "divisive" decision depends in part on whether "most people" would now agree that it should be overruled. Either the demise of opposition or its progression to substantial popular agreement apparently is required to allow the Court to reconsider a divisive decision. How such agreement would be ascertained, short of a public opinion poll, the joint opinion does not say. But surely even the suggestion is totally at war with the idea of "legitimacy" in whose name it is invoked. The Judicial Branch derives its legitimacy, not from following public opinion, but from deciding by its best lights whether legislative enactments of the popular branches of Government comport with the Constitution. The doctrine of stare decisis is an adjunct of this duty, and should be no more subject to the vagaries of public opinion than is the basic judicial task.

There are other reasons why the joint opinion's discussion of legitimacy is unconvincing as well. In assuming that the Court is perceived as "surrender[ing] to political pressure" when it overrules a controversial decision, the joint opinion forgets that there are two sides to any controversy. The joint opinion asserts that, in order to protect its legitimacy, the Court must refrain from overruling a controversial decision lest it be viewed as favoring those who oppose the decision. But a decision to adhere to prior precedent is subject to the same criticism, for in such a case one can easily argue that the Court is responding to those who have demonstrated in favor of the original deci-

sion. The decision in *Roe* has engendered large demonstrations, including repeated marches on this Court and on Congress, both in opposition to and in support of that opinion. A decision either way on *Roe* can therefore be perceived as favoring one group or the other. But this perceived dilemma arises only if one assumes, as the joint opinion does, that the Court should make its decisions with a view toward speculative public perceptions. If one assumes instead, as the Court surely did in both *Brown* and *West Coast Hotel*, that the Court's legitimacy is enhanced by faithful interpretation of the Constitution irrespective of public opposition, such self-engendered difficulties may be put to one side.

. . .

The end result of the joint opinion's paeans of praise for legitimacy is the enunciation of a brand new standard for evaluating state regulation of a woman's right to abortion—the "undue burden" standard. As indicated above, *Roe v. Wade* adopted a "fundamental right" standard under which state regulations could survive only if they met the requirement of "strict scrutiny." While we disagree with that standard, it at least had a recognized basis in constitutional law at the time *Roe* was decided. The same cannot be said for the "undue burden" standard, which is created largely out of whole cloth by the authors of the joint opinion. It is a standard which even today does not command the support of a majority of this Court. And it will not, we believe, result in the sort of "simple limitation," easily applied, which the joint opinion anticipates. In sum, it is a standard which is not built to last.

In evaluating abortion regulations under that standard, judges will have to decide whether they place a "substantial obstacle" in the path of a woman seeking an abortion. In that this standard is based even more on a judge's subjective determinations than was the trimester framework, the standard will do nothing to prevent "judges from roaming at large in the constitutional field" guided only by their personal views. Because the undue burden standard is plucked from nowhere, the question of what is a "substantial obstacle" to abortion will undoubtedly engender a variety of conflicting views. . . .

. . .

The sum of the joint opinion's labors in the name of *stare decisis* and "legitimacy" is this: *Roe v. Wade* stands as a sort of judicial Potemkin Village, which may be pointed out to passersby as a monument to importance of adhering to precedent. But behind the facade, an entirely new method of analysis, without any roots in constitutional law, is imported to decide the constitutionality of state laws regulating abortion. Neither *stare decisis* nor "legitimacy" are truly served by such an effort.

We have stated above our belief that the Constitution does not subject state abortion regulations to heightened scrutiny. Accordingly, we think that the correct analysis is that set forth by the plurality opinion in *Webster*. A woman's interest in having an abortion is a form of liberty protected by the Due Process Clause, but States may regulate abortion procedures in ways rationally related to a legitimate state interest.

III

[Rehnquist agreed with the Joint Opinion that the Act's informed consent and parental consent provisions should be upheld.]

. . .

Because this is a facial challenge to the Act, it is insufficient for petitioners to show that the [spousal] notification provision "might operate unconstitutionally under some conceivable set of circumstances." Thus, it is not enough for petitioners to show that, in some "worst-case" circumstances, the notice provision will operate as a grant of veto power to husbands. Because they are making a facial challenge to the provision, they must "show that no set of circumstances exists under which the [provision] would be valid." This they have failed to do. . . .

The question before us is therefore whether the spousal notification requirement rationally furthers any legitimate state interests. We conclude that it does. First, a husband's interests in procreation within marriage and in the potential life of his unborn child are certainly substantial ones. The State itself has legitimate interests both in protecting these interests of the father and in protecting the potential life of the fetus, and the spousal notification requirement is reasonably related to advancing those state interests. By providing that a husband will usually know of his spouse's intent to have an abortion, the provision makes it more likely that the husband will participate in deciding the fate of his unborn child, a possibility that might otherwise have been denied him. This participation might in some cases result in a decision to proceed with the pregnancy. . . .

The State also has a legitimate interest in promoting "the integrity of the marital relationship." This Court has previously recognized "the importance of the marital relationship in our society." In our view, the spousal notice requirement is a rational attempt by the State to improve truthful communication between spouses and encourage collaborative decisionmaking, and thereby fosters marital integrity. . . . [I]t is unrealistic to assume that every husband-wife relationship is either (1) so perfect that this type of truthful and important communication will take place as a matter of course, or (2) so imperfect that, upon notice, the husband will react selfishly, violently, or contrary to the best interests of his wife. The spousal notice provision will admittedly be unnecessary in some circumstances, and possibly harmful in others, but "the existence of particular cases in which a feature of a statute performs no function (or is even counterproductive) ordinarily does not render the statute unconstitutional or even constitutionally suspect." *Thornburgh v. American College of Obstetricians and Gynecologists* (WHITE, J., dissenting). The Pennsylvania Legislature was in a position to weigh the likely benefits of the provision against its likely adverse effects, and presumably concluded, on balance, that the provision would be beneficial. Whether this was a wise decision or not, we cannot say that it was irrational. We therefore conclude that the spousal notice provision comports with the Constitution.

[Rehnquist concluded that the Act's recordkeeping and reporting requirements also rationally further legitimate state interests.]

. . .

IV

For the reasons stated, we therefore would hold that each of the challenged provisions of the Pennsylvania statute is consistent with the Constitution. It bears emphasis that our conclusion in this regard does not carry with it any necessary approval of these regulations. Our task is, as always, to decide only whether the challenged provisions of a law comport with the United States Constitution. If, as we believe, these do, their wisdom as a matter of public policy is for the people of Pennsylvania to decide.

Justice SCALIA, with whom THE CHIEF JUSTICE, Justice WHITE, and Justice THOMAS join, concurring in the judgement in part and dissenting in part.

My views on this matter are unchanged from those I set forth in my separate opinions in *Webster v. Reproductive Health Services* and *Ohio v. Akron Center for Reproductive Health*. The States may, if they wish, permit abortion-on-demand, but the Constitution does not *require* them to do so. The permissibility of abortion, and the limitations upon it, are to be resolved like most important questions in our democracy; by citizens trying to persuade one another and then voting. . . . A State's choice between two positions on which reasonable people can disagree is constitutional even when (as is often the case) it intrudes upon a "liberty" in the absolute sense. Laws against bigamy, for example—which entire societies of reasonable people disagree with—intrude upon men and women's liberty to marry and live with one another. But bigamy happens not to be a liberty specially "protected" by the Constitution.

That is, quite simply, the issue in this case: not whether the power of a woman to abort her unborn child is a "liberty" in the absolute sense; or even whether it is a liberty of great importance to many women. Of course it is both. The issue is whether it is a liberty protected by the Constitution of the United States. I am sure it is not. I reach that conclusion not because of anything so exalted as my views concerning the "concept of existence, of meaning, of the universe, and of the mystery of human life." Rather, I reach it for the same reason I reach the conclusion that bigamy is not constitutionally protected—because of two simple facts: (1) the Constitution says absolutely nothing about it, and (2) the longstanding traditions of American society have permitted it to be legally proscribed.

. . .

Beyond that brief summary of the essence of my position, I will not swell the United States Reports with repetition of what I have said before; and applying the rational basis test, I would uphold the Pennsylvania statute in its entirety. I must, however, respond to a few of the more outrageous arguments in today's opinion, which it is beyond human nature to have unanswered. I shall discuss each of them under a quotation from the Court's opinion to which they pertain.

"The inescapable fact is that adjudication of substantive due process claims may call upon the Court in interpreting the Constitution to exercise that same capacity which by tradition courts always have exercised: reasoned judgment."

Assuming that the question before us is to be resolved at such a level of philosophical abstraction, in such isolation from the traditions of American society, as by simply applying "reasoned judgment," I do not see how that could possibly have produced the answer the Court arrived at in *Roe v. Wade*. Today's opinion describes the methodology of *Roe*, quite accurately, as weighing against the woman's interest the State's "'important and legitimate interest in protecting the potentiality of human life.'" But "reasoned judgment" does not begin by begging the question, as *Roe* and subsequent cases unquestionably did by assuming that what the State is protecting is the mere "potentiality of human life." The whole argument of abortion opponents is that what the Court calls the fetus and what others call the unborn child *is a human life*. Thus, whatever answer *Roe* came up with after conducting its "balancing" is bound to be wrong, unless it is correct that the human fetus is in some critical sense merely potentially human. There is of

course no way to determine that as a legal matter; it is in fact a value judgment. Some societies have considered newborn children not yet human, or the incompetent elderly no longer so.

The authors of the joint opinion, of course, do not squarely contend that *Roe v. Wade* was a *correct* application of "reasoned judgment"; merely that it must be followed, because of *stare decisis*. But in their exhaustive discussion of all the factors that go into the determination of when *stare decisis* should be observed and when disregarded, they never mention "how wrong was the decision on its face?" Surely, if "[t]he Court's power lies . . . in its legitimacy, a product of substance and perception," the "substance" part of the equation demands that plain error be acknowledged and eliminated. *Roe* was plainly wrong—even on the Court's methodology of "reasoned judgment," and even more so (of course) if the proper criteria of text and tradition are applied.

The emptiness of the "reasoned judgment" that produced *Roe* is displayed in plain view by the fact that, after more than 19 years of effort by some of the brightest (and most determined) legal minds in the country, after more than 10 cases upholding abortion rights in this Court, and after dozens upon dozens of *amicus* briefs submitted in this and other cases, the best the Court can do to explain how it is that the word "liberty" *must* be thought to include the right to destroy human fetuses is to rattle off a collection of adjectives that simply decorate a value judgment and conceal a political choice. . . . Those adjectives might be applied, for example, to homosexual sodomy, polygamy, adult incest, and suicide, all of which are equally "intimate" and "deep[ly] personal" decisions involving "personal autonomy and bodily integrity," and all of which can constitutionally be proscribed because it is our unquestionable constitutional tradition that they are proscribable. It is not reasoned judgment that supports the Court's decision; only personal predilection. . . .

"Liberty finds no refuge in jurisprudence of doubt."

One might have feared to encounter this august and sonorous phrase in an opinion defending the real *Roe v. Wade*, rather than the revised version fabricated today by the authors of the joint opinion. The shortcomings of *Roe* did not include lack of clarity: Virtually all regulation of abortion before the third trimester was invalid. But to come across this phrase in the joint opinion—which calls upon federal district judges to apply an "undue burden" standard as doubtful in application as it is unprincipled in origin—is really more than one should have to bear.

. . .

The ultimately standardless nature of the "undue burden" inquiry is a reflection of the underlying fact that the concept has no principled or coherent legal basis. . . . I agree, indeed I have forcefully urged, that a law of general applicability which places only an incidental burden on a fundamental right does not infringe that right, but that principle does not establish the quite different (and quite dangerous) proposition that a law which directly regulates a fundamental right will not be found to violate the Constitution unless it imposes an "undue burden." It is that, of course, which is at issue here: Pennsylvania has consciously and directly regulated conduct that our cases have held is constitutionally protected. The appropriate analogy, therefore, is that of a state law requiring purchasers of religious books to endure a 24-hour waiting period, or to pay a nominal additional tax of 1 [cent]. The joint opinion cannot possibly be correct in suggesting that we would uphold such legislation on the ground that it does not impose a "substantial obstacle" to the exercise of First Amendment rights. The "undue burden" standard is not at all the generally applicable principle the joint opinion pretends it to be; rather, it is a unique concept created specially for this case, to preserve some judicial foothold in this illgotten territory. In claiming otherwise, the three Justices show their willingness to place all constitutional rights at risk in the effort to preserve what they deem the "central holding in *Roe*."

. . .

To the extent I can discern any meaningful content in the "undue burden" standard as applied in the joint opinion, it appears to be that a State may not regulate abortion in such a way as to reduce significantly its incidence. Thus, despite flowery rhetoric about the State's "substantial" and "profound" interest in "potential human life," and criticism of *Roe* for undervaluing that interest, the joint opinion permits the State to pursue that interest only so long as it is not too successful. . . . Reason finds no refuge in this jurisprudence of confusion.

"While we appreciate the weight of the arguments . . . that *Roe* should be overruled, the reservations any of us may have in reaffirming the central holding of *Roe* are outweighed by the explication of individual liberty we have given combined with the force of *stare decisis*."

The Court's reliance upon *stare decisis* can best be described as contrived. It insists upon the necessity of adhering not to all of *Roe*, but only to what it calls the "central holding." It seems to me that stare decisis ought to be applied even to the doctrine of *stare decisis*, and I confess never to have heard of this new, keep-what-you-want-and-throw-away-the-rest version. I wonder whether, as applied to *Marbury*

v. Madison, for example, the new version of *stare decisis* would be satisfied if we allowed courts to review the constitutionality of only those statutes that (like the one in *Marbury*) pertain to the jurisdiction of the courts.

I am certainly not in a good position to dispute that the Court has saved the "central holding" of *Roe*, since to do that effectively I would have to know what the Court has saved, which in turn would require me to understand (as I do not) what the "undue burden" test means. I must confess, however, that I have always thought, and I think a lot of other people have always thought, that the arbitrary trimester framework, which the Court today discards, was quite as central to *Roe* as the arbitrary viability test, which the Court today retains. It seems particularly ungrateful to carve the trimester framework out of the core of *Roe*, since its very rigidity (in sharp contrast to the utter indeterminability of the "undue burden" test) is probably the only reason the Court is able to say, in urging *stare decisis*, that *Roe* "has in no sense proven 'unworkable.'"

"Where, in the performance of its judicial duties, the Court decides a case in such a way as to resolve the sort of intensely divisive controversy reflected in *Roe* . . . , its decision has a dimension that the resolution of the normal case does not carry. It is the dimension present whenever the Court's interpretation of the Constitution calls the contending sides of a national controversy to end their national division by accepting a common mandate rooted in the Constitution."

The Court's description of the place of *Roe* in the social history of the United States is unrecognizable. Not only did *Roe* not, as the Court suggests, *resolve* the deeply divisive issue of abortion; it did more than anything else to nourish it, by elevating it to the national level where it is infinitely more difficult to resolve. National politics were not plagued by abortion protests, national abortion lobbying, or abortion marches on Congress, before *Roe v. Wade* was decided. Profound disagreement existed among our citizens over the issue—as it does over other issues, such as the death penalty—but that disagreement was being worked out at the state level. As with many other issues, the division of sentiment within each State was not as closely balanced as it was among the population of the Nation as a whole, meaning not only that more people would be satisfied with the results of state-by-state resolution, but also that those results would be more stable. Pre-*Roe* moreover, political compromise was possible.

Roe's mandate for abortion-on-demand destroyed the compromises of the past, rendered compromise impossible for the future, and required the entire issue to be resolved uniformly, at the national level. At the same time, *Roe* created a vast new class of abortion consumers and abortion proponents by eliminating the moral opprobrium that had attached to the act. ("If the Constitution *guarantees* abortion, how can it be bad?"—not an accurate line of thought, but a natural one.) Many favor all of those developments, and it is not for me to say that they are wrong. But to portray Roe as the statesmanlike "settlement" of a divisive issue, a jurisprudential Peace of Westphalia that is worth preserving, is nothing less than Orwellian. *Roe* fanned into life an issue that has inflamed our national politics in general, and has obscured with its smoke the selection of Justices to this Court in particular, ever since. And by keeping us in the abortion-umpiring business, it is the perpetuation of that disruption, rather than of any *pax Roeana*, that the Court's new majority decrees.

"[To] overrule under fire ... would subvert the Court's legitimacy....

To all those who will be ... tested by following, the Court implicitly undertakes to remain steadfast....

"[The American people's] belief in themselves as ... a people [who aspire to live according to the rule of law] is not readily separate from their understanding of the Court invested with the authority to decide their constitutional cases and speak before all others for their constitutional ideals. If the Court's legitimacy should be undermined, then, so would the country be in its very ability to see itself through its constitutional ideals."

The imperial Judiciary lives. It is instructive to compare this Nietzschean vision of us unelected, life-tenured judges—leading a Volk who will be "tested by following," and whose very "belief in themselves" is mystically bound up in their "understanding" of a Court that "speak[s] before all others for their constitutional ideals"—with the somewhat more modest role envisioned for these lawyers by the Founders.

> "The judiciary ... has ... no direction either of the strength or of the wealth of the society, and can take no active resolution whatever. It may truly be said to have neither FORCE nor WILL but merely judgment...." The Federalist No. 78.

Or, again, to compare this ecstasy of a Supreme Court in which there is, especially on controversial matters, no shadow of change or hint of alteration ... with the more democratic views of a more humble man:

> "[T]he candid citizen must confess that if the policy of the Government upon vital questions affecting the whole people is to be irrevocably fixed by decisions of the Supreme Court, ... the people will have ceased to be their own rulers, having to that extent practically resigned their Government into the hands of that eminent tribunal." A. Lincoln, First Inaugural Address (Mar. 4, 1861).

. . .

I cannot agree with, indeed I am appalled by, the Court's suggestion that the decision whether to stand by an erroneous constitutional decision must be strongly influenced—*against* overruling, no less—by the substantial and continuing public opposition the decision has generated. The Court's judgment that any other course would "subvert the Court's legitimacy" must be another consequence of reading the error-filled history book that described the deeply divided country brought together by *Roe*. In my history-book, the Court was covered with dishonor and deprived of legitimacy by *Dred Scott v. Sandford*, an erroneous (and widely opposed) opinion that it did not abandon, rather than by *West Coast Hotel Co. v. Parrish*, which produced the famous "switch in time" from the Court's erroneous (and widely opposed) constitutional opposition to the social measures of the New Deal. (Both *Dred Scott* and one line of the cases resisting the New Deal rested upon the concept of "substantive due process" that the Court praises and employs today. Indeed, *Dred Scott* was "very possibly the first application of substantive due process in the Supreme Court, the original precedent for *Lochner v. New York* and *Roe v. Wade*." D. Currie, The Constitution in the Supreme Court 271 (1985).

But whether it would "subvert the Court's legitimacy" or not, the notion that we would decide a case differently from the way we otherwise would have in order to show that we can stand firm against public disapproval is frightening. It is a bad enough idea, even in the head of someone like me, who believes that the text of the Constitution, and our traditions, say what they say and there is no fiddling with them. But when it is in the mind of a Court that believes the Constitution has an evolving meaning; that the Ninth Amendment's reference to "othe[r]" rights is not a disclaimer, but a charter for action; and that the function of this Court is to "speak before all others for [the people's] constitutional ideals" unrestrained by meaningful text or tradition—then the notion that the Court must adhere to a decision for as long as the decision faces "great opposition" and the Court is "under fire" acquires a character of almost czarist arrogance. We are offended by these marchers who descend upon us, every year on the anniversary of *Roe*, to protest our saying that the Constitution requires what our society has never thought the Constitution requires. These people who refuse to be "tested by following" must be taught a lesson. We have no Cossacks, but at least we can stubbornly refuse to abandon an erroneous opinion that we might otherwise change—to show how little they intimidate us.

... Instead of engaging in the hopeless task of predicting public perception—a job not for lawyers but for political campaign managers—the Justices should do what is legally right by asking two questions (1) Was *Roe* correctly decided? (2) Has *Roe* succeeded in producing a settled body of law? If the answer to both questions is no, *Roe* should undoubtedly be overruled.

There is a poignant aspect to today's opinion. Its length, and what might be called its epic tone, suggest that its authors believe they are bringing to an end a troublesome era in the history of our Nation and of our Court....

There comes vividly to mind a portrait by Emanuel Leutze that hangs in the Harvard Law School: Roger Brooke Taney, painted in 1859, the 82nd year of his life, the 24th of his Chief Justiceship, the second after his opinion in *Dred Scott*. He is all in black, sitting in a shadowed red armchair, left hand resting upon a pad of paper in his lap, right hand hanging limply, almost lifelessly, beside the inner arm of the chair. He sits facing the viewer, and staring straight out. There seems to be on his face, and in his deep-set eyes, an expression of profound sadness and disillusionment. Perhaps he always looked that way, even when dwelling upon the happiest of thoughts. But those of us who know how the lustre of his great Chief Justiceship came to be eclipsed by Dred Scott cannot help believing that he had that case—its already apparent consequences for the Court, and its soon-to-be-played-out consequences for the Nation—burning on his mind. I expect that two years earlier he, too, had thought himself "call[ing] the contending sides of national controversy to end their national division by accepting a common mandate rooted in the Constitution."

It is no more realistic for us in this case, than it was for him in that, to think that an issue of the sort they both involved—an issue involving life and death, freedom and subjugation—can be "speedily and finally settled" by the Supreme Court, as President James Buchanan in his inaugural address said the issue of slavery in the territories would be. Quite to the contrary, by foreclosing all democratic outlet for the deep passions this issue arouses, by banishing the issue from the political forum that gives all participants, even the losers, the satisfaction of a fair hearing and an honest fight, by continuing the imposition of a rigid national rule instead of allowing for regional differences, the Court merely prolongs and intensifies the anguish.

We should get out of this area, where we have no right to be, and where we do neither ourselves nor the country any good by remaining.

Although the joint opinion claimed to retain *Roe*'s "essential holding," it discarded a substantial portion of the *Roe* decision. It rejected *Roe*'s holding that the right to terminate a pregnancy is fundamental; that state restrictions on abortion should therefore be subjected to strict scrutiny; and that abortion regulation should be analyzed under the trimester framework. The joint opinion replaced *Roe*'s fundamental rights analysis with the undue burden standard. Moreover, the joint opinion underscored the state's interest in protecting the life of the fetus from the outset of the pregnancy. The Court's four most conservative justices (Rehnquist, Scalia, Thomas and White) agreed; but they would have overturned *Roe* altogether. Justice Blackmun, the author of the *Roe* opinion, was the sole defender of the full extent of constitutional protection that *Roe* guaranteed. After *Casey*, future abortion jurisprudence will focus on defining what constitutes an "unduly burdensome" interference with abortion, as well as the battle over the retention of *Roe*.

DER: The abortion cases following *Roe* demonstrate that the Court's understanding of privacy has significant limitations. Critics of the concept of privacy note that framing the abortion right as a right merely to be shielded from state intrusion into private choices provides no basis for a constitutional claim to public support for abortions. As the Court explained in *Harris v. McRae*, and affirmed in *Webster* and *Casey*, "although government may not place obstacles in the path of a woman's exercise of her freedom of choice, it need not remove those not of its own creation." Moreover, *Casey*'s undue burden standard allows states to place additional hurdles in the path of poor women seeking abortion services. The Court upheld, for example, Pennsylvania's 24-hour waiting period despite evidence that it increased the cost and risk of delay for low-income women and those living in rural areas. It appears that the justices consider unduly burdensome only those absolute obstacles to choice, such as a husband's veto, that prevent even affluent women from obtaining abortions.

The Court's interpretation of privacy makes abortion a private privilege for those who can afford it, rather than a public right. First, the abstract freedom to choose is of meager value without meaningful options from which to choose and the ability to effectuate one's choice. The traditional concept of privacy makes the false presumption that the right to choose is contained entirely within the individual and not circumscribed by the material conditions of the individual's life. Second, the abstract freedom of self-definition is of little help to someone who lacks the resources to realize the person she envisions or whose emergent self is continually beaten down by social forces. Defining the guarantee of personhood as no more than shielding a sphere of personal decisions from the reach of government—merely ensuring the individual's "right to be let alone"—may be inadequate to protect the dignity and autonomy of the poor and oppressed.

The definition of privacy as a purely negative right serves to exempt the state from any obligation to ensure the social conditions and resources necessary for self-determination and autonomous decisionmaking. Must privacy doctrine sever the government's negative obligations from its affirmative responsibilities in guaranteeing the rights of personhood? An alternative concept of liberty guaranteed by the due process clause includes not only the negative proscription against government coercion, but also the affirmative duty of government to protect the individual's personhood from degradation and to facilitate the processes of choice and self-determination. This approach shifts the focus of privacy theory from state nonintervention to the goal of an affirmatively autonomous and flourishing life.[156]

RLW: Had the Court construed *Roe* as requiring the government to pay for abortions, the Court might have exceeded the limits of political tolerance. Medicaid costs, already high, would have increased. Pro-Life activists, already distressed about the availability of abortion, would have been incensed about the expenditure of federal and state tax dollars to finance a procedure that they regard as murder.

DEL: Results like those in *Maher* and *Harris* make it difficult to sort out whether it is principle or moral preferences that are being prioritized in the name of fundamental law. In asserting that government need not underwrite the exercise of a right or liberty, even if obligated to respect it, the Court reaffirms a general constitutional reality. Although freedom of the press or the right to counsel are comprehensively assured in the abstract, for instance, the extent to which the guarantees actually may be enjoyed is a function of personal resources. Whether an individual actually publishes or broadcasts, or is the beneficiary of high quality legal representation, depends primarily upon his or her access to wealth.

Insofar as they are rooted in the sense that freedom extends to all, but the power to exercise it is relative and not apt for redistribution unless directed by the political process, *Maher* and *Harris* reflect a normative understanding of the nature of rights and liberties.

---

[156] *See* LAURENCE H. TRIBE, AMERICAN CONSTITUTIONAL LAW 1305 (2d ed. 1988); Dorothy E. Roberts, *Punishing Drug Addicts Who Have Babies: Women of Color, Equality, and The Right of Privacy*, 104 HARV. L. REV. 1419, 1476–81 (1991); Robin West, *Progressive and Conservative Constitutionalism*, 88 MICH. L. REV. 641, 707 (1990).

Those who argue that the state has an affirmative obligation to ensure equal enjoyment of a right or liberty tout a legitimate political order, as a matter of vision, but it is a system that has yet to be established in fact under the existing constitutional regime. It is unnecessary to redefine or argue the nature of rights or liberties, however, to doubt decisions such as *Maher* and *Harris*. The seeds of doctrinal inadequacy are planted in the very assertion that, even though government may not be obligated to eliminate barriers that are a function of economic or social condition, it "may not place obstacles in the path of a woman's freedom to exercise her choice." Realistically, it makes no difference that a woman is influenced in her decision-making by state action that prohibits or induces. Government payments to buy silence on a political issue, for instance, would represent no less an affront to the First Amendment than more traditional forms of restraint. Similarly, a subsidization policy that favors full-term pregnancies over abortion can be viewed as a constitutionally significant abridgment.

A fundamental problem with the *Maher* and *Harris* decisions is not that they do not take a legitimate constitutional cue. The dilemma is that more than one valid cue exists—rights and freedoms are not to be redistributed as an exercise of judicial management vs. government may not influence a women's choice—but no credible basis has been articulated for preferring one outcome-determinative starting point over the other.

e. Family Liberty

The decision in *Meyer v. Nebraska*, protecting the right of parents to direct their children's education, has stood as precedent for a due process right to form families and to conduct family life free from unjustified government interference. More recently, the Court has been called upon to determine the scope and source of the family's freedom from state regulation. The doctrine of family liberty is subject to the same criticisms as the Court's application of privacy in *Griswold v. Connecticut* and *Roe v. Wade*, that judicial enforcement of unenumerated due process liberties exceeds constitutional prerogatives. Yet it can be argued that the Reconstruction origins of the Fourteenth Amendment provide strong support for its special concern for family autonomy:

> Slavery . . . required that men, women and children be bound more surely by ties of ownership than by ties of kinship. Slavery supported itself by annulment of marital, parental and procreative rights.

> Drafters and advocates of the Fourteenth Amendment had vivid impressions of what it meant to be denied rights of family, for the denial of those rights was a hallmark of slavery in the United States. These men and women regarded the denial of family liberty as a vice of slavery that inverted concepts of human dignity, citizenship and natural law. And they regarded the Fourteenth Amendment as the instrument with which to re-enshrine family liberty as an inalienable aspect of national citizenship and natural law.[157]

One context in which the Court has explored the meaning of family liberty is the extent of constitutional protection for living arrangements that violate local zoning ordinances. In *Village of Belle Terre v. Boraas*, the Court upheld a New York village ordinance that restricted land use to single-family dwellings.[158] The ordinance defined "family" to include all persons related by blood, adoption, or marriage, who lived together as a single-housekeeping unit. It prohibited occupancy by any group of three

---

[157] Peggy Cooper Davis, *Neglected Stories and The Lawfulness of Roe v, Wade*, 28 HARV. C.R.-C.L. L. REV. 299, 309 (1993) (citations omitted).

[158] Village of Belle Terre v. Boraas, 416 U.S. 1 (1974).

or more persons, such as the students to whom Mr. Boraas wished to rent, who were not related in this way. The Court rejected Boraas's due process claim, concluding that the zoning law "involve[d] no 'fundamental' right guaranteed by the Constitution, such as . . . the right of association or any rights of privacy." Although the right of privacy protected decisions about marriage and procreation, it did not extend to all decisions about the people with whom we wish to live.

Two years later, in *Moore v. City of East Cleveland*, the Court considered whether its rejection of a due process claim in *Belle Terre* applied to living arrangements that did involve a family. Inez Moore's family did not fit any of the few categories of related individuals East Cleveland included in its definition of "family." The city's housing ordinance essentially restricted occupancy of dwellings to nuclear families. Mrs. Moore violated the ordinance by living with her two adult sons and their children because her two grandsons were first cousins and not brothers. She was sentenced to five days in jail and a $25 fine.

The justices divided as to whether Mrs. Moore's plight rose to constitutional significance. Justice Powell's plurality opinion distinguished *Belle Terre* and held that the ordinance violated the Due Process Clause of the Fourteenth Amendment. *Moore* concerned the liberty to live as a family, similar to the family rights protected in other substantive due process decisions. The dissenters, however, saw the plurality's excursion beyond marriage, procreation, and child rearing as a dangerous due process precedent. Mrs. Moore's interest in sharing living space with her grandchildren simply did not compare in fundamental importance to the aspects of family life the Court had already included in the right of privacy. Finding a fundamental right to family living arrangements also seemed to have limitless potential for judicial intrusion in local land use regulations; as Justice Stewart wondered, how far does an "extended family" extend?

Moore v. City of East Cleveland, Ohio
431 U.S. 494 (1976)

MR. JUSTICE POWELL announced the judgment of the Court, and delivered an opinion in which MR. JUSTICE BRENNAN, MR. JUSTICE MARSHALL, and MR. JUSTICE BLACKMUN joined.

. . .

II

The city argues that our decision in *Village of Belle Terre v. Boraas* requires us to sustain the ordinance attacked here. . . . But one overriding factor sets this case apart from *Belle Terre*. The ordinance there affected only *unrelated* individuals. It expressly allowed all who were related by "blood, adoption, or marriage" to live together, and in sustaining the ordinance we were careful to note that it promoted "family needs" and "family values." East Cleveland, in contrast, has chosen to regulate the occupancy of its housing by slicing deeply into the family itself. This is no mere incidental result of the ordinance. On its face it selects certain categories of relatives who may live together and declares that others may not. In particular, it makes a crime of a grandmother's choice to live with her grandson in circumstances like those presented here.

When a city undertakes such intrusive regulation of the family . . . the usual judicial deference to the legislature is inappropriate. "This Court has long recognized that freedom of personal choice in matters of marriage and family life is one of the liberties protected by the Due Process Clause of the Fourteenth Amendment." *Cleveland Board of Education v. LaFleur*, 414 U.S. 632, 639–640 (1974). A host of cases, tracing their lineage to *Meyer v. Nebraska*, and *Pierce v. Society of Sisters*, have consistently acknowledged a "private realm of family life which the state cannot enter." Of course, the family is not beyond regulation. But when the government intrudes on choices concerning family living arrangements, this Court must examine carefully the importance of the governmental interests advanced and the extent to which they are served by the challenged regulation.

When thus examined, this ordinance cannot survive. The city seeks to justify it as a means of preventing overcrowding, minimizing traffic and parking congestion, and avoiding an undue financial burden on East Cleveland's school system. Although these are legitimate goals, the ordinance before us serves them marginally, at best. For example, the ordinance permits any family consisting only of husband, wife, and unmarried children to live together, even if the family contains a half dozen licensed drivers, each with his or her own car. At the same time it forbids an adult brother and sister to share a household, even if both faithfully use public transportation. The ordinance would permit a grandmother to live with a single dependent son and children, even if his school-age children number a dozen, yet it forces Mrs. Moore to find another dwelling for her grandson John, simply because of the presence of his uncle and cousin in the same household. We need not labor the point. Section 1341.08 has but a tenuous relation to alleviation of the conditions mentioned by the city.

III

The city would distinguish the cases based on *Meyer* and *Pierce*. It points out that none of them "gives grandmothers any fundamental rights with respect to grandsons," and suggests that any constitutional right to live together as a family extends only to the nuclear family—essentially a couple and their dependent children.

To be sure, these cases did not expressly consider the family relationship presented here. They were immediately concerned with freedom of choice with respect to childbearing, or with the rights of parents to the custody and companionship of their own children, or with traditional parental authority in matters of child rearing and education. But unless we close our eyes to the basic reasons why certain rights associated with the family have been accorded shelter under the Fourteenth Amendment's Due Process Clause, we cannot avoid applying the force and rationale of these precedents to the family choice involved in this case.

Understanding those reasons requires careful attention to this Court's function under the Due Process Clause. . . . Substantive due process has at times been a treacherous field for this Court. There are risks when the judicial branch gives enhanced protection to certain substantive liberties without the guidance of the more specific provisions of the Bill of Rights. As the history of the *Lochner* era demonstrates, there is reason for concern lest the only limits to such judicial intervention become the predilections of those who happen at the time to Members of this Court. That history counsels caution and restraint. But it does not counsel abandonment, nor does it require what the city urges here: cutting off any protection of family rights at the first convenient, if arbitrary boundary—the boundary of the nuclear family.

Appropriate limits on substantive due process come not from drawing arbitrary lines but rather from careful "respect for the teachings of history [and] solid recognition of the basic values that underlie our society." *Griswold v. Connecticut*, (Harlan, J., concurring). Our decisions established that the Constitution protects the sanctity of the family precisely because the institution of the family is deeply rooted in this Nation's history and tradition. It is through the family that we inculcate and pass down many of our most cherished values, moral and cultural.

Ours is by no means a tradition limited to respect for the bonds uniting the members of the nuclear family. The tradition of uncles, aunts, cousins, and especially grandparents sharing a household along with parents and children has roots equally venerable and equally deserving of constitutional recognition. Over the years millions of our citizens have grown up in just such an environment, and most, surely, have profited from it. Even if conditions of modern society have brought about a decline in extended family households, they have not erased the accumulated wisdom of civilization, gained over the centuries and honored throughout our history, that supports a larger conception of the family. Out of choice, necessity, or a sense of family responsibility, it has been common for close relatives to draw together and participate in the duties and the satisfactions of a common home. Decisions concerning child rearing, which *Yoder, Meyer, Pierce* and other cases have recognized as entitled to constitutional protection, long have been shared with grandparents or other relatives who occupy the same household—indeed who may take on major responsibility for the rearing of the children. Especially in times of adversity, such as the death of a spouse or economic need, the broader family has tended to come together for mutual sustenance and to maintain or rebuild a secure home life. This is apparently what happened here.

Whether or not such a household is established because of personal tragedy, the choice of relatives in this degree of kinship to live together may not lightly be denied by the State. *Pierce* struck down an Oregon law requiring all children to attend the State's public schools, holding that the Constitution "excludes any general power of the State to standardize its children by forcing them to accept instruction from public teachers only." By the same token the Constitution prevents East Cleveland from standardizing its children—and its adults—by forcing all to live in certain narrowly defined family patterns.

Reversed.

MR. JUSTICE BRENNAN, with whom MR. JUSTICE MARSHALL joins, concurring.

. . . I write only to underscore the cultural myopia of the arbitrary boundary drawn by the

East Cleveland ordinance in the light of the tradition of the American home that has been a feature of our society since our beginning as a Nation. . . . The line drawn by this ordinance displays a depressing insensitivity toward the economic and emotional needs of a very large part of our society.

In today's America, the "nuclear family" is the pattern so often found in much of white suburbia. The Constitution cannot be interpreted, however, to tolerate the imposition by government upon the rest of us of white suburbia's preference in patterns of family living. The "extended family" that provided generations of early Americans with social services and economic and emotional support in times of hardship, and was the beachhead for successive waves of immigrants who populated our cities, remains not merely still a pervasive living pattern, but under the goad of brutal economic necessity, a prominent pattern—virtually a means of survival—for large numbers of the poor and deprived minorities of our society. For them compelled pooling of scant resources requires compelled sharing of a household.

The "extended" form is especially familiar among black families. . . .

I do not wish to be understood as implying that East Cleveland's enforcement of its ordinance is motivated by a racially discriminatory purpose: The record of this case would not support that implication. But the prominence of other than nuclear families among ethnic and racial minority groups, including our black citizens, surely demonstrates that the "extended family" pattern remains a vital tenet of our society. It suffices that in prohibiting this pattern of family living as a means of achieving its objectives, appellee city has chosen a device that deeply intrudes into family associational rights that historically have been central, and today remain central, to a large proportion of our population.

. . .

MR. JUSTICE STEVENS, concurring in the judgment.

In my judgment the critical question presented by this case is whether East Cleveland's housing ordinance is a permissible restriction on appellant's right to use her own property as she sees fit.

. . .

MR. CHIEF JUSTICE BURGER, dissenting.

It is unnecessary for me to reach the difficult constitutional issue this case presents. Appellant's deliberate refusal to use a plainly adequate administrative remedy provided by the city should foreclose her from pressing in this Court any constitutional objections to the city's zoning ordinance. . . .

. . .

MR. JUSTICE STEWART, with whom MR. JUSTICE REHNQUIST joins, dissenting.

. . .

In my view, the appellant's claim that the ordinance in question invades constitutionally protected rights of association and privacy is in large part answered by the *Belle Terre* decision. . . .

The *Belle Terre* decision . . . disposes of the appellant's contentions to the extent they focus not on her blood relationships with her sons and grandsons but on more general notions about the "privacy of the home." Her suggestion that every person has a constitutional right permanently to share his residence with whomever he pleases, and that such choices are "beyond the province of legitimate governmental intrusion," amounts to the same argument that was made and found unpersuasive in *Belle Terre*.

To be sure, the ordinance involved in *Belle Terre* did not prevent blood relatives from occupying the same dwelling, and the Court's decision in that case does not, therefore, foreclose the appellant's arguments based specifically on the ties of kinship present in this case. Nonetheless, I would hold, for the reasons that follow, that the existence of those ties does not elevate either the appellant's claim of associational freedom or her claim of privacy to a level invoking constitutional protection.

. . .

Although the appellant's desire to share a single-dwelling unit also involves "private family life" in a sense, that desire can hardly be equated with any of the interests protected in [*Roe, Griswold, Meyer,* and *Pierce*]. The ordinance about which the appellant complains did not impede her choice to have or not to have children, and it did not dictate to her how her own children were to be nurtured and reared. The ordinance clearly does not prevent parents from living together or living with their unemancipated offspring.

But even though the Court's previous cases are not directly in point, the appellant contends that the importance of the "extended family" in American society requires us to hold that her decision to share her residence with her grandsons may not be interfered with by the State. This decision, like the decisions involved in bearing and raising children, is said to be an aspect of "family life" also entitled to substantive protection under the Constitution. Without pausing to inquire how far under this argument an "extended family" might extend, I cannot agree. When the Court has found that the Fourteenth Amendment placed a substantive limitation on a State's power to regulate, it has been in those rare cases in which the personal interests at issue have been deemed "'implicit in the concept of ordered liberty.'"

The interest that the appellant may have in permanently sharing a single kitchen and a suite of contiguous rooms with some of her relatives simply does not rise to that level. To equate this interest with the fundamental decisions to marry and to bear and raise children is to extend the limited substantive contours of the Due Process Clause beyond recognition.

. . .

MR. JUSTICE WHITE, dissenting.

. . .

Although the Court regularly proceeds on the assumption that the Due Process Clause has more than a procedural dimension, we must always bear in mind that the substantive context of the Clause is suggested neither by its language nor by preconstitutional history; that content is nothing more than the accumulated product of judicial interpretation of the Fifth and Fourteenth Amendments. This is not to suggest, at this point, that any of these cases should be overruled, or that the process by which they were decided was illegitimate or even unacceptable, but only to underline Mr. Justice Black's constant reminder to his colleagues that the Court has no license to invalidate legislation which it thinks merely arbitrary or unreasonable. And no one was more sensitive than Mr. Justice Harlan to any suggestion that his approach to the Due Process Clause would lead to judges "roaming at large in the constitutional field." *Griswold v. Connecticut.* No one proceeded with more caution than he did when the validity of state or federal legislation was challenged in the name of the Due Process Clause.

This is surely the preferred approach. That the Court has ample precedent for the creation of new constitutional rights should not lead it to repeal the process at will. The Judiciary, including this Court, is the most vulnerable and comes the nearest to illegitimacy when it deals with judge-made constitutional law having little or no cognizable roots in the language or even design of the Constitution. Realizing that the present construction of the Due Process Clause represents a major judicial gloss on its terms, as well as on the anticipation of the Framers, and that much of the underpinnings for the broad, substantive application of the Clause disappeared in the conflict between the Executive and the Judiciary in the 1930's and 1940's, the Court should be extremely reluctant to breathe still further substantive content into the Due Process Clause so as to strike down legislation adopted by a State or city to promote its welfare. Whenever the Judiciary does so, it unavoidably pre-empts for itself another part of the governance of the country without express constitutional authority.

. . .

. . . Under our cases, the Due Process Clause extends substantial protection to various phases of family life, but none requires that the claim made here be sustained. I cannot believe that the interest in residing with more than one set of grandchildren is one that calls for any kind of heightened protection under the Due Process Clause. To say that one has a personal right to live with all, rather than some, of one's grandchildren and that this right is implicit in ordered liberty is, as my Brother STEWART says, "to extend the limited substantive contours of the Due Process Clause beyond recognition." The present claim is hardly one of which it could be said that "neither liberty nor justice would exist if [it] were sacrificed." . . . The suggested view would broaden enormously the horizons of the Clause; and, if the interest involved here is any measure of what the States would be forbidden to regulate, the courts would be substantively weighing and very likely invalidating a wide range of measures that Congress and state legislatures think appropriate to respond to a changing economic and social order.

. . .

DER: *Moore* is an important decision because it recognizes constitutional limits on government interference in nontraditional families. The state should not have the power to impose upon all of us the majority's narrow and biased definition of the proper family form. The concept of family liberty, protected by the Fourteenth Amendment, safeguards from repressive government action aspects of family life that are essential to personal freedom. These are freedoms that should not be subject to the moral dictates of the majority.

But the limits of *Moore*'s reasoning are more striking than its possibilities. First, the Court limited its protection of families to individuals related by blood. Presumably, Mrs. Moore would have lost her claim if she took a neighbor's child into her home—a family pattern also deeply rooted in the history of the Black community. Moreover, the Court's rationale for protecting Mrs. Moore's family seems just as useful for enforcing government regimentation of families as for opposing it. The Court paradoxically based its support of Mrs. Moore's defiance of the zoning ordinance on her ultimate conformance to the "Nation's history and tradition." This test offers little protection, for example, for single mothers and their children or gay and lesbian families, who fail to conform to traditional notions of the family. The Court's focus on preserving personal choice in the private sphere of family life also neglected the family's important political role. The majority therefore failed to answer Justice Stewart's objection to extending constitutional protection to "those who assert no interest other than the gratification, convenience, and economy of sharing the same residence." Forming families serves more than personal whims. The family is a social institution that serves the important political ends of preparing citizens to participate in the life of the community and protecting family members from social and government forces. Protecting the autonomous individual within the family neglects the importance of family relationships. Ironically, by isolating the individual from her family connections, this interpretation of liberty denies the importance of the family as itself a shield against government power. The Fourteenth Amendment's protection of personal liberty should include the family's role in resisting tradition, as well as conforming to it.

DEL: The *Moore* decision is a source of dissatisfaction on virtually all fronts. Because the judgment was not supported by a majority point of view, Justice Powell's opinion for the prevailing plurality is essentially precatory. Even so, it represents a significant entry into the competition over what analytical role model should govern fundamental rights analysis. The plurality's determination that the "sanctity of the family . . . is deeply rooted in this Nation's history and tradition" may be accurate in the abstract. The Court's inclination to extend the scope of a family's "sanctity" only to the point of blood or marital relationships, however, seems no less arbitrary than a distinction between nuclear and extended families. To the extent that the state may favor housing second cousins under the same roof, but deny joint living accommodations to persons who may have a more significant personal relationship or an arrangement driven by need or charity, the logic of the liberty interest is hard to grasp.

Unsatisfactory too in Powell's analysis is the continuing fixation on what is rooted in the nation's history and tradition. Justice White notes that such a reference point vests the Court with "far too expansive [a] charter," insofar as what is deeply rooted is arguable and what deserves constitutional protection is even more debatable. It is possible to argue, however, that the focus upon history and tradition can be constraining to the point of crippling means of progress. Because society is a dynamic rather than static condition, a commitment to preserving history and tradition actually could translate into a true Lochnerist renaissance. Such would be the result if the established order, in the name of history and tradition, were to be protected against innovation and change demanded by the political process. To the extent progress may require liberation from history and tradition, as has been demonstrated in the nation's passage beyond official segregation, attention to such concerns may be problematic not only because of the potential for overreaching but for underachieving.

Perplexing too is the debate between Justices Brennan and Stewart over the inspiration for the regulatory scheme. Brennan stresses the "senseless" and "eccentric" nature of the exclusion, which he characterizes as an exercise in "cultural myopia" reflecting "a distressing insensitivity toward the economic and emotional needs of a very large part of our society." Noting how the extended family is essential to the survival of many impoverished and black families, he concludes that the Constitution does not "tolerate the imposition by government upon the rest of us of white suburbia's preference in patterns of family living." Responding to the allegation of cultural myopia and imperialism, Justice Stewart points out that the community is predominantly black in its population and governance.

In reality, both sides may miss the real cultural issue. The observation that the community is primarily African-American seems to assume the absence of diversity in values and attitudes among members of a racial group. Depiction of the ordinance as a function of myopia associated with white suburban values, however, misses the real cultural imperative of middle-class blacks attempting to insulate themselves from lifestyles associated with lower-class conditions.[159] Constitutional intolerance of the regulation in *Moore* is unsettling to the extent that the Court, in upholding an ordinance excluding more than two unrelated persons from living together in a white suburban community, was moved by the imperatives of "family values, youth values, and the blessings of the quiet seclusion and clean air [that] make the area a sanctuary for people."[160] Insofar as case law facilitates the values of white suburbanites in defining acceptable living arrangements in their neighborhoods, but cramps other communities' power to order their priorities similarly, the Court's own work might be viewed as an exercise in cultural myopia and elitism. Viewed in its totality, the debate in *Moore* reflects a competition between moral perspectives in which neither the standards, stakes nor context of the debate are identified with adequate clarity. Little wonder that so many have found so much about *Moore* that is unsatisfactory.

---

[159] See Burt, *The Constitution of the Family*, 1979 SUP. CT. REV. 329, 389 (1979).
[160] Belle Terre v. Boraas, 416 U.S. 1, 9 (1974).

The Court in *Moore* struck down the city ordinance because it unconstitutionally intruded upon a family tradition—the extended family. In *Michael H v. Gerald D.*, the Court *upheld* a California statute in the face of a due process challenge because the statute safeguarded a family tradition—the marital unit. Under the California law at issue, a child born to a married woman living with her husband was presumed to be a child of the marriage. This marital presumption of paternity has its roots in the common law rules of parentage, which became codified in state statutes. At common law, a woman was the legal mother of the child to whom she gave birth. This rule was expressed in the maxim, *mater est quam gestatio demonstrat*: She is the mother whom the bearing designates. A man, on the other hand, could obtain parental rights only through marriage. *Pater est quam nuptiae demonstrat*: He is the father whom marriage designates.[161] A child born to unwed parents was *"filius nullius"*—the son (or daughter) of no one. Thus, common law denied unwed biological fathers paternity rights and established a presumption that a mother's husband was the father of her children. Whether the presumption is rebuttable varies by state and typically can be challenged only by the mother or her husband, and then only in limited circumstances. Some states, including California, have abolished the presumption, allowing the unwed father to petition for visitation and custody.

The Court considered in four cases prior to *Michael H. v. Gerald D.* whether unwed fathers have a constitutionally protected interest in their relationships with their children.[162] Taken together, these cases produced a general standard for determining unwed fathers' claims to parental rights: although an unwed father's biological link to his child does not, in and of itself, guarantee him a constitutional stake in his relationship with that child, that link combined with a substantial relationship with the child and the child's mother may be sufficient to do so. The Court granted the unwed biological fathers in *Stanley v. Illinois* and *Caban v. Mohammed* parental rights because they had formed such relationships, while the fathers in *Quilloin v. Walcott* and *Lehr v. Robertson*, who were denied parental rights, had not. The Court explained in *Lehr* that "[t]he significance of the biological connection is that it offers the natural father an opportunity that no other male possesses to develop a relationship with his offspring."

---

[161] 1 WILLIAM BLACKSTONE, COMMENTARIES *434.
[162] Stanley v. Illinois, 405 U.S. 645 (1972); Quilloin v. Walcott, 434 U.S. 246 (1978); Caban v. Mohammed, 441 U.S. 380 (1979); and Lehr v. Robertson, 463 U.S. 248 (1983).

Michael H. involved two Fourteenth Amendment challenges to the marital presumption of paternity. Michael H. claimed that the presumption violated his due process rights to establish his paternity of a child born to the wife of another man. The child, Victoria, claimed that the presumption violated her constitutional right to maintain a relationship with her biological father.

Michael H. v. Gerald D.
491 U.S. 110 (1989)

JUSTICE SCALIA announced the judgment of the Court and delivered an opinion, in which THE CHIEF JUSTICE joins, and in all but footnote 6 of which JUSTICE O'CONNOR and JUSTICE KENNEDY join.

. . .

I

The facts of this case are, we must hope, extraordinary. On May 9, 1976, in Las Vegas, Nevada, Carole D., an international model, and Gerald D., a top executive in a French oil company, were married. The couple established a home in Playa del Rey, California, in which they resided as husband and wife when one or the other was not out of the country on business. In the summer of 1978, Carole became involved in an adulterous affair with a neighbor, Michael H. In September 1980, she conceived a child, Victoria D., who was born on May 11, 1981. Gerald was listed as father on the birth certificate and has always held Victoria out to the world as his daughter. Soon after delivery of the child, however, Carole informed Michael that she believed he might be the father.

In the first three years of her life, Victoria remained always with Carole, but found herself within a variety of quasifamily units. In October 1981, Gerald moved to New York City to pursue his business interests, but Carole chose to remain in California. At the end of that month, Carole and Michael had blood tests of themselves and Victoria, which showed a 98.07% probability that Michael was Victoria's father. [From January to March 1982], Carole visited Michael in St. Thomas, where his primary business interests were based. There Michael held Victoria out as his child. . . .

In November 1982, rebuffed in his attempts to visit Victoria, Michael filed a filiation action in California Superior Court to establish his paternity and right to visitation. . . . [Victoria's court-appointed attorney and guardian *ad litem*] filed a cross-complaint asserting that if she had more than one psychological or de facto father, she was entitled to maintain her filial relationship, with all of the attendant rights, duties, and obligations, with both. . . . [F]rom

March through July 1983, Carole was again living with Gerald in New York. In August, however, she returned to California [and] became involved once against with Michael. . . .

For the ensuing eight months, when Michael was not in St. Thomas he lived with Carole and Victoria in Carole's apartment in Los Angeles and held Victoria out as his daughter. . . . In June 1984, Carole reconciled with Gerald and joined him in New York, where they now live with Victoria and two other children since born into the marriage.

In May 1984, Michael and Victoria, through her guardian *ad litem*, sought visitation rights for Michael. . . . On October 19, 1984, Gerald, who had intervened in the action, moved for summary judgment on the ground that under Cal. Evid. Code § 621 there were no triable issues of fact as to Victoria's paternity. . . . [The California Superior Court granted Gerald's motion for summary judgment and the California Court of Appeal affirmed the judgment.]

. . .

III

We address first the claims of Michael. At the outset, it is necessary to clarify what he sought and what he was denied. California law, like nature itself, makes no provision for dual fatherhood. Michael was seeking to be declared the father of Victoria. The immediate benefit he evidently sought to obtain from that status was visitation rights. But if Michael were successful in being declared the father, other rights would follow—most importantly, the right to be considered as the parent who should have custody, a status which "embrace[s] the sum of parental rights with respect to the rearing of a child, including the child's care; the right to the child's services and earnings; the right to direct the child's activities; the right to make decisions regarding the control, education, and health of the child; and the right, as well as the duty, to prepare the child for additional obligations, which includes the teaching of moral standards, religious beliefs, and elements of good citizenship." 4 California Family Law § 60.02[1][b]. All parental rights, including visitation, were automatically denied by denying Michael status as the father. . . .

. . .

Michael contends as a matter of substantive due process that, because he has established a parental relationship with Victoria, protection of Gerald's and Carole's marital union is an insufficient state interest to support termination of that relationship. This argument is, of course, predicated on the assertion that Michael has a constitutionally protected liberty interest in his relationship with Victoria.

It is an established part of our constitutional jurisprudence that the term "liberty" in the Due Process Clause extends beyond freedom from physical restraint. Without that core textual meaning as a limitation, defining the scope of the Due Process Clause "has at times been a treacherous field for this Court," giving "reason for concern lest the only limits to . . . judicial intervention become the predilections of those who happen at the time to be Members of this Court." *Moore v. East Cleveland.* . . . In an attempt to limit and guide interpretation of the Clause, we have insisted not merely that the interest denominated as a "liberty" be "fundamental" (a concept that, in isolation, is hard to objectify), but also that it be an interest traditionally protected by our society. As we have put it, the Due Process Clause affords only those protections "so rooted in the traditions and conscience of our people as to be ranked as fundamental." Our cases reflect "continual insistence upon respect for the teachings of history [and] solid recognition of the basic values that underlie our society. . . ." *Griswold v. Connecticut* (Harlan, J., concurring in judgment).

This insistence that the asserted liberty interest be rooted in history and tradition is evident, as elsewhere, in our cases according constitutional protection to certain parental rights. Michael reads the landmark case of *Stanley v. Illinois*, 405 U.S. 645 (1972), and the subsequent cases of *Quilloin v. Walcott*, 434 U.S. 246 (1978), *Caban v. Mohammed*, 441 U.S. 380 (1979), and *Lehr v. Robertson*, 463 U.S. 248 (1983), as establishing that a liberty interest is created by biological fatherhood plus an established parental relationship—factors that exist in the present case as well. We think that distorts the rationale of those cases. As we view them, they rest not upon such isolated factors but upon the historic respect—indeed, sanctity would not be too strong a term—traditionally accorded to the relationships that develop within the unitary family. In *Stanley*, for example, we forbade the destruction of such a family when, upon the death of the mother, the State had sought to remove children from the custody of a father who had lived with and supported them and their mother for 18 years. As

Justice Powell stated for the plurality in *Moore v. East Cleveland*: "Our decisions establish that the Constitution protects the sanctity of the family precisely because the institution of the family is deeply rooted in this Nation's history and tradition."

Thus, the legal issue in the present case reduces to whether the relationship between persons in the situation of Michael and Victoria has been treated as a protected family unit under the historic practices of our society, or whether on any other basis it has been accorded special protection. We think it impossible to find that it has. In fact, quite to the contrary, our traditions have protected the marital family (Gerald, Carole, and the child they acknowledge to be theirs) against the sort of claim Michael asserts.[4]

The presumption of legitimacy was a fundamental principle of the common law. H. Nicholas, Adulturine Bastardy 1 (1836). Traditionally, that presumption could be rebutted only by proof that a husband was incapable of procreation or had had no access to his wife during the relevant period. As explained by Blackstone, nonaccess could only be proved "if the husband be out of the kingdom of England (or, as the law somewhat loosely phrases it, *extra quatuor maria* [beyond the four seas]) for above nine months. . . ." 1 Blackstone's Commentaries 456 (J. Chitty ed. 1826). And, under the common law both in England and here, "neither husband nor wife [could] be a witness to prove access or nonaccess." J. Schouler, Law of the Domestic Relations § 225, p. 306 (3d ed. 1882). The primary policy rationale underlying the common law's severe restrictions on rebuttal of the presumption appears to have been an aversion to declaring children illegitimate, thereby depriving them of rights of inheritance and succession, and likely making them wards of the state. A secondary policy concern was the interest in promoting the "peace and tranquillity of States and families," a goal that is

---

[4] JUSTICE BRENNAN insists that in determining whether a liberty interest exists we must look at Michael's relationship with Victoria in isolation, without reference to the circumstance that Victoria's mother was married to someone else when the child was conceived, and that that woman and her husband wish to raise the child as their own. We cannot imagine what compels this strange procedure of looking at the act which is assertedly the subject of a liberty interest in isolation from its effect upon other people—rather like inquiring whether there is a liberty interest in firing a gun where the case at hand happens to involve its discharge into another person's body. The logic of JUSTICE BRENNAN's position leads to the conclusion that if Michael had begotten Victoria by rape, that fact would in no way affect his possession of a liberty interest in his relationship with her.

obviously impaired by facilitating suits against husband and wife asserting that their children are illegitimate. . . .

We have found nothing in the older sources, nor in the older cases, addressing specifically the power of the natural father to assert parental rights over a child born into a woman's existing marriage with another man. Since it is Michael's burden to establish that such a power (at least where the natural father has established a relationship with the child) is so deeply embedded within our traditions as to be a fundamental right, the lack of evidence alone might defeat his case. But the evidence shows that even in modern times—when, as we have noted, the rigid protection of the marital family has in other respects been relaxed—the ability of a person in Michael's position to claim paternity has not been generally acknowledged. . . .

Moreover, even if it were clear that one in Michael's position generally possesses, and has generally always possessed, standing to challenge the marital child's legitimacy, that would still not establish Michael's case. . . . What Michael asserts here is a right to have himself declared the natural father *and thereby to obtain parental prerogatives.* What he must establish, therefore, is not that our society has traditionally allowed a natural father in his circumstances to establish paternity, but that it has traditionally accorded such a father parental rights, or at least has not traditionally denied them. What counts is whether the States in fact award substantive parental rights to the natural father of a child conceived within, and born into, an extant marital union that wishes to embrace the child. We are not aware of a single case, old or new, that has done so. This is not the stuff of which fundamental rights qualifying as liberty interests are made.[6]

· · ·

[6] JUSTICE BRENNAN criticizes our methodology in using historical traditions specifically relating to the rights of an adulterous natural father, rather than inquiring more generally "whether parenthood is an interest that historically has received our attention and protection." There seems to us no basis for the contention that this methodology is "nove[l]." For example, in . . . *Roe v. Wade,* we spent about a fifth of our opinion negating the proposition that there was a longstanding tradition of laws proscribing abortion.

We do not understand why, having rejected our focus upon the societal tradition regarding the natural father's rights vis-a-vis a child whose mother is married to another man, JUSTICE BRENNAN would choose to focus instead upon "parenthood." Why should the relevant category not be even more general—perhaps "family relationships"; or "personal relationships"; or even "emotional attachments in general"? Though the dissent has no basis for the level of generality it would select, we do: We refer to

We do not accept JUSTICE BRENNAN'S criticism that this result "squashes" the liberty that consists of "the freedom not to conform." It seems to us that reflects the erroneous view that there is only one side to this controversy—that one disposition can expand a "liberty" of sorts without contracting an equivalent "liberty" on the other side. Such a happy choice is rarely available. Here, to provide protection to an adulterous natural father is to deny protection to a marital father, and vice versa. If Michael has a "freedom not to conform" (whatever that means), Gerald must equivalently have a "freedom to conform." One of them will pay a price for asserting that "freedom"—Michael by being unable to act as father of the child he has adulterously begotten, or Gerald by being unable to preserve the integrity of the traditional family unit he and Victoria have established. Our disposition does not choose between these two "freedoms," but leaves that to the people of California. JUSTICE BRENNAN'S approach chooses one of them as the constitutional imperative, on no apparent basis except that the unconventional is to be preferred.

---

the most specific level at which a relevant tradition protecting, or denying protection to, the asserted right can be identified. If, for example, there were no societal tradition, either way, regarding the rights of the natural father of a child adulterously conceived, we would have to consult, and (if possible) reason from, the traditions regarding natural fathers in general. But there is such a more specific tradition, and it unqualifiedly denies protection to such a parent.

One would think that JUSTICE BRENNAN would appreciate the value of consulting the most specific tradition available, since he acknowledges that "[e]ven if we can agree . . . that 'family' and 'parenthood' are part of the good life, it is absurd to assume that we can agree on the content of those terms and destructive to pretend that we do." Because such general traditions provide such imprecise guidance, they permit judges to dictate rather than discern the society's views. The need, if arbitrary decisionmaking is to be avoided, to adopt the most specific tradition as the point of reference—or at least to announce, as JUSTICE BRENNAN declines to do, some other criterion for selecting among the innumerable relevant traditions that could be consulted—is well enough exemplified by the fact that in the present case JUSTICE BRENNAN'S opinion and JUSTICE O'CONNOR'S opinion, which disapproves this footnote, *both* appeal to tradition, but on the basis of the tradition they select reach opposite results. Although assuredly having the virtue (if it be that) of leaving judges free to decide as they think best when the unanticipated occurs, a rule of law that binds neither by text nor by any particular, identifiable tradition is no rule of law at all.

Finally, we may note that this analysis is not inconsistent with the result in cases such as *Griswold v. Connecticut* or *Eisenstadt v. Baird.* None of those cases acknowledged a longstanding and still extant societal tradition withholding the very right pronounced to be the subject of a liberty interest and then rejected it. JUSTICE BRENNAN must do so here. . . .

IV

We have never had occasion to decide whether a child has a liberty interest, symmetrical with that of her parent, in maintaining her filial relationship. We need not do so here because, even assuming that such a right exists, Victoria's claim must fail. Victoria's due process challenge is, if anything, weaker than Michael's. Her basic claim is not that California has erred in preventing her from establishing that Michael, not Gerald, should stand as her legal father. Rather, she claims a due process right to maintain filial relationships with both Michael and Gerald. This assertion merits little discussion, for, whatever the merits of the guardian ad litem's belief that such an arrangement can be of great psychological benefit to a child, the claim that a State must recognize multiple fatherhood has no support in the history or traditions of this country. . . .

The judgment of the California Court of Appeal is
Affirmed.

JUSTICE O'CONNOR, with whom JUSTICE KENNEDY joins, concurring in part.

I concur in all but footnote 6 of JUSTICE SCALIA'S opinion. This footnote sketches a mode of historical analysis to be used when identifying liberty interests protected by the Due Process Clause of the Fourteenth Amendment that may be somewhat inconsistent with our past decisions in this area. See *Griswold v. Connecticut, Eisenstadt v. Baird.* On occasion the Court has characterized relevant traditions protecting asserted rights at levels of generality that might not be "the most specific level" available. See *Loving v. Virginia*, 388 U.S. 1, 12 (1967); *Turner v. Safley*, 482 U.S. 78, 94 (1987). I would not foreclose the unanticipated by the prior imposition of a single mode of historical analysis.

JUSTICE STEVENS, concurring in the judgment.

. . .

. . . I do not agree with JUSTICE SCALIA'S analysis. He seems to reject the possibility that a natural father might ever have a constitutionally protected interest in his relationship with a child whose mother was married to, and cohabiting with, another man at the time of the child's conception and birth. I think cases like *Stanley v. Illinois* and *Caban v. Mohammed* demonstrate that enduring "family" relationships may develop in unconventional settings. I therefore would not foreclose the possibility that a constitutionally protected relationship between a natural father and his child might exist in a case like this. Indeed, I am willing to assume for the purpose of deciding this case that Michael's relationship with Victoria is strong enough to give him a constitutional right to try to convince a trial judge that Victoria's best interest would be served by granting him visitation rights. . . .

Under the circumstances of the case before us, Michael was given a fair opportunity to show that he is Victoria's natural father, that he had developed a relationship with her, and that her interests would be served by granting him visitation rights. On the other hand, the record also shows that after its rather shaky start, the marriage between Carole and Gerald developed a stability that now provides Victoria with a loving and harmonious family home. In the circumstances of this case, I find nothing fundamentally unfair about the exercise of a judge's discretion that, in the end, allows the mother to decide whether her child's best interests would be served by allowing the natural father visitation privileges. Because I am convinced that the trial judge had the authority under state law both to hear Michael's plea for visitation rights and to grant him such rights if Victoria's best interests so warranted, I am satisfied that the California statutory scheme is consistent with the Due Process Clause of the Fourteenth Amendment.

. . .

JUSTICE BRENNAN, with whom JUSTICE MARSHALL and JUSTICE BLACKMUN join, dissenting.

In a case that has yielded so many opinions as has this one, it is fruitful to begin by emphasizing the common ground shared by a majority of this Court. Five Members of the Court refuse to foreclose "the possibility that a natural father might ever have a constitutionally protected interest in his relationship with a child whose mother was married to, and cohabiting with, another man at the time of the child's conception and birth." . . . Four Members of the Court agree that Michael H. has a liberty interest in his relationship with Victoria, and one assumes for purposes of this case that he does.

In contrast, only one other Member of the Court fully endorses JUSTICE SCALIA'S view of the proper method of analyzing questions arising under the Due Process Clause. Nevertheless, because the plurality opinion's exclusively historical analysis portends a significant and unfortunate departure from our prior cases and from sound constitutional decisionmaking, I devote a substantial portion of my discussion to it.

I

Once we recognized that the "liberty" protected by the Due Process Clause of the Fourteenth Amendment encompasses more than freedom from bodily restraint, as today's plurality opinion emphasizes, the concept was cut loose from one natural limitation on its meaning. This innovation paved the way, so the plurality hints, for judges to substitute their own preferences for those of elected officials. Dissatisfied with this supposedly unbridled and uncertain state of affairs, the plurality casts about for another limitation on the concept of liberty.

It finds this limitation in "tradition." Apparently oblivious to the fact that this concept can be as malleable and as elusive as "liberty" itself, the plurality pretends that tradition places a discernible border around the Constitution. The pretense is seductive; it would be comforting to believe that a search for "tradition" involves nothing more idiosyncratic or complicated than poring through dusty volumes on American history. Yet, as JUSTICE WHITE observed in his dissent in *Moore v. East Cleveland*, "What the deeply rooted traditions of the country are is arguable." Indeed, wherever I would begin to look for an interest "deeply rooted in the country's traditions," one thing is certain: I would not stop (as does the plurality) at Bracton, or Blackstone, or Kent, or even the American Law Reports in conducting my search. Because reasonable people can disagree about the content of particular traditions, and because they can disagree even about which traditions are relevant to the definition of "liberty," the plurality has not found the objective boundary that it seeks.

Even if we could agree, moreover, on the content and significance of particular traditions, we still would be forced to identify the point at which a tradition becomes firm enough to be relevant to our definition of liberty and the moment at which it becomes too obsolete to be relevant any longer. The plurality supplies no objective means by which we might make these determinations. Indeed, as soon as the plurality sees signs that the tradition upon which it bases its decision (the laws denying putative fathers like Michael standing to assert paternity) is crumbling, it shifts ground and says that the case has nothing to do with that tradition, after all. "[W]hat is at issue here," the plurality asserts after canvassing the law on paternity suits, "is not entitlement to a state pronouncement that Victoria was begotten by Michael." But that is precisely what is at issue here, and the plurality's last-minute denial of this fact dramatically illustrates the subjectivity of its own analysis.

It is ironic that an approach so utterly dependent on tradition is so indifferent to our precedents. Citing barely a handful of this Court's numerous decisions defining the scope of the liberty protected by the Due Process Clause to support its reliance on tradition, the plurality acts as though English legal treatises and the American Law Reports always have provided the sole source for our constitutional principles. They have not. Just as common-law notions no longer define the "property" that the Constitution protects, neither do they circumscribe the "liberty" that it guarantees. On the contrary, "'[l]iberty' and 'property' are broad and majestic terms. They are among the '[g]reat [constitutional] concepts . . . purposely left to gather meaning from experience. . . . [T]hey relate to the whole domain of social and economic fact, and the statesmen who founded this Nation knew too well that only a stagnant society remains unchanged.'" *Board of Regents of State Colleges v. Roth*, 408 U.S. 564, 571 (1972), quoting *National Ins. Co. v. Tidewater Co.*, 337 U.S. 582, 646 (1949) (Frankfurter, J., dissenting).

It is not that tradition has been irrelevant to our prior decisions. Throughout our decisionmaking in this important area runs the theme that certain interests and practices—freedom from physical restraint, marriage, childbearing, childrearing, and others—form the core of our definition of "liberty." Our solicitude for these interests is partly the result of the fact that the Due Process Clause would seem an empty promise if it did not protect them, and partly the result of the historical and traditional importance of these interests in our society. In deciding cases arising under the Due Process Clause, therefore, we have considered whether the concrete limitation under consideration impermissibly impinges upon one of these more generalized interests.

Today's plurality, however, does not ask whether parenthood is an interest that historically has received our attention and protection; the answer to that question is too clear for dispute. Instead, the plurality asks whether the specific variety of parenthood under consideration—a natural father's relationship with a child whose mother is married to another man—has enjoyed such protection.

If we had looked to tradition with such specificity in past cases, many a decision would have reached a different result. Surely the use of contraceptives by unmarried couples, *Eisenstadt*, or even by married couples, *Griswold*; the freedom from corporal punishment in schools, *Ingraham v. Wright*, 430 U.S. 651 (1977); the freedom from an arbitrary transfer from a prison to a psychiatric institution, *Vitek v. Jones*, 445 U.S. 480 (1980); and even the right to raise one's natural but illegitimate children, *Stanley*, were not "interest[s] traditionally protected by our society," at the time of their consideration by this Court. If we had asked, therefore, in *Eisenstadt, Griswold, Ingraham, Vitek*, or *Stanley* itself whether the specific interest under consideration had been traditionally protected, the answer would have been a resounding "no." That we did not ask this question in those cases highlights the novelty of the interpretive method that the plurality opinion employs today.

The plurality's interpretive method is more than novel; it is misguided. It ignores the good reasons for limiting the role of "tradition" in interpreting the Constitution's deliberately capacious language. In the plurality's constitutional universe, we may not take notice of the fact that the original reasons for the conclusive presumption of paternity are out of place in a world in which blood tests can prove virtually beyond a shadow of a doubt who sired a particular child and in which the fact of illegitimacy no longer plays the burdensome and stigmatizing role it once did. Nor, in the plurality's world, may we deny "tradition" its full scope by pointing out that the rationale for the conventional rule has changed over the years, as has the rationale for Cal. Evid. Code Ann. § 621; instead, our task is simply to identify a rule denying the asserted interest and not to ask whether the basis for that rule—which is the true reflection of the values undergirding it—has changed too often or too recently to call the rule embodying that rationale a "tradition." Moreover, by describing the decisive question as whether Michael's and Victoria's interest is one that has been "traditionally *protected by* our society," rather than one that society traditionally has thought important (with or without protecting it), and by suggesting that our sole function is to "*discern* the society's views," the plurality acts as if the only purpose of the Due Process Clause is to confirm the importance of interests already protected by a majority of the States. Transforming the protection afforded by the Due Process Clause into a redundancy mocks those who, with care and purpose, wrote the Fourteenth Amendment.

In construing the Fourteenth Amendment to offer shelter only to those interests specifically protected by historical practice, moreover, the plurality ignores the kind of society in which our Constitution exists. We are not an assimilative, homogeneous society, but a facilitative, pluralistic one, in which we must be willing to abide someone else's unfamiliar or even repellent practice because the same tolerant impulse protects our own idiosyncracies. Even if we can agree, therefore, that "family" and "parenthood" are part of the good life, it is absurd to assume that we can agree on the content of those terms and destructive to pretend that we do. In a community such as ours, "liberty" must include the freedom not to conform. The plurality today squashes this freedom by requiring specific approval from history before protecting anything in the name of liberty.

The document that the plurality construes today is unfamiliar to me. It is not the living charter that I have taken to be our Constitution; it is instead a stagnant, archaic, hidebound document steeped in the prejudices and superstitions of a time long past. *This* Constitution does not recognize that times change,

does not see that sometimes a practice or rule outlives its foundations. I cannot accept an interpretive method that does such violence to the charter that I am bound by oath to uphold.

II

The plurality's reworking of our interpretive approach is all the more troubling because it is unnecessary. This is not a case in which we face a "new" kind of interest, one that requires us to consider for the first time whether the Constitution protects it. On the contrary, we confront an interest—that of a parent and child in their relationship with each other—that was among the first that this Court acknowledged in its cases defining the "liberty" protected by the Constitution, see, e.g., *Meyer v. Nebraska, Skinner v. Oklahoma*, and I think I am safe in saying that no one doubts the wisdom or validity of those decisions. Where the interest under consideration is a parent-child relationship, we need not ask, over and over again, whether that interest is one that society traditionally protects.

Thus, to describe the issue in this case as whether the relationship existing between Michael and Victoria "has been treated as a protected family unit under the historic practices of our society, or whether on any other basis it has been accorded special protection," is to reinvent the wheel. The better approach—indeed, the one commanded by our prior cases and by common sense—is to ask whether the specific parent-child relationship under consideration is close enough to the interests that we already have protected to be deemed an aspect of "liberty" as well. On the facts before us, therefore, the question is not what "level of generality" should be used to describe the relationship between Michael and Victoria, but whether the relationship under consideration is sufficiently substantial to qualify as a liberty interest under our prior cases.

. . .

The evidence is undisputed that Michael, Victoria, and Carole did live together as a family; that is, they shared the same household, Victoria called Michael "Daddy," Michael contributed to Victoria's support, and he is eager to continue his relationship with her. Yet they are not, in the plurality's view, a "unitary family," whereas Gerald, Carole, and Victoria do compose such a family. The only difference between these two sets of relationships, however, is the fact of marriage. The plurality, indeed, expressly recognizes that marriage is the critical fact in denying Michael a constitutionally protected stake in his relationship with Victoria: no fewer than six times, the plurality refers to Michael as the "adulterous natural father" (emphasis added) or the like. However, the very premise of Stanley and the cases following it is that marriage is not decisive in answering the question whether the Constitution protects the parental relationship under consideration. These cases are, after all, important precisely because they involve the rights of unwed fathers. . . .

The plurality's exclusive rather than inclusive definition of the "unitary family" is out of step with other decisions as well. This pinched conception of "the family," crucial as it is in rejecting Michael's and Victoria's claims of a liberty interest, is jarring in light of our many cases preventing the States from denying important interests or statuses to those whose situations do not fit the government's narrow view of the family. . . .

. . .

IV

The atmosphere surrounding today's decision is one of make-believe. Beginning with the suggestion that the situation confronting us here does not repeat itself every day in every corner of the country, moving on to the claim that it is tradition alone that supplies the details of the liberty that the Constitution protects, and passing finally to the notion that the Court always has recognized a cramped vision of "the family," today's decision lets stand California's pronouncement that Michael—whom blood tests show to a 98 percent probability to be Victoria's father—is not Victoria's father. When and if the Court awakes to reality, it will find a world very different from the one it expects.

JUSTICE WHITE, with whom JUSTICE BRENNAN joins, dissenting.

California law, as the plurality describes it, tells us that, except in limited circumstances, California declares it to be "*irrelevant* for paternity purposes whether a child conceived during, and born into, an existing marriage was begotten by someone other than the husband." This I do not accept, for the fact that Michael H. is the biological father of Victoria is to me highly relevant to whether he has rights, as a father or otherwise, with respect to the child. Because I believe that Michael H. has a liberty interest that cannot be denied without due process of the law, I must dissent.

I

Like JUSTICES BRENNAN, MARSHALL, BLACKMUN, and STEVENS, I do not agree with the plurality opinion's conclusion that a natural father can never "have a constitutionally protected interest in his relationship with a child whose mother was married to, and cohabiting with, another man at the time of the child's conception and birth." Prior cases here have recognized the liberty interest of a father in his relationship with his child. In none of

these cases did we indicate that the father's rights were dependent on the marital status of the mother or biological father. The basic principle enunciated in the Court's unwed father cases is that an unwed father who has demonstrated a sufficient commitment to his paternity by way of personal, financial, or custodial responsibilities has a protected liberty interest in a relationship with his child.

We have not before faced the question of a biological father's relationship with his child when the child was born while the mother was married to another man. On several occasions however, we have considered whether a biological father has a constitutionally cognizable interest in an opportunity to establish paternity. . . .

. . .

In the case now before us, Michael H. is not a father unwilling to assume his responsibilities as a parent. To the contrary, he is a father who has asserted his interests in raising and providing for his child since the very time of the child's birth. The facts in this case satisfy the *Lehr* criteria, which focused on the relationship between father and child, not on the relationship between father and mother. Under *Lehr* a "mere biological relationship" is not enough, but in light of Carole's vicissitudes, what more could Michael have done? It is clear enough that Michael more than meets the mark in establishing the constitutionally protected liberty interest discussed in *Lehr* and recognized in *Stanley v. Illinois*, and *Caban v. Mohammed*. He therefore has a liberty interest entitled to protection under the Due Process Clause of the Fourteenth Amendment.

II

California plainly denies Michael this protection, by refusing him the opportunity to rebut the State's presumption that the mother's husband is the father of the child. California law not only deprives Michael of a legal parent-child relationship with his daughter Victoria but even denies him the opportunity to introduce blood-test evidence to rebut the demonstrable fiction that Gerald is Victoria's father. . . .

The interest in protecting a child from the social stigma of illegitimacy lacks any real connection to the facts of a case where a father is seeking to establish, rather than repudiate, paternity. The "stigma of illegitimacy" argument harks back to ancient common law when there were no blood tests to ascertain that the husband could not "by the laws of nature" be the child's father. . . . I see no reason to debate the plurality's multilingual explorations into "spousal nonaccess" and ancient policy concerns behind bastardy laws. It may be true that a child conceived in an extramarital relationship would be considered a "bastard" in the literal sense of the word, but whatever stigma remains in today's society is far less compelling in the context of a child of a married mother, especially when there is a father asserting paternity and seeking a relationship with his child. It is hardly rare in this world of divorce and remarriage for a child to live with the "father" to whom her mother is married, and still have a relationship with her biological father.

The State's professed interest in the preservation of the existing marital unit is a more significant concern. To be sure, the intrusion of an outsider asserting that he is the father of a child whom the husband believes to be his own would be disruptive to say the least. On the facts of this case, however, Gerald was well aware of the liaison between Carole and Michael. The conclusive presumption of evidentiary rule § 621 virtually eliminates the putative father's chances of succeeding in his effort to establish paternity, but it by no means prevents him from asserting the claim. It may serve as a deterrent to such claims but does not eliminate the threat. Further, the argument that the conclusive presumption preserved the sanctity of the marital unit had more sway in a time when the husband was similarly prevented from challenging paternity.

. . .

As the Court has said: "The significance of the biological connection is that it offers the natural father an opportunity that no other male possesses to develop a relationship with his offspring. If he grasps that opportunity and accepts some measure of responsibility for the child's future, he may enjoy the blessings of the parent-child relationship and make uniquely valuable contributions to the child's development." *Lehr.* It is as if this passage was addressed to Michael. Yet the plurality today recants. Michael eagerly grasped the opportunity to have a relationship with his daughter (he lived with her; he declared her to be his child; he provided financial support for her) and still, with today's opinion, his opportunity has vanished. He has been rendered a stranger to his child.

. . .

f. Homosexuality and Sexual Privacy

Are sexual orientation and sexual expression aspects of personhood that are protected from state interference under substantive due process? In *Bowers v. Hardwick*, the Supreme Court considered whether homosexuals' sexual conduct was protected by the right of privacy against criminal prohibition by state sodomy laws. By the time of *Bowers*, the gay rights movement had raised Americans' consciousness about attitudes about homosexuality and had opposed laws and practices that disadvantage gays and lesbians. Many date the birth of this movement to the "Stonewall Rebellion" on June 27, 1969, when gay male patrons of the Stonewall Bar in New York City threw bottles and stones in response to police harassment. The *Bowers* decision, upholding the Georgia sodomy statute, appeared to foreclose homosexuals' claims for constitutional protection based on due process liberty. Hardwick did not challenge the Georgia law based on the Eighth or Ninth Amendments or the Equal Protection Clause, and the Court's holding did not extend to those constitutional provisions.

Michael Hardwick was arrested in the bedroom of his own home while engaging in consensual oral sex with another man. He was charged with violating a Georgia criminal statute, which provided that "[a] person commits the offense of sodomy when he performs or submits to any sexual act involving the sex organs of one person and the mouth or anus of another." When the district attorney decided to drop the charges, Hardwick brought a federal suit challenging the constitutionality of the Georgia statute insofar as it criminalized consensual sexual activity. Although the Georgia statute's prohibition applied equally to heterosexual and homosexual conduct, the Supreme Court addressed only its application to homosexuals. The case is therefore significant—although not controlling—not only with respect to its holding regarding sodomy statutes, but also with respect to the constitutionality of other laws that discriminate against homosexuals, in areas such as adoption, child custody, and marriage.

Bowers became a case concerning the due process rights of homosexuals in part because of the way Hardwick framed his constitutional claim. His complaint alleged that the law placed him "and all other practicing homosexuals in imminent danger of arrest, prosecution, and imprisonment."[163] Hardwick was thus able to avoid the fate of his co-plaintiffs, a married couple, whose claim that the sodomy law deterred them from engaging in prohibited private sexual activity was dismissed for lack of standing. (It was highly unlikely that the police would arrest a married, heterosexual couple engaged in conduct comparable to Hardwick's.) Moreover, Hardwick's lawyers were gay rights activists specifically interested in challenging the Georgia sodomy law as it applied to homosexuals.[164]

The Court's opinion in *Bowers* again interpreted the due process clause to protect only traditionally recognized rights from legislative interference. Justice White invoked the history of the prohibition against sodomy in order to discern the Framers' intentions regarding the scope of Fourteenth Amendment protection. Even if we accept this originalist interpretation, however, it is not clear what conclusion it yields since Hardwick's conduct probably was *not* a crime when the Fourteenth Amendment was adopted. It appears that American courts did not interpret criminal sodomy statutes to prohibit fellatio, the conduct for which Hardwick was arrested, until after 1897.[165] As several commentators have noted, "[t]raditions can be described at varying levels of generality."[166] The Court might look to, for example, a tradition of punishing fellatio, a tradition of criminalizing "deviant" sexual activity, or a tradition of respect for intimate associations. The Justices' opinions reflect these divergent possibilities for identifying the tradition—and liberty—at stake in the case.

---

[163] Complaint 15, Joint Appendix at 5, Bowers v. Hardwick, 478 U.S. 186 (1986) (No. 85–140).

[164] Anne B. Goldstein, *Reasoning About Homosexuality: A Commentary on Janet Halley's "Reasoning About Sodomy: Act and Identity in and After Bowers v. Hardwick*, 79 Va. L. Rev. 1781, 1791 n.54 (1993).

[165] Anne B. Goldstein, *History, Homosexuality and Political Values: Searching for the Hidden Determinants of Bowers v, Hardwick*, 9 Yale L.J. 1073, 1082–85 (1988).

[166] Cass R. Sunstein, *Sexual Orientation and the Constitution: A Note on the Relationship between Due Process and Equal Protection*, 55 U. Chi. L. Rev. 1161, 1173 (1988); *See also* Laurence H. Tribe and Michael C. Dorf, *Levels of Generality in the Definition of Rights*, 57 U. Chi. L. Rev. 1057 (1990).

Bowers v. Hardwick
478 U.S. 186 (1986)

Justice White delivered the opinion of the Court.

. . .

This case does not require a judgment on whether laws against sodomy between consenting adults in general, or between homosexuals in particular, are wise or desirable. It raises no question about the right or propriety of state legislative decisions to repeal their laws that criminalize homosexual sodomy, or of state-court decisions invalidating those laws on state constitutional grounds. The issue presented is whether the Federal Constitution confers a fundamental right upon homosexuals to engage in sodomy and hence invalidates the laws of the many States that still make such conduct illegal and have done so for a very long time. The case also calls for some judgment about the limits of the Court's role in carrying out its constitutional mandate.

We first register our disagreement with the Court of Appeals and with respondent [Hardwick] that the Court's prior cases have construed the Constitution to confer a right of privacy that extends to homosexual sodomy and for all intents and purposes have decided this case. The reach of this line of cases was sketched in *Carey v. Population Services International. Pierce v. Society of Sisters* and *Meyer v. Nebraska* were described as dealing with child rearing and education; *Prince v. Massachusetts* with family relationships; *Skinner v.*

Oklahoma ex rel. Williamson with procreation; *Loving v. Virginia* with marriage; *Griswold v. Connecticut* and *Eisenstadt v. Baird* with contraception; and *Roe v. Wade* with abortion. The latter three cases were interpreted as construing the Due Process Clause of the Fourteenth Amendment to confer a fundamental individual right to decide whether or not to beget or bear a child.

Accepting the decisions in these cases and the above description of them, we think it evident that none of the rights announced in those cases bears any resemblance to the claimed constitutional right of homosexuals to engage in acts of sodomy that is asserted in this case. No connection between family, marriage, or procreation on the one hand and homosexual activity on the other has been demonstrated, either by the Court of Appeals or by respondent. Moreover, any claim that these cases nevertheless stand for the proposition that any kind of private sexual conduct between consenting adults is constitutionally insulated from state proscription is unsupportable. Indeed, the Court's opinion in *Carey* twice asserted that the privacy right, which the *Griswold* line of cases found to be one of the protections provided by the Due Process Clause, did not reach so far.

Precedent aside, however, respondent would have us announce, as the Court of Appeals did, a fundamental right to engage in homosexual sodomy. This we are quite unwilling to do. It is true that despite the language of the Due Process Clauses of the Fifth and Fourteenth Amendments, which appears to focus only on the processes by which life, liberty, or property is taken, the cases are legion in which those Clauses have been interpreted to have substantive content, subsuming rights that to a great extent are immune from federal or state regulation or proscription. Among such cases are those recognizing rights that have little or no textual support in the constitutional language. *Meyer*, *Prince*, and *Pierce* fall in this category, as do the privacy cases from Griswold to *Carey*.

Striving to assure itself and the public that announcing rights not readily identifiable in the Constitution's text involves much more than the imposition of the Justices' own choice of values on the States and the Federal Government, the Court has sought to identify the nature of the rights qualifying for heightened judicial protection. In *Palko v. Connecticut*, 302 U.S. 319, 325, 326 (1937), it was said that this category includes those fundamental liberties that are "implicit in the concept of ordered liberty," such that "neither liberty nor justice would exist if [they] were sacrificed." A different description of fundamental liberties appeared in *Moore v. East Cleveland* (opinion of

POWELL, J.), where they are characterized as those liberties that are "deeply rooted in this Nation's history and tradition."

It is obvious to us that neither of these formulations would extend a fundamental right to homosexuals to engage in acts of consensual sodomy. Proscriptions against that conduct have ancient roots. Sodomy was a criminal offense at common law and was forbidden by the laws of the original 13 States when they ratified the Bill of Rights. In 1868, when the Fourteenth Amendment was ratified, all but 5 of the 37 States in the Union had criminal sodomy laws. In fact, until 1961, all 50 States outlawed sodomy, and today, 24 States and the District of Columbia continue to provide criminal penalties for sodomy performed in private and between consenting adults. Against this background, to claim that a right to engage in such conduct is "deeply rooted in this Nation's history and tradition" or "implicit in the concept of ordered liberty" is, at best, facetious.

Nor are we inclined to take a more expansive view of our authority to discover new fundamental rights imbedded in the Due Process Clause. The Court is most vulnerable and comes nearest to illegitimacy when it deals with judge-made constitutional law having little or no cognizable roots in the language or design of the Constitution. That this is so was painfully demonstrated by the face-off between the Executive and the Court in the 1930's, which resulted in the repudiation of much of the substantive gloss that the Court had placed on the Due Process Clauses of the Fifth and Fourteenth Amendments. There should be, therefore, great resistance to expand the substantive reach of those Clauses, particularly if it requires redefining the category of rights deemed to be fundamental. Otherwise, the Judiciary necessarily takes to itself further authority to govern the country without express constitutional authority. The claimed right pressed on us today falls far short of overcoming this resistance.

Respondent, however, asserts that the result should be different where the homosexual conduct occurs in the privacy of the home. He relies on *Stanley v. Georgia*, 394 U.S. 557 (1969), where the Court held that the First Amendment prevents conviction for possessing and reading obscene material in the privacy of one's home: "If the First Amendment means anything, it means that a State has no business telling a man, sitting alone in his house, what books he may read or what films he may watch."

Stanley did protect conduct that would not have been protected outside the home, and it partially prevented the enforcement of state obscenity laws; but the decision was firmly grounded in the First Amendment. The right pressed upon us here has no similar support in the text of the Constitution, and it does not qualify for recognition under the prevailing principles for construing the Fourteenth Amendment. Its limits are also difficult to discern. Plainly enough, otherwise illegal conduct is not always immunized whenever it occurs in the home. Victimless crimes, such as the possession and use of illegal drugs, do not escape the law where they are committed at home. *Stanley* itself recognized that its holding offered no protection for the possession in the home of drugs, firearms, or stolen goods. And if respondent's submission is limited to the voluntary sexual conduct between consenting adults, it would be difficult, except by fiat, to limit the claimed right to homosexual conduct while leaving exposed to prosecution adultery, incest, and other sexual crimes even though they are committed in the home. We are unwilling to start down that road.

Even if the conduct at issue here is not a fundamental right, respondent asserts that there must be a rational basis for the law and that there is none in this case other than the presumed belief of a majority of the electorate in Georgia that homosexual sodomy is immoral and unacceptable. This is said to be an inadequate rationale to support the law. The law, however, is constantly based on notions of morality, and if all laws representing essentially moral choices are to be invalidated under the Due Process Clause, the courts will be very busy indeed. Even respondent makes no such claim, but insists that majority sentiments about the morality of homosexuality should be declared inadequate. We do not agree, and are unpersuaded that the sodomy laws of some 25 States should be invalidated on this basis.

Accordingly, the judgment of the Court of Appeals is Reversed.

CHIEF JUSTICE BURGER, concurring.

I join the Court's opinion, but I write separately to underscore my view that in constitutional terms there is no such thing as a fundamental right to commit homosexual sodomy.

As the Court notes, the proscriptions against sodomy have very "ancient roots." Decisions of individuals relating to homosexual conduct have been subject to state intervention throughout the history of Western civilization. Condemnation of those practices is firmly rooted in Judeo-Christian moral and ethical standards. Homosexual sodomy was a capital crime under Roman law. During the English Reformation when powers of the ecclesiastical courts were transferred to the King's Courts, the first English statute criminalizing sodomy was passed. Blackstone described "the infamous *crime against nature*" as an offense of "deeper malignity" than rape, a heinous act "the very mention of which is a disgrace to human nature," and "a crime not fit to be

named." The common law of England, including its prohibition of sodomy, became the received law of Georgia and the other Colonies. In 1816 the Georgia Legislature passed the statute at issue here, and that statute has been continuously in force in one form or another since that time. To hold that the act of homosexual sodomy is somehow protected as a fundamental right would be to cast aside millennia of moral teaching.

This is essentially not a question of personal "preferences" but rather of the legislative authority of the State. I find nothing in the Constitution depriving a State of the power to enact the statute challenged here.

JUSTICE POWELL, concurring.

I join the opinion of the Court. I agree with the Court that there is no fundamental right—*i.e.*, no substantive right under the Due Process Clause—such as that claimed by respondent Hardwick, and found to exist by the Court of Appeals. This is not to suggest, however, that respondent may not be protected by the Eighth Amendment of the Constitution. The Georgia statute at issue in this case, authorizes a court to imprison a person for up to 20 years for a single private, consensual act of sodomy. In my view, a prison sentence for such conduct—certainly a sentence of long duration—would create a serious Eighth Amendment issue. . . .

. . .

JUSTICE BLACKMUN, with whom JUSTICE BRENNAN, JUSTICE MARSHALL, and JUSTICE STEVENS join, dissenting.

This case is no more about "a fundamental right to engage in homosexual sodomy," as the Court purports to declare, ante, at 191, than *Stanley v. Georgia*, was about a fundamental right to watch obscene movies, or *Katz v. United States*, 389 U.S. 347 (1967), was about a fundamental right to place interstate bets from a telephone booth. Rather, this case is about "the most comprehensive of rights and the right most valued by civilized men," namely, "the right to be let alone." *Olmstead v. United States*, 277 U.S. 438, 478 (1928) (Brandeis, J., dissenting).

The statute at issue denies individuals the right to decide for themselves whether to engage in particular forms of private, consensual sexual activity. . . . I believe we must analyze respondent Hardwick's claim in the light of the values that underlie the constitutional right to privacy. If that right means anything, it means that, before Georgia can prosecute its citizens for making choices about the most intimate aspects of their lives, it must do more than assert that the choice they have made is an "'abominable crime not fit to be named among Christians.'"

. . .

II

"Our cases long have recognized that the Constitution embodies a promise that a certain private sphere of individual liberty will be kept largely beyond the reach of government." *Thornburgh v. American College of Obstetricians & Gynecologists*. In construing the right to privacy, the Court has proceeded along two somewhat distinct, albeit complementary, lines. First, it has recognized a privacy interest with reference to certain *decisions* that are properly for the individual to make. Second, it has recognized a privacy interest with reference to certain *places* without regard for the particular activities in which the individuals who occupy them are engaged. The case before us implicates both the decisional and the spatial aspects of the right to privacy.

A

The Court concludes today that none of our prior cases dealing with various decisions that individuals are entitled to make free of governmental interference "bears any resemblance to the claimed constitutional right of homosexuals to engage in acts of sodomy that is asserted in this case." While it is true that these cases may be characterized by their connection to protection of the family, the Court's conclusion that they extend no further than this boundary ignores the warning in *Moore v. East Cleveland* against "[closing] our eyes to the basic reasons why certain rights associated with the family have been accorded shelter under the Fourteenth Amendment's Due Process Clause." We protect those rights not because they contribute, in some direct and material way, to the general public welfare, but because they form so central a part of an individual's life. "[The] concept of privacy embodies the 'moral fact that a person belongs to himself and not others nor to society as a whole.'" *Thornburgh* (STEVENS, J., concurring), quoting Fried, Correspondence, 6 Phil. & Pub. Affairs 288–289 (1977). And so we protect the decision whether to marry precisely because marriage "is an association that promotes a way of life, not causes; a harmony in living, not political faiths; a bilateral loyalty, not commercial or social projects." *Griswold*. We protect the decision whether to have a child because parenthood alters so dramatically an individual's self-definition, not because of demographic considerations or the Bible's command to be fruitful and multiply. And we protect the family because it contributes so powerfully to the happiness of individuals, not because of a preference for stereotypical households. The Court recognized in *Roberts* [*v. United States Jaycees*] that the "ability independently to define one's identity that is central to any concept of liberty" cannot truly be exercised in a vacuum; we all

depend on the "emotional enrichment from close ties with others."

Only the most willful blindness could obscure the fact that sexual intimacy is "a sensitive, key relationship of human existence, central to family life, community welfare, and the development of human personality," *Paris Adult Theatre I v. Slaton*. The fact that individuals define themselves in a significant way through their intimate sexual relationships with others suggests, in a Nation as diverse as ours, that there may be many "right" ways of conducting those relationships, and that much of the richness of a relationship will come from the freedom an individual has to *choose* the form and nature of these intensely personal bonds.

The Court claims that its decision today merely refuses to recognize a fundamental right to engage in homosexual sodomy; what the Court really has refused to recognize is the fundamental interest all individuals have in controlling the nature of their intimate associations with others.

B

The behavior for which Hardwick faces prosecution occurred in his own home, a place to which the Fourth Amendment attaches special significance. The Court's treatment of this aspect of the case is symptomatic of its overall refusal to consider the broad principles that have informed our treatment of privacy in specific cases. Just as the right to privacy is more than the mere aggregation of a number of entitlements to engage in specific behavior, so too, protecting the physical integrity of the home is more than merely a means of protecting specific activities that often take place there. . . .

. . .

The central place that *Stanley* gives Justice Brandeis' dissent in *Olmstead*, a case raising no First Amendment claim, shows that *Stanley* rested as much on the Court's understanding of the Fourth Amendment as it did on the First. . . . "The right of the people to be secure in their . . . houses," expressly guaranteed by the Fourth Amendment, is perhaps the most "textual" of the various constitutional provisions that inform our understanding of the right to privacy, and thus I cannot agree with the Court's statement that "[t]he right pressed upon us here has no . . . support in the text of the Constitution." Indeed, the right of an individual to conduct intimate relationships in the intimacy of his or her own home seems to me to be the heart of the Constitution's protection of privacy.

III

The Court's failure to comprehend the magnitude of the liberty interests at stake in this case leads it to slight the question whether petitioner, on behalf of the State, has justified Georgia's infringement on these interests. I believe that neither of the two general justifications for § 16-6-2 that petitioner has advanced warrants dismissing respondent's challenge for failure to state a claim.

First, petitioner asserts that the acts made criminal by the statute may have serious adverse consequences for "the general public health and welfare," such as spreading communicable diseases or fostering other criminal activity. Inasmuch as this case was dismissed by the District Court on the pleadings, it is not surprising that the record before us is barren of any evidence to support petitioner's claim. In light of the state of the record, I see no justification for the Court's attempt to equate the private, consensual sexual activity at issue here with the "possession in the home of drugs, firearms, or stolen goods," to which *Stanley* refused to extend its protection. None of the behavior so mentioned in *Stanley* can properly be viewed as "[v]ictimless": drugs and weapons are inherently dangerous, and for property to be "stolen," someone must have been wrongfully deprived of it. Nothing in the record before the Court provides any justification for finding the activity forbidden by § 16-6-2 to be physically dangerous, either to the persons engaged in it or to others.

The core of petitioner's defense of § 16-6-2, however, is that respondent and others who engage in the conduct prohibited by § 16-6-2 interfere with Georgia's exercise of the "'right of the Nation and of the States to maintain a decent society.'" Essentially, petitioner argues, and the Court agrees, that the fact that the acts described in § 16-6-2 "for hundreds of years, if not thousands, have been uniformly condemned as immoral" is a sufficient reason to permit a State to ban them today.

I cannot agree that either the length of time a majority has held its convictions or the passions with which it defends them can withdraw legislation from this Court's scrutiny. As Justice Jackson wrote so eloquently for the Court in *West Virginia Board of Education v. Barnette*, 319 U.S. 624, 641–642 (1943), "we apply the limitations of the Constitution with no fear that freedom to be intellectually and spiritually diverse or even contrary will disintegrate the social organization.... [F]reedom to differ is not limited to things that do not matter much. That would be a mere shadow of freedom. The test of its substance is the right to differ as to things that touch the heart of the existing order." It is precisely because the issue raised by this case touches the heart of what makes individuals what they are that we should be especially sensitive to the rights of those whose choices upset the majority.

The assertion that "traditional Judeo-Christian values proscribe" the conduct involved, cannot provide an adequate justification for § 16-6-2. That certain, but by no means all, religious groups condemn the behavior at issue gives the State no license to impose their judgments on the entire citizenry. The legitimacy of secular legislation depends instead on whether the State can advance some justification for its law beyond its conformity to religious doctrine. Thus, far from buttressing his case, petitioner's invocation of Leviticus, Romans, St. Thomas Aquinas, and sodomy's heretical status during the Middle Ages undermines his suggestion that § 16-6-2 represents a legitimate use of secular coercive power. A State can no more punish private behavior because of religious intolerance than it can punish such behavior because of racial animus.... No matter how uncomfortable a certain group may make the majority of this Court, we have held that "[m]ere public intolerance or animosity cannot constitutionally justify the deprivation of a person's physical liberty." *O'Connor v. Donaldson*, 422 U.S. 563, 575 (1975).

. . .

JUSTICE STEVENS, with whom JUSTICE BRENNAN and JUSTICE MARSHALL join, dissenting.

Like the statute that is challenged in this case, the rationale of the Court's opinion applies equally to the prohibited conduct regardless of whether the parties who engage in it are married or unmarried, or are of the same or different sexes. Sodomy was condemned as an odious and sinful type of behavior during the formative period of the common law. That condemnation was equally damning for heterosexual and homosexual sodomy. Moreover, it provided no special exemption for married couples. The license to cohabit and to produce legitimate offspring simply did not include any permission to engage in sexual conduct that was considered a "crime against nature."

The history of the Georgia statute before us clearly reveals this traditional prohibition of heterosexual, as well as homosexual, sodomy. Indeed, at one point in the 20th century, Georgia's law was construed to permit certain sexual conduct between homosexual women even though such conduct was prohibited between heterosexuals. The history of the statutes cited by the majority as proof for the proposition that sodomy is not constitutionally protected, similarly reveals a prohibition on heterosexual, as well as homosexual, sodomy.

Because the Georgia statute expresses the traditional view that sodomy is an immoral kind of conduct regardless of the identity of the persons who engage in it, I believe that a proper analysis of its constitutionality requires consideration of two questions: First, may a State totally prohibit the described conduct by means of a neutral law applying without exception to all persons subject to its jurisdiction? If not, may the State save the statute by announcing that it will only enforce the law against homosexuals? . . .

I

Our prior cases make two propositions abundantly clear. First, the fact that the governing majority in a State has traditionally viewed a particular practice as immoral is not a sufficient reason for upholding a law prohibiting the practice; neither history nor tradition could save a law prohibiting miscegenation from constitutional attack. Second, individual decisions by married persons, concerning the intimacies of their physical relationship, even when not intended to produce offspring, are a form of "liberty" protected by the Due Process Clause of the Fourteenth Amendment. *Griswold*. Moreover, this protection extends to intimate choices by unmarried as well as married persons. *Carey; Eisenstadt*.

. . .

Society has every right to encourage its individual members to follow particular traditions in expressing affection for one another and in gratifying their personal desires. It, of course, may prohibit an individual from imposing his will on another to satisfy his own selfish interests. It also may prevent an individual from interfering with, or violating, a legally sanctioned and protected relationship, such as marriage. And it may explain the relative advantages and disadvantages of different forms of intimate expression. But when individual married couples are isolated from observation by others, the way in which they voluntarily choose to conduct their intimate relations is a matter for them—not the State—to decide. The essential "liberty" that animated the development of the law in cases like *Griswold*, *Eisenstadt*, and *Carey* surely embraces the right to engage in nonreproductive, sexual conduct that others may consider offensive or immoral.

Paradoxical as it may seem, our prior cases thus establish that a State may not prohibit sodomy within "the sacred precincts of marital bedrooms," or, indeed, between unmarried heterosexual adults. In all events, it is perfectly clear that the State of Georgia may not totally prohibit the conduct proscribed by § 16-6-2 of the Georgia Criminal Code.

II

If the Georgia statute cannot be enforced as it is written—if the conduct it seeks to prohibit is a protected form of liberty for the vast majority of Georgia's citizens—the State must assume the burden of justifying a selective application of its law. Either the persons to whom Georgia seeks to apply its statute do not have the same interest in "liberty" that others have, or there must be a reason why the State may be permitted to apply a generally applicable law to certain persons that it does not apply to others.

The first possibility is plainly unacceptable. Although the meaning of the principle that "all men are created equal" is not always clear, it surely must mean that every free citizen has the same interest in "liberty" that the members of the majority share. . . .

The second possibility is similarly unacceptable. A policy of selective application must be supported by a neutral and legitimate interest—something more substantial than a habitual dislike for, or ignorance about, the disfavored group. Neither the State nor the Court has identified any such interest in this case. The Court has posited as a justification for the Georgia statute "the presumed belief of a majority of the electorate in Georgia that homosexual sodomy is immoral and unacceptable." But the Georgia electorate has expressed no such belief—instead, its representatives enacted a law that presumably reflects the belief that all sodomy is immoral and unacceptable. Unless the Court is prepared to conclude that such a law is constitutional, it may not rely on the work product of the Georgia Legislature to support its holding. For the Georgia statute does not single out homosexuals as a separate class meriting special disfavored treatment.

. . .

DER: Although the judicial excesses of economic due process led to its demise, substantive due process remains a vital, if criticized, constitutional doctrine in the realm of family. Does substantive due process in the family avoid the dangers of substantive due process in the market? The concept of family liberty has the potential of protecting nontraditional families from legislative standardization. It has become a conservative force, however, in the hands of conservative judges. Family liberty gives the Court the power to protect family decisions that conform to a traditional conception of family roles that have subordinated women, homosexuals, and minorities. As feminist critics of the right of privacy have noted, protecting the liberty of autonomous individuals in the family may perpetuate the unequal family relationships that already exist. Sanctioning the liberty of certain family members may only allow them to continue suppressing others. While family privacy shields the family from state intervention, intervention may be necessary to protect less powerful family members from harms such as domestic violence. Just as substantive economic due process shielded traditional social structures from legislative reform, family due process can preserve traditional family relationships against the forces of social change. Thus, privacy may impose repressive conceptions of the family rather than liberate us from them.

Surely the majority in *Bowers* and plurality in *Michael H.* must be wrong in their assertion that the due process clause protects only family practices prevalent at the time of the Fourteenth Amendment's enactment, for this interpretation would preserve antimiscegenation laws, women's confinement to the home, and nonrecognition of children born out of wedlock. The Court must ultimately determine which traditions are worthy of upholding and which are not. Justice White (who wrote the majority opinion in *Bowers*, but dissented in *Michael H.*) apparently believed that the tradition condemning homosexuality was more valuable than that denying parental rights to unwed fathers. White's difference of opinion about these two traditions reflects as much "judicial predilection" as decisions based on other standards for determining fundamental liberties.

The Court's interpretation of the Fourteenth Amendment—grounded in subordinating traditions—makes substantive due process profoundly conservative, if not affirmatively repressive. Laws criminalizing sodomy and abortion and imposing the marital presumption are all examples of state intervention in the family that enforce traditional, patriarchal relationships. As we learned from the social horrors of economic due process, granting individuals liberty without concern for societal inequities will inevitably benefit the powerful. We can reject the economic due process of *Lochner* while embracing the personal due process of *Roe* and *Moore* because we distinguish between the social and political values that were upheld in the two cases. The Court should apply family liberty in order to reject, rather than preserve, traditions that have subjugated people based on race, gender, class, and sexual orientation.

RLW: *Bowers* is inconsistent with *Roe* and the Court's earlier privacy decisions. If the right of privacy includes the right to decide whether to carry a baby to term, should it not also include the right to choose one's sexual partner? The latter decision is one of the most intimate and private decisions in a person's life.

DEL: It is hard to ignore the homophobic spirit of the *Bowers* opinion, and even less the homophobic letter of Chief Justice Burger's concurrence. Difficult to resist too is Justice Blackmun's dissenting observation in *Hardwick* "that depriving individuals of the right to choose for themselves how to conduct their intimate relationships poses a far greater threat to the values most deeply rooted in our nation's history than tolerance of nonconformity could ever do." It is difficult to figure how the right of privacy amounts to much if it does not protect personal decisions or orientations not cut from a dominant mold. It is fair to ask, however, why a community that is offended by any lifestyle, orientation or behavior should be *constitutionally* barred from exercising its police power in a proscriptive fashion? Reference to an indeterminate right of privacy seems rather conclusory, and the suggestion that the right defines itself broadly enough seems inadequate, especially when the real issue is the state of the society's moral development. If animus toward, disapproval of, or discomfort with gays and lesbians are common cultural factors in a given community, advertence to a right of privacy seems more an incantation than an explanation of why citizens cannot account for their moral visions and needs. A sense that such cultural perspective is retarded or subordinating does not substitute for reasoning that supports broadening the contours of the right of privacy or explain in a constitutional way why a community may not trade on its fears, apprehensions or ignorance.

The *Hardwick* and *Michael H.* decisions also exemplify nicely how manipulative analysis can be even by those who object to allegedly neo-Lochnerist exercises. In *Michael*

M., Justice Scalia refined the inquiry into the nation's history and traditions by requiring that the interest claimed as fundamental be examined at its highest level of specificity rather than abstraction. The analytical choice ratifies the Court's decision in *Hardwick* that a "fundamental right to engage in homosexual sodomy," rather than "the right to be let alone," was at stake. In *Michael H.*, Scalia asserts, "what counts" is not the status of natural father but his role in conceiving a child as the consequence of an extramarital affair. A primary failure of *Hardwick* and *Michael H.* is announcing than the higher level of specificity is "what counts," but not explaining why it is a more logical reference point than the higher level of abstraction. Insofar as the standard is outcome-determinative-- with a higher level of abstraction favoring recognition of a right as fundamental and the higher level of specificity a precursor to repudiation of a constitutional interest—some amplification for the prioritization is in order. What these decisions ultimately suggest, given the analytical choices they reflect, is that the case against Lochnerist type adventur- ism itself can indulge the subjectivism and ideological filtration that it condemns.

PAH: What is revealed in the recent family liberty and sexual privacy rulings, as in the Court's recent interpretations of the Fourteenth Amendment Equal Protection Clause, is what Professor Girardeau Spann has described as the "veiled majoritarian nature of the Supreme Court,"[1] challenging the countermajoritarian image often associated with the traditional model of judicial review. The Court's reliance on narrowly defined traditions and intolerance for difference in these cases contradicts any notion of the Court as the protector of minority interests, reflecting instead a view that principled Constitutional analysis requires the Court to forsake preferences of those whose life experiences are at the social margins.

---

[1] Girardeau Spann, *Pure Politics*, 88 MICH. L. REV. 1971 (1990).

g. The "Right to Die"

As medical science has improved the technological means for prolonging life, states have had to grapple with patients' requests to "die with dignity" by refusing life-sustain- ing medical treatment and even by taking affirmative steps to end their own lives. The right to refuse medical treatment, commonly referred to as the "right to die," has its foundation in common law traditions that respect patient autonomy and bodily integ- rity. The doctrine of informed consent, for example, requires physicians to obtain per- mission for any medical procedure after disclosing to the patient the risks involved. Indeed, medical treatment without consent constituted a crime. In the words of Justice Cardozo: "Every human being of adult years and sound mind has a right to determine what shall be done with his own body; and a surgeon who performs an operation without his patient's consent commits an assault. . . . "[167] At common law, even the touching of one person by another without consent and without legal justification was a battery. The patient's right *not* to consent to medical treatment flows logically from the require- ment that physicians obtain informed consent.

Over the last several decades, state courts and legislatures have increasingly ac- cepted claims that competent adults have a right to terminate life-sustaining medical treatment and even to euthanasia. State courts have taken diverse approaches in find- ing a right to refuse treatment, relying primarily on state constitutions, statutes, and common law. Some early cases involved patients who refused medical treatment forbid- den by their religious beliefs, thus implicating First Amendment rights as well as

---

[167] Schloendorff v. New York Hospital, 211 N.Y. 125, 127, 105 N.E. 92, 93 (1914).

common-law rights of patient autonomy. The seminal decision in *In re Quinlan*[168] arose when Karen Quinlan entered a persistent vegetative state and her father sought judicial approval to disconnect her respirator. The New Jersey Supreme Court granted the relief, holding that Karen had a right to terminate treatment protected by the right of privacy under the United States Constitution.

More recently, courts have considered the more difficult issue of whether the Constitution protects assisted suicide or voluntary, active euthanasia, where an individual takes affirmative steps to end her life. In a lawsuit filed on behalf of a woman dying of cancer, a man dying of AIDS, and a man suffering from emphysema, the United States Court of Appeals for the Ninth Circuit held that Washington state's statute prohibiting physician-assisted suicide of terminally ill patients who wish to hasten their death was unconstitutional because it placed an undue burden on the exercise of a Fourteenth Amendment liberty interest.[169] In a case considering charges brought against Dr. Jack Kevorkian for assisting in patient suicides, the Michigan Supreme Court held that the federal Constitution's Due Process Clause does not prohibit states from imposing criminal penalties on individuals who assist others in committing suicide.[170] In 1994, Oregon became the first state to allow assisted suicide when voters approved a ballot initiative permitting physicians after a fifteen day waiting period to prescribe lethal medication to terminally ill adult patients who have expressed the desire to die. A federal judge preliminarily enjoined implementation of the initiative, finding serious constitutional questions about its legality and a great threat of irreparable injury.[171]

In *Cruzan v. Director, Missouri Department of Health*, the Supreme Court considered for the first time whether the United States Constitution conferred a right to terminate life-sustaining medical treatment. Certain key aspects of "the right to die" make it easily comparable to the right to an abortion. The decision whether to terminate one's life ranks high with the decision whether to give birth as a critical aspect of personhood and self-determination. Moreover, both forced pregnancy and forced medical treatment can be seen as violations of physical autonomy. Indeed, denying a patient's request to terminate treatment results in an affirmative physical invasion into the patient's body. Thus, like the right to an abortion, the right to terminate medical treatment implicates the due process freedom from bodily restraint and intrusion, as well as its protection of life-defining decisions. As with the right to an abortion, the state asserts an opposing interest in sustaining human life.

On the other hand, there are significant differences between terminating a pregnancy and terminating one's life—differences which may lead to opposite conclusions about the Constitution's protection of each practice. The state's interest in preserving the life of a fully developed human being may be stronger and less controversial than its interest in protecting the potential life of a fetus. The danger of terminating the life of an individual for the wrong reasons or without adequate proof of the patient's free, informed, and competent choice may outweigh the liberty interest in ending one's life. Professor Seth F. Kreimer summarizes the reasons why he believes the rationales of *Roe* and *Casey* do not support a constitutional right to die as follows:

> The value of self-determination in situations of intimate and personal moral conflict is engaged by claims for assisted suicide in ways that differ significantly from the abortion cases. Assisted suicide and voluntary active

---

[168] 70 N.J. 10, 355 A.2d 647, *cert. denied sub nom.* Garger v. New Jersey, 429 U.S. 922 (1976).

[169] Compassion in Dying v. Washington, No. 94-35534 (9th Cir. March 6, 1996).

[170] People v. Kevorkian, 447 Mich. 436, 527 N.W.2d 714 (1994). *See also* Seth F. Kreimer, *Does Pro-Choice Mean Pro-Kevorkian? An Essay on Roe, Casey, and The Right to Die*, 44 AM. U. L. REV. 803, 805 (1995).

[171] Lee v. Oregon, Civ. No. 94–6467-HO (D. Or. Dec. 27, 1994).

euthanasia, unlike abortion, involve the extinction of what all involved agree is a human life. The societal values attached to avoiding the killing of those who do not desire to die, whether because of medical error, the effects of a blurring of norms, or the pervasive connection between treatable clinical depression and suicide are absent in the case of abortion.

Legalization of euthanasia and assisted suicide, unlike abortion, raises the specter or an increasingly cost-conscious medical system advertently or unconsciously tracking vulnerable populations away from expensive and personally demanding medical treatment or palliative care toward less expensive and easier medical suicide. Desperately ill citizens may feel themselves forced to justify their decision to remain alive. And unlike legalized abortion, the prospect of medical suicide threatens to taint pervasively the relations between doctor and patient.

The principles of bodily autonomy that undergird *Casey*, guard against the "plenary override" of a citizen's considered choices regarding her own body. Yet both the moral force of the prohibitions against killing conceded human beings and the practical dangers of legalizing assisted suicide provide justifications for interference, which are absent in the case of abortion.

Finally, the concerns of women's equality that are implicated by abortion are absent from the arguments for assisted suicide or euthanasia. Indeed, while the prohibition of assistance denies to some handicapped individuals the practical option of suicide available to the nonhandicapped, it also arguably shields other handicapped individuals against lethal abuses to which they are disproportionately vulnerable.[172]

These arguments might also support drawing a clear line between a right to resist bodily invasion in the form of medical treatment and a right to demand lethal medical attention.

Cruzan is also a case about the constitutionality of state procedures for determining requests to terminate treatment. The Missouri Supreme Court had denied the request by Nancy Cruzan's parents to withdraw their daughter's artificial feeding and hydration equipment. The question before the United States Supreme Court was whether the federal Constitution prohibits Missouri from making its decision the way it did. For critics of judicial activism, the "right to die," like the right to an abortion, invites the Court to interfere in an area that is best left for resolution by state legislatures. According to this view, the fundamental liberty to terminate medical treatment is also a judicial invention, without adequate support in the language of the Constitution or the history of the Nation.

---

[172] Kreimer, supra note 170, at 809–10.

Cruzan v. Director, Missouri Department of Health
497 U.S. 261 (1990)

CHIEF JUSTICE REHNQUIST delivered the opinion of the Court.

Petitioner Nancy Beth Cruzan was rendered incompetent as a result of severe injuries sustained during an automobile accident. Copetitioners Lester and Joyce Cruzan, Nancy's parents and coguardians, sought a court order directing the withdrawal of their daughter's artificial feeding and hydration equipment after it became apparent that she had virtually no chance of recovering her cognitive faculties.

The Supreme Court of Missouri held that because there was no clear and convincing evidence of Nancy's desire to have lifesustaining treatment withdrawn under such circumstances, her parents lacked authority to effectuate such a request.

. . .

. . . The principle that a competent person has a constitutionally protected liberty interest in refusing unwanted medical treatment may be inferred from our prior decisions. In *Jacob-*

son v. *Massachusetts*, 197 U.S. 11, 24–30 (1905), for instance, the Court balanced an individual's liberty interest in declining an unwanted smallpox vaccine against the State's interest in preventing disease. Decisions prior to the incorporation of the Fourth Amendment into the Fourteenth Amendment analyzed searches and seizures involving the body under the Due Process Clause and were thought to implicate substantial liberty interests.

Just this Term, in the course of holding that a State's procedures for administering antipsychotic medication to prisoners were sufficient to satisfy due process concerns, we recognized that prisoners possess "a significant liberty interest in avoiding the unwanted administration of antipsychotic drugs under the Due Process Clause of the Fourteenth Amendment." *Washington v. Harper*, 494 U.S. 210, 221–222 (1990).

But determining that a person has a "liberty interest" under the Due Process Clause does not end the inquiry; "whether respondent's constitutional rights have been violated must be determined by balancing his liberty interests against the relevant state interests."

Petitioners insist that under the general holdings of our cases, the forced administration of life-sustaining medical treatment, and even of artificially delivered food and water essential to life, would implicate a competent person's liberty interest. Although we think the logic of the cases discussed above would embrace such a liberty interest, the dramatic consequences involved in refusal of such treatment would inform the inquiry as to whether the deprivation of that interest is constitutionally permissible. But for purposes of this case, we assume that the United States Constitution would grant a competent person a constitutionally protected right to refuse lifesaving hydration and nutrition.

Petitioners go on to assert that an incompetent person should possess the same right in this respect as is possessed by a competent person....

The difficulty with petitioners' claim is that in a sense it begs the question: An incompetent person is not able to make an informed and voluntary choice to exercise a hypothetical right to refuse treatment or any other right. Such a "right" must be exercised for her, if at all, by some sort of surrogate. Here, Missouri has in effect recognized that under certain circumstances a surrogate may act for the patient in electing to have hydration and nutrition withdrawn in such a way as to cause death, but it has established a procedural safeguard to assure that the action of the surrogate conforms as best it may to the wishes expressed by the patient while competent. Missouri requires that evidence of the incompetent's wishes as to the withdrawal of treatment be proved by clear and convincing evidence. The question, then,

is whether the United States Constitution forbids the establishment of this procedural requirement by the State. We hold that it does not.

Whether or not Missouri's clear and convincing evidence requirement comports with the United States Constitution depends in part on what interests the State may properly seek to protect in this situation. Missouri relies on its interest in the protection and preservation of human life, and there can be no gainsaying this interest. As a general matter, the States—indeed, all civilized nations—demonstrate their commitment to life by treating homicide as a serious crime. Moreover, the majority of States in this country have laws imposing criminal penalties on one who assists another to commit suicide. We do not think a State is required to remain neutral in the face of an informed and voluntary decision by a physically able adult to starve to death.

But in the context presented here, a State has more particular interests at stake. The choice between life and death is a deeply personal decision of obvious and overwhelming finality. We believe Missouri may legitimately seek to safeguard the personal element of this choice through the imposition of heightened evidentiary requirements. It cannot be disputed that the Due Process Clause protects an interest in life as well as an interest in refusing life-sustaining medical treatment. Not all incompetent patients will have loved ones available to serve as surrogate decisionmakers. And even where family members are present, "[t]here will, of course, be some unfortunate situations in which family members will not act to protect a patient." A State is entitled to guard against potential abuses in such situations. Similarly, a State is entitled to consider that a judicial proceeding to make a determination regarding an incompetent's wishes may very well not be an adversarial one, with the added guarantee of accurate factfinding that the adversary process brings with it. Finally, we think a State may properly decline to make judgments about the "quality" of life that a particular individual may enjoy, and simply assert an unqualified interest in the preservation of human life to be weighed against the constitutionally protected interests of the individual.

In our view, Missouri has permissibly sought to advance these interests through the adoption of a "clear and convincing" standard of proof to govern such proceedings. . . .

We think it self-evident that the interests at stake in the instant proceedings are more substantial, both on an individual and societal level, than those involved in a run-of-the-mine civil dispute. But not only does the standard of proof reflect the importance of a particular adjudication, it also serves as "a societal judgment about how the risk of error should be distributed between the litigants." The more stringent the burden of proof a party must bear, the more that party bears the risk of an erroneous decision. We believe that Missouri may permissibly place an increased risk of an erroneous decision on those seeking to terminate an incompetent individual's life-sustaining treatment. An erroneous decision not to terminate results in a maintenance of the status quo; the possibility of subsequent developments such as advancements in medical science, the discovery of new evidence regarding the patient's intent, changes in the law, or simply the unexpected death of the patient despite the administration of life-sustaining treatment at least create the potential that a wrong decision will eventually be corrected or its impact mitigated. An erroneous decision to withdraw life-sustaining treatment, however, is not susceptible of correction. . . .

. . .

Petitioners alternatively contend that Missouri must accept the "substituted judgment" of close family members even in the absence of substantial proof that their views reflect the views of the patient. . . . But we do not think the Due Process Clause requires the State to repose judgment on these matters with anyone but the patient herself. Close family members may have a strong feeling—a feeling not at all ignoble or unworthy, but not entirely disinterested, either—that they do not wish to witness the continuation of the life of a loved one which they regard as hopeless, meaningless, and even degrading. But there is no automatic assurance that the view of close family members will necessarily be the same as the patient's would have been had she been confronted with the prospect of her situation while competent. All of the reasons previously discussed for allowing Missouri to require clear and convincing evidence of the patient's wishes lead us to conclude that the State may choose to defer only to those wishes, rather than confide the decision to close family members.

The judgment of the Supreme Court of Missouri is

Affirmed.

JUSTICE O'CONNOR, concurring.

I agree that a protected liberty interest in refusing unwanted medical treatment may be inferred from our prior decisions and that the refusal of artificially delivered food and water is encompassed within that liberty interest. I write separately to clarify why I believe this to be so.

As the Court notes, the liberty interest in refusing medical treatment flows from decisions involving the State's invasions into the body. Because our notions of liberty are inextricably entwined with our idea of physical freedom and self-determination, the Court has often deemed state incursions into the body repugnant to the interests protected by the Due Process Clause. . . . The State's imposition of medical treatment on an unwilling competent adult necessarily involves some form of restraint and intrusion. A seriously ill or dying patient whose wishes are not honored may feel a captive of the machinery required for life-sustaining measures or other medical interventions. Such forced treatment may burden that individual's liberty interests as much as any state coercion.

The State's artificial provision of nutrition and hydration implicates identical concerns. Artificial feeding cannot readily be distinguished from other forms of medical treatment. Whether or not the techniques used to pass food and water into the patient's alimentary tract are termed "medical treatment," it is clear they all involve some degree of intrusion and restraint. Feeding a patient by means of a nasogastric tube requires a physician to pass a long flexible tube through the patient's nose, throat, and esophagus and into the stomach. . . . Requiring a competent adult to endure such procedures against her will burdens the patient's liberty, dignity, and freedom to determine the course of her own treatment. Accordingly, the liberty guaranteed by the Due Process Clause must protect, if it protects anything, an individual's deeply personal decision to reject medical treatment, including the artificial delivery of food and water.

I also write separately to emphasize that the Court does not today decide the issue whether a State must also give effect to the decisions of a surrogate decisionmaker. In my view, such a duty may well be constitutionally required to protect the patient's liberty interest in refusing medical treatment. Few individuals provide explicit oral or written instructions regarding their intent to refuse medical treatment should they become incompetent. States which decline to consider any evidence other than such instructions may frequently fail to honor a patient's intent. Such failures might be avoided if the State considered an equally probative source of evidence: the patient's appointment of a proxy to make health care decisions on her behalf. . . .

Today's decision, holding only that the Constitution permits a State to require clear and convincing evidence of Nancy Cruzan's desire to have artificial hydration and nutrition withdrawn, does not preclude a future determination that the Constitution requires the States to implement the decisions of a patient's duly appointed surrogate. Nor does it prevent States from developing other approaches for protecting an incompetent individual's liberty interest in refusing medical treatment. Today we decide only that one State's practice does not violate the Constitution; the more challenging task of crafting appropriate procedures for safeguarding incompetents' liberty interests is entrusted to the "laboratory" of the States in the first instance.

JUSTICE SCALIA, concurring.

The various opinions in this case portray quite clearly the difficult, indeed agonizing, questions that are presented by the constantly increasing power of science to keep the human body alive for longer than any reasonable person would want to inhabit it. The States have begun to grapple with these problems through legislation. I am concerned, from the tenor of today's opinions, that we are poised to confuse that enterprise as successfully as we have confused the enterprise of legislating concerning abortion—requiring it to be conducted against a background of federal constitutional imperatives that are unknown because they are being newly crafted from Term to Term. That would be a great misfortune.

While I agree with the Court's analysis today, and therefore join in its opinion, I would have preferred that we announce, clearly and promptly, that the federal courts have no business in this field; that American law has always accorded the State the power to prevent, by force if necessary, suicide—including suicide by refusing to take appropriate measures necessary to preserve one's life; that the point at which life becomes "worthless," and the point at which the means necessary to preserve it become "extraordinary" or "inappropriate," are neither set forth in the Constitution nor known to the nine Justices of this Court any better than they are known to nine people picked at random from the Kansas City telephone directory; and hence, that even when it is demonstrated by clear and convincing evidence that a patient no longer wishes certain measures to be taken to preserve his or her life, it is up to the citizens of Missouri to decide, through their elected representatives, whether that wish will be honored. It is quite impossible (because the Constitution says nothing about the matter) that those citizens will decide upon a line less lawful than the one we would choose; and it is unlikely (because we know no more about "life and death" than they do) that they will decide upon a line less reasonable.

The text of the Due Process Clause does not protect individuals against deprivations of liberty *simpliciter*. It protects them against deprivations of liberty "without due process of law." To determine that such a deprivation would not occur if Nancy Cruzan were forced to take nourishment against her will, it is unnecessary to reopen the historically recurrent debate over whether "due process" includes substantive restrictions. It is at least true that no "substantive due process" claim can be maintained unless the claimant demonstrates that the State has deprived him of a right historically and traditionally protected against state interference. That cannot possibly be established here.

At common law in England, a suicide—defined as one who "deliberately puts an end to

his own existence, or commits any unlawful malicious act, the consequence of which is his own death," was criminally liable. Although the States abolished the penalties imposed by the common law (i. e., forfeiture and ignominious burial), they did so to spare the innocent family and not to legitimize the act. Case law at the time of the adoption of the Fourteenth Amendment generally held that assisting suicide was a criminal offense. . . .

. . .

The dissents of JUSTICES BRENNAN and STEVENS make a plausible case for our intervention here only by embracing—the latter explicitly and the former by implication—a political principle that the States are free to adopt, but that is demonstrably not imposed by the Constitution. "[T]he State," says JUSTICE BRENNAN, "has no legitimate general interest in someone's life, completely abstracted from the interest of the person living that life, that could outweigh the person's choice to avoid medical treatment." One who accepts it must also accept, I think, that the State has no such legitimate interest that could outweigh "the person's choice to put an end to her life." . . . For insofar as balancing the relative interests of the State and the individual is concerned, there is nothing distinctive about accepting death through the refusal of "medical treatment," as opposed to accepting it through the refusal of food, or through the failure to shut off the engine and get out of the car after parking in one's garage after work. Suppose that Nancy Cruzan were in precisely the condition she is in today, except that she could be fed and digest food and water without artificial assistance. How is the State's "interest" in keeping her alive thereby increased, or her interest in deciding whether she wants to continue living reduced? It seems to me, in other words, that JUSTICE BRENNAN'S position ultimately rests upon the proposition that it is none of the State's business if a person wants to commit suicide. JUSTICE STEVENS is explicit on the point: "Choices about death touch the core of liberty. . . . [N]ot much may be said with confidence about death unless it is said from faith, and that alone is reason enough to protect the freedom to conform choices about death to individual conscience." This is a view that some societies have held, and that our States are free to adopt if they wish. But it is not a view imposed by our constitutional traditions, in which the power of the State to prohibit suicide is unquestionable.

What I have said above is not meant to suggest that I would think it desirable, if we were sure that Nancy Cruzan wanted to die, to keep her alive by the means at issue here. I assert only that the Constitution has nothing to say about the subject. To raise up a constitutional right here we would have to create out of nothing (for it exists neither in text nor tradition) some constitutional principle whereby, although the State may insist that an individual come in out of the cold and eat food, it may not insist that he take medicine; and although it may pump his stomach empty of poison he has ingested, it may not fill his stomach with food he has failed to ingest. Are there, then, no reasonable and humane limits that ought not to be exceeded in requiring an individual to preserve his own life? There obviously are, but they are not set forth in the Due Process Clause. What assures us that those limits will not be exceeded is the same constitutional guarantee that is the source of most of our protection—what protects us, for example, from being assessed a tax of 100% of our income above the subsistence level, from being forbidden to drive cars, or from being required to send our children to school for 10 hours a day, none of which horribles are categorically prohibited by the Constitution. Our salvation is the Equal Protection Clause, which requires the democratic majority to accept for themselves and their loved ones what they impose on you and me. This Court need not, and has no authority to, inject itself into every field of human activity where irrationality and oppression may theoretically occur, and if it tries to do so it will destroy itself.

JUSTICE BRENNAN, with whom JUSTICE MARSHALL and JUSTICE BLACKMUN join, dissenting.

. . .

. . . Because I believe that Nancy Cruzan has a fundamental Right to be free of unwanted artificial nutrition and hydration, which right is not outweighed by any interests of the State, and because I find that the improperly biased procedural obstacles imposed by the Missouri Supreme Court impermissibly burden that right, I respectfully dissent. Nancy Cruzan is entitled to choose to die with dignity.

I

. . .

The question before this Court is a relatively narrow one: whether the Due Process Clause allows Missouri to require a now-incompetent patient in an irreversible persistent vegetative state to remain on life support absent rigorously clear and convincing evidence that avoiding the treatment represents the patient's prior, express choice. If a fundamental right is at issue, Missouri's rule of decision must be scrutinized under the standards this Court has always applied in such circumstances. As we said in *Zablocki v. Redhail*, 434 U.S. 374, 388, (1978), if a requirement imposed by a State "significantly interferes with the exercise of a fundamental right, it cannot be upheld unless it is supported by sufficiently important state interests and is closely tailored to effectuate only those interests." . . . An evidentiary rule, just as a substantive prohibition,

must meet these standards if it significantly burdens a fundamental liberty interest. . . .

The starting point for our legal analysis must be whether a competent person has a constitutional right to avoid unwanted medical care. Earlier this Term, this Court held that the Due Process Clause of the Fourteenth Amendment confers a significant liberty interest in avoiding unwanted medical treatment. *Washington v. Harper*. Today, the Court concedes that our prior decisions "support the recognition of a general liberty interest in refusing medical treatment." The Court, however, avoids discussing either the measure of that liberty interest or its application by assuming, for purposes of this case only, that a competent person has a constitutionally protected liberty interest in being free of unwanted artificial nutrition and hydration. . . . But if a competent person has a liberty interest to be free of unwanted medical treatment, as both the majority and JUSTICE O'CONNOR concede, it must be fundamental. . . .

The right to be free from medical attention without consent, to determine what shall be done with one's own body, is deeply rooted in this Nation's traditions, as the majority acknowledges. This right has long been "firmly entrenched in American tort law" and is securely grounded in the earliest common law. . . .

. . .

No material distinction can be drawn between the treatment to which Nancy Cruzan continues to be subject—artificial nutrition and hydration—and any other medical treatment. The technique to which Nancy Cruzan is subject—artificial feeding through a gastrostomy tube—involves a tube implanted surgically into her stomach through incisions in her abdominal wall. . . .

Nor does the fact that Nancy Cruzan is now incompetent deprive her of her fundamental rights. . . . As the majority recognizes, the question is not whether an incompetent has constitutional rights, but how such rights may be exercised.

II

The right to be free from unwanted medical attention is a right to evaluate the potential benefit of treatment and its possible consequences according to one's own values and to make a personal decision whether to subject oneself to the intrusion. For a patient like Nancy Cruzan, the sole benefit of medical treatment is being kept metabolically alive. Neither artificial nutrition nor any other form of medical treatment available today can cure or in any way ameliorate her condition. Irreversibly vegetative patients are devoid of thought, emotion, and sensation; they are permanently and completely unconscious. . . .

There are also affirmative reasons why someone like Nancy might choose to forgo artificial nutrition and hydration under these circumstances. Dying is personal. And it is profound. For many, the thought of an ignoble end, steeped in decay, is abhorrent. A quiet, proud death, bodily integrity intact, is a matter of extreme consequence. . . .

Although the right to be free of unwanted medical intervention, like other constitutionally protected interests, may not be absolute, no state interest could outweigh the rights of an individual in Nancy Cruzan's position. Whatever a State's possible interests in mandating life-support treatment under other circumstances, there is no good to be obtained here by Missouri's insistence that Nancy Cruzan remain on life-support systems if it is indeed her wish not to do so. Missouri does not claim, nor could it, that society as a whole will be benefited by Nancy's receiving medical treatment. No third party's situation will be improved and no harm to others will be averted.

The only state interest asserted here is a general interest in the preservation of life. But the State has no legitimate general interest in someone's life, completely abstracted from the interest of the person living that life, that could outweigh the person's choice to avoid medical treatment. . . . Thus, the State's general interest in life must accede to Nancy Cruzan's particularized and intense interest in self-determination in her choice of medical treatment. There is simply nothing legitimately within the State's purview to be gained by superseding her decision.

. . .

III

This is not to say that the State has no legitimate interests to assert here. As the majority recognizes, Missouri has a *parens patriae* interest in providing Nancy Cruzan, now incompetent, with as accurate as possible a determination of how she would exercise her rights under these circumstances. Second, if and when it is determined that Nancy Cruzan would want to continue treatment, the State may legitimately assert an interest in providing that treatment. But until Nancy's wishes have been determined, the only state interest that may be asserted is an interest in safeguarding the accuracy of that determination.

Accuracy, therefore, must be our touchstone. Missouri may constitutionally impose only those procedural requirements that serve to enhance the accuracy of a determination of Nancy Cruzan's wishes or are at least consistent with an accurate determination. The Missouri "safeguard" that the Court upholds today does not meet that standard. The determination needed in this context is whether the incompetent person would choose to live in a persistent vegetative state on life support or to avoid this medical treatment. Missouri's rule of decision imposes a markedly asymmetrical evidentiary burden. Only evidence of specific statements of treatment choice made by the patient when competent is admissible to support a finding that the patient, now in a persistent vegetative state, would wish to avoid further medical treatment. Moreover, this evidence must be clear and convincing. No proof is required to support a finding that the incompetent person would wish to continue treatment.

. . .

The majority claims that the allocation of the risk of error is justified because it is more important not to terminate life support for someone who would wish it continued than to honor the wishes of someone who would not. An erroneous decision to terminate life support is irrevocable, says the majority, while an erroneous decision not to terminate "results in a maintenance of the status quo." But, from the point of view of the patient, an erroneous decision in either direction is irrevocable. An erroneous decision to terminate artificial nutrition and hydration, to be sure, will lead to failure of that last remnant of physiological life, the brain stem, and result in complete brain death. An erroneous decision not to terminate life support, however, robs a patient of the very qualities protected by the right to avoid unwanted medical treatment. His own degraded existence is perpetuated; his family's suffering is protracted; the memory he leaves behind becomes more and more distorted.

. . .

Finally, I cannot agree with the majority that where it is not possible to determine what choice an incompetent patient would make, a State's role as *parens patriae* permits the State automatically to make that choice itself. . . . A State's inability to discern an incompetent patient's choice still need not mean that a State is rendered powerless to protect that choice. But I would find that the Due Process Clause prohibits a State from doing more than that. A State may ensure that the person who makes the decision on the patient's behalf is the one whom the patient himself would have selected to make that choice for him. And a State may exclude from consideration anyone having improper motives. But a State generally must either repose the choice with the person whom the patient himself would most likely have chosen as proxy or leave the decision to the patient's family.

. . .

JUSTICE STEVENS, dissenting.

. . .

It is perhaps predictable that courts might undervalue the liberty at stake here. Because death is so profoundly personal, public reflection upon it is unusual. As this sad case shows, however, such reflection must become more common if we are to deal responsibly with the modern circumstances of death. Medical advances have altered the physiological conditions of death in ways that may be alarming: Highly invasive treatment may perpetuate human existence through a merger of body and machine that some might reasonably regard as an insult to life rather than as its continuation. But those same advances, and the reorganization of medical care accompanying the new science and technology, have also transformed the political and social conditions of death: People are less likely to die at home, and more likely to die in relatively public places, such as hospitals or nursing homes.

Ultimate questions that might once have been dealt with in intimacy by a family and its physician have now become the concern of institutions. When the institution is a state hospital, as it is in this case, the government itself becomes involved. Dying nonetheless remains a part of "the life which characteristically has its place in the home," *Poe v. Ullman* (Harlan, J., dissenting). The "integrity of that life is something so fundamental that it has been found to draw to its protection the principles of more than one explicitly granted Constitutional right," *id.*, and our decisions have demarcated a "private realm of family life which the state cannot enter." *Prince v. Massachusetts*, 321 U.S. 158, 166–167 (1944). The physical boundaries of the home, of course, remain crucial guarantors of the life within it. Nevertheless, this Court has long recognized that the liberty to make the decisions and choices constitutive of private life is so fundamental to our "concept of ordered liberty," that those choices must occasionally be afforded more direct protection.

. . .

It is against this background of decisional law, and the constitutional tradition which it illuminates, that the right to be free from unwanted life-sustaining medical treatment must be understood. That right presupposes no abandonment of the desire for life. Nor is it reducible to a protection against batteries undertaken in the name of treatment, or to a guarantee against the infliction of bodily discomfort. Choices about death touch the core of liberty. Our duty, and the concomitant freedom, to come to terms with the conditions of our own mortality are undoubtedly "so rooted in the traditions and conscience of our people as to be ranked as fundamental," *Snyder v. Massachusetts*, and indeed are essential incidents of the unalienable rights to life and liberty endowed us by our Creator.

The more precise constitutional significance of death is difficult to describe; not much may be said with confidence about death unless it is said from faith, and that alone is reason

enough to protect the freedom to conform choices about death to individual conscience. We may also, however, justly assume that death is not life's simple opposite, or its necessary terminus, but rather its completion. Our ethical tradition has long regarded an appreciation of mortality as essential to understanding life's significance. It may, in fact, be impossible to live for anything without being prepared to die for something. . . .

To be constitutionally permissible, Missouri's intrusion upon these fundamental liberties must, at a minimum, bear a reasonable relationship to a legitimate state end. Missouri asserts that its policy is related to a state interest in the protection of life. In my view, however, it is an effort to define life, rather than to protect it, that is the heart of Missouri's policy. Missouri insists, without regard to Nancy Cruzan's own interests, upon equating her life with the biological persistence of her bodily functions. . . .

. . .

My disagreement with the Court is . . . unrelated to its endorsement of the clear and convincing standard of proof for cases of this kind. Indeed, I agree that the controlling facts must be established with unmistakable clarity. The critical question, however, is not how to prove the controlling facts but rather what proven facts should be controlling. In my view, the constitutional answer is clear: The best interests of the individual, especially when buttressed by the interests of all related third parties, must prevail over any general state policy that simply ignores those interests. Indeed, the only apparent secular basis for the State's interest in life is the policy's persuasive impact upon people other than Nancy and her family. Yet, "[a]lthough the State may properly perform a teaching function," and although that teaching may foster respect for the sanctity of life, the State may not pursue its project by infringing constitutionally protected interests for "symbolic effect." *Carey v. Population Services International* (STEVENS, J., concurring in part and concurring in judgment). The failure of Missouri's policy to heed the interests of a dying individual with respect to matters so private is ample evidence of the policy's illegitimacy.

Only because Missouri has arrogated to itself the power to define life, and only because the Court permits this usurpation, are Nancy Cruzan's life and liberty put into disquieting conflict. If Nancy Cruzan's life were defined by reference to her own interests, so that her life expired when her biological existence ceased serving any of her own interests, then her constitutionally protected interest in freedom from unwanted treatment would not come into conflict with her constitutionally protected interest in life. Conversely, if there were any evidence that Nancy Cruzan herself defined life to encompass every form of biological persistence by a human being, so that the continuation of treatment would serve Nancy's own liberty, then once again there would be no conflict between life and liberty. The opposition of life and liberty in this case are thus not the result of Nancy Cruzan's tragic accident, but are instead the artificial consequence of Missouri's effort, and this Court's willingness, to abstract Nancy Cruzan's life from Nancy Cruzan's person.

. . .

The Cruzan family's continuing concern provides a concrete reminder that Nancy Cruzan's interests did not disappear with her vitality or her consciousness. However commendable may be the State's interest in human life, it cannot pursue that interest by appropriating Nancy Cruzan's life as a symbol for its own purposes. Lives do not exist in abstraction from persons, and to pretend otherwise is not to honor but to desecrate the State's responsibility for protecting life. A State that seeks to demonstrate its commitment to life may do so by aiding those who are actively struggling for life and health. In this endeavor, unfortunately, no State can lack for opportunities: There can be no need to make an example of tragic cases like that of Nancy Cruzan.

PART II

THE DISTRIBUTION OF NATIONAL POWERS

There is no "Separation of Powers" clause in the Constitution. Rather we draw the meaning of separation of powers from the structure of national government and our understanding of what the Framers contemplated in the establishment of the three separate branches of national government and a system of checks and balances. Separation of powers is defined by the political resolution of interbranch disputes about the allocation of power as well as by the doctrine which has evolved in separation of powers problems confronted by the Supreme Court.

The doctrine of separation of powers which has emerged from Court cases does not reflect a consistent approach and thus the resolutions of disputes appears more ad hoc than principled. Perhaps because the doctrine is ill defined, at times the Court has been reluctant to address separation of challenges, consequently avoiding unprincipled confrontation with the political branches involved in a dispute. Indeed among those cases that have been decided by the Court, few have touched upon the critical issues—like the power to commit troops to battle—prompting some commentators to contend that separation of powers is better understood as political accommodation in conflicts about the authority to exercise power. The Court, moreover, has been criticized for making political decisions in response to separation of powers problems masked in lawyers' language, without offering principled analysis for its conclusions and for inconsistently applying doctrine to address pragmatic concerns in a way that defeats the formulation of a consistent theory. Sometimes the Court's effort to resolve separation of power disputes seem to result in its earlier intrusion into the process of political accommodation than was contemplated by a structure of interacting branches. In this way it can be said that the Court's decision about whether or when to intervene in disputes about the exercise of power by one of the political branches itself presents concerns about separation of power.

Part of the lack of clarity and controversy about the meaning of separation of powers stems from the Court's continuing sally about the approach to be taken in analyzing separation of powers cases. The differences in approaches center on which sources are available to determine whether power is within the domain of the executive, legislative, or judicial branches and whether separation or coordination is seen as the predominant value found in the structural framework. The principal approaches taken by the Court—formalism and functionalism[1]—roughly correspond to strict interpretation and pragmatic interpretation theories of constitutional law.

---

[1] Commentators have used different words to capture the differences in these analyses: "devolutionary" versus "evolutionary," see Stephen Carter, *The Independent Counsel Mess*, 102 HARV. L. REV. 105, 108–112 (1988); "neoclassical" versus pragmatic, *see* Geoffrey P. Miller, *Independent Agencies*, 1986 SUP. CT. REV. 41; "originalist" versus "nonoriginalist," see Paul Brest, *The Misconceived Quest for the Original Understanding*, 60 B.U. L. REV. 204, 205–224 (1980): judicial literalism versus interpretation; *see* Elliot, *Why Our Separation of Powers Jurisprudence Is So Abysmal*, 57 GEO. WASH. L. REV. 506, 511 (1989); formal versus functional, *see* Peter L. Strauss, *Was There a Baby in the Bath Water? A Comment on the Supreme Court's Legislative Veto Decision*, 1983 DUKE L.J. 789, 817 (1983).

A. Establishing a Framework for Considering Power Relationships

The text of the Constitution allocates the national power among the legislative, executive, and judicial branches, in a framework providing for separation of functions as well as interlocking checks on the accretion of power. In article I, Congress is vested with "[a]ll legislative powers." In article II, the President, assisted by departments, is to carry out the "executive powers." In article III, the Supreme Court, and such "inferior courts" as Congress shall establish, is vested with the "judicial power." This language itself reflects the Framers' interest in limiting the opportunities for any branch to accumulate too much power and thereby abuse the authority vested in it to act. Although the Framers were concerned about the weakness of the Confederation, they continued to be reluctant to concentrate power in the national government. In their view, a consequence of too much accumulation of power was the loss of liberty of the citizens being governed. The structural framework the Framers agreed upon was more complex than reflected in the functional division of powers.

Whereas the intent to allocate authority among the branches is demonstrated in the language vesting power, creating spheres of operation within the legislative, executive and judicial branches, other provisions reflect a commitment to intermixing power. Through language requiring interaction among the branches there results a web of interrelated functions or checks and balances. In article I, for example, "[a]ll legislative Powers" are vested in Congress; but section 7 of article I requires that for a bill duly passed by both legislative chambers to become law, it must be presented for signature—or disapproved—by the President. Article II provides that "the executive Power shall be vested in a President"; however section 2 of that article requires the advice and consent of the Senate for the President to make Treaties and to appoint officers and "Congress may by Law invest the Appointment of such inferior Officers, as they think proper, in the President alone, in the Courts of Law, or in the Heads of Departments." The powers to make war similarly are parsed and assigned to the branches.

Notwithstanding the vesting language, the breadth and limits of each branch's authority are textually undefined, inviting a degree of fluidity. The concept of separation of powers attributable to our Constitution thus contemplates a structure which provides for both a division and a sharing of power, a governmental framework which in practice creates tension and invites accommodation by the political branches. The assertion of one branch's authority often either implicates a resulting diminishment of authority of another branch, or is dependent on the cooperation of others. The resulting opportunities for political accommodation as well as conflict among the branches clearly has affected the willingness of courts to intervene in disputes about the allocation of power and authority between the political branches. In fact, relatively few cases have been decided by the Court which shed light on the sources and limits of power, particularly that of the Executive, its relationship to the power of Congress, and to the Judiciary.[2] Of course, the Court's decisions about whether its intervention is required by the Constitution or represents an unwarranted intrusion into the domain of the political branches raise questions about the meaning of separation of powers. In addition, the Court's reluctance may stem from the fact that what we know about the framing process suggests that the structure agreed upon was not the product of broad consensus about the objectives of separation but rather represents a pragmatic accommodation of a number of concerns including the fear of tyranny, preservation of liberty and efficiency of action by the government. That accommodation has been difficult to capture in an intelligible standard.

---

[2] Marbury v. Madison, 5 U.S. (1 Cranch) 137 (1803) reflects a conflict between Congress and the Court and the Executive and the Court.

1. How the Framers Conceived Separation of Powers

Commentators reflecting on what the Framers intended and what happened to the separation of powers during the first years of government[3] underscore the difficulties of creating a structure which at once responded to the weaknesses of the Articles of Confederation and to the Framers' concerns about tyranny and distrust of government. Those difficulties required a separation of powers doctrine which has been called at once "tentative, reflective, suggestive, contradictory, and incomplete."[4]

Much of what we have come to understand as what the Framers originally intended relates to debates about the adoption of state constitutions between 1776 and 1787.[5] The view adopted by a number of states in their own constitutions was that separation of functions was essential to free government, because it protected liberty by avoiding the usurpation of power by the respective departments, and it preserved the independence of the citizenry because tyranny by one department was avoided. But the government these constitutions framed was also designed to promote balance, coordination and cooperation.

The concept of separation of powers we attribute to the Framers is also drawn from debate among late eighteenth century political philosophers about how best to protect liberty, as well as about the challenge of adapting institutions of mixed government to the doctrine of popular sovereignty. In addition, as Professor Casper has observed, distrust resulting from the fact that the former colonists were highly stratified also affected their evolving conception of governmental power. In short, a number of competing interests and concerns were conveniently captured in the words "separation of powers." The distinct yet interdependent branches of government that became the structure proposed in the Constitution was hardly a product of one cohesive theory of government or of one agreed upon governmental framework.

The debate at the constitutional convention confirms that no consensus existed as to the precise institutional arrangement that would satisfy all proponents of such an uncertain doctrine.[6] The Constitution, itself, contained no express provision for separation of power. James Madison writing The Federalist No. 47, defended the document against criticism that it therefore did not satisfy the requirements of separation, noting that some mixing or coordination among the branches was both practically necessary and not contrary to the teachings of Montesquieu. The Senate, moreover, rejected amendments subsequently proposed by Madison and others intended to confirm the "principle" of separation. Professor Casper attributes the amendments' rejection by the Senate to the Senators' concern for protecting their own power base by ensuring that the Senate had some role in effectuating the work assigned to other branches. Thus such areas as selecting the President and the assignment of the appointments power were contested until the end of deliberations about the Constitution. Professor Casper concludes that there was no clear agreement about the meaning of the doctrine of separations of powers other than that it was necessary to protect against tyranny and to provide a structural framework by which the institutional arrangements reflecting an uncertain doctrine could be accommodated.

---

[3] *See* Gerhard Casper, *An Essay in Separation of Powers: Some Early Versions and Practices*, 30 WM. & MARY L. REV. 211 (1989).

[4] P. KURKLAND, FELIX FRANKFURTER ON THE SUPREME COURT (1970), cited in Gerhard Casper, *An Essay in Separation of Powers: Some Early Versions and Practices*, 30 WM. & MARY L. REV. 211, 212 (1989).

[5] *See, e.g.*, Russell Osgood, *Early Versions and Practice of Separation of Powers: A Comment*, 30 WM. & MARY L. REV. 279 (1989).

[6] *See, e.g.*, Casper, *supra* note 3.

In addition, early instances of interaction among the branches in the conduct of affairs, particularly those of Congress and the President, shaped the nascent governmental structures, creating models for interbranch conduct which were neither compelled by any conception of separation of powers nor derived from language in the Constitution, but were instead affected by practical and political considerations of the day as well as concern for efficiency.[7] Many of the behavioral models have lasted through time and serve to inform our understanding of separation of powers but do not necessarily flow from any essential meaning of the concept.

As in the period in which the Constitution was framed, in the first administration under it, separation of powers appeared to incorporate notions of separation found in contemporary political philosophy and reflected the profound distrust of power, and also pragmatic interest in governmental coordination and cooperation. Invocation of the doctrine was often rhetorical, a means of legitimizing a promoter's own structural preferences, rather than clarifying the necessary institutional arrangements that might satisfy the doctrine or identifying the goals of a particular system of government.[8] As one commentator has observed about the early years: "Separation of powers notions played a supportive role but the views were not doctrinaire; in part because there was no clear doctrine."[9]

2. Sources of Executive Authority

In 1863, with the advent of the Civil War, the Court decided the *Prize Cases*[10] challenging President Lincoln's authority to establish the blockade of southern ports. Despite the fact that war had not been declared by Congress, the Court majority of five to four reasoned that Lincoln had authority as Commander-in-Chief to control the militia and consequently to execute the blockade. Emphasizing that the Constitution allocated to Congress the power to declare war, the four justices who dissented argued that the executive's action was not explicitly authorized and was a usurpation of the Congress' power. Although commentators have argued that the war clause is one provision which clearly assigns authority to Congress,[11] other provisions (like the president's assignment as Commander in Chief) as well as structural implications[12] provide sources of power upon which to claim executive authority to act. "Madison and Hamilton who presumably knew something about the original intent, came to contradictory conclusions within a few years of the Constitutional Convention,"[13] and in an exchange of letters under the names Pacificus and Helvidius debated their views.

---

[7] *See* William Gwynn, *The Indeterminacy of the Separation of Powers in the Age of the Framers*, 30 WM. AND MARY L. REV. 263, 263 (1989).

[8] *Id.* at 265.

[9] Casper, *supra* note 3 at 261.

[10] 67 U.S. (2 Black) 635 (1863).

[11] *See, e.g.*, John H. Ely, *Suppose Congress Wanted a War Powers Act that Worked?*, 88 COLUM. L. REV. 1379 (1988).

[12] *See, e.g.*, HAROLD H. KOH, THE NATIONAL SECURITY CONSTITUTION: SHARING POWER AFTER THE IRAN-CONTRA AFFAIR 68 (1990) ("there lurks within our constitutional system an identifiable National Security Constitution, a normative vision of the foreign-policy-making process that emerges only partially from the text of the Constitution itself").

[13] Charles A. Lofgren, *War-Making Under the Constitution: The Original Understanding*, 81 YALE L.J. 672, 673 (1972). Madison reasoned that foreign affairs power could be used to commit the country to war. Thus he argued that Congress, which had the power to declare war, also must have power in foreign affairs. Hamilton argued that the foreign affairs power was inherently executive in nature. EDWARD CORWIN, THE PRESIDENT: OFFICE AND POWER 177–81 (4th ed. 1957). Presidents have justified military intervention on theories of self-defense, neutrality, and collective security. JOHN E. NOWAK & RONALD D. ROTUNDA, CONSTITUTIONAL LAW 221 (4th ed. 1991).

The debate about the limits of executive authority has continued in more modern times with little doctrinal clarity able to be drawn from the cases. The Court's responses to the question of executive authority to act in the cases which it has decided exposes the indeterminacy of separation of powers doctrine not simply because what is in fact vested in the executive is less clear than for other branches (*i.e.*, defining what is "executive" has proven difficult) but also because in confronting the practical need for national leadership, confidence, and swift action in crises, the courts (and commentators) have differed in their analyses as to whether separation of powers creates formal and functional limits on or provides justification for the President's authority to act.

The most-cited modern authority, *Youngstown Sheet & Tube Co. v. Sawyer*, presents the range of competing methods of analyzing separation of powers. Formalist and functional methodologies compete in the justifications for invalidating the steps taken by President Truman offered by the majority and concurring opinions, and the strongly worded dissents emphasizing the exigencies of the circumstances. The opinions concerning the sources and limits of executive action in that case are notably lacking in controlling judicial precedents. This is not only because cases are few in number which actually address significant separation of powers issues, but also, as Professor William Gwynn has argued, the Framers' lack of clarity as to the reasons for separation continues today—"lawyers and judges continue to invoke the doctrine without . . . an idea of the values to be maximized by separating the exercise of legislative, executive, and judicial powers."[14]

Although Congress never formally declared war, the United States entered an armed conflict, which President Truman labeled "police action," with North Korea in response to North Korea's June 1950 attack on South Korea. Congress authorized the deployment of armed forces and funds to support the military action. During the conflict, to avert a nation-wide strike of steel workers in April 1952, President Truman issued an Executive Order directing the Secretary of Commerce to seize and operate most of the country's steel mills. The Order included findings that his action was necessary to avert a national catastrophe which would inevitably result from a stoppage of steel production with implications in the country's ongoing military action. The Order was not based upon any specific statutory authority.

The Secretary issued an order seizing the mills and directing their presidents to operate them as managers in accordance with the Secretary's regulations and directions. President Truman reported these events to Congress, which took no action. The steel companies sued the Secretary in federal district court, seeking a declaratory judgment as to the constitutional validity of the Executive Order and injunctive relief from the Secretary's action. The district court issued a preliminary injunction and the Court of Appeals stayed the action.

---

[14] Gwynn, *supra* note 7, at 265.

Youngstown Sheet & Tube Co. v. Sawyer
(Steel Seizure Case)
343 U.S. 579 (1952)

MR. JUSTICE BLACK delivered the opinion of the Court.

We are asked to decide whether the President was acting within his constitutional power when he issued an order directing the Secretary of Commerce to take possession of and operate most of the Nation's steel mills. The mill owners argue that the President's order amounts to lawmaking, a legislative function which the Constitution has expressly confided to the Congress and not to the President. The Government's position is that the order was made on findings of the President that his action was necessary to avert a national catastrophe which would inevitably result from a stoppage of steel production, and that in meeting this grave emergency the President was acting within the aggregate of his constitutional powers as the Nation's Chief Executive and the Commander in Chief of the Armed Forces of the United States.

In the latter part of 1951, a dispute arose between the steel companies and their employees over terms and conditions that should be included in new collective bargaining agreements. Long-continued conferences failed to resolve the dispute. On December 18, 1951, the employees' representative, United Steelworkers of America, C.I.O., gave notice of an intention to strike when the existing bargaining agreements expired on December 31. The indispensability of steel as a component of substantially all weapons and other war materials led the President to believe that the proposed work stoppage would immediately jeopardize our national defense and that governmental seizure of the steel mills was necessary in order to assure the continued availability of steel. Reciting these considerations for his action, the President, a few hours before the strike was to begin, issued Executive Order 10340. The order directed the Secretary of Commerce to take possession of most of the steel mills and keep them running. The Secretary immediately issued his own possessory orders, calling upon the presidents of the various seized companies to serve as operating managers for the United States. They were directed to carry on their activities in accordance with regulations and directions of the Secretary. The next morning the President sent a message to Congress reporting his action. Twelve days later he sent a second message. Congress has taken no action.

Obeying the Secretary's orders under protest, the companies brought proceedings against him in the District Court. Their complaints charged that the seizure was not authorized by an act of Congress or by any constitutional provisions. The United States asserted that a strike disrupting steel production for even a brief period would so endanger the wellbeing and safety of the Nation that the President had 'inherent power' to do what he had done—power 'supported by the Constitution, by historical precedent, and by court decisions.' The District Court on April 30 issued a preliminary injunction restraining the Secretary from 'continuing the seizure and possession of the plant.' On the same day the Court of Appeals stayed the District Court's injunction.

II.

The President's power, if any, to issue the order must stem either from an act of Congress or from the Constitution itself. There is no stat-

ute that expressly authorizes the President to take possession of property as he did here. Nor is there any act of Congress to which our attention has been directed from which such a power can fairly be implied. Indeed, we do not understand the Government to rely on statutory authorization for this seizure. There are two statutes which do authorize the President to take both personal and real property under certain conditions. However, the Government admits that these conditions were not met and that the President's order was not rooted in either of the statutes.

Moreover, the use of the seizure technique to solve labor disputes in order to prevent work stoppages was not only unauthorized by any congressional enactment; prior to this controversy, Congress had refused to adopt that method of settling labor disputes. When the Taft-Hartley Act was under consideration in 1947, Congress rejected an amendment which would have authorized such governmental seizures in cases of emergency. Apparently it was thought that the technique of seizure, like that of compulsory arbitration, would interfere with the process of collective bargaining. Consequently, the plan Congress adopted in that Act did not provide for seizure under any circumstances. Instead, the plan sought to bring about settlements by use of the customary devices of mediation, conciliation, investigation by boards of inquiry, and public reports. In some instances temporary injunctions were authorized to provide cooling-off periods. All this failing, unions were left free to strike after a secret vote by employees as to whether they wished to accept their employers' final settlement offer.

It is clear that if the President had authority to issue the order he did, it must be found in some provisions of the Constitution. And it is not claimed that express constitutional language grants this power to the President. The contention is that presidential power should be implied from the aggregate of his powers under the Constitution. Particular reliance is placed on provisions in Article II which say that 'The executive Power shall be vested in a President'; that 'he shall take Care that the Laws be faithfully executed'; and that he 'shall be Commander in Chief of the Army and Navy of the United States.'

The order cannot properly be sustained as an exercise of the President's military power as Commander in Chief of the Armed Forces. The Government attempts to do so by citing a number of cases upholding broad powers in military commanders engaged in day-to-day fighting in a theater of war. Even though 'theater of war' be an expanding concept, we cannot with faithfulness to our constitutional system hold that the Commander in Chief of the

Armed Forces has the ultimate power as such to take possession of private property in order to keep labor disputes from stopping production. This is a job for the Nation's lawmakers, not for its military authorities.

Nor can the seizure order be sustained because of the several constitutional provisions that grant executive power to the President. In the framework of our Constitution, the President's power to see that the laws are faithfully executed refutes the idea that he is to be a lawmaker. The Constitution limits his functions in the lawmaking process to the recommending of laws he thinks wise and the vetoing of laws he thinks bad. And the Constitution is neither silent nor equivocal about who shall make laws which the President is to execute. The first section of the first article says that 'All legislative Powers herein granted shall be vested in a Congress of the United States.' After granting many powers to the Congress, Article I goes on to provide that Congress may 'make all Laws which shall be necessary and proper for carrying into Execution the foregoing Powers and all other Powers vested by this Constitution in the Government of the United States, or in any Department or Officer thereof.'

The preamble of the order itself, like that of many statutes, sets out reasons why the President believes certain policies should be adopted, proclaims these policies as rules of conduct to be followed, and again, like a statute, authorizes a government official to promulgate additional rules and regulations consistent with the policy proclaimed and needed to carry that policy into execution. The power of Congress to adopt such public policies as those proclaimed by the order is beyond question. It can authorize the taking of private property for public use. It can make laws regulating the relationships between employers and employees, prescribing rules designed to settle labor disputes, and fixing wages and working conditions in certain fields of our economy. The Constitution does not subject this law making power of Congress to presidential or military supervision or control.

It is said that other Presidents without congressional authority have taken possession of private business enterprises in order to settle labor disputes. But even if this be true, Congress has not thereby lost its exclusive constitutional authority to make laws necessary and proper to carry out the powers vested by the Constitution.

The Founders of this Nation entrusted the law making power to the Congress alone in both good and bad times. It would do no good to recall the historical events, the fears of power and the hopes for freedom that lay behind their choice. This seizure order cannot stand.

The judgment of the District Court is affirmed.

Mr. Justice FRANKFURTER, concurring.

Although the considerations relevant to the legal enforcement of the principle of separation of powers seem to me more complicated and flexible than may appear from what Mr. Justice BLACK has written, I join his opinion because I thoroughly agree with the application of the principle to the circumstances of this case.

A constitutional democracy like ours is perhaps the most difficult of man's social arrangements to manage successfully. The Founders of this Nation acted on the conviction that the experience of man sheds a good deal of light on his nature. It sheds a good deal of light not merely on the need for effective power, if a society is to be at once cohesive and civilized, but also on the need for limitations on the power of governors over the governed.

To that end they rested the structure of our central government on the system of checks and balances. For them the doctrine of separation of powers was not mere theory; it was a felt necessity. The experience through which the world has passed in our own day has made vivid the realization that the Framers of our Constitution were not inexperienced doctrinaires. The accretion of dangerous power does not come in a day. It does come, however slowly, from the generative force of unchecked disregard of the restrictions that fence in even the most disinterested assertion of authority.

The pole-star for constitutional adjudications is John Marshall's greatest judicial utterance that 'it is a constitution we are expounding.' *McCulloch v. Maryland*, 4 Wheat. 316, 407. That requires both a spacious view in applying an instrument of government 'made for an undefined and expanding future,' and as narrow a delimitation of the constitutional issues as the circumstances permit. Not the least characteristic of great statesmanship which the Framers manifested was the extent to which they did not attempt to bind the future. It is no less incumbent upon this Court to avoid putting fetters upon the future by needless pronouncements today.

Marshall's admonition is especially relevant when the Court is required to give legal sanctions to an underlying principle of the Constitution—that of separation of powers. The issue before us can be met, and therefore should be, without attempting to define the President's powers comprehensively. The judiciary may, as this case proves, have to intervene in determining where authority lies as between the democratic forces in our scheme of government. But in doing so we should be wary and humble.

Congress has frequently—at least 16

times since 1916—specifically provided for executive seizure of production, transportation, communications, or storage facilities. In every case it has qualified this grant of power with limitations and safeguards. This body of enactments demonstrates that Congress deemed seizure so drastic a power as to require that it be carefully circumscribed whenever the President was vested with this extraordinary authority.

Congress in 1947 was again called upon to consider whether governmental seizure should be used to avoid serious industrial shutdowns. Congress decided against conferring such power generally and in advance, without special congressional enactment to meet each particular need. Proponents as well as the opponents of the bill which became the Labor Management Relations Act of 1947 clearly understood that as a result of that legislation the only recourse for preventing a shutdown in any basic industry, after failure of mediation, was Congress. On a balance of considerations Congress chose not to lodge this power in the President. Congress made a conscious choice of policy in a field full of perplexity and peculiarly within legislative responsibility for choice.

It cannot be contended that the President would have had power to issue this order had Congress explicitly negated such authority in formal legislation. But it is now claimed that the President has seizure power by virtue of the Defense Production Act of 1950 and its Amendments. And the claim is based on the occurrence of new events—Korea and the need for stabilization. Absence of authority in the President to deal with a crisis does not imply want of power in the Government. Conversely the fact that power exists in the Government does not vest it in the President. The need for new legislation does not enact it. Nor does it repeal or amend existing law.

It is one thing to draw an intention of Congress from general language and to say that Congress would have explicitly written what is inferred, where Congress has not addressed itself to a specific situation. It is quite impossible, however, when Congress did specifically address itself to a problem, as Congress did to that of seizure, to find secreted in the interstices of legislation the very grant of power which Congress consciously withheld. To find authority so explicitly withheld is not merely to disregard in a particular instance the clear will of Congress. It is to disrespect the whole legislative process and the constitutional division of authority between President and Congress.

Apart from his vast share of responsibility for the conduct of our foreign relations, the embracing function of the President is that 'he shall take Care that the Laws be faithfully exe-

cuted. . . . ' The nature of that authority has for me been comprehensively indicated by Mr. Justice Holmes. 'The duty of the President to see that the laws be executed is a duty that does not go beyond the laws or require him to achieve more than Congress sees fit to leave within his power.' The powers of the President are not as particularized as are those of Congress. But unenumerated powers do not mean undefined powers.

Deeply embedded traditional ways of conducting government cannot supplant the Constitution or legislation, but they give meaning to the words of a text or supply them. It is an inadmissibly narrow conception of American constitutional law to confine it to the words of the Constitution and to disregard the gloss which life has written upon them. In short, a systematic, unbroken, executive practice, long pursued to the knowledge of the Congress and never before questioned, engaged in by Presidents who have also sworn to uphold the Constitution, making as it were such exercise of power part of the structure of our government, may be treated as a gloss on 'executive Power' vested in the President.

In his eleven seizures of industrial facilities, President Wilson acted, or at least purported to act, under authority granted by Congress. Thus his seizures cannot be adduced as interpretations by a President of his own powers in the absence of statute. Down to the World War II period, then, the record is barren of instances comparable to the one before us. Of twelve seizures by President Roosevelt prior to the enactment of the War Labor Disputes Act in June, 1943, three were sanctioned by existing law, and six others were effected after Congress, on December 8, 1941, had declared the existence of a state of war. Reliance on the powers that flow from declared war has been commendably disclaimed by the Solicitor General. Thus the list of executive assertions of the power of seizure in circumstances comparable to the present reduces to three in the six-month period from June to December of 1941. These three isolated instances do not come to us sanctioned by long-continued acquiescence of Congress giving decisive weight to a construction by the Executive of its powers.

Mr. Justice Jackson, concurring in the judgment and opinion of the court.

Just what our forefathers did envision, or would have envisioned had they foreseen modern conditions, must be divined from materials almost as enigmatic as the dreams Joseph was called upon to interpret for Pharaoh. A century and a half of partisan debate and scholarly speculation yields no net result but only supplies more or less apt quotations from respected sources on each side of any question. They largely cancel each other. And court decisions are indecisive because of the judicial practice of dealing with the largest questions in the most narrow way.

The actual art of governing under our Constitution does not and cannot conform to judicial definitions of the power of any of its branches based on isolated clauses or even single Articles torn from context. While the Constitution diffuses power the better to secure liberty, it also contemplates that practice will integrate the dispersed powers into a workable government. It enjoins upon its branches separateness but interdependence, autonomy but reciprocity. Presidential powers are not fixed but fluctuate, depending upon their disjunction or conjunction with those of Congress.

1. When the President acts pursuant to an express or implied authorization of Congress, his authority is at its maximum, for it includes all that he possesses in his own right plus all that Congress can delegate. In these circumstances, and in these only, may he be said (for what it may be worth), to personify the federal sovereignty. A seizure executed by the President pursuant to an Act of Congress would be supported by the strongest of presumptions and the widest latitude of judicial interpretation, and the burden of persuasion would rest heavily upon any who might attack it.

2. When the President acts in absence of either a congressional grant or denial of authority, he can only rely upon his own independent powers, but there is a zone of twilight in which he and Congress may have concurrent authority, or in which its distribution is uncertain. Therefore, congressional inertia, indifference or quiescence may sometimes, at least as a practical matter, enable, if not invite, measures on independent presidential responsibility. In this area, any actual test of power is likely to depend on the imperatives of events and contemporary imponderables rather than on abstract theories of law.

3. When the President takes measures incompatible with the expressed or implied will of Congress, his power is at its lowest ebb, for then he can rely only upon his own constitutional powers minus any constitutional powers of Congress over the matter. Courts can sustain exclusive Presidential control in such a case only by disabling the Congress from acting upon the subject. Presidential claim to a power at once so conclusive and preclusive must be scrutinized with caution, for what is at stake is the equilibrium established by our constitutional system.

Into which of these classifications does this executive seizure of the steel industry fit? It is conceded that no congressional authorization exists for this seizure. Can it then be defended under flexible tests available to the second category? Congress has not left seizure of private

property an open field but has covered it by three statutory policies inconsistent with this seizure. This leaves the current seizure to be justified only by the severe tests under the third grouping, where it can be supported only by any remainder of executive power after subtraction of such powers as Congress may have over the subject. In short, we can sustain the President only by holding that seizure of such strike-bound industries is within his domain and beyond control by Congress.

The Solicitor General seeks the power of seizure in three clauses of the Executive Article, the first reading, "The executive Power shall be vested in a President of the United States of America." I cannot accept the view that this clause is a grant in bulk of all conceivable executive power but regard it as an allocation to the presidential office of the generic powers thereafter stated.

The clause on which the Government next relies is that "The President shall be Commander in Chief of the Army and Navy of the United States."[The] argument tendered at our bar [is] that the President having, on his own responsibility, sent American troops abroad derives from that act "affirmative power" to seize the means of producing a supply of steel for them. Nothing in our Constitution is plainer than that declaration of a war is entrusted only to Congress. Of course, a state of war may in fact exist without a formal declaration. But no doctrine that the Court could promulgate would seem to me more sinister and alarming than that a President whose conduct of foreign affairs is so largely controlled, and often even is unknown, can vastly enlarge his mastery over the internal affairs of the country by his own commitment of the Nation's armed forces to some foreign venture.

The third clause in which the Solicitor General finds seizure powers is that "he shall take Care that the Laws be faithfully executed." That authority must be matched against words of the Fifth Amendment that "No person shall be deprived of life, liberty or property, without due process of law." One gives a governmental authority that reaches so far as there is law, the other gives a private right that authority shall go no farther. These signify about all there is of the principle that ours is a government of laws, not men, and that we submit ourselves to rulers only if under rules.

The Solicitor General lastly grounds support of the seizure upon nebulous, inherent powers never expressly granted but said to have accrued to the office from the customs and claims of preceding administrations. The plea is for a resulting power to deal with a crisis or emergency according to the necessities of the case, the unarticulated assumption being that necessity knows no law.

Loose and irresponsible use of adjectives colors all non-legal and much legal discussion of presidential powers. "Inherent" powers, "implied" powers, "incidental" powers, "plenary" powers, "war" powers and "emergency" powers are used, often interchangeably and without fixed or ascertainable meanings.

The vagueness and generality of the clauses that set forth presidential powers afford a plausible basis for pressures within and without an administration for presidential action beyond that supported by those whose responsibility it is to defend his actions in court. The claim of inherent and unrestricted presidential powers has long been a persuasive dialectical weapon in political controversy. [A] judge cannot accept self-serving press statements of the attorney for one of the interested parties as authority in answering a constitutional question, even if the advocate was himself. But prudence has counseled that actual reliance on such nebulous claims stop short of provoking a judicial test.

Congress may and has granted extraordinary authorities which lie dormant in normal times but may be called into play by the Executive in war or upon proclamation of a national emergency. The public may know the extent and limitations of the powers that can be asserted, and persons affected may be informed from the statute of their rights and duties.

In view of the ease, expedition and safety with which Congress can grant and has granted large emergency powers, certainly ample to embrace this crisis, I am quite unimpressed with the argument that we should affirm possession of them without statute. Such power either has no beginning or it has no end. If it exists, it need submit to no legal restraint. I am not alarmed that it would plunge us straightaway into dictatorship, but it is at least a step in that wrong direction.

Executive power has the advantage of concentration in a single head in whose choice the whole Nation has a part, making him the focus of public hopes and expectations. In drama, magnitude and finality his decisions so far overshadow any others that almost alone he fills the public eye and ear. No other personality in public life can begin to compete with him in access to the public mind through modern methods of communications. By his prestige as head of state and his influence upon public opinion he exerts a leverage upon those who are supposed to check and balance his power which often cancels their effectiveness.

Moreover, rise of the party system has made a significant extraconstitutional supplement to real executive power. Party loyalties and interests, sometimes more binding than law, extend his effective control into branches of government other than his own and he often may win, as a political leader, what he cannot command under the Constitution. I cannot be brought to believe that this country will suffer if the Court refuses further to aggrandize the presidential office, already so potent and so relatively immune from judicial review, at the expense of Congress.

But I have no illusion that any decision by this Court can keep power in the hands of Congress if it is not wise and timely in meeting its problems. A crisis that challenges the President equally, or perhaps primarily, challenges Congress. We may say that power to legislate for emergencies belongs in the hands of Congress, but only Congress itself can prevent power from slipping through its fingers. With all its defects, delays and inconveniences, men have discovered no technique for long preserving free government except that the Executive be under the law, and that the law be made by parliamentary deliberations.

CHIEF JUSTICE VINSON, with whom MR. JUSTICE REED and MR. JUSTICE MINTON join, dissenting.

The President of the United States directed the Secretary of Commerce to take temporary possession of the Nation's steel mills during the existing emergency because 'a work stoppage would immediately jeopardize and imperil our national defense and the defense of those joined with us in resisting aggression, and would add to the continuing danger of our soldiers, sailors and airmen engaged in combat in the field.' Because we cannot agree that affirmance is proper on any ground, and because of the transcending importance of the questions presented not only in this critical litigation but also to the powers the President and of future Presidents to act in time of crisis, we are compelled to register this dissent.

I.

The Defense Production Act was extended in 1951, a Senate Committee noting that in the dislocation caused by the programs for purchase of military equipment 'lies the seed of an economic disaster that might well destroy the military might we are straining to build.' Even before Korea, steel production at levels above theoretical 100% capacity was not capable of supplying civilian needs alone. Since Korea, the tremendous military demand for steel has far exceeded the increases in productive capacity. This Committee emphasized that the shortage of steel, even with the mills operating at full capacity, coupled with increased civilian purchasing power, presented grave danger of disastrous inflation.

II.

Under this view, the President is left powerless at the very moment when the need for action may be most pressing and when no one, other than he, is immediately capable of action. He is left powerless because a power not expressly given to Congress is nevertheless found to rest exclusively with Congress. The whole of the 'executive Power' is vested in the President. Before entering office, the President swears that he 'will faithfully execute the Office of President of the United States, and will to the best of [his] Ability, preserve, protect and defend the Constitution of the United States.' Art. II, § 1. The Presidency was deliberately fashioned as an office of power and independence. Of course, the Framers created no autocrat capable of arrogating any power unto himself at any time. But neither did they create an automaton impotent to exercise the powers of Government at a time when the survival of the Republic itself may be at stake.

Marshall admonished, that the Constitution is 'intended to endure for ages to come, and consequently, to be adapted to the various crises of human affairs,' and that '[i]ts means are adequate to its ends.' Cases do arise presenting questions which could not have been foreseen by the Framers. In such cases, the Constitution has been treated as a living document adaptable to new situations.

III.

A review of executive action demonstrates that our Presidents have on many occasions exhibited the leadership contemplated by the Framers when they made the President Commander in Chief, and imposed upon him the trust to 'take Care that the Laws be faithfully executed.' With or without explicit statutory authorization, Presidents have at such times dealt with national emergencies by acting promptly and resolutely to enforce legislative programs, at least to save those programs until Congress could act.

The President is the active agent, not of Congress, but of the Nation. As such he performs the duties which the Constitution lays upon him immediately, and as such, also, he executes the laws and regulations adopted by Congress. He is the agent of the people of the United States, deriving all his powers from them and responsible directly to them. In no sense is he the agent of Congress. He obeys and executes the laws of Congress, not because Congress is enthroned in authority over him, but because the Constitution directs him to do so. Therefore it follows that in ways short of making laws or disobeying them, the Executive may be under a grave constitutional duty to act for the national protection in situations not covered by the acts of Congress, and in which, even, it may not be said that his action is the direct expression of any particular one of the independent powers which are granted to him specifically by the Constitution.

The fact that temporary executive seizures of industrial plants to meet an emergency have not been directly tested in this Court furnishes not the slightest suggestion that such actions have been illegal. Rather, the fact that Congress and the courts have consistently recognized and given their support to such executive action indicates that such a power of seizure has been accepted throughout our history.

VI.

Faced with the duty of executing the defense programs which Congress had enacted and the disastrous effects that any stoppage in steel production would have on those programs, the President acted to preserve those programs by seizing the steel mills. There is no question that the possession was other than temporary in character and subject to congressional direction—either approving, disapproving or regulating the manner in which the mills were to be administered and returned to the owners. The President immediately informed Congress of his action and clearly stated his intention to abide by the legislative will. In this case the President acted in full conformity with his duties under the Constitution. Accordingly, we would reverse the order of the District Court.

The *Youngstown* opinions concerning how to define the limits of executive power expose the terms of the debate about separation of powers. Justice Black's opinion concludes that the presidential order was a usurpation of the legislative power in which the lawmaking power is vested. For him, because there exists no explicit textual support for the executive action in the vesting clause or elsewhere in the Constitution, and no law of Congress authorizing such an executive act, the President cannot act. Fear of governmental tyranny and the concomitant incursions on liberty requires vigilant policing of the boundaries by the Court under Justice Black's analysis. The concurring opinion of Justice Jackson is more flexible than this clause-bound approach. Reflecting his own pragmatic understanding of political accommodation as well as the Framers' use of checks and balances as a means of protecting against tyranny, Justice Jackson begins with but looks beyond explicit delegations found in the text to define power in light of interbranch dependence and function. Dissenters joining then-Chief Justice Vinson, on the other hand, are prepared to recognize the pragmatic needs for executive action in emergency which in practice define the boundary of power available to the executive. The explanations the dissenters offer to justify the presidential action stress the practical need for discretion which they conclude is available to the President, as the nation's leader. The dissenters find in the constitutional text and inferences to be drawn therefrom executive authority to respond whereas the concurrences conclude in these circumstances that Congress has expressly denied the President the recourse taken.

PAH: Although they agree with the outcome he reaches, both Justice Jackson and Justice Frankfurter acknowledge that Justice Black's focus on text alone is too narrow to describe modern government. The pragmatic considerations each of them offer in order to assess the validity of action taken by the Executive have proven more useful than the rigid boundary setting of Justice Black in reviewing Executive action in subsequent cases, although both Justice Jackson and Justice Frankfurter agree that in this context the President overstepped his bounds. Though the concurring opinions—like the dissenting one—stress that the Constitution is a living document adaptable to changing circumstances, they share Justice Black's concern about the dangers of tyranny that can arise when a branch accumulates power, dangers which were contemplated by the Framers in providing separation. But they emphasize that the tension which is a product of the structural checks and balances also serves the interest of preventing tyranny.

Justice Black reasons that the actions of President Truman offend the Constitution because they are "law making" reserved to the Congress. His conclusion is built on the express textual provisions defining the legislative and executive functions which he argues resolve the question of whether the President has the power to act. In fact, although the Constitution grants to Congress "[a]ll legislative powers" and vests the President with "executive" power and the Supreme Court with "judicial power of the United States," it does not tell us the meaning of "legislative," "executive" and "judicial."[15] Looking back to the Constitution's framing, Professor Gwyn has argued that the concepts of "executive" and "legislative" in seventeenth century political philosophy referred not to single functions, but to multifunctional power. Moreover, William Gwynn argues, there is little consensus even today as to which government actions belong to each type of organization.[16] This argument challenges the assumptions of a formalist or clause-bound interpretation that boundaries of power available to be exercised by the executive or other branch can be drawn with scientific precision by reference to the language vesting in each branch authority to act. Formalists, however, also look to history and practice at the time of the constitutional framing as a way of clarifying whether a given action is encompassed within one or another of the branch's bound-

---

[15] Notably, Professor Gwyn points out that during the seventeenth century, the term "executive power" usually included what has been labeled "judicial power" since the eighteenth century. *See also* GORDON S. WOOD, THE CREATION OF THE AMERICAN REPUBLIC, 1776–1787 (1969).

[16] *See* Gwyn, *supra* note 7, at 267. Justice Scalia would clearly disagree. For his view of the allocation of power, see his dissent in *Morrison v. Olson, infra,* p. 264.

aries of power. Thus they seek certainty in the Framers' design as a means of imposing discipline in a more complex modern world.

It is also notable that Justice Black views the power allocated to the executive in seriatim fashion and not cumulatively. Thus for example, the presidential power as Commander in Chief does not supplement the executive power, increasing the President's reach; rather, each power is measured separately in consideration of whether presidential action is justified.

Although he concurs in the judgment and opinion written by Justice Black, Justice Jackson offers a more fluid image of power in his concurrence, emphasizing that the Constitution contemplates diffusion of power to secure liberty and is best understood in the context of practical workings of government. Justice Jackson's opinion establishes three categories for analyzing the constitutionality of presidential action: (1) presidential acts pursuant to authority delegated by Congress; (2) presidential acts in the absence of a congressional grant or denial of authority; and (3) presidential acts against congressional will. Justice Jackson considers President Truman's action under category three of his analysis because no statute authorized the President's seizure and Congress had rejected making this alternative available in the relevant statutory provisions. According to Justice Jackson, such presidential action must be justified by clear warrant of constitutional authority. Justice Jackson concludes that none of the specific constitutional powers asserted by the President—the grant of executive power, the Commander in Chief clause, or the faithful execution clause—is sufficient, standing alone, to authorize the seizure. Because he refuses in these circumstances to recognize "inherent," "implied" war or emergency power, Justice Jackson finds the President's action to be invalid because it lacks constitutional basis. Under the tripartite analysis Justice Jackson constructs it is not clear that inherent authority is never recognized; he concludes, however, it is not able to be invoked here where Congress has the capability of authorizing the action and chose not to do so.

Justice Jackson's acknowledgment of a "twilight zone" of power seems to respond to the observations attributed to Professor Gwynn about the ill defined contours of executive power. For Justice Jackson defining government is less the science that Justice Black's formalist analysis reflects than an art.[17] Jackson's grouping of powers, describing the legal consequences of executive action as stemming from understandings about its core functions as well as from express or implied authorization of executive action by Congress and establishing presumptions about legitimacy, has become a prominent way of resolving conflicts about the allocation of power between the political branches.[18] But it is not without controversy. How, we can ask, does Congress' expression of will (or inferences to be drawn from its legislative expression) *constitutionally* support an accretion of executive power if an action taken by the President is not in any sense "executive" in nature? Can Congress, for example, delegate to the President (or any other body) its "law making" power?

As he invokes separation of powers to invalidate President Truman's action, Justice Jackson, informed by his own experiences in the executive branch of the government from 1934 to 1941, as Assistant Attorney General, Solicitor General and Attorney General of the United States,[19] admits that "paper powers" and "real powers" of the

---

[17] *Youngstown*, 343 U.S. at 635 (Jackson, J., concurring).

[18] In Dames & Moore v. Regan, 453 U.S. 654, 661 (1981), then-Justice Rehnquist cited Justice Jackson's concurrence with approval, observing that it "brings together as much combination of analysis and common sense as there is in this area."

[19] For a brief account of the impact of Justice Jackson's life experiences on his perspective as Judge, written by Justice Rehnquist, *see*, *Robert H. Jackson: A Perspective Twenty-Five Years Later*, 44 ALA. L. REV. 533 (1980).

branches are not the same. He concludes: "We may say that power to legislate for emergencies belongs in the hands of Congress, but only Congress itself can prevent power from slipping through its fingers."[20] Under this reasoning what effect does the Supreme Court's conclusion that President Truman lacked the power to act in this case have on the allocation of power?

Like Justice Black and Justice Jackson, Justice Frankfurter rejects governmental efficiency as an appropriate constitutional consideration, a value which is, in contrast, recognized by the dissenters in defining authority to act, particularly in the context of emergency or war. The pragmatic need for swift response and strong national leadership is rejected by the majority as a constitutionally sound basis for action in light of the Framers' concern about tyranny that can result from the accretion of power. Thus they view separation of powers as a prophylactic measure,[21] a tool for the court to police the balance of power among the branches because of the natural tendency of government to assume more power. The Court's boundary patrol concerns well intentioned exercises of national power as well as unintended incursions which are likely to be condoned politically, particularly in times of emergency or war. The fear is that in these contexts, when the balance of power shifts, the liberty of the citizenry is eventually jeopardized, perhaps subtly and incrementally, but significantly for separation of powers purposes. The majority thus sees the Court's role to maintain the boundaries intended by the Framers for the protection of liberty. However, while they viewed the action taken by the President as outside the range of constitutional and statutory choices, both Justices Frankfurter and Jackson are prepared to acknowledge that the constitutional framework and allocation of power effectively change over time through accommodation by the political branches.

Although Justice Frankfurter shares Justice Black's purpose to prevent abuse by confining each branch to its assigned, separate domain, he candidly acknowledges that what is to be understood as "executive," "legislative" or "judicial" is a product of history and practice as well as text. It follows that the question of abuse of power cannot be resolved without an appreciation of the historical "gloss"—the way the constitutional framework has consistently operated. How can such a gloss be consistent with the notion of limited government and a written constitution? Justice Frankfurter's recognition of a gloss seems to promote a kind of adverse possession theory of power accumulation, affecting our understanding of governmental authority to act.

A consistent dispute among commentators grappling with this "gloss" of power explanation concerns the grounds for asserting that authority has been affected by institutional practice. How many instances of executive action are necessary for the Court to recognize a gloss in order to incorporate the power? What kind of steps must be taken to ensure that the "natural tendency" of one branch to seek more power is overcome by another branch which claims the Constitution commits that power to it?

Pragmatists like the dissenters in *Youngstown* view the establishment of rigid boundaries between the branches as neither constitutionally required nor necessary to prevent abuses of government. Like Justice Frankfurter and Justice Jackson, the dissenters are not persuaded that explicit allocation of authority in the Constitution is always a realistic measure of executive authority. Pragmatic functionalists argue that even if the need for policing the structural boundaries was important because of concern about tyranny in the Framers' minds, that concern is outdated or at least diminished in the interest of efficiency, particularly in crisis. Indeed, they argue, efficiency was a competing concern of the Framers inasmuch as they constructed a national

---

[20] *Youngstown*, 343 U.S. at 654.

[21] Martin H. Redish & Elizabeth Cisar, *"If Angels Were to Govern"*: The Need for Pragmatic Formalism in Separation of Powers Theory*, 41 Duke L.J. 449, 452 (1991).

framework for government which responded to the failure of the Articles of Confederation. Moreover, as President Lincoln said of his own arguable usurpation of power during the civil war conflict, in an emergency situation we can loose the country in an effort to save the Constitution.[22] Skeptical that the structural and practical checks and balances provide adequate protection, formalists are concerned that this pragmatic assessment of needs and efficiency offer no constitutional limits except the context of emergency.

Justice Frankfurter refers to Justice Marshall's admonition to interpret the Constitution as a living document. Is Justice Black's literal, formalist approach at odds with that admonition? It can be argued that fear of tyranny—the usurpation of authority—leads formalists like Justice Black to enforce constitutional language which suggests any plausible "clear" boundary without duly considering the ultimate effect on government or the practical impact on liberty of citizens. Rejecting Justice Black's formalist approach, some commentators (like Justice Jackson) challenge the certainty formalists find in the constitutional text, arguing that the relevant constitutional provisions confer only an allusion of certainty in separation of powers cases since there is no separation clause. It has been said, in fact, that developing a jurisprudence of separation of powers which rests on discrete passages or words found in the Constitution alone does injustice to the concept of separation of powers since—"[i]n a sense, the "text" in separation of powers law is everything that the Framers did and said in making the original Constitution plus the history of our government since the founding."[23] In this way judicial dependence on formal textual boundaries in decisions about the allocation of power among the branches, without more, represents as much the Court's abdication of interpretive responsibility as formalists charge pragmatists are guilty of doing in ignoring the text.[24]

Undaunted by the absence of express language authorizing presidential action in *Youngstown*, the dissenters find inherent authority in the President. The source of that authority lies for them in the nature and duties of the executive. How does this rationale for Presidential action differ from that asserted for Congress by Justice Marshall in *McCulloch*? Is it reasonable to conclude that Congress and not the executive has inherent or implied authority to act? *See McCulloch* and *United States v. Nixon*, discussed *infra*.

DEL: The debate between the formalists and functionalists, when scopes of power are at stake, parallels the disagreement between interpretivists and noninterpretivists, when fundamental rights are at issue. As a primary exponent of formalism and interpretivism, Justice Black makes perhaps the definitive case for the interests of certainty and minimal judicial discretion in delineating powers and rights. For those who would have the judiciary assume an expansive role in amplifying the Constitution's meaning, because it is a living

---

[22] In the Prize Cases, 67 U.S. (2 Black) 635 (1886), the Supreme Court upheld the power of the President to establish the blockade of southern states despite the fact that war had not been declared by Congress. *Id.* at 668, 670. Notably, one commentator has acknowledged that: "there were widespread violations of individual rights that took place when President Lincoln assumed the inordinate level of power." Reddish & Cisar, *supra* note 21, at 473 (describing suspension of the writ of habeas corpus on April 27, 1861, leading to the military arrests of thousands of citizens and subsequently authorization of military commissions to try civilians.)

[23] E. Donald Elliot, *Why Our Separation of Powers Jurisprudence Is So Abysmal*, 57 GEO. WASH. L. REV. 506, 508 (1989).

[24] *See* Suzanna Sherry, *Separation of Powers, Asking a Different Question*, 30 WM. & MARY L. REV. 279, 289 (1989).

document or "a *Constitution* that we are expounding," Black's theory of review results in neither a dead letter nor an inability to expound. Investment in his analytical model, however, at least should be prefaced by some critical evaluation—especially if reflecting an absolutist perspective. Perhaps a greater challenge to formalistic methodology would arise if the steel industry maintained its position against seizure even as enemy forces approached American soil. At some point, it would seem that even the most ardent formalist might want to reconsider his or her thinking if circumstances presented a choice between defending the nation and maintaining ideological purity. Ironically for the formalist, such a dilemma might translate into choosing between defending the Constitution and defending a constitutional theory. To the extent any concession was made on the basis of exigency, functionalism would prevail and the professed formalist would be unmasked as a pragmatist whose attention to circumstance was simply more difficult to trigger.

DER: The division between formalist and functionalist approaches to separation of powers may not always be so clear. Some formalist arguments limiting executive power might be motivated by functionalist concerns. The separation of powers doctrine protects citizens' liberty by guarding against the ability of any one branch of government from assuming unbridled power. If the text of the Constitution carefully assigned the authority to take particular actions with this end in mind, then following the text ultimately serves the function of safeguarding citizens from totalitarian abuse. Thus, if, as Justice Douglas noted, the Constitution specifically allocates to Congress the power of raising revenues to compensate for public takings, the President cannot have an "inherent" power that contradicts that constitutional grant to Congress. Finding inherent powers unsettles the intricate balance that the Framers orchestrated when they originally distributed constitutional activities among the branches. This functionalist explanation of the formalist approach falls apart, however, if Congress and the President have historically struck a balance not contemplated by the Constitution's text.

The Court's treatment of separation of powers cases has been called a methodological "tug-of-war."[25] As you read the history and consider the cases which follow, consider whether either approach—the essentially pragmatic functionalism or the more clausebound formalism—offers a useful analytical framework for the Court.

B. Locating Constitutional Boundaries of Executive Power

1. Foreign Affairs

The *Youngstown* case centered on presidential action aimed at resolving a domestic labor dispute. In foreign affairs controversies the clause-bound limits on executive action framed in Justice Black's opinion in *Youngstown* have given way to judicial acknowledgment of the need for broad latitude and discretion in the President as a necessary consequence of national leadership in foreign affairs. This discretion has roots in the concept of executive authority of article II and in the president's duty to take care that laws are faithfully executed.

In *United States v. Curtiss-Wright Export Corp.*[26], the Supreme Court upheld a presidential embargo on arms sales to Paraguay and Bolivia made pursuant to a joint resolution of Congress. The arms merchants who were indicted for violating the ban demurred to the indictment, asserting that the joint resolution unconstitutionally dele-

---

[25] Note, *Separation of Powers: No Longer Simply Hanging in the Balance*, 79 Geo. L.J. 173, 173 (1990).

[26] 299 U.S. 304 (1936).

gated legislative power to the President. The Court recognized that the federal government had very expansive foreign affairs powers. To Justice Sutherland such power though unenumerated, flowed from sovereignty. Having acknowledged expansive power in the federal government, Justice Sutherland located the authority to exercise the power in the executive branch. Referring to Justice Marshall's argument before the House of Representatives on March 7, 1800, Justice Sutherland stated that "[t]he President is the sole organ of the nation in external relations, and its sole representative with foreign nations."

In *Curtiss-Wright*, the Court's assertion of "the very delicate, plenary and exclusive power of the President as the sole organ of the federal government in the field of international relations,"[27] was unnecessary since there was no conflict about power between Congress and the President in that case; the Court had ruled that Congress authorized the presidential action. Since *Curtiss-Wright*, however, the notion persists that the constitutional presidential authority is more expansive in the foreign affairs area than in domestic,[28] and courts have been more deferential to claims of independent executive power undertaken in the foreign affairs context, emphasizing the need for leadership, confidentiality and external sovereignty.

The difference in treatment of executive power in a domestic as contrasted with a foreign affairs context again reveals competing understandings of separation of powers which continue to affect analysis of claims of power. Whereas the separation of powers approach reflected in Justice Black's opinion in *Youngstown* emphasizes concern about tyranny, the usurpation of power and the consequent danger to liberty of citizens resulting from the unchecked exercise of power, the approach reflected in *Curtiss-Wright* focuses on the notion of separating governmental functions in order to promote efficiency and effective government. These efficiency concerns, moreover, have sometimes led courts to defer to pragmatic adjustments in the structural framework by the political branches in domestic as well as foreign contexts, relying on the political branches to resolve potential power conflicts through accommodation. In settings where there has been accommodation courts have sometimes been reluctant to intrude. This judicial reluctance to intervene—particularly in disputes about executive action in foreign affairs—has been grounded in the doctrine of political questions or concerns about justiciability.[29]

Some commentators have argued that the Court's reticence contributes to the lack of a well developed analytical model for considering separation of powers.[30] Many important issues bearing on separation of powers have been avoided by the Court. Other writers have observed that political and power relationships, not judicial decisions, determine the validity and shape of our system.[31] Professor Entin notes:

---

[27] 299 U.S. at 319–20.

[28] Notably, Justice Sutherland in *Curtiss-Wright* argued that the President is really the successor of the British Crown, *see* 299 U.S. 304, 316–29 (1936), an observation criticized as historically inaccurate, *see* Russell K. Osgood, *Early Versions and Practices of Separation of Powers: A Comment*, 30 WM & MARY L. REV. 279, 285 (1989). A similar position was rejected in *Youngstown* by Justice Jackson in his concurrence.

[29] *See* JESSE CHOPER, JUDICIAL REVIEW AND THE NATIONAL POLITICAL PROCESS 273–314 (1980) (arguing for making separation of powers a political question). The doctrine of ripeness and nonjusticiability has been applied to avoid judicial involvement in controversies related to the use of military force in international conflicts.

[30] Elliott, *supra* note 23, at 507.

[31] Professor Gewirtz argues, for example, that the truly important separation of powers issues have not been addressed by the court and that those that have have been wrongly decided because they are not the ones that have the greatest meaning. Paul Gewirtz, *Realism in Separation of Powers Thinking*, 30 WM. & MARY L. REV. 343 (1989).

At a more fundamental level, the quest for ultimate judicial resolution of constitutional turf battles between Congress and the President has undesirable consequences for the nation as a whole. Separation of powers disputes implicate fundamental questions respecting the role of government, questions that rarely receive detailed attention in Supreme Court opinions. Excessive reliance upon the Court deceives us into thinking that these disputes are purely constitutional in nature and that only the Justices can resolve them. Demanding judicial resolution improperly diminishes the role of the political branches in interpreting the Constitution, and emphasizing the constitutionality of a proposal diverts attention from its often dubious wisdom.[32]

The hostage crisis and conflict with Iran in the late seventies and early eighties provide a context for considering not only the role of the president in foreign affairs but also the Supreme Court's role in validating presidential authority utilizing separation of powers analysis.

After the seizure of American personnel as hostages in Tehran, on November 14, 1979, President Carter invoked the International Emergency Economic Powers Act (IEEPA) and declared a national emergency. As a way of ensuring the preservation of assets, the President blocked the removal or transfer of all property and interests in property of the Government of Iran under the United States jurisdiction. The Treasury Department implemented regulations which essentially froze all Iranian assets.

Subsequently, on January 19, 1981, the Americans held hostage were released by Iran pursuant to an agreement worked out by the executive branch of the United States. The plaintiffs in *Dames & Moore v. Regan* challenged the constitutional and legal authority of the President's actions preceding negotiations concerning the hostages and in effectuating the agreement which led to the hostages' release. In reading the response of the Court, consider whether it can be said that the opinion of Justice Rehnquist is faithful to *Youngstown* in its rationale concerning the constitutional validity of the deal.

---

[32] Jonathan L. Entin, *Separation of Powers, The Political Branches, and the Limits of Judicial Review*, 51 OHIO ST. L.J. 175, 176–77 (1990).

Dames & Moore v. Regan
453 U.S. 654 (1981)

JUSTICE REHNQUIST delivered the opinion of the Court.

The questions presented by this case touch fundamentally upon the matter in which our Republic is to be governed. . . . We have had the benefit of commentators such as John Jay, Alexander Hamilton, and James Madison writing in The Federalist Papers at the Nation's very inception, the benefit of astute foreign observers of our system such as Alexis de Tocqueville and James Bryce writing during the first century of the Nation's existence, and the benefit of many other treatises as well as more than 400 volumes of reports of decisions of this Court. As these writings reveal it is doubtless both futile and perhaps dangerous to find any epigrammatical explanation of how this country has been governed. Indeed, as Justice Jackson noted, "[a] judge . . . may be surprised at the poverty of really useful and unambiguous authority applicable to concrete problems of executive power as they actually present themselves." *Youngstown Sheet & Tube Co. v. Sawyer* (concurring opinion).

Our decision today will not dramatically alter this situation, for the Framers "did not make the judiciary the overseer of our government." We are confined to a resolution of the dispute presented to us. That dispute involves various Executive Orders and regulations by which the President nullified attachments and liens on Iranian assets in the United States, directed that these assets be transferred to Iran, and suspended claims against Iran that may be presented to an International Claims Tribunal. This action was taken in an effort to comply with an Executive Agreement between the United States and Iran. We granted certiorari before judgment in this case, and set an expedited briefing and argument schedule, because lower courts had reached conflicting conclusions on the validity of the President's actions and, as the Solicitor General informed us, unless the Government acted by July 19, 1981, Iran could consider the United States to be in breach of the Executive Agreement.

But before turning to the facts and law which we believe determine the result in this case, we stress that the expeditious treatment of the issues involved by all of the courts which have considered the President's actions makes us acutely aware of the necessity to rest decision on the narrowest possible ground capable of deciding the case. This does not mean that reasoned analysis may give way to judicial fiat. It does mean that the statement of Justice Jackson—that we decide difficult cases presented to us by virtue of our commissions, not our competence—is especially true here. We attempt to lay down no general "guidelines" covering other situations not involved here, and attempt to confine the opinion only to the very questions necessary to decision of the case.

Perhaps it is because it is so difficult to reconcile the definition of Art. III judicial power with the broad range of vitally important day-to-day questions regularly decided by Congress or the Executive, without either challenge or interference by the Judiciary, that the decisions of the Court in this area have been rare, episodic, and afford little precedential value for subsequent cases. The tensions present in any exercise of executive power under the tri-partite system of Federal Government established by the Constitution have been reflected in opinions by Members of this Court more than once. The Court stated in *United States v. Curtiss-Wright Export Corp.*, . . . :

> "[W]e are here dealing not alone with an authority vested in the President by an exertion of legislative power, but with such an authority plus the very delicate, plenary and exclusive power of the President as the sole organ of the federal government in the field of international relations—a power which does not require as a basis for its exercise an act of Congress, but which, of course, like every other governmental power, must be exercised in subordination to the applicable provisions of the Constitution."

And yet 16 years later, Justice Jackson in his concurring opinion in *Youngstown, supra,* which both parties agree brings together as much combination of analysis and common sense as there is in this area, focused not on the "plenary and exclusive power of the President" but rather responded to a claim of virtually unlimited powers for the Executive by noting: "The example of such unlimited executive power that must have most impressed the forefathers was the prerogative exercised by George III, and the description of its evils in the Declaration of Independence leads me to doubt that they were creating their new Executive in his image."

As we now turn to the factual and legal issues in this case, we freely confess that we are obviously deciding only one more episode in the never-ending tension between the President exercising the executive authority in a world that presents each day some new challenge with which he must deal and the Constitution under which we all live and which no one disputes embodies some sort of system of checks and balances.

I

On November 4, 1979, the American Embassy in Tehran was seized and our diplomatic personnel were captured and held hostage. In response to that crisis, President Carter, acting pursuant to the International Emergency Economic Powers Act, 91 Stat. 1626, 50 U.S.C. §§ 1701–1706 (1976 ed., Supp. III) (hereinafter IEEPA), declared a national emergency on November 14, 1979, and blocked the removal or transfer of "all property and interests in property of the Government of Iran, its instrumentalities and controlled entities and the Central Bank of Iran which are or become subject to the jurisdiction of the United States. . . ." President Carter authorized the Secretary of the Treasury to promulgate regulations carrying out the blocking order. On November 15, 1979, the Treasury Department's Office of Foreign Assets Control issued a regulation providing that "[u]nless licensed or authorized . . . any attachment, judgment, decree, lien, execution, garnishment, or other judicial process is null and void with respect to any property in which on or since [November 14, 1979,] there existed an interest of Iran." The regulations also made clear that any licenses or authorizations granted could be "amended, modified, or revoked at any time."

On December 19, 1979, petitioner Dames & Moore filed suit in the United States District Court for the Central District of California against the Government of Iran, the Atomic Energy Organization of Iran, and a number of Iranian banks. In its complaint, petitioner alleged that its wholly owned subsidiary, Dames & Moore International, S. R. L., was a party to a written contract with the Atomic Energy Organization, and that the subsidiary's entire interest in the contract had been assigned to petitioner. Petitioner contended, however, that it was owed

$3,436,694.30 plus interest for services performed under the contract prior to the date of termination. The District Court issued orders of attachment directed against property of the defendants, and the property of certain Iranian banks was then attached to secure any judgment that might be entered against them.

On January 20, 1981, the Americans held hostage were released by Iran pursuant to an Agreement entered into the day before and embodied in two Declarations of the Democratic and Popular Republic of Algeria. The Agreement stated that "[i]t is the purpose of [the United States and Iran] . . . to terminate all litigation as between the Government of each party and the nationals of the other, and to bring about the settlement and termination of all such claims through binding arbitration." In furtherance of this goal, the Agreement called for the establishment of an Iran-United States Claims Tribunal which would arbitrate any claims not settled within six months. Awards of the Claims Tribunal are to be "final and binding" and "enforceable . . . in the courts of any nation in accordance with its laws." Under the Agreement, the United States is obligated

> "to terminate all legal proceedings in United States courts involving claims of United States persons and institutions against Iran and its state enterprises, to nullify all attachments and judgments obtained therein, to prohibit all further litigation based on such claims, and to bring about the termination of such claims through binding arbitration." Id., at 22.

In addition, the United States must "act to bring about the transfer" by July 19, 1981, of all Iranian assets held in this country by American banks. Id., at 24–25. One billion dollars of these assets will be deposited in a security account and used to satisfy awards rendered against Iran by the Claims Tribunal.

On January 19, 1981, President Carter issued a series of Executive Orders implementing the terms of the agreement.

On February 24, 1981, President Reagan issued an Executive Order in which he "ratified" the January 19th Executive Orders. Moreover, he "suspended" all "claims which may be presented to the . . . Tribunal" and provided that such claims "shall have no legal effect in any action now pending in any court of the United States." The suspension of any particular claim terminates if the Claims Tribunal determines that it has no jurisdiction over that claim; claims are discharged for all purposes when the Claims Tribunal either awards some recovery and that amount is paid, or determines that no recovery is due.

II

The parties and the lower courts, confronted with the instant questions, have all agreed that much relevant analysis is contained in *Youngstown Sheet & Tube Co. v. Sawyer*. Justice Black's opinion recognized that "[t]he President's power, if any, to issue the order must stem either from an act of Congress or from the Constitution itself." Justice Jackson's concurring opinion elaborated in a general way the consequences of different types of interaction between the two democratic branches in assessing Presidential authority to act in any given case. When the President acts pursuant to an express or implied authorization from Congress, he exercises not only his powers but also those delegated by Congress. In such a case the executive action "would be supported by the strongest of presumptions and the widest latitude of judicial interpretation, and the burden of persuasion would rest heavily upon any who might attack it." When the President acts in the absence of congressional authorization he may enter "a zone of twilight in which he and Congress may have concurrent authority, or in which its distribution is uncertain." In such a case the analysis becomes more complicated, and the validity of the President's action, at least so far as separation-of-powers principles are concerned, hinges on a consideration of all the circumstances which might shed light on the views of the Legislative Branch toward such action, including "congressional inertia, indifference or quiescence." Finally, when the President acts in contravention of the will of Congress, "his power is at its lowest ebb," and the Court can sustain his actions "only by disabling the Congress from acting upon the subject."

Although we have in the past found and do today find Justice Jackson's classification of executive actions into three general categories analytically useful, we should be mindful of Justice Holmes' admonition, quoted by Justice Frankfurter in *Youngstown, supra*, that "[t]he great ordinances of the Constitution do not establish and divide fields of black and white." Justice Jackson himself recognized that his three categories represented "a somewhat over-simplified grouping," and it is doubtless the case that executive action in any particular instance falls, not neatly in one of three pigeon-holes, but rather at some point along a spectrum running from explicit congressional authorization to explicit congressional prohibition. This is particularly true as respects cases such as the one before us, involving responses to international crises the nature of which Congress can hardly have been expected to anticipate in any detail.

III

In nullifying post-November 14, 1979, attachments and directing those persons holding blocked Iranian funds and securities to transfer them to the Federal Reserve Bank of New York for ultimate transfer to Iran, President Carter cited five sources of express or inherent power. The Government, however, has principally relied on § 203 of the IEEPA, as authorization for these actions. Section 1702(a)(1) provides in part:

"At the times and to the extent specified in section 1701 of this title, the President may, under such regulations as he may prescribe, by means of instructions, licenses, or otherwise—

"(A) investigate, regulate, or prohibit—

"(i) any transactions in foreign exchange,

"(ii) transfers of credit or payments between, by, through, or to any banking institution, to the extent that such transfers or payments involve any interest of any foreign country or a national thereof,

"(iii) the importing or exporting of currency or securities, and

"(B) investigate, regulate, direct and compel, nullify, void, prevent or prohibit, any acquisition, holding, withholding, use, transfer, withdrawal, transportation, importation or exportation of, or dealing in, or exercising any right, power, or privilege with respect to, or transactions involving, any property in which any foreign country or a national thereof has any interest; "by any person, or with respect to any property, subject to the jurisdiction of the United States."

The Government contends that the acts of "nullifying" the attachments and ordering the "transfer" of the frozen assets are specifically authorized by the plain language of the above statute.

Petitioner contends that we should ignore the plain language of this statute because an examination of its legislative history as well as the history of § 5(b) of the Trading With the Enemy Act (hereinafter TWEA), from which the pertinent language of § 1702 is directly drawn, reveals that the statute was not intended to give the President such extensive power over the assets of a foreign state during times of national emergency. According to petitioner, once the President instituted the November 14, 1979, blocking order, § 1702 authorized him "only to continue the freeze or to discontinue controls."

We do not agree and refuse to read out of § 1702 all meaning to the words "transfer," "compel," or "nullify." [W]e think both the legislative history and cases interpreting the TWEA fully sustain the broad authority of the Executive when acting under this congressional grant of power.

Because the President's action in nulli-fying the attachments and ordering the transfer of the assets was taken pursuant to specific congressional authorization, it is "supported by the strongest of presumptions and the widest latitude of judicial interpretation, and the burden of persuasion would rest heavily upon any who might attack it." *Youngstown* (Jackson, J., concurring). Under the circumstances of this case, we cannot say that petitioner has sustained that heavy burden. A contrary ruling would mean that the Federal Government as a whole lacked the power exercised by the President, and that we are not prepared to say.

IV

Although we have concluded that the IEEPA constitutes specific congressional authorization to the President to nullify the attachments and order the transfer of Iranian assets, there remains the question of the President's authority to suspend claims pending in American courts. Such claims have, of course, an existence apart from the attachments which accompanied them. In terminating these claims through Executive Order No. 12294 the President purported to act under authority of both the IEEPA and 22 U.S.C. § 1732, the so-called "Hostage Act."

We conclude that although the IEEPA authorized the nullification of the attachments, it cannot be read to authorize the suspension of the claims. The claims of American citizens against Iran are not in themselves transactions involving Iranian property or efforts to exercise any rights with respect to such property. An in personam lawsuit, although it might eventually be reduced to judgment and that judgment might be executed upon, is an effort to establish liability and fix damages and does not focus on any particular property within the jurisdiction. The terms of the IEEPA therefore do not authorize the President to suspend claims in American courts.

The Hostage Act, passed in 1868, provides:

"Whenever it is made known to the President that any citizen of the United States has been unjustly deprived of his liberty by or under the authority of any foreign government, it shall be the duty of the President forthwith to demand of that government the reasons of such imprisonment; and if it appears to be wrongful and in violation of the rights of American citizenship, the President shall forthwith demand the release of such citizen, and if the release so demanded is unreasonably delayed or refused, the President shall use such means, not amounting to acts of war, as he may think necessary and proper to obtain or effectuate the release; and all the facts and proceedings relative thereto shall as soon as practicable be communicated by the President to Congress."

We are reluctant to conclude that this provision constitutes specific authorization to the President to suspend claims in American courts. Although the broad language of the Hostage Act suggests it may cover this case, there are several difficulties with such a view. The legislative history indicates that the Act was passed in response to a situation unlike the recent Iranian crisis. Congress in 1868 was concerned with the activity of certain countries refusing to recognize the citizenship of naturalized Americans traveling abroad, and repatriating such citizens against their will. These countries were not interested in returning the citizens in exchange for any sort of ransom. This also explains the reference in the Act to imprisonment "in violation of the rights of American citizenship." Although the Iranian hostage-taking violated international law and common decency, the hostages were not seized out of any refusal to recognize their American citizenship—they were seized precisely because of their American citizenship. The legislative history is also somewhat ambiguous on the question whether Congress contemplated Presidential action such as that involved here or rather simply reprisals directed against the offending foreign country and *its* citizens.

Concluding that neither the IEEPA nor the Hostage Act constitutes specific authorization of the President's action suspending claims, however, is not to say that these statutory provisions are entirely irrelevant to the question of the validity of the President's action. We think both statutes highly relevant in the looser sense of indicating congressional acceptance of a broad scope for executive action in circumstances such as those presented in this case. [T]he IEEPA delegates broad authority to the President to act in times of national emergency with respect to property of a foreign country. The Hostage Act similarly indicates congressional willingness that the President have broad discretion when responding to the hostile acts of foreign sovereigns.

Although we have declined to conclude that the IEEPA or the Hostage Act directly authorizes the President's suspension of claims for the reasons noted, we cannot ignore the general tenor of Congress' legislation in this area in trying to determine whether the President is acting alone or at least with the acceptance of Congress. As we have noted, Congress cannot anticipate and legislate with regard to every possible action the President may find it necessary to take or every possible situation in which he might act. Such failure of Congress specifically to delegate authority does not, "especially . . . in the areas of foreign policy and national security," imply "congressional disapproval" of action taken by the Executive. On the contrary, the enactment of legislation closely related to the question of the President's authority in a particular case which

evinces legislative intent to accord the President broad discretion may be considered to "invite" "measures on independent presidential responsibility," *Youngstown* (Jackson, J., concurring). At least this is so where there is no contrary indication of legislative intent and when, as here, there is a history of congressional acquiescence in conduct of the sort engaged in by the President. It is to that history which we now turn.

Not infrequently in affairs between nations, outstanding claims by nationals of one country against the government of another country are "sources of friction" between the two sovereigns. To resolve these difficulties, nations have often entered into agreements settling the claims of their respective nationals. The United States has repeatedly exercised its sovereign authority to settle the claims of its nationals against foreign countries. Though those settlements have sometimes been made by treaty, there has also been a longstanding practice of settling such claims by executive agreement without the advice and consent of the Senate. Under such agreements, the President has agreed to renounce or extinguish claims of United States nationals against foreign governments in return for lump-sum payments or the establishment of arbitration procedures. To be sure, many of these settlements were encouraged by the United States claimants themselves, since a claimant's only hope of obtaining any payment at all might lie in having his Government negotiate a diplomatic settlement on his behalf. It is clear that the practice of settling claims continues today. Since 1952, the President has entered into at least 10 binding settlements with foreign nations, including an $80 million settlement with the People's Republic of China.

Crucial to our decision today is the conclusion that Congress has implicitly approved the practice of claim settlement by executive agreement. This is best demonstrated by Congress' enactment of the International Claims Settlement Act of 1949. The Act had two purposes: (1) to allocate to United States nationals funds received in the course of an executive claims settlement with Yugoslavia, and (2) to provide a procedure whereby funds resulting from future settlements could be distributed. To achieve these ends Congress created the International Claims Commission, now the Foreign Claims Settlement Commission, and gave it jurisdiction to make final and binding decisions with respect to claims by United States nationals against settlement funds. By creating a procedure to implement future settlement agreements, Congress placed its stamp of approval on such agreements. Indeed, the legislative history of the Act observed that the United States was seeking settlements with countries and that the bill contemplated settlements of a similar nature in the future.

Over the years Congress has frequently amended the International Claims Settlement Act to provide for particular problems arising out of settlement agreements, thus demonstrating Congress' continuing acceptance of the President's claim settlement authority. As with legislation involving other executive agreements, Congress did not question the fact of the settlement or the power of the President to have concluded it. Congress recently amended the International Claims Settlement Act to facilitate the settlement of claims against Vietnam. Finally, the legislative history of the IEEPA further reveals that Congress has accepted the authority of the Executive to enter into settlement agreements. Though the IEEPA was enacted to provide for some limitation on the President's emergency powers, Congress stressed that "[n]othing in this act is intended . . . to interfere with the authority of the President to [block assets], or to impede the settlement of claims of U. S. citizens against foreign countries."

In addition to congressional acquiescence in the President's power to settle claims, prior cases of this Court have also recognized that the President does have some measure of power to enter into executive agreements without obtaining the advice and consent of the Senate. In *United States v. Pink*, 315 U.S. 203 (1942), for example, the Court upheld the validity of the Litvinov Assignment, which was part of an Executive Agreement whereby the Soviet Union assigned to the United States amounts owed to it by American nationals so that outstanding claims of other American nationals could be paid. The Court explained that the resolution of such claims was integrally connected with normalizing United States' relations with a foreign state:

> "Power to remove such obstacles to full recognition as settlement of claims of our nationals . . . certainly is a modest implied power of the President. . . . No such obstacle can be placed in the way of rehabilitation of relations between this country and another nation, unless the historic conception of the powers and responsibilities . . . is to be drastically revised."

In light of all of the foregoing—the inferences to be drawn from the character of the legislation Congress has enacted in the area, such as the IEEPA and the Hostage Act, and from the history of acquiescence in executive claims settlement—we conclude that the President was authorized to suspend pending claims pursuant to Executive Order No. 12294. As Justice Frankfurter pointed out in Youngstown, "a systematic, unbroken, executive practice, long pursued to the knowledge of the Congress and never before questioned . . . may be

treated as a gloss on 'Executive Power' vested in the President by § 1 of Art. II." Past practice does not, by itself, create power, but "long-continued practice, known to and acquiesced in by Congress, would raise a presumption that the [action] had been [taken] in pursuance of its consent. . . ." Such practice is present here and such a presumption is also appropriate. In light of the fact that Congress may be considered to have consented to the President's action in suspending claims, we cannot say that action exceeded the President's powers.

Our conclusion is buttressed by the fact that the means chosen by the President to settle the claims of American nationals provided an alternative forum, the Claims Tribunal, which is capable of providing meaningful relief. Moreover, it is important to remember that we have already held that the President has the *statutory* authority to nullify attachments and to transfer the assets out of the country. The President's power to do so does not depend on his provision of a forum whereby claimants can recover on those claims. The fact that the President has provided such a forum here means that the claimants are receiving something in return for the suspension of their claims, namely, access to an international tribunal before which they may well recover something on their claims. Because there does appear to be a real "settlement" here, this case is more easily analogized to the more traditional claim settlement cases of the past.

Just as importantly, Congress has not disapproved of the action taken here. Though Congress has held hearings on the Iranian Agreement itself, Congress has not enacted legislation, or even passed a resolution, indicating its displeasure with the Agreement. Quite the contrary, the relevant Senate Committee has stated that the establishment of the Tribunal is "of vital importance to the United States."

Finally, we re-emphasize the narrowness of our decision. We do not decide that the President possesses plenary power to settle claims, even as against foreign governmental entities. "The sheer magnitude of such a power, considered against the background of the diversity and complexity of modern international trade, cautions against any broader construction of authority than is necessary." *Chas T. Main Int'l, Inc. v. Khuzestan Water & Power Authority*, 651 F.2d, at 814. But where, as here, the settlement of claims has been determined to be a necessary incident to the resolution of a major foreign policy dispute between our country and another, and where, as here, we can conclude that Congress acquiesced in the President's action, we are not prepared to say that the President lacks the power to settle such claims.

The judgment of the District Court is accordingly affirmed, and the mandate shall issue forthwith.

Drawing upon language not only from *Curtiss-Wright* but also from the opinion of Justice Jackson in *Youngstown*, Justice Rehnquist upholds the actions of President Carter, asserting not only that the President's nullification of liens and attachments which were effectuated by the plaintiffs is valid but also that the President has authority to suspend private actions on claims like those held by the plaintiffs against Iran, directing the claims to be presented to an International Claims Tribunal. Justice Rehnquist disclaims any purpose in resolving this case favorably to the President, to lay down "general guidelines" covering other executive actions, and candidly alludes to the "necessities of the day" in justifying the Court's decision. The opinion suggests that separation of powers is less principled than an effort to provide legitimacy to "ad hoc political adjustments"[33] resulting from events like the hostage crisis.

In support of his conclusion Justice Rehnquist utilizes Justice Jackson's three categories of executive actions, emphasizing the fluidity of Jackson's analysis of executive power. He adds that the challenges to the President's actions must be assessed against the background of the international crisis to which President Carter was responding—"the nature of which Congress can hardly have been expected to anticipate in any detail."[34] He consequently considers the challenge to the nullification of attachments and transfer of frozen Iranian assets not merely in terms of express or inherent power of the President but also unconstrained by specific congressional authorizations for rendering attachments "revocable" or "contingent" in effect.

Even if the President's authority to nullify the attachments and order the transfer of assets is sustainable against a separation of powers challenge, there are considerable barriers to suspending claims pending in American courts. The terms of the IEEPA do not authorize the President to take such action, nor realistically, can the so-called Hostage Act of 1868 be construed as providing general authority for the executive action challenged in *Dames & Moore*. Justice Rehnquist, nevertheless, concludes that the President's actions are valid because both statutes indicate congressional acceptance of a broad executive discretion in response to such circumstances of national emergency.[35] Thus Justice Rehnquist reasons that the failure of Congress specifically to delegate authority in the areas of foreign policy and national security does not check executive action, at least where there is a history of congressional acquiescence to similar executive action. Justice Rehnquist finds that this acquiescence to executive power lies in Congress' implicit approval of the practice of settling claims by executive agreement—its failure to object to such a practice even when it has had the opportunity to do so in the past.

How is Justice Rehnquist's conclusion justified in principle? Would Justice Jackson agree that the "general tenor" of congressional legislation supports the President's action? Is his reliance on acquiescence by Congress consistent with the "gloss" to which Justice Frankfurter refers in *Youngstown*? Certainly Justice Rehnquist's analysis is more consistent with the concept of "a government of separated institutions sharing powers"[36] than with a conception of strict separation.

---

[33] *See* Arthur S. Miller, *Dames & Moore v. Regan: A Political Decision by a Political Court*, 29 U.C.L.A. L. Rev. 1104 1107 (1982).

[34] 453 U.S. at 669.

[35] 453 U.S. at 677.

[36] R. Neustadt, Presidential Power 26 (rev. ed. 1980).

PAH: Although the outcome may be desirable given the context of the crisis, *Dames & Moore* offers little more than justification for a political decision and does little to clarify the doctrine of separation of powers. The need for swift action and leadership in a hostage crisis involving another government is clear and the *Dames & Moore* case presents a challenging context for considering whether the Court can make a principled response that gives meaning to separation of powers beyond the case. It raises the question of what role the judiciary, the most insulated branch of national government, should play in defining the lines of authority in foreign affairs and domestic crises. How should we address concerns about institutional competence to make decisions about the dangers of one branch accumulating too much power: Are questions about the limits of authority better defined by the "democratic" branches than by an isolated judicial umpire?[37] For many commentators deference to political accommodations is a consequence of the fact that neither formalism, emphasizing separateness, nor pragmatic balancing or functionalism seem to have provided the Court with principled means of resolving separation of power controversies.[38]

Whereas a "minimalist" version of the Constitution may be at odds with what the Framers intended, some writers argue that separation of powers is an outmoded concept and that today the structure derived from it unduly impedes government from functioning. They assert that, in part as a product of the political accommodations the structure of checks and balances invites, separation as the Framers envisioned it is today not possible. Even if the president wants to lead, the president is often inhibited because of lack of cooperation from Congress; on the other hand, Congress often feels no compunction to provide policy-focused direction because of lethargy, lack of organization, or lack of direction. Some commentators believe that the party system has promoted politicians' interest in being elected rather than governing. Especially when a congressional majority is of a different party from the President, neither can be held accountable for its own failures by the voting electorate.[39] How do these observations affect your assessment of Justice Rehnquist's reasoning concerning the practice of the executive and acquiescence by Congress?

Although there were previous decisions supporting the authority of the President to interfere with litigation pending in American courts,[40] the President's suspension of claims in this context was supported neither by express authorization of Congress nor by treaty. In the context of this uncontemplated crisis, Justice Rehnquist looks to the "general tenor" of Congress' legislation in the area and Congress' "acceptance" of executive settlement authority in the past. In contrast, in *Youngstown* Justice Black invalidated President Truman's takeover of the steel mills, refusing to acknowledge that a real emergency existed and construing Congressional silence on the matter to reflect the absence of presidential authority.

Dames & Moore, like *Youngstown* and many of the cases involving separation of powers challenges to governmental institutions exercising authority, affects individual rights of citizens—here property interests. Indeed, Justice Jackson in *Youngstown* acknowledged the connection between limitations on executive authority to act which are the concern of separation of powers analysis and due process rights which shield private individuals from governmental action under the Fifth Amendment. Professor Rebecca

---

[37] *See, e.g.,* Arthur S. Miller, *From Compromise to Confrontation: Separation of Powers in the Reagan Era,* 57 GEO. WASH. L. REV. 401 (1989) (noting increase in lower court cases since 1960 which discuss the concept of separation of powers.)

[38] *See* Arthur S. Miller, *Dames & Moore v. Regan: A Political Decision by a Political Court,* 29 UCLA L. REV. 1104, 1107 (1982).

[39] *See* Lloyd N. Cutler, *To Form a Government, in* SEPARATION OF POWERS: DOES IT STILL WORK? (Robert A. Goldwin & Art Kaufman eds. 1986); Donald L. Robinson, *The Renewal of American Constitutionalism,* cited in *id.* Redish & Cisar, *Pragmatic Formalism, supra* note 21.

[40] *See, e.g.,* Haig v. Agee, 453 U.S. 280 (1981) *See also* United States v. Pink, 315 U.S. 203 (1942) (settlement of claims arising from recognition of the Litinov Assignment).

Brown has argued that in separation of powers controversies courts should focus on the governmental action's impact on private rights because that consideration can provide coherence which is presently lacking in modern separation of powers analysis.[41] Would such a focus on the impact of private claims affect the outcome of *Dames & Moore*? Significantly, Justice Rehnquist admits that in other settings where settlement of citizens' claims had occurred, the citizens themselves supported settlement.

As a pragmatic response, the *Dames & Moore* Court's decision to uphold the President's action rather than to permit the expectations of future private litigation to obstruct the resolution of the hostage situation seems justified. As a constitutional proposition, however, the President's authority to settle international claims by executive agreement may be accepted[42] but it has not been established that the President through executive agreement can extinguish a litigant's right to sue.[43] *Youngstown* and *Dames & Moore*, read together, leave open the opportunity for the President to establish authority to act because of congressional acquiescence, but do not provide clarity about the situations when the Court will acknowledge the gloss of practice to have occurred. The Court in *Dames & Moore* is candid about the fact that the crisis provided a context for evaluating the challenge to presidential action but it provides little guidance as to how to distinguish the significance of this context from others in which the Court has refused to do so.

Dames & Moore raises the issue presented by Justice Jackson's approach in *Youngstown* as to how Congress and the President, acting together, constitutionally validate executive action when the power exercised is not able to be classified as within the power vested in the executive branch. Justice Jackson found such an exercise "supported by the strongest of presumptions and the widest latitude of judicial interpretation."[44] A less pragmatic formalist would argue that executive action which is validated by addition or subtraction of Congress destroys "separation" of branch powers[45] except in the circumstances where Congress is authorizing implementation of policy. The Court's willingness (notwithstanding its nondelegation doctrine) to condone broad delegations of policy-making power by Congress to the President and the creation of independent administrative agencies, is discussed *supra*.

Justice Rehnquist's analysis draws upon Justice Jackson's analytical grouping of executive powers to validate President Carter's action in circumstances where the action taken was not explicitly authorized by Congress. Is Rehnquist's reasoning as to why the actions of the president were legal persuasive? Notably, Justice Rehnquist, who clerked for Justice Jackson at the time of the *Youngstown* decision later characterized Justice

---

[41] Rebecca L. Brown, *Separated Powers and Ordered Liberty*, 139 U. PA. L. REV. 1513 (1991) (exploring the relationship between "ordered liberty" and separation of powers and proposing a "countermajoritarian" model for considering separation of powers controversies).

[42] Treaties, which are executive agreements which have been formulated and given effect with the advice and consent of the Senate, are authorized in the Constitution under article II, section 2, clause 2. In several ways Presidents have asserted authority to enter other international agreements without formal congressional approval pursuant to the treaty-making requirements or law-making requirements of article I, section 7. Presidents have claimed authority: (1) drawn from express presidential power, such as commander in chief, or other exclusive power such as the power to receive foreign ambassadors and recognize foreign governments; (2) in pursuance of an authorization contained in a treaty; and (3) derived from prior congressional authorizations or steps approving presidential action by Congress. *See* JOHN E. NOWAK & RONALD D. ROTUNDA, CONSTITUTIONAL LAW 215–16 (4th ed. 1991).

[43] *See* Wilson v. Girard, 354 U.S. 524 (1957) (sustained agreement permitting trial of citizen in a Japanese court.); Seery v. United States, 127 F. Supp. 601, 607 (Ct. Cl. 1955), cert. denied, 359 U.S. 943 (1959); Reid v. Covert, 354 U.S. 1 (1954).

[44] 453 U.S. at 668 (quoting Youngstown Sheet & Tube Co. v. Sawyer, 343 U.S. 579, 637 (1952).

[45] *See* Redish & Cisar, *supra* note 21, at 486.

Jackson's approach in that case as "yet to be surpassed in its statesmanlike and lawyerlike analysis of the executive branch,"[46] and a product of common sense and experience in the executive branch. It is questionable however, whether a principle emerges from this case applicable to less threatening settings. Indicative of a more general theoretical vacuum in the area of separation of powers, the Court seems to shift between its functional or pragmatic approach to disputes and a formal, more clause-bound method of analysis, creating conflicting precedents for future courts.

DEL: Apart from the mixed signals radiated by the Court's decisions, but no less confounding, is the uncertainty over what constitutes acquiescence. Given the extensive gray area that exists in delineating presidential and congressional power, many controversies over executive action have the potential to turn on whether legislative action can be established. In *Dames & Moore*, the Court did not insist upon a specific congressional acquiescence with the seizure of Iranian assets. Rather, it was satisfied that such acquiescence could be inferred from other circumstances concerning other nations. The willingness to operate at a higher level of generalization, when executive power is at stake, contrasts with recent trends in the area of fundamental rights that disfavor abstraction and insist upon analytical specificity.[47] Although the *Sawyer* scenario may be distinguishable on grounds legislation had specifically prohibited the president's action, the argument for acquiescence could rest upon the fact that the president had notified Congress of his intention and given it the opportunity to stop him. The legislature, by not challenging him, might be seen as ratifying or consenting to the seizure. Like the scope of presidential and legislative powers themselves, the contours of acquiescence seem to be determined not by any overarching definition but in catalogue or registry fashion.

DER: Not only does the Court leave open the question of what constitutes congressional acquiescence, it also vacillates on the significance of congressional silence in the first place. Does Congress' failure to enact legislation authorizing executive action mean that the President is barred from acting or that Congress has acquiesced in the President's exercise of power? In the steel seizure case, a majority of Justices interpreted Congress' silence as an expression of intent to forbid President Truman from seizing the mills. In *Dames v. Moore*, on the other hand, Justice Rehnquist reasoned that Congress' silence permitted President Carter's seizure of Iranian assets. Professor Laurence Tribe argues that determining separation of powers questions on the basis of congressional silence is constitutionally dubious, particularly when it is treated as a bar to presidential authority: "[T]he internal system of checks and balances is thwarted because legislative silences are not subject to presidential veto, and external political accountability is diminished since Congress cannot realistically be held accountable by the electorate for laws it 'enacts' by silence."[48]

---

[46] *Id.* at 539.

[47] *See* Part I, at 176.

[48] Laurence Tribe, Constitutional Law 240 (1988). *See generally* Laurence Tribe, Constitutional Choices 29–44 (1985).

The Court's lack of a principled statement of limits on the executive power in the foreign affairs context has led some commentators to argue political accommodation is preferable, at least in this area. A consequence of this political accommodation is that the balance of power can shift to the most assertive branch. Particularly in the context of foreign affairs, where the need to act quickly in response to crises has been fairly accepted, the presidential power has evolved as far-reaching with virtually no objection from Congress, at least until the Vietnam war. In the domestic context, the Watergate controversy presented the specter of an "Imperial Presidency"[49] and an opportunity for the Court to address the balance of power as it relates to the privileges and immunities of office.

2. Privileges and Immunities of Office

The question of the president's amenability to process has been at the center of a few challenges to executive action in the courts as well as in proceedings in Congress. Yet only a few cases have directly addressed the set of issues raised by it, among them justiciability, political question, immunity and privilege. During the presidency of George Washington, Executive Privilege was asserted by the President to withhold information from Congress. By the 1790's Congress had recognized some Executive authority to withhold information which was sensitive.[50] The impeachment proceedings in connection with Watergate, however, raised the long-lingering issue of whether Congress' disagreement with the President over whether information was privileged is justiciable or a controversy to be resolved in the political arena.[51]

Nowhere in the text of the Constitution is there any reference to executive privilege. In contrast, Article I, § 5, cl. 3, the Speech or Debate Clause, provides Congress authority to keep secret certain information relating to its business and deliberations.[52] There is little to suggest that the Framers clearly intended the president or executive department to enjoy a similar privilege. In the constitutional debates delegates expressed concern about the dangers of unchecked power in the executive in support of provisions designed to limit authority by requiring cooperation and coordination with Congress (for example, in Art. II, § 2, cl. 2) and established impeachment as a means of restraining presidential action (Art. II, § 4, cl 6–7).

James Wilson told the Pennsylvania Ratification Convention:

> The Executive power is better to be trusted when it has no screen. Sir, we have a responsibility in the person for our President; he cannot act improperly, and hide either his negligence or inattention; he cannot roll upon any other person the weight of his criminality. . . . Add to all this, that officer is placed high, and is possessed of power far from being contemptible, yet not a *single privilege* is annexed to his character.[53]

In the trial of Aaron Burr, the Vice President during Jefferson's first term who was charged with treason in a scheme involving the purchase of property in the newly acquired Louisiana Territory, the issue of executive privilege was squarely before the court. Burr was the target of great hostility by Jefferson, who barely won the presidential race against Burr for a second term. During the trial, in response to President Jefferson's refusal to release a letter from General Wilkinson, a confidante and aide

---

[49] ARTHUR A. SCHLESINGER, JR., THE IMPERIAL PRESIDENCY III (1973). The title of this book has proven useful to describe not only President Nixon's assumption of broad power in the domestic arena but also to describe the "siphoning" of power by other Presidents in the area of foreign affairs.

[50] *See* DANIEL N. HOFFMAN, GOVERNMENTAL SECRECY AND THE FOUNDING FATHERS 104–18 (1981).

[51] *See* Senate Select Comm. v. Nixon, 366 F. Supp. 51 (D.D.C. 1973); Senate Select Comm. on Presidential Campaign Activity v. Nixon, 370 F. Supp. 521 (D.D.C. 1974), *aff'd*, 498 F.2d 725 (D.C.Cir. 1974).

[52] *See* Powell v. McCormack, 395 U.S. 486 (1969).

[53] Elliot, THE DEBATES IN THE SEVERAL STATE CONVENTIONS OF THE ADOPTION OF THE FEDERAL CONSTITUTION 480 (2d ed 1836), quoted in Archibald Cox, *Executive Privilege,* 122 U. PA. L. REV. 1383, 1391 (1974).

to Burr, Chief Justice John Marshall, sitting as trial judge in that case, countered that the President can be subpoenaed, examined as a witness, and required to produce papers. Justice Marshall reasoned that the president's circumstances were distinguishable from the prerogatives of a monarch. Consequently, immunity from the legal process which was afforded the King did not extend to the President in a government of laws such as was contemplated by the Constitution.[54] However, Justice Marshall emphasized special deference to be accorded requests by the President to be excused from producing documents or offering testimony:

> Although subject to the general rules which apply to others, [he] may have sufficient motives for declining to produce a particular paper, and those motives may be such as to restrain the court from enforcing its production . . . . The occasion for demanding it ought, in such a case, be very strong, and to be fully shown to the court before its production could be insisted on.[55]

A few other cases preceding the Watergate controversy had directly addressed other aspects of the president's amenability to the judicial process in controversies not involving Congress.[56] In a suit aimed at enjoining President Andrew Johnson from implementing certain Reconstruction laws, *Mississippi v. Johnson*, the question arose whether a President could be compelled to act or was exempt from judicial process. Chief Justice Chase for a unanimous Court ruled that in enforcing the Reconstruction Acts the President would be exercising duties that were "purely executive and political,"[57] and thus outside the jurisdiction of the Court to enforce. Chief Justice Chase emphasized the confrontation among the three branches such enforcement would impose: obeying the Court's injunction could subject the president to impeachment for failure to enforce the laws. If the President sought protection from the Court, the Court and the Senate would be in conflict. Chief Justice Chase observed: "[T]he Congress is the legislative department of the government; the President is the executive department. Neither can be restrained in its action by the judicial department; though the acts of both, when performed, are, in proper cases, subject to its cognizance."[58] In *Youngstown,* the issue of presidential immunity from a judicial proceeding was circumvented by the litigants who sued the Secretary of Commerce, Henry Sawyer.

---

[54] 25 F. Cas. at 34. *See also* Federalist No. 77.
[55] United States v. Burr, 25 F. Cas. 187, 191–92 (c.c. Va. 1807).
[56] Notably, Marbury v. Madison includes some discussion of the issue.
[57] 71 U.S. (4 Wall.) 475, 499.
[58] *Id.* at 500.

PAH: There are conflicting concerns which explain the reluctance of courts to resolve the question of amenability to suit. On the one hand, the President, like other individuals, is not above the law, and thus the Court's traditional role in the resolution of legal disputes consistently should extend to matters concerning the President.[59] The Court's independence and its insulation from politics further supports its role in resolving controversies concerning the President, particularly as a check on governmental abuse. On the other hand, the institutional confrontation which results when the Court compels the President to act implicates separation of powers considerations about the intrusion of one branch into the affairs of a co-equal branch, acknowledged in *Marbury*, and intragovernmental conflict. Moreover, because the President is seen as the nation's leader, the representative of sovereign power, there is special concern about subjecting him to process dictated

---

[59] *See* Marbury v. Madison 5 U.S. (1 Cranch) 137 (1803).

by the judicial branch in the course of his exercising leadership. Most importantly, because the Constitution expressly makes a commitment to political accountability of the President through the provisions for congressional impeachment and removal, there is the sense that the judicial forum is an inappropriate forum for the resolution of disputes concerning the President.

In *United States v. Nixon*, the Court avoided reaching the general issue of amenability, narrowly focusing on the availability of a generalized assertion of executive privilege in the context of a criminal prosecution. Following indictments alleging violation of federal statutes by White House staff and political supporters of the President, a special prosecutor who was appointed to direct the criminal investigation of the burglary of the Democratic National Committee's headquarters obtained a subpoena directing the President to produce tape recordings, papers, and other materials relating to the pending trial.[60] The material concerned conversations with aides and advisors. President Nixon, who was not indicted but was named by the grand jury as an unindicted co-conspirator, claimed executive privilege in a motion to quash the subpoena. The district court, treating the requested material as presumptively privileged, ruled that the Special Prosecutor had made a sufficient showing to rebut the presumption and issued an order for *in camera* examination of the subpoenaed material. The court stayed its order pending appellate review and the President sought review by the court of appeals. The Special Prosecutor immediately filed a petition for writ of certiorari before judgment and the President filed a cross petition for the writ. The Court granted both petitions "because of the public importance of the issues presented and the need for their prompt resolution."[61]

---

[60] As news exposing the Nixon Administration's involvement in the Watergate burglary unfolded, it came to light that the Administration kept tapes of meetings and phone calls conducted in the oval office. This knowledge resulted in three cases wherein access to the tapes was sought. An attempt by Congress to obtain the tapes eventually produced a negotiated settlement in which the President agreed to turn over some of the material requested, but only after two sets of judicial proceedings, see Senate Select Committee on Presidential Campaign Activities v. Nixon, 498 F.2d 725 (D.C. Cir. 1974). Special Prosecutor Archibald Cox sought judicial compulsion to release the tapes when a grand jury impaneled to bring indictments against key participants in Watergate sought them to determine who might be culpable. Nixon appealed the trial court's order to turn over the tapes and a divided court of appeals affirmed. The President chose not to appeal but to negotiate a settlement with Special Prosecutor Cox. When the Special Prosecutor refused the White House's compromise offer, Nixon ordered him fired for his refusal. Attorney General Elliot Richardson refused to comply, contending that he had made assurances to the Senate during his confirmation hearings that the Special Prosecutor would enjoy independence and would be fired only in the event of grave acts of misconduct. After Richardson resigned, William Ruckelshaus, next in line of authority, also refused to fire Cox and President Nixon fired Ruckelshaus for failing to act upon the President's order. Finally, Acting Attorney General Robert Bork was ordered to fire Cox and he complied. Calls for impeachment followed this series of events dubbed the "Saturday Night Massacre" and Congress laid plans for impeachment proceedings. Attempting to placate Congress and the public, the Justice Department named a new special prosecutor, Leon Jaworski. Jaworski subsequently initiated the third action seeking access to the tapes in response to the grand jury indictments. The expedited certiorari, an extraordinary response, followed from the lower court's ordering in that case that the tapes be produced.

[61] United States v. Nixon, 418 U.S., 683, 687 (1974). The *Nixon* case was argued on July 8, 1974 and decided on July 24, 1994.

United States v. Nixon
418 U.S. 683 (1974)

Mr. Chief Justice BURGER delivered the opinion of the Court.

This litigation presents for review the denial of a motion, filed in the District Court on behalf of the President of the United States, in the case of *United States v. Mitchell*, to quash a third-party subpoena duces tecum issued by the United States District Court for the District of Columbia, pursuant to Fed.Rule Crim.Proc. 17(c). The subpoena directed the President to produce certain tape recordings and documents relating to his conversations with aides and advisers. The court rejected the President's claims of absolute executive privilege, of lack of jurisdiction, and of failure to satisfy the requirements of Rule 17(c). The President appealed to the Court of Appeals. We granted both the United States' petition for certiorari before judgment and also the President's cross-petition for certiorari before judgment.

On March 1, 1974, a grand jury of the United States District Court for the District of Columbia returned an indictment charging seven named individuals with various offenses, including conspiracy to defraud the United States and to obstruct justice. Although he was not designated as such in the indictment, the grand jury named the President, among others, as an unindicted co-conspirator. On April 18, 1974, upon motion of the Special Prosecutor, a subpoena duces tecum was issued pursuant to Rule 17(c) to the President. This subpoena required the production, in advance of the September 9 trial date, of certain tapes, memoranda, papers, transcripts or other writings relating to certain precisely identified meetings between the President and others. The Special Prosecutor was able to fix the time, place, and persons present at these discussions because the White House daily logs and appointment records had been delivered to him. On April 30, the President publicly released edited transcripts of 43 conversations; portions of 20 conversations subject to subpoena in the present case were included. On May 1, 1974, the President's counsel filed a 'special appearance' and a motion to quash the subpoena under Rule 17(c). This motion was accompanied by a formal claim of privilege.

On May 20, 1974, the District Court denied the motion to quash and protective orders. It further ordered 'the President or any subordinate officer, official, or employee with custody or control of the documents or objects subpoenaed,' to deliver to the District Court, on or before May 31, 1974, the originals of all subpoenaed items, as well as an index and analysis of those items, together with tape copies of those portions of the subpoenaed recordings for which transcripts had been released to the public by the President on April 30. The District Court rejected jurisdictional challenges based on a contention that the dispute was nonjusticiable because it was between the Special Prosecutor and the Chief Executive and hence 'intra-executive' in character; it also rejected the contention that the Judiciary was without authority to review an assertion of executive privilege by the President. The court's rejection of the first challenge was based on the authority and powers vested in the Special Prosecutor by the regulation promulgated by the Attorney General; the court concluded that a justiciable controversy was presented. The second challenge was held to be foreclosed by the decision in *Nixon v. Sirica*, 487 F.2d 700 (D.C. Cir. 1973).

The District Court held that the judiciary, not the President, was the final arbiter of a claim of executive privilege. The court concluded that under the circumstances of this case the presumptive privilege was overcome by the Special Prosecutor's prima facie 'demonstration of need sufficiently compelling to warrant judicial examination in chambers. . . . ' 377 F.Supp., at 1330. The court held, finally, that the Special Prosecutor had satisfied the requirements of Rule 17(c). The District Court stayed its order pending appellate review on condition that review was sought before 4 p.m., May 24. The court further provided that matters filed under seal remain under seal when transmitted as part of the record.

On May 24, 1974, the President filed a timely notice of appeal from the District Court order, and the certified record from the District Court was docketed in the United States Court of Appeals for the District of Columbia Circuit. On the same day, the President also filed a petition for writ of mandamus in the Court of Appeals seeking review of the District Court order.

Later on May 24, the Special Prosecutor also filed, in this Court, a petition for a writ of certiorari before judgment. On May 31, the petition was granted with an expedited briefing schedule. 417 U.S. 927. On June 6, the President filed, under seal, a cross-petition for writ of certiorari before judgment. This cross-petition was granted and the case was set for argument on July 8, 1974.

I

JURISDICTION

The threshold question presented is whether the May 20, 1974, order of the District Court was an appealable order. The Court of Appeals jurisdiction under 28 U.S.C. § 1291 encompasses only 'final decisions of the district courts.' Since the appeal was timely filed and all other procedural requirements were met, the petition is properly before this Court for consideration if the District Court order was final. 28 U.S.C. §§ 1254(1), 2101(e).

The finality requirement of 28 U.S.C. § 1291 embodies a strong congressional policy against piecemeal reviews, and against obstructing or impeding an ongoing judicial proceeding by interlocutory appeals. *See, e.g., Cobbledick v. United States*, 309 U.S. 323, 324–326 (1940). This requirement ordinarily promotes judicial efficiency and hastens the ultimate termination of litigation. In applying this principle to an order denying a motion to quash and requiring the production of evidence pursuant to a subpoena duces tecum, it has been repeatedly held that the order is not final and hence not appealable. *United States v. Ryan*, 402 U.S. 530, 532 (1971); *Cobbledick v. United States, supra; Alexander v. United States*, 201 U.S. 117 (1906). This Court has 'consistently held that the necessity for expedition in the administration of the criminal law justifies putting one who seeks to resist the production of desired information to a choice between compliance with a trial court's order to produce prior to any review of that order, and resistance to that order with the concomitant possibility of an adjudication of contempt if his claims are rejected on appeal.' *United States v. Ryan, supra*, 402 U.S., at 533.

The requirement of submitting to contempt, however, is not without exception and in some instances the purposes underlying the finality rule require a different result. The traditional contempt avenue to immediate appeal is peculiarly inappropriate due to the unique setting in which the question arises. To require a President of the United States to place himself in the posture of disobeying an order of a court merely to trigger the procedural mechanism for review of the ruling would be unseemly, and would present an unnecessary occasion for constitutional confrontation between two branches of the Government. Similarly, a federal judge should not be placed in the posture of issuing a citation to a President simply in order to invoke review. The issue whether a President can be cited for contempt could itself engender protracted litigation, and would further delay both review on the merits of his claim of privilege and the ultimate termination of the underlying criminal action for which his

evidence is sought. These considerations lead us to conclude that the order of the District Court was an appealable order.

II

JUSTICIABILITY

In the District Court, the President's counsel argued that the court lacked jurisdiction to issue the subpoena because the matter was an intra-branch dispute between a subordinate and superior officer of the Executive Branch and hence not subject to judicial resolution. That argument has been renewed in this Court with emphasis on the contention that the dispute does not present a 'case' or 'controversy' which can be adjudicated in the federal courts. The President's counsel argues that the federal courts should not intrude into areas committed to the other branches of Government. He views the present dispute as essentially a 'jurisdictional' dispute within the Executive Branch which he analogizes to a dispute between two congressional committees. Since the Executive Branch has exclusive authority and absolute discretion to decide whether to prosecute a case, Confiscation Cases, 7 Wall. 454 (1869); *United States v. Cox*, 342 F.2d 167, 171 (CA5), cert. denied sub nom. *Cox v. Hauberg*, 381 U.S. 935 (1965), it is contended that a President's decision is final in determining what evidence is to be used in a given criminal case. Although his counsel concedes that the President has delegated certain specific powers to the Special Prosecutor, he has not 'waived nor delegated to the Special Prosecutor the President's duty to claim privilege as to all materials . . . which fall within the President's inherent authority to refuse to disclose to any executive officer.' Brief for the President 42. The Special Prosecutor's demand for the items therefore presents, in the view of the President's counsel, a political question under *Baker v. Carr*, 369 U.S. 186 (1962), since it involves a 'textually demonstrable' grant of power under Art. II.

The mere assertion of a claim of an 'intra-branch dispute,' without more, has never operated to defeat federal jurisdiction; justiciability does not depend on such a surface inquiry. In *United States v. ICC*, 337 U.S. 426 (1949), the Court observed, 'courts must look behind names that symbolize the parties to determine whether a justiciable case or controversy is presented.' Id. at 430.

Our starting point is the nature of the proceeding for which the evidence is sought—here a pending criminal prosecution. It is a judicial proceeding in a federal court alleging violation of federal laws and is brought in the name of the United States as sovereign. *Berger v. United States*, 295 U.S. 78, 88 (1935). Under the authority of Art. II, § 2, Congress has vested in the Attorney General the power to conduct the criminal litigation of the United States Government. 28 U.S.C. § 516. It has also vested in him the power to appoint subordinate officers to assist him in the discharge of his duties. 28 U.S.C. §§ 509, 510, 515, 533. Acting pursuant to those statutes, the Attorney General has delegated the authority to represent the United States in these particular matters to a Special Prosecutor with unique authority and tenure. The regulation gives the Special Prosecutor explicit power to contest the invocation of executive privilege in the process of seeking evidence deemed relevant to the performance of these specially delegated duties. 38 Fed. Reg. 30739, as amended by 38 Fed. Reg. 32805.

So long as this regulation is extant it has the force of law. *In United States ex rel. Accardi v. Shaughnessy*, 347 U.S. 260 (1954), regulations of the Attorney General delegated certain of his discretionary powers to the Board of Immigration Appeals and required that Board to exercise its own discretion on appeals in deportation cases. The Court held that so long as the Attorney General's regulations remained operative, he denied himself the authority to exercise the discretion delegated to the Board even though the original authority was his and he could reassert it by amending the regulations. *Service v. Dulles*, 354 U.S. 363 (1957), and *Vitarelli v. Seaton*, 359 U.S. 535 (1959), reaffirmed the basic holding of *Accardi*.

Here, as in *Accardi*, it is theoretically possible for the Attorney General to amend or revoke the regulation defining the Special Prosecutor's authority. But he has not done so. So long as this regulation remains in force the Executive Branch is bound by it, and indeed the United States as the sovereign composed of the three branches is bound to respect and to enforce it. Moreover, the delegation of authority to the Special Prosecutor in this case is not an ordinary delegation by the Attorney General to a subordinate officer: with the authorization of the President, the Acting Attorney General provided in the regulation that the Special Prosecutor was not to be removed without the 'consensus' of eight designated leaders of Congress.

The demands of and the resistance to the subpoena present an obvious controversy in the ordinary sense, but that alone is not sufficient to meet constitutional standards. In the constitutional sense, controversy means more than disagreement and conflict; rather it means the kind of controversy courts traditionally resolve. Here at issue is the production or nonproduction of specified evidence deemed by the Special Prosecutor to be relevant and admissible in a pending criminal case. It is sought by one official of the Executive Branch within the scope of his express authority; it is resisted by the Chief Executive on the ground of his duty to preserve the confidentiality of the communications of the President. Whatever the correct answer on the merits, these issues are 'of a type which are traditionally justiciable.' *United States v. ICC*, 337 U.S. at 430. The independent Special Prosecutor with his asserted need for the subpoenaed material in the underlying criminal prosecution is opposed by the President with his steadfast assertion of privilege against disclosure of the material. This setting assures there is 'that concrete adverseness which sharpens the presentation of issues upon which the court so largely depends for illumination of difficult constitutional questions'. *Baker v. Carr*, 369 U.S. at 204. Moreover, since the matter is one arising in the regular course of a federal criminal prosecution, it is within the traditional scope of Art. III power. Id., at 198.

In light of the uniqueness of the setting in which the conflict arises, the fact that both parties are officers of the Executive Branch cannot be viewed as a barrier to justiciability. It would be inconsistent with the applicable law and regulation, and the unique facts of this case to conclude other than that the Special Prosecutor has standing to bring this action and that a justiciable controversy is presented for decision.

III

THE CLAIM OF PRIVILEGE

A

[W]e turn to the claim that the subpoena should be quashed because it demands 'confidential conversations between a President and his close advisors that it would be inconsistent with the public interest to produce.' App. 48a. The first contention is a broad claim that the separation of powers doctrine precludes judicial review of a President's claim of privilege. The second contention is that if he does not prevail on the claim of absolute privilege, the court should hold as a matter of constitutional law that the privilege prevails over the subpoena duces tecum.

In the performance of assigned constitutional duties each branch of the Government must initially interpret the Constitution, and the interpretation of its powers by any branch is due great respect from the others. The President's counsel, as we have noted, reads the Constitution as providing an absolute privilege of confidentiality for all Presidential communications. Many decisions of this Court, however, have unequivocally reaffirmed the holding of *Marbury v. Madison*, that '[i]t is emphatically the province and duty of the judicial department to say what the law is.'

No holding of the Court has defined the scope of judicial power specifically relating to the enforcement of a subpoena for confidential Presidential communications for use in a criminal prosecution, but other exercises of power by the Executive Branch and the Legislative Branch have been found invalid as in conflict with the Constitution. *Powell v. McCormack*, 395 U.S. 486 (1969); *Youngstown, Sheet & Tube Co. v. Sawyer*, 343 U.S. 579 (1952). In a series of cases, the Court interpreted the explicit immunity conferred by express provisions of the Constitution on Members of the House and Senate by the Speech or Debate Clause, U.S. Const. Art. I, § 6. *Doe v. McMillan*, 412 U.S. 306 (1973); *Gravel v. United States*, 408 U.S. 606 (1972); *United States v. Brewster*, 408 U.S. 501 (1972); *United States v. Johnson*, 383 U.S. 169 (1966). Since this Court has consistently exercised the power to construe and delineate claims arising under express powers, it must follow that the Court has authority to interpret claims with respect to powers alleged to derive from enumerated powers.

Our system of government 'requires that federal courts on occasion interpret the Constitution in a manner at variance with the construction given the document by another branch.' *Powell v. McCormack, supra*, 395 U.S. at 549. And in *Baker v. Carr*, 369 U.S., at 211 the Court stated:

> '[D]eciding whether a matter has in any measure been committed by the Constitution to another branch of government, or whether the action of that branch exceeds whatever authority has been committed, is itself a delicate exercise in constitutional interpretation, and is a responsibility of this Court as ultimate interpreter of the Constitution.'

Notwithstanding the deference each branch must accord the others, the 'judicial Power of the United States' vested in the federal courts by Art. III, § 1, of the Constitution can no more be shared with the Executive Branch than the Chief Executive, for example, can share with the Judiciary the veto power, or the Congress share with the Judiciary the power to override a Presidential veto. Any other conclusion would be contrary to the basic concept of separation of powers and the checks and balances that flow from the scheme of a tripartite government. The Federalist, No. 47, p. 313 (S. Mittell ed. 1938). We therefore reaffirm that it is the province and duty of this Court 'to say what the law is' with respect to the claim of privilege presented in this case.

B

In support of his claim of absolute privilege, the President's counsel urges two grounds, one of which is common to all governments and one of which is peculiar to our system of separation of powers. The first ground is the valid need for protection of communications between high Government officials and those who advise and assist them in the performance of their manifold duties; the importance of this confidentiality is too plain to require further discussion. Human experience teaches that those who expect public dissemination of their remarks may well temper candor with a concern for appearances and for their own interests to the detriment of the decisionmaking process.[15] Whatever the nature of the privilege of confidentiality of Presidential communications in the exercise of Art. II powers, the privilege can be said to derive from the supremacy of each branch within its own assigned area of constitutional duties. Certain powers and privileges flow from the nature of enumerated powers;[16] the protection of the confidentiality of Presidential communications has similar constitutional underpinnings.

The second ground asserted by the President's counsel in support of the claim of absolute privilege rests on the doctrine of separation of powers. Here it is argued that the independence of the Executive Branch within its own sphere, *Humphrey's Executor v. United States*, 295 U.S. 602, 629–630 (1935); *Kilbourn v. Thompson*, 103 U.S. 168, 190–191 (1881), insulates a President from a judicial subpoena in an ongoing criminal prosecution, and thereby protects confidential Presidential communications.

However, neither the doctrine of separation of powers, nor the need for confidentiality of high-level communications, without more, can sustain an absolute, unqualified Presidential privilege of immunity from judicial process under all circumstances. The President's need

---

[15] There is nothing novel about governmental confidentiality. The meetings of the Constitutional Convention in 1787 were conducted in complete privacy. 1 M. Farrand, The Records of the Federal Convention of 1787, pp. xi–xxv (1911). Moreover, all records of those meetings were sealed for more than 30 years after the Convention. See 3 Stat. 475, 15th Cong., 1st Sess., Res. 8 (1818). Most of the Framers acknowledged that without secrecy no constitution of the kind that was developed could have been written. C. WARREN, THE MAKING OF THE CONSTITUTION 134–139 (1937).

[16] The Special Prosecutor argues that there is no provision in the Constitution for a Presidential privilege as to the President's communications corresponding to the privilege of Members of Congress under the Speech or Debate Clause. But the silence of the Constitution on this score is not dispositive. 'The rule of constitutional interpretation announced in McCulloch v. Maryland, 4 Wheat. 316, 4 L.Ed. 579, that that which was reasonably appropriate and relevant to the exercise of a granted power was to be considered as accompanying the grant, has been so universally applied that it suffices merely to state it.' Marshall v. Gordon, 243 U.S. 521, 537 (1917).

for complete candor and objectivity from advisers calls for great deference from the courts. However, when the privilege depends solely on the broad, undifferentiated claim of public interest in the confidentiality of such conversations, a confrontation with other values arises. Absent a claim of need to protect military, diplomatic, or sensitive national security secrets, we find it difficult to accept the argument that even the very important interest in confidentiality of Presidential communications is significantly diminished by production of such material for in camera inspection with all the protection that a district court will be obliged to provide.

The impediment that an absolute, unqualified privilege would place in the way of the primary constitutional duty of the Judicial Branch to do justice in criminal prosecutions would plainly conflict with the function of the courts under Art. III. In designing the structure of our Government and dividing and allocating the sovereign power among three coequal branches, the Framers of the Constitution sought to provide a comprehensive system, but the separate powers were not intended to operate with absolute independence.

'While the Constitution diffuses power the better to secure liberty, it also contemplates that practice will integrate the dispersed powers into a workable government. It enjoins upon its branches separateness but interdependence, autonomy but reciprocity.' *Youngstown Sheet & Tube Co. v. Sawyer*, 343 U.S. at 635 (Jackson, J., concurring).

To read the Art. II powers of the President as providing an absolute privilege as against a subpoena essential to enforcement of criminal statutes on no more than a generalized claim of the public interest in confidentiality of nonmilitary and nondiplomatic discussions would upset the constitutional balance of 'a workable government' and gravely impair the role of the courts under Art. III.

C

Since we conclude that the legitimate needs of the judicial process may outweigh Presidential privilege, it is necessary to resolve those competing interests in a manner that preserves the essential functions of each branch. The right and indeed the duty to resolve that question does not free the Judiciary from according high respect to the representations made on behalf of the President. *United States v. Burr*, 25 F.Cas.187, 190, 191–192.

The expectation of a President to the confidentiality of his conversations and correspondence, like the claim of confidentiality of judicial deliberations, for example, has all the values to which we accord deference for the privacy of all citizens and, added to those values,

is the necessity for protection of the public interest in candid, objective, and even blunt or harsh opinions in Presidential decisionmaking. A President and those who assist him must be free to explore alternatives in the process of shaping policies and making decisions and to do so in a way many would be unwilling to express except privately. These are the considerations justifying a presumptive privilege for Presidential communications. The privilege is fundamental to the operation of Government and inextricably rooted in the separation of powers under the Constitution.[17] In *Nixon v. Sirica*, 487 F.2d 700 (D.C. Cir. 1973), the Court of Appeals held that such Presidential communications are 'presumptively privileged,' *id.* at 717, and this position is accepted by both parties in the present litigation. We agree with Mr. Chief Justice Marshall's observation, therefore, that '[i]n no case of this kind would a court be required to proceed against the president as against an ordinary individual.' *United States v. Burr*, 25 F.Cas. at 192.

But this presumptive privilege must be considered in light of our historic commitment to the rule of law. This is nowhere more profoundly manifest than in our view that 'the twofold aim [of criminal justice] is that guilt shall not escape or innocence suffer.' *Berger v. United States*, 295 U.S. at 88. We have elected to employ an adversary system of criminal justice in which the parties contest all issues before a court of law. The need to develop all relevant facts in the adversary system is both fundamental and comprehensive. The ends of criminal justice would be defeated if judgments were to be founded on a partial or speculative presentation of the facts. The very integrity of the judicial system and public confidence in the system depend on full disclosure of all the facts, within the framework of the rules of evidence. To ensure that justice is done, it is imperative to the function of courts that compulsory process be available for the production of evidence needed either by the prosecution or by the defense.

Only recently the Court restated the ancient proposition of law, albeit in the context of a grand jury inquiry rather than a trial, "that 'the public . . . has a right to every man's evidence,' except for those persons protected by a constitutional, common-law, or statutory privilege, *United States v. Bryan*, 339 U.S. 323, 331 (1950)." The privileges referred to by the Court are designed to protect weighty and legitimate

---

[17] 'Freedom of communication vital to fulfillment of the aims of wholesome relationships is obtained only by removing the specter of compelled disclosure. . . . [G]overnment . . . needs open but protected channels for the kind of plain talk that is essential to the quality of its functioning.' Carl Zeiss Stiftung v. V. E. B. Carl Zeiss, Jena, 40 F.R.D. 318, 325 (D.C. 1966).

competing interests. Thus, the Fifth Amendment to the Constitution provides that no man 'shall be compelled in any criminal case to be a witness against himself.' And, generally, an attorney or a priest may not be required to disclose what has been revealed in professional confidence. These and other interests are recognized in law by privileges against forced disclosure, established in the Constitution, by statute, or at common law [but are not] expansively construed, for they are in derogation of the search for truth.

In this case the President challenges a subpoena served on him as a third party requiring the production of materials for use in a criminal prosecution; he does so on the claim that he has a privilege against disclosure of confidential communications. He does not place his claim of privilege on the ground they are military or diplomatic secrets. As to these areas of Art. II duties the courts have traditionally shown the utmost deference to Presidential responsibilities. In *C. & S. Air Lines v. Waterman S.S. Corp.*, 333 U.S. 103 (1948) dealing with Presidential authority involving foreign policy considerations, the Court said:

'The President, both as Commander-in-Chief and as the Nation's organ for foreign affairs, has available intelligence services whose reports are not and ought not to be published to the world. It would be intolerable that courts, without the relevant information, should review and perhaps nullify actions of the Executive taken on information properly held secret.'

In *United States v. Reynolds,* 345 U.S. 1 (1953), dealing with a claimant's demand for evidence in a Tort Claims Act case against the Government, the Court said:

'It may be possible to satisfy the court, from all the circumstances of the case, that there is a reasonable danger that compulsion of the evidence will expose military matters which, in the interest of national security, should not be divulged. When this is the case, the occasion for the privilege is appropriate, and the court should not jeopardize the security which the privilege is meant to protect by insisting upon an examination of the evidence, even by the judge alone, in chambers.'

Id. at 10. No case of the Court, however, has extended this high degree of deference to a President's generalized interest in confidentiality.

The right to the production of all evidence at a criminal trial similarly has constitutional dimensions. The Sixth Amendment explicitly confers upon every defendant in a criminal trial the right 'to be confronted with the witnesses against him' and 'to have compulsory process for obtaining witnesses in his favor.' Moreover, the Fifth Amendment also guarantees that no person shall be deprived of liberty without due process of law. It is the manifest duty of the courts to vindicate those guarantees, and to accomplish that it is essential that all relevant and admissible evidence be produced.

In this case we must weigh the importance of the general privilege of confidentiality of Presidential communications in performance of the President's responsibilities against the inroads of such a privilege on the fair administration of criminal justice.[19] The interest in preserving confidentiality is weighty indeed and entitled to great respect. However, we cannot conclude that advisers will be moved to temper the candor of their remarks by the infrequent occasions of disclosure because of the possibility that such conversations will be called for in the context of a criminal prosecution.

On the other hand, the allowance of the privilege to withhold evidence that is demonstrably relevant in a criminal trial would cut deeply into the guarantee of due process of law and gravely impair the basic function of the courts. A President's acknowledged need for confidentiality in the communications of his office is general in nature, whereas the constitutional need for production of relevant evidence in a criminal proceeding is specific and central to the fair adjudication of a particular criminal case in the administration of justice. Without access to specific facts a criminal prosecution may be totally frustrated. The President's broad interest in confidentiality of communications will not be vitiated by disclosure of a limited number of conversations preliminarily shown to have some bearing on the pending criminal cases.

We conclude that when the ground for asserting privilege as to subpoenaed materials sought for use in a criminal trial is based only on the generalized interest in confidentiality, it cannot prevail over the fundamental demands of due process of law in the fair administration of criminal justice. The generalized assertion of privilege must yield to the demonstrated, specific need for evidence in a pending criminal trial.

D

If a President concludes that compliance with a subpoena would be injurious to the pub-

---

[19] We are not here concerned with the balance between the President's generalized interest in confidentiality and the need for relevant evidence in civil litigation, nor with that between the confidentiality interest and congressional demands for information, nor with the President's interest in preserving state secrets. We address only the conflict between the President's assertion of a generalized privilege of confidentiality and the constitutional need for relevant evidence in criminal trials.

lic interest he may properly, as was done here, invoke a claim of privilege on the return of the subpoena. Upon receiving a claim of privilege from the Chief Executive, it became the further duty of the District Court to treat the subpoenaed material as presumptively privileged and to require the Special Prosecutor to demonstrate that the Presidential material was 'essential to the justice of the [pending criminal] case.' *United States v. Burr*, 25 F.Cas. at 192. Here the District Court treated the material as presumptively privileged, proceeded to find that the Special Prosecutor had made a sufficient showing to rebut the presumption, and ordered an in camera examination of the subpoenaed material. On the basis of our examination of the record we are unable to conclude that the District Court erred in ordering the inspection. Accordingly we affirm the order of the District Court that subpoenaed materials be transmitted to that court. We now turn to the important question of the District Court's responsibilities in conducting the in camera examination of Presidential materials or communications delivered under the compulsion of the subpoena duces tecum.

E

'[T]he guard, furnished to [the President] to protect him from being harassed by vexatious and unnecessary subpoenas, is to be looked for in the conduct of a court after those subpoenas have issued; not in any circumstance which is to precede their being issued.' *United States v. Burr, supra*, at 34. Statements that meet the test of admissibility and relevance must be isolated; all other material must be excised. At this stage the District Court is not limited to representations of the Special Prosecutor as to the evidence sought by the subpoena; the material will be available to the District Court. It is elementary that in camera inspection of evidence is always a procedure calling for scrupulous protection against any release or publication of material not found by the court, at that stage, probably admissible in evidence and relevant to the issues of the trial for which it is sought. That being true of an ordinary situation, it is obvious that the District Court has a very heavy responsibility to see to it that Presidential conversations, which are either not relevant or not admissible, are accorded that high degree of respect due the President of the United States. Mr. Chief Justice Marshall, sitting as a trial judge in the Burr case, supra, was extraordinarily careful to point out that '[i]n no case of this kind would a court be required to proceed against the president as against an ordinary individual.' 25 F.Cas. at 192. Marshall's statement cannot be read to mean in any sense that a President is above the law, but relates to the singularly unique role under Art. II of a President's communications and activities, related to the performance of duties under that Article. Moreover, a President's communications and activities encompass a vastly wider range of sensitive material than would be true of any 'ordinary individual.' It is therefore necessary in the public interest to afford Presidential confidentiality the greatest protection consistent with the fair administration of justice. The need for confidentiality even as to idle conversations with associates in which casual reference might be made concerning political leaders within the country or foreign statesmen is too obvious to call for further treatment. We have no doubt that the District Judge will at all times accord to Presidential records that high degree of deference suggested in *United States v. Burr, supra* and will discharge his responsibility to see to it that until released to the Special Prosecutor no in camera material is revealed to anyone. This burden applies with even greater force to excised material; once the decision is made to excise, the material is restored to its privileged status and should be returned under seal to its lawful custodian.

Since this matter came before the Court during the pendency of a criminal prosecution, and on representations that time is of the essence, the mandate shall issue forthwith.

Affirmed.

Mr. Justice Rehnquist took no part in the consideration or decision of these cases.

At trial, the President's counsel had argued that this was an internal dispute among members of the Executive Branch and thus there was no justiciable controversy before the court and the dispute was a political question. Moreover, he contended that the Special Prosecutor did not enjoy the necessary standing to obtain the materials in the courts. The rationale presented by the President was thus that the Court's intervention was an inappropriate interference with the affairs of the Executive. A second argument centered on Executive Privilege. Positing that the Constitution vests all the Executive power within the Executive Branch, the President argued that a constitutionally protected privilege exists as part of the President's inherent authority, to be invoked exclusively by him. The President's counsel contended that the privilege was so fundamentally a part of the executive office that there was no need for explicitness as was the case in the Speech or Debate Clause for Congress.

In its opinion, the Court ruled that a justiciable controversy existed and recognized the doctrine of Executive Privilege. The Court thus apparently accepted the Government's contention that the appointment of the Special Prosecutor with the understanding that he could litigate to obtain materials meant he was suing as a representative of the sovereign state and not as the Executive.

Whereas the Court rejected the President's contention that an absolute privilege existed, it affirmed the existence of a privilege of confidentiality which it characterized as flowing both from the needs of government and enumerated powers, and to be drawn from separation of powers and the Executive branch's independence. Having recognized that a qualified privilege presumptively exists, the Court asserted its institutional competence to determine whether the privilege protected most communications, emphasizing the availability of *in camera* review. The Court drew the line at "military, diplomatic, or sensitive national security secrets."[62]

The Court rejected the President's ability to offer a mere generalizable interest in confidentiality as a basis for nondisclosure, at least in the context of a criminal trial. It drew authority for determining the applicability of the privilege in areas outside of the military, diplomacy, and national security context in the statement drawn from *Marbury* that it "is emphatically the province and the duty of the judicial department to say what the law is."

Once the qualified privilege is recognized as available to the President, it does not necessarily follow that the Court is the appropriate branch to determine its applicability in a given context. It may be that Justice Burger's position, also expressed by Justice Marshall in the *Burr* case, is concerned with establishing the "independence" of the judicial branch; but this position seems somewhat contradictory of the need for special deference to the President also recognized in these cases.

---

[62] 418 U.S. at 706.

PAH: Although the Court was prepared to recognize a public interest in maintaining a presumption of privacy in presidential communications, its balancing approach left unsettled under what circumstances recognition of the privilege would result in nondisclosure even in less publicly focused criminal proceedings, the more so in noncriminal proceedings. It narrowed its holding: "We address only the conflict between the President's assertion of a *generalized privilege of confidentiality* and the constitutional need for relevant evidence in criminal trials."[63] Its careful outlining of the protections offered by *in camera* inspection suggests that in other cases the balance might well tip in favor of disclosure, utilizing these protections. But it did not explain why such protections would not also satisfy the concerns about military, diplomatic or national security secrets.

Nixon's holding was explicitly linked to considerations in the context of a criminal proceeding. Yet the process values it recognized could easily extend to civil suits as well, leading to *in camera* review in those cases. On the other hand, *Nixon* can be read as leaving unprotected communications that are merely defended by self-serving assertions of privilege but extending protection in almost any case where a more specific ground is offered. The latter reading is consistent with the Court's emphasis on the narrow holding of the case, as well as the special deference it accorded to the President.

---

[63] *Id.* at 712 n.19.

Following the Court's decision, the Executive Branch released the tapes, including the conversation tape confirming that Richard Nixon was involved in the Watergate burglary's cover up. On August 9, 1974, Richard Nixon resigned the presidency. The Senate had commenced impeachment proceedings. A spate of writers has criticized the Court's premature ruling in the face of the political alternatives for resolving this controversy, questioning whether the public interest was in fact served by the Court's early ruling.

The impact of the case is also unclear. *United States v. Nixon* establishes that the President is not immune from suit but under an assortment of theories the President can nevertheless continue to avoid suit. Although there have been numerous actions by private and government litigants against presidents since *Nixon*, questions remain about the propriety of suing and when the executive is to be held responsive to litigant's demands, in part a reflection of courts' continued reluctance to intrude in certain areas of executive decision making. For example, the courts have continued to abstain in controversies arising when the President asserts he is acting in his capacity as Commander in Chief and leader in foreign affairs.[64] Whereas the qualified privilege approach recognized in *Nixon* can be seen as a means for the Court to assert its own institutional competence to police the executive without unduly intruding into its affairs, in practice the decision may ultimately serve to further isolate the office of president from accountability to the public,[65] by shrouding the office in secrecy.

Three other cases concerning the Nixon Administration bear on the question of the reach of privilege or immunity of the executive. In *Nixon v. Administrator of General Services*[66] the former President challenged the constitutionality of a federal statute, the Presidential Recordings and Materials Preservation Act. The Act directed the Administrator of the General Services Administration to take custody of the presidential papers of the former President, promulgate regulations for orderly processing and screening by archivists, return papers which are personal in nature, and determine the conditions for public access of those materials retained. The Court rejected the former President's contention that the regulation of the disposition of the materials violated separation of powers. It stated:

> [I]n determining whether the act disrupts the proper balance between the coordinate branches, the proper inquiry focuses on the extent to which it prevents the Executive Branch from accomplishing its constitutionally assigned functions. . . . Only where the potential for disruption is present must we then determine whether the impact is justified by an overriding need to promote objectives within the constitutional authority of Congress.

---

[64] *See, e.g.*, Goldwater v. Carter, 444 U.S. 361 (1979), *vacating and remanding for dismissal*, 617 F.2d 687, 697 (D.C. Cir. 19798); Crockett v. Reagan, 720 F.2d 1355 (D.C. Cir. 1983), *cert. denied* 467 U.S. 1251 (1984) (suit regarding military activities in El Salvador nonjusticiable political question); Lowry v. Reagan, 676 F.Supp. 333 (D.D.C. 1987) (suit to compel compliance with War Powers Resolution nonjusticiable).

[65] During the Reagan Administration claims of executive privilege were challenged in a number of cases involving requests for documents in congressional oversight proceedings and testimonial and documentary requests in criminal litigation. *See e.g.*, *Note*, U.S. v. Nixon, *Twenty Years After: The Good, the Bad and the Ugly—an Exploration of Executive Privilege*, 154 N. ILL. U. L. REV. 251, 280–97 (1993). Compare ANATOMY OF AN UNDECLARED WAR: CONGRESSIONAL CONFERENCE ON THE PENTAGON PAPERS (Patricia A. Krause ed. 1972) (attacking dishonesty of several presidential administrations for hiding facts of Vietnam conflict from Congress and arguing Congress cannot depend upon the Executive Branch to provide information upon which it can fulfill its constitutional oversight role.)

[66] 433 U.S. 425 (1977).

The Act gave the Executive Branch control of the papers and therefore a claim of undue disruption of executive functions was not supported.

The Court rejected the former President's claims that the presidential privilege shields the papers from archival scrutiny and that the Act violated presidential privilege. It recognized that the presidential privilege was available to incumbents but the fact that neither President Ford (who had signed the Act) nor President Carter supported the claims "detracts from the weight of [Nixon's] contentions that the Act intrudes into the executive function and the needs of the Executive Branch." Observing that the scope of the privilege extended under the act corresponded to that recognized in *United States v. Nixon*, and that the act included a screening process that was unlikely to impair confidentiality, the Court concluded that the limited intrusion was justified in light of the substantial public interest in the "American people's ability to reconstruct and come to terms with their history [and] the desire to restore public confidence in our political processes by preserving materials as a source for facilitating a full airing of the events leading to appellant's resignation." Balanced against the presidential claims of privilege were these public interests as well as Congress' interest in having the materials available because of "Congress' need to understand how those political processes had in fact operated in order to gauge the necessity for remedial legislation." Significantly, then-Justice Burger, the author of *United States v. Nixon*, dissented, contending that the Act violated the Court's doctrine of presidential privilege.

In *Nixon v. Fitzgerald*,[67] a case arising out of an alleged retaliatory discharge of an Air Force employee, the Court concluded that "a former President of the United States is entitled to absolute immunity from damages liability predicated on his official acts. We consider this immunity a functionally mandated incident of the President's unique office, rooted in the constitutional tradition of separation of powers and supported by our history." It added "we think it appropriate to recognize absolute Presidential immunity from damages liability for acts within the 'outer perimeter' of his official responsibility." Although the dissenters argued that the presidential office is thereby clothe[d] with sovereign immunity, placing it above the law,"[68] the majority emphasized "other incentives to avoid misconduct"; among them the constitutional remedy of impeachment exists as well as "constant scrutiny by the press," as well as "a desire to earn re-election, . . . and a President's traditional concern for his historical stature."

On the same day in *Harlow v. Fitzgerald*[69] the Court concluded that except in exceptional circumstances, where the need for a derivative claim to Presidential immunity arises because of the function they are performing, executive officials, including senior aides and advisers to the President, are merely entitled to qualified immunity. "A derivative claim to a Presidential immunity would be strongest in such 'central' Presidential domains as foreign policy and national security, in which the president could not discharge his singularly vital mandate without delegating functions nearly as sensitive as his own."[70]

---

[67] 457 U.S. 731 (1982).
[68] 457 U.S, at 767 (White, J., dissenting).
[69] 457 U.S. 800 (1982).
[70] 457 U.S. at 812 n.19.

PAH: If the claim of confidentiality flows from the Constitution as *United States v. Nixon* establishes, the grounds supporting Congress's authority to regulate the privilege should be carefully considered. It is questionable in *Nixon v. Administrator of General Services* whether the Court struck the proper balance between the constitutionally based privilege and the interests of the public which it recognized. Justice Rehnquist argued in dissent that the Act would frustrate candid discourse among presidential advisors and foreign heads of state and would have the effect of restraining, not promoting, dissemination of information. Of course, the result of the decision is not surprising in the context of Watergate, but how does it measure against *Fitzgerald*?

The Court's decision to accord the President absolute instead of a qualified privilege in damage actions is consistent with its longstanding reluctance to exercise jurisdiction over the president. Justice Powell in *Fitzgerald* noted that "[a] Court before exercising jurisdiction, must balance the Constitutional weight of the interest served against the dangers of intrusion on the authority and function of the Executive Branch." The outcome of "interest-balancing" in these cases may seem to turn on the values preferred by the judge writing the opinion. Notably, Justice Powell expressed concern that the president is a likely target of civil suits and could be distracted from his duties to the detriment of the nation. However, the Court left open the possibility that Congress could create a statutory cause of action against the president for damages.

DEL: Although rooted in *Marbury v. Madison*, and thus in the proposition that the Court has the power "to say what the law is," the decision in *United States v. Nixon* generated profoundly different political consequences. The *Marbury* ruling against the midnight Federalist appointments was hailed by Jeffersonians as a triumph for them, even though the long-term result was an expansion of judicial power and curtailment of presidential authority. Although the *Nixon* decision helped prompt the president's resignation from office, it actually enhanced presidential authority to the extent it determined that executive privilege was grounded in the Constitution itself. The *Nixon* decision itself exemplifies how even the etching of boundaries between branches of government may be driven by the balancing methods that define so much constitutional analysis. Executive privilege may prevail provided no competing consideration, such as the imperatives of the criminal justice system, presents a significant enough demand to the contrary. Some lower courts have indicated that countervailing interests may outweigh a generalized claim of executive privilege in the civil arena when, for instance, the United States is a plaintiff.[71] A meaningful standard, that helps identify the functional equivalent of a "demonstrated, specific need for evidence in a pending criminal trial" for purposes of determining when the presumption of privilege is overcome, is difficult to discern from existing case law.

---

[71] *E.g.*, United States v. Gates, 35 F.R.D. 524, 529 (D.D.C. 1964).

C. Defining Limits of Congressional Delegation of Power

In the 1980's the Supreme Court heard a number of separation of powers cases and its responses were sufficiently confused to prompt the observation that "political and power relationships, not judicial decisions . . . determine the validity and shape of our system of checks and balances."[72] For a time, however, the Court seemed intent upon reconsidering its deference to congressional judgment about how to deploy its authority and asserting some judicial responsibility in policing separation of powers to restore a balance of power as it had earlier in the case of presidential authority.

Although some justices threatened to do so, the Court did not resurrect the nondelegation doctrine. In the Court's "laissez faire" period, in response to the New Deal, the Roosevelt Administration's federal economic and social programs designed to address the Depression, the Court had questioned the broad delegation of authority by Congress to independent agencies and to the Executive Department's administrative agencies. The Roosevelt Administration contended that the economic and social crisis required

---

[72] E. Donald Elliot, 57 Geo. Wash. L. Rev. 506 (1989).

that flexibility and discretion rest in administrative authorities to create the details capable of responding to the complex conditions of the Depression. The Court, however, viewed its role as to identify whether "essential" legislative functions were performed by Congress or abdicated by delegations of authority to other decision makers. Thus the Court was prepared to obstruct the implementation of the New Deal because it believed the Constitution did not condone the distribution of federal authority envisaged in the legislative program.

A.L.A. Schechter Poultry Corp. v. United States
295 U.S. 495 (1935)

Mr. Chief Justice HUGHES delivered the opinion of the Court.

Petitioners were convicted in the District Court of the United States for the Eastern District of New York on eighteen counts of an indictment charging violations of what is known as the 'Live Poultry Code,' and on an additional count for conspiracy to commit such violations. By demurrer to the indictment and appropriate motions on the trial, the defendants contended (1) that the code had been adopted pursuant to an unconstitutional delegation by Congress of legislative power.

New York City is the largest live poultry market in the United States. Ninety-six percent of the live poultry there marketed comes from other states. Three-fourths of this amount arrives by rail and is consigned to commission men or receivers. Most of these freight shipments (about 75 per cent) come in at the Manhattan Terminal of the New York Central Railroad, and the remainder at one of the four terminals in New Jersey serving New York City. The commission men transact by far the greater part of the business on a commission basis, representing the shippers as agents, and remitting to them the proceeds of sale, less commissions, freight, and handling charges. Otherwise, they buy for their own account. They sell to slaughterhouse operators who are also called market-men.

The defendants are slaughterhouse operators of the latter class. A.L.A. Schechter Poultry Corporation and Schechter Live Poultry Market are corporations conducting wholesale poultry slaughterhouse markets in Brooklyn, New York City. Defendants ordinarily purchase their live poultry from commission men at the West Washington Market in New York City or at the railroad terminals serving the city, but occasionally they purchase from commission men in Philadelphia. They buy the poultry for slaughter and resale. After the poultry is trucked to their slaughterhouse markets in Brooklyn, it is there sold, usually within twenty-four hours, to retail poultry dealers and butchers who sell directly to consumers. The poultry purchased from defendants is immediately slaughtered, prior to delivery, by shochtim in defendants' employ. Defendants do not sell poultry in interstate commerce.

The 'Live Poultry Code' was promulgated under section 3 of the National Industrial Recovery Act. That section—the pertinent provisions of which are set forth in the margin—authorizes the President to approve 'codes of fair competition.' Such a code may be approved for a trade or industry, upon application by one or more trade or industrial associations or groups, if the President finds (1) that such associations or groups 'impose no inequitable restrictions on admission to membership therein and are truly representative,' and (2) that such codes are not designed 'to promote monopolies or to eliminate or oppress small enterprises and will not operate to discriminate against them, and will tend to effectuate the policy' of Title 1 of the Act. Such codes 'shall not permit monopolies or monopolistic practices.' As a condition of his approval, the President may 'impose such conditions (including requirements for the making of reports and the keeping of accounts) for the protection of consumers, competitors, employees, and others, and in furtherance of the public interest, and may provide such exceptions to and exemptions from the provisions of such code as the President in his discretion deems necessary to effectuate the policy herein declared.' Where such a code has not been approved, the President may prescribe one, either on his own motion or on complaint. Violation of any provision of a code (so approved or prescribed) 'in any transaction in or affecting interstate or foreign commerce' is made a misdemeanor punishable by a fine of not more than $500 for each offense, and each day the violation continues is to be deemed a separate offense.

The 'Live Poultry Code' was approved by the President on April 13, 1934. The declared purpose is 'To effect the policies of title I of the National Industrial Recovery Act.' The Code established a code for fair competition for the live poultry industry of the metropolitan area in and about the City of New York.' The 'industry' is defined as including 'every person engaged in the business of selling, purchasing for resale, transporting, or handling and/or slaughtering live poultry, from the time such poultry comes into the New York metropolitan area to the time it is first sold in slaughtered form,' and such 'related branches' as may from time to time be included by amendment. Employers are styled 'members of the industry,' and the term employee is defined to embrace 'any and all persons engaged in the industry, however compensated,' except 'members.'

The Code fixes the number of hours for workdays. It provides that no employee, with certain exceptions, shall be permitted to work in excess of forty (40) hours in any one week, and that no employees, save as stated, 'shall be paid in any pay period less than at the rate of fifty (50) cents per hour.' The article containing 'general labor provisions' prohibits the employment of any person under 16 years of age, and declares that employees shall have the right of 'collective bargaining' and freedom of choice with respect to labor organizations, in the terms of section 7(a) of the Act.

Provision is made for administration through an 'industry advisory committee,' to be selected by trade associations and members of the industry, and a 'code supervisor,' to be appointed, with the approval of the committee, by agreement between the Secretary of Agriculture and the Administrator for Industrial Recovery.

The seventh article, containing 'trade practice provisions,' prohibits various practices which are said to constitute 'unfair methods of competition.' The final article provides for verified reports, such as the Secretary or Administrator may require, '(1) for the protection of consumers, competitors, employees, and others, and in furtherance of the public interest, and (2) for the determination by the Secretary or Administrator of the extent to which the declared policy of the act is being effectuated by this code.'

The President approved the code by an executive order [No. 6675—A] in which he found that the application for his approval had been duly made in accordance with the provisions of Title 1 of the National Industrial Recovery Act; that there had been due notice and hearings; that the code constituted 'a code of fair competition' as contemplated by the act and complied with its pertinent provisions and that the code would tend 'to effectuate the policy of Congress as declared in section 1 of Title I.' The executive order also recited that the Secretary of Agriculture and the Administrator of the National Industrial Recovery Act had rendered separate reports as to the provisions within their respective jurisdictions.

[Defendants were convicted under a number of different counts.]

First. We are told that the provision of the statute authorizing the adoption of codes must be viewed in the light of the grave national crisis with which Congress was confronted. Undoubtedly, the conditions to which power is addressed are always to be considered when the exercise of power is challenged. Extraordinary conditions may call for extraordinary remedies. But the argument necessarily stops short of an attempt to justify action which lies outside the sphere of constitutional authority. Extraordinary conditions do not create or enlarge constitutional power. The Constitution established a national government with powers deemed to be adequate, as they have proved to be both in war and peace, but these powers of the national government are limited by the constitutional grants. Those who act under these grants are not at liberty to transcend the imposed limits because they believe that more or different power is necessary. Such assertions of extra-constitutional authority were anticipated and precluded by the explicit terms of the Tenth Amendment—'The powers not delegated to the United States by the Constitution, nor prohibited by it to the States, are reserved to the States respectively, or to the people.'

The further point is urged that the national crisis demanded a broad and intensive co-operative effort by those engaged in trade and industry, and that this necessary co-operation was sought to be fostered by permitting them to initiate the adoption of codes. But the statutory plan is not simply one for voluntary effort. It does not seek merely to endow voluntary trade or industrial associations or groups with privileges or immunities. It involves the coercive exercise of the law-making power. The codes of fair competition which the statute attempts to authorize are codes of laws. Violations of the provisions of the codes are punishable as crimes.

Second. We recently had occasion to review the pertinent decisions and the general principles which govern the determination of this question. *Panama Refining Company v. Ryan*, 293 U.S. 388. The Constitution provides that 'All legislative powers herein granted shall be vested in a Congress of the United States, which shall consist of a Senate and House of Representatives.' Art. 1, § 1. And the Congress is authorized 'To make all Laws which shall be necessary and proper for carrying into Execution' its general powers. Art. 1, § 8, par. 18. The Congress is not permitted to abdicate or to transfer to others the essential legislative functions with which it is thus vested. We have repeatedly recognized the necessity of adapting legislation to complex conditions involving a host of details with which the national legislature cannot deal directly. We pointed out in the *Panama Company* case that the Constitution has never been regarded as denying to Congress the necessary resources of flexibility and practicality, which will enable it to perform its function in laying down policies and establishing standards, while leaving to selected instrumentalities the making of subordinate rules within prescribed limits and the determination of facts to which the policy as declared by the Legislature is to apply. But we said that the constant recognition of the necessity and validity of such provisions, and the wide range of administrative authority which has been developed by means of them, cannot be allowed to obscure the limitations of the authority to delegate, if our constitutional system is to be maintained. *Id.* at 421.

Accordingly, we look to the statute to see whether Congress has overstepped these limitations—whether Congress in authorizing 'codes of fair competition' has itself established the standards of legal obligation, thus performing its essential legislative function, or, by the failure to enact such standards, has attempted to transfer that function to others.

The aspect in which the question is now presented is distinct from that which was before us in the case of the *Panama Company*. There, the subject of the statutory prohibition was defined. National Industrial Recovery Act, § 9(c), [15 USCA § 709(c)]. That subject was the transportation in interstate and foreign commerce of petroleum and petroleum products which are produced or withdrawn from storage in excess of the amount permitted by state authority. The question was with respect to the range of discretion given to the President in prohibiting that transportation. *Id.* at 414, 415, 430. As to the 'codes of fair competition,' under section 3 of the act, the question is more fundamental. It is whether there is any adequate definition of the subject to which the codes are to be addressed.

What is meant by 'fair competition' as the term is used in the Act? Does it refer to a category established in the law, and is the authority to make codes limited accordingly? Or is it used as a convenient designation for whatever set of laws the formulators of a code for a particular trade or industry may propose and the President may approve (subject to certain restrictions), or the President may himself prescribe, as being wise and beneficent provisions for the government of the trade or industry in order to accomplish the broad purposes of rehabilitation, correction, and expansion which are stated in the first section of title 1?

The act does not define 'fair competition.' 'Unfair competition,' as known to the common law, is a limited concept. Primarily, and strictly, it relates to the palming off of one's goods as those of a rival trader. But it is evident that in its widest range, 'unfair competition,' as it has been understood in the law, does not reach the objectives of the codes which are authorized by the National Industrial Recovery Act. The codes may, indeed, cover conduct which existing law condemns, but they are not limited to conduct of that sort. The Government does not contend that the Act contemplates such a limitation. It would be opposed both to the declared purposes of the act and to its administrative construction.

For a statement of the authorized objectives and content of the 'codes of fair competition,' we are referred repeatedly to the 'Declaration of Policy' in section 1 of Title 1 of the Recovery Act. Thus the approval of a code by the President is conditioned on his finding that it 'will tend to effectuate the policy of this title.' Section 3(a) [of the act, 15 USCA § 703(a)]. The President is authorized to impose such conditions 'for the protection of consumers, competitors, employees, and others, and in furtherance of the public interest, and may provide such exceptions to and exemptions from the provisions of such code, as the President in his discretion deems necessary to effectuate the policy herein declared.' *Id.* The 'policy herein declared' is manifestly that set forth in section 1. That declaration embraces a broad range of objectives. Among them we find the elimination of 'unfair competitive practices.' But, even if this clause were to be taken to relate to practices which fall under the ban of existing law, either common law or statute, it is still only one of the authorized aims described in section 1. It is there declared to be 'the policy of Congress'—'to remove obstructions to the free flow of interstate and foreign commerce which tend to diminish the amount thereof; and to provide for the general welfare by promoting the organization of industry for the purpose of cooperative action among trade groups, to induce and maintain united action of labor and management under adequate governmental sanctions and supervision, to eliminate unfair competitive practices, to promote the fullest possible utilization of the present productive capacity of industries, to avoid undue restriction of production (except as may be temporarily required), to increase the consumption of industrial and agricultural products by increasing purchasing power, to reduce and relieve unemployment, to improve standards of labor, and otherwise to rehabilitate industry and to conserve natural resources.'

Under section 3, whatever 'may tend to effectuate' these general purposes may be included in the 'codes of fair competition.' We think the conclusion is inescapable that the authority sought to be conferred by section 3 was not merely to deal with 'unfair competitive practices' which offend against existing law, and could be the subject of judicial condemnation without further legislation, or to create administrative machinery for the application of established principles of law to particular instances of violation. Rather, the purpose is clearly disclosed to authorize new and controlling prohibitions through codes of laws which would embrace what the formulators would propose, and what the President would approve or prescribe, as wise and beneficent measures for the government of trades and industries in order to bring about their rehabilitation, correction, and development, according to the general declaration of policy in section 1. Codes of laws of this sort are styled 'codes of fair competition.'

We find no real controversy upon this point and we must determine the validity of the code in question in this aspect. As the government candidly says in its brief: 'The words 'policy of this title' clearly refer to the 'policy' which Congress declared in the section entitled 'Declaration of Policy'—Section 1. All of the policies there set forth point toward a single goal—the rehabilitation of industry and the industrial recovery which unquestionably was the major policy of Congress in adopting the National Industrial Recovery Act.' And that this is the controlling purpose of the code now before us appears both from its repeated declarations to that effect and from the scope of its requirements. It will be observed that its provisions as to the hours and wages of employees and its 'general labor provisions' were placed in separate articles, and these were not included in the article on 'trade practice provisions' declaring what should be deemed to constitute 'unfair methods of competition.'

The government urges that the codes will 'consist of rules of competition deemed fair for each industry by representative members of that industry—by the persons most vitally concerned and most familiar with its problems.' Instances are cited in which Congress has availed itself of such assistance; as, e.g., in the exercise of its authority over the public domain, with respect to the recognition of local customs or rules of miners as to mining claims, or, in matters of a more or less technical nature, as in designating the standard height of drawbars. But would it be seriously contended that Congress could delegate its legislative authority to trade or industrial associations or groups so as to empower them to enact the laws they deem to be wise and beneficent for the rehabilitation and expansion of their trade or industries? Could trade or industrial associations or groups be constituted legislative bodies for that

purpose because such associations or groups are familiar with the problems of their enterprises? And could an effort of that sort be made valid by such a preface of generalities as to permissible aims as we find in section 1 of title 1? The answer is obvious. Such a delegation of legislative power is unknown to our law, and is utterly inconsistent with the constitutional prerogatives and duties of Congress.

The question, then, turns upon the authority which section 3 of the Recovery Act vests in the President to approve or prescribe. But Congress cannot delegate legislative power to the President to exercise an unfettered discretion to make whatever laws he thinks may be needed or advisable for the rehabilitation and expansion of trade or industry. See *Panama Refining Co. v. Ryan*, *supra*, and cases there reviewed.

Accordingly we turn to the Recovery Act to ascertain what limits have been set to the exercise of the President's discretion. *First*, the President, as a condition of approval, is required to find that the trade or industrial associations or groups which propose a code 'impose no inequitable restrictions on admission to membership' and are 'truly representative.' That condition, however, relates only to the status of the initiators of the new laws and not to the permissible scope of such laws. *Second*, the President is required to find that the code is not 'designed to promote monopolies or to eliminate or oppress small enterprises and will not operate to discriminate against them.' And to this is added a proviso that the code 'shall not permit monopolies or monopolistic practices.' But these restrictions leave virtually untouched the field of policy envisaged by section 1, and, in that wide field of legislative possibilities, the proponents of a code, refraining from monopolistic designs, may roam at will, and the President may approve or disapprove their proposals as he may see fit. That is the precise effect of the further finding that the President is to make—that the code 'will tend to effectuate the policy of this title.' While this is called a finding, it is really but a statement of an opinion as to the general effect upon the promotion of trade or industry of a scheme of laws. These are the only findings which Congress has made essential in order to put into operation a legislative code having the aims described in the 'Declaration of Policy.'

Nor is the breadth of the President's discretion left to the necessary implications of this limited requirement as to his findings. As already noted, the President in approving a code may impose his own conditions, adding to or taking from what is proposed, as 'in his discretion' he thinks necessary 'to effectuate the policy' declared by the act. Of course, he has no less liberty when he prescribes a code on his own motion or on complaint, and he is free to prescribe one if a code has not been approved. The act provides for the creation by the President of administrative agencies to assist him, but the action or reports of such agencies, or of his other assistants—their recommendations and findings in relation to the making of codes—have no sanction beyond the will of the President, who may accept, modify, or reject them as he pleases. Such recommendations or findings in no way limit the authority which section 3 undertakes to vest in the President with no other conditions than those there specified. And this authority relates to a host of different trades and industries, thus extending the President's discretion to all the varieties of laws which he may deem to be beneficial in dealing with the vast array of commercial and industrial activities throughout the country.

Such a sweeping delegation of legislative power finds no support in the decisions upon which the government especially relies.

Section 3 of the Recovery Act is without precedent. It supplies no standards for any trade, industry, or activity. It does not undertake to prescribe rules of conduct to be applied to particular states of fact determined by appropriate administrative procedure. Instead of prescribing rules of conduct, it authorizes the making of codes to prescribe them. For that legislative undertaking, section 3 sets up no standards, aside from the statement of the general aims of rehabilitation, correction, and expansion described in section 1. In view of the scope of that broad declaration and of the nature of the few restrictions that are imposed, the discretion of the President in approving or prescribing codes, and thus enacting laws for the government of trade and industry throughout the country, is virtually unfettered. We think that the code-making authority thus conferred is an unconstitutional delegation of legislative power.

We are of the opinion that the attempt through the provisions of the code to fix the hours and wages of employees of defendants in their intrastate business was not a valid exercise of federal power.

We hold the code provisions here in question to be invalid and that the judgment of conviction must be reversed.

Mr. Justice CARDOZO, concurring.

The delegated power of legislation which has found expression in this code is not canalized within banks that keep it from overflowing. It is unconfined and vagrant, if I may borrow my own words in an earlier opinion. *Panama Refining Co. v. Ryan*, 293 U.S. 388, 440.

This court has held that delegation may be unlawful, though the act to be performed is definite and single, if the necessity, time, and occasion of performance have been left in the end to the discretion of the delegate. *Panama Refining Co. v. Ryan, supra.* I thought that ruling went too far. I pointed out in an opinion that there had been 'no grant to the Executive of any roving commission to inquire into evils and then, upon discovering them, do anything he pleases.' 293 U.S. 388 at p. 435. Choice, though within limits, had been given him 'as to the occasion, but none whatever as to the means.' Here, in the case before us, is an attempted delegation not confined to any single act nor to any class or group of acts identified or described by reference to a standard. Here in effect is a roving commission to inquire into evils and upon discovery correct them.

I have said that there is no standard, definite or even approximate, to which legislation must conform. Let me make my meaning more precise. If codes of fair competition are codes eliminating 'unfair' methods of competition ascertained upon inquiry to prevail in one industry or another, there is no unlawful delegation of legislative functions when the President is directed to inquire into such practices and denounce them when discovered. For many years a like power has been committed to the Federal Trade Commission with the approval of this court in a long series of decisions. Delegation in such circumstances is born of the necessities of the occasion. The industries of the country are too many and diverse to make it possible for Congress, in respect of matters such as these, to legislate directly with adequate appreciation of varying conditions. Nor is the substance of the power changed because the President may act at the instance of trade or industrial associations having special knowledge of the facts. Their function is strictly advisory; it is the *imprimatur* of the President that begets the quality of law. When the task that is set before one is that of cleaning house, it is prudent as well as usual to take counsel of the dwellers.

But there is another conception of codes of fair competition, their significance and function, which leads to very different consequences, though it is one that is struggling now for recognition and acceptance. By this other conception a code is not to be restricted to the elimination of business practices that would be characterized by general acceptation as oppressive or unfair. It is to include whatever ordinances may be desirable or helpful for the well-being or prosperity of the industry affected. In that view, the function of its adoption is not merely negative, but positive; the planning of improvements as well as the extirpation of abuses. What is fair, as thus conceived, is not something to be contrasted with what is unfair or fraudulent or tricky. The extension becomes as wide as the field of industrial regulation. If that conception shall prevail, anything that Congress may do within the limits of the commerce clause for the betterment of business may be done by the President upon the recommendation of a trade association by calling it a code. This is delegation running riot. No such plenitude of power is susceptible of transfer. The statute, however, aims at nothing less, as one can learn both from its terms and from the administrative practice under it. Nothing less is aimed at by the code now submitted to our scrutiny.

But there is another objection, far-reaching and incurable, aside from any defect of unlawful delegation.

If this code had been adopted by Congress itself, and not by the President on the advice of an industrial association, it would even then be void, unless authority to adopt it is included in the grant of power 'to regulate commerce with foreign nations, and among the several States.' United States Constitution, Art. 1, § 8, cl. 3.

I find no authority in that grant for the regulation of wages and hours of labor in the intrastate transactions that make up the defendants' business. As to this feature of the case, little can be added to the opinion of the court. There is a view of causation that would obliterate the distinction between what is national and what is local in the activities of commerce. Motion at the outer rim is communicated perceptibly, though minutely, to recording instruments at the center. A society such as ours 'is an elastic medium which transmits all tremors throughout its territory; the only question is of their size.' Per Learned Hand, J., in the court below. The law is not indifferent to considerations of degree. Activities local in their immediacy do not become interstate and national because of distant repercussions. What is near and what is distant may at times be uncertain. There is no penumbra of uncertainty obscuring judgment here. To find immediacy or directness here is to find it almost everywhere. If centripetal forces are to be isolated to the exclusion of the forces that oppose and counteract them, there will be an end to our federal system.

I am authorized to state that Mr. Justice STONE joins in this opinion.

Although theoretically under the nondelegation theory agencies and officials were constitutionally limited to filling in details of congressional policy, in practice restrictions on the scope of power that could be delegated have all but disappeared. In only two cases—*Schechter* and *Panama Refining Co. v. Ryan*[73]—did the Court find the congressional delegation unconstitutional. In other cases, the Court has concluded that legislation was not forbidden, reasoning that Congress had laid down an "intelligible principle" to which the person or body authorized to fix rules was directed to conform, curbing discretion.[74] Despite sweeping delegations of legislative, judicial and executive authority to independent expert bodies and administrative agencies, and to the executive department, the Court has consistently concluded the delegation is constitutional. Now familiar legislated formulations like "just and reasonable,"[75] "public interest,"[76] "public convenience, interest, or necessity,"[77] and "unfair methods of competition"[78] were sustained as providing adequately defined standards to guide administrative discretion in decision-making. On the other hand, in no case has the Court rejected the

---

[73] 293 U.S. 388 (1935).

[74] Notably, even on the same day that *Schechter* was handed down, the Court upheld the creation of the Federal Trade Commission, an agency with powers which the Court defined as quasi legislative and quasi judicial and which included Commissioners who did not serve at the pleasure of the President. Humphrey's Executor v. United States, 295 U.S. 602, 628–29 (1935).

[75] Tagg Bros. & Moorhead v. United States, 280 U.S. 420 (1930).

[76] New York Central Securities Corp. v. United States, 287 U.S., 12 (1932).

[77] Federal Radio Comm'n v. Nelson Bros. Bond & Mortgage Co., 289 U.S. 266, 285 (1933).

[78] FTC v. Gratz, 253 U.S. 421 (1920).

nondelegation doctrine. Recently, in *National Cable Television Ass'n v. United States,*[79] the Court used the doctrine to narrowly interpret a statute to avoid concluding that it was a forbidden delegation of authority. The doctrine itself, however, has undergone some changes since its early use as the Court has struggled to sustain legislative action that leaves much of the details of policy-making to the Executive Branch or other decision makers. Reviewing the validity of a price control measure which was adopted as a temporary wartime measure "in the interest of the national defense and security," the Court redefined the circumstances in which it would override Congress.

---

[79] 415 U.S. 336 (1974). In Industrial Union Dep't. v. American Petroleum Inst., 448 U.S. 607, 671–88 (1980); and American Textile Manufacturers Inst. v. Donovan, 452 U.S. 490, 543–48 (1981) (Rehnquist, J. and Burger, C.J., dissenting) Justice Rehnquist concluded that the delegation was unconstitutional. In another case he identified three important functions which the nondelegation doctrine serves:

> First, . . . it ensures to the extent consistent with orderly governmental administration that important choices of social policy are made by Congress, the branch of our Government most responsive to the popular will. Second, the doctrine guarantees that, to the extent Congress finds it necessary to delegate authority, it provides the recipient of that authority with an "intelligible principle" to guide the exercise of the delegated discretion. Third . . . the doctrine ensures that courts charged with reviewing the exercise of delegated legislative discretion will be able to test that exercise against ascertainable standards.

Industrial Union Dep't v. American Petroleum Inst., 448 U.S. 607, 685–86 (1980) (Rehnquist, J., concurring) (citations omitted).

Yakus v. United States
321 U.S. 414 (1944)

Opinion of the Court by Chief Justice Stone, announced by Mr. Roberts.

The question for our decision [is] whether the Emergency Price Control Act of January 30, 1942 involves an unconstitutional delegation to the Price Administrator of the legislative power of Congress to control prices.

Petitioners in both of these cases were tried and convicted by the District Court for Massachusetts upon several counts of indictments charging violation of §§ 4(a) and 205(b) of the Act by the willful sale of wholesale cuts of beef at prices above the maximum prices prescribed by [regulations].

I.

The Emergency Price Control Act provides for the establishment of the Office of Price Administration under the direction of a Price Administrator appointed by the President, and sets up a comprehensive scheme for the promulgation by the Administrator of regulations or orders fixing such maximum prices of commodities and rents as will effectuate the purposes of the Act and conform to the standards which it prescribes. The Act was adopted as a temporary wartime measure, and provides in § 1(b) for its termination on June 30, 1943, unless sooner terminated by Presidential proclamation or concurrent resolution of Congress. By the amendatory act of October 2, 1942, it was extended to June 30, 1944.

Section 1(a) declares that the Act is 'in the interest of the national defense and security and necessary to the effective prosecution of the present war', and that its purposes are: 'to stabilize prices and to prevent speculative, unwarranted, and abnormal increases in prices and rents; to eliminate and prevent profiteering, hoarding, manipulation, speculation, and other disruptive practices resulting from abnormal market conditions or scarcities caused by or contributing to the national emergency; to assure that defense appropriations are not dissipated by excessive prices; to protect persons with relatively fixed and limited incomes, consumers, wage earners, investors, and persons dependent on life insurance, annuities, and pensions, from undue impairment of their standard of living; to prevent hardships to persons engaged in business, . . . and to the Federal, State, and local governments, which would result from abnormal increases in prices; to assist in securing adequate production of commodities and facilities; to prevent a post emergency collapse of values. . . .'

The standards which are to guide the Administrator's exercise of his authority to fix prices, so far as now relevant, are prescribed by § 2(a) and by § 1 of the amendatory Act of October 2, 1942, and Executive Order 9250. By § 2(a) the Administrator is authorized, after consultation with representative members of the industry so far as practicable, to promulgate regulations fixing prices of commodities which 'in his judgment will be generally fair and equitable and will effectuate the purposes of this Act' when, in his judgment, their prices 'have risen or threaten to rise to an extent or in a manner inconsistent with the purposes of this Act.'

The section also directs that

So far as practicable, in establishing any maximum price, the Administrator shall ascertain and give due consideration to the prices prevailing between October 1 and October 15, 1941 (or if, in the case of any commodity, there are no prevailing prices between such dates, or the prevailing prices between such dates are not generally representative because of abnormal or seasonal market conditions or other cause, then to the prices prevailing during the nearest two-week period in which, in the judgment of the Administrator, the prices for such commodity are generally representative) . . . and shall make adjustments for such relevant factors as he may determine and deem to be of general applicability, including. . . . Speculative fluctuations, general increases or decreases in costs of production, distribution, and transportation, and general increases or decreases in profits earned by sellers of the commodity or commodities, during and subsequent to the year ended October 1, 1941.

By the Act of October 2, 1942, the President is directed to stabilize prices, wages and salaries 'so far as practicable' on the basis of the levels which existed on September 15, 1942, except as otherwise provided in the Act. By Title I, § 4 of Executive Order No. 9250, he has directed 'all departments and agencies of the Government' 'to stabilize the cost of living in accordance with the Act of October 2, 1942.'

That Congress has constitutional authority to prescribe commodity prices as a war emergency measure, and that the Act was adopted by Congress in the exercise of that power, are not questioned here, and need not now be considered save as they have a bearing on the procedural features of the Act later to be considered which are challenged on constitutional grounds.

Congress enacted the Emergency Price Control Act in pursuance of a defined policy and required that the prices fixed by the Administrator should further that policy and conform to standards prescribed by the Act. The boundaries of the field of the Administrator's permissible action are marked by the statute. It directs that the prices fixed shall effectuate the declared policy of the Act to stabilize commodity prices so as to prevent wartime inflation and its enumerated disruptive causes and effects. In addition the prices established must be fair and equitable, and in fixing them the Administrator is directed to give due consideration, so far as practicable, to prevailing prices during the designated base period, with prescribed administrative adjustments to compensate for enumerated disturbing factors affecting prices. In short the purposes of the Act specified in § 1 denote the objective to be sought by the Administrator in fixing prices—the prevention of inflation and its enumerated consequences. The standards set out in § 2 define the boundaries within which prices having that purpose must be fixed. It is enough to satisfy the statutory requirements that the Administrator finds that the prices fixed will tend to achieve that objective and will conform to those standards, and that the courts in an appropriate proceeding can see that substantial basis for those findings is not wanting.

The Act is thus an exercise by Congress of its legislative power. In it Congress has stated the legislative objective, has prescribed the method of achieving that objective—maximum price fixing—and has laid down standards to guide the administrative determination of both the occasions for the exercise of the price-fixing power, and the particular prices to be established.

The Act is unlike the National Industrial Recovery Act considered in *Schechter Poultry Corp. v. United States*, 295 U.S. 495 which proclaimed in the broadest terms its purpose 'to rehabilitate industry and to conserve natural resources.' It prescribed no method of attaining that end save by the establishment of codes of fair competition, the nature of whose permissible provisions was left undefined. It provided no standards to which those codes were to conform. The function of formulating the codes was delegated, not to a public official responsible to Congress or the Executive, but to private individuals engaged in the industries to be regulated.

The Constitution as a continuously operative charter of government does not demand the impossible or the impracticable. It does not require that Congress find for itself every fact upon which it desires to base legislative action or that it make for itself detailed determinations which it has declared to be prerequisite to the application of the legislative policy to particular facts and circumstances impossible for Congress itself properly to investigate. The essentials of the legislative function are the determination of the legislative policy and its formulation and promulgation as a defined and binding rule of conduct—here the rule, with penal sanctions, that prices shall not be greater than those fixed by maximum price regulations which conform to standards and will tend to further the policy which Congress has established. These essentials are preserved when Congress has specified the basic conditions of fact upon whose existence or occurrence, ascertained from relevant data by a designated administrative agency, it directs that its statutory command shall be effective. It is no objection that the determination of facts and the inferences to be drawn from them in the light of the statutory standards and declaration of policy call for the exercise of judgment, and for the formulation of subsidiary administrative policy within the prescribed statutory framework.

Nor does the doctrine of separation of powers deny to Congress power to direct that an administrative officer properly designated for that purpose have ample latitude within which he is to ascertain the conditions which Congress has made prerequisite to the operation of its legislative command. Acting within its constitutional power to fix prices it is for Congress to say whether the data on the basis of which prices are to be fixed are to be confined within a narrow or a broad range. In either case the only concern of courts is to ascertain whether the will of Congress has been obeyed. This depends not upon the breadth of the definition of the facts or conditions which the administrative officer is to find but upon the determination whether the definition sufficiently marks the field within which the Administrator is to act so that it may be known whether he has kept within it in compliance with the legislative will.

As we have said: 'The Constitution has never been regarded as denying to the Congress the necessary resources of flexibility and practicality . . . to perform its function.' *Currin v. Wallace, supra*, [306 U.S. at] 15. Only if we could say that there is an absence of standards for guidance of the Administrator's action, so that it would be impossible in a proper proceeding to ascertain whether the will of Congress has been obeyed, would we be justified in overriding its choice of means for effecting its declared purpose of preventing inflation.

The standards prescribed by the present Act, with the aid of the 'statement of the considerations' required to be made by the Administrator, are sufficiently definite and precise to enable Congress, the courts and the public to ascertain whether the Administrator, in fixing the designated prices, has conformed to those standards. Hence we are unable to find in them an unauthorized delegation of legislative power.

Affirmed.

In *Panama Refining Co. v. Ryan*, the Court acknowledged:

undoubtedly legislation must often be adapted to complex conditions involving a host of details with which the national legislature cannot deal directly. The Constitution has never been regarded as denying to the Congress the necessary resources of flexibility and practicality, which will enable it to perform its function in laying down policies and establishing standards, while leaving to selected instrumentalities the making of subordinate rules within prescribed limits and the determination of facts to which the policy as declared by the legislature is to apply. Without capacity to give authorizations of that sort we should have the anomaly of a legislative power which in many circumstances calling for its exertion would be but a futility.[80]

---

[80] 293 U.S. at 249.

[81] KENNETH DAVIS, SUPPLEMENT TO ADMINISTRATIVE LAW TREATISE 151 (1982).

PAH: Practically abandoning the position that Congress could not constitutionally delegate legislative power, the Court reformulated the principle into the proposition that Congress could not delegate without meaningful standards.[81] Whereas the nondelegation principle began as a recognition that the Constitution required Congress to retain independent and exclusive legislature power, the focus has shifted to considering the kind of discretion available to the agent to whom the details of policy has been assigned and to the kind of functions that the agent was left to perform. However, the line between conferring discretion as to execution—the mark of executive power—and offering unbounded delegation of power to make law is not always clear. The Court has been willing to ignore the distinction, citing *McCulloch* for the proposition that Congress is authorized to select the means to a legitimate end as part of its expansive powers, including conferring broad power to decision makers other than Congress, the President or the judiciary.

As scholars such as Professor Carter point out, independent agencies—whether agencies implementing executive authority outside the control of the executive or wielding a mixture of legislative executive or judicial power—are conceptually inconsistent with the tripartite structure of government. The Supreme Court has never provided a constitutional rationale for their existence although it has responded when Congress has asserted power to retain some oversight over their decision making.

DEL: If resurrection of the Tenth Amendment as a check on the commerce power (after a half century of dormancy)[82] reflects a mounting backlash against centralized federal authority in the post-New Deal era, revisitation of delegation principles would not be a surprising development. The notion that faceless bureaucrats in Washington have preempted the consent of the governed represents a concern that predates but merges with agendas favoring term limits for legislators, an end to unfunded federal mandates to the states, a reinvigorated takings clause and general deregulation. Given contemporary political concerns and movements, a broad delegation doctrine presents itself as a logical target for litigative assault.

RLW: Since the 1930s, the Court has been extremely deferential to Congress on delegation issues. "[R]estrictions on the scope of the power that could be delegated diminished and all but disappeared."[83] In many cases, "the 'intelligible principle' through which agencies have attained enormous control over the economic affairs of the country was held to include such formulations as 'just and reasonable,' 'public interest,' 'public convenience, interest, or necessity,' and 'unfair methods of competition.'"[84]

Because of these broad delegations, administrative agencies have been allowed to assume broad powers. As the D.C. Circuit observed, "administrative agencies may well have a more far-reaching effect on the daily lives of all citizens than do the combined actions of the executive, legislative and judicial branches. . . ."[85] This assertion is borne out by the size of the Code of Federal Regulations which has grown to 208 volumes.

The growth of administrative power is not solely attributable to the demise of the unlawful delegation doctrine. The "Switch of '37" allowed Congress to assume ever greater authority under the commerce clause, and much of that power was delegated to administrative agencies. An equally important development was the creation of so-called "independent agencies"—independent in the sense that they are run by officials with a measure of freedom from Presidential control.[86] As Justice Jackson recognized, "administrative bodies . . . have become a veritable fourth branch of the Government, which has deranged our three-branch legal theories. . . ."[87] The Court's recent decision in *United States v.*

---

[82] *See* Part III, *infra.*

[83] INS v. Chadha, 462 U.S. 919, 985 (1983)

[84] *Id.*

[85] Ballerina Pen Co. v. Kunzig, 433 F. 2d 1204, 1207–08 (D.C. Cir. 1970), *cert. denied*, 401 U.S. 950 (1971).

[86] *See* Humphrey's Executor v. United States, 295 U.S. 602 (1935).

[87] Federal Trade Commission v. Ruberoid Co., 343 U.S. 470, 487 (1952) (Jackson, J., dissenting).

Lopez,[88] as well as Congress' effort to restrain administrative authority, may slow or reverse the growth of administrative power.

---

[88] 115 S. Ct. 1624 (1995).

D. Defining the Limits of Congressional Continued Oversight

Until the 1980's the Court did not attempt to reign in administrative agencies, thereby acquiescing in Congress' willingness to authorize them to accrue so much decision making power that "[t]hey have become a veritable fourth branch of the Government."[89] These cases raise for consideration whether the original checks and balances contemplated by the Framers adequately address contemporary concerns about mingling legislative and executive power in one body and about the accretion of responsibility in the President. While deferring to Congress even when it passed "laws requiring broad-scale policy making before execution"[90] the Court did begin to focus on the constitutionality of alternative congressional efforts to check the President. In the "legislative veto" the Court found an improper congressional mechanism.

---

[89] FTC v. Ruberoid Co., 343 U.S. 470, 487 (1952) (Jackson, J., dissenting). By 1974, Justice Marshall observed that the nondelegation doctrine "is surely as moribund as the substantive due process approach of the same era . . . if not more so." Federal Power Comm'n v. New England Power Co. 415 U.S. 345, 352–53 (Marshall J., concurring).

[90] Abner Greene, *Checks and Balances in an Era of Presidential Lawmaking*, 61 U. CHI. L. REV. 123, 154 (1994).

Immigration and Naturalization Service v. Chadha
462 U.S. 919 (1983)

Chief Justice BURGER delivered the opinion of the Court.

We granted certiorari in . . . a challenge to the constitutionality of the provision in § 244(c)(2) of the Immigration and Nationality Act, 8 U.S.C. § 1254(c)(2), authorizing one House of Congress, by resolution, to invalidate the decision of the Executive Branch, pursuant to authority delegated by Congress to the Attorney General of the United States, to allow a particular deportable alien to remain in the United States.

I

Chadha is an East Indian who was born in Kenya and holds a British passport. He was lawfully admitted to the United States in 1966 on a nonimmigrant student visa. His visa expired on June 30, 1972. On October 11, 1973, the District Director of the Immigration and Naturalization Service ordered Chadha to show cause why he should not be deported for having "remained in the United States for a longer time than permitted." App. 6. Pursuant to § 242(b) of the Immigration and Nationality

Act (Act), 8 U.S.C. § 1252(b), a deportation hearing was held before an immigration judge on January 11, 1974. Chadha conceded that he was deportable for overstaying his visa and the hearing was adjourned to enable him to file an application for suspension of deportation under § 244(a)(1) of the Act, 8 U.S.C. § 1254(a)(1). Section 244(a)(1), at the time in question provided:

"As hereinafter prescribed in this section, the Attorney General may, in his discretion, suspend deportation and adjust the status to that of an alien lawfully admitted for permanent residence, in the case of an alien who applies to the Attorney General for suspension of deportation and—

(1) is deportable under any law of the United States except the provisions specified in paragraph (2) of this subsection; has been physically present in the United States for a continuous period of not less than seven years immediately preceding the date of such application, and proves that during all of such period he was and

is a person of good moral character; and is a person whose deportation would, in the opinion of the Attorney General, result in extreme hardship to the alien or to his spouse, parent, or child, who is a citizen of the United States or an alien lawfully admitted for permanent residence."

After Chadha submitted his application for suspension of deportation, the deportation hearing was resumed on February 7, 1974. On the basis of evidence adduced at the hearing, affidavits submitted with the application, and the results of a character investigation conducted by the INS, the Immigration Judge, on June 25, 1974, ordered that Chadha's deportation be suspended. The Immigration Judge found that Chadha met the requirements of § 244(a)(1): he had resided continuously in the United States for over seven years, was of good moral character, and would suffer "extreme hardship" if deported.

Pursuant to § 244(c)(1) of the Act, 8 U.S.C. § 1254(c)(1), the Immigration Judge suspended Chadha's deportation and a report of the suspension was transmitted to Congress. Section 244(c)(1) provides:

"Upon application by any alien who is found by the Attorney General to meet the requirements of subsection (a) of this section the Attorney General may in his discretion suspend deportation of such alien. If the deportation of any alien is suspended under the provisions of this subsection, a complete and detailed statement of the facts and pertinent provisions of law in the case shall be reported to the Congress with the reasons for such suspension. Such reports shall be submitted on the first day of each calendar month in which Congress is in session."

Once the Attorney General's recommendation for suspension of Chadha's deportation was conveyed to Congress, Congress had the power under § 244(c)(2) of the Act, 8 U.S.C. § 1254(c)(2), to veto[2] the Attorney General's de-

termination that Chadha should not be deported. Section 244(c)(2) provides:

"(2) In the case of an alien specified in paragraph (1) of subsection (a) of this subsection—if during the session of the Congress at which a case is reported, or prior to the close of the session of the Congress next following the session at which a case is reported, either the Senate or the House of Representatives passes a resolution stating in substance that it does not favor the suspension of such deportation, the Attorney General shall thereupon deport such alien or authorize the alien's voluntary departure at his own expense under the order of deportation in the manner provided by law. If, within the time above specified, neither the Senate nor the House of Representatives shall pass such a resolution, the Attorney General shall cancel deportation proceedings."

The June 25, 1974 order of the Immigration Judge suspending Chadha's deportation remained outstanding as a valid order for a year and a half. For reasons not disclosed by the record, Congress did not exercise the veto authority reserved to it under § 244(c)(2) until the first session of the 94th Congress. This was the final session in which Congress, pursuant to § 244(c)(2), could act to veto the Attorney General's determination that Chadha should not be deported. The session ended on December 19, 1975. Absent Congressional action, Chadha's deportation proceedings would have been cancelled after this date and his status adjusted to that of a permanent resident alien. See 8 U.S.C. § 1254(d).

On December 12, 1975, Representative Eilberg, Chairman of the Judiciary Subcommittee on Immigration, Citizenship, and International Law, introduced a resolution opposing "the granting of permanent residence in the United States to [six] aliens," including Chadha. The resolution was referred to the House Committee on the Judiciary. On December 16, 1975, the resolution was discharged from further consideration by the House Committee on the Judiciary and submitted to the House of Representatives for a vote. The resolution had not been printed and was not made available to other Members of the House prior to or at the time it was voted on. So far as the record before us shows, the House consideration of the resolution was based on Representative Eilberg's statement from the floor that

"[i]t was the feeling of the committee, after reviewing 340 cases, that the aliens contained in the resolution [Chadha and five others] did not meet these statutory requirements, particularly as it relates to hardship; and it is the opinion of the committee that their deportation should not be suspended."

---

[2] In constitutional terms, "veto" is used to describe the President's power under Art. I, § 7 of the Constitution. *See* Black's Law Dictionary 1403 (5th ed. 1979). It appears, however, that Congressional devices of the type authorized by § 244(c)(2) have come to be commonly referred to as a "veto." *See, e.g.*, Martin, *The Legislative Veto and the Responsible Exercise of Congressional Power*, 68 VA. L. REV. 253 (1982); Miller and Knapp, *The Congressional Veto: Preserving the Constitutional Framework*, 52 IND. L.J. 367 (1977). We refer to the Congressional "resolution" authorized by § 244(c)(2) as a "one-House veto" of the Attorney General's decision to allow a particular deportable alien to remain in the United States.

The resolution was passed without debate or recorded vote.[3] Since the House action was pursuant to § 244(c)(2), the resolution was not treated as an Article I legislative act; it was not submitted to the Senate or presented to the President for his action.

After the House veto of the Attorney General's decision to allow Chadha to remain in the United States, the Immigration Judge reopened the deportation proceedings to implement the House order deporting Chadha. Chadha moved to terminate the proceedings on the ground that § 244(c)(2) is unconstitutional. The Immigration Judge held that he had no authority to rule on the constitutional validity of § 244(c)(2). On November 8, 1976, Chadha was ordered deported pursuant to the House action.

Chadha appealed the deportation order to the Board of Immigration Appeals again contending that § 244(c)(2) is unconstitutional. The Board held that it had "no power to declare unconstitutional an act of Congress" and Chadha's appeal was dismissed.

---

[3] It is not at all clear whether the House generally, or Subcommittee Chairman Eilberg in particular, correctly understood the relationship between H.R.Res. 926 and the Attorney General's decision to suspend Chadha's deportation. Exactly one year previous to the House veto of the Attorney General's decision in this case, Representative Eilberg introduced a similar resolution disapproving the Attorney General's suspension of deportation in the case of six other aliens. H.R.Res. 1518, 93d Cong., 2d Sess. The following colloquy occurred on the floor of the House: Mr. EILBERG. Mr. Speaker, these aliens have been found to be deportable and the Special Inquiry Officer's decision denying suspension of deportation has been reversed by the Board of Immigration Appeals. We are complying with the law since all of these decisions have been referred to us for approval or disapproval, and there are hundreds of cases in this category. In these six cases however, we believe it would be grossly improper to allow these people to acquire the status of permanent resident aliens.
Mr. WYLIE. In other words, the gentleman has been working with the Attorney General's office?
Mr. EILBERG. Yes.
Mr. WYLIE. This bill then is in fact a confirmation of what the Attorney General intends to do?
Mr. EILBERG. The gentleman is correct insofar as it relates to the determination of deportability which has been made by the Department of Justice in these cases.
Mr. WYLIE. Mr. Speaker, I withdraw my reservation of objection."
120 Cong.Rec. 41412 (1974).
Clearly, this was an obfuscation of the effect of a veto under § 244(c)(2). Such a veto in no way constitutes "a confirmation of what the Attorney General intends to do." To the contrary, such a resolution was meant to overrule and set aside, or "veto," the Attorney General's determination that, in a particular case, cancellation of deportation would be appropriate under the standards set forth in § 244(a)(1).

Pursuant to § 106(a) of the Act, 8 U.S.C. § 1105a(a), Chadha filed a petition for review of the deportation order in the United States Court of Appeals for the Ninth Circuit. The Immigration and Naturalization Service agreed with Chadha's position before the Court of Appeals and joined him in arguing that § 244(c)(2) is unconstitutional. In light of the importance of the question, the Court of Appeals invited both the Senate and the House of Representatives to file briefs *amici curiae*.

After full briefing and oral argument, the Court of Appeals held that the House was without constitutional authority to order Chadha's deportation; accordingly it directed the Attorney General "to cease and desist from taking any steps to deport this alien based upon the resolution enacted by the House of Representatives." *Chadha v. INS,* 634 F.2d 408, 436 (9th Cir. 1980). The essence of its holding was that § 244(c)(2) violates the constitutional doctrine of separation of powers.

II

Before we address the important question of the constitutionality of the one-House veto provision of § 244(c)(2), we first consider several challenges to the authority of this Court to resolve the issue raised.

F

Case or Controversy

It is contended that this is not a genuine controversy but "a friendly, non-adversary, proceeding," *Ashwander v. TVA,* 297 U.S., at 346 (Brandeis, J., concurring), upon which the Court should not pass. This argument rests on the fact that Chadha and the INS take the same position on the constitutionality of the one-House veto. But it would be a curious result if, in the administration of justice, a person could be denied access to the courts because the Attorney General of the United States agreed with the legal arguments asserted by the individual.

A case or controversy is presented by these cases. First, from the time of Congress' formal intervention, the concrete adverseness is beyond doubt. Congress is both a proper party to defend the constitutionality of § 244(c)(2) and a proper petitioner under 28 U.S.C. 1254(1). Second, prior to Congress' intervention, there was adequate Art. III adverseness even though the only parties were INS and Chadha. . . .[T]he INS's agreement with the Court of Appeals' decision that § 244(c)(2) is unconstitutional does not affect that agency's "aggrieved" status for the purposes of appealing that decision under 28 U.S.C. 1252. For similar reasons, the INS's agreement with Chadha's position does not alter the fact that the INS would have deported Chadha absent the Court of Appeals' judgment.

Of course, there may be prudential, as opposed to Art. III, concerns about sanctioning the adjudication of these cases in the absence of any participant supporting the validity of § 244(c)(2). The Court of Appeals properly dispelled any such concerns by inviting and accepting briefs form both Houses of Congress. We have long held that Congress is the proper party to defend the validity of a statute when an agency of government, as a defendant charged with enforcing the statute agrees with plaintiffs that the statute is inapplicable or unconstitutional.

G

Political Question

It is also argued that these cases present a nonjusticiable political question because Chadha is merely challenging Congress' authority under the Naturalization Clause, U.S. Const. Art. I, § 8, cl. 4, and the Necessary and Proper Clause, U.S. Const. art. I, § 8, cl. 18. It is argued that Congress' Article I power "To Establish an uniform Rule of Naturalization," combined with the Necessary and Proper Clause, grants it unreviewable authority over the regulation of aliens. The plenary authority of Congress over aliens under Art. I, § 8, cl. 4, is not open to question, but what is challenged here is whether Congress has chosen a constitutionally permissible means of implementing that power. As we made clear in *Buckley v. Valeo*, 424 U.S. 1 (1976): "Congress has plenary authority in all cases in which it has substantive legislative jurisdiction, *McCulloch v. Maryland*, 4 Wheat. 316 (1819), so long as the exercise of that authority does not offend some other constitutional restriction."

As identified in *Baker v. Carr*, 369 U.S. 186, 217 (1962), a political question may arise when any one of the following circumstances is present:

> "a textually demonstrable constitutional commitment of the issue to a coordinate political department; or a lack of judicially discoverable and manageable standards for resolving it; or the impossibility of deciding without an initial policy determination of a kind clearly for nonjudicial discretion; or the impossibility of a court's undertaking independent resolution without expressing lack of the respect due coordinate branches of government; or an unusual need for unquestioning adherence to a political decision already made; or the potentiality of embarrassment from multifarious pronouncements by various departments on one question."

Congress apparently directs its assertion of nonjusticiability to the first of the *Baker* factors by asserting that Chadha's claim is "an assault on the legislative authority to enact Section 244(c)(2)." But if this turns the question into a political question virtually every challenge to the constitutionality of a statute would be a political question. Chadha indeed argues that one House of Congress cannot constitutionally veto the Attorney General's decision to allow him to remain in this country. No policy underlying the political question doctrine suggests that Congress or the Executive, or both acting in concert and in compliance with Art. I, can decide the constitutionality of a statute; that is a decision for the courts.

Other *Baker* factors are likewise inapplicable to this case. As we discuss more fully below, Art. I provides the "judicially discoverable and manageable standards" of *Baker* for resolving the question presented by these cases. Those standards forestall reliance by this Court on nonjudicial "policy determinations" or any showing of disrespect for a coordinate branch. Similarly, if Chadha's arguments are accepted, § 244(c)(2) cannot stand, and, since the constitutionality of that statute is for this Court to resolve, there is no possibility of "multifarious pronouncements" on this question.

It is correct that this controversy may, in a sense, be termed "political." But the presence of constitutional issues with significant political overtones does not automatically invoke the political question doctrine. Resolution of litigation challenging the constitutional authority of one of the three branches cannot be evaded by courts because the issues have political implications in the sense urged by Congress. *Marbury v. Madison*, was also a "political" case, involving as it did claims under a judicial commission alleged to have been duly signed by the President but not delivered. But "courts cannot reject as 'no law suit' a bona fide controversy as to whether some action denominated 'political' exceeds constitutional authority." *Baker v. Carr, supra,* at 217.

III

A

We turn now to the question whether action of one House of Congress under § 244(c)(2) violates strictures of the Constitution. We begin, of course, with the presumption that the challenged statute is valid. Its wisdom is not the concern of the courts; if a challenged action does not violate the Constitution, it must be sustained:

> "Once the meaning of an enactment is discerned and its constitutionality determined, the judicial process comes to an end. We do not sit as a committee of review, nor are we vested with the power of veto." *Tennessee Valley Authority v. Hill*, 437 U.S. 153, 194–195 (1978).

By the same token, the fact that a given law or procedure is efficient, convenient, and useful in facilitating functions of government, standing alone, will not save it if it is contrary to the Constitution. Convenience and efficiency are not the primary objectives—or the hallmarks—of democratic government and our inquiry is sharpened rather than blunted by the fact that congressional veto provisions are appearing with increasing frequency in statutes which delegate authority to executive and independent agencies:

> "Since 1932, when the first veto provision was enacted into law, 295 congressional veto-type procedures have been inserted in 196 different statutes as follows: from 1932 to 1939, five statutes were affected; from 1940–49, nineteen statutes; between 1950–59, thirty-four statutes; and from 1960–69, forty-nine. From the year 1970 through 1975, at least one hundred sixty-three such provisions were included in eighty-nine laws." Abourezk, The Congressional Veto: A Contemporary Response to Executive Encroachment on Legislative Prerogatives, 52 Ind. L.Rev. 323, 324 (1977). . . .

Justice WHITE undertakes to make a case for the proposition that the one-House veto is a useful "political invention," and we need not challenge that assertion. We can even concede this utilitarian argument although the long range political wisdom of this "invention" is arguable. It has been vigorously debated and it is instructive to compare the views of the protagonists. See, *e.g.*, Javits & Klein, Congressional Oversight and the Legislative Veto: A Constitutional Analysis, 52 N.Y.U. L. Rev. 455 (1977), and Martin, The Legislative Veto and the Responsible Exercise of Congressional Power, 68 Va. L.Rev. 253 (1982). But policy arguments supporting even useful "political inventions" are subject to the demands of the Constitution which defines powers and, with respect to this subject, sets out just how those powers are to be exercised.

Explicit and unambiguous provisions of the Constitution prescribe and define the respective functions of the Congress and of the Executive in the legislative process. Since the precise terms of those familiar provisions are critical to the resolution of this case, we set them out verbatim. Article I provides:

> "All legislative Powers herein granted shall be vested in a Congress of the United States, which shall consist of a Senate *and* a House of Representatives." Art. I, § 1. (Emphasis added).
>
> "Every Bill which shall have passed the House of Representatives *and* the Senate, *shall*, before it becomes a Law, be presented to the President of the United States; . . . " Art. I, § 7, cl. 2. (Emphasis added).
>
> "Every Order, Resolution, or Vote to which the Concurrence of the Senate and House of Representatives may be necessary (except on a question of Adjournment) *shall be* presented to the President of the United States; and before the Same shall take Effect, *shall be* approved by him, or being disapproved by him, *shall be* repassed by two thirds of the Senate and House of Representatives, according to the Rules and Limitations prescribed in the Case of a Bill." Art. I, § 7, cl. 3. (Emphasis added).

These provisions of Art. I are integral parts of the constitutional design for the separation of powers. We have recently noted that "[t]he principle of separation of powers was not simply an abstract generalization in the minds of the Framers: it was woven into the documents that they drafted in Philadelphia in the summer of 1787." *Buckley v. Valeo.* Just as we relied on the textual provision of Art. II, § 2, cl. 2, to vindicate the principle of separation of powers in *Buckley*, we find that the purposes underlying the Presentment Clauses, Art. I, § 7, cls. 2, 3, and the bicameral requirement of Art. I, § 1 and § 7, cl. 2, guide our resolution of the important question presented in this case. The very structure of the articles delegating and separating powers under Arts. I, II, and III exemplify the concept of separation of powers and we now turn to Art. I.

B

The Presentment Clauses

The records of the Constitutional Convention reveal that the requirement that all legislation be presented to the President before becoming law was uniformly accepted by the Framers. Presentment to the President and the Presidential veto were considered so imperative that the draftsmen took special pains to assure that these requirements could not be circumvented. During the final debate on Art. I, § 7, cl. 2, James Madison expressed concern that it might easily be evaded by the simple expedient of calling a proposed law a "resolution" or "vote" rather than a "bill." [2 M. Farrand, The Records of the Federal Convention of 1787 301–302.] As a consequence, Art. I, § 7, cl. 3 was added. [*Id.*, at 304–305.]

The decision to provide the President with a limited and qualified power to nullify proposed legislation by veto was based on the profound conviction of the Framers that the powers conferred on Congress were the powers to be most carefully circumscribed. It is beyond doubt that lawmaking was a power to be shared by both Houses and the President. In

The Federalist No. 73 (H. Lodge ed. 1888), Hamilton focused on the President's role in making laws:

> "If even no propensity had ever discovered itself in the legislative body to invade the rights of the Executive, the rules of just reasoning and theoretic propriety would of themselves teach us that the one ought not to be left to the mercy of the other, but ought to possess a constitutional and effectual power of self-defense."

Id., at 457-458. See also The Federalist No. 51.

The President's role in the lawmaking process also reflects the Framers' careful efforts to check whatever propensity a particular Congress might have to enact oppressive, improvident, or ill-considered measures. The President's veto role in the legislative process was described later during public debate on ratification:

> "It establishes a salutary check upon the legislative body, calculated to guard the community against the effects of faction, precipitancy, or of any impulse unfriendly to the public good which may happen to influence a majority of that body.... The primary inducement to conferring the power in question upon the Executive is to enable him to defend himself; the secondary one is to increase the chances in favor of the community against the passing of bad laws through haste, inadvertence, or design." The Federalist No. 73, *supra*, at 458 (A. Hamilton)....

The Court also has observed that the Presentment Clauses serve the important purpose of assuring that a "national" perspective is grafted on the legislative process:

> "The President is a representative of the people just as the members of the Senate and of the House are, and it may be, at some times, on some subjects, that the President elected by all the people is rather more representative of them all than are the members of either body of the Legislature whose constituencies are local and not countrywide...." *Myers v. United States, supra,* [272 U.S.], at 123.

C

Bicameralism

The bicameral requirement of Art. I, §§ 1, 7 was of scarcely less concern to the Framers than was the Presidential veto and indeed the two concepts are interdependent. By providing that no law could take effect without the concurrence of the prescribed majority of the Members of both Houses, the Framers reemphasized their belief, already remarked upon in connection with the Presentment Clauses, that legislation should not be enacted unless it has been carefully and fully considered by the Nation's elected officials. In the Constitutional Convention debates on the need for a bicameral legislature, James Wilson, later to become a Justice of this Court, commented:

> "Despotism comes on mankind in different shapes. Sometimes in an Executive, sometimes in a military, one. Is there danger of a Legislative despotism? Theory & practice both proclaim it. If the Legislative authority be not restrained, there can be neither liberty nor stability; and it can only be restrained by dividing it within itself, into distinct and independent branches. In a single house there is no check, but the inadequate one, of the virtue & good sense of those who compose it." 1 [M. Farrand,] *supra*, at 254.

Hamilton argued that a Congress comprised of a single House was antithetical to the very purposes of the Constitution. Were the Nation to adopt a Constitution providing for only one legislative organ, he warned:

> "[W]e shall finally accumulate, in a single body, all the most important prerogatives of sovereignty, and thus entail upon our posterity one of the most execrable forms of government that human infatuation ever contrived. Thus we should create in reality that very tyranny which the adversaries of the new Constitution either are, or affect to be, solicitous to avert." The Federalist No. 22, [*supra*, at 135].

This view was rooted in a general skepticism regarding the fallibility of human nature later commented on by Joseph Story:

> "Public bodies, like private persons, are occasionally under the dominion of strong passions and excitements; impatient, irritable, and impetuous.... If [a legislature] feels no check but its own will, it rarely has the firmness to insist upon holding a question long enough under its own view, to see and mark it in all its bearings and relations to society." 1 J. Story, *supra*, at 383–384.

These observations are consistent with what many of the Framers expressed, none more cogently than Hamilton in pointing up the need to divide and disperse power in order to protect liberty:

> "In republican government, the legislative authority necessarily predominates. The remedy for this inconvenience is to divide the legislature into different branches; and to render them, by different modes of election and different principles of action, as little connected with each other as the nature of their common functions and their common dependence on the society will admit." The Federalist No. 51, *supra*, at 324.

See also The Federalist No. 62.

However familiar, it is useful to recall that apart from their fear that special interests could be favored at the expense of public needs, the Framers were also concerned, although not of one mind, over the apprehensions of the smaller states. Those states feared a commonality of interest among the larger states would work to their disadvantage; representatives of the larger states, on the other hand, were skeptical of a legislature that could pass laws favoring a minority of the people. See 1 M. Farrand, 176–177, 484–491. It need hardly be repeated here that the Great Compromise, under which one House was viewed as representing the people and the other the states, allayed the fears of both the large and small states.

We see therefore that the Framers were acutely conscious that the bicameral requirement and the Presentment Clauses would serve essential constitutional functions. The President's participation in the legislative process was to protect the Executive Branch from Congress and to protect the whole people from improvident laws. The division of the Congress into two distinctive bodies assures that the legislative power would be exercised only after opportunity for full study and debate in separate settings. The President's unilateral veto power, in turn, was limited by the power of two-thirds of both Houses of Congress to overrule a veto thereby precluding final arbitrary action of one person. See 1 [M. Farrand, supra, at 99–104.] It emerges clearly that the prescription for legislative action in Art. I, §§ 1, 7 represents the Framers' decision that the legislative power of the Federal government be exercised in accord with a single, finely wrought and exhaustively considered, procedure.

IV

The Constitution sought to divide the delegated powers of the new federal government into three defined categories, legislative, executive and judicial, to assure, as nearly as possible, that each Branch of government would confine itself to its assigned responsibility. The hydraulic pressure inherent within each of the separate Branches to exceed the outer limits of its power, even to accomplish desirable objectives, must be resisted.

Although not "hermetically" sealed from one another, *Buckley v. Valeo,* supra, 424 U.S., at 121, the powers delegated to the three Branches are functionally identifiable. When any Branch acts, it is presumptively exercising the power the Constitution has delegated to it. See *J. W. Hampton & Co. v. United States,* 276 U.S. 394, 406 (1928). When the Executive acts, it presumptively acts in an executive or administrative capacity as defined in Art. II. And when, as here, one House of Congress purports

to act, it is presumptively acting within its assigned sphere.

Beginning with this presumption, we must nevertheless establish that the challenged action under § 244(c)(2) is of the kind to which the procedural requirements of Art. I, § 7 apply. Not every action taken by either House is subject to the bicameralism and presentment requirements of Art I. Whether actions taken by either House are, in law and fact, an exercise of legislative power depends not on their form but upon "whether they contain matter which is properly to be regarded as legislative in its character and effect." S. Rep. No. 1335, 54th Cong., 2d Sess., 8 (1897).

Examination of the action taken here by one House pursuant to § 244(c)(2) reveals that it was essentially legislative in purpose and effect. In purporting to exercise power defined in Art. I, § 8, cl. 4 to "establish an uniform Rule of Naturalization," the House took action that had the purpose and effect of altering the legal rights, duties and relations of persons, including the Attorney General, Executive Branch officials and Chadha, all outside the legislative branch. Section 244(c)(2) purports to authorize one House of Congress to require the Attorney General to deport an individual alien whose deportation otherwise would be cancelled under § 244. The one-House veto operated in this case to overrule the Attorney General and mandate Chadha's deportation; absent the House action, Chadha would remain in the United States. Congress has *acted* and its action has altered Chadha's status.

The legislative character of the one-House veto in these cases is confirmed by the character of the Congressional action it supplants. Neither the House of Representatives nor the Senate contends that, absent the veto provision in § 244(c)(2), either of them, or both of them acting together, could effectively require the Attorney General to deport an alien once the Attorney General, in the exercise of legislatively delegated authority, had determined the alien should remain in the United States. Without the challenged provision in § 244(c)(2), this could have been achieved, if at all, only by legislation requiring deportation. Similarly, a veto by one House of Congress under § 244(c)(2) cannot be justified as an attempt at amending the standards set out in § 244(a)(1), or as a repeal of § 244 as applied to Chadha. Amendment and repeal of statutes, no less than enactment, must conform with Art. I.

The nature of the decision implemented by the one-House veto in this case further manifests its legislative character. After long experience with the clumsy, time consuming private bill procedure, Congress made a deliberate choice to delegate to the Executive Branch, and specifically to the Attorney General, the authority to allow deportable aliens to remain in this country in certain specified circumstances. It is not disputed that this choice to delegate authority is precisely the kind of decision that can be implemented only in accordance with the procedures set out in Art. I. Disagreement with the Attorney General's decision on Chadha's deportation—that is, Congress' decision to deport Chadha—no less than Congress' original choice to delegate to the Attorney General the authority to make that decision, involves determinations of policy that Congress can implement in only one way; bicameral passage followed by presentment to the President. Congress must abide by its delegation of authority until that delegation is legislatively altered or revoked.

Finally, we see that when the Framers intended to authorize either House of Congress to act alone and outside of its prescribed bicameral legislative role, they narrowly and precisely defined the procedure for such action. There are but four provisions in the Constitution, explicit and unambiguous, by which one House may act alone with the unreviewable force of law, not subject to the President's veto:

(a) The House of Representatives alone was given the power to initiate impeachments. Art. I, § 2, cl. 5;

(b) The Senate alone was given the power to conduct trials following impeachment on charges initiated by the House and to convict following trial. Art. I, § 3, cl. 6;

(c) The Senate alone was given final unreviewable power to approve or to disapprove presidential appointments. Art. II, § 2, cl. 2;

(d) The Senate alone was given unreviewable power to ratify treaties negotiated by the President. Art. II, § 2, cl. 2.

Clearly, when the Draftsmen sought to confer special powers on one House, independent of the other House, or of the President, they did so in explicit, unambiguous terms. These carefully defined exceptions from presentment and bicameralism underscore the difference between the legislative functions of Congress and other unilateral but important and binding one-House acts provided for in the Constitution. These exceptions are narrow, explicit, and separately justified; none of them authorize the action challenged here. On the contrary, they provide further support for the conclusion that Congressional authority is not to be implied and for the conclusion that the veto provided for in § 244(c)(2) is not authorized by the constitutional design of the powers of the Legislative Branch.

Since it is clear that the action by the House under § 244(c)(2) was not within any of the express constitutional exceptions authorizing one House to act alone, and equally clear that it was an exercise of legislative power, that action was subject to the standards prescribed in Article I.[22] The bicameral requirement, the Presentment Clauses, the President's veto, and Congress' power to override a veto were intended to erect enduring checks on each Branch and to protect the people from the improvident exercise of power by mandating certain prescribed steps. To preserve those checks, and maintain the separation of powers, the carefully defined limits on the power of each Branch must not be eroded. To accomplish what has been attempted by one House of Congress in this case requires action in conformity with the express procedures of the Constitution's prescription for legislative action: passage by a majority of both Houses and presentment to the President.

The veto authorized by § 244(c)(2) doubtless has been in many respects a convenient shortcut; the "sharing" with the Executive by Congress of its authority over aliens in this

---

[22] Justice POWELL's position is that the one-House veto in this case is a judicial act and therefore unconstitutional as beyond the authority vested in Congress by the Constitution. We agree that there is a sense in which one-House action pursuant to § 244(c)(2) has a judicial cast, since it purports to "review" Executive action. In this case, for example, the sponsor of the resolution vetoing the suspension of Chadha's deportation argued that Chadha "did not meet [the] statutory requirements" for suspension of deportation. To be sure, it is normally up to the courts to decide whether an agency has complied with its statutory mandate. But the attempted analogy between judicial action and the one-House veto is less than perfect. Federal courts do not enjoy a roving mandate to correct alleged excesses of administrative agencies; we are limited by Art. III to hearing cases and controversies and no justiciable case or controversy was presented by the Attorney General's decision to allow Chadha to remain in this country. We are aware of no decision, and Justice POWELL has cited none, where a federal court has reviewed a decision of the Attorney General suspending deportation of an alien pursuant to the standards set out in § 244(a)(1). This is not surprising, given that no party to such action has either the motivation or the right to appeal from it. As Justice WHITE correctly notes, "the courts have not been given the authority to review whether an alien should be given permanent status; review is limited to whether the Attorney General has properly applied the statutory standards for" denying a request for suspension of deportation. *Foti v. INS*, 375 U.S. 217 (1963), relied on by Justice POWELL, addressed only "whether a refusal by the Attorney General to grant a suspension of deportation is one of these 'final orders of deportation' of which direct review by Courts of Appeals is authorized under § 106(a) of the Act." *Id.*, at 221. Thus, Justice POWELL's statement that the one-House veto in this case is "clearly adjudicatory," simply is not supported by his accompanying assertion that the House has "assumed a function ordinarily entrusted to the federal courts." *Ibid.* We are satisfied that the one-House veto is legislative in purpose and effect and subject to the procedures set out in Art. I.

manner is, on its face, an appealing compromise. In purely practical terms, it is obviously easier for action to be taken by one House without submission to the President; but it is crystal clear from the records of the Convention, contemporaneous writings and debates, that the Framers ranked other values higher than efficiency. There is unmistakable expression of a determination that legislation by the national Congress be a step-by-step, deliberate and deliberative process.

The choices we discern as having been made in the Constitutional Convention impose burdens on governmental processes that often seem clumsy, inefficient, even unworkable, but those hard choices were consciously made by men who had lived under a form of government that permitted arbitrary governmental acts to go unchecked. With all the obvious flaws of delay, untidiness, and potential for abuse, we have not yet found a better way to preserve freedom than by making the exercise of power subject to the carefully crafted restraints spelled out in the Constitution.

V

We hold that the Congressional veto provision in § 244(c)(2) is severable from the Act and that it is unconstitutional. Accordingly, the judgment of the Court of Appeals is

Affirmed.

Justice POWELL, concurring in the judgment.

The Court's decision, based on the Presentment Clauses, Art. I, § 7, cls. 2 and 3, apparently will invalidate every use of the legislative veto. The breadth of this holding gives one pause. Congress has included the veto in literally hundreds of statutes, dating back to the 1930s. Congress clearly views this procedure as essential to controlling the delegation of power to administrative agencies. One reasonably may disagree with Congress' assessment of the veto's utility, but the respect due its judgment as a coordinate branch of Government cautions that our holding should be no more extensive than necessary to decide this case. In my view, the case may be decided on a narrower ground. When Congress finds that a particular person does not satisfy the statutory criteria for permanent residence in this country it has assumed a judicial function in violation of the principle of separation of powers. Accordingly, I concur only in the judgment.

I

A

The Framers perceived that "[t]he accumulation of all powers legislative, executive and judiciary in the same hands, whether of one, a few or many, and whether hereditary, self appointed, or elective, may justly be pronounced the very definition of tyranny." The

Federalist No. 47, p. 324 (J. Cooke ed. 1961) (J. Madison). Theirs was not a baseless fear. Under British rule, the colonies suffered the abuses of unchecked executive power that were attributed, at least popularly, to an hereditary monarchy. See Levi, Some Aspects of Separation of Powers, 76 Colum.L.Rev. 369, 374 (1976); The Federalist No. 48. During the Confederation, the States reacted by removing power from the executive and placing it in the hands of elected legislators. But many legislators proved to be little better than the Crown. "The supremacy of legislatures came to be recognized as the supremacy of faction and the tyranny of shifting majorities. The legislatures confiscated property, erected paper money schemes, [and] suspended the ordinary means of collecting debts." Levi, [76 Colum. L.Rev., at 374–375].

One abuse that was prevalent during the Confederation was the exercise of judicial power by the state legislatures. The Framers were well acquainted with the danger of subjecting the determination of the rights of one person to the "tyranny of shifting majorities." Jefferson observed that members of the General Assembly in his native Virginia had not been prevented from assuming judicial power, and "'[t]hey have accordingly in many instances decided rights which should have been left to judiciary controversy.'" The Federalist, supra, at 336 (emphasis in the original).

It was to prevent the recurrence of such abuses that the Framers vested the executive, legislative, and judicial powers in separate branches. Their concern that a legislature should not be able unilaterally to impose a substantial deprivation on one person was expressed not only in this general allocation of power, but also in more specific provisions, such as the Bill of Attainder Clause, Art. I, § 9, cl. 3. As the Court recognized in United States v. Brown, 381 U.S. 437, 442 (1965), "the Bill of Attainder Clause was intended not as a narrow, technical . . . prohibition, but rather as an implementation of the separation of powers, a general safeguard against legislative exercise of the judicial function, or more simply—trial by legislature." This Clause, and the separation of powers doctrine generally, reflect the Framers' concern that trial by a legislature lacks the safeguards necessary to prevent the abuse of power.

On its face, the House's action appears clearly adjudicatory. The House did not enact a general rule; rather it made its own determination that six specific persons did not comply with certain statutory criteria. It thus undertook the type of decision that traditionally has been left to other branches. Even if the House did not make a de novo determination, but simply reviewed the Immigration and Naturalization Service's findings, it still assumed a function ordinarily entrusted to the federal courts.

The impropriety of the House's assumption of this function is confirmed by the fact that its action raises the very danger the Framers sought to avoid—the exercise of unchecked power. In deciding whether Chadha deserves to be deported, Congress is not subject to any internal constraints that prevent it from arbitrarily depriving him of the right to remain in this country. Unlike the judiciary or an administrative agency, Congress is not bound by established substantive rules. Nor is it subject to the procedural safeguards, such as the right to counsel and a hearing before an impartial tribunal, that are present when a court or an agency adjudicates individual rights. The only effective constraint on Congress' power is political, but Congress is most accountable politically when it prescribes rules of general applicability. When it decides rights of specific persons, those rights are subject to "the tyranny of a shifting majority."

Chief Justice Marshall observed: "It is the peculiar province of the legislature to prescribe general rules for the government of society; the application of those rules would seem to be the duty of other departments." *Fletcher v. Peck*, 6 Cranch 87, 136, 3 L.Ed. 162 (1810). In my view, when Congress undertook to apply its rules to Chadha, it exceeded the scope of its constitutionally prescribed authority. I would not reach the broader question whether legislative vetoes are invalid under the Presentment Clauses.

Justice WHITE, dissenting.

Today the Court not only invalidates § 244(c)(2) of the Immigration and Nationality Act, but also sounds the death knell for nearly 200 other statutory provisions in which Congress has reserved a "legislative veto." For this reason, the Court's decision is of surpassing importance. And it is for this reason that the Court would have been well advised to decide the cases, if possible, on the narrower grounds of separation of powers, leaving for full consideration the constitutionality of other congressional review statutes operating on such varied matters as war powers and agency rulemaking, some of which concern the independent regulatory agencies.

The prominence of the legislative veto mechanism in our contemporary political system and its importance to Congress can hardly be overstated. It has become a central means by which Congress secures the accountability of executive and independent agencies. Without the legislative veto, Congress is faced with a Hobson's choice: either to refrain from delegating the necessary authority, leaving itself with a hopeless task of writing laws with the requisite specificity to cover endless special circumstances across the entire policy landscape, or in the alternative, to abdicate its law-making function to the Executive Branch and independent agencies.

I

The legislative veto developed initially in response to the problems of reorganizing the sprawling government structure created in response to the Depression. Over the years, the provision was used extensively. Presidents submitted 115 reorganization plans to Congress of which 23 were disapproved by Congress pursuant to legislative veto provisions.

Shortly after adoption of the Reorganization Act of 1939, 53 Stat. 561, Congress and the President applied the legislative veto procedure to resolve the delegation problem for national security and foreign affairs. World War II occasioned the need to transfer greater authority to the President in these areas. The legislative veto offered the means by which Congress could confer additional authority while preserving its own constitutional role. During World War II, Congress enacted over 30 statutes conferring powers on the Executive with legislative veto provisions. President Roosevelt accepted the veto as the necessary price for obtaining exceptional authority.

Over the quarter century following World War II, Presidents continued to accept legislative vetoes by one or both Houses as constitutional, while regularly denouncing provisions by which congressional Committees reviewed Executive activity. The legislative veto balanced delegations of statutory authority in new areas of governmental involvement: the space program, international agreements on nuclear energy, tariff arrangements, and adjustment of federal pay rates.

During the 1970's the legislative veto was important in resolving a series of major constitutional disputes between the President and Congress over claims of the President to broad impoundment, war, and national emergency powers. The key provision of the War Powers Resolution, 50 U.S.C. § 1544(c), authorizes the termination by concurrent resolution of the use of armed forces in hostilities. A similar measure resolved the problem posed by Presidential claims of inherent power to impound appropriations. Congressional Budget and Impoundment Control Act of 1974, 31 U.S.C. § 1403. These statutes were followed by others resolving similar problems.

In the energy field, the legislative veto served to balance broad delegations in legislation emerging from the energy crisis of the 1970's. In the educational field, it was found that fragmented and narrow grant programs "inevitably lead to Executive-Legislative confrontations" because they ineptly limited the Commissioner of Education's authority. S. Rep. No. 763 [93d Cong., 2d Sess.] 69 (1974). The response was to grant the Commissioner of Education rulemaking authority, subject to a legislative veto. In the trade regulation area, the veto preserved congressional authority over the Federal Trade Commission's broad mandate to make rules to prevent businesses from engaging in "unfair or deceptive acts or practices in commerce."

Even this brief review suffices to demonstrate that the legislative veto is more than "efficient, convenient, and useful." It is an important if not indispensable political invention that allows the President and Congress to resolve major constitutional and policy differences, assures the accountability of independent regulatory agencies, and preserves Congress' control over lawmaking. Perhaps there are other means of accommodation and accountability, but the increasing reliance of Congress upon the legislative veto suggests that the alternatives to which Congress must now turn are not entirely satisfactory.

The history of the legislative veto also makes clear that it has not been a sword with which Congress has struck out to aggrandize itself at the expense of the other branches—the concerns of Madison and Hamilton. Rather, the veto has been a means of defense, a reservation of ultimate authority necessary if Congress is to fulfill its designated role under Art. I as the Nation's lawmaker. While the President has often objected to particular legislative vetoes, generally those left in the hands of congressional Committees, the Executive has more often agreed to legislative review as the price for a broad delegation of authority. To be sure, the President may have preferred unrestricted power, but that could be precisely why Congress thought it essential to retain a check on the exercise of delegated authority.

II

For all these reasons, the apparent sweep of the Court's decision today is regrettable. The Court's Art. I analysis appears to invalidate all legislative vetoes irrespective of form or subject. Because the legislative veto is commonly found as a check upon rulemaking by administrative agencies and upon broad-based policy decisions of the Executive Branch, it is particularly unfortunate that the Court reaches its decision in a case involving the exercise of a veto over deportation decisions regarding particular individuals. Courts should always be wary of striking statutes as unconstitutional; to strike an entire class of statutes based on consideration of a somewhat atypical and more readily indictable exemplar of the class is irresponsible.

If the legislative veto were as plainly unconstitutional as the Court strives to suggest, its broad ruling today would be more comprehensible. But, the constitutionality of the legislative veto is anything but clear-cut. The issue divides scholars, courts, Attorneys General, and the two other branches of the National Government. If the veto devices so flagrantly disregarded the requirements of Art. I as the Court today suggests, I find it incomprehensible that Congress, whose Members are bound by oath to uphold the Constitution, would have placed these mechanisms in nearly 200 separate laws over a period of 50 years.

The Constitution does not directly authorize or prohibit the legislative veto. Thus, our task should be to determine whether the legislative veto is consistent with the purposes of Art. I and the principles of separation of powers which are reflected in that Article and throughout the Constitution. We should not find the lack of a specific constitutional authorization for the legislative veto surprising, and I would not infer disapproval of the mechanism from its absence. From the summer of 1787 to the present the Government of the United States has become an endeavor far beyond the contemplation of the Framers. Only within the last half century has the complexity and size of the Federal Government's responsibilities grown so greatly that the Congress must rely on the legislative veto as the most effective if not the only means to insure their role as the Nation's lawmakers. But the wisdom of the Framers was to anticipate that the Nation would grow and new problems of governance would require different solutions. Accordingly, our Federal Government was intentionally chartered with the flexibility to respond to contemporary needs without losing sight of fundamental democratic principles.

III

The Court maintains that the provisions of § 244(c)(2) are inconsistent with the requirement of bicameral approval, implicit in Art. I, § 1, and the requirement that all bills and resolutions that require the concurrence of both Houses be presented to the President, Art. I, § 7, cls. 2 and 3. I would not hesitate to strike an action of Congress in the form of a concurrent resolution which constituted an exercise of original lawmaking authority. I agree with the Court that the President's qualified veto power is a critical element in the distribution of powers under the Constitution, widely endorsed among the Framers, and intended to serve the President as a defense against legislative encroachment and to check the "passing of bad laws through haste, inadvertence, or design." The Federalist No. 73, [at 458] (A. Hamilton). The records of the Convention reveal that it is the first purpose which figured most prominently but I acknowledge the vitality of the second. *Id.*, at 443. I also agree that the bicameral approval required by Art. I, §§ 1, 7 "was of scarcely less concern to the Framers than was the Presidential veto," and that the need to divide and disperse legislative power figures significantly in our scheme of Government. . . .

It does not, however, answer the constitutional question before us. The power to exercise a legislative veto is not the power to write new law without bicameral approval or Presidential consideration. The veto must be authorized by statute and may only negative what an Executive department or independent agency has proposed. On its face, the legislative veto no more allows one House of Congress to make law than does the Presidential veto confer such power upon the President.

A

The terms of the Presentment Clauses suggest only that bills and their equivalent are subject to the requirements of bicameral passage and presentment to the President.

Although the Clause does not specify the actions for which the concurrence of both Houses is "necessary," the proceedings at the Philadelphia Convention suggest its purpose was to prevent Congress from circumventing the presentation requirement in the making of new legislation. James Madison observed that if the President's veto was confined to bills, it could be evaded by calling a proposed law a "resolution" or "vote" rather than a "bill." Accordingly, he proposed that "or resolve" should be added after "bill" in what is now clause 2 of § 7. 2 M. Farrand, The Records of the Federal Convention of 1787 [at 301–302]. After a short discussion on the subject, the amendment was rejected. On the following day, however, Randolph renewed the proposal in the substantial form as it now appears, and the motion passed. *Id.*, at 304–305; The chosen language, Madison's comment, and the brevity of the Convention's consideration, all suggest a modest role was intended for the Clause and no broad restraint on congressional authority was contemplated. See Stewart, Constitutionality of the Legislative Veto, 13 Harv.J.Legis. 593, 609–611 (1976). This reading is consistent with the historical background of the Presentation Clause itself which reveals only that the Framers were concerned with limiting the methods for enacting new legislation. The Framers were aware of the experience in Pennsylvania where the legislature had evaded the requirements attached to the passing of legislation by the use of "resolves," and the criticisms directed at this practice by the Council of Censors. There is no record that the Convention contemplated, let alone intended, that these Art. I requirements would someday be invoked to restrain the scope of congressional authority pursuant to duly enacted law.

When the Convention did turn its attention to the scope of Congress' lawmaking power, the Framers were expansive. The Necessary and Proper Clause, Art. I, § 8, cl. 18, vests Congress with the power "to make all Laws which shall be necessary and proper for carrying into Execution the foregoing Powers [the enumerated powers of § 8], and all other Powers vested by this Constitution in the Government of the United States, or in any Department or Officer thereof." It is longsettled that Congress may "exercise its best judgment in the selection of measures, to carry into execution the constitutional powers of the government," and "avail itself of experience, to exercise its reason, and to accommodate its legislation to circumstances." *McCulloch v. Maryland*, 4 Wheat. 316, 415–416, 420 (1819).

B

The Court heeded this counsel in approving the modern administrative state. The Court's holding today that all legislative-type action must be enacted through the lawmaking process ignores that legislative authority is routinely delegated to the Executive Branch, to the independent regulatory agencies, and to private individuals and groups.

"The rise of administrative bodies probably has been the most significant legal trend of the last century. . . . They have become a veritable fourth branch of the Government, which has deranged our three-branch legal theories. . . . " *Federal Trade Commission v. Ruberoid Co.*, 343 U.S. 470, 487 (1952) (Jackson, J. dissenting).

This Court's decisions sanctioning such delegations make clear that Article I does not require all action with the effect of legislation to be passed as a law.

The wisdom and the constitutionality of these broad delegations are matters that still have not been put to rest. But for present purposes, these cases establish that by virtue of congressional delegation, legislative power can be exercised by independent agencies and Executive departments without the passage of new legislation. For some time, the sheer amount of law—the substantive rules that regulate private conduct and direct the operation of government—made by the agencies has far outnumbered the lawmaking engaged in by Congress through the traditional process. There is no question but that agency rulemaking is lawmaking in any functional or realistic sense of the term.

If Congress may delegate lawmaking power to independent and executive agencies, it is most difficult to understand Art. I as prohibiting Congress from also reserving a check on legislative power for itself. Absent the veto, the agencies receiving delegations of legislative or quasi-legislative power may issue regulations having the force of law without bicameral approval and without the President's signature. It is thus not apparent why the reservation of a veto over the exercise of that legislative power must be subject to a more exacting test. In both cases, it is enough that the initial statutory authorizations comply with the Art. I requirements.

Nor are there strict limits on the agents that may receive such delegations of Legislative authority so that it might be said that the legislature can delegate authority to others but not to itself. While most authority to issue rules and regulations is given to the Executive Branch and the independent regulatory agencies, statutory delegations to private persons have also passed this Court's scrutiny. The Court's decision today suggests that Congress may place a "veto" power over suspensions of deportation in private hands or in the hands of an independent agency, but is forbidden to reserve such authority for itself. Perhaps this odd result could be justified on other constitutional grounds, such as the separation of powers, but certainly it cannot be defended as consistent with the Court's view of the Art. I presentment and bicameralism commands.[20]

The Court's opinion in the present case comes closest to facing the reality of administrative lawmaking in considering the contention that the Attorney General's action in suspending deportation under § 244 is itself a legislative act. The Court posits that the Attorney General is acting in an Art. II enforcement capacity under § 244. This characterization is at odds with *Mahler v. Eby*, 264 U.S. 32 (1924), where the power conferred on the Executive to deport aliens was considered a delegation of legislative power. The Court suggests, however, that the Attorney General acts in an Art. II capacity because "[t]he courts when a case or controversy arises, can always 'ascertain whether the will of Congress has been obeyed,'" *Yakus v. United States*, 321 U.S. 414, 425 (1944), and can enforce adherence to statutory standards." This assumption is simply wrong. On the other hand the Court's reasoning does persuasively explain why a resolution of disapproval under § 244(c)(2) need not again be subject to the bicameral process. Because it serves

only to check the Attorney General's exercise of the suspension authority granted by § 244, the disapproval resolution—unlike the Attorney General's action—"cannot reach beyond the limits of the statute that created it—a statute duly enacted pursuant to Art. I."

If the effective functioning of a complex modern government requires the delegation of vast authority which, by virtue of its breadth, is legislative or "quasi-legislative" in character, I cannot accept that Art. I—which is, after all, the source of the nondelegation doctrine—should forbid Congress to qualify that grant with a legislative veto.

The Court also takes no account of perhaps the most relevant consideration: However resolutions of disapproval under § 244(c)(2) are formally characterized, in reality, a departure from the status quo occurs only upon the concurrence of opinion among the House, Senate, and President. Reservations of legislative authority to be exercised by Congress should be upheld if the exercise of such reserved authority is consistent with the distribution of and limits upon legislative power that Art. I provides.

The central concern of the presentment and bicameralism requirements of Art. I is that when a departure from the legal status quo is undertaken, it is done with the approval of the President and both Houses of Congress—or, in the event of a Presidential veto, a two-thirds majority in both Houses. This interest is fully satisfied by the operation of § 244(c)(2). The President's approval is found in the Attorney General's action in recommending to Congress that the deportation order for a given alien be suspended. The House and the Senate indicate their approval of the Executive's action by not passing a resolution of disapproval within the statutory period. Thus, a change in the legal status quo—the deportability of the alien—is consummated only with the approval of each of the three relevant actors. The disagreement of any one of the three maintains the alien's pre-existing status: the Executive may choose not to recommend suspension; the House and Senate may each veto the recommendation. The effect on the rights and obligations of the affected individuals and upon the legislative system is precisely the same as if a private bill were introduced but failed to receive the necessary approval.

Section 244(c)(2) fully effectuates the purposes of the bicameralism and presentation requirements. I now briefly consider possible objections to the analysis.

First, it may be asserted that Chadha's status before legislative disapproval is one of nondeportation and that the exercise of the veto, unlike the failure of a private bill, works a

---

[20] As the Court acknowledges, the "provisions of Art. I are integral parts of the constitutional design for the separation of powers." Ante, at 2781. But these separation of power concerns are that legislative power be exercised by Congress, executive power by the President, and judicial power by the Courts. A scheme which allows delegation of legislative power to the President and the departments under his control, but forbids a check on its exercise by Congress itself obviously denigrates the separation of power concerns underlying Article I. To be sure, the doctrine of separation of powers is also concerned with checking each branch's exercise of its characteristic authority. Section 244(c)(2) is fully consistent with the need for checks upon Congressional authority, infra, at 2783–2784, and the legislative veto mechanism, more generally is an important check upon Executive authority, supra, at 2793–2796.

change in the status quo. This position plainly ignores the statutory language. At no place in § 244 has Congress delegated to the Attorney General any final power to determine which aliens shall be allowed to remain in the United States. Congress has retained the ultimate power to pass on such changes in deportable status. By its own terms, § 244(a) states that whatever power the Attorney General has been delegated to suspend deportation and adjust status is to be exercisable only "[a]s hereinafter prescribed in this section." Subsection (c) is part of that section. A grant of "suspension" does not cancel the alien's deportation or adjust the alien's status to that of a permanent resident alien. A suspension order is merely a "deferment of deportation," *McGrath v. Kristensen*, 340 U.S. 162, 168 (1950), which can mature into a cancellation of deportation and adjustment of status only upon the approval of Congress—by way of silence—under § 244(c)(2). Only then does the statute authorize the Attorney General to "cancel deportation proceedings" § 244(c)(2), and "record the alien's lawful admission for permanent residence. . . . " § 244(d). The Immigration and Naturalization Service's action, on behalf of the Attorney General, "cannot become effective without ratification by Congress. . . ." Until that ratification occurs, the executive's action is simply a recommendation that Congress finalize the suspension—in itself, it works no legal change.

Second, it may be said that this approach leads to the incongruity that the two-House veto is more suspect than its one-House brother. Although the idea may be initially counterintuitive, on close analysis, it is not at all unusual that the one-House veto is of more certain constitutionality than the two-House version. If the Attorney General's action is a proposal for legislation, then the disapproval of but a single House is all that is required to prevent its passage. Because approval is indicated by the failure to veto, the one-House veto satisfies the requirement of bicameral approval. The two-House version may present a different question. The concept that "neither branch of Congress, when acting separately, can lawfully exercise more power than is conferred by the Constitution on the whole body . . . is fully observed."

Third, it may be objected that Congress cannot indicate its approval of legislative change by inaction. In the Court of Appeals' view, inaction by Congress "could equally imply endorsement, acquiescence, passivity, indecision or indifference. . . ." This objection appears more properly directed at the wisdom of the legislative veto than its constitutionality. The Constitution does not and cannot guarantee that legislators will carefully scrutinize legislation and deliberate before acting. In a democracy it is the electorate that holds the legislators accountable for the wisdom of their choices. It is hard to maintain that a private bill receives any greater individualized scrutiny than a resolution of disapproval under § 244(c)(2). Certainly the legislative veto is no more susceptible to this attack than the Court's increasingly common practice of according weight to the failure of Congress to disturb an Executive or independent agency's action.

IV

The Court of Appeals struck § 244(c)(2) as violative of the constitutional principle of separation of powers. It is true that the purpose of separating the authority of Government is to prevent unnecessary and dangerous concentration of power in one branch. For that reason, the Framers saw fit to divide and balance the powers of Government so that each branch would be checked by the others. Virtually every part of our constitutional system bears the mark of this judgment.

But the history of the separation-of-powers doctrine is also a history of accommodation and practicality. Apprehensions of an overly powerful branch have not led to undue prophylactic measures that handicap the effective working of the National Government as a whole. The Constitution does not contemplate total separation of the three branches of Government. *Buckley v. Valeo*, 424 U.S. 1, 121 (1976).

Our decisions reflect this judgment. As already noted, the Court, recognizing that modern government must address a formidable agenda of complex policy issues, countenanced the delegation of extensive legislative authority to Executive and independent agencies. *J. W. Hampton & Co. v. United States*, 276 U.S. 394, 406 (1928). The separation-of-powers doctrine has heretofore led to the invalidation of Government action only when the challenged action violated some express provision in the Constitution. Because we must have a workable efficient government, this is as it should be.

This is the teaching of *Nixon v. Administrator of General Services*, 433 U.S. 425 (1977), which, in rejecting a separation-of-powers objection to a law requiring that the Administrator take custody of certain Presidential papers, set forth a framework for evaluating such claims:

"[I]n determining whether the Act disrupts the proper balance between the coordinate branches, the proper inquiry focuses on the extent to which it prevents the Executive Branch from accomplishing its constitutionally assigned functions. *United States v. Nixon*, 418 U.S. [683] at 711–712. Only where the potential for disruption is present must we then determine whether that impact is justified by an overriding need to promote objectives within the constitutional authority of Congress."

Id. at 443.

Section 244(c)(2) survives this test. The legislative veto provision does not "prevent the Executive Branch from accomplishing its constitutionally assigned functions." First, it is clear that the Executive Branch has no "constitutionally assigned" function of suspending the deportation of aliens. "'[O]ver no conceivable subject is the legislative power of Congress more complete than it is over' the admission of aliens." Nor can it be said that the inherent function of the Executive Branch in executing the law is involved. The *Steel Seizure Case* resolved that the Art. II mandate for the President to execute the law is a directive to enforce the law which Congress has written. *Youngstown Sheet & Tube Co. v. Sawyer*, 343 U.S. 579 (1952). "The duty of the President to see that the laws be executed is a duty that does not go beyond the laws or require him to achieve more than Congress sees fit to leave within his power." *Myers v. United States*, 272 U.S., at 177 (Holmes, J., dissenting); *Id.*, at 247 (Brandeis, J., dissenting). Here, § 244 grants the executive only a qualified suspension authority and it is only that authority which the President is constitutionally authorized to execute.

Moreover, the Court believes that the legislative veto we consider today is best characterized as an exercise of legislative or quasi-legislative authority. Under this characterization, the practice does not, even on the surface, constitute an infringement of executive or judicial prerogative. The Attorney General's suspension of deportation is equivalent to a proposal for legislation. The nature of the Attorney General's role as recommendatory is not altered because § 244 provides for congressional action through disapproval rather than by ratification. In comparison to private bills, which must be initiated in the Congress and which allow a Presidential veto to be overridden by a two-thirds majority in both Houses of Congress, § 244 augments rather than reduces the Executive Branch's authority. So under-

stood, congressional review does not undermine, as the Court of Appeals thought, the "weight and dignity" that attends the decisions of the Executive Branch.

Nor does § 244 infringe on the judicial power, as JUSTICE POWELL would hold. Section 244 makes clear that Congress has reserved its own judgment as part of the statutory process. Congressional action does not substitute for judicial review of the Attorney General's decisions. The Act provides for judicial review of the refusal of the Attorney General to suspend a deportation and to transmit a recommendation to Congress. But the courts have not been given the authority to review whether an alien should be given permanent status; review is limited to whether the Attorney General has properly applied the statutory standards for essentially denying the alien a recommendation that his deportable status be changed by the Congress. Moreover, there is no constitutional obligation to provide any judicial review whatever for a failure to suspend deportation.

I do not suggest that all legislative vetoes are necessarily consistent with separation-of-powers principles. A legislative check on an inherently executive function, for example, that of initiating prosecutions, poses an entirely different question. But the legislative veto device here—and in many other settings—is far from an instance of legislative tyranny over the Executive. It is a necessary check on the unavoidably expanding power of the agencies, both Executive and independent, as they engage in exercising authority delegated by Congress.

V

I regret that I am in disagreement with my colleagues on the fundamental questions that these cases present. But even more I regret the destructive scope of the Court's holding. It reflects a profoundly different conception of the Constitution than that held by the courts which sanctioned the modern administrative state. Today's decision strikes down in one fell swoop provisions in more laws enacted by Congress than the Court has cumulatively invalidated in its history. I must dissent.

In *Chadha*, the majority's decision that article I prohibits Congress from reserving a check on the legislative power for itself is built on its view that "[t]he very structure of the Articles delegating and separating powers under Arts. I, II, and III exemplifies the concept of separation of powers."[91] The Court thus reads the presentment clauses, Art. I, § 7, cls. 2 and 3, and the bicameral requirement of Art. I, § 1, and § 7, cl. 2, as necessary to provide a check on any legislative action taken which can be considered "lawmaking" by requiring the formal steps of engaging the President and each House

---

[91] 462 U.S. at 946.

in the process of making law. Those concerns which the majority attribute to the Framers about providing adequate checks on the legislature by dispersing and dividing authority become more complex seen against the background of the modern administrative state. Avoiding direct confrontation with the question of delegation, the Court has begun to focus on the alternative ways Congress has sought to control the decision maker to which the discretion is accorded. Commentators had disagreed about whether one such vehicle, the legislative veto, is a valid means of curbing administrative discretion and securing accountability of the executive and independent agencies.[92]

Dissenting from the Court's conclusion that the formal lawmaking provisions are required, Justice White argued that its rejection of the legislative veto mechanism (at least a one-house veto procedure) removes a practical, convenient and useful means of assuring accountability and preserving Congress' institutional role. Justice White based his conclusion in substantial part on the "increasing reliance of Congress upon the legislative veto" and on the fact that the President and Congress have themselves been able to resolve constitutional and policy differences by means of it, thereby avoiding confrontations.[93]

Since, as Justice White observes, the Constitution does not directly authorize or prohibit the legislative veto, how should the issue be resolved? The difference between the majority and Justice White's dissent lies in competing views about whether the action Congress reserves in its initial lawmaking must be characterized as "law making." The majority concludes that section 244(a)(c)(2) is "essentially legislative in purpose and effect" because it alters legal rights or the status of a person whose deportation otherwise would be canceled under the law. Thus the section must comply with the formal law making requirements set forth in Article I of the Constitution.

Justice White responds that the legislative step is merely a step in the first "law making" action. Moreover, any change in the legal status quo is undertaken only with the approval of the President and both Houses, and no change in the alien's pre-existing status occurs if any one of the three disagrees. Under this analysis, the Attorney General's action is in the form of a proposal for change and the one-House disapproval is all that is required to prevent its passage.[94] The fact that the formal requirements of lawmaking found in the bicameral and presentment provisions of Article I are not followed is not determinative under this functional approach, which emphasizes that the effect on the constitutional distribution of power between the legislature and the executive is negligible—or even well served by the alternative process. From a functional standpoint because there is no "undue interference" with the performance of constitutionally assigned functions of another branch, nor alteration of the balance of authority among the branches, the Court should defer to the legislature's judgment about the means to effectuate a legitimate end.

---

[92] In his concurrence Justice White provides citations to a host of writers who had written favorably and unfavorably about the legislative veto. *See* Chadha, 462 U.S. at 918–19 n.12.

[93] 462 U.S. at 972–74.

[94] Of course, under this approach a two-house veto presents a more difficult question. *See* 462 U.S. at 997.

PAH: Although Justice White's explanation as to why the challenged legislative provision meets the formal law-making requirements set forth by the majority seems tortured, the majority's analysis that presentment and bicameralism requirements flow from such provisions seems unduly rigid and flies in the face of longstanding practice.[95] Legislative vetoes

---

[95] *See* 462 U.S. at 960 (Powell, J. concurring); *id.* at 968–73 (White, J. dissenting). Recall the discussion of acquiescence and the gloss of power of the *Steel Seizure Case*, *supra.*

have been utilized by Congress for the last 25 years and are often approved by the executive as a price of obtaining far-reaching, policy-making discretion. However, given the sense of lack of even-handedness that lurks in this case, it is not surprising that the majority reached the *result* it did; the potential for abuse of such actions, particularly one-house provisions such as was present in this case, was not lost on the majority nor on Justice Powell, whose analysis focuses on the functionally "judicial" nature of the action affecting Mr. Chadha. The majority's reasoning that the legislative veto should fail because of its avoidance of a constitutionally assigned check on congressional power designed by the Framers required a broad sweep, implicating legislative vetoes irrespective of form or subject. As an attempt to reinstate the original understanding of checks and balances contemplated by the Framers, the majority's analysis may be questionable given the complexities of government and the reality of a post-nondelegation world.[96] Does the Court's rationale, resting on concern about the danger of accumulation of power and unchecked encroachment on functions of the executive posed by the legislative veto comport with reality?

DEL: The *Chadha* ruling represents a particularly profound reiteration of the judiciary's power "to say what the law is." It indicates that even when the political branches reach an accommodation that responds to imperatives of practicality, the Court may prioritize constitutional technicality over constitutional glossing. Notwithstanding a jointly framed response by the executive and legislative branches to modern realities of governance that strain the consent of the governed, the Court has been unrelenting in its position. As subsequent case law has demonstrated, the legislative veto has been repudiated even when used against independent regulatory agencies and approval of both houses of Congress was required.[97] With no reference to (or perhaps an interest in) an overarching theory of separation of powers review, analysis veered sharply toward formalism and away from functionalism.

DER: *Chadha* may have been the Court's attempt to curb what was perceived as excessive congressional delegation of authority to agencies, commissions, and departments. The legislative veto facilitated broader delegations because skeptical legislators could rely on their ability to reverse particular agency decisions they disagreed with. Without the legislative veto many existing delegations might not have been able to attract enough votes in Congress. By invalidating legislative vetoes, then, the Court may have made it harder in practice for Congress to pass statutes delegating its power to others.

---

[96] Abner S. Greene, *Checks and Balances in an Era of Presidential Lawmaking*, 61 U. Chi. L. Rev. 123, 126 (1994). Though not upholding all legislative vetoes, Abner Greene proposes to validate certain legislative efforts to regulate presidential control of agency officials or reject presidential action by a majority vote of both Houses because they would restore a proper balance of power that is both consonant with the original view of checks and balances and appropriately takes account of contemporary underenforcement of nondelegation theory. *Id.* at 128 & n.128.

[97] Process Gas Consumers Group v. Consumers Energy Council of America, 463 U.S. 1216 (1983).

The determined shift away from a functional approach and deference to congressional judgment about institutional arrangements and about deploying its authority reflected in *Chadha* was subsequently tested in the Court's treatment of the question of the authority to remove and limit executive control of officers. The Court has considered several cases challenging the statutory allocation of authority over administrative officers. In later cases considerations of efficiency and workable government overcame the formalist determination to return the system of checks and balances to a model resembling what the Framers intended.[98]

In *Bowsher v. Synar*,[99] the Court, following *Chadha*, utilized a formalist approach to strike parts of the Gramm-Rudman-Hollings Deficit Reduction Act.[100] Under the Act the Comptroller General was given the power to resolve conflicts between the Office of Management and Budget, and the Congressional Budget Office regarding budget cuts. The Act also authorized the Comptroller General to make necessary cuts in the budget if these agencies could not balance the budget. Concluding that the Act delegated to the officer "executive" power, then-Chief Justice Burger reasoned that Congress' reservation of the power to remove the Comptroller General by joint resolution demonstrated that it "retained control over the execution of the Act and therefore unconstitutionally intruded in the executive function."[101]

Concluding that the statute posed no real danger of accretion of congressional power, Justice White, again dissenting, charged that the majority's position "that, outside of the impeachment process, any 'direct' congressional role in the removal of officers charged with the execution of law" was unconstitutional is rigid and contrary to separation of powers.[102] In his view, the decision as to whether to vest executive powers in an officer removable by joint resolution or of permitting an unelected official to revise the congressional budget is for the Congress and the President to work out through the legislative process. "The role of this Court should be limited to determining whether the Act so alters the balance of authority among the branches of government as to pose a genuine threat to the basic division between the lawmaking power and the power to execute the law."[103] In subsequent cases, the Court appears to have moved away from the formalist model. In *Morrison v. Olson*, the Court upheld the constitutionality of provisions of the Ethics in Government Act, permitting judicial appointment of special prosecutors to investigate and prosecute allegations of criminal wrongdoing in the executive branch and insulating the independent counsel from discharge by the executive without cause.

---

[98] Stephen Carter eschews the terms functionalism and formalism and employs "evolutionary" and "de-evolutionary" to describe the competing strands of jurisprudence or traditions the Supreme Court has utilized in resolving separation of powers controversies. *See, e.g.*, Stephen Carter, *From Sick Chicken to Synar: The Evolution and Subsequent De-Evolution of the Separation of Powers*, 1987 B.Y.U. L. REV. 719 (1987).

[99] 478 U.S. 714 (1986).

[100] Balanced Budget and Emergency Deficit Control Act of 1985, Pub. L. 99–177, 99 Stat. 1038.1.

[101] In contrast, in Commodity Futures Trading Commission v. Schor, 478 U.S. 833 (1986), decided the same day as *Bowsher*, Justice O'Connor, writing for the majority, used a functional analysis to determine whether the Commodity Futures Trading Commission had jurisdiction to decide common-law counterclaims arising out of state law claims. Justice O'Connor decided that, on balance, the congressional delegation of power to the agency to adjudicate such claims did not impermissibly intrude on the judicial province. *Id.* at 851–52.

[102] 478 U.S. at 776.

[103] *Id.* Justice Stevens concurred in the judgment of the majority, reasoning that the authority delegated to the Comptroller General to cut the budget was legislative and therefore required Article I presentment and bicameralism procedures. *Id.* at 757–58.

Morrison v. Olson
487 U.S. 654 (1988)

CHIEF JUSTICE REHNQUIST delivered the opinion of the Court.

This case presents us with a challenge to the independent counsel provisions of the Ethics in Government Act of 1978, 28 U.S.C. §§ 49, 591 *et seq.* (1982 ed., Supp. V). We hold today that these provisions of the Act do not violate the Appointments Clause of the Constitution, Art. II, § 2, cl. 2, or the limitations of Article III, nor do they impermissibly interfere with the President's authority under Article II in violation of the constitutional principle of separation of powers.

I

Briefly stated, Title VI of the Ethics in Government Act allows for the appointment of an "independent counsel" to investigate and, if appropriate, prosecute certain high-ranking Government officials for violations of federal criminal laws. The Act requires the Attorney General, upon receipt of information that he determines is "sufficient to constitute grounds to investigate whether any person [covered by the Act] may have violated any Federal criminal law," to conduct a preliminary investigation of the matter. When the Attorney General has completed this investigation, or 90 days has elapsed, he is required to report to a special court (the Special Division) created by the Act "for the purpose of appointing independent counsels."[3] If the Attorney General determines that "there are no reasonable grounds to believe that further investigation is warranted," then he must notify the Special Division of this result. In such a case, "the division of the court shall have no power to appoint an independent counsel." § 592(b)(1). If, however, the Attorney General has determined that there are "reasonable grounds to believe that further investigation or prosecution is warranted," then he "shall apply to the division of the court for the appointment of an independent counsel." The Attorney General's application to the court "shall contain sufficient information to assist the [court] in selecting an independent counsel and in defining that independent counsel's prosecutorial jurisdiction." § 592(d). Upon receiving this application, the Special Division "shall appoint an appropriate independent counsel and shall define that independent counsel's prosecutorial jurisdiction." § 593(b).

With respect to all matters within the independent counsel's jurisdiction, the Act grants the counsel "full power and independent authority to exercise all investigative and prosecutorial functions and powers of the Department of Justice, the Attorney General, and any other officer or employee of the Department of Justice." § 594(a). The functions of the independent counsel include conducting grand jury proceedings and other investigations, participating in civil and criminal court proceedings and litigation, and appealing any decision in any case in which the counsel participates in an official capacity. §§ 594(a)(1)–(3). Under § 594(a)(9), the counsel's powers include "initiating and conducting prosecutions in any court of competent jurisdiction, framing and signing indictments, filing information, and handling all aspects of any case, in the name of the United States." The counsel may appoint employees, § 594(c), may request and obtain assistance from the Department of Justice, § 594(d), and may accept referral of matters from the Attorney General if the matter falls within the counsel's jurisdiction as defined by the Special Division, § 594(e). An independent counsel has "full authority to dismiss matters within [his or her] prosecutorial jurisdiction without conducting an investigation or at any subsequent time before prosecution, if to do so would be consistent" with Department of Justice policy. § 594(g).

Two statutory provisions govern the length of an independent counsel's tenure in office. The first defines the procedure for removing an independent counsel. Section 596(a)(1) provides:

> "An independent counsel appointed under this chapter may be removed from office, other than by impeachment and conviction, only by the personal action of the Attorney General and only for good cause, physical disability, mental incapacity, or any other condition that substantially impairs the performance of such independent counsel's duties."

If an independent counsel is removed pursuant to this section, the Attorney General is required to submit a report to both the Special Division and the Judiciary Committees of the Senate and the House "specifying the facts

---

[3] The Special Division is a division of the United States Court of Appeals for the District of Columbia Circuit. 28 U.S.C. § 49 (1982 ed., Supp. V). The court consists of three circuit court judges or justices appointed by the Chief Justice of the United States. One of the judges must be a judge of the United States Court of Appeals for the District of Columbia Circuit, and no two of the judges may be named to the Special Division from a particular court. The judges are appointed for 2-year terms, with any vacancy being filled only for the remainder of the 2-year period. *Ibid.*

found and the ultimate grounds for such removal." § 596(a)(2). Under the current version of the Act, an independent counsel can obtain judicial review of the Attorney General's action by filing a civil action in the United States District Court for the District of Columbia. Members of the Special Division "may not hear or determine any such civil action or any appeal of a decision in any such civil action." The reviewing court is authorized to grant reinstatement or "other appropriate relief." § 596(a)(3).

The other provision governing the tenure of the independent counsel defines the procedures for "terminating" the counsel's office. Under § 596(b)(1), the office of an independent counsel terminates when he or she notifies the Attorney General that he or she has completed or substantially completed any investigations or prosecutions undertaken pursuant to the Act. In addition, the Special Division, acting either on its own or on the suggestion of the Attorney General, may terminate the office of an independent counsel at any time if it finds that "the investigation of all matters within the prosecutorial jurisdiction of such independent counsel . . . have been completed or so substantially completed that it would be appropriate for the Department of Justice to complete such investigations and prosecutions." § 596(b)(2).

Finally, the Act provides for congressional oversight of the activities of independent counsel. An independent counsel may from time to time send Congress statements or reports on his or her activities. § 595(a)(2). The "appropriate committees of the Congress" are given oversight jurisdiction in regard to the official conduct of an independent counsel, and the counsel is required by the Act to cooperate with Congress in the exercise of this jurisdiction. § 595(a)(1). The counsel is required to inform the House of Representatives of "substantial and credible information which [the counsel] receives . . . that may constitute grounds for an impeachment." § 595(c). In addition, the Act gives certain congressional committee members the power to "request in writing that the Attorney General apply for the appointment of an independent counsel." § 592(g)(1). The Attorney General is required to respond to this request within a specified time but is not required to accede to the request. § 592(g)(2).

The proceedings in this case provide an example of how the Act works in practice. In 1982, two Subcommittees of the House of Representatives issued subpoenas directing the Environmental Protection Agency (EPA) to produce certain documents relating to the efforts of the EPA and the Land and Natural Resources Division of the Justice Department to enforce the "Superfund Law." At that time, appellee Olson was the Assistant Attorney General for the Office of Legal Counsel (OLC), appellee Schmults was Deputy Attorney General,

and appellee Dinkins was the Assistant Attorney General for the Land and Natural Resources Division. Acting on the advice of the Justice Department, the President ordered the Administrator of EPA to invoke executive privilege to withhold certain of the documents on the ground that they contained "enforcement sensitive information." The Administrator obeyed this order and withheld the documents. In response, the House voted to hold the Administrator in contempt, after which the Administrator and the United States together filed a lawsuit against the House. The conflict abated in March 1983, when the administration agreed to give the House Subcommittees limited access to the documents.

The following year, the House Judiciary Committee began an investigation into the Justice Department's role in the controversy over the EPA documents. During this investigation, appellee Olson testified before a House Subcommittee. Both before and after that testimony, the Department complied with several Committee requests to produce certain documents. Other documents were at first withheld, although these documents were eventually disclosed by the Department after the Committee learned of their existence. In 1985, the majority members of the Judiciary Committee published a lengthy report on the Committee's investigation. The report not only criticized various officials in the Department of Justice for their role in the EPA executive privilege dispute, but it also suggested that appellee Olson had given false and misleading testimony to the Subcommittee on March 10, 1983, and that appellees Schmults and Dinkins had wrongfully withheld certain documents from the Committee, thus obstructing the Committee's investigation. The Chairman of the Judiciary Committee forwarded a copy of the report to the Attorney General with a request, pursuant to 28 U.S.C. § 592(c), that he seek the appointment of an independent counsel to investigate the allegations. . . .

The Attorney General chose to apply to the Special Division for the appointment of an independent counsel solely with respect to appellee Olson. The Attorney General accordingly requested appointment of an independent counsel to investigate whether Olson's March 10, 1983, testimony "regarding the completeness of [OLC's] response to the Judiciary Committee's request for OLC documents, and regarding his knowledge of EPA's willingness to turn over certain disputed documents to Congress, violated 18 U.S.C. § 1505, § 1001, or any other provision of federal criminal law." Attorney General Report, at 2–3. The Attorney General also requested that the independent counsel have authority to investigate "any other matter related to that allegation."

On April 23, 1986, the Special Division appointed James C. McKay as independent counsel to investigate "whether the testimony of . . . Olson and his revision of such testimony on March 10, 1983, violated either 18 U.S.C. § 1505 or § 1001, or any other provision of federal law." McKay later resigned as independent counsel, and on May 29, 1986, the Division appointed appellant Morrison as his replacement, with the same jurisdiction.

In January 1987, appellant asked the Attorney General pursuant to § 594(e) to refer to her as "related matters" the Committee's allegations against appellees Schmults and Dinkins. The Attorney General refused to refer the matters, concluding that his decision not to request the appointment of an independent counsel in regard to those matters was final under § 592(b)(1). Appellant then asked the Special Division to order that the matters be referred to her under § 594(e). On April 2, 1987, the Division ruled that the Attorney General's decision not to seek appointment of an independent counsel with respect to Schmults and Dinkins was final and unreviewable under § 592(b)(1), and that therefore the court had no authority to make the requested referral. *In re Olson*, 260 U.S. App. D.C. 168, 818 F.2d 34. The court ruled, however, that its original grant of jurisdiction to appellant was broad enough to permit inquiry into whether Olson may have conspired with others, including Schmults and Dinkins, to obstruct the Committee's investigation.

Following this ruling, in May and June 1987, appellant caused a grand jury to issue and serve subpoenas *ad testificandum* and *duces tecum* on appellees. All three appellees moved to quash the subpoenas, claiming, among other things, that the independent counsel provisions of the Act were unconstitutional and that appellant accordingly had no authority to proceed. On July 20, 1987, the District Court upheld the constitutionality of the Act and denied the motions to quash. The court subsequently ordered that appellees be held in contempt . . . for continuing to refuse to comply with the subpoenas. The Court stayed the effect of its contempt orders pending expedited appeal.

A divided Court of Appeals reversed. *In re Sealed Case*, 267 U.S. App. D.C. 178, 838 F.2d 476 (1988). The majority ruled first that an independent counsel is not an "inferior Officer" of the United States for purposes of the Appointments Clause. Accordingly, the court found the Act invalid because it does not provide for the independent counsel to be nominated by the President and confirmed by the Senate, as the Clause requires for "principal" officers. The court then went on to consider several alternative grounds for its conclusion that the statute was unconstitutional. In the majority's view, the Act also violates the Appoint-

ments Clause insofar as it empowers a court of law to appoint an "inferior" officer who performs core executive functions; the Act's delegation of various powers to the Special Division violates the limitations of Article III; the Act's restrictions on the Attorney General's power to remove an independent counsel violate the separation of powers; and finally, the Act interferes with the Executive Branch's prerogative to "take care that the Laws be faithfully executed," Art. II, § 3. The dissenting judge was of the view that the Act was constitutional. We now reverse.

III

The Appointments Clause of Article II reads as follows:

> "[The President] shall nominate, and by and with the Advice and Consent of the Senate, shall appoint Ambassadors, other public Ministers and Consuls, Judges of the Supreme Court, and all other Officers of the United States, whose Appointments are not herein otherwise provided for, and which shall be established by Law: but the Congress may by Law vest the Appointment of such inferior Officers, as they think proper, in the President alone, in the Courts of Law, or in the Heads of Departments." U.S. Const., Art. II, § 2, cl. 2.

The parties do not dispute that "[t]he Constitution for purposes of appointment . . . divides all its officers into two classes." As we stated in *Buckley v. Valeo*, 424 U.S. 1, 132 (1976): "Principal officers are selected by the President with the advice and consent of the Senate. Inferior officers Congress may allow to be appointed by the President alone, by the heads of departments, or by the Judiciary." The initial question is, accordingly, whether appellant is an "inferior" or a "principal" officer. If she is the latter, as the Court of Appeals concluded, then the Act is in violation of the Appointments Clause.

The line between "inferior" and "principal" officers is one that is far from clear, and the Framers provided little guidance into where it should be drawn. We need not attempt here to decide exactly where the line falls between the two types of officers, because in our view appellant clearly falls on the "inferior officer" side of that line. Several factors lead to this conclusion.

First, appellant is subject to removal by a higher Executive Branch official. Although appellant may not be "subordinate" to the Attorney General (and the President) insofar as she possesses a degree of independent discretion to exercise the powers delegated to her under the Act, the fact that she can be removed by the Attorney General indicates that she is to some degree "inferior" in rank and authority. Second, appellant is empowered by the Act to perform only certain, limited duties. An independent counsel's role is restricted primarily to investigation and, if appropriate, prosecution for certain federal crimes. Admittedly, the Act delegates to appellant "full power and independent authority to exercise all investigative and prosecutorial functions and powers of the Department of Justice," § 594(a), but this grant of authority does not include any authority to formulate policy for the Government or the Executive Branch, nor does it give appellant any administrative duties outside of those necessary to operate her office. The Act specifically provides that in policy matters appellant is to comply to the extent possible with the policies of the Department. § 594(f).

Third, appellant's office is limited in jurisdiction. Not only is the Act itself restricted in applicability to certain federal officials suspected of certain serious federal crimes, but an independent counsel can only act within the scope of the jurisdiction that has been granted by the Special Division pursuant to a request by the Attorney General. Finally, appellant's office is limited in tenure. There is concededly no time limit on the appointment of a particular counsel. Nonetheless, the office of independent counsel is "temporary" in the sense that an independent counsel is appointed essentially to accomplish a single task, and when that task is over the office is terminated, either by the counsel herself or by action of the Special Division. Unlike other prosecutors, appellant has no ongoing responsibilities that extend beyond the accomplishment of the mission that she was appointed for and authorized by the Special Division to undertake. In our view, these factors relating to the "ideas of tenure, duration . . . and duties" of the independent counsel, . . . are sufficient to establish that appellant is an "inferior" officer in the constitutional sense.

This conclusion is consistent with our few previous decisions that considered the question whether a particular Government official is a "principal" or an "inferior" officer. . . . [T]his is consistent with our reference in *United States v. Nixon*, 418 U.S. 683, 694, 696 (1974), to the office of Watergate Special Prosecutor—whose authority was similar to that of appellant, see *id.*, at 694, n. 8—as a "subordinate officer."

This does not, however, end our inquiry under the Appointments Clause. Appellees argue that even if appellant is an "inferior" officer, the Clause does not empower Congress to place the power to appoint such an officer outside the Executive Branch. They contend that the Clause does not contemplate congressional authorization of "interbranch appointments," in which an officer of one branch is appointed by officers of another branch. The relevant language of the Appointments Clause . . . admits of no limitation on interbranch appointments.

Indeed, the [language] seems clearly to give Congress significant discretion to determine whether it is "proper" to vest the appointment of, for example, executive officials in the "courts of Law." We recognized as much in one of our few decisions in this area, . . . where we stated:

> "It is no doubt usual and proper to vest the appointment of inferior officers in that department of the government, executive or judicial, or in that particular executive department to which the duties of such officers appertain. But there is no absolute requirement to this effect in the Constitution; and, if there were, it would be difficult in many cases to determine to which department an office properly belonged. . . .
>
> "But as the Constitution stands, the selection of the appointing power, as between the functionaries named, is a matter resting in the discretion of Congress. And, looking at the subject in a practical light, it is perhaps better that it should rest there, than that the country should be harassed by the endless controversies to which a more specific direction on this subject might have given rise." [*Ex parte* Siebold, 100 U.S. at 397-98].

[T]here is very little, if any, express discussion of the propriety of interbranch appointments in our decisions, and we see no reason now to depart from the holding of *Siebold* that such appointments are not proscribed by the excepting clause.

We also note that the history of the Clause provides no support for appellees' position. [T]here was little or no debate on the question whether the [Appointment] Clause empowers Congress to provide for interbranch appointments, and there is nothing to suggest that the Framers intended to prevent Congress from having that power.

We do not mean to say that Congress' power to provide for interbranch appointments of "inferior officers" is unlimited. In addition to separation- of-powers concerns, which would arise if such provisions for appointment had the potential to impair the constitutional functions assigned to one of the branches, . . . Congress' decision to vest the appointment power in the courts would be improper if there was some "incongruity" between the functions normally performed by the courts and the performance of their duty to appoint. In this case, however, we do not think it impermissible for Congress to vest the power to appoint independent counsel in a specially created federal court. We thus disagree with the Court of Appeals' conclusion that there is an inherent incongruity about a court having the power to appoint prosecutorial officers. We have recognized that courts may appoint private attorneys to act as prosecutor for judicial contempt judgments. *See Young v. United States ex rel. Vuitton et Fils S.A.*, 481 U.S. 787 (1987). In *Go-Bart Importing Co. v. United States*, 282 U.S. 344 (1931), we approved court appointment of United States commissioners, who exercised certain limited prosecutorial powers. In *Siebold*, as well, we indicated that judicial appointment of federal marshals, who are "executive officer[s]," would not be inappropriate. Congress, of course was concerned when it created the office of independent counsel with the conflicts of interest that could arise in situations when the Executive Branch is called upon to investigate its own high-ranking officers. If it were to remove the appointing authority from the Executive Branch, the most logical place to put it was in the Judicial Branch. In the light of the Act's provision making the judges of the Special Division ineligible to participate in any matters relating to an independent counsel they have appointed, 28 U.S.C. § 49(f) (1982 ed., Supp. V) we do not think that appointment of the independent counsel by the court runs afoul of the constitutional limitation on "incongruous" interbranch appointments.

IV

Appellees next contend that the powers vested in the Special Division by the Act conflict with Article III of the Constitution. We have long recognized that by the express provision of Article III, the judicial power of the United States is limited to "Cases" and "Controversies." *See Muskrat v. United States*, 219 U.S. 346, 356 (1911). As a general rule, we have broadly stated that "executive or administrative duties of a nonjudicial nature may not be imposed on judges holding office under Art. III of the Constitution." . . . The purpose of this limitation is to help ensure the independence of the Judicial Branch and to prevent the Judiciary from encroaching into areas reserved for the other branches. *See United States Parole Comm'n v. Geraghty*, 445 U.S. 388, 396 (1980). With this in mind, we address in turn the various duties given to the Special Division by the Act.

[T]he Act vests in the Special Division the power to choose who will serve as independent counsel and the power to define his or her jurisdiction. § 593(b). Clearly, once it is accepted that the Appointments Clause gives Congress the power to vest the appointment of officials such as the independent counsel in the "courts of Law," there can be no Article III objection to the Special Division's exercise of that power, as the power itself derives from the Appointments Clause, a source of authority for judicial action that is independent of Article III. Appellees contend, however, that the Division's Appointments Clause powers do not encompass the power to define the independent counsel's ju-

risdiction. We disagree. In our view, Congress' power under the Clause to vest the "Appointment" of inferior officers in the courts may, in certain circumstances, allow Congress to give the courts some discretion in defining the nature and scope of the appointed official's authority. Particularly when, as here, Congress creates a temporary "office" the nature and duties of which will by necessity vary with the factual circumstances giving rise to the need for an appointment in the first place, it may vest the power to define the scope of the office in the court as an incident to the appointment of the officer pursuant to the Appointments Clause. This said, we do not think that Congress may give the Division *unlimited* discretion to determine the independent counsel's jurisdiction. In order for the Division's definition of the counsel's jurisdiction to be truly "incidental" to its power to appoint, the jurisdiction that the court decides upon must be demonstrably related to the factual circumstances that gave rise to the Attorney General's investigation and request for the appointment of the independent counsel in the particular case.

The Act also vests in the Special Division various powers and duties in relation to the independent counsel that, because they do not involve appointing the counsel or defining his or her jurisdiction, cannot be said to derive from the Division's Appointments Clause authority.

Leaving aside for the moment the Division's power to terminate an independent counsel, we do not think that Article III absolutely prevents Congress from vesting miscellaneous powers in the Special Division pursuant to the Act. As we observed above, one purpose of the broad prohibition upon the courts' exercise of "executive or administrative duties of a nonjudicial nature," *Buckley*, 424 U.S., at 123 is to maintain the separation between the Judiciary and the other branches of the Federal Government by ensuring that judges do not encroach upon executive or legislative authority or undertake tasks that are more properly accomplished by those branches. In this case, the miscellaneous powers described above do not impermissibly trespass upon the authority of the Executive Branch. Some of these allegedly "supervisory" powers conferred on the court are passive: the Division merely "receives" reports from the counsel or the Attorney General, it is not entitled to act on them or to specifically approve or disapprove of their contents. Other provisions of the Act do require the court to exercise some judgment and discretion, but the powers granted by these provisions are themselves essentially ministerial. The Act simply does not give the Division the power to "supervise" the independent counsel in the exercise of his or her investigative or prosecutorial authority. And, the functions that the Special Division is empowered to perform are not inherently "Executive"; indeed, they are directly analogous to functions that federal judges perform in other contexts, such as deciding whether to allow disclosure of matters occurring before a grand jury, see Fed. Rule Crim.Proc. 6(e), deciding to extend a grand jury investigation, Rule 6(g), or awarding attorney's fees, see, *e.g.*, 42 U.S.C. § 1988.

We are more doubtful about the Special Division's power to terminate the office of the independent counsel pursuant to § 596(b)(2). As appellees suggest, the power to terminate, especially when exercised by the Division on its own motion, is "administrative" to the extent that it requires the Special Division to monitor the progress of proceedings of the independent counsel and come to a decision as to whether the counsel's job is "completed." § 596(b)(2). It also is not a power that could be considered typically "judicial," as it has few analogues among the court's more traditional powers. Nonetheless, we do not, as did the Court of Appeals, view this provision as a significant judicial encroachment upon executive power or upon the prosecutorial discretion of the independent counsel.

We think that the Court of Appeals overstated the matter when it described the power to terminate as a "broadsword and . . . rapier" that enables the court to "control the pace and depth of the independent counsel's activities." 267 U.S.App.D.C., at 217, 838 F.2d, at 515. The provision has not been tested in practice, and we do not mean to say that an adventurous special court could not reasonably construe the provision as did the Court of Appeals; but it is the duty of federal courts to construe a statute in order to save it from constitutional infirmities, see, e.g., *Commodity Futures Trading Comm'n v. Schor*, 478 U.S. 833, 841 (1986), and to that end we think a narrow construction is appropriate here. The termination provisions of the Act do not give the Special Division anything approaching the power to remove the counsel while an investigation or court proceeding is still underway—this power is vested solely in the Attorney General. As we see it, "termination" may occur only when the duties of the counsel are truly "completed" or "so substantially completed" that there remains no need for any continuing action by the independent counsel. It is basically a device for removing from the public payroll an independent counsel who has served his or her purpose, but is unwilling to acknowledge the fact. So construed, the Special Division's power to terminate does not pose a sufficient threat of judicial intrusion into matters that are more properly within the Executive's authority to require that the Act be invalidated as inconsistent with Article III.

Nor do we believe, as appellees contend,

that the Special Division's exercise of the various powers specifically granted to it under the Act poses any threat to the "impartial and independent federal adjudication of claims within the judicial power of the United States." *Commodity Futures Trading Comm'n v. Schor, supra*, at 850. We reach this conclusion for two reasons. First, the Act as it currently stands gives the Special Division itself no power to review any of the actions of the independent counsel or any of the actions of the Attorney General with regard to the counsel. Accordingly, there is no risk of partisan or biased adjudication of claims regarding the independent counsel by that court. Second, the Act prevents members of the Special Division from participating in "any judicial proceeding concerning a matter which involves such independent counsel while such independent counsel is serving in that office or which involves the exercise of such independent counsel's official duties, regardless of whether such independent counsel is still serving in that office." 28 U.S.C. § 49(f) (1982 ed., Supp. V). We think both the special court and its judges are sufficiently isolated . . . from the review of the activities of the independent counsel so as to avoid any taint of the independence of the Judiciary such as would render the Act invalid under Article III.

V

We now turn to consider whether the Act is invalid under the constitutional principle of separation of powers. Two related issues must be addressed: The first is whether the provision of the Act restricting the Attorney General's power to remove the independent counsel to only those instances in which he can show "good cause," taken by itself, impermissibly interferes with the President's exercise of his constitutionally appointed functions. The second is whether, taken as a whole, the Act violates the separation of powers by reducing the President's ability to control the prosecutorial powers wielded by the independent counsel.

A

Two Terms ago we had occasion to consider whether it was consistent with the separation of powers for Congress to pass a statute that authorized a Government official who is removable only by Congress to participate in what we found to be "executive powers." *Bowsher v. Synar*, 478 U.S. 714, 730 (1986). We held in *Bowsher* that "Congress cannot reserve for itself the power of removal of an officer charged with the execution of the laws except by impeachment." *Id.*, at 726. A primary antecedent for this ruling was our 1926 decision in *Myers v. United States*, 272 U.S. 52 (1926). *Myers* had considered the propriety of a federal statute by which certain postmasters of the United States could be removed by the President only "by and with the advice and consent of the Senate." There too, Congress' attempt to involve itself in the removal of an executive official was found to be sufficient grounds to render the statute invalid. As we observed in *Bowsher*, the essence of the decision in *Myers* was the judgment that the Constitution prevents Congress from "draw[ing] to itself ... the power to remove or the right to participate in the exercise of that power. To do this would be to go beyond the words and implications of the [Appointments Clause] and to infringe the constitutional principle of the separation of governmental powers." *Myers, supra,* at 161.

Unlike both *Bowsher* and *Myers*, this case does not involve an attempt by Congress itself to gain a role in the removal of executive officials other than its established powers of impeachment and conviction. The Act instead puts the removal power squarely in the hands of the Executive Branch; an independent counsel may be removed from office, "only by the personal action of the Attorney General, and only for good cause." § 596(a)(1). There is no requirement of congressional approval of the Attorney General's removal decision, though the decision is subject to judicial review. § 596(a)(3). In our view, the removal provisions of the Act make this case more analogous to *Humphrey's Executor v. United States*, 295 U.S. 602 (1935), and *Wiener v. United States*, 357 U.S. 349 (1958), than to *Myers* or *Bowsher*.

In *Humphrey's Executor*, the issue was whether a statute restricting the President's power to remove the Commissioners of the Federal Trade Commission (FTC) only for "inefficiency, neglect of duty, or malfeasance in office" was consistent with the Constitution. 295 U.S., at 619. We stated that whether Congress can "condition the [President's power of removal] by fixing a definite term and precluding a removal except for cause, will depend upon the character of the office." *Id.,* at 631. Contrary to the implication of some dicta in *Myers*, the President's power to remove Government officials simply was not "all-inclusive in respect of civil officers with the exception of the judiciary provided for by the Constitution." 295 U.S., at 629. At least in regard to "quasi-legislative" and "quasi-judicial" agencies such as the FTC, "[t]he authority of Congress, in creating [such] agencies, to require them to act in discharge of their duties independently of executive control ... includes, as an appropriate incident, power to fix the period during which they shall continue in office, and to forbid their removal except for cause in the meantime." *Ibid.* In *Humphrey's Executor*, we found it "plain" that the Constitution did not give the President "illimitable power of removal" over the officers of independent agencies.

Appellees contend that *Humphrey's Executor* and *Wiener* are distinguishable from this case because they did not involve officials who performed a "core executive function." They argue that our decision in *Humphrey's Executor* rests on a distinction between "purely executive" officials and officials who exercise "quasi-legislative" and "quasi-judicial" powers. In their view, when a "purely executive" official is involved, the governing precedent is *Myers,* not *Humphrey's Executor. See Humphrey's Executor, supra,* 295 U.S. at 628. And, under *Myers,* the President must have absolute discretion to discharge "purely" executive officials at will. *See Myers,* 272 U.S. at 132–134.

We undoubtedly did rely on the terms "quasi-legislative" and "quasi-judicial" to distinguish the officials involved in *Humphrey's Executor* and *Wiener* from those in *Myers,* but our present considered view is that the determination of whether the Constitution allows Congress to impose a "good cause"-type restriction on the President's power to remove an official cannot be made to turn on whether or not that official is classified as "purely executive." The analysis contained in our removal cases is designed not to define rigid categories of those officials who may or may not be removed at will by the President,[28] but to ensure that Congress does not interfere with the President's exercise of the "executive power" and his constitutionally appointed duty to "take care that the laws

---

[28] The difficulty of defining such categories of "executive" or "quasi-legislative" officials is illustrated by a comparison of our decisions in cases such as Humphrey's Executor, Buckley v. Valeo, 424 U.S. 1, 140–141 (1976), and Bowsher, supra, 478 U.S., at 732–734. In Buckley, we indicated that the functions of the Federal Election Commission are "administrative," and "more legislative and judicial in nature," and are "of kinds usually performed by independent regulatory agencies or by some department in the Executive Branch under the direction of an Act of Congress." 424 U.S., at 140–141. In Bowsher, we found that the functions of the Comptroller General were "executive" in nature, in that he was required to "exercise judgment concerning facts that affect the application of the Act," and he must "interpret the provisions of the Act to determine precisely what budgetary calculations are required." 478 U.S. at 733. Compare this with the description of the FTC's powers in *Humphrey's Executor*, which we stated "occupie[d] no place in the executive department": "The [FTC] is an administrative body created by Congress to carry into effect legislative policies embodied in the statute in accordance with the legislative standard therein prescribed, and to perform other specified duties as a legislative or as a judicial aid." 295 U.S., at 628. As Justice WHITE noted in his dissent in *Bowsher*, it is hard to dispute that the powers of the FTC at the time of *Humphrey's Executor* would at the present time be considered "executive," at least to some degree. *See* 478 U.S. at 761, n. 3.

be faithfully executed" under Article II. [T]he characterization of the agencies in *Humphrey's Executor* and *Wiener* as "quasi-legislative" or "quasi-judicial" in large part reflected our judgment that it was not essential to the President's proper execution of his Article II powers that these agencies be headed up by individuals who were removable at will. We do not mean to suggest that an analysis of the functions served by the officials at issue is irrelevant. But the real question is whether the removal restrictions are of such a nature that they impede the President's ability to perform his constitutional duty, and the functions of the officials in question must be analyzed in that light.

Considering for the moment the "good cause" removal provision in isolation from the other parts of the Act at issue in this case, we cannot say that the imposition of a "good cause" standard for removal by itself unduly trammels on executive authority. There is no real dispute that the functions performed by the independent counsel are "executive" in the sense that they are law enforcement functions that typically have been undertaken by officials within the Executive Branch. As we noted above, however, the independent counsel is an inferior officer under the Appointments Clause, with limited jurisdiction and tenure and lacking policymaking or significant administrative authority. Although the counsel exercises no small amount of discretion and judgment in deciding how to carry out his or her duties under the Act, we simply do not see how the President's need to control the exercise of that discretion is so central to the functioning of the Executive Branch as to require as a matter of constitutional law that the counsel be terminable at will by the President.

Nor do we think that the "good cause" removal provision at issue here impermissibly burdens the President's power to control or supervise the independent counsel, as an executive official, in the execution of his or her duties under the Act. This is not a case in which the power to remove an executive official has been completely stripped from the President, thus providing no means for the President to ensure the "faithful execution" of the laws. Rather, because the independent counsel may be terminated for "good cause," the Executive, through the Attorney General, retains ample authority to assure that the counsel is competently performing his or her statutory responsibilities in a manner that comports with the provisions of the Act.

B

The final question to be addressed is whether the Act, taken as a whole, violates the principle of separation of powers by unduly interfering with the role of the Executive Branch. Time and again we have reaffirmed the importance in our constitutional scheme of the separation of governmental powers into the three coordinate branches. See, *e.g.*, *Bowsher v. Synar*, 478 U.S. at 725 (citing *Humphrey's Executor*, 295 U.S. at 629–630). As we stated in *Buckley v. Valeo*, 424 U.S. 1 (1976), the system of separated powers and checks and balances established in the Constitution was regarded by the Framers as "a self-executing safeguard against the encroachment or aggrandizement of one branch at the expense of the other." *Id.*, at 122. We have not hesitated to invalidate provisions of law which violate this principle. See *id.* at 123. On the other hand, we have never held that the Constitution requires that the three branches of Government "operate with absolute independence." *United States v. Nixon*, 418 U.S. at 707; see also *Nixon v. Administrator of General Services*, 433 U.S. 425, 442 (1977). In the often-quoted words of Justice Jackson:

> "While the Constitution diffuses power the better to secure liberty, it also contemplates that practice will integrate the dispersed powers into a workable government. It enjoins upon its branches separateness but interdependence, autonomy but reciprocity."
> *Youngstown Sheet & Tube Co. v. Sawyer*, 343 U.S. 579, 635 (1952) (concurring opinion).

We observe first that this case does not involve an attempt by Congress to increase its own powers at the expense of the Executive Branch. Cf. *Commodity Futures Trading Comm'n v. Schor*, 478 U.S. at 856. Unlike some of our previous cases, most recently *Bowsher v. Synar*, this case simply does not pose a "dange[r] of congressional usurpation of Executive Branch functions." 478 U.S. at 727; see also *INS v. Chadha*, 462 U.S. 919, 958 (1983). Indeed, with the exception of the power of impeachment—which applies to all officers of the United States—Congress retained for itself no powers of control or supervision over an independent counsel. The Act does empower certain Members of Congress to request the Attorney General to apply for the appointment of an independent counsel, but the Attorney General has no duty to comply with the request, although he must respond within a certain time limit. § 529(g). Other than that, Congress' role under the Act is limited to receiving reports or other information and oversight of the independent counsel's activities, § 595(a), functions that we have recognized generally as being incidental to the legislative function of Congress. See *McGrain v. Daugherty*, 273 U.S. 135, 174 (1927).

Similarly, we do not think that the Act

works any *judicial* usurpation of properly executive functions. As should be apparent from our discussion of the Appointments Clause above, the power to appoint inferior officers such as independent counsel is not in itself an "executive" function in the constitutional sense, at least when Congress has exercised its power to vest the appointment of an inferior office in the "courts of Law." We note nonetheless that under the Act the Special Division has no power to appoint an independent counsel *sua sponte*; it may only do so upon the specific request of the Attorney General, and the courts are specifically prevented from reviewing the Attorney General's decision not to seek appointment, § 592(f). In addition, once the court has appointed a counsel and defined his or her jurisdiction, it has no power to supervise or control the activities of the counsel.

Finally, we do not think that the Act "impermissibly undermine[s]" the powers of the Executive Branch, *Schor, supra,* [478 U.S.] at 856, or "disrupts the proper balance between the coordinate branches [by] prevent[ing] the Executive Branch from accomplishing its constitutionally assigned functions," *Nixon v. Administrator of General Services, supra,* [433 U.S.] at 443. It is undeniable that the Act reduces the amount of control or supervision that the Attorney General and, through him, the President exercises over the investigation and prosecution of a certain class of alleged criminal activity. The Attorney General is not allowed to appoint the individual of his choice; he does not determine the counsel's jurisdiction; and his power to remove a counsel is limited. Nonetheless, the Act does give the Attorney General several means of supervising or controlling the prosecutorial powers that may be wielded by an independent counsel. Most importantly, the Attorney General retains the power to remove the counsel for "good cause," a power that we have already concluded provides the Executive with substantial ability to ensure that the laws are "faithfully executed" by an independent counsel.

. . . The decision of the Court of Appeals is therefore

Reversed.

Justice KENNEDY took no part in the consideration or decision of this case.

Justice SCALIA, dissenting.

It is the proud boast of our democracy that we have "a government of laws and not of men." Many Americans are familiar with that phrase; not many know its derivation. It comes from Part the First, Article XXX, of the Massachusetts Constitution of 1780, which reads in full as follows:

"In the government of this Commonwealth, the legislative department shall never exercise the executive and judicial powers, or either of them: The executive shall never exercise the legislative and judicial powers, or either of them: The judicial shall never exercise the legislative and executive powers, or either of them: to the end it may be a government of laws and not of men."

The Framers of the Federal Constitution similarly viewed the principle of separation of powers as the absolutely central guarantee of a just Government.

The principle of separation of powers is expressed in our Constitution in the first section of each of the first three Articles. Article I, § 1, provides that "[a]ll legislative Powers herein granted shall be vested in a Congress of the United States, which shall consist of a Senate and House of Representatives." Article III, § 1, provides that "[t]he judicial Power of the United States, shall be vested in one supreme Court, and in such inferior Courts as the Congress may from time to time ordain and establish." And the provision at issue here, Art. II, § 1, cl. 1, provides that "[t]he executive Power shall be vested in a President of the United States of America."

[As Madison recognized in Federalist No. 51, pp. 321–22] "In republican government, the legislative authority necessarily predominates. The remedy for this inconveniency is to divide the legislature into different branches; and to render them, by different modes of election and different principles of action, as little connected with each other as the nature of their common functions and their common dependence on the society will admit. . . . As the weight of the legislative authority requires that it should be thus divided, the weakness of the executive may require, on the other hand, that it should be fortified." *Id.,* at 322–323.

The major "fortification" provided, of course, was the veto power. But in addition to providing fortification, the Founders conspicuously and very consciously declined to sap the Executive's strength in the same way they had weakened the Legislature: by dividing the executive power. Proposals to have multiple executives, or a council of advisers with separate authority were rejected. Thus, while "[a]ll legislative Powers herein granted shall be vested in a Congress of the United States, which shall consist of a Senate *and* House of Representatives," U.S. Const., Art. I, § 1 (emphasis added), "[t]he executive Power shall be vested in a *President of the United States,*" Art. II, § 1, cl. 1 (emphasis added).

That is what this suit is about. Power. The allocation of power among Congress, the President, and the courts in such fashion as to preserve the equilibrium the Constitution sought to establish—so that "a gradual concentration of the several powers in the same department," Federalist No. 51, p. 321 (J. Madison), can effectively be resisted. Frequently an issue of this sort will come before the Court clad, so to speak, in sheep's clothing: the potential of the asserted principle to effect important change in the equilibrium of power is not immediately evident, and must be discerned by a careful and perceptive analysis. But this wolf comes as a wolf.

[B]y the application of this statute in the present case, Congress has effectively compelled a criminal investigation of a high-level appointee of the President in connection with his actions arising out of a bitter power dispute between the President and the Legislative Branch. Mr. Olson may or may not be guilty of a crime; we do not know. But we do know that the investigation of him has been commenced not . . . because the President or his authorized subordinates believe . . . that an investigation is likely to unearth a violation worth prosecuting; but only because the Attorney General cannot affirm, as Congress demands, that there are *no reasonable grounds to believe* that further investigation is warranted. The decisions regarding the scope of that further investigation, its duration, and, finally, whether or not prosecution should ensue, are likewise beyond the control of the President and his subordinates.

II

If to describe this case is not to decide it, the concept of a government of separate and coordinate powers no longer has meaning. The Court devotes most of its attention to such relatively technical details as the Appointments Clause and the removal power, addressing briefly and only at the end of its opinion the separation of powers. I think that has it backwards. Our opinions are full of the recognition that it is the principle of separation of powers, and the inseparable corollary that each department's "defense must . . . be made commensurate to the danger of attack," Federalist No. 51, p. 322 (J. Madison), which gives comprehensible content to the Appointments Clause, and determines the appropriate scope of the removal power. Thus, while I will subsequently discuss why our appointments and removal jurisprudence does not support today's holding, I begin with a consideration of the fountainhead of that jurisprudence, the separation and equilibration of powers.

[A premise that underlies this deliberation is that] where the issue pertains to separation of powers, and the political branches are (as here) in disagreement, neither can be presumed correct. As one of the interested and coordinate parties to the underlying constitutional dispute, Congress, no more than the President, is entitled to the benefit of the doubt.

To repeat, Article II, § 1, cl. 1, of the Constitution provides: "The executive Power shall be vested in a President of the United States." As I described at the outset of this opinion, this does not mean *some* of the executive power, but *all* of the executive power.

The Court concedes that "[t]here is no real dispute that the functions performed by the independent counsel are 'executive'," though it qualifies that concession by adding "in the sense that they are law enforcement functions that typically have been undertaken by officials within the Executive Branch." The qualifier adds nothing but atmosphere. In what *other* sense can one identify "the executive Power" that is supposed to be vested in the President (unless it includes everything the Executive Branch is given to do) *except* by reference to what has always and everywhere—if conducted by government at all—been conducted never by the legislature, never by the courts, and always by the executive. There is no possible doubt that the independent counsel's functions fit this description. Governmental investigation and prosecution of crimes is a quintessentially executive function.

The statute before us deprives the President of exclusive control over that quintessentially executive activity: The Court does not, and could not possibly, assert that it does not. That is indeed the whole object of the statute. Instead, the Court points out that the President, through his Attorney General, has at least *some* control. That concession is alone enough to invalidate the statute, but I cannot refrain from pointing out that the Court greatly exaggerates the extent of that "some" Presidential control. "Most importan[t]" among these controls, the Court asserts, is the Attorney General's "power to remove the counsel for 'good cause.' " This is somewhat like referring to shackles as an effective means of locomotion. As we recognized in *Humphrey's Executor v. United States*, 295 U.S. 602 (1935) limiting removal power to "good cause" is an impediment to, not an effective grant of, Presidential control. We said that limitation was necessary with respect to members of the Federal Trade Commission, which we found to be "an agency of the legislative and judicial departments," and "wholly disconnected from the executive department," id., at 630, because "it is quite evident that one who holds his office only during the pleasure of another, cannot be depended upon to maintain an attitude of independence against the latter's will." Id., at 629. What we in *Humphrey's Executor* found to be a means of eliminating Presidential control, the Court today considers the "most importan[t]" means of assuring Presidential control. Congress, of course, operated under no such illusion when it enacted this statute, describing the "good cause" limitation as "protecting the independent counsel's ability to act independently of the President's direct control" since it permits removal only for "misconduct." H.R. Conf. Rep. 100-452, p. 37 (1987).

Moving on to the presumably "less important" controls that the President retains, the Court notes that no independent counsel may be appointed without a specific request from the Attorney General. As I have discussed above, the condition that renders such a request mandatory (inability to find "no reasonable grounds to believe" that further investigation is warranted) is so insubstantial that the Attorney General's discretion is severely confined. And once the referral is made, it is for the Special Division to determine the scope and duration of the investigation. See 28 U.S.C. § 593(b) (1982 ed., Supp. V). And in any event, the limited power over referral is irrelevant to the question whether, *once appointed*, the independent counsel exercises executive power free from the President's control. Finally, the Court points out that the Act directs the independent counsel to abide by general Justice Department policy, except when not "possible." See 28 U.S.C. § 594(f) (1982 ed., Supp. V). The exception alone shows this to be an empty promise. Even without that, however, one would be hard put to come up with many investigative or prosecutorial "policies" (other than those imposed by the Constitution or by Congress through law) that are absolute. [T]he balancing of various legal, practical, and political considerations, none of which is absolute, is the very essence of prosecutorial discretion. To take this away is to remove the core of the prosecutorial function, and not merely "some" Presidential control.

As I have said, however, it is ultimately irrelevant how *much* the statute reduces Presidential control. The case is over when the Court acknowledges, as it must, that "[i]t is undeniable that the Act reduces the amount of control or supervision that the Attorney General and, through him, the President exercises over the investigation and prosecution of a certain class of alleged criminal activity." It effects a revolution in our constitutional jurisprudence for the Court, once it has determined that (1) purely executive functions are at issue here, and (2) those functions have been given to a person whose actions are not fully within the supervision and control of the President, nonetheless to proceed further to sit in judgment of whether "the President's need to control the exercise of [the independent counsel's] discretion is so *central* to the functioning of the Executive Branch" as to require complete control, . . . whether the conferral of his powers upon someone else "sufficiently deprives the President of control over

the independent counsel to interfere impermissibly with [his] constitutional obligation to ensure the faithful execution of the laws," . . . and whether "the Act give[s] the Executive Branch *sufficient* control over the independent counsel to ensure that the President is able to perform his constitutionally assigned duties." [Emphasis added by Justice Scalia.] It is not for us to determine, and we have never presumed to determine, how much of the purely executive powers of government must be within the full control of the President. The Constitution prescribes that they *all* are.

Is it unthinkable that the President should have such exclusive power, even when alleged crimes by him or his close associates are at issue? No more so than that Congress should have the exclusive power of legislation, even when what is at issue is its own exemption from the burdens of certain laws. See Civil Rights Act of 1964, Title VII, 42 U.S.C. § 2000e et seq. (prohibiting "employers," not defined to include the United States, from discriminating on the basis of race, color, religion, sex, or national origin). No more so than that this Court should have the exclusive power to pronounce the final decision on justiciable cases and controversies, even those pertaining to the constitutionality of a statute reducing the salaries of the Justices. See *United States v. Will*, 449 U.S. 200, 211–217 (1980). A system of separate and coordinate powers necessarily involves an acceptance of exclusive power that can theoretically be abused. While the separation of powers may prevent us from righting every wrong, it does so in order to ensure that we do not lose liberty.

The Court has, nonetheless, replaced the clear constitutional prescription that the executive power belongs to the President with a "balancing test." What are the standards to determine how the balance is to be struck, that is, how much removal of Presidential power is too much? The most amazing feature of the Court's opinion is that it does not even purport to give an answer. It simply *announces*, with no analysis, that the ability to control the decision whether to investigate and prosecute the President's closest advisers, and indeed the President himself, is not "so central to the functioning of the Executive Branch" as to be constitutionally required to be within the President's control. Apparently it is so because we say it is so. Having abandoned as the basis for our decisionmaking the text of Article II that "the executive Power" must be vested in the President, the Court does not even attempt to craft a *substitute* criterion—a "justiciable standard," see, *e.g.*, *Baker v. Carr*, 369 U.S. 186, 210 (1962).

In the Ethics in Government Act, Congress sought to foster impartial investigations of high level executive officers. The Act was one of a series of statutes, including the War Powers Resolution of 1973, the Federal Election Campaign Act amendments of 1974, and the Presidential Recordings and Materials Preservation Act of 1974, considered by the Court in cases challenging congressional efforts to limit the power of the executive in the early seventies.[104] Under the formalist analysis which had been utilized by the Court in *Chadha* and *Bowsher*, the Court would be more concerned about whether these legislative efforts to control the executive disrupted the formal structure designed by the Framers. Thus, in the case of *Morrison*, even if insulation of the independent counsel was desirable because of fears about presidential overreaching, particularly after the Watergate controversy, "[s]uch fears, however, rational, do not by themselves warrant a distortion of the Framers' work."[105] To determine whether the special prosecutor could be free of control of the President, formalist analysis in this case begins with the text: under Article II, the executive power is vested in a single individual, the President. This textual provision proposes a unitary executive and thus the statutory framework offends the Constitution if the prosecutorial and investigatory powers are powers attributable to the Executive and placed in the control of another branch. Although there may be alternative understandings found in history, the well understood tradition is for prosecutorial and investigatory powers to be essentially executive.[106]

To determine whether the appointment is required to be made by the President, the formalist considers whether the independent counsel is a principal officer (to be appointed by the Executive under Article II, § 2 cl. 2) or an inferior one. Even if an officer is considered inferior, the issue remains in which branch the Congress may constitutionally vest the appointment. Thus Congress could most clearly provide legislatively that it make an appointment of an inferior officer whose function is "quasi legislative." Consistent with a formalist approach, in *Buckley v. Valeo* the Court found there to be an implied interbranch appointment barrier arising out of the constitutional appointment provision. Consequently, for Congress to provide for an interbranch appointment would be insupportable and disruptive of separation requirements.

In *Morrison*, Justice Rehnquist, however, concluded that Congress' power to provide for the interbranch appointments of inferior officers would offend separation of powers only if it "impair[s] the functions assigned to one of the branches."[107] The majority's conclusions do not focus on the disruptions to the design but rather bow to the policy judgment that the independent counsel be insulated to a certain extent from the control of the Executive. Despite the tradition of locating prosecutorial functions in the Executive, the *Morrison* Court concluded that for separation of powers purposes the challenged law left the Executive with limited but sufficient control for the counsel not to be disruptive of the constitutional balance.

---

[104] *See* Stephen Carter, *The Independent Counsel Mess*, 102 Harv. L. Rev. 105 (1988).

[105] Buckley v. Valeo, 424 U.S. 1, 134 (1976) (reviewing Federal Election Campaign Act amendments).

[106] Professor Carter, for example, notes that there is some evidence that the prosecutorial function was *not* attached to the executive during the Framers' times, although prosecutorial power resting in the executive branch serves the divided government notion in separation of powers that the power to make laws, execute them and adjudicate controversies lies in separate hands. Carter, *supra,* 102 Harv. L. Rev. at 127–29.

[107] Buckley v. Valeo, 424 U.S. 1, 126 (1976) (whether the officer's authority is significant).

PAH: Although the analysis is questionable from a formalist vantage point, *Morrison* can be read in line with a number of cases, beginning with *Humphrey's Executor v. United*

States,[108] in which the Court considered challenges to the authority of Congress to establish independent agencies, to appoint officers of those agencies and to protect them from presidential removal. In *Humphrey's Executor,* the Court assumed the constitutionality of independent agencies and ruled that Congress had authority to limit the president's ability to remove an appointee, even when the appointee's power is partly executive. (Was it significant that the President who sought to fire the Federal Trade Commission official in *Humphrey's Executor* was President Roosevelt and his reason was that Humphrey was resistant to his New Deal program?) The Court reasoned (though weakly) that since Congress had constituted the agency with "quasi" legislative and "quasi" judicial as well as "quasi" executive power, the agency was not located in the Executive Branch. According to the Court, it followed that the President's ability to remove the officer or to have him serve as "at his pleasure" would upset the independence Congress intended for the commission.

Humphrey's Executor has been sharply criticized for its failure to provide reasoned support for its assertion of the constitutionality of independent agencies created by Congress. The additional proposition that because Congress has the power to create agencies, it can provide an officer with "some" executive authority who is nevertheless free of the power of removal by the President is questionable in light of separation of powers requirements. Article II's vesting of the executive power in the Executive, as well as the President's duty to "take care that laws be faithfully executed,"[109] have been construed by critics of *Humphrey's Executor* and other cases to require control by the President of officers performing executive functions. The Court, however, has continued to defer to congressional judgment about the necessity for independent administrative agencies as well as to congressional decisions to place limitations on executive power to interfere with agency functions.

According to Professor Stephen Carter, regardless of your view of limitations Congress can constitutionally impose on executive power over independent agencies, it is troublesome to extend this line of reasoning to *Morrison*, since the independent counsel position can properly be characterized as an "arm or an eye of the executive:"[110]

> To make the counsel fit the independent agency model, the Justices were forced to lump together all executive authority as one malleable whole, and to test restrictions on that authority only for the degree of their intrusiveness. In so doing, the Court presented the Congress with what Justice Scalia called "an invitation . . . to experiment."
>
> Already wending its way through the Congress is a proposal for a special environmental prosecutor to handle those cases too explosive to leave to politically accountable officials. What might be next? [P]erhaps the Congress, angered by the direction and policies of the Justice Department . . . could decree (over the President's likely veto) that the entire Justice Department is to become an independent agency, like the FTC, thereby placing all criminal prosecution beyond direct presidential control. Nor is there any reason to think that *Morrison* is limited to situations involving prosecution. . . . Thus if the Congress determines that foreign policy is too important a matter to be left to the politically expedient judgment of

---

[108] 295 U.S. 602 (1935).

[109] *See e.g.,* Carter *supra*, 102 Harv. L. Rev. 105; Strauss *supra*, 1983 Duke L. J. 789. Miller, *supra*, 1986 Sup. Ct Rep. 58. The inference is drawn that because the executive power vests in the President, administrative agencies have executive power flowing from the "original font of executive power" in the president and not from Congress when it creates them. Thus the President should have a broad degree of authority over the administrative agencies.

[110] 295 U.S. at 628.

the White House, it might command the independence of the Department of State . . . placing under its command a commission of experts nominated by the President and confirmed by the Senate. The Department of Defense . . . might be next.

And because the Congress is able to specify not only the tenure of office of executive employees but also their functions, it may not be too far-fetched to wonder whether the President—who, after all, does almost every thing through aides—might be stripped of a substantial part of even his inherent constitutional authority. . . . The trouble with *Morrison* is that it provides no reliable guide for answering questions . . . The reader is left with the uneasy sense that there may, in fact, be no rule at all, and that the principal practical restraint on the Congress is its own discretion. . . . And perhaps there is, at this late date, no escape [from the slippery slope leading] from the line of cases permitting the Congress to vest executive authority in agencies beyond presidential control. In that case, it may be that legislative government, with a profoundly weaker executive, is indeed what the future holds, or at least, that nothing more than the wisdom and discretion of one-third-plus-one of the members of either House of the Congress will be available to prevent the legislature from taking us there. [I]f government by independent agency is indeed our future, it would be nice to get there by constitutional amendment rather than legislative fiat."[111]

Professor Carter argues that the Court should apply its formalist reasoning and confront the question of constitutionality of independent agencies, particularly the independence of executive officers from executive control.

Are you convinced that the Court's review of this issue would resolve the concerns he has expressed? Notably, Justice Scalia, the dissenter in *Morrison*, has characterized the formalist decisions of the eighties as representing a period of "renewed respectability" for the nondelegation doctrine.[112] Even if it is practically feasible for the Court today to restore the institutional separation and structural checks believed to have been contemplated by the Framers (such as the rule of nondelegation) it does not necessarily follow that liberty is thereby promoted or better served.

---

[111] Carter, *supra* 102 HARV. L. REV. at 134–35.

[112] ANTONIN SCALIA, A NOTE ON THE BENZENE CASE, Reg., July-Aug. 1980, at 25, 27.

The shift toward the functionalist approach in *Morrison* seemed to continue in *Mistretta v. United States*.[113] In that case the Court upheld the appointment of federal judges to the Federal Sentencing Commission, which was given responsibility to create sentencing guidelines and report its progress to Congress. The Court concluded for purposes of separation of powers analysis that the commission was located in the judicial branch. It made this conclusion acknowledging that the Commission did not exercise judicial power, that it is accountable to Congress, and that its members are subject to limited power of removal by the President.

---

[113] 109 S. Ct. 647 (1989).

Mistretta v. United States
488 U.S. 361 (1988)

Justice BLACKMUN delivered the opinion of the Court.

In this litigation, we granted certiorari before judgment in the United States Court of Appeals for the Eighth Circuit in order to consider the constitutionality of the Sentencing Guidelines promulgated by the United States Sentencing Commission. The Commission is a body created under the Sentencing Reform Act of 1984 (Act). The United States District Court for the Western District of Missouri ruled that the Guidelines were constitutional.

I

A

Background

For almost a century, the Federal Government employed in criminal cases a system of indeterminate sentencing. Statutes specified the penalties for crimes but nearly always gave the sentencing judge wide discretion to decide whether the offender should be incarcerated and for how long, whether he should be fined and how much, and whether some lesser restraint, such as probation, should be imposed instead of imprisonment or fine. This indeterminate-sentencing system was supplemented by the utilization of parole, by which an offender was returned to society under the "guidance and control" of a parole officer.

Both indeterminate sentencing and parole were based on concepts of the offender's possible, indeed probable, rehabilitation, a view that it was realistic to attempt to rehabilitate the inmate and thereby to minimize the risk that he would resume criminal activity upon his return to society. It obviously required the judge and the parole officer to make their respective sentencing and release decisions upon their own assessments of the offender's amenability to rehabilitation. As a result, the court and the officer were in positions to exercise, and usually did exercise, very broad discretion. This led almost inevitably to the conclusion on the part of a reviewing court that the sentencing judge "sees more and senses more" than the appellate court; thus, the judge enjoyed the "superiority of his nether position," for that court's determination as to what sentence was appropriate met with virtually unconditional deference on appeal. The decision whether to parole was also "predictive and discretionary." The correction official possessed almost absolute discretion over the parole decision.

Historically, federal sentencing—the function of determining the scope and extent of punishment—never has been thought to be assigned by the Constitution to the exclusive jurisdiction of any one of the three Branches of Government. Congress, of course, has the power to fix the sentence for a federal crime, and the scope of judicial discretion with respect to a sentence is subject to congressional control. Congress early abandoned fixed-sentence rigidity, however, and put in place a system of ranges within which the sentencer could choose the precise punishment. Congress delegated almost unfettered discretion to the sentencing judge to determine what the sentence should be within the customarily wide range so selected. This broad discretion was further enhanced by the power later granted the judge to suspend the sentence and by the resulting growth of an elaborate probation system. Also, with the advent of parole, Congress moved toward a "three-way sharing" of sentencing responsibility by granting corrections personnel in the Executive Branch the discretion to release a prisoner before the expiration of the sentence imposed by the judge. Thus, under the indeterminate-sentence system, Congress defined the maximum, the judge imposed a sentence within the statutory range (which he usually could replace with probation), and the Executive Branch's parole official eventually determined the actual duration of imprisonment.

Serious disparities in sentences, however, were common. Rehabilitation as a sound penological theory came to be questioned and, in any event, was regarded by some as an unattainable goal for most cases. In 1958, Congress authorized the creation of judicial sentencing institutes and joint councils, . . . to formulate standards and criteria for sentencing. In 1973, the United States Parole Board adopted guidelines that established a "customary range" of confinement. Congress in 1976 endorsed this initiative through the Parole Commission and Reorganization Act, . . . an attempt to envision for the Parole Commission a role, at least in part, "to moderate the disparities in the sentencing practices of individual judges." That Act, however, did not disturb the division of sentencing responsibility among the three Branches. The judge continued to exercise discretion and to set the sentence within the statutory range fixed by Congress, while the prisoner's actual release date generally was set by the Parole Commission.

This proved to be no more than a way station. Fundamental and widespread dissatisfaction with the uncertainties and the disparities continued to be expressed. Congress had wrestled with the problem for more than a decade when, in 1984, it enacted the sweeping reforms that are at issue here.

Helpful in our consideration and analysis of the statute is the Senate Report on the 1984 legislation. The Report referred to the "outmoded rehabilitation model" for federal criminal sentencing, and recognized that the efforts of the criminal justice system to achieve rehabilitation of offenders had failed. It observed that the indeterminate-sentencing system had two "unjustifi[ed]" and "shameful" consequences. The first was the great variation among sentences imposed by different judges upon similarly situated offenders. The second was the uncertainty as to the time the offender would spend in prison. Each was a serious impediment to an evenhanded and effective operation of the criminal justice system. The Report went on to note that parole was an inadequate device for overcoming these undesirable consequences. This was due to the division of authority between the sentencing judge and the parole officer who often worked at cross purposes; to the fact that the Parole Commission's own guidelines did not take into account factors Congress regarded as important in sentencing, such as the sophistication of the offender and the role the offender played in an offense committed with others, and to the fact that the Parole Commission had only limited power to adjust a sentence imposed by the court. [S. Rep. No. 98-225 (1983), U.S. Code Cong. & Admin. News 1984]

Before settling on a mandatory-guideline system, Congress considered other competing proposals for sentencing reform. It rejected strict determinate sentencing because it concluded that a guideline system would be successful in reducing sentence disparities while retaining the flexibility needed to adjust for unanticipated factors arising in a particular case. The Judiciary Committee rejected a proposal that would have made the sentencing guidelines only advisory.

B

The Act

The Act, as adopted, revises the old sentencing process in several ways:

1. It rejects imprisonment as a means of promoting rehabilitation, 28 U.S.C. § 994(k), and it states that punishment should serve retributive, educational, deterrent, and incapacitative goals, 18 U.S.C. § 3553(a)(2).

2. It consolidates the power that had been exercised by the sentencing judge and the Parole Commission to decide what punishment an offender should suffer. This is done by creating the United States Sentencing Commission, directing that Commission to devise guidelines to be used for sentencing, and prospectively abolishing the Parole Commission. 28 U.S.C. §§ 991, 994, and 995(a)(1).

3. It makes all sentences basically determinate. A prisoner is to be released at the completion of his sentence reduced only by any credit earned by good behavior while in custody. 18 U.S.C. §§ 3624(a) and (b).

4. It makes the Sentencing Commission's guidelines binding on the courts, although it preserves for the judge the discretion to depart from the guideline applicable to a particular case if the judge finds an aggravating or mitigating factor present that the Commission did not adequately consider when formulating guidelines. §§ 3553(a) and (b). The Act also requires the court to state its reasons for the sentence imposed and to give "the specific reason" for imposing a sentence different from that described in the guideline. § 3553(c).

5. It authorizes limited appellate review of the sentence. It permits a defendant to appeal a sentence that is above the defined range, and it permits the Government to appeal a sentence that is below that range. It also permits either side to appeal an incorrect application of the guideline. §§ 3742(a) and (b).

Thus, guidelines were meant to establish a range of determinate sentences for categories of offenses and defendants according to various specified factors, "among others." 28 U.S.C. §§ 994(b), (c), and (d). The maximum of the range ordinarily may not exceed the minimum by more than the greater of 25% or six months, and each sentence is to be within the limit provided by existing law. §§ 994(a) and (b)(2).

C

The Sentencing Commission

The Commission is established "as an independent commission in the judicial branch of the United States." § 991(a). It has seven voting members (one of whom is the Chairman) appointed by the President "by and with the advice and consent of the Senate." "At least three of the members shall be Federal judges selected after considering a list of six judges recommended to the President by the Judicial Conference of the United States." *Ibid.* No more than four members of the Commission shall be members of the same political party. The Attorney General, or his designee, is an ex officio non-voting member. The Chairman and other members of the Commission are subject to removal by the President "only for neglect of duty or malfeasance in office or for other good cause shown." *Ibid.* Except for initial staggering of terms, a voting member serves for six years and may not serve more than two full terms. §§ 992(a) and (b).

D

The Responsibilities of the Commission

In addition to the duty the Commission has to promulgate determinative-sentence guidelines, it is under an obligation periodically to "review and revise" the guidelines. § 994(o). It is to "consult with authorities on, and individual and institutional representatives of, various aspects of the Federal criminal justice system." . . . It must report to Congress "any amendments of the guidelines." § 994(p). It is to make recommendations to Congress whether the grades or maximum penalties should be modified. § 994(r). It must submit to Congress at least annually an analysis of the operation of the guidelines. § 994(w). It is to issue "general policy statements" regarding their application. § 994(a)(2). And it has the power to "establish general policies . . . as are necessary to carry out the purposes" of the legislation § 995(a)(1); to "monitor the performance of probation officers" with respect to the guidelines, § 995(a)(9); to "devise and conduct periodic training programs of instruction in sentencing techniques for judicial and probation personnel" and others, § 995(a)(18); and to "perform such other functions as are required to permit Federal courts to meet their responsibilities" as to sentencing, § 995(a)(22).

We note, in passing, that the monitoring function is not without its burden. Every year, with respect to each of more than 40,000 sentences, the federal courts must forward, and the Commission must review, the presentence report, the guideline worksheets, the tribunal's sentencing statement, and any written plea agreement.

II

This Litigation

On December 10, 1987, John M. Mistretta (petitioner) and another were indicted in the United States District Court for the Western District of Missouri on three counts centering in a cocaine sale. Mistretta moved to have the promulgated Guidelines ruled unconstitutional on the grounds that the Sentencing Commission was constituted in violation of the established doctrine of separation of powers, and that Congress delegated excessive authority to the Commission to structure the Guidelines. . . .

The District Court rejected petitioner's delegation argument on the ground that, despite the language of the statute, the Sentencing Commission "should be judicially characterized as having Executive Branch status," and that the Guidelines are similar to substantive rules promulgated by other agencies. The court also rejected petitioner's claim that the Act is unconstitutional because it requires Article III federal judges to serve on the Commission. The court stated, however, that its opinion "does not imply that I have no serious doubts about some parts of the Sentencing Guidelines and the legality of their anticipated operation." [682 F. Supp. at 1035.]

Petitioner had pleaded guilty to the first count of his indictment (conspiracy and agreement to distribute cocaine, in violation of 21 U.S.C. §§ 846 and 841(b)(1)(B)). . . . Petitioner was sentenced under the Guidelines. . . .

Petitioner filed a notice of appeal to the Eighth Circuit, but both petitioner and the United States, pursuant to this Court's Rule 18, petitioned for certiorari before judgment. Because of the "imperative public importance" of the issue, as prescribed by the Rule, and because of the disarray among the Federal District Courts, we granted those petitions.

III

Delegation of Power

Petitioner argues that in delegating the power to promulgate sentencing guidelines for every federal criminal offense to an independent Sentencing Commission, Congress has granted the Commission excessive legislative discretion in violation of the constitutionally based nondelegation doctrine. We do not agree.

The nondelegation doctrine is rooted in the principle of separation of powers that underlies our tripartite system of Government. [W]e long have insisted that "the integrity and maintenance of the system of government ordained by the Constitution" mandate that Congress generally cannot delegate its legislative power to another Branch. . . . We also have recognized, however, that the separation-of-powers principle, and the nondelegation doctrine in particular, do not prevent Congress from obtaining the assistance of its coordinate Branches. In a passage now enshrined in our jurisprudence, Chief Justice Taft, writing for the Court, explained our approach to such cooperative ventures: "In determining what [Congress] may do in seeking assistance from another branch, the extent and character of that assistance must be fixed according to common sense and the inherent necessities of the government co-ordination." . . . So long as Congress "shall lay down by legislative act an intelligible principle to which the person or body authorized to [exercise the delegated authority] is directed to conform, such legislative action is not a forbidden delegation of legislative power." [*J. W. Hampton, Jr. & Co. v. United States*, 276 U.S. 394, 406, 409 (1928).]

Applying this "intelligible principle" test to congressional delegations, our jurisprudence has been driven by a practical understanding that in our increasingly complex society, replete with ever changing and more technical problems, Congress simply cannot do its job absent an ability to delegate power under broad general directives. . . . "The Constitution has never been regarded as denying to the Congress the necessary resources of flexibility and practicality, which will enable it to perform its function." *Panama Refining Co. v.*

Ryan, 293 U.S. 388, 421 (1935). Accordingly, this Court has deemed it "constitutionally sufficient if Congress clearly delineates the general policy, the public agency which is to apply it, and the boundaries of this delegated authority."

Until 1935, this Court never struck down a challenged statute on delegation grounds. After invalidating in 1935 two statutes as excessive delegations, we have upheld, again without deviation, Congress' ability to delegate power under broad standards.

In light of our approval of these broad delegations, we harbor no doubt that Congress' delegation of authority to the Sentencing Commission is sufficiently specific and detailed to meet constitutional requirements.

... Congress prescribed the specific tool—the guidelines system—for the Commission to use in regulating sentencing. More particularly, Congress directed the Commission to develop a system of "sentencing ranges" applicable "for each category of offense involving each category of defendant." Congress instructed the Commission that these sentencing ranges must be consistent with pertinent provisions of Title 18 of the United States Code and could not include sentences in excess of the statutory maxima. Congress also required that for sentences of imprisonment, "the maximum of the range established for such a term shall not exceed the minimum of that range by more than the greater of 25 percent or 6 months, except that, if the minimum term of the range is 30 years or more, the maximum may be life imprisonment." Moreover, Congress directed the Commission to use current average sentences "as a starting point" for its structuring of the sentencing ranges.

To guide the Commission in its formulation of offense categories, Congress directed it to consider seven factors: the grade of the offense; the aggravating and mitigating circumstances of the crime; the nature and degree of the harm caused by the crime; the community view of the gravity of the offense; the public concern generated by the crime; the deterrent effect that a particular sentence may have on others; and the current incidence of the offense. § 994(c)(7). Congress set forth 11 factors for the Commission to consider in establishing categories of defendants. These include the offender's age, education, vocational skills, mental and emotional condition, physical condition (including drug dependence), previous employment record, family ties and responsibilities, community ties, role in the offense, criminal history, and degree of dependence upon crime for a livelihood. § 994(d)(1). Congress also prohibited the Commission from considering the "race, sex, national origin, creed, and socioeconomic status of offenders," § 994(d), and instructed that the guidelines should reflect the "general inappropriateness" of considering certain other factors, such as current unemployment, that might serve as proxies for forbidden factors, § 994(e).

In addition to these overarching constraints, Congress provided even more detailed guidance to the Commission about categories of offenses and offender characteristics. Congress directed that guidelines require a term of confinement at or near the statutory maximum for certain crimes of violence and for drug offenses, particularly when committed by recidivists. § 994(h). Congress further directed that the Commission assure a substantial term of imprisonment for an offense constituting a third felony conviction, for a career felon, for one convicted of a managerial role in a racketeering enterprise, for a crime of violence by an offender on release from a prior felony conviction, and for an offense involving a substantial quantity of narcotics. § 994(i). Congress also instructed "that the guidelines reflect ... the general appropriateness of imposing a term of imprisonment" for a crime of violence that resulted in serious bodily injury. On the other hand, Congress directed that guidelines reflect the general inappropriateness of imposing a sentence of imprisonment "in cases in which the defendant is a first offender who has not been convicted of a crime of violence or an otherwise serious offense." § 994(j). Congress also enumerated various aggravating and mitigating circumstances, such as, respectively, multiple offenses or substantial assistance to the Government, to be reflected in the guidelines. §§ 994(l) and (h). In other words, although Congress granted the Commission substantial discretion in formulating guidelines, in actuality it legislated a full hierarchy of punishment—from near maximum imprisonment, to substantial imprisonment, to some imprisonment, to alternatives—and stipulated the most important offense and offender characteristics to place defendants within these categories.

The Commission does have discretionary authority to determine the relative severity of federal crimes and to assess the relative weight of the offender characteristics that Congress listed for the Commission to consider. The Commission also has significant discretion to determine which crimes have been punished too leniently, and which too severely. Congress has called upon the Commission to exercise its judgment about which types of crimes and which types of criminals are to be considered similar for the purposes of sentencing.

But our cases do not at all suggest that delegations of this type may not carry with them the need to exercise judgment on matters of policy. In *Yakus v. United States*, 321 U.S. 414 (1944), the Court upheld a delegation to the Price Administrator to fix commodity fair and equitable and will effectuate the purposes of this Act" to stabilize prices and avert speculation. In *Yakus*, the Court laid down the applicable principle:

> "It is no objection that the determination of facts and the inferences to be drawn from them in the light of the statutory standards and declaration of policy call for the exercise of judgment, and for the formulation of subsidiary administrative policy within the prescribed statutory framework. . . .
>
> * * *
>
> ". . . Only if we could say that there is an absence of standards for the guidance of the Administrator's action, so that it would be impossible in a proper proceeding to ascertain whether the will of Congress has been obeyed, would we be justified in overriding its choice of means for effecting its declared purpose. . . . " 321 U.S. 425-26.

Congress has met that standard here. The Act sets forth more than merely an "intelligible principle" or minimal standards. One court has aptly put it: "The statute outlines the policies which prompted establishment of the Commission, explains what the Commission should do and how it should do it, and sets out specific directives to govern particular situations." *United States v. Chambless*, 680 F. Supp. 793, 796 (E.D. La. 1988).

Developing proportionate penalties for hundreds of different crimes by a virtually limitless array of offenders is precisely the sort of intricate, labor-intensive task for which delegation to an expert body is especially appropriate. Although Congress has delegated significant discretion to the Commission to draw judgments from its analysis of existing sentencing practice and alternative sentencing models, "Congress is not confined to that method of executing its policy which involves the least possible delegation of discretion to administrative officers." *Yakus v. United States*, [*supra*] at 425-26.

IV

Separation of Powers

Having determined that Congress has set forth sufficient standards for the exercise of the Commission's delegated authority, we turn to Mistretta's claim that the Act violates the constitutional principle of separation of powers.

This Court consistently has given voice to, and has reaffirmed, the central judgment of the Framers of the Constitution that, within our political scheme, the separation of governmental powers into three coordinate Branches is essential to the preservation of liberty. . . .

In applying the principle of separated powers in our jurisprudence, we have sought to give life to Madison's view of the appropriate relationship among the three coequal Branches. Accordingly, we have recognized, as Madison admonished at the founding, that while our Constitution mandates that "each of the three general departments of government [must remain] entirely free from the control or coercive influence, direct or indirect, of either of the others," the Framers did not require—and indeed rejected—the notion that the three Branches must be entirely separate and distinct. Madison, defending the Constitution against charges that it established insufficiently separate Branches, addressed the point directly. Separation of powers, he wrote, "d[oes] not mean that these [three] departments ought to have no *partial agency* in, or no *controul* over the acts of each other," but rather "that where the *whole* power of one department is exercised by the same hands which possess the *whole* power of another department, the fundamental principles of a free constitution, are subverted." The Federalist No. 47, pp. 325-326 (J. Cooke ed. 1961) (emphasis in original). Madison recognized that our constitutional system imposes upon the Branches a degree of overlapping responsibility, a duty of interdependence as well as independence the absence of which "would preclude the establishment of a Nation capable of governing itself effectively." *Buckley v. Valeo*, 424 U.S. 1, 121 (1976).

It is concern of encroachment and aggrandizement that has animated our separation-of-powers jurisprudence and aroused our vigilance against the "hydraulic pressure inherent within each of the separate Branches to exceed the outer limits of its power." Accordingly, we have not hesitated to strike down provisions of law that either accrete to a single Branch powers more appropriately diffused among separate Branches or that undermine the authority and independence of one or another coordinate Branch.

In *Nixon v. Administrator of General Services, supra,* upholding, against a separation-of-powers challenge, legislation providing for the General Services Administration to control Presidential papers after resignation, we described our separation-of-powers inquiry as focusing "on the extent to which [a provision of law] prevents the Executive Branch from accomplishing its constitutionally assigned functions." In cases specifically involving the Judicial Branch, we have expressed our vigilance against two dangers: first, that the Judicial Branch neither be assigned nor allowed "tasks that are more properly accomplished by [other] branches," *Morrison v. Olson*, 487 U.S. at 680-81, and, second, that no provision of law "impermissibly threatens the institutional integrity of the Judicial Branch." *Commodity Futures Trading Comm'n v. Schor*, 478 U.S. at 851.

Mistretta argues that the Act suffers from each of these constitutional infirmities. He argues that Congress, in constituting the Commission as it did, effected an unconstitutional accumulation of power within the Judicial Branch while at the same time undermining the Judiciary's independence and integrity. Specifically, petitioner claims that in delegating to an independent agency within the Judicial Branch the power to promulgate sentencing guidelines, Congress unconstitutionally has required the Branch, and individual Article III judges, to exercise not only their judicial authority, but legislative authority—the making of sentencing policy—as well. Such rulemaking authority, petitioner contends, may be exercised by Congress, or delegated by Congress to the Executive, but may not be delegated to or exercised by the Judiciary....

At the same time, petitioner asserts, Congress unconstitutionally eroded the integrity and independence of the Judiciary by requiring Article III judges to sit on the Commission, by requiring that those judges share their rulemaking authority with nonjudges, and by subjecting the Commission's members to appointment and removal by the President. According to petitioner, Congress, consistent with the separation of powers, may not upset the balance among the Branches by co-opting federal judges into the quintessentially political work of establishing sentencing guidelines, by subjecting those judges to the political whims of the Chief Executive, and by forcing judges to share their power with nonjudges.

"When this Court is asked to invalidate a statutory provision that has been approved by both Houses of the Congress and signed by the President, particularly an Act of Congress that confronts a deeply vexing national problem, it should only do so for the most compelling constitutional reasons." Although the unique composition and responsibilities of the Sentencing Commission give rise to serious concerns about a disruption of the appropriate balance of governmental power among the coordinate Branches, we conclude, upon close inspection, that petitioner's fears for the fundamental structural protections of the Constitution prove, at least in this case, to be "more smoke than fire," and do not compel us to invalidate Congress' considered scheme for resolving the seemingly intractable dilemma of excessive disparity in criminal sentencing.

A

Location of the Commission

The Sentencing Commission unquestionably is a peculiar institution within the framework of our Government. Although placed by the Act in the Judicial Branch, it is not a court and does not exercise judicial power. Rather, the Commission is an "independent" body comprised of seven voting members including at least three federal judges, entrusted by Congress with the primary task of promulgating sentencing guidelines. Our constitutional principles of separated powers are not violated, however, by mere anomaly or innovation. Setting to one side, for the moment, the question whether the composition of the Sentencing Commission violates the separation of powers, we observe that Congress' decision to create an independent rulemaking body to promulgate sentencing guidelines and to locate that body within the Judicial Branch is not unconstitutional unless Congress has vested in the Commission powers that are more appropriately performed by the other Branches or that undermine the integrity of the Judiciary.

According to express provision of Article III, the judicial power of the United States is limited to "Cases" and "Controversies." In implementing this limited grant of power, we have refused to issue advisory opinions or to resolve disputes that are not justiciable. These doctrines help to ensure the independence of the Judicial Branch by precluding debilitating entanglements between the Judiciary and the two political Branches, and prevent the Judiciary from encroaching into areas reserved for the other Branches by extending judicial power to matters beyond those disputes "traditionally thought to be capable of resolution through the judicial process."

Nonetheless, we have ... approved the assumption of some nonadjudicatory activities by the Judicial Branch. In keeping with Justice Jackson's *Youngstown* admonition that the separation of powers contemplates the integration of dispersed powers into a workable Government, we have recognized the constitutionality of a "twilight area" in which the activities of the separate Branches merge.

That judicial rulemaking, at least with respect to some subjects, falls within this twilight area is no longer an issue for dispute. None of our cases indicate that rulemaking *per se* is a function that may not be performed by an entity within the Judicial Branch, either because rulemaking is inherently nonjudicial or because it is a function exclusively committed to the Executive Branch. On the contrary, we specifically have held that Congress, in some circumstances, may confer rulemaking authority on the Judicial Branch. In *Sibbach v. Wilson & Co.*, 312 U.S. 1 (1941), we upheld a challenge to certain rules promulgated under the Rules Enabling Act of 1934, which conferred upon the Judiciary the power to promulgate federal rules of civil procedure. We observed: "Congress has undoubted power to regulate the practice and procedure of federal courts, and may exercise that power by delegating to this or other federal courts authority to make rules not inconsistent with the statutes or constitution of the United States." [*Id.*] at 9-10. Pursuant to this power to delegate rulemaking authority to the Judicial Branch, Congress expressly has authorized this Court to establish rules for the conduct of its own business and to prescribe rules of procedure for lower federal courts in bankruptcy cases, in other civil cases, and in criminal cases, and to revise the Federal Rules of Evidence.

Our approach to other nonadjudicatory activities that Congress has vested either in federal courts or in auxiliary bodies within the Judicial Branch has been identical to our approach to judicial rulemaking: consistent with the separation of powers, Congress may delegate to the Judicial Branch nonadjudicatory functions that do not trench upon the prerogatives of another Branch and that are appropriate to the central mission of the Judiciary. Following this approach, we specifically have upheld not only Congress' power to confer on the Judicial Branch the rulemaking authority contemplated in the various enabling Acts, but also to vest in judicial councils authority to "make 'all necessary orders for the effective and expeditious administration of the business of the courts.'" Though not the subject of constitutional challenge, by established practice we have recognized Congress' power to create the Judicial Conference of the United States, the Rules Advisory Committees that it oversees, and the Administrative Office of the United States Courts whose myriad responsibilities include the administration of the entire probation service. These entities, some of which are comprised of judges, others of judges and nonjudges, still others of nonjudges only, do not exercise judicial power in the constitutional sense of deciding cases and controversies, but they share the common purpose of providing for the fair and efficient fulfillment of responsibilities that are properly the province of the Judiciary. Thus, although the judicial power of the United States is limited by express provision of Article III to "Cases" and "Controversies," we have never held, and have clearly disavowed in practice, that the Constitution prohibits Congress from assigning to courts or auxiliary bodies within the Judicial Branch administrative or rulemaking duties that, in the words of Chief Justice Marshall, are "necessary and proper . . . for carrying into execution all the judgments which the judicial department has power to pronounce." *Wayman v. Southard,* 10 Wheat at 22. . . .

In light of this precedent and practice, we can discern no separation-of-powers impediment to the placement of the Sentencing Commission within the Judicial Branch. As we described at the outset, the sentencing function long has been a peculiarly shared responsibility among the Branches of Government and has never been thought of as the exclusive constitutional province of any one Branch. For more than a century, federal judges have enjoyed wide discretion to determine the appropriate sentence in individual cases and have exercised special authority to determine the sentencing factors to be applied in any given case. Indeed, the legislative history of the Act makes clear that Congress' decision to place the Commission within the Judicial Branch reflected Congress' "strong feeling" that sentencing has been and should remain "primarily a judicial function."

Petitioner nonetheless objects that the analogy between the Guidelines and the rules of procedure is flawed: Although the Judicial Branch may participate in rulemaking and administrative work that is "procedural" in nature, it may not assume, it is said, the "substantive" authority over sentencing policy that Congress has delegated to the Commission. Such substantive decisionmaking, petitioner contends, entangles the Judicial Branch in essentially political work of the other Branches and unites both judicial and legislative power in the Judicial Branch.

We do not believe, however, that the significantly political nature of the Commission's work renders unconstitutional its placement within the Judicial Branch. Our separation-of-powers analysis does not turn on the labeling of an activity as "substantive" as opposed to "procedural," or "political" as opposed to "judicial." Rather, our inquiry is focused on the "unique aspects of the congressional plan at issue and its practical consequences in light of the larger concerns that underlie Article III." In this case, the "practical consequences" of locating the Commission within the Judicial Branch pose no threat of undermining the integrity of the Judicial Branch or of expanding the powers of the Judiciary beyond constitutional bounds by uniting within the Branch the political or quasi-legislative power of the Commission with the judicial power of the courts.

First, although the Commission is located in the Judicial Branch, its powers are not united with the powers of the Judiciary in a way that has meaning for separation-of-powers analysis. Whatever constitutional problems might arise if the powers of the Commission were vested in a court, the Commission is not a court, does not exercise judicial power, and is not controlled by or accountable to members of the Judicial Branch. The Commission, on which members of the Judiciary may be a minority, is an independent agency in every relevant sense. In contrast to a court's exercising judicial power, the Commission is fully accountable to Congress, which can revoke or amend any or all of the Guidelines as it sees fit either within the 180-day waiting period, or at any time. In contrast to a court, the Commission's members are subject to the President's limited powers of removal. In contrast to a court, its rulemaking is subject to the notice and comment requirements of the Administrative Procedure Act. While we recognize the continuing vitality of Montesquieu's admonition: "'Were the power of judging joined with the legislative, the life and liberty of the subject would be exposed to arbitrary controul,'" The Federalist No. 47 [*supra* at 326], because Congress vested the power to promulgate sentencing guidelines in an independent agency, not a court, there can be no serious argument that Congress combined legislative and judicial power within the Judicial Branch.

Second, although the Commission wields rulemaking power and not the adjudicatory power exercised by individual judges when passing sentence, the placement of the Sentencing Commission in the Judicial Branch has not increased the Branch's authority. Prior to the passage of the Act, the Judicial Branch, as an aggregate, decided precisely the questions assigned to the Commission: what sentence is appropriate to what criminal conduct under what circumstances. It was the everyday business of judges, taken collectively, to evaluate and weigh the various aims of sentencing and to apply those aims to the individual cases that came before them. The Sentencing Commission does no more than this, albeit basically through the methodology of sentencing guidelines, rather than entirely individualized sentencing determinations. Accordingly, in placing the Commission in the Judicial Branch, Congress cannot be said to have aggrandized the authority of that Branch or to have deprived the Executive Branch of a power it once possessed. Indeed, because the Guidelines have the effect of promoting sentencing within a narrower range than was previously applied, the power of the Judicial Branch is, if anything, somewhat diminished by the Act. And, since Congress did not unconstitutionally delegate its own authority, the Act does not unconstitutionally diminish Congress' authority.

Nor do the Guidelines, though substantive, involve a degree of political authority inappropriate for a nonpolitical Branch. Although the Guidelines are intended to have substantive effects on public behavior (as do the rules of procedure), they do not bind or regulate the primary conduct of the public or vest in the Judicial Branch the legislative responsibility for establishing minimum and maximum penalties for every crime. They do no more than fetter the discretion of sentencing judges to do what they have done for generations—impose sentences within the broad limits established by Congress. Given their limited reach, the special role of the Judicial Branch in the field of sentencing, and the fact that the Guidelines are promulgated by an independent agency and not a court, it follows that as a matter of "practical consequences" the location of the Sentencing Commission within the Judicial Branch simply leaves with the Judiciary what long has belonged to it.

In sum, since substantive judgment in the field of sentencing has been and remains appropriate to the Judicial Branch, and the methodology of rulemaking has been and remains appropriate to that Branch, Congress' considered decision to combine these functions in an independent Sentencing Commission and to locate that Commission within the Judicial Branch does not violate the principle of separation of powers.

B

Composition of the Commission

We now turn to petitioner's claim that Congress' decision to require at least three federal judges to serve on the Commission and to require those judges to share their authority with nonjudges undermines the integrity of the Judicial Branch.

The Act provides in part: "At least three of [the Commission's] members shall be Federal judges selected [by the President] after considering a list of six judges recommended to the President by the Judicial Conference of the United States." 28 U.S.C. § 991(a). Petitioner urges us to strike down the Act on the ground that its requirement of judicial participation on the Commission unconstitutionally conscripts individual federal judges for political service and thereby undermines the essential impartiality of the Judicial Branch. We find Congress' requirement of judicial service somewhat troublesome, but we do not believe that the Act impermissibly interferes with the functioning of the Judiciary.

The text of the Constitution contains no prohibition against the service of active federal judges on independent commissions such as that established by the Act. The Constitution does include an Incompatibility Clause applicable to national legislators:

> "No Senator or Representative shall, during the Time for which he was elected, be appointed to any civil Office under the Authority of the United States, which shall have been created, or the Emoluments whereof shall have been increased during such time; and no Person holding any Office under the United States, shall be a Member of either House during his Continuance in Office." U.S. Const., Art. I, § 6, cl. 2.

No comparable restriction applies to judges, and we find it at least inferentially meaningful that at the Constitutional Convention two prohibitions against plural officeholding by members of the Judiciary were proposed, but did not reach the floor of the Convention for a vote.

Our inferential reading that the Constitution does not prohibit Article III judges from undertaking extrajudicial duties finds support in the historical practice of the Founders after ratification. Our early history indicates that the Framers themselves did not read the Constitution as forbidding extrajudicial service by federal judges. The first Chief Justice, John Jay, served simultaneously as Chief Justice and as Ambassador to England, where he negotiated the treaty that bears his name. Oliver Ellsworth served simultaneously as Chief Justice and as Minister to France. While he was Chief Justice, John Marshall served briefly as Secretary of State and was a member of the Sinking Fund Commission with responsibility for refunding the Revolutionary War debt.

All these appointments were made by the President with the "Advice and Consent" of the Senate. Thus, at a minimum, both the Executive and Legislative Branches acquiesced in the assumption of extrajudicial duties by judges. In addition, although the records of Congress contain no reference to the confirmation debate, Charles Warren, in his history of this Court, reports that the Senate specifically rejected by a vote of 18 to 8 a resolution proposed during the debate over Jay's nomination to the effect that such extrajudicial service was "contrary to the spirit of the Constitution." This contemporaneous practice by the Founders themselves is significant evidence that the constitutional principle of separation of powers does not absolutely prohibit extrajudicial service.

[Although we have not specifically addressed the constitutionality of extrajudicial service . . . our precedents suggest that Congress may] authorize a federal judge, in an individual capacity, to perform an executive function without violating the separation of powers.

In light of the foregoing history and precedent, we conclude that the principle of separation of powers does not absolutely prohibit Article III judges from serving on commissions such as that created by the Act. The judges serve on the Sentencing Commission not pursuant to their status and authority as Article III judges, but solely because of their appointment by the President as the Act directs. Such power as these judges wield as Commissioners is not judicial power; it is administrative power derived from the enabling legislation. Just as the nonjudicial members of the Commission act as administrators, bringing their experience and wisdom to bear on the problems of sentencing disparity, so too the judges, uniquely qualified on the subject of sentencing, assume a wholly administrative role upon entering into the deliberations of the Commission. In other words, the Constitution, at least as a *per se* matter, does not forbid judges to wear two hats; it merely forbids them to wear both hats at the same time.

This is not to suggest, of course, that every kind of extrajudicial service under every circumstance necessarily accords with the Constitution. That the Constitution does not absolutely prohibit a federal judge from assuming extrajudicial duties does not mean that every extrajudicial service would be compatible with, or appropriate to, continuing service on the bench; nor does it mean that Congress may require a federal judge to assume extrajudicial duties as long as the judge is assigned those duties in an individual, not judicial, capacity. The ultimate inquiry remains whether a particular extrajudicial assignment undermines the integrity of the Judicial Branch.

With respect to the Sentencing Commission, we understand petitioner to argue that the service required of at least three judges presents two distinct threats to the integrity of the Judicial Branch. Regardless of constitutionality, this mandatory service, it is said, diminishes the independence of the Judiciary. It is further claimed that the participation of judges on the Commission improperly lends judicial prestige and an aura of judicial impartiality to the Commission's political work. The involvement of Article III judges in the process of policymaking, petitioner asserts, "'[w]eakens confidence in the disinterestedness of the judicatory functions.'"

In our view, petitioner significantly overstates the mandatory nature of Congress' directive that at least three members of the Commission shall be federal judges, as well as the effect of this service on the practical operation of the Judicial Branch. Service on the Commission by any particular judge is voluntary. The Act does not conscript judges for the Commission. No Commission member to date has been appointed without his consent and we have no reason to believe that the Act confers upon the President any authority to force a judge to serve on the Commission against his will. Accordingly, we simply do not face the question whether Congress may require a particular judge to undertake the extrajudicial duty of serving on the Commission. In *Chandler v. Judicial Council*, we found "no constitutional obstacle preventing Congress from vesting in the Circuit Judicial Councils, as administrative bodies," authority to administer "'the business of the courts within [each] circuit.'" [398 U.S. 74, 86 n.7]. Indeed, Congress has created numerous nonadjudicatory bodies, such as the Judicial Conference, that are composed entirely, or in part, of federal judges. Accordingly, absent a more specific threat to judicial independence, the fact that Congress has included federal judges on the Commission does not itself threaten the integrity of the Judicial Branch.

Moreover, we cannot see how the service of federal judges on the Commission will have a constitutionally significant practical effect on the operation of the Judicial Branch. We see no reason why service on the Commission should result in widespread judicial recusals. That federal judges participate in the promulgation of guidelines does not affect their or other judges' ability impartially to adjudicate sentencing issues. While in the abstract a proliferation of commissions with congressionally mandated judiciary participation might threaten judicial independence by exhausting the resources of the Judicial Branch, that danger is far too remote for consideration here.

We are somewhat more troubled by petitioner's argument that the Judiciary's entanglement in the political work of the Commission undermines public confidence in the disinterestedness of the Judicial Branch. While the problem of individual bias is usually cured through recusal, no such mechanism can overcome the appearance of institutional partiality that may arise from judiciary involvement in the making of policy. The legitimacy of the Judicial Branch ultimately depends on its reputation for impartiality and nonpartisanship. That reputation may not be borrowed by the political Branches to cloak their work in the neutral colors of judicial action.

Although it is a judgment that is not without difficulty, we conclude that the participation of federal judges on the Sentencing Commission does not threaten, either in fact or in appearance, the impartiality of the Judicial Branch. We are drawn to this conclusion by one paramount consideration: that the Sentencing Commission is devoted exclusively to the development of rules to rationalize a process that has been and will continue to be performed exclusively by the Judicial Branch. In our view, this is an essentially neutral endeavor and one in which judicial participation is peculiarly appropriate. Judicial contribution to the enterprise of creating rules to limit the discretion of sentencing judges does not enlist the resources or reputation of the Judicial Branch in either the legislative business of determining what conduct should be criminalized or the executive business of enforcing the law. Rather, judicial participation on the Commission ensures that judicial experience and expertise will inform the promulgation of rules for the exercise of the Judicial Branch's own business—that of passing sentence on every criminal defendant. To this end, Congress has provided, not inappropriately, for a significant judicial voice on the Commission.

[As part of dispersed powers] into a workable government, Congress may enlist the assistance of judges in the creation of rules to govern the Judicial Branch. Our principle of separation of powers anticipates that the coordinate Branches will converse with each other on matters of vital common interest. While we have some reservation that Congress required such a dialogue in this case, the Constitution does not prohibit Congress from enlisting federal judges to present a uniquely judicial view on the uniquely judicial subject of sentencing.

Finally, we reject petitioner's argument that the mixed nature of the Commission violates the Constitution by requiring Article III judges to share judicial power with nonjudges. As noted earlier, the Commission is not a court and exercises no judicial power. Thus, the Act does not vest Article III power in nonjudges or require Article III judges to share their power with nonjudges.

C

Presidential Control

The Act empowers the President to appoint all seven members of the Commission with the advice and consent of the Senate. The Act further provides that the President shall make his choice of judicial appointees to the Commission after considering a list of six judges recommended by the Judicial Conference of the United States. The Act also grants the President authority to remove members of the Commission, although "only for neglect of duty or malfeasance in office or for other good cause shown." 28 U.S.C. § 991(a).

Mistretta argues that this power of Presidential appointment and removal prevents the Judicial Branch from performing its constitutionally assigned functions. Although we agree with petitioner that the independence of the Judicial Branch must be "jealously guarded" against outside interference, and that, as Madison admonished at the founding, "neither of [the Branches] ought to possess directly or indirectly, an overruling influence over the others in the administration of their respective powers," The Federalist [*supra*] No. 48, p. 332, we do not believe that the President's appointment and removal powers over the Commission afford him influence over the functions of the Judicial Branch or undue sway over its members.

The notion that the President's power to appoint federal judges to the Commission somehow gives him influence over the Judicial Branch or prevents, even potentially, the Judicial Branch from performing its constitutionally assigned functions is fanciful. We have never considered it incompatible with the functioning of the Judicial Branch that the President has the power to elevate federal judges from one level to another or to tempt judges away from the bench with Executive Branch positions. The mere fact that the President within his appointment portfolio has positions that may be attractive to federal judges does not, of itself, corrupt the integrity of the Judiciary. Were the impartiality of the Judicial Branch so easily subverted, our constitutional system of tripartite Government would have failed long ago. We simply cannot imagine that federal judges will comport their actions to the wishes of the President for the purpose of receiving an appointment to the Sentencing Commission.

The President's removal power over Commission members poses a similarly negligible threat to judicial independence. Even if removed from the Commission, a federal judge appointed to the Commission would continue, absent impeachment, to enjoy tenure "during good Behaviour" and a full judicial salary. Also, the President's removal power under the Act is limited. In order to safeguard the independence of the Commission from executive control, Congress specified in the Act that the President may remove the Commission members only for good cause. Under these circumstances, we see no risk that the President's limited removal power will compromise the impartiality of Article III judges serving on the Commission and, consequently, no risk that the Act's removal provision will prevent the Judicial Branch from performing its constitution-ally assigned function of fairly adjudicating cases and controversies.

The judgment of United States District Court for the Western District of Missouri is affirmed.

It is so ordered.

Justice SCALIA, dissenting.

Today's decision follows the regrettable tendency of our recent separation-of-powers jurisprudence to treat the Constitution as though it were no more than a generalized prescription that the functions of the Branches should not be commingled too much—how much is too much is to be determined—case-by-case, by this Court. The Constitution is not that. Rather, as its name suggests, it is a prescribed structure, a framework, for the conduct of government. In designing that structure the framers *themselves* considered how much commingling was, in the generality of things, acceptable, and set forth their conclusions in the document.

PAH: *Morrison* and *Mistretta* demonstrate that a functional analysis remains attractive to the Court in at least some circumstances and that legislative efforts to promote efficient and workable government will not automatically fail. A functional analysis permits the Court to sustain legislative delegation of power even if the designated actor is insulated from executive control or there is diffusion of governmental functions in an official or agency. Formalists' concerns about the effects on liberty of accumulated power may not be as compelling in such cases.[114]

DEL: Taken as a whole, the separation of powers cases reflect the influence of both formalism and functionalism. Like the cyclical shifts from interpretivism to noninterpretivism in the area of fundamental rights, the competing value systems seem locked in an eternal struggle for dominance. Notwithstanding the fervor of the debate, and voluminous and sometimes exotic output of commentators, a final resolution seems no closer today than it was two centuries ago.

---

[114] *See, e.g.,* Greene, *supra,* 61 U. CHI. L. REV. 123 (attempting to extract a coherent principle from recent cases, he posits as a framework that Congress may give away legislative power and insulate such delegated power from total presidential control but Congress may neither draw executive power to itself nor seek to legislate outside the Art. I, sec. 7 framework); Todd D. Peterson, *Prosecuting Executive Branch Officials for Contempt of Congress,* 66 N.Y.U. L. REV. 563 (1991) (noting distinction between statutory accumulation and diffusion of power is that in the former there may be substantial impact on individual liberty).

E. Congressional Power to Enforce and Expand Constitutional Rights

Theoretically, it seems consistent with the Framer's design of three co-equal branches that Congress would have the power independently to determine the constitutionality of legislation. Although Madison viewed the Judiciary as having principal authority for the exposition of laws and the Constitution, as a member of the House of Representatives, Madison said to his colleagues that it was their duty "to take care that the powers of the Constitution be preserved."[115] Those serving in the early Congresses were of the view that "Congress, as an independent branch of government, had both independent authority and duty to decide constitutional questions."[116] The fundamental principle often attributed to *Marbury v. Madison*, that the Court is the ultimate expositor of the Constitution, casts doubt on the role of Congress in discerning and providing remedies for constitutional wrongdoing.

1. Power to Enforce and Expand the Reconstruction Amendments

The Court itself has recognized that the Thirteenth, Fourteenth, and Fifteenth Amendments which were added during Reconstruction were designed to change the federal/state balance of power, affording the federal government the authority to develop and implement a plan for moving toward freedom and equality for Black Americans. It is indisputable that a primary purpose of the amendments was to provide Congress with authority to enforce and implement the amendments' rights. Both the Thirteenth Amendment, which prohibits slavery, and the Fifteenth Amendment, which guarantees all citizens the vote, include a provision like the Fourteenth Amendment's section 5, stating that: "Congress shall have power to enforce, by appropriate legislation, the provisions of this article." Relying on this language, Congress has asserted its power in each of these "enforcement" provisions to enact legislation beyond the boundaries of rights defined by the Court.

The *Civil Rights Cases* narrowly construed the reach of the Thirteenth and Fourteenth Amendments in their application to private racial discrimination. Although the Court held that the Thirteenth Amendment's prohibition of slavery restricts both private and governmental action, in the *Civil Rights Cases* the Court limited Congress' ability to define and remedy the badges of slavery. Justice Bradley also took a narrow view of the power of Congress to enforce the Fourteenth Amendment under its section 5 power. Noting that section 5 of the Fourteenth Amendment invests Congress with power to enforce it by appropriate legislation, Justice Bradley asked:

> To enforce what? To enforce the prohibition. To adopt appropriate legislation for correcting the effects of such prohibited state laws and state acts, and thus to render them effectually null and void, and innocuous. This is the legislative power conferred upon congress, and this is the whole of it. It does not invest congress with power to legislate upon subjects which are within the domain of state legislation; but to provide modes of relief against state legislation, or state action, of the kind referred to. It does not authorize congress to create a code of municipal law for the regulation of private rights; but to provide modes of redress against the operation of state laws, and the action of state officers, executive or judicial, when they are subversive of the fundamental rights specified in the amendment. . . .

Dissenting, Justice Harlan argued that both the Thirteenth and Fourteenth Amendments conferred power on Congress to legislate directly, at least reaching private individuals engaged in quasi-public businesses:

> The supreme law of the land has decreed that no authority shall be exercised in this country upon the basis of discrimination, in respect of civil condition of servitude. To that decrease—for the due enforcement of which, by appropriate legislation, Congress has been invested with express power—every one must

---

[115] Stephen F. Ross, *Legislative Enforcement of Equal Protection*, 72 MINN. L. REV. 311, 313 n.10 (quoting Annals of Cong. 500) (Joseph Gates ed., 1789).
[116] *Id.*

bow, whatever may have been, or whatever now are, his individual views as to the wisdom or policy, either of the recent changes in the fundamental law, or of the legislation which has been enacted to give them effect. . . .

Almost 100 years later, in *Jones v. Alfred H. Mayer Co.*[117] the Court upheld a provision of the Civil Rights Act of 1866 prohibiting race discrimination in private transactions involving real and personal property. The Court held that the provision "bars *all* racial discrimination, private as well as public, in the sale or rental of property and so construed, it was a valid exercise of the power of Congress to enforce the thirteenth amendment. The Court reasoned that Congress' power to enforce the amendment under section two's enabling clause "clothed 'Congress with power to pass *all laws necessary and proper for abolishing all badges and incidents of slavery in the United States.*'"[118] In support of its reasoning that Congress' authority stemmed from the enabling clause, the Court quoted Senator Trumbull, Chairman of the Judiciary Committee which brought the thirteenth amendment to the floor of the Senate: "Who is to decide what that appropriate legislation is to be? The Congress of the United States; and it is for Congress to adopt such appropriate legislation as it may think proper, so that it be a means to accomplish the end." The Court held in a later case, *Runyon v. McCrary,*[119] that in another provision of the 1866 Act, Congress could prohibit racial discrimination in the making and enforcing of contracts, thereby constitutionally reaching purely private acts.

In a series of cases involving voting rights, the Court also accepted congressional power to identify and prohibit discriminatory conduct and thereby to extend the meaning of the Fourteenth and Fifteenth Amendments. Prior to enactment of the Voting Rights Act of 1965, racially discriminatory voting practices could only be identified and removed on a case-by-case basis, at great cost and with little impact. In the 1965 Act Congress sought to promote systemic change by prohibiting certain qualifications and requirements for voting. In *South Carolina v. Katzenbach,*[120] the Court upheld section 4(a) and (b) of the Voting Rights Act of 1965 which temporarily suspended literacy tests in states or political subdivisions with less than fifty per cent of the persons of voting age registered to vote. South Carolina contended that the provision invaded the state's province to regulate voter qualifications and election procedures. The Court found authority for the provision in the Fifteenth Amendment, § 2. Ten years earlier, in *Lassiter v. Northampton County Board of Elections,*[121] the Court had concluded that a state may, consistent with the fifteenth amendment, condition the right of suffrage on literacy tests. However, in *South Carolina*, the Court reasoned that Congress' elimination of case-by-case adjudication in the 1965 Voting Rights Act, based on Congress' conclusion that litigation had been inadequate to stem widespread and persistent vote discrimination, appropriately led Congress to focus on the victims of Fifteenth Amendment violations. The Court emphasized Congress' primary role in enforcement under the Fifteenth Amendment and its broad discretion to select appropriate relief without regard to available judicial remedies.

The Court also upheld the legislative provision for approval of new state voting regulations since

"Congress knew that some of the States covered had resorted to the extraordinary stratagem of contriving new rules . . . for the sole purpose of perpetuating voting discrimination in the face of adverse federal court decrees. Congress had

---

[117] 392 U.S. 409 (1968).
[118] 392 U.S. at 439 (emphasis in the original).
[119] 427 U.S. 160 (1976).
[120] 383 U.S. 301 (1966).
[121] 360 U.S. 45 (1959).

reason to suppose that these States might try similar maneuvers in the future in order to evade the remedies for voting discrimination contained in the Act itself. Under the compulsion of these unique circumstances, Congress responded in a permissibly decisive manner."

"After enduring nearly a century of widespread resistance to the Fifteenth Amendment, Congress has marshalled an array of potent weapons against the evil, with the authority of the Attorney General to employ them effectively. We here hold that the portions of the Voting Rights Act properly before us are a valid means for carrying out the commands of the Fifteenth Amendment."

Ruling that the Necessary and Proper clause of Article I and § 2 of the Fifteenth Amendment were coextensive, the Court quoted from *McCulloch*: "Let the end be legitimate, let it be within the scope of the constitution, and all means which are appropriate, which are plainly adapted to that end, which are not prohibited, but consistent with the letter and the spirit of the constitution are constitutional."

In *Katzenbach v. Morgan*,[122] another voting rights case, the Court concluded that § 5 of the Fourteenth Amendment authorized section 4(e) of the Voting Rights Act, which invalidated New York State's literacy test as applied to persons who had completed the sixth grade in Puerto Rico.

---

[122] 384 U.S. 641 (1966).

Katenzenbach v. Morgan
384 U.S. 641 (1966)

Mr. Justice BRENNAN delivered the opinion of the Court.

These cases concern the constitutionality of § 4(e) of the Voting Rights Act of 1965. That law, in the respects pertinent in these cases, provides that no person who has successfully completed the sixth primary grade in a public school in, or a private school accredited by, the Commonwealth of Puerto Rico in which the language of instruction was other than English shall be denied the right to vote in any election because of his inability to read or write English. Appellees, registered voters in New York City, brought this suit to challenge the constitutionality of § 4(e) insofar as it *pro tanto* prohibits the enforcement of the election laws of New York requiring an ability to read and write English as a condition of voting. Under these laws many of the several hundred thousand New York City residents who have migrated there from the Commonwealth of Puerto Rico had previously been denied the right to vote, and appellees attack § 4(e) insofar as it would enable many of these citizens to vote. Pursuant to § 14(b) of the Voting Rights Act of 1965, appellees commenced this proceeding in the District Court for the District of Columbia seeking a declaration that § 4(e) is invalid and an injunction prohibiting appellants, the Attorney General of the United States and the New York City Board of Elections, from either enforcing or complying with § 4(e). A three-judge district court was designated. Upon cross motions for summary judgment, that court, one judge dissenting, granted the declaratory and injunctive relief appellees sought. The court held that in enacting § 4(e) Congress exceeded the powers granted to it by the Constitution and therefore usurped powers reserved to the States by the Tenth Amendment. Appeals were taken directly to this Court, and we noted probable jurisdiction. We reverse. We hold that, in the application challenged in these cases, § 4(e) is a proper exercise of the powers granted to Congress by § 5 of the Fourteenth Amendment and that by force of the Supremacy Clause, Article VI, the New York English literacy requirement cannot be enforced to the extent that it is inconsistent with § 4(e).

Under the distribution of powers effected by the Constitution, the States establish qualifications for voting for state officers, and the qualifications established by the States for voting for members of the most numerous branch of the state legislature also determine who may vote for United States Representatives and Senators. But, of course, the States have no power to grant or withhold the franchise on conditions that are forbidden by the Fourteenth Amendment, or any other provision of the Constitution. Such exercises of state power are no more immune to the limitations of the Fourteenth Amendment than any other state action. The Equal Protection Clause itself has been held to forbid some state laws that restrict the right to vote.

The Attorney General of the State of New York argues that an exercise of congressional power under § 5 of the Fourteenth Amendment that prohibits the enforcement of a state law can only be sustained if the judicial branch determines that the state law is prohibited by the provisions of the Amendment that Congress sought to enforce. More specifically, he urges that § 4(e) cannot be sustained as appropriate legislation to enforce the Equal Protection Clause unless the judiciary decides—even with the guidance of a congressional judgment—that the application of the English literacy requirement prohibited by § 4(e) is forbidden by the Equal Protection Clause itself. We disagree. Neither the language nor history of § 5 supports such a construction. As was said with regard to § 5 in *Ex parte Virginia*, 100 U.S. 339, 345 'It is the power of Congress which has been enlarged. Congress is authorized to enforce the prohibitions by appropriate legislation. Some legislation is contemplated to make the amendments fully effective.' A construction of § 5 that would require a judicial determination that the enforcement of the state law precluded by Congress violated the Amendment, as a condition of sustaining the congressional enactment, would depreciate both congressional resourcefulness and congressional responsibility for implementing the Amendment. It would confine the legislative power in this context to the insignificant role of abrogating only those state laws that the judicial branch was prepared to adjudge unconstitutional, or of merely informing the judgment of the judiciary by particularizing the 'majestic generalities' of § 1 of the Amendment.

By including § 5 the draftsmen sought to grant to Congress, by a specific provision applicable to the Fourteenth Amendment, the same broad powers expressed in the Necessary and Proper Clause, Art. I, § 8, cl. 18. The classic formulation of the reach of those powers was established by Chief Justice Marshall in *McCulloch v. Maryland*:

> 'Let the end be legitimate, let it be within the scope of the constitution, and all means which are appropriate, which are plainly adapted to that end, which are not prohibited, but consist with the letter and spirit of the constitution, are constitutional.

Ex parte Virginia, decided 12 years after the adoption of the Fourteenth Amendment, held that congressional power under § 5 had this same broad scope:

> 'Whatever legislation is appropriate, that is, adapted to carry out the objects the amendments have in view, whatever tends to enforce submission to the prohibitions they contain, and to secure to all persons the enjoyment of perfect equality of civil rights and the equal protection of the laws against State denial or invasion, if not prohibited, is brought within the domain of congressional power.'

Section 2 of the Fifteenth Amendment grants Congress a similar power to enforce by 'appropriate legislation' the provisions of that amendment; and we recently held in *State of South Carolina v. Katzenbach*, 383 U.S. 301, 326, that '[t]he basic test to be applied in a case involving § 2 of the Fifteenth Amendment is the same as in all cases concerning the express powers of Congress with relation to the reserved powers of the States.' That test was identified as the one formulated in *McCulloch v. Maryland*. Thus the *McCulloch v. Maryland* standard is the measure of what constitutes 'appropriate legislation' under § 5 of the Fourteenth Amendment. Correctly viewed, § 5 is a positive grant of legislative power authorizing Congress to exercise its discretion in determining whether and what legislation is needed to secure the guarantees of the Fourteenth Amendment.

We therefore proceed to the consideration whether § 4(e) is 'appropriate legislation' to enforce the Equal Protection Clause, that is, under the *McCulloch v. Maryland* standard, whether § 4(e) may be regarded as an enactment to enforce the Equal Protection Clause, whether it is 'plainly adapted to that end' and whether it is not prohibited by but is consistent with 'the letter and spirit of the constitution.'

There can be no doubt that § 4(e) may be regarded as an enactment to enforce the Equal Protection Clause. Congress explicitly declared that it enacted § 4(e) 'to secure the rights under the fourteenth amendment of persons educated in American-flag schools in which the predominant classroom language was other than English.' The persons referred to include those who have migrated from the Commonwealth of Puerto Rico to New York and who have been denied the right to vote because of their inability to read and write English, and the Fourteenth Amendment rights referred to include those emanating from the Equal Protection Clause. More specifically, § 4(e) may be viewed as a measure to secure for the Puerto Rican community residing in New York nondiscriminatory treatment by government—both in the imposition of voting qualifications and the provision or administration of governmental services, such as public schools, public housing and law enforcement.

Section 4(e) may be readily seen as 'plainly adapted' to furthering these aims of the Equal Protection Clause. The practical effect of § 4(e) is to prohibit New York from denying the right to vote to large segments of its Puerto Rican community. Congress has thus prohibited the State from denying to that community the right that is 'preservative of all rights.' *Yick Wo v. Hopkins*, 118 U.S. 356, 370. This enhanced political power will be helpful in gaining non-discriminatory treatment in public services for the entire Puerto Rican community. Section 4(e) thereby enables the Puerto Rican minority better to obtain 'perfect equality of civil rights and the equal protection of the laws.' It was well within congressional authority to say that this need of the Puerto Rican minority for the vote warranted federal intrusion upon any state interests served by the English literacy requirement. It was for Congress, as the branch that made this judgment, to assess and weigh the various conflicting considerations—the risk or pervasiveness of the discrimination in governmental services, the effectiveness of eliminating the state restriction on the right to vote as a means of dealing with the evil, the adequacy or availability of alternative remedies, and the nature and significance of the state interests that would be affected by the nullification of the English literacy requirement as applied to residents who have successfully completed the sixth grade in a Puerto Rican school. It is not for us to review the congressional resolution of these factors. It is enough that we be able to perceive a basis upon which the Congress might resolve the conflict as it did.

The result is no different if we confine our inquiry to the question whether § 4(e) was merely legislation aimed at the elimination of an invidious discrimination in establishing voter qualifications. We are told that New York's English literacy requirement originated in the desire to provide an incentive for non-English speaking immigrants to learn the English language and in order to assure the intelligent exercise of the franchise. Yet Congress might well have questioned, in light of the many exemptions provided, and some evidence suggesting that prejudice played a prominent role in the enactment of the requirement, whether these were actually the interests being served. Congress might have also questioned whether denial of a right deemed so precious and fundamental in our society was a necessary or appropriate means of encouraging persons to learn English, or of furthering the goal of an intelligent exercise of the franchise. Finally, Congress might well have concluded that as a means of furthering the intelligent exercise of the franchise, an ability to read or understand Spanish is as effective as ability to read English for those to whom Spanish-language newspapers and Spanish-language radio and television programs are available to inform them of election issues and governmental affairs. Since Congress undertook to legis-

late so as to preclude the enforcement of the state law, and did so in the context of a general appraisal of literacy requirements for voting, *see* State of *South Carolina v. Katzenbach*, *supra*, to which it brought a specially informed legislative competence, it was Congress' prerogative to weigh these competing considerations. Here again, it is enough that we perceive a basis upon which Congress might predicate a judgment that the application of New York's English literacy requirement to deny the right to vote to a person with a sixth grade education in Puerto Rican schools in which the language of instruction was other than English constituted an invidious discrimination in violation of the Equal Protection Clause.

There remains the question whether the congressional remedies adopted in § 4(e) constitute means which are not prohibited by, but are consistent 'with the letter and spirit of the constitution.' The only respect in which appellees contend that § 4(e) fails in this regard is that the section itself works an invidious discrimination in violation of the Fifth Amendment by prohibiting the enforcement of the English literacy requirement only for those educated in American-flag schools (schools located within United States jurisdiction) in which the language of instruction was other than English, and not for those educated in schools beyond the territorial limits of the United States in which the language of instruction was also other than English. This is not a complaint that Congress, in enacting § 4(e), has unconstitutionally denied or diluted anyone's right to vote but rather that Congress violated the Constitution by not extending the relief effected in § 4(e) to those educated in non-American-flag schools.

Section 4(e) does not restrict or deny the franchise but in effect extends the franchise to persons who otherwise would be denied it by state law. Thus we need not decide whether a state literacy law conditioning the right to vote on achieving a certain level of education in an American-flag school (regardless of the language of instruction) discriminates invidiously against those educated in non-American-flag schools. We need only decide whether the challenged limitation on the relief effected in § 4(e) was permissible. In deciding that question, the principle that calls for the closest scrutiny of distinctions in laws *denying* fundamental rights, see n. 15, *supra*, is inapplicable; for the distinction challenged by appellees is presented only as a limitation on a reform measure aimed at eliminating an existing barrier to the exercise of the franchise. Rather, in deciding the constitutional propriety of the limitations in such a reform measure we are guided by the familiar principles that a 'statute is not invalid under the Constitution because it might have gone farther than it did,' *Roschen v. Ward*, 279 U.S. 337, 339, that a legislature need not 'strike at all evils at the same time,' *Semler v. Dental Examiners*, 294 U.S. 608, 610, and that 'reform may take one step at a time, addressing itself to the phase of the problem which seems most acute to the legislative mind,' *Williamson v. Lee Optical Co.*, 348 U.S. 483, 489.

Guided by these principles, we are satisfied that appellees' challenge to this limitation in § 4(e) is without merit. In the context of the case before us, the congressional choice to limit the relief effected in § 4(e) may, for example, reflect Congress' greater familiarity with the quality of instruction in American-flag schools, a recognition of the unique historic relationship between the Congress and the Commonwealth of Puerto Rico, an awareness of the Federal Government's acceptance of the desirability of the use of Spanish as the language of instruction in Commonwealth schools, and the fact that Congress has fostered policies encouraging migration from the Commonwealth to the States. We have no occasion to determine in this case whether such factors would justify a similar distinction embodied in a voting-qualification law that denied the franchise to persons educated in non-American-flag schools. We hold only that the limitation on relief effected in § 4(e) does not constitute a forbidden discrimination since these factors might well have been the basis for the decision of Congress to go 'no farther than it did.'

We therefore conclude that § 4(e), in the application challenged in this case, is appropriate legislation to enforce the Equal Protection Clause and that the judgment of the District Court must be and hereby is reversed.

Reversed.

Mr. Justice HARLAN, whom Mr. Justice STEWART joins, dissenting.

Worthy as its purposes may be thought by many, I do not see how § 4(e) of the Voting Rights Act of 1965, can be sustained except at the sacrifice of fundamentals in the American constitutional system—the separation between the legislative and judicial function and the boundaries between federal and state political authority. By the same token I think that the validity of New York's literacy test, a question which the Court considers *only* in the context of the federal statute, must be upheld. It will conduce to analytical clarity if I discuss the second issue first.

I.

This case presents a straightforward Equal Protection problem. Appellant, a resident and citizen of New York, sought to register to vote but was refused registration because she failed to meet the New York English literacy qualification respecting eligibility for the franchise. She maintained that although she could not read or write English, she had been born and educated in Puerto Rico and was liter-

ate in Spanish. She alleges that New York's statute requiring satisfaction of an English literacy test is an arbitrary and irrational classification that violates the Equal Protection Clause at least as applied to someone who, like herself, is literate in Spanish.

Any analysis of this problem must begin with the established rule of law that the franchise is essentially a matter of state concern, subject only to the overriding requirements of various federal constitutional provisions dealing with the franchise, *e.g.*, the Fifteenth, Seventeenth, Nineteenth, and Twenty-fourth Amendments, and, as more recently decided, to the general principles of the Fourteenth Amendment.

The Equal Protection Clause of the Fourteenth Amendment, which alone concerns us here, forbids a State from arbitrarily discriminating among different classes of persons. Of course it has always been recognized that nearly all legislation involves some sort of classification, and the equal protection test applied by this Court is a narrow one: a state enactment or practice may be struck down under the clause only if it cannot be justified as founded upon a rational and permissible state policy.

It is suggested that a different and broader equal protection standard applies in cases where 'fundamental liberties and rights are threatened,' . . . which would require a State to show a need greater than mere rational policy to justify classifications in this area. No such dual-level test has ever been articulated by this Court, and I do not believe that any such approach is consistent with the purposes of the Equal Protection Clause, with the overwhelming weight of authority, or with well-established principles of federalism which underlie the Equal Protection Clause.

Thus for me, applying the basic equal protection standard, the issue in this case is whether New York has shown that its English-language literacy test is reasonably designed to serve a legitimate state interest. I think that it has.

In 1959, in *Lassiter v. Northampton Election Bd.*, *supra*, this Court dealt with substantially the same question and resolved it unanimously in favor of the legitimacy of a state literacy qualification. There a North Carolina English literacy test was challenged. We held that there was 'wide scope' for State qualifications of this sort. Dealing with literacy tests generally, the Court there held:

'The ability to read and write . . . has some relation to standards designed to promote intelligent use of the ballot. . . . Literacy and intelligence are obviously not synonymous. Illiterate people may be intelligent voters. Yet in our society where newspapers, periodicals, books, and other printed matter canvass and debate campaign issues, a State might conclude that only those who are literate should exercise the franchise. ... It was said last century in Massachusetts that a literacy test was designed to insure an 'independent and intelligent' exercise of the right of suffrage. North Carolina agrees. We do not sit in judgment on the wisdom of that policy. We cannot say, however, that it is not an allowable one measured by constitutional standards.'

I believe the same interests recounted in *Lassiter* indubitably point toward upholding the rationality of the New York voting test. It is true that the issue here is not so simply drawn between literacy *per se* and illiteracy. Appellant alleges that she is literate in Spanish, and that she studied American history and government in United States Spanish-speaking schools in Puerto Rico. She alleges further that she is 'a regular reader of the New York City Spanish-language daily newspapers and other periodicals, which ... provide proportionately more coverage of government and politics than do most English-language newspapers,' and that she listens to Spanish-language radio broadcasts in New York which provide full treatment of governmental and political news. It is thus maintained that whatever may be the validity of literacy tests *per se* as a condition of voting, application of such a test to one literate in Spanish, in the context of the large and politically significant Spanish-speaking community in New York, serves no legitimate state interest, and is thus an arbitrary classification that violates the Equal Protection Clause.

Although to be sure there is a difference between a totally illiterate person and one who is literate in a foreign tongue, I do not believe that this added factor vitiates the constitutionality of the New York statute. Accepting appellant's allegations as true, it is nevertheless also true that the range of material available to a resident of New York literate only in Spanish is much more limited than what is available to an English-speaking resident, that the business of national, state, and local government is conducted in English, and that propositions, amendments, and offices for which candidates are running listed on the ballot are likewise in English. It is also true that most candidates, certainly those campaigning on a national or statewide level make their speeches in English. New York may justifiably want its voters to be able to understand candidates directly rather than through possibly imprecise translations or summaries reported in a limited number of Spanish news media. It is noteworthy that the Federal Government requires literacy in English as a prerequisite to naturalization, ... attesting to the national view of its importance

as a prerequisite to full integration into the American political community. Relevant too is the fact that the New York English test is not complex, that it is fairly administered, and that New York maintains free adult education classes which appellant and members of her class are encouraged to attend. Given the State's legitimate concern with promoting and safeguarding the intelligent use of the ballot, and given also New York's long experience with the process of integrating non-English-speaking residents into the mainstream of American life, I do not see how it can be said that this qualification for suffrage is unconstitutional. I would uphold the validity of the New York statute, unless the federal statute prevents that result, the question to which I now turn.

II.

The Morgan Cases

These cases involve the same New York suffrage restriction discussed above, but the challenge here comes not in the form of a suit to enjoin enforcement of the state statute, but in a test of the constitutionality of a federal enactment which declares that 'to secure the rights under the fourteenth amendment of persons educated in American-flag schools in which the predominant classroom language was other than English, it is necessary to prohibit the States from conditioning the right to vote of such persons on ability to read, write, understand, or interpret any matter in the English language.' Section 4(e) of the Voting Rights Act of 1965. Section 4(e) declares that anyone who has successfully completed six grades of schooling in an 'American-flag' school, in which the primary language is not English, shall not be denied the right to vote because of an inability to satisfy an English literacy test. Although the statute is framed in general terms, so far as has been shown it applies in actual effect only to citizens of Puerto Rican background, and the Court so treats it.

The pivotal question in this instance is what effect the added factor of a congressional enactment has on the straight equal protection argument dealt with above. The Court declares that since § 5 of the Fourteenth Amendment gives to the Congress power to 'enforce' the prohibitions of the Amendment by 'appropriate' legislation, the test for judicial review of any congressional determination in this area is simply one of rationality; that is, in effect, was Congress acting rationally in declaring that the New York statute is irrational? Although § 5 most certainly does give to the Congress wide powers in the field of devising remedial legislation to effectuate the Amendment's prohibition on arbitrary state action. I believe the Court has confused the issue of how much enforcement power Congress possesses under § 5 with the distinct issue of what questions are appropriate for congressional determination and what questions are essentially judicial in nature.

When recognized state violations of federal constitutional standards have occurred, Congress is of course empowered by § 5 to take appropriate remedial measures to redress and prevent the wrongs. But it is a judicial question whether the condition with which Congress has thus sought to deal is in truth an infringement of the Constitution, something that is the necessary prerequisite to bringing the § 5 power into play at all. Thus, in *Ex parte Virginia, supra*, involving a federal statute making it a federal crime to disqualify anyone from jury service because of race, the Court first held as a matter of constitutional law that 'the Fourteenth Amendment secures, among other civil rights, to colored men, when charged with criminal offenses against a State, an impartial jury trial, by jurors indifferently selected or chosen without discrimination against such jurors because of their color.' Only then did the Court hold that to enforce this prohibition upon state discrimination, Congress could enact a criminal statute of the type under consideration.

The question here is not whether the statute is appropriate remedial legislation to cure an established violation of a constitutional command, but whether there has in fact been an infringement of that constitutional command, that is, whether a particular state practice or, as here, a statute is so arbitrary or irrational as to offend the command of the Equal Protection Clause of the Fourteenth Amendment. That question is one for the judicial branch ultimately to determine. Were the rule otherwise, Congress would be able to qualify this Court's constitutional decisions under the Fourteenth and Fifteenth Amendments let alone those under other provisions of the Constitution, by resorting to congressional power under the Necessary and Proper Clause. In view of this Court's holding in *Lassiter, supra*, that an English literacy test is a permissible exercise of state supervision over its franchise, I do not think it is open to Congress to limit the effect of that decision as it has undertaken to do by § 4(e). In effect the Court reads § 5 of the Fourteenth Amendment as giving Congress the power to define the *substantive* scope of the Amendment. If that indeed be the true reach of § 5, then I do not see why Congress should not be able as well to exercise its § 5 'discretion' by enacting statutes so as in effect to dilute equal protection and due process decisions of this Court. In all such cases there is room for reasonable men to differ as to whether or not a denial of equal protection or due process has occurred, and the final decision is one

of judgment. Until today this judgment has always been one for the judiciary to resolve.

I do not mean to suggest in what has been said that a legislative judgment of the type incorporated in § 4(e) is without any force whatsoever. Decisions on questions of equal protection and due process are based not on abstract logic, but on empirical foundations. To the extent 'legislative facts' are relevant to a judicial determination, Congress is well equipped to investigate them, and such determinations are of course entitled to due respect. In *South Carolina v. Katzenbach, supra*, such legislative findings were made to show that racial discrimination in voting was actually occurring. Similarly, in *Heart of Atlanta Motel, Inc. v. United States*, and *Katzenbach v. McClung*, this Court upheld Title II of the Civil Rights Act of 1964 under the Commerce Clause. There again the congressional determination that racial discrimination in a clearly defined group of public accommodations did effectively impede interstate commerce was based on 'voluminous testimony,' which had been put before the Congress and in the context of which it passed remedial legislation.

But no such factual data provide a legislative record supporting § 4(e) by way of showing that Spanish-speaking citizens are fully as capable of making informed decisions in a New York election as are English-speaking citizens. Nor was there any showing whatever to support the Court's alternative argument that § 4(e) should be viewed as but a remedial measure designed to cure or assure against unconstitutional discrimination of other varieties, e.g., in 'public schools, public housing and law enforcement,' to which Puerto Rican minorities might be subject in such communities as New York. There is simply no legislative record supporting such hypothesized discrimination of the sort we have hitherto insisted upon when congressional power is brought to bear on constitutionally reserved state concerns.

Thus, we have here not a matter of giving deference to a congressional estimate, based on its determination of legislative facts, bearing upon the validity *vel non* of a statute, but rather what can at most be called a legislative announcement that Congress believes a state law to entail an unconstitutional deprivation of equal protection. Although this kind of declaration is of course entitled to the most respectful consideration, coming as it does from a concurrent branch and one that is knowledgeable in matters of popular political participation, I do not believe it lessens our responsibility to decide the fundamental issue of whether in fact the state enactment violates federal constitutional rights.

In assessing the deference we should give to this kind of congressional expression of policy, it is relevant that the judiciary has always given to congressional enactments a presumption of validity. However, it is also a canon of judicial review that state statutes are given a similar presumption. Whichever way this case is decided, one statute will be rendered inoperative in whole or in part, and although it has been suggested that this Court should give somewhat more deference to Congress than to a state legislature, such a simple weighing of presumptions is hardly a satisfying way of resolving a matter that touches the distribution of state and federal power in an area so sensitive as that of the regulation of the franchise. Rather it should be recognized that while the Fourteenth Amendment is a 'brooding omnipresence' over all state legislation, the substantive matters which it touches are all within the primary legislative competence of the States. Federal authority, legislative no less than judicial, does not intrude unless there has been a denial by state action of Fourteenth Amendment limitations, in this instance a denial of equal protection. At least in the area of primary state concern a state statute that passes constitutional muster under the judicial standard of rationality should not be permitted to be set at naught by a mere contrary congressional pronouncement unsupported by a legislative record justifying that conclusion.

To deny the effectiveness of this congressional enactment is not of course to disparage Congress' exertion of authority in the field of civil rights; it is simply to recognize that the Legislative Branch like the other branches of federal authority is subject to the governmental boundaries set by the Constitution. To hold, on this record, that § 4(e) overrides the New York literacy requirement seems to me tantamount to allowing the Fourteenth Amendment to swallow the State's constitutionally ordained primary authority in this field. For if Congress by what, as here, amounts to mere *ipse dixit* can set that otherwise permissible requirement partially at naught I see no reason why it could not also substitute its judgment for that of the States in other fields of their exclusive primary competence as well.

I would affirm the judgments in each of these cases.

Justice Brennan's opinion first reads section 4(e) as an appropriate exercise of Congress' remedial power under section 5 of the Fourteenth Amendment. He disagrees with the state's attorney general that the power to act under section five is limited to what is forbidden by section 1 of the Fourteenth Amendment itself. Thus he reasons that Congress' power to enforce the amendment can properly include the elimination of the English literacy requirement as a means of promoting nondiscriminatory treatment in public services for the Puerto Rican community under *McCulloch v. Maryland*. This is so despite the fact that the conduct which is being promoted is beyond the scope of section 1 of the Fourteenth Amendment and is in an area of traditional state autonomy under the Constitution.

Justice Brennan's second rationale, that Congress can disagree with the Court concerning the reach of the Fourteenth Amendment, is more controversial as an exceptionally broad assertion of congressional power. Is it consistent with *Marbury v. Madison* that "[i]t is emphatically the province and duty of the judicial department to say what the law is"? Notably, in footnote 10 of *Katzenbach*, the majority emphasizes that Congress' power to "enforce" the Fourteenth Amendment does not include the power to "restrict, abrogate or dilute" its guarantees,[123] a concern addressed by Justice Harlan in his dissent.

Justice Harlan argues that Congress' power is limited to remedying violations of the fourteenth amendment determined by the Court: "Were the rule otherwise, Congress would be able to qualify this Court's constitutional decisions under the Fourteenth and Fifteenth Amendments, let alone those under other provisions of the Constitution, by resorting to congressional power under the Necessary and Proper Clause." Thus Justice Harlan rests his conclusion in part out of concern that a construction recognizing congressional power to "ratchet up" equal protection through legislation could also be used by Congress to "rachet down" or dilute equal protection if it is Congress' will. But Justice Harlan's effort to cabin congressional power may also prove

---

[123] *Morgan*, 384 U.S. at 651 n.10.

troublesome since it is built upon distinguishing remedial from interpretive provisions. As Professor Cohen observes: "In close cases, hewing the line between permissible remedial measures and impermissible interpretation may depend . . . on the ability of the congressional staff to supply the appropriate testimony in hearings and to draft a statutory preamble picking the proper theory."[124] Do separation of powers concerns support Justice Harlan's position? Read broadly, *Katzenbach* suggests that Congress has the power to directly challenge the finality of the Court's decisions in areas related to civil rights. Professor Gordon avoids conflict about the respective roles of judiciary and legislature raised by the language from *Marbury v. Madison* by distinguishing normative and empirical components of constitutional decision making:

> The empirical component consists of the "legislative facts" which are gathered, arranged, debated, and evaluated by the legislative body as a basis for the law. If a rational basis may be found for the existence of such facts, the Court generally leaves legislative facts undisturbed, deferring to the legislature as a superior fact-finding body. The normative component is the expression of the Court's judgment as to whether the statute is compatible with the standard which the Court has found or read into the Constitution. . . . The familiar words of *Marbury v. Madison* mean only that Congress cannot alter the normative component of a judicial decision.[125]

Professor Gordon, however, is not as persuaded by the majority's one-way "ratchet" theory, that Congress has the power in legislating to give an expansive reading, even where the Court has declined to do so, but is not able to give a limited reading of the substantive guarantees of the fourteenth amendment:

> If the word "enforce" in section 5, on which Justice Brennan seems to rely in *Morgan* connotes that Congress may authoritatively declare the substantive meaning of section 1, it is not evident how the connotation may be confined so as to authorize Congress to act only in one direction. The weakness of the textual support is not overcome by analytical necessity. To the contrary, if congress's entitlement rests on its far-flung and multi-faceted experience with national problems and its superior competency as a fact-finder and empirical decision maker, the superiority ought to cut both ways.[126]

It can be countered, however, that while the Supreme Court may defer to Congress when it "ratchets up" equal protection guarantees, the Court "should never defer to any legislative determination which restricts those rights without making its own investigation and characterization of the interests affected. . . . "[127] Thus to prevent the kind of battle between the Court and Congress that Justice Harlan feared, the ratchet theory could be interpreted as requiring the Court to invalidate congressional restrictions of constitutional rights.[128]

---

[124] William Cohen, *Congressional Power to Interpret Due Process and Equal Protection*, 27 STAN. L. REV. 603 (1975).

[125] Irving A. Gordon, *The Nature and Uses of Congressional Power Under Section Five of the Fourteenth Amendment to Overcome Decisions of the Supreme Court*, 72 NW. U.L. REV. 656 (1977).

[126] *Id.* at 656.

[127] Archibald Cox, *The Role of Congress in Constitutional Determinations*, 40 U. CIN. L. REV. 199, 253 (1971).

[128] *See* Matt Pawa, *When the Supreme Court Restricts Constitutional Rights, Can Congress Save Us? An Examination of Section 5 of the Fourteenth Amendment*, 141 U. PA. L. REV. 1029, 1062–63 & n.218 (citing S. Rep. No. 321, 102d Cong., 2d sess. 30 (1992) which argues that the Human Life Bill introduced in the 97th Congress would have violated the ratchet effect by restricting the rights of women).

DEL: The debate over the Fourteenth Amendment's ratcheting potential, like that over the Civil Rights Act of 1964,[129] is a captive of the *Civil Rights Cases* decision in 1883 that articulated the Court's (nation's) impatience with the intractable problem of race. In determining that Congress' power under Section 5 was coextensive with the scope of section 1, and thus invalidating the Civil Rights Act of 1875, the Court reduced legislative ability to reckon with the legacy of slavery. Holding congressional initiative hostage to judicial interpretation may have been partially offset by the judiciary's eventual intervention on behalf of "discrete and insular minorities" who were formally excluded from or underrepresented in the political process. It is a crucial consideration, however, to the extent that Congress strives through to account for the nation's legacy of racial discrimination. At the point that the political process has been pried open not only by constitutional case law but federal votings rights legislation, and the brokering potential of previously excluded minorities has been enhanced accordingly, a revisitation of long-standing premises may be in order. To the extent that Reconstruction represented primarily a legislative project, and among other things reflected a distrust of the judiciary and further discrediting of the *Dred Scott* decision, history may suggest some extra latitude is in order for Congress in enforcing the Fourteenth Amendment.

---

[129] *See* Part IV.

In *City of Rome v. United States*,[130] the Court held that Congress could prohibit electoral schemes with discriminatory effects even as the Court itself concluded on the same day that such schemes were not themselves violative of the Fifteenth Amendment.[131] Justice Marshall stated:

> [T]he Act's ban on electoral changes that are discriminatory in effect is an appropriate method of promoting the purposes of the Fifteenth Amendment, even if it is assumed the Amendment prohibits only intentional discrimination in voting. Congress could rationally have concluded that, because electoral changes by jurisdictions with a demonstrable history of intentional racial discrimination in voting created the risk of purposeful discrimination, it was proper to prohibit changes that have a discriminatory impact. [P]rinicples of federalism that might otherwise be an obstacle to congressional authority are necessarily overridden by the power to enforce the Civil War amendments 'by appropriate legislation.' Those Amendments were specifically designed as an expansion of federal power and an intrusion on state sovereignty.[132]

The Supreme Court has grappled with the reach of congressional power under the enforcement provisions of the Reconstruction Amendments in several other cases since *Morgan v. Katzenbach*. In *Oregon v. Mitchell*,[133] the Court considered challenges to the 1970 Voting Rights Act in which Congress attempted to lower the voting age from 21 to 18 in federal and state elections, to extend its prohibition of literacy tests to all state and federal elections for five years, and to eliminate state residency requirements in presidential elections. Although its vote was fractured on the question of age requirements in state and federal elections, the Court unanimously upheld the literacy test prohibition as a proper means of implementing the Fifteenth Amendment under § 2. In *Mitchell* Justice Brennan emphasized that Congress' superior fact-finding capability

---

[130] 446 U.S. 156 (1980).
[131] Mobile v. Bolden, 446 U.S. 55 (1980).
[132] 446 U.S. at 158.
[133] 400 U.S. 112 (1970).

as compared with the states' led the Court to defer to federal policy choices over state choices; similarly, the Court would bow to the choices of Congress instead of the Court's in light of Congress' capacity for fact-finding. Although he dissented, Justice Harlan acknowledged that since Congress had established a factual basis for finding discrimination and that literacy tests could be tools of discrimination, in constructing a remedy Congress "may paint with a much broader brush" than the Court which is restrained by the "judicial function of deciding individual cases and controversies upon individual records."[134] Thus from the standpoint of institutional competence and constitutional authority, Justice Harlan seemed to agree that Congress was the appropriate branch to address such widespread practices.

The *Mitchell* Court, however, was divided on the issue of lowering the voting age to eighteen, suggesting there is disagreement among the justices concerning the scope of Congress' power under the Fourteenth Amendment. Four justices decided that both provisions for lowering the voting age in state and federal elections were valid because Congress could find that age discrimination violated the Equal Protection Clause. Four justices believed the provisions were unconstitutional and Justice Black reasoned that the provision relating to the voting age in federal elections was valid because it was authorized by Article I, § 4. Noting that Article I, § 2, among other provisions of the Constitution, reserves to states the power to set qualifications for voters in state and local elections, Justice Black argued that Congress inappropriately invaded the states' province in legislating age requirements for state elections without legislative findings that the legislation was needed to remedy race discrimination. He added: "On the other hand, where Congress legislates in a domain not exclusively reserved by the Constitution to the States, its enforcement power need not be tied so closely to the goal of eliminating discriminations on account of race."[135] Thus four justices reasoned that Congress can find age discrimination to be a violation of the Equal Protection Clause for which its remedial power can be used, three justices believed that Congress cannot remedy age discrimination under the Equal Protection Clause and one justice seemed most concerned about federalism limitations, equivocating on the issue of whether Congress' expansive enforcement power was tied to "discrimination on account of race."

The Court also recognized far-reaching congressional remedial power in *Fullilove v. Klutznick*.[136] Reviewing the broad treatment of Congress' power in the voting rights cases, the Court upheld a program requiring ten per cent of federal funds granted for

---

[134] 400 U.S. at 284.

[135] 400 U.S. at 130. In City of Rome v. United States, 446 U.S. 156, 179 (1980), discussed *supra*, and Fitzpatrick v. Bitzer, 427 U.S. 445, 456 (1976), a gender discrimination case, the Court rejected the view that federalism concerns limit Congress's enforcement powers under the Civil War amendments. *But cf.* Gregory v. Ashcroft, 111 S. Ct. 2395 (1991), in which state judges lost their challenge to the state's mandatory retirement provision because the Court concluded that principles of federalism required the Age Discrimination in Employment Act (ADEA) to be interpreted utilizing a "plain statement rule." Although the Commerce Clause was implicated in *Gregory*, the Court noted that one could argue that federalism concerns which might compel one result under the Commerce Clause would not be compelled if Congress had enacted the ADEA pursuant to its power under section 5 of the fourteenth amendment. The Court stated, however, "this Court has never held that the [fourteenth] amendment may be applied in complete disregard for a State's constitutional powers." 111 S. Ct. at 2401. Although *Gregory* seems to reflect the Court's continued concern about federalism, its impact may be limited. Gregory's rule of construction would not affect cases where Congress has utilized its section 5 enforcement power clearly stating its intent to abrogate federalism. Moreover, contrary to the suggestion in *Gregory* noted above, the Court has acknowledged that the Reconstruction Acts were intended to redefine the federal/state balance.

[136] 448 U.S. 448 (1980).

local public work projects to be used by the state or local grantee to procure supplies or services from minority businesses. Then-Chief Justice Burger, joined by Justices Powell and White, concluded that the objectives of the program, to remedy past discrimination perpetuated by prevailing procurement practices, were within congressional power under the Fourteenth Amendment. In a separate opinion emphasizing the competency of Congress to make findings, Justice Powell said:

> the issue here turns on the scope of congressional power, and Congress has been given a unique constitutional role in the enforcement of the post-Civil War amendments. In this case, where Congress determined that minority contractors were victims of purposeful discrimination and where Congress chose a reasonably necessary means to effectuate its purpose, I find no constitutional reason to invalidate [the program].

In *Metro Broadcasting v. FCC*[137] the Court found Congress' use of race-conscious measures to prevent future discrimination authorized by section 5 of the Fourteenth Amendment. Rejecting the application of section 5 to administrative agencies, Justice O'Connor nonetheless acknowledged "considerable latitude, presenting special concerns for judicial review when [Congress] exercises its 'unique remedial powers under section 5. . . .'" Notably, Justice O'Connor distinguished *City of Richmond v. J.A. Croson*,[138] in which the Court invalidated a local affirmative action plan modeled after the plan upheld in *Fullilove*. In *Croson*, Justice O'Connor had stated that Congress' "power to 'enforce' may at times also include the power to define situations which *Congress* determines threaten principles of equality and to adopt prophylactic rules to deal with those situations."[139] More recently, in the affirmative action cases, the Court appears to be less willing to defer to Congress' judgment about the appropriate remedial response to persistent racial discrimination. *See* Part IV *supra*.

F. Allocating the Power Between the Congress and the President to Make War

Debate about the authority to commit the nation to war and the war-making roles of the political branches has, for the most part, been conducted outside the courts. Questions related to the meaning of war-related, enumerated powers of the President (such as action taken in his capacity as Commander in Chief and as the repository of executive power) and of Congress (such as its power to raise and provide armies, to lay and collect taxes for the common defense, and to declare war), as well as questions related to the coordination of responsibilities, have tended to be treated as political or nonjusticiable questions, not ripe for review. The Supreme Court has refrained from deciding such questions even when there are plausible grounds to proceed.[140] Thus, as commentators have acknowledged, one of the most compelling areas for considering separation of powers has been left to political accommodation and consequently has been unavailable to sharpen or promote a principled analysis of separation of powers by courts.[141]

---

[137] 110 S.Ct. 2997 (1990).

[138] 488 U.S. 469 (1990).

[139] 488 U.S. at 490.

[140] *See, e.g.*, Orlando v. Laird, 443 F.2d 1039 (2d Cir.), *cert. denied*, 404 U.S. 869 (1971); Mora v. McNamara, 387 F.2d 664 (D.C. Cir.), *cert. denied*, 389 U.S. 934 (1967); Luftig v. McNamara, 373 F.2d 664 (D.C. Cir.), *cert. denied*, 387 U.S. 945 (1967).

[141] *See, e.g.*, Paul Gewirtz, *Realism in Separation of Powers Thinking*, 30 Wm. & Mary L. Rev. 343, 345–47 (1989).

1. Textual Support for War Power

The textual references to powers allocated between the President and Congress provide no clear resolution of the competing claims to authorize (or prevent) war. Proponents of broad presidential claims to war powers have often pointed to the fact that the text of Article II provides that "the whole Executive power" is vested in the President.[142] In contrast, Article I states that "[a]ll legislative Powers herein granted shall be vested in a Congress. . . . " Because the powers granted Congress are then carefully delineated in § 8, proponents of broad presidential authority have argued that the Framers intended the flow of power to the President to be fluid, enabling the President to be responsive to events requiring national leadership and discretion.[143] On the other hand, the Necessary and Proper Clause provides Congress with authority to make all appropriate laws for carrying into execution the powers of the coordinate branches, authority traditionally interpreted as extending farther than to the specific objects of legislative power enumerated, though not curtailing the powers of the other branches.

In claiming powers specifically related to matters of war or necessary to its commitment, each of the political branches can assert only incomplete express authority, suggesting once again that the Framers intended mutuality and coordination. Thus the President who is Commander in Chief, who has been seen as the principal instrument of government in foreign affairs, and who has the duty to see that the laws be faithfully executed, can assert authority to commit troops to battle in order to repel attacks but lacks power to declare war. Congress, on the other hand, is allocated not only the power to declare war but also the power to raise taxes, raise armies and provide for the common defense and general welfare, but its authorizations ultimately depend upon the leadership of the Commander in Chief.

2. Framing History

The historical background does not neatly resolve contradictory claims to war powers since, as in other controversies concerning separation of powers, the proponents of competing positions buttress their arguments by referring to selected isolated observations of the Framers and perceptions of the colonists at the time of the Constitutional Framing, that substantiate their positions. Advocates of broad Congressional power point to the colonists' view of "the executive magistracy [a]s the natural enemy, the legislative assembly the natural friend of liberty . . . "[144] and to observations about the authority to "declare" war, such as the following made by Wilson:

> The power of declaring wars, and the other powers connected with it, are vested in congress. To provide and maintain a navy—to make rules for its government—to grant letters of marque and reprisal—to make rules concerning captures—to raise and support armies—to establish rules for their regulation—to provide for organizing . . . the militia, and for calling them forth in the service of the Union—all these are powers naturally connected with the power of declaring war. All these powers, therefore, are vested in Congress.[145]

---

[142] *See, e.g,* David Lewittes, *Constitutional Separation of War Powers: Protecting Public and Private Liberty,* 57 Brook. L. Rev. 1083, 1087–89 (1992) (citing The Prize Cases, 67 U.S. (2 Black) 635, 668 (1862).

[143] *See* Myers v. United States, 272 U.S. 52 (1926) (quoting Alexander Hamilton's formulation of this argument in addressing President's Washington's Neutrality Proclamation during the war between Great Britain and France).

[144] Raoul Berger, *War-making by the President,* 121 U. Pa. L. Rev. 29, 32 (1972), quoting E. Corwin, The President: Office and Powers 4 (3d ed. 1948).

[145] 1 J.Wilson, Works 433, quoted in Berger, *supra* at 36.

Emphasizing the duties imposed on the President to preserve the nation, and that the international arena requires prompt, direct unity of action, proponents of broad discretionary power of the President in foreign affairs and war argue that the President's discretion is limited, politically, through the impeachment process and the desire to be re-elected. They refer to observations like that recorded by Madison:

> Secrecy, vigor & despatch are not the principal properties reqd. in the Executive. Important as these are, that of responsibility is more so, which can only be preserved; by leaving it singly to discharge its functions.[146]

3. The "Gloss" of Practice

In the Vietnam conflict and in subsequent "police actions," Presidents have relied on the practice of other Presidents throughout history of committing armed forces to action without consulting with or obtaining congressional authorization. During the Vietnam crisis, in a supporting legal memorandum, the State Department cited 125 instances in which Presidents had committed forces. In many cases the intervention could be regarded as action taken short of committing war, such as protecting United States nationals in foreign territory and "neutral" action which could be undertaken pursuant to the executive power.[147] In others, Congress ratified the actions of the President or itself issued a declaration of war.

A previously noted incident of presidential war making, validated by the Court, occurred during the Civil War. President Lincoln linked his role as Commander in Chief to his duty to execute laws and to preserve peace to authorize his blockade in retaliation of the Confederate Army's firing on Fort Sumter in South Carolina. The Supreme Court in *The Prize Cases*[148] stated that although

> Congress alone has the power to initiate or declare a national or foreign war . . . [i]f a war be made by invasion of a foreign nation, the President is . . . bound to resist force by force. He does not initiate the war, but is bound to accept the challenge without waiting for any special legislative authority. And whether the hostile party be a foreign invader, or states organized in rebellion, it is none the less a war, although declaration of it be *'unilateral.'*

The Court recognized that the President has power to assess whether force is required and to what degree it is necessary in the conflict. Because Lincoln's response can be viewed as a presidential reaction to a "sudden attack" on American soil while Congress was not in session, some commentators consider President Lincoln's actions taken in self defense as within his constitutional duty to protect national interests, relying on Lincoln's own expression of the constrained powers of the President in response to actions taken by President Polk while Lincoln was in Congress:

> Allow the President to invade a neighboring nation whenever he shall deem it necessary to repel an invasion, and you . . . allow him to make war at his pleasure. . . . The Provision of the Constitution giving war-making power to Congress was dictated by the [fact that] Kings had always been involving and

---

[146] Madison's Notes of Debates in the Federal Convention of 1787 at 81 (John Dickensian) (Gouverneur Morris) (Ohio U. Pres. rev. ed. 1984), quoted in David Lewittes, *Constitutional Separation of War Powers: Protecting Public and Private Liberty*, 57 BROOK. L. REV. 1083, 1112 & n. 121 (1992).

[147] Office of the Legal Advisor, U.S. Dept. of State, *The Legality of the United States Participation in the Defense of Vietnam*, reprinted in 75 YALE L.J. 1085, 1101 (1966).

[148] 67 U.S. (2 Black) 635 (1862).

impoverishing their people in wars . . . and they resolved to frame the Constitution that no one man should hold the power of bringing oppression upon us.[149]

---

[149] Berger, *War-Making, supra*, at 65, citing Wormuth, The Vietnam War: The President versus the Constitution, in 2 The Vietnam War and International Law 711, 713–17 (R. Falk ed. 1969). Justice Story wrote in Martin v. Mott, 25 U.S. (12 Wheaton) 19, 29 (1827) "the power to provide for repelling invasions includes the power to provide against the attempt and danger of invasion, as the necessary and proper means to effectuate the object. One of the best means to repel invasion is to provide the requisite force for action before the invader himself has reached the soil."

PAH: Recent Presidents have used Congress' failure to challenge President Truman's "police action" in South Korea to support the independent authority of the executive to become involved in sustained military conflicts abroad. Often they have sought congressional authorization through joint resolutions while continuing to argue that there is independent authority for the President to deploy troops because of regional security or other international executive agreements or treaties obligating the United States to become involved for the collective defense of the region. The executive branch has argued that inherent power on the part of the President to act in foreign affairs, acknowledged by Justice Sutherland in *United States v. Curtiss-Wright Export Corp.*, extends to such deployment of troops. Significantly, the proposition that the President possess implied or inherent power to act was rejected not only by Justice Black but also, arguably, by Justice Jackson, who refused to draw the analogy between the presidency and monarchy which Justice Sutherland found useful in characterizing the President's need for discretion in foreign affairs in *Curtiss-Wright*. Scholars have challenged Justice Sutherland's characterization as historically unfounded in light of the expressed concerns of the Framers about too much executive power in the executive which led them to vest the power to "*declare*" or commence war in Congress.[150] But commentators acknowledge that in practice modern Presidents assume wide-wielding power in foreign affairs, including deployment of troops short of full-scale war.

The Framers' concern about protecting the nation from hasty deployment of troops by Presidents seems today to be built on outmoded concepts of war. While it is certain that the Framers were not willing to confer unbridled discretion to commit the nation to war as a prerogative of presidential office, given the gloss of practice and the realities of modern war, the constitutional text provides Congress and the President with an "invitation to struggle."[151]

---

[150] For contrasting interpretations of the shift made by joint motion from Gerry and Madison to substitute "declare" for "make" war in the text of the Constitution, which Berger argues was out of the concern about the Executive's need to repel sudden attacks, see Berger, *War-Making* 121 U. PA. L. REV. at 39–41 (1972).

[151] EDWARD S. CORWIN, THE PRESIDENTIAL OFFICE AND POWERS 171 (4th rev. ed. 1957).

4. Undeclared War

The creation of regional and global organizations for collective security such as the League of Nations and the United Nations as well as the experience of world war in this century led Professor Eagleton to observe:

> The science of warfare has itself been greatly changed; the interrelationships between states have become much more numerous, more complicated, and more important; and the community of nations has developed an organization and has accepted new principles through which it attempts to control the right to make war. These forces have all had their impact upon the declaration of war;

and recent happenings raise doubt as to whether war will ever again be declared by beligerents. Under these changed circumstances, the declaration of war seems to be regarded by some as an anachronism to be discarded.[152]

No other conflict more dramatically framed the issues of the sources of authority for Presidents to commit troops without a declaration of War by Congress than the continued use of troops in Vietnam. President Johnson relied upon his role as Commander in Chief, congressional ratification of the Southeast Asia Treaty, the Charter of the United Nations, and a 1964 resolution by Congress, the Gulf of Tolkin Resolution, which he read as giving broad discretion to the President to initiate war in the region, to justify military involvement which lasted more than a decade and resulted in the commitment of a half million troops, a hundred billion dollars and fifty thousand deaths of Americans.[153] In an effort to restore what many citizens perceived as the intended constitutional balance between congressional and presidential authority to make war, Congress, over the President's veto, passed the War Powers Resolution.

---

[152] Clyde Eagleton, *The Form and Function of the Declaration of War*, 32 AM. J. INT'L L. 19, 19 (1938).

[153] William Van Alstyne, *Congress, The President, and the Power to Declare War: A Requiem for Vietnam*, 121 U. PA. L. REV. 1, 2 (1972).

War Powers Resolution
Pub. L.93–148, 87 Stat. 555

Sec. 2. (a) It is the purpose of this joint resolution to fulfill the intent of the framers of the Constitution of the United States and insure that the collective judgment of both the Congress and the President will apply to the introduction of United States Armed Forces in hostilities, or into situations where imminent involvement in hostilities is clearly indicated by the circumstances, and to the continued use of such forces in hostilities or in such situations.

(b) Under article I, section 8, of the Constitution, it is specifically provided that the Congress shall have the power to make all laws necessary and proper for carrying into execution, not only its own powers but also other powers vested by the Constitution in the Government of the United States, or in any department or officer thereof.

(c) The constitutional powers of the President as Commander-in-Chief to introduce United States Armed Forces into hostilities, or into situations where imminent involvement in hostilities is clearly indicated by the circumstances, are exercised only pursuant to (1) a declaration of war, (2) specific statutory authorization, or (3) a national emergency created by attack upon the United States, its territories or possessions, or its armed forces.

Consultation

Sec. 3. The President in every possible instance shall consult with Congress before introducing United States Armed Forces into hostilities or into situations where imminent involvement in hostilities is clearly indicated by the circumstances, and after every such introduction shall consult regularly with the Congress until United States Armed Forces are no longer engaged in hostilities or have been removed from such situations.

Reporting

Sec. 4 (a) In the absence of a declaration of war, in any case in which United States Armed Forces are introduced—

(1) into hostilities or into situations where imminent involvement in hostilities is clearly indicated by the circumstances;

(2) into the territory, airspace or waters of a foreign nation, while equipped for combat, except for deployments which relate solely to supply, replacement, repair, or training of such forces; or

(3) in numbers which substantially enlarge United States Armed Forces equipped for combat already located in a foreign nation; the President shall submit within 48 hours to the Speaker of the House of Representatives and to the President pro tempore of the Senate a report, in writing, setting forth—

(A) the circumstance necessitating the introduction of United States Armed Forces;

(B) the constitutional and legislative authority under which such introduction took place; and

(C) the estimated scope and duration of the hostilities or involvement.

(b) The President shall provide other such information as the Congress may request in the fulfillment of its responsibilities with respect to committing the Nation to war and to the use of United States Armed Forces abroad.

(c) Whenever United States Armed Forces are introduced into hostilities or into any situation described in subsection (a) of this section, the President shall, so long as such armed forces continue to be engaged in such hostilities or situation, report to the Congress periodically on the status of such hostilities or situation as well as on the scope and duration of such hostilities or situation, but in no event shall he report to the Congress less often than once every six months.

Sec. 5.(b) Within sixty calendar days after a report is submitted or is required to be submitted pursuant to section 4(a)(1), whichever is earlier, the President shall terminate any use of United States Armed Forces with respect to which such report was submitted (or required to be submitted), unless the Congress (1) has declared war or has enacted a specific authorization for such use of United States Armed Forces, (2) has extended by law such sixty-day period, or (3) is physically unable to meet as a result of an armed attack upon the United States. Such sixty-day period shall be extended for not more than an additional thirty days if the President determines and certifies to the Congress in writing that unavoidable military necessity respecting the safety of United States Armed Forces requires the continued use of such armed forces in the course of bringing about a prompt removal of such forces.

(c) Notwithstanding subsection (b), at any time that United States Armed Forces are engaged in hostilities outside the territory of the United States, its possessions and territories without a declaration of war or specific statutory authorization, such forces shall be removed by the President if the Congress so directs by concurrent resolution.

Interpretation of Joint Resolution

Sec. 8.(a) Authority to introduce United States Armed Forces into hostilities or into situation wherein involvement in hostilities is clearly indicated by the circumstances shall not be inferred—

(1) from any provision of law (whether or not in effect before the date of the enactment of this joint resolution), including any provision contained in any appropriations Act, unless such provision specifically authorizes the introduction of United States Armed Forces into hostilities or into such situation and states that it is intended to constitute specific statutory authorization within the meaning of this joint resolution; or

(2) from any treaty heretofore or hereafter ratified unless such treaty is implemented by legislation specifically authorizing the introduction of United States Armed Forces into hostilities or into such situation within the meaning of his joint [resolution].

(b) Nothing in this joint resolution—

(1) is intended to alter the constitutional authority of the Congress or of the President, or the provisions of existing treaties; or

(2) shall be construed as granting any authority to the President with respect to the introduction of United States Armed Forces into hostilities by the circumstances which authority he would not have had in the absence of this joint [resolution].

An essential issue raised by the War Powers Resolutions is whether Congress can mandate collective participation in this manner. Notably, no President has formally invoked the War Powers Resolution although Presidents have consulted with Congress about deployment of troops. Even a President who shares the view that war making requires the coordinated participation of Congress and the President is likely to be concerned about preserving the President's discretion to act in crises. A related consideration concerns accountability. In several provisions of the Resolution, Congress outlines consequences which will result from a failure to comply. Consider whether there are available to Congress recourses which were not available to it in the absence of the Resolution. The reporting provisions, which provide a set of timetables from which expectations about coordinated action can be measured, have been essentially ignored by Presidents.

PAH: It is not surprising that no President has formally submitted to the War Powers Resolution. It sets rigid timetables and allocates responsibilities in a way that contradicts the fluid conception of coordinated power that is implied in the Constitution and that has proven favorable to the Executive. Although the Resolution attempts to delineate Congress' vision of the appropriate arrangements for sharing information and coordinating war-making steps, Presidents have consistently taken positions that are inconsistent with that vision, asserting that the Constitution (particularly read with the gloss of practice) makes available power to act unilaterally in the context of war. The effort to freeze a framework for understanding the respective roles of the political branches, moreover, seems at odds with the idea that the Framers contemplated—indeed invited—struggle between the political branches in this area to ensure that the commitment of troops would not occur without reflection and without the support of the citizens. Congress' purpose, to restore to the war-making context a balance of power between the President and Congress can be separated from the details of the Resolution. This reaffirmation of an active role in war-making in the language of the Resolution becomes meaningful, however, only if accompanied by political will. Moreover, although the Resolution sets up standards for compliance, it is unlikely that the Court will intervene in disputes about authority which are raised in the document. Notably, section 5(c) of the resolution, which purports to force the President to withdraw armed forces, has the "purpose and effect or altering rights, duties and relations of persons, including . . . Executive Branch officials," and consequently, under *Chadha*, is unconstitutional unless it is subject to the presidential veto.

Public reaction and, ultimately, impeachment, remain options available to prod presidential engagement in a partnership reflected in the spirit if not the express terms of the War Powers Resolution.

G. Formalism vs. Functionalism—Defining the Court's Role in Future Controversies

Commentators have disagreed about the significance of the Court's participation in modern controversies implicating separation of powers. Much of the disagreement concerns whether the Court is capable of devising an approach to resolving conflicts about the allocation of constitutional power among the branches which is more than ad hoc and outcome-focused or justificatory. The unexplained, shifting preference for formalism and functionalism by the Court fuels the disagreement and invites the observation that political resolution of separation of power claims is not only consistent with the constitutional framework, it avoids damage to the institutional integrity of the Court which can occur when the Court renders decisions which lack a consistently applied analytical framework. For those who believe there continues to be a role for the Court in resolving conflicts about political power arrangements, the challenge is to define an appropriate analytical focus that is not perceived as merely favoring one branch over the other or protecting "institutional turf."[154]

---

[154] Some critics of the Supreme Court's role in separation of powers cases assert that decisions are often result-driven, though not necessarily decided on the basis of "liberal" or "conservative" camps. Advancement of preferred institutional interests may explain the results of cases. For example, some scholars have argued that recent Court rulings favor the President, Congress or the Court, Erwin Chemerinsky, *A Paradox Without a Principle: A Comment on the Burger Court's Jurisprudence in Separation of Powers Cases*, 60 S. CAL. L. REV. 1083, 1085–86 (1987). As in the case of *Dames & Moore*, where Justice Rehnquist candidly acknowledged that the exigencies of the hostage crisis affected decision making, weakening the precedential value of the Court's disposition beyond the context, in some cases, the specter of political result-driven impetus for the Court's decision lurks. For example, Watergate and the resulting Saturday night massacre spawned political support for independent counsel legislation which Congress passed and which was implemented. The subsequent constitutional challenge to the legislation presented the problem of overturning convictions which likely led the Court to reach a decision upholding the sentencing commission in *Morrison*.

PAH: Both formalism and functionalism offer insights that are important in the resolution of conflicting constitutional power claims, but each approach seems deficient in light of our understanding of the design and the reality of modern government. The formalists' account of separation of powers and the constitutional structure it supports relies on particular provisions of the text and other documents reflecting the Framers' design for government. Emphasizing the Framers' concern about tyranny, formalists demand strict adherence to the functional boundaries separating the branches of government and the understanding that, except for the provisions expressly spelled out by the Framers, each branch should exercise its own powers. Formalists do not question whether strict construction promoting separated functions preserves liberty. They view as sacrosanct that the Framers chose separation as a preventative method of guaranteeing liberty for citizens by means of limited and separated government. Constitutional provisions are construed by formalists as marking boundaries from which the courts can formulate ascertainable standards and thereby exercise their constitutional role of safeguarding against the accretion of power. Formalists often give a nod to *Marbury* to support this view.

Functionalist critics argue that this analytical approach is mechanical and projects a notion of "scientific" precision in distinguishing governmental functions that is not available now or at the time of the Framing. Because formalism emphasizes maintaining the framework contemplated by the Framers through literal adherence to the details of each Constitutional provision, it minimizes the value of efficiency or workable government that was also envisioned by the Framers in their structural plan. As a consequence, commentators have criticized formalism as having the potential for strait-jacketing government, penalizing the very political accommodation that was invited by the Framers and promoting intrusion by courts in matters in which they are not competent (nor constitutionally assigned) to address. Functionalists here often nod toward *McCulloch* and deference to political policymaking that serves to restrain the Court. Critics of formalism are skeptical of the fundamental assumption that liberty is unquestionably served by drawing distinct lines of branch autonomy, suggesting that courts are capable of a more searching inquiry as to whether the public good is served than formalism permits. Thus although functionalists are often more willing to defer to legislative or executive determinations about the proper accommodation of power, they are also willing to have courts consider whether, all things considered, political arrangements result in disruption or encroachments on functions which are "undue."[155]

Functionalism conceives the constitutional framework as more fluid than formalism. Proponents of a functionalist approach emphasize the Framers' reliance on checks and balances to promote coordination and efficiency rather than the preservation of power and branch independence as the Framers may have conceived. Because functionalists tend to defer to legislative judgment about the political arrangements which will promote the constitutional plan and accommodate the needs of modern government in a complex world, they have been characterized as majoritarian in outlook. However, formalists often reject legislative checks which are designed to control the accumulation of power in the executive branch. Thus to some extent both can be considered "majoritarian," though favoring different political institutions. Similarly, whereas critics of functionalism argue that their deference to political decisionmaking is an abdication of judicial responsibility, both functionalists and formalists can be considered activists—formalists in their willingness to overrule politically preferred arrangements, functionalists in their exercise of "boundless" discretion in balancing interests to determine whether there has occurred "undue" encroachment or disruption of another branch's functions which impedes its ability to perform its constitutional duty.

---

[155] *See, e.g., Morrison,* 108 S. Ct. at 2620 (Justice White, quoting United States v. Nixon, 418 U.S. at 707).

Despite hyperbole about differences in approaches which has accompanied the "tug of war" waged between the formalists and functionalists in resolving separation of power controversies, the distinctions in the approaches are most often a matter of degree. The functionalists' emphasis on efficiency or effectiveness of government operation presumes that political accommodation serves those interests; but functionalism is not blind to the need for maintaining boundaries. The formalists' attention to isolated textual limitations and express formal checks is built on the assumption that the legislative and executive autonomy is best preserved by disciplined adherence to established limitations; but formalism also contemplates some degree of flexibility.[156] Both approaches are designed to promote liberty and preserve the Constitution though formalists and functionalists conceive of different institutional roles to accomplish those objectives.

Recognition of the deficiencies and strengths of both approaches has led some commentators to propose an amalgam of the two approaches in response to separation of power controversies. Martin Redish and Elizabeth Cisar argue that what is needed is a "'street-smart' mode of interpretation, growing out of a recognition of the dangers to which a more 'functional' or 'balancing' analysis in the separation of powers context may create." Seeking to retain the "meaningful limitations" they believe is available in formalism as well as preserving the "prophylactic nature" of protection of that approach, they advocate injecting functionalism's "pragmatic nature" in two ways:

> Initially pragmatic factors lead to the choice of formalism in the first place: No conceivable alternative adequately guards against the dangers that the system of separation of powers was adopted to avoid. Secondly, pragmatism influences how the differing concepts of branch power are ultimately to be defined. . . . In other words, the Court's role in separation of powers cases should be limited to determining whether the challenged branch falls within the definition of that branch's constitutionally derived powers—executive, legislative, or judicial. If the answer is yes, the branch's action is constitutional; if the answer is no, the action is unconstitutional. No other questions are to be asked; no other countervailing factors are to be considered.[157]

Thus, to use one example, in *Morrison v. Olson* the "pragmatic formalist" would look at the power to investigate and prosecute high government officials for certain criminal activity which the independent counsel is authorized to do under the Act and conclude that the power the independent counsel exercises is "executive"; that determination would lead to a determination that the legislation is an unconstitutional vesting of executive power in the judicial branch.[158]

Ms. Cisar and Professor Redish further caution, however, that the Court should not then engage in the "ad hoc balancing" of functionalism, weighing unquantifiable harms to separation of powers interests against interests in efficiency because this approach undermines the "key structural assumptions of separation of powers theory—that it will be impossible (at least until it is too late) to determine whether or not a particular breach of branch separation will seriously threaten the core political values of accountability, diversity, and checking."[159] Of course, the difficulty in this approach lies in the capacity of courts to define power that is conferred by legislation or assumed by any member of

---

[156] "As we have said, 'The Constitution has never been regarded as denying to the Congress the necessary resources of flexibility and practicality . . . to perform its function.'" Yakus v. United States, 321 U.S. 414, 425 (1944).

[157] 41 DUKE L.J. at 454–55.

[158] *Id.* at 490.

[159] *Id.* at 490–91.

a branch as clearly able to be characterized as "executive," "legislative" or "judicial."[160] The discipline which Redish and Cisar claim to be able to achieve by defining a power is not nearly as easily obtainable as they suggest and a judge may be swayed—consciously or unconsciously—to define power about which there may be some doubt, affected by the consideration of whether an encroachment on another branch's power is "undue." Indeed another proponent of a combined approach, Professor Keith Werhan, suggests that a "two-step" analysis *should consciously* be undertaken—much as was actually taken in *Morrison*. Justice Rehnquist focused on text and history of the appointments clause in an effort to resolve the controversy about whether the power exercised by the independent counsel under the Act was "executive"; he then moved to the second step of considering whether there had been an undue encroachment on power only after the first step was unsuccessful in clearly resolving the question of the kind of power being exercised.[161]

The quest for ascertainable standards has led other scholars to look away from these competing approaches. Professor Rebecca Brown has criticized the functionalism and formalism debate:

> This debate goes wrong because it hangs in midair, moored to no grander objective than the abstract merits of the two relatively mechanical theories themselves—in the end no more than a question of where the proper point lies on the lexibility/determinacy matrix.[162]

Unlike some scholars who have become disaffected with the debate, urging judicial abstention at least in some circumstances,[163] Professor Brown posits that when fundamental policy choices affect personal interests, the Court is remiss in not intervening. Often separation of powers cases in which the Court has been willing to intervene reflect due process interests in "even-handed" government. Professor Rebecca Brown argues that consideration of individual rights provides a rational structure for articles I, II, and III and that recognition of the value of individual liberty in resolving structural issues can bring coherence to separation of powers analysis which is presently missing. Similarly, Paul Verkuil suggests that we focus attention on the relationship of separation of powers and other constitutional concepts like due process and bill of attainder, because they provide tools of analysis which have an intelligible foundation, and avoid the present ad hoc nature of separation of powers analysis.[164]

---

[160] As James Madison is often quoted as saying: "no skill in the science of government has yet been able to discriminate and define, with sufficient certainty, its three great provinces—the legislative, executive, and judiciary; or even the privileges and powers of the different legislative branches." The Federalist No. 37, (mod. Lib 1941) at 229 (James Madison).

[161] Keith Werhan, *Toward an Eclectic Approach to Separation of Powers: Morrison v. Olson Examined*, 16 Hastings Const. L.Q. 393 1989). Martin Redish and Elizabeth Cisar would respond that regardless of the difference in view about the definition of power being exercised by the independent counsel, this approach permits the Court to engage in the ad hoc balancing that it is not competent to perform.

[162] Rebecca L. Brown, *Separated Powers and Ordered Liberty*, 139 U. Pa. L. Rev. 1513, 1530.

[163] *See, e.g.*, Jesse Choper, Judicial Review and the National Political Process 55–59, 263 (1980); Carter, *supra* 102 Harv. L. Rev. 105 (advocating limited abstention); *see also* Myers v. United States, 272 U.S. 52, 177 (1926) (dissenting opinion of Justice Holmes), cited in Brown, *supra*, 139 U. Pa. L. Rev. at 1529 n.65.

[164] *See, e.g.*, Paul Verkuil, *Separation of Powers, The Rule of Law and the Idea of Independence*, 30 Wm. & Mary L. Rev. 301, 308-13 (1989). In her article Professor Brown suggests that it is not surprising that the individual rights revolution of the sixties was followed in the seventies and eighties by renewed interest in the separation of powers doctrine. Brown, *supra*, 139 U. Pa. L. Rev. 1514 (analysis should focus on concepts (such as due process clause) which concern conflict of interest and fairness).

Professor Brown argues that separation of powers jurisprudence has failed to clarify how the public good (besides preservation of government for governments own sake) ought to be served. Scholars therefore have often been left to rationalize results or to seek some coherence in an area without a consistent theoretical foundation. Professor Carter and others have charged that this incoherence is in substantial part the result of the Court's avoidance of the constitutional issues raised by independent administrative agencies and the Court's willingness implicitly to adjust the framework of tripartite federal government to permit the creation of this "fourth branch." While it can be said that the Court's ambivalence about its role in condoning broad delegation of national power to unelected decision makers has affected separation of powers jurisprudence, it is not nearly as clear to others as it is to Professor Carter that the Court is capable of policing the delicate balance of relationships conceived in separation of powers.

PART III

POWER TO REGULATE OR AFFECT THE ECONOMY

A. Federal Power

The Constitution explicitly gives Congress the power to regulate commerce "among" the several states. The decision to vest this power in the federal government was not taken lightly. Under the Articles of Confederation, the states reserved the commerce power to themselves. Moreover, although the Articles gave Congress some control over foreign affairs, the Articles specifically prohibited Congress from entering into treaties limiting the states' power over commerce or their right to tax imports and exports.

The Articles of Confederation did not provide the basis for a sound economy. The states used their powers to protect their own economies at the expense of their neighbors, and there "grew up a conflict of commercial regulations, destructive to the harmony of the States, and fatal to their commercial interests abroad."[1] Many states imposed economic sanctions, including taxes and tariffs, on trade from other states. By 1875–76, the nation was mired in a recession caused by "a high national debt, increasing trade deficits, and economic infighting."[2]

As the economic situation worsened, many began to call for a convention to amend the Articles of Confederation. This convention, which convened in 1786, was supposed to propose amendments giving the federal government increased power over commerce. But, when the delegates finally met, they quickly realized that more drastic change was needed and called for a second convention to make more sweeping changes. This second convention, which ultimately became known as the Constitutional Convention, produced our present Constitution.

Under the Constitution, Congress was specifically given the power "to regulate commerce with foreign nations, and among the several states, and with the Indian Tribes."

1. Seminal Principles

The Constitution did not define the phrase "among the several states." That task was left to the courts.

---

[1] Gibbons v. Ogden, 22 U.S. (9 Wheat) 1 (1824) (Johnson, J., concurring).
[2] DANIEL A. FARBER & SUZANNA SHERRY, A HISTORY OF THE AMERICAN CONSTITUTION 25 (1990)

Gibbons v. Ogden
22 U.S. 1 (1824)

[The New York Legislature enacted a statute giving Robert Livingston and Robert Fulton the exclusive right to operate steamboats in New York waters. The license was enforced by strict penalties. Thereafter, Livingston and Fulton granted Aaron Ogden a license to operate a ferry between New York City and various points in New Jersey.

Under an act of Congress, Thomas Gibbons obtained a license to navigate steamboats in the same waters. When Gibbons began operating two competing steamboats, Ogden sought and obtained an injunction prohibiting the steamboats from operating in the State of New York. When the injunction was affirmed by the New York courts, Gibbons appealed to the U.S. Supreme Court.]

Mr. Chief Justice MARSHALL delivered the opinion of the Court.

. . .

The appellant contends that this decree is erroneous, because the laws which purport to give the exclusive privilege it sustains, are repugnant to . . . that clause in the constitution which authorizes Congress to regulate commerce.

. . .

The words are, "Congress shall have power to regulate commerce with foreign nations, and among the several States, and with the Indian tribes."

. . .

If commerce does not include navigation, the government of the Union has no direct power over that subject, and can make no law prescribing what shall constitute American vessels, or requiring that they shall be navigated by American seamen. Yet this power has been exercised from the commencement of the government, has been exercised with the consent of all, and has been understood by all to be a commercial regulation. All America understands, and has uniformly understood, the word "commerce," to comprehend navigation. . . .

. . .

The word used in the constitution, then, comprehends, and has been always understood to comprehend, navigation within its meaning; and a power to regulate navigation, is as expressly granted, as if that term had been added to the word "commerce."

To what commerce does this power extend? The constitution informs us, to commerce "with foreign nations, and among the several States, and with the Indian tribes."

. . .

The subject to which the power is next applied, is to commerce "among the several States." The word "among" means intermingled with. A thing which is among others, is intermingled with them. Commerce among the States, cannot stop at the external boundary line of each State, but may be introduced into the interior.

It is not intended to say that these words comprehend that commerce, which is completely internal, which is carried on between man and man in a State, or between different parts of the same State, and which does not extend to or affect other States. Such a power would be inconvenient, and is certainly unnecessary.

Comprehensive as the word "among" is, it may very properly be restricted to that commerce which concerns more States than one. The phrase is not one which would probably have been selected to indicate the completely interior traffic of a State, because it is not an apt phrase for that purpose; and the enumeration of the particular classes of commerce, to which the power was to be extended, would not have been made, had the intention been to extend the power to every description. The enumeration presupposes something not enumerated; and that something, if we regard the language or the subject of the sentence, must be the exclusively internal commerce of a State. The genius and character of the whole government seem to be, that its action is to be applied to all the external concerns of the nation, and to those internal concerns which affect the States generally; but not to those which are completely within a particular State, which do not affect other States, and with which it is not necessary to interfere, for the purpose of executing some of the general powers of the government. The completely internal commerce of a State, then, may be considered as reserved for the State itself.

But, in regulating commerce with foreign nations, the power of Congress does not stop at the jurisdictional lines of the several States. It would be a very useless power, if it could not pass those lines. The commerce of the United States with foreign nations, is that of the whole United States. Every district has a right to participate in it. The deep streams which penetrate our country in every direction, pass through the interior of almost every State in the Union, and furnish the means of exercising this right. If Congress has the power to regulate it, that power must be exercised whenever the subject exists. If it exists within the States, if a foreign voyage may commence or terminate at a port within a State, then the power of Congress may be exercised within a State.

This principle is, if possible, still more clear, when applied to commerce "among the several States." They either join each other, in which case they are separated by a mathematical line, or they are remote from each other, in which case other States lie between them. What is commerce "among" them; and how is it to be conducted? Can a trading expedition between two adjoining States, commence and terminate outside of each? And if the trading intercourse be between two States remote from each other, must it not commence in one, terminate in the other, and probably pass through a third? Commerce among the States must, of necessity, be commerce with the States. In the regulation of trade with the Indian tribes, the action of the law, especially when the constitution was made, was chiefly within a State. The power of Congress, then, whatever it may be, must be exercised within the territorial jurisdiction of the several States. The sense of the nation on this subject, is unequivocally manifested by the provisions made in the laws for transporting goods, by land, between Baltimore and Providence, between New York and Philadelphia, and between Philadelphia and Baltimore.

We are now arrived at the inquiry—What is this power?

It is the power to regulate; that is, to prescribe the rule by which commerce is to be governed. This power, like all others vested in Congress, is complete in itself, may be exercised to its utmost extent, and acknowledges no limitations, other than are prescribed in the constitution. These are expressed in plain terms, and do not affect the questions which arise in this case, or which have been discussed at the bar. If, as has always been understood, the sovereignty of Congress, though limited to specified objects, is plenary as to those objects, the power over commerce with foreign nations, and among the several States, is vested in Congress as absolutely as it would be in a single government, having in its constitution the same restrictions on the exercise of the power as are found in the constitution of the United States. The wisdom and the discretion of Congress, their identity with the people, and the influence which their constituents possess at elections, are, in this, as in many other instances, as that, for example, of declaring war, the sole restraints on which they have relied, to secure them from its abuse. They are the restraints on which the people must often rely solely, in all representative governments.

The power of Congress, then, comprehends navigation, within the limits of every State in the Union; so far as that navigation may be, in any manner, connected with "commerce with foreign nations, or among the several States, or with the Indian tribes." It may, of consequence, pass the jurisdictional line of New York, and act upon the very waters to which the prohibition now under consideration applies.

. . .

Gibbons' Impact. "The effects of the decision were at once felt in the waters of New York and the other States."[3] "Shortly after the fourteenth of March, the newspapers of the North carried this item: 'Yesterday the Steamboat *United States*, . . . entered New York in triumph, with streamers flying, and a large company of passengers exulting in the decision of the United States Supreme Court against the New York monopoly. She fired a salute which was loudly returned by huzzas from the wharves.'"[4] "A representative Southern paper spoke of 'the immense public advantages that flow from the decision. The fare in the steamboats that ply between New York and New Haven has been reduced from five to three dollars.'"[5] "Shortly over a year after the decision, *Niles Register* reported that the number of steamboats plying from New York had increased from six to forty-three."[6] "[T]he chief importance of the case in the eyes of the public of that day was its effect in shattering the great monopoly against which they had been struggling for fifteen years."[7]

Despite *Gibbons'* expansive language, the Court did not always construe the commerce clause broadly during the nineteenth century. *Paul v. Virginia*[8] involved a Virginia statute which discriminated against insurance companies incorporated in other states. The statute was challenged as repugnant to the federal commerce power. In an opinion delivered by Mr. Justice Field, the Court rejected the challenge concluding that "[i]ssuing a policy of insurance is not a transaction of commerce" so the commerce clause does not reach it:

> The policies are simple contracts of indemnity against loss by fire, entered into between the corporations and the assured, for a consideration paid by the

---

[3] 2 C. WARREN, THE SUPREME COURT IN UNITED STATES HISTORY 75 (1922).
[4] *Id.*
[5] *Id.*
[6] *Id.*
[7] *Id.* at 76.
[8] 75 U.S. (8 Wall.) 168 (1868).

latter. . . . They are not commodities to be shipped or forwarded from one State to another, and then put up for sale. They are like other personal contracts between parties which are completed by their signature and the transfer of the consideration. Such contracts are not inter-state transactions, though the parties may be domiciled in different States. The policies do not take effect—are not executed contracts—until delivered by the agent in Virginia. They are, then, local transactions, and are governed by the local law. They do not constitute a part of the commerce between the States any more than a contract for the purchase and sale of goods in Virginia by a citizen of New York whilst in Virginia would constitute a portion of such commerce.

In some early decisions, the Court held that the states retained control over their internal commerce. *Kidd v. Pearson*[9] involved an Iowa statute that prohibited the manufacture of liquor. The statute was applied to an Iowa company that sold all of its product in other states. In an opinion written by Mr. Justice Lamar, the Court upheld the Iowa law:

> [Congress' power over commerce] does not comprehend the purely internal domestic commerce of a state, which is carried on between man and man within a state or between different parts of the same state. . . . The completely internal commerce of a state, then, may be considered as reserved for the state itself. . . .
>
> . . .
>
> We find . . . [that the statute's] avowed object is to prevent, not the carrying of intoxicating liquors out of the state, but to prevent their manufacture, except for specified purposes, within the state. It is true that, notwithstanding its purposes and ends are restricted to the jurisdictional limits of the state of Iowa, and apply to transactions wholly internal and between its own citizens, its effects may reach beyond the state, by lessening the amount of intoxicating liquors exported. But it does not follow that, because the products of a domestic manufacture may ultimately become the subjects of interstate commerce, at the pleasure of the manufacturer, the legislation of the state respecting such manufacture is an attempted exercise of the power to regulate commerce exclusively conferred upon congress. . . .

However, some nineteenth century decisions took a more expansive view of commerce's power. *The Daniel Ball*[10] involved a steamer that travelled routes wholly within the State of Michigan, but which carried merchandise being transported to, or from, other states. The question was whether a federal safety regulation applied to the steamer. In an opinion written by Mr. Justice Field, the Court concluded that the regulation applied:

> [W]e are unable to draw any clear and distinct line between the authority of Congress to regulate an agency employed in commerce between the States, when that agency extends through two or more States, and when it is confined in its action entirely within the limits of a single State. If its authority does not extend to an agency in such commerce, when that agency is confined within the limits of a State, its entire authority over interstate commerce may be defeated. Several agencies combining, each taking up the commodity transported at the boundary line at one end of a State, and leaving it at the boundary line at the other end, the Federal jurisdiction would be entirely ousted, and the constitutional provision would become a dead letter.

---

[9] 128 U.S. 1 (1888).
[10] 77 U.S. 557 (1870).

2. Early Twentieth Century Analysis

When the Constitution was ratified, the United States was a largely agrarian society. By the end of the nineteenth century, the economy was in a period of dramatic industrial transition.

Industrialization produced profound changes in the U.S. economy. The development of railroads, and eventually cars, allowed people and goods to move freely across state borders. This movement meant that many commercial problems which had formerly been more local in nature were increasingly becoming national problems. As a result, Congress began to assume a more active regulatory role passing the Interstate Commerce Act, the Sherman Antitrust Act and a host of other legislation.

Congress' more aggressive posture forced the Court to confront difficult questions regarding the scope of Congress' power. It did so in several cases decided early in the twentieth century. In some of these cases, the Court took a broad view of federal power. In other cases, the Court took a more restrictive view.

Champion v. Ames
(The Lottery Case)
188 U.S. 321 (1903)

[Appellant Champion was indicted for conspiring to transport Paraguayan lottery tickets across state lines in violation of federal law. After his arrest, Champion sought a writ of habeas corpus on the basis that the law prohibiting the transportation of lottery tickets was unconstitutional.]

Mr. Justice Harlan delivered the opinion of the court:

The appellant insists that the carrying of lottery tickets from one state to another state by an express company engaged in carrying freight and packages from state to state, although such tickets may be contained in a box or package, does not constitute, and cannot by any act of Congress be legally made to constitute, commerce among the states within the meaning of the . . . Constitution . . .; consequently, that Congress cannot make it an offense to cause such tickets to be carried from one state to another.

. . .

[Our prior precedent] show[s] that commerce among the states embraces navigation, intercourse, communication, traffic, the transit of persons, and the transmission of messages by telegraph. They also show that the power to regulate commerce among the several states is vested in Congress as absolutely as it would be in a single government, having in its constitution the same restrictions on the exercise of the power as are found in the Constitution of the United States; that such power is plenary, complete in itself, and may be exerted by Congress to its utmost extent, subject only to such limitations as the Constitution imposes upon the exercise of the powers granted by it; and that in determining the character of the regulations to be adopted Congress has a large discretion which is not to be controlled by the courts, simply because, in their opinion, such regulations may not be the best or most effective that could be employed.

. . .

It was said in argument that lottery tickets are not of any real or substantial value in themselves, and therefore are not subjects of commerce. [W]e cannot accept as accurate the broad statement that such tickets are of no value. Upon their face they showed that the lottery company offered a large capital prize, to be paid to the holder of the ticket winning the prize at the drawing advertised to be held at Asuncion, Paraguay. . . .

We are of opinion that lottery tickets are subjects of traffic, and therefore are subjects of commerce, and the regulation of the carriage of such tickets from state to state, at least by independent carriers, is a regulation of commerce among the several states.

But it is said that the statute in question does not regulate the carrying of lottery tickets from state to state, but by punishing those who cause them to be so carried Congress in effect prohibits such carrying; that in respect of the carrying from one state to another of articles or things that are, in fact, or according to usage in business, the subjects of commerce, the authority given Congress was not to *prohibit*, but only to *regulate*. This view was earnestly pressed at the bar by learned counsel, and must be examined.

It is to be remarked that the Constitution does not define what is to be deemed a legitimate regulation of interstate commerce. In *Gibbons v. Ogden* it was said that the power to regulate such commerce is the power to prescribe the rule by which it is to be governed. But this general observation leaves it to be determined, when the question comes before the court, whether Congress, in prescribing a particular rule, has exceeded its power under the Constitution. While our government must be acknowledged by all to be one of enumerated powers, the Constitution does not attempt to set forth all the means by which such powers may be carried into execution. It leaves to Congress a large discretion as to the means that may be employed in executing a given power. The sound construction of the Constitution, this court has said, "must allow to the national legislature that discretion, with respect to the means by which the powers it confers are to be carried into execution, which will enable that body to perform the high duties assigned to it, in the manner most beneficial to the people. Let the end be legitimate, let it be within the scope of the Constitution, and all means which are appropriate, which are plainly adapted to that end, which are not prohibited, but consist with the letter and spirit of the Constitution, are constitutional."

We have said that the carrying from state to state of lottery tickets constitutes interstate commerce, and that the regulation of such commerce is within the power of Congress under the Constitution. Are we prepared to say that a provision which is, in effect, a *prohibition* of the carriage of such articles from state to state is not a fit or appropriate mode for the *regulation* of that particular kind of commerce? If lottery traffic, *carried on through interstate commerce*, is a matter of which Congress may take cognizance and over which its power may be exerted, can it be possible that it must tolerate the traffic, and simply regulate the manner in which it may be carried on? Or may not Congress, for the protection of the people of all the states, and under the power to regulate interstate commerce, devise such means, within the scope of the Constitution, and not prohibited by it, as will drive that traffic out of commerce among the states?

In determining whether regulation may not under some circumstances properly take the from or have the effect of prohibition, the nature of the interstate traffic which it was sought by the act of May 2d, 1895, to suppress cannot be overlooked. When enacting that statute Congress no doubt shared the views upon the subject of lotteries heretofore expressed by this court. In *Phalen v. Virginia*, 8 How. 163, 168, after observing that the suppression of nuisances injurious to public health or moral-ity is among the most important duties of government, this court said: "Experience has shown that the common forms of gambling are comparatively innocuous when placed in contrast with the widespread pestilence of lotteries. The former are confined to a few persons and places, but the latter infests the whole community; it enters every dwelling; it reaches every class; it preys upon the hard earnings of the poor; it plunders the ignorant and simple." . . .

If a State, when considering legislation for the suppression of lotteries within its own limits, may properly take into view the evils that inhere in the raising of money, in that mode, why may not Congress, invested with the power to regulate commerce among the several states, provide that such commerce shall not be polluted by the carrying of lottery tickets from one state to another? In this connection it must not be forgotten that the power of Congress to regulate commerce among the states is plenary, is complete in itself, and is subject to no limitations except such as may be found in the Constitution. What provision in that instrument can be regarded as limiting the exercise of the power granted? What clause can be cited which, in any degree, countenances the suggestion that one may, of right, carry or cause to be carried from one state to another that which will harm the public morals? We cannot think of any clause of that instrument that could possibly be invoked by those who assert their right to send lottery tickets from state to state except the one providing that no person shall be deprived of his liberty without due process of law. We have said that the liberty protected by the Constitution embraces the right to be free in the enjoyment of one's faculties; "to be free to use them in all lawful ways; to live and work where he will; to earn his livelihood by any lawful calling; to pursue any livelihood or avocation, and for that purpose to enter into all contracts which may be proper." *Allgeyer v. Louisiana*, 165 U.S. 578, 589. But surely it will not be said to be a part of anyone's liberty, as recognized by the supreme law of the land, that he shall be allowed to introduce into commerce among the states an element that will be confessedly injurious to the public morals.

If it be said that the act of 1894 is inconsistent with the 10th Amendment, reserving to the states respectively, or to the people, the powers not delegated to the United States, the answer is that the power to regulate commerce among the states has been expressly delegated to Congress.

Besides, Congress, by that act, does not assume to interfere with traffic or commerce in lottery tickets carried on exclusively within the limits of any state, but has in view only commerce of that kind among the several states. It has not assumed to interfere with the completely internal affairs of any state, and has only legislated in respect of a matter which concerns the people of the United States. As a state may, for the purpose of guarding the morals of its own people, forbid all sales of lottery tickets within its limits, so Congress, for the purpose of guarding the people of the United States against the "widespread pestilence of lotteries" and to protect the commerce which concerns all the states, may prohibit the carrying of lottery tickets from one state to another. In legislating upon the subject of the traffic in lottery tickets, as carried on through interstate commerce, Congress only supplemented the action of those states—perhaps all of them—which, for the protection of the public morals, prohibit the drawing of lotteries, as well as the sale or circulation of lottery tickets, within their respective limits. It said, in effect, that it would not permit the declared policy of the states, which sought to protect their people against the mischiefs of the lottery business, to be overthrown or disregarded by the agency of interstate commerce. We should hesitate long before adjudging that an evil of such appalling character, carried on through interstate commerce, cannot be met and crushed by the only power competent to that end. We say competent to that end, because Congress alone has the power to occupy, by legislation, the whole field of interstate commerce. . . .

That regulation may sometimes appropriately assume the form of prohibition is also illustrated by the case of diseased cattle, transported from one state to another. Such cattle may have, notwithstanding their condition, a value in money for some purposes, and yet it cannot be doubted that Congress, under its power to regulate commerce, may either provide for their being inspected before transportation begins, or, in its discretion, may prohibit their being transported from one state to another. . . .

. . .

It is said, however, that if, in order to suppress lotteries carried on through interstate commerce, Congress may exclude lottery tickets from such commerce, that principle leads necessarily to the conclusion that Congress may arbitrarily exclude from commerce among the states any article, commodity, or thing, of whatever kind or nature, or however useful or valuable, which it may choose, no matter with what motive, to declare shall not be carried from one state to another. It will be time enough to consider the constitutionality of such legislation when we must do so. . . .

The whole subject is too important, and the questions suggested by its consideration are too difficult of solution, to justify any attempt to lay down a rule for determining in advance the validity of every statute that may be enacted under the commerce clause. We decide nothing more in the present case than that lottery tickets are subjects of traffic among those who choose to sell or buy them; that the carriage of such tickets by independent carriers from one state to another is therefore interstate commerce; that under its power to regulate commerce among the several states Congress—subject to the limitations imposed by the Constitution upon the exercise of the powers granted—has plenary authority over such commerce, and may prohibit the carriage of such tickets from state to state; and that legislation to that end, and of that character, is not inconsistent with any limitation or restriction imposed upon the exercise of the powers granted to Congress.

The judgment is affirmed.

Mr. Chief Justice Fuller, with whom concur Mr. Justice Brewer, Mr. Justice Shiras, and Mr. Justice Peckham, dissenting:

Doubtless an act prohibiting the carriage of lottery matter would be necessary and proper to the execution of a power to suppress lotteries; but that power belongs to the states and not to Congress. To hold that Congress has general police power would be to hold that it may accomplish objects not intrusted to the general government, and to defeat the operation of the 10th Amendment, declaring that "the powers not delegated to the United States by the Constitution, nor prohibited by it to the states, are reserved to the states respectively, or to the people."

. . .

Is the carriage of lottery tickets from one state to another commercial intercourse?

The lottery ticket purports to create contractual relations, and to furnish the means of enforcing a contract right.

This is true of insurance policies, and both are contingent in their nature. Yet this court has held that the issuing of fire, marine, and life insurance policies, in one state, and sending them to another, to be there delivered to the insured on payment of premium, is not interstate commerce. *Paul v. Virginia*, 8 Wall. 168. . . .

. . .

If a lottery ticket is not an article of commerce, how can it become so when placed in an envelope or box or other covering, and transported by an express company? To say that the mere carrying of an article which is not an article of commerce in and of itself nevertheless becomes such the moment it is to be transported from one state to another, is to transform a non-commercial article into a commercial one simply because it is transported. I cannot conceive that any such result can properly follow.

It would be to say that everything is an

article of commerce the moment it is taken to be transported from place to place, and of interstate commerce if from state to state.

An invitation to dine, or to take a drive, or a note of introduction, all become articles of commerce under the ruling in this case, by being deposited with an express company for transportation. This in effect breaks down all the differences between that which is, and that which is not, an article of commerce, and the necessary consequence is to take from the states all jurisdiction over the subject so far as interstate communication is concerned. It is a long step in the direction of wiping out all traces of state lines, and the creation of a centralized government.

Does the grant to Congress of the power to regulate interstate commerce import the absolute power to prohibit it?

. . .

The power to prohibit the transportation of diseased animals and infected goods over railroads or on steamboats is an entirely different thing, for they would be in themselves injurious to the transaction of interstate commerce, and, moreover, are essentially commercial in their nature. And the exclusion of diseased persons rests on different ground, for nobody would pretend that persons could be kept off the trains because they were going from one state to another to engage in the lottery business. However enticing that business may be, we do not understand these pieces of paper themselves can communicate bad principles by contact.

. . .

I regard this decision as inconsistent with the views of the framers of the Constitution, and of Marshall, its great expounder. . . .

. . .

The Lottery Case established the broad principle that Congress can ban items from interstate commerce. This principle was reaffirmed in *McDermott v. Wisconsin*,[11] a case that involved a federal statute making it a crime to sell improperly labelled food products. McDermott allegedly sold improperly labelled syrup. When he was indicted, he sought to challenge the federal law as beyond Congress' authority. In an opinion delivered by Mr. Justice Day, the Court upheld the law:

> That Congress has ample power in this connection is no longer open to question. That body has the right not only to pass laws which shall regulate legitimate commerce among the states and with foreign nations, but has full power to keep the channels of such commerce free from the transportation of illicit or harmful articles, to make such as are injurious to the public health outlaws of such commerce, and to bar them from the facilities and privileges thereof. . . .
>
> . . .
>
> The object of the statute is to prevent the misuse of the facilities of interstate commerce in conveying to and placing before the consumer misbranded and adulterated articles of medicine or food, and in order that its protection may be afforded to those who are intended to receive its benefits, the brands regulated must be upon the packages intended to reach the purchaser. This is the only practical or sensible construction of the act . . . we think the requirements of the act as so construed clearly within the powers of Congress. . . .

---

[11] 228 U.S. 115 (1913).

Houston, East & West Texas Railway Company v. United States
234 U.S. 342 (1914)

Mr. Justice Hughes delivered the opinion of the court:

These suits were brought in the commerce court by the Houston, East & West Texas Rail-way Company and the Houston & Shreveport Railroad Company, and by the Texas & Pacific Railway Company, respectively, to set aside an order of the Interstate Commerce Commission, dated March 11, 1912, upon the ground that it exceeded the Commission's authority. . . .

. . .

The Interstate Commerce Commission found that the interstate class rates out of Shreveport to named Texas points were unreasonable, and it established maximum class rates for this traffic. These rates, we understand, were substantially the same as the class rates fixed by the Railroad Commission of Texas, and charged by the carriers, for transportation for similar distances in that state. The Interstate Commerce Commission also found that the carriers maintained "higher rates from Shreveport to points in Texas" than were in force "from cities in Texas to such points under substantially similar conditions and circumstances," and that thereby "an unlawful and undue preference and advantage" was given to the Texas cities, and a "discrimination" that was "undue and unlawful" was effected against Shreveport. In order to correct this discrimination, the carriers were directed to desist from charging higher rates for the transportation of any commodity from Shreveport to Dallas and Houston, respectively, and intermediate points than were contemporaneously charged for the carriage of such commodity from Dallas and Houston toward Shreveport for equal distances, as the Commission found that relation of rates to be reasonable.

. . .

[Appellants object] that, as the discrimination found by the Commission to be unjust arises out of the relation of intrastate rates, maintained under state authority, to interstate rates that have been upheld as reasonable, its correction was beyond the Commission's power. Manifestly the order might be complied with, and the discrimination avoided, either by reducing the interstate rates from Shreveport to the level of the competing intrastate rates, or by raising these intrastate rates to the level of the interstate rates, or by such reduction in the one case and increase in the other as would result in equality. But it is urged that, so far as the interstate rates were sustained by the Commission as reasonable, the Commission was without authority to compel their reduction in order to equalize them with the lower intrastate rates. . . .

. . .

First. It is unnecessary to repeat what has frequently been said by this court with respect to the complete and paramount character of the power confided to Congress to regulate commerce among the several states. It is of the essence of this power that, where it exists, it dominates. Interstate trade was not left to be destroyed or impeded by the rivalries of local government. The purpose was to make impos-

sible the recurrence of the evils which had overwhelmed the Confederation, and to provide the necessary basis of national unity by insuring "uniformity of regulation against conflicting and discriminating state legislation." By virtue of the comprehensive terms of the grant, the authority of Congress is at all times adequate to meet the varying exigencies that arise, and to protect the national interest by securing the freedom of interstate commercial intercourse from local control. *Gibbons v. Ogden*, 9 Wheat. 1, 196, 224.

Congress is empowered to regulate,—that is, to provide the law for the government of interstate commerce; to enact "all appropriate legislation" for its "protection and advancement"; to adopt measures "to promote its growth and insure its safety"; "to foster, protect, control, and restrain." Its authority, extending to these interstate carriers as instruments of interstate commerce, necessarily embraces the right to control their operations in all matters having such a close and substantial relation to interstate traffic that the control is essential or appropriate to the security of that traffic, to the efficiency of the interstate service, and to the maintenance of conditions under which interstate commerce may be conducted upon fair terms and without molestation or hindrance. As it is competent for Congress to legislate to these ends, unquestionably it may seek their attainment by requiring that the agencies of interstate commerce shall not be used in such manner as to cripple, retard, or destroy it. The fact that carriers are instruments of intrastate commerce, as well as of interstate commerce, does not derogate from the complete and paramount authority of Congress over the latter, or preclude the Federal power from being exerted to prevent the intrastate operations of such carriers from being made a means of injury to that which has been confided to Federal care. Wherever the interstate and intrastate transactions of carriers are so related that the government of the one involves the control of the other, it is Congress, and not the state, that is entitled to prescribe the final and dominant rule, for otherwise Congress would be denied the exercise of its constitutional authority, and the state, and not the nation, would be supreme within the national field. . . .

. . .

. . . Congress, in the exercise of its paramount power, may prevent the common instrumentalities of interstate and intrastate commercial intercourse from being used in their intrastate operations to the injury of interstate commerce. This is not to say that Congress possesses the authority to regulate the internal commerce of a state, as such, but that it does possess the power to foster and protect interstate commerce, and to take all measures necessary or appropriate to that end, although intrastate transactions of interstate carriers may thereby be controlled.

This principle is applicable here. We find no reason to doubt that Congress is entitled to keep the highways of interstate communication open to interstate traffic upon fair and equal terms. That an unjust discrimination in the rates of a common carrier, by which one person or locality is unduly favored as against another under substantially similar conditions of traffic, constitutes an evil, is undeniable; and where this evil consists in the action of an interstate carrier in unreasonably discriminating against interstate traffic over its line, the authority of Congress to prevent it is equally clear. It is immaterial, so far as the protecting power of Congress is concerned, that the discrimination arises from intrastate rates as compared with interstate rates. The use of the instrument of interstate commerce in a discriminatory manner so as to inflict injury upon that commerce, or some part thereof, furnishes abundant ground for Federal intervention. Nor can the attempted exercise of state authority alter the matter, where Congress has acted, for a state may not authorize the carrier to do that which Congress is entitled to forbid and has forbidden.

. . .

The decree of the Commerce Court is affirmed in each case.

Affirmed.

Stafford v. Wallace[12] involved a challenge to the Packers and Stockyards Act of 1921 which prohibited packers from engaging in a variety of improper trade practices. Pursuant to the Act, the Secretary of Agriculture proposed rules prohibiting, among other things, misleading reports to depress or enhance prices, prescribing proper feed and care of livestock, and forbidding a commission man to sell livestock to another in whose business he is interested, without disclosing such interest to his principal. The Court upheld the law:

> [The] reasonable fear by Congress that such acts, usually lawful and affecting only intrastate commerce when considered alone, will probably and more or less constantly be used in conspiracies against interstate commerce or constitute a direct and undue burden on it, expressed in this remedial legislation, serves the same purpose as the intent charged in the Swift indictment to bring acts of a similar character into the current of interstate commerce for federal restraint. Whatever amounts to more or less constant practice, and threatens to obstruct or unduly to burden the freedom of interstate commerce is within the regulatory power of Congress under the commerce clause, and it is primarily for Congress to consider and decide the fact of the danger and meet it. This court will certainly not substitute its judgment for that of Congress in such a matter unless the relation of the subject to interstate commerce and its effect upon it are clearly nonexistent.

---

[12] 258 U.S. 495 (1922).

Hammer v. Dagenhart
247 U.S. 251 (1918)

Mr. Justice DAY delivered the opinion of the Court.

. . .

The controlling question for decision is: Is it within the authority of Congress in regulating commerce among the states to prohibit the transportation in interstate commerce of manufactured goods, the product of a factory in which, within thirty days prior to their removal therefrom, children under the age of fourteen have been employed or permitted to work, or children between the ages of fourteen and sixteen years have been employed or permitted to work more than eight hours in any day, or more than six days in any week, or after the hour of 7 o'clock p.m., or before the hour of 6 o'clock a.m.?

The power essential to the passage of this act, the government contends, is found in the commerce clause of the Constitution which authorizes Congress to regulate commerce with foreign nations and among the states.

In *Gibbons v. Ogden*, 9 Wheat. 1, Chief Justice Marshall, speaking for this court, and defining the extent and nature of the commerce power, said, "It is the power to regulate; that is, to prescribe the rule by which commerce is to be governed." In other words, the power is one to control the means by which commerce is carried on, which is directly the contrary of the assumed right to forbid commerce from moving and thus destroying it as to particular commodities. But it is insisted that adjudged cases in this court establish the doctrine that the power to regulate given to Congress incidentally includes the authority to prohibit the movement of ordinary commodities and therefore that the subject is not open for discussion. The cases demonstrate the contrary. They rest upon the character of the particular subjects dealt with and the fact that the scope of governmental authority, state or national, possessed over them is such that the authority to prohibit is as to them but the exertion of the power to regulate.

The first of these cases is *Champion v. Ames*, 188 U.S. 321, the so-called Lottery Case, in which it was held that Congress might pass a law having the effect to keep the channels of commerce free from use in the transportation of tickets used in the promotion of lottery schemes. In *Hipolite Egg Co. v. United States*, 220 U.S. 45, this court sustained the power of Congress to pass the Pure Food and Drug Act . . . which prohibited the introduction into the states by means of interstate commerce of impure foods and drugs. In *Hoke v. United States*, 227 U.S. 308, this court sustained the constitutionality of the so-called "White Slave Traffic Act, whereby the transportation of a woman in interstate commerce for the purpose of prostitution was forbidden. . . . In *Caminetti v. United States*, 242 U.S. 470, we held that Congress might prohibit the transportation of women in interstate commerce for the purposes of debauchery and kindred purposes. In *Clark Distilling Co. v. Western Maryland Railway Co.*, 242 U.S. 311, the power of Congress over the transportation of intoxicating liquors was sustained. . . .

. . .

In each of these instances the use of interstate transportation was necessary to the accomplishment of harmful results. In other words, although the power over interstate transportation was to regulate, that could only

be accomplished by prohibiting the use of the facilities of interstate commerce to effect the evil intended.

This element is wanting in the present case. The thing intended to be accomplished by this statute is the denial of the facilities of interstate commerce to those manufacturers in the states who employ children within the prohibited ages. The act in its effect does not regulate transportation among the states, but aims to standardize the ages at which children may be employed in mining and manufacturing within the states. The goods shipped are of themselves harmless. The act permits them to be freely shipped after thirty days from the time of their removal from the factory. When offered for shipment, and before transportation begins, the labor of their production is over, and the mere fact that they were intended for interstate commerce transportation does not make their production subject to federal control under the commerce power.

Commerce "consists of intercourse and traffic . . . and includes the transportation of persons and property, as well as the purchase, sale and exchange of commodities." The making of goods and the mining of coal are not commerce, nor does the fact that these things are to be afterwards shipped, or used in interstate commerce, make their production a part thereof. *Delaware, Lackawanna & Western R.R. Co. v. Yurkonis*, 238 U.S. 439.

Over interstate transportation, or its incidents, the regulatory power of Congress is ample, but the production of articles, intended for interstate commerce, is a matter of local regulation. "When the commerce begins is determined, not by the character of the commodity, nor by the intention of the owner to transfer it to another state for sale, nor by his preparation of it for transportation, but by its actual delivery to a common carrier for transportation, or the actual commencement of its transfer to another state." Mr. Justice Jackson in *Re Greene* (C.C.) 52 Fed. 113. If it were otherwise, all manufacture intended for interstate shipment would be brought under federal control to the practical exclusion of the authority of the states, a result certainly not contemplated by the framers of the Constitution when they vested in Congress the authority to regulate commerce among the States. *Kidd v. Pearson*, 128 U.S. 1, 21.

It is further contended that the authority of Congress may be exerted to control interstate commerce in the shipment of childmade goods because of the effect of the circulation of such goods in other states where the evil of this class of labor has been recognized by local legislation, and the right to thus employ child labor has been more rigorously restrained than in the state of production. In other words, that the unfair competition, thus engendered, may be controlled by closing the channels of interstate commerce to manufacturers in those states where the local laws do not meet what Congress deems to be the more just standard of other states.

There is no power vested in Congress to require the states to exercise their police power so as to prevent possible unfair competition. Many causes may cooperate to give one state, by reason of local laws or conditions, an economic advantage over others. The commerce clause was not intended to give to Congress a general authority to equalize such conditions. In some of the states laws have been passed fixing minimum wages for women, in others the local law regulates the hours of labor of women in various employments. Business done in such states may be at an economic disadvantage when compared with states which have no such regulations; surely, this fact does not give Congress the power to deny transportation in interstate commerce to those who carry on business where the hours of labor and the rate of compensation for women have not been fixed by a standard in use in other states and approved by Congress.

The grant of power of Congress over the subject of interstate commerce was to enable it to regulate such commerce, and not to give it authority to control the states in their exercise of the police power over local trade and manufacture.

The grant of authority over a purely federal matter was not intended to destroy the local power always existing and carefully reserved to the states in the Tenth Amendment to the Constitution.

Police regulations relating to the internal trade and affairs of the states have been uniformly recognized as within such control. "This," said this court in *United States v. Dewitt*, 9 Wall. 41, 45, "has been so frequently declared by this court, results so obviously from the terms of the Constitution, and has been so fully explained and supported on former occasions, that we think it unnecessary to enter again upon the discussion." See *Keller v. United States*, 213 U.S. 138, 144, 145, 146.

In the judgment which established the broad power of Congress over interstate commerce, Chief Justice Marshall said: "They [inspection laws] act upon the subject, before it becomes an article of foreign commerce, or of commerce among the states, and prepare it for that purpose. They form a portion of that immense mass of legislation, which embraces everything within the territory of a state, not surrendered to the general government; all of which can be most advantageously exercised by the states themselves. Inspection laws, quarantine laws, health laws of every description, as well as laws for regulating the internal commerce of a state, and those which respect turnpike roads, ferries, etc., are component parts of this mass."

. . .

That there should be limitations upon the right to employ children in mines and factories in the interest of their own and the public welfare, all will admit. That such employment is generally deemed to require regulation is shown by the fact that the brief of counsel states that every state in the Union has a law upon the subject, limiting the right to thus employ children. In North Carolina, the state wherein is located the factory in which the employment was had in the present case, no child under twelve years of age is permitted to work.

It may be desirable that such laws be uniform, but our federal government is one of enumerated powers; "this principle," declared Chief Justice Marshall in *McCulloch v. Maryland*, "is universally admitted."

A statute must be judged by its natural and reasonable effect. The control by Congress over interstate commerce cannot authorize the exercise of authority not entrusted to it by the Constitution. *Pipe Line Case*, 234 U.S. 548, 560. The maintenance of the authority of the states over matters purely local is as essential to the preservation of our institutions as is the conservation of the supremacy of the federal power in all matters entrusted to the nation by the federal Constitution.

In interpreting the Constitution it must never be forgotten that the nation is made up of states to which are entrusted the powers of local government. And to them and to the people the powers not expressly delegated to the national government are reserved. *Lane County v. Oregon*. The power of the states to regulate their purely internal affairs by such laws as seem wise to the local authority is inherent and has never been surrendered to the general government. *New York v. Miln*. To sustain this statute would not be in our judgment a recognition of the lawful exertion of congressional authority over interstate commerce, but would sanction an invasion by the federal power of the control of a matter purely local in its character, and over which no authority has been delegated to Congress in conferring the power to regulate commerce among the states.

We have neither authority nor disposition to question the motives of Congress in enacting this legislation. The purposes intended must be attained consistently with constitutional limitations and not by an invasion of the powers of the states. This court has no more important function than that which devolves upon it the obligation to preserve inviolate the constitutional limitations upon the exercise of authority federal and state to the end that each may continue to discharge, harmoniously with the other, the duties entrusted to it by the Constitution.

In our view the necessary effect of this act is, by means of a prohibition against the movement in interstate commerce of ordinary commercial commodities to regulate the hours of labor of children in factories and mines within the states, a purely state authority. Thus the act in a two-fold sense is repugnant to the Constitution. It not only transcends the authority delegated to Congress over commerce but also exerts a power as to a purely local matter to which the federal authority does not extend. The far reaching result of upholding the act cannot be more plainly indicated than by pointing out that if Congress can thus regulate matters entrusted to local authority by prohibition of the movement of commodities in interstate commerce, all freedom of commerce will be at an end, and the power of the states over local matters may be eliminated, and thus our system of government be practically destroyed.

For these reasons we hold that this law exceeds the constitutional authority of Congress. It follows that the decree of the District Court must be

Affirmed.

Mr. Justice HOLMES, dissenting.

The single question in this case is whether Congress has power to prohibit the shipment in interstate or foreign commerce of any product of a cotton mill situated in the United States, in which within thirty days before the removal of the product children under fourteen have been employed, or children between fourteen and sixteen have been employed more than eight hours in a day, or more than six days in any week, or between seven in the evening and six in the morning. The objection urged against the power is that the States have exclusive control over their methods of production and that Congress cannot meddle with them, and taking the proposition in the sense of direct intermeddling I agree to it and suppose that no one denies it. But if an act is within the powers specifically conferred upon Congress, it seems to me that it is not made any less constitutional because of the indirect effects that it may have, however obvious it may be that it will have those effects, and that we are not at liberty upon such grounds to hold it void.

[T]he statute in question is within the power expressly given to Congress if considered only as to its immediate effects and that if invalid it is so only upon some collateral ground. The statute confines itself to prohibiting the carriage of certain goods in interstate or foreign commerce. Congress is given power to regulate such commerce in unqualified terms. It would not be argued today that the power to regulate does not include the power to prohibit. Regulation means the prohibition of something, and when interstate commerce is the matter to be regulated I cannot doubt that the regulation may prohibit any part of such commerce that Congress sees fit to forbid. At all events it is established by the Lottery Case and others that have followed it that a law is not beyond the regulative power of Congress merely because it prohibits certain transportation out and out. *Champion v. Ames*, 188 U.S. 321, 355, 359. So I repeat that this statute in its immediate operation is clearly within the Congress's constitutional power.

The question then is narrowed to whether the exercise of its otherwise constitutional power by Congress can be pronounced unconstitutional because of its possible reaction upon the conduct of the States in a matter upon which I have admitted that they are free from direct control. I should have thought that that matter had been disposed of so fully as to leave no room for doubt. I should have thought that the most conspicuous decisions of this Court had made it clear that the power to regulate commerce and other constitutional powers could not be cut down or qualified by the fact that it might interfere with the carrying out of the domestic policy of any State.

. . .

[I]f there is any matter upon which civilized countries have agreed—far more unanimously than they have with regard to intoxicants and some other matters over which this country is now emotionally aroused—it is the evil of premature and excessive child labor. I should have thought that if we were to introduce our own moral conceptions where in my opinion they do not belong, this was preeminently a case for upholding the exercise of all its powers by the United States.

. . .

The Act does not meddle with anything belonging to the States. They may regulate their internal affairs and their domestic commerce as they like. But when they seek to send their products across the State line they are no longer within their rights. If there were no Constitution and no Congress their power to cross the line would depend upon their neighbors. Under the Constitution such commerce belongs not to the States but to Congress to regulate. It may carry out its views of public policy whatever indirect effect they may have upon the activities of the States. Instead of being encountered by a prohibitive tariff at her boundaries the State encounters the public policy of the United States which it is for Congress to express. The public policy of the United States is shaped with a view to the benefit of the nation as a whole. If, as has been the case within the memory of men still living, a State should take a different view of the propriety of sustaining a lottery from that which generally prevails, I cannot believe that the fact would require a different decision from that reached in *Champion v. Ames*. Yet in that case it would be said with quite as much force as in this that Congress was attempting to intermeddle with the State's domestic affairs. The national welfare as understood by Congress may require a different attitude within its sphere from that of some self-seeking State. It seems to me entirely constitutional for Congress to enforce its understanding by all the means at its command.

3. The Constitutional Crisis

In 1929, the stock market crashed and the country settled into a prolonged period of economic depression. In 1932, President Franklin Delano Roosevelt (FDR) was elected on the promise of a "New Deal." The situation facing FDR and the country was grim. In 1931, the year before FDR was elected, more than 2,000 banks had failed.[13] By the winter of 1932–33, shortly before FDR assumed office, "one-fourth of the nation's work force was unemployed"[14] and the price of wheat had dropped by "nearly 90 percent."[15] Industrial output had fallen by 60%.

FDR took office demanding "action, and action now."[16] One of his first acts was to call an extraordinary session of Congress to begin five days after his inauguration. During this session, the House passed eleven major bills with "a total of forty hours of debate."[17] During his first hundred days, Roosevelt managed to push through Congress a host of bills regulating financial markets, creating federal works programs, and regulating prices and wages. Included in this mass of legislation were the Agricultural Adjustment Act, the Bituminous Coal Act, the Farm Relief Act, the Emergency Farm Mortgage Act, the National Industrial Recovery Act, the Railway Pension Act, and the Truth-in-Securities Act. These acts were hostilely received by the federal courts.

---

[13] ROBERT S. MCELVAINE, THE GREAT DEPRESSION 137 (1984).

[14] *Id.* at 134.

[15] *Id.* at 135.

[16] *Id.* at 140.

[17] *Id.* at 140–47.

Carter v. Carter Coal Co.
298 U.S. 238 (1936)

Mr. Justice SUTHERLAND delivered the opinion of the Court.

. . .

Without repeating the long and involved provisions with regard to the fixing of minimum prices, it is enough to say that the act confers the power to fix the minimum price of coal at each and every coal mine in the United States, with such price variations as the board may deem necessary and proper. There is also a provision authorizing the commission, when deemed necessary in the public interest, to establish maximum prices in order to protect the consumer against unreasonably high prices.

. . .

The labor provisions of the code, found in part 3 of the same section, require that in order to effectuate the purposes of the act the district boards and code members shall accept specified conditions contained in the code . . . [including maximum daily and weekly hours and wage rates].

. . .

. . . It is no longer open to question that the general government, unlike the states, *Hammer v. Dagenhart*, 247 U.S. 251, 275, possesses no inherent power in respect of the internal affairs of the states; and emphatically not with regard to legislation. The question in respect of the inherent power of that government as to the external affairs of the Nation and in the field of international law is a wholly different matter which it is not necessary now to consider. . . .

The determination of the Framers Convention and the ratifying conventions to preserve complete and unimpaired state self-government in all matters not committed to the general government is one of the plainest facts which emerges from the history of their deliberations. And adherence to that determination is incumbent equally upon the federal government and the states. State powers can neither be appropriated on the one hand nor abdicated on the other. As this court said in *Texas v. White*, 7 Wall. 700, 725, "The preservation of the States, and the maintenance of their governments, are as much within the design and care of the Constitution as the preservation of the Union and the maintenance of the National government. The Constitution, in all its provisions, looks to an indestructible Union, composed of indestructible States." Every journey to a forbidden end begins with the first step; and the danger of such a step by the federal government in the direction of taking over the powers of the states is that the end of the journey may find the states so despoiled of their powers, or—what may amount to the same thing—so relieved of the responsibilities which possession of the powers necessarily enjoins, as to reduce them to little more than geographical subdivisions of the national domain. It is safe to say that if, when the Constitution was under consideration, it had been thought that any such danger lurked behind its plain words, it would never have been ratified.

. . .

Since the validity of the act depends upon whether it is a regulation of interstate commerce, the nature and extent of the power conferred upon Congress by the commerce clause becomes the determinative question in this branch of the case. . . . In exercising the authority conferred by this clause of the Constitution, Congress is powerless to regulate anything which is not commerce, as it is powerless to do anything about commerce which is not regulation. . . .

. . .

The distinction between manufacture and commerce was discussed in *Kidd v. Pearson*, 128 U.S. 1, 20, and it was said:

"No distinction is more popular to the common mind, or more clearly expressed in economic and political literature, than that between manufactures and commerce. Manufacture is transformation—the fashioning of raw materials into a change of form for use. The functions of commerce are different. . . . If it be held that the term includes the regulation of all such manufactures as are intended to be the subject of commercial transactions in the future, it is impossible to deny that it would also include all productive industries that contemplate the same thing. The result would be

that congress would be invested, to the exclusion of the states, with the power to regulate, not only manufacture, but also agriculture, horticulture, stock-raising, domestic fisheries, mining,—in short, every branch of human industry. For is there one of them that does not contemplate, more or less clearly, an interstate or foreign market? Does not the wheat-grower of the northwest, and the cotton-planter of the south, plant, cultivate, and harvest his crop with an eye on the prices at Liverpool, New York, and Chicago? The power being vested in congress and denied to the states, it would follow as an inevitable result that the duty would devolve on congress to regulate all of these delicate, multiform, and vital interests,—interests which in their nature are, and must be, local in all the details of their successful management."

. . .

We have seen that the word "commerce" is the equivalent of the phrase "intercourse for the purposes of trade." Plainly, the incidents leading up to and culminating in the mining of coal do not constitute such intercourse. The employment of men, the fixing of their wages, hours of labor, and working conditions, the bargaining in respect of these things—whether carried on separately or collectively—each and all constitute intercourse for the purposes of production, not of trade. The latter is a thing apart from the relation of employer and employee, which in all producing occupations is purely local in character. Extraction of coal from the mine is the aim and the completed result of local activities. Commerce in the coal mined is not brought into being by force of these activities, but by negotiations, agreements and circumstances entirely apart from production. Mining brings the subject-matter of commerce into existence. Commerce disposes of it.

A consideration of the foregoing, and of many cases which might be added to those already cited, renders inescapable the conclusion that the effect of the labor provisions of the act, including those in respect of minimum wages, wage agreements, collective bargaining, and the Labor Board and its powers, primarily falls upon production and not upon commerce; and confirms the further resulting conclusion that production is a purely local activity. It follows that none of these essential antecedents of production constitutes a transaction in or forms any part of interstate commerce. *Schechter Poultry Corp. v. United States, supra*, 295 U.S. 495, at page 542 et seq. Everything which moves in interstate commerce has had a local origin. Without local production somewhere, interstate commerce, as now carried on, would practically disappear. Nevertheless, the local character of mining, of manufacturing, and of crop growing is a fact, and remains a fact, whatever may be done with the products.

. . .

That the production of every commodity intended for interstate sale and transportation has some effect upon interstate commerce may be, if it has not already been, freely granted; and we are brought to the final and decisive inquiry, whether here that effect is direct, as the "Preamble" recites, or indirect. The distinction is not formal, but substantial in the highest degree, as we pointed out in the *Schechter Case, supra,* 295 U.S. 495, at page 546 et seq. "If the commerce clause were construed," we there said, "to reach all enterprises and transactions which could be said to have an indirect effect upon interstate commerce, the federal authority would embrace practically all the activities of the people, and the authority of the state over its domestic concerns would exist only by sufferance of the federal government. Indeed, on such a theory, even the development of the state's commercial facilities would be subject to federal control." It was also pointed out, 295 U.S. 495, at page 548, that "the distinction between direct and indirect effects of intrastate transactions upon interstate commerce must be recognized as a fundamental one, essential to the maintenance of our constitutional system."

Whether the effect of a given activity or condition is direct or indirect is not always easy to determine. The word "direct" implies that the activity or condition invoked or blamed shall operate proximately—not mediately, remotely, or collaterally—to produce the effect. It connotes the absence of an efficient intervening agency or condition. And the extent of the effect bears no logical relation to its character. The distinction between a direct and an indirect effect turns, not upon the magnitude of either the cause or the effect, but entirely upon the manner in which the effect has been brought about. If the production by one man of a single ton of coal intended for interstate sale and shipment, and actually so sold and shipped, affects interstate commerce indirectly, the effect does not become direct by multiplying the tonnage, or increasing the number of men employed, or adding to the expense or complexities of the business, or by all combined. It is quite true that rules of law are sometimes qualified by considerations of degree, as the government argues. But the matter of degree has no bearing upon the question here, since that question is not—What is the extent of the local activity or condition, or the extent of the effect produced upon interstate commerce? but—What is the relation between the activity or condition and the effect?

Much stress is put upon the evils which come from the struggle between employers and employees over the matter of wages, working conditions, the right of collective bargaining, etc., and the resulting strikes, curtailment, and irregularity of production and effect on prices; and it is insisted that interstate commerce is greatly affected thereby. But, in addition to what has just been said, the conclusive answer is that the evils are all local evils over which the federal government has no legislative control. The relation of employer and employee is a local relation. At common law, it is one of the domestic relations. The wages are paid for the doing of local work. Working conditions are obviously local conditions. The employees are not engaged in or about commerce, but exclusively in producing a commodity. And the controversies and evils, which it is the object of the act to regulate and minimize, are local controversies and evils affecting local work undertaken to accomplish that local result. Such effect as they may have upon commerce, however extensive it may be, is secondary and indirect. An increase in the greatness of the effect adds to its importance. It does not alter its character.

. . .

The decrees in Nos. 636, 649, and 650 must be reversed and the causes remanded for further consideration in conformity with this opinion. The decree in No. 651 will be affirmed.

It is so ordered.

. . .

Mr. Justice CARDOZO (dissenting in Nos. 636, 649, and 650, and in No. 651 Concurring in the result).

. . .

(1) With reference to the first objection, the obvious and sufficient answer is, so far as the act is directed to interstate transactions, that sales made in such conditions constitute interstate commerce, and do not merely "affect" it. To regulate the price for such transactions is to regulate commerce itself, and not alone its antecedent conditions or its ultimate consequences. . . .

Regulation of prices being an exercise of the commerce power in respect of interstate transactions, the question remains whether it comes within that power as applied to intrastate sales where interstate prices are directly or intimately affected. Mining and agriculture and manufacture are not interstate commerce considered by themselves, yet their relation to that commerce may be such that for the protection of the one there is need to regulate the other. Sometimes it is said that the relation must be "direct" to bring that power into play. . . . "[D]irect" and "indirect," even if accepted as sufficient, must not be read too narrowly. . . .

. . .

What has been said in this regard is said with added certitude when complainants' business is considered in the light of the statistics exhibited in the several records. In No. 636, the Carter case, the complainant has admitted that "substantially all" (over 97 1/2 per cent.) of the sales of the Carter Company are made in interstate commerce. In No. 649 the percentages of intrastate sales are, for one of the complaining companies, 25 per cent., for another 1 per cent., and for most of the others 2 per cent. or 4. The Carter Company has its mines in West Virginia; the mines of the other companies are located in Kentucky. In each of those states, moreover, coal from other regions is purchased in large quantities, and is thus brought into competition with the coal locally produced. Plainly, it is impossible to say either from the statute itself or from any figures laid before us that interstate sales will not be prejudicially affected in West Virginia and Kentucky if intrastate prices are maintained on a lower level. . . .

. . .

[At the time of the enactment of this statute in August, 1935,] [o]verproduction was at a point where free competition had been degraded into anarchy. Prices had been cut so low that profit had become impossible for all except a lucky handful. Wages came down along with prices and with profits. There were strikes, at times nation-wide in extent, at other times spreading over broad areas and many mines, with the accompaniment of violence and bloodshed and misery and bitter feeling. The sordid tale is unfolded in many a document and treatise. During the twenty-three years between 1913 and 1935, there were nineteen investigations or hearings by Congress or by specially created commissions with reference to conditions in the coal mines. The hope of betterment was faint unless the industry could be subjected to the compulsion of a code. In the weeks immediately preceding the passage of this act the country was threatened once more with a strike of ominous proportions. The plight of the industry was not merely a menace to owners and to mine workers, it was and had long been a menace to the public, deeply concerned in a steady and uniform supply of a fuel so vital to the national economy.

Congress was not condemned to inaction in the face of price wars and wage wars so pregnant with disaster. Commerce had been choked and burdened; its normal flow had been diverted from one state to another; there had been bankruptcy and waste and ruin alike for capital and for labor. . . . There is testimony in these records, testimony even by the assailants of the statute, that only through a system of regulated prices can the industry be stabilized and set upon the road of orderly and peaceful progress. If further facts are looked for, they are narrated in the findings as well as in Congressional Reports and a mass of public records. After making every allowance for difference of opinion as to the most efficient cure, the student of the subject is confronted with the indisputable truth that there were ills to be corrected, and ills that had a direct relation to the maintenance of commerce among the states without friction or diversion. An evil existing, and also the power to correct it, the lawmakers were at liberty to use their own discretion in the selection of the means.

. . .

Carter involved only one of many setbacks for FDR's "New Deal." In *Panama Refining Co. v. Ryan*,[18] the Court struck down Section 9(c) of the National Industrial Recovery Act (NIRA) of 1933 on unlawful delegation grounds. In *A.L.A. Schechter Poultry Corp. v. United States*,[19] the Court struck down other sections of the NIRA. In all, the Court struck down four major pieces of legislation (the National Industrial Recovery Act, Bituminous Coal Act, Agricultural Adjustment Act and Railway Pension Act). In addition, the federal courts issued hundreds of injunctions against New Deal legislation.

Decisions like *Panama Refining* and *Schechter*, coupled with the Court's restrictive interpretation of the Commerce Clause in *Carter Coal Co.* and *Schechter*, angered President Roosevelt, who viewed the Court as an obstacle to his reform program. At the time, several major pieces of legislation had not been ruled on by the courts, including the National Labor Relations Act, the Social Security Act, and the Public Utility Holding Act. Roosevelt was worried that the Court would strike them down too.

Following his landslide reelection victory in the 1936 elections, President Roosevelt decided to move against the Court. Roosevelt's vehicle was the now infamous "Court

---

[18] 293 U.S. 388 (1935).
[19] 295 U.S. 495 (1935).

Packing Plan," which would have altered the Court's membership (and, presumably, its decisions) by adding additional members to the Court. The Plan provided that, when a judge or justice of any federal court reached the age of seventy without availing himself of the opportunity to retire on a pension, a new member could be appointed by the President then in office. The appointment would be made in the manner prescribed by the Constitution: nomination by the President with confirmation by the Senate.[20] At the time, six justices were age 70 or older. If the plan had passed, the Court's membership would have expanded to 15 members, giving Roosevelt a majority of members sympathetic to his positions.

The Court Packing plan died in Congress. Many questioned the wisdom and constitutionality of the plan believing that it would upset the balance of powers between the three branches. The debate was effectively moot once the Court rendered its decision in *NLRB v. Jones & Laughlin Steel Corp.*

---

[20] *See* Leuchtenburg, *The Origins of Franklin D. Roosevelt's "Court Packing" Plan*, 1966 SUP. CT. REV. 347–94.

NLRB v. Jones & Laughlin Steel Corp.
301 U.S. 1 (1937)

[The National Labor Relations Board (NLRB) concluded that Jones & Laughlin Steel Corp. had engaged in the unfair labor practice of discharging employees in order to interfere with their union organizing activities. The NLRB ordered Jones & Laughlin to cease and desist from such practices, to offer reinstatement to ten of the employees named, to make good their losses in pay, and to post notices that it would not discharge or discriminate against members or prospective members of the union. The Court of Appeals refused to enforce the order, holding it lay beyond the scope of federal power.]

Mr. Chief Justice HUGHES delivered the opinion of the Court.

. . .

Contesting the ruling of the Board, the respondent argues . . . that the act can have no application to the respondent's relations with its production employees because they are not subject to regulation by the federal government. . . .

. . .

[T]he Labor Board concluded that the works in Pittsburgh and Aliquippa "might be likened to the heart of a self-contained, highly integrated body. They draw in the raw materials from Michigan, Minnesota, West Virginia, Pennsylvania in part through arteries and by means controlled by the respondent; they transform the materials and then pump them out to all parts of the nation through the vast mechanism which the respondent has elaborated."

To carry on the activities of the entire steel industry, 33,000 men mine ore, 44,000 men mine coal, 4,000 men quarry limestone, 16,000 men manufacture coke, 343,000 men manufacture steel, and 83,000 men transport its product. Respondent has about 10,000 employees in its Aliquippa plant, which is located in a community of about 30,000 persons.

. . .

First. The Scope of the Act.—The act is challenged in its entirety as an attempt to regulate all industry, thus invading the reserved powers of the States over their local concerns. It is asserted that the references in the act to interstate and foreign commerce are colorable at best; that the act is not a true regulation of such commerce or of matters which directly affect it, but on the contrary has the fundamental object of placing under the compulsory supervision of the federal government all industrial labor relations within the nation. . . .

. . .

There can be no question that the commerce thus contemplated by the act (aside from that within a Territory or the District of Columbia) is interstate and foreign commerce in the constitutional sense. The act also defines the term "affecting commerce" section 2(7), 29 U.S.C.A. § 152(7):

The term "affecting commerce" means in commerce, or burdening or obstructing commerce or the free flow of commerce, or having led or tending to lead to a labor dispute burdening or obstructing commerce or the free flow of commerce.

This definition is one of exclusion as well as inclusion. The grant of authority to the

Board does not purport to extend to the relationship between all industrial employees and employers. Its terms do not impose collective bargaining upon all industry regardless of effects upon interstate or foreign commerce. It purports to reach only what may be deemed to burden or obstruct that commerce and, thus qualified, it must be construed as contemplating the exercise of control within constitutional bounds. It is a familiar principle that acts which directly burden or obstruct interstate or foreign commerce, or its free flow, are within the reach of the congressional power. Acts having that effect are not rendered immune because they grow out of labor disputes. It is the effect upon commerce, not the source of the injury, which is the criterion. *Second Employers' Liability Cases (Mondou v. New York, N.H. & H.R. Co.)*, 223 U.S. 1, 51. Whether or not particular action does affect commerce in such a close and intimate fashion as to be subject to federal control, and hence to lie within the authority conferred upon the Board, is left by the statute to be determined as individual cases arise. We are thus to inquire whether in the instant case the constitutional boundary has been passed.

. . .

. . . The congressional authority to protect interstate commerce from burdens and obstructions is not limited to transactions which can be deemed to be an essential part of a "flow" of interstate or foreign commerce. Burdens and obstructions may be due to injurious action springing from other sources. The fundamental principle is that the power to regulate commerce is the power to enact "all appropriate legislation" for its "protection or advancement" (*The Daniel Ball*, 10 Wall. 557, 564); to adopt measures "to promote its growth and insure its safety" (County of *Mobile v. Kimball*, 102 U.S. 691, 696, 697); "to foster, protect, control, and restrain." (*Second Employers' Liability Cases, supra*, 223 U.S. 1, at page 47. That power is plenary and may be exerted to protect interstate commerce "no matter what the source of the dangers which threaten it." *Second Employers' Liability Cases*, 223 U.S. 1, at page 51; *Schechter Corporation v. United States, supra*. Although activities may be intrastate in character when separately considered, if they have such a close and substantial relation to interstate commerce that their control is essential or appropriate to protect that commerce from burdens and obstructions, Congress cannot be denied the power to exercise that control. Undoubtedly the scope of this power must be considered in the light of our dual system of government and may not be extended so as to embrace effects upon interstate commerce so indirect and remote that to embrace them, in view of our complex society, would effectually obliterate the distinction between what is na-

tional and what is local and create a completely centralized government. The question is necessarily one of degree. As the Court said in *Board of Trade of City of Chicago v. Olsen, supra*, 262 U.S. 1, at page 37, repeating what had been said in *Stafford v. Wallace, supra*: "Whatever amounts to more or less constant practice, and threatens to obstruct or unduly to burden the freedom of interstate commerce is within the regulatory power of Congress under the commerce clause, and it is primarily for Congress to consider and decide the fact of the danger and to meet it."

. . .

[T]he fact that the employees here concerned were engaged in production is not determinative. The question remains as to the effect upon interstate commerce of the labor practice involved. In the *Schechter Case, supra*, we found that the effect there was so remote as to be beyond the federal power. To find "immediacy or directness" there was to find it "almost everywhere," a result inconsistent with the maintenance of our federal system. In the *Carter Case, supra*, the Court was of the opinion that the provisions of the statute relating to production were invalid upon several grounds. . . .

[Giving] full weight to respondent's contention with respect to a break in the complete continuity of the "stream of commerce" by reason of respondent's manufacturing operations, the fact remains that the stoppage of those operations by industrial strife would have a most serious effect upon interstate commerce. In view of respondent's far-flung activities, it is idle to say that the effect would be indirect or remote. It is obvious that it would be immediate and might be catastrophic. We are asked to shut our eyes to the plainest facts of our national life and to deal with the question of direct and indirect effects in an intellectual vacuum. Because there may be but indirect and remote effects upon interstate commerce in connection with a host of local enterprises throughout the country, it does not follow that other industrial activities do not have such a close and intimate relation to interstate commerce as to make the presence of industrial strife a matter of the most urgent national concern. When industries organize themselves on a national scale, making their relation to interstate commerce the dominant factor in their activities, how can it be maintained that their industrial labor relations constitute a forbidden field into which Congress may not enter when it is necessary to protect interstate commerce from the paralyzing consequences of industrial war? We have often said that interstate commerce itself is a practical conception. It is equally true that interferences with that commerce must be appraised by a judgment that does not ignore actual experience.

Experience has abundantly demonstrated that the recognition of the right of employees to self-organization and to have representatives of their own choosing for the purpose of collective bargaining is often an essential condition of industrial peace. Refusal to confer and negotiate has been one of the most prolific causes of strife. This is such an outstanding fact in the history of labor disturbances that it is a proper subject of judicial notice and requires no citation of instances. . . .

These questions have frequently engaged the attention of Congress and have been the subject of many inquiries. The steel industry is one of the great basic industries of the United States, with ramifying activities affecting interstate commerce at every point. The Government aptly refers to the steel strike of 1919–1920 with its far-reaching consequences. The fact that there appears to have been no major disturbance in that industry in the more recent period did not dispose of the possibilities of future and like dangers to interstate commerce which Congress was entitled to foresee and to exercise its protective power to forestall. It is not necessary again to detail the facts as to respondent's enterprise. Instead of being beyond the pale, we think that it presents in a most striking way the close and intimate relation which a manufacturing industry may have to interstate commerce and we have no doubt that Congress had constitutional authority to safeguard the right of respondent's employees to self-organization and freedom in the choice of representatives for collective bargaining.

. . .

Our conclusion is that the order of the Board was within its competency and that the act is valid as here applied. . . .

Reversed and remanded.

Mr. Justice McReynolds delivered the following dissenting opinion [which was joined by Justices Van Devanter, Sutherland and Butler].

. . .

The Court as we think departs from well-established principles followed in *Schechter Poultry Corporation v. United States*, 295 U.S. 495 (1935), and *Carter v. Carter Coal Co.*, 298 U.S. 238 (1936). Upon the authority of those decisions, the Circuit Courts of Appeals of the Fifth, Sixth and Second Circuits in the causes now before us have held the power of Congress under the commerce clause does not extend to relations between employers and their employees engaged in manufacture, and therefore the act conferred upon the National Labor Relations Board no authority in respect of matters covered by the questioned orders. . . .

. . .

Any effect on interstate commerce by the discharge of employees shown here would be indirect and remote in the highest degree, as consideration of the facts will show. In No. 419 ten men out of ten thousand were discharged; in the other cases only a few. The immediate effect in the factor may be to create discontent among all those employed and a strike may follow, which, in turn, may result in reducing production, which ultimately may reduce the volume of goods moving in interstate commerce. By this chain of indirect and progressively remote events we finally reach the evil with which it is said the legislation under consideration undertakes to deal. A more remote and indirect interference with interstate commerce or a more definite invasion of the powers reserved to the states is difficult, if not impossible, to imagine.

. . .

Justice Roberts, who had voted to strike down federal action in *Carter Coal*, voted to sustain it in *Jones & Laughlin*.

Following the *Jones & Laughlin* decision, support for the Court packing plan waned. Senator Joseph Robinson developed a modified plan which appeared to have a good chance of passage. But when he died suddenly of a heart attack, the plan was voted down.[21]

4.   The "Post-Switch" Expansion of Federal Power

Following *Jones & Laughlin*, the Court upheld a number of federal statutes. In these cases, the Court construed the scope of federal power broadly.

---

[21] *Id.*

United States v. Darby
312 U.S. 100 (1941)

Mr. Justice STONE delivered the opinion of the Court.

The two principal questions raised by the record in this case are, first, whether Congress has constitutional power to prohibit the shipment in interstate commerce of lumber manufactured by employees whose wages are less than a prescribed minimum or whose weekly hours of labor at that wage are greater than a prescribed maximum, and, second, whether it has power to prohibit the employment of workmen in the production of goods "for interstate commerce" at other than prescribed wages and hours. A subsidiary question is whether in connection with such prohibitions Congress can require the employer subject to them to keep records showing the hours worked each day and week by each of his employees including those engaged "in the production and manufacture of goods to wit, lumber, for interstate commerce."

. . .

The indictment charges that appellee is engaged, in the state of Georgia, in the business of acquiring raw materials, which he manufactures into finished lumber with the intent, when manufactured, to ship it in interstate commerce to customers outside the state, and that he does in fact so ship a large part of the lumber so produced. . . .

. . .

While manufacture is not of itself interstate commerce the shipment of manufactured goods interstate is such commerce and the prohibition of such shipment by Congress is indubitably a regulation of the commerce. The power to regulate commerce is the power "to prescribe the rule by which commerce is to be governed." *Gibbons v. Ogden*, 9 Wheat. 1, 196. It extends not only to those regulations which aid, foster and protect the commerce, but embraces those which prohibit it. *Reid v. Colorado*, 187 U.S. 137; *Lottery Case (Champion v. Ames)*, 188 U.S. 321. It is conceded that the power of Congress to prohibit transportation in interstate commerce includes noxious articles, *Lottery Case, supra; Hipolite Egg Co. v. United States*, 220 U.S. 45; stolen articles, *Brooks v. United States*, 267 U.S. 432; kidnapped persons, *Gooch v. United States*, 297 U.S. 124, and articles such as intoxicating liquor or convict made goods, traffic in which is forbidden or restricted by the laws of the state of destination. *Kentucky Whip & Collar Co. v. Illinois Central R. Co.*, 299 U.S. 334.

But it is said that the present prohibition falls within the scope of none of these categories; that while the prohibition is nominally a regulation of the commerce its motive or purpose is regulation of wages and hours of persons engaged in manufacture, the control of which has been reserved to the states and upon which Georgia and some of the states of destination have placed no restriction; that the effect of the present statute is not to exclude the prescribed articles from interstate commerce in aid of state regulation as in *Kentucky Whip & Collar Co. v. Illinois Central R. Co.*, but instead, under the guise of a regulation of interstate commerce, it undertakes to regulate wages and hours within the state contrary to the policy of the state which has elected to leave them unregulated.

The power of Congress over interstate commerce "is complete in itself, may be exercised to its utmost extent, and acknowledges no limitations, other than are prescribed by the constitution." *Gibbons v. Ogden, supra,* 9 Wheat. 196. That power can neither be enlarged nor diminished by the exercise or nonexercise of state power. Congress, following its own conception of public policy concerning the restrictions which may appropriately be imposed on interstate commerce, is free to exclude from the commerce articles whose use in the states for which they are destined it may conceive to be injurious to the public health, morals or welfare, even though the state has not sought to regulate their use. *Reid v. Colorado, supra; Lottery Case, supra.*

Such regulation is not a forbidden invasion of state power merely because either its motive or its consequence is to restrict the use of articles of commerce within the states of destination and is not prohibited unless by other Constitutional provisions. It is no objection to the assertion of the power to regulate interstate commerce that its exercise is attended by the same incidents which attend the exercise of the police power of the states. . . .

The motive and purpose of the present regulation are plainly to make effective the Congressional conception of public policy that interstate commerce should not be made the instrument of competition in the distribution of goods produced under substandard labor conditions, which competition is injurious to the commerce and to the states from and to which the commerce flows. The motive and purpose of a regulation of interstate commerce are matters for the legislative judgment upon the exercise of which the Constitution places no restriction and over which the courts are given no control. McCray v. United States, 195 U.S. 27. "The judicial cannot prescribe to the legislative departments of the government limitations upon the exercise of its acknowledged power." *Veazie Bank v. Fenno*, 8 Wall. 533, 548. Whatever their motive and purpose, regulations of commerce which do not infringe some constitutional prohibition are within the plenary power conferred on Congress by the Commerce Clause. Subject only to that limitation, presently to be considered, we conclude that the prohibition of the shipment interstate of goods produced under the forbidden substandard labor conditions is within the constitutional authority of Congress.

In the more than a century which has elapsed since the decision of *Gibbons v. Ogden*, these principles of constitutional interpretation have been so long and repeatedly recognized by this Court as applicable to the Commerce Clause, that there would be little occasion for repeating them now were it not for the decision of this Court twenty-two years ago in *Hammer v. Dagenhart*, 247 U.S. 251. In that case it was held by a bare majority of the Court over the powerful and now classic dissent of Mr. Justice Holmes setting forth the fundamental issues involved, that Congress was without power to exclude the products of child labor from interstate commerce. The reasoning and conclusion of the Court's opinion there cannot be reconciled with the conclusion which we have reached, that the power of Congress under the Commerce Clause is plenary to exclude any article from interstate commerce subject only to the specific prohibitions of the Constitution.

Hammer v. Dagenhart has not been followed. The distinction on which the decision was rested that Congressional power to prohibit interstate commerce is limited to articles which in themselves have some harmful or deleterious property—a distinction which was novel when made and unsupported by any provision of the Constitution—has long since been abandoned. *Brooks v. United States, supra*. The thesis of the opinion that the motive of the prohibition or its effect to control in some measure the use or production within the states of the article thus excluded from the commerce can operate to deprive the regulation of its constitutional authority has long since ceased to have force. *Reid v. Colorado, supra*. And finally we have declared "The authority of the Federal Government over interstate commerce does not differ in extent or character from that retained by the states over intrastate commerce." *United States v. Rock Royal Co-Operative, Inc.*, 307 U.S. 533, 569.

The conclusion is inescapable that *Hammer v. Dagenhart*, was a departure from the principles which have prevailed in the interpretation of the commerce clause both before and since the decision and that such vitality,

as a precedent, as it then had has long since been exhausted. It should be and now is overruled.

. . . Section 15(a)(2) and §§ 6 and 7 require employers to conform to the wage and hour provisions with respect to all employees engaged in the production of goods for interstate commerce. As appellee's employees are not alleged to be "engaged in interstate commerce" the validity of the prohibition turns on the question whether the employment, under other than the prescribed labor standards, of employees engaged in the production of goods for interstate commerce is so related to the commerce and so affects it as to be within the reach of the power of Congress to regulate it.

To answer this question we must at the outset determine whether the particular acts charged in the counts which are laid under § 15(a)(2) as they were construed below, constitute "production for commerce" within the meaning of the statute. As the Government seeks to apply the statute in the indictment, and as the court below construed the phrase "produced for interstate commerce," it embraces at least the case where an employer engaged, as are appellees, in the manufacture and shipment of goods in filling orders of extrastate customers, manufactures his product with the intent or expectation that according to the normal course of his business all or some part of it will be selected for shipment to those customers.

Without attempting to define the precise limits of the phrase, we think the acts alleged in the indictment are within the sweep of the statute. The obvious purpose of the Act was not only to prevent the interstate transportation of the proscribed product, but to stop the initial step toward transportation, production with the purpose of so transporting it. Congress was not unaware that most manufacturing businesses shipping their product in interstate commerce make it in their shops without reference to its ultimate destination and then after manufacture select some of it for shipment interstate and some intrastate according to the daily demands of their business, and that it would be practically impossible, without disrupting manufacturing businesses, to restrict the prohibited kind of production to the particular pieces of lumber, cloth, furniture or the like which later move in interstate rather than intrastate commerce.

The recognized need of drafting a workable statute and the well-known circumstances in which it was to be applied are persuasive of the conclusion, which the legislative history supports, that the "production for commerce" intended includes at least production of goods, which, at the time of production, the employer, according to the normal course of his business, intends or expects to move in interstate commerce although, through the exigencies of the business, all of the goods may not thereafter actually enter interstate commerce.

There remains the question whether such restriction on the production of goods for commerce is a permissible exercise of the commerce power. The power of Congress over interstate commerce is not confined to the regulation of commerce among the states. It extends to those activities intrastate which so affect interstate commerce or the exercise of the power of Congress over it as to make regulation of them appropriate means to the attainment of a legitimate end, the exercise of the granted power of Congress to regulate interstate commerce. *See* McCulloch v. Maryland, 4 Wheat. 316, 421.

. . .

But it does not follow that Congress may not by appropriate legislation regulate intrastate activities where they have a substantial effect on interstate commerce. *See Santa Cruz Fruit Packing Co. v. National Labor Relations Board*, 303 U.S. 453, 466. A recent example is the National Labor Relations Act, 29 U.S.C.A. § 151 et seq., for the regulation of employer and employee relations in industries in which strikes, induced by unfair labor practices named in the Act, tend to disturb or obstruct interstate commerce. *See National Labor Relations Board v. Jones & Laughlin Steel Corp.*, 301 U.S. 1, 38, 40. But long before the adoption of the National Labor Relations Act, this Court had many times held that the power of Congress to regulate interstate commerce extends to the regulation through legislative action of activities intrastate which have a substantial effect on the commerce or the exercise of the Congressional power over it.

. . .

Congress, having by the present Act adopted the policy of excluding from interstate commerce all goods produced for the commerce which do not conform to the specified labor standards, . . . may choose the means reasonably adapted to the attainment of the permitted end, even though they involve control of intrastate activities. Such legislation has often been sustained with respect to powers, other than the commerce power granted to the national government, when the means chosen, although not themselves within the granted power, were nevertheless deemed appropriate aids to the accomplishment of some purpose within an admitted power of the national government. *See Ruppert, Inc., v. Caffey*, 251 U.S. 264. A familiar like exercise of power is the regulation of intrastate transactions which are so commingled with or related to interstate commerce that all must be regulated if the interstate commerce is to be effectively controlled. *Shreveport Case*, 234 U.S. 342. . . .

. . .

The means adopted by § 15(a)(2) for the protection of interstate commerce by the suppression of the production of the condemned goods for interstate commerce is so related to the commerce and so affects it as to be within the reach of the commerce power. *See Currin v. Wallace, supra*, 306 U.S. 11. Congress, to attain its objective in the suppression of nationwide competition in interstate commerce by goods produced under substandard labor conditions, has made no distinction as to the volume or amount of shipments in the commerce or of production for commerce by any particular shipper or producer. It recognized that in present day industry, competition by a small part may affect the whole and that the total effect of the competition of many small producers may be great. See H. Rept. No. 2182, 75th Cong. 1st Sess., p. 7. The legislation aimed at a whole embraces all its parts.

So far as *Carter v. Carter Coal Co.*, 298 U.S. 238, is inconsistent with this conclusion, its doctrine is limited in principle by the decisions under the Sherman Act and the National Labor Relations Act, which we have cited and which we follow. . . .

Our conclusion is unaffected by the Tenth Amendment which provides: "The powers not delegated to the United States by the Constitution, nor prohibited by it to the States, are reserved to the States respectively, or to the people." The amendment states but a truism that all is retained which has not been surrendered. There is nothing in the history of its adoption to suggest that it was more than declaratory of the relationship between the national and state governments as it had been established by the Constitution before the amendment or that its purpose was other than to allay fears that the new national government might seek to exercise powers not granted, and that the states might not be able to exercise fully their reserved powers. . . .

From the beginning and for many years the amendment has been construed as not depriving the national government of authority to resort to all means for the exercise of a granted power which are appropriate and plainly adapted to the permitted end. *Martin v. Hunter's Lessee*, 1 Wheat. 304, 324, 325; *McCulloch v. Maryland, supra*, 4 Wheat. 405, 406.

. . .

We have considered, but find it unnecessary to discuss other contentions.

Reversed.

Darby was unanimously decided. The four justices who had dissented in *Jones and Laughlin* had all left the Court. Three (Van Devanter, Sutherland & McReynolds) had retired and one had died (Butler). Within the short space of 5 years, the Supreme Court had not only altered its interpretation of the commerce clause, but the Court's new view had "swept the field."

In the same year that *Jones & Laughlin* was decided, the Court reaffirmed its *Lottery Case* holding in *Kentucky Whip & Collar Co. v. Illinois Cent. R. Co.*[22] *Kentucky Whip* involved a federal law which made it unlawful knowingly to transport in interstate or foreign commerce goods made by convict labor in violation of state law. The Court concluded that Congress had the power to exclude such goods from interstate commerce:

> Petitioner's argument necessarily recognizes that in certain circumstances an absolute prohibition of interstate transportation is constitutional regulation. The power to prohibit interstate transportation has been upheld by this Court in relation to diseased live stock, lottery tickets, commodities owned by the interstate carrier transporting them, except such as may be required in the conduct of its business as a common carrier, adulterated and misbranded articles, under the Pure Food and Drugs Act, women, for immoral purposes, intoxicating liquors, diseased plants, stolen motor vehicles, and kidnaped persons.
>
> . . .
>
> The anticipated evil or harm may proceed from something inherent in the subject of transportation as in the case of diseased or noxious articles, which are unfit for commerce. Or the evil may lie in the purpose of the transportation, as in the case of lottery tickets, or the transportation of women for immoral purposes. The prohibition may be designed to give effect to the policies of the Congress in relation to the instrumentalities of interstate commerce, as in the case of commodities owned by interstate carriers. And, while the power to regulate interstate commerce resides in the Congress, which must determine its own policy, the Congress may shape that policy in the light of the fact that the transportation in interstate commerce, if permitted, would aid in the frustration of valid state laws for the protection of persons and property.
>
> The contention is inadmissible that the Act of Congress is invalid merely because the horse collars and harness which petitioner manufactures and sells are useful and harmless articles. . . .

Mulford v. Smith[23] involved a challenge to the Agricultural Adjustment Act which imposed marketing quotas on flue-cured tobacco. The quotas allocated marketing rights to existing growers, and prohibited the sale of tobacco in excess of those quotas. In an opinion written by Mr. Justice Roberts, the Court upheld the law:

> The record discloses that at least two-thirds of all flue-cured tobacco sold at auction warehouses is sold for immediate shipment to an interstate or foreign destination. In Georgia nearly one hundred per cent. [sic] of the tobacco so sold is purchased by extrastate purchasers. In markets where tobacco is sold to both interstate and intrastate purchasers it is not known, when the grower places his tobacco on the warehouse floor for sale, whether it is destined for interstate or intrastate commerce. Regulation to be effective, must, and therefore may constitutionally, apply to all sales. This court has recently declared that sales of tobacco by growers through warehousemen to purchasers for removal outside the state constitute interstate commerce. Any rule, such as that

---

[22] 299 U.S. 334 (1937).
[23] 307 U.S. 38 (1939).

embodied in the Act, which is intended to foster, protect and conserve that commerce, or to prevent the flow of commerce from working harm to the people of the nation, is within the competence of Congress. Within these limits the exercise of the power, the grant being unlimited in its terms, may lawfully extend to the absolute prohibition of such commerce, and a fortiori to limitation of the amount of a given commodity which may be transported in such commerce. The motive of Congress in exerting the power is irrelevant to the validity of the legislation.

Maryland v. Wirtz[24] involved the Fair Labor Standards Act of 1938 which required all employers to pay employees "engaged in commerce or in the production of goods for commerce" a certain minimum hourly wage, and to pay at a higher rate for work in excess of a certain maximum number of hours per week. In an opinion written by Mr. Justice Harlan, the Court upheld the law:

> [W]here we find that the legislators . . . have a rational basis for finding a chosen regulatory scheme necessary to the protection of commerce, our investigation is at an end.

There was obviously a "rational basis" for the logical inference that the pay and hours of production employees affect a company's competitive position.

The logical inference does not stop with production employees. When a company does an interstate business, its competition with companies elsewhere is affected by all its significant labor costs, not merely by the wages and hours of those employees who have physical contact with the goods in question. Consequently, it is not surprising that this Court has already explicitly recognized that Congress' original choice to extend the Act only to certain employees of interstate enterprises was not constitutionally compelled; rather, Congress decided, at that time, "not to enter areas which it might have occupied (under the commerce power)." *Kirschbaum Co. v. Walling*, 316 U.S. 517, 522.

---

[24] 392 U.S. 183 (1968).

Wickard v. Filburn
317 U.S. 111 (1942)

Mr. Justice JACKSON delivered the opinion of the Court.

[A]ppellee . . . sought to enjoin enforcement against himself of the marketing penalty imposed by the amendment of May 26, 1941, to the Agricultural Adjustment Act of 1938, upon that part of his 1941 wheat crop which was available for marketing in excess of the marketing quota established for his farm. He also sought a declaratory judgment that the wheat marketing quota provisions of the Act as amended and applicable to him were unconstitutional because not sustainable under the Commerce Clause. . . .

. . .

The appellee for many years past has owned and operated a small farm in Montgomery County, Ohio, maintaining a herd of dairy cattle, selling milk, raising poultry, and selling poultry and eggs. It has been his practice to raise a small acreage of winter wheat, sown in the Fall and harvested in the following July; to sell a portion of the crop; to feed part to poultry and livestock on the farm, some of which is sold; to use some in making flour for home consumption; and to keep the rest for the following seeding. . . .

In July of 1940, pursuant to the Agricultural Adjustment Act of 1938, as then amended, there were established for the appellee's 1941 crop a wheat acreage allotment of 11.1 acres and a normal yield of 20.1 bushels of wheat an acre. He was given notice of such allotment in July of 1940 before the Fall planting of his 1941 crop of wheat, and again in July of 1941, before it was harvested. He sowed, however, 23 acres, and harvested from his 11.9 acres of excess acreage 239 bushels, which under the terms of the Act as amended on May 26, 1941, constituted farm marketing excess, subject to a penalty of 49 cents a bushel, or $117.11 in all. The appellee has not paid the penalty and he has not postponed or avoided it by storing the excess under regulations of the Secretary of Agriculture, or by delivering it up to the Secretary. The Committee, therefore, refused him a marketing card, which was, under the terms of Regulations promulgated by the Secretary, necessary to protect a buyer from liability to the penalty and upon its protecting lien.

The general scheme of the Agricultural Adjustment Act of 1938 as related to wheat is to control the volume moving in interstate and foreign commerce in order to avoid surpluses and shortages and the consequent abnormally low or high wheat prices and obstructions to commerce. Within prescribed limits and by prescribed standards the Secretary of Agriculture is directed to ascertain and proclaim each year a national acreage allotment for the next crop of wheat, which is then apportioned to the states and their counties, and is eventually broken up into allotments for individual farms. Loans and payments to wheat farmers are authorized in stated circumstances.

. . .

II.

It is urged that under the Commerce Clause of the Constitution, Article I, § 8, clause 3, Congress does not possess the power it has in this instance sought to exercise. The question would merit little consideration since our decision in *United States v. Darby*, 312 U.S. 100 . . . sustaining the federal power to regulate production of goods for commerce except for the fact that this Act extends federal regulation to production not intended in any part for commerce but wholly for consumption on the farm. The Act includes a definition of "market" and its derivatives so that as related to wheat in addition to its conventional meaning it also means to dispose of "by feeding (in any form) to poultry or livestock which, or the products of which, are sold, bartered, or exchanged, or to be so disposed of." Hence, marketing quotas not only embrace all that may be sold without penalty but also what may be consumed on the premises. Wheat produced on excess acreage is designated as "available for marketing" as so defined and the penalty is imposed thereon. Penalties do not depend upon whether any part of the wheat either within or without the quota is sold or intended to be sold. The sum of this is that the Federal Government fixes a quota including all that the farmer may harvest for sale or for his own farm needs, and declares

that wheat produced on excess acreage may neither be disposed of nor used except upon payment of the penalty or except it is stored as required by the Act or delivered to the Secretary of Agriculture.

Appellee says that this is a regulation of production and consumption of wheat. Such activities are, he urges, beyond the reach of Congressional power under the Commerce Clause, since they are local in character, and their effects upon interstate commerce are at most "indirect." In answer the Government argues that the statute regulates neither production nor consumption, but only marketing; and, in the alternative, that if the Act does go beyond the regulation of marketing it is sustainable as a "necessary and proper" implementation of the power of Congress over interstate commerce.

The Government's concern lest the Act be held to be a regulation of production or consumption rather than of marketing is attributable to a few dicta and decisions of this Court which might be understood to lay it down that activities such as "production," "manufacturing," and "mining" are strictly "local" and, except in special circumstances which are not present here, cannot be regulated under the commerce power because their effects upon interstate commerce are, as matter of law, only "indirect." Even today, when this power has been held to have great latitude, there is no decision of this Court that such activities may be regulated where no part of the product is intended for interstate commerce or intermingled with the subjects thereof. We believe that a review of the course of decision under the Commerce Clause will make plain, however, that questions of the power of Congress are not to be decided by reference to any formula which would give controlling force to nomenclature such as "production" and "indirect" and foreclose consideration of the actual effects of the activity in question upon interstate commerce.

. . .

Whether the subject of the regulation in question was "production," "consumption," or "marketing" is . . . not material for purposes of deciding the question of federal power before us. That an activity is of local character may help in a doubtful case to determine whether Congress intended to reach it. The same consideration might help in determining whether in the absence of Congressional action it would be permissible for the state to exert its power on the subject matter, even though in so doing it to some degree affected interstate commerce. But even if appellee's activity be local and though it may not be regarded as commerce, it may still, whatever its nature, be reached by Congress if it exerts a substantial economic effect on interstate commerce and this irrespective of whether such effect is what might at some earlier time have been defined as "direct" or "indirect."

The parties have stipulated a summary of the economics of the wheat industry. Commerce among the states in wheat is large and important. Although wheat is raised in every state but one, production in most states is not equal to consumption. Sixteen states on average have had a surplus of wheat above their own requirements for feed, seed, and food. Thirty-two states and the District of Columbia, where production has been below consumption, have looked to these surplus-producing states for their supply as well as for wheat for export and carryover.

The wheat industry has been a problem industry for some years. Largely as a result of increased foreign production and import restrictions, annual exports of wheat and flour from the United States during the ten-year period ending in 1940 averaged less than 10 per cent of total production, while during the 1920's they averaged more than 25 per cent. The decline in the export trade has left a large surplus in production which in connection with an abnormally large supply of wheat and other grains in recent years caused congestion in a number of markets; tied up railroad cars; and caused elevators in some instances to turn away grains, and railroads to institute embargoes to prevent further congestion.

Many countries, both importing and exporting, have sought to modify the impact of the world market conditions on their own economy. Importing countries have taken measures to stimulate production and self-sufficiency. The four large exporting countries of Argentina, Australia, Canada, and the United States have all undertaken various programs for the relief of growers. Such measures have been designed in part at least to protect the domestic price received by producers. Such plans have generally evolved towards control by the central government.

In the absence of regulation the price of wheat in the United States would be much affected by world conditions. During 1941 producers who cooperated with the Agricultural Adjustment program received an average price on the farm of about $1.16 a bushel as compared with the world market price of 40 cents a bushel.

Differences in farming conditions, however, make these benefits mean different things to different wheat growers. There are several large areas of specialization in wheat, and the concentration on this crop reaches 27 percent of the crop land, and the average harvest runs as high as 155 acres. Except for some use of wheat as stock feed and for seed, the practice is to sell the crop for cash. Wheat from such areas constitutes the bulk of the interstate commerce therein.

On the other hand, in some New England states less than one percent of the crop land is devoted to wheat, and the average harvest is less than five acres per farm. In 1940 the average percentage of the total wheat production that was sold in each state as measured by value ranged from 29 per cent thereof in Wisconsin to 90 per cent in Washington. Except in regions of large-scale production, wheat is usually grown in rotation with other crops; for a nurse crop for grass seeding; and as a cover crop to prevent soil erosion and leaching. Some is sold, some kept for seed, and a percentage of the total production much larger than in areas of specialization is consumed on the farm and grown for such purpose. Such farmers, while growing some wheat, may even find the balance of their interest on the consumer's side.

The effect of consumption of homegrown wheat on interstate commerce is due to the fact that it constitutes the most variable factor in the disappearance of the wheat crop. Consumption on the farm where grown appears to vary in an amount greater than 20 per cent of average production. The total amount of wheat consumed as food varies but relatively little, and use as seed is relatively constant.

The maintenance by government regulation of a price for wheat undoubtedly can be accomplished as effectively by sustaining or increasing the demand as by limiting the supply. The effect of the statute before us is to restrict the amount which may be produced for market and the extent as well to which one may forestall resort to the market by producing to meet his own needs. That appellee's own contribution to the demand for wheat may be trivial by itself is not enough to remove him from the scope of federal regulation where, as here, his contribution, taken together with that of many others similarly situated, is far from trivial. . . .

It is well established by decisions of this Court that the power to regulate commerce includes the power to regulate the prices at which commodities in that commerce are dealt in and practices affecting such prices. One of the primary purposes of the Act in question was to increase the market price of wheat and to that end to limit the volume thereof that could affect the market. It can hardly be denied that a factor of such volume and variability as home-consumed wheat would have a substantial influence on price and market conditions. This may arise because being in marketable condition such wheat overhangs the market and if induced by rising prices tends to flow into the market and check price increases. But if we assume that it is never marketed, it supplies a need of the man who grew it which would otherwise be reflected by purchases in the open market. Home-grown wheat in this sense competes with wheat in commerce. The stimulation of commerce is a use of the regulatory function quite as definitely as prohibitions or restrictions thereon. This record leaves us in no doubt that Congress may properly have considered that wheat consumed on the farm where grown if wholly outside the scheme of regulation would have a substantial effect in defeating and obstructing its purpose to stimulate trade therein at increased prices.

It is said, however, that this Act, forcing some farmers into the market to buy what they could provide for themselves, is an unfair promotion of the markets and prices of specializ-

ing wheat growers. It is of the essence of regulation that it lays a restraining hand on the self interest of the regulated and that advantages from the regulation commonly fall to others. The conflicts of economic interest between the regulated and those who advantage by it are wisely left under our system to resolution by the Congress under its more flexible and responsible legislative process. Such conflicts rarely lend themselves to judicial determination. And with the wisdom, workability, or fairness, of the plan of regulation we have nothing to do.

. . .

Reversed.

Two years later, in *United States v. South-Eastern Underwriters Ass'n*,[25] the Court overturned *Paul v. Virginia* insofar as that case held that insurance policies do not constitute commerce within the meaning of the Commerce Clause. *South-Eastern* involved an indictment for violations of the Sherman Act. Since the indictments were based on conduct involving insurance policies, appellees argued that the Sherman Act could not be applied to them because "the business of fire insurance is not commerce." The Court disagreed:

[I]t would indeed be difficult now to hold that no activities of any insurance company can ever constitute interstate commerce so as to make it subject to such regulation;—activities which, as part of the conduct of a legitimate and useful commercial enterprise, may embrace integrated operations in many states and involve the transmission of great quantities of money, documents, and communications across dozens of state lines.

---

[25] 322 U.S. 533 (1944).

RLW: *Wickard's* holding was striking given the scope of prior precedent. Many commentators suggested that, if Congress could reach a small wheat farmer because of the aggregate effect of all small farmers on interstate commerce, Congress could reach virtually anything.

DEL: Such commentary has proved accurate in its prophecy. Although the *Darby* and *Wickard* cases made possible subsequent interpretations that vastly expanded the reach of Congress' power under the commerce clause, it would be the Court's rulings beginning in the 1960s that not only actualized fully but perhaps even exceeded the potential of the New Deal decisions. Over the course of this century in particular, standards of review have been notable primarily for their malleability and manipulability. Notwithstanding the narrower perception of commerce related by the Court in the *Dagenhart* era, the standard of review on its face was hardly outcome-determinative. Distinguishing between direct and indirect effects is a highly subjective exercise so, depending upon perspective, child labor regulation as easily could be understood as within the purview of commerce as beyond it. Given the forces that redefined the Court in the 1930s, it seems safe to say that analytical criteria were relatively inconsequential for purposes of defining eventual understanding of the commerce power's breadth.

DER: *Wickard* represents a transformation of the meaning of "private" and "local" in the economic arena. The Court's broadened understanding of private business matters reflects *Lochner*'s demise. It exemplifies the rejection of the *Lochner* Court's protection of private economic liberty, in favor of expanding governmental power over citizens' economic transactions. The Court also recognized a more complicated and interrelated economic universe in which not only local market decisions affected the national economy, but foreign economic decisions influenced American prices and market conditions. In this context, few economic transactions can be characterized as purely private or local. Effective federal economic policy could no longer be isolationist at either the national or international levels. This broader understanding of private and local transactions facilitated the enforcement of civil rights legislation decades later in cases such as *Heart of Atlanta Motel* and *McClung* which recognized that even the discriminatory actions of small businesses could have an impact on the highly public and national issue of Black citizens' ability to participate fully in American society.

PAH: While I agree that the establishment of the reach of commerce power in cases like *Wickard* has served important commercial and social interests in the twentieth century, in this area, like others where the court has been willing to defer to political judgment about the exercise of governmental power, it can be argued that some oversight role is preferable to none. Requiring Congress to make findings demonstrating a rational basis for a decision to exercise commerce power and to demonstrate the activity's substantial connection with commerce is appropriate and consistent with the court's reviewing power. This kind of limited oversight is consistent with federalism and separation of powers concerns, fosters accountability and, in my view, is preferable to the Court's eventual tack of using the Tenth Amendment to police the exercise of commerce power.

5. Modern Cases

In the wake of decisions like *Darby* and *Wickard*, the federal government's power over the U.S. economy increased dramatically. The federal government began to assert control over such diverse matters as consumer safety, energy, agriculture, aviation travel, civil rights, drugs, labor, commerce, securities, and banking, to name a few. Until 1995, Supreme Court decisions readily sustained broad assertions of power.

a. Environmental Cases

Hodel v. Virginia Surface Mining and Reclamation Association, Inc.
452 U.S. 264 (1981)

Justice MARSHALL delivered the opinion of the Court.

These cases arise out of a pre-enforcement challenge to the constitutionality of the Surface Mining Control and Reclamation Act of 1977. . . . In these appeals, we consider whether Congress, in adopting the Act, exceeded its powers under the Commerce Clause of the Constitution. . . .

The Surface Mining Act is a comprehensive statute designed to "establish a nationwide program to protect society and the environment from the adverse effects of surface coal mining operations." 30 U.S.C. § 1202(a). . . . Section 501(a) directs the Secre-tary to promulgate regulations establishing an interim regulatory program during which mine operators will be required to comply with some of the Act's performance standards. . . . Included among those selected standards are requirements governing: (a) restoration of land after mining to its prior condition; (b) restoration of land to its approximate original contour; (c) segregation and preservation of topsoil; (d) minimization of disturbance to the hydrologic balance; (e) construction of coal mine waste piles used as dams and embankments; (f) revegetation of mined areas; and (g) spoil disposal. . . .

. . .

[A]ppellees . . . insist that the Act's principal goal is regulating the use of private lands within the borders of the States and not, as the District Court found, regulating the interstate commerce effects of surface coal mining. Consequently, appellees contend that the ultimate issue presented is "whether land as such is subject to regulation under the Commerce Clause, i.e. whether land can be regarded as 'in commerce.'" Brief for Virginia Surface Mining & Reclamation Association, Inc., et al. 12 (emphasis in original). In urging us to answer "no" to this question, appellees emphasize that the Court has recognized that land-use regulation is within the inherent police powers of the States and their political subdivisions. . . .

[The] task of a court that is asked to determine whether a particular exercise of congressional power is valid under the Commerce Clause is relatively narrow. The court must defer to a congressional finding that a regulated activity affects interstate commerce, if there is any rational basis for such a finding. *Heart of Atlanta Motel, Inc. v. United States*, 379 U.S. 241, 258 (1964); *Katzenbach v. McClung*, 379 U.S. 294, 303–304 (1964). This established, the only remaining question for judicial inquiry is whether "the means chosen by [Congress] must be reasonably adapted to the end permitted by the Constitution." *Heart of Atlanta Motel, Inc. v. United States, supra*, at 262. The judicial task is at an end once the court determines that Congress acted rationally in adopting a particular regulatory scheme.

. . .

[W]hen Congress has determined that an activity affects interstate commerce, the courts need inquire only whether the finding is rational. Here, the District Court properly deferred to Congress' express findings, set out in the Act itself, about the effects of surface coal mining on interstate commerce. Section 101(c), 30 U.S.C. § 1201(c) (1976 ed., Supp. III), recites the congressional finding that "many surface mining operations result in disturbances of surface areas that burden and adversely affect commerce and the public welfare by destroying or diminishing the utility of land for commercial, industrial, residential, recreational, agricultural, and forestry purposes, by causing erosion and landslides, by contributing to floods, by polluting the water, by destroying fish and wildlife habitats, by impairing natural beauty, by damaging the property of citizens, by creating hazards dangerous to life and property by degrading the quality of life in local communities, and by counteracting governmental programs and efforts to conserve soil, water, and other natural resources."

The legislative record provides ample support for these statutory findings. The Surface Mining Act became law only after six years of the most thorough legislative consideration. Committees of both Houses of Congress held extended hearings during which vast amounts of testimony and documentary evidence about the effects of surface mining on our Nation's environment and economy were brought to Congress' attention. . . .

. . .

Appellees do not, in general, dispute the validity of the congressional findings. Rather, appellees' contention is that the "rational basis" test should not apply in this case because the Act regulates land use, a local activity not affecting interstate commerce. But even assuming that appellees correctly characterize the land use regulated by the Act as a "local" activity, their argument is unpersuasive.

The denomination of an activity as a "local" or "intrastate" activity does not resolve the question whether Congress may regulate it under the Commerce Clause. As previously noted, the commerce power "extends to those activities intrastate which so affect interstate commerce, or the exertion of the power of Congress over it, as to make regulation of them appropriate means to the attainment of a legitimate end, the effective execution of the granted power to regulate interstate commerce." *United States v. Wrightwood Dairy Co.*, 315 U.S., at 119. This Court has long held that Congress may regulate the conditions under which goods shipped in interstate commerce are produced where the "local" activity of producing these goods itself affects interstate commerce. Appellees do not dispute that coal is a commodity that moves in interstate commerce. Here, Congress rationally determined that regulation of surface coal mining is necessary to protect interstate commerce from adverse effects that may result from that activity. This congressional finding is sufficient to sustain the Act as a valid exercise of Congress' power under the Commerce Clause.

Moreover, the Act responds to a congressional finding that nationwide "surface mining and reclamation standards are essential in order to insure that competition in interstate commerce among sellers of coal produced in different States will not be used to undermine the ability of the several States to improve and maintain adequate standards on coal mining operations within their borders." 30 U.S.C. § 1201(g) (1976 ed., Supp. III). The prevention of this sort of destructive interstate competition is a traditional role for congressional action under the Commerce Clause. In *United States v. Darby, supra*, the Court used a similar rationale to sustain the imposition of federal minimum wage and maximum hour regulations on a manufacturer of goods shipped in interstate commerce. The Court explained that the statute implemented Congress' view that "interstate commerce should not be made the instrument of competition in the distribution of goods produced under substandard labor conditions, which competition is injurious to the commerce and to the states from and to which the commerce flows." *Id.* 312 U.S., at 115. The same rationale applies here to support the conclusion that the Surface Mining Act is within the authority granted to Congress by the Commerce Clause.

Finally, we agree with the lower federal courts that have uniformly found the power conferred by the Commerce Clause broad enough to permit congressional regulation of activities causing air or water pollution, or other environmental hazards that may have effects in more than one State. Appellees do not dispute that the environmental and other problems that the Act attempts to control can properly be addressed through Commerce Clause legislation. In these circumstances, it is difficult to find any remaining foundation for appellees' argument that, because it regulates a particular land use, the Surface Mining Act is beyond congressional Commerce Clause authority. Accordingly, we turn to the question whether the means selected by Congress were reasonable and appropriate.

. . .

Justice POWELL, concurring.

The Surface Mining Act mandates an extraordinarily intrusive program of federal regulation and control of land use and land reclamation, activities normally left to state and local governments. But the decisions of this Court over many years make clear that, under the Commerce Clause, Congress has the power to enact this legislation.

. . .

The Switch of '37 bought with it the demise of the non-delegation doctrine. Decisions like *Panama Refining* and *Schechter*, which limited Congress' power to delegate, were effectively overruled. In later cases, the Court sustained increasingly broad assertions of power. Consider the following language from *INS v. Chadha*:[26]

> [In] practice, . . . restrictions on the scope of the power that could be delegated diminished and all but disappeared. . . . [T]he "intelligible principle" through which agencies have attained enormous control over the economic affairs of the country was held to include such formulations as "just and reasonable," *Tagg Bros. & Moorhead v. United States*, 280 U.S. 420 (1930), "public interest," *New York Central Securities Corp. v. United States*, 287 U.S. 12 (1932), "public convenience, interest, or necessity," *Federal Radio Comm. v. Nelson Bros. Bond & Mortgage Co.*, 289 U.S. 266 (1933), and "unfair methods of competition." *FTC v. Gratz*, 253 U.S. 421 (1920).

---

[26] 462 U.S. 919, 985 (1983).

RLW: Decisions like *Hodel* have led to dramatic growth in the scope of administrative power as Congress has delegated more and more power to administrative agencies. As the D.C. Circuit recently noted, "administrative agencies may well have a more far-reaching effect on the daily lives of all citizens than do the combined actions of the executive, legislative and judicial branches. . . ."[27] The growth of agency power is reflected in the size of the Code of Federal Regulations, which now includes 208 volumes.

While the growth of administrative power may have been necessary, and perhaps inevitable, that growth has not been without costs. Justice Jackson stated that "[t]he rise of administrative bodies probably has been the most significant legal trend of the last century. . . . They have become a veritable fourth branch of the Government, which has deranged our three-branch legal theories. . . ."[28]

---

[27] Ballerina Pen Co. v. Kunzig, 433 F.2d 1204, 1207–08 (D.C. Cir. 1970), cert. denied, 401 U.S. 950 (1971).

[28] Federal Trade Commission v. Ruberoid Co., 343 U.S. 470, 487 (1952) (Jackson, J. dissenting).

The Switch of '37 did not abrogate political checks on the scope of federal power. To the extent that Congress is unhappy with the growth of federal regulation, it can rein in that growth or even reduce it. As the 1994 elections reveal, the ballot box can influence Congress' actions.

DEL: Even if the emergence of administrative agencies represents a significant trend of the past century, its "deranging" consequences are debatable given the choices available. The growth of administrative bodies, at both the federal and state level, responds to a society that has grown not just in size but complexity. The political order's response to the challenge of change has been to create resources of expertise and management attending to details that would overload a single legislative body. Given the challenge that governance of modern society presents, it is hard to imagine any systemic adaptation that would not derange original "three branch legal theories." Strict maintenance of that initial structure might have engendered the most deranging consequences of all.

PAH: One of the most notable aspects of the rise of the administrative state has been the absence of an emerging coherent judicial approach to separation of powers concerns. As it has struggled to formulate rational limits on decision making authority the Court has sought support in a constitutional model which no longer reflects the structure of government today.

b. Civil Rights

Congress has also passed various civil rights statutes using its commerce power.

Heart of Atlanta Motel, Inc. v. United States
379 U.S. 241 (1964)

Mr. Justice CLARK delivered the opinion of the Court

. . .

Appellant owns and operates the Heart of Atlanta Motel which has 216 rooms available to transient guests. The motel is located on Courtland Street, two blocks from downtown Peachtree Street. It is readily accessible to interstate highways 75 and 85 and state highways 23 and 41. Appellant solicits patronage from outside the State of Georgia through various national advertising media, including magazines of national circulation; it maintains over 50 billboards and highway signs within the State, soliciting patronage for the motel; it accepts convention trade from outside Georgia and approximately 75% of its registered guests are from out of State. Prior to passage of the Act the motel had followed a practice of refusing to rent rooms to Negroes, and it alleged that it intended to continue to do so. In an effort to perpetuate that policy this suit was filed.

The appellant contends [, inter alia,] that Congress in passing this Act exceeded its power to regulate commerce under Art. I, § 8,

cl. 3, of the Constitution of the United States. . . .

. . .

Title [II of the 1964 Civil Rights Act] is divided into seven sections beginning with § 201(a) which provides that: "All persons shall be entitled to the full and equal enjoyment of the goods, services, facilities, privileges, advantages, and accommodations of any place of public accommodation, as defined in this section, without discrimination or segregation on the ground of race, color, religion, or national origin."

. . .

It is admitted that the operation of the motel brings it within the provisions of § 201(a) of the Act and that appellant refused to provide lodging for transient Negroes because of their race or color and that it intends to continue that policy unless restrained.

The sole question posed is, therefore, the constitutionality of the Civil Rights Act of 1964 as applied to these facts. The legislative history of the Act indicates that Congress based the Act on § 5 and the Equal Protection Clause of the Fourteenth Amendment as well as its power to regulate interstate commerce under Art. I, § 8, cl. 3, of the Constitution.

The Senate Commerce Committee made it quite clear that the fundamental object of Title II was to vindicate "the deprivation of personal dignity that surely accompanies denials of equal access to public establishments." At the same time, however, it noted that such an objective has been and could be readily achieved "by congressional action based on the commerce power of the Constitution." S.Rep. No. 872, *supra*, at 16—17. Our study of the legislative record, made in the light of prior cases, has brought us to the conclusion that Congress possessed ample power in this regard, and we have therefore not considered the other grounds relied upon. This is not to say that the remaining authority upon which it acted was not adequate, a question upon which we do not pass, but merely that since the commerce power is sufficient for our decision here we have considered it alone. . . .

. . .

While the Act as adopted carried no congressional findings the record of its passage through each house is replete with evidence of the burdens that discrimination by race or color places upon interstate commerce. . . . This testimony included the fact that our people have become increasingly mobile with millions of people of all races traveling from State to State; that Negroes in particular have been the subject of discrimination in transient accommodations, having to travel great distances to secure the same; that often they have been unable to obtain accommodations and have had to call upon friends to put them up overnight; and that these conditions had become so acute as to require the listing of available lodging for Negroes in a special guidebook which was itself "dramatic testimony to the difficulties" Negroes encounter in travel. These exclusionary practices were found to be nationwide, the Under Secretary of Commerce testifying that there is "no question that this discrimination in the North still exists to a large degree" and in the West and Midwest as well. This testimony indicated a qualitative as well as quantitative effect on interstate travel by Negroes. The former was the obvious impairment of the Negro traveler's pleasure and convenience that resulted when he continually was uncertain of finding lodging. As for the latter, there was evidence that this uncertainty stemming from racial discrimination had the effect of discouraging travel on the part of a substantial portion of the Negro community. This was the conclusion not only of the Under Secretary of Commerce but also of the Administrator of the Federal Aviation Agency who wrote the Chairman of the Senate Commerce Committee that it was his "belief that air com-

merce is adversely affected by the denial to a substantial segment of the traveling public of adequate and desegregated public accommodations." We shall not burden this opinion with further details since the voluminous testimony presents overwhelming evidence that discrimination by hotels and motels impedes interstate travel.

. . .

The power of Congress to deal with these obstructions depends on the meaning of the Commerce Clause. Its meaning was first enunciated 140 years ago by the great Chief Justice John Marshall in *Gibbons v. Ogden*, 9 Wheat. 1 (1824). . . .

That the "intercourse" of which the Chief Justice spoke included the movement of persons through more States than one was settled as early as 1849, in the *Passenger Cases (Smith v. Turner)*, 7 How. 283, where Mr. Justice McLean stated: "That the transportation of passengers is a part of commerce is not now an open question." At 401. Again in 1913 Mr. Justice McKenna, speaking for the Court, said: "Commerce among the states, we have said, consists of intercourse and traffic between their citizens, and includes the transportation of persons and property." *Hoke v. United States*, 227 U.S. 308, 320. And only four years later in 1917 in *Caminetti v. United States*, 242 U.S. 470, Mr. Justice Day held for the Court: "The transportation of passengers in interstate commerce, it has long been settled, is within the regulatory power of Congress, under the commerce clause of the Constitution, and the authority of Congress to keep the channels of interstate commerce free from immoral and injurious uses has been frequently sustained, and is no longer open to question." At 491. Nor does it make any difference whether the transportation is commercial in character. *Id.*, at 484–486. In *Morgan v. Com. of Virginia*, 328 U.S. 373 (1946), Mr. Justice Reed observed as to the modern movement of persons among the States: "The recent changes in transportation brought about by the coming of automobiles (do) not seem of great significance in the problem. People of all races travel today more extensively than in 1878 when this Court first passed upon state regulation of racial segregation in commerce. (It but) emphasizes the soundness of this Court's early conclusion in *Hall v. De Cuir*, 95 U.S. 485."

. . .

In framing Title II of this Act Congress was also dealing with what it considered a moral problem. But that fact does not detract from the overwhelming evidence of the disruptive effect that racial discrimination has had on commercial intercourse. It was this burden which empowered Congress to enact appropriate legislation, and, given this basis for the exercise of its power, Congress was not restricted by the fact that the particular obstruction to interstate commerce with which it was dealing was also deemed a moral and social wrong.

It is said that the operation of the motel here is of a purely local character. But, assuming this to be true, "(i)f it is interstate commerce that feels the pinch, it does not matter how local the operation which applies the squeeze." *United States v. Women's Sportswear Mfg. Ass'n*, 336 U.S. 460, 464 (1949). As Chief Justice Stone put it in *United States v. Darby, supra:* "The power of Congress over interstate commerce is not confined to the regulation of commerce among the states. It extends to those activities intrastate which so affect interstate commerce or the exercise of the power of Congress over it as to make regulation of them appropriate means to the attainment of a legitimate end, the exercise of the granted power of Congress to regulate interstate commerce. *See* McCulloch v. Maryland, 4 Wheat. 316, 421. Thus the power of Congress to promote interstate commerce also includes the power to regulate the local incidents thereof, including local activities in both the States of origin and destination, which might have a substantial and harmful effect upon that commerce. One need only examine the evidence which we have discussed above to see that Congress may—as it has—prohibit racial discrimination by motels serving travelers, however "local" their operations may appear.

. . .

We, therefore, conclude that the action of the Congress in the adoption of the Act as applied here to a motel which concededly serves interstate travelers is within the power granted it by the Commerce Clause of the Constitution, as interpreted by this Court for 140 years. It may be argued that Congress could have pursued other methods to eliminate the obstructions it found in interstate commerce caused by racial discrimination. But this is a matter of policy that rests entirely with the Congress not with the courts. How obstructions in commerce may be removed—what means are to be employed—is within the sound and exclusive discretion of the Congress. It is subject only to one caveat—that the means chosen by it must be reasonably adapted to the end permitted by the Constitution. We cannot say that its choice here was not so adapted. The Constitution requires no more.

Affirmed.

Katzenbach v. McClung
379 U.S. 294 (1964)

Mr. Justice CLARK delivered the opinion of the Court.

This case was argued with No. 515, *Heart of Atlanta Motel v. United States*, decided this date, 379 U.S. 241, in which we upheld the constitutional validity of Title II of the Civil Rights Act of 1964 against an attack by hotels, motels, and like establishments. This complaint for injunctive relief against appellants attacks the constitutionality of the Act as applied to a restaurant. . . .

. . .

Ollie's Barbecue is a family-owned restaurant in Birmingham, Alabama, specializing in barbecued meats and homemade pies, with a seating capacity of 220 customers. It is located on a state highway 11 blocks from an interstate one and a somewhat greater distance from railroad and bus stations. The restaurant caters to a family and white-collar trade with a take-out service for Negroes. It employs 36 persons, two-thirds of whom are Negroes.

In the 12 months preceding the passage of the Act, the restaurant purchased locally approximately $150,000 worth of food, $69,683 or 46% of which was meat that it bought from a local supplier who had procured it from outside the State. The District Court expressly found that a substantial portion of the food served in the restaurant had moved in interstate commerce. The restaurant has refused to serve Negroes in its dining accommodations since its original opening in 1927, and since July 2, 1964, it has been operating in violation of the Act. The court below concluded that if it were required to serve Negroes it would lose a substantial amount of business.

. . .

Ollie's Barbecue admits that it is covered by these provisions of the Act. The Government makes no contention that the discrimination at the restaurant was supported by the State of Alabama. There is no claim that interstate travelers frequented the restaurant. The sole question, therefore, narrows down to whether Title II, as applied to a restaurant annually receiving about $70,000 worth of food which has moved in commerce, is a valid exercise of the power of Congress. The Government has contended that Congress had ample basis upon which to find that racial discrimination at restaurants which receive from out of state a substantial portion of the food served does, in fact, impose commercial burdens of national magnitude upon interstate commerce. The appellees' major argument is directed to this premise. They urge that no such basis existed. It is to that question that we now turn.

. . .

As we noted in *Heart of Atlanta Motel* both Houses of Congress conducted prolonged hearings on the Act. And, as we said there, while no formal findings were made, which of course are not necessary, it is well that we make mention of the testimony at these hearings the better to understand the problem before Congress and determine whether the Act is a reasonable and appropriate means toward its solution. The record is replete with testimony of the burdens placed on interstate commerce by racial discrimination in restaurants. A comparison of per capita spending by Negroes in restaurants, theaters, and like establishments indicated less spending, after discounting income differences, in areas where discrimination is widely practiced. This condition, which was especially aggravated in the South, was attributed in the testimony of the Under Secretary of Commerce to racial segregation. See Hearings before the Senate Committee on Commerce on S. 1732, 88th Cong., 1st Sess., 695. This diminutive spending springing from a refusal to serve Negroes and their total loss as customers has, regardless of the absence of direct evidence, a close connection to interstate commerce. The fewer customers a restaurant enjoys the less food it sells and consequently the less it buys. In addition, the Attorney General testified that this type of discrimination imposed "an artificial restriction on the market" and interfered with the flow of merchandise. In addition, there were many references to discriminatory situations causing wide unrest and having a depressant effect on general business conditions in the respective communities.

Moreover there was an impressive array of testimony that discrimination in restaurants had a direct and highly restrictive effect upon interstate travel by Negroes. This resulted, it was said, because discriminatory practices prevent Negroes from buying prepared food served on the premises while on a trip, except in isolated and unkempt restaurants and under most unsatisfactory and often unpleasant conditions. This obviously discourages travel and obstructs interstate commerce for one can hardly travel without eating. Likewise, it was said, that discrimination deterred professional, as well as skilled, people from moving into areas where such practices occurred and thereby caused industry to be reluctant to establish there. S. Rep. No. 872, *supra*, at 18–19.

We believe that this testimony afforded ample basis for the conclusion that established restaurants in such areas sold less interstate goods because of the discrimination, that inter-

state travel was obstructed directly by it, that business in general suffered and that many new businesses refrained from establishing there as a result of it. Hence the District Court was in error in concluding that there was no connection between discrimination and the movement of interstate commerce. The court's conclusion that such a connection is outside "common experience" flies in the face of stubborn fact.

It goes without saying that, viewed in isolation, the volume of food purchased by Ollie's Barbecue from sources supplied from out of state was insignificant when compared with the total foodstuffs moving in commerce. But, as our late Brother Jackson said for the Court in *Wickard v. Filburn*, 317 U.S. 111 (1942): "That appellee's own contribution to the demand for wheat may be trivial by itself is not enough to remove him from the scope of federal regulation where, as here, his contribution, taken together with that of many others similarly situated, is far from trivial." At 127–128.

We noted in *Heart of Atlanta Motel* that a number of witnesses attested to the fact that racial discrimination was not merely a state or regional problem but was one of nationwide scope. Against this background, we must conclude that while the focus of the legislation was on the individual restaurant's relation to interstate commerce, Congress appropriately considered the importance of that connection with the knowledge that the discrimination was but "representative of many others throughout the country, the total incidence of which if left unchecked may well become far-reaching in its harm to commerce." *Polish National Alliance of U.S. v. National Labor Relations Board*, 322 U.S. 643, 648 (1944).

. . .

Much is said about a restaurant business being local but "even if appellee's activity be local and though it may not be regarded as commerce, it may still, whatever its nature, be reached by Congress if it exerts a substantial economic effect on interstate commerce. . . ." *Wickard v. Filburn, supra*, at 125. The activities that are beyond the reach of Congress are "those which are completely within a particular State, which do not affect other States, and with which it is not necessary to interfere, for the purpose of executing some of the general powers of the government." *Gibbons v. Ogden*, 9 Wheat. 1, 195 (1824). This rule is as good today as it was when Chief Justice Marshall laid it down almost a century and a half ago.

. . .

The appellees contend that Congress has arbitrarily created a conclusive presumption that all restaurants meeting the criteria set out in the Act "affect commerce." Stated another way, they object to the omission of a provision for a case-by-case determination—judicial or administrative—that racial discrimination in a particular restaurant affects commerce.

But Congress' action in framing this Act was not unprecedented. In *United States v. Darby*, 312 U.S. 100, 657 (1941), this Court held constitutional the Fair Labor Standards Act of 1938. There Congress determined that the payment of substandard wages to employees engaged in the production of goods for commerce, while not itself commerce, so inhibited it as to be subject to federal regulation. The appellees in that case argued, as do the appellees here, that the Act was invalid because it included no provision for an independent inquiry regarding the effect on commerce of substandard wages in a particular business. . . .

. . .

Here, as there, Congress has determined for itself that refusals of service to Negroes have imposed burdens both upon the interstate flow of food and upon the movement of products generally. Of course, the mere fact that Congress has said when particular activity shall be deemed to affect commerce does not preclude further examination by this Court. But where we find that the legislators, in light of the facts and testimony before them, have a rational basis for finding a chosen regulatory scheme necessary to the protection of commerce, our investigation is at an end. The only remaining question—one answered in the affirmative by the court below—is whether the particular restaurant either serves or offers to serve interstate travelers or serves food a substantial portion of which has moved in interstate commerce.

. . .

Confronted as we are with the facts laid before Congress, we must conclude that it had a rational basis for finding that racial discrimination in restaurants had a direct and adverse effect on the free flow of interstate commerce. Insofar as the sections of the Act here relevant are concerned, §§ 201(b)(2) and (c), Congress prohibited discrimination only in those establishments having a close tie to interstate commerce, i.e., those, like the McClungs', serving food that has come from out of the State. We think in so doing that Congress acted well within its power to protect and foster commerce in extending the coverage of Title II only to those restaurants offering to serve interstate travelers or serving food, a substantial portion of which has moved in interstate commerce. . . .

The Civil Rights Act of 1964, as here applied, we find to be plainly appropriate in the resolution of what the Congress found to be a national commercial problem of the first magnitude. We find it in no violation of any express limitations of the Constitution and we therefore declare it valid.

The judgment is therefore reversed.

Reversed.

c. Crime

Historically, the states have passed virtually all basic criminal legislation including murder, robbery, rape, and assault statutes. Congress has passed some criminal statutes, but most federal statutes have concerned crimes against the federal government (filing a false tax return) or criminal activity that crossed state lines (*e.g.*, *The Lottery Cases*).

Perez v. United States
402 U.S. 146 (1971)

Mr. Justice DOUGLAS delivered the opinion of the Court.

The question in this case is whether Title II of the Consumer Credit Protection Act, 82 Stat. 159, 18 U.S.C. § 891 et seq. (1964 ed., Supp. V), as construed and applied to petitioner, is a permissible exercise by Congress of its powers under the Commerce Clause of the Constitution. . . .

Petitioner is one of the species commonly known as "loan sharks" which Congress found are in large part under the control of "organized crime." "Extortionate credit transactions" are defined as those characterized by the use or threat of the use of "violence or other criminal means" in enforcement. There was ample evidence showing petitioner was a "loan shark" who used the threat of violence as a method of collection. He loaned money to one Miranda, owner of a new butcher shop, making a $1,000 advance to be repaid in installments of $105 per week for 14 weeks. After paying at this rate for six or eight weeks, petitioner increased the weekly payment to $130. In two months Miranda asked for an additional loan of $2,000 which was made, the agreement being that Miranda was to pay $205 a week. In a few weeks petitioner increased the weekly payment to

$330. When Miranda objected, petitioner told him about a customer who refused to pay and ended up in a hospital. So Miranda paid. In a few months petitioner increased his demands to $500 weekly which Miranda paid, only to be advised that at the end of the week petitioner would need $1,000. Miranda made that payment by not paying his suppliers; but, faced with a $1,000 payment the next week, he sold his butcher shop. Petitioner pursued Miranda, first making threats to Miranda's wife and then telling Miranda he could have him castrated. When Miranda did not make more payments, petitioner said he was turning over his collections to people who would not be nice but who would put him in the hospital if he did not pay. Negotiations went on, Miranda finally saying he could only pay $25 a week. Petitioner said that was not enough, that Miranda should steal or sell drugs if necessary to get the money to pay the loan, and that if he went to jail it would be better than going to a hospital with a broken back or legs. He added, "I could have sent you to the hospital, you and your family, any moment I want with my people."

Petitioner's arrest followed. Miranda, his wife, and an employee gave the evidence against petitioner who did not testify or call any witnesses. Petitioner's attack was on the constitutionality of the Act, starting with a motion to dismiss the indictment.

The constitutional question is a substantial one.

. . .

The House debates include a long article from the New York Times Magazine for January 28, 1968, on the connection between the "loan shark" and organized crime. The gruesome and stirring episodes related have the following as a prelude: "The loan shark, then, is the indispensable 'moneymover' of the underworld. He takes 'black' money tainted by its derivation from the gambling or narcotics rackets and turns it 'white' by funneling it into channels of legitimate trade. In so doing, he exacts usurious interest that doubles the black-white money in no time; and, by his special decrees, by his imposition of impossible penalties, he greases the way for the underworld takeover of entire businesses."

There were objections on constitutional grounds. Congressman Eckhardt of Texas said: "Should it become law, the amendment would take a long stride by the Federal Government toward occupying the field of general criminal law and toward exercising a general Federal police power; and it would permit prosecution in Federal as well as State courts of a typically State offense. 'I believe that Alexander Hamilton, though a federalist, would be astonished that such a deep entrenchment on the rights of the States in performing their most funda-

mental function should come from the more conservative quarter of the House.'"

Senator Proxmire presented to the Senate the Conference Report approving essentially the "loan shark" provision suggested by Congressman McDade, saying: "Once again these provisions raised serious questions of Federal-State responsibilities. Nonetheless, because of the importance of the problem, the Senate conferees agreed to the House provision. Organized crime operates on a national scale. One of the principal sources of revenue of organized crime comes from loan sharking. If we are to win the battle against organized crime we must strike at their source of revenue and give the Justice Department additional tools to deal with the problem. The problem simply cannot be solved by the States alone. We must bring into play the full resources of the Federal Government."

The Commerce Clause reaches, in the main, three categories of problems. First, the use of channels of interstate or foreign commerce which Congress deems are being misused, as, for example, the shipment of stolen goods or of persons who have been kidnaped. Second, protection of the instrumentalities of interstate commerce, as for example, the destruction of an aircraft, or persons or things in commerce, as, for example, thefts from interstate shipments. Third, those activities affecting commerce. It is with this last category that we are here concerned.

Chief Justice Marshall in *Gibbons v. Ogden*, 9 Wheat. 1, 195, said: "The genius and character of the whole government seem to be, that its action is to be applied to all the external concerns of the nation, and to those internal concerns which affect the States generally; but not to those which are completely within a particular State, which do not affect other States, and with which it is not necessary to interfere, for the purpose of executing some of the general powers of the government. The completely Internal commerce of a State, then, may be considered as reserved for the State itself."

. . .

". . . (E)ven if appellee's activity be local and though it may not be regarded as commerce, it may still, whatever its nature, be reached by Congress if it exerts a substantial economic effect on interstate commerce, and this irrespective of whether such effect is what might at some earlier time have been defined as 'direct' or 'indirect.'" 317 U.S., at 125.

. . .

Where the class of activities is regulated and that class is within the reach of federal power, the courts have no power "to excise, as trivial, individual instances" of the class. *Maryland v. Wirtz*, 392 U.S. 183, 193.

Extortionate credit transactions, though purely intrastate, may in the judgment of Congress affect interstate commerce. In an analogous situation, Mr. Justice Holmes, speaking for a unanimous Court, said: "(W)hen it is necessary in order to prevent an evil to make the law embrace more than the precise thing to be prevented it may do so." *Westfall v. United States*, 274 U.S. 256, 259. In that case an officer of a state bank which was a member of the Federal Reserve System issued a fraudulent certificate of deposit and paid it from the funds of the state bank. It was argued that there was no loss to the Reserve Bank. Mr. Justice Holmes replied, "But every fraud like the one before us weakens the member bank and therefore weakens the System." *Id.*, at 259. In the setting of the present case there is a tie-in between local loan sharks and interstate crime.

The findings by Congress are quite adequate on that ground. The McDade Amendment in the House, as already noted, was the one ultimately adopted. As stated by Congressman McDade it grew out of a "profound study of organized crime, its ramifications and its implications" undertaken by some 22 Congressmen in 1966—1967. 114 Cong. Rec. 14391. The results of that study were included in a report, The Urban Poor and Organized Crime, submitted to the House on August 29, 1967, which revealed that "organized crime takes over $350 million a year from America's poor through loan-sharking alone." See 113 Cong. Rec. 24460—24464. Congressman McDade also relied on The Challenge of Crime in a Free Society, A Report by the President's Commission on Law Enforcement and Administration of Justice (February 1967) which stated that loan sharking was "the second largest source of revenue for organized crime," *id.*, at 189, and is one way by which the underworld obtains control of legitimate businesses. *Id.*, at 190.

The Congress also knew about New York's Report, An Investigation of the Loan Shark Racket (1965). See 114 Cong.Rec. 1428—1431. That report shows the loan shark racket is controlled by organized criminal syndicates, either directly or in partnership with independent operators; that in most instances the racket is organized into three echelons, with the top underworld "bosses" providing the money to their principal "lieutenants," who in turn distribute the money to the "operators" who make the actual individual loans; that loan sharks serve as a source of funds to bookmakers, narcotics dealers, and other racketeers; that victims of the racket include all classes, rich and poor, businessmen and laborers; that the victims are often coerced into the commission of criminal acts in order to repay their loans; that through loan sharking the organized underworld has obtained control of legitimate businesses, including securities brokerages and banks which are then exploited; and that "(e)ven where extortionate credit transactions are purely intrastate in character, they nevertheless directly affect interstate and foreign commerce."

. . .

The essence of all these reports and hearings was summarized and embodied in formal congressional findings. They supplied Congress with the knowledge that the loan shark racket provides organized crime with its second most lucrative source of revenue, exacts millions from the pockets of people, coerces its victims into the commission of crimes against property, and causes the takeover by racketeers of legitimate businesses. See generally 114 Cong. Rec. 14391, 14392, 14395, 14396.

We have mentioned in detail the economic, financial, and social setting of the problem as revealed to Congress. We do so not to infer that Congress need make particularized findings in order to legislate. We relate the history of the Act in detail to answer the impassioned plea of petitioner that all that is involved in loan sharking is a traditionally local activity. It appears, instead, that loan sharking in its national setting is one way organized interstate crime holds its guns to the heads of the poor and the rich alike and syphons funds from numerous localities to finance its national operations.

Affirmed.

Mr. Justice STEWART, dissenting.

Congress surely has power under the Commerce Clause to enact criminal laws to protect the instrumentalities of interstate commerce, to prohibit the misuse of the channels or facilities of interstate commerce, and to prohibit or regulate those intrastate activities that have a demonstrably substantial effect on interstate commerce. But under the statute before us a man can be convicted without any proof of interstate movement, of the use of the facilities of interstate commerce, or of facts showing that his conduct affected interstate commerce. I think the Framers of the Constitution never intended that the National Government might define as a crime and prosecute such wholly local activity through the enactment of federal criminal laws.

In order to sustain this law we would, in my view, have to be able at the least to say that Congress could rationally have concluded that loan sharking is an activity with interstate attributes that distinguish it in some substantial respect from other local crime. But it is not enough to say that loan sharking is a national problem, for all crime is a national problem. It is not enough to say that some loan sharking has interstate characteristics, for any crime may have an interstate setting. And the circumstance that loan sharking has an adverse impact on interstate business is not a distinguishing attribute, for interstate business suffers from almost all criminal activity, be it shoplifting or violence in the streets.

Because I am unable to discern any rational distinction between loan sharking and other local crime, I cannot escape the conclusion that this statute was beyond the power of Congress to enact. The definition and prosecution of local, intrastate crime are reserved to the States under the Ninth and Tenth Amendments.

RLW: After *Perez*, it seemed that Congress was free to pass broad-based criminal legislation. Indeed, pushed to its logical extreme, *Perez* permitted Congress to pass broad-based criminal statutes on diverse subjects such as murder, rape, and robbery. For political and practical reasons, Congress largely has refrained from doing so, limiting itself to specific problems (*e.g.*, access to abortion clinics).

DEL: A particularly striking feature of commerce power jurisprudence over the course of the twentieth century has been the radical fluctuation of doctrine and result. Until the mid-1930s, the question was whether the Court would acknowledge any federal interest beyond the transportation process itself. Until 1995, the question was whether any activity would be found unrelated to commerce and thus beyond Congress' purview. Renewed attention to the Tenth Amendment, noted in the following discussion of *Lopez*, so far represents less a reversal of course than a marking of outer limits. A power that initially was understood as essential for establishing a viable economic union, and conferred as an exception to norms that limited the national government's reach, thus has proved to be a primary facilitator of centralized management and policy-making.

DER: Recent commerce power cases certainly represent a victory of expansive federal policy-making over the concern for limiting Congress' power to regulate local activities. One's conclusion as to whether this development is justified may depend on one's political persuasion, school of constitutional interpretation, or view of the proper balance between federal and state power. Although approval of expanded federal regulation may reflect agreement with the substance of federal policies, there are other bases for judging the growth of national government. Given the Framers' emphasis on restricting federal authority over the states (to which the Commerce Clause was an exception), strict interpretationists might claim that the Court's current understanding of the clause distorts its original scope. On the other hand, some commentators have argued that the congressional political process ensures ample state representation and therefore adequately protects against federal arrogation of state authority. In other words, the Constitution entrusts the political process—and not the federal courts—with the task of limiting national power.

6. A Revolution in the Offing?

In 1995, the Supreme Court did the unthinkable: it struck down a federal statute on Commerce Clause grounds for the first time in more than half-a-century.

United States v. Lopez
115 S. Ct. 1624 (1995)

Chief Justice REHNQUIST delivered the opinion of the Court.

In the Gun-Free School Zones Act of 1990, Congress made it a federal offense "for any individual knowingly to possess a firearm at a place that the individual knows, or has reasonable cause to believe, is a school zone." 18 U.S.C. § 922(q)(1)(A) (1988 ed., Supp. V). The Act neither regulates a commercial activity nor contains a requirement that the possession be connected in any way to interstate commerce. We hold that the Act exceeds the authority of Congress "[t]o regulate Commerce . . . among the several States. . . ." U.S. Const., Art. I, § 8, cl. 3.

On March 10, 1992, respondent, who was then a 12th-grade student, arrived at Edison High School in San Antonio, Texas, carrying a concealed .38 caliber handgun and five bullets. Acting upon an anonymous tip, school authorities confronted respondent, who admitted that he was carrying the weapon. He was arrested and charged . . . with violating the Gun-Free School Zones Act of 1990. 18 U.S.C. § 922(q)(1)(A) (1988 ed., Supp. V).[1]

[We] start with first principles. The Constitution creates a Federal Government of enumerated powers. See U.S. Const., Art. I, § 8. As James Madison wrote, "[t]he powers delegated by the proposed Constitution to the federal government are few and defined. Those which are to remain in the State governments are numerous and indefinite." The Federalist No. 45, pp. 292–293 (C. Rossiter ed. 1961). . . .

The Constitution delegates to Congress the power "[t]o regulate Commerce with foreign Nations, and among the several States, and with the Indian Tribes." U.S. Const., Art. I, § 8, cl. 3. The Court, through Chief Justice Marshall, first defined the nature of Congress' commerce power in Gibbons v. Ogden, 9 Wheat. 1, 189–190, 6 L.Ed. 23 (1824): "Commerce, undoubtedly, is traffic, but it is something more: it is intercourse. It describes the commercial intercourse between nations, and parts of nations, in all its branches, and is regulated by prescribing rules for carrying on that intercourse." The commerce power "is the power to regulate; that is, to prescribe the rule by which commerce is to be governed. This power, like all others vested in Congress, is complete in itself, may be exercised to its utmost extent, and acknowledges no limitations, other than are prescribed in the constitution." Id., at 196. The Gibbons Court, however, acknowledged that limitations on the commerce power are inherent in the very language of the Commerce Clause. "It is not intended to say that these words comprehend that commerce, which is completely internal, which is carried on between man and man in a State, or between different parts of the same State, and which does not extend to or affect other States. Such a power would be inconvenient, and is certainly unnecessary. "Comprehensive as the word 'among' is, it may very properly be restricted to that commerce which concerns more States

than one. . . . The enumeration presupposes something not enumerated; and that something, if we regard the language or the subject of the sentence, must be the exclusively internal commerce of a State." Id., at 194–195.

For nearly a century thereafter, the Court's Commerce Clause decisions dealt but rarely with the extent of Congress' power, and almost entirely with the Commerce Clause as a limit on state legislation that discriminated against interstate commerce. Under this line of precedent, the Court held that certain categories of activity such as "production," "manufacturing," and "mining" were within the province of state governments, and thus were beyond the power of Congress under the Commerce Clause.

In 1887, Congress enacted the Interstate Commerce Act, 24 Stat. 379, and in 1890, Congress enacted the Sherman Antitrust Act, 26 Stat. 209, as amended, 15 U.S.C. § 1 et seq. These laws ushered in a new era of federal regulation under the commerce power. When cases involving these laws first reached this Court, we imported from our negative Commerce Clause cases the approach that Congress could not regulate activities such as "production," "manufacturing," and "mining." See, e.g., Carter v. Carter Coal Co., 298 U.S. 238, 304 (1936). Simultaneously, however, the Court held that, where the interstate and intrastate aspects of commerce were so mingled together that full regulation of interstate commerce required incidental regulation of intrastate commerce, the Commerce Clause authorized such regulation. See, e.g., Houston, E. & W.T.R. Co. v. United States, 234 U.S. 342 (1914).

. . .

Jones & Laughlin Steel, Darby, and Wickard ushered in an era of Commerce Clause jurisprudence that greatly expanded the previously defined authority of Congress under that Clause. In part, this was a recognition of the great changes that had occurred in the way business was carried on in this country. Enterprises that had once been local or at most regional in nature had become national in scope. But the doctrinal change also reflected a view that earlier Commerce Clause cases artificially had constrained the authority of Congress to regulate interstate commerce.

But even these modern-era precedents which have expanded congressional power under the Commerce Clause confirm that this power is subject to outer limits. In Jones & Laughlin Steel, the Court warned that the scope of the interstate commerce power "must be considered in the light of our dual system of government and may not be extended so as to embrace effects upon interstate commerce so indirect and remote that to embrace them, in

---

[1] The term "school zone" is defined as "in, or on the grounds of, a public, parochial or private school" or "within a distance of 1,000 feet from the grounds of a public, parochial or private school." § 921(a)(25).

view of our complex society, would effectually obliterate the distinction between what is national and what is local and create a completely centralized government." 301 U.S., at 37. Since that time, the Court has heeded that warning and undertaken to decide whether a rational basis existed for concluding that a regulated activity sufficiently affected interstate commerce. *See, e.g., Hodel v. Virginia Surface Mining & Reclamation Assn., Inc.*, 452 U.S. 264, 276–280 (1981).

Similarly, in *Maryland v. Wirtz*, 392 U.S. 183 (1968), the Court reaffirmed that "the power to regulate commerce, though broad indeed, has limits" that "[t]he Court has ample power" to enforce. *Id.*, at 196, overruled on other grounds, *National League of Cities v. Usery*, 426 U.S. 833 (1976), overruled by *Garcia v. San Antonio Metropolitan Transit Authority*, 469 U.S. 528 (1985). In response to the dissent's warnings that the Court was powerless to enforce the limitations on Congress' commerce powers because "[a]ll activities affecting commerce, even in the minutest degree, [*Wickard*], may be regulated and controlled by Congress," 392 U.S., at 204 (Douglas, J., dissenting), the *Wirtz* Court replied that the dissent had misread precedent as "[n]either here nor in *Wickard* has the Court declared that Congress may use a relatively trivial impact on commerce as an excuse for broad general regulation of state or private activities," *id.*, at 197, n. 27. Rather, "[t]he Court has said only that where a general regulatory statute bears a substantial relation to commerce, the de minimis character of individual instances arising under that statute is of no consequence." *Ibid.*

Consistent with this structure, we have identified three broad categories of activity that Congress may regulate under its commerce power. *Perez v. United States, supra*, at 150. First, Congress may regulate the use of the channels of interstate commerce. *See, e.g., Darby*, 312 U.S., at 114. Second, Congress is empowered to regulate and protect the instrumentalities of interstate commerce, or persons or things in interstate commerce, even though the threat may come only from intrastate activities. *See, e.g., Shreveport Rate Cases*, 234 U.S. 342 (1914). Finally, Congress' commerce authority includes the power to regulate those activities having a substantial relation to interstate commerce, *Jones & Laughlin Steel*, 301 U.S., at 37, *i.e.*, those activities that substantially affect interstate commerce. *Wirtz, supra*, at 196, n.27.

Within this final category, admittedly, our case law has not been clear whether an activity must "affect" or "substantially affect" interstate commerce in order to be within Congress' power to regulate it under the Commerce Clause. *Compare Preseault v. ICC*, 494 U.S. 1,

17 (1990), with *Wirtz, supra*, at 196, n. 27. We conclude, consistent with the great weight of our case law, that the proper test requires an analysis of whether the regulated activity "substantially affects" interstate commerce.

We now turn to consider the power of Congress, in the light of this framework, to enact § 922(q). The first two categories of authority may be quickly disposed of: § 922(q) is not a regulation of the use of the channels of interstate commerce, nor is it an attempt to prohibit the interstate transportation of a commodity through the channels of commerce; nor can § 922(q) be justified as a regulation by which Congress has sought to protect an instrumentality of interstate commerce or a thing in interstate commerce. Thus, if § 922(q) is to be sustained, it must be under the third category as a regulation of an activity that substantially affects interstate commerce.

First, we have upheld a wide variety of congressional Acts regulating intrastate economic activity where we have concluded that the activity substantially affected interstate commerce. Examples include the regulation of intrastate coal mining, intrastate extortionate credit transactions, restaurants utilizing substantial interstate supplies, and hotels catering to interstate guests, and production and consumption of home-grown wheat. These examples are by no means exhaustive, but the pattern is clear. Where economic activity substantially affects interstate commerce, legislation regulating that activity will be sustained.

Even *Wickard*, which is perhaps the most far reaching example of Commerce Clause authority over intrastate activity, involved economic activity in a way that the possession of a gun in a school zone does not. . . .

Section 922(q) is a criminal statute that by its terms has nothing to do with "commerce" or any sort of economic enterprise, however broadly one might define those terms.[3] Section 922(q) is not an essential part of a larger regulation of economic activity, in which the regulatory scheme could be undercut unless the intrastate activity were regulated. It cannot, therefore, be sustained under our cases upholding regulations of activities that arise out of or are connected with a commercial transaction, which viewed in the aggregate, substantially affects interstate commerce.

Second, § 922(q) contains no jurisdictional element which would ensure, through case-by-case inquiry, that the firearm possession in question affects interstate commerce. For ex-

---

[3] Under our federal system, the "'States possess primary authority for defining and enforcing the criminal law.'" Brecht v. Abrahamson, 113 S.Ct. 1710, 1720 (1993) (quoting Engle v. Isaac, 456 U.S. 107, 128 (1982)).

ample, in *United States v. Bass*, 404 U.S. 336 (1971), the Court interpreted former 18 U.S.C. § 1202(a), which made it a crime for a felon to "receiv[e], posses[s], or transpor[t] in commerce or affecting commerce . . . any firearm." 404 U.S., at 337. The Court interpreted the possession component of § 1202(a) to require an additional nexus to interstate commerce both because the statute was ambiguous and because "unless Congress conveys its purpose clearly, it will not be deemed to have significantly changed the federal-state balance." *Id.*, at 349. The *Bass* Court set aside the conviction because although the Government had demonstrated that Bass had possessed a firearm, it had failed "to show the requisite nexus with interstate commerce." *Id.*, at 347. The Court thus interpreted the statute to reserve the constitutional question whether Congress could regulate, without more, the "mere possession" of firearms. *See id.*, at 339, n.4. Unlike the statute in *Bass*, § 922(q) has no express jurisdictional element which might limit its reach to a discrete set of firearm possessions that additionally have an explicit connection with or effect on interstate commerce.

Although as part of our independent evaluation of constitutionality under the Commerce Clause we of course consider legislative findings, and indeed even congressional committee findings, regarding effect on interstate commerce, *see, e.g., Preseault v.* ICC, 494 U.S. 1, 17 (1990), the Government concedes that "[n]either the statute nor its legislative history contain[s] express congressional findings regarding the effects upon interstate commerce of gun possession in a school zone." We agree with the Government that Congress normally is not required to make formal findings as to the substantial burdens that an activity has on interstate commerce. *See* McClung, 379 U.S., at 304. But to the extent that congressional findings would enable us to evaluate the legislative judgment that the activity in question substantially affected interstate commerce, even though no such substantial effect was visible to the naked eye, they are lacking here.[4]

The Government argues that Congress has accumulated institutional expertise regarding the regulation of firearms through previous enactments. *Cf. Fullilove v. Klutznick,*

[4] We note that on September 13, 1994, President Clinton signed into law the Violent Crime Control and Law Enforcement Act of 1994, Pub.L. 103–322, 108 Stat. 1796. Section 320904 of that Act, *id.*, at 2125, amends § 922(q) to include congressional findings regarding the effects of firearm possession in and around schools upon interstate and foreign commerce. The Government does not rely upon these subsequent findings as a substitute for the absence of findings in the first instance.

448 U.S. 448, 503 (1980) (Powell, J., concurring). We agree, however, with the Fifth Circuit that importation of previous findings to justify § 922(q) is especially inappropriate here because the "prior federal enactments or Congressional findings [do not] speak to the subject matter of section 922(q) or its relationship to interstate commerce. Indeed, section 922(q) plows thoroughly new ground and represents a sharp break with the long-standing pattern of federal firearms legislation." 2 F.3d, at 1366.

The Government's essential contention, in fine, is that we may determine here that § 922(q) is valid because possession of a firearm in a local school zone does indeed substantially affect interstate commerce. The Government argues that possession of a firearm in a school zone may result in violent crime and that violent crime can be expected to affect the functioning of the national economy in two ways. First, the costs of violent crime are substantial, and, through the mechanism of insurance, those costs are spread throughout the population. *See United States v. Evans*, 928 F.2d 858, 862 (CA9 1991). Second, violent crime reduces the willingness of individuals to travel to areas within the country that are perceived to be unsafe. *Cf. Heart of Atlanta Motel*, 379 U.S., at 253. The Government also argues that the presence of guns in schools poses a substantial threat to the educational process by threatening the learning environment. A handicapped educational process, in turn, will result in a less productive citizenry. That, in turn, would have an adverse effect on the Nation's economic well-being. As a result, the Government argues that Congress could rationally have concluded that § 922(q) substantially affects interstate commerce.

We pause to consider the implications of the Government's arguments. The Government admits, under its "costs of crime" reasoning, that Congress could regulate not only all violent crime, but all activities that might lead to violent crime, regardless of how tenuously they relate to interstate commerce. Similarly, under the Government's "national productivity" reasoning, Congress could regulate any activity that it found was related to the economic productivity of individual citizens: family law (including marriage, divorce, and child custody), for example. Under the theories that the Government presents in support of § 922(q), it is difficult to perceive any limitation on federal power, even in areas such as criminal law enforcement or education where States historically have been sovereign. Thus, if we were to accept the Government's arguments, we are hard-pressed to posit any activity by an individual that Congress is without power to regulate.

Although Justice BREYER argues that acceptance of the Government's rationales would not authorize a general federal police power, he is unable to identify any activity that the States may regulate but Congress may not. . . .

[I]f Congress can, pursuant to its Commerce Clause power, regulate activities that adversely affect the learning environment, then, a fortiori, it also can regulate the educational process directly. Congress could determine that a school's curriculum has a "significant" effect on the extent of classroom learning. As a result, Congress could mandate a federal curriculum for local elementary and secondary schools because what is taught in local schools has a significant "effect on classroom learning," and that, in turn, has a substantial effect on interstate commerce.

Justice BREYER rejects our reading of precedent and argues that "Congress . . . could rationally conclude that schools fall on the commercial side of the line." Again, Justice BREYER'S rationale lacks any real limits because, depending on the level of generality, any activity can be looked upon as commercial. . . .

[A] determination whether an intrastate activity is commercial or noncommercial may in some cases result in legal uncertainty. But, so long as Congress' authority is limited to those powers enumerated in the Constitution, and so long as those enumerated powers are interpreted as having judicially enforceable outer limits, congressional legislation under the Commerce Clause always will engender "legal uncertainty." . . . The Constitution mandates this uncertainty by withholding from Congress a plenary police power that would authorize enactment of every type of legislation. *See* U.S. Const., Art. I, § 8. Congress has operated within this framework of legal uncertainty ever since this Court determined that it was the judiciary's duty "to say what the law is." *Marbury v. Madison*, 1 Cranch. 137, 177, 2 L.Ed. 60 (1803) (Marshall, C.J.). Any possible benefit from eliminating this "legal uncertainty" would be at the expense of the Constitution's system of enumerated powers.

[The] possession of a gun in a local school zone is in no sense an economic activity that might, through repetition elsewhere, substantially affect any sort of interstate commerce. Respondent was a local student at a local school; there is no indication that he had recently moved in interstate commerce, and there is no requirement that his possession of the firearm have any concrete tie to interstate commerce.

To uphold the Government's contentions here, we would have to pile inference upon inference in a manner that would bid fair to convert congressional authority under the Commerce Clause to a general police power of the sort retained by the States. Admittedly, some of our prior cases have taken long steps down that road, giving great deference to congressional action. The broad language in these opinions has suggested the possibility of additional expansion, but we decline here to proceed any further. To do so would require us to conclude that the Constitution's enumeration of powers does not presuppose something not enumerated, *cf. Gibbons v. Ogden, supra,* at 195, and that there never will be a distinction between what is truly national and what is truly local, *cf. Jones & Laughlin Steel, supra,* at 30. This we are unwilling to do.

For the foregoing reasons the judgment of the Court of Appeals is
Affirmed.

Justice KENNEDY, with whom Justice O'CONNOR joins, concurring.

. . .

The statute before us upsets the federal balance to a degree that renders it an unconstitutional assertion of the commerce power, and our intervention is required. As THE CHIEF JUSTICE explains, unlike the earlier cases to come before the Court here neither the actors nor their conduct have a commercial character, and neither the purposes nor the design of the statute have an evident commercial nexus. The statute makes the simple possession of a gun within 1,000 feet of the grounds of the school a criminal offense. In a sense any conduct in this interdependent world of ours has an ultimate commercial origin or consequence, but we have not yet said the commerce power may reach so far. If Congress attempts that extension, then at the least we must inquire whether the exercise of national power seeks to intrude upon an area of traditional state concern.

An interference of these dimensions occurs here, for it is well established that education is a traditional concern of the States. *Milliken v. Bradley*, 418 U.S. 717, 741–742 (1974). The proximity to schools, including of course schools owned and operated by the States or their subdivisions, is the very premise for making the conduct criminal. In these circumstances, we have a particular duty to insure that the federal-state balance is not destroyed.

While it is doubtful that any State, or indeed any reasonable person, would argue that it is wise policy to allow students to carry guns on school premises, considerable disagreement exists about how best to accomplish that goal. In this circumstance, the theory and utility of our federalism are revealed, for the States may perform their role as laboratories for experimentation to devise various solutions where the best solution is far from clear. . . .

If a State or municipality determines that harsh criminal sanctions are necessary and wise to deter students from carrying guns on school premises, the reserved powers of the States are sufficient to enact those measures.

Indeed, over 40 States already have criminal laws outlawing the possession of firearms on or near school grounds. *See, e.g.*, Alaska Stat.-Ann. §§ 11.61.195(a)(2)(A), 11.61.220(a)(4)(A) (Supp.1994).

Other, more practicable means to rid the schools of guns may be thought by the citizens of some States to be preferable for the safety and welfare of the schools those States are charged with maintaining. These might include inducements to inform on violators where the information leads to arrests or confiscation of the guns, programs to encourage the voluntary surrender of guns with some provision for amnesty, penalties imposed on parents or guardians for failure to supervise the child, laws providing for suspension or expulsion of gun-toting students, or programs for expulsion with assignment to special facilities.

The statute now before us forecloses the States from experimenting and exercising their own judgment in an area to which States lay claim by right of history and expertise, and it does so by regulating an activity beyond the realm of commerce in the ordinary and usual sense of that term. . . .

Justice THOMAS, concurring.

[I] write separately to observe that our case law has drifted far from the original understanding of the Commerce Clause. In a future case, we ought to temper our Commerce Clause jurisprudence in a manner that both makes sense of our more recent case law and is more faithful to the original understanding of that Clause.

We have said that Congress may regulate not only "Commerce . . . among the several states," U.S. Const., Art. I, § 8, cl. 3, but also anything that has a "substantial effect" on such commerce. This test, if taken to its logical extreme, would give Congress a "police power" over all aspects of American life. Unfortunately, we have never come to grips with this implication of our substantial effects formula. Although we have supposedly applied the substantial effects test for the past 60 years, we always have rejected readings of the Commerce Clause and the scope of federal power that would permit Congress to exercise a police power; our cases are quite clear that there are real limits to federal power. *See New York v. United States*, 112 S.Ct. 2408, 2417 (1992). . . .

In an appropriate case, I believe that we must further reconsider our "substantial effects" test with an eye toward constructing a standard that reflects the text and history of the Commerce Clause without totally rejecting our more recent Commerce Clause jurisprudence.

[My] goal is simply to show how far we have departed from the original understanding and to demonstrate that the result we reach today is by no means "radical." I also want to point out the necessity of refashioning a coherent test that does not tend to "obliterate the distinction between what is national and what is local and create a completely centralized government." *Jones & Laughlin Steel Corp., supra*, at 37.

I

At the time the original Constitution was ratified, "commerce" consisted of selling, buying, and bartering, as well as transporting for these purposes. *See* 1 S. Johnson, A Dictionary of the English Language 361 (4th ed. 1773). In fact, when Federalists and Anti-Federalists discussed the Commerce Clause during the ratification period, they often used trade (in its selling/bartering sense) and commerce interchangeably.

As one would expect, the term "commerce" was used in contradistinction to productive activities such as manufacturing and agriculture. . . .

[I]nterjecting a modern sense of commerce into the Constitution generates significant textual and structural problems. For example, one cannot replace "commerce" with a different type of enterprise, such as manufacturing. When a manufacturer produces a car, assembly cannot take place "with a foreign nation" or "with the Indian Tribes." Parts may come from different States or other nations and hence may have been in the flow of commerce at one time, but manufacturing takes place at a discrete site. Agriculture and manufacturing involve the production of goods; commerce encompasses traffic in such articles.

. . .

The Constitution not only uses the word "commerce" in a narrower sense than our case law might suggest, it also does not support the proposition that Congress has authority over all activities that "substantially affect" interstate commerce. The Commerce Clause does not state that Congress may "regulate matters that substantially affect commerce with foreign Nations, and among the several States, and with the Indian Tribes." In contrast, the Constitution itself temporarily prohibited amendments that would "affect" Congress' lack of authority to prohibit or restrict the slave trade or to enact unproportioned direct taxation. U.S. Const., Art. V. Clearly, the Framers could have drafted a Constitution that contained a "substantially affects interstate commerce" clause had that been their objective.

In addition to its powers under the Commerce Clause, Congress has the authority to enact such laws as are "necessary and proper" to carry into execution its power to regulate commerce among the several States. U.S. Const., Art. I, § 8, cl. 18. But on this Court's understanding of congressional power under these two Clauses, many of Congress' other enumerated powers under Art. I, § 8 are wholly superfluous. After all, if Congress may regulate all matters that substantially affect commerce, there is no need for the Constitution to specify that Congress may enact bankruptcy laws, or coin money and fix the standard of weights and measures, or punish counterfeiters of United States coin and securities. Likewise, Congress would not need the separate authority to establish post offices and post roads, or to grant patents and copyrights, or to "punish Piracies and Felonies committed on the high Seas." It might not even need the power to raise and support an Army and Navy, for fewer people would engage in commercial shipping if they thought that a foreign power could expropriate their property with ease. Indeed, if Congress could regulate matters that substantially affect interstate commerce, there would have been no need to specify that Congress can regulate international trade and commerce with the Indians. As the Framers surely understood, these other branches of trade substantially affect interstate commerce.

Put simply, much if not all of Art. I, § 8 (including portions of the Commerce Clause itself) would be surplusage if Congress had been given authority over matters that substantially affect interstate commerce. An interpretation of cl. 3 that makes the rest of § 8 superfluous simply cannot be correct. Yet this Court's Commerce Clause jurisprudence has endorsed just such an interpretation: the power we have accorded Congress has swallowed Art. I, § 8.

[Our] construction of the scope of congressional authority has the additional problem of coming close to turning the Tenth Amendment on its head. . . .

II

[The] comments of Hamilton and others about federal power reflected the well-known truth that the new Government would have only the limited and enumerated powers found in the Constitution. *See, e.g.,* 2 Debates 267–268 (A. Hamilton at New York convention); The Federalist No. 45, at 313 (J. Madison). Agriculture and manufacture, since they were not surrendered to the Federal Government, were state concerns. Even before the passage of the Tenth Amendment, it was apparent that Congress would possess only those powers "herein granted" by the rest of the Constitution. U.S. Const., Art. I, § 1.

Where the Constitution was meant to grant federal authority over an activity substantially affecting interstate commerce, the Constitution contains an enumerated power over that particular activity. . . .

In short, the Founding Fathers were well aware of what the principal dissent calls " 'economic . . . realities.' " Even though the boundary between commerce and other matters may ignore "economic reality" and thus seem arbitrary or artificial to some, we must nevertheless respect a constitutional line that does not grant Congress power over all that substantially affects interstate commerce.

III

. . .

A

. . . From an early moment, the Court rejected the notion that Congress can regulate everything that affects interstate commerce. That the internal commerce of the States and the numerous state inspection, quarantine, and health laws had substantial effects on interstate commerce cannot be doubted. Nevertheless, they were not "surrendered to the general government."

Of course, the principal dissent is not the first to misconstrue *Gibbons*. For instance, the Court has stated that *Gibbons* "described the federal commerce power with a breadth never yet exceeded." *Wickard v. Filburn*, 317 U.S. 111, 120 (1942). I believe that this misreading stems from two statements in *Gibbons*.

. . .

B

I am aware of no cases prior to the New Deal that characterized the power flowing from the Commerce Clause as sweepingly as does our substantial effects test. My review of the case law indicates that the substantial effects test is but an innovation of the 20th century.

[As] recently as 1936, the Court continued to insist that the Commerce Clause did not reach the wholly internal business of the States. The Federal Government simply could not reach such subjects regardless of their effects on interstate commerce.

These cases all establish a simple point: from the time of the ratification of the Constitution to the mid-1930's, it was widely understood that the Constitution granted Congress only limited powers, notwithstanding the Commerce Clause. Moreover, there was no question that activities wholly separated from business, such as gun possession, were beyond the reach of the commerce power. If anything, the "wrong turn" was the Court's dramatic departure in the 1930's from a century and a half of precedent.

IV

[T]he substantial effects test suffers from the further flaw that it appears to grant Congress a police power over the Nation. When asked at oral argument if there were any limits to the Commerce Clause, the Government was at a loss for words. Likewise, the principal dissent insists that there are limits, but it cannot muster even one example. Indeed, the dissent implicitly concedes that its reading has no limits when it criticizes the Court for "threaten[ing] legal uncertainty in an area of law that . . . seemed reasonably well settled." The one advantage of the dissent's standard is certainty: it is certain that under its analysis everything may be regulated under the guise of the Commerce Clause.

The substantial effects test suffers from this flaw, in part, because of its "aggregation principle." . . .

The aggregation principle is clever, but has no stopping point. Suppose all would agree that gun possession within 1,000 feet of a school does not substantially affect commerce, but that possession of weapons generally (knives, brass knuckles, nunchakus, etc.) does. Under our substantial effects doctrine, even though Congress cannot single out gun possession, it can prohibit weapon possession generally. But one always can draw the circle broadly enough to cover an activity that, when taken in isolation, would not have substantial effects on commerce. Under our jurisprudence, if Congress passed an omnibus "substantially affects interstate commerce" statute, purporting to regulate every aspect of human existence, the Act apparently would be constitutional. Even though particular sections may govern only trivial activities, the statute in the aggregate regulates matters that substantially affect commerce.

V

This extended discussion of the original understanding and our first century and a half of case law does not necessarily require a wholesale abandonment of our more recent opinions. It simply reveals that our substantial effects test is far removed from both the Constitution and from our early case law and that the Court's opinion should not be viewed as "radical" or another "wrong turn" that must be corrected in the future. The analysis also suggests that we ought to temper our Commerce Clause jurisprudence.

Unless the dissenting Justices are willing to repudiate our long-held understanding of the limited nature of federal power, I would think that they too must be willing to reconsider the substantial effects test in a future case. If we wish to be true to a Constitution that does not cede a police power to the Federal Government, our Commerce Clause's boundaries simply cannot be "defined" as being "'commensurate with the national needs'" or self-

consciously intended to let the Federal Government "'defend itself against economic forces that Congress decrees inimical or destructive of the national economy.'" See post, at 1662–1663 (BREYER, J., dissenting) (quoting North American Co. v. SEC, 327 U.S. 686, 705 (1946)). Such a formulation of federal power is no test at all: it is a blank check.

At an appropriate juncture, I think we must modify our Commerce Clause jurisprudence. Today, it is easy enough to say that the Clause certainly does not empower Congress to ban gun possession within 1,000 feet of a school.

Justice STEVENS, dissenting.

The welfare of our future "Commerce with foreign Nations, and among the several States," U.S. Const., Art. I, § 8, cl. 3, is vitally dependent on the character of the education of our children. . . .

Guns are both articles of commerce and articles that can be used to restrain commerce. Their possession is the consequence, either directly or indirectly, of commercial activity. In my judgment, Congress' power to regulate commerce in firearms includes the power to prohibit possession of guns at any location because of their potentially harmful use; it necessarily follows that Congress may also prohibit their possession in particular markets. The market for the possession of handguns by school-age children is, distressingly, substantial. Whether or not the national interest in eliminating that market would have justified federal legislation in 1789, it surely does today.

Justice SOUTER, dissenting.

[The] practice of deferring to rationally based legislative judgments "is a paradigm of judicial restraint." FCC v. Beach Communications, Inc., 113 S.Ct. 2096, 2101 (1993). In judicial review under the Commerce Clause, it reflects our respect for the institutional competence of the Congress on a subject expressly assigned to it by the Constitution and our appreciation of the legitimacy that comes from Congress's political accountability in dealing with matters open to a wide range of possible choices. See id., at 2101–2102.

It was not ever thus, however, as even a brief overview of Commerce Clause history during the past century reminds us. The modern respect for the competence and primacy of Congress in matters affecting commerce developed only after one of this Court's most chastening experiences, when it perforce repudiated an earlier and untenably expansive conception of judicial review in derogation of congressional commerce power. A look at history's sequence will serve to show how today's decision tugs the Court off course, leading it to suggest opportunities for further developments that would be at odds with the rule of restraint to which the Court still wisely states adherence.

I

[T]he period from the turn of the century to 1937 is better noted for a series of cases applying highly formalistic notions of "commerce" to invalidate federal social and economic legislation. . . .

These restrictive views of commerce subject to congressional power complemented the Court's activism in limiting the enforceable scope of state economic regulation. It is most familiar history that during this same period the Court routinely invalidated state social and economic legislation under an expansive conception of Fourteenth Amendment substantive due process. The fulcrums of judicial review in these cases were the notions of liberty and property characteristic of laissez-faire economics, whereas the Commerce Clause cases turned on what was ostensibly a structural limit of federal power, but under each conception of judicial review the Court's character for the first third of the century showed itself in exacting judicial scrutiny of a legislature's choice of economic ends and of the legislative means selected to reach them.

It was not merely coincidental, then, that sea changes in the Court's conceptions of its authority under the Due Process and Commerce Clauses occurred virtually together, in 1937. . . .

In the years following these decisions, deference to legislative policy judgments on commercial regulation became the powerful theme under both the Due Process and Commerce Clauses, and in due course that deference became articulate in the standard of rationality review. . . .

II

There is today, however, a backward glance at both the old pitfalls, as the Court treats deference under the rationality rule as subject to gradation according to the commercial or noncommercial nature of the immediate subject of the challenged regulation. The distinction between what is patently commercial and what is not looks much like the old distinction between what directly affects commerce and what touches it only indirectly. And the act of calibrating the level of deference by drawing a line between what is patently commercial and what is less purely so will probably resemble the process of deciding how much interference with contractual freedom was fatal. Thus, it seems fair to ask whether the step taken by the Court today does anything but portend a return to the untenable jurisprudence from which the Court extricated itself almost 60 years ago. The answer is not reassur-

ing. To be sure, the occasion for today's decision reflects the century's end, not its beginning. But if it seems anomalous that the Congress of the United States has taken to regulating school yards, the act in question is still probably no more remarkable than state regulation of bake shops 90 years ago. In any event, there is no reason to hope that the Court's qualification of rational basis review will be any more successful than the efforts at substantive economic review made by our predecessors as the century began. Taking the Court's opinion on its own terms, Justice BREYER has explained both the hopeless porosity of "commercial" character as a ground of Commerce Clause distinction in America's highly connected economy, and the inconsistency of this categorization with our rational basis precedents from the last 50 years.

Further glosses on rationality review, moreover, may be in the offing. Although this case turns on commercial character, the Court gestures toward two other considerations that it might sometime entertain in applying rational basis scrutiny (apart from a statutory obligation to supply independent proof of a jurisdictional element): does the congressional statute deal with subjects of traditional state regulation, and does the statute contain explicit factual findings supporting the otherwise implicit determination that the regulated activity substantially affects interstate commerce? Once again, any appeal these considerations may have depends on ignoring the painful lesson learned in 1937, for neither of the Court's suggestions would square with rational basis scrutiny.

A

The Court observes that the Gun-Free School Zones Act operates in two areas traditionally subject to legislation by the States, education and enforcement of criminal law. The suggestion is either that a connection between commerce and these subjects is remote, or that the commerce power is simply weaker when it touches subjects on which the States have historically been the primary legislators. Neither suggestion is tenable. As for remoteness, it may or may not be wise for the National Government to deal with education, but Justice BREYER has surely demonstrated that the commercial prospects of an illiterate State or Nation are not rosy, and no argument should be needed to show that hijacking interstate shipments of cigarettes can affect commerce substantially, even though the States have traditionally prosecuted robbery. And as for the notion that the commerce power diminishes the closer it gets to customary state concerns, that idea has been flatly rejected, and not long ago. The commerce power, we have often observed, is plenary . . . .

B

There remain questions about legislative findings. The Court of Appeals expressed the view that the result in this case might well have been different if Congress had made explicit findings that guns in schools have a substantial effect on interstate commerce, and the Court today does not repudiate that position. Might a court aided by such findings have subjected this legislation to less exacting scrutiny (or, put another way, should a court have deferred to such findings if Congress had made them)? The answer to either question must be no, although as a general matter findings are important and to be hoped for in the difficult cases.

. . .

III

Because Justice BREYER's opinion demonstrates beyond any doubt that the Act in question passes the rationality review that the Court continues to espouse, today's decision may be seen as only a misstep, its reasoning and its suggestions not quite in gear with the prevailing standard, but hardly an epochal case. I would not argue otherwise, but I would raise a caveat. Not every epochal case has come in epochal trappings. *Jones & Laughlin* did not reject the direct-indirect standard in so many words; it just said the relation of the regulated subject matter to commerce was direct enough. But we know what happened.

I respectfully dissent.

Justice BREYER, with whom Justice STEVENS, Justice SOUTER, and Justice GINSBURG join, dissenting.

. . .

[W]e must ask whether Congress could have had a rational basis for finding a significant (or substantial) connection between gun-related school violence and interstate commerce. . . . As long as one views the commerce connection, not as a "technical legal conception," but as "a practical one," *Swift & Co. v. United States*, 196 U.S. 375, 398 (1905) (Holmes, J.), the answer to this question must be yes. Numerous reports and studies—generated both inside and outside government—make clear that Congress could reasonably have found the empirical connection that its law, implicitly or explicitly, asserts.

For one thing, reports, hearings, and other readily available literature make clear that the problem of guns in and around schools is widespread and extremely serious. These materials report, for example, that four percent of American high school students (and six percent of inner-city high school students) carry a gun to school at least occasionally, Centers for Disease Control 2342; that 12 percent of urban high school students have had guns fired at them; that 20 percent of those students have been threatened with guns; and that, in any 6-month period, several hundred thousand schoolchildren are victims of violent crimes in or near their schools. And, they report that this widespread violence in schools throughout the Nation significantly interferes with the quality of education in those schools. *See, e.g.*, House Judiciary Committee Hearing 44 (1990); U.S. Dept. of Health 118–119 (1978). Based on reports such as these, Congress obviously could have thought that guns and learning are mutually exclusive. Senate Labor and Human Resources Committee Hearing 39 (1993). And, Congress could therefore have found a substantial educational problem—teachers unable to teach, students unable to learn—and concluded that guns near schools contribute substantially to the size and scope of that problem.

Having found that guns in schools significantly undermine the quality of education in our Nation's classrooms, Congress could also have found, given the effect of education upon interstate and foreign commerce, that gun-related violence in and around schools is a commercial, as well as a human, problem. Education, although far more than a matter of economics, has long been inextricably intertwined with the Nation's economy. . . . Scholars estimate that nearly a quarter of America's economic growth in the early years of this century is traceable directly to increased schooling; that investment in "human capital" (through spending on education) exceeded investment in "physical capital" by a ratio of almost two to one; and that the economic returns to this investment in education exceeded the returns to conventional capital investment.

In recent years the link between secondary education and business has strengthened, becoming both more direct and more important. Scholars on the subject report that technological changes and innovations in management techniques have altered the nature of the workplace so that more jobs now demand greater educational skills. . . .

Increasing global competition also has made primary and secondary education economically more important. . . . Congress has said, when writing other statutes, that "functionally or technologically illiterate" Americans in the work force "erod[e]" our economic "standing in the international marketplace," Pub.L. 100–418, § 6002(a)(3), 102 Stat. 1469, and that "our Nation is . . . paying the price of scientific and technological illiteracy, with our productivity declining, our industrial base ailing, and our global competitiveness dwindling." H.R.Rep. No. 98–6, pt. 1, p. 19 (1983).

Finally, there is evidence that, today more

than ever, many firms base their location decisions upon the presence, or absence, of a work force with a basic education. . . .

The economic links I have just sketched seem fairly obvious. Why then is it not equally obvious, in light of those links, that a widespread, serious, and substantial physical threat to teaching and learning also substantially threatens the commerce to which that teaching and learning is inextricably tied? That is to say, guns in the hands of six percent of inner-city high school students and gun-related violence throughout a city's schools must threaten the trade and commerce that those schools support. The only question, then, is whether the latter threat is (to use the majority's terminology) "substantial." And, the evidence of (1) the extent of the gun-related violence problem, (2) the extent of the resulting negative effect on classroom learning, and (3) the extent of the consequent negative commercial effects, when taken together, indicate a threat to trade and commerce that is "substantial." At the very least, Congress could rationally have concluded that the links are "substantial."

Specifically, Congress could have found that gun-related violence near the classroom poses a serious economic threat (1) to consequently inadequately educated workers who must endure low paying jobs, and (2) to communities and businesses that might (in today's "information society") otherwise gain, from a well-educated work force, an important commercial advantage of a kind that location near a railhead or harbor provided in the past. Congress might also have found these threats to be no different in kind from other threats that this Court has found within the commerce power, such as the threat that loan sharking poses to the "funds" of "numerous localities," *Perez v. United States*, 402 U.S., at 157, and that unfair labor practices pose to instrumentalities of commerce. As I have pointed out, Congress has written that "the occurrence of violent crime in school zones" has brought about a "decline in the quality of education" that "has an adverse impact on interstate commerce and the foreign commerce of the United States." 18 U.S.C.A. §§ 922(q)(1)(F), (G) (Nov.1994 Supp.). The violence-related facts, the educational facts, and the economic facts, taken together, make this conclusion rational. And, because under our case law, the sufficiency of the constitutionally necessary Commerce Clause link between a crime of violence and interstate commerce turns simply upon size or degree, those same facts make the statute constitutional.

To hold this statute constitutional is not to "obliterate" the "distinction of what is national and what is local," *ante*, at 1633; nor is it to hold

that the Commerce Clause permits the Federal Government to "regulate any activity that it found was related to the economic productivity of individual citizens," to regulate "marriage, divorce, and child custody," or to regulate any and all aspects of education. . . .

In sum, a holding that the particular statute before us falls within the commerce power would not expand the scope of that Clause. Rather, it simply would apply preexisting law to changing economic circumstances. It would recognize that, in today's economic world, gun-related violence near the classroom makes a significant difference to our economic, as well as our social, well-being. In accordance with well-accepted precedent, such a holding would permit Congress "to act in terms of economic . . . realities," would interpret the commerce power as "an affirmative power commensurate with the national needs," and would acknowledge that the "commerce clause does not operate so as to render the nation powerless to defend itself against economic forces that Congress decrees inimical or destructive of the national economy." *North American Co. v. SEC*, 327 U.S. 686, 705 (1946).

III

The majority's holding—that § 922 falls outside the scope of the Commerce Clause—creates three serious legal problems. First, the majority's holding runs contrary to modern Supreme Court cases that have upheld congressional actions despite connections to interstate or foreign commerce that are less significant than the effect of school violence. . . .

The second legal problem the Court creates comes from its apparent belief that it can reconcile its holding with earlier cases by making a critical distinction between "commercial" and noncommercial "transaction[s]." That is to say, the Court believes the Constitution would distinguish between two local activities, each of which has an identical effect upon interstate commerce, if one, but not the other, is "commercial" in nature. As a general matter, this approach fails to heed this Court's earlier warning not to turn "questions of the power of Congress" upon "formula[s]" that would give "controlling force to nomenclature such as 'production' and 'indirect' and foreclose consideration of the actual effects of the activity in question upon interstate commerce." *Wickard, supra*, 317 U.S., at 120. . . .

More importantly, if a distinction between commercial and noncommercial activities is to be made, this is not the case in which to make it. The majority clearly cannot intend such a distinction to focus narrowly on an act of gun possession standing by itself, for such a reading could not be reconciled with either the civil rights cases or *Perez*—in each of those cases the specific transaction (the race-based exclusion, the use of force) was not itself "commercial." And, if the majority instead means to distinguish generally among broad categories of activities, differentiating what is educational from what is commercial, then, as a practical matter, the line becomes almost impossible to draw. Schools that teach reading, writing, mathematics, and related basic skills serve both social and commercial purposes, and one cannot easily separate the one from the other. American industry itself has been, and is again, involved in teaching. When, and to what extent, does its involvement make education commercial? Does the number of vocational classes that train students directly for jobs make a difference? Does it matter if the school is public or private, nonprofit or profit-seeking? Does it matter if a city or State adopts a voucher plan that pays private firms to run a school? Even if one were to ignore these practical questions, why should there be a theoretical distinction between education, when it significantly benefits commerce, and environmental pollution, when it causes economic harm? *See Hodel v. Virginia Surface Mining & Reclamation Assn., Inc.*, 452 U.S. 264 (1981).

Regardless, if there is a principled distinction that could work both here and in future cases, Congress (even in the absence of vocational classes, industry involvement, and private management) could rationally conclude that schools fall on the commercial side of the line. . . .

The third legal problem created by the Court's holding is that it threatens legal uncertainty in an area of law that, until this case, seemed reasonably well settled. Congress has enacted many statutes (more than 100 sections of the United States Code), including criminal statutes, that use the words "affecting commerce" to define their scope, and other statutes that contain no jurisdictional language at all, *see, e.g.*, 18 U.S.C. § 922(o)(1). Do these, or similar, statutes regulate noncommercial activities? If so, would that alter the meaning of "affecting commerce" in a jurisdictional element? More importantly, in the absence of a jurisdictional element, are the courts nevertheless to take *Wickard*, 317 U.S., at 127–128 (and later similar cases) as inapplicable, and to judge the effect of a single noncommercial activity on interstate commerce without considering similar instances of the forbidden conduct? However these questions are eventually resolved, the legal uncertainty now created will restrict Congress' ability to enact criminal laws aimed at criminal behavior that, considered problem by problem rather than instance by instance, seriously threatens the economic, as well as social, well-being of Americans.

. . .

Does *Lopez* overturn *Hodel, Heart of Atlanta, Katzenbach* and *Perez*, and return commerce clause jurisprudence to that of the pre-Switch era? Or does it do something less? Is *Lopez* simply a "shot across Congress' bow?" Do you agree with Justice Thomas that a more radical restructuring of the Court's commerce clause jurisprudence is necessary?

B. State Power to Regulate

Do the states also have the power to regulate commerce? As we saw in the last chapter, during the first third of this century, the Supreme Court construed the Tenth Amendment as giving the states a reserved power over "purely local" commerce. Although Congress controlled commerce "among" the states, it was precluded from violating the states' reserved power. Following the Switch of 1937, the distinction between "local" commerce and commerce "among" the states began to disappear. Under decisions like *Wickard* and *Perez*, the federal government assumed much broader authority over both interstate and local commerce. Moreover, the Court began to treat the Tenth Amendment as a truism thereby depriving states of their reserved power over commerce.

In the post-Switch era, the federal courts have faced quite different questions regarding the scope of state power. Most post-Switch cases involve "dormant" power situations—situations in which the federal government has the power to regulate a subject, but has not done so (or has done so incompletely). In these dormant power situations, does the commerce clause contain negative implications for state power which preclude states from regulating? In other words, is the federal commerce power "exclusive" so that the states are precluded from regulating an area within federal authority even in the absence of federal regulation? Or do the states have "concurrent" jurisdiction so that they are also free to regulate? If concurrent power exists, what limits apply to state power?

The Constitution provides little guidance on these issues. Article I, § 8, explicitly gives Congress the power to regulate commerce "among" the several states, but the Constitution does not say whether the states can also regulate commerce. That issue was left to the courts.

1. Early Cases

Several early Supreme Court decisions discussed whether the federal government's authority over commerce was exclusive or concurrent.

Gibbons v. Ogden
22 U.S. 1 (1824)

[In this case, the Court held that Congress' authority over commerce allowed it to license a steamboat which travels between New York and New Jersey. The Court struck down an exclusive license that New York had issued on supremacy clause grounds. The Court did not resolve the question of whether, in the absence of a conflict between the state and federal license, the state was free to regulate and license navigation. The Court did make the following statements in dicta.]

Mr. Chief Justice MARSHALL delivered the opinion of the Court, and, after stating the case, proceeded as follows:

. . .

[I]t has been urged with great earnestness, that, although the power of Congress to regulate commerce with foreign nations, and among the several States, be co-extensive with the subject itself, and have no other limits than are prescribed in the constitution, yet the States may severally exercise the same power, within their respective jurisdictions. In support of this argument, it is said, that they possessed it as an inseparable attribute of sovereignty, before the formation of the constitution, and still retain it, except so far as they have surrendered it by that instrument; that this principle results from the nature of the government, and is secured by the tenth amendment; that an affirmative grant of power is not exclusive, unless in its own nature it be such that the continued exercise of it by the former possessor is inconsistent with the grant, and that this is not of that description.

. . .

The grant of the power to lay and collect taxes is, like the power to regulate commerce, made in general terms, and has never been understood to interfere with the exercise of the same power by the State; and hence has been drawn an argument which has been applied to the question under consideration. But the two grants are not, it is conceived, similar in their terms or their nature. Although many of the powers formerly exercised by the States, are transferred to the government of the Union, yet the State governments remain, and constitute a most important part of our system. The power of taxation is indispensable to their existence, and is a power which, in its own nature, is capable of residing in, and being exercised by, different authorities at the same time. . . .

. . .

[I]nspection laws are said to be regulations of commerce, and are certainly recognized in the constitution, as being passed in the exercise of a power remaining with the States.

That inspection laws may have a remote and considerable influence on commerce, will not be denied; but that a power to regulate commerce is the source from which the right to pass them is derived, cannot be admitted. The object of inspection laws, is to improve the quality of articles produced by the labour of a country; to fit them for exportation; or, it may be, for domestic use. They act upon the subject before it becomes an article of foreign commerce, or of commerce among the States, and prepare it for that purpose. They form a portion of that immense mass of legislation, which embraces every thing within the territory of a State, not surrendered to the general government: all which can be most advantageously exercised by the States themselves. Inspection laws, quarantine laws, health laws of every description, as well as laws for regulating the internal commerce of a State, and those which respect turnpike roads, ferries, &c., are component parts of this mass.

No direct general power over these objects is granted to Congress; and, consequently, they remain subject to State legislation. If the legislative power of the Union can reach them, it must be for national purposes; it must be where the power is expressly given for a special purpose, or is clearly incidental to some power which is expressly given. . . .

. . .

It has been contended by the counsel for the appellant, that, as the word "to regulate" implies in its nature, full power over the thing to be regulated, it excludes, necessarily, the action of all others that would perform the same operation on the same thing. That regulation is designed for the entire result, applying to those parts which remain as they were, as well as to those which are altered. It produces a uniform whole, which is as much disturbed and deranged by changing what the regulating power designs to leave untouched, as that on which it has operated.

There is great force in this argument, and the Court is not satisfied that it has been refuted.

. . .

RLW: Note how broadly Chief Justice Marshall conceives the federal government's authority to regulate commerce in *Gibbons*: "the word 'to regulate' implies in its nature, full power over the thing to be regulated, it excludes, necessarily, the action of all others that would perform the same operation on the same thing." If the courts gave this language full effect today, given holdings like *Wickard* and *Perez*, the states would have very little power to regulate commerce. States might not be allowed to pass the inspection laws which Marshall suggested were within the scope of their authority.

Marshall characterizes inspection laws as acting "upon the subject before it becomes an article of foreign commerce, or of commerce among the States, and [to] prepare it for that purpose." As a result, "[i]nspection laws, quarantine laws, health laws of every description, as well as laws for regulating the internal commerce of a State" are within the scope of state authority. "No direct general power over these objects is granted to Congress." In light of later decisions, this statement is probably untrue.

Plumley v. Commonwealth of Massachusetts[29] reinforced the notion that the states retained control over certain internal matters. Plumley was convicted of violating a Massachusetts law prohibiting the sale of adulterated oleomargarine. Following his incarceration, Plumley sought a writ of habeas corpus. The Court, in an opinion written by Mr. Justice Harlan, denied the writ holding that the Massachusetts law did not violate Congress' commerce power:

[Massachusetts] does not prohibit the manufacture or sale of all oleomargarine, but only such as is colored in imitation of yellow butter produced from pure unadulterated milk or cream of such milk. . . . The statute seeks to suppress false pretenses and to promote fair dealing in the sale of an article of food. It compels the sale of oleomargarine for what it really is, by preventing its sale for what it is not.

. . .

If there be any subject over which it would seem the states ought to have plenary control, and the power to legislate in respect to which, it ought not to be supposed, was intended to be surrendered to the general government, it is the protection of the people against fraud and deception in the sale of food products. Such legislation may, indeed, indirectly or incidentally affect trade in such products transported from one state to another state. But that circumstance does not show that laws of the character alluded to are inconsistent with the power of congress to regulate commerce among the states. . . .

---

[29] 155 U.S. 461 (1894).

DEL: The *Gibbons* Court's indication, that Congress' authority to regulate commerce implied "full power of the thing to be regulated," was not pushed to its interpretative extreme. The Federalist values of the Marshall Court, although indelibly etched by decisions such as *Gibbons*, eventually were harmonized with the imperatives of federalism. Case law rendered by the Taney Court acknowledged not only the vastness of congressional power to regulate commerce but concurrent state interests. Doctrine thus became a function of accommodation that would be driven by standards that screened for regulatory logic and eventually balanced interests.

Cooley v. Board of Wardens
53 U.S. 299 (1851)

[A Pennsylvania law required all ships to use local pilots when they navigated in the Delaware River. Any ship that failed to employ a local pilot was required to pay a penalty. Plaintiff paid the penalty, and then sued for restitution claiming that the local pilot law conflicted with Congress' power to regulate commerce. Pennsylvania defended relying, in part, on a 1789 federal law giving states the power to enact local pilot laws.]

Mr. Justice CURTIS delivered the opinion of the court.

. . .

[W]e are brought directly and unavoidably to the consideration of the question, whether the grant of the commercial power to Congress, did per se deprive the states of all power to regulate pilots. This question has never been decided by this court, nor, in our judgment, has any case depending upon all the considerations which must govern this one, come before this court. The grant of commercial power to Congress does not contain any terms which expressly exclude the states from exercising an authority over its subject-matter. If they are excluded it must be because the nature of the power, thus granted to Congress, requires that a similar authority should not exist in the states. . . .

[T]he power to regulate commerce, embraces a vast field, containing not only many, but exceedingly various subjects, quite unlike in their nature; some imperatively demanding a single uniform rule, operating equally on the commerce of the United States in every port; and some, like the subject now in question, as imperatively demanding that diversity, which alone can meet the local necessities of navigation.

Either absolutely to affirm, or deny that the nature of this power requires exclusive legislation by Congress, is to lose sight of the nature of the subjects of this power, and to assert concerning all of them, what is really applicable but to a part. Whatever subjects of this power are in their nature national, or admit only of one uniform system, or plan of regulation, may justly be said to be of such a nature as to require exclusive legislation by Congress. That this cannot be affirmed of laws for the regulation of pilots and pilotage is plain. The act of 1789 contains a clear and authoritative declaration by the first Congress, that the nature of this subject is such, that until Congress should find it necessary to exert its power, it should be left to the legislation of the states; that it is local and not national; that it is likely to be the best provided for, not by one system, or plan of regulations, but by as many as the legislative discretion of the several states should deem applicable to the local peculiarities of the ports within their limits.

Viewed in this light, so much of this act of 1789 as declares that pilots shall continue to be regulated "by such laws as the states may respectively hereafter enact for that purpose," instead of being held to be inoperative, as an attempt to confer on the states a power to legislate, of which the Constitution had deprived them, is allowed an appropriate and important signification. It manifests the understanding of Congress, at the outset of the government, that the nature of this subject is not such as to require its exclusive legislation. The practice of the states, and of the national government, has been in conformity with this declaration, from the origin of the national government to this time; and the nature of the subject when examined, is such as to leave no doubt of the superior fitness and propriety, not to say the absolute necessity, of different systems of regulation, drawn from local knowledge and experience, and conformed to local wants. How then can we say, that by the mere grant of power to regulate commerce, the states are deprived of all the power to legislate on this subject, because from the nature of the power the legislation of Congress must be exclusive. . . .

It is the opinion of a majority of the court that the mere grant to Congress of the power to regulate commerce, did not deprive the states of power to regulate pilots, and that although Congress has legislated on this subject, its legislation manifests an intention, with a single exception, not to regulate this subject, but to leave its regulation to the several states. To these precise questions, which are all we are called on to decide, this opinion must be understood to be confined. It does not extend to the question what other subjects, under the commercial power, are within the exclusive control of Congress, or may be regulated by the states in the absence of all congressional legislation; nor to the general question how far any regulation of a subject by Congress, may be deemed to operate as an exclusion of all legislation by the states upon the same subject. . . .

We have not adverted to the practical consequences of holding that the states possess no power to legislate for the regulation of pilots, though in our apprehension these would be of the most serious importance. For more than sixty years this subject has been acted on by the states, and the systems of some of them created and of others essentially modified during that period. To hold that pilotage fees and penalties demanded and received during that time, have been illegally exacted, under color of void laws, would work an amount of mischief which a clear conviction of constitutional duty, if entertained, must force us to occasion, but which could be viewed by no just mind without deep regret. Nor would the mischief be limited to the past. If Congress were now to pass a law adopting the existing state laws, if enacted without authority, and in violation of the Constitution, it would seem to us to be a new and questionable mode of legislation.

If the grant of commercial power in the Constitution has deprived the states of all power to legislate for the regulation of pilots, if their laws on this subject are mere usurpations upon the exclusive power of the general government, and utterly void, it may be doubted whether Congress could, with propriety, recog-

nize them as laws, and adopt them as its own acts; and how are the legislatures of the states to proceed in future, to watch over and amend these laws, as the progressive wants of a growing commerce will require, when the members of those legislatures are made aware that they cannot legislate on this subject without violating the oaths they have taken to support the Constitution of the United States?

We are of opinion that this state law was enacted by virtue of a power, residing in the state to legislate; that it is not in conflict with any law of Congress; that it does not interfere with any system which Congress has established by making regulations, or by intentionally leaving individuals to their own unrestricted action; that this law is therefore valid, and the judgment of the Supreme Court of Pennsylvania in each case must be affirmed.

Mr. Justice McLean [dissenting].

. . .

If the states had not the power to enact pilot laws, as connected with foreign commerce, in 1789, when did they get it? . . . Is it derived from the act of 1789, that pilots shall continue to be regulated "in conformity with such laws as the states may respectively hereafter enact?" . . . Congress may adopt the laws of a state, but it cannot enable a state to legislate. In other words, it cannot transfer to a state legislative powers. . . .

. . .

[The majority concludes that state regulation is appropriate] because the subject [of this legislation] is more appropriate for state than federal action; and consequently, it must be presumed the Constitution cannot have intended to inhibit state action. This is not a rule by which the Constitution is to be construed. It can receive but little support from the discussions which took place on the adoption of the Constitution, and none at all from the earlier decisions of this court.

. . .

RLW: *Cooley* rejects the exclusivity approach articulated in *Gibbons*. But *Cooley* offers little guidance on how to determine whether a matter is national or local in character.

Congressional Authorization. Can Congress authorize the states to exercise regulatory authority which they would not have in the absence of congressional authorization? In *Leisy v. Hardin,*[30] the Court held that although "a state may provide for the security of the lives, limbs, health, and comfort of persons and the protection of property so situated," the Court concluded that "as the grant of the power to regulate commerce

---

[30] 135 U.S. 100 (1890).

among the states, so far as one system is required, is exclusive, the states cannot exercise that power without the assent of congress." But, in *Prudential Ins. Co. v. Benjamin*,[31] the Court upheld a South Carolina tax imposed on foreign insurance companies as a condition of doing business in the state. The tax was equal to three per cent of the aggregate premiums received from business done in South Carolina without reference to its interstate or local character. No similar tax was imposed on South Carolina corporations. The Court concluded that a federal law authorized the tax:

> [W]e are not required to determine whether South Carolina's tax would be valid in the dormancy of Congress' power. For Congress has expressly stated its intent and policy in the Act. And, for reasons to be stated, we think that the declaration's effect is clearly to sustain the exaction and that this can be done without violating any constitutional provision.
>
> . . .
>
> [Congress'] purpose was . . . [to remove] obstructions which might be thought to flow from its own power, whether dormant or exercised, except as otherwise expressly provided in the Act itself or in future legislation. The other was by declaring expressly and affirmatively that continued state regulation and taxation of this business is in the public interest and that the business and all who engage in it "shall be subject to" the laws of the several states in these respects.

2. Burdens on Interstate Commerce

In dormant power situations, when a state decides to regulate commerce, what is the role of the federal courts? Some argue that the federal courts should be deferential to state legislation. If Congress disagrees with state legislation, it can pass a law overriding that legislation. Others argue that the courts should actively review state laws, and should strike down laws that burden interstate commerce. Which approach is preferable?

---

[31] 328 U.S. 408 (1946).

South Carolina State Highway Department v. Barnwell Bros.
303 U.S. 177 (1938)

Mr. Justice STONE delivered the opinion of the Court.

Act No. 259 of the General Assembly of South Carolina, of April 28, 1933, prohibits use on the state highways of motor trucks and "semi-trailer motor trucks" whose width exceeds 90 inches, and whose weight including load exceeds 20,000 pounds. . . . The principal question for decision is whether these prohibitions impose an unconstitutional burden upon interstate commerce.

. . .

[Congress] has not undertaken to regulate the weight and size of motor vehicles in interstate motor traffic and has left undisturbed whatever authority in that regard the states have retained under the Constitution.

While the constitutional grant to Congress of power to regulate interstate commerce has been held to operate of its own force to curtail state power in some measure, . . . there are matters of local concern, the regulation of which unavoidably involves some regulation of interstate commerce but which, because of their local character and their number and diversity, may never be fully dealt with by Congress. Notwithstanding the commerce clause, such regulation in the absence of congressional action has for the most part been left to the states by the decisions of this Court, subject to the other applicable constitutional restraints.

. . .

[T]he present case affords no occasion for saying that the bare possession of power by Congress to regulate the interstate traffic forces the states to conform to standards which Congress might, but has not adopted, or curtails their power to take measures to insure the safety and conservation of their highways which may be applied to like traffic moving intrastate. Few subjects of state regulation are so peculiarly of local concern as is the use of state highways. There are few, local regulation of which is so inseparable from a substantial effect on interstate commerce. Unlike the railroads, local highways are built, owned, and maintained by the state or its municipal subdivisions. The state has a primary and immediate concern in their safe and economical administration. The present regulations, or any others of like purpose, if they are to accomplish their end, must be applied alike to interstate and intrastate traffic both moving in large volume over the highways. The fact that they affect alike shippers in interstate and intrastate commerce in large number within as well as without the state is a safeguard against their abuse.

[The states] may not, under the guise of regulation, discriminate against interstate commerce. But, "In the absence of national legislation especially covering the subject of interstate commerce, the state may rightly prescribe uniform regulations adapted to promote safety upon its highways and the conservation of their use, applicable alike to vehicles moving in interstate commerce and those of its own citizens." *Morris v. Duby*, 274 U.S. 135, 143. . . . This Court has often sustained the exercise of that power, although it has burdened or impeded interstate commerce. It has upheld weight limitations lower than those presently imposed, applied alike to motor traffic moving interstate and intrastate. Restrictions favoring passenger traffic over the carriage of interstate merchandise by truck have been similarly sustained, as has the exaction of a reasonable fee for the use of the highways.

. . .

Congress, in the exercise of its plenary power to regulate interstate commerce, may determine whether the burdens imposed on it by state regulation, otherwise permissible, are too great, and may, by legislation designed to secure uniformity or in other respects to protect the national interest in the commerce, curtail to some extent the state's regulatory power. But that is a legislative, not a judicial, function, to be performed in the light of the congressional judgment of what is appropriate regulation of interstate commerce, and the extent to which, in that field, state power and local interests should be required to yield to the national authority and interest. In the absence of such legislation the judicial function, under the commerce clause, Const. art. 1, § 8, cl. 3, as well as the Fourteenth Amendment, stops with the inquiry whether the state Legislature in adopting regulations such as the present has acted within its province, and whether the means of regulation chosen are reasonably adapted to the end sought.

Here the first inquiry has already been re-solved by our decisions that a state may impose nondiscriminatory restrictions with respect to the character of motor vehicles moving in interstate commerce as a safety measure and as a means of securing the economical use of its highways. In resolving the second, courts do not sit as Legislatures, either state or national. They cannot act as Congress does when, after weighing all the conflicting interests, state and national, it determines when and how much the state regulatory power shall yield to the larger interests of a national commerce. And in reviewing a state highway regulation where Congress has not acted, a court is not called upon, as are state Legislatures, to determine what, in its judgment, is the most suitable restriction to be applied of those that are possible, or to choose that one which in its opinion is best adapted to all the diverse interests affected. When the action of a Legislature is within the scope of its power, fairly debatable questions as to its reasonableness, wisdom, and propriety are not for the determination of courts, but for the legislative body, on which rests the duty and responsibility of decision. This is equally the case when the legislative power is one which may legitimately place an incidental burden on interstate commerce. It is not any the less a legislative power committed to the states because it affects interstate commerce, and courts are not any the more entitled, because interstate commerce is affected, to substitute their own for the legislative judgment.

Since the adoption of one weight or width regulation, rather than another, is a legislative, not a judicial, choice, its constitutionality is not to be determined by weighing in the judicial scales the merits of the legislative choice and rejecting it if the weight of evidence presented in court appears to favor a different standard. Being a legislative judgment it is presumed to be supported by facts known to the Legislature unless facts judicially known or proved preclude that possibility. Hence, in reviewing the present determination, we examine the record, not to see whether the findings of the court below are supported by evidence, but to ascertain upon the whole record whether it is possible to say that the legislative choice is without rational basis. *Standard Oil Co. v. Marysville, supra; Borden's Farm Products Co. v. Ten Eyck*, 297 U.S. 251, 263. Not only does the record fail to exclude that possibility but it shows affirmatively that there is adequate support for the legislative judgment.

. . .

The regulatory measures taken by South Carolina are within its legislative power. They do not infringe the Fourteenth Amendment, and the resulting burden on interstate commerce is not forbidden.

Reversed.

Southern Pac. Co. v. Arizona
325 U.S. 761 (1945)

Mr. Chief Justice STONE delivered the opinion of the Court.

The Arizona Train Limit Law of May 16, 1912 makes it unlawful for any person or corporation to operate within the state a railroad train of more than fourteen passenger or seventy freight cars. . . .

. . .

For a hundred years it has been accepted constitutional doctrine that the commerce clause, without the aid of Congressional legislation, thus affords some protection from state legislation inimical to the national commerce, and that in such cases, where Congress has not acted, this Court, and not the state legislature, is under the commerce clause the final arbiter of the competing demands of state and national interests. *Cooley v. Board of Wardens, supra.*

[There] has thus been left to the states wide scope for the regulation of matters of local state concern, even though it in some measure affects the commerce, provided it does not materially restrict the free flow of commerce across state lines, or interfere with it in matters with respect to which uniformity of regulation is of predominant national concern.

Hence the matters for ultimate determination here are the nature and extent of the burden which the state regulation of interstate trains, adopted as a safety measure, imposes on interstate commerce, and whether the relative weights of the state and national interests involved are such as to make inapplicable the rule, generally observed, that the free flow of interstate commerce and its freedom from local restraints in matters requiring uniformity of regulation are interests safeguarded by the commerce clause from state interference.

. . .

The findings show that the operation of long trains, that is trains of more than fourteen passenger and more than seventy freight cars, is standard practice over the main lines of the railroads of the United States, and that, if the length of trains is to be regulated at all, national uniformity in the regulation adopted, such as only Congress can prescribe, is practically indispensable to the operation of an efficient and economical national railway system. On many railroads passenger trains of more than fourteen cars and freight trains of more than seventy cars are operated, and on some systems freight trains are run ranging from one hundred and twenty-five to one hundred and sixty cars in length. Outside of Arizona, where the length of trains is not restricted, appellant runs a substantial proportion of long trains. In 1939 on its comparable route for through traffic through Utah and Nevada from 66 to 85% of its freight trains were over 70 cars in length and over 43% of its passenger trains included more than fourteen passenger cars.

In Arizona, approximately 93% of the freight traffic and 95% of the passenger traffic is interstate. Because of the Train Limit Law appellant is required to haul over 30% more trains in Arizona than would otherwise have been necessary. . . .

. . .

The unchallenged findings leave no doubt that the Arizona Train Limit Law imposes a serious burden on the interstate commerce conducted by appellant. It materially impedes the movement of appellant's interstate trains through that state and interposes a substantial obstruction to the national policy proclaimed by Congress, to promote adequate, economical and efficient railway transportation service. Enforcement of the law in Arizona, while train lengths remain unregulated or are regulated by varying standards in other states, must inevitably result in an impairment of uniformity of efficient railroad operation because the railroads are subjected to regulation which is not uniform in its application. Compliance with a state statute limiting train lengths requires interstate trains of a length lawful in other states to be broken up and reconstituted as they enter each state according as it may impose varying limitations upon train lengths. The alternative is for the carrier to conform to the lowest train limit restriction of any of the states through which its trains pass, whose laws thus control the carriers' operations both within and without the regulating state.

[At] present the seventy freight car laws are enforced only in Arizona and Oklahoma, with a fourteen car passenger car limit in Arizona. The record here shows that the enforcement of the Arizona statute results in freight trains being broken up and reformed at the California border and in New Mexico, some distance from the Arizona line. Frequently it is not feasible to operate a newly assembled train from the New Mexico yard nearest to Arizona, with the result that the Arizona limitation governs the flow of traffic as far east as El Paso, Texas. For similar reasons the Arizona law often controls the length of passenger trains all the way from Los Angeles to El Paso.

If one state may regulate train lengths, so may all the others, and they need not prescribe the same maximum limitation. The practical effect of such regulation is to control train operations beyond the boundaries of the state exacting it because of the necessity of breaking up and reassembling long trains at the nearest terminal points before entering and after leaving the regulating state. The serious impediment to the free flow of commerce by the local regulation of train lengths and the practical necessity that such regulation, if any, must be prescribed by a single body having a nationwide authority are apparent.

The trial court found that the Arizona law had no reasonable relation to safety, and made train operation more dangerous. Examination of the evidence and the detailed findings makes it clear that this conclusion was rested on facts found which indicate that such increased danger of accident and personal injury as may result from the greater length of trains is more than offset by the increase in the number of accidents resulting from the larger number of trains when train lengths are reduced. In considering the effect of the statute as a safety measure, therefore, the factor of controlling significance for present purposes is not whether there is basis for the conclusion of the Arizona Supreme Court that the increase in length of trains beyond the statutory maximum has an adverse effect upon safety of operation. The decisive question is whether in the circumstances the total effect of the law as a safety measure in reducing accidents and casualties is so slight or problematical as not to outweigh the national interest in keeping interstate commerce free from interferences which seriously impede it and subject it to local regulation which does not have a uniform effect on the interstate train journey which it interrupts.

The principal source of danger of accident from increased length of trains is the resulting increase of "slack action" of the train. Slack action is the amount of free movement of one car before it transmits its motion to an adjoining coupled car. This free movement results from the fact that in railroad practice cars are loosely coupled, and the coupling is often combined with a shock-absorbing device, a "draft gear," which, under stress, substantially increases the free movement as the train is started or stopped. Loose coupling is necessary to enable the train to proceed freely around curves and is an aid in starting heavy trains, since the application of the locomotive power to the train operates on each car in the train successively, and the power is thus utilized to start only one car at a time.

The slack action between cars due to loose couplings varies from seven-eighths of an inch to one and one-eighth inches and, with the added free movement due to the use of draft gears, may be as high as six or seven inches between cars. The length of the train increases the slack since the slack action of a train is the total of the free movement between its several

cars. The amount of slack action has some effect on the severity of the shock of train movements, and on freight trains sometimes results in injuries to operatives, which most frequently occur to occupants of the caboose. The amount and severity of slack action, however, are not wholly dependent upon the length of train, as they may be affected by the mode and conditions of operation as to grades, speed, and load. And accidents due to slack action also occur in the operation of short trains. On comparison of the number of slack action accidents in Arizona with those in Nevada, where the length of trains is now unregulated, the trial court found that with substantially the same amount of traffic in each state the number of accidents was relatively the same in long as in short train operations. While accidents from slack action do occur in the operation of passenger trains, it does not appear that they are more frequent or the resulting shocks more severe on long than on short passenger trains. Nor does it appear that slack action accidents occurring on passenger trains, whatever their length, are of sufficient severity to cause serious injury or damage.

. . .

Upon an examination of the whole case the trial court found that "if short-train operation may or should result in any decrease in the number or severity of the 'slack' or 'slack-surge' type of accidents or casualties, such decrease is substantially more than offset by the increased number of accidents and casualties from other causes that follow the arbitrary limitation of freight trains to 70 cars * * * and passenger trains to 14 cars."

We think, as the trial court found, that the Arizona Train Limit Law, viewed as a safety measure, affords at most slight and dubious advantage, if any, over unregulated train lengths, because it results in an increase in the number of trains and train operations and the consequent increase in train accidents of a character generally more severe than those due to slack action. Its undoubted effect on the commerce is the regulation, without securing uniformity, of the length of trains operated in interstate commerce, which lack is itself a primary cause of preventing the free flow of commerce by delaying it and by substantially increasing its cost and impairing its efficiency. In these respects the case differs from those where a state, by regulatory measures affecting the commerce, has removed or reduced safety hazards without substantial interference with the interstate movement of trains. . . .

. . .

Here we conclude that the state does go too far. Its regulation of train lengths, admittedly obstructive to interstate train operation, and having a seriously adverse effect on transportation efficiency and economy, passes beyond what is plainly essential for safety since it does not appear that it will lessen rather than increase the danger of accident. Its attempted regulation of the operation of interstate trains cannot establish nation-wide control such as is essential to the maintenance of an efficient transportation system, which Congress alone can prescribe. The state interest cannot be preserved at the expense of the national interest by an enactment which regulates interstate train lengths without securing such control, which is a matter of national concern. To this the interest of the state here asserted is subordinate.

. . .

Reversed.

Mr. Justice BLACK, dissenting.

. . .

Before the state trial judge finally determined that the dangers found by the legislature in 1912 no longer existed, he heard evidence over a period of 5 1/2 months which appears in about 3000 pages of the printed record before us. It then adopted findings of fact submitted to it by the railroad, which cover 148 printed pages, and conclusions of law which cover 5 pages. . . . This new pattern of trial procedure makes it necessary for a judge to hear all the evidence offered as to why a legislature passed a law and to make findings of fact as to the validity of those reasons. If under today's ruling a court does make findings, as to a danger contrary to the findings of the legislature, and the evidence heard "lends support" to those findings, a court can then invalidate the law. In this respect, the Arizona County Court acted, and this Court today is acting, as a "super-legislature."

Even if this method of invalidating legislative acts is a correct one, I still think that the "findings" of the state court do not authorize today's decision. That court did not find that there is no unusual danger from slack movements in long trains. It did decide on disputed evidence that the long train "slack movement" dangers were more than offset by prospective dangers as a result of running a larger number of short trains, since many people might be hurt at grade crossings. There was undoubt-

edly some evidence before the state court from which it could have reached such a conclusion. There was undoubtedly as much evidence before it which would have justified a different conclusion.

Under those circumstances, the determination of whether it is in the interest of society for the length of trains to be governmentally regulated is a matter of public policy. Someone must fix that policy—either the Congress, or the state, or the courts. A century and a half of constitutional history and government admonishes this Court to leave that choice to the elected legislative representatives of the people themselves, where it properly belongs both on democratic principles and the requirements of efficient government.

. . .

There have been many sharp divisions of this Court concerning its authority, in the absence of congressional enactment, to invalidate state laws as violating the Commerce Clause. . . . That discussion need not be renewed here, because even the broadest exponents of judicial power in this field have not heretofore expressed doubt as to a state's power, absent a paramount congressional declaration, to regulate interstate trains in the interest of safety. . . .

. . .

When we finally get down to the gist of what the Court today actually decides, it is this: Even though more railroad employees will be injured by "slack action" movements on long trains than on short trains, there must be no regulation of this danger in the absence of "uniform regulations." That means that no one can legislate against this danger except the Congress; and even though the Congress is perfectly content to leave the matter to the different state legislatures, this Court, on the ground of "lack of uniformity," will require it to make an express avowal of that fact before it will permit a state to guard against that admitted danger.

. . .

Mr. Justice DOUGLAS, dissenting.

My view has been that the courts should intervene only where the state legislation discriminated against interstate commerce or was out of harmony with laws which Congress had enacted. . . .

RLW: Note how differently the Court perceives its role in the *Barnwell* and *Southern Pacific* cases. Which approach is better? One can argue that, in the absence of federal action, the federal courts should be deferential to state legislation. If the states decide to regulate (as Arizona did in the *Southern Pacific* case), and Congress does not like what the states have done, Congress can pass a law overriding the state law. Moreover, if a state law unreasonably burdens commerce (*e.g.*, the Arizona law), it is reasonable to assume that those adversely affected by the law (in this case, the national railroad companies) will urge Congress to pass override legislation. If Congress decides not to pass such legislation, why should the courts intervene? The countervailing argument is that Congress does not have time to individually consider, and legislate on, all of the burdens that states may place on commerce.

The troubling thing about the *Southern Pacific* case was the scope of review. As Justice Black, notes in his dissent, the trial court heard 5½ months of testimony and compiled a 3000-page record before ruling on the validity of Arizona's law. One might question whether this type of review is appropriate for a federal court.

DEL: Notwithstanding the Court's rhetoric of deference, its review in both *Barnwell* and *Southern Pacific* was independent and probing. The difference in outcomes was attributable not to analytical methodology but to perceptions of legislative wisdom. To the extent that the review in *Barnwell* may appear less aggressive, it is only because the Court agreed with the state's thinking. The outcome should not obscure the reality that, in both instances, the Court independently evaluated the sensibility of transportation safety rules. If such regulation is truly disruptive, as the Court alleges in *Southern Pacific*, powerful economic concerns have all the incentive they need and Congress has the power it needs to displace state law through a federal enactment. So long as the political process is thusly functional, it is appropriate to raise the questions that Justice Black does about the judiciary's role.

DER: Given the wisdom in many cases of state safety regulation where Congress has failed to act, the ability of Congress to intercede when necessary, and the courts' arguable incompetence in this area, we might well ask why there should be a dormant commerce clause at all. When would the courts ever be better forums than Congress for judging whether state laws interfere with federal authority over interstate commerce? The argument that courts are more capable than Congress of handling frequent conflicts seems less persuasive in light of the over-burdened judicial system—especially when trials may last for months and then proceed through years of appeals. Besides, couldn't Congress often pass a single law that would preclude numerous conflicting state regulations? Another answer might be that the Court is uniquely positioned to weigh the benefits of the state regulation against its threat to interstate commerce. But the Court's role is not to be more sympathetic to state interests than Congress. Since dormant commerce clause cases arise only where Congress has refrained from exercising its power to enact superseding federal legislation, the Court's main function is to move more aggressively against state interests than Congress has. Finally, the Court might be more sensitive than Congress to out-of-state interests that are unrepresented in the regulating state's political process. Still, there is a strong argument that the Constitution simply does not authorize the courts to "legislate" in place of Congress.

Southern Pacific was followed by *Bibb v. Navajo Freight Lines, Inc.*,[32] which involved an Illinois statute requiring the use of a contoured rear fender mudguard on trucks and trailers operated in Illinois. Illinois' contour mudflap differed from the conventional or straight mudflap permitted in 45 States and required in Arkansas.

In passing the law, the Illinois legislature relied on evidence that contour flaps promote safety by preventing trucks from throwing debris onto the windshields of passing cars and following vehicles. The District Court found that it was "conclusively shown that the contour mud flap possesses no advantages over the conventional or straight mud flap previously required in Illinois and presently required in most of the

---

[32] 359 U.S. 520 (1959).

states," and that "there is rather convincing testimony that use of the contour flap creates hazards previously unknown to those using the highways."

In an opinion written by Mr. Justice Douglas, the Court struck down the Illinois law:

> ... State control of the width and weight of motor trucks and trailers sustained in *South Carolina State Highway Dept. v. Barnwell Bros.,* involved nice questions of judgment concerning the need of those regulations so far as the issue of safety was concerned. ... The matter of safety was said to be one essentially for the legislative judgment; and the burden of redesigning or replacing equipment was said to be a proper price to exact from interstate and intrastate motor carriers alike. ...
>
> ...
>
> This is one of those cases—few in number—where local safety measures that are nondiscriminatory place an unconstitutional burden on interstate commerce. This conclusion is especially underlined by the deleterious effect which the Illinois law will have on the "interline" operation of interstate motor carriers. The conflict between the Arkansas regulation and the Illinois regulation also suggests that this regulation of mudguards is not one of those matters "admitting of diversity of treatment, according to the special requirements of local conditions," to use the words of Chief Justice Hughes in *Sproles v. Binford.* A State which insists on a design out of line with the requirements of almost all the other States may sometimes place a great burden of delay and inconvenience on those interstate motor carriers entering or crossing its territory. Such a new safety device—out of line with the requirements of the other States—may be so compelling that the innovating State need not be the one to give way. But the present showing—balanced against the clear burden on commerce—is far too inconclusive to make this mudguard meet that test.
>
> We deal not with absolutes but with questions of degree. The state legislatures plainly have great leeway in providing safety regulations for all vehicles—interstate as well as local. Our decisions so hold. Yet the heavy burden which the Illinois mudguard law places on the interstate movement of trucks and trailers seems to us to pass the permissible limits even for safety regulations.

Raymond Motor Transportation, Inc. v. Rice[33] involved a Wisconsin law limiting the length and configuration of trucks operated in that state. The law prohibited the pulling of double-trailers, as well as any rig longer than 55 feet in length (absent a special permit). The evidence revealed that many trucking companies preferred to use double-trailers, and that they were allowed to do so in surrounding states provided that the rigs were 65 feet in length or shorter. The evidence also revealed that the Wisconsin law was disruptive, and raised trucking costs. The Court struck down the law:

> [T]he regulations impose a substantial burden on the interstate movement of goods. The regulations substantially increase the cost of such movement, a fact which is not, as the District Court thought, entirely irrelevant. In addition, the regulations slow the movement of goods in interstate commerce by forcing appellants to haul doubles across the State separately, to haul doubles around the State altogether, or to incur the delays caused by using singles instead of

---

[33] 434 U.S. 429 (1978).

doubles to pick up and deliver goods. Finally, the regulations prevent appellants from accepting interline transfers of 65-foot doubles for movement through Wisconsin from carriers that operate only in the 33 States where the doubles are legal. In our view, the burden imposed on interstate commerce by Wisconsin's regulations is no less than that imposed by the statute invalidated in *Bibb*.

3. Discrimination Against Interstate Commerce

The *Southern Pacific* balancing test is commonly applied to state regulations that impose burdens on interstate commerce. Do different rules apply when a state discriminates against interstate commerce in favor of local interests?

a. Incoming Commerce

Baldwin v. G.A.F. Seelig, Inc.
294 U.S. 511 (1935)

Mr. Justice CARDOZO delivered the opinion of the Court.

. . .

G.A.F. Seelig, Inc. is engaged in business as a milk dealer in the city of New York. It buys its milk, including cream, in Fair Haven, Vt., from the Seelig Creamery Corporation, which in turn buys from the producers on the neighboring farms. The milk is transported to New York by rail in 40-quart cans; the daily shipment amounting to about 200 cans of milk and 20 cans of cream. Upon arrival in New York about 90 per cent. is sold to customers in the original cans; the buyers being chiefly hotels, restaurants, and stores. About 10 per cent. is bottled in New York, and sold to customers in bottles. By concession title passes from the Seelig Creamery to G.A.F. Seelig, Inc., at Fair Haven, Vt. For convenience the one company will be referred to as the Creamery and the other as Seelig.

The New York Milk Control Act, with the aid of regulations made thereunder, has set up a system of minimum prices to be paid by dealers to producers. . . . From the farms of New York the inhabitants of the so-called Metropolitan milk district, comprising the city of New York and certain neighboring communities, derive about 70 per cent. of the milk requisite for their use. To keep the system unimpaired by competition from afar, the act has a provision whereby the protective prices are extended to that part of the supply (about 30 per cent.) which comes from other states. The substance of the provision is that, so far as such a prohibition is permitted by the Constitution, there shall be no sale within the state of milk bought outside unless the price paid to the producers was one that would be lawful upon a like transaction within the state. . . .

Seelig buys its milk from the Creamery in Vermont at prices lower than the minimum payable to producers in New York. The Commissioner of Farms and Markets refuses to license the transaction of its business unless it signs an agreement to conform to the New York statute and regulations in the sale of the imported product. This the applicant declines to do. . . .

. . .

New York has no power to project its legislation into Vermont by regulating the price to be paid in that state for milk acquired there. So much is not disputed. New York is equally without power to prohibit the introduction within her territory of milk of wholesome quality acquired in Vermont, whether at high prices or at low ones. This again is not disputed. Accepting those postulates, New York asserts her power to outlaw milk so introduced by prohibiting its sale thereafter if the price that has been paid for it to the farmers of Vermont is less than would be owing in like circumstances to farmers in New York. The importer in that view may keep his milk or drink it, but sell it he may not.

Such a power, if exerted, will set a barrier to traffic between one state and another as effective as if customs duties, equal to the price differential, had been laid upon the thing transported. Imposts or duties upon commerce with other countries are placed, by an express prohibition of the Constitution, beyond the power of a state, "except what may be absolutely necessary for executing its inspection Laws." Constitution, art. 1, § 10, cl. 2; *Woodruff v. Parham*, 8 Wall. 123. Imposts and duties upon interstate commerce are placed beyond the power of a state, without the mention of an exception, by the provision committing commerce of that order to the power of the Congress. Constitution, art. 1, § 8, cl. 3. "It is the established doctrine of this court that a state may not, in any form or under any guise, directly burden the prosecution of interstate business." *International Textbook Co. v. Pigg*, 217 U.S. 91, 112. Nice distinctions have been made at times between direct and indirect burdens. They are irrelevant when the avowed purpose of the obstruction, as well as its necessary tendency, is to suppress or mitigate the consequences of competition between the states. Such an obstruction is direct by the very terms of the hypothesis. We are reminded in the opinion below that a chief occasion of the commerce clauses was "the mutual jealousies and aggressions of the States, taking form in customs barriers and other economic retaliation." Farrand, Records of the Federal Convention, vol. II, p. 308; vol. III, pp. 478, 547, 548; the Federalist, No. XLII; Curtis, History of the Constitution, vol. 1, p. 502; Story on the Constitution, § 259. If New York, in order to promote the economic welfare of her farmers, may guard them against competition with the cheaper prices of Vermont, the door has been opened to rivalries and reprisals that were meant to be averted by subjecting commerce between the states to the power of the nation.

The argument is pressed upon us, however, that the end to be served by the Milk Control Act is something more than the economic welfare of the farmers or of any other class or classes. The end to be served is the maintenance of a regular and adequate supply of pure and wholesome milk; the supply being put in jeopardy when the farmers of the state are unable to earn a living income. *Nebbia v. New York, supra*. Price security, we are told, is only a special form of sanitary security; the economic motive is secondary and subordinate; the state intervenes to make its inhabitants healthy, and not to make them rich. On that assumption we are asked to say that intervention will be upheld as a valid exercise by the state of its internal police power, though there is an incidental obstruction to commerce between one state and another. This would be to eat up the rule under the guise of an exception. Economic welfare is always related to health, for there can be no health if men are starving. Let such an exception be admitted, and all that a state will have to do in times of stress and strain is to say that its farmers and merchants and workmen must be protected against competition from without, lest they go upon the poor relief lists or perish altogether. To give entrance to that excuse would be to invite a speedy end of our national solidarity. The Constitution was framed under the dominion of a political philosophy less parochial in range. It was framed upon the theory that the peoples of the several states must sink or swim together, and that in the long run prosperity and salvation are in union and not division.

We have dwelt up to this point upon the argument of the state that economic security for farmers in the milk shed may be a means of assuring to consumers a steady supply of a food of prime necessity. There is, however, another argument which seeks to establish a relation between the well-being of the producer and the quality of the product. We are told that farmers who are underpaid will be tempted to save the expense or sanitary precautions. This temptation will affect the farmers outside New York as well as those within it. For that reason, the exclusion of milk paid for in Vermont below the New York minimum will tend, it is said, to impose a higher standard of quality and thereby promote health. We think the argument will not avail to justify impediments to commerce between the states. There is neither evidence nor presumption that the same minimum prices established by order of the board for producers in New York are necessary also for producers in Vermont. But apart from such defects of proof, the evils springing from uncared for cattle must be remedied by measures of repression more direct and certain than the creation of a parity of prices between New York and other states. Appropriate certificates may be exacted from farmers in Vermont and elsewhere; milk may be excluded if necessary safeguards have been omitted; but commerce between the states is burdened unduly when one state regulates by indirection the prices to be paid to producers in another, in the faith that augmentation of prices will lift up the level of economic welfare, and that this will stimulate the observance of sanitary requirements in the preparation of the product. The next step would be to condition importation upon proof of a satisfactory wage scale in factory or shop, or even upon proof of the profits of the business. Whatever relation there may be between earnings and sanitation is too remote and indirect to justify obstructions to the normal flow of commerce in its movement between states. One state may not put pressure of that sort upon others to reform their economic standards. If farmers or manufacturers in Vermont are abandoning farms or factories, or are failing to maintain them properly, the Legislature of Vermont and not that of New York must supply the fitting remedy.

. . . Subject to the paramount power of the Congress, a state may regulate the importation of unhealthy swine or cattle or decayed or noxious foods. *Crossman v. Lurman*, 192 U.S. 189; *Savage v. Jones*, 225 U.S. 501. Things such as these are not proper subjects of commerce, and there is no unreasonable interference when they are inspected and excluded. So a state may protect its inhabitants against the fraudulent substitution, by deceptive coloring or otherwise, of one article for another. *Plumley v. Massachusetts*, 155 U.S. 461. It may give protection to travelers against the dangers of overcrowded highways and protection to its residents against unnecessary noises. . . . None of these statutes—inspection laws, game laws, laws intended to curb fraud or exterminate disease—approaches in drastic quality the statute here in controversy which would neutralize the economic consequences of free trade among the states.

. . .

[O]ne state in its dealings with another may not place itself in a position of economic isolation. Formulas and catchwords are subordinate to this overmastering requirement. Neither the power to tax nor the police power may be used by the state of destination with the aim and effect of establishing an economic barrier against competition with the products of another state or the labor of its residents. Restrictions so contrived are an unreasonable clog upon the mobility of commerce. They set up what is equivalent to a rampart of customs duties designed to neutralize advantages belonging to the place of origin. They are thus hostile in conception as well as burdensome in result. . . .

. . .

RLW: *Baldwin's* analysis, which prohibits states from discriminating against interstate commerce, supplements the *Southern Pacific* balancing test. When a state seeks to promote a valid health and safety interest, on a non-discriminatory basis, the *Southern Pacific* balancing test applies. But, when a state discriminates against interstate commerce, its actions are presumptively invalid. As the Court stated in *Gibbons*, "[i]f there was any one object riding over every other in the adoption of the Constitution, it was to keep the commercial intercourse among the states free from all invidious and partial restraints." The Court routinely strikes down such restraints.

DEL: Curiously, perhaps, the Court has upheld use taxes that eliminate the price advantage of an out-of-state producer or distributor operating beyond the reach of a state's sales tax.[34] Whether denominated as a state-imposed tariff or tax, such measures have the effect of discouraging out-of-state purchases by creating official filters or barriers to trade. Unless the degree of burden is considered a significant difference, or the reason for one law is more acceptable than the other, it is difficult to perceive in the case law much of a distinction for constitutional purposes.

DER: While the Court has routinely invalidated state laws that *discriminate* against interstate commerce, it has also routinely upheld state laws serving a legitimate social purpose that only incidentally restrict access to local markets. Health, environmental and deceptive trade practices regulations may discourage out-of-state business, but they do not necessarily give local enterprises an unfair advantage over out-of-state competition. Moreover, these regulations are designed to protect public safety, not to maximize local profits. It may be argued that, like health and safety regulations, use taxes do not *discriminate* against out-of-state business; rather, they ensure that all sales connected to the state must bear roughly equivalent tax burdens. On the other hand, use taxes differ from health and safety regulations in that they have an economic, rather than social, purpose.

PAH: As Justice Scalia has aptly pointed out,[35] the court's decisions "leave open the possibility that a state may validate a statute that discriminates against interstate commerce by showing that it advances a legitimate local purpose that cannot adequately be served by reasonable nondiscriminatory alternatives." Thus the court imposes on the state the obligation of showing that economic protectionism is not the objective. And, as cases like *City of Philadelphia* reflect, it is not always clear who is actually being benefitted by alleged protectionism.

---

[34] Henneford v. Silas Mason Co., 300 U.S. 577 (1937).
[35] New Energy Co. of Indiana v. Limbach, 486 U.S. 269 (1988).

Welton v. State of Missouri[36] illustrates the Court's approach. That case involved a Missouri statute which required peddlers to have licenses except for peddlers who sold goods which were grown, produced, or manufactured in Missouri. The Court struck down the law as a discrimination against interstate commerce:

> The general power of the State to impose taxes in the way of licenses upon all pursuits and occupations within its limits is admitted, but, like all other powers, must be exercised in subordination to the requirements of the Federal Constitution. . . .
>
> . . .
>
> The power which insures uniformity of commercial regulation must cover the property which is transported as an article of commerce from hostile or interfering legislation, until it has mingled with and become a part of the general property of the country, and subjected like it to similar protection, and to no greater burdens. If, at any time before it has thus become incorporated into the mass of property of the state or nation, it can be subjected to any restrictions by State legislation, the object of investing the control in Congress may be entirely defeated. . . .

---

[36] 91 U.S. 275 (1875).

RLW: The Court has had difficulty determining whether a given law discriminates against interstate commerce. In most instances, the state does not proclaim an intention to discriminate on the face of the statute. On the contrary, the state usually articulates health and safety considerations. In cases like *Baldwin*, the Court concludes that the health and safety interests mask an intent to discriminate.

DEL: Inquiry into discriminatory purpose is a notoriously treacherous exercise. *The* purpose of legislation not only tends to be elusive but illusory. Legislators often support policies for diverse and even conflicting reasons. If an illicit motive inspires a lawmaker's vote, moreover, articulation of a more acceptable reason is all that is required to mask the truth. Even if a discriminatory motive is discerned, the question then becomes how much protectionism is sufficient to invalidate a law. Is it enough that one legislature was so motivated, or must it be established that a majority of the legislative body was so influenced? Curious too is why some of those who doubt the utility of motive-based inquiry in the dormant commerce clause cases and other settings continue to invest in it for equal protection purposes.

DER: Legislative motive is irrelevant to dormant commerce clause cases since the Constitution's concern is with state interference with interstate commerce, not lawmakers' state of mind. The question to be answered is whether the state regulation gives local businesses an unfair advantage over out-of-state competitors—regardless of the justification articulated by state legislators. Courts should be concerned with the discriminatory *consequences* of legislation. The statute in *Welton* on its face plainly discriminated against interstate commerce by exempting local products from the restriction it imposed on the sale of out-of-state goods. But even regulations that are facially neutral may have this discriminatory effect. On the other hand, regulations that burden in-state and out-of-state enterprises alike in order to serve a legitimate social purpose are valid despite an incidental burden on trade. In either case, searching the motives of lawmakers does not advance the inquiry.

Hunt v. Washington State Apple Advertising Commission[37] involved a North Carolina statute which required "all closed containers of apples sold, offered for sale, or
shipped into the State to bear 'no grade other than the applicable U.S. grade or standard.'" The law was passed to eliminate "confusion" and "deception" caused by the fact
that seven states had their own grading systems, and it was difficult for consumers
to know and understand all the systems. The Washington State Apple Advertising
Commission challenged the law insofar as it prohibited the display of Washington State
apple grades. The Court struck down the law:

> [T]he challenged statute has the practical effect of not only burdening inter-
> state sales of Washington apples, but also discriminating against them. This
> discrimination takes various forms. The first, and most obvious, is the statute's
> consequence of raising the costs of doing business in the North Carolina market
> for Washington apple growers and dealers, while leaving those of their North
> Carolina counterparts unaffected. . . .
>
> Second, the statute has the effect of stripping away from the Washington
> apple industry the competitive and economic advantages it has earned for
> itself through its expensive inspection and grading system. The record demon-
> strates that the Washington apple-grading system has gained nationwide
> acceptance in the apple trade. Indeed, it contains numerous affidavits from
> apple brokers and dealers located both inside and outside of North Carolina
> who state their preference, and that of their customers, for apples graded
> under the Washington, as opposed to the USDA, system because of the
> former's greater consistency, its emphasis on color, and its supporting manda-
> tory inspections. . . .
>
> Third, by prohibiting Washington growers and dealers from marketing ap-
> ples under their State's grades, the statute has a leveling effect which insidi-
> ously operates to the advantage of local apple producers. As noted earlier, the
> Washington State grades are equal or superior to the USDA grades in all corre-
> sponding categories. Hence, with free market forces at work, Washington sell-
> ers would normally enjoy a distinct market advantage vis-a-vis local producers
> in those categories where the Washington grade is superior. . . . Such "down-
> grading" offers the North Carolina apple industry the very sort of protection
> against competing out-of-state products that the Commerce Clause was de-
> signed to prohibit. . . .
>
> . . .
>
> The several States unquestionably possess a substantial interest in protect-
> ing their citizens from confusion and deception in the marketing of foodstuffs,
> but the challenged statute does remarkably little to further that laudable goal
> at least with respect to Washington apples and grades. The statute, as already
> noted, permits the marketing of closed containers of apples under no grades
> at all. . . . Since the statute does nothing at all to purify the flow of information
> at the retail level, it does little to protect consumers against the problems it
> was designed to eliminate. . . .
>
> In addition, it appears that nondiscriminatory alternatives to the outright
> ban of Washington State grades are readily available. For example, North Caro-
> lina could effectuate its goal by permitting out-of-state growers to utilize state
> grades only if they also marked their shipments with the applicable USDA
> label. . . .

---

[37] 432 U.S. 333 (1977).

Edwards v. State of California[38] concerned a California law which made it illegal to bring, or assist in bringing, an indigent person into the state with knowledge of the indigency. Edwards was charged with transporting his wife's brother from Texas to California. Edwards knew that his brother-in-law was indigent. The Court struck down the California law:

> [I]t is settled beyond question that the transportation of persons is "commerce," within the meaning of [the commerce clause].
>
> [The] State asserts that the huge influx of migrants into California in recent years has resulted in problems of health, morals, and especially finance, the proportions of which are staggering. It is not for us to say that this is not true. . . .
>
> But this does not mean that there are no boundaries to the permissible area of State legislative activity. There are. And none is more certain than the prohibition against attempts on the part of any single State to isolate itself from difficulties common to all of them by restraining the transportation of persons and property across its borders. . . .

Healy v. Beer Institute[39] involved a Connecticut law which required out-of-state shippers of beer to affirm that their posted prices for beer sold to Connecticut wholesalers were, at the moment of posting, no higher than the prices at which those products are sold in the bordering States of Massachusetts, New York, and Rhode Island. In an opinion written by Mr. Justice Blackmun, the Court struck down the law:

> [I]f Connecticut may enact a contemporaneous affirmation statute, so may each of the border States and, indeed, so may every other State in the Nation. . . . The short-circuiting of normal pricing decisions based on local conditions would be carried to a national scale if a significant group of States enacted contemporaneous affirmation statutes that linked in-state prices to the lowest price in any State in the country. This kind of potential regional and even national regulation of the pricing mechanism for goods is reserved by the Commerce Clause to the Federal Government and may not be accomplished piecemeal through the extraterritorial reach of individual state statutes.
>
> . . .
>
> The Connecticut statute, moreover, violates the Commerce Clause in a second respect: On its face, the statute discriminates against brewers and shippers of beer engaged in interstate commerce. . . . By its plain terms, the Connecticut affirmation statute applies solely to interstate brewers or shippers of beer, that is, either Connecticut brewers who sell both in Connecticut and in at least one border State or out-of-state shippers who sell both in Connecticut and in at least one border State. . . .

Chief Justice Rehnquist, joined by two other justices, dissented:

> The Connecticut statute here is markedly different from the New York statute condemned in *Baldwin.* Connecticut has no motive to favor local brewers over out-of-state brewers, because there are no local brewers. Its motive—unchallenged here—is to obtain from out-of-state brewers prices for Connecticut retailers and Connecticut beer drinkers as low as those charged by the brewers in neighboring States. Connecticut does not seek to erect any sort of tariff barrier to exclude out-of-state beer; its residents will drink out-of-state

---

[38] 314 U.S. 160 (1941).
[39] 491 U.S. 324 (1989).

beer if they drink beer at all, and the State simply wishes its inhabitants to be treated as favorably as those of neighboring States by the brewers who sell interstate. . . .

Neither the parties nor the Court points to any concrete evidence that the Connecticut regulation will have any effect on the beer prices charged in other States, much less a constitutionally impermissible one. It is merely assumed that consumers in the neighboring States possess "competitive advantages" over Connecticut consumers. . . . [T]his view is simply the Court's personal forecast about the business strategies that distributors may use to set their prices in light of regulatory obligations in various States. . . .

Dean Milk Co. v. Madison
340 U.S. 349 (1951)

Mr. Justice CLARK delivered the opinion of the Court.

This appeal challenges the constitutional validity of two sections of an ordinance of the City of Madison, Wisconsin, regulating the sale of milk and milk products within the municipality's jurisdiction. One section in issue makes it unlawful to sell any milk as pasteurized unless it has been processed and bottled at an approved pasteurization plant within a radius of five miles from the central square of Madison. Another section, which prohibits the sale of milk, or the importation, receipt or storage of milk for sale, in Madison unless from a source of supply possessing a permit issued after inspection by Madison officials, is attacked insofar as it expressly relieves municipal authorities from any duty to inspect farms located beyond twenty-five miles from the center of the city.

Appellant is an Illinois corporation engaged in distributing milk and milk products in Illinois and Wisconsin. It contended below, as it does here, that both the five-mile limit on pasteurization plants and the twenty-five-mile limit on sources of milk violate the Commerce Clause and the Fourteenth Amendment to the Federal Constitution. . . .

The City of Madison is the county seat of Dane County. Within the county are some 5,600 dairy farms with total raw milk production in excess of 600,000,000 pounds annually and more than ten times the requirements of Madison. Aside from the milk supplied to Madison, fluid milk produced in the county moves in large quantities to Chicago and more distant consuming areas, and the remainder is used in making cheese, butter and other products. At the time of trial the Madison milkshed was not of "Grade A" quality by the standards recommended by the United States Public Health Service, and no milk labeled "Grade A" was distributed in Madison.

The area defined by the ordinance with respect to milk sources encompasses practically all of Dane County and includes some 500 farms which supply milk for Madison. Within the five-mile area for pasteurization are plants of five processors, only three of which are engaged in the general wholesale and retail trade in Madison. Inspection of these farms and plants is scheduled once every thirty days and is performed by two municipal inspectors, one of whom is full-time. The courts below found that the ordinance in question promotes convenient, economical and efficient plant inspection.

Appellant purchases and gathers milk from approximately 950 farms in northern Illinois and southern Wisconsin, none being within twenty-five miles of Madison. Its pasteurization plants are located at Chemung and Huntley, Illinois, about 65 and 85 miles respectively from Madison. Appellant was denied a license to sell its products within Madison solely because its pasteurization plants were more than five miles away.

It is conceded that the milk which appellant seeks to sell in Madison is supplied from farms and processed in plants licensed and inspected by public health authorities of Chicago, and is labeled "Grade A" under the Chicago ordinance which adopts the rating standards recommended by the United States Public Health Service. Both the Chicago and Madison ordinances, though not the sections of the latter here in issue, are largely patterned after the Model Milk Ordinance of the Public Health Service. However, Madison contends and we assume that in some particulars its ordinance is more rigorous than that of Chicago.

Upon these facts we find it necessary to determine only the issue raised under the Commerce Clause, for we agree with appellant that the ordinance imposes an undue burden on interstate commerce.

This is not an instance in which an enactment falls because of federal legislation which, as a proper exercise of paramount national power over commerce, excludes measures which might otherwise be within the police power of the states. There is no pertinent national regulation by the Congress, and statutes enacted for the District of Columbia indicate that Congress has recognized the appropriateness of local regulation of the sale of fluid milk. D.C.Code, 1940, §§ 33—301 et seq. It is not contended, however, that Congress has authorized the regulation before us.

Nor can there be objection to the avowed purpose of this enactment. We assume that difficulties in sanitary regulation of milk and milk products originating in remote areas may present a situation in which "upon a consideration of all the relevant facts and circumstances it appears that the matter is one which may appropriately be regulated in the interest of the safety, health and well-being of local communities * * *." *Parker v. Brown*, 1943, 317 U.S. 341, 362—363. We also assume that since Congress has not spoken to the contrary, the subject matter of the ordinance lies within the sphere of state regulation even though interstate commerce may be affected.

But this regulation, like the provision invalidated in *Baldwin v. G.A.F. Seelig, Inc.*, *supra*, in practical effect excludes from distribution in Madison wholesome milk produced and pasteurized in Illinois. "The importer . . . may keep his milk or drink it, but sell it he may not." *Id.*, 294 U.S. at page 521. In thus erecting an economic barrier protecting a major local industry against competition from without the State, Madison plainly discriminates against interstate commerce.[4] This it cannot do, even in the exercise of its unquestioned power to protect the health and safety of its people, if reasonable nondiscriminatory alternatives, adequate to conserve legitimate local interests, are available. A different view, that the ordinance is valid simply because it professes to be a health measure, would mean that the Commerce Clause of itself imposes no limitations on state action other than those laid down by the Due Process Clause, save for the rare instance where a state artlessly discloses an avowed purpose to discriminate against interstate goods. Our issue then is whether the discrimination inherent in the Madison ordinance can be justified in view of the character of the local interests and the available methods of protecting them.

It appears that reasonable and adequate alternatives are available. If the City of Madi-

son prefers to rely upon its own officials for inspection of distant milk sources, such inspection is readily open to it without hardship for it could charge the actual and reasonable cost of such inspection to the importing producers and processors. Moreover, appellee Health Commissioner of Madison testified that as proponent of the local milk ordinance he had submitted the provisions here in controversy and an alternative proposal based on § 11 of the Model Milk Ordinance recommended by the United States Public Health Service. The model provision imposes no geographical limitation on location of milk sources and processing plants but excludes from the municipality milk not produced and pasteurized conformably to standards as high as those enforced by the receiving city. In implementing such an ordinance, the importing city obtains milk ratings based on uniform standards and established by health authorities in the jurisdiction where production and processing occur. The receiving city may determine the extent of enforcement of sanitary standards in the exporting area by verifying the accuracy of safety ratings of specific plants or of the milkshed in the distant jurisdiction through the United States Public Health Service, which routinely and on request spot checks the local ratings. The Commissioner testified that Madison consumers "would be safeguarded adequately" under either proposal and that he had expressed no preference. The milk sanitarian of the Wisconsin State Board of Health testified that the State Health Department recommends the adoption of a provision based on the Model Ordinance. Both officials agreed that a local health officer would be justified in relying upon the evaluation by the Public Health Service of enforcement conditions in remote producing areas.

To permit Madison to adopt a regulation not essential for the protection of local health interests and placing a discriminatory burden on interstate commerce would invite a multiplication of preferential trade areas destructive of the very purpose of the Commerce Clause. Under the circumstances here presented, the regulation must yield to the principle that "one state in its dealings with another may not place itself in a position of economic isolation." *Baldwin v. G.A.F. Seelig, Inc.*, *supra*, 294 U.S. at page 527.

For these reasons we conclude that the judgment below sustaining the five-mile provision as to pasteurization must be reversed.

. . .

Judgment vacated and cause remanded.

Mr. Justice BLACK, with whom Mr. Justice DOUGLAS and Mr. Justice MINTON concur, dissenting.

. . .

---

[4] It is immaterial that Wisconsin milk from outside the Madison area is subjected to the same proscription as that moving in interstate commerce. Cf. Brimmer v. Rebman, 1891, 138 U.S. 78.

[B]oth state courts below found that § 7.21 represents a good-faith attempt to safeguard public health by making adequate sanitation inspection possible. While we are not bound by these findings, I do not understand the Court to overturn them. Therefore, the fact that § 7.21, like all health regulations, imposes some burden on trade, does not mean that it "discriminates" against interstate commerce.

This health regulation should not be invalidated merely because the Court believes that alternative milk-inspection methods might insure the cleanliness and healthfulness of Dean's Illinois milk. . . . No case is cited, and I have found none, in which a bona fide health law was struck down on the ground that some other method of safeguarding health would be as good as, or better than, the one the Court was called on to review. In my view, to use this ground now elevates the right to traffic in commerce for profit above the power of the people to guard the purity of their daily diet of milk.

. . .

One of the Court's proposals is that Madison require milk processors to pay reasonable inspection fees at the milk supply "sources." Experience shows, however, that the fee method gives rise to prolonged litigation over the calculation and collection of the charges. *E.g., Sprout v. City of South Bend,* 277 U.S. 163.

The Court's second proposal is that Madison adopt § 11 of the "Model Milk Ordinance." The state courts made no findings as to the relative merits of this inspection ordinance and the one chosen by Madison. The evidence indicates to me that enforcement of the Madison law would assure a more healthful quality of milk than that which is entitled to use the label of "Grade A" under the Model Ordinance. Indeed, the United States Board of Public Health, which drafted the Model Ordinance, suggests that the provisions are "minimum" standards only. . . .

Furthermore, the Model Ordinance would force the Madison health authorities to rely on "spot checks" by the United States Public Health Service to determine whether Chicago enforced its milk regulations. The evidence shows that these "spot checks" are based on random inspection of farms and pasteurization plants: the United States Public Health Service rates the ten thousand or more dairy farms in the Chicago milkshed by a sampling of no more than two hundred farms. The same sampling technique is employed to inspect pasteurization plants. There was evidence that neither the farms supplying Dean with milk nor Dean's pasteurization plants were necessarily inspected in the last "spot check" of the Chicago milkshed made two years before the present case was tried.

From what this record shows, and from what it fails to show, I do not think that either of the alternatives suggested by the Court would assure the people of Madison as pure a supply of milk as they receive under their own ordinance. . . .

RLW: This case is interesting because the Court concludes that Madison's ordinance discriminates against interstate commerce in spite of the existence of valid health and safety interests. Does the Court strictly apply either a *Southern Pacific* or *Baldwin* approach?

DEL: The *Dean Milk* decision, thanks largely to Justice Black's dissent, returns us to constitutional law's most pervasive question—what is the role of the judiciary? Even if the Court's power "to say what the law is" can be granted, *Dean Milk*, like *Southern Pacific* in the transportation regulation area or the right of privacy cases that define modern substantive due process review, invariably draws attention to the reference points that the judiciary may factor in developing constitutional law. Especially when the state's regulatory interest is perceptible, it is worth considering whether the judiciary is better suited for processing the interests and ordering the priorities that generate policy. Assessment of whether milk can be as effectively inspected by means other than what the state has adopted requires expertise beyond what a legal education provides. If such a role is acceptable, it may be that judges should be certified according not only to their legal knowledge and ability but to whether they qualify for service on a health and safety review board or its functional equivalent.

DER: In *Dean Milk Co.* the Court augmented the Commerce Clause test by assessing not only the state's purpose in passing the regulation but also the necessity of the method which the state used to achieve its purpose. Even a regulation with a valid objective may be struck down if reasonable nondiscriminatory alternatives that adequately serve the state's aim are available. This type of two-part inquiry is characteristic of strict scrutiny review which the Court routinely applies in First Amendment, Equal Protection, and right of privacy cases. Judging the necessity or practical consequences of legislation is not beyond courts' competence, although it may require judges to learn bodies of knowledge quite different from legal doctrine. *Brown v. Board of Education*, for example, required the Court to learn about the effects of segregated education upon the minds of school children. In *New York Times v. Sullivan*, the Court had to evaluate the impact of large libel judgments on the editorial judgments of newspapers. Many other constitutional cases similarly require the courts to examine complicated questions involving medicine, economics, art, the environment, psychology, and so on. The critical question is not whether judges are capable of digesting this information, for they are certainly just as capable of understanding diverse subjects as members of Congress or state legislatures. Rather, we must ask whether the Constitution gives judges the *institutional* authority to decide these issues. If the Commerce Clause delegates part of the responsibility of ensuring unrestrained trade to the courts, then there is nothing perverse about judges investigating the practical effects of state regulation on interstate commerce.

Consider *Maine v. Taylor*,[40] involving a Maine statute which prohibited the importation of live baitfish. The purpose of the law was to prevent foreign baitfish from infecting the native baitfish population with disease. Taylor was indicted under the Lacey Act, a federal statute, for bringing 158,000 live baitfish into Maine. That Act prohibited the import, export, transport, sale, receipt, acquisition, or purchase "in interstate or foreign commerce [of] . . . any fish or wildlife taken, possessed, transported, or sold in violation of any law or regulation of any State or in violation of any foreign law." Taylor challenged the Maine law, on which the federal prosecution was based, on the theory that Maine's law discriminated against interstate commerce. In an opinion written by Mr. Justice Blackmun, the Court upheld the law:

> Maine's statute restricts interstate trade in the most direct manner possible, blocking all inward shipments of live baitfish at the State's border. [This] fact alone does not render the law unconstitutional. The limitation imposed by the Commerce Clause on state regulatory power "is by no means absolute," and "the States retain authority under their general police powers to regulate matters of 'legitimate local concern,' even though interstate commerce may be affected."
>
> [Statutes which discriminate against interstate commerce] are subject to more demanding scrutiny. [If] a state law is shown to discriminate against interstate commerce "either on its face or in practical effect," the burden falls on the State to demonstrate both that the statute "serves a legitimate local purpose," and that this purpose could not be served as well by available nondiscriminatory means.
>
> [No] matter how one describes the abstract issue whether "alternative means could promote this local purpose as well without discriminating against interstate commerce," *Hughes v. Oklahoma*, 441 U.S., at 336, the more specific question whether scientifically accepted techniques exist for the sampling and inspection of live baitfish is one of fact, and the District Court's finding that such techniques have not been devised cannot be characterized as clearly erroneous. Indeed, the record probably could not support a contrary finding. Two prosecu-

---

[40] 477 U.S. 131 (1986).

tion witnesses testified to the lack of such procedures, and appellee's expert conceded the point, although he disagreed about the need for such tests. . . .

Mr. Justice Stevens dissented:

There is something fishy about this case. Maine is the only State in the Union that blatantly discriminates against out-of-state baitfish by flatly prohibiting their importation. Although golden shiners are already present and thriving in Maine (and, perhaps not coincidentally, the subject of a flourishing domestic industry), Maine excludes golden shiners grown and harvested (and, perhaps not coincidentally sold) in other States. This kind of stark discrimination against out-of-state articles of commerce requires rigorous justification by the discriminating State. . . .

In *Breard v. City of Alexandria*,[41] a regional representative of Keystone Readers Service, Inc., a Pennsylvania corporation, was arrested while engaged in door-to-door solicitations for nationally known magazines in the City of Alexandria, Louisiana. The arrest was based on his failure to obtain the prior consent of residence owners as required by statute. The Court upheld the law:

When there is a reasonable basis for legislation to protect the social, as distinguished from the economic, welfare of a community, it is not for this Court because of the Commerce Clause to deny the exercise locally of the sovereign power of Louisiana. Changing living conditions or variations in the experiences or habits of different communities may well call for different legislative regulations as to methods and manners of doing business. Powers of municipalities are subject to control by the states. Their judgment of local needs is made from a more intimate knowledge of local conditions than that of any other legislative body. We cannot say that this ordinance of Alexandria so burdens or impedes interstate commerce as to exceed the regulatory powers of that city.

Mr. Chief Justice Vinson, joined by Mr. Justice Douglas, dissented:

In passing upon other ordinances affecting solicitors, this Court has not hesitated in noting the economic fact that "the 'real competitors' of (solicitors) are, among others, the local retail merchants." *Nippert v. Richmond, supra*, 327 U.S. at page 433. The Court acknowledges "effective competition" between solicitors and the local retail merchants, but is deliberate in its refusal to appraise the practical effect of this ordinance as a deterrent to interstate commerce, 341 U.S. 639. I think it plain that a "blanket prohibition" upon appellant's solicitation discriminates against and unduly burdens interstate commerce in favoring local retail merchants. "Whether or not it was so intended, those are its necessary effects." *Nippert v. Richmond, supra*, 327 U.S. at page 434. . . .

---

[41] 341 U.S. 622 (1951).

Philadelphia v. New Jersey
437 U.S. 617 (1978)

Mr. Justice STEWART delivered the opinion of the Court.

A New Jersey law prohibits the importation of most "solid or liquid waste which originated or was collected outside the territorial limits of the State. . . . " In this case we are required to decide whether this statutory prohibition violates the Commerce Clause of the United States Constitution.

. . .

Immediately affected by [this law] were the operators of private landfills in New Jersey, and several cities in other States that had agreements with these operators for waste disposal. They brought suit against New Jersey and its Department of Environmental Protection in state court, attacking the statute and regulations on a number of state and federal grounds....

. . .

[W]e reject the state court's suggestion that the banning of "valueless" out-of-state wastes by ch. 363 implicates no constitutional protection. Just as Congress has power to regulate the interstate movement of these wastes, States are not free from constitutional scrutiny when they restrict that movement.

. . .

The crucial inquiry, therefore, must be directed to determining whether ch. 363 is basically a protectionist measure, or whether it can fairly be viewed as a law directed to legitimate local concerns, with effects upon interstate commerce that are only incidental.

The purpose of ch. 363 is set out in the statute itself as follows: "The Legislature finds and determines that . . . the volume of solid and liquid waste continues to rapidly increase, that the treatment and disposal of these wastes continues to pose an even greater threat to the quality of the environment of New Jersey, that the available and appropriate landfill sites within the State are being diminished, that the environment continues to be threatened by the treatment and disposal of waste which originated or was collected outside the State, and that the public health, safety and welfare require that the treatment and disposal within this State of all wastes generated outside of the State be prohibited."

The New Jersey Supreme Court accepted this statement of the state legislature's purpose. The state court additionally found that New Jersey's existing landfill sites will be exhausted within a few years; that to go on using these sites or to develop new ones will take a heavy environmental toll, both from pollution and from loss of scarce open lands; that new techniques to divert waste from landfills to other methods of disposal and resource recovery processes are under development, but that these changes will require time; and finally, that "the extension of the lifespan of existing landfills, resulting from the exclusion of out-of-state waste, may be of crucial importance in preventing further virgin wetlands or other undeveloped lands from being devoted to landfill purposes." 68 N.J., at 460–465. Based on these findings, the court concluded that ch. 363 was designed to protect, not the State's economy, but its environment, and that its substan-

tial benefits outweigh its "slight" burden on interstate commerce. *Id.*, at 471–478.

The appellants strenuously contend that ch. 363, "while outwardly cloaked 'in the currently fashionable garb of environmental protection,' . . . is actually no more than a legislative effort to suppress competition and stabilize the cost of solid waste disposal for New Jersey residents. . . . " They cite passages of legislative history suggesting that the problem addressed by ch. 363 is primarily financial: Stemming the flow of out-of-state waste into certain landfill sites will extend their lives, thus delaying the day when New Jersey cities must transport their waste to more distant and expensive sites.

The appellees, on the other hand, deny that ch. 363 was motivated by financial concerns or economic protectionism. In the words of their brief, "[n]o New Jersey commercial interests stand to gain advantage over competitors from outside the state as a result of the ban on dumping out-of-state waste." Noting that New Jersey landfill operators are among the plaintiffs, the appellee's brief argues that "[t]he complaint is not that New Jersey has forged an economic preference for its own commercial interests, but rather that it has denied a small group of its entrepreneurs an economic opportunity to traffic in waste in order to protect the health, safety and welfare of the citizenry at large."

This dispute about ultimate legislative purpose need not be resolved, because its resolution would not be relevant to the constitutional issue to be decided in this case. Contrary to the evident assumption of the state court and the parties, the evil of protectionism can reside in legislative means as well as legislative ends. Thus, it does not matter whether the ultimate aim of ch. 363 is to reduce the waste disposal costs of New Jersey residents or to save remaining open lands from pollution, for we assume New Jersey has every right to protect its residents' pocketbooks as well as their environment. And it may be assumed as well that New Jersey may pursue those ends by slowing the flow of all waste into the State's remaining landfills, even though interstate commerce may incidentally be affected. But whatever New Jersey's ultimate purpose, it may not be accomplished by discriminating against articles of commerce coming from outside the State unless there is some reason, apart from their origin, to treat them differently. Both on its face and in its plain effect, ch. 363 violates this principle of nondiscrimination.

The Court has consistently found parochial legislation of this kind to be constitutionally invalid, whether the ultimate aim of the legislation was to assure a steady supply of milk by erecting barriers to allegedly ruinous outside competition, or to create jobs by keeping industry within the State, or to preserve the State's financial resources from depletion by fencing out indigent immigrants. In each of these cases, a presumably legitimate goal was sought to be achieved by the illegitimate means of isolating the State from the national economy.

Also relevant here are the Court's decisions holding that a State may not accord its own inhabitants a preferred right of access over consumers in other States to natural resources located within its borders. *West, Attorney General of Oklahoma v. Kansas Natural Gas Co.*, 221 U.S. 229; *Pennsylvania v. West Virginia*, 262 U.S. 553. These cases stand for the basic principle that a "State is without power to prevent privately owned articles of trade from being shipped and sold in interstate commerce on the ground that they are required to satisfy local demands or because they are needed by the people of the State." *Foster-Fountain Packing Co. v. Haydel, supra*, 278 U.S. at 10.

The New Jersey law at issue in this case falls squarely within the area that the Commerce Clause puts off limits to state regulation. On its face, it imposes on out-of-state commercial interests the full burden of conserving the State's remaining landfill space. It is true that in our previous cases the scarce natural resource was itself the article of commerce, whereas here the scarce resource and the article of commerce are distinct. But that difference is without consequence. In both instances, the State has overtly moved to slow or freeze the flow of commerce for protectionist reasons. It does not matter that the State has shut the article of commerce inside the State in one case and outside the State in the other. What is crucial is the attempt by one State to isolate itself from a problem common to many by erecting a barrier against the movement of interstate trade.

The appellees argue that not all laws which facially discriminate against out-of-state commerce are forbidden protectionist regulations. In particular, they point to quarantine laws, which this Court has repeatedly upheld even though they appear to single out interstate commerce for special treatment. *See Baldwin v. G.A.F. Seelig, Inc., supra*, 294 U.S., at 525; *Bowman v. Chicago & Northwestern R. Co.*, 125 U.S., at 489. In the appellees' view, ch. 363 is analogous to such health-protective measures, since it reduces the exposure of New Jersey residents to the allegedly harmful effects of landfill sites.

It is true that certain quarantine laws have not been considered forbidden protection-

ist measures, even though they were directed against out-of-state commerce. *See Asbell v. Kansas*, 209 U.S. 251; *Reid v. Colorado*, 187 U.S. 137. But those quarantine laws banned the importation of articles such as diseased livestock that required destruction as soon as possible because their very movement risked contagion and other evils. Those laws thus did not discriminate against interstate commerce as such, but simply prevented traffic in noxious articles, whatever their origin.

The New Jersey statute is not such a quarantine law. There has been no claim here that the very movement of waste into or through New Jersey endangers health, or that waste must be disposed of as soon and as close to its point of generation as possible. The harms caused by waste are said to arise after its disposal in landfill sites, and at that point, as New Jersey concedes, there is no basis to distinguish out-of-state waste from domestic waste. If one is inherently harmful, so is the other. Yet New Jersey has banned the former while leaving its landfill sites open to the latter. The New Jersey law blocks the importation of waste in an obvious effort to saddle those outside the State with the entire burden of slowing the flow of refuse into New Jersey's remaining landfill sites. That legislative effort is clearly impermissible under the Commerce Clause of the Constitution.

Today, cities in Pennsylvania and New York find it expedient or necessary to send their waste into New Jersey for disposal, and New Jersey claims the right to close its borders to such traffic. Tomorrow, cities in New Jersey may find it expedient or necessary to send their waste into Pennsylvania or New York for disposal, and those States might then claim the right to close its borders to such traffic. The Commerce Clause will protect New Jersey in the future, just as it protects her neighbors now, from efforts by one State to isolate itself in the stream of interstate commerce from a problem shared by all. The judgment is

Reversed.

Mr. Justice Rehnquist, with whom The Chief Justice joins, dissenting.

. . .

The Court recognizes that States can prohibit the importation of items "'which, on account of their existing condition, would bring in and spread disease, pestilence, and death, such as rags or other substances infected with the germs of yellow fever or the virus of smallpox, or cattle or meat or other provisions that are diseased or decayed or otherwise, from their condition and quality, unfit for human use or consumption.'" *Bowman v. Chicago & Northwestern R. Co.*, 125 U.S. 465, 489 (1888). As the Court points out, such "quarantine laws have not been considered forbidden protectionist measures, even though they were directed against out-of-state commerce." *Ante*, at 2538.

In my opinion, these cases are dispositive of the present one. Under them, New Jersey may require germ-infected rags or diseased meat to be disposed of as best as possible within the State, but at the same time prohibit the importation of such items for disposal at the facilities that are set up within New Jersey for disposal of such material generated within the State. The physical fact of life that New Jersey must somehow dispose of its own noxious items does not mean that it must serve as a depository for those of every other State. Similarly, New Jersey should be free under our past precedents to prohibit the importation of solid waste because of the health and safety problems that such waste poses to its citizens. The fact that New Jersey continues to, and indeed must continue to, dispose of its own solid waste does not mean that New Jersey may not prohibit the importation of even more solid waste into the State. I simply see no way to distinguish solid waste, on the record of this case, from germ-infected rags, diseased meat, and other noxious items.

The Court's effort to distinguish these prior cases is unconvincing. It first asserts that the quarantine laws which have previously been upheld "banned the importation of articles such as diseased livestock that required destruction as soon as possible because their very movement risked contagion and other evils." *Ante*, at 2538. . . . Solid waste which is a health hazard when it reaches its destination may in all likelihood be an equally great health hazard in transit.

. . .

Second, the Court implies that the challenged laws must be invalidated because New Jersey has left its landfills open to domestic waste. But, as the Court notes, this Court has repeatedly upheld quarantine laws "even though they appear to single out interstate commerce for special treatment." . . .

The Supreme Court of New Jersey expressly found that ch. 363 was passed "to preserve the health of New Jersey residents by keeping their exposure to solid waste and landfill areas to a minimum." 68 N.J. 451, 473. The Court points to absolutely no evidence that would contradict this finding by the New Jersey Supreme Court. . . .

Exxon Corp. v. Maryland[42] involved a Maryland law which provided that a producer or refiner of petroleum products (1) may not operate any retail service station within the State, and (2) must extend all "voluntary allowances" uniformly to all service stations it supplies. The law was designed to prevent refiners from discriminating in favor of their company-owned stations in times of shortage. In an opinion written by Mr. Justice Stevens, the Court upheld the law:

> Plainly, the Maryland statute does not discriminate against interstate goods, nor does it favor local producers and refiners. Since Maryland's entire gasoline supply flows in interstate commerce and since there are no local producers or refiners, such claims of disparate treatment between interstate and local commerce would be meritless. Appellants, however, focus on the retail market arguing that the effect of the statute is to protect in-state independent dealers from out-of-state competition. They contend that the divestiture provisions "create a protected enclave for Maryland independent dealers. . . . " As support for this proposition, they rely on the fact that the burden of the divestiture requirements falls solely on interstate companies. But this fact does not lead, either logically or as a practical matter, to a conclusion that the State is discriminating against interstate commerce at the retail level.
>
> As the record shows, there are several major interstate marketers of petroleum that own and operate their own retail gasoline stations. These interstate dealers, who compete directly with the Maryland independent dealers, are not affected by the Act because they do not refine or produce gasoline. In fact, the Act creates no barriers whatsoever against interstate independent dealers; it does not prohibit the flow of interstate goods, place added costs upon them, or

---

[42] 437 U.S. 117 (1978).

distinguish between in-state and out-of-state companies in the retail market. . . .

Mr. Justice Blackmun concurred:

[G]iven the structure of the retail gasoline market in Maryland, the effect of §§ (b) and (c) is to exclude a class of predominantly out-of-state gasoline retailers while providing protection from competition to a class of nonintegrated retailers that is overwhelmingly composed of local businessmen. . . .

· · ·

With discrimination proved against interstate commerce, the burden falls upon the State to justify the distinction with legitimate state interests that cannot be vindicated with more evenhanded regulation. . . .

In sum, the State has asserted before this Court only a vague interest in preserving competition in its retail gasoline market. It has not shown why its interest cannot be vindicated by legislation less discriminatory toward out-of-state retailers. It therefore has not met its burden to justify the discrimination inherent in §§ (b) and (c), and they violate the Commerce Clause.

Minnesota v. Clover Leaf Creamery Co.[43] involved a Minnesota law which banned the retail sale of milk in plastic nonreturnable, nonrefillable containers, but permitted such sale in other nonreturnable, nonrefillable containers, such as paperboard milk cartons. The law was passed for environmental reasons including concerns regarding solid waste management disposal, energy waste, and depletion of natural resources presented by plastic containers. The Court upheld the law:

Minnesota's statute does not effect "simple protectionism," but "regulates evenhandedly" by prohibiting all milk retailers from selling their products in plastic, nonreturnable milk containers, without regard to whether the milk, the containers, or the sellers are from outside the State. This statute is therefore unlike statutes discriminating against interstate commerce, which we have consistently struck down.

· · ·

The burden imposed on interstate commerce by the statute is relatively minor. Milk products may continue to move freely across the Minnesota border, and since most dairies package their products in more than one type of containers, the inconvenience of having to conform to different packaging requirements in Minnesota and the surrounding States should be slight. . . .

· · ·

Even granting that the out-of-state plastics industry is burdened relatively more heavily than the Minnesota pulpwood industry, we find that this burden is not "clearly excessive" in light of the substantial state interest in promoting conservation of energy and other natural resources and easing solid waste disposal problems. . . . We find these local benefits ample to support Minnesota's decision under the Commerce Clause. Moreover, we find that no approach with "a lesser impact on interstate activities," *Pike v. Bruce Church, Inc., supra*, at 142, is available. Respondents have suggested several alternative statutory schemes, but these alternatives are either more burdensome on commerce than the Act (as, for example, banning all nonreturnables) or less likely to be effective (as, for example, providing incentives for recycling).

---

[43] 449 U.S. 456 (1981).

Reciprocity Provisions. Great Atlantic & Pacific Tea Co., Inc. v. Cottrell[44] involved a Mississippi law which prohibited the sale of foreign milk and milk products in Mississippi unless the foreign state accepted Grade A milk and milk products produced and processed in Mississippi on a reciprocal basis. A Louisiana milk producer, who was denied entry to the Mississippi market because Louisiana did not give Mississippi milk reciprocity, challenged the Mississippi law. The Louisiana milk met Mississippi's health standards. In an opinion written by Mr. Justice Brennan, the Court struck down the Mississippi law:

> The second prong of appellee's argument that the reciprocity requirement promotes trade between the States draws upon Mississippi's allegations that Louisiana is itself violating the Commerce Clause by refusing to admit milk produced in Mississippi. . . . Hence, the reciprocity agreement, it is argued, is a legitimate means by which Mississippi may seek to gain access to Louisiana markets for its own producers as a condition to allowing Louisiana milk to be sold in Mississippi. We cannot agree.
>
> [T]o the extent, if any, that Louisiana is unconstitutionally burdening the flow of milk in interstate commerce by erecting and enforcing economic trade barriers to protect its own producers from competition under the guise of health regulations, the Commerce Clause itself creates the necessary reciprocity: Mississippi and its producers may pursue their constitutional remedy by suit in state or federal court challenging Louisiana's actions as violative of the Commerce Clause.
>
> . . .
>
> Accordingly, we hold that the mandatory character of the reciprocity requirement of § 11 unduly burdens the free flow of interstate commerce and cannot be justified as a permissible exercise of any state power.

Cottrell was followed by *New Energy Co. of Indiana v. Limbach*, 486 U.S. 269 (1988). *Limbach* involved an Ohio statute which awarded a tax credit against the Ohio motor vehicle fuel sales tax for each gallon of ethanol sold (as a component of gasohol) by fuel dealers, but only if the ethanol was produced in Ohio or in a State that grants similar tax advantages to ethanol produced in Ohio. New Energy Co., an Indiana firm which manufactured ethanol, challenged the law. Because Indiana did not provide similar benefits to Ohio ethanol producers, New Energy was not entitled to the Ohio credit. In an opinion written by Mr. Justice Scalia, the Court struck down the law:

> The Ohio provision at issue here explicitly deprives certain products of generally available beneficial tax treatment because they are made in certain other States, and thus on its face appears to violate the cardinal requirement of nondiscrimination. . . .
>
> It is true that in *Cottrell* and *Sporhase* the effect of a State's refusal to accept the offered reciprocity was total elimination of all transport of the subject product into or out of the offering State; whereas in the present case the only effect of refusal is that the out-of-state product is placed at a substantial commercial disadvantage through discriminatory tax treatment. That makes no difference for purposes of Commerce Clause analysis. In the leading case of *Baldwin v. G.A.F. Seelig, Inc.*, 294 U.S. 511 (1935), the New York law excluding out-of-state milk did not impose an absolute ban, but rather allowed importation and sale so long as the initial purchase from the dairy farmer was made at or above the New York State-mandated price. In other words, just as the

---

[44] 424 U.S. 366 (1976).

appellant here, in order to sell its product in Ohio, only has to cut its profits by reducing its sales price below the market price sufficiently to compensate the Ohio purchaser-retailer for the foregone tax credit, so also the milk wholesaler-distributor in *Baldwin*, in order to sell its product in New York, only had to cut its profits by increasing its purchase price above the market price sufficiently to meet the New York-prescribed minimum. We viewed the New York law as "an economic barrier against competition" that was "equivalent to a rampart of customs duties." *Id.*, at 527. . . .

[The] Commerce Clause does not prohibit all state action designed to give its residents an advantage in the marketplace, but only action of that description in connection with the State's regulation of interstate commerce. Direct subsidization of domestic industry does not ordinarily run afoul of that prohibition; discriminatory taxation of out-of-state manufacturers does. Of course, even if the Indiana subsidy were invalid, retaliatory violation of the Commerce Clause by Ohio would not be acceptable.

Sporhase v. Nebraska[45] was yet another reciprocity case, involving a state law that restricted the withdrawal of ground water from any well within Nebraska intended for use in an adjoining State. Nebraska allowed water to be withdrawn from the ground, for use in another state, only if the other state provided reciprocity to Nebraskans regarding the use of its water. Although the Court struck down the reciprocity provision, the Court indicated that it would have upheld the statute had Nebraska simply prohibited the transport of water out of state:

> Ground water overdraft is a national problem and Congress has the power to deal with it on that scale.
>
> . . .
>
> The . . . purpose [of] § 46–613.01 is to conserve and preserve diminishing sources of ground water. The purpose is unquestionably legitimate and highly important, and the other aspects of Nebraska's ground water regulation demonstrate that it is genuine.
>
> . . .
>
> [I]n the absence of a contrary view expressed by Congress, we are reluctant to condemn as unreasonable, measures taken by a State to conserve and preserve for its own citizens this vital resource in times of severe shortage. . . .

Mr. Justice Rehnquist dissented:

> . . .
>
> [If] the State allows indiscriminate intrastate commercial dealings in a particular resource, it may have a difficult task proving that an outright prohibition on interstate commercial dealings is not such a discrimination. I had thought that this was the basis for this Court's decisions in *Hughes v. Oklahoma*, 441 U.S. 322 (1979), *Pennsylvania v. West Virginia*, 262 U.S. 553 (1923), and *West v. Kansas Natural Gas Co.*, 221 U.S. 229 (1911). In each case, the State permitted a natural resource to be reduced to private possession, permitted an intrastate market to exist in that resource, and either barred interstate commerce entirely or granted its residents a commercial preference.

b. Outgoing Commerce

Do different rules apply when states regulate outgoing commerce as opposed to incoming commerce?

---

[45] 458 U.S. 941 (1982).

H. P. Hood & Sons v. Du Mond
336 U.S. 525 (1949)

Mr. Justice JACKSON delivered the opinion of the Court.

This case concerns the power of the State of New York to deny additional facilities to acquire and ship milk in interstate commerce where the grounds of denial are that such limitation upon interstate business will protect and advance local economic interests.

H.P. Hood & Sons, Inc., a Massachusetts corporation, has long distributed milk and its products to inhabitants of Boston. That city obtains about 90% of its fluid milk from states other than Massachusetts. Dairies located in New York State since about 1900 have been among the sources of Boston's supply, their contribution having varied but during the last ten years approximately 8%. The area in which Hood has been denied an additional license to make interstate purchases has been developed as a part of the Boston milkshed from which both the Hood Company and a competitor have shipped to Boston.

The state courts have held and it is conceded here that Hood's entire business in New York, present and proposed, is interstate commerce. This Hood has conducted for some time by means of three receiving depots, where it takes raw milk from farmers. The milk is not processed in New York but is weighed, tested and, if necessary, cooled and on the same day shipped as fluid milk to Boston. These existing plants have been operated under license from the State and are not in question here as the State has licensed Hood to continue them. The controversy concerns a proposed additional plant for the same kind of operation at Greenwich, New York.

. . .

[The Commissioner denied Hood a permit for the additional plant.] The Commissioner's denial was based on further provisions of this section which require him to be satisfied "that the issuance of the license will not tend to a destructive competition in a market already adequately served, and that the issuance of the license will be in the public interest."

Upon the hearing pursuant to the statute, milk dealers competing with Hood as buyers in the area opposed licensing the proposed Greenwich plant. They complained that Hood, by reason of conditions under which it sold in Boston, had competitive advantages under applicable federal milk orders, Boston health regulations, and OPA ceiling prices. There was also evidence of a temporary shortage of supply in the Troy, New York market during the fall and winter of 1945—46. The Commissioner was urged not to allow Hood to compete for additional supplies to milk or to take on producers then delivering to other dealers.

The Commissioner found that Hood, if licensed at Greenwich, would permit its present suppliers, at their option, to deliver at the new plant rather than the old ones and for a substantial number this would mean shorter hauls and savings in delivery costs. The new plant also would attract twenty to thirty producers, some of whose milk Hood anticipates will or may be diverted from other buyers. Other large milk distributors have plants within the general area and dealers serving Troy obtain milk in the locality. He found that Troy was inadequately supplied during the preceding short season.

. . .

Production and distribution of milk are so intimately related to public health and welfare that the need for regulation to protect those interests has long been recognized and is, from a constitutional standpoint, hardly controversial. Also, the economy of the industry is so eccentric that economic controls have been found at once necessary and difficult. . . . As the states extended their efforts to control various phases of export and import also, questions were raised as to limitations on state power under the Commerce Clause of the Constitution.

. . .

[New] York's regulations, designed to assure producers a fair price and a responsible purchaser, and consumers a sanitary and modernly equipped handler, are not challenged here but have been complied with. It is only additional restrictions, imposed for the avowed purpose and with the practical effect of curtailing the volume of interstate commerce to aid local economic interests, that are in question here. . . .

Our decision in a milk litigation most relevant to the present controversy deals with the converse of the present situation. *Baldwin v. G.A.F. Seelig, Inc.*, 294 U.S. 511. In that case, New York placed conditions and limitations on the local sale of milk imported from Vermont designed in practical effect to exclude it, while here its order proposes to limit the local facilities for purchase of additional milk so as to withhold milk from export. The State agreed then, as now, that the Commerce Clause prohibits it from directly curtailing movement of milk into or out of the State. But in the earlier case, it contended that the same result could be accomplished by controlling delivery, bottling and sale after arrival, while here it says it can do so by curtailing facilities for its purchase and receipt before it is shipped out. In neither case is the measure supported by health or safety considerations but solely by protection of local economic interests, such as supply for local consumption and limitation of competition. This Court unanimously rejected the State's contention in the Seelig case and held that the Commerce Clause, even in the absence or congressional action, prohibits such regulations for such ends.

[We recognize] . . . broad power in the State to protect its inhabitants against perils to health or safety, fraudulent traders and highway hazards even by use of measures which bear adversely upon interstate commerce. But . . . the State may not promote its own economic advantages by curtailment or burdening of interstate commerce.

. . .

This distinction between the power of the State to shelter its people from menaces to their health or safety and from fraud, even when those dangers emanate from interstate commerce, and its lack of power to retard, burden or constrict the flow of such commerce for their economic advantage, is one deeply rooted in both our history and our law.

. . .

This principle that our economic unit is the Nation, which alone has the gamut of powers necessary to control of the economy, including the vital power of erecting customs barriers against foreign competition, has as its corollary that the states are not separable economic units. . . . This Court has not only recognized this disability of the state to isolate its own economy as a basis for striking down parochial legislative policies designed to do so, but it has recognized the incapacity of the state to protect its own inhabitants from competition as a reason for sustaining particular exercises of the commerce power of Congress to reach matters in which states were so disabled.

The material success that has come to inhabitants of the states which make up this federal free trade unit has been the most impressive in the history of commerce, but the established interdependence of the states only emphasizes the necessity of protecting interstate movement of goods against local burdens and repressions. We need only consider the consequences if each of the few states that produce copper, lead, high-grade iron ore, timber, cotton, oil or gas should decree that industries located in that state shall have priority. What fantastic rivalries and dislocations and reprisals would ensue if such practices were begun! Or suppose that the field of discrimination and retaliation be industry. May Michigan provide that automobiles cannot be taken out of that State until local dealers' demands are fully met? Would she not have every argument in the favor of such a statute that can be offered in support of New York's limiting sales of milk for out-of-state shipment to protect the economic interests of her competing dealers and local consumers? Could Ohio then pounce upon the rubber-tire industry, on which she has a substantial grip, to retaliate for Michigan's auto monopoly?

Our system, fostered by the Commerce Clause, is that every farmer and every craftsman shall be encouraged to produce by the certainty that he will have free access to every market in the Nation, that no home embargoes will withhold his export, and no foreign state will by customs duties or regulations exclude them. Likewise, every consumer may look to the free competition from every producing area in the Nation to protect him from exploitation by any. Such was the vision of the Founders; such has been the doctrine of this Court which has given it reality.

. . .

Since the statute as applied violates the Commerce Clause and is not authorized by federal legislation pursuant to that Clause, it cannot stand. The judgment is reversed and the cause remanded for proceedings not inconsistent with this opinion. It is so ordered.

Reversed and remanded.

Mr. Justice FRANKFURTER, with whom Mr. Justice RUTLEDGE joins, dissenting.

. . .

[I]n the absence of federal regulation, it is sometimes—of course not always—of greater importance that local interests be protected than that interstate commerce be not touched.

. . .

[The] milk industry is peculiarly subject to internecine warfare, as this Court recognized in sustaining against due-process attack the precursor of New York's present milk-control law. *Nebbia v. People of State of New York*, 291 U.S. 502. A picture of ruthless and wasteful competition was painted in that case as in each of the other cases in which the Court has upheld the regulation of the milk industry. *United States v. Rock Royal Co-operative*, 307 U.S. 533; *H.P. Hood & Sons v. United States*, 307 U.S. 588. And so far as appears, State action to maintain the price structure in conjunction with complementary regulation by the Secretary of Agriculture is no less necessary for the dairy industry than for the raisin industry. *Compare Parker v. Brown*, 317 U.S. 341. In view of the importance that we have hitherto found in regulation of the economy of agriculture, I cannot understand the justification for assigning, as a matter of law, so much higher a place to milk dealers' standards of bookkeeping than to the economic well-being of their industry.

. . .

Broadly stated, the question is whether a State can withhold from interstate commerce a product derived from local raw materials upon a determination by an administrative agency that there is a local need for it. . . . It is arguable, moreover, that the Commissioner was actuated not by preference for New York consumers, but by the aim of stabilizing the supply of all the local markets, including Boston as well as Troy, served by the New York milkshed. It may also be that he had in mind the potentially harmful competitive effect of efforts by dealers supplying the Troy market to repair by attracting new producers, the aggravation of Troy's shortage which would result from the diversion to Boston of part of Troy's supply. These too are matters as to which more light would be needed if it were now necessary to decide the question.

. . .

Mr. Justice BLACK, dissenting.

. . .

[I]t seems to me that here as in the Eisenberg case, this Court should not pit its legal judgment against a legislative judgment that is in harmony with the views of persons who have devoted their lives to a practical study of the milk problem.

. . .

The sole immediate result of today's holding is that petitioner will be allowed to operate a new milk plant in New York. This consequence standing alone is of no great importance. But there are other consequences of importance. It is always a serious thing for this Court to strike down a statewide law. It is more serious when the state law falls under a new rule which will inescapably narrow the area in which states can regulate and control local business practices found inimical to the public welfare. The gravity of striking down state regulations is immeasurably increased when it results as here in leaving a no-man's land immune from any effective regulation whatever. It is dangerous to assume that the aggressive cupidity of some need never be checked by government in the interest of all.

. . .

. . . While I have doubt about the wisdom of this New York law, I do not conceive it to be the function of this Court to revise that state's economic judgments. Any doubt I may have concerning the wisdom of New York's law is far less, however, than is my skepticism concerning the ability of the Federal Government to reach out and effectively regulate all the local business activities in the forty-eight states.

I would leave New York's law alone.

Pike v. Bruce Church, Inc.
397 U.S. 137 (1970)

Mr. Justice STEWART delivered the opinion of the Court.

[T]he Arizona Fruit and Vegetable Standardization Act . . . requires that, with certain exceptions, all cantaloupes grown in Arizona and offered for sale must "be packed in regular compact arrangement in closed standard containers approved by the supervisor. . . ." . . . [Appellee, who grew cantaloupes in both Arizona and California, had its Arizona cantaloupes packed at its plant in nearby California. Appellee sued to enjoin enforcement of the Act.].

. . .

Although the criteria for determining the validity of state statutes affecting interstate commerce have been variously stated, the general rule that emerges can be phrased as follows: Where the statute regulates even-handedly to effectuate a legitimate local public interest, and its effects on interstate commerce are only incidental, it will be upheld unless the burden imposed on such commerce is clearly excessive in relation to the putative local benefits. *Huron Portland Cement Co. v. City of Detroit*, 362 U.S. 440, 443. If a legitimate local

purpose is found, then the question becomes one of degree. And the extent of the burden that will be tolerated will of course depend on the nature of the local interest involved, and on whether it could be promoted as well with a lesser impact on interstate activities. Occasionally the Court has candidly undertaken a balancing approach in resolving these issues, but more frequently it has spoken in terms of "direct" and "indirect" effects and burdens.

At the core of the Arizona Fruit and Vegetable Standardization Act are the requirements that fruits and vegetables shipped from Arizona meet certain standards of wholesomeness and quality, and that they be packed in standard containers in such a way that the outer layer or exposed portion of the pack does not "materially misrepresent" the quality of the lot as a whole. The impetus for the Act was the fear that some growers were shipping inferior or deceptively packaged produce, with the result that the reputation of Arizona growers generally was being tarnished and their financial return concomitantly reduced. It was to prevent this that the Act was passed in 1929. The State has stipulated that its primary purpose is to promote and preserve the reputation of Arizona growers by prohibiting deceptive packaging.

We are not, then, dealing here with "state legislation in the field of safety where the propriety of local regulation has long been recognized," or with an Act designed to protect consumers in Arizona from contaminated or unfit goods. Its purpose and design are simply to protect and enhance the reputation of growers within the State. These are surely legitimate state interests. We have upheld a State's power to require that produce packaged in the State be packaged in a particular kind of receptacle. And we have recognized the legitimate interest of a State in maximizing the financial return to an industry within it. Therefore, as applied to Arizona growers who package their produce in Arizona, we may assume the constitutional validity of the Act. We may further assume that Arizona has full constitutional power to forbid the misleading use of its name on produce that was grown or packed elsewhere. And, to the extent the Act forbids the shipment of contaminated or unfit produce, it clearly rests on sure footing. For, as the Court has said, such produce is "not the legitimate subject of trade or commerce, nor within the protection of the commerce clause of the Constitution." *Sligh v. Kirkwood, supra*, 237 U.S., at 60.

But application of the Act through the appellant's order to the appellee company has a far different impact, and quite a different purpose. The cantaloupes grown by the company at Parker are of exceptionally high quality. The company does not pack them in Arizona and cannot do so without making a capital expenditure of approximately $200,000. It transports them in bulk to nearby Blythe, California, where they are sorted, inspected, packed, and shipped in containers that do not identify them as Arizona cantaloupes, but bear the name of their California packer. The appellant's order would forbid the company to pack its cantaloupes outside Arizona, not for the purpose of keeping the reputation of its growers unsullied, but to enhance their reputation through the reflected good will of the company's superior produce. The appellant, in other words, is not complaining because the company is putting the good name of Arizona on an inferior or deceptively packaged product, but because it is not putting that name on a product that is superior and well packaged. As the appellant's brief puts the matter, "It is within Arizona's legitimate interest to require that interstate cantaloupe purchasers be informed that this high quality Parker fruit was grown in Arizona."

Although it is not easy to see why the other growers of Arizona are entitled to benefit at the company's expense from the fact that it produces superior crops, we may assume that the asserted state interest is a legitimate one. But the State's tenuous interest in having the company's cantaloupes identified as originating in Arizona cannot constitutionally justify the requirement that the company build and operate an unneeded $200,000 packing plant in the State. The nature of that burden is, constitutionally, more significant than its extent. For the Court has viewed with particular suspicion state statutes requiring business operations to be performed in the home State that could more efficiently be performed elsewhere. Even where the State is pursuing a clearly legitimate local interest, this particular burden on commerce has been declared to be virtually per se illegal.

The appellant argues that the above cases are different because they involved statutes whose express or concealed purpose was to preserve or secure employment for the home State, while here the statute is a regulatory one and there is no hint of such a purpose. But in *Toomer v. Witsell, supra*, the Court indicated that such a burden upon interstate commerce is unconstitutional even in the absence of such a purpose. In *Toomer* the Court held invalid a South Carolina statute requiring that owners of shrimp boats licensed by the State to fish in the maritime belt off South Carolina must unload and pack their catch in that State before "shipping or transporting it to another State." What we said there applies to this case as well: "There was also uncontradicted evidence that appellants' costs would be materially increased by the necessity of having their shrimp unloaded and packed in South Carolina ports rather than at their home bases in Georgia where they maintain their own docking, warehousing, refrigeration and packing facilities. In addition, an inevitable concomitant of a statute requiring that work be done in South Carolina, even though that be economically disadvantageous to the fishermen, is to divert to South Carolina employment and business which might otherwise go to Georgia; the necessary tendency of the statute is to impose an artificial rigidity on the economic pattern of the industry." 334 U.S., at 403—404.

While the order issued under the Arizona statute does not impose such rigidity on an entire industry, it does impose just such a straitjacket on the appellee company with respect to the allocation of its interstate resources. Such an incidental consequence of a regulatory scheme could perhaps be tolerated if a more compelling state interest were involved. But here the State's interest is minimal at best—certainly less substantial than a State's interest in securing employment for its people.

If the Commerce Clause forbids a State to require work to be done within its jurisdiction to promote local employment, then surely it cannot permit a State to require a person to go into a local packing business solely for the sake of enhancing the reputation of other producers within its borders.

The judgment is affirmed.

Hughes v. Oklahoma[46] involved an Oklahoma law which prohibited the transportation or shipment of minnows, for sale outside the state, which were seined or procured within Oklahoma. Appellant Hughes was charged with transporting to Texas a load of natural minnows purchased from a minnow dealer in Oklahoma. In an opinion written by Mr. Justice Brennan, the Court struck down the Oklahoma law:

> Oklahoma argues that § 4–115(B) serves a legitimate local purpose in that it is "readily apparent as a conservation measure." The State's interest in maintaining the ecological balance in state waters by avoiding the removal of inordinate numbers of minnows may well qualify as a legitimate local purpose. . . . But [a] State may no longer "keep the property, if the sovereign so chooses, always within its jurisdiction for every purpose." *Greer v. Connecticut*, 161 U.S., at 530. . . .
>
> Far from choosing the least discriminatory alternative, Oklahoma has chosen to "conserve" its minnows in the way that most overtly discriminates against interstate commerce. The State places no limits on the numbers of minnows that can be taken by licensed minnow dealers; nor does it limit in any way how these minnows may be disposed of within the State. Yet it forbids the transportation of any commercially significant number of natural minnows out of the State for sale. . . .

Mr. Justice Rehnquist, joined by Chief Justice Burger, dissented:

> Contrary to the view of the Court, I do not think that Oklahoma's regulation of the commercial exploitation of natural minnows either discriminates against out-of-state enterprises in favor of local businesses or that it burdens the interstate commerce in minnows. At least, no such showing has been made on the record before us. This is not a case where a State's regulation permits residents to export naturally seined minnows but prohibits nonresidents from so doing. No person is allowed to export natural minnows for sale outside of Oklahoma; the statute is evenhanded in its application. The State has not used its power to protect its own citizens from outside competition. . . . [N]otwithstanding the Court's protestations to the contrary, Oklahoma has not blocked the flow of interstate commerce in minnows at the State's borders. Appellant, or anyone else, may freely export as many minnows as he wishes, so long as the minnows so transported are hatchery minnows and not naturally seined minnows. On this record, I simply fail to see how interstate commerce in minnows, the commodity at issue here, is impeded in the least by Oklahoma's regulatory scheme.

Cities Service Gas Co. v. Peerless Oil & Gas Co.[47] involved an Oklahoma law which established a minimum wellhead price for natural gas produced in Oklahoma and sold interstate. In an opinion written by Mr. Justice Clark, the Court upheld the law:

> That a legitimate local interest is at stake in this case is clear. A state is justifiably concerned with preventing rapid and uneconomic dissipation of one of its chief natural resources. . . .

---

[46] 441 U.S. 322 (1979).
[47] 340 U.S. 179 (1950).

[In] a field of this complexity with such diverse interests involved, we cannot say that there is a clear national interest so harmed that the state price-fixing orders here employed fall within the ban of the Commerce Clause. Nor is it for us to consider whether Oklahoma's unilateral efforts to conserve gas will be fully effective.

H.P. Hood & Sons v. Du Mond, 1949, 336 U.S. 525, is not inconsistent with this result. . . . The vice in the regulation invalidated by Hood was solely that it denied facilities to a company in interstate commerce on the articulated ground that such facilities would divert milk supplies needed by local consumers; in other words, the regulation discriminated against interstate commerce. There is no such problem here. The price regulation applies to all gas taken from the field, whether destined for interstate or intrastate consumers.

Parker v. Brown[48] involved the California Agricultural Prorate Act which established a marketing program for the 1940 raisin crop. The declared purpose of the Act was to "conserve the agricultural wealth of the State" and to "prevent economic waste in the marketing of agricultural crops" of the state. At the time, virtually all raisins consumed in the United States, and nearly one-half of the world crop, were produced in Raisin Proration Zone No. 1 in California. Between 90 and 95 per cent of the raisins grown in California were ultimately shipped in interstate or foreign commerce. The program limited the ability of producers to sell their grapes. The Court upheld the law:

Examination of the evidence in this case and of available data of the raisin industry in California, of which we may take judicial notice, leaves no doubt that the evils attending the production and marketing of raisins in that state present a problem local in character and urgently demanding state action for the economic protection of those engaged in one of its important industries. [T]he industry, with a large increase in acreage and the attendant fall in price, has been unable to market its product and has been compelled to sell at less than parity prices and in some years at prices regarded by students of the industry as less than the cost of production.

The history of the industry at least since 1929 is a record of a continuous search for expedients which would stabilize the marketing of the raisin crop and maintain a price standard which would bring fair return to the producers. . . .

[T]he adoption of legislative measures to prevent the demoralization of the industry by stabilizing the marketing of the raisin crop is a matter of state as well as national concern and, in the absence of inconsistent Congressional action, is a problem whose solution is peculiarly within the province of the state. In the exercise of its power the state has adopted a measure appropriate to the end sought. The program was not aimed at nor did it discriminate against interstate commerce, although it undoubtedly affected the commerce by increasing the interstate price of raisins and curtailing interstate shipments to some undetermined extent. The effect on the commerce is not greater, and in some instances was far less, than that which this Court has held not to afford a basis for denying to the states the right to pursue a legitimate state end.

[W]hatever effect the operation of the California program may have on interstate commerce, it is one which it has been the policy of Congress to aid and encourage through federal agencies in conformity to the Agricultural Marketing Agreement Act, and § 302 of the Agricultural Adjustment Act. Nor is the effect on the commerce greater than or substantially different in kind from that contemplated by the stabilization programs authorized by federal statutes. . . .

---

[48] 317 U.S. 341 (1943).

4. Preemption

Southern Pacific and *Baldwin* involve "dormant" power situations in which the federal government has the power to regulate a subject, but has chosen not to exercise its power. What happens if the federal government has exercised its power? *Gibbons* holds that, if the federal government has regulated a subject within the scope of its authority, and there is a conflict between the federal law and a state law, the state law is invalid by virtue of the supremacy clause.

In some situations, both the federal government and the states have regulated a subject, but their laws do not conflict. Does the mere existence of federal regulation require invalidation of state laws on the same subject? In other words, does the federal law "preempt" the state law?

Pacific Gas and Electric Co. v. State Energy Resources Conservation & Development Commission
461 U.S. 190 (1983)

Justice WHITE delivered the opinion of the Court.

The turning of swords into plowshares has symbolized the transformation of atomic power into a source of energy in American society. To facilitate this development the federal government relaxed its monopoly over fissionable materials and nuclear technology, and in its place, erected a complex scheme to promote the civilian development of nuclear energy, while seeking to safeguard the public and the environment from the unpredictable risks of a new technology. Early on, it was decided that the states would continue their traditional role in the regulation of electricity production. The interrelationship of federal and state authority in the nuclear energy field has not been simple; the federal regulatory structure has been frequently amended to optimize the partnership.

This case emerges from the intersection of the federal government's efforts to ensure that nuclear power is safe with the exercise of the historic state authority over the generation and sale of electricity. At issue is whether provisions in the 1976 amendments to California's Warren-Alquist Act, which condition the construction of nuclear plants on findings by the State Energy Resources Conservation and Development Commission that adequate storage facilities and means of disposal are available for nuclear waste, are preempted by the Atomic Energy Act of 1954.

I

A nuclear reactor must be periodically refueled and the "spent fuel" removed. This spent fuel is intensely radioactive and must be carefully stored. The general practice is to store the fuel in a water-filled pool at the reactor site. For many years, it was assumed that this fuel

would be reprocessed; accordingly, the storage pools were designed as short-term holding facilities with limited storage capacities. As expectations for reprocessing remained unfulfilled, the spent fuel accumulated in the storage pools, creating the risk that nuclear reactors would have to be shut down. This could occur if there were insufficient room in the pool to store spent fuel and also if there were not enough space to hold the entire fuel core when certain inspections or emergencies required unloading of the reactor. In recent years, the problem has taken on special urgency. Some 8,000 metric tons of spent nuclear fuel have already accumulated, and it is projected that by the year 2000 there will be some 72,000 metric tons of spent fuel. Government studies indicate that a number of reactors could be forced to shut down in the near future due to the inability to store spent fuel.

There is a second dimension to the problem. Even with water-pools adequate to store safely all the spent fuel produced during the working lifetime of the reactor, permanent disposal is needed because the wastes will remain radioactive for thousands of years. A number of long-term nuclear waste management strategies have been extensively examined. These range from sinking the wastes in stable deep seabeds, to placing the wastes beneath ice sheets in Greenland and Antarctica, to ejecting the wastes into space by rocket. The greatest attention has been focused on disposing of the wastes in subsurface geologic repositories such as salt deposits. Problems of how and where to store nuclear wastes has engendered considerable scientific, political, and public debate. There are both safety and economic aspects to the nuclear waste issue: first, if not properly stored, nuclear wastes might leak and endanger both the environment and human health; second, the lack of a long-term disposal option increases the risk that the insufficiency of interim storage space for spent fuel will lead to reactor-shutdowns, rendering nuclear energy an unpredictable and uneconomical adventure.

The California laws at issue here are responses to these concerns. In 1974, California adopted the Warren-Alquist State Energy Resources Conservation and Development Act. The Act requires that a utility seeking to build in California any electric power generating plant, including a nuclear power plant, must apply for certification to the State Energy Resources and Conservation Commission (Energy Commission). The Warren-Alquist Act was amended in 1976 to provide additional state regulation of new nuclear power plant construction.

Two sections of these amendments are before us. Section 25524.1(b) provides that before additional nuclear plants may be built, the Energy Commission must determine on a case-by-case basis that there will be "adequate capacity" for storage of a plant's spent fuel rods "at the time such nuclear facility requires such ... storage." The law also requires that each utility provide continuous, on-site, "full core reserve storage capacity" in order to permit storage of the entire reactor core if it must be removed to permit repairs of the reactor. In short, § 25524.1(b) addresses the interim storage of spent fuel.

Section 25524.2 deals with the long-term solution to nuclear wastes. This section imposes a moratorium on the certification of new nuclear plants until the Energy Commission "finds that there has been developed and that the United States through its authorized agency has approved and there exists a demonstrated technology or means for the disposal of high-level nuclear waste." "Disposal" is defined as a "method for the permanent and terminal disposition of high-level nuclear waste ... " Cal.Pub.Res.Code § 25524.2(a), (c). Such a finding must be reported to the state legislature, which may nullify it.

. . .

It is well-established that within Constitutional limits Congress may preempt state authority by so stating in express terms. Absent explicit preemptive language, Congress' intent to supersede state law altogether may be found from a "scheme of federal regulation so pervasive as to make reasonable the inference that Congress left no room to supplement it," "because the Act of Congress may touch a field in which the federal interest is so dominant that the federal system will be assumed to preclude enforcement of state laws on the same subject," or because "the object sought to be obtained by the federal law and the character of obligations

imposed by it may reveal the same purpose." *Fidelity Federal Savings & Loan Ass'n v. de la Cuesta*, 102 S.Ct. 3014, 3022 (1982). Even where Congress has not entirely displaced state regulation in a specific area, state law is preempted to the extent that it actually conflicts with federal law. Such a conflict arises when "compliance with both federal and state regulations is a physical impossibility," *Florida Lime & Avocado Growers, Inc. v. Paul*, 373 U.S. 132, 142–143 (1963), or where state law "stands as an obstacle to the accomplishment and execution of the full purposes and objectives of Congress." *Hines v. Davidowitz*, 312 U.S. 52, 67 (1941).

. . .

Even a brief perusal of the Atomic Energy Act reveals that, despite its comprehensiveness, it does not at any point expressly require the States to construct or authorize nuclear power plants or prohibit the States from deciding, as an absolute or conditional matter, not to permit the construction of any further reactors. Instead, petitioners argue that the Act is intended to preserve the federal government as the sole regulator of all matters nuclear, and that § 25524.2 falls within the scope of this impliedly preempted field. But as we view the issue, Congress, in passing the 1954 Act and in subsequently amending it, intended that the federal government should regulate the radiological safety aspects involved in the construction and operation of a nuclear plant, but that the States retain their traditional responsibility in the field of regulating electrical utilities for determining questions of need, reliability, cost and other related state concerns.

Need for new power facilities, their economic feasibility, and rates and services, are areas that have been characteristically governed by the States. . . . "Congress legislated here in a field which the States have traditionally occupied ... so we start with the assumption that the historic police powers of the States were not to be superseded by the Federal Act unless that was the clear and manifest purpose of Congress." *Rice v. Santa Fe Elevator Corp.*, *supra*, 331 U.S., at 230.

The Atomic Energy Act must be read, however, against another background. . . . The Atomic Energy Act of 1954, 42 U.S.C. §§ 2011–2281 (1976), grew out of Congress' determination that the national interest would be best served if the Government encouraged the private sector to become involved in the development of atomic energy for peaceful purposes under a program of federal regulation and licensing. See H.R.Rep. No. 2181, 83d Cong., 2d Sess., 1–11 (1954). The Act implemented this policy decision by providing for licensing of private construction, ownership, and operation of commercial nuclear power reactors. *Duke*

Power Co. v. Carolina Environmental Study Group, Inc., 438 U.S., at 63. The AEC, however, was given exclusive jurisdiction to license the transfer, delivery, receipt, acquisition, possession and use of nuclear materials. 42 U.S.C. §§ 2014, (e), (z), (aa), 2061–2064, 2071- 2078, 2091–99, 2111–14 (1976 and Supp. IV 1980). Upon these subjects, no role was left for the states.

The Commission, however, was not given authority over the generation of electricity itself, or over the economic question whether a particular plant should be built. We observed in *Vermont Yankee, supra*, 435 U.S., at 550, that "The Commission's prime area of concern in the licensing context, . . . is national security, public health, and safety." *See also Power Reactor Development Corp. v. International Union of Electrical, Radio and Machine Workers*, 367 U.S. 396, 415 (1961). The Nuclear Regulatory Commission (NRC), which now exercises the AEC's regulatory authority, does not purport to exercise its authority based on economic considerations, 10 CFR § 8.4, and has recently repealed its regulations concerning the financial qualifications and capabilities of a utility proposing to construct and operate a nuclear power plant. 47 Fed. Reg. 13751. In its notice of rule repeal, the NRC stated that utility financial qualifications are only of concern to the NRC if related to the public health and safety. It is almost inconceivable that Congress would have left a regulatory vacuum; the only reasonable inference is that Congress intended the states to continue to make these judgments. Any doubt that ratemaking and plant-need questions were to remain in state hands was removed by § 271, 42 U.S.C. § 2018 which provided: "Nothing in this chapter shall be construed to affect the authority or regulations of any Federal, State or local agency with respect to the generation, sale, or transmission of electric power produced through the use of nuclear facilities licensed by the Commission. . . . "

. . .

This account indicates that from the passage of the Atomic Energy Act in 1954, through several revisions, and to the present day, Congress has preserved the dual regulation of nuclear-powered electricity generation: the federal government maintains complete control of the safety and "nuclear" aspects of energy generation; the states exercise their traditional authority over the need for additional generating capacity, the type of generating facilities to be licensed, land use, ratemaking, and the like.

The above is not particularly controversial. But deciding how § 25524.2 is to be construed and classified is a more difficult proposition. At the outset, we emphasize that the statute does not seek to regulate the construc-tion or operation of a nuclear powerplant. It would clearly be impermissible for California to attempt to do so, for such regulation, even if enacted out of non-safety concerns, would nevertheless directly conflict with the NRC's exclusive authority over plant construction and operation. Respondents appear to concede as much. Respondents do broadly argue, however, that although safety regulation of nuclear plants by states is forbidden, a state may completely prohibit new construction until its safety concerns are satisfied by the federal government. We reject this line of reasoning. State safety regulation is not preempted only when it conflicts with federal law. Rather, the federal government has occupied the entire field of nuclear safety concerns, except the limited powers expressly ceded to the states. When the federal government completely occupies a given field or an identifiable portion of it, as it has done here, the test of preemption is whether "the matter on which the state asserts the right to act is in any way regulated by the federal government." *Rice v. Santa Fe Elevator Corp.*, *supra*, 331 U.S., at 236. A state moratorium on nuclear construction grounded in safety concerns falls squarely within the prohibited field. Moreover, a state judgment that nuclear power is not safe enough to be further developed would conflict directly with the countervailing judgment of the NRC, see, infra, at 1729–1730, that nuclear construction may proceed notwithstanding extant uncertainties as to waste disposal. A state prohibition on nuclear construction for safety reasons would also be in the teeth of the Atomic Energy Act's objective to insure that nuclear technology be safe enough for widespread development and use—and would be preempted for that reason. *Infra*, at 1731–1732.

That being the case, it is necessary to determine whether there is a non-safety rationale for § 25524.2. California has maintained, and the Court of Appeals agreed, that § 25524.2 was aimed at economic problems, not radiation hazards. The California Assembly Committee On Resources, Land Use, and Energy, which proposed a package of bills including § 25524.2, reported that the waste disposal problem was "largely economic or the result of poor planning, not safety related." Reassessment of Nuclear Energy in California: A Policy Analysis of Proposition 15 and its Alternatives (1976) (Reassessment Report) at 18 (emphasis in original). The Committee explained that the lack of a federally approved method of waste disposal created a "clog" in the nuclear fuel cycle. Storage space was limited while more nuclear wastes were continuously produced. Without a permanent means of disposal, the nuclear waste problem could become critical leading to unpredictably high costs to contain the problem or, worse, shutdowns in reactors. "Waste disposal safety," the Reassessment Report notes, "is not directly addressed by the bills, which ask only that a method [of waste disposal] be chosen and accepted by the federal government." *Id.*, at 156.

[W]e accept California's avowed economic purpose as the rationale for enacting § 25524.2. Accordingly, the statute lies outside the occupied field of nuclear safety regulation.

B

Petitioners' second major argument concerns federal regulation aimed at the nuclear waste disposal problem itself. It is contended that § 25524.2 conflicts with federal regulation of nuclear waste disposal, with the NRC's decision that it is permissible to continue to license reactors, notwithstanding uncertainty surrounding the waste disposal problem, and with Congress' recent passage of legislation directed at that problem.

[The] NRC's imprimatur, however, indicates only that it is safe to proceed with such plants, not that it is economically wise to do so. Because the NRC order does not and could not compel a utility to develop a nuclear plant, compliance with both it and § 25524.2 are possible. Moreover, because the NRC's regulations are aimed at insuring that plants are safe, not necessarily that they are economical, § 25524.2 does not interfere with the objective of the federal regulation.

Nor has California sought through § 25524.2 to impose its own standards on nuclear waste disposal. The statute accepts that it is the federal responsibility to develop and license such technology. As there is no attempt on California's part to enter this field, one which is occupied by the federal government, we do not find § 25524.2 preempted any more by the NRC's obligations in the waste disposal field than by its licensing power over the plants themselves.

. . .

C

Finally, it is strongly contended that § 25524.2 frustrates the Atomic Energy Act's purpose to develop the commercial use of nuclear power. It is well established that state law is preempted if it "stands as an obstacle to the accomplishment of the full purposes and objectives of Congress." *Hines v. Davidowitz*, 312 U.S. 52, 67 (1941).

There is little doubt that a primary purpose of the Atomic Energy Act was, and continues to be, the promotion of nuclear power. The Act itself states that it is a program "to encourage widespread participation in the development and utilization of atomic energy for peaceful purposes to the maximum extent consistent with the common defense and security and with the health and safety of the public." 42 U.S.C. § 2013(b). . . .

. . .

The Court of Appeals is right, however, that the promotion of nuclear power is not to be accomplished "at all costs." The elaborate licensing and safety provisions and the continued preservation of state regulation in traditional areas belie that. Moreover, Congress has allowed the States to determine—as a matter of economics—whether a nuclear plant vis-a-vis a fossil fuel plant should be built. The decision of California to exercise that authority does not, in itself, constitute a basis for preemption.

. . .

The judgment of the Court of Appeals is
Affirmed.

City of Burbank v. Lockheed Air Terminal, Inc.[49] involved a Burbank, California ordinance which made it unlawful for a so-called "pure jet aircraft" to take off from the Hollywood-Burbank Airport between 11 p.m. of one day and 7 a.m. the next day, and making it unlawful for the operator of an airport to allow any such aircraft to take off from that airport during such periods. The only regularly scheduled flight affected by the ordinance was an intrastate flight of Pacific Southwest Airlines originating in Oakland, California, and departing from Hollywood-Burbank Airport for San Diego every Sunday night at 11:30. In an opinion written by Mr. Justice Douglas, the Court concluded the ordinance was preempted by the Federal Aviation Act of 1958 and the Noise Control Act of 1972:

There is, to be sure, no express provision of pre-emption in the 1972 Act. That, however, is not decisive. . . . It is the pervasive nature of the scheme of

---

[49] 411 U.S. 624 (1973).

federal regulation of aircraft noise that leads us to conclude that there is preemption. As Mr. Justice Jackson stated, concurring in *Northwest Airlines, Inc. v. Minnesota*, 322 U.S. 292: "Federal control is intensive and exclusive. Planes do not wander about in the sky like vagrant clouds. They move only by federal permission, subject to federal inspection, in the hands of federally certified personnel and under an intricate system of federal commands. The moment a ship taxis onto a runway it is caught up in an elaborate and detailed system of controls."

[Control] of noise is of course deep-seated in the police power of the States. Yet the pervasive control vested in EPA and in FAA under the 1972 Act seems to us to leave no room for local curfews or other local controls. . . . [This area] requires a uniform and exclusive system of federal regulation if the congressional objectives underlying the Federal Aviation Act are to be fulfilled.

Mr. Justice Rehnquist, joined by two other justices, dissented:

The history of congressional action in this field demonstrates, I believe, an affirmative congressional intent to allow local regulation. But even if it did not go that far, that history surely does not reflect "the clear and manifest purpose of Congress" to prohibit the exercise of "the historic police powers of the States" which our decisions require before a conclusion of implied preemption is reached. . . .

Hines v. Davidowitz[50] concerned the validity of Pennsylvania's Alien Registration Act. Among other things, the Act required all aliens 18 years of age or over to register with the state, pay a $1 annual registration fee, and carry an alien identification card. Following passage of the Pennsylvania Act, Congress enacted a federal Alien Registration Act requiring a single registration of aliens 14 years of age and over and requiring detailed information. The federal act did not require aliens to carry a registration card. The Court struck down the Pennsylvania law:

[W]hether or not registration of aliens is of such a nature that the Constitution permits only of one uniform national system, it cannot be denied that the Congress might validly conclude that such uniformity is desirable. The legislative history of the Act indicates that Congress was trying to steer a middle path, realizing that any registration requirement was a departure from our traditional policy of not treating aliens as a thing apart, but also feeling that the Nation was in need of the type of information to be secured. Having the constitutional authority so to do, it has provided a standard for alien registration in a single integrated and all-embracing system in order to obtain the information deemed to be desirable in connection with aliens. When it made this addition to its uniform naturalization and immigration laws, it plainly manifested a purpose to do so in such a way as to protect the personal liberties of law-abiding aliens through one uniform national registration system, and to leave them free from the possibility of inquisitorial practices and police surveillance that might not only affect our international relations but might also generate the very disloyalty which the law has intended guarding against. Under these circumstances, the Pennsylvania Act cannot be enforced.

Mr. Justice Stone dissented:

[We] must take it that Congress was not unaware that some nineteen states have statutes or ordinances requiring some form of registration for aliens, seven

---

[50] 312 U.S. 52 (1941).

of them dating from the last war. The repeal of this legislation is not to be inferred from the silence of Congress in enacting a law which at no point conflicts with the state legislation and is harmonious with it.

Pennsylvania v. Nelson[51] involved the Pennsylvania Sedition Act which prohibited sedition against both Pennsylvania and the U.S. government. Nelson was charged with uttering sedition against the U.S. Nelson challenged the Pennsylvania Act as contravening the Smith Act of 1940, a federal law which prohibited the knowing advocacy of the overthrow of the Government of the United States by force and violence. The Court again struck down the Pennsylvania law:

> Since we find that Congress has occupied the field to the exclusion of parallel state legislation, that the dominant interest of the Federal Government precludes state intervention, and that administration of state Acts would conflict with the operation of the federal plan, we are convinced that the decision of the Supreme Court of Pennsylvania is unassailable.

Mr. Justice Reed, joined by two other justices, dissented:

> Congress has not, in any of its statutes relating to sedition, specifically barred the exercise of state power to punish the same Acts under state law. . . .
>
> We look upon the Smith Act as a provision for controlling incitements to overthrow by force and violence the Nation, or any State, or any political subdivision of either. Such an exercise of federal police power carries, we think, no such dominancy over similar state powers as might be attributed to continuing federal regulations concerning foreign affairs or coinage, for example. In the responsibility of national and local governments to protect themselves against sedition, there is no "dominant interest."

Askew v. American Waterways Operators, Inc.[52] involved Florida's Oil Spill Prevention and Pollution Control Act, which imposed strict liability for any damage incurred by the State or private persons as a result of an oil spill in the State's territorial waters. Liability was imposed on spills from any waterfront facility used for drilling for oil or handling the transfer or storage of oil (terminal facility) and from any ship destined for or leaving such facility.

Each owner or operator of a terminal facility or ship subject to the Act was required to establish evidence of financial responsibility by insurance or a surety bond. In addition, the Florida Act required the state's Department of Natural Resources to regulate containment gear and other equipment which must be maintained by ships and terminal facilities for the prevention of oil spills.

Several months prior to the enactment of the Florida Act, Congress enacted the Water Quality Improvement Act of 1970 which subjected shipowners and terminal facilities to liability without fault up to $14,000,000 and $8,000,000, respectively, for cleanup costs incurred by the Federal Government as a result of oil spills. It also authorized the President to promulgate regulations requiring ships and terminal facilities to maintain equipment for the prevention of oil spills.

The Court upheld the Florida law:

> [We] find no constitutional or statutory impediment to permitting Florida, in the present setting of this case, to establish any "requirement or liability" concerning the impact of oil spillages on Florida's interests or concerns.

---

[51] 350 U.S. 497 (1956).
[52] 411 U.S. 325 (1973).

. . .

While the Federal Act is concerned only with actual cleanup costs incurred by the Federal Government, the State of Florida is concerned with its own cleanup costs. Hence there need be no collision between the Federal Act and the Florida Act because, as noted, the Federal Act presupposes a coordinated effort with the States, and any federal limitation of liability runs to "vessels," not to shore "facilities." That is one of the reasons why the Congress decided that the Federal Act does not pre-empt the States from establishing either "any requirement or liability" respecting oil spills.

Moreover, since Congress dealt only with "cleanup" costs, it left the States free to impose "liability" in damages for losses suffered both by the States and by private interests. The Florida Act imposes liability without fault. So far as liability without fault for damages to state and private interests is concerned, the police power has been held adequate for that purpose. . . .

[The] provision of the Florida Act requiring the licensing of terminal facilities, a traditional state concern, creates no conflict per se with federal legislation. Section 1171(b)(1) of the Federal Act provides that federal permits will not be issued to terminal facility operators or owners unless the applicant first supplies a certificate from the State that his operation "will be conducted in a manner which will not violate applicable water quality standards."

5. State As a Market Participant

In some instances, the states do not try to regulate commerce. Instead, they intervene in commercial markets and become "market participants." Do different rules apply when a state acts as a market participant rather then as a market regulator?

Reeves, Inc. v. Stake
447 U.S. 429 (1980)

Mr. Justice BLACKMUN delivered the opinion of the Court.

The issue in this case is whether, consistent with the Commerce Clause, the State of South Dakota, in a time of shortage, may confine the sale of the cement it produces solely to its residents.

In 1919, South Dakota [built] a cement plant . . . in response to recent regional cement shortages that "interfered with and delayed both public and private enterprises," and that were "threatening the people of this state." *Eakin v. South Dakota State Cement Comm'n*, 44 S.D. 268, 272 (1921). . . . The plant, however, located at Rapid City, soon produced more cement than South Dakotans could use. Over the years, buyers in no less than nine nearby States purchased cement from the State's plant. Between 1970 and 1977, some 40% of the plant's output went outside the State.

The plant's list of out-of-state cement buyers included petitioner Reeves, Inc. Reeves is a ready-mix concrete distributor organized under Wyoming law and with facilities in Buffalo, Gillette, and Sheridan, Wyo. From the beginning of its operations in 1958, and until 1978, Reeves purchased about 95% of its cement from the South Dakota plant. In 1977, its purchases were $1,172,000. In turn, Reeves has supplied three northwestern Wyoming counties with more than half their ready-mix concrete needs. For 20 years the relationship between Reeves and the South Dakota cement plant was amicable, uninterrupted, and mutually profitable.

As the 1978 construction season approached, difficulties at the plant slowed production. Meanwhile, a booming construction industry spurred demand for cement both regionally and nationally. The plant found itself unable to meet all orders. Faced with the same type of "serious cement shortage" that inspired the plant's construction, the Commission "reaffirmed its policy of supplying all South Dakota customers first and to honor all contract commitments, with the remaining volume allocated on a first come, first served basis."

Reeves, which had no pre-existing long-term supply contract, was hit hard and quickly by this development. On June 30, 1978, the plant informed Reeves that it could not continue to fill Reeves' orders, and on July 5, it turned away a Reeves truck. Unable to find another supplier, Reeves was forced to cut production by 76% in mid-July.

. . .

[T]he Commerce Clause responds principally to state taxes and regulatory measures impeding free private trade in the national marketplace. There is no indication of a constitutional plan to limit the ability of the States themselves to operate freely in the free market. The precedents comport with this distinction.

Restraint in this area is also counseled by considerations of state sovereignty, the role of each State "'as guardian and trustee for its people,'" *Heim v. McCall*, 239 U.S. 175, 191 (1915), quoting *Atkin v. Kansas*, 191 U.S. 207, 222–223 (1903), and "the long recognized right of trader or manufacturer, engaged in an entirely private business, freely to exercise his own independent discretion as to parties with whom he will deal." *United States v. Colgate & Co.*, 250 U.S. 300, 307 (1919). Moreover, state proprietary activities may be, and often are, burdened with the same restrictions imposed on private market participants. Evenhandedness suggests that, when acting as proprietors, States should similarly share existing freedoms from federal constraints, including the inherent limits of the Commerce Clause. Finally, as this case illustrates, the competing considerations in cases involving state proprietary action often will be subtle, complex, politically charged, and difficult to assess under traditional Commerce Clause analysis. Given these factors, *Alexandria Scrap* wisely recognizes that, as a rule, the adjustment of interests in this context is a task better suited for Congress than this Court.

South Dakota, as a seller of cement, unquestionably fits the "market participant" label. . . . Thus, the general rule of *Alexandria Scrap* plainly applies here. . . .

In finding a Commerce Clause violation, the District Court emphasized "that the Commission . . . made an election to become part of the interstate commerce system." App. 28. The gist of this reasoning, repeated by petitioner here, is that [h]aving long exploited the interstate market, South Dakota should not be permitted to withdraw from it when a shortage arises. This argument is not persuasive. It is somewhat self-serving to say that South Dakota has "exploited" the interstate market. An equally fair characterization is that neighboring States long have benefitted from South Dakota's foresight and industry. . . .

. . .

[P]etitioner protests that South Dakota's preference for its residents responds solely to the "non-governmental objectiv[e]" of protectionism. Therefore, petitioner argues, the policy is per se invalid. *See Philadelphia v. New Jersey*, 437 U.S. 617, 624 (1978).

We find the label "protectionism" of little help in this context. The State's refusal to sell to buyers other than South Dakotans is "protectionist" only in the sense that it limits benefits generated by a state program to those who fund the state treasury and whom the State was created to serve. Petitioner's argument apparently also would characterize as "protectionist" rules restricting to state residents the enjoyment of state educational institutions, energy generated by a state-run plant, police and fire protection, and agricultural improvement and business development programs. Such policies, while perhaps "protectionist" in a loose sense, reflect the essential and patently unobjectionable purpose of state government—to serve the citizens of the State.

Second, petitioner echoes the District Court's warning: "If a state in this union, were allowed to hoard its commodities or resources for the use of their own residents only, a drastic situation might evolve. For example, Pennsylvania or Wyoming might keep their coal, the northwest its timber, and the mining states their minerals. The result being that embargo may be retaliated by embargo and commerce would be halted at state lines." *See, e.g., Baldwin v. Montana Fish & Game Comm'n*, 436 U.S. 371, 385–386 (1978). This argument, although rooted in the core purpose of the Commerce Clause, does not fit the present facts. Cement is not a natural resource, like coal, timber, wild game, or minerals. *Cf. Hughes v. Oklahoma*, 441 U.S. 322 (1979) (minnows); *Philadelphia v. New Jersey, supra* (landfill sites); *Pennsylvania v. West Virginia*, 262 U.S. 553 (1923) (natural gas); *West v. Kansas Natural Gas Co.*, 221 U.S. 229 (1911) (same). It is the end product of a complex process whereby a costly physical plant and human labor act on raw materials. South Dakota has not sought to limit access to the State's limestone or other materials used to make cement. Nor has it restricted the ability of private firms or sister States to set up plants within its borders. Moreover, petitioner has not suggested that South Dakota possesses unique access to the materials needed to produce cement. Whatever limits might exist on a State's ability to invoke the *Alexandria Scrap* exemption to hoard resources which by happenstance are found there, those limits do not apply here.

Third, it is suggested that the South Dakota program is infirm because it places South Dakota suppliers of ready-mix concrete at a competitive advantage in the out-of-state market; Wyoming suppliers, such as petitioner, have little chance against South Dakota suppliers who can purchase cement from the

State's plant and freely sell beyond South Dakota's borders.

The force of this argument is seriously diminished, if not eliminated by several considerations. The argument necessarily implies that the South Dakota scheme would be unobjectionable if sales in other States were totally barred. It therefore proves too much, for it would tolerate even a greater measure of protectionism and stifling of interstate commerce than the challenge system allows. Nor is it to be forgotten that *Alexandria Scrap* approved a state program that "not only . . . effectively protect[ed] scrap processors with existing plants in Maryland from the pressures of competitors with nearby out-of-state plants, but [that] implicitly offer[ed] to extend similar protection to any competitor . . . willing to erect a scrap processing facility within Maryland's boundaries." 391 F.Supp., at 63. Finally, the competitive plight of out-of-state ready-mix suppliers cannot be laid solely at the feet of South Dakota. It is attributable as well to their own States' not providing or attracting alternative sources of supply and to the suppliers' own failure to guard against shortages by executing long-term supply contracts with the South Dakota plant.

In its last argument, petitioner urges that, had South Dakota not acted, free market forces would have generated an appropriate level of supply at free market prices for all buyers in the region. Having replaced free market forces, South Dakota should be forced to replicate how the free market would have operated under prevailing conditions.

This argument appears to us to be simplistic and speculative. The very reason South Dakota built its plant was because the free market had failed adequately to supply the region with cement. There is no indication, and no way to know, that private industry would have moved into petitioner's market area, and would have ensured a supply of cement to petitioner either prior to or during the 1978 construction season. Indeed, it is quite possible that petitioner would never have existed—far less operated successfully for 20 years—had it not been for South Dakota cement.

We conclude, then, that the arguments for invalidating South Dakota's resident-preference program are weak at best. Whatever residual force inheres in them is more than offset by countervailing considerations of policy and fairness. Reversal would discourage similar state projects, even though this project demonstrably has served the needs of state residents and has helped the entire region for more than a half century. Reversal also would rob South Dakota of the intended benefit of its foresight, risk, and industry. Under these circumstances, there is no reason to depart from the general rule of *Alexandria Scrap*.

The judgment of the United States Court of Appeals is affirmed.

It is so ordered.

Mr. Justice POWELL, with whom Mr. Justice BRENNAN, Mr. Justice WHITE, and Mr. Justice STEVENS join, dissenting.

[South Dakota's] policy represents precisely the kind of economic protectionism that the Commerce Clause was intended to prevent. The Court, however, finds no violation of the Commerce Clause, solely because the State produces the cement. I agree with the Court that the State of South Dakota may provide cement for its public needs without violating the Commerce Clause. But I cannot agree that South Dakota may withhold its cement from interstate commerce in order to benefit private citizens and businesses within the State.

The need to ensure unrestricted trade among the States created a major impetus for the drafting of the Constitution. "The power over commerce . . . was one of the primary objects for which the people of America adopted their government. . . . " *Gibbons v. Ogden*, 9 Wheat. 1, 190 (1824). Indeed, the Constitutional Convention was called after an earlier convention on trade and commercial problems proved inconclusive. In the subsequent debate over ratification, Alexander Hamilton emphasized the importance of unrestricted interstate commerce: "An unrestrained intercourse between the States themselves will advance the trade of each, by an interchange of their respective productions. . . . Commercial enterprise will have much greater scope, from the diversity in the productions of different States. When the staple of one fails . . . it can call to its aid the staple of another." The Federalist, No. 11, p. 71 (J. Cooke ed., 1961) (A. Hamilton).

The Commerce Clause has proved an effective weapon against protectionism. The Court has used it to strike down limitations on access to local goods, be they animal, vegetable, or mineral. Only this Term, the Court held unconstitutional a Florida statute designed to exclude out-of-state investment advisers. As we observed in *Hughes v. Alexandria Scrap Corp.*, 426 U.S. 794, 803 (1976), "this Nation is a common market in which state lines cannot be made barriers to the free flow of both raw materials and finished goods in response to the economic laws of supply and demand."

This case presents a novel constitutional question. The Commerce Clause would bar legislation imposing on private parties the type of restraint on commerce adopted by South Dakota. Conversely, a private business constitutionally could adopt a marketing policy that excluded customers who come from another State. This case falls between those polar situations. The State, through its Commission, engages in a commercial enterprise and restricts its own interstate distribution. The question is whether the Commission's policy should be treated like state regulation of private parties or like the marketing policy of a private business.

The application of the Commerce Clause to this case should turn on the nature of the governmental activity involved. If a public enterprise undertakes an "integral operatio[n] in areas of traditional governmental functions," *National League of Cities v. Usery*, 426 U.S. 833, 852 (1976), the Commerce Clause is not directly relevant. If, however, the State enters the private market and operates a commercial enterprise for the advantage of its private citizens, it may not evade the constitutional policy against economic Balkanization.

This distinction derives from the power of governments to supply their own needs, and from the purpose of the Commerce Clause itself, which is designed to protect "the natural functioning of the interstate market," *Hughes v. Alexandria Scrap Corp., supra*, at 806. In procuring goods and services for the operation of government, a State may act without regard to the private marketplace and remove itself from the reach of the Commerce Clause. But when a State itself becomes a participant in the private market for other purposes, the Constitution forbids actions that would impede the flow of interstate commerce. These categories recognize no more than the "constitutional line between the State as government and the State as trader." *New York v. United States*, 326 U.S. 572, 579 (1946).

The Court holds that South Dakota, like a private business, should not be governed by the Commerce Clause when it enters the private market. But precisely because South Dakota is a State, it cannot be presumed to behave like an enterprise "'engaged in an entirely private business.'" A State frequently will respond to market conditions on the basis of political rather than economic concerns. To use the Court's terms, a State may attempt to act as a "market regulator" rather than a "market participant." In that situation, it is a pretense to equate the State with a private economic actor. State action burdening interstate trade is no less state action because it is accomplished by a public agency authorized to participate in the private market.

The threshold issue is whether South Dakota has undertaken integral government operations in an area of traditional governmental functions, or whether it has participated in the marketplace as a private firm. If the latter characterization applies, we also must determine whether the State Commission's marketing policy burdens the flow of interstate trade. This analysis highlights the differences between the state action here and that before the Court in *Hughes v. Alexandria Scrap Corp.*

[T]he marketing policy of the South Dakota Cement Commission has cut off interstate trade. The State can raise such a bar when it enters the market to supply its own needs. In order to ensure an adequate supply of cement for public uses, the State can withhold from interstate commerce the cement needed for public projects.

The State, however, has no parallel justification for favoring private, in-state customers over out-of-state customers. In response to political concerns that likely would be inconsequential to a private cement producer, South Dakota has shut off its cement sales to customers beyond its borders. That discrimination constitutes a direct barrier to trade "of the type forbidden by the Commerce Clause, and involved in previous cases.... " *Alexandria Scrap*, 426 U.S., at 810. The effect on interstate trade is the same as if the state legislature had imposed the policy on private cement producers. The Commerce Clause prohibits this severe restraint on commerce.

I share the Court's desire to preserve state sovereignty. But the Commerce Clause long has been recognized as a limitation on that sovereignty, consciously designed to maintain a national market and defeat economic provincialism. The Court today approves protectionist state policies. In the absence of contrary congressional action, those policies now can be implemented as long as the State itself directly participates in the market.

By enforcing the Commerce Clause in this case, the Court would work no unfairness on the people of South Dakota. They still could reserve cement for public projects and share in whatever return the plant generated. They could not, however, use the power of the State to furnish themselves with cement forbidden to the people of neighboring States.

The creation of a free national economy was a major goal of the States when they resolved to unite under the Federal Constitution. The decision today cannot be reconciled with that purpose.

Consider, again, *New Energy Co. of Indiana v. Limbach*,[53] which involved an Ohio statute that awarded a tax credit against the Ohio motor vehicle fuel sales tax for each

---

[53] 486 U.S. 269 (1988).

gallon of ethanol sold (as a component of gasohol) by fuel dealers, but only if the ethanol was produced in Ohio or in a State that grants similar tax advantages to ethanol produced in Ohio. Might the law have been upheld on a market participant theory? The Court, in an opinion written by Mr. Justice Scalia, refused to apply that theory:

> The market-participant doctrine has no application here. The Ohio action ultimately at issue is neither its purchase nor its sale of ethanol, but its assessment and computation of taxes—a primeval governmental activity. To be sure, the tax credit scheme has the purpose and effect of subsidizing a particular industry, as do many dispositions of the tax laws. That does not transform it into a form of state participation in the free market. Our opinion in *Alexandria Scrap, supra*, a case on which appellees place great reliance, does not remotely establish such a proposition. There we examined, and upheld against Commerce Clause attack on the basis of the market-participant doctrine, a Maryland cash subsidy program that discriminated in favor of in-state auto-hulk processors. The purpose of the program was to achieve the removal of unsightly abandoned autos from the State, *id.*, 426 U.S., at 796–797, and the Court characterized it as proprietary rather than regulatory activity, based on the analogy of the State to a private purchaser of the auto hulks, *id.*, at 808–810. We have subsequently observed that subsidy programs unlike that of *Alexandria Scrap* might not be characterized as proprietary. We think it clear that Ohio's assessment and computation of its fuel sales tax, regardless of whether it produces a subsidy, cannot plausibly be analogized to the activity of a private purchaser.

South-Central Timber Development, Inc. v. Wunnicke
467 U.S. 82 (1984)

Justice WHITE delivered the opinion of the Court with respect to Parts I and II, and delivered an opinion with respect to Parts III and IV, in which Justice BRENNAN, Justice BLACKMUN, and Justice STEVENS joined.

We granted certiorari in this case to review a decision of the Court of Appeals for the Ninth Circuit that held that Alaska's requirement that timber taken from state lands be processed within the State prior to export was "implicitly authorized" by Congress and therefore does not violate the Commerce Clause. We hold that it was not authorized and reverse the judgment of the Court of Appeals.

. . .

Our cases make clear that if a State is acting as a market participant, rather than as a market regulator, the dormant Commerce Clause places no limitation on its activities. The precise contours of the market-participant doctrine have yet to be established, however, the doctrine having been applied in only three cases of this Court to date.

The most recent of this Court's cases developing the market-participant doctrine is *White v. Massachusetts Council of Construction Employers, Inc., supra*, in which the Court sustained against a Commerce Clause challenge an executive order of the Mayor of Boston that required all construction projects funded in whole or in part by city funds or city-administered funds to be performed by a work force of at least 50% city residents. The Court rejected the argument that the city was not entitled to the protection of the doctrine because the order had the effect of regulating employment contracts between public contractors and their employees. 103 S.Ct., at 1046, n.7. Recognizing that "there are some limits on a state or local government's ability to impose restrictions that reach beyond the immediate parties with which the government transacts business," the Court found it unnecessary to define those limits because "[e]veryone affected by the order [was], in a substantial if informal sense, "working for the city." The fact that the employees were "working for the city" was "crucial" to the market-participant analysis in *White*. *United Building and Construction Trades Council v. Mayor of Camden*, 104 S.Ct. 1020 (1984).

The State of Alaska contends that its primary-manufacture requirement fits squarely within the market-participant doctrine, arguing that "Alaska's entry into the market may be viewed as precisely the same type of subsidy to local interests that the Court found unobjectionable in *Alexandria Scrap.*" However, when Maryland became involved in the scrap market it was as a purchaser of scrap; Alaska, on the other hand, participates in the timber market, but imposes conditions downstream in the timber-processing market. Alaska is not merely subsidizing local timber processing in an amount "roughly equal to the difference between the price the timber would fetch in the absence of such a requirement and the amount the state actually receives." Ibid. If the State directly subsidized the timber-processing industry by such an amount, the purchaser would retain the option of taking advantage of the subsidy by processing timber in the State or forgoing the benefits of the subsidy and exporting unprocessed timber. Under the Alaska requirement, however, the choice is made for him: if he buys timber from the State he is not free to take the timber out of state prior to processing.

The State also would have us find *Reeves* controlling. It states that "*Reeves* made it clear that the Commerce Clause imposes no limitation on Alaska's power to choose the terms on which it will sell its timber." Such an unrestrained reading of *Reeves* is unwarranted. Although the Court in *Reeves did* strongly endorse the right of a State to deal with whomever it chooses when it participates in the market, it did not—and did not purport to—sanction the imposition of any terms that the State might desire. For example, the Court expressly noted in *Reeves* that "Commerce Clause scrutiny may well be more rigorous when a restraint on foreign commerce is alleged," 447 U.S., at 438; that a natural resource "like coal, timber, wild game, or minerals," was not involved, but instead the cement was "the end product of a complex process whereby a costly physical plant and human labor act on raw materials," *id.*, at 443–444; and that South Dakota did not bar resale of South Dakota cement to out-of-state purchasers, *id.*, at 444, n.17. In this case, all three of the elements that were not present in *Reeves*—foreign commerce, a natural resource, and restrictions on resale—are present.

Finally, Alaska argues that since the Court in *White* upheld a requirement that reached beyond "the boundary of formal privity of contract," 103 S.Ct., at 1046, n.7, then, a fortiori, the primary-manufacture requirement is permissible, because the State is not regulating contracts for resale of timber or regulating the buying and selling of timber, but is instead "a seller of timber, pure and simple." Yet it is clear that the State is more than merely a seller of timber. In the commercial context, the seller usually has no say over, and no interest in, how the product is to be used after sale; in this case, however, payment for the timber does not end the obligations of the purchaser, for, despite the fact that the purchaser has taken delivery of the timber and has paid for it, he cannot do with it as he pleases. Instead, he is obligated to deal with a stranger to the contract after completion of the sale.

That privity of contract is not always the outer boundary of permissible state activity does not necessarily mean that the Commerce Clause has no application within the boundary of formal privity. The market-participant doctrine permits a State to influence "a discrete, identifiable class of economic activity in which [it] is a major participant." *White v. Massachusetts Council of Construction Workers, Inc.*, 103 S.Ct., at 1046, n.7. Contrary to the State's contention, the doctrine is not carte blanche to impose any conditions that the State has the economic power to dictate, and does not validate any requirement merely because the State imposes it upon someone with whom it is in contractual privity.

The limit of the market-participant doctrine must be that it allows a State to impose burdens on commerce within the market in which it is a participant, but allows it to go no further. The State may not impose conditions, whether by statute, regulation, or contract, that have a substantial regulatory effect outside of that particular market. Unless the "market" is relatively narrowly defined, the doctrine has the potential of swallowing up the rule that States may not impose substantial burdens on interstate commerce even if they act with the permissible state purpose of fostering local industry.

At the heart of the dispute in this case is disagreement over the definition of the market. Alaska contends that it is participating in the processed timber market, although it acknowledges that it participates in no way in the actual processing. South-Central argues, on the other hand, that although the State may be a participant in the timber market, it is using its leverage in that market to exert a regulatory effect in the processing market, in which it is not a participant. We agree with the latter position.

There are sound reasons for distinguishing between a State's preferring its own residents in the initial disposition of goods when it is a market participant and a State's attachment of restrictions on dispositions subsequent to the goods coming to rest in private hands. First, simply as a matter of intuition a State market participant has a greater interest as a "private trader" in the immediate transaction than it has in what its purchaser does with the goods after the State no longer has an interest in them. The common law recognized such a notion in the doctrine of restraints on alienation. Similarly, the antitrust laws place limits on vertical restraints. It is no defense in an action charging vertical trade restraints that the same end could be achieved through vertical integration; if it were, there would be virtually no antitrust scrutiny of vertical arrangements. We reject the contention that a State's action as a market regulator may be upheld against Commerce Clause challenge on the ground that the State could achieve the same end as a market participant. We therefore find it unimportant for present purposes that the State could support its processing industry by selling only to Alaska processors, by vertical integration, or by direct subsidy.

Second, downstream restrictions have a greater regulatory effect than do limitations on the immediate transaction. Instead of merely choosing its own trading partners, the State is attempting to govern the private, separate economic relationships of its trading partners; that is, it restricts the post-purchase activity of the purchaser, rather than merely the purchasing activity. In contrast to the situation in *White*, this restriction on private economic activity takes place after the completion of the parties' direct commercial obligations, rather than during the course of an ongoing commercial relationship in which the city retained a continuing proprietary interest in the subject of the contract. In sum, the State may not avail itself of the market-participant doctrine to immunize its downstream regulation of the timber-processing market in which it is not a participant.

. . .

The judgment of the Court of Appeals is reversed and the case is remanded for proceedings consistent with the opinion of this Court.

It is so ordered.

Justice REHNQUIST, with whom Justice O'CONNOR joins, dissenting.

. . .

The contractual term at issue here no more transforms Alaska's sale of timber into "regulation" of the processing industry than the resident-hiring preference imposed by the city of Boston in *White v. Massachusetts Council of Const. Employers*, 103 S.Ct. 1042 (1983), constituted regulation of the construction industry. Alaska is merely paying the buyer of the timber indirectly, by means of a reduced price, to hire Alaska residents to process the timber. Under existing precedent, the State could accomplish that same result in any number of ways. For example, the State could choose to sell its timber only to those companies that maintain active primary-processing plants in Alaska. *Reeves, Inc. v. Stake*, 447 U.S. 429 (1980). Or the State could directly subsidize the primary-processing industry within the State. *Hughes v. Alexandria Scrap Corp.*, 426 U.S. 794 (1976). The State could even pay to have the logs processed and then enter the market only to sell processed logs. It seems to me unduly formalistic to conclude that the one path chosen by the State as best suited to promote its concerns is the path forbidden it by the Commerce Clause.

6. Interstate Privileges and Immunities

Article IV, § 2, contains the Interstate Privileges and Immunities Clause: "The Citizens of each State shall be entitled to all Privileges and Immunities of Citizens in the several States." This clause was designed to ensure that states would not discriminate against the citizens of other states because of their citizenship in those states.

The privileges and immunities clause does not require states to treat non-residents in exactly the same way that they treat their own citizens. Nor does it impose an absolute ban on discrimination by one state against the citizens of another. States can treat the citizens of other states differently in some instances.

Baldwin v. Fish and Game Commission of Montana
436 U.S. 371 (1978)

Mr. Justice BLACKMUN delivered the opinion of the Court.

This case presents issues, under the Privileges and Immunities Clause of the Constitution's Art. IV, § 2, and the Equal Protection Clause of the Fourteenth Amendment, as to

the constitutional validity of disparities, as between residents and nonresidents, in a State's hunting license system.

Appellant Lester Baldwin is a Montana resident. He also is an outfitter holding a state license as a hunting guide. The majority of his customers are nonresidents who come to Montana to hunt elk and other big game. Appellants Carlson, Huseby, Lee and Moris are residents of Minnesota. They have hunted big game, particularly elk, in Montana in past years and wish to continue to do so. . . .

The relevant facts are not in any real controversy and many of them are agreed:

A. For the 1975 hunting season, a Montana resident could purchase a license solely for elk for $4. The nonresident, however, in order to hunt elk, was required to purchase a combination license at a cost of $151; this entitled him to take one elk and two deer.

For the 1976 season, the Montana resident could purchase a license solely for elk for $9. The nonresident, in order to hunt elk was required to purchase a combination license at a cost of $225; this entitled him to take one elk, one deer, one black bear, and game birds, and to fish with hook and line. A resident was not required to buy any combination of licenses, but if he did, the cost to him of all the privileges granted by the nonresident combination license was $30. The nonresident thus paid 7 1/2 times as much as the resident, and if the nonresident wished to hunt only elk, he paid 25 times as much as the resident.

. . .

Montana maintains significant populations of big game, including elk, deer, and antelope. Its elk population is one of the largest in the United States. Elk are prized by big-game hunters who come from near and far to pursue the animals for sport. The quest for big game has grown in popularity. During the 10-year period from 1960 to 1970 licenses issued by Montana increased by approximately 67% for residents and by approximately 530% for nonresidents.

Owing to its successful management programs for elk, the State has not been compelled to limit the overall number of hunters by means of drawings or lotteries as have other States with harvestable elk populations. Elk are not hunted commercially in Montana. Nonresident hunters seek the animal for its trophy value; the trophy is the distinctive set of antlers. The interest of resident hunters more often may be in the meat. Elk are now found in the mountainous regions of western Montana and are generally not encountered in the eastern two-thirds of the State where the plains prevail. During the summer the animals move to higher elevations and lands that are largely federally owned. In the late fall they move down to lower privately owned lands that provide the winter habitat necessary to their survival. During the critical midwinter period elk are often supported by ranchers.

Elk management is expensive. In regions of the State with significant elk population,

more personnel time of the Fish and Game Commission is spent on elk than on any other species of big game.

. . .

Privileges and immunities. Appellants strongly urge here that the Montana licensing scheme for the hunting of elk violates the Privileges and Immunities Clause of Art. IV, § 2, of our Constitution. That Clause is not one the contours of which have been precisely shaped by the process and wear of constant litigation and judicial interpretation over the years since 1789.

. . .

When the Privileges and Immunities Clause has been applied to specific cases, it has been interpreted to prevent a State from imposing unreasonable burdens on citizens of other States in their pursuit of common callings within the State, *Ward v. Maryland*, 12 Wall. 418 (1871); in the ownership and disposition of privately held property within the State, *Blake v. McClung*, 172 U.S. 239 (1898); and in access to the courts of the State, *Canadian Northern R. Co. v. Eggen*, 252 U.S. 553 (1920).

It has not been suggested, however, that state citizenship or residency may never be used by a State to distinguish among persons. Suffrage, for example, always has been understood to be tied to an individual's identification with a particular State. No one would suggest that the Privileges and Immunities Clause requires a State to open its polls to a person who declines to assert that the State is the only one where he claims a right to vote. The same is true as to qualification for an elective office of the State. *Kanapaux v. Ellisor*, 419 U.S. 891 (1974). Nor must a State always apply all its laws or all its services equally to anyone, resident or nonresident, who may request it so to do. *Canadian Northern R. Co. v. Eggen, supra.* Some distinctions between residents and nonresidents merely reflect the fact that this is a Nation composed of individual States, and are permitted; other distinctions are prohibited because they hinder the formation, the purpose, or the development of a single Union of those States. Only with respect to those "privileges" and "immunities" bearing upon the vitality of the Nation as a single entity must the State treat all citizens, resident and nonresident, equally. Here we must decide into which category falls a distinction with respect to access to recreational big-game hunting.

Many of the early cases embrace the concept that the States had complete ownership over wildlife within their boundaries, and, as well, the power to preserve this bounty for their citizens alone. It was enough to say "that in regulating the use of the common property of the citizens of [a] state, the legislature is [not] bound to extend to the citizens of all the other states the same advantages as are secured to their own citizens." *Corfield v. Coryell*, 6 F.Cas. 546, 552 (No. 3,230) (CC ED Pa. 1825). It appears to have been generally accepted that although the States were obligated to treat all those within their territory equally in most respects, they were not obliged to share those things they held in trust for their own people. In *Corfield*, a case the Court has described as "the first, and long the leading, explication of the [Privileges and Immunities] Clause," *see Austin v. New Hampshire*, 420 U.S., at 661, Mr. Justice Washington, sitting as Circuit Justice, although recognizing that the States may not interfere with the "right of a citizen of one state to pass through, or to reside in any other state, for purposes of trade, agriculture, professional pursuits, or otherwise; to claim the benefit of the writ of habeas corpus; to institute and maintain actions of any kind in the courts of the state; to take, hold and dispose of property, either real or personal," 6 F.Cas., at 552, nonetheless concluded that access to oyster beds determined to be owned by New Jersey could be limited to New Jersey residents. This holding, and the conception of state sovereignty upon which it relied, formed the basis for similar decisions during later years of the 19th century. *E.g., McCready v. Virginia*, 94 U.S. 391 (1877). . . .

In more recent years, however, the Court has recognized that the States' interest in regulating and controlling those things they claim to "own," including wildlife, is by no means absolute. States may not compel the confinement of the benefits of their resources, even their wildlife, to their own people whenever such hoarding and confinement impedes interstate commerce. *Foster-Fountain Packing Co. v. Haydel*, 278 U.S. 1 (1928). Nor does a State's control over its resources preclude the proper exercise of federal power. *Douglas v. Seacoast Products, Inc.*, 431 U.S. 265 (1977). And a State's interest in its wildlife and other resources must yield when, without reason, it interferes with a nonresident's right to pursue a livelihood in a State other than his own, a right that is protected by the Privileges and Immunities Clause. *Toomer v. Witsell*, 334 U.S. 385 (1948).

. . .

Does the distinction made by Montana between residents and nonresidents in establishing access to elk hunting threaten a basic right in a way that offends the Privileges and Immunities Clause? Merely to ask the question seems to provide the answer. We repeat much of what already has been said above: Elk hunting by nonresidents in Montana is a recreation and a sport. In itself—wholly apart from license fees—it is costly and obviously available only to the wealthy nonresident or to the one

so taken with the sport that he sacrifices other values in order to indulge in it and to enjoy what it offers. It is not a means to the nonresident's livelihood. The mastery of the animal and the trophy are the ends that are sought; appellants are not totally excluded from these. The elk supply, which has been entrusted to the care of the State by the people of Montana, is finite and must be carefully tended in order to be preserved.

Appellants' interest in sharing this limited resource on more equal terms with Montana residents simply does not fall within the purview of the Privileges and Immunities Clause. Equality in access to Montana elk is not basic to the maintenance or well-being of the Union. Appellants do not—and cannot—contend that they are deprived of a means of a livelihood by the system or of access to any part of the State to which they may seek to travel. We do not decide the full range of activities that are sufficiently basic to the livelihood of the Nation that the States may not interfere with a nonresident's participation therein without similarly interfering with a resident's participation. Whatever rights or activities may be "fundamental" under the Privileges and Immunities Clause, we are persuaded, and hold, that elk hunting by nonresidents in Montana is not one of them.

. . .

The judgment of the District Court is affirmed.

It is so ordered.

Mr. Justice BRENNAN, with whom Mr. Justice WHITE and Mr. Justice MARSHALL join, dissenting.

. . .

I think the time has come to confirm explicitly that which has been implicit in our modern privileges and immunities decisions, namely that an inquiry into whether a given right is "fundamental" has no place in our analysis of whether a State's discrimination against nonresidents—who "are not represented in the [discriminating] State's legislative halls," *Austin v. New Hampshire, supra*, at 662—violates the Clause. Rather, our primary concern is the State's justification for its discrimination. Drawing from the principles announced in *Toomer* and *Mullaney*, a State's discrimination against nonresidents is permissible where (1) the presence or activity of nonresidents is the source or cause of the problem or effect with which the State seeks to deal, and (2) the discrimination practiced against nonresidents bears a substantial relation to the problem they present. Although a State has no burden to prove that its laws are not violative of the Privileges and Immunities Clause, its mere assertion that the discrimination practiced against nonresidents is justified by the peculiar problem nonresidents present will not prevail in the face of a prima facie showing that the discrimination is not supportable on the asserted grounds. This requirement that a State's unequal treatment of nonresidents be reasoned and suitably tailored furthers the federal interest in ensuring that "a norm of comity," *Austin v. New Hampshire, supra,* 420 U.S., at 660, prevails throughout the Nation while simultaneously guaranteeing to the States the needed leeway to draw viable distinctions between their citizens and those of other States.

It is clear that under a proper privileges and immunities analysis Montana's discriminatory treatment of nonresident big-game hunters in this case must fall. Putting aside the validity of the requirement that nonresident hunters desiring to hunt elk must purchase a combination license that resident elk hunters need not buy, there are three possible justifications for charging nonresident elk hunters an amount at least 7.5 times the fee imposed on resident big-game hunters. The first is conservation. The State did not attempt to assert this as a justification for its discriminatory licensing scheme in the District Court, and apparently does not do so here. Indeed, it is difficult to see how it could consistently with the first prong of a modern privileges and immunities analysis. First, there is nothing in the record to indicate that the influx of nonresident hunters created a special danger to Montana's elk or to any of its other wildlife species. In the most recent year for which statistics are available, 1974–1975, there were 198,411 resident hunters in Montana and only 31,406 nonresident hunters. Nonresidents thus constituted only 13% of all hunters pursuing their sport in the State. Moreover, as the Court recognizes, *ante,* at 1856 n.10, the number of nonresident big-game hunters has never approached the 17,000 limit set by statute, presumably as a precautionary conservation measure. Second, if Montana's discriminatorily high big-game license fee is an outgrowth of general conservation policy to discourage elk hunting, this too fails as a basis for the licensing scheme. Montana makes no effort similarly to inhibit its own resi-

dents. As we said in *Douglas v. Seacoast Products, Inc.,* 431 U.S. 265, 285 n.21 (1977), "[a] statute that leaves a State's residents free to destroy a natural resource while excluding aliens or nonresidents is not a conservation law at all."

The second possible justification for the fee differential Montana imposes on nonresident elk hunters—the one presented in the District Court and principally relied upon here—is a cost justification. Appellants have never contended that the Privileges and Immunities Clause requires that identical fees be assessed residents and nonresidents. They recognize that *Toomer* and *Mullaney* allow additional charges to be made on nonresidents based on both the added enforcement costs the presence of nonresident hunters imposes on Montana and the State's conservation expenditures supported by resident-borne taxes. Their position throughout this litigation has been that the higher fee extracted from nonresident elk hunters is not a valid effort by Montana to recoup state expenditures on their behalf, but a price gouged from those who can satisfactorily pursue their avocation in no other State in the Union. The licensing scheme, appellants contend, is simply an attempt by Montana to shift the costs of its conservation efforts, however commendable they may be, onto the shoulders of nonresidents who are powerless to help themselves at the ballot box. The District Court agreed, finding that "[o]n a consideration of [the] evidence . . . and with due regard to the presumption of constitutionality . . . the ratio of 7.5 to 1 cannot be justified on any basis of cost allocation." *Montana Outfitters Action Group v. Fish & Game Comm'n,* 417 F.Supp. 1005, 1008 (Mont.1976). This finding is not clearly erroneous, *United States v. United States Gypsum Co.,* 333 U.S. 364, 394–395 (1948), and the Court does not intimate otherwise. Montana's attempt to cost-justify its discriminatory licensing practices thus fails under the second prong of a correct privileges and immunities analysis—that which requires the discrimination a State visits upon nonresidents to bear a substantial relation to the problem or burden they pose.

. . .

Toomer v. Witsell[54] involved a South Carolina law which regulated commercial shrimp fishing in the three-mile maritime belt off the coast of that state. Among other things, the law imposed a $2,500-per-boat fee on non-residents while imposing a $25 fee on residents. Georgia shrimpers challenged the law as a violation of the interstate privileges and immunities clause. The Court struck down the law:

---

[54] 334 U.S. 385 (1948).

[A]ppellees mention, without further elucidation, the fishing methods used by non-residents, the size of their boats, and the allegedly greater cost of enforcing the laws against them. One statement in the appellees' brief might also be construed to mean that the State's conservation program for shrimp requires expenditure of funds beyond those collected in license fees—funds to which residents and not non-residents contribute. Nothing in the record indicates that non-residents use larger boats or different fishing methods than residents, that the cost of enforcing the laws against them is appreciably greater, or that any substantial amount of the State's general funds is devoted to shrimp conservation. But assuming such were the facts, they would not necessarily support a remedy so drastic as to be a near equivalent of total exclusion. The State is not without power, for example, to restrict the type of equipment used in its fisheries, to graduate license fees according to the size of the boats, or even to charge non-residents a differential which would merely compensate the State for any added enforcement burden they may impose or for any conservation expenditures from taxes which only residents pay. We would be closing our eyes to reality, we believe, if we concluded that there was a reasonable relationship between the danger represented by non-citizens, as a class, and the severe discrimination practiced upon them.

. . .

Hicklin v. Orbeck
437 U.S. 518 (1978)

Mr. Justice BRENNAN delivered the opinion of the Court.

In 1972, professedly for the purpose of reducing unemployment in the State, the Alaska Legislature passed an Act entitled "Local Hire Under State Leases." Alaska Stat.Ann. §§ 38.40.010 to 38.40.090 (1977). The key provision of "Alaska Hire," as the Act has come to be known, is the requirement that "all oil and gas leases, easements or right-of-way permits for oil or gas pipeline purposes, unitization agreements, or any renegotiation of any of the preceding to which the state is a party" contain a provision "requiring the employment of qualified Alaska residents" in preference to nonresidents. Alaska Stat.Ann. § 38.40.030(a) (1977). This employment preference is administered by providing persons meeting the statutory requirements for Alaskan residency with certificates of residence—"resident cards"—that can be presented to an employer covered by the Act as proof of residency. 8 Alaska Admin. Code 35.015 (1977). Appellants [were] desirous of securing jobs covered by the Act but unable to qualify for the necessary resident cards. . . .

Appellants' principal challenge to Alaska Hire is made under the Privileges and Immunities Clause of Art. IV, § 2. . . .

Appellants' appeal to the protection of the Clause is strongly supported by this Court's decisions holding violative of the Clause state discrimination against nonresidents seeking to ply their trade, practice their occupation, or pursue a common calling within the State. For example, in *Ward v. Maryland*, 12 Wall. 418 (1871), a Maryland statute regulating the sale of most goods in the city of Baltimore fell to the privileges and immunities challenge of a New Jersey resident against whom the law discriminated. The statute discriminated against nonresidents of Maryland in several ways: It required nonresident merchants to obtain licenses in order to practice their trade without requiring the same of certain similarly situated Maryland merchants; it charged nonresidents a higher license fee than those Maryland residents who were required to secure licenses; and it prohibited both resident and nonresident merchants from using nonresident salesmen, other than their regular employees, to sell their goods in the city. In holding that the statute violated the Privileges and Immunities Clause, the Court observed that "the clause plainly and unmistakably secures and protects the right of a citizen of one State to pass into any other State of the Union for the purpose of engaging in lawful commerce, trade, or business without molestation." *Id.*, at 430. *Ward* thus recognized that a resident of one State is constitutionally entitled to travel to another State for purposes of employment free from discriminatory restrictions in favor of state residents imposed by the other State.

[E]ven where the presence or activity of nonresidents causes or exacerbates the problem the State seeks to remedy, there must be a "reasonable relationship between the danger represented by non-citizens, as a class, and the ... discrimination practiced upon them." *Id.*, at 399. *Toomer's* analytical framework was confirmed in *Mullaney v. Anderson*, 342 U.S. 415 (1952), where it was applied to invalidate a scheme used by the Territory of Alaska for the licensing of commercial fishermen in territorial waters; under that scheme residents paid a license fee of only $5 while nonresidents were charged $50.

Even assuming that a State may validly attempt to alleviate its unemployment problem by requiring private employers within the State to discriminate against nonresidents—an assumption made at least dubious by *Ward*—it is clear that under the *Toomer* analysis reaffirmed in *Mullaney*, Alaska Hire's discrimination against nonresidents cannot withstand scrutiny under the Privileges and Immunities Clause. For although the statute may not violate the Clause if the State shows "something to indicate that noncitizens constitute a peculiar source of the evil at which the statute is aimed." *Toomer v. Witsell, supra*, 334 U.S. at 398, and, beyond this, the State "has no burden to prove that its laws are not violative of the ... Clause," *Baldwin v. Montana Fish and Game Comm'n*, 436 U.S. at 402 (Brennan, J., dissenting), certainly no showing was made on this record that nonresidents were "a peculiar source of the evil." Alaska Hire was enacted to remedy, namely, Alaska's "uniquely high unemployment." Alaska Stat.Ann. § 38.40.020 (1977). What evidence the record does contain indicates that the major cause of Alaska's high unemployment was not the influx of nonresidents seeking employment, but rather the fact that a substantial number of Alaska's jobless residents—especially the unemployed Eskimo and Indian residents—were unable to secure employment either because of their lack of education and job training or because of their geographical remoteness from job opportunities; and that the employment of nonresidents threatened to deny jobs to Alaska residents only to the extent that jobs for which untrained residents were being prepared might be filled by nonresidents before the residents' training was completed.

Moreover, even if the State's showing is accepted as sufficient to indicate that nonresidents were "a peculiar source of evil," *Toomer* and *Mullaney* compel the conclusion that Alaska Hire nevertheless fails to pass constitutional muster. For the discrimination the Act works against nonresidents does not bear a substantial relationship to the particular "evil" they are said to present. Alaska Hire simply grants all Alaskans, regardless of their employment status, education, or training, a flat employment preference for all jobs covered by the Act. A highly skilled and educated resident who has never been unemployed is entitled to precisely the same preferential treatment as the unskilled, habitually unemployed Arctic Eskimo enrolled in a job-training program. If Alaska is to attempt to ease its unemployment problem by forcing employers within the State to discriminate against nonresidents—again, a policy which may present serious constitutional questions—the means by which it does so must be more closely tailored to aid the unemployed the Act is intended to benefit. Even if a statute granting an employment preference to unemployed residents or to residents enrolled in job-training programs might be permissible, Alaska Hire's across-the-board grant of a job preference to all Alaskan residents clearly is not.

Relying on *McCready v. Virginia*, 94 U.S. 391 (1877), however, Alaska contends that because the oil and gas that are the subject of Alaska Hire are owned by the State, this ownership, of itself, is sufficient justification for the Act's discrimination against nonresidents, and takes the Act totally without the scope of the Privileges and Immunities Clause. As the State sees it "the privileges and immunities clause [does] not apply, and was never meant to apply, to decisions by the states as to how they would permit, if at all, the use and distribution of the natural resources which they own. . . . " Brief for Appellees 20 n.14. We do not agree that the fact that a State owns a resource, of itself, completely removes a law concerning that resource from the prohibitions of the Clause. Although some courts, including the court below, have read *McCready* as creating an "exception" to the Privileges and Immunities Clause, we have just recently confirmed that "[i]n more recent years . . . the Court has recognized that the States' interest in regulating and controlling those things they claim to 'own' . . . is by no means absolute." *Baldwin v. Montana Fish and Game Comm'n*, 436 U.S., at 385. Rather than placing a statute completely beyond the Clause, a State's ownership of the property with which the statute is concerned is a factor—although often the crucial factor—to be considered in evaluating whether the statute's discrimination against noncitizens violates the Clause. Dispositive though this factor may be in many cases in which a State discriminates against nonresidents, it is not dispositive here.

[But] Alaska Hire extends to employers who have no connection whatsoever with the State's oil and gas, perform no work on state land, have no contractual relationship with the State, and receive no payment from the

State. . . . Moreover, the Act's coverage is not limited to activities connected with the extraction of Alaska's oil and gas. It encompasses, as emphasized by the dissent below, "employment opportunities at refineries and in distribution systems utilizing oil and gas obtained under Alaska leases." 565 P.2d, at 171. The only limit of any consequence on the Act's reach is the requirement that "the activity which generates the employment must take place inside the state." Although the absence of this limitation would be noteworthy, its presence hardly is; for it simply prevents Alaska Hire from having what would be the surprising effect of requiring potentially covered out-of-state employers to discriminate against residents of their own State in favor of nonresident Alaskans. In sum, the Act is an attempt to force virtually all businesses that benefit in some way from the economic ripple effect of Alaska's decision to develop its oil and gas resources to bias their employment practices in favor of the State's residents. We believe that Alaska's ownership of the oil and gas that is the subject matter of Alaska Hire simply constitutes insufficient justification for the pervasive discrimination against nonresidents that the Act mandates.

· · ·

[Prior precedent establishes] that the Commerce Clause circumscribes a State's ability to prefer its own citizens in the utilization of natural resources found within its borders,

but destined for interstate commerce. Like Louisiana's shrimp in *Foster Packing*, Alaska's oil and gas here are bound for out-of-state consumption. Indeed, the construction of the Trans-Alaska Pipeline, on which project appellants' nonresidency has prevented them from working, was undertaken expressly to accomplish this end. Although the fact that a state-owned resource is destined for interstate commerce does not, of itself, disable the State from preferring its own citizens in the utilization of that resource, it does inform analysis under the Privileges and Immunities Clause as to the permissibility of the discrimination the State visits upon nonresidents based on its ownership of the resource. Here, the oil and gas upon which Alaska hinges its discrimination against nonresidents are of profound national importance. On the other hand, the breadth of the discrimination mandated by Alaska Hire goes far beyond the degree of resident bias Alaska's ownership of the oil and gas can justifiably support. The confluence of these realities points to but one conclusion: Alaska Hire cannot withstand constitutional scrutiny. As Mr. Justice Cardozo observed in *Baldwin v. G.A.F. Seelig, Inc.*, 294 U.S. 511, 523 (1935), the Constitution "was framed upon the theory that the peoples of the several states must sink or swim together, and that in the long run prosperity and salvation are in union and not division."

Reversed.

Supreme Court of New Hampshire v. Piper[55] involved a New Hampshire Supreme Court rule which limited membership in the New Hampshire bar to state residents. Kathryn Piper, who lived in Lower Waterford, Vermont, about 400 yards from the New Hampshire border, applied to take the February 1980 New Hampshire bar examination. Following an investigation, the Board of Bar Examiners found that Piper was of good moral character and met the other requirements for admission. She was allowed to take the bar examination and passed, but was told that she would have to establish a home address in New Hampshire before she could become a member of the bar. In an opinion written by Mr. Justice Powell, the Court struck down the rule:

> There is nothing in *Ward, Toomer*, or *Hicklin* suggesting that the practice of law should not be viewed as a "privilege" under Art. IV, § 2. Like the occupations considered in our earlier cases, the practice of law is important to the national economy. As the Court noted in *Goldfarb v. Virginia State Bar*, 421 U.S. 773, 788, the "activities of lawyers play an important part in commercial intercourse."
>
> The lawyer's role in the national economy is not the only reason that the opportunity to practice law should be considered a "fundamental right." . . . Out-of-state lawyers may—and often do—represent persons who raise unpopular federal claims. In some cases, representation by nonresident counsel may be the only means available for the vindication of federal rights. . . .

---

[55] 470 U.S. 274 (1985).

. . .

Because, under Griffiths, a lawyer is not an "officer" of the State in any political sense, there is no reason for New Hampshire to exclude from its bar nonresidents. We therefore conclude that the right to practice law is protected by the Privileges and Immunities Clause.

. . .

There is no evidence to support appellant's claim that nonresidents might be less likely to keep abreast of local rules and procedures. Nor may we assume that a nonresident lawyer—any more than a resident—would disserve his clients by failing to familiarize himself with the rules. As a practical matter, we think that unless a lawyer has, or anticipates, a considerable practice in the New Hampshire courts, he would be unlikely to take the bar examination and pay the annual dues of $125.

We also find the appellant's second justification to be without merit, for there is no reason to believe that a nonresident lawyer will conduct his practice in a dishonest manner. The nonresident lawyer's professional duty and interest in his reputation should provide the same incentive to maintain high ethical standards as they do for resident lawyers. . . .

There is more merit to the appellant's assertion that a nonresident member of the bar at times would be unavailable for court proceedings. . . . [But o]ne may assume that a high percentage of nonresident lawyers willing to take the state bar examination and pay the annual dues will reside in places reasonably convenient to New Hampshire. Furthermore, in those cases where the nonresident counsel will be unavailable on short notice, the State can protect its interests through less restrictive means. The trial court, by rule or as an exercise of discretion, may require any lawyer who resides at a great distance to retain a local attorney who will be available for unscheduled meetings and hearings.

The final reason advanced by appellant is that nonresident members of the state bar would be disinclined to do their share of pro bono and volunteer work. Perhaps this is true to a limited extent, particularly where the member resides in a distant location. We think it is reasonable to believe, however, that most lawyers who become members of a state bar will endeavor to perform their share of these services. . . .

In summary, appellant neither advances a "substantial reason" for its discrimination against nonresident applicants to the bar, nor demonstrates that the discrimination practiced bears a close relationship to its proffered objectives.

. . .

United Building and Construction Trades Council of Camden County v. City of Camden[56] involved a Camden, New Jersey ordinance which required that at least 40% of the employees of contractors and subcontractors working on city construction projects be Camden residents. A resident was defined as anyone who lives in the City of Camden without regard to the length of residency. The Court concluded that the privileges and immunities clause applies to cities, but held that the clause did not prohibit Camden's law:

The conclusion that Camden's ordinance discriminates against a protected privilege does not, of course, end the inquiry. We have stressed in prior cases

---

[56] 465 U.S. 208 (1984).

that "[l]ike many other constitutional provisions, the privileges and immunities clause is not an absolute." *Toomer v. Witsell*, 334 U.S. 385, 396 (1948). It does not preclude discrimination against citizens of other States where there is a "substantial reason" for the difference in treatment. "[T]he inquiry in each case must be concerned with whether such reasons do exist and whether the degree of discrimination bears a close relation to them." As part of any justification offered for the discriminatory law, nonresidents must somehow be shown to "constitute a peculiar source of the evil at which the statute is aimed."

The city of Camden contends that its ordinance is necessary to counteract grave economic and social ills. Spiralling unemployment, a sharp decline in population, and a dramatic reduction in the number of businesses located in the city have eroded property values and depleted the city's tax base. The resident hiring preference is designed, the city contends, to increase the number of employed persons living in Camden and to arrest the "middle class flight" currently plaguing the city. The city also argues that all non-Camden residents employed on city public works projects, whether they reside in New Jersey or Pennsylvania, constitute a "source of the evil at which the statute is aimed." That is, they "live off" Camden without "living in" Camden. Camden contends that the scope of the discrimination practiced in the ordinance, with its municipal residency requirement, is carefully tailored to alleviate this evil without unreasonably harming nonresidents, who still have access to 60% of the available positions.

Every inquiry under the Privileges and Immunities Clause "must . . . be conducted with due regard for the principle that the states should have considerable leeway in analyzing local evils and in prescribing appropriate cures." *Toomer v. Witsell*, 334 U.S. 385, 396 (1948). This caution is particularly appropriate when a government body is merely setting conditions on the expenditure of funds it controls. *See supra*, at 1028. . . .

[W]e find it impossible to evaluate Camden's justification on the record as it now stands. No trial has ever been held in the case. No findings of fact have been made. The Supreme Court of New Jersey certified the case for direct appeal after the brief administrative proceedings that led to approval of the ordinance by the State Treasurer. It would not be appropriate for this Court either to make factual determinations as an initial matter or to take judicial notice of Camden's decay. We, therefore, deem it wise to remand the case to the New Jersey Supreme Court. . . .

Justice Blackmun dissented:

. . .

[T]he Framers meant to foreclose any one State from denying citizens of other States the same "privileges and immunities" accorded its own citizens. *See Austin v. New Hampshire*, 420 U.S., at 660–661.

. . .

While the Framers thus conceived of the Privileges and Immunities Clause as an instrument for frustrating discrimination based on state citizenship, there is no evidence of any sort that they were concerned by intrastate discrimination based on municipal residence. The most obvious reason for this is also the most simple one: by the time the Constitution was enacted, such discrimination was rarely practiced and even more rarely successful. . . .

PART IV

EQUALITY CONCEPTS

As a consequence of slavery, the Civil War and its aftermath, and the decades following *Brown v. Board of Education*, the meaning of equality in constitutional jurisprudence has undergone extraordinary change. As others have observed,[1] the Preamble's opening words "We the People" suggest that a community of individuals was being created with a government respectful of all members. Membership, however, was not all inclusive. The original Constitution's express provisions for equality, moreover, were conflicting: Article IV, § 2's privileges and immunities clause certainly was designed to capture some notion of equality. In *Corfield v. Coryell*[2] Circuit Justice Washington interpreted the clause to secure to citizens of each state "those privileges and immunities which are, in their nature, fundamental: which belong, of right to the citizens of all free governments; and which have at all times, been enjoyed by the citizens of the several states which compose this union, from the time of their becoming free, independent, and sovereign." The clause was subsequently interpreted as establishing a rule against discrimination "plac[ing] the citizens of each State upon the same footing with citizens of other States, so far as the advantages resulting from citizenship in those States are concerned . . . insur[ing] them in other States the same freedom possessed by the citizens of those States in the acquisition and enjoyment of property and in the pursuit of happiness; and secur[ing] to them in other States the equal protection of the laws."[3]

This interstate privileges and immunities provision by its terms was applicable to *citizens* of the states—thus equality conceived at the time extended essentially to white males. Other provisions of the original Constitution made clear that the Framers were not willing to take on the issue of slavery. *See* Article I, § 2, cl. 3 (defining a slave as three-fifths of a white man for purposes of political representation and taxation); Article I, § 9, cl. 1 (preventing legislative interference with the slave trade until 1808). Article IV, § 2 provided that slaves who had escaped would be returned to their masters.

Moreover, subsequent judicial decision making clarified the position of blacks as beyond the pale of the community of citizens which was the focus of constitutional rhetoric about equality. *Strader v. Graham*,[4] held that a black person's legal status was to be determined by the law of the state in which he resided and federal courts were bound by that law. In *Dred Scott v. Sandford*,[5] Justice Taney, speaking for a majority of the Court, ruled inter alia that the Constitution did not contemplate citizenship for slaves who had "no rights or privileges but such as those who held the power and the Government might choose to grant them." The Court held further that neither slaves nor their descendants—even if freed—could be considered citizens of any state for jurisdictional purposes.

The Civil War led to changes in the Constitution including a reformulation of the

---

[1] E.g., Angela Harris, *Race and Essentialism in Feminist Theory, 42* STAN. L. REV 581 (1990); Barbara Flagg, *"Was Blind but Now I See": White Consciousness and The Requirement of Discriminatory Intent*, 91MICH. L. REV. 953 (1993).

[2] 4 Wash. C.C. 371 (C.C.E.D. Pa. 1823).

[3] Paul v. Virginia, 75 U.S. (8 Wall.) 168, 180 (1868).

[4] 51 U.S. (10 How.) 82 (1850).

[5] 60 U.S. (19 How.) 393 (1856).

relationship of state and national citizenship as well as a rethinking of individual rights and equality in the Reconstruction Amendments and statutes which were passed following the abrogation of slavery.

By its language, the Fourteenth Amendment (if not the Thirteenth Amendment) had the potential to radically transform the Constitution. Section 1 redefined citizenship and rights, overruling *Dred Scott* by stating that persons born in the United States are citizens of the country and the states in which they reside. The second sentence stated: "No state shall make or enforce any law which shall abridge the privileges or immunities of the citizens of the United States: nor shall any State deprive any person of life, liberty, or property, without due process of law; nor deny to any person within its jurisdiction the equal protection of the law." Section 5 of the Amendment authorized Congress to enforce the provisions of the Amendment "by appropriate legislation." (See Part II, *supra*)

Legal historians, however, have continued to debate the purposes and intentions of the Fourteenth Amendment's framers and the nature of Reconstruction. Although the Reconstruction Amendments, including the Thirteenth, Fourteenth, and Fifteenth Amendments, were the work of Republicans many of whom had been active in the pre-War antislavery movement,[6] some historians have pointed out that antislavery advocates were not necessarily in agreement with abolitionism. Read expansively, the Fourteenth Amendment has been viewed as drafted by radical Republicans who intended to give it sufficient breadth to prohibit racial segregation and grant the right to vote, guaranteeing equality and other unspecified rights. More narrow readings focus on the pragmatic interests of "mainstream Republican leaders" whose central purpose "was to hold the party together, retain political power, and thereby preserve a political climate in which the North's capitalist economy could continue to flourish and grow."[7] In this view the amendment was not intended to give blacks the right to vote or to prohibit segregation. Noting the confusion and contradictions uncovered by other legal historians, Professor Nelson concludes that the "present impasse" results from scholars "asking questions of twentieth-century significance that cannot be answered by historical inquiry"—questions that either never occurred to the framers or were left unresolved by them.[8] He adds:

> "Although my reading of the many sources on the framing and ratification of the amendment has uncovered a rich debate on virtually every issue that would subsequently come before the Supreme Court, the participants in this debate never agreed on how section one would apply to those issues. The framers of the Fourteenth Amendment simply never took advantage of the many opportunities they had to specify its precise boundaries. But the ambiguities of the amendment for purposes of today's doctrinal issues should not lead to a conclusion that the amendment has no meaning for its supporters. It did have meaning. But the meaning the amendment had for them existed on a conceptual level different from the doctrinal level on which most scholars have tended to examine it, and this meaning can only be recovered though a more genuinely historical analysis than those scholars have employed.
>
> . . .

---

[6] *See* DANIEL FARBER AND SUZANNA SHERRY, A HISTORY OF THE AMERICAN CONSTITUTION 253 (1990).

[7] WILLIAM E. NELSON, THE FOURTEENTH AMENDMENT 3 (1988). *See also* DANIEL A. FARBER & SUZANNA SHERRY, A HISTORY OF THE AMERICAN CONSTITUTION 253–96 (discussing the antislavery position of Republicans as not opposed to the maintenance of slavery in the South.)

[8] Nelson at 6.

Those who adopted the Fourteenth Amendment did not design it to provide judges with a determinative text for resolving [the conflict between protection of individual rights by the judiciary and the free exercise of legislative power] in a narrow doctrinal fashion. They wrote the amendment for a very different audience and purpose: to reaffirm the lay public's longstanding rhetorical commitment to general principles of equality, individual rights, and local self-rule. . . . The Supreme Court began to elaborate doctrines resolving issues of priority only when a flood of cases in the closing decades of the nineteenth century made the inevitability of conflict fully apparent."

Following ratification of the Fourteenth Amendment, as Congress considered the Civil Rights laws in 1870, 1871, and 1875, as well as the Fifteenth Amendment, debate about the meaning of the Fourteenth Amendment did not clarify its meaning. "A few Republicans would speak in support of the amendment or the pending enforcement legislation and in so doing would typically present different interpretations of the amendment's meaning; then the party as a whole would vote overwhelmingly in support of the matter at hand without the individual members identifying the interpretation they preferred," leaving disparate views.[9]

In a 5-4 decision by the Supreme Court in the *Slaughter-House Cases*,[10] the first case interpreting the Fourteenth Amendment by the Court, the Equal Protection Clause was read by Justice Miller to apply only to race discrimination. In dissent, Justice Field, on the other hand, argued that section one conferred on each individual "fundamental rights, privileges, and immunities . . . as a free man and a free citizen [and] as a citizen of the United States." Such rights were only "subject to such restraints as equally affected all others" and "without other restraint than such as equally affects all persons." Thus Justice Field concluded that the states could regulate rights federally protected by enactment of the Fourteenth Amendment but only if the state regulation was reasonable, that is, applied generally and equally to all. He therefore would have invalidated the Louisiana legislation creating a monopoly at issue in the *Slaughter-House Cases* because it regulated the right of butchers to engage in their occupation in an unreasonable way. In contrast to the other dissenters who found other privileges and immunities absolutely protected, Justice Field would have read the amendment as granting the right to equality at least as to matters of fundamental importance.

Seeking to constrict the Fourteenth Amendment from becoming a broad charter for increasing federal power and control of the states, Justice Miller, writing for the majority, stated:"We doubt very much whether any action of a State not directed by way of discrimination against the Negroes as a class, or on account of their race, will ever be held to come within the purview" of equal protection.

In the majority's view, the privileges and immunities clause was to be read narrowly and did not apply to ordinary civil rights which were traditionally protected by state law. That interpretation seems at odds with the intentions of the amendment's proponents both in terms of the implications of the amendment's coverage of other groups, such as Chinese, Indians, women, religious minorities and Northern whites, as well as with the notion that section one was to extend power of the federal government to protect basic common law rights of property and contract.[11]

---

[9] Nelson at 148.

[10] 83 U.S. (16 Wall.) 36 (1873).

[11] Nelson at 163. *See also* FARBER & SHERRY, *supra*, at 300–01 (discussing changes in the views about the relationship between the individual citizen and the national government which were a consequence of the Civil war, "a war for the primary allegiance of the citizen" to the federal government).

The meaning of equal protection as it relates to racial discrimination as well as to other governmental activity has continued to perplex the Court. Historically, after *Slaughter-House Cases*, outside of extreme cases of race-focused governmental decision making, the primary vehicle for protecting individual rights against state and local action became the Due Process Clause of the Fourteenth Amendment. The Equal Protection Clause, like the Privileges and Immunities Clause, was left narrowly cabined by the *Slaughter-House Cases*. Indeed, with the demise of substantive due process, in reviewing social and economic legislation against equal protection challenges, the Court applied the prevailing due process rationality standard of review. With the advent of the school desegregation movement spurred by *Brown v. Board of Education*[12], however, a two-tiered standard of review began to emerge: strict scrutiny was applied to racial and other "suspect" classification schemes and to cases in which fundamental rights were implicated. In most cases, however, a lax "rationality" standard for reviewing challenged governmental action was applied by the Court, with such deference to both the classification crafted and governmental objective chosen that victory for the government was almost always assured.

Notably, although the language of the Fourteenth Amendment concerns states, equal protection as a concept has been applied to the federal government by courts utilizing the due process clause of the Fifth Amendment. In reviewing federal legislation, however, courts have sometimes suggested that Congress is not held to the same limitations on discrimination as the states.[13] But the Court has stated that the Fifth Amendment's protection against the legislature's withholding of the right to life, liberty and property "tends to secure equality of law," *Truax v. Corrigan*, 257 U.S. 312, 331 (1921), and that amendment bars racially discriminatory treatment. *Korematsu v. United States*, 323 U.S. 214 (1944).[14]

A.   Introduction to Equal Protection Scrutiny

In the last quarter century, beginning with *Brown v. Board of Education*, the Court has relied on the Equal Protection Clause as a vehicle for protecting a variety of rights and interests against governmental action. Scarcely 25 years earlier, the Equal Protection Clause had been called by Justice Holmes "the usual last resort of constitutional arguments" in *Buck v. Bell*.[15]

Almost all governmental action is discriminatory in that it imposes burdens or obligations on or confers benefits to some but not other individuals. Whether the distinction in treatment is unlawful because it violates the guarantee intended by this clause of the Fourteenth Amendment depends on the meaning of "equal protection." Thus at one level, equal protection jurisprudence concerns the ways in which government may classify people. "The government can classify persons or 'draw lines' in according benefits and burdens but in the creation of laws or application of them allocations cannot be based upon impermissible criteria or arbitrarily used to burden a group of individuals."[16] Rather equal protection of laws requires that similarly situated people be treated similarly.

As Ronald Dworkin has pointed out, defining equal treatment can prove trouble-

---

[12] 347 U.S. 483 (1954).

[13] *See, e.g.*, Steward Machine Co. v. Davis, 301 U.S. 548 (1937).

[14] In Bolling v. Sharpe, 347 U.S. 497 (1954) racial segregation of public schools of the District of Columbia was held to violate the due process clause of the Fifth Amendment.

[15] 274 U.S. 200 (1927). *See* Section B, *infra*.

[16] Nowak & Rotunda at 570. For a discussion of the doctrine of reasonable classification and their test of similarity which determines the reasonableness of a classification. *See* Tussman and TenBroek, *The Equal Protection of the Laws,* 37 CALIF. L. REV. 341(1949).

some: For some it means "the right to an equal distribution of some opportunity or resource or burden," and for others the right "to be treated with the same respect and concern as anyone else."[17] Moreover, the question of who is "similarly situated" or different for purposes of equal protection analysis depends upon the point of view or points of comparison. Feminists have criticized traditional legal assumptions about difference which draw upon unstated norms for purposes of comparison, creating an illusion of objectivity and "categories that bury their perspective and wrongly imply a natural fit with the world . . . Legal treatment of difference thus tends to treat as unproblematic the point of view from which difference is seen, assigned, or ignored, rather than acknowledging that the problem of difference can be described and understood form multiple points of view."[18] In contrast, as Angela Harris observes, the inevitable danger of categorization is that it generalizes and thereby tends to essentialize the experience of some individuals and groups and to negate the experiences of others. For example, Professor Harris challenges the notion that women's experience can be isolated and described independently of race, class, sexual orientation, and other realities of experience, and charges that feminist legal theory's critique of objectivity ignores and silences groups like black women.[19]

---

[17] RONALD DWORKIN, TAKING RIGHTS SERIOUSLY 227 (1977).

[18] Martha Minow, *Supreme Court—Forward Justice Engendered*, 101 HARV. L. REV. 10, 13-14 (1987). Angela Harris also remarks that claims that the Declaration of Independence or Preamble of the United States Constitution speaks for an entire and united nation are false because "this voice does not speak for everyone, but for a political faction trying to constitute itself as a unit of many disparate voices; its power last[ing] only as long as the contradictory voices remain silenced." Angela Harris, *Race and Essentialism in Feminist Theory*, 42 STAN. L. REV. 581, 583 (1990).

[19] 42 STAN. L. REV. at 585.

Railway Express Agency v. New York
336 U.S. 106 (1949)

Mr. Justice DOUGLAS delivered the opinion of the Court. Section 124 of the Traffic Regulations of the City of New York promulgated by the Police Commissioner provides:

'No person shall operate, or cause to be operated, in or upon any street an advertising vehicle; provided that nothing herein contained shall prevent the putting of business notices upon business delivery vehicles, so long as such vehicles are engaged in the usual business or regular work of the owner and not used merely or mainly for advertising.'

Appellant is engaged in a nation-wide express business. It operates about 1,900 trucks in New York City and sells the space on the exterior sides of these trucks for advertising. That advertising is for the most part unconnected with its own business. It was convicted in the magistrates court and fined. The judgment of conviction was sustained in the Court of Special Sessions. The Court of Appeals affirmed without opinion by a divided vote.

The Court of Special Sessions concluded that advertising on vehicles using the streets of New York City constitutes a distraction to vehicle drivers and to pedestrians alike and therefore affects the safety of the public in the use of the streets. We do not sit to weigh evidence on the due process issue in order to determine whether the regulation is sound or appropriate; nor is it our function to pass judgment on its wisdom. We would be trespassing on one of the most intensely local and specialized of all municipal problems if we held that this regulation had no relation to the traffic problem of New York City. It is the judgment of the local authorities that it does have such a relation. And nothing has been advanced which shows that to be palpably false.

The question of equal protection of the laws is pressed more strenuously on us. It is pointed out that the regulation draws the line between advertisements of products sold by the owner of the truck and general advertisements. It is argued that unequal treatment on the basis of such a distinction is not justified by the aim and purpose of the regulation. It is said, for example, that one of appellant's trucks carrying the advertisement of a commercial house would not cause any greater distraction of pedestrians and vehicle drivers than if the commercial house carried the same advertisement on its own truck. Yet the regulation allows the latter to do what the former is forbidden from doing. It is therefore contended that the classification which the regulation makes has no relation to the traffic problem since a violation turns not on what kind of advertisements are carried on trucks but on whose trucks they are carried.

That, however, is a superficial way of analyzing the problem, even if we assume that it is premised on the correct construction of the regulation. The local authorities may well have concluded that those who advertised their own wares on their trucks do not present the same traffic problem in view of the nature or extent of the advertising which they use. It would take a degree of omniscience which we lack to say that such is not the case. If that judgment is correct, the advertising displays that are exempt have less incidence on traffic than those of appellants.

We cannot say that that judgment is not an allowable one. Yet if it is, the classification has relation to the purpose for which it is made and does not contain the kind of discrimination against which the Equal Protection Clause affords protection. It is by such practical considerations based on experience rather than by theoretical inconsistencies that the question of equal protection is to be answered. And the fact that New York City sees fit to eliminate from traffic this kind of distraction but does not touch what may be even greater ones in a different category, such as the vivid displays on Times Square, is immaterial. It is no requirement of equal protection that all evils of the same genus be eradicated or none at all. Affirmed.

Mr. Justice JACKSON, concurring.

There are two clauses of the Fourteenth Amendment which this Court may invoke to invalidate ordinances by which municipal governments seek to solve their local problems. One says that no state shall 'deprive any person of life, liberty, or property, without due process of law'. The other declares that no state shall 'deny to any person within its jurisdiction the equal protection of the laws.'

The burden should rest heavily upon one who would persuade us to use the due process clause to strike down a substantive law or ordinance. Even its provident use against municipal regulations frequently disables all government—state, municipal and federal—from dealing with the conduct in question because the requirement of due process is also applicable to State and Federal Governments. Invalidation of a statute or an ordinance on due process grounds leaves ungoverned and ungovernable conduct which many people find objectionable.

Invocation of the equal protection clause, on the other hand, does not disable any governmental body from dealing with the subject at hand. It merely means that the prohibition or regulation must have a broader impact. I regard it as a salutary doctrine that cities, states and the Federal Government must exercise their powers so as not to discriminate between their inhabitants except upon some reasonable differentiation fairly related to the object of regulation. This equality is not merely abstract justice. The framers of the Constitution knew that there is no more effective practical guaranty against arbitrary and unreasonable government than to require that the principles of law which officials would impose upon a minority must be imposed generally. Conversely, nothing opens the door to arbitrary action so effectively as to allow those officials to pick and choose only a few to whom they will apply legislation and thus to escape the political retribution that might be visited upon them if larger numbers were affected. Courts can take no better measure to assure that laws will be just than to require that laws be equal in operation. Hence, for my part, I am more receptive to attack on local ordinances for denial of equal protection than for denial of due process, while the Court has more often used the latter clause.

In this case, if the City of New York should assume that display of any advertising on vehicles tends and intends to distract the attention of persons using the highways and to increase the dangers of its traffic, I should think it fully within its constitutional powers to forbid it all. The same would be true if the City should undertake to eliminate or minimize the hazard by any generally applicable restraint, such as limiting the size, color, shape or perhaps to some extent the contents of vehicular advertising. Instead of such general regulation of advertising, however, the City seeks to reduce the hazard only by saying that while some may, others may not exhibit such appeals. The same display, for example, advertising cigarettes, which this appellant is forbidden to carry on its trucks, may be carried on the trucks of a cigarette dealer and might on the trucks of this appellant if it dealt in cigarettes. And almost an identical advertisement, certainly one of equal size, shape, color and appearance, may be carried by this appellant if it proclaims its own offer to transport cigarettes. But it may not be carried so long as the message is not its own but a cigarette dealer's offer to sell the same cigarettes.

The City urges that this applies equally to all persons of a permissible classification, because all that it does is (1) forbid all inhabitants of New York City from engaging in the business of selling and advertising space on trucks which move as part of the city traffic; (2) forbid all truck owners from incidentally employing their vehicles for such purpose, with the exception that all truck owners can advertise their own business on their own trucks. It is argued that, while this does not eliminate vehicular advertising, it does eliminate such advertising for hire and to this extent cuts down the hazard sought to be controlled.

That the difference between carrying on any business for hire and engaging in the same activity on one's own is a sufficient one to sustain some types of regulations of the one that is not applied to the other, is almost elementary. But it is usual to find such regulations applied to the very incidents wherein the two classes present different problems, such as in charges, liability and quality of service.

The difference, however, is invoked here to sustain a discrimination in a problem in which two classes present identical dangers. The courts of New York have declared the sole nature and purpose of the regulation before us is to reduce traffic hazards. There is not even a pretense here that the traffic hazard created by the advertising which is forbidden is in any manner or degree more hazardous than that which is [exempted].

I do not think differences of treatment under law should be approved on classification because of differences unrelated to the legislative purpose. The equal protection clause ceases to assure either equality or protection if it is avoided by any conceivable difference that can be pointed out between those bound and those left free. The differentiation must have an appropriate relation to the object of the legislation or ordinance.

There is a real difference between doing in self-interest and doing for hire, so that it is one thing to tolerate action from those who act on their own and it is another thing to permit the same action to be promoted for a price.

While I do not think highly of this type of regulation, that is not my business, and in view of the control I would concede to cities to protect citizens in quiet and orderly use for their proper purposes of the highways and public places, I think the judgment below must be affirmed.

The Court's inquiry as to the reasonableness of a legislative classification in an equal protection challenge is similar to the Court's consideration of whether there exists a rational relationship between governmental means and ends in economic due process challenges. In considering whether there is sufficient rationality in traditional equal protection analysis, however, the focus is on the over-inclusiveness or under-inclusiveness of the classification and the relationship of the classification to some legitimate end. A law is under-inclusive when it benefits or burdens one group in pursuit of an objective but excludes others who should have been included. A law is over-inclusive when it burdens or benefits those intended but also applies to others not similarly situated as those targeted by the governmental action. Often, as in this case, legislation can be both over-inclusive—sweeping too broadly—and under-inclusive—not reaching all who should have been reached in pursuit of the objective.

As Justice Douglas' opinion underscores, similar to what it does in its modern economic due process review, in challenges to social and economic legislation the Court defers to legislative judgment and merely requires some congruence between the classification and a permissible governmental purpose. Justice Douglas thus dismisses the contention that the regulation should fail because there is no meaningful distinction between advertisements of products sold by truck owners and general advertisements, leaving to the legislature the consideration whether the classification bears some relation to the problem the regulation was designed to address and concluding that the ordinance "does not contain the kind of discrimination against which the Equal Protection Clause affords protection." In addition, the fact that the ordinance does not address other distractions contributing to the traffic problem is not offensive under his analysis. How are Justice Douglas' conclusions consistent with the proposition that the Equal Protection Clause requires similar treatment for those similarly situated?

Justice Jackson appears to struggle to find a "reasonable differentiation fairly related to the object of regulation," based on the nature and purpose of the regulation he finds to be identified by the courts of New York—the reduction of traffic hazards created by distraction of persons using the highways. It should be obvious that the determination of rationality is affected by how the purpose of the law is defined. It is also affected by the willingness to tolerate imperfection in the political process of identifying the appropriate classification scheme to accomplish the objective. In economic regulations, the Court has been willing to recognize that "reform may take one step at a time, addressing itself to the phases of the problem which seems most acute to the legislative mind." *Williamson v. Lee Optical of Oklahoma.*[20] How can a court distinguish between a legislative effort to address a problem "one step at a time" and unreasonable discrimination violative of equal protection? Notably, in *Williamson* the legislature had created specific exemptions from its general requirements for the sale and advertisement of eyeware having the effect of benefitting some, but not other sellers and outfitters of eye glasses.

---

[20] 348 U.S. 483 (1955).

PAH: The highly deferential rationality test offered in the *REA* case and typically applied in cases challenging economic and social regulation not only permits the government to identify any purpose which will likely support the classification (including ends not necessarily contemplated when the legislature enacted the law); the Court will also consider whether there exists any permissible purpose contemplatable but not formulated by the government against which the rationality of the classification scheme can be measured. If the purpose inquiry is taken seriously by the Court, shouldn't the Court require that the legislative steps undertaken to address the purpose be reasonable and not merely rationally furthering any permissible state objective? Surely the one step at a time justification is a pragmatic recognition of political negotiation. But the Court's willingness to defer to the political process in the identification of a legitimate purpose as well as its uncritical acceptance of any classification which even somewhat furthers that end invite arbitrary governmental action to go unchallenged.

DEL: Equal protection review since *Carolene Products*, like substantive due process analysis, has reflected the murkiness of an uncertain response to the *Lochner* era. Figuring when the judiciary should intervene and undo the will of the political process is vexing both for the courts and a general culture steeped (sometimes mistakenly) in principles of majoritarianism. What commenced as a two-tier level of review—strict scrutiny for classifications categorically perceived as dubious and disinterest in any other classifications—has evolved into a further source of confoundment to the extent glossed by an intermediate level of review. The *Slaughter-House Cases* Court doubted, in initially assessing the equal protection guarantee, "whether any action of a State not directed by way of discrimination against the Negroes as a class, or on account of their race, will ever be held to come within the purview of this provision."[21] From attention to discrete and insular minorities (who actually may have more political power than those who are neither discrete nor insular),[22] to stigmatization theory grounded in dubious social science data and elevated attention to the interest of majorities (in the context of gender and affirmative action), equal protection theory has stumbled upon and beyond its original understanding. Ill-defined and rather shoddily anchored, analytical criteria mirror a historical tension among competing values of liberty, equality, majoritarianism and group identity. Racial classifica-

---

[21] Slaughter-House Cases, 83 U.S. 36, 81 (1873).
[22] Bruce A. Ackerman, *Beyond Carolene Products*, 98 Harv. L. Rev. 713 (1985).

tions aside, concern that equal protection analysis is not rigorous enough and allows too many opportunities for arbitrary governmental action may reflect a worry that is exaggerated. Although legislative wisdom may be debatable or dubious, law-making does not operate in a vacuum. Because the political process responds to perceived needs, problems or interests, for better or for worse, the chances for legislation that is arbitrary in the real sense of the word (as opposed to misconceived or miscalibrated) are slim. Whether the judiciary should play a more meaningful role in reviewing legislative output simply reprises the question of whether the institution's function should include that of a perfecting agent.

Massachusetts Board of Retirement v. Murgia
427 U.S. 307 (1976)

Per Curiam.

This case presents the question whether the provision of Mass. Gen. Laws Ann. c. 32 §26(3)(a)(1969), that a uniformed state police officer "shall be retired . . . upon attaining age fifty," denies appellee police officer equal protection of the laws in violation of the Fourteenth Amendment.

Appellee Robert Murgia was an officer in the Uniformed Branch of the Massachusetts State Police. The Massachusetts Board of Retirement retired him upon this 50th birthday.

The primary function of the Uniformed Branch of the Massachusetts State Police is to protect persons and property and maintain law and order. Specifically, uniformed officers participate in controlling prison and civil disorders, respond to emergencies and natural disasters, patrol highways in marked cruisers, investigate crime, apprehend criminal suspects, and provide backup support for local law enforcement personnel. As the District Court observed, "service in this branch is, or can be arduous.: "[H]igh versatility is required, with few, if any, backwaters available for the partially superannuated." Thus, "even [appellee's] experts concede that there is a general relationship between advancing age and decreasing physical ability to respond to the demands of the job."

These considerations prompt the requirement that uniformed state police officers pass a comprehensive physical examination biennially until age 40. After that, until mandatory retirement at age 50, uniformed officers must pass annually a more rigorous examination, including an electrocardiogram and tests for gastrointestinal bleeding. Appellee Murgia passed such an examination four months before he was retired, and there is no dispute that, when he retired, his excellent physical and mental health still rendered him capable of performing the duties of a uniformed officer.

The record includes the testimony of three physicians: that of the State Police Surgeon, who testified to the physiological and psychological demands involved in the performance of uniformed police functions; that of an associated professor of medicine, who testified generally to the relationship between aging and the ability to perform under stress; and that of a surgeon, who also testified to aging and the ability safely to perform police functions. The testimony clearly established that the risk of physical failure, particularly in the cardiovascular system increases with age, and that the number of individuals in a given age group incapable of performing stress functions increases with the age of the group. The testimony also recognized that particular individuals over 50 could be capable of safely performing the functions of uniformed officers. The associate professor of medicine, who was a witness for the appellee, further testified that evaluating the risk of cardiovascular failure in a given individual would require a number of detailed studies. . . .

We need state only briefly our reasons for agreeing that strict scrutiny is not the proper test for determining whether the mandatory retirement provision denies appellee equal protection. [E]qual protection analysis requires strict scrutiny of a legislative classification only when the classification impermissibly interferes with the exercise of a fundamental right or operates to the peculiar disadvantage of a suspect class. Mandatory retirement at age 50 under the Massachusetts statute involves neither situation.

This Court's decisions give no support for the proposition that a right of governmental employment *per se* is fundamental. Accordingly, we have expressly stated that a standard less than strict scrutiny "has consistently been applied to state legislation restricting the availability of employment opportunities."

Nor does the class of uniformed state police officers over 50 constitute a suspect class for purposes of equal protection analysis. The treatment of the aged in this Nation has not been wholly free of discrimination [but] such persons, unlike, say, those who have been discriminated against on the basis of race or national origin, have not experienced a "history of purposeful unequal treatment" or been subject to unique disabilities on the basis of stereotyped characteristics not truly indicative of their abilities. The class subject to the compulsory retirement feature of the Massachusetts statute consists of uniformed state police officers over the age of 50. It cannot be said to discriminate only against the elderly. Rather, it draws the line at a certain age in middle life. But even old age does not define a "discrete and insular" group in need of "extraordinary protection from the majoritarian process." Instead it marks a stage that each of us will reach if we live out our normal life span.

Under the circumstances, it is unnecessary to subject the State's resolution of competing interests in this case to the degree of critical examination that our cases under the Equal Protection Clause recently have characterized as "strict judicial scrutiny."

In this case, the Massachusetts statute clearly meets the requirements of the Equal Protection Clause, for the State's classification rationally furthers the purpose identified by the State. Through mandatory retirement at age 50, the legislature seeks to protect the public by assuring physical preparedness of its uniformed police. Since physical ability generally declines with age, mandatory retirement at 50 serves to remove from police service those whose fitness for uniformed work presumptively has diminished with age. This clearly is rationally related to the State's objective. There is no indication that § 26(3)(a) has the effect of excluding from service so few officers who are in fact unqualified as to render age 50 a criterion wholly unrelated to the objective of the statute.

That the State chooses not to determine fitness more precisely through individualized testing after age 50 is not to say that the objective of assuring physical fitness is not rationally furthered by a maximum-age limitation. It is only to say that with regard to the interest of all concerned, the State perhaps has not chosen the best means to accomplish this purpose.

We do not make light of the substantial economic and psychological effects premature and compulsory retirement can have on an individual; nor do we denigrate the ability of elderly citizens to continue to contribute to society. The problems of retirement have been well documented and are beyond serious dispute. But "[w]e do not decide today that the [Massachusetts statute] is wise, that it best fulfills the relevant social and economic objectives that

[Massachusetts] might ideally espouse, or that a more just and humane system could not be devised.' We decide only that the system enacted by the Massachusetts Legislature does not deny appellee equal protection of the laws.

The judgment is reversed.

Mr. Justice MARSHALL, dissenting:

Although there are signs that its grasp on the law is weakening, the rigid two-tier model still holds sway as the Court's articulated description of the equal protection test. Again, I must object to its perpetuation. The model's two fixed modes of analysis, strict scrutiny and mere rationality, simply do not describe the inquiry that the Court has undertaken—or should undertake—in equal protection cases. Rather, the inquiry has been more sophisticated and the Court should admit as much. It has focused upon the character of the classification in question, the relative importance to individuals in the class discriminated against of the governmental benefits that they do not receive, and the state interests asserted in support of the classification.

Although the court adheres to the two-tier model, it has apparently lost interest in recognizing further "fundamental" rights and "suspect" classes. In my view, this result is the natural consequence of the limitations of the Court's traditional equal protection analysis. If a statute invades a "fundamental" right or discriminates against a "suspect" class, it is subject to strict scrutiny. If a statute is subject to strict scrutiny, the statute always, or nearly always, is struck down. Quite obviously, the only critical decision is whether strict scrutiny should be invoked at all. It should be no surprise, then, that the Court is hesitant to expand the number of categories of rights and classes subject to strict scrutiny, when each expansion involves the invalidation of virtually every classification bearing upon a newly covered category.

But however understandable the Court's hesitancy to invoke strict scrutiny, all remaining legislation should not drop into the bottom tier, and be measured by the mere rationality test. For that test, too, when applied as articulated, leaves little doubt about the outcome; the challenged legislation is always upheld. It cannot be gainsaid that there remain rights, not now classified as "fundamental" that remain vital to the flourishing of a free society, and classes, not now classified as "suspect," that are unfairly burdened by invidious discrimination unrelated to the individual worth of their members. Whatever we call these rights and classes, we simply cannot forgo all judicial protection against discrimination legislation bearing upon them, but for the rare instances when the legislative choice can be termed "wholly irrelevant" to the legislative goal.

While the Court's traditional articulation of the rational-basis test does suggest just such an abdication, happily the Court's deeds have not matched its words. Time and again, met with cases touching upon the prized rights and burdened classes, the Court has acted only after a reasonably probing look at the legislative goals and means, and at the significance of the personal rights and interests invaded.

But there are problems with deciding cases based on factors not encompassed by the applicable standards. First the approach is rudderless, affording no notice to interested parties of the standards governing particular cases and given no firm guidance to judges who, as a consequence, must assess the constitutionality of legislation before them on an *ad hoc* basis. Second, and not unrelatedly, the approach is unpredictable and requires holding this Court to standards it has never publicly adopted. Thus the approach presents the danger, that as I suggest has happened here, relevant factors will be misapplied or ignored. All interests not "fundamental" and all classes not "suspect" are not the same; and it is time for the Court to drop the pretense that, for purposes of the Equal Protection Clause, they are.

The danger of the Court's verbal adherence to the rigid two-tier test, despite its effective repudiation of that test in the cases, is demonstrated by its efforts here. There is simply no reason why a statute that tells able-bodied police officers, ready and willing to work, that they no longer have the right to earn a living in their chosen profession merely because they are 50 years old should be judged by the same minimal standards of rationality that were used to test economic legislation that discriminates against business interests. Yet, the Court today not only invokes the minimal level of scrutiny, it wrongly adheres to it. Analysis of the three factors I have identified above—the importance of the governmental benefits denied, the character of the class, and the asserted state interests—demonstrates the Court's error.

Whether "'fundamental' or not, 'the right of the individual . . . to engage in any of the common occupations of life'" has been repeatedly recognized by this Court as falling within the concept of liberty guaranteed by the Fourteenth Amendment.

[I] agree that the purpose of the mandatory retirement law is legitimate, and indeed compelling. The Commonwealth has every reason to assure that its state police officers are of sufficient physical strength and health to perform their jobs. In my view, however, the means chosen, the forced retirement of officers at age 50, is so over-inclusive that it must fall.

[T]he only members of the state police still on the force at age 50 are those who have been determined—repeatedly—by the Commonwealth to be physically fit for the job. Yet all of these physically fit officers are automatically terminated at age 50. Thus the Commonwealth is in the position of already individually testing its police officers for physical fitness, conceding that such testing is adequate to determine the physical ability of an officer to continue on the job, and conceding that that ability may continue after age 50. I see no reason at all for automatically terminating those officers who reach the age of 50; indeed, that action seems the height of irrationality.

The majority in *Murgia* expresses certainty that "strict scrutiny" should be unavailable in this case because neither a suspect class is affected nor a fundamental right implicated in the mandatory retirement measure. The majority argues in part that the troopers are not members of a suspect class because the determinative age for mandatory retirement does not implicate elderliness by drawing the line at middle-age. The majority further argues, however, that growing old is inevitable, affecting everyone and not a discrete group. If you agree with Justice Marshall that this group is burdened with invidious discrimination does the majority's approach to equal protection provide an adequate response? Notably, the majority seems confident that the legislature will eventually consider whatever inequities such a group claims it experiences and determine whether it requires a legislative response.[23] Even though government employment has not been considered a "fundamental right" in due process cases, Justice Marshall argues for a more "probing look" at the legislative goals and means as well as consideration of the significance of the personal rights and interests invaded in these circumstances. Justice Marshall is concerned that the two-tiered analysis in equal

---

[23] *See* JOHN H. ELY, DEMOCRACY AND DISTRUST (1980).

protection is outcome determinative and that, as a result, the Court's concern about disrupting the legislative process has naturally made it reluctant to identify classes as "suspect" or rights "fundamental" because the consequence is the invalidation of governmental decisionmaking. Justice Marshall concludes that a two-tier analysis leads to judicial abdication of its protective role in equal protection cases. He argues, moreover, that the Court has never really adhered to a two-tiered analysis, undertaking a more searching inquiry of the relationship between the means chosen and end purported to be served when decisionmaking adversely affects a group which has experienced a history of invidious treatment in the political arena and when the interests at stake are significant though not necessarily "fundamental." In Justice Marshall's view, however, the failure of the Court to admit to a "sliding scale" review, more closely scrutinizing political decisionmaking which impacts on disfavored groups and important interests, is most disturbing. In his view it invites arbitrary decisionmaking by courts. Consider Justice Marshall's concerns as you read the *Cleburne* case, *infra*.

PAH: The difference between the approaches to equal protection challenges taken by the majority and dissent essentially concerns questions about judicial authority.[24] Confining judicial inquiry into political decisionmaking to "mere rationality" review requires the Court to virtually rubber-stamp what has been decided (unless "wholly unrelated to a legitimate purpose") and suggests that majoritarian rule is superior to virtually all constitutional values, including equality and respect envisioned in the Equal Protection Clause.[25] The Court's reluctance to intrude is not a necessary consequence of separation of powers since that concept envisions cooperation as well as independence of the branches of government. Functionally, there is nothing inconsistent with separation of powers for the court to have a more actively searching role considering whether there is a reasonable relationship between the classification scheme and a legitimate government end. It may be, however, that the majority is not persuaded that a "sliding scale" analysis in equal protection provides greater certainty or protects against arbitrary decision making by the courts.

Arguably the "hands-off" attitude of the Court is less justified in equal protection cases, where discrimination is alleged, than in the due process context, where the wisdom of the political decision is being challenged. And, as Justice Jackson suggested in the *REA* case it is less disruptive for the court to invalidate legislation by invoking the Equal Protection Clause because it does not disable any governmental body from dealing with the subject but merely requires a broader impact to ensure that government does "not . . . discriminate . . . except upon some reasonable differentiation fairly related to the object of regulation."[26]

DEL: The Constitution itself, given the structural safeguards it establishes against raw majoritarianism, radiates a fundamental message that majoritarian rule is not a categorically preferred value. Deference to the political process does not necessarily translate into sanctification of majoritarianism. It may reflect a sense, for instance, that courts have less expertise or are less competent (given their resources and decisional style) to resolve thorny issues that require brokering and compromise. A degree of deference to the political

---

[24] Owen Fiss for example challenges the decisionmaking hierarchy created by footnote 4 of Carolene Products, suggesting that democratic decisionmaking is not exclusively majoritarian. *See Foreword: Traces of Self-Government*; Guido Calabresi, *Foreword: Antidiscrimination and Constitutional Accountability (What the Bork-Brennan Debate Ignores*, 105 HARV. L. REV. 1 (1991).

[25] *See* Kenneth Karst, *Paths to Belonging: The Constitution and Cultural Identity*, 64 N.C.L. REV. 304 (1986).

[26] 336 U.S. at 112. *See* Calabresi, *supra,* 105 HARV. L. REV. 1 (1991).

process and to the imperatives of federalism actually might provide room, presently missing because of aggressive equal protection review, for the testing and implementing of innovative methods that allow race-conscious initiatives for reckoning with racial reality. Justice Jackson's observation that equal protection review is less intrusive than due process analysis may be apt in the abstract. Whether it is accurate in reality, however, depends upon the standard of review. Scrutiny that was strict in theory but consistently fatal in fact, for instance, would be no less preclusive merely because performed in the cause of equal protection.

City of Cleburne v. Cleburne Living Center
473 U.S. 432 (1985)

Justice WHITE delivered the opinion of the Court.

A Texas city denied a special use permit for the operation of a group home for the mentally retarded, acting pursuant to a municipal zoning ordinance requiring permits for such homes. The Court of Appeals for the Fifth Circuit held that mental retardation is a "quasi-suspect" classification and that the ordinance violated the Equal Protection Clause because it did not substantially further an important governmental purpose. We hold that a lesser standard of scrutiny is appropriate, but conclude that under that standard the ordinance is invalid as applied in this case.

I

In July 1980, respondent Jan Hannah purchased a building with the intention of leasing it to Cleburne Living Center, Inc. (CLC), for the operation of a group home for the mentally retarded. It was anticipated that the home would house 13 retarded men and women, who would be under the constant supervision of CLC staff members. The house had four bedrooms and two baths, with a half bath to be added. CLC planned to comply with all applicable state and federal regulations.

The city informed CLC that a special use permit would be required for the operation of a group home at the site, and CLC accordingly submitted a permit application. In response to a subsequent inquiry from CLC, the city explained that under the zoning regulations applicable to the site, a special use permit, renewable annually, was required for the construction of "[h]ospitals for the insane or feeble-minded, or alcoholic [sic] or drug addicts, or penal or correctional institutions." The city had determined that the proposed group home should be classified as a "hospital for the feebleminded." After holding a public hearing on CLC's application, the City Council voted 3 to 1 to deny a special use permit.

CLC then filed suit in Federal District Court against the city and a number of its officials, alleging, *inter alia,* that the zoning ordinance was invalid on its face and as applied because it discriminated against the mentally retarded in violation of the equal protection rights of CLC and its potential residents. The District Court found that "[i]f the potential residents of the Featherston Street home were not mentally retarded, but the home was the same in all other respects, its use would be permitted under the city's zoning ordinance," and that the City Council's decision "was motivated primarily by the fact that the residents of the home would be persons who are mentally retarded." Even so, the District Court held the ordinance and its application constitutional. Concluding that no fundamental right was implicated and that mental retardation was neither a suspect nor a quasi-suspect classification, the court employed the minimum level of judicial scrutiny applicable to equal protection claims. The court deemed the ordinance, as written and applied, to be rationally related to the city's legitimate interests in "the legal responsibility of CLC and its residents, . . . the safety and fears of residents in the adjoining neighborhood," and the number of people to be housed in the home.

The Court of Appeals for the Fifth Circuit reversed, determining that mental retardation was a quasi-suspect classification and that it should assess the validity of the ordinance under intermediate-level scrutiny. Because mental retardation was in fact relevant to many legislative actions, strict scrutiny was not appropriate. But in light of the history of "unfair and often grotesque mistreatment" of the retarded, discrimination against them was "likely to reflect deep-seated prejudice." In addition, the mentally retarded lacked political power, and their condition was immutable. The court considered heightened scrutiny to be particularly appropriate in this case, because the city's ordinance withheld a benefit which, although not fundamental, was very important to the mentally retarded. Without group homes, the court stated, the retarded could never hope to integrate themselves into the community. Applying the test that it considered appropriate, the court held that the ordinance was invalid on its face because it did not substantially further any important governmental interests. The Court of Appeals went on to hold that the ordinance was also invalid as applied. Rehearing en banc was denied with six judges dissenting in an opinion urging en banc consideration of the panel's adoption of a heightened standard of review. We granted certiorari.

II

The Equal Protection Clause of the Fourteenth Amendment is essentially a direction that all persons similarly situated should be treated alike. Section 5 of the Amendment empowers Congress to enforce this mandate, but absent controlling congressional direction, the courts have themselves devised standards for determining the validity of state legislation or other official action that is challenged as denying equal protection. The general rule is that legislation is presumed to be valid and will be sustained if the classification drawn by the statute is rationally related to a legitimate state interest. When social or economic legislation is at issue, the Equal Protection Clause allows the States wide latitude, and the Constitution presumes that even improvident decisions will eventually be rectified by the democratic processes.

The general rule gives way, however, when a statute classifies by race, alienage, or national origin. These factors are so seldom relevant to the achievement of any legitimate state interest that laws grounded in such considerations are deemed to reflect prejudice and antipathy—a view that those in the burdened class are not as worthy or deserving as others. For these reasons and because such discrimination is unlikely to be soon rectified by legislative means, these laws are subjected to strict scrutiny and will be sustained only if they are suitably tailored to serve a compelling state interest.

We have declined, however, to extend heightened review to differential treatment based on age:

> "While the treatment of the aged in this Nation has not been wholly free of discrimination, such persons, unlike, say, those who have been discriminated against on the basis of race or national origin, have not experienced a 'history of purposeful unequal treatment' or been subjected to unique disabilities on the basis of stereotyped characteristics not truly indicative of their abilities."

The lesson of *Murgia* is that where individuals in the group affected by a law have distinguishing characteristics relevant to interests the State has the authority to implement, the courts have been very reluctant, as they should be in our federal system and with our respect for the separation of powers, to closely scrutinize legislative choices as to whether, how, and to what extent those interests should be pursued. In such cases, the Equal Protection Clause requires only a rational means to serve a legitimate end.

III

Against this background, we conclude for several reasons that the Court of Appeals erred in holding mental retardation a quasi-suspect classification calling for a more exacting standard of judicial review than is normally accorded economic and social legislation. First, it is undeniable, and it is not argued otherwise here, that those who are mentally retarded have a reduced ability to cope with and function in the everyday world. Nor are they all cut from the same pattern: as the testimony in this record indicates, they range from those whose disability is not immediately evident to those who must be constantly cared for. They are thus different, immutably so, in relevant respects, and the States' interest in dealing with and providing for them is plainly a legitimate one. How this large and diversified group is to be treated under the law is a difficult and often a technical matter, very much a task for legislators guided by qualified professionals and not by the perhaps ill-informed opinions of the judiciary. Heightened scrutiny inevitably involves substantive judgments about legislative decisions, and we doubt that the predicate for such judicial oversight is present where the classification deals with mental retardation.

Second, the distinctive legislative response, both national and state, to the plight of those who are mentally retarded demonstrates not only that they have unique problems, but also that the lawmakers have been addressing their difficulties in a manner that belies a continuing antipathy or prejudice and a corresponding need for more intrusive oversight by the judiciary. Thus, the Federal Government has not only outlawed discrimination against the mentally retarded in federally funded programs, but it has also provided the retarded with the right to receive "appropriate treatment, services, and habilitation" in a setting that is "least restrictive of [their] personal liberty." In addition, the Government has conditioned federal education funds on a State's assurance that retarded children will enjoy an education that, "to the maximum extent appropriate," is integrated with that of nonmentally retarded children. The Government has also facilitated the hiring of the mentally retarded into the federal civil service by exempting them from the requirement of competitive examination. The State of Texas has similarly enacted legislation that acknowledges the special status of the mentally retarded by conferring certain rights upon them, such as "the right to live in the least restrictive setting appropriate to [their] individual needs and abilities," including "the right to live . . . in a group home."

Such legislation thus singling out the retarded for special treatment reflects the real and undeniable differences between the retarded and others. That a civilized and decent society expects and approves such legislation indicates that governmental consideration of those differences in the vast majority of situations is not only legitimate but also desirable. It may be, as CLC contends, that legislation designed to benefit, rather than disadvantage, the retarded would generally withstand examination under a test of heightened scrutiny. The relevant inquiry, however, is whether heightened scrutiny is constitutionally mandated in the first instance. Even assuming that many of these laws could be shown to be substantially related to an important governmental purpose, merely requiring the legislature to justify its efforts in these terms may lead it to refrain from acting at all.

Third, the legislative response, which could hardly have occurred and survived without public support, negates any claim that the mentally retarded are politically powerless in the sense that they have no ability to attract the attention of the lawmakers. Any minority can be said to be powerless to assert direct control over the legislature, but if that were a criterion for higher level scrutiny by the courts, much economic and social legislation would now be suspect.

Fourth, if the large and amorphous class of the mentally retarded were deemed quasi-suspect for the reasons given by the Court of Appeals, it would be difficult to find a principled way to distinguish a variety of other groups who have perhaps immutable disabilities setting them off from others, who cannot themselves mandate the desired legislative responses, and who can claim some degree of prejudice from at least part of the public at large. One need mention in this respect only the aging, the disabled, the mentally ill, and the infirm. We are reluctant to set out on that course, and we decline to do so.

Doubtless, there have been and there will continue to be instances of discrimination against the retarded that are in fact invidious, and that are properly subject to judicial correction under constitutional norms. But the appropriate method of reaching such instances is not to create a new quasi-suspect classification and subject all governmental action based on that classification to more searching evaluation. Rather, we should look to the likelihood that governmental action premised on a particular classification is valid as a general matter, not merely to the specifics of the case before us. Because mental retardation is a characteristic that the government may legitimately take into account in a wide range of decisions, and because both State and Federal Governments have recently committed themselves to assisting the retarded, we will not presume that any given legislative action, even one that disadvantages retarded individuals, is rooted in considerations that the Constitution will not tolerate.

Our refusal to recognize the retarded as a quasi-suspect class does not leave them entirely unprotected from invidious discrimination. To withstand equal protection review, legislation that distinguishes between the mentally retarded and others must be rationally related to a legitimate governmental purpose. This standard, we believe, affords government the latitude necessary both to pursue policies designed to assist the retarded in realizing their full potential, and to freely and efficiently engage in activities that burden the retarded in what is essentially an incidental manner. The State may not rely on a classification whose relationship to an asserted goal is so attenuated as to render the distinction arbitrary or irrational. Furthermore, some objectives—such as "a bare . . . desire to harm a politically unpopular group,"—are not legitimate state interests. Beyond that, the mentally retarded, like others, have and retain their substantive constitutional rights in addition to the right to be treated equally by the law.

IV

We turn to the issue of the validity of the zoning ordinance insofar as it requires a special use permit for homes for the mentally retarded. We inquire first whether requiring a special use permit for the Featherston home in the circumstances here deprives respondents of the equal protection of the laws. If it does, there will be no occasion to decide whether the special use permit provision is facially invalid where the mentally retarded are involved, or to put it another way, whether the city may never insist on a special use permit for a home for the mentally retarded in an R-3 zone. This is the preferred course of adjudication since it enables courts to avoid making unnecessarily broad constitutional judgments.

The constitutional issue is clearly posed. The city does not require a special use permit in an R-3 zone for apartment houses, multiple dwellings, boarding and lodging houses, fraternity or sorority houses, dormitories, apartment hotels, hospitals, sanitariums, nursing homes for convalescents or the aged (other than for the insane or feebleminded or alcoholics or drug addicts), private clubs or fraternal orders, and other specified uses. It does, however, insist on a special permit for the Featherston home, and it does so, as the District Court found, because it would be a facility for the mentally retarded. May the city require the permit for this facility when other care and multiple-dwelling facilities are freely permitted?

It is true, as already pointed out, that the mentally retarded as a group are indeed different from others not sharing their misfortune, and in this respect they may be different from those who would occupy other facilities that would be permitted in an R-3 zone without a special permit. But this difference is largely irrelevant unless the Featherston home and those who would occupy it would threaten legitimate interests of the city in a way that other permitted uses such as boarding houses and hospitals would not. Because in our view the record does not reveal any rational basis for believing that the Featherston home would pose any special threat to the city's legitimate interests, we affirm the judgment below insofar as it holds the ordinance invalid as applied in this case.

The judgment of the Court of Appeals is affirmed insofar as it invalidates the zoning ordinance as applied to the Featherston home. The judgment is otherwise vacated, and the case is remanded.

It is so ordered.

Justice STEVENS with whom THE CHIEF JUSTICE joins, concurring.

Our cases reflect a continuum of judgmental responses to differing classifications which have been explained in opinions by terms ranging from "strict scrutiny" at one extreme to "rational basis" at the other. I have never been persuaded that these so-called "standards" adequately explain the decisional process. Cases involving classifications based on alienage, illegal residency, illegitimacy, gender, age, or—as in this case—mental retardation, do not fit well into sharply defined classifications.

Justice MARSHALL, with whom Justice BRENNAN and Justice BLACKMUN join, concurring in the judgment in part and dissenting in part.

The Court holds that all retarded individuals cannot be grouped together as the "feebleminded" and deemed presumptively unfit to live in a community. Underlying this holding is the principle that mental retardation *per se* cannot be a proxy for depriving retarded people of their rights and interests without regard to variations in individual ability. With this holding and principle I agree. The Equal Protection Clause requires attention to the capacities and needs of retarded people as individuals.

I cannot agree, however, with the way in which the Court reaches its result or with the narrow, as-applied remedy it provides for the city of Cleburne's equal protection violation. The Court holds the ordinance invalid on rational-basis grounds and disclaims that anything special, in the form of heightened scrutiny, is taking place. Yet Cleburne's ordinance surely would be valid under the traditional rational-basis test applicable to economic and commercial regulation. In my view, it is important to articulate, as the Court does not, the facts and principles that justify subjecting this zoning ordinance to the searching review—the heightened scrutiny—that actually leads to its invalidation. Moreover, in invalidating Cleburne's exclusion of the "feebleminded" only as applied to respondents, rather than on its face, the Court radically departs from our equal protection precedents. Because I dissent from this novel and truncated remedy, and because I cannot accept the Court's disclaimer that no "more exacting standard" than ordinary rational-basis review is being applied, I [concur in the judgment in part and dissent in part].

The majority rejects the use of a different standard than "rationality" in this case, reasoning that, unlike race and ethnicity which has been viewed with suspicion as a basis for governmental determination of who should receive benefits or be burdened by governmental action, mental retardation as a characteristic may legitimately be taken into account. The majority makes this conclusion while acknowledging deepseated prejudice of a group has led that Court to require the government to show important interests at stake in order to burden that group. Purporting to apply the "minimum level scrutiny" the Court nonetheless invalidates the ordinance at issue in *Cleburne*. As the concurring judges suggest, however, the rationality review in *Cleburne* seems more searching than the Court's review of other economic and social regulations such as *REA*. The Court's additional justification for using mere rationality review, that extending a more searching standard of review to the mentally retarded would require it to provide similar protection to other groups, seems hollow in the face of its conclusion and apparently more "biting" consideration of the basis for governmental decision making in this case. As you read the race and gender cases to follow, review the *Cleburne* case and consider whether you support the Court's effort to distinguish mental retardation. *See also Carolene Products*[27] footnote 4. Notably, in both *Murgia* and *Cleburne* the Court emphasizes the amorphousness of the groups, suggesting that legislatures are better capable than courts to determine whether the group characteristics are relevant in the distribution of benefits and burdens.[28]

---

[27] 304 U.S. 144, 152-53 n.4(1938).

[28] *See* Calabresi, *supra*, 105 HARV. L. REV. 1; *see also* Minow, *supra*, 101 HARV. L. REV. 10; (arguing that legislation should not be sustained if it confirms the distribution of power in ways that harm the less powerful and benefit the more powerful).

PAH: One can read recent cases such as *Cleburne* in one of two ways: either the Court has determined to perform a more searching inquiry of governmental action affecting economic and social matters than the "drop dead" or rubber stamping reminiscent of rationality review in *REA*, or the application of the rationality review it undertakes is, as Justice Marshall suggests, affected by the kind of group impacted and the importance of the benefit being offered or withheld. One would be hard pressed to suggest that the lax review accorded social and economic legislation in the early seventies, see, e.g., *Dandridge v. Williams*,[29] is being applied in *Murgia* or *Cleburne*. The treatment in cases concerning "purely" economic regulation or the distribution of government benefits, however, still seem to reveal a toothless rationality review. See e.g., *Nordlinger v. Hahn*.[30] (statewide ballot initiative known as Proposition 13 imposing limits on real property taxes upheld against equal protection challenge despite legislative difference in treatment between newer and older home owners.)

DEL: The fact that cases such as *Cleburne* can be read in two ways (at least) indicates the analytical morass in which equal protection review functions. Rulings like *Cleburne* that announce a standard of review, yet stray from it, may seem unprincipled when viewed in isolation. Surveyed in context, however, they further illuminate a historical reality of judicial review characterized by professions of not second-guessing legislative wisdom but sometimes finding it difficult to avoid trumping the political process with its own set of values or sense of "simple justice."

---

[29] Dandridge v. Williams 397 U.S. 471 (1970)(statutory distinction will not be set aside if any set of facts reasonably may be conceived to justify it.)

[30] 505 U.S. 1 (1992).

B. Race

1. Race and the Union's Formation

The Constitutional Convention in 1787 represented an effort to create order out of the political chaos and economic conflict that characterized post-Revolutionary experience under the Articles of Confederation. In attempting "to form a more perfect Union,"[31] the republic's founders deliberated upon and resolved a multiplicity of difficult issues including the relative strength of each state within the federal system and

---

[31] U.S. CONST. pmbl.

protectionist state practices that burdened commercial intercourse among the several states. The most divisive controversy among the Constitution's framers, however, concerned slavery. As James Madison noted, sectional friction was attributable partly to climate but principally [to] the effects of [states] having or not having slaves. These two causes concur in forming the great division of interests in the U. States. It did not lie between the large [and] small states; it lay, between the Northern [and] Southern states.[32]

Although not debated at the feverish level of the mid-nineteenth century, the slavery issue was divisive enough to put the union's formation at risk. The Georgia and South Carolina delegations in particular struck a hard line posture of refusing to participate in any political union requiring divestiture of slavery.[33] Although a minority, the ardent pro-slavery delegates were vociferous and tenacious in promoting their interests. As one historian has noted, "(w)henever this group apprehended a danger to slavery, its members raised a protest, made a deal or threatened to start packing. Through bluster, compromise, and political blackmail over the question of the union itself, they secured power and protection for slavery."[34] Despite significant anti-slavery sentiment, the overarching imperative of forming a viable union drove a compromise. The net result was a Constitution structured in terms that neither endorsed nor prohibited but accommodated slavery. Although leaving the question of slavery for each state to resolve, the Constitution included several significant concessions to the Georgia and South Carolina delegations. Representation in the House was based upon a population count that recognized a slave as three-fifths of a person,[35] direct taxes among the states were to be apportioned similarly,[36] Congress was prohibited until 1808 from banning the importation of slaves[37] and free states were obligated to return upon an owner's request any slave that escaped.[38]

Opposition to slavery melted when confronted with the reality that a new union rested upon the institution's accommodation. George Mason had advocated a federal role in curbing the spread of slavery but eventually acknowledged the "great difficulties and infelicity to be now deprived" of the institution.[39] Although perhaps grounded more in rationalization than reality, some backed away from their opposition to slavery on grounds that it was a terminal institution.[40] Given the interests at stake in 1787, historians have concluded that formal termination of slavery was simply not in the constitutional deck of cards. As Winthrop Jordan has noted, "propositions on this stead would have sent half the delegates packing."[41] Even if the framers had known the full consequences of their compromise on the slavery issue, Derrick Bell suggests that the framers' output would not have been different.

---

[32] 1 M. FARRAND, THE RECORDS OF THE FEDERAL CONVENTION OF 1787 486 (1937).

[33] DON E. FEHRENBACHER, THE DRED SCOTT CASE 2-27 (1978).

[34] PAUL FINKELMAN, AN IMPERFECT UNION 23 (1981).

[35] U.S. CONST. art. I, § 2[3].

[36] *Id.*

[37] *Id.*, art. I, § 9[1].

[38] *Id.*, art. IV, § 2[3].

[39] I J. ELLIOTT, THE DEBATES IN THE SEVERAL STATE CONVENTIONS OF THE ADOPTION OF THE FEDERAL CONSTITUTION, v.4, at 100 (1941).

[40] In the Massachusetts ratification proceeding, Thomas Dawes asserted that "[i]t would not do to abolish slavery . . . [but] it . . . will die of a consumption." *Id.*, v.2, at 41.

[41] WINTHROP JORDAN, WHITE OVER BLACK: AMERICAN ATTITUDES TOWARD THE NEGRO 323 (1968).

Derrick A. Bell, Jr.
And We Are Not Saved (1987)*

. . .
The Chronicle of the Constitutional Contradiction

AT THE END of a journey back millions of light-years, I found myself standing quietly at the podium at the Constitutional convention of 1787. It was late afternoon, and hot in that late summer way that makes it pleasant to stroll down a shaded country lane, but mighty oppressive in a large, crowded meeting room, particularly one where the doors are closed and locked to ensure secrecy.

The three dozen or so convention delegates looked tired. They had doubtless been meeting all day and now, clustered in small groups, were caucusing with their state delegations. So intense were their discussions that the few men who looked my way did not seem to see me. They knew this was a closed meeting, and thus could not readily take in the appearance, on what had just been an empty platform, of a tall stranger—a stranger who was not only a woman but also, all too clearly, black.

Though I knew I was protected by extraordinary forces, my hands were wet with nervous perspiration. Then I remembered why I was there. Taking a deep breath, I picked up the gavel and quickly struck the desktop twice, hard.

"Gentlemen," I said, "my name is Geneva Crenshaw, and I appear here to you as a representative of the late twentieth century to test whether the decisions you are making today might be altered if you were to know their future disastrous effect on the nation's people, both white and black."

For perhaps ten seconds, there was a shocked silence. Then the chamber exploded with shouts, exclamations, oaths. I fear the delegates' expressions of stunned surprise did no honor to their distinguished images. A warm welcome would have been too much to expect, but their shock at my sudden presence turned into an angry commotion unrelieved by even a modicum of curiosity.

The delegates to the Constitutional Convention were, in the main, young and vigorous. When I remained standing, unmoved by their strong language and dire threats, several particularly robust delegated charged toward the platform, determined to carry out the shouted orders: "Eject the Negro woman at once!"

Suddenly the hall was filled with the sound of martial music, blasting trumpets, and a deafening roll of snare drums. At the same time—as the delegates were almost upon me—a cylinder composed of thin vertical bars of red, white, and blue light descended swiftly and silently from the high ceiling, nicely encapsulating the podium and me.

The self-appointed ejection party neither slowed nor swerved, a courageous act they soon regretted. As each man reached and tried to pass through the transparent light shield, there was a loud hiss, quite like the sound that electrified bug zappers make on a warm summer evening. While not lethal, the shock each attacker received was sufficiently strong to knock him to the floor, stunned and shaking.

The injured delegates all seemed to recover quickly, except one who had tried to pierce the light shield with his sword. The weapon instantly glowed red hot and burned his hand. At that point, several delegates tried to rush out of the room either to escape or to seek help—but neither doors nor windows would open.

"Gentlemen," I repeated, but no one heard me in the turmoil of shouted orders, cries of outrage, and efforts to sound the alarm to those outside. Scanning the room, I saw a swarthy delegate cock his long pistol, aim carefully, and fire directly at me. But the ball hit the shield, ricocheted back into the room, and shattered an inkwell, splattering my intended assassin with red ink.

At that, one of the delegates, raising his hand roared, "Silence" and then turned to me. "Woman! Who are you and by what authority do you interrupt this gathering?"

"Gentlemen," I began, "delegates"—then paused and, with a slight smile, added, "fellow citizens, I—like some of you—am a Virginian, my forefathers having labored on the land holdings of your fellow patriot, the Honorable Thomas Jefferson. I have come to urge that, in your great work here, you not restrict the sweep of Mr. Jefferson's self-evident truths that all men are equal and endowed by the Creator with inalienable rights, including 'Life, Liberty and the pursuit of Happiness.'" It was, I thought, a clever touch to invoke the name of Thomas Jefferson who, then serving as American minister to France, was not a member of the Virginia delegation. But my remark could not overcome the offense of my presence.

"How dare you insert yourself in these deliberations?" a delegate demanded.

"I dare," I said, "because slavery is an evil that Jefferson, himself a slave owner and unconvinced that Africans are equal to whites, nevertheless found involved 'a perpetual exercise of the most boisterous passions, the most unremitting despotism on the one part, and degrading submissions on the other.' Slavery, Jefferson has written, brutalizes slave owner as well as slave and, worst of all, tends to undermine the 'only firm basis' of liberty, the conviction in the minds of the people that liberty is 'the gift of God.'

"Gentlemen, it was also Thomas Jefferson who, considering the evil of slavery, wrote" 'I tremble for my country when I reflect that God is just; that his justice cannot sleep forever.'"

There was a hush in the group. No one wanted to admit it, but the ambivalence on the slavery issue expressed by Jefferson obviously had meaning for at least some of those in the hall. It seemed the right moment to prove both that I was a visitor from the future and that Jefferson's troubled concern for his country had not been misplaced. In quick, broad strokes, I told them of the country's rapid growth, of how slavery had expanded rather than withered of its own accord, and finally of how its continued presence bred first suspicion and then enmity between those in the South who continued to rely on a plantation economy and those Northerners committed to industrial development using white wage workers. The entry into the Union of each new state, I explained, further dramatized the disparity between North and South. Inevitably, the differences led to armed conflict—a civil war that, for all its bloody costs, did not settle those differences, and they remain divisive even as we celebrate our two-hundredth anniversary as one nation.

"The stark truth is that the racial grief that persists today," I ended, "originated in the slavery institutionalized in the document you are drafting. Is this, gentlemen, an achievement for which you wish to be remembered?"

Oblivious to my plea, a delegate tried what he likely considered a sympathetic approach. "Geneva, be reasonable. Go and leave us to work. We have heard the petitions of Africans and of abolitionists speaking in their behalf. Some here are sympathetic to these pleas for freedom. Others are not. But we have debated this issue at length, and after three months of difficult negotiations, compromises have been reached, decisions made, language drafted and approved. The matter is settled. Neither you nor whatever powers have sent you here can undo what is done."

I was not to be put off so easily. "Sirs," I said, "I have come to tell you that the matter of slavery will not be settled by your compromises. And even when it is ended by armed conflict and domestic turmoil far more devastating than that you hope to avoid here, the potential evil of giving priority to property over human rights will remain. Can you not address the contradiction in your words and deeds?"

"There is no contradiction," replied another delegate. "Gouverneur Morris of Pennsylvania, the Convention's most outspoken opponent of slavery, has admitted that 'life and liberty were generally said to be of more value, than property, . . . [but] an accurate view of the matter would nevertheless prove that property was the main object of Society.'"

"A contradiction," another delegate added, "would occur were we to follow the course you urge. We are not unaware of the moral issues raised by slavery, but we have no response to the delegate from South Carolina, General Charles Cotesworth Pinckney, who has admonished us that 'property in slaves should not be exposed to danger under a Govt. instituted for the protection of property.'"

"Of what value is a government that does not secure its citizens in their persons and their property?" inquired another delegate. "Government, as Mr. Pierce Butler from South Carolina has maintained here,' was instituted principally for the protection of property and was itself . . . supported by property.' Property, he reminded us, was 'the great object of government; the great cause of war; the great means of carrying it on. And the whole South Carolina delegation joined him in making it clear that 'the security the Southern states want is that their Negroes may not be taken from them.'"

"Your deliberations here have been secret," I replied. "And yet history has revealed what you here would hide. The Southern delegates have demanded the slavery compromises as their absolute precondition to forming a new government."

"And why should it not be so?" a delegate in the rear called out. "I do not represent the Southern point of view, and yet their rigidity on the slavery issue is wholly natural, stemming as it does from the commitment of their economy to labor-intensive agriculture. We are not surprised by the determined bargaining of the Georgia and South Carolina delegations, nor distressed that our Southern colleagues, in seeking the protection they have gained, seem untroubled by doubts about the policy and morality of slavery and the slave trade."

"Then," I countered, "you are not troubled by the knowledge that this document will be defended by your Southern colleagues in the South Carolina ratification debates, by admissions that 'Negroes were our wealth, our only resource'?"

"Why, in God's name," the delegate responded, "should we be troubled by the truth, candidly stated? They have said no less in these chambers. General Charles Cotesworth Pinckney has flatly stated that 'South Carolina and Georgia cannot do without slaves.' And his cousin and fellow planter, Charles Pinckney, has added, 'The blacks are the laborers, the peasants of the Southern states.'"

At this, an elderly delegate arose and rapped his cane on his chair for attention. "Woman, we would have you gone from this place. But if a record be made, that record should show that the economic benefits of slavery do not accrue only to the South. Plantation states provide a market for Northern factories, and the New England shipping industry and merchants participate in the slave trade. Northern states, moreover, utilize slaves in the fields, as domestics, and even as soldiers to defend against Indian raids."

I shook my head. "Here you are then! Representatives from large and small states, slave states and those that have abolished slavery, all of you are protecting your property interests at the cost of your principles."

There was no response. The transparent shield protected my person, served as a language translator smoothing the differences in English usage, and provided a tranquilizing effect as it shimmered softly in the hot and humid room. Evidently, even this powerful mechanism could not bring the delegates to reassess their views on the slavery issue.

I asked, "Are you not concerned with the basic contradiction in your position: that you, who have gathered here in Philadelphia from each state in the confederacy, in fact represent and constitute major property holders? Do you not mind that your slogans of liberty and individual rights are basically guarantees that neither a strong government nor the masses will be able to interfere with your property rights and those of your class? This contradiction between what you espouse and what you here protect will be held against you by future citizens of this nation."

"Unless we continue on our present course," a delegate called out, "there will be no nation whose origins can be criticized. These sessions were called because the country is teetering between anarchy and bankruptcy. The nation cannot meet its debts. And only a year ago, thousands of poor farmers in Massachusetts and elsewhere took up arms against the government."

"Indeed," I said, "I am aware of Shay's Rebellion, led by Daniel Shay, a former officer who served with distinction in the war against England. According to historians of my time, the inability of Congress to respond to Massachusetts's appeal for help provided 'the final argument to sway many Americans in favor of a stronger federal government.' I understand the nature of the crisis that brings you here, but the compromises you make on the slavery issue are——"

"Young woman!" interrupted one of the older delegates. "Young woman, you say you understand. But I tell you that it is 'nearly impossible for anybody who has not been on the spot to conceive (from any description) what the delicacy and danger of our situation... [has] been. I am President of this Convention, drafted to the task against my wishes. I am here and I am ready to embrace any tolerable compromise that... [is] competent to save us from impending ruin.'"

While so far I had recognized none of the delegates, the identify of this man—seated off by himself, and one of the few who had remained quiet through the bedlam that broke out after my arrival—was unmistakable.

"Thank you, General Washington," I responded. "I know that you, though a slave owner, are opposed to slavery. And yet you have said little during these meetings—to prevent, one may assume, your great prestige from unduly influencing debate. Future historians will say of your silence that you recognize that for you to throw the weight of your opinion against slavery might so hearten the opponents of the system, while discouraging its proponents, as to destroy all hope of compromise. This would prevent the formation of the Union, and the Union, for you is essential."

I will not respond to these presumptions," said General Washington, "but I will tell you now what I will say to others at a later time. There are in the new form some things, I will readily acknowledge, that never did, and I am persuaded never will, obtain my cordial approbation; but I did then conceive, and do now most firmly believe, that in the aggregate it is the best constitution, that can be obtained at this epoch, and that this, or a dissolution, awaits our choice, and is the only alternative."

"Do you recognize," I asked, "that in order to gain unity among yourselves, your slavery compromises sacrifice freedom for Africans who live amongst you and work for you? Such sacrifices of the rights of one group of human beings will, unless arrested here, become a difficult-to-break pattern in the nation's politics."

"Did you not listen to the general?" This man, I decided, must be James Madison. As the delegates calmed down, he had returned to a prominent seat in the front of the room directly in front of the podium. It was from this vantage point that he took notes of the proceedings which, when finally released in 1840, became the best record of the Convention.

"I expect," Madison went on, "that many will question why I have agreed to the Constitution. And, like General Washington, I will answer: 'because I thought it safe to the liberties of the people, and the best that could be obtained from the jarring interests of States, and the miscellaneous opinions of Politicians; and because experience has proved that the real danger to America & to liberty lies in the defect of *energy & stability* in the present establishments of the United States.'"

"Do not think," added a delegate from Massachusetts, "that this Convention has come easily to its conclusions on the matter that concerns you. Gouverneur Morris from Pennsylvania has said to us in the strongest terms: 'Domestic slavery is the most prominent feature in the aristocratic countenance of the proposed Constitution.' He warned again and again that 'the people of Pennsylvania will never agree to a representation of Negroes.'

"Many of us shared Mr. Morris's concern about basing apportionment on slaves as insisted by the Southern delegates. I recall with great sympathy his questions:

Upon what principle is it that the slaves shall be computed in the representation? Are they men? Then make them citizens & let them vote? Are they property? Why then is no other property included? . . .

The admission of slaves into the Representation when fairly explained comes to this: that the inhabitant of Georgia and S.C. who goes to the Coast of Africa, and in defiance of the most sacred laws of humanity tears away his fellow creatures from their dearest connections & damns them to the most cruel bondage, shall have more votes in a Govt. instituted for protection of the rights of mankind, then the Citizen of Pa or N. Jersey who views with a laudable horror, so nefarious a practice.

"I tell you woman, this Convention was not unmoved at these words of Mr. Morris's only a few weeks ago."

"Even so," I said, "the Convention has acquiesced when representatives of the Southern states adamantly insisted that the proposed new government not interfere with their property in slaves. And is it not so that, beyond a few speeches, the representatives of the Northern states have been, at best, ambivalent on the issue?"

"And why not?" interjected another delegate. "Slavery has provided the wealth that made independence possible. The profits from slavery funded the Revolution. It cannot be denied. At the time of the Revolution, the goods for which the United States demanded freedom were produced in very large measure by slave labor. Desperately needing assistance from other countries, we purchases this aid from France with tobacco produced mainly by slave labor. The nation's economic well-being depended on the institution, and its preservation is essential if the Constitution we are drafting is to be more than a useless document. At least, that is how we view the crisis we face."

To pierce the delegates' adamant front, I called on the oratorical talents that have, in the twentieth century, won me both praise and courtroom battles: "The real crisis you face should not be resolved by your recognition of slavery, an evil whose immorality will pollute the nation as it now stains your document. Despite your resort to euphemisms like *persons* to keep out of the Constitution such words as *slave* and *slavery*, you cannot evade the consequences of the ten different provisions you have placed in the Constitution for the purpose of protection property in slaves.

"Woman!" a delegate shouted from the rear of the room. "Explain to us how you, a black, have gotten free of your chains and gained the audacity to come here and teach white men anything."

I smiled, recognizing the eternal question. "Audacity," I replied, "is an antidote to your arrogance. Be assured: my knowledge, despite my race, is far greater than yours."

"But if my race and audacity offend you, then listen to your contemporaries who have opposed slavery in most moving terms. With all due respect, there are few in this company whose insight exceeds that of Abigail Adams who wrote her husband, John, during the Revolutionary War: 'I wish most sincerely there was not a slave in the province; it always appeared a most iniquitous scheme to me to fight ourselves for what we are daily robbing and plundering from those who have as good a right to freedom as we have.' Mrs. Adams's wish is, as you know, shared by many influential Americans who denounce slavery as a corrupting and morally unjustifiable practice.

"Gentlemen," I continued, "how can you disagree with the view of the Maryland delegate Luther Martin that the slave trade and 'three-fifths' compromises' ought to be considered as a solemn mockery of, and insult to that God whose protection we had then implored, and . . . who views with equal eye the poor African slave and his American master'? I can tell you that Mr. Martin will not only abandon these deliberations and refuse to sign the Constitution but also oppose its ratification in Maryland. And further, he will, in his opposition, expose the deal of the committee on which he served, under which New England states agreed to give the slave trade a twenty-year immunity from federal restrictions in exchange for Southern votes to eliminate restrictions on navigation acts. What is more, he will write that, to the rest of the world, it must appear 'absurd and disgraceful to the last degree, that we should *except* from the exercise of that power [to regulate commerce], the *only branch of commerce* which is *unjustifiable in its nature,* and *contrary to the rights of mankind.*'"

"Again, woman," a Northern delegate assured me, "we have heard and considered all those who oppose slavery. Despite the remonstrations of the abolitionists—of whom few, I must add, believe Negroes to be the equal of white men, and even fewer would want the blacks to remain in this land were slavery abandoned—we have acted as we believe the situation demands."

"I cannot believe," I said, "that even a sincere belief in the superiority of the white race should suffice to condone so blatant a contradiction of your hallowed ideals."

"It should be apparent by now," said the delegate who had shot at me, but had now recovered his composure and shed his inkstained coat, "that we do not care what you think. Furthermore, if your people actually had the sensitivities of real human beings, you would realize that you are not wanted here and would have the decency to leave."

"I will not leave!" I said steadily, and waited while the delegates conferred.

Finally, a delegate responded to my challenge. "You have, by now, heard enough to realize that we have not lightly reached the compromises on slavery you so deplore. Perhaps we, with the responsibility of forming a radically new government in perilous times, see more clearly than is possible for you in hindsight that the unavoidable cost of our labors will be the need to accept and live with what you call a contradiction."

The delegate had gotten to his feet, and was walking slowly toward me as he spoke. "This contradiction is not lost on us. Surely we know, even though we are at pains not to mention it, that we have sacrificed the rights of some in the belief that this involuntary forfeiture is necessary to secure the rights for others in a society espousing, as its basic principle, the liberty of all."

He was standing directly in front of the shield now, ignoring its gentle hum, disregarding its known danger. "It grieves me," he continued, "that your presence here confirms my worst fears about the harm done to your people because the Constitution, while claiming to speak in an unequivocal voice, in fact promises freedom to whites and condemns blacks to slavery. But what alternative do we have? Unless we here frame a constitution that can first gain our signatures and then win ratification by the states, we shall soon have no nation. For better or worse, slavery has been the backbone of our economy, the source of much of our wealth. It was condoned in the colonies and recognized in the Articles of Confederation. The majority of the delegates to this convention own slaves and must have that right protected if they and their states are to be included in the new government."

He paused and then asked, more out of frustration than defiance, "What better compromise on this issue can you offer than that which has been fashioned over so many hours of heated debate?"

The room was silent. The delegate, his statement made, his question presented, turned and walked slowly back to his seat. A few from his state touched his hand as he passed. Then all eyes turned to me.

I thanked the delegate for his question and then said, "The processes by which Northern states are even now abolishing slavery are known to you all. What is lacking here is not legislative skill but the courage to recognize the evil of holding blacks in slavery—an evil that would be quickly and universally condemned were the subjects of bondage members of the Caucasian race. You fear that unless the slavery of blacks is recognized and given protection, the nation will not survive. And my message is that the compromises you are making here mean that the nation's survival will always be in doubt. For now in my own day, after two hundred years and despite bloody wars and the earnest efforts of committed people, the racial contradiction you sanction in this document remains and threatens to tear this country apart."

"Mr. Chairman," said a delegate near the podium whose accent indicated that he was from the deep South, "this discussion grows tiresome and I resent to my very soul the presence in our midst of this offspring of slaves. If she accurately predicts the future fate of her race in this country, then our protection of slave property, which we deem essential for our survival, is easier to justify than in some later time when, as she implies, Negroes remain subjugated even without the threats we face."

"Hear! Hear! shouted a few delegates. "Bravo, Colonel!"

"It's all hypocrisy!" the Colonel shouted, his arms flailing the air, "sheer hypocrisy! Our Northern colleagues bemoan slavery while profiting from it as much as we in the South, meanwhile avoiding its costs and dangers. And our friends from Virginia, where slavery began, urge the end of importation—not out of humanitarian motivations, as their speeches suggest, but because they have sufficient slaves, and expect the value of their property will increase if further imports are barred.

"Mr. George Mason, of the Virginia delegation, in his speech opposing the continued importation of slaves expressed fear that, if not barred, the people of Western lands, already crying for slaves, could get them through South Carolina and Georgia. He moans that: 'Slavery discourages arts & manufactures. The poor despise labor when performed by slaves. They prevent the immigration of Whites, who really enrich & strengthen a Country. They produce the most pernicious effect on manners.' Furthermore, according to Mr. Mason, 'every master of slaves is born a petty tyrant. They bring the judgment of heaven on a Country . . . [and] by an inevitable chain of causes & effects providence punishes national sins, by national calamities.'

"This, Mr. Chairman, is nothing but hypocrisy or, worse, ignorance of history. We speak easily today of liberty, but the rise of liberty and equality in this country has been accompanied by the rise of slavery. The Negress who has seized our podium by diabolical force charges that we hold blacks slaves because we view them as inferior. Inferior in every way they surely are, but they were not slaves when Virginia was a new colony 150 years ago. Or, at least, their status was hardly worse then the luckless white indentured servants brought here from debtors' prisons and the poverty-ridden streets of England. Neither slave nor servant lived very long in that harsh, fever-ridden clime."

The Colonel, so close to the podium, steadfastly refused to speak to me or even to acknowledge my presence.

"In the beginning," he went on, "life was harsh, but the coming of tobacco to Virginia in 1617 turned a struggling colony into a place where great wealth could be made relative quickly. To ultimate the labor-intense crop, large numbers of mainly white, male servants, indentured to their masters for a period of years, were imported. Blacks, too, were brought to the colony, both as slaves and as servants. They generally worked, ate, and slept with the white servants.

"As the years passed, more and more servants lived to gain their freedom, despite the practice of extending terms for an offense, large or small. They soon became a growing, poverty-stricken class, some of whom resigned themselves to working for wages; others preferred a meager living on dangerous frontier land or a hand-to-mouth existence, roaming from one county to another, renting a bit of land here, squatting on some there, dodging the tax collector, drinking, quarrelling, stealing hogs, and enticing servants to run away with them."

"It is not extraordinary to suggest that the planters and those who governed Virginia were caught in a dilemma—a dilemma more like the contradiction we are accused of building into the Constitution than may at first meet the eye. They needed workers to maintain production in their fields, but young men were soon rebellious, without either land of their own or women, who were not seen fit to work the fields. Moreover, the young workers were armed and had to be armed to repel attacks from Indians by land and from privateers and petty-thieving pirates by sea.

"The worst fears of Virginia's leaders were realized when, in 1676, a group of these former servants returned from a fruitless expedition against the Indians to attack their rulers in what was called Bacon's Rebellion. Governor William Berkeley bemoaned his lot in terms that defined the problem: 'How miserable that man is that Governes a People wher six parts of seaven at least are Poore Endebted Discontented and Armed.'

"The solution came naturally and without decision. The planters purchased more slaves and imported fewer English servants. Slaves were more expensive initially, but their terms did not end, and their owners gained the benefits of the slaves' offspring. Africans, easily identified by color, could not hope to run away without being caught. The fear of pain and death could be and was substituted for the extension of terms as an incentive to force the slaves to work. They were not armed and could be held in chains.

"The fear of slave revolts increased as reliance on slavery grew and racial antipathy became more apparent. But this danger, while real, was less than that from restive and armed freedmen. Slaves did not have rising expectations, and no one told them they had rights. They had lost their freedom. Moreover, a woman could be made to work and have children every two years, thereby adding to the income of her master. Thus, many more women than indentured servants were imported.

"A free society divided between large landholders and small was much less driven by antagonisms than one divided between landholders and landless, masterless men. With the freedmen's expectations, sobriety, and status restored, he was no longer a man to be feared. That fact, together with the presence of a growing mass of alien slave, tended to draw the white settlers closer together and to reduce the importance of the class difference between yeoman farmer and large plantation owner.

"Racial fears tended to lessen the economic and political differences between rich and poor whites. And as royal officials and tax collectors became more oppressive, both groups joined forces in protesting the import taxes on tobacco which provided income for the high and low. The rich began to look to their less wealthy neighbors for political support against the English government and in local elections.

"Wealthy whites, of course, retained all their former prerogatives, but the creation of a black subclass enabled poor whites to identify with and support the policies of the upper class. With the safe economic advantage provided by their slaves, large landowners were willing to grant poor whites a larger role in the political process."

"So, Colonel," I interrupted, "you are saying that slavery for blacks not only provided wealth for rich whites but, paradoxically, led also to greater freedom for poor whites. One of our twentieth-century historians, Edmund Morgan, has explained this paradox of slave owners espousing freedom and liberty:

Aristocrats could more safely preach equality in a slave society than in a free one. Slaves did not become leveling mobs, because their owners would see to it that they had no chance to. The apostrophes to equality were not addressed to them. And because Virginia's labor force was composed mainly of slaves, who had been isolated by race and removed from the political equation, the remaining free laborers and tenant farmers were too few in number to constitute a serious threat to the superiority of the men who assured them of their equality.

"In effect," I concluded, "what I call a contradiction here was deemed a solution then. Slavery enabled the rich to keep their lands, arrested discontent and repression of other Englishmen, strengthened their rights and nourished their attachment to liberty. But the solution, as Professor Morgan said, 'put an end to the process of turning Africans into Englishmen. The rights of Englishmen were preserved by destroying the rights of Africans.'"

"Do you charge that our belief in individual liberty is feigned?" demanded a Virginian, outraged.

"It was Professor Morgan's point," I replied, "not that 'a belief in republican equality had to rest on slavery, but only that in Virginia (and probably in other southern colonies) it did. The most ardent American republicans were Virginians, and their ardor was not unrelated to their power over the men and women they held in bondage.'"

And now, for the first time, the Colonel looked at me, amazed. "my thoughts on this slavery matter have confounded my mind for many years, and yet you summarize them in a few paragraphs. I must, after all, thank you." He walked back to his seat in a daze, neither commended nor condemned by his colleagues. Most, indeed, were deep in thought—but for a few delegates I noticed trying desperately to signal to passersby in the street. But I could not attend to them: my time, I knew, must be growing short.

"The Colonel," I began again, "has performed a valuable service. He has delineated the advantages of slavery as an institution in this country. And your lengthy debates here are but prelude to the struggles that will follow your incorporation of this moral evil into the nation's basic law."

"Woman! We implore you to allow us to continue our work. While we may be inconsistent about the Negro problem, we are convinced that this is the only way open to us. You asked that we let your people go. We cannot do that and still preserve the potential of this nation for good—a potential that requires us to recognize here and now what later generations may condemn as evil. And as we talk I wonder—are the problems of race in your time equally paradoxical?"

I longed to continue the debate, but never got the chance. Apparently someone outside had finally understood the delegates' signals for help, and had summoned the local militia. Hearing some commotion beyond the window, I turned to see a small cannon being rolled up, pointing straight at me. Then, in quick succession, the cannoneer lighted the fuse; the delegates dived under their desks; the cannon fired; and, with an ear-splitting roar, the cannonball broke against the light shield and splintered leaving me and the shield intact.

I knew then my mission was over, and I returned to the twentieth century.

2. Slavery: The Constitutional Convention's Unfinished Business

Ratification of the Constitution established a union but did not resolve the issue of slavery. The idea that slavery would wither as an institution was refuted as the slave population increased during the early eighteenth century. Anticipated noninterference in each other's affairs proved elusive for slave and non-slave jurisdictions, as territorial expansion and the problem of fugitive slaves generated conflict and eventually destroyed the myth that the institution of slavery implicated and affected only those states and territories where it was permitted. As the union expanded to comprehend new territories and states, slavery became an increasingly thorny and divisive issue. With Missouri and Maine statehood held hostage by opposing camps, Congress in 1819 adopted the Missouri Compromise which drew a geographical bright line westward above which slavery would be prohibited and below which it would be allowed.[42]

Like the framers of the Constitution, Congress had attempted to finesse an issue

---

[42] Donald E. Lively, The Constitution and Race 12 (1992).

that increasingly allowed little middle ground. Territorial expansion heightened the political stakes insofar as slave states envisioned the possibility that their relative power in the union might be diluted and their ability to resist anti-slavery sentiment eventually might diminish. Emergence of the abolitionist movement during the 1830s exacerbated the sense of vulnerability and inspired attention to constitutional theory that would fortify the southern position. As radical abolitionists challenged what they perceived as a pro-slavery document that could be repaired only by the union's dissolution, and other strains of abolitionism favored as high a wall as possible between federal policy and slavery or tinkered with the notion that the privileges and immunities clause and due process clause could provide a basis for eliminating slavery,[43] new pro-slavery interpretations of the Constitution began to emerge. Southern legislators, for instance, maintained that the federal government was an agent of the several states and thus duty bound to support their institutions including slavery.[44] They also suggested that slave owner rights were protected by the due process clause of the Fifth Amendment.[45] Attention to the Constitution as a reference point for settling the controversy, despite the framers calculated bypass of the slavery question, demonstrated not only the magnitude of the stakes but the political process' futility in reckoning with the issue.

During the first few decades of the nineteenth century, the Supreme Court resolved several controversies that implicated aspects of slavery[46] but heard no real challenge to the institution. Although characterizing the international slave trade as an "inhuman traffic . . . contrary to the laws of nature,"[47] which the nation at least formally had disengaged itself from in 1808,[48] case law generally was constructed upon the premises of state determination and federal noninterference. Consistent with such analysis was the Court's resolution of a fugitive slave controversy in *Prigg v. Pennsylvania*. The *Prigg* case arose when a Maryland slave catcher entered Pennsylvania and removed a woman, who was the daughter of slaves but never herself claimed as a slave, and her children who had been born on free soil. Like some other northern states, Pennsylvania had enacted legislation allowing alleged fugitive slaves to be detained only by judicial officers, requiring strict proof of ownership and making private capture of a suspected fugitive a crime. At issue in *Prigg* was fugitive slave legislation enacted by Congress in 1793. In striking down the state law, on grounds it conflicted with the federal statute, the Court accommodated recaption processes that could result in the seizure of free blacks who were afforded no due process. Central to the decision was the conclusion that fugitive slave matters were within the federal government's exclusive jurisdiction.[49] Although the result was unpopular in the North, where anti-kidnapping laws had been enacted, it also was unsettling to the South insofar as it suggested that slavery was a federal rather than state interest. Sensitive to the possibility that federal power could be used against the institution, even if exercised protectively within the context of *Prigg*, Chief Justice Taney authored a concurring opinion previewing his analysis fifteen years later when the Court would attempt to resolve the slavery issue once and for all.

---

[43] DONALD E. LIVELY, THE CONSTITUTION AND RACE 13-14 (1992).

[44] DON E. FEHRENBACHER, THE DRED SCOTT CASE 122 (1978).

[45] *Id.*

[46] *E.g.*, The Josefa Segunda, 18 U.S. 338 (1820)(upholding congressional ban on importation of slaves).

[47] The Antelope, 23 U.S. 66, 120 (1825).

[48] Despite a congressional ban upon importing slaves, trade continued to thrive due to lax enforcement. PAUL FINKELMAN, AN IMPERFECT UNION 26 (1981).

[49] Prigg v. Pennsylvania, 41 U.S. 539, 616–17 (1842).

Prigg v. Pennsylvania
41 U.S. 536 (1842)

. . .

TANEY, CH. J.—I concur in the opinion pronounced by the court, that the law of Pennsylvania, under which the plaintiff in error was indicted, is unconstitutional and void; and that the judgment against him must be reversed. But as the questions before us arise upon the constitution of the United States, and as I do not assent to all the principles contained in the opinion just delivered, it is proper to state the points on which I differ.

I agree entirely in all that is said in relation to the right of the master, by virtue of the third clause of the second section of the fourth article of the constitution of the United States, to arrest his fugitive slave in any state wherein he may find him. He has a right, peaceably, to take possession of him, and carry him away, without any certificate or warrants from a judge of the district or circuit court of the United States, or from any magistrate of the state; and whoever resists or obstructs him, is a wrongdoer: and every state law which proposes directly or indirectly, to authorize such resistance or obstruction, is null and void, and affords no justification to the individual or the officer of the state who acts under it. This right of the master being given by the constitution of the United States, neither congress nor a state legislature can, by any law or regulation, impair it or restrict it.

I concur also in all that is contained in the opinion concerning the power of congress to protect the citizens of the slave-holding states, in the enjoyment of this right; and to provide by law an effectual remedy to enforce it, and to inflict penalties upon those who shall violate its provisions; and no state is authorized to pass any law, that comes in conflict in any respect with the remedy provided by congress. . . .

But, as I understand the opinion of the court, it goes further, and decides, that the power to provide a remedy for this right is vested exclusively in congress; and that all laws upon the subject, passed by a state, since the adoption of the constitution of the United States, are null and void; even although they were intended, in good faith, to protect the owner in the exercise of his rights of property, and do not conflict in any degree with the act of congress. . . . so exclusively vested in congress, that no state, since the adoption of the constitution, can pass any law in relation to it. In other words, according to the opinion just delivered, the state authorities are prohibited from interfering, for the purpose of protecting the right of the master, and aiding him in the recovery of his property. I think, the states are not prohibited; and that, on the contrary, it is enjoined upon them as a duty, to protect and support the owner, when he is endeavoring to obtain possession of his property found within their respective territories. The language used in the constitution does not, in my judgment, justify the construction given to it by the court. It contains no words prohibiting the several states from passing laws to enforce this right. . . .

The constitution of the United States, and every article and clause in it, is a part of the law of every state in the Union; and is the paramount law. The right of the master, therefore, to seize his fugitive slave, is the law of each state; and no state has the power to abrogate or alter it. And why may not a state protect a right of property, acknowledged by its own paramount law? Besides, the laws of the different states, in all other cases, constantly protect the citizens of other states in their rights of property, when it is found within their respective territories; and no one doubts their power to do so. And in the absence of any express prohibition, I perceive no reason for establishing, by implication, a different rule in this instance; where, by the national compact, this right of property is recognized as an existing right in every state of the Union.

. . .

The *Prigg* decision was significant in catalyzing awareness in the North that the institution of slavery implicated not just a region but the entire nation. Contemporaneously with the Court's ruling, William Lloyd Garrison wrote that allowing a slave owner to scour any corner of the nation for recaption "establish[es] the constitutionality of slavery in every State in the Union."[50] The immediate practical effect of the *Prigg* decision was less severe than its critics anticipated. Pursuant to the Court's dicta, to

---

[50] PAUL FINKELMAN, AN IMPERFECT UNION 172 (1981)(quoting William Lloyd Garrison, *The Liberator*, Mar. 11, 1842.

the effect that it could not require states "to carry into effect the duties of the national government" and state judges could enforce federal law "unless prohibited by state legislation,"[51] several states enacted laws forbidding judicial enforcement of the federal law. Having heightened awareness of slavery as a national rather than mere regional phenomenon, the net effect of the *Prigg* decision was to deepen sectional antagonism. As part of the Compromise of 1850, which also prohibited the slave trade in the District of Columbia, admitted California as a free state and organized Utah and New Mexico as slave territories, Congress attempted to repair damage to the fugitive slave law by creating a federal bureau charged with enforcement.[52] Inadequate resources limited its efficacy.

Continuing controversy over the status of new territories and states increasingly challenged and eventually paralyzed the political process. Conflict over the Kansas and Nebraska territories escalated into extensive violence, and was suffused with chicanery, as pro-slave and anti-slave interests vied to advance their competing agendas. From that experience emerged the Republican Party, which became notable for its touting of free soil principles—the position essentially being that slavery should be limited to those states and territories where it already existed. The Democratic Party was fractured between northern and southern interests which, although advocating resolution of the slavery question within each territory pursuant to the doctrine of popular sovereignty, differed on the timing for the decision.[53] With congressional machinery frozen by the absence of a middle ground satisfactory to both sides, the Supreme Court in 1857 offered what many anticipated as a final constitutional solution to the slavery question. The case of *Dred Scott v. Sandford* concerned a slave family that claimed freedom as a consequence of having lived with its owner for extended periods of time in a free state and territory. Although the Court could have resolved the case on jurisdictional or choice of law grounds, it reckoned with general questions of citizenship, congressional power in the territories and rights of slave owners.

---

[51] *Id.* at 615–16, 625.

[52] DONALD E. LIVELY, THE CONSTITUTION AND RACE 23 (1992).

[53] *Id.* at 25–26.

Dred Scott v. Sandford
60 U.S. 393 (1857)

This case was brought up, by writ of error, from the Circuit Court of the United States for the district of Missouri.

It was an action of trespass *vi et armis* instituted in the Circuit court by Scott against Sandford.

Prior to the institution of the present suit, an action was brought by Scott for his freedom in the Circuit Court of St. Louis county, (State court,) where there was a verdict and judgment in his favor. On a writ of error to the Supreme Court of the State, the judgment below was reversed, and the case remanded to the Circuit Court, where it was continued to await the decision of the case now in question.

The declaration of Scott contained three counts: one, that Sandford had assaulted the plaintiff; one, that he had assaulted Harriet

Scott, his wife; and one, that he had assaulted Eliza Scott and Lizzie Scott, his children.

And the said John F. A. Sandford, in his own proper person, comes and says that this court ought not to have or take further cognizance of the action aforesaid, because he says the said cause of action, and each and every of them, (if any such have accrued to the said Dred Scott,) accrued to the said Dred Scott out of the jurisdiction of this courts of the State of Missouri, for that, to wit: the said plaintiff, Dred Scott, is not a citizen of the State of Missouri, as alleged in his declaration, because he is a Negro of African descent; his ancestors were of pure African blood, and were brought into this country and sold as Negro slaves, and this the said Sandford is ready to verify. Wherefore, he prays judgment whether this court can or will take further cognizance of the action aforesaid. . . .

. . .

In the year 1834, the plaintiff was a Negro slave belonging to Dr. Emerson, who was a surgeon in the army of the United States. In that year, 1834, said Dr. Emerson took the plaintiff from the State of Missouri to the military post at Rock Island, in the State of Illinois, and held him there as a slave until the month of April or May, 1836. At the time last mentioned, said Dr. Emerson removed the plaintiff from said military post at Rock Island to the military post at Fort Snelling, situate on the west bank of the Mississippi river, in the Territory known as Upper Louisiana, acquired by the United States from France, and situate north of the latitude of thirty-six degrees thirty minutes north, and north of the State of Missouri. Said Dr. Emerson held the plaintiff in slavery at said Fort Snelling, from said last-mentioned date until the year 1838.

In the year 1835, Harriet, who is named in the second count of the plaintiff's declaration, was the Negro slave of Major Taliaferre, who belonged to the army of the United States. In that year, 1835, said Major Taliaferre took said Harriet to said Fort Snelling, a military post, situated as hereinbefore stated, and kept her there as a slave until the year 1836, and then sold and delivered her as a slave at said Fort Snelling unto the said Dr. Emerson hereinbefore named. Said Dr. Emerson held said Harriet in slavery at said Fort Snelling unit the year 1838.

In the year 1836, the plaintiff and said Harriet at said Fort Snelling, with the consent of said Dr. Emerson, who then claimed to be their master and owner, intermarried, and took each other for husband and wife. Eliza and Lizzie, named in the third count of the plaintiff's declaration, are the fruit of that marriage. Eliza is about fourteen years old, and was born on board the steamboat Gipsey, north of the north line of the State of Missouri, and upon the river Mississippi. Lizzie is about seven years old, and was born in the State of Missouri, at the military post called Jefferson Barracks.

In they year 1838, said Dr. Emerson removed the plaintiff and said Harriet and their said daughter Eliza, from said Fort Snelling to the State of Missouri, where they have ever since resided.

Before the commencement of this suit, said Dr. Emerson sold and conveyed the plaintiff, said Harriet, Eliza, and Lizzie, to the defendant, as slaves, and the defendant has ever since claimed to hold them and each of them as slaves.

At the times mentioned in the plaintiff's declaration, the defendant, claiming to be owner as aforesaid, laid his hands upon said plaintiff, Harriet, Eliza, and Lizzie, and imprisoned them, doing in this respect, however, no more than what he might lawfully do if they were of right his slaves at such times.

. . .

TANEY, CHIEF JUSTICE,

we proceed to examine the case as presented by the pleadings.

The words "people of the United States" and "citizens" are synonymous terms, and mean the same thing. They both describe the political body who, according to our republican institutions, form the sovereignty, and who hold the power and conduct the Government through their representatives. They are what we familiarly call the "sovereign people," and every citizen is one of this people, and a constituent member of this sovereignty. The question before us is, whether the class of persons described in the plea in abatement compose a portion of this people, and are constituent members of this sovereignty? We think they are not, and that they are not included, and were not intended to be included, under the word "citizens" in the Constitution, and can therefore claim none of the rights and privileges which that instrument provides for and secures to citizens of the United States. On the contrary, they were at that time considered as a subordinate and inferior class of beings, who had been subjugated by the dominant race, and, whether emancipated or not, yet remained subject to their authority, and had no rights or privileges but such as those who held the power and the Government might choose to grant them.

It is not the province of the court to decide upon the justice or injustice, the policy or impolicy, of these laws. The decision of that question belonged to the political or law-making power; to those who formed the sovereignty and framed the Constitution. The duty of the court is, to interpret the instrument they have framed, with the best lights we can obtain on the subject, and to administer it as we find it, according to its true intent and meaning when it was adopted.

In discussing this question, we must not confound the rights of citizenship which a State may confer within its own limits, and the rights of citizenship as a member of the Union. It does not by any means follow, because he has all the rights and privileges of a citizen of a State, that he must be a citizen of the United States. He may have all of the rights and privileges of the citizen of a State, and yet not be entitled to the rights and privileges of a citizen in any other State. For, previous to the adoption of the constitution of the United States, every State had the undoubted right to confer on whomsoever it pleased, the character of citizen, and to endow him with all its rights. But this character of course was confined to the boundaries of the State, and gave him no rights or privileges in other States beyond those secured to him by the laws of nations and the comity of States. Nor have the several States surrendered the power of conferring these rights and privileges by adopting the Constitution of the United States. Each State may still confer them upon an alien, or any one it thinks proper, or upon any class or description of persons; yet he would not be a citizen in the sense in which that word is used in the Constitution of the United States, nor entitled to sue as such in one of its courts, nor to the privileges and immunities of a citizen in the other States. The rights which he would acquire would be restricted to the State which gave them. . . .

The question then arises, whether the provisions of the Constitution, in relation to the personal rights and privileges to which the citizen of a State should be entitled, embraced the Negro African race, at that time in this country, or who might afterwards be imported, who had then or should afterwards be made free in any State; and to put it in the power of a single State to make him a citizen of the United States, and endow him with the full rights of citizenship in every other State without their consent? . . .

It is true, every person, and every class and description of persons, who were at the time of the adoption of the Constitution recognized as citizens in the several States, became also citizens of this new political body; but none other; it was formed by them, and for them and their posterity, but for no one else. And the personal rights and privileges guaranteed to citizens of this new sovereignty were intended to embrace those only who were then members of the several State communities, or who should afterwards by birthright or otherwise become members, according to the provisions of the Constitution and the principles on which it was founded. It was the union of those who were at that time members of distinct and separate political communities into one political family, whose power, for certain specified purposes, was to extend over the whole territory of the United States. And it gave to each citizen rights and privileges outside of his State which he did not before possess, and placed him in every other State upon a perfect equality with its own citizens as to rights of person and rights of property; it made him a citizen of the United States.

It becomes necessary, therefore, to determine who were citizens of the several States when the Constitution was adopted. And in order to do this, we must recur to the Governments and institutions of the thirteen colonies, when they separated from Great Britain and formed new sovereignties, and took their places in the family of independent nations. We must inquire who, at that time, were recognized as the people or citizens of a State, whose rights and liberties had been outraged by the English Government; and who declared their independence, and assumed the powers of Government to defend their rights by force of arms.

In the opinion of the court, the legislation and histories of the times, and the language used in the Declaration of Independence, show, that neither the class of persons who had been imported as slaves, nor their descendants, whether they had become free or not, were then acknowledged as a part of the people, nor intended to be included in the general words used in that memorable instrument.

It is difficult at this day to realize the state of public opinion in relation to that unfortunate race, which prevailed in the civilized and enlightened portions of the world at the time of the Declaration of Independence, and when the Constitution of United States was framed and adopted. But the public history of every European nation displays it in a manner too plain to be mistaken.

They had for more than a century before been regarded as beings of an inferior order, and altogether unfit to associate with the white race, either in social or political relations; and so far inferior, that they had no rights which the white man was bound to respect; and that the Negro might justly and lawfully be reduced to slavery for his benefit. He was bought and sold, and treated as an ordinary article of merchandise and traffic, whenever a profit could be made by it. This opinion was at that time fixed and universal in the civilized portion of the white race. It was regarded as an axiom in morals as well as in politics, which no one thought of disputing or supposed to be open to dispute; and men in every grade and position in society daily and habitually acted upon it in their private pursuits, as well as in matters of public concern, without doubting for a moment the correctness of this opinion.

And in no nation was this opinion more firmly fixed or more uniformly acted upon than by the English Government and English people. They not only seized them on the coast of Africa, and sold them or held them in slavery for their own use; but they took them as ordinary articles of merchandise to every country where they could make a profit on them, and were far more extensively engaged in this commerce than any other nation in the world.

The opinion thus entertained and acted upon in England was naturally impressed upon the colonies they founded on this side of the Atlantic. And, accordingly, a Negro of the African race was regarded by them as an article of property and held, and bought and sold as such, in every one of the thirteen colonies which united in the Declaration of Independence, and afterwards formed the Constitution of the United States. The slaves were more or less numerous in the different colonies, as slave labor was found more or less profitable. But no one seems to have doubted the correctness of the prevailing opinion of the time.

. . .

The language of the Declaration of Independence is equally conclusive:

It begins by declaring that, "when in the course of human events it becomes necessary for one people to dissolve the political bands which have connected them with another, and to assume among the powers of the earth the separate and equal station to which the laws of nature and nature's God entitle them, a decent respect for the opinions of mankind requires that they should declare the causes which impel them to the separation."

It then proceeds to say: "We hold these truths to be self-evident: that all men are created equal; that they are endowed by their Creator with certain unalienable rights; that among them is life, liberty, and the pursuit of happiness; that to secure these rights, Governments are instituted, deriving their just powers from the consent of the governed."

The general words above quoted would seem to embrace the whole human family, and if they were used in a similar instrument at this day would be so understood. But it is too clear for dispute, that the enslaved African race were not intended to be included, and formed no part of the people who framed and adopted this declaration; for if the language, as understood in that day, would embrace them, the conduct of the distinguished men who framed the Declaration of Independence would have been utterly and flagrantly inconsistent with the principles they asserted; and instead of the sympathy of mankind, to which they so confidently appealed, they would have deserved and received universal rebuke and reprobation.

Yet the men who framed this declaration were great men—high in literary acquirements—high in their sense of honor, and incapable of asserting principles inconsistent with those on which they were acting. They perfectly understood the meaning of the language they used, and how it would be understood by others; and they knew that it would not in any part of the civilized world be supposed to embrace the Negro race, which, by common consent, had been excluded from civilized Governments and the family of nations, and doomed to slavery. They spoke and acted according to the then established doctrines and principles, and in the ordinary language of the day, and no one misunderstood them. The unhappy black race were separated from the white by indelible marks, and laws long before established, and were never thought of or spoken of except as property, and when the claims of the owner or the profit of the trader were supposed to need protection.

This state of public opinion had undergone no change when the Constitution was adopted, as is equally evident from its provisions and language.

The brief preamble sets forth by whom it was formed, for what purposes, and for whose benefit and protection. It declares that it is formed by the *people* of the United States: that is to say, by those who were members of the different political communities in the several States; and its great object is declared to be to secure the blessings of liberty to themselves and their posterity. It speaks in general terms of the *people* of the United States, and of *citizens* of the several States, when it is providing for the exercise of the powers granted or the privileges accrued to the citizen. It does not define what description of persons are intended to be included under these terms, or who shall be regarded as a citizen and one of the people. It uses them as terms so well understood, that no further description or definition was necessary. . . . All we mean to say on this point is, that, as there is no express regulation in the Constitution defining the power which the General Government may exercise over the person or property of a citizen in a Territory thus acquired, the court must necessarily look to the provisions and principles of the Constitution, and its distribution of powers, for the rules and principles by which its decisions must be governed.

. . .

. . . [T]he rights of property are united with the rights of person, and placed on the same ground by the fifth amendment to the Constitution, which provides that no person shall be deprived of life, liberty, and property, without due process of law. And an act of Congress which deprives a citizen of the United States of his liberty or property, merely because he came himself or brought his property into a particular Territory of the United States, and who had committed no offence against the laws, could hardly be dignified with the name of due process of law.

. . .

. . . And if the Constitution recognizes the right of property of the master in a slave, and makes no distinction between that description of property and other property owned by a citizen, no tribunal, acting under the authority of the United States, whether it be legislative, executive, or judicial, has a right to draw such a distinction, or deny to it the benefit of the provisions and guarantees which have been provided for the protection of private property against the encroachments of the Government.

Now, as we have already said in an earlier part of this opinion, upon a different point, the right of property in a slave is distinctly and expressly affirmed in the Constitution. The right to traffic in it, like an ordinary article of merchandise and property, was guarantied to the citizens of the United States, in every State that might desire it, for twenty years. And the Government in express terms is pledged to protect it in all future time, if the slave escapes from his owner. This is done in plain words—too plain to be understood. And no word can be found in the Constitution which gives Congress a greater power over slave property, or which entitles property of that kind to less protection than property of any other description. The only power conferred is the power coupled with the duty of guarding and protecting the owner in his rights.

...

Instead of settling the slavery issue, the *Dred Scott* decision further fueled sectional animus. Strident as criticism was in the North, most of it was directed toward the Court's cramped reading of federal power to regulate territories. In the elections of 1858 and 1860, Republican Party candidates stressed the obligation to respect fugitive slave laws and the institution of slavery itself where it existed.[54] Critical reaction included little if any attention to liberty or equality interests, and even less to the idea of racial mixing as evidenced by Lincoln's reference to a "natural disgust in the minds of nearly all white people to the idea of an indiscriminate amalgamation of the white and black races."[55]

---

[54] *Id.* at 31–32.

[55] Don E. Fehrenbacher, The Dred Scott Case 436 (1978).

DEL: The *Dred Scott* decision has been described as "the most frequently overturned decision history."[56] The need to stamp it out more than once suggests that its spiritual vitality survived its formal eradication. Systematic exclusion, segregation and discrimination on the basis of race during and long after Reconstruction attest to that aftermath. The virtual disappearance of the *Dred Scott* decision from modern constitutional law textbooks and casebooks intimates that it is essentially a historical relic or, in the words of some observers, a "derelict[] of constitutional law."[57] Such a conclusion distorts history and reality. The ideology of *Dred Scott*, if not its result, is as relevant in the modern era as it was prior to the Civil War. A century later, in declaring official segregation in education unconstitutional, the Supreme Court was challenging essentially the same values that inspired *Dred Scott*. Its progeny include not only the Court's endorsement of formal segregation until the middle of this century but the massive delay, resistance and evasion that characterized response to Court-ordered desegregation. Over the course of two centuries, in which the republic has accommodated slavery as the cost of forming a union, countenanced comprehensive systems of state-sanctioned racism for a century following slavery's abolition, allowed virtual evisceration of the desegregation mandate and rejected attention to race as a means of reckoning with racism, the *Dred Scott* decision seems more normative than exceptional. Given the historical context, a stronger case exists for the proposition that the Court's decision in *Brown v. Board of Education* is the real constitutional "derelict."

DER: *Dred Scott* asked the enduring question of American constitutional history: Will the law guarantee Americans of African descent the full rights and privileges of citizenship?

---

[56] Derrick Bell, Race, Racism and American Law 21 (1973).

[57] Edwin Meese III, *The Law of the Constitution*, 61 Tul. L. Rev. 979, 989 (1987)(quoting Philip Kurland, Politics, the Constitution and the Warren Court 186 (1970).

That question is as relevant to the political life of the country today as it was in 1857. American law, culture, and ideology persist in finding new ways to explain the anomaly of slavery, followed by continued second-class citizenship, existing in a republic founded on a revolutionary commitment to liberty and equality. The ideology underlying *Dred Scott*—that Blacks and whites constitute two radically distinct and unequal races—was sanctioned by law even after the *Brown* decision. The Court did not invalidate antimiscegenation laws, designed to maintain a rule of racial purity, until its decision in *Loving v. Virginia* less than thirty years ago.[58]

If the Constitution requires a positive response to that fundamental question, then how is equality of citizenship to be accomplished? *Dred Scott* denied equal rights to Blacks, but had the advantage of a straight-forward treatment of race. Subsequent Court decisions have avoided forthrightly confronting white supremacy and imposed instead a "color-blind" standard. The Court's color-blind approach pretends that racial equality can be achieved by treating all individuals in a neutral fashion without regard to race. Colorblindness overlooks systemic racial discrimination resulting from entrenched institutional barriers to equality, thereby helping to perpetuate the racial status quo in America.

PAH: Notwithstanding the language of the fourteenth amendment, no response to the inequality fostered by *Dred Scott*—not the separate-but-equal-is-inherently-unequal analysis of *Brown* nor the colorblindness approach which the Court built upon it in the late twentieth century—has secured equal citizenship for African Americans. As Kenneth Karst has argued, constitutional decisions promoting equal citizenship should protect the choice of a group member to turn inward for nourishment and support and the choice to use group identity to participate fully in the institutions of the wider society.[59] For African Americans, the citizenship explicitly deprived in *Dred Scott*, has never been extended except at the price of sacrificing their connection to a group identity. The color-blind approach of the Court purports to protect African Americans from the stigma and stereotypes that made the Court's reasoning in *Dred Scott* assailable. What it actually does, however, is to legitimatize unconscious race discrimination and reinforce the notion that any inequality that persists is the fault of Blacks who individually do not measure up and of the group which cannot "get beyond" race.[60]

---

[58] 388 U.S. 1 (1967).

[59] Karst, supra, 64 N.C.L. Rev. at 361.

[60] Robert Seidman, Brown and Miranda, 80 Calif. L. Rev. 673, 717 (1992) (rationale of Brown made the demand for equality satisfied by whites making facilities legally nonseparate without effectively changing power arrangements); see also Barbara Flagg, "Was Blind but Now I see": White Race Consciousness and the Requirement of Discriminatory Intent, 91 Mich. L. Rev. 953, 987–88 (1993) (presumption of race neutrality ignores possibility that government decision-making criteria reflect white-specific characteristics, attitudes, or experiences, affording substantial advantages to whites while reassuring them that the unfortunate history of race discrimination is largely behind us).

Even if the base for criticism of the *Dred Scott* decision was relatively narrow at the time, it was profound enough to present a significant challenge to the Court's authority. When a state court freed two persons convicted in a federal court for aiding runaway slaves, Taney in *Ableman v. Booth* stressed the imperatives of respect for its decisions if a national union was to be preserved.[61] The 1860 presidential election in significant part became a referendum upon the *Dred Scott* decision, with southern

---

[61] Ableman v. Booth, 62 U.S. 506 (1859).

Democrats maintaining that the slavery issue had been resolved, northern Democrats asserting that the scope of congressional power over the territories was not fully resolved but could be in a subsequent decision and Republicans challenging the ruling's legitimacy.[62] The political fortunes of 1860 negated the *Dred Scott* decision for practical purposes, as President Lincoln and Congress ignored it. In 1862, Congress repealed the Fugitive Slave Act, prohibited slavery in the District of Columbia and enacted confiscation laws intended to remove slaves from their masters. President Lincoln in 1863 issued the Emancipation Proclamation which, although largely symbolic, indicated that the federal interest had evolved toward an abolitionist position.

3. Reconstruction: Toward a More Perfect Union

As the Civil War drew toward its conclusion, attention began to turn toward reconstruction of the union. Early thinking included the possibility of proceeding without constitutional amendment. Although the Emancipation Proclamation had been predicated upon the president's war power, that basis was inadequate for purposes of supporting a general and enduring proscription against slavery. Awareness of the dubious premises of emancipation generated interest in and eventual conviction to amend the Constitution in terms that irrefutably condemned slavery.

The Thirteenth Amendment not only prohibited slavery but empowered Congress to enforce its terms "by appropriate legislation."[63] What it accounted for beyond slavery, if anything, was a subject of debate. Lincoln's view, that the amendment incorporated the guarantees recited in the Declaration of Independence, failed to carry the day.[64] The notion that civil rights flowed incidentally from the Thirteenth Amendment, or could be secured by legislation enacted by Congress thereunder, was tested almost immediately by post-ratification experience in the South. The rise of Black Codes reintroduced slavery in function after it had been defeated in form. The impact of constitutional change was diminished profoundly, therefore, by laws that

> forbade blacks from pursuing certain occupations of professions, . . . forbade owning firearms or weapons; controlled the movement of blacks by systems of passes; required proof of residence; prohibited the congregation of groups of blacks; restricted blacks from residing in certain areas; . . . specified an etiquette of deference to whites . . . forbade racial intermarriage and provided the death penalty for blacks raping white women, while omitting special provisions for whites raping black women . . . [and] excluded blacks from jury duty, public office, and voting.[65]

Despite a newly established federal interest in freedom, the Black Codes thus represented an effort to reinvent pre-war master-servant relationships to the extent possible within the new constitutional order. Differences that had split the union and engendered armed conflict thus rebounded back to the political process.

As the Joint Committee on Reconstruction commenced its work in 1865, it did so with the recognition that civil rights and equality would not be actualized without further legal initiative. Not only the Black Codes, but southern harassment of unionists and interference with the remedial efforts of the Freedmen's Bureau, disclosed significant undermining of the new federal interest. President Johnson's position, that the Thirteenth Amendment achieved no more than the abolition of slavery, identified a need for further legal reform if civil rights and equality were to be accounted for mean-

---

[62] Donald E. Lively, The Constitution and Race 32.

[63] U.S. Const. amend. XIII.

[64] Harold Hyman, A More Perfect Union 278 (1973).

[65] Harold Hyman and William Wiecek, Equal Justice under the Law 319 (1982).

ingfully at the national level.[66] Such a reckoning was to occur within the context of prevailing racial realities. Notwithstanding the constitutional commitment to prohibit slavery, attention to the liberty and equality interests of persons of African descent was filtered through dominant notions of white supremacy. Insofar as civil rights could not be catalogued in a consensual fashion, moreover, accounting for them was affected significantly by differences over their nature and scope and racial attitudes.

Notwithstanding the arguments of some that civil rights must be defined as broadly as the Bill of Rights and Declaration of Independence, a more certain common denominator was the proposition that civil rights included those privileges and immunities incidental to the status of a free person. Essential for meaningful participation in civil society were those rights and liberties that facilitated material self-development and the assurance of equal standing before the law. Responding to the immediate aftermath of the war, therefore, the Reconstruction Congress enacted the Civil Rights Act of 1866 which provided that

> there shall be no discrimination in civil rights or immunities . . . on account of race . . . but the inhabitants of every race . . . shall have the same rights to make and enforce contracts, to sue, be parties, and give evidence, to inherit, purchase, lease, sell, hold and convey real and personal property, and to full and equal benefit of all laws and proceedings for the security of persons and property, and shall be subject to like punishment.[67]

Conspicuously missing from the Civil Rights Act of 1866 was the right to vote, an omission which many of its supporters explained as intentional.[68] To have included the right to vote would have imposed a profound change not only upon the political structure of the South but much of the North where many states denied the franchise to persons of African descent. The limited objectives of the 1866 act were amplified by the House Chair of the Joint Committee on Reconstruction, who observed that the legislation did not mean "that in all things, civil, social, political, all citizens, without distinction of race or color, shall be equal. . . . By no means can [civil rights and immunities] be so construed. . . . Nor do they mean that all citizens shall sit on juries, or that their children shall attend the same schools."[69]

The relatively discrete focus of the Civil Rights Act of 1866 is useful for purposes of understanding the pitch of the Fourteenth Amendment as initially conceived. Concern that the enactment might be undone, if politically unrepentant southern states returned to the union and mustered enough votes to repeal it, engendered attention to its fortification. President Johnson's rationale for his unsuccessful veto of the 1866 act, moreover, enhanced concern that the law might be susceptible to constitutional challenge.[70] To secure the federal interest in civil rights beyond the normal political processes, therefore, the Fourteenth Amendment was framed and ratified.

Both the breadth and content of the Fourteenth Amendment have been the subject of enduring debate. Although some of its architects and supporters urged an expansive reading of the amendment so as to incorporate rights and equality interests set forth in the Bill of Rights and Declaration of Independence, others merely understood it as a constitutionalization of the Civil Rights Act of 1866. A common denominator was that "(v)irtually every speaker in the debates on the Fourteenth Amendment—Republi-

---

[66] *Id.* at 389.
[67] Cong. Globe, 39th Cong., 1st Sess. 474 (1866).
[68] DONALD E. LIVELY, THE CONSTITUTION AND RACE 47 (1992).
[69] Cong. Globe at 1117 (Rep. Wilson).
[70] KENNETH KARST, BELONGING TO AMERICA 51 (1989).

cans and Democrats alike—said or agreed that [it] was designed to embody or incorporate the Civil Rights Act."[71] Debate also has persisted on whether the privileges and immunities clause, due process clause and equal protection clause have significant independent meaning. One perspective is that the privileges and immunities clause housed the rights secured by the Civil Rights Act of 1866, the due process clause guaranteed access to judicial process and the equal protection clause prohibited discrimination against the newly minted federal rights.[72] Competing against that view is the notion that the framers made no real effort to distinguish the function of the three clauses and "the section in its entirety was taken to guarantee equality in the enjoyment of the rights of citizenship."[73] Eventual resolution of those divergent understandings was to be a function of judicial review.

Before the Supreme Court ventured into the new constitutional territory, however, one more reconstruction plank was added to the nation's charter. What was politically impossible when the Fourteenth Amendment was being framed and ratified became politically expedient if not imperative shortly thereafter. Given compounding evidence of southern intransigence, and signs of impatience with the slow and costly process of reconstruction, extension of the right to vote to persons of African descent became an attractive option. The Fifteenth Amendment elicited support not only from those whose view of the Fourteenth Amendment was more expansive than political circumstance allowed at the time but also for those who wished to accelerate the reconstruction process. The common premise was that the right to vote would be the best security for federal civil rights, because fear of electoral retribution would deter potential abuse by officials.[74] Further achievements of reconstruction included federal laws prohibiting public or private interference with the right to vote,[75] deprivation of civil rights under the color of state law and denial of equal protection by private action[76] and proscribing discrimination in certain public venues.[77] Notwithstanding its formal achievements, Reconstruction's significance diminished by lax enforcement, eventual repeal of much voting rights legislation and judicial interpretations that gutted the Civil Rights Act of 1875.[78]

a. Reconstruction and the Court

The political changes wrought by Reconstruction soon commanded the Supreme Court's attention. Previewing several decades of review, that largely deferred to state interests in maintaining racial separation and invested in the ideology of white supremacy, the Court in *Blylew v. United States* considered whether a federal court could hear a criminal case "affecting persons" who could not enforce their rights secured by the Civil Rights Act of 1866. Despite the 1866 act's provision for such an action, and the state's refusal to prosecute because of a law prohibiting persons of one race from testifying against a defendant of another race, the Court determined that the federal court had no jurisdiction. Among other things, it found that because the victims were deceased they no longer were "persons affected."

---

[71] HOWARD J. GRAHAM, EVERYMAN'S CONSTITUTION 291 n.73 (1968).

[72] RAOUL BERGER, GOVERNMENT BY JUDICIARY 18 (1977).

[73] KENNETH KARST at 18.

[74] DONALD E. LIVELY, THE CONSTITUTION AND RACE 54 (1992).

[75] Enforcement Act of 1870, 16 Stat. 170 (1870).

[76] Ku Klux Klan Act, 17 Stat. 13 (1871), subsequently codified as 42 U.S.C. §§ 1983, 1985(3).

[77] Civil Rights Act of 1875, 18 Stat. 335 (1875).

[78] *Id.* at 55.

Blylew v. United States
80 U.S. 581 (1872)

By the Revised Statutes of Kentucky, published A.D. 1860, it is enacted:

"That a slave, Negro, or Indian, shall be a competent witness in the case of the commonwealth for or against a slave, Negro or Indian, or in a civil case to which only Negroes or Indians are parties, *but in no other case.*"

. . .

In this state of things, Congress on the 9th April, 1866, passed an act entitled "An act to protect all persons in the United States in their civil rights, and furnish the means of their vindication." The first section of that act declared all persons born in the United States, and not subject to any foreign power, excluding Indians not taxed, to be citizens of the United States, and it enacted that:

"Such citizens of every race and color, shall have the same right in every State and Territory in the United States to make and enforce contracts, to sue, be parties and *give evidence*, to inherit, purchase, lease, sell, hold, and convey real and personal property, and to *full and equal benefit of all laws and proceedings for the security of person and property as is enjoyed by white citizens*, and shall be subject to like punishment, pains, and penalties, and to none other any law, statute, ordinance, regulation, or custom to the contrary notwithstanding."

. . .

In this state of things, two persons, Blylew and Kennard, were indicted October 7th, 1868, in the Circuit Court for the District of Kentucky, for the murder, on the 29th of August preceding, within that district, of a colored woman named Lucy Armstrong. The indictment contained three counts, all of them charging the murder in the usual form of indictments for that offence, and with sufficient certainty. But, in order to show jurisdiction in the Circuit Court of the United States, an averment was made in the first count that the said Lucy Armstrong was a citizen of the United States having been born therein, and not subject to any foreign power; that she was of the African race, and was above the age of seventy-five years; that Blylew and Kennard (the persons indicted) were white persons, each of them at the time of the alleged killing and murder above the age of eighteen years; that the said killing and murder, done and committed, as averred, were seen and witnessed by one Richard Foster, and one Laura Foster, citizens of the United States, having been born therein and not subject to any foreign power, both of the African race; and that the said Lucy Armstrong, Richard Foster, and Laura Foster were then and there denied the right to testify

against the said Blylew and Kennard or either of them, concerning the said killing and murder, in the courts and judicial tribunals of the State of Kentucky, solely on the account of their race and color. . . .

The murder for which the defendants were convicted, and as they now sought to show illegally, had been one of peculiar atrocity. A number of witnesses testified that on a summer evening of 1868 (August 29th), towards eleven o'clock, at the cabin of a colored man named Jack Foster, there were found the dead bodies of the said Jack, of Sallie Foster, his wife, and of Lucy Armstrong, for the murder of whom Blylew and Kennard stood convicted; this person a blind woman, over ninety years old, and the mother of Mrs. Foster; all persons of color; their bodies yet warm. Lucy Armstrong was wounded in the head; her head cut open as with a broad-axe. Jack Foster and Sallie, his wife, were cut in several places, almost to pieces. Richard Foster, a son of Jack, who was in this seventeenth year, was found about two hundred yards from the house of his father, at the house of a Mr. Nichols, whither he had crawled from the house of his father, mortally wounded by an instrument corresponding to one used in the killing of Lucy Armstrong, Jack and Sallie Foster. He died two days afterwards from the effects of his wounds aforesaid, having made a dying declaration tending to fix the crime on Blylew and Kennard. Two young children, girls, one aged ten years and the other thirteen (this last, the Laura Foster above mentioned), asleep in a trundle-bed, escaped, and the latter was a witness on the trial.

Evidence was produced on the part of the United States, that a short time previous to the murder, Kennard was heard to declare, in presence of Blylew, "that he (Kennard) thought there would soon be another war about the niggers; that when it did come he intended to go to killing niggers, and he was not sure that he would not begin his work of killing them before the war should actually commence."

We are thus brought to the question whether a criminal prosecution for a public offence is a cause "affecting," within the meaning of the act of Congress, persons who may be called to testify therein. Obviously the only parties to such a cause are the government and the persons indicted. They alone can be reached by any judgment that may be announced. . . .

It will be observed that this statute prohibits the testimony of colored persons either for or against a white person in any civil or criminal cause to which he may be a party. If, therefore, they are persons affected by the cause, whenever they might be witnesses were they competent to testify, it follows that in any suit between white citizens, jurisdiction might be taken by the Federal courts whenever it was alleged that a citizen of the African race was or might be an important witness. And such an allegation might always be made. So in all criminal prosecutions against white persons a similar allegation would call into existence the like jurisdiction. We cannot think that such was the purpose of Congress in the statute of April 9th 1866. It would seem rather to have been to afford protection to persons of the colored race by giving to the Federal courts jurisdiction of cases, the decision of which might injuriously affect them either in their personal, relative, or property rights, whenever, they are denied by the State courts any of the rights mentioned and assured to them in the first section of the act.

. . .

In view of these considerations we are of opinion that the case now before us is not within the provisions of the act of April 9th, 1866, and that the Circuit Court had not jurisdiction of the crime of murder committed in the district of Kentucky, merely because two persons who witnessed the murder were citizens of the African race, and for that reason incompetent by the law of Kentucky to testify in the courts of that State. They are not persons affected by the cause.

We need hardly add the jurisdiction of the Circuit Court is not sustained by the fact averred in the indictment that Lucy Armstrong, the person murdered, was a citizen of the African race, and for that reason denied the right to testify in the Kentucky courts. In no sense can she be said to be affected by the cause. Manifestly the act refers to persons in existence. She was the victim of the frightful outrage which give rise to the cause, but she is beyond being affected by the cause itself. . . .

MR. JUSTICE BRADLEY, with whom concurred MR. JUSTICE SWAYNE, dissenting. . . .

. . . The cause is one affecting the person murdered, as well as the whole class of persons to which she belonged. . . .

To deprive a whole class of the community of this right, to refuse their evidenced and their sworn complaints, is to brand them with a badge of slavery; is to expose them to wanton insults and fiendish assaults; is to leave their lives, their families, and their property unprotected by law. It gives unrestricted license and impunity to vindictive outlaws and felons to rush upon these helpless people and kill and slay them at will, as was done in these case. To say that actions or prosecutions intended for the redress of such outrages are not "causes affecting persons" who are the victims of them, is to take, it seems to me, a view of the law too narrow, too technical, and too forgetful of the liberal objects it had in view. If, in such a raid as I have supposed, a colored person is merely wounded or maimed, but is still capable of making complaint, and on appearing to do so, has the doors of justice shut in his face on the ground that he is a colored person, and cannot testify against a white citizen, it seems to me almost a stultification of the law to say that the case is not within its scope. Let us read it once more: "The District Courts shall, concurrently with the Circuit Courts, have cognizance of all causes, civil and *criminal*, affecting persons who are denied or cannot enforce in the courts or judicial tribunals of the State or locality where they may be, any of the rights secured to them by the first section of this act.:

In the case above supposed is within the act (as it assuredly must be), does it cease to be so when the violence offered is so great as to deprive the victim of life? Such a construction would be a premium on murder. If mere violence offered to a colored person (who, by the law of Kentucky, was denied the privilege of complaint), gives the United States court jurisdiction, when such violence is short of being fatal, that jurisdiction cannot cease when death is the result. The reason for its existence is stronger than before. If it would have been a cause affecting him when living, it will be a cause affecting him though dead. The object of prosecution and punishment is to *prevent* crime, as well as to vindicate public justice. The fear of it, the anticipation of it, stands between the assassin and his victim like a vindictive shade. It arrests his arm, and loosens the dagger from his grasp. Should not the colored man have the aegis of this protection to guard his life, as well as to guard his limbs, or his property? Should he not enjoy it in equal degree with the white citizen? In a large and just sense, can a prosection for his murder affect him any less than a prosection for an assault upon him? He is interested in both alike. *They are his protection against violence and wrong.* At all events it cannot be denied that the entire class of persons under disability is affected by prosecutions for wrongs done to one of their number, in which they are not permitted to testify in the State courts. . . .

A year after the *Blylew* decision, the Court in the *Slaughter-House Cases* discussed the core purpose of the Fourteenth Amendment and its equal protection guarantee.

Slaughter-House Cases
83 U.S. 36 (1873)

. . .

"Nor shall any State deny to any person within its jurisdiction the equal protection of the laws."

In the light of history of these amendments, and the pervading purpose of them, which we have already discussed, it is not difficult to give a meaning to this clause. The existence of laws in the States where the newly emancipated Negroes resided, which discriminated with gross injustice and hardship against them as a class, was the evil to be remedied by this clause, and by it such laws are forbidden.

If, however, the States did not conform their laws to its requirements, then by the fifth section of the article of amendment Congress was authorized to enforce it by suitable legislation. We doubt very much whether any action of a State not directed by way of discrimination against the Negroes as a class, or on account of their race, will ever be held to come within the purview of this provision. It is so clearly a provision for that race and that emergency, that a strong case would be necessary for its application to any other. But as it is a State that is to be dealt with, and not alone the validity of its laws, we may safely leave that matter until Congress shall have exercised its power, or some case of State oppression, by denial of equal justice in its courts, shall have claimed a decision at our hands. We find no such case in the one before us, and do not deem it necessary to go over the argument again, as it may have relation to this particular clause of the amendment.

The Court's initial examination of the Fourteenth Amendment in a racially significant context concerned the scope of congressional power to enforce it. Reviewing federal law protecting civil rights against private interference, in the wake of a political dispute in Louisiana that resulted in the massacre of numerous black persons,[79] the Court determined that such concerns were within the province of the states.[80] In reviewing the substantive guarantees of the Fourteenth Amendment itself for the first time, however, the Court characterized the provision's central concern with establishing a "right to exemption" from laws that reflected racial animus, implied inferiority in civil society or reduced to the status "of a subject race."[81] In *Strauder v. West Virginia*, the Court thus struck down a state law excluding blacks from juries.

---

[79] The Colfax Massacre, which occurred the day before the Court's decision in the *Slaughter-House Cases*, is recounted in CHARLES FAIRMAN, VII HISTORY OF THE SUPREME COURT OF THE UNITED STATES, RECONSTRUCTION AND REUNION, pt. 2, at 261-62 (1987).

[80] United States v. Cruikshank, 92 U.S. 542, 555 (1876). The *Cruikshank* decision was cited to seven years later when the Court determined that a federal prosecution of state law enforcement officials, charged with conspiring to deny equal protection of the laws in connection with beating a black prisoner to death, encroached upon a traditional state interest. United States v. Harris, 106 U.S. 629, 639 (1883).

[81] Strauder v. West Virginia, 100 U.S. 303, 308 (1879).

Strauder v. West Virginia
100 U.S. 303 (1879)

. . .

MR. JUSTICE STRONG delivered the opinion of the Court.

. . .

In this court, several errors have been assigned, and the controlling questions underlying them all are, first, whether, by the Constitution and laws of the United States, every citizen of the United States has a right to a trial of an indictment against him by a jury selected and impanelled without discrimination against his race or color, because of race or color; and, second, if he is such a right, and is denied its enjoyment by the State in which he is indicted, may he cause the case to be removed into the Circuit Court of the United States?

The questions are important, for they demand a construction of the recent amendments of the Constitution. If the defendant has a right to have a jury selected for the trial of his case without discrimination against all persons of his race or color, because of their race or color, the right, if not created, is protected by those amendments and the legislation of Congress under them. The Fourteenth Amendment ordains that "all persons born or naturalized in the United States and subject to the jurisdiction thereof are citizens of the United States and of the State wherein they reside. No State shall make or enforce any laws which shall abridge the privileges or immunities of citizens of the United States, nor shall any State deprive any person of life, liberty, or property, without due process of law, nor deny to any person within its jurisdiction the equal protection of the laws."

This is one of a series of constitutional provisions having a common purpose; namely, securing to a race recently emancipated, a race that through many generations had been held in slavery, all the civil rights that the superior race enjoy. The true spirit and meaning of the amendments, as we said in the *Slaughter-House Cases*, cannot be understood without keeping in view the history of the times when they were adopted, and the general objects they plainly sought to accomplish. At the time when they were incorporated into the Constitution, it required little knowledge of human nature to anticipate that those who had long been regarded as an inferior and subject race would, when suddenly raised to the rank of citizenship, be looked upon with jealousy and positive dislike, and that State laws might be enacted or enforced to perpetuate the distinctions that had before existed. Discriminations against them had been habitual. It was well known that in some States laws making such discriminations then existed, and others might well be expected. The colored race, as a race, was abject and ignorant, and in that condition was unfitted to command the respect of those who had superior intelligence. Their training had left them mere children, and as such they needed the protection which a wise government extends to those who are unable to protect themselves. They especially needed protection against unfriendly action in the States where

they were resident. It was in view of these considerations the Fourteenth Amendment was framed and adopted. It was designed to assure to the colored race the enjoyment of all the civil rights that under the law are enjoyed by white persons, and to give to that race the protection of the general government, in that enjoyment, whenever it should be denied by the States. It not only gave citizenship and the privileges of citizenship to persons of color, but it denied to any State the power to withhold from them the equal protection of the laws, and authorized Congress to enforce its provisions by appropriate legislation. . . .

If this is the spirit and meaning of the amendment, whether it means more or not, is to be construed liberally, to carry out the purposes of its framers. It ordains that no State shall make or enforce any laws which shall abridge the privileges or immunities of citizens of the United States (evidently referring to the newly made citizens, who, being citizens of the United States, are declared to be also citizens of the United States, are declared to be also citizens of the State in which they reside). It ordains that no State shall deprive any person of life, liberty, or property, without due process of law, or deny to any person within its jurisdiction the equal protection of the laws. What is this but declaring that the law in the States shall be the same for the black as for the white; that all persons, whether colored or white, shall stand equal before the laws of the States, and, in regard to the colored race, for whose protection the amendment was primarily designed, that no discrimination shall be made against them by law because of their color? The words of the amendment, it is true, are prohibitory, but they contain a necessary implication of a positive immunity, or right, most valuable to the colored race,—the right to exemption from unfriendly legislation against them distinctively as colored,—exemption from legal discriminations, implying inferiority in civil society, lessening the security of their enjoyment of the rights which others enjoy, and discriminations which are steps towards reducing them to the condition of a subject race.

. . .

. . . [T]he state of West Virginia, discriminating in the selection of jurors, as it does, against Negroes because of their color, amounts to a denial of the equal protection of the laws to a colored man when he is put upon trial for an alleged offence against the State. . . .

Contemporaneous with the *Strauder* decision, the Court in *Ex parte Virginia*, determined that exclusion of blacks from juries pursuant to a judge's order also violated the Fourteenth Amendment. The Court stressed that "(w)hoever, by virtue of public position under a State government deprives another of property, life, or liberty without due process of law, or denies or takes away the equal protection of the laws, violates the constitutional inhibition."[82] Insofar as neither state law nor official action overtly discriminated on the basis of race, however, the Court refused to find a constitutional violation. Notwithstanding evidence that no black person ever had served on a jury in a county where two African-American defendants were convicted by all white juries, the Court in *Virginia v. Rives* distinguished between security from official discrimination and "a right to have the jury composed in part of colored men."[83]

The spirit of *Strauder*, reflected by the Court's sense that the Fourteenth Amendment spoke to the condition of a group "unable to protect [itself] ... [and] especially need[ing] protection against unfriendly action in the States where they were resident,"[84] proved to be short-lived. In reviewing the constitutionality of the Civil Rights Act of 1875, which prohibited discrimination in "accommodations, advantages, facilities, and privileges of inns, public conveyances on land or water, theaters and other places of public amusement," the Court's analysis evinced little if any fidelity to the command that the Fourteenth Amendment should "be construed liberally, to carry out the purposes of its framers."[85] To the contrary, the tone of its decision in the *Civil Rights Cases* was consistent with a sense of fatigue with the Thirteenth and Fourteenth Amendment's imperatives. In determining that federal legislative power to enforce the Fourteenth Amendment was coextensive with the terms of Section One, and thus limited to regulation of state action, the Court expressed concern that "Congress [otherwise would] take the place of the State Legislatures and ... supersede them ... [by] establish[ing] a code of municipal law regulative of all private rights between man and men in society."[86] The Court rejected both Thirteenth and Fourteenth Amendment arguments for a broader exercise of congressional power, stressing that the "slavery argument" was run "into the ground" if applied "to every act of discrimination."

---

[82] Ex parte Virginia, 100 U.S. 339, 347 (1879).

[83] Virginia v. Rives, 100 U.S. 313, 322-23 (1879).

[84] Strauder v. West Virginia, 100 U.S. 303, 306 (1879).

[85] *Id.* at 307.

[86] Civil Rights Cases, 109 U.S. 3, 13-14 (1883).

Civil Rights Cases
109 U.S. 3 (1883)

. . .

When a man has emerged from slavery, and by the aid of beneficent legislation has shaken off the inseparable concomitants of that state, there must be some stage in the progress of his elevation when he takes the rank of a mere citizen, and ceases to be the special favorite of the laws, and when his rights as a citizen, *or a man*, are to be protected in the ordinary modes by which other men's rights are protected. There were thousands of free colored people in this country before the abolition of slavery, enjoying all the essential rights of life, liberty and property the same as white citizens; yet no one, at that time, thought that it was any invasion of his personal status as a freeman because he was not admitted to all the privileges enjoyed by the white citizens, or because he was subjected to discriminations in the enjoyment of accommodations in inns, public conveyances and places of amusement. Mere discriminations on account of race or color were not regarded as badges of slavery. If, since that time, the enjoyment of equal rights in all these respects has become established by constitutional enactment, it is not by force of the Thirteenth Amendment (which merely abolishes slavery), but by force of the Thirteenth and Fifteenth Amendments.

. . . That there are burdens and disabilities which constitute badges of slavery and servitude, and that the power to enforce by appropriate legislation the Thirteenth Amendment may be exerted by legislation of a direct and primary character, for the eradication, not simply of the institution, but of its badges and incidents, are propositions which ought to be deemed indisputable. They lie at the foundation of the Civil Rights Act of 1866. Whether that act was authorized by the Thirteenth Amendment alone, without the support which it subsequently received from the Fourteenth Amendment, after the adoption of which it was re-enacted with some additions, my brethren do not consider it necessary to inquire. But I submit, with all respect to them, that its constitutionality is conclusively shown by their opinion. They admit, as I have said, that the Thirteenth Amendment established freedom: that there are burdens and disabilities, the necessary incidents of slavery, which constitute its substance and visible form; that Congress, by the act of 1866, passed in view of the Thirteenth Amendment, before the Fourteenth was adopted, undertook to remove certain burdens and disabilities, the necessary incidents of slavery, and to secure to all citizens of every race and color, and without regard to previous servitude, those fundamental rights which are the essence of civil freedom, namely, the same right to make and enforce contracts, to sue, be parties, give evidence, and to inherit, purchase, lease, sell, and convey property as is enjoyed by white citizens; that under the Thirteenth Amendment, Congress has to do with slavery and its incidents; and that legislation, so far as necessary or proper to eradicate all forms and incidents of slavery and involuntary servitude, may be direct and primary, operating upon the acts of individuals, whether sanctioned by State legislation or not. . . .

As perceived by Justice Harlan, who dissented from the Court's decision, the majority's understanding transformed the Thirteenth and Fourteenth Amendments into guarantees of an illusory nature.

But what was secured to colored citizens of the United States—as between them and their respective States—by the national grant to them of State citizenship? With what rights, privileges, or immunities did this grant invest them? There is one, if there be no other—exemption from race discrimination in respect of any civil right belonging to citizens of the white race in the same State. That, surely, is their constitutional privilege when within the jurisdiction of other States. And such must be their constitutional right, in their own State, unless the recent amendments be splendid baubles, thrown out to delude those who deserved fair and generous treatment at the hands of the nation. Citizenship in this country necessarily imports at least equality of civil rights among citizens of every race in the same State. It is fundamental in American citizenship that, in respect of such rights, there shall be no discrimination by the State, or its officers, or by individuals or corporations exercising public functions or authority, against any citizen because of his race or previous conditions of servitude. . . .

Harlan warned that "there cannot be, in this republic, any class of human beings in practical subjugation to another class, with power in the latter to dole out to the former just such privileges as they may choose to grant."[87] Case law for several decades after the *Civil Rights Cases* accommodated official oppression, exclusion and discrimination on the basis of race, however, and actualized Harlan's concern that the Reconstruction Amendments were merely "splendid baubles, thrown out to delude those who deserved fair and generous treatment at the hands of the Nation."[88]

4.   Separate but Equal

From the late nineteenth century through the mid-twentieth century, official segregation was the dominant legal aspect of the nation's racial landscape. Like slavery, segregation insinuated itself throughout the entire republic even though its formal operation was primarily a regional phenomenon. The federal government which accommodated southern custom by allowing military officers to bring their slaves into free states and territories prior to the Civil War, for instance, was similarly inspired to segregate the armed forces until 1948. Official segregation itself was borrowed from the North which, although prohibiting slavery, comprehensively managed opportunity, status and rights on the basis of race. Before and after the Fourteenth Amendment's ratification, segregation in public education was upheld by state courts in northern states.

---

[87] *Id.* at 62 (Harlan, J., dissenting).
[88] *Id.* at 48 (Harlan, J., dissenting).

Roberts v. City of Boston,
59 Mass. 198 (1850)

SHAW, C. J.

. . .

By the agreed statement of facts, it appears, that the defendants support a class of schools called primary schools, to the number of about one hundred and sixty, designed for the instruction of children of both sexes, who are between the ages of four and sevens years. Two of these schools are appropriated by the primary school committee, having charge of that class of schools, to the exclusive instruction of colored children, and the residue to the exclusive instruction of white children.

The plaintiff, by her father, took proper measures to obtain admission into one of these schools appropriated to white children, but pursuant to the regulations of the committee, and in conformity therewith, she was not admitted. Either of the schools appropriated to colored children was open to her; the nearest of which was about a fifth of a mile or seventy rods distant from her father's house than the nearest primary school. It further appears, by the facts agreed, that the committee having charge of that class of schools had, a short time previously to the plaintiffs application, adopted a resolution, upon a report of a committee, that in the opinion of that board, a continuance of the separate schools for colored children, and the regular attendance of all such children upon the schools, is not only legal and just, but is best adapted to promote the instruction of that class of the population.

. . .

. . . The plaintiff had access to a school, set apart for colored children, as well conducted in all respects, and as fitted, in point of capacity and qualification of the instructors, to advance the education of children under seven years old, as the other primary schools; the objection is, that the schools thus open to the plaintiff are exclusively appropriated to colored children, and are at a greater distance from her home. Under these circumstances, has the plaintiff been unlawfully excluded from public school instruction? Upon the best consideration we have been able to give the subject, the court are all of opinion that she has not.

. . .

It will be considered, that this is a question of power, or of the legal authority of the committee intrusted by the city with this department of public instruction; because, if they are the legal authority, the expediency of exercising it in any particular way is exclusively with them.

The great principle, advanced by the learned and eloquent advocate of the plaintiff, is, that by the constitution and law of Massachusetts, all persons without distinction of age or sex, birth or color, origin or condition, are equal before the law, This, as a broad general principle, such as ought to appear in a declaration of rights, is perfectly sound; it is not only expressed in terms, but pervades and animates the whole spirit of our constitution of free government. But, when this great principle comes to be applied to the actual and various conditions of persons in society, it will not warrant that assertion that men and women are legally clothed with the same civil and political powers, and that children and adults are legally to have the same functions and be subject to the same treatment, but only that the rights of all, as they are settled and regulate by law, are equally entitled to the paternal consideration and protection of the law, for their maintenance and security. What those rights are, to which individuals, in the variety or circumstances by which they are surrounded in society, are entitled, must depend on laws adapted to their respective relations and conditions.

Conceding, therefore, in the fullest manner, that colored persons, the descendants of Africans, are entitled by law, in this commonwealth, to equal rights, constitutional and political, civil and social, the question then arises, whether the regulation in question, which provides separate schools for children, is a violation of any of these rights.

. . .

. . . In towns of a large territory, over which the inhabitants are thinly settled, an arrangement or classification going far into detail, providing different schools for pupils of different ages, of each sex, and the like, would require the pupils to go such long distances from their homes to the schools, that it would be quite unreasonable. But in Boston, where more than one hundred thousand inhabitants live within a space so small, that it would be scarcely an inconvenience to require a boy of good health to traverse daily the whole extent of it, a system of distribution and classification may be adopted and carried into effect, which may be useful and beneficial in its influence on the character of the schools, and in its adaptation to the improvement and advancement of the great purpose of education, and at the same time practicable and reasonable in its operation.

In the absence of special legislation on this subject, the law has vested the power in the committee to regulate the system of distribution and classification; and when this power is reasonably exercised, without being abused or perverted by colorable pretenses, the decision of the committee must be deemed conclusive. The committee, apparently upon great deliberation, has come to the conclusion, that the good of both classes of schools will be best promoted, by maintaining the separate primary schools for colored and for white children, and we can perceive no ground to doubt, that this is the honest result of their experience and judgment.

It is urged, that this maintenance of separate schools tends to deepen and perpetuate the odious distinction of caste founded in a deep-rooted prejudice in public opinion. This prejudice if it exists, is not created by law, and probably cannot be changed by law. Whether this distinction and prejudice, existing in the opinion and feelings of the community, would not be as effectually fostered by compelling colored and white children to associate together in the same schools, may well be doubted; at all events, it is a fair and proper question for the committee to consider and decide upon, having in view the best interests of both classes of children placed under their superintendence, and we cannot say, that their decision upon it is not founded on just grounds of reason and experience, and in the results of a discriminating and honest judgment.

The increased distance, to which the plaintiff was obliged to go to school from her father's house, is not such, in our opinion, as to render the regulation in question unreasonable, still less illegal.

On the whole the court are of opinion, that upon the facts stated, the action cannot be maintained.

As noted previously, similar results were reached in northern courts even after the Fourteenth Amendment's ratification.[89] Although transplanted from the North, official segregation flourished as an effective method of maintaining racial advantage in the post-slavery era. From their inception in the 1880s, Jim Crow laws evolved rapidly into a comprehensive scheme of racial management. In 1896, the Supreme Court determined that prescriptive segregation was a reasonable exercise of a state's police power and thus offended neither the Thirteenth nor Fourteenth Amendment.

---

[89] *E.g.*, State v. McCann, 21 Ohio St. 198 (1872).

Plessy v. Ferguson
163 U.S. 537 (1896)

. . .

MR. JUSTICE BROWN, after stating the case, delivered the opinion of the Court.

This case turns upon the constitutionality of an act of the General Assembly of the States of Louisiana, passed in 1890, providing for separate railway carriages for the white and colored races.

. . .

The petition for the writ of prohibition averred that petitioner was seven-eighths Caucasian and one eighth African blood; that the mixture of colored blood was not discernible in him, and that he was entitled to every right, privilege and immunity secured to citizens of the United States of the white race; and that, upon such theory, he took possession of a vacant seat in a coach where passengers of the white race were accommodated, and was ordered by the conductor to vacate said coach and take a seat in another assigned to persons of the colored race, and having refused to comply with such demand he was forcibly ejected with the aid of a police officer, and imprisoned in the parish jail to answer a charge of having violated the above act.

. . .

The object of the amendment was undoubtedly to enforce the absolute equality of the two races before the law, but in the nature of things it could not have been intended to abolish distinctions based upon color, or to enforce social, as distinguished from political equality, or a commingling of the two races upon terms unsatisfactory to either. Laws permitting, and even requiring, their separation in places where they are liable to be brought into contact do not necessarily imply the inferiority of either race to the other, and have been generally, if not universally, recognized as within the competency of the state legislatures in the exercise of their police power. The most common instance of this is connected with the establishment of separate schools for white and colored children, which has been held to be a valid exercise of the legislative power even by courts of States where the political rights of the colored races have been longest and most earnestly enforced.

One of the earliest of these cases is that of *Roberts v. City of Boston*, . . . in which the Supreme Judicial Court of Massachusetts held that the general school committee of Boston had power to make provision for the instruction of colored children in separate schools established exclusively for them, and to prohibit their attendance upon the other schools.

Similar laws have been enacted by Congress under its general power of legislation over the District of Columbia, Rev. Stat. D.C. §§ 231, 282, 310, 319, as well as by the legislatures of many of the States, and have been generally, if not uniformly, sustained by the courts. *State v.* McCann, 21 Ohio St. 198; *Lehen v. Brummell*, 15 S.W. Rep. 765; *Ward v. Flood*, 48 California, 36; *Berfonneau v. School Directors*, 3 Woods, 177; *People v. Gallagher*, 93 N.Y. 433; *Cory v. Carter*, 43 Indiana, 327; *Dawson v. Lee,* 83 Kentucky 49.

Laws forbidding the intermarriage of the two races may be said in a technical sense to interfere with the freedom of contract, and yet have been universally recognized as within the police power of the State.

It is claimed by the plaintiff in error that, in any mixed community, the reputation of belonging to the dominant race, in this instance the white race, is *property*, in the same sense that a right of action, or of inheritance, is property. Conceding this to be so, for the purposes of this case, we are unable to see how this statute deprives him of, or in any way affects his right to, such property. If he be a white man and assigned to a colored coach, he may have his action for damages against the company for being deprived of his so called property. Upon the other hand, if he be a colored man and be so assigned, he has been deprived of no property, since he is not lawfully entitled to the reputation of being a white man.

In this connection, it is also suggested by the learned counsel for the plaintiff in error that the same argument that will justify the state legislature in requiring railways to provide separate accommodations for the two races will also authorize them to require separate cars to be provided for people whose hair is of a certain color, or who are aliens, or who belong to certain nationalities, or to enact laws requiring colored people to walk upon one side of the street, and white people upon the other, or requiring white men's houses to be painted white, and colored men's black, or their vehicles or business signs to be of different colors, upon the theory that one side of the street is as good as the other, or that a house or vehicle of one color is as good as one of another color. The reply to all this is that every exercise of the police power must be reasonable, and extend only to such laws as are enacted in good faith for the promotion for the public good, and not for the annoyance of oppression of a particular class. . . .

So far, then, as a conflict with the Fourteenth Amendment is concerned, the case reduces itself to the question whether the statute of Louisiana is a reasonable regulation, and with respect to this there must necessarily be a large discretion on the part of the legislature. In determining the question of reasonableness it is at liberty to act with reference to the established usages, customs and traditions of the people, and with a view of the promotion of their comfort, and the preservation of the public peace and good order. Gauged by this standard, we cannot say that a law which authorizes or even requires the separation of the two races in public conveyances is unreasonable, or more obnoxious to the Fourteenth Amendment than the acts of Congress requiring separate schools for colored children in the District of Columbia, the constitutionality of which does not seem to have been questioned, or the corresponding acts of state legislatures.

We consider the underlying fallacy of the plaintiff's argument to consist in the assumption that the enforced separation of the two races stamps the colored race with a badge of inferiority. If this be so, it is not by reason of anything found in the act, but solely because the colored race chooses to put that construction upon it. The argument necessarily assumes that if, as has been more than once the case, and is not unlikely to be so again, the colored race should become the dominant power in the state legislature, and should enact a law in precisely similar terms, it would thereby relegate the white races to an inferior position. We imagine that the white race, at least, would not acquiesce in this assumption. The argument also assumes that social prejudices may be overcome by legislation, and that equal rights cannot be secured to the Negro except by an enforced commingling of the two races. We cannot accept this proposition. If the two races are to meet upon terms of social equality, it must be the result of natural affinities, a mutual appreciation of each other's merits and a voluntary consent of individuals. . . .

When the government, therefore, has sourced to each of its citizens equal rights before the law and equal opportunities for improvement and progress, it has accomplished the end for which it was organized and performed all of the functions respecting social advantages with which it is endowed." Legislation is powerless to eradicate racial instincts or to abolish distinctions based upon physical differences, and the attempt to do so can only result in accentuating the difficulties of the present situation. If the civil and political rights of both races be equal one cannot be inferior to the other civilly or politically. If one race be inferior to the other socially, the Constitution of the United States cannot put them upon the same plane.

It is true that the question of the proportion of colored blood necessary to constitute a colored person, as distinguished from a white person, is one upon which there is a difference of opinion in the different States, some holding that any visible admixture of black blood stamps the person as belonging to the colored race, others that it depends upon the preponderance of blood, and still others that the predominance of white blood must only be in the proportion of three fourths. But those are questions to be determined under the laws of each State and are not properly put in issue in this case. Under the allegations of his petition it may undoubtedly become a question of importance whether, under the laws of Louisiana, the petitioner belongs to the white or colored race.

The judgment of the court below is, therefore,

Affirmed.

MR. JUSTICE HARLAN dissenting.

. . .

It was said in argument that the statute of Louisiana does not discriminate against either race, but prescribes a rule applicable alike to white and colored citizens. But this argument does not meet the difficulty. Every one knows that the statute in question had its origin in the purpose, not so much to exclude colored people from railroad cars occupied by blacks, as to exclude colored people from coaches occupied by or assigned to white persons. Railroad corporations of Louisiana did not make discrimination among whites in the matter of accommodation for travellers. The thing to accomplish was, under the guise of giving equal accommodation for whites and blacks, to compel the latter to keep to themselves while travelling in railroad passenger coaches. No one would be so wanting in candor as to assert the contrary. The fundamental objection, therefore, to the statute is that it interferes with the personal freedom of citizens. "Personal liberty," it has been well said, "consists in the power of locomotion, of changing situation, or removing one's person to whatsoever places one's own inclination may direct, without imprisonment or restraint, unless by due course of law." If a white man and a black man choose to occupy the same public conveyance on a public highway, it is their right to do so, and no government, proceeding alone on grounds of race, can prevent it without infringing the personal liberty of each.

. . .

. . . Mr. Sedgwick correctly states the rule when he says that the legislative intention being clearly ascertained, "the courts have no other duty to perform than to execute the legislative will, without any regard to their views as to the wisdom or justice of the particular enactment." Stat. & Const. Constr. 321. There is a dangerous tendency in these latter days to enlarge the functions of the courts, by means of judicial interference with the will of the people as expressed by the legislature. Our institutions have the distinguishing characteristic that the three departments of government are coordinate and separate. Each must keep within the limits defined by the Constitution. And the courts best discharge their duty by executing the will of the law-making power, constitutionally expressed, leaving the results of legislation to be dealt with by the people through their representatives. Statutes must always have a reasonable construction. Sometimes they are to be construed strictly; sometimes, liberally, in order to carry out the legislative will. But however construed, the intent of the legislature is to be respected, if the particular statute in question is valid, although the courts, looking at the public interests, may conceive the statute to be both unreasonable and impolitic. If the power exists to enact a statute, that ends the matter so far as the courts are concerned. The adjudged cases in which statutes have been held to be void, because unreasonable, are those in which the means employed by the legislature were not at all germane to the end to which the legislature was competent.

The white race deems itself to be the dominant race in this country. And so it is, in prestige, in achievements, in education, in wealth and in power. So, I doubt not, it will continue to be for all time, if it remains true to its great heritage and holds fast to the principles of constitutional liberty. But in view of the Constitution, in the eye of the law, there is in this country no superior, dominant, ruling class of citizens. There is no caste here. Our Constitution is color-blind, and neither knows nor tolerates classes among citizens. In respect of civil rights, all citizens are equal before the law. The humblest is the peer of the most powerful. The law regards man as man, and takes no account of his surroundings or of this color when his civil rights as guaranteed by the supreme law of the land are involved. It is, therefore, to be regretted that this high tribunal, the final expositor of the fundamental law of the land, has reached the conclusion that it is competent for a State to regulate the enjoyment by citizens of their civil rights solely upon the basis of race.

In my opinion, the judgment this day rendered will, in time, prove to be quite as pernicious as the decision made by this tribunal in the *Dred Scott case*. It was adjudged in that case that the descendants of Africans who were imported into this country and sold as slavers were not included nor intended to be included under the word "citizens" in the Constitution, and could not claim any of the rights and privileges which that instrument provided for and secured to citizens of the United States; that at the time of the adoption of the Constitution they were "considered as a subordinate and inferior class of beings, who had been subjugated by the dominant race, and, whether emancipated or not, yet remained subject to their authority, and had no rights or privileges but such as those who held the power and the government might choose to grant them." The recent amendments of the Constitution, by one of which the blacks of this country were made citizens of the United States and of the States in which they respectively reside, and whose privileges and immunities, as citizens, the States are forbidden to abridge. Sixty millions of whites are in no danger from the presence here of eight millions of blacks. The destinies of the two races, in this country, are indissolubly linked together, and the interests of both require that the common government of all shall not permit the seeds of race hate to be planted under the sanction of law. What can more certainly arouse race hate, what more certainly create and perpetuate a feeling of distrust between these races, than state enactments, which, in fact, proceed on the ground that colored citizens are so inferior and degraded that they cannot be allowed to sit in public coaches occupied by white citizens? That, as all will admit, is the real meaning of such legislation as was enacted in Louisiana.

. . .

There is a race so different from our own that we do not permit those belonging to it to become citizens of the United States. Persons belonging to it are, with few exceptions, absolutely excluded from our country. I allude to the Chinese race. But by the statute in question, a Chinaman can ride in the same passenger coach with white citizens of the United States, while citizens of the black race in Louisiana, many of whom, perhaps, risked their lives for the preservation of the Union, who are entitled, by law, to participate in the political control of the State and nation, who are not excluded, by law or by reason of their race, from public stations of any kind, and who have all the legal rights that belong to white citizens, are yet declared to be criminals, liable to imprisonment, if they ride in a public coach occupied by citizens of the white race. It is scarcely just to say that a colored citizen should not object to occupying a public coach assigned to his own race. He does not object, nor, perhaps, would he object to separate coaches for his race, if his rights under the law were recognized. But he objects, and ought never to cease objecting to the proposition, that citizens of the white and black races can be adjudged criminals because they sit, or claim the right to sit, in the same public coach on a public highway.

The arbitrary separation of citizens, on the basis of race, while they are on a public highway, is a badge of servitude wholly inconsistent with the civil freedom and the equality before the law established by the Constitution. It cannot be justified upon any legal grounds.

If evils will result from the commingling of the two races upon public highways established for the benefit of all, they will be infinitely less than those that will surely come from state legislation regulating the enjoyment of civil rights upon the basis of race. We boast of the freedom enjoyed by our people above all other peoples. But it is difficult to reconcile that boast with a state of the law which, practically puts the brand of servitude and degradation upon a large class of our fellow-citizens, our equals before the law. The thin disguise of "equal" accommodations for passengers in railroad coaches will not mislead any one, nor atone for the wrong this day done.

DEL: The *Plessy* decision, like *Dred Scott*, tends to be dismissed by modern perspectives as a "derelict[] of constitutional law."[90] It is Justice Harlan's dissent, stressing that the Constitution allows "no caste" and "is color-blind," that reflexively is adverted to now as representing the Fourteenth Amendment's true meaning. Harlan's argument thus has been referenced in modern Fourteenth Amendment analysis to support the proposition that race-conscious remedies, designed to reckon with the nation's legacy of discrimination including much of what was facilitated by *Plessy* itself, are at odds with color-blind constitutional principles.[91] Such reliance may be misplaced, insofar as Harlan's assessment was in the context of legislation that burdened a discrete racial group instead of attempting

---

[90] *See supra* note 27.
[91] *E.g.*, Metro Broadcasting, Inc. v. FCC, 499 U.S. 547, 637 (1991)(Kennedy, J., dissenting); Fullilove v. Klutznick, 448 U.S. 448, 522-23 (1980).

to remedy group disadvantage. Harlan's message itself was not disengaged from a racist ideology, as evidenced by its author's certainty that the white race would remain "dominant" if it merely adhered to "principles of constitutional liberty." The logical inference of Harlan's observation was that, even in an unregulated marketplace, whites would be dominant "in prestige, in achievements, in education, in wealth, and in power." Such thinking provides some meaningful insight not only into the inspiring racial ideology of the moment but of the virtually impossible circumstances within which the Fourteenth Amendment was asked to operate by those challenging official segregation. The majority's reasoning may have been disingenuously driven to the extent that it concluded that any inference of inferiority was drawn "not by reason of anything found in the act but solely because the colored race chooses to put that construction on it."[92] Taking that analysis seriously required blindness to the reality that the ideology of inherent white superiority and black inferiority was "being stridently trumpeted . . . from the press, the pulpit, and the platform, as well as from the legislative halls of the South."[93] The Court itself identified a person's white status as a property right that merited protection.[94] For all of its racist inspiration, the *Plessy* decision was right on two significant points. First, the regulation was a reasonable exercise of the police power at least insofar as reasonableness was assessed from the perspective of moral development relevant to the Fourteenth Amendment. As evidenced by the framers rather discrete vision of the amendment's purpose, reinforced by the *Civil Rights Cases* Court's dismissal of racially exclusionary practices as "mere discriminations,"[95] formal segregation in the social arena simply was not to be taken seriously. Second, in noting that the law was "powerless to eradicate social instincts or to abolish distinctions based upon physical differences,"[96] the Court provided insight into the law's limited capacity to change hearts and minds. At a time when legal reform largely is tapped out as a basis for racial progress, and formal segregation largely has been superseded by functional segregation, whatever progress there may be in eradicating racially significant "social instincts" will be the function not of legal but moral development.

DER: Both the *Plessy* majority opinion and Justice Harlan's dissent distinguished between the political and social equality of the races. The majority reasoned that Blacks' civil rights guaranteed by the Fourteenth Amendment did not encompass social amalgamation with whites. Similarly, Justice Harlan observed that whites would remain socially dominant despite Blacks' equality before the law. It is true that the law alone cannot transform individuals' racial prejudices and preferences that govern much of American social life. But the law's limitations are often used as an excuse for judges to disregard racist practices altogether. Recognizing the difficulty of changing racial prejudice becomes a rationale for acquiescing in it. To some extent, racial bias, categorized as social rather than political, is seen to immunize harmful practices from legal scrutiny. Certainly, the *Plessy* Court's reference to "social instincts" was an attempt to rationalize a practice that degraded Black citizens and denied them equal liberty of movement. A contemporary example is the argument that hate speech should be protected under the First Amendment for its racist motivation rather than punished for its injury to its victims. Courts may be powerless to change invidious attitudes about African Americans, but that is no reason for the law to ignore their consequences. Moreover, legal inaction encourages these attitudes to flourish by appearing to give them official approval.

---

[92] Plessy v. Ferguson, 163 U.S. 537, 551 (1896).
[93] Leonard W. Levy, Plessy v. Ferguson, in CIVIL RIGHTS AND EQUALITY 174 (Kenneth Karst ed. 1989).
[94] Plessy v. Ferguson, 163 U.S. at 549.
[95] Civil Rights Cases, 109 U.S. 3, 25 (1883).
[96] Plessy v. Ferguson, 163 U.S. at 551-52.

PAH: While it is true that modern supporters of a color-blind approach to the Constitution often point to Justice Harlan's dissent in *Plessy v. Ferguson* as the legacy upon which their interpretation of the Fourteenth Amendment rests, it bears noting, as Professor Aleinikoff reminds us,[97] that Justice Harlan's opinion is a text of another era, "speak[ing] the language of 'the fundamental rights of citizens,' 'liberty,' and 'civil rights.' It is an attack, not on the use of racial classifications, but on a social system based on an idealogy of white supremacy." Thus, rather than supporting a color-blind reading of the Fourteenth Amendment that disallows race-conscious measures but condones laws that operate to continue "freedom-limiting subordination" of African Americans, Justice Harlan's dissent concerns "the meaning of freedom embodied in the Thirteenth Amendment and the nature and scope of rights inhering in national citizenship as embodied in the Fourteenth Amendment."[98] Under this reasoning, what was offensive was the infringement of the right of mobility of the recently freed slaves (a freedom which is inherent in national citizenship) which resulted from a racial classification scheme which was motivated and had the effect of maintaining a race-based caste system, subjugating the recently freed slaves.

This interpretation of Justice Harlan's dissent in *Plessy* has implications beyond understanding 19th-century thinking; it offers support for rethinking the *color-blind* interpretation of *Brown*, so popular in political arenas and in recent Supreme Court cases. It also responds to the conservative attack on affirmative action as unlawful reverse discrimation because it is race-conscious. This connection between liberty and citizenship flowing from an understanding of the meaning of the Thirteenth *and* Fourteenth Amendments is a reasonable alternative to the impoverished understanding of equality that is portrayed in the *color-blind* reading of the *Plessy* dissent currently attributed to Justice Harlan.

---

[97] T. Alexander Aleinikoff, Re-reading Justice Harlan's Dissent in Plessy v. Ferguson: Freedom, Antiracism, and Citizenship, 1992 U. Ill. L. Rev. 961 (1992). Notably, nowhere in the text of the *Plessy* dissent does Justice Harlan argue that the Fourteenth Amendment should be understood as establishing a norm of color-blindness. 1992 U. Ill. L. Rev. at 963.

[98] Id. at 963-64.

Considered by itself and in context, the *Plessy* decision heralded a significant redirection of Fourteenth Amendment interest. A year later, in a case also arising out of Louisiana, the Court struck down a law regulating the insurance industry on grounds it interfered with economic liberty. The decision, in *Allgeyer v. Louisiana*,[99] previewed the rise of substantive due process review which for the next four decades held social and economic legislation hostage to the Fourteenth Amendment. Before and even after the demise of economic rights doctrine, and notwithstanding what the *Slaughter-House* and *Strauder* Courts had characterized as "the one pervading purpose" of the Fourteenth Amendment,[100] standards of review remained generally accommodating toward official segregation.

The real meaning of the separate but equal doctrine soon revealed itself in *Plessy's* progeny. In *Cumming v. Richmond County Board of Education*, the Court examined a school board's decision to close a black high school as a solution to its shortage of funds. In determining whether the white high school should be shut down for purposes of equality, the Court in an opinion authored by Justice Harlan determined that such a resolution would deny an education to white students without providing any benefit to black students.

---

[99] 165 U.S. 575 (1897).

[100] Strauder v. West Virginia, 100 U.S. 303, 307 (1879)(quoting Slaughter-House Cases, 83 U.S. 36, 71 (1873).

Cumming v. Richmond County Board of Education
175 U.S. 529 (1899)

The petitioners . . . alleged that they were persons of color and parents of children of school age lawfully entitled to the full benefit of any system of high schools organized or maintained by the Board; that up to the time of the said tax levy and for many years continuously prior thereto, the Board maintained a system of high schools in Richmond County in which the colored school population had the same educational advantages as the white school population, but on July 10, 1897, it withdrew from and denied to the colored school population any participation in the educational facilities of a high school system in the county and had voted to continue to deny to that population any admission to or participation in such educational facilities; and that at the time of such withdrawal and denial the petitioners respectively had children attending the colored high school then existing, but who were now debarred from participation in the benefits of a public high school education though petitioners were being taxed therefor. They averred that the action of the Board of Education was a denial of the equal protection of the laws secured by the Constitution of the United States, and that it was inequitable, illegal and unconstitutional for the Board to levy upon or for the tax collector to collect from them any tax for the educational purposes of the county, from the benefits of which the petitioners in the persons of their children of school age were excluded and debarred. . . .

MR. JUSTICE HARLAN, after stating the facts as above, delivered the opinion of the Court.

. . .

The plaintiffs in error complain that the Board of Education used the funds in its hands to assist in maintaining a high school for white children without providing a similar school for colored children. The substantial relief asked is an injunction that would either impair the efficiency of the high school provided for white children or compel the Board to close it. But if that were done, the result would only be to take from white children educational privileges enjoyed by them, without giving to colored children additional opportunities for the education furnished in high schools. The colored school children of the county would not be advanced in the matter of their education by a decree compelling the defendant Board to cease giving support to a high school for white children. The Board had before it the question whether it should maintain, under its control, a high school for about sixty colored children or withhold the benefits of education in primary schools from three hundred children of the same race. It was impossible, the Board believed, to give educational facilities to the three hundred colored children who were unprovided for, if it maintained a separate school for the sixty children who wished to have a high school education. Its decision was in the interest of the greater number of colored children, leaving the smaller number to obtain a high school education in existing private institutions at an expense beyond that incurred in the high school discontinued by the Board.

The *Cumming* decision indicated that the separate but equal doctrine was concerned almost exclusively with its first half. By refusing to penalize provision of secondary education on a racially exclusive basis, the Court diminished any incentive for equalization. Funding of public education over the next several decades evidenced gross disparities consistent with the logical implications of the *Cumming* decision. In 1915, for instance, South Carolina invested ten times more money in white students than black students.[101] By 1954, despite the commitment of many states to increase funding of black schools as segregation was under mounting challenge, expenditures on public education in the South averaged $165 per white student and $115 per black student.[102]

The Court's disinterest in reckoning with racially exclusionary and discriminatory practices was especially notable over the first few decades of the twentieth century. Even flagrant constitutional violations were countenanced pursuant to the sense that meaningful relief only could come from the political process. Such was the Court's

---

[101] ANTHONY LEWIS, PORTRAIT OF A DECADE: THE SECOND AMERICAN REVOLUTION 29 (1964).
[102] *Id.*

response when black voters in Alabama, systematically prohibited from registering to vote, alleged a Fifteenth Amendment violation.

Giles v. Harris
189 U.S. 475 (1903)

Mr. Justice Holmes delivered the opinion of the Court.

. . .

The allegations of the bill may be summed up as follows. The plaintiff is subject to none of the disqualifications set forth in the constitution of Alabama and is entitled to vote—entitled, as the bill plainly means, under the constitution as it is. He applied in March, 1902, for registration as a voter, and was refused arbitrarily on the ground of his color, together with large numbers of other duly qualified Negroes, while all white men were registered. The same thing was done all over the State. Under section 187 of article 8 of the Alabama constitution persons registered January 1, 1903, remain electors for life unless they become disqualified by certain crimes, etc., while after that date severer tests come into play which would exclude, perhaps, a large part of the black race. Therefore, by the refusal, the plaintiff and the other Negroes excluded were deprived not only of their vote at an election which has taken place since the bill was filed, but of the permanent advantage incident to registration before 1903. The white men generally are registered for good under the easy test and the black men are likely to be kept out in the future as in the past. This refusal to register the blacks was part of a general scheme to disfranchise them, to which the defendants and the State itself, according to the bill, were parties. The defendants accepted their office for the purpose of carrying out the scheme. The part taken by the State, that is, by the white population which framed the constitution, consisted in shaping that instrument so as to give opportunity and effect to the wholesale fraud which has been practiced.

The difficulties which we cannot overcome are two, and the first is this: The plaintiff alleges that the whole registration scheme of the Alabama constitution is a fraud upon the Constitution of the United States, and asks us to declare it void. But of course he could not maintain a bill for a mere declaration in the air. He does not try to do so, but asks to be registered as a party qualified under the void instrument. If then we accept the conclusion which it is the chief purpose of the bill to maintain, how can we make the court a party to the unlawful scheme by accepting and adding another voter to its fraudulent lists? . . .

The other difficulty is of a different sort, and strictly reinforces the argument that equity cannot undertake now, any more than it has in the past, to enforce political rights, and also the suggestion that state constitutions were not left unmentioned in § 1979 by accident. In determining whether a court of equity can take jurisdiction, one of the first questions is what it can do to enforce any order that it may make. This is alleged to be the conspiracy of a State, although the State is not and could not be made a party to the bill. The Circuit Court has no constitutional power to control its action by any direct means. And if we leave the State out of consideration, the court has as little practical power to deal with the people of the State in a body. The bill imports that the great mass of the white population intends to keep the blacks from voting. To meet such an intent something more than ordering the plaintiff's name to be inscribed upon the lists of 1902 will be needed. If the conspiracy and the intent exist, a name on a piece of paper will not defeat them. Unless we are prepared to supervise the voting in that State by officers of the court, it seems to us that all that the plaintiff could get from equity would be an empty form. Apart from damages to the individual, relief from a great political wrong, if done, as alleged, by the people of a State and the State itself, must be given by them or by the legislative and political department of the government of the United States.

Appearances of equality were allowed to prevail over reality when, in *McCabe v. Atchison, Topeka & Santa Fe Railway Co.*, the Court considered whether an injunction should be entered in response to a law providing that railroads need not afford blacks sleeping, dining and chair cars to the extent market demand was insignificant. Although noting that the "volume of traffic" consideration was "without merit," the Court determined that the complainants themselves had not requested such accommodations and thus had not established that they were without an adequate remedy at law.[103]

---

[103] McCabe v. Atchison, Topeka & Santa Fe Railway Co., 235 U.S. 151, 161-63 (1914).

McCabe v. Atchison, Topeka & Santa Fe Railway Company
235 U.S. 151 (1914)

MR. JUSTICE HUGHES delivered the opinion of the Court.

The legislature of the State of Oklahoma passed an act known as the 'Separate Coach law.' It provided that 'every railway company . . . doing business in this State, as a common carrier of passengers for hire' should 'provide separate coaches or compartments, for the accommodation of the white and Negro races, which separate coaches or cars' should 'be equal in all points of comfort and convenience'; that at passenger depots, there should be maintained 'separate waiting rooms,' likewise with equal facilities; that the term Negro, as used in the act, should include every person of African descent, as defined by the state constitution; and that each compartment of a railway coach 'divided by a good and substantial wooden partition, with a door therein, shall be deemed a separate coach' within the meaning of the statute.

It was further provided that nothing contained in the act should be construed to prevent railway companies 'from hauling sleeping cars, dining or chair cars attached to their trains to be used exclusively by either white or Negro passengers, separately but not jointly'.

. . .

. . . It is not questioned that the meaning is that the carriers may provide sleeping cars, dining cars and chair cars exclusively for white persons and provide no similar accommodations for Negroes. The reasoning is that there may not be enough persons of African descent seeking these accommodations to warrant the outlay in providing them. Thus, the Attorney General of the State, in the brief filed by him in support of the law, urges that "the plaintiffs must show that their own travel is in such quantity and of such kind as to actually afford the roads the same profits, not per man, but per car, as does the white traffic, or, sufficient profit to justify the furnishing of the facility, and that in such case they are not supplied with separate cars containing the same. This they have not attempted. What vexes the plaintiffs is the limited market value they offer for such accommodations. Defendants are not by

law compelled to furnish chair cars, diners nor sleepers, except when the market offered reasonably demands the facility." And in the brief of counsel for the appellees, it is stated that the members of the legislature "were undoubtedly familiar with the character and extent of travel of persons of African descent in the State of Oklahoma and were of the opinion that there was no substantial demand for Pullman car and dining car service for persons of the African race in the intrastate travel" in that State.

This argument with respect to volume of traffic seems to us to be without merit. It makes the constitutional right depend upon the number of persons who may be discriminated against, whereas the essence of the constitutional right is that it is a personal one. Whether or not particular facilities shall be provided may doubtless be conditioned upon there being a reasonable demand therefor, but, if facilities are provided, substantial equality of treatment of persons traveling under like conditions cannot be refused. It is the individual who is entitled to the equal protection of the laws, and if he is denied by a common carrier, acting in the matter under the authority of a state law, a facility or convenience in the course of his journey which under substantially the same circumstances is furnished to another traveler, he may properly complain that his constitutional privilege has been invaded.

There is, however, an insuperable obstacle to the granting of the relief sought by this bill. It was filed as we have seen, by five persons against five railroad corporations to restrain them from complying with the state statute. . . . But we are dealing here with the case of the complainants, and nothing is shown to entitle them to an injunction. It is an elementary principle that, in order to justify the granting of this extraordinary relief, the complainant's need of it, and the absence of an adequate remedy at law, must clearly appear. The complainant cannot succeed because someone else may be hurt. . . .

. . . It is not alleged that any one of the complainants has ever traveled on any one of the five railroads, or has ever requested transportation on any of them; or that any one of the complainants has ever requested that accommodations be furnished to him in any sleeping cars, dining cars or chair cars; or that any of these five companies has ever notified any one of these complainants that such accommodations would not be furnished to him, when furnished to others, upon reasonable request and payment of the customary charge. Nor is there anything to show that in case any of these complainants offers himself as a passenger on any of these roads and is refused accommodations equal to those afforded to others on a like journey, he will not have an adequate remedy at law. . . .

To the extent segregation was successfully challenged during the early part of the twentieth century, it was a function of economic rights doctrine rather than equality analysis. In *Berea College v. Commonwealth of Kentucky*, the Court upheld a state law prohibiting racially mixed education at private schools and colleges. Although the Court rejected the notion of a right or freedom to teach being at stake, Justice Harlan suggested that the law not only denied a liberty interest protected by the Fourteenth Amendment but deviated extensively from basic principles of equality.

Berea College v. Commonwealth of Kentucky
211 U.S. 45 (1908)

On October 8, 1904, the grand jury of Madison County, Kentucky, presented in the Circuit Court of that county an indictment, charging:

"The said Berea College, being a corporation duly incorporated under the laws of the State of Kentucky, and owning maintaining and operating a college, school and institution of learning, known as 'Berea College,' located in the town of Berea, Madison County, Kentucky, did unlawfully and willfully permit and receive both the white and Negro races as pupils for instruction in said college, school and institution of learning."

This indictment was found under an act . . . whose first section reads:

"Sec. 1. That it shall be unlawful for any person, corporation or association of persons to maintain or operate any college, school or institution where persons of the white and Negro races are both received as pupils for instruction, and any person or corporation who shall operate or maintain any such college, school or institution shall be fined $1,000, and any person or corporation who may be convicted of violating the provisions of this act shall be fined $100 for each day they may operate said school, college or institution after such conviction."

On a trial the defendant was found, guilty and sentenced to pay fine of one thousand dollars. . . .

MR. JUSTICE BREWER, after making the foregoing statement, delivered the opinion of the court.

There is no dispute as to the facts. That the act does not violate the constitution of Kentucky is settled by the decision of its highest court, and the single question for our consideration is whether it conflicts with the Federal Constitution. The Court of Appeals discussed at some length the general power of the State in respect to the separation of the two races. It also ruled that "the right to teach white and Negro children in a private school at the same time and place is not a property right. Besides, appellant as a corporation created by this State has no natural right to teach at all. Its right to teach is such as the State sees fit to give to it. The State may withhold it altogether, or qualify it.

[T]he decision by a state court of the extent and limitation of the powers conferred by the State upon one of its own corporations is of a purely local nature. In creating a corporation a State may withhold powers which may be exercised by and cannot be denied to in individual. It is under no obligation to treat both alike. In granting corporate powers the legislature may deem that the best interests of the State would be subserved by some restriction, and the corporation may not plead that in spite of the restriction it has more or greater powers because the citizen has. "The granting of such right or privilege [the right or privilege to be a corporation] rests entirely in the discretion of the State, and, of course, when granted, may be accompanied with such conditions as its legislature may judge most befitting to its interests and policy." The act of 1904 forbids "any person, corporation or association of persons to maintain or operate any college," etc. Such a statute may conflict with the Federal Constitution in denying to individuals powers which they may rightfully exercise, and yet, at the same time, be valid as to a corporation created by the State. . . .

Mr. Justice Harlan, dissenting.

. . .

The capacity to impart instruction to others is given by the Almighty for beneficent purposes and its use may not be forbidden or interfered with by Government—certainly not, unless such instruction is, in its nature, harmful to the public morals or imperils the public safety. The right to impart instruction, harmless in itself or beneficial to those who receive it, is a substantial right of property—especially, where the services are tendered for compensation. But even if such right be not strictly a property right, it is, beyond question, part of one's liberty as guaranteed against hostile state action by the Constitution of the United States. This court has more than once said that the liberty guaranteed by the Fourteenth Amendment embraces "the right of the citizen to be free in the enjoyment of all his faculties," and "to be free to use them in all lawful ways." If pupils, of whatever race—cer-

tainly, if they be citizens—choose with the consent of their parents or voluntarily to sit together in a private institution of learning while receiving instruction which is not in its nature harmful or dangerous to the public, no government, whether Federal or state, can legally forbid their coming together, or being together temporarily, for such an innocent purpose. . . .

. . . Have we become so inoculated with prejudice of race that an American government, professedly based on the principles of freedom, and charged with the protection of all citizens alike, can make distinctions between such citizens in the matter of their voluntary meeting for innocent purposes simply because of their respective races? Further, if the lower court be right, then a State may make it a crime for white and colored persons to frequent the same market places at the same time, or appear in an assemblage of citizens convened to consider questions of a public or political nature in which all citizens, without regard to race, are equally interested. Many other illustrations might be given to show the mischievous, not to say cruel, character of the statute in question and how inconsistent such legislation is with the great principle of the equality of citizens before the law.

The *Berea College* decision illustrated how pervasive official management of racial relations and conditions had become under the separate but equal doctrine. Economic rights doctrine, rather than equality principles, proved effective in challenging a city ordinance requiring to the extent possible segregation by neighborhood block for purposes of residence and assembly.

Buchanan v. Warley
245 U.S. 60 (1917)

Mr. Justice Day delivered the opinion of the Court.

. . .

. . . This ordinance prevents the occupancy of a lot in the City of Louisville by a person of color in a block where the greater number of residences are occupied by white persons; where such a majority exists colored persons are excluded. This interdiction is based wholly upon color; simply that and nothing more. In effect, premises situated as are those in question in the so-called white block are effectively debarred from sale to persons of color, because if sold they cannot be occupied by the purchaser nor by him sold to another of the same color.

This drastic measure is sought to be justified under the authority of the State in the ex-

ercise of the police power. It is said such legislation tends to promote the public peace by preventing racial conflicts; that it tends to maintain racial purity; that it prevents the deterioration of property owned and occupied by white people, which deterioration it is contended, is sure to follow the occupancy of adjacent premises by persons of color.

. . . The Fourteenth Amendment protects life, liberty, and property from invasion by the States without due process of law. Property is more than the mere thing which a person owns. It is elementary that it includes the right to acquire, use, and dispose of it. The Constitution protects these essential attributes of property. Property consists of the free use, enjoyment, and disposal of a person's acquisitions without control or diminution save by the law of the land.

. . .

The concrete question here is: May the occupancy, and, necessarily, the purchase and sale of property of which occupancy is an incident, be inhibited by the States, or by one of its municipalities, solely because of the color of the proposed occupant of the premises? That one may dispose of his property, subject only to the control of lawful enactments curtailing that right in the public interest, must be conceded. The question now presented makes it pertinent to enquire into the constitutional right of the white man to sell his property to a colored man, having in view the legal status of the purchaser and occupant. . . .

That there exists a serious and difficult problem arising from a feeling of race hostility which the law is powerless to control, and to which it must give a measure of consideration, may be freely admitted. But its solution cannot be promoted by depriving citizens of their constitutional rights and privileges.

. . .

The case presented does not deal with an attempt to prohibit the amalgamation of the races. The right which the ordinance annulled was the civil right of a white man to dispose of his property if he saw fit to do so to a person of color and of a colored person to make such disposition to a white person. It is urged that this proposed segregation will promote the public peace by preventing race conflicts. Desirable as this is, and important as is the preservation of the public peace, this aim cannot be accomplished by laws or ordinances which right created or protected by the Federal Constitution.

It is said that such acquisitions by colored persons depreciate property owned in the neighborhood by white persons. But property may be acquired by undesirable white neighbors or put to disagreeable though lawful uses with like results.

We think this attempt to prevent the alienation of the property in question to a person of color was not a legitimate exercise of the police power of the State, and is in direct violation of the fundamental law enacted in the Fourteenth Amendment of the Constitution preventing state interference with property rights except by due process of law. That being the case the ordinance cannot stand.

Official segregation established itself as a methodology for separating white persons not only from blacks but from other racial or ethnic groups. When a citizen of Chinese descent challenged a Mississippi law placing his daughter in a black school, the Court in *Gong Lum v. Rice* determined that

we can not think that the question is any different or that any different result can be reached, . . . where the issue is as between white pupils and the pupils of the yellow races. The decision is within the discretion of the state in regulating its public schools and does not conflict with the Fourteenth Amendment.[104]

a. The Challenge to Prescriptive Segregation

Against a backdrop of hardened regulatory methodology and persistent judicial endorsement of it, the National Association for Advancement of Colored People (NAACP) commenced an organized challenge to the separate but equal doctrine. Under the leadership of Charles Houston and Thurgood Marshall, the NAACP developed a two part strategy for attacking official segregation of public education. Although initially targeting tangible inequalities, their plan was to demonstrate eventually that the separate but equal doctrine was inimical to the equal protection guarantee. Litigative demands for "absolute and complete equalization of curricula, faculty and physical equipment in white and black schools" were calculated to impose such an "extreme cost of maintaining two equal systems [that it] would eventually destroy segregation."[105] The initial focus was on graduate and professional education. As Marshall explained

the university level was the best place to begin a campaign that had as its ultimate objective the total elimination of segregation in public institutions in

---

[104] Gong Lum v. Rice, 275 U.S. 78 (1925).

[105] Thurgood Marshall, *An Evaluation of Recent Efforts to Achieve Racial Integration in Education through Resort to the Courts*, 21 J. NEGRO EDUC. 316, 318 (1952).

the United States. In the first place, at the university level no provision for Negro education was a rule rather than the exception. Then, too, the difficulties incident to providing equal educational opportunities even within the scope of the "separate but equal " doctrine were insurmountable. To provide separate medical schools, law schools, engineering schools, and graduate schools with all the variety of offerings available at most state universities would be an almost financial impossibility.[106]

The first of the NAACP's legal successes occurred when a state court ordered admission of a black student to Maryland's only public law school. Finding effectively that Maryland must provide racially integrated legal education, if it did not provide a separate opportunity to nonwhites,[107] the decision previewed the NAACP's initial success before the Supreme Court.

---

[106] *Id.* at 319.
[107] Pearson v. Murray, 182 A. 590, 594 (Md. 1936).

Missouri ex Rel. Gaines v. Canada
305 U.S. 337 (1938)

MR. CHIEF JUSTICE HUGHES delivered the opinion of the Court.

Petitioner Lloyd Gaines, a Negro, was refused admission to the School of Law at the State University of Missouri. Asserting that this refusal constituted a denial by the State of the equal protection of the laws in violation of the Fourteenth Amendment of the Federal Constitution, petitioner brought this action for mandamus to compel the curators of the University to admit him. . . .

In answering petitioner's contention that this discrimination constituted a denial of his constitutional right, the state court has fully recognized the obligation of the State to provide Negroes with advantages for higher education substantially equal to the advantages afforded to white students. The State has sought to fulfill that obligation by furnishing equal facilities in separate schools, a method the validity of which has been sustained by our decisions. Respondents' counsel have appropriately emphasized the special solicitude of the State for higher education of Negroes as shown in the establishment of Lincoln University, a state institution well conducted on a plane state with the University of Missouri so far as the offered courses are concerned. It is said that Missouri is a pioneer in that field and is the only State in the Union which has established a separate university for Negroes on the same basis as the state university for white students. But, commendable as is that action, the fact remains that instruction in law for Negroes is not now afforded by the State, either at Lincoln University or elsewhere within the State, and that the State excludes Negroes from the advantages of the law school it has established at the University of Missouri.

It is manifest that this discrimination, if not relieved by the provision we shall presently discuss, would constitute a denial of equal protection. . . .

The state court stresses the advantages that are afforded by the law schools of the adjacent States,—Kansas, Nebraska, Iowa and Illinois,—which admit non-resident Negroes. The court considered that these were schools of high standing where one desiring to practice law in Missouri can get "as sound, comprehensive, valuable legal education" as in the University of Missouri; that the system of education in the former is the same as that in the latter and is designed to give the students a basis for the practice of law in any State where the Anglo-American system of law obtains; that the law school of the University of Missouri does not specialize in Missouri law and that the course of study and the case book used in the five schools are substantially identical. Petitioner insists that for one intending to practice in Missouri there are special advantages in attending a law school there, both in relation to the opportunities for the particular study of Missouri law and for the observation of the local courts, and also in view of the prestige of the Missouri law school among the citizens of the State, his prospective clients. Proceeding with its examination of relative advantages, the state court found that the difference in distances to be traveled afforded no substantial ground of complaint and that there was an adequate appropriate full tuition fees which petitioner would have to pay.

We think that these matters are beside the point. The basic consideration is not as to what sort of opportunities other States provide, or whether they are as good as those in Missouri, but as to what opportunities Missouri itself furnishes to white students and denies to Negroes solely upon the ground of color. The admissibility of laws separating the races in the enjoyment of privileges afforded by the State rests wholly upon the equality of the privileges which the laws give to the separated groups within the State. The question here is not of a duty of the State to supply legal training, or of the quality of the training which it does supply, but of its duty when it provides such training to furnish it to the residents of the State upon the basis of an equality of right. By the operation of the laws of Missouri a privilege has been created for white law students which is denied to Negroes by reason of their race. The white resident is afforded legal education within the State; the Negro resident having the same qualifications is refused it there and must go outside the State to obtain it. That is a denial of the equality of legal right to the enjoyment of the privilege which the State has set up, and the provision for the payment of tuition fees in another State does not remove the discrimination.

The equal protection of the laws is "a pledge of the protection of equal laws." Manifestly, the obligation of the State to give the protection of equal laws can be performed only where its laws operate, that is, within its own jurisdiction. It is there that the equality of legal right must be maintained. That obligation is imposed by the Constitution upon the States severally as governmental entities,—each responsible for its own laws establishing the rights and duties of persons within its borders. It is an obligation the burden of which cannot be cast by one State upon another, and no State can be excused from performance by what another State may do or fail to do. That separate responsibility of each State within its own sphere is of the essence of statehood maintained under our dual system. It seems to be implicit in respondents' argument that if other States did not provide courses for legal education, it would nevertheless be the constitutional duty of Missouri when it supplied such courses for white students to make equivalent

provision for Negroes. But that plain duty would exist because it rested upon the State independently of the action of other States. We find it impossible to conclude that what otherwise would be an unconstitutional discrimination, with respect to the legal right to the enjoyment of opportunities within the State, can be justified by requiring resort to opportunities elsewhere. That resort may mitigate the inconvenience of the discrimination but cannot serve to validate it.

. . . We are of the opinion that the ruling was error, and that petitioner was entitled to be admitted to the law school of the State University in the absence of other and proper provision for his legal training within the State.

. . .

Separate opinion of MR. JUSTICE McREYNOLDS.

. . .

For a long time Missouri has acted upon the view that the best interest of her people demands separation of whites and Negroes in schools. Under the opinion just announced, I presume she may abandon her law school and thereby disadvantage her white citizens without improving petitioner's opportunities for legal instruction; or she may break down the settled practice concerning separate schools and thereby, as indicated by experience, damnify both races. Whether by some other course it may be possible for her to avoid condemnation is matter for conjecture.

The State has offered to provide the Negro petitioner opportunity for study of the law—if perchance that is the thing really desired—by paying his tuition at some nearby school of good standing. This is far from unmistakable disregard of his rights and in the circumstances is enough to satisfy any reasonable demand for specialized training. It appears that never before has a Negro applied for admission to [law school in Missouri].

The problem presented obviously is a difficult and highly practical one. A fair effort to solve it has been made by offering adequate opportunity for study when sought in good faith. The State should not be unduly hampered through theorization inadequately restrained by experience.

. . .

Prior to 1954, the Court evidenced little interest in reexamining the pivotal notion of *Plessy* that official segregation did not imply the inferiority of a given race. Presented in *Sipuel v. Board of Regents* with circumstances identical to those reviewed in *Gaines*, the Court heard arguments that challenged the constitutional integrity of prescriptive segregation itself. Marshall asserted that such methods "preserve a caste system which is based upon race and color. It is designed and intended to perpetuate the slave tradition. . . . 'Separate' and 'equal' can not be used conjunctively in a situation of this kind; there can be no separate equality."[108] The Court declined the NAACP's invitation to declare segregation unconstitutional and ordered the state to provide a separate law school or admit African-American students to the state university.[109] When the Court refused to press the state to achieve more than sectioning off a part of the state capitol building and denominating it a law school for black students,[110] the NAACP's strategy appeared to have stalled short not only of dismantling segregation but of achieving meaningful equalization.[111]

The ice upon which the separate but equal doctrine skated was thinned by two decisions in 1950. In *Sweatt v. Painter*, the Court agreed with the NAACP's argument that attention to tangible differences in education was not enough to equalize education.

---

[108] RICHARD KLUGER, SIMPLE JUSTICE 259 (quoting Brief for Appellant).
[109] Sipuel v. Board of Regents, 332 U.S. 631, 633 (1948).
[110] Fisher v. Hurst, 333 U.S. 147 (1948).
[111] Pearson v. Murray, 182 A. 590, 594 (Md. 1936).

Sweatt v. Painter
339 U.S. 629 (1950)

MR. CHIEF JUSTICE VINSON delivered the opinion of the Court.

. . . To what extent does the Equal Protection Clause of the Fourteenth Amendment limit the power of a state to distinguish between students of different races in professional and graduate education in a state university? Broader issues have been urged for our consideration, but we adhere to the principle of deciding constitutional questions only in the context of the particular case before the Court. . . .

In the instant case, petitioner filed an application for admission to the University of Texas Law School for the February, 1946 term. His application was rejected solely because he is a Negro. Petitioner thereupon brought this suit for mandamus against the appropriate school officials, respondents here, to compel his admission. At that time, there was no law school in Texas which admitted Negroes.

. . .

The University of Texas Law School, from which petitioner was excluded, was staffed by a faculty of sixteen full-time and three part-time professors, some of whom are nationally recognized authorities in their field. Its student body numbered 850. The library contained over 65,000 volumes. Among the other facilities available to the students were a law review, moot court facilities, scholarship funds, and Order of the Coif affiliation. The school's alumni occupy the most distinguished positions in the private practice of the law and in the public life of the State. It may properly be

considered one of the nation's ranking law schools.

The law school for Negroes which was to have opened in February, 1947, would have had no independent faculty or library. The teaching was to be carried on by four members of the University of Texas Law School faculty, who were to maintain their offices at the University of Texas while teaching at both institutions. Few of the 10,000 volumes ordered for the library had arrived; nor was there any full-time librarian. The school lacked accreditation.

Since the trial of this case, respondents report the opening of a law school at the Texas State University for Negroes. It is apparently on the road to full accreditation. It has a faculty of five full-time professors; a student body of 23; a library of some 16,500 volumes serviced by a full-time staff; a practice court and legal aid association; and one alumnus who has become a member of the Texas Bar.

Whether the University of Texas Law School is compared with the original or the new law school for Negroes, we cannot find substantial equality in the educational opportunities offered white and Negro law students by the State. In terms of number of the faculty, variety of courses and opportunity for specialization, size of the student body, scope of the library, availability of law review and similar activities, the University of Texas Law School is superior. What is more important, the University of Texas Law School possess to a far greater degree those qualities which are incapable of objective measurement but which make for greatness in a law school. Such qualities, to name but a few, include reputation of the faculty, experience of the administration, position and influence of the alumni, standing in the community, traditions and prestige. It is difficult to believe that one who had a free choice between these law schools would consider the question close.

Moreover, although the law is a highly learned profession, we are well aware that it is an intensely practical one. The law school, the proving ground for legal learning and practice, cannot be effective in isolation from the individuals and institutions with which the law interacts. Few students and no one who has practiced law would choose to study in an academic vacuum, removed from the interplay of ideas and the exchange of views with which the law is concerned. The law school to which Texas is willing to admit petitioner excludes from its student body members of the racial groups which number 85% of the population of the State and include most of the lawyers, witnesses, jurors, judges and other officials with whom petitioner will inevitably be dealing when he becomes a member of the Texas Bar. With such a substantial and significant segment of society excluded, we cannot conclude that the education offered petitioner is substantially equal to that which he would receive if admitted to the University of Texas Law School.

It may be argued that excluding petitioner from that school is no different from excluding white students from the new law school. This contention overlooks realities. It is unlikely that a member of a group so decisively in the majority, attending a school with rich traditions and prestige which only a history of consistently maintained excellence could command, would claim that the opportunities afforded him for legal education were unequal to those held open to petitioner. . . .

In accordance with these cases, petitioner may claim his full constitutional right: legal education equivalent to that offered by the State to students of other races. Such education is not available to him in a separate law school as offered by the State. We cannot, therefore, agree with respondents that the doctrine of *Plessy v. Ferguson*, requires affirmance of the judgment below. Nor need we reach petitioner's contention that *Plessy v. Ferguson* should be reexamined in the light of contemporary knowledge respecting the purposes of the Fourteenth Amendment and the effects of racial segregation.

We hold that the Equal Protection Clause of the Fourteenth Amendment requires that petitioner be admitted to the University of Texas Law School. . . .

The *Sweatt* decision was significant because the state not only offered legal education at a racially separate institution but pledged significant resources for equalization purposes. Consistent with the *Sweatt* ruling was the Court's determination, in *McLaurin v. Oklahoma State Regents for Higher Education*, that study conditions for a black student, admitted to a racially exclusive graduate school pursuant to a court order, must be the same as for white students.

McLaurin v. Oklahoma State Regents for Higher Education
339 U.S. 637 (1950)

MR. CHIEF JUSTICE VINSON delivered the opinion of the Court.

In this case, we are faced with the question whether a state may, after admitting a student to graduate instruction in its state university, afford him different treatment from other students solely because of his race. . . .

Appellant is a Negro citizen of Oklahoma. Possessing a Master's Degree, he applied for admission to the University of Oklahoma in order to pursue studies and courses leading to a Doctorate in Education. At that time his application was denied, solely because of his race. . . . [F]ollowing a district court ruling that

the State had a Constitutional duty to provide him with the education he sought as soon as it provided that education for applicants of any other group. . . .

[T]he Oklahoma legislature amended its statutes to permit the admission of Negroes to institutions of higher learning attended by white students, in cases where such institutions offered courses not available in the Negro schools. The amendment provided, however, that in such cases the program of instruction "shall be given at such colleges or institutions of higher education upon a segregated basis." Appellant was thereupon admitted to the University of Oklahoma Graduate School. In apparent conformity with the amendment, his admission was made subject to "such rules and regulations as to segregation as the President of the University shall consider to afford to Mr. G. W. McLaurin substantially equal educational opportunities as are afforded to other persons seeking the same education in the Graduate College," a condition which does not appear to have been withdrawn. Thus he was required to sit apart at a designated desk in an anteroom adjoining the classroom; to sit at a designated desk on the mezzanine floor of the library, but not to use the desks in the regular reading room; and to sit at a designated table and to eat at a different time from the other students in the school cafeteria.

. . .

In the interval between the decision of the court below and the hearing in this Court, the treatment afforded appellant was altered. For some time, the section of the classroom in which appellant sat was surrounded by a rail on which there was a sign stating, "Reserved For Colored," but these have been removed. He is now assigned to a seat in the classroom in a row specified for colored students; he is assigned to a table in the library on the main floor; and he is permitted to eat at the same time in the cafeteria as other students, although here again he is assigned to a special table.

These restrictions were obviously imposed in order to comply, as nearly as could be, with the statutory requirements of Oklahoma. But they signify that the State, in administering the facilities it affords for professional and graduate study, sets McLaurin apart from the other students. The result is that appellant is handicapped in his pursuit of effective graduate instruction. Such restrictions impair and inhibit his ability to study, to engage in discus-

sions and exchange views with other students, and, in general, to learn his profession.

Our society grows increasingly complex, and our need for trained leaders increases correspondingly. Appellant's case represents, perhaps, the epitome of that need, for he is attempting to obtain an advanced degree in education, to become, by definition, a leader and trainer of others. Those who will come under his guidance and influence must be directly affected by the education he receives. Their own education and development will necessarily suffer to the extent that his training is unequal to that of his classmates. State-imposed restrictions which produce such inequalities cannot be sustained.

It may be argued that appellant will be in no better position when these restrictions are removed, for he may still be set apart by his fellow students. This we think irrelevant. There is a vast difference—a Constitutional difference—between restrictions imposed by the state which prohibit the intellectual commingling of students, and the refusal of individuals to commingle where the state presents no such bar. The removal of the state restrictions will not necessarily abate individual and group predilections, prejudices and choices. But at the very least, the state will not be depriving appellant of the opportunity to secure acceptance by his fellow students on his own merits.

We conclude that the conditions under which this appellant is required to receive his education deprive him of his personal and present right to the equal protection of the laws. We hold that under these circumstances the Fourteenth Amendment precludes differences in treatment by the state based upon race. Appellant, having been admitted to a state-supported graduate school, must receive the same treatment at the hands of the state as students of other races. . . .

Although the NAACP effectively had succeeded in desegregating professional and graduate education in those jurisdictions where it had been challenged, the separate but equal doctrine survived generally intact. Its eventual demise was a function of personnel turnover on the Supreme Court and the emergence of more exacting standards of review for racial classifications. The appointment of Earl Warren as chief justice in 1953 brought leadership favoring a more aggressive review of the *Plessy* principle. Doctrine also had evolved from the premise in 1927 that equal protection claims were "the last resort of constitutional arguments"[112] to the possibility at least that "prejudice against discrete and insular minorities may be a special condition, which tends seriously to curtail the operation of th[e] political processes ordinarily relied upon to protect minorities, and which may call for a correspondingly more search-

---

[112] Buck v. Bell, 274 U.S. 200, 208 (1927).

ing inquiry."[113] The possibility that racial classification would be more strictly reviewed was actualized, at least in theory, in *Korematsu v. United States*.

---

[113] United States v. Carolene Products Co., 304 U.S. 144, 154 n.4 (1938).

Korematsu v. United States
323 U.S. 214 (1944)

MR. JUSTICE BLACK, delivered the opinion of the Court. The petitioner, an American citizen of Japanese descent, was convicted in a federal district court for remaining in San Leandro, California, a Military Area," contrary to Civilian Exclusion Order No. 34 of the Commanding General of the Western Command, U. S. Army, which directed that after May 9, 1942, all persons of Japanese ancestry should be excluded from that area. No question was raised as to petitioner's loyalty to the United States. The Circuit Court of Appeals affirmed, and the importance of the constitutional question involved caused us to grant certiorari.

It should be noted, to begin with, that all legal restrictions which curtail the civil rights of a single racial group are immediately suspect. That is not to say that all such restrictions are unconstitutional. It is to say that courts must subject them to the most rigid scrutiny. Pressing public necessity may sometimes justify the existence of such restrictions; racial antagonism never can.

It is said that we are dealing here with the case of imprisonment of a citizen in a concentration camp solely because of his ancestry, without evidence or inquiry concerning his loyalty and good disposition towards the United States. Our task would be simple, our duty clear, were this a case involving the imprisonment of a loyal citizen in a concentration camp because of racial prejudice. Regardless of the true nature of the assembly and relocation centers—and we deem it unjustifiable to call them concentration camps with all the ugly connotations that term implies—we are dealing specifically with nothing but an exclusion order. To cast this case into outlines of racial prejudice, without reference to the real military dangers which were presented, merely confuses the issue. Korematsu was not excluded from the Military Area because of hostility to him or his race. He *was* excluded because we are at war with the Japanese Empire, because the properly constituted military authorities feared an invasion of our West Coast and felt constrained to take proper security measures, because they decided that the military urgency of the situation demanded that all citizens of Japanese ancestry be segregated from the West Coast temporarily, and finally, because Congress, reposing its confidence in this time of war in our military leader—as inevitably it must—determined that they should have the power to do just this. There was evidence of disloyalty on the part of some, the military authorities considered that the need for action was great, and time was short. We cannot—by availing ourselves of the calm perspective of hindsight—now say that at that time these actions were unjustified.

MR. JUSTICE MURPHY, dissenting.

This exclusion of "all persons of Japanese ancestry, both alien and non-alien," from the Pacific Coast are on a plea of military necessity in the absence of martial law ought not to be approved. Such exclusion goes over "the very brink of constitutional power" and falls into the ugly abyss of racism.

In dealing with matters relating to the prosecution and progress of a war, we must accord great respect and consideration to the judgments of the military authorities who are on the scene and who have full knowledge of the military facts. The scope of their discretion must, as a matter of necessity and common sense, be wide. And their judgments ought not to be overruled lightly by those whose training and duties ill-equip them to deal intelligently with matters so vital to the physical security of the nation.

At the same time, however, it is essential that there be definite limits to military discretion, especially where martial law has not been declared. Individuals must not be left impoverished of their constitutional rights on a plea of military necessity that has neither substance nor military support. Thus, like other claims conflicting with the asserted constitutional rights of the individual, the military claim must subject itself to the judicial process of having its reasonableness determined and its conflicts with other interests reconciled. "What are the allowable limits of military discretion, and whether or not they have been overstepped in a particular case, are judicial questions."

The judicial test of whether the Government, on a plea of military necessity, can validly deprive an individual of any of his constitutional rights is whether the deprivation is reasonably related to a public danger that is so "immediate, imminent, and impending" as not to admit of delay and not to permit the intervention of ordinary constitutional processes to alleviate the danger.

. . .

Justification for the exclusion is sought . . . upon questionable racial and sociological grounds not ordinarily within the realm of expert military judgment, supplemented by certain semi-military conclusions drawn from an unwarranted use of circumstantial evidence. Individuals of Japanese ancestry are condemned because they are said to be "a large, unassimilated, tightly knit racial group, bound to an enemy nation by strong ties of race, culture, custom and religion." They are claimed to be given to "emperor worshipping ceremonies" and to "dual citizenship." Japanese language schools and allegedly pro-Japanese organizations are cited as evidence of possible group disloyalty, together with facts as to certain persons being educated and residing at length in Japan. It is intimated that many of these individuals deliberately resided "adjacent to strategic points," thus enabling them "to carry into execution a tremendous program of sabotage on a mass scale should any considerable number of them have been inclined to do so." The need for protective custody is also asserted. The report refers without identity to "numerous incidents of violence" as well as to other admittedly unverified or cumulative incidents. From this, plus certain other events not shown to have been connected with the Japanese Americans, it is concluded that the "situation was fraught with danger to the Japanese population itself" and that the general public "was ready to take matters into its own hands." Finally, it is intimated, though not directly charged or proved, that persons of Japanese ancestry were responsible for three minor isolated shelling and bombings of the Pacific Coast area, as well as for unidentified radio transmissions and night signalling.

The main reasons relied upon by those responsible for the forced evacuation, therefore, do not prove a reasonable relation between the group characteristics of Japanese Americans and the dangers of invasion, sabotage and espionage. The reasons appear, instead, to be largely an accumulation of much of the misinformation, half-truths and insinuations that for years have been directed against Japanese Americans by people with racial and economic prejudice—the same people who have been among the foremost advocates of the evacuation. A military judgment based upon such racial and sociological considerations is not entitled to the great weight ordinarily given to the judgments based upon strictly military considerations. Especially is this so when every

charge relative to race, religion, culture, geographical location, and legal and economic status has been substantially discredited by independent studies made by experts in these matters.

The military necessity which is essential to the validity of the evacuation order thus resolves itself into a few intimations that certain individuals actively aided the enemy, from which it is inferred that the entire group of Japanese Americans could not be trusted to be or remain loyal to the United States. No one denies, of course, that there were some disloyal persons of Japanese descent on the Pacific Coast who did all in their power to aid their ancestral land. Similar disloyal activities have been engaged in by many persons of German, Italian and even more pioneer stock in our country. But to infer that examples of individual disloyalty prove group disloyalty and justify discriminatory action against the entire group is to deny that under our system of law individual guilt is the sole basis for deprivation of rights. Moreover, this inference, which is at the very heart of the evacuation orders, has been used in support of the abhorrent and despicable treatment of minority groups by the dictatorial tyrannies which this nation is now pledged to destroy. To give constitutional sanction to that inference in this case, however well-intentioned may have been the military command on the Pacific Coast, is to adopt one of the cruelest of the rationales used by our enemies to destroy the dignity of the individual and to encourage and open the door to discriminatory actions against other minority groups in the passions of tomorrow.

. . .

I dissent, therefore, from this legalization of racism. Racial discrimination in any form and in any degree has no justifiable part whatever in our democratic way of life. It is unattractive in any setting but it is utterly revolting among a free people who have embraced the principles set forth in the Constitution of the United States. All residents of this nation are kin in some way by blood or culture to a foreign land. Yet they are primarily and necessarily a part of the new and distinct civilization of the United States. They must accordingly be treated at all times as the heirs of the American experiment and as entitled to all the rights and freedoms guaranteed by the Constitution.

MR. JUSTICE JACKSON, dissenting.

. . .

Much is said of the danger to liberty from the Army program for deporting and detaining these citizens of Japanese extraction. But a judicial construction of the due process clause that will sustain this order is a far more subtle blow to liberty than the promulgation of the order itself. A military order, however unconstitutional, is not apt to last longer than the military emergency. Even during that period a succeeding commander may revoke it all. But once a judicial opinion rationalizes such an order to show that it conforms to the Constitution, or rather rationalizes the Constitution to show that the Constitution sanctions such an order, the Court for all time has validated the principle of racial discrimination in criminal procedure and of transplanting American citizens. The principle then lies about like a loaded weapon ready for the hand of any authority that can bring forward a plausible claim of an urgent need. Every repetition imbeds that principle more deeply in our law and thinking and expands it to new purposes. All who observe the work of courts are familiar with what Judge Cardozo described as "the tendency of a principle to expand itself to the limit of its logic." A military commander may overstep the bounds of constitutionality, and it is an incident. But if we review and approve, that passing incident becomes the doctrine of the Constitution. There it has a generative power of its own, and all that it creates will be in its own image. Nothing better illustrates this danger than does the Court's opinion in this case. . . .

Although upholding the wartime relocation of persons of Japanese descent, the Court determined that any legal burden upon the civil rights of a racial group was suspect.[114]

b. Prelude to Desegregation

Warren's appointment as Chief Justice occurred one year after the Court first heard arguments in *Brown v. Board of Education*. The *Brown* case actually consolidated for review the decisions of courts in Kansas, Delaware, Virginia and South Carolina that rejected arguments for repudiating the *Plessy* doctrine at the elementary level of public education. The South Carolina case was particularly dramatic, as the plaintiffs, their supporters and Marshall himself were subject to threats and intimidation.[115] The district court majority focused upon unequal conditions in the education of white and black students and reiterated the separate but equal doctrine's vitality.[116] The decision elicited a dissenting opinion criticizing the court for evading the real issue and concluding that segregated education was an extension of the "warped thinking" of "white supremacy" and an exercise in *"per se inequality."*[117]

---

[114] Korematsu v. United States, 323 U.S. 214, 216 (1944).

[115] For an account of the terrorist and other tactics used to dissuade the attack on segregated schools in Clarendon County, South Carolina, *see* CARL ROWAN, DREAM MAKERS, DREAM BREAKERS: THE LIFE OF THURGOOD MARSHALL 248 (1993).

[116] Briggs v. Elliott, 98 F. Supp. 529, 531-38 (E.D.S.C. 1951).

[117] *Id.* at 542, 548 (Waring, J., dissenting)(emphasis in original).

Briggs v. Elliott
98 F. Supp. 529 (E.D.S.C. 1951)

PARKER, Circuit Judge.
. . .

At the beginning of the hearing the defendants admitted upon the record that "the educational facilities, equipment, curricula and opportunities afforded in School District No. 22 for colored pupils are not substantially equal to those afforded for white pupils." The evidence offered in the case fully sustains this admission. The defendants contend, however, that the district is one of the rural school districts which has not kept pace with urban districts in providing educational facilities for the children of either race, and that the inequalities have resulted from limited resources and from the disposition of the school officials to spend the limited funds available "for the most immediate demands rather than in the light of the overall picture." They state that under the leadership of Governor Byrnes the Legislature of South Carolina has made provision for a bond issue of $75,000,000 with a three per cent sales tax to support it for the purpose of equalizing education opportunities and facilities throughout the state and of meeting the problem of providing equal educational opportunities for Negro children where this had not been done. They have offered evidence to show that this education program is going forward and that under it the educational facilities in the district will be greatly improved for both races and that Negro children will be afforded educational facilities and opportunities in all respects equal to those afforded white children.

There can be no question but that where separate schools are maintained for Negroes and whites, the educational facilities and opportunities afforded by them must be equal. The state may not deny to any person within its jurisdiction the equal protection of the laws, says the Fourteenth Amendment; and this means that, when the state undertakes public education, it may not discriminate against any individual on account of race but must offer equal opportunity to all ...

Plaintiffs ask that, in addition to granting them relief on account of the inferiority of the educational facilities furnished them, we hold that segregation of the races in the public schools, as required by the Constitution and statutes of South Carolina, is of itself a denial of the equal protection of the laws guaranteed by the Fourteenth Amendment, and that we enjoin the enforcement of the constitutional provision and statute requiring it and by our injunction require defendants to admit Negroes to schools to which white students are admitted within the district. We think, however, that segregation of the races in the public schools, so long as equality of rights is preserved, is a matter of legislative policy for the several states, with which the federal courts are powerless to interfere.

. . .

Only a little over a year ago, the question was before the Court of Appeals of the District of Columbia in *Carr v. Corning*, a case involving the validity of segregation within the District, and the whole matter was exhaustively explored in the light of history and the pertinent decisions in an able opinion by Judge Prettyman, who said:

"It is urged that the separation of the races is itself, apart from equality or inequality of treatment, forbidden by the Constitution. The question thus posed is whether the Constitution lifted this problem out of the hands of all legislatures and settled it. We do not think it did. Since the beginning of human history, no circumstances has given rise to more difficult and delicate problems than has the coexistence of different races in the same area. Centuries of bitter experience in all parts of the world have proved that the problem is insoluble by

force of any sort. The same history shows that it is soluble by the patient processes of community experience. Such problems lie naturally in the field of legislation, a method susceptible of experimentation, of development, of adjustment to the current necessities in a variety of community circumstance. We do not believe that the makers of the first ten Amendments in 1789 or of the Fourteenth Amendment in 1866 meant to foreclose legislative treatment of the problem in this country.

"This is not to decry efforts to reach that state of common existence which is the obvious highest good in our concept of civilization. It is merely to say that the social and economic interrelationship of two races living together is a legislative problem, as yet not solved, and is not a problem solved fully, finally and unequivocally by a fiat enacted many years ago. We must remember that on this particular point we are interpreting a constitution and not enacting a statute.

"We are not unmindful of the debates which occurred in Congress relative to the Civil Rights Act of April 9, 1866, the Fourteenth Amendment, and the Civil Rights Act of March 1, 1875. But the actions of Congress, the discussion in the Civil Rights cases, and the fact that in 1862, 1864, 1866 and 1874, as we shall point out in a moment, enacted legislation which specifically provided for separation of the races in the schools of the District of Columbia, conclusively support our view of the Amendment and its effect.

Plaintiffs rely upon expressions contained in opinions relating to professional education such as *Sweatt v. Painter*, [and] *McLaurin v. Oklahoma State Regents*, . . .

The problem of segregation as applied to graduate and professional education is essentially different from that involved in segregation in education at the lower levels. In the graduate and professional schools the problem is one of affording equal educational facilities to persons sui juris and of mature personality. Because of the great expense of such education and the importance of the professional contacts established while carrying on the educational process, it is difficult for the state to maintain segregated schools for Negroes in this field which will afford them opportunities for education and professional advancement equal to those afforded by the graduate and professional schools maintained for white persons. What the courts have said, and all they have said in the cases upon which plaintiffs rely is that, notwithstanding these difficulties, the opportunity afforded the Negro student must be equal to that afforded the white student and that the schools established for furnishing this instruction to white persons must be opened to Negroes if this is necessary to give them the equal opportunity which the Constitution requires.

The problem of segregation at the common school level is a very different one. At this level, as good education can be afforded in Negro schools as in white schools and the thought of establishing professional contacts does not enter into the picture. Moreover, education at this level is not a matter of voluntary choice on the part of the student but of compulsion by the state. The student is taken from the control of the family during school hours by compulsion of law and placed in control of the school, where he must associate with his fellow students. The law thus provides that the school shall supplement the work of the parent in the training of the child and in doing so it is entering a delicate field and one fraught with tensions and difficulties. In formulating educational policy at the common school level, therefore, the law must take account, not merely of the matter of affording instruction to the student, but also of the wishes of the parent as to the upbringing of the child and his associates in the formative period of childhood and adolescence. If public education is to have the support of the people through their legislatures, it must not go contrary to what they deem for the best interests of their children.

There is testimony to the effect that mixed schools will give better education and a better understanding of the community in which the child is to live than segregated schools. There is testimony, on the other hand, that mixed schools will result in racial friction and tension and that the only practical way of conducting public education in South Carolina is with segregated schools. The questions thus presented are not questions of constitutional right but of legislative policy, which must be formulated, not in vacuo or with doctrinaire disregard of existing conditions, but in realistic approach to the situations to which it is to be applied. In some states, the legislatures may well decide that segregation in public schools should be abolished, in others that it should be maintained—all depending upon the relationships existing between the races and the tensions likely to be produced by an attempt to educate the children of the two races together in the same schools. The federal courts would be going far outside their constitutional function were they to attempt to prescribe educational policies for the states in such matters, however, desirable such policies might be in the opinion of some sociologists or educators. For the federal courts to do so would result, not only in interference with local affairs by an agency of the federal government, but also in the substitution of the judicial for the legislative process in what is essentially a legislative matter.

. . .

We conclude, therefore, that if equal facilities are offered, segregation of the races in the public schools as prescribed by the Constitution and laws of South Carolina is not of itself violative of the Fourteenth Amendment. We think that this conclusion is supported by overwhelming authority which we are not at liberty to disregard on the basis of theories advanced by a few educators and sociologists. Even if we felt at liberty to disregard other authorities, we may not ignore the unreversed decisions of the Supreme Court of the United States which are squarely on point and conclusive of the question before us. . . .

To this we may add that, when seventeen states and the Congress of the United States have for more than three-quarters of a century required segregation of the races in the public schools, and when this has received the approval of the leading appellate courts of the country including the unanimous approval of the Supreme Court of the United States at a time when that court included Chief Justice Taft and Justices Stone, Holmes and Brandeis, it is a late day to say that such segregation is violative of fundamental constitutional rights. It is hardly reasonable to suppose that legislative bodies over so wide a territory, including the Congress of the United States, and great judges of high courts have knowingly defied the Constitution for so long a period or that they have acted in ignorance of the meaning of its provisions. The constitutional principle is the same now that it has been throughout this period; and if conditions have changed so that segregation is no longer wise, this is a matter for the legislatures and not for the courts. The members of the judiciary have no more right to read their ideas of sociology into the Constitution than their ideas of economics.

. . .

WARING, District Judge (dissenting).

This case has been brought for the express and declared purpose of determining the right of the State of South Carolina, in its public schools, to practice segregation according to race.

The case came on for a trial upon the issues as presented in the complaint and answer. But upon the call of the case, defendants' counsel announced that they wished to make a statement on behalf of the defendants making certain admissions and praying that the Court make a finding as to inequalities in respect to buildings, equipment, facilities, curricula and other aspects of the schools provided for children in School District 22 in Clarendon county and giving the public authorities time to formulate plans for ending such inequalities. In this statement defendants claim that they never had intended to discriminate against any of the pupils and although they had filed an answer to the complaint, some five months ago, denying inequalities they now admit that they had found some; but rely upon the fact that subsequent to the institution of this suit, James F. Byrnes, the Governor of South Carolina, had stated in his inaugural address that the State must take steps to provide money for improving educational facilities and that thereafter, the legislature had adopted certain legislation. They stated that they hoped that in time they would obtain money as a result of the foregoing and improve the school situation.

This statement was allowed to be filed and considered as an amendment to the answer.

By this maneuver, the defendants have endeavored to induce this Court to avoid the primary purpose of the suit. And if the Court should follow this suggestion and fail to meet the issues raised by merely considering this case in the light of another "separate but equal" case, the entire purpose and reason for the institution of the case and the convening of a three-judge court would be voided. The 66 plaintiffs in this cause have brought this suit at what must have cost much in effort and financial expenditures. They are here represented by 6 attorneys, all, save one, practicing lawyers from without the State of South Carolina and coming here from a considerable distance. The plaintiffs have brought a large number of witnesses exclusive of themselves. As a matter of fact, they called and examined 11 witnesses. They said that they had a number more coming who did not arrive in time owing to the shortening of the proceedings and they also stated that they had on hand and had contemplated calling a large number of other witnesses but this became unnecessary by reason of the foregoing admissions by defendants. It certainly appears that large expenses must have been caused by the institution of this case and great efforts expended in gathering data, making a study of the issues involved, interviewing and bringing numerous witnesses, some of whom are foremost scientists in America. And in addition to all of this, these 66 plaintiffs have not merely expended their time and money in order to test this important Constitutional question, but they have shown unexampled courage in bringing and presenting this cause at their own expense in the face of the long established and age-old pattern of the way of life which the State of South Carolina has adopted and practiced and lived in since and as a result of the institution of human slavery.

If a case of this magnitude can be turned aside and a court refuse to hear these basic issues by the mere device of admission that some buildings, blackboards, lighting fixtures and toilet facilities are unequal but that they may be remedied by the spending of a few dollars then, indeed people in the plight in which these plaintiffs are, have no adequate remedy or forum in which to air their wrongs. If this method of judicial evasion be adopted, these very infant plaintiffs now pupils in Clarendon County will probably be bringing suits for their children and grandchildren decades or rather generations hence in an effort to get for their descendants what are today denied to them. If they are entitled to any rights as American citizens, they are entitled to have these rights now and not in the future. And no excuse can be made to deny them these rights which are theirs under the Constitution and laws of America by the use of the false doctrine and patter called "separate but equal" and it is the duty of the Court to meet these issues simply and factually and without fear, sophistry and evasion. If this be the measure of justice to be meted out to them, then, indeed, hundred, nay thousands, of cases will have to be brought and in each case thousands of dollars will have to be spent for the employment of legal talent and scientific testimony and then the cases will be turned aside, postponed or eliminated by devices such as this.

We should be unwilling to straddle or avoid this issue and if the suggestion made by these defendants is to be adopted as the type of justice to be meted out by this Court, then I want no part of it.

. . .

Let us now come to consider whether the Constitution and Laws of the State of South Carolina which we have heretofore quoted are in conflict with the true meaning and intendment of this Fourteenth Amendment. The whole discussion of race and ancestry has been intermingled with sophistry and prejudice. What possible definition can be found for the so-called white race, Negro race or other races? Who is to decide and what is the test? For years, there was much talk of blood and taint of blood. Science tells us that there are but four kinds of blood: A, B, AB and O and these are found in Europeans, Asiatics, Africans, Americans and others. And so we need not further consider the irresponsible and baseless references to preservation of "Caucasian blood." So then, what test are we going to use in opening our school doors and labeling them "white" and "Negro"? The law of South Carolina considers a person of one-eighth African ancestry to be a Negro. Why this proportion? Is it based upon any reason: anthropological, historical or ethical? And how are the trustees to know who are "whites" and who are "Negroes"? If it is dangerous and evil for a white child to be associated with another child, one of whose great-grandparents was of African descent, is it not equally dangerous for one with a one-sixteenth percentage? And if the State has decided that there is danger in contact between the whites and Negroes, isn't it requisite and proper that the State furnish a series of schools one for each of these percentages? If the idea is perfect racial equality in educational systems, why should children of pure African descent be brought in contact with children of one-half, one-fourth, or one-eighth such ancestry? To ask these questions is sufficient answer to them. The whole thing is unreasonable, unscientific and based upon unadulterated prejudice. We see the results of all of this warped thinking in the poor under-privileged and frightened attitude of so many of the Negroes in the southern states; and in the sadistic insistence of the "white supremacists" in declaring that their will must be imposed irrespective of rights of other citizens. This claim of "white supremacy," while fantastic and without foundation, is rally believed by them for we have had repeated declarations from leading politicians and governors of this state and other states declaring that "white supremacy" will be endangered by the abolition of segregation. There are present threats, including those of the present Governor of this state, going to the extent of saying that all public education may be abandoned if the courts should grant true equality in educational facilities. . . . There is absolutely no reasonable explanation for racial prejudice. It is all caused by unreasoning emotional reactions and these are gained in early childhood. Let the little child's mind be poisoned by prejudice of this kind and it is practically impossible to ever remove these impressions however many years he may have of teaching by philosophers, religious leaders or patriotic citizens. If segregation is wrong then the place to stop it is in the first grade and not in graduate colleges. *Segregation is per se inequality.*

As heretofore shown, the courts of this land have stricken down discrimination in higher education and have declared unequivocally that segregation is not equality. But these decisions have pruned away only the noxious fruits. Here in this case, we are asked to strike its very root. Or rather, to change the metaphor, we are asked to strike at the cause of infection and not merely at the symptoms of disease. And if the courts of this land are to render justice under the laws without fear or favor, justice for all men and all kinds of men, the time to do it is now and the place is in the elementary schools where our future citizens learn their first lesson to respect the dignity of the individual in a democracy.

To me the situation is clear and important, particularly at this time when our national leaders are called upon to show to the world that our democracy means what it says and that it is a true democracy and there is no under-cover suppression of the rights of any of our citizens because of the pigmentation of their skins. And I had hoped that this Court would take this view of the situation and make a clear cut declaration that the State of South Carolina should follow the intendment and meaning of the Constitution of the United States and that it shall not abridge the privileges accorded to or deny equal protection of its laws to any of its citizens. But since the majority of this Court feel otherwise, and since I cannot concur with them or join in the proposed decree, this opinion is filed as a dissent.

5. The Desegregation Principle

Judge Waring's dissenting characterization of segregation as *"per se* inequality," in *Briggs*, previewed the Supreme Court's determination in *Brown v. Board of Education* that "(s)eparate educational facilities are inherently unequal."[118] Following initial argument in its 1952 term, the Court requested reargument the following year on the intent of the Fourteenth Amendment's framers. Relevant historical context included a contemporaneous congressional decision to segregate public schools in the District of Columbia and the operation of racially separate educational systems in many ratifying states.[119] The *Brown* Court, however, concluded that history was unrevealing for purposes of resolving the constitutional question in 1954.

---

[118] Brown v. Board of Education, 347 U.S. 483, 495 (1954).
[119] DONALD E. LIVELY, THE CONSTITUTION AND RACE 47, 89 (1992).

Brown v. Board of Education
347 U.S. 483 (1954)

MR. CHIEF JUSTICE WARREN delivered the opinion of the Court.

These cases come to us from the States of Kansas, South Carolina, Virginia, and Delaware. They are premised on different facts and different local conditions, but a common legal question justifies their consideration together in this consolidated opinion.

In each of the cases, minors of the Negro race, through their legal representatives, seek the aid of the courts in obtaining admission to the public schools of their community on a non-segregated basis. In each instance, they had been denied admission to schools attended by white children under laws requiring or permitting segregation according to race. This segregation was alleged to deprive the plaintiffs of the equal protection of the laws under the Fourteenth Amendment. In each of the cases other than the Delaware case, a three-judge federal district court denied relief to the plaintiffs on the so-called "separate but equal" doctrine announced by this Court in *Plessy v. Ferguson*, 103 U.S. 537. Under that doctrine, equality of treatment is accorded when the races are provided substantially equal facilities, even though these facilities be separate. In the Delaware case, the Supreme Court of Delaware adhered to that doctrine, but ordered that the plaintiffs be admitted to the white schools because of their superiority to the Negro schools.

The plaintiffs contend that segregated public schools are not "equal" and cannot be made "equal," and that hence they are deprived of the equal protection of the laws. Because of the obvious importance of the question presented, the Court took jurisdiction. Argument was heard in the 1952 Term, and reargument was heard this Term on certain questions propounded by the Court.

Reargument was largely devoted to the circumstances surrounding the adoption of the Fourteenth Amendment in 1868, It covered exhaustively consideration of the Amendment in Congress, ratification by the states, then existing practices in racial segregation, and the views of proponents and opponents of the Amendment. This discussion and our own investigation convince us that, although these sources cast some light, it is not enough to resolve the problem with which we are faced. At best, they are inconclusive. The most avid proponents of the post-War Amendments undoubtedly intended them to remove all legal distinctions among "all persons born or naturalized in the United States. Their opponents, just as certainly, were antagonistic to both the letter and the spirit of the Amendments and

wished them to have the most limited effect. What others in Congress and the state legislatures had in mind cannot be determined with any degree of certainly.

An additional reason for the inconclusive nature of the Amendment's history, with respect to segregated sensors, is the status of public education at that time. In the South, the movement toward free common schools, supported by general taxation, had not yet taken hold. Education of white children was largely in the hands of private groups. Education of Negroes was almost non-existent, and practically all of the race were illiterate. In fact, any education of Negroes was forbidden by law in some states. Today, in contrast, many Negroes have achieved outstanding success in the arts and sciences as well as in the business and professional world. It is true that public school education at the time of the Amendment had advanced further in the North, but the effect of the Amendment on Northern States was generally ignored in the congressional debates. Even in the North, the conditions of public education did not approximate those existing today. The curriculum was usually rudimentary; ungraded schools were common in rural areas; the school term was but three months a year in many states; and compulsory school attendance was virtually unknown. As a consequence, it is not surprising that there should be so little in the history of the Fourteenth Amendment relating to its intended effect on public education. . . .

In approaching this problem, we cannot turn the clock back to 1868 when the Amendment was adopted, or even to 1800 when Plessy v. *Ferguson* was written. We must consider public education in the light of its full development and its present place in American life throughout the Nation. Only in this way can it be determined if segregation in public schools deprives these plaintiffs of the equal protection of the laws.

Today, education is perhaps the most important function of state and local governments. Compulsory school attendance laws and the great expenditures for education both demonstrate our recognition of the importance of education to our democratic society. It is required in the performance of our most basic public responsibilities, even service in the armed forces. It is the very foundation of good citizenship. Today it is a principal instrument in awakening the child to cultural values, in preparing him for later professional training, and in helping him to adjust normally to his environment. In these days, it is doubtful that any child may reasonably be expected to succeed in life if he is denied the opportunity of an education. Such an opportunity, where the state has undertaken to provide it, is a right which must be made available to all on equal terms.

We come then to the question presented: Does segregation of children in public schools solely on the basis of race, even though the physical facilities and other "tangible" factors may be equal, deprive the children of a minority group of equal educational opportunities? We believe that it does. ... Such considerations apply with added force to children in grade and high schools. To separate them from others of similar age and qualifications solely because of their race generates a feeling of inferiority as to their status in the community that may affect their hearts and minds in a way unlikely ever to be undone. The effect of this separation on their educational opportunities was well stated by a finding in the Kansas case by a court which nevertheless felt compelled to rule against the Negro plaintiffs:

"Segregation of white and colored children in public schools has a detrimental effect upon the colored children. The impact is greater when it has the sanction of the law; for the policy of separating the races is usually interpreted as denoting the inferiority of the Negro group. A sense of inferiority affects the activation of a child to learn. Segregation with the sanction of law, therefore, has a tendency to [retard] the educational and mental development of Negro children and to deprive them of some of the benefits they would receive in a racially integrated school system."

Whatever may have been the extent of psychological knowledge at the time of *Plessy v. Fergu-son*, this finding is amply supported by modern authority. Any language in *Plessy v. Ferguson* contrary to this finding is rejected.

We conclude that in the field of public education the doctrine of "separate but equal" has no place. Separate educational facilities are inherently unequal. Therefore, we hold that the plaintiffs and others similarly situated for whom the actions have been brought are, by reason of the segregation complained of, deprived of the equal protection of the laws guaranteed by the Fourteenth Amendment. This disposition makes unnecessary any discussion whether such segregation also violates the Due Process Clause of the Fourteenth Amendment.

Because these are class actions, because of the wide applicability of this decision, and because of the great variety of local conditions, the formulation of decrees in these cases presents problems of considerable complexity. On reargument, the consideration of appropriate relief was necessarily subordinated to the primary question—the constitutionality of segregation in public education. We have now announced that such segregation is a denial of the equal protection of the laws. In order that we may have the full assistance of the parties in formulating decrees, the cases will be restored to the docket, and the parties are requested to present further argument on Questions 4 and 5 previously propounded by the Court for the reargument this Term. The Attorney General of the United States is again invited to participate. The Attorneys General of the states requiring or permitting segregation in public education will also be permitted to appear as *amici curiae* upon request to do so by September 15, 1954, and submission of briefs by October 1, 1954.

DEL: It is not an exaggeration to refer to the *Brown* decision as a primary constitutional landmark. Although the ruling is a source of endless discussion, an especially intriguing aspect of the decision is the challenge it has presented to interpretivists. For all of his insistence upon strict constitutional color-blindness, for instance, Justice Scalia makes an exception for race-conscious desegregative relief to the extent a Fourteenth Amendment violation is established. Robert Bork has argued that the choice in 1954 was between desegregation, which was disfavored by the Fourteenth Amendment's framers, and abandonment of the equal protection guarantee altogether. Given the options, Bork claims that he is satisfied that the Court made the right choice. Reality is that, if the framers disfavored racially mixed schools, the principled originalist position should be that *Brown* was wrong. To the extent that discrimination was prohibited in those areas of concern to the framers, namely with respect to economic liberty and standing before the courts, the equal protection clause would still operate albeit in conformance with the relatively narrow focus of its originators. It may be that *Brown* can be criticized on grounds that it stigmatizes in its own way, by suggesting that the self-esteem of nonwhite students depends upon their acceptance by and acceptability to white students. The decision also might be questioned on grounds that it put all equal protection eggs in the desegregation basket and wrongly assumed that future decisions would stick with its premises against all odds and resistance. Insofar as desegregation demands have wound down and segregation persists, without any constitutional significance, it may be that the Court traded away too much when it abandoned the doctrine not only of separate but of equal. Those whose ideology logically should beget criticism of *Brown* have been notably shy in expressing themselves and have engaged in major intellectual gymnastics to rationalize it. The ultimate fate of *Brown*, if not the decision itself, should be a primary illuminating agent for the elementary interpretivist concern with the risk of accelerating the law beyond the state of moral development.

DER: The law is generally conservative, responding to social movements rather than leading them. The *Brown* decision could not have occurred had legal advocates, social activists, and international scrutiny not prevailed upon the moral conscience of the nation. On the other hand, judicial inaction for fear of "accelerating the law beyond the state of moral development" merely aids in the perpetuation of racial inequality. The Court would have betrayed the Constitution had it upheld segregation on the ground that whites were morally unprepared for equality in schooling. The *Brown* decision stands as a landmark in constitutional jurisprudence because it attempted to give substance to the Fourteenth Amendment command of racial equality in the face of conflicting social convention. It also recognized the injury inflicted by the message of racial subordination: segregated education defined Blacks as inferior and excluded them from social participation. But the Court mischaracterized the injury inflicted by racial separation by focusing on its psychological harm to Black school children rather than its institutional function. The breakdown of school desegregation efforts evidences not only a failure of will, but also the inadequacy of an integrationist remedy. Fifty years after *Brown*, American schools remain largely segregated, with stark disparities between suburban and inner-city schools. Despite decades of court challenges, per-pupil spending in San Antonio, Texas, for example, ranges from $2000 in the poorest districts to $19,000 in the richest.[120] An alternative educational policy emphasizes Black citizens' control over their own school funds and administration rather than simple reassignment of pupils, teachers, and administrators. Challenging present school financing schemes that help to create unequal educational opportunities would also be a more fruitful strategy.[121] Moreover, since current de facto segregation results largely from neighborhood segregation the former will disappear only through a national commitment to fair housing—a task far more monumental than bussing students between school districts. That the Court has been unwilling to mandate measures that would more effectively promote equality in schooling lends support to Derrick Bell's "interest convergence" thesis: "The interest of blacks in achieving racial equality will be accommodated only when it converges with the interests of whites" and does not significantly threaten white supremacy.[122]

PAH: In addition to its pronouncemant that "separate but equal is inherently unequal," *Brown* emphasized the importance of education in attaining equal citizenship. Read with

---

[120] Jonathan Kozol, Savage Inequalities: Children in America's Schools 223 (1991).

[121] The Supreme Court has upheld school financing schemes based on local property taxes that help to create gross disparities among schools. *See* San Antonio Indep. Sch. Dist. v. Rodriguez, 411 U.S. 1, 55 (1973) (holding that the Texas school-financing system did not violate the equal protection clause). State constitutions may provide a stronger claim to equal education. *See, e.g.*, Abbott v. Burke, 575 A.2d 359, 408–410 (1990) (striking down New Jersey school-aid formula as a violation of the state constitution and mandating increased funding for poor districts).

[122] Derrick Bell, *Brown and the Interest-Convergence Dilemma*, in Shades of Brown: New Perspectives on School Desegregation 91, 95 (Derrick Bell ed., 1980).

this in mind, the evil of segregation lies in its unreasonable—caste-maintaining—restriction on a fundamental liberty, basic to citizenship-building.[123] This is a reading, by the way, consistent with the dissent of Justice Harlan in *Plessy* as well as the Court's opinion in *Bolling v. Sharpe* which follows. Because the Court in *Brown* drew upon the social science data demonstrating the psychological damage to Black children who experienced segregated schooling to prove the constitutional violation, and did not recognize the benefits of a diverse environment to whites, however, it left open the implication of superiority of the white race (as did Justice Harlan in the dissent in *Plessy*).[124]

The focus on a color-blind meaning of equal protection and subsequent refusal of courts following the Warren Court era to recognize fundamental rights and interests—including education, recognized as the lynchpin of good citizenship—have created confusion about what were the promises of *Brown* and the goals of the civil rights movement that followed. For many whites—conservative and liberal—the notion of a color-blind society is attractive because it responds to the individual's interest in autonomy and agency; it also fosters a sense of community, a sense of group membership in the body politic recognized in "We the People," by eliminating the race-based barrier to it.[125] It also seems consistent with Dr. Martin Luther King's invitation to create a world where you are judged by your character and not the color of your skin, and the civil rights movement model of a diverse group of individuals hand-in-hand fighting the evil of state-sanctioned segregation personified by Bull Connor's attacking police dogs.

The reality is, however, that most Blacks continue to experience group-based racism, if not isolation, in schools and work and living arrangements and thus equal justice and respect has not been attained by the elimination of explicit Jim Crow. The social reality of inequality makes the individualistic and communitarian reasons for promoting color-blindness unattractive to some African Americans and other minorities who view themselves as victims of group-based discrimination.

For many Blacks, the Court's motivation in refusing to recognize that the Equal Protection clause requires a legal response to persistent social inequality is questionable. The Court's continued references in *Brown* and its progeny of the inherent inequality of separate schools and other institutions while rejecting the use of race-focused tools for eliminating racial isolation and its effects seems to condemn blacks to second-class status and promotes disrespect, not equality. Thus the Court's reticence suggests willingness to participate in perpetuating exclusion—by choice, abandoning its role as protector of minority interests, particularly under the Equal Protection clause.

---

[123] This reading draws upon the re-interpretation of the Plessy dissent urged by T. Alexander Aleinokoff in Re-reading Plessy, supra.

[124] See 1992 Ill. L. Rev. at 972 &n. 48 (noting parallels between Brown and Justice Harlan's dissent in Plessy.)

[125] For a fuller discussion of trhe idividualistic and communitarian approaches to racial difference, see, e.g., Adeno Addis, In Defense of Crookedness, 1992 U. Ill. L. Rev. 947, 952–53.

The challenge to prescriptive segregation of public education in *Brown* succeeded on equal protection grounds. Racially separate schools in the District of Columbia, however, were contested on Fifth Amendment rather than Fourteenth Amendment grounds. Notwithstanding the textual absence of an equal protection guarantee in the Fifth Amendment, the Court effectively read such a provision into the due process clause.

Bolling v. Sharpe
347 U.S. 497 (1954)

MR. CHIEF JUSTICE WARREN delivered the opinion of the Court.

. . .

We have this day held that the Equal Protection Clause of the Fourteenth Amendment prohibits the states from maintaining racially segregated public schools. The legal problem in the District of Columbia is somewhat different, however. The Fifth Amendment, which is applicable in the District of Columbia, does not contain an equal protection clause as does the Fourteenth Amendment which applies only to the states. But the concepts of equal protection and due process, both stemming from our American ideal of fairness, are not mutually exclusive. The "equal protection of the laws" is a more explicit safeguard of prohibited unfairness than "due process of law," and, therefore, we do not imply that the two are always interchangeable phrases. But, as this Court has recognized, discrimination may be so unjustifiable as to be violative of due process.

Classifications based solely upon race must be scrutinized with particular care, since they are contrary to our traditions and hence constitutionally suspect. As long ago as 1896, this Court declared the principle "that the Constitution of the United States, in its present form forbids, so far as civil and political rights are concerned discrimination by the General Government, or by the States, against any citizen because of his race." And in *Buchanan v. Warley*, 245 U.S. 60, the Court held that a statute which limited the right of a property owner to convey his property to a person of another race was, as an unreasonable discrimination, a denial of due process of law.

Although the Court has not assumed to define "liberty with any great precision, that term is not confined to mere freedom from bodily restraint. Liberty under law extends to the full range of conduct which the individual is free to pursue, and it cannot be restricted except for a proper governmental objective. Segregation in public education is not reasonably related to any proper governmental objective, and thus it imposes on Negro children of the District of Columbia a burden that constitutes an arbitrary deprivation of their liberty in violation of the Due Process Clause.

In view of our decision that the Constitution prohibits the states from maintaining racially segregated public schools, it would be unthinkable that the same Constitution would impose a lesser duty on the Federal Government. We hold that racial segregation in the public schools of the District of Columbia is a denial of the due process of law guaranteed by the Fifth Amendment to the Constitution. . . .

The determination that official segregation in education violated the Constitution was as electric a decision in its own way as the *Dred Scott* decision a century prior. Both the *Brown* and *Dred Scott* Courts were confronted with the same problem of achieving compliance from the political branches and the public. To defuse anticipated resistance, the *Brown* Court invited affected states to provide input on how relief should be framed. In formulating relief a year later, the Court attempted to balance the interests of plaintiffs in obtaining prompt relief and of the public in a well-conceived restructuring of the educational order.

Brown v. Board of Education
349 U.S. 294 (1955)

MR CHIEF JUSTICE WARREN delivered the opinion of the Court.

These cases were decided on May 17, 1954. The opinions of that date, declaring the fundamental principle that racial discrimination in public education is unconstitutional, are incorporated herein by reference. All provisions to federal, state, or local law requiring or permit-ting such discrimination must yield to this principle. There remains for consideration the manner in which relief is to be accorded.

Full implementation of these constitutional principles may require solution of varied local school problems. School authorities have the primary responsibility for educating, assessing, and solving these problems; courts will have to consider whether the action of school authorities constitutes good faith implementation of the governing constitutional principles. Because of their proximity to local conditions and the possible need for further hearings, the courts which originally heard these cases can best perform this judicial appraisal. Accordingly, we believe it appropriate to remand the cases to those courts.

In fashioning and effectuating the decrees, the courts will be guided by equitable principles. Traditionally, equity has been characterized by a practical flexibility in shaping its remedies and by a facility for adjusting and reconciling public and private needs. These cases call for the exercise of these traditional attributes of equity power. At stake is the personal interest of the plaintiffs in admission to public schools as soon as practicable on a nondiscriminatory basis. To effectuate this interest may call for elimination of a variety of obstacles in making the transition to school systems operated in accordance with the constitutional principles act forth in our May 17, 1954, decision. Courts of equity may properly take into account the public interest in the elimination of such obstacles in a systematic and effective manner. But it should go without saying that the vitality of these constitutional

principles cannot be allowed to yield simply because of disagreement with them.

While giving weight to these public and private considerations, the courts will require that the defendants make a prompt and reasonable start toward full compliance with our May 17, 1954, ruling. Once such a start has been made, the courts may find that additional time is necessary to carry out the ruling in an effective manner. The burden rests upon the defendants to establish that such time is necessary in the public interest and is consistent with good faith compliance at the earliest practicable date. To that end, the courts may consider problems related to administration, arising from the physical condition of the school plant, the school transportation system, personnel, revision of school districts and attendance areas into compact units to achieve a system of determining admission to the public schools on a nonracial basis, and revision of local laws and regulations which may be necessary in solving the foregoing problems. They will also consider the adequacy of any plans the defendants may propose to meet these problems and to effectuate a transition to a racially nondiscriminatory school system. During this period of transition, the courts will retain jurisdiction of these cases.

. . .

As anticipated by the Court, implementation would be effected through and monitored primarily by local federal courts that would factor the idiosyncrasies of diverse communities into orders that would achieve desegregation "with all deliberate speed." Response to the desegregation mandate, however, was characterized by widespread evasion, resistance and delay. Facilitating maintenance of the status quo were lower court decisions that read the *Brown* mandate in especially cramped terms. On remand, for instance, the district court in *Briggs v. Elliott* determined that neither the Constitution nor the Supreme Court required action beyond a formal change in the law.

Briggs v. Elliott
132 F. Supp. 776 (E.D.S.C. 1955)

PER CURIAM.

. . .

Whatever may have been the views of this court as to the law when the case was originally before us, it is our duty now to accept the law as declared by the Supreme Court.

Having said this, it is important that we point out exactly what the Supreme Court has decided and what it has not decided in this case. It has not decided that the federal courts are to take over or regulate the public schools of the states. It has not decided that the states

must mix persons of different races in the schools or must require them to attend schools or must deprive them of the right of choosing the schools they attend. What it has decided, and all that it has decided, is that a state may not deny to any person on account of race the right to attend any school that it maintains. This, under the decision of the Supreme Court, the state may not do directly or indirectly; but if the schools which it maintains are open to children of all races, no violation of the Constitution is involved even though the children of different races voluntarily attend different schools, as they attend different churches. Nothing in the Constitution or in the decision of the Supreme Court takes away from the people freedom to choose the schools they attend. The Constitution, in other words, does not require integration. It merely forbids discrimination. It does not forbid such segregation as occurs as the result of voluntary action. It merely forbids the use of governmental power to enforce segregation. The Fourteenth Amendment is a limitation upon the exercise of power by the state or state agencies, not a limitation upon the freedom of individuals. . . .

a. The First Decade of *Brown*: Evasion, Resistance and Delay

The legacy of *Brown* during its first decade was one of practical nonachievement. Ten years after the initial *Brown* decision, only two percent of African-American students in the South attended schools where white students exceeded their numbers.[126] Such results were facilitated by a combination of inaction, half-hearted effort and outright resistance. The first desegregation case to reach the Court was significant not only for its challenge to the *Brown* mandate but to the power of the judiciary. In *Cooper v. Aaron*, the Court heard a request by a local school board to delay implementation of its desegregation plan because of profound tension and conflict within the community. A significant dimension of the case was a state law, relieving students from having to attend racially mixed schools, enacted pursuant to a constitutional amendment prioritizing legislative judgment over "the Unconstitutional desegregation decisions . . . of the United States Supreme Court."[127] Notwithstanding the disruptive circumstances, and consequent fallout for the educational process, the Court refused to have the desegregation held hostage to official agitation.

---

[126] BUREAU OF THE CENSUS, U.S. DEPT. OF COMMERCE, STATISTICAL ABSTRACT OF THE UNITED STATES 124 (1974).

[127] Cooper v. Aaron, 358 U.S. 1, 8–9 (1957)(quoting Ark. Const. amend. 44).

Cooper v. Aaron
358 U.S. 1 (1958)

Opinion of the Court by THE CHIEF JUSTICE, MR. JUSTICE BLACK, MR. JUSTICE FRANKFURTER, MR. JUSTICE DOUGLAS, MR. JUSTICE BURTON, MR. JUSTICE CLARK, MR. JUSTICE HARLAN, MR. JUSTICE BRENNAN, and MR.JUSTICE WHITTAKER.

. . .

While the School Board was . . . going forward with its preparation for desegregating the Little Rock school system, other state authorities, in contrast, were actively pursuing a program designed to perpetuate in Arkansas the system of racial segregation which this Court had held violated the Fourteenth Amendment. First came, in November 1956, an amendment to the State Constitution flatly commanding the Arkansas General Assembly to oppose "in every Constitutional manner the Unconstitutional desegregation decisions of May 17, 1954 and May 31, 1955 of the United States Supreme Court," Ark. Const., Amend. 44, and, through the initiative, a pupil assignment law, Ark. Stat. 80-1519 to 80-1524. Pursuant to this state constitutional command, a law relieving school children from compulsory attendance at racially mixed schools, Ark. Stat. 80-1525, and a law establishing a State Sovereignty Commission, Ark. Stat. 6-801 to 6-824, were enacted by the General Assembly in February 1957.

On September 2, 1957, the day before . . . Negro students were to enter Central High, the school authorities were met with drastic opposing action on the part of the Governor of Arkansas who dispatched units of the Arkansas National Guard to the Central High School grounds and placed the school "off limits" to colored students. . . .

The Board's petition for postponement in this proceeding states: "The effect of that action [of the Governor] was to harden the core of opposition to the Plan and cause many persons who theretofore had reluctantly accepted the Plan to believe there was some power in the State of Arkansas which, when exerted, could nullify the Federal law and permit disobedience of the decree of this [District] Court, and from that date hostility to the Plan was increased and criticism of the officials of the [School] District has become more bitter and unrestrained." The Governor's action caused the School Board to request the Negro students on September 2 not to attend the high school "until the legal dilemma was solved." The next day, September 3, 1957, the Board petitioned the District Court for instructions, and the court, after a hearing, found that the Board's request of the Negro students to stay away from the high school had been made because of the stationing of the military guards by the state authorities. The court determined that this was not a reason for departing from the approved plan, and ordered the School Board and Superintendent to proceed with it.

On the morning of the next day, September 4, 1957, the Negro children attempted to enter the high school but, as the District Court later found, units of the Arkansas National Guard "acting pursuant to the Governor's order, stood shoulder to shoulder at the school grounds and thereby forcibly prevented the 9 Negro students . . . from entering," as they continued to do every school day during the following three weeks. . . . (T)he District Court found that the School Board's plan had been obstructed by the Governor through the use of National Guard troops, and granted a preliminary injunction on September 20, 1957, enjoining the Governor and the officers of the Guard from preventing the attendance of Negro children at Central High School, and from otherwise obstructing or interfering with the orders of the court in connection with the plan. The National Guard was then withdrawn from the school.

The next school day was Monday, September 23, 1957. The Negro children entered the high school that morning under the protection of the Little Rock Police Department and members of the Arkansas State Police. But the officers caused the children to be removed from the school during the morning because they had difficulty controlling a large and demonstrating crowd which had gathered at the high school. On September 25, however, the President of the United States dispatched federal troops to Central High School and admission of the Negro students to the school was thereby effected. Regular army troops continued at the high School until November 27, 1957. They were then replaced by federalized National Guardsmen who remained throughout the balance of the school year. Eight of the Negro students remained in attendance at the school throughout the school year.

We come now to the aspect of the proceedings presently before us. On February 20, 1958, the School Board and the Superintendent of Schools filed a petition in the District Court seeking a postponement of their program for desegregation. Their position in essence was that because of extreme public hostility, which they stated had been engendered largely by the official attitudes and action of the Governor and the Legislature, the maintenance of a sound educational program at Central High School, with the Negro students in attendance, would be impossible. The Board therefore proposed that the Negro students already admitted to the school be withdrawn and sent to segregated schools, and that all further steps to carry out the Board's desegregation program be postponed for a period later suggested by the Board to be two and one-half years.

After a hearing the District Court granted the relief requested by the Board. . . .

. . .

In affirming the judgment of the Court of Appeals which reversed the District Court we have accepted without reservation the position of the School Board, the Superintendent of Schools, and their counsel that they displayed entire good faith in the conduct of these proceedings and in dealing with the unfortunate and distressing sequence of events which has been outlined. We likewise have accepted the findings of the District Court as to the conditions at Central High School during the 1957-1958 school year, and also the findings that the educational progress of all the students, white and colored, of that school has suffered and will continue to suffer if the conditions which prevailed last year are permitted to continue.

The significance of these findings, however, is to be considered in light of the fact, indisputably revealed by the record before us, that the conditions they depict are directly traceable to the actions of legislators and executive officials of the State of Arkansas, taken in their official capacities, which reflect their own determination to resist this Court's decision in the Brown case and which have brought about violent resistance to that decision in Arkansas. . . .

One may well sympathize with the position of the Board in the face of the frustrating conditions which have confronted it, but, regardless of the Board's good faith, the actions of the other state agencies responsible for those conditions compel us to reject the Board's legal position. . . .

The constitutional rights of respondents are not to be sacrificed or yielded to the violence and disorder which have followed upon the actions of the Governor and Legislature. As this Court said some 41 years ago in a unanimous opinion in a case involving another aspect of racial segregation: "It is urged that this proposed segregation will promote the public peace by preventing race conflicts. Desirable as this is, and important as is the preservation of the public peace, this aim cannot be accomplished by laws or ordinances which deny rights created or protected by the Federal Constitution." *Buchanan v. Warley*, 245 U.S. 60, 81. Thus law and order are not here to be preserved by depriving the Negro children of their constitutional rights. . . .

The *Cooper* decision represented a significant doctrinal showdown between the Court and the state. Crucial to the outcome, and to the Court's authority, and the efficacy of its mandate, was support from the political branches of the federal government. Despite his reservations about the wisdom of the *Brown* decision itself, President Eisenhower's dispatch of federal troops to Little Rock to enforce desegregation provided essential backup for what otherwise would have been empty constitutional rhetoric.

The aftermath of *Cooper* on a broader level was not much different from what preceded it. Through the late 1960s, the Court persistently invalidated plans that fell short of compliance with or constituted an outright evasion of its mandate. Methods that failed to pass constitutional muster included desegregation of one school grade per year,[128] closure of the public school system coupled with subsidization of private schooling,[129] freedom of choice plans,[130] and partition[131] or subdivision[132] of school districts. Contributing to the slow pace of desegregation were not just intimidation, resistance, and underachievement but the resource disadvantage of potential plaintiffs. For the most part, desegregation was not achievable without a court order which required the identification and underwriting of plaintiffs who would bring the case and persist against the realities of intimidation and protracted appeals. The NAACP itself, as the primary agent of litigative change, was the target of state efforts to put it out of the desegregation business. In *NAACP v. Button*, the Court referenced the First Amendment to invalidate construction of a Virginia law which was the basis for a finding that the NAACP's activities constituted illegal solicitation of clients.[133]

b. Beyond "All Deliberate Speed"

The Court's mounting frustration with noncompliance prompted it to ratchet remedial standards upward. The second decade of the desegregation era thus commenced with a determination that "[t]he time for mere 'deliberate' speed has run out."[134] School systems not yet in compliance with the *Brown* mandate thus were directed to formulate a "plan that promises realistically to work, and promises realistically to work *now*."[135] Without additional leverage to achieve compliance, however, the higher standard would have been an exercise in rhetoric. Critical to meaningful progress was intervention of the political branches of the federal government on behalf of the desegregation mandate. Enforcement objectives were facilitated significantly by legislation that empowered the Department of Justice to bring desegregation lawsuits and the conditioning of federal funds for education upon compliance with the *Brown* mandate.[136] Through the late 1960s, the primary emphasis was upon immediate desegregative results.

---

[128] Rogers v. Paul, 382 U.S. 198 (1965).

[129] Griffin v. County School Board of Prince Edward County, 377 U.S. 218 (1964).

[130] Green v. County School Board of New Kent County, Virginia, 391 U.S. 430 (1968).

[131] United States v. Scotland Neck City Board of Education, 407 U.S. 484 (1972).

[132] Wright v. City Council of Emporia, 407 U.S. 451 (1972).

[133] NAACP v. Button, 371 U.S. 415 (1963).

[134] Griffin v. County School Board of Prince Edward County, 377 U.S. 218, 234 (1964).

[135] Green v. County School Board of New Kent County, Virginia, 391 U.S. at 439 (emphasis in original).

[136] DONALD E. LIVELY, THE CONSTITUTION AND RACE 116 (1992).

Green v. County School Board
of New Kent County, Virginia
391 U.S. 430 (1968)

MR. JUSTICE BRENNAN delivered the opinion of the Court.

The question for decision is whether, under all the circumstances here, respondent School Board's adoption of a 'freedom-of-choice' plan which allows a pupil to choose his own public school constitutes adequate compliance with the Board's responsibility 'to achieve a system of determining admission to the public schools on a non-racial basis.'

The segregated system was initially established and maintained under the compulsion of Virginia constitutional and statutory provisions mandating racial segregation in public education. The respondent School Board continued the segregated operation of the system after the *Brown* decisions, presumably on the authority of several statutes enacted by Virginia in resistance to those decisions. Some of these statutes were held to be unconstitutional on their face or as applied. One statute, the Pupil Placement Act, not repealed until 1966, divested local boards of authority to assign children to particular schools and placed that authority in a State Pupil Placement Board. Under that Act children were each year automatically reassigned to the school previously attended unless upon their application the State Board assigned them to another school; students seeking enrollment for the first time were also assigned at the discretion of the State Board. To September 1964, no Negro pupil had applied for admission to the New Kent school under this statute and no white pupil had applied for admission to the Watkins school. . . .

The School Board initially sought dismissal of this suit on the ground that petitioners had failed to apply to the State Board for assignment to New Kent school. However on August 2, 1965, five months after the suit was brought, respondent School Board, in order to remain eligible for federal financial aid, adopted a 'freedom-of-choice' plan for desegregating the schools. Under that plan, each pupil, except those entering the first and eighth grades, may annually choose between the New Kent and Watkins schools and pupils not making a choice are assigned to the school previously attended; first and eighth grade pupils must affirmatively choose a school. . . .

The pattern of separate 'white' and "Negro' schools in New Kent County school system established under compulsion of state laws is precisely the pattern of segregation to which *Brown I* and *Brown II* were particularly addressed, and which *Brown I* declared unconsti-

tutionally denied Negro school children equal protection of the laws. Racial identification of the system's schools was complete, extending not just to the composition of student bodies at the two schools but to every facet of school operations—faculty, staff, transportation, extracurricular activities and facilities. In short, the State, acting through the local school board and school officials, organized and operated a dual system, part 'white' and part 'Negro."

It was such dual systems that 14 years ago *Brown I* held unconstitutional and a year later *Brown II* 'to effectuate a transition to a racially nondiscriminatory school system." . . .

. . . The transition to a unitary, nonracial system of public education was and is the ultimate end to be brought about; it was because of the 'complexities arising from the transition to a system of public education freed of racial discrimination' that we provided for 'all deliberate speed' in the implementation of the principles of *Brown I*. Thus we recognized the task would necessarily involve solution of 'varied local school problems.' In referring to the 'personal interest of the plaintiffs in admission to public schools as soon as practicable on a nondiscriminatory basis,' we also noted that '(t)o effectuate this interest may call for elimination of a variety of obstacles in making the transition.' Yet we emphasized that the constitutional rights of Negro children required school officials to bear the burden of establishing that additional time to carry out the ruling in an effective manner' is necessary in the public interest and is consistent with good faith compliance at the earliest practicable date.' . . .

It is against this background that 13 years after *Brown II* commanded the abolition of dual systems we must measure the effectiveness of respondent School Board's 'freedom-of-choice' plan to achieve that end. The School Board contends that it has fully discharged its obligation by adopting a plan by which every student, regardless of race, may 'freely' choose the school he will attend. The Board attempts to cast the issue in its broadest form by arguing that its 'freedom-of-choice' plan may be faulted only by reading the Fourteenth Amendment as universally requiring 'compulsory integration,' a reading it insists the wording of the Amendment will not support. . . . In the context of the state-imposed segregated pattern of long standing, the fact that in 1965 the Board opened the doors of the former 'white' school to Negro children and of the 'Negro' school to white children merely begins, not ends, our inquiry whether the Board has taken steps adequate to abolish its dual, segregated system. *Brown II* was a call for the dismantling of well-entrenched dual systems tempered by an awareness that complex and multifaceted problems would arise which would require time and flexibility for a successful resolution. School boards such as the respondent then operating state-compelled dual systems were nevertheless clearly charged with the affirmative duty to take whatever steps might be necessary to convert to a unitary system in which racial discrimination would be eliminated root and branch. The constitutional rights of Negro school children articulated in *Brown I* permit no less than this; and it was to this end that *Brown II* commanded school boards to bend their efforts. In determining whether respondent School Board met that command by adopting its 'freedom-of-choice' plan, it is relevant that this first step did not come until some 11 years after *Brown I* was decided and 10 years after *Brown II* directed the making of a 'prompt

and reasonable start.' This deliberate perpetuation of the unconstitutional dual system can only have compounded the harm of such a system. Such delays are no longer tolerable, for 'the governing constitutional principles no longer bear the imprint of newly enunciated doctrine.' Moreover, a plan that at this late date fails to provide meaningful assurance of prompt and effective disestablishment of a dual system is also intolerable. 'The time for mere 'deliberate speed' has run out,' 'the context in which we must interpret and apply this language (of *Brown II*) to plans for desegregation has been significantly altered.' The burden on a school board today is to come forward with a plan that promises realistically to work, and promises realistically to work now.
... We do not hold that a 'freedom-of-choice' plan might of itself be unconstitutional, although that argument has been urged upon us. Rather, all we decide today is that in desegregating a dual system a plan utilizing 'freedom of choice' is not an end in itself ...

Consensus within the federal government regarding the nature and scope of desegregation remedies began to fracture toward the end of the 1960s. Concern with the demands of desegregation manifested itself as a primary issue in the 1968 presidential campaign. The independent candidacy of George Wallace was premised in significant part upon hostility to the *Brown* legacy. Richard Nixon's campaign included a promise to appoint personnel to the Court who would be less aggressive in selecting remedies such as busing to achieve desegregation. Both pitches had significant appeal beyond the South, where attention was being directed to segregated schools especially in major cities of the North and West. Against such a backdrop, the Court in *Swann v. Charlotte-Mecklenburg Board of Education* amplified the responsibilities of state officials and the judiciary's own power in achieving desegregation.

Swann v. Charlotte-Mecklenburg Board of Education
402 U.S. 1 (1970)

Mr. Chief Justice Burger delivered the opinion of the Court.
We granted certiorari in this case to review important issues as to the duties of school authorities and the scope of powers of federal courts under this Court's mandates to eliminate racially separate public schools established and maintained by state action. ...
Nearly 17 years ago this Court held, in explicit terms, that state-imposed segregation by race in public schools denies equal protection of the laws. At no time has the Court deviated in the slightest degree from that holding or its constitutional under-pinnings. ...
Over the 16 years since *Brown II*, many difficulties were encountered in implementa-

tion of the basic constitutional requirement that the State not discriminate between public school children on the basis of their race. Nothing in our national experience prior to 1955 prepared anyone for dealing with changes and adjustments of the magnitude and complexity encountered since then. Deliberate resistance of some to the Court's mandates has impeded the good-faith efforts of others to bring school systems into compliance. The detail and nature of these dilatory tactics have been noted frequently by this Court and other courts.
By the time the Court considered *Green v. County School Board* ... very little progress had been made in many areas where dual school systems had historically been main-

tained by operation of state laws. In *Green*, the Court was confronted with a record of a freedom-of-choice program that the District Court had found to operate in fact to preserve a dual system more than a decade after Brown II. While acknowledging that a freedom-of-choice concept could be a valid remedial measure in some circumstances, its failure to be effective in *Green* required that:

> "The burden on a school board today is to come forward with a plan that promises realistically to work ... *now* ... until it is clear that state-imposed segregation has been completely removed."

The problems encountered by the district courts and courts of appeals make plain that we should now try to amplify guidelines, however incomplete and imperfect, for the assistance of school authorities and courts. The failure of local authorities to meet their constitutional obligations aggravated the massive problem of converting from the state-enforced discrimination of racially separate school systems. This process has been rendered more difficult by changes since 1954 in the structure and patterns of communities, the growth of student population, movement of families, and other changes, some of which had marked impact on school planning, sometimes neutralizing or negating remedial action before it was fully implemented. Rural areas accustomed for half a century to the consolidated school systems implemented by bus transportation could make adjustments more readily than metropolitan areas with dense and shifting population, numerous schools, congested and complex traffic patterns.

The objective today remains to eliminate from the public schools all vestiges of state-imposed segregation. . . .

If school authorities fail in their affirmative obligations under these holdings, judicial authority may be invoked. Once a right and a violation have been shown, the scope of a district court's equitable powers to remedy past wrongs is broad, for breadth and flexibility are inherent in equitable remedies. . . .

This allocation of responsibility once made, the Court attempted from time to time to provide some guidelines for the exercise of the district judge's discretion and for the reviewing function of the courts of appeals. However, a school desegregation case does not differ fundamentally from other cases involving the framing of equitable remedies to repair the denial of a constitutional right. The task is to correct, by a balancing of the individual and collective interests, the condition that offends the Constitution.

In seeking to define even in broad and general terms how far this remedial power extends it is important to remember that judicial powers may be exercised only on the basis of a constitutional violation. Remedial judicial authority does not put judges automatically in the shoes of school authorities whose powers are plenary. Judicial authority enters only when local authority defaults.

School authorities are traditionally charged with broad power to formulate and implement educational policy and might well conclude, for example, that in order to prepare students to live in a pluralistic society each school should have a prescribed ratio of Negro to white students reflecting the proportion for the district as a whole. To do this as an educational policy is within the broad discretionary powers of school authorities; absent a finding of a constitutional violation, however, that would not be within the authority of a federal court. As with any equity case, the nature of the violation determines the scope of the remedy. In default by the school authorities of their obligation to proffer acceptable remedies, a district court has broad power to fashion a remedy that will assure a unitary school system. . . .

We turn now to the problem of defining with more particularity the responsibilities of school authorities in desegregating a state-enforced dual school system in light of the Equal Protection Clause. Although the several related cases before us are primarily concerned with problems of student assignment, it may be helpful to begin with a brief discussion of other aspects of the process.

In *Green,* we pointed out that existing policy and practice with regard to faculty, staff, transportation, extracurricular activities, and facilities were among the most important indicia of a segregated system.

Independent of student assignment, where it is possible to identify a "white school" or a "Negro school" simply by reference to the racial composition of teachers and staff, the quality of school buildings and equipment, or the organization of sports activities, a *prima facie* case of violation of substantive constitutional rights under the Equal Protection Clause is shown.

When a system has been dual in these respects, the first remedial responsibility of school authorities is to eliminate invidious racial distinctions. With respect to such matters as transportation, supporting personnel, and extracurricular activities, no more than this may be necessary. Similar corrective action must be taken with regard to the maintenance of buildings and the distribution of equipment. In these areas, normal administrative practice should produce schools of like quality, facilities, and staffs. Something more must be said, however, as to faculty assignment and new school construction.

The construction of new schools and the closing of old ones are two of the most important functions of local school authorities and also two of the most complex. They must decide questions of location and capacity in light of population growth, finances, land values, site availability, through an almost endless list of factors to be considered. The result of this will be a decision which, when combined with one technique or another of student assignment, will determine the racial composition of the student body in each school in the system. Over the long run, the consequences of the choices will be far reaching. People gravitate toward school facilities, just as schools are located in response to the needs of people. The location of schools may thus influence the patterns of residential development of a metropolitan area and have important impact on composition of inner-city neighborhoods.

In the past, choices in this respect have been used as a potent weapon for creating or maintaining a state-segregated school system. In addition to the classic pattern of building schools specifically intended for Negro or white students, school authorities have sometimes, since *Brown,* closed schools which appeared likely to become racially mixed through changes in neighborhood residential patterns. This was sometimes accompanied by building new schools in the areas of white suburban expansion farthest from Negro population centers in order to maintain the separation of the races with a minimum departure from the formal principles of "neighborhood zoning." Such a policy does more than simply influence the short-run composition of the student body of a new school. It may well promote segregated residential patterns which, when combined with "neighborhood zoning," further lock the school system into the mold of separation of the races. Upon a proper showing a district court may consider this in fashioning a remedy.

In ascertaining the existence of legally imposed school segregation, the existence of a pattern of school construction and abandonment is thus a factor of great weight. In devising remedies where legally imposed segregation has been established, it is the responsibility of local authorities and district courts to see to it that future school construction and abandonment are not used and do not serve to perpetuate or reestablish the dual system. When necessary, district courts should retain jurisdiction to assure that these responsibilities are carried out.

The central issue in this case is that of student assignment, and there are essentially four problem areas:

(1) to what extent racial balance or racial quotas may be used as an implement in a remedial order to correct a previously segregated system;

(2) whether every all-Negro and all-white school must be eliminated as an indispensable part of a remedial process of desegregation;

(3) what the limits are, if any, on the rearrangement of school districts and attendance zones, as a remedial measure; and

(4) what the limits are, if any, on the use of transportation facilities to correct state-enforced racial school segregation.

(1) Racial Balances or Racial Quotas.

The constant theme and thrust of every holding from *Brown I* to date is that state-enforced separation of races in public schools is discrimination that violates the Equal Protection Clause. The remedy commanded was to dismantle dual school systems.

We are concerned in these cases with the elimination of the discrimination inherent in the dual school systems, not with myriad factors of human existence which can cause discrimination in a multitude of ways on racial, religious, or ethnic grounds. The target of the cases from *Brown I* to the present was the dual school system. The elimination of racial discrimination in public schools is a large task and one that should not be retarded by efforts to achieve broader purposes lying beyond the jurisdiction of school authorities. One vehicle can carry only a limited amount of baggage. It would not serve the important objective of *Brown I* to seek to use school desegregation cases for purposes beyond their scope, although desegregation of schools ultimately will have impact on other forms of discrimination. We do not reach in this case the question whether a showing that school segregation is a consequence of other types of state action, without any discriminatory action by the school authorities, is a constitutional violation requiring remedial action by a school desegregation decree. This case does not present that question and we therefore do not decide it.

Our objective in dealing with the issues presented by these cases is to see that school authorities exclude no pupil of a racial minority from any school, directly or indirectly, on account of race; it does not and cannot embrace all the problems of racial prejudice, even when those problems contribute to disproportionate racial concentrations in some schools. . . .

As the voluminous record in this case shows, the predicate for the District Court's use of the 71%-29% ratio was twofold: first, its express finding, approved by the Court of Appeals and not challenged here, that a dual school system had been maintained by the school authorities at least until 1969; second, its finding, also approved by the Court of Appeals, that the school board had totally defaulted in its acknowledged duty to come forward with an acceptable plan of its own, notwithstanding the patient efforts of the District Judge who, on at least three occasions, urged the board to submit plans. As the statement of facts shows, these findings are abundantly supported by the record . . .

We see therefore that the use made of mathematical ratios was no more than a starting point in the process of shaping a remedy, rather than an inflexible requirement. From that starting point the District Court proceeded to frame a decree that was within its discretionary powers, as an equitable remedy for the particular circumstances. As we said in *Green*, a school authority's remedial plan or a district court's remedial decree is to be judged by its effectiveness. Awareness of the racial composition of the whole school system is likely to be a useful starting point in shaping a remedy to correct past constitutional violations. In sum, the very limited use made of mathematical ratios was within the equitable remedial discretion of the District Court.

(2) One-race Schools.

The record in this case reveals the familiar phenomenon that in metropolitan areas minority groups are often found concentrated in one part of the city. In some circumstances certain schools may remain all or largely of one race until new schools can be provided or neighborhood patterns change. Schools all or predominately of one race in a district of mixed population will require close scrutiny to determine that school assignments are not part of state-enforced segregation.

In light of the above, it should be clear that the existence of some small number of one-race, or virtually one-race, schools within a district is not in and of itself the mark of a system that still practices segregation by law. The district judge or school authorities should make every effort to achieve the greatest possible degree of actual desegregation and will thus necessarily be concerned with the elimination of one-race schools. No *per se* rule can adequately embrace all the difficulties reconciling the competing interests involved. . . .

An optional majority-to-minority transfer provision has long been recognized as a useful part of every desegregation plan. Provision for optional transfer of those in the majority racial group of a particular school to other schools where they will be in the minority is an indispensable remedy for those students willing to transfer to other schools in order to lessen the impact on them of the state-imposed stigma of segregation. In order to be effective, such a transfer arrangement must grant the transferring student free transportation and space must be made available in the school to which he desires to move. . . .

(3) Remedial Altering of Attendance Zones.

The maps submitted in these cases graphically demonstrate that one of the principal tools employed by school planners and by courts to break up the dual school system has been a frank—and sometimes drastic—gerrymandering of school districts and attendance zones. An additional step was pairing, "clustering," or "grouping" of schools with attendance assignments made deliberately to accomplish the transfer of Negro students out of formerly segregated Negro schools and transfer of white students to formerly all-Negro schools. More often than not, these zones are neither compact " nor contiguous; indeed they may be on opposite ends of the city. As an interim corrective measure, this cannot be said to be beyond the broad remedial powers of a court. . . .

Absent a constitutional violation there would be no basis for judicially ordering assignment of students on a racial basis. All things being equal, with no history of discrimination, it might well be desirable to assign pupils to schools nearest their homes. But all things are not equal in a system that has been deliberately constructed and maintained to enforce racial segregation. The remedy for such segregation may be administratively awkward, inconvenient, and even bizarre in some situations and may impose burdens on some; but all awkwardness and inconvenience cannot be avoided in the interim period when remedial adjustments are being made to eliminate the dual school systems.

No fixed or even substantially fixed guidelines can be established as to how far a court can go, but it must be recognized that there are limits. The objective is to dismantle the dual school system. . . .

In this area, we must of necessity rely to a large extent, as this Court has for more than 16 years, on the informed judgment of the district courts in the first instance and on courts of appeals.

We hold that the pairing and grouping of noncontiguous school zones is a permissible tool and such action is to be considered in light of the objectives sought. . . .

(4) Transportation of Students.

The scope of permissible transportation of students as all implement of a remedial decree has never been defined by this Court and by the very nature of the problem it cannot be defined with precision. No rigid guidelines as to student transportation can be given for application to the infinite variety of problems presented in thousands of situations. Bus transportation has been an integral part of the public education system for years, and was perhaps the single most important factor in the transition from the one-room schoolhouse to the consolidated school. Eighteen million of the

Nation's public school children, approximately 39%, were transported to their schools by bus in 1969-1970 in all parts of the country. . . .

An objection to transportation of students may have validity when the time or distance of travel is so great as to either risk the health of the children or significantly impinge on the educational process. District courts must weigh the soundness of any transportation plan in light of what is said in subdivisions (1), (2), and (3) above. It hardly needs stating that the limits on time of travel will vary with many factors, but probably with none more than the age of the students. The reconciliation of competing values in a desegregation case is, of course, a difficult task with many sensitive facets but fundamentally no more so than remedial measures courts of equity have traditionally employed.

At some point, these school authorities and others like them should have achieved full compliance with this Court's decision in *Brown I*. The systems would then be "unitary" . . . school authorities nor district courts are constitutionally required to make year-by-year adjustments of the racial composition of student bodies once the affirmative duty to desegregate has been accomplished and racial discrimination through official action is eliminated from the system. This does not mean that federal courts are without power to deal with future problems; but in the absence of a showing that either the school authorities or some other agency of the State has deliberately attempted to fix or alter demographic patterns to affect the racial composition of the schools, further intervention by a district court should not be necessary. . . .

c. Limiting the Reach of *Brown*

Defining moments in the long-term meaning of *Brown* occurred in the early 1970s, by which time the Supreme Court had experienced significant change in personnel and leadership. As attention expanded to racially segregated schools in the North and West, the Court considered whether conditions there offended the Fourteenth Amendment. Resulting were a series of decisions that profoundly limited the reach and duration of the desegregation mandate. In *Keyes v. School District No. 1*, the Court drew a distinction between what it characterized as *de jure* and *de facto* segregation.

Keyes v. School District No. 1, Denver, Colorado
413 U.S. 189 (1973)

MR. JUSTICE BRENNAN delivered the opinion of the Court.

This school desegregation case concerns the Denver, Colorado, school system. That system has never been operated under a constitutional or statutory provision that mandated or permitted racial segregation in public education. Rather, the gravamen of this action, brought in June 1969 in the District Court for the District of Colorado by parents of Denver schoolchildren, is that respondent School Board alone, by use of various techniques such as the manipulation of student attendance zones, schoolsite selection and a neighborhood school policy, created or maintained racially or ethnically (or both racially and ethnically) segregated schools throughout the school district, entitling petitioners to a decree directing desegregation of the entire school district.

. . .

This is not a case, . . . where a statutory dual system has ever existed. Nevertheless,

where plaintiffs prove that the school authorities have carried out a systematic program of segregation affecting a substantial portion of the students, schools, teachers, and facilities within the school system, it is only common sense to conclude that there exists a predicate for a finding of the existence of a dual school system. Several considerations support this conclusion. First, it is obvious that a practice of concentrating Negroes in certain schools by structuring attendance zones or designating "feeder" schools on the basis of race has the reciprocal effect of keeping other nearby schools predominantly white. Similarly, the practice of building a school—such as the Barrett Elementary School in this case—to a certain size and in a certain location, "with conscious knowledge that it would be a segregated school," 303 F. Supp., at 295, has a substantial reciprocal effect on the racial composition of other nearby schools. So also, the use of mobile classrooms, the drafting of student transfer policies, the transportation of students, and the assignment of faculty and staff, on racially identifiable bases, have the clear effect of earmarking schools according to their racial composition, and this, in turn, together with the elements of student assignment and school construction, may have a profound reciprocal effect on the racial composition of residential neighborhoods within a metropolitan area, thereby causing further racial concentration within the schools. . . .

. . .

. . . [W]e hold that a finding of intentionally segregative school board actions in a meaningful portion of a school system, as in this case, creates a presumption that other segregated schooling within the system is not adventitious. It establishes, in other words, a *prima facie* case of unlawful segregative design on the part of school authorities, and shifts to those authorities the burden of proving that other segregated schools within the system are not also the result of intentionally segregative actions. This is true even if it is determined that different areas of the school district should be viewed independently of each other because, even in that situation, there is high probability that where school authorities have effectuated an intentionally segregative policy in a meaningful portion of the school system, similar impermissible considerations have motivated their actions in other areas of the system. We emphasize that the differentiating factor between *de jure* segregation and so-called *de facto* segregation to which we referred in *Swann* is purpose or intent to segregate. Where school authorities have been found to have practiced purposeful segregation in part of a school system, they may be expected to oppose system-wide desegregation, as did the respondents in this case, on the ground that their purposefully segregative actions were isolated and individual events, thus leaving plaintiffs with the burden of proving otherwise. But at that point where an intentionally segregative policy is practiced in a meaningful or significant segment of a school system, as in this case, the school authorities cannot be heard to argue that plaintiffs have proved only "isolated and individual" unlawfully segregative actions. In that circumstance, it is both fair and reasonable to require that the school authorities bear the burden of showing that their actions as to other segregated schools within the system were not also motivated by segregative intent. . . . Indeed, to say that a system has a "history of segregation is merely to say that a pattern of intentional segregation has been established in the past. Thus, be it a statutory dual system or an allegedly unitary system where a meaningful portion of the system is found to be intentionally segregated, the existence of subsequent or other segregated schooling within the same system justifies a rule imposing on the school authorities the burden of proving that this segregated schooling is not also the result of intentionally segregative acts.

In discharging that burden, it is not enough, of course, that the school authorities rely upon some allegedly logical, racially neutral explanation for their actions. Their burden is to adduce proof sufficient to support a finding that segregative intent was not among the factors that motivated their actions. The courts below attributed much significance to the fact that many of the Board's actions in the core city area antedated our decision in *Brown*. We reject any suggestion that remoteness in time has any relevance to the issue of intent. If the actions of school authorities were to any degree motivated by segregative intent and the segregation resulting from those actions continues to exist, the fact of remoteness in time certainly does not make those actions any less "intentional.". . . We [have] made it clear, however, that a connection between past segregative acts and past segregative acts and present segregation may be present even when not apparent and that close examination is required before concluding that the connection does not exist. Intentional school segregation in the past may have been a factor in creating a natural environment for the growth of further segregation. Thus, if respondent School Board cannot disprove segregative intent, it can rebut the prima facie case only by showing that its past segregative acts did not create or contribute to the current segregated condition of the core city schools.

. . .

MR. JUSTICE DOUGLAS, concurring.

. . .

I think it is time to state that there is no constitutional difference between *de jure* and *de facto* segregation, for each is the product of state actions or policies. If a "neighborhood" or "geographical" unit has been created along racial lines by reason of the play of restrictive covenants that restrict certain areas to "the elite," leaving the "undesirables" to move elsewhere, there is state action in the constitutional sense because the force of law is placed behind those covenants.

There is state action in the constitutional sense when public funds are dispersed by urban development agencies to build racial ghettoes.

Where the school district is racially mixed and the races are segregated in separate schools, where black teachers are assigned almost exclusively to black schools, where the school board closed existing schools located in fringe areas and built new schools in black areas and in distant white areas, where the school board continued the "neighborhood" school policy at the elementary level, these actions constitute state action. They are of a kind quite distinct from the classical *de jure* type of school segregation. Yet calling them *de facto* is a misnomer, as they are only more subtle types of state action that create or maintain a wholly or partially segregated school system.

When a State forces, aids, or abets, or helps create a racial "neighborhood," it is a travesty of justice to treat that neighborhood as sacrosanct in the sense that its creation is free from the taint of state action.

The Constitution and Bill of Rights have described the design of a pluralistic society. The individual has the right to seek such comparisons as he desires. But a State is barred from creating by one device or another ghettoes that determine the school one is compelled to attend.

MR. JUSTICE POWELL concurring in part and dissenting in part.

. . .

The situation in Denver is generally comparable to that in other large cities across the country in which there is a substantial minority population and where desegregation has not been ordered by the federal courts. There is segregation in the schools of many of these cities fully as pervasive as that in southern cities prior to the desegregation decrees of the past decade and a half. The focus of the school desegregation problem has now shifted from the South to the country as a whole. Unwilling and footdragging as the process was in most places, substantial progress toward achieving integration has been made in Southern States. No comparable progress has been made in many nonsouthern cities with large minority populations primarily because of the *de facto / de jure* distinction nurtured by the courts and accepted complacently by many of the same voices which denounced the evils of segregated schools in the South. But if our national concern is for those who attend such schools, rather than for perpetuating a legalism rooted in history rather than present reality, we must recognize that the evil of operating separate schools is no less in Denver than in Atlanta.

. . .

. . . I would not, however, perpetuate the *de jure / de facto* distinction nor would I leave to petitioners the initial tortuous effort of identifying "segregative acts" and deducing "segregative intent." I would hold, quite simply, that where segregated public schools exist within a school district to a substantial degree, there is a prima facie case that the duly constituted public authorities (I will usually refer to them collectively as the "school board") are sufficiently responsible to warrant imposing upon them a nationally applicable burden to demonstrate they nevertheless are operating a genuinely integrated school system.

. . .

Having school boards operate an integrated school system provides the best assurance of meeting the constitutional requirement that racial discrimination, subtle or otherwise, will find no place in the decisions of public school officials. Courts judging past school board actions with a view to their *general integrative effect* will be best able to assure an absence of such discrimination while avoiding the murky, subjective judgments inherent in the Court's search for "segregative intent." Any test resting on so nebulous and elusive an element as a school board's segregative "intent" provides inadequate assurance that minority children will not be shortchanged in the decisions of those entrusted with the nondiscriminatory operation of our public schools.

. . .

This Court has recognized repeatedly that it is "extremely difficult for a court to ascertain the motivation, or collection of different motivations, that lie behind a legislative enactment." Whatever difficulties exist with regard to a single statute will be compounded in a judicial review of years of administration of a large and complex school system. Every act of a school board and school administration, and indeed every failure to act where an affirmative action is indicated, must now be subject to scrutiny. The most routine decisions with respect to the operation of schools, made almost daily, can affect in varying degrees the extent to which schools are initially segregated, remain in that condition, are desegregated, or—for the long term future—are likely to be one or the other. These decisions include action or nonaction with respect to school building construction and location; the timing of building new schools and their size; the closing and consolidation of schools; the drawing or gerrymandering of student attendance zones; the extent to which a neighborhood policy is enforced; the recruitment, promotion and assignment of faculty and supervisory personnel; policies with respect to transfers from one school to another; whether, and to what extent, special schools will be provided, where they will be located, and who will qualify to attend them; the determination of curriculum, including whether there will be "tracks" that lead primarily to college or to vocational training, and the routing of students into these tracks; and even decisions as to social, recreational, and athletic policies.

. . .

Rather than continue to prop up a distinction no longer grounded in principle, and contributing to the consequences indicated above, we should acknowledge that whenever public school segregation exists to a substantial degree there is prima facie evidence of a constitutional violation by the responsible school board. . . .

DEL: The *Keyes* decision established a profoundly important limiting principle with respect to desegregation duties. Constitutional responsibility was conditioned upon proof of official segregative intent. Although successfully established in *Keyes*, such purpose would prove itself elusive in the future. As Justice Powell noted in his opinion, reflecting the administrative expertise of a former school board official, wrongful purpose easily could be obscured by the opportunities for subtlety available to administrators. The distinction between *de jure* and *de facto* segregation, in any event, is more artificial than real. Although the North may not have been governed by the comprehensive system of racial segregation characterizing the South, it used the law creatively and effectively to achieve racial separation especially with respect to residence. As black migration accelerated from the South, in response to the magnetic appeal of northern factories during the first half of this century, established white communities responded with restrictive covenants and other exclusionary practices. Such methods were facilitated by federal lending policies which considered the mixing of "inharmonious racial groups" an "adverse influence" and thus a basis for denying loan support.[137] Siting decisions with respect to schools and public housing, school construction, closure and staffing policies and the distribution of urban development funds also, as Justice Douglas noted, contributed to segregation outside the South.[138]

At bottom, the *de jure—de facto* distinction is the functional analogue of proximate causation in tort theory. Because modern segregated conditions in the North and West connect up with official policy, the principle establishes a cut-off point for constitutional liability. The reality is that racial segregation was and is a defining feature of public education on a national basis. If the desegregation premise was to be developed seriously, understanding was necessary that the cause of racially separate conditions was rooted in a racist legacy that, regardless of its different dimensions geographically, implicated the same concern identified in by *Brown* in 1954 and *Strauder* in 1879 with stigmatization.

DER: Professor Lively is correct that *Keyes* presents an unrealistic and restricted understanding of government's segregative intent. Proof of racial motivation should center on institutional practices rather than on individual officials' thoughts. But even if a case of wrongful purpose could not be made, the Court should nevertheless provide a remedy for the injury of de facto segregated schools. According to the Court's reasoning, the goal of the Fourteenth Amendment is to penalize individual instances of official racial animus. But the goal of the Civil Rights Amendments should be much more radical and far-reaching: it is to eradicate the vestiges of slavery and second-class citizenship and to ensure Black Americans equal participation in the national community. That goal is violated by a segregated school system that provides an inferior education to Black students, regardless of the motives of government officials. The requirement that plaintiffs show discriminatory intent is one of the major stumbling blocks to racial equality in the Court's constitutional jurisprudence.

PAH: As I have indicated in earlier comments, I believe that the purpose of the Civil War Amendments to eliminate second-class citizenship has been subverted by the Court's preoccupation with color-blindness. The insistence upon proof of segregative intent similarly blunts the quest for equal citizenship and damages the cause of racial justice. Courts are required to ignore whether governmental action continues to subordinate the rights and interests of African Americans, and to leave some racial discrimination not recognized as wrong and unremediated even when governmental motives are suspect. This is so despite the fact (as we recognize also in Torts) actors are taken to contemplate the probable consequences of their acts.

---

[137] PAUL JACOBS, PRELUDE TO RIOT: A VIEW OF URBAN AMERICA FROM THE BOTTOM 140 (1967).
[138] Keyes v. School District No. 1, 413 U.S. 189, 216 (1973)(Douglas, J., concurring)

A de facto/de jure distinction puts the burden on the victims of inequality to prove that their circumstances result from intentional conduct, focusing attention away from harm affecting them. The implication is that racism and racial inequality are not national problems but aberrations, even, perhaps, that societal interests are not served by eradicating inequality. Both color-blindness and segregative intent suggest that there lies a clear demarcation between bad, racist conduct and "neutral" conduct which may have untoward consequences not attributable to morally objectionable conduct. The reality is that the racism is so subtly and pervasively part of our social construction and institutional decision making that addressig merely intentional racism does not meaningfully reach significant governmental acts resposible for perpetuating inequality.[139]

By requiring segregative intent by the government the Court does avoid judging the substantive fairness of the governmental decision making, thereby purporting to minimize the intrusion of the Court in review.[140] In part this concern about intrusion arose from the development of a tiered and rigid equal protection analysis that made scrutiny of race-based classification schemes "'strict' in theory and fatal in fact."[141] But it results in the failure forthrightly to recognize the impact of race in continuing inequality of citizens.

---

[139] See, e.g., Charles Lawrence, III *The Id, the Ego, and Equal Protection: Reckoning with Unconscious Racism,* 39 STAN. L. REV. 317 (1987). Some authorities have argued that the Court has in fact relaxed the connection between intnet and actual motivation in the school desegregation area. Thus, for example, by allowing plaintiffs in *Keyes* to transfer itent from part of the district to the whole, the Court found they had satisfied the requirement of showing the district had acted purposefully to segregate Denver schools. Once intent de jure segregatio is shown the Court holds a district to an effects standard in requiring the district to eradicate vestiges of discrimination. But once unitariness is found the level of intent required is higher, resting on a showing of actual and recent discriminatory motivation. *See* Daniel R. Ortiz, *The Myth of Intent* 41 STAN. L. REV. 1105, 1131–34 (1989).

[140] Proponents of intent requirements are usually process-oriented, believing that the Court should work to keep the government's decision making process pure, striking laws only when they reflect a discriminatory animus. See, e.g., John Hart Ely, Democracy and Distruct (1980); Paul Brest, *Palmer v. Thompson: An Approach to the Problem of Unconstitutional Legislative Motive,* 1971 SUP. CT. REV. 95.

[141] Gerald Gunther, *The Supreme Court 1971 Term—Foreword: In Search of Evolving Doctrine of a Changing Court: A Model for a Newer Equal Protection,* 86 HARV. L. REV. 1, 8 (1972).

Having established the notion of *de facto* segregation, the Court determined that a logical extension of the principle required preclusion of interdistrict remedies implicating primarily suburban communities that had evolved to a large extent in the post-segregation era. Notwithstanding that desegregation fueled white flight from urban centers, the Court in *Milliken v. Bradley* stressed that relief could reach no further than the district within which the constitutional violation occurred.

Milliken v. Bradley
417 U.S. 717 (1974)

MR. CHIEF JUSTICE BURGER delivered the opinion of the Court.

We granted certiorari in these consolidated cases to determine whether a federal court may impose a multidistrict, areawide remedy to a single-district *de jure* segregation problem absent any finding that the other included school districts have failed to operate unitary school systems within their districts, absent any claim or finding that the boundary lines of any affected school district were established with the purpose of fostering racial segregation in public schools, absent any finding that the included districts committed acts which effected segregation within the other districts, and absent a meaningful opportunity for the included neighboring school districts to present evidence or be heard on the propriety of a multidistrict remedy or on the question of constitutional violations by those neighboring districts.

. . .

. . . The controlling principle consistently expounded in our holdings is that the scope of the remedy is determined by the nature and extent of the constitutional violation. *Swann.* Before the boundaries of separate and autonomous school districts may be set aside by consolidating the separate units for remedial purposes or by imposing a cross district remedy, it must first be shown that there has been a constitutional violation within one district that produces a significant segregative effect in another district. Specifically, it must be shown that racially discriminatory acts of the state or local school districts, or of a single school district have been a substantial cause of interdistrict segregation. Thus an interdistrict remedy might be in order where the racially discriminatory acts of one or more school districts caused racial segregation in an adjacent district, or where district lines have been deliberately drawn on the basis of race. In such circumstances an interdistrict remedy would be appropriate to eliminate the interdistrict segregation directly caused by the constitutional violation and interdistrict effect, there is no constitutional wrong calling for an interdistrict remedy.

The record before us voluminous as it is, contains evidence of *de jure* segregated conditions only in the Detroit schools; indeed, that was the theory on which the litigation was initially based and on which the District Court took evidence. With no showing of significant violation by the 53 outlying school districts and no evidence of any interdistrict violation or effect, the court went beyond the original theory of the case as framed by the pleadings and mandated a metropolitan area remedy. To approve the remedy ordered by the court would impose on the outlying districts, not shown to have committed any constitutional violation, a wholly impermissible remedy based on a standard not hinted at in *Brown I* and *II* or any holding of this Court.

In dissent, MR. JUSTICE WHITE and MR. JUSTICE MARSHALL undertake to demonstrate that agencies having statewide authority participated in maintaining the dual school system found to exist in Detroit. They are apparently of the view that once such participation

is shown, the District Court should have a relatively free hand to reconstruct school districts outside of Detroit in fashioning relief. Our assumption, *arguendo*, that state agencies did participate in the maintenance of the Detroit system, should make it clear that it is not on this point that we part company. The difference between us arises instead from established doctrine laid down by our cases [which] addressed the issue of constitutional wrong in terms of an established geographic and administrative school system populated by both Negro and white children. In such a context, terms such as "unitary" and "dual" systems, and "racially identifiable schools," have meaning, and the necessary federal authority to remedy the constitutional wrong is firmly established. But the remedy is necessarily designed, as all remedies are, to restore the victims of discriminatory conduct to the position they would have occupied in the absence of such conduct. Disparate treatment of white and Negro students occurred within the Detroit school system, and not elsewhere, and on this record the remedy must be limited to that system. The constitutional right of the Negro respondents residing in Detroit is to attend a unitary school system in that district. Unless petitioners drew the district lines in a discriminatory fashion, or arranged for white students residing in the Detroit district to attend schools in Oakland and Macom Counties, they were under no constitutional duty to make provisions for Negro students to do so. The view of the dissenters, that the existence of a dual system in *Detroit* can be made the basis for a decree requiring cross-district transportation of pupils, cannot be supported on the grounds that it represents merely the devising of a suitable flexible remedy for the violation of rights already established by our prior decisions. It can be supported only by drastic expansion of the constitutional right itself, an expansion without any support in either constitutional principle or precedent.

MR. JUSTICE DOUGLAS, dissenting.

. . .

When we rule against the metropolitan area remedy we take a step that will likely put the problems of the blacks and our society back to the period that antedated the "separate but equal" regime of *Plessy v. Ferguson*. The reason is simple.

The inner core of Detroit is now rather solidly black, and the blacks, we know, in many instances are likely to be poorer, just as were the Chicanos in *San Antonio School District v. Rodriguez*. By that decision the poorer school districts must pay their own way. It is therefore a foregone conclusion that we have now given the States a formula whereby the poor must pay their own way.

Today's decision, given *Rodriguez*, means that there is no violation of the Equal Protection Clause though the schools are segregated by race and though the black schools are not only "separate" but "inferior."

So far as equal protection is concerned we are now in a dramatic retreat from the 7-to-1 decision in 1896 that blacks could be segregated in public facilities, provided they received equal treatment.

As I indicated in *Keyes v. School District No. 1, Denver, Colorado,* there is so far as the school cases go no constitutional difference between *de facto* and *de jure* segregation. Each school board performs state action for Fourteenth Amendment purposes when it draws the lines that confine it to a given area, when it builds schools at particular sites, or when it allocates students. The creation of the school districts in Metropolitan Detroit either maintained existing segregation or caused additional segregation. Restrictive covenants maintained by state action or inaction build black ghettos. It is state action when public funds are dispensed by housing agencies to build racial ghettos. Where a community is racially mixed and school authorities segregate schools, or assign black teachers to black schools or close schools in fringe areas and build new schools in black areas and in more distant white areas, the State creates and nurtures a segregated school system, just as surely as did those States involved in *Brown v. Board of Education*, when they maintained dual school systems.

All these conditions and more were found by the District Court to exist. The issue is not whether there should be racial balance but whether the State's use of various devices that end up with black schools and white schools brought the Equal Protection Clause into effect.... It is conceivable that ghettos develop on their own without any hint of state action. But since Michigan by one device or another has over the years created black school districts and white school districts, the task of equity is to provide a unitary system for the affected area where, as here, the State washes its hands of its own creations.

MR. JUSTICE WHITE, with whom MR. JUSTICE DOUGLAS, MR. JUSTICE BRENNAN, and MR. JUSTICE MARSHALL join, dissenting.

The District Court and the Court of Appeals found that over a long period of years those in charge of the Michigan public schools engaged in various practices calculated to effect the segregation of the Detroit school system. The Court does not question these findings, nor could it reasonably do so. Neither does it question the obligation of the federal courts to devise a feasible and effective remedy. But it promptly cripples the ability of the judiciary to perform this task, which is of fundamental importance to our constitutional system, by fashioning a strict rule that remedies in school cases must stop at the school district line unless certain other conditions are met. As applied here, the remedy for unquestioned violations of the protection rights of Detroit's Negroes by the Detroit School Board and the State of Michigan must be totally confined to the limits of the school district and may not reach into adjoining or surrounding districts unless and until it is proved there has been some sort of "interdistrict violation"—unless unconstitutional actions of the Detroit School Board have had a segregative impact on other districts, or unless the segregated condition of the Detroit schools has itself been influenced by segregative practices in those surrounding districts into which it is proposed to extend the remedy.

Regretfully, and for several reasons, I can join neither the Court's judgment nor its opinion. The core of my disagreement is that deliberate acts of segregation and their consequences will go unremedied, not because a remedy would be infeasible or unreasonable in terms of the usual criteria governing school desegregation cases, but because an effective remedy would cause what the Court considers to be undue administrative inconvenience to the State. The result is that the State of Michigan, the entity at which the Fourteenth Amendment is directed, has successfully insulated itself from its duty to provide effective desegregation remedies by vesting sufficient power over its public schools in its local school districts. If this is the case in Michigan, it will be the case in most States.

. . .

I am even more mystified as to how the Court can ignore the legal reality that the constitutional violations, even if occurring locally, were committed by governmental entities for which the State is responsible and that it is the State that must respond to the command of the Fourteenth Amendment. An interdistrict remedy for the infringements that occurred in this case is well within the confines and powers of the State, which is the governmental entity ultimately responsible for desegregating its schools....

. . .

Finally, I remain wholly unpersuaded by the Court's assertion that "the remedy is necessarily designed, as all remedies are, to restore the victims of discriminatory conduct to the position they would have occupied in the absence of such conduct." In the first place, under this premise the court's judgment is itself infirm; for had the Detroit school system not followed an official policy of segregation throughout the 1950's and 1960's, Negroes and whites would have been going to school together. There would have been no, or at least not as many, recognizable Negro schools and no, or at least not as many, white schools, but "just schools," and neither Negroes nor whites would have suffered from the effects of segregated education, with all its short-comings. . . .

MR. JUSTICE MARSHALL, with whom MR. JUSTICE DOUGLAS, MR.JUSTICE BRENNAN, and MR. JUSTICE WHITE join, dissenting.

In *Brown v. Board of Education,* this Court held that segregation of children in public schools on the basis of race deprives minority group children of equal educational opportunities and therefore denies them the equal protection of the laws under the Fourteenth Amendment. This Court recognized then that remedying decades of segregation in public education would not be an easy task. Subsequent event's unfortunately, have seen that prediction bear bitter fruit. But however imbedded old ways, however ingrained old prejudices, this Court has not been diverted from its appointed task of making "a living truth" of our constitutional ideal of equal justice under law.

After 20 years of small, often difficult steps toward that great end, the Court today takes a giant step backwards. Notwithstanding a record showing widespread and pervasive racial segregation in the educational system provided by the State of Michigan for children in Detroit, this Court holds that the District Court was powerless to require the State to remedy its constitutional violation in any meaningful fashion. Ironically purporting to base its result on the principle that scope of the remedy in a desegregation case should be determined by the nature and the extent of the constitutional violation, the Court's answer is to provide no remedy at all for the violation proved in this case, thereby guaranteeing that Negro children in Detroit will receive the same separate and inherently unequal education in the future as they have been unconstitutionally afforded in the past.

I cannot subscribe to this emasculation of our constitutional guarantee of equal protection of the laws and must respectfully dissent. Our precedents, in my view, firmly establish that where, as here, state-imposed segregation has been demonstrated, it becomes the duty of the State to eliminate root and branch all vestiges of racial discrimination and to achieve the greatest possible degree of actual desegregation. I agree with both the District Court and the Court of Appeals that, under the facts of this case, this duty cannot be fulfilled unless the State of Michigan involves outlying metropolitan area school districts in its desegregation remedy. Furthermore, I perceive no basis either in law or in the practicalities of the situation justifying the State's interposition of school district boundaries as absolute barriers to the implementation of an effective desegregation remedy. Under established and frequently used Michigan procedures, school district lines are both flexible and permeable for a wide variety of purposes, and there is no reason why they must now stand in the way of meaningful desegregation relief.

The rights at issue in this case are too fundamental to be abridged on grounds as superficial as those relied on by the majority today. We deal here with the right of all of our children, whatever their race, to an equal start in life and to an equal opportunity to reach their full potential as citizens. Those children who have been denied that right in the past deserve better than to see fences thrown up to deny them that right in the future. Our Nation, I fear, will be ill served by the Court's refusal to remedy separate and unequal education, for unless our children begin to learn together, there is little hope that our people will ever learn to live together.

. . .

Under Michigan law a "school district is an agency of the City or State Government." It is "a legal division of territory, created by the State for educational purposes, to which the State has granted such powers as are deemed necessary to permit the district to function as a State agency." Racial discrimination by the school district, an agency of the State, is therefore racial discrimination by the State itself, forbidden by the Fourteenth Amendment.

Vesting responsibility with the State of Michigan for Detroit's segregated schools is particularly appropriate as Michigan, unlike some other States, operates a single statewide system of education rather than several separate and independent local school systems. The majority's emphasis on local governmental control and local autonomy of school districts in Michigan will come as a surprise to those with any familiarity with that State's system of education. School districts are not separate and distinct sovereign entities under Michigan law, but rather are "'auxiliaries of the States.'" subject to its "absolute power."

. . .

In sum, several factors in this case coalesce to support the District Court's ruling that it was the State of Michigan itself, not simply the Detroit Board of Education, which bore the obligation of curing the condition of segregation within the Detroit city schools. The actions of the State itself directly contributed to Detroit's segregation. Under the Fourteenth Amendment, the State is ultimately responsible for the actions of its local agencies. And, finally, given the structure of Michigan's educational system, Detroit's segregation cannot be viewed as the problem of an independent and separate entity. Michigan operates a single statewide system of education, a substantial part of which was shown to be segregated in this case.

... [E]ven if a plan were adopted which, at its outset, provided in every school a 65% Negro-35% white racial mix in keeping with the Negro-white proportions of the total student population, such a system would, in short order, devolve into an all-Negro system. The net result would be a continuation of the all-Negro schools which were the hallmarks of Detroit's former dual system of one-race schools.

Under our decisions, it was clearly proper for the District Court to take into account the so-called "white flight" from the city schools which would be forthcoming from any Detroit-only decree. The court's prediction of white flight was well supported by expert testimony based on past experience in other cities undergoing desegregation relief. We ourselves took the possibility of white flight into account in evaluating the effectiveness of a desegregation plan in *Wright*, where we relied on the District Court's finding that if the city of Emporia were allowed to withdraw from the existing system, leaving a system with a higher proportion of Negroes, it "'may be anticipated that the proportion of whites in county schools may drop as those who can register in private academies'...." One cannot ignore the white-flight problem, for where legally imposed segregation has been established, the District Court has the responsibility to see to it not only that the dual system is terminated at once but also that future events do not serve to perpetuate or re-establish segregation.

Because of the already high and rapidly increasing percentage of Negro students in the Detroit system, as well as the prospect of white flight, a Detroit-only plan simply has no hope of achieving actual desegregation. Under such a plan white and Negro students will not go to school together. Instead, Negro children will continue to attend all-Negro schools. The very evil that *Brown I* was aimed at will not be cured, but will be perpetuated for the future.

. . .

The State must also bear part of the blame for the white flight to the suburbs which would be forthcoming from a Detroit-only decree and would render such a remedy ineffective. Having created a system where whites and Negroes were intentionally kept apart so that they could not become accustomed to learning together, the State is responsible for the fact that many whites will react to the dismantling of that segregated system by attempting to flee to the suburbs. Indeed, by limiting the District Court to a Detroit-only remedy and allowing that flight to the suburbs to succeed, the Court today allows the State to profit from its own wrong and to perpetuate for years to come the separation of the races it achieved in the past by purposeful state action.

The majority asserts, however, that involvement of outlying districts would do violence to the accepted principle that "the nature of the violation determines the scope of the remedy." *Swann*. Not only is the majority's attempt to find in this single phrase the answer to the complex and difficult questions presented in this case hopelessly simplistic, but more important, the Court reads these words in a manner which perverts their obvious meaning. The nature of a violation determines the scope of the remedy simply because the function of any remedy is to cure the violation to which it is addressed. In school segregation cases, as in other equitable causes, a remedy which effectively cures the violation is what is required. No more is necessary, but we can tolerate no less. To read this principle as barring a district court form imposing the only effective remedy for past segregation and remitting the court to a patently ineffective alternative is, in my view, to turn a simple commonsense rule into a cruel and meaningless paradox. Ironically, by ruling out an interdistrict remedy, the only relief which promises to cure segregation in the Detroit public schools, the majority flouts the very principle on which it purports to rely.

. . .

It is a hollow remedy indeed where "after supposed 'desegregation' the schools remained segregated in fact." We must do better than "'substitute ... one segregated school system for another segregated school system.'" To suggest, as does the majority, that a Detroit-only plan somehow remedies the effects of *de jure* segregation not the races is, in my view, to make a solemn mockery of *Brown I*'s holding that separate educational facilities are inherently unequal and of *Swann's* unequivocal mandate that the answer to *de jure* segregation is the greatest possible degree of actual desegregation.

. . .

Desegregation is not and was never expected to be an easy task. Racial attitudes ingrained in our Nation's childhood and adolescence are not quickly thrown aside in its middle years. But just as the inconvenience of some cannot be allowed to stand in the way of the rights of others, so public opposition, no matter how strident, cannot be permitted to divert this Court from the enforcement of the constitutional principles at issue in this case. Today's holding, I fear, is more a reflection of a perceived public mood that we have gone far enough in enforcing the Constitution's guarantee of equal justice than it is the product of neutral principles of law. In the short run, it may seem to be the easier course to allow our great metropolitan areas to be divided up each into two cities—one white, the other black—but it is a course, I predict, our people will ultimately regret. I dissent.

DEL: The *Milliken* decision profoundly limited the potential for meaningful desegregation in urban areas. It effectively constructed a safe harbor for suburbs which to the extent they had virtually no history, much less one that included segregative practices, could insulate themselves from remedial obligations. Insofar as Michigan itself had contributed to segregated conditions in Detroit, the refusal to impose constitutional responsibility on the state's subdivisions seems dubious. Compounding a sense of analytical irregularity was the Court's repudiation of the trial court's findings of fact. With the *Milliken* decision, the Court's attitude changed from criticizing lower courts for holding back to admonishing them for being too enthusiastic on the desegregation front. As white persons and wealth rushed out of urban centers, predominantly black schools were left without the human and economic resources to desegregate or equalize. The *Milliken* decision, at least in those communities that experienced racially significant demographic change, facilitated reversion to educational conditions that not only were separate but unequal.

DER: The consequences of the *Milliken* decision for millions of Black children powerfully demonstrate the inadequacy of the desegregation remedy. Making desegregation the only response to separate and unequal schooling left inferior inner-city schools with no recourse after whites abandoned the cities. *Brown* taught the perverse lesson that we can expect schools in America to provide a decent education only if they are attended by white children.

PAH: *Milliken* demonstrates the Court's use of intent doctrine to insulate classifications like wealth, which are *cohorts* of race, from treatment as *proxies* for race and thereby subjecting them to strict scrutiny.[142] The racial impact of demographic changes in housing patterns crossing the borders of the city to the suburb is clear but correlates with wealth. Because market allocations are the foundation of our society, discrimination based on wealth is less likely to be subjected to judicial intervention. Thus, despite the State's ultimate responsibility for educating its citizens, the Court was not prepared to recognize a constitutional violation that would require an interdistrict remedy which would disrupt local autonomy and market-driven distribution of benefits like education. As Professor Ortiz argues,[143] this case exposes a hierarchy of values driving equal protection analysis; equality is balanced against property and other interests favoring maintenance of the status quo.

---

[142] *See* Ortiz, *supra* at 1139–40.
[143] *Id.*

In *Pasadena City Board of Education v. Spangler*, the Court reiterated its message in *Swann* that desegregation was a finite duty. Once unitary status was achieved, therefore, no further remedial obligations would exist unless intentional resegregation was established.

Pasadena City Board of Education v. Spangler
427 U.S. 424 (1976)

. . . Following the [first year of a desegregation order], black student enrollment at one Pasadena school exceeded 50% of that school's total enrollment. The next year, four Pasadena schools exceeded this 50% black enrollment fig-ure; and at the time of the hearing on petitioners' motion some five schools, in a system of 32 regular schools, were ostensibly in violation of the District Court's "no majority of any minority" requirement. . . . The fact that black student enrollment at 5 out of 32 of the regular Pasadena schools came to exceed 50% during the 4-year period from 1970 to 1974 apparently resulted from people randomly moving into, out of, and around the PUSD area. This quite normal pattern of human migration resulted in some changes in the demographics of Pasadena's residential patterns, with resultant shifts in the racial makeup of some of the schools. But as these shifts were not attributed to any segregative actions on the part of the petitioners, we think this case comes squarely within the sort of situation foreseen in *Swann*:

> "It does not follow that the communities served by [unitary] systems will remain demographically stable, for in a growing, mobile society, few will do so. Neither school authorities nor district courts are constitutionally required to make year-by-year adjustments of the racial composition of student bodies once the affirmative duty to desegregate has been accomplished and racial discrimination through official action is eliminated from the system."

... In this case the District Court approved a plan designed to obtain racial neutrality in the attendance of students at Pasadena's public schools. No one disputes that the initial implementation of this plan accomplished *that* objective. That being the case, the District Court was not entitled to require the PUSD to rearrange its attendance zones each year so as to ensure that the racial mix desired by the court was maintained in perpetuity. For having once implemented a racially neutral attendance pattern in order to remedy the perceived constitutional violations on the part of the defen-

dants, the District Court had fully performed its function of providing the appropriate remedy for previous racially discriminatory attendance patterns. . . .

MR. JUSTICE MARSHALL, with whom MR. JUSTICE BRENNAN joins, dissenting.

I cannot agree with the Court that the District Court's refusal to modify the "no majority of any minority" provision of its order was erroneous. Because at the time of the refusal "racial discrimination through official action," had apparently not yet been eliminated from the Pasadena school system, it is my view that the District Court did not abuse its discretion in refusing to dissolve a major part of its order.

In denying petitioners' motion for modification of the 1970 desegregation order, the District Court described a 3-year pattern of opposition by a number of the members of the Board of Education of both the spirit and letter of the Pasadena Plan. If found that "the Pasadena Plan has not had the cooperation from the Board that permits a realistic measurement of its educational success or failure." Moreover, the 1974 Board of Education submitted to the District Court an alternative to the Pasadena Plan, which, at least in the mind of one member of the court of Appeals, "would very likely result in rapid resegregation.; I agree with Judge Ely that there is "abundant evidence upon which the district judge, in the reasonable exercise of his discretion, could rightly determine that the 'dangers' which induced the original determination of constitutional infringements in Pasadena have not diminished sufficiently to require modification or dissolution of the original Order."

The *Keyes, Milliken* and *Spangler* decisions significantly narrowed the desegregation mandate's meaning. To the extent that the Court could identify dual school systems that had not been dismantled after *Brown*, it still affirmed a duty to desegregate.[144] Increasingly, however, post-*Brown* jurisprudence included concern with the wisdom of compulsory desegregation.

---

[144] Columbus Board of Education v. Penick, 443 U.S. 449 (1979); Dayton Board of Education v. Brinkman, 443 U.S. 526 (1979).

d. Second Thoughts About *Brown*

Columbus Board of Education v. Penick
443 U.S. 449 (1979)

MR. JUSTICE POWELL, dissenting . . .

There are unintegrated schools in every major urban area in the country that contains

a substantial minority population. This condition results primarily from familiar segregated housing patterns, which—in turn—are caused by social, economic, and demographic forces for which no school board is responsible. These causes of the greater part of the school segregation problem are not newly discovered. Nearly a decade ago, Professor Bickel wrote:

"In most of the larger urban areas, demographic conditions are such that no policy that a court can order, and a school board, a city or even a state has the capability to put into effect, will in fact result in the foreseeable future in racially balanced public schools. Only a reordering of the environment involving economic and social policy on the broadest conceivable front might have an appreciable impact." A. Bickel, The Supreme Court and the Idea of Progress 132, and n. 47 (1970).

Federal courts, including this Court today, continue to ignore these indisputable facts. Relying upon fictions and presumptions in school cases that are irreconcilable with principles of equal protection law applied in all other cases, federal courts prescribe systemwide remedies without relation to the causes of the segregation found to exist, and implement their decrees by requiring extensive transportation of children of all school ages.

The type of state-enforced segregation that *Brown I* properly condemned no longer exists in this country. . . .

. . .

Holding the school boards of these two cities responsible for *all* of the segregation in the Dayton and Columbus systems and prescribing fixed racial ratios in every school as the constitutionally required remedy necessarily implies a belief that the same school boards—under court supervision—will be capable of bringing about and maintaining the desired racial balance in each of these schools. The experience in city after city demonstrates that this is an illusion. The process of resegregation, stimulated by resentment against judicial coercion and concern as to the effect of court supervision of education, will follow today's decisions as surely as it has in other cities subjected to similar sweeping decrees.

The orders affirmed today typify intrusions on local and professional authorities that affect adversely the quality of education. They require an extensive reorganization of both school systems, including the reassignment of almost half of the 96,000 students in the Columbus system and the busing of some 15,000 students in Dayton. They also require reassignments of teachers and other staff personnel, reorganization of grade structures, and the closing of certain schools. The orders substantially dismantle and displace neighborhood schools in the face of compelling economic and educational reasons for preserving them. This wholesale substitution of judicial legislation for the judgments of elected officials and professional educators derogates the entire process of public education. Moreover, it constitutes a serious interference with the private decisions of parents as to how their children will be educated. These harmful consequences are the inevitable by products of a judicial approach that ignores other relevant factors in favor of an exclusive focus on racial balance in every school.

These harmful consequences, moreover, in all likelihood will provoke responses that will defeat the integrative purpose of the courts' orders. Parents, unlike school officials, are not bound by these decrees and may frustrate them through the simple expedient of withdrawing their children from a public school system in which they have lost confidence. In spite of the substantial costs often involved in relocation of the family or in resort to private education, experience demonstrates that many parents view these alternatives as preferable to submitting their children to court-run school systems. . . .

At least where inner-city populations comprise a large proportion of racial minorities and surrounding suburbs remain white, conditions that exist in most large American cities, the demonstrated effect of compulsory integration is a substantial exodus of whites from the system. It would be unfair and misleading to attribute this phenomenon to a racist response to integration per se. It is at least as likely that the exodus is in substantial part a natural reaction to the displacement of professional and local control that occurs when courts go into the business of restructuring and operating school systems.

Nor will this resegregation be the only negative effect of court-coerced integration on minority children. Public schools depend on community support for their effectiveness. When substantial elements of the community are driven to abandon these schools, their quality tends to decline, sometimes markedly. Members of minority groups, who have relied especially on education as a means of advancing themselves, also are likely to react to this decline in quality by removing their children from public schools. As a result, public school enrollment increasingly will become limited to children from families that either lack the resources to choose alternatives or are indifferent to the quality of education. The net effect is an overall deterioration in public education, the one national resource that traditionally has made this country a land of opportunity for diverse ethnic and racial groups.

After all, and in spite of what many view as excessive government regulation, we are a free society—perhaps the most free of any in the world. Our people instinctively resent coercion, and perhaps most of all when it affects their children and the opportunities that only education afford them. It is now reasonably clear that the goal of diversity that we call integration, if it is to be lasting and conducive to quality education, must have the support of parents who so frequently have the option to choose where their children will attend school. Courts, of course, should confront discrimination wherever it is found to exist. But they should recognize limitations on judicial action inherent in our system and also the limits of effective judicial power. The primary and continuing responsibility for public education, including the bringing about and maintaining of desired diversity, must be left with school officials and public authorities.

Building upon his misgivings about desegregation methodology, Justice Powell a year after *Penick* amplified his views and attracted further support for his position.

Estes v. Metropolitan Branch of the Dallas NAACP
444 U.S. 437 (1980)

MR. JUSTICE POWELL, with whom MR. JUSTICE STEWART andMR. JUSTICE REHNQUIST join, dissenting [from dismissal of certiorari]

The Court today dismisses the writs previously granted in this litigation and thereby reinstates the ruling of the Court of Appeals. The suit now will be returned to the District Court for elaboration of that court's conclusions on the feasibility of extensive busing to achieve racial balance in the Dallas public schools. The Court of Appeals directed the trial court to supplement the record with formal studies of the anticipated times and distances of likely bus routes, and to make additional findings on desegregation in the city's high schools.

. . .

I believe that two rules provide the basic outline for responsible exercise of the courts' equitable powers in school desegregation cases. First, "the nature of the desegregation remedy is to be determined by the nature and scope of the constitutional violation." The constitutional deprivation must be identified accurately, and the remedy must be related closely to that deprivation. Otherwise, a desegregation order may exceed both the power and the competence of courts. Second, "[t]he measure of any desegregation plan is its effectiveness." A court must act decisively to remove purposeful segregation, but it also must avoid the danger of inciting resegregation by unduly disrupting the public schools.

. . .

. . . In large cities, the principal cause of segregation in the schools is residential segregation, which results largely from demographic and economic conditions over which school authorities have no control. In cases since *Green*, the Court has stated explicitly that the existence of "predominantly white or predominantly black [schools,] without more . . . does not offend the Constitution." It is puzzling that many trial and appellate courts continue to misapply *Green* and largely to ignore more recent statements on this issue.

The important distinction is between "desegregated" schools and "integrated" schools. There can be no legitimate claim that "racial balance" in the public schools is constitutionally required. Rather, the Constitution mandates that no school system be structured to segregate the races. . . .

. . .

The pursuit of racial balance at any cost—the unintended legacy of *Green*--is without Constitutional or social justification. Out of zeal to remedy one evil, courts may encourage or set the stage for other evils. By acting against one-race schools, courts may produce one-race school systems. Parents with school-age children are highly motivated to seek access to schools perceived to afford quality education. A desegregation plan without community support, typically one with objectionable transportation requirements and continuing judicial oversight, accelerates the exodus to the suburbs of families able to move. The children of families remaining in the area affected by the court's decree are denied the opportunity to be part of an ethnically diverse student body. See *Parents Assn. of Andrew Jackson High School v. Ambach*. The general quality of the schools also tends to decline when substantial elements of the community abandon them.

The effects of resegregation can be even broader, reaching beyond the quality of education in the inner city to the life of the community. When the more economically advantaged citizens leave the city, the tax base shrinks and all city services suffer. And students whose parents elect to live beyond the reach of the court decree lose the benefits of attending ethnically diverse schools, an experience that prepares a child for citizenship in our pluralistic society.

. . .

Doubt about the wisdom of the Court's mission, a generation after the *Brown* decision, may have been most succinctly put by Justice Rehnquist who in 1980 observed that "(e)ven if the Constitution required it, and it were possible for the federal courts to do it, no equitable decrees can fashion an 'Emerald City' where all races, ethnic groups, and persons of various income levels live side by side in a large metropolitan area."[145]

e. Desegregation "to the Extent Practicable"

Four decades after the *Brown* case first was brought to the Court's attention, the Court further altered the terms of constitutional responsibility. In *Board of Education of Oklahoma City Public Schools v. Dowell*, the Court not only reminded that desegregation decrees were not to operate in perpetuity but stressed that eradication of past discrimination was to be achieved "to the extent practicable."[146] Such language reflected a change in tone and expectations from previous insistence upon eliminating such vestiges "root and branch."[147]

---

[145] Cleveland Board of Education v. Reed, 445 U.S. 935 (1980).

[146] Board of Education of Oklahoma City Public Schools v. Dowell, 111 S. Ct. 630, 636 (1991).

[147] *E.g.*, Green v. School Board of New Kent County, Virginia, 391 U.S. 430, 438 (1969).

Board of Education of Oklahoma City Public Schools v. Dowell
498 U.S. 237 (1991)

CHIEF JUSTICE REHNQUIST delivered the opinion of the court.

. . .

From the very first, federal supervision of local school systems was intended as a temporary measure to remedy past discrimination. *Brown* considered the "complexities arising from the *transition* to a system of public education freed of racial discrimination" in holding that the implementation of desegregation was to proceed "with all deliberate speed." . . .

Green also spoke of the *"transition* to a unitary, nonracial system of public education." Considerations based on the allocation of powers within our federal system, we think, support our view that quoted language from *Swift* does not provide the proper standard to apply to injunctions entered in school desegregation cases. Such decrees, unlike the one in *Swift*, are not intended to operate in perpetuity. Local control over the education of children allows citizens to participate in decisionmaking, and allows innovation so that school programs can fit local needs. . . .

. . .

A district court need not accept at face value the profession of a school board which has intentionally discriminated that it will cease to do so in the future. But in deciding whether to modify or dissolve a desegregation decree, a school board's compliance with previous court orders is obviously relevant. In this case the original finding of *de jure* segregation was entered in 1961, the injunctive decree from which the Board seeks relief was entered in 1972, and the Board complied with the decree in good faith until 1985. Not only do the personnel of school boards change over time, but the same passage of time enables the District Court to observe the good faith of the school board in complying the decree. The test espoused by the Court of Appeals would condemn a school district, once governed by a board which intentionally discriminated, to judicial tutelage for the indefinite future. Neither the principles governing the entry and dissolution of injunctive decrees nor the commands of the Equal Protection Clause of the Fourteenth Amendment, require any such Draconian result.

. . .

JUSTICE MARSHALL, with whom JUSTICE BLACKMUN and JUSTICE STEVENS join, dissenting.

Oklahoma gained statehood in 1907. For the next 65 years, the Oklahoma City School Board maintained segregated schools—initially relying on laws requiring dual school systems; thereafter, by exploiting residential segregation that had been created by legally enforced restrictive covenants. In 1972—18 years after this Court first found segregated schools unconstitutional—a federal court finally interrupted this cycle, enjoining the Oklahoma City School Board to implement a specific plan for achieving actual desegregation of its schools.

The practical question now before us is whether, 13 years after that injunction was imposed, the same School Board should have been allowed to return many of its elementary schools to their former one-race status. The majority today suggests that 13 years of desegregation was enough. The Court remands the case for further evaluation of whether the purposes of the injunctive decree were achieved sufficient to justify the decree's dissolution. However, the inquiry it commends to the District Court fails to recognize explicitly the threatened reemergence of one-race schools as a relevant "vestige" of de jure segregation.

In my view, the standard for dissolution of a school desegregation decree must reflect the central aim of our school desegregation precedents. In Brown ... a unanimous court declared that racially "[s]eparate educational facilities are inherently unequal." This holding rested on the Court's recognition that state-sponsored segregation conveys a message of "inferiority as to th[e] status [of Afro-American school children] in the community that may affect their hearts and minds in a way unlikely ever to be undone." Remedying this evil and preventing its recurrence were the motivations animating our requirement that formerly de jure segregated school districts take all feasible steps to eliminate racially identifiable schools.

I believe a desegregation decree cannot be lifted so long as conditions likely to inflict the stigmatic injury condemned in Brown I persist and there remain feasible methods of eliminating such conditions. Because the record here shows, and the Court of Appeals found, that feasible steps could be taken to avoid one-race schools, it is clear that the purposes of the decree have not yet been achieved and the Court of Appeals' reinstatement of the decree should be affirmed. I therefore dissent. In order to assess the full consequence of lifting the decree at issue in this case, it is necessary to explore more fully than does the majority the history of racial segregation in the Oklahoma City schools. This history reveals nearly unflagging resistance by the Board to judicial efforts to dismantle the City's dual education system.

When Oklahoma was admitted to the Union in 1907, its Constitution mandated separation of Afro-American children from all other races in the public school system. In addition to laws enforcing segregation in the schools, racially restrictive covenants, supported by state and local law, established a segregated residential pattern in Oklahoma City. Petitioner Board of Education of Oklahoma City (Board) exploited this residential segregation to enforce school segregation, locating "all-Negro" schools in the heart of the City's northeast quadrant, in which the majority of the City's Afro-American citizens resided.

Matters did not change in Oklahoma City after this Court's decision in Brown I and Brown v. Board of Education (Brown II). Although new school boundaries were established at that time, the Board also adopted a resolution allowing children to continue in the schools in which they were placed or to submit transfer requests that would be considered on a case-by-case basis.

Parents of Afro-American children relegated to schools in the northeast quadrant filed suit against the Board in 1961. Finding that the Board's special transfer policy was "designed to perpetuate and encourage segregation," the District Court struck down the policy as a violation of the Equal Protection Clause. Undeterred, the Board proceeded to adopt another special transfer policy which, as the District Court found in 1965, had virtually the same effect as the prior policy—"perpetuat[ion] [of] a segregated system." Because it allowed thousands of white children each year to transfer to schools in which their race was the majority, this transfer policy undermined any potential desegregation.

Thus, by 1972, 11 years after the plaintiffs had filed suit and 18 years after our decision in Brown I, the School Board continued to resist integration and in some respects the Board had worsened the situation. Four years after this Court's admonition to formerly de jure segregated school districts to come forward with realistic plans for immediate relief, the Board still had offered no meaningful plan of its own. Instead, "[i]t rationalize[d] its intransigence on the constitutionally unsound basis that public opinion [was] opposed to any further desegregation." The District Court concluded: "This litigation has been frustratingly interminable, not because of insuperable difficulties of implementation of the commands of the Supreme Court ... and the Constitution ... but because of the unpardonable recalcitrance of the ... Board." Consequently, the District Court ordered the Board to implement the only available plan that exhibited the promise of achieving actual desegregation— ...

In 1975, after a mere three years of operating under the [desegregation plan] the Board filed a "Motion to Close Case," arguing that it had "'eliminated all vestiges of state imposed racial discrimination in its school system.'" In 1977, the District Court granted the Board's motion and issued an "Order Terminating Case."

The Board continued to operate under the Plan until 1985, when it implemented the Student Reassignment Plan (SRP). The SRP superimposed attendance zones over some residentially segregated areas. As a result, considerable racial imbalance reemerged in 33 of 64 elementary schools in the Oklahoma City system with student bodies either greater than 90% Afro-American or greater than 90% non-Afro-American. More specially, 11 of the schools ranged from 96.9% to 99.7% Afro-American, and approximately 44% of all Afro-American children in grades K–4 were assigned to these virtually all-Afro-American schools.

I agree with the majority that the proper standard for determining whether a school desegregation decree should be dissolved is whether the purposes of the desegregation litigation, as incorporated in the decree, have been fully achieved. I strongly disagree with the majority, however, on what must be shown to demonstrate that a decree's purposes have been fully realized. In my view, a standard for dissolution of a desegregation decree must take into account the unique harm associated with a system of racially identifiable schools and must expressly demand the elimination of such schools.

Our pointed focus in *Brown I* upon the stigmatic injury caused by segregated schools explains our unflagging insistence that formerly *de jure* segregated school districts extinguish all vestiges of school segregation. The concept of stigma also gives us guidance as to what conditions must be eliminated before a decree can be deemed to have served its purpose.

. . .

Similarly, avoiding reemergence of the harm condemned in *Brown I* accounts for the Court's insistence on remedies that insure lasting integration of formerly segregated systems. Such school districts are required to "make every effort to achieve the *greatest possible degree of actual desegregation* and [to] be concerned with the elimination of one-race schools."

Just as it is central to the standard for evaluating the formation of a desegregation decree, so should the stigmatic injury associated with segregated schools be central to the standard for dissolving a decree. . . .

The majority suggests a more vague and, I fear, milder standard. Ignoring the harm

identified in *Brown I*, the majority asserts that the District Court should find that the purposes of the decree have been achieved so long as "the Oklahoma City School District [is now] being operated in compliance with the commands of the Equal Protection Clause" and "it [is] unlikely that the school board would return to its former ways." . . .

By focusing heavily on present and future compliance with the Equal Protection Clause, the majority's standard ignores how the stigmatic harm identified in *Brown I* can persist even after the State ceases actively to enforce segregation. It was not enough in *Green*, for example, for the school district to withdraw its own enforcement of segregation, leaving it up to individual children and their families to "choose" which school to attend. For it was clear under the circumstances that these choices would be shaped by and perpetuate the state-created message of racial inferiority associated with the school district's historical involvement in segregation. In sum, our school-desegregation jurisprudence establishes that the *effects* of past discrimination remain chargeable to the school district regardless of its lack of continued enforcement of segregation, and the remedial decree is required until those effects have been finally eliminated.

Applying the standard I have outlined, I would affirm the Court of Appeals' decision ordering the District Court to restore the desegregation decree. For it is clear on this record that removal of the decree will result in a significant number of racially identifiable schools that could be eliminated.

. . .

The majority equivocates on the effect to be given to the reemergence of racially identifiable schools. It instructs the District Court to consider whether those "'most important indicia of a segregated system'" have been eliminated, reciting the facets of segregated school operations identified in *Green*—"'faculty, staff, transportation, extra-curricular activities and facilities.'" And, by rendering "*res nova*" the issue whether *residential* segregation in Oklahoma City is a vestige of former *school* segregation, the majority accepts at least as a theoretical possibility that vestiges may exist beyond those identified in *Green*. Nonetheless, the majority hints that the District Court could ignore the effect of residential segregation in perpetuating racially identifiable schools if the court finds residential segregation to be "the result of private decisionmaking and economics." Finally, the majority warns against the application of a standard that would subject formerly segregated school districts to the "Draconian" fate of "judicial tutelage for the indefinite future."

This equivocation is completely unsatisfying. First, it is well established that school segregation "may have a profound reciprocal effect on the racial composition of residential neighborhoods." The record in this case amply demonstrates this form of complicity in residential segregation on the part of the Board. The District Court found as early as 1965 that the Board's use of neighborhood schools "serve[d] to . . . exten[d] areas of Negro housing, destroying in the process already integrated neighborhoods and thereby increasing the number of segregated schools." It was because of the School Board's responsibility for residential segregation that the District Court refused to permit the Board to superimpose a neighborhood plan over the racially isolated northeast quadrant.

Second, there is no basis for the majority's apparent suggestion that the result should be different if residential segregation is now perpetuated by "private decisionmaking." The District Court's conclusion that the racial identify of the northeast quadrant now subsists because of "personal preference[s]," pays insufficient attention to the roles of the State, local officials, and the Board in creating what are now self-perpetuating patterns of residential segregation. Even more important, it fails to account for the *unique* role of the School Board in creating "all-Negro" schools clouded by the stigma of segregation—schools to which white parents would not opt to send their children. That such negative "personal preferences" exist should not absolve a school district that played a role in creating such "preferences"

from its obligation to desegregate the schools to the maximum extent possible.

I also reject the majority's suggestion that the length of federal judicial supervision is a valid factor in assessing a dissolution. The majority is correct that the Court has never contemplated perpetual judicial oversight of former *de jure* segregated school districts. Our jurisprudence requires, however, that the job of school desegregation be fully completed and maintained so that the stigmatic harm identified in *Brown I* will not recur upon lifting the decree. Any doubt on the issue whether the School Board has fulfilled its remedial obligations should be resolved in favor of the Afro-American children affected by this litigation.

In its concern to spare local school boards the "Draconian" fate of "indefinite" "judicial tutelage," the majority risks subordination of the constitutional rights of Afro-American children to the interest of school board autonomy.

. . .

Consistent with the mandate of *Brown I*, our cases have imposed on school districts an unconditional duty to eliminate *any* condition that perpetuates the message of racial inferiority inherent in the policy of state-sponsored segregation. The racial identifiability of a district's schools is such a condition. Whether this "vestige" of state-sponsored segregation will persist cannot simply be ignored at the point where a district with a history of state-sponsored school segregation, racial separation, in my view, *remains* inherently unequal.

Consistent with the obligation to desegregate to the extent practicable, the Court in *Freeman v. Pitts*, determined that a school district was obligated "to achieve maximum practicable desegregation."[148] It also indicated that courts could withdraw from supervision of desegregation cases on an incremental basis.[149]

---

[148] Freeman v. Pitts, 112 S. Ct. 1430, 1447–48 (1992).

[149] *Id.* at 1445.

Freeman v. Pitts
112 S. Ct. 1430 (1992)

JUSTICE KENNEDY delivered the opinion of the Court.

. . .

[The District Court found that the DeKalb County, Georgia school system (DCSS) had achieved unitary status] with regard to student assignments, transportation, physical facilities, and extracurricular activities, and ruled that it would order no further relief in

those areas. The District Court stopped short of dismissing the case, however, because it found that DCSS was not unitary in every respect. The court said that vestiges of the dual system remain in the areas of teacher and principal assignments, resource allocation, and quality of education. DCSS was ordered to take measures to address the remaining problems.

. . .

Proper resolution of any desegregation case turns on a careful assessment of its facts. *Green*. Here, as in most cases where the issue is the degree of compliance with a school desegregation decree, a critical beginning point is the degree of racial imbalance in the school district, that is to say a comparison of the proportion of majority to minority students in individual schools with the proportions of the races in the district as a whole. This inquiry is fundamental, for under the former *de jure* regimes racial exclusion was both the means and the end of a policy motivated by disparagement of or hostility towards the disfavored race. . . .

Today, we make explicit the rationale that was central in *Spangler*. A federal court in a school desegregation case has the discretion to order an incremental or partial withdrawal of its supervision and control. This discretion drives both from the constitutional authority which justified its intervention in the first instance and its ultimate objectives in formulating the decree. The authority of the court is invoked at the outset to remedy particular constitutional violations. In construing the remedial authority of the district courts, we have been guided by the principles that "judicial powers may be exercised only on the basis of a constitutional violation," and that "the nature of the violation determines the scope of the remedy." A remedy is justifiable only insofar as it advances the ultimate objective of alleviating the initial constitutional violation.

We have said that the court's end purpose must be to remedy the violation and in addition to restore state and local authorities to the control of a school system that is operating in compliance with the Constitution. *Milliken v. Bradley*, ("[T]he federal courts in devising a remedy must take into account the interests of state and local authorities in managing their own affairs, consistent with the Constitution"). Partial relinquishment of judicial control, where justified by the facts of the case, can be an important and significant step in fulfilling the district court's duty to return the operations and control of schools to local authorities. In *Dowell*, we emphasized that federal judicial supervision of local school systems was intended as a "temporary measure." Although this temporary measure has lasted decades, the ultimate objective has not changed—to return school districts to the control of local authorities. Just as a court has the obligation at the outset of a desegregation decree to structure a plan so that all available resources of the court are directed to comprehensive supervision of its decree, so too must a court provide an orderly means for withdrawing from control when it is shown that the school district has attained the requisite degree of compliance. A transition phase in which control is relinquished in a gradual way is an appropriate means to this end.

. . .

We hold that, in the course of supervising desegregation plans, federal courts have the authority to relinquish supervision and control of school districts in incremental stages, before full compliance has been achieved in every area of school operations. While retaining jurisdiction over the case, the court may determine that it will not order further remedies in areas where the school district is in compliance with the decree. That is to say, upon a finding that a school system subject to a court-supervised desegregation plan is in compliance in some but not all areas, the court in appropriate cases may return control to the school system in those areas where compliance has been achieved, limiting further judicial supervision to operations that are not yet in full compliance with the court decree. In particular, the district court may determine that it will not order further remedies in the area of student assignments where racial imbalance is not traceable, in a proximate way, to constitutional violations.

A court's discretion to order the incremental withdrawal of its supervision in a school desegregation case must be exercised in a manner consistent with the purposes and objectives of its equitable power. Among the factors which must inform the sound discretion of the court in ordering partial withdrawal are the following: whether retention of judicial control is necessary or practicable to achieve compliance with the decree in other facets of the school system; and whether the school district has demonstrated, to the public and to the parents and students of the once disfavored race, its good faith commitment to the whole of the court's decree and to those provisions of the law and the constitution that were the predicate for judicial intervention in the first instance.

In considering these factors a court should give particular attention to the school system's record of compliance. A school system is better positioned to demonstrate its good-faith commitment to a constitutional course of action when its policies form a consistent pattern of lawful conduct directed to eliminating earlier violations. And with the passage of time the degree to which racial imbalances continue to represent vestiges of a constitutional violation may diminish, and the practicability and efficacy of various remedies can be evaluated with more precision. . . .

The Court of Appeals was mistaken in ruling that our opinion in *Swann* requires "awkward," "inconvenient" and "even bizarre" measures to achieve racial balance in student assignments in the late phases of carrying out a decree, when the imbalance is attributable neither to the prior *de jure* system nor to a later violation by the school district but rather to independent demographic forces. . . .

The desegregation decree was designed to achieve maximum practicable desegregation. Its central remedy was the closing of black schools and the reassignment of pupils to neighborhood schools, with attendance zones that achieved racial balance. The plan accomplished its objective in the first year of operation, before dramatic demographic changes altered residential patterns. For the entire 17-year period the respondents raised no substantial objection to the basic student assignment system, as the parties and the District Court concentrated on other mechanisms to eliminate the *de jure* taint.

Where resegregation is a product not of state action but of private choices, it does not have constitutional implications. It is beyond the authority and beyond the practical ability of the federal courts to try to counteract these kinds of continuous and massive demographic shifts. To attempt such results would require ongoing and never-ending supervision by the courts of school districts simply because they were once *de jure* segregated. Residential housing choices, and their attendant effects on the racial composition of schools, present an ever-changing pattern, one difficult to address through judicial remedies.

In one sense of the term, vestiges of past segregation by state decree do remain in our society and in our schools. Past wrongs to the black race, wrongs committed by the State and in its name, are a stubborn fact of history. And stubborn facts of history linger and persist. But though we cannot escape our history, neither must we overstate its consequences in fixing legal responsibilities. The vestiges of segregation that are the concern of the law in a school case may be subtle and intangible but nonetheless they must be so real that they have a causal link to the *de jure* violation being remedied. It is simply not always the case that demographic forces causing population change bear any real and substantial relation to a *de jure* violation. And the law need not proceed on that premise.

As the *de jure* violation becomes more remote in time and these demographic changes intervene, it becomes less likely that a current racial imbalance in a school district is a vestige of the prior *de jure* system. The causal link between current conditions and the prior violation is even more attenuated if the school district has demonstrated its good faith. In light of its finding that the demographic changes in DeKalb County are unrelated to the prior violation, the District Court was correct to entertain the suggestion that DCSS had no duty to achieve systemwide racial balance in the student population.

Both *Dowell* and *Freeman* illuminated the Court's mounting interest in downsizing the judiciary's role in the desegregative process. Impatience with remedial foot-dragging by the late 1960s had inspired constitutional demands for relief that promised "to work now" and delineation of expansive judicial powers to command results. Confronted with a lower court's management of an urban school district that insisted upon an expensive and expansive magnet school system, the Court seized the opportunity for significantly scaling back the judiciary's monitoring function.

Missouri v. Jenkins
115 S. Ct. 2038 (1995)

CHIEF JUSTICE REHNQUIST delivered the opinion of the Court.

As this school desegregation litigation enters its 18th year, we are called upon again to review the decisions of the lower courts. In this case, the State of Missouri has challenged the District Court's order of salary increases for virtually all instructional and noninstructional staff within the Kansas City, Missouri, School District (KCMSD) and the District Court's order requiring the State to continue to fund remedial "quality education" programs because student achievement levels were still "at or below national norms at many grade levels."

I

A general overview of this litigation is necessary for proper resolution of the issues upon which we granted certiorari. This case has been before the same United States District Judge since 1977. In that year, the KCMSD, the school board, and the children of two school board members brought suit against the State and other defendants. Plaintiffs alleged that the State, the surrounding suburban school districts (SSD's), and various federal agencies had caused and perpetuated a system of racial segregation in the schools of the Kansas City metropolitan area. The District Court realigned the KCMSD as a nominal defendant and certified as a class, present and future KCMSD students. The KCMSD brought a cross-claim against the State for its failure to eliminate the vestiges of its prior dual school system.

After a trial that lasted 7½ months, the District Court dismissed the case against the federal defendants and the SSD's, but determined that the State and the KCMSD were liable for an intradistrict violation, i.e., they had operated a segregated school system within the KCMSD. The District Court determined that prior to 1954 "Missouri mandated segregated schools for black and white children." Furthermore, the KCMSD and the State had failed in their affirmative obligations to eliminate the vestiges of the State's dual school system within the KCMSD.

In June 1985, the District Court issued its first remedial order and established as its goal the "elimination of all vestiges of state imposed segregation." The District Court determined that "segregation had caused a system wide reduction in student achievement in the schools of the KCMSD." The District Court made no particularized findings regarding the extent that student achievement had been reduced or what portion of that reduction was attributable to segregation. The District Court also identified 25 schools within the KCMSD that had enrollments of 90% or more black students.

The District Court, pursuant to plans submitted by the KCMSD and the State, ordered a wide range of quality education programs for all students attending the KCMSD. First, the District Court ordered that the KCMSD be restored to an AAA classification, the highest classification awarded by the State Board of Education. Second, it ordered that the number of students per class be reduced so that the student-to-teacher ratio was below the level required for AAA standing. The District Court justified its reduction in class size as

> "an essential part of any plan to remedy the vestiges of segregation in the KCMSD. Reducing class size will serve to remedy the vestiges of past segregation by increasing individual attention and instruction, as well as increasing the potential for desegregative educational experiences for KCMSD students by maintaining and attracting non-minority enrollment."

The District Court also ordered programs to expand educational opportunities for all

KCMSD students: full-day kindergarten; expanded summer school; before- and after-school tutoring; and an early childhood development program. Finally, the District Court implemented a state-funded "effective schools" program that consisted of substantial yearly cash grants to each of the schools within the KCMSD. Under the "effective schools" program, the State was required to fund programs at both the 25 racially identifiable schools as well as the 43 other schools within the KCMSD.

The KCMSD was awarded an AAA rating in the 1987–1988 school year, and there is no dispute that since that time it has "'maintained and greatly exceeded AAA requirements.'" The total cost for these quality education programs has exceeded $220 million.

The District Court also set out to desegregate the KCMSD but believed that "to accomplish desegregation within the boundary lines of a school district whose enrollment remains 68.3% black is a difficult task." Because it had found no interdistrict violation, the District Court could not order mandatory interdistrict redistribution of students between the KCMSD and the surrounding SSD's. The District Court refused to order additional mandatory student reassignments because they would "increase the instability of the KCMSD and reduce the potential for desegregation." Relying on favorable precedent from the Eighth Circuit, the District Court determined that "achievement of AAA status, improvement of the quality of education being offered at the KCMSD schools, magnet schools, as well as other components of this desegregation plan can serve to maintain and hopefully attract non-minority student enrollment."

In November 1986, the District Court approved a comprehensive magnet school and capital improvements plan and held the State and the KCMSD jointly and severally liable for its funding. Under the District Court's plan, every senior high school, every middle school, and one-half of the elementary schools were converted into magnet schools. The District Court adopted the magnet-school program to "provide a greater educational opportunity to all KCMSD students," and because it believed "that the proposed magnet plan [was] so attractive that it would draw non-minority students from the private schools who have abandoned or avoided the KCMSD, and draw in additional non-minority students from the suburbs." The District Court felt that "the long-term benefit of all KCMSD students of a greater educational opportunity in an integrated environment is worthy of such an investment." Since its inception, the magnet school program has operated at a cost, including magnet transportation, in excess of $448 million. In April 1993, the District Court considered, but ultimately rejected, the plaintiffs' and the KCMSD's proposal seeking approval of a long-range magnet renewal program that included a 10-year budget of well over $500 million, funded by the State and the KCMSD on a joint-and-several basis.

. . .

In September 1987, the District Court adopted, for the most part, KCMSD's long-range capital improvements plan at a cost in excess of $187 million. The plan called for the renovation of approximately 55 schools, the closure of 18 facilities, and the construction of 17 new schools. The District Court rejected what it referred to as the "'patch and repair' approach proposed by the State" because it "would not achieve suburban comparability or the visual attractiveness sought by the Court as it would result in floor coverings with unsightly sections of mismatched carpeting and tile, and individual walls possessing different shades of paint." The District Court reasoned that "if the KCMSD schools underwent the limited renovation proposed by the State, the schools would continue to be unattractive and substandard, and would certainly serve as a deterrent to parents considering enrolling their children in KCMSD schools." As of 1990, the District Court had ordered $260 million in capital improvements. Since then, the total cost of capital improvements ordered has soared to over $540 million.

As part of its desegregation plan, the District Court has ordered salary assistance to the KCMSD. In 1987, the District Court initially ordered salary assistance only for teachers within the KCMSD. Since that time, however, the District Court has ordered salary assistance to all but three of the approximately 5,000 KCMSD employees. The total cost of this component of the desegregation remedy since 1987 is over $200 million.

The District Court's desegregation plan has been described as the most ambitious and expensive remedial program in the history of school desegregation. The annual cost per pupil at the KCMSD far exceeds that of the neighboring SSD's or of any school district in Missouri. Nevertheless, the KCMSD, which has pursued a "friendly adversary" relationship with the plaintiffs, has continued to propose ever more expensive programs. As a result, the desegregation costs have escalated and now are approaching an annual cost of $200 million. These massive expenditures have financed

"high schools in which every classroom will have air conditioning, an alarm system, and 15 microcomputers; a 2,000-square-foot planetarium; green houses and vivariums; a 25-acre farm with an air-conditioned meeting room for 104 people; a Model United Nations wired for language translation; broadcast capable radio and television studios with an editing and animation lab; a temperature controlled art gallery; movie editing and screening rooms; a 3,500-square-foot dust-free diesel mechanics room; 1,875-square-foot elementary school animal rooms for use in a zoo project; swimming pools; and numerous other facilities."

Not surprisingly, the cost of this remedial plan has "far exceeded KCMSD's budget, or for that matter, its authority to tax." The State, through the operation of joint-and-several liability, has borne the brunt of these costs. The District Court candidly has acknowledged that it has "allowed the District planners to dream" and "provided the mechanism for those dreams to be realized." In short, the District Court "has gone to great lengths to provide KCMSD with facilities and opportunities not available anywhere else in the country."

II

With this background, we turn to the present controversy. First, the State has challenged the District Court's requirement that it fund salary increases for KCMSD instructional and noninstructional staff. The State claimed that funding for salaries was beyond the scope of the District Court's remedial authority. Second, the State has challenged the District Court's order requiring it to continue to fund the remedial quality education programs for the 1992–1993 school year. The State contended that under *Freeman v. Pitts*, it had achieved partial unitary status with respect to the quality education programs already in place. As a result, the State argued that the District Court should have relieved it of responsibility for funding those programs.

The District Court rejected the State's arguments. It first determined that the salary increases were warranted because "high quality personnel are necessary not only to implement specialized desegregation programs intended to 'improve educational opportunities and reduce racial isolation' . . . but also to 'ensure that there is no diminution in the quality of its regular academic program.'" Its "ruling [was] grounded in remedying the vestiges of segregation by improving the desegregative attractiveness of the KCMSD." The District Court did not address the State's *Freeman* arguments; nevertheless, it ordered the State to continue to fund the quality education programs for the 1992–1993 school year.

The Court of Appeals denied rehearing en blanc, with five judges dissenting. . . .

Because of the importance of the issues, we granted certiorari to consider the following:

(1) whether the District Court exceeded its constitutional authority when it granted salary increases to virtually all instructional and noninstructional employees of the KCMSD, and (2) whether the District Court properly relied upon the fact that student achievement test scores had failed to rise to some unspecified level when it declined to find that the State had achieved partial unitary status as to the quality education programs.

. . .

The ultimate inquiry is "'whether the [constitutional violator] has complied in good faith with the desegregation decree since it was entered, and whether the vestiges of past discrimination have been eliminated to the extent practicable.'"

Proper analysis of the District Court's orders challenged here, then, must rest upon their serving as proper means to the end of restoring the victims of discriminatory conduct to the position they would have occupied in the absence of that conduct and their eventual restoration of "state and local authorities to the control of a school system that is operating in compliance with the Constitution." We turn to that analysis.

The State argues that the order approving salary increases is beyond the District Court's authority because it was crafted to serve an "interdistrict goal," in spite of the fact that the constitutional violation in this case is "intradistrict" in nature. "The nature of the desegregation remedy is to be determined by the nature and scope of the constitutional violation." The proper response to an intradistrict violation is an intradistrict remedy, that serves to eliminate the racial identity of the schools within the effected school district by eliminating, as far as practicable, the vestiges of *de jure* segregation in all facets of their operations.

Here, the District Court has found, and the Court of Appeals has affirmed, that this case involved no interdistrict constitutional violation that would support interdistrict relief. Thus, the proper response by the District Court should have been to eliminate to the extent practicable the vestiges of prior de jure segregation within the KCMSD: a system-wide reduction in student achievement and the existence of 25 racially identifiable schools with a population of over 90% black students.

The District Court and Court of Appeals, however, have felt that because the KCMSD's enrollment remained 68.3% black, a purely intradistrict remedy would be insufficient. But, as noted in *Milliken I*, we have rejected the suggestion "that schools which have a majority of Negro students are not 'desegregated' whatever the racial makeup of the school district's population and however neutrally the district lines have been drawn and administered."

Instead of seeking to remove the racial identity of the various schools within the KCMSD, the District Court has set out on a program to create a school district that was equal to or superior to the surrounding SSD's. Its remedy has focused on "desegregative attractiveness," coupled with "suburban comparability." Examination of the District Court's reliance on "desegregative attractiveness" and "suburban comparability" is instructive for our ultimate resolution of the salary-order issue.

The purpose of desegregative attractiveness has been not only to remedy the system-wide reduction in student achievement, but also to attract nonminority students not presently enrolled in the KCMSD. This remedy has included an elaborate program of capital improvements, course enrichment, and extracurricular enhancement not simply in the formerly identifiable black schools, but in schools throughout the district. The District Court's remedial orders have converted every senior high school, every middle school, and one-half of the elementary schools in the KCMSD into "magnet" schools. The District Court's remedial order has all but made the KCMSD itself into a magnet district.

We previously have approved of intradistrict desegregation remedies involving magnet schools. Magnet schools have the advantage of encouraging voluntary movement of students within a school district in a pattern that aids desegregation on a voluntary basis, without requiring extensive busing and redrawing of district boundary lines. As a component in an intradistrict remedy, magnet schools also are attractive because they promote desegregation while limiting the withdrawal of white student enrollment that may result from mandatory student reassignment.

The District Court's remedial plan in this case, however, is not designed solely to redistribute the students within the KCMSD in order to eliminate racially identifiable schools within the KCMSD. Instead, its purpose is to attract nonminority students from outside the KCMSD schools. But this inter district goal is beyond the scope of the intradistrict violation identified by the District Court. In effect, the District Court has devised a remedy to accomplish indirectly what it admittedly lacks the remedial authority to mandate directly: the interdistrict transfer of students.

. . .

What we meant in *Milliken I* by an interdistrict violation was a violation that caused segregation between adjoining districts. Nothing in *Milliken I* suggests that the District Court in that case could have circumvented the limits on its remedial authority by requiring the State of Michigan, a constitutional violator, to implement a magnet program designed to achieve the same interdistrict transfer of students that we held was beyond its remedial authority. Here, the District Court has done just that: created a magnet district of the KCMSD in order to serve the interdistrict goal of attracting nonminority students from the surrounding SSD's and redistributing them within the KCMSD. The District Court's pursuit of "desegregative attractiveness" is beyond the scope of its broad remedial authority.

. . .

The District Court's pursuit of "desegregative attractiveness" cannot be reconciled with our cases placing limitations on a district court's remedial authority. It is certainly theoretically possible that the greater the expenditure per pupil within the KCMSD, the more likely it is that some unknowable number of nonminority students not presently attending schools in the KCMSD will choose to enroll in those schools. Under this reasoning, however, every increased expenditure, whether it be for teachers, noninstructional employees, books, or buildings, will make the KCMSD in some way more attractive, and thereby perhaps induce nonminority students to enroll in its schools. But this rationale is not susceptible to any objective limitation. This case provides numerous examples demonstrating the limitless authority of the District Court operating under this rationale. In short, desegregative attractiveness has been used "as the hook on which to hang numerous policy choices about improving the quality of education in general within the KCMSD."

. . .

The District Court's pursuit of the goal of "desegregative attractiveness" results in so many imponderables and is so far removed from the task of eliminating the racial identifiability of the schools within the KCMSD that we believe it is beyond the admittedly broad discretion of the District Court. In this posture, we conclude that the District Court's order of salary increases, which was "grounded in remedying the vestiges of segregation by improving the desegregative attractiveness of the KCMSD," is simply too far removed from an acceptable implementation of a permissible means to remedy previous legally mandated segregation.

Similar considerations lead us to conclude that the District Court's order requiring the State to continue to fund the quality education programs because student achievement levels were still "at or below national norms at many grade levels" cannot be sustained. The State does not seek from this Court a declaration of partial unitary status with respect to the quality education programs. It challenges the requirement of indefinite funding of a quality education program until national norms are met, based on the assumption that while a mandate for significant educational improvement, both in teaching and in facilities, may have been justified originally, its indefinite extension is not.

. . .

But this clearly is not the appropriate test to be applied in deciding whether a previously segregated district has achieved partially unitary status. . . . The basic task of the District Court is to decide whether the reduction in achievement by minority students attributable to prior de jure segregation has been remedied to the extent practicable. Under our precedents, the State and the KCMSD are "entitled to a rather precise statement of [their] obligations under a desegregation decree." Although the District Court has determined that "segregation has caused a system wide reduction in achievement in the schools of the KCMSD," it never has identified the incremental effect that segregation has had on minority student achievement or the specific goals of the quality education programs.

In reconsidering this order, the District Court should apply our three-part test from *Freeman v. Pitts*. The District Court should consider that the State's role with respect to the quality education programs has been limited to the funding, not the implementation, of those programs. As all the parties agree that improved achievement on test scores is not necessarily required for the State to achieve partial unitary status as to the quality education programs, the District Court should sharply limit, if not dispense with, its reliance on this factor. Just as demographic changes independent of de jure segregation will affect the racial composition of student assignments, so too will numerous external factors beyond the control of the KCMSD and the State affect minority student achievement. So long as these external factors are not the result of segregation, they do not figure in the remedial calculus. Insistence upon academic goals unrelated to the effects of legal segregation unwarrantably postpones the day when the KCMSD will be able to operate on its own.

The District Court also should consider that many goals of its quality education plan already have been attained: the KCMSD now is equipped with "facilities and opportunities not available anywhere else in the country." KCMSD schools received an AAA rating eight years ago, and the present remedial programs have been in place for seven years. It may be that in education, just as it may be in economics, a "rising tide lifts all boats," but the remedial quality education program should be tailored to remedy the injuries suffered by the victims of prior de jure segregation. Minority students in kindergarten through grade 7 in the KCMSD always have attended AAA-rated schools; minority students in the KCMSD that previously attended schools rated below AAA have since received remedial education programs for a period of up to seven years.

On remand, the District Court must bear in mind that its end purpose is not only "to remedy the violation" to the extent practicable, but also "to restore state and local authorities to the control of a school system that is operating in compliance with the Constitution."

The judgment of the Court of Appeals is reversed.

. . .

JUSTICE O'CONNOR, concurring.

. . .

What the District Court did in this case, however, and how it transgressed the constitutional bounds of its remedial powers, is to make desegregative attractiveness the underlying goal of its remedy for the specific purpose of reversing the trend of white flight. However troubling that trend may be, remedying it is within the District Court's authority only if it is "directly caused by the constitutional violation." . . . The Court and the dissent attempt to reconcile the different statements by the lower courts as to whether white flight was caused by segregation or desegregation. Whether the white exodus that has resulted in a school district that is 68% black was caused by the District Court's remedial orders or by natural, if unfortunate, demographic forces, we have it directly from the District Court that the segregative effects of KCMSD's constitutional violation did not transcend its geographical boundaries. In light of that finding, the District Court cannot order remedies seeking to rectify regional demographic trends that go beyond the nature and scope of the constitutional violation.

This case, like other school desegregation litigation, is concerned with "the elimination of the discrimination inherent in the dual school systems, not with myriad factors of human existence which can cause discrimination in a multitude of ways on racial, religious, or ethnic grounds." Those myriad factors are not readily corrected by judicial intervention, but are best addressed by the representative branches; time and again, we have recognized the ample authority legislatures possess to combat racial injustice, It is true that where such legislative efforts classify persons on the basis of their race, we have mandated strict judicial scrutiny to ensure that the personal right to equal protection of the laws has not been infringed. It is only by applying strict scrutiny that we can distinguish between unconstitutional discrimination and narrowly tailored remedial programs that legislatures may enact to further the compelling governmental interest in redressing the effects of past discrimination.

Courts, however, are different. The necessary restrictions on our jurisdiction and authority contained in Article III of the Constitution limit the judiciary's institutional capacity to prescribe palliatives for societal ills. The unfortunate fact of racial imbalance and bias in our society, however pervasive or invidious, does not admit of judicial intervention absent a constitutional violation. . . .

In this case, it may be the "myriad factors of human existence," that have prompted the white exodus from KCMSD, and the District Court cannot justify its transgression of the above constitutional principles simply by invoking desegregative attractiveness. The Court today discusses desegregative attractiveness only insofar as it supports the salary increase order under review, and properly refrains from addressing the propriety of all the remedies that the District Court has ordered, revised, and extended in the 18-year history of this case. These remedies may also be improper to the extent that they serve the same goals of desegregative attractiveness and suburban comparability that we hold today to be impermissible, and, conversely, the District Court may be able to justify some remedies without reliance on these goals. But these are questions that the Court rightly leaves to be answered on remand. For now, it is enough to affirm the principle that "the nature of the desegregation remedy is to be determined by the nature and scope of the constitutional violation."

For these reasons, I join the opinion of the Court.

JUSTICE THOMAS, concurring.

It never ceases to amaze me that the courts are so willing to assume that anything that is predominantly black must be inferior. Instead of focusing on remedying the harm done to those black schoolchildren injured by segregation, the District Court here sought to convert the Kansas City, Missouri, School District (KCMSD) into a "magnet district" that would reverse the "white flight" caused by desegregation. In this respect, I join the Court's decision concerning the two remedial issues presented for review. I write separately, however, to add a few thoughts with respect to the overall course of this litigation. In order to evaluate the scope of the remedy, we must understand the scope of the constitutional violation and the nature of the remedial powers of the federal courts.

Two threads in our jurisprudence have produced this unfortunate situation, in which a District Court has taken it upon itself to experiment with the education of the KCMSD's black youth. First, the court has read our cases to support the theory that black students suffer an unspecified psychological harm from segregation that retards their mental and educational development. This approach not only relies upon questionable social science research rather than constitutional principle, but it also rests on an assumption of black inferiority. Second, we have permitted the federal courts to exercise virtually unlimited equitable powers to remedy this alleged constitutional violation. The exercise of this authority has trampled upon principles of federalism and the separation of powers and has freed courts to pursue other agendas unrelated to the narrow purpose of precisely remedying a constitutional harm.

I

A

The mere fact that a school is black does not mean that it is the product of a constitutional violation. A "racial imbalance does not itself establish a violation of the Constitution." Instead, in order to find unconstitutional segregation, we require that plaintiffs "prove all of the essential elements of de jure segregation—that is, stated simply, a current condition of segregation resulting from intentional state action directed specifically to the [allegedly segregated] schools."

Without more, the District Court's findings could not have supported a finding of liability against the state. It should by now be clear that the existence of one-race schools is not by itself an indication that the State is practicing segregation. The continuing "racial isolation" of schools after de jure segregation has ended may well reflect voluntary housing choices or other private decisions. Here, for instance, the demography of the entire KCMSD has changed considerably since 1954. Though blacks accounted for only 18.9% of KCMSD's enrollment in 1954, by 1983–1984 the school district was 67.7% black. That certain schools are overwhelmingly black in a district that is now more than two-thirds black is hardly a sure sign of intentional state action.

. . . The District Court therefore rested the State's liability on the simple fact that the State had intentionally created the dual school system before 1954, and had failed to fulfill "its affirmative duty of disestablishing a dual school system subsequent to 1954." . . .

In order for a "vestige" to supply the ground for an exercise of remedial authority, it must be clearly traceable to the dual school system. The "vestiges of segregation that are the concern of the law in a school case may be subtle and intangible but nonetheless they must be so real that they have a causal link to the de jure violation being remedied." District Courts must not confuse the consequences of de jure segregation with the results of larger social forces or of private decisions. "It is simply not always the case that demographic forces

causing population change bear any real and substantial relation to a de jure violation." As state-enforced segregation recedes farther into the past, it is more likely that "these kinds of continuous and massive demographic shifts," will be the real source of racial imbalance or of poor educational performance in a school district. And as we have emphasized, "it is beyond the authority and beyond the practical ability of the federal courts to try to counteract" these social changes.

When a district court holds the State liable for discrimination almost 30 years after the last official state action, it must do more than show that there are schools with high black populations or low test scores. Here, the district judge did not make clear how the high black enrollments in certain schools were fairly traceable to the State of Missouri's actions. I do not doubt that Missouri maintained the despicable system of segregation until 1954. But I question the District Court's conclusion that because the State had enforced segregation until 1954, its actions, or lack thereof, proximately caused the "racial isolation" of the predominantly black schools in 1984. In fact, where, as here, the finding of liability comes so late in the day, I would think it incumbent upon the District Court to explain how more recent social or demographic phenomena did not cause the "vestiges." This the District Court did not do.

B

Without a basis in any real finding of intentional government action, the District Court's imposition of liability upon the State of Missouri improperly rests upon a theory that racial imbalances are unconstitutional. That is, the court has "indulged the presumption, often irrebuttable in practice, that a presently observed [racial] imbalance has been proximately caused by intentional state action during the prior de jure era." In effect, the court found that racial imbalances constituted an ongoing constitutional violation that continued to inflict harm on black students. This position appears to rest upon the idea that any school that is black is inferior, and that blacks cannot succeed without the benefit of the company of whites.

The District Court's willingness to adopt such stereotypes stemmed from a misreading of our earliest school desegregation case. In *Brown v. Board of Education*, the Court noted several psychological and sociological studies purporting to show that de jure segregation harmed black students by generating "a feeling of inferiority" in them. Seizing upon this passage in *Brown I*, the District Court asserted that "forced segregation ruins attitudes and is inherently unequal." The District Court suggested that this inequality continues in full force even after the end of de jure segregation:

> "The general attitude of inferiority among blacks produces low achievement which ultimately limits employment opportunities and causes poverty. While it may be true that poverty results in low achievement regardless of race, it is undeniable that most poverty-level families are black. The District stipulated that as of 1977 they had not eliminated all the vestiges of the prior dual system. The Court finds the inferior education indigenous of the state-compelled dual school system has lingering effects in the [KCMSD]."

Thus, the District Court seemed to believe that black students in the KCMSD would continue to receive an "inferior education" despite the end of de jure segregation, as long as de facto segregation persisted. As the District Court later concluded, compensatory educational programs were necessary "as a means of remedying many of the educational problems which go hand in hand with racially isolated minority student populations." Such assumptions and any social science research upon which they rely certainly cannot form the basis upon which we decide matters of constitutional principle.[2]

It is clear that the District Court misunderstood the meaning of *Brown I*. *Brown I* did not say that "racially isolated" schools were inherently inferior; the harm that it identified was tied purely to de jure segregation, not de facto segregation. Indeed, *Brown I* itself did not need to rely upon any psychological or social-science research in order to announce the simple, yet fundamental truth that the Government cannot discriminate among its citizens on the basis of race. As the Court's unanimous opinion indicated: "In the field of public education the doctrine of 'separate but equal' has no place. Separate educational facilities are inherently unequal." At the heart of this interpretation of the Equal Protection Clause lies the principle that the Government must treat citizens as individuals, and not as members of racial, ethnic or religious groups. It is for this reason that we must subject all racial classifications to the strictest of scrutiny, which (aside

from two decisions rendered in the midst of wartime), has proven automatically fatal.

Segregation was not unconstitutional because it might have caused psychological feelings of inferiority. Public school systems that separated blacks and provided them with superior educational resources—making blacks "feel" superior to whites sent to lesser schools—would violate the Fourteenth Amendment, whether or not the white students felt stigmatized, just as do school systems in which the positions of the races are reversed. Psychological injury or benefit is irrelevant to the question whether state actors have engaged in intentional discrimination—the critical inquiry for ascertaining violations of the Equal Protection Clause. The judiciary is fully competent to make independent determinations concerning the existence of state action without the unnecessary and misleading assistance of the social sciences.

Regardless of the relative quality of the schools, segregation violated the Constitution because the State classified students based on their race. Of course, segregation additionally harmed black students by relegating them to schools with substandard facilities and resources. But neutral policies, such as local school assignments, do not offend the Constitution when individual private choices concerning work or residence produce schools with high black populations. The Constitution does not prevent individuals from choosing to live together, to work together, or to send their children to school together, so long as the State does not interfere with their choices on the basis of race.

Given that desegregation has not produced the predicted leaps forward in black educational achievement, there is no reason to think that black students cannot learn as well when surrounded by members of their own race as when they are in an integrated environment. Indeed, it may very well be that what has been true for historically black colleges is true for black middle and high schools. Despite their origins in "the shameful history of state-enforced segregation," these institutions can be "both a source of pride to blacks who have attended them and a source of hope to black families who want the benefits of . . . learning for their children.'" Because of their "distinctive histories and traditions," black schools can function as the center and symbol of black communities, and provide examples of independent black leadership, success, and achievement.

Thus, even if the District Court had been on firmer ground in identifying a link between the KCMSD's pre-1954 de jure segregation and the present "racial isolation" of some of the district's schools, mere de facto segregation (unac-

---

[2] The studies cited in *Brown I* have received harsh criticism. Moreover, there simply is no conclusive evidence that desegregation either has sparked a permanent jump in the achievement scores of black children, or has remedied any psychological feelings of inferiority black schoolchildren might have had. Although the gap between black and white test scores has narrowed over the past two decades, it appears that this has resulted more from gains in the socioeconomic status of black families than from desegregation.

companied by discriminatory inequalities in educational resources) does not constitute a continuing harm after the end of de jure segregation. "Racial isolation" itself is not a harm; only state-enforced segregation is. After all, if separation itself is a harm, and if integration therefore is the only way that blacks can receive a proper education, then there must be something inferior about blacks. Under this theory, segregation injures blacks because blacks, when left on their own, cannot achieve. To my way of thinking, that conclusion is the result of a jurisprudence based upon a theory of black inferiority.

This misconception has drawn the courts away from the important goal in desegregation. The point of the Equal Protection Clause is not to enforce strict race-mixing, but to ensure that blacks and whites are treated equally by the State without regard to their skin color. The lower courts should not be swayed by the easy answers of social science, nor should they accept the findings, and the assumptions, of sociology and psychology at the price of constitutional principle.

II

. . .

The District Court's unwarranted focus on the psychological harm to blacks and on racial imbalances has been only half of the tale. Not only did the court subscribe to a theory of injury that was predicated on black inferiority, it also married this concept of liability to our expansive approach to remedial powers. We have given the federal courts the freedom to use any measure necessary to reverse problems—such as racial isolation or low educational achievement—that have proven stubbornly resistant to government policies. We have not permitted constitutional principles such as federalism or the separation of powers to stand in the way of our drive to reform the schools. Thus, the District Court here ordered massive expenditures by local and state authorities, without congressional or executive authorization and without any indication that such measures would attract whites back to KCMSD or raise KCMSD test scores. The time has come for us to put the genie back in the bottle.

A

. . .

It is perhaps understandable that we permitted the lower courts to exercise such sweeping powers. Although we had authorized the federal courts to work toward "a system of determining admission to the public schools on a nonracial basis" in *Brown II* resistance to *Brown I* produced little desegregation by the time we decided *Green v. School Board of New Kent County*. Our impatience with the pace of desegregation and with the lack of a good-faith effort on the part of school boards led us to approve such extraordinary remedial measures. But such powers should have been temporary and used only to overcome the widespread resistance to the dictates of the Constitution. The judicial overreaching we see before us today perhaps is the price we now pay for our approval of such extraordinary remedies in the past.

. . .

B

Such extravagant uses of judicial power are at odds with the history and tradition of the equity power and the Framers' design. The available historical records suggest that the Framers did not intend federal equitable remedies to reach as broadly as we have permitted. Anticipating the growth of our modern doctrine, the Anti-Federalists criticized the Constitution because it might be read to grant broad equitable powers to the federal courts. In response, the defenders of the Constitution "sold" the new framework of government to the public by espousing a narrower interpretation of the equity power. When an attack on the Constitution is followed by an open Federalist effort to narrow the provision, the appropriate conclusion is that the drafters and ratifiers of the Constitution approved the more limited construction offered in response.

. . .

C

Two clear restraints on the use of the equity power—federalism and the separation of powers—derive from the very form of our Government. Federal courts should pause before using their inherent equitable powers to intrude into the proper sphere of the States. We have long recognized that education is primarily a concern of local authorities. "Local autonomy of school districts is a vital national tradition." A structural reform decree eviscerates a State's discretionary authority over its own program and budgets and forces state officials to reallocate state resources and funds to the desegregation plan at the expense of other citizens, other government programs, and other institutions not represented in court. When District Courts seize complete control over the schools, they strip state and local governments of one of their most important governmental responsibilities, and thus deny their existence as independent governmental entities.

Federal courts do not possess the capabilities of state and local governments in addressing difficult educational problems. State and local school officials not only bear the responsibility for educational decisions, they also are better equipped than a single federal judge to make the day-to-day policy, curricular, and funding choices necessary to bring a school district into compliance with the Constitution. Federal courts simply cannot gather sufficient information to render an effective decree, have limited resources to induce compliance, and cannot seek political and public support for their remedies. When we presume to have the institutional ability to set effective educational, budgetary, or administrative policy, we transform the least dangerous branch into the most dangerous one.

The separation of powers imposes additional restraints on the judiciary's exercise of its remedial powers. To be sure, this is not a case of one branch of Government encroaching on the prerogatives of another, but rather of the power of the Federal Government over the States. Nonetheless, what the federal courts cannot do at the federal level they cannot do against the States; in either case, Article III courts are constrained by the inherent constitutional limitations on their powers. There simply are certain things that courts, in order to remain courts, cannot and should not do. There is no difference between courts running school systems or prisons and courts running executive branch agencies.

In this case, not only did the district court exercise the legislative power to tax, it also engaged in budgeting, staffing, and educational decisions, in judgments about the location and aesthetic quality of the schools, and in administrative oversight and monitoring. These functions involve a legislative or executive, rather than a judicial, power. . . .

It is perhaps not surprising that broad equitable powers have crept into our jurisprudence, for they vest judges with the discretion to escape the constraints and dictates of the law and legal rules. But I believe that we must impose more precise standards and guidelines on the federal equitable power, not only to restore predictability to the law and reduce judicial discretion, but also to ensure that constitutional remedies are actually targeted toward those who have been injured.

D

The dissent's approval of the District Court's treatment of salary increases is typical of this Court's failure to place limits on the equitable remedial power. . . .

Contrary to the dissent's conclusion, the District Court's remedial orders are in tension with two common-sense principles. First, the District Court retained jurisdiction over the implementation and modification of the remedial decree, instead of terminating its involvement after issuing its remedy. Although briefly mentioned in *Brown II* as a temporary measure

to overcome local resistance to desegregation ("during this period of transition, the courts will retain jurisdiction"), this concept of continuing judicial involvement has permitted the District Courts to revise their remedies constantly in order to reach some broad, abstract, and often elusive goal. Not only does this approach deprive the parties of finality and a clear understanding of their responsibilities, but it also tends to inject the judiciary into the day-to-day management of institutions and local policies—a function that lies outside of our Article III competence.

Much of the District Court's overreaching in this case occurred because it employed this hit-or-miss method to shape, and reshape, its remedial decree. Using its authority of continuing jurisdiction, the Court pursued its goal of decreasing "racial isolation" regardless of the cost or of the difficulties of engineering demographic changes. Wherever possible, district courts should focus their remedial discretion on devising and implementing a unified remedy in a single decree. This method would still provide the lower courts with substantial flexibility to tailor a remedy to fit a violation, and courts could employ their contempt power to ensure compliance. To ensure that they do not overstep the boundaries of their Article III powers, however, district courts should refrain from exercising their authority in a manner that supplants the proper sphere reserved to the political branches, who have a coordinate duty to enforce the Constitution's dictates, and to the States, whose authority over schools we have long sought to preserve. Only by remaining aware of the limited nature of its remedial powers, and by giving the respect due to other governmental authorities, can the Judiciary ensure that its desire to do good will not tempt it into abandoning its limited role in our constitutional Government.

Second, the District Court failed to target its equitable remedies in this case specifically to cure the harm suffered by the victims of segregation. Of course, the initial and most important aspect of any remedy will be to eliminate any invidious racial distinctions in matters such as student assignments, transportation, staff, resource allocation, and activities. This element of most desegregation decrees is fairly straightforward and has not produced many examples of overreaching by the district courts. It is the "compensatory" ingredient in many desegregation plans that has produced many of the difficulties in the case before us.

Having found that segregation "has caused a system wide reduction in student achievement in the schools of the KCMSD," the District Court ordered the series of magnet school plans, educational programs, and capital improvements that the Court criticizes today because of their interdistrict nature. In ordering these programs, the District Court exceeded its authority by benefitting those who were not victims of discriminatory conduct. KCMSD as a whole may have experienced reduced achievement levels, but raising the test scores of the entire district is a goal that is not sufficiently tailored to restoring the victims of segregation to the position they would have occupied absent discrimination. A school district cannot be discriminated against on the basis of its race, because a school district has no race. It goes without saying that only individuals can suffer from discrimination, and only individuals can receive the remedy.

Of course, a district court may see fit to order necessary remedies that have the side effect of benefitting those who were not victims of segregation. But the court cannot order broad remedies that indiscriminately benefit a school district as a whole, rather than the individual students who suffered from discrimination. Not only do such remedies tend to indicate "efforts to achieve broader purposes lying beyond" the scope of the violation, but they also force state and local governments to work toward the benefit of those who have suffered no harm from their actions.

To ensure that district courts do not embark on such broad initiatives in the future, we should demand that remedial decrees be more precisely designed to benefit only those who have been victims of segregation. Race-conscious remedies for discrimination not only must serve a compelling governmental interest (which is met in desegregation cases), but also must be narrowly tailored to further that interest. In the absence of special circumstances, the remedy for de jure segregation ordinarily should not include educational programs for students who were not in school (or were even alive) during the period of segregation. Although I do not doubt that all KCMSD students benefit from many of the initiatives ordered by the court below, it is for the democratically accountable state and local officials to decide whether they are to be made available even to those who were never harmed by segregation.

III

This Court should never approve a State's efforts to deny students, because of their race, an equal opportunity for an education. But the federal courts also should avoid using racial equality as a pretext for solving social problems that do not violate the Constitution. It seems apparent to me that the District Court undertook the worthy task of providing a quality education to the children of KCMSD. As far as I can tell, however, the District Court sought to bring new funds and facilities into the KCMSD by finding a constitutional violation on the part of the State where there was none. Federal courts should not lightly assume that States have caused "racial isolation" in 1984 by maintaining a segregated school system in 1954. We must forever put aside the notion that simply because a school district today is black, it must be educationally inferior.

Even if segregation were present, we must remember that a deserving end does not justify all possible means. The desire to reform a school district, or any other institution, cannot so captivate the Judiciary that it forgets its constitutionally mandated role. Usurpation of the traditionally local control over education not only takes the judiciary beyond its proper sphere, it also deprives the States and their elected officials of their constitutional powers. At some point, we must recognize that the judiciary is not omniscient, and that all problems do not require a remedy of constitutional proportions.

DISSENT: JUSTICE SOUTER, with whom JUSTICE STEVENS, JUSTICE GINSBURG, and JUSTICE BREYER join, dissenting.

The Court's process of orderly adjudication has broken down in this case. The Court disposes of challenges to only two of the District Court's many discrete remedial orders by declaring that the District Court erroneously provided an interdistrict remedy for an intradistrict violation. In doing so, it resolves a foundational issue going to one element of the District Court's decree that we did not accept for review in this case, that we need not reach in order to answer the questions that we did accept for review, and that we specifically refused to consider when it was presented in a prior petition for certiorari. Since, under these circumstances, the respondent school district and pupils naturally came to this Court without expecting that a fundamental premise of a portion of the District Court's remedial order would become the focus of the case, the essence of the Court's misjudgment in reviewing and repudiating that central premise lies in its failure to have warned the respondents of what was really at stake. This failure lulled the respondents into addressing the case without sufficient attention to the foundational issue, and their lack of attention has now infected the Court's decision.

No one on the Court has had the benefit of briefing and argument informed by an appreciation of the potential breadth of the ruling. The deficiencies from which we suffer have led the Court effectively to overrule a unanimous constitutional precedent of 20 years standing, which was not even addressed in argument, was mentioned merely in passing by one of the parties, and discussed by another of them only in a misleading way.

The Court's departures from the practices

that produce informed adjudication would call for dissent even in a simple case. But in this one, with a trial history of more than 10 years of litigation, the Court's failure to provide adequate notice of the issue to be decided (or to limit the decision to issues on which certiorari was clearly granted) rules out any confidence that today's result is sound, either in fact or in law.

I

. . .

. . . [T]he State presented, and we agreed to review, these two questions:

"1. Whether a remedial educational desegregation program providing greater educational opportunities to victims of past de jure segregation than provided anywhere else in the country nonetheless fails to satisfy the Fourteenth Amendment (thus precluding a finding of partial unitary status) solely because student achievement in the District, as measured by results on standardized test scores, has not risen to some unspecified level?

"2. Whether a federal court order granting salary increases to virtually every employee of a school district—including non-instructional personnel—as a part of a school desegregation remedy conflicts with applicable decisions of this court which require that remedial components must directly address and relate to the constitutional violation and be tailored to cure the condition that offends the Constitution?"

These questions focus on two discrete issues: the extent to which a district court may look at students' test scores in determining whether a school district has attained partial unitary status as to its *Milliken* II educational programs, and whether the particular salary increases ordered by the District Court constitute a permissible component of its remedy.

The State did not go beyond these discrete issues, and it framed no broader, foundational question about the validity of the District Court's magnet concept. The Court decides, however, that it can reach that question of its own initiative, and it sees no bar to this course in the provision of this Court's Rule 14.1 that "only the questions set forth in the petition, or fairly included therein, will be considered. . . ." The broader issue, the Court claims, is "fairly included" in the State's salary question. But that claim does not survive scrutiny.

. . .

If there is any doubt about the lack of fairness and prudence displayed by the Court, it should disappear upon seeing two things: first, how readily the questions presented can be answered on their own terms, without giving any countenance to the State's now successful attempt to "'smuggle additional questions into a case after we granted certiorari,'" and, second,

how the Court's decision to go beyond those questions to address an issue not adequately briefed or argued by one set of parties leads it to render an opinion anchored in neither the findings and evidence contained in the record, nor in controlling precedent, which is squarely at odds with the Court's holding today.

II

A

The test score question as it comes to us is one of word play, not substance. . . . (W)hat is important here is that none of the District Court's or Court of Appeals's opinions or orders requires a certain level of test scores before unitary status can be found, or indicates that test scores are the only thing standing between the State and a finding of unitary status as to the KCMSD's *Milliken II* programs. Indeed, the opinion concurring in the denial of rehearing en banc below (not mentioned by the Court, although it is certainly more probative of the governing law in the Eighth Circuit than the dissenting opinion on which the Court does rely) expressly disavows any dispositive role for test scores.

. . .

If, then, test scores do not explain why there was no finding of unitary status as to the *Milliken II* programs, one may ask what does explain it. The answer is quite straightforward. The Court of Appeals refused to order the District Court to enter a finding of partial unitary status as to the KCMSD's *Milliken II* programs (and apparently, the District Court did not speak to the issue itself) simply because the State did not attempt to make the showing required for that relief. As the Court recognizes, we have established a clear set of procedures to be followed by governmental entities seeking the partial termination of a desegregation decree. . . .

While the Court recognizes the three-part showing that the State must make under *Freeman* in order to get a finding of partial unitary status, it fails to acknowledge that the State did not even try to make a Freeman showing in the litigation leading up to the District Court's Order of June 17, 1992. . . .

The State did not claim that implementation of the *Milliken II* component of the decree had remedied the reduction in student achievement in the KCMSD to the extent practicable; it simply argued that various Milliken II programs had been implemented. . . .

Thus, it was the State's failure to meet or even to recognize its burden under *Freeman* that led the Court of Appeals to reject the suggestion that it make a finding of partial unitary status as to the district's *Milliken II* education programs.

Examining only the first *Freeman* prong, there can be no doubt that the Court of Appeals was correct. *Freeman* and *Dowell* make it entirely clear that the central focus of this prong of the unitary status enquiry is on effects: to the extent reasonably possible, a constitutional violator must remedy the ills caused by its actions before it can be freed of the court-ordered obligations it has brought upon itself. Under the logic of the State's arguments to the District Court, the moment the *Milliken II* programs were put in place, the State was at liberty to walk away from them, no matter how great the remaining consequences of segregation for educational quality or how great the potential for curing them if State funding continued.

Looking ahead, if indeed the State believes itself entitled to a finding of partial unitary status on the subject of educational programs, there is an orderly procedural course for it to follow. It may frame a proper motion for partial unitary status, and prepare to make a record sufficient to allow the District Court and the Court of Appeals to address the continued need for and efficacy of the *Milliken II* programs.

In the development of a proper unitary status record, test scores will undoubtedly play a role. It is true, as the Court recognizes, that all parties to this case agree that it would be error to require that the students in a school district attain the national average test score as a prerequisite to a finding of partial unitary status, if only because all sorts of causes independent of the vestiges of past school segregation might stand in the way of the goal. That said, test scores will clearly be relevant in determining whether the improvement programs have cured a deficiency in student achievement to the practicable extent. The District Court has noted (in the finding that the Court would read as a dispositive requirement for unitary status) that while students' scores have shown a trend of improvement, they remain at or below national norms. The significance of this fact is subject to assessment. Depending, of course, on other facts developed in the course of unitary status proceedings, the improvement to less than the national average might reasonably be taken to show that education programs are having a good effect on student achievement, and that further improvement can be expected. On the other hand, if test score changes were shown to have flattened out, that might suggest the impracticability of any additional remedial progress. While the significance of scores is thus open to judgment, the judgment is not likely to be very sound unless it is informed by more of a record than we have in front of us, and the Court's admonition that the District Court should "sharply limit" its reliance on test scores, should be viewed in this light.

B

The other question properly before us has to do with the propriety of the District Court's recent salary orders. While the Court suggests otherwise, the District Court did not ground its orders of salary increases solely on the goal of attracting students back to the KCMSD. From the start, the District Court has consistently treated salary increases as an important element in remedying the systemwide reduction in student achievement resulting from segregation in the KCSMD. As noted above, the Court does not question this remedial goal, which we expressly approved in *Milliken II*. The only issue, then, is whether the salary increases ordered by the District Court have been reasonably related to achieving that goal, keeping in mind the broad discretion enjoyed by the District Court in exercising its equitable powers.

. . .

It is the District Court's 1992 and 1993 orders that are before us, and it is difficult to see how the District Court abused its discretion in either instance. The District Court had evidence in front of it that adopting the State's position and discontinuing desegregation funding for salary levels would result in their abrupt drop to 1986–1987 levels, with the resulting disparity between teacher pay in the district and the nationwide level increasing to as much as 40–45 percent, and a mass exodus of competent employees likely taking place. Faced with this evidence, the District Court found that continued desegregation funding of salaries, and small increases in those salaries over time, were essential to the successful implementation of its remedial scheme, including the elevation of student achievement.

The Court of Appeals affirmed the District Court's orders on the basis of these findings, again taking special note of the importance of adequate salaries to the remedial goal of improving student achievement.

. . .

There is nothing exceptionable in the lower courts' findings about the relationship between salaries and the District Court's remedial objectives, and certainly nothing in the record suggests obvious error as to the amounts of the increases ordered. If it is tempting to question the place of salary increases for administrative and maintenance personnel in a desegregation order, the Court of Appeals addressed the temptation in specifically affirming the District Court's finding that such personnel are critical to the success of the desegregation effort, and did so in the circumstances of a district whose schools have been plagued by leaking roofs, defective lighting, and reeking lavatories. As for teachers' increases, the District Court and the Court of Appeals were beyond reproach in finding and affirming that in order to remedy the educational deficits flowing from segregation in the KCMSD, "those persons charged with implementing the [remedial] plan [must] be the most qualified persons reasonably attainable.

Indeed, the Court does not question the District Court's salary orders insofar as they relate to the objective of raising the level of student achievement in the KCMSD, but rather overlooks that basis for the orders altogether. The Court suggests that the District Court rested its approval of salary increases only on the object of drawing students into the district's schools, and rejects the increases for that reason. It seems clear, however, that the District Court and the Court of Appeals both viewed the salary orders as serving two complementary but distinct purposes, and to the extent that the District Court concludes on remand that its salary orders are justified by reference to the quality of education alone, nothing in the Court's opinion precludes those orders from remaining in effect.

III

The two discrete questions that we actually accepted for review are, then, answerable on their own terms without any need to consider whether the District Court's use of the magnet school concept in its remedial plan is itself constitutionally vulnerable. The capacity to deal thus with the questions raised, coupled with the unfairness of doing otherwise without warning, are enough to demand a dissent.

But there is more to fuel dissent. On its face, the Court's opinion projects an appealing pragmatism in seeming to cut through the details of many facts by applying a rule of law that can claim both precedential support and intuitive sense, that there is error in imposing an interdistrict remedy to cure a merely intradistrict violation. Since the District Court has consistently described the violation here as solely intradistrict, and since the object of the magnet schools under its plan includes attracting students into the district from other districts, the Court's result seems to follow with the necessity of logic, against which arguments about detail or calls for fair warning may not carry great weight.

The attractiveness of the Court's analysis disappears, however, as soon as we recognize two things. First, the District Court did not mean by an "intradistrict violation" what the Court apparently means by it today. The District Court meant that the violation within the KCMSD had not led to segregation outside of it, and that no other school districts had played a part in the violation. It did not mean that the violation had not produced effects of any sort beyond the district. Indeed, the record that we have indicates that the District Court understood that the violation here did produce effects spanning district borders and leading to greater segregation within the KCMSD, the reversal of which the District Court sought to accomplish by establishing magnet schools. Insofar as the Court assumes that this was not so in fact, there is at least enough in the record to cast serious doubt on its assumption. Second, the Court violates existing case law even on its own apparent view of the facts, that the segregation violation within the KCMSD produced no proven effects, segregative or otherwise, outside it. Assuming this to be true, the Court's decision that the rule against interdistrict remedies for intradistrict violations applies to this case, solely because the remedy here is meant to produce effects outside the district in which the violation occurred, is flatly contrary to established precedent.

. . .

A

. . .

The Court, . . . rejects the findings of the District Court, endorsed by the Court of Appeals, that segregation led to white flight from the KCMSD, and does so at the expense of another accepted norm of our appellate procedure. We have long adhered to the view that "[a] court of law, such as this Court is, rather than a court for correction of errors in factfinding, cannot undertake to review concurrent findings of fact by two courts below in the absence of a very obvious and exceptional showing of error." The Court fails to show any exceptional circumstance present here, however: it relies on a "contradiction" that is not an obvious contradiction at all, and on an arbitrary "supposition" that "'white flight' may result from desegregation, not de jure segregation," a supposition said to be bolstered by the District Court's statement that there was "an abundance of evidence that many residents of the KCMSD left the district and moved to the suburbs because of the district's efforts to integrate its schools."

The doubtful contradiction is said to exist between the District Court's findings, on the one hand, that segregation caused white flight to the SSDs, and the Court of Appeals's conclusion, on the other, that the District Court "made specific findings that negate current significant interdistrict effects. . . .'" Any impression of contradiction quickly disappears, however, when the Court of Appeals's statement is read in context:

"The [district] court explicitly recognized that [to consolidate school districts] under *Milliken* [I] 'there must be evidence of a constitutional violation in one district that produces a significant segregative effect in another district.' ... The district court thus dealt not only with the issue of whether the SSDs were constitutional violators but also whether there were significant interdistrict segregative effects. When it did so, it made specific findings that negate current significant interdistrict effects. ..."

It is clear that, in this passage, the Court of Appeals was summarizing the District Court's findings that the constitutional violations within the KCMSD had not produced any segregative effects in other districts. While the Court of Appeals did not repeat the word "segregative" in its concluding sentence, there is nothing to indicate that it was referring to anything but segregative effects, and there is in fact nothing in the District Court's own statements going beyond its finding that the State and the KCMSD's actions did not lead to segregative effects in the SSDs. There is, in turn, no contradiction between this finding and the District Court's findings about white flight: while white flight would have produced significant effects in other school districts, in the form of greatly increased numbers of white students, those effects would not have been segregative beyond the KCMSD, as the departing students were absorbed into wholly unitary systems.

Without the contradiction, the Court has nothing to justify its rejection of the District Court's finding that segregation caused white flight but its supposition that flight results from integration, not segregation. The supposition, and the distinction on which it rests, are untenable. At the more obvious level, there is in fact no break in the chain of causation linking the effects of desegregation with those of segregation. There would be no desegregation orders and no remedial plans without prior unconstitutional segregation as the occasion for issuing and adopting them, and an adverse reaction to a desegregation order is traceable in fact to the segregation that is subject to the remedy. When the Court quotes the District Court's reference to abundant evidence that integration caused flight to the suburbs, then, it quotes nothing inconsistent with the District Court's other findings that segregation had caused the flight. The only difference between the statements lies in the point to which the District Court happened to trace the causal sequence.

The unreality of the Court's categorical distinction can be illustrated by some examples. There is no dispute that before the District Court's remedial plan was placed into ef-

fect the schools in the unreformed segregated system were physically a shambles:

"The KCMSD facilities still have numerous health and safety hazards, educational environment hazards, functional impairments, and appearance impairments. The specific problems include: inadequate lighting; peeling paint and crumbling plaster on ceilings, walls and corridors; loose tiles, torn floor coverings; odors resulting from unventilated restrooms with rotted, corroded toilet fixtures; noisy classrooms due to lack of adequate acoustical treatment; lack of off street parking and bus loading for parents, teachers and students; lack of appropriate space for many cafeterias, libraries and classrooms; faulty and antiquated heating and electrical systems; damaged and inoperable lockers; and inadequate fire safety systems. The conditions at Paseo High School are such that even the principal stated that he would not send his own child to that facility."

The cost of turning this shambles into habitable schools was enormous, as anyone would have seen long before the District Court ordered repairs. Property tax-paying parents of white children, seeing the handwriting on the wall in 1985, could well have decided that the inevitable cost of clean-up would produce an intolerable tax rate and could have moved to escape it. The District Court's remedial orders had not yet been put in place. Was the white flight caused by segregation or desegregation? The distinction has no significance.

Another example makes the same point. After *Brown*, white parents likely came to understand that the practice of spending more on white schools than on black ones would be stopped at some point. If they were unwilling to raise all expenditures to match the customary white school level, they must have expected the expenditures on white schools to drop to the level of those for the segregated black schools or to some level in between. If they thus believed that the white schools would deteriorate they might then have taken steps to establish private white schools, starting a practice of local private education that has endured. Again, what sense does it make to say of this example that the cause of white private education was desegregation (not yet underway), rather than the segregation that led to it?

I do not claim that either of these possible explanations would ultimately turn out to be correct, for any such claim would head me down the same road the Court is taking, of resolving factual issues independently of the trial court without warning the respondents that the full evidentiary record bearing on the issue should be identified for us. My point is only that the Court is on shaky grounds when it assumes that prior segregation and later desegregation are separable in fact as causes of "white flight," that the flight can plausibly be said to result from desegregation alone, and that therefore as a matter of fact the "intradistrict" segregation violation lacked the relevant consequences outside the district required to justify the District Court's magnet concept. With the arguable plausibility of each of these assumptions seriously in question, it is simply rash to reverse the concurrent factual findings of the District Court and the Court of Appeals. All the judges who spoke to the issue below concluded that segregated schooling in the KCMSD contributed to the exodus of white students from the district. . . .

The reality is that the Court today overturns the concurrent factual findings of the District Court and the Court of Appeals without having identified any circumstance in the record sufficient to warrant such an extraordinary course of action.

JUSTICE GINSBURG, dissenting.

I join Justice Souter's illuminating dissent and emphasize a consideration key to this controversy.

The Court stresses that the present remedial programs have been in place for seven years. But compared to more than two centuries of firmly entrenched official discrimination, the experience with the desegregation remedies ordered by the District Court has been evanescent.

In 1724, Louis XV of France issued the Code Noir, the first slave code for the Colony of Louisiana, an area that included Missouri.

When Missouri entered the Union in 1821, it entered as a slave State.

Before the Civil War, Missouri law prohibited the creation or maintenance of schools for educating blacks: "No person shall keep or teach any school for the instruction of Negroes or mulattoes, in reading or writing, in this State."

Beginning in 1865, Missouri passed a series of laws requiring separate public schools for blacks. The Missouri Constitution first permitted, then required, separate schools.

After this Court announced its decision in *Brown* Missouri's Attorney General declared these provisions mandating segregated schools unenforceable. The statutes were repealed in 1957 and the constitutional provision was rescinded in 1976. Nonetheless, thirty years after Brown, the District Court found that "the inferior education indigenous of the state-compelled dual school system has lingering effects in the Kansas City, Missouri School District." The District Court concluded that "the State . . . cannot defend its failure to affirmatively act to eliminate the structure and effects of its past dual system on the basis of restrictive state law." Just ten years ago, in June 1985, the District Court issued its first remedial order.

Today, the Court declares illegitimate the goal of attracting nonminority students to the Kansas City, Missouri, School District, and thus stops the District Court's efforts to integrate a school district that was, in the 1984/1985 school year, sorely in need and 68.3% black. Given the deep, inglorious history of segregation in Missouri, to curtail desegregation at this time and in this manner is an action at once too swift and too soon.

DEL: The *Jenkins* decision's significance owes not just to its determinations but how those results were achieved. As in *Milliken v. Bradley*, when the Court narrowed *Brown's* potential by largely precluding interdistrict remediation, the *Jenkins* Court rejected lower court findings of fact. The factual adjustment, coupled with an eagerness to resolve important issues minus an extensive record, may indicate a result-orientation consistent with what rulings in *Dowell* and *Freeman* previewed. The *Keyes-Milliken-Spangler* trilogy collectively narrowed the substantive grounds for desegregation claims. Taken together, *Dowell-Freeman-Jenkins* extend foreclosure to process. The *Jenkins* decision in particular represents a triumph of perspective, previewed 15 years prior in the dissenting perspectives of Justices Rehnquist and Powell.[150] If *Jenkins* is the terminal point for the desegregation experience, *Brown's* legacy comprehends much rhetoric, disruption and false hope for the sake of ritual. Four decades later, *Brown* effectively denotes

---

[150] *See supra* pp. 502–05.

an exercise in illusion and a tribute to formalism evidencing the limits of moral direction by means of legal reform.[151]

PAH The public school desegregation cases demonstrate that the equal protection analysis adopted by the Court masks but does not constrain discretion available in judicial review. Beyond suggesting the limits of moral direction, these cases indicate that the Court more often than not uses its discretion to serve majoritarian interests. Both the Court's selection of intent over effect principles as a means of defining equal protection violations as well as the Court's recognition of the limits of remediation expose an "esseial majoritarian nature of the Court" challenging countermajoritarian assumption of judicial review.[152]

---

[151] GIRARDEAU A. SPANN, PURE POLITICS IN CRITICAL RACE THEORY: THE CUTTING EDGE 27 (Richard Delgado, ed.)

[152] *Id.* at 1448.

f. Higher Education Revisited

Even as constitutional standards have narrowed and devolved, the Court has identified vestiges of discrimination rooted in a segregative past. More than half a century after the NAACP focused upon tertiary schooling as its starting point for contesting official segregation, the Court in *United States v. Fordice* revisited racial duality in higher education.

United States v. Fordice
112 S. Ct. 2727 (1992)

JUSTICE WHITE delivered the opinion of the Court.

In 1954, this Court held that the concept of "'separate but equal'" has no place in the field of public education. *Brown v. Board of Education (Brown I)*. . . . The following year, the Court ordered an end to segregated public education, "with all deliberate speed." *Brown v. Board of Education (Brown II)*. . . .

Mississippi launched its public university system in 1848 by establishing the University of Mississippi, an institution dedicated to the higher education exclusively of white persons. In succeeding decades, the State erected additional post-secondary, single-race educational facilities. Alcorn State University opened its doors in 1871 as "an agricultural college for the education of Mississippi's black youth." Creation of four more exclusively white institutions followed: Mississippi State University (1880), Mississippi University for Women (1885), University of Southern Mississippi (1912), and Delta State University (1925). The State added two more solely black institutions in 1940 and 1950: in the former year, Jackson State University, which was charged with training "black teachers for the black public schools," and in the latter year, Mississippi Valley State Uni-

versity, whose functions were to educate teachers primarily for rural and elementary schools and to provide vocational instruction to black students.

Despite this Court's decisions in *Brown I* and *Brown II*, Mississippi's policy of *de jure* segregation continued. The first black student was not admitted to the University of Mississippi until 1962, and then only by court order. . . . For the next 12 years the segregated public university system in the State remained largely intact. . . . By the mid-1980's, 30 years after *Brown*, more than 99 per cent of Mississippi's white students were enrolled at University of Mississippi, Mississippi State, Southern Mississippi, Delta State, and Mississippi University for Women. The student bodies at these universities remained predominantly white, averaging between 80 and 91 percent white students. Seventy-one percent of the State's black students attended Jackson State, Alcorn State, and Mississippi Valley, where the racial composition ranged from 92 to 99 percent black. . . . The Court of Appeals concluded that the State had fulfilled its affirmative obligation to disestablish its prior *de jure* segregated system by adopting and implementing race-neutral policies governing its college and university system. Because students seeking higher education had "real freedom" to choose the institution of their choice, the State need do no more. Even though neutral policies and free choice were not enough to dismantle a dual system of primary or secondary schools, the Court of Appeals thought that universities "differ in character fundamentally" from lower levels of schools. . . .

We do not agree with the Court of Appeals or the District Court, that the adoption and implementation of race-neutral policies alone suffice to demonstrate that the State has completely abandoned its prior dual system. That college attendance is by choice and not by assignment does not mean that a race-neutral admissions policy cures the constitutional violation of a dual system. In a system based on choice, student attendance is determined not simply by admissions policies, but also by many other factors. Although some of these factors clearly cannot be attributed to State policies, many can be. Thus, even after a State dismantles its segregative admissions policy, there may still be state action that is traceable to the State's prior *de jure* segregation and that continues to foster segregation. The Equal Protection Clause is offended by "sophisticated as well as simple-minded modes of discrimination." If policies traceable to the *de jure* system are still in force and have discriminatory effects, those policies too must be reformed to the extent practicable and consistent with sound educational practices.

Had the Court of Appeals applied the correct legal standard, it would have been apparent from the undisturbed factual findings of the District Court that there are several surviving aspects of Mississippi's prior dual system which are constitutionally suspect; for even though such policies may be race-neutral on their face, they substantially restrict a person's choice of which institution to enter and they contribute to the racial identifiability of the eight public universities. Mississippi must justify these policies or eliminate them.

. . .

We deal first with the current admissions policies of Mississippi's public universities. As the District Court found, the three flagship historically white universities in the system—University of Mississippi, Mississippi State University, and University of Souther Mississippi-enacted policies in 1963 requiring all entrants to achieve a minimum composite score of 15 on the American College Testing Program (ACT). The court described the "discriminatory taint" of this policy, an obvious reference to the fact that, at the time, the average ACT score for white students was 18 and the average score for blacks was 7. . . .

The present admission standards are not only traceable to the de jure system and were originally adopted for a discriminatory purpose, but they also have present discriminatory effects. Every Mississippi resident under 21 seeking admission to the university system must take the ACT. Any applicant who scores at least 15 qualifies for automatic admission to any of the five historically white institutions except Mississippi University for Women, which requires a score of 18 for automatic admission unless the student has a 3.0 high school grade average. Those scoring less than 15 but at least 13 automatically qualify to enter Jackson State University, Alcorn State University, and Mississippi Valley State University. Without doubt, these requirements restrict the range of choices of entering students as to which institution they may attend in a way that perpetuates segregation. Those scoring 13 or 14, with some exceptions, are excluded from the five historically white universities and if they want a higher education must go to one of the historically black institutions or attend junior college with hope of transferring to a historically white institution. Proportionately more blacks than whites face this choice: in 1985, 72 percent of Mississippi's white high school seniors achieved an ACT composite score of 15 or better, while less than 30 percent of black high school seniors earned that score. It is not surprising then that Mississippi's universities remain predominantly identifiable by race.

. . .

A second aspect of the present system that necessitates further inquiry is the widespread duplication of programs. . . . It can hardly be denied that such duplication was part and parcel of the prior dual system of higher education—the whole notion of "separate but equal" required duplicative programs in two sets of schools—and that the present unnecessary duplication is a continuation of that practice. *Brown* and its progeny established that the burden of proof falls on the State, and not the aggrieved plaintiffs, to establish that it has dismantled its prior *de jure* system. *Brown II.* The court's holding that petitioners could not establish the constitutional defect of unnecessary duplication, therefore, improperly shifted the burden from the State. . . .

In 1981, the State assigned certain missions to Mississippi's public universities as they then exited. It classified University of Mississippi, Mississippi State, and Southern Mississippi as "comprehensive" universities having the most varied programs and offering graduate degrees. Two of the historically white institutions, Delta State University and Mississippi University for Women, along with two of the historically black institutions, Alcorn State University and Mississippi Valley State

University, were designated as "regional" universities with more limited programs and devoted primarily to undergraduate education. Jackson State University was classified as an "urban" university whose mission was defined by its urban location.

The institutional mission designations adopted in 1981 have as their antecedents the policies enacted to perpetuate racial separation during the *de jure* segregated regime. The Court of Appeals expressly disagreed with the District Court by recognizing that the "inequalities among the institutions largely follow the mission designations, and the mission designations to some degree follow the historical racial assignments." It nevertheless upheld this facet of the system as constitutionally acceptable based on the existence of good-faith racially neutral policies and procedures. That different missions are assigned to the universities surely limits to some extent an entering student's choice as to which university to seek admittance. While the courts below both agreed that the classification and mission assignments were made without discriminatory purpose, the Court of Appeals found that the record "supports the plaintiffs' argument that the mission designations had the effect of maintaining the more limited program scope at the historically black universities." We do not suggest that absent discriminatory purpose the assignment of different missions to various institutions in a State's higher education system would raise an equal protection issue where one or more of the institutions become or remain predominantly black or white. But here the issue is whether the State has sufficiently dismantled its prior dual system; and when combined with the differential admission practices and unnecessary program duplication, it is likely that the mission designations interfere with student choice and tend to perpetuate the segregated system. On remand, the court should inquire whether it would be practicable and consistent with sound educational practices to eliminate any such discriminatory effects of the State's present policy of mission assignments.

Fourth, the State attempted to bring itself into compliance with the Constitution by continuing to maintain and operate all eight higher educational institutions. The existence of eight instead of some lesser number was undoubtedly occasioned by State laws forbidding the mingling of the races. And as the District Court recognized, continuing to maintain all eight universities in Mississippi is wasteful and irrational. The District Court pointed especially to the facts that Delta State and Mississippi Valley are only 35 miles apart and that only 20 miles separate Mississippi State and Mississippi University for Women. It was evident to the District Court that "the defendants undertake to fund more institutions of higher learning than are justified by the amount of financial resources available to the state," but the court concluded that such fiscal irresponsibility was a policy choice of the legislature rather than a feature of a system subject to constitutional scrutiny.

Unquestionably, a larger rather than a smaller number of institutions from which to choose in itself makes for different choices, particularly when examined in the light of other factors present in the operation of the system, such as admissions, program duplication, and institutional mission designations. Though certainly closure of one or more institutions would decrease the discriminatory effects of the present system, based on the present record we are unable to say whether such action is constitutionally required. Because the former *de jure* segregated system of public universities in Mississippi impeded the free choice of prospective students, the State in dismantling that system must take the necessary steps to ensure that this choice now is truly free. The full range of policies and practices must be examined with this duty in mind. That an institution is predominantly white or black does not in itself make out a constitutional violation. But surely the State may not leave in place policies rooted in its prior officially-segregated system that serve to maintain the racial identifiability of its universities if those policies can practicably be eliminated without eroding sound educational policies.

If we understand private petitioners to press us to order the upgrading of Jackson State, Alcorn State, and Mississippi Valley solely so that they may be publicly financed, exclusively black enclaves by private choice, we reject that request. The State provides these facilities for all its citizens and it has not met its burden under *Brown* to take affirmative steps to dismantle its prior *de jure* system when it perpetuates a separate, but "more equal" one. Whether such an increase in funding is necessary to achieve a full dismantlement under the standards we have outlined, however, is a different question, and one that must be addressed on remand.

. . .

JUSTICE THOMAS, concurring.

"We must rally to the defense of our schools. We must repudiate this unbearable assumption of the right to kill institutions unless they conform to one narrow standard." W.E.B. Du Bois, Schools, 13 The Crisis 111, 112 (1917).

I agree with the Court that a State does not satisfy its obligation to dismantle a dual system of higher education merely by adopting race-neutral policies for the future administration of that system. Today, we hold that "[i]f policies traceable to the de jure system are still in force and have discriminatory effects, those policies too must be reformed to the extent practicable and consistent with sound educational policies." I agree that this statement defines the appropriate standard to apply in the higher-education context. I write separately to emphasize that this standard is far different from the one adopted to govern the grade-school context in *Green v. New Kent County School Bd.,* and its progeny. In particular, because it does not compel the elimination of all observed racial imbalance, it portends neither the destruction of historically black colleges nor the severing of those institutions from their distinctive histories and traditions. From the beginning, we have recognized that desegregation remedies cannot be designed to ensure the elimination of any remnant at any price, but rather must display "a practical flexibility" and "a facility for adjusting and reconciling public and private needs." Quite obviously, one compelling need to be considered is the *educational* need of the present and future *students* in the Mississippi university system, for whose benefit the remedies will be crafted.

In particular, we do not foreclose the possibility that there exists "sound educational justification" for maintaining historically black colleges as such. Despite the shameful history of stated-enforced segregation, these institutions have survived and flourished. Indeed, they have expanded as opportunities for blacks to enter historically white institutions have expanded. Between 1954 and 1980, for example, enrollment at historically black colleges increased from 70,000 to 200,000 students, while degrees awarded increased 13,000 to 32,000.

I think it undisputable that these institutions have succeeded in part because of their distinctive histories and traditions; for many, historically black colleges have become "a symbol of the highest attainments of black culture." Obviously, a State cannot maintain such traditions by closing particular institutions, historically white or historically black, to particular racial groups. Nonetheless, it hardly follows that a State cannot operate a diverse assortment of institutions—including historically black institutions—open to all on a race-neutral basis but with established traditions and programs that might disproportionately appeal to one race or another. No one, I image, would argue that such institutional diversity is without "sound educational justification," or that it is even remotely akin to program duplication, which is designed to separate the races for the sake of separating the races. The Court at least hints at the importance of this value when it distinguishes *Green* in part on the ground that colleges and universities "are not fungible." Although I agree that a State is not

constitutionally required to maintain its historically black institutions as such, I do not understand our opinion to hold that a State is forbidden from doing so. It would be ironic, to say the least, if the institutions that sustained blacks during segregation were themselves destroyed in an effort to combat its vestiges.

JUSTICE SCALIA, concurring in the judgment in part and dissenting in part.

. . .

Before evaluating the Court's handiwork, it is no small task simply to comprehend it. The Court sets forth not one, but seemingly two different tests for ascertaining compliance with *Brown I*—though in the last analysis they come to the same. The Court initially announces the following test, . . . its opinion: all policies (i) "traceable to [the State's] prior [de jure] system" (ii) "that continue to have segregative effects—whether by influencing student enrollment decisions or by fostering segregation in other facets of the university system—" must be eliminated (iii) to the extent "practicabl[e]" and (iv) consistent with "sound educational" practices. When the Court comes to applying its test, however, . . . of the opinion, "influencing student enrollment decisions" is not merely one example of a "segregative effec[t]," but is elevated to an independent and essential requirement of its own. The policies that must be eliminated are those that (i) are legacies of the dual system, (ii) "contribute to the racial identifiability" of the State's universities and in addition (iii) do so in a way that "substantially restrict[s] a person's choice of which institution to enter."

What the Court means by "substantially restrict[ing] a person's choice of which institution to enter" is not clear. . . .

Whether one consults the Court's description of what it purports to be doing, . . . or what the Court actually does, . . . one must conclude that the Court is essentially applying to universities the amorphous standard adopted for primary and secondary schools in *Green.* Like that case, today's, decision places upon the State the ordinarily unsustainable burden of proving the negative proposition that it is not responsible for extant racial disparity in enrollment. . . . *Green* requires school boards to prove that racially identifiable schools are *not* the consequence of past or present discriminatory state action; today's opinion requires state university administrators to prove that racially identifiable schools are not the consequence of any practice or practices (in such impromptu "aggregation" as might strike the fancy of a district judge) held over from the prior *de jure* regime. This will imperil virtually any practice or program plaintiffs decide to challenge—just as *Green* has—so long as racial imbalance remains. . . .

The constitutional evil of the "separate but equal" regime that we confronted in *Brown I* was that blacks were told to go to one set of schools, whites to another. What made this "evenhanded" racial partitioning offensive to equal protection was its implicit stigmatization of minority students: "To separate [black students] from others of similar age and qualifications solely because of their race generates a feeling of inferiority as to their status in the community that may affect their hearts and minds in a way unlikely ever to be undone." In the context of higher education, a context in which students decide whether to attend school and if so where, the only unconstitutional derivations of that bygone system are those that limit access on discriminatory bases; for only they have the potential to generate the harm *Brown I* condemned, and only they have the potential to deny students equal access to the best public education a State has to offer. Legacies of the dual system that permit (or even incidentally facilitate) free choice of racially identifiable schools—while still assuring each individual student the right to attend whatever school he wishes—do not have these consequences.

. . .

It is my view that the requirement of compelled integration (whether by student assignment, as in *Green* itself, or by elimination of nonintegrated options, as the Court today effected decrees) does not apply to higher education. Only one aspect of an historically segregated university system need be eliminated: discriminatory admissions standards. The burden is upon the formerly *de jure* system to show that that has been achieved. Once that has been done, however, it is not just unprecedented, but illogical as well, to establish that former *de jure* States continue to deny equal protection of the law to students whose choices among public university offerings are unimpeded by discriminatory barriers. Unless one takes the position that *Brown I* required States not only to provide equal access to their universities but also to correct lingering disparities between them, that is, to remedy institutional noncompliance with the "equal" requirement of *Plessy*, a State is in compliance with *Brown I* once it established that it has dismantled all discriminatory barriers to its public universities. Having done that, a State is free to govern its public institutions of higher learning as it will, unless it is convicted of discriminating anew—which requires both discriminatory intent and discriminatory causation.

I must add a few words about the unanticipated consequences of today's decision. Among petitioners' contentions is the claim that the Constitution requires Mississippi to correct funding disparities between its HBIs and HWIs. The Court rejects that, as I think it should, since it is students and not colleges that are guaranteed equal protection of the laws. But to say that the Constitution does not require equal funding is not to say that the Constitution prohibits it. The citizens of a State may conclude that if certain of their public educational institutions are used predominantly by whites and others predominantly by blacks, it is desirable to fund those institutions more or less equally.

Ironically enough, however, today's decision seems to prevent adoption of such a conscious policy. What the Court says about duplicate programs is as true of equal funding: the requirement "was part and parcel of the prior dual system." Moreover, equal funding, like program duplication, facilitates continued segregation—enabling students to attend schools where their own race predominates without paying a penalty in the quality of education. Nor could such an equal-funding policy be saved on the basis that it serves what the Court calls a "sound educational justification." The only conceivable educational value it furthers is that of fostering schools in which blacks receive their education in a "majority" setting; but to acknowledge that as a "value" would contradict the compulsory-integration philosophy that underlies *Green*. Just as vulnerable, of course, would be all other programs that have the effect of facilitating the continued existence of predominantly black institutions: elevating an HBI to comprehensive status; offering a so-called Afrocentric curriculum, as has been done recently on an experimental basis in some secondary and primary schools, preserving eight separate which is perhaps Mississippi's single policy most segregative in effect; or providing funding for HBIs which does just that.

But this predictable impairment of HBIs should come as no surprise: for incidentally facilitating—indeed, even tolerating—the continued existence of HBIs is not what the court's test is about, and has never been what *Green* is about. What the Court's test is designed to achieve is the elimination of predominantly black institutions. While that may be good social policy, the present petitioners I suspect, would not agree; and there is much to be said for the Court of Appeals' perception . . . that "if no [state] authority exists to deny [the student] the right to attend the institution of his choice, he is done a severe disservice by remedies which, in seeking to maximize integration, minimize diversity and vitiate his choices" But whether or not the Court's antagonism to unintegrated schooling is good policy, it is assuredly not good constitutional law. There is nothing unconstitutional about a "black" school in the sense, not of a school that blacks must attend and that whites cannot, but of a school that, as a consequence of private choice in residence or in school selection, contains, and has long contained, a large black majority. In a perverse way, in fact, the insistence, whether explicit or implicit, that such institutional not be permitted to endure perpetuates the very stigma of black inferiority that *Brown I* sought to destroy.

. . .

I would not predict, however, that today's opinion will succeed in producing the same result as *Green*—viz., compelling the States to compel racial "balance" in their schools—because of several practical imperfections: because of the Court deprives district judges of the most efficient (and perhaps the only effective) *Green* remedy, mandatory student assignment, because some contradictory elements of the opinion (its suggestion, for example, that Mississippi's mission designations foster, rather than deter, segregation) will prevent clarity of application; and because the virtually standardless discretion conferred upon district judges will permit them to do pretty much what they please. What I do predict is a number of years of litigation-driven confusion and destabilization in the university systems of all the formerly *de jure* States, that will benefit neither blacks nor whites, neither predominantly black institutions nor predominantly white ones. Nothing good will come of this judicially ordained turmoil, except the public recognition that any Court that would knowingly impose it must hate segregation. We must find some other way of making that point.

DEL: The *Dowell* and *Freeman* decisions have both substantive and symbolic significance. The *Freeman* decision was the first desegregation ruling after Justice Marshall's resignation. Four decades after the *Brown* Court unanimously found racially separate education "inherently unequal," the *Freeman* Court determined unanimously that the desegregation mandate had to accommodate "stubborn facts of history [that] linger and persist."[153] With such a winding down of the *Brown* era, it is not unreasonable to wonder what was achieved beyond a rather bombastic but ultimately underachieving constitutional ritual. Justice Marshall correctly observed that the devolution of *Brown* "guarantee[d] that Negro children . . . will receive the same separate and inherently unequal education in the future as they have been unconstitutionally afforded in the past."[153] It may be true that the *Brown* Court could not have envisioned the significant cultural realities of suburban development and personal mobility that soon challenged the operation of the desegregation mandate. History itself provided strong evidence that, in Marshall's words, desegregation was not "to be an easy task."[154] The *Brown* decision was reached against a backdrop of experience that included systematic evasion of every previous effort to achieve racial reform as a function of law. As the NAACP launched its attack on segregated schools, a significant dissenting perspective was raised by W.E.B. DuBois who wrote that "[o]ther things being equal, the [racially] mixed school is the broader, more natural basis for the education of all youth, [but] things seldom are equal, and in that case, sympathy, knowledge, and the truth outweigh all that the mixed school can offer."[155] The desegregation experience, despite some notable successes, has underachieved and perhaps been a function of fundamental miscalculation. Too often, where desegregation has been ordered, persisting discrimination has resulted in a more insidious internalized racial regimen in which students are sorted pursuant to stereotype. For African-American students whose desegregated experience exposes them more directly to racism, DuBois' skepticism has special relevance. Perhaps the most fundamental mistake in light of history, however, was the expectation that formal legal change could alter racial reality in a moral sense. A key lesson of the desegregation era is that racial progress, especially for the future, is primarily a function of moral progress rather than legal development.

---

[153] Milliken v. Bradley, 418 U.S. 717, 782 (1974)(Marshall, J., dissenting).

[154] *Id.* at 814.

[155] W. E. B. DuBois, *Does the Negro Need Separate Schools?*, 4 J. Negro Educ. 328, 335 (1935).

RLW: Interestingly enough, following the *Fordice* decision, Mississippi proposed to close some of its HBI's and to merge them with other institutions of higher education. A number of African-American leaders objected to closure arguing that HBI's perform a unique function and should be preserved as a separate educational system.

DER: Despite the monumental failure of the Court's desegregation efforts, *Brown* made an important jurisprudential contribution by recognizing the immorality of state-imposed segregation and demanding that the law live up to the Constitution's moral demands. Its mistake lies not in commanding that the law accomplish too much, but in refusing to provide a strong enough remedy for America's moral failure. As Martin Luther King, Jr. observed, "[t]he law may not be able to make a man love me, but at least it can keep him from lynching me."[156] Black school children should not have to wait for a change in white citizens' attitudes about them in order to receive an equal education. Rather, the Court has an obligation to help to eradicate—whether through desegregation orders, equality in school financing, community control of schools, or other means—the persistent reality of second-class schooling for most Black students.

PAH I believe it is logical to view *Brown's* contribution to be the Court's recognition of the immorality of state-imposed segregation that has the effect of subordinating rights of Blacks and nevertheless support the claims of the individual plaintiffs in *Fordice* seeking to upgrade and continue the historically Black colleges as part of the Mississippi system. As I have argued earlier, *Brown* emphasized the importance of education for attaining equal citizenship but its approach of focusing on the damage to African American children resulting from racial isolation left open the implication of white superiority. The color-blind doctrine which has emerged from *Brown* is thus not always consistent with the equal citizenship goals of African Americans and other traditionally subordinated groups who seek to draw substantive meaning in the Civil War amendments.

---

[156] Quoted in ALAN F. WESTIN & BARRY MAHONEY, THE TRIAL OF MARTIN LUTHER KING 41 (1974).

g.   The Logical Extensions of *Brown*

Given the dimensions of the *Brown* litigation, the decision technically was limited to prescriptive segregation in the context of public education. Its logic radiated inexorably to other venues and contexts, however, as the Court summarily struck down official segregation in a broad spectrum of public settings and circumstances.[157] Official policy representing a vestige of overtly racist ideology also was subject to constitutional defeasance.

---

[157] E.g., Schiro v. Bynum, 375 U.S. 395 (1964)(per curiam) (public auditoriums); Turner v. City of Memphis, 369 U.S. 350 (1962)(public restaurants); New Orleans Park Development Assn. v. Detiege, 358 U.S. 54 (1958)(per curiam)(public parks); Mayor of Baltimore v. Dawson, 350 U.S. 877 (1955)(public beaches).

Loving v. Virginia,
388 U.S. 1 (1967)

MR. CHIEF JUSTICE WARREN delivered the opinion of the Court.

This case presents a constitutional question never addressed by this Court: whether a statutory scheme adopted by the State of Virginia to prevent marriages between persons solely on the basis of racial classifications violates the Equal Protection and Due Process Clauses of the Fourteenth Amendment. For reasons which seem to us to reflect the central meaning of those constitutional commands, we conclude that these statutes cannot stand consistently with the Fourteenth Amendment.

. . .

Virginia is now one of 16 States which prohibit and punish marriages on the basis of racial classifications. Penalties for miscegenation arose as an incident to slavery and have been common in Virginia since the colonial period. The present statutory scheme dates from the adoption of the Racial Integrity Act of 1924, passed during the period of extreme nativism which followed the end of the First World War. The central features of this Act, and current Virginia law, are the absolute prohibition of a "white person" marrying other than another "white person," a prohibition against issuing marriage licenses until the issuing official is satisfied that the applicants' statements as to their race are correct, certificate of "racial composition" to be kept by both local and state registrars, and the carrying forward of earlier prohibitions against racial intermarriage.

In upholding the constitutionality of these provisions in the decision below, the Supreme Court of Appeals of Virginia referred to its 1955 decision . . . [in which it] concluded that the State's legitimate purpose were "to preserve the racial integrity of its citizens," and to prevent "the corruption of blood," "a mongrel bred of citizens," and "the obliteration of racial pride," obviously an endorsement of the doctrine of White Supremacy. The court also reasoned that marriage has traditionally been subject to state regulation without federal intervention, and, consequently, the regulation of marriage should be left to exclusive state control by the Tenth Amendment.

. . .

There can be no question but that Virginia's miscegenation statutes rest solely upon distinctions drawn according to race. The statutes proscribe generally accepted conduct if engaged in by members of different races. Over the years, this Court has consistently repudiated "[d]istinctions between citizens solely because of their ancestry" as being "odious to a free people whose institutions are founded upon the doctrine of equality." At the very least, the Equal Protection Clause demands that racial classifications, especially suspect in criminal statutes, be subjected to the "most rigid scrutiny," and, if they are ever to be upheld, they must be shown to be necessary to the accomplishment of some permissible state objective, independent of the racial discrimination which it was the object of the Fourteenth Amendment to eliminate. Indeed, two members of this Court have already stated that they "cannot conceive of a valid legislative purpose . . . which makes the color of a person's skin the test of whether his conduct is a criminal offense."

There is patently no legitimate overriding purpose independent of invidious racial discrimination which justifies this classification. The fact that Virginia prohibits only interracial marriages involving white persons demonstrates that the racial classifications must stand on their own justification, as measures designed to maintain White Supremacy. We have consistently denied the constitutionality of measures which restrict the rights of citizens on account of race. There can be no doubt that restricting the freedom to marry solely because of racial classifications violates the central meaning of the Equal Protection Clause.

These statutes also deprive the Lovings of liberty without due process of law in violation of the Due Process Clause of the Fourteenth Amendment. The freedom to marry has long been recognized as one of the vital personal rights essential to the orderly pursuit of happiness by free men.

Marriage is one of the "basic civil rights of man," fundamental to our very existence and survival. To deny this fundamental freedom on so unsupportable a basis as the racial classifications embodied in these statutes, classifications so directly subversive of the principle of equality at the heart of the Fourteenth Amendment, is surely to deprive all the State's citizens of liberty without due process of law. The Fourteenth Amendment requires that the freedom of choice to marry not be restricted by invidious racial discriminations. Under our Constitution, the freedom to marry, or not marry, a person of another race resides with the individual and cannot be infringed by the State.

These convictions must be reversed.

Consistent with the equal protection analysis of *Loving*, the Court determined that child custody decisions could not be referenced to race[158] and that a state law requiring disclosure of a candidate's race on election ballots offended the equal protection guarantee.[159]

---

[158] Palmore v. Sidoti, 466 U.S. 429 (1984).

[159] Anderson v. Martin, 375 U.S. 399 (1964).

h. Integration Maintenance

A discrete but significant offshoot of the *Brown* era has been the legitimacy of policy calculated to preserve desegregation achievements. Although the Court has stressed that constitutional responsibilities abate with the elimination of dual school systems to the extent possible, some school districts have adopted integration maintenance policies that themselves have been the object of litigation. Given the relative scarcity of white students in many urban districts and concern with "tipping points" that, once reached will accelerate their flight from the school district, some systems have imposed restrictions on minority enrollment options and transfers for purposes of maintaining racial balance.[160] The net result, in an effort to preserve even a semblance of integration, has been racially disparate opportunities with respect to choice and the relegation of large numbers of minority students to predominantly minority schools. A similarly motivated strategy has established neighborhood schools for primary school students as a prelude to their assignment to racially mixed secondary schools. In reviewing a school board policy stressing the objective of minimizing white flight, the district court determined that public racial attitude was a permissible consideration.[161] Notwithstanding previous assertions that desegregation imperatives could not accommodate resistance,[162] dominant attitude and behavior have been allowable considerations so far in the framing of integration maintenance policy. Such policies have elicited criticism for elevating integration methodology to a point that its real objectives are forgotten.

Voluntary efforts to achieve or maintain racial balance in public schools have inspired efforts in some instance to restrict the availability of remedies. Review of such conditions has yielded mixed results. In *Washington v. Seattle School District*, the Court invalidated a state constitutional amendment prohibiting the use of busing to achieve integrative objectives.

---

[160] *E.g.*, Parent Assn. of Andrew Jackson High School v. Ambach, 598 F.2d 705 (2d Cir. 1984).

[161] Riddick v. School Board of Norfolk, 627 F. Supp. 814, 824 (E.D. Va. 1984), *aff'd*, 784 F.2d 521 (4th Cir.), *cert. denied*, 479 U.S. 938 (1986).

[162] *E.g.*, Cooper v. Aaron, 358 U.S. 1, 16–18 (1957).

Washington v. Seattle School District No. 1
458 U.S. 457 (1982)

JUSTICE BLACKMUN delivered the opinion of the Court.

We are presented here with an extraordinary question: whether an elected local school board may use the Fourteenth Amendment to defend its program of busing for integration from attack by the State.

Seattle School District No. 1 (District), which is largely coterminous with the city of Seattle Wash., is charged by state law with administering 112 schools and educating approximately 54,000 public school students. About 37% of these children are of Negro, Asian, American Indian, or Hispanic ancestry. Be-

cause segregated housing patterns in Seattle have created racially imbalanced schools, the District historically has taken steps to alleviate the isolation of minority students; since 1963, it has permitted students to transfer from their neighborhood schools to help cure the District's racial imbalance.

Despite these efforts, the District in 1977 came under increasing pressure to accelerate its program of desegregation. . . . The District therefore concluded that mandatory reassignment of students was necessary if racial isolation in its schools was to be eliminated. Accordingly, in March 1978, the School Board enacted the so-called "Seattle Plan" for desegregation. The plan, which makes extensive use of busing and mandatory reassignments, desegregates elementary schools by "pairing" and "trading" predominantly minority with predominantly white attendance areas, and by basing student assignments on attendance zones rather than on race. . . .

The desegregation program, implemented in the 1978-79 academic year, apparently was effective: the District Court found that the Seattle Plan "has substantially reduced the number of racially imbalanced schools in the district and has substantially reduced the percentage of minority students in those schools which remain racially imbalanced."

In late 1977, shortly before the Seattle Plan was formally adopted by the District, a number of Seattle residents who opposed the segregation strategies being discussed by the School Board formed an organization called the Citizens for Voluntary Integration Committee (CiVIC). This organization, which the District Court found "was formed because of its founders' opposition to The Seattle Plan," attempted to enjoin implementation of the Board's mandatory desegregation program through litigation in state court; when these efforts failed, CiVIC drafted a statewide initiative designed to terminate the use of mandatory busing for purposes of racial integration. This proposal, known as Initiative 350, provided that "no school board . . . shall directly or indirectly require any student to attend a school other than the school which is geographically nearest or next nearest the student's place of residence . . . and which offers the course of study pursued by such student. . . ."

[T]wo months after the Seattle Plan went into effect, Initiative 350 passed by a substantial margin, drawing almost 66% of the vote statewide. The initiative failed to attract majority support in two state legislative districts, both in Seattle. In the city as a whole, however, the initiative passed with some 61% of the vote. . . .

[L]aws structuring political institutions or allocating political power according to "neutral principles"—such as the executive veto, or the typically burdensome requirements for amending state constitutions—are not subject to equal protection attack, though they may "make it more difficult for minorities to achieve favorable legislation." Because such laws make it more difficult for every group in the community to enact comparable laws, they "provid[e] a just framework within which the diverse political groups in our society may fairly compete." Thus, the political majority may generally restructure the political process to place obstacles in the path of everyone seeking to secure the benefits of governmental action. But

a different analysis is required when the State allocates governmental power nonneutrally, by explicitly using the racial nature of a decision to determine the decisionmaking process. State action of this kind, the Court said, "places special burdens on racial minorities within the governmental process, thereby "making it more difficult for certain racial and religious minorities [than for other members of the community] to achieve legislation that is in their interest." . . . The initiative removes the authority to address a racial problem—and only a racial problem—from the existing decisionmaking body, in such a way as to burden minority interests. Those favoring the elimination of de facto school segregation now must seek relief from the state legislature, or from the statewide electorate. Yet authority over all other student assignment decisions, as well as over most other areas of educational policy, remains vested in the local school board. Indeed, by specifically exempting from initiative 350's proscriptions most nonracial reasons for assigning students away from their neighborhood schools, the initiative expressly requires those championing school integration to surmount a considerably higher hurdle than persons seeking comparable legislative action. [T]he community's political mechanisms are modified to place effective decisionmaking authority over a racial issue at a different level of government. In a very obvious sense, the initiative thus "disadvantages those who would benefit from laws barring" de facto desegregation "as against those who . . . would otherwise regulate" student assignment decisions; "the reality is that the law's impact falls on the minority." [H]ere, the power to enact racial legislation has been reallocated. In each case, the effect of the challenged action was to redraw decisionmaking authority over racial matters—and only racial matters—in such a way as to place comparative burdens on minorities. [W]e have little difficulty concluding that Initiative 350 worked a major reordering of the State's educational decisionmaking process. Before adoption of the initiative, the power to determine what programs would most appropriately fill a school district's educational needs-including programs involving student assignment and desegregation—was firmly committed to the local board's discretion. The question whether to provide an integrated learning environment rather than a system of neighborhood schools surely involved a decision of that sort. After passage of Initiative 350, authority over all but one of those areas remained in the hands of the local board. By placing power over desegregative busing at the state level, then, Initiative 350 plainly "differentiates between the treatment of problems involving racial matters and that afforded other problems in the same area."

The District Court and the Court of Appeals similarly concluded that the initiative restructured the Washington political process, and we see no reason to challenge the determinations of courts familiar with local law.

That we reach this conclusion should come as no surprise, for when faced with a similar educational scheme in *Milliken* the Court concluded that the actions of a local school board could not be attributed to the State that had created it. [T]he Court, noting that "[n]o single tradition in public education is more deeply rooted than local control over the operation of schools," concluded that the "Michigan educational structure ... in common with most States, provides for a large measure of local control." Relying on this analysis, the Court determined that a Michigan school board's assignment policies could not be attributed to the State, and therefore declined to permit interdistrict busing as a remedy for one school district's acts of unconstitutional segregation. If local school boards operating under a similar statutory structure are considered separate entities for purposes of constitutional adjudication when they make segregative assignment decisions, it is difficult to see why a different analysis should apply when a local board's desegregative policy is at issue.

To be sure, "the simple repeal or modification of desegregation or antidiscrimination laws, without more, never has ben viewed as embodying a presumptively invalid racial classification." *Crawford v. Los Angeles Board of Education.* ...

Initiative 350, however, works something more than the "mere repeal" of a desegregation law by the political entity that created it. It burdens all future attempts to integrate Washington schools in districts throughout the State, by lodging decisionmaking authority over the question at a new and remote level of government. ...

JUSTICE POWELL, with whom THE CHIEF JUSTICE, JUSTICE REHNQUIST, and JUSTICE O'CONNOR join, dissenting.

The people of the State of Washington, by a two-to-one vote, have adopted a neighborhood school policy. The policy is binding on local school districts but in no way affects the authority of state or federal courts to order school transportation to remedy violations of the Fourteenth Amendment. Nor does the policy affect the power of local school districts to establish voluntary transfer programs for racial integration or for any other purpose.

. . .

I dissent from the Court's unprecedented intrusion into the structure of a state government. The School Districts in this case were under no federal constitutional obligation to adopt mandatory busing programs. The State of Washington, the governmental body ultimately responsible for the provision of public education, has determined that certain mandatory busing programs are detrimental to the education of its children. "[T]he Fourteenth Amendment leaves the State free to distribute the powers of government as they will between their legislative and judicial branches." In my view, that Amendment leaves the States equally free to decide matters of concern to the State at the state, rather than local, level of government.

. . .

[A] State may choose to run its schools from the state legislature or through local school boards just as it may choose to address the matter of race relations at the state or local level. There is no constitutional requirement that the State establish or maintain local institutions of government or that it delegate particular powers to these bodies. The only relevant constitutional limitation on a State's freedom to order its political institutions is that it may not do so in a fashion designed to "plac[e] special burdens or racial minorities within the governmental process." [I]n the absence of a prior constitutional violation, the States are under no constitutional duty to adopt integration programs in their schools, and certainly they are under no duty to establish a regime of mandatory busing. Nor does the Federal Constitution require that particular decisions concerning the schools or any other matter be made on the local as opposed to the state level. It does not require the States to establish local governmental bodies or to delegate unreviewable authority to them.

Application of these settled principles demonstrates the serious error of today's decision—an error that cuts deeply into the heretofore unquestioned right of a State to structure the decisionmaking authority of its government. In this case, by Initiative 350, the State has adopted a policy of racial neutrality in student assignments. The policy in no way interferes with the power of state or federal courts to remedy constitutional violations. And if such a policy had been adopted by any of the School Districts in this litigation there could have been no question that the policy was constitutional.

Under today's decision this heretofore undoubted supreme authority of a State's electorate is to be curtailed whenever a school board—indeed any other state board or local instrumentality—adopts a race-specific program that arguable benefits racial minorities. Once such a program is adopted, only the local or subordinate entity that approved it will have authority to change it. The Court offers no authority or relevant explanation for this extraordinary subordination of the ultimate sovereign power of a State to act with respect to racial matters by subordinate bodies. It is a strange notion—alien to our system—that local governmental bodies can forever preempt the ability of a State—the sovereign power—to address a matter of compelling concern to the State. The Constitution of the United States does not require such a bizarre result.

This is certainly not a case where a State—in moving to change a locally adopted policy—has established a racially discriminatory requirement. Initiative 350 does not impede enforcement of the Fourteenth Amendment. If a Washington school district should be found to have established a segregated school system, Initiative 350 will place no barrier in the way of a remedial busing order. Nor does Initiative 350 authorize or approve segregation in any form or degree. It is neutral on its face, and racially neutral as public policy. Children of all races benefit from neighborhood schooling, just as children of all races benefit from exposure to "'ethnic and racial diversity in the classroom.'". . .

Finally, Initiative 350 places no "special burdens on racial minorities within the governmental process," such that interference with the State's political process at work. It does not alter that process in any respect. It does not alter require, for example, that all matters dealing with race—or with integration in the schools—must henceforth be submitted to a referendum of the people. The State has done mo more than precisely what the Court has said that it should do: It has "resolved through the political process" the "desirability and efficacy of [mandatory] school desegregation" where there has been no unlawful segregation.

The political process in Washington, as in other States, permits persons who are dissatisfied at a local level to appeal to the state legislature or the people of the State for redress. It permits the people of a State to pre-empt local policies, and to formulate new programs and regulations. Such a process is inherent in the continued sovereignty of the States. This is our system. Any time a State chooses to address a major issue some persons or groups may be disadvantaged. In a democratic system there are winners and losers. But there is no inherent unfairness in this and certainly no constitutional violation.

We are asked to decide the wisdom of a state policy that limits the ability of local school districts to adopt—on their own volition-mandatory reassignments for racial balance. We must decide only whether the Federal Constitution permits the State to adopt such a policy. The School Districts in this case were under no federal constitutional obligation to adopt mandatory busing. Absent such an obligation, the State—exercising its sovereign authority over all subordinate agencies—should be free to reject this debatable restriction on liberty. But today's decision denies this right to a State. In this case, it deprives the State of Washington of all opportunity to address the unresolved questions resulting from extensive mandatory busing. The Constitution does not dictate to the States at what level of government decisions affecting the public schools must be taken. It certainly does not strip the States of their sovereignty. It therefore does not authorize today's intrusion into the State's internal structure.

A constitutional amendment in California, prohibiting state courts from ordering busing unless a Fourteenth Amendment violation was established, was upheld.

Crawford v. Board of Education
of the City of Los Angeles
458 U.S. 527 (1982)

JUSTICE POWELL delivered the opinion of the Court.

An amendment to the California Constitution provides that state courts shall not order mandatory pupil assignment or transportation unless a federal court would do so to remedy a violation of the Equal Protection Clause of the Fourteenth Amendment of the United States Constitution. The question for our decision is whether this provision is itself in violation of the Fourteenth Amendment.

In November 1979 the voters of the State of California ratified Proposition I, an amendment to the Due Process and Equal Protection Clauses of the State Constitution. Proposition I conforms the power of state courts to order busing to that exercised by the federal courts under the Fourteenth Amendment:

"[No court of this state may impose upon the State of California or any public entity, board, or official any obligation or responsibility with respect to the use of pupil school assignment or pupil transportation, (1) except to remedy a specific violation by such party that would also constitute a violation of the Equal Protection Clause of the 14th Amendment to the United States Constitution, and (2) unless a federal court would be permitted under federal decisional law to impose that obligation or responsibility upon such party to remedy the specific violation of the Equal Protection Clause. . . ."

Following approval of Proposition I, the District asked the Superior Court to halt all mandatory reassignment and busing of pupils. On May 19, 1980, the court denied the District's application. The court reasoned that Proposition I was of no effect in this case in light of the court's 1970 finding of de jure segregation by the District in violation of the Fourteenth Amendment. Shortly thereafter, the court ordered implementation of a revised desegregation plan, one that . . . substantially relied upon mandatory pupil reassignment and transportation.

We agree with the California Court of Appeal in rejecting the contention that once a State chooses to do "more" than the Fourteenth Amendment requires, it may never recede. We reject an interpretation of the Fourteenth Amendment so destructive of a State's democratic processes and of its ability to experiment. This interpretation has no support in the decisions of this Court.

Proposition I does not inhibit enforcement of any federal law or constitutional requirement. Quite the contrary, by its plain language the Proposition seeks only to embrace the requirements of the Federal Constitutional with respect to mandatory school assignments and transportation. It would be paradoxical to conclude that by adopting the Equal Protection Clause of the Fourteenth Amendment, the voters of the State thereby had violated it. Moreover, even after Proposition I, the California Constitution still imposes a greater duty of desegregation than does the Federal Constitution. The state courts of California continue to have an obligation under state law to order segregated school districts to use voluntary desegregation techniques, whether or not there has been a finding of intentional segregation. The school districts themselves retain a state-law obligation to take reasonably feasible steps to desegregate, and they remain free to adopt reassignment and busing plans to effectuate desegregation.

Nonetheless, petitioners contend that Proposition I is unconstitutional on its face. They argue that Preposition I employs an "explicit racial classification" and imposes a "race-specific" burden on minorities seeking to vindicate state-created rights. By limiting the power of state courts to enforce the state-created right to desegregated schools petitioners contend,

Proposition I creates a "dual court system" that discriminates on the basis of race. They emphasize that other state-created rights may be vindicated by the state courts without limitation on remedies. Petitioners argue that the "dual court system" created by Proposition I is unconstitutional unless supported by a compelling state interest.

Were we to hold that the mere repeal of race-related legislation is unconstitutional, we would limit seriously the authority of States to deal with the problems of our heterogeneous population. States would be committed irrevocably to legislation that has proved unsuccessful or even harmful in practice. And certainly the purposes of the Fourteenth Amendment would not be advanced by an interpretation that discouraged the States from providing greater protection to racial minorities. Nor would the purposes of the Amendment be furthered by requiring the States to maintaining legislation designed to ameliorate race relations or to protect racial minorities but which has produced just the opposite effects. Yet these would be the results of requiring a State to maintain legislation that has proved unworkable or harmful when the State was under no obligation to adopt the legislation in the first place. Moreover and relevant to this case, we would not interpret the Fourteenth Amendment to require the people of a State to adhere to a judicial construction of their State Constitution when that Constitution itself vests final authority in the people.

Nor can it be said that Proposition I distorts the political process for racial reasons or that it allocates governmental or judicial power on the basis of a discriminatory principle. "The Constitution does not require things which are different in fact or opinion to be treated in law as though they were the same." Remedies appropriate in one area of legislation may not be desirable in another. The remedies available for violation of the antitrust laws, for example, are different than those available for violation of the Civil Rights Acts. Yet a "dual court system"—one for the racial majority and one for the racial minority—is not established simply because civil rights remedies are different from those available in other areas.

Surely it was constitutional for the California Supreme Court to caution that although "in some circumstances busing will be an appropriate and useful element in a desegregation plan," in other circumstances "its 'costs,' both in financial and educational terms, will render its use inadvisable." It was equally constitutional for the people of the State to determine that the standard of the Fourteenth Amendment was more appropriate for California courts to apply in desegregation cases than the standard repealed by Proposition I.

In short, having gone beyond the requirements of the Federal Constitution, the State was free to return in part to the standard prevailing generally throughout the United States. It could have conformed its laws to the Federal Constitution in every respect. That it chose to pull back only in part, and by preserving a greater right to desegregation than exists under the Federal Constitution, most assuredly does not render the Proposition unconstitutional on its face.

. . .

Under decisions of this Court, a law neutral on its face still may be unconstitutional if motivated by a discriminatory purpose. In determining whether such a purpose was the motivating factor, the racially disproportionate effect of official action provides "an 'important starting point.'"

Proposition I in no way purports to limit the power of state courts to remedy the effects of intentional segregation with its accompanying stigma. The benefits of neighborhood schooling are racially neutral. This manifestly is true in Los Angeles where over 75% of the public school body is composed of groups viewed as racial minorities. Moreover, the Proposition simply removes one means of achieving the state-created right to desegregated education. School districts retain the obligation to alleviate segregation regardless of cause. And the state courts still may order desegregation measures other than pupil school assignment or pupil transportation. . . . Even if we could assume that Proposition I had a disproportionate adverse effect on racial minorities, we see no reason to challenge the Court of Appeal's conclusion that the voters of the State were not motivated by a discriminatory purpose.

In this case the Proposition was approved by an overwhelming majority of the electorate. It received support from members of all races. The purposes of the Proposition are stated in its text and are legitimate, nondiscriminatory objectives. In these circumstances, we will not dispute the judgment of the Court of Appeal or impugn the motives of the State's electorate.

. . .

JUSTICE BLACKMUN, with whom JUSTICE BRENNAN joins, concurring.

While I join the opinion of the Court, I write separately to address what I believe are the critical distinctions between this case and *Washington v. Seattle School District No. 1.* The Court distortions of the political process have special implications for attempts to achieve equal protection of the laws. Thus the Court has found particularly pernicious those classifications that threaten the ability of minorities to involve themselves in the process of self-government, for if laws are not drawn

within a "just framework," it is unlikely that they will be drawn on just principals.

The Court's conclusion in *Seattle* followed inexorably from these considerations. . . .

In my view, something significantly different is involved in this case. State courts do not create the rights they enforce; those rights originate elsewhere—in the state legislature, in the State's political subdivisions, or in the State's political subdivisions, or in the state constitution itself. When one of those rights is repealed, and therefore is rendered unenforceable in the courts, that action hardly can be said to restructure the State's decisionmaking mechanism. While the California electorate may have made it more difficult to achieve desegregation when it enacted Proposition I, to my mind it did so not by working a structural change in the political process so much as by simply repealing the right to invoke a judicial busing remedy. . . .

JUSTICE MARSHALL, dissenting.

. . . Because I fail to see how a fundamental redefinition of the governmental decisionmaking structure with respect to the same racial issue can be unconstitutional when the State seeks to remove the authority from local school boards, yet constitutional when the State attempts to achieve the same result by limiting the power of its courts, I must dissent from the Court's decision to uphold Proposition I.

In order to understand fully the implications of the Court's action today, it is necessary to place the facts concerning the adoption of Proposition I in their proper context. Nearly two decades ago, a unanimous California Supreme Court declared that "[t]he segregation of school children into separate schools because of their race, even though the physical facilities and the methods and quality of instruction in the several schools may be equal, deprives the children of the minority group of equal opportunities for education and denies them equal protection and due process of the law." Recognizing that the "right to an equal opportunity for education and the harmful consequences of segregation" do not differ according to the cause of racial isolation, the California Supreme Court declined to adopt the distinction between de facto and de jure segregation engrafted by this Court on the Fourteenth Amendment. Instead, the court clearly held that "school boards [must] take steps, insofar as reasonably feasible, to alleviate racial imbalance in schools regardless of its cause."

Like so many other decisions protecting the rights of minorities, California's decision to eradicate the evils of segregation regardless of cause has not been a popular one. In the nearly two decades since the State Supreme Court's decision in *Jackson*, there have been repeated attempts to restrain school boards and courts from enforcing this constitutional guarantee by means of mandatory student transfers or assignments.

Finally, in 1979, the people of California enacted Proposition I. That Proposition, like all of the previous initiatives, effectively deprived California courts of the ability to enforce the state constitutional guarantee that minority children will not attend racially isolated schools by use of what may be "the sole and exclusive means of eliminating racial segregation in the schools," mandatory student assignment and transfer. Unlike the earlier attempts to accomplish this objective, however, Proposition I does not purport to prevent mandatory assignments and transfers when such measures are predicated on a violation of the Federal Constitution. Therefore, the only question presented by this case is whether the fact that mandatory transfers may still be made to vindicate federal constitutional rights saves this initiative from the constitutional infirmity presented in the previous attempts to accomplish this same objective. In my view, the recitation of the obvious—that a state constitutional amendment does not override federal constitutional guarantees—cannot work to deprive minority children in California of their federally protected right to the equal protection of the laws.

Nor can there be any doubt that Proposition I works a substantial reallocation of state power. Prior to the enactment of Proposition I, those seeking to vindicate the rights enumerated by the Supreme Court, just as those interested in attaining any other educational objective, followed a two-stage procedure. First, California's minority community could attempt to convince the local school board voluntarily to comply with its constitutional obligation to take reasonable feasible steps to eliminate racial isolation in the public schools. If the board was either unwilling or unable to carry out its constitutional duty, those seeking redress could petition the California state courts to require school officials to live up to their obligations. Busing could be required as part of a judicial remedial order. . . . Proposition I eliminates by fiat the second stage: the ability of California courts to order meaningful compliance with the requirements of the State Constitution. After the adoption of Proposition I, the only method of enforcing against a recalcitrant school board the state constitutional duty to eliminate racial isolation is to petition either the state legislature or the electorate as a whole. Clearly, the rules of the game have been significantly changed for those attempting to vindicate this state constitutional right.

. . .

As in *Seattle*, . . . Proposition I's repeal of the state court's enforcement powers was the work of an independent governmental entity, and not of the state courts themselves. That this repeal drastically alters the substantive rights granted by existing policy is patently obvious from the facts of this litigation. By prohibiting California courts from ordering mandatory student assignment when necessary to eliminate racially isolated schools, Proposition I has placed an enormous barrier between minority children and the effective enjoyment of their constitutional rights, a barrier that is not placed in the path of those who seek to vindicate other rights granted by state law. This Court's precedents demonstrate that, absent a compelling state interest, which respondents have hardly demonstrated, such a discriminatory barrier cannot stand. . . . The fact that California attempts to cloak its discrimination in the mantel of the Fourteenth Amendment does not alter this result. Although it might seem "paradoxical" to some Members of this Court that a referendum that adopts the wording of the Fourteenth Amendment might violate it, the paradox is specious. Because of the Supremacy Clause, Proposition I would have precisely the same legal effect if it contained no reference to the Fourteenth Amendment. . . .

In this case, the reallocation of power occurs in the judicial process—the major arena minorities have used to ensure the protection of rights "in their interest." Certainly, . . . *Seattle* cannot be distinguished on the ground that they concerned the reallocation of legislative power, whereas Proposition I redistributes the inherent power of a court to tailor the remedy to the violation. As we have long recognized, courts too often have been "the sole practicable avenue open to a minority to petition for redress of grievances." It is no wonder, as the present case amply illustrates, that whatever progress has been made towards the elimination of de facto segregation has come from the California courts. Indeed, Proposition I, by denying full access to the only branch of government that has been willing to address this issue meaningfully, is far worse for those seeking to vindicate the plainly unpopular cause of racial integration in the public schools than a simple reallocation of an often unavailable and unresponsive legislative process.

Proposition I is in some sense "better" than the Washington initiative struck down in *Seattle*. In their generosity, California voters have allowed those seeking racial balance to petition the very school officials who have steadfastly maintained the color line at the schoolhouse door to comply voluntarily with their continuing state constitutional duty to desegregate. At the same time, the voters have deprived minorities of the only method of redress that has proved effective—the full remedial powers of the state judiciary. In the name of the State's "ability to experiment," the Court today allows this placement of yet another burden in the path of those seeking to counter the effects of nearly three centuries of racial prejudice. Because this decision is neither justified by our prior decisions nor consistent with our duty to guarantee all citizens the equal protection of the laws, I must dissent.

6. Motive-Based Inquiry: The Requirement of Discriminatory Purpose

Consistent with emergence of the *de jure—de facto* distinction in the context of school desegregation case law, equal protection doctrine has been conditioned by the threshold requirement of proving discriminatory purpose. Insofar as discriminatory intent is palpable on the face of regulation, as it was with respect to prescriptive segregation, the evidentiary requirement is not imposing. Because overt segregation and discrimination largely is a historic relic, that has been supplanted by more subtle methodologies, proving wrongful purpose is more vexing. Even before *Plessy*, the Court determined that discrimination may exist even though a law or policy is racially neutral on its face. In reviewing a city ordinance, prohibiting laundries in buildings constructed of wood but enforced exclusively against persons of Chinese descent, the Court determined that

> an administration directed so exclusively against a particular class of persons as to warrant and require the conclusion that, whatever may have been the intent of the ordinances as adopted, they are applied with a mind so unequal and oppressive as to amount to a practical denial by the State of equal protection. . . . Though the law itself be fair on its face and impartial in appearance, yet, if it is applied and administered by public authority with an evil eye and an unequal hand, so as practically to make unjust and illegal discriminations between persons in similar circumstances, material to their rights, the denial of equal justice is still within the prohibition of the Constitution.[163]

Although well-established that the Court may scratch the surface of a law or policy to determine whether it is wrongly inspired, it also is settled that racially disproportionate effect by itself is constitutionally insignificant. In *Washington v. Davis*, the Court determined that the racially disparate consequences of a city's police hiring practices did not by themselves constitute an equal protection violation.

---

[163] Yick Wo v. Hopkins, 118 U.S. 356, 373–74 (1886).

Washington v. Davis
426 U.S. 229 (1976)

Mr. Justice White delivered the opinion of the Court.

This case involves the validity of a qualifying test administered to applicants for positions as police officers in the District of Columbia Metropolitan Police Department. The test was sustained by the District Court but invalidated by the Court of Appeals. We are in agreement with the District Court and hence reverse the judgment of the Court of Appeals.

This action began on April 10, 1970, when two Negro police officers filed suit against the then Commissioner of the District of Columbia, the Chief of the District's Metropolitan Police Department, and the Commissioners of the United States Civil Service Commission. An amended complaint, filed December 10, alleged that the promotion policies of the Department were racially discriminatory and sought a declaratory judgment and an injunction. The respondents Harley and Sellers were permitted to intervene, their amended complaint asserting that their applications to become officers in the Department had been rejected, and that the Department's recruiting procedures (discriminated on the basis of race against black applicants by a series of practices including, but not limited to, a written personnel test which excluded a disproportionately high number of Negro applicants. These practices were asserted to violate respondents' rights under the due process clause of the Fifth Amendment to the United States Constitution. . . .

According to the findings and conclusions of the District Court, to be accepted by the Department and to enter an intensive 17-week training program, the police recruit was required to satisfy certain physical and character standards, to be a high school graduate or its equivalent, and to receive a grade of at least 40 out of 80 on "Test 21," which is "an examination that is used generally throughout the federal service," which "was developed by the Civil Service Commission, not the Police Department," and which was "designed to test verbal ability, vocabulary, reading and comprehension."

The validity of Test 21 was the sole issue before the court on the motions for summary judgment. The District Court noted that there was no claim of "an intentional discrimination or purposeful discriminatory acts" but only a claim that Test 21 bore no relationship to job performance and "has a highly discriminatory impact in screening out black candidates. Respondents' evidence, the District Court said, warranted three conclusions: "(a) The number of black police officers, while substantial, is not proportionate to the population mix of the city. (b) A higher percentage of blacks fail the Test than whites. (c) The Test has not been validated to establish its reliability for measuring subsequent job performance." . . .

As the Court of Appeals understood Title VII, employees or applicants proceeding under it need not concern themselves with the employer's possibly discriminatory purpose but instead may focus solely on the racially differential impact of the challenged hiring or promotion practices. This is not the constitutional rule. We have never held that the constitutional standard for adjudicating claims of invidious racial discrimination is identical to the standards applicable under Title VII, and we decline to do so today.

The central purpose of the Equal Protection Clause of the Fourteenth Amendment is the prevention of official conduct discriminating on the basis of race. It is also true that the Due Process Clause of the Fifth Amendment contains an equal protection component prohibiting the United States from invidiously dis-

criminating between individuals or groups. *Bolling v. Sharpe,* 347 U. S. 497 (1954). But our cases have not embraced the proposition that a law or other official act, without regard to whether it reflects a racially discriminatory purpose, is unconstitutional solely because it has a racially disproportionate impact. . . .

The school desegregation cases have . . . adhered to the basic equal protection principle that the invidious quality of a law claimed to be racially discriminatory must ultimately be traced to a racially discriminatory purpose. That there are both predominantly black and predominantly white schools in a community is not alone violative of the Equal Protection Clause. The essential element of *de jure* segregation is "a current condition of segregation resulting from intentional state action." "The differentiating factor between de jure segregation and so-called *de facto* segregation . . . *is purpose* or *intent* to segregate." . . . The Court has also recently rejected allegations of racial discrimination based solely on the statistically disproportionate racial impact of various provisions of the Social Security Act because "[t]he acceptance of appellants' constitutional theory would render suspect each difference in treatment among the grant classes, however lacking in racial motivation and however otherwise rational the treatment might be." *Jefferson v. Hackney*, 406 U.S. 535, 548 (1972). . . .

This is not to say that the necessary discriminatory racial purpose must be express or appear on the face of the statute, or that a law's disproportionate impact is irrelevant in cases involving Constitution-based claims of racial discrimination. A statute, otherwise neutral on its face, must not be applied so as invidiously to discriminate on the basis of race. . . .

Necessarily, an invidious discriminatory purpose may often be inferred from the totality of the relevant facts, including the fact, if it is true, that the law bears more heavily on one race than another. It is also not infrequently true that the discriminatory impact—in the jury cases for example, the total or seriously disproportionate exclusion of Negroes from jury cases—may for all practical purposes demonstrate unconstitutionality because in various circumstances the discrimination is very difficult to explain on nonracial grounds. Nevertheless, we have not held that a law, neutral on its face and serving ends otherwise within the power of government to pursue, is invalid under the Equal Protection Clause simply because it may affect a greater proportion of one race than of another. Disproportionate impact is not irrelevant, but it is not the sole touchstone of an invidious racial discrimination forbidden by the Constitution. Standing alone, it does not trigger the rule, . . . that racial classifications are to be subjected to the strictest scrutiny and are justifiable only by the weightiest of considerations.

As an initial matter, we have difficulty understanding how a law establishing a racially neutral qualification for employment is nevertheless racially discriminatory and denies "any person . . . equal protection of the laws" simply because a greater proportion of Negroes fail to qualify than members of other racial or ethnic groups. Had respondents, along with all others who had failed Test 21, whether white or black, brought an action claiming that the test denied each of them equal protection of the laws as compared with those who had passed with high enough scores to qualify them as police recruits, it is most unlikely that their challenge would have been sustained. Test 21, which is administered generally to prospective Government employees, concededly seeks to ascertain whether those who take it have acquired a particular level of verbal skill; and it is untenable that the Constitution prevents the Government from seeking modestly to upgrade the communicative abilities of its employees rather than to be satisfied with some lower level of competence, particularly where the job requires special ability to communicate orally and in writing. Respondents, as Negroes, could no more successfully claim that the test denied them equal protection than could white applicants who also failed. The conclusion would not be different in the face of proof that more Negroes than whites had been disqualified by Test 21. That other Negroes also failed to score well would, alone, not demonstrate that respondents individually were being denied equal protection of the laws by the application of an otherwise valid qualifying test being administered to prospective police recruits.

Nor on the facts of the case before us would the disproportionate impact of Test 21 warrant the conclusion that it is a purposeful device to discriminate against Negroes and hence an infringement of the constitutional rights of respondents as well as other black applicants. As we have said, the test is neutral on its face and rationally may be said to serve a purpose the Government is constitutionally empowered to pursue. Even agreeing with the District Court that the differential racial effect of Test 21 called for further inquiry, we think the District Court correctly held that the affirmative efforts of the Metropolitan Police Department to recruit black officers, the changing racial composition of the recruit classes and of the force in general, and the relationship of the test to the training program negated any inference that the Department discriminated on the basis of race or that "a police officer qualifies on the color of his skin rather than ability." . . .

Under Title VII, Congress provided that when hiring and promotion practices disqualifying substantially disproportionate numbers of blacks are challenged, discriminatory purpose need not be proved, and that it is an insufficient response to demonstrate some rational basis for the challenged practices. It is necessary, in addition, that they be "validated" in terms of job performance in any one of several ways, perhaps by ascertaining the minimum skill, ability, or potential necessary for the position at issue and determining whether the qualifying tests are appropriate for the selection of qualified applicants for the job in question. However this process proceeds, it involves a more probing judicial review of, and less deference to, the seemingly reasonable acts of administrators and executives than is appropriate under the Constitution where special racial impact, without discriminatory purpose, is claimed. We are not disposed to adopt this more rigorous standard for the purposes of applying the Fifth and the Fourteenth Amendments in cases such as this.

A rule that a statute designed to serve neutral ends is nevertheless invalid, absent compelling justification, if in practice it benefits or burdens one race more than another would be far reaching and would raise serious questions about, and perhaps invalidate, a whole range of tax, welfare, public service, regulatory, and licensing statutes that may be more burdensome to the poor and to the average black than to the more affluent white.

Given that rule, such consequences would perhaps be likely to follow. However, in our view, extension of the rule beyond those areas where it is already applicable by reason of statute, such as in the field of public employment, should await legislative prescription. . . .

A year after *Davis*, the Court reaffirmed its investment in discriminatory motive criteria. Its decision, in *Village of Arlington Heights v. Metropolitan Housing Development Corp.*, was notable for setting forth some of the evidentiary factors that might support a finding of illicit purpose.

Village of Arlington Heights v. Metropolitan Housing Development Corp.
429 U.S. 252 (1977)

Our decision last Term in *Washington v. Davis*, made it clear that official action will not be held unconstitutional solely because it results in a racially disproportionate impact. "Disproportionate impact is not irrelevant, but it is not the sole touchstone of an invidious racial discrimination." Proof of racially discriminatory intent or purpose is required to show a violation of the Equal Protection Clause. Although some contrary indications may be drawn from some of our cases," the holding in *Davis* reaffirmed a principle well established in a variety of contexts.

Davis does not require a plaintiff to prove that the challenged action rested solely on racially discriminatory purposes. Rarely can it be said that a legislature or administrative body operating under a broad mandate made a decision motivated solely by a single concern, or even that a particular purpose was the "dominant" or "primary" one. In fact, it is because legislators and administrators are properly concerned with balancing numerous competing considerations that courts refrain from reviewing the merits of their decisions, absent a showing of arbitrariness or irrationality. But racial discrimination is not just another competing consideration. When there is a proof that a discriminatory purpose has been a motivating factor in the decision, this judicial deference is no longer justified.

Determining whether invidious discriminatory purpose was a motivating factor demands a sensitive inquiry into such circumstantial and direct evidence of intent as may be available. The impact of the official action—whether it "bears more heavily on one race than another,"—may provide an important starting point. Sometimes a clear pattern, unexplainable on grounds other than race, emerges from the effect of the state action even when the governing legislation appears neutral on its face. The evidentiary inquiry is then relatively easy. But such cases are rare. Absent a [stark] pattern . . . impact alone is not determinative," and the Court must look to other evidence.

The historical background of the decision is one evidentiary source, particularly if it reveals a series of official actions taken for invidious purposes. The specific sequence of events leading up to the challenged decision also may shed some light on the decisionmaker's purposes. For example, if the property involved here always had been zoned R-5 but suddenly was changed to R-3 when the town learned of MHDC's plans to erect integrated housing, we would have a far different case. Departures from the normal procedural sequence also might afford evidence that improper purposes are playing a role. Substantive departures too may be relevant, particularly if the factors usually considered important by the decisionmaker strongly favor a decision contrary to the one reached.

The legislative or administrative history may be highly relevant, especially where there are contemporary statements by members of the decisionmaking body, minutes of its meetings, its reports. In some extraordinary instances the members might be called to the stand at trial to testify concerning the purpose of the official action, although even then such testimony frequently will be barred by privilege.

The foregoing summary identifies, without purporting to be exhaustive, subjects of proper inquiry in determining whether racially discriminatory intent existed. With these in mind, we now address the case before us.

. . .

The *Arlington Heights* decision did not speak directly to whether foreseeability of disproportionate consequence could be a basis for establishing discriminatory purpose. Two years later, in the context of alleged gender discrimination, the Court rejected arguments that foreseeability was a legitimate basis for identifying illegal motive. *See Personnel Administrator of Massachusetts v. Feeney*, 442 U.S. 256 (1979), *infra.*

The Court's reluctance to correlate an equal protection violation to statistics alone was accentuated in *McCleskey v. Kemp*. Reviewing a study of the racially disparate operation of the death penalty in Georgia, both with respect to prosecutorial and sentencing decisions, the Court concluded that the numbers did not speak for themselves.

McCleskey v. Kemp
481 U.S. 279 (1987)

JUSTICE POWELL delivered the opinion of the Court.

This case presents the question whether a complex statistical study that indicates a risk that racial considerations enter into capital sentencing determinations proves that petitioner McCleskey's capital sentence is unconstitutional under the Eighth or Fourteenth Amendment.

McCleskey, a black man, was convicted of two counts of armed robbery and one count of murder in the Superior Court of Fulton County, Georgia, on October 12, 1978. McCleskey's convictions arose out of the robbery of a furniture store and the killing of a white police officer during the course of the robbery. . . . McCleskey offered no mitigating evidence. The jury recommended that he be sentenced to death on the murder charge and to consecutive life sentences on the armed robbery charges. The court followed the jury's recommendation and sentenced McCleskey to death. . . .

McCleskey . . . filed a petition for a writ of habeas corpus in the Federal District Court for the Northern District of Georgia. His petition raised 18 claims, one of which was that the Georgia capital sentencing process is administered in a racially discriminatory manner in violation of the Eighth and Fourteenth Amendments to the United States Constitution. In support of his claim, McCleskey proffered a statistical study performed by Professors David C. Baldus, Charles Pulaski, and George Woodworth (the Baldus study) that purports to show a disparity in the imposition of the death sentence in Georgia based on the race of the murder victim and, to a lesser extent, the race of the defendant. The Baldus study is actually two sophisticated statistical studies that examine over 2,000 murder cases that occurred in Georgia during the 1970's. The raw numbers collected by Professor Baldus indicate that defendants charged with killing white persons received the death penalty in 11% of the cases, but defendants charged with killing blacks received the death penalty in only 1% of the cases. The raw numbers also indicate a reverse racial disparity according to the race of the defendant: 4% of the black defendants received the death penalty, as opposed to 7% of the white defendants.

Baldus also divided the cases according to the combination of the race of the defendant and the race of the victim. He found that the death penalty was assessed in 22% of the cases involving black defendants and white victims; 8% of the cases involving white defendants and white victims; 1% of the cases involving black defendants and black victims; and 3% of the cases involving white defendants and black victims. Similarly, Baldus found that prosecutors sought the death penalty in 70% of the cases involving black defendants and white victims; 32% of the cases involving white defendants and white victims; 15% of the cases involving black defendants and black victims; and 19% of the cases involving white defendants and black victims.

Baldus subjected his data to an extensive analysis, taking account of 230 variables that could have explained the disparities on nonracial grounds. One of his models concludes that, even if after taking account of 39 nonracial variables, defendants charged with killing white victims were 4.3 times as likely to receive a death sentence as defendants charged with killing blacks. According to this model, black defendants were 1.1 times as likely to receive a death sentence as other defendants. Thus, the Baldus study indicates that black defendants, such as McCleskey, who kill white victims have the greatest likelihood of receiving the death penalty. . . .

McCleskey's first claim is that the Georgia capital punishment statute violates the Equal Protection Clause of the Fourteenth Amendment. He argues that race has infected the administration of Georgia's statute in two ways: persons who murder whites are more likely to be sentenced to death than persons who murder blacks, and black murderers are more likely to be sentenced to death than white murderers.

[T]o prevail under the Equal Protection Clause, McCleskey must prove that the decisionmakers in *his* case acted with discriminatory purpose. He offers no evidence specific to his own case that would support an inference that racial considerations played a part in his sentence.

Although statistical proof normally must present a "stark" pattern to be accepted as the sole proof of discriminatory intent under the Constitution, "[b]ecause of the nature of the jury-selection task, . . . we have permitted a finding of constitutional violation even when the statistical pattern does not approach [such] extremes."

But the nature of the capital sentencing decision, and the relationship of the statistics to that decision, are fundamentally different from the corresponding elements in the venire-selection or Title VII cases. Most importantly, each particular decision to impose the death penalty is made by a petit jury selected from a properly constituted venire. Each jury is unique in its composition, and the Constitution requires that its decision rest on consideration of innumerable factors that vary according to the characteristics of the individual defendant and the facts of the particular capital offense. Thus, the application of an inference drawn from the general statistics to a specific decision in a trial and "sentencing simply is not comparable to the application of an inference drawn from general statistics to a specific venire-selection or Title VII case. In those cases, the statistics relate to fewer entities, and fewer variables are relevant to, the challenged decisions.

Another important difference between the cases in which we have accepted statistics as proof of discriminatory intent and this case is that, in the venire-selection and Title VII contexts, the decisionmaker has an opportunity to explain the statistical disparity. . . . Here, the State has no practical opportunity to rebut the Baldus study. "[C]ontrolling considerations of . . . public policy," dictate that jurors "cannot be called . . . to testify to the motives and influences that led to their verdict." Similarly, the policy considerations behind a prosecutor's traditionally "wide discretion" suggest the impropriety of our requiring prosecutors to defend their decisions to seek death penalties, "often years after they were made." . . .

Finally, McCleskey's statistical proffer must be viewed in the context of his challenge. McCleskey challenges decisions at the heart of the State's criminal justice system. "[O]ne of society's most basic tasks is that of protecting the lives of its citizens and one of the most basic ways in which it achieves the task is through criminal laws against murder." Implementation of these laws necessarily requires discretionary judgments. Because discretion is essential to the criminal justice process, we would demand exceptionally clear proof before we would infer that the discretion has been abused. The unique nature of the decisions at issue in this case also counsels against adopting such an inference from the disparities indicated by the Baldus study. Accordingly, we hold that the Baldus study is clearly insufficient to support an inference that any of the decisionmakers in McCleskey's case acted with discriminatory purpose.

McCleskey also suggests that the Baldus study proves that the State as a whole has acted with a discriminatory purpose. He appears to argue that the State has violated the Equal Protection Clause by adopting the capital punishment statute and allowing it to remain in force despite its allegedly discriminatory application. But "'[d]iscriminatory purpose' . . . implies more than intent as volition or intent as awareness of consequences. It implies that the decisionmaker, in this case a state legislature, selected or reaffirmed a particular course of action at least in part 'because of,' not merely 'in spite of,' its adverse effects upon an identifiable group." For this claim to prevail, McCleskey would have to prove that the Georgia Legislature enacted or maintained the death penalty statute *because of* an anticipated racially discriminatory effect. There was no evidence then, and there is none now, that the Georgia Legislature enacted the capital punishment statute to further a racially discriminatory purpose.

Nor has McCleskey demonstrated that the legislature maintains the capital punishment statute because of the racially disproportionate impact suggested by the Baldus study. As legislatures necessarily have wide discretion in the choice of criminal laws and penalties, and as there were legitimate reasons for the Georgia Legislature to adopt and maintain capital punishment, we will not infer a discriminatory purpose on the part of the State of Georgia." Accordingly, we reject McCleskey's equal protection claims.

To evaluate McCleskey's challenge, we must examine exactly what the Baldus study may show. Even Professor Baldus does not contend that his statistics *prove* that race enters into any capital sentencing decisions or that race was a factor in McCleskey's particular case. Statistics at most may show only a likelihood that a particular factor entered into some decisions. There is, of course, some risk of racial prejudice influencing a jury's decision in a criminal case. There are similar risks that other kinds of prejudice will influence other criminal trials. The question "is at what point that risk becomes constitutionally unacceptable," McCleskey asks us to accept the likelihood allegedly shown by the Baldus study as the constitutional measure of an unacceptable risk of racial prejudice influencing capital sentencing decisions. This we decline to do.

Because of the risk that the factor of race may enter the criminal justice process, we have engaged in "unceasing efforts" to eradicate racial prejudice from our criminal justice system. Our efforts have been guided by our recognition that "the inestimable privilege of trial by jury is a vital principle, underlying the whole administration of criminal justice." Thus, it is the jury that is a criminal defendant's fundamental "protection of life and liberty against race or color prejudice." Specifically, a capital sentencing jury representative of a criminal defendants community assures a "'diffused impartiality.'"

McCleskey's argument that the Constitution condemns the discretion allowed decisionmakers in the Georgia capital sentencing system is antithetical to the fundamental role of discretion in our criminal justice system. Discretion in the criminal justice system offers substantial benefits to the criminal defendant. Not only can a jury decline to impose the death sentence, it can decline to convict or choose to convict of a lesser offense. . . . Similarly, the capacity of prosecutorial discretion to provide individualized justice is "firmly entrenched in American law." As we have noted, a prosecutor can decline to charge, offer a plea bargain, or decline to seek a death sentence in any particular case.

Of course, the power to be lenient [also] is the power to discriminate," but a capital punishment system that did not allow for discretionary acts of leniency "would be totally alien to our notions of criminal justice." . . . Where the discretion that is fundamental to our criminal process is involved, we decline to assume that what is unexplained is invidious. In light of the safeguards designed to minimize racial bias in the process, the fundamental value of jury trial in our criminal justice system, and the benefits that discretion provides to criminal defendants, we hold that the Baldus study does not demonstrate a constitutionally significant risk of racial bias affecting the Georgia capital sentencing process.

JUSTICE BRENNAN, with whom JUSTICE MARSHALL joins, and with whom JUSTICE BLACKMUN and JUSTICE STEVENS join in all but Part I, dissenting.

. . .

At some point in this case, Warren McCleskey doubtless asked his lawyer whether a jury was likely to sentence him to die. A candid reply to this question would have been disturbing. First, counsel would have to tell McCleskey that few of the details of the crime or of McCleskey's past criminal conduct were more important than the fact that his victim was white. Furthermore, counsel would feel bound to tell McCleskey that defendants charged with killing white victims in Georgia are 4.3 times as likely to be sentenced to death as defendants charged with killing blacks. In addition, frankness would compel the disclosure that it was more likely than not that the race of McCleskey's victim would determine whether he received a death sentence: 6 of every 11 defendants convicted of killing a white person would not have received the death penalty if their victims had been black, while, among defendants with aggravating and mitigating factors comparable to McCleskey's, 20 of every 34 would not have been sentenced to die if their victims had been black. Finally, the assessment would not be complete without the information that cases involving black defendants and white victims are more likely to result in a death sentence than cases featuring any other racial combination of defendant and victim. The story could be told in a variety of ways, but McCleskey could not fail to grasp its

essential narrative line: there was a significant chance that race would play a prominent role in determining if he lived or died.

The Court today holds that Warren McCleskey's sentence was constitutionally imposed. It finds no fault in a system in which lawyers must tell their clients that race casts a large shadow on the capital sentencing process. The Court arrives at this conclusion by stating that the Baldus study cannot "prove that race enters into any capital sentencing decisions or that race was a factor in McCleskey's particular case. Since, according to Professor Baldus, we cannot say "to a moral certainty" that race influenced a decision, we can identify only "a likelihood that a particular factor entered into some decisions," and "a discrepancy that appears to correlate with race." This "likelihood" and "discrepancy," holds the Court, is insufficient to establish a constitutional violation. . . .

The Baldus study indicates that, after taking into account some 230 nonracial factors that might legitimately influence a sentencer, the jury *more likely than not* would have spared McCleskey's life had his victim been black. The study distinguishes between those cases in which (1) the jury exercises virtually no discretion because the strength or weakness of aggravating factors usually suggests that only one outcome is appropriate, and (2) cases reflecting an "intermediate" level of aggravation, in which the jury has considerable discretion in choosing a sentence. McCleskey's case falls into the intermediate range. In such cases, death is imposed in 34% of white-victim crimes and 14% of black-victim crimes, a difference of 139% in the rate of imposition of the death penalty. In other words, just under 59%—almost 6 in 10—defendants comparable to McCleskey would not have received the death penalty if their victims had been black.

Furthermore, even examination of the sentencing system as a whole, factoring in those cases in which the jury exercises little discretion, indicates the influence of race on capital sentencing. For the Georgia system as a whole, race accounts for a six percentage point difference in the rate at which capital punishment is imposed. Since death is imposed in 11% of all white-victim cases, the rate in comparably aggravated black-victim cases is 5%. The rate of capital sentencing in a white-victim case is thus 120% greater than the rate in a black-victim case. Put another way, over half—55%—of defendants in white-victim crimes in Georgia would not have been sentenced to die if their victims had been black. Of the more than 200 variables potentially relevant to a sentencing decision, race of the victim is a powerful explanation for variation in death sentence rates—as powerful as nonracial aggravating factors such as a prior murder conviction or acting as the principal planner of the homicide.

These adjusted figures are only the most conservative indication of the risk that race will influence the death sentences of defendants in Georgia. Data unadjusted for the mitigating or aggravating effect of other factors show an even more pronounced disparity by race. The capital sentencing rate for all white-victim cases was almost 11 *times* greater than the rate for black-victim cases. Furthermore, blacks who kill whites are sentenced to death at nearly *22 times* the rate of blacks who kill blacks, and more than 7 time's the rate of whites who kill blacks. In addition, prosecutors seek the death penalty for 70% of black defendants with white victims, but for only 15% of black defendants with black victims, and only 19% of white defendants with black victims. Since our decision upholding the Georgia capital sentencing system in *Gregg,* the State has executed seven persons. All of the seven were convicted of killing whites, and six of the seven executed were black. Such execution figures are especially striking in light of the fact that, during the period encompassed by the Baldus study, only 9.2% of Georgia homicides involved black defendants and white victims, while 60.7% involved black victims.

McCleskey's statistics have particular force because most of them are the product of sophisticated multiple-regression analysis. Such analysis is designed precisely to identify patterns in the aggregate, even though we may not be able to reconstitute with certainty any individual decision that goes to make up that pattern. Multiple-regression analysis is particularly well suited to identify the influence of impermissible considerations in sentencing, since it is able to control for permissible factors that may explain an apparent arbitrary pattern. . . .

The statistical evidence in this case thus relentlessly documents the risk that McCleskey's sentence was influenced by racial considerations. This evidence shows that there is a better than even chance in Georgia that race will influence the decision to impose the death penalty: a majority of defendants in white-victim crimes would not have been sentenced to die if their victims had been black. . . .

Evaluation of McCleskey's evidence cannot rest solely on the numbers themselves. We must also ask whether the conclusion suggested by those numbers is consonant with our understanding of history and human experience. Georgia's legacy of a race-conscious criminal justice system, as well as this Court's own recognition of the persistent danger that racial attitudes may affect criminal proceedings, indicates that McCleskey's claim is not a fanciful product of mere statistical artifice.

For many years, Georgia operated openly and formally precisely the type of dual system the evidence shows is still effectively in place. The criminal law expressly differentiated between crimes committed by and against blacks and whites, distinctions whose lineage traced back to the time of slavery. During the colonial period, black slaves who killed whites in Georgia, regardless of whether in self-defense or in defense of another, were automatically executed.

By the time of the Civil War, a dual system of crime and punishment was well established in Georgia. . . .

This Court has invalidated portions of the Georgia capital sentencing system three times over the past 15 years. . . .

History and its continuing legacy . . . buttress the probative force of McCleskey's statistics. Formal dual criminal laws may no longer be in effect, and intentional discrimination may no longer be prominent. Nonetheless, . . . "subtle, less consciously held racial attitudes" continue to be of concern, and the Georgia system gives such attitudes considerable room to operate. The conclusions drawn from McCleskey's statistical evidence are therefore consistent with the lessons of social experience. . . .

At the time our Constitution was framed 200 years ago this year, blacks "had for more than a century before been regarded as beings of an inferior race, either in social or political relations; and so far inferior, that they had no rights which the white man was bound to respect." Only 130 years ago, this Court relied on these observations to deny American citizenship to blacks. A mere three generations ago, this Court sanctioned "racial segregation, stating that "[i]f one race be inferior to the other socially, the Constitution of the United States cannot put them upon the same plane."

In more recent times, we have sought to free ourselves from the burden of this history. Yet it has been scarcely a generation since this Court's first decision striking down racial segregation, and barely two decades since the legislative prohibition of racial discrimination in major domains of national life. These have been honorable steps, but we cannot pretend that in three decades we have completely escaped the grip of a historical legacy spanning centuries. Warren McCleskey's evidence confronts us with the subtle and persistent influence of the past. His message is a disturbing one to a society that has formally repudiated racism, and a frustrating one to a Nation accustomed to regarding its destiny as the product of its own will. Nonetheless, we ignore him at our peril, for we remain imprisoned by the past as long as we deny its influence in the present.

It is tempting to pretend that minorities

on death row share a fate in no way connected to our own, that our treatment of them sounds no echoes beyond the chambers in which they die. Such an illusion is ultimately corrosive, for the reverberations of injustice are not so easily confined. "The destinies of the two races in this country are indissolubly linked together," and the way in which we choose those who will die reveals the depth of moral commitment among the living.

The Court's decision today will not change what attorneys in Georgia tell other Warren McCleskeys about their chances of execution. Nothing will soften the harsh message they must convey, nor alter the prospect that race undoubtedly will continue to be a topic of discussion. McCleskey's evidence will not have obtained judicial acceptance, but that will not affect what is said on death row. However many criticisms of today's decision may be tendered, these painful conversations will serve as the most eloquent dissents of all.

a. Racial Disparities and Eighth Amendment Implications

The claim that juries impose the death penalty in an arbitrary and racially discriminatory fashion also raises Eighth Amendment concerns. The Supreme Court considered the question whether capital punishment violated the Eighth Amendment's prohibition of cruel and unusual punishments in its 1972 decision in *Furman v. Georgia*. *Furman* was the culmination of several decades of an organized movement to abolish the death penalty in America, with roots dating back to the eighteenth century. By the turn of the twentieth century most states had rejected the common law's mandatory imposition of capital punishment for all murders. The abolition effort focused at first on legislative reform and was successful in eliminating the death penalty in several states, although the vast majority of states retained capital punishment. In the 1950s the movement shifted to a litigation strategy, directed principally by the NAACP Legal Defense Fund, aimed at convincing the federal courts that the death penalty was unconstitutional. There was a notable and steady decline in the number of executions, from a high of 200 in 1935 to 1 in 1966. A 1966 Gallup Poll reported 47 percent of the American public opposed the death penalty, compared to 42 percent in favor of it.[164] At the time *Furman* came before the Court, the abolitionist campaign had achieved a de facto death penalty moratorium, with the last execution in the United States before the *Furman* decision taking place in 1967.

Only a year prior to *Furman*, the Court rejected the argument that leaving capital sentencing completely to jury discretion violated the due process clause. In *McGautha v. California* the Court concluded: "In light of history, experience, and the present limitations of human knowledge, we find it quite impossible to say that committing to the untrammeled discretion of the jury the power to pronounce life or death in capital cases is offensive to anything in the Constitution."[165] The Court reasoned that states had "adopted the method of forthrightly granting juries the discretion which they had been exercising in fact" and that it would be pointless to require legislatures to impose upon jurors a statement of appropriate factors or general standards to guide their decisions.

Despite the holding in *McGautha*, a bare majority of justices ruled in *Furman* that the death penalty, as then administered, violated the Eighth Amendment. Unable to agree upon a rationale for the death penalty's unconstitutionality, the Court issued a brief *per curiam* decision. Each of the justices filed separate concurring and dissenting opinions, amounting to 232 pages in all. Only two members of the Court—Justices Brennan and Marshall—concluded that the Eighth Amendment prohibits capital pun-

[164] President's Commission on Law Enforcement and Administration of Justice, Task Force Report: The Courts (1967).
[165] 402 U.S. 183, 207–08 (1971).

ishment for all crimes and under all circumstances. Justices Douglas, White and Stewart reasoned that prevailing capital sentencing practices violated the Eighth Amendment because they were arbitrary and capricious. While Douglas emphasized the exclusive imposition of the death penalty upon the poor, racial minorities, and other disempowered groups, White and Stewart stressed its infrequent and freakish application. The dissenting justices disagreed with the majority's view of the Court's constitutional role in evaluating the excessiveness of punishments. That job, the dissenters argued, was largely reserved for state legislatures, especially in light of the long-standing acceptance of capital punishment in America.

All of the *Furman* opinions explored whether the origins of the Eighth Amendment and American citizens' sentiments about capital punishment over centuries shed any light on the question whether the death penalty now amounted to a "cruel and unusual" punishment. Justice Marshall's opinion provided the most detailed history of both the Eighth Amendment and the enforcement of capital punishment in the United States.

Furman v. Georgia
408 U.S. 238 (1972)

MR. JUSTICE MARSHALL, concurring.

The Eighth Amendment's ban against cruel and unusual punishments derives from English law. In 1583, John Whitgift, Archbishop of Canterbury, turned the High Commission into a permanent ecclesiastical court, and the Commission began to use torture to extract confessions from persons suspected of various offenses. Sir Robert Beale protested that cruel and barbarous torture violated Magna Carta, but his protests were made in vain.

Cruel punishments were not confined to those accused of crimes, but were notoriously applied with even greater relish to those who were convicted. Blackstone described in ghastly detail the myriad of inhumane forms of punishment imposed on persons found guilty of any of a large number of offenses. Death, of course, was the usual result.

The treason trials of 1685—the "Bloody Assizes"—which followed an abortive rebellion by the Duke of Monmouth, marked the culmination of the parade of horrors, and most historians believe that it was this event that finally spurred the adoption of the English Bill of Rights containing the progenitor of our prohibition against cruel and unusual punishments. The conduct of Lord Chief Justice Jeffreys at those trials has been described as an "insane lust for cruelty" which was "stimulated by orders from the King" (James II). The assizes received wide publicity from Puritan pamphleteers and doubtless had some influence on the adoption of a cruel and unusual punishments clause. . . .

. . .

Whether the English Bill of Rights prohibition against cruel and unusual punishments

is properly read as a response to excessive or illegal punishments, as a reaction to barbaric and objectionable modes of punishment, or as both, there is no doubt whatever that in borrowing the language and in including it in the Eighth Amendment, our Founding Fathers intended to outlaw torture and other cruel punishments.

The precise language used in the Eighth Amendment first appeared in America on June 12, 1776, in Virginia's "Declaration of Rights," § 9 of which read: "That excessive bail ought not to be required, nor excessive fines imposed, nor cruel and unusual punishments inflicted." This language was drawn verbatim from the English Bill of Rights of 1689. Other States adopted similar clauses, and there is evidence in the debates of the various state conventions that were called upon to ratify the Constitution of great concern for the omission of any prohibition against torture or other cruel punishments.

The Virginia Convention offers some clues as to what the Founding Fathers had in mind in prohibiting cruel and unusual punishments. At one point George Mason advocated the adoption of a Bill of Rights, and Patrick Henry concurred, stating:

. . .

"In this business of legislation, your members of Congress will loose the restriction of not imposing excessive fines, demanding excessive bail, and inflicting cruel and unusual punishments. These are prohibited by your declaration of rights. What has distinguished our ancestors?—That they would not admit of tortures, or cruel and barbarous punishment. But Congress may introduce the practice of the civil law, in preference to that of the common law. They may introduce the practice of France, Spain, and Germany—of torturing, to extort a confession of the crime. They will say that they might as well draw examples from those countries as from Great Britain, and they will tell you that there is such a necessity of strengthening the arm of government, that they must have a criminal equity, and extort confession by torture, in order to punish with still more relentless severity. We are then lost and undone."

Henry's statement indicates that he wished to insure that "relentless severity" would be prohibited by the Constitution. Other expressions with respect to the proposed Eighth Amendment by Members of the First Congress indicate that they shared Henry's view of the need for and purpose of the Cruel and Unusual Punishments Clause.

Thus, the history of the clause clearly establishes that it was intended to prohibit cruel punishments. We must now turn to the case law to discover the manner in which courts have given meaning to the term "cruel."

II

This Court did not squarely face the task of interpreting the cruel and unusual punishments language for the first time until *Wilkerson v. Utah*, 99 U.S. 130 (1879), although the language received a cursory examination in several prior cases. In *Wilkerson* the Court unanimously upheld a sentence of public execution by shooting imposed pursuant to a conviction for premeditated murder. . . . To determine whether the punishment under attack was unnecessarily cruel, the Court examined the history of the Utah Territory and the then-current writings on capital punishment, and compared this Nation's practices with those of other countries. It is apparent that the Court felt it could not dispose of the question simply by referring to traditional practices; instead, it felt bound to examine developing thought.

[After discussing several intervening Eighth Amendment cases, Justice Marshall turned to the landmark case of *Weems v. United States*, 217 U.S. 349 (1910)].

Weems, an officer of the Bureau of Coast Guard and Transportation of the United States Government of the Philippine Islands, was convicted of falsifying a "public and official document." He was sentenced to 15 years' incarceration at hard labor with chains on his ankles, to an unusual loss of his civil rights, and to perpetual surveillance. Called upon to determine whether this was a cruel and unusual punishment, the Court found that it was. The Court emphasized that the Constitution was not an "ephemeral" enactment, or one "designed to meet passing occasions." Recognizing that "[t]ime works changes, [and] brings into existence new conditions and purposes[,]" the Court commented that "[i]n the application of a constitution . . . our contemplation cannot be only of what has been, but of what may be."

In striking down the penalty imposed on Weems, the Court examined the punishment in relation to the offense, compared the punishment to those inflicted for other crimes and to those imposed in other jurisdictions, and concluded that the punishment was excessive. Justices White and Holmes dissented and argued that the cruel and unusual prohibition was meant to prohibit only those things that were objectionable at the time the Constitution was adopted.

Weems is a landmark case because it represents the first time that the Court invalidated a penalty prescribed by a legislature for a particular offense. The Court made it plain beyond any reasonable doubt that excessive punishments were as objectionable as those that were inherently cruel. . . .

III

Perhaps the most important principle in analyzing "cruel and unusual" punishment questions is one that is reiterated again and again in the prior opinions of the Court: i.e., the cruel and unusual language "must draw its meaning from the evolving standards of decency that mark the progress of a maturing society." Thus, a penalty that was permissible at one time in our Nation's history is not necessarily permissible today.

The fact, therefore, that the Court, or individual Justices, may have in the past expressed an opinion that the death penalty is constitutional is not now binding on us. . . .

There is no holding directly in point, and the very nature of the Eighth Amendment would dictate that unless a very recent decision existed, *stare decisis* would bow to changing values, and the question of the constitutionality of capital punishment at a given moment in history would remain open.

. . .

[S]ince capital punishment is not a recent phenomenon, if it violates the Constitution, it does so because it is excessive or unnecessary, or because it is abhorrent to currently existing moral values.

We must proceed to the history of capital punishment in the United States.

IV

. . .

By 1500, English law recognized eight major capital crimes: Treason, petty treason (killing of husband by his wife), murder, larceny, robbery, burglary, rape, and arson. Tudor and Stuart kings added many more crimes to the list of those punishable by death, and by 1688 there were nearly 50. George II (1727–1760) added nearly 36 more, and George III (1760–1820) increased the number by 60.

By shortly after 1800, capital offenses numbered more than 200 and not only included crimes against person and property, but even some against the public peace. While England may, in retrospect, look particularly brutal, Blackstone points out that England was fairly civilized when compared to the rest of Europe.

Capital punishment was not as common a penalty in the American Colonies. "The Capital Lawes of New-England," dating from 1636, were drawn by the Massachusetts Bay Colony and are the first written expression of capital offenses known to exist in this country. These laws make the following crimes capital offenses: idolatry, witchcraft, blasphemy, murder, assault in sudden anger, sodomy, buggery, adultery, statutory rape, rape, manstealing, perjury in a capital trial, and rebellion. Each crime is accompanied by a reference to the Old Testament to indicate its source. . . .

By the 18th century, the list of crimes became much less theocratic and much more secular. In the average colony, there were 12 capital crimes. This was far fewer than existed in England, and part of the reason was that there was a scarcity of labor in the Colonies. Still, there were many executions, because "[w]ith county jails inadequate and insecure, the criminal population seemed best controlled by death, mutilation, and fines." . . .

In 1776 the Philadelphia Society for Relieving Distressed Prisoners organized, and it was followed 11 years later by the Philadelphia Society for Alleviating the Miseries of Public Prisons. These groups pressured for reform of all penal laws, including capital offenses. Dr. Benjamin Rush soon drafted America's first reasoned argument against capital punishment, entitled An Enquiry into the Effects of Public Punishments upon Criminals and upon Society. In 1793, William Bradford, the Attorney General of Pennsylvania and later Attorney General of the United States, conducted "An Enquiry How Far the Punishment of Death is Necessary in Pennsylvania." He concluded that it was doubtful whether capital punishment was at all necessary, and that until more information could be obtained, it should be immediately eliminated for all offenses except high treason and murder.

. . .

During the 1830's, there was a rising tide of sentiment against capital punishment. In 1834, Pennsylvania abolished public executions, and two years later, The Report on Capital Punishment Made to the Maine Legislature was published. It led to a law that prohibited the executive from issuing a warrant for execution within one year after a criminal was sentenced by the courts. . . . The law spread throughout New England and led to Michigan's being the first State to abolish capital punishment in 1846.

Anti-capital punishment feeling grew in the 1840's as the literature of the period pointed out the agony of the condemned man and expressed the philosophy that repentance atoned for the worst crimes, and that true repentance derived, not from fear, but from harmony with nature.

By 1850, societies for abolition existed in Massachusetts, New York, Pennsylvania, Tennessee, Ohio, Alabama, Louisiana, Indiana, and Iowa. New York, Massachusetts, and Pennsylvania constantly had abolition bills before their legislatures. In 1852, Rhode Island followed in the footsteps of Michigan and partially abolished capital punishment. Wisconsin totally abolished the death penalty the following year. Those States that did not abolish the death penalty greatly reduced its scope, and "[f]ew states outside the South had more than one or two . . . capital offenses" in addition to treason and murder.

. . .

One great success of the abolitionist movement in the period from 1830–1900 was almost complete elimination of mandatory capital punishment. Before the legislatures formally gave juries discretion to refrain from imposing the death penalty, the phenomenon of "jury nullification," in which juries refused to convict in cases in which they believed that death was an inappropriate penalty, was experienced. Tennessee was the first State to give juries discretion, but other States quickly followed suit. Then, Rep. Curtis of New York introduced a federal bill that ultimately became law in 1897 which reduced the number of federal capital offenses from 60 to 3 (treason, murder, and rape) and gave the jury sentencing discretion in murder and rape cases.

By 1917, 12 States had become abolitionist jurisdictions. But, under the nervous tension of World War I, four of these States reinstituted capital punishment and promising movements in other States came grinding to a halt. During the period following the First World War, the abolitionist movement never regained its momentum.

. . .

In recent years there has been renewed interest in modifying capital punishment. . . . At the present time, 41 States, the District of Columbia, and other federal jurisdictions authorize the death penalty for at least one crime. It would be fruitless to attempt here to categorize the approach to capital punishment taken by the various States. It is sufficient to note that murder is the crime most often punished by death, followed by kidnaping and treason. Rape is a capital offense in 16 States and the federal system.

The foregoing history demonstrates that capital punishment was carried from Europe to America but, once here, was tempered considerably. At times in our history, strong abolitionist movements have existed. But, they have never been completely successful, as no more than one-quarter of the States of the Union have, at any one time, abolished the death penalty. They have had partial success, however, especially in reducing the number of capital crimes, replacing mandatory death sentences with jury discretion, and developing more humane methods of conducting executions.

This is where our historical foray leads. The question now to be faced is whether American society has reached a point where abolition is not dependent on a successful grass roots movement in particular jurisdictions, but is demanded by the Eighth Amendment. . . .

Furman v. Georgia
408 U.S. 238 (1972)

PER CURIAM.

. . . Certiorari was granted limited to the following question: "Does the imposition and carrying out of the death penalty in (these cases) constitute cruel and unusual punishment in violation of the Eighth and Fourteenth Amendments?" The Court holds that the imposition and carrying out of the death penalty in these cases constitute cruel and unusual punishment in violation of the Eighth and Fourteenth Amendments. The judgment in each case is therefore reversed insofar as it leaves undisturbed the death sentence imposed, and the cases are remanded for further proceedings.

So ordered.

MR. JUSTICE DOUGLAS, MR. JUSTICE BRENNAN, MR. JUSTICE STEWART, MR. JUSTICE WHITE, and MR. JUSTICE MARSHALL have filed separate opinions in support of the judgments. THE CHIEF JUSTICE [BURGER], MR. JUSTICE BLACKMUN, MR. JUSTICE POWELL, and MR. JUSTICE REHNQUIST have filed separate dissenting opinions.

MR. JUSTICE DOUGLAS, concurring.

In these three cases the death penalty was imposed, one of them for murder, and two for rape. In each the determination of whether the penalty should be death or a lighter punishment was left by the State to the discretion of the judge or of the jury. . . .

. . .

It has been assumed in our decisions that punishment by death is not cruel, unless the manner of execution can be said to be inhuman and barbarous. It is also said in our opinions that the proscription of cruel and unusual punishments "is not fastened to the obsolete, but may acquire meaning as public opinion becomes enlightened by a humane justice." *Weems v. United States*. A like statement was made in *Trop v. Dulles*, that the Eighth Amendment "must draw its meaning from the evolving standards of decency that mark the progress of a maturing society."

. . .

It would seem to be incontestable that the death penalty inflicted on one defendant is "unusual" if it discriminates against him by reason of his race, religion, wealth, social position, or class, or if it is imposed under a procedure that gives room for the play of such prejudices.

There is evidence that the provision of the English Bill of Rights of 1689, from which the language of the Eighth Amendment was taken, was concerned primarily with selective or irregular application of harsh penalties and that its aim was to forbid arbitrary and discriminatory penalties of a severe nature. . . .

The English Bill of Rights, enacted December 16, 1689, stated that "excessive bail ought not to be required, nor excessive fines imposed, nor cruel and unusual punishments inflicted." These were the words chosen for our Eighth Amendment. A like provision had been in Virginia's Constitution of 1776 and in the constitutions of seven other States. . . .

The words "cruel and unusual" certainly include penalties that are barbaric. But the words, at least when read in light of the English proscription against selective and irregular use of penalties, suggest that it is "cruel and unusual" to apply the death penalty—or any other penalty—selectively to minorities whose numbers are few, who are outcasts of society, and who are unpopular, but whom society is willing to see suffer though it would not countenance general application of the same penalty across the board. . . .

. . .

We are now imprisoned in the *McGautha* holding. Indeed the seeds of the present cases are in *McGautha*. Juries (or judges, as the case may be) have practically untrammeled discretion to let an accused live or insist that he die.

. . .

There is increasing recognition of the fact that the basic theme of equal protection is implicit in "cruel and unusual" punishments. "A penalty . . . should be considered 'unusually' imposed if it is administered arbitrarily or discriminatorily." The same authors add that "[t]he extreme rarity with which applicable death penalty provisions are put to use raises a strong inference of arbitrariness." The President's Commission of Law Enforcement and Administration of Justice recently concluded:

> "Finally there is evidence that the imposition of the death sentence and the exercise of dispensing power by the courts and the executive follow discriminatory patterns. The death sentence is disproportionately imposed and carried out on the poor, the Negro, and the members of unpopular groups."

. . .

We cannot say from facts disclosed in [the] records that these defendants were sentenced to death because they were black. Yet our task is not restricted to an effort to divine what motives impelled these death penalties. Rather, we deal with a system of law and of justice that leaves to the uncontrolled discretion of judges or juries the determination whether defendants committing these crimes should die or be imprisoned. Under these laws no standards govern the selection of the penalty. People live or die, dependent on the whim of one man or of 12.

. . .

Those who wrote the Eighth Amendment knew what price their forebears had paid for a system based, not on equal justice, but on discrimination. In those days the target was not the blacks or the poor, but the dissenters, those who opposed absolutism in government, who struggled for a parliamentary regime, and who opposed governments' recurring efforts to foist a particular religion on the people. But the tool of capital punishment was used with vengeance against the opposition and those unpopular with the regime. One cannot read this history without realizing that the desire for equality was reflected in the ban against "cruel and unusual punishments" contained in the Eighth Amendment.

. . .

A law that stated that anyone making more than $50,000 would be exempt from the death penalty would plainly fall, as would a law that in terms said that blacks, those who never went beyond the fifth grade in school, those who made less than $3000 a year, or those who were unpopular or unstable should be the only people executed. A law which in the

overall view reaches that result in practice has no more sanctity than a law which in terms provides the same.

Thus, these discretionary statutes are unconstitutional in their operation. They are pregnant with discrimination and discrimination is an ingredient not compatible with the idea of equal protection of the laws that is implicit in the ban on "cruel and unusual" punishments.

Any law which is nondiscriminatory on its face may be applied in such a way as to violate the Equal Protection Clause of the Fourteenth Amendment. *Yick Wo v. Hopkins.* Such conceivably might be the fate of a mandatory death penalty, where equal or lesser sentences were imposed on the elite, a harsher one on the minorities or members of the lower castes. Whether a mandatory death penalty would otherwise be constitutional is a question I do not reach.

MR. JUSTICE BRENNAN, concurring.

. . .

I

We have very little evidence of the Framers' intent in including the Cruel and Unusual Punishments Clause among those restraints upon the new Government enumerated in the Bill of Rights. The absence of such a restraint from the body of the Constitution was alluded to, so far as we now know, in the debates of only two of the state ratifying conventions. In the Massachusetts convention, Mr. Holmes protested:

> "What gives an additional glare of horror to these gloomy circumstances is the consideration, that Congress have to ascertain, point out, and determine, what kind of punishments shall be inflicted on persons convicted of crimes. They are nowhere restraining from inventing the most cruel and unheard-of punishments, and annexing them to crimes; and there is no constitutional check on them, but that racks and gibbets may be amongst the most mild instruments of their discipline." 2 J. Elliot's Debates 111 (2d ed. 1876).

Holmes' fear that Congress would have unlimited power to prescribe punishments for crimes was echoed by Patrick Henry at the Virginia convention. . . .

. . . [I]t is quite clear that Holmes and Henry focused wholly upon the necessity to restrain the legislative power. Because they recognized "that Congress have to ascertain, point out, and determine, what kinds of punishments shall be inflicted on persons convicted of crimes," they insisted that Congress must be limited in its power to punish. Accordingly, they called for a "constitutional check" that would ensure that "when we come to punishments, no latitude ought to be left, nor dependence put on the virtue of representatives."

. . .

Several conclusions . . . emerge from the history of the adoption of the Clause. We know that the Framers' concern was directed specifically at the exercise of legislative power. They included in the Bill of Rights a prohibition upon "cruel and unusual punishments" precisely because the legislature would otherwise have had the unfettered power to prescribe punishments for crimes. Yet we cannot now know exactly what the Framers thought "cruel and unusual punishments" were. Certainly they intended to ban torturous punishments, but the available evidence does not support the further conclusion that *only* torturous punishments were to be outlawed. . . . Nor did they intend simply to forbid punishments considered "cruel and unusual" at the time. The "import" of the Clause is, indeed, "indefinite," and for good reason. A constitutional provision "is enacted, it is true, from an experience of evils, but its general language should not, therefore, be necessarily confined to the form that evil had theretofore taken. Time works changes, brings into existence new conditions and purposes. Therefore a principle, to be vital, must be capable of wider application than the mischief which gave it birth." *Weems v. United States.*

It was almost 80 years before this Court had occasion to refer to the Clause. These early cases, as the Court pointed out in *Weems v. United States*, did not undertake to provide "an exhaustive definition" of "cruel and unusual punishments." Most of them proceeded primarily by "looking backwards for examples by which to fix the meaning of the clause," concluding simply that a punishment would be "cruel and unusual" if it were similar to punishments considered "cruel and unusual" at the time the Bill of Rights was adopted. . . .

Had this "historical" interpretation of the Cruel and Unusual Punishments Clause prevailed, the Clause would have been effectively read out of the Bill of Rights. As the Court noted in *Weems v. United States*, this interpretation led Story to conclude "that the provision 'would seem to be wholly unnecessary in a free government, since it is scarcely possible that any department of such a government should authorize or justify such atrocious conduct.'"..

But this Court in *Weems* decisively repudiated the "historical" interpretation of the Clause. The Court, returning to the intention of the Framers, "rel[ied] on the conditions which existed when the Constitution was adopted." And the Framers knew "that government by the people, instituted by the Constitution, would not imitate the conduct of arbitrary monarchs. The abuse of power might, indeed,

be apprehended, but not that it would be manifested in provisions or practices which would shock the sensibilities of men." The Clause, then, guards against "[t]he abuse of power." . . .

II

Ours would indeed be a simple task were we required merely to measure a challenged punishment against those that history has long condemned. That narrow and unwarranted view of the Clause, however, was left behind with the 19th century. Our task today is more complex. We know "that the words of the [Clause] are not precise, and that their scope is not static." We know, therefore, that the Clause "must draw its meaning from the evolving standards of decency that mark the progress of a maturing society." That knowledge, of course, is but the beginning of the inquiry.

. . .

At bottom, the Cruel and Unusual Punishments Clause prohibits the infliction of uncivilized and inhuman punishments. The State, even as it punishes, must treat its members with respect for their intrinsic worth as human beings. A punishment is "cruel and unusual," therefore, if it does not comport with human dignity.

. . .

The primary principle is that a punishment must not be so severe as to be degrading to the dignity of human beings. Pain, certainly, may be a factor in the judgment. The infliction of an extremely severe punishment will often entail physical suffering. Yet the Framers also knew "that there could be exercises of cruelty by laws other than those which inflicted bodily pain or mutilation." . . .

. . .

In determining whether a punishment comports with human dignity, we are aided also by a second principle inherent in the Clause—that the State must not arbitrarily inflict a severe punishment. This principle derives from the notion that the State does not respect human dignity when, without reason, it inflicts upon some people a severe punishment that it does not inflict upon others. Indeed, the very words "cruel and unusual punishments" imply condemnation of the arbitrary infliction of severe punishments. And, as we now know, the English history of the Clause reveals a particular concern with the establishment of a safeguard against arbitrary punishments.

. . .

A third principle inherent in the Clause is that a severe punishment must not be unacceptable to contemporary society. Rejection by society, of course, is a strong indication that a severe punishment does not comport with human dignity. In applying this principle, however, we must make certain that the judicial determination is as objective as possible.

. . .

The question under this principle, then, is whether there are objective indicators from which a court can conclude that contemporary society considers a severe punishment unacceptable. Accordingly, the judicial task is to review the history of a challenged punishment and to examine society's present practices with respect to its use. Legislative authorization, of course, does not establish acceptance. The acceptability of a severe punishment is measured, not by its availability, for it might become so offensive to society as never to be inflicted, but by its use.

The final principle inherent in the Clause is that a severe punishment must not be excessive. A punishment is excessive under this principle if it is unnecessary: The infliction of a severe punishment by the State cannot comport with human dignity when it is nothing more than the pointless infliction of suffering. If there is a significantly less severe punishment adequate to achieve the purposes for which the punishment is inflicted, the punishment inflicted is unnecessary and therefore excessive.

. . . Although the determination that a severe punishment is excessive may be grounded in a judgment that it is disproportionate to the crime, the more significant basis is that the punishment serves no penal purpose more effectively than a less severe punishment. . . .

. . .

Since the Bill of Rights was adopted, this Court has adjudged only three punishments to be within the prohibition of the Clause. *See Weems v. United States* (12 years in chains at hard and painful labor); *Trop v. Dulles* (expatriation); *Robinson v. California* (imprisonment for narcotics addiction). Each punishment, of course, was degrading to human dignity, but of none could it be said conclusively that it was fatally offensive under one or the other of the principles. Rather, these "cruel and unusual punishments" seriously implicated several of the principles, and it was the application of the principles in combination that supported the judgment. That, indeed, is not surprising. The function of these principles, after all, is simply to provide means by which a court can determine whether a challenged punishment comports with human dignity. They are, therefore, interrelated, and in most cases it will be their convergence that will justify the conclusion that a punishment is "cruel and unusual." The test, then, will ordinarily be a cumulative one: If a punishment is unusually severe, if there is a strong probability that it is inflicted arbitrarily, if it is substantially rejected by con-

temporary society, and if there is no reason to believe that it serves any penal purpose more effectively than some less severe punishment, then the continued infliction of that punishment violates the command of the Clause that the State may not inflict inhuman and uncivilized punishments upon those convicted of crimes.

III

The punishment challenged in these cases is death. . . .

The question . . . is whether the deliberate infliction of death is today consistent with the command of the Clause that the State may not inflict punishments that do not comport with human dignity. I will analyze the punishment of death in terms of the principles set out above and the cumulative test to which they lead. . . . Under these principles and this test, death is today a "cruel and unusual" punishment. I therefore

. . .

Death is truly an awesome punishment. The calculated killing of a human being by the State involves, by its very nature, a denial of the executed person's humanity. The contrast with the plight of a person punished by imprisonment is evident. An individual in prison does not lose "the right to have rights." A prisoner retains, for example, the constitutional rights to the free exercise of religion, to be free of cruel and unusual punishments, and to treatment as a "person" for purposes of due process of law and the equal protection of the laws. A prisoner remains a member of the human family. Moreover, he retains the right of access to the courts. His punishment is not irrevocable. Apart from the common charge, grounded upon the recognition of human fallibility, that the punishment of death must inevitably be inflicted upon innocent men, we know that death has been the lot of men whose convictions were unconstitutionally secured in view of later, retroactively applied, holdings of this Court. The punishment itself may have been unconstitutionally inflicted, yet the finality of death precludes relief. An executed person has indeed "lost the right to have rights." As one 19th century proponent of punishing criminals by death declared, "When a man is hung, there is an end of our relations with him. His execution is a way of saying, 'You are not fit for this world, take your chance elsewhere.'"

In comparison to all other punishments today, then, the deliberate extinguishment of human life by the State is uniquely degrading to human dignity. I would not hesitate to hold, on that ground alone, that death is today a "cruel and unusual" punishment, were it not that death is a punishment of longstanding usage and acceptance in this country. I therefore turn to the second principle—that the State may not arbitrarily inflict an unusually severe punishment.

The outstanding characteristic of our present practice of punishing criminals by death is the infrequency with which we resort to it. The evidence is conclusive that death is not the ordinary punishment for any crime.

There has been a steady decline in the infliction of this punishment in every decade since the 1930's, the earliest period for which accurate statistics are available. In the 1930's, executions averaged 167 per year; in the 1940's, the average was 128; in the 1950's, it was 72; and in the years 1960–1962, it was 48. There have been a total of 46 executions since then, 36 of them in 1963–1964. Yet our population and the number of capital crimes committed have increased greatly over the past four decades. The contemporary rarity of the infliction of this punishment is thus the end result of a long-continued decline. . . .

When a country of over 200 million people inflicts an unusually severe punishment no more than 50 times a year, the inference is strong that the punishment is not being regularly and fairly applied. To dispel it would indeed require a clear showing of nonarbitrary infliction.

Although there are no exact figures available, we know that thousands of murders and rapes are committed annually in States where death is an authorized punishment for those crimes. However the rate of infliction is characterized—as "freakishly" or "spectacularly" rare, or simply as rare—it would take the purest sophistry to deny that death is inflicted in only a minute fraction of these cases. How much rarer, after all, could the infliction of death be?

When the punishment of death is inflicted in a trivial number of the cases in which it is legally available, the conclusion is virtually inescapable that it is being inflicted arbitrarily. Indeed, it smacks of little more than a lottery system. The States claim, however, that this rarity is evidence not of arbitrariness, but of informed selectivity: Death is inflicted, they say, only in "extreme" cases.

No one has yet suggested a rational basis that could differentiate in those terms the few who die from the many who go to prison. Crimes and criminals simply do not admit of a distinction that can be drawn so finely as to explain, on that ground, the execution of such a tiny sample of those eligible. Certainly the laws that provide for this punishment do not attempt to draw that distinction; all cases to which the laws apply are necessarily "extreme." Nor is the distinction credible in fact. If, for example, petitioner Furman or his crime illustrates the "extreme," then nearly all murderers and their murders are also "extreme."[48] Furthermore, our procedures in death cases, rather than resulting in the selection of "extreme" cases for this punishment, actually sanction an arbitrary selection. For this Court has held that juries may, as they do, make the decision whether to impose a death sentence wholly unguided by standards governing that decision. *McGautha v. California.* In other words, our procedures are not constructed to guard against the totally capricious selection of criminals for the punishment of death.

. . .

When there is a strong probability that an unusually severe and degrading punishment is being inflicted arbitrarily, we may well expect that society will disapprove of its infliction. I turn, therefore, to the third principle. An examination of the history and present operation of the American practice of punishing criminals by death reveals that this punishment has been almost totally rejected by contemporary society.

I cannot add to my Brother MARSHALL'S comprehensive treatment of the English and American history of this punishment. I emphasize, however, one significant conclusion that emerges from that history. From the beginning of our Nation, the punishment of death has stirred acute public controversy. Although pragmatic arguments for and against the punishment have been frequently advanced, this longstanding and heated controversy cannot be explained solely as the result of differences over the practical wisdom of a particular government policy. At bottom, the battle has been waged on moral grounds. The country has debated whether a society for which the dignity of the individual is the supreme value can, without a fundamental inconsistency, follow the practice of deliberately putting some of its members to death. . . .

. . .

---

[48] The victim surprised Furman in the act of burglarizing the victim's home in the middle of the night. While escaping, Furman killed the victim with one pistol shot fired through the closed kitchen door from the outside. At the trial, Furman gave his version of the killing: "They got me charged with murder and I admit, I admit going to these folks' home and they did caught me in there and I was coming back out, backing up and there was a wire down there on the floor. I was coming out backwards and fell back and I didn't intend to kill nobody. I didn't know they was behind the door. The gun went off and I didn't know nothing about no murder until they arrested me, and when the gun went off I was down on the floor and I got up and ran. That's all to it." The Georgia Supreme Court accepted that version. . . .
About Furman himself, the jury knew only that he was black and that, according to his statement at trial, he was 26 years old and worked at "Superior Upholstery." It took the jury one hour and 35 minutes to return a verdict of guilt and a sentence of death.

The progressive decline in, and the current rarity of, the infliction of death demonstrate that our society seriously questions the appropriateness of this punishment today. The States point out that many legislatures authorize death as the punishment for certain crimes and that substantial segments of the public, as reflected in opinion polls and referendum votes, continue to support it. Yet the availability of this punishment through statutory authorization, as well as the polls and referenda, which amount simply to approval of that authorization, simply underscores the extent to which our society has in fact rejected this punishment. When an unusually severe punishment is authorized for wide-scale application but not, because of society's refusal, inflicted save in a few instances, the inference is compelling that there is a deep-seated reluctance to inflict it. Indeed, the likelihood is great that the punishment is tolerated only because of its disuse. . . .

The final principle to be considered is that an unusually severe and degrading punishment may not be excessive in view of the purposes for which it is inflicted. This principle, too, is related to the others. When there is a strong probability that the State is arbitrarily inflicting an unusually severe punishment that is subject to grave societal doubts, it is likely also that the punishment cannot be shown to be serving any penal purpose that could not be served equally well by some less severe punishment.

The States' primary claim is that death is a necessary punishment because it prevents the commission of capital crimes more effectively than any less severe punishment. . . .

Proponents of this argument necessarily admit that its validity depends upon the existence of a system in which the punishment of death is invariably and swiftly imposed. Our system, of course, satisfies neither condition. A rational person contemplating a murder or rape is confronted, not with the certainty of a speedy death, but with the slightest possibility that he will be executed in the distant future. The risk of death is remote and improbable; in contrast, the risk of long-term imprisonment is near and great. In short, whatever the speculative validity of the assumption that the threat of death is a superior deterrent, there is no reason to believe that as currently administered the punishment of death is necessary to deter the commission of capital crimes. . . .

. . .

In sum, the punishment of death is inconsistent with all four principles: Death is an unusually severe and degrading punishment; there is a strong probability that it is inflicted arbitrarily; its rejection by contemporary society is virtually total; and there is no reason to

believe that it serves any penal purpose more effectively than the less severe punishment of imprisonment. The function of these principles is to enable a court to determine whether a punishment comports with human dignity. Death, quite simply, does not.

IV

When this country was founded, memories of the Stuart horrors were fresh and severe corporal punishments were common. Death was not then a unique punishment. The practice of punishing criminals by death, moreover, was widespread and by and large acceptable to society. Indeed, without developed prison systems, there was frequently no workable alternative. Since that time successive restrictions, imposed against the background of a continuing moral controversy, have drastically curtailed the use of this punishment. Today death is a uniquely and unusually severe punishment. When examined by the principles applicable under the Cruel and Unusual Punishments Clause, death stands condemned as fatally offensive to human dignity. The punishment of death is therefore "cruel and unusual," and the States may no longer inflict it as a punishment for crimes.

MR. JUSTICE STEWART, concurring.

The penalty of death differs from all other forms of criminal punishment, not in degree but in kind. It is unique in its total irrevocability. It is unique in its rejection of rehabilitation of the convict as a basic purpose of criminal justice. And it is unique, finally, in its absolute renunciation of all that is embodied in our concept of humanity.

For these and other reasons, at least two of my Brothers have concluded that the infliction of the death penalty is constitutionally impermissible in all circumstances under the Eight and Fourteenth Amendments. Their case is a strong one. But I find it unnecessary to reach the ultimate question they would decide.

. . .

I cannot agree that retribution is a constitutionally impermissible ingredient in the imposition of punishment. The instinct for retribution is part of the nature of man, and channeling that instinct in the administration of criminal justice serves an important purpose in promoting the stability of a society governed by law. When people begin to believe that organized society is unwilling or unable to impose upon criminal offenders the punishment they "deserve," then there are sown the seeds of anarchy—of self-help, vigilante justice, and lynch law.

The constitutionality of capital punishment in the abstract is not, however, before us in these cases. . . .

Instead, the death sentences now before us

are the product of a legal system that brings them, I believe, within the very core of the Eighth Amendment's guarantee against cruel and unusual punishments, a guarantee applicable against the States through the Fourteenth Amendment. In the first place, it is clear that these sentences are "cruel" in the sense that they excessively go beyond, not in degree but in kind, the punishments that the state legislatures have determined to be necessary. In the second place, it is equally clear that these sentences are "unusual" in the sense that the penalty of death is infrequently imposed for murder, and that its imposition for rape is extraordinarily rare. But I do not rest by conclusion upon these two propositions alone.

These death sentences are cruel and unusual in the same way that being struck by lightning is cruel and unusual. For, of all the people convicted of rapes and murders in 1967 and 1968, many just as reprehensible as these, the petitioners are among a capriciously selected random handful upon whom the sentence of death has in fact been imposed. My concurring Brothers have demonstrated that, if any basis can be discerned for the selection of these few to be sentenced to die, it is the constitutionally impermissible basis of race. But racial discrimination has not been proved, and I put it to one side. I simply conclude that the Eighth and Fourteenth Amendments cannot tolerate the infliction of a sentence of death under legal systems that permit this unique penalty to be so wantonly and so freakishly imposed.

MR. JUSTICE WHITE, concurring.

The facial constitutionality of statutes requiring the imposition of the death penalty for first-degree murder, for more narrowly defined categories of murder, or for rape would present quite different issues under the Eighth Amendment than are posed by the cases before us. In joining the Court's judgments, therefore, I do not at all intimate that the death penalty is unconstitutional *per se* or that there is no system of capital punishment that would comport with the Eighth Amendment. That question, ably argued by several of my Brethren, is not presented by these cases and need not be decided.

. . .

I begin with what I consider a near truism: that the death penalty could so seldom be imposed that it would cease to be a credible deterrent or measurably to contribute to any other end of punishment in the criminal justice system. It is perhaps true that no matter how infrequently those convicted of rape or murder are executed, the penalty so imposed is not disproportionate to the crime and those executed may deserve exactly what they received. It would also be clear that executed defendants are finally and completely incapacitated from

again committing rape or murder or any other crime. But when imposition of the penalty reaches a certain degree of infrequency, it would be very doubtful that any existing general need for retribution would be measurably satisfied. Nor could it be said with confidence that society's need for specific deterrence justifies death for so few when for so many in like circumstances life imprisonment or shorter prison terms are judged sufficient, or that community values are measurably reinforced by authorizing a penalty so rarely invoked.

Most important, a major goal of the criminal law—to deter others by punishing the convicted criminal—would not be substantially served where the penalty is so seldom invoked that it ceases to be the credible threat essential to influence the conduct of others. . . .

. . . At the moment that [the death penalty] ceases realistically to further these purposes, however, the emerging question is whether its imposition in such circumstances would violate the Eighth Amendment. It is my view that it would, for its imposition would then be the pointless and needless extinction of life with only marginal contributions to any discernible social or public purposes. A penalty with such negligible returns to the State would be patently excessive and cruel and unusual punishment violative of the Eighth Amendment.

It is also my judgment that this point has been reached with respect to capital punishment as it is presently administered under the statutes involved in these cases. Concededly, it is difficult to prove as a general proposition that capital punishment, however administered, more effectively serves the ends of the criminal law than does imprisonment. But however that may be, I cannot avoid the conclusion that as the statutes before us are now administered, the penalty is so infrequently imposed that the threat of execution is too attenuated to be of substantial service to criminal justice.

. . .

MR. JUSTICE MARSHALL, concurring.

. . .

V

In order to assess whether or not death is an excessive or unnecessary penalty, it is necessary to consider the reasons why a legislature might select it as punishment for one or more offenses, and examine whether less severe penalties would satisfy the legitimate legislative wants as well as capital punishment. If they would, then the death penalty is unnecessary cruelty, and, therefore, unconstitutional.

There are six purposes conceivably served by capital punishment: retribution, deterrence, prevention of repetitive criminal acts, encouragement of guilty pleas and confessions, eugenics, and economy. These are considered *seriatim* below.

A. . . . The fact that the State may seek retribution against those who have broken its laws does not mean that retribution may then become the State's sole end in punishing. Our jurisprudence has always accepted deterrence in general, deterrence of individual recidivism, isolation of dangerous persons, and rehabilitation as proper goals of punishment. Retaliation, vengeance, and retribution have been roundly condemned as intolerable aspirations for a government in a free society. Punishment as retribution has been condemned by scholars for centuries, and the Eighth Amendment itself was adopted to prevent punishment from becoming synonymous with vengeance.

. . .

B. The most hotly contested issue regarding capital punishment is whether it is better than life imprisonment as a deterrent to crime.

While the contrary position has been argued, it is my firm opinion that the death penalty is a more severe sanction than life imprisonment. . . .

It must be kept in mind, then, that the question to be considered is not simply whether capital punishment is a deterrent, but whether it is a better deterrent than life imprisonment.

. . .

[Justice Marshall discussed at length an influential study on the death penalty's deterrent effect—Thorsten Sellin, The Death Penalty: A Report for the Model Penal Code Project of the American Law Institute (1959).] Sellin's statistics demonstrate that there is no correlation between the murder rate and the presence or absence of the capital sanction. He compares States that have similar characteristics and finds that irrespective of their position on capital punishment, they have similar murder rates. . . .

Sellin also concludes that abolition and/or reintroduction of the death penalty had no effect on the homicide rates of the various States involved. This conclusion is borne out by others who have made similar inquiries and by the experience of other countries. . . .

Statistics also show that the deterrent effect of capital punishment is no greater in those communities where executions take place than in other communities. In fact, there is some evidence that imposition of capital punishment may actually encourage crime, rather than deter it. . . .

. . .

In light of the massive amount of evidence before us, I see no alternative but to conclude that capital punishment cannot be justified on the basis of its deterrent effect.

[Justice Marshall also rejected arguments that the death penalty prevents recidivism, encourages guilty pleas and confessions, offers eugenic benefits, and reduces state expenditures.]

. . .

E. There is but one conclusion that can be drawn from all of this—*i.e.*, the death penalty is an excessive and unnecessary punishment that violates the Eighth Amendment. . . . The point has now been reached at which deference to the legislatures is tantamount to abdication of our judicial roles as factfinders, judges, and ultimate arbiters of the Constitution. We know that at some point the presumption of constitutionality accorded legislative acts gives way to a realistic assessment of those acts. This point comes when there is sufficient evidence available so that judges can determine, not whether the legislature acted wisely, but whether it had any rational basis whatsoever for acting. We have this evidence before us now. There is no rational basis for concluding that capital punishment is not excessive. It therefore violates the Eighth Amendment.

VI

In addition, even if capital punishment is not excessive, it nonetheless violates the Eighth Amendment because it is morally unacceptable to the people of the United States at this time in their history.

In judging whether or not a given penalty is morally acceptable, most courts have said that the punishment is valid unless "it shocks the conscience and sense of justice of the people."

. . . [T]he question with which we must deal is not whether a substantial proportion of American citizens would today, if polled, opine that capital punishment is barbarously cruel, but whether they would find it to be so in the light of all information presently available.

It has often been noted that American citizens know almost nothing about capital punishment. Some of the conclusions arrived at in the preceding section and the supporting evidence would be critical to an informed judgment on the morality of the death penalty: *e.g.*, that the death penalty is no more effective a deterrent than life imprisonment, that convicted murderers are rarely executed, but are usually sentenced to a term in prison; that convicted murderers usually are model prisoners, and that they almost always become law-abiding citizens upon their release from prison; that the costs of executing a capital offender exceed the costs of imprisoning him for life; that while in prison, a convict under sentence of death performs none of the useful functions that life prisoners perform; that no attempt is made in the sentencing process to ferret out likely recidivists for execution; and that the death penalty may actually stimulate criminal activity.

This information would almost surely convince the average citizen that the death penalty was unwise, but a problem arises as to whether it would convince him that the penalty was morally reprehensible. This problem arises from the fact that the public's desire for retribution, even though this is a goal that the legislature cannot constitutionally pursue as its sole justification for capital punishment, might influence the citizenry's view of the morality of capital punishment. The solution to the problem lies in the fact that no one has ever seriously advanced retribution as a legitimate goal of our society. . . . I cannot believe that at this stage in our history, the American people would ever knowingly support purposeless vengeance. Thus, I believe that the great mass of citizens would conclude on the basis of the material already considered that the death penalty is immoral and therefore unconstitutional.

But, if this information needs supplementing, I believe that the following facts would serve to convince even the most hesitant of citizens to condemn death as a sanction: capital punishment is imposed discriminatorily against certain identifiable classes of people; there is evidence that innocent people have been executed before their innocence can be proved; and the death penalty wreaks havoc with our entire criminal justice system. . . .

VII

. . .

In striking down capital punishment, this Court does not malign our system of government. On the contrary, it pays homage to it. Only in a free society could right triumph in difficult times, and could civilization record its magnificent advancement. In recognizing the humanity of our fellow beings, we pay ourselves the highest tribute. We achieve "a major milestone in the long road up from barbarism" and join the approximately 70 other jurisdictions in the world which celebrate their regard for civilization and humanity by shunning capital punishment.

MR. CHIEF JUSTICE BURGER, with whom MR. JUSTICE BLACKMUN, MR. JUSTICE POWELL, and MR. JUSTICE REHNQUIST join, dissenting.

. . .

I

It we were possessed of legislative power, I would either join with MR. JUSTICE BRENNAN and MR. JUSTICE MARSHALL or, at the very least, restrict the use of capital punishment to a small category of the most heinous crimes. Our constitutional inquiry, however, must be divorced from personal feelings as to the morality and efficacy of the death penalty, and be confined to the meaning and applicability of the uncertain language of the Eighth Amendment. There is no novelty in being called upon to interpret a constitutional provision that is less than self-defining, but, of all our fundamental guarantees, the ban on "cruel and unusual punishments" is one of the most difficult to translate into judicially manageable terms. The widely divergent views of the Amendment expressed in today's opinions reveal the haze that surrounds this constitutional command. Yet it is essential to our role as a court that we not seize upon the enigmatic character of the guarantee as an invitation to enact our personal predilections into law.

. . .

From every indication, the Framers of the Eighth Amendment intended to give the phrase a meaning far different from that of its English precursor. The records of the debates in several of the state conventions called to ratify the 1789 draft Constitution submitted prior to the addition of the Bill of Rights show that the Framers' exclusive concern was the absence of any ban on tortures. The later inclusion of the "cruel and unusual punishment" clause was in response to these objections. There was no discussion of the interrelationship of the terms "cruel" and "unusual," and there is nothing in the debates supporting the inference that the Founding Fathers would have been receptive to torturous or excessively cruel punishments even if usual in character or authorized by law.

. . .

I do not suggest that the presence of the word "unusual" in the Eighth Amendment is merely vestigial, having no relevance to the constitutionality of any punishment that might be devised. But where, as here, we consider a punishment well known to history, and clearly authorized 'by legislative enactment, it disregards the history of the Eighth Amendment and all the judicial comment that has followed to rely on the term "unusual" as affecting the outcome of [prior Eighth Amendment] cases. Instead, I view these cases as turning on the single question whether capital punishment is "cruel" in the constitutional sense. The term "unusual" cannot be read as limiting the ban on "cruel" punishments or as somehow expanding the meaning of the term "cruel." For this reason I am unpersuaded by the facile argument that since capital punishment has always been cruel in the everyday sense of the word, and has become unusual due to decreased use, it is, therefore, now "cruel and unusual."

II

Counsel for petitioners properly concede that capital punishment was not impermissibly cruel at the time of the adoption of the Eighth Amendment. Not only do the records of the debates indicate that the Founding Fathers were limited in their concern to the prevention of torture, but it is also clear from the language of the Constitution itself that there was no thought whatever of the elimination of capital punishment. . . .

In the 181 years since the enactment of the Eighth Amendment, not a single decision of this Court has cast the slightest shadow of a doubt on the constitutionality of capital punishment. In rejecting Eighth Amendment attacks on particular modes of execution, the Court has more than once implicitly denied that capital punishment is impermissibly "cruel" in the constitutional sense. . . . Nonetheless, the Court has now been asked to hold that a punishment clearly permissible under the Constitution at the time of its adoption and accepted as such by every member of the Court until today, is suddenly so cruel as to be incompatible with the Eighth Amendment.

. . .

I do not suggest that the validity of legislatively authorized punishments presents no justiciable issue under the Eighth Amendment, but, rather, that the primacy of the legislative role narrowly confines the scope of judicial inquiry. Whether or not provable, and whether or not true at all times, in a democracy the legislative judgment is presumed to embody the basic standards of decency prevailing in the society. This presumption can only be negated by unambiguous and compelling evidence of legislative default.

III

There are no obvious indications that capital punishment offends the conscience of society to such a degree that our traditional deference to the legislative judgment must be abandoned. It is not a punishment such as burning at the stake that everyone would ineffably find to be repugnant to all civilized standards. Nor is it a punishment so roundly condemned that only a few aberrant legislatures have retained it on the statute books. Capital punishment is authorized by statute in 40 States, the District of Columbia, and in the federal courts for the commission of certain crimes. On four occasions in the last 11 years Congress has added to the list of federal crimes punishable by death. In looking for reliable indicia of contemporary attitude, none more trustworthy has been advanced.

. . .

Counsel for petitioners . . . argue, in effect, that the number of cases in which the death penalty is imposed, as compared with the number of cases in which it is statutorily available, reflects a general revulsion toward the penalty that would lead to its repeal if only it were more generally and widely enforced. It cannot be gainsaid that by the choice of juries—and sometimes judges—the death penalty is imposed in far fewer than half the cases in which it is available. To go further and characterize the rate of imposition as "freakishly rare," as petitioners insist, is unwarranted hyperbole. And regardless of its characterization, the rate of imposition does not impel the conclusion that capital punishment is now regarded as intolerably cruel or uncivilized.

. . .

. . . The selectivity of juries in imposing the punishment of death is properly viewed as a refinement on, rather than a repudiation of, the statutory authorization for that penalty. Legislatures prescribe the categories of crimes for which the death penalty should be available, and, acting as "the conscience of the community," juries are entrusted to determine in individual cases that the ultimate punishment is warranted. . . .

. . .

The rate of imposition of death sentences falls far short of providing the requisite unambiguous evidence that the legislatures of 40 States and the Congress have turned their backs on current or evolving standards of decency in continuing to make the death penalty available. For, if selective imposition evidences a rejection of capital punishment in those cases where it is not imposed, it surely evidences a correlative affirmation of the penalty in those cases where it is imposed. Absent some clear indication that the continued imposition of the death penalty on a selective basis is violative of prevailing standards of civilized conduct, the Eighth Amendment cannot be said to interdict its use.

IV

Capital punishment has also been attacked as violative of the Eighth Amendment on the ground that it is not needed to achieve legitimate penal aims and is thus "unnecessarily cruel." As a pure policy matter, this approach has much to recommend it, but it seeks to give a dimension to the Eighth Amendment that it was never intended to have and promotes a line of inquiry that this Court has never before pursued.

. . .

Apart from isolated uses of the word "unnecessary," nothing in the cases suggests that it is for the courts to make a determination of the efficacy of punishments. The decision in *Weems v. United States* is not to the contrary. . . . Under any characterization of the holding, it is readily apparent that the decision grew out of the Court's overwhelming abhorrence of the imposition of the particular penalty for the particular crime; it was making an essentially moral judgment, not a dispassionate assessment of the need for the penalty. . . . Thus, apart from the fact that the Court in *Weems* concerned itself with the crime committed as well as the punishment imposed, the case marks no departure from the largely unarticulable standard of extreme cruelty. However intractable that standard may be, that is what the Eighth Amendment is all about. The constitutional provision is not addressed to social utility and does not command that enlightened principles of penology always be followed.

V

Today the Court has not ruled that capital punishment is *per se* violative of the Eighth Amendment; nor has it ruled that the punishment is barred for any particular class or classes of crimes. The substantially similar concurring opinions of MR. JUSTICE STEWART and MR. JUSTICE WHITE, which are necessary to support the judgment setting aside petitioners' sentences, stop short of reaching the ultimate question. The actual scope of the Court's ruling, which I take to be embodied in these concurring opinions, is not entirely clear. This much, however, seems apparent: if the legislatures are to continue to authorize capital punishment for some crimes, juries and judges can no longer be permitted to make the sentencing determination in the same manner they have in the past. This approach—not urged in oral arguments or briefs —misconceives the nature of the constitutional command against "cruel and unusual punishments," disregards controlling case law, and demands a rigidity in capital cases which, if possible of achievement, cannot be regarded as a welcome change. Indeed the contrary seems to be the case.

. . . The Amendment is not concerned with the process by which a State determines that a particular punishment is to be imposed in a particular case. And the Amendment most assuredly does not speak to the power of legislatures to confer sentencing discretion on juries, rather than to fix all sentences by statute.

. . .

While I would not undertake to make a definitive statement as to the parameters of the Court's ruling, it is clear that if state legislatures and the Congress wish to maintain the availability of capital punishment, significant statutory changes will have to be made. Since the two pivotal concurring opinions turn on the assumption that the punishment of death is now meted out in a random and unpredictable manner, legislative bodies may seek to bring their laws into compliance with the Court's ruling by providing standards for juries and judges to follow in determining the sentence in capital cases or by more narrowly defining the crimes for which the penalty is to be imposed. If such standards can be devised or the crimes more meticulously defined, the result cannot be detrimental. . . . But even assuming that suitable guidelines can be established, there is no assurance that sentencing patterns will change so long as juries are possessed of the power to determine the sentence or to bring in a verdict of guilt on a charge carrying a lesser sentence; juries have not been inhibited in the exercise of these powers in the past. Thus, unless the Court in *McGautha* misjudged the experience of history, there is little reason to believe that sentencing standards in any form will substantially alter the discretionary character of the prevailing system of sentencing in capital cases. That system may fall short of perfection, but it is yet to be shown that a different system would produce more satisfactory results.

Real change could clearly be brought about if legislatures provided mandatory death sentences in such a way as to deny juries the opportunity to bring in a verdict on a lesser charge; under such a system, the death sentence could only be avoided by a verdict of acquittal. If this is the only alternative that the legislatures can safely pursue under today's ruling, I would have preferred that the Court opt for total abolition.

. . .

MR. JUSTICE BLACKMUN, dissenting.

I join the respective opinions of THE CHIEF JUSTICE, MR. JUSTICE POWELL, and MR. JUSTICE REHNQUIST, and add only the following, somewhat personal, comments.

Cases such as these provide for me an excruciating agony of the spirit. I yield to no one in the depth of my distaste, antipathy, and, indeed, abhorrence, for the death penalty, with all its aspects of physical distress and fear and of moral judgment exercised by finite minds. That distaste is buttressed by a belief that capital punishment serves no useful purpose that can be demonstrated. For me, it violates childhood's training and life's experiences, and is not compatible with the philosophical convictions I have been able to develop. It is antagonistic to any sense of "reverence for life." Were I a legislator, I would vote against the death penalty for the policy reasons argued by counsel for the respective petitioners and expressed and adopted in the several opinions filed by the Justices who vote to reverse these judgments.

. . .

The several concurring opinions acknowledge, as they must, that until today capital punishment was accepted and assumed as not unconstitutional *per se* under the Eighth Amendment or the Fourteenth Amendment. . . .

Suddenly, however, the course of decision is now the opposite way, with the Court evidently persuaded that somehow the passage of time has taken us to a place of greater maturity and outlook. The argument, plausible and high-sounding as it may be, is not persuasive, for it is only one year since *McGautha* . . . and we have been presented with nothing that demonstrates a significant movement of any kind in [this] brief period[ ]. The Court has just decided that it is time to strike down the death penalty. . . .

. . .

. . . Our task here, as must so frequently be emphasized and re-emphasized, is to pass upon the constitutionality of legislation that has been enacted and that is challenged. This is the sole task for judges. We should not allow our personal preferences as to the wisdom of legislative and congressional action, or our distaste for such action, to guide our judicial decision in cases such as these. The temptations to cross that policy line are very great. In fact, as today's decision reveals, they are almost irresistible.

. . .

Although personally I may rejoice at the Court's result, I find it difficult to accept or to justify as a matter of history, of law, or of constitutional pronouncement. I fear the Court has overstepped. It has sought and has achieved an end.

MR. JUSTICE POWELL, with whom THE CHIEF JUSTICE, MR. JUSTICE BLACKMUN, and MR. JUSTICE REHNQUIST join, dissenting.

. . .

. . . It is important to keep in focus the enormity of the step undertaken by the Court today. Not only does it invalidate hundreds of state and federal laws, it deprives those jurisdictions of the power to legislate with respect to capital punishment in the future, except in a manner consistent with the cloudily outlined views of those Justices who do not purport to undertake total abolition. Nothing short of an amendment to the United States Constitution can reverse the Court's judgments. Meanwhile, all flexibility is foreclosed. The normal democratic process, as well as the opportunities for the several States to respond to the will of their people expressed through ballot referenda (as in Massachusetts, Illinois, and Colorado), is now shut off.

The sobering disadvantage of constitutional adjudication of this magnitude is the universality and permanence of the judgment. The enduring merit of legislative action is its responsiveness to the democratic process, and to revision and change: mistaken judgments may be corrected and refinements perfected. . . .

. . . [A]s a matter of policy and precedent, this is a classic case for the exercise of our oft-announced allegiance to judicial restraint. I know of no case in which greater gravity and delicacy have attached to the duty that this Court is called on to perform whenever legislation—state or federal—is challenged on constitutional grounds. It seems to me that the sweeping judicial action undertaken today reflects a basic lack of faith and confidence in the democratic process. Many may regret, as I do, the failure of some legislative bodies to address the capital punishment issue with greater frankness or effectiveness. Many might decry their failure either to abolish the penalty entirely or selectively, or to establish standards for its enforcement. But impatience with the slowness, and even the unresponsiveness, of legislatures is no justification for judicial intrusion upon their historic powers. . . .

MR. JUSTICE REHNQUIST, with whom THE CHIEF JUSTICE, MR. JUSTICE BLACKMUN, and MR. JUSTICE POWELL join, dissenting.

. . .

The very nature of judicial review . . . makes the courts the least subject to Madisonian check in the event that they shall, for the best of motives, expand judicial authority beyond the limits contemplated by the Framers. It is for this reason that judicial self-restraint is surely an implied, if not an expressed, condition of the grant of authority of judicial review. The Court's holding in these cases has been reached, I believe, in complete disregard of that implied condition.

As Chief Justice Burger's dissenting opinion in *Furman* anticipated, most state legislatures attempted to salvage their death penalty statutes in the wake of *Furman*. Despite the NAACP Legal Defense Fund's death penalty moratorium, support for the death penalty remained high. At the time of *Furman*, there were over 600 inmates sitting on death row whose executions had been stymied by litigation. Two Gallup polls conducted in 1972 showed that a majority of Americans once again favored the death penalty. The *Furman* opinions left open two alternatives for limiting jury discretion: (1) statutes that made capital punishment mandatory for certain crimes and (2) statutes that specified factors to be weighed and procedures to be followed in determining which defendants deserved to be sentenced to death. By 1976, 35 states and the United

States Congress had passed new death penalty legislation, evenly divided between those which imposed mandatory capital punishment and those which provided guidelines and procedural safeguards. Georgia followed the second route by amending its capital punishment statute to specify 10 statutory aggravating circumstances, one of which must be found by the jury to exist beyond a reasonable doubt before a death sentence could be imposed. In addition, the jury was authorized to consider any other appropriate aggravating or mitigating circumstances. Although the jury was not required to find any mitigating circumstance in order to make a binding recommendation of mercy, it had to find a *statutory* aggravating circumstance before recommending a sentence of death.

After determining that the death penalty does not invariably violate the Constitution, a majority of justices in *Gregg v. Georgia* concluded that the Georgia capital sentencing scheme satisfied the Eighth Amendment requirements suggested in *Furman*. Now the majority displayed the concern for judicial restraint and respect for legislative judgment that characterized the dissenting opinions in *Furman*.

Gregg v. Georgia,
428 U.S. 153 (1976)

Judgment of the Court, and opinion of MR. JUSTICE STEWART, MR. JUSTICE POWELL, and MR. JUSTICE STEVENS, announced by MR. JUSTICE STEWART.

The issue in this case is whether the imposition of the sentence of death for the crime of murder under the law of Georgia violates the Eighth and Fourteenth Amendments.

I

The petitioner, Troy Gregg, was charged with committing armed robbery and murder. In accordance with Georgia procedure in capital cases, the trial was in two stages, a guilt stage and a sentencing stage. . . . The jury found the petitioner guilty of two counts of armed robbery and two counts of murder.

At the penalty stage, which took place before the same jury, . . . [t]he trial judge instructed the jury that it could recommend either a death sentence or a life prison sentence on each count. . . . Finding [two of the statutory aggravating circumstances], the jury returned verdicts of death on each count.

The Supreme Court of Georgia affirmed the convictions and the imposition of the death sentences for murder. . . .

. . .

III

We address initially the basic contention that the punishment of death for the crime of murder is, under all circumstances, "cruel and unusual" in violation of the Eighth and Fourteenth Amendments of the Constitution. In Part IV of this opinion, we will consider the sentence of death imposed under the Georgia statutes at issue in this case.

The Court on a number of occasions has both assumed and asserted the constitutionality of capital punishment. In several cases that assumption provided a necessary foundation for the decision, as the Court was asked to decide whether a particular method of carrying out a capital sentence would be allowed to stand under the Eighth Amendment. But until *Furman v. Georgia* the Court never confronted squarely the fundamental claim that the punishment of death always, regardless of the enormity of the offense or the procedure followed in imposing the sentence, is cruel and unusual punishment in violation of the Constitution. Although this issue was presented and addressed in *Furman,* it was not resolved by the Court. . . . We now hold that the punishment of death does not invariably violate the Constitution.

. . .

Of course, the requirements of the Eighth Amendment must be applied with an awareness of the limited role to be played by the courts. This does not mean that judges have no role to play, for the Eighth Amendment is a restraint upon the exercise of legislative power. . . . But, while we have an obligation to insure that constitutional bounds are not overreached, we may not act as judges as we might as legislators. . . .

Therefore, in assessing a punishment selected by a democratically elected legislature against the constitutional measure, we presume its validity. We may not require the legislature to select the least severe penalty possible so long as the penalty selected is not cruelly inhumane or disproportionate to the crime involved. And a heavy burden rests on those who would attack the judgment of the representatives of the people.

This is true in part because the constitutional test is intertwined with an assessment of contemporary standards and the legislative judgment weighs heavily in ascertaining such standards. "[I]n a democratic society legislatures, not courts, are constituted to respond to the will and consequently the moral values of the people." *Furman v. Georgia* (BURGER, C. J., dissenting). The deference we owe to the decisions of the state legislatures under our federal system is enhanced where the specification of punishments is concerned, for "these are peculiarly questions of legislative policy. Caution is necessary lest this Court become, "under the aegis of the Cruel and Unusual Punishment Clause, the ultimate arbiter of the standards of criminal responsibility . . . throughout the country." *Powell v. Texas*, 392 U.S. 514, 533 (1968) (plurality opinion). . . .

. . .

Four years ago, the petitioners in *Furman* and its companion cases predicated their argument primarily upon the asserted proposition that standards of decency had evolved to the point where capital punishment no longer could be tolerated. The petitioners in those cases said, in effect, that the evolutionary process had come to an end, and that standards of decency required that the Eighth Amendment be construed finally as prohibiting capital punishment for any crime regardless of its depravity and impact on society. . . .

The petitioners in the capital cases before the Court today renew the "standards of decency" argument, but developments during the four years since *Furman* have undercut substantially the assumptions upon which their argument rested. Despite the continuing debate, dating back to the 19th century, over the morality and utility of capital punishment, it is now evident that a large proportion of American society continues to regard it as an appropriate and necessary criminal sanction.

The most marked indication of society's endorsement of the death penalty for murder is the legislative response to *Furman*. . . . [A]ll of the post-*Furman* statutes make clear that capital punishment itself has not been rejected by the elected representatives of the people.

. . .

The jury also is a significant and reliable objective index of contemporary values because it is so directly involved. . . . It may be true that evolving standards have influenced juries in recent decades to be more discriminating in imposing the sentence of death. But the relative infrequency of jury verdicts imposing the death sentence does not indicate rejection of capital punishment *per se*. Rather, the reluctance of juries in many cases to impose the sentence may well reflect the humane feeling that this most irrevocable of sanctions should be reserved for a small number of extreme cases. Indeed, the actions of juries in many States since *Furman* are fully compatible with the legislative judgments, reflected in the new statutes, as to the continued utility and necessity of capital punishment in appropriate cases. At the close of 1974 at least 254 persons had been sentenced to death since *Furman*, and by the end of March 1976, more than 460 persons were subject to death sentences.

As we have seen, however, the Eighth Amendment demands more than that a challenged punishment be acceptable to contemporary society. The Court also must ask whether it comports with the basic concept of human dignity at the core of the Amendment. Although we cannot "invalidate a category of penalties because we deem less severe penalties adequate to serve the ends of penology," *Furman v. Georgia*, (Powell, J., dissenting), the sanction imposed cannot be so totally without penological justification that it results in the gratuitous infliction of suffering.

The death penalty is said to serve two principal social purposes: retribution and deterrence of capital crimes by prospective offenders.

In part, capital punishment is an expression of society's moral outrage at particularly offensive conduct. This function may be unappealing to many, but it is essential in an ordered society that asks its citizens to rely on legal processes rather than self-help to vindicate their wrongs. . . .

Statistical attempts to evaluate the worth of the death penalty as a deterrent to crimes by potential offenders have occasioned a great deal of debate. The results simply have been inconclusive. . . .

. . .

The value of capital punishment as a deterrent of crime is a complex factual issue the resolution of which properly rests with the legislatures, which can evaluate the results of statistical studies in terms of their own local conditions and with a flexibility of approach that is not available to the courts. . . .

In sum, we cannot say that the judgment of the Georgia Legislature that capital punishment may be necessary in some cases is clearly wrong. Considerations of federalism, as well as respect for the ability of a legislature to evaluate, in terms of its particular State, the moral consensus concerning the death penalty and its social utility as a sanction, require us to conclude, in the absence of more convincing evidence, that the infliction of death as a punishment for murder is not without justification and thus is not unconstitutionally severe.

Finally, we must consider whether the punishment of death is disproportionate in relation to the crime for which it is imposed. There is no question that death as a punishment is unique in its severity and irrevocability. When a defendant's life is at stake, the Court has been particularly sensitive to insure that every safeguard is observed. But we are concerned here only with the imposition of capital punishment for the crime of murder, and when a life has been taken deliberately by the offender, we cannot say that the punishment is invariably disproportionate to the crime. It is an extreme sanction, suitable to the most extreme of crimes.

. . .

IV

We now consider whether Georgia may impose the death penalty on the petitioner in this case.

. . .

Furman mandates that where discretion is afforded a sentencing body on a matter so grave as the determination of whether a human life should be taken or spared, that discretion must be suitably directed and limited so as to minimize the risk of wholly arbitrary and capricious action.

. . .

Jury sentencing has been considered desirable in capital cases in order "to maintain a link between contemporary community values and the penal system a link without which the determination of punishment could hardly reflect 'the evolving standards of decency that mark the progress of a maturing society.'" But it creates special problems. Much of the information that is relevant to the sentencing decision may have no relevance to the question of guilt, or may even be extremely prejudicial to a fair determination of that question. This problem, however, is scarcely insurmountable. Those who have studied the question suggest that a bifurcated procedure one in which the question of sentence is not considered until the determination of guilt has been made is the best answer. . . .

But the provision of relevant information under fair procedural rules is not alone sufficient to guarantee that the information will be properly used in the imposition of punishment, especially if sentencing is performed by a jury. Since the members of a jury will have had little, if any, previous experience in sentencing, they are unlikely to be skilled in dealing with the information they are given. To the extent that this problem is inherent in jury sentencing, it may not be totally correctable. It seems clear, however, that the problem will be alleviated if the jury is given guidance regarding the factors about the crime and the defendant that the State, representing organized society, deems particularly relevant to the sentencing decision.

. . .

While some have suggested that standards to guide a capital jury's sentencing deliberations are impossible to formulate, the fact is that such standards have been developed. When the drafters of the Model Penal Code faced this problem, they concluded "that it is within the realm of possibility to point to the main circumstances of aggravation and of mitigation that should be weighed *and weighed against each other* when they are presented in a concrete case." While such standards are by necessity somewhat general, they do provide guidance to the sentencing authority and thereby reduce the likelihood that it will impose a sentence that fairly can be called capricious or arbitrary. Where the sentencing authority is required to specify the factors it relied upon in reaching its decision, the further safeguard of meaningful appellate review is available to ensure that death sentences are not imposed capriciously or in a freakish manner.

In summary, the concerns expressed in *Furman* that the penalty of death not be imposed in an arbitrary or capricious manner can be met by a carefully drafted statute that ensures that the sentencing authority is given adequate information and guidance. As a general proposition these concerns are best met by a system that provides for a bifurcated proceeding at which the sentencing authority is apprised of the information relevant to the imposition of sentence and provided with standards to guide its use of the information.

[The Court next concluded that Georgia's capital-sentencing procedures met these constitutional standards.]

. . .

The basic concern of *Furman* centered on those defendants who were being condemned to death capriciously and arbitrarily. Under the procedures before the Court in that case, sentencing authorities were not directed to give attention to the nature or circumstances of the crime committed or to the character or record of the defendant. Left unguided, juries imposed the death sentence in a way that could only be called freakish. The new Georgia sentencing procedures, by contrast, focus the jury's attention on the particularized nature of the crime and the particularized characteristics of the individual defendant. While the jury is permitted to consider any aggravating or mitigating circumstances, it must find and identify at least one statutory aggravating factor before it may impose a penalty of death. In this way the jury's discretion is channeled. No longer can a jury wantonly and freakishly impose the death sentence; it is always circumscribed by the legislative guidelines. In addition, the review function of the Supreme Court of Georgia affords additional assurance that the concerns that prompted our decision in Furman are not present to any significant degree in the Georgia procedure applied here.

For the reasons expressed in this opinion, we hold that the statutory system under which Gregg was sentenced to death does not violate the Constitution. Accordingly, the judgment of the Georgia Supreme Court is affirmed.

MR. JUSTICE WHITE, with whom THE CHIEF JUSTICE and MR. JUSTICE REHNQUIST join, concurring in the judgment.

. . .

. . . Petitioner argues that, as in Furman, the jury is still the sentencer; that the statutory criteria to be considered by the jury on the issue of sentence under Georgia's new statutory scheme are vague and do not purport to be all-inclusive; and that, in any event, there are No circumstances under which the jury is required to impose the death penalty. Consequently, the petitioner argues that the death penalty will inexorably be imposed in as discriminatory, standardless, and rare a manner as it was imposed under the scheme declared invalid in Furman.

. . .

Petitioner's argument that there is an unconstitutional amount of discretion in the system which separates those suspects who receive the death penalty from those who receive life imprisonment, a lesser penalty, or are acquitted or never charged seems to be in final analysis an indictment of our entire system of justice. Petitioner has argued in effect that no matter how effective the death penalty may be as a punishment, government, created and run as it must be by humans, is inevitably incompetent to administer it. This cannot be accepted as a proposition of constitutional law. Imposition of the death penalty is surely an awesome responsibility for any system of justice and those who participate in it. Mistakes will be made and discriminations will occur which will be difficult to explain. However, one of society's most basic tasks is that of protecting the lives of its citizens and one of the most basic ways in which it achieves the task is through criminal laws against murder. I decline to interfere with the manner in which Georgia has chosen to enforce such laws on what is simply an assertion of lack of faith in the ability of the system of justice to operate in a fundamentally fair manner.

. . .

[JUSTICE BLACKMUN concurred in the judgment for the reasons expressed in his dissenting opinion in Furman.]

MR. JUSTICE BRENNAN, dissenting.

. . .

In Furman v. Georgia (concurring), I read "evolving standards of decency" as requiring focus upon the essence of the death penalty itself and not primarily or solely upon the procedures under which the determination to inflict the penalty upon a particular person was made. . . . That continues to be my view. For the Clause forbidding cruel and unusual punishments under our constitutional system of government embodies in unique degree moral principles restraining the punishments that our civilized society may impose on those persons who transgress its laws. . . .

This Court inescapably has the duty, as the ultimate arbiter of the meaning of our Constitution, to say whether, when individuals condemned to death stand before our Bar, "moral concepts" require us to hold that the law has progressed to the point where we should declare that the punishment of death, like punishments on the rack, the screw, and the wheel, is no longer morally tolerable in our civilized society. . . . [F]oremost among the "moral concepts" recognized in our cases and inherent in the Clause is the primary moral principle that the state, even as it punishes, must treat its citizens in a manner consistent with their intrinsic worth as human beings—a punishment must not be so severe as to be degrading to human dignity. A judicial determination whether the punishment of death comports with human dignity is therefore not only permitted but compelled by the Clause. . . .

. . .

MR. JUSTICE MARSHALL, dissenting.

In Furman v. Georgia (concurring opinion), I set forth at some length my views on the basic issue presented to the Court in these cases. The death penalty, I concluded, is a cruel and unusual punishment prohibited by the Eighth and Fourteenth Amendments. That continues to be my view.

. . . My sole purposes here are to consider the suggestion that my conclusion in Furman has been undercut by developments since then, and briefly to evaluate the basis for my Brethen's holding that the extinction of life is a permissible form of punishment under the Cruel and Unusual Punishments Clause.

. . .

. . . In Furman, I observed that the American people are largely unaware of the information critical to a judgment on the morality of the death penalty, and concluded that if they were better informed they would consider it shocking, unjust, and unacceptable. A recent study, conducted after the enactment of the post-*Furman* statutes, has confirmed that the American people know little about the death penalty, and that the opinions of an informed public would differ significantly from those of a public unaware of the consequences and effects of the death penalty.[1]

Even assuming, however, that the post-*Furman* enactment of statutes authorizing the death penalty renders the prediction of the view of an informed citizenry an uncertain basis for a constitutional decision, the enactment of those statutes has no bearing whatsoever on the conclusion that the death penalty is unconstitutional because it is excessive. An excessive penalty is invalid under the Cruel

---

[1] Sarat & Vidmar, *Public Opinion, The Death Penalty, and the Eighth Amendment: Testing the Marshall Hypothesis*, 1976 Wis. L. Rev. 171.

and Unusual Punishments Clause "even though popular sentiment may favor" it. . . .

. . .

. . . The mere fact that the community demands the murderer's life in return for the evil he has done cannot sustain the death penalty, for as JUSTICES STEWART, POWELL, and STEVENS remind us, "the Eighth Amendment demands more than that a challenged punishment be acceptable to contemporary society." To be sustained under the Eighth Amendment, the death penalty must "compor[t] with the basic concept of human dignity at the core of the Amendment"; the objective in imposing it must be "[consistent] with our respect for the dignity of [other] men." Under these standards, the taking of life "because the wrongdoer deserves it" surely must fall, for such a punishment has as its very basis the total denial of the wrongdoer's dignity and worth.

. . .

DER: Like the majority in *McClesky*, the majority in *Gregg* recognized that the Eighth Amendment challenge to the death penalty was potentially an indictment of the entire criminal justice system. Finding that racial discrimination stemming from jury discretion violated the Constitution would mean opening non-capital criminal trials to constitutional challenge, as well. Yet the fear of "too much justice" offers no excuse to uphold the death penalty in the face of overwhelming evidence that juries continue to impose sentences in a freakish and biased fashion. Two decades of death penalty cases after *Gregg* have made it even clearer that this problem cannot be fixed by judicial and legislative tinkering with capital sentencing guidelines. The Court could easily contain its invalidation of the death penalty by distinguishing executions from other punishments based on their finality, brutality, and infrequency.

On the same day that the Court upheld capital sentencing schemes that specified aggravating and mitigating circumstances, it rejected the alternative of mandatory death sentences for all first-degree murders. In *Woodson v. North Carolina*, Justice Stewart (joined by Justices Powell and Stevens) reasoned that mandatory death sentences failed to allow for the particularized consideration of relevant information about the defendant and the circumstances of the crime that the Eighth Amendment requires.[166] Mandating that juries impose capital punishment, therefore, "treats all persons convicted of a designated offense not as uniquely human beings, but as members of a faceless, undifferentiated mass to be subjected to the blind infliction of the penalty of death." Besides, Stewart noted, since juries were likely to resist imposing the death penalty in many first-degree murder cases, "mandatory statutes enacted in response to *Furman* have simply papered over the problem of unguided and unchecked jury discretion."[167] Justices Brennan and Marshall contributed the deciding votes on the basis of their absolute opposition to the death penalty.

The most appalling racial disparities in capital sentencing occurred in rape cases.

---

[166] 428 U.S. 280, 303–04 (1976).
[165] *Id.* at 302.

The entire history of punishment for rape in America was entangled with the repression of African Americans, a history starkly reflected in the death penalty statistics. Between 1930 and 1972, 89 percent of all those executed for rape were Black men who raped white women.[168] During that period in Georgia, 58 of 61 defendants executed for rape were Black.[169] No man had ever been executed for raping a Black woman. A year after its decision in *Gregg*, the Court held in *Coker v. Georgia* that the death penalty "is grossly disproportionate and excessive punishment for the crime of rape and is therefore forbidden by the Eighth Amendment."[170] Overlooking the history of racial bias, the plurality (Justices White, Stewart, Blackmun, and Stevens) reasoned that, although rape deserves serious punishment, "in terms of moral depravity and of the injury to the person and to the public, it does not compare with murder." Justices Brennan, Marshall, and Powell concurred in result, with Brennan and Marshall holding to their position that the death penalty is *per se* unconstitutional. Chief Justice Burger dissented in an opinion joined by Justice Rehnquist.

The *Gregg* decision precipitated numerous cases calling for Supreme Court evaluation of states' post-*Furman* capital sentencing schemes. In *Lockett v. Ohio*,[171] the Court considered a statute that required that, once the jury found any of seven aggravating circumstances, it must impose the death penalty unless one of three specified mitigating factors was also present. In a 7–1 decision, the Court held that the statute violated the Eighth Amendment because it precluded jurors from considering as a mitigating factor *any* aspect of the defendant's character or crime that the defendant proffers. The facts of Lockett highlighted the death penalty's arbitrary potential: Sandra Lockett was sentenced to death for a murder committed in the course of a robbery while she sat in the getaway car. The state's key witness against Lockett was her partner who actually committed the murder, but escaped the death penalty pursuant to a plea bargain.

The Court's capital sentencing decisions soon evinced a tension between *Furman*'s requirement of guided jury discretion and *Woodson*'s and *Lockett*'s concern for juror consideration of all relevant mitigating evidence. How can a single capital sentencing scheme reconcile the seemingly incompatible constitutional commands to limit jury discretion on the one hand and to allow individualized sentencing on the other? Although the Court has attempted to balance these competing interests, Justices Scalia and Blackmun have argued that the tension is in fact irreconcilable. Scalia and Blackmun reached opposite conclusions, however, about the proper outcome of this impasse. Blackmun, in a dramatic reversal of his position in *Furman* and subsequent cases, determined that the conflicting messages of *Furman* and *Lockett* proved that the death penalty could not be administered in a constitutional fashion. Scalia, on the other hand, contends that the incompatibility of the two lines of cases should lead to overruling *Lockett*, rather than abolishing the death penalty altogether. In a caustic concurrence in *Walton v. Arizona*, Scalia quipped that acknowledging this "inherent tension" in the Court's decisions "is rather like saying there was perhaps an inherent tension between the Allies and the Axis powers in World War II. And to refer to the two lines as pursuing 'twin objectives' is rather like referring to the twin objectives of good and evil."[172] After concluding that "[t]he mandatory imposition of death—without

---

[168] Marvin E. Wolfgang, *Racial Discrimination in the Death Sentence for Rape*, in Executions in America 109, 113 (William J. Bowers ed. 1974).

[169] Marvin E. Wolfgang & Marc Reidel, *Rape, Race, and the Death Penalty in Georgia*, 45 Am. J. Orthopsychiatry 658, 663 (1975).

[170] 433 U.S. 584, 595 (1977).

[171] 438 U.S. 586 (1978).

[172] 497 U.S. 639, 664 (1990).

sentencing discretion—for a crime which States have traditionally punished with death cannot possibly violate the Eighth Amendment," Scalia declared that he would no longer vote "to uphold an Eighth Amendment claim that the sentencer's discretion has been unlawfully restricted."

Shortly before stepping down from the Court, Justice Blackmun expressed his passionate condemnation of the Court's post-*Furman* death penalty decisions. Dissenting from the Court's denial of certiorari in *Callins v. Collins*,[173] Blackmun wrote:

> On February 23, 1994, at approximately 1:00 a.m., Bruce Edwin Callins will be executed by the State of Texas. Intravenous tubes attached to his arms will carry the instrument of death, a toxic fluid designed specifically for the purpose of killing human beings. The witnesses, standing a few feet away, will behold Callins, no longer a defendant, an appellant, or a petitioner, but a man, strapped to a guerney, and seconds away from extinction.
>
> . . .
>
> . . . Twenty years have passed since this Court declared that the death penalty must be imposed fairly, and with reasonable consistency, or not at all, see *Furman v. Georgia*, and, despite the effort of the States and courts to devise legal formulas and procedural rules to meet this daunting challenge, the death penalty remains fraught with arbitrariness, discrimination, caprice, and mistake. . . . . Experience has taught us that the constitutional goal of eliminating arbitrariness and discrimination from the administration of death can never be achieved without compromising an equally essential component of fundamental fairness—individualized sentencing. See *Lockett v. Ohio*.
>
> It is tempting, when faced with conflicting constitutional commands, to sacrifice one for the other or to assume that an acceptable balance between them already has been struck. In the context of the death penalty, however, such jurisprudential maneuvers are wholly inappropriate. . . . .
>
> To be fair, a capital sentencing scheme must treat each person convicted of a capital offense with that "degree of respect due the uniqueness of the individual." *Lockett* (plurality opinion). That means affording the sentencer the power and discretion to grant mercy in a particular case, and providing avenues for the consideration of any and all relevant mitigating evidence that would justify a sentence less than death. Reasonable consistency, on the other hand, requires that the death penalty be inflicted evenhandedly, in accordance with reason and objective standards, rather than by whim, caprice, or prejudice. Finally, because human error is inevitable, and because our criminal justice system is less than perfect, searching appellate review of death sentences and their underlying convictions is a prerequisite to a constitutional death penalty scheme.
>
> On their face, these goals of individual fairness, reasonable consistency, and absence of error appear to be attainable. . . . Yet, in the death penalty area, this Court, in my view, has engaged in a futile effort to balance these constitutional demands, and now is retreating not only from the *Furman* promise of consistency and rationality, but from the requirement of individualized sentencing as well. Having virtually conceded that both fairness and rationality cannot be achieved in the administration of the death penalty, see *McCleskey v. Kemp*, the Court has chosen to deregulate the entire enterprise, replacing, it would seem, substantive constitutional requirements with mere aesthetics, and abdicating its statutorily and constitutionally imposed duty to provide meaningful judicial oversight to the administration of death by the States.
>
> From this day forward, I no longer shall tinker with the machinery of death.

---

[173] 114 S. Ct. 1127 (1994).

For more than 20 years I have endeavored—indeed, I have struggled—along with a majority of this Court, to develop procedural and substantive rules that would lend more than the mere appearance of fairness to the death penalty endeavor. Rather than continue to coddle the Court's delusion that the desired level of fairness has been achieved and the need for regulation eviscerated, I feel morally and intellectually obligated simply to concede that the death penalty experiment has failed. It is virtually self-evident to me now that no combination of procedural rules or substantive regulations ever can save the death penalty from its inherent constitutional deficiencies. The basic question—does the system accurately and consistently determine which defendants "deserve" to die?—cannot be answered in the affirmative. It is not simply that this Court has allowed vague aggravating circumstances to be employed, relevant mitigating evidence to be disregarded, and vital judicial review to be blocked. The problem is that the inevitability of factual, legal, and moral error gives us a system that we know must wrongly kill some defendants, a system that fails to deliver the fair, consistent, and reliable sentences of death required by the Constitution.

There is a heightened need for fairness in the administration of death. This unique level of fairness in born of the appreciation that death truly is different from all other punishments a society inflicts upon its citizens. . . . While the risk of mistake in the determination of the appropriate penalty may be tolerated in other areas of the criminal law, "in capital cases the fundamental respect for humanity underlying the Eighth Amendment . . . requires consideration of the character and record of the individual offender and the circumstances of the particular offense as a constitutionally indispensable part of the process of inflicting the penalty of death." *Woodson v. North Carolina.*

. . .

Yet, as several Members of the Court have recognized, there is a real "tension" between the need for fairness to the individual and the consistency promised in *Furman.* On the one hand, discretion in capital sentencing must be "'controlled by clear and objective standards so as to produce non-discriminatory [and reasoned] application.'" *Gregg.* On the other hand, the Constitution also requires that the sentencer be able to consider "any relevant mitigating evidence regarding the defendant's character and background, and the circumstances of the particular offense." The power to consider mitigating evidence that would warrant a sentence less than death is meaningless unless the sentencer has the discretion and authority to dispense mercy based on that evidence. Thus, the Constitution, by requiring a heightened degree of fairness to the individual, and also a greater degree of equality and rationality in the administration of death, demands sentencer discretion that is at once generously expanded and severely restricted.

. . .

The theory underlying . . . *Lockett* is that an appropriate balance can be struck between the *Furman* promise of consistency and the *Lockett* requirement of individualized sentencing if the death penalty is conceptualized as consisting of two distinct stages. In the first stage of capital sentencing, the demands of *Furman* are met by "narrowing" the class of death-eligible offenders according to objective, fact-bound characteristics of the defendant or the circumstances of the offense. Once the pool of death-eligible defendants has been reduced, the sentencer retains the discretion to consider whatever relevant mitigating evidence the defendant chooses to offer.

Over time, I have come to conclude that even this approach is unacceptable: It simply reduces, rather than eliminates, the number of people subject to arbitrary sentencing. It is the decision to sentence a defendant to death—not merely the decision to make a defendant eligible for death—that may not be arbitrary. While one might hope that providing the sentencer with as much relevant mitigating evidence as possible will lead to more rational and consistent sentences, experience has taught otherwise. It seems that the decision whether a human being should live or die is so inherently subjective—rife with all of life's understandings, experiences, prejudices, and passions—that it inevitably defies the rationality and consistency required by the Constitution.

The arbitrariness inherent in the sentencer's discretion to afford mercy is exacerbated by the problem of race. Even under the most sophisticated death penalty statutes, race continues to play a major role in determining who should live and who should die. Perhaps it should not be surprising that the biases and prejudices that infect society influence the determination of who is sentenced to death, even within the narrower pool of death-eligible defendants selected according to objective standards. . . . . "The power to be lenient [also] is the power to discriminate.'" *McClesky v. Kemp.*

. . .

. . . In my view, the proper course when faced with irreconcilable constitutional commands is not to ignore one or the other, nor to pretend that the dilemma does not exist, but to admit the futility of the effort to harmonize them. This means accepting the fact that the death penalty cannot be administered in accord with our Constitution.

Justice Scalia responded to Justice Blackmun in his concurrence in the Court's denial of Callins' petition for review:

Justice Blackmun dissents from the denial of certiorari in this case with a statement explaining why the death penalty "as currently administered" is contrary to the Constitution of the United States. That explanation often refers to "intellectual, moral and personal" perceptions, but never the text and tradition of the Constitution. It is the latter rather than the former that ought to control. The Fifth Amendment provides that "[n]o person shall be held to answer for a capital . . . crime, unless on a presentment or indictment of a Grand Jury, . . . nor be deprived of life . . . without due process of law." This clearly permits the death penalty to be imposed, and establishes beyond doubt that the death penalty is not one of the "cruel and unusual punishments" prohibited by the Eighth Amendment.

As Justice Blackmun describes, however, over the years since 1972 this Court has attached to the imposition of the death penalty two quite incompatible sets of commands: the sentencer's discretion to impose death must be closely confined, but the sentencer's discretion not to impose death (to extend mercy) must be unlimited. These commands were invented without benefit of any textual or historical support; they are the product of just such "intellectual, moral, and personal" perceptions as Justice Blackmun expresses today. . . .

Though Justice Blackmun joins those of us who have acknowledged the incompatibility of the Court's *Furman* and *Lockett-Eddings* lines of jurisprudence, he unfortunately draws the wrong conclusion. . . . Surely a different conclusion commends itself—to wit, that at least one of these judicially announced irreconcilable commands which cause the Constitution to prohibit what its text explicitly permits must be wrong.

Convictions in opposition to the death penalty are often passionate and deeply held. That would be no excuse for reading them into the Constitution that does not contain them, even if they represented the convictions of a majority of Americans. Much less is there any excuse for using that course to thrust a minority's view upon the people. Justice Blackmun begins his statement by describing with poignancy the death of a convicted murderer by lethal injection. He chooses, as the case in which to make that statement, one of the less brutal of the murders that regularly come before us—the murder of a man ripped by a bullet suddenly and unexpectedly, with no opportunity to prepare himself and his affairs, and left to bleed to death on the floor of a tavern. The death-by-injection which Justice Blackmun describes looks pretty desirable next to that. . . . If the people conclude that such . . . brutal deaths may be deterred by capital punishment; indeed, if they merely conclude that justice requires such brutal deaths to be avenged by capital punishment; the creation of false, untextual and unhistorical contradictions within "the Court's Eighth Amendment jurisprudence" should not prevent them.

b. Discriminatory Purpose and the Thirteenth Amendment

Despite the indication in *Arlington Heights* that "historical background" was relevant to determining discriminatory purpose,[174] the tradition of a dual criminal justice system and disparate advice that a defense attorney logically would provide white and black defendants in capital cases were apparently too nonspecific to satisfy the majority in *McCleskey v. Kemp.* A similar result was achieved in the Thirteenth Amendment context, when the Court in *Memphis v. Greene* determined that a street barrier erected to divert predominantly black traffic around a white neighborhood was not a function of invidious motive.[175] In finding a racially neutral justification for the barrier, the Court dismissed the historical significance of the wall in a community not far removed from a long tradition of prescriptive racial segregation.

---

[174] Village of Arlington Heights v. Metropolitan Housing Development Corp., 429 U.S. 252, 265 (1977).

[175] Memphis v. Greene, 451 U.S. 100, 126–27 (1981).

Memphis v. Greene
451 U.S. 100 (1981)

The question presented is whether a decision by the city of Memphis to close the north end of West Drive, a street that traverses a white residential community, violated . . . the Thirteenth Amendment to the United States Constitution. The city's action was challenged by respondents, who resided in a predominantly black area to the north.

The area to the north of Hein Park is predominantly black. All of the homes in Hein Park were owned by whites when the decision to close the street was made.

. . .

In a complaint filed against the city and various officials in the United States District Court for the Western District of Tennessee on April 1, 1974, three individuals and two civic associations, suing on behalf of a class of residents north of Jackson Ave. and west of Springdale St., alleged that the closing was unconsti-

tutional and prayed for an injunction requiring the city to keep West Drive open for through traffic. The District Court granted a motion to dismiss, holding that the complaint, as amended, failed to allege any injury to the plaintiffs' own property or any disparate racial effect, and that they had no standing as affected property owners to raise procedural objections to the city's action.

The United States Court of Appeals for the Sixth Circuit reversed. . . .

The first of the four factual predicates for the Court of Appeals' holding relates to the effect of the closing on black residents and is squarely rooted in the District Court's findings. Judge McRae expressly found that the City Council action "will have disproportionate impact on certain black citizens." He described the traffic that will be diverted by the closing as "overwhelming black," and noted that the white residents of West Drive will have less inconvenience. We must note, however, that although neither Judge McRae nor the Court of Appeals focused on the extent of the inconvenience to residents living north of Jackson Ave., the record makes it clear that such inconvenience will be minimal. A motorist southbound on Springdale St. could continue south on West Drive for only a half mile before the end of West Drive at Overton Park would necessitate a turn. Thus unless the motorist is going to Overton Park, the only effect of the street closing for traffic proceeding south will be to require a turn sooner without lengthening the entire trip or requiring any more turns. Moreover, even the motorist going to Overton Park had to make a turn from West Drive and a short drive down North Parkway to reach the entrance to the park. The entire trip from Springdale St. to the park will be slightly longer with West Drive closed, but it will not be significantly less convenient. Thus although it is correct that the motorists who will be inconvenienced by the closing are primarily black, the extent of the inconvenience is not great.

As for the Court of Appeals' second point, the court attached greater significance to the closing as a "barrier" between two neighborhoods than appears warranted by the record. The physical barrier is a curb that will not impede the passage of municipal vehicles. Moreover, because only one of the several streets entering Hein Park is closed to vehicular traffic, the other streets will provide ample access to the residences in Hein Park. The diversion of through traffic around the Hein Park residential area affects the diverted motorists, but does not support the suggestion that such diversion will limit the social perceived or commercial contact between residents of neighboring communities. The Court of Appeals' reference to protecting the neighborhood from "undesirable" outside influences may be read as suggesting that the court viewed the closure as motivated by the racial attitude of the residents of Hein Park. The District Court's findings do not support that view of the record. Judge McRae expressly discounted the racial composition of the traffic on West Drive in evaluating its undesirable character; he noted that "excessive traffic in any residential neighborhood has public welfare factors such as safety, noise, and litter, regardless of the race of the traffic and the neighborhood. The transcript of the City Council hearings indicates that the residents of West Drive perceived the traffic to be a problem because of the number and speed of the cars traveling down West Drive. Even if the statements of the residents of West Drive are discounted as self-serving, there is no evidence that the closing was motivated by any

racially exclusionary desire. The City Council members who favored the closing expressed concerns similar to those of the West Drive residents. Those who opposed the resolution did so because they believed that a less drastic response to the traffic problems would be adequate and that the closing would create a dangerous precedent. The one witness at trial who testified that "someone" soliciting signatures for a petition favoring the closure had described the traffic on West Drive as "undesirable traffic," stated that the solicitor mentioned excess traffic and danger to children as reasons for signing. Unlike the Court of Appeals we therefore believe that the "undesirable" character of the traffic flow must be viewed as a factor supporting, rather than undermining, the validity of the closure decision. . . . Finally, the Court of Appeals was not justified in inferring that the closure would cause "an economic depreciation in the property values in the predominantly black residential area. . . . " The only expert testimony credited by the District Court on that issue was provided by a real estate broker called by the plaintiffs. His expert opinion, as summarized by the District Court, was that "there would not be a decrease in value experienced by property owners located to the north of West Drive because of the closure." After the witness had expressed that opinion, he admittedly speculated that some property owners to the north might be envious of the better housing that they could not afford and therefore might be less attentive to the upkeep of their own property, which in turn "could have a detrimental effect on the property values in the future." In our opinion the District Court correctly refused to find an adverse impact on black property values based on that speculation.

In summary, then, the critical facts established by the record are these: The city's decision to close West Drive was motivated by its interest in protecting the safety and tranquility of a residential neighborhood. The procedures followed in making the decision were fair and were not affected by any racial or other impermissible factors. The city has conferred a benefit on certain white property owners but there is no reason to believe that it would refuse to confer a comparable benefit on black property owners. The closing has not affected the value of property owned by black citizens, but it has caused some slight inconvenience to black motorists.

Under the Court's recent decisions in *Washington v. Davis*, and *Arlington Heights v. Metropolitan Housing Dev. Corp.*, the absence of proof of discriminatory intent forecloses any claim that the official action challenged in this case violates the Equal Protection Clause of the Fourteenth Amendment. Petitioners ask us to hold that respondents' claims under . . . the Thirteenth Amendment are likewise barred by the absence of proof of discriminatory purpose. We note initially that the coverage of both § 1982 and the Thirteenth Amendment is significantly different from the coverage of the Fourteenth Amendment. The prohibitions of the latter apply only to official action. . . . [I]t has long been settled that the Thirteenth Amendment "is not a mere prohibition of State laws establishing or upholding slavery, but an absolute declaration that slavery or involuntary servitude shall not exist in any part of the United States." . . . Thus, although respondents challenge official action in this case, the provisions of the law on which the challenge is based cover certain private action as well. Rather than confront prematurely the rather general question whether the Thirteenth Amendment requires proof of a specific unlawful purpose, we first consider the extent to which either provision applies at all to this street closing case.

. . .

In relevant part, the Thirteenth Amendment provides:

"Neither slavery nor involuntary servitude, except as a punishment for crime whereof the party shall have been duly convicted, shall exist within the United States, or any place subject to their jurisdiction."

In this case respondents challenge the conferring of a benefit upon white citizens by a measure that places a burden on black citizens as an unconstitutional "badge of slavery." . . .

. . .

We begin our examination of respondents' Thirteenth Amendment argument by reiterating the conclusion that the record discloses no racially discriminatory motive on the part of the City Council. Instead, the record demonstrates that the interests that did motivate the Council are legitimate. Proper management of the flow of vehicular traffic within a city requires the accommodation of a variety of conflicting interests: the motorist's interest in unhindered access to his destination, the city's interest in the efficient provision of municipal services, the commercial interest in adequate parking, the residents' interest in relative quiet, and the pedestrians' interest in safety. Local governments necessarily exercise wide discretion in making the policy decisions that accommodate these interests.

In this case the city favored the interests of safety and tranquility. As a matter of constitutional law a city's power to adopt rules that will avoid anticipated traffic safety problems is the same as its power to correct those hazards that have been revealed by actual events. The decision to reduce the flow of traffic on West Drive was motivated, in part, by an interest in the safety of children walking to school. That interest is equally legitimate whether it provides support for an arguably unnecessary preventive measure or for a community's reaction to a tragic accident that adequate planning might have prevented.

The residential interest in comparative tranquility is also unquestionably legitimate. That interest provides support for zoning regulations, designed to protect a "quiet place where yards are wide, people few, and motor vehicles restricted. . . . " and for the accepted view that a man's home is his castle. The interest in privacy has the same dignity in a densely populated apartment complex, or in an affluent neighborhood of single-family homes. In either context, the protection of the individual interest may involve the imposition of some burdens on the general public.

Whether the individual privacy interests of the residents of Hein Park, coupled with the interest in safety, should be considered strong enough to overcome the more general interest in the use of West Drive as a thoroughfare is the type of question that a multitude of local governments must resolve every day. Because there is no basis for concluding that the interests favored by the city in its decision were contrived or pretextual, the District Court correctly concluded that it had no authority to review the wisdom of the city's policy decision. The interests motivating the city's action are thus sufficient to justify an adverse impact on motorists who are somewhat inconvenienced by the street closing. That inconvenience cannot be equated to an actual restraint on the liberty of black citizens that is in any sense comparable to the odious practice the Thirteenth Amendment was designed to eradicate. The argument that the closing violates the Amendment must therefore rest, not on the actual consequences of the closing, but rather on the symbolic significance of the fact that most of the drivers who will be inconvenienced by the action are black.

But the inconvenience of the drivers is a function of where they live and where they regularly drive—not a function of their race, the hazards and the inconvenience that the closing is intended to minimize are a function of the number of vehicles involved, not the race of their drivers or of the local residents. Almost any traffic regulation—whether it be a temporary detour during construction, a speed limit, a one-way street, or a no-parking sign—may have a differential impact on residents of adjacent or nearby neighborhoods. Because urban neighborhoods are so frequently characterized by a common ethnic or racial heritage, a regulation's adverse impact on a particular neighborhood will often have a disparate effect on an identifiable ethnic or racial group. To regard an inevitable consequence of that kind as a form of stigma so severe as to violate the Thirteenth Amendment would trivialize the great purpose of that charter of freedom. Proper respect for the dignity of the residents of any neighborhood requires that they accept the same burdens as well as the same benefits of citizenship regardless of their racial or ethnic origin. . . .

JUSTICE WHITE concurring in the judgment.

JUSTICE MARSHALL, with whom JUSTICE BRENNAN and JUSTICE BLACKMUN join, dissenting.

This case is easier than the majority makes it appear. Petitioner city of Memphis, acting at the behest of white property owners, has closed the main thoroughfare between an all-white enclave and a predominantly Negro area of the city. The stated explanation for the closing is of a sort all too familiar: "protecting the safety and tranquility of a residential neighborhood" by preventing "undesirable traffic" from entering it. Too often in our Nation's history, statements such as these have been little more than code phrases for racial discrimination, but apparently not, after today's decision, forbidden discrimination. The majority, purporting to rely on the evidence developed at trial, concludes that the city's stated interests are sufficient to justify erection of the barrier. Because I do not believe that either the Constitution or federal law permits a city to carve out racial enclaves I dissent.

. . .

In order to determine "whether the State 'in any of its manifestations' has become significantly involved in private discriminations," it is necessary to "sif[t] facts and weig[h] circumstances'" so that "'nonobvious involvement of the State in private conduct [can] be attributed its true significance.'" The key to the majority's conclusion is the view that it takes of the facts, and consequently I will review the relevant parts of the record in some detail.

The majority treats this case as involving nothing more than a dispute over a city's race-neutral decision to place a barrier across a road. My own examination of the record suggests, however, that far more is at stake here than a simple street closing. The picture that emerges from a more careful review of the records is one of a white community, disgruntled over sharing its street with Negroes, taking legal measures to keep out the "undesirable traffic," and of a city, heedless of the harm to its Negro citizens, acquiescing in the plan.

. . .

I readily accept much of the majority's summary of the circumstances that led to this litigation. I would, however, begin by emphasizing three critical facts. First, as the District Court found, Hein Park "was developed well before World War II as an exclusive residential neighborhood for white citizens and these characteristics have been maintained." Second, the area to the north of Hein Park, like the "undesirable traffic" that Hein Park wants to keep out, is predominantly Negro. And third, the closing of West Drive stems entirely from the efforts of residents of Hein Park. Up to this point, the majority and I are in agreement. But we part company over our characterizations of the evidence developed in the course of the trial of this case. At the close of the evidence, the trial court described this as "a situation where an all white neighborhood is seeking to stop the traffic from an overwhelming black neighborhood from coming through their street." In the legal and factual context before us, I find that a revealing summary of the case. The majority apparently does not.

. . .

The majority does not seriously dispute the first of the four facts relied on by the Court of Appeals. In fact it concedes that the trial court "clearly concluded . . . that the adverse impact on blacks was greater than on whites." The majority suggests, however, that this "impact" is limited to the "inconvenience" that will be suffered by drivers who live in the predominantly Negro area north of Hein Park and who will no longer be able to drive through the subdivision. This, says the majority, is because residents of the area north of Hein Park will still be able to get where they are going; they will just have to go a little out of their way and thus will take a little longer to complete the trip.

This analysis ignores the plain and powerful symbolic message of the "inconvenience." Many places to which residents of the area north of Hein Park would logically drive lie to the south of the subdivision. Until the closing of West Drive, the most direct route for those who lived on or near Springdale St. was straight down West Drive. Now the Negro drivers are being told in essence: "You must take the long way around because you don't live in this 'protected' white neighborhood." Negro residents of the area north of Hein Park testified at trial that this is what they thought the city was telling them by closing West Drive. Even the District Court, which granted judgment for petitioners, conceded that "[o]bviously, the black people north of [Hein Park] . . . are being told to stay out of the subdivision." In my judgment, this message constitutes a far greater adverse impact on respondents than the majority would prefer to believe.

The majority also does not challenge the Sixth Circuit's second finding, that the barrier is being erected at the point of contact of the two communities. Nor could it do so, because the fact is not really in dispute. The Court attempts instead to downplay the significance of this barrier by calling it "a curb that will not impede the passage of municipal vehicles." But that is beside the point. Respondents did not bring this suit to challenge the exclusion of municipal vehicles from Hein Park. Their goal is to preserve access for their own vehicles. But in fact, they may not even be able to preserve access for their own persons. The city is creating the barrier across West Drive by deeding public property to private landowners. Nothing will prevent the residents of Hein Park from excluding "undesirable" pedestrians as well as vehicular traffic if they so choose. What is clear is that there will be a barrier to traffic that is to be erected precisely at the point where West Drive (and thus, all-white Hein Park) ends and Springdale St. (and the mostly Negro section) begins.

The psychological effect of this barrier is likely to be significant. In his unchallenged expert testimony in the trial court, Dr. Marvin Feit, a professor of psychiatry at the University of Tennessee, predicted that the barrier between West Drive and Springdale St. will reinforce feelings abut the city's "favoritism" toward whites and will "serve as a monument to racial hostility." The testimony of Negro residents and of a real estate agent familiar with the area provides powerful support for this prediction. As the District Court put it: "[Y]ou are not going to be able to convince those black people out there that they didn't do it because they were black. They are helping a white neighborhood. Now, that is a problem that somebody is going to have to live with. . . . " I cannot subscribe to the majority's apparent view that the city's erection of this "monument to racial hostility" amounts to nothing more than a "slight inconvenience." Thus, unlike the majority, I do not minimize the significance of the barrier itself in determining the harm respondents will suffer from its erection.

The majority does not attempt to question the third conclusion by the Court of Appeals, that the closing of West Drive is intended as a protection of Hein Park against "undesirable" outside influences. . . . A proper reading of the record demonstrates to the contrary that respondents produced at trial precisely the kind of evidence of intent that we deemed probative in *Arlington Heights v. Metropolitan Housing Dev. Corp.* . . .

The term "undesirable traffic" first entered this litigation through the trial testimony of Sarah Terry. Terry, a West Drive resident who opposed the closing testified that she was urged to support the barrier by an individual who explained to her that "the traffic on the street was undesirable traffic." The majority apparently reads the term "undesirable" as referring to the prospect of having any traffic at all on West Drive. But the common-sense understanding of Terry's testimony must be that the word "undesirable" was meant to describe the traffic that was actually using the street, as opposed to any traffic that might use it. Of course, the traffic that was both actually using the street and would be affected by the barrier was predominantly Negro.

. . .

. . . In particular, despite an unambiguous requirement that applications for street closings be signed by "all" owners of property abutting on the thoroughfare to be closed, the city here permitted this application to go through without the signature or the consent of Sarah Terry. Perhaps more important, the city gave no notice to the Negro property owners living north of Hein Park that the Planning Commission was considering an application to close West Drive. The Planning Commission held its hearing without participation by any of the affected Negro residents and it declined to let them examine the file on the West Drive closing. It gave no notice that the City Council would be considering the issue. When respondents found out about it, they sought to state their case. But the Council gave opponents of the proposal only 15 minutes, even though some members objected that that was not enough time. Furthermore, although the majority treats West Drive as just another closing, it is, according to the city official in charge of closings, the only time the city has ever closed a street for traffic control purposes. . . . And it cannot be disputed that all parties were aware of the disparate racial impact of the erection of the barrier. The city of Memphis, moreover, has an unfortunate but very real history of racial segregation—a history that has in the past led to intercession by this Court. All these factors represent precisely the kind of evidence that we said in *Arlington Heights* was relevant to an inquiry into motivation. Regardless of whether this evidence is viewed as conclusive, it can hardly be stated with accuracy that "no evidence" exists. Most important, I believe that the findings of the District Court and the record in this case fully support the Court of Appeals' conclusion that Negro property owners are likely to suffer economic harm as a result of the construction of the barrier. . . .

In sum, I cannot agree with the majority's suggestion that "[t]he injury to respondents established by the record is the requirement that one public street rather than another must be used for certain trips within the city," and that this requirement amounts to no more than "some slight inconvenience." Indeed, as should be clear from the foregoing, the problem is less the closing of West Drive in particular than the establishment of racially determined districts which the closing effects. I can only agree with the Court of Appeals, which viewed the city's action as nothing more than "one more of the many humiliations which society has historically visited" on Negro citizens. In my judgment, respondents provided ample evidence that erection of the challenged barrier will harm them in several significant ways. Respondents are being sent a clear, though sophisticated, message that because of their race, they are to stay out of the all-white enclave of Hein Park and should instead take the long way around in reaching their destinations to the south. Combined with this message are the prospects of increased police harassment and of a decline in their property values. It is on the basis of these facts, all firmly established by record, that I evaluate the legal question presented by this case. . . . In short, I conclude that the plain language of § 1982 and its legislative history show that the harm established by a fair reading of this record falls within the prohibition of the statute. Because the Court of Appeals reached the same conclusion, I would affirm its judgment.

In light of my disposition of the statutory question, I would ordinarily find it unnecessary to consider the merits of the Thirteenth Amendment. But I cannot let the court's discussion of the constitutional claim pass without comment. The majority reserves until another case the issue whether § 1 of the Amendment by its own force bans "badges and incidents of slavery" because, in its view, "a review of the justification for the official action challenged in this case demonstrates that its disparate impact on black citizens could not . . . be fairly characterized as a badge or incident of slavery." For reasons that I have already indicated, I believe that the degree of harm to respondents from the erection of a barrier at the end of West Drive far exceeds the minimal inconvenience found by the majority. Assuming with the majority that the Amendment would, even without implementing legislation, ban more than the mere practice of slavery, I would conclude that official action causing harm of the magnitude suffered here plainly qualifies as a "badge or incident" of slavery, at least as those terms were understood by the

Reconstruction Congress. When the Thirteenth Amendment was being debated, supporters and opponents alike acknowledge that it would have the effect of striking down racial discrimination in a wide variety of areas. . . . Congress did not believe it was doing more than spelling out the guarantees implicit in § 1 of the Thirteenth Amendment. Because that Congress included so many of those who had a hand in drafting the Thirteenth Amendment, would give its judgment considerable deference. Consequently, I would hold that because the closing of West Drive is forbidden on these facts by § 1982, it is a fortiori a violation of the Thirteenth Amendment as well. Of course, this should not be taken as an argument that Congress cannot under § 2 of the Thirteenth Amendment enact legislation forbidding more than would § 1 of the Civil Rights Act of 1866. I also do not mean to imply that all municipal decisions that affect Negroes adversely and benefit whites are prohibited by the Thirteenth Amendment. I would, however, insist that the government carry a heavy burden of justification before I would sustain against Thirteenth Amendment challenge conduct as egregious as erection of a barrier to prevent predominantly Negro traffic from entering a historically all-white neighborhood. For reasons that I have already stated, I do not believe that the city has discharged that burden in this case, and for that reason I would hold that the erection of the barrier at the end of the West Drive amounts to a badge or incident of slavery forbidden by the Thirteenth Amendment.

. . .

I end, then, where I began. Given the majority's decision to characterize this case as a mere policy decision on the part of the city of Memphis to close a street for valid municipal reasons, the conclusion that it reaches follows inevitably. But the evidence in this case, combined with a dab of common sense, paints a far different picture from the one emerging from the majority's opinion. In this picture a group of white citizens has decided to act to keep Negro citizens from traveling through their urban "utopia," and the city has placed its seal of approval on the scheme. It is this action that I believe is forbidden, and it is for that reason that I dissent.

PAH: The majority in *Greene* views the physical barrier and street closing as a mere inconvenience, one of a myriad of inconsequential burdens on citizens as a byproduct of political decision making. Justice Marshall, challenges the Court's characterization, unpacking the "mere inconvenience" to expose stigmatizing official action. As then-Professor (now Judge) Guido Calabresi reminds us, stigmatic actions aren't necessarily heavily burdensome disadvantages but can justify judicial intervention if it "reinforces the very sort of discriminatory attitudes and treatment that earned the group its disfavored status in the first place."[176] Both Justic Marshall (and Professor Calabresi) argue that the Court is justified in taking a closer look—demanding a heavier burden potentially stigmatizing official action. In contrast to the court's blindness to racial reality in this context, recall that in the school desegregation cases, the Court had legitmated challenges to remedial efforts, considering the tendency for the action to incite racial hostility of whites.[177]

---

[176] Guido Calabresi, The Supreme Court 1990 Term: Foreword: Antidiscrimination and Constitutional Accountability (What the Bork-Brennan Debate Ignores), 105 HARV. L. REV. 80, 99 (1991).

[177] See e.g., Columbus Board of Educ. v. Penick, 443 U.S. 449 (1979) (white exodus); Estes v. Metropolitan Branch of the Dallas NAACP, 444 U.S. 437 (1980)(danger of exciting resegregation).

c. "Appearances" That Matter

Since the Court's investment in motive-referenced standards, equal protection success has been limited primarily to those instances in which discriminatory purpose is evident upon the face or from the history of a challenged law or policy. Striking down a state law disenfranchising persons convicted of certain crimes in *Hunter v. Underwood*, for instance, the Court referenced a historical record evidencing that it was a relic of official segregation enacted for a nakedly discriminatory purpose.[178] In *Shaw v. Reno*, what the Court described as a redistricting scheme "so bizarre on its face that it is 'unexplainable on grounds other than race,'" gave rise to strict scrutiny.[179] At issue was a North Carolina reapportionment plan crafting two majority-black districts for the House of Representatives. As the court noted, one district had "been compared to a 'Rohrshach ink-blot test and a bug splattered on a windshield.'"[180] The other was "even more unusually shaped . . . [being] approximately 160 miles long, . . . for much of its length no wider than the I-85 corridor, . . . [and contoured] in snake-like fashion through tobacco country, financial centers, and manufacturing areas 'until it gobbles in enough enclaves of black neighborhoods."[181] The unusually shaped district was begotten in significant part by the Attorney General of the United States' objection, under the Voting Rights Act of 1965, to a plan providing for one majority-black congressional district in the state.

---

[178] Hunter v. Underwood, 471 U.S. 222, 233 (1985).

[179] Shaw v. Reno, 113 S. Ct. 2816, 2825 (1993).

[180] *Id.* at 2820.

[181] *Id.* at 2820–21.

Shaw v. Reno
113 S. Ct. 2816 (1993)

No inquiry into legislative purpose is necessary when the racial classification appears on the face of the statute. Express racial classifications are immediately suspect because "[a]bsent searching judicial inquiry . . . , there is simply no way of determining what classifications are 'benign' or 'remedial' and what classifications are in fact motivated by illegitimate notions of racial inferiority or simple racial politics." ("[A] purportedly preferential race assignment may in fact disguise a policy that perpetuates disadvantageous treatment of the plan's supposed beneficiaries").

Classification of citizens solely on the basis of race "are by their very nature odious to a free people whose institutions are founded upon the doctrine of equality." They threaten to stigmatize individuals by reason of their membership in a racial group and to incite racial hostility. Accordingly, we have held that the Fourteenth

Amendment requires state legislation that expressly distinguishes among citizens because of their race to be narrowly tailored to further a compelling governmental interest.

These principles apply not only to legislation that contains explicit racial distinctions, but also to those "rare" statutes that, although race-neutral, are, on their face, "unexplainable on grounds other than race."

Appellants contend that redistricting legislation that is so bizarre on its face that it is "unexplainable on grounds other than race," demands the same close scrutiny that we give other state laws that classify citizens by race. Our voting rights precedents support that conclusion.

[W]e believe that reapportionment is one area in which appearances do matter. A reapportionment plan that includes in one district individuals who belong to the same race, but who are otherwise separated by geographical and political boundaries, and who may have little in common with one another but the color of their skin, bears an uncomfortable resemblance to political apartheid. It reinforces the perception that members of the same racial group—regardless of their age, education, economic status, or the community in which they live—think alike, share the same political interests, and will prefer the same candidates at the polls. We have rejected such perceptions elsewhere as impermissible racial stereotypes.

The message that such districting sends to elected representatives is equally pernicious. When a district obviously is created solely to effectuate the perceived common interests of one racial group, elected officials are more likely to believe that their primary obligation is to represent only the members of that group, rather than their constituency as a whole. This is altogether antithetical to our system of representative democracy. . . .

For these reasons, we conclude that a plaintiff challenging a reapportionment statute under the Equal Protection Clause may state a claim by alleging that the legislation, though race-neutral on its face, rationally cannot be understood as anything other than an effort to separate voters into different districts on the basis of race, and that the separation lacks sufficient justification. It is unnecessary for us to decide whether or how a reapportionment plan that, on its face, can be explained in nonracial terms successfully could be challenged. Thus, we express no view as to whether "the intentional creation of minority-majority districts, without more" always gives rise to an equal protection claim. We hold only that, on the facts of this case, plaintiffs have stated a claim sufficient to defeat the state appellees' motion to dismiss.

. . .

. . . Today we hold only that appellants have stated a claim under the Equal Protection Clause by alleging that the North Carolina General Assembly adopted a reapportionment scheme so irrational on its face that it can be understood only as an effort to segregate voters into separate voting districts because of their race, and that the separation lacks sufficient justification. If the allegation of racial gerrymandering remains uncontradicted, the District Court further must determine whether the North Carolina plan is narrowly tailored to further a compelling governmental interest. Accordingly, we reverse the judgment of the District Court and remand the case for further proceedings consistent with this opinion.

. . .

JUSTICE WHITE, with whom JUSTICE BLACKMUN and JUSTICE STEVENS join, dissenting.

. . .

The grounds for my disagreement with the majority are simply stated: appellants have not presented a cognizable claim, because they have not alleged a cognizable injury. To date, we have held that only two types of state voting practices could give rise to a constitutional claim. The first involves direct and outright deprivation of the right to vote, for example by means of a poll tax or literacy test. Plainly, this variety is not implicated by appellants' allegations and need not detain us further. The second type of unconstitutional practice is that which "affects the political strength of various groups," in violation of the Equal Protection Clause. As for this latter category, we have insisted that members of the political or racial group demonstrate that the challenged action have the intent and effect of unduly diminishing their influence on the political process. Although this severe burden has limited the number of successful suits, it was adopted for sound reasons.

. . .

. . . The State has made no mystery of its intent, which was to . . . improv[e] the minority group's prospects of electing a candidate of its choice. I doubt that this constitutes a discriminatory purpose as defined in the Court's equal protection cases—i.e., an intent to aggravate "the unequal distribution of electoral power." But even assuming that it does, there is no question that appellants have not alleged the requisite discriminatory effects. Whites constitute roughly 76 percent of the total population and 79 percent of the voting age population in North Carolina. Yet, under the State's plan, they still constitute a voting majority in 10 (or 83 percent) of the 12 congressional districts. Though they might be dissatisfied at the prospect of casting a vote for a losing candidate—a lot shared by many, including a disproportionate number of minority voters—surely they cannot complain of discriminatory treatment.

Although I disagree with the holding that appellants' claim is cognizable, the Court's discussion of the level of scrutiny it requires warrants a few comments. I have no doubt that a State's compliance with the Voting Rights Act clearly constitutes a compelling interest. . . . Here, the Attorney General objected to the State's plan on the ground that it failed to draw a second minority-majority district for what appeared to be pretextual reasons. Rather than challenge this conclusion, North Carolina chose to draw the second district. . . . (A) State is entitled to take such action.

The Court, while seemingly agreeing with this position, warns that the State's redistricting effort must be "narrowly tailored" to further its interest in complying with the law. It is evident to me, however, that what North Carolina did was precisely tailored to meet the objection of the Attorney General to its prior plan. Hence, I see no need for a remand at all, even accepting the majority's basic approach to this case.

Furthermore, how it intends to manage this standard, I do no know. Is it more "narrowly tailored" to create an irregular minority-majority district as opposed to one that is compact but harms other State interests such as incumbency protection or the representation of rural interests? Of the following two options—creation of two minority-majority district—is one "narrowly tailored" and the other not? Once the Attorney General has found that a proposed redistricting change violates § 5's nonretrogression principle in that it will abridge a racial minority's right to vote, does "narrow tailoring" mean that the most the State can do is preserve the status quo? Or can it maintain that change, while attempting to enhance minority voting power in some other manner? This small sample only begins to scratch the surface of the problems raised by the majority's test. But it suffices to illustrate the unworkability of a standard that is divorced from any measure of constitutional harm. In that, State efforts to remedy minority vote dilution are wholly unlike what typically has been labeled "affirmative action." To the extent that no other racial group is injured, remedying a Voting Rights Act violation does not involve preferential treatment. It involves, instead, an attempt to equalize treatment, and to provide minority voters with an effective voice in the political process. The Equal Protection Clause of the constitution, surely, does not stand in the way.

Since I do not agree that petitioners alleged an Equal Protection violation and because the Court of Appeals faithfully followed the Court's prior cases, I dissent and would affirm the judgment below.

JUSTICE BLACKMUN, dissenting.

I join JUSTICE WHITE's dissenting opinion. . . . I . . . agree that the conscious use of race in redistricting does not violate the Equal Protection Clause unless the effect of the redistricting plan is to deny a particular group equal access to the political process or to minimize its voting strength unduly. It is particularly ironic that the case in which today's majority chooses to abandon settled law and to recognize for the first time this "analytically distinct" constitutional claim, is a challenge by white voters to the plan under which North Carolina has sent black representatives to Congress for the first time since Reconstruction. I dissent.

JUSTICE STEVENS, dissenting.

For the reasons stated by JUSTICE WHITE the decision of the District Court should be affirmed. . . .

. . . Unlike other contexts in which we have addressed the State's conscious use of race, electoral districting calls for decisions that nearly always require some consideration of race for legitimate reasons where there is a racially mixed population. As long as members of racial groups have the commonality of interest implicit in our ability to talk about concepts like "minority voting strength," and "dilution of minority votes," and as long as racial bloc voting takes place, legislators will have to take race into account in order to avoid dilution of minority voting strength in the districting plans they adopt. . . .

A second distinction between districting and most other governmental decisions in which race has figured is that those other decisions using racial criteria characteristically occur in circumstances in which the use of race to the advantage of one person is necessarily at the obvious expense of a member of a different race. Thus, for example, awarding government contracts on a racial basis excludes certain firms from competition on racial grounds. . . .

In districting, by contrast, the mere placement of an individual in one district instead of another denies no one a right or benefit provided to others. All citizens may register, vote, and be represented. In whatever district, the individual voter has a right to vote in each election, and the election will result in the voter's representation. As we have held, one's constitutional rights are not violated merely because the candidate one supports loses the election or because a group (including a racial group) to which one belongs winds up with a representative from outside that group. . . . Presumably because the legitimate consideration of race in a districting decision is usually inevitable under the Voting Rights Act when communities are racially mixed, however, and because, without more, it does not result in diminished political effectiveness for anyone, we have not taken the approach of applying the usual standard of such heightened "scrutiny" to race-based districting decisions. To be sure, as the Court says, it would be logically possible to apply strict scrutiny to these cases (and to uphold those uses of race that are permissible. But just because there frequently will be a constitutionally permissible use of race in electoral districting, as exemplified by the consideration of race to comply with the Voting Rights Act (quite apart from the consideration of race to remedy a violation of the Act or the Constitution), it has seemed more appropriate for the court to identify impermissible uses by describing particular effects sufficiently serious to justify recognition under the Fourteenth Amendment, the purpose and effect of the districting must be to devalue the effectiveness of a voter compared to what, as a group member, he would otherwise be able to enjoy.

A consequence of this categorical approach is the absence of any need for further searching "scrutiny" once it has been shown that a given districting decision has a purpose and effect falling within one of those categories. If a cognizable harm like dilution or the abridgment of the right to participate in the electoral process is shown, the districting plan violates the Fourteenth Amendment. If not, it does not. Under this approach, in the absence of an allegation of such cognizable harm, there is no need for further scrutiny because a gerrymandering claim cannot be proven without the element of harm. Nor if dilution is proven is there any need for further constitutional scrutiny; there has never been a suggestion that such use of race could be justified under any type of scrutiny, since the dilution of the right to vote can not be said to serve any legitimate governmental purpose.

The court offers no adequate justification for treating the narrow category of bizarrely shaped district claims differently form other districting claims. The only justification I can imagine would be the preservation of "sound districting principles," we have held that such principles are not constitutionally required, with the consequence that their absence cannot justify the distinct constitutional regime put in place by the Court today. Since there is no justification for the departure here from the principles that continue to govern electoral districting cases generally in accordance with our prior decisions, I would not respond to the seeming egregiousness of the redistricting now before us by untethering the concept of racial gerrymander in such a case from the concept of harm exemplified by dilution. In the absence of an allegation of such harm, I would affirm the judgment of the District Court. I respectfully dissent.

The Court says its new cause of action is justified by what I understand to be some ingredients of stigmatic harm, and by a "threa[t] . . . to our system of representative democracy," both caused by the mere adoption of a districting plan with the elements I have described in the text. To begin with, the complaint nowhere alleges any type of stigmatic harm. Putting that to one side, it seems utterly implausible to me to presume, as the Court does, that North Carolina's creation of this strangely-shaped minority-majority district "generates" within the white plaintiffs here anything comparable to "a feeling of inferiority as to their status in the community that may affect their hearts and minds in a way unlikely ever to be undone." As for representative democracy, I have difficulty seeing how it is threatened (indeed why it is not, rather, enhanced) by districts that are not even alleged to dilute anyone's vote.

The *Shaw* Court, in noting that "[c]lassifications of citizens on the basis of race 'are by their very nature odious to a free people whose institutions are founded upon the doctrine of equality,'" encapsulized a baseline principle of the post-segregation era. Given a model of reviewing racial classifications that has been characterized as "strict in theory, fatal in fact,"[182] some have wondered whether any legal distinction on the basis of race (beyond those necessary to remedy identified discrimination) could survive constitutional scrutiny. Although never the basis for a majority determination, some justices have indicated that "a social emergency rising to the level of imminent danger to life and limb—for example, a prison race riot, requiring temporary segregation of inmates," might survive Fourteenth Amendment review.[183]

---

[182] Gerald Gunther, *In Search of Evolving Doctrine on a Changing Court: A Model for a Newer Equal Protection*, 86 HARV. L. REV. 1, 8 (1972).

[183] City of Richmond v. J. A. Croson Co. 488 U.S. 469, 521 (1989)(Scalia, J., concurring), citing Lee v. Washington, 390 U.S. 333, 334 (1968)(Black, J., concurring).

In *Shaw*, the Court refrained from determining whether purposeful creation of minority-majority districts by itself generated an equal protection claim. Two years later, in *Miller v. Johnson*, it concluded that redistricting driven predominantly by attention to race violated the Fourteenth Amendment. As in *Shaw*, and consistent with its review of racial preferences (*see infra* pp. 597-632), the Court condemned such plans as sources of stigma.

Miller v. Johnson
115 S.Ct. 2475 (1995)

JUSTICE KENNEDY delivered the opinion of the Court.

The constitutionality of Georgia's congressional redistricting plan is at issue here. In *Shaw v. Reno*, we held that a plaintiff states a claim under the Equal Protection Clause by alleging that a state redistricting plan, on its face, has no rational explanation save as an effort to separate voters on the basis of race. The question we now decide is whether Georgia's new Eleventh District gives rise to a valid equal protection claim under the principles announced in *Shaw*, and, if so, whether it can be sustained nonetheless as narrowly tailored to serve a compelling governmental interest.

I

A

The Equal Protection Clause of the Fourteenth Amendment provides that no State shall "deny to any person within its jurisdiction the equal protection of the laws." Its central mandate is racial neutrality in governmental decisionmaking. See, e.g., *Loving v. Virginia*, 388 U.S. 1 (1967). Though application of this imperative raises difficult questions, the basic principle is straightforward: "Racial and ethnic distinctions of any sort are inherently suspect and thus call for the most exacting judicial examination. . . . This perception of racial and ethnic distinctions is rooted in our Nation's constitutional and demographic history." This rule obtains with equal force regardless of "the race of those burdened or benefited by a particular classification." Laws classifying citizens on the basis of race cannot be upheld unless they are narrowly tailored to achieving a compelling state interest.

In *Shaw v. Reno*, we recognized that these equal protection principles govern a State's drawing of congressional districts, though, as our cautious approach there discloses, application of these principles to electoral districting is a most delicate task. Our analysis began from the premise that "laws that explicitly distinguish between individuals on racial grounds fall within the core of [the Equal Protection Clause's] prohibition." This prohibition extends not just to explicit racial classifications, but also to laws neutral on their face but "'unexplainable on grounds other than race.'" Applying this basic Equal Protection analysis in the voting rights context, we held that "redistricting legislation that is so bizarre on its face that it is 'unexplainable on grounds other than race,' . . . demands the same close scrutiny that we give other state laws that classify citizens by race."

This case requires us to apply the principles articulated in *Shaw* to the most recent congressional redistricting plan enacted by the State of Georgia.

B

In 1965, the Attorney General designated Georgia a covered jurisdiction under § 4(b) of the Voting Rights Act. In consequence, § 5 of the Act requires Georgia to obtain either administrative preclearance by the Attorney General or approval by the United States District Court for the District of Columbia of any change in a "standard, practice, or procedure with respect to voting" made after November 1, 1964. The preclearance mechanism applies to congressional redistricting plans, see, e.g., *Beer v. United States*, and requires that the proposed change "not have the purpose and will not have the effect of denying or abridging the right to vote on account of race or color." "The purpose of § 5 has always been to insure that no voting-procedure changes would be made that would lead to a retrogression in the position of racial minorities with respect to their effective exercise of the electoral franchise."

[The congressional districting plan at

issue is] the so-called "max-black" plan, drafted by the American Civil Liberties Union (ACLU) for the [Georgia] General Assembly's black caucus. The key to the ACLU's plan was the "Macon/Savannah trade." The dense black population in the Macon region would be transferred from the Eleventh District to the Second, converting the Second into a majority-black district, and the Eleventh District's loss in black population would be offset by extending the Eleventh to include the black populations in Savannah.

. . . The black population of Meriwether County was gouged out of the Third District and attached to the Second District by the narrowest of land bridges; Effingham and Chatham Counties were split to make way for the Savannah extension, which itself split the City of Savannah; and the plan as a whole split 26 counties, 23 more than the existing congressional districts."

The new plan also enacted the Macon/Savannah swap necessary to create a third majority-black district. The Eleventh District lost the black population of Macon, but picked up Savannah, thereby connecting the black neighborhoods of metropolitan Atlanta and the poor black populace of coastal Chatham County, though 260 miles apart in distance and worlds apart in culture. In short, the social, political and economic makeup of the Eleventh District tells a tale of disparity, not community. As the attached appendices attest,

> "the populations of the Eleventh are centered around four discrete, widely spaced urban centers that have absolutely nothing to do with each other, and stretch the district hundreds of miles across rural counties and narrow swamp corridors." "The dense population centers of the approved Eleventh District were all majority-black, all at the periphery of the district, and in the case of Atlanta, Augusta and Savannah, all tied to a sparsely populated rural core by even less populated land bridges. Extending from Atlanta to the Atlantic, the Eleventh covered 6,784.2 square miles, splitting eight counties and five municipalities along the way."

> The Almanac of American Politics has this to say about the Eleventh District: "Geographically, it is a monstrosity, stretching from Atlanta to Savannah. Its core is the plantation country in the center of the state, lightly populated, but heavily black. It links by narrow corridors the black neighborhoods in Augusta, Savannah and southern DeKalb County."

Elections were held under the new congressional redistricting plan on November 4, 1992, and black candidates were elected to Congress from all three majority-black districts. On January 13, 1994, appellees, five white voters from the Eleventh District, filed this action against various state officials in the United States District Court for the Southern District of Georgia. As residents of the challenged Eleventh District, all appellees had standing. Their suit alleged that Georgia's Eleventh District was a racial gerrymander and so a violation of the Equal Protection Clause as interpreted in *Shaw v. Reno*. A three-judge court was convened pursuant to 28 U.S.C. § 2284, and the United States and a number of Georgia residents intervened in support of the defendant-state officials.

A majority of the District Court panel agreed that the Eleventh District was invalid under *Shaw*, with one judge dissenting. . . .

. . .

II

A

Finding that the "evidence of the General Assembly's intent to racially gerrymander the Eleventh District is overwhelming, and practically stipulated by the parties involved," the District Court held that race was the predominant, overriding factor in drawing the Eleventh District. Appellants do not take issue with the court's factual finding of this racial motivation. Rather, they contend that evidence of a legislature's deliberate classification of voters on the basis of race cannot alone suffice to state a claim under *Shaw*. They argue that, regardless of the legislature's purposes, a plaintiff must demonstrate that a district's shape is so bizarre that it is unexplainable other than on the basis of race, and that appellees failed to make that showing here. Appellants' conception of the constitutional violation misapprehends our holding in *Shaw* and the Equal Protection precedent upon which *Shaw* relied.

. . . Just as the State may not, absent extraordinary segregate citizens on the basis of race in its public parks, buses, golf courses, beaches, and schools, so did we recognize in *Shaw* that it may not separate its citizens into different voting districts on the basis of race. The idea is a simple one: "At the heart of the Constitution's guarantee of equal protection lies the simple command that the Government must treat citizens 'as individuals, not "as simply components of a racial, religious, sexual or national class."'" When the State assigns voters on the basis of race, it engages in the offensive and demeaning assumption that voters of a particular race, because of their race, "think alike, share the same political interests, and will prefer the same candidates at the polls."

Race-based assignments "embody stereotypes that treat individuals as the product of their race, evaluating their thoughts and efforts—their very worth as citizens—according to a criterion barred to the Government by history and the Constitution."They also cause society serious harm. As we concluded in *Shaw*:

"Racial classifications with respect to voting carry particular dangers. Racial gerrymandering, even for remedial purposes, may balkanize us into competing racial factions; it threatens to carry us further from the goal of a political system in which race no longer matters—a goal that the Fourteenth and Fifteenth Amendments embody, and to which the Nation continues to aspire. It is for these reasons that race-based districting by our state legislatures demands close judicial scrutiny."

Our observation in *Shaw* of the consequences of racial stereotyping was not meant to suggest that a district must be bizarre on its face before there is a constitutional violation. Nor was our conclusion in Shaw that in certain instances a district's appearance (or, to be more precise, its appearance in combination with certain demographic evidence) can give rise to an equal protection claim, a holding that bizarreness was a threshold showing, as appellants believe it to be. Our circumspect approach and narrow holding in *Shaw* did not erect an artificial rule barring accepted equal protection analysis in other redistricting cases. Shape is relevant not because bizarreness is a necessary element of the constitutional wrong or a threshold requirement of proof, but because it may be persuasive circumstantial evidence that race for its own sake, and not other districting principles, was the legislature's dominant and controlling rationale in drawing its district lines. The logical implication, as courts applying *Shaw* have recognized, is that parties may rely on evidence other than bizarreness to establish race-based districting.

Our reasoning in *Shaw* compels this conclusion. We recognized in *Shaw* that, outside the districting context, statutes are subject to strict scrutiny under the Equal Protection Clause not just when they contain express racial classifications, but also when, though race neutral on their face, they are motivated by a racial purpose or object. In the rare case, where the effect of government action is a pattern "'unexplainable on grounds other than race,'" "the evidentiary inquiry is . . . relatively easy." As early as *Yick Wo v. Hopkins*, the Court recognized that a laundry permit ordinance was administered in a deliberate way to exclude all Chinese from the laundry business; and in

Gomillion v. Lightfoot, the Court concluded that the redrawing of Tuskegee, Alabama's municipal boundaries left no doubt that the plan was designed to exclude blacks. Even in those cases, however, it was the presumed racial purpose of state action, not its stark manifestation, that was the constitutional violation. Patterns of discrimination as conspicuous as these are rare, and are not a necessary predicate to a violation of the Equal Protection Clause. In the absence of a pattern as stark as those in *Yick Wo* or *Gomillion*, "impact alone is not determinative, and the Court must look to other evidence" of race-based decisionmaking.

Shaw applied these same principles to redistricting. "In some exceptional cases, a reapportionment plan may be so highly irregular that, on its face, it rationally cannot be understood as anything other than an effort to 'segregate . . . voters' on the basis of race." In other cases, where the district is not so bizarre on its face that it discloses a racial design, the proof will be more "difficult." Although it was not necessary in *Shaw* to consider further the proof required in these more difficult cases, the logical import of our reasoning is that evidence other than a district's bizarre shape can be used to support the claim.

Appellants and some of their amici argue that the Equal Protection Clause's general proscription on race-based decisionmaking does not obtain in the districting context because redistricting by definition involves racial considerations. Underlying their argument are the very stereotypical assumptions the Equal Protection Clause forbids. It is true that redistricting in most cases will implicate a political calculus in which various interests compete for recognition, but it does not follow from this that individuals of the same race share a single political interest. The view that they do is "based on the demeaning notion that members of the defined racial groups ascribe to certain 'minority views' that must be different from those of other citizens," the precise use of race as a proxy the Constitution prohibits. . . .

In sum, we make clear that parties alleging that a State has assigned voters on the basis of race are neither confined in their proof to evidence regarding the district's geometry and makeup nor required to make a threshold showing of bizarreness. Today's case requires us further to consider the requirements of the proof necessary to sustain this equal protection challenge.

B

. . . Redistricting legislatures will, for example, almost always be aware of racial demographics; but it does not follow that race predominates in the redistricting process. The distinction between being aware of racial considerations and being motivated by them may be difficult to make. This evidentiary difficulty, together with the sensitive nature of redistricting and the presumption of good faith that must be accorded legislative enactments, requires courts to exercise extraordinary caution in adjudicating claims that a state has drawn district lines on the basis of race. The plaintiff's burden is to show, either through circumstantial evidence of a district's shape and demographics or more direct evidence going to legislative purpose, that race was the predominant factor motivating the legislature's decision to place a significant number of voters within or without a particular district. To make this showing, a plaintiff must prove that the legislature subordinated traditional race-neutral districting principles, including but not limited to compactness, contiguity, respect for political subdivisions or communities defined by actual shared interests, to racial considerations. Where these or other race-neutral considerations are the basis for redistricting legislation, and are not subordinated to race, a state can "defeat a claim that a district has been gerrymandered on racial lines." These principles inform the plaintiff's burden of proof at trial. Of course, courts must also recognize these principles, and the intrusive potential of judicial intervention into the legislative realm, when assessing under the Federal Rules of Civil Procedure the adequacy of a plaintiff's showing at the various stages of litigation and determining whether to permit discovery or trial to proceed.

In our view, the District Court applied the correct analysis, and its finding that race was the predominant factor motivating the drawing of the Eleventh District was not clearly erroneous. The court found it was "exceedingly obvious" from the shape of the Eleventh District, together with the relevant racial demographics, that the drawing of narrow land bridges to incorporate within the District outlying appendages containing nearly 80% of the district's total black population was a deliberate attempt to bring black populations into the district. Although by comparison with other districts the geometric shape of the Eleventh District may not seem bizarre on its face, when its shape is considered in conjunction with its racial and population densities, the story of racial gerrymandering seen by the District Court becomes much clearer. Although this evidence is quite compelling, we need not determine whether it was, standing alone, sufficient to establish a *Shaw* claim that the Eleventh District is unexplainable other than by race. The District Court had before it considerable additional evidence showing that the General Assembly was motivated by a predominant, overriding desire to assign black populations to the Eleventh District and thereby permit the creation of a third majority-black district in the Second.

The court found that "it became obvious," both from the Justice Department's objection letters and the three preclearance rounds in general, "that [the Justice Department] would accept nothing less than abject surrender to its maximization agenda." . . .

In light of its well-supported finding, the District Court was justified in rejecting the various alternative explanations offered for the District. Although a legislature's compliance with "traditional districting principles such as compactness, contiguity, and respect for political subdivisions" may well suffice to refute a claim of racial gerrymandering, appellants cannot make such a refutation where, as here, those factors were subordinated to racial objectives. Georgia's Attorney General objected to the Justice Department's demand for three majority-black districts on the ground that to do so the State would have to "violate all reasonable standards of compactness and contiguity." This statement from a state official is powerful evidence that the legislature subordinated traditional districting principles to race . . .

Nor can the State's districting legislation be rescued by mere recitation of purported communities of interest. The evidence was compelling "that there are no tangible 'communities of interest' spanning the hundreds of miles of the Eleventh District." A comprehensive report demonstrated the fractured political, social, and economic interests within the Eleventh District's black population. It is apparent that it was not alleged shared interests but rather the object of maximizing the District's black population and obtaining Justice Department approval that in fact explained the General Assembly's actions. . . .

Race was, as the District Court found, the predominant, overriding factor explaining the General Assembly's decision to attach to the Eleventh District various appendages containing dense majority-black populations. As a result, Georgia's congressional redistricting plan cannot be upheld unless it satisfies strict scrutiny, our most rigorous and exacting standard of constitutional review.

III

To satisfy strict scrutiny, the State must demonstrate that its districting legislation is narrowly tailored to achieve a compelling interest. There is a "significant state interest in eradicating the effects of past racial discrimination." The State does not argue, however, that it created the Eleventh District to remedy past discrimination, and with good reason: there is little doubt that the State's true interest in designing the Eleventh District was creating a third majority-black district to satisfy the Justice Department's preclearance demands. Whether or not in some cases compliance with the Voting Rights Act, standing alone, can provide a compelling interest independent of any interest in remedying past discrimination, it cannot do so here. As we suggested in *Shaw*, compliance with federal antidiscrimination laws cannot justify race-based districting where the challenged district was not reasonably necessary under a constitutional reading and application of those laws. The congressional plan challenged here was not required by the Voting Rights Act under a correct reading of the statute.

. . . It is . . . safe to say that the congressional plan enacted in the end was required in order to obtain preclearance. It does not follow, however, that the plan was required by the substantive provisions of the Voting Rights Act.

We do not accept the contention that the State has a compelling interest in complying with whatever preclearance mandates the Justice Department issues. When a state governmental entity seeks to justify race-based remedies to cure the effects of past discrimination, we do not accept the government's mere assertion that the remedial action is required. Rather, we insist on a strong basis in evidence of the harm being remedied. . . . Our presumptive skepticism of all racial classifications, prohibits us as well from accepting on its face the Justice Department's conclusion that racial districting is necessary under the Voting Rights Act. Where a State relies on the Department's determination that race-based districting is necessary to comply with the Voting Rights Act, the judiciary retains an independent obligation in adjudicating consequent equal protection challenges to ensure that the State's actions are narrowly tailored to achieve a compelling interest. Were we to accept the Justice Department's objection itself as a compelling interest adequate to insulate racial districting from constitutional review, we would be surrendering to the Executive Branch our role in enforcing the constitutional limits on race-based official action. We may not do so.

. . . When the Justice Department's interpretation of the Act compels race-based districting, it by definition raises a serious constitutional question. . . .

Instead of grounding its objections on evidence of a discriminatory purpose, it would appear the Government was driven by its policy of maximizing majority-black districts. Although the Government now disavows having had that policy, and seems to concede its impropriety, the District Court's well-documented factual finding was that the Department did adopt a maximization policy and followed it in objecting to Georgia's first two plans. One of the two Department of Justice line attorneys overseeing the Georgia preclearance process himself disclosed that "what we did and what I did specifically was to take a . . . map of the State of Georgia shaded for race, shaded by minority concentration, and overlay the districts that were drawn by the State of Georgia and see how well those lines adequately reflected black voting strength." In utilizing § 5 to require States to create majority-minority districts wherever possible, the Department of Justice expanded its authority under the statute beyond what Congress intended and we have upheld.

. . .

IV

The Voting Rights Act, and its grant of authority to the federal courts to uncover official efforts to abridge minorities' right to vote, has been of vital importance in eradicating invidious discrimination from the electoral process and enhancing the legitimacy of our political institutions. Only if our political system and our society cleanse themselves of that discrimination will all members of the polity share an equal opportunity to gain public office regardless of race. As a Nation we share both the obligation and the aspiration of working toward this end. The end is neither assured nor well served, however, by carving electorates into racial blocs. "If our society is to continue to progress as a multiracial democracy, it must recognize that the automatic invocation of race stereotypes retards that progress and causes continued hurt and injury." It takes a shortsighted and unauthorized view of the Voting Rights Act to invoke that statute, which has played a decisive role in redressing some of our worst forms of discrimination, to demand the very racial stereotyping the Fourteenth Amendment forbids.

. . .

The judgment of the District Court is affirmed, and the case is remanded for further proceedings consistent with this decision.

JUSTICE O'CONNOR, concurring.

I understand the threshold standard the Court adopts—"that the legislature subordinated traditional race-neutral districting principles . . . to racial considerations,"—to be a demanding one. To invoke strict scrutiny, a plaintiff must show that the State has relied on race in substantial disregard of customary and traditional districting practices. Those practices provide a crucial frame of reference and therefore constitute a significant governing principle in cases of this kind. . . .

. . .

JUSTICE STEVENS, dissenting.

JUSTICE GINSBURG has explained why the District Court's opinion on the merits was erroneous and why this Court's law-changing decision will breed unproductive litigation. I join her excellent opinion without reservation. I add these comments because I believe the respondents in these cases, have not suffered any legally cognizable injury.

. . .

The Court . . . equat[es] the injury it imagines respondents have suffered with the injuries African Americans suffered under segregation. The heart of respondents' claim, by the Court's account, is that "a State's assignment of voters on the basis of race," violates the Equal Protection Clause for the same reason a State may not "segregate citizens on the basis of race in its public parks, buses, golf courses, beaches, and schools. This equation, however, fails to elucidate the elusive *Shaw* injury. Our desegregation cases redressed the exclusion of black citizens from public facilities reserved for whites. In this case, in contrast, any voter, black or white, may live in the Eleventh District. What respondents contest is the inclusion of too many black voters in the District as drawn. In my view, if respondents allege no vote dilution, that inclusion can cause them no conceivable injury.

The Court's equation of *Shaw* claims with our desegregation decisions is inappropriate for another reason. In each of those cases, legal segregation frustrated the public interest in diversity and tolerance by barring African Americans from joining whites in the activities at issue. The districting plan here, in contrast, serves the interest in diversity and tolerance by increasing the likelihood that a meaningful number of black representatives will add their voices to legislative debates. "There is no moral or constitutional equivalence between a policy that is designed to perpetuate a caste system and one that seeks to eradicate racial subordination." That racial integration of the sort attempted by Georgia now appears more vulnerable to judicial challenge than some policies alleged to perpetuate racial bias, is anomalous, to say the least.

Equally distressing is the Court's equation of traditional gerrymanders, designed to maintain or enhance a dominant group's power, with a dominant group's decision to share its power with a previously underrepresented group. In my view, districting plans violate the Equal Protection Clause when they "serve no purpose other than to favor one segment—whether racial, ethnic, religious, economic, or political—that may occupy a position of strength at a particular point in time, or to disadvantage a politically weak segment of the community." In contrast, I do not see how a districting plan that favors a politically weak group can violate equal protection. The Constitution does not mandate any form of proportional representation, but it certainly permits a State to adopt a policy that promotes fair representation of different groups. . . .

The Court's refusal to distinguish an enactment that helps a minority group from enactments that cause it harm is especially unfortunate at the intersection of race and voting, given that African Americans and other disadvantaged groups have struggled so long and so hard for inclusion in that most central exercise of our democracy. I have long believed that treating racial groups differently from other identifiable groups of voters, as the Court does today, is itself an invidious racial classification. Racial minorities should receive neither more nor less protection than other groups against gerrymanders. A fortiori, racial minorities should not be less eligible than other groups to benefit from districting plans the majority designs to aid them.

. . .

JUSTICE GINSBURG, with whom JUSTICES STEVENS and BREYER join, and with whom JUSTICE SOUTER joins except as to Part III-B, dissenting.

. . .

II

A

Before *Shaw v. Reno*, this Court invoked the Equal Protection Clause to justify intervention in the quintessentially political task of legislative districting in two circumstances: to enforce the one-person-one-vote requirement, and to prevent dilution of a minority group's voting strength.

In *Shaw*, the Court recognized a third basis for an equal protection challenge to a State's apportionment plan. The Court wrote cautiously, emphasizing that judicial intervention is exceptional: "Strict [judicial] scrutiny" is in order, the Court declared, if a district is "so extremely irregular on its face that it rationally can be viewed only as an effort to segregate the races for purposes of voting."

"Extrem[e] irregularity" was evident in *Shaw*, the Court explained. . . . The problem in Shaw was not the plan architects' consideration of race as relevant in redistricting. Rather, in the Court's estimation, it was the virtual exclusion of other factors from the calculus. Traditional districting practices were cast aside, the Court concluded, with race alone steering placement of district lines.

B

The record before us does not show that race similarly overwhelmed traditional districting practices in Georgia. Although the Georgia General Assembly prominently considered race in shaping the Eleventh District, race did not crowd out all other factors, as the Court found it did in North Carolina's delineation of the Shaw district.

In contrast to the snake-like North Carolina district inspected in *Shaw*, Georgia's Eleventh District is hardly "bizarre," "extremely irregular," or "irrational on its face." Instead, the Eleventh District's design reflects significant consideration of "traditional districting factors (such as keeping political subdivisions intact) and the usual political process of compromise and trades for a variety of nonracial reasons." The District covers a core area in central and eastern Georgia, and its total land area of 6,780 square miles is about average for the State. The border of the Eleventh District runs 1,184 miles, in line with Georgia's Second District, which has a 1,243-mile border, and the State's Eighth District, with a border running 1,155 miles.

Nor does the Eleventh District disrespect the boundaries of political subdivisions. Of the 22 counties in the District, 14 are intact and 8 are divided. . . .

Evidence at trial similarly shows that considerations other than race went into determining the Eleventh District's boundaries. . . .

Georgia's Eleventh District, in sum, is not an outlier district shaped without reference to familiar districting techniques. Tellingly, the District that the Court's decision today unsettles is not among those on a statistically calculated list of the 28 most bizarre districts in the United States, a study prepared in the wake of our decision in *Shaw*.

C

The Court suggests that it was not Georgia's legislature, but the U.S. Department of Justice, that effectively drew the lines, and that Department officers did so with nothing but race in mind. Yet the "Max-Black" plan advanced by the Attorney General was not the plan passed by the Georgia General Assembly.

And although the Attorney General refused preclearance to the first two plans approved by Georgia's legislature, the State was not thereby disarmed; Georgia could have demanded relief from the Department's objections by instituting a civil action in the United States District Court for the District of Columbia, with ultimate review in this Court. Instead of pursuing that avenue, the State chose to adopt the plan here in controversy—a plan the State forcefully defends before us. We should respect Georgia's choice by taking its position on brief as genuine.

D

Along with attention to size, shape, and political subdivisions, the Court recognizes as an appropriate districting principle, "respect for . . . communities defined by actual shared interests." The Court finds no community here, however, because a report in the record showed "fractured political, social, and economic interests within the Eleventh District's black population."

To accommodate the reality of ethnic bonds, legislatures have long drawn voting districts along ethnic lines. Our Nation's cities are full of districts identified by their ethnic character—Chinese, Irish, Italian, Jewish, Polish, Russian, for example. . . . The creation of ethnic districts reflecting felt identity is not ordinarily viewed as offensive or demeaning to those included in the delineation.

III

To separate permissible and impermissible use of race in legislative apportionment, the Court orders strict scrutiny for districting plans "predominantly motivated" by race. No longer can a State avoid judicial oversight by giving—as in this case—genuine and measurable consideration to traditional districting practices. Instead, a federal case can be mounted whenever plaintiffs plausibly allege that other factors carried less weight than race. This invitation to litigate against the State seems to me neither necessary nor proper.

A

The Court derives its test from diverse opinions on the relevance of race in contexts distinctly unlike apportionment. The controlling idea, the Court says, is "'the simple command [at the heart of the Constitution's guarantee of equal protection] that the Government must treat citizens as individuals, not as simply components of a racial, religious, sexual or national class.'" *But cf. Strauder v. West Virginia*, 100 U.S. 303, 307, (1880) (pervading purpose of post-Civil War Amendments was to bar discrimination against once-enslaved race).

In adopting districting plans, . . . States do not treat people as individuals. Apportionment schemes, by their very nature, assemble people in groups. States do not assign voters to districts based on merit or achievement, standards States might use in hiring employees or engaging contractors. Rather, legislators classify voters in groups—by economic, geographical, political, or social characteristics—and then "reconcile the competing claims of [these] groups."

That ethnicity defines some of these groups is a political reality. Until now, no constitutional infirmity has been seen in districting Irish or Italian voters together, for example, so long as the delineation does not abandon familiar apportionment practices. If Chinese-Americans and Russian-Americans may seek and secure group recognition in the delineation of voting districts, then African-Americans should not be dissimilarly treated. Otherwise, in the name of equal protection, we would shut out "the very minority group whose history in the United States gave birth to the Equal Protection Clause."

B

Under the Court's approach, judicial review of the same intensity, i.e., strict scrutiny, is in order once it is determined that an apportionment is predominantly motivated by race. It matters not at all, in this new regime, whether the apportionment dilutes or enhances minority voting strength. As very recently observed, however, "there is no moral or constitutional equivalence between a policy that is designed to perpetuate a caste system and one that seeks to eradicate racial subordination."

Special circumstances justify vigilant judicial inspection to protect minority voters—circumstances that do not apply to majority voters. A history of exclusion from state politics left racial minorities without clout to extract provisions for fair representation in the lawmaking forum. The equal protection rights of minority voters thus could have remained unrealized absent the Judiciary's close surveillance. The majority, by definition, encounters no such blockage. White voters in Georgia do not lack means to exert strong pressure on their state legislators. The force of their numbers is itself a powerful determiner of what the

legislature will do that does not coincide with perceived majority interests.

State legislatures like Georgia's today operate under federal constraints imposed by the Voting Rights Act—constraints justified by history and designed by Congress to make once-subordinated people free and equal citizens. But these federal constraints do not leave majority voters in need of extraordinary judicial solicitude. The Attorney General, who administers the Voting Rights Act's preclearance requirements, is herself a political actor. She has a duty to enforce the law Congress passed, and she is no doubt aware of the political cost of venturing too far to the detriment of majority voters. Majority voters, furthermore, can press the State to seek judicial review if the Attorney General refuses to preclear a plan that the voters favor. Finally, the Act is itself a political measure, subject to modification in the political process.

C

The Court's disposition renders redistricting perilous work for state legislatures. Statutory mandates and political realities may require States to consider race when drawing district lines. But today's decision is a counterforce; it opens the way for federal litigation if "traditional . . . districting principles" arguably were accorded less weight than race. Genuine attention to traditional districting practices and avoidance of bizarre configurations seemed, under *Shaw*, to provide a safe harbor. In view of today's decision, that is no longer the case.

Only after litigation—under either the Voting Rights Act, the Court's new *Miller* standard, or both—will States now be assured that plans conscious of race are safe. Federal judges in large numbers may be drawn into the fray. This enlargement of the judicial role is unwarranted. The reapportionment plan that resulted from Georgia's political process merited this Court's approbation, not its condemnation. Accordingly, I dissent.

DEL: The Court's hard-line rhetoric against racial politics rings hollow when examined in context with a national history defined by such considerations. From the constitutional compromise that counted slaves as three-fifths of a person for representational and tax purposes to modern voting practices reflecting tribal allegiance, racial politics have been rooted in the nation's traditions. Although less enthusiastic about ferreting out the vestiges of racial discrimination in the context of education, the Court has dedicated itself to purging race from the electoral process—a commitment to using judicial power to define or impose a moral vision that is mystifying when the lesson of *Brown*'s devolution is considered. Critical reaction to the *Johnson* decision may be a function of whether a functionally segregated society is perceived as a temporary waystation or final destination for the republic. Maximum-minority districting may represent an investment in short-term gain at the risk of long-term interests. In creating a ceiling of safe minority districts, the method actually may marginalize minorities by discounting their brokering and coalition-building potential in racially diverse districts. The flip side of some safe districts for minorities is even more safe districts for predominantly white suburbanites who are further empowered to pursue a course of insularity. Given the net result of such a trade-off, it is not surprising that the Republican Party suspended its profound animus toward racial criteria and with the NAACP coorchestrated maximum-minority redistricting strategy.

Batson v. Kentucky
476 U.S. 79 (1986)

. . .

Purposeful racial discrimination in selection of the venire violates a defendant's right to equal protection because it denies him the protection that a trial by jury is intended to secure. "The very idea of a jury is a body . . . composed of the peers or equals of the person whose rights it is selected or summoned to determine; that is, of his neighbors, fellows, associates, persons having the same legal status in society as that which he holds."

The petit jury has occupied a central position in our system of justice by safeguarding a person accused of crime against the arbitrary exercise of power by prosecutor or judge. Those on the venire must be "indifferently chosen," to secure the defendant's right under the Fourteenth Amendment to "protection of life and liberty against race or color prejudice."

Racial discrimination in selection of jurors harms not only the accused whose life or liberty they are summoned to try. Competence to serve as a juror ultimately depends on an assessment of individual qualifications and ability impartially to consider evidence presented at a trial. A person's race simply "is unrelated to his fitness as a juror." As long ago as *Strauder*, therefore, the Court recognized that participation in jury service on account of his race, the State unconstitutionally discriminated against the excluded juror.

The harm from discriminatory jury selection extends beyond that inflicted on the defendant and the excluded juror to touch the entire community. Selection procedures that purposefully exclude black persons from juries undermine public confidence in the fairness of our system of justice. Discrimination within the judicial system is most pernicious because it is "a stimulant to that race prejudice which is an impediment to securing to [black citizens] that equal justice which the law aims to secure to all others." [A] defendant may establish a prima facie purposeful discrimination in selection of the petit jury solely on evidence concerning the prosecutor's exercise of peremptory challenges at the defendant's trial. To establish

such a case, the defendant first must show that he is a member of a cognizable racial group, and that the prosecutor has exercised peremptory challenges to remove from the venire members of the defendant's race. Second, the defendant is entitled to rely on the fact, as to which there can be no dispute, that peremptory challenges constitute a jury selection practice that permits "those to discriminate who are of a mind to discriminate." Finally, the defendant must show that these facts and any other relevant circumstances raise an inference that the prosecutor used that practice to exclude the veniremen from the petit jury on account of their race. This combination of factors in the empaneling of the petit jury, as in the selection of the venire, raises the necessary inference of purposeful discrimination.

In deciding whether the defendant has made the requisite showing, the trial court should consider all relevant circumstances. For example, a "pattern" of strikes against black jurors included in the particular venire might give rise to an inference of discrimination. Similarly, the prosecutor's questions and statements during *voir dire* examination and in exercising his challenges may support or refute an inference of discriminatory purpose. These examples are merely illustrative. We have confidence that trial judges, experienced in supervising *voir dire,* will be able to decide if the circumstances concerning the prosecutor's use of peremptory challenges creates a prima facie case of discrimination against black jurors.

Once the defendant makes a prima facie showing, the burden shifts to the State to come forward with a neutral explanation for challenging black jurors. Though this requirement imposes a limitation in some cases on the full peremptory character of the historic challenge, we emphasize that the prosecutor's explanation need not rise to the level justifying exercise of a challenge for cause. But the prosecutor may not rebut the defendant's prima facie case of discrimination by stating merely that he challenged jurors of the defendant's race on the assumption—or his intuitive judgment—that they would be partial to the defendant because of their shared race.

Just as the Equal Protection Clause forbids the States to exclude black persons from the venire on the assumption that blacks as a group are unqualified to serve as jurors, *supra,* so it forbids the States to strike black veniremen on the assumption that they will be biased in a particular case simply because the defendant is black. The core guarantee of equal protection, ensuring citizens that their State will not discriminate on account of race, would be meaningless were we to approve the exclusion of jurors on the basis of such assumptions, which arise solely from the jurors' race. Nor may the prosecutor rebut the defendant's case merely by denying that he had a discriminatory motive or "affirm[ing] [his] good faith in making individual selections." If these general assertions were accepted as rebutting a defendant's prima facie case, the Equal Protection Clause "would be but a vain and illusory requirement." The prosecutor therefore must articulate a neutral explanation related to the particular case to be tried." The trial court then will have the duty to determine if the defendant has established purposeful discriminations.

JUSTICE REHNQUIST, with whom THE CHIEF JUSTICE joins, dissenting.

. . .

I cannot subscribe to the Court's unprecedented use of the Equal Protection Clause to restrict the historic scope of the peremptory challenge, which has been described as "a necessary part of trial by jury. In my view, there is simply nothing "unequal" about the State's using its peremptory challenges to strike blacks from the jury in cases involving black defendants, so long as such challenges are also used to exclude whites in cases involving white defendants, Hispanics in cases involving Hispanic defendants, Asians in cases involving Asian defendants, and so on. This case-specific use of peremptory challenges by the State does not single out blacks, or members of any other race for that matter, for discriminatory treatment. Such use of peremptories is at best based upon seat-of-the-pants instincts, which are undoubtedly crudely stereotypical and may in many cases be hopelessly mistaken. But as long as they are applied across-the-board to jurors of all races and nationalities, I do not see—and the Court most certainly has not explained—how their use violates the Equal Protection Clause.

. . .

The prohibition upon race-dependent use of peremptory challenges has expanded into a comprehensive bar. Noting that "racial exclusion in this official forum compounds the racial insult inherent in judging a citizen by the color of his or her skin," the Court in *Edmonson v. Leesville Concrete Co.* extended the *Batson* principle to civil trials.[184] Justice O'Connor, joined by Chief Justice Rehnquist and Justice Scalia, dissented on grounds that "[t]he peremptory is, by design an enclave of private action" and thus not constitutionally significant.[185] In *Georgia v. McCollum*, the Court determined that race-conscious peremptory strikes by a criminal defendant were impermissible.[186] As Justice Blackmun put it for the majority, "public confidence" is no less "undermined where a defendant, assisted by racially discriminatory peremptory strikes, obtains an acquittal."[187] Justices O'Connor and Scalia dissented on grounds that a peremptory challenge by a criminal defendant did not constitute state action and that the majority was compounding a bad decision in *Edmonson* by extending it to an illogical conclusion.[188] Although concurring in the result, Justice Thomas warned that the decision put black criminal defendants at greatest risk and they would "rue the day that this Court ventured down the road that inexorably will lead to the elimination of peremptory strikes."[189]

---

[184] Edmonson v. Leesville Concrete Co., 111 S. Ct. 2077, 2080 (1991).

[185] *Id.* at 2090 (O'Connor, J., dissenting).

[186] Georgia v. McCollum, 112 S.Ct. 2348, 2359 (1992).

[187] *Id.* at 2354.

[188] *Id.* at 2361–63 (O'Connor, J., dissenting); *id.* at 2364–65 (Scalia, J., dissenting).

[189] *Id.* at 2360 (Thomas, J., concurring). *See also id.* at 2364 (O'Connor, J., concurring).

DEL: The Court's decisions on peremptory challenges are based on the premise that race cannot matter, even though in the real world it does matter. Unquestionably, peremptory challenges historically have been used to exclude minorities pursuant to the sense that members of a certain group are more likely to view circumstances one way than members of another group. The opportunity to stereotype, however, cuts both ways. Given a history of problematic attitudes by the dominant racial group toward minorities, the opportunity to stereotype should not be lightly discarded. Especially in modern circumstances, where racism exists but is difficult to pinpoint in a particular case, peremptory challenges that are a function of racial hunches may perform a legitimate function. Wholesale dispensing with race-conscious peremptory challenges seems not only to defeat the purpose of the methodology but is oblivious to the real world where race-dependent perception and judgment is normative rather than exceptional.

PAH: In this area as in other parts of equal protection jurisprudence colorblindness has trumped other considerations. A concept of representative participation of citizens is only weakly reflected in *Batson* and subsequent peremptory challenge cases through the reaffirmation of a randomness requirement. As I have argued elsewhere, a preoccupation with developing a 'neutral' selection process, including a color-blind and gender-neutral focus, can devalue the significance of social differences, and can preclude the possibility of meaningful exchange and the sharing of decision-making power. However, to promote authentic representative participation I would favor eliminating all peremptory challenges, and focus on developing selection criteria which would enhance the cross-sectional requirement and on increasing the participatory role of jurors in the trial process.[190]

DEL: By holding doctrine captive to motive requirements, the Court essentially has limited the equal protection guarantee's utility to circumstances where race dependence speaks for itself—as in the case of affirmative action. Even though suggesting that history is relevant to the discernment of wrongful purpose, the Court has discounted significant indications of such motive. In *McCleskey*, as Justice Brennan noted, the reality of a dual criminal justice system was not distant and persisted insofar as defense counsel undoubtedly would have to provide racially disparate advice to capital clients. Investment in motive-based standards is troublesome because of their disutility and the reasons for rejecting them in other constitutional contexts. Identifying wrongful purpose is next to impossible at a time when discrimination is subtly practiced and wrongdoers are sophisticated in the methodology of covering their tracks. Even to the extent possible to identify a discriminatory motive of a policy-maker, it is problematic to figure its significance in the context of a collective decision-making body. Especially puzzling is why those who have been so quick to resist motive-based inquiry in other constitutional settings have embraced it in the equal protection context. In the dormant commerce clause setting, Justice Rehnquist maintained that a search for discriminatory intent was an illusory exercise.[191] Justice Scalia, in the establishment clause area, persuasively demonstrated the multitude of reasons for a legislator's vote that would be inscrutable.[192] In refusing to use motive-based criteria in the First Amendment context, to discern content discrimination, the Court stressed that the constitutional "stakes are sufficiently high . . . to eschew guesswork."[193] One possible inference from the Court's referencing of equal protection doctrine to motive is that the stakes are not "sufficiently high."

Some critics have proposed abandoning motive-based inquiry in the equal protection

---

[190] Phoebe A. Haddon, *Rethinking the Jury*, 3 Wm & Mary Bill of Rights J. 29, 94–105 (1994).

[191] Kassel v. Consolidated Freightways Corp., 450 U.S. 662, 702–03 (1981)(Rehnquist, J., dissenting).

[192] Edwards v. Aguillard, 482 U.S. 578, 284–85 (1987)(Scalia, J., dissenting).

[193] United States v. O'Brien, 391 U.S. 367, 384 (1968).

context in favor of criteria that are better able to discern modern variants of discrimination. Charles Lawrence, noting that standards are referenced to racial realities largely consigned to the past, has suggested attention to the racial significance of official action as a means of reckoning with subtle discrimination and unconscious racism.[194] Expectations that results would change significantly pursuant to an altered standard of review, however, may be misplaced if not naive. It at least is questionable whether a Court, unable to identify the connection between constitutionally significant history and the racially disproportionate operation of the death penalty in Georgia or the significance of traffic barriers separating white and black neighborhoods in a community not long removed from prescriptive segregation, would perform any more sensitively in attempting to discern racially stigmatizing policy or action. It is at least "ironic," as Justice Blackmun put it,[195] that constitutional radar has failed when minority claims have been pressed against a backdrop of discriminatory history and experience yet has been especially sensitive in responding to a redistricting plan perceived simply as "bizarre." When more sympathetically utilized, as it was by Justice Brennan in establishing the *de jure* segregation prerequisite, motive-based inquiry actually has been successful in identifying discriminatory purpose that was not entirely overt.[196] If the problem ultimately is one of awareness and understanding, it is doubtful whether much progress can be expected from formalistic solutions. As in other racially significant areas, further achievement hinges more upon the slow but more certain dividends of education than upon legalistic expediencies.

DER: Equal protection analyses have divided into two visions of equality—one that is informed by an "antidiscrimination" principle, the other by an "antisubordination" principle. The antidiscrimination principle identifies the primary threat to equality as the government's "failure to treat Black people as individuals without regard to race."[197] The goal of the antidiscrimination approach is to ensure that all members of society are treated in a color-blind or race-neutral fashion. This view of equality, by focusing on the process by which government decisions are made, judges the legitimacy of state action from the *perpetrator's* perspective.[198] The Supreme Court not only subscribes to the antidiscrimination principle, but gives it a very narrow interpretation. The Court confines discrimination prohibited by the Constitution to state conduct performed with a discriminatory intent. As one commentator has noted, "the Justices have demanded proof . . . that officials were 'out to get' a person or group on account of race."[199]

The antisubordination approach, on the other hand, recognizes that racial subjugation is not maintained solely through the racially antagonistic acts of individual officials. It instead views social patterns and institutions that perpetuate the inferior status of Blacks as the primary threats to equality. The goal of antisubordination law would be to dismantle racial hierarchy by eliminating state action or inaction that effectively preserves Black subordination. Rather than requiring victims to prove distinct instances of discriminating behavior accompanied by wrongful purpose, the antisubordination approach considers the concrete effects of government policy on the substantive condition of the disempowered. Although we cannot expect the law to work a miraculous transformation of Americans'

---

[194] Charles Lawrence III, *The Id, the Ego and Equal Protection: Reckoning with Unconscious Racism*, 39 Stan. L. Rev. 317 (1987).

[195] Shaw v. Reno, 113 S.Ct. 2816, 2846 (1993)(Blackmun, J., dissenting).

[196] Keyes v. School District No. 1, 413 U.S. 189, 208–09 (1973).

[197] Paul R. Dimond, *The Anti-Caste Principle—Toward a Constitutional Standard for Review of Race Cases*, 30 Wayne L. Rev. 1, 1 (1983).

[198] Alan Freeman, *Legitimizing Racial Discrimination Through Antidiscrimination Law: A Critical Review of Supreme Court Doctrine*, 62 Minn. L. Rev. 1049, 1952–57 (1978).

[199] Randall Kennedy, McClesky v. Kemp, *Race, Capital Punishment, and the Supreme Court*, 101 Harv. L. Rev. 1388, 1405 (1988).

attitudes, the antisubordination view of equality would yield more effective results. Moreover, the antisubordination approach is more faithful to the historical origins of the Civil War amendments, which were drafted specifically to eradicate "the badges and incidents" of racial hierarchy.[200]

PAH: Both the Supreme Court's discriminatory intent requirement and its preoccupation with color blindness permit the perpetuation of racial inequality by condoning racially discriminatory practices which are built on historical and continuing assumptions of the moral inequality of the races.[201] The antidiscrimination view of equality which they promote limits the legal capacity to attack present consequences of racial subordination. Not only has the antidiscrimination approach limited the steps the government is required to take to address inequality, but in recent voting rights cases (and in affirmative action cases discussed below), the Court has also narrowly limited the steps government can affirmatively employ to alleviate the disadvantaging effects of past discrimination. These cases are all the more disturbing because they suggest a willingness on the part of the court to overturn pragmatic majoritarian judgment about how to alleviate societal discrimination—intruding in areas where the Court has traditionally deferred to the political process and in a manner in which the court has been unwilling to undertake to address political decision making which operates to injure African Americans and other disempowered groups. In this way the Court's actions seem more political than principled.

Noting that most of the "major advances that racial minorities have made since manumission have . . . come from the representative branches" Professor Girardeau Spann has argued that the Supreme Court's action has not consistently supported minority interests but rather has made concessions only when the political climate has been conducive to such concessions.[202] He therefore urges minorities to concentrate equality-promoting activities on the representative branches since "minorities are more likely to secure concessions from an overtly political branch of government than from one whose political dimensions are covert." However, he acknowledges: "[O]ne might object to this asserted preference for the representative branches by arguing that if the actions of each branch are ultimately determined by majoritarian political preferences, it should not matter which branch minorities choose as the focus of their political efforts. Therein lies the dilemma."[203]

DEL: The antisubordination principle accurately reflects the essential meaning of the Thirteenth and Fourteenth Amendments, as further amplified by the Civil Rights Act of 1866 and the *Strauder* Court's seminal recognition that official action "implying inferiority" was constitutionally impermissible. However, invocation of core meaning is inconsequential (as post-Reconstruction and post-*Brown* experiences indicate) minus standards and applications that respond to actual racial dynamics. To the extent conditioned by threshold criteria demanding proof of intent, or brigaded with review that skirts or fails to understand subordinating factors, an anti-subordination principle will be no more productive than an anti-discrimination principle. Because either reference point can be conditioned by standards that reflect the limits of prevailing morality, it should not be surprising when energy poured into legal reform has an impact that is heavily discounted by standards of review and interpretations.

---

[200] *See* Civil Rights Cases, 109 U.S. 3, 20 (1883).

[201] *See* Perry, *Modern Equal Protection: A Conconceptualization and Appraisal*, 79 Colum. L. Rev. 1023, 1040 (1979).

[202] Girardeau A. Spann, *Pure Politics*, 88 Mich. L. Rev. 1971 (1990). Professor Spann's observations about the majoritarian influences are reminiscent of the interest convergence analysis of Professor Derrick Bell. Derrick Bell, *Brown v. Board of Education and the Interest-Convergence Dilemma*, 93 Harv. L. Rev. 518 (1980).

[203] *Id.*

7. A Color Blind Constitution: The Controversy Over Racial Preferences

The principle of constitutional color blindness historically has been either nonexistent or elusive. Law and morality at the republic's inception accommodated slavery in the South and the formal derogation of the civil and political status of African-Americans in the North. Although the Thirteenth Amendment defeated slavery in form, and the Fourteenth and Fifteenth Amendments challenged formal restrictions upon aspects of liberty and equality in the civil and political arenas, official segregation defined the racial landscape through the middle of the twentieth century. For more than half of its existence, the Fourteenth Amendment has allowed formal racial exclusion of or discrimination against those who were the primary object of the provision's concern. In attempting to remedy the nation's legacy of segregation in public schools, *Brown* and its progeny responded in color-conscious terms that took race into account for purposes of achieving racial balance.

As a proposed means of undoing the consequences of racial discrimination, systems of preference upon the basis of race began to emerge during the 1960s in a variety of contexts. Racially preferential admissions programs in higher education, hiring and retention plans in the workplace and government contracting and licensing schemes ultimately became the focus of Fourteenth Amendment attention. After a decade of doctrinal uncertainty, the Court eventually articulated a comprehensive standard of constitutional color blindness.[204] After determining that racial classifications are suspect regardless of whether they are intended to burden or remediate,[205] it promptly identified an exception to the rule and upheld racial preferences in the broadcast licensing process.[206] A few years later, the Court repudiated that "surprising turn."[207]

The Court's initial response to the constitutional debate was to bypass a decision on the merits. In *DeFunis v. Odegaard*, it determined that a controversy over a law school's preferential admissions program was moot.[208] Justice Brennan's dissent criticized the Court for using principles of avoiding constitutional decisions as the means for side-stepping a difficult case. As he put it, "few constitutional questions in recent history have stirred as much debate."[209] Four years later, the Court revisited the issue in the context of a state-supported medical school's preferential admissions program. The result, in *Regents of the University of California v. Bakke*, was a fragmented Court and majority support only for the proposition that racial diversity legitimately could be factored into the admissions process provided that it was not the exclusive consideration.[210]

---

[204] Richmond v. J. A. Croson Co., 488 U.S. 469, 498–500 (1989).

[205] *Id.*

[206] Metro Broadcasting, Inc. v. FCC, 497 U.S. 547, 565 (1990) (congressionally mandated preferences on the basis of race permissible insofar as they substantially promote important governmental objectives).

[207] Adarand Constructors, Inc. v. Pena, 115 S. Ct. 2097, 2111 (1995).

[208] De Funis v. Odegaard, 416 U.S. 312 (1974).

[209] *Id.* at 350 (Brennan, J., dissenting).

[210] Regents of the University of California v. Bakke, 438 U.S. 265, 320 (1978)(opinion of Powell, J.); *id.* at 325–26 (Brennan, White, Marshall and Blackmun, JJ., concurring and dissenting).

Donald E. Lively,
The Constitution And Race 138–41 (1992)*

In *Regents of the University of California v. Bakke*, the Court examined a preferential admissions program at a state medical school. The institution had established criteria which set aside positions for designated racial or ethnic minorities. The respondent, a white male, maintained that he was denied admission as a consequence of the policy. The California Supreme Court, finding the program at odds with the state constitution, Title VI of the Civil Rights Act of 1964, and equal protection, accordingly ordered the school to admit the respondent. The U.S. Supreme Court affirmed the decision but did so on grounds that did not conclusively answer the constitutional question. Four justices determined that the special admissions program breached neither the equal protection guarantee nor Title VI of the Civil Rights Act of 1964. Four justices avoided the constitutional issue altogether and discerned a violation of Title VI. Justice Powell concluded that the program was generally at odds with the equal protection guarantee and Title VI. Unlike the four justices who discerned a statutory violation, Powell maintained that neither Title VI nor the Constitution barred all race-conscious programs. His refusal to foreclose such classifications entirely was significant because it was the one constitutional point in the decision that commanded majority support.

On the critical question of what the appropriate standard of review should be, Powell refused to join the four justices who found the program constitutionally permissible. Instead of a bifurcated level of review contingent on the nature of the classification, he asserted that any racial favoritism, even if characterized as benign, should be subject to strict review. The level of judicial scrutiny employed in evaluating a policy or action is critical to the outcome of a case. To the extent a mere rationality standard operates, as in the assessment of general economic regulation, review is highly deferential and the contested law generally is upheld. When the Court engages in strict scrutiny, the challenged enactment or provision must be justified by compelling reasons and must minimally burden constitutional interests. Such exacting review, characterizing analysis of racial classifications, tends to be unforgiving. In between strict and rationality criteria is an intermediate standard of review, used when gender and other classifications are implicated, which is reducible to a balancing of constitutional and governmental interests. In advocating rigorous judicial scrutiny of the special admissions program, Powell did not make clear whether he meant review that, as applied since 1954, was "strict in theory, and fatal in fact." Confusing the issue somewhat was his mixing of "compelling interest" language of an intermediate standard. Because a less rigorous level of review was urged by other justices whom he did not join, it may be logical to infer that Powell intended all racial classifications to be reviewed pursuant to the most exacting standards.

Having identified what he considered the appropriate level of scrutiny, Powell determined whether a compelling reason existed for the special admissions program. The university had offered four justifications that included enrolling a minimum number of students from certain racial or ethnic groups, eliminating discrimination, improving health care in disadvantaged communities, and maintaining a diverse student body. Powell considered each point seriatim. First, he determined that the objective of admitting a fixed proportion of designated minorities, whether identified in terms of quotas or goals, was "facially invalid." Although acknowledging a valid state interest in accounting for "identified discrimination," he concluded that remediation requires legislative or judicial findings of prior wrongdoing by the pertinent institution or program. Such determinations had not been made, nor did he consider the school itself authorized to make them on its own. Third, Powell criticized the assumption that minority students necessarily would practice in and thereby improve the quality of health care in disadvantaged communities. Even if that goal might reflect a profound interest, he found no evidence that the "special admissions program is needed or geared to promote that goal." Finally, Powell determined that the aim of general diversification represented a compelling interest. Although disapproving of diversification based on racial or ethnic considerations exclusively, he concluded that "students with a particular background—whether it be ethnic, geographic, culturally advantaged or disadvantaged—may bring to a professional school of medicine experiences, outlooks and ideas that enrich the training of its student body and better equip its graduates to render with understanding their vital service to humanity."

Given four votes for a manifestly race-conscious policy and Powell's approval of race as a factor within a general diversification policy, majority support existed at least for the latter premise. The Court did not exempt any racial classification from close scrutiny for compliance but left open the possibility of limited con-

---

* Reprinted with permission.

sideration of race. Although the policy itself was deficient under the Fourteenth Amendment, the state had a constitutional "interest that legitimately may be served by a properly devised admissions program involving the competitive consideration of race and ethnic origin."

Justice Brennan, joined by Justices White, Marshall, and Blackmun, urged a more relaxed standard of review on the grounds that the Court should not impede initiatives calculated to eliminate discrimination against minorities. For Brennan, the process defect rationale of strict scrutiny was inapt because whites were neither traditionally excluded from nor underrepresented in the political process and their interests were thus unlikely to be slighted. Because even benign-appearing classifications might stereotype or stigmatize a discrete group, and because race constituted an immutable characteristic, Brennan did not advocate entirely deferential review. Rather, he proposed an intermediate standard that would have required a careful examination of but a more favorable disposition toward racial preferences. As Brennan put it:

> to justify such a classification an important and articulated purpose for its use must be shown. In addition, any statute must be stricken that stigmatizes any group or that singles out those least well represented in the political process to bear the brunt of a benign program. Thus our review under the Fourteenth Amendment should be strict—not " 'strict' in theory and fatal in fact," because it is stigma that causes fatality—but strict and searching nonetheless.

Brennan thus proposed a version of "strict" review friendlier to remedial policy and aims but not insensitive to possible abuse or misuse of racial classifications. Specifically, any preferential policy would have to be justified by an important interest outweighing its burdens and narrowly tailored to avoid stigmatizing consequences. From Brennan's perspective, remediation of societal discrimination was a significant interest that outweighed any harm to members of the majority race. Nor did he consider the special admissions policy a source of stigma insofar as the respondent would not "in any sense [be] stamped as inferior by [his] rejection.

In a separate opinion, Justice Marshall noted the nation's legacy of racial discrimination, which from his viewpoint justified race-dependent attention. Noting that the Court a century earlier had foreclosed "several affirmative action programs after the Civil War," he expressed his "fear that we have come full circle." Justice Blackmun maintained that racial discrimination could not be effectively reckoned with absent policies that directly and explicitly confronted its consequences. He accordingly observed that "[i]n order to get beyond racism, we must first take account of race."

A third analysis was provided by a plurality of four justices who, focusing solely on the statutory permissibility of the program, asserted that federal law required strict neutrality. In an opinion joined by Chief Justice Burger and Justices Rehnquist and Stewart, Justice Stevens opined that Title VI and its legislative history required strict colorblindness.

The *Bakke* decision did not establish a consensus with respect to the standard of review that should be employed in assessing racial preferences intended to benefit minorities. Nor was any clarification provided when the Court revisited the subject in *Fullilove v. Klutznick.* The Court in *Fullilove* upheld a congressionally mandated set aside program requiring ten percent minority participation in public works programs.[211] In an opinion joined by Justices White and Powell, Chief Justice Burger determined that the program's aims were within Congress' power but did not clearly indicate whether a strict or relaxed standard of review should be utilized.[212] Justices Brennan, Marshall and Blackmun, who voted to uphold the program, advocated a standard of review focused upon whether the preferential program was substantially related to achievement of an important governmental interest.[213] In a dissenting opinion, Justices Stewart and Rehnquist urged a standard of absolute constitutional color

---

[211] Fullilove v. Klutznick, 448 U.S. 448 (1980).
[212] *Id.* at 480 (Burger, C.J., White and Powell, JJ.).
[213] *Id.* at 517–22 (Brennan, Marshall and Blackmun, JJ., concurring).

blindness against which the congressional scheme failed.[214] Justice Stevens dissented separately on grounds that the program was supported by inadequate evidence.[215] He left open the possibility of supporting racial preferences to the extent used to account for past "unfair treatment" or to support groups who experience a competitive disadvantage.[216]

Movement toward a majority position on the appropriate standard of review was evidenced in *Wygant v. Jackson Board of Education.* In *Wygant,* the Court struck down a preferential layoff scheme that was part of a collective bargaining agreement entered into by teachers and the school board.[217] The preferential position of recently hired minority teachers represented an interest in defusing a history of racial problems in the school system, providing minority role models and "alleviat[ing] the effects of societal discrimination."[218] Four justices, in an opinion authored by Justice Powell, endorsed heightened review and determined that the justifications advanced for the preferential hiring scheme were inadequate. The plurality specifically determined that the reference to societal discrimination was "too amorphous a basis for imposing a racially classified remedy"[219] and race-conscious programs could not operate without "some showing of prior discrimination to the government unit involved."[220] Especially contrasted with the more diffuse effect of hiring preferences, the Court found that the impact of a preferential layoff program upon "innocent individuals" was too profound.[221]

In a concurring opinion, Justice O'Connor suggested that prior discrimination should not absolutely bar voluntary plans but noted an evolving position toward limited allowance of racially preferential methods.[222] Justice Marshall, in a dissent joined by Justices Brennan and Blackmun, criticized the Court for impeding a consensual solution to the school system's problem that was negotiated in a forum more adept at resolving the "thorny problems" at stake.[223] He also objected to the constitutional exclusion of race from other factors that were allowed to supersede seniority in the layoff plan.[224] In a separate dissent, Justice Stevens suggested that racial preferences might be justified by forward-looking interests in educating children for a diverse world.[225] He also expressed concern with the evolution toward comprehensive color blind standards insofar as they failed to distinguish between "the inclusionary decision [which] is consistent with the principle that all men are created equal; [and] the exclusionary decision [which] is at war with that principle."[226]

Even as judicial thinking coalesced toward a stricter standard of review, evidence surfaced that disagreement existed with respect to the scope of preferential permissibility. In *United States v. Paradise,* the Court reviewed a court-ordered quota system intended to remedy a history of discriminatory employment practices by the Alabama state police. Following more than a decade of noncompliance with previous orders, the lower court had required as a temporary measure that at least half of future promotions

---

[214] *Id.* at 522–32 (Stewart and Rehnquist, JJ., dissenting).

[215] *Id.* at 538–41.

[214] *Id.* at 553 (Stevens, J., dissenting).

[217] Wygant v. Jackson Board of Education, 476 U.S. 267 (1986).

[218] *Id.* at 276 (plurality opinion).

[219] *Id.*

[220] *Id.*

[221] *Id.* at 282–83.

[222] *Id.* at 287–90 (O'Connor, J., concurring).

[223] *Id.* at 312 (Marshall, J. dissenting).

[224] *Id.* at 308 (Marshall, J. dissenting).

[225] *Id.* at 315 (Stevens, J., dissenting).

[226] *Id.* at 316–17 (Stevens, J., dissenting).

to the rank of corporal be set aside for African-American troopers. Without articulating a particular standard of review, Justice Brennan, on behalf of a plurality, determined that the quota would survive strict scrutiny.[227] Compelling factors referenced in support of the preference were the need to undo the effects of past and present discrimination, the inefficacy of other methods of relief, the availability of waiver provisions, the minimal burden on third parties and the limited scope and duration of the remedy that only postponed promotions for qualified whites.[228] Justices Powell and Stevens in separate concurrences emphasized the history of noncompliance with previous court orders as relevant factors.[229] Joined by Chief Justice Rehnquist and Justice Scalia, Justice O'Connor dissented on grounds that the plan could not survive strict scrutiny.[230] The dissenters criticized the quota as an "in terrorem" exercise toward achieving an objective that could be reached better by methods including appointment of a trustee to monitor promotion practices and use of contempt procedures.[231]

A decade after *Bakke*, the Court invested in the premise that all racial classifications regardless of purpose are suspect and should be strictly scrutinized. Four justices, in *City of Richmond v. J. A. Croson Co.*, determined that racial preferences were not constitutionally permissible unless narrowly responsive to a constitutional violation.[232] Complementing Justice O'Connor's plurality opinion was Justice Scalia's concurrence that reflected an even less tolerant view of remedial classifications. In a dissenting opinion joined by Justices Brennan and Blackmun, Justice Marshall criticized the decision as an exercise in "cynicism" and blindness to racial reality.[233]

---

[227] United States v. Paradise, 480 U.S. 149, 185–86 (1987)(plurality opinion).

[228] *Id.* at 171–86.

[229] *Id.* at 186 (Powell, J. concurring); *id.* at 193 (Stevens, J., concurring).

[230] *Id.* at 198–99.

[231] *Id.* at 200 (O'Connor, J., dissenting).

[232] Richmond v. J. A. Croson Co., 488 U.S. 469, 509 (1989).

[233] *Id.* at 740–43 (Marshall, J., dissenting).

Richmond v J.A. Croson Co.
488 U.S. 469 (1989)

JUSTICE O'CONNOR announced the judgment of the Court and delivered the opinion of the Court with respect to Parts I, III-B, and IV, an opinion with respect to Part II, in which THE CHIEF JUSTICE and JUSTICE WHITE join, and an opinion with respect to Parts III-A and V, in which THE CHIEF JUSTICE, JUSTICE WHITE, and JUSTICE KENNEDY join.

In this case, we confront once again the tension between the Fourteenth Amendment's guarantee of equal treatment to all citizens, and the use of race-based measures to ameliorate the effects of past discrimination on the opportunities enjoyed by members of minority groups in our society. . . .

I

On April 11, 1983, the Richmond City Council adopted the Minority Business Utilization Plan (the Plan). The Plan required prime contractors to whom the city awarded construction contracts to subcontract at least 30% of the dollar amount of the contract to one or more Minority Business Enterprises (MBE's). . . .

The Plan defined an MBE as "[a] business at least fifty-one (51) percent of which is owned and controlled . . . by minority group members." "Minority group members" were defined as "[c]itizens of the United States who are Blacks, Spanish-speaking, Orientals, Indians, Eskimos or Aleuts." There was no geographic limit to the Plan; an otherwise qualified MBE from anywhere in the United States could avail itself of the 30% set-aside. The Plan declared that it was "remedial" in nature, and enacted "for the purpose of promoting wider participation by minority business enterprises in the construction of public projects." . . .

There was no direct evidence of race discrimination on the part of the city in letting contracts or any evidence that the city's prime contractors had discriminated against minority-owned subcontractors....

II

Appellant and its supporting *amici rely* heavily on *Fullilove* for the proposition that a city council, like Congress, need not make specific findings of discrimination to engage in race-conscious relief. Thus, appellant argues "[i]t would be a perversion of federalism to hold that the federal government has a compelling interest in remedying the effects of racial discrimination in its own public works program, but a city government does not."

What appellant ignores is that Congress, unlike any State or political subdivision, has a specific constitutional mandate to enforce the dictates of the Fourteenth Amendment. The power to "enforce" may at times also include the power to define situations which *Congress* determines threaten principles of equality and to adopt prophylactic rules to deal with those situations.... The Civil War Amendments themselves worked a dramatic change in the balance between congressional and state power over matters of race. Speaking of the Thirteenth and Fourteenth Amendments in *Ex parte Virginia*, 100 U. S. 339, 345 (1880), the Court stated: "They were intended to be, what they really are, limitations of the powers of the States and enlargements of the power of Congress."

That Congress may identify and redress the effects of society-wide discrimination does not mean that, a *fortiori,* the States and their political subdivisions are free to decide that such remedies are appropriate. Section 1 of the Fourteenth Amendment is an explicit *constraint* on state power, and the States must undertake any remedial efforts in accordance with that provision. To hold otherwise would be to cede control over the content of the Equal Protection Clause to the 50 state legislatures and their myriad political subdivisions. The mere recitation of a benign or compensatory purpose for the use of a racial classification would essentially entitle the States to exercise the full power of Congress under § 5 of the Fourteenth Amendment and insulate any racial classification from judicial scrutiny under § 1. We believe that such a result would be contrary to the intentions of the Framers of the Fourteenth Amendment, who desired to place clear limits on the States' use of race as a criterion for legislative action, and to have the federal courts enforce those limitations....

It would seem equally clear, however, that a state or local subdivision (if delegated the authority from the State) has the authority to eradicate the effects of private discrimination within its own legislative jurisdiction. This authority must, of course, be exercised within the constraints of § 1 of the Fourteenth Amendment.... As a matter of state law, the city of Richmond has legislative authority over its procurement policies, and can use its spending powers to remedy private discrimination, if it identifies that discrimination with the particularity required by the Fourteenth Amendment....

The Equal Protection Clause of the Fourteenth Amendment provides that "no State shall . . . deny to *any person* within its jurisdiction the equal protection of the laws." (Emphasis added.) As this Court has noted in the past, the "rights created by the first section of the Fourteenth Amendment are, by its terms, guaranteed to the individual. The rights established are personal rights."

III

A

The Richmond Plan denies certain citizens the opportunity to compete for a fixed percentage of public contracts based solely upon their race. To whatever racial group these citizens belong, their "personal rights" to be treated with equal dignity and respect are implicated by a rigid rule erecting race as the sole criterion in an aspect of public decisionmaking.

Absent searching judicial inquiry into the justification for such race-based measures, there is simply no way of determining what classifications are "benign" or "remedial" and what classifications are in fact motivated by illegitimate notions of racial inferiority or simple racial politics. Indeed, the purpose of strict scrutiny is to "smoke out" illegitimate uses of race by assuring that the legislative body is pursuing a goal important enough to warrant use of a highly suspect tool. The test also ensures that the means chosen "fit" this compelling goal so closely that there is little or no possibility that the motive for the classification was illegitimate racial prejudice or stereotype.

Classifications based on race carry a danger of stigmatic harm. Unless they are strictly reserved for remedial settings, they may in fact promote notions of racial inferiority and lead to a politics of racial hostility. We thus reaffirm the view expressed by the plurality in *Wygant* that the standard of review under the Equal Protection Clause is not dependent on the race of those burdened or benefited by a particular classification.

Our continued adherence to the standard of review employed in Wygant does not, as JUSTICE MARSHALL's dissent suggests, indicate that we view "racial discrimination as largely a phenomenon of the past" or that "government bodies need no longer preoccupy themselves with rectifying racial injustice." As we indicate, . . . [s]tates and their local divisions have many legislative weapons at their disposal both to punish and prevent present discrimination and to remove arbitrary barriers to minority advancement. Rather, our interpretation of § 1 stems from our agreement with the view expressed by Justice Powell in *Bakke* that "[t]he guarantee of equal protection cannot mean one thing when applied to one individual and something else when applied to a person of another color."

Under the standard proposed by JUSTICE MARSHALL's dissent, "race-conscious classifications designed to further remedial goals are forthwith subject to a relaxed standard of review. How the dissent arrives at the legal conclusion that a racial classification is "designed to further remedial goals," without first engaging in an examination of the factual basis for its enactment and the nexus between its scope and that factual basis, we are not told. However, once the "remedial" conclusion is reached, the dissent's standard is singularly deferential, and bears little resemblance to the close examination of legislative purpose we have engaged in when reviewing classifications based either on race or gender. The dissent's watered-down version of equal protection review effectively assures that race will always be relevant in American life, and that the "ultimate goal" of "eliminat[ing] entirely from governmental decisionmaking such irrelevant factors as a human being's race," will never be achieved.

Even were we to accept a reading of the guarantee of equal protection under which the level of scrutiny varies according to the ability of different groups to defend their interests in the representative process, heightened scrutiny would still be appropriate in the circumstances of this case. One of the central arguments for applying a less exacting standard to "benign" racial classifications is that such measures essentially involve a choice made by dominant racial groups to disadvantage themselves. If one aspect of the judiciary's role under the Equal Protection Clause is to protect "discrete and insular minorities" from majoritarian prejudice or indifference, some maintain that these concerns are not implicated when the "white majority" places burdens upon itself.

In this case, blacks constitute approximately 50% of the population of the city of Richmond. Five of the nine seats on the city council are held by blacks. The concern that a political majority will more easily act to the disadvantage of a minority based on unwarranted assumptions or incomplete facts would seem to militate for, not against, the application of heightened judicial scrutiny in this case. . . .

B

. . . Like the "role model" theory employed in *Wygant*, a generalized assertion that there has been past discrimination in an entire industry provides no guidance for a legislative body to determine the precise scope of the injury it seeks to remedy. It "has no logical stopping point." "Relief " for such an ill-defined wrong could extend until the percentage of public contracts awarded to MBE's in Richmond mirrored the percentage of minorities in the population as a whole.

Appellant argues that it is attempting to remedy various forms of past discrimination that are alleged to be responsible for the small number of minority businesses in the local contracting industry. Among these the city cites the exclusion of blacks from skilled construction trade unions and training programs. This past discrimination has prevented them "from following the traditional path from laborer to entrepreneur." The city also lists a host of nonracial factors which would seem to face a member of any racial group attempting to establish a new business enterprise, such as deficiencies in working capital, inability to meet bonding requirements, unfamiliarity with bidding procedures and disability caused by an inadequate track record.

While there is no doubt that the sorry history of both private and public discrimination in this country has contributed to a lack of opportunities for black entrepreneurs, this observation, standing alone, cannot justify a rigid racial quota in the awarding of public contracts in Richmond, Virginia. Like the claim that discrimination in primary and secondary schooling justifies a rigid racial preference in medical school admissions, an amorphous claim that there has been past discrimination in a particular industry cannot justify the use of an unyielding racial quota.

It is sheer speculation how many minority firms there would be in Richmond absent past societal discrimination, just as it was sheer speculation how many minority medical students would have been admitted to the medical school at Davis absent past discrimination in educational opportunities. Defining these sorts of injuries as "identified discrimination" would give local governments license to create a patchwork of racial preferences based on statistical generalizations about any particular field of endeavor.

These defects are readily apparent in this case. The 30% quota cannot in any realistic sense be tied to any injury suffered by anyone. The District Court relied upon five predicate "facts" in reaching its conclusion that there was an adequate basis for the 30% quota: (1) the ordinance declares itself to be remedial; (2) several proponents of the measure stated their views that there had been past discrimination in the construction industry; (3) minority businesses received 0.67% of prime contracts from the city while minorities constituted 50% of the city's population; (4) there were very few minority contractors in local and state contractors' associations; and (5) in 1977, Congress made a determination that the effects of past discrimination had stifled minority participation in the construction industry nationally.

None of these "findings," singly or together, provide the city of Richmond with a "strong basis in evidence for its conclusion that remedial action was necessary." . . . There is nothing approaching a prima facie case of a constitutional or statutory violation by *anyone* in the Richmond construction industry.

The District Court accorded great weight to the fact that the city council designated the Plan as "remedial." But the mere recitation of a "benign" or legitimate purpose for a racial classification is entitled to little or no weight.

Racial classifications are suspect, and that means that simple legislative assurances of good intention cannot suffice. . . .

Finally, the city and the District Court relied on Congress' finding in connection with the set-aside approved in *Fullilove* that there had been nationwide discrimination in the construction industry. The probative value of these findings for demonstrating the existence of discrimination in Richmond is extremely limited. By its inclusion of a waiver procedure in the national program addressed in *Fullilove*, Congress explicitly recognized that the scope of the problem would vary from market area to market area. . . .

Moreover, as noted above, Congress was exercising its powers under § 5 of the Fourteenth Amendment in making a finding that past discrimination would cause federal funds to be distributed in a manner which reinforced prior patterns of discrimination. While the States and their subdivisions may take remedial action when they possess evidence that their own spending practices are exacerbating a pattern of prior discrimination, they must identify that discrimination, public or private, with some specificity before they may use race-conscious relief. Congress has made national findings that there has been societal discrimination in a host of fields. If all a state or local government need do is find a congressional report on the subject to enact a set-aside program, the constraints of the Equal Protection Clause will, in effect, have been rendered a nullity. . . .

In sum, none of the evidence presented by the city points discrimination in the Richmond construction to any identified industry. We, therefore, hold that the city has failed to rest in apportioning public contracting opportunities on the basis of race. To accept Richmond's claim that past societal discrimination alone can serve as the basis for rigid racial prefer-

ences would be to open the door to competing claims for "remedial relief" for every disadvantaged group. The dream of a Nation of equal citizens in a society where race is irrelevant to personal opportunity and achievement would be lost in a mosaic of shifting preferences based on inherently unmeasurable claims of past wrongs. "Courts would be asked to evaluate the extent of the prejudice and consequent harm suffered by various minority groups. Those whose societal injury is thought to exceed some arbitrary level of tolerability then would be entitled to preferential classifications. . . . " We think such a result would be contrary to both the letter and spirit of a constitutional provision whose central command is equality.

The foregoing analysis applies only to the inclusion of blacks within the Richmond set-aside program. There is ab*solutely no evidence* of past discrimination against Spanish-speaking, Oriental, Indian, Eskimo, or Aleut persons in any aspect of the Richmond construction industry. The District Court took judicial notice of the fact that the vast majority of " minority" persons in Richmond were black. . . .

It may well be that Richmond has never had an Aleut or Eskimo citizen. The random inclusion of racial groups that, as a practical matter, may never have suffered from discrimination in the construction industry in Richmond suggests that perhaps the city's purpose was not in fact to remedy past discrimination.

If a 30% set-aside was "narrowly tailored" to compensate black contractors for past discrimination, one may legitimately ask why they are forced to share this "remedial relief" with an Aleut citizen who moves to Richmond tomorrow? The gross overinclusiveness of Richmond's racial preference strongly impugns the city's claim of remedial motivation.

IV

As noted by the court below, it is almost impossible to assess whether the Richmond Plan is narrowly tailored to remedy prior discrimination since it is not linked to identified discrimination in any way. We limit ourselves to two observations in this regard.

First, there does not appear to have been any consideration of the use of race-neutral means to increase minority business participation in city contracting. Many of the barriers to minority participation in the construction industry relied upon by the city to justify a racial classification appear to be race neutral. If MBE's disproportionately lack capital or cannot meet bonding requirements, a race-neutral program of city financing for small firms would, *a fortiori,* lead to greater minority participation. The principal opinion in *Fullilove* found that Congress had carefully examined and rejected race-neutral alternatives before enacting the MBE set-aside. There is no evidence in this record that the Richmond City Council has considered any alternatives to a race-based quota.

Second, the 30% quota cannot be said to be narrowly tailored to any goal, except perhaps outright racial balancing. It rests upon the "completely unrealistic" assumption that minorities will choose a particular trade in lockstep proportion to their representation in the local population.

. . .

V

Nothing we say today preludes a state or local entity from taking action to rectify the effects of identified discrimination within its jurisdiction. If the city of Richmond had evidence before it that nonminority contractors were systematically excluding minority businesses from subcontracting opportunities, it could take action to end the discriminatory exclusion. Where there is a significant statistical disparity between the number of qualified minority contractors willing and able to perform a particular service and the number of such contractors actually engaged by the locality or the locality's prime contractors, an inference of discriminatory exclusion could arise. Under such circumstances, the city could act to dismantle the closed business system by taking appropriate measures against those who discriminate on the basis of race or other illegitimate criteria. In the extreme case, some form of narrowly tailored racial preference might be necessary to break down patterns of deliberate exclusion.

Nor is local government powerless to deal with individual instances of racially motivated refusals to employ minority contractors. Where such discrimination occurs, a city would be justified in penalizing the discriminator and providing appropriate relief to the victim of such discrimination. Moreover, evidence of a pattern of individual discriminatory acts can, if supported by appropriate statistical proof, lend support to a local government's determination that broader remedial relief is justified.

Even in the absence of evidence of discrimination, the city has at its disposal a whole array of race-neutral devices to increase the accessibility of city contracting opportunities to small entrepreneurs of all races. Simplification of bidding, procedures, relaxation of bonding requirements, and training and financial aid for disadvantaged entrepreneurs of all races would open the public contracting market to all those who have suffered the effects of past societal discrimination or neglect. Many of the formal barriers to new entrants may be the product of bureaucratic inertia more than actual necessity, and may have a dispropor-

tionate effect on the opportunities open to new minority firms. Their elimination or modification would have little detrimental effect on the city's interests and would serve to increase the opportunities available to minority business without classifying individuals on the basis of race. The city may also act to prohibit discrimination in the provision of credit or bonding by local suppliers and banks. Business as usual should not mean business pursuant to the unthinking exclusion of certain members of our society from its rewards.

In the case at hand, the city has not ascertained how many minority enterprises are present in the local construction market nor the level of their participation in city construction projects. The city points to no evidence that qualified minority contractors have been passed over for city contracts or subcontracts either as a group or in any individual case. Under such circumstances, it is simply impossible to say that the city has demonstrated "a strong basis in evidence for its conclusion that remedial action was necessary."

Proper findings in this regard are necessary to define both the scope of the injury and the extent of the remedy necessary to cure its effects. Such findings also serve to assure all citizens that the deviation from the norm of equal treatment of all racial and ethnic groups is a temporary matter, a measure taken in the service of the goal of equality itself. Absent such findings, there is a danger that a racial classification is merely the product of unthinking stereotypes or a form of racial politics. . . . Because the city of Richmond has failed to identify the need for remedial action in the awarding of its public construction contracts, its treatment of its citizens on a racial basis violates the dictates of the Equal Protection Clause. Accordingly, the judgment of the Court of Appeals for the Fourth Circuit is

Affirmed.

JUSTICE STEVENS, concurring in part and concurring in the judgment.

A central purpose of the Fourteenth Amendment is to further the national goal of equal opportunity for all our citizens. In order to achieve that goal we must learn from our past mistakes, but I believe the Constitution requires us to evaluate our policy decisions—including those that govern the relationships among different racial and ethnic groups—primarily by studying their probable impact on the future. I therefore do not agree with the premise that seems to underlie today's decision, . . . that a governmental decision that rests on a racial classification is never permissible except as a remedy for a past wrong. I do, however, agree with the Court's explanation of why the Richmond ordinance cannot be justified as a remedy for past discrimination, and therefore join Parts I, III-B and IV of the Court's opinion and judgment. I write separately to emphasize three aspects of the case that are of special importance to me.

First, the city makes no claim that the public interest in the efficient performance of its construction contracts will be served by granting a preference to minority-business enterprises. This case is therefore completely unlike *Wygant*, in which I though it quite obvious that the school board had reasonably concluded that an integrated faculty could provide educational benefits to the entire student body that could not be provided by an all-white, or nearly all-white, faculty. As I point out in my dissent in that case, even if we completely disregard our history of racial injustice, race is not always irrelevant to sound governmental decision-making. In the case of public contracting, however, if we disregard the past, there is not even an arguable basis for suggesting that the race of a subcontractor or general contractor should have any relevance to his or her access to the market.

Second, this litigation involves an attempt by a legislative body, rather than a court, to fashion a remedy for a past wrong. Legislatures are primarily policymaking bodies that promulgate rules to govern future conduct. The constitutional prohibitions against the enactment of *ex post facto* laws and bills of attainder reflect a valid concern about the use of the political process to punish or characterize past conduct of private citizens. It is the judicial system, rather than the legislative process, that is best equipped to identify past wrongdoers and to fashion remedies that will create the conditions that presumably would have existed had no wrong been committed. Thus, in cases involving the review of judicial remedies imposed against persons who have been proved guilty of violations of law, I would allow the courts in racial discrimination cases the same broad discretion that chancellors enjoy in other areas of the law.

Third, instead of engaging in a debate over the proper standard of review to apply in affirmative-action litigation, I believe its more constructive to try to identify the characteristics of the advantaged and disadvantaged classes that may justify their disparate treatment. In this case that approach convinces me that, instead of carefully identifying the characteristics of the two classes of contractors that are respectively favored and disfavored by its ordinance, the Richmond City Council has merely engaged in the type of stereotypical analysis that is a hallmark of violations of the Equal Protection Clause. Whether we look at the class of persons benefited by the ordinance or at the disadvantaged class, the same conclusion emerges.

The justification for the ordinance is the fact that in the past white contractors—and presumably other white citizens in Richmond—have discriminated against black contractors. The class of persons benefited by the ordinance is not, however, limited to victims of such discrimination—it encompasses persons who have never been in business in Richmond as well as minority contractors who may have been guilty of discriminating against members of other minority groups. Indeed, for all the record shows, all of the minority-business enterprises that have benefited from the ordinance may be firms that have prospered notwithstanding the discriminatory conduct that may have harmed other minority firms years ago. Ironically, minority firms that have survived in the competitive struggle, rather than those that have perished, are most likely to benefit from an ordinance of this kind.

The ordinance is equally vulnerable because of its failure to identify the characteristics of the disadvantaged class of white contractors that justify the disparate treatment. That class unquestionably includes some white contractors who are guilty of past discrimination against blacks, but it is only habit, rather than evidence or analysis, that makes it seem acceptable to assume that every white contractor covered by the ordinance shares in that guilt. Indeed, even among those who have discriminated in the past, it must be assumed that at least some of them have complied with the city ordinance that has made such discrimination unlawful since 1975. Thus, the composition of the disadvantaged class of white contractors presumably includes some who have been guilty of unlawful discrimination before it was forbidden by law, and some who have never discriminated against anyone on the basis of race. Imposing a common burden on such a disparate class merely because each member of the class is of the same race stems from reliance on a stereotype rather than fact or reason.

There is a special irony in the stereotypical thinking that prompts legislation of this kind. Although it stigmatizes the disadvantaged class with the unproven charge of past racial discrimination, it actually imposes a greater stigma on its supposed beneficiaries. . . .

Parts I, III-B, and IV of the Court's opinion, and in the judgment.

JUSTICE KENNEDY, concurring in part and concurring in the judgment.

I join all but Part II of JUSTICE O'CONNOR'S opinion and give this further explanation.

Part II examines our case law upholding congressional power to grant preferences based on overt and explicit classification by race. See *Fullilove v. Klutznick,* 448 U. S. 448 (1980). With the acknowledgment that the summary in Part II is both precise and fair, I must decline to join it. The process by which a law that is an equal protection violation when enacted by a State becomes transformed to an equal protection guarantee when enacted by Congress poses a difficult proposition for me; but as it is not before us, any reconsideration of that issue must await some further case. . . .

JUSTICE SCALIA, concurring in the judgment.

I agree with much of the Court's opinion, and, in particular, with JUSTICE O'CONNOR'S conclusion that strict scrutiny must be applied to all governmental classification by race, whether or not its asserted purpose is "remedial" or "benign." I do not agree, however, with JUSTICE O'CONNOR's dictum suggesting that, despite the Fourteenth Amendment, state and local governments may in some circumstances discriminate on the basis of race in order (in a broad sense) "to ameliorate the effects of past discrimination." The benign purpose of compensating for social disadvantages, whether they have been acquired by reason of prior discrimination or otherwise, can no more be pursued by the illegitimate means of racial discrimination than can other assertedly benign purposes we have repeatedly rejected. The difficulty of overcoming the effects of past discrimination is as nothing compared with the difficulty of eradicating from our society the source of those effects, which is the tendency—fatal to a Nation such as ours—to classify and judge men and women on the basis of their country of origin or the color of their skin. A solution to the first problem that aggravates the second is no solution at all. I share the view expressed by Alexander Bickel that "[t]he lesson of the great decisions of the Supreme Court and the lesson of contemporary history have been the same for at least a generation: discrimination on the basis of race is illegal, immoral, unconstitutional, inherently wrong, and destructive of democratic society." At least where state or local action is at issue, only a social emergency rising to the level of imminent danger to life and limb—for example, a prison race riot, requiring temporary segregation of inmates, can justify an exception to the principle embodied in the Fourteenth Amendment that "[o]ur Constitution is colorblind, and neither knows nor tolerates classes among citizens, . . . We have in some contexts approved the use of racial classifications by the Federal Government to remedy the effects of past discrimination. I do not believe that we must or should extend those holdings to the States. . . . What the record shows, in other words, is that racial discrimination against any group finds a more ready expression at the state and local than at the federal level. To the children of the Founding Fathers, this should come as no surprise. An acute awareness of the heightened danger of oppression from political factions in small, rather than large, political units dates to the very beginning of our national history.

As James Madison observed in support of the proposed Constitution's enhancement of national powers:

"The smaller the society, the fewer probably will be the distinct parties and interests composing it; the fewer the distinct parties and interests, the more frequently will a majority be found of the same party; and the smaller the number of individuals composing a majority, and the smaller the compass within which they are placed, the more easily will they concert and execute then plan of oppression. . . .

The prophesy of these words came to fruition in Richmond in the enactment of a set-aside clearly and directly beneficial to the dominant political group, which happens also to be the dominant racial group. The same thing has no doubt happened before in other cities (though the racial basis of the preference has rarely been made textually explicit)—and blacks have often been on the receiving end of the injustice. Where injustice is the game, however, turnabout is not fair play.

In my view there is only one circumstance in which the States may act *by race* to "undo the effects of past discrimination": where that is necessary to eliminate their own maintenance of a system of unlawful racial classification. If, for example, a state agency has a discriminatory pay scale compensating black employees in all positions' at 20% less than their nonblack counterparts, it may assuredly promulgate an order raising the salaries of "all black employees" to eliminate the differential. This distinction explains our school desegregation cases, in which we have made plain that States and localities sometimes have an obligation to adopt race-conscious remedies. While there is no doubt that those cases have taken into account the continuing "effects" of previously mandated racial school assignment, we have held those effects to justify a race-conscious remedy only because we have concluded, in that context, that they perpetuate a "dual school system." . . .

A State can, of course, act "to undo the effects of past discrimination" in many permissible ways that do not involve classification by race. In the particular field of state contracting, for example, it may adopt a preference for small businesses, or even for new businesses—which would make it easier for those previously excluded by discrimination to enter the field. Such programs may well have racially disproportionate impact, but they are not based on race. And, of course, a State may "undo the effects of past discrimination" in the sense of giving the identified victim of state discrimination that which it wrongfully denied him—for example, giving to a previously rejected black applicant the job that, by reason of discrimination, had been awarded to a white applicant, even if this means terminating the latter's employment. In such a context, the white jobholder is not being selected for disadvantageous treatment because of his race, but because he was wrongfully awarded a job to which another is entitled. That is worlds apart from the system here, in which those to be disadvantaged are identified solely by race.

I agree with the Court's dictum that a fundamental distinction must be drawn between the effects of "societal" discrimination and the effects of "identified" discrimination, and that the situation would be different if Richmond's plan were "tailored" to identify those particular bidders who "suffered from the effects of past discrimination by the city or prime contractors." In my view, however, the reason that would make a difference is not, as the Court states, that it would justify race-conscious action—but rather that it would enable race-neutral remediation. Nothing prevents Richmond from according a contracting preference to identified victims of discrimination. While most of the beneficiaries might be black, neither the beneficiaries nor those disadvantaged by the preference would be identified on the basis of their race. In other words, far from justifying racial classification, identification of actual victims of discrimination makes it less supportable than ever, because more obviously unneeded.

In his final book, Professor Bickel wrote:

"[A] racial quota derogates the human dignity and individuality of all to whom it is applied; it is invidious in principle as well as in practice. Moreover, it can easily be turned against those it purports to help. The history of the racial quota is a history of subjugation, not beneficence. Its evil lies not in its name, but in its effects: a quota is a divider of society, a creator of castes, and it is all the worse for its racial base, especially in a society desperately striving for an equality that will make race irrelevant."

Those statements are true and increasingly prophetic. Apart from their societal effects, however, which are "in the aggregate disastrous," it is important not to lose sight of the fact that even "benign" racial quotas have individual victims, whose very real injustice we ignore whenever we deny them enforcement of their right not to be disadvantaged on the basis of race. As Justice Douglas observed: "A DeFunis who is entitled to no advantage by virtue of that fact; nor is he subject to any disability, no matter what his race or color. Whatever his race, he had a constitutional right to have his application considered on its individual merits in a racially neutral manner." When we depart from this American principle we play with fire, and much more than an occasional DeFunis, Johnson, or Croson burns.

It is plainly true that in our society blacks have suffered discrimination immeasurably greater than any directed at other racial groups. But those who believe that racial preferences can help to "even the score" display, and reinforce, a manner of thinking by race that was the source of the injustice and that will, if it endures within our society, be the source of more injustice still. The relevant proposition is not that it was blacks, or Jews, or Irish who were discriminated against, but that it was individual men and women, "created equal," who were discriminated against. And the relevant resolve is that that should never happen again. Racial preferences appear to "even the score" (in some small degree) only if one embraces the proposition that our society is appropriately viewed as divided into races, making it right that an injustice rendered in the past to a black man should be compensated for by discriminating against a white. Nothing is worth that embrace. Since blacks have been disproportionately disadvantaged by racial discrimination, any race-neutral remedial program aimed at the disadvantaged as such will have a disproportionately beneficial impact on blacks. Only such a program, and not one that operates on the basis of race, is in accord with the letter and the spirit of our Constitution.

Since I believe that the appellee here had a constitutional right to have its bid succeed or fail under a decisionmaking process uninfected with racial bias, I concur in the judgment of the Court.

JUSTICE MARSHALL, with whom JUSTICE BRENNAN and JUSTICE BLACKMUN join, dissenting.

It is a welcome symbol of racial progress when the former capital of the Confederacy acts forthrightly to confront the effects of racial discrimination in its midst. In my view, nothing in the Constitution can be construed to prevent Richmond, Virginia, from allocating a portion of its contracting dollars for businesses owned or controlled by members of minority groups. Indeed, Richmond's set-aside program is indistinguishable in all meaningful respects from—and in fact was patterned upon—the federal set-aside plan which this Court upheld in *Fullilove*.

A majority of this Court holds today, however, that the Equal Protection Clause of the Fourteenth Amendment blocks Richmond's initiative. The essence of the majority's position is that Richmond has failed to catalog adequate findings to prove that past discrimination has impeded minorities from joining or participating fully in Richmond's construction contracting industry. I find deep irony in second-guessing Richmond's judgment on this point. As much as any municipality in the United States, Richmond knows what racial discrimination is; a century of decisions by this and other federal courts has richly documented the city's disgraceful history of public and private racial discrimination. In any event, the Richmond City Council *has* supported its determination that minorities have been wrongly excluded from local construction contracting. Its proof includes statistics showing that minority-owned businesses have received virtually no city contracting dollars and rarely if ever belonged to area trade associations; testimony by municipal officials that discrimination has been widespread in the local construction industry; and the same exhaustive and widely publicized federal studies relied on in *Fullilove,* studies which showed that pervasive discrimination in the Nation's tight-knit construction industry had operated to exclude minorities from public contracting. These are precisely the types of statistical and testimonial evidence which, until today, this Court had credited in cases approving of race-conscious measures designed to remedy past discrimination.

More fundamentally, today's decision marks a deliberate and giant step backward in this Court's affirmative-action jurisprudence. Cynical of one municipality's attempt to redress the effects of past racial discrimination in a particular industry, the majority launches a grapeshot attack on race-conscious remedies in general. The majority's unnecessary pronouncements will inevitably discourage or prevent governmental entities, particularly States and localities, from acting to rectify the scourge of past discrimination. This is the harsh reality of the majority's decision, but it is not the Constitution's command.

As an initial matter, the majority takes an exceedingly myopic view of the factual predicate on which the Richmond City Council relied when it passed the Minority Business Utilization Plan. The majority analyzes Richmond's initiative as if it were based solely upon the facts about local construction and contracting practices adduced during the city council session at which the measure was enacted. In so doing, the majority downplays the fact that the city council had before it a rich trove of evidence that discrimination in the Nation's construction industry had seriously impaired the competitive position of businesses owned or controlled by members of minority groups. It is only against this backdrop of documented national discrimination, however, that the local evidence adduced by Richmond can be properly understood. The majority's refusal to recognize that Richmond has proved itself no exception to the dismaying pattern of national exclusion which Congress so painstakingly identified infects its entire analysis of this case. . . .

The members of the Richmond City Council were well aware of these exhaustive congressional findings, a point the majority, tellingly, elides. The transcript of the session at which the council enacted the local set-aside initiative contains numerous references to the 6-year-old congressional set-aside program, to the evidence of nationwide discrimination barriers described above, and to the Fullilove decision itself. . . .

The city council's members also heard testimony that, although minority groups made up half of the city's population, only 0.67% of the $24.6 million which Richmond had dispensed in construction contracts during the five years ending in March 1983 had gone to minority-owned prime contractors. They heard testimony that the major Richmond area construction trade associations had virtually no minorities among their hundreds of members. Finally, they heard testimony from city officials as to the exclusionary history of the local construction industry. As the District Court noted, not a single person who testified before the city council denied that discrimination in Richmond's construction industry had been widespread. So long as one views Richmond's local evidence of discrimination against the backdrop of systematic nationwide racial discrimination which Congress had so painstakingly identified in this very industry, this case is readily resolved. . . . My view has long been that race-conscious classifications designed to further remedial goals "must serve important governmental objectives and must be substantially related to achievement of those objectives" in order to withstand constitutional scrutiny. Analyzed in terms of this two-pronged standard, Richmond's set-side, like the federal program on which it was modeled, is "plainly constitutional."

Turning first to the governmental interest inquiry, Richmond has two powerful interests in setting aside a portion of public contracting funds for minority-owned enterprises. The first is the city's interest in eradicating the effects of past racial discrimination. It is far too late in the day to doubt that remedying such discrimination is a compelling, let alone an important, interest. . . .

Richmond has a second compelling interest in setting aside, where possible, a portion of its contracting dollars. That interest is the prospective one of preventing the city's own spending decisions from reinforcing and perpetuating the exclusionary effects of past discrimination.

The majority pays only lipservice to this additional governmental interest. But our decisions have often emphasized the danger of the government tacitly adopting, encouraging, or furthering, racial discrimination even by its own routine operations. . . .

The majority is wrong to trivialize the continuing impact of government acceptance or use of private institutions or structures. once wrought by discrimination. When government channels all its contracting funds to a white-dominated community of established contractors whose racial homogeneity is the product of private discrimination, it does more than place its *imprimatur* on the practices which forged and which continue to define that community. It also provides a measurable boost to those economic entities that have thrived within it, while denying important economic benefits to those entities which, but for prior discrimination, might well be better qualified to receive valuable government contracts. In my view, the interest in ensuring that the government does not reflect and reinforce prior private discrimination in dispensing public contracts is every bit as strong as the interest in eliminating private discrimination—an interest which this Court has repeatedly deemed compelling. . . . The more government bestows its rewards on those persons or businesses that were positioned to thrive during a period of private racial discrimination, the tighter the deadhand grip of prior discrimination becomes on the present and future. Cities like Richmond may not be constitutionally required to adopt set-aside plans. But there can be no doubt that when Richmond acted affirmatively to stem the perpetuation of patterns of discrimination through its own decisionmaking, it served an interest of the highest order.

The remaining question with respect to the "governmental interest" prong of equal protection analysis is whether Richmond has proffered satisfactory proof of past racial discrimination to support its twin interests in remediation and in, governmental nonperpetuation.

The varied body of evidence in which Richmond relied provides a "strong," "firm," and "unquestionable" basis upon which the city council could determine that the effects of past racial discrimination warranted a remedial and prophylactic governmental response. . . .

Richmond's reliance on localized, industry-specific findings is a far cry from the reliance on generalized "societal discrimination" which the majority decries as a basis for remedial action. But characterizing the plight of Richmond's minority contractors as mere "societal discrimination" is not the only respect in which the majority's critique shows an unwillingness to come to grips with why construction contracting in Richmond is essentially a whites-only enterprise. The majority also takes the disingenuous approach of disaggregating Richmond's local evidence, attacking it piecemeal, and thereby concluding that no *single* piece of evidence adduced by the city, "standing alone," suffices to prove past discrimination. But items of evidence do not, of course, "stan[d] alone" or exist in alien juxtaposition; they necessarily work together, reinforcing or contradicting each other. . . . it is true that, when the factual predicate needed to be proved is one of *present* discrimination, we have generally credited statistical contrasts between the racial composition of a work force and the general population as proving discrimination only where this contrast revealed "gross statistical disparities." But this principle does not impugn Richmond's statistical contrast, for two reasons. First, considering how minuscule the share of Richmond public construction contracting dollars received by minority-owned businesses is, it is hardly unreasonable to conclude that this case involves a "gross statistical disparit[y]." There are roughly equal numbers of minorities and nonminorities in Richmond—yet minority-owned businesses receive *one-seventy-fifth* of the public contracting funds that other businesses receive.

Second, and more fundamentally, where the issue is not present discrimination but rather whether past discrimination has resulted in the continuing *exclusion* of minorities from a historically tight-knit industry, a contrast between population and work force is entirely appropriate to help gauge the degree of the exclusion. . . . This contrast is especially illuminating in cases, like this, where a main avenue of introduction into the work force—here, membership in the trade associations whose members presumably train apprentices and help them procure subcontracting assignments—is itself grossly dominated by nonminorities. The majority's assertion that, the city "does not even know how many MBE's in the relevant market are qualified," is thus entirely beside the point. If Richmond indeed has a monochromatic contracting community, this most likely reflects the lingering power of past exclusionary practices. Certainly this is the explanation Congress has found persuasive at the national level. The city's requirement that prime public contractors set aside 30% of their subcontracting assignments for minority-owned enterprises, subject to the ordinance's provision for waivers where minority-owned enterprises are unavailable or unwilling to participate, is designed precisely to ease minority contractors into the industry.

The majority's perfunctory dismissal of the testimony of Richmond's appointed and elected leaders is also deeply disturbing. These officials—including council members, a former mayor, and the present city manager—asserted that race discrimination in area contracting had been widespread, and that the set-aside ordinance was a sincere and necessary attempt to eradicate the effects of this discrimination. The majority, however, states that where racial classifications are concerned, "simple legislative assurances of good intention cannot suffice." It similarly discounts as minimally probative the city council's designation of its set-aside plan as remedial. "[B]lind judicial deference to legislative or executive pronouncements," the majority explains, "has no place in equal protection analysis."

No one, of course, advocates "blind judicial deference" to the findings of the city council or the testimony of city leaders. The majority's suggestion that wholesale deference is what Richmond seeks is a classic straw-man argument. But the majority's trivialization of the testimony of Richmond's leaders is dismaying in a far more serious respect. By disregarding the testimony of local leaders and the judgment of local government, the majority does violence to the very principles of comity within our federal system which this Court has long championed. Local officials, by virtue of their proximity to, and their expertise with, local affairs, are exceptionally well qualified to make determinations of public good "within their respective sphere of authority." The majority, however, leaves any traces of comity behind in its headlong rush to strike down Richmond's race-conscious measure.

Had the majority paused for a moment on the facts of the Richmond experience, it would have discovered that the city's leadership is deeply familiar with what racial discrimination is. The members of the Richmond City Council have spent long years witnessing multifarious acts of discrimination, including, but not limited to, the deliberate diminution of black residents' voting rights, resistance to school desegregation, and publicly sanctioned housing discrimination. Numerous decisions of federal courts chronicle this disgraceful recent history. . . .

When the legislatures and leaders of cities with histories of pervasive discrimination testify that past discrimination has infected one of their industries, armchair cynicism like that exercised by the majority has no place. [The majority, however, leaves any traces of comity behind in its headlong rush to strike down Richmond's race-conscious measure.]

. . . The majority concedes that Congress established nothing less than a "presumption" that minority contracting firms have been disadvantaged by prior discrimination. The majority, inexplicably, would forbid Richmond to "share" in this information, and permit only

Congress to take note of these ample findings. In thus requiring that Richmond's local evidence be severed from the context in which it was prepared, the majority would require cities seeking to eradicate the effects of past discrimination within their borders to reinvent the evidentiary wheel and engage in unnecessarily duplicative, costly, and time-consuming fact-finding.

No principle of federalism or of federal power, however, forbids a state or local government to draw upon a nationally relevant historical record prepared by the Federal Government. . . . Of course, Richmond could have built an even more compendious record of past discrimination, one including additional stark statistics and additional individual accounts of past discrimination. But nothing in the Fourteenth Amendment imposes such onerous documentary obligations upon States and localities once the reality of past discrimination is apparent.

In my judgment, Richmond's set-aside plan also comports with the second prong of the equal protection inquiry, for it is substantially related to the interests it seeks to serve in remedying past discrimination and in ensuring that municipal contract procurement does not perpetuate that discrimination. The most striking aspect of the city's ordinance is the similarity it bears to the "appropriately limited" federal set-aside provision upheld in Fullilove. Like the federal provision, Richmond's is limited to five years in duration, ibid., and was not renewed when it came up for reconsideration in 1988. Like the federal provision, Richmond's contains a waiver provision freeing from its subcontracting requirements those nonminority firms that demonstrate that they cannot comply with its provisions. Like the federal provision, Richmond's has a minimal impact on innocent third parties. While the measure affects 30% of public contracting dollars, that translates to only 3% of overall Richmond area contracting.

Finally, like the federal provision, Richmond's does not interfere with any vested right of a contractor to a particular contract; instead it operates entirely prospectively. Richmond's initiative affects only future economic arrangements and imposes only a diffuse burden on nonminority competitors—here, businesses owned or controlled by nonminorities which seek subcontracting work on public construction projects. . . .

Today, for the first time, a majority of this Court has adopted strict scrutiny as its standard of Equal Protection Clause review of race-conscious remedial measures. This is an unwelcome development. A profound difference separates governmental actions that themselves are racist, and governmental actions that seek to remedy the effects of prior racism or to prevent neutral governmental activity from perpetuating the effects of such racism.

Racial classifications "drawn on the presumption that one race is inferior to another or because they put the weight of government behind racial hatred and separatism" warrant the strictest judicial scrutiny because of the very irrelevance of these rationales. By contrast, racial classifications drawn for the purpose of remedying the effects of discrimination that itself was race based have a highly pertinent basis: the tragic and indelible fact that discrimination against blacks and other racial minorities in this Nation has pervaded our Nation's history and continues to scar our society.

In concluding that remedial classifications warrant no different standard of review under the Constitution than the most brutal and repugnant forms of state-sponsored racism, a majority of this Court signals that it regards racial discrimination as largely a phenomenon of the past, and that government bodies need no longer preoccupy themselves with rectifying racial injustice. I, however, do not believe this Nation is anywhere close to eradicating racial discrimination or its vestiges. In constitutionalizing its wishful thinking, the majority today does a grave disservice not only to those victims of past and present racial discrimination in this Nation whom government has sought to assist, but also to this Court's long tradition of approaching issues of race with the utmost sensitivity.

I am also troubled by the majority's assertion that, even if it did not believe generally in strict scrutiny of race-based remedial measures, "the circumstances of this case" require this Court to look upon the Richmond City Council's measure with the strictest scrutiny. The sole such circumstance which the majority cites, however, is the fact that blacks in Richmond are a "dominant racial grou[p]" in the city. In support of this characterization of dominance, the majority observes that "blacks constitute approximately 50% of the population of the city of Richmond" and that "[f]ive of the nine seats on the City Council are held by blacks."

While I agree that the numerical and political supremacy of a given racial group is a factor bearing upon the level of scrutiny to be applied, this Court has never held that numerical inferiority, standing alone, makes a racial group "suspect" and thus entitled to strict scrutiny review. Rather, we have identified other "traditional indicia of suspectness": whether a group has been "saddled with such disabilities, or subjected to such a history of purposeful unequal treatment, or relegated to such a position of political powerlessness as to command extraordinary protection from the majoritarian political process."

It cannot seriously be suggested that nonminorities in Richmond have any "history of purposeful unequal treatment." Nor is there any indication that they have any of the disabilities that have characteristically afflicted those groups this Court has deemed suspect. Indeed, the numerical and political dominance of nonminorities within the State of Virginia and the Nation as a whole provides an enormous political check against the "simple racial politics" at the municipal level which the majority fears. If the majority really believes that groups like Richmond's nonminorities, which constitute approximately half the population but which are outnumbered even marginally in political fora, are deserving of suspect class status for these reasons alone, this Court's decisions denying suspect status to women, and to persons with below-average incomes, stand on extremely shaky ground.

In my view, the "circumstances of this case," underscore the importance of *not* subjecting to a strict scrutiny straitjacket the increasing number of cities which have recently come under minority leadership and are eager to rectify, or at least prevent the perpetuation of, past racial discrimination. In many cases, these cities will be the ones with the most in the way of prior discrimination to rectify. Richmond's leaders had just witnessed decades of publicly sanctioned racial discrimination in virtually all walks of life—discrimination amply documented in decisions of the federal judicially. This history of "purposefully unequal treatment" forced upon minorities, not imposed by them, should raise an inference that minorities in Richmond had much to remedy—and that the 1983 set-aside was undertaken with sincere remedial goals in mind, not "simple racial Politics." . . .

Today's decision, finally, is particularly noteworthy for the daunting standard it imposes upon States and local contemplating the use of race-conscious measures to eradicate present effects of prior discrimination and prevent its perpetuation. The majority restricts the use of such measures to situations in which a State or locality can put forth "a prima facie case of constitutional or statutory violation." In so doing, the majority calls into question the validity of the business set-asides which dozens of municipalities across this Nation have adopted on the authority of *Fullilove.* . . .

To the degree that this parsimonious standard is grounded on a view that either § 1 or § 5 of the Fourteenth Amendment substantially disempowered States and localities from remedying past racial discrimination, the majority is seriously mistaken. With respect, first, to § 5, our precedents have never suggested that this provision—or, for that matter, its companion federal-empowerment provisions in the

Thirteenth and Fifteenth Amendments—was meant to pre-empt or limit police power to undertake race-conscious remedial measures. . . .

As for § 1, it is too late in the day to assert seriously that the Equal Protection Clause prohibits States—or for that matter, the Federal Government, to whom the equal protection guarantee has largely been applied,—from enacting race-conscious remedies. Our cases in the areas of school desegregation, voting rights, and affirmative action have demonstrated time and again that race is constitutionally germane, precisely because race remains dismayingly relevant in American life.

In adopting its prima facie standard for States and localities, the majority closes its eyes to this constitutional history and social reality. So, too, does JUSTICE SCALIA. He would further limit consideration of race to those cases in which States find it "necessary to eliminate their own maintenance of a system of unlawful racial classification"—a "distinction" which, he states, "explains our school desegregation cases." But this Court's remedy-stage school desegregation decisions cannot so conveniently be cordoned off. These decisions (like those involving voting rights and affirmative action) stand for the same broad principles of equal protection which Richmond seeks to vindicate in this case: all persons have equal worth, and it is permissible, given a sufficient factual predicate and appropriate tailoring, for government to take account of race to eradicate the present effects of race-based subjugation denying that basic equality. JUSTICE SCALIA'S artful distinction allows him to avoid having to repudiate "our school desegregation cases," ibid., but, like the arbitrary limitation on race-conscious relief adopted by the majority, his approach "would freeze the status quo that is the very target" of the remedial actions of States and localities. . . .

The fact is that Congress' concern in passing the reconstruction Amendments, and particularly their congressional authorization provisions, was that States would *not* adequately respond to racial violence or discrimination against newly freed slaves. To interpret any aspect of these Amendments as proscribing state remedial responses to these very problems turns the Amendments on their heads. . . .

In short, there is simply no credible evidence that the Framers of the Fourteenth Amendment sought "to transfer the security and protection of all the civil rights . . . from the States to the Federal government. The three Reconstruction Amendments undeniably "worked a dramatic change in the balance between congressional and state power," they forbade state-sanctioned slavery, forbade the state-sanctioned denial of the right to vote, and

(until the content of the Equal Protection Clause was substantially applied to the Federal Government through the Due Process Clause of the Fifth Amendment) uniquely forbade States to deny equal protection. The Amendments also specifically empowered the Federal Government to combat discrimination at a time when the breadth of federal power under the Constitution was less apparent than it is today. But nothing in the Amendments themselves, or in our long history of interpreting or applying those momentous charters, suggests that States, exercising their police power, are in any way constitutionally inhibited from working alongside the Federal Government in the fight against discrimination and its effects.

The majority today sounds a full-scale retreat from the Court's longstanding solicitude to race-conscious remedial efforts "directed toward deliverance of the century-old promise of equality of economic opportunity." The new and restrictive tests it applies scuttle one city's effort to surmount its discriminatory past, and imperil those of dozens more localities. I, however, profoundly disagree with the cramped vision of the Equal Protection Clause which the majority offers today and with its application of that vision to Richmond, Virginia's, laudable set-aside plan. The battle against pernicious racial discrimination or its effects is nowhere near won. I must dissent.

JUSTICE BLACKMUN, with whom JUSTICE BRENNAN joins, dissenting.

I join JUSTICE MARSHALL'S perceptive and incisive opinion revealing great sensitivity toward those who have suffered the pains of economic discrimination in the construction trades for so long.

I never thought that I would live to see the day when the city of Richmond, Virginia, the cradle of the Old Confederacy, sought on its own, within a narrow confine, to lessen the stark impact of persistent discrimination. But Richmond, to its great credit, acted. Yet this Court, the supposed bastion of equality strikes down Richmond's efforts as though discrimination had never existed or was not demonstrated in this particular litigation. JUSTICE MARSHALL convincingly discloses the fallacy and the shallowness of that approach. History is irrefutable, even though one might sympathize with those who—though possibly innocent in themselves—benefit from the wrongs of past decades.

So the Court today regresses. I am confident, however, that, given time, it one day again will do its best to fulfill the great promises of the Constitution's Preamble and of the guarantees embodied in the Bill of Rights—a fulfillment that would make this Nation very special.

Emergence of a majority standard, requiring strict scrutiny of all racial classifications, did not establish an absolute prohibition against racially preferential methods. As the O'Connor plurality indicated, race-conscious policy is allowable to the extent necessary to remedy a Fourteenth Amendment violation.[234] The availability of such relief, however, is conditioned by the vexing requirement of having to prove intentional discrimination.[235]

---

[234] *Id.* at 729 (plurality opinion).
[235] *See* notes 113–30 and accompanying text.

DEL: Taken individually or collectively, the Supreme Court's arguments against racial preferences are not terribly impressive. In *Croson*, the Court acknowledged the "nation's sorry history of public and private racial discrimination."[236] It concluded, however, that a general accounting for societal discrimination is impermissible because the methodology of preference stigmatizes and perpetuates stereotypes and fosters racial politics.[237] Even if the beneficiaries of racial preferences are viewed as having succeeded because of a special break rather than because of talent, such attitudes may be defeated by actual performance. More importantly, stigma and stereotype precede preferential methodology which attempts to undo them even if at the risk of temporarily exacerbating them. Racial preferences also might be viewed as a means of breaking down stigma and stereotype insofar as white males, who traditionally have benefited from an unlevel playing field, would no longer have their success tainted by the exclusion of potential competition. To hold preferential programs and policies responsible for racial politics both exaggerates and discriminates. Reality is that from the framing of the Constitution, to the Black Codes, to official segregation and to the devolution of the desegregation principle—not to mention historical and contemporary voting behavior—racial politics have been a central societal reality. Prohibiting race-conscious brokering in the political process—especially as voting rights reform has made the legislative branch more open and responsive to minority needs—seems an exercise in traditional exclusion on the basis of race. If concern is with innocent victims, as earlier decisions have suggested,[238] the Court again discounts historical reality. Given a racial legacy which includes an understanding that "the reputation of belonging . . . to the white race, is property,"[239] the notion of innocent victims must compete against a legacy of inherited racial advantage.

The failure of the Court to articulate a persuasive rationale against racial preferences does not mean that none exists. Insofar as such methods depend upon the willingness of the majority to make racial concessions, they perpetuate a misplaced habit of reliance upon good will and interest that historically has proved either impermanent or nonexistent. The phenomenon of racial fatigue, that facilitated the unwinding of Reconstruction and desegregation process, indicates that minority dependence upon majority favors offers rather low returns. To the extent minorities trade in victimization, moreover, it becomes even more difficult to escape majority control. Equally if not more dangerous is the possibility that preferential systems will create ceilings rather than floors for opportunity. If faculty hiring practices at American law schools are representative, a danger appears to be a sense that after a bout of minority hiring in recent years the imperatives of diversity have been satisfied and life can return to normal. If such a mentality survives, the result will have been another triumph of formalism achieving at most a token quota system. Such an

---

[236] City of Richmond v. J. A. Croson Co., 488 U.S. 469, 499 (1989).
[237] *Id.* at 493.
[238] Wygant v. Jackson Board of Education, 476 U.S. 267, 280–83 (1986)(plurality opinion).
[239] Plessy v. Ferguson, 163 U.S. 537, 549 (1896).

outcome would compound the mystery over why reaction to preferential methodology has been so powerfully negative when its impact is so slight.[240] Further legitimized would be doubts about the wisdom of reliance upon legal innovation to fix an acute societal pathology.

RLW: Professor Lively may be right about the wisdom of relying on "legal innovation to fix an acute societal pathology," but affirmative actions programs suffer from their own "pathology." These programs encourage society to continue dividing itself into racial classes, and to continue judging people based on the color of their skin rather than the content of their character. Moreover, because affirmative action programs distribute benefits and opportunities on the basis of an immutable characteristic, they inevitably breed anger, resentment and racial disharmony.[241] This is particularly true today when many programs effectively require the use of quotas (whether or not the preference is stated as a quota). Despite Professor Lively's assertion, these programs have not had slight impact.

As a remedy for past wrongs, affirmative action is a very rough remedy. It does not directly seek to punish the original wrongdoer. Rather, it seeks to stigmatize and hold back an entire racial group because of the perceived sins of their ancestors, whether or not one's ancestors actually sinned by participating in slavery or segregation. Benefits and opportunities are also denied to Caucasians from economically disadvantaged backgrounds even though these individuals have suffered societal oppression of a different sort.

The affirmative action remedy is equally rough on the beneficiary side of the equation. Affirmative action programs extend benefits to some individuals who did not suffer (and whose ancestors did not suffer) from slavery or segregation in this country (*e.g.*, black immigrants). In one case of which I'm aware, a black woman whose family held black slaves in a Caribbean country was the beneficiary of an affirmative action program in this country. Moreover, most affirmative action programs are not designed to help those African-Americans who suffered the worst from racial discrimination in this country. Employers and universities, anxious to recruit "qualified" African-Americans (or Hispanics) without wholesale reductions in standards, disproportionately recruit African-Americans (and Hispanics) from middle, upper-middle, or upper-class backgrounds (*e.g.,* an extremely wealthy African-American friend's son was recently given a full scholarship to Harvard University). Employers and academic institutions, having relieved their consciences by recruiting more advantaged African-Americans (or Hispanics), are content to leave the poorest African-Americans (and Hispanics) mired in poverty with far less to show from preferences, quotas and financial aid.

Another problem with affirmative action is that it stigmatizes those it seeks to help. When members of one (or some) races are recruited under radically different standards, others may wonder about the competency of those recruited under lower standards. For example, the University of Louisville has an official policy statement which requires all units to give "qualified" African-American faculty candidates preference over all other faculty candidates. Even if another candidate has outstanding or even sensational qualifications, the African-American *must* be given the job. Understandably, African-American faculty members wonder whether others question their abilities and qualifications. When an African-American fails in the classroom, racial stereotypes are reinforced.

It would be far better to replace existing race based programs with programs that favor

---

[240] Randall Kennedy, *Persuasion and Distrust: A Comment on the Affirmative Action Debate,* 99 Harv. L. Rev. 1327, 1334 (1986).

[241] Some try to justify affirmative action on the basis that it promotes "diversity." So the argument goes, "diversity" is a value in and of itself because it brings different perspectives. In most cases, the diversity argument is fraudulent. Many "diversity" programs focus narrowly on race and ethnicity. At the University of Louisville, administrators sometimes justify giving preferences to a single race (African-Americans) on "diversity" grounds. No effort is made to consider the myriad of other factors which constitute "diversity" including "intellectual diversity."

the economically disadvantaged. That approach would extend opportunities and benefits to those who need them the most. Moreover, although disadvantaged programs would disproportionately favor African-Americans (and Hispanics), those programs would generate less hostility since they function on a race neutral basis. The need for speech codes and other means of suppressing hostility might disappear. Moreover, society would be better served by helping those who need help rather than by doling out benefits, preferences and financial aid to the children of African-American (and Hispanic) professionals.

DER: I agree with Professor Lively's assessment of the weakness of the Court's arguments against racial preferences. The Court's color-blind standard, that invalidates any government action taking race into account, distorts the meaning of the Equal Protection Clause and the objectives of race-conscious remedies designed to enforce it. The Fourteenth Amendment's goal is not racial neutrality; it is to eradicate the imbalance of group power and privilege. The fact that white businesses in Richmond received over 99 percent of all city contracts evidenced the stark power imbalance in that city spawned by centuries of racial discrimination. Ignoring this question of power permitted the Court to treat state-sponsored racism that subjugated a disempowered group the same as state remedial programs designed to eliminate such inequality. But the former violates the Fourteenth Amendment's prohibition of racial hierarchy, while the latter does not. White businessmen in Richmond clearly did not constitute a subordinated class in need of Fourteenth Amendment protection. The Court's affirmative action to preserve their entrenched power turned the Fourteenth Amendment's equality mandate on its head.

Both Professor Lively's and Professor Weaver's account of a rationale for invalidating affirmative action programs also mischaracterize the purpose of these programs, as well as the reason for hostility towards them. Race-conscious remedies need not result from the pleading of victims for favors from the majority. They respond to minorities' justified demands, made most effectively by political mobilization, to eliminate the unfair privileges of race. Richmond's set-aside program, for example, was not an instance of "minority dependence upon majority favors," but an effort by the Black majority on the city council finally to dismantle the historical hold that white businesses had on city contracting. The *Croson* decision thus protected the interests of whites "against both the economic aspirations of black contractors and the political effectiveness of black leaders and constituents."[242]

Hostility towards affirmative action programs cannot justify demolishing them. Why do these programs "breed anger, resentment and racial disharmony," as Professor Weaver contends? Many individuals who have come to expect the institutionalized advantages of being white in America understandably take offense at any diminution in this power. The backlash against programs designed to integrate Blacks into the national economy, including the dismantling of Reconstruction and of the 1960s War on Poverty, constitutes an aggressive fight to retain the advantages of whiteness rather than "racial fatigue." Cheryl Harris convincingly argues that *Croson* treats white Americans' expectation of a superior status as the basis for a valid claim to special constitutional protection: "Essentially, Croson's claim was an assertion of the property interest in whiteness."[243] Ending race-conscious remedies for this reason caters to white individuals' hostility at losing some of the historical privileges of their race. Like the Court's anemic enforcement of the desegregation mandate, abolishing affirmative action programs allows the interests of whites to supersede the requirements of equality.

Professor Weaver mischaracterizes the purpose of affirmative action as punishing

---

[242] Linda S. Greene, *Race in the 21st Century: Equality Through Law?*, 64 TUL. L. REV. 1515, 1533 (1990).

[243] Cheryl I. Harris, *Whiteness as Property*, 106 HARV. L. REV. 1707, 1775 (1993).

innocent whites for the "sins" of slavery and segregation committed by their ancestors. Rather, it attempts to remove present barriers to Black economic participation that are rooted in this past and from which white Americans currently benefit. It is a surprising proposition that the beneficiaries of historical wrongs have an inviolable claim to their tainted property. As Patricia Williams noted, "[i]f a thief steals so that his children may live in luxury and the law returns his ill-gotten gain to its rightful owner, the children cannot complain that they have been deprived of what they did not own."[244] More important, the goal of equal citizenship and just distribution of resources justifies unsettling hiring standards and the expectations of white applicants. Affirmative action, if allowed to thrive, would reallocate economic benefits in a way that better resembles a society free of racial discrimination. The alternative is the unacceptable status quo where nearly all city contracts, corporate jobs, and, no doubt, faculty positions at the University of Louisville are reserved for whites only.

Weaver is correct that race-conscious remedies have not reached the most disadvantaged African Americans and members of other groups (although the benefits are more widespread than Weaver suggests).[245] But affirmative action programs were not designed to solve the problem of poverty. The answer to this limitation is to craft additional remedies for economic, as well as racial, injustice. Nor does the perverse manipulation of affirmative action programs to limit minority participation justify abandoning these programs altogether. Employers' imposition of minority hiring ceilings and use of empty jargon to create the false impression of progress should be challenged with increased scrutiny of actual results.

RLW: Professor Roberts's passionate defense of affirmative action reflects the anger of more advantaged African-Americans (and Hispanics) "who have come to expect the institutionalized advantages" of affirmative action and who "take offense" at any attempt to diminish this advantage by shifting benefits to the truly disadvantaged.

PAH: We live in a world in which racial and gender inequality is deeply imbedded in the social structure. Statistics document that despite antidiscrimination laws extreme disparity persists between whites and blacks as well as men and women.[246] The "power" gap is especially pronounced,[247] yet opponents of affirmative action, like Professor Weaver, take the position that our Constitution is color blind and thus race-focused affirmative action is constitutionally suspect. This position condemns blacks and other subordinated minorities to continue to suffer isolating inequality because of disabilities created by societal prejudice without redress beyond "race-neutral" governmental policies. The implication is that the public interest in maintaining the illusion of a colorblind society outweighs the interest in eradicating societal discrimination and its consequent harms.

I call the color blind approach merely an illusion because the reality is that race cannot be ignored. Professor Weaver ignores the complexities of *Brown* when he argues that our constitution should be interpreted as color blind. As David Strauss has set forth in THE MYTH OF COLORBLINDNESS,[248] the prohibition of discrimination that was the focus of *Brown* is not a color blind requirement. Rather the prohibition requirement forces us to treat race

---

[244] Patricia Williams, *The Obliging Shell*, in ALCHEMY OF RACE AND RIGHTS 101 (1991).

[245] *See* GERTRUDE EZORSKY, RACISM AND JUSTICE: THE CASE FOR AFFIRMATIVE ACTION 63- 65 (1991) (citing studies demonstrating increased job opportunities among Blacks in blue-collar work as a result of affirmative action).

[264] *See, e.g, Women and Minorities Still Face 'Glass Ceiling'* NY TIMES Mar. 15, 1995.

[247] *See e.g.* Robert Sedler, *The Constitution and the Consequences of the Social History of Racism,* 40 ARK. L. REV. 677 (1989).

[248] 1986 SUP. CT. REV. 99.

differently than we normally would and different from other bases for classifying people. To attack race-conscious affirmative efforts to eliminate subordinating discrimination because they move us away from color blindness ignores the fact that "race is already before our eyes."[249] As Professor David Strauss explains it:

'Race is a very visible characteristic, and it correlates to some extent with other characteristics. Left to their own devices, people will notice the correlations and attribute characteristics to people on the basis of their race."[250]

Professor Roberts has persuasively responded to the argument that the rights of innocent victims are jeopardized by affirmative action, pointing out that the assumptions of white privilege are what is shaken—a necessary step in the elimination of racial and gender inequality. Professor Strauss points out:

There is unquestionably an undertone in the affirmative Action debate that affirmative action is different from nondiscrimination because affirmative action causes innocent people to suffer. The assertion that there is a difference i[s] [sic] incorrect. Prohibiting discrimination also causes, and has caused, innocent people to suffer. And so far as I am aware, no one has justified that suffering of these victims of nondiscrimination in a way that would not also justify the suffering of victims of affirmative action.'

What opponents of affirmative action *have* argued is that discrimination for which government ought to be held responsible should be limited because other changes would impact the lives of those benefitting from the present order. Disrupting that order is not justified by the equality claims of African Americans or other subordinated groups. From the perspective of citizens who continue to experience inequality (and who see that the beneficiaries of the present order are overwhelmingly white and male), this *racially determined preference* for preserving the existing social order is hidden in the myth of color blindness.

Affirmative action *like* the prohibition against discrimination expressed in *Brown* are color-conscious measures designed to avoid the results of a society where racism is deeply imbedded. Like the prohibition against discrimination, affirmative action reflects a decision to give special treatment to race in order to deal with a serious social problem.

Professor Strauss asserts that the myth of color blindness "at its worst" suggests that a posture of race-neutrality despite persistent inequality "is the correct state of affairs from which any deviation is wrong."[251] Like him, I question why that base-line *necessarily* exists. Rather than denying the acceptability of race-conscious action we ought to focus on continuing the discourse, begun in *Brown* about why discrimination is wrong, considering in particular why continuing disparity between the races is not destructive of the Fourteenth Amendment equality principles *Brown* was to promote. By placing the burdens of evidence and persuasion on those who have experienced social and economic disparities to explain why deviations from colorblindness are constitutionally justified we avoid this troubling, yet potentially transformative interpretive work.

---

[249] *Id.* at 131.
[250] DAVID STRAUSS, THE MYTH OF COLORBLINDNESS, 1986 SUP. CT. REV. at 114.
[251] *Id.* at 132.

One year after the *Croson* decision, it appeared that a safe harbor was established for racial preferences that were congressionally mandated. In *Metro Broadcasting, Inc. v. FCC*, the Court upheld regulations that gave designated minorities a preference in broadcast licensing proceedings. Noting that the policies were prescribed by Congress, Justice Brennan authored a majority opinion endorsing a less demanding standard of review than used in *Croson*.[252] Responding to the majority's determination that congressionally mandated "benign racial classifications" were constitutionally permissible,[253] four dissenting justices criticized what they perceived as an unwarranted departure from the strict scrutiny demands of *Croson*.[254] Justice Kennedy further asserted that the majority was repeating the "fundamental error of the *Plessy* Court" pursuant to "a similar confidence in its ability to identify 'benign' discrimination."[255] From his perspective, validation of the preferential policy represented a neo-apartheid exercise.[256]

In *Adarand Constructors, Inc. v. Pena*, the Court reversed the equal protection course of *Metro Broadcasting* and determined that racial preferences—whether formulated by federal or state government—must be strictly scrutinized.

---

[252] Metro Broadcasting, Inc. v. FCC, 497 U.S. 547 600 (1990).

[253] *Id*. at 565.

[254] *Id*. at 603–10 (O'Connor, J., dissenting, joined by Rehnquist, C.J. and Scalia and Kennedy, J.J.).

[255] *Id*. at 634–35 (Kennedy, J., dissenting).

[256] *Id*. at 635.

Adarand Constructors, Inc. v. Pena
115 S.Ct. 2097 (1995)

JUSTICE O'CONNOR announced the judgment of the Court and delivered an opinion with respect to Parts I, II, III-A, III-B, III-D, and IV, which is for the Court except insofar as it might be inconsistent with the views expressed in JUSTICE SCALIA's concurrence, and an opinion with respect to Part III-C in which JUSTICE KENNEDY joins.

Petitioner Adarand Constructors, Inc., claims that the Federal Government's practice of giving general contractors on government projects a financial incentive to hire subcontractors controlled by "socially and economically disadvantaged individuals," and in particular, the Government's use of race-based presumptions in identifying such individuals, violates the equal protection component of the Fifth Amendment's Due Process Clause. The Court of Appeals rejected Adarand's claim. We conclude, however, that courts should analyze cases of this kind under a different standard of review than the one the Court of Appeals applied. We therefore vacate the Court of Appeals' judgment and remand the case for further proceedings.

I

In 1989, the Central Federal Lands Highway Division (CFLHD), which is part of the United States Department of Transportation (DOT), awarded the prime contract for a highway construction project in Colorado to Mountain Gravel & Construction Company. Mountain Gravel then solicited bids from subcontractors for the guardrail portion of the contract. Adarand, a Colorado-based highway construction company specializing in guardrail work, submitted the low bid. Gonzales Construction Company also submitted a bid.

The prime contract's terms provide that Mountain Gravel would receive additional compensation if it hired subcontractors certified as small businesses controlled by "socially and economically disadvantaged individuals." Gonzales is certified as such a business; Adarand is not. Mountain Gravel awarded the subcontract to Gonzales, despite Adarand's low bid, and Mountain Gravel's Chief Estimator has submitted an affidavit stating that Mountain Gravel would have accepted Adarand's bid, had it not been for the additional payment it received by hiring Gonzales instead. Federal law requires that a subcontracting clause similar to the one used here must appear in most federal agency contracts, and it also requires the clause to state that "the contractor shall presume that socially and economically disadvantaged individuals include Black Americans, Hispanic Americans, Native Americans, Asian Pacific Americans, and other minorities, or any other individual found to be disadvantaged by the [Small Business] Administration pursuant. . . . Adarand claims that the presumption set forth in that statute discriminates on the basis of race in violation of the Federal Government's Fifth Amendment obligation not to deny anyone equal protection of the laws.

. . . The Small Business Act, declares it to be "the policy of the United States that small business concerns, [and] small business concerns owned and controlled by socially and economically disadvantaged individuals, . . . shall have the maximum practicable opportunity to participate in the performance of contracts let by any Federal agency." The Act defines "socially disadvantaged individuals" as "those who have been subjected to racial or ethnic prejudice or cultural bias because of their identity as a member of a group without regard to their individual qualities," and it defines "economically disadvantaged individuals" as "those socially disadvantaged individuals whose ability to compete in the free enterprise system has been impaired due to diminished capital and credit opportunities as compared to others in the same business area who are not socially disadvantaged."

. . . [T]he Act establishes "the Government-wide goal for participation by small business concerns owned and controlled by socially and economically disadvantaged individuals" at "not less than 5 percent of the total value of all prime contract and subcontract awards for each fiscal year." It also requires the head of each Federal agency to set agency-specific goals for participation by businesses controlled by socially and economically disadvantaged individuals.

The Small Business Administration (SBA) has implemented these statutory directives in a variety of ways, two of which are relevant here. One is the "8(a) program," which is available to small businesses controlled by socially and economically disadvantaged individuals as the SBA has defined those terms. The 8(a) program confers a wide range of benefits on participating businesses. To participate in the 8(a) program, a business must be "small," and it must be 51% owned by individuals who qualify as "socially and economically disadvantaged," § 124.103. The SBA presumes that Black, Hispanic, Asian Pacific, Subcontinent Asian, and Native Americans, as well as "members of other groups designated from time to time by SBA," are "socially disadvantaged." It also allows any individual not a member of a listed group to prove social disadvantage "on the basis of clear and convincing evidence." Social disadvantage is not enough to establish eligibility, however; SBA also requires each 8(a) program participant to prove "economic disadvantage."

The other SBA program relevant to this case is the "8(d) subcontracting program," which unlike the 8(a) program is limited to eligibility for subcontracting provisions like the one at issue here. In determining eligibility, the SBA presumes social disadvantage based on membership in certain minority groups, just

as in the 8(a) program, and again appears to require an individualized, although "less restrictive," showing of economic disadvantage. A different set of regulations, however, says that members of minority groups wishing to participate in the 8(d) subcontracting program are entitled to a race-based presumption of social and economic disadvantage. We are left with some uncertainty as to whether participation in the 8(d) subcontracting program requires an individualized showing of economic disadvantage. In any event, in both the 8(a) and the 8(d) programs, the presumptions of disadvantage are rebuttable if a third party comes forward with evidence suggesting that the participant is not, in fact, either economically or socially disadvantaged.

The contract giving rise to the dispute in this case came about as a result of the Surface Transportation and Uniform Relocation Assistance Act of 1987, a DOT appropriations measure. Section 106(c)(1) of STURAA provides that "not less than 10 percent" of the appropriated funds "shall be expended with small business concerns owned and controlled by socially and economically disadvantaged individuals." STURAA adopts the Small Business Act's definition of "socially and economically disadvantaged individual," including the applicable race-based presumptions, and adds that "women shall be presumed to be socially and economically disadvantaged individuals for purposes of this subsection." STURAA also requires the Secretary of Transportation to establish "minimum uniform criteria for State governments to use in certifying whether a concern qualifies for purposes of this subsection." The Secretary has done so. . . . Those regulations say that the certifying authority should presume both social and economic disadvantage (i.e., eligibility to participate) if the applicant belongs to certain racial groups, or is a woman. As with the SBA programs, third parties may come forward with evidence in an effort to rebut the presumption of disadvantage for a particular business.

The operative clause in the contract in this case reads as follows:

"Subcontracting. This subsection is supplemented to include a Disadvantaged Business Enterprise (DBE) Development and Subcontracting Provision as follows:

"Monetary compensation is offered for awarding subcontracts to small business concerns owned and controlled by socially and economically disadvantaged individuals. . . .

"A small business concern will be considered a DBE after it has been certified as such by the U.S. Small Business Administration or any State Highway Agency. Certification by other Government agencies, counties, or cities may be acceptable on an individual basis provided the Contracting Officer has determined the certifying agency has an acceptable and viable DBE certification program. If the Contractor requests payment under this provision, the Contractor shall furnish the engineer with acceptable evidence of the subcontractor(s) DBE certification and shall furnish one certified copy of the executed subcontract(s).

. . .

"The Contractor will be paid an amount computed as follows:

"1. If a subcontract is awarded to one DBE, 10 percent of the final amount of the approved DBE subcontract, not to exceed 1.5 percent of the original contract amount.

"2. If subcontracts are awarded to two or more DBEs, 10 percent of the final amount of the approved DBE subcontracts, not to exceed 2 percent of the original contract amount." To benefit from this clause, Mountain Gravel had to hire a subcontractor who had been certified as a small disadvantaged business by the SBA, a state highway agency, or some other certifying authority acceptable to the Contracting Officer. Any of the three routes to such certification described above—SBA's 8(a) or 8(d) program, or certification by a State under the DOT regulations—would meet that requirement. . . .

After losing the guardrail subcontract to Gonzales, Adarand filed suit against various federal officials in the United States District Court for the District of Colorado, claiming that the race-based presumptions involved in the use of subcontracting compensation clauses violate Adarand's right to equal protection. The District Court granted the Government's motion for summary judgment. The Court of Appeals for the Tenth Circuit affirmed. It understood our decision in *Fullilove v. Klutznick*, to have adopted "a lenient standard, resembling intermediate scrutiny, in assessing" the constitutionality of federal race-based action. Applying that "lenient standard," as further developed in *Metro Broadcasting, Inc. v. FCC*, the Court of Appeals upheld the use of subcontractor compensation clauses. We granted certiorari.

. . .

III

The Government urges that "the Subcontracting Compensation Clause program is . . . a program based on disadvantage, not on race," and thus that it is subject only to "the most relaxed judicial scrutiny." Brief for Respondents 26. To the extent that the statutes and regulations involved in this case are race neu-

tral, we agree. The Government concedes, however, that "the race-based rebuttable presumption used in some certification determinations under the Subcontracting Compensation Clause" is subject to some heightened level of scrutiny. The parties disagree as to what that level should be. (We note, incidentally, that this case concerns only classifications based explicitly on race, and presents none of the additional difficulties posed by laws that, although facially race neutral, result in racially disproportionate impact and are motivated by a racially discriminatory purpose. *Washington v. Davis.*

Adarand's claim arises under the Fifth Amendment to the Constitution, which provides that "No person shall . . . be deprived of life, liberty, or property, without due process of law." Although this Court has always understood that Clause to provide some measure of protection against arbitrary treatment by the Federal Government, it is not as explicit a guarantee of equal treatment as the Fourteenth Amendment, which provides that "No State shall . . . deny to any person within its jurisdiction the equal protection of the laws" (emphasis added). Our cases have accorded varying degrees of significance to the difference in the language of those two Clauses. We think it necessary to revisit the issue here.

A

Through the 1940s, this Court had routinely taken the view in non-race-related cases that, "unlike the Fourteenth Amendment, the Fifth contains no equal protection clause and it provides no guaranty against discriminatory legislation by Congress." . . .

. . .

In *Bolling v. Sharpe*, the Court for the first time explicitly questioned the existence of any difference between the obligations of the Federal Government and the States to avoid racial classifications. *Bolling* did note that "the 'equal protection of the laws' is a more explicit safeguard of prohibited unfairness than 'due process of law.'" But *Bolling* then concluded that, "in view of [the] decision that the Constitution prohibits the states from maintaining racially segregated public schools, it would be unthinkable that the same Constitution would impose a lesser duty on the Federal Government."

Bolling's facts concerned school desegregation, but its reasoning was not so limited. The Court's observations that "distinctions between citizens solely because of their ancestry are by their very nature odious," and that "all legal restrictions which curtail the civil rights of a single racial group are immediately suspect," carry no less force in the context of federal action than in the context of action by the States—indeed, they first appeared in cases concerning action by the Federal Government. . . .

. . . Thus, in 1975, the Court stated explicitly that "this Court's approach to Fifth Amendment equal protection claims has always been precisely the same as to equal protection claims under the Fourteenth Amendment." *Weinberger v. Wiesenfeld*, 420 U.S. 636, 638, n. 2; *Buckley v. Valeo*, 424 U.S. 1, 93, 46 L. Ed. 2d 659, 96 S. Ct. 612 (1976). We do not understand a few contrary suggestions appearing in cases in which we found special deference to the political branches of the Federal Government to be appropriate, to detract from this general rule.

B

. . .

With *Croson*, the Court finally agreed that the Fourteenth Amendment requires strict scrutiny of all race-based action by state and local governments. But *Croson* of course had no occasion to declare what standard of review the Fifth Amendment requires for such action taken by the Federal Government. *Croson* observed simply that the Court's "treatment of an exercise of congressional power in *Fullilove* cannot be dispositive here," because *Croson*'s facts did not implicate Congress' broad power under § 5 of the Fourteenth Amendment. Thus, some uncertainty persisted with respect to the standard of review for federal racial classifications. . . .

Despite lingering uncertainty in the details, however, the Court's cases through *Croson* had established three general propositions with respect to governmental racial classifications. First, skepticism: "any preference based on racial or ethnic criteria must necessarily receive a most searching examination."' Second, consistency: "the standard of review under the Equal Protection Clause is not dependent on the race of those burdened or benefited by a particular classification," all racial classifications reviewable under the Equal Protection Clause must be strictly scrutinized. And third, congruence: "equal protection analysis in the Fifth Amendment area is the same as that under the Fourteenth Amendment." Taken together, these three propositions lead to the conclusion that any person, of whatever race, has the right to demand that any governmental actor subject to the Constitution justify any racial classification subjecting that person to unequal treatment under the strictest judicial scrutiny. Justice Powell's defense of this conclusion bears repeating here:

"If it is the individual who is entitled to judicial protection against classifications

based upon his racial or ethnic background because such distinctions impinge upon personal rights, rather than the individual only because of his membership in a particular group, then constitutional standards may be applied consistently. Political judgments regarding the necessity for the particular classification may be weighed in the constitutional balance, but the standard of justification will remain constant. This is as it should be, since those political judgments are the product of rough compromise struck by contending groups within the democratic process. When they touch upon an individual's race or ethnic background, he is entitled to a judicial determination that the burden he is asked to bear on that basis is precisely tailored to serve a compelling governmental interest. The Constitution guarantees that right to every person regardless of his background.

A year later, however, the Court took a surprising turn. *Metro Broadcasting, Inc. v. FCC*, involved a Fifth Amendment challenge to two race-based policies of the Federal Communications Commission. In Metro Broadcasting, the Court repudiated the long-held notion that "it would be unthinkable that the same Constitution would impose a lesser duty on the Federal Government" than it does on a State to afford equal protection of the laws. It did so by holding that "benign" federal racial classifications need only satisfy intermediate scrutiny, even though Croson had recently concluded that such classifications enacted by a State must satisfy strict scrutiny. "Benign" federal racial classifications, the Court said, "—even if those measures are not 'remedial' in the sense of being designed to compensate victims of past governmental or societal discrimination—are constitutionally permissible to the extent that they serve important governmental objectives within the power of Congress and are substantially related to achievement of those objectives." The Court did not explain how to tell whether a racial classification should be deemed "benign," other than to express "confidence that an 'examination of the legislative scheme and its history' will separate benign measures from other types of racial classifications."

Applying this test, the Court first noted that the FCC policies at issue did not serve as a remedy for past discrimination. Proceeding on the assumption that the policies were nonetheless "benign," it concluded that they served the "important governmental objective" of "enhancing broadcast diversity," and that they were "substantially related" to that objective. It therefore upheld the policies.

By adopting intermediate scrutiny as the standard of review for congressionally mandated "benign" racial classifications, *Metro Broadcasting* departed from prior cases in two significant respects. First, it turned its back on *Croson's* explanation of why strict scrutiny of all governmental racial classifications is essential:

> "Absent searching judicial inquiry into the justification for such race-based measures, there is simply no way of determining what classifications are 'benign' or 'remedial' and what classifications are in fact motivated by illegitimate notions of racial inferiority or simple racial politics. Indeed, the purpose of strict scrutiny is to 'smoke out' illegitimate uses of race by assuring that the legislative body is pursuing a goal important enough to warrant use of a highly suspect tool. The test also ensures that the means chosen 'fit' this compelling goal so closely that there is little or no possibility that the motive for the classification was illegitimate racial prejudice or stereotype."

We adhere to that view today, despite the surface appeal of holding "benign" racial classifications to a lower standard, because "it may not always be clear that a so-called preference is in fact benign." "More than good motives should be required when government seeks to allocate its resources by way of an explicit racial classification system."

Second, *Metro Broadcasting* squarely rejected one of the three propositions established by the Court's earlier equal protection cases, namely, congruence between the standards applicable to federal and state racial classifications, and in so doing also undermined the other two—skepticism of all racial classifications, and consistency of treatment irrespective of the race of the burdened or benefited group. Under *Metro Broadcasting*, certain racial classifications should be treated less skeptically than others; and the race of the benefited group is critical to the determination of which standard of review to apply. Metro Broadcasting was thus a significant departure from much of what had come before it.

The three propositions undermined by *Metro Broadcasting* all derive from the basic principle that the Fifth and Fourteenth Amendments to the Constitution protect persons, not groups. It follows from that principle that all governmental action based on race—a group classification long recognized as "in most circumstances irrelevant and therefore prohibited,"—should be subjected to detailed judicial inquiry to ensure that the personal right to equal protection of the laws has not been infringed. These ideas have long been central to this Court's understanding of equal protection, and holding "benign" state and federal racial classifications to different standards does not square with them. "[A] free people whose institutions are founded upon the doctrine of equality,"should tolerate no retreat from the principle that government may treat people differently because of their race only for the most compelling reasons. Accordingly, we hold today that all racial classifications, imposed by whatever federal, state, or local governmental actor, must be analyzed by a reviewing court under strict scrutiny. In other words, such classifications are constitutional only if they are narrowly tailored measures that further compelling governmental interests. To the extent that *Metro Broadcasting* is inconsistent with that holding, it is overruled.

In dissent, Justice Stevens criticizes us for "delivering a disconcerting lecture about the evils of governmental racial classifications." With respect, we believe his criticisms reflect a serious misunderstanding of our opinion.

Justice Stevens concurs in our view that courts should take a skeptical view of all governmental racial classifications. He also allows that "nothing is inherently wrong with applying a single standard to fundamentally different situations, as long as that standard takes relevant differences into account." What he fails to recognize is that strict scrutiny does take "relevant differences" into account—indeed, that is its fundamental purpose. The point of carefully examining the interest asserted by the government in support of a racial classification, and the evidence offered to show that the classification is needed, is precisely to distinguish legitimate from illegitimate uses of race in governmental decisionmaking. . . .

Justice Stevens chides us for our "supposed inability to differentiate between 'invidious' and 'benign' discrimination," because it is in his view sufficient that "people understand the difference between good intentions and bad." But, as we have just explained, the point of strict scrutiny is to "differentiate between" permissible and impermissible governmental use of race. And Justice Stevens himself has already explained in his dissent in Fullilove why "good intentions" alone are not enough to sustain a supposedly "benign" racial classification: "Even though it is not the actual predicate for this legislation, a statute of this kind inevitably is perceived by many as resting on an assumption that those who are granted this special preference are less qualified in some respect that is identified purely by their race. Because that perception—especially when fostered by the Congress of the United States—can only exacerbate rather than reduce racial prejudice, it will delay the time when race will become a truly irrelevant, or at least insignificant, factor. Unless Congress clearly articulates the need and basis for a racial classification, and also tailors the classification to its justification, the Court should not uphold this kind of statute." . . .

. . . According to Justice Stevens, our view of consistency "equates remedial preferences with invidious discrimination," and ignores the difference between "an engine of oppression" and an effort "to foster equality in society," or, more colorfully, "between a 'No Trespassing' sign and a welcome mat," post, at 2, 4. It does nothing of the kind. The principle of consistency simply means that whenever the government treats any person unequally because of his or her race, that person has suffered an injury that falls squarely within the language and spirit of the Constitution's guarantee of equal protection. It says nothing about the ultimate validity of any particular law; that determination is the job of the court applying strict scrutiny. The principle of consistency explains the circumstances in which the injury requiring strict scrutiny occurs. The application of strict scrutiny, in turn, determines whether a compelling governmental interest justifies the infliction of that injury.

. . .

C

"Although adherence to precedent is not rigidly required in constitutional cases, any departure from the doctrine of stare decisis demands special justification." In deciding whether this case presents such justification, we recall Justice Frankfurter's admonition that "stare decisis is a principle of policy and not a mechanical formula of adherence to the latest decision, however recent and questionable, when such adherence involves collision with a prior doctrine more embracing in its scope, intrinsically sounder, and verified by experience." Remaining true to an "intrinsically sounder" doctrine established in prior cases better serves the values of stare decisis than would following a more recently decided case inconsistent with the decisions that came before it; the latter course would simply compound the recent error and would likely make the unjustified break from previously established doctrine complete. In such a situation,

"special justification" exists to depart from the recently decided case.

As we have explained, *Metro Broadcasting* undermined important principles of this Court's equal protection jurisprudence, established in a line of cases stretching back over fifty years. Those principles together stood for an "embracing" and "intrinsically sound" understanding of equal protection "verified by experience," namely, that the Constitution imposes upon federal, state, and local governmental actors the same obligation to respect the personal right to equal protection of the laws. This case therefore presents precisely the situation described by Justice Frankfurter. . . .

D

Our action today makes explicit what Justice Powell thought implicit in the *Fullilove* lead opinion: federal racial classifications, like those of a State, must serve a compelling governmental interest, and must be narrowly tailored to further that interest. Of course, it follows that to the extent (if any) that *Fullilove* held federal racial classifications to be subject to a less rigorous standard, it is no longer controlling. But we need not decide today whether the program upheld in *Fullilove* would survive strict scrutiny as our more recent cases have defined it.

Some have questioned the importance of debating the proper standard of review of race-based legislation. But we agree with Justice Stevens that, "because racial characteristics so seldom provide a relevant basis for disparate treatment, and because classifications based on race are potentially so harmful to the entire body politic, it is especially important that the reasons for any such classification be clearly identified and unquestionably legitimate," and that "racial classifications are simply too pernicious to permit any but the most exact connection between justification and classification." We think that requiring strict scrutiny is the best way to ensure that courts will consistently give racial classifications that kind of detailed examination, both as to ends and as to means. *Korematsu* demonstrates vividly that even "the most rigid scrutiny" can sometimes fail to detect an illegitimate racial classification. Any retreat from the most searching judicial inquiry can only increase the risk of another such error occurring in the future.

Finally, we wish to dispel the notion that strict scrutiny is "strict in theory, but fatal in fact." The unhappy persistence of both the practice and the lingering effects of racial discrimination against minority groups in this country is an unfortunate reality, and government is not disqualified from acting in response to it. As recently as 1987, for example, every Justice of this Court agreed that the Alabama Department of Public Safety's "pervasive, systematic, and obstinate discriminatory conduct" justified a narrowly tailored race-based remedy. When race-based action is necessary to further a compelling interest, such action is within constitutional constraints if it satisfies the "narrow tailoring" test this Court has set out in previous cases.

IV

. . .

. . . The question whether any of the ways in which the Government uses subcontractor compensation clauses can survive strict scrutiny, and any relevance distinctions such as these may have to that question, should be addressed in the first instance by the lower courts.

Accordingly, the judgment of the Court of Appeals is vacated, and the case is remanded for further proceedings consistent with this opinion.

. . .

JUSTICE SCALIA, concurring in part and concurring in the judgment.

I join the opinion of the Court, except Part III-C, and except insofar as it may be inconsistent with the following: In my view, government can never have a "compelling interest" in discriminating on the basis of race in order to "make up" for past racial discrimination in the opposite direction. Individuals who have been wronged by unlawful racial discrimination should be made whole; but under our Constitution there can be no such thing as either a creditor or a debtor race. That concept is alien to the Constitution's focus upon the individual, and its rejection of dispositions based on race, or based on blood. To pursue the concept of racial entitlement—even for the most admirable and benign of purposes—is to reinforce and preserve for future mischief the way of thinking that produced race slavery, race privilege and race hatred. In the eyes of government, we are just one race here. It is American.

It is unlikely, if not impossible, that the challenged program would survive under this understanding of strict scrutiny, but I am content to leave that to be decided on remand.

JUSTICE THOMAS, concurring in part and concurring in the judgment.

I agree with the majority's conclusion that strict scrutiny applies to all government classifications based on race. I write separately, however, to express my disagreement with the premise underlying Justice Stevens' and Justice Ginsburg's dissents: that there is a racial paternalism exception to the principle of equal protection. I believe that there is a "moral [and] constitutional equivalence," between laws designed to subjugate a race and those that distribute benefits on the basis of race in order to foster some current notion of equality. Government cannot make us equal; it can only recognize, respect, and protect us as equal before the law.

That these programs may have been motivated, in part, by good intentions cannot provide refuge from the principle that under our Constitution, the government may not make distinctions on the basis of race. As far as the Constitution is concerned, it is irrelevant whether a government's racial classifications are drawn by those who wish to oppress a race or by those who have a sincere desire to help those thought to be disadvantaged. There can be no doubt that the paternalism that appears to lie at the heart of this program is at war with the principle of inherent equality that underlies and infuses our Constitution. *See* Declaration of Independence ("We hold these truths to be self-evident, that all men are created equal, that they are endowed by their Creator with certain unalienable Rights, that among these are Life, Liberty, and the pursuit of Happiness").

These programs not only raise grave constitutional questions, they also undermine the moral basis of the equal protection principle. Purchased at the price of immeasurable human suffering, the equal protection principle reflects our Nation's understanding that such classifications ultimately have a destructive impact on the individual and our society. Unquestionably, "invidious [racial] discrimination is an engine of oppression." It is also true that "remedial" racial preferences may reflect "a desire to foster equality in society." But there can be no doubt that racial paternalism and its unintended consequences can be as poisonous and pernicious as any other form of discrimination. So-called "benign" discrimination teaches many that because of chronic and apparently immutable handicaps, minorities cannot compete with them without their patronizing indulgence. Inevitably, such programs engender attitudes of superiority or, alternatively, provoke resentment among those who believe that they have been wronged by the government's use of race. These programs stamp minorities with a badge of inferiority and may cause them to develop dependencies or to adopt an attitude that they are "entitled" to preferences. . . .

In my mind, government-sponsored racial discrimination based on benign prejudice is just as noxious as discrimination inspired by malicious prejudice.* In each instance, it is racial discrimination, plain and simple.

JUSTICE STEVENS, with whom JUSTICE GINSBURG joins, dissenting.

Instead of deciding this case in accordance with controlling precedent, the Court today delivers a disconcerting lecture about the evils of governmental racial classifications. For its text the Court has selected three propositions, represented by the bywords "skepticism," "consistency," and "congruence." I shall comment on each of these propositions, then add a few words about stare decisis, and finally explain why I believe this Court has a duty to affirm the judgment of the Court of Appeals.

I

The Court's concept of skepticism is, at least in principle, a good statement of law and of common sense. Undoubtedly, a court should be wary of a governmental decision that relies upon a racial classification. "Because racial characteristics so seldom provide a relevant basis for disparate treatment, and because classifications based on race are potentially so harmful to the entire body politic," a reviewing court must satisfy itself that the reasons for any such classification are "clearly identified and unquestionably legitimate." ... (A)s the opinions in *Fullilove* demonstrate, substantial agreement on the standard to be applied in deciding difficult cases does not necessarily lead to agreement on how those cases actually should or will be resolved. In my judgment, because uniform standards are often anything but uniform, we should evaluate the Court's comments on "consistency," "congruence," and stare decisis with the same type of skepticism that the Court advocates for the underlying issue.

II

The Court's concept of "consistency" assumes that there is no significant difference between a decision by the majority to impose a special burden on the members of a minority race and a decision by the majority to provide a benefit to certain members of that minority notwithstanding its incidental burden on some members of the majority. In my opinion that assumption is untenable. There is no moral or constitutional equivalence between a policy that is designed to perpetuate a caste system

---

* It should be obvious that every racial classification helps, in a narrow sense, some races and hurts others. As to the races benefitted, the classification could surely be called "benign." Accordingly, whether a law relying upon racial taxonomy is "benign" or "malign," or on distinctions found only in the eye of the beholder.

and one that seeks to eradicate racial subordination. Invidious discrimination is an engine of oppression, subjugating a disfavored group to enhance or maintain the power of the majority. Remedial race-based preferences reflect the opposite impulse: a desire to foster equality in society. No sensible conception of the Government's constitutional obligation to "govern impartially," should ignore this distinction.

To illustrate the point, consider our cases addressing the Federal Government's discrimination against Japanese Americans during World War II. The discrimination at issue in those cases was invidious because the Government imposed special burdens—a curfew and exclusion from certain areas on the West Coast—on the members of a minority class defined by racial and ethnic characteristics. Members of the same racially defined class exhibited exceptional heroism in the service of our country during that War. Now suppose Congress decided to reward that service with a federal program that gave all Japanese-American veterans an extraordinary preference in Government employment. If Congress had done so, the same racial characteristics that motivated the discriminatory burdens in *Hirabayashi* and *Korematsu* would have defined the preferred class of veterans. Nevertheless, "consistency" surely would not require us to describe the incidental burden on everyone else in the country as "odious" or "invidious" as those terms were used in those cases. We should reject a concept of "consistency" that would view the special preferences that the National Government has provided to Native Americans since 1834 as comparable to the official discrimination against African Americans that was prevalent for much of our history.

The consistency that the Court espouses would disregard the difference between a "No Trespassing" sign and a welcome mat. It would treat a Dixiecrat Senator's decision to vote against Thurgood Marshall's confirmation in order to keep African Americans off the Supreme Court as on a par with President Johnson's evaluation of his nominee's race as a positive factor. It would equate a law that made black citizens ineligible for military service with a program aimed at recruiting black soldiers. An attempt by the majority to exclude members of a minority race from a regulated market is fundamentally different from a subsidy that enables a relatively small group of newcomers to enter that market. An interest in "consistency" does not justify treating differences as though they were similarities.

The Court's explanation for treating dissimilar race-based decisions as though they were equally objectionable is a supposed inability to differentiate between "invidious" and "benign" discrimination. But the term "affirmative action" is common and well understood. Its presence in everyday parlance shows that people understand the difference between good intentions and bad. As with any legal concept, some cases may be difficult to classify, but our equal protection jurisprudence has identified a critical difference between state action that imposes burdens on a disfavored few and state action that benefits the few "in spite of" its adverse effects on the many.

Indeed, our jurisprudence has made the standard to be applied in cases of invidious discrimination turn on whether the discrimination is "intentional," or whether, by contrast, it merely has a discriminatory "effect." Surely this distinction is at least as subtle, and at least as difficult to apply, as the usually obvious distinction between a measure intended to benefit members of a particular minority race and a measure intended to burden a minority race. A state actor inclined to subvert the Constitution might easily hide bad intentions in the guise of unintended "effects"; but I should think it far more difficult to enact a law intending to preserve the majority's hegemony while casting it plausibly in the guise of affirmative action for minorities.

Nothing is inherently wrong with applying a single standard to fundamentally different situations, as long as that standard takes relevant differences into account. For example, if the Court in all equal protection cases were to insist that differential treatment be justified by relevant characteristics of the members of the favored and disfavored classes that provide a legitimate basis for disparate treatment, such a standard would treat dissimilar cases differently while still recognizing that there is, after all, only one Equal Protection Clause. Under such a standard, subsidies for disadvantaged businesses may be constitutional though special taxes on such businesses would be invalid. But a single standard that purports to equate remedial preferences with invidious discrimination cannot be defended in the name of "equal protection."

Moreover, the Court may find that its new "consistency" approach to race-based classifications is difficult to square with its insistence upon rigidly separate categories for discrimination against different classes of individuals. For example, as the law currently stands, the Court will apply "intermediate scrutiny" to cases of invidious gender discrimination and "strict scrutiny" to cases of invidious race discrimination, while applying the same standard for benign classifications as for invidious ones. If this remains the law, then today's lecture about "consistency" will produce the anomalous result that the Government can more easily enact affirmative-action programs to remedy discrimination against women than it can enact affirmative-action programs to remedy discrimination against African Americans —even though the primary purpose of the Equal Protection Clause was to end discrimination against the former slaves. When a court becomes preoccupied with abstract standards, it risks sacrificing common sense at the altar of formal consistency.

As a matter of constitutional and democratic principle, a decision by representatives of the majority to discriminate against the members of a minority race is fundamentally different from those same representatives' decision to impose incidental costs on the majority of their constituents in order to provide a benefit to a disadvantaged minority. Indeed, as I have previously argued, the former is virtually always repugnant to the principles of a free and democratic society, whereas the latter is, in some circumstances, entirely consistent with the ideal of equality. By insisting on a doctrinaire notion of "consistency" in the standard applicable to all race-based governmental actions, the Court obscures this essential dichotomy.

III

The Court's concept of "congruence" assumes that there is no significant difference between a decision by the Congress of the United States to adopt an affirmative-action program and such a decision by a State or a municipality. In my opinion that assumption is untenable. It ignores important practical and legal differences between federal and state or local decisionmakers. These differences have been identified repeatedly and consistently both in opinions of the Court and in separate opinions authored by members of today's majority. Thus, in *Metro Broadcasting, Inc. v. FCC*, we identified the special "institutional competence" of our National Legislature.... We recalled the several opinions in *Fullilove* that admonished this Court to "'approach our task with appropriate deference to the Congress, a co-equal branch charged by the Constitution with the power to "provide for the . . . general Welfare of the United States" and "to enforce, by appropriate legislation," the equal protection guarantees of the Fourteenth Amendment.' . . .

The majority in *Metro Broadcasting* and the plurality in *Fullilove* were not alone in relying upon a critical distinction between federal and state programs. In his separate opinion Justice Scalia discussed the basis for this distinction. He observed that "it is one thing to permit racially based conduct by the Federal Government—whose legislative powers concerning matters of race were explicitly enhanced by the Fourteenth Amendment,—and quite another to permit it by the precise entities against whose conduct in matters of race that Amendment was specifically directed. Continuing, Justice Scalia explained why a "sound distinction between federal and state (or local) action based on race rests not only upon the substance of the Civil War Amendments, but upon social reality and governmental theory."

. . .

Presumably, the majority is now satisfied that its theory of "congruence" between the substantive rights provided by the Fifth and Fourteenth Amendments disposes of the objection based upon divided constitutional powers. But it is one thing to say (as no one seems to dispute) that the Fifth Amendment encompasses a general guarantee of equal protection as broad as that contained within the Fourteenth Amendment. It is another thing entirely to say that Congress' institutional competence and constitutional authority entitles it to no greater deference when it enacts a program designed to foster equality than the deference due a State legislature. The latter is an extraordinary proposition; and, as the foregoing discussion demonstrates, our precedents have rejected it explicitly and repeatedly.

In my judgment, the Court's novel doctrine of "congruence" is seriously misguided. Congressional deliberations about a matter as important as affirmative action should be accorded far greater deference than those of a State or municipality.

IV

The Court's concept of stare decisis treats some of the language we have used in explaining our decisions as though it were more important than our actual holdings. In my opinion that treatment is incorrect.

This is the third time in the Court's entire history that it has considered the constitutionality of a federal affirmative-action program. On each of the two prior occasions, the first in 1980, and the second in 1990, *Metro Broadcasting*, the Court upheld the program. Today the Court explicitly overrules *Metro Broadcasting* (at least in part), and undermines *Fullilove* by recasting the standard on which it rested and by calling even its holding into question. By way of explanation, Justice O'Connor advises the federal agencies and private parties that have made countless decisions in reliance on those cases that "we do not depart from the fabric of the law; we restore it." A skeptical observer might ask whether this pronouncement is a faithful application of the doctrine of stare decisis. A brief comment on each of the two ailing cases may provide the answer.

In the Court's view, our decision in Metro Broadcasting was inconsistent with the rule announced in *Croson*. But two decisive distinctions separate those two cases. First, *Metro Broadcasting* involved a federal program, whereas *Croson* involved a city ordinance. *Metro Broadcasting* thus drew primary support from *Fullilove*, which predated *Croson* and which *Croson* distinguished on the grounds of the federal-state dichotomy that the majority today discredits. Although members of today's majority trumpeted the importance of that distinction in *Croson*, they now reject it in the name of "congruence." It is therefore quite wrong for the Court to suggest today that overruling *Metro Broadcasting* merely restores the status quo ante, for the law at the time of that decision was entirely open to the result the Court reached. Today's decision is an unjustified departure from settled law.

Second, *Metro Broadcasting*'s holding rested on more than its application of "intermediate scrutiny." Indeed, I have always believed that, labels notwithstanding, the FCC program we upheld in that case would have satisfied any of our various standards in affirmative-action cases—including the one the majority fashions today. What truly distinguishes *Metro Broadcasting* from our other affirmative-action precedents is the distinctive goal of the federal program in that case. Instead of merely seeking to remedy past discrimination, the FCC program was intended to achieve future benefits in the form of broadcast diversity. Reliance on race as a legitimate means of achieving diversity was first endorsed by Justice Powell in *Bakke*. . . .

. . . [P]rior to *Metro Broadcasting*, the interest in diversity had been mentioned in a few opinions, but it is perfectly clear that the Court had not yet decided whether that interest had sufficient magnitude to justify a racial classification. *Metro Broadcasting*, of course, answered that question in the affirmative. The majority today overrules *Metro Broadcasting* only insofar as it is "inconsistent with [the] holding" that strict scrutiny applies to "benign" racial classifications promulgated by the Federal Government. The proposition that fostering diversity may provide a sufficient interest to justify such a program is not inconsistent with the Court's holding today—indeed, the question is not remotely presented in this case—and I do not take the Court's opinion to diminish that aspect of our decision in *Metro Broadcasting*.

The Court's suggestion that it may be necessary in the future to overrule *Fullilove* in order to restore the fabric of the law, is even more disingenuous than its treatment of *Metro Broadcasting*. For the Court endorses the "strict scrutiny" standard that Justice Powell applied in *Bakke*, and acknowledges that he applied that standard in *Fullilove* as well. The

Court thus adopts a standard applied in Fullilove at the same time it questions that case's continued vitality and accuses it of departing from prior law. I continue to believe that the *Fullilove* case was incorrectly decided, but neither my dissent nor that filed by Justice Stewart, contained any suggestion that the issue the Court was resolving had been decided before. As was true of *Metro Broadcasting*, the Court in *Fullilove* decided an important, novel, and difficult question. Providing a different answer to a similar question today cannot fairly be characterized as merely "restoring" previously settled law.

V

The Court's holding in *Fullilove* surely governs the result in this case. The Public Works Employment Act of 1977, which this Court upheld in *Fullilove*, is different in several critical respects from the portions of the Small Business Act and the Surface Transportation and Uniform Relocation Assistance Act of 1987, challenged in this case. Each of those differences makes the current program designed to provide assistance to disadvantaged business enterprises (DBE's) significantly less objectionable than the 1977 categorical grant of $ 400 million in exchange for a 10% set-aside in public contracts to "a class of investors defined solely by racial characteristics." In no meaningful respect is the current scheme more objectionable than the 1977 Act. Thus, if the 1977 Act was constitutional, then so must be the SBA and STURAA. Indeed, even if my dissenting views in *Fullilove* had prevailed, this program would be valid.

Unlike the 1977 Act, the present statutory scheme does not make race the sole criterion of eligibility for participation in the program. Race does give rise to a rebuttable presumption of social disadvantage which, at least under STURAA, gives rise to a second rebuttable presumption of economic disadvantage. But a small business may qualify as a DBE, by showing that it is both socially and economically disadvantaged, even if it receives neither of these presumptions. Thus, the current preference is more inclusive than the 1977 Act because it does not make race a necessary qualification.

More importantly, race is not a sufficient qualification. Whereas a millionaire with a long history of financial successes, who was a member of numerous social clubs and trade associations, would have qualified for a preference under the 1977 Act merely because he was an Asian American or an African American, neither the SBA nor STURAA creates any such anomaly. The DBE program excludes members of minority races who are not, in fact, socially or economically disadvantaged. The presumption of social disadvantage reflects the unfortunate fact that irrational racial prejudice—along with its lingering effects—still survives. The presumption of economic disadvantage embodies a recognition that success in the private sector of the economy is often attributable, in part, to social skills and relationships. Unlike the 1977 set-asides, the current preference is designed to overcome the social and economic disadvantages that are often associated with racial characteristics. If, in a particular case, these disadvantages are not present, the presumptions can be rebutted. The program is thus designed to allow race to play a part in the decisional process only when there is a meaningful basis for assuming its relevance. In this connection, I think it is particularly significant that the current program targets the negotiation of subcontracts between private firms. The 1977 Act applied entirely to the award of public contracts, an area of the economy in which social relationships should be irrelevant and in which proper supervision of government contracting officers should preclude any discrimination against particular bidders on account of their race. In this case, in contrast, the program seeks to overcome barriers of prejudice between private parties—specifically, between general contractors and subcontractors. The SBA and STURAA embody Congress' recognition that such barriers may actually handicap minority firms seeking business as subcontractors from established leaders in the industry that have a history of doing business with their golfing partners. Indeed, minority subcontractors may face more obstacles than direct, intentional racial prejudice: they may face particular barriers simply because they are more likely to be new in the business and less likely to know others in the business. Given such difficulties, Congress could reasonably find that a minority subcontractor is less likely to receive favors from the entrenched businesspersons who award subcontracts only to people with whom—or with whose friends—they have an existing relationship. This program, then, if in part a remedy for past discrimination, is most importantly a forward-looking response to practical problems faced by minority subcontractors.

The current program contains another forward-looking component that the 1977 set-asides did not share. Section 8(a) of the SBA provides for periodic review of the status of DBE's, and DBE status can be challenged by a competitor at any time under any of the routes to certification. Such review prevents ineligible firms from taking part in the program solely because of their minority ownership, even when those firms were once disadvantaged but have since become successful. The emphasis on review also indicates the Administration's anticipation that after their presumed disadvantages have been overcome, firms will "graduate" into a status in which they will be able to compete for business, including prime contracts, on an equal basis. As with other phases of the statutory policy of encouraging the formation and growth of small business enterprises, this program is intended to facilitate entry and increase competition in the free market.

Significantly, the current program, unlike the 1977 set-aside, does not establish any requirement—numerical or otherwise—that a general contractor must hire DBE subcontractors. The program we upheld in Fullilove required that 10% of the federal grant for every federally funded project be expended on minority business enterprises. In contrast, the current program contains no quota. Although it provides monetary incentives to general contractors to hire DBE subcontractors, it does not require them to hire DBE's, and they do not lose their contracts if they fail to do so. The importance of this incentive to general contractors (who always seek to offer the lowest bid) should not be underestimated; but the preference here is far less rigid, and thus more narrowly tailored, than the 1977 Act.

Finally, the record shows a dramatic contrast between the sparse deliberations that preceded the 1977 Act, and the extensive hearings conducted in several Congresses before the current program was developed. However we might evaluate the benefits and costs —both fiscal and social—of this or any other affirmative-action program, our obligation to give deference to Congress' policy choices is much more demanding in this case than it was in *Fullilove*. If the 1977 program of race-based set-asides satisfied the strict scrutiny dictated by Justice Powell's vision of the Constitution—a vision the Court expressly endorses today—it must follow as night follows the day that the Court of Appeals' judgment upholding this more carefully crafted program should be affirmed.

VI

My skeptical scrutiny of the Court's opinion leaves me in dissent. The majority's concept of "consistency" ignores a difference, fundamental to the idea of equal protection, between oppression and assistance. The majority's concept of "congruence" ignores a difference, fundamental to our constitutional system, between the Federal Government and the States. And the majority's concept of stare decisis ignores the force of binding precedent. I would affirm the judgment of the Court of Appeals.

JUSTICE SOUTER, with whom JUSTICE GINSBURG and JUSTICE BREYER join, dissenting.

. . .

. . . [T]he Court's very recognition today that strict scrutiny can be compatible with the survival of a classification so reviewed demonstrates that our concepts of equal protection enjoy a greater elasticity than the standard categories might suggest. . . .

In assessing the degree to which today's holding portends a departure from past practice, it is . . . worth noting that nothing in today's opinion implies any view of Congress's § 5 power and the deference due its exercise that differs from the views expressed by the *Fullilove* plurality. The Court simply notes the observation in *Croson* "that the Court's 'treatment of an exercise of congressional power in *Fullilove* cannot be dispositive here,' because *Croson*'s facts did not implicate Congress' broad power under § 5 of the Fourteenth Amendment," and explains that there is disagreement among today's majority about the extent of the § 5 power. There is therefore no reason to treat the opinion as affecting one way or another the views of § 5 power, described as "broad," "unique," and "unlike [that of] any state or political subdivision." Thus, today's decision should leave § 5 exactly where it is as the source of an interest of the national government sufficiently important to satisfy the corresponding requirement of the strict scrutiny test.

Finally, I should say that I do not understand that today's decision will necessarily have any effect on the resolution of an issue that was just as pertinent under *Fullilove*'s unlabeled standard as it is under the standard of strict scrutiny now adopted by the Court. The Court has long accepted the view that constitutional authority to remedy past discrimination is not limited to the power to forbid its continuation, but extends to eliminating those effects that would otherwise persist and skew the operation of public systems even in the absence of current intent to practice any discrimination. . . .

When the extirpation of lingering discriminatory effects is thought to require a catch-up mechanism, like the racially preferential inducement under the statutes considered here, the result may be that some members of the historically favored race are hurt by that remedial mechanism, however innocent they may be of any personal responsibility for any discriminatory conduct. When this price is considered reasonable, it is in part because it is a price to be paid only temporarily; if the justification for the preference is eliminating the effects of a past practice, the assumption is that the effects will themselves recede into the past, becoming attenuated and finally disappearing. Thus, Justice Powell wrote in his concurring opinion in Fullilove that the "temporary nature of this remedy ensures that a race-conscious program will not last longer than the discriminatory effects it is designed to eliminate."

Surely the transition from the *Fullilove* plurality view (in which Justice Powell joined) to today's strict scrutiny (which will presumably be applied as Justice Powell employed it) does not signal a change in the standard by which the burden of a remedial racial preference is to be judged as reasonable or not at any given time. If in the District Court Adarand had chosen to press a challenge to the reasonableness of the burden of these statutes, more than a decade after *Fullilove* had examined such a burden, I doubt that the claim would have fared any differently from the way it will now be treated on remand from this Court.

JUSTICE GINSBURG, with whom JUSTICE BREYER joins, dissenting.

I

. . .

The divisions in this difficult case should not obscure the Court's recognition of the persistence of racial inequality and a majority's acknowledgment of Congress' authority to act affirmatively, not only to end discrimination, but also to counteract discrimination's lingering effects. Those effects, reflective of a system of racial caste only recently ended, are evident in our workplaces, markets, and neighborhoods. Job applicants with identical resumes, qualifications, and interview styles still experience different receptions, depending on their race. White and African-American consumers still encounter different deals. People of color looking for housing still face discriminatory treatment by landlords, real estate agents, and mortgage lenders. Minority entrepreneurs sometimes fail to gain contracts though they are the low bidders, and they are sometimes refused work even after winning contracts. Bias both conscious and unconscious, reflecting traditional and unexamined habits of thought, keeps up barriers that must come down if equal opportunity and nondiscrimination are ever genuinely to become this country's law and practice.

Given this history and its practical consequences, Congress surely can conclude that a carefully designed affirmative action program may help to realize, finally, the "equal protection of the laws" the Fourteenth Amendment has promised since 1868.

II

The lead opinion uses one term, "strict scrutiny," to describe the standard of judicial review for all governmental classifications by race. But that opinion's elaboration strongly suggests that the strict standard announced is indeed "fatal" for classifications burdening groups that have suffered discrimination in our society. That seems to me, and, I believe, to the Court, the enduring lesson one should draw from *Korematsu v. United States*, for in that case, scrutiny the Court described as "most rigid," nonetheless yielded a pass for an odious, gravely injurious racial classification. A *Korematsu*-type classification, as I read the opinions in this case, will never again survive scrutiny: such a classification, history and precedent instruct, properly ranks as prohibited.

For a classification made to hasten the day when "we are just one race," however, the lead opinion has dispelled the notion that "strict scrutiny" is "'fatal in fact.'" Properly, a majority of the Court calls for review that is searching, in order to ferret out classifications in reality malign, but masquerading as benign. The Court's once lax review of sex-based classifications demonstrates the need for such suspicion. Today's decision thus usefully reiterates that the purpose of strict scrutiny "is precisely to distinguish legitimate from illegitimate uses of race in governmental decisionmaking," "to 'differentiate between' permissible and impermissible governmental use of race," to distinguish "'between a "No Trespassing" sign and a welcome mat.'" . . .

***

While I would not disturb the programs challenged in this case, and would leave their improvement to the political branches, I see today's decision as one that allows our precedent to evolve, still to be informed by and responsive to changing conditions.

The *Adarand* decision as presented communicates a sense of certitude, if not finality, lacking in prior opinions on the subject. Even if providing a firm answer with respect to the appropriate standard of review, the Court leaves room for maneuvering on what constitutes a compelling justification. The Court's air of resolution, moreover, is not well-oxygenated. Although insisting on strict scrutiny, the Court disowns the notion that the standard translates into "strict in theory, but fatal in fact." Even if narrowed, therefore, the opportunity for race-conscious methods at least in theory is not foreclosed. Given a critical mass of juridical animus toward racial preferences, at least as the Court is presently constituted, it is difficult to imagine much constitutional room for overt attention to racial disadvantage in the real world. Heightening that impression is the actuality that the program struck down in *Adarand* seemed more responsive than previously upheld policies to demands for focus beyond exclusive attention to race and for narrowly tailored initiatives that avoid conferring windfall benefits upon nondisadvantaged individuals.

DEL: Viewed in its best light, the *Adarand* decision has a quixotic quality. A significant degree of charity is required, however, to view the ruling in its best light. The Court's primary reasoning represents a challenge to logic. At precisely the same time that the Court was vilifying racial preferences, the United States was demanding managed access to Japanese markets traditionally closed to American products by standards that historically have rigged the system against imports. A central tenet of the *Adarand* ruling, that group preferences are stigmatizing when used to reckon with racial disadvantage, has yet to be articulated in the debate over remedial preferences for American trade interests. It is somewhat mystifying why remedial initiatives for trade, that favor Americans as a group, should be sought so vigorously if policy referenced to categorical status imprints such profound stigma. Incongruously, *Adarand's* repudiation of race as a permissible reference point for official policy—even as group-conscious preference is permitted with respect to seniority, veterans and other categories—recreates race as an exclusionary classification. If Justice Thomas' point about the *Brown* Court (to the effect that its findings of stigma rested on shoddy social science data) is to be taken seriously, it follows that the *Adarand* Court has committed a more egregious error by assuming and asserting as mere dogma that racial preferences are stigmatizing. To the extent that the Court touts a color-blind constitution, it accelerates the law beyond the culture's moral development. For all its professions of restraint, therefore, the court when racial reality is implicated seems immersed in an exercise of Platonic guardianship.

At least as significant as the law's coursing pursuant to *Adarand* are some new dimensions of jurisprudential dialogue. In dissenting, Justice Ginsberg laments the majority's lack of historical appreciation. She thus criticizes a perspective that, because of its failure to factor the nation's racially significant legacy, generates case law that is the function of myopia and real-world detachment. As a counterpoint to Ginsberg, Justice Thomas challenges what he characterizes as the racial paternalism underlying group-referenced management of opportunity. It is a useful role model for general discussion that, although disagreeing fundamentally, both Ginsberg and Thomas offer insights of validity and utility and enhance a debate that for all of its rhetorical fireworks had become somewhat stale. Whether Ginsberg's assessment can receive a serious hearing is questionable, given a societal context in which convenient labels such as "quota queen" substitute for serious thought. Among Thomas' handicaps to being taken seriously on the subject is the sense of many critics that, as a beneficiary of affirmative action, he should be estopped from criticizing it. Such reaction equates with the proposition, for instance, that a professor who benefited from tenure should not be heard to assert upon further reflection that the system is corrupt, is an impediment to faculty diversification and should be abolished. If progress is dependent upon real dialogue, achievement depends upon transcending preliminary skirmishes, twisted characterizations and ad hoc standards regarding who is qualified to speak. Given a backdrop of moral underachievement in accounting for equal opportunity, general risk-aversion toward openly and honestly debating racial issues, and racially significant legal reform and initiative being at a point of diminishing returns, further accounting for equality interests depends upon broadening and deepening the debate beyond "affirmative action" and refocusing attention upon underlying realities constituting the nation's still unfinished racial business.

C. Gender Discrimination

Despite language of the Fourteenth Amendment which guaranteed to "[a]ll persons born or naturalized in the United States" citizenship and prohibited states from denying "any person" equal protection of the laws, the Court did not interpret the amendment as transforming the state's treatment of women in the nineteenth century.[257] In fact, the amendment's second section refers to "male" citizens in formulating how representatvies shall be apportioned, confirming the existing "gendered" political order. Traditionally, the Court relied on biological differences between men and women to justify laws bottomed on gender-based distinctions in the allocation of benefits and burdens by the state. Laws which confirmed social roles of women and men, depriving women of independence from their husbands, and leaving them outside the political community, were said to flow from "natural" differences between the sexes and the demands of motherhood and family, and were treated as presumptively valid.

1. Judicial Deference to Traditional Images of Gender-Based Distinctions

In *Bradwell v. Illinois*,[258] the Court upheld an Illinois law denying Myra Bradwell the right to practice law. Writing for the majority Justice Miller concluded that the law did not deprive Myra Bradwell, a married woman, of any of the privileges and immunities of United States citizenship. Joined by Justices Swayne and Justice Feld, Justice Bradley stated in a concurring opinion:

> [T]he civil law, as well as nature herself, has always recognized a wide difference in the respective spheres and destinies of man and woman. Man is, or should be, woman's protector and defender. The natural and proper timidity and delicacy which belongs to the female sex evidently unfits it for many of the occupations of civil life. The constitution of the family organization, which is founded in the divine ordinance, as well as in the nature of things, indicates the domestic sphere as that which properly belongs to the domain and functions of womanhood. The harmony, not to say, identity, of interests and views which belong, or should belong, to the family institution is repugnant to the idea of a woman adopting a distinct and independent career from that of her husband. So firmly fixed was this sentiment in the founders of the common law that it became a maxim of that system of jurisprudence that a woman had no legal existence separate from her husband.
>
> It is true that many women are unmarried and not affected by any of the duties, complications, and incapacities arising out of the married state, but these are exceptions to the general rule. The paramount destiny and mission of woman are to fulfill the noble and benign offices of wife and mother. This is the law of the Creator. And the rules of civil society must be adapted to the general constitution of things.
>
> The humane movements of modern society, which have for their object the multiplication of avenues for human's advancement, and of occupations adapted to her conditions and sex, have my heartiest concurrence. But I am not prepared to say that it is one of her fundamental rights and privileges to

---

[257] The Constitution's gender neutral references to "citizen" and "persons" were not interpreted as changing the common-law assumptions about the political and social status of women. *See, e.g.*, Mary Becker, *The Politics of Women's Wrongs and the Bill of Rights: A Bicentennial Perspective*, 59 U. Chi. L. Rev. 453 (1992); M. Norton, Liberty's Daughters: The Revolutionary Experience of America Women, 1750–1800 (1980).

[258] 83 U.S. (16 Wall.) 130 (1873).

be admitted into every office and position, including those which require highly special qualifications and demanding special responsibilities. In the nature of things it is not every citizen of every age, sex and condition that is qualified for every calling and position. It is the prerogative of the legislator to prescribe regulations founded on nature, reason, and experience for the due admission of qualified persons to professions and callings demanding special skill and confidence. This fairly belongs to the police power of the State; and in my view of the peculiar characteristics, destiny, and mission of woman, it is within the province of the legislature to ordain that offices, positions, and callings shall be filled and discharged by men.

A year later, in *Minor v. Happersett*,[259] the Supreme Court also ruled that states could deny women the right to vote without violating the privileges and immunities of national citizenship. It added:"[ce]rtainly, if the courts can consider any question settled, this is one. For nearly ninety years the people have acted upon the idea that the Constitution, when it conferred citizenship, did not necessarily confer the right of suffrage." The Nineteenth Amendment overturned that decision.

In due process challenges to state protective laws limiting hours for women and children (often raised by businesses, *not* women) and in response to equal protection arguments mounted to defeat statutes that provided wage and hour differentials, the Supreme Court generally upheld the legislation. In *Muller v. Oregon*[260] the Court concluded that the state had a compelling interest in protecting women. The conclusion rested on empirical arguments set forth in a brief filed on behalf of the National Consumer's League by Louis Brandeis. Noting that the "woman's physical structure and the performance of maternal functions place her at a disadvantage in the struggle for subsistence," the Court stated:

> [H]istory discloses the fact that woman has always been dependent upon man. [S]he has been looked upon in the courts as needing especial care that her rights may be preserved. . . . Differentiated by these matters from the other sex, she is properly placed in a class by herself, and legislation is not necessary for men and could not be sustained. It is impossible to close one's eyes to the fact that she still looks to her brother and depends upon him."

Citing *Muller*, Justice Holmes turned down an equal protection challenge to a statute exempting laundries operated by two or fewer women from a licensing charge, noting that the occupation was commonly regarded by people as woman's work and that "the Fourteenth Amendment does not interfere by creating a fictitious equality where there is a real difference."

2.   Rational Basis Review

As it developed its deferential rationality review of social and economic equal protection claims, the Court appeared unwilling to find gender-based discrimination claims subject to special protection.

---

[259] 88 U.S. (21 Wall.) 162 (1874).
[260] 208 U.S. 412 (1908).

Goesart v. Cleary
335 U.S. 464 (1948)

Mr. Justice Frankfurter delivered the opinion of the Court.

As part of the Michigan system for controlling the sale of liquor, bartenders are required to be licensed in all cities having a population of 50,000, or more, but no female may be so licensed unless she be "the wife or daughter of the male owner of a liquor establishment." [Plaintiff claims] Michigan cannot forbid females generally from being barmaids and at the same time make an exception in favor of the wives and daughters of the owners of liquor establishments. To ask whether or not the Equal Protection of the Laws Clause barred Michigan from making the classification the State has made between wives and daughters of owner of liquor places and wives and daughters of non-owners, is one of those rare instances where to state the question is in effect to answer it.

We are, to be sure, dealing with a historic calling. We meet the alewife, sprightly and ribald in Shakespeare, but centuries before him she played a role in the social life of England. The Fourteenth Amendment did not tear history up by the roots, and the regulation of the liquor traffic is one of the oldest and most untrammeled of legislative powers. Michigan could, beyond question, forbid all women from working behind a bar. This is so despite the vast changes in the social and legal position of women. The fact that women may now have achieved the virtues that men have long practiced, does not preclude the States from drawing a sharp line between the sexes.

While Michigan may deny to all women opportunities for bartending, Michigan cannot play favorites among women without rhyme or reasons. . . . Since bartending by women may, in the allowable legislative judgment, give rise to moral and social problems against which it may devise preventive measures, the legislature need not go to the full length of prohibition if it believes that as to a defined group of females other factors are operating which either eliminate or reduce the moral and social problems otherwise calling for prohibition. Michigan evidently believes that the oversight assured through ownership of a bar by a barmaid's husband or father minimizes hazards that may confront a barmaid. . . . This court is certainly not in a position to gainsay such belief by the Michigan legislature. . . .

Mr. JUSTICE RUTLEDGE, with whom Mr. JUSTICE DOUGLAS and Mr. JUSTICE MURPHY join, dissenting . . .

The statute arbitrarily discriminates between male and female owners of liquor establishments. A male owner, although he himself is always absent from his bar, may employ his wife and daughter as barmaids. A female owner may neither work as a barmaid herself nor employ her daughter in that position, even if a man is always present in the establishment to keep order. This inevitable result of the classification belies the assumption that the statute was motivated by a legislative solicitude for the moral and physical well-being of women who, but for the law, would be employed as barmaids. Since there could be no other conceivable justification for such discrimination against women owners of liquor establishments, the statute should be held invalid as a denial of equal protection.

Judicial deference to paternalistic (i.e., protective) treatment of women continued well into the twentieth century. For example, the Warren Court, in *Hoyt v. Florida*[261] upheld a Florida statute which excluded women from jury service unless they expressly requested to be included on jury lists.

3. Evolution of a Heightened Standard of Review for Gender-Based Discrimination

Consideration of the Supreme Court's struggle with questions of gender difference in modern constitutional jurisprudence concerning gender discrimination should be made against the background of the civil rights movement of the sixties and the dialogue about sameness and difference in feminist writing of the seventies. Its responses

---

[261] 368 U.S. 57 (1961). Taylor v. Louisiana, 419 U.S. 522 (1975) overturned *Hoyt*. The Court concluded that exclusion of women from jury service in criminal cases deprived defendants of their rights to an impartial jury drawn from a fair cross-section of the community.

also reflect difficulties which are a consequence of the Court's treatment of challenges to racial inequalities.[262]

In *Reed v. Reed*,[263] the plaintiff challenged the Idaho probate code which accorded men a mandatory preference over women when persons of the same class of entitlement applied for appointment as administrator of a decedent's estate. The Idaho Supreme Court upheld the constitutionality of the statute against the contention by the mother of an intestate minor decedent that it violated equal protection in discriminating against her on the ground of gender. Justice Burger, writing for the majority stated:

> In applying th[e Equal Protection] clause, this Court has consistently recognized that the Fourteenth Amendment does not deny to States the power to treat different classes of persons in different ways . . . . The Equal Protection Clause does, however, deny to States the power to legislate that different treatment be accorded to persons placed by a statute into different classes on the basis of criteria wholly unrelated to the objective of that statute. A classification 'must be reasonable, not arbitrary, and must rest upon some ground of difference having a fair and substantial relation to the object of the legislation, so that all persons similarly circumstanced shall be treated alike.' The question presented by this case, then, is whether a difference in the sex of competing applicants for letters of administration bears a rational relationship to a state objective that is sought to be advanced by the operation of [the statute].
>
> Clearly the objective of reducing the workload on probate courts by eliminating one class of contests is not without legitimacy. The crucial question, however, is whether [the statute] advances that objective in a manner consistent with the command of the Equal Protection Clause. We hold that it does not. To give a mandatory preference to members of either sex over members of the other, merely to accomplish the elimination of hearings on the merits, is to make the very kind of arbitrary legislative choice forbidden by the Equal Protection Clause. [W]hatever may be said as to the positive values of avoiding intrafamily controversy, the choice in this context may not lawfully be mandated solely on the basis of sex. . . .

The Court in *Reed* purports to apply a rational basis test in the tradition of *REA*, *supra*. Its language clarifying the level of scrutiny as considering whether the classification "rest[s] upon some ground of difference having a fair and substantial relation to the object of the legislation, so that all persons similarly circumstanced shall be treated alike" suggests a more searching level of review. Notably, the state's interest in administrative convenience as well as the interest in avoiding intrafamily controversy are rejected when accomplished by gender-based preferential treatment.

---

[262] For example, Professor Kathryn Abrams has noted the civil rights movement's influence on the agenda of the women's movement, including borrowing of integrationist strategy by the women's movement in workplace and the similarities of group conflicts). *See e.g.* Kathryn Abrams, *Title VII and the Complex Female Subject,* 92 MICH. L. REV. 2479 (1994). *See also* Joan C. Williams, *Deconstructing Gender,* 87 MICH. L. REV. 797 (1989) (deinstitutionalizing gender).

[263] 404 U.S. 71 (1971).

a. Middle-Tier Scrutiny

Frontiero v. Richardson
411 U.S. 677 (1973)

Mr. JUSTICE BRENNAN announced the judgment of the Court in an opinion in which Mr. JUSTICE DOUGLAS, Mr. JUSTICE WHITE, and Mr. JUSTICE MARSHALL join.

The question before us concerns the right of a female member of the uniformed services to claim her spouse as a 'dependent' for the purposes of obtaining increased quarters allowances and medical and dental benefits under 37 U.S.C. §§ 401, 403, and 10 U.S.C. §§ 1072, 1076, on an equal footing with male members. Under these statutes, a serviceman may claim his wife as a 'dependent' without regard to whether she is in fact dependent upon him for any part of her support. A servicewoman, on the other hand, may not claim her husband as a 'dependent' under these programs unless he is in fact dependent upon her for over one-half of his support. Thus, the question for decision is whether this difference in treatment constitutes an unconstitutional discrimination against servicewomen in violation of the Due Process Clause of the Fifth Amendment. A three-judge District Court for the Middle District of Alabama, one judge dissenting, rejected this contention and sustained the constitutionality of the provisions of the statutes making this distinction. . . . We reverse.

I

In an effort to attract career personnel through reenlistment, Congress established, in 37 U.S.C. § 401 et seq., and 10 U.S.C. § 1071 et seq., a scheme for the provision of fringe benefits to members of the uniformed services on a competitive basis with business and industry. Thus, under 37 U.S.C. § 403, a member of the uniformed services with dependents is entitled to an increased 'basic allowance for quarters' and, under 10 U.S.C. § 1076, a member's dependents are provided comprehensive medical and dental care.

Appellant Sharron Frontiero, a lieutenant in the United States Air Force, sought increased quarters allowances, and housing and medical benefits for her husband, appellant Joseph Frontiero, on the ground that he was her 'dependent.' Although such benefits would automatically have been granted with respect to the wife of a male member of the uniformed services, appellant's application was denied because she failed to demonstrate that her husband was dependent on her for more than one-half of his support. Appellants then com-

menced this suit, contending that, by making this distinction, the statutes unreasonably discriminate on the basis of sex in violation of the Due Process Clause of the Fifth Amendment. In essence, appellants asserted that the discriminatory impact of the statutes is twofold: first, as a procedural matter, a female member is required to demonstrate her spouse's dependency, while no such burden is imposed upon male members; and, second, as a substantive matter, a male member who does not provide more than one-half of his wife's support receives benefits, while a similarly situated female member is denied such benefits. Appellants therefore sought a permanent injunction against the continued enforcement of these statutes and an order directing the appellees to provide Lieutenant Frontiero with the same housing and medical benefits that a similarly situated male member would receive.

Although the legislative history of these statutes sheds virtually no light on the purposes underlying the differential treatment accorded male and female members, a majority of the three-judge District Court surmised that Congress might reasonably have concluded that, since the husband in our society is generally the 'breadwinner' in the family—and the wife typically the 'dependent' partner—'it would be more economical to require married female members claiming husbands to prove actual dependency than to extend the presumption of dependency to such members.' Indeed, given the fact that approximately 99% of all members of the uniformed services are male, the District Court speculated that such differential treatment might conceivably lead to a 'considerable saving of administrative expense and manpower.'

II

At the outset, appellants contend that classifications based upon sex, like classifications based upon race, alienage, and national origin, are inherently suspect and must therefore be subjected to close judicial scrutiny. We agree and, indeed, find at least implicit support for such an approach in our unanimous decision only last Term in Reed v. Reed.

In *Reed*, the Court considered the constitutionality of an Idaho statute providing that, when two individuals are otherwise equally entitled to appointment as administrator of an estate, the male applicant must be preferred to the female. Appellant, the mother of the deceased . . . claimed that this statute, by giving a mandatory preference to males over females [in the same entitlement class] without regard to their individual qualifications, violated the Equal Protection Clause of the Fourteenth Amendment.

The Court noted that the Idaho statute . . . establishes a classification subject to scrutiny under the Equal Protection Clause.' Under 'traditional' equal protection analysis, a legislative classification must be sustained unless it is 'patently arbitrary' and bears no rational relationship to a legitimate governmental interest.

In an effort to meet this standard, appellee contended that the statutory scheme was a reasonable measure designed to reduce the workload on probate courts by eliminating one class of contests. Moreover, appellee argued that the mandatory preference for male applicants was in itself reasonable since 'men [are] as a rule more conversant with business affairs than . . . women.' Indeed, appellee maintained that 'it is a matter of common knowledge, that women still are not engaged in politics, the professions, business or industry to the extent that men are.' And the Idaho Supreme Court, in upholding the constitutionality of this statute, suggested that the Idaho Legislature might reasonably have 'concluded that in general men are better qualified to act as an administrator than are women.'

Despite these contentions, however, the Court held the statutory preference for male applicants unconstitutional. In reaching this result, the Court implicitly rejected appellee's apparently rational explanation of the statutory scheme, and concluded that, by ignoring the individual qualifications of particular applicants, the challenged statute provide 'dissimilar treatment for men and women who are . . . similarly situated.' The Court therefore held that, even though the State's interest in achieving administrative efficiency 'is not without some legitimacy,' '[t]o give a mandatory preference to members of either sex over members of the other, merely to accomplish the elimination of hearings on the merits, is to make the very kind of arbitrary legislative choice forbidden by the [Constitution]. . . . ' This departure from 'traditional' rational-basis analysis with respect to sex-based classifications is clearly justified.

There can be no doubt that our Nation has had a long and unfortunate history of sex discrimination. Traditionally, such discrimination was rationalized by an attitude of 'romantic paternalism' which, in practical effect, put women, not on a pedestal, but in a cage.

As a result of notions such as these, our statute books gradually became laden with gross, stereotyped distinctions between the sexes and, indeed, throughout much of the 19th century the position of women in our society was, in many respects, comparable to that of blacks under the pre-Civil War slave codes. Neither slaves nor women could hold office, serve on juries, or bring suit in their own names, and married women traditionally were denied the legal capacity to hold or convey property or to serve as legal guardians of their own children. And although blacks were guaranteed the right to vote in 1870, women were denied even that right—which is itself 'preservative of other basic civil and political rights'—until adoption of the Nineteenth Amendment half a century later.

It is true, of course, that the position of women in America has improved markedly in recent decades. Nevertheless, it can hardly be doubted that, in part because of the high visibility of the sex characteristic, women still face pervasive, although at times more subtle, discrimination in our educational institutions, in the job market and, perhaps most conspicuously, in the political arena.

Moreover, since sex, like race and national origin, is an immutable characteristic determined solely by the accident of birth, the imposition of special disabilities upon the members of a particular sex because of their sex would seem to violate 'the basic concept of our system that legal burdens should bear some relationship to individual responsibility. . . .' And what differentiates sex from such non-suspect statuses as intelligence or physical disability, and aligns it with the recognized suspect criteria, is that the sex characteristic frequently bears no relation to ability to perform or contribute to society. As a result, statutory distinctions between the sexes often have the effect of inviduously relegating the entire class of females to inferior legal status without regard to the actual capabilities of its individual members.

We might also note that, over the past decade, Congress has itself manifested an increasing sensitivity to sex-based classifications. In Title VII of the Civil Rights Act of 1964, for example, Congress expressly declared that no employer, labor union, or other organization subject to the provisions of the Act shall discriminate against any individual on the basis of 'race, color, religion, sex, or national origin.' Similarly, the Equal Pay Act of 1963 provides that no employer covered by the Act 'shall discriminate . . . between employees on the basis of sex.' And § 1 of the Equal Rights Amendment, passed by Congress on March 22, 1972, and submitted to the legislatures of the States for ratification, declares that '[e]quality of rights under the law shall not be denied or abridged by the United States or by any State on account of sex.' Thus, Congress itself has concluded that classifications based upon sex are inherently invidious, and this conclusion of a coequal branch of Government is not without significance to the question presently under consideration.

With these considerations in mind, we can only conclude that classifications based upon sex, like classifications based upon race, alienage, or national origin, are inherently suspect, and must therefore be subjected to strict judicial scrutiny. Applying the analysis mandated by that stricter standard of review, it is clear that the statutory scheme now before us is constitutionally invalid.

III

The sole basis of the classification established in the challenged statutes is the sex of the individuals involved. Thus, under [the relevant statutory provisions], a female member of the uniformed services seeking to obtain housing and medical benefits for her spouse must prove his dependency in fact, whereas no such burden is imposed upon male members. In addition, the statutes operate so as to deny benefits to a female member, such as appellant Sharron Frontiero, who provides less than one-half of her spouse's support, while at the same time granting such benefits to a male member who likewise provides less than one-half of his spouse's support. Thus, to this extent at least, it may fairly be said that these statutes command 'dissimilar treatment for men and women who are . . . similarly situated.'

Moreover, the Government concedes that the differential treatment accorded men and women under these statutes serves no purpose other than mere 'administrative convenience.' In essence, the Government maintains that, as an empirical matter, wives in our society frequently are dependent upon their husbands, while husbands rarely are dependent upon their wives. Thus, the Government argues that Congress might reasonably have concluded that it would be both cheaper and easier simply conclusively to presume that wives of male members are financially dependent upon their husbands, while burdening female members with the task of establishing dependency in fact.

The Government offers no concrete evidence, however, tending to support its view that such differential treatment in fact saves the Government any money. In order to satisfy the demands of strict judicial scrutiny, the Government must demonstrate, for example, that it is actually cheaper to grant increased benefits with respect to *all* male members, than it is to determine which male members are in fact entitled to such benefits and to grant increased benefits only to those members whose wives actually meet the dependency requirement. Here, however, there is substantial evidence that, if put to the test, many of the wives of male members would fail to qualify for benefits. And in light of the fact that the dependency determination with respect to the

husbands of female members is presently made solely on the basis of affidavits rather than through the more costly hearing process, the Government's explanation of the statutory scheme is, to say the least, questionable.

In any case, our prior decisions make clear that, although efficacious administration of governmental programs is not without some importance, 'the Constitution recognizes higher values than speed and efficiency.' And when we enter the realm of 'strict judicial scrutiny,' there can be no doubt that 'administrative convenience' is not a shibboleth, the mere recitation of which dictates constitutionality. On the contrary, any statutory scheme which draws a sharp line between the sexes, solely for the purpose of achieving administrative convenience, necessarily commands 'dissimilar treatment for men and women who are . . . similarly situated,' and therefore involves the 'very kind of arbitrary legislative choice forbidden by the [Constitution]. . . . ' We therefore conclude that, by according differential treatment to male and female members of the uniformed services for the sole purpose of achieving administrative convenience, the challenged statutes violate the Due Process Clause of the Fifth Amendment insofar as they require a female member to prove the dependency of her husband.

Reversed.

Mr. JUSTICE STEWART concurs in the judgment, agreeing that the statutes before us work an invidious discrimination in violation of the Constitution.

Mr. JUSTICE REHNQUIST dissents.

Mr. JUSTICE POWELL, with whom THE CHIEF JUSTICE and Mr. JUSTICE BLACKMUN join, concurring in the judgment.

I agree that the challenged statutes constitute an unconstitutional discrimination against servicewomen in violation of the Due Process Clause of the Fifth Amendment, but I cannot join the opinion of Mr. JUSTICE BRENNAN, which would hold that all classifications based upon sex, 'like classifications based upon race, alienage, and national origin,' are 'inherently suspect and must therefore be subjected to close judicial scrutiny.' It is unnecessary for the Court in this case to characterize sex as a suspect classification, with all of the far-reaching implications of such a holding. *Reed v. Reed*, which abundantly supports our decision today, did not add sex to the narrowly limited group of classifications which are inherently suspect. In my view, we can and should decide this case on the authority of *Reed* and reserve for the future any expansion of its rationale.

There is another, and I find compelling, reason for deferring a general categorizing of sex classifications as invoking the strictest test of judicial scrutiny. The Equal Rights Amendment, which if adopted will resolve the substance of this precise question, has been approved by the Congress and submitted for ratification by the States. If this Amendment is duly adopted, it will represent the will of the people accomplished in the manner prescribed by the Constitution. By acting prematurely and unnecessarily, as I view it, the Court has assumed a decisional responsibility at the very time when state legislatures, functioning within the traditional democratic process, are debating the proposed Amendment. It seems to me that this reaching out to pre-empt by judicial action a major political decision which is currently in process of resolution does not reflect appropriate respect for duly prescribed legislative processes.

There are times when this Court, under our system, cannot avoid a constitutional decision on issues which normally should be resolved by the elected representatives of the people. But democratic institutions are weakened, and confidence in the restraint of the Court is impaired, when we appear unnecessarily to decide sensitive issues of broad social and political importance at the very time they are under consideration within the prescribed constitutional processes.

Justice Brennan's plurality opinion in *Frontiero* interprets *Reed* as adopting a strict scrutiny approach to gender-based discrimination which he characterizes as "inherently suspect," like race-based discrimination. Justice Powell's reading of *Reed* does not agree with that characterization, but uses the *Reed* analysis to strike the legislation. *Frontiero* was subsequently read as introducing an intermediate standard of review, applicable in examining gender-based claims of discrimination in violation of equal protection.[264]

Justice Brennan's rationale for departing from rationality review is that like race, gender is "an immutable characteristic determined solely by accident of birth" and women in our society, like African Americans, have suffered historically from "stereotyped distinctions" leading to social and political disabilities. "[I]ncreasing sensitivity" by Congress to gender-based distinctions, Justice Brennan argues, should result in the stricter standard of review by the Court. In contrast, Justice Powell concludes Congress' approval of the Equal Rights Amendment and its submission to the states for ratification, should lead the Court to "defer[] a general categorizing of sex classifications as invoking the strictest test of judicial scrutiny." Do Justice Powell's concerns implicate separation of powers concerns? Concerns about original intent of the Fourteenth Amendment framers?

Recall that in *City of Cleburne, supra,* Justice White argued against recognizing mental retardation as a quasi-suspect classification (as the Court began to characterize its treatment of gender differentials)—despite immutability—because the mentally retarded as a group lacked discreteness and insularity which characterized racial and ethnic groups. Women, in contrast may be considered a discrete group, but not an insular minority. Justice White, in *Cleburne,* appeared concerned about extending heightened review to groups which are not discrete and insular minorities, since "heightened scrutiny inevitably involves substantive judgments about legislative decisions." The Court doubted "the predicate for such judicial oversight" of classification schemes concerning the mentally retarded, in addition, because of the national and state legislative response to the plight of the mentally retarded, suggesting that the need for judicial oversight was thereby rendered unnecessary. These observations seem to reflect judicial reluctance to engage in a searching review under equal protection because of the risk of undue intrusion into areas more appropriately left to political branches to resolve. Why is this reluctance not present in most affirmative action cases?

---

[264] *See, e.g.,* Gerald Gunther, *In Search of Evolving Doctrine on a Changing Court: A Model for a Newer Equal Protection,* 86 HARV. L. REV. 1 (1972); John E. Nowak, Realigning the Standards of Review Under the Equal Protection Guarantee—Prohibited, Neutral and Permissive Classifications, 62 GEO. L.J. 1071 (1974).

Consider in the following cases whether the Court's approach in gender-based cases of treating claims between the extremes of rational basis review and strict scrutiny offers a satisfactory, balanced response to competing interests.

PAH: *Frontiero* invited women's rights advocates to look upon the Court as a potentially responsive forum for challenging gender inequalities (notwithstanding the legacy of *Bradwell* and *Goesart*). This alternative became increasingly important when, by 1978, political support for the Equal Rights Amendment foundered. Ironically, despite the failure of the ERA, white women have benefitted from the intermediate level of scrutiny of the Court—arguably more than African Americans who were "protected" by strict scrutiny review from even well intentioned political decision making designed to address social and political inequities. Under intermediate level of review, theoretically women have the possibility of benefitting from deference to "benign" political decisionmaking as well as obtaining more biting consideration of plausible but suspicious grounds for majoritarian decisionmaking. Thus in addition to permitting the Court to bow to political judgments about measures which are designed to eliminate gender inequalities which are a product of historical gender-based subordination of women, intermediate scrutiny has been used by the Court to "place the burden of justification upon the party defending the law or rule in court" when laws and rules have a disproportionately negative effect upon one sex,"[265] overturning legislation even when there is some basis for political decisionmaking where there lurks stigmatizing stereotypes.[266] Of course, as the following cases suggest, the Court has not always been able to move away from the sexist approaches of the past. Perhaps because of the litigation experiences of African Americans which preceded it, the feminist legal movement though not without disagreement about the meaning of equal treatment, has attempted to define its agenda. As Wendy Webster Williams has observed:

> "the goal of the feminist legal movement that began in the early seventies is not and never was the integration of women into a male world any more than it has been to build a separate but better place for women. Rather, the goal has been to break down the legal barriers that restricted each sex to its predefined role and created a hierarchy based on gender. The ability to challenge covert as well as overt gender sorting laws is essential both for challenging in court a male defined set of structures and institutions and for requiring their reconstitution to reflect the full range of our human concerns."[267]

DEL: As with racial progress under the law, the role of the judiciary in breaking down barriers of gender tends to be overstated. History in both the areas of race and gender indicates that the courts are an unreliable partner for any group that seeks satisfaction or relief that is not forthcoming from the political process itself. Relevant jurisprudence over the past half century in part reaffirms the notion that "equal protection as it spreads out tends to lift all to the level of the most favored."[268] It also constitutes a perversion, however,

---

[265] Wendy Webster Williams, *Equality's Riddle: Pregnancy and the Equal Treatment/Special Treatment Debate*, 13 N.Y.U. Rev. L. & Soc. Change 325, 329–31 (1984–85).

[266] *See, e.g.,* Guido Calabresi, *Foreword: Antidiscrimination and Constitutional Accountability (What the Bork-Brennan Debate Ignores)*, 105 Harv. L. Rev. 80, 100 (1991)(under antidiscrimination approach to judicial review even "protective" legislation can raise issues suitable for judicial resolution because of stigma-reinforcing effect).

[267] Wendy Webster Williams, *supra* note 265.

[268] Charles Fairman, Vii History of the Supreme Court of the United States, Reconstruction and Reunion, pt. 2, at 134 (1987).

to the extent that equal protection standards of review have become friendlier to women as a group than to racial minorities. The net result is that litigative methods which generated the *Brown* era have been copied and coopted to the point that the equal protection guarantee is more serviceable to racial and gender majorities than minorities. It is a consequence that is difficult to comprehend, notwithstanding a profound legacy of gender-based discrimination and oppression, when the political and economic circumstances and clout of traditionally disadvantaged minorities are compared with women.

b. What Differences Are "Real"?

An essential problem in cases challenging the Court to strike state measures as gender-based discrimination concerns identifying the appropriate norm against which gender equality should be assessed. On the one hand, the attack on traditional jurisprudence can be made by focusing on distinctions which are the product of stereotype depriving women of treatment as equal citizens entitled to the same benefits and burdens of men. On the other hand, a jurisprudence built on notions of gender sameness devalues significant differences and ignores inequalities that are deeply imbedded in the social order. Some modern feminists argue that—like colorblindness in the context of challenges to racial inequality—sameness jurisprudence ignores existing structural subordination of women and perpetuates social and political inequality by using the experiences of men as the norm against which to measure rights. The Court's movement in the 1970's from a rationality standard to closer scrutiny framed the feminist debate about sameness and difference.

Craig v. Boren
429 U.S. 190 (1976)

MR. JUSTICE BRENNAN delivered the opinion of the Court.

The interaction of two sections of an Oklahoma statute, Okla. Stat., Tit. 37, §§ 241 and 245 prohibits the sale of "nonintoxicating" 3.2% beer to males under the age of 21 and to females under the age of 18. The question to be decided is whether such a gender-based differential constitutes a denial to males 18–20 years of age of the equal protection of the laws in violation of the Fourteenth Amendment.

This action was brought in the District Court . . . by appellant Craig, a male then between 18 and 21 years of age, and appellant Whitener, a licensed vendor of 3.2% beer [seeking] declaratory and injunctive relief against enforcement of the gender-based differential on the ground that it constituted invidious discrimination against males 18–20 years of age.

. . .

II

A

Before 1972, Oklahoma defined the commencement of civil majority at age 18 for females and age 21 for males. In contrast, females were held criminally responsible as adults at age 18 and males at age 16. After the Court of Appeals for the Tenth Circuit held in 1972, on the authority of *Reed v. Reed,* that the age distinction was unconstitutional for purposes of establishing criminal responsibility as adults, the Oklahoma Legislature fixed age 18 as applicable to both males and females. In 1972, 18 also was established as the age of majority for males and females in civil matters, except that §§ 241 and 245 of the 3.2% beer statute were simultaneously codified to create an exception to the gender-free rule.

Analysis may appropriately begin with the reminder that *Reed* emphasized that statutory classifications that distinguish between males and females are "subject to scrutiny under the Equal Protection Clause." To withstand constitutional challenge, previous cases establish that classifications by gender must serve important governmental objectives and must be substantially related to achievement of those objectives. Thus, in *Reed,* the objectives of "reducing the workload on probate courts," and "avoiding intrafamily controversy," were deemed of insufficient importance to sustain use of an overt gender criterion in the appointment of administrators of intestate decedents' estates. Decisions following *Reed* similarly have rejected administrative ease and convenience as sufficiently important objectives to justify gender-based classifications. . . .

Reed v. Reed has also provided the underpinning for decisions that have invalidated statutes employing gender as an inaccurate proxy for other, more germane bases of classification. Hence, "archaic and overbroad" generalizations, *Schlesinger v. Ballard*, concerning the financial position of servicewomen, *Frontiero v. Richardson*, and working women, *Weinberger v. Wiesenfeld*, could not justify use of a gender line in determining eligibility for certain governmental entitlements. Similarly, increasingly outdated misconceptions concerning the role of females in the home rather than in the "marketplace and world of ideas" were rejected as loose-fitting characterizations incapable of supporting state statutory schemes that were premised upon their accuracy. In light of the weak congruence between gender and the characteristic or trait that gender purported to represent, it was necessary that the legislatures choose either to realign their substantive laws in a gender-neutral fashion, or to adopt procedures for identifying those instances where the sex-centered generalization actually comported with fact.

. . . We turn then to the question whether, under *Reed*, the difference between males and females with respect to the purchase of 3.2% beer warrants the differential in age drawn by the Oklahoma statute. We conclude that it does not.

. . .

C

We accept for purposes of discussion the District Court's identification of the objective underlying §§ 241 and 245 as the enhancement of traffic safety. Clearly, the protection of public health and safety represents an important function of state and local governments. However, appellees' statistics in our view cannot support the conclusion that the gender-based distinction closely serves to achieve that objective and therefore the distinction cannot under *Reed* withstand equal protection challenge.

The appellees introduced a variety of statistical surveys. First, an analysis of arrest statistics for 1973 demonstrated that 18–20-year-old male arrests for "driving under the influence" and "drunkenness" substantially exceeded female arrests for that same age period. Similarly, youths aged 17–21 were found to be overrepresented among those killed or injured in traffic accidents, with males again numerically exceeding females in this regard. Third, a random roadside survey in Oklahoma City revealed that young males were more inclined to drive and drink beer than were their female

counterparts. Fourth, Federal Bureau of Investigation nationwide statistics exhibited a notable increase in arrests for "driving under the influence." Finally, statistical evidence gathered in other jurisdictions, particularly Minnesota and Michigan, was offered to corroborate Oklahoma's experience by indicating the pervasiveness of youthful participation in motor vehicle accidents following the imbibing of alcohol. . . .

Even were this statistical evidence accepted as accurate, it nevertheless offers only a weak answer to the equal protection question presented here. The most focused and relevant of the statistical surveys, arrests of 18–20-year-olds for alcohol-related driving offenses, exemplifies the ultimate unpersuasiveness of this evidentiary record. Viewed in terms of the correlation between sex and the actual activity that Oklahoma seeks to regulate—driving while under the influence of alcohol—the statistics broadly establish that .18% of females and 2% of males in that age group were arrested for that offense. While such a disparity is not trivial in a statistical sense, it hardly can form the basis for employment of a gender line as a classifying device. Certainly if maleness is to serve as a proxy for drinking and driving, a correlation of 2% must be considered an unduly tenuous "fit." Indeed, prior cases have consistently rejected the use of sex as a decisionmaking factor even though the statutes in question certainly rested on far more predictive empirical relationships than this.

Moreover, the statistics exhibit a variety of other shortcomings that seriously impugn their value to equal protection analysis. Setting aside the obvious methodological problems,[14] the surveys do not adequately justify the salient features of Oklahoma's gender-

---

[14] The very special stereotypes that find reflection in age-differential laws, are likely substantially to distort the accuracy of these comparative statistics. Hence "reckless" young men who drink and drive are transformed into arrest statistics, whereas their female counterparts are chivalrously escorted home. *See, e.g.,* W. RECKLESS & B., KAY, THE FEMALE OFFENDER 4,7,13,16–17 (Report to Pres. Comm'n on Law Enforcement & Admin. of Justice, 1967) Moreover, the Oklahoma surveys, gathered under a regime where the age-differential law in question has been in effect, are lacking in controls necessary for appraisal of the actual effectiveness of their male 3.2% beer prohibition. In this regard, the disproportionately high arrest statistics for young males—and, indeed, the growing alcohol-related arrest figures for all ages and sexes—simply may be taken to document the relative futility of controlling driving behavior by the 3.2 beer statute and like legislation, although we obviously have no means of estimating how many individuals, if any, actually were prevented from drinking by these laws.

based traffic-safety law. None purports to measure the use and dangerousness of 3.2% beer as opposed to alcohol generally, a detail that is of particular importance since, in light of its low alcohol level, Oklahoma apparently considers the 3.2% beverage to be "nonintoxicating." Moreover, many of the studies, while graphically documenting the unfortunate increase in driving while under the influence of alcohol, make no effort to relate their findings to age-sex differentials as involved here. Indeed, the only survey that explicitly centered its attention upon young drivers and their use of beer—albeit apparently not of the diluted 3.2% variety—reached results that hardly can be viewed as impressive in justifying either a gender or age classification.[16]

There is no reason to belabor this line of analysis. It is unrealistic to expect either members of the judiciary or state officials to be well versed in the rigors of experimental or statistical technique. But this merely illustrates that proving broad sociological propositions by statistics is a dubious business, and one that inevitably is in tension with the normative philosophy that underlies the Equal Protection Clause. Suffice to say that the showing offered by the appellees does not satisfy us that sex represents a legitimate, accurate proxy for the regulation of drinking and driving. In fact, when it is further recognized that Oklahoma's statute prohibits only the selling of 3.2% beer to young males and not their drinking the beverage once acquired (even after purchase by their 18–20-year-old female companions), the relationship between gender and traffic safety becomes far too tenuous to satisfy Reed's requirement that the gender-based difference be substantially related to achievement of the statutory objective.

We hold, therefore, that under *Reed,* Oklahoma's 3.2% beer statute invidiously discriminates against males 18–20 years of age.

---

[16] The random roadside survey of drivers conducted in Oklahoma City during August of 1972 found that 78% of drivers under 20 were male. Turning to an evaluation of their drinking habits and factoring nondrinkers, 84% of the males versus 77% of the females expressed a preference for beer. Further 16.5% of the men and 11.4% of the women had consumed some alcoholic beverage within two hours of the interview. Finally, a blood alcohol concentration greater than .01% was discovered in 14.6% of the males compared to 11.5% of the females. . . . Plainly these statistical disparities between the sexes are not substantial. Moreover, when the 18–20 age boundaries are lifted and all drivers analyzed, the 1972 roadside survey indicates that male drinking rose slightly whereas female exposure to alcohol remained relatively constant.[T]his survey provides little support for a gender line among teenagers and actually runs counter to the imposition of drinking restrictions based upon age.

. . .

We conclude that the gender-based differential constitutes a denial of the equal protection of the laws to males aged 18–20 and reverse the judgment of the District Court.

It is so ordered.

Mr. Justice Powell, concurring.

. . . I join the opinion of the Court as I am in general agreement with it. I do have reservations as to some of the discussion concerning the appropriate standard for equal protection analysis and the relevance of the statistical evidence. Accordingly, I add this concurring statement.

. . . I find it unnecessary, in deciding this case, to read [Reed] as broadly as some of the Court's language may imply. *Reed* and subsequent cases involving gender-based classifications make clear that the Court subjects such classifications to a more critical examination than is normally applied when "fundamental" constitutional rights and "suspect classes" are not present.

I view this as a relatively easy case. No one questions the legitimacy or importance of the asserted governmental objective: the promotion of highway safety. The decision of the case turns on whether the state legislature, by the classification it has chosen, has adopted a means that bears a "'fair and substantial relation'" to this objective.

It seems to me that the statistics offered by appellees and relied upon by the District Court do tend generally to support the view that young men drive more, possibly are inclined to drink more, and—for various reasons—are involved in more accidents than young women. Even so, I am not persuaded that these facts and the inferences fairly drawn from them justify this classification based on a three-year age differential between the sexes, and especially one that is so easily circumvented as to be virtually meaningless. Putting it differently, this gender-based classification does not bear a fair and substantial relation to the object of the legislation.

Mr. Justice Stevens, concurring.

There is only one Equal Protection Clause. It requires every State to govern impartially. It does not direct the courts to apply one standard of review in some cases and a different standard in other cases. Whatever criticism may be leveled at a judicial opinion implying that there are at least three such standards applies with the same force to a double standard.

I am inclined to believe that what has become known as the two-tiered analysis of equal protection claims does not describe a completely logical method of deciding cases, but rather is a method the Court has employed to explain decisions that actually apply a single standard in a reasonably consistent fashion. I also suspect that a careful explanation of the reasons motivating particular decisions may contribute more to an identification of that standard than an attempt to articulate it in all-encompassing terms. . . .

MR. JUSTICE REHNQUIST, dissenting.

The Court's disposition of this case is objectionable on two grounds. First is its conclusion that *men* challenging a gender-based statute which treats them less favorably than women may invoke a more stringent standard of judicial review than pertains to most other types of classifications. Second is the Court's enunciation of this standard, without citation to any source, as being that "classifications by gender must serve *important* governmental objectives and must be *substantially* related to achievement of those objectives." The only redeeming feature of the Court's opinion, to my mind, is that it apparently signals a retreat by those who joined the plurality opinion in *Frontiero v. Richardson,* from their view that sex is a "suspect" classification for purposes of equal protection analysis. I think the Oklahoma statute challenged here need pass only the "rational basis" equal protection analysis expounded in cases such as *McGowan v. Maryland* and *Williamson v. Lee Optical Co.* and I believe that it is constitutional under that analysis.

Justice Brennan gives short shrift to the data supporting the legislative determination in *Craig*, arguing that such proof of broad sociological arguments is 'in tension with the normative philosophy" of Equal Protection. Under this approach (in contrast with the more deferential rationality-based review) merely rational correlations established by statistics are insufficient to support gender-based differentials. However, under intermediate review, support for gender-based classifications will not always prove fatal.

Geduldig v. Aiello
417 U.S. 484 (1974)

Mr. JUSTICE STEWART delivered the opinion of the Court.

For almost 30 years California has administered a disability insurance system that pays benefits to persons in private employment who are temporarily unable to work because of disability not covered by workmen's compensation. The appellees brought this action to challenge the constitutionality of a provision of the California program that, in defining 'disability,' excludes from coverage certain disabilities resulting from pregnancy. . . . On the appellees' motion for summary judgment, the District Court, by a divided vote, held that this provision of the disability insurance program violates the Equal Protection Clause of the Fourteenth Amendment, and therefore enjoined its continued enforcement. . . .

I

California's disability insurance system is funded entirely from contributions deducted from the wages of participating employees. Participation in the program is mandatory unless the employees are protected by a voluntary private plan approved by the State. Each employee is required to contribute one percent of his salary, up to an annual maximum of $85. These contributions are placed in the Unemployment Compensation Disability Fund, which is established and administered as a special trust fund within the state treasury. It is from this Disability Fund that benefits under the program are paid.

An individual is eligible for disability benefits if, during a one-year base period prior to his disability, he has contributed one percent of a minimum income of $300 to the Disability Fund. In the event he suffers a compensable disability, the individual can receive a 'weekly benefit amount' of between $25 and $105, depending on the amount he earned during the highest quarter of the base period. Benefits are not paid until the eighth day of disability, unless the employee is hospitalized, in which case benefits commence on the first day of hospitalization. In addition to the 'weekly benefit amount,' a hospitalized employee is entitled to receive 'additional benefits' of $12 per day of hospitalization. 'Weekly benefit amounts' for any one disability are payable for 26 weeks so long as the total amount paid does not exceed one-half of the wages received during the base period. 'Additional benefits' for any one disability are paid for a maximum of 20 days.

In return for his one-percent contribution to the Disability Fund, the individual employee is insured against the risk of disability stemming from a substantial number of 'mental or physical illness[es] and mental or physical injur[ies].' It is not every disabling condition, however, that triggers the obligation to pay benefits under the program. As already noted, for example, any disability of less than eight days' duration is not compensable, except when the employee is hospitalized. Conversely, no benefits are payable for any single disability beyond 26 weeks. Further, disability is not compensable if it results from the individual's court commitment as a dipsomaniac, drug addict, or sexual psychopath. Finally, [the section] excludes from coverage certain disabilities that are attributable to pregnancy. It is this provision that is at issue in the present case.

. . .

At all times relevant to this case, the Unemployment Insurance Code provided:

'Disability' or 'disabled' includes both mental or physical illness and mental or physical injury. An individual shall be deemed disabled in any day in which, because of his physical or mental condition, he is unable to perform his regular or customary work. *In no case shall the term 'disability' or 'disabled' include any injury or illness caused by or arising in connection with pregnancy up to the termination of such pregnancy and for a period of 28 days thereafter.'* (Emphasis added).

. . .

The issue before the Court on this appeal is whether the California disability insurance program invidiously discriminates against Jaramillo and others similarly situated by not paying insurance benefits for disability that accompanies normal pregnancy and childbirth.

II

It is clear that California intended to establish this benefit system as an insurance program that was to function essentially in accordance with insurance concepts. . . . The Disability Fund is wholly supported by the one percent of wages annually contributed by participating employees. At oral argument, counsel for the appellant informed us that in recent years between 90% and 103% of the revenue to the Disability Fund has been paid out in disability and hospital benefits. This history strongly suggests that the one-percent contribution rate, in addition to being easily computable, bears a close and substantial relationship to the level of benefits payable and to the disability risks insured under the program.

Over the years California has demonstrated a strong commitment not to increase the contribution rate above the one-percent level. The State has sought to provide the broadest possible disability protection that would be affordable by all employees, including those with very low incomes. Because any larger percentage or any flat dollar-amount rate of contribution would impose an increasingly regressive levy bearing most heavily upon those with the lowest incomes, the State has resisted any attempt to change the required contribution from the one-percent level. The program is thus structured, in terms of the level of benefits and the risks insured, to maintain the solvency of the Disability Fund at a one-percent annual level of contribution.

In ordering the State to pay benefits for disability accompanying normal pregnancy and delivery, the District Court acknowledged the State's contention 'that coverage of these disabilities is so extraordinarily expensive that it would be impossible to maintain a program supported by employee contributions if these disabilities are included.' There is considerable disagreement between the parties with respect to how great the increased costs would actually be, but they would clearly be substantial. For purposes of analysis the District Court accepted the State's estimate, which was in excess of $100 million annually, and stated: '[I]t is clear that including these disabilities would not destroy the program. The increased costs could be accommodated quite easily by making reasonable changes in the contribution rate, the maximum benefits allowable, and the other variables affecting the solvency of the program.'

Each of these 'variables'—the benefit level deemed appropriate to compensate employee disability, the risks selected to be insured under the program, and the contribution rate chosen to maintain the solvency of the program and at the same time to permit low-income employees to participate with minimal personal sacrifice—represents a policy determination by the State. The essential issue in this case is whether the Equal Protection Clause requires such policies to be sacrificed or compromised in order to finance the payment of benefits to those whose disability is attributable to normal pregnancy and delivery.

We cannot agree that the exclusion of this disability from coverage amounts to invidious discrimination under the Equal Protection Clause. California does not discriminate with respect to the persons or groups which are eligible for disability insurance protection under the program. The classification challenged in this case relates to the asserted underinclusiveness of the set of risks that the State has selected to insure. Although California has created a program to insure most risks of employment disability, it has not chosen to insure all such risks, and this decision is reflected in the level of annual contributions exacted from participating employees. This Court has held that, consistently with the Equal Protection Clause, a State 'may take one step at a time, addressing itself to the phase of the problem which seems most acute to the legislative mind. . . . The legislature may select one phase of one field and apply a remedy there, neglecting the others. . . . Particularly with respect to social welfare programs, so long as the line drawn by the State is rationally supportable, the courts will not interpose their judgment as to the appropriate stopping point. The Equal Protection Clause does not require that a State must choose between attacking every aspect of a problem or not attacking the problem at all.'

The District Court suggested that moderate alterations in what it regarded as 'variables' of the disability insurance program could be made to accommodate the substantial expense required to include normal pregnancy within the program's protection. The same can be said, however, with respect to the other expensive class of disabilities that are excluded from coverage—short-term disabilities. If the Equal Protection Clause were thought to compel disability payments for normal pregnancy, it is hard to perceive why it would not also compel payments for short-term disabilities suffered by participating employees.

It is evident that a totally comprehensive program would be substantially more costly than the present program and would inevitably require state subsidy, a higher rate of employee contribution, a lower scale of benefits for those suffering insured disabilities, or some combination of these measures. There is nothing in the Constitution, however, that requires the State to subordinate or compromise its legitimate interests solely to create a more comprehensive social insurance program than it already has.

The State has a legitimate interest in maintaining the self-supporting nature of its insurance program. Similarly, it has an interest in distributing the available resources in such a way as to keep benefit payments at an adequate level for disabilities that are covered, rather than to cover all disabilities inadequately. Finally, California has a legitimate concern in maintaining the contribution rate at a level that will not unduly burden participating employees, particularly low-income employees who may be most in need of the disability insurance.

These policies provide an objective and wholly noninvidious basis for the State's decision not to create a more comprehensive insurance program than it has. There is no evidence in the record that the selection of the risks insured by the program worked to discriminate against any in terms of the aggregate risk protection derived by that group or class from the program.[20] There is no risk from which men are protected and women are not. Likewise, there is no risk from which women are protected and men are not.

The appellee simply contends that, although she has received insurance protection equivalent to that provided all other participating employees, she has suffered discrimination because she encountered a risk that was outside the program's protection. For the reasons we have stated, we hold that this contention is not a valid one under the Equal Protection Clause of the Fourteenth Amendment.

The judgment of the District Court is reversed.

JUSTICE BRENNAN, with whom Mr. JUSTICE DOUGLAS and Mr. JUSTICE MARSHALL join, dissenting.

The Court today rejects appellees' equal protection claim and upholds the exclusion of normal-pregnancy-related disabilities from coverage under California's disability insurance program on the ground that the legislative classification rationally promotes the State's legitimate cost-saving interests in 'maintaining the self-supporting nature of its insurance program[,] . . . distributing the available resources in such a way as to keep benefit payments at an adequate level for disabilities that are covered, . . . [and] maintaining the contribution rate at a level that will not unduly burden participating employees.'. . .

. . .

---

[20] The California insurance program does not exclude anyone from benefit eligibility because of gender but merely removes one physical condition—pregnancy—from the list of compensable disabilities . While it is true that only women can become pregnant, it does not follow that every legislative classification concerning pregnancy is a sex-based classification like those considered in *Reed, supra*, and *Frontiero, supra* . Normal pregnancy is an objectively identifiable physical condition with unique characteristics. Absent a showing that distinctions involving pregnancy are mere pretexts designed to effect an invidious discrimination against the members of one sex of the other, lawmakers are constitutionally free to include or exclude pregnancy from the coverage of legislation such as this on any reasonable basis just as with respect to any physical condition. . . .

Disabilities caused by pregnancy . . . like other physically disabling conditions covered by the Code, require medical care, often include hospitalization, anesthesia and surgical procedures, and many involve genuine risk to life. Moreover, the economic effects cause by pregnancy-related disabilities are functionally indistinguishable from the effects caused by any other disability: wages are lost due to a physical inability to work, and medical expenses are incurred for the delivery of the child and for post-partum care. In my view, by singling out for less favorable treatment a gender-linked disability peculiar to women, the State has created a double standard for disability compensation: a limitation is imposed upon the disabilities suffered for which women workers may recover, while men receive full compensation for all disabilities suffered, including those that effect only or primarily their sex, such as prostatectomies, circumcision, hemophilia, and gout. . . . Such dissimilar treatment of men and women, on the basis of physical characteristics inextricably linked to one sex, inevitably constitutes sex discrimination.

Because I believe that *Reed v. Reed*, and *Frontiero v. Richardson*, mandate a stricter standard of scrutiny which the State's classification fails to satisfy, I respectfully dissent.

Justice Stewart concludes that no gender discrimination in violation of the Equal Protection Clause occurs when the state determines to remove pregnancy from the list of compensable disabilities because the classification (pregnant women and nonpregnant men and women) is not gender-based. Contrast Justice Brennan's view that dissimilar treatment of men and women "on the basis of physical characteristics inextricably linked to one sex" constitutes unlawful discrimination. He reasons that the state has created a double standard, imposing a limitation on recovery from disabilities which women can incur which does not exist for men. Notably, Justice Stewart's rationality approach avoids the sameness vs. difference conundrum. The difference in conclusions by Justices Stewart and Brennan can be viewed as disagreement about what constitutes gender discrimination; is it preferable to consider their contradictory conclusions a consequence of the stringency of their respective constitutional standards?

Professor Lucinda Finley has called equality analysis a trap for women, particularly in issues which appear to turn on biology, like pregnancy, because as judges undertake to search for sameness they apply an analysis that is "inherently male:"

> The search for sameness is built around male norms, so that what is male is the standard for measurement. For women, the application of equality analysis means that so long as women are just like men, or are willing to ascribe to male values and standards, the law will assist them in doing so. But where women appear to be truly different from men—in their capacity to become pregnant and their traditional relegation to the sphere of childbearing—they may be legally penalized in the public sphere of the workplace for not being men. Equality analysis is of little use to women who would like to question the male-oriented values and norms upon which the workplace is built."[269]

---

[269] Lucinda Finley, *Transcending Equality Theory: A Way Out of the Maternity and the Workplace Debate,* 86 COLUM. L. REV. 1118, 1181–82 (1986)

Michael M. v. Superior Court Sonoma County

450 U.S. 464 (1981)

Justice REHNQUIST announced the judgment of the Court and delivered an opinion, in which THE CHIEF JUSTICE, Justice STEWART, and Justice POWELL joined.

The question presented in this case is whether California's "statutory rape" law violates the Equal Protection Clause of the Fourteenth Amendment. Section 261.5 defines unlawful sexual intercourse as "an act of sexual intercourse accomplished with a female not the wife of the perpetrator, where the female is under the age of 18 years." The statute thus makes men alone criminally liable for the act of sexual intercourse.

In July 1978, a complaint was filed in the Municipal Court of Sonoma County, Cal., alleging that petitioner, then a 17½-year-old male, had had unlawful sexual intercourse with a female under the age of 18, in violation of § 261.5. The evidence, adduced at a preliminary hearing showed that at approximately midnight on June 3, 1978, petitioner and two friends approached Sharon, a 16 1/2 -year-old female, and her sister as they waited at a bus stop. Petitioner and Sharon, who had already been drinking, moved away from the others and began to kiss. After being struck in the face for rebuffing petitioner's initial advances, Sharon submitted to sexual intercourse with petitioner. Prior to trial, petitioner sought to set aside the information on both state and federal constitutional grounds, asserting that § 261.5 unlawfully discriminated on the basis of gender. The trial court and the California Court of Appeal denied petitioner's request for relief and petitioner sought review in the Supreme Court of California.

The Supreme Court held that "section 261.5 discriminates on the basis of sex because only females may be victims, and only males may violate the section." The court then subjected the classification to "strict scrutiny," stating that it must be justified by a compelling state interest. It found that the classification was "supported not by mere social convention but by the immutable physiological fact that it is the female exclusively who can become pregnant." Canvassing "the tragic human costs of illegitimate teenage pregnancies," including the large number of teenage abortions, the increased medical risk associated with teenage pregnancies, and the social consequences of teenage childbearing, the court concluded that the State has a compelling interest in preventing such pregnancies. Because males alone can "physiologically cause the result which the law properly seeks to avoid," the court further held that the gender classification was readily justified as a means of identifying offender and victim. For the reasons stated below, we affirm the judgment of the California Supreme Court.

As is evident from our opinions, the Court has had some difficulty in agreeing upon the proper approach and analysis in cases involving challenges to gender-based classifications. The issues posed by such challenges range from issues of standing, to the appropriate standard of judicial review for the substantive classification. Unlike the California Supreme Court, we have not held that gender-based classifications are "inherently suspect" and thus we do not apply so-called "strict scrutiny" to those classifications. Our cases have held, however, that the traditional minimum rationality test takes on a somewhat "sharper focus" when gender-based classifications are challenged. In *Reed v. Reed*, for example, the Court stated that a gender-based classification will be upheld if it bears a "fair and substantial relationship" to legitimate state ends, while in *Craig v. Boren*, the Court restated the test to require the classification to bear a "substantial relationship" to "important governmental objectives."

Underlying these decisions is the principle that a legislature may not "make overbroad generalizations based on sex which are entirely unrelated to any differences between men and women or which demean the ability or social status of the affected class." But because the Equal Protection Clause does not "demand that a statute necessarily apply equally to all persons" or require "'things which are different in fact . . . to be treated in law as though they were the same,'" this Court has consistently upheld statutes where the gender classification is not invidious, but rather realistically reflects the fact that the sexes are not similarly situated in certain circumstances. As the Court has stated, a legislature may "provide for the special problems of women."

Applying those principles to this case, the fact that the California Legislature criminalized the act of illicit sexual intercourse with a minor female is a sure indication of its intent or purpose to discourage that conduct. Precisely why the legislature desired that result is of course somewhat less clear. This Court has long recognized that "[i]nquiries into congressional motives or purposes are a hazardous matter," and the search for the "actual" or "primary" purpose of a statute is likely to be elusive. Here, for example, the individual legislators may have voted for the statute for a variety of reasons. Some legislators may have been concerned about preventing teenage pregnancies, others about protecting young females from physical injury or from the loss of "chastity," and still others about promoting various religious and moral attitudes towards premarital sex.

The justification for the statute offered by

the State, and accepted by the Supreme Court of California, is that the legislature sought to prevent illegitimate teenage pregnancies. That finding, of course, is entitled to great deference. And although our cases establish that the State's asserted reason for the enactment of a statute may be rejected, if it "could not have been a goal of the legislation," this is not such a case.

We are satisfied not only that the prevention of illegitimate pregnancy is at least one of the "purposes" of the statute, but also that the State has a strong interest in preventing such pregnancy. At the risk of stating the obvious, teenage pregnancies, which have increased dramatically over the last two decades, have significant social, medical, and economic consequences for both the mother and her child, and the State. Of particular concern to the State is that approximately half of all teenage pregnancies end in abortion. And of those children who are born, their illegitimacy makes them likely candidates to become wards of the State.

[In a footnote, Justice Rehnquist notes that] the California Legislature considered and rejected proposals to render § 261.5 gender neutral, thereby ratifying the judgment of the California Supreme Court. That is enough to answer petitioner's contention that the statute was the "'accidental by-product of a traditional way of thinking about females.'" Certainly this decision of the California Legislature is as good a source as is this Court in deciding what is "current" and what is "outmoded" in the perception of women.

We need not be medical doctors to discern that young men and young women are not similarly situated with respect to the problems and the risks of sexual intercourse. Only women may become pregnant, and they suffer disproportionately the profound physical, emotional and psychological consequences of sexual activity. The statute at issue here protects women from sexual intercourse at an age when those consequences are particularly severe.

The question thus boils down to whether a State may attack the problem of sexual intercourse and teenage pregnancy directly by prohibiting a male from having sexual intercourse with a minor female.[8] We hold that such a statute is sufficiently related to the State's objectives to pass constitutional muster.

Because virtually all of the significant harmful and inescapably identifiable consequences of teenage pregnancy fall on the young female, a legislature acts well within its authority when it elects to punish only the participant who, by nature, suffers few of the consequences of his conduct. It is hardly unreasonable for a legislature acting to protect minor females to exclude them from punishment. Moreover, the risk of pregnancy itself constitutes a substantial deterrence to young females. No similar natural sanctions deter males. A criminal sanction imposed solely on males thus serves to roughly "equalize" the deterrents on the sexes.

We are unable to accept petitioner's contention that the statute is impermissibly underinclusive and must, in order to pass judicial scrutiny, be *broadened* so as to hold the female as criminally liable as the male. It is argued that this statute is not *necessary* to deter teenage pregnancy because a gender-neutral statute, where both male and female would be subject to prosecution, would serve that goal equally well. The relevant inquiry, however, is not whether the statute is drawn as precisely as it might have been, but whether the line chosen by the California Legislature is within constitutional limitations.

In any event, we cannot say that a gender-neutral statute would be as effective as the statute California has chosen to enact. The State persuasively contends that a gender-neutral statute would frustrate its interest in effective enforcement. Its view is that a female is surely less likely to report violations of the statute if she herself would be subject to criminal prosecution. In an area already fraught with prosecutorial difficulties, we decline to hold that the Equal Protection Clause requires a legislature to enact a statute so broad that it may well be incapable of enforcement.[10]

---

[8] We do not understand petitioner to question a State's authority to make sexual intercourse among teenagers a criminal act, at least on a gender-neutral basis. In *Carey v. Population Services International*, four Members of the Court assumed for the purposes of that case that a State may regulate the sexual behavior of minors, while four other Members of the Court more emphatically stated that such regulation would be permissible. The Court has long recognized that a State has even broader authority to protect the physical, mental, and moral well-being of its youth, than of its adults.

[10] Where such differing speculations as to the effect of a statute are plausible, we think it appropriate to defer to the decision of the California Supreme Court, "armed as it was with the knowledge of the facts and circumstances concerning the passage and potential impact of [the statute], and familiar with the milieu in which that provision would operate."

It should be noted that two of the three cases relied upon by Justice BRENNAN's dissent are readily distinguishable from the instant one. In both *Navedo v. Preisser* and *Meloon v. Helgemoe*, the respective governments asserted that the purpose of the statute was to protect young women from physical injury. Both courts rejected the justification on the grounds that there had been no showing that young females are more likely than males to suffer physical injury from sexual intercourse. They further held, contrary to our decision, that pregnancy prevention was not a "plausible" purpose of the legislation. Thus neither

We similarly reject petitioner's argument that § 261.5 is impermissibly overbroad because it makes unlawful sexual intercourse with prepubescent females, who are, by definition, incapable of becoming pregnant. Quite apart from the fact that the statute could well be justified on the grounds that very young females are particularly susceptible to physical injury from sexual intercourse, it is ludicrous to suggest that the Constitution requires the California Legislature to limit the scope of its rape statute to older teenagers and exclude young girls.

There remains only petitioner's contention that the statute is unconstitutional as it is applied to him because he, like Sharon, was under 18 at the time of sexual intercourse. Petitioner argues that the statute is flawed because it presumes that as between two persons under 18, the male is the culpable aggressor. We find petitioner's contentions unpersuasive. Contrary to his assertions, the statute does not rest on the assumption that males are generally the aggressors. It is instead an attempt by a legislature to prevent illegitimate teenage pregnancy by providing an additional deterrent for men. The age of the man is irrelevant since young men are as capable as older men of inflicting the harm sought to be prevented.

In upholding the California statute we also recognize that this is not a case where a statute is being challenged on the grounds that it "invidiously discriminates" against females. To the contrary, the statute places a burden on males which is not shared by females. But we find nothing to suggest that men, because of past discrimination or peculiar disadvantages, are in need of the special solicitude of the courts. Nor is this a case where the gender classification is made "solely for . . . administrative convenience," as in *Frontiero v. Richardson,* or rests on "the baggage of sexual stereotypes" as in *Orr v. Orr.* As we have held, the statute instead reasonably reflects the fact that the consequences of sexual intercourse and pregnancy fall more heavily on the female than on the male.

Accordingly, the judgment of the California Supreme Court is affirmed.

Justice STEWART, concurring.

Section 261.5, on its face, classifies on the basis of sex. A male who engages in sexual intercourse with an underage female who is not his wife violates the statute; a female who engages in sexual intercourse with an underage male who is not her husband does not. The petitioner contends that this state law, which punishes only males for the conduct in question, violates his Fourteenth Amendment right to the equal protection of the law. The Court today correctly rejects that contention.

A

At the outset, it should be noted that the statutory discrimination, when viewed as part of the wider scheme of California law, is not as clearcut as might at first appear. Females are not freed from criminal liability in California for engaging in sexual activity that may be harmful. It is unlawful, for example, for any person, of either sex, to molest, annoy, or contribute to the delinquency of anyone under 18 years of age. All persons are prohibited from committing "any lewd or lascivious act," including consensual intercourse, with a child under 14. And members of both sexes may be convicted for engaging in deviant sexual acts with anyone under 18. Finally, females may be brought within the proscription of § 261.5 itself, since a female may be charged with aiding and abetting its violation.

Section 261.5 is thus but one part of a broad statutory scheme that protects all minors from the problems and risks attendant upon adolescent sexual activity. To be sure, § 261.5 creates an additional measure of punishment for males who engage in sexual intercourse with females between the ages of 14 and 17. The question then is whether the Constitution prohibits a state legislature from imposing this *additional* sanction on a gender-specific basis.

B

We have recognized that in certain narrow circumstances men and women are *not* similarly situated; in these circumstances a gender classification based on clear differences between the sexes in not invidious, and a legislative classification realistically based upon those differences is not unconstitutional. "[G]ender-based classifications are not invariably invalid. When men and women are not in fact similarly situated in the area covered by the legislation in question, the Equal Protection Clause is not violated."

Applying these principles to the classification enacted by the California Legislature, it is readily apparent that § 261.5 does not violate the Equal Protection Clause. Young women and men are not similarly situated with respect to the problems and risk associated with intercourse and pregnancy, and the statute is realistically related to the legitimate state purpose of reducing those problems and risks.

---

court reached the issue presented here, whether the statute is substantially related to the prevention of teenage pregnancy. Significantly, *Meloon* has been severely limited. Here, of course, even Justice BRENNAN's dissent does not dispute that young women suffer disproportionately the deleterious consequences of illegitimate pregnancy.

E

The Equal Protection Clause does not mean that the physiological differences between men and women must be disregarded. While those differences must never be permitted to become a pretext for invidious discrimination, no such discrimination is presented by this case. The Constitution surely does not require a State to pretend that demonstrable differences between men and women do not really exist.

Justice BLACKMUN, concurring in the judgment.

It is gratifying that the plurality recognizes that "[a]t the risk of stating the obvious, teenage pregnancies . . . have increased dramatically over the last two decades" and "have significant social, medical, and economic consequences for both the mother and her child, and the State." There have been times when I have wondered whether the Court was capable of this perception, particularly when it has struggled with the different but not unrelated problems that attend abortion issues.

I . . . cannot vote to strike down the California statutory rape law, for I think it is a sufficiently reasoned and constitutional effort to control the problem at its inception.

Justice BRENNAN, with whom Justices WHITE and MARSHALL join, dissenting.

It is disturbing to find the Court so splintered on a case that presents such a straightforward issue: Whether the admittedly gender-based classification in Cal.Penal Code Ann. § 261.5 bears a sufficient relationship to the State's asserted goal of preventing teenage pregnancies to survive the "mid-level" constitutional scrutiny mandated by *Craig v. Boren.* Applying the analytical framework provided by our precedents, I am convinced that there is only one proper resolution of this issue: the classification must be declared unconstitutional. [The State has not shown that Cal.-Penal Code § 261.5 is any more effective than a gender-neutral law would be in determining minor females from engaging in sexual intercourse. It has therefore not met its burden of proving that the statutory classification is substantially related to the achievement of its asserted goal.] [E]ven assuming that prevention of teenage pregnancy is an important governmental objective and that it is in fact an objective of § 261.5, California still has the burden of proving that there are fewer teenage pregnancies under its gender-based statutory rape law than there would be if the law were gender neutral. To meet this burden, the State must show that because its statutory rape law punishes only males, and not females, it more effectively deters minor females from having sexual intercourse.

. . .

[T]here are at least two flaws in the State's assertion that law enforcement problems created by a gender-neutral statutory rape law would make such a statute less effective than a gender-based statute in deterring sexual activity.

First, the experience of other jurisdictions, and California itself, belies the plurality's conclusion that a gender-neutral statutory rape law "may well be incapable of enforcement." . . .

. . .

The second flaw . . . is that even assuming that a gender-neutral statute would be more difficult to enforce, the State has still not shown that those enforcement problems would make such a statute less effective than a gender-based statute in deterring minor females from engaging in sexual intercourse. Common sense, however, suggests that a gender-neutral law subjects both men and women to criminal sanctions and thus arguably has a deterrent effect on twice as many potential violators. . . .

III

Until very recently, no California court or commentator had suggested that the purpose of California's statutory rape law was to protect young women from the risk of pregnancy. Indeed the historical development of § 261.5 demonstrates that the law was initially enacted on the premise that young women, in contrast to young men, were to be deemed legally incapable of consenting to an act of sexual intercourse. Because their chastity was considered particularly precious, those young women were felt to be uniquely in need of . . . protection [while] men were assumed to be capable of making such decisions for themselves.

It is perhaps because the gender classification in California's statutory rape law was initially designed to further these outmoded sexual stereotypes, rather than to reduce the incidence of teenage pregnancies, that the State has been unable to demonstrate a substantial relationship between the classification and its newly asserted goal . . . But whatever the reason, the State has not shown that [the statute] is any more effective than a gender-neutral law would be in deterring minor females from engaging in sexual intercourse. It has therefore not met its burden of proving that the statutory classification is substantially related to the achievement of its asserted goal.

I would hold that § 261.5 violates the Equal Protection Clause of the Fourteenth Amendment, and I would reverse the judgment of the California Supreme Court.

Justice STEVENS, dissenting.

Local custom and belief—rather than statutory laws of venerable but doubtful ancestry—will determine the volume of sexual activity among unmarried teenagers. The empirical evidence cited by the plurality demonstrates the futility of the notion that a statutory prohibition will significantly affect the volume of that activity or provide a meaningful solution to the problems created by it. Nevertheless, as a matter of constitutional power, unlike my Brother BRENNAN, I would have no doubt about the validity of a state law prohibiting all unmarried teenagers from engaging in sexual intercourse. The societal interests in reducing the incidence of venereal disease and teenage pregnancy are sufficient, in my judgment, to justify a prohibition of conduct that increases the risk of those harms.

My conclusion that a nondiscriminatory prohibition would be constitutional does not help me answer the question whether a prohibition applicable to only half of the joint participants in the risk-creating conduct is also valid. It cannot be true that the validity of a total ban is an adequate justification for a selective prohibition; otherwise, the constitutional objection to discriminatory rules would be meaningless. The question in this case is whether the difference between males and females justifies this statutory discrimination based entirely on sex.

In this case, the fact that a female confronts a greater risk of harm than a male is a reason for applying the prohibition to her—not a reason for granting her a license to use her own judgment on whether or not to assume the risk. Surely, if we examine the problem from the point of view of society's interest in preventing the risk-creating conduct from occurring at all, it is irrational to exempt 50% of the potential violators. And, if we view the government's interest as that of a *parens patriae* seeking to protect its subjects from harming themselves, the discrimination is actually perverse. Would a rational parent making rules for the conduct of twin children of opposite sex simultaneously forbid the son and authorize the daughter to engage in conduct that is especially harmful to the daughter? That is the effect of this statutory classification.

If pregnancy or some other special harm is suffered by one of the two participants in the prohibited act, that special harm no doubt would constitute a legitimate mitigating factor in deciding what, if any, punishment might be appropriate in a given case. But from the standpoint of fashioning a general preventive rule—or, indeed, in determining appropriate punishment when neither party in fact has suffered any special harm—I regard a total exemption for the members of the more endangered class as utterly irrational.

In my opinion, the only acceptable justification for a general rule requiring disparate treatment of the two participants in a joint act must be a legislative judgment that one is more guilty than the other. The risk-creating conduct that this statute is designed to prevent requires the participation of two persons—one male and one female.

Even if my logic is faulty and there actually is some speculative basis for treating equally guilty males and females differently, I still believe that any such speculative justification would be outweighed by the paramount interest in evenhanded enforcement of the law. A rule that authorizes punishment of only one of two equally guilty wrongdoers violates the essence of the constitutional requirement that the sovereign must govern impartially.

I respectfully dissent.

PAH: As in some of the earlier cases (like *Mueller*), the decisions in *Michael M* expose the Courts' preoccupation with biological characteristics as the measure of sameness or difference in gender cases. None of the opinions satisfactorily address the fact that existing social inequality, shorn of outdated, oppressive stereotypes, make the circumstances for young women and men different. For many feminists (and others concerned about equality) the potential for reinforcing traditional "breeder-victim" images makes the "protective" posture of the majority troublesome.[270]

DEL: The *Michael M.* decision descends at least in spirit from the paternalistic jurisprudence of *Bradwell* and *Mueller*. It is a result that casts doubt upon the assertion that, because the Equal Rights Amendment was rejected, the judiciary should be more receptive to women's equal protection claims. The *Michael M.* mind-set suggests that a less

---

[270] *See, e.g.*, Wendy Webster Williams, *The Equality Crisis: Reflections on Culture, Courts and Feminism*, 7 WOMEN'S RTS. L. REP. 175 (1982). *See also* Ruth Colker, *Anti-Subordination Above All: Sex, Race, and Equal Protection*, 61 N.Y.U. L. REV. 1003 (1986).

regulated political process, pried open by the Nineteenth Amendment and increasingly responsive to the influence of women, may be more beneficial to group interests and aspirations that traditionally have been subordinated. It is a primary lesson of the *Lochner* era, that should not be lost on a group that constitutes an electoral majority if gender were the sole reference point, that the judiciary may be an agent of obstruction rather than progress even when the political process wishes to move ahead.

DER: Feminist theorizing has long grappled with describing the nature of differences between men and women. According to this framework, the "difference" approach emphasizes gender disparities and advocates different treatment for women. The "sameness" approach minimizes differences between the sexes and advocates the same treatment for men and women based on gender neutrality. Proponents of this latter view fear that acknowledging gender differences in power or biology perpetuates negative female stereotypes and roles. Other feminists, however, have demonstrated that the very framing of gender equality in terms of sameness and difference ignores an underlying male standard, as well as the systemic subordination of women. Instead of either glorifying or ignoring innate differences between men and women, we should focus instead on eradicating society's use of gender differences to keep women in an inferior political status.

Rostker v. Goldberg
453 U.S. 57 (1981)

Justice REHNQUIST delivered the opinion of the Court.

The question presented is whether the Military Selective Service Act, 50 U.S.C. App. § 451 *et seq.,* violates the Fifth Amendment to the United States Constitution in authorizing the President to require the registration of males and not females.

I

Congress is given the power under the Constitution "To raise and support Armies," "To provide and maintain a Navy," and "To make Rules for the Government and Regulation of the land and naval Forces." Art. I, § 8, cls. 12–14. Pursuant to this grant of authority Congress has enacted the Military Selective Service Act. Section 3 of the Act empowers the President, by proclamation, to require the registration of "every male citizen" and male resident aliens between the ages of 18 and 26. The purpose of this registration is to facilitate any eventual conscription: pursuant to § 4(a) of the Act, those persons required to register under § 3 are liable for training and service in the Armed Forces.

In early 1980, President Carter determined that it was necessary to reactivate the draft registration process.

Congress agreed that it was necessary to reactivate the registration process, and allocated funds for that purpose in a Joint Resolution which passed the House on April 22 and the Senate on June 12. The Resolution did not allocate all the funds originally requested by the President, but only those necessary to register males. Although Congress considered the question at great length, it declined to amend the MSSA to permit the registration of women.

II

Whenever called upon to judge the constitutionality of an Act of Congress—"the gravest and most delicate duty that this Court is called upon to perform," the Court accords "great weight to the decisions of Congress." The Congress is a coequal branch of government whose Members take the same oath we do to uphold the Constitution of the United States. The customary deference accorded the judgments of Congress is certainly appropriate when, as here, Congress specifically considered the question of the Act's constitutionality.

This is not, however, merely a case involving the customary deference accorded congressional decisions. The case arises in the context of Congress' authority over national defense and military affairs, and perhaps in no other area has the Court accorded Congress greater deference. In rejecting the registration of women, Congress explicitly relied upon its constitutional powers under Art. I, § 8, cls. 12–14. The "specific findings" section of the Report of the Senate Armed Services Committee, later adopted by both Houses of Congress, began by stating:

"Article I, section 8 of the Constitution commits exclusively to the Congress the powers to raise and support armies, provide and maintain a Navy, and make rules for Government and regulation of the land and naval forces, and pursuant to these powers it lies within the discretion of the Congress to determine the occasions for expansion of our Armed Forces, and the means best suited to such expansion should it prove necessary."

This Court has consistently recognized Congress' "broad constitutional power" to raise and regulate armies and navies. As the Court noted in considering a challenge to the selective service laws: "The constitutional power of Congress to raise and support armies and to make all laws necessary and proper to that end is broad and sweeping."

Not only is the scope of Congress' constitutional power in this area broad, but the lack of competence on the part of the courts is marked. In Gilligan v. Morgan, the Court noted: "[I]t is difficult to conceive of an area of governmental activity in which the courts have less competence. The complex, subtle, and professional decisions as to the composition, training, equipping, and control of a military force are essentially professional military judgments, subject *always* to civilian control of the Legislative and Executive Branches."

Congress remains subject to the limitations of the Due Process Clause, but the tests and limitations to be applied may differ because of the military context. We of course do not abdicate our ultimate responsibility to decide the constitutional question, but simply recognize that the Constitution itself requires such deference to congressional choice. In deciding the question before us we must be particularly careful not to substitute our judgment of what is desirable for that of Congress, or our own evaluation of evidence for a reasonable evaluation by the Legislative Branch. The reconciliation between the deference due Congress and our own constitutional responsibility is perhaps best instanced in *Schlesinger v. Ballard*, where we stated:

"This Court has recognized that 'it is the primary business of armies and navies to fight or be ready to fight wars should the occasion arise.' The responsibility for determining how best our Armed Forces shall attend to that business rests with Congress, see U.S.Const. Art. I, § 8, cls. 12–14, and with the President. See U.S.-Const., Art. II, § 2, cl. 1. We cannot say that, in exercising its broad constitutional power here, Congress has violated the Due Process Clause of the Fifth Amendment."

Or, as put a generation ago in a case not involving any claim of gender-based discrimination:

"[J]udges are not given the task of running the Army. The responsibility for setting up channels through which . . . grievances can be considered and fairly settled rests upon the Congress and upon the President of the United States and his subordinates. The Military constitutes a specialized community governed by a separate discipline from that of the civilian. Orderly government requires that the judiciary be as scrupulous not to interfere with legitimate Army matters as the Army must be scrupulous not to intervene in judicial matters."

Schlesinger v. Ballard did not purport to apply a different equal protection test because of the military context, but did stress the deference due congressional choices among alternatives in exercising the congressional authority to raise and support armies and make rules for their governance. It is apparent that Congress was fully aware not merely of the many facts and figures presented to it by witnesses who testified before its Committees, but of the current thinking as to the place of women in the Armed Services. In such a case, we cannot ignore Congress' broad authority conferred by the Constitution to raise and support armies when we are urged to declare unconstitutional its studied choice of one alternative in preference to another for furthering that goal.

III

This case is quite different from several of the gender-based discrimination cases we have considered in that, despite appellees' assertions, Congress did not act "unthinkingly" or "reflexively and not for any considered reason." The question of registering women for the draft not only received considerable national attention and was the subject of wide-ranging public debate, but also was extensively considered by Congress in hearings, floor debate, and in committee. Hearings held by both Houses of Congress in response to the President's request for authorization to register women adduced extensive testimony and evidence concerning the issue.

The House declined to provide for the registration of women when it passed the Joint Resolution allocating funds for the Selective Service System. When the Senate considered the Joint Resolution, it defeated, after extensive debate, an amendment which in effect would have authorized the registration of women. As noted earlier, Congress in H.J.Res. 521 only authorized funds sufficient to cover the registration of males. The Report of the Senate Committee on Appropriations on H.J.Res. 521 noted that the amount authorized was below the President's request "due to the Committee's decision not to provide $8,500,000 to register women," and that "[t]he amount recommended by the Committee would allow for registration of young men only."

The foregoing clearly establishes that the decision to exempt women from registration was not the " 'accidental by-product of a traditional way of thinking about females.' " In Michael M., we rejected a similar argument because of action by the California Legislature considering and rejecting proposals to make a statute challenged on discrimination grounds gender-neutral. The cause for rejecting the argument is considerably stronger here. The issue was considered at great length, and Congress clearly expressed its purpose and intent.

For the same reasons we reject appellees' argument that we must consider the constitutionality of the MSSA solely on the basis of the views expressed by Congress in 1948, when the MSSA was first enacted in its modern form. Contrary to the suggestions of appellees and various *amici,* reliance on the legislative history of Joint Resolution 521 and the activity of the various Committees of the 96th Congress considering the registration of women does not violate sound principles that appropriations legislation should not be considered as modifying substantive legislation. Congress did not change the MSSA in 1980, but it did thoroughly reconsider the question of exempting women from its provisions, and its basis for doing so. The 1980 legislative history is, therefore, highly relevant in assessing the constitutional validity of the exemption.

Congress determined that any future draft, which would be facilitated by the registration scheme, would be characterized by a need for combat troops. The Senate Report explained, in a specific finding later adopted by both Houses, that "[i]f mobilization were to be ordered in a wartime scenario, the primary manpower need would be for combat replacements." This conclusion echoed one made a year before by the same Senate Committee. As Senator Jepsen put it, "the shortage would be in the combat arms. That is why you have drafts." Congress' determination that the need would be for combat troops if a draft took place was sufficiently supported by testimony adduced at the hearings so that the courts are not free to make their own judgment on the question. The purpose of registration, therefore, was to prepare for a draft *of combat troops.*

Women as a group, however, unlike men as a group, are not eligible for combat. The restrictions on the participation of women in combat in the Navy and Air Force are statutory. Under 10 U.S.C. § 6015, "women may not be assigned to duty on vessels or in aircraft that are engaged in combat missions," and under 10 U.S.C. § 8549 female members of the Air Force "may not be assigned to duty in aircraft engaged in combat missions." The Army and Marine Corps preclude the use of women in combat as a matter of established policy. Congress specifically recog-

nized and endorsed the exclusion of women from combat in exempting women from registration. The President expressed his intent to continue the current military policy precluding women from combat, and appellees present their argument concerning registration against the background of such restrictions on the use of women in combat. Consistent with the approach of this Court in *Schlesinger v. Ballard,* we must examine appellees' constitutional claim concerning registration with these combat restrictions firmly in mind.

The existence of the combat restrictions clearly indicates the basis for Congress' decision to exempt women from registration. The purpose of registration was to prepare for a draft of combat troops. Since women are excluded from combat, Congress concluded that they would not be needed in the event of a draft, and therefore decided not to register them. As [the district] court put it: "Congress could not constitutionally require registration under the MSSA of only black citizens or only white citizens, or single out any political or religious group simply because those groups contain sufficient persons to fill the needs of the Selective Service System." This reasoning is beside the point. The reason women are exempt from registration is not because military needs can be met by drafting men. This is not a case of Congress arbitrarily choosing to burden one of two similarly situated groups, such as would be the case with an all-black or all-white, or an all-Catholic or all-Lutheran, or an all-Republican or all-Democratic registration. Men and women, because of the combat restrictions on women, are simply not similarly situated for purposes of a draft or registration for a draft.

Congress' decision to authorize the registration of only men, therefore, does not violate the Due Process Clause. The exemption of women from registration is not only sufficiently but also closely related to Congress' purpose in authorizing registration. The fact that Congress and the Executive have decided that women should not serve in combat fully justifies Congress in not authorizing their registration, since the purpose of registration is to develop a pool of potential combat troops. As was the case in *Schlesinger v. Ballard, supra,* "the gender classification is not invidious, but rather realistically reflects the fact that the sexes are not similarly situated" in this case. *Michael M.* The Constitution requires that Congress treat similarly situated persons similarly, not that it engage in gestures of superficial equality.

In holding the MSSA constitutionally invalid the District Court relied heavily on the President's decision to seek authority to register women and the testimony of members of the Executive Branch and the military in support of that decision. As stated by the administration's witnesses before Congress, however, the President's "decision to ask for authority to register women is based on equity." This was also the basis for the testimony by military officials. The Senate Report, evaluating the testimony before the Committee, recognized that "[t]he argument for registration and induction of women . . . is not based on military necessity, but on consideration of equity." Congress was certainly entitled, in the exercise of its constitutional powers to raise and regulate armies and navies, to focus on the question of military need rather than "equity." As Senator Nunn of the Senate Armed Services Committee put it:

> "Our committee went into very great detail. We found that there was no military necessity cited by any witnesses for the registration of females.
>
> "The main point that those who favored the registration of females made was that they were in favor of this because of the equality issue, which is, of course, a legitimate view. But as far as military necessity, and that is what we are primarily, I hope, considering in the overall registration bill, there is no military necessity for this."

Although the military experts who testified in favor of registering women uniformly opposed the actual drafting of women there was testimony that in the event of a draft of 650,000 the military could absorb some 80,000 female inductees. The 80,000 would be used to fill non-combat positions, freeing men to go to the front. In relying on this testimony in striking down the MSSA, the District Court, palpably exceeded its authority when it ignored Congress' considered response to this line of reasoning.

In the first place, assuming that a small number of women could be drafted for noncombat roles, Congress simply did not consider it worth the added burdens of including women in draft and registration plans. "It has been suggested that all women be registered, but only a handful actually be inducted in an emergency. The Committee finds this a confused and ultimately unsatisfactory solution." As the Senate Committee recognized a year before, "training would be needlessly burdened by women recruits who could not be used in combat." It is not for this Court to dismiss such problems as insignificant in the context of military preparedness and the exigencies of a future mobilization.

Congress also concluded that whatever the need for women for noncombat roles during mobilization, whether 80,000 or less, it could be met by volunteers.

Most significantly, Congress determined that staffing noncombat positions with women during a mobilization would be positively detrimental to the important goal of military flexibility.

> " . . . [T]here are other military reasons that preclude very large numbers of women

from serving. Military flexibility requires that a commander be able to move units or ships quickly. Units or ships not located at the front or not previously scheduled for the front nevertheless must be able to move into action if necessary. In peace and war, significant rotation of personnel is necessary. We should not divide the military into two groups—one in permanent combat and one in permanent support. Large numbers of non-combat positions must be available to which combat troops can return for duty before being redeployed."

In sum, Congress carefully evaluated the testimony that 80,000 women conscripts could be usefully employed in the event of a draft and rejected it in the permissible exercise of its constitutional responsibility. The District Court was quite wrong in undertaking an independent evaluation of this evidence, rather than adopting an appropriately deferential examination of Congress' evaluation of that evidence.

In light of the foregoing, we conclude that Congress acted well within its constitutional authority when it authorized the registration of men, and not women, under the Military Selective Service Act. The decision of the District Court holding otherwise is accordingly

Reversed.

JUSTICE WHITE, with whom JUSTICE BRENNAN joins, dissenting.

I assume what has not been challenged in this case—that excluding women from combat positions does not offend the Constitution. Granting that, it is self-evident that if during mobilization for war, all noncombat military positions must be filled by combat-qualified personnel available to be moved into combat positions, there would be no occasion whatsoever to have any women in the Army, whether as volunteers or inductees. The Court appears to say, that Congress concluded as much and that we should accept that judgment even though the view of the Executive Branch, including the responsible military services, is to the contrary. The Court's position in this regard is most unpersuasive. I perceive little, if any, indication that Congress itself concluded that every position in the military, no matter how far removed from combat, must be filled, with combat-ready men.

. . . I cannot agree with the Court, that Congress concluded or that the legislative record indicates that each of the services could rely on women volunteers to fill all the positions for which they might be eligible in the event of mobilization.

As I understand the record, in order to secure the personnel it needs during mobilization, the Government cannot rely on volunteers and must register and draft not only to fill combat positions and those noncombat positions that must be filled by combat-trained men, but also to secure the personnel needed for jobs that can be performed by persons ineligible for combat without diminishing military effectiveness. The claim is that in providing for the latter category of positions, Congress is free to register and draft only men. I discern no adequate justification for this kind of discrimination between men and women. Accordingly, with all due respect, I dissent.

Justice MARSHALL, with whom Justice BRENNAN joins, dissenting.

The Court today places its imprimatur on one of the most potent remaining public expressions of "ancient canards about the proper role of women." It upholds a statute that requires males but not females to register for the draft, and which thereby categorically excludes women from a fundamental civic obligation. Because I believe the Court's decision is inconsistent with the Constitution's guarantee of equal protection of the laws, I dissent.

It bears emphasis . . . that the only question presented by this case is whether the exclusion of women from registration . . . contravenes the equal protection component of the Due Process Clause of the Fifth Amendment. [W]e are not called upon to decide whether either men or women can be drafted at all, whether they must be drafted in equal numbers, in what order they should be drafted, or, once inducted, how they are to be trained for their respective functions. In addition, this case does not involve a challenge to the statutes or policies that prohibit female members of the Armed Forces from serving in combat. . . .

VI

After reviewing the discussion and findings contained in the Senate Report, the most I am able to say of the Report is that it demonstrates that drafting *very large* numbers of women would frustrate the achievement of a number of important governmental objectives that relate to the ultimate goal of maintaining "an adequate armed strength . . . to insure the security of this Nation."[T]he discussion and findings in the Senate Report do not enable the Government to carry its burden of demonstrating that *completely* excluding women from the draft by excluding them from registration substantially furthers important governmental objectives.

In concluding that the Government has carried its burden in this case, the Court adopts "an appropriately deferential examination of *Congress'* evaluation of [the] evidence,"(emphasis in the original). The majority then proceeds to supplement Congress' actual findings with those the Court apparently believes Congress could (and should) have made. Beyond that, the Court substitutes hollow shibboleths about "deference to legislative decisions" for constitutional analysis. It is as if the majority has lost sight of the fact that "it is the responsibility of this Court to act as the ultimate interpreter of the Constitution." Congressional enactments in the area of military affairs must, like all other laws, be *judged* by the standards of the Constitution.

Furthermore, "[w]hen it appears that an Act of Congress conflicts with [a constitutional] provisio[n], we have no choice but to enforce the paramount commands of the Constitution. We are sworn to do no less. . . . [T]he Court today "pushes back the limits of the Constitution" to accommodate an Act of Congress.

The majority's deference to Congress is sharply criticized by Justice Marshall as inconsistent with principled review and applicable equal protection analysis. Compare, for example, the treatment of federal legislation in *Frontiero, supra*. The Court's willingness to defer in gender inequality controversies, as manifested in this case, might be a product of its view that decisions about how to distinguish *real* from irrelevant differences are so contentious that they should be left for political resolution. *See, e.g., City of Cleburne, supra*.

Consider the impact of the political defeat of the Equal Rights Amendment on gender discrimination challenges confronted by the Court. The Constitutional Amendment passed by Congress in 1972 stated:

Section 1. Equality of rights under the law shall not be denied of abridged by the United States or any State on account of sex.

Section 2. The Congress shall have the power to enforce, by appropriate legislation, the provisions of this article.

Section 3. This amendment shall take effect two years after the date of ratification.

By 1978, 35 states had ratified the amendment. Congress extended the seven-year ratification to June 1982 but the necessary number of ratifying states never emerged. In fact, several states which had previously ratified the amendment rescinded their ratification.

PAH: In *Korematsu, supra,* the Court deferred to the judgment of military authorities of military necessity and national security, devaluing the equal protection claims of the Japanese interned in camps against their will and ignoring that the internment was grossly over- and under-inclusive. The rhetoric of strict scrutiny analysis applied there rang hollow, as Justice Marshall suggests that the rhetoric of review rings here. Recent affirmative action cases, particularly *Adarand, supra,* would suggest that a principled application of the equal protection doctrine to congressional acts would not support the degree of deference the Court accords Congress in this case. We are left with the impression of wide-ranging discretion available to the Court in equal protection cases, wielded through its decision to bow or defer to other branches or to federalism concerns and through its formulation of the standard of review, and operating here to reinforce the cultural tradition of treating men and women differently.

DEL: Justice Holmes once described the equal protection guarantee as "the last resort of constitutional argument."[271] The *Brown* era, which many contemporary academics were conditioned by, suggested a different norm. Modern standards of review, however, have imposed usually insurmountable threshold hurdles (such as proving discriminatory motive), and case law categorically distinguishes between men and women for purposes of armed service or statutory rape. Viewed in historical context, contemporary equal protection doctrine tends to be guided more by the compass of Holmes than of *Brown.*

In part because of the sameness/difference controversy and the legacy of oppressive "protective" governmental decision-making affecting women, it may be unclear who is "benefitted" or "burdened" by governmental action.[272] A related problem arises in the context of affirmative action.

---

[271] Buck v. Bell, 274 U.S. 200, 208 (1927).

[272] *Compare, e.g.,* Weinberger v. Wisenfeld, 420 U.S. 636 (1975) (Court struck provision according social security benefits to both minor children and widow of decedent, but not to fathers of children of deceased wives), *with e.g.,* Kahn v. Shevin, 416 U.S. 351 (1974)(widower's challenge to Florida statute granting widows, but not widowers, $500 annual tax exemption upheld under traditional rationality review since law was "reasonably designed to further the state policy of cushioning financial impact of spousal loss upon sex for which loss imposes a disproportionately heavy burden). More recently, in Wengler v. Druggist Mutual Insurance Co., 446 U.S. 142 (1980) the Court (with a dissent by Justice Rehnquist), held unconstitutional a workers' compensation law providing death benefits to widows of men who died of work-related accidents without proof of dependency on the husband's earnings but required such proof of dependency for recovery by widowers. The Court concluded that the measure both devalued the women's role as provider and unjustifiably deprived surviving males by using gender as a proxy for dependency.

4. Gender-Focused Disparate Impact

Personnel Administrator of Massachusetts v. Feeney
442 U.S. 256 (1979)

MR. JUSTICE STEWART delivered the opinion of the Court.

This case presents a challenge to the constitutionality of the Massachusetts veterans' preference statute, on the ground that it discriminates against women in violation of the Equal Protection Clause of the Fourteenth Amendment. Under ch. 31, § 23, all veterans who qualify for state civil service positions must be considered for appointment ahead of any qualifying nonveterans. The preference operates overwhelmingly to the advantage of males.

The appellee Helen B. Feeney is not a veteran. She brought this action alleging that the absolute-preference formula inevitably operates to exclude women from consideration for the best Massachusetts civil service jobs and thus unconstitutionally denies them the equal protection of the laws. The three-judge District Court agreed, one judge dissenting.

The District Court found that the absolute preference afforded by Massachusetts to veterans has a devastating impact upon the employment opportunities of women. Although it found that the goals of the preference were worthy and legitimate and that the legislation had not been enacted for the purpose of discriminating against women, the court reasoned that its exclusionary impact upon women was nonetheless so severe as to require the State to further its goals through a more limited form of preference. Finding that a more modest preference formula would readily accommodate the State's interest in aiding veterans, the court declared ch. 31, § 23, unconstitutional and enjoined its operation.

[T]his Court vacated the judgment and remanded the case for further consideration in light of our intervening decision in *Washington v. Davis*. The *Davis* case held that a neutral law does not violate the Equal Protection Clause solely because it results in a racially disproportionate impact; instead the disproportionate impact must be traced to a purpose to discriminate on the basis of race.

Upon remand, the District Court, one judge concurring and one judge again dissenting, concluded that a veterans' hiring preference is inherently nonneutral because it favors a class from which women have traditionally been excluded, and that the consequences of the Massachusetts absolute-preference formula for the employment opportunities of women were too inevitable to have been "unintended." Accordingly, the court reaffirmed its original judgment. The Attorney General again appealed to this Court.

I

A

The Federal Government and virtually all of the States grant some sort of hiring preference to veterans. The Massachusetts preference, which is loosely termed an "absolute lifetime" preference, is among the most generous. It applies to all positions in the State's classified civil service, which constitute approximately 60% of the public jobs in the State. It is available to "any person, male or female, including a nurse," who was honorably discharged from the United States Armed Forces after at least 90 days of active service, at least one day of which was during "wartime." Persons who are deemed veterans and who are otherwise qualified for a particular civil service job may exercise the preference at any time and as many times as they wish.

Rank on the eligible list and availability for employment are the sole factors that determine which candidates are considered for appointment to an official civil service position. When a public agency has a vacancy, it requisitions a list of "certified eligibles" from the state personnel division. Under formulas prescribed by civil service rules, a small number of candidates from the top of an appropriate list, three if there is only one vacancy, are certified. The appointing agency is then required to choose from among these candidates. Although the veterans' preference thus does not guarantee that a veteran will be appointed, it is obvious that the preference gives to veterans who achieve passing scores a well-nigh absolute advantage.

B

During her 12-year tenure as a public employee, Ms. Feeney took and passed a number of open competitive civil service examinations. On several she did quite well, receiving in 1971 the second highest score on an examination for a job with the Board of Dental Examiners, and in 1973 the third highest on a test for an Administrative Assistant position with a mental health center. Her high scores, however, did not win her a place on the certified eligible list. Because of the veterans' preference, she was ranked sixth behind five male veterans on the Dental Examiner list. She was not certified, and a lower scoring veteran was eventually appointed. On the 1973 examination, she was placed in a position on the list behind 12 male veterans, 11 of whom had lower scores. Following the other examinations that she took, her name was similarly ranked below those of veterans who had achieved passing grades.

Ms. Feeney's interest in securing a better job in state government did not wane. Having been consistently eclipsed by veterans, however, she eventually concluded that further competition for civil service positions of interest to veterans would be futile. In 1975, shortly after her civil defense job was abolished, she commenced this litigation.

C

The veterans' hiring preference in Massachusetts, as in other jurisdictions, has traditionally been justified as a measure designed to reward veterans for the sacrifice of military service, to ease the transition from military to civilian life, to encourage patriotic service, and to attract loyal and well-disciplined people to civil service occupations. The Massachusetts law dates back to 1884, when the State, as part of its first civil service legislation, gave a statutory preference to civil service applicants who were Civil War veterans if their qualifications were equal to those of nonveterans. This tie-breaking provision blossomed into a truly absolute preference in 1895, when the State enacted its first general veterans' preference law and exempted veterans from all merit selection requirements. In response to a challenge brought by a male nonveteran, this statute was declared violative of state constitutional provisions guaranteeing that government should be for the "common good" and prohibiting hereditary titles.

The current veterans' preference law has its origins in an 1896 statute, enacted to meet the state constitutional standards enunciated in *Brown v. Russell.* That statute limited the absolute preference to veterans who were otherwise qualified. A closely divided Supreme Judicial Court, in an advisory opinion issued the same year, concluded that the preference embodied in such a statute would be valid. In 1919, when the preference was extended to cover the veterans of World War I, the formula was further limited to provide for a priority in eligibility, in contrast to an absolute preference in hiring.

Since 1919, the preference has been repeatedly amended to cover persons who served in subsequent wars, declared or undeclared. Over the years it has been subjected to repeated legal challenges, see *Hutcheson v. Director of Civil Service, supra* (collecting cases), to criticism by civil service reform groups. The present case is apparently the first to challenge the Massachusetts veterans' preference on the simple ground that it discriminates on the basis of sex.

D

The first Massachusetts veterans' preference statute defined the term "veterans" in gender-neutral language. Women who have served in official United States military units during wartime, then, have always been entitled to the benefit of the preference. In addition, Massachusetts, through a 1943 amendment to the definition of "wartime service," extended the preference to women who served in unofficial auxiliary women's units.

When the first general veterans' preference statute was adopted in 1896, there were no women veterans. . . .

. . . Notwithstanding the apparent attempts by Massachusetts to include as many military women as possible within the scope of the preference, the statute today benefits an overwhelmingly male class. This is attributable in some measure to the variety of federal statutes, regulations, and policies that have restricted the number of women who could enlist in the United States Armed Forces, and largely to the simple fact that women have never been subjected to a military draft.

When this litigation was commenced, then, over 98% of the veterans in Massachusetts were male; only 1.8% were female. And over one-quarter of the Massachusetts popula-

tion were veterans. During the decade between 1963 and 1973 when the appellee was actively participating in the State's merit selection system, 47,005 new permanent appointments were made in the classified official service. Forty-three percent of those hired were women, and 57% were men. Of the women appointed, 1.8% were veterans, while 54% of the men had veteran status. A large unspecified percentage of the female appointees were serving in lower paying positions for which males traditionally had not applied. On each of 50 sample eligible lists that are part of the record in this case, one or more women who would have been certified as eligible for appointment on the basis of test results were displaced by veterans whose test scores were lower.

At the outset of this litigation appellants conceded that for "many of the permanent positions for which males and females have competed" the veterans' preference has "resulted in a substantially greater proportion of female eligibles than male eligibles" not being certified for consideration. The impact of the veterans' preference law upon the public employment opportunities of women has thus been severe. This impact lies at the heart of the appellee's federal constitutional claim.

II

The sole question for decision on this appeal is whether Massachusetts, in granting an absolute lifetime preference to veterans, has discriminated against women in violation of the Equal Protection Clause of the Fourteenth Amendment.

A

The equal protection guarantee of the Fourteenth Amendment does not take from the States all power of classification. Most laws classify, and many affect certain groups unevenly, even though the law itself treats them no differently from all other members of the class described by the law. When the basic classification is rationally based, uneven effects upon particular groups within a class are ordinarily of no constitutional concern. The calculus of effects, the manner in which a particular law reverberates in a society, is a legislative and not a judicial responsibility. In assessing an equal protection challenge, a court is called upon only to measure the basic validity of the legislative classification. When some other independent right is not at stake and when there is no "reason to infer antipathy," it is presumed that "even improvident decisions will eventually be rectified by the democratic process . . .".

Certain classifications, however, in themselves supply a reason to infer antipathy. Race is the paradigm. A racial classification, regardless of purported motivation, is presumptively invalid and can be upheld only upon an extraordinary justification. This rule applies as well to a classification that is ostensibly neutral but is an obvious pretext for racial discrimination. But, as was made clear in *Washington v. Davis* and *Arlington Heights v. Metropolitan Housing Dev. Corp.*, even if a neutral law has a disproportionately adverse effect upon a racial minority, it is unconstitutional under the Equal Protection Clause only if that impact can be traced to a discriminatory purpose.

Classifications based upon gender, not unlike those based upon race, have traditionally been the touchstone for pervasive and often subtle discrimination. This Court's recent cases teach that such classifications must bear a close and substantial relationship to important governmental objectives, and are in many settings unconstitutional. Although public employment is not a constitutional right, and the States have wide discretion in framing employee qualifications, these precedents dictate that any state law overtly or covertly designed to prefer males over females in public employment would require an exceedingly persuasive justification to withstand a constitutional challenge under the Equal Protection Clause of the Fourteenth Amendment.

B

The cases of *Washington v. Davis* and *Arlington Heights v. Metropolitan Housing Dev. Corp.*, recognize that when a neutral law has a disparate impact upon a group that has historically been the victim of discrimination, an unconstitutional purpose may still be at work. But those cases signaled no departure from the settled rule that the Fourteenth Amendment guarantees equal laws, not equal results. *Davis* upheld a job-related employment test that white people passed in proportionately greater numbers than Negroes, for there had been no showing that racial discrimination entered into the establishment or formulation of the test. *Arlington Heights* upheld a zoning board decision that tended to perpetuate racially segregated housing patterns, since, apart from its effect, the board's decision was shown to be nothing more than an application of a constitutionally neutral zoning policy. Those principles apply with equal force to a case involving alleged gender discrimination.

When a statute gender-neutral on its face is challenged on the ground that its effects upon women are disproportionally adverse, a two-fold inquiry is thus appropriate. The first question is whether the statutory classification is indeed neutral in the sense that it is not gender based. If the classification itself, covert or overt, is not based upon gender, the second question is whether the adverse effect reflects invidious gender-based discrimination. In this second inquiry, impact provides an "important starting point," but purposeful discrimination is "the condition that offends the Constitution."

It is against this background of precedent that we consider the merits of the case before us.

III

A

The appellee has conceded that ch. 31, § 23, is neutral on its face. She has also acknowledged that state hiring preferences for veterans are not *per se* invalid, for she has limited her challenge to the absolute lifetime preference that Massachusetts provides to veterans. The District Court made two central findings that are relevant here: first, that ch. 31, § 23, serves legitimate and worthy purposes; second, that the absolute preference was not established for the purpose of discriminating against women. The appellee has thus acknowledged and the District Court has thus found that the distinction between veterans and nonveterans drawn by ch. 31, § 23, is not a pretext for gender discrimination. The appellee's concession and the District Court's finding are clearly correct.

If the impact of this statute could not be plausibly explained on a neutral ground, impact itself would signal that the real classification made by the law was in fact not neutral. But there can be but one answer to the question whether this veteran preference excludes significant numbers of women from preferred state jobs because they are women or because they are nonveterans. Apart from the facts that the definition of "veterans" in the statute has always been neutral as to gender and that Massachusetts has consistently defined veteran status in a way that has been inclusive of women who have served in the military, this is not a law that can plausibly be explained only as a gender-based classification. Indeed, it is not a law that can rationally be explained on that ground. Veteran status is not uniquely male. Although few women benefit from the preference, the nonveteran class is not substantially all female. To the contrary, significant numbers of nonveterans are men, and all nonveterans—male as well as female—are placed at a disadvantage. Too many men are affected by ch. 31, § 23, to permit the inference that the statute is but a pretext for preferring men over women.

Moreover, as the District Court implicitly found, the purposes of the statute provide the surest explanation for its impact. Just as there are cases in which impact alone can unmask an invidious classification, there are others, in which—notwithstanding impact—the legitimate noninvidious purposes of a law cannot be missed. This is one. The distinction made by ch. 31, § 23, is, as it seems to be, quite simply between veterans and nonveterans, not between men and women.

B

The dispositive question, then, is whether the appellee has shown that a gender-based discriminatory purpose has, at least in some measure, shaped the Massachusetts veterans' preference legislation. As did the District Court, she points to two basic factors which in her view distinguish ch. 31, § 23, from the neutral rules at issue in the *Washington v. Davis* and *Arlington Heights* cases. The first is the nature of the preference, which is said to be demonstrably gender-biased in the sense that it favors a status reserved under federal military policy primarily to men. The second concerns the impact of the absolute lifetime preference upon the employment opportunities of women, an impact claimed to be too inevitable to have been unintended. The appellee contends that these factors, coupled with the fact that the preference itself has little if any relevance to actual job performance, more than suffice to prove the discriminatory intent required to establish a constitutional violation.

The contention that this veterans' preference is "inherently nonneutral" or "gender-biased" presumes that the State, by favoring veterans, intentionally incorporated into its public employment policies the panoply of sex-based and assertedly discriminatory federal laws that have prevented all but a handful of women from becoming veterans. There are two serious difficulties with this argument. First, it is wholly at odds with the District Court's central finding that Massachusetts has not offered a preference to veterans for the purpose of discriminating against women. Second, it cannot be reconciled with the assumption made by both the appellee and the District Court that a more limited hiring preference for veterans could be sustained. Taken together, these difficulties are fatal.

To the extent that the status of veteran is one that few women have been enabled to achieve, every hiring preference for veterans, however modest or extreme, is inherently gender-biased. If Massachusetts by offering such a preference can be said intentionally to have incorporated into its state employment policies the historical gender-based federal military personnel practices, the degree of the preference would or should make no constitutional difference. Invidious discrimination does not become less so because the discrimination accomplished is of a lesser magnitude. Discriminatory intent is simply not amenable to calibration. It either is a factor that has influenced the legislative choice or it is not. The District Court's conclusion that the absolute veterans' preference was not originally enacted or subsequently reaffirmed for the purpose of giving an advantage to males as such necessarily compels the conclusion that the State intended

nothing more than to prefer "veterans." Given this finding, simple logic suggests that an intent to exclude women from significant public jobs was not at work in this law. To reason that it was, by describing the preference as "inherently nonneutral" or "gender-biased," is merely to restate the fact of impact, not to answer the question of intent.

To be sure, this case is unusual in that it involves a law that by design is not neutral. The law overtly prefers veterans as such. As opposed to the written test at issue in *Davis*, it does not purport to define a job-related characteristic. To the contrary, it confers upon a specifically described group—perceived to be particularly deserving—a competitive head start. But the District Court found, and the appellee has not disputed, that this legislative choice was legitimate. The basic distinction between veterans and nonveterans, having been found not gender-based, and the goals of the preference having been found worthy, ch. 31 must be analyzed as is any other neutral law that casts a greater burden upon women as a group than upon men as a group. The enlistment policies of the Armed Services may well have discriminated on the basis of sex. But the history of discrimination against women in the military is not on trial in this case.

The appellee's ultimate argument rests upon the presumption, common to the criminal and civil law, that a person intends the natural and foreseeable consequences of his voluntary actions. The decision to grant a preference to veterans was of course "intentional." So, necessarily, did an adverse impact upon nonveterans follow from that decision. And it cannot seriously be argued that the Legislature of Massachusetts could have been unaware that most veterans are men. It would thus be disingenuous to say that the adverse consequences of this legislation for women were unintended, in the sense that they were not volitional or in the sense that they were not foreseeable.

"Discriminatory purpose," however, implies more than intent as volition or intent as awareness of consequences. It implies that the decisionmaker, in this case a state legislature, selected or reaffirmed a particular course of action at least in part "because of," not merely "in spite of," its adverse effects upon an identifiable group. Yet nothing in the record demonstrates that this preference for veterans was originally devised or subsequently re-enacted because it would accomplish the collateral goal of keeping women in a stereotypic and predefined place in the Massachusetts Civil Service. When the totality of legislative actions establishing and extending the Massachusetts veterans' preference are considered, the law remains what it purports to be: a preference for veterans of either sex over nonveterans of either sex, not for men over women.

IV

Veterans' hiring preferences represent an awkward—and, many argue, unfair—exception to the widely shared view that merit and merit alone should prevail in the employment policies of government. After a war, such laws have been enacted virtually without opposition. During peacetime, they inevitable have come to be viewed in many quarters as undemocratic and unwise. Absolute and permanent preferences, as the troubled history of this law demonstrates, have always been subject to the objection that they give the veteran more than a square deal. But the Fourteenth Amendment "cannot be made a refuge from ill-advised . . . laws." The substantial edge granted to veterans by ch. 31, § 23, may reflect unwise policy. The appellee, however, has simply failed to demonstrate that the law in any way reflects a purpose to discriminate on the basis of sex.

The judgment is reversed, and the case is remanded for further proceedings consistent with this opinion.

It is so ordered.

Mr. Justice STEVENS, with whom Mr. Justice WHITE joins, concurring.

While I concur in the Court's opinion, I confess that I am not at all sure that there is any difference between the two questions posed. If a classification is not overtly based on gender, I am inclined to believe the question whether it is covertly gender based is the same as the question whether its adverse effects reflect invidious gender-based discrimination. However the question is phrased, for me the answer is largely provided by the fact that the number of males disadvantaged by Massachusetts' veterans' preference (1,867,000) is sufficiently large—and sufficiently close to the number of disadvantaged females (2,954,000)—to refute the claim that the rule was intended to benefit males as a class over females as a class.

Mr. JUSTICE MARSHALL, with whom Mr. JUSTICE BRENNAN joins, dissenting.

Although acknowledging that in some circumstances, discriminatory intent may be inferred from the inevitable or foreseeable impact of a statute, the Court concludes that no such intent has been established here. I cannot agree. In my judgment, Massachusetts' choice of an absolute veterans' preference system evinces purposeful gender-based discrimination. And because the statutory scheme bears no substantial relationship to a legitimate governmental objective, it cannot withstand scrutiny under the Equal Protection Clause.

In the instant case, the impact of the Massachusetts statute on women is undisputed. . . . Because less than 2% of the women in Massachusetts are veterans, the absolute-preference formula has rendered desirable state civil service employment an almost exclusively male prerogative. As the District Court recognized, this consequence follows foreseeably, indeed inexorably, from the long history of policies severely limiting women's participation in the military. Although neutral in form, the statute is anything but neutral in application. . . . Where the foreseeable impact of a facially neutral policy is so disproportionate, the burden should rest on the State to establish that sex-based considerations played no part in the choice of the particular legislative scheme.

Clearly that burden was not sustained here. The legislative history of the statute reflects the Commonwealth's patent appreciation of the impact the preference system would have on women, and an equally evident desire to mitigate that impact only with respect to certain traditionally female occupations. Until 1971, the statue and implementing civil service regulations exempted from operation of the preference any job requisitions "especially calling for women." In practice, this exemption, coupled with the absolute preference for veterans, has created a gender-based civil service hierarchy, with women occupying low-grade clerical and secretarial jobs and men holding more responsible and remunerative positions. . . .

Such a statutory scheme both reflects and perpetuates precisely the kind of archaic assumptions about women's roles which we have previously held invalid. Particularly when viewed against the range of less discriminatory alternatives available to assist veterans, Massachusetts' choice of a formula that so severely restricts public employment opportunities for women cannot reasonably be thought gender-neutral.

Where a particular statutory scheme visits substantial hardship on a class long subject to discrimination, the legislation cannot be sustained unless "carefully tuned to alternative considerations." Here, there are a wide variety of less discriminatory means by which Massachusetts could effect its compensatory purposes. [Instead] the Massachusetts statute exacts a substantial price from a discrete group of individuals who have long been subject to employment discrimination, and who, "because of circumstances totally beyond their control, have [had] little if any chance of becoming members of the preferred class."

As Justice Stevens has noted in *Washington v. Davis, supra,* the line between discriminatory purpose and impact is not as bright as the majority proposes. Although the *Feeney* majority argued that foreseeability of adverse gender impact "is not a synonym for proof," Justice Marshall viewed the fact that the best jobs are almost exclusively held by men as flowing "inexorably, from the long history of policies severely limiting women's participation in the military." Justice Marshall argues that when a scheme burdens a class long subject to discrimination, the offending measure should not be sustained unless "carefully tuned to alternative considerations." Scholars have long debated the value implications and constitutional support for the requirement of intent in equal protection analysis.[273]

---

[273] *See, e.g.*, Guido Calabresi, *Foreword: Antidiscrimination and Constitutional Accountability (What the Bork-Brennan Debate Ignores)*,105 HARV. L. REV. 801 (proposing antidiscrimination principle which is presumptively violated when legislation works to impose a significant practical disadvantage or burden on a politically disfavored group or reinforces discriminatory attitudes and treatment that earned the group its disfavored status); Daniel R. Ortiz, *The Myth of Intent in Equal Protection*, 41 STAN. L. REV. 1105, 1109, 1134–51 (1989) (noting the controversial assumptions of motivation-focused analysis and arguing that intent requirement masks value judgments and insulates some interests from being challenged under equal protection).

PAH: The majority in *Feeney* expresses confidence that the political process will eventually correct any "improvident decisions" arguably insulating its value judgments through the use of intent requirements.[274] Consistent with the majority view are the comments of John Hart Ely, made in 1980:[275]

> The very stereotypes that give rise to laws "protecting" women by barring them from various activities are under daily and publicized attack, and are the subject of equally spirited defense. Given such open discussion of the traditional stereotypes, the claim that the numerical majority is being "dominated," that women are in effect "slaves" who have no realistic choice but to assimilate the stereotypes, is one it has become impossible to maintain except at the most inflated rhetorical level. . . .
>
> In fact I may be wrong in supposing that because women now are in a position to protect themselves they will, that we are thus unlikely to see in the future the sort of official gender discrimination that has marked our past. But if women don't protect themselves from sex discrimination in the future, it won't be because they can't. It will rather be because for one reason or another—substantive disagreement or most likely the assignment of a low priority to the issue—they don't choose to . . . Many of us may condemn such a choice as benighted on the merits, but that is not a constitutional argument.

This process-centered approach seems to dismiss or trivialize the notion that gender subordination, like racial marginalization, is pervasive and part of the unconscious background in which political and social decisions are made.[276]

DEL: Gender discrimination and subordination are historical realities that cannot be denied. In a culture fundamentally primed and motivated by self-interest, however, it seems myopic to expect much change to be driven by constitutional review—especially given an agent of interpretation whose aggressive use of the equal protection guarantee tends

---

[274] *See* Daniel Ortiz, *supra.*
[275] DEMOCRACY AND DISTRUST 164–179 (1980).
[276] *See e.g.*, Charles Lawrence, *The Id, the Ego, and Equal Protection: Reckoning with Unconscious Racism*, 39 STAN. L. REV. 317 (1987).

to be aberrational rather than normative and accommodating of rather than unsettling to the established order. The *Brown* experience itself suggests that doctrinal revision is achievable but also a precedent for a next stage in which power relationships are reestablished pursuant to glossed standards of review and limiting principles. For all of the debate over equality, Fourteenth Amendment jurisprudence has become a primary arena for group struggles over power. Incantations that the equal protection guarantee protects individuals rather than groups have not dispelled agendas by majorities or minorities framed in tribally-referenced redistributive ways. Viewed in such context, equal protection claims from any quarter have the potential not only to account for real oppression but to be a front for aspirations of raw power.

5. Scrutiny of Other Group-Based Treatment

As the Court acknowledged in *City of Cleburne, supra,* there has been a decided reluctance to extend heightened scrutiny—the intermediate level as well as the searching scrutiny applied in cases concerning race-focused treatment—to other groups. During the Warren Court era, however, a number of cases arose in which the majority of the Court—or, some judges, in settings where consensus could not be achieved—used language suggesting that a heightened standard of review was being applied or concluded that justifications traditionally acceptable in a mere rationality inquiry were insufficient because of the disfavored political status of the group affected by the classification. The Court often reasoned that there were grounds for expanding heightened equal protection scrutiny because the classification was analogous to race or gender, implicating a discrete and insular group as was recognized in the famous footnote 4 of *Carolene Products*.[277] On the one hand, in many of these cases, the Court forthrightly recognized or hinted that more demanding consideration of the grounds for differential treatment arose because the interests of the group affected by the classification were important—even fundamental. On the other hand, there was often substantial disagreement about the appropriate standard of review to be applied, even where agreement could be reached on the challenge's outcome. Adding to confusion, particularly because of the Court's reluctance to add other contexts in which strict or intermediate scrutiny would apply, some justices seemed less than forthcoming about the level of

---

[277] Having severely narrowed the degree of scrutiny accorded economic regulations, deferring to political decision making, the Court in footnote 4 of *United States v. Carolene Products* acknowledged the possibility of a contrasting scrutinizing role for courts in protecting civil liberties:

There may be narrower scope for operation of the presumption of constitutionality when legislation appears on its face to be within a specific prohibition of the Constitution, such as those of the first ten amendments, which are deemed equally specific when held to be embraced within the Fourteenth Amendment. . . .

It is unnecessary to consider now whether legislation which restricts those political processes which can ordinarily be expected to bring about repeal of undesirable legislation, is to be subjected to more exacting judicial scrutiny under the general prohibitions of the Fourteenth Amendment than are most other types of legislation. . . .

Nor need we enquire whether similar considerations enter into the review of statutes directed at particular religious . . . or national . . . or racial minorities[;] whether prejudice against discrete and insular minorities may be a special condition, which tends seriously to curtail the operation of those political processes ordinarily to be relied upon to protect minorities, and which may call for a correspondingly more searching judicial inquiry. . . .

304 U.S. 144, 152 n.4 (1983).

review they were prepared to employ. The possibility was left open that the rationality review the Court undertook had become "biting" or, as Justice Marshall charged, the Court was actually applying a "sliding-scale" which took account of rights and classification schemes without relying on a formally tiered form of analysis.

In this section the focus is on grounds the Court has found available to support or reject the application of intermediate or strict scrutiny of the treatment of identifiable groups whose interests have been adversely affected by governmental action. The section following will briefly discuss the Court's treatment of fundamental rights in equal protection claims.

a. Alienage

In *Graham v. Richardson*,[278] welfare benefits were conditioned upon citizenship or the recipient's having lived in the United States for a substantial number of years. Noting the broad discretion available to states in the area of economics and social welfare to classify as long as the classification has reasonable basis, the Court stated:

> "But the Court's decisions have established that classifications based on alienage like those based on race, are inherently suspect and subject to close judicial scrutiny. Aliens as a class are a prime example of a 'discrete and insular' minority for whom such heightened judicial solicitude is appropriate. Accordingly . . . 'the power of the state to apply its laws exclusively to its alien inhabitants as a class is confined within narrow limits.'"

The Court rejected the justification offered by Arizona and Pennsylvania for the legislative preference for citizens and long-time resident aliens, that States had a "special public interest" in favoring their own citizens over aliens in the distribution of limited resources:

> 'It is true that this Court on occasion has upheld state statutes that treat citizens and noncitizens differently, the distinction having been that such laws were necessary to protect special interests of the State or its citizens. Thus in *Truax v. Raich*, 329 U.S. 33 (1915), the Court, in striking down an Arizona statute restricting employment of aliens, emphasized that '[t]he discrimination defined by the act does not pertain to the regulation or distribution of the public domain, or of the common property or resources of the people of the State, the enjoyment of which may be limited to its citizens as against both aliens and the citizens of other States.' . . . On the same theory, the Court has upheld statutes that, in the absence of overriding treaties limit the right of noncitizens to engage in exploitation of a State's natural resources, restrict the devolution of property to aliens, or deny to aliens the right to acquire and own land.
>
> Whatever may be the contemporary vitality of the special interest doctrine in other contexts . . .
>
> . . . we conclude that a State's desire to preserve limited welfare benefits for its own citizens is inadequate to justify . . . making noncitizens ineligible for public assistance and . . . restricting benefits to citizens and longtime resident aliens."

Notably, the Court's conclusion was unaffected by characterizing the governmental benefit as a "right" or "privilege." It added:

> "a State has a valid interest in preserving the fiscal integrity of its programs. It may legitimately attempt to limit its expenditures, whether for public assistance, public education, or any other program. But a State may not accomplish such a purpose by invidious distinctions between classes of its citizens. . . . The saving of welfare costs cannot justify an otherwise invidious classification. . . .

---

[278] 403 U.S. 365 (1971).

> Since an alien as well as a citizen is a 'person' for equal protection purposes, a concern for fiscal integrity is no more compelling a justification for the questioned classification in these cases.

It found justification for limiting expenses "particularly inappropriate and unreasonable when the discriminated class consists of aliens [, who] like citizens, may pay taxes . . . may be called into armed forces [and] may live within a state for many years, work[ing] and contribut[ing] to the economic growth of the state."

The statutes in *Graham v. Richardson* were also found to encroach on federal power over noncitizens and the expressed congressional policy permitting permanent residence and assuring full and equal benefits of state laws.

Faced with an economic downturn, California and other states have recently targeted immigrants who reside in the state illegally as unfairly tapping scarce resources which the state prefers to make available to citizens. California's now-famous Proposition 187 sought to address the problem by (among other things) depriving illegal immigrants of educational, welfare and certain emergency hospital benefits made available to legal residents. Although *Graham* may be distinguishable in some respects, doesn't it provide support for a challenge to such official action by state or local government?[279] Notably the immigrants in *Graham* were lawfully residing in the state and congressional policy supported their presence. Is this distinction between that case and recent targeting of illegal immigrants fatal? See *Plyler v. Doe*, infra.

In two cases following *Graham v. Richardson* the Court seemed willing to invalidate restrictions on immigrant rights in the work environment. *See Sugarman v. Dougall*[280] (legislative scheme which was "flat statutory prohibition against the employment of aliens in competitive classified civil service," reaching positions in nearly the full range of jobs, violates equal protection); and a companion case, *In re Griffiths*[281] (state's total exclusion of aliens from practice of law by making them ineligible to take the state bar examination violate equal protection, despite "undoubted interest in high professional standards" among lawyers and wide freedom of state to gauge the fitness of an applicant to practice law.) The Court in *Griffiths* emphasized that lawyers "are not officials of government or "so close to the core of the political process" that they are considered government policy formulators. Thus employment restrictions on immigrants practicing law could not be justified by the state's "governing prerogatives." In later cases, the Court qualified these holdings. Thus, in *Foley v. Connelie*,[282] the Court upheld a state requirement that state troopers be United States citizens because "[p]olice officers very clearly fall within the category of 'important nonelective [officials] who participate directly in the . . . execution . . . of broad public policy.'" Although it acknowledged that cases following *Graham* had required close scrutiny where governmental action "struck at the noncitizens' ability to exist in the community" and seemed inconsistent with congressional determination to permit aliens permanent residence, it found it inappropriate to require "every statutory exclusion of aliens to clear the high hurdle of "strict scrutiny, " because of the "historic values of citizenship." The Court thus concluded that the scrutiny would not be as demanding where "we deal with matters firmly within a State's constitutional prerogatives," adding:

---

[279] At the time of this writing a district court had concluded that portions of the immigration initiative providing for classification, notification, and reporting were preempted by federal immigration law; provisions barring illegal immigrants from public social welfare services were invalid since they clashed with superseding federal regulatory authority; and the ban on public elementary and secondary education violated equal protection. League of United Latin American Citizens v. Wilson, 908 F. Supp. 755 (C.D. Cal. 1995).

[280] 413 U.S. 634 (1973).

[281] 413 U.S. 717 (1973) .

[282] 435 U.S. 291(1978).

"The essence of our holdings . . . is that although we extend to aliens the right to education and public welfare, along with the ability to earn a livelihood and engage in licensed professions, the right to govern is reserved to citizens. . . . The police function fulfills a most fundamental obligation of government to its constituency. . . . [In] the enforcement and execution of the laws the police function is one where citizenship bears a rational relationship to the special demands of the particular position."

In *Ambach v. Noirwick*,[283] the Court continued in this vein, upholding the state's prohibiting teaching certification to applicants who did not demonstrate an intention to apply for citizenship. It stated that public school teaching is a "governmental function" and thus falls within the "exception to the general standard applicable to classification based on alienage," and requires only a rational relationship be shown between the governmental action and a legitimate interest.

As regards immigrants subject to federal regulations, the reach of the Fifth Amendment has not always been read as coextensive with the equal protection requirements applied to the states. In *Hampton v. Mow Sun Wong*,[284] the Court held unconstitutional a Civil Service Commission regulation barring resident aliens from employment in federal competitive civil service. The Court concluded that *Sugarman* and *Griffiths*, though relevant, were not controlling since "overriding national interests may justify selective federal [civil] service even though an identical state requirement may not be valid. However, although interests like the national authority over immigration and nationalization concerns may justify a citizenship requirement, the Court concluded the federal power over noncitizens is not so plenary that an agency may "subject all resident aliens to different substantive rules than those applied to citizens." Such a flat prohibition might be a valid exercise of the foreign affairs power of the President or Congress but is not available to sustain adoption of a regulation by an entity such as the civil service commission. The Court in *Matthew v. Diaz*,[285] upheld a federal statute denying immigrants age 65 and over eligibility for Medicare benefits unless they have applied for permanent residence and have resided in the United States for five years. The Court distinguished *Graham* as concerning the relationship between noncitizens and the States, rather than noncitizens and the federal government.

Reflecting some ambivalence toward heightened review which is "fatal in fact," the Court appears to have moved away from treating alienage unquestionably as a status requiring heightened review, like nationality and race; *see Korematsu, supra*, instead tending to focus on the rationality of attaching citizenship as a condition for attaining a benefit from the State or federal government. The result is that the Court will uphold exclusionary statutes which are not merely protectionist but are rationalized by the State as reserving sovereign functions or functions which "go to the heart of representative government"[286] to citizens. Justice Rehnquist had argued, while dissenting in *Graham* and *Griffiths*, that the Constitution itself classifies on the basis of citizenship. He found "a marked difference between a status of conditions such as . . . national origin, or race, which cannot be altered by an individual," and the situation of immigrants who, if they wished, could become citizens. Are you persuaded that a constitutional distinction should be made between laws focused on alienage as contrasted with nation-

---

[283] 412 U.S. 68 (1979). *See also* Nyquist v. Manclet, 432 U.S. 1 (1977)(exclusion of aliens from eligibility for state financial aid for higher education struck under strict scrutiny analysis.

[284] 426 U.S. 567 (1976).

[285] 426 U.S. 567 (1976).

[286] Bernal v. Fainter, 467 U.S. 216 (1984)(invalidating citizenship requirement to become notary public because functions are clerical).

ality, ethnicity or race classifications? In addition to the considerations offered by Justice Rehnquist, the Court in cases like *Graham* seemed concerned about prejudice against noncitizens rendering them politically powerless. The political disadvantage of some immigrants—particular white, English-speaking ones—stems from noncitizenship and the consequential lack of the right to vote on decisions which have the potential to affect their interests. For some noncitizens, however, the roots and branches of political disadvantage may be more complex. It bears noting the link between ethnicity- or nationality-related prejudice and alienage-focused political action.[287] Indeed for a substantial part of the twentieth century immigration restrictions were aimed at attracting English-speaking and other white immigrants and keeping out "unassimilable" immigrants, including those from eastern and southern Europe, and from Japan. State laws restricting or denying to immigrants who were ineligible for citizenship the right to acquire and own property (aimed principally at the Japanese) were upheld by the United States Supreme Court, and unquestioned until *Oyama v. California.*[288] In *Oyama*, the Court invalidated a state-law statutory presumption imposed against the interests of property owners whose conveyances were paid by noncitizens who were themselves ineligible to own property. The law had been aimed at preventing the Japanese from circumventing state laws which prevented them from owning property by purchasing land in the name of children or other eligible holders. In *Takahashi v. Fish & Game Commission*,[289] the Court also struck a state provision barring issuance of commercial fishing license to any person ineligible for citizenship.[290]

More recently, the Court has confronted the possibility that language is used as a proxy for ethnicity or national origin discrimination. *See Hernandez v. New York*[291] (rejecting *Batson*-connected claim that peremptory challenge of Latino jurors violated equal protection).

b. Legitimacy

In 1968 in two cases[292] the Court struck statutory provisions treating children born outside of marriage differently than children who were the product of a marriage, utilizing language that suggested more than mere rationality review was being applied. Justice Douglas speaking for the Court noted the Court had been "extremely sensitive when it comes to basic civil rights" and called the discrimination at issue "invidious" despite the history and tradition of legal distinction based on "Wedlock." The Court

---

[287] For an account of the hostile treatment of Chinese and Japanese immigrants see PETER IRONS, JUSTICE AT WAR 9–13 (1983). The nativist movement in California aimed at excluding Chinese in the late 1800's was directed toward the Japanese in the 1920's. Federal law at the time the anti-Japanese movement began still limited naturalization to aliens who were either "free white persons" or "persons of African descent, " though some American-born Japanese had become citizens. Professor Irons chronicles the federal and state political action directed against the Japanese which were supported by the state and federal courts.

[288] 332 U.S. 633 (1948).

[289] 334 U.S. 410 (1948).

[290] In Fuji v. State, 38 Cal. 2d 718, 242 P.2d 617 (1952), the California Supreme Court declared invalid the state provision prohibiting ownership of land by aliens ineligible for citizenship, citing the Supreme Court disapproval in *Oyama* and *Takahashi* of the Court's earlier alien land cases.

[291] 500 U.S. 352 (1991). *See* e.g., Deborah Ramirez, *Excluded Voices: The Disenfranchisement of Ethic Groups from Jury Service*, 1993 WIS. L. REV. 761.

[292] *See* Levy v. Louisiana, 391 U.S. 68 (1968)(striking state provision for damage suit for mother's wrongful death available to marital but nonmarital offspring) ; Glona v. American Guarantee & Liability Ins. Co., 391 U.S. 73 (1968)(invalidating state provision permitting parent to sue for wrongful death of marital, but not nonmarital offspring).

recognized in subsequent cases that nonmarital children are often the victims of societal disdain and rejected the argument that disparate treatment fostered the State's interest in marriage,[293] but in some contexts was willing to find a rational basis for the state's disposition.[294] Applying intermediate scrutiny in later cases, the Court sustained some legislative distinctions between marital and nonmarital children, often in decisions fracturing the Court and making coherence in this area unlikely. In *Lalli v. Lalli*,[295] the Court upheld a statute limiting inheritance to a child adjudged by a state court to be the offspring of the intestate, although a state cannot constitutionally deny intestate succession to nonmarital children of the father.[296] In connection with child support, in *Clark v. Jeter*[297] the Court invalidated a six-year statute of limitations for establishing paternity and struck a measure limiting the obligation to support children who have established paternity.[298]

A problematic area has been the question of whether equal protection requires that a father consent to the adoption of nonmarital children. In *Caban v. Mohammed*,[299] the Court held that a state law that accorded the mother but not the father the right to block adoption violated equal protection on the basis of gender distinction. In *Caban* the father had lived with the children as their father. A distinction between mothers and fathers was sustained in *Parham v. Hughes*[300] on the basis that the gender based distinction there was not invidious because the father had taken no steps to legitimate the child. In *Lehr v, Robertson*,[301] the Court concluded that the state law adequately protected the opportunity of the putative father to establish a relationship with his child and thus the entering of the adoption order without notice to the father was not a denial of equal protection for differential treatment of the parents.

Although the status classification based on illegitimacy, like race, is not within the control of the person affected and illegitimates have experienced a history of stigmatized treatment, it is clear that the Court has not applied the strict scrutiny reserved for racial classifications. The level of scrutiny appears to comport roughly with the "middle tier" scrutinization associated with gender.[302]

c. Other Groups

In other contexts, the Court has refused to formally acknowledge that social or political disfavor warrant heightened scrutiny by the courts. As has been discussed earlier, the Court has not been willing to view age classifications as suspect or demanding heightened review, upholding state and federal mandatory retirement provisions.[303] Is age sufficiently distinguishable from the *Carolene Products* prototype of race and ethnicity because of the power able to be wielded by individual group members—like

---

[293] *See* Weber v. Aetna Casualty & Surety Co., 406 U.S. 164 (1972).

[294] *See, e.g.,* Labine v. Vincent, 401 U.S. 532 (1971)(provision of Louisiana probate law which bars nonmarital child who is not legitimated or adopted by the father from sharing equally with the marital offspring in the intestate's estate does not offend equal protection.)

[295] 439 U.S. 259 (1978).

[296] Trimble v. Gordon, 430 U.S. 762 (1977).

[297] 486 U.S. 456 (1988).

[298] Gomez v. Perez, 409 U.S. 535 (1973).

[299] 441 U.S. 380 (1979).

[300] 441 U.S. 347 (1979).

[301] 463 U.S. 248 (1983).

[302] The Supreme Court, 1976 Term, 91 HARV. L. REV. 70 (1977)(noting that gender classifications are viewed as more invidious than illegitimacy).

[303] *See* Massachusetts Board of Retirement v. Murgia, 427 U.S. 307 (1979). Similarly, the Court upheld a mandatory retirement provision for federal foreign service employees in *Vance v. Bradley*, 440 U.S. 93 (1979).

judges? Notably —like women, who meet some but not all of the *Carolene Products* conditions, the older people are discrete—but are not an insular group. But isn't there danger that in the political process decisions about older people will be built upon "stereotype not truly indicative of their abilities"? Is historical prejudice and stereotypical treatment a more meaningful way of determining that some judicial protection is warranted than consideration of the discreteness and insularity of the group at issue?

The Court has not forthrightly decided whether heightened equal protection should extend to classifications based on sexual orientation. The majority in *Bowers v. Hardwick*[304] upheld a Georgia sodomy statute against a due process challenge, as applied to homosexual conduct.[305] Because of the violence-provoking hostility and history of discrimination against gays and lesbians in society some lower courts have found sexual orientation quasi-suspect.[306] In *City of Cleburne*, discussed *supra*, the Court found that, despite a history of disfavored treatment of and prejudice against the mentally retarded, political efforts to address their problems offered sufficient protection. How should courts treat the fact of some local legislative efforts to outlaw discrimination based on sexual orientation? What about the fact that some of those efforts have been subsequently overturned by voter referendum?[307]

Political controversy about whether to exclude gays from the military, flamed by conflict between military authorities who supported the exclusion on the basis of national security and the Clinton Administration's election promise to address the issue, led to a compromise policy requiring homosexual service personnel to refrain from homosexual conduct and to be silent about their sexual orientation or risk expulsion under a rebuttable presumption that a gay or lesbian service person would act on expressed sexual interest. Lower courts have disagreed as to whether such a policy, labeled "Don't Ask, Don't Tell," adequately meets equal protection and speech concerns.[308] Another controversial question is raised by state laws excluding gay and lesbian couples from marrying.[309]

How should lesbians and other individuals who experience a "double bind" because of membership in more than one disfavored group be protected? Women of color have noted that their experiences of gender and racial discrimination are not adequately captured in the Court's construction of gender inequality or in its approach to race.[310]

d.   Wealth

Notwithstanding some cases which appeared to be concerned about drawing distinctions based on wealth, the Court has not found wealth classifications entitled to heightened review. Instead the Court has maintained its position of deferring to the

---

[304] 478 U.S. 186 (1986).

[305] Justice Blackmun was prompted to argue that the singling out of homosexuals under the sodomy statute offended equal protection.

[306] *See* Watkins v. United States Army, 847 F.2d 132 (9th Circuit 1989).

[307] *See* Romer v. Evans (No. 94-1039).

[308] *See* Able v. United States, No. 94 CV 0974 (EDNY Mar. 30, 1995)(Invalidating 'Don't Ask Don't Tell Directive on free speech grounds); Thomasson v. Perry, No. 95–252-A (ED Va. 1995)(no infringement on first amendment rights). The scholarship on sexual orientation has been extensive. *See e.g.,* Elvia Arriola, *Sexual Identity and the Constitution: Homosexual Persons as a Discrete and Insular Minority,* 10 Women's Rts. L. Rep. 143 (1988); *Note, The Constitutional Status of Sexual Orientation: Homosexuality as a Suspect Classification,* 98 Harv. L. Rev. 1285 (1985).

[309] *See* William Eskridge, *A Social Constructionist History of Same-Sex Marriages,* U. Va. L. Rev. (1993).

[310] *See* Judy Scales-Trent, *Black Women and the Constitution: Finding Our Place, Asserting Our Rights,* 24 Harv. C.R.-C.L. L. Rev. 9 (1989). *See also* Harris, Essentialism, *supra.*

political forum for the resolution of appropriate classification schemes to address the myriad social and economic problems despite the adverse impact on the poor.[311] In cases dealing with the poor's right to counsel,[312], and access to the judicial process for resolution of disputes,[313] and voting,[314] judicial scrutiny has occurred but especially in later cases the basis of protection stemmed from the "fundamental rights" at stake.

In *Dandridge v. Williams*,[315] the Court upheld a state regulation in connection with the State's participation in the federal Aid to Families with Dependent Children (AFDC) program, imposing a ceiling on the amount of monthly grants available to a family for each child in a family. Justice Marshall, joined by Justice Brennan, disagreed with the equal protection analysis of the Court majority and its conclusion, without searching review of the justifications, that "a solid foundation for the regulation can be found in the State's legitimate interest in encouraging employment and in avoiding discrimination between welfare families and families of the working poor." Arguing that the case "defies easy characterization in terms of one or the other [equal protection] tests," Justice Marshall noted that "the literally vital interests of a powerless minority—poor families without breadwinners—is far removed from the area of business regulation." He urged forthright recognition of a "sliding-scale" analysis in which "concentration must be placed upon the character of the classification in question, the relative importance to individuals in the class discriminated against of the governmental benefits that they do not receive, and the asserted state interests in support of the classification."

Reaffirming this position in the context of a zoning decision adversely affecting the mentally retarded, in *City of Cleburne* Justice Marshall stated: "I have long believed the level of scrutiny employed in an equal protection case should vary with 'the constitutional and societal importance of the interest adversely affected and the recognized invidiousness of the basis upon which the particular classification is drawn.'"[316] The Court's reluctance to move away from a formal tiered approach and its reticence to expand classes and rights warranting stricter scrutiny under the intermediate and strict tiers of review were criticized as not promoting predictability and offering little guidance to judges who are left to an ad hoc basis of review. What are the disadvantages of recognizing this "sliding scale" approach to equal protection? Certainly the Court engages in balancing interests in other areas of constitutional analysis.

Similar concerns have led Justice Stevens to argue that there is but one Equal Protection Clause. In *City of Cleburne* Justice Stevens considered the appropriate test to be whether "an impartial lawmaker could logically believe that the classification would serve a legitimate public purpose that transcends the harm to the disadvantaged class."

D.   The Fundamental Rights Strand of Equal Protection—Right to Travel, Voting and Education

Despite the Court's unwillingness to identify new rights "vital to the flourishing of a free society" which justify strict scrutiny, in several areas the Court's fundamental rights analysis has shaped equal protection jurisprudence and significantly contributed to our concept of equality. This discussion is intended to be a brief survey since much

---

[311] *See e.,g.*, Dandridge v. Williams, 397 U.S. 471 (1970)(ceiling on welfare assistance disadvantaging larger families upheld by Court utilizing rational basis review.)

[312] *See, e.g.*, Argersinger v. Hamlin, 407 U.S. 25 (1972).

[313] *See, e.g.* Boddie v. Connecticut, 401 U.S. 371 (1971).

[314] *See, e.g.*, Harper v. Virginia Board of Elections, 383 U.S. 663 (1966).

[315] 397 U.S. 471 (1970).

[316] 473 U.S. 432, 460 (1985).

of what can be discussed can be understood in the context of the Court's struggle to define its modern substantive due process analysis. *See* Part I *supra*.

1.   The Right to Travel

In *Shapiro v. Thompson*[317] the Court overturned statutory provisions denying welfare benefits to claimants who failed to meet the required one-year waiting period. The Court concluded that the classification constituted an "invidious discrimination." It rejected the states' justification of the waiting-period as a protective device to preserve fiscal integrity of state public assistance programs, finding "weighty evidence that exclusion from the jurisdiction of the poor who need or may need relief was the specific objective of these provisions."

The Court acknowledged that the one-year waiting period was well suited to discourage the influx of poor families who would burden the system, adding that "the purpose of inhibiting migration by needy persons into the State is constitutionally impermissible. . . . The constitutional right to travel from one State to another . . . occupies a position fundamental to the concept of our Federal Union. It is a right that has been firmly established and repeatedly recognized." In the context of rejecting arguments about various administrative convenience and governmental efficiencies served by the provisions, the majority used language indicating that the Court would require a compelling state interest and a consideration of less drastic alternatives before sustaining such legislation which infringed on the right to travel.

Later cases implicating the right of travel suggest that a "compelling governmental interest" test did not endure. While durational residency requirements have been overturned because of their infringement on the right to travel recognized in *Shapiro* in the voting context, *see*, e.g., *Dunn v. Blumstein*,[318] and as a condition for county-supported nonemergency hospitalization or medical care, *see*, *Memorial Hospital v. Maricopa County*,[319] in other contexts durational residency requirements have been upheld on the basis that the impingement on travel was not present or the consequence minimal in comparison to the state's interests.[320] In *Maricopa County*, the Court stated: "Although any durational residence requirement impinges to some extent on the right to travel, the Court in *Shapiro* did not declare such requirements to be per se unconstitutional. [A] classification which 'operates to *penalize* those persons . . . who have exercised their constitutional right of interstate migration,' must be justified by a compelling state interest . . . ." The Court further qualified earlier holdings by pointing out that some waiting periods (such as for attaining lower college tuition) would not be considered penalties, as in *Shapiro*, where there was "denial of the basic 'necessities of life." Separate opinions written by Justice Marshall, Justice Douglas, and Justice Rehnquist reflected disagreement about the level of scrutiny required in such a case.

Subsequently, in *Sosna v. Iowa*[321] Justice Rehnquist over the dissent of three justices concluded that a durational requirement for filing for divorce was justified by the interest in the state in having adequate connections with the parties and because domestic regulations were viewed as a "virtually exclusive province of the State." The Court reasoned that in this case the claimant was "not irretrievably foreclosed from

---

[317] 394 U.S. 618 (1969).

[318] 405 U.S. 330 (1972).

[319] 415 U.S. 250 (1974).

[320] *See, e.g.*, Sosna v. Iowa, 419 U.S. 393 (1975)(one-year durational residency requirement for filing for divorce causes only delay and does not foreclose right; state has interests in individual filing divorce to have connections with it before permitting divorce to be filed particularly in light of custody, property rights and other issues of concern to this and other states.)

[321] 419 U.S. 393 (1975).

obtaining some part of what she sought" but rather access to the courts was delayed. Justices Marshall and Brennan accused the Court majority of "ad hoc balancing of the respective interests of state and divorce plaintiff. In *Jones v. Helms*[322] the Court rejected a right to travel claim asserted by a criminal defendant who claimed the State's enhancement of criminal punishment for parental child abandonment if the parent leaves the state from a misdemeanor to a felony was unconstitutional. The Court noted that engaging in criminal conduct qualified defendant's right.

In contrast to durational requirements bona fide continuing residence requirements have been upheld, as in *McCarthy v. Philadelphia Civil Service Commission*.[323] For a majority in *Zobel v. Williams*,[324] Alaska's efforts to create fixed distinctions between classes of *bona fide* residents, based on how long they have been in the State, for the purposes of determining rights and benefits of the State were troublesome under *Shapiro*. Justice O'Connor, however, found the distribution scheme offensive to the Privileges and Immunities Clause of Article VI, because it imposes one of the "disabilities of alienage."

In *Attorney General of New York v. Soto-Lopez*,[325] over the dissent of Justice O'Connor and two others, the Court following *Zobel,* concluded that a one-time preference in civil service employment opportunities offered solely to resident veterans who lived in the state at the time of military service, violated equal protection. Whereas Justice Brennan applied strict scrutiny requiring a compelling state interest because of the provisions's impingement on travel, Justices White and Burger, concurring in the judgment relied on a rationality review of the equal protection claim.

2. Voting

In 1962, *Baker v. Carr*,[326] recognized the equal protection clause as the source of a right to vote and run for elective office. That amendment became the principal means of challenging measures which have the effect of denying or diluting the right to vote. Notably, the original constitutional scheme contemplated that the franchise be available to a limited segment of the population (white propertied men) and not universal suffrage. The Constitution, moreover, left it to the States to determine who should vote in state and national elections.[327]

Before the adoption of the Civil War Amendments, most states denied the franchise to African Americans and to women. The Fourteenth Amendment did not explicitly forbid the continuation of discrimination. The Fifteenth Amendment prohibited the "right of citizens of the United States to vote [being] denied or abridged by the United States or by any State on account of race, color, or previous condition of servitude," but did not extend the franchise to women. *See Minor v. Happersett*, discussed *supra*. Following ratification in 1920, the Nineteenth Amendment provided that the "right of any citizen to vote shall not be denied or abridged by the United States or by any State on account of sex. Other amendments in the twentieth century extended the franchise more universally and set forth minimum qualifications affecting federal elections. The Seventeenth Amendment in 1913 provided that two United States Senators from each state be elected by the people for six years and have one vote and that "[t]he electors in each State shall have the qualifications requisite for electors of the most numerous branch of the State Legislatures. The Twenty-fourth and Twenty-sixth amendments,

---

[322] 452 U.S. 412 (1981).
[323] 424 U.S. 645 (1976).
[324] 457 U.S. 55 (1982).
[325] 476 U.S. 898 (1986).
[326] 369 U.S. 186 (1962).
[327] *See* Art. I, §1, Cl. 1; Art. I, § 4, cl. 1; Art. II, § 1; Art. I, § 3.

respectively, removed poll tax qualifications on the franchise right and extended the franchise to any citizen eighteen or older.

The Amendments reflect a scheme whereby States continue to set voting qualifications, subject to constitutional restrictions on limiting the vote because of age, gender, race and ability to pay tax and subject to congressional authority under all but the Seventeenth Amendment to enact appropriate enforcing legislation. For a discussion of the Court's interpretation of this enforcement authority *see* Part I, *supra*.

Having struggled with the question of justiciability in *Baker v. Carr*, discussed *infra*, utilizing the Fourteenth Amendment equal protection clause the Court has taken an active role in clearing the channels of political participation.

Reynolds v. Sims
377 U.S. 533 (1964)

MR. CHIEF JUSTICE WARREN delivered the opinion of the Court.

Involved in these cases are ... appeals [concerning the district court's invalidation] under the Equal Protection Clause .. [of] two legislatively proposed plans for the apportionment of seats in the two houses of the Alabama Legislature, and ordering into effect a temporary reapportionment plan comprised of parts of the proposed but judicially disapproved measures. ...

Plaintiffs below alleged that the last apportionment of the Alabama Legislature was based on the 1900 federal census, despite the requirement of the State Constitution that the legislature be reapportioned decennially. They asserted that, since the population growth in the State from 1900 to 1960 had been uneven, Jefferson and other counties were now victims of serious discrimination with respect to the allocation of legislative representation. As a result of the failure of the legislature to reapportion itself, plaintiffs asserted, they were denied "equal suffrage in free and equal elections ... and the equal protection of the laws" in violation of the Alabama Constitution and the Fourteenth Amendment to the Federal Constitution. The complaint asserted that plaintiffs had no other adequate remedy, and that they had exhausted all forms of relief other than that available through the federal courts. They alleged that the Alabama Legislature had established a pattern of prolonged inaction from 1911 to the present which "clearly demonstrates that no reapportionment ... shall be effected"; that representation at any future constitutional convention would be established by the legislature, making it unlikely that the membership of any such convention would be fairly representative; and that, while the Alabama Supreme Court had found that the legislature had not complied with the State Consti-

tution in failing to reapportion according to population decennially, that court had nevertheless indicated that it would not interfere with matters of legislative reapportionment.

Undeniably the Constitution of the United States protects the right of all qualified citizens to vote, in state as well as in federal elections. A consistent line of decisions by this Court in cases involving attempts to deny or restrict the right of suffrage has made this indelibly clear. It has been repeatedly recognized that all qualified voters have a constitutionally protected right to vote, *Ex parte Yarbrough* and to have their votes counted. In *Mosley* the Court stated that it is "as equally unquestionable that the right to have one's vote counted is as open to protection ... as the right to put a ballot in a box." The right to vote can neither be denied outright, nor destroyed by alteration of ballots, nor diluted by ballot-box stuffing. As the Court stated in *Classic*, "Obviously included within the right to choose, secured by the Constitution, is the right of qualified voters within a state to cast their ballots and have them counted. ... " Racially based gerrymandering, and the conducting of white primaries, both of which result in denying to some citizens their right to vote, have been held to be constitutionally impermissible. And history has seen a continuing expansion of the scope of the right of suffrage in this country. The right to vote freely for the candidate of one's choice is of the essence of a democratic society, and any restrictions on that right strike at the heart of representative government. And the right of suffrage can be denied by a debasement or dilution of the weight of a citizen's vote just as effectively as by wholly prohibiting the free exercise of the franchise.

. . .

In *Gray v. Sanders* we held that the Georgia county unit system, applicable in statewide primary elections, was unconstitutional since it resulted in a dilution of the weight of the votes of certain Georgia voters merely because of where they resided. . . .

In *Wesberry v. Sanders*, decided earlier this Term, we held that attacks on the constitutionality of congressional districting plans enacted by state legislatures do not present nonjusticiable questions and should not be dismissed generally for "want of equity." We determined that the constitutional test for the validity of congressional districting schemes was one of substantial equality of population among the various districts established by a state legislature for the election of members of the Federal House of Representatives.

In that case we decided that an apportionment of congressional seats which "contracts the value of some votes and expands that of others" is unconstitutional, since "the Federal Constitution intends that when qualified voters elect members of Congress each vote be given as much weight as any other vote . . . ." We concluded that the constitutional prescription for election of members of the House of Representatives "by the People," construed in its historical context, "means that as nearly as is practicable one man's vote in a congressional election is to be worth as much as another's." . . . We found further, in Wesberry, that "our Constitution's plain objective" was that "of making equal representation for equal numbers of people the fundamental goal. . . . " We concluded by stating:

> "No right is more precious in a free country than that of having a voice in the election of those who make the laws under which, as good citizens, we must live. Other rights, even the most basic, are illusory if the right to vote is undermined. Our Constitution leaves no room for classification of people in a way that unnecessarily abridges this right."

Gray and *Wesberry* are of course not dispositive of or directly controlling on our decision in these cases involving state legislative apportionment controversies. Admittedly, those decisions, in which we held that, in statewide and in congressional elections, one person's vote must be counted equally with those of all other voters in a State, were based on different constitutional considerations and were addressed to rather distinct problems. But neither are they wholly inapposite. *Gray*, though not determinative here since involving the weighting of votes in statewide elections, established the basic principle of equality among voters within a State, and held that voters cannot be classified, constitutionally, on the basis of where they live, at least with respect to voting in statewide elections. And our decision in *Wesberry* was of course grounded on that language of the Constitution which prescribes that members of the Federal House of Representatives are to be chosen "by the People," while attacks on state legislative apportionment schemes, such as that involved in the instant cases, are principally based on the Equal Protection Clause of the Fourteenth Amendment. Nevertheless, *Wesberry* clearly established that the fundamental principle of representative government in this country is one of equal representation for equal numbers of people, without regard to race, sex, economic status, or place of residence within a State. Our problem, then, is to ascertain, in the instant cases, whether there are any constitutionally cognizable principles which would justify departures from the basic standard of equality among voters in the apportionment of seats in state legislatures.

III.

A predominant consideration in determining whether a State's legislative apportionment scheme constitutes an invidious discrimination violative of rights asserted under the Equal Protection Clause is that the rights allegedly impaired are individual and personal in nature. . . . Like *Skinner v. Oklahoma*, such a case "touches a sensitive and important area of human rights," and "involves one of the basic civil rights of man," presenting questions of alleged "invidious discriminations . . . against groups or types of individuals in violation of the constitutional guaranty of just and equal laws." Undoubtedly, the right of suffrage is a fundamental matter in a free and democratic society. Especially since the right to exercise the franchise in a free and unimpaired manner is preservative of other basic civil and political rights, any alleged infringement of the right of citizens to vote must be carefully and meticulously scrutinized. Almost a century ago, in *Yick Wo v. Hopkins*, the Court referred to "the political franchise of voting" as "a fundamental political right, because preservative of all rights."

Legislators represent people, not trees or acres. Legislators are elected by voters, not farms or cities or economic interests. As long as ours is a representative form of government, and our legislatures are those instruments of government elected directly by and directly representative of the people, the right to elect legislators in a free and unimpaired fashion is a bedrock of our political system. It could hardly be gainsaid that a constitutional claim had been asserted by an allegation that certain otherwise qualified voters had been entirely prohibited from voting for members of their state legislature. And, if a State should provide that the votes of citizens in one part of the State should be given two times, or five times, or 10 times the weight of votes of citizens in another part of the State, it could hardly be contended that the right to vote of those residing in the disfavored areas had not been effectively diluted. It would appear extraordinary to suggest that a State could be constitutionally permitted to enact a law providing that certain of the State's voters could vote two, five, or 10 times for their legislative representatives, while voters living elsewhere could vote only once. And it is inconceivable that a state law to the effect that, in counting votes for legislators, the votes of citizens in one part of the State would be multiplied by two, five, or 10, while the votes of persons in another area would be counted only at face value, could be constitutionally sustainable. Of course, the effect of state legislative districting schemes which give the same number of representatives to unequal numbers of constituents is identical. Overweighting and overvaluation of the votes of those living here has the certain effect of dilution and undervaluation of the votes of those living there. The resulting discrimination against those individual voters living in disfavored areas is easily demonstrable mathematically. Their right to vote is simply not the same right to vote as that of those living in a favored part of the State. Two, five, or 10 of them must vote before the effect of their voting is equivalent to that of their favored neighbor. Weighting the votes of citizens differently, by any method or means, merely because of where they happen to reside, hardly seems justifiable.

Logically, in a society ostensibly grounded on representative government, it would seem reasonable that a majority of the people of a State could elect a majority of that State's legislators. To conclude differently, and to sanction minority control of state legislative bodies, would appear to deny majority rights in a way that far surpasses any possible denial of minority rights that might otherwise be thought to result. Since legislatures are responsible for enacting laws by which all citizens are to be governed, they should be bodies which are collectively responsive to the popular will. And the concept of equal protection has been traditionally viewed as requiring the uniform treatment of persons standing in the same relation to the governmental action questioned or challenged. With respect to the allocation of legislative representation, all voters, as citizens of a State, stand in the same relation regardless of where they live. Any suggested criteria for the differentiation of citizens are insufficient to justify any discrimination, as to the weight of

their votes, unless relevant to the permissible purposes of legislative apportionment. Since the achieving of fair and effective representation for all citizens is concededly the basic aim of legislative apportionment, we conclude that the Equal Protection Clause guarantees the opportunity for equal participation by all voters in the election of state legislators. Diluting the weight of votes because of place of residence impairs basic constitutional rights under the Fourteenth Amendment just as much as invidious discriminations based upon factors such as race, or economic status. Our constitutional system amply provides for the protection of minorities by means other than giving them majority control of state legislatures. And the democratic ideals of equality and majority rule, which have served this Nation so well in the past, are hardly of any less significance for the present and the future.

We are told that the matter of apportioning representation in a state legislature is a complex and many-faceted one. We are advised that States can rationally consider factors other than population in apportioning legislative representation. We are admonished not to restrict the power of the States to impose differing views as to political philosophy on their citizens. We are cautioned about the dangers of entering into political thickets and mathematical quagmires. Our answer is this: a denial of constitutionally protected rights demands judicial protection; our oath and our office require no less of us. . . . Population is, of necessity, the starting point for consideration and the controlling criterion for judgment in legislative apportionment controversies. A citizen, a qualified voter, is no more nor no less so because he lives in the city or on the farm. This is the clear and strong command of our Constitution's Equal Protection Clause. This is an essential part of the concept of a government of laws and not men. This is at the heart of Lincoln's vision of "government of the people, by the people, [and] for the people." The Equal Protection Clause demands no less than substantially equal state legislative representation for all citizens, of all places as well as of all races.

IV.

We hold that, as a basic constitutional standard, the Equal Protection Clause requires that the seats in both houses of a bicameral state legislature must be apportioned on a population basis. Simply stated, an individual's right to vote for state legislators is unconstitutionally impaired when its weight is in a substantial fashion diluted when compared with votes of citizens living in other parts of the State. Since, under neither the existing apportionment provisions nor either of the proposed plans was either of the houses of the Alabama Legislature apportioned on a population basis, the District Court correctly held that all three of these schemes were constitutionally invalid.

V.

. . . The system of representation in the two Houses of the Federal Congress is one ingrained in our Constitution, as part of the law of the land. It is one conceived out of compromise and concession indispensable to the establishment of our federal republic. Arising from unique historical circumstances, it is based on the consideration that in establishing our type of federalism a group of formerly independent States bound themselves together under one national government. Admittedly, the original 13 States surrendered some of their sovereignty in agreeing to join together "to form a more perfect Union." But at the heart of our constitutional system remains the concept of separate and distinct governmental entities which have delegated some, but not all, of their formerly held powers to the single national government. The fact that almost threefourths of our present States were never in fact independently sovereign does not detract from our view that the so-called federal analogy is inapplicable as a sustaining precedent for state legislative apportionments.

Political subdivisions of States —counties, cities, or whatever—never were and never have been considered as sovereign entities. Rather, they have been traditionally regarded as subordinate governmental instrumentalities created by the State to assist in the carrying out of state governmental functions. . . . The relationship of the States to the Federal Government could hardly be less analogous. . . .

Since we find the so-called federal analogy inapposite to a consideration of the constitutional validity of state legislative apportionment schemes, we necessarily hold that the Equal Protection Clause requires both houses of a state legislature to be apportioned on a population basis. The right of a citizen to equal representation and to have his vote weighted equally with those of all other citizens in the election of members of one house of a bicameral state legislature would amount to little if States could effectively submerge the equalpopulation principle in the apportionment of seats in the other house. If such a scheme were permissible, an individual citizen's ability to exercise an effective voice in the only instrument of state government directly representative of the people might be almost as effectively thwarted as if neither house were apportioned on a population basis.

We do not believe that the concept of bicameralism is rendered anachronistic and meaningless when the predominant basis of representation in the two state legislative bodies is required to be the same — population. A prime reason for bicameralism, modernly considered, is to insure mature and deliberate consideration of, and to prevent precipitate action on, proposed legislative measures. Simply because the controlling criterion for apportioning representation is required to be the same in both houses does not mean that there will be no differences in the composition and complexion of the two bodies. Different constituencies can be represented in the two houses. One body could be composed of single-member districts while the other could have at least some multimember districts. The length of terms of the legislators in the separate bodies could differ. The numerical size of the two bodies could be made to differ, even significantly, and the geographical size of districts from which legislators are elected could also be made to differ. And apportionment in one house could be arranged so as to balance off minor inequities in the representation of certain areas in the other house. In summary, these and other factors could be, and are presently in many States, utilized to engender differing complexions and collective attitudes in the two bodies of a state legislature, although both are apportioned substantially on a population basis.

VI.

By holding that as a federal constitutional requisite both houses of a state legislature must be apportioned on a population basis, we mean that the Equal Protection Clause requires that a State make an honest and good faith effort to construct districts, in both houses of its legislature, as nearly of equal population as is practicable. We realize that it is a practical impossibility to arrange legislative districts so that each one has an identical number of residents, or citizens, or voters. Mathematical exactness or precision is hardly a workable constitutional requirement.

. . . Thus, we proceed to state here only a few rather general considerations which appear to us to be relevant.

A State may legitimately desire to maintain the integrity of various political subdivisions, insofar as possible, and provide for compact districts of contiguous territory in designing a legislative apportionment scheme. Valid considerations may underlie such aims. Indiscriminate districting, without any regard for political subdivision or natural or historical boundary lines, may be little more than an open invitation to partisan gerrymandering. Single-member districts may be the rule in one State, while another State might desire to achieve some flexibility by creating multimember or floterial districts. Whatever the means of accomplishment, the overriding objective must be substantial equality of population among the various districts, so that the vote of any citizen is approximately equal in weight to that of any other citizen in the State.

[N]either history alone, nor economic or other sorts of group interests, are permissible factors in attempting to justify disparities from population-based representation. Citizens, not history or economic interests, cast votes. Considerations of area alone provide an insufficient justification for deviations from the equal-population principle. Again, people, not land or trees or pastures, vote. Modern developments and improvements in transportation and communications make rather hollow, in the mid-1960's, most claims that deviations from population-based representation can validly be based solely on geographical considerations. Arguments for allowing such deviations in order to insure effective representation for sparsely settled areas and to prevent legislative districts from becoming so large that the availability of access of citizens to their representatives is impaired are today, for the most part, unconvincing.

A consideration that appears to be of more substance in justifying some deviations from population-based representation in state legislatures is that of insuring some voice to political subdivisions, as political subdivisions. Several factors make more than insubstantial claims that a State can rationally consider according political subdivisions some independent representation in at least one body of the state legislature, as long as the basic standard of equality of population among districts is maintained. Local governmental entities are frequently charged with various responsibilities incident to the operation of state government. In many States much of the legislature's activity involves the enactment of so-called local legislation, directed only to the concerns of particular political subdivisions. And a State may legitimately desire to construct districts along political subdivision lines to deter the possibilities of gerrymandering. However, permitting deviations from population-based representation does not mean that each local governmental unit or political subdivision can be given separate representation, regardless oᶠ population. Carried too far, a scheme of giving at least one seat in one house to each political subdivision (for example, to each county) could easily result, in many States, in a total subversion of the equal-population principle in that legislative body. . . .

VIII.

That the Equal Protection Clause requires that both houses of a state legislature be apportioned on a population basis does not mean that States cannot adopt some reasonable plan for periodic revision of their apportionment schemes. Decennial reapportionment appears to be a rational approach to readjustment of legislative representation in order to take into account population shifts and growth. . . . . In substance, we do not regard the Equal Protection Clause as requiring daily, monthly, annual or biennial reapportionment, so long as a State has a reasonably conceived plan for periodic readjustment of legislative representation. While we do not intend to indicate that decennial reapportionment is a constitutional requisite, compliance with such an approach would clearly meet the minimal requirements for maintaining a reasonably current scheme of legislative representation.

Affirmed and remanded.

[Justice Clark and Steward concurred and Justice Harlan dissented.]

The Court's decision in *Reynolds* provoked a spate of litigation as States struggled to reapportion legislatures in accordance with its standards. The Court construed the one person, one vote requirement strictly and often state constructions which did not promote mathematically equal districts risked disapproval. In the seventies, however, the Court shifted attention from mathematical standards to more searching consideration of whether unfair representation schemes to favor incumbents or interests groups, or dilute the voting power of minorities were being effectuated.

3. Education

In the school financing controversy the Court was pressed to reconsider its two-tiered analysis of Equal Protection analysis in response to gross disparities in Texas' scheme allocating funds to wealthy and poor school districts in the state. Texas' scheme built on local property taxes imposed by school districts was similar to those of states across the country. Faced with the potential drain of judicial resources which would occur if it reached a decision that the disparities which were a consequence of such schemes were unconstitutional, the Court chose to avoid recognizing education as a fundamental interest warranting judicial intervention to address the inequalities in available funding. Consider whether the Court's resolution of the controversies in *Rodriguez* and *Plyler v. Doe* which follows is consistent with equal protection precedents and persuasive in their treatment of important "non" fundamental interests.

San Antonio Independent School District v. Rodriguez
411 U.S. 1 (1973)

MR. JUSTICE POWELL delivered the opinion of the Court.

This suit attacking the Texas system of financing public education was initiated by Mexican-American parents whose children attend the elementary and secondary schools in . . . an urban school district in San Antonio, Texas. They brought a class action on behalf of school children throughout the State who are members of minority groups or who are poor and reside in school districts having a low property tax base. Named as defendants were the State Board of Education, the Commissioner of Education, the State Attorney General, and the Bexar County (San Antonio) Board of Trustees. . . . [W]e reverse the decision of the District Court [holding the Texas school finance system unconstitutional.]

I

. . .

Until recent times, Texas was a predominantly rural State and its population and property wealth were spread relatively evenly across the State. Sizable differences in the value of assessable property between local school districts became increasingly evident as the State became more industrialized and as rural-to-urban population shifts became more pronounced. The location of commercial and industrial property began to play a significant role in determining the amount of tax resources available to each school district. These growing disparities in population and taxable property between districts were responsible in part for increasingly notable differences in levels of local expenditure for education.

. . .

Recognizing the need for increased state funding to help offset disparities in local spending and to meet Texas' changing educational requirements, the state legislature in the late 1940's undertook a thorough evaluation of public education with an eye toward major reform.

In 1947, an 18-member committee, composed of educators and legislators, was appointed to explore alternative systems in other States and to propose a funding scheme that would guarantee a minimum or basic educational offering to each child and that would help overcome interdistrict disparities in taxable resources. The Committee's efforts led to the passage of the . . . Texas Minimum Foundation School Program. Today, this Program accounts for approximately half of the total educational expenditures in Texas.

The Program calls for state and local contributions to a fund earmarked specifically for teacher salaries, operating expenses, and transportation costs. The State, supplying funds from its general revenues, finances approximately 80% of the Program, and the school districts are responsible—as a unit—for providing the remaining 20%. The districts' share, known as the Local Fund Assignment, is apportioned among the school districts under a formula designed to reflect each district's relative taxpaying ability. The Assignment is first divided among Texas' 254 counties pursuant to a complicated economic index that takes into account the relative value of each county's contribution to the State's total income from manufacturing, mining, and agricultural activities. It also considers each county's relative share of all payrolls paid within the State and, to a lesser extent, considers each county's share of all property in the State. Each county's assignment is then divided among its school districts on the basis of each district's share of assessable property within the county. The district, in turn, finances its share of the Assignment out of revenues from local property taxation.

The design of this complex system was twofold. First, it was an attempt to assure that the Foundation Program would have an equalizing influence on expenditure levels between school districts by placing the heaviest burden on the school districts most capable of paying.

Second, the Program's architects sought to establish a Local Fund Assignment that would force every school district to contribute to the education of its children but that would not by itself exhaust any district's resources. Today every school district does impose a property tax from which it derives locally expendable funds in excess of the amount necessary to satisfy its Local Fund Assignment under the Foundation Program.

. . .

The school district in which appellees reside, the Edgewood Independent School District, has been compared throughout this litigation with the Alamo Heights Independent School District. This comparison between the least and most affluent districts in the San Antonio area serves to illustrate the manner in which the dual system of finance operates and to indicate the extent to which substantial disparities exist despite the State's impressive progress in recent years. Edgewood is one of seven public school districts in the metropolitan area. . . . The district is situated in the core-city sector of San Antonio in a residential neighborhood that has little commercial or industrial property. The residents are predominantly of Mexican-American descent: approximately 90% of the student population is Mexican-American and over 6% is Negro. The average assessed property value per pupil is $5,960—the lowest in the metropolitan area—and the median family income ($4,686) is also the lowest. At an equalized tax rate of $1.05 per $100 of assessed property—the highest in the metropolitan area—the district contributed $26 to the education of each child for the 1967–1968 school year above its Local Fund Assignment for the Minimum Foundation Program. The Foundation Program contributed $222 per pupil for a state-local total of $248. Federal funds added another $108 for a total of $356 per pupil.

. . .

Alamo Heights is the most affluent school district in San Antonio. Its six schools, housing approximately 5,000 students, are situated in a residential community quite unlike the Edgewood District. The school population is predominantly "Anglo," having only 18% Mexican-Americans and less than 1% Negroes. The assessed property value per pupil exceeds $49,000, and the median family income is $8,001. In 1967–1968 the local tax rate of $.85 per $100 of valuation yielded $333 per pupil over $225 provided from that Program, the district was able to supply $558 per student. Supplemented by a $36 per-pupil grant from federal sources, Alamo Heights spent $594 per pupil.

. . .

[S]ubstantial interdistrict disparities in school expenditures found by the District Court to prevail in San Antonio and in varying degrees throughout the State still exist. And it was these disparities, largely attributable to differences in the amounts of money collected through local property taxation, that led the District Court to conclude that Texas' dual system of public school financing violated the Equal Protection Clause. The District Court held that the Texas system discriminates on the basis of wealth in the manner in which education is provided for its people. Finding that wealth is a "suspect" classification and that education is a "fundamental" interest, the District Court held that the Texas system could be sustained only if the State could show that it was premised upon some compelling state interest. On this issue the court concluded that "[n]ot only are defendants unable to demonstrate compelling state interests . . . they fail even to establish a reasonable basis for these classifications."

Texas virtually concedes that its historically rooted dual system of financing education could not withstand the strict judicial scrutiny that this Court has found appropriate in reviewing legislative judgments that interfere with fundamental constitutional rights or that involve suspect classifications. If, as previous decisions have indicated, strict scrutiny means that the State's system is not entitled to the usual presumption of validity, that the State rather than the complainants must carry a "heavy burden of justification," that the State must demonstrate that its educational system has been structured with "precision," and is "tailored" narrowly to serve legitimate objectives and that it has selected the "less drastic means" for effectuating its objectives, the Texas financing system and its counterpart in virtually every other State will not pass muster. [T]he State defends the system's rationality with vigor and disputes the District Court's finding that it lacks a "reasonable basis."

. . .

II

The District Court [found wealth discrimination and] reasoned, based on decisions of this Court affirming the undeniable importance of education, that there is a fundamental right to education and that, absent some compelling state justification, the Texas system could not stand.

We are unable to agree that this case, which in significant aspects is *sui generis,* may be so neatly fitted into the conventional mosaic of constitutional analysis under the Equal Protection Clause. Indeed, for the several reasons that follow, we find neither the suspect-classification nor the fundamental-interest analysis persuasive.

A

The wealth discrimination discovered by the District Court in this case, and by several other courts that have recently struck down school-financing laws in other States, is quite unlike any of the forms of wealth discrimination heretofore reviewed by this Court. Rather than focusing on the unique features of the alleged discrimination, the courts in these cases have virtually assumed their findings of a suspect classification through a simplistic process of analysis: since, under the traditional systems of financing public schools, some poorer people receive less expensive educations than other more affluent people, these systems discriminate on the basis of wealth. This approach largely ignores the hard threshold questions, including whether it makes a difference for purposes of consideration under the Constitution that the class of disadvantaged "poor" cannot be identified or defined in customary equal protection terms, and whether the relative—rather than absolute—nature of the asserted deprivation is of significant consequence. Before a State's laws and the justifications for the classifications they create are subjected to strict judicial scrutiny, we think these threshold considerations must be analyzed more closely than they were in the court below.

. . . The Texas system of school financing might be regarded as discriminating (1) against "poor" persons whose incomes fall below some identifiable level of poverty or who might be characterized as functionally "indigent," or (2) against those who are relatively poorer than others, or (3) against all those who, irrespective of their personal incomes, happen to reside in relatively poorer school districts. Our task must be to ascertain whether, in fact, the Texas system has been shown to discriminate on any of these possible bases and, if so, whether the resulting classification may be regarded as suspect.

[In] precedents of this Court . . . [t]he individuals, or groups of individuals, who constituted the class discriminated against . . . shared two distinguishing characteristics: because of their impecunity they were completely unable to pay for some desired benefit, and as a consequence, they sustained an absolute deprivation of a meaningful opportunity to enjoy that benefit. In *Griffin v. Illinois*, and its progeny, the Court invalidated state laws that prevented an indigent criminal defendant from acquiring a transcript, or an adequate substitute for a transcript, for use at several stages of the trial and appeal process. The payment require-

ments in each case were found to occasion *de facto* discrimination against those who, because of their indigency, were totally unable to pay for transcripts. And the Court in each case emphasized that no constitutional violation would have been shown if the State had provided some "adequate substitute" for a full stenographic transcript. . . .

. . .

Only appellees' first possible basis for describing the class disadvantaged by the Texas school-financing system—discrimination against a class of definably "poor" persons—might arguably meet the criteria established in these prior cases. Even a cursory examination, however, demonstrates that neither of the two distinguishing characteristics of wealth classifications can be found here. First, in support of their charge that the system discriminates against the "poor," appellees have made no effort to demonstrate that it operates to the peculiar disadvantage of any class fairly definable as indigent, or as composed of persons whose incomes are beneath any designated poverty level. Indeed, there is reason to believe that the poorest families are not necessarily clustered in the poorest property districts. A recent and exhaustive study of school districts in Connecticut concluded that "[i]t is clearly incorrect . . . to contend that the 'poor' live in 'poor' districts . . . Thus, the major factual assumption of Serrano—that the educational financing system discriminates against the 'poor'—is simply false in Connecticut." Defining "poor" families as those below the Bureau of the Census "poverty level," the Connecticut study found, not surprisingly, that the poor were clustered around commercial and industrial areas—those same areas that provide the most attractive sources of property tax income for school districts. Whether a similar pattern would be discovered in Texas is not known, but there is no basis on the record in this case for assuming that the poorest people —defined by reference to any level of absolute impecunity—are concentrated in the poorest districts.

Second, neither appellees nor the District Court addressed the fact that, unlike each of the foregoing cases, lack of personal resources has not occasioned an absolute deprivation of the desired benefit. The argument here is not that the children in districts having relatively low assessable property values are receiving no public education; rather, it is that they are receiving a poorer quality education than that available to children in districts having more assessable wealth. Apart from the unsettled and disputed question whether the quality of education may be determined by the amount of money expended for it a sufficient answer to appellees' argument is that, at least where wealth is involved, the Equal Protection Clause does not require absolute equality or precisely equal advantages. Nor, indeed, in view of the infinite variables affecting the educational process, can any system assure equal quality of education except in the most relative sense. Texas asserts that the Minimum Foundation Program provides an "adequate" education for all children in the State. By providing 12 years of free public-school education, and by assuring teachers, books, transportation, and operating funds, the Texas Legislature has endeavored to "guarantee, for the welfare of the state as a whole, that all people shall have at least an adequate program of education. This is what is meant by 'A Minimum Foundation Program of Education.'" The State repeatedly asserted in its briefs in this Court that it has fulfilled this desire and that it now assures "every child in every school district an adequate education." No proof was offered at trial persuasively discrediting or refuting the State's assertion.

. . .

[I]t is clear that appellees' suit asks this Court to extend its most exacting scrutiny to review a system that allegedly discriminates against a large, diverse, and amorphous class, unified only by the common factor of residence in districts that happen to have less taxable wealth than other districts. The system of alleged discrimination and the class it defines have none of the traditional indicia of suspectness: the class is not saddled with such disabilities, or subjected to such a history of purposeful unequal treatment, or relegated to such a position of political powerlessness as to command extraordinary protection from the majoritarian political process.

[Appellees] also assert that the State's system impermissibly interferes with the exercise of a "fundamental" right and that accordingly the prior decisions of this Court require the application of the strict standard of judicial review. It is this question—whether education is a fundamental right, in the sense that it is among the rights and liberties protected by the Constitution—which has so consumed the attention of courts and commentators in recent years.

B

In *Brown v. Board of Education*, a unanimous Court recognized that "education is perhaps the most important function of state and local governments." [As *Brown* stated:]

> "It is required in the performance of our most basic public responsibilities, even service in the armed forces. It is the very foundation of good citizenship. Today it is

a principal instrument in awakening the child to cultural values, in preparing him for later professional training, and in helping him to adjust normally to his environment. In these days, it is doubtful that any child may reasonably be expected to succeed in life if he is denied the opportunity of an education. Such an opportunity, where the state has undertaken to provide it, is a right which must be made available to all on equal terms."

Nothing this Court holds today in any way detracts from our historic dedication to public education. We are in complete agreement with the conclusion of the three-judge panel below that "the grave significance of education both to the individual and to our society" cannot be doubted. But the importance of a service performed by the State does not determine whether it must be regarded as fundamental for purposes of examination under the Equal Protection Clause. Mr. Justice Harlan, dissenting from the Court's application of strict scrutiny to a law impinging upon the right of interstate travel, admonished that "[v]irtually every state statute affects important rights." In his view, if the degree of judicial scrutiny of state legislation fluctuated depending on a majority's view of the importance of the interest affected, we would have gone "far toward making this Court a 'super-legislature.'" We would, indeed, then be assuming a legislative role and one for which the Court lacks both authority and competence. . . .

. . .

[I]n *Dandridge v. Williams*, the Court's explicit recognition of the fact that the "administration of public welfare assistance . . . involves the most basic economic needs of impoverished human beings," provided no basis for departing from the settled mode of constitutional analysis of legislative classifications involving questions of economic and social policy. As in the case of housing, the central importance of welfare benefits to the poor was not an adequate foundation for requiring the State to justify its law by showing some compelling state interest.

The lesson of these cases in addressing the question now before the Court is plain. It is not the province of this Court to create substantive constitutional rights in the name of guaranteeing equal protection of the laws. Thus, the key to discovering whether education is "fundamental" is not to be found in comparisons of the relative societal significance of education as opposed to subsistence or housing. Nor is it to be found by weighing whether education is as important as the right to travel. Rather, the answer lies in assessing whether there is a right to education explicitly or implicitly guaranteed by the Constitution.

Education, of course, is not among the rights afforded explicit protection under our Federal Constitution. Nor do we find any basis for saying it is implicitly so protected. As we have said, the undisputed importance of education will not alone cause this Court to depart from the usual standard for reviewing a State's social and economic legislation. It is appellees' contention, however, that education is distinguishable from other services and benefits provided by the State because it bears a peculiarly close relationship to other rights and liberties accorded protection under the Constitution. Specifically, they insist that education is itself a fundamental personal right because it is essential to the effective exercise of First Amendment freedoms and to intelligent utilization of the right to vote. In asserting a nexus between speech and education, appellees urge that the right to speak is meaningless unless the speaker is capable of articulating his thoughts intelligently and persuasively. The "marketplace of ideas" is an empty forum for those lacking basic communicative tools. Likewise, they argue that the corollary right to receive information becomes little more than a hollow privilege when the recipient has not been taught to read, assimilate, and utilize available knowledge.

A similar line of reasoning is pursued with respect to the right to vote. Exercise of the franchise, it is contended, cannot be divorced from the educational foundation of the voter. The electoral process, if reality is to conform to the democratic ideal, depends on an informed electorate: a voter cannot cast his ballot intelligently unless his reading skills and thought processes have been adequately developed.

We . . . have never presumed to possess either the ability or the authority to guarantee to the citizenry the most *effective* speech or the most *informed* electoral choice. That these may be desirable goals of a system of freedom of expression and of a representative form of government is not to be doubted. . . . But they are not values to be implemented by judicial intrusion into otherwise legitimate state activities.

Even if it were conceded that some identifiable quantum of education is a constitutionally protected prerequisite to the meaningful exercise of either right, we have no indication that the present levels of educational expenditure in Texas provide an education that falls short. Whatever merit appellees' argument might have if a State's financial scheme occasioned an absolute denial of educational opportunities to any of its children, that argument provides

no basis for finding an interference with fundamental rights where only relative differences in spending levels are involved and where—as is true in the present case—no charge fairly could be made that the system fails to provide each child with an opportunity to acquire the basic minimal skills necessary for the enjoyment of the rights of speech and of full participation in the political process.

Furthermore, the logical limitations on appellees' nexus theory are difficult to perceive. How, for instance, is education to be distinguished from the significant personal interests in the basics of decent food and shelter? Empirical examination might well buttress an assumption that the ill-fed, ill-clothed, and ill-housed are among the most ineffective participants in the political process, and that they derive the least enjoyment from the benefits of the First Amendment. If so, appellees' thesis would cast serious doubt on [previous] authority.

. . . The present case, in another basic sense, is significantly different from any of the cases in which the Court has applied strict scrutiny to state or federal legislation touching upon constitutionally protected rights. Each of our prior cases involved legislation which "deprived," "infringed," or "interfered" with the free exercise of some such fundamental personal right or liberty. A critical distinction between those cases and the one now before us lies in what Texas is endeavoring to do with respect to education. [As Justice Brennan observed in *Katzenbach v. Morgan:*]

> [I]n deciding the constitutional propriety of the limitations in such a reform measure we are guided by the familiar principles that a 'statute is not invalid under the Constitution because it might have gone farther than it did,' . . . that a legislature need not 'strike at all evils at the same time,' . . . and that 'reform may take one step at a time, addressing itself to the phase of the problem which seems most acute to the legislative mind . . .'"

. . .

It should be clear, for the reasons stated above and in accord with the prior decisions of this Court, that this is not a case in which the challenged state action must be subjected to the searching judicial scrutiny reserved for laws that create suspect classifications or impinge upon constitutionally protected rights.

We need not rest our decision, however, solely on the inappropriateness of the strict-scrutiny test. A century of Supreme Court adjudication under the Equal Protection Clause affirmatively supports the application of the traditional standard of review, which requires only that the State's system be shown to bear some rational relationship to legitimate state purposes. This case represents far more than a challenge to the manner in which Texas provides for the education of its children. We have here nothing less than a direct attack on the way in which Texas has chosen to raise and disburse state and local tax revenues. We are asked to condemn the State's judgment in conferring on political subdivisions the power to tax local property to supply revenues for local interests. In so doing, appellees would have the Court intrude in an area in which it has traditionally deferred to state legislatures. This Court has often admonished against such interferences with the State's fiscal policies under the Equal Protection Clause:

"The broad discretion as to classification possessed by a legislature in the field of taxation has long been recognized.... [The] passage of time has only served to underscore the wisdom of that recognition of the large area of discretion which is needed by a legislature in formulating sound tax policies.... It has ... been pointed out that in taxation, even more than in other fields, legislatures possess the greatest freedom in classification. Since the members of a legislature necessarily enjoy a familiarity with local conditions which this Court cannot have, the presumption of constitutionality can be overcome only by the most explicit demonstration that a classification is a hostile and oppressive discrimination against particular persons and classes...."

Madden v. Kentucky.

. . .

In addition to matters of fiscal policy, this case also involves the most persistent and difficult questions of educational policy, another area in which this Court's lack of specialized knowledge and experience counsels against premature interference with the informed judgments made at the state and local levels. Education, perhaps even more than welfare assistance, presents a myriad of "intractable economic, social, and even philosophical problems." The very complexity of the problems of financing and managing a statewide public school system suggests that "there will be more than one constitutionally permissible method of solving them," and that, within the limits of rationality, "the legislature's efforts to tackle the problems" should be entitled to respect. On even the most basic questions in this area the scholars and educational experts are divided. Indeed, one of the major sources of controversy concerns the extent to which there is a demon-

strable correlation between educational expenditures and the quality of education—an assumed correlation underlying virtually every legal conclusion drawn by the District Court in this case. Related to the questioned relationship between cost and quality is the equally unsettled controversy as to the proper goals of a system of public education. And the question regarding the most effective relationship between state boards of education and local school boards, in terms of their respective responsibilities and degrees of control, is now undergoing searching re-examination. The ultimate wisdom as to these and related problems of education is not likely to be divined for all time even by the scholars who now so earnestly debate the issues. In such circumstances, the judiciary is well advised to refrain from imposing on the States inflexible constitutional restraints that could circumscribe or handicap the continued research and experimentation so vital to finding even partial solutions to educational problems and to keeping abreast of ever-changing conditions.

It must be remembered, also, that every claim arising under the Equal Protection Clause has implications for the relationship between national and state power under our federal system. . . .

Reversed.

MR. JUSTICE STEWART, concurring.

. . .

Unlike other provisions of the Constitution, the Equal Protection Clause confers no substantive rights and creates no substantive liberties. The function of the Equal Protection Clause, rather, is simply to measure the validity of *classifications* created by state laws.

There is hardly a law on the books that does not affect some people differently than others. But the basic concern of the Equal Protection Clause is with the state legislation whose purpose or effect is to create discrete and objectively identifiable classes.... The Equal Protection Clause is offended only by laws that are invidiously discriminatory—only by classifications that are wholly arbitrary or capricious. . . .

MR. JUSTICE BRENNAN, dissenting.

Although I agree with my Brother WHITE that the Texas statutory scheme is devoid of any rational basis, and for that reason is violative of the Equal Protection Clause, I also record my disagreement with the Court's rather distressing assertion that a right may be deemed "fundamental" for the purposes of equal protection analysis only if it is "explicitly or implicitly guaranteed by the Constitution." As my Brother MARSHALL convincingly demonstrates, our prior cases stand for the proposition that "fundamentality" is, in large measure, a function of the right's importance in terms of the effectuation of those rights which are in fact constitutionally guaranteed. Thus, "[a]s the nexus between the specific constitutional guarantee and the nonconstitutional interest draws closer, the nonconstitutional interest becomes more fundamental and the degree of judicial scrutiny applied when the interest is infringed on a discriminatory basis must be adjusted accordingly."

Here, there can be no doubt that education is inextricably linked to the right to participate in the electoral process and to the rights of free speech and association guaranteed by the First Amendment. This being so, any classification affecting education must be subjected to strict judicial scrutiny, and since even the State concedes that the statutory scheme now before us cannot pass constitutional muster under this stricter standard of review, I can only conclude that the Texas school-financing scheme is constitutionally invalid.

MR. JUSTICE WHITE, with whom MR. JUSTICE DOUGLAS and MR. JUSTICE BRENNAN join, dissenting.

. . .

The Equal Protection Clause permits discriminations between classes but requires that the classification bear some rational relationship to a permissible object sought to be attained by the statute. It is not enough that the Texas system before us seeks to achieve the valid, rational purpose of maximizing local initiative; the means chosen by the State must also be rationally related to the end sought to be achieved. . . . [As the Court recognized in *Weber v. Casualty Surety Co.,*] "[T]his Court requires, at a minimum, that a statutory classification bear some rational relationship to a legitimate state purpose."

Neither Texas nor the majority heeds this rule. If the State aims at maximizing local initiative and local choice, by permitting school districts to resort to the real property tax if they choose to do so, it utterly fails in achieving its purpose in districts with property tax bases so low that there is little if any opportunity for interested parents, rich or poor, to augment school district revenues. Requiring the State to establish only that unequal treatment is in furtherance of a permissible goal, without also requiring the State to show that the means chosen to effectuate that goal are rationally re-

lated to its achievement, makes equal protection analysis no more than an empty gesture. In my view, the parents and children in Edgewood, and in like districts, suffer from an invidious discrimination violative of the Equal Protection Clause. . . .

MR. JUSTICE MARSHALL, with whom MR. JUSTICE DOUGLAS concurs, dissenting.

The Court today decides, in effect, that a State may constitutionally vary the quality of education which it offers its children in accordance with the amount of taxable wealth located in the school districts within which they reside. . . .

In my judgment, the right of every American to an equal start in life, so far as the provision of a state service as important as education is concerned, is far too vital to permit state discrimination on grounds as tenuous as those presented by this record. Nor can I accept the notion that it is sufficient to remit these appellees to the vagaries of the political process which, contrary to the majority's suggestion, has proved singularly unsuited to the task of providing a remedy for this discrimination. I for one, am unsatisfied with the hope of an ultimate "political" solution sometime in the indefinite future while, in the meantime, countless children unjustifiably receive inferior educations that "may affect their hearts and minds in a way unlikely ever to be undone." I must therefore respectfully dissent.

II

By [utilizing] nothing more than that lenient standard of rationality which we have traditionally applied to discriminatory state action in the context of economic and commercial matters . . . the Court avoids the telling task of searching for a substantial state interest which the Texas financing scheme, with its variations in taxable district property wealth, is necessary to further. I cannot accept such an emasculation of the Equal Protection Clause in the contest of this case [and must once more voice my disagreement with] the Court's rigidified approach to equal protection analysis. . . . A principled reading of what this Court has done reveals that it has applied a spectrum of standards in reviewing discrimination allegedly violative of the Equal Protection Clause.

Plyler v. Doe
457 U.S. 202 (1982)

JUSTICE BRENNAN delivered the opinion of the Court.

The question presented by these cases is

whether, consistent with the Equal Protection Clause of the Fourteenth Amendment, Texas may deny to undocumented school-age children the free public education that it provides to children who are citizens of the United States or legally admitted aliens.

I

Since the late 19th century, the United States has restricted immigration into this country. Unsanctioned entry into the United States is a crime, and those who have entered unlawfully are subject to deportation. But despite the existence of these legal restrictions, a substantial number of persons have succeeded in unlawfully entering the United States, and now live within various States, including the State of Texas.

In May 1975, the Texas Legislature revised its education laws to withhold from local school districts any state funds for the education of children who were not "legally admitted" into the United States. The 1975 revision also authorized local school districts to deny enrollment in their public schools to children not "legally admitted" to the country. These cases involve constitutional challenges to those provisions.

The Fourteenth Amendment provides that "[no] State shall . . . deprive any person of life, liberty, or property, without due process of law; nor deny to any person within its jurisdiction the equal protection of the laws." Appellants argue at the outset that undocumented aliens, because of their immigration status, are not "persons within the jurisdiction" of the State of Texas, and that they therefore have no right to the equal protection of Texas law. We reject this argument. Whatever his status under the immigration laws, an alien is surely a "person" in any ordinary sense of that term. Aliens, even aliens whose presence in this country is unlawful, have long been recognized as "persons" guaranteed due process of law by the Fifth and Fourteenth Amendments.

. . .

To permit a State to employ the phrase "within its jurisdiction" in order to identify subclasses of persons whom it would define as beyond its jurisdiction, thereby relieving itself of the obligation to assure that its laws are designed and applied equally to those persons, would undermine the principal purpose for which the Equal Protection Clause was incorporated in the Fourteenth Amendment. The Equal Protection Clause was intended to work nothing less than the abolition of all caste-based and invidious class-based legislation. That objective is fundamentally at odds with the power the State asserts here to classify persons subject to its laws as nonetheless excepted from its protection.

. . .

Sheer incapability or lax enforcement of the laws barring entry into this country, coupled with the failure to establish an effective bar to the employment of undocumented aliens, has resulted in the creation of a substantial "shadow population" of illegal migrants—numbering in the millions—within our borders. This situation raises the specter of a permanent caste of undocumented resident aliens, encouraged by some to remain here as a source of cheap labor, but nevertheless denied the benefits that our society makes available to citizens and lawful residents. The existence of such an underclass presents most difficult problems for a Nation that prides itself on adherence to principles of equality under law.

The children who are plaintiffs in these cases are special members of this underclass. Persuasive arguments support the view that a State may withhold its beneficence from those whose very presence within the United States is the product of their own unlawful conduct. These arguments do not apply with the same force to classifications imposing disabilities on the minor *children* of such illegal entrants. At the least, those who elect to enter our territory by stealth and in violation of our law should be prepared to bear the consequences, including, but not limited to, deportation. But the children of those illegal entrants are not comparably situated. Their "parents have the ability to conform their conduct to societal norms," and presumably the ability to remove themselves from the State's jurisdiction; but the children who are plaintiffs in these cases "can affect neither their parents' conduct nor their own status." Even if the State found it expedient to control the conduct of adults by acting against their children, legislation directing the onus of a parent's misconduct against his children does not comport with fundamental conceptions of justice.

"[Visiting] . . . condemnation on the head of an infant is illogical and unjust. Moreover, imposing disabilities on the . . . child is contrary to the basic concept of our system that legal burdens should bear some relationship to individual responsibility or wrongdoing. Obviously, no child is responsible for his birth and penalizing the . . . child is an ineffectual—as well as unjust—way of deterring the parent."

Public education is not a "right" granted to individuals by the Constitution. But neither is it merely some governmental "benefit" indistinguishable from other forms of social welfare legislation. Both the importance of education in maintaining our basic institutions, and the lasting impact of its deprivation on the life of the child, mark the distinction. . . . We cannot ignore the significant social costs borne by our Nation when select groups are denied the means to absorb the values and skills upon which our social order rests.

In addition to the pivotal role of education in sustaining our political and cultural heritage, denial of education to some isolated group of children poses an affront to one of the goals of the Equal Protection Clause: the abolition of governmental barriers presenting unreasonable obstacles to advancement on the basis of individual merit. Paradoxically, by depriving the children of any disfavored group of an education, we foreclose the means by which that group might raise the level of esteem in which it is held by the majority. But more directly, "education prepares individuals to be self-reliant and self-sufficient participants in society." Illiteracy is an enduring disability. The inability to read and write will handicap the individual deprived of a basic education each and every day of his life. The inestimable toll of that deprivation on the social, economic, intellectual, and psychological well-being of the individual, and the obstacle it poses to individual achievement, make it most difficult to reconcile the cost or the principle of a status-based denial of basic education with the framework of equality embodied in the Equal Protection Clause.

These well-settled principles allow us to determine the proper level of deference to be afforded [this provision]. Undocumented aliens cannot be treated as a suspect class because their presence in this country in violation of federal law is not a "constitutional irrelevancy." Nor is education a fundamental right; a State need not justify by compelling necessity every variation in the manner in which education is provided to its population. But more is involved in these cases than the abstract question whether [the provision] discriminates against a suspect class, or whether education is a fundamental right. [The statute] imposes a lifetime hardship on a discrete class of children not accountable for their disabling status. The stigma of illiteracy will mark them for the rest of their lives. By denying these children a basic education, we deny them the ability to live within the structure of our civic institutions, and foreclose any realistic possibility that they will contribute in even the smallest way to the progress of our Nation. In determining the [statute's] rationality, we may appropriately take into account its costs to the Nation and to the innocent children who are its victims. In light of these countervailing costs, the discrimination contained can hardly be considered rational unless it furthers some substantial goal of the State.

IV

It is the State's principal argument, and apparently the view of the dissenting Justices, that the undocumented status of these children vel non establishes a sufficient rational basis for denying them benefits that a State might choose to afford other residents. The State notes that while other aliens are admitted "on an equality of legal privileges with all citizens under non-discriminatory laws," the asserted right of these children to an education can claim no implicit congressional imprimatur. Indeed, in the State's view, Congress' apparent disapproval of the presence of these children within the United States, and the evasion of the federal regulatory program that is the mark of undocumented status, provides authority for its decision to impose upon them special disabilities. Faced with an equal protection challenge respecting the treatment of aliens, we agree that the courts must be attentive to congressional policy; the exercise of congressional power might well affect the State's prerogatives to afford differential treatment to a particular class of aliens. But we are unable to find in the congressional immigration scheme any statement of policy that might weigh significantly in arriving at an equal protection balance concerning the State's authority to deprive these children of an education.

The Constitution grants Congress the power to "establish an uniform Rule of Naturalization." Art. I., § 8, cl. 4. Drawing upon this power, upon its plenary authority with respect to foreign relations and international commerce, and upon the inherent power of a sovereign to close its borders, Congress has developed a complex scheme governing admission to our Nation and status within our borders. The obvious need for delicate policy judgments has counseled the Judicial Branch to avoid intrusion into this field. But . . . the States enjoy no power with respect to the classification of aliens. This power is "committed to the political branches of the Federal Government." Although it is "a routine and normally legitimate part" of the business of the Federal Government to classify on the basis of alien status and to "take into account the character of the relationship between the alien and this country," only rarely are such matters relevant to legislation by a State.

To be sure, like all persons who have entered the United States unlawfully, these children are subject to deportation. But there is no assurance that a child subject to deportation will ever be deported. An illegal entrant might be granted federal permission to continue to reside in this country, or even to become a citizen. In light of the discretionary federal power to grant relief from deportation, a State cannot realistically determine that any particular undocumented child will in fact be deported until after deportation proceedings have been completed. It would of course be most difficult for the State to justify a denial of education to a child enjoying an inchoate federal permission to remain.

We are reluctant to impute to Congress the intention to withhold from these children, for so long as they are present in this country through no fault of their own, access to a basic education. In other contexts, undocumented status, coupled with some articulable federal policy, might enhance state authority with respect to the treatment of undocumented aliens. But in the area of special constitutional sensitivity presented by these cases, and in the absence of any contrary indication fairly discernible in the present legislative record, we perceive no national policy that supports the State in denying these children an elementary education. The State may borrow the federal classification. But to justify its use as a criterion for its own discriminatory policy, the State must demonstrate that the classification is reasonably adapted to the purposes for which the state desires to use it.

V

Appellants argue that the classification at issue furthers an interest in the "preservation of the state's limited resources for the education of its lawful residents." Of course, a concern for the preservation of resources standing alone can hardly justify the classification used in allocating those resources. The State must do more than justify its classification with a concise expression of an intention to discriminate. Apart from the asserted state prerogative to act against undocumented children solely on the basis of their undocumented status—an asserted prerogative that carries only minimal force in the circumstances of these cases—we discern three colorable state interests.

First, appellants appear to suggest that the State may seek to protect itself from an influx of illegal immigrants. While a State might have an interest in mitigating the potentially harsh economic effects of sudden shifts in population, [the statute] hardly offers an effective method of dealing with an urgent demographic or economic problem. There is no evidence in the record suggesting that illegal entrants impose any significant burden on the State's economy. To the contrary, the available evidence suggests that illegal aliens underutilize public services, while contributing their labor to the local economy and tax money to the state fisc. The dominant incentive for illegal entry into the State of Texas is the availability of employment; few if any illegal immigrants come to this country, or presumably to the State of Texas, in order to avail themselves of a free education. Thus, even making the doubtful assumption that the net impact of illegal aliens on the economy of the State is negative, we think it clear that "[charging] tuition to undocumented children constitutes a ludicrously ineffectual attempt to stem the tide of illegal immigration," at least when compared with the alternative of prohibiting the employment of illegal aliens.

Second, while it is apparent that a State may "not . . . reduce expenditures for education by barring [some] arbitrarily chosen class of children from its schools," appellants suggest that undocumented children are appropriately singled out for exclusion because of the special burdens they impose on the State's ability to provide high-quality public education. But the record in no way supports the claim that exclusion of undocumented children is likely to improve the overall quality of education in the State. In terms of educational cost and need, however, undocumented children are "basically indistinguishable" from legally resident alien children.

Finally, appellants suggest that undocumented children are appropriately singled out because their unlawful presence within the United States renders them less likely than other children to remain within the boundaries of the State, and to put their education to productive social or political use within the State. Even assuming that such an interest is legitimate, it is an interest that is most difficult to quantify. The State has no assurance that any child, citizen or not, will employ the education provided by the State within the confines of the State's borders. In any event, the record is clear that many of the undocumented children disabled by this classification will remain in this country indefinitely, and that some will become lawful residents or citizens of the United States. It is difficult to understand precisely what the State hopes to achieve by promoting the creation and perpetuation of a subclass of illiterates within our boundaries, surely adding to the problems and costs of unemployment, welfare, and crime. It is thus clear that whatever savings might be achieved by denying these children an education, they are wholly insubstantial in light of the costs involved to these children, the State, and the Nation.

VI

If the State is to deny a discrete group of innocent children the free public education that it offers to other children residing within its borders, that denial must be justified by a showing that it furthers some substantial state interest. No such showing was made here. Accordingly, the judgment of the Court of Appeals in each of these cases is

Affirmed.

JUSTICE MARSHALL, concurring.

While I join the Court opinion, I do so without in any way retreating from my opinion in *San Antonio Independent School District v. Rodriguez,* I continue to believe that an individual's interest in education is fundamental, and that this view is amply supported "by the unique status accorded public education by our society, and by the close relationship between education and some of our most basic constitutional values." Furthermore, I believe that the facts of these cases demonstrate the wisdom of rejecting a rigidified approach to equal protection analysis, and of employing an approach that allows for varying levels of scrutiny depending upon "the constitutional and societal importance of the interest adversely affected and the recognized invidiousness of the basis upon which the particular classification is drawn."

JUSTICE BLACKMUN, concurring.

I join the opinion and judgment of the Court. Like JUSTICE POWELL, I believe that the children involved in this litigation "should not be left on the streets uneducated." . . . I write separately, however, because in my view the nature of the interest at stake is crucial to the proper resolution of these cases. . . .

I joined JUSTICE POWELL's opinion in *Rodriguez* and I continue to believe that it provides the appropriate model for resolving most equal protection disputes. [However] I believe the Court's experience has demonstrated that the *Rodriguez* formulation does not settle every issue of "fundamental" rights arising under the Equal Protection Clause. Only a pendant would insist that there are *no* meaningful distinctions among the multitude of social and political interests regulated by the States, and *Rodriguez* does not stand for quite so absolute a proposition. . . .

In my view when the State provides an education for some and denies it to others, it immediately and inevitably creates class distinctions of a type fundamentally inconsistent with . . . the Equal Protection Clause. In a sense .. the denial of an education is the analogue of denial of the right to vote. This conclusion is fully consistent with *Rodriguez.*

JUSTICE POWELL, concurring.

Although the analogy is not perfect, our holding today does find support in decisions of this Court with respect to the status of illegitimates. In *Weber v. Aetna Casualty & Surety Co,* we said: "visiting . . . condemnation on the head of an infant" for the misdeeds of the parents is illogical, unjust, and "contrary to the basic concept of our system that legal burdens should bear some relationship to individual responsibility or wrongdoing."

. . .

In my view, the State's denial of education to these children bears no substantial relation to any substantial state interest. . . . [I]t hardly can be argued rationally that anyone benefits from the creation within our borders of a subclass of illiterate alien persons many of whom will remain in the State, adding to the problems and costs of both State and National Governments attendant upon employment, welfare and crime.

[JUSTICES BURGER, WHITE, REHNQUIST and O'CONNOR dissent, arguing for a rationality review in this case since concededly no suspect class or fundamental right is present].

In *Martinez v. Bynum*[328] the Court rejected a challenge to a state law denying tuition-free admission to a local public school to students living in the district without parents or guardians for the primary purpose of attending school. The Court found the law to be a bona fide residence requirement which did not burden the right of interstate travel.

San Antonio v. Rodriguez seeks to distinguish education and other "non fundamental" though important rights from those rights protected because of implicit or explicit constitutional guarantees. Doesn't the Court's willingness to find constitutional support for protecting voting and rejection of education suggest more discretion in "finding" constitutional guarantees than the Court suggests? Notably, the Court seeks (weakly) to make a distinction between *Plyler* and *Rodriguez* on the basis that a complete denial of an important (though "non fundamental") right to some groups warrants scrutiny

---

[328] 461 U.S. 321 (1983).

which is not called for where some opportunity to enjoy the right exists. Scholars have noted that the rationale of *Rodriguez*, if logically extended and consistently applied would result in disqualification of other well settled guarantees like the right to travel, procreation and privacy.[329] On the other hand, education has been analogized to other services for which we have not imposed a governmental obligation to dispense equally.[330]

---

[329] *See, e.g.,* Goodpaster, *The Constitution and Fundamental Rights,* 15 ARIZ. 479, 502 (1973).

[330] *See* Philip Kurland, *Equal Educational Opportunity: The Limits of Constitutional Jurisprudence Undefined,* 35 U. CHI. L. REV. 583 (1968).

PART V

THE FIRST AMENDMENT

A. Freedom of Speech and Association

The First Amendment's simple mandate, "Congress shall make no law . . . abridging the freedom of speech," leaves wide latitude for interpretation. Scholars have debated not only what the purpose of the First Amendment should be, but also what the intent of its framers was. Historical evidence regarding the eighteenth century understanding of freedom of expression has yielded divergent conclusions. Indeed, one of the most prominent First Amendment historians, Leonard Levy, has himself changed his views concerning the extent of early Americans' respect for freedom of speech. In *Legacy of Suppression: Freedom of Speech and Press in Early American History*, published in 1960, Levy challenged the conventional wisdom that the First Amendment was intended to abolish the English common law suppression of dissent and to protect citizens' freedom of expression. Rather, Levy concluded that numerous seditious speech prosecutions during the seventeenth century left colonists with little experience of liberty of expression. The framers, therefore, had a very limited view of freedom of expression, understanding it to mean only freedom from prior restraint; their rejection of the doctrine of seditious libel did not occur until the battle over the Sedition Act of 1798, seven years *after* the First Amendment was ratified. Levy argued further that the First Amendment was intended as a restraint on Congress that reserved the regulation of speech and press to the states, rather than as a guarantee of free expression. Thus, the First Amendment, according to Levy, "was motivated far less by a desire to give immunity to political expression than by a solicitude for states' rights and the federal principle."[1]

Two decades later, Levy revised his assessment, conceding that "Americans respected freedom of expression far more than theoreticians and legalists acknowledged before 1798."[2] More recent historical investigation has revealed a dramatic expansion of the colonists' freedom to criticize government by the end of the seventeenth century.[3] This growth in freedom of speech established the foundation for eighteenth-century dissent against English authority, as well as the First Amendment's intellectual justification. Although colonial Americans may not have expected the legal right to free expression we value today, they were accustomed to robust and uninhibited political discourse, especially in the press.

Other scholars have argued that the First Amendment incorporated the framers' vision of freedom of speech as a critical piece of the democratic structure established by the Constitution. Under a civil republican view, associated with Thomas Jefferson, free speech is the foundation for self-government, ensuring the ability of citizens to fulfill their decisionmaking role as the true rulers of a democracy.[4] Intelligent determi-

---

[1] Leonard Levy, Introduction, FREEDOM OF PRESS FROM ZENGER to JEFFERSON lix (Leonard Levy ed. 1966).

[2] LEONARD LEVY, EMERGENCE OF A FREE PRESS xi (1985). *See also* Leonard W. Levy, *The Legacy Reexamined*, 37 STAN. L. REV. 767 (1985).

[3] LARRY D. ELDRIDGE, A DISTANT HERITAGE: THE GROWTH OF FREE SPEECH IN EARLY AMERICA (1994).

[4] ALEXANDER MEIKLEJOHN, FREE SPEECH AND ITS RELATION TO SELF-GOVERNMENT (1948); Owen M. Fiss, *Why the State?*, 100 HARV. L. REV. 781 (1987); Cass R. Sunstein, *Free Speech Now*, 59 U. CHI. L. REV. 255 (1992).

nation of public issues by citizens, as envisioned by the Constitution's democratic structure, requires widespread and informed popular deliberation. In addition, James Madison advocated the "American idea" of speech that ensures limitations and dispersals of the government's power over expression in response to the people's distrust of concentrated power.[5] In Madison's words, "[T]he censorial power is in the people over the Government, and not the Government over the people."[6]

There is also evidence that the Framers intended that the free exchange of ideas among citizens would serve as a check against government abuses. A letter of the Continental Congress to the inhabitants of Quebec in 1774 stated this objective:

> The last right we shall mention, regards the freedom of the press. The importance of this consists, besides the advancement of truth, science, morality, and arts in general, in its diffusion of liberal sentiments on the administration of Government, its ready communication of thoughts between subjects, and its consequential promotion of union among them, whereby oppressive officers are shamed or intimidated, into more honourable and just modes of conducting affairs.[7]

Until very recently, First Amendment scholars devoted little attention to the period between the Sedition Act of 1798 and the Espionage Act of 1917. The Supreme Court did not begin developing a clear First Amendment jurisprudence until the turn of this century. Part of the reason was that the Court did not hold that the Fourteenth Amendment made the First Amendment applicable to the states until its 1925 decision in *Gitlow v. New York*.[8] The Court of the nineteenth-century understood the First Amendment to restrain only the exercise of power by the *federal* government.[9] The states therefore remained free from federal constitutional limits to restrict speech according to their own laws and common law principles. During the nineteenth century, states and municipalities brutally suppressed the speech of abolitionists, Civil War protesters, labor reformers, anarchists, and other political dissenters. There was no freedom of expression for freed slaves in the South. The Supreme Court rarely scrutinized federal restraints on speech, as well, prior to World War I.

In *Patterson v. Colorado*, decided in 1907, the Court upheld the criminal contempt conviction of the Democratic editor-in-chief of two newspapers which condemned in a series of articles, cartoons, and editorials the Republican judges on the Colorado Supreme Court for their invalidation of amendments to the state constitution.[10] Justice Holmes explained that the Fourteenth Amendment did not limit the state's punishment of contempt, nor did the First Amendment apply to Patterson's conviction:

> We leave undecided the question whether there is to be found in the Fourteenth Amendment a prohibition similar to that in the First. But even if we were to assume that freedom of speech and freedom of press were protected from abridgment on the part not only of the United States but also of the States, still we should be far from the conclusion that the plaintiff in error would have

---

[5] William T. Mayton, *Seditious Libel and the Lost Guarantee of a Freedom of Expression*, 84 COLUM. L. REV. 91 (1984); William T. Mayton, *From a Legacy of Suppression to the "Metaphor of the Fourth Estate,"* 39 STAN. L. REV. 139 (1986).

[6] 4 ANNALS OF CONGRESS 934 (1794), quoted in New York Times v. Sullivan, 376 U.S. 254, 275 (1964).

[7] 1 JOURNALS OF THE CONTINENTAL CONGRESS 108 (1774), quoted in Roth v. United States, 354 U.S. 476, 484 (1957).

[8] Gitlow v. New York, 268 U.S. 652 (1925).

[9] *See* United States v. Cruikshank, 92 U.S. 542 (1875).

[10] Patterson v. Colorado, 205 U.S. 454 (1907).

us reach. In the first place, the main purpose of such constitutional provisions is "to prevent all such *previous restraints* upon publications as had been practiced by other governments," and they do not prevent the subsequent punishment of such as may be deemed contrary to the public welfare.

Justice Harlan disagreed with both the Court's refusal to extend the protection of speech to the states and its limited understanding of the First Amendment.

As the First Amendment guaranteed the rights of free speech and of free press against hostile action by the United States, it would seem clear that when the Fourteenth Amendment prohibited the States from impairing or abridging the privileges of citizens of the United States it necessarily prohibited the States from impairing or abridging the constitutional rights of such citizens to free speech and press. But the court announces that it leaves undecided [that] specific question. . . . It yet proceeds to say that the main purpose of such constitutional provisions was to prevent all such *"previous* restraints." . . . I cannot assent to that view, if it be meant that the legislature may impair or abridge the rights of a free press and of free speech whenever it thinks that the public welfare requires that to be done. The public welfare cannot override constitutional privileges, and if the rights of free speech and press are, in their essence, attributes of national citizenship, as I think they are, then neither Congress nor any State since the adoption of the Fourteenth Amendment can, by legislative enactments or by judicial action, impair or abridge them.

The experience of state government suppression of dissident speech began to transform the Court's understanding of the First Amendment as simply a restraint on federal power. The incorporation of the First Amendment in 1925 reflected the perspective gained during Reconstruction that local majorities could be as just as dangerous to free expression as federal abuses of state interests.

The gloss of the Fourteenth Amendment experience on the First Amendment text has important doctrinal implications. As the paradigmatic speech in need of constitutional protection shifts from a localist criticizing the central government to a Unionist defending its Reconstruction policies, carpetbagging federal judges appointed in Washington, D.C. become more trustworthy guardians of First Amendment freedoms than localist juries.[11]

When Professor Zechariah Chafee published the first treatise devoted to freedom of speech in 1920, he commented, "[t]he cases are too few, too varied in their character and often too easily solved, to develop any definite boundary between lawful and unlawful speech. . . . Nearly every free speech decision . . . appears to have been decided largely by intuition."[12] The Court itself declared, "[n]o important case involving free speech was decided by this Court prior to *Schenck v. United*."[13] The justices began crafting a body of First Amendment principles in 1919 as if the Court had remained silent on freedom of speech for one hundred and twenty years.[14]

Recently First Amendment scholars have challenged Chafee's assessment of the paucity of free speech precedents. They have uncovered a substantial body of litigation, legal scholarship, and organized defense of free speech arising from a variety of contro-

---

[11] Akhil Reed Amar, *The Bill of Rights*, 101 YALE L.J. 1193, 1280 (1992).

[12] ZECHARIAH CHAFEE, FREEDOM OF SPEECH 16 (1920).

[13] Dennis v. United States, 341 U.S. 494, 494 (1951).

[14] *See* Michael T. Gibson, *The Supreme Court and Freedom of Expression from 1791 to 1917*, 55 FORDHAM L. REV. 263 (1986).

versies in the generation before World War I.[15] Although the Supreme Court decided few First Amendment cases during this period, its postwar decisions were issued in a context of intense debate about the meaning of freedom of speech. Libertarians organized opposition to censorship imposed by the Comstock Act, passed by Congress in 1873, that prohibited circulation of obscene materials through the mails, and prosecutions of anarchist speech following an anarchist's assassination of President McKinley in 1901. The Free Speech League, founded in 1902 and incorporated in 1911, advocated a theory of free speech for all viewpoints and aided a variety of activists in trouble for their dissident speech. The Free Speech League declared that it was committed "to maintain the right of free speech against all encroachments" and opposed "every form of governmental censorship over any method for the expression, communication or transmission of ideas, whether by use of previous inhibition or subsequent punishment."[16] The Free Speech League never garnered widespread support for its position, but its literature, demonstrations, lectures, and court battles reached a substantial audience during the first two decades of the twentieth century.

1. Punishing Harmful Speech

A major part of First Amendment interpretation involves identifying speech that the Constitution does *not* protect. The Supreme Court has recognized that the government may punish some types of speech because of their content. These categories of speech—advocacy of illegal action, libel, obscenity, and fighting words—fall outside the usual constitutional safeguards because their messages cause social harm. At the same time, the Court has grappled with defining these categories narrowly enough to avoid punishment of protected speech based on official disagreement with its message. Does a dissident's advocacy of radical social change constitute punishable incitement of illegal action or protected political speech? When should false and defamatory publications be subject to a libel judgment or be constitutionally privileged? Does the state's ban on sexually explicit material represent its legitimate concern for public morality or an illegitimate enforcement of an official viewpoint? When do hostile communications inflict socially worthless "verbal assaults" and when do they merely express offensive ideas?

a. Advocacy of Illegal Action

America's intervention in World War I propelled the Court into serious consideration of the First Amendment's protection of political dissent. America's war effort led to the massive use of federal power to restrict expression. The Espionage Act of 1917 made it a crime to obstruct the draft or to cause, or attempt to cause, insubordination in the military. Socialists and conscientious objectors were arrested for distributing literature and making speeches that opposed involvement in the war on the ground that they violated the Espionage Act. These cases raised the question whether their opposition to the war constituted advocacy protected by the First Amendment or unprotected incitement of illegal action.

One possibility was to analyze these cases under the criminal law of attempt, rather than the First Amendment. A criminal attempt to interfere with the war effort would

---

[15] MARK A. GRABER, TRANSFORMING FREE SPEECH: THE AMBIGUOUS LEGACY OF CIVIL LIBERTARIANISM (1991); Alexis J. Alexander, *The Formative Period of First Amendment Theory, 1870–1915*, 24 AM. J.L. HIST. 56 (1980); David M. Rabban, *The First Amendment in Its Forgotten Years*, 90 YALE L.J. 514 (1981); David M. Rabban, *The Emergence of Modern First Amendment Doctrine*, 50 U. CHI. L. REV. 1205 (1983); David M. Rabban, *The Free Speech League, the ACLU, and Changing Conceptions of Free Speech in American History*, 45 STAN. L. REV. 47 (1992).

[16] Rabban, The Free Speech League, *Supra* note 15, at 72, 80.

be punishable, despite the defendant's use of speech to accomplish his aim. At that time, speech constituted a criminal attempt if its natural and reasonable tendency was to bring about the illegal result. At the same time, a generation of constitutional scholars and activists prior to World War I had debated the extent of freedom of expression and produced a strong defense of radical libertarian protection for political speech. The American Union Against Militarism, founded in 1917, established a national Civil Liberties Bureau to defend the free speech rights of conscientious objectors, which became the American Civil Liberties Union in 1920. A zealous proponent of the absolutist position was the activist Theodore Schroeder, secretary of the Free Speech League, and author of *"Obscene" Literature and Constitutional Law: A Forensic Defense of Freedom of The Press* (1911) and *Free Speech for Radicals* (1916). Schroeder argued that the First Amendment protected seditious advocacy, including socialist dogma, and asked rhetorically, "Can a man under our Constitution guaranteeing liberty of speech and press be properly punished for his fruitless advocacy of crime?"[17]

In *Schenck v. United States*, a unanimous Court easily upheld the conviction of the general secretary of the Socialist Party for conspiring to violate the Espionage Act by distributing antiwar leaflets to enlisted men.

---

[17] Theodore Schroeder, *On Suppressing the Advocacy of Crime*, 1 MOTHER EARTH 7, 13 (Jan., 1907); Theodore Schroeder, *Historical Interpretation of Freedom of Speech and of the Press*, 70 CENT. L.J. 184, 185 (1910).

Schenck v. United States
249 U.S. 47 (1919)

MR. JUSTICE HOLMES delivered the opinion of the court.

. . .

According to the testimony Schenck said he was general secretary of the Socialist party and had charge of the Socialist headquarters from which the documents were sent. He identified a book found there as the minutes of the Executive Committee of the party. The book showed a resolution of August 13, 1917, that 15,000 leaflets should be printed on the other side of one of them in use, to be mailed to men who had passed exemption boards, and for distribution. Schenck personally attended to the printing. On August 20 the general secretary's report said "Obtained new leaflets from printer and started work addressing envelopes" &c.; and there was a resolve that Comrade Schenck be allowed $125 for sending leaflets through the mail. He said that he had about fifteen or sixteen thousand printed. There were files of the circular in question in the inner office which he said were printed on the other side of the one sided circular and were there for distribution. Other copies were proved to have been sent through the mails to drafted men. . . . The document in question upon its first printed side recited the first section of the Thirteenth Amendment, said that the idea embodied in it was violated by the Conscription Act and that a conscript is little better than a convict. In impassioned language it intimated that conscription was despotism in its worst form and a monstrous wrong against humanity in the interest of Wall Street's chosen few. It said "Do not submit to intimidation," but in form at least confined itself to peaceful measures such as a petition for the repeal of the act. The other and later printed side of the sheet was headed "Assert Your Rights." It stated reasons for alleging that any one violated the Constitution when he refused to recognize "your right to assert your opposition to the draft," and went on "If you do not assert and support your rights, you are helping to deny or disparage rights which it is the solemn duty of all citizens and residents of the United States to retain." It described the arguments on the other side as coming from cunning politicians and a mercenary capitalist press, and even silent consent to the conscription law as helping to support an infamous conspiracy. It denied the power to send our citizens away to foreign shores to shoot up the people of other lands, and added that words could not express the condemnation such cold-blooded ruthlessness deserves, &c., &c., winding up "You must do your share to maintain, support and uphold the rights of the people of this country." Of course the documents would not have been sent unless it had been intended to have some effect, and we do not see what effect it could be expected to have upon persons subject to the draft except to influence them to obstruct the carrying of it out. The defendants do not deny that the jury might find against them on this point.

But it is said, suppose that was the tendency of this circular, it is protected by the First Amendment to the Constitution. Two of the strongest expressions are said to be quoted respectively from well-known public men. It well may be that the prohibition of laws abridging the freedom of speech is not confined to previous restraints, although to prevent them may have been the main purpose, as intimated in *Patterson v. Colorado.* We admit that in many places and in ordinary times the defendants in saying all that was said in the circular would have been within their constitutional rights. But the character of every act depends upon the circumstances in which it is done. The most stringent protection of free speech would not protect a man in falsely shouting fire in a theater and causing a panic. It does not even protect a man from an injunction against uttering words that may have all the effect of force. The question in every case is whether the words used are used in such circumstances and are of such a nature as to create a clear and present danger that they will bring about the substantive evils that Congress has a right to prevent. It is a question of proximity and degree. When a nation is at war many things that might be said in time of peace are such a hindrance to its effort that their utterance will not be endured so long as men fight and that no Court could regard them as protected by any constitutional right. It seems to be admitted that if an actual obstruction of the recruiting service were proved, liability for words that produced that effect might be enforced. The statute of 1917 in § 4 punishes conspiracies to obstruct as well as actual obstruction. If the act, (speaking, or circulating a paper,) its tendency and the intent with which it is done are the same, we perceive no ground for saying that success alone warrants making the act a crime. . . .

Judgments affirmed.

The Court also affirmed the convictions under the Espionage Act of anti-war protesters in two companion cases, *Debs v. United States,*[18] and *Frohwerk v. United States.*[19] *Debs* involved the conviction of Eugene V. Debs, a Socialist leader who ran for President from jail in 1920, for an antiwar speech. To put the case in historical perspective, Harry Kalven later observed that the conviction of Debs was "somewhat as though George McGovern had been sent to prison for his criticism of the [Vietnam] war."[20] (A more contemporary analogy might be the imprisonment of Jerry Brown for his opposition to America's intervention in the Gulf War.) Holmes's opinion in *Debs* failed to employ the "clear and present danger" phrase, judging Debs's words by their "natural tendency and reasonably probable effect."

These three Espionage cases immediately sparked a debate among constitutional scholars and jurists about the amount of protection Holmes's clear and present danger test afforded political speech. In the first major law review article on the First Amendment, *Freedom of Speech in War Time*, Zechariah Chaffee applauded the clear and present danger test for prohibiting government from punishing speech for its "bad tendency" to produce unlawful acts.[21] Although it affirmed the convictions, moreover, the *Schenck* opinion acknowledged that the First Amendment protects more than prior restraints. Others, including Judge Learned Hand and Professor Ernst Freund, criticized Holmes's opinions for disregarding the value of political dissent in a democracy.[22] Theodore Schroeder of The Free Speech League later argued that "Holmes set the clock

---

[18] 249 U.S. 211 (1919).

[19] 249 U.S. 204 (1919).

[20] Harry Kalven, Jr., *Professor Ernst Freund and* Debs v. United States, 40 U. Chi. L. Rev. 235, 237 (1973).

[21] Zechariah Chafee, Jr., *Freedom of Speech in War Time*, 32 Harv. L. Rev. 932, 967 (1919).

[22] Harry Kalven, Jr., *Professor Ernst Freund and* Debs v. United States, 40 U. Chi. L. Rev. 235 (1973); Gerald Gunther, *Learned Hand and the Origins of Modern First Amendment Doctrine: Some Fragments of History*, 27 Stan. L. Rev. 719 (1975).

back many centuries by his 'clear and present danger' test of intellectual liberty."[23] Holmes, far from announcing a new, speech-protective standard, "simply continued the prewar reliance on the alleged 'bad tendency' of speech to justify its punishment."[24]

Two years prior to the *Schenck* decision, Judge Hand had construed the Espionage Act more narrowly in a case concerning the New York Postmaster's refusal to deliver a "revolutionary journal" called "The Masses" on the ground that it interfered with the war effort.[25] In *Masses Publishing Co. v. Patten*, Judge Hand preliminarily enjoined the Postmaster from excluding the journal from the mails. He held that the Espionage Act's prohibitions extended only to words "which have no purport but to counsel the violation of law," such as "language that directly advocated resistance to the draft"; the Act did not punish speech that did no more than "arouse a seditious disposition." Hand reasoned that the government's interpretation of the Act would justify suppression of all opinion criticizing government policies:

> ... It would contradict the normal assumption of democratic government that the suppression of hostile criticism does not turn upon the justice of its substance or the decency and propriety of its temper. Assuming that the power to repress such opinion may rest in Congress in the throes of a struggle for the very existence of the state, its exercise is so contrary to the use and wont of our people that only the clearest expression of such a power justified the conclusion that it was intended. ...
>
> ... Detestation of existing policies is easily transformed into forcible resistance of the authority which puts them in execution, and it would be folly to disregard the causal relation between the two. Yet to assimilate agitation, legitimate as such, with direct incitement to violent resistance, is to disregard the tolerance of all methods of political agitation which in normal times is a safeguard of free government.

Hand's decision was immediately reversed by the Second Circuit.

Eight months after his opinions in *Schenck, Debs, and Frohwerk*, Holmes took a striking turn in his understanding of freedom of speech. In *Abrams v. United States*, the Court upheld the convictions of five Bolshevik sympathizers under a 1918 amendment to the Espionage Act making it a crime to, among other things, urge curtailment of military production with intent to hinder the war effort with Germany. The defendants had printed in a basement in New York City 5000 leaflets in English and Yiddish opposing American intervention in Russia. They had thrown some of the leaflets from a window of a building where one of the defendants worked and distributed the rest in the city. Holmes wrote a passionate dissent, defending the defendants' freedom of speech.

Some commentators characterize Holmes's dissent as a conversion; others as an evolutionary step. Holmes may have been influenced by his correspondence with Learned Hand, from the summer of 1918 to the spring of 1921, in which Hand impressed upon Holmes the more tolerant approach to free speech Hand had expressed in his *Masses* opinion.[26] Whatever the explanation for the change in Holmes's perspective, his *Abrams* dissent provided a philosophical foundation for freedom of speech that influenced the development of First Amendment doctrine for years to come.

---

[23] RABBAN, THE FREE SPEECH LEAGUE 55, *quoting* Letter from Theodore Schroeder to Max Lerner (June 18, 1951).

[24] RABBAN, THE FREE SPEECH LEAGUE 50.

[25] Masses Publishing Co. v. Patten, 244 F. 535 (S.D.N.Y.), *rev'd*, 246 F. 24 (2d Cir. 1917).

[26] Gerald Gunther, *Learned Hand and the Origins of Modern First Amendment Doctrine: Some Fragments of History*, 27 STAN. L. REV. 719 (1975).

Abrams v. United States
250 U.S. 616 (1919)

Mr. Justice Clarke delivered the opinion of the court.

. . .

All of the five defendants were born in Russia. They were intelligent, had considerable schooling, and at the time they were arrested they had lived in the United States terms varying from five to ten years, but none of them had applied for naturalization. Four of them testified as witnesses in their own behalf and of these, three frankly avowed that they were "rebels," "revolutionists," "anarchists," that they did not believe in government in any form, and they declared that they had no interest whatever in the Government of the United States. The fourth defendant testified that he was a "socialist" and believed in "a proper kind of government, not capitalistic," but in his classification the Government of the United States was "capitalistic."

. . .

. . . [I]t is argued, somewhat faintly, that the acts charged against the defendants were not unlawful because within the protection of that freedom of speech and of the press which is guaranteed by the First Amendment to the Constitution of the United States, and that the entire Espionage Act is unconstitutional because in conflict with that Amendment.

This contention is sufficiently discussed and is definitely negatived in *Schenck v. United States* . . . and in *Frohwerk v. United States*.

. . .

The first of the two articles attached to the indictment is conspicuously headed, "The Hypocrisy of the United States and her Allies." After denouncing President Wilson as a hypocrite and a coward because troops were sent into Russia, it proceeds to assail our Government in general, saying:

"His [the President's] shameful, cowardly silence about the intervention in Russia reveals the hypocrisy of the plutocratic gang in Washington and vicinity."

It continues:

"He [the President] is too much of a coward to come out openly and say: 'We capitalistic nations cannot afford to have a proletarian republic in Russia.'"

Among the capitalistic nations Abrams testified the United States was included.

Growing more inflammatory as it proceeds, the circular culminates in:

"The Russian Revolution cries: Workers of the World! Awake! Rise! Put down your enemy and mine!

"Yes! friends, there is only one enemy of the workers of the world and that is CAPITALISM."

This is clearly an appeal to the "workers" of this country to arise and put down by force the Government of the United States which they characterize as their "hypocritical," "cowardly" and "capitalistic" enemy.

It concludes:

"Awake! Awake, you Workers of the World!

"REVOLUTIONISTS."

The second of the articles was printed in the Yiddish language and in the translation is headed, "Workers—Wake up." After referring to "his Majesty, Mr. Wilson, and the rest of the gang; dogs of all colors!", it continues:

"Workers, Russian emigrants, you who had the least belief in the honesty of *our* Government," which defendants admitted referred to the United States Government, "must now throw away all confidence, must spit in the face the false, hypocritic, military propaganda which has fooled you so relentlessly, calling forth your sympathy, your help, to the prosecution of the war."

The purpose of this obviously was to persuade the persons to whom it was addressed to turn a deaf ear to patriotic appeals in behalf of the Government of the United States, and to cease to render it assistance in the prosecution of the war.

It goes on:

"With the money which you have loaned, or are going to loan them, they will make bullets not only for the Germans, but also for the Workers Soviets of Russia. *Workers in the ammunition factories, you are producing bullets, bayonets, cannon, to murder not only the Germans, but also your dearest, best, who are in Russia and are fighting for freedom.*"

It will not do to say, as is now argued, that the only intent of these defendants was to prevent injury to the Russian cause. Men must be held to have intended, and to be accountable for, the effects which their acts were likely to produce. Even if their primary purpose and intent was to aid the cause of the Russian Revolution, the plan of action which they adopted necessarily involved, before it could be realized, defeat of the war program of the United States, for the obvious effect of this appeal, if it should become effective, as they, hoped it might, would be to persuade persons of character such as those whom they regarded themselves as addressing, not to aid government loans and not to work in ammunition factories, where their work would produce "bullets, bayonets, cannon" and other munitions of war, the use of which would cause the "murder" of Germans and Russians.

Again, the spirit becomes more bitter as it proceeds to declare that—

"America and her Allies have betrayed (the Workers). Their robberish aims are clear to all men. The destruction of the Russian Revolution, that is the politics of the march to Russia.

"*Workers, our reply to the barbaric intervention has to be a general strike! An open challenge* only will let the Government know that not only the Russian Worker fights for freedom, but also *here in America lives the spirit of Revolution.*"

This is not an attempt to bring about a change of administration by candid discussion, for no matter what may have incited the outbreak on the part of the defendant anarchists, the manifest purpose of such a publication was to create an attempt to defeat the war plans of the Government of the United States, by bringing upon the country the paralysis of a general strike, thereby arresting the production of all munitions and other things essential to the conduct of the war.

. . .

These excerpts sufficiently show, that while the immediate occasion for this particular outbreak of lawlessness, on the part of the defendant alien anarchists, may have been resentment caused by our Government sending troops into Russia as a strategic operation against the Germans on the eastern battle front, yet the plain purpose of their propaganda was to excite, at the supreme crisis of the war, disaffection, sedition, riots, and, as they hoped, revolution, in this country for the purpose of embarrassing and if possible defeating the military plans of the Government in Europe. . . . Thus it is clear not only that some evidence but that much persuasive evidence was before the jury tending to prove that the defendants were guilty as charged. . . . and under the long established rule of law herein before stated the judgment of the District Court must be

Affirmed.

MR. JUSTICE HOLMES dissenting.

. . .

I never have seen any reason to doubt that the questions of law that alone were before this Court in the cases of *Schenck, Frohwerk* and *Debs* were rightly decided. I do not doubt for a moment that by the same reasoning that would justify punishing persuasion to murder, the United States constitutionally may punish speech that produces or is intended to produce a clear and imminent danger that it will bring about forthwith certain substantive evils that the United States constitutionally may seek to prevent. The power undoubtedly is greater in time of war than in time of peace because war opens dangers that do not exist at other times.

But as against dangers peculiar to war, as against others, the principle of the right to free speech is always the same. It is only the present danger of immediate evil or an intent to bring it about that warrants Congress in setting a limit to the expression of opinion where private rights are not concerned. Congress certainly cannot forbid all effort to change the mind of the country. Now nobody can suppose that the surreptitious publishing of a silly leaflet by an unknown man, without more, would present any immediate danger that its opinions would hinder the success of the government arms or have any appreciable tendency to do so. Publishing those opinions for the very purpose of obstructing however, might indicate a greater danger and at any rate would have the quality of an attempt. . . . But it seems pretty clear to me that nothing less than that would bring these papers within the scope of this law. An actual intent in the sense that I have explained is necessary to constitute an attempt, where a further act of the same individual is required to complete the substantive crime. . . . An intent to prevent interference with the revolution in Russia might have been satisfied without any hindrance to carrying on the war in which we were engaged.

I do not see how anyone can find the intent required by the statute in any of the defendants' words. The second leaflet is the only one that affords even a foundation for the charge, and there, without invoking the hatred of German militarism expressed in the former one, it is evident from the beginning to the end that the only object of the paper is to help Russia and stop American intervention there against the popular government—not to impede the United States in the war that it was carrying on. To say that two phrases taken literally might import a suggestion of conduct that would have interference with the war as an indirect and probably undesired effect seems to me by no means enough to show an attempt to produce that effect.

. . .

In this case sentences of twenty years imprisonment have been imposed for the publishing of two leaflets that I believe the defendants had as much right to publish as the Government has to publish the Constitution of the United States now vainly invoked by them. Even if I am technically wrong and enough can be squeezed from these poor and puny anonymities to turn the color of legal litmus paper; I will add, even if what I think the necessary intent were shown; the most nominal punishment seems to me all that possibly could be inflicted, unless the defendants are to be made to suffer not for what the indictment alleges but for the creed that they avow—a creed that I believe to be the creed of ignorance and immaturity when honestly held, as I see no reason to doubt that it was held here, but which, although made the subject of examination at the trial, no one has a right even to consider in dealing with the charges before the Court.

Persecution for the expression of opinions seems to me perfectly logical. If you have no doubt of your premises or your power and want a certain result with all your heart you naturally express your wishes in law and sweep away all opposition. To allow opposition by speech seems to indicate that you think the speech impotent, as when a man says that he has squared the circle, or that you do not care whole-heartedly for the result, or that you doubt either your power or your premises. But when men have realized that time has upset many fighting faiths, they may come to believe even more than they believe the very foundations of their own conduct that the ultimate good desired is better reached by free trade in ideas—that the best test of truth is the power of the thought to get itself accepted in the competition of the market, and that truth is the only ground upon which their wishes safely can be carried out. That at any rate is the theory of our Constitution. It is an experiment, as all life is an experiment. Every year if not every day we have to wager our salvation upon some prophecy based upon imperfect knowledge. While that experiment is part of our system I think that we should be eternally vigilant against attempts to check the expression of opinions that we loathe and believe to be fraught with death, unless they so imminently threaten immediate interference with the lawful and pressing purposes of the law that an immediate check is required to save the country. I wholly disagree with the argument of the Government that the First Amendment left the common law as to seditious libel in force. History seems to me against the notion. I had conceived that the United States through many years had shown its repentance for the Sedition Act of 1798, by repaying fines that it imposed. Only the emergency that makes it immediately dangerous to leave the correction of evil counsels to time warrants making any exception to the sweeping command, "Congress shall make no law . . . abridging the freedom of speech." Of course I am speaking only of expressions of opinion and exhortations, which were all that were uttered here, but I regret that I cannot put into more impressive words my belief that in their conviction upon this indictment the defendants were deprived of their rights under the Constitution of the United States.

MR. JUSTICE BRANDEIS concurs with the foregoing opinion.

Justice Holmes invoked the "free trade in ideas" as the theoretical foundation for freedom of speech. The marketplace of ideas metaphor has since dominated the Supreme Court's interpretation of the First Amendment. The marketplace imagery was foreshadowed by Milton's *Areopagitica*, written nearly three centuries earlier, which based freedom of expression in the search for Truth.[27] The marketplace of ideas theory posits that speech should be protected from government interference because exposing the public to different viewpoints is the best way to discover truth. Truth will prevail ultimately in public debate, the theory goes, wherein all ideas are allowed to compete freely.

In the first three decades of this century most states enacted criminal laws aimed at dangerous political action. In 1902, a year after an anarchist's assassination of President McKinley, New York passed the first state antisedition law. The New York Criminal Anarchy Law prohibited actual or attempted violence or conspiracies to commit violence, as well as advocacy of "criminal anarchy," defined as "the doctrine that organized government should be overthrown by force or violence." In *Gitlow v. New York*, the Court reviewed the conviction of a member of the Socialist Party for distributing 16,000 copies of a "Left Wing Manifesto" that advocated a "Communist Revolution" through class struggle and mass political strikes.[28] The Court assumed that freedom of speech was among the liberties protected by the Fourteenth Amendment from state

---

[27] *See* JOHN MILTON, AREOPAGITICA (1644) *reprinted in* THE TRADITION OF FREEDOM 28 (Milton Mayer ed., 1957); *see also* David Cole, *Agon at Agora: Creative Misreadings in First Amendment Tradition*, 95 YALE L.J. 857, 876 (1986).

[28] Gitlow v. New York, 268 U. S. 652 (1925).

impairment, but upheld Gitlow's conviction. The Court reasoned that it need not apply the clear and present danger test because the New York legislature had already determined the harmful potential of anarchist advocacy:

> By enacting the present statute the State has determined, through its legislative body, that utterances advocating the overthrow of organized government by force, violence and unlawful means, are so inimical to the general welfare and involve such danger of substantive evil that they may be penalized in the exercise of its police power. That determination must be given great weight. . . . That utterances inciting to the overthrow of organized government by unlawful means, present a sufficient danger of substantive evil to bring their punishment within the range of legislative discretion is clear. Such utterances, by their very nature, involve danger to the public peace and to the security of the State. They threaten breaches of the peace and ultimate revolution. And the immediate danger is none the less real and substantial, because the effect of a given utterance cannot be accurately foreseen. The State cannot reasonably be required to measure the danger from every utterance in a nice balance of a jeweler's scale. A single revolutionary spark may kindle a fire that, smoldering for a time, may burst into a sweeping and destructive conflagration.

Justices Holmes and Brandeis dissented on the ground that the publication did not meet the clear and present danger test, noting "[e]very idea is an incitement."

In *Whitney v. California*, the Court considered the constitutionality of state syndicalism laws. Charlotte Anita Whitney was convicted of violating the California Criminal Syndicalism Act, which provided:

> "Section 1. The term 'criminal syndicalism' as used in this act is hereby defined as any doctrine or precept advocating, teaching or aiding and abetting the commission of crime, sabotage (which word is hereby defined as meaning willful and malicious physical damage or injury to physical property), or unlawful acts of force and violence or unlawful methods of terrorism as a means of accomplishing a change in industrial ownership or control or effecting any political change.
> "Sec. 2. Any person who: . . . 4. Organizes or assists in organizing, or is or knowingly becomes a member of, any organization, society, group or assemblage of persons organized or assembled to advocate, teach or aid and abet criminal syndicalism; . . . Is guilty of a felony and punishable by imprisonment."

The evidence at trial showed that Whitney participated in a convention held in Oakland in November, 1919, for the purpose of organizing a California branch of the Communist Labor Party, as well as meetings in San Jose and San Francisco. As a member of the Resolutions Committee, she signed a resolution recognizing "the value of political action as a means of spreading communist propaganda" and proclaiming that "the capture of political power, locally or nationally by the revolutionary working class can be of tremendous assistance to the workers in their struggle of emancipation." Whitney stated at her trial that she was then a member of the Communist Labor Party.

The Court held that the Syndicalism Act did not violate Whitney's rights of free speech, assembly, and association. But, *Whitney* is remembered for Justice Brandeis's concurring opinion which, like Holmes's *Abrams* dissent, set out a rationale for the Constitution's protection of speech. While Holmes emphasized the role of free expression in the search for truth, Brandeis emphasized its role in the functioning of an effective democracy.

Whitney v. California
274 U.S. 357 (1927)

MR. JUSTICE SANFORD delivered the opinion of the Court.

. . .

That the freedom of speech which is secured by the Constitution does not confer an absolute right to speak, without responsibility, whatever one may choose, or an unrestricted and unbridled license giving immunity for every possible use of language and preventing the punishment of those who abuse this freedom; and that a State in the exercise of its police power may punish those who abuse this freedom by utterances inimical to the public welfare, tending to incite to crime, disturb the public peace, or endanger the foundations of organized government and threaten its overthrow by unlawful means, is not open to question. *Gitlow v. New York.* . . . Every presumption is to be indulged in favor of the validity of the statute; and it may not be declared unconstitutional unless it is an arbitrary or unreasonable attempt to exercise the authority vested in the State in the public interest.

The essence of the offense denounced by the Act is the combining with others in an association for the accomplishment of the desired ends through the advocacy and use of criminal and unlawful methods. It partakes of the nature of a criminal conspiracy. That such united and joint action involves even greater danger to the public peace and security than the isolated utterances and acts of individuals is clear. We cannot hold that, as here applied, the Act is an unreasonable or arbitrary exercise of the police power of the State, unwarrantably infringing any right of free speech, assembly or association, or that those persons are protected from punishment by the due process clause who abuse such rights by joining and furthering an organization thus menacing the peace and welfare of the State.

. . .

MR. JUSTICE BRANDEIS (concurring.)

Miss Whitney was convicted of the felony of assisting in organizing, in the year 1919, the Communist Labor Party of California, of being a member of it, and of assembling with it. These acts are held to constitute a crime, because the party was formed to teach criminal syndicalism. The statute which made these acts a crime restricted the right of free speech and of assembly theretofore existing. The claim is that the statute, as applied, denied to Miss Whitney the liberty guaranteed by the Fourteenth Amendment.

The felony which the statute created is a crime very unlike the old felony of conspiracy or the old misdemeanor of unlawful assembly.

The mere act of assisting in forming a society for teaching syndicalism, of becoming a member of it, or assembling with others for that purpose is given the dynamic quality of crime. There is guilt although the society may not contemplate immediate promulgation of the doctrine. Thus the accused is to be punished, not for attempt, incitement or conspiracy, but for a step in preparation, which, if it threatens the public order at all, does so only remotely. The novelty in the prohibition introduced is that the statute aims, not at the practice of criminal syndicalism, nor even directly at the preaching of it, but at association with those who propose to preach it.

. . . [A]lthough the rights of free speech and assembly are fundamental, they are not in their nature absolute. Their exercise is subject to restriction, if the particular restriction proposed is required in order to protect the state from destruction or from serious injury, political, economic or moral. That the necessity which is essential to a valid restriction does not exist unless speech would produce, or is intended to produce, a clear and imminent danger of some substantive evil which the state constitutionally may seek to prevent has been settled. See *Schenck v. United States.*

It is said to be the function of the Legislature to determine whether at a particular time and under the particular circumstances the formation of, or assembly with, a society organized to advocate criminal syndicalism constitutes a clear and present danger of substantive evil; and that by enacting the law here in question the Legislature of California determined that question in the affirmative. Compare *Gitlow v. New York.* The Legislature must obviously decide, in the first instance, whether a danger exists which calls for a particular protective measure. But where a statute is valid only in case certain condition exist, the enactment of the statute cannot alone establish the facts which are essential to its validity. . . .

This Court has not yet fixed the standard by which to determine when a danger shall be deemed clear; how remote the danger may be and yet be deemed present; and what degree of evil shall be deemed sufficiently substantial to justify resort to abridgment of free speech and assembly as the means of protection. To reach sound conclusions on these matters, we must bear in mind why a state is, ordinarily, denied the power to prohibit dissemination of social, economic and political doctrine which a vast majority of its citizens believes to be false and fraught with evil consequence.

Those who won our independence believed

that the final end of the state was to make men free to develop their faculties; and that in its government the deliberative forces should prevail over the arbitrary. They valued liberty both as an end and as a means. They believed liberty to be the secret of happiness and courage to be the secret of liberty. They believed that freedom to think as you will and to speak as you think are means indispensable to the discovery and spread of political truth; that without free speech and assembly discussion would be futile; that with them, discussion affords ordinarily adequate protection against the dissemination of noxious doctrine; that the greatest menace to freedom is an inert people; that public discussion is a political duty; and that this should be a fundamental principle of the American government. They recognized the risks to which all human institutions are subject. But they knew that order cannot be secured merely through fear of punishment for its infraction; that it is hazardous to discourage thought, hope and imagination; that fear breeds repression; that repression breeds hate; that hate menaces stable government; that the path of safety lies in the opportunity to discuss freely supposed grievances and proposed remedies; and that the fitting remedy for evil counsels is good ones. Believing in the power of reason as applied through public discussion, they eschewed silence coerced by law—the argument of force in its worst form. Recognizing the occasional tyrannies of governing majorities, they amended the Constitution so that free speech and assembly should be guaranteed.

Fear of serious injury cannot alone justify suppression of free speech and assembly. Men feared witches and burnt women. It is the function of speech to free men from the bondage of irrational fears. To justify suppression of free speech there must be reasonable ground to fear that serious evil will result if free speech is practiced. There must be reasonable ground to believe that the danger apprehended is imminent. There must be reasonable ground to believe that the evil to be prevented is a serious one. Every denunciation of existing law tends in some measure to increase the probability that there will be violation of it. Condonation of a breach enhances the probability. Expressions of approval add to the probability. Propagation of the criminal state of mind by teaching syndicalism increases it. Advocacy of lawbreaking heightens it still further. But even advocacy of violation, however reprehensible morally, is not a justification for denying free speech where the advocacy falls short of incitement and there is nothing to indicate that the advocacy would be immediately acted on. The wide difference between advocacy and incitement, between preparation and attempt, between assembling and conspiracy, must be borne in mind. In order to support a finding of clear and present danger it must be shown either that immediate serious violence was to be expected or was advocated, or that the past conduct furnished reason to believe that such advocacy was then contemplated.

Those who won our independence by revolution were not cowards. They did not fear political change. They did not exalt order at the cost of liberty. To courageous, self-reliant men, with confidence in the power of free and fearless reasoning applied through the processes of popular government, no danger flowing from speech can be deemed clear and present, unless the incidence of the evil apprehended is so imminent that it may befall before there is opportunity for full discussion. If there be time to expose through discussion the falsehood and fallacies, to avert the evil by the processes of education, the remedy to be applied is more speech, not enforced silence. Only an emergency can justify repression. Such must be the rule if authority is to be reconciled with freedom. Such, in my opinion, is the command of the Constitution. It is therefore always open to Americans to challenge a law abridging free speech and assembly by showing that there was no emergency justifying it.

Moreover, even imminent danger cannot justify resort to prohibition of these functions essential to effective democracy, unless the evil apprehended is relatively serious. Prohibition of free speech and assembly is a measure so stringent that it would be inappropriate as the means for averting a relatively trivial harm to society. . . . The fact that speech is likely to result in some violence or in destruction of property is not enough to justify its suppression. There must be the probability of serious injury to the State. Among free men, the deterrents ordinarily to be applied to prevent crime are education and punishment for violations of the law, not abridgment of the rights of free speech and assembly.

. . . Whenever the fundamental rights of free speech and assembly are alleged to have been invaded, it must remain open to a defendant to present the issue whether there actually did exist at the time a clear danger, whether the danger, if any, was imminent, and whether the evil apprehended was one so substantial as to justify the stringent restriction interposed by the Legislature. The legislative declaration, like the fact that the statute was passed and was sustained by the highest court of the State, creates merely a rebuttable presumption that these conditions have been satisfied.

Whether in 1919, when Miss Whitney did the things complained of, there was in California such clear and present danger of serious evil, might have been made the important issue in the case. . . . I am unable to assent to the suggestion in the opinion of the court that assembling with a political party, formed to advocate the desirability of a proletarian revolution by mass action at some date necessarily far in the future, is not a right within the protection of the Fourteenth Amendment. In the present case, however, there was other testimony which tended to establish the existence of a conspiracy, on the part of members of the International Workers of the World, to commit present serious crimes, and likewise to show that such a conspiracy would be furthered by the activity of the society of which Miss Whitney was a member. Under these circumstances the judgment of the State court cannot be disturbed.

MR. JUSTICE HOLMES joins in this opinion.

After World War II, anti-communist sentiment swept the country and the federal government took steps to combat "subversive" activities. Senator Joseph McCarthy waged a campaign of weeding out Communists from government, education, and other professions. Congress enacted the Smith Act, modeled after the New York criminal anarchy law, that made it a crime to "knowingly or willfully advocate, abet, advise, or teach the duty, necessity, desirability, or propriety of overthrowing or destroying the government of the United States by force or violence. . . . " In a series of decisions between 1951 and 1961, the Supreme Court upheld the constitutionality of the Smith Act and determined its permissible scope under the First Amendment.

Dennis v. United States, decided in 1951, involved the convictions of the top leaders of the American Communist Party for violating the conspiracy provisions of the Smith Act.[29] The Court applied the clear and present danger test as interpreted by Judge Learned Hand in his opinion below: "In each case [courts] must ask whether the gravity of the 'evil,' discounted by its improbability, justifies such invasion of free speech as is necessary to avoid the danger." This version of the clear and present danger test represented a substantial watering-down of the version in *Schenck*: it eliminated the requirement that the danger be "clear," minimized the importance of "present," and increased the weight of the "evil." The *Schenck* clear and present danger test could not mean, the Court reasoned, that "before the Government may act, it must wait until the putsch is about to be executed, the plans have been laid and the signal is awaited." The Court concluded that the defendants' conspiracy to organize the Communist Party and to advocate the overthrow of the United States government met the less stringent test and upheld the convictions.

In his dissent, Justice Douglas stressed the First Amendment's protection of teaching political doctrine, even that which contradicts American ideals. These defendants were convicted of organizing people to teach Marxist-Leninist doctrine contained in books by Stalin, Marx and Engels, not "the techniques of sabotage, the assassination of the President, the filching of documents from public files, the planting of bombs, the art of street warfare."

By the time the Supreme Court decided the other Smith Act cases, Joseph McCarthy had died and opposition to his tactics had grown. In its 1957 decision, *Yates v. United States*, the Court reversed the conspiracy convictions of fourteen "second-string" Communist Party officials.[30] The Court narrowed the holding in *Dennis*, stating that the Smith Act did not prohibit "advocacy and teaching of forcible overthrow, as an abstract principle, divorced from any effort to instigate action to that end." In 1961, the Court decided two cases concerning convictions under the Smith Act's "membership clause," which prohibited becoming a member of a group that advocates the overthrow of the government. The Court upheld the constitutionality of the clause in *Scales v.*

---

[29] Dennis v. United States, 341 U.S. 494 (1951).
[30] Yates v. United States, 354 U.S. 298 (1957).

United States, in which the defendant was the chairman of the Communist Party in North and South Carolina, but reversed the conviction of a communist worker in *Noto v. United States* for insufficient evidence of his illegal advocacy.[31]

The Court once again restated the clear and present danger test in a case arising out of a Ku Klux Klan rally. In *Brandenburg v. Ohio*, the Court reversed the conviction of a Klan leader under an Ohio syndicalism statute that was nearly identical to the California law the Court had upheld in *Whitney*. *Whitney* was explicitly overruled.

---

[31] Scales v. United States, 367 U.S. 203 (1961); Noto v. United States, 367 U.S. 290 (1961).

Brandenburg v. Ohio
395 U.S. 444 (1968)

PER CURIAM.

The appellant, a leader of a Ku Klux Klan group, was convicted under the Ohio Criminal Syndicalism statute for "advocat[ing] . . . the duty, necessity, or propriety of crime, sabotage, violence, or unlawful methods of terrorism as a means of accomplishing industrial or political reform" and for "voluntarily assembl[ing] with any society, group, or assemblage of persons formed to teach or advocate the doctrines of criminal syndicalism." He was fined $1,000 and sentenced to one to 10 years' imprisonment. The appellant challenged the constitutionality of the criminal syndicalism statute under the First and Fourteenth Amendments to the United States Constitution, but the intermediate appellate court of Ohio affirmed his conviction without opinion. The Supreme Court of Ohio dismissed his appeal, sua sponte, "for the reason that no substantial constitutional question exists herein." . . . We reverse.

The record shows that a man, identified at trial as the appellant, telephoned an announcer-reporter on the staff of a Cincinnati television station and invited him to come to a Ku Klux Klan "rally" to be held at a farm in Hamilton County. With the cooperation of the organizers, the reporter and a cameraman attended the meeting and filmed the events. Portions of the films were later broadcast on the local station and on a national network.

The prosecution's case rested on the films and on testimony identifying the appellant as the person who communicated with the reporter and who spoke at the rally. The State also introduced into evidence several articles appearing in the film, including a pistol, a rifle, a shotgun, ammunition, a Bible, and a red hood worn by the speaker in the films.

One film showed 12 hooded figures, some of whom carried firearms. They were gathered around a large wooden cross, which they burned. No one was present other than the participants and the newsmen who made the film.

Most of the words uttered during the scene were incomprehensible when the film was projected, but scattered phrases could be understood that were derogatory of Negroes and, in one instance, of Jews.[1] Another scene on the same film showed the appellant, in Klan regalia, making a speech. The speech, in full, was as follows:

"This is an organizers' meeting. We have had quite a few members here today which are—we have hundreds, hundreds of members throughout the State of Ohio. I can quote from a newspaper clipping from the Columbus, Ohio Dispatch, five weeks ago Sunday morning. The Klan has more members in the State of Ohio than does any other organization. We're not a revengent organization, but if our President, our Congress, our Supreme Court, continues to suppress the white, Caucasian race, it's possible that there might have to be some revengeance taken.

"We are marching on Congress July the Fourth, four hundred thousand strong. From there we are dividing into two groups, one group to march on St. Augustine, Florida, the other group to march into Mississippi. Thank you."

---

[1] The significant portions that could be understood were:
"How far is the nigger going to—yeah."
"This is what we are going to do to the niggers."
"A dirty nigger."
"Send the Jews back to Israel."
"Let's give them back to the dark garden."
"Save America."
"Let's go back to constitutional betterment."
"Bury the niggers."
"We intend to do our part."
"Give us our state rights."
"Freedom for the whites."
"Nigger will have to fight for every inch he gets from now on."

The second film showed six hooded figures one of whom, later identified as the appellant, repeated a speech very similar to that recorded on the first film. The reference to the possibility of "revengeance" was omitted, and one sentence was added: "Personally, I believe the nigger should be returned to Africa, the Jew returned to Israel." Though some of the figures in the films carried weapons, the speaker did not.

The Ohio Criminal Syndicalism Statute was enacted in 1919. From 1917 to 1920, identical or quite similar laws were adopted by 20 States and two territories. In 1927, this Court sustained the constitutionality of California's Criminal Syndicalism Act, the text of which is quite similar to that of the laws of Ohio. *Whitney v. California*. The Court upheld the statute on the ground that, without more, "advocating" violent means to effect political and economic change involves such danger to the security of the State that the State may outlaw it. But *Whitney* has been thoroughly discredited by later decisions. See *Dennis v. United States*. These later decisions have fashioned the principle that the constitutional guarantees of free speech and free press do not permit a State to forbid or proscribe advocacy of the use of force or of law violation except where such advocacy is directed to inciting or producing imminent lawless action and is likely to incite or produce such action.[2] As we said in *Noto v. United States*, "the mere abstract teaching . . . of the moral propriety or even moral necessity for a resort to force and violence, is not the same as preparing a group for violent action and steeling it to such action." A statute which fails to draw this distinction impermissibly intrudes upon the freedoms guaranteed by the First and Fourteenth Amendments. It sweeps within its condemnation speech which our Constitution has immunized from governmental control.

Measured by this test, Ohio's Criminal Syndicalism Act cannot be sustained. The Act punishes persons who "advocate or teach the duty, necessity, or propriety" of violence "as a means of accomplishing industrial or political reform"; or who publish or circulate or display any book or paper containing such advocacy; or who "justify" the commission of violent acts

"with intent to exemplify, spread or advocate the propriety of the doctrines of criminal syndicalism"; or who "voluntarily assemble" with a group formed "to teach or advocate the doctrines of criminal syndicalism." Neither the indictment nor the trial judge's instructions to the jury in any way refined the statute's bald definition of the crime in terms of mere advocacy not distinguished from incitement to imminent lawless action.

Accordingly, we are here confronted with a statute which, by its own words and as applied, purports to punish mere advocacy and to forbid, on pain of criminal punishment, assembly with others merely to advocate the described type of action. Such a statute falls within the condemnation of the First and Fourteenth Amendments. The contrary teaching of *Whitney v. California* cannot be supported, and that decision is therefore overruled.

Reversed.

MR. JUSTICE BLACK, concurring.

I agree with the views expressed by MR. JUSTICE DOUGLAS in his concurring opinion in this case that the "clear and present danger" doctrine should have no place in the interpretation of the First Amendment. I join the Court's opinion, which, as I understand it, simply cites *Dennis v. United States*, but does not indicate any agreement on the Court's part with the "clear and present danger" doctrine on which *Dennis* purported to rely.

MR. JUSTICE DOUGLAS, concurring.

. . .

. . . I see no place in the regime of the First Amendment for any "clear and present danger" test, whether strict and tight as some would make it, or free-wheeling as the Court in *Dennis* rephrased it.

When one reads the opinions closely and sees when and how the "clear and present danger" test has been applied, great misgivings are aroused. First, the threats were often loud but always puny and made serious only by judges so wedded to the status quo that critical analysis made them nervous. Second, the test was so twisted and perverted in *Dennis* as to make the trial of those teachers of Marxism an all-out political trial which was part and parcel of the cold war that has eroded substantial parts of the First Amendment.

. . .

One's beliefs have long been thought to be sanctuaries which government could not invade. . . . The lines drawn by the Court between the criminal act of being an "active" Communist and the innocent act of being a nominal or inactive Communist mark the difference only between deep and abiding belief and casual or uncertain belief. But I think that all matters of belief are beyond the reach of subpoenas or the probings of investigators.

---

[2] It was on the theory that the Smith Act embodied such a principle and that it had been applied only in conformity with it that this Court sustained the Act's constitutionality. *Dennis v. United States.* That this was the basis for *Dennis* was emphasized in *Yates v. United States*, in which the Court overturned convictions for advocacy of the forcible overthrow of the Government under the Smith Act, because the trial judge's instructions had allowed conviction for mere advocacy, unrelated to its tendency to produce forcible action.

That is why the invasions of privacy made by investigating committees were notoriously unconstitutional. That is the deep-seated fault in the infamous loyalty-security hearings which, since 1947 when President Truman launched them, have processed 20,000,000 men and women. Those hearings were primarily concerned with one's thoughts, ideas, beliefs, and convictions. They were the most blatant violations of the First Amendment we have ever known.

The line between what is permissible and not subject to control and what may be made impermissible and subject to regulation is the line between ideas and overt acts.

The example usually given by those who would punish speech is the case of one who falsely shouts fire in a crowded theatre.

This is, however, a classic case where speech is brigaded with action. They are indeed inseparable and a prosecution can be launched for the overt acts actually caused. Apart from rare instances of that kind, speech is, I think, immune from prosecution. Certainly there is no constitutional line between advocacy of abstract ideas as in *Yates* and advocacy of political action as in *Scales*. The quality of advocacy turns on the depth of the conviction; and government has no power to invade that sanctuary of belief and conscience.

DER: The clear and present danger test provides inadequate protection for radical political speech. Although *Brandenburg v. Ohio* overruled *Whitney v. California* and greatly narrowed the clear and present danger test, it affirmed the Court's reasoning in *Dennis v. United States* and *Scales v. United States*. The current version of the clear and present danger test, then, still allows punishment of political activists based on their teachings and membership in radical political organizations, without evidence of action towards an illegal end. The test appears to have originated from the law of attempt liability that applied to ordinary criminal cases. It may indeed be appropriate when a defendant incites or solicits others to commit a crime that has no political implications. But the Supreme Court's decisions applying the clear and present danger test involved speech challenging the government's policies and advocating political change. Unlike advocacy of crime in the non-political context, they invoke important First Amendment concerns which the Court failed sufficiently to acknowledge. As the Court recognized in its landmark libel decision, *New York Times v. Sullivan*, criticism of the government lies at the heart of the First Amendment's purpose and requires ample "breathing space." There is extra danger that the state will attempt to stifle radical dissent that contests its decisions and even its legitimacy, and that in times of political turmoil juries will become especially hostile to dissident opinions. The clear and present danger test, even after *Brandenburg*, does not protect political speech from this peril.

DEL: For all the tightening up of clear and present danger principles since *Dennis* that help limit government's ability to overpredict harm, the standard is still susceptible to perversion in times when society is fearful, anxious or paranoid. Attention to imminence and likelihood may represent significant clarifying and limiting principles in the abstract, but it is unclear whether it would have avoided the persecutorial excesses of the Great Red Scare in the 1920s or the McCarthyism of the 1950s. Unless the society is confident enough in its own stability and survival to invest in the absolute protections urged by Justices Black and Douglas, it is doubtful that expressive freedom can be insulated from the moods and mentalities that accompany crises imagined and real.

b. Libel

The colonists valued an individual's good reputation and commonly punished instances of defamation. The preamble to a 1647 Rhode Island statute, for example, stated, "[a] good name is better than precious ointment and slanderers are worse than dead flies to corrupt and alter the savour thereof." Of even greater concern to colonial authorities was "seditious speech"—speech that slandered the government. Seditious speech fell into three categories.[32] *Scandalum magnatum* meant deriding high public officials or "great men," such as nobles, judges, governors, and ministers. These scandalous words included charges of incompetence, unfairness or disloyalty, as well as personal insults. In 1687, for example, Cornelius Jones was convicted of "diverse, base, ignominious, vile and reproachful speeches" against Edmund Andros, governor of the Dominion of New England, and sentenced to receive twenty-one "stripes on the bare skin, well laid on."[33] Seditious speech was a misdemeanor, but slander of the king might be judged as treason—a capital offense.

Second, colonial authorities punished as seditious criticism of government laws, practices, and policies. Colonists were commonly prosecuted, for example, for complaining about the colony laws and the levying of taxes. In 1678, the Connecticut General Court fined John Wheeler five pounds for complaining that New London County officials "sit here to pick men's pockets."[34] The colonists nevertheless had a legal avenue of complaint through proper appeals and petitions to courts and government bodies. Finally, colonial authorities prosecuted citizens who spread "false news" that endangered the government. A 1671 Maryland statute, for example, provided for a fine or corporal punishment for "any such idle and busy-headed person [who] shall forge or maliciously publish or invent any false reports or tales of any of his Lordship's Justices."[35]

The tradition of seditious libel survived the ratification of the First Amendment. In 1798, the Federalists passed The Sedition Act, which made it a crime, punishable by a $5,000 fine and five years in prison, to "write, print, utter or publish . . . any false, scandalous and malicious writings against the government of the United States, or either House of Congress . . . or the President . . . with intent to defame . . . or to bring them into contempt or disrepute; or to excite against them . . . the hatred of the good people of the United States." The Federalists, under President Adams, obtained convictions of their political opponents for three years, until the Act expired by its own terms in 1801. One laborer was imprisoned for two years for erecting a sign that read, "NO STAMP ACT, NO SEDITION . . . DOWNFALL TO THE TYRANTS OF AMERICA, PEACE AND RETIREMENT TO THE PRESIDENT."[36] President Jefferson pardoned all those convicted under the Act, and the government repaid their fines.

Although the Supreme Court never considered the constitutionality of The Sedition Act, the law of seditious libel was a critical theme of the Court's opinion in the landmark First Amendment case, *New York Times v. Sullivan*. The issue before the Court was whether the First Amendment afforded protection from libel judgments for speech that defamed government officials. It considered this issue against the backdrop not only of the seditious libel law, but also a long tradition of state protection of citizens' reputations. At the time of the Court's *New York Times* decision, the law of libel was governed by state law. Justice White's dissent in a subsequent case, *Gertz v. Robert Welch, Inc.*, summarized the body of state libel law that the Supreme Court began to disassemble in *New York Times*:

> In 1938, the Restatement of Torts reflected the historic rule that publication in written form of defamatory material—material tending "so to harm the reputation of another as to lower him in the estimation of the community or to deter third persons from associating or dealing with him"—subjected the publisher

---

[32] Eldridge, A Distant Heritage, *supra* note 3, at 10.

[33] *Id.*

[34] *Id.* at 15.

[35] *Id.* at 30.

[36] David Kairys, *Freedom of Speech*, in The Politics of Law: A Progressive Critique 146 (David Kairys ed., 1990).

to liability although no special harm to reputation was actually proved. Truth was a defense, and some libels were privileged; but, given a false circulation, general damage to reputation was presumed and damages could be awarded by the jury, along with any special damages such as pecuniary loss and emotional distress. At the very least, the rule allowed the recovery of nominal damages for any defamatory publication actionable *per se* and thus performed "a vindicatory function by enabling the plaintiff publicly to brand the defamatory publication as false. . . . "

. . . At the heart of the libel-and-slander-*per-se* damage scheme lay the award of general damages for loss of reputation. They were granted without special proof because the judgment of history was that the content of the publication itself was so likely to cause injury and because "in many cases the effect of defamatory statements is so subtle and indirect that it is impossible directly to trace the effects thereof in loss to the person defamed." Punitive damages were recoverable upon proof of special facts amounting to express malice.

The state rules governing libel operated without federal interference on the presumption that defamatory falsehoods were not constitutionally protected speech. Libel was one of the categories of speech which the Court in 1942, in *Chaplinsky v. New Hampshire*, declared outside the scope of the First Amendment.[37] Ten years later, the Court in *Beauharnais v. Illinois* confirmed this exemption of libel by upholding a conviction under a statute prohibiting dissemination of materials promoting racial or religious hatred.[38] The Court reasoned that the defendant's defamatory statements about Negroes constituted unprotected libel of a group. The Supreme Court had never before found that the First Amendment placed any limits on libel judgments.

The *New York Times* case arose out of the civil rights struggles in the South during the 1960s. The advertisement at issue, appearing in the New York Times under the heading "Heed Their Rising Voices," solicited contributions for Dr. Martin Luther King, Jr. and other civil rights protesters who faced opposition from local authorities. Huge libel judgments, along with police dogs, fire hoses, and arrest warrants, had proven to be a powerful weapon for curbing dissent in the hands of Southern officials. At stake "was the ability, or the willingness, of the American press to go on covering the racial conflict in the Court as it had been doing."[39] Although the First Amendment may have originally contemplated reservation of libel law to the states, the tumultuous events unfolding in the South made clear the danger to free speech of unrestrained state power. The *New York Times* decision initiated a new approach to libel law that involves the federal courts in crafting rules that satisfy First Amendment concerns.

---

[37] Chaplinsky v. New Hampshire, 315 U.S. 568 (1942).
[38] Beauharnais v. Illinois, 343 U.S. 250 (1952).
[39] Anthony Lewis, New York Times v. Sullivan *Reconsidered: Time to Return to "The Central Meaning of the First Amendment*," 83 COLUM. L. REV. 603, 605 (1983).

New York Times Co. v. Sullivan
376 U.S. 254 (1964)

MR. JUSTICE BRENNAN delivered the opinion of the Court.

We are required in this case to determine for the first time the extent to which the constitutional protections for speech and press limit a State's power to award damages in a libel action brought by a public official against critics of his official conduct.

Respondent L. B. Sullivan is one of the three elected Commissioners of the City of

Montgomery, Alabama. He testified that he was "Commissioner of Public Affairs and the duties are supervision of the Police Department, Fire Department, Department of Cemetery and Department of Scales." He brought this civil libel action against the four individual petitioners, who are Negroes and Alabama clergymen, and against petitioner the New York Times Company, a New York corporation which publishes the New York Times, a daily newspaper. A jury in the Circuit Court of Montgomery County awarded him damages of $500,000, the full amount claimed, against all the petitioners, and the Supreme Court of Alabama affirmed.

Respondent's complaint alleged that he had been libeled by statements in a full-page advertisement that was carried in the New York Times on March 29, 1960. Entitled "Heed Their Rising Voices," the advertisement began by stating that "As the whole world knows by now, thousands of Southern Negro students are engaged in widespread non-violent demonstrations in positive affirmation of the right to live in human dignity as guaranteed by the U.S. Constitution and the Bill of Rights." It went on to charge that "in their efforts to uphold these guarantees, they are being met by an unprecedented wave of terror by those who would deny and negate that document which the whole world looks upon as setting the pattern for modern freedom. . . ." Succeeding paragraphs purported to illustrate the "wave of terror" by describing certain alleged events. The text concluded with an appeal for funds for three purposes: support of the student movement, "the struggle for the right-to-vote," and the legal defense of Dr. Martin Luther King, Jr., leader of the movement, against a perjury indictment then pending in Montgomery.

The text appeared over the names of 64 persons, many widely known for their activities in public affairs, religion, trade unions, and the performing arts. Below these names, and under a line reading "We in the south who are struggling daily for dignity and freedom warmly endorse this appeal," appeared the names of the four individual petitioners and of 16 other persons, all but two of whom were identified as clergymen in various Southern cities. The advertisement was signed at the bottom of the page by the "Committee to Defend Martin Luther King and the Struggle for Freedom in the South," and the officers of the Committee were listed.

Of the 10 paragraphs of text in the advertisement, the third and a portion of the sixth were the basis of respondent's claim of libel. They read as follows:

Third paragraph:

"In Montgomery, Alabama, after students sang 'My Country, 'Tis of Thee' on the State Capitol steps, their leaders were expelled from school, and truckloads of police armed with shotguns and tear-gas ringed the Alabama State College Campus. When the entire student body protested to state authorities by refusing to re-register, their dining hall was padlocked in an attempt to starve them into submission."

Sixth paragraph:

"Again and again the Southern violators have answered Dr. King's peaceful protests with intimidation and violence. They have bombed his home almost killing his wife and child. They have assaulted his person. They have arrested him seven times—for 'speeding,' 'loitering' and similar 'offenses.' And now they have charged him with 'perjury'—a *felony* under which they could imprison him for *ten years*. . . . "

Although neither of these statements mentions respondent by name, he contended that the word "police" in the third paragraph referred to him as the Montgomery Commissioner who supervised the Police Department, so that he was being accused of "ringing" the campus with police. He further claimed that the paragraph would be read as imputing to the police, and hence to him, the padlocking of the dining hall in order to starve the students into submission.

As to the sixth paragraph, he contended that since arrests are ordinarily made by the police, the statement "They have arrested [Dr. King] seven times" would be read as referring to him; he further contended that the "They" who did the arresting would be equated with the "They" who committed the other described acts and with the "Southern violators." Thus, he argued, the paragraph would be read as accusing the Montgomery police, and hence him, of answering Dr. King's protests with "intimidation and violence," bombing his home, assaulting his person, and charging him with perjury. Respondent and six other Montgomery residents testified that they read some or all of the statements as referring to him in his capacity as Commissioner.

It is uncontroverted that some of the statements contained in the two paragraphs were not accurate descriptions of events which occurred in Montgomery. Although Negro students staged a demonstration on the State Capitol steps, they sang the National Anthem and not "My Country, 'Tis of Thee." Although nine students were expelled by the State Board of Education, this was not for leading the demonstration at the Capitol, but for demanding service at a lunch counter in the Montgomery County Courthouse on another day. Not the entire student body, but most of it, had protested the expulsion, not by refusing to register, but by boycotting classes on a single day; virtually all the students did register for the ensuing semester. The campus dining hall was not padlocked on any occasion, and the only students who may have been barred from eating there were the few who had neither signed a preregistration application nor requested temporary meal tickets. Although the police were deployed near the campus in large numbers on three occasions, they did not at any time "ring" the campus, and they were not called to the campus in connection with the demonstration on the State Capitol steps, as the third paragraph implied. Dr. King had not been arrested seven times, but only four; and although he claimed to have been assaulted some years earlier in connection with his arrest for loitering outside a courtroom, one of the officers who made the arrest denied that there was such an assault.

. . .

Respondent made no effort to prove that he suffered actual pecuniary loss as a result of the alleged libel. . . .

. . .

The trial judge submitted the case to the jury under instructions that the statements in the advertisement were "libelous per se" and were not privileged, so that petitioners might be held liable if the jury found that they had published the advertisement and that the statements were made "of and concerning" respondent. The jury was instructed that, because the statements were libelous per se, "the law . . . implies legal injury from the bare fact of publication itself," "falsity and malice are presumed," "general damages need not be alleged or proved but are presumed," and "punitive damages may be awarded by the jury even though the amount of actual damages is neither found nor shown." . . .

. . .

. . . We reverse the judgment. We hold that the rule of law applied by the Alabama courts is constitutionally deficient for failure to provide the safeguards for freedom of speech and of the press that are required by the First and Fourteenth Amendments in a libel action brought by a public official against critics of his official conduct. We further hold that under the proper safeguards the evidence presented in this case is constitutionally insufficient to support the judgment for respondent.

Under Alabama law as applied in this case, a publication is "libelous per se" if the words "tend to injure a person . . . in his reputation" or to "bring [him] into public contempt"; the trial court stated that the standard was met if the words are such as to "injure him in his public office, or impute misconduct to him

in his office, or want of official integrity, or want of fidelity to a public trust. . . . " The jury must find that the words were published "of and concerning" the plaintiff, but where the plaintiff is a public official his place in the governmental hierarchy is sufficient evidence to support a finding that his reputation has been affected by statements that reflect upon the agency of which he is in charge. Once "libel per se" has been established, the defendant has no defense as to stated facts unless he can persuade the jury that they were true in all their particulars. . . .

Respondent relies heavily, as did the Alabama courts, on statements of this Court to the effect that the Constitution does not protect libelous publications. Those statements do not foreclose our inquiry here. None of the cases sustained the use of libel laws to impose sanctions upon expression critical of the official conduct of public officials. . . . In deciding the question now, we are compelled by neither precedent nor policy to give any more weight to the epithet "libel" than we have to other "mere labels" of state law. Like insurrection, contempt, advocacy of unlawful acts, breach of the peace, obscenity, solicitation of legal business, and the various other formulae for the repression of expression that have been challenged in this Court, libel can claim no talismanic immunity from constitutional limitations. It must be measured by standards that satisfy the First Amendment.

. . .

Thus we consider this case against the background of a profound national commitment to the principle that debate on public issues should be uninhibited, robust, and wide-open, and that it may well include vehement, caustic, and sometimes unpleasantly sharp attacks on government and public officials. The present advertisement, as an expression of grievance and protest on one of the major public issues of our time, would seem clearly to qualify for the constitutional protection. The question is whether it forfeits that protection by the falsity of some of its factual statements and by its alleged defamation of respondent.

Authoritative interpretations of the First Amendment guarantees have consistently refused to recognize an exception for any test of truth—whether administered by judges, juries, or administrative officials—and especially one that puts the burden of proving truth on the speaker. The constitutional protection does not turn upon "the truth, popularity, or social utility of the ideas and beliefs which are offered." As Madison said, "Some degree of abuse is inseparable from the proper use of every thing; and in no instance is this more true than in that of the press." "[E]rroneous statement is inevitable in free debate, and it must be protected if the freedoms of expression are to have the "breathing space" that they "need . . . to survive," *N.A.A.C.P. v. Button*, [371 U.S. 415, 433 (1963)]. . . .

Injury to official reputation affords no more warrant for repressing speech that would otherwise be free than does factual error. Where judicial officers are involved, this Court has held that concern for the dignity and reputation of the courts does not justify the punishment as criminal contempt of criticism of the judge or his decision. This is true even though the utterance contains "half-truths" and "misinformation." Such repression can be justified, if at all, only by a clear and present danger of the obstruction of justice. If judges are to be treated as "men of fortitude, able to thrive in a hardy climate," surely the same must be true of other government officials, such as elected city commissioners. Criticism of their official conduct does not lose its constitutional protection merely because it is effective criticism and hence diminishes their official reputations.

If neither factual error nor defamatory content suffices to remove the constitutional shield from criticism of official conduct, the combination of the two elements is no less inadequate. This is the lesson to be drawn from the great controversy over the Sedition Act of 1798, which first crystallized a national awareness of the central meaning of the First Amendment. . . . The Act allowed the defendant the defense of truth, and provided that the jury were to be judges both of the law and the facts. Despite these qualifications, the Act was vigorously condemned as unconstitutional in an attack joined in by Jefferson and Madison. In the famous Virginia Resolutions of 1798, the General Assembly of Virginia resolved that it

> "doth particularly protest against the palpable and alarming infractions of the Constitution, in the two late cases of the 'Alien and Sedition Acts,' passed at the last session of Congress. . . . [The Sedition Act] exercises . . . a power not delegated by the Constitution, but, on the contrary, expressly and positively forbidden by one of the amendments thereto—a power which, more than any other, ought to produce universal alarm, because it is levelled against the right of freely examining public characters and measures, and of free communication among the people thereon, which has ever been justly deemed the only effectual guardian of every other right."

Madison prepared the Report in support of the protest. His premise was that the Constitution created a form of government under which "The people, not the government, possess the absolute sovereignty." The structure of the government dispersed power in reflection of the people's distrust of concentrated power, and of power itself at all levels. This form of government was "altogether different" from the British form, under which the Crown was sovereign and the people were subjects. "Is it not natural and necessary, under such different circumstances," he asked, "that a different degree of freedom in the use of the press should be contemplated?" Earlier, in a debate in the House of Representatives, Madison had said: "If we advert to the nature of Republican Government, we shall find that the censorial power is in the people over the Government, and not in the Government over the people." Of the exercise of that power by the press, his Report said: "In every state, probably, in the Union, the press has exerted a freedom in canvassing the merits and measures of public men, of every description, which has not been confined to the strict limits of the common law. On this footing the freedom of the press has stood; on this foundation it yet stands. . . . " The right of free public discussion of the stewardship of public officials was thus, in Madison's view, a fundamental principle of the American form of government.

Although the Sedition Act was never tested in this Court, the attack upon its validity has carried the day in the court of history. Fines levied in its prosecution were repaid by Act of Congress on the ground that it was unconstitutional. Calhoun, reporting to the Senate on February 4, 1836, assumed that its invalidity was a matter "which no one now doubts." Jefferson, as President, pardoned those who had been convicted and sentenced under the Act and remitted their fines, stating: "I discharged every person under punishment or prosecution under the sedition law, because I considered, and now consider, that law to be a nullity, as absolute and as palpable as if Congress had ordered us to fall down and worship a golden image." Letter to Mrs. Adams, July 22, 1804. The invalidity of the Act has also been assumed by Justices of this Court. These views reflect a broad consensus that the Act, because of the restraint it imposed upon criticism of government and public officials, was inconsistent with the First Amendment.

. . .

What a State may not constitutionally bring about by means of a criminal statute is likewise beyond the reach of its civil law of libel. The fear of damage awards under a rule such as that invoked by the Alabama courts here may be markedly more inhibiting than the fear of prosecution under a criminal statute. . . . The judgment awarded in this case—without the need for any proof of actual pecuniary loss—was one thousand times greater than the maximum fine provided by the Alabama criminal statute, and one hundred times greater than that provided by the Sedition Act. And since there is no double-jeopardy limitation applicable to civil lawsuits, this is not the only judgment that may be awarded against petitioners for the same publication. Whether or not a newspaper can survive a succession of such judgments, the pall of fear and timidity imposed upon those who would give voice to public criticism is an atmosphere in which the First Amendment freedoms cannot survive. . . .

The state rule of law is not saved by its allowance of the defense of truth. . . . A rule compelling the critic of official conduct to guarantee the truth of all his factual assertions—and to do so on pain of libel judgments virtually unlimited in amount—leads to . . . "self-censorship." Allowance of the defense of truth, with the burden of proving it on the defendant, does not mean that only false speech will be deterred. Even courts accepting this defense as an adequate safeguard have recognized the difficulties of adducing legal proofs that the alleged libel was true in all its factual particulars. Under such a rule, would-be critics of official conduct may be deterred from voicing their criticism, even though it is believed to be true and even though it is in fact true, because of doubt whether it can be proved in court or fear of the expense of having to do so. They tend to make only statements which "steer far wider of the unlawful zone." The rule thus dampens the vigor and limits the variety of public debate. It is inconsistent with the First and Fourteenth Amendments.

The constitutional guarantees require, we think, a federal rule that prohibits a public official from recovering damages for a defamatory falsehood relating to his official conduct unless he proves that the statement was made with "actual malice"—that is, with knowledge that it was false or with reckless disregard of whether it was false or not. . . .

Such a privilege for criticism of official conduct is appropriately analogous to the protection accorded a public official when he is sued for libel by a private citizen. In *Barr v. Matteo,* 360 U.S. 564, this court held the utterance of a federal official to be absolutely privileged if made "within the outer perimeter" of his duties. The States accord the same immunity to statements of their highest officers, although some differentiate their lesser officials and qualify the privilege they enjoy. But all hold that all officials are protected unless actual malice can be proved. The reason for the official privilege is said to be that the threat of damage suits would otherwise "inhibit the fearless, vigorous, and effective administration of policies of government" and "dampen the ardor of all but the most resolute, or the most irresponsible, in the unflinching discharge of their du-

ties." *Barr v. Matteo.* Analogous considerations support the privilege for the citizen-critic of government. It is as much his duty to criticize as it is the official's duty to administer. See *Whitney v. California* (concurring opinion of Mr. Justice Brandeis). As Madison said, "the censorial power is in the people over the Government, and not in the Government over the people." It would give public servants an unjustified preference over the public they serve, if critics of official conduct did not have a fair equivalent of the immunity granted to the officials themselves.

We conclude that such a privilege is required by the First and Fourteenth Amendments.

We hold today that the Constitution delimits a State's power to award damages for libel in actions brought by public officials against critics of their official conduct. Since this is such an action, the rule requiring proof of actual malice is applicable. . . .

Since respondent may seek a new trial, we deem that considerations of effective judicial administration require us to review the evidence in the present record to determine whether it could constitutionally support a judgment for respondent. This Court's duty is not limited to the elaboration of constitutional principles; we must also in proper cases review the evidence to make certain that those principles have been constitutionally applied. . . . Applying these standards, we consider that the proof presented to show actual malice lacks the convincing clarity which the constitutional standard demands, and hence that it would not constitutionally sustain the judgment for respondent under the proper rule of law.

. . .

MR. JUSTICE BLACK, with whom MR. JUSTICE DOUGLAS joins, concurring.

I concur in reversing this half-million-dollar judgment against the New York Times Company and the four individual defendants. In reversing the Court holds that "the Constitution delimits a State's power to award damages for libel in actions brought by public officials against critics of their official conduct." I base my vote to reverse on the belief that the First and Fourteenth Amendments not merely "delimit" a State's power to award damages to "public officials against critics of their official conduct" but completely prohibit a State from exercising such a power. The Court goes on to hold that a State can subject such critics to damages if "actual malice" can be proved against them. "Malice," even as defined by the Court, is an elusive, abstract concept, hard to prove and hard to disprove. The requirement that malice be proved provides at best an evanescent protection for the right critically to discuss public affairs and certainly does not measure up to the sturdy safeguard embodied in the First Amendment. Unlike the Court, therefore, I vote to reverse exclusively on the ground that the Times and the individual defendants had an absolute, unconditional constitutional right to publish in the Times advertisement their criticisms of the Montgomery agencies and officials. . . .

The half-million-dollar verdict does give dramatic proof, however, that state libel laws threaten the very existence of an American press virile enough to publish unpopular views on public affairs and bold enough to criticize the conduct of public officials. The factual background of this case emphasizes the imminence and enormity of that threat. One of the acute and highly emotional issues in this country arises out of efforts of many people, even including some public officials, to continue state-commanded segregation of races in the public schools and other public places, despite our several holdings that such a state practice is forbidden by the Fourteenth Amendment. Montgomery is one of the localities in which widespread hostility to desegregation has been manifested. This hostility has sometimes extended itself to persons who favor desegregation, particularly to so-called "outside agitators," a term which can be made to fit papers like the Times, which is published in New York. . . . Moreover, this technique for harassing and punishing a free press—now that it has been shown to be possible—is by no means limited to cases with racial overtones; it can be used in other fields where public feelings may make local as well as out-of-state newspapers easy prey for libel verdict seekers.

In my opinion the Federal Constitution has dealt with this deadly danger to the press in the only way possible without leaving the free press open to destruction—by granting the press an absolute immunity for criticism of the way public officials do their public duty. Stopgap measures like those the Court adopts are in my judgment not enough. This record certainly does not indicate that any different verdict would have been rendered here whatever the Court had charged the jury about "malice," "truth," "good motives," "justifiable ends," or any other legal formulas which in theory would protect the press. Nor does the record indicate that any of these legalistic words would have caused the courts below to set aside or to reduce the half-million-dollar verdict in any amount.

. . .

We would, I think, more faithfully interpret the First Amendment by holding that at the very least it leaves the people and the press free to criticize officials and discuss public affairs with impunity. This Nation of ours elects many of its important officials; so do the States, the municipalities, the counties, and even many precincts. These officials are responsible to the people for the way they perform their duties. While our Court has held that some kinds of speech and writings, such as "obscenity" and "fighting words" are not expression within the protection of the First Amendment, freedom to discuss public affairs and public officials is unquestionably, as the Court today holds, the kind of speech the First Amendment was primarily designed to keep within the area of free discussion. To punish the exercise of this right to discuss public affairs or to penalize it through libel judgments is to abridge or shut off discussion of the very kind most needed. This Nation, I suspect, can live in peace without libel suits based on public discussions of public affairs and public officials. But I doubt that a country can live in freedom where its people can be made to suffer physically or financially for criticizing their government, its actions, or its officials. . . .

. . .

MR. JUSTICE GOLDBERG, with whom MR. JUSTICE DOUGLAS joins, concurring in the result.

The Court today . . . rules that the Constitution gives citizens and newspapers a "conditional privilege" immunizing nonmalicious misstatements of fact regarding the official conduct of a government officer. The impressive array of history and precedent marshaled by the Court, however, confirms my belief that the Constitution affords greater protection than that provided by the Court's standard to citizen and press in exercising the right of public criticism.

In my view, the First and Fourteenth Amendments to the Constitution afford to the citizen and to the press an absolute, unconditional privilege to criticize official conduct despite the harm which may flow from excesses and abuses. The prized American right "to speak one's mind" about public officials and affairs needs "breathing space to survive." The right should not depend upon a probing by the jury of the motivation of the citizen or press. The theory of our Constitution is that every citizen may speak his mind and every newspaper express its view on matters of public concern and may not be barred from speaking or publishing because those in control of government think that what is said or written is unwise, unfair, false, or malicious. In a democratic society, one who assumes to act for the citizens in an executive, legislative, or judicial capacity must expect that his official acts will be commented upon and criticized. Such criticism cannot, in my opinion, be muzzled or deterred by the courts at the instance of public officials under the label of libel.

. . .

If the government official should be immune from libel actions so that his ardor to serve the public will not be dampened and "fearless, vigorous, and effective administration of policies of government" not be inhibited, then the citizen and the press should likewise be immune from libel actions for their criticism of official conduct. Their ardor as citizens will thus not be dampened and they will be free "to applaud or to criticize the way public employees do their jobs, from the least to the most important." If liability can attach to political criticism because it damages the reputation of a public official as a public official, then no critical citizen can safely utter anything but faint praise about the government or its officials. The vigorous criticism by press and citizen of the conduct of the government of the day by the officials of the day will soon yield to silence if officials in control of government agencies, instead of answering criticisms, can resort to friendly juries to forestall criticism of their official conduct.

The conclusion that the Constitution affords the citizen and the press an absolute privilege for criticism of official conduct does not leave the public official without defenses against unsubstantiated opinions or deliberate misstatements. "Under our system of government, counterargument and education are the weapons available to expose these matters, not abridgment . . . of free speech. . . . " *Wood v. Georgia*, 370 U.S. 375, 389. The public official certainly has equal if not greater access than most private citizens to media of communication. . . .

After its *New York Times* decision, the Court had to decide the scope of the privilege it had added to state libel law. The justices disagreed dramatically in their approaches to the general problem of reconciling the law of defamation with the First Amendment. Three years after *New York Times*, a majority of justices in *Curtis Publishing Co. v. Butts* and its companion, *Associated Press v. Walker*, agreed to extend the actual malice requirement to libel actions brought by public figures—people who are "intimately involved in the resolution of important public questions or, by reason of their fame, shape events in areas of concern to society at large."[40] The Court reasoned that public figures have access to the media "both to influence policy and to counter criticism of their views and activities."

The Court then addressed the issue whether the *New York Times* privilege should extend even further—to defamation actions brought by ordinary citizens. In *Rosenbloom v. Metromedia, Inc.*, the justices announced their views in five separate opinions, none of which commanded more than three votes.[41] A plurality of justices (Brennan, Burger, and Blackmun) advocated extending the *New York Times* test to defamatory statements concerning matters of public interest, "without regard to whether the persons involved are famous or anonymous." In his opinion for the plurality, Brennan rejected the distinction between private plaintiffs versus public officials or figures: "If a matter is a subject of public or general interest, it cannot suddenly become less so merely because a private individual is involved, or because in some sense the individual did not 'voluntarily' choose to become involved." Another approach varied the level of constitutional privilege for defamatory falsehood with the status of the person defamed. And a third view, shared by Douglas and Black, would grant to the press and broadcast media absolute immunity from liability for defamation.

When the Court heard *Gertz v. Robert Welch, Inc.* it was thus faced with a number of options. Should it adopt the plurality approach in *Rosenbloom*, extending the *New York Times* privilege to defamation of *private* individuals? Or should it expand First Amendment protection even further, as Justices Black and Douglas advocated? At the other extreme, should the Court stay out of the business of defining the rules for ordinary defamation actions, an area of law traditionally developed by state courts and legislatures? And, if the federal Constitution did apply to this area, how much latitude should be left to states in protecting private reputations from defamation?

While the justices' opinions in *New York Times v. Sullivan* presented a strong

---

[40] Curtis Publishing Co. v. Butts and Associated Press v. Walker, 388 U.S. 130 (1967).
[41] *Rosenbloom v. Metromedia, Inc.,* 403 U.S. 29 (1971).

defense of freedom of speech based on citizens' right to criticize government officials, the opinions in *Gertz* weighed more heavily the countervailing state interest in compensating private citizens for injury to reputation. The Court accommodated states' efforts to protect private reputations by articulating a standard located between the "drastic alternatives of the *New York Times* privilege and the common law of strict liability for defamatory error." After *Gertz*, however, ordinary state libel cases were no longer immune from federal free speech concerns.

Gertz v. Robert Welch, Inc.
418 U.S. 323 (1974)

MR. JUSTICE POWELL delivered the opinion of the Court.

This Court has struggled for nearly a decade to define the proper accommodation between the law of defamation and the freedoms of speech and press protected by the First Amendment. With this decision we return to that effort. We granted certiorari to reconsider the extent of a publisher's constitutional privilege against liability for defamation of a private citizen.

I

In 1968 a Chicago policeman named Nuccio shot and killed a youth named Nelson. The state authorities prosecuted Nuccio for the homicide and ultimately obtained a conviction for murder in the second degree. The Nelson family retained petitioner Elmer Gertz, a reputable attorney, to represent them in civil litigation against Nuccio.

Respondent publishes American Opinion, a monthly outlet for the views of the John Birch Society. Early in the 1960's the magazine began to warn of a nationwide conspiracy to discredit local law enforcement agencies and create in their stead a national police force capable of supporting a Communist dictatorship. . . . In March 1969 respondent published [an] article under the title "FRAME-UP: Richard Nuccio And The War On Police." The article purports to demonstrate that the testimony against Nuccio at his criminal trial was false and that his prosecution was part of the Communist campaign against the police.

Notwithstanding petitioner's remote connection with the prosecution of Nuccio, respondent's magazine portrayed him as an architect of the "frame-up." According to the article, the police file on petitioner took "a big, Irish cop to lift." The article stated that petitioner had been an official of the "Marxist League for Industrial Democracy, originally known as the Intercollegiate Socialist Society, which has advocated the violent seizure of our government." It labeled Gertz a "Leninist" and a "Communist-fronter." It also stated that

Gertz had been an officer of the National Lawyers Guild, described as a Communist organization that "probably did more than any other outfit to plan the Communist attack on the Chicago police during the 1968 Democratic Convention."

These statements contained serious inaccuracies. The implication that petitioner had a criminal record was false. Petitioner had been a member and officer of the National Lawyers Guild some 15 years earlier, but there was no evidence that he or that organization had taken any part in planning the 1968 demonstrations in Chicago. There was also no basis for the charge that petitioner was a "Leninist" or a "Communist-fronter." And he had never been a member of the "Marxist League for Industrial Democracy" or the "Intercollegiate Socialist Society."

. . .

Petitioner filed a diversity action for libel in the United States District Court for the Northern District of Illinois. He claimed that the falsehoods published by respondent injured his reputation as a lawyer and a citizen. . . . Because some statements in the article constituted libel per se under Illinois law, the court submitted the case to the jury under instructions that withdrew from its consideration all issues save the measure of damages. The jury awarded $ 50,000 to petitioner.

Following the jury verdict and on further reflection, the District Court concluded that the *New York Times* standard should govern this case even though petitioner was not a public official or public figure. It accepted respondent's contention that that privilege protected discussion of any public issue without regard to the status of a person defamed therein. Accordingly, the court entered judgment for respondent notwithstanding the jury's verdict. This conclusion anticipated the reasoning of a plurality of this Court in *Rosenbloom v. Metromedia, Inc.*, 403 U.S. 29 (1971).

Petitioner appealed to contest the applicability of the *New York Times* standard to this case. . . . [T]he Court of Appeals for the Seventh Circuit . . . agreed with the District Court that respondent could assert the constitutional privilege because the article concerned a matter of public interest, citing this Court's intervening decision in *Rosenbloom v. Metromedia, Inc.* . . . . The Court of Appeals therefore affirmed. For the reasons stated below, we reverse.

II

The principal issue in this case is whether a newspaper or broadcaster that publishes defamatory falsehoods about an individual who is neither a public official nor a public figure may claim a constitutional privilege against liability for the injury inflicted by those statements. . . .

. . .

III

We begin with the common ground. Under the First Amendment there is no such thing as a false idea. However pernicious an opinion may seem, we depend for its correction not on the conscience of judges and juries but on the competition of other ideas. But there is no constitutional value in false statements of fact. Neither the intentional lie nor the careless error materially advances society's interest in "uninhibited, robust, and wide-open" debate on public issues. *New York Times Co.* They belong to that category of utterances which "are no essential part of any exposition of ideas, and are of such slight social value as a step to truth that any benefit that may be derived from them is clearly outweighed by the social interest in order and morality." *Chaplinsky.*

Although the erroneous statement of fact is not worthy of constitutional protection, it is nevertheless inevitable in free debate. . . . And punishment of error runs the risk of inducing a cautious and restrictive exercise of the constitutionally guaranteed freedoms of speech and press. Our decisions recognize that a rule of strict liability that compels a publisher or broadcaster to guarantee the accuracy of his factual assertions may lead to intolerable self-censorship. Allowing the media to avoid liability only by proving the truth of all injurious statements does not accord adequate protection to First Amendment liberties. . . . The First Amendment requires that we protect some falsehood in order to protect speech that matters.

The need to avoid self-censorship by the news media is, however, not the only societal value at issue. If it were, this Court would have embraced long ago the view that publishers and broadcasters enjoy an unconditional and indefeasible immunity from liability for defamation. See *New York Times Co.* (Black, J., concurring). Such a rule would, indeed, obviate the fear that the prospect of civil liability for injurious falsehood might dissuade a timorous press from the effective exercise of First Amendment freedoms. Yet absolute protection for the communications media requires a total sacrifice of the competing value served by the law of defamation.

The legitimate state interest underlying the law of libel is the compensation of individuals for the harm inflicted on them by defamatory falsehood. We would not lightly require the State to abandon this purpose, for, as MR. JUSTICE STEWART has reminded us, the individual's right to the protection of his own good name

> "reflects no more than our basic concept of the essential dignity and worth of every human being—a concept at the root of any decent system of ordered liberty. The protection of private personality, like the protection of life itself, is left primarily to the individual States under the Ninth and Tenth Amendments. But this does not mean that the right is entitled to any less recognition by this Court as a basic of our constitutional system." *Rosenblatt v. Baer*, 383 U.S. 75, 92 (1966) (concurring opinion).

Some tension necessarily exists between the need for a vigorous and uninhibited press and the legitimate interest in redressing wrongful injury. As Mr. Justice Harlan stated, "some antithesis between freedom of speech and press and libel actions persists, for libel remains premised on the content of speech and limits the freedom of the publisher to express certain sentiments, at least without guaranteeing legal proof of their substantial accuracy." *Curtis Publishing Co. v. Butts.* In our continuing effort to define the proper accommodation between these competing concerns, we have been especially anxious to assure to the freedoms of speech and press that "breathing space" essential to their fruitful exercise. To that end this Court has extended a measure of strategic protection to defamatory falsehood.

The *New York Times* standard defines the level of constitutional protection appropriate to the context of defamation of a public person. Those who, by reason of the notoriety of their achievements or the vigor and success with which they seek the public's attention, are properly classed as public figures and those who hold governmental office may recover for injury to reputation only on clear and convincing proof that the defamatory falsehood was made with knowledge of its falsity or with reckless disregard for the truth. This standard administers an extremely powerful antidote to the inducement to media self-censorship of the common-law rule of strict liability for libel and slander. And it exacts a correspondingly high price from the victims of defamatory falsehood. Plainly many deserving plaintiffs, including some intentionally subjected to injury, will be unable to surmount the barrier of the *New York Times* test. Despite this substantial abridgment of the state law right to compensation for wrongful hurt to one's reputation, the Court has concluded that the protection of the *New York Times* privilege should be available to publishers and broadcasters of defamatory falsehood concerning public officials and public figures. We think that these decisions are correct, but we do not find their holdings justified solely by reference to the interest of the press and broadcast media in immunity from liability. Rather, we believe that the *New York Times* rule states an accommodation between this concern and the limited state interest present in the context of libel actions brought by public persons. For the reasons stated below, we conclude that the state interest in compensating injury to the reputation of private individuals requires that a different rule should obtain with respect to them.

. . .

. . . [W]e have no difficulty in distinguishing among defamation plaintiffs. The first remedy of any victim of defamation is self-help—using available opportunities to contradict the lie or correct the error and thereby to minimize its adverse impact on reputation. Public officials and public figures usually enjoy significantly greater access to the channels of effective communication and hence have a more realistic opportunity to counteract false statements than private individuals normally enjoy. Private individuals are therefore more vulnerable to injury, and the state interest in protecting them is correspondingly greater.

More important than the likelihood that private individuals will lack effective opportunities for rebuttal, there is a compelling normative consideration underlying the distinction between public and private defamation plaintiffs. An individual who decides to seek governmental office must accept certain necessary consequences of that involvement in public affairs. He runs the risk of closer public scrutiny than might otherwise be the case. And society's interest in the officers of government is not strictly limited to the formal discharge of official duties. As the Court pointed out in *Garrison v. Louisiana*, 379 U.S., at 77, the public's interest extends to "anything which might touch on an official's fitness for office. . . . "

Those classed as public figures stand in a similar position. Hypothetically, it may be possible for someone to become a public figure through no purposeful action of his own, but the instances of truly involuntary public figures must be exceedingly rare. For the most part those who attain this status have assumed roles of special prominence in the affairs of society. Some occupy positions of such persuasive power and influence that they are deemed public figures for all purposes. More commonly, those classed as public figures have thrust themselves to the forefront of particular public controversies in order to influence the resolution of the issues involved. In either event, they invite attention and comment.

Even if the foregoing generalities do not obtain in every instance, the communications media are entitled to act on the assumption that public officials and public figures have voluntarily exposed themselves to increased risk of injury from defamatory falsehood concerning them. No such assumption is justified with respect to a private individual. He has not accepted public office or assumed an "influential role in ordering society." *Curtis Publishing Co. v. Butts* (Warren, C. J., concurring in result). He has relinquished no part of his interest in the protection of his own good name, and consequently he has a more compelling call on the courts for redress of injury inflicted by defamatory falsehood. Thus, private individuals are not only more vulnerable to injury than public officials and public figures; they are also more deserving of recovery.

For these reasons we conclude that the States should retain substantial latitude in their efforts to enforce a legal remedy for defamatory falsehood injurious to the reputation of a private individual. The extension of the *New York Times* test proposed by the *Rosenbloom* plurality would abridge this legitimate state interest to a degree that we find unacceptable. And it would occasion the additional difficulty of forcing state and federal judges to decide on an *ad hoc* basis which publications address issues of "general or public interest" and which do not—to determine, in the words of Mr. Justice Marshall, "what information is relevant to self-government." *Rosenbloom v. Metromedia, Inc.* We doubt the wisdom of committing this task to the conscience of judges. Nor does the Constitution require us to draw so thin a line between the drastic alternatives of the New York Times privilege and the common law of strict liability for defamatory error. . . .

We hold that, so long as they do not impose liability without fault, the States may define for themselves the appropriate standard of liability for a publisher or broadcaster of defamatory falsehood injurious to a private individual. This approach provides a more equitable boundary between the competing concerns involved here. It recognizes the strength of the legitimate state interest in compensating private individuals for wrongful injury to reputation, yet shields the press and broadcast media from the rigors of strict liability for defamation. At least this conclusion obtains where, as here, the substance of the defamatory statement "makes substantial danger to reputation apparent." This phrase places in perspective the conclusion we announce today. Our inquiry would involve considerations somewhat different from those discussed above if a State purported to condition civil liability on a factual misstatement whose content did not warn a reasonably prudent editor or broadcaster of its defamatory potential. Such a case is not now before us, and we intimate no view as to its proper resolution.

IV

Our accommodation of the competing values at stake in defamation suits by private individuals allows the States to impose liability on the publisher or broadcaster of defamatory falsehood on a less demanding showing than that required by *New York Times*. This conclusion is not based on a belief that the considerations which prompted the adoption of the *New York Times* privilege for defamation of public officials and its extension to public figures are wholly inapplicable to the context of private individuals. Rather, we endorse this approach in recognition of the strong and legitimate state interest in compensating private individuals for injury to reputation. But this countervailing state interest extends no further than compensation for actual injury. For the reasons stated below, we hold that the States may not permit recovery of presumed or punitive damages, at least when liability is not based on a showing of knowledge of falsity or reckless disregard for the truth.

The common law of defamation is an oddity of tort law, for it allows recovery of purportedly compensatory damages without evidence of actual loss. Under the traditional rules pertaining to actions for libel, the existence of injury is presumed from the fact of publication. Juries may award substantial sums as compensation for supposed damage to reputation without any proof that such harm actually occurred. The largely uncontrolled discretion of juries to award damages where there is no loss unnecessarily compounds the potential of any system of liability for defamatory falsehood to inhibit the vigorous exercise of First Amendment freedoms. Additionally, the doctrine of presumed damages invites juries to punish unpopular opinion rather than to compensate individuals for injury sustained by the publication of a false fact. More to the point, the States have no substantial interest in securing for plaintiffs such as this petitioner gratuitous awards of money damages far in excess of any actual injury.

. . .

We also find no justification for allowing awards of punitive damages against publishers and broadcasters held liable under state-defined standards of liability for defamation. In most jurisdictions jury discretion over the amounts awarded is limited only by the gentle rule that they not be excessive. Consequently, juries assess punitive damages in wholly unpredictable amounts bearing no necessary relation to the actual harm caused. And they remain free to use their discretion selectively to punish expressions of unpopular views. Like the doctrine of presumed damages, jury discretion to award punitive damages unnecessarily exacerbates the danger of media self-censorship, but, unlike the former rule, punitive damages are wholly irrelevant to the state interest that justifies a negligence standard for private defamation actions. They are not compensation for injury. Instead, they are private fines levied by civil juries to punish reprehensible conduct and to deter its future occurrence. In short, the private defamation plaintiff who establishes liability under a less demanding standard than that stated by *New York Times* may recover only such damages as are sufficient to compensate him for actual injury.

V

Notwithstanding our refusal to extend the *New York Times* privilege to defamation of private individuals, respondent contends that we should affirm the judgment below on the ground that petitioner is either a public official or a public figure. There is little basis for the former assertion. . . . Respondent's suggestion would sweep all lawyers under the *New York Times* rule as officers of the court and distort the plain meaning of the "public official" category beyond all recognition. We decline to follow it.

Respondent's characterization of petitioner as a public figure raises a different question. That designation may rest on either of two alternative bases. In some instances an individual may achieve such pervasive fame or notoriety that he becomes a public figure for all purposes and in all contexts. More commonly, an individual voluntarily injects himself or is drawn into a particular public controversy and thereby becomes a public figure for a limited range of issues. In either case such persons assume special prominence in the resolution of public questions. . . . Absent clear evidence of general fame or notoriety in the community, and pervasive involvement in the affairs of society, an individual should not be deemed a public personality for all aspects of his life. It is preferable to reduce the public-figure question to a more meaningful context by looking to the nature and extent of an individual's participation in the particular controversy giving rise to the defamation.

In this context it is plain that petitioner was not a public figure. He played a minimal role at the coroner's inquest, and his participation related solely to his representation of a private client. He took no part in the criminal prosecution of Officer Nuccio. Moreover, he never discussed either the criminal or civil litigation with the press and was never quoted as having done so. He plainly did not thrust himself into the vortex of this public issue, nor did he engage the public's attention in an attempt to influence its outcome. . . .

We therefore conclude that the *New York Times* standard is inapplicable to this case and that the trial court erred in entering judgment for respondent. Because the jury was allowed to impose liability without fault and was permitted to presume damages without proof of injury, a new trial is necessary. We reverse and remand for further proceedings in accord with this opinion.

[Justice Blackmun's concurring opinion is omitted.]

MR. CHIEF JUSTICE BURGER, dissenting.

. . .

Agreement or disagreement with the law as it has evolved to this time does not alter the fact that it has been orderly development with a consistent basic rationale. In today's opinion the Court abandons the traditional thread so far as the ordinary private citizen is concerned and introduces the concept that the media will be liable for negligence in publishing defamatory statements with respect to such persons. . . . I am frank to say I do not know the parameters of a "negligence" doctrine as applied to the news media. Conceivably this new doctrine could inhibit some editors, as the dissents of MR. JUSTICE DOUGLAS and MR. JUSTICE BRENNAN suggest. But I would prefer to allow this area of law to continue to evolve as it has up to now with respect to private citizens rather than embark on a new doctrinal theory which has no jurisprudential ancestry.

. . .

MR. JUSTICE DOUGLAS, dissenting.

. . .

There can be no doubt that a State impinges upon free and open discussion when it sanctions the imposition of damages for such discussion through its civil libel laws. Discussion of public affairs is often marked by highly charged emotions, and jurymen, not unlike us all, are subject to those emotions. It is indeed this very type of speech which is the reason for the First Amendment since speech which arouses little emotion is little in need of protection. The vehicle for publication in this case was the American Opinion, a most controversial periodical which disseminates the views of the John Birch Society, an organization which many deem to be quite offensive. The subject matter involved "Communist plots," "conspiracies against law enforcement agencies," and the killing of a private citizen by the police. With any such amalgam of controversial elements pressing upon the jury, a jury determination, unpredictable in the most neutral circumstances, becomes for those who venture to discuss heated issues, a virtual roll of the dice separating them from liability for often massive claims of damage.

It is only the hardy publisher who will engage in discussion in the face of such risk, and the Court's preoccupation with proliferating standards in the area of libel increases the risks. It matters little whether the standard be articulated as "malice" or "reckless disregard of the truth" or "negligence," for jury determinations by any of those criteria are virtually unreviewable. This Court, in its continuing delineation of variegated mantles of First Amendment protection, is, like the potential publisher, left with only speculation on how jury findings were influenced by the effect the subject matter of the publication had upon the minds and viscera of the jury. The standard announced today leaves the States free to "define for themselves the appropriate standard of liability for a publisher or broadcaster" in the circumstances of this case. This of course leaves the simple negligence standard as an option, with the jury free to impose damages upon a finding that the publisher failed to act as "a reasonable man." With such continued erosion of First Amendment protection, I fear that it may well be the reasonable man who refrains from speaking.

Since in my view the First and Fourteenth Amendments prohibit the imposition of damages upon respondent for this discussion of public affairs, I would affirm the judgment below.

MR. JUSTICE BRENNAN, dissenting.

. . . I adhere to my view expressed in *Rosenbloom v. Metromedia, Inc.* that we strike the proper accommodation between avoidance of media self-censorship and protection of individual reputations only when we require States to apply the *New York Times Co. v. Sullivan* knowing-or-reckless-falsity standard in civil libel actions concerning media reports of the involvement of private individuals in events of public or general interest.

. . .

We recognized in *New York Times Co. v. Sullivan* that a rule requiring a critic of official conduct to guarantee the truth of all of his factual contentions would inevitably lead to self-censorship when publishers, fearful of being unable to prove truth or unable to bear the expense of attempting to do so, simply eschewed printing controversial articles. Adoption, by many States, of a reasonable-care standard in cases where private individuals are involved in matters of public interest—the probable result of today's decision—will likewise lead to self-censorship since publishers will be required carefully to weigh a myriad of uncertain factors before publication. The reasonable-care standard is "elusive"; it saddles the press with "the intolerable burden of guessing how a jury might assess the reasonableness of steps taken by it to verify the accuracy of every reference to a name, picture or portrait." Under a reasonable-care regime, publishers and broadcasters will have to make pre-publication judgments about juror assessment of such diverse considerations as the size, operating procedures, and financial condition of the newsgathering system, as well as the relative costs and benefits of instituting less frequent and more costly reporting at a higher level of accuracy.

On the other hand, the uncertainties which the media face under today's decision are largely avoided by the *New York Times* standard. I reject the argument that my *Rosenbloom* view improperly commits to judges the task of determining what is and what is not an issue of "general or public interest." . . . The public interest is necessarily broad; any residual self-censorship that may result from the uncertain contours of the "general or public interest" concept should be of far less concern to publishers and broadcasters than that occasioned by state laws imposing liability for negligent falsehood.

. . . I would affirm the judgment of the Court of Appeals.

MR. JUSTICE WHITE, dissenting.

For some 200 years—from the very founding of the Nation—the law of defamation and right of the ordinary citizen to recover for false publication injurious to his reputation have been almost exclusively the business of state courts and legislatures. . . . The law governing the defamation of private citizens remained untouched by the First Amendment because, until relatively recently, the consistent view of the Court was that libelous words constitute a class of speech wholly unprotected by the First Amendment, subject only to limited exceptions carved out since 1964.

But now, using that Amendment as the chosen instrument, the Court, in a few printed pages, has federalized major aspects of libel law by declaring unconstitutional in important respects the prevailing defamation law in all or most of the 50 States. . . . I assume these sweeping changes will be popular with the press, but this is not the road to salvation for a court of law. As I see it, there are wholly insufficient grounds for scuttling the libel laws of the States in such wholesale fashion, to say nothing of deprecating the reputation interest of ordinary citizens and rendering them power-

less to protect themselves. I do not suggest that the decision is illegitimate or beyond the bounds of judicial review, but it is an ill-considered exercise of the power entrusted to this Court, particularly when the Court has not had the benefit of briefs and argument addressed to most of the major issues which the Court now decides. I respectfully dissent.

. . .

The Court does not contend, and it could hardly do so, that those who wrote the First Amendment intended to prohibit the Federal Government, within its sphere of influence in the Territories and the District of Columbia, from providing the private citizen a peaceful remedy for damaging falsehood. At the time of the adoption of the First Amendment, many of the consequences of libel law already described had developed, particularly the rule that libels and some slanders were so inherently injurious that they were actionable without special proof of damage to reputation. As the Court pointed out in *Roth v. United States*, 10 of the 14 States that had ratified the Constitution by 1792 had themselves provided constitutional guarantees for free expression, and 13 of the 14 nevertheless provided for the prosecution of libels. Prior to the Revolution, the American Colonies had adopted the common law of libel. Contrary to some popular notions, freedom of the press was sharply curtailed in colonial America. Seditious libel was punished as a contempt by the colonial legislatures and as a criminal offense in the colonial courts.

Scant, if any, evidence exists that the First Amendment was intended to abolish the common law of libel, at least to the extent of depriving ordinary citizens of meaningful redress against their defamers. On the contrary,

> "[it] is conceded on all sides that the common-law rules that subjected the libeler to responsibility for the private injury, or the public scandal or disorder occasioned by his conduct, are not abolished by the protection extended to the press in our constitutions." 2 T. Cooley, Constitutional Limitations 883 (8th ed. 1927).

Moreover . . . these common-law actions did not abridge freedom of the press. . . .

. . .

The central meaning of *New York Times*, and for me the First Amendment as it relates to libel laws, is that seditious libel—criticism of government and public officials—falls beyond the police power of the State. In a democratic society such as ours, the citizen has the privilege of criticizing his government and its officials. But neither *New York Times* nor its progeny suggest that the First Amendment intended in all circumstances to deprive the private citizen of his historic recourse to redress published falsehoods damaging to reputation or that, contrary to history and precedent, the Amendment should now be so interpreted. Simply put, the First Amendment did not confer a "license to defame the citizen." W. Douglas, The Right of the People 36 (1958).

. . .

In these circumstances, the law has heretofore put the risk of falsehood on the publisher where the victim is a private citizen and no grounds of special privilege are invoked. The Court would now shift this risk to the victim, even though he has done nothing to invite the calumny, is wholly innocent of fault, and is helpless to avoid his injury. I doubt that jurisprudential resistance to liability without fault is sufficient ground for employing the First Amendment to revolutionize the law of libel, and in my view, that body of legal rules poses no realistic threat to the press and its service to the public. The press today is vigorous and robust. To me, it is quite incredible to suggest that threats of libel suits from private citizens are causing the press to refrain from publishing the truth. I know of no hard facts to support that proposition, and the Court furnishes none.

The communications industry has increasingly become concentrated in a few powerful hands operating very lucrative businesses reaching across the Nation and into almost every home. Neither the industry as a whole nor its individual components are easily intimidated, and we are fortunate that they are not. Requiring them to pay for the occasional damage they do to private reputation will play no substantial part in their future performance or their existence.

. . .

It is difficult for me to understand why the ordinary citizen should himself carry the risk of damage and suffer the injury in order to vindicate First Amendment values by protecting the press and others from liability for circulating false information. This is particularly true because such statements serve no purpose whatsoever in furthering the public interest or the search for truth but, on the contrary, may frustrate that search and at the same time inflict great injury on the defenseless individual. The owners of the press and the stockholders of the communications enterprises can much better bear the burden. And if they cannot, the public at large should somehow pay for what is essentially a public benefit derived at private expense.

. . .

I fail to see how the quality or quantity of public debate will be promoted by further emasculation of state libel laws for the benefit of the news media. If anything, this trend may provoke a new and radical imbalance in the communications process. It is not at all inconceivable that virtually unrestrained defamatory remarks about private citizens will discourage them from speaking out and concerning themselves with social problems. This would turn the First Amendment on its head. David Riesman, writing in the midst of World War II on the fascists' effective use of defamatory attacks on their opponents, commented: "Thus it is that the law of libel, with its ecclesiastic background and domestic character, its aura of heart-balm suits and crusading nineteenth-century editors, becomes suddenly important for modern democratic survival." Democracy and Defamation: Fair Game and Fair Comment I, 42 Col. L. Rev. 1085, 1088 (1942).

. . .

Freedom and human dignity and decency are not antithetical. Indeed, they cannot survive without each other. Both exist side-by-side in precarious balance, one always threatening to overwhelm the other. Our experience as a Nation testifies to the ability of our democratic institutions to harness this dynamic tension. One of the mechanisms seized upon by the common law to accommodate these forces was the civil libel action tried before a jury of average citizens. . . .

. . . Whether or not the course followed by the majority is wise, and I have indicated my doubts that it is, our constitutional scheme compels a proper respect for the role of the States in acquitting their duty to obey the Constitution. Finding no evidence that they have shirked this responsibility, particularly when the law of defamation is even now in transition, I would await some demonstration of the diminution of freedom of expression before acting.

For the foregoing reasons, I would reverse the judgment of the Court of Appeals and reinstate the jury's verdict.

After *Gertz* does it matter whether or not a defamatory statement involves a matter of public concern? The Court considered this question in *Dun & Bradstreet, Inc. v. Greenmoss Builders, Inc.*[42] Dun & Bradstreet, a credit reporting agency, sent a report to five subscribers indicating—falsely—that Greenmoss Builders, a construction con-

---

[42] 472 U.S. 749 (1985).

tractor, had filed a voluntary petition for bankruptcy. Greenmoss Builders brought a defamation action in Vermont state court and the jury returned a verdict in its favor, awarding the company $50,000 in presumed damages and $300,000 in punitive damages. The trial court granted Dun & Bradstreet's petition for a new trial, however, because it had failed to charge the jury to apply the *Gertz* standard. The Vermont Supreme Court reversed on the ground that "the media protections outlined in *Gertz* are inapplicable to nonmedia defamation actions." Emphasizing the state's interest in providing remedies for defamation, the United States Supreme Court affirmed: "In light of the reduced constitutional value of speech involving no matters of public concern, we hold that the state interest adequately supports awards of presumed and punitive damages—even absent a showing of 'actual malice'." Since the credit report was "speech solely in the individual interest of the speaker and its specific business audience," it merited no constitutional privilege.

The concern about creating sufficient "breathing space" for free expression raised in *New York Times v. Sullivan* arises in tort contexts besides libel. The Court has held that the First Amendment affords special privileges to the press against liability arising from other types of injury, including emotional distress and disclosure of private facts.

In *Hustler Magazine v. Falwell*, the Court considered whether government officials and public figures offended by a media parody could avoid the *New York Times* actual malice requirement by suing for the tort of intentional infliction of emotional distress rather than libel.[43] Jerry Falwell, the nationally known minister who founded the Moral Majority, sued Hustler Magazine over a parody of an advertisement for Campari Liqueur entitled, "Jerry Falwell talks about his first time," modeled after actual advertisements that played on the sexual double entendre of the subject of "first times." The parody contained a fabricated interview with Falwell in which he stated that his "first time" was during a drunken incestuous rendezvous with his mother in an outhouse. The jury found against Falwell on his libel claim on the ground that the parody could not reasonably be understood as describing actual facts about him. The jury awarded him both compensatory and punitive damages, however, for his intentional infliction of emotional distress claim. The Court of Appeals for the Fourth Circuit affirmed the judgment, reasoning that the *New York Times* standard was satisfied by the state law requirement that the plaintiff prove intentional or reckless infliction of emotional distress.

The Supreme Court emphasized the First Amendment's protection of outrageous speech occurring in public debate and the importance of parodies and cartoons in the American tradition of political criticism.

> Generally speaking the law does not regard the intent to inflict emotional distress as one which should receive much solicitude, and it is quite understandable that most if not all jurisdictions have chosen to make it civilly culpable where the conduct in question is sufficiently "outrageous." But in the world of debate about public affairs, many things done with motives that are less than admirable are protected by the First Amendment. . . . "Debate on public issues will not be uninhibited if the speaker must run the risk that it will be proved in court that he spoke out of hatred; even if he did speak out of hatred, utterances honestly believed contribute to the free interchange of ideas and the ascertainment of truth." Thus while such a bad motive may be deemed controlling for purposes of tort liability in other areas of the law, we think the First Amendment prohibits such a result in the area of public debate about public figures.
>
> Were we to hold otherwise, there can be little doubt that political cartoon-

---

[43] Hustler Magazine v. Falwell, 485 U.S. 46 (1988).

ists and satirists would be subjected to damages awards without any showing that their work falsely defamed its subject. . . . The appeal of the political cartoon or caricature is often based on exploration of unfortunate physical traits or politically embarrassing events—an exploration often calculated to injure the feelings of the subject of the portrayal. The art of the cartoonist is often not reasoned or evenhanded, but slashing and one-sided. . . .

Respondent contends, however, that the caricature in question here was so "outrageous" as to distinguish it from more traditional political cartoons. There is no doubt that the caricature of respondent and his mother published in Hustler is at best a distant cousin of [traditional] political cartoons, and a rather poor relation at that. If it were possible by laying down a principles standard to separate the one from the other, public discourse would probably suffer little or no harm. But we doubt that there is any such standard, and we are quite sure that the pejorative description "outrageous" does not supply one. "Outrageousness" in the area of political and social discourse has an inherent subjectiveness about it which would allow a jury to impose liability on the basis of the jurors' tastes or views, or perhaps on the basis of their dislike of a particular expression. . . .

Given this First Amendment interest in preserving uninhibited political debate, the Court held that "public figures and public officials may not recover for the tort of intentional infliction of emotional distress by reason of publications such as the one here at issue without showing in addition that the publication contains a false statement of fact which was made with 'actual malice'."

Part of the reason that the Hustler parody was protected by the First Amendment was that it did not contain a false statement of fact. Indeed, it did not contain *any* statement of fact. Although truth is a defense in libel actions, truthful statements of fact by the media may cause other types of injury for which individuals seek damages, such as the emotional distress caused by disclosure of private information. In *Florida Star v. B.J.F.*, a jury found the Florida Star newspaper civilly liable for publishing the name of a rape victim in violation of a state statute making such disclosures unlawful.[44] Florida Star argued that truthful publication may *never* be punished consistent with the First Amendment. The Court settled on a narrower rule, explaining that "the sensitivity and significance of the interests presented in clashes between First Amendment and privacy rights counsel relying on limited principles that sweep no more broadly than the appropriate context of the instant case." The limited First Amendment principle the Court applied was: "[I]f a newspaper lawfully obtains truthful information about a matter of public significance then state officials may not constitutionally punish publication of the information, absent a need to further a state interest of the highest order." The Court reversed the judgment against Florida Star because the newspaper had lawfully obtained the rape victim's name from a publicly released police report; the article in which the name appeared concerned an important public matter—the commission and investigation of a violent crime; and the state had failed to demonstrate its commitment to preserving rape victims' privacy. Moreover, the Florida statute swept too broadly, automatically imposing liability upon publication regardless of the defendants' level of culpability and the circumstances of the disclosure.

c. Obscenity

American governments have long attempted to maintain a moral society by prohibiting immoral speech. This was a primary concern of colonial leaders who enacted laws

---

[44] Florida Star v. B.J.F., 491 U.S. 524 (1989).

regulating sexual activity, including speech. Every colony passed statutes outlawing vulgar or obscene language, as well as profane and blasphemous words.[45] A 1691 Virginia law, for example, prohibited "swearing, cursing, profaning God's holy name, Sabbath abusing, drunkenness, fornication and adultery." A 1698 New Jersey law banned "all sorts of lewdness and profane behavior in word or action."

Most of the states that had ratified the Constitution by 1792 punished the crime of blasphemy or profanity despite the guarantees of free expression in their constitutions, and Massachusetts expressly prohibited the "Composing, Writing, Printing or Publishing, of any Filthy Obscene or Profane Song, Pamphlet, Libel or Mock-Sermon, in Imitation or in Mimicking of Preaching, or any other part of Divine Worship." Pennsylvania obtained the first reported obscenity conviction in 1815 under its common law.[46] In 1821 Vermont enacted the first state law prohibiting the publication or sale of "lewd or obscene" material, and federal legislation barring the importation of similar matter passed in 1842.[47]

These early obscenity laws were few in number and rarely enforced. In the late nineteenth century, however, both federal and state governments began to take an active interest in the suppression of obscenity. By the turn of the century at least thirty states had enacted some type of general prohibition on the dissemination of obscene materials, and by the time of the Court's 1957 decision in *Roth v. United States* no state was without some restriction of obscenity.

The federal government alone enacted twenty obscenity laws between 1842 and 1956. In 1873, Congress passed legislation which made it a crime to circulate obscene materials through the mails. Officially titled "An Act for the Suppression of Trade in, and Circulation of, obscene Literature and Articles of immoral Use," the statute became popularly known as the Comstock Act. Anthony Comstock had lobbied for passage of the law and, as special agent of the Post Office, oversaw its enforcement until his death in 1915. Under his broad conception of "obscenity" (which the statute did not define), Comstock confiscated sexually related material, blasphemy, and information about contraceptives, and prosecuted their distributors. He could boast in 1913 that he had destroyed 160 tons of obscene literature during his reign.[48]

Although Comstock generally exempted literary classics not marketed for their sexual content, he targeted scientific and philosophical works about sex as well as commercial pornography. For example, in 1877 Comstock prosecuted Ezra Heywood for distributing the anarchist pamphlet *Cupid's Yokes*, which proclaimed "the Natural Right and Necessity of Sexual Self-Government."[49] *Cupid's Yokes* defended the individual's right to "free love" governed by the "bonds of affection," rather than the state regulation of marriage. Heywood was convicted of violating the Comstock Act, and was fined and sentenced to two years in jail. A rally protesting the conviction at Boston's Faneuil Hall on August 1, 1878, drawing between 4000 and 6000 people, as well as numerous petitions, prompted President Hayes to pardon Heywood six months after his imprisonment.

It is likely that Heywood lost his court appeal on First Amendment grounds because of the Supreme Court's intervening decision in *Ex Parte Jackson*, 96 U.S. 727 (1877). *Ex Parte Jackson* upheld the constitutionality of a federal statute that prohibited the mailing of lottery advertisements. The Court reasoned that Congress' power to determine what materials can be mailed entailed a power to determine what can be excluded;

---

[45] ELDRIDGE, A DISTANT HERITAGE, *supra* note 3, at 6.

[46] *See* Commonwealth v. Sharpless, 2 S. & R. 91 (1815).

[47] *See* Laws of Vermont, 1824, c. XXXII, No. 1, § 23; Tariff Act of 1842, § 28, 5 Stat. 566.

[48] Rabban, *The Free Speech League*, *supra* note 15, at 57.

[49] *Id.* at 61–64.

the First Amendment did not require the Post Office to furnish "facilities for the distribution of matter deemed injurious to the public morals." Subsequent federal court decisions involving obscenity prosecutions under the Comstock Act borrowed the test of obscenity from an 1868 English decision, *The Queen v. Hicklin*: "[w]hether the tendency of the matter charged as obscenity is to deprave and corrupt those whose minds are open to such immoral influences, and into whose hands a publication of this sort may fall."

This history provided what seemed to the Supreme Court in *Roth v. United States* a "universal judgment that obscenity should be restrained." In *Roth*, the Court addressed the constitutionality of convictions for advertising and circulating obscene material under both federal and California law. The Court approached the issue by asking whether obscenity was protected speech at all, or whether—like libel—it fell outside the First Amendment's safeguards.

Roth v. United States
354 U.S. 476 (1957)

MR. JUSTICE BRENNAN delivered the opinion of the Court.

. . .

The dispositive question is whether obscenity is utterance within the area of protected speech and press. Although this is the first time the question has been squarely presented to this Court, either under the First Amendment or under the Fourteenth Amendment, expressions found in numerous opinions indicate that this Court has always assumed that obscenity is not protected by the freedoms of speech and press.

The guaranties of freedom of expression in effect in 10 of the 14 States which by 1792 had ratified the Constitution, gave no absolute protection for every utterance. Thirteen of the 14 States provided for the prosecution of libel, and all of those States made either blasphemy or profanity, or both, statutory crimes. As early as 1712, Massachusetts made it criminal to publish "any filthy, obscene, or profane song, pamphlet, libel or mock sermon" in imitation or mimicking of religious services. Thus, profanity and obscenity were related offenses.

In light of this history, it is apparent that the unconditional phrasing of the First Amendment was not intended to protect every utterance. This phrasing did not prevent this Court from concluding that libelous utterances are not within the area of constitutionally protected speech. *Beauharnais v. Illinois*. At the time of the adoption of the First Amendment, obscenity law was not as fully developed as libel law, but there is sufficiently contemporaneous evidence to show that obscenity, too, was outside the protection intended for speech and press.

The protection given speech and press was fashioned to assure unfettered interchange of ideas for the bringing about of political and social changes desired by the people. . . . All ideas having even the slightest redeeming social importance—unorthodox ideas, controversial ideas, even ideas hateful to the prevailing climate of opinion—have the full protection of the guaranties, unless excludable because they encroach upon the limited area of more important interests. But implicit in the history of the First Amendment is the rejection of obscenity as utterly without redeeming social importance. This rejection for that reason is mirrored in the universal judgment that obscenity should be restrained, reflected in the international agreement of over 50 nations, in the obscenity laws of all of the 48 States, and in the 20 obscenity laws enacted by the Congress from 1842 to 1956. This is the same judgment expressed by this Court in *Chaplinsky v. New Hampshire*:

> " . . . There are certain well-defined and narrowly limited classes of speech, the prevention and punishment of which have never been thought to raise any Constitutional problem. These include *the lewd and obscene. . . . It has been well observed that such utterances are no essential part of any exposition of ideas, and are of such slight social value as a step to truth that any benefit that may be derived from them is clearly outweighed by the social interest in order and morality. . . .* " (Emphasis added.)

We hold that obscenity is not within the area of constitutionally protected speech or press.

It is strenuously urged that these obscenity statutes offend the constitutional guaranties because they punish incitation to impure sexual *thoughts*, not shown to be related to any overt antisocial conduct which is or may be incited in the persons stimulated to such *thoughts*. In *Roth*, the trial judge instructed the jury: "The words 'obscene, lewd and lascivious' as used in the law, signify that form of immorality which has relation to sexual impurity and has a tendency to excite lustful *thoughts*." (Emphasis added.) . . . It is insisted that the constitutional guaranties are violated because convictions may be had without proof either that obscene material will perceptibly create a clear and present danger of antisocial conduct, or will probably induce its recipients to such conduct. But, in light of our holding that obscenity is not protected speech, the complete answer to this argument is in the holding of this Court in *Beauharnais v. Illinois*:

> "Libelous utterances not being within the area of constitutionally protected speech, it is unnecessary, either for us or for the State courts, to consider the issues behind the phrase 'clear and present danger.' Certainly no one would contend that obscene speech, for example, may be punished only upon a showing of such circumstances. Libel, as we have seen, is in the same class."

However, sex and obscenity are not synonymous. Obscene material is material which deals with sex in a manner appealing to prurient interest.[20] The portrayal of sex, *e.g.*, in art, literature and scientific works, is not itself sufficient reason to deny material the constitutional protection of freedom of speech and press. Sex, a great and mysterious motive force in human life, has indisputably been a subject of absorbing interest to mankind through the ages; it is one of the vital problems of human interest and public concern. . . . It is therefore vital that the standards for judging obscenity safeguard the protection of freedom of speech and press for material which does not treat sex in a manner appealing to prurient interest.

The early leading standard of obscenity allowed material to be judged merely by the effect of an isolated excerpt upon particularly susceptible persons. *Regina v. Hicklin*, L.R. 3 Q.B. 360 [1868]. Some American courts adopted this standard but later decisions have rejected it and substituted this test: whether to the average person, applying contemporary community standards, the dominant theme of the material taken as a whole appeals to prurient interest. The *Hicklin* test, judging obscenity by the effect of isolated passages upon the most susceptible persons, might well encompass material legitimately treating with sex, and so it must be rejected as unconstitutionally restrictive of the freedoms of speech and press. On the other hand, the substituted standard provides safeguards adequate to withstand the charge of constitutional infirmity.

. . .

The judgments are

Affirmed.

[Chief Justice Warren's concurring opinion is omitted.]

Mr. Justice Harlan, . . . dissenting in [*Roth*].

. . .

We are faced here with the question whether the federal obscenity statute, as construed and applied in this case, violates the First Amendment to the Constitution. To me, this question is of quite a different order than one where we are dealing with state legislation under the Fourteenth Amendment. I do not think it follows that state and federal powers in this area are the same, and that just because the State may suppress a particular utterance, it is automatically permissible for the Federal Government to do the same. . . .

. . . Whether a particular limitation on speech or press is to be upheld because it subserves a paramount governmental interest must, to a large extent, I think, depend on whether that government has, under the Constitution, a direct substantive interest, that is, the power to act, in the particular area involved.

The Federal Government has, for example, power to restrict seditious speech directed against it, because that Government certainly has the substantive authority to protect itself against revolution. But in dealing with obscenity we are faced with the converse situation, for the interests which obscenity statutes purportedly protect are primarily entrusted to the care, not of the Federal Government, but of the States. Congress has no substantive power over sexual morality. Such powers as the Federal Government has in this field are but incidental to its other powers, here the postal power, and are not of the same nature as those possessed by the States, which bear direct responsibility for the protection of the local moral fabric.

. . .

Not only is the federal interest in protecting the Nation against pornography attenuated, but the dangers of federal censorship in this field are far greater than anything the States may do. . . . Different States will have

---

[20] *I.e.*, material having a tendency to excite lustful thoughts. Webster's New International Dictionary (Unabridged, 2d ed., 1949) defines prurient, in pertinent part, as follows:

" . . . Itching; longing; uneasy with desire or longing; of persons, having itching, morbid, or lascivious longings; of desire, curiosity, or propensity, lewd. . . . " . . .

different attitudes toward the same work of literature. The same book which is freely read in one State might be classed as obscene in another. And it seems to me that no overwhelming danger to our freedom to experiment and to gratify our tastes in literature is likely to result from the suppression of a borderline book in one of the States, so long as there is no uniform nation-wide suppression of the book, and so long as other States are free to experiment with the same or bolder books.... But the dangers to free thought and expression are truly great if the Federal Government imposes a blanket ban over the Nation on such a book. The prerogative of the States to differ on their ideas of morality will be destroyed, the ability of States to experiment will be stunted.

. . .

MR. JUSTICE DOUGLAS, with whom MR. JUSTICE BLACK concurs, dissenting.

When we sustain these convictions, we make the legality of a publication turn on the purity of thought which a book or tract instills in the mind of the reader. I do not think we can approve that standard and be faithful to the command of the First Amendment....

. . .

The tests by which these convictions were obtained require only the arousing of sexual thoughts. Yet the arousing of sexual thoughts and desires happens every day in normal life in dozens of ways.... The test of obscenity the Court endorses today gives the censor free range over a vast domain. To allow the State to step in and punish mere speech or publication that the judge or the jury thinks has an *undesirable* impact on thoughts but that is not shown to be a part of unlawful action is drastically to curtail the First Amendment. As recently stated by two of our outstanding authorities on obscenity, "The danger of influencing a change in the current moral standards of the community, or of shocking or offending readers, or of stimulating sex thoughts or desires apart from objective conduct, can never justify the losses to society that result from interference with literary freedom." Lockhart & McClure, Literature, The Law of Obscenity and the Constitution, 38 Minn.L.Rev. 295, 387.

If we were certain that impurity of sexual thoughts impelled to action, we would be on less dangerous ground in punishing the distributors of this sex literature. But it is by no means clear that obscene literature, as so defined, is a significant factor in influencing substantial deviations from the community standards.... The absence of dependable information on the effect of obscene literature on human conduct should make us wary. It should put us on the side of protecting society's interest in literature, except and unless it can

be said that the particular publication has an impact on action that the government can control.

. . .

Any test that turns on what is offensive to the community's standards is too loose, too capricious, too destructive of freedom of expression to be squared with the First Amendment. Under that test, juries can censor, suppress, and punish what they don't like, provided the matter relates to "sexual impurity" or has a tendency "to excite lustful thoughts." This is community censorship in one of its worst forms. It creates a regime where in the battle between the literati and the Philistines, the Philistines are certain to win. If experience in this field teaches anything, it is that "censorship of obscenity has almost always been both irrational and indiscriminate." . . .

I do not think that the problem can be resolved by the Court's statement that "obscenity is not expression protected by the First Amendment." With the exception of *Beauharnais v. Illinois*, none of our cases has resolved problems of free speech and free press by placing any form of expression beyond the pale of the absolute prohibition of the First Amendment. Unlike the law of libel, wrongfully relied on in *Beauharnais*, there is no special historical evidence that literature dealing with sex was intended to be treated in a special manner by those who drafted the First Amendment. In fact, the first reported court decision in this country involving obscene literature was in 1821. I reject too the implication that problems of freedom of speech and of the press are to be resolved by weighing against the values of free expression, the judgment of the Court that a particular form of that expression has "no redeeming social importance." The First Amendment, its prohibition in terms absolute, was designed to preclude courts as well as legislatures from weighing the values of speech against silence. The First Amendment puts free speech in the preferred position.

Freedom of expression can be suppressed if, and to the extent that, it is so closely brigaded with illegal action as to be an inseparable part of it. As a people, we cannot afford to relax that standard. For the test that suppresses a cheap tract today can suppress a literary gem tomorrow. All it need do is to incite a lascivious thought or arouse a lustful desire. The list of books that judges or juries can place in that category is endless.

I would give the broad sweep of the First Amendment full support. I have the same confidence in the ability of our people to reject noxious literature as I have in their capacity to sort out the true from the false in theology, economics, politics, or any other field.

A major point of contention between the majority and dissenting justices in *Roth* was whether obscenity laws punished mere thoughts which the government found objectionable, thereby violating the First Amendment. The majority acknowledged this possibility, but avoided it by citing dicta in *Beauharnais v. Illinois* that the government need not show that *unprotected* speech actually poses a clear and present danger of inciting harmful action. Justice Douglas, on the other hand, stressed that the First Amendment prohibits punishment of speech without evidence of its association with illegal conduct; obscenity's arousal of lascivious thoughts, according to Douglas, was constitutionally insufficient to justify government censorship. The Court focused on this question of government thought control in *Stanley v. Georgia*. Because Stanley was arrested for possessing obscene movies in the privacy of his own home, the government could not demonstrate the social harms it argued arose from the public circulation of obscenity.

Stanley v. Georgia
394 U.S. 557 (1969)

MR. JUSTICE MARSHALL delivered the opinion of the Court.

An investigation of appellant's alleged bookmaking activities led to the issuance of a search warrant for appellant's home. Under authority of this warrant, federal and state agents secured entrance. They found very little evidence of bookmaking activity, but while looking through a desk drawer in an upstairs bedroom, one of the federal agents, accompanied by a state officer, found three reels of eight-millimeter film. Using a projector and screen found in an upstairs living room, they viewed the films. The state officer concluded that they were obscene and seized them. Since a further examination of the bedroom indicated that appellant occupied it, he was charged with possession of obscene matter and placed under arrest. He was later indicted for "knowingly hav[ing] possession of . . . obscene matter" in violation of Georgia law. Appellant was tried before a jury and convicted. The Supreme Court of Georgia affirmed.

. . . Appellant argues here, and argued below, that the Georgia obscenity statute, insofar as it punishes mere private possession of obscene matter, violates the First Amendment, as made applicable to the States by the Fourteenth Amendment. For reasons set forth below, we agree that the mere private possession of obscene matter cannot constitutionally be made a crime.

. . .

It is true that *Roth* does declare, seemingly without qualification, that obscenity is not protected by the First Amendment. That statement has been repeated in various forms in subsequent cases. However, neither *Roth* nor any subsequent decision of this Court dealt with the precise problem involved in the pres-

ent case. . . . In this context, we do not believe that this case can be decided simply by citing *Roth*. *Roth* and its progeny certainly do mean that the First and Fourteenth Amendments recognize a valid governmental interest in dealing with the problem of obscenity. But the assertion of that interest cannot, in every context, be insulated from all constitutional protections. . . . *Roth* and the cases following it discerned such an "important interest" in the regulation of commercial distribution of obscene material. That holding cannot foreclose an examination of the constitutional implications of a statute forbidding mere private possession of such material.

It is now well established that the Constitution protects the right to receive information and ideas. . . . This right to receive information and ideas, regardless of their social worth, is fundamental to our free society. Moreover, in the context of this case—a prosecution for mere possession of printed or filmed matter in the privacy of a person's own home—that right takes on an added dimension. For also fundamental is the right to be free, except in very limited circumstances, from unwanted governmental intrusions into one's privacy. . . .

These are the rights that appellant is asserting in the case before us. He is asserting the right to read or observe what he pleases—the right to satisfy his intellectual and emotional needs in the privacy of his own home. He is asserting the right to be free from state inquiry into the contents of his library. Georgia contends that appellant does not have these rights, that there are certain types of materials that the individual may not read or even possess. Georgia justifies this assertion by arguing that the films in the present case are obscene. But we think that mere categorization of these films as "obscene" is insufficient justification for such a drastic invasion of personal liberties guaranteed by the First and Fourteenth Amendments. Whatever may be the justifications for other statutes regulating obscenity, we do not think they reach into the privacy of one's own home. If the First Amendment means anything, it means that a State has no business telling a man, sitting alone in his own house, what books he may read or what films he may watch. Our whole constitutional heritage rebels at the thought of giving government the power to control men's minds.

And yet, in the face of these traditional notions of individual liberty, Georgia asserts the right to protect the individual's mind from the effects of obscenity. We are not certain that this argument amounts to anything more than the assertion that the State has the right to control the moral content of a person's thoughts. To some, this may be a noble purpose, but it is wholly inconsistent with the philosophy of the First Amendment. . . . Nor is it relevant that obscene materials in general, or the particular films before the Court, are arguably devoid of any ideological content. The line between the transmission of ideas and mere entertainment is much too elusive for this Court to draw, if indeed such a line can be drawn at all. Whatever the power of the state to control public dissemination of ideas inimical to the public morality, it cannot constitutionally premise legislation on the desirability of controlling a person's private thoughts.

Perhaps recognizing this, Georgia asserts that exposure to obscene materials may lead to deviant sexual behavior or crimes of sexual violence. There appears to be little empirical basis for that assertion. But more important, if the State is only concerned about printed or filmed materials inducing antisocial conduct, we believe that in the context of private consumption of ideas and information we should adhere to the view that "[a]mong free men, the deterrents ordinarily to be applied to prevent crime are education and punishment for violations of the law. . . ." *Whitney v. California* (Brandeis, J., concurring). Given the present state of knowledge, the State may no more pro-

hibit mere possession of obscene matter on the ground that it may lead to antisocial conduct than it may prohibit possession of chemistry books on the ground that they may lead to the manufacture of homemade spirits.

It is true that in *Roth* this Court rejected the necessity of proving that exposure to obscene material would create a clear and present danger of antisocial conduct or would probably induce its recipients to such conduct. But that case dealt with public distribution of obscene materials and such distribution is subject to different objections. For example, there is always the danger that obscene material might fall into the hands of children, or that it might intrude upon the sensibilities or privacy of the general public. No such dangers are present in this case.

Finally, we are faced with the argument that prohibition of possession of obscene materials is a necessary incident to statutory schemes prohibiting distribution. That argument is based on alleged difficulties of proving an intent to distribute or in producing evidence of actual distribution. We are not convinced that such difficulties exist, but even if they did we do not think that they would justify infringement of the individual's right to read or observe what he pleases. Because that right is so fundamental to our scheme of individual liberty, its restriction may not be justified by the need to ease the administration of otherwise valid criminal laws.

We hold that the First and Fourteenth Amendments prohibit making mere private possession of obscene material a crime. *Roth* and the cases following that decision are not impaired by today's holding. As we have said, the States retain broad power to regulate obscenity; that power simply does not extend to mere possession by the individual in the privacy of his own home. Accordingly, the judgment of the court below is reversed and the case is remanded for proceedings not inconsistent with this opinion.

[Concurring opinions by JUSTICES BLACK and STEWART are omitted.]

In the fifteen years following its decision in *Roth*, no majority of Justices was able to agree on a standard for obscenity. The Court needed a test that specified what elements distinguished obscenity from other sexually explicit but constitutionally protected speech, as well as ensured that government regulation of the former did not lead to suppression of the latter. In *Memoirs v. Massachusetts*, a plurality of three Justices set out a test for obscenity which some members of the Court thought contradicted the holding in *Roth*.[50] *Memoirs* required three elements for material to be ob-

---

[50] Memoirs v. Massachusetts, 383 U.S. 413 (1966).

scene: "it must be established that (a) the dominant theme of the material taken as a whole appeals to a prurient interest in sex; (b) the material is patently offensive because if affronts contemporary community standards relating to the description or representation of sexual matters; and (c) the material is utterly without redeeming social value." Rather than presume that obscenity was without social value, the *Memoirs* test required the government to prove it. The *Memoirs* test, however, never commanded a majority of the Court.

The justices also differed as to the extent of federal power to curb obscenity. Justices Black and Douglas contended that the First Amendment prohibited government from regulating *any* sexually oriented material on the ground that it was obscene. Justice Harlan maintained that the federal government had limited constitutional power to control the distribution of obscenity, while the states had wide latitude to ban obscenity based on rationally established criteria. Justice Stewart believed that both federal and state power was limited to suppressing "hard core" pornography.

Without an agreed upon test for determining obscenity, the Court began the practice of summarily reversing convictions for the dissemination of materials that at least five Justices, applying their separate tests, found to be protected by the First Amendment. Beginning with *Redrup v. New York* in 1967, the Court decided thirty-one obscenity cases using this procedure.[51] Justice Stewart declared that, despite the difficulty of defining a test for obscenity, "I know it when I see it."[52] Chief Justice Burger complained that this means of disposing of obscenity cases cast the Court "in the role of an unreviewable board of censorship for the 50 States, subjectively judging each piece of material brought before us."[53] In 1973, the Court decided two obscenity cases—*Paris Adult Theatre I v. Slaton* and *Miller v. California*—that set out a new test for obscenity and that confirmed the government's power to prohibit the public distribution of obscenity even to consenting adults.

---

[51] Redrup v. New York, 386 U.S. 767 (1967).
[52] Jacobellis v. Ohio, 378 U.S. 184, 197 (1964) (Stewart, J. concurring).
[53] Miller v. California, 413 U.S. 15, 22 n.3 (1973).

Paris Adult Theatre I v. Slaton
413 U.S. 49 (1973)

MR. CHIEF JUSTICE BURGER delivered the opinion of the Court.

Petitioners are two Atlanta, Georgia, movie theaters and their owners and managers, operating in the style of "adult" theaters. On December 28, 1970, respondents, the local state district attorney and the solicitor for the local state trial court, filed civil complaints in that court alleging that petitioners were exhibiting to the public for paid admission two allegedly obscene films, contrary to Georgia Code Ann. § 26–2101. The two films in question, "Magic Mirror" and "It All Comes Out in the End," depict sexual conduct characterized by the Georgia Supreme Court as "hard core pornography" leaving "little to the imagination." ... [T]he trial judge dismissed respondents' complaints.... On appeal, the Georgia

Supreme Court unanimously reversed....

. . .

We categorically disapprove the theory, apparently adopted by the trial judge, that obscene, pornographic films acquire constitutional immunity from state regulation simply because they are exhibited for consenting adults only. This holding was properly rejected by the Georgia Supreme Court. Although we have often pointedly recognized the high importance of the state interest in regulating the exposure of obscene materials to juveniles and unconsenting adults, this Court has never declared these to be the only legitimate state interests permitting regulation of obscene material. The States have a long-recognized legitimate interest in regulating the use of obscene material in local commerce and in all places of public accommodation, as long as these regulations do not run afoul of specific constitutional prohibitions. . . .

In particular, we hold that there are legitimate state interests at stake in stemming the tide of commercialized obscenity, even assuming it is feasible to enforce effective safeguards against exposure to juveniles and to passersby. Rights and interests "other than those of the advocates are involved." These include the interest of the public in the quality of life and the total community environment, the tone of commerce in the great city centers, and, possibly, the public safety itself. The Hill-Link Minority Report of the Commission on Obscenity and Pornography indicates that there is at least an arguable correlation between obscene material and crime. Quite apart from sex crimes, however, there remains one problem of large proportions aptly described by Professor Bickel:

"It concerns the tone of the society, the mode, or to use terms that have perhaps greater currency, the style and quality of life, now and in the future. A man may be entitled to read an obscene book in his room, or expose himself indecently there. . . . We should protect his privacy. But if he demands a right to obtain the books and pictures he wants in the market, and to foregather in public places—discreet, if you will, but accessible to all—with others who share his tastes, *then to grant him his right is to affect the world about the rest of us, and to impinge on other privacies.* Even supposing that each of us can, if he wishes, effectively avert the eye and stop the ear (which, in truth, we cannot), what is commonly read and seen and heard and done intrudes upon us all, want it or not." 22 The Public Interest 25–26 (Winter 1971). (Emphasis added.) . . .

But, it is argued, there are no scientific data which conclusively demonstrate that exposure to obscene material adversely affects men and women or their society. It is urged on behalf of the petitioners that, absent such a demonstration, any kind of state regulation is "impermissible." We reject this argument. It is not for us to resolve empirical uncertainties underlying state legislation, save in the exceptional case where that legislation plainly impinges upon rights protected by the Constitution itself. . . .

From the beginning of civilized societies, legislators and judges have acted on various unprovable assumptions. Such assumptions underlie much lawful state regulation of commercial and business affairs. The same is true of the federal securities and antitrust laws and a host of federal regulations. On the basis of these assumptions both Congress and state legislatures have, for example, drastically re-

stricted associational rights by adopting antitrust laws, and have strictly regulated public expression by issuers of and dealers in securities, profit sharing "coupons," and "trading stamps," commanding what they must and must not publish and announce. Understandably those who entertain an absolutist view of the First Amendment find it uncomfortable to explain why rights of association, speech, and press should be severely restrained in the marketplace of goods and money, but not in the marketplace of pornography.

Likewise, when legislatures and administrators act to protect the physical environment from pollution and to preserve our resources of forests, streams, and parks, they must act on such imponderables as the impact of a new highway near or through an existing park or wilderness area. . . . The fact that a congressional directive reflects unprovable assumptions about what is good for the people, including imponderable aesthetic assumptions, is not a sufficient reason to find that statute unconstitutional.

If we accept the unprovable assumption that a complete education requires the reading of certain books, and the well nigh universal belief that good books, plays, and art lift the spirit, improve the mind, enrich the human personality, and develop character, can we then say that a state legislature may not act on the corollary assumption that commerce in obscene books, or public exhibitions focused on obscene conduct, have a tendency to exert a corrupting and debasing impact leading to antisocial behavior? . . . The sum of experience, including that of the past two decades, affords an ample basis for legislatures to conclude that a sensitive, key relationship of human existence, central to family life, community welfare, and the development of human personality, can be debased and distorted by crass commercial exploitation of sex. Nothing in the Constitution prohibits a State from reaching such a conclusion and acting on it legislatively simply because there is no conclusive evidence or empirical data.

It is argued that individual "free will" must govern, even in activities beyond the protection of the First Amendment and other constitutional guarantees of privacy, and that government cannot legitimately impede an individual's desire to see or acquire obscene plays, movies, and books. We do indeed base our society on certain assumptions that people have the capacity for free choice. Most exercises of individual free choice—those in politics, religion, and expression of ideas—are explicitly protected by the Constitution. Totally unlimited play for free will, however, is not allowed in our or any other society. . . . States are told by some that they must await a "laissez-faire" market solution to the obscenity-pornography problem, paradoxically "by people who have never otherwise had a kind word to say for laissez-faire," particularly in solving urban, commercial, and environmental pollution problems.

The States, of course, may follow such a "laissez-faire" policy and drop all controls on commercialized obscenity, if that is what they prefer, just as they can ignore consumer protection in the marketplace, but nothing in the Constitution *compels* the States to do so with regard to matters falling within state jurisdiction. "We do not sit as a superlegislature to determine the wisdom, need, and propriety of laws that touch economic problems, business affairs, or social conditions." *Griswold v. Connecticut.*
. . .

It is also argued that the State has no legitimate interest in "control [of] the moral content of a person's thoughts," *Stanley v. Georgia,* and we need not quarrel with this. But we reject the claim that the State of Georgia is here attempting to control the minds or thoughts of those who patronize theaters. Preventing unlimited display or distribution of obscene material, which by definition lacks any serious literary, artistic, political, or scientific value as communication, *Miller v. California,* is distinct from a control of reason and the intellect. Where communication of ideas, protected by the First Amendment, is not involved, or the particular privacy of the home protected by *Stanley,* or any of the other "areas or zones" of constitutionally protected privacy, the mere fact that, as a consequence, some human "utterances" or "thoughts" may be incidentally affected does not bar the State from acting to protect legitimate state interests. The fantasies of a drug addict are his own and beyond the reach of government, but government regulation of drug sales is not prohibited by the Constitution.

Finally, petitioners argue that conduct which directly involves "consenting adults" only has, for that sole reason, a special claim to constitutional protection. Our Constitution establishes a broad range of conditions on the exercise of power by the States, but for us to say that our Constitution incorporates the proposition that conduct involving consenting adults only is always beyond state regulation, is a step we are unable to take.[15] Commercial

exploitation of depictions, descriptions, or exhibitions of obscene conduct on commercial premises open to the adult public falls within a State's broad power to regulate commerce and protect the public environment. The issue in this context goes beyond whether someone, or even the majority, considers the conduct depicted as "wrong" or "sinful." The States have the power to make a morally neutral judgment that public exhibition of obscene material, or commerce in such material, has a tendency to injure the community as a whole, to endanger the public safety, or to jeopardize in Mr. Chief Justice Warren's words, the States' "right . . . to maintain a decent society." *Jacobellis v. Ohio,* 378 U.S., at 199 (dissenting opinion).

To summarize, we have today reaffirmed the basic holding of *Roth v. United States,* that obscene material has no protection under the First Amendment. See *Miller v. California.* We have directed our holdings, not at thoughts or speech, but at depiction and description of specifically defined sexual conduct that States may regulate within limits designed to prevent infringement of First Amendment rights. . . . In this case we hold that the States have a legitimate interest in regulating commerce in obscene material and in regulating exhibition of obscene material in places of public accommodation, including so-called "adult" theaters from which minors are excluded. In light of these holdings, nothing precludes the State of Georgia from the regulation of the allegedly obscene material exhibited in Paris Adult Theatre I or II, provided that the applicable Georgia law, as written or authoritatively interpreted by the Georgia courts, meets the First Amendment standards set forth in *Miller v. California.* The judgment is vacated and the case remanded to the Georgia Supreme Court for further proceedings not inconsistent with this opinion and *Miller v. California.*

MR. JUSTICE DOUGLAS, dissenting.

My Brother BRENNAN is to be commended for seeking a new path through the thicket which the Court entered when it undertook to sustain the constitutionality of obscenity laws and to place limits on their application. I have expressed on numerous occasions my disagreement with the basic decision that held that "obscenity" was not protected by the First Amendment. I disagreed also with the definitions that evolved. Art and literature reflect tastes; and tastes, like musical appreciation, are hardly reducible to precise definitions. That is one reason I have always felt that "obscenity" was not an exception to the First Amendment. For mat-

---

[15] The state statute books are replete with constitutionally unchallenged laws against prostitution, suicide, voluntary self-mutilation, brutalizing "bare fist" prize fights, and duels, although these crimes may only directly involve "consenting adults." Statutes making bigamy a crime surely cut into an individual's freedom to associate, but few today seriously claim such statutes violate the First Amendment or any other constitutional provision. . . . As Professor Irving Kristol has observed: "Bearbaiting and cockfighting are prohibited only in part out of compassion for the suffering animals; the main reason they were

abolished was because it was felt that they debased and brutalized the citizenry who flocked to witness such spectacles." On the Democratic Idea in America 33 (1972).

ters of taste, like matters of belief, turn on the idiosyncrasies of individuals. They are too personal to define and too emotional and vague to apply. . . .

The other reason I could not bring myself to conclude that "obscenity" was not covered by the First Amendment was that prior to the adoption of our Constitution and Bill of Rights the Colonies had no law excluding "obscenity" from the regime of freedom of expression and press that then existed. I could find no such laws; and more important, our leading colonial expert, Julius Goebel, could find none, J. Goebel, Development of Legal Institutions (1946); J. Goebel, Felony and Misdemeanor (1937). So I became convinced that the creation of the "obscenity" exception to the First Amendment was a legislative and judicial *tour de force*; that if we were to have such a regime of censorship and punishment, it should be done by constitutional amendment.

People are, of course, offended by many offerings made by merchants in this area. They are also offended by political pronouncements, sociological themes, and by stories of official misconduct. The list of activities and publications and pronouncements that offend someone is endless. Some of it goes on in private; some of it is inescapably public, as when a government official generates crime, becomes a blatant offender of the moral sensibilities of the people, engages in burglary, or breaches the privacy of the telephone, the conference room, or the home. Life in this crowded modern technological world creates many offensive statements and many offensive deeds. There is no protection against offensive ideas, only against offensive conduct.

"Obscenity" at most is the expression of offensive ideas. There are regimes in the world where ideas "offensive" to the majority (or at least to those who control the majority) are suppressed. There life proceeds at a monotonous pace. Most of us would find that world offensive. One of the most offensive experiences in my life was a visit to a nation where bookstalls were filled only with books on mathematics and books on religion.

I am sure I would find offensive most of the books and movies charged with being obscene. But in a life that has not been short, I have yet to be trapped into seeing or reading something that would offend me. I never read or see the materials coming to the Court under charges of "obscenity," because I have thought the First Amendment made it unconstitutional for me to act as a censor. I see ads in bookstores and neon lights over theaters that resemble bait for those who seek vicarious exhilaration. As a parent or a priest or as a teacher I would have no compunction in edging my children or wards away from the books and movies that did no more than excite man's base instincts. But I

never supposed that government was permitted to sit in judgment on one's tastes or belief—save as they involved action within the reach of the police power of government.

. . .

Mr. Justice Brennan, with whom Mr. Justice Stewart and Mr. Justice Marshall join, dissenting.

. . .

Our experience with the *Roth* approach has certainly taught us that the outright suppression of obscenity cannot be reconciled with the fundamental principles of the First and Fourteenth Amendments. For we have failed to formulate a standard that sharply distinguishes protected from unprotected speech, and out of necessity, we have resorted to the *Redrup* approach, which resolves cases as between the parties, but offers only the most obscure guidance to legislation, adjudication by other courts, and primary conduct. By disposing of cases through summary reversal or denial of certiorari we have deliberately and effectively obscured the rationale underlying the decisions. It comes as no surprise that judicial attempts to follow our lead conscientiously have often ended in hopeless confusion.

Of course, the vagueness problem would be largely of our own creation if it stemmed primarily from our failure to reach a consensus on any one standard. But after 16 years of experimentation and debate I am reluctantly forced to the conclusion that none of the available formulas, including the one announced today, can reduce the vagueness to a tolerable level while at the same time striking an acceptable balance between the protections of the First and Fourteenth Amendments, on the one hand, and on the other the asserted state interest in regulating the dissemination of certain sexually oriented materials. Any effort to draw a constitutionally acceptable boundary on state power must resort to such indefinite concepts as "prurient interest," "patent offensiveness," "serious literary value," and the like. The meaning of these concepts necessarily varies with the experience, outlook, and even idiosyncrasies of the person defining them. Although we have assumed that obscenity does exist and that we "know it when [we] see it," *Jacobellis v. Ohio* (Stewart, J., concurring), we are manifestly unable to describe it in advance except by reference to concepts so elusive that they fail to distinguish clearly between protected and unprotected speech. . . . These considerations suggest that no one definition, no matter how precisely or narrowly drawn, can possibly suffice for all situations, or carve out fully suppressible expression from all media without also creating a substantial risk of encroachment upon the guarantees of the Due Process Clause and the First Amendment.

. . . In this context, even the most painstaking efforts to determine in advance whether certain sexually oriented expression is obscene must inevitably prove unavailing. For the insufficiency of the notice compels persons to guess not only whether their conduct is covered by a criminal statute, but also whether their conduct falls within the constitutionally permissible reach of the statute. The resulting level of uncertainty is utterly intolerable, not alone because it makes "[b]ookselling ... a hazardous profession," *Ginsberg v. New York* (Fortas, J., dissenting), but as well because it invites arbitrary and erratic enforcement of the law.

. . .

The problems of fair notice and chilling protected speech are very grave standing alone. But it does not detract from their importance to recognize that a vague statute in this area creates a third, although admittedly more subtle, set of problems. These problems concern the institutional stress that inevitably results where the line separating protected from unprotected speech is excessively vague. In *Roth* we conceded that "there may be marginal cases in which it is difficult to determine the side of the line on which a particular fact situation falls. ..." Our subsequent experience demonstrates that almost every case is "marginal." And since the "margin" marks the point of separation between protected and unprotected speech, we are left with a system in which almost every obscenity case presents a constitutional question of exceptional difficulty. . . . .

. . .

As a result of our failure to define standards with predictable application to any given piece of material, there is no probability of regularity in obscenity decisions by state and lower federal courts. That is not to say that these courts have performed badly in this area or paid insufficient attention to the principles we have established. The problem is, rather, that one cannot say with certainty that material is obscene until at least five members of this Court, applying inevitably obscure standards, have pronounced it so. The number of obscenity cases on our docket gives ample testimony to the burden that has been placed upon this Court.

. . .

The severe problems arising from the lack of fair notice, from the chill on protected expression, and from the stress imposed on the state and federal judicial machinery persuade me that a significant change in direction is urgently required. . . .

. . .

Our experience since *Roth* requires us not only to abandon the effort to pick out obscene material on a case-by-case basis, but also to reconsider a fundamental postulate of *Roth*: that there exists a definable class of sexually oriented expression that may be totally suppressed by the Federal and State Governments. Assuming that such a class of expression does in fact exist, I am forced to conclude that the concept of "obscenity" cannot be defined with sufficient specificity and clarity to provide fair notice to persons who create and distribute sexually oriented materials, to prevent substantial erosion of protected speech as a byproduct of the attempt to suppress unprotected speech, and to avoid very costly institutional harms. Given these inevitable side effects of state efforts to suppress what is assumed to be *unprotected* speech, we must scrutinize with care the state interest that is asserted to justify the suppression. For in the absence of some very substantial interest in suppressing such speech, we can hardly condone the ill effects that seem to flow inevitably from the effort.

. . .

Because we assumed—incorrectly, as experience has proved—that obscenity could be separated from other sexually oriented expression without significant costs either to the First Amendment or to the judicial machinery charged with the task of safeguarding First Amendment freedoms, we had no occasion in *Roth* to probe the asserted state interest in curtailing unprotected, sexually oriented speech. Yet, as we have increasingly come to appreciate the vagueness of the concept of obscenity, we have begun to recognize and articulate the state interests at stake. . . .

The opinions in *Redrup* and *Stanley* reflected our emerging view that the state interests in protecting children and in protecting unconsenting adults may stand on a different footing from the other asserted state interests. It may well be, as one commentator has argued, that "exposure to [erotic material] is for some persons an intense emotional experience. A communication of this nature, imposed upon a person contrary to his wishes, has all the characteristics of a physical assault. . . . [And it] constitutes an invasion of his privacy. . . . "[24] Similarly, if children are "not possessed of that full capacity for individual choice which is the presupposition of the First Amendment guarantees," *Ginsberg v. New York* (Stewart, J., concurring), then the State may have a substantial interest in precluding the flow of obscene materials even to consenting juveniles.

But, whatever the strength of the state interests in protecting juveniles and unconsenting adults from exposure to sexually oriented materials, those interests cannot be asserted in defense of the holding of the Georgia Supreme Court in this case. That court assumed for the purposes of its decision that the films in issue

---

[24] T. EMERSON, THE SYSTEM OF FREEDOM OF EXPRESSION 496 (1970).

were exhibited only to persons over the age of 21 who viewed them willingly and with prior knowledge of the nature of their contents. And on that assumption the state court held that the films could still be suppressed. The justification for the suppression must be found, therefore, in some independent interest in regulating the reading and viewing habits of consenting adults.

. . .

If, as the Court today assumes, "a state legislature may . . . act on the . . . assumption that commerce in obscene books, or public exhibitions focused on obscene conduct, have a tendency to exert a corrupting and debasing impact leading to antisocial behavior," then it is hard to see how state-ordered regimentation of our minds can ever be forestalled. For if a State, in an effort to maintain or create a particular moral tone, may prescribe what its citizens cannot read or cannot see, then it would seem to follow that in pursuit of that same objective a State could decree that its citizens must read certain books or must view certain films. However laudable its goal—and that is obviously a question on which reasonable minds may differ—the State cannot proceed by means that violate the Constitution. . . . Even a legitimate, sharply focused state concern for

the morality of the community cannot, in other words, justify an assault on the protections of the First Amendment. Where the state interest in regulation of morality is vague and ill defined, interference with the guarantees of the First Amendment is even more difficult to justify.

In short, while I cannot say that the interests of the State—apart from the question of juveniles and unconsenting adults—are trivial or nonexistent, I am compelled to conclude that these interests cannot justify the substantial damage to constitutional rights and to this Nation's judicial machinery that inevitably results from state efforts to bar the distribution even of unprotected material to consenting adults. I would hold, therefore, that at least in the absence of distribution to juveniles or obtrusive exposure to unconsenting adults, the First and Fourteenth Amendments prohibit the State and Federal Governments from attempting wholly to suppress sexually oriented materials on the basis of their allegedly "obscene" contents. Nothing in this approach precludes those governments from taking action to serve what may be strong and legitimate interests through regulation of the manner of distribution of sexually oriented material.

. . .

Miller v. California
413 U.S. 15 (1973)

Mr. Chief Justice Burger delivered the opinion of the Court.

This is one of a group of "obscenity-pornography" cases being reviewed by the Court in a re-examination of standards enunciated in earlier cases involving what Mr. Justice Harlan called "the intractable obscenity problem."

Appellant conducted a mass mailing campaign to advertise the sale of illustrated books, euphemistically called "adult" material. After a jury trial, he was convicted of violating California Penal Code § 311.2(a), a misdemeanor, by knowingly distributing obscene matter,[1]

---

[1] At the time of the commission of the alleged offense, . . . §§ 311.2(a) and 311 of the California Penal Code read in relevant part:

. . . "(a) 'Obscene' means that to the average person, applying contemporary standards, the predominant appeal of the matter, taken as a whole, is to prurient interest, i.e., a shameful or morbid interest in nudity, sex, or excretion, which goes substantially beyond customary limits of candor in description or representation of such matters and is matter which is utterly without redeeming social importance." . . .

and the Appellate Department, Superior Court of California, County of Orange, summarily affirmed the judgment without opinion. Appellant's conviction was specifically based on his conduct in causing five unsolicited advertising brochures to be sent through the mail in an envelope addressed to a restaurant in Newport Beach, California. The envelope was opened by the manager of the restaurant and his mother. They had not requested the brochures; they complained to the police.

The brochures advertise four books entitled "Intercourse," "Man-Woman," "Sex Orgies Illustrated," and "An Illustrated History of Pornography," and a film entitled "Marital Intercourse." While the brochures contain some descriptive printed material, primarily they consist of pictures and drawings very explicitly depicting men and women in groups of two or more engaging in a variety of sexual activities, with genitals often prominently displayed.

I

This case involves the application of a State's criminal obscenity statute to a situation in which sexually explicit materials have been thrust by aggressive sales action upon unwilling recipients who had in no way indicated any desire to receive such materials. This Court has recognized that the States have a legitimate interest in prohibiting dissemination or exhibition of obscene material when the mode of dissemination carries with it a significant danger of offending the sensibilities of unwilling recipients or of exposure to juveniles. It is in this context that we are called on to define the standards which must be used to identify obscene material that a State may regulate without infringing on the First Amendment as applicable to the States through the Fourteenth Amendment.

. . . [S]ince the Court now undertakes to formulate standards more concrete than those in the past, it is useful for us to focus on two of the landmark cases in the somewhat tortured history of the Court's obscenity decisions. In *Roth v. United States*, the Court sustained a conviction under a federal statute punishing the mailing of "obscene, lewd, lascivious or filthy . . . " materials. The key to that holding was the Court's rejection of the claim that obscene materials were protected by the First Amendment. . . .

Nine years later, in *Memoirs v. Massachusetts*, 383 U.S. 413 (1966), the Court veered sharply away from the *Roth* concept and, with only three Justices in the plurality opinion, articulated a new test of obscenity. . . . While *Roth* presumed "obscenity" to be "utterly without redeeming social importance," *Memoirs* required that to prove obscenity it must be affirmatively established that the material is "utterly without redeeming social value." Thus, even as they repeated the words of *Roth*, the *Memoirs* plurality produced a drastically altered test that called on the prosecution to prove a negative, i.e., that the material was "utterly without redeeming social value"—a burden virtually impossible to discharge under our criminal standards of proof. Such considerations caused Mr. Justice Harlan to wonder if the "utterly without redeeming social value" test had any meaning at all. See *Memoirs v. Massachusetts* (Harlan, J., dissenting).

Apart from the initial formulation in the *Roth* case, no majority of the Court has at any given time been able to agree on a standard to determine what constitutes obscene, pornographic material subject to regulation under the States' police power. We have seen "a variety of views among the members of the Court unmatched in any other course of constitutional adjudication." *Interstate Circuit, Inc. v. Dallas*, 390 U.S., at 704–705 (Harlan, J., concurring and dissenting). This is not remarkable, for in the area of freedom of speech and press the courts must always remain sensitive to any infringement on genuinely serious liter-

ary, artistic, political, or scientific expression. This is an area in which there are few eternal verities.

The case we now review was tried on the theory that the California Penal Code § 311 approximately incorporates the three-stage *Memoirs* test. But now the *Memoirs* test has been abandoned as unworkable by its author [Justice Brennan], and no Member of the Court today supports the *Memoirs* formulation.

II

This much has been categorically settled by the Court, that obscene material is unprotected by the First Amendment. . . . We acknowledge, however, the inherent dangers of undertaking to regulate any form of expression. State statutes designed to regulate obscene materials must be carefully limited. As a result, we now confine the permissible scope of such regulation to works which depict or describe sexual conduct. That conduct must be specifically defined by the applicable state law, as written or authoritatively construed. A state offense must also be limited to works which, taken as a whole, appeal to the prurient interest in sex, which portray sexual conduct in a patently offensive way, and which, taken as a whole, do not have serious literary, artistic, political, or scientific value.

The basic guidelines for the trier of fact must be: (a) whether "the average person, applying contemporary community standards" would find that the work, taken as a whole, appeals to the prurient interest; (b) whether the work depicts or describes, in a patently offensive way, sexual conduct specifically defined by the applicable state law; and (c) whether the work, taken as a whole, lacks serious literary, artistic, political, or scientific value. We do not adopt as a constitutional standard the "*utterly* without redeeming social value" test of *Memoirs v. Massachusetts*; that concept has never commanded the adherence of more than three Justices at one time.[7] If a state law that regulates obscene material is thus limited, as written or construed, the First Amendment values applicable to the States through the Fourteenth Amendment are adequately protected by the ultimate power of appellant courts to conduct an independent review of constitutional claims when necessary.

We emphasize that it is not our function to propose regulatory schemes for the States. That must await their concrete legislative ef-

---

[7] "A quotation from Voltaire in the flyleaf of a book will not constitutionally redeem an otherwise obscene publication. . . . " Kois v. Wisconsin, 408 U.S., 229, 231 (1972). We also reject, as a constitutional standard, the ambiguous concept of "social importance."

forts. It is possible, however, to give a few plain examples of what a state statute could define for regulation under part (b) of the standard announced in this opinion:

(a) Patently offensive representations or descriptions of ultimate sexual acts, normal or perverted, actual or simulated.

(b) Patently offensive representation or descriptions of masturbation, excretory functions, and lewd exhibition of the genitals.

Sex and nudity may not be exploited without limit by films or pictures exhibited or sold in places of public accommodation any more than live sex and nudity can be exhibited or sold without limit in such public places. At a minimum, prurient, patently offensive depiction or description of sexual conduct must have serious literary, artistic, political, or scientific value to merit First Amendment protection. For example, medical books for the education of physicians and related personnel necessarily use graphic illustrations and descriptions of human anatomy. In resolving the inevitably sensitive questions of fact and law, we must continue to rely on the jury system, accompanied by the safeguards that judges, rules of evidence, presumption of innocence, and other protective features provide, as we do with rape, murder, and a host of other offenses against society and its individual members.

. . .

Under the holdings announced today, no one will be subject to prosecution for the sale or exposure of obscene materials unless these materials depict or describe patently offensive "hard core" sexual conduct specifically defined by the regulating state law, as written or construed. We are satisfied that these specific prerequisites will provide fair notice to a dealer in such materials that his public and commercial activities may bring prosecution. If the inability to define regulated materials with ultimate, god-like precision altogether removes the power of the States or the Congress to regulate, then "hard core" pornography may be exposed without limit to the juvenile, the passerby, and the consenting adult alike. . . .

. . .

It is certainly true that the absence, since *Roth*, of a single majority view of this Court as to proper standards for testing obscenity has placed a strain on both state and federal courts. But today, for the first time since *Roth* was decided in 1957, a majority of this Court has agreed on concrete guidelines to isolate "hard core" pornography from expression protected by the First Amendment. Now we may abandon the casual practice of *Redrup v. New York*, 386 U.S. 767 (1967), and attempt to provide positive guidance to federal and state courts alike.

This may not be an easy road, free from difficulty. But no amount of "fatigue" should lead us to adopt a convenient "institutional" rationale—an absolutist, "anything goes" view of the First Amendment—because it will lighten our burdens. . . . Nor should we remedy "tension between state and federal courts" by arbitrarily depriving the States of a power reserved to them under the Constitution, a power which they have enjoyed and exercised continuously from before the adoption of the First Amendment to this day. . . .

III

Under a National Constitution, fundamental First Amendment limitations on the powers of the States do not vary from community to community, but this does not mean that there are, or should or can be, fixed, uniform national standards of precisely what appeals to the "prurient interest" or is "patently offensive." These are essentially questions of fact, and our Nation is simply too big and too diverse for this Court to reasonably expect that such standards could be articulated for all 50 States in a single formulation, even assuming the prerequisite consensus exists. When triers of fact are asked to decide whether "the average person, applying contemporary community standards" would consider certain materials "prurient," it would be unrealistic to require that the answer be based on some abstract formulation. The adversary system, with lay jurors as the usual ultimate factfinders in criminal prosecutions, has historically permitted triers of fact to draw on the standards of their community, guided always by limiting instructions on the law. To require a State to structure obscenity proceedings around evidence of a national "community standard" would be an exercise in futility.

. . .

We conclude that neither the State's alleged failure to offer evidence of "national standards," nor the trial court's charge that the jury consider state community standards, were constitutional errors. Nothing in the First Amendment requires that a jury must consider hypothetical and unascertainable "national standards" when attempting to determine whether certain materials are obscene as a matter of fact. . . .

It is neither realistic nor constitutionally sound to read the First Amendment as requiring that the people of Maine or Mississippi accept public depiction of conduct found tolerable in Las Vegas, or New York City. People in different States vary in their tastes and attitudes, and this diversity is not to be strangled by the absolutism of imposed uniformity. . . . [T]he primary concern with requiring a jury to apply the standard of "the average person, applying contemporary community standards" is to be certain that, so far as material is not aimed at a deviant group, it will be judged by its impact on an average person, rather than a particularly susceptible or sensitive person—or indeed a totally insensitive one. We hold that the requirement that the jury evaluate the materials with reference to "contemporary standards of the State of California" serves this protective purpose and is constitutionally adequate.

IV

The dissenting Justices sound the alarm of repression. But, in our view, to equate the free and robust exchange of ideas and political debate with commercial exploitation of obscene material demeans the grand conception of the First Amendment and its high purposes in the historic struggle for freedom.... The First Amendment protects works which, taken as a whole, have serious literary, artistic, political, or scientific value, regardless of whether the government or a majority of the people approve of the ideas these works represent. "The protection given speech and press was fashioned to assure unfettered interchange of *ideas* for the bringing about of political and social changes desired by the people," *Roth* (emphasis added). But the public portrayal of hard-core sexual conduct for its own sake, and for the ensuing commercial gain, is a different matter.

There is no evidence, empirical or historical, that the stern 19th century American censorship of public distribution and display of material relating to sex in any way limited or affected expression of serious literary, artistic, political, or scientific ideas. On the contrary, it is beyond any question that the era following Thomas Jefferson to Theodore Roosevelt was an "extraordinarily vigorous period," not just in economics and politics, but in *belles lettres* and in "the outlying fields of social and political philosophies." We do not see the harsh hand of censorship of ideas—good or bad, sound or unsound—and "repression" of political liberty lurking in every state regulation of commercial exploitation of human interest in sex.

. . .

Mr. Justice Douglas, dissenting.

. . .

Today the Court retreats from the earlier formulations of the constitutional test and undertakes to make new definitions. This effort, like the earlier ones, is earnest and well intentioned. The difficulty is that we do not deal with constitutional terms, since "obscenity" is not mentioned in the Constitution or Bill of Rights. And the First Amendment makes no such exception from "the press" which it undertakes to protect nor, as I have said on other occasions, is an exception necessarily implied, for there was no recognized exception to the free press at the time the Bill of Rights was adopted which treated "obscene" publications differently from other types of papers, magazines, and books. So there are no constitutional guidelines for deciding what is and what is not "obscene." The Court is at large because we deal with tastes and standards of literature. What shocks me may be sustenance for my neighbor. What causes one person to boil up in rage over one pamphlet or movie may reflect only his neurosis, not shared by others. We deal here with a regime of censorship which, if adopted, should be done by constitutional amendment after full debate by the people.

. . .

The idea that the First Amendment permits government to ban publications that are "offensive" to some people puts an ominous gloss on freedom of the press. That test would make it possible to ban any paper or any journal or magazine in some benighted place. The First Amendment was designed "to invite dispute," to induce "a condition of unrest," to "create dissatisfaction with conditions as they are," and even to stir "people to anger." The idea that the First Amendment permits punishment for ideas that are "offensive" to the particular judge or jury sitting in judgment is astounding. No greater leveler of speech or literature has ever been designed. To give the power to the censor, as we do today, is to make a sharp and radical break with the traditions of a free society. The First Amendment was not fashioned as a vehicle for dispensing tranquilizers to the people. Its prime function was to keep debate open to "offensive" as well as to "staid" people. The tendency throughout history has been to subdue the individual and to exalt the power of government. The use of the standard "offensive" gives authority to government that cuts the very vitals out of the First Amendment. As is intimated by the Court's opinion, the materials before us may be garbage. But so is much of what is said in political campaigns, in the daily press, on TV, or over the radio. By reason of the First Amendment—and solely because of it—speakers and publishers have not been threatened or subdued because their thoughts and ideas may be "offensive" to some.

. . .

We deal with highly emotional, not rational, questions. To many the Song of Solomon is obscene. I do not think we, the judges, were ever given the constitutional power to make definitions of obscenity. If it is to be defined, let the people debate and decide by a constitutional amendment what they want to ban as obscene and what standards they want the legislatures and the courts to apply. Perhaps the people will decide that the path towards a mature, integrated society requires that all ideas competing for acceptance must have no censor. Perhaps they will decide otherwise. Whatever the choice, the courts will have some guidelines. Now we have none except our own predilections.

Mr. Justice Brennan, with whom Mr.

JUSTICE STEWART and MR. JUSTICE MARSHALL join, dissenting.

    . . . I need not now decide whether a statute might be drawn to impose, within the requirements of the First Amendment, criminal penalties for the precise conduct at issue here. For it is clear that under my dissent in *Paris Adult Theatre, I*, the statute under which the prosecution was brought is unconstitutionally overbroad, and therefore invalid on its face. . . .

Very recently, courts have considered whether other types of sexually-explicit speech are harmful enough or characterized by so little social value to warrant inclusion, along with obscenity, among the categories of speech outside First Amendment protection. It has been argued that pornography which does not meet the test for obscenity may nevertheless be prohibited because of its exploitation and subordination of women and children.

In *New York v. Ferber*, the Court validated a New York statute that prohibits the dissemination of material showing children actually engaged in sexual conduct, regardless of whether the material is obscene.[54] *Ferber* involved the conviction of a seller of films showing young boys masturbating. The Court reasoned that states are entitled to "greater leeway in the regulation of pornographic depiction of children" because of the surpassing importance of the state's interest in preventing the sexual exploitation of children and because the distribution of this material is itself related to child sexual abuse. Disseminating child pornography produces a permanent record of children's participation in the sexual activity, further harming the children, and prohibiting distribution is the only way effectively to halt the initial production of the material. The Court therefore recognized child pornography as a category of material outside the protection of the First Amendment. In articulating a test for this unprotected category the Court "adjusted" the *Miller* standard for obscenity: "A trier of fact need not find that the material appeals to the prurient interest of the average person; it is not required that the sexual conduct portrayed be done so in a patently offensive manner; and the material at issue need not be considered as a whole. We note that the distribution of descriptions or other depictions of sexual conduct, not otherwise obscene, which do not involve live performances or photographic or other visual reproduction of live performances, retains First Amendment protection."

Far more controversial than the Court's holding in *Ferber* is the argument that pornography that subordinates women may be banned consistent with the First Amendment. This argument, initially advocated by feminists Catharine MacKinnon and Andrea Dworkin, sparked a heated debate among feminists, as well legislators and constitutional scholars. The anti-pornography camp argues that pornography is a political practice that subordinates women by eroticizing women's inequality and men's power over women. The anti-censorship camp argues that pornography is valuable sexual expression whose censoring will undermine the interests of women and other less powerful groups who benefit from broad speech rights.

---

[54] New York v. Ferber, 458 U.S. 747 (1982).

American Booksellers Association, Inc. v. Hudnut
771 F.2d 323 (7th Cir. 1985), affirmed, 475 U.S. 1001 (1986)

EASTERBROOK, Circuit Judge.

    Indianapolis enacted an ordinance defining "pornography" as a practice that discriminates against women. "Pornography" is to be redressed through the administrative and judicial methods used for other discrimination. The City's definition of "pornography" is considerably different from "obscenity," which the Supreme Court has held is not protected by the First Amendment.

. . .

"Pornography" under the ordinance is "the graphic sexually explicit subordination of women, whether in pictures or in words, that also includes one or more of the following:

(1) Women are presented as sexual objects who enjoy pain or humiliation; or

(2) Women are presented as sexual objects who experience sexual pleasure in being raped; or

(3) Women are presented as sexual objects tied up or cut up or mutilated or bruised or physically hurt, or as dismembered or truncated or fragmented or severed into body parts; or

(4) Women are presented as being penetrated by objects or animals; or

(5) Women are presented in scenarios of degradation, injury, abasement, torture, shown as filthy or inferior, bleeding, bruised, or hurt in a context that makes these conditions sexual; or

(6) Women are presented as sexual objects for domination, conquest, violation, exploitation, possession, or use, or through postures or positions of servility or submission or display."

. . .

The Indianapolis ordinance does not refer to the prurient interest, to offensiveness, or to the standards of the community. It demands attention to particular depictions, not to the work judged as a whole. It is irrelevant under the ordinance whether the work has literary, artistic, political, or scientific value. The City and many amici point to these omissions as virtues. They maintain that pornography influences attitudes, and the statute is a way to alter the socialization of men and women rather than to vindicate community standards of offensiveness. And as one of the principal drafters of the ordinance has asserted, "if a woman is subjected, why should it matter that the work has other value?" Catharine A. Mac-Kinnon, *Pornography, Civil Rights, and Speech,* 20 Harv.Civ.Rts.—Civ.Lib.L.Rev. 1, 21 (1985).

Civil rights groups and feminists have entered this case as amici on both sides. Those supporting the ordinance say that it will play an important role in reducing the tendency of men to view women as sexual objects, a tendency that leads to both unacceptable attitudes and discrimination in the workplace and violence away from it. Those opposing the ordinance point out that much radical feminist literature is explicit and depicts women in ways forbidden by the ordinance and that the ordinance would reopen old battles. It is unclear how Indianapolis would treat works from James Joyce's *Ulysses* to Homer's *Iliad*; both depict women as submissive objects for conquest and domination.

We do not try to balance the arguments for and against an ordinance such as this. The ordinance discriminates on the ground of the content of the speech. Speech treating women in the approved way—in sexual encounters "premised on equality" (MacKinnon)—is lawful no matter how sexually explicit. Speech treating women in the disapproved way—as submissive in matters sexual or as enjoying humiliation—is unlawful no matter how significant the literary, artistic, or political qualities of the work taken as a whole. The state may not ordain preferred viewpoints in this way. The Constitution forbids the state to declare one perspective right and silence opponents.

I

The ordinance contains four prohibitions. People may not "traffic" in pornography, "coerce" others into performing in pornographic works, or "force" pornography on anyone. Anyone injured by someone who has seen or read pornography has a right of action against the maker or seller.

Trafficking is defined in § 16–3(g)(4) as the "production, sale, exhibition, or distribution of pornography." The offense excludes exhibition in a public or educational library, but a "special display" in a library may be sex discrimination. Section 16–3(g)(4)(C) provides that the trafficking paragraph "shall not be construed to make isolated passages or isolated parts actionable."

. . .

A woman aggrieved by trafficking in pornography may file a complaint "as a woman acting against the subordination of women" with the office of equal opportunity. . . .

. . .

III

"If there is any fixed star in our constitutional constellation, it is that no official, high or petty, can prescribe what shall be orthodox in politics, nationalism, religion, or other matters of opinion or force citizens to confess by word or act their faith therein." *West Virginia State Board of Education v. Barnette*, 319 U.S. 624, 642 (1943). Under the First Amendment the government must leave to the people the evaluation of ideas. Bald or subtle, an idea is as powerful as the audience allows it to be. A belief may be pernicious—the beliefs of Nazis led to the death of millions, those of the Klan to the repression of millions. A pernicious belief may prevail. Totalitarian governments today rule much of the planet, practicing suppression of billions and spreading dogma that may enslave others. One of the things that separates our society from theirs is our absolute right to propagate opinions that the government finds wrong or even hateful.

. . .

Under the ordinance graphic sexually explicit speech is "pornography" or not depending on the perspective the author adopts. Speech that "subordinates" women and also, for example, presents women as enjoying pain, humiliation, or rape, or even simply presents women in "positions of servility or submission or display" is forbidden, no matter how great the literary or political value of the work taken as a whole. Speech that portrays women in positions of equality is lawful, no matter how graphic the sexual content. This is thought control. It establishes an "approved" view of women, of how they may react to sexual encounters, of how the sexes may relate to each other. Those who espouse the approved view may use sexual images; those who do not, may not.

Indianapolis justifies the ordinance on the ground that pornography affects thoughts. Men who see women depicted as subordinate are more likely to treat them so. Pornography is an aspect of dominance.[1] It does not persuade people so much as change them. It works by socializing, by establishing the expected and the permissible. In this view pornography is not an idea; pornography is the injury.

There is much to this perspective. Beliefs are also facts. People often act in accordance with the images and patterns they find around

---

[1] "Pornography constructs what a woman is in terms of its view of what men want sexually. . . . Pornography's world of equality is a harmonious and balanced place. Men and women are perfectly complementary and perfectly bipolar. . . . All the ways men love to take and violate women, women love to be taken and violated. . . . What pornography *does* goes beyond its content: It eroticizes hierarchy, it sexualizes inequality. It makes dominance and submission sex. Inequality is its central dynamic; the illusion of freedom coming together with the reality of force is central to its working. . . . [P]ornography is neither harmless fantasy nor a corrupt and confused misrepresentation of an otherwise neutral and healthy sexual situation. It institutionalizes the sexuality of male supremacy, fusing the erotization of dominance and submission with the social construction of male and female. . . . Men treat women as who they see women as being. Pornography constructs who that is. Men's power over women means that the way men see women defines who women can be. Pornography . . . is a sexual reality." MacKinnon (emphasis in original). *See also* ANDREA DWORKIN, PORNOGRAPHY: MEN POSSESSING WOMEN (1981). A national commission in Canada recently adopted a similar rationale for controlling pornography. Special Commission on Pornography and Prostitution, 1 PORNOGRAPHY AND PROSTITUTION IN CANADA 49–59 (Canadian Government Publishing Centre 1985).

them. People raised in a religion tend to accept the tenets of that religion, often without independent examination. People taught from birth that black people are fit only for slavery rarely rebelled against that creed; beliefs coupled with the self-interest of the masters established a social structure that inflicted great harm while enduring for centuries. Words and images act at the level of the subconscious before they persuade at the level of the conscious. Even the truth has little chance unless a statement fits within the framework of beliefs that may never have been subjected to rational study.

Therefore we accept the premises of this legislation. Depictions of subordination tend to perpetuate subordination. The subordinate status of women in turn leads to affront and lower pay at work, insult and injury at home, battery and rape on the streets.[2] In the language of the legislature, "[p]ornography is central in creating and maintaining sex as a basis of discrimination. Pornography is a systematic practice of exploitation and subordination based on sex which differentially harms women. The bigotry and contempt it produces, with the acts of aggression it fosters, harm women's opportunities for equality and rights [of all kinds]." Indianapolis Code § 16–1(a)(2).

Yet this simply demonstrates the power of pornography as speech. All of these unhappy effects depend on mental intermediation. Pornography affects how people see the world, their fellows, and social relations. If pornography is what pornography does, so is other speech. Hitler's orations affected how some Germans saw Jews. Communism is a world view, not simply a *Manifesto* by Marx and Engels or a set of speeches. Efforts to suppress communist speech in the United States were based on the belief that the public acceptability of

---

[2] MacKinnon's article collects empirical work that supports this proposition. The social science studies are very difficult to interpret, however, and they conflict. Because much of the effect of speech comes through a process of socialization, it is difficult to measure incremental benefits and injuries caused by particular speech. Several psychologists have found, for example, that those who see violent, sexually explicit films tend to have more violent thoughts. But how often does this lead to actual violence? National commissions on obscenity here, in the United Kingdom, and in Canada have found that it is not possible to demonstrate a direct link between obscenity and rape or exhibitionism. . . . In saying that we accept the finding that pornography as the ordinance defines it leads to unhappy consequences, we mean only that there is evidence to this effect, that this evidence is consistent with much human experience, and that as judges we must accept the legislative resolution of such disputed empirical questions.

such ideas would increase the likelihood of totalitarian government. Religions affect socialization in the most pervasive way. The opinion in *Wisconsin v. Yoder*, 406 U.S. 205 (1972), shows how a religion can dominate an entire approach to life, governing much more than the relation between the sexes. Many people believe that the existence of television, apart from the content of specific programs, leads to intellectual laziness, to a penchant for violence, to many other ills. The Alien and Sedition Acts passed during the administration of John Adams rested on a sincerely held belief that disrespect for the government leads to social collapse and revolution—a belief with support in the history of many nations. Most governments of the world act on this empirical regularity, suppressing critical speech. In the United States, however, the strength of the support for this belief is irrelevant. Seditious libel is protected speech unless the danger is not only grave but also imminent. See *New York Times Co. v. Sullivan.*

Racial bigotry, anti-Semitism, violence on television, reporters' biases—these and many more influence the culture and shape our socialization. None is directly answerable by more speech, unless that speech too finds its place in the popular culture. Yet all is protected as speech, however insidious. Any other answer leaves the government in control of all of the institutions of culture, the great censor and director of which thoughts are good for us.

Sexual responses often are unthinking responses, and the association of sexual arousal with the subordination of women therefore may have a substantial effect. But almost all cultural stimuli provoke unconscious responses. Religious ceremonies condition their participants. Teachers convey messages by selecting what not to cover; the implicit message about what is off limits or unthinkable may be more powerful than the messages for which they present rational argument. Television scripts contain unarticulated assumptions. People may be conditioned in subtle ways. If the fact that speech plays a role in a process of conditioning were enough to permit governmental regulation, that would be the end of freedom of speech.

. . .

. . . [T]he image of pain is not necessarily pain. In *Body Double*, a suspense film directed by Brian DePalma, a woman who has disrobed and presented a sexually explicit display is murdered by an intruder with a drill. The drill runs through the woman's body. The film is sexually explicit and a murder occurs—yet no one believes that the actress suffered pain or died. In *Barbarella* a character played by Jane Fonda is at times displayed in sexually explicit ways and at times shown "bleeding, bruised, [and] hurt in a context that makes these conditions sexual"—and again no one believes that Fonda was actually tortured to make the film. In *Carnal Knowledge* a woman grovels to please the sexual whims of a character played by Jack Nicholson; no one believes that there was a real sexual submission, and the Supreme Court held the film protected by the First Amendment. *Jenkins v. Georgia*, 418 U.S. 153 (1974). And this works both ways. The description of women's sexual domination of men in *Lysistrata* was not real dominance. Depictions may affect slavery, war, or sexual roles, but a book about slavery is not itself slavery, or a book about death by poison a murder.

Much of Indianapolis's argument rests on the belief that when speech is "unanswerable," and the metaphor that there is a "marketplace of ideas" does not apply, the First Amendment does not apply either. The metaphor is honored; Milton's *Aeropagitica* and John Stewart Mill's *On Liberty* defend freedom of speech on the ground that the truth will prevail, and many of the most important cases under the First Amendment recite this position. The Framers undoubtedly believed it. As a general matter it is true. But the Constitution does not make the dominance of truth a necessary condition of freedom of speech. To say that it does would be to confuse an outcome of free speech with a necessary condition for the application of the amendment.

A power to limit speech on the ground that truth has not yet prevailed and is not likely to prevail implies the power to declare truth. At some point the government must be able to say (as Indianapolis has said): "We know what the truth is, yet a free exchange of speech has not driven out falsity, so that we must now prohibit falsity." If the government may declare the truth, why wait for the failure of speech? Under the First Amendment, however, there is no such thing as a false idea, *Gertz v. Robert Welch, Inc.*, so the government may not restrict speech on the ground that in a free exchange truth is not yet dominant.

We come, finally, to the argument that pornography is "low value" speech, that it is enough like obscenity that Indianapolis may prohibit it. Some cases hold that speech far removed from politics and other subjects at the core of the Framers' concerns may be subjected to special regulation. E.g., *FCC v. Pacifica Foundation*, 438 U.S. 726 (1978); *Young v. American Mini Theatres, Inc.*, 427 U.S. 50, 67–70 (1976) (plurality opinion); *Chaplinsky v. New Hampshire.* These cases do not sustain statutes that select among viewpoints, however. . . .

At all events, "pornography" is not low value speech within the meaning of these cases. Indianapolis seeks to prohibit certain speech because it believes this speech influences social relations and politics on a grand scale, that it controls attitudes at home and in the legislature. This precludes a characterization of the speech as low value. True, pornography and obscenity have sex in common. But Indianapolis left out of its definition any reference to literary, artistic, political, or scientific value. The ordinance applies to graphic sexually explicit subordination in works great and small.[3] The Court sometimes balances the

value of speech against the costs of its restriction, but it does this by category of speech and not by the content of particular works. Indianapolis has created an approved point of view and so loses the support of these cases.

Any rationale we could imagine in support of this ordinance could not be limited to sex discrimination. Free speech has been on balance an ally of those seeking change. Governments that want stasis start by restricting speech. Culture is a powerful force of continuity; Indianapolis paints pornography as part of the culture of power. Change in any complex system ultimately depends on the ability of outsiders to challenge accepted views and the reigning institutions. Without a strong guarantee of freedom of speech, there is no effective right to challenge what is.

[Senior Circuit Judge Swygert's concurring opinion is omitted.]

---

[3] Indianapolis briefly argues that *Beauharnais v. Illinois*, which allowed a state to penalize "group libel," supports the ordinance. In *Collin v. Smith*, [578 F.2d 1197 (7th Cir.), *cert. denied*, 439 U.S. 916 (1978)], we concluded that cases such as *New York Times v. Sullivan* had so washed away the foundations of Beauharnais that it could not be considered authoritative. If we are wrong in this, however, the case still does not support the ordinance. It is not clear that depicting women as subordinate in sexually explicit ways, even combined with a depiction of pleasure in rape, would fit within the definition of a group libel. The well received film SWEPT AWAY used explicit sex, plus taking pleasure in rape, to make a political statement, not to defame. Work must be an insult or slur for its own sake to come within the ambit of *Beauharnais*, and a work need not be scurrilous at all to be "pornography" under the ordinance.

DER: The Supreme Court's acknowledgment of the assumed social harms caused by obscenity supports its exclusion of obscenity from First Amendment protection. Recognizing the government's interest in preventing these harms, however, also justifies upholding bans on pornography and on viewing obscene materials in one's home. The alleged harm to the morals of society from obscenity must result from the effect it has on people's thoughts—unless we are to believe that obscenity has a direct, unmediated impact on the body. That harm occurs whether obscenity is consumed in a public theater or in the privacy of one's home. If this harm is constitutionally sufficient to justify censorship, then the harm to women from pornography should be sufficient to justify censorship. Pornography causes as much harm to our social environment as obscenity.

Conversely, the view that punishment of pornography constitutes unconstitutional viewpoint discrimination supports the invalidation of obscenity statutes, as well as the Indianapolis ordinance. Bans on obscenity also express a point of view about sexual morality. The court decisions finding it constitutional for the government to censor obscenity in movie theaters but not bedrooms and to punish sexually explicit material that is immoral but not subordinating are hopelessly contradictory.

The opinions in *Miller* and *Hudnut*, moreover, both demonstrate a willful blindness to the social realities. In *Miller*, the Supreme Court exhibited extreme historical ignorance when it claimed there was no evidence of "the harsh hand of censorship of ideas" during the nineteenth century suppression of obscenity. Under the Comstock Act, the federal government repressed political opinion about reproduction, sexuality, and marriage, as well as information about contraceptives. There are good reasons for concern about bans on pornography in the name of women's liberation, but there are better reasons for such bans than for the prohibition of obscenity. MacKinnon and Dworkin's argument in favor of censoring pornography is based not only on the view of women that pornography expresses but also on claims about its relationship to concrete conditions of sex inequality. If the Indianapolis civil rights statute violates the First Amendment, then obscenity laws do so more blatantly.

DEL: What is striking about the Court's presumptuousness in the obscenity cases is not the phenomenon itself but how the majority of the justices view it as a source of analytical pride. The observation in *Paris Adult Theatre*, that "[f]rom the beginning of civilized societies, legislators and judges have acted on various unprovable assumptions,"[55] provides little assurance that wholesale abandonment of any First Amendment interests has been sensibly or sensitively achieved. Justice Brennan, who authored the majority opinion in *Roth*, eventually wised up to its deficiencies and struck a sensible balance that protects children and unconsenting adults.

The railings of MacKinnon and Dworkin, in an effort to stem the tide of pornography, graphically demonstrate the risks of having any group or institution pass judgment upon what is fit to read or view. They assert a cause and effect relationship between pornography and subordination that rests upon evidence that is flimsy at worst and debatable at best. Competing against their risk assessment is the experience of other nations that have easy access to pornography and relatively fewer incidents of sex crimes and abuses. Given the reality that the evidence is not as clear as they might like it to be, the MacKinnon-Dworkin agenda seems reducible not to an empirical premise but to an opinion that prioritizes prudishness over prurience. Such attitudes are well-grounded in socially conservative thought and work effectively to reinforce traditional notions of women as fragile and in need of special guardianship. Whatever satisfaction they may take in successfully convincing other nation's to define law according to their protective methods should be qualified by a reality that is particularly ominous. The Canadian experience, under MacKinnon and Dworkin-inspired anti-pornography law, has been most notable for its suppression of literature reflecting gay, lesbian and feminist perspectives. Barely a few years into the legal regime they successfully urged, half of the nation's feminist bookstores had been the target of police raids and seizures. It is mystifying why those whose complaint is a patriarchal society rush toward enhancing the established order's power and control over what is read, heard and viewed. Modern advocacy of pornography control has more aspects of a power game than an equality agenda. The imperative for courts, legislators and all interested bystanders should be that, so long as the debate is driven by ideology rather than science, the risks of overreaching and even subordination are more profound in the context of authoritative selection rather than autonomous determination.

---

[55] Paris Adult Theatre I v. Slaton, 413 U.S. 49, 61 (1973).

d. Fighting Words

Colonial authorities attempted to maintain proper social hierarchies by controlling improper verbal exchanges.

> Punishment for presumptuous or abusive language to "betters" was ubiquitous. Servants everywhere risked extension of their indentures and other penalties for being disrespectful to their masters. Children (especially in New England) faced the rigors of the law in deriding their parents. And wives were expected to be properly submissive to their husbands . . . and not use abusive or reviling language toward them. Margaret Jones, an early Virginia colonist offers but one of many examples. In 1626 she and John Butterfield "had a falling out," as a witness described it, over who should be allowed to gather peas from a nearby plot. A witness "found her with her hair about her ears," and she later railed at her husband and called him a "base rascal" for his apparent lack of concern over her condition. . . . [T]he Virginia General Court ordered the

woman tied to the back of a boat and dragged up and down the James River for her words and behavior.[56]

A modern day New Jersey prosecutor charged Marion Palendrano with a similar common law crime—being a Common Scold—arising out of her heated spats with her neighbors.[57] Corpus Juris Secundum defines a common scold as a "troublesome and angry woman, who, by brawling and wrangling among her neighbors, breaks the public peace, increases discord, and becomes a nuisance to the neighborhood."[58] Blackstone specified that the punishment for women who committed this crime was to be placed in a scolding or ducking stool and plunged into the water.[59] Although Mrs. Palendrano's caustic words to her neighbors seemed to fit the common law definition of being a common scold, the New Jersey judge dismissed the charge as unconstitutionally vague.

It appears that lower-level officials, who represented the most objectionable aspects of colonial government, regularly endured abusive language as they collected taxes, made arrests, and levied attachments.[60] Sometimes colonial authorities punished angry citizens for their words, in an effort to keep the peace and to preserve the integrity of governmental institutions. In 1665, for example, Joan Ford received nine lashes for calling a constable "horn headed rogue and slow headed rogue." John Nason was fined 1.10 pounds for "bidding the constable of Kittery go shit and his warrant too."[61]

Chaplinsky committed a similar offense when he shouted at a Rochester, New Hampshire city marshal who attempted to stop the Jehovah's Witness from distributing religious literature on a street corner. The Court might have viewed Chaplinsky's words as criticism of a government official and, therefore, particularly worthy of First Amendment protection. Instead, the Court emphasized the slight social value and injurious potential of Chaplinsky's "fighting words," which placed them among those categories of speech that fall outside the First Amendment's concerns.

---

[56] ELDRIDGE, A DISTANT HERITAGE, *supra* note 3, at 7.

[57] *See* State v. Palendrano, 120 N.J. Super. 336, 293 A.2d 747 (1972).

[58] 15A C.J.S. Common Scold S 1, p. 81.

[59] IV BLACKTONE, COMMENTARIES ON THE LAWS OF ENGLAND 168 (7th ed. 1775).

[60] ELDRIDGE, A DISTANT HERITAGE, *supra* note 3, at 8.

[61] *Id.*

Chaplinsky v. State of New Hampshire
315 U.S. 568 (1942)

MR. JUSTICE MURPHY delivered the opinion of the Court.

Appellant, a member of the sect known as Jehovah's Witnesses, was convicted in the municipal court of Rochester, New Hampshire, for violation of Chapter 378, Section 2, of the Public Laws of New Hampshire:

"No person shall address any offensive, derisive or annoying word to any other person who is lawfully in any street or other public place, nor call him by any offensive or derisive name, nor make any noise or exclamation in his presence and hearing with intent to deride, offend or annoy him, or to prevent him from pursuing his lawful business or occupation."

The complaint charged that appellant "with force and arms, in a certain public place in said city of Rochester, to wit, on the public sidewalk on the easterly side of Wakefield Street, near unto the entrance of the City Hall, did unlawfully repeat, the words following, addressed to the complainant, that is to say, 'You are a God damned racketeer' and 'a damned Fascist and the whole government of Rochester are Fascists or agents of Fascists,' the same being offensive, derisive and annoying words and names."

Upon appeal there was a trial *de novo* of appellant before a jury in the Superior Court. He was found guilty and the judgment of conviction was affirmed by the Supreme Court of the State.

. . .

There is no substantial dispute over the facts. Chaplinsky was distributing the literature of his sect on the streets of Rochester on a busy Saturday afternoon. Members of the local citizenry complained to the City Marshal, Bowering, that Chaplinsky was denouncing all religion as a "racket." Bowering told them that Chaplinsky was lawfully engaged, and then warned Chaplinsky that the crowd was getting restless. Some time later a disturbance occurred and the traffic officer on duty at the busy intersection started with Chaplinsky for the police station, but did not inform him that he was under arrest or that he was going to be arrested. On the way they encountered Marshal Bowering who had been advised that a riot was under way and was therefore hurrying to the scene. Bowering repeated his earlier warning to Chaplinsky, who then addressed to Bowering the words set forth in the complaint.

Chaplinsky's version of the affair was slightly different. He testified that when he met Bowering, he asked him to arrest the ones responsible for the disturbance. In reply Bowering cursed him and told him to come along. Appellant admitted that he said the words charged in the complaint with the exception of the name of the Deity.

. . .

Appellant assails the statute as a violation of all three freedoms, speech, press and worship, but only an attack on the basis of free speech is warranted. . . .

Allowing the broadest scope to the language and purpose of the Fourteenth Amendment, it is well understood that the right of free speech is not absolute at all times and under all circumstances. There are certain well-defined and narrowly limited classes of speech, the prevention and punishment of which has never been thought to raise any Constitutional problem. These include the lewd and obscene, the profane, the libelous, and the insulting or "fighting" words—those which by their very utterance inflict injury or tend to incite an immediate breach of the peace. It has been well observed that such utterances are no essential part of any exposition of ideas, and are of such slight social value as a step to truth that any benefit that may be derived from them is clearly outweighed by the social interest in order and morality. "Resort to epithets or personal abuse is not in any proper sense communication of information or opinion safeguarded by the Constitution, and its punishment as a

criminal act would raise no question under that instrument." *Cantwell v. Connecticut*, 310 U.S. 296, 309–310 [1940].

. . .

On the authority of its earlier decisions, the state court declared that the statute's purpose was to preserve the public peace, no words being "forbidden except such as have a direct tendency to cause acts of violence by the person to whom, individually, the remark is addressed." It was further said: "The word 'offensive' is not to be defined in terms of what a particular addressee thinks. . . . The test is what men of common intelligence would understand would be words likely to cause an average addressee to fight. . . . The English language has a number of words and expressions which by general consent are 'fighting words' when said without a disarming smile. . . . Such words, as ordinary men know, are likely to cause a fight. So are threatening, profane or obscene revilings. Derisive and annoying words can be taken as coming within the purview of the statute as heretofore interpreted only when they have this characteristic of plainly tending to excite the addressee to a breach of the peace. . . . The statute, as construed, does no more than prohibit the face-to-face words plainly likely to cause a breach of the peace by the addressee, words whose speaking constitute a breach of the peace by the speaker—including 'classical fighting words', words in current use less 'classical' but equally likely to cause violence, and other disorderly words, including profanity, obscenity and threats."

We are unable to say that the limited scope of the statute as thus construed contravenes the constitutional right of free expression. It is a statute narrowly drawn and limited to define and punish specific conduct lying within the domain of state power, the use in a public place of words likely to cause a breach of the peace. . . .

Nor can we say that the application of the statute to the facts disclosed by the record substantially or unreasonably impinges upon the privilege of free speech. Argument is unnecessary to demonstrate that the appellations "damn racketeer" and "damn Fascist" are epithets likely to provoke the average person to retaliation, and thereby cause a breach of the peace.

. . .

Affirmed.

The *Chaplinsky* opinion might support the state's power, unrestrained by the First Amendment, to punish any words which others find provocative or offensive. In *Cohen v. California*, the Court narrowed the category of unprotected "fighting words" to foreclose that interpretation.

Cohen v. California
403 U.S. 15 (1971)

MR. JUSTICE HARLAN delivered the opinion of the Court.

This case may seem at first blush too inconsequential to find its way into our books, but the issue it presents is of no small constitutional significance.

Appellant Paul Robert Cohen was convicted in the Los Angeles Municipal Court of violating that part of California Penal Code § 415 which prohibits "maliciously and willfully disturb[ing] the peace or quiet of any neighborhood or person . . . by . . . offensive conduct. . . ." He was given 30 days' imprisonment. The facts upon which his conviction rests are detailed in the opinion of the Court of Appeal of California, Second Appellate District, as follows:

> "On April 26, 1968, the defendant was observed in the Los Angeles County Courthouse in the corridor outside of division 20 of the municipal court wearing a jacket bearing the words 'Fuck the Draft' which were plainly visible. There were women and children present in the corridor. The defendant was arrested. The defendant testified that he wore the jacket knowing that the words were on the jacket as a means of informing the public of the depth of his feelings against the Vietnam War and the draft.

> "The defendant did not engage in, nor threaten to engage in, nor did anyone as the result of his conduct in fact commit or threaten to commit any act of violence. The defendant did not make any loud or unusual noise, nor was there any evidence that he uttered any sound prior to his arrest."

In affirming the conviction the Court of Appeal held that "offensive conduct" means "behavior which has a tendency to provoke others to acts of violence or to in turn disturb the peace," and that the State had proved this element because, on the facts of this case, "[i]t was certainly reasonably foreseeable that such conduct might cause others to rise up to commit a violent act against the person of the defendant or attempt to forcibly remove his jacket." The California Supreme Court declined review by a divided vote. . . . We now reverse.

. . .

I

In order to lay hands on the precise issue which this case involves, it is useful first to canvass various matters which this record does not present.

The conviction quite clearly rests upon the asserted offensiveness of the *words* Cohen used to convey his message to the public. The only "conduct" which the State sought to punish is the fact of communication. Thus, we deal here with a conviction resting solely upon "speech," not upon any separately identifiable conduct which allegedly was intended by Cohen to be perceived by others as expressive of particular views but which, on its face, does not necessarily convey any message and hence arguably could be regulated without effectively repressing Cohen's ability to express himself. Further, the State certainly lacks power to punish Cohen for the underlying content of the message the inscription conveyed. At least so long as there is no showing of an intent to incite disobedience to or disruption of the draft, Cohen could not, consistently with the First and Fourteenth Amendments, be punished for asserting the evident position on the inutility or immorality of the draft his jacket reflected.

Appellant's conviction, then, rests squarely upon his exercise of the "freedom of speech" protected from arbitrary governmental interference by the Constitution and can be justified, if at all, only as a valid regulation of the manner in which he exercised that freedom, not as a permissible prohibition on the substantive message it conveys. This does not end the inquiry, of course, for the First and Fourteenth Amendments have never been thought to give absolute protection to every individual to speak whenever or wherever he pleases or to use any form of address in any circumstances that he chooses. In this vein, too, however, we think it important to note that several issues typically associated with such problems are not presented here.

In the first place, Cohen was tried under a statute applicable throughout the entire State. Any attempt to support this conviction on the ground that the statute seeks to preserve an appropriately decorous atmosphere in the courthouse where Cohen was arrested must fail in the absence of any language in the statute that would have put appellant on notice that certain kinds of otherwise permissible speech or conduct would nevertheless, under California law, not be tolerated in certain places. No fair reading of the phrase "offensive conduct" can be said sufficiently to inform the ordinary person that distinctions between certain locations are thereby created.[3]

---

[3] It is illuminating to note what transpired when Cohen entered a courtroom in the building. He removed his jacket and stood with it folded over his arm. Meanwhile, a policeman sent the presiding

In the second place, as it comes to us, this case cannot be said to fall within those relatively few categories of instances where prior decisions have established the power of government to deal more comprehensively with certain forms of individual expression simply upon a showing that such a form was employed. This is not, for example, an obscenity case. Whatever else may be necessary to give rise to the States' broader power to prohibit obscene expression, such expression must be, in some significant way, erotic. *Roth v. United States*. It cannot plausibly be maintained that this vulgar allusion to the Selective Service System would conjure up such psychic stimulation in anyone likely to be confronted with Cohen's crudely defaced jacket.

This Court has also held that the States are free to ban the simple use, without a demonstration of additional justifying circumstances, of so-called "fighting words," those personally abusive epithets which, when addressed to the ordinary citizen, are, as a matter of common knowledge, inherently likely to provoke violent reaction. *Chaplinsky v. New Hampshire*. While the four-letter word displayed by Cohen in relation to the draft is not uncommonly employed in a personally provocative fashion, in this instance it was clearly not "directed to the person of the hearer." No individual actually or likely to be present could reasonably have regarded the words on appellant's jacket as a direct personal insult. Nor do we have here an instance of the exercise of the State's police power to prevent a speaker from intentionally provoking a given group to hostile reaction. There is, as noted above, no showing that anyone who saw Cohen was in fact violently aroused or that appellant intended such a result.

Finally, in arguments before this Court much has been made of the claim that Cohen's distasteful mode of expression was thrust upon unwilling or unsuspecting viewers, and that the State might therefore legitimately act as it did in order to protect the sensitive from otherwise unavoidable exposure to appellant's crude form of protest. Of course, the mere presumed presence of unwitting listeners or viewers does not serve automatically to justify curtailing all speech capable of giving offense. While this Court has recognized that government may properly act in many situations to prohibit intrusion into the privacy of the home of unwelcome views and ideas which cannot be totally banned from the public dialogue, we have at the same time consistently stressed that "we

are often 'captives' outside the sanctuary of the home and subject to objectionable speech." The ability of government, consonant with the Constitution, to shut off discourse solely to protect others from hearing it is, in other words, dependent upon a showing that substantial privacy interests are being invaded in an essentially intolerable manner. Any broader view of this authority would effectively empower a majority to silence dissidents simply as a matter of personal predilections.

In this regard, persons confronted with Cohen's jacket were in a quite different posture than, say, those subjected to the raucous emissions of sound trucks blaring outside their residences. Those in the Los Angeles courthouse could effectively avoid further bombardment of their sensibilities simply by averting their eyes. And, while it may be that one has a more substantial claim to a recognizable privacy interest when walking through a courthouse corridor than, for example, strolling through Central Park, surely it is nothing like the interest in being free from unwanted expression in the confines of one's own home. Given the subtlety and complexity of the factors involved, if Cohen's "speech" was otherwise entitled to constitutional protection, we do not think the fact that some unwilling "listeners" in a public building may have been briefly exposed to it can serve to justify this breach of the peace conviction where, as here, there was no evidence that persons powerless to avoid appellant's conduct did in fact object to it, and where that portion of the statute upon which Cohen's conviction rests evinces no concern, either on its face or as construed by the California courts, with the special plight of the captive auditor, but, instead, indiscriminately sweeps within its prohibitions all "offensive conduct" that disturbs "any neighborhood or person."

II

Against this background, the issue flushed by this case stands out in bold relief. It is whether California can excise, as "offensive conduct," one particular scurrilous epithet from the public discourse, either upon the theory of the court below that its use is inherently likely to cause violent reaction or upon a more general assertion that the States, acting as guardians of public morality, may properly remove this offensive word from the public vocabulary.

The rationale of the California court is plainly untenable. At most it reflects an "undifferentiated fear or apprehension of disturbance [which] is not enough to overcome the right to freedom of expression." *Tinker v. Des Moines Indep. Community School Dist.*, 393 U.S. 503, 508 (1969). We have been shown no evidence that substantial numbers of citizens are stand-

---

judge a note suggesting that Cohen be held in contempt of court. The judge declined to do so and Cohen was arrested by the officer only after he emerged from the courtroom.

ing ready to strike out physically at whoever may assault their sensibilities with execrations like that uttered by Cohen. There may be some persons about with such lawless and violent proclivities, but that is an insufficient base upon which to erect, consistently with constitutional values, a governmental power to force persons who wish to ventilate their dissident views into avoiding particular forms of expression. The argument amounts to little more than the self-defeating proposition that to avoid physical censorship of one who has not sought to provoke such a response by a hypothetical coterie of the violent and lawless, the States may more appropriately effectuate that censorship themselves.

Admittedly, it is not so obvious that the First and Fourteenth Amendments must be taken to disable the States from punishing public utterance of this unseemly expletive in order to maintain what they regard as a suitable level of discourse within the body politic. We think, however, that examination and reflection will reveal the shortcomings of a contrary viewpoint.

At the outset, we cannot overemphasize that, in our judgment, most situations where the State has a justifiable interest in regulating speech will fall within one or more of the various established exceptions, discussed above but not applicable here, to the usual rule that governmental bodies may not prescribe the form or content of individual expression. Equally important to our conclusion is the constitutional backdrop against which our decision must be made. The constitutional right of free expression is powerful medicine in a society as diverse and populous as ours. It is designed and intended to remove governmental restraints from the arena of public discussion, putting the decision as to what views shall be voiced largely into the hands of each of us, in the hope that use of such freedom will ultimately produce a more capable citizenry and more perfect polity and in the belief that no other approach would comport with the premise of individual dignity and choice upon which our political system rests. See *Whitney v. California* (Brandeis, J., concurring).

To many, the immediate consequence of this freedom may often appear to be only verbal tumult, discord, and even offensive utterance. These are, however, within established limits, in truth necessary side effects of the broader enduring values which the process of open debate permits us to achieve. That the air may at times seem filled with verbal cacophony is, in this sense not a sign of weakness but of strength. We cannot lose sight of the fact that, in what otherwise might seem a trifling and annoying instance of individual distasteful abuse of a privilege, these fundamental societal values are truly implicated. That is why

"[w]holly neutral futilities . . . come under the protection of free speech as fully as do Keats' poems or Donne's sermons," *Winters v. New York*, 333 U.S. 507, 528 (1948) (Frankfurter, J., dissenting), and why "so long as the means are peaceful, the communication need not meet standards of acceptability," *Organization for a Better Austin v. Keefe*, 402 U.S. 415, 419 (1971).

Against this perception of the constitutional policies involved, we discern certain more particularized considerations that peculiarly call for reversal of this conviction. First, the principle contended for by the State seems inherently boundless. How is one to distinguish this from any other offensive word? Surely the State has no right to cleanse public debate to the point where it is grammatically palatable to the most squeamish among us. Yet no readily ascertainable general principle exists for stopping short of that result were we to affirm the judgment below. For, while the particular four-letter word being litigated here is perhaps more distasteful than most others of its genre, it is nevertheless often true that one man's vulgarity is another's lyric. Indeed, we think it is largely because governmental officials cannot make principled distinctions in this area that the Constitution leaves matters of taste and style so largely to the individual.

Additionally, we cannot overlook the fact, because it is well illustrated by the episode involved here, that much linguistic expression serves a dual communicative function: it conveys not only ideas capable of relatively precise, detached explication, but otherwise inexpressible emotions as well. In fact, words are often chosen as much for their emotive as their cognitive force. We cannot sanction the view that the Constitution, while solicitous of the cognitive content of individual speech has little or no regard for that emotive function which practically speaking, may often be the more important element of the overall message sought to be communicated. Indeed, as Mr. Justice Frankfurter has said, "[o]ne of the prerogatives of American citizenship is the right to criticize public men and measures—and that means not only informed and responsible criticism but the freedom to speak foolishly and without moderation." *Baumgartner v. United States*, 322 U.S. 665, 673–674 (1944).

Finally, and in the same vein, we cannot indulge the facile assumption that one can forbid particular words without also running a substantial risk of suppressing ideas in the process. Indeed, governments might soon seize upon the censorship of particular words as a convenient guise for banning the expression of unpopular views. We have been able, as noted above, to discern little social benefit that might result from running the risk of opening the door to such grave results.

It is, in sum, our judgment that, absent a more particularized and compelling reason for its actions, the State may not, consistently with the First and Fourteenth Amendments, make the simple public display here involved of this single four-letter expletive a criminal offense. Because that is the only arguably sustainable rationale for the conviction here at issue, the judgment below must be

Reversed.

MR. JUSTICE BLACKMUN, with whom THE CHIEF JUSTICE and Mr. JUSTICE BLACK join [dissenting].

. . .

Cohen's absurd and immature antic, in my view, was mainly conduct and little speech. The California Court of Appeal appears so to have described it, and I cannot characterize it otherwise. Further, the case appears to me to be well within the sphere of *Chaplinsky v. New Hampshire*, where Mr. Justice Murphy, a known champion of First Amendment freedoms, wrote for a unanimous bench. As a consequence, this Court's agonizing over First Amendment values seems misplaced and unnecessary.

Paralleling the debate about the antipornography laws is a debate about the constitutionality of efforts to curb "hate speech"—degrading or threatening expressions directed at individuals on the basis of their race, ethnic background, gender, sexual orientation or religion. In the wake of increased instances of hate speech across the country, college administrators, employers, and local legislators have implemented regulations penalizing this type of expression. A number of constitutional scholars defended these restrictions, arguing that targeted slurs constitute an act of terror that helps to perpetuate racial and other forms of inequality in our society. Hate speech, they contend, not only inflicts an immediate injury—a "verbal slap in the face"—but also deters members of historically subordinated groups from living where they choose, travelling freely, participating in the political life of the community, and otherwise engaging in constitutionally protected freedoms. Opponents of hate speech regulations argue that they chill valuable expression and are ineffective at promoting racial equality.

The chances that a hate speech regulation will be declared constitutional are greatly enhanced if it restricts only speech within a category that is not protected by the First Amendment. St. Paul, Minnesota attempted to immunize its Bias-Motivated Crime ordinance in this way by punishing expression that constituted unprotected fighting words. The Court nevertheless invalidated the ordinance as a violation of the First Amendment. Although all of the justices agreed that the law was unconstitutional, they vehemently disagreed on a rationale.

R.A.V. v. City of St. Paul, Minnesota
112 S. Ct. 2538 (1992)

Justice SCALIA delivered the opinion of the Court.

In the predawn hours of June 21, 1990, petitioner and several other teenagers allegedly assembled a crudely-made cross by taping together broken chair legs. They then allegedly burned the cross inside the fenced yard of a black family that lived across the street from the house where petitioner was staying. Although this conduct could have been punished under any of a number of laws, one of the two provisions under which respondent city of St. Paul chose to charge petitioner (then a juvenile) was the St. Paul Bias-Motivated Crime Ordinance, which provides:

"Whoever places on public or private property a symbol, object, appellation, characterization or graffiti, including, but not limited to, a burning cross or Nazi swastika, which one knows or has reasonable grounds to know arouses anger, alarm or resentment in others on the basis of race, color, creed, religion or gender commits disorderly conduct and shall be guilty of a misdemeanor."

Petitioner moved to dismiss this count on the ground that the St. Paul ordinance was substantially overbroad and impermissibly content-based and therefore facially invalid under the First Amendment. The trial court granted this motion, but the Minnesota Supreme Court reversed. That court rejected petitioner's overbreadth claim because, as construed in prior Minnesota cases, the modifying phrase "arouses anger, alarm or resentment in others" limited the reach of the ordinance to conduct that amounts to "fighting words," *i.e.*, "conduct that itself inflicts injury or tends to incite immediate violence ... " (citing *Chaplinsky v. New Hampshire*), and therefore the ordinance reached only expression "that the first amendment does not protect." The court also concluded that the ordinance was not impermissibly content-based because, in its view, "the ordinance is a narrowly tailored means toward accomplishing the compelling governmental interest in protecting the community against bias-motivated threats to public safety and order."

I

In construing the St. Paul ordinance, we are bound by the construction given to it by the Minnesota court. Accordingly, we accept the Minnesota Supreme Court's authoritative statement that the ordinance reaches only those expressions that constitute "fighting words" within the meaning of *Chaplinsky*. ...

The First Amendment generally prevents government from proscribing speech, or even expressive conduct, because of disapproval of the ideas expressed. Content-based regulations are presumptively invalid. From 1791 to the present, however, our society, like other free but civilized societies, has permitted restrictions upon the content of speech in a few limited areas, which are "of such slight social value as a step to truth that any benefit that may be derived from them is clearly outweighed by the social interest in order and morality." *Chaplinsky*.

We have sometimes said that these categories of expression are "not within the area of constitutionally protected speech," or that the "protection of the First Amendment does not extend" to them. Such statements must be taken in context, however, and are no more literally true than is the occasionally repeated shorthand characterizing obscenity "as not being speech at all." What they mean is that these areas of speech can, consistently with the First Amendment, be regulated *because of their constitutionally proscribable content* (obscenity, defamation, etc.)—not that they are categories of speech entirely invisible to the Constitution, so that they may be made the vehicles for content discrimination unrelated to their distinctively proscribable content. Thus, the government may proscribe libel; but it may not make the further content discrimination of proscribing only libel critical of the govern-

ment. We recently acknowledged this distinction in *Ferber*, where, in upholding New York's child pornography law, we expressly recognized that there was no "question here of censoring a particular literary theme. ... "

Our cases surely do not establish the proposition that the First Amendment imposes no obstacle whatsoever to regulation of particular instances of such proscribable expression, so that the government "may regulate [them] freely." That would mean that a city council could enact an ordinance prohibiting only those legally obscene works that contain criticism of the city government or, indeed, that do not include endorsement of the city government. Such a simplistic, all-or-nothing-at-all approach to First Amendment protection is at odds with common sense and with our jurisprudence as well. It is not true that "fighting words" have at most a "*de minimis*" expressive content, or that their content is *in all respects* "worthless and undeserving of constitutional protection"; sometimes they are quite expressive indeed. We have not said that they constitute "no part of the expression of ideas," but only that they constitute "no *essential* part of any exposition of ideas." *Chaplinsky* (emphasis added).

The proposition that a particular instance of speech can be proscribable on the basis of one feature (*e.g.*, obscenity) but not on the basis of another (*e.g.*, opposition to the city government) is commonplace, and has found application in many contexts. We have long held, for example, that nonverbal expressive activity can be banned because of the action it entails, but not because of the ideas it expresses—so that burning a flag in violation of an ordinance against outdoor fires could be punishable, whereas burning a flag in violation of an ordinance against dishonoring the flag is not. Similarly, we have upheld reasonable "time, place, or manner" restrictions, but only if they are "justified without reference to the content of the regulated speech." And just as the power to proscribe particular speech on the basis of a noncontent element (*e.g.*, noise) does not entail the power to proscribe the same speech on the basis of a content element; so also, the power to proscribe it on the basis of one content element (*e.g.*, obscenity) does not entail the power to proscribe it on the basis of *other* content elements.

In other words, the exclusion of "fighting words" from the scope of the First Amendment simply means that, for purposes of that Amendment, the unprotected features of the words are, despite their verbal character, essentially a "nonspeech" element of communication. Fighting words are thus analogous to a noisy sound truck: Each is, as Justice Frankfurter recognized, a "mode of speech," both can be used to convey an idea; but neither has, in and of itself, a claim upon the First Amendment. As with the sound truck, however, so also with fighting words: The government may not regulate use based on hostility—or favoritism—towards the underlying message expressed.

. . .

Even the prohibition against content discrimination that we assert the First Amendment requires is not absolute. It applies differently in the context of proscribable speech than in the area of fully protected speech. The rationale of the general prohibition, after all, is that content discrimination "rais[es] the specter that the Government may effectively drive certain ideas or viewpoints from the marketplace." But content discrimination among various instances of a class of proscribable speech often does not pose this threat.

When the basis for the content discrimination consists entirely of the very reason the entire class of speech at issue is proscribable, no significant danger of idea or viewpoint discrimination exists. Such a reason, having been adjudged neutral enough to support exclusion of the entire class of speech from First Amendment protection, is also neutral enough to form the basis of distinction within the class. To illustrate: A State might choose to prohibit only that obscenity which is the most patently offensive *in its prurience—i.e.*, that which involves the most lascivious displays of sexual activity. But it may not prohibit, for example, only that obscenity which includes offensive *political* messages. And the Federal Government can criminalize only those threats of violence that are directed against the President—since the reasons why threats of violence are outside the First Amendment (protecting individuals from the fear of violence, from the disruption that fear engenders, and from the possibility that the threatened violence will occur) have special force when applied to the person of the President. But the Federal Government may not criminalize only those threats against the President that mention his policy on aid to inner cities. And to take a final example (one mentioned by Justice STEVENS), a State may choose to regulate price advertising in one industry but not in others, because the risk of fraud (one of the characteristics of commercial speech that justifies depriving it of full First Amendment protection) is in its view greater there. But a State may not prohibit only that commercial advertising that depicts men in a demeaning fashion.

Another valid basis for according differential treatment to even a content-defined subclass of proscribable speech is that the subclass happens to be associated with particular "secondary effects" of the speech, so that the regulation is "*justified* without reference to the content of the . . . speech," *Renton v. Playtime Theatres, Inc.*, 475 U.S. 41, 48 (1986). A State could, for example, permit all obscene live performances except those involving minors. Moreover, since words can in some circumstances violate laws directed not against speech but against conduct (a law against treason, for example, is violated by telling the enemy the nation's defense secrets), a particular content-based subcategory of a proscribable class of speech can be swept up incidentally within the reach of a statute directed at conduct rather than speech. Thus, for example, sexually derogatory "fighting words," among other words, may produce a violation of Title VII's general prohibition against sexual discrimination in employment practices. Where the government does not target conduct on the basis of its expressive content, acts are not shielded from regulation merely because they express a discriminatory idea or philosophy.

These bases for distinction refute the proposition that the selectivity of the restriction is "even arguably 'conditioned upon the sovereign's agreement with what a speaker may intend to say.'" There may be other such bases as well. Indeed, to validate such selectivity (where totally proscribable speech is at issue) it may not even be necessary to identify any particular "neutral" basis, so long as the nature of the content discrimination is such that there is no realistic possibility that official suppression of ideas is afoot. (We cannot think of any First Amendment interest that would stand in the way of a State's prohibiting only those obscene motion pictures with blue-eyed actresses.) Save for that limitation, the regulation of "fighting words," like the regulation of noisy speech, may address some offensive instances and leave other, equally offensive, instances alone.

II

Applying these principles to the St. Paul ordinance, we conclude that, even as narrowly construed by the Minnesota Supreme Court, the ordinance is facially unconstitutional. Although the phrase in the ordinance, "arouses anger, alarm or resentment in others," has been limited by the Minnesota Supreme Court's construction to reach only those symbols or displays that amount to "fighting words," the remaining, unmodified terms make clear that the ordinance applies only to "fighting words" that insult, or provoke violence, "on the basis of race, color, creed, religion or gender." Displays containing abusive invective, no matter how vicious or severe, are permissible unless they are addressed to one of the specified disfavored topics. Those who wish to use "fighting words" in connection with other ideas—to express hostility, for example, on the basis of political affiliation, union membership, or homosexuality—are not covered. The First Amendment does not permit St. Paul to impose special prohibitions on those speakers who express views on disfavored subjects.

In its practical operation, moreover, the ordinance goes even beyond mere content discrimination, to actual viewpoint discrimination. Displays containing some words—odious racial epithets, for example—would be prohibited to proponents of all views. But "fighting words" that do not themselves invoke race, color, creed, religion, or gender—aspersions upon a person's mother, for example—would seemingly be usable *ad libitum* in the placards of those arguing *in favor* of racial, color, etc. tolerance and equality, but could not be used by that speaker's opponents. One could hold up a sign saying, for example, that all "anti-Catholic bigots" are misbegotten; but not that all "papists" are, for that would insult and provoke violence "on the basis of religion." St. Paul has no such authority to license one side of a debate to fight freestyle, while requiring the other to follow Marquis of Queensbury Rules.

What we have here, it must be emphasized, is not a prohibition of fighting words that are directed at certain persons or groups (which would be *facially* valid if it met the requirements of the Equal Protection Clause); but rather, a prohibition of fighting words that contain (as the Minnesota Supreme Court repeatedly emphasized) messages of "bias-motivated" hatred and in particular, as applied to this case, messages "based on virulent notions of racial supremacy." One must wholeheartedly agree with the Minnesota Supreme Court that "[i]t is the responsibility, even the obligation, of diverse communities to confront such notions in whatever form they appear," but the manner of that confrontation cannot consist of selective limitations upon speech. St. Paul's brief asserts that a general "fighting words" law would not meet the city's needs because only a content-specific measure can communicate to minority groups that the "group hatred" aspect of such speech "is not condoned by the majority." The point of the First Amendment is that majority preferences must be expressed in some fashion other than silencing speech on the basis of its content.

Despite the fact that the Minnesota Supreme Court and St. Paul acknowledge that the ordinance is directed at expression of group hatred, Justice STEVENS suggests that this "fundamentally misreads" the ordinance. It is directed, he claims, not to speech of a particular content, but to particular "injur[ies]" that are "qualitatively different" from other injuries. This is word-play. What makes the anger, fear, sense of dishonor, etc. produced by violation

of this ordinance distinct from the anger, fear, sense of dishonor, etc. produced by other fighting words is nothing other than the fact that it is caused by a distinctive idea, conveyed by a distinctive message. The First Amendment cannot be evaded that easily. It is obvious that the symbols which will arouse "anger, alarm or resentment in others on the basis of race, color, creed, religion or gender" are those symbols that communicate a message of hostility based on one of these characteristics. . . .

The content-based discrimination reflected in the St. Paul ordinance comes within neither any of the specific exceptions to the First Amendment prohibition we discussed earlier, nor within a more general exception for content discrimination that does not threaten censorship of ideas. It assuredly does not fall within the exception for content discrimination based on the very reasons why the particular class of speech at issue (here, fighting words) is proscribable. As explained earlier, the reason why fighting words are categorically excluded from the protection of the First Amendment is not that their content communicates any particular idea, but that their content embodies a particularly intolerable (and socially unnecessary) mode of expressing whatever idea the speaker wishes to convey. St. Paul has not singled out an especially offensive mode of expression—it has not, for example, selected for prohibition only those fighting words that communicate ideas in a threatening (as opposed to a merely obnoxious) manner. Rather, it has proscribed fighting words of whatever manner that communicate messages of racial, gender, or religious intolerance. Selectivity of this sort creates the possibility that the city is seeking to handicap the expression of particular ideas. That possibility would alone be enough to render the ordinance presumptively invalid, but St. Paul's comments and concessions in this case elevate the possibility to a certainty.

. . .

Finally, St. Paul and its *amici* defend the conclusion of the Minnesota Supreme Court that, even if the ordinance regulates expression based on hostility towards its protected ideological content, this discrimination is nonetheless justified because it is narrowly tailored to serve compelling state interests. Specifically, they assert that the ordinance helps to ensure the basic human rights of members of groups that have historically been subjected to discrimination, including the right of such group members to live in peace where they wish. We do not doubt that these interests are compelling, and that the ordinance can be said to promote them. But the "danger of censorship" presented by a facially content-based statute, requires that that weapon be employed only where it is *"necessary* to serve the asserted [compelling] interest." The existence of adequate content-neutral alternatives thus "undercut[s] significantly" any defense of such a statute, casting considerable doubt on the government's protestations that "the asserted justification is in fact an accurate description of the purpose and effect of the law." The dispositive question in this case, therefore, is whether content discrimination is reasonably necessary to achieve St. Paul's compelling interests; it plainly is not. An ordinance not limited to the favored topics, for example, would have precisely the same beneficial effect. In fact the only interest distinctively served by the content limitation is that of displaying the city council's special hostility towards the particular biases thus singled out. That is precisely what the First Amendment forbids. The politicians of St. Paul are entitled to express that hostility—but not through the means of imposing unique limitations upon speakers who (however benightedly) disagree.

* * *

Let there be no mistake about our belief that burning a cross in someone's front yard is reprehensible. But St. Paul has sufficient means at its disposal to prevent such behavior without adding the First Amendment to the fire.

. . .

Justice WHITE, with whom Justice BLACKMUN and Justice O'CONNOR join, and with whom Justice STEVENS joins except as to Part I(A), concurring in the judgment.

I agree with the majority that the judgment of the Minnesota Supreme Court should be reversed. However, our agreement ends there.

This case could easily be decided within the contours of established First Amendment law by holding, as petitioner argues, that the St. Paul ordinance is fatally overbroad because it criminalizes not only unprotected expression but expression protected by the First Amendment. . . .

. . .

But in the present case, the majority casts aside long-established First Amendment doctrine without the benefit of briefing and adopts an untried theory. This is hardly a judicious way of proceeding, and the Court's reasoning in reaching its result is transparently wrong.

I

A

This Court's decisions have plainly stated that expression falling within certain limited categories so lacks the values the First Amendment was designed to protect that the Constitution affords no protection to that expres-

sion. . . . Thus, as the majority concedes, this Court has long held certain discrete categories of expression to be proscribable on the basis of their content. . . . All of these categories are content based. But the Court has held that First Amendment does not apply to them because their expressive content is worthless or of *de minimis* value to society. We have not departed from this principle, emphasizing repeatedly that, "within the confines of [these] given classification[s], the evil to be restricted so overwhelmingly outweighs the expressive interests, if any, at stake, that no process of case-by-case adjudication is required." *Ferber.* This categorical approach has provided a principled and narrowly focused means for distinguishing between expression that the government may regulate freely and that which it may regulate on the basis of content only upon a showing of compelling need.

Today, however, the Court announces that earlier Courts did not mean their repeated statements that certain categories of expression are "not within the area of constitutionally protected speech." The present Court submits that such clear statements "must be taken in context" and are not "literally true."

To the contrary, those statements meant precisely what they said: The categorical approach is a firmly entrenched part of our First Amendment jurisprudence. . . . Nevertheless, the majority holds that the First Amendment protects those narrow categories of expression long held to be undeserving of First Amendment protection—at least to the extent that lawmakers may not regulate some fighting words more strictly than others because of their content. The Court announces that such content-based distinctions violate the First Amendment because "the government may not regulate use based on hostility—or favoritism—towards the underlying message expressed." Should the government want to criminalize certain fighting words, the Court now requires it to criminalize all fighting words.

To borrow a phrase, "Such a simplistic, all-or-nothing-at-all approach to First Amendment protection is at odds with common sense and with our jurisprudence as well." It is inconsistent to hold that the government may proscribe an entire category of speech because the content of that speech is evil; but that the government may not treat a subset of that category differently without violating the First Amendment; the content of the subset is by definition worthless and undeserving of constitutional protection.

The majority's observation that fighting words are "quite expressive indeed," is no answer. Fighting words are not a means of exchanging views, rallying supporters, or registering a protest; they are directed against individuals to provoke violence or to inflict injury. Therefore, a ban on all fighting words or on a subset of the fighting words category would restrict only the social evil of hate speech, without creating the danger of driving viewpoints from the marketplace.

Therefore, the Court's insistence on inventing its brand of First Amendment underinclusiveness puzzles me. The overbreadth doctrine has the redeeming virtue of attempting to avoid the chilling of protected expression, but the Court's new "underbreadth" creation serves no desirable function. Instead, it permits, indeed invites, the continuation of expressive conduct that in this case is evil and worthless in First Amendment terms, until the city of St. Paul cures the underbreadth by adding to its ordinance a catch-all phrase such as "and all other fighting words that may constitutionally be subject to this ordinance."

Any contribution of this holding to First Amendment jurisprudence is surely a negative one, since it necessarily signals that expressions of violence, such as the message of intimidation and racial hatred conveyed by burning a cross on someone's lawn, are of sufficient value to outweigh the social interest in order and morality that has traditionally placed such fighting words outside the First Amendment. Indeed, by characterizing fighting words as a form of "debate," the majority legitimates hate speech as a form of public discussion.

Furthermore, the Court obscures the line between speech that could be regulated freely on the basis of content (*i.e.*, the narrow categories of expression falling outside the First Amendment) and that which could be regulated on the basis of content only upon a showing of a compelling state interest (*i.e.*, all remaining expression). By placing fighting words, which the Court has long held to be valueless, on at least equal constitutional footing with political discourse and other forms of speech that we have deemed to have the greatest social value, the majority devalues the latter category.

B

In a second break with precedent, the Court refuses to sustain the ordinance even though it would survive under the strict scrutiny applicable to other protected expression. Assuming, *arguendo*, that the St. Paul ordinance is a content-based regulation of protected expression, it nevertheless would pass First Amendment review under settled law upon a showing that the regulation "'is necessary to serve a compelling state interest and is narrowly drawn to achieve that end.'" St. Paul has urged that its ordinance, in the words of the majority, "helps to ensure the basic human rights of members of groups that have histori-

cally been subjected to discrimination. . . ." The Court expressly concedes that this interest is compelling and is promoted by the ordinance. Nevertheless, the Court treats strict scrutiny analysis as irrelevant to the constitutionality of the legislation. . . . Under the majority's view, a narrowly drawn, content-based ordinance could never pass constitutional muster if the object of that legislation could be accomplished by banning a wider category of speech. This appears to be a general renunciation of strict scrutiny review, a fundamental tool of First Amendment analysis.

. . .

C

The Court has patched up its argument with an apparently nonexhaustive list of *ad hoc* exceptions, in what can be viewed either as an attempt to confine the effects of its decision to the facts of this case, or as an effort to anticipate some of the questions that will arise from its radical revision of First Amendment law.

For instance, if the majority were to give general application to the rule on which it decides this case, today's decision would call into question the constitutionality of the statute making it illegal to threaten the life of the President. Surely, this statute, by singling out certain threats, incorporates a content-based distinction; it indicates that the Government especially disfavors threats against the President as opposed to threats against all others. But because the Government could prohibit all threats and not just those directed against the President, under the Court's theory, the compelling reasons justifying the enactment of special legislation to safeguard the President would be irrelevant, and the statute would fail First Amendment review.

To save the statute, the majority has engrafted the following exception onto its newly announced First Amendment rule: Content-based distinctions may be drawn within an unprotected category of speech if the basis for the distinctions is "the very reason the entire class of speech at issue is proscribable." . . . The exception swallows the majority's rule. Certainly, it should apply to the St. Paul ordinance, since "the reasons why [fighting words] are outside the First Amendment . . . have special force when applied to [groups that have historically been subjected to discrimination]."

To avoid the result of its own analysis, the Court suggests that fighting words are simply a mode of communication, rather than a content-based category, and that the St. Paul ordinance has not singled out a particularly objectionable mode of communication. Again, the majority confuses the issue. A prohibition on fighting words is not a time, place, or manner restriction; it is a ban on a class of speech that conveys an overriding message of personal injury and imminent violence, a message that is at its ugliest when directed against groups that have long been the targets of discrimination. Accordingly, the ordinance falls within the first exception to the majority's theory.

As its second exception, the Court posits that certain content-based regulations will survive under the new regime if the regulated subclass "happens to be associated with particular 'secondary effects' of the speech . . . ," which the majority treats as encompassing instances in which "words can . . . violate laws directed not against speech but against conduct . . . " Again, there is a simple explanation for the Court's eagerness to craft an exception to its new First Amendment rule: Under the general rule the Court applies in this case, Title VII hostile work environment claims would suddenly be unconstitutional.

Title VII makes it unlawful to discriminate "because of [an] individual's race, color, religion, sex, or national origin," and the regulations covering hostile workplace claims forbid "sexual harassment," which includes "[u]nwelcome sexual advances, requests for sexual favors, and other verbal or physical conduct of a sexual nature" which creates "an intimidating, hostile, or offensive working environment." The regulation does not prohibit workplace harassment generally; it focuses on what the majority would characterize as the "disfavored topi[c]" of sexual harassment. In this way, Title VII is similar to the St. Paul ordinance that the majority condemns because it "impose[s] special prohibitions on those speakers who express views on disfavored subjects." Under the broad principle the Court uses to decide the present case, hostile work environment claims based on sexual harassment should fail First Amendment review; because a general ban on harassment in the workplace would cover the problem of sexual harassment, any attempt to proscribe the subcategory of sexually harassing expression would violate the First Amendment.

Hence, the majority's second exception, which the Court indicates would insulate a Title VII hostile work environment claim from an underinclusiveness challenge because "sexually derogatory 'fighting words' . . . may produce a violation of Title VII's general prohibition against sexual discrimination in employment practices." But application of this exception to a hostile work environment claim does not hold up under close examination.

First, the hostile work environment regulation is not keyed to the presence or absence of an economic *quid pro quo*, but to the impact of the speech on the victimized worker. Consequently, the regulation would no more fall within a secondary effects exception than does the St. Paul ordinance. Second, the majority's focus on the statute's general prohibition on discrimination glosses over the language of the specific regulation governing hostile working environment, which reaches beyond any "incidental" effect on speech.

. . .

II

Although I disagree with the Court's analysis, I do agree with its conclusion: The St. Paul ordinance is unconstitutional. However, I would decide the case on overbreadth grounds.

. . .

I agree with petitioner that the ordinance is invalid on its face. Although the ordinance as construed reaches categories of speech that are constitutionally unprotected, it also criminalizes a substantial amount of expression that—however repugnant—is shielded by the First Amendment.

In attempting to narrow the scope of the St. Paul antibias ordinance, the Minnesota Supreme Court relied upon two of the categories of speech and expressive conduct that fall outside the First Amendment's protective sphere: words that incite "imminent lawless action," *Brandenburg v. Ohio*, and "fighting" words, *Chaplinsky v. New Hampshire*. The Minnesota Supreme Court erred in its application of the *Chaplinsky* fighting words test and consequently interpreted the St. Paul ordinance in a fashion that rendered the ordinance facially overbroad.

In construing the St. Paul ordinance, the Minnesota Supreme Court drew upon the definition of fighting words that appears in *Chaplinsky*—words "which by their very utterance inflict injury or tend to incite an immediate breach of the peace." However, the Minnesota court was far from clear in identifying the "injur[ies]" inflicted by the expression that St. Paul sought to regulate. Indeed, the Minnesota court emphasized (tracking the language of the ordinance) that "the ordinance censors only those displays that one knows or should know will create anger, alarm or resentment based on racial, ethnic, gender or religious bias." I therefore understand the court to have ruled that St. Paul may constitutionally prohibit expression that "by its very utterance" causes "anger, alarm or resentment."

Our fighting words cases have made clear, however, that such generalized reactions are not sufficient to strip expression of its constitutional protection. The mere fact that expressive activity causes hurt feelings, offense, or resentment does not render the expression unprotected.

In the First Amendment context, "[c]riminal statutes must be scrutinized with particular care; those that make unlawful a substantial amount of constitutionally protected conduct may be held facially invalid even if they also have legitimate application." The St. Paul antibias ordinance is such a law. Although the ordinance reaches conduct that is unprotected, it also makes criminal expressive conduct that causes only hurt feelings, offense, or resentment, and is protected by the First Amendment. The ordinance is therefore fatally overbroad and invalid on its face.

III

Today, the Court has disregarded two established principles of First Amendment law without providing a coherent replacement theory. Its decision is an arid, doctrinaire interpretation, driven by the frequently irresistible impulse of judges to tinker with the First Amendment. The decision is mischievous at best and will surely confuse the lower courts. I join the judgment, but not the folly of the opinion.

Justice BLACKMUN, concurring in the judgment.

I regret what the Court has done in this case. The majority opinion signals one of two possibilities: it will serve as precedent for future cases, or it will not. Either result is disheartening.

In the first instance, by deciding that a State cannot regulate speech that causes great harm unless it also regulates speech that does not (setting law and logic on their heads), the Court seems to abandon the categorical approach, and inevitably to relax the level of scrutiny applicable to content-based laws. As Justice WHITE points out, this weakens the traditional protections of speech. If all expressive activity must be accorded the same protection, that protection will be scant. The simple reality is that the Court will never provide child pornography or cigarette advertising the level of protection customarily granted political speech. If we are forbidden from categorizing, as the Court has done here, we shall reduce protection across the board. It is sad that in its effort to reach a satisfying result in this case, the Court is willing to weaken First Amendment protections.

In the second instance is the possibility that this case will not significantly alter First Amendment jurisprudence, but, instead, will be regarded as an aberration—a case where the Court manipulated doctrine to strike down an ordinance whose premise it opposed, namely, that racial threats and verbal assaults are of greater harm than other fighting words. I fear that the Court has been distracted from its proper mission by the temptation to decide the issue over "politically correct speech" and "cultural diversity," neither of which is presented here. If this is the meaning of today's opinion, it is perhaps even more regrettable.

I see no First Amendment values that are compromised by a law that prohibits hoodlums from driving minorities out of their homes by burning crosses on their lawns, but I see great harm in preventing the people of Saint Paul from specifically punishing the race-based fighting words that so prejudice their community.

I concur in the judgment, however, because I agree with Justice WHITE that this particular ordinance reaches beyond fighting words to speech protected by the First Amendment.

Justice STEVENS, with whom Justice WHITE and Justice BLACKMUN join as to Part I, concurring in the judgment.

Conduct that creates special risks or causes special harms may be prohibited by special rules. Lighting a fire near an ammunition dump or a gasoline storage tank is especially dangerous; such behavior may be punished more severely than burning trash in a vacant lot. Threatening someone because of her race or religious beliefs may cause particularly severe trauma or touch off a riot, and threatening a high public official may cause substantial social disruption; such threats may be punished more severely than threats against someone based on, say, his support of a particular athletic team. There are legitimate, reasonable, and neutral justifications for such special rules.

This case involves the constitutionality of one such ordinance. Because the regulated conduct has some communicative content—a message of racial, religious or gender hostility—the ordinance raises two quite different First Amendment questions. Is the ordinance "overbroad" because it prohibits too much speech? If not, is it "underbroad" because it does not prohibit enough speech?

In answering these questions, my colleagues today wrestle with two broad principles: first, that certain "categories of expression [including 'fighting words'] are 'not within the area of constitutionally protected speech'"; and second, that "[c]ontent-based regulations [of expression] are presumptively invalid." Although in past opinions the Court has repeated both of these maxims, it has—quite rightly—adhered to neither with the absolutism suggested by my colleagues. Thus, while I agree that the St. Paul ordinance is unconstitutionally overbroad for the reasons stated in Part II of Justice WHITE's opinion, I write separately to suggest how the allure of absolute principles has skewed the analysis of both the majority and concurring opinions.

I

Fifty years ago, the Court articulated a categorical approach to First Amendment jurisprudence. *Chaplinsky*. . . .

The Court today revises this categorical approach. It is not, the Court rules, that certain "categories" of expression are "unprotected," but rather that certain "elements" of expression are wholly "proscribable." To the Court, an expressive act, like a chemical compound, consists of more than one element. Although the act may be regulated because it contains a proscribable element, it may not be regulated on the basis of another (nonproscribable) element it also contains. Thus, obscene antigovernment speech may be regulated because it is obscene, but not because it is antigovernment. It is this revision of the categorical approach that allows the Court to assume that the St. Paul ordinance proscribes only fighting words, while at the same time concluding that the ordinance is invalid because it imposes a content-based regulation on expressive activity.

. . .

I am, however, even more troubled by the second step of the Court's analysis—namely, its conclusion that the St. Paul ordinance is an unconstitutional content-based regulation of speech. Drawing on broadly worded *dicta*, the Court establishes a near-absolute ban on content-based regulations of expression and holds that the First Amendment prohibits the regulation of fighting words by subject matter. Thus, while the Court rejects the "all-or-nothing-at-all" nature of the categorical approach, it promptly embraces an absolutism of its own: within a particular "proscribable" category of expression, the Court holds, a government must either proscribe all speech or no speech at all. This aspect of the Court's ruling fundamentally misunderstands the role and constitutional status of content-based regulations on speech, conflicts with the very nature of First Amendment jurisprudence, and disrupts well-settled principles of First Amendment law.

. . .

Our First Amendment decisions have created a rough hierarchy in the constitutional protection of speech. Core political speech occupies the highest, most protected position; commercial speech and nonobscene, sexually explicit speech are regarded as a sort of second-class expression; obscenity and fighting words receive the least protection of all. Assuming that the Court is correct that this last class of speech is not wholly "unprotected," it certainly does not follow that fighting words and obscenity receive the same sort of protection afforded core political speech. Yet in ruling that proscribable speech cannot be regulated based on subject matter, the Court does just that. Perversely, this gives fighting words *greater* protection than is afforded commercial speech. If Congress can prohibit false advertising directed at airline passengers without also prohibiting false advertising directed at bus passengers and if a city can prohibit political advertisements in its buses while allowing other advertisements, it is ironic to hold that a city cannot regulate fighting words based on "race, color, creed, religion or gender" while leaving unregulated fighting words based on "union membership or homosexuality." The Court today turns First Amendment law on its head: Communication that was once entirely unprotected (and that still can be wholly proscribed) is now entitled to greater protection than commercial speech—and possibly greater protection than core political speech.

Perhaps because the Court recognizes these perversities, it quickly offers some *ad hoc* limitations on its newly extended prohibition on content-based regulations. First, the Court states that a content-based regulation is valid "[w]hen the content discrimination is based upon the very reason the entire class of speech . . . is proscribable." . . . Just as Congress may determine that threats against the President entail more severe consequences than other threats, so St. Paul's City Council may determine that threats based on the target's race, religion, or gender cause more severe harm to both the target and to society than other threats. This latter judgment—that harms caused by racial, religious, and gender-based invective are qualitatively different from that caused by other fighting words—seems to me eminently reasonable and realistic.

Next, the Court recognizes that a State may regulate advertising in one industry but not another because "the risk of fraud (one of the characteristics that justifies depriving [commercial speech] of full First Amendment protection . . .)" in the regulated industry is "greater" than in other industries. . . . Certainly a legislature that may determine that the risk of fraud is greater in the legal trade than in the medical trade may determine that the risk of injury or breach of peace created by race-based threats is greater than that created by other threats.

Similarly, it is impossible to reconcile the Court's analysis of the St. Paul ordinance with its recognition that "a prohibition of fighting words that are directed at certain persons or groups . . . would be facially valid." A selective proscription of unprotected expression designed to protect "certain persons or groups" (for example, a law proscribing threats directed at the elderly) would be constitutional if it were based on a legitimate determination that the harm created by the regulated expression differs from that created by the unregulated expression (that is, if the elderly are more severely injured by threats than are the nonelderly). Such selective protection is no different from a law prohibiting minors (and only minors) from obtaining obscene publications. St.

Paul has determined—reasonably in my judgment—that fighting-word injuries "based on race, color, creed, religion or gender" are qualitatively different and more severe than fighting-word injuries based on other characteristics. Whether the selective proscription of proscribable speech is defined by the protected target ("certain persons or groups") or the basis of the harm (injuries "based on race, color, creed, religion or gender") makes no constitutional difference: what matters is whether the legislature's selection is based on a legitimate, neutral, and reasonable distinction.

In sum, the central premise of the Court's ruling—that "[c]ontent-based regulations are presumptively invalid"—has simplistic appeal, but lacks support in our First Amendment jurisprudence. To make matters worse, the Court today extends this overstated claim to reach categories of hitherto unprotected speech and, in doing so, wreaks havoc in an area of settled law. Finally, although the Court recognizes exceptions to its new principle, those exceptions undermine its very conclusion that the St. Paul ordinance is unconstitutional. Stated directly, the majority's position cannot withstand scrutiny.

II

Although I agree with much of Justice WHITE's analysis, I do not join Part I-A of his opinion because I have reservations about the "categorical approach" to the First Amendment. These concerns . . . lead me to find Justice WHITE's response to the Court's analysis unsatisfying.

Admittedly, the categorical approach to the First Amendment has some appeal: either expression is protected or it is not—the categories create safe harbors for governments and speakers alike. But this approach sacrifices subtlety for clarity and is, I am convinced, ultimately unsound. As an initial matter, the concept of "categories" fits poorly with the complex reality of expression. Few dividing lines in First Amendment law are straight and unwavering, and efforts at categorization inevitably give rise only to fuzzy boundaries. . . .

Moreover, the categorical approach does not take seriously the importance of context. The meaning of any expression and the legitimacy of its regulation can only be determined in context. Whether, for example, a picture or a sentence is obscene cannot be judged in the abstract, but rather only in the context of its setting, its use, and its audience. Similarly, although legislatures may freely regulate most nonobscene child pornography, such pornography that is part of "a serious work of art, a documentary on behavioral problems, or a medical or psychiatric teaching device," may be entitled to constitutional protection. . . . The

categorical approach sweeps too broadly when it declares that all such expression is beyond the protection of the First Amendment.

Perhaps sensing the limits of such an all-or-nothing approach, the Court has applied its analysis less categorically than its doctrinal statements suggest. The Court has recognized intermediate categories of speech (for example, for indecent nonobscene speech and commercial speech) and geographic categories of speech (public fora, limited public fora, nonpublic fora) entitled to varying levels of protection. The Court has also stringently delimited the categories of unprotected speech. . . . In short, the history of the categorical approach is largely the history of narrowing the categories of unprotected speech.

This evolution, I believe, indicates that the categorical approach is unworkable and the quest for absolute categories of "protected" and "unprotected" speech ultimately futile. . . .

III

As the foregoing suggests, I disagree with both the Court's and part of Justice WHITE's analysis of the constitutionality [of the] St. Paul ordinance. Unlike the Court, I do not believe that all content-based regulations are equally infirm and presumptively invalid; unlike Justice WHITE, I do not believe that fighting words are wholly unprotected by the First Amendment. To the contrary, I believe our decisions establish a more complex and subtle analysis, one that considers the content and context of the regulated speech, and the nature and scope of the restriction on speech. Applying this analysis and assuming *arguendo* (as the Court does) that the St. Paul ordinance is not overbroad, I conclude that such a selective, subject-matter regulation on proscribable speech is constitutional.

Not all content-based regulations are alike; our decisions clearly recognize that some content-based restrictions raise more constitutional questions than others. Although the Court's analysis of content-based regulations cannot be reduced to a simple formula, we have considered a number of factors in determining the validity of such regulations.

First, as suggested above, the scope of protection provided expressive activity depends in part upon its content and character. . . . The protection afforded expression turns as well on the context of the regulated speech. . . . The nature of a contested restriction of speech also informs our evaluation of its constitutionality. . . . Finally, in considering the validity of content-based regulations we have also looked more broadly at the scope of the restrictions.

All of these factors play some role in our evaluation of content-based regulations on expression. Such a multi-faceted analysis cannot be conflated into two dimensions. Whatever the allure of absolute doctrines, it is just too simple to declare expression "protected" or "unprotected" or to proclaim a regulation "content-based" or "content-neutral."

In applying this analysis to the St. Paul ordinance, I assume *arguendo*—as the Court does—that the ordinance regulates only fighting words and therefore is not overbroad. Looking to the content and character of the regulated activity, two things are clear. First, by hypothesis the ordinance bars only low-value speech, namely, fighting words. By definition such expression constitutes "no essential part of any exposition of ideas, and [is] of such slight social value as a step to truth that any benefit that may be derived from [it] is clearly outweighed by the social interest in order and morality." *Chaplinsky*. Second, the ordinance regulates "expressive conduct [rather] than . . . the written or spoken word."

Looking to the context of the regulated activity, it is again significant that the statute (by hypothesis) regulates only fighting words. Whether words are fighting words is determined in part by their context. Fighting words are not words that merely cause offense; fighting words must be directed at individuals so as to "by their very utterance inflict injury." By hypothesis, then, the St. Paul ordinance restricts speech in confrontational and potentially violent situations. The case at hand is illustrative. The cross-burning in this case—directed as it was to a single African-American family trapped in their home—was nothing more than a crude form of physical intimidation. That this cross-burning sends a message of racial hostility does not automatically endow it with complete constitutional protection.

Significantly, the St. Paul ordinance regulates speech not on the basis of its subject matter or the viewpoint expressed, but rather on the basis of the *harm* the speech causes. In this regard, the Court fundamentally misreads the St. Paul ordinance. The Court describes the St. Paul ordinance as regulating expression "addressed to one of [several] specified disfavored *topics*," (emphasis supplied), as policing "disfavored *subjects*," (emphasis supplied), and as "prohibit[ing] . . . speech solely on the basis of the *subjects* the speech addresses" (emphasis supplied). Contrary to the Court's suggestion, the ordinance regulates only a subcategory of expression that causes injuries based on "race, color, creed, religion or gender," not a subcategory that involves discussions that concern those characteristics. The ordinance, as construed by the Court, criminalizes expression that "one knows . . . [by its very utterance inflicts injury on] others on the basis of race, color, creed, religion or gender." In this regard, the ordinance resembles the child pornography law at issue in *Ferber*, which in effect singled out child pornography because those publications caused far greater harms than pornography involving adults.

Moreover, even if the St. Paul ordinance did regulate fighting words based on its subject matter, such a regulation would, in my opinion, be constitutional. As noted above, subject-matter based regulations on commercial speech are widespread and largely unproblematic. As we have long recognized, subject-matter regulations generally do not raise the same concerns of government censorship and the distortion of public discourse presented by viewpoint regulations. Thus, in upholding subject-matter regulations we have carefully noted that viewpoint-based discrimination was not implicated. . . .

. . .

The St. Paul ordinance is evenhanded. In a battle between advocates of tolerance and advocates of intolerance, the ordinance does not prevent either side from hurling fighting words at the other on the basis of their conflicting ideas, but it does bar both sides from hurling such words on the basis of the target's "race, color, creed, religion or gender." To extend the Court's pugilistic metaphor, the St. Paul ordinance simply bans punches "below the belt" —*by either party*. It does not, therefore, favor one side of any debate.

Finally, it is noteworthy that the St. Paul ordinance is, as construed by the Court today, quite narrow. The St. Paul ordinance does not ban all "hate speech," nor does it ban, say, all cross-burnings or all swastika displays. Rather it only bans a subcategory of the already narrow category of fighting words. Such a limited ordinance leaves open and protected a vast range of expression on the subjects of racial, religious, and gender equality. As construed by the Court today, the ordinance certainly does not "'raise the specter that the Government may effectively drive certain ideas or viewpoints from the marketplace.'" Petitioner is free to burn a cross to announce a rally or to express his views about racial supremacy, he may do so on private property or public land, at day or at night, so long as the burning is not so threatening and so directed at an individual as to "by its very [execution] inflict injury." Such a limited proscription scarcely offends the First Amendment.

In sum, the St. Paul ordinance (as construed by the Court) regulates expressive activity that is wholly proscribable and does so not on the basis of viewpoint, but rather in recognition of the different harms caused by such activity. Taken together, these several considerations persuade me that the St. Paul ordinance is not an unconstitutional content-based regulation of speech. Thus, were the ordinance not overbroad, I would vote to uphold it.

DER: In *R.A.V. v. City of St. Paul*, Justice Scalia pretends that the Court has not allowed government to ban speech based on its content. He asserts that the lack of protection afforded categories of speech such as fighting words and obscenity really reflect their "nonspeech" elements, analogizing them to the noise made by sound trucks. In fact, the Court has recognized that some messages are harmful enough and possess so little social value that they may be prohibited. Viewing obscenity in public may be censored, not because it is conduct, but because the Court believes its message leads to social immorality. Fighting words may be punished because the Court believes their message to the target will provoke a fight or cause immediate injury. Ignoring this truth about First Amendment jurisprudence avoids addressing the values that underlie decisions distinguishing between which speech deserves protection and which speech does not.

Scalia's objection that the St. Paul ordinance singles out words based on their "distinctive idea, conveyed by a distinctive message" is true of obscenity laws and statutes prohibiting fighting words in general. His comparison of the St. Paul ordinance with Title VII's prohibition of sexually derogatory fighting words demonstrates this point. Both types of disfavored speech are similar to harmful conduct in the sense that they do not invite argumentation, but seek to cause a direct injury to the target. Indeed sexually derogatory fighting words are less conduct than burning a cross. Both nevertheless constitute speech with a harmful message.

Given this history of upholding government's restrictions of harmful messages, it is odd that the majority opposed St. Paul's effort to single out race-based fighting words—already unworthy of protection—because of their particular harms to disadvantaged groups. The only explanation is that the justices simply did not understand or value the harm involved. Burning a cross is a particularly injurious mode of expressing racial animosity. Terroristic threats are in no sense a debate about the merits of tolerance versus bigotry. Or, to put it more cynically, the justices simply disagreed with the St. Paul legislature about the degree of harm caused by racial threats. It seems highly suspicious that the conservative Justice Scalia, usually preoccupied with keeping the Court from interfering with state regulation, would go to the extreme of reworking established First Amendment doctrine in order to overturn a city ordinance designed to "ensure the basic human rights of members of groups that have historically been subjected to discrimination." St. Paul's determination that threats based on a target's race, religion or gender cause more severe harm to both the target and to society than other threats seems precisely the type of legislative judgment that Scalia typically wants to preserve from federal judicial intrusion. It can only be that Scalia is offended by this judgment, thus making his opinion *less* neutral than the concurring opinions.

DEL: Reading Justice Scalia's opinion in *R.A.V.* is hard to do without having words like disingenuous, unprincipled or manipulative come to mind. On initial blush, concern for viewpoint discrimination, when unprotected expression is at stake, seems to fit somewhere between eccentric and absurd. Using such an analytical role model, a law prohibiting only some forms of obscenity or defamation would be deficient because it was not sufficiently comprehensive. Scalia's reasoning may have more application to the case that was not, rather than the case that was, if his concern is with setting up a barrier to hate speech codes that single out minorities for protection. Especially when traditional overbreadth analysis provided a perfectly adequate basis for invalidating the ordinance, the radical doctrine espoused by Scalia is as mystifying as it is misplaced.

The Court's decision in *RAV* threw into question penalty enhancement statutes enacted by several states to address the problem of bias-motivated violence. Wisconsin, for example, passed a provision that increased by several years the maximum penalty for certain offenses whenever the defendant "[i]ntentionally selects the person against whom the crime . . . is committed . . . because of the race, religion, color, disability, sexual orientation, national origin or ancestry of that person. . . . " Relying on *RAV*, the Wisconsin Supreme Court reversed Todd Mitchell's sentence for aggravated battery, which had been enhanced pursuant to the above statute because he intentionally selected his victim based on race. The evidence at trial showed that at the time of the assault Mitchell was part of a group of young black men and boys who had been discussing the movie "Mississippi Burning," in which a white man beat a black boy who was praying. When a white boy approached the group, Mitchell said, "There goes a white boy; go get him," and the group severely beat the boy and stole his tennis shoes. The Wisconsin Supreme Court reasoned that, because the only reason for the penalty enhancement is the defendant's discriminatory motive, the statute in effect punishes offenders' bigoted beliefs. The statute, the Court concluded, violated Mitchell's First Amendment rights by "punishing what the legislature has deemed to be offensive thought."

In *Wisconsin v. Mitchell*,[62] the Supreme Court held, in a unanimous opinion delivered by Chief Justice Rehnquist, that the First Amendment did not prohibit the penalty enhancement. The Court noted that sentencing judges traditionally have considered a wide variety of factors in addition to evidence bearing on guilt in determining sentences, including the defendant's motive. Motive played the same role under the Wisconsin statute as it does under federal and state antidiscrimination laws, which the Court has upheld as permissible content-neutral regulations of conduct. Moreover, the First Amendment does not prohibit the evidentiary use of speech to establish the elements of a crime or to prove motive.

The Court distinguished *RAV* in the following passage:

> . . . [W]hereas the ordinance struck down in *RAV* was explicitly directed at expression (*i.e.*, "speech" or "messages"), the statute in this case is aimed at conduct unprotected by the First Amendment.
>
> Moreover, the Wisconsin statute singles out for enhancement bias-inspired conduct because this conduct is thought to inflict greater individual and societal harm. For example, according to the State and its *amici*, bias-motivated crimes are more likely to provoke retaliatory crimes, inflict distinct emotional harms on their victims, and incite community unrest. The State's desire to redress these perceived harms provides adequate explanation for its penalty-enhancement provision over and above mere disagreement with offenders' beliefs or biases. . . .
>
> . . . Mitchell argues (and the Wisconsin Supreme Court agreed) that the statute is "overbroad" because evidence of the defendant's prior speech or associations may be used to prove that the defendant intentionally selected his victim on account of the victim's protected status. Consequently, the argument goes, the statute impermissibly chills free expression with respect to such matters by those concerned about the possibility of enhanced sentences if they should in the future commit a criminal offense covered by the statute. We find no merit in this contention.
>
> The sort of chill envisioned here is far more attenuated and unlikely than that contemplated in traditional "overbreath" cases. We must conjure up a vision of a Wisconsin citizen suppressing his unpopular bigoted opinions for fear that if he later commits an offense covered by the statute, these opinions will be offered at trial to establish that he selected his victim on account of the

---

[62] 508 U.S. 476 (1993).

victim's protected status, thus qualifying him for penalty-enhancement. . . . This is simply too speculative a hypothesis to support Mitchell's overbreath claim.

2. Symbolic and Unconventional Modes of Speech

Speakers often use a great deal of conduct to get their message across. To some extent, all speech involves conduct: the act of verbal expression requires bodily movement, and may be augmented by further conduct such as driving a sound truck or standing on a soap box on a street corner. Our image of the traditional political speaker probably includes the conduct of passing out leaflets, marching in the street, or carrying placards. Speakers also use less conventional means of communication that rely on the symbolic message of their conduct. The cases that follow involve speakers who claimed First Amendment protection for destroying a draft card, sleeping in a national park, and burning an American flag. These dissenters argued that the laws prohibiting their conduct were unconstitutional because their unlawful acts conveyed a political message. Obviously the claim that one's prohibited conduct communicates a message will not automatically invoke the First Amendment. A dissident who bombs the State House in protest of the legislature's recent enactment has no First Amendment defense. Yet many instances of symbolic speech that violate statutes regulating conduct raise serious First Amendment concerns.

The cases in the preceding section concerned the government's power to prohibit speech based on its message. Cases involving symbolic speech concern government attempts to regulate speech based on its non-communicative impact, rather than its message. The government argued in the first set of cases that it was justified in preventing the speaker's harmful message. Here, the government argues that it does not seek to prevent the speaker's message at all. Unfortunately, in restricting the speaker's method of expression, state regulation of symbolic speech often does abridge the speaker's ability to deliver her message.

One way to resolve this conflict might be to try to divide the particular instance of symbolic speech into separate expression and conduct components. The eminent First Amendment scholar Thomas Emerson proposed that the Court decide the constitutionality of restrictions on symbolic speech by determining which element—speech or conduct—predominates.[63] More recently, scholars have observed that it is impossible to divide up symbolic expression in this way: burning a draft card in protest, for example, "is an undifferentiated whole, 100% action and 100% expression, and to outlaw the act is therefore necessarily to regulate both elements."[64] In the leading case, *United States v. O'Brien*, the Court focused on the interest which the government asserted to justify the challenged regulation.

Among the conflicts that marked the 1960s was the vociferous debate about America's involvement in the Vietnam War. The military's draft effort precipitated many forms of opposition, including massive demonstrations and the flight of conscientious objectors to Canada. Many of the First Amendment cases concerning protest against the war involved symbolic speech, including draft-card burning, flag desecration, armband wearing, unauthorized use of a military uniform, and damaging Selective Service records.[65] Congress addressed the practice of draft card burning in 1965 by passing an

---

[63] Thomas Emerson, The System of Freedom of Expression 80–89 (1970).

[64] John Ely, *Flag Desecration: A Case Study in the Roles of Categorization and Balancing in First Amendment Analysis*, 88 Harv. L. Rev. 1482 (1975).

[65] *See* Norman Dorsen, Paul Bender & Burt Neuborne, Political and Civil Rights in the United States, vol. 1, 56 (1976).

amendment to the statute regulating registration for the draft that made mutilation of draft cards a crime. In this context, the Court provided a test for determining whether the government could punish symbolic speech, consistent with the First Amendment, for violating a statute directed at the speech's conduct.

United States v. O'Brien
391 U.S. 367 (1968)

MR. CHIEF JUSTICE WARREN delivered the opinion of the Court.

On the morning of March 31, 1966, David Paul O'Brien and three companions burned their Selective Service registration certificates on the steps of the South Boston Courthouse. A sizable crowd, including several agents of the Federal Bureau of Investigation, witnessed the event. Immediately after the burning, members of the crowd began attacking O'Brien and his companions. An FBI agent ushered O'Brien to safety inside the courthouse. After he was advised of his right to counsel and to silence, O'Brien stated to FBI agents that he had burned his registration certificate because of his beliefs, knowing that he was violating federal law. He produced the charred remains of the certificate, which, with his consent, were photographed.

For this act, O'Brien was indicted, tried, convicted, and sentenced in the United States District Court for the District of Massachusetts. He did not contest the fact that he had burned the certificate. He stated in argument to the jury that he burned the certificate publicly to influence others to adopt his antiwar beliefs, as he put it, "so that other people would reevaluate their positions with Selective Service, with the armed forces, and reevaluate their place in the culture of today, to hopefully consider my position."

The indictment upon which he was tried charged that he "willfully and knowingly did mutilate, destroy, and change by burning . . . [his] Registration Certificate (Selective Service System Form No. 2); in violation of Title 50, App., United States Code, Section 462(b)." Section 462(b) is part of the Universal Military Training and Service Act of 1948. Section 462(b)(3), one of six numbered subdivisions of § 462(b), was amended by Congress in 1965 (adding the words italicized below), so that at the time O'Brien burned his certificate an offense was committed by any person,

"who forges, alters, *knowingly destroys, knowingly mutilates*, or in any manner changes any such certificate. . . . " (Italics supplied.)

. . .

II.

O'Brien first argues that the 1965 Amendment is unconstitutional as applied to him because his act of burning his registration certificate was protected "symbolic speech" within the First Amendment. His argument is that the freedom of expression which the First Amendment guarantees includes all modes of "communication of ideas by conduct," and that his conduct is within this definition because he did it in "demonstration against the war and against the draft."

We cannot accept the view that an apparently limitless variety of conduct can be labeled "speech" whenever the person engaging in the conduct intends thereby to express an idea. However, even on the assumption that the alleged communicative element in O'Brien's conduct is sufficient to bring into play the First Amendment, it does not necessarily follow that the destruction of a registration certificate is constitutionally protected activity. This Court has held that when "speech" and "nonspeech" elements are combined in the same course of conduct, a sufficiently important governmental interest in regulating the nonspeech element can justify incidental limitations on First Amendment freedoms. To characterize the quality of the governmental interest which must appear, the Court has employed a variety of descriptive terms: compelling; substantial; subordinating; paramount; cogent; strong. Whatever imprecision inheres in these terms, we think it clear that a government regulation is sufficiently justified if it is within the constitutional power of the Government; if it furthers an important or substantial governmental interest; if the governmental interest is unrelated to the suppression of free expression; and if the incidental restriction on alleged First Amendment freedoms is no greater than is essential to the furtherance of that interest. We find that the 1965 Amendment to § 12(b)(3) of the Universal Military Training and Service Act meets all of these requirements, and consequently that O'Brien can be constitutionally convicted for violating it.

The constitutional power of Congress to raise and support armies and to make all laws necessary and proper to that end is broad and sweeping. The power of Congress to classify and conscript manpower for military service is "beyond question." Pursuant to this power, Congress may establish a system of registration for individuals liable for training and service, and may require such individuals within reason to cooperate in the registration system. The issuance of certificates indicating the registration and eligibility classification of individuals is a legitimate and substantial administrative aid in the functioning of this system. And legislation to insure the continuing availability of issued certificates serves a legitimate and substantial purpose in the system's administration.

O'Brien's argument to the contrary is necessarily premised upon his unrealistic characterization of Selective Service certificates. He essentially adopts the position that such certificates are so many pieces of paper designed to notify registrants of their registration or classification, to be retained or tossed in the wastebasket according to the convenience or taste of the registrant. Once the registrant has received notification, according to this view, there is no reason for him to retain the certificates. O'Brien notes that most of the information on a registration certificate serves no notification purpose at all; the registrant hardly needs to be told his address and physical characteristics. We agree that the registration certificate contains much information of which the registrant needs no notification. This circumstance, however, does not lead to the conclusion that the certificate serves no purpose, but that, like the classification certificate, it serves purposes in addition to initial notification. Many of these purposes would be defeated by the certificates' destruction or mutilation. Among these are:

1. The registration certificate serves as proof that the individual described thereon has registered for the draft. . . .

2. The information supplied on the certificates facilitates communication between registrants and local boards, simplifying the system and benefiting all concerned. . . .

3. Both certificates carry continual reminders that the registrant must notify his local board of any change of address, and other specified changes in his status. . . .

4. The regulatory scheme involving Selective Service certificates includes clearly valid prohibitions against the alteration, forgery, or similar deceptive misuse of certificates. The destruction or mutilation of certificates obviously increases the difficulty of detecting and tracing abuses such as these. Further, a mutilated certificate might itself be used for deceptive purposes.

The many functions performed by Selective Service certificates establish beyond doubt that Congress has a legitimate and substantial interest in preventing their wanton and unrestrained destruction and assuring their continuing availability by punishing people who knowingly and wilfully destroy or mutilate them. And we are unpersuaded that the pre-existence of the nonpossession regulations in any way negates this interest.

. . .

It is equally clear that the 1965 Amendment specifically protects this substantial governmental interest. We perceive no alternative means that would more precisely and narrowly assure the continuing availability of issued Selective Service certificates than a law which prohibits their wilful mutilation or destruction. The 1965 Amendment prohibits such conduct and does nothing more. In other words, both the governmental interest and the operation of the 1965 Amendment are limited to the noncommunicative aspect of O'Brien's conduct. The governmental interest and the scope of the 1965 Amendment are limited to preventing harm to the smooth and efficient functioning of the Selective Service System. When O'Brien deliberately rendered unavailable his registration certificate, he wilfully frustrated this governmental interest. For this noncommunicative impact of his conduct, and for nothing else, he was convicted.

. . .

In conclusion, we find that because of the Government's substantial interest in assuring the continuing availability of issued Selective Service certificates, because amended § 462(b) is an appropriately narrow means of protecting this interest and condemns only the independent noncommunicative impact of conduct within its reach, and because the noncommunicative impact of O'Brien's act of burning his registration certificate frustrated the Government's interest, a sufficient governmental interest has been shown to justify O'Brien's conviction.

III.

O'Brien finally argues that the 1965 Amendment is unconstitutional as enacted because what he calls the "purpose" of Congress was "to suppress freedom of speech." We reject this argument because under settled principles the purpose of Congress, as O'Brien uses that term, is not a basis for declaring this legislation unconstitutional.

It is a familiar principle of constitutional law that this Court will not strike down an otherwise constitutional statute on the basis of an alleged illicit legislative motive. . . .

Inquiries into congressional motives or purposes are a hazardous matter. When the issue is simply the interpretation of legislation, the Court will look to statements by legislators for guidance as to the purpose of the legislature, because the benefit to sound decision-making in this circumstance is thought sufficient to risk the possibility of misreading Congress' purpose. It is entirely a different matter when we are asked to void a statute that is, under well-settled criteria, constitutional on its face, on the basis of what fewer than a handful of Congressmen said about it. What motivates one legislator to make a speech about a statute is not necessarily what motivates scores of others to enact it, and the stakes are sufficiently high for us to eschew guesswork. We decline to void essentially on the ground that it is unwise legislation which Congress had the undoubted power to enact and which could be reenacted in its exact form if the same or another legislator made a "wiser" speech about it.

. . .

MR. JUSTICE MARSHALL took no part in the consideration or decision of these cases.

MR. JUSTICE HARLAN, concurring.

The crux of the Court's opinion, which I join, is of course its general statement, that:

> "a government regulation is sufficiently justified if it is within the constitutional power of the Government; if it furthers an important or substantial governmental interest; if the governmental interest is unrelated to the suppression of free expres-

sion; and if the incidental restriction on alleged First Amendment freedoms is no greater than is essential to the furtherance of that interest."

I wish to make explicit my understanding that this passage does not foreclose consideration of First Amendment claims in those rare instances when an "incidental" restriction upon expression, imposed by a regulation which furthers an "important or substantial" governmental interest and satisfies the Court's other criteria, in practice has the effect of entirely preventing a "speaker" from reaching a significant audience with whom he could not otherwise lawfully communicate. This is not such a case, since O'Brien manifestly could have conveyed his message in many ways other than by burning his draft card.

MR. JUSTICE DOUGLAS, dissenting.

The Court states that the constitutional power of Congress to raise and support armies is "broad and sweeping" and that Congress' power "to classify and conscript manpower for military service is 'beyond question.'" This is undoubtedly true in times when, by declaration of Congress, the Nation is in a state of war. The underlying and basic problem in this case, however, is whether conscription is permissible in the absence of a declaration of war. . . .

. . . [T]he instant case [should be restored] to the calendar for reargument on the question of the constitutionality of a peacetime draft. . . .

Two decades after *United States v. O'Brien*, the Court applied the test that the Court articulated in *O'Brien* to the federal government's ban on a demonstration concerning a more contemporary national issue—the plight of the homeless in America. In *Clark v. Community for Creative Non-Violence*, the Court noted the similarity between the *O'Brien* test and the test for time, place, and manner restrictions (which are the subject of Section 4b *infra*). Like the abridgement of symbolic speech, state regulations governing speech's time, place, and manner are directed at the speaker's method, rather than the message. Punishing symbolic speech, however, prohibits speakers' chosen form of expression, which may be uniquely associated with the message they intend to communicate. By collapsing the *O'Brien* test and the test for time, place, and manner restrictions, the Court modified the last step of the *O'Brien* standard—whether the incidental restriction on speech is no greater than essential to further the government's interest.

Clark v. Community for Creative Non-Violence
468 U.S. 288 (1984)

JUSTICE WHITE delivered the opinion of the Court.

The issue in this case is whether a Na-

tional Park Service regulation prohibiting camping in certain parks violates the First Amendment when applied to prohibit demonstrators from sleeping in Lafayette Park and the Mall in connection with a demonstration intended to call attention to the plight of the homeless. We hold that it does not and reverse the contrary judgment of the Court of Appeals.

I

The Interior Department, through the National Park Service, is charged with responsibility for the management and maintenance of the National Parks and is authorized to promulgate rules and regulations for the use of the parks in accordance with the purposes for which they were established. The network of National Parks includes the National Memorial-core parks, Lafayette Park and the Mall, which are set in the heart of Washington, D.C., and which are unique resources that the Federal Government holds in trust for the American people. Lafayette Park is a roughly seven-acre square located across Pennsylvania Avenue from the White House. . . . The Mall is a stretch of land running westward from the Capitol to the Lincoln Memorial some two miles away. It includes the Washington Monument, a series of reflecting pools, trees, lawns, and other greenery. . . .

Under the regulations involved in this case, camping in National Parks is permitted only in campgrounds designated for that purpose. No such campgrounds have ever been designated in Lafayette Park or the Mall. . . .

In 1982, the Park Service issued a renewable permit to respondent Community for Creative Non-Violence (CCNV) to conduct a wintertime demonstration in Lafayette Park and the Mall for the purpose of demonstrating the plight of the homeless. The permit authorized the erection of two symbolic tent cities: 20 tents in Lafayette Park that would accommodate 50 people and 40 tents in the Mall with a capacity of up to 100. The Park Service, however, relying on the above regulations, specifically denied CCNV's request that demonstrators be permitted to sleep in the symbolic tents.

CCNV and several individuals then filed an action to prevent the application of the anti-camping regulations to the proposed demonstration, which, it was claimed, was not covered by the regulation. It was also submitted that the regulations were unconstitutionally vague, had been discriminatorily applied, and could not be applied to prevent sleeping in the tents without violating the First Amendment. The District Court granted summary judgment in favor of the Park Service. The Court of Appeals, sitting en banc, reversed. The eleven judges produced six opinions. Six of the judges believed that application of the regulations so as to prevent sleeping in the tents would infringe the demonstrators' First Amendment right of free expression. The other five judges

disagreed and would have sustained the regulations as applied to CCNV's proposed demonstration. We granted the Government's petition for certiorari, and now reverse.

II

We need not differ with the view of the Court of Appeals that overnight sleeping in connection with the demonstration is expressive conduct protected to some extent by the First Amendment.[5] We assume for present purposes, but do not decide, that such is the case, cf. *United States v. O'Brien*, but this assumption only begins the inquiry. Expression, whether oral or written or symbolized by conduct, is subject to reasonable time, place, and manner restrictions. We have often noted that restrictions of this kind are valid provided that they are justified without reference to the content of the regulated speech, that they are narrowly tailored to serve a significant governmental interest, and that they leave open ample alternative channels for communication of the information.

It is also true that a message may be delivered by conduct that is intended to be communicative and that, in context, would reasonably be understood by the viewer to be communicative. Symbolic expression of this kind may be forbidden or regulated if the conduct itself may constitutionally be regulated, if the regulation is narrowly drawn to further a substantial governmental interest, and if the interest is unrelated to the suppression of free speech. *United States v. O'Brien.*

Petitioners submit, as they did in the Court of Appeals, that the regulation forbidding sleeping is defensible either as a time, place, or manner restriction or as a regulation of symbolic conduct. We agree with that assessment. The permit that was issued authorized the demonstration but required compliance with 36 CFR § 50.19 (1983), which prohibits "camping" on park lands, that is, the use of park lands for living accommodations, such as sleeping, storing personal belongings, making fires, digging, or cooking. These provisions, in-

---

[5] We reject the suggestion of the plurality below, however, that the burden on the demonstrators is limited to "the advancement of a plausible contention" that their conduct is expressive. Although it is common to place the burden upon the Government to justify impingements on First Amendment interests, it is the obligation of the person desiring to engage in assertedly expressive conduct to demonstrate that the First Amendment even applies. To hold otherwise would be to create a rule that all conduct is presumptively expressive. In the absence of a showing that such a rule is necessary to protect vital First Amendment interests, we decline to deviate from the general rule that one seeking relief bears the burden of demonstrating that he is entitled to it.

cluding the ban on sleeping, are clearly limitations on the manner in which the demonstration could be carried out. That sleeping, like the symbolic tents themselves, may be expressive and part of the message delivered by the demonstration does not make the ban any less a limitation on the manner of demonstrating, for reasonable time, place, and manner regulations normally have the purpose and direct effect of limiting expression but are nevertheless valid. Neither does the fact that sleeping, *arguendo*, may be expressive conduct, rather than oral or written expression, render the sleeping prohibition any less a time, place, or manner regulation. To the contrary, the Park Service neither attempts to ban sleeping generally nor to ban it everywhere in the Parks. It has established areas for camping and forbids it elsewhere, including Lafayette Park and the Mall. Considered as such, we have very little trouble concluding that the Park Service may prohibit overnight sleeping in the parks involved here.

The requirement that the regulation be content neutral is clearly satisfied. The courts below accepted that view, and it is not disputed here that the prohibition on camping, and on sleeping specifically, is content neutral and is not being applied because of disagreement with the message presented. Neither was the regulation faulted, nor could it be, on the ground that without overnight sleeping the plight of the homeless could not be communicated in other ways. The regulation otherwise left the demonstration intact, with its symbolic city, signs, and the presence of those who were willing to take their turns in a day-and-night vigil. Respondents do not suggest that there was, or is, any barrier to delivering to the media, or to the public by other means, the intended message concerning the plight of the homeless.

It is also apparent to us that the regulation narrowly focuses on the Government's substantial interest in maintaining the parks in the heart of our Capital in an attractive and intact condition, readily available to the millions of people who wish to see and enjoy them by their presence. To permit camping—using these areas as living accommodations—would be totally inimical to these purposes, as would be readily understood by those who have frequented the National Parks across the country and observed the unfortunate consequences of the activities of those who refuse to confine their camping to designated areas.

It is urged by respondents, and the Court of Appeals was of this view, that if the symbolic city of tents was to be permitted and if the demonstrators did not intend to cook, dig, or engage in aspects of camping other than sleeping, the incremental benefit to the parks could not justify the ban on sleeping, which was here an expressive activity said to enhance the message concerning the plight of the poor and homeless. We cannot agree. In the first place, we seriously doubt that the First Amendment requires the Park Service to permit a demonstration in Lafayette Park and the Mall involving a 24-hour vigil and the erection of tents to accommodate 150 people. Furthermore, although we have assumed for present purposes that the sleeping banned in this case would have an expressive element, it is evident that its major value to this demonstration would be facilitative. Without a permit to sleep, it would be difficult to get the poor and homeless to participate or to be present at all. This much is apparent from the permit application filed by respondents: "Without the incentive of sleeping space or a hot meal, the homeless would not come to the site." The sleeping ban, if enforced, would thus effectively limit the nature, extent, and duration of the demonstration and to that extent ease the pressure on the Parks.

Beyond this, however, it is evident from our cases that the validity of this regulation need not be judged solely by reference to the demonstration at hand. Absent the prohibition on sleeping, there would be other groups who would demand permission to deliver an asserted message by camping in Lafayette Park. Some of them would surely have as credible a claim in this regard as does CCNV, and the denial of permits to still others would present difficult problems for the Park Service. With the prohibition, however, as is evident in the case before us, at least some around-the-clock demonstrations lasting for days on end will not materialize, others will be limited in size and duration, and the purposes of the regulation will thus be materially served. Perhaps these purposes would be more effectively and not so clumsily achieved by preventing tents and 24-hour vigils entirely in the core areas. But the Park Service's decision to permit non-sleeping demonstrations does not, in our view, impugn the camping prohibition as a valuable, but perhaps imperfect, protection to the parks. If the Government has a legitimate interest in ensuring that the National Parks are adequately protected, which we think it has, and if the parks would be more exposed to harm without the sleeping prohibition than with it, the ban is safe from invalidation under the First Amendment as a reasonable regulation on the manner in which a demonstration may be carried out. . . .

. . .

Contrary to the conclusion of the Court of Appeals, the foregoing analysis demonstrates that the Park Service regulation is sustainable under the four-factor standard of *United States v. O'Brien, supra*, for validating a regulation of expressive conduct, which, in the last analysis is little, if any, different from the standard applied to time, place, and manner restrictions.[8] No one contends that aside from its impact on speech a rule against camping or overnight sleeping in public parks is beyond the constitutional power of the Government to enforce. And for the reasons we have discussed above, there is a substantial government interest in conserving park property, an interest that is plainly served by, and requires for its implementation, measures such as the proscription of sleeping that are designed to limit the wear and tear on park properties. That interest is unrelated to suppression of expression.

We are unmoved by the Court of Appeals' view that the challenged regulation is unnecessary, and hence invalid, because there are less speech-restrictive alternatives that could have satisfied the government interest in preserving park lands. There is no gainsaying that preventing overnight sleeping will avoid a measure of actual or threatened damage to Lafayette Park and the Mall. The Court of Appeals' suggestions that the Park Service minimize the possible injury by reducing the size, duration, or frequency of demonstrations would still curtail the total allowable expression in which demonstrators could engage, whether by sleeping or otherwise, and these suggestions represent no more than a disagreement with the Park Service over how much protection the core parks require or how an acceptable level of preservation is to be attained. We do not believe, however, that either *United States v. O'Brien* or the time, place, and manner decisions assign to the judiciary the authority to replace the Park Service as the manager of the Nation's parks or endow the judiciary with the competence to judge how much protection of park lands is wise and how that level of conservation is to be attained.

Accordingly, the judgment of the Court of Appeals is

Reversed.

[CHIEF JUSTICE BURGER's concurring opinion is omitted.]

JUSTICE MARSHALL, with whom Justice BRENNAN joins, dissenting.

---

[8] Reasonable time, place, and manner restrictions are valid even though they directly limit oral or written expression. It would be odd to insist on a higher standard for limitations aimed at regulable conduct and having only an incidental impact on speech. Thus, if the time, place, and manner restriction on expressive sleeping, if that is what is involved in this case, sufficiently and narrowly serves a substantial enough governmental interest to escape First Amendment condemnation, it is untenable to invalidate it under *O'Brien* on the ground that the governmental interest is insufficient to warrant the intrusion on First Amendment concerns or that there is an inadequate nexus between the regulation and the interest sought to be served. . . .

The Court's disposition of this case is marked by two related failings. First, the majority is either unwilling or unable to take seriously the First Amendment claims advanced by respondents. Contrary to the impression given by the majority, respondents are not supplicants seeking to wheedle an undeserved favor from the Government. They are citizens raising issues of profound public importance who have properly turned to the courts for the vindication of their constitutional rights. Second, the majority misapplies the test for ascertaining whether a restraint on speech qualifies as a reasonable time, place, and manner regulation. In determining what constitutes a sustainable regulation, the majority fails to subject the alleged interests of the Government to the degree of scrutiny required to ensure that expressive activity protected by the First Amendment remains free of unnecessary limitations.

I

The proper starting point for analysis of this case is a recognition that the activity in which respondents seek to engage—sleeping in a highly public place, outside, in the winter for the purpose of protesting homelessness—is symbolic speech protected by the First Amendment. The majority assumes, without deciding, that the respondents' conduct is entitled to constitutional protection. The problem with this assumption is that the Court thereby avoids examining closely the reality of respondents' planned expression. The majority's approach denatures respondents' asserted right and thus makes all too easy identification of a government interest sufficient to warrant its abridgement. A realistic appraisal of the competing interests at stake in this case requires a closer look at the nature of the expressive conduct at issue and the context in which that conduct would be displayed.

In late autumn of 1982, respondents sought permission to conduct a round-the-clock demonstration in Lafayette Park and on the Mall. Part of the demonstration would include homeless persons sleeping outside in tents without any other amenities. Respondents sought to begin their demonstration on a date full of ominous meaning to any homeless person: the first day of winter. Respondents were similarly purposeful in choosing demonstration sites. . . .

Missing from the majority's description [of these sites] is any inkling that Lafayette Park and the Mall have served as the sites for some of the most rousing political demonstrations in the Nation's history. It is interesting to learn, I suppose, that Lafayette Park and the Mall were both part of Major Pierre L'Enfant's original plan for the capital. Far more pertinent, however, is that these areas constitute, in the Government's words, "a fitting and powerful forum for political expression and political protest."

The primary purpose for making sleep an integral part of the demonstration was "to re-enact the central reality of homelessness," and to impress upon public consciousness, in as dramatic a way as possible, that homelessness is a widespread problem, often ignored, that confronts its victims with life-threatening deprivations. As one of the homeless men seeking to demonstrate explained: "Sleeping in Lafayette Park or on the Mall, for me, is to show people that conditions are so poor for the homeless and poor in this city that we would actually sleep outside in the winter to get the point across."

In a long line of cases, this Court has afforded First Amendment protection to expressive conduct that qualifies as symbolic speech. In light of the surrounding context, respondents' proposed activity meets the qualifications. The Court has previously acknowledged the importance of context in determining whether an act can properly be denominated as "speech" for First Amendment purposes and has provided guidance concerning the way in which courts should "read" a context in making this determination. The leading case is *Spence v. Washington*, 418 U.S. 405 (1974), where this Court held that displaying a United States flag with a peace symbol attached to it was conduct protected by the First Amendment. The Court looked first to the intent of the speaker—whether there was an "intent to convey a particularized message"—and second to the perception of the audience—whether "the likelihood was great that the message would be understood by those who viewed it." Here respondents clearly intended to protest the reality of homelessness by sleeping outdoors in the winter in the near vicinity of the magisterial residence of the President of the United States. In addition to accentuating the political character of their protest by their choice of location and mode of communication, respondents also intended to underline the meaning of their protest by giving their demonstration satirical names. Respondents planned to name the demonstration on the Mall "Congressional Village," and the demonstration in Lafayette Park, "Reaganville II."

Nor can there be any doubt that in the surrounding circumstances the likelihood was great that the political significance of sleeping in the parks would be understood by those who viewed it. Certainly the news media understood the significance of respondents' proposed activity; newspapers and magazines from around the Nation reported their previous sleep-in and their planned display. Ordinary citizens, too, would likely understand the political message intended by respondents. This likelihood stems from the remarkably apt fit between the activity in which respondents seek to engage and the social problem they seek to highlight. By using sleep as an integral part of their mode of protest, respondents "can express with their bodies the poignancy of their plight. They can physically demonstrate the neglect from which they suffer with an articulateness even Dickens could not match." *Community for Creative Non-Violence v. Watt*, 227 U.S. App. D.C. 19, 34, 703 F.2d 586, 601 (1983) (Edwards, J. concurring).

It is true that we all go to sleep as part of our daily regimen and that, for the most part, sleep represents a physical necessity and not a vehicle for expression. But these characteristics need not prevent an activity that is normally devoid of expressive purpose from being used as a novel mode of communication. Sitting or standing in a library is a commonplace activity necessary to facilitate ends usually having nothing to do with making a statement. Moreover, sitting or standing is not conduct that an observer would normally construe as expressive conduct. However, for Negroes to stand or sit in a "whites only" library in Louisiana in 1965 was powerfully expressive; in that particular context, those acts became "monuments of protest" against segregation. . . .

. . .

II

Although sleep in the context of this case is symbolic speech protected by the First Amendment, it is nonetheless subject to reasonable time, place, and manner restrictions. I agree with the standard enunciated by the majority: "[R]estrictions of this kind are valid provided that they are justified without reference to the content of the regulated speech, that they are narrowly tailored to serve a significant governmental interest, and that they leave open ample alternative channels for communication of the information."[6] I conclude, however, that the regulations at issue in this case, as applied to respondents, fail to satisfy this standard.

According to the majority, the significant government interest advanced by denying respondents' request to engage in sleep-speech is the interest in "maintaining the parks in the heart of our capital in an attractive and intact condition, readily available to the millions of people who wish to see and enjoy them by their presence." That interest is indeed significant.

---

[6] I also agree with the majority that no substantial difference distinguishes the test applicable to time, place, and manner restrictions and the test articulated in *United States v. O'Brien*.

However, neither the Government nor the majority adequately explains how prohibiting respondents' planned activity will substantially further that interest.

The majority's attempted explanation begins with the curious statement that it seriously doubts that the First Amendment requires the Park Service to permit a demonstration in Lafayette Park and the Mall involving a 24-hour vigil and the erection of tents to accommodate 150 people. I cannot perceive why the Court should have "serious doubts" regarding this matter and it provides no explanation for its uncertainty. Furthermore, even if the majority's doubts were well-founded, I cannot see how such doubts relate to the problem at hand. The issue posed by this case is not whether the Government is constitutionally compelled to permit the erection of tents and the staging of a continuous 24-hour vigil; rather, the issue is whether any substantial government interest is served by banning sleep that is part of a political demonstration.

. . .

The majority's second argument is comprised of the suggestion that, although sleeping contains an element of expression, "its major value to [respondents'] demonstration would have been facilitative." While this observation does provide a hint of the weight the Court attached to respondents' First Amendment claims it is utterly irrelevant to whether the Government's ban on sleeping advances a substantial government interest.

The majority's third argument is based upon two claims. The first is that the ban on sleeping relieves the Government of an administrative burden because, without the flat ban, the process of issuing and denying permits to other demonstrators asserting First Amendment rights to sleep in the parks "would present difficult problems for the Park Service." The second is that the ban on sleeping will increase the probability that "some around-the-clock demonstrations for days on end will not materialize, [that] others will be limited in size and duration, and that the purpose of the regulation will thus be materially served," that purpose being "to limit the wear and tear on park properties."

The flaw in these two contentions is that neither is supported by a factual showing that evinces a real, as opposed to a merely speculative, problem. . . .

In short, there are no substantial government interests advanced by the Government's regulations as applied to respondents. All that the Court's decision advances are the prerogatives of a bureaucracy that over the years has shown an implacable hostility toward citizens' exercise of First Amendment rights.

III

The disposition of this case impels me to make two additional observations. First, in this case, as in some others involving time, place, and manner restrictions, the Court has dramatically lowered its scrutiny of governmental regulations once it has determined that such regulations are content neutral. The result has been the creation of a two-tiered approach to First Amendment cases: while regulations that turn on the content of the expression are subjected to a strict form of judicial review, regulations that are aimed at matters other than expression receive only a minimal level of scrutiny. The minimal scrutiny prong of this two-tiered approach has led to an unfortunate diminution of First Amendment protection. By narrowly limiting its concern to whether a given regulation creates a content-based distinction, the Court has seemingly overlooked the fact that content-neutral restrictions are also capable of unnecessarily restricting protected expressive activity. To be sure, the general prohibition against content-based regulations is an essential tool of First Amendment analysis. It helps to put into operation the well-established principle that "government may not grant the use of a forum to people whose views it finds acceptable, but deny use to those wishing to express less favored or more controversial views." *Police Department of the City of Chicago v. Mosley*, 408 U.S. 92, 95–96 (1972). The Court, however, has transformed the ban against content-distinctions from a floor that offers all persons at least equal liberty under the First Amendment into a ceiling that restricts persons to the protection of First Amendment equality—but nothing more.[14] The consistent imposition of silence upon all may fulfill the dictates of an even-handed content-neutrality. But it offends our "profound national commitment to the principle that debate on public issues should be unin-

---

[14] Furthermore, a content-neutral regulation does not necessarily fall with random or equal force upon different groups or different points of view. A content-neutral regulation that restricts an inexpensive mode of communication will fall most heavily upon relatively poor speakers and the points of view that such speakers typically espouse. This sort of latent inequality is very much in evidence in this case for respondents lack the financial means necessary to buy access to more conventional modes of persuasion.

A disquieting feature about the disposition of this case is that it lends credence to the charge that judicial administration of the First Amendment, in conjunction with a social order marked by large disparities in wealth and other sources of power, tends systematically to discriminate against efforts by the relatively disadvantaged to convey their political ideas. . . .

hibited, robust, and wide-open." *New York Times Co. v. Sullivan.*

Second, the disposition of this case reveals a mistaken assumption regarding the motives and behavior of government officials who create and administer content-neutral regulations. The Court's salutary skepticism of governmental decisionmaking in First Amendment matters suddenly dissipates once it determines that a restriction is not content-based. The Court evidently assumes that the balance struck by officials is deserving of deference so long as it does not appear to be tainted by content discrimination. What the Court fails to recognize is that public officials have strong incentives to overregulate even in the absence of an intent to censor particular views. This incentive stems from the fact that of the two groups whose interests officials must accommodate—on the one hand, the interests of the general public and on the other, the interests of those who seek to use a particular forum for First Amendment activity—the political power of the former is likely to be far greater than that of the latter.

. . .

DER: Footnote 14 of Justice Marshall's dissenting opinion in *Clark v. Community for Creative Non-Violence* is a powerful critique of the Court's First Amendment jurisprudence that centers on government neutrality. Although relegated to a footnote, it presents an approach to the First Amendment radically different from that of the majority. Marshall forcefully demonstrates that the focus on government neutrality actually discriminates against the least powerful members of society and reinforces social inequalities. Requiring nothing more from the government than a neutral interest leaves intact the existing inequalities of resources. Impeding the form of expression is likely to have greater impact on the poor and powerless who have fewer alternative avenues of communication available to them. The reliance on neutral principles thus serves as a shield that allows the Court to avoid confronting imbalances in the power to communicate.

In addition, the focus on content-neutrality—a standard supposedly designed to guard against government censorship of ideas—actually serves as a rationale for government restrictions of speech. Once the government can articulate a neutral, non-speech justification for its abridgement of expression, the Court is likely to uphold the regulation without further concern for speakers' interest in communicating their message. The Court's collapsing of the *O'Brien* test and the test for time, place, and manner regulations further weakens the rights of symbolic speakers. Unlike time, place and manner restrictions, punishing symbolic speech prohibits the speakers' preferred form of conveying their ideas. Because the form of symbolic speech is intimately—and perhaps uniquely—associated with the message, its prohibition may censor the message itself. The Court should not only reinstitute the final prong of the *O'Brien* test but give it more force, requiring the government to prove that it could not achieve its non-speech interest through a less restrictive means.

DEL: Devitalization of the *O'Brien* formula is disturbing not only because it discounts the value of symbolic speech but because the standard of review was not that protective to begin with. It was both a virtue and vice of *O'Brien* that the Court refused an inquiry into official purpose. Such investigation is notoriously futile, because intent may not be a singular phenomenon and in any event can be easily masked. Suppressive designs may have been identified in *O'Brien*, but enshrinement of such analysis would have tipped regulators to the reality that successful regulation in the future hinged upon camouflaging their true motives. It is no more satisfactory, however, to allow the government room to suppress dissenters by hiding behind an allegedly avowed primary interest that is unrelated to speech. As is typically the case with the elusive search for motive, perceptions of what is dominant and incidental may be a function of convenience rather than honesty. Government's power to cramp speech should rest not on its dexterity in fabricating neutral appearing reasons but on the basis of whether it has demonstrated compelling regulatory reasons.

The type of symbolic speech that has generated the most controversy and the most Supreme Court decisions is desecration and other uses of the American flag. Because of the long history of reverence for the flag, manifested in holidays, pledges, anthems, and ceremonies, both federal and state governments have relentlessly attempted to protect it from desecration. Dissidents have found the flag a powerful symbol to use in expressing their opposition to American policies and defenders of the flag have just as vehemently supported anti-desecration statutes against First Amendment challenge.

For two decades, the Supreme Court avoided squarely resolving the constitutionality of a statute that punished someone for desecrating an American flag as a means of political protest. In *Street v. New York*, the defendant accompanied the act of burning a flag with the words, "We don't need no damned flag" and "[i]f they let that happen to Meredith we don't need an American flag."[66] The Court held that since the defendant might have been convicted solely on the basis of his words, the conviction violated the First Amendment.

Nor did the Court reach the constitutionality of punishing flag desecration in *Spence v. Washington*, which involved the conviction of a college student who displayed the flag with a peace symbol made of black tape affixed to it.[67] The Court held that the student's conduct was protected by the First Amendment, noting that the student did not permanently disfigure the flag and was not charged under a desecration statute. Finally, in *Smith v. Goguen*, the Court reversed the conviction under a Massachusetts flag-misuse statute of a man who wore a small flag on the seat of his pants.[68] The Court held that the statute's prohibition of treating the flag "contemptuously" was unconstitutionally broad and vague.

The question of First Amendment protection of flag desecration presented itself squarely in *Texas v. Johnson*. The justices' opinions displayed a passionate disagreement over whether dissidents' use of the American flag to convey their message raises unique government concerns. The majority, applying the *O'Brien* test, concluded that the government's interest was improperly related to suppressing the speaker's message. The dissent, on the other hand, understood the symbolic value of the flag as an important national good and therefore emphasized the government's justifiable interest in protecting the flag from desecration.

---

[66] Street v. New York, 394 U.S. 576 (1969).
[67] Spence v. Washington, 418 U.S. 405 (1974).
[68] Smith v. Goguen, 415 U.S. 566 (1974).

Texas v. Johnson
491 U.S. 397 (1989)

JUSTICE BRENNAN delivered the opinion of the Court.

After publicly burning an American flag as a means of political protest, Gregory Lee Johnson was convicted of desecrating a flag in violation of Texas law. This case presents the question whether his conviction is consistent with the First Amendment. We hold that it is not.

I

While the Republican National Convention was taking place in Dallas in 1984, respondent Johnson participated in a political demonstration dubbed the "Republican War Chest Tour." As explained in literature distributed by the demonstrators and in speeches made by them, the purpose of this event was to protest the policies of the Reagan administration and of certain Dallas-based corporations. The demonstrators marched through the Dallas streets, chanting political slogans and stopping at several corporate locations to stage "die-ins" intended to dramatize the consequences of nuclear war. On several occasions they spray-painted the walls of buildings and overturned potted plants, but Johnson himself took no part in such activities. He did, however, accept an American flag handed to him by a fellow protestor who had taken it from a flagpole outside one of the targeted buildings.

The demonstration ended in front of Dallas City Hall, where Johnson unfurled the American flag, doused it with kerosene, and set it on fire. While the flag burned, the protestors chanted: "America, the red, white, and blue, we spit on you." After the demonstrators dispersed, a witness to the flag burning collected the flag's remains and buried them in his backyard. No one was physically injured or threatened with injury, though several witnesses testified that they had been seriously offended by the flag burning.

Of the approximately 100 demonstrators, Johnson alone was charged with a crime. The only criminal offense with which he was charged was the desecration of a venerated object in violation of Tex. Penal Code Ann. § 42.09(a)(3)(1989).[1] After a trial, he was convicted, sentenced to one year in prison, and fined $ 2,000. The Court of Appeals for the Fifth District of Texas at Dallas affirmed Johnson's conviction, but the Texas Court of Criminal Appeals reversed, holding that the State could not, consistent with the First Amendment, punish Johnson for burning the flag in these circumstances.

. . .

II

Johnson was convicted of flag desecration for burning the flag rather than for uttering insulting words. This fact somewhat complicates our consideration of his conviction under the First Amendment. We must first determine whether Johnson's burning of the flag constituted expressive conduct, permitting him to invoke the First Amendment in challenging his conviction. If his conduct was expressive, we next decide whether the State's regulation is related to the suppression of free expression. See, *e.g.*, *United States v. O'Brien*. If the State's regulation is not related to expression, then the less stringent standard we announced in

United States v. O'Brien for regulations of non-communicative conduct controls. If it is, then we are outside of *O'Brien*'s test, and we must ask whether this interest justifies Johnson's conviction under a more demanding standard. A third possibility is that the State's asserted interest is simply not implicated on these facts, and in that event the interest drops out of the picture.

The First Amendment literally forbids the abridgment only of "speech," but we have long recognized that its protection does not end at the spoken or written word. While we have rejected "the view that an apparently limitless variety of conduct can be labeled 'speech' whenever the person engaging in the conduct intends thereby to express an idea," *United States v. O'Brien*, we have acknowledged that conduct may be "sufficiently imbued with elements of communication to fall within the scope of the First and Fourteenth Amendments."

In deciding whether particular conduct possesses sufficient communicative elements to bring the First Amendment into play, we have asked whether "[a]n intent to convey a particularized message was present, and [whether] the likelihood was great that the message would be understood by those who viewed it." *Spence v. Washington*. Hence, we have recognized the expressive nature of students' wearing of black armbands to protest American military involvement in Vietnam; of a sit-in by blacks in a "whites only" area to protest segregation; of the wearing of American military uniforms in a dramatic presentation criticizing American involvement in Vietnam; and of picketing about a wide variety of causes.

Especially pertinent to this case are our decisions recognizing the communicative nature of conduct relating to flags. Attaching a peace sign to the flag; refusing to salute the flag; and displaying a red flag, we have held, all may find shelter under the First Amendment. That we have had little difficulty identifying an expressive element in conduct relating to flags should not be surprising. The very purpose of a national flag is to serve as a symbol of our country; it is, one might say, "the one visible manifestation of two hundred years of nationhood." Thus, we have observed:

> "[T]he flag salute is a form of utterance. Symbolism is a primitive but effective way of communicating ideas. The use of an emblem or flag to symbolize some system, idea, institution, or personality, is a short cut from mind to mind. Causes and nations, political parties, lodges and ecclesiastical groups seek to knit the loyalty of their followings to a flag or banner, a color

---

[1] Texas Penal Code Ann. § 42.09 (1989) provides in full:

"§ 42.09. Desecration of Venerated Object

"(a) A person commits an offense if he intentionally or knowingly desecrates:

"(1) a public monument;

"(2) a place of worship or burial; or

"(3) a state or national flag.

"(b) For purposes of this section, 'desecrate' means deface, damage, or otherwise physically mistreat in a way that the actor knows will seriously offend one or more persons likely to observe or discover his action.

"(c) An offense under this section is a Class A misdemeanor."

or design." [*West Virginia Board of Education v. Barnette*, 319 U.S. 624, 632 (1943).]

Pregnant with expressive content, the flag as readily signifies this Nation as does the combination of letters found in "America."

We have not automatically concluded, however, that any action taken with respect to our flag is expressive. Instead, in characterizing such action for First Amendment purposes, we have considered the context in which it occurred. . . .

The State of Texas conceded for purposes of its oral argument in this case that Johnson's conduct was expressive conduct. . . . Johnson burned an American flag as part—indeed, as the culmination—of a political demonstration that coincided with the convening of the Republican Party and its renomination of Ronald Reagan for President. The expressive, overtly political nature of this conduct was both intentional and overwhelmingly apparent. At his trial, Johnson explained his reasons for burning the flag as follows: "The American Flag was burned as Ronald Reagan was being renominated as President. And a more powerful statement of symbolic speech, whether you agree with it or not, couldn't have been made at that time. It's quite a just position [juxtaposition]. We had new patriotism and no patriotism." In these circumstances, Johnson's burning of the flag was conduct "sufficiently imbued with elements of communication" to implicate the First Amendment.

III

The government generally has a freer hand in restricting expressive conduct than it has in restricting the written or spoken word. It may not, however, proscribe particular conduct because it has expressive elements. . . . It is, in short, not simply the verbal or nonverbal nature of the expression, but the governmental interest at stake, that helps to determine whether a restriction on that expression is valid.

Thus, although we have recognized that where "'speech' and 'nonspeech' elements are combined in the same course of conduct, a sufficiently important governmental interest in regulating the nonspeech element can justify incidental limitations on First Amendment freedoms," *O'Brien*, we have limited the applicability of *O'Brien*'s relatively lenient standard to those cases in which "the governmental interest is unrelated to the suppression of free expression." In stating, moreover, that *O'Brien*'s test "in the last analysis is little, if any, different from the standard applied to time, place, or manner restrictions," *Clark*, we have highlighted the requirement that the governmental interest in question be unconnected to

expression in order to come under *O'Brien*'s less demanding rule.

In order to decide whether *O'Brien*'s test applies here, therefore, we must decide whether Texas has asserted an interest in support of Johnson's conviction that is unrelated to the suppression of expression. If we find that an interest asserted by the State is simply not implicated on the facts before us, we need not ask whether *O'Brien*'s test applies. The State offers two separate interests to justify this conviction: preventing breaches of the peace and preserving the flag as a symbol of nationhood and national unity. We hold that the first interest is not implicated on this record and that the second is related to the suppression of expression.

A

Texas claims that its interest in preventing breaches of the peace justifies Johnson's conviction for flag desecration. However, no disturbance of the peace actually occurred or threatened to occur because of Johnson's burning of the flag. Although the State stresses the disruptive behavior of the protestors during their march toward City Hall, it admits that "no actual breach of the peace occurred at the time of the flagburning or in response to the flagburning." The State's emphasis on the protestors' disorderly actions prior to arriving at City Hall is not only somewhat surprising given that no charges were brought on the basis of this conduct, but it also fails to show that a disturbance of the peace was a likely reaction to Johnson's conduct. The only evidence offered by the State at trial to show the reaction to Johnson's actions was the testimony of several persons who had been seriously offended by the flag burning.

The State's position, therefore, amounts to a claim that an audience that takes serious offense at particular expression is necessarily likely to disturb the peace and that the expression may be prohibited on this basis. Our precedents do not countenance such a presumption. On the contrary, they recognize that a principal "function of free speech under our system of government is to invite dispute. It may indeed best serve its high purpose when it induces a condition of unrest, creates dissatisfaction with conditions as they are, or even stirs people to anger." *Terminiello v. Chicago*, 337 U.S. 1, 4 (1949). It would be odd indeed to conclude both that "if it is the speaker's opinion that gives offense, that consequence is a reason for according it constitutional protection," *FCC v. Pacifica Foundation*, 438 U.S. 726, 745 (1978) (opinion of Stevens, J.), *and* that the government may ban the expression of certain disagreeable ideas on the unsupported presumption that their very disagreeableness will provoke violence.

Nor does Johnson's expressive conduct fall within that small class of "fighting words" that are "likely to provoke the average person to retaliation, and thereby cause a breach of the peace." *Chaplinsky v. New Hampshire*. No reasonable onlooker would have regarded Johnson's generalized expression of dissatisfaction with the policies of the Federal Government as a direct personal insult or an invitation to exchange fisticuffs.

We thus conclude that the State's interest in maintaining order is not implicated on these facts. The State need not worry that our holding will disable it from preserving the peace. We do not suggest that the First Amendment forbids a State to prevent "imminent lawless action." *Brandenburg*. And, in fact, Texas already has a statute specifically prohibiting breaches of the peace, which tends to confirm that Texas need not punish this flag desecration in order to keep the peace.

B

The State also asserts an interest in preserving the flag as a symbol of nationhood and national unity. In *Spence*, we acknowledged that the government's interest in preserving the flag's special symbolic value "is directly related to expression in the context of activity" such as affixing a peace symbol to a flag. We are equally persuaded that this interest is related to expression in the case of Johnson's burning of the flag. The State, apparently, is concerned that such conduct will lead people to believe either that the flag does not stand for nationhood and national unity, but instead reflects other, less positive concepts, or that the concepts reflected in the flag do not in fact exist, that is, that we do not enjoy unity as a Nation. These concerns blossom only when a person's treatment of the flag communicates some message, and thus are related "to the suppression of free expression" within the meaning of *O'Brien*. We are thus outside of *O'Brien*'s test altogether.

IV

It remains to consider whether the State's interest in preserving the flag as a symbol of nationhood and national unity justifies Johnson's conviction.

As in *Spence*, "[w]e are confronted with a case of prosecution for the expression of an idea through activity," and "[a]ccordingly, we must examine with particular care the interests advanced by [petitioner] to support its prosecution." Johnson was not, we add, prosecuted for the expression of just any idea; he was prosecuted for his expression of dissatisfaction with the policies of this country, expression situated at the core of our First Amendment values.

Moreover, Johnson was prosecuted because he knew that his politically charged expression would cause "serious offense." If he had burned the flag as a means of disposing of it because it was dirty or torn, he would not have been convicted of flag desecration under this Texas law: federal law designates burning as the preferred means of disposing of a flag "when it is in such condition that it is no longer a fitting emblem for display," and Texas has no quarrel with this means of disposal. The Texas law is thus not aimed at protecting the physical integrity of the flag in all circumstances, but is designed instead to protect it only against impairments that would cause serious offense to others. . . .

Whether Johnson's treatment of the flag violated Texas law thus depended on the likely communicative impact of his expressive conduct. . . . We must therefore subject the State's asserted interest in preserving the special symbolic character of the flag to "the most exacting scrutiny."

Texas argues that its interest in preserving the flag as a symbol of nationhood and national unity survives this close analysis. Quoting extensively from the writings of this Court chronicling the flag's historic and symbolic role in our society, the State emphasizes the "'special place'" reserved for the flag in our Nation. The State's argument is not that it has an interest simply in maintaining the flag as a symbol of *something*, no matter what it symbolizes; indeed, if that were the State's position, it would be difficult to see how that interest is endangered by highly symbolic conduct such as Johnson's. Rather, the State's claim is that it has an interest in preserving the flag as a symbol of *nationhood* and *national unity*, a symbol with a determinate range of meanings. According to Texas, if one physically treats the flag in a way that would tend to cast doubt on either the idea that nationhood and national unity are the flag's referents or that national unity actually exists, the message conveyed thereby is a harmful one and therefore may be prohibited.

If there is a bedrock principle underlying the First Amendment, it is that the government may not prohibit the expression of an idea simply because society finds the idea itself offensive or disagreeable.

We have not recognized an exception to this principle even where our flag has been involved. In *Street v. New York*, 394 U.S. 576 (1969), we held that a State may not criminally punish a person for uttering words critical of the flag. Rejecting the argument that the conviction could be sustained on the ground that Street had "failed to show the respect for our national symbol which may properly be demanded of every citizen," we concluded that "the constitutionally guaranteed 'freedom to be intellectually . . . diverse or even contrary,' and the 'right to differ as to things that touch the heart of the existing order,' encompass the freedom to express publicly one's opinions about our flag, including those opinions which are defiant or contemptuous." Nor may the government, we have held, compel conduct that would evince respect for the flag. "To sustain the compulsory flag salute we are required to say that a Bill of Rights which guards the individual's right to speak his own mind, left it open to public authorities to compel him to utter what is not in his mind." [*Barnette*.]

In holding in *Barnette* that the Constitution did not leave this course open to the government, Justice Jackson described one of our society's defining principles in words deserving of their frequent repetition: "If there is any fixed star in our constitutional constellation, it is that no official, high or petty, can prescribe what shall be orthodox in politics, nationalism, religion, or other matters of opinion or force citizens to confess by word or act their faith therein." In *Spence*, we held that the same interest asserted by Texas here was insufficient to support a criminal conviction under a flag-misuse statute for the taping of a peace sign to an American flag. "Given the protected character of [Spence's] expression and in light of the fact that no interest the State may have in preserving the physical integrity of a privately owned flag was significantly impaired on these facts," we held, "the conviction must be invalidated."

In short, nothing in our precedents suggests that a State may foster its own view of the flag by prohibiting expressive conduct relating to it. To bring its argument outside our precedents, Texas attempts to convince us that even if its interest in preserving the flag's symbolic role does not allow it to prohibit words or some expressive conduct critical of the flag, it does permit it to forbid the outright destruction of the flag. The State's argument cannot depend here on the distinction between written or spoken words and nonverbal conduct. That distinction, we have shown, is of no moment where the nonverbal conduct is expressive, as it is here, and where the regulation of that conduct is related to expression, as it is here. In addition, both *Barnette* and *Spence* involved expressive conduct, not only verbal communication, and both found that conduct protected.

Texas' focus on the precise nature of Johnson's expression, moreover, misses the point of our prior decisions: their enduring lesson, that the government may not prohibit expression simply because it disagrees with its message, is not dependent on the particular mode in which one chooses to express an idea. If we were to hold that a State may forbid flag burning wherever it is likely to endanger the flag's symbolic role, but allow it wherever burning a flag promotes that role—as where, for example, a person ceremoniously burns a dirty flag—we would be saying that when it comes to impairing the flag's physical integrity, the flag itself may be used as a symbol—as a substitute for the written or spoken word or a "short cut from mind to mind"—only in one direction. We would be permitting a State to "prescribe what shall be orthodox" by saying that one may burn the flag to convey one's attitude toward it and its referents only if one does not endanger the flag's representation of nationhood and national unity.

. . .

. . . To conclude that the government may permit designated symbols to be used to communicate only a limited set of messages would be to enter territory having no discernible or defensible boundaries. Could the government, on this theory, prohibit the burning of state flags? Of copies of the Presidential seal? Of the Constitution? In evaluating these choices under the First Amendment, how would we decide which symbols were sufficiently special to warrant this unique status? To do so, we would be forced to consult our own political preferences, and impose them on the citizenry, in the very way that the First Amendment forbids us to do.

There is, moreover, no indication—either in the text of the Constitution or in our cases interpreting it—that a separate juridical category exists for the American flag alone. Indeed, we would not be surprised to learn that the persons who framed our Constitution and wrote the Amendment that we now construe were not known for their reverence for the Union Jack. The First Amendment does not guarantee that other concepts virtually sacred to our Nation as a whole—such as the principle that discrimination on the basis of race is odious and destructive—will go unquestioned in the market-place of ideas. See *Brandenburg v. Ohio*. We decline, therefore, to create for the flag an exception to the joust of principles protected by the First Amendment.

It is not the State's ends, but its means, to which we object. It cannot be gainsaid that there is a special place reserved for the flag in this Nation, and thus we do not doubt that the government has a legitimate interest in making efforts to "preserv[e] the national flag as an unalloyed symbol of our country." We reject the suggestion, urged at oral argument by counsel for Johnson, that the government lacks "any state interest whatsoever" in regulating the manner in which the flag may be displayed. Congress has, for example, enacted precatory regulations describing the proper treatment of the flag, and we cast no doubt on the legitimacy of its interest in making such recommendations. To say that the government has an interest in encouraging proper treatment of the flag, however, is not to say that it may criminally punish a person for burning a flag as a means of political protest.

We are fortified in today's conclusion by our conviction that forbidding criminal punishment for conduct such as Johnson's will not endanger the special role played by our flag or the feelings it inspires. To paraphrase Justice Holmes, we submit that nobody can suppose that this one gesture of an unknown man will change our Nation's attitude towards its flag. See *Abrams v. United States* (Holmes, J., dissenting). Indeed, Texas' argument that the burning of an American flag "'is an act having a high likelihood to cause a breach of the peace,'" and its statute's implicit assumption that physical mistreatment of the flag will lead to "serious offense," tend to confirm that the flag's special role is not in danger; if it were, no one would riot or take offense because a flag had been burned.

. . .

The way to preserve the flag's special role is not to punish those who feel differently about these matters. It is to persuade them that they are wrong. . . . And, precisely because it is our flag that is involved, one's response to the flag burner may exploit the uniquely persuasive power of the flag itself. We can imagine no more appropriate response to burning a flag than waving one's own, no better way to counter a flag burner's message than by saluting the flag that burns, no surer means of preserving the dignity even of the flag that burned than by—as one witness here did—according its remains a respectful burial. We do not consecrate the flag by punishing its desecration, for in doing so we dilute the freedom that this cherished emblem represents.

. . .

[JUSTICE KENNEDY's concurring opinion is omitted].

CHIEF JUSTICE REHNQUIST, with whom JUSTICE WHITE and JUSTICE O'CONNOR join, dissenting.

In holding this Texas statute unconstitutional, the Court ignores Justice Holmes' familiar aphorism that "a page of history is worth a volume of logic." *New York Trust Co. v. Eisner*, 256 U.S. 345, 349 (1921). For more than 200 years, the American flag has occupied a unique position as the symbol of our Nation, a uniqueness that justifies a governmental prohibition against flag burning in the way respondent Johnson did here.

At the time of the American Revolution, the flag served to unify the Thirteen Colonies at home, while obtaining recognition of national sovereignty abroad. . . . During that time, there were many colonial and regimental flags, adorned with such symbols as pine trees, beavers, anchors, and rattlesnakes, bearing slogans such as "Liberty or Death," "Hope," "An Appeal to Heaven," and "Don't Tread on Me." The first distinctive flag of the Colonies was the "Grand Union Flag"—with 13 stripes and a British flag in the left corner—which was flown for the first time on January 2, 1776, by troops of the Continental Army around Boston. By June 14, 1777, after we declared our independence from England, the Continental Congress resolved:

> "That the flag of the thirteen United States be thirteen stripes, alternate red and white: that the union be thirteen stars, white in a blue field, representing a new constellation." 8 Journal of the Continental Congress 1774–1789.

One immediate result of the flag's adoption was that American vessels harassing British shipping sailed under an authorized national flag. Without such a flag, the British could treat captured seamen as pirates and hang them summarily; with a national flag, such seamen were treated as prisoners of war.

During the War of 1812, British naval forces sailed up Chesapeake Bay and marched overland to sack and burn the city of Washington. They then sailed up the Patapsco River to invest the city of Baltimore, but to do so it was first necessary to reduce Fort McHenry in Baltimore Harbor. Francis Scott Key, a Washington lawyer, had been granted permission by the British to board one of their warships to negotiate the release of an American who had been taken prisoner. That night, waiting anxiously on the British ship, Key watched the British fleet firing on Fort McHenry. Finally, at daybreak, he saw the fort's American flag still flying; the British attack had failed. Intensely moved, he began to scribble on the back of an envelope the poem that became our national anthem. . . .

The American flag played a central role in our Nation's most tragic conflict, when the North fought against the South. The lowering of the American flag at Fort Sumter was viewed as the start of the war. The Southern States, to formalize their separation from the Union, adopted the "Stars and Bars" of the Confederacy. The Union troops marched to the sound of "Yes We'll Rally Round The Flag Boys, We'll Rally Once Again." President Abraham Lincoln refused proposals to remove from the American flag the stars representing the rebel States, because he considered the conflict not a war between two nations but an attack by 11 States against the National Government. By war's end, the American flag again flew over "an indestructible union, composed of indestructible states."

. . .

In the First and Second World Wars, thousands of our countrymen died on foreign soil fighting for the American cause. At Iwo Jima in the Second World War, United States Marines fought hand to hand against thousands of Japanese. By the time the Marines reached the top of Mount Suribachi, they raised a piece of pipe upright and from one end fluttered a flag. That ascent had cost nearly 6,000 American lives. The Iwo Jima Memorial in Arlington National Cemetery memorializes that event. President Franklin Roosevelt authorized the use of the flag on labels, packages, cartons, and containers intended for export as lend-lease aid, in order to inform people in other countries of the United States' assistance.

During the Korean war, the successful amphibious landing of American troops at Inchon was marked by the raising of an American flag within an hour of the event. Impetus for the enactment of the Federal Flag Desecration Statute in 1967 came from the impact of flag burnings in the United States on troop morale in Vietnam. Representative L. Mendel Rivers, then Chairman of the House Armed Services Committee, testified that "[t]he burning of the flag . . . has caused my mail to increase 100 percent from the boys in Vietnam, writing me and asking me what is going on in America." Representative Charles Wiggins stated: "The public act of desecration of our flag tends to undermine the morale of American troops. That this finding is true can be attested by many Members who have received correspondence from servicemen expressing their shock and disgust of such conduct."

The flag symbolizes the Nation in peace as well as in war. It signifies our national presence on battleships, airplanes, military installations, and public buildings from the United States Capitol to the thousands of county courthouses and city halls throughout the country. Two flags are prominently placed in our courtroom. Countless flags are placed by the graves of loved ones each year on what was first called Decoration Day, and is now called Memorial Day. The flag is traditionally placed on the casket of deceased members of the Armed Forces, and it is later given to the deceased's family. Congress has provided that the flag be flown at half-staff upon the death of the President, Vice President, and other government officials "as a mark of respect to their memory." The flag identifies United States merchant ships, and "[t]he laws of the Union protect our commerce wherever the flag of the country may float."

No other American symbol has been as universally honored as the flag. In 1931, Congress declared "The Star-Spangled Banner" to be our national anthem. In 1949, Congress declared June 14th to be Flag Day. In 1987, John Philip Sousa's "The Stars and Stripes Forever" was designated as the national march. Congress has also established "The Pledge of Allegiance to the Flag" and the manner of its deliverance. The flag has appeared as the principal symbol on approximately 33 United States postal stamps and in the design of at least 43 more, more times than any other symbol.

Both Congress and the States have enacted numerous laws regulating misuse of the American flag. Until 1967, Congress left the regulation of misuse of the flag up to the States. Now, however, 18 U. S. C. § 700(a) provides that:

> "Whoever knowingly casts contempt upon any flag of the United States by publicly mutilating, defacing, defiling, burning, or trampling upon it shall be fined not more than $ 1,000 or imprisoned for not more than one year, or both."

Congress has also prescribed, *inter alia*, detailed rules for the design of the flag, the time and occasion of flag's display, the position and manner of its display, respect for the flag, and conduct during hoisting, lowering, and passing of the flag. With the exception of Alaska and Wyoming, all of the States now have statutes prohibiting the burning of the flag. . . .

The American flag, then, throughout more than 200 years of our history, has come to be the visible symbol embodying our Nation. It does not represent the views of any particular political party, and it does not represent any particular political philosophy. The flag is not simply another "idea" or "point of view" competing for recognition in the marketplace of ideas. Millions and millions of Americans regard it with an almost mystical reverence regardless of what sort of social, political, or philosophical beliefs they may have. I cannot agree that the First Amendment invalidates the Act of Congress, and the laws of 48 of the 50 States, which make criminal the public burning of the flag.

. . .

. . . [I]t may equally well be said that the public burning of the American flag by Johnson was no essential part of any exposition of ideas, and at the same time it had a tendency to incite a breach of the peace. Johnson was free to make any verbal denunciation of the flag that he wished; indeed, he was free to burn the flag in private. He could publicly burn other symbols of the Government or effigies of political leaders. He did lead a march through the streets of Dallas, and conducted a rally in front of the Dallas City Hall. He engaged in a "die-in" to protest nuclear weapons. He shouted out various slogans during the march, including: "Reagan, Mondale which will it be? Either one means World War III"; "Ronald Reagan, killer of the hour, Perfect example of U. S. power"; and "red, white and blue, we spit on you, you stand for plunder, you will go under." For none of these acts was he arrested or prosecuted; it was only when he proceeded to burn publicly an American flag stolen from its rightful owner that he violated the Texas statute.

The Court could not, and did not, say that Chaplinsky's utterances were not expressive phrases—they clearly and succinctly conveyed an extremely low opinion of the addressee. The same may be said of Johnson's public burning of the flag in this case; it obviously did convey Johnson's bitter dislike of his country. But his act, like Chaplinsky's provocative words, conveyed nothing that could not have been conveyed and was not conveyed just as forcefully in a dozen different ways. As with "fighting words," so with flag burning, for purposes of the First Amendment: It is "no essential part of any exposition of ideas, and [is] of such slight social value as a step to truth that any benefit that may be derived from [it] is clearly outweighed" by the public interest in avoiding a probable breach of the peace. . . .

The result of the Texas statute is obviously to deny one in Johnson's frame of mind one of many means of "symbolic speech." Far from being a case of "one picture being worth a thousand words," flag burning is the equivalent of an inarticulate grunt or roar that, it seems fair to say, is most likely to be indulged in not to express any particular idea, but to antagonize others. Only five years ago we said in *City Council of Los Angeles v. Taxpayers for Vincent*, 466 U.S. 789, 812 (1984), that "the First Amendment does not guarantee the right to employ every conceivable method of communication at all times and in all places." The Texas statute deprived Johnson of only one rather inarticulate symbolic form of protest—a form of protest that was profoundly offensive to many—and left him with a full panoply of other symbols and every conceivable form of verbal expression to express his deep disapproval of national policy. Thus, in no way can it be said that Texas is punishing him because his hearers—or any other group of people—were profoundly opposed to the message that he sought to convey. Such opposition is no proper basis for restricting speech or expression under the First Amendment. It was Johnson's use of this particular symbol, and not the idea that he sought to convey by it or by his many other expressions, for which he was punished.

. . .

The Court concludes its opinion with a regrettably patronizing civics lecture, presumably addressed to the Members of both Houses of Congress, the members of the 48 state legislatures that enacted prohibitions against flag burning, and the troops fighting under that flag in Vietnam who objected to its being burned: "The way to preserve the flag's special role is not to punish those who feel differently about these matters. It is to persuade them that they are wrong." The Court's role as the final expositor of the Constitution is well established, but its role as a Platonic guardian admonishing those responsible to public opinion as if they were truant schoolchildren has no similar place in our system of government. The cry of "no taxation without representation" animated those who revolted against the English Crown to found our Nation—the idea that those who submitted to government should have some say as to what kind of laws would be passed. Surely one of the high purposes of a democratic society is to legislate against conduct that is regarded as evil and profoundly offensive to the majority of people—whether it be murder, embezzlement, pollution, or flag burning.

Our Constitution wisely places limits on powers of legislative majorities to act, but the declaration of such limits by this Court "is, at all times, a question of much delicacy, which ought seldom, if ever, to be decided in the affirmative, in a doubtful case." *Fletcher v. Peck*, 6 Cranch 87, 128 (1810) (Marshall, C. J.). Uncritical extension of constitutional protection to the burning of the flag risks the frustration of the very purpose for which organized governments are instituted. The Court decides that the American flag is just another symbol, about which not only must opinions pro and con be tolerated, but for which the most minimal public respect may not be enjoined. The government may conscript men into the Armed Forces where they must fight and perhaps die for the flag, but the government may not prohibit the public burning of the banner under which they fight. I would uphold the Texas statute as applied in this case.

JUSTICE STEVENS, dissenting.

As the Court analyzes this case, it presents the question whether the State of Texas, or indeed the Federal Government, has the power to prohibit the public desecration of the American flag. The question is unique. In my judgment rules that apply to a host of other symbols, such as state flags, armbands, or various privately promoted emblems of political or commercial identity, are not necessarily controlling. Even if flag burning could be considered just another species of symbolic speech under the logical application of the rules that the Court has developed in its interpretation of the First Amendment in other contexts, this case has an intangible dimension that makes those rules inapplicable.

A country's flag is a symbol of more than "nationhood and national unity." It also signifies the ideas that characterize the society that has chosen that emblem as well as the special history that has animated the growth and power of those ideas. The fleurs-de-lis and the tricolor both symbolized "nationhood and national unity," but they had vastly different meanings. The message conveyed by some flags—the swastika, for example—may survive long after it has outlived its usefulness as a symbol of regimented unity in a particular nation.

So it is with the American flag. It is more than a proud symbol of the courage, the determination, and the gifts of nature that transformed 13 fledgling Colonies into a world power. It is a symbol of freedom, of equal opportunity, of religious tolerance, and of good will for other peoples who share our aspirations. The symbol carries its message to dissidents both at home and abroad who may have no interest at all in our national unity or survival.

The value of the flag as a symbol cannot be measured. Even so, I have no doubt that the interest in preserving that value for the future is both significant and legitimate. Conceivably that value will be enhanced by the Court's conclusion that our national commitment to free expression is so strong that even the United States as ultimate guarantor of that freedom is without power to prohibit the desecration of its unique symbol. But I am unpersuaded. The creation of a federal right to post bulletin boards and graffiti on the Washington Monument might enlarge the market for free expression, but at a cost I would not pay. Similarly, in my considered judgment, sanctioning the public desecration of the flag will tarnish its value—both for those who cherish the ideas for which it waves and for those who desire to don the robes of martyrdom by burning it. That tarnish is not justified by the trivial burden on free expression occasioned by requiring that an available, alternative mode of expression—including uttering words critical of the flag,—be employed.

It is appropriate to emphasize certain propositions that are not implicated by this case. The statutory prohibition of flag desecration does not "prescribe what shall be orthodox in politics, nationalism, religion, or other matters of opinion or force citizens to confess by word or act their faith therein." *West Virginia Board of Education v. Barnette.* The statute does not compel any conduct or any profession of respect for any idea or any symbol.

Nor does the statute violate "the government's paramount obligation of neutrality in its regulation of protected communication." *Young v. American Mini Theatres, Inc.*, 427 U.S. 50, 70 (1976) (plurality opinion). The content of respondent's message has no relevance whatsoever to the case. The concept of "desecration" does not turn on the substance of the message the actor intends to convey, but rather on whether those who view the act will take serious offense. Accordingly, one intending to convey a message of respect for the flag by burning it in a public square might nonetheless be guilty of desecration if he knows that others—perhaps simply because they misperceive the intended message—will be seriously offended. Indeed, even if the actor knows that all possible witnesses will understand that he intends to send a message of respect, he might still be guilty of desecration if he also knows that this understanding does not lessen the offense taken by some of those witnesses. Thus, this is not a case in which the fact that "it is the speaker's opinion that gives offense" provides a special "reason for according it constitutional protection," *FCC v. Pacifica Foundation* (plurality opinion). The case has nothing to do with "disagreeable ideas." It involves disagreeable conduct that, in my opinion, diminishes the value of an important national asset.

The Court is therefore quite wrong in blandly asserting that respondent "was prosecuted for his expression of dissatisfaction with the policies of this country, expression situated at the core of our First Amendment values." Respondent was prosecuted because of the method he chose to express his dissatisfaction with those policies. Had he chosen to spray-paint—or perhaps convey with a motion picture projector—his message of dissatisfaction on the facade of the Lincoln Memorial, there would be no question about the power of the Government to prohibit his means of expression. The prohibition would be supported by the legitimate interest in preserving the quality of an important national asset. Though the asset at stake in this case is intangible, given its unique value, the same interest supports a prohibition on the desecration of the American flag.

The ideas of liberty and equality have been an irresistible force in motivating leaders like Patrick Henry, Susan B. Anthony, and Abraham Lincoln, schoolteachers like Nathan Hale and Booker T. Washington, the Philippine Scouts who fought at Bataan, and the soldiers who scaled the bluff at Omaha Beach. If those ideas are worth fighting for—and our history demonstrates that they are—it cannot be true that the flag that uniquely symbolizes their power is not itself worthy of protection from unnecessary desecration.

I respectfully dissent.

3. More Regulable Speech

Apart from prohibitions of speech that deserves no First Amendment protection, such as obscenity and fighting words, must government restrictions of expression always meet the same high standard of judicial scrutiny? Do nude dancing, commercial advertisements, and campaign financing, for example, deserve the same degree of protection as "pure" political speech? The Court has not treated all types of speech equally; some are more regulable than others. In coming to this approach, the Court has grappled with a tension created by our varying respect for different kinds of expression. On the one hand, according different categories of protected speech different levels of value risks importing the majority's invidious preferences, based on its objection to the speaker or the message, into First Amendment jurisprudence. On the other hand, treating all speech the same risks diminishing the extent of protection for the kind of speech that is most valuable (typically identified as political speech).

a. Indecent Speech

As indicated by the section on obscenity, indecent speech that is not obscene has long been regulated by the government. In *Barnes v. Glen Theatre, Inc.*, the Court considered the constitutionality of South Bend, Indiana's prohibition of nude dancing under the state public indecency statute. The statute prohibited engaging in sexual intercourse or deviate sexual conduct, genital fondling, and appearing in a state of nudity in a public place. Because the Court saw the statute as a general regulation of conduct—public nudity—with some incidental restriction of expressive activity, it applied the four-prong *O'Brien* test. But the ban on nude dancing raised two principal First Amendment issues: first, is nude dancing speech within the meaning of the First Amendment? If so, may the government justify its infringement of this speech based on the state's interest in moral decency? Although *Barnes* concerns what some might consider the trivial topic of topless dancing, it grapples with fundamental questions about the nature of protected speech and the scope of First Amendment limits on government's power to enforce morality. Clearly a majority of the justices believed that, although art is a form of protected expressive conduct, some types of art deserve greater protection than others.

The opinions also demonstrate the difficulty of distinguishing the expression from the conduct in expressive conduct. This is why the justices disagreed about whether the statute was "unrelated to the suppression of free expression." The majority thought that South Bend could constitutionally punish the *nudity* component of nude dancing, despite the protected erotic *message* conveyed by the dancers. The dissenting justices, on the other hand, felt that the two could not be separated: the nudity was itself an expressive element of the dancing. Indeed, it was precisely because of the erotic message that the nudity communicated that South Bend sought to prohibit the dancing.

Barnes v. Glen Theatre, Inc.
501 U.S. 560 (1991)

CHIEF JUSTICE REHNQUIST delivered the opinion of the Court.

Respondents are two establishments in South Bend, Indiana, that wish to provide totally nude dancing as entertainment, and individual dancers who are employed at these establishments. They claim that the First Amendment's guarantee of freedom of expres-sion prevents the State of Indiana from enforcing its public indecency law to prevent this form of dancing. We reject their claim.

. . .

Several of our cases contain language suggesting that nude dancing of the kind involved here is expressive conduct protected by the First Amendment.... These statements support the conclusion of the Court of Appeals that nude dancing of the kind sought to be performed here is expressive conduct within the outer perimeters of the First Amendment, though we view it as only marginally so. This, of course, does not end our inquiry. We must determine the level of protection to be afforded to the expressive conduct at issue, and must determine whether the Indiana statute is an impermissible infringement of that protected activity.

Indiana, of course, has not banned nude dancing as such, but has proscribed public nudity across the board. The Supreme Court of Indiana has construed the Indiana statute to preclude nudity in what are essentially places of public accommodation such as the Glen Theatre and the Kitty Kat Lounge. In such places, respondents point out, minors are excluded and there are no non-consenting viewers. Respondents contend that while the state may license establishments such as the ones involved here, and limit the geographical area in which they do business, it may not in any way limit the performance of the dances within them without violating the First Amendment. The petitioner contends, on the other hand, that Indiana's restriction on nude dancing is a valid "time, place or manner" restriction under cases such as *Clark v. Community for Creative Non-Violence.*

The "time, place, or manner" test was developed for evaluating restrictions on expression taking place on public property which had been dedicated as a "public forum," although we have on at least one occasion applied it to conduct occurring on private property. See *Renton v. Playtime Theatres, Inc.* In *Clark* we observed that this test has been interpreted to embody much the same standards as those set forth in *United States v. O'Brien,* and we turn, therefore, to the rule enunciated in *O'Brien.*

. . .

Applying the four-part *O'Brien* test enunciated above, we find that Indiana's public indecency statute is justified despite its incidental limitations on some expressive activity. The public indecency statute is clearly within the constitutional power of the State and furthers substantial governmental interests. It is impossible to discern, other than from the text of the statute, exactly what governmental interest the Indiana legislators had in mind when they enacted this statute, for Indiana does not record legislative history, and the state's highest court has not shed additional light on the statute's purpose. Nonetheless, the statute's purpose of protecting societal order and morality is clear from its text and history. Public indecency statutes of this sort are of ancient origin, and presently exist in at least 47 States. Public indecency, including nudity, was a crim-

inal offense at common law, and this Court recognized the common-law roots of the offense of "gross and open indecency" in *Winters v. New York*, 333 U.S. 507, 515 (1948). Public nudity was considered an act *malum en se*. Public indecency statutes such as the one before us reflect moral disapproval of people appearing in the nude among strangers in public places.

This public indecency statute follows a long line of earlier Indiana statutes banning all public nudity. The history of Indiana's public indecency statute shows that it predates barroom nude dancing and was enacted as a general prohibition. At least as early as 1831, Indiana had a statute punishing "open and notorious lewdness, or . . . any grossly scandalous and public indecency." A gap during which no statute was in effect was filled by the Indiana Supreme Court in *Ardery v. State*, 56 Ind. 328 (1877), which held that the court could sustain a conviction for exhibition of "privates" in the presence of others. The court traced the offense to the Bible story of Adam and Eve. In 1881, a statute was enacted that would remain essentially unchanged for nearly a century:

> "Whoever, being over fourteen years of age, makes an indecent exposure of his person in a public place, or in any place where there are other persons to be offended or annoyed thereby, . . . is guilty of public indecency. . . . " 1881 Ind. Acts, ch. 37, § 90.

The language quoted above remained unchanged until it was simultaneously repealed and replaced with the present statute in 1976.

This and other public indecency statutes were designed to protect morals and public order. The traditional police power of the States is defined as the authority to provide for the public health, safety, and morals, and we have upheld such a basis for legislation. . . .

This interest is unrelated to the suppression of free expression. Some may view restricting nudity on moral grounds as necessarily related to expression. We disagree. It can be argued, of course, that almost limitless types of conduct—including appearing in the nude in public—are "expressive," and in one sense of the word this is true. People who go about in the nude in public may be expressing something about themselves by so doing. But the court rejected this expansive notion of "expressive conduct" in *O'Brien*, saying:

> "We cannot accept the view that an apparently limitless variety of conduct can be labeled 'speech' whenever the person engaging in the conduct intends thereby to express an idea."

. . .

Respondents contend that even though prohibiting nudity in public generally may not be related to suppressing expression, prohibiting the performance of nude dancing is related to expression because the state seeks to prevent its erotic message. Therefore, they reason that the application of the Indiana statute to the nude dancing in this case violates the First Amendment, because it fails the third part of the *O'Brien* test, viz: the governmental interest must be unrelated to the suppression of free expression.

But we do not think that when Indiana applies its statute to the nude dancing in these nightclubs it is proscribing nudity because of the erotic message conveyed by the dancers. Presumably numerous other erotic performances are presented at these establishments and similar clubs without any interference from the state, so long as the performers wear a scant amount of clothing. Likewise, the requirement that the dancers don pasties and a G-string does not deprive the dance of whatever erotic message it conveys; it simply makes the message slightly less graphic. The perceived evil that Indiana seeks to address is not erotic dancing, but public nudity. The appearance of people of all shapes, sizes and ages in the nude at a beach, for example, would convey little if any erotic message, yet the state still seeks to prevent it. Public nudity is the evil the state seeks to prevent, whether or not it is combined with expressive activity.

This conclusion is buttressed by a reference to the facts of *O'Brien*. . . . It was assumed that O'Brien's act in burning the certificate had a communicative element in it sufficient to bring into play the First Amendment, but it was for the noncommunicative element that he was prosecuted. So here with the Indiana statute; while the dancing to which it was applied had a communicative element, it was not the dancing that was prohibited, but simply its being done in the nude.

The fourth part of the *O'Brien* test requires that the incidental restriction on First Amendment freedom be no greater than is essential to the furtherance of the governmental interest. As indicated in the discussion above, the governmental interest served by the text of the prohibition is societal disapproval of nudity in public places and among strangers. The statutory prohibition is not a means to some greater end, but an end in itself. It is without cavil that the public indecency statute is "narrowly tailored;" Indiana's requirement that the dancers wear at least pasties and a G-string is modest, and the bare minimum necessary to achieve the state's purpose.

The judgment of the Court of Appeals accordingly is

Reversed.

JUSTICE SCALIA, concurring in the judgment.

I agree that the judgment of the Court of Appeals must be reversed. In my view, however, the challenged regulation must be upheld, not because it survives some lower level of First-Amendment scrutiny, but because, as a general law regulating conduct and not specifically directed at expression, it is not subject to First-Amendment scrutiny at all.

I

. . . On its face, [Indiana's public indecency statute] is not directed at expression in particular. As Judge Easterbrook put it in his dissent below: "Indiana does not regulate dancing. It regulates public nudity. . . . Almost the entire domain of Indiana's statute is unrelated to expression, unless we view nude beaches and topless hot dog vendors as speech." *Miller v. Civil City of South Bend*, 904 F.2d 1081, 1120 (CA7 1990) (Easterbrook, J., dissenting). The intent to convey a "message of eroticism" (or any other message) is not a necessary element of the statutory offense of public indecency; nor does one commit that statutory offense by conveying the most explicit "message of eroticism," so long as he does not commit any of the four specified acts in the process.

Indiana's statute is in the line of a long tradition of laws against public nudity, which have never been thought to run afoul of traditional understanding of "the freedom of speech." Public indecency—including public nudity—has long been an offense at common law. Indiana's first public nudity statute, Rev. Laws of Indiana, ch. 26, § 60 (1831), predated by many years the appearance of nude barroom dancing. It was general in scope, directed at all public nudity, and not just at public nude expression; and all succeeding statutes, down to the present one, have been the same. Were it the case that Indiana in *practice* targeted only expressive nudity, while turning a blind eye to nude beaches and unclothed purveyors of hot dogs and machine tools, it might be said that what posed as a regulation of conduct in general was in reality a regulation of only communicative conduct. Respondents have adduced no evidence of that. Indiana officials have brought many public indecency prosecutions for activities having no communicative element.

The dissent confidently asserts, that the purpose of restricting nudity in public places in general is to protect nonconsenting parties from offense; and argues that since only consenting, admission-paying patrons see respondents dance, that purpose cannot apply and the only remaining purpose must relate to the communicative elements of the performance. Perhaps the dissenters believe that "offense to others" *ought* to be the only reason for restricting nudity in public places generally, but there is no basis for thinking that our society has ever shared that Thoreauvian "you-may- do- what -you -like - so - long - as - it - does - not-injure-someone-else" beau ideal—much less for thinking that it was written into the Constitution. The purpose of Indiana's nudity law would be violated, I think, if 60,000 fully consenting adults crowded into the Hoosier-dome to display their genitals to one another, even if there were not an offended innocent in the crowd. Our society prohibits, and all human societies have prohibited, certain activities not because they harm others but because they are considered, in the traditional phrase, "*contra bonos mores*," i.e., immoral. In American society, such prohibitions have included, for example, sadomasochism, cock-fighting, bestiality, suicide, drug use, prostitution, and sodomy. While there may be great diversity of view on whether various of these prohibitions should exist (though I have found few ready to abandon, in principle, all of them) there is no doubt that, absent specific constitutional protection for the conduct involved, the Constitution does not prohibit them simply because they regulate "morality." The purpose of the Indiana statute, as both its text and the manner of its enforcement demonstrate, is to enforce the traditional moral belief that people should not expose their private parts indiscriminately, regardless of whether those who see them are disedified. Since that is so, the dissent has no basis for positing that, where only thoroughly edified adults are present, the purpose must be repression of communication.

II

Since the Indiana regulation is a general law not specifically targeted at expressive conduct, its application to such conduct does not in my view implicate the First Amendment.

The First Amendment explicitly protects "the freedom of speech [and] of the press"—oral and written speech—not "expressive conduct." When any law restricts speech, even for a purpose that has nothing to do with the suppression of communication (for instance, to reduce noise, to regulate election campaigns, or to prevent littering, we insist that it meet the high, First-Amendment standard of justification. But virtually *every* law restricts conduct, and virtually *any* prohibited conduct can be performed for an expressive purpose—if only expressive of the fact that the actor disagrees with the prohibition. It cannot reasonably be demanded, therefore, that every restriction of expression incidentally produced by a general law regulating conduct pass normal First-Amendment scrutiny, or even—as some of our cases have suggested,—that it be justified by

an "important or substantial" government interest. Nor do our holdings require such justification: we have never invalidated the application of a general law simply because the conduct that it reached was being engaged in for expressive purposes and the government could not demonstrate a sufficiently important state interest.

This is not to say that the First Amendment affords no protection to expressive conduct. Where the government prohibits conduct *precisely because of its communicative attributes*, we hold the regulation unconstitutional. . . .

. . .

III

While I do not think the plurality's conclusions differ greatly from my own, I cannot entirely endorse its reasoning. The plurality purports to apply to this general law, insofar as it regulates this allegedly expressive conduct, an intermediate level of First Amendment scrutiny: the government interest in the regulation must be "'important or substantial.'" As I have indicated, I do not believe such a heightened standard exists. I think we should avoid wherever possible, moreover, a method of analysis that requires judicial assessment of the "importance" of government interests—and especially of government interests in various aspects of morality.

. . .

[*Paris Adult Theatre I v.*] *Slaton* involved an exhibition which, since it was obscene and at least to some extent public, was unprotected by the First Amendment; the State's prohibition could therefore be invalidated only if it had no rational basis. We found that the State's "right . . . to maintain a decent society" provided a "legitimate" basis for regulation—even as to obscene material viewed by consenting adults. I would uphold the Indiana statute on precisely the same ground: moral opposition to nudity supplies a rational basis for its prohibition, and since the First Amendment has no application to this case no more than that is needed.

* * *

Indiana may constitutionally enforce its prohibition of public nudity even against those who choose to use public nudity as a means of communication. The State is regulating conduct, not expression, and those who choose to employ conduct as a means of expression must make sure that the conduct they select is not generally forbidden. For these reasons, I agree that the judgment should be reversed.

[JUSTICE SOUTER's concurring opinion is omitted.]

JUSTICE WHITE, with whom Justice MARSHALL, Justice BLACKMUN, and Justice STEVENS join, dissenting.

The first question presented to us in this case is whether nonobscene nude dancing performed as entertainment is expressive conduct protected by the First Amendment. The Court of Appeals held that it is, observing that our prior decisions permit no other conclusion. Not surprisingly, then, the Court now concedes that "nude dancing of the kind sought to be performed here is expressive conduct within the outer perimeters of the First Amendment. . . ." This is no more than recognizing, as the Seventh Circuit observed, that dancing is an ancient art form and "inherently embodies the expression and communication of ideas and emotions." *Miller v. Civil City of South Bend*, 904 F.2d 1081, 1087 (1990) (en banc).

. . .

The Court's analysis is erroneous in several respects. Both the Court and Justice SCALIA in his concurring opinion overlook a fundamental and critical aspect of our cases upholding the States' exercise of their police powers. None of the cases they rely upon, including *O'Brien* . . . , involved anything less than truly *general* proscriptions on individual conduct. In *O'Brien*, for example, individuals were prohibited from destroying their draft cards at any time and in any place, even in completely private places such as the home. By contrast, in this case Indiana does not suggest that its statute applies to, or could be applied to, nudity wherever it occurs, including the home. . . . By contrast, in this case Indiana does not suggest that its statute applies to, or could be applied to, nudity wherever it occurs, including the home. We do not understand the Court or Justice SCALIA to be suggesting that Indiana could constitutionally enact such an intrusive prohibition, nor do we think such a suggestion would be tenable in light of our decision in *Stanley v. Georgia*, in which we held that States could not punish the mere possession of obscenity in the privacy of one's own home.

We are told by the Attorney General of Indiana that, in *State v. Baysinger*, 272 Individual. 236, 397 N.E.2d 580 (1979), the Indiana Supreme Court held that the statute at issue here cannot and does not prohibit nudity as a part of some larger form of expression meriting protection when the communication of ideas is involved. Petitioners also state that the evils sought to be avoided by applying the statute in this case would not obtain in the case of theatrical productions, such as *Salome* or *Hair*. Neither is there any evidence that the State has attempted to apply the statute to nudity in performances such as plays, ballets or operas. . . .

Thus, the Indiana statute is not a *general* prohibition of the type we have upheld in prior cases. As a result, the Court's and Justice SCALIA'S simple references to the State's general interest in promoting societal order and morality is not sufficient justification for a statute which concededly reaches a significant amount of protected expressive activity. Instead, in applying the *O'Brien* test, we are obligated to carefully examine the reasons the State has chosen to regulate this expressive conduct in a less than general statute. In other words, when the State enacts a law which draws a line between expressive conduct which is regulated and nonexpressive conduct of the same type which is not regulated, *O'Brien* places the burden on the State to justify the distinctions it has made. Closer inquiry as to the purpose of the statute is surely appropriate.

Legislators do not just randomly select certain conduct for proscription; they have reasons for doing so and those reasons illuminate the purpose of the law that is passed. Indeed, a law may have multiple purposes. The purpose of forbidding people from appearing nude in parks, beaches, hot dog stands, and like public places is to protect others from offense. But that could not possibly be the purpose of preventing nude dancing in theaters and barrooms since the viewers are exclusively consenting adults who pay money to see these dances. The purpose of the proscription in these contexts is to protect the viewers from what the State believes is the harmful message that nude dancing communicates. This is why *Clark v. Community for Creative Non-Violence* is of no help to the State: "In *Clark* . . . the damage to the parks was the same whether the sleepers were camping out for fun, were in fact homeless, or wished by sleeping in the park to make a symbolic statement on behalf of the homeless." 904 F.2d, at 1103 (Posner, J., concurring). That cannot be said in this case: the perceived damage to the public interest caused by appearing nude on the streets or in the parks, as I have said, is not what the State seeks to avoid in preventing nude dancing in theaters and taverns. There the perceived harm is the communicative aspect of the erotic dance. . . .

The Court nevertheless holds that the third requirement of the *O'Brien* test, that the governmental interest be unrelated to the suppression of free expression, is satisfied because in applying the statute to nude dancing, the State is not "proscribing nudity because of the erotic message conveyed by the dancers." The Court suggests that this is so because the State does not ban dancing that sends an erotic message; it is only nude erotic dancing that is forbidden. The perceived evil is not erotic dancing but public nudity, which may be prohibited despite any incidental impact on expressive activity. This analysis is transparently erroneous.

In arriving at its conclusion, the Court concedes that nude dancing conveys an erotic message and concedes that the message would be muted if the dancers wore pasties and G-strings. Indeed, the emotional or erotic impact of the dance is intensified by the nudity of the performers. As Judge Posner argued in his thoughtful concurring opinion in the Court of Appeals, the nudity of the dancer is an integral part of the emotions and thoughts that a nude dancing performance evokes. The sight of a fully clothed, or even a partially clothed, dancer generally will have a far different impact on a spectator than that of a nude dancer, even if the same dance is performed. The nudity is itself an expressive component of the dance, not merely incidental "conduct." . . .

This being the case, it cannot be that the statutory prohibition is unrelated to expressive conduct. Since the State permits the dancers to perform if they wear pasties and G-strings but forbids nude dancing, it is precisely because of the distinctive, expressive content of the nude dancing performances at issue in this case that the State seeks to apply the statutory prohibition. It is only because nude dancing performances may generate emotions and feelings of eroticism and sensuality among the spectators that the State seeks to regulate such expressive activity, apparently on the assumption that creating or emphasizing such thoughts and ideas in the minds of the spectators may lead to increased prostitution and the degradation of women. But generating thoughts, ideas, and emotions is the essence of communication. The nudity element of nude dancing performances cannot be neatly pigeonholed as mere "conduct" independent of any expressive component of the dance.

That fact dictates the level of First Amendment protection to be accorded the performances at issue here. . . . Content based restrictions "will be upheld only if narrowly drawn to accomplish a compelling governmental interest." . . .

That the performances in the Kitty Kat Lounge may not be high art, to say the least, and may not appeal to the Court, is hardly an excuse for distorting and ignoring settled doctrine. The Court's assessment of the artistic merits of nude dancing performances should not be the determining factor in deciding this case. In the words of Justice Harlan, "it is largely because governmental officials cannot make principled decisions in this area that the Constitution leaves matters of taste and style so largely to the individual." *Cohen v. California.* "[W]hile the entertainment afforded by a nude ballet at Lincoln Center to those who can pay the price may differ vastly in content (as viewed by judges) or in quality (as viewed by critics), it may not differ in substance from the dance viewed by the person who . . . wants some 'entertainment' with his beer or shot of rye." *Salem Inn, Inc. v. Frank*, 501 F.2d 18, 21, n. 3 (CA2 1974), aff'd in part, *Doran v. Salem Inn, Inc.*, 422 U.S. 922 (1975).

The Court . . . do[es] not go beyond saying that the state interests asserted here are important and substantial. But even if there were compelling interests, the Indiana statute is not narrowly drawn. If the State is genuinely concerned with prostitution and associated evils, . . . it can adopt restrictions that do not interfere with the expressiveness of nonobscene nude dancing performances. For instance, the State could perhaps require that, while performing, nude performers remain at all times a certain minimum distance from spectators, that nude entertainment be limited to certain hours, or even that establishments providing such entertainment be dispersed throughout the city. Likewise, the State clearly has the authority to criminalize prostitution and obscene behavior. Banning an entire category of expressive activity, however, generally does not satisfy the narrow tailoring requirement of strict First Amendment scrutiny.

. . .

b.   Commercial Speech

Another type of speech that has traditionally received less First Amendment attention is commercial speech, or speech which proposes a commercial transaction. Although even political speech often involves a financial element—the speaker at a political rally, for example, may be paid an honorarium for her service—commercial speech "relate[s] solely to the economic interests of the speaker and its audience."[69] The Supreme Court at one time reasoned that this primary market motivation deprived commercial advertising of the usual First Amendment protection from government regulation. In *Valentine v. Chrestensen*, the Court unanimously upheld an ordinance

---

[69] Central Hudson Gas & Electric Corporation. v. Public Service Comm'n, 447 U.S. 557 (1980).

that prohibited the circulation of advertisements in the streets, refusing to enjoin its enforcement against the distribution of a leaflet promoting the commercial exhibition of a former Navy submarine.[70]

The *Chrestensen* dictum denying commercial speech First Amendment protection was later abandoned. Since a great deal of fully protected speech has a commercial motivation, the fact that an advertiser seeks financial gain cannot by itself eliminate First Amendment concerns. Moreover, advertising serves many of the purposes that other types of speech serve by providing useful information to citizens. In *Bigelow v. Virginia*, for example, the Court reversed the conviction of a newspaper editor who violated a Virginia statute by printing an advertisement for a New York abortion referral agency.[71] The decision had limited applicability to most commercial speech since the Court stressed that the advertisement contained information about the availability of abortions and therefore concerned the public's "constitutional interests." A year later, however, the Court issued a landmark decision resting on the value of commercial speech and the dangers of government paternalism towards its citizens. *Virginia State Board of Pharmacy v. Virginia Citizens Consumer Council, Inc.* invalidated a Virginia statute prohibiting licensed pharmacists from advertising the prices of prescription drugs.

---

[70] Valentine v. Chrestensen, 316 U.S. 52 (1942).
[71] Bigelow v. Virginia, 421 U.S. 809 (1975).

Virginia State Board of Pharmacy
v.
Virginia Citizens Consumer Council, Inc.
425 U.S. 748 (1976)

MR. JUSTICE BLACKMUN delivered the opinion of the Court.

The plaintiff-appellees in this case attack, as violative of the First and Fourteenth Amendments, that portion of § 54–524.35 of Va. Code Ann. (1974), which provides that a pharmacist licensed in Virginia is guilty of unprofessional conduct if he "(3) publishes, advertises or promotes, directly or indirectly, in any manner whatsoever, any amount, price, fee, premium, discount, rebate or credit terms . . . for any drugs which may be dispensed only by prescription." . . .

I

. . .

Inasmuch as only a licensed pharmacist may dispense prescription drugs in Virginia, advertising or other affirmative dissemination of prescription drug price information is effectively forbidden in the State. Some pharmacies refuse even to quote prescription drug prices over the telephone. The Board's position, however, is that this would not constitute an unprofessional publication. It is clear, nonetheless, that all advertising of such prices, in the normal sense, is forbidden. The prohibition does not extend to nonprescription drugs, but neither is it confined to prescriptions that the pharmacist compounds himself. Indeed, about 95% of all prescriptions now are filled with dosage forms prepared by the pharmaceutical manufacturer.

II

. . .

The present . . . attack on the statute is one made not by one directly subject to its prohibition, that is, a pharmacist, but by prescription drug consumers who claim that they would greatly benefit if the prohibition were lifted and advertising freely allowed. The plaintiffs are an individual Virginia resident who suffers from diseases that require her to take prescription drugs on a daily basis, and two nonprofit organizations. Their claim is that the First Amendment entitles the user of prescription drugs to receive information that pharmacists wish to communicate to them through advertising and other promotional means, concerning the prices of such drugs.

Certainly that information may be of value. Drug prices in Virginia, for both prescription and nonprescription items, strikingly vary from outlet to outlet even within the same locality. It is stipulated, for example, that in Richmond "the cost of 40 Achromycin tablets ranges from $2.59 to $6.00, a difference of 140% (Sic)," and that in the Newport News-Hampton area the cost of tetracycline ranges from $1.20 to $9.00, a difference of 650%.

. . .

III

The question first arises whether, even assuming that First Amendment protection attaches to the flow of drug price information, it is a protection enjoyed by the appellees as recipients of the information, and not solely, if at all, by the advertisers themselves who seek to disseminate that information.

Freedom of speech presupposes a willing speaker. But where a speaker exists, as is the case here, the protection afforded is to the communication, to its source and to its recipients both. This is clear from the decided cases. In *Lamont v. Postmaster General*, 381 U.S. 301 (1965), the Court upheld the First Amendment rights of citizens to receive political publications sent from abroad. More recently, in *Kleindienst v. Mandel*, 408 U.S. 753, 762–763 (1972), we acknowledged that this Court has referred a First Amendment right to "receive information and ideas," and that freedom of speech "'necessarily protects the right to receive.'" And in *Procunier v. Martinez*, 416 U.S. 396, 408–409 (1974), where censorship of prison inmates' mail was under examination, we thought it unnecessary to assess the First Amendment rights of the inmates themselves, for it was reasoned that such censorship equally infringed the rights of noninmates to whom the correspondence was addressed. There are numerous other expressions to the same effect in the Court's decisions. See, e. g., *Red Lion Broadcasting Co. v. FCC; Stanley v. Georgia; Griswold v. Connecticut*. If there is a right to advertise, there is a reciprocal right to receive the advertising, and it may be asserted by these appellees.

IV

The appellants contend that the advertisement of prescription drug prices is outside the protection of the First Amendment because it is "commercial speech." There can be no question that in past decisions the Court has given some indication that commercial speech is unprotected. In *Valentine v. Chrestensen* [316 U.S. 52 (1942)], the Court upheld a New York statute that prohibited the distribution of any "handbill, circular . . . or other advertising matter whatsoever in or upon any street." The Court concluded that, although the First Amendment would forbid the banning of all communication by handbill in the public tho-

roughfares, it imposed "no such restraint on government as respects purely commercial advertising." Further support for a "commercial speech" exception to the First Amendment may perhaps be found in *Breard v. Alexandria*, 341 U.S. 622 (1951), where the Court upheld a conviction for violation of an ordinance prohibiting door-to-door solicitation of magazine subscriptions. The Court reasoned: "The selling . . . brings into the transaction a commercial feature," and it distinguished *Martin v. Struthers*, [319 U.S. 141 (1943)], where it had reversed a conviction for door-to-door distribution of leaflets publicizing a religious meeting, as a case involving "no element of the commercial." Moreover, the Court several times has stressed that communications to which First Amendment protection was given were *not* "purely commercial." *New York Times Co. v. Sullivan*.

Since the decision in *Breard*, however, the Court has never *denied* protection on the ground that the speech in issue was "commercial speech." That simplistic approach, which by then had come under criticism or was regarded as of doubtful validity by Members of the Court, was avoided in *Pittsburgh Press Co. v. Human Relations Comm'n*, 413 U.S. 376 (1973). There the Court upheld an ordinance prohibiting newspapers from listing employment advertisements in columns according to whether male or female employees were sought to be hired. The Court, to be sure, characterized the advertisements as "classic examples of commercial speech," and a newspaper's printing of the advertisements as of the same character. The Court, however, upheld the ordinance on the ground that the restriction it imposed was permissible because the discriminatory hirings proposed by the advertisements, and by their newspaper layout, were themselves illegal.

Last Term, in *Bigelow v. Virginia*, 421 U.S. 809 (1975), the notion of unprotected "commercial speech" all but passed from the scene. We reversed a conviction for violation of a Virginia statute that made the circulation of any publication to encourage or promote the processing of an abortion in Virginia a misdemeanor. The defendant had published in his newspaper the availability of abortions in New York. The advertisement in question, in addition to announcing that abortions were legal in New York, offered the services of a referral agency in that State. We rejected the contention that the publication was unprotected because it was commercial. *Chrestensen*'s continued validity was questioned and its holding was described as "distinctly a limited one" that merely upheld "a reasonable regulation of the manner in which commercial advertising could be distributed." We concluded that "the Virginia courts erred in their assumptions that advertising, as such, was entitled to no First Amendment protection," and we observed that the "relationship of speech to the marketplace of products or of services does not make it valueless in the marketplace of ideas."

...

... [T]he question whether there is a First Amendment exception for "commercial speech" is squarely before us. Our pharmacist does not wish to editorialize on any subject, cultural, philosophical, or political. He does not wish to report any particularly newsworthy fact, or to make generalized observations even about commercial matters. The "idea" he wishes to communicate is simply this: "I will sell you the X prescription drug at the Y price." Our question, then, is whether this communication is wholly outside the protection of the First Amendment.

V

We begin with several propositions that already are settled or beyond serious dispute. It is clear, for example, that speech does not lose its First Amendment protection because money is spent to project it, as in a paid advertisement of one form or another. Speech likewise is protected even though it is carried in a form that is "sold" for profit, and even though it may involve a solicitation to purchase or otherwise pay or contribute money.

If there is a kind of commercial speech that lacks all First Amendment protection, therefore, it must be distinguished by its content. Yet the speech whose content deprives it of protection cannot simply be speech on a commercial subject. No one would contend that our pharmacist may be prevented from being heard on the subject of whether, in general, pharmaceutical prices should be regulated, or their advertisement forbidden. Nor can it be dispositive that a commercial advertisement is noneditorial, and merely reports a fact. Purely factual matter of public interest may claim protection.

Our question is whether speech which does "no more than propose a commercial transaction," is so removed from any "exposition of ideas," and from "'truth, science, morality, and arts in general, in its diffusion of liberal sentiments on the administration of Government,'" that it lacks all protection. Our answer is that it is not.

Focusing first on the individual parties to the transaction that is proposed in the commercial advertisement, we may assume that the advertiser's interest is a purely economic one. That hardly disqualifies him from protection under the First Amendment. The interests of the contestants in a labor dispute are primarily economic, but it has long been settled that both the employee and the employer are protected by the First Amendment when they express themselves on the merits of the dispute in order to influence its outcome. We know of no requirement that, in order to avail themselves of First Amendment protection, the parties to a labor dispute need address themselves to the merits of unionism in general or to any subject beyond their immediate dispute. It was observed in *Thornhill* [*v. Alabama*, 310 U.S. 88 (1940),] that "the practices in a single factory may have economic repercussions upon a whole region and affect widespread systems of marketing." Since the fate of such a "single factory" could as well turn on its ability to advertise its product as on the resolution of its labor difficulties, we see no satisfactory distinction between the two kinds of speech.

As to the particular consumer's interest in the free flow of commercial information, that interest may be as keen, if not keener by far, than his interest in the day's most urgent political debate. Appellees' case in this respect is a convincing one. Those whom the suppression of prescription drug price information hits the hardest are the poor, the sick, and particularly the aged. A disproportionate amount of their income tends to be spent on prescription drugs; yet they are the least able to learn, by shopping from pharmacist to pharmacist, where their scarce dollars are best spent. When drug prices vary as strikingly as they do, information as to who is charging what becomes more than a convenience. It could mean the alleviation of physical pain or the enjoyment of basic necessities.

Generalizing, society also may have a strong interest in the free flow of commercial information. Even an individual advertisement, though entirely "commercial," may be of general public interest. The facts of decided cases furnish illustrations: advertisements stating that referral services for legal abortions are available; that a manufacturer of artificial furs promotes his product as an alternative to the extinction by his competitors of fur-bearing mammals; and that a domestic producer advertises his product as an alternative to imports that tend to deprive American residents of their jobs. Obviously, not all commercial messages contain the same or even a very great public interest element. There are few to which such an element, however, could not be added. Our pharmacist, for example, could cast himself as a commentator on store-to-store disparities in drug prices, giving his own and those of a competitor as proof. We see little point in requiring him to do so, and little difference if he does not.

Moreover, there is another consideration that suggests that no line between publicly "interesting" or "important" commercial advertising and the opposite kind could ever be drawn. Advertising, however tasteless and excessive it sometimes may seem, is nonetheless dissemination of information as to who is producing and selling what product, for what reason, and at what price. So long as we preserve a predominantly free enterprise economy, the allocation of our resources in large measure will be made through numerous private economic decisions. It is a matter of public interest that those decisions, in the aggregate, be intelligent and well informed. To this end, the free flow of commercial information is indispensable. And if it is indispensable to the proper allocation of resources in a free enterprise system, it is also indispensable to the formation of intelligent opinions as to how that system ought to be regulated or altered. Therefore, even if the First Amendment were thought to be primarily an instrument to enlighten public decisionmaking in a democracy, we could not say that the free flow of information does not serve that goal.

Arrayed against these substantial individual and societal interests are a number of justifications for the advertising ban. These have to do principally with maintaining a high degree of professionalism on the part of licensed pharmacists. Indisputably, the State has a strong interest in maintaining that professionalism. It is exercised in a number of ways for the consumer's benefit. There is the clinical skill involved in the compounding of drugs, although, as has been noted, these now make up only a small percentage of the prescriptions filled. Yet, even with respect to manufacturer-prepared compounds, there is room for the pharmacist to serve his customer well or badly. Drugs kept too long on the shelf may lose their efficacy or become adulterated. They can be packaged for the user in such a way that the same results occur. The expertise of the pharmacist may supplement that of the prescribing physician, if the latter has not specified the amount to be dispensed or the directions that are to appear on the label. The pharmacist, a specialist in the potencies and dangers of drugs, may even be consulted by the physician as to what to prescribe. . . . A pharmacist who has a continuous relationship with his customer is in the best position, of course, to exert professional skill for the customer's protection.

Price advertising, it is argued, will place in jeopardy the pharmacist's expertise and, with it, the customer's health. It is claimed that the aggressive price competition that will result from unlimited advertising will make it impossible for the pharmacist to supply professional services in the compounding, handling, and dispensing of prescription drugs. Such services are time consuming and expensive; if competitors who economize by eliminating them are permitted to advertise their resulting lower prices, the more painstaking and conscientious pharmacist will be forced either to fol-

low suit or to go out of business. It is also claimed that prices might not necessarily fall as a result of advertising. If one pharmacist advertises, others must, and the resulting expense will inflate the cost of drugs. It is further claimed that advertising will lead people to shop for their prescription drugs among the various pharmacists who offer the lowest prices, and the loss of stable pharmacist-customer relationships will make individual attention and certainly the practice of monitoring impossible. Finally, it is argued that damage will be done to the professional image of the pharmacist. This image, that of a skilled and specialized craftsman, attracts talent to the profession and reinforces the better habits of those who are in it. Price advertising, it is said, will reduce the pharmacist's status to that of a mere retailer.

. . .

The challenge now made, however, is based on the First Amendment. This casts the Board's justifications in a different light, for on close inspection it is seen that the State's protectiveness of its citizens rests in large measure on the advantages of their being kept in ignorance. The advertising ban does not directly affect professional standards one way or the other. It affects them only through the reactions it is assumed people will have to the free flow of drug price information. There is no claim that the advertising ban in any way prevents the cutting of corners by the pharmacist who is so inclined. That pharmacist is likely to cut corners in any event. The only effect the advertising ban has on him is to insulate him from price competition and to open the way for him to make a substantial, and perhaps even excessive, profit in addition to providing an inferior service. The more painstaking pharmacist is also protected but, again, it is a protection based in large part on public ignorance.

It appears to be feared that if the pharmacist who wishes to provide low cost, and assertedly low quality, services is permitted to advertise, he will be taken up on his offer by too many unwitting customers. They will choose the low-cost, low-quality service and drive the "professional" pharmacist out of business. They will respond only to costly and excessive advertising, and end up paying the price. They will go from one pharmacist to another, following the discount, and destroy the pharmacist-customer relationship. They will lose respect for the profession because it advertises. All this is not in their best interests, and all this can be avoided if they are not permitted to know who is charging what.

There is, of course, an alternative to this highly paternalistic approach. That alternative is to assume that this information is not in itself harmful, that people will perceive their own best interests if only they are well enough informed, and that the best means to that end is to open the channels of communication rather than to close them. If they are truly open, nothing prevents the "professional" pharmacist from marketing his own assertedly superior product, and contrasting it with that of the low-cost, high-volume prescription drug retailer. But the choice among these alternative approaches is not ours to make or the Virginia General Assembly's. It is precisely this kind of choice, between the dangers of suppressing information, and the dangers of its misuse if it is freely available, that the First Amendment makes for us. Virginia is free to require whatever professional standards it wishes of its pharmacists; it may subsidize them or protect them from competition in other ways. But it may not do so by keeping the public in ignorance of the entirely lawful terms that competing pharmacists are offering. In this sense, the justifications Virginia has offered for suppressing the flow of prescription drug price information, far from persuading us that the flow is not protected by the First Amendment, have reinforced our view that it is. We so hold.

VI

In concluding that commercial speech, like other varieties, is protected, we of course do not hold that it can never be regulated in any way. Some forms of commercial speech regulation are surely permissible. We mention a few only to make clear that they are not before us and therefore are not foreclosed by this case.

There is no claim, for example, that the prohibition on prescription drug price advertising is a mere time, place, and manner restriction. We have often approved restrictions of that kind provided that they are justified without reference to the content of the regulated speech, that they serve a significant governmental interest, and that in so doing they leave open ample alternative channels for communication of the information. Whatever may be the proper bounds of time, place, and manner restrictions on commercial speech, they are plainly exceeded by this Virginia statute, which singles out speech of a particular content and seeks to prevent its dissemination completely.

Nor is there any claim that prescription drug price advertisements are forbidden because they are false or misleading in any way. Untruthful speech, commercial or otherwise, has never been protected for its own sake. Obviously, much commercial speech is not provably false, or even wholly false, but only deceptive or misleading. We foresee no obstacle to a State's dealing effectively with this problem. The First Amendment, as we construe it today, does not prohibit the State from insuring that the stream of commercial information flow cleanly as well as freely.

Also, there is no claim that the transactions proposed in the forbidden advertisements are themselves illegal in any way. Finally, the special problems of the electronic broadcast media are likewise not in this case.

What is at issue is whether a State may completely suppress the dissemination of concededly truthful information about entirely lawful activity, fearful of that information's effect upon its disseminators and its recipients. Reserving other questions, we conclude that the answer to this one is in the negative.

. . .

MR. JUSTICE STEVENS took no part in the consideration or decision of this case.

[MR. CHIEF JUSTICE BURGER's and JUSTICE STEWART's concurring opinions are omitted.]

MR. JUSTICE REHNQUIST, dissenting.

The logical consequences of the Court's decision in this case, a decision which elevates commercial intercourse between a seller hawking his wares and a buyer seeking to strike a bargain to the same plane as has been previously reserved for the free marketplace of ideas, are far reaching indeed. Under the Court's opinion the way will be open not only for dissemination of price information but for active promotion of prescription drugs, liquor, cigarettes, and other products the use of which it has previously been thought desirable to discourage. Now, however, such promotion is protected by the First Amendment so long as it is not misleading or does not promote an illegal product or enterprise. In coming to this conclusion, the Court has overruled a legislative determination that such advertising should not be allowed and has done so on behalf of a consumer group which is not directly disadvantaged by the statute in question. This effort to reach a result which the Court obviously considers desirable is a troublesome one, for two reasons. It extends standing to raise First Amendment claims beyond the previous decisions of this Court. It also extends the protection of that Amendment to purely commercial endeavors which its most vigorous champions on this Court had thought to be beyond its pale.

. . .

The Court speaks of the consumer's interest in the free flow of commercial information, particularly in the case of the poor, the sick, and the aged. It goes on to observe that "society also may have a strong interest in the free flow of commercial information." One need not disagree with either of these statements in order to feel that they should presumptively be the concern of the Virginia Legislature, which sits to balance these and other claims in the process of making laws such as the one here under attack. The Court speaks of the importance in a "predominantly free enterprise economy" of intelligent and well-informed decisions as to allocation of resources. While there is again much to be said for the Court's observation as a matter of desirable public policy, there is certainly nothing in the United States Constitution which requires the Virginia Legislature to hew to the teachings of Adam Smith in its legislative decisions regulating the pharmacy profession.

. . .

The Court concedes that legislatures may prohibit false and misleading advertisements, and may likewise prohibit advertisements seeking to induce transactions which are themselves illegal. In the final footnote the opinion tosses a bone to the traditionalists in the legal and medical professions by suggesting that because they sell services rather than drugs the holding of this case is not automatically applicable to advertising in those professions. But if the sole limitation on permissible state proscription of advertising is that it may not be false or misleading, surely the difference between pharmacists' advertising and lawyers' and doctors' advertising can be only one of degree and not of kind. I cannot distinguish between the public's right to know the price of drugs and its right to know the price of title searches or physical examinations or other professional services for which standardized fees are charged. . . .

. . .

There are undoubted difficulties with an effort to draw a bright line between "commercial speech" on the one hand and "protected speech" on the other, and the Court does better to face up to these difficulties than to attempt to hide them under labels. In this case, however, the Court has unfortunately substituted for the wavering line previously thought to exist between commercial speech and protected speech a no more satisfactory line of its own—that between "truthful" commercial speech, on the one hand, and that which is "false and misleading" on the other. The difficulty with this line is not that it wavers, but on the contrary that it is simply too Procrustean to take into account the congeries of factors which I believe could, quite consistently with the First and Fourteenth Amendments, properly influence a legislative decision with respect to commercial advertising.

The Court insists that the rule it lays down is consistent even with the view that the First Amendment is "primarily an instrument to enlighten public decisionmaking in a democracy." I had understood this view to relate to public decisionmaking as to political, social, and other public issues, rather than the decision of a particular individual as to whether to purchase one or another kind of shampoo. It is undoubtedly arguable that many people in the country regard the choice of shampoo as just as important as who may be elected to local, state, or national political office, but that does not automatically bring information about competing shampoos within the protection of the First Amendment. It is one thing to say that the line between strictly ideological and political commentaries and other kinds of commentary is difficult to draw, and that the mere fact that the former may have in it an element of commercialism does not strip it of First Amendment protection. But it is another thing to say that because that line is difficult to draw, we will stand at the other end of the spectrum and reject out of hand the observation of so dedicated a champion of the First Amendment as Mr. Justice Black that the protections of that Amendment do not apply to a "'merchant' who goes from door to door 'selling pots.'" *Breard v. City of Alexandria* (dissenting).

In the case of "our" hypothetical pharmacist, he may now presumably advertise not only the prices of prescription drugs, but may attempt to energetically promote their sale so long as he does so truthfully. Quite consistently with Virginia law requiring prescription drugs to be available only through a physician, "our" pharmacist might run any of the following representative advertisements in a local newspaper:

> "Pain getting you down? Insist that your physician prescribe Demerol. You pay a little more than for aspirin, but you get a lot more relief."
>
> "Can't shake the flu? Get a prescription for Tetracycline from your doctor today."
>
> "Don't spend another sleepless night. Ask your doctor to prescribe Seconal without delay."

Unless the State can show that these advertisements are either actually untruthful or misleading, it presumably is not free to restrict in any way commercial efforts on the part of those who profit from the sale of prescription drugs to put them in the widest possible circulation. But such a line simply makes no allowance whatever for what appears to have been a considered legislative judgment in most States that while prescription drugs are a necessary and vital part of medical care and treatment, there are sufficient dangers attending their widespread use that they simply may not be promoted in the same manner as hair creams, deodorants, and toothpaste. The very real dangers that general advertising for such drugs might create in terms of encouraging, even though not sanctioning, illicit use of them by individuals for whom they have not been prescribed, or by generating patient pressure upon physicians to prescribe them, are simply not dealt with in the Court's opinion. If prescription drugs may be advertised, they may be advertised on television during family viewing time. Nothing we know about the acquisitive instincts of those who inhabit every business and profession to a greater or lesser extent gives any reason to think that such persons will not do everything they can to generate demand for these products in much the same manner and to much the same degree as demand for other commodities has been generated.

Both Congress and state legislatures have by law sharply limited the permissible dissemi-nation of information about some commodities because of the potential harm resulting from those commodities, even though they were not thought to be sufficiently demonstrably harmful to warrant outright prohibition of their sale. Current prohibitions on television advertising of liquor and cigarettes are prominent in this category, but apparently under the Court's holding so long as the advertisements are not deceptive they may no longer be prohibited.

. . .

Virginia Pharmacy Board gave commercial speech unprecedented First Amendment protection. The Court, however, did not erase entirely the distinction between commercial speech and non-commercial speech. Rather, the Court pointed out "commonsense differences between speech that does no more than propose a commercial transaction" and other varieties of speech. For one thing, the Court noted that the First Amendment afforded no protection to false or misleading commercial speech, or to advertisements of illegal activities. Thus, although *Virginia Board of Pharmacy* ended the absolute exclusion of commercial speech from the First Amendment, it left open the possibility that content-based restrictions on this type of speech might be more easily justified. In *Central Hudson Gas & Electric Corporation. v. Public Service Commission of New York*, the Court announced a new test to determine the constitutionality of government regulations of commercial speech.

Central Hudson Gas & Electric Corporation v. Public Service Commission of New York
447 U.S. 557 (1980)

MR. JUSTICE POWELL delivered the opinion of the Court.

This case presents the question whether a regulation of the Public Service Commission of the State of New York violates the First and Fourteenth Amendments because it completely bans promotional advertising by an electrical utility.

I

In December 1973, the Commission, appellee here, ordered electric utilities in New York State to cease all advertising that "promot[es] the use of electricity." . . . The Commission declared all promotional advertising contrary to the national policy of conserving energy. It acknowledged that the ban is not a perfect vehicle for conserving energy. For example, the Commission's order prohibits promotional advertising to develop consumption during periods when demand for electricity is low. . . . Still, the Commission adopted the restriction because it was deemed likely to "result in some dampening of unnecessary growth" in energy consumption.

The Commission's order explicitly permitted "informational" advertising designed to encourage "*shifts* of consumption" from peak demand times to periods of low electricity demand. Informational advertising would not seek to increase aggregate consumption, but would invite a leveling of demand throughout any given 24-hour period. . . .

. . .

. . . The Commission's order was upheld by the trial court and at the intermediate appellate level. The New York Court of Appeals affirmed. It found little value to advertising in "the non-competitive market in which electric corporations operate." . . .

II

The Commission's order restricts only commercial speech, that is, expression related solely to the economic interests of the speaker and its audience. The First Amendment, as applied to the States through the Fourteenth Amendment, protects commercial speech from unwarranted governmental regulation. *Vir-*

ginia Pharmacy Board. Commercial expression not only serves the economic interest of the speaker, but also assists consumers and furthers the societal interest in the fullest possible dissemination of information. In applying the First Amendment to this area, we have rejected the "highly paternalistic" view that government has complete power to suppress or regulate commercial speech. "[P]eople will perceive their own best interests if only they are well enough informed, and . . . the best means to that end is to open the channels of communication rather than to close them. . . . " *Id.* Even when advertising communicates only an incomplete version of the relevant facts, the First Amendment presumes that some accurate information is better than no information at all.

Nevertheless, our decisions have recognized "the 'commonsense' distinction between speech proposing a commercial transaction, which occurs in an area traditionally subject to government regulation, and other varieties of speech." *Ohralik v. Ohio State Bar Assn.*, 436 U.S. 447, 455–456 (1978). The Constitution therefore accords a lesser protection to commercial speech than to other constitutionally guaranteed expression. The protection available for particular commercial expression turns on the nature both of the expression and of the governmental interests served by its regulation.

The First Amendment's concern for commercial speech is based on the informational function of advertising. Consequently, there can be no constitutional objection to the suppression of commercial messages that do not accurately inform the public about lawful activity. The government may ban forms of communication more likely to deceive the public than to inform it, or commercial speech related to illegal activity.[6]

. . .

In commercial speech cases, . . . a four-part analysis has developed. At the outset, we must determine whether the expression is protected by the First Amendment. For commercial speech to come within that provision, it at least must concern lawful activity and not be misleading. Next, we ask whether the asserted governmental interest is substantial. If both

inquiries yield positive answers, we must determine whether the regulation directly advances the governmental interest asserted, and whether it is not more extensive than is necessary to serve that interest.

III

We now apply this four-step analysis for commercial speech to the Commission's arguments in support of its ban on promotional advertising.

A

The Commission does not claim that the expression at issue either is inaccurate or relates to unlawful activity. Yet the New York Court of Appeals questioned whether Central Hudson's advertising is protected commercial speech. Because appellant holds a monopoly over the sale of electricity in its service area, the state court suggested that the Commission's order restricts no commercial speech of any worth. The court stated that advertising in a "noncompetitive market" could not improve the decisionmaking of consumers. The court saw no constitutional problem with barring commercial speech that it viewed as conveying little useful information.

This reasoning falls short of establishing that appellant's advertising is not commercial speech protected by the First Amendment. Monopoly over the supply of a product provides no protection from competition with substitutes for that product. Electric utilities compete with suppliers of fuel oil and natural gas in several markets, such as those for home heating and industrial power. . . . Each energy source continues to offer peculiar advantages and disadvantages that may influence consumer choice. For consumers in those competitive markets, advertising by utilities is just as valuable as advertising by unregulated firms.

Even in monopoly markets, the suppression of advertising reduces the information available for consumer decisions and thereby defeats the purpose of the First Amendment. The New York court's argument appears to assume that the providers of a monopoly service or product are willing to pay for wholly ineffective advertising. Most businesses—even regulated monopolies—are unlikely to underwrite promotional advertising that is of no interest or use to consumers. Indeed, a monopoly enterprise legitimately may wish to inform the public that it has developed new services or terms of doing business. A consumer may need information to aid his decision whether or not to use the monopoly service at all, or how much of the service he should purchase. . . .

B

The Commission offers two state interests as justifications for the ban on promotional ad-

---

[6] In most other contexts, the First Amendment prohibits regulation based on the content of the message. Two features of commercial speech permit regulation of its content. First, commercial speakers have extensive knowledge of both the market and their products. Thus, they are well situated to evaluate the accuracy of their messages and the lawfulness of the underlying activity. In addition, commercial speech, the offspring of economic self-interest, is a hardy breed of expression that is not "particularly susceptible to being crushed by overbroad regulation."

vertising. The first concerns energy conservation. Any increase in demand for electricity—during peak or off-peak periods—means greater consumption of energy. The Commission argues, and the New York court agreed, that the State's interest in conserving energy is sufficient to support suppression of advertising designed to increase consumption of electricity. In view of our country's dependence on energy resources beyond our control, no one can doubt the importance of energy conservation. Plainly, therefore, the state interest asserted is substantial.

The Commission also argues that promotional advertising will aggravate inequities caused by the failure to base the utilities' rates on marginal cost. The utilities argued to the Commission that if they could promote the use of electricity in periods of low demand, they would improve their utilization of generating capacity. The Commission responded that promotion of off-peak consumption also would increase consumption during peak periods. If peak demand were to rise, the absence of marginal cost rates would mean that the rates charged for the additional power would not reflect the true costs of expanding production. Instead, the extra costs would be borne by all consumers through higher overall rates. Without promotional advertising, the Commission stated, this inequitable turn of events would be less likely to occur. The choice among rate structures involves difficult and important questions of economic supply and distributional fairness. The State's concern that rates be fair and efficient represents a clear and substantial governmental interest.

C

Next, we focus on the relationship between the State's interests and the advertising ban. Under this criterion, the Commission's laudable concern over the equity and efficiency of appellant's rates does not provide a constitutionally adequate reason for restricting protected speech. The link between the advertising prohibition and appellant's rate structure is, at most, tenuous. The impact of promotional advertising on the equity of appellant's rates is highly speculative. Advertising to increase off-peak usage would have to increase peak usage, while other factors that directly affect the fairness and efficiency of appellant's rates remained constant. Such conditional and remote eventualities simply cannot justify silencing appellant's promotional advertising.

In contrast, the State's interest in energy conservation is directly advanced by the Commission order at issue here. There is an immediate connection between advertising and demand for electricity. Central Hudson would not contest the advertising ban unless it believed that promotion would increase its sales. Thus, we find a direct link between the state interest in conservation and the Commission's order.

D

We come finally to the critical inquiry in this case: whether the Commission's complete suppression of speech ordinarily protected by the First Amendment is no more extensive than necessary to further the State's interest in energy conservation. The Commission's order reaches all promotional advertising, regardless of the impact of the touted service on overall energy use. But the energy conservation rationale, as important as it is, cannot justify suppressing information about electric devices or services that would cause no net increase in total energy use. In addition, no showing has been made that a more limited restriction on the content of promotional advertising would not serve adequately the State's interests. . . .

The Commission's order prevents appellant from promoting electric services that would reduce energy use by diverting demand from less efficient sources, or that would consume roughly the same amount of energy as do alternative sources. In neither situation would the utility's advertising endanger conservation or mislead the public. To the extent that the Commission's order suppresses speech that in no way impairs the State's interest in energy conservation, the Commission's order violates the First and Fourteenth Amendments and must be invalidated.

The Commission also has not demonstrated that its interest in conservation cannot be protected adequately by more limited regulation of appellant's commercial expression. To further its policy of conservation, the Commission could attempt to restrict the format and content of Central Hudson's advertising. It might, for example, require that the advertisements include information about the relative efficiency and expense of the offered service, both under current conditions and for the foreseeable future. In the absence of a showing that more limited speech regulation would be ineffective, we cannot approve the complete suppression of Central Hudson's advertising.

. . .

Accordingly, the judgment of the New York Court of Appeals is

Reversed.

[MR. JUSTICE BRENNAN's concurring opinion is omitted.]

MR. JUSTICE BLACKMUN, with whom MR. JUSTICE BRENNAN joins, concurring in the judgment.

I agree with the Court that the Public Service Commission's ban on promotional advertising of electricity by public utilities is inconsistent with the First and Fourteenth

Amendments. I concur only in the Court's judgment, however, because I believe the test now evolved and applied by the Court is not consistent with our prior cases and does not provide adequate protection for truthful, nonmisleading, noncoercive commercial speech.

The Court asserts that "a four-part analysis has developed" from our decisions concerning commercial speech.... I agree with the Court that this level of intermediate scrutiny is appropriate for a restraint on commercial speech designed to protect consumers from misleading or coercive speech, or a regulation related to the time, place, or manner of commercial speech. I do not agree, however, that the Court's four-part test is the proper one to be applied when a State seeks to suppress information about a product in order to manipulate a private economic decision that the State cannot or has not regulated or outlawed directly.

Since the Court, without citing empirical data or other authority, finds a "direct link" between advertising and energy consumption, it leaves open the possibility that the State may suppress advertising of electricity in order to lessen demand for electricity. I, of course, agree with the Court that, in today's world, energy conservation is a goal of paramount national and local importance. I disagree with the Court, however, when it says that suppression of speech may be a permissible means to achieve that goal....

. . .

I seriously doubt whether suppression of information concerning the availability and price of a legally offered product is ever a permissible way for the State to "dampen" demand for or use of the product. Even though "commercial" speech is involved, such a regulatory measure strikes at the heart of the First Amendment. This is because it is a covert attempt by the State to manipulate the choices of its citizens, not by persuasion or direct regulation, but by depriving the public of the information needed to make a free choice. As the Court recognizes, the State's policy choices are insulated from the visibility and scrutiny that direct regulation would entail and the conduct of citizens is molded by the information that government chooses to give them.

If the First Amendment guarantee means anything, it means that, absent clear and present danger, government has no power to restrict expression because of the effect its message is likely to have on the public. Our cases indicate that this guarantee applies even to commercial speech....

. . .

Our prior references to the "'commonsense differences'" between commercial speech and other speech "'suggest that a different degree

of protection is necessary to insure that the flow of truthful and legitimate commercial information is unimpaired.'" *Linmark Associates, Inc. v. Willingboro*, [431 U.S. 85, 98 (1977)], quoting *Virginia Pharmacy Board*. We have not suggested that the "commonsense differences" between commercial speech and other speech justify relaxed scrutiny of restraints that suppress truthful, nondeceptive, noncoercive commercial speech. The differences articulated by the Court, justify a more permissive approach to regulation of the manner of commercial speech for the purpose of protecting consumers from deception or coercion, and these differences explain why doctrines designed to prevent "chilling" of protected speech are inapplicable to commercial speech. No differences between commercial speech and other protected speech justify suppression of commercial speech in order to influence public conduct through manipulation of the availability of information. . . .

It appears that the Court would permit the State to ban all direct advertising of air conditioning, assuming that a more limited restriction on such advertising would not effectively deter the public from cooling its homes. In my view, our cases do not support this type of suppression. If a governmental unit believes that use or overuse of air conditioning is a serious problem, it must attack that problem directly, by prohibiting air conditioning or regulating thermostat levels. Just as the Commonwealth of Virginia may promote professionalism of pharmacists directly, so too New York may *not* promote energy conservation "by keeping the public in ignorance." *Virginia Pharmacy Board*.

MR. JUSTICE STEVENS, with whom MR. JUSTICE BRENNAN joins, concurring in the judgment.

Because "commercial speech" is afforded less constitutional protection than other forms of speech, it is important that the commercial speech concept not be defined too broadly lest speech deserving of greater constitutional protection be inadvertently suppressed. The issue in this case is whether New York's prohibition on the promotion of the use of electricity through advertising is a ban on nothing but commercial speech.

In my judgment one of the two definitions the Court uses in addressing that issue is too broad and the other may be somewhat too narrow. The Court first describes commercial speech as "expression related solely to the economic interests of the speaker and its audience." Although it is not entirely clear whether this definition uses the subject matter of the speech or the motivation of the speaker as the limiting factor, it seems clear to me that it encompasses speech that is entitled to the maximum protection afforded by the First Amendment. Neither a labor leader's exhortation to strike, nor an economist's dissertation on the money supply, should receive any lesser protection because the subject matter concerns only the economic interests of the audience. Nor should the economic motivation of a speaker qualify his constitutional protection; even Shakespeare may have been motivated by the prospect of pecuniary reward. Thus, the Court's first definition of commercial speech is unquestionably too broad.

The Court's second definition refers to "'speech proposing a commercial transaction.'" A salesman's solicitation, a broker's offer, and a manufacturer's publication of a price list or the terms of his standard warranty would unquestionably fit within this concept. Presumably, the definition is intended to encompass advertising that advises possible buyers of the availability of specific products at specific prices and describes the advantages of purchasing such items. Perhaps it also extends to other communications that do little more than make the name of a product or a service more familiar to the general public. Whatever the precise contours of the concept, and perhaps it is too early to enunciate an exact formulation, I am persuaded that it should not include the entire range of communication that is embraced within the term "promotional advertising."

This case involves a governmental regulation that completely bans promotional advertising by an electric utility. This ban encompasses a great deal more than mere proposals to engage in certain kinds of commercial transactions. It prohibits all advocacy of the immediate or future use of electricity. It curtails expression by an informed and interested group of persons of their point of view on questions relating to the production and consumption of electrical energy—questions frequently discussed and debated by our political leaders. For example, an electric company's advocacy of the use of electric heat for environmental reasons, as opposed to wood-burning stoves, would seem to fall squarely within New York's promotional advertising ban and also within the bounds of maximum First Amendment protection. The breadth of the ban thus exceeds the boundaries of the commercial speech concept, however that concept may be defined.

The justification for the regulation is nothing more than the expressed fear that the audience may find the utility's message persuasive. Without the aid of any coercion, deception, or misinformation, truthful communication may persuade some citizens to consume more electricity than they otherwise would. I assume that such a consequence would be undesirable and that government may therefore prohibit and punish the unnecessary or excessive use

of electricity. But if the perceived harm associated with greater electrical usage is not sufficiently serious to justify direct regulation, surely it does not constitute the kind of clear and present danger that can justify the suppression of speech.

. . .

In sum, I concur in the result because I do not consider this to be a "commercial speech" case. Accordingly, I see no need to decide whether the Court's four-part analysis, adequately protects commercial speech—as properly defined—in the face of a blanket ban of the sort involved in this case.

MR. JUSTICE REHNQUIST, dissenting.

. . .

I

. . .

While this Court has stated that the "capacity [of speech] for informing the public does not depend upon the identity of its source," *First National Bank of Boston v. Bellotti*, 435 U.S. 765, 777 (1978), the source of the speech nevertheless may be relevant in determining whether a given message is protected under the First Amendment. When the source of the speech is a state-created monopoly such as this, traditional First Amendment concerns, if they come into play at all, certainly do not justify the broad interventionist role adopted by the Court today. . . .

. . .

The state-created monopoly status of a utility arises from the unique characteristics of the services that a utility provides. As recognized in *Cantor v. Detroit Edison Co.*, 428 U.S. 579, 595–596 (1976), "public utility regulation typically assumes that the private firm is a natural monopoly and that public controls are necessary to protect the consumer from exploitation." The consequences of this natural monopoly in my view justify much more wide-ranging supervision and control of a utility under the First Amendment than this Court held in *Bellotti* to be permissible with regard to ordinary corporations. . . . A utility, by contrast fulfills a function that serves special public interests as a result of the natural monopoly of the service provided. Indeed, the extensive regulations governing decisionmaking by public utilities suggest that for purposes of First Amendment analysis, a utility is far closer to a state-controlled enterprise than is an ordinary corporation. Accordingly, I think a State has broad discretion in determining the statements that a utility may make in that such statements emanate from the entity created by the State to provide important and unique public services. And a state regulatory body charged with the oversight of these types of services may reasonably decide to impose on the utility a special duty to conform its conduct to the agency's conception of the public interest. Thus I think it is constitutionally permissible for it to decide that promotional advertising is inconsistent with the public interest in energy conservation. I also think New York's ban on such advertising falls within the scope of permissible state regulation of an economic activity by an entity that could not exist in corporate form, say nothing of enjoy monopoly status, were it not for the laws of New York.

II

This Court has previously recognized that although commercial speech may be entitled to First Amendment protection, that protection is not as extensive as that accorded to the advocacy of ideas.... The Court's decision today fails to give due deference to this subordinate position of commercial speech. The Court in so doing returns to the bygone era of *Lochner v. New York*, in which it was common practice for this Court to strike down economic regulations adopted by a State based on the Court's own notions of the most appropriate means for the State to implement its considered policies.

I had thought by now it had become well established that a State has broad discretion in imposing economic regulations....

The Court today holds not only that commercial speech is entitled to First Amendment protection, but also that when it is protected a State may not regulate it unless its reason for doing so amounts to a "substantial" governmental interest, its regulation "directly advances" that interest, and its manner of regulation is "not more extensive than necessary" to serve the interest. The test adopted by the Court thus elevates the protection accorded commercial speech that falls within the scope of the First Amendment to a level that is virtually indistinguishable from that of noncommercial speech. I think the Court in so doing has effectively accomplished the "devitalization" of the First Amendment....

I doubt there would be any question as to the constitutionality of New York's conservation effort if the Public Service Commission had chosen to raise the price of electricity, to condition its sale on specified terms, or to restrict its production. In terms of constitutional values, I think that such controls are virtually indistinguishable from the State's ban on promotional advertising.

An ostensible justification for striking down New York's ban on promotional advertising is that this Court has previously "rejected the 'highly paternalistic' view that government has complete power to suppress or regulate commercial speech.... Whatever the merits of this view, I think the Court has carried its logic too far here.

The view apparently derives from the Court's frequent reference to the "marketplace of ideas," which was deemed analogous to the commercial market in which a laissez-faire policy would lead to optimum economic decision-making under the guidance of the "invisible hand." ... While it is true that an important objective of the First Amendment is to foster the free flow of information, identification of speech that falls within its protection is not aided by the metaphorical reference to a "marketplace of ideas." There is no reason for believing that the marketplace of ideas is free from market imperfections any more than there is to believe that the invisible hand will always lead to optimum economic decisions in the commercial market. Indeed, many types of speech have been held to fall outside the scope of the First Amendment, thereby subject to governmental regulation, despite this Court's references to a marketplace of ideas. It also has been held that the government has a greater interest in regulating some types of protected speech than others.... The Court similarly has recognized that false and misleading commercial speech is not entitled to any First Amendment protection.

The above examples illustrate that in a number of instances government may constitutionally decide that societal interests justify the imposition of restrictions on the free flow of information. When the question is whether a given commercial message is protected, I do not think this Court's determination that the information will "assist" consumers justifies judicial invalidation of a reasonably drafted state restriction on such speech when the restriction is designed to promote a concededly substantial state interest. I consequently disagree with the Court's conclusion that the societal interest in the dissemination of commercial information is sufficient to justify a restriction on the State's authority to regulate promotional advertising by utilities; indeed, in the case of a regulated monopoly, it is difficult for me to distinguish "society" from the state legislature and the Public Service Commission. Nor do I think there is any basis for concluding that individual citizens of the State will recognize the need for and act to promote energy conservation to the extent the government deems appropriate, if only the channels of communication are left open. Thus, even if I were to agree that commercial speech is entitled to some First Amendment protection, I would hold here that the State's decision to ban promotional advertising, in light of the substantial state interest at stake, is a constitutionally permissible exercise of its power to adopt regulations designed to promote the interests of its citizens.

. . .

I remain of the view that the Court unlocked a Pandora's Box when it "elevated" commercial speech to the level of traditional political speech by according it First Amendment protection in *Virginia Pharmacy Board v. Vir-*

ginia Citizens Consumer Council. The line between "commercial speech," and the kind of speech that those who drafted the First Amendment had in mind, may not be a technically or intellectually easy one to draw, but it surely produced far fewer problems than has the development of judicial doctrine in this area since *Virginia Pharmacy Board*. For in the world of political advocacy and its marketplace of ideas, there is no such thing as a "fraudulent" idea: there may be useless proposals, totally unworkable schemes, as well as very sound proposals that will receive the imprimatur of the "marketplace of ideas" through our majoritarian system of election and representative government. The free flow of information is important in this context not because it will lead to the discovery of any objective "truth," but because it is essential to our system of self-government.

The notion that more speech is the remedy to expose falsehood and fallacies is wholly out of place in the commercial bazaar, where if applied logically the remedy of one who was defrauded would be merely a statement, available upon request, reciting the Latin maxim *"caveat emptor."* But since "fraudulent speech" in this area is to be remediable under *Virginia Pharmacy Board*, the remedy of one defrauded is a lawsuit or an agency proceeding based on common-law notions of fraud that are separated by a world of difference from the realm of politics and government. What time, legal decisions, and common sense have so widely severed, I declined to join in *Virginia Pharmacy Board*, and regret now to see the Court reaping the seeds that it there sowed. For in a democracy, the economic is subordinate to the political, a lesson that our ancestors learned long ago, and that our descendants will undoubtedly have to relearn many years hence.

III

The Court concedes that the state interest in energy conservation is plainly substantial, as is the State's concern that its rates be fair and efficient. It also concedes that there is a direct link between the Commission's ban on promotional advertising and the State's interest in conservation. The Court nonetheless strikes down the ban on promotional advertising because the Commission has failed to demonstrate, under the final part of the Court's four-part test, that its regulation is no more extensive than necessary to serve the State's interest. In reaching this conclusion, the Court conjures up potential advertisements that a utility might make that conceivably would result in net energy savings. . . .

. . . Until I have mastered electrical engineering and marketing, I am not prepared to contradict by virtue of my judicial office those who assume that the ban will be successful in making a substantial contribution to conservation efforts. And I doubt that any of this Court's First Amendment decisions justify striking down the Commission's order because more steps toward conservation could have been made. This is especially true when, as here, the Commission lacks authority over oil dealers.

The Court concludes that the Commission's ban on promotional advertising must be struck down because it is more extensive than necessary: it may result in the suppression of advertising by utilities that promotes the use of electrical devices or services that cause no net increase in total energy use. The Court's reasoning in this regard, however, is highly speculative. . . . Ordinarily it is the role of the State Public Service Commission to make factual determinations concerning whether a device or service will result in a net energy savings and, if so, whether and to what extent state law permits dissemination of information about the device or service. Otherwise, as here, this Court will have no factual basis for its assertions. . . . Even assuming that the Court's speculation is correct, I do not think it follows that facial invalidation of the ban is the appropriate course. . . .

Central Hudson resurrected the critical question of commercial speech which *Virginia Pharmacy Board* had apparently put to rest: May the state promote the interests of its citizens by denying them information? May the government prohibit advertising because it fears that the public will find it persuasive? *Virginia Pharmacy Board* rejected this view of commercial speech regulation as paternalistic and suggested that commercial speech was no longer exempt from the First Amendment's distrust of government prohibition of harmful messages. The majority in *Central Hudson* concluded that New York could not reduce citizens' wasteful demand for electricity by prohibiting promotional advertising. Although *Central Hudson* ultimately struck down the Commission regulation, its reasoning suggested that government restriction of advertising promoting a lawful activity might be permissible in another case.

In *Posadas de Puerto Rico Associates v. Tourism Company of Puerto Rico*, the Court did sustain a regulation of commercial speech based on the government's interest in preventing the public from receiving a message the government deemed harmful. The majority reasoned that the legislature could shield Puerto Rican residents from casino advertising because it might induce them to gamble and need not rely on its own "counterspeech" to discourage gambling. The majority rejected the argument that the public has the right to hear competing messages about the benefits and evils of gambling and decide for itself whether or not to frequent casinos. It also rejected Justice Stevens' argument in *Central Hudson* that, if the legislature has not declared the activity at issue illegal, the activity is not harmful enough to justify restrictions on advertising. The majority's decidedly paternalistic view of government's interest in regulating commercial speech is a dramatic departure from the Court's reasoning in *Virginia Pharmacy Board.*

Posadas de Puerto Rico Associates
v.
Tourism Company of Puerto Rico
478 U.S. 328 (1986)

JUSTICE REHNQUIST delivered the opinion of the Court.

In this case we address the facial constitutionality of a Puerto Rico statute and regulations restricting advertising of casino gambling aimed at the residents of Puerto Rico. Appellant Posadas de Puerto Rico Associates, doing business in Puerto Rico as Condado Holiday Inn Hotel and Sands Casino, filed suit against appellee Tourism Company of Puerto Rico in the Superior Court of Puerto Rico, San Juan Section. Appellant sought a declaratory judgment that the statute and regulations, both facially and as applied by the Tourism Company, impermissibly suppressed commercial speech in violation of the First Amendment and the equal protection and due process guarantees of the United States Constitution. . . .

In 1948, the Puerto Rico Legislature legalized certain forms of casino gambling. The Games of Chance Act of 1948 (Act) authorized the playing of roulette, dice, and card games in licensed "gambling rooms." Bingo and slot machines were later added to the list of authorized games of chance under the Act. . . . The Act also provided that "[n]o gambling room shall be permitted to advertise or otherwise offer their facilities to the public of Puerto Rico."

. . . The two regulations at issue in this case were originally issued in 1957 for the purpose of implementing the advertising restrictions contained in § 8 of the Act. Regulation 76–218 basically reiterates the language of § 8. Regulation 76a-1(7), as amended in 1971, provides in pertinent part:

"No concessionaire, nor his agent or employee is authorized to advertise the gambling parlors to the public in Puerto Rico. The advertising of our games of chance is hereby authorized through newspapers, magazines, radio, television and other publicity media outside Puerto Rico subject to the prior editing and approval by the Tourism Development Company of the advertisement to be submitted in draft to the Company."

. . .

Because this case involves the restriction of pure commercial speech which does "no more than propose a commercial transaction," *Virginia Pharmacy Board v. Virginia Citizens Consumer Council, Inc.*, our First Amendment analysis is guided by the general principles identified in *Central Hudson Gas & Electric Corp. v. Public Service Comm'n of New York.* Under *Central Hudson*, commercial speech receives a limited form of First Amendment protection so long as it concerns a lawful activity and is not misleading or fraudulent. Once it is determined that the First Amendment applies to the particular kind of commercial speech at issue, then the speech may be restricted only if the government's interest in doing so is substantial, the restrictions directly advance the government's asserted interest, and the restrictions are no more extensive than necessary to serve that interest.

The particular kind of commercial speech at issue here, namely, advertising of casino gambling aimed at the residents of Puerto Rico, concerns a lawful activity and is not misleading or fraudulent, at least in the abstract. We must therefore proceed to the three remaining steps of the *Central Hudson* analysis in order to determine whether Puerto Rico's advertising restrictions run afoul of the First Amendment. The first of these three steps involves an assessment of the strength of the government's interest in restricting the speech. The interest at stake in this case, as determined by the Superior Court, is the reduction of demand for casino gambling by the residents of Puerto Rico. Appellant acknowledged the existence of this interest in its February 24, 1982, letter to the Tourism Company. ("The legislators wanted the tourists to flock to the casinos to gamble, but not our own people"). The Tourism Company's brief before this Court explains the legislature's belief that "[e]xcessive casino gambling among local residents . . . would produce serious harmful effects on the health, safety and welfare of the Puerto Rican citizens, such as the disruption of moral and cultural patterns, the increase in local crime, the fostering of prostitution, the development of corruption, and the infiltration of organized crime." These are some of the very same concerns, of course, that have motivated the vast majority of the 50 States to prohibit casino gambling. We have no difficulty in concluding that the Puerto Rico Legislature's interest in the health, safety, and welfare of its citizens constitutes a "substantial" governmental interest.

The last two steps of the *Central Hudson* analysis basically involve a consideration of the "fit" between the legislature's ends and the means chosen to accomplish those ends. Step three asks the question whether the challenged restrictions on commercial speech "directly advance" the government's asserted interest. In the instant case, the answer to this question is clearly "yes." The Puerto Rico Legislature obviously believed, when it enacted the advertising restrictions at issue here, that advertising of casino gambling aimed at the residents of Puerto Rico would serve to increase the demand for the product advertised. We think the legislature's belief is a reasonable one, and the fact that appellant has chosen to litigate this case all the way to this Court indicates that appellant shares the legislature's view.

Appellant argues, however, that the challenged advertising restrictions are underinclusive because other kinds of gambling such as horse racing, cockfighting, and the lottery may be advertised to the residents of Puerto Rico. Appellant's argument is misplaced for two reasons. First, whether other kinds of gambling are advertised in Puerto Rico or not, the restrictions on advertising of casino gambling "directly advance" the legislature's interest in reducing demand for games of chance. Second, the legislature's interest, as previously identified, is not necessarily to reduce demand for all games of chance, but to reduce demand for casino gambling. According to the Superior Court, horse racing, cockfighting, "picas," or small games of chance at fiestas, and the lottery "have been traditionally part of the Puerto Rican's roots," so that "the legislator could have been more flexible than in authorizing more sophisticated games which are not so widely sponsored by the people." In other words, the legislature felt that for Puerto Ricans the risks associated with casino gambling were significantly greater than those associated with the more traditional kinds of gambling in Puerto Rico. In our view, the legislature's separate classification of casino gambling, for purposes of the advertising ban, satisfies the third step of the *Central Hudson* analysis.

We also think it clear beyond peradventure that the challenged statute and regulations satisfy the fourth and last step of the *Central Hudson* analysis, namely, whether the restrictions on commercial speech are no more extensive than necessary to serve the government's interest. The narrowing constructions of the advertising restrictions announced by the Superior Court ensure that the restrictions will not affect advertising of casino gambling aimed at tourists, but will apply only to such advertising when aimed at the residents of Puerto Rico. Appellant contends, however, that the First Amendment requires the Puerto Rico Legislature to reduce demand for casino gambling among the residents of Puerto Rico not by suppressing commercial speech that might *encourage* such gambling, but by promulgating additional speech designed to *discourage* it. We reject this contention. We think it is up to the legislature to decide whether or not such a "counterspeech" policy would be as effective in reducing the demand for casino gambling as a restriction on advertising. The legislature could conclude, as it apparently did here, that residents of Puerto Rico are already aware of the risks of casino gambling, yet would nevertheless be induced by widespread advertising to engage in such potentially harmful conduct.

In short, we conclude that the statute and regulations at issue in this case, as construed by the Superior Court, pass muster under each prong of the *Central Hudson* test. We therefore hold that the Supreme Court of Puerto Rico properly rejected appellant's First Amendment claim.

Appellant argues, however, that the challenged advertising restrictions are constitutionally defective under our decisions in *Carey v. Population Services International*, 431 U.S. 678 (1977), and *Bigelow v. Virginia*, 421 U.S. 809 (1975). In *Carey*, this Court struck down a ban on any "advertisement or display" of contraceptives, and in *Bigelow*, we reversed a criminal conviction based on the advertisement of an abortion clinic. We think appellant's argument ignores a crucial distinction between the *Carey* and *Bigelow* decisions and the instant case. In *Carey* and *Bigelow*, the underlying conduct that was the subject of the advertising restrictions was constitutionally protected and could not have been prohibited by the State. Here, on the other hand, the Puerto Rico Legislature surely could have prohibited casino gambling by the residents of Puerto Rico altogether. In our view, the greater power to completely ban casino gambling necessarily includes the lesser power to ban advertising of casino gambling, and *Carey* and *Bigelow* are hence inapposite.

Appellant also makes the related argument that, having chosen to legalize casino gambling for residents of Puerto Rico, the legislature is prohibited by the First Amendment from using restrictions on advertising to accomplish its goal of reducing demand for such gambling. We disagree. In our view, appellant has the argument backwards. As we noted in the preceding paragraph, it is precisely because the government could have enacted a wholesale prohibition of the underlying conduct that it is permissible for the government to take the less intrusive step of allowing the conduct, but reducing the demand through restrictions on advertising. It would surely be a Pyrrhic victory for casino owners such as appellant to gain recognition of a First Amendment right to advertise their casinos to the residents of Puerto Rico, only to thereby force the legislature into banning casino gambling by residents altogether. It would just as surely be a strange constitutional doctrine which would concede to the legislature the authority to totally ban a product or activity, but deny to the legislature the authority to forbid the stimulation of demand for the product or activity through advertising on behalf of those who would profit from such increased demand. Legislative regulation of products or activities deemed harmful, such as cigarettes, alcoholic beverages, and prostitution, has varied from outright prohibition on the one hand, to legalization of the product or activity with restrictions on stimulation of its demand on the other hand. To rule out the latter, intermediate kind of response would require more than we find in the First Amendment.

. . .

JUSTICE BRENNAN, with whom JUSTICE MARSHALL and JUSTICE BLACKMUN join, dissenting.

I

. . .

I see no reason why commercial speech should be afforded less protection than other types of speech where, as here, the government seeks to suppress commercial speech in order to deprive consumers of accurate information concerning lawful activity. Commercial speech is considered to be different from other kinds of protected expression because advertisers are particularly well suited to evaluate "the accuracy of their messages and the lawfulness of the underlying activity," *Central Hudson*, and because "commercial speech, the offspring of economic self-interest, is a hardy breed of expression that is not 'particularly susceptible to being crushed by overbroad regulation.'" However, no differences between commercial and other kinds of speech justify protecting commercial speech less extensively where, as here, the government seeks to manipulate private behavior by depriving citizens of truthful information concerning lawful activities. . . . Accordingly, I believe that where the government seeks to suppress the dissemination of nonmisleading commercial speech relating to legal activities, for fear that recipients will act on the information provided, such regulation should be subject to strict judicial scrutiny.

II

The Court, rather than applying strict scrutiny, evaluates Puerto Rico's advertising ban under the relaxed standards normally used to test government regulation of commercial speech. Even under these standards, however, I do not believe that Puerto Rico constitutionally may suppress all casino advertising directed to its residents. . . . [T]he Court does little more than defer to what it perceives to be the determination by Puerto Rico's Legislature that a ban on casino advertising aimed at residents is reasonable. The Court totally ignores the fact that commercial speech is entitled to substantial First Amendment protection, giving the government unprecedented authority to eviscerate constitutionally protected expression.

A

The Court asserts that the Commonwealth has a legitimate and substantial interest in discouraging its residents from engaging in casino gambling. . . . Neither the statute on its face nor the legislative history indicates that the Puerto Rico Legislature thought that serious harm would result if residents were allowed to engage in casino gambling; indeed, the available evidence suggests exactly the opposite. Puerto Rico has legalized gambling casinos, and permits its residents to patronize them. Thus, the Puerto Rico Legislature has determined that permitting residents to engage in casino gambling will not produce the "serious harmful effects" that have led a majority of States to ban such activity. Residents of Puerto Rico are also permitted to engage in a variety of other gambling activities—including horse racing, "picas," cockfighting, and the Puerto

Rico lottery—all of which are allowed to advertise freely to residents. Indeed, it is surely not farfetched to suppose that the legislature chose to restrict casino advertising not because of the "evils" of casino gambling, but because it preferred that Puerto Ricans spend their gambling dollars on the Puerto Rico lottery. In any event, in light of the legislature's determination that serious harm will *not* result if residents are permitted and *encouraged* to gamble, I do not see how Puerto Rico's interest in discouraging its residents from engaging in casino gambling can be characterized as "substantial," even if the legislature had actually asserted such an interest which, of course, it has not.

The Court nevertheless sustains Puerto Rico's advertising ban because the legislature *could* have determined that casino gambling would seriously harm the health, safety, and welfare of the Puerto Rican citizens. This reasoning is contrary to this Court's long-established First Amendment jurisprudence. When the government seeks to place restrictions upon commercial speech, a court may not, as the Court implies today, simply speculate about valid reasons that the government might have for enacting such restrictions. Rather, the government ultimately bears the burden of justifying the challenged regulation, and it is incumbent upon the government to *prove* that the interests it seeks to further are real and substantial. . . .

B

Even assuming that appellee could show that the challenged restrictions are supported by a substantial governmental interest, this would not end the inquiry into their constitutionality. Appellee must still demonstrate that the challenged advertising ban directly advances Puerto Rico's interest in controlling the harmful effects allegedly associated with casino gambling. The Court proclaims that Puerto Rico's legislature "obviously believed . . . that advertising of casino gambling aimed at the residents of Puerto Rico would serve to increase the demand for the product advertised." However, even assuming that an advertising ban would effectively reduce residents' patronage of gambling casinos, it is not clear how it would directly advance Puerto Rico's interest in controlling the "serious harmful effects" the Court associates with casino gambling. In particular, it is unclear whether banning casino advertising aimed at residents would affect local crime, prostitution, the development of corruption, or the infiltration of organized crime. Because Puerto Rico actively promotes its casinos to tourists, these problems are likely to persist whether or not residents are also encouraged to gamble. Absent some showing that a ban on advertising aimed only at residents will directly advance Puerto Rico's interest in controlling the harmful effects allegedly associated with casino gambling, Puerto Rico may not constitutionally restrict protected expression in that way.

C

Finally, appellees have failed to show that Puerto Rico's interest in controlling the harmful effects allegedly associated with casino gambling "cannot be protected adequately by more limited regulation of appellant's commercial expression." Rather than suppressing constitutionally protected expression, Puerto Rico could seek directly to address the specific harms thought to be associated with casino gambling. Thus, Puerto Rico could continue carefully to monitor casino operations to guard against "the development of corruption, and the infiltration of organized crime." It could vigorously enforce its criminal statutes to combat "the increase in local crime [and] the fostering of prostitution." It could establish limits on the level of permissible betting, or promulgate additional speech designed to discourage casino gambling among residents, in order to avoid the "disruption of moral and cultural patterns," that might result if residents were to engage in excessive casino gambling. Such measures would directly address the problems appellee associates with casino gambling, while avoiding the First Amendment problems raised where the government seeks to ban constitutionally protected speech.

. . . Where the government seeks to restrict speech in order to advance an important interest, it is not, contrary to what the Court has stated, "up to the legislature" to decide whether or not the government's interest might be protected adequately by less intrusive measures. Rather, it is incumbent upon the government to prove that more limited means are not sufficient to protect its interests, and for a court to decide whether or not the government has sustained this burden. In this case, nothing suggests that the Puerto Rico Legislature ever considered the efficacy of measures other than suppressing protected expression. More importantly, there has been no showing that alternative measures would inadequately safeguard the Commonwealth's interest in controlling the harmful effects allegedly associated with casino gambling. Under these circumstances, Puerto Rico's ban on advertising clearly violates the First Amendment.

. . .

JUSTICE STEVENS, with whom JUSTICE MARSHALL and JUSTICE BLACKMUN join, dissenting.

The Court concludes that "the greater power to completely ban casino gambling necessarily includes the lesser power to ban advertising of casino gambling." Whether a State may ban all advertising of an activity that it permits but could prohibit—such as gambling, prostitution, or the consumption of marijuana or liquor—is an elegant question of constitutional law. It is not, however, appropriate to address that question in this case because Puerto Rico's rather bizarre restraints on speech are so plainly forbidden by the First Amendment.

Puerto Rico does not simply "ban advertising of casino gambling." Rather, Puerto Rico blatantly discriminates in its punishment of speech depending on the publication, audience, and words employed. . . .

With respect to the publisher, in stark, unabashed language, the Superior Court's construction favors certain identifiable publications and disfavors others. If the publication (or medium) is from outside Puerto Rico, it is very favored indeed. . . . If the publication is native to Puerto Rico, however—the San Juan Star, for instance—it is subject to a far more rigid system of restraints and controls regarding the manner in which a certain form of speech (casino ads) may be carried in its pages. Unless the Court is prepared to uphold an Illinois regulation of speech that subjects the New York Times to one standard and the Chicago Tribune to another, I do not understand why it is willing to uphold a Puerto Rico regulation that applies one standard to the New York Times and another to the San Juan Star.

With respect to the audience, the newly construed regulations plainly discriminate in terms of the intended listener or reader. Casino advertising must be "addressed to tourists." It must not "invite the residents of Puerto Rico to visit the casino." The regulation thus poses what might be viewed as a reverse privileges and immunities problem: Puerto Rico's residents are singled out for disfavored treatment in comparison to all other Americans. But nothing so fancy is required to recognize the obvious First Amendment problem in this kind of audience discrimination. I cannot imagine that this Court would uphold an Illinois regulation that forbade advertising "addressed" to Illinois residents while allowing the same advertiser to communicate his message to visitors and commuters; we should be no more willing to uphold a Puerto Rico regulation that forbids advertising "addressed" to Puerto Rico residents.

With respect to the message, the regulations now take one word of the English language—"casino"—and give it a special opprobrium. Use of that suspicious six-letter word is permitted only "where the trade name of the hotel is used even though it may contain a reference to the casino." The regulations explicitly include an important provision—"that the word casino is never used alone nor specified." . . . Singling out the use of a particular word for official sanctions raises grave First Amendment concerns, and Puerto Rico has utterly failed to justify the disfavor in which that particular six-letter word is held.

. . .

DEL: The *Posadas* notwithstanding its analytical rhetoric, deflates the standard of review articulated in *Central Hudson*. The Court refused to probe the state's interest, the relationship between means and ends, and availability of less restrictive methodologies. It thus discounted the standard of review to the point of being indistinguishable from a mere rationality criterion. Such analysis contradicts the understanding, in *Virginia Board of Pharmacy*, that commercial speech has significant social value.

c. Campaign Financing, Corporations, and the Political Process

It is well-established that Congress has power under the Constitution to regulate the election of federal officers, including the President and the Vice President. Over a century ago, the Court held in *Ex parte Yarbrough* that this congressional power includes the authority to protect the elective processes against the "two great natural and historical enemies of all republics, open violence and insidious corruption."[72] The Court reasoned that "[i]f this government is anything more than a mere aggregation of delegated agents of other states and governments, each of which is superior to the general government, it must have the power to protect the elections on which its existence depends, from violence and corruption," the latter being the consequence of "the free use of money in elections, arising from the vast growth of recent wealth. . . . " The Court repeated its approval of campaign regulation in *Burroughs v. United States*, upholding the Federal Corrupt Practices Act of 1925, which, among other things, re-

---

[72] Ex parte Yarbrough, 110 U.S. 651, 658 (1884).

quired political committees to keep records and file reports concerning all contributions and expenditures received and made by political committees for the purposes of influencing the election of candidates for federal office.[73] The Court deferred to the conclusion of Congress that public disclosure of contributions would discourage the corrupt use of money to influence elections: "The power of Congress to protect the election of President and Vice President from corruption being clear, the choice of means to that end present a question primarily addressed to the judgment of Congress."

More recently, the Watergate investigations raised similar public concern about the corruption of election campaigns. A major source of corruption was campaign financing characterized by large contributions that might influence the future policies of elected officials, as well as large expenditures by candidates that gave them an unfair advantage over less wealthy opponents. In 1974, Congress attempted to rid the federal electoral process of these corrupting influences by passing amendments to the Federal Election Campaign Act of 1971. The Amendments regulated four aspects of campaign financing: a) they limited the amount of political contributions to candidates for federal elective office by an individual or a group; b) they limited the amount of expenditures by individuals or groups "relative to a clearly identified candidate" and by a candidate from his personal or family funds, as well as placed limitations on overall campaign expenditures; c) they required political committees to keep detailed records of contributions and expenditures and to file quarterly reports; and d) they created the eight-member Federal Election Commission as the administering agency with recordkeeping, adjudicatory, and enforcement powers. An amendment of the Internal Revenue Code provides for public subsidies to presidential election campaigns.

A group of political candidates, organizations, parties, and potential contributors—ranging from the Committee for a Constitutional Presidency–McCarthy '76 to the Conservative Party of the State of New York—filed a lawsuit in the District Court for the District of Columbia seeking both a declaratory judgment that the major provisions of the Act were unconstitutional and an injunction against enforcement of those provisions. The critical question before the Court was whether the contribution and expenditure limitations violated candidates' and contributors' freedom of speech. Although election campaigns clearly concerned political speech, it was debatable whether or not spending money on campaigns constituted speech at all. Moreover, even if the regulations infringed constitutionally protected speech, they did so without regard to political message. After rejecting the argument that the *O'Brien* test applied, the Court had to decide whether the government's interest in protecting the electoral process from corruption overcame the strict scrutiny standard. The Court distinguished between the speaker and government interests at stake in the case of contributions on the one hand and expenditures on the other.

---

[73] Burroughs v. United States, 290 U.S. 534, 546–548 (1934).

Buckley v. Valeo
424 U.S. 1 (1976)

PER CURIAM.

. . .

I. CONTRIBUTION AND EXPENDITURE LIMITATIONS

. . .

The constitutional power of Congress to regulate federal elections is well established and is not questioned by any of the parties in this case. Thus, the critical constitutional questions presented here go not to the basic power of Congress to legislate in this area, but to whether the specific legislation that Congress has enacted interferes with First Amendment freedoms.

A. General Principles

The Act's contribution and expenditure limitations operate in an area of the most fundamental First Amendment activities. Discussion of public issues and debate on the qualifications of candidates are integral to the operation of the system of government established by our Constitution. The First Amendment affords the broadest protection to such political expression in order "to assure [the] unfettered interchange of ideas for the bringing about of political and social changes desired by the people." *Roth v. United States.* . . . In a republic where the people are sovereign, the ability of the citizenry to make informed choices among candidates for office is essential, for the identities of those who are elected will inevitably shape the course that we follow as a nation. . . . The First Amendment protects political association as well as political expression. . . .

It is with these principles in mind that we consider the primary contentions of the parties with respect to the Act's limitations upon the giving and spending of money in political campaigns. Those conflicting contentions could not more sharply define the basic issues before us. Appellees contend that what the Act regulates is conduct, and that its effect on speech and association is incidental at most. Appellants respond that contributions and expenditures are at the very core of political speech, and that the Act's limitations thus constitute restraints on First Amendment liberty that are both gross and direct.

. . .

We'cannot share the view that the present Act's contribution and expenditure limitations are comparable to the restrictions on conduct upheld in *O'Brien*. The expenditure of money simply cannot be equated with such conduct as destruction of a draft card. Some forms of communication made possible by the giving and spending of money involve speech alone, some involve conduct primarily, and some involve a combination of the two. Yet this Court has never suggested that the dependence of a communication on the expenditure of money operates itself to introduce a nonspeech element or to reduce the exacting scrutiny required by the First Amendment. . . .

Even if the categorization of the expenditure of money as conduct were accepted, the limitations challenged here would not meet the *O'Brien* test because the governmental interests advanced in support of the Act involve "suppressing communication." The interests served by the Act include restricting the voices of people and interest groups who have money to spend and reducing the overall scope of federal election campaigns. Although the Act does not focus on the ideas expressed by persons or groups subject to its regulations, it is aimed in part at equalizing the relative ability of all voters to affect electoral outcomes by placing a ceiling on expenditures for political expression by citizens and groups. Unlike *O'Brien*, where the Selective Service System's administrative interest in the preservation of draft cards was wholly unrelated to their use as a means of communication, it is beyond dispute that the interest in regulating the alleged "conduct" of giving or spending money "arises in some measure because the communication allegedly integral to the conduct is itself thought to be harmful."

. . .

A restriction on the amount of money a person or group can spend on political communication during a campaign necessarily reduces the quantity of expression by restricting the number of issues discussed, the depth of their exploration, and the size of the audience reached. This is because virtually every means of communicating ideas in today's mass society requires the expenditure of money. The distribution of the humblest handbill or leaflet entails printing, paper, and circulation costs. Speeches and rallies generally necessitate hiring a hall and publicizing the event. The electorate's increasing dependence on television, radio, and other mass media for news and information has made these expensive modes of communication indispensable instruments of effective political speech.

The expenditure limitations contained in the Act represent substantial rather than merely theoretical restraints on the quantity and diversity of political speech. The $1,000 ceiling on spending "relative to a clearly identified candidate," would appear to exclude all citizens and groups except candidates, political parties, and the institutional press from any significant use of the most effective modes of communication. Although the Act's limitations on expenditures by campaign organizations and political parties provide substantially greater room for discussion and debate, they would have required restrictions in the scope of a number of past congressional and Presidential campaigns and would operate to constrain campaigning by candidates who raise sums in excess of the spending ceiling.

By contrast with a limitation upon expenditures for political expression, a limitation upon the amount that any one person or group may contribute to a candidate or political committee entails only a marginal restriction upon the contributor's ability to engage in free communication. A contribution serves as a general expression of support for the candidate and his views, but does not communicate the underlying basis for the support. The quantity of communication by the contributor does not increase perceptibly with the size of his contribution, since the expression rests solely on the undifferentiated, symbolic act of contributing. At most, the size of the contribution provides a very rough index of the intensity of the contributor's support for the candidate. A limitation on the amount of money a person may give to a candidate or campaign organization thus involves little direct restraint on his political communication, for it permits the symbolic expression of support evidenced by a contribution but does not in any way infringe the contributor's freedom to discuss candidates and issues. While contributions may result in political expression if spent by a candidate or an association to present views to the voters, the transformation of contributions into political debate involves speech by someone other than the contributor.

Given the important role of contributions in financing political campaigns, contribution restrictions could have a severe impact on political dialogue if the limitations prevented candidates and political committees from amassing the resources necessary for effective advocacy. There is no indication, however, that the contribution limitations imposed by the Act would have any dramatic adverse effect on the funding of campaigns and political associations. The overall effect of the Act's contribution ceilings is merely to require candidates and political committees to raise funds from a greater number of persons and to compel people who would otherwise contribute amounts greater than the statutory limits to expend such funds on direct political expression, rather than to reduce the total amount of money potentially available to promote political expression.

The Act's contribution and expenditure limitations also impinge on protected associational freedoms. Making a contribution, like joining a political party, serves to affiliate a person with a candidate. In addition, it enables like-minded persons to pool their resources in furtherance of common political goals. The Act's contribution ceilings thus limit one important means of associating with a candidate or committee, but leave the contributor free to become a member of any political association and to assist personally in the association's efforts on behalf of candidates. And the Act's contribution limitations permit associations and candidates to aggregate large sums of money to promote effective advocacy. By contrast, the Act's $1,000 limitation on independent expenditures "relative to a clearly identified candidate" precludes most associations from effectively amplifying the voice of their adherents, the original basis for the recognition of First Amendment protection of the freedom of association. See *NAACP v. Alabama.* . . .

In sum, although the Act's contribution and expenditure limitations both implicate fundamental First Amendment interests, its expenditure ceilings impose significantly more severe restrictions on protected freedoms of political expression and association than do its limitations on financial contributions.

B. Contribution Limitations

1. The $1,000 Limitation on Contributions by Individuals and Groups to Candidates and Authorized Campaign Committees.

. . .

Appellees argue that the Act's restrictions on large campaign contributions are justified by three governmental interests. According to the parties and *amici,* the primary interest served by the limitations and, indeed, by the Act as a whole, is the prevention of corruption and the appearance of corruption spawned by the real or imagined coercive influence of large financial contributions on candidates' positions and on their actions if elected to office. Two "ancillary" interests underlying the Act are also allegedly furthered by the $1,000 limits on contributions. First, the limits serve to mute the voices of affluent persons and groups in the election process and thereby to equalize the relative ability of all citizens to affect the outcome of elections. Second, it is argued, the ceilings may to some extent act as a brake on the skyrocketing cost of political campaigns and thereby serve to open the political system more widely to candidates without access to sources of large amounts of money.

It is unnecessary to look beyond the Act's primary purpose—to limit the actuality and appearance of corruption resulting from large individual financial contributions in order to find a constitutionally sufficient justification for the $1,000 contribution limitation. Under a system of private financing of elections, a candidate lacking immense personal or family wealth must depend on financial contributions from others to provide the resources necessary to conduct a successful campaign. The increasing importance of the communications media and sophisticated mass-mailing and polling operations to effective campaigning make the raising of large sums of money an ever more essential ingredient of an effective candidacy. To the extent that large contributions are given to secure a political *quid pro quo* from current and potential office holders, the integrity of our system of representative democracy is undermined. Although the scope of such pernicious practices can never be reliably ascertained, the deeply disturbing examples surfacing after the 1972 election demonstrate that the problem is not an illusory one.

Of almost equal concern as the danger of actual *quid pro quo* arrangements is the impact of the appearance of corruption stemming from public awareness of the opportunities for abuse inherent in a regime of large individual financial contributions. . . .

The Act's $1,000 contribution limitation focuses precisely on the problem of large campaign contributions—the narrow aspect of political association where the actuality and potential for corruption have been identified—while leaving persons free to engage in independent political expression, to associate actively through volunteering their services, and to assist to a limited but nonetheless substantial extent in supporting candidates and committees with financial resources. Significantly, the Act's contribution limitations in themselves do not undermine to any material degree the potential for robust and effective discussion of candidates and campaign issues by individual citizens, associations, the institutional press, candidates, and political parties.

We find that, under the rigorous standard of review established by our prior decisions, the weighty interests served by restricting the size of financial contributions to political candidates are sufficient to justify the limited effect upon First Amendment freedoms caused by the $1,000 contribution ceiling.

. . .

C. Expenditure Limitations

The Act's expenditure ceilings impose direct and substantial restraints on the quantity of political speech. The most drastic of the limitations restricts individuals and groups, including political parties that fail to place a candidate on the ballot, to an expenditure of $1,000 "relative to a clearly identified candidate during a calendar year." Other expenditure ceilings limit spending by candidates, their campaigns, and political parties in connection with election campaigns. It is clear that a primary effect of these expenditure limitations is to restrict the quantity of campaign speech by individuals, groups, and candidates. The restrictions, while neutral as to the ideas expressed, limit political expression "at the core of our electoral process and of the First Amendment freedoms."

1. The $1,000 Limitation on Expenditures "Relative to a Clearly Identified Candidate"

Section 608(e)(1) provides that "[n]o person may make any expenditure . . . relative to a clearly identified candidate during a calendar year which, when added to all other expenditures made by such person during the year advocating the election or defeat of such candidate, exceeds $1,000." The plain effect of § 608(e)(1) is to prohibit all individuals, who are neither candidates nor owners of institutional press facilities, and all groups, except political parties and campaign organizations, from voicing their views "relative to a clearly identified candidate" through means that entail aggregate expenditures of more than $1,000 during a calendar year. The provision, for example, would make it a federal criminal offense for a person or association to place a single one-quarter page advertisement "relative to a clearly identified candidate" in a major metropolitan newspaper.

. . .

The discussion in Part I-A, explains why the Act's expenditure limitations impose far greater restraints on the freedom of speech and association than do its contribution limitations. The markedly greater burden on basic freedoms caused by § 608(e)(1) thus cannot be sustained simply by invoking the interest in maximizing the effectiveness of the less intrusive contribution limitations. Rather, the constitutionality of § 608(e)(1) turns on whether the governmental interests advanced in its support satisfy the exacting scrutiny applicable to limitations on core First Amendment rights of political expression.

We find that the governmental interest in preventing corruption and the appearance of corruption is inadequate to justify § 608(e)(1)'s ceiling on independent expenditures. First, assuming, *arguendo*, that large independent expenditures pose the same dangers of actual or apparent *quid pro quo* arrangements as do large contributions, § 608(e)(1) does not provide an answer that sufficiently relates to the elimination of those dangers. Unlike the contribution limitations' total ban on the giving of large amounts of money to candidates, § 608(e)(1) prevents only some large expenditures. So long as persons and groups eschew expenditures that in express terms advocate the election or defeat of a clearly identified candidate, they are free to spend as much as they want to promote the candidate and his views. . . .

Second, quite apart from the shortcomings of § 608(e)(1) in preventing any abuses generated by large independent expenditures, the independent advocacy restricted by the provision does not presently appear to pose dangers of real or apparent corruption comparable to those identified with large campaign contributions. . . .

While the independent expenditure ceiling thus fails to serve any substantial governmental interest in stemming the reality or appearance of corruption in the electoral process, it heavily burdens core First Amendment expression. For the First Amendment right to "'speak one's mind . . . on all public institutions'" includes the right to engage in " 'vigorous advocacy' no less than 'abstract discussion.'" *New York Times Co. v. Sullivan.* Advocacy of the election or defeat of candidates for federal office is no less entitled to protection under the First Amendment than the discussion of political policy generally or advocacy of the passage or defeat of legislation.

It is argued, however, that the ancillary governmental interest in equalizing the relative ability of individuals and groups to influence the outcome of elections serves to justify the limitation on express advocacy of the election or defeat of candidates imposed by § 608(e)(1)'s expenditure ceiling. But the concept that government may restrict the speech of some elements of our society in order to enhance the relative voice of others is wholly foreign to the First Amendment, which was designed "to secure 'the widest possible dissemination of information from diverse and antagonistic sources,'" and "'to assure unfettered interchange of ideas for the bringing about of political and social changes desired by the people.'" *New York Times Co. v. Sullivan.* The First Amendment's protection against governmental abridgment of free expression cannot properly be made to depend on a person's financial ability to engage in public discussion.

For the reasons stated, we conclude that § 608(e)(1)'s independent expenditure limitation is unconstitutional under the First Amendment.

2. Limitation on Expenditures by Candidates from Personal or Family Resources

. . .

The ceiling on personal expenditures by candidates on their own behalf, like the limitations on independent expenditures contained in § 608(e)(1), imposes a substantial restraint on the ability of persons to engage in protected First Amendment expression. The candidate, no less than any other person, has a First Amendment right to engage in the discussion of public issues and vigorously and tirelessly to advocate his own election and the election of other candidates. Indeed, it is of particular importance that candidates have the unfettered opportunity to make their views known so that the electorate may intelligently evaluate the candidates' personal qualities and their positions on vital public issues before choosing among them on election day. Mr. Justice Brandeis' observation that in our country "public discussion is a political duty," *Whitney v. California* (concurring opinion), applies with spe-

cial force to candidates for public office. Section 608(a)'s ceiling on personal expenditures by a candidate in furtherance of his own candidacy thus clearly and directly interferes with constitutionally protected freedoms.

The primary governmental interest served by the Act—the prevention of actual and apparent corruption of the political process—does not support the limitation on the candidate's expenditure of his own personal funds. As the Court of Appeals concluded: "Manifestly, the core problem of avoiding undisclosed and undue influence on candidates from outside interests has lesser application when the monies involved come from the candidate himself or from his immediate family." Indeed, the use of personal funds reduces the candidate's dependence on outside contributions and thereby counteracts the coercive pressures and attendant risks of abuse to which the Act's contribution limitations are directed.

The ancillary interest in equalizing the relative financial resources of candidates competing for elective office, therefore, provides the sole relevant rationale for § 608(a)'s expenditure ceiling. That interest is clearly not sufficient to justify the provision's infringement of fundamental First Amendment rights. First, the limitation may fail to promote financial equality among candidates. A candidate who spends less of his personal resources on his campaign may nonetheless outspend his rival as a result of more successful fundraising efforts. Indeed, a candidate's personal wealth may impede his efforts to persuade others that he needs their financial contributions or volunteer efforts to conduct an effective campaign. Second, and more fundamentally, the First Amendment simply cannot tolerate § 608(a)'s restriction upon the freedom of a candidate to speak without legislative limit on behalf of his own candidacy. We therefore hold that § 608(a)'s restriction on a candidate's personal expenditures is unconstitutional.

3. Limitations on Campaign Expenditures

No governmental interest that has been suggested is sufficient to justify the restriction on the quantity of political expression imposed by § 608(c)'s campaign expenditure limitations. The major evil associated with rapidly increasing campaign expenditures is the danger of candidate dependence on large contributions. The interest in alleviating the corrupting influence of large contributions is served by the Act's contribution limitations and disclosure provisions rather than by § 608(c)'s campaign expenditure ceilings. The Court of Appeals' assertion that the expenditure restrictions are necessary to reduce the incentive to circumvent direct contribution limits is not persuasive. There is no indication that the substantial criminal penalties for violating the contribution ceilings combined with the political repercussion of such violations will be insufficient to police the contribution provisions. . . .

The interest in equalizing the financial resources of candidates competing for federal office is no more convincing a justification for restricting the scope of federal election campaigns. Given the limitation on the size of outside contributions, the financial resources available to a candidate's campaign, like the number of volunteers recruited, will normally vary with the size and intensity of the candidate's support. There is nothing invidious, improper, or unhealthy in permitting such funds to be spent to carry the candidate's message to the electorate. Moreover, the equalization of permissible campaign expenditures might serve not to equalize the opportunities of all candidates, but to handicap a candidate who lacked substantial name recognition or exposure of his views before the start of the campaign.

The campaign expenditure ceilings appear to be designed primarily to serve the governmental interests in reducing the allegedly skyrocketing costs of political campaigns. Appellees and the Court of Appeals stressed statistics indicating that spending for federal election campaigns increased almost 300% between 1952 and 1972 in comparison with a 57.6% rise in the consumer price index during the same period. Appellants respond that during these years the rise in campaign spending lagged behind the percentage increase in total expenditures for commercial advertising and the size of the gross national product. In any event, the mere growth in the cost of federal election campaigns in and of itself provides no basis for governmental restrictions on the quantity of campaign spending and the resulting limitation on the scope of federal campaigns. The First Amendment denies government the power to determine that spending to promote one's political views is wasteful, excessive, or unwise. In the free society ordained by our Constitution it is not the government, but the people individually as citizens and candidates and collectively as associations and political committees who must retain control over the quantity and range of debate on public issues in a political campaign.

For these reasons we hold that § 608(c) is constitutionally invalid.

In sum, the provisions of the Act that impose a $1,000 limitation on contributions to a single candidate, § 608(b)(1), a $5,000 limitation on contributions by a political committee to a single candidate, § 608(b)(2), and a $25,000 limitation on total contributions by an individual during any calendar year, § 608(b)(3), are constitutionally valid. These limitations, along with the disclosure provisions, constitute the Act's primary weapons against the reality or appearance of improper influence stemming from the dependence of candidates on large campaign contributions. The contribution ceilings thus serve the basic governmental interest in safeguarding the integrity of the electoral process without directly impinging upon the rights of individual citizens and candidates to engage in political debate and discussion. By contrast, the First Amendment requires the invalidation of the Act's independent expenditure ceiling, § 608(e)(1), its limitation on a candidate's expenditures from his own personal funds, § 608(a), and its ceilings on overall campaign expenditures, § 608(c). These provisions place substantial and direct restrictions on the ability of candidates, citizens, and associations to engage in protected political expression, restrictions that the First Amendment cannot tolerate.

[The Court also upheld the Act's disclosure and recordkeeping provisions and the Internal Revenue Code's subsidies for federal presidential campaigns.]

Mr. Chief Justice Burger, concurring in part and dissenting in part.

. . .

I agree fully with that part of the Court's opinion that holds unconstitutional the limitations the Act puts on campaign expenditures which "place substantial and direct restrictions on the ability of candidates, citizens, and associations to engage in protected political expression, restrictions that the First Amendment cannot tolerate." Yet when it approves similarly stringent limitations on contributions, the Court ignores the reasons it finds so persuasive in the context of expenditures. For me contributions and expenditures are two sides of the same First Amendment coin.

By limiting campaign contributions, the Act restricts the amount of money that will be spent on political activity and does so directly. Appellees argue, as the Court notes, that these limits will "act as a brake on the skyrocketing cost of political campaigns." . . . Limiting contributions, as a practical matter, will limit expenditures and will put an effective ceiling on the amount of political activity and debate that the Government will permit to take place. The argument that the ceiling is not, after all, very low as matters now stand gives little comfort for the future, since the Court elsewhere notes the rapid inflation in the cost of political campaigning.

The Court attempts to separate the two communicative aspects of political contributions—the "moral" support that the gift itself conveys, which the Court suggests is the same whether the gift is $10 or $10,000, and the fact that money translates into communication. The Court dismisses the effect of the limitations on the second aspect of contributions: "[T]he transformation of contributions into political debate involves speech by someone other than the contributor." On this premise that contribution limitations restrict only the speech of "someone other than the contributor" rests the Court's justification for treating contributions differently from expenditures. The premise is demonstrably flawed; the contribution limitations will, in specific instances, limit exactly the same political activity that the expenditure ceilings limit, and at least one of the "expenditure" limitations the Court finds objectionable operates precisely like the "contribution" limitations.

The Court's attempt to distinguish the communication inherent in political *contributions* from the speech aspects of political expenditures simply "will not wash." We do little but engage in word games unless we recognize that people—candidates and contributors—spend money on political activity because they wish to communicate ideas, and their constitutional interest in doing so is precisely the same whether they or someone else utters the words.

. . .

Moreover, the Act or so much as the Court leaves standing creates significant inequities. A candidate with substantial personal resources is now given by the Court a clear advantage over his less affluent opponents, who are constrained by law in fundraising, because the Court holds that the "First Amendment cannot tolerate" any restrictions on spending. Minority parties, whose situation is difficult enough under an Act that excludes them from public funding, are prevented from accepting large single-donor contributions. . . . Minor parties must now compete for votes against two major parties whose expenditures will be vast. Finally, the Act's distinction between contributions in money and contributions in services remains, with only the former being subject to any limits. . . .

The Court's piecemeal approach fails to give adequate consideration to the integrated nature of this legislation. A serious question is raised, which the Court does not consider: when central segments, key operative provisions, of this Act are stricken, can what remains function in anything like the way Congress intended? The incongruities are obvious. . . . All candidates can now spend freely; affluent candidates, after today, can spend their own money without limit; yet, contributions for the ordinary candidate are severely restricted in amount—and small contributors are deterred. I cannot believe that Congress would have enacted a statutory scheme containing such incongruous and inequitable provisions.

. . .

MR. JUSTICE WHITE, concurring in part and dissenting in part.

. . .

I

. . . [T]he limitations on contributions and expenditures are challenged as invalid abridgments of the right of free speech protected by the First Amendment. I would reject these challenges. I am in agreement with the Court's judgment upholding the limitations on contributions. I dissent, however, from the Court's view that the expenditure limitations of 18 U.S.C. § 608(c) and (e) violate the First Amendment.

Concededly, neither the limitations on contributions nor those on expenditures directly or indirectly purport to control the content of political speech by candidates or by their supporters or detractors. What the Act regulates is giving and spending money, acts that have First Amendment significance not because they are themselves communicative with respect to the qualifications of the candidate, but because money may be used to defray the expenses of speaking or otherwise communicating about the merits or demerits of federal candidates for election. The act of giving money to political candidates, however, may have illegal or other undesirable consequences: it may be used to secure the express or tacit understanding that the giver will enjoy political favor if the candidate is elected. Both Congress and this Court's cases have recognized this as a mortal danger against which effective preventive and curative steps must be taken.

Since the contribution and expenditure limitations are neutral as to the content of speech and are not motivated by fear of the consequences of the political speech of particular candidates or of political speech in general, this case depends on whether the nonspeech interests of the Federal Government in regulating the use of money in political campaigns are sufficiently urgent to justify the incidental effects that the limitations visit upon the First Amendment interests of candidates and their supporters.

Despite its seeming struggle with the standard by which to judge this case, this is essentially the question the Court asks and answers in the affirmative with respect to the limitations on contributions which individuals and political committees are permitted to make to federal candidates. . . . The congressional judgment, which I would also accept, was that other steps must be taken to counter the corrosive effects of money in federal election campaigns.

It would make little sense to me, and apparently made none to Congress, to limit the amounts an individual may give to a candidate or spend with his approval but fail to limit the amounts that could be spent on his behalf. Yet the Court permits the former while striking down the latter limitation. No more than $1,000 may be given to a candidate or spent at his request or with his approval or cooperation; but otherwise, apparently, a contributor is to be constitutionally protected in spending unlimited amounts of money in support of his chosen candidate or candidates.

Let us suppose that each of two brothers

spends $1 million on TV spot announcements that he has individually prepared and in which he appears, urging the election of the same named candidate in identical words. One brother has sought and obtained the approval of the candidate; the other has not. The former may validly be prosecuted under § 608(e); under the Court's view, the latter may not, even though the candidate could scarcely help knowing about and appreciating the expensive favor. For constitutional purposes it is difficult to see the difference between the two situations. I would take the word of those who know—that limiting independent expenditures is essential to prevent transparent and widespread evasion of the contribution limits.

Proceeding from the maxim that "money talks," the Court finds that the expenditure limitations will seriously curtail political expression by candidates and interfere substantially with their chances for election. The Court concludes that the Constitution denies Congress the power to limit campaign expenses; federal candidates—and I would suppose state candidates, too—are to have the constitutional right to raise and spend unlimited amounts of money in quest of their own election.

As an initial matter, the argument that money is speech and that limiting the flow of money to the speaker violates the First Amendment proves entirely too much. Compulsory bargaining and the right to strike, both provided for or protected by federal law, inevitably have increased the labor costs of those who publish newspapers, which are in turn an important factor in the recent disappearance of many daily papers. Federal and state taxation directly removes from company coffers large amounts of money that might be spent on larger and better newspapers. The antitrust laws are aimed at preventing monopoly profits and price fixing, which gouge the consumer. It is also true that general price controls have from time to time existed and have been applied to the newspapers or other media. But it has not been suggested, nor could it be successfully, that these laws, and many others, are invalid because they siphon off or prevent the accumulation of large sums that would otherwise be available for communicative activities.

In any event, as it should be unnecessary to point out, money is not always equivalent to or used for speech, even in the context of political campaigns. . . . The judgment of Congress was that reasonably effective campaigns could be conducted within the limits established by the Act and that the communicative efforts of these campaigns would not seriously suffer. In this posture of the case, there is no sound basis for invalidating the expenditure limitations, so long as the purposes they serve are legitimate and sufficiently substantial, which in my view they are.

. . . [T]he expenditure limit imposed on candidates plays its own role in lessening the chance that the contribution ceiling will be violated. Without limits on total expenditures, campaign costs will inevitably and endlessly escalate. Pressure to raise funds will constantly build and with it the temptation to resort in "emergencies" to those sources of large sums, who, history shows, are sufficiently confident of not being caught to risk flouting contribution limits. Congress would save the candidate from this predicament by establishing a reasonable ceiling on all candidates. . . .

I have little doubt in addition that limiting the total that can be spent will ease the candidate's understandable obsession with fundraising, and so free him and his staff to communicate in more places and ways unconnected with the fundraising function. There is nothing objectionable—indeed it seems to me a weighty interest in favor of the provision in the attempt to insulate the political expression of federal candidates from the influence inevitably exerted by the endless job of raising increasingly large sums of money. I regret that the Court has returned them all to the treadmill.

It is also important to restore and maintain public confidence in federal elections. It is critical to obviate or dispel the impression that federal elections are purely and simply a function of money, that federal offices are bought and sold or that political races are reserved for those who have the facility and the stomach for doing whatever it takes to bring together those interests, groups, and individuals that can raise or contribute large fortunes in order to prevail at the polls.

. . .

. . . Similarly, § 608(a) tends to equalize access to the political arena, encouraging the less wealthy, unable to bankroll their own campaigns, to run for political office.

As with the campaign expenditure limits, Congress was entitled to determine that personal wealth ought to play a less important role in political campaigns than it has in the past. Nothing in the First Amendment stands in the way of that determination.

. . .

MR. JUSTICE MARSHALL, concurring in part and dissenting in part.

I join in all of the Court's opinion except Part I-C-2, which deals with 18 U.S.C. § 608(a). . . .

To be sure, § 608(a) affects the candidate's exercise of his First Amendment rights. But unlike the other expenditure limitations contained in the Act and invalidated by the Court—the limitation on independent expenditures relative to a clearly identified candidate, § 608(e), and the limitations on overall candidate expenditures, § 608(c)—the limitations on expenditures by candidates from personal resources contained in § 608(a) need never prevent the speaker from spending another dollar to communicate his ideas. Section 608(a) imposes no overall limit on the amount a candidate can spend; it simply limits the "contribution" a candidate may make to his own campaign. The candidate remains free to raise an unlimited amount in contributions from others. . . .

The Court views "[t]he ancillary interest in equalizing the relative financial resources of candidates" as the relevant rationale for § 608(a), and deems that interest insufficient to justify § 608(a). In my view the interest is more precisely the interest in promoting the reality and appearance of equal access to the political arena. Our ballot-access decisions serve as a reminder of the importance of the general interest in promoting equal access among potential candidates. . . .

One of the points on which all Members of the Court agree is that money is essential for effective communication in a political campaign. It would appear to follow that the candidate with a substantial personal fortune at his disposal is off to a significant "headstart." Of course, the less wealthy candidate can potentially overcome the disparity in resources through contributions from others. But ability to generate contributions may itself depend upon a showing of a financial base for the campaign or some demonstration of pre-existing support, which in turn is facilitated by expenditures of substantial personal sums. Thus the wealthy candidate's immediate access to a substantial personal fortune may give him an initial advantage that his less wealthy opponent can never overcome. And even if the advantage can be overcome, the perception that personal wealth wins elections may not only discourage potential candidates without significant personal wealth from entering the political arena, but also undermine public confidence in the integrity of the electoral process.

. . .

[Mr. Justice Blackmun dissented from the holding that the contribution limitations were valid: "I am not persuaded that the Court makes, or indeed is able to make, a principled constitutional distinction between the contribution limitations, on the one hand, and the expenditure limitations on the other, that are involved here."]

[Mr. Justice Rehnquist, concurred in the Court's holdings on contribution and expenditure limitations.]

DER: The central theme of *Buckley v. Valeo*, that the "First Amendment's protection against governmental abridgment of free expression cannot properly be made to depend on a person's financial ability to engage in public discussion" has very different meanings depending upon the baseline for constitutional protection. The Court views pre-existing wealth as the baseline which the government may not disturb. This approach interprets the First Amendment as shielding wealthy people's ability to use their money towards their expressive purposes. The case might have reached a different result, however, if the Court saw the First Amendment goal as structuring political campaigns so that personal wealth has less impact on citizens' ability to participate in public discussion. This view would be more concerned about the First Amendment imbalances stemming from gross economic inequality. On the one hand some individuals, groups and institutions can amass enormous sums of money in order to influence public debates, while most citizens simply cannot afford to participate.

The dissenting justices' points about the incongruities produced by the *per curiam* decision have merit. It does seem contradictory, for example, to restrict the amount a candidate may receive from outside contributions, but allow her to spend millions of dollars of personal wealth on her own campaign. These incongruities result from the Court's extremely narrow view of the problem of wealth in the electoral process in particular and for the meaning of free expression in general. The Court understood the problem of wealth as corruption of individual candidates, rather than its distortion of the entire democratic system. It saw spending money as an individual act of expression, rather than a reflection of the gross imbalances of communication resources in our society. The Court therefore recognized the problem of corruption stemming from too much spending on others' campaigns, but it failed to see the problem of exclusion of the poor—or even middle-class—from campaigns for lack of money. This narrow focus is part of the Court's general refusal to consider the broader implications of the maldistribution of wealth on citizens' ability to enjoy First Amendment freedoms.

DEL: The Court's distinction between expenditures and contributions, on grounds the latter is marginally relevant to First Amendment interests, is problematic. It is a categorical overstatement to assert that contributions represent undifferentiated support rather than a direct statement of values. If the political system's corruption is attributed to the distorting consequences of money, moreover, distinctions between expenditures and contributions are senseless. Forcing candidates to broaden their base of fund-raising actually has made the political process even more hostage to the imperatives of money. The need to raise capital from multiple sources has become a primary preoccupation that diverts elected officials from their duties. If the net effect is that a politician ends up in the pockets of several key supporters instead of one, and attention to official responsibilities are compromised by the heightened demands for holding on to office, reform is cosmetic at best and counter-productive at worst.

Principle that defers to expenditures, on grounds they are more closely tied to First Amendment values, has the net effect of reconfiguring the methods of corruption. Such doctrine increases the influence of political action committees and enhances the likelihood of special interest politics. It also facilitates the nationalization of local politics, as funds must be raised from groups whose interest is driven by a single issue rather than regional concern. Viewed in a broader context, the analysis adds to the factors that over the course of the past several decades have jeopardized federalism. Like "adoption of the Seventeenth Amendment (providing for direct election of Senators), the weakening of political parties on the local level, and the rise of national media," the Court's narrow view of what corrupts the electoral process helps make "Congress increasingly less representative of state and local interests, and more likely to be responsive to the demands of various national constituencies."[74]

---

[74] Garcia v. San Antonio Metropolitan Transit Authority, 469 U.S. 528, 565 n.9 (1985)(Powell, J., dissenting).

The Court continued to grapple with the problems created by the influence of concentrated wealth on the democratic process. The ability of corporations in particular to use the aggregation of capital to sway elections has long been a source of concern. American campaign finance reform was originally addressed to the concentration of corporate wealth during the post-Civil War era. In 1894, Elihu Root proposed restricting corporate campaign contributions before the New York Constitutional Convention in order to "prevent . . . the great railroad companies, the great insurance companies, the great telephone companies, the great aggregations of wealth from using their corporate funds, directly or indirectly, to send members of the legislature to these halls in order to vote for their protection and advancement of their interests as against those of the public."[75] Congress passed the Tillman Act of 1907 to combat the distorting influence of corporate wealth on the electoral process. The Act initially only prohibited corporations from contributing money to candidates for federal office, but was expanded through additional statutes to prohibit both corporations and unions from making expenditures as well as contributions in connection with federal campaigns.

The Supreme Court avoided reaching the constitutionality of these restrictions by construing them very narrowly. In the first case to address the campaign spending laws, *United States v. Congress of Industrial Organizations*, the Court interpreted the Federal Corrupt Practices Act not to apply to a union's endorsement of a congressional

---

[75] Elihu Root, Addresses on Government and Citizenship 143 (1916) quoted in United States v. UAW, 352 U.S. 567, 571 (1957).

candidate in its regular newspaper.[76] Similarly, in *Pipefitters Local Union No, 562 v. United States*, the Court construed the Act to bar only expenditures from general treasuries, which were not voluntarily donated by stockholders and union members.[77] The Court thus neglected Congress' goal of eliminating the influence of corporate and union wealth on elections, emphasizing instead Congress' secondary concern with protecting the views of minority shareholders and union members.[78] This interpretation corresponded with the provision in the Federal Election Campaign Act of 1971 that permitted corporations and unions to establish separate segregated funds with money voluntarily donated for political expenditures.

The Court did not address the First Amendment rights of corporations until its 1978 decision in *First National Bank of Boston v. Bellotti*.[79] The Court struck down a Massachusetts criminal statute prohibiting corporate expenditures to influence the vote in any referendum "other than one materially affecting any of the property, business or assets of the corporation," except those concerning the taxation of individuals. The Court rejected the state's argument that corporate spending distorts the electoral process and violates the rights of minority shareholders, reasoning that corporate speech is as valuable as the speech of individuals. The *Bellotti* Court explained:

> "If the speakers here were not corporations, no one would suggest that the State could silence their proposed speech. It is the type of speech indispensable to decisionmaking in a democracy, and this is no less true because the speech comes from a corporation rather than an individual. The inherent worth of the speech in terms of its capacity for informing the public does not depend upon the identity of its source, whether corporation, association, union, or individual."

Justices White and Rehnquist dissented on the ground that the state's creation of corporations, which afforded them special legal advantages, justified greater government regulation of corporate speech.

The Court re-opened the possibility for state restrictions on corporate campaign expenditures in *FEC v. Massachusetts Citizens for Life, Inc.*[80] Massachusetts Citizens for Life, a nonprofit corporation that supported pro-life candidates and legislation, challenged the Federal Election Campaign Act's requirement that corporations finance political expenditures through special segregated funds rather than treasury funds. The Court held that the provision was unconstitutional because it posed too burdensome an administrative hurdle on the political expression of small, nonprofit corporations. But it articulated a test for the constitutionality of restrictions on corporate expenditures that the Court applied four years later to uphold a Michigan campaign finance law. *Austin v. Michigan Chamber of Commerce* concerned the combined issues of government regulations of corporate speech and campaign financing. The Court in *Austin* not only distinguished *MCFL*, but for the first time acknowledged the systemic problem for free expression created by "the corrosive and distorting effects of immense aggregations of wealth that are accumulated with the help of the corporate form."

---

[76] United States v. Congress of Industrial Organization, 335 U.S. 106 (1948).

[77] Pipefitters Local Union No. 562 v. United States, 407 U.S. 385 (1972).

[78] See David Cole, *First Amendment Antitrust: The End of Laissez-Faire in Campaign Finance*, 9 YALE L. & POLICY REV. 236, 254–78 (1991).

[79] 435 U.S. 765 (1978).

[80] FEC v. Massachusetts Citizens for Life, Inc., 479 U.S. 238 (1986).

Austin v. Michigan Chamber of Commerce
494 U.S. 652 (1990)

JUSTICE MARSHALL delivered the opinion of the Court.

In this appeal, we must determine whether § 54(1) of the Michigan Campaign Finance Act violates either the First or the Fourteenth Amendment to the Constitution. Section 54(1) prohibits corporations from using corporate treasury funds for independent expenditures in support of, or in opposition to, any candidate in elections for state office. . . . In response to a challenge brought by the Michigan State Chamber of Commerce (Chamber), the Sixth Circuit held that § 54(1) could not be applied to the Chamber, a Michigan nonprofit corporation, without violating the First Amendment. Although we agree that expressive rights are implicated in this case, we hold that application of § 54(1) to the Chamber is constitutional because the provision is narrowly tailored to serve a compelling state interest. Accordingly, we reverse the judgment of the Court of Appeals.

I

. . . . The issue before us is only the constitutionality of the State's ban on independent expenditures. The Act defines "expenditure" as "a payment, donation, loan, pledge, or promise of payment of money or anything of ascertainable monetary value for goods, materials, services, or facilities in assistance of, or in opposition to, the nomination or election of a candidate." An expenditure is considered independent if it is "not made at the direction of, or under the control of, another person and if the expenditure is not a contribution to a committee." The Act exempts from this general prohibition against corporate political spending any expenditure made from a segregated fund. A corporation may solicit contributions to its political fund only from an enumerated list of persons associated with the corporation.

The Chamber, a nonprofit Michigan corporation, challenges the constitutionality of this statutory scheme. The Chamber comprises more than 8,000 members, three-quarters of whom are for-profit corporations. The Chamber's general treasury is funded through annual dues required of all members. Its purposes, as set out in the bylaws, are to promote economic conditions favorable to private enterprise; to analyze, compile, and disseminate information about laws of interest to the business community and to publicize to the government the views of the business community on such matters; to train and educate its members; to foster ethical business practices; to collect data on, and investigate matters of, social, civic, and

economic importance to the State; to receive contributions and to make expenditures for political purposes and to perform any other lawful political activity; and to coordinate activities with other similar organizations.

In June 1985 Michigan scheduled a special election to fill a vacancy in the Michigan House of Representatives. Although the Chamber had established and funded a separate political fund, it sought to use its general treasury funds to place in a local newspaper an advertisement supporting a specific candidate. As the Act made such an expenditure punishable as a felony, the Chamber brought suit in District Court for injunctive relief against enforcement of the Act, arguing that the restriction on expenditures is unconstitutional under both the First and the Fourteenth Amendments.

. . .

II

To determine whether Michigan's restriction on corporate political expenditures may constitutionally be applied to the Chamber, we must ascertain whether it burdens the exercise of political speech and, if it does, whether it is narrowly tailored to serve a compelling state interest. *Buckley v. Valeo.* Certainly, the use of funds to support a political candidate is "speech"; independent campaign expenditures constitute "political expression 'at the core of our electoral process and of the First Amendment freedoms.'" The mere fact that the Chamber is a corporation does not remove its speech from the ambit of the First Amendment. See, e.g., *First National Bank of Boston v. Bellotti.*

A

This Court concluded in *FEC v. Massachusetts Citizens for Life, Inc.*, 479 U.S. 238 (1986) (*MCFL*), that a federal statute requiring corporations to make independent political expenditures only through special segregated funds burdens corporate freedom of expression. The Court reasoned that the small nonprofit corporation in that case would face certain organizational and financial hurdles in establishing and administering a segregated political fund. For example, the statute required the corporation to appoint a treasurer for its segregated fund, keep records of all contributions, file a statement of organization containing information about the fund, and update that statement periodically. In addition, the corporation was permitted to solicit contributions to its segregated fund only from "members," which did not include persons who merely contributed to or indicated support for the organization. These hurdles "impose[d] administrative costs that many small entities [might] be unable to bear" and "create[d] a disincentive for such organizations to engage in political speech."

Despite the Chamber's success in administering its separate political fund, Michigan's segregated fund requirement still burdens the Chamber's exercise of expression because "the corporation is not free to use its general funds for campaign advocacy purposes." The Act imposes requirements similar to those in the federal statute involved in *MCFL*: a segregated fund must have a treasurer; and its administrators must keep detailed accounts of contributions, and file with state officials a statement of organization. In addition, a nonprofit corporation like the Chamber may solicit contributions to its political fund only from members, stockholders of members, officers or directors of members, and the spouses of any of these persons. Although these requirements do not stifle corporate speech entirely, they do burden expressive activity. Thus, they must be justified by a compelling state interest.

B

The State contends that the unique legal and economic characteristics of corporations necessitate some regulation of their political expenditures to avoid corruption or the appearance of corruption. State law grants corporations special advantages—such as limited liability, perpetual life, and favorable treatment of the accumulation and distribution of assets—that enhance their ability to attract capital and to deploy their resources in ways that maximize the return on their shareholders' investments. These state-created advantages not only allow corporations to play a dominant role in the Nation's economy, but also permit them to use "resources amassed in the economic marketplace" to obtain "an unfair advantage in the political marketplace." As the Court explained in *MCFL*, the political advantage of corporations is unfair because

> "[t]he resources in the treasury of a business corporation . . . are not an indication of popular support for the corporation's political ideas. They reflect instead the economically motivated decisions of investors and customers. The availability of these resources may make a corporation a formidable political presence, even though the power of the corporation may be no reflection of the power of its ideas."

We therefore have recognized that "the compelling governmental interest in preventing corruption support[s] the restriction of the influence of political war chests funneled through the corporate form."

The Chamber argues that this concern about corporate domination of the political process is insufficient to justify a restriction on independent expenditures. Although this Court has distinguished these expenditures from direct contributions in the context of federal laws regulating individual donors, *Buckley*, it has also recognized that a legislature might demonstrate a danger of real or apparent corruption posed by such expenditures when made by corporations to influence candidate elections. Regardless of whether this danger of "financial *quid pro quo*" corruption may be sufficient to justify a restriction on independent expenditures, Michigan's regulation aims at a different type of corruption in the political arena: the corrosive and distorting effects of immense aggregations of wealth that are accumulated with the help of the corporate form and that have little or no correlation to the public's support for the corporation's political ideas. The Act does not attempt "to equalize the relative influence of speakers on elections;" rather, it ensures that expenditures reflect actual public support for the political ideas espoused by corporations. We emphasize that the mere fact that corporations may accumulate large amounts of wealth is not the justification for § 54; rather, the unique state-conferred corporate structure that facilitates the amassing of large treasuries warrants the limit on independent expenditures. Corporate wealth can unfairly influence elections when it is deployed in the form of independent expenditures, just as it can when it assumes the guise of political contributions. We therefore hold that the State has articulated a sufficiently compelling rationale to support its restriction on independent expenditures by corporations.

C

We next turn to the question whether the Act is sufficiently narrowly tailored to achieve its goal. We find that the Act is precisely targeted to eliminate the distortion caused by corporate spending while also allowing corporations to express their political views. Contrary to the dissents' critical assumptions, the Act does not impose an absolute ban on all forms of corporate political spending but permits corporations to make independent political expenditures through separate segregated funds. Because persons contributing to such funds understand that their money will be used solely for political purposes, the speech generated accurately reflects contributors' support for the corporation's political views.

The Chamber argues that § 54(1) is substantially overinclusive, because it includes within its scope closely held corporations that do not possess vast reservoirs of capital. . . . Although some closely held corporations, just as some publicly held ones, may not have accumulated significant amounts of wealth, they receive from the State the special benefits conferred by the corporate structure and present the potential for distorting the political process. This potential for distortion justifies § 54(1)'s general applicability to all corporations. The section therefore is not substantially overbroad.

III

The Chamber contends that even if the Campaign Finance Act is constitutional with respect to for-profit corporations, it nonetheless cannot be applied to a nonprofit ideological corporation like a chamber of commerce. In *MCFL*, we held that the nonprofit organization there had "features more akin to voluntary political associations than business firms, and therefore should not have to bear burdens on independent spending solely because of [its] incorporated status." In reaching that conclusion, we enumerated three characteristics of the corporation that were "essential" to our holding. Because the Chamber does not share these crucial features, the Constitution does not require that it be exempted from the generally applicable provisions of § 54(1).

The first characteristic of Massachusetts Citizens for Life, Inc., that distinguished it from ordinary business corporations was that the organization "was formed for the express purpose of promoting political ideas, and cannot engage in business activities." . . . In contrast, the Chamber's bylaws set forth more varied purposes, several of which are not inherently political. For instance, the Chamber compiles and disseminates information relating to social, civic, and economic conditions, trains and educates its members, and promotes ethical business practices. Unlike MCFL's, the Chamber's educational activities are not expressly tied to political goals; many of its seminars, conventions, and publications are politically neutral and focus on business and economic issues. . . . The Chamber's nonpolitical activities therefore suffice to distinguish it from MCFL in the context of this characteristic.

We described the second feature of *MCFL* as the absence of "shareholders or other persons affiliated so as to have a claim on its assets or earnings. This ensures that persons connected with the organization will have no economic disincentive for disassociating with it if they disagree with its political activity." Although the Chamber also lacks shareholders, many of its members may be similarly reluctant to withdraw as members even if they disagree with the Chamber's political expression, because they wish to benefit from the Chamber's nonpolitical programs and to establish contacts with other members of the business community. The Chamber's political agenda is sufficiently distinct from its educational and outreach programs that members who disagree with the former may continue to pay dues to participate in the latter. Justice KENNEDY ignores these disincentives for withdrawing as a member of the Chamber, stating only that "[o]ne need not become a member . . . to earn a living." Certainly, members would be disinclined to terminate their involvement with the organization on the basis of less extreme disincentives than the loss of employment. Thus, we are persuaded that the Chamber's members are more similar to shareholders of a business corporation than to the members of MCFL in this respect.

The final characteristic upon which we relied in *MCFL* was the organization's independence from the influence of business corporations. On this score, the Chamber differs most greatly from the Massachusetts organization. MCFL was not established by, and had a policy of not accepting contributions from, business corporations. Thus it could not "serv[e] as [a] condui[t] for the type of direct spending that creates a threat to the political marketplace." In striking contrast, more than three-quarters of the Chamber's members are business corporations, whose political contributions and expenditures can constitutionally be regulated by the State. See *Buckley v. Valeo*. . . . Because the Chamber accepts money from for-profit corporations, it could, absent application of § 54(1), serve as a conduit for corporate political spending. In sum, the Chamber does not possess the features that would compel the State to exempt it from restriction on independent political expenditures.

. . .

Michigan identified as a serious danger the significant possibility that corporate political expenditures will undermine the integrity of the political process, and it has implemented a narrowly tailored solution to that problem. By requiring corporations to make all independent political expenditures through a separate fund made up of money solicited expressly for political purposes, the Michigan Campaign Finance Act reduces the threat that huge corporate treasuries amassed with the aid of favorable state laws will be used to influence unfairly the outcome of elections. The Michigan Chamber of Commerce does not exhibit the characteristics identified in *MCFL* that would require the State to exempt it from a generally applicable restriction on independent corporate expenditures. We therefore reverse the decision of the Court of Appeals.

JUSTICE BRENNAN, concurring.

I join the Court's opinion. As one of the "Orwellian" "censor[s]" derided by the dissents (SCALIA, J.); and as the author of our recent decision in *FEC v. Massachusetts Citizens for Life, Inc.*, I write separately to explain my views in this case.

The Michigan law at issue is not an across-the-board prohibition on political participation by corporations or even a complete ban on corporate political expenditures. Rather, the statute merely requires those corporations wishing to make independent expenditures in support of candidates to do so through segregated funds or political action committees (PAC's) rather than directly from their corporate treasuries. As the dissents observe, this restriction still must be analyzed with great solicitude and care, because independent expenditures constitute expression "'at the core of our electoral process and of the First Amendment freedoms.'" *Buckley v. Valeo*. I believe, however, that the dissents significantly overstate their case in several important respects and that the Court's decision today is faithful to our prior opinions in the campaign financing area, particularly *MCFL*.

. . .

The PAC requirement may be unconstitutional as applied to some corporations because they do not present the dangers at which expenditure limitations are aimed. Indeed, we determined that Massachusetts Citizens for Life—the antiabortion advocacy organization at issue in *MCFL*—fell into this category. We nevertheless predicted that the class of exempt organizations would be small, and we set out three features of *MCFL* that were "essential" to our holding that it could not be bound by the restriction on independent spending. . . .

The majority today persuasively demonstrates that the situation in this case is markedly different from that in *MCFL*. The Michigan State Chamber of Commerce (Chamber) is first and foremost a business association, not a political advocacy organization. The Michigan statute advances the interest identified in *MCFL* in two distinct ways, by preventing both the Chamber *and other business corporations* from using the funds of other persons for purposes that those persons may not support. First, the state law protects the small businessperson who does not wish his or her dues to be spent in support of political candidates, but who nevertheless wishes to maintain an association with the Chamber because of the myriad benefits it provides that are unrelated to its political activities. . . .

In addition, the Michigan law protects dissenting shareholders of business corporations that are members of the Chamber to the extent that such shareholders oppose the use of their money, paid as dues to the Chamber out of general corporate treasury funds, for political campaigns. . . .

The Michigan law is concededly "underinclusive" insofar as it does not ban other types of political expenditures to which a dissenting Chamber member or corporate shareholder might object. The particular provision at issue prohibits corporations from using treasury funds only for making independent expenditures in support of, or in opposition to, any candidate in state elections. A corporation remains free, for example, to use general treasury funds to support an initiative proposal in a state referendum. See *First National Bank of Boston v. Bellotti*.

I do not find this underinclusiveness fatal, for several reasons. First, as the dissents recognize, discussions on candidate elections lie "at the heart of political debate." But just as speech interests are at their zenith in this area, so too are the interests of unwilling Chamber members and corporate shareholders forced to subsidize that speech. The State's decision to focus on this especially sensitive context is a justifiable one. Second, in light of our decisions in *Bellotti* . . . and related cases, a State cannot prohibit corporations from making many other types of political expenditures. One purpose of the underinclusiveness inquiry is to ensure that the proffered state interest actually underlies the law.

JUSTICE STEVENS, concurring.

In my opinion the distinction between individual expenditures and individual contributions that the Court identified in *Buckley v. Valeo*, should have little, if any, weight in reviewing corporate participation in candidate elections. In that context, I believe the danger of either the fact, or the appearance, of quid pro quo relationships provides an adequate justification for state regulation of both expenditures and contributions. Moreover, as we recognized in *First National Bank of Boston v. Bellotti*, there is a vast difference between lobbying and debating public issues on the one hand, and political campaigns for election to public office on the other. Accordingly, I join the Court's opinion and judgment.

JUSTICE SCALIA, dissenting.

"Attention all citizens. To assure the fairness of elections by preventing disproportionate expression of the views of any single powerful group, your Government has decided that the following associations of persons shall be prohibited from speaking or writing in support of any candidate: _____." In permitting Michigan to make private corporations the first object of this Orwellian announcement, the Court today endorses the principle that too much speech is an evil that the democratic majority can proscribe. I dissent because that principle is contrary to our case law and incompatible with the absolutely central truth of the First Amendment: that government cannot be trusted to assure, through censorship, the "fairness" of political debate.

I

A

The Court's opinion says that political speech of corporations can be regulated because "[s]tate law grants [them] special advantages," and because this "unique state-conferred corporate structure . . . facilitates the amassing of large treasuries." This analysis seeks to create one good argument by combining two bad ones. Those individuals who form that type of voluntary association known as a corporation are, to be sure, given special advantages—notably, the immunization of their personal fortunes from liability for the actions of the association—that the State is under no obligation to confer. But so are other associations and private individuals given all sorts of special advantages that the State need not confer, ranging from tax breaks to contract awards to public employment to outright cash subsidies. It is rudimentary that the State cannot exact as the price of those special advantages the forfeiture of First Amendment rights. The categorical suspension of the right of any person, or of any association of persons, to speak out on political matters must be justified by a compelling state need. That is why the Court puts forward its second bad argument, the fact that corporations "amas[s] large treasuries." But that alone is also not sufficient justification for the suppression of political speech, unless one thinks it would be lawful to prohibit men and women whose net worth is above a certain figure from endorsing political candidates. Neither of these two flawed arguments is improved by combining them and saying, as the Court in effect does, that "since the State gives special advantages to these voluntary associations, and since they thereby amass vast wealth, they may be required to abandon their right of political speech."

. . .

We held in *Buckley v. Valeo* . . . that independent expenditures to express the political views of individuals and associations do not raise a sufficient threat of corruption to justify prohibition. . . . *Buckley v. Valeo* should not be overruled, because it is entirely correct. The contention that prohibiting overt advocacy for or against a political candidate satisfies a "compelling need" to avoid "corruption" is easily dismissed. . . . Independent advocacy, moreover, unlike contributions, "may well provide little assistance to the candidate's campaign and indeed may prove counterproductive," thus reducing the danger that it will be exchanged "as a *quid pro quo* for improper commitments from the candidate." The latter point seems even more plainly true with respect to corporate advocates than it is with respect to individuals. I expect I could count on the fingers of one hand the candidates who would generally welcome, much less negotiate for, a formal endorsement by AT&T or General Motors. The advocacy of such entities that have "amassed great wealth" will be effective only to the extent that it brings

to the people's attention *ideas* which—despite the invariably self-interested and probably uncongenial source—strike them as true.

The Court does not try to defend the proposition that independent advocacy poses a substantial risk of political "corruption," as English speakers understand that term. Rather, it asserts that that concept (which it defines as "'financial *quid pro quo*' corruption," is really just a narrow subspecies of a hitherto unrecognized genus of political corruption. "Michigan's regulation," we are told, "aims at a different type of corruption in the political arena: the corrosive and distorting effects of immense aggregations of wealth that are accumulated with the help of the corporate form and that have little or no correlation to the public's support for the corporations's political ideas." Under this mode of analysis, virtually anything the Court deems politically undesirable can be turned into political corruption—by simply describing its effects as politically "corrosive," which is close enough to "corruptive" to qualify. It is sad to think that the First Amendment will ultimately be brought down not by brute force but by poetic metaphor.

The Court's opinion ultimately rests upon that proposition whose violation constitutes the "New Corruption": Expenditures must "reflect actual public support for the political ideas espoused." This illiberal free-speech principle of "one man, one minute" was proposed and soundly rejected in *Buckley*. . . . But it can be said that I have not accurately quoted today's decision. It does not endorse the proposition that government may ensure that expenditures "reflect actual public support for the political ideas espoused," but only the more limited proposition that government may ensure that expenditures "reflect actual public support for the political ideas espoused *by corporations*." The limitation is of course entirely irrational. Why is it perfectly all right if advocacy by an individual billionaire is out of proportion with "actual public support" for his positions?

B

JUSTICE BRENNAN'S concurrence would have us believe that the prohibition adopted by Michigan and approved by the Court is a paternalistic measure to protect the corporate shareholders of America. . . .

But even if the object of the prohibition could plausibly be portrayed as the protection of shareholders (which the Court's opinion, at least, does not even assert), that would not suffice as a "compelling need" to support this blatant restriction upon core political speech. A person becomes a member of that form of association known as a for-profit corporation in order to pursue economic objectives, *i.e.*, to make money. . . . Thus, in joining such an association, the shareholder knows that management may take any action that is ultimately in accord with what the majority (or a specified supermajority) of the shareholders wishes, so long as that action is designed to make a profit. That is the deal. The corporate actions to which the shareholder exposes himself, therefore, include many things that he may find politically or ideologically uncongenial: investment in South Africa, operation of an abortion clinic, publication of a pornographic magazine, or even publication of a newspaper that adopts absurd political views and makes catastrophic political endorsements. . . . It seems to me entirely fanciful, in other words, to suggest that the Michigan statute makes any significant contribution toward insulating the exclusively profit-motivated shareholder from the rude world of politics and ideology.

II

I would not do justice to the significance of today's decision to discuss only its lapses from case precedent and logic. Infinitely more important than that is its departure from long-accepted premises of our political system regarding the benevolence that can be expected of government in managing the arena of public debate, and the danger that is to be anticipated from powerful private institutions that compete with government, and with one another, within that arena.

Perhaps the Michigan law before us here has an unqualifiedly noble objective—to "equalize" the political debate by preventing disproportionate expression of corporations' points of view. . . . The premise of our Bill of Rights, however, is that there are some things—even some seemingly *desirable* things—that government cannot be trusted to do. The very first of these is establishing the restrictions upon speech that will assure "fair" political debate. The incumbent politician who says he welcomes full and fair debate is no more to be believed than the entrenched monopolist who says he welcomes full and fair competition. Perhaps the Michigan Legislature was genuinely trying to assure a "balanced" presentation of political views; on the other hand, perhaps it was trying to give unincorporated unions (a not insubstantial force in Michigan) political advantage over major employers. Or perhaps it was trying to assure a "balanced" presentation because it knows that with evenly balanced speech incumbent officeholders generally win. The fundamental approach of the First Amendment, I had always thought, was to assume the worst, and to rule the regulation of political speech "for fairness' sake" simply out of bounds.

I doubt that those who framed and adopted the First Amendment would agree that avoiding the New Corruption, that is, calibrating political speech to the degree of public opinion that supports it, is even a *desirable* objective, much less one that is important enough to qualify as a compelling state interest. Those Founders designed, of course, a system in which popular ideas would ultimately prevail; but also, through the First Amendment, a system in which true ideas could readily become popular. For the latter purpose, the calibration that the Court today endorses is precisely backwards: To the extent a valid proposition has scant public support, it should have wider rather than narrower public circulation. I am confident, in other words, that Jefferson and Madison would not have sat at these controls; but if they did, they would have turned them in the opposite direction.

Ah, but then there is the special element of corporate wealth: What would the Founders have thought of that? They would have endorsed, I think, what Tocqueville wrote in 1835:

"When the members of an aristocratic community adopt a new opinion or conceive a new sentiment, they give it a station, as it were, beside themselves, upon the lofty platform where they stand; and opinions or sentiments so conspicuous to the eyes of the multitude are easily introduced into the minds or hearts of all around. In democratic countries the governing power alone is naturally in a condition to act in this manner; but it is easy to see that its action is always inadequate, and often dangerous. . . . No sooner does a government attempt to go beyond its political sphere and to enter upon this new track than it exercises, even unintentionally, an insupportable tyranny. Worse still will be the case if the government really believes itself interested in preventing all circulation of ideas; it will then stand motionless and oppressed by the heaviness of voluntary torpor. Governments, therefore, should not be the only active powers; associations ought, in democratic nations, to stand in lieu of those powerful private individuals whom the equality of conditions has swept away." 2 A. de Tocqueville, Democracy in America 109.

While Tocqueville was discussing "circulation of ideas" in general, what he wrote is also true of candidate endorsements in particular. To eliminate voluntary associations—not only including powerful ones, but especially including powerful ones—from the public debate is either to augment the always dominant power of government or to impoverish the public debate. The case at hand is a good enough example. Why should the Michigan voters in the 93d House District be deprived of the information that private associations owning and operating a vast percentage of the industry of the State, and employing a large number of its citizens, believe that the election of a particular candidate is important to their prosperity? Contrary to the Court's suggestion, the same point cannot effectively be made through corporate PACs to which individuals may voluntarily contribute. It is important to the message that it represents the views of Michigan's leading corporations *as corporations*, occupying the "lofty platform" that they do within the economic life of the State—not just the views of some other voluntary associations to which some of the corporations' shareholders belong.

Despite all the talk about "corruption and the appearance of corruption"—evils that are not significantly implicated and that can be avoided in many other ways—it is entirely obvious that the object of the law we have approved today is not to prevent wrongdoing but to prevent speech. Since those private associations known as corporations have so much money, they will speak so much more, and their views will be given inordinate prominence in election campaigns. This is not an argument that our democratic traditions allow—neither with respect to individuals associated in corporations nor with respect to other categories of individuals whose speech may be "unduly" extensive (because they are rich) or "unduly" persuasive (because they are movie stars) or "unduly" respected (because they are clergymen). The premise of our system is that there is no such thing as too much speech—that the people are not foolish but intelligent, and will separate the wheat from the chaff. As conceded in Lincoln's aphorism about fooling "all of the people some of the time," that premise will not invariably accord with reality; but it will assuredly do so more often than the premise the Court today embraces: that a healthy democratic system can survive the legislative power to prescribe how much political speech is too much, who may speak, and who may not.

Justice KENNEDY, with whom JUSTICE O'CONNOR and JUSTICE SCALIA join, dissenting.

The majority opinion validates not one censorship of speech but two. One is Michigan's content-based law which decrees it a crime for a nonprofit corporate speaker to endorse or oppose candidates for Michigan public office. By permitting the statute to stand, the Court upholds a direct restriction on the independent expenditure of funds for political speech for the first time in its history.

The other censorship scheme, I most regret to say, is of our own creation. It is value-laden, content-based speech suppression that permits some nonprofit corporate groups, but not others, to engage in political speech. After failing to disguise its animosity and distrust for the particular kind of political speech here at issue—the qualifications of a candidate to understand economic matters—the Court adopts a rule that allows Michigan to stifle the voices of some of the most respected groups in public life on subjects central to the integrity of our democratic system. Each of these schemes is repugnant to the First Amendment and contradicts its central guarantee, the freedom to speak in the electoral process. I dissent.

I

. . .

A

The State has conceded that among those communications prohibited by its statute are the publication by a nonprofit corporation of its own assessment of a candidate's voting record. With the *imprimatur* of this Court, it is now a felony in Michigan for the Sierra Club, or the American Civil Liberties Union, or the Michigan Chamber of Commerce, to advise the public how a candidate voted on issues of urgent concern to its members. In both practice and theory, the prohibition aims at the heart of political debate.

As the majority must acknowledge, and as no party contests, the advertisement in this case is a paradigm of political speech. The Michigan statute bans it, however, along with all other communications by nonprofit corporate speakers that carry an inference of support for, or opposition to, a candidate, on the sole ground that the speaker is organized in corporate form. The Act operates to prohibit information essential to the ability of voters to evaluate candidates. In my view, this speech cannot be restricted.

Far more than the interest of the Chamber is at stake. We confront here society's interest in free and informed discussion on political issues, a discourse vital to the capacity for self-government. . . .

First, the Act prohibits corporations from speaking on a particular subject, the subject of candidate elections. It is a basic precept that the State may not confine speech to certain subjects. Content-based restrictions are the essence of censorial power.

Second, the Act discriminates on the basis of the speaker's identity. Under the Michigan law, any person or group other than a corporation may engage in political debate over candidate elections; but corporations, even nonprofit corporations that have unique views of vital importance to the electorate, must remain mute. Our precedents condemn this censorship.

The protection afforded core political speech is not diminished because the speaker is a nonprofit corporation. Even in the case of a for-profit corporation, we have upheld the right to speak on ballot issues. *Bellotti.*

. . .

B

The second censorship scheme validated by today's holding is the one imposed by the Court. In *FEC v. Massachusetts Citizens for Life, Inc.*, a First Amendment right to use corporate treasury funds was recognized for the nonprofit corporation then before us. Those who thought that the First Amendment exists to protect all points of view in candidate elections will be disillusioned by the Court's opinion today; for that protection is given only to a preferred class of nonprofit corporate speakers: small, single issue nonprofit corporations that pass the Court's own vague test for determining who are the favored participants in the electoral process. There can be no doubt that if a State were to enact a statute empowering an administrative board to determine which corporations could place candidate advertisements in newspapers and which could not, with authority to enforce the guidelines the Court adopts today to distinguish between the Massachusetts Citizens for Life and the Michigan Chamber of Commerce, the statute would be held unconstitutional. The First Amendment does not permit courts to exercise speech suppression authority denied to legislatures.

. . .

II

The Act does not meet our standards for laws that burden fundamental rights. The State cannot demonstrate that a compelling interest supports its speech restriction, nor can it show that its law is narrowly tailored to the purported statutory end. Restrictions on independent expenditures are unconstitutional if they fail to meet both of these standards. *Buckley v. Valeo*; *First National Bank of Boston v. Bellotti*; *MCFL*. The majority opinion cannot establish either of these predicate conditions for the speech restriction imposed by the State.

A

Our cases acknowledge the danger that corruption poses for the electoral process, but draw a line in permissible regulation between payments to candidates ("contributions") and payments or expenditures to express one's own views ("independent expenditures"). Today's decision abandons this distinction and threatens once-protected political speech. . . . The proper analysis must follow our cases on independent expenditures. We have established that limitations on independent political expenditures are subject to exacting First Amendment scrutiny. . . .

The majority almost admits that, in the case of independent expenditures, the danger of a political quid pro quo is insufficient to justify a restriction of this kind. Since the specter of corruption, which had been "the only legitimate and compelling government interes[t] thus far identified for restricting campaign finances," is missing in this case, the majority invents a new interest: combating the "corrosive and distorting effects of immense aggregations of wealth," accumulated in corporate form without shareholder or public support. The majority styles this novel interest as simply a different kind of corruption, but has no support for its assertion. While it is questionable whether such imprecision would suffice to justify restricting political speech by for-profit corporations, it is certain that it does not apply to nonprofit entities.

. . .

The regulatory mechanism adopted by the Michigan statute is aimed at reducing the quantity of political speech, a rationale endorsed by today's majority. The First Amendment rests on quite the opposite theory. . . . In *Buckley* and *Bellotti*, . . . we rejected the argument that the expenditure of money to increase the quantity of political speech somehow fosters corruption. The key to the majority's reasoning appears to be that because some corporate speakers are well supported and can buy press space or broadcast time to express their ideas, government may ban all corporate speech to ensure that it will not dominate political debate. The argument is flawed in at least two respects. First, the statute is overinclusive because it covers all groups which use the corporate form, including all nonprofit corporations. Second, it assumes that the government has a legitimate interest in equalizing the relative influence of speakers.

With regard to nonprofit corporations in particular, there is no reason to assume that the corporate form has an intrinsic flaw that makes it corrupt, or that all corporations possess great wealth, or that all corporations can buy more media coverage for their views than can individuals or other groups. There is no reason to conclude that independent speech by a corporation is any more likely to dominate the political arena than speech by the wealthy individual, protected in *Buckley v. Valeo*, or by the well-funded PAC, protected in [*FEC v. National Conservative Political Action Committee*, 470 U.S. 480 (1985)](protecting speech rights of PAC's against expenditure limitations).

In addition, the notion that the government has a legitimate interest in restricting the quantity of speech to equalize the relative influence of speakers on elections is antithetical to the First Amendment.... That those who can afford to publicize their views may succeed in the political arena as a result does not detract from the fact that they are exercising a First Amendment right. As we stated in *Bellotti*, paid advocacy "may influence the outcome of the vote; this would be its purpose. But the fact that advocacy may persuade the electorate is hardly a reason to suppress it." The suggestion that the government has an interest in shaping the political debate by insulating the electorate from too much exposure to certain views is incompatible with the First Amendment....

...

B

...

To create second-class speakers that can be stifled on the subject of candidate qualifications is to silence some of the most significant participants in the American public dialogue, as evidenced by the *amici* briefs filed on behalf of the Chamber of Commerce by the American Civil Liberties Union, the Center for Public Interest Law, the American Medical Association, the National Association of Realtors, the American Insurance Association, the National Organization for Women, Greenpeace Action, the National Abortion Rights Action League, the National Right to Work Committee, the Planned Parenthood Federation of America, the Fund for the Feminist Majority, the Washington Legal Foundation, and the Allied Educational Foundation. I reject any argument based on the idea that these groups and their views are not of importance and value to the self-fulfillment and self-expression of their members, and to the rich public dialogue that must be the mark of any free society. To suggest otherwise is contrary to the American political experience and our own judicial knowledge.

It is a distinctive part of the American character for individuals to join associations to enrich the public dialogue. The theme of group identity is part of the history of American democracy. See, *e.g.*, The Federalist No. 10 (J. Madison).

Finally, the majority's conclusion that the statute is not overinclusive because independent expenditures by nonprofit corporations may be assumed to have a pernicious, distorting effect on political processes does not withstand the rigorous scrutiny applicable to bans on speech.... The reality, of course, is that some groups and organizations, particularly those with many members, may find that the nonprofit corporate form is the only feasible way of organizing so that they can transmit important views to the public as a whole. Because the unincorporated association structure carries with it a high risk of personal liability for members and operates in an uncertain legal climate, groups often prefer to organize in nonprofit corporate form....

DER: The negative view of First Amendment rights led to two problems in *Austin*. First, the court had to target an aspect of corporate speech that was not really the source of corruption. The Court relied on the state-conferred corporate structure, rather than corporations' accumulation of wealth, in order to maintain *Buckley*'s prohibition of government redistribution. Although the Court may not interfere with corporations' private money, it may regulate corporate advantages created by the state. As in *Buckley*, the Court viewed wealth as a *corrupting*, but not a *distorting* influence. *Government* interference in the marketplace of ideas —not *private* maldistributions of wealth—constitutes the only First Amendment distortion that the Court may address. Thus, it is only the corporation's legal structure, and not its capital, that justifies First Amendment concern. Despite Scalia's objection, the Court has held in other contexts that the State may "exact as the price of special advantages [the State confers] the forfeiture of First Amendment rights." The Court allows government substantial control over speech on its property and it has held that the government can prohibit speech about certain topics in programs that are publicly financed. This reliance on corporate structure enabled the Court to reconcile its holding with the reasoning of *Buckley*, but it limited the redistributional potential of *Austin* to speech by corporations.

Second, the Court was forced to address the problem of economic inequality by denying speech rather than by supporting it. Because the First Amendment does not require government affirmatively to finance speech, the Court was left no option but to limit the speech of corporations. Ironically, it is more compatible with prevalent constitutional doctrine to censor speech than to fund it.

DEL: The *Austin* decision tortures the logic of a problematic doctrine. The Court generally has stood by the proposition that officially "restrict[ing] the speech of some elements of our society in order to enhance the relative voice of others is wholly foreign to the First Amendment."[81] Even if disinterest in the distribution of power in the information marketplace is a constitutional norm, the Court has upheld redistributive methods when convinced that a significant enough interest was at stake. The scarcity of spectrum space which limits access to the broadcast medium, for instance, has been referenced in justifying a dilution of editorial autonomy in favor of the public's right to receive diverse views.[82] As a consequence, regulation compelling broadcasters to provide fair and balanced coverage of important public issues has been upheld.[83] If redistribution of expressive power can be justified by the imperative of informed self-governance, it is difficult to comprehend why such methods cause the Court to pull its punches when the essence of self-governance itself is at stake.

---

[81] First National Bank of Boston v. Bellotti, 435 U.S. 765, 790–91 (1978) (quoting Buckley v. Valeo, 424 U.S. 1, 48–49 (1976).

[82] *E.g.*, Red Lion Broadcasting Co. v. Federal Communications Commission, 395 U.S. 367, 388–90 (1969).

[83] *Id.*

Bellotti and *Austin* concerned First Amendment limitations on the government's power to regulate a corporation's speech. The Supreme Court recently addressed the issue of First Amendment limitations on a corporation's power to regulate the speech of others. *Lebron v. National Railroad Passenger Corp.*[84] extended the First Amendment to a corporation created by Congress in furtherance of government objectives and over which the federal government retained substantial control. The artist Michael A. Lebron sought to display in Philadelphia's Penn Station his photomontage criticizing the Coors family for its support of right-wing causes. When the National Railroad Passenger Corporation (Amtrak) rejected Lebron's display because of its political nature, Lebron claimed that the corporation violated his right to free expression.

The First Amendment, of course, protects citizens against *government* restrictions on speech, and does not apply to private business decisions. The Court held, however, that Amtrak is an agency or instrumentality of the United States for purposes of individual rights guaranteed by the Constitution. Amtrak was created by the Rail Passenger Services Act of 1970 to avert the threatened extinction of passenger trains. The Act assigned the appointment of a majority of Amtrak's board of directors to the President. The Court remanded the case to the Court of Appeals to decide whether Amtrak's refusal to display Lebron's billboard violated the First Amendment. Only Justice O'Connor dissented from the decision, on the ground that Lebron had failed to claim in the courts below and in his petition for certiorari that Amtrak was a government entity.

4. Speech in the Public Forum

a. Public Forum Doctrine

In the late nineteenth century it was well-established that city governments had broad power to regulate speech under bylaws "relating to the public safety and good

---

[84] 115 S.Ct. 961 (1995).

order of their inhabitants."[85] State courts often held that a municipality's duty to promote the general welfare outweighed a speaker's right to use the public streets. A number of state court decisions issued at the turn of the century upheld convictions of socialists for violating city ordinances banning street gatherings.[86] When Professor J.L. Fitts gave a "Free Street Lecture on Socialism" in Atlanta, calling on people to "lawfully assembl[e] to discuss our condition and needs," the court rejected his First Amendment claim: "Professor Fitts has confused in his mind the constitutional right of freedom of speech with an imaginary, though non-existing right to hold public meetings and make speeches in the public streets."[87] Because the United States Supreme Court had not yet held that the First Amendment applied to the states, it found no constitutional basis for overriding the state police power reasonably to promote the general enjoyment of public land through its licensing scheme.

In 1895, Oliver Wendell Holmes, then sitting on the Massachusetts Supreme Court, reviewed the conviction of Reverend William F. Davis for attempting to preach on the Boston Common in violation of a city ordinance that prohibited all public speaking on public grounds without a permit from the mayor. The Boston authorities may have resented Reverend Davis's espousal of the Social Gospel promoting social responsibility and opposing corruption of city officials.[88] Holmes upheld the ordinance as a proper regulation of the city's property. The United States Supreme Court unanimously endorsed Holmes's view.

---

[85] John Dillon, Commentaries on the Law of Municipal Corporations 423 (2d ed. 1873).

[86] Alexander, *The Formative Period of First Amendment Theory, supra* note 15, at 71–72.

[87] Fitts v. City of Atlanta, 49 S.E. 793, 795 (1905).

[88] David Kairys, *Freedom of Speech,* in The Politics of Law: A Progressive Critique 237 (David Kairys ed., 2d ed. 1990).

Davis v. Massachusetts
167 U.S. 43 (1897)

Mr. Justice White, after stating the case, delivered the opinion of the court.

In the brief of counsel for plaintiff in error many presumed errors are elaborately discussed, all of which, when analyzed, rest on the assumption that there was a right in the plaintiff in error to use the common of the city of Boston free from legislative or municipal control or regulation. It is argued that—

"Boston Common is the property of the inhabitants of the city of Boston, and dedicated to the use of the people of that city and the public in many ways, and the preaching of the gospel there has been, from time immemorial to a recent period, one of these ways. For the making of this ordinance in 1862, and its enforcement against preaching since 1885, no reason whatever has been or can be shown."

The record, however, contains no evidence showing the manner in which the ordinance in question had been previously enforced, nor does it include any proof whatever as to the nature of the ownership in the common from which it can be deduced that the plaintiff in error had any particular right to use the common apart from the general enjoyment, which he was entitled, as a citizen, to avail himself of along with others, and to the extent only which the law permitted. On the contrary, the legislative act and the ordinance passed in pursuance thereof, previously set out in the statement of facts, show an assumption by the state of control over the common in question. Indeed, the Supreme Judicial Court, in affirming the conviction, placed its conclusion upon the express ground that the common was absolutely under the control of the legislature, which, in the exercise of its discretion, could limit the use to the extent deemed by it advisable, and could and did delegate to the municipality the power to assert such authority. The court said:

"There is no evidence before us to show that the power of the legislature over the common is less than its power over any other park dedicated to the use of the public, or over public streets, the legal title to which is in a city or town. As representative of the public, it may and does exercise control over the use which the public may make of such places, and it may and does delegate more of less of such control to the city or town immediately concerned. For the legislature absolutely or conditionally to forbid public speaking in a highway or public park is no more an infringement of the rights of a member of the public than for the owner of a private house to forbid it in his house. When no proprietary rights interfere, the legislature may end the right of the public to enter upon the public place by putting an end to the dedication to public uses. So it may take the less step of limiting the public use to certain purposes. . . . "

It is, therefore, conclusively determined there was no right in the plaintiff in error to use the common except in such mode and subject to such regulations as the legislature in its wisdom may have deemed proper to prescribe. The Fourteenth Amendment to the Constitution of the United States does not destroy the power of the states to enact police regulations as to the subjects within their control, and does not have the effect of creating a particular and personal right in the citizen to use public property in defiance of the constitution and laws of the State.

. . .

Affirmed.

At the turn of the century, labor organizers, suffragists, and other political activists challenged restrictions on their use of the public streets. A notable example is the "free-speech fights" of the Industrial Workers of the World (I.W.W.). From 1909 to 1915, the Wobblies conducted a nationwide campaign to defy denials by city officials of their freedom to organize migratory workers on public streets, sidewalks, and parks.[89] Thousands of supporters were arrested, jailed, beaten by guards, and attacked by vigilantes for violating city ordinances that prohibited public meetings. The Wobblies often succeeded in obtaining the repeal of these ordinances.

Forty years after *Davis v. Massachusetts*, the Supreme Court had changed its understanding of speech in public places. *Hague v. CIO* arose when political boss Frank Hague denied the Committee of Industrial Organization (CIO) permits to distribute literature and hold outdoor assemblies to disseminate information about the National Labor Relations Act in Jersey City, New Jersey.[90] The Court voided the city's permit system. Justice Roberts's plurality opinion presented an eloquent and often-repeated—though largely ahistorical—account of the importance of speech in the public forum:

> Wherever the title of streets and parks may rest, they have immemorially been held in trust for the use of the public and, time out of mind, have been used for purposes of assembly, communicating thoughts between citizens, and discussing public questions. Such use of the streets and public places has, from ancient times, been a part of the privileges, immunities, rights, and liberties of citizens.

It appears that Justice Roberts borrowed this language from Reverend Davis's losing argument in *Davis v. Massachusetts*.

That same year, in *Schneider v. State*, the Court examined further the nature of government interests that might justify restricting citizens' liberty to use the public streets and parks and those that would not.

---

[89] *Id.*

[90] Hague v. CIO, 307 U.S. 496 (1939).

Schneider v. State
308 U.S. 147 (1939)

MR. JUSTICE ROBERTS delivered the opinion of the Court.

Four cases are here, each of which presents the question whether regulations embodied in a municipal ordinance [forbidding distribution of handbills on the street, door-to-door, or in public] abridge the freedom of speech and of the press secured against state invasion by the Fourteenth Amendment of the Constitution.

. . .

Although a municipality may enact regulations in the interest of the public safety, health, welfare or convenience, these may not abridge the individual liberties secured by the Constitution to those who wish to speak, write, print or circulate information or opinion.

Municipal authorities, as trustees for the public, have the duty to keep their communities' streets open and available for movement of people and property, the primary purpose to which the streets are dedicated. So long as legislation to this end does not abridge the constitutional liberty of one rightfully upon the street to impart information through speech or the distribution of literature, it may lawfully regulate the conduct of those using the streets. For example, a person could not exercise this liberty by taking his stand in the middle of a crowded street, contrary to traffic regulations, and maintain his position to the stoppage of all traffic; a group of distributors could not insist upon a constitutional right to form a cordon across the street and to allow no pedestrian to pass who did not accept a tendered leaflet; nor does the guarantee of freedom of speech or of the press deprive a municipality of power to enact regulations against throwing literature broadcast in the streets. Prohibition of such conduct would not abridge the constitutional liberty since such activity bears no necessary relationship to the freedom to speak, write, print or distribute information or opinion.

This court has characterized the freedom of speech and that of the press as fundamental personal rights and liberties. The phrase is not an empty one and was not lightly used. It reflects the belief of the framers of the Constitution that exercise of the rights lies at the foundation of free government by free men. It stresses, as do many opinions of this court, the importance of preventing the restriction of enjoyment of these liberties.

In every case, therefore, where legislative abridgment of the rights is asserted, the courts should be astute to examine the effect of the challenged legislation. Mere legislative preferences or beliefs respecting matters of public convenience may well support regulation directed at other personal activities, but be insufficient to justify such as diminishes the exercise of rights so vital to the maintenance of democratic institutions. And so, as cases arise, the delicate and difficult task falls upon the courts to weigh the circumstances and to appraise the substantiality of the reasons advanced in support of the regulation of the free enjoyment of the rights.

. . .

The motive of the legislation under attack . . . is held by the courts below to be the prevention of littering of the streets and, although the alleged offenders were not charged with themselves scattering paper in the streets, their convictions were sustained upon the theory that distribution by them encouraged or resulted in such littering. We are of opinion that the purpose to keep the streets clean and of good appearance is insufficient to justify an ordinance which prohibits a person rightfully on a public street from handing literature to one willing to receive it. Any burden imposed upon the city authorities in cleaning and caring for the streets as an indirect consequence of such distribution results from the constitutional protection of the freedom of speech and press. This constitutional protection does not deprive a city of all power to prevent street littering. There are obvious methods of preventing littering. Amongst these is the punishment of those who actually throw papers on the streets.

. . .

It is suggested that the Los Angeles and Worcester ordinances are valid because their operation is limited to streets and alleys and leaves persons free to distribute printed matter in other public places. But, as we have said, the streets are natural and proper places for the dissemination of information and opinion; and one is not to have the exercise of his liberty of expression in appropriate places abridged on the plea that it may be exercised in some other place.

While it affects others, the Irvington ordinance . . . affects all those, who, like the petitioner, desire to impart information and opinion to citizens at their homes. If it covers the petitioner's activities it equally applies to one who wishes to present his views on political, social or economic questions. The ordinance is not limited to those who canvass for private profit; nor is it merely the common type of ordinance requiring some form of registration or license of hawkers, or peddlers. It is not a general ordinance to prohibit trespassing. It bans unlicensed communication of any views or the advocacy of any cause from door to door, and permits canvassing only subject to the power of a police officer to determine, as a censor, what literature may be distributed from house to house and who may distribute it. . . .

. . . [P]amphlets have proved most effective instruments in the dissemination of opinion. And perhaps the most effective way of bringing them to the notice of individuals is their distribution at the homes of the people. On this method of communication the ordinance imposes censorship, abuse of which engendered the struggle in England which eventuated in the establishment of the doctrine of the freedom of the press embodied in our Constitution. To require a censorship through license which makes impossible the free and unhampered distribution of pamphlets strikes at the very heart of the constitutional guarantees. Conceding that fraudulent appeals may be

made in the name of charity and religion, we hold a municipality cannot, for this reason, require all who wish to disseminate ideas to present them first to police authorities for their consideration and approval, with a discretion in the police to say some ideas may, while others may not, be carried to the homes of citizens; some persons may, while others may not, disseminate information from house to house. Frauds may be denounced as offenses and punished by law. Trespasses may similarly be forbidden. If it is said that these means are less efficient and convenient than bestowal of power on police authorities to decide what information may be disseminated from house to house, and who may impart the information, the answer is that considerations of this sort do not empower a municipality to abridge freedom of speech and press.

. . .

Reversed.

During the 1960s the civil rights movement tested the Court's opening of government property to citizens for speech purposes. Thousands of civil rights protesters were arrested and convicted for participating in rallies, marches, and sit-ins in public places. In a series of cases reversing such convictions, the Court upheld a limited right of the public to demonstrate in the streets and in government buildings, especially where vague state statutes allowed prosecutions based on the anti-segregation viewpoint of the speakers. *Edwards v. South Carolina* reversed breach of the peace convictions for the orderly carrying of anti-segregation placards on the grounds of the state capitol.[91] *Cox v. Louisiana* reversed the convictions of demonstrators for obstructing a public passageway near the Baton Rouge courthouse.[92] And *Brown v. Louisiana* reversed the breach of the peace convictions of demonstrators who had conducted a silent vigil in a public library.[93] Professor Harry Kalven's influential 1965 article entitled *The Concept of the Public Forum: Cox v. Louisiana* helped to bring public forum analysis to even greater prominence. Kalven argued eloquently that citizens' access to public spaces was essential for freedom of expression: "[I]n an open democratic society the streets, the parks, and other public places are an important facility for public discussion and political process. They are in brief a public forum that the citizen can commandeer; the generosity and empathy with which such facilities are made available is an index of freedom."[94]

The Court made clear in *Adderley v. Florida*, however, that the First Amendment does not deprive the government of the power to preserve its property for its intended use. The Court narrowly upheld trespass convictions of students who held a peaceful demonstration in a jail driveway. The dissenting opinion in *Adderley* highlighted the injustice of confining protest to conventional means that are convenient to the government and available only to the wealthy.

---

[91] Edwards v. South Carolina, 373 U.S. 229 (1963).

[92] Cox v. Louisiana, 379 U.S. 536 (1965).

[93] 383 U.S. 131 (1966) (plurality opinion).

[94] Harry Kalven, *The Concept of the Public Forum:* Cox v. Louisiana, 1965 SUP. CT. REV. 1, 11–12.

Adderley v. Florida
385 U.S. 39 (1966)

MR. JUSTICE BLACK delivered the opinion of the Court.

Petitioners, Harriett Louise Adderley and 31 other persons, were convicted by a jury in a joint trial in the County Judge's Court of Leon County, Florida, on a charge of "trespass with a malicious and mischievous intent" upon the premises of the county jail contrary to § 821.18 of the Florida statutes. . . . . Petitioners, apparently all students of the Florida A. & M. University in Tallahassee, had gone from the school to the jail about a mile away, along with many other students, to "demonstrate" at the jail their protests of arrests of other protesting students the day before, and perhaps to protest more generally against state and local policies and practices of racial segregation, including segregation of the jail. The county sheriff, legal custodian of the jail and jail grounds, tried to persuade the students to leave the jail grounds. When this did not work, he notified them that they must leave, that if they did not leave he would arrest them for trespassing, and that if they resisted he would charge them with that as well. Some of the students left but others, including petitioners, remained and they were arrested. On appeal the convictions were affirmed by the Florida Circuit Court and then by the Florida District Court of Appeal. . . . [P]etitioners contend[ ] that, in view of petitioners' purpose to protest against jail and other segregation policies, their conviction denied them "rights of free speech [and] assembly. . . ." ...

Petitioners have insisted from the beginning of this case that it is controlled by and must be reversed because of our prior cases of *Edwards v. South Carolina* and *Cox v. Louisiana*. We cannot agree.

The *Edwards* case, like this one, did come up when a number of persons demonstrated on public property against their State's segregation policies. They also sang hymns and danced, as did the demonstrators in this case. But here the analogies to this case end. In *Edwards*, the demonstrators went to the South Carolina State Capitol grounds to protest. In this case they went to the jail. Traditionally, state capitol grounds are open to the public. Jails, built for security purposes, are not. The demonstrators at the South Carolina Capitol went in through a public driveway and as they entered they were told by state officials there that they had a right as citizens to go through the State House grounds as long as they were peaceful. Here the demonstrators entered the jail grounds through a driveway used only for jail purposes and without warning to or per-

mission from the sheriff. More importantly, South Carolina sought to prosecute its State Capitol demonstrators by charging them with the common-law crime of breach of the peace. This Court in *Edwards* took pains to point out at length the indefinite, loose, and broad nature of this charge; indeed, this Court pointed out . . . that the South Carolina Supreme Court had itself declared that the "breach of the peace" charge is "not susceptible of exact definition." South Carolina's power to prosecute . . . would have been different had the State proceeded under a "precise and narrowly drawn regulatory statute evincing a legislative judgment that certain specific conduct be limited or proscribed" such as, for example, "limiting the periods during which the State House grounds were open to the public. . . . " The South Carolina breach-of-the-peace statute was thus struck down as being so broad and all-embracing as to jeopardize speech, press, assembly and petition. . . . And it was on this same ground of vagueness that in *Cox v. Louisiana* the Louisiana breach-of-the-peace law used to prosecute Cox was invalidated.

The Florida trespass statute under which these petitioners were charged cannot be challenged on this ground. It is aimed at conduct of one limited kind, that is, for one person or persons to trespass upon the property of another with a malicious and mischievous intent. There is no lack of notice in this law, nothing to entrap or fool the unwary.

. . .

. . . The sheriff, as jail custodian, had power, as the state courts have here held, to direct that this large crowd of people get off the grounds. There is not a shred of evidence in this record that this power was exercised, or that its exercise was sanctioned by the lower courts, because the sheriff objected to what was being sung or said by the demonstrators or because he disagreed with the objectives of their protest. The record reveals that he objected only to their presence on that part of the jail grounds reserved for jail uses. There is no evidence at all that on any other occasion had similarly large groups of the public been permitted to gather on this portion of the jail grounds for any purpose. Nothing in the Constitution of the United States prevents Florida from even-handed enforcement of its general trespass statute against those refusing to obey the sheriff's order to remove themselves from what amounted to the curtilage of the jailhouse. The State, no less than a private owner of property, has power to preserve the property under its control for the use to which it is lawfully dedicated. For this reason there is no merit to the petitioners' argument that they had a constitutional right to stay on the property, over the jail custodian's objections, because this "area chosen for the peaceful civil rights demonstration was not only 'reasonable' but also particularly appropriate. . . . " Such an argument has as its major unarticulated premise the assumption that people who want to propagandize protests or views have a constitutional right to do so whenever and however and wherever they please. That concept of constitutional law was vigorously and forthrightly rejected in two of the cases petitioners rely on, *Cox v. Louisiana*. We reject it again. The United States Constitution does not forbid a State to control the use of its own property for its own lawful nondiscriminatory purpose.

These judgments are

Affirmed.

MR. JUSTICE DOUGLAS, with whom THE CHIEF JUSTICE [WARREN], MR. JUSTICE BRENNAN, and MR. JUSTICE FORTAS concur, dissenting.

The First Amendment, applicable to the States by reason of the Fourteenth provides that "Congress shall make no law . . . abridging . . . the right of the people peaceably to assemble, and to petition the Government for a redress of grievances." These rights, along with religion, speech, and press, are preferred rights of the Constitution, made so by reason of that explicit guarantee and what Edmond Cahn in Confronting Injustice (1966) referred to as "The Firstness of the First Amendment." With all respect, therefore, the Court errs in treating the case as if it were an ordinary trespass case or an ordinary picketing case.

The jailhouse, like an executive mansion, a legislative chamber, a courthouse, or the statehouse itself is one of the seats of governments whether it be the Tower of London, the Bastille, or a small county jail. And when it houses political prisoners or those who many think are unjustly held, it is an obvious center for protest. The right to petition for the redress of grievances has an ancient history and is not limited to writing a letter or sending a telegram to a congressman; it is not confined to appearing before the local city council, or writing letters to the President or Governor or Mayor. Conventional methods of petitioning may be, and often have been, shut off to large groups of our citizens. Legislators may turn deaf ears; formal complaints may be routed endlessly through a bureaucratic maze; courts may let the wheels of justice grind very slowly. Those who do not control television and radio, those who cannot afford to advertise in newspapers or circulate elaborate pamphlets may have only a more limited type of access to public officials. Their methods should not be condemned as tactics of obstruction and harassment as

long as the assembly and petition are peaceable, as these were.

There is no question that petitioners had as their purpose a protest against the arrest of Florida A.&M. students for trying to integrate public theatres. The sheriff's testimony indicates that he well understood the purpose of the rally. The petitioners who testified unequivocally stated that the group was protesting the arrests, and state and local policies of segregation, including segregation of the jail. This testimony was not contradicted or even questioned. The fact that no one gave a formal speech, that no elaborate handbills were distributed, and that the group was not laden with signs would seem to be immaterial. Such methods are not the *sine qua non* of petitioning for the redress of grievances. The group did sing "freedom" songs. And history shows that a song can be a powerful tool of protest. There was no violence; no threat of violence; no attempted jail break; no storming of a prison; no plan or plot to do anything but protest. The evidence is uncontradicted that the petitioners' conduct did not upset the jailhouse routine; things went on as they normally would. None of the group entered the jail. Indeed, they moved back from the entrance as they were instructed. There was no shoving, no pushing, no disorder or threat of riot. . . .

We do violence to the First Amendment when we permit this "petition for redress of grievances" to be turned into a trespass action. It does not help to analogize this problem to the problem of picketing. Picketing is a form of protest usually directed against private interests. I do not see how rules governing picketing in general are relevant to this express constitutional right to assemble and to petition for redress of grievances. In the first place the jailhouse grounds were not marked with "NO TRESPASSING!" signs, nor does respondent claim that the public was generally excluded from the grounds. Only the sheriff's fiat transformed lawful conduct into an unlawful trespass. To say that a private owner could have done the same if the rally had taken place on private property is to speak of a different case, as an assembly and a petition for redress of grievances run to government, not to private proprietors.

The Court forgets that prior to this day our decisions have drastically limited the application of state statutes inhibiting the right to go peacefully on public property to exercise First Amendment rights. . . . *Hague v. CIO*.

Such was the case of *Edwards v. South Carolina*, where aggrieved people "peaceably assembled at the site of the State Government" to express their grievances to the citizens of the State as well as to the legislature. *Edwards* was in the tradition of *Cox v. New Hampshire*, where the public streets were said to be "immemorially associated" with "the right of assembly and the opportunities for the communication of thought and the discussion of public questions." When we allow Florida to construe her "malicious trespass" statute to bar a person from going on property knowing it is not his own and to apply that prohibition to public property, we discard *Cox* and *Edwards*. Would the case be any different if, as is common, the demonstration took place outside a building which housed both the jail and the legislative body? I think not.

There may be some public places which are so clearly committed to other purposes that their use for the airing of grievances is anomalous. There may be some instances in which assemblies and petitions for redress of grievances are not consistent with other necessary purposes of public property. A noisy meeting may be out of keeping with the serenity of the statehouse or the quiet of the courthouse. No one, for example, would suggest that the Senate gallery is the proper place for a vociferous protest rally. And in other cases it may be necessary to adjust the right to petition for redress of grievances to the other interests inhering in the uses to which the public property is normally put. But this is quite different from saying that all public places are off limits to people with grievances. And it is farther yet from saying that the "custodian" of the public property in his discretion can decide when public places shall be used for the communication of ideas, especially the constitutional right to assemble and petition for redress of grievances. For to place such discretion in any public official, be he the "custodian" of the public property or the local police commissioner, is to place those who assert their First Amendment rights at his mercy. It gives him the awesome power to decide whose ideas may be expressed and who shall be denied a place to air their claims and

petition their government. Such power is out of step with all our decisions prior to today where we have insisted that before a First Amendment right may be curtailed under the guise of a criminal law, any evil that may be collateral to the exercise of the right, must be isolated and defined in a "narrowly drawn" statute lest the power to control excesses of conduct be used to suppress the constitutional right itself.

That tragic consequence happens today when a trespass law is used to bludgeon those who peacefully exercise a First Amendment right to protest to government against one of the most grievous of all modern oppressions which some of our States are inflicting on our citizens.

. . .

Today a trespass law is used to penalize people for exercising a constitutional right. Tomorrow a disorderly conduct statute, a breach-of-the-peace statute, a vagrancy statute will be put to the same end. It is said that the sheriff did not make the arrests because of the views which petitioners espoused. That excuse is usually given, as we know from the many cases involving arrests of minority groups for breaches of the peace, unlawful assemblies, and parading without a permit. The charge against William Penn, who preached a nonconformist doctrine in a street in London, was that he caused "a great concourse and tumult of people" and contempt of the King and "to the great disturbance of his peace." That was in 1670. In modern times, also, such arrests are usually sought to be justified by some legitimate function of government. Yet by allowing these orderly and civilized protests against injustice to be suppressed, we only increase the forces of frustration which the conditions of second-class citizenship are generating amongst us.

By the 1970s, the concept of the public forum was firmly entrenched; it was clear that the extent of First Amendment protection afforded speech depends on the location where the speech occurs. In its 1983 decision *Perry Educational Association v. Perry Local Educators' Association*, the Court provided a comprehensive analysis of speech on government property by distinguishing three types of forums.[95] First, in "quintessential" public forums—"places which by long tradition or by government fiat have been devoted to assembly and debate," such as parks, streets, and sidewalks—the Court strictly scrutinizes content-based regulations of protected speech to determine whether they are narrowly drawn to serve a compelling state interest. Second, the Court also applies strict scrutiny to "designated" public forums which the government has opened "for use by the public as a place for expressive activity," such as a public school meeting facility or a state fairground. Unlike in the case of traditional public forums, however, the government may later choose to close a public forum in this second category. Finally,

---

[95] Perry Educ. Ass'n v. Perry Local Educators Ass'n, 460 U.S. 37 (1983).

in a nonpublic forum "which is not by tradition or designation for public communication," the government may exclude speakers based on the content of their message. In other words, the government may grant access to nonpublic forums based on the subject matter of the expression or the speaker's identity, without meeting the strict scrutiny test. The Court has with rare exception upheld viewpoint-neutral restrictions on access to nonpublic forums on the ground that they reasonably furthered the government's interest in preserving the property for the non-speech use to which it was dedicated.

The government is forbidden in any forum from punishing speech based on viewpoint discrimination—its disagreement with the opinions expressed by the speaker. Even in a nonpublic forum, the government may not admit supporters of a particular political position while excluding their opponents. The difficulty in distinguishing between content and viewpoint discrimination, however, sometimes makes it hard to tell when the government has crossed the line. In *Perry Educational Association*, for example, the Court held that a collective bargaining agreement that granted access to school mailboxes to the union elected to represent teachers while denying access to the losing union did not violate the First Amendment. The Court reasoned that the mail boxes were not public forums and that the school district could grant access only to organizations engaged in official school business. An equally plausible interpretation of the exclusion of the rival union, however, was that the school district distinguished between the two unions based on their viewpoints.

b. Time, Place and Manner Restrictions

One way in which the Court has reconciled the interests of speakers to use public forums with the interests of government to maintain the orderly use of its property is to permit the state to impose content-neutral time, place and manner restrictions on speech activities. These restrictions regulate the form of speech and not the content of its message. Thus, even speech in traditional public forums may be subject to government limits on time, place and manner, provided the regulation is content neutral, promotes a substantial government interest, and allows the speakers adequate alternative means of communicating their message. Typical time, place and manner regulations include licensing schemes for parades in public streets, restrictions on the hours of door-to-door solicitation, or even-handed limits on the location of sidewalk picketing.

The government also imposes time, place and manner restrictions on speech in nontraditional public forums. For example, in *Heffron v. International Society for Krishna Consciousness, Inc.*, the Court validated the requirement that a religious organization, the Krishna Society, confine its solicitation of donations and distribution of religious literature at a Minnesota State Fair to a licensed booth on the fairgrounds.[96] The Court reasoned that the rule was a valid time, place and manner regulation since it allocated booths in a nondiscriminatory manner, served the state's significant interest in maintaining the orderly movement of crowds at the fair, and was the only way, short of granting the Krishna Society special privileges, to achieve this goal.

---

[96] Heffron v. International Society for Krishna Consciousness, Inc., 452 U.S. 640 (1981).

Frisby v. Schultz
487 U.S. 474 (1988)

JUSTICE O'CONNOR delivered the opinion of the Court.

Brookfield, Wisconsin, has adopted an ordi- nance that completely bans picketing "before or about" any residence. This case presents a facial First Amendment challenge to that ordinance.

I

Brookfield, Wisconsin, is a residential suburb of Milwaukee with a population of approximately 4,300. The appellees, Sandra C. Schultz and Robert C. Braun, are individuals strongly opposed to abortion and wish to express their views on the subject by picketing on a public street outside the Brookfield residence of a doctor who apparently performs abortions at two clinics in neighboring towns. Appellees and others engaged in precisely that activity, assembling outside the doctor's home on at least six occasions between April 20, 1985, and May 20, 1985, for periods ranging from one to one and a half hours. The size of the group varied from 11 to more than 40. The picketing was generally orderly and peaceful; the town never had occasion to invoke any of its various ordinances prohibiting obstruction of the streets, loud and unnecessary noises, or disorderly conduct. Nonetheless, the picketing generated substantial controversy and numerous complaints.

The town therefore resolved to enact an ordinance to restrict the picketing. . . . The ordinance itself recites the primary purpose of this ban: "the protection and preservation of the home" through assurance "that members of the community enjoy in their homes and dwellings a feeling of well-being, tranquility, and privacy." The Town Board believed that a ban was necessary because it determined that "the practice of picketing before or about residences and dwellings causes emotional disturbance and distress to the occupants . . . [and] has as its object the harassing of such occupants." The ordinance also evinces a concern for public safety, noting that picketing obstructs and interferes with "the free use of public sidewalks and public ways of travel."

. . .

II

The antipicketing ordinance operates at the core of the First Amendment by prohibiting appellees from engaging in picketing on an issue of public concern. Because of the importance of "uninhibited, robust, and wide-open" debate on public issues, *New York Times Co. v. Sullivan*, we have traditionally subjected restrictions on public issue picketing to careful scrutiny. Of course, "[e]ven protected speech is not equally permissible in all places and at all times." *Cornelius v. NAACP Legal Defense & Educational Fund, Inc.*, 473 U.S. 788, 799 (1985).

To ascertain what limits, if any, may be placed on protected speech, we have often focused on the "place" of that speech, considering the nature of the forum the speaker seeks to employ. Our cases have recognized that the standards by which limitations on speech must be evaluated "differ depending on the character of the property at issue." *Perry Education Assn. v. Perry Local Educators' Assn.*, 460 U.S. 37, 44 (1983). Specifically, we have identified three types of fora: "the traditional public forum, the public forum created by government designation, and the nonpublic forum." *Cornelius.*

The relevant forum here may be easily identified: appellees wish to picket on the public streets of Brookfield. Ordinarily, a determination of the nature of the forum would follow automatically from this identification; we have repeatedly referred to public streets as the archetype of a traditional public forum. "[T]ime out of mind" public streets and sidewalks have been used for public assembly and debate, the hallmarks of a traditional public forum. Appellants, however, urge us to disregard these "cliches." They argue that the streets of Brookfield should be considered a nonpublic forum. Pointing to the physical narrowness of Brookfield's streets as well as to their residential character, appellants contend that such streets have not by tradition or designation been held open for public communication.

We reject this suggestion. Our prior holdings make clear that a public street does not lose its status as a traditional public forum simply because it runs through a residential neighborhood. . . . [O]ur decisions identifying public streets and sidewalks as traditional public fora are not accidental invocations of a "cliche," but recognition that "[w]herever the title of streets and parks may rest, they have immemorially been held in trust for the use of the public." *Hague v. CIO.* No particularized inquiry into the precise nature of a specific street is necessary; all public streets are held in the public trust and are properly considered traditional public fora. Accordingly, the streets of Brookfield are traditional public fora. The residential character of those streets may well inform the application of the relevant test, but it does not lead to a different test; the antipicketing ordinance must be judged against the stringent standards we have established for restrictions on speech in traditional public fora:

> "In these quintessential public for[a], the government may not prohibit all communicative activity. For the State to enforce a content-based exclusion it must show that its regulation is necessary to serve a compelling state interest and that it is narrowly drawn to achieve that end. . . . The State may also enforce regulations of the time, place, and manner of expression which are content-neutral, are narrowly tailored to serve a significant government interest, and leave open ample alternative channels of communication." *Perry.*

As *Perry* makes clear, the appropriate level of scrutiny is initially tied to whether the statute distinguishes between prohibited and permitted speech on the basis of content.... [W]e accept the lower courts' conclusion that the Brookfield ordinance is content neutral. Accordingly, we turn to consider whether the ordinance is "narrowly tailored to serve a significant government interest" and whether it "leave[s] open ample alternative channels of communication."

Because the last question is so easily answered, we address it first. Of course, before we are able to assess the available alternatives, we must consider more carefully the reach of the ordinance. The precise scope of the ban is not further described within the text of the ordinance, but in our view the ordinance is readily subject to a narrowing construction that avoids constitutional difficulties. Specifically, the use of the singular form of the words "residence" and "dwelling" suggests that the ordinance is intended to prohibit only picketing focused on, and taking place in front of, a particular residence.... This narrow reading is supported by the representations of counsel for the town at oral argument, which indicate that the town takes, and will enforce, a limited view of the "picketing" proscribed by the ordinance. Thus, generally speaking, "picketing would be having the picket proceed on a definite course or route in front of a home." The picket need not be carrying a sign, but in order to fall within the scope of the ordinance the picketing must be directed at a single residence. General marching through residential neighborhoods, or even walking a route in front of an entire block of houses, is not prohibited by this ordinance. Accordingly, we construe the ban to be a limited one; only focused picketing taking place solely in front of a particular residence is prohibited.

So narrowed, the ordinance permits the more general dissemination of a message. As appellants explain, the limited nature of the prohibition makes it virtually self-evident that ample alternatives remain:

> "Protestors have not been barred from the residential neighborhoods. They may enter such neighborhoods, alone or in groups, even marching.... They may go door-to-door to proselytize their views. They may distribute literature in this manner ... or through the mails. They may contact residents by telephone, short of harassment."

We readily agree that the ordinance preserves ample alternative channels of communication and thus move on to inquire whether the ordinance serves a significant government interest. We find that such an interest is identified within the text of the ordinance itself: the protection of residential privacy.

"The State's interest in protecting the well-being, tranquility, and privacy of the home is certainly of the highest order in a free and civilized society." *Carey v. Brown*, 447 U.S. [455, 471 (1980)]. Our prior decisions have often remarked on the unique nature of the home, "the last citadel of the tired, the weary, and the sick," *Gregory v. Chicago*, 394 U.S. 111, 125 (1969) (Black, J., concurring), and have recognized that "[p]reserving the sanctity of the home, the one retreat to which men and women can repair to escape from the tribulations of their daily pursuits, is surely an important value." *Carey*.

One important aspect of residential privacy is protection of the unwilling listener. Although in many locations, we expect individuals simply to avoid speech they do not want to hear, cf. *Cohen v. California*, the home is different. Instead, a special benefit of the privacy all citizens enjoy within their own walls, which the State may legislate to protect, is an ability to avoid intrusions. Thus, we have repeatedly held that individuals are not required to welcome unwanted speech into their own homes and that the government may protect this freedom.

. . .

It remains to be considered, however, whether the Brookfield ordinance is narrowly tailored to protect only unwilling recipients of the communications. A statute is narrowly tailored if it targets and eliminates no more than the exact source of the "evil" it seeks to remedy. *City Council of Los Angeles v. Taxpayers for Vincent*, 466 U.S. 789, 808–810 (1984). A complete ban can be narrowly tailored, but only if each activity within the proscription's scope is an appropriately targeted evil. For example, in *Taxpayers for Vincent* we upheld an ordinance that banned all signs on public property because the interest supporting the regulation, an esthetic interest in avoiding visual clutter and blight, rendered each sign an evil. Complete prohibition was necessary because "the substantive evil—visual blight—[was] not merely a possible byproduct of the activity, but [was] created by the medium of expression itself."

The same is true here. The type of focused picketing prohibited by the Brookfield ordinance is fundamentally different from more generally directed means of communication that may not be completely banned in residential areas. In such cases "the flow of information [is not] into ... household[s], but to the public." *Organization for a Better Austin v. Keefe*, 402 U.S. 415, 420 (1971). Here, in contrast, the picketing is narrowly directed at the household, not the public. The type of picketers banned by the Brookfield ordinance generally do not seek to disseminate a message to the general public, but to intrude upon the targeted resident, and to do so in an especially offensive way. Moreover, even if some such picketers have a broader communicative purpose, their activity nonetheless inherently and offensively intrudes on residential privacy. The devastating effect of targeted picketing on the quiet enjoyment of the home is beyond doubt. . . .

In this case, for example, appellees subjected the doctor and his family to the presence of a relatively large group of protesters on their doorstep in an attempt to force the doctor to cease performing abortions. But the actual size of the group is irrelevant; even a solitary picket can invade residential privacy. The offensive and disturbing nature of the form of the communication banned by the Brookfield ordinance thus can scarcely be questioned.

The First Amendment permits the government to prohibit offensive speech as intrusive when the "captive" audience cannot avoid the objectionable speech. The target of the focused picketing banned by the Brookfield ordinance is just such a "captive." The resident is figuratively, and perhaps literally, trapped within the home, and because of the unique and subtle impact of such picketing is left with no ready means of avoiding the unwanted speech. Thus, the "evil" of targeted residential picketing, "the very presence of an unwelcome visitor at the home," *Carey* (REHNQUIST, J., dissenting), is "created by the medium of expression itself." Accordingly, the Brookfield ordinance's complete ban of that particular medium of expression is narrowly tailored.

Of course, this case presents only a facial challenge to the ordinance. Particular hypothetical applications of the ordinance—to, for example, a particular resident's use of his or her home as a place of business or public meeting, or to picketers present at a particular home by invitation of the resident—may present somewhat different questions. . . .

Because the picketing prohibited by the Brookfield ordinance is speech directed primarily at those who are presumptively unwilling to receive it, the State has a substantial and justifiable interest in banning it. The nature and scope of this interest make the ban narrowly tailored. The ordinance also leaves open ample alternative channels of communication and is content neutral. Thus, largely because of its narrow scope, the facial challenge to the ordinance must fail. The contrary judgment of the Court of Appeals is

Reversed.

JUSTICE WHITE, concurring in the judgment.

I agree with the Court that an ordinance which only forbade picketing before a single residence would not be unconstitutional on its face. If such an ordinance were applied to the kind of picketing that appellees carried out here, it clearly would not be invalid under the First Amendment, for the picketing in this case involved large groups of people, ranging at various times from 11 individuals to more than 40. I am convinced, absent more than this record indicates, that if some single-residence picketing by smaller groups could not be forbidden, the range of possibly unconstitutional application of such an ordinance would not render it substantially overbroad and thus unconstitutional on its face.

. . .

. . . In my view, if the ordinance were construed to forbid all picketing in residential neighborhoods, the overbreadth doctrine would render it unconstitutional on its face and hence prohibit its enforcement against those, like appellees, who engage in single-residence picketing. At least this would be the case until the ordinance is limited in some authoritative manner. Because the representations made in this Court by the town's legal officer create sufficient doubts in my mind, however, as to how the ordinance will be enforced by the town or construed by the state courts, I would put aside the overbreadth approach here, sustain the ordinance as applied in this case, which the Court at least does, and await further developments.

JUSTICE BRENNAN, with whom JUSTICE MARSHALL joins, dissenting.

The Court today sets out the appropriate legal tests and standards governing the question presented, and proceeds to apply most of them correctly. Regrettably, though, the Court errs in the final step of its analysis, and approves an ordinance banning significantly more speech than is necessary to achieve the government's substantial and legitimate goal. Accordingly, I must dissent.

The ordinance before us absolutely prohibits picketing "before or about" any residence in the town of Brookfield, thereby restricting a manner of speech in a traditional public forum. Consequently, as the Court correctly states, the ordinance is subject to the well-settled time, place, and manner test: the restriction must be content and viewpoint neutral, leave open ample alternative channels of communication, and be narrowly tailored to further a substantial governmental interest.

Assuming one construes the ordinance as the Court does, I agree that the regulation reserves ample alternative channels of communication. I also agree with the Court that the town has a substantial interest in protecting its residents' right to be left alone in their homes. It is, however, critical to specify the precise scope of this interest. The mere fact that speech takes place in a residential neighborhood does not automatically implicate a residential privacy interest. It is the intrusion of speech into the home or the unduly coercive nature of a particular manner of speech around the home that is subject to more exacting regulation.... A crowd of protesters need not be permitted virtually to imprison a person in his or her own house merely because they shout slogans or carry signs. But so long as the speech remains outside the home and does not unduly coerce the occupant, the government's heightened interest in protecting residential privacy is not implicated.

The foregoing distinction is crucial here because it directly affects the last prong of the time, place, and manner test: whether the ordinance is narrowly tailored to achieve the governmental interest. I do not quarrel with the Court's reliance on *City Council of Los Angeles v. Taxpayers for Vincent* for the proposition that a blanket prohibition of a manner of speech in particular public fora may nonetheless be "narrowly tailored" if in each case the manner of speech forbidden necessarily produces the very "evil" the government seeks to eradicate. However, the application of this test requires that the government demonstrate that the offending aspects of the prohibited manner of speech cannot be separately, and less intrusively, controlled. Thus here, if the intrusive and unduly coercive elements of residential picketing can be eliminated without simultaneously eliminating residential picketing completely, the Brookfield ordinance fails the *Vincent* test.

Without question there are many aspects of residential picketing that, if unregulated, might easily become intrusive or unduly coercive. Indeed, some of these aspects are illustrated by this very case. As the District Court found, before the ordinance took effect up to 40 sign-carrying, slogan-shouting protesters regularly converged on Dr. Victoria's home and, in addition to protesting, warned young children not to go near the house because Dr. Victoria was a "baby killer." Further, the throng repeatedly trespassed onto the Victorias' property and at least once blocked the exits to their home. Surely it is within the government's power to enact regulations as necessary to prevent such intrusive and coercive abuses. Thus, for example, the government could constitutionally regulate the number of residential picketers, the hours during which a residential picket may take place, or the noise level of such a picket. In short, substantial regulation is permitted to neutralize the intrusive or unduly coercive aspects of picketing around the home. But to say that picketing may be substantially regulated is not to say that it may be prohibited in its entirety. Once size, time, volume, and the like have been controlled to ensure that the picket is no longer intrusive or

coercive, only the speech itself remains, conveyed perhaps by a lone, silent individual, walking back and forth with a sign. Such speech, which no longer implicates the heightened governmental interest in residential privacy, is nevertheless banned by the Brookfield law. Therefore, the ordinance is not narrowly tailored.

...

A flaw in the Court's reasoning is that it assumes that the intrusive elements of a residential picket are "inherent." However, in support of this crucial conclusion the Court only briefly examines the effect of a narrowly tailored ordinance: "[E]ven a solitary picket can invade residential privacy...." The Court's reference to the Carey dissent, its sole support for this assertion, conjures up images of a "lurking" stranger, secreting himself or herself outside a residence like a thief in the night, threatening physical harm. This hardly seems an apt depiction of a solitary picket, especially at midafternoon, whose presence is objectionable because it is notorious. Contrary to the Court's declaration in this regard, it seems far more likely that a picketer who truly desires only to harass those inside a particular residence will find that goal unachievable in the face of a narrowly tailored ordinance substantially limiting, for example, the size, time, and volume of the protest. If, on the other hand, the picketer intends to communicate generally, a carefully crafted ordinance will allow him or her to do so without intruding upon or unduly harassing the resident. Consequently, the discomfort to which the Court must refer is merely that of knowing there is a person outside who disagrees with someone inside. This may indeed be uncomfortable, but it does not implicate the town's interest in residential privacy and therefore does not warrant silencing speech.

A valid time, place, or manner law neutrally regulates speech only to the extent necessary to achieve a substantial governmental interest, and no further. Because the Court is unwilling to examine the Brookfield ordinance in light of the precise governmental interest at issue, it condones a law that suppresses substantially more speech than is necessary. I dissent.

JUSTICE STEVENS, dissenting.
"GET WELL CHARLIE—OUR TEAM NEEDS YOU."

In Brookfield, Wisconsin, it is unlawful for a fifth grader to carry such a sign in front of a residence for the period of time necessary to convey its friendly message to its intended audience.

...

I do not believe we advance the inquiry by rejecting ... the "... argument that residential streets are something less than public fora." The streets in a residential neighborhood that has no sidewalks are quite obviously a different type of forum than a stadium or a public park. Attaching the label "public forum" to the area in front of a single family dwelling does not help us decide whether the town's interest in the safe and efficient flow of traffic or its interest in protecting the privacy of its citizens justifies denying picketers the right to march up and down the streets at will.

Two characteristics of picketing—and of speech more generally—make this a difficult case. First, it is important to recognize that, "[l]ike so many other kinds of expression, picketing is a mixture of conduct and communication." *NLRB v. Retail Store Employees*, 447 U.S. 607, 618–619 (1980) (STEVENS, J., concurring in part and concurring in result). If we put the speech element to one side, I should think it perfectly clear that the town could prohibit pedestrians from loitering in front of a residence. On the other hand, it seems equally clear that a sign carrier has a right to march past a residence—and presumably pause long enough to give the occupants an opportunity to read his or her message—regardless of whether the reader agrees, disagrees, or is simply indifferent to the point of view being expressed. Second, . . . [p]icketing is a form of speech that, by virtue of its repetition of message and often hostile presentation, may be disruptive of an environment irrespective of the substantive message conveyed.

The picketing that gave rise to the ordinance enacted in this case was obviously intended to do more than convey a message of opposition to the character of the doctor's practice; it was intended to cause him and his family substantial psychological distress. As the record reveals, the picketers' message was repeatedly redelivered by a relatively large group—in essence, increasing the volume and intrusiveness of the same message with each repeated assertion. As is often the function of picketing, during the periods of protest the doctor's home was held under a virtual siege. I do not believe that picketing for the sole purpose of imposing psychological harm on a family in the shelter of their home is constitutionally protected. I do believe, however, that the picketers have a right to communicate their strong opposition to abortion to the doctor, but after they have had a fair opportunity to communicate that message, I see little justification for allowing them to remain in front of his home and repeat it over and over again simply to harm the doctor and his family. Thus, I agree that the ordinance may be constitutionally applied to the kind of picketing that gave rise to its enactment.

On the other hand, the ordinance is unquestionably "overbroad" in that it prohibits some communication that is protected by the First Amendment. . . . In this case the overbreadth is unquestionably "real." Whether or not it is "substantial" in relation to the "plainly legitimate sweep" of the ordinance is a more difficult question. My hunch is that the town will probably not enforce its ban against friendly, innocuous, or even brief unfriendly picketing, and that the Court may be right in concluding that its legitimate sweep makes its overbreadth insubstantial. But there are two countervailing considerations that are persuasive to me. The scope of the ordinance gives the town officials far too much discretion in making enforcement decisions; while we sit by and await further developments, potential picketers must act at their peril. Second, it is a simple matter for the town to amend its ordinance and to limit the ban to conduct that unreasonably interferes with the privacy of the home and does not serve a reasonable communicative purpose. Accordingly, I respectfully dissent.

The year following its decision in *Frisby v. Schultz* the Court clarified the narrow tailoring requirement of the time, place and manner test.

Ward v. Rock Against Racism
491 U.S. 781 (1989)

JUSTICE KENNEDY delivered the opinion of the Court.

In the southeast portion of New York City's Central Park, about 10 blocks upward from the park's beginning point at 59th Street, there is an amphitheater and stage structure known as the Naumberg Acoustic Bandshell. The bandshell faces west across the remaining width of the park. In close proximity to the bandshell, and lying within the directional path of its sound, is a grassy open area called the Sheep Meadow. The city has designated the Sheep Meadow as a quiet area for passive recreations like reclining, walking, and reading. Just beyond the park, and also within the potential sound range of the bandshell, are the apartments and residences of Central Park West.

This case arises from the city's attempt to regulate the volume of amplified music at the bandshell so the performances are satisfactory to the audience without intruding upon those who use the Sheep Meadow or live on Central Park West and in its vicinity.

The city's regulation requires bandshell performers to use sound-amplification equipment and a sound technician provided by the city. The challenge to this volume control technique comes from the sponsor of a rock concert. The trial court sustained the noise control measures, but the Court of Appeals for the Second Circuit reversed. . . .

. . .

Music is one of the oldest forms of human expression. From Plato's discourse in the Republic to the totalitarian state in our own times, rulers have known its capacity to appeal to the intellect and to the emotions, and have censored musical compositions to serve the needs of the state. The Constitution prohibits any like attempts in our own legal order. Music, as a form of expression and communication, is protected under the First Amendment. In the case before us the performances apparently consisted of remarks by speakers, as well as rock music, but the case has been presented as one in which the constitutional challenge is to the city's regulation of the musical aspects of the concert; and, based on the principle we have stated, the city's guideline must meet the demands of the First Amendment. The parties do not appear to dispute that proposition.

We need not here discuss whether a municipality which owns a bandstand or stage facility may exercise, in some circumstances, a proprietary right to select performances and control their quality. Though it did demonstrate its own interest in the effort to insure high quality performances by providing the equipment in question, the city justifies its guideline as a regulatory measure to limit and control noise. Here the bandshell was open, apparently, to all performers; and we decide the case as one in which the bandshell is a public forum for performances in which the government's right to regulate expression is subject to the protections of the First Amendment. Our cases make clear, however, that even in a public forum the government may impose reasonable restrictions on the time, place, or manner of protected speech, provided the restrictions "are justified without reference to the content of the regulated speech, that they are narrowly tailored to serve a significant governmental interest, and that they leave open ample alternative channels for communication of the information." *Clark v. Community for Creative Non-Violence*. We consider these requirements in turn.

A

The principal inquiry in determining content neutrality, in speech cases generally and in time, place, or manner cases in particular, is whether the government has adopted a regulation of speech because of disagreement with the message it conveys. The government's purpose is the controlling consideration. A regulation that serves purposes unrelated to the content of expression is deemed neutral, even if it has an incidental effect on some speakers or messages but not others. Government regulation of expressive activity is content neutral so long as it is *"justified* without reference to the content of the regulated speech." *Community for Creative Non-Violence* (emphasis added).

The principal justification for the sound-amplification guideline is the city's desire to control noise levels at bandshell events, in order to retain the character of the Sheep Meadow and its more sedate activities, and to avoid undue intrusion into residential areas and other areas of the park. This justification for the guideline "ha[s] nothing to do with content," and it satisfies the requirement that time, place, or manner regulations be content neutral.

The only other justification offered below was the city's interest in "ensur[ing] the quality of sound at Bandshell events." Respondent urges that this justification is not content neutral because it is based upon the quality, and thus the content, of the speech being regulated. In respondent's view, the city is seeking to assert artistic control over performers at the bandshell by enforcing a bureaucratically determined, value-laden conception of good sound. . . .

While respondent's arguments that the government may not interfere with artistic judgment may have much force in other contexts, they are inapplicable to the facts of this case. The city has disclaimed in express terms any interest in imposing its own view of appropriate sound mix on performers. . . . On this record, the City's concern with sound quality extends only to the clearly content-neutral goals of ensuring adequate sound amplification and avoiding the volume problems associated with inadequate sound mix. Any governmental attempt to serve purely esthetic goals by imposing subjective standards of acceptable sound mix on performers would raise serious First Amendment concerns, but this case provides us with no opportunity to address those questions. . . .

. . .

B

The city's regulation is also "narrowly tailored to serve a significant governmental inter-

844 Part V: The First Amendment

est." Despite respondent's protestations to the contrary, it can no longer be doubted that government "ha[s] a substantial interest in protecting its citizens from unwelcome noise." *City Council of Los Angeles v. Taxpayers for Vincent.* This interest is perhaps at its greatest when government seeks to protect "'the well-being, tranquility, and privacy of the home,'" *Frisby v. Schultz,* but it is by no means limited to that context, for the government may act to protect even such traditional public forums as city streets and parks from excessive noise.

We think it also apparent that the city's interest in ensuring the sufficiency of sound amplification at bandshell events is a substantial one. The record indicates that inadequate sound amplification has had an adverse affect on the ability of some audiences to hear and enjoy performances at the bandshell. The city enjoys a substantial interest in ensuring the ability of its citizens to enjoy whatever benefits the city parks have to offer, from amplified music to silent meditation.

The Court of Appeals recognized the city's substantial interest in limiting the sound emanating from the bandshell. The court concluded, however, that the city's sound-amplification guideline was not narrowly tailored to further this interest, because "it has not [been] shown . . . that the requirement of the use of the city's sound system and technician was the least intrusive means of regulating the volume." In the court's judgment, there were several alternative methods of achieving the desired end that would have been less restrictive of respondent's First Amendment rights.

The Court of Appeals erred in sifting through all the available or imagined alternative means of regulating sound volume in order to determine whether the city's solution was "the *least intrusive means*" of achieving the desired end. This "less-restrictive-alternative analysis . . . has never been a part of the inquiry into the validity of a time, place, and manner regulation." *Regan v. Time, Inc.,* 468 U.S. 641, 657 (1984) (opinion of WHITE, J.). Instead, our cases quite clearly hold that restrictions on the time, place, or manner of protected speech are not invalid "simply because there is some imaginable alternative that might be less burdensome on speech." *United States v. Albertini,* 472 U.S. 675, 689 (1985).

The Court of Appeals apparently drew its least-intrusive-means requirement from *United States v. O'Brien,* the case in which we established the standard for judging the validity of restrictions on expressive conduct. The court's reliance was misplaced, however, for we have held that the *O'Brien* test "in the last analysis is little, if any, different from the standard applied to time, place, or manner restrictions." *Community for Creative Non-Violence. . . .*

Lest any confusion on the point remain, we reaffirm today that a regulation of the time, place, or manner of protected speech must be narrowly tailored to serve the government's legitimate, content-neutral interests but that it need not be the least restrictive or least intrusive means of doing so. Rather, the requirement of narrow tailoring is satisfied "so long as the . . . regulation promotes a substantial government interest that would be achieved less effectively absent the regulation." *United States v. Albertini.* To be sure, this standard does not mean that a time, place, or manner regulation may burden substantially more speech than is necessary to further the government's legitimate interests. Government may not regulate expression in such a manner that a substantial portion of the burden on speech does not serve to advance its goals. So long as the means chosen are not substantially broader than necessary to achieve the government's interest, however, the regulation will not be invalid simply because a court concludes that the government's interest could be adequately served by some less-speech-restrictive alternative. . . .

It is undeniable that the city's substantial interest in limiting sound volume is served in a direct and effective way by the requirement that the city's sound technician control the mixing board during performances. Absent this requirement, the city's interest would have been served less well, as is evidenced by the complaints about excessive volume generated by respondent's past concerts. The alternative regulatory methods hypothesized by the Court of Appeals reflect nothing more than a disagreement with the city over how much control of volume is appropriate or how that level of control is to be achieved. The Court of Appeals erred in failing to defer to the city's reasonable determination that its interest in controlling volume would be best served by requiring bandshell performers to utilize the city's sound technician.

The city's second content-neutral justification for the guideline, that of ensuring "that the sound amplification [is] sufficient to reach all listeners within the defined concert ground," also supports the city's choice of regulatory methods. By providing competent sound technicians and adequate amplification equipment, the city eliminated the problems of inexperienced technicians and insufficient sound volume that had plagued some bandshell performers in the past. No doubt this concern is not applicable to respondent's concerts, which apparently were characterized by more-than-adequate sound amplification. But that fact is beside the point, for the validity of the regulation depends on the relation it bears to the overall problem the government seeks to correct, not on the extent to which it furthers the government's interests in an individual case. Here, the regulation's effectiveness must be judged by considering all the varied groups that use the bandshell, and it is valid so long as the city could reasonably have determined that its interests overall would be served less effectively without the sound-amplification guideline than with it. Considering these proffered justifications together, therefore, it is apparent that the guideline directly furthers the city's legitimate governmental interests and that those interests would have been less well served in the absence of the sound-amplification guideline.

. . .

C

The final requirement, that the guideline leave open ample alternative channels of communication, is easily met. Indeed, in this respect the guideline is far less restrictive than regulations we have upheld in other cases, for it does not attempt to ban any particular manner or type of expression at a given place or time. Rather, the guideline continues to permit expressive activity in the bandshell, and has no effect on the quantity or content of that expression beyond regulating the extent of amplification. That the city's limitations on volume may reduce to some degree the potential audience for respondent's speech is of no consequence, for there has been no showing that the remaining avenues of communication are inadequate.

. . .

Justice Blackmun concurs in the result.

Justice Marshall, with whom Justice Brennan and Justice Stevens join, dissenting.

No one can doubt that government has a substantial interest in regulating the barrage of excessive sound that can plague urban life. Unfortunately, the majority plays to our shared impatience with loud noise to obscure the damage that it does to our First Amendment rights. Until today, a key safeguard of free speech has been government's obligation to adopt the least intrusive restriction necessary to achieve its goals. By abandoning the requirement that time, place, and manner regulations must be narrowly tailored, the majority replaces constitutional scrutiny with mandatory deference. The majority's willingness to give government officials a free hand in achieving their policy ends extends so far as to permit, in this case, government control of speech in advance of its dissemination. Because New York City's Use Guidelines (Guidelines) are not narrowly tailored to serve its interest in regulating loud noise, and because they constitute an impermissible prior restraint, I dissent.

I

. . .

My complaint is with the majority's serious distortion of the narrow tailoring requirement. Our cases have not, as the majority asserts, "clearly" rejected a less-restrictive-alternative test. On the contrary, just last Term, we held that a statute is narrowly tailored only "if it targets and eliminates no more than the exact source of the 'evil' it seeks to remedy." *Frisby v. Schultz*. While there is language in a few opinions which, taken out of context, supports the majority's position, in practice, the Court has interpreted the narrow tailoring requirement to mandate an examination of alternative methods of serving the asserted governmental interest and a determination whether the greater efficacy of the challenged regulation outweighs the increased burden it places on protected speech. . . .

The Court's past concern for the extent to which a regulation burdens speech more than would a satisfactory alternative is noticeably absent from today's decision. The majority requires only that government show that its interest cannot be served as effectively without the challenged restriction. It will be enough, therefore, that the challenged regulation advances the government's interest only in the slightest, for any differential burden on speech that results does not enter the calculus. Despite its protestations to the contrary, the majority thus has abandoned the requirement that restrictions on speech be narrowly tailored in any ordinary use of the phrase. Indeed, after today's decision, a city could claim that bans on handbill distribution or on door-to-door solicitation are the most effective means of avoiding littering and fraud, or that a ban on loudspeakers and radios in a public park is the most effective means of avoiding loud noise. Logically extended, the majority's analysis would permit such far-reaching restrictions on speech.

. . . The Court of Appeals examined "how much control of volume is appropriate [and] how that level of control is to be achieved," but the majority admonishes that court for doing so, stating that it should have "defer[red] to the city's reasonable determination." The majority thus instructs courts to refrain from examining how much speech may be restricted to serve an asserted interest and how that level of restriction is to be achieved. If a court cannot engage in such inquiries, I am at a loss to understand how a court can ascertain whether the government has adopted a regulation that burdens substantially more speech than is necessary.

Had the majority not abandoned the narrow tailoring requirement, the Guidelines could not possibly survive constitutional scrutiny. Government's interest in avoiding loud sounds cannot justify giving government total control over sound equipment, any more than its interest in avoiding litter could justify a ban on handbill distribution. In both cases, government's legitimate goals can be effectively and less intrusively served by directly punishing the evil—the persons responsible for excessive sounds and the persons who litter. Indeed, the city concedes that it has an ordinance generally limiting noise but has chosen not to enforce it.

By holding that the Guidelines are valid time, place, and manner restrictions, notwithstanding the availability of less intrusive but effective means of controlling volume, the majority deprives the narrow tailoring requirement of all meaning. Today, the majority enshrines efficacy but sacrifices free speech.

. . .

DER: Justice Marshall's fears expressed in *Clark v. Community for Creative Non-Violence*, that the content-neutrality requirement had become a ceiling, rather than a minimum, of speech protection are even more exaggerated in *Ward's* version of the time, place and manner test. *Ward* turns the requirement that the restriction be narrowly tailored on its head. Instead of a test that ensures the *least* amount of infringement on speech necessary to fulfill the government's non-speech objectives, the *Ward* test favors restrictions that will impose the *most* amount of infringement. The regulation that serves the government's interests best is likely to interfere the most with the speaker's interests. Short of banning the speech altogether, it will always serve the state's interests perfectly to have one of its bureaucrats monitor the performance. Ultimately, the *Ward* test allows any restriction that serves a government purpose other than restricting the content of speech.

DEL: The *Ward* decision illustrates how time, place and manner analysis has become a method of judicial deference that enables government to insinuate itself deeply into the business of expressive control. The lowered standard of review, when regulation channels rather than suppresses speech, affords meaningful opportunities for government to affect the style and efficacy of expression. Merely requiring a regulation to promote "a substantial government interest that would be achieved less effectively absent the regulation" makes a mockery of the demand for narrow tailoring. So deferential to regulatory interests is time, place and manner doctrine in *Ward* that it accommodated a system of prior restraint. Even if the city's sound technician had not performed unsatisfactorily from the perspective of performers, the role is difficult to distinguish from a censorship board that in its actual performance has seldom refused to license a film or other form of expression. The Court has determined that "any system of prior restraint of expression carries a heavy presumption against its constitutional validity."[97] Relaxed standards for assessing time, place or manner regulation provide a mechanism for indulging such methodology, however, despite historical understanding that the central guarantee of freedom of the press "consists in laying no previous restraints upon publications."[98]

In *Ladue v. Gilleo*,[99] the Court unanimously invalidated a town ordinance that banned all residential signs, with some exemptions, in order to minimize visual clutter. The case arose when police advised Ms. Gilleo that the sign on her front law, bearing the message, "Say No to War in the Persian Gulf, Call Congress Now," violated the ordinance. The Court reasoned that the ordinance virtually eliminated an important and distinct medium of expression. Unlike the residential picketing ordinance in *Frisby*, this ban could not be justified as a time, place and manner restriction. Possible

---

[97] New York Times Co. v. United States, 403 U.S. 713, 713 (1971) (per curiam).
[98] Near v. Minnesota, 283 U.S. 697, 713 (1931).
[99] 114 S. Ct. 2038 (1994).

alternatives, such as handbills and newspaper advertisements, were inadequate substitutes for displaying a message on one's own property, which uniquely conveys information about the speaker's identify. Moreover, the audience intended to be reached by residential signs—one's neighbors and visitors—could not be reached as well by these other means of communication.

c. Regulating the Secondary Effects of Speech

In *City of Renton v. Playtime Theatres, Inc.*, a case involving the zoning of adult movie theaters, the Court examined the nature of the interest that government may assert in defending a time, place and manner regulation. Ten years earlier, in *Young v. American Mini Theatres*, the Court had upheld Detroit "Anti-Skid Row" ordinances that restricted the location of adult book stores and movie theaters, holding that, in order to preserve the character of its neighborhoods, "the State may legitimately use the content of these materials as the basis for placing them in a different classification from other motion pictures."[100] The *Renton* Court concluded that the zoning ordinance was content-neutral by focusing on the government's interest in combatting the theaters' "secondary effects," rather than the message of the movies they displayed. Although *Renton* concerned speech on *private* property, rather than in a public forum, the Court analyzed the ordinance at issue as a form of time, place, and manner regulation. *Renton*'s "secondary effects" analysis, therefore, may be relevant to the constitutionality of time, place, and manner restrictions of speech on public property, as well.

Indeed, two years after the *Renton* decision, a majority of justices suggested in *Boos v. Barry* that the government might justify a regulation that restricted even political speech in a public forum based on the secondary effects of the speech.[101] *Boos v. Barry* struck down part of a District of Columbia ordinance that prohibited the display of any sign within 500 feet of a foreign embassy that tends to bring the foreign government into "public odium" or "public disrepute." In distinguishing *Renton*, Justice O'Connor, joined by Justices Stevens and Scalia, wrote: "Respondents and the United States do not point to the 'secondary effects' of picket signs in front of embassies. They do not point to congestion, to interference with ingress or egress, to visual clutter, or to the need to protect the dignity of foreign diplomatic personnel by shielding them from speech that is critical of their government. . . . Because the display clause regulates speech due to its potential primary impact, we conclude it must be considered content-based." Justices Rehnquist, White and Blackmun voted to uphold the ordinance on the basis of Judge Bork's opinion below, which also suggested that a *Renton* secondary effects analysis might apply to political speech in public forums.[102] Justice Brennan, joined by Justice Marshall, concurred in Justice O'Connor's conclusion that the ordinance was content-based, but contested the "assumption that the *Renton* analysis applies not only outside the context of businesses purveying sexually explicit materials but even to political speech."

---

[100] Young v. American Mini-Theatres, Inc., 427 U.S. 50 (1976).
[101] Boos v. Barry, 485 U.S. 312 (1988).
[102] *See* Finzer v. Barry, 798 F.2d 1450, 1469–70 n. 15 (D.C. Cir. 1986).

City of Renton v. Playtime Theatres, Inc.
475 U.S. 41 (1986)

JUSTICE REHNQUIST delivered the opinion of the Court.

This case involves a constitutional challenge to a zoning ordinance, enacted by appellant city of Renton, Washington, that prohibits adult motion picture theaters from locating within 1,000 feet of any residential zone, single- or multiple-family dwelling, church, park, or school. Appellees, Playtime Theatres, Inc., and Sea-First Properties, Inc., filed an action in the United States District Court for the Western District of Washington seeking a declaratory judgment that the Renton ordinance violated the First and Fourteenth Amendments and a permanent injunction against its enforcement. The District Court ruled in favor of Renton and denied the permanent injunction, but the Court of Appeals for the Ninth Circuit reversed and remanded for reconsideration. We . . . now reverse the judgment of the Ninth Circuit.

. . .

In our view, the resolution of this case is largely dictated by our decision in *Young v. American Mini Theatres, Inc.* There, although five Members of the Court did not agree on a single rationale for the decision, we held that the city of Detroit's zoning ordinance, which prohibited locating an adult theater within 1,000 feet of any two other "regulated uses" or within 500 feet of any residential zone, did not violate the First and Fourteenth Amendments. The Renton ordinance, like the one in *American Mini Theatres*, does not ban adult theaters altogether, but merely provides that such theaters may not be located within 1,000 feet of any residential zone, single- or multiple-family dwelling, church, park, or school. The ordinance is therefore properly analyzed as a form of time, place, and manner regulation.

Describing the ordinance as a time, place, and manner regulation is, of course, only the first step in our inquiry. This Court has long held that regulations enacted for the purpose of restraining speech on the basis of its content presumptively violate the First Amendment. On the other hand, so-called "content-neutral" time, place, and manner regulations are acceptable so long as they are designed to serve a substantial governmental interest and do not unreasonably limit alternative avenues of communication.

At first glance, the Renton ordinance, like the ordinance in *American Mini Theatres*, does not appear to fit neatly into either the "content-based" or the "content-neutral" category. To be sure, the ordinance treats theaters that specialize in adult films differently from other kinds of theaters. Nevertheless, as the District Court concluded, the Renton ordinance is aimed not at the *content* of the films shown at "adult motion picture theatres," but rather at the *secondary effects* of such theaters on the surrounding community. The District Court found that the City Council's *"predominate concerns"* were with the secondary effects of adult theaters, and not with the content of adult films themselves. But the Court of Appeals . . . held that this was not enough to sustain the ordinance. According to the Court of Appeals, if *"a motivating factor"* in enacting the ordinance was to restrict respondents' exercise of First Amendment rights the ordinance would be invalid, apparently no matter how small a part this motivating factor may have played in the City Council's decision. This view of the law was rejected in *United States v. O'Brien,* the very case that the Court of Appeals said it was applying. . . .

The District Court's finding as to "predominate" intent, left undisturbed by the Court of Appeals, is more than adequate to establish that the city's pursuit of its zoning interests here was unrelated to the suppression of free expression. The ordinance by its terms is designed to prevent crime, protect the city's retail trade, maintain property values, and generally "protec[t] and preserv[e] the quality of [the city's] neighborhoods, commercial districts, and the quality of urban life," not to suppress the expression of unpopular views. As JUSTICE POWELL observed in *American Mini Theatres,* "[i]f [the city] had been concerned with restricting the message purveyed by adult theaters, it would have tried to close them or restrict their number rather than circumscribe their choice as to location."

In short, the Renton ordinance is completely consistent with our definition of "content-neutral" speech regulations as those that "are *justified* without reference to the content of the regulated speech." The ordinance does not contravene the fundamental principle that underlies our concern about "content-based" speech regulations: that "government may not grant the use of a forum to people whose views it finds acceptable, but deny use to those wishing to express less favored or more controversial views."

It was with this understanding in mind that, in *American Mini Theatres,* a majority of this Court decided that, at least with respect to businesses that purvey sexually explicit materials, zoning ordinances designed to combat the undesirable secondary effects of such businesses are to be reviewed under the standards applicable to "content-neutral" time, place, and manner regulations. JUSTICE STEVENS, writing for the plurality, concluded that the city of Detroit was entitled to draw a distinction between adult theaters and other kinds of theaters "without violating the government's paramount obligation of neutrality in its regulation of protected communication," noting that "[i]t is th[e] secondary effect which these zoning ordinances attempt to avoid, not the dissemination of 'offensive' speech." . . .

The appropriate inquiry in this case, then, is whether the Renton ordinance is designed to serve a substantial governmental interest and allows for reasonable alternative avenues of communication. It is clear that the ordinance meets such a standard. As a majority of this Court recognized in *American Mini Theatres*, a city's "interest in attempting to preserve the quality of urban life is one that must be accorded high respect." Exactly the same vital governmental interests are at stake here.

The Court of Appeals ruled, however, that because the Renton ordinance was enacted without the benefit of studies specifically relating to "the particular problems or needs of Renton," the city's justifications for the ordinance were "conclusory and speculative." We think the Court of Appeals imposed on the city an unnecessarily rigid burden of proof. The record in this case reveals that Renton relied heavily on the experience of, and studies produced by, the city of Seattle. In Seattle, as in Renton, the adult theater zoning ordinance was aimed at preventing the secondary effects caused by the presence of even one such theater in a given neighborhood. . . .

We hold that Renton was entitled to rely on the experiences of Seattle and other cities, and in particular on the "detailed findings" summarized in the Washington Supreme Court's *Northend Cinema* opinion, in enacting its adult theater zoning ordinance. The First Amendment does not require a city, before enacting such an ordinance, to conduct new studies or produce evidence independent of that already generated by other cities, so long as whatever evidence the city relies upon is reasonably believed to be relevant to the problem that the city addresses. That was the case here. Nor is our holding affected by the fact that Seattle ultimately chose a different method of adult theater zoning than that chosen by Renton, since Seattle's choice of a different remedy to combat the secondary effects of adult theaters does not call into question either Seattle's identification of those secondary effects or the relevance of Seattle's experience to Renton.

We also find no constitutional defect in the method chosen by Renton to further its substantial interests. Cities may regulate adult theaters by dispersing them, as in Detroit, or by effectively concentrating them, as in Renton. "It is not our function to appraise the wisdom of [the city's] decision to require adult theaters to be separated rather than concentrated in the same areas. . . . [T]he city must be allowed a reasonable opportunity to experiment with solutions to admittedly serious problems." *American Mini Theatres*. Moreover, the Renton ordinance is "narrowly tailored" to affect only that category of theaters shown to produce the unwanted secondary effects. . . .

Respondents contend that the Renton ordinance is "under-inclusive," in that it fails to regulate other kinds of adult businesses that are likely to produce secondary effects similar to those produced by adult theaters. On this record the contention must fail. There is no evidence that, at the time the Renton ordinance was enacted, any other adult business was located in, or was contemplating moving into, Renton. . . . That Renton chose first to address the potential problems created by one particular kind of adult business in no way suggests that the city has "singled out" adult theaters for discriminatory treatment. We simply have no basis on this record for assuming that Renton will not, in the future, amend its ordinance to include other kinds of adult businesses that have been shown to produce the same kinds of secondary effects as adult theaters.

Finally, turning to the question whether the Renton ordinance allows for reasonable alternative avenues of communication, we note that the ordinance leaves some 520 acres, or more than five percent of the entire land area of Renton, open to use as adult theater sites. The District Court found, and the Court of Appeals did not dispute the finding, that the 520 acres of land consists of "[a]mple, accessible real estate," including "acreage in all stages of development from raw land to developed, industrial, warehouse, office, and shopping space that is criss-crossed by freeways, highways, and roads."

Respondents argue, however, that some of the land in question is already occupied by existing businesses, that "practically none" of the undeveloped land is currently for sale or lease, and that in general there are no "commercially viable" adult theater sites within the 520 acres left open by the Renton ordinance. The Court of Appeals accepted these arguments, concluded that the 520 acres was not truly "available" land, and therefore held that the Renton ordinance "would result in a substantial restriction" on speech.

We disagree with both the reasoning and the conclusion of the Court of Appeals. That respondents must fend for themselves in the real estate market, on an equal footing with other prospective purchasers and lessees, does not give rise to a First Amendment violation.

And although we have cautioned against the enactment of zoning regulations that have "the effect of suppressing, or greatly restricting access to, lawful speech," we have never suggested that the First Amendment compels the Government to ensure that adult theaters, or any other kinds of speech-related businesses for that matter, will be able to obtain sites at bargain prices. In our view, the First Amendment requires only that Renton refrain from effectively denying respondents a reasonable opportunity to open and operate an adult theater within the city, and the ordinance before us easily meets this requirement.

In sum, we find that the Renton ordinance represents a valid governmental response to the "admittedly serious problems" created by adult theaters. Renton has not used "the power to zone as a pretext for suppressing expression," but rather has sought to make some areas available for adult theaters and their patrons, while at the same time preserving the quality of life in the community at large by preventing those theaters from locating in other areas. This, after all, is the essence of zoning. Here, as in *American Mini Theatres*, the city has enacted a zoning ordinance that meets these goals while also satisfying the dictates of the First Amendment. The judgment of the Court of Appeals is therefore

Reversed.

JUSTICE BLACKMUN concurs in the result.

JUSTICE BRENNAN, with whom JUSTICE MARSHALL joins, dissenting.

Renton's zoning ordinance selectively imposes limitations on the location of a movie theater based exclusively on the content of the films shown there. The constitutionality of the ordinance is therefore not correctly analyzed under standards applied to content-neutral time, place, and manner restrictions. But even assuming that the ordinance may fairly be characterized as content neutral, it is plainly unconstitutional under the standards established by the decisions of this Court. Although the Court's analysis is limited to cases involving "businesses that purvey sexually explicit materials," and thus does not affect our holdings in cases involving state regulation of other kinds of speech, I dissent.

I

. . .

The fact that adult movie theaters may cause harmful "secondary" land-use effects may arguably give Renton a compelling reason to regulate such establishments; it does not mean, however, that such regulations are content neutral. Because the ordinance imposes special restrictions on certain kinds of speech on the basis of content, I cannot simply accept, as the Court does, Renton's claim that the ordi-

nance was not designed to suppress the content of adult movies. . . . In this case, both the language of the ordinance and its dubious legislative history belie the Court's conclusion that "the city's pursuit of its zoning interests here was unrelated to the suppression of free expression."

A

The ordinance discriminates on its face against certain forms of speech based on content. Movie theaters specializing in "adult motion pictures" may not be located within 1,000 feet of any residential zone, single- or multiple-family dwelling, church, park, or school. Other motion picture theaters, and other forms of "adult entertainment," such as bars, massage parlors, and adult bookstores, are not subject to the same restrictions. This selective treatment strongly suggests that Renton was interested not in controlling the "secondary effects" associated with adult businesses, but in discriminating against adult theaters based on the content of the films they exhibit. The Court ignores this discriminatory treatment, declaring that Renton is free "to address the potential problems created by one particular kind of adult business," and to amend the ordinance in the future to include other adult enterprises. However, because of the First Amendment interests at stake here, this one-step-at-a-time analysis is wholly inappropriate. . . .

B

Shortly *after* this lawsuit commenced, the Renton City Council amended the ordinance, adding a provision explaining that its intention in adopting the ordinance had been "to promote the City of Renton's great interest in protecting and preserving the quality of its neighborhoods, commercial districts, and the quality of urban life through effective land use planning." The amended ordinance also lists certain conclusory "findings" concerning adult entertainment land uses that the Council purportedly relied upon in adopting the ordinance. The city points to these provisions as evidence that the ordinance was designed to control the secondary effects associated with adult movie theaters, rather than to suppress the content of the films they exhibit. However, the "legislative history" of the ordinance strongly suggests otherwise.

. . .

The City Council conducted no studies, and heard no expert testimony, on how the protected uses would be affected by the presence of an adult movie theater, and never considered whether residents' concerns could be met by "restrictions that are less intrusive on protected forms of expression." As a result, any "findings" regarding "secondary effects" caused by adult movie theaters, or the need to adopt specific locational requirements to combat such effects, were not "findings" at all, but purely speculative conclusions. Such "findings" were not such as are required to justify the burdens the ordinance imposed upon constitutionally protected expression.

. . .

In sum, the circumstances here strongly suggest that the ordinance was designed to suppress expression, even that constitutionally protected, and thus was not to be analyzed as a content-neutral time, place, and manner restriction. The Court allows Renton to conceal its illicit motives, however, by reliance on the fact that other communities adopted similar restrictions. The Court's approach largely immunizes such measures from judicial scrutiny, since a municipality can readily find other municipal ordinances to rely upon, thus always retrospectively justifying special zoning regulations for adult theaters. Rather than speculate about Renton's motives for adopting such measures, our cases require the conclusion that the ordinance, like any other content-based restriction on speech, is constitutional "only if the [city] can show that [it] is a precisely drawn means of serving a compelling [governmental] interest." Only this strict approach can insure that cities will not use their zoning powers as a pretext for suppressing constitutionally protected expression.

Applying this standard to the facts of this case, the ordinance is patently unconstitutional. Renton has not shown that locating adult movie theaters in proximity to its churches, schools, parks, and residences will necessarily result in undesirable "secondary effects," or that these problems could not be effectively addressed by less intrusive restrictions.

II

Even assuming that the ordinance should be treated like a content-neutral time, place, and manner restriction, I would still find it unconstitutional. . . .

The Court finds that the ordinance was designed to further Renton's substantial interest in "preserv[ing] the quality of urban life." As explained above, the record here is simply insufficient to support this assertion. The city made no showing as to how uses "protected" by the ordinance would be affected by the presence of an adult movie theater. Thus, the Renton ordinance is clearly distinguishable from the Detroit zoning ordinance upheld in *Young v. American Mini Theatres, Inc.* . . . Here, the Renton Council was aware only that some residents had complained about adult movie theaters, and that other localities had adopted special zoning restrictions for such establishments. These are not "facts" sufficient to justify the burdens the ordinance imposed upon constitutionally protected expression.

Finally, the ordinance is invalid because it does not provide for reasonable alternative avenues of communication. The District Court found that the ordinance left 520 acres in Renton available for adult theater sites, an area comprising about five percent of the city. However, the Court of Appeals found that because much of this land was already occupied, "[l]imiting adult theater uses to these areas is a substantial restriction on speech." Many "available" sites are also largely unsuited for use by movie theaters. Again, these facts serve to distinguish this case from *American Mini Theaters*, where there was no indication that the Detroit zoning ordinance seriously limited the locations available for adult businesses.

Despite the evidence in the record, the Court reasons that the fact "[t]hat respondents must fend for themselves in the real estate market, on an equal footing with other prospective purchasers and lessees, does not give rise to a First Amendment violation." However, respondents are not on equal footing with other prospective purchasers and lessees, but must conduct business under severe restrictions not imposed upon other establishments. The Court also argues that the First Amendment does not compel "the government to ensure that adult theaters, or any other kinds of speech-related businesses for that matter, will be able to obtain sites at bargain prices." However, respondents do not ask Renton to guarantee low-price sites for their businesses, but seek only a reasonable opportunity to operate adult theaters in the city. By denying them this opportunity, Renton can effectively ban a form of protected speech from its borders. . . .

DER: *Renton* potentially adds another dimension to the progression from *Clark* to *Ward* that weakened the test for content-neutral time, place, and manner restrictions on speech. While *Ward* substantially watered down the narrowly tailored prong, *Renton* weakened the requirement that the government present a content-neutral justification. By focusing entirely on the government's justification, rather than the regulations's effect on speech, the time, place, and manner test allows government substantial freedom to interfere with speakers' preferred means of getting their message across. The secondary effects test makes it even easier for the government to explain its regulation in content-neutral terms.

The Court eased the government's burden in two ways. First, it provided the government with a simple, non-speech rationale. Second, it reduced the amount of proof the government must have in order to demonstrate that the asserted secondary effects of speech will actually occur. Indeed, it is permissible for government attorneys to concoct a non-speech justification, without the benefit of hearings, *after* the legislation is enacted. Thus, the Court has turned the requirement of a non-speech government justification into an easy excuse for infringing speech.

The secondary effects test may be less troublesome if confined to certain, "less valuable" speech. However, the Court did not confine its analysis to adult movie theatres, and language in *Boos v. Barry* suggests its broader application. If we substitute adult movies with another type of speech—say, political rallies—and crime and lower property values with other secondary effects—say, noise, congestion, and visual clutter, the potential dangers of the *Renton* test become obvious.

The Court could have followed three possible avenues in addressing Renton's concerns about adult movie theatres. First, it could have acknowledged that the zoning ordinance targeted these theatres because of the content of the movies, and therefore was subject to strict scrutiny. Second, the Court could have determined that this type of speech is less valuable or more regulable because it is less central to First Amendment concerns, and therefore subject the zoning ordinance to a lower standard of scrutiny. Finally, the Court could take the route that it did—further dilute the time, place, and manner test to allow the city more easily to defend its ordinance. Either of the first two alternatives would have been preferable to a far-reaching theory that upholds government pretexts for restricting speech based on its objectionable content.

DEL: The Court's decisions, upholding the zoning of adult movie theaters and similar property uses, illuminates how official control inspired by concern with content can masquerade as time, place and manner regulation. In *Young v. American Mini Theatres, Inc.*, Justice Stevens observed that "few of us would march our sons and daughters off to war to preserve the citizen's right to see 'Specified Sexual Activities' exhibited in the theaters of our choice."[103] Time, place and manner regulation, that commenced as a narrow allowance for efficient but content-neutral management of public fora, thus has expanded into a premise for official value judgment that is explicitly content-conscious.

---

[103] Young v. American Mini Theatres, Inc., 427 U.S. 50, 70 (1976).

d. New Public Forums

The public forum doctrine originated in Justice Roberts's declaration that the government has immemorially held the streets and parks in trust for public expression. It is well-established that the First Amendment guarantees freedom of speech in the "quintessential" traditional public forums of parks, streets and sidewalks. But are citizens subject to state discretion in their use of all other government property besides these traditional forums, as long as it is applied neutrally? It can be argued that times have changed since Justice Roberts's famous dictum and that additional modern public forums are now just as important to robust freedom of expression as traditional ones. In *International Society for Krishna Consciousness, Inc. v. Lee* the Supreme Court considered whether the concept of the traditional public forum should be extended to airport terminals. In the end, however, the justices' divergent opinions depended more on whether they believed the speech at issue was compatible with the intended use of the airport than on whether they classified airports as traditional public forums.

International Society for Krishna Consciousness, Inc. v. Lee
112 S. Ct. 2701 & 2711 (1992)

Chief Justice REHNQUIST delivered the opinion of the Court.

In this case we consider whether an airport terminal operated by a public authority is a public forum and whether a regulation prohibiting solicitation in the interior of an airport terminal violates the First Amendment.

The relevant facts in this case are not in dispute. Petitioner International Society for Krishna Consciousness, Inc. (ISKCON) is a not-for-profit religious corporation whose members perform a ritual known as *sankirtan*. The ritual consists of " 'going into public places, disseminating religious literature and soliciting funds to support the religion.' " The primary purpose of this ritual is raising funds for the movement.

Respondent Walter Lee . . . was the police superintendent of the Port Authority of New York and New Jersey and was charged with enforcing the regulation at issue. The Port Authority owns and operates three major airports in the greater New York City area: John F. Kennedy International Airport (Kennedy), La Guardia Airport (La Guardia), and Newark International Airport (Newark). The three airports collectively form one of the world's busiest metropolitan airport complexes. . . . The terminals are generally accessible to the general public and contain various commercial establishments such as restaurants, snack stands, bars, newsstands, and stores of various types. Virtually all who visit the terminals do so for purposes related to air travel. These visitors principally include passengers, those meeting or seeing off passengers, flight crews, and terminal employees.

The Port Authority has adopted a regulation forbidding within the terminals the repetitive solicitation of money or distribution of literature. . . . The regulation governs only the terminals; the Port Authority permits solicitation and distribution on the sidewalks outside the terminal buildings. The regulation effectively prohibits petitioner from performing *sankirtan* in the terminals. As a result, petitioner brought suit seeking declaratory and injunctive relief under 42 U.S.C. § 1983, alleging that the regulation worked to deprive them of rights guaranteed under the First Amendment. [A divided panel of the Court of Appeals concluded that the terminals were not public fora, and that the ban on solicitation was reasonable, but that the ban on distribution was not.]

. . .

It is uncontested that the solicitation at issue in this case is a form of speech protected under the First Amendment. But it is also well settled that the government need not permit all forms of speech on property that it owns and controls. Where the government is acting as a proprietor, managing its internal operations, rather than acting as lawmaker with the power to regulate or license, its action will not be subjected to the heightened review to which its actions as a lawmaker may be subject. Thus, we have upheld a ban on political advertisements in city-operated transit vehicles, *Lehman v. City of Shaker Heights*, 418 U.S. 298 (1974), even though the city permitted other types of advertising on those vehicles. Similarly, we have permitted a school district to limit access to an internal mail system used to communicate with teachers employed by the district. *Perry Education Assn. v. Perry Local Educators' Ass'n*, 460 U.S. 37 (1983).

These cases reflect, either implicitly or explicitly, a "forum-based" approach for assessing restrictions that the government seeks to place on the use of its property. Under this approach, regulation of speech on government property that has traditionally been available for public expression is subject to the highest scrutiny. Such regulations survive only if they are narrowly drawn to achieve a compelling state interest. The second category of public property is the designated public forum, whether of a limited or unlimited character—property that the state has opened for expressive activity by part or all of the public. Regulation of such property is subject to the same limitations as that governing a traditional public forum. Finally, there is all remaining public property. Limitations on expressive activity conducted on this last category of property must survive only a much more limited review. The challenged regulation need only be reasonable, as long as the regulation is not an effort to suppress the speaker's activity due to disagreement with the speaker's view.

The parties do not disagree that this is the proper framework. Rather, they disagree whether the airport terminals are public fora or nonpublic fora. They also disagree whether the regulation survives the "reasonableness" review governing nonpublic fora, should that prove the appropriate category. Like the Court of Appeals, we conclude that the terminals are nonpublic fora and that the regulation reasonably limits solicitation.

The suggestion that the government has a high burden in justifying speech restrictions relating to traditional public fora made its first appearance in *Hague v. Committee for Industrial Organization*. We confirmed this observation in *Frisby v. Schultz*, where we held that a residential street was a public forum.

Our recent cases provide additional guidance on the characteristics of a public forum. In *Cornelius [v. NAACP Legal Defense and Educational Fund, Inc.*, 473 U.S. 788 (1985)], we noted that a traditional public forum is property that has as "a principal purpose . . . the free exchange of ideas." Moreover, consistent with the notion that the government—like other property owners—"has power to preserve the property under its control for the use to which it is lawfully dedicated," the government does not create a public forum by inaction. Nor is a public forum created "whenever members of the public are permitted freely to visit a place owned or operated by the Government." The decision to create a public forum must instead be made "by intentionally opening a nontraditional forum for public discourse." Finally, we have recognized that the location of property also has bearing because separation from acknowledged public areas may serve to indicate that the separated property is a special enclave, subject to greater restriction.

These precedents foreclose the conclusion that airport terminals are public fora. Reflecting the general growth of the air travel industry, airport terminals have only recently achieved their contemporary size and character. But given the lateness with which the modern air terminal has made its appearance, it hardly qualifies for the description of having "immemorially . . . time out of mind" been held in the public trust and used for purposes of expressive activity. *Hague*. Moreover, even within the rather short history of air transport, it is only "[i]n recent years [that] it has become a common practice for various religious and non-profit organizations to use commercial airports as a forum for the distribution of literature, the solicitation of funds, the proselytizing of new members, and other similar activities." Thus, the tradition of airport activity does not demonstrate that airports have historically been made available for speech activity. Nor can we say that these particular terminals, or airport terminals generally, have been intentionally opened by their operators to such activity; the frequent and continuing litigation evidencing the operators' objections belies any such claim. In short, there can be no argument that society's time-tested judgment, expressed through acquiescence in a continuing practice, has resolved the issue in petitioner's favor.

Petitioner attempts to circumvent the history and practice governing airport activity by pointing our attention to the variety of speech activity that it claims historically occurred at various "transportation nodes" such as rail stations, business stations, wharves, and Ellis Island. Even if we were inclined to accept petitioner's historical account describing speech activity at these locations, an account respondent contests, we think that such evidence is of little import for two reasons. First, much of the evidence is irrelevant to *public* fora analysis, because sites such as business and rail terminals traditionally have had *private* ownership. The development of privately owned parks that ban speech activity would not change the public fora status of publicly held parks. But the reverse is also true. The practices of privately held transportation centers do not bear on the government's regulatory authority over a publicly owned airport.

Second, the relevant unit for our inquiry is an airport, not "transportation nodes" generally. When new methods of transportation develop, new methods for accommodating that transportation are also likely to be needed. And with each new step, it therefore will be a new inquiry whether the transportation necessities are compatible with various kinds of expressive activity. To make a category of "transportation nodes," therefore, would unjustifiably elide what may prove to be critical differences of which we should rightfully take account. . . .

The differences among such facilities are unsurprising since . . . airports are commercial establishments funded by users fees and designed to make a regulated profit and where nearly all who visit do so for some travel related purpose. As commercial enterprises, airports must provide services attractive to the marketplace. In light of this, it cannot fairly be said that an airport terminal has as a principal purpose "promoting the free exchange of ideas." To the contrary, the record demonstrates that Port Authority management considers the purpose of the terminals to be the facilitation of passenger air travel, not the promotion of expression. . . . Although many airports have expanded their function beyond merely contributing to efficient air travel, few have included among their purposes the designation of a forum for solicitation and distribution activities. Thus, we think that neither by tradition nor purpose can the terminals be described as satisfying the standards we have previously set out for identifying a public forum.

The restrictions here challenged, therefore, need only satisfy a requirement of reasonableness. We reiterate what we stated in [*United States v. Kokinda*, 497 U.S. 720 (1990)], the restriction "'need only be reasonable; it need not be the most reasonable or the only reasonable limitation.'" We have no doubt that under this standard the prohibition on solicitation passes muster.

We have on many prior occasions noted the disruptive effect that solicitation may have on business. "Solicitation requires action by those who would respond: The individual solicited must decide whether or not to contribute (which itself might involve reading the solicitor's literature or hearing his pitch), and then, having decided to do so, reach for a wallet, search it for money, write a check, or produce a credit card." *Kokinda.* Passengers who wish to avoid the solicitor may have to alter their path, slowing both themselves and those around them. The result is that the normal flow of traffic is impeded. This is especially so in an airport, where "air travelers, who are often weighted down by cumbersome baggage . . . may be hurrying to catch a plane or to arrange ground transportation." Delays may be particularly costly in this setting, as a flight missed by only a few minutes can result in hours worth of subsequent inconvenience.

In addition, face-to-face solicitation presents risks of duress that are an appropriate target of regulation. The skillful, and unprincipled, solicitor can target the most vulnerable, including those accompanying children or those suffering physical impairment and who cannot easily avoid the solicitation. The unsavory solicitor can also commit fraud through concealment of his affiliation or through deliberate efforts to shortchange those who agree to purchase. Compounding this problem is the fact that, in an airport, the targets of such activity frequently are on tight schedules. This in turn makes such visitors unlikely to stop and formally complain to airport authorities. As a result, the airport faces considerable difficulty in achieving its legitimate interest in monitoring solicitation activity to assure that travelers are not interfered with unduly.

. . .

The inconveniences to passengers and the burdens on Port Authority officials flowing from solicitation activity may seem small, but viewed against the fact that "pedestrian congestion is one of the greatest problems facing the three terminals," the Port Authority could reasonably worry that even such incremental effects would prove quite disruptive. Moreover, "the justification for the Rule should not be measured by the disorder that would result from granting an exemption solely to ISKCON." For if petitioner is given access, so too must other groups. . . .

For the foregoing reasons, the judgment of the Court of Appeals sustaining the ban on solicitation in Port Authority terminals is
Affirmed.

[A separate *per curiam* decision affirmed the Court of Appeals' holding that the ban on distribution of literature in the terminals is invalid under the First Amendment.]

Chief Justice REHNQUIST, with whom Justice WHITE, Justice SCALIA and Justice THOMAS join, dissenting.

. . .

. . . The risks and burdens posed by leafletting are quite similar to those posed by solicitation. The weary, harried, or hurried traveler may have no less desire and need to avoid delays generated by having literature foisted upon him than he does to avoid delays from a financial solicitation. And while a busy passenger perhaps may succeed in fending off a leafletter with minimal disruption to himself by agreeing simply to take the proffered material, this does not completely ameliorate the dangers of congestion flowing from such leafletting. Others may choose not simply to accept the material but also to stop and engage the leafletter in debate, obstructing those who follow. Moreover, those who accept material may often simply drop it on the floor once out of the leafletter's range, creating an eyesore, a safety hazard, and additional clean-up work for airport staff.

. . .

Justice O'CONNOR, concurring. . . .

I . . . agree that publicly owned airports are not public fora. Unlike public streets and parks, both of which our First Amendment jurisprudence has identified as "traditional public fora," airports do not count among their purposes the "free exchange of ideas;" they have not "by long tradition or by government fiat . . . been devoted to assembly and debate;" nor have they "time out of mind, . . . been used for purposes of . . . communicating thoughts between citizens, and discussing public questions." Although most airports do not ordinarily restrict public access, "[p]ublicly owned or operated property does not become a 'public forum' simply because members of the public are permitted to come and go at will." . . . There is little doubt that airports are among those publicly owned facilities that could be closed to all except those who have legitimate business there. Public access to airports is thus not "inherent in the open nature of the locations," as it is for most streets and parks, but is rather a "matter of grace by government officials." I also agree with the Court that the Port Authority has not expressly opened its airports to the types of expression at issue here, and therefore has not created a "limited" or "designated" public forum relevant to this case.

For these reasons, the Port Authority's restrictions on solicitation and leafletting within the airport terminals do not qualify for the strict scrutiny that applies to restriction of speech in public fora. That airports are not public fora, however, does not mean that the government can restrict speech in whatever way it likes. "The Government, even when acting in its proprietary capacity, does not enjoy absolute freedom from First Amendment constraints." *Kokinda*. . . . Moreover, we have consistently stated that restrictions on speech in nonpublic fora are valid only if they are "reasonable" and "not an effort to suppress expression merely because public officials oppose the speaker's view." The determination that airports are not public fora thus only begins our inquiry.

"The reasonableness of the Government's restriction [on speech in a nonpublic forum] must be assessed in light of the purpose of the forum and all the surrounding circumstances." *Cornelius*. "'[C]onsideration of a forum's special attributes is relevant to the constitutionality of a regulation since the significance of the governmental interest must be assessed in light of the characteristic nature and function of the particular forum involved.'" *Kokinda*. In this case, the "special attributes" and "surrounding circumstances" of the airports operated by the Port Authority are determinative. Not only has the Port Authority chosen not to limit access to the airports under its control, it has created a huge complex open to travelers and nontravelers alike. The airports house restaurants, cafeterias, snack bars, coffee shops, cocktail lounges, post offices, banks, telegraph offices, clothing shops, drug stores, food stores, nurseries, barber shops, currency exchanges, art exhibits, commercial advertising displays, bookstores, newsstands, dental offices and private clubs. The International Arrivals Building at JFK Airport even has two branches of Bloomingdale's.

We have said that a restriction on speech in a nonpublic forum is "reasonable" when it is "consistent with the [government's] legitimate interest in 'preserv[ing] the property . . . for the use to which it is lawfully dedicated.'" *Perry*. Ordinarily, this inquiry is relatively straightforward, because we have almost always been confronted with cases where the fora at issue were discrete, single-purpose facilities. The Port Authority urges that this case is no different and contends that it, too, has dedicated its airports to a single purpose—facilitating air travel—and that the speech it seeks to prohibit is not consistent with that purpose. But the wide range of activities promoted by the Port Authority is no more directly related to facilitating air travel than are the types of activities in which ISKCON wishes to engage. In my view, the Port Authority is operating a shopping mall as well as an airport. The reasonable-

ness inquiry, therefore, is not whether the restrictions on speech are "consistent with . . . preserving the property" for air travel, but whether they are reasonably related to maintaining the multipurpose environment that the Port Authority has deliberately created.

Applying that standard, I agree . . . that the ban on solicitation is reasonable. Face-to-face solicitation is incompatible with the airport's functioning in a way that the other, permitted activities are not. . . . The record in this case confirms that the problems of congestion and fraud that we have identified with solicitation in other contexts have also proved true in the airports' experience. Because airports' users are frequently facing time constraints, and are traveling with luggage or children, the ban on solicitation is a reasonable means of avoiding disruption of an airport's operation.

In my view, however, the regulation banning leafletting—or, in the Port Authority's words, the "continuous or repetitive . . . distribution of . . . printed or written material"—cannot be upheld as reasonable on this record. I therefore concur in the judgment . . . striking down that prohibition. While the difficulties posed by solicitation in a nonpublic forum are sufficiently obvious that its regulation may "rin[g] of common-sense," the same is not necessarily true of leafletting. To the contrary, we have expressly noted that leafletting does not entail the same kinds of problems presented by face-to-face solicitation. Specifically, "[o]ne need not ponder the contents of a leaflet or pamphlet in order mechanically to take it out of someone's hand. . . . 'The distribution of literature does not require that the recipient stop in order to receive the message the speaker wishes to convey; instead the recipient is free to read the message at a later time.'" *Kokinda*. With the possible exception of avoiding litter, it is difficult to point to any problems intrinsic to the act of leafletting that would make it naturally incompatible with a large, multipurpose forum such as those at issue here.

We have only once before considered restrictions on speech in a nonpublic forum that sustained the kind of extensive, nonforum-related activity found in the Port Authority airports, and I believe that case is instructive. In *Greer v. Spock*, 424 U.S. 828 (1976), the Court held that even though certain parts of a military base were open to the public, they still did not constitute a public forum in light of "'the historically unquestioned power of [a] commanding officer summarily to exclude civilians from the area of his command.'" The Court then proceeded to uphold a regulation banning the distribution of literature without the prior approval of the base commander. In so doing, the Court "emphasized" that the regulation on leafletting did "not authorize the Fort Dix authorities to prohibit the distribution of conventional political campaign literature." Rather, the Court explained, "[t]he only publications that a military commander may disapprove are those that he finds constitute 'a clear danger to [military] loyalty, discipline, or morale' " and that "[t]here is nothing in the Constitution that disables a military commander from acting to avert what he perceives to be a clear danger to the loyalty, discipline, or morale of troops on the base under his command." In contrast, the regulation at issue in this case effects an absolute prohibition and is not supported by any independent justification outside of the problems caused by the accompanying solicitation.

Moreover, the Port Authority has not offered any justifications or record evidence to support its ban on the distribution of pamphlets alone. Its argument is focused instead on the problems created when literature is distributed in conjunction with a solicitation plea. . . . Because I cannot see how peaceful pamphleteering is incompatible with the multipurpose environment of the Port Authority airports, I cannot accept that a total ban on that activity is reasonable without an explanation as to why such a restriction "preserv[es] the property" for the several uses to which it has been put.

Of course, it is still open for the Port Authority to promulgate regulations of the time, place, and manner of leafletting which are "content-neutral, narrowly tailored to serve a significant government interest, and leave open ample alternative channels of communication." For example, during the many years that this litigation has been in progress, the Port Authority has not banned *sankirtan* completely from JFK International Airport, but has restricted it to a relatively uncongested part of the airport terminals, the same part that houses the airport chapel. In my view, that regulation meets the standards we have applied to time, place, and manner restrictions of protected expression.

. . .

Justice KENNEDY, with whom Justice BLACKMUN, Justice STEVENS, and Justice SOUTER join as to Part I, concurring in the judgment.

While I concur in the judgment affirming in this case, my analysis differs in substantial respects from that of the Court. In my view the airport corridors and shopping areas outside of the passenger security zones, areas operated by the Port Authority, are public forums, and speech in those places is entitled to protection against all government regulation inconsistent with public forum principles. The Port Authority's blanket prohibition on the distribution or sale of literature cannot meet those stringent standards, and I agree it is invalid under the First and Fourteenth Amendments. The Port Authority's rule disallowing in-person solicitation of money for immediate payment, however, is in my view a narrow and valid regulation of the time, place, and manner of protected speech in this forum, or else is a valid regulation of the nonspeech element of expressive conduct. I would sustain the Port Authority's ban on solicitation and receipt of funds.

I

An earlier opinion expressed my concern that "[i]f our public forum jurisprudence is to retain vitality, we must recognize that certain objective characteristics of Government property and its customary use by the public may control" the status of the property. *United States v. Kokinda* (KENNEDY, J., concurring in judgment). The case before us does not heed that principle. Our public forum doctrine ought not to be a jurisprudence of categories rather than ideas or convert what was once an analysis protective of expression into one which grants the government authority to restrict speech by fiat. I believe that the Court's public forum analysis in this case is inconsistent with the values underlying the speech and press clauses of the First Amendment.

Our public forum analysis has its origins in Justice Roberts' rather sweeping dictum in *Hague v. Committee for Industrial Organization*. The doctrine was not stated with much precision or elaboration, though, until our more recent decisions in *Perry Education Assn. v. Perry Local Educators' Assn. and Cornelius v. NAACP Legal Defense & Educational Fund, Inc.* These cases describe a three part analysis to designate government-owned property as either a traditional public forum, a designated public forum, or a nonpublic forum. The Court today holds that traditional public forums are limited to public property which have as "'a principal purpose . . . the free exchange of ideas'"; and that this purpose must be evidenced by a long-standing historical practice of permitting speech. The Court also holds that designated forums consist of property which the government intends to open for public discourse. All other types of property are, in the Court's view, nonpublic forums (in other words, not public forums), and government-imposed restrictions of speech in these places will be upheld so long as reasonable and viewpoint-neutral. . . .

This analysis is flawed at its very beginning. It leaves the government with almost unlimited authority to restrict speech on its property by doing nothing more than articulating a non-speech-related purpose for the area, and it leaves almost no scope for the development of new public forums absent the rare approval of the government. The Court's error lies in its conclusion that the public-forum status of public property depends on the government's defined purpose for the property, or on an explicit decision by the government to dedicate the property to expressive activity. In my view, the inquiry must be an objective one, based on the actual, physical characteristics and uses of the property. The fact that in our public-forum cases we discuss and analyze these precise characteristics tends to support my position.

The First Amendment is a limitation on government, not a grant of power. Its design is to prevent the government from controlling speech. Yet under the Court's view the authority of the government to control speech on its property is paramount, for in almost all cases the critical step in the Court's analysis is a classification of the property that turns on the government's own definition or decision, unconstrained by an independent duty to respect the speech its citizens can voice there. The Court acknowledges as much, by reintroducing today into our First Amendment law a strict doctrinal line between the proprietary and regulatory functions of government which I thought had been abandoned long ago. [C]ompare *Davis v. Massachusetts* with *Hague v. Committee for Industrial Organization; Schneider v. State.*

The Court's approach is contrary to the underlying purposes of the public forum doctrine. The liberties protected by our doctrine derive from the Assembly, as well as the Speech and Press Clauses of the First Amendment, and are essential to a functioning democracy. Public places are of necessity the locus for discussion of public issues, as well as protest against arbitrary government action. At the heart of our jurisprudence lies the principle that in a free nation citizens must have the right to gather and speak with other persons in public places. The recognition that certain government-owned property is a public forum provides open notice to citizens that their freedoms may be exercised there without fear of a censorial government, adding tangible reinforcement to the idea that we are a free people.

. . .

The Court's analysis rests on an inaccurate view of history. The notion that traditional public forums are property which have public discourse as their principal purpose is a most doubtful fiction. The types of property that we have recognized as the quintessential public forums are streets, parks, and sidewalks. It would seem apparent that the principal purpose of streets and sidewalks, like airports, is to facilitate transportation, not public discourse, and we have recognized as much. Similarly, the purpose for the creation of public parks may be as much for beauty and open space as for discourse. Thus under the Court's analysis, even the quintessential public forums would appear to lack the necessary elements of what the Court defines as a public forum.

The effect of the Court's narrow view of the first category of public forums is compounded by its description of the second purported category, the so-called "designated" forum. The requirements for such a designation are so stringent that I cannot be certain whether the category has any content left at all. In any event, it seems evident that under the Court's analysis today few if any types of property other than those already recognized as public forums will be accorded that status.

The Court's answer to these objections appears to be a recourse to history as justifying its recognition of streets, parks, and sidewalks, but apparently no other types of government property, as traditional public forums. The Court ignores the fact that the purpose of the public forum doctrine is to give effect to the broad command of the First Amendment to protect speech from governmental interference. The jurisprudence is rooted in historic practice, but it is not tied to a narrow textual command limiting the recognition of new forums. In my view the policies underlying the doctrine cannot be given effect unless we recognize that open, public spaces and thoroughfares which are suitable for discourse may be public forums, whatever their historical pedigree and without concern for a precise classification of the property. . . . Without this recognition our forum doctrine retains no relevance in times of fast-changing technology and increasing insularity. In a country where most citizens travel by automobile, and parks all too often become locales for crime rather than social intercourse, our failure to recognize the possibility that new types of government property may be appropriate forums for speech will lead to a serious curtailment of our expressive activity.

One of the places left in our mobile society that is suitable for discourse is a metropolitan airport. It is of particular importance to recognize that such spaces are public forums because in these days an airport is one of the few government-owned spaces where many persons have extensive contact with other members of the public. Given that private spaces of similar character are not subject to the dictates of the First Amendment, it is critical that we preserve these areas for protected speech. In my view, our public forum doctrine must recognize this reality, and allow the creation of public forums which do not fit within the narrow tradition of streets, sidewalks, and parks. We have allowed flexibility in our doctrine to meet changing technologies in other areas of constitutional interpretation, see, *e.g.*, *Katz v. United*

States, 389 U.S. 347 (1967), and I believe we must do the same with the First Amendment.

I agree with the Court that government property of a type which by history and tradition has been available for speech activity must continue to be recognized as a public forum. In my view, however, constitutional protection is not confined to these properties alone. Under the proper circumstances I would accord public forum status to other forms of property, regardless of its ancient or contemporary origins and whether or not it fits within a narrow historic tradition. If the objective, physical characteristics of the property at issue and the actual public access and uses which have been permitted by the government indicate that expressive activity would be appropriate and compatible with those uses, the property is a public forum. The most important considerations in this analysis are whether the property shares physical similarities with more traditional public forums, whether the government has permitted or acquiesced in broad public access to the property, and whether expressive activity would tend to interfere in a significant way with the uses to which the government has as a factual matter dedicated the property. In conducting the last inquiry, courts must consider the consistency of those uses with expressive activities in general, rather than the specific sort of speech at issue in the case before it; otherwise the analysis would be one not of classification but rather of case-by-case balancing, and would provide little guidance to the State regarding its discretion to regulate speech. Courts must also consider the availability of reasonable time, place, and manner restrictions in undertaking this compatibility analysis. The possibility of some theoretical inconsistency between expressive activities and the property's uses should not bar a finding of a public forum, if those inconsistencies can be avoided through simple and permitted regulations.

· · ·

Under this analysis, it is evident that the public spaces of the Port Authority's airports are public forums. First, the District Court made detailed findings regarding the physical similarities between the Port Authority's airports and public streets. These findings show that the public spaces in the airports are broad, public thoroughfares full of people and lined with stores and other commercial activities. An airport corridor is of course not a street, but that is not the proper inquiry. The question is one of physical similarities, sufficient to suggest that the airport corridor should be a public forum for the same reasons that streets and sidewalks have been treated as public forums by the people who use them.

Second, the airport areas involved here are open to the public without restriction. Plaintiffs do not seek access to the secured areas of the airports, nor do I suggest that these areas would be public forums. And while most people who come to the Port Authority's airports do so for a reason related to air travel, either because they are passengers or because they are picking up or dropping off passengers, this does not distinguish an airport from streets or sidewalks, which most people use for travel. Further, the group visiting the airports encompasses a vast portion of the public: In 1986 the Authority's three airports served over 78 million passengers. It is the very breadth and extent of the public's use of airports that makes it imperative to protect speech rights there. . . .

Third, and perhaps most important, it is apparent from the record, and from the recent history of airports, that when adequate time, place, and manner regulations are in place, expressive activity is quite compatible with the uses of major airports. The Port Authority's primary argument to the contrary is that the problem of congestion in its airports' corridors makes expressive activity inconsistent with the airports' primary purpose, which is to facilitate air travel. The First Amendment is often inconvenient. But that is besides the point. Inconvenience does not absolve the government of its obligation to tolerate speech. The Authority makes no showing that any real impediments to the smooth functioning of the airports cannot be cured with reasonable time, place, and manner regulations. . . . And in fact expressive activity has been a commonplace feature of our Nation's major airports for many years, in part because of the wide consensus among the Courts of Appeals, prior to the decision in this case, that the public spaces of airports are public forums. . . .

. . . The first challenged Port Authority regulation establishes a flat prohibition on "[t]he sale or distribution of flyers, brochures, pamphlets, books or any other printed or written material," if conducted within the airport terminal, "in a continuous or repetitive manner." We have long recognized that the right to distribute flyers and literature lies at the heart of the liberties guaranteed by the Speech and Press Clauses of the First Amendment. The Port Authority's rule, which prohibits almost all such activity, is among the most restrictive possible of those liberties. The regulation is in fact so broad and restrictive of speech, Justice O'CONNOR finds it void even under the standards applicable to government regulations in nonpublic forums. I have no difficulty deciding the regulation cannot survive the far more stringent rules applicable to regulations in public forums. The regulation is not drawn in narrow terms and it does not leave open ample alternative channels for communication. The

Port Authority's concerns with the problem of congestion can be addressed through narrow restrictions on the time and place of expressive activity. I would strike down the regulation as an unconstitutional restriction of speech.

II

It is my view, however, that the Port Authority's ban on the "solicitation and receipt of funds" within its airport terminals should be upheld under the standards applicable to speech regulations in public forums. The regulation may be upheld as either a reasonable time, place, and manner restriction, or as a regulation directed at the nonspeech element of expressive conduct. The two standards have considerable overlap in a case like this one.

. . .

I am in full agreement with the statement of the Court that solicitation is a form of protected speech. If the Port Authority's solicitation regulation prohibited all speech which requested the contribution of funds, I would conclude that it was a direct, content-based restriction of speech in clear violation of the First Amendment. The Authority's regulation does not prohibit all solicitation, however; it prohibits the "solicitation and receipt of funds." I do not understand this regulation to prohibit all speech that solicits funds. It reaches only personal solicitations for immediate payment of money. Otherwise, the "receipt of funds" phrase would be written out of the provision. The regulation does not cover, for example, the distribution of preaddressed envelopes along with a plea to contribute money to the distributor or his organization. As I understand the restriction it is directed only at the physical exchange of money, which is an element of conduct interwoven with otherwise expressive solicitation. In other words, the regulation permits expression that solicits funds, but limits the manner of that expression to forms other than the immediate receipt of money.

So viewed, I believe the Port Authority's rule survives our test for speech restrictions in the public forum. In-person solicitation of funds, when combined with immediate receipt of that money, creates a risk of fraud and duress which is well recognized, and which is different in kind from other forms of expression or conduct. Travelers who are unfamiliar with the airport, perhaps even unfamiliar with this country, its customs and its language, are an easy prey for the money solicitor. I agree in full with the Court's discussion of these dangers. . . . Because the Port Authority's solicitation ban is directed at these abusive practices and not at any particular message, idea, or form of speech, the regulation is a content-neutral rule serving a significant government interest. . . .

To survive scrutiny, the regulation must be drawn in narrow terms to accomplish its end and leave open ample alternative channels for communication. Regarding the former requirement, we have held that to be narrowly tailored a regulation need not be the least restrictive or least intrusive means of achieving an end. The regulation must be reasonable, and must not burden substantially more speech than necessary. *Ward.* Under this standard the solicitation ban survives with ease, because it prohibits only solicitation of money for immediate receipt. The regulation does not burden any broader category of speech or expressive conduct than is the source of the evil sought to be avoided. And in fact, the regulation is even more narrow because it only prohibits such behavior if conducted in a continuous or repetitive manner. The Port Authority has made a reasonable judgment that this type of conduct raises the most serious concerns, and it is entitled to deference. . . .

I have little difficulty in deciding that the Port Authority has left open ample alternative channels for the communication of the message which is an aspect of solicitation. As already discussed, the Authority's rule does not prohibit all solicitation of funds: It restricts only the manner of the solicitation, or the conduct associated with solicitation, to prohibit immediate receipt of the solicited money. Requests for money continue to be permitted, and in the course of requesting money solicitors may explain their cause, or the purposes of their organization, without violating the regulation. . . .

For these reasons I agree that the Court of Appeals should be affirmed in full in finding the Port Authority's ban on the distribution or sale of literature unconstitutional, but upholding the prohibition on solicitation and immediate receipt of funds.

Justice SOUTER, with whom Justice BLACKMUN and Justice STEVENS join, concurring . . . and dissenting. . . .

I

. . . I agree with Justice KENNEDY's view of the rule that should determine what is a public forum and with his conclusion that the public areas of the airports at issue here qualify as such. The designation of a given piece of public property as a traditional public forum must not merely state a conclusion that the property falls within a static category including streets, parks, sidewalks and perhaps not much more, but must represent a conclusion that the property is no different in principle from such examples, which we have previously described as "archetypes" of property from which the government was and is powerless to exclude speech. To treat the class of such forums as closed by their description as "traditional," taking that word merely as a charter for examining the history of the particular public property claimed as a forum, has no warrant in a Constitution whose values are not to be left behind in the city streets that are no longer the only focus of our community life. If that were the line of our direction, we might as well abandon the public forum doctrine altogether.

Nor is that a Scylla without Charybdis. Public forum analysis is stultified not only by treating its archetypes as closed categories, but by treating its candidates so categorically as to defeat their identification with the archetypes. We need not say that all "transportation nodes" or all airports are public forums in order to find that certain metropolitan airports are. Thus, the enquiry may and must relate to the particular property at issue and not necessarily to the "precise classification of the property." . . .

. . .

II

From the Court's conclusion . . . , however, sustaining the total ban on solicitation of money for immediate payment, I respectfully dissent. "We have held the solicitation of money by charities to be fully protected as the dissemination of ideas. It is axiomatic that, although fraudulent misrepresentation of facts can be regulated, the dissemination of ideas cannot be regulated to prevent it from being unfair or unreasonable." *Riley v. National Federation of Blind of N.C., Inc.*, 487 U.S. 781, 803 (1988) (SCALIA, J., concurring in part and concurring in judgment).

Even if I assume arguendo that the ban on the petitioners' activity at issue here is both content neutral and merely a restriction on the manner of communication, the regulation must be struck down for its failure to satisfy the requirements of narrow tailoring to further a significant state interest, and availability of "ample alternative channels for communication."

As Justice KENNEDY's opinion indicates, the respondent comes closest to justifying the restriction as one furthering the government's interest in preventing coercion and fraud. The claim to be preventing coercion is weak to start with. While a solicitor can be insistent, a pedestrian on the street or airport concourse can simply walk away or walk on. In any event, we have held in a far more coercive context than this one, that of a black boycott of white stores in Claiborne County, Mississippi, that "Speech does not lose its protected character . . . simply

because it may embarrass others or coerce them into action." *NAACP v. Claiborne Hardware Co.*, 458 U.S. 886, 910 (1982). Since there is here no evidence of any type of coercive conduct, over and above the merely importunate character of the open and public solicitation, that might justify a ban, the regulation cannot be sustained to avoid coercion.

As for fraud, our cases do not provide government with plenary authority to ban solicitation just because it could be fraudulent. "Broad prophylactic rules in the area of free expression are suspect," and more than a laudable intent to prevent fraud is required to sustain the present ban. The evidence of fraudulent conduct here is virtually nonexistent. . . .

Even assuming a governmental interest adequate to justify some regulation, the present ban would fall when subjected to the requirement of narrow tailoring. Thus, in *Schaumburg [v. Citizens for a Better Environment*, 444 U.S. 620 (1980)] we said:

"The Village's legitimate interest in preventing fraud can be better served by measures less intrusive than a direct prohibition on solicitation. Fraudulent misrepresentations can be prohibited and the penal laws used to punish such conduct directly. Efforts to promote disclosure of the finances of charitable organizations also may assist in preventing fraud by informing the public of the ways in which their contributions will be employed. Such measures may help make contribution decisions more informed, while leaving to individual choice the decision whether to contribute. . . . " . . .

Finally, I do not think the Port Authority's solicitation ban leaves open the "ample" channels of communication required of a valid content-neutral time, place and manner restriction. A distribution of preaddressed envelopes is unlikely to be much of an alternative. The practical reality of the regulation, which this Court can never ignore, is that it shuts off a uniquely powerful avenue of communication for organizations like the International Society for Krishna Consciousness, and may, in effect, completely prohibit unpopular and poorly funded groups from receiving funds in response to protected solicitation.

Accordingly, I would reverse the judgment of the Court of Appeals and strike down the ban on solicitation.

DER: Public forum doctrine has become a way for the majority to restrict the places where dissidents may speak. The Court approaches citizens' right to speak on public property based on the government's lack of any duty to provide for speech rather than on the government's affirmative duty to respect speech. Even those justices willing to recognize new public forums require speech to be compatible with government purposes. This standard focuses on the government's needs for the property rather than the speakers' need to use the property to get their message across. The justices' approach harks back to the Court's emphasis in *Davis v. Massachusetts* on the government's proprietary interests, having lost the speech-protective spirit of the opinion in *Schneider*. The *Schneider* Court opened up the principal public forums of its day—streets, sidewalks, and parks—and rejected government justifications based on mere efficiency and convenience. A true respect for the rights of the masses of people to use public property for expression would have to reflect the dramatic technological changes that have occurred since *Schneider* was written in 1939.

DEL: A striking feature of the *Heffron* decision is a seeming concern that, for all the touting of the virtues of a system of expressive freedom, too much opportunity for the airing of expression is a negative. Pointing out that a state fair is a temporary event, has a dedicated purpose and has significant safety concerns identifies specific characteristics that distinguish it from a public street. All public venues, including streets contrasted with parks, vary from one another with respect to some aspect of nature or structure. Even acknowledging differences with respect to those particularities, it remains unclear what the principle is that enables the Court to define what is a public forum and what is not. Manifest in the Court's drift, however, is doctrine that is friendlier to regulatory concerns than expressive interests.

e. Injunctions

Madsen v. Women's Health Center, Inc., like *Frisby v. Schultz*, arose out of controversy surrounding picketing by pro-life activists. In the decade preceding the Court's decision in *Madsen*, there were thousands of reported incidents of violence at clinics that provide abortions and at related sites. Congress responded by passing the Freedom of Access to Clinics Entrance Act of 1994.[104] Various courts upheld injunctions against activities by anti-abortion protesters as a content-neutral means of protecting women's access to abortion services.[105] In securing the rights of women seeking an abortion, courts issuing injunctions must also guard against the danger of chilling all speakers who wish to express the same views as those who have broken the law.

The speakers in *Madsen*, unlike those in *Frisby*, had violated a court injunction that restricted their activities near a clinic that performed abortions, rather than violating a city ordinance. The Court considered whether an injunction directed at the speech of particular parties in the public forum poses more or less of a threat to First Amendment concerns than a statute applied generally to the public. The opinions in *Madsen* presented three different approaches to this question.

---

[104] Pub. L. No. 103–258, 108 Stat. 694 (1994), 18 U.S.C. § 248.

[105] *See, e.g.,* Northeast Women's Ctr., Inc. v. McMonagle, 939 F.2d 57 (3d Cir. 1991); Portland Feminist Women's Health Ctr. v. Advocates for Life, Inc., 859 F.2d 681 (9th Cir. 1988).

Madsen v. Women's Health Center, Inc.
114 S. Ct. 2516 (1994)

CHIEF JUSTICE REHNQUIST delivered the opinion of the Court.

Petitioners challenge the constitutionality of an injunction entered by a Florida state court which prohibits antiabortion protestors from demonstrating in certain places and in various ways outside of a health clinic that performs abortions. We hold that the establishment of a 36-foot buffer zone on a public street from which demonstrators are excluded passes muster under the First Amendment, but that several other provisions of the injunction do not.

I

Respondents operate abortion clinics throughout central Florida. Petitioners and other groups and individuals are engaged in activities near the site of one such clinic in Melbourne, Florida. They picketed and demonstrated where the public street gives access to the clinic. In September 1992, a Florida state court permanently enjoined petitioners from blocking or interfering with public access to the clinic, and from physically abusing persons entering or leaving the clinic. Six months later, respondents sought to broaden the injunction, complaining that access to the clinic was still impeded by petitioners' activities and that such activities had also discouraged some potential patients from entering the clinic, and had deleterious physical effects on others. The trial court thereupon issued a broader injunction, which is challenged here.

The court found that, despite the initial injunction, protesters continued to impede access to the clinic by congregating on the paved portion of the street—Dixie Way—leading up to the clinic, and by marching in front of the clinic's driveways. It found that as vehicles heading toward the clinic slowed to allow the protesters to move out of the way, "sidewalk counselors" would approach and attempt to give the vehicle's occupants antiabortion literature. The number of people congregating varied from a handful to 400, and the noise varied from singing and chanting to the use of loudspeakers and bullhorns.

The protests, the court found, took their toll on the clinic's patients. A clinic doctor testified that, as a result of having to run such a gauntlet to enter the clinic, the patients "manifested a higher level of anxiety and hypertension causing those patients to need a higher level of sedation to undergo the surgical procedures, thereby increasing the risk associated with such procedures." The noise produced by the protestors could be heard within the clinic, causing stress in the patients both during surgical procedures and while recuperating in the recovery rooms. And those patients who turned away because of the crowd to return at a later date, the doctor testified, increased their health risks by reason of the delay.

Doctors and clinic workers, in turn, were not immune even in their homes. Petitioners picketed in front of clinic employees' residences; shouted at passerby; rang the doorbells of neighbors and provided literature identifying the particular clinic employee as a "baby killer." Occasionally, the protestors would confront minor children of clinic employees who were home alone.

This and similar testimony led the state court to conclude that its original injunction had proved insufficient "to protect the health, safety and rights of women in Brevard and Seminole County, Florida, and surrounding counties seeking access to [medical and counseling] services." The state court therefore amended its prior order, enjoining a broader array of activities. The amended injunction prohibits petitioners from engaging in the following acts:

"(1) At all times on all days, from entering the premises and property of the Aware Woman Center for Choice [the Melbourne clinic]. . . .

"(2) At all times on all days, from blocking, impeding, inhibiting, or in any other manner obstructing or interfering with access to, ingress into and egress from any building or parking lot of the Clinic.

"(3) At all times on all days, from congregating, picketing, patrolling, demonstrating or entering that portion of public right-of-way or private property within [36] feet of the property line of the Clinic. . . . [The injunction included certain exceptions to the buffer zone.]

"(4) During the hours of 7:30 a.m. through noon, on Mondays through Saturdays, during surgical procedures and recovery periods, from singing, chanting, whistling, shouting, yelling, use of bullhorns, auto horns, sound amplification equipment or other sounds or images observable to or within earshot of the patients inside the Clinic.

"(5) At all times on all days, in an area within [300] feet of the Clinic, from physically approaching any person seeking the services of the Clinic unless such person indicates a desire to communicate by approaching or by inquiring of the [petitioners]. . . .

"(6) At all times on all days, from approaching, congregating, picketing, patrolling, demonstrating or using bullhorns or other sound amplification equipment within [300] feet of the residence of any of the [respondents'] employees, staff, owners or agents, or blocking or attempting to block, barricade, or in any other manner, temporarily or otherwise, obstruct the entrances, exits or driveways of the residences of any of the [respondents'] employees, staff, owners or agents. The [petitioners] and those acting in concert with them are prohibited from inhibiting or impeding or attempting to impede, temporarily or otherwise, the free ingress or egress of persons to any street that provides the sole access to the street on which those residences are located.

"(7) At all times on all days, from physically abusing, grabbing, intimidating, harassing, touching, pushing, shoving, crowding or assaulting persons entering or leaving, working at or using services at the [respondents'] Clinic or trying to gain access to, or leave, any of the homes of owners, staff or patients of the Clinic.

"(8) At all times on all days, from harassing, intimidating or physically abusing, assaulting or threatening any present or former doctor, health care professional, or other staff member, employee or volunteer who assists in providing services at the [respondents'] Clinic.

"(9) At all times on all days, from encouraging, inciting, or securing other persons to commit any of the prohibited acts listed herein."

. . .

II

We begin by addressing petitioners' contention that the state court's order, because it is an injunction that restricts only the speech of antiabortion protesters, is necessarily content or viewpoint based. Accordingly, they argue, we should examine the entire injunction under the strictest standard of scrutiny. We disagree. To accept petitioners' claim would be to classify virtually every injunction as content or viewpoint based. An injunction, by its very nature, applies only to a particular group (or individuals) and regulates the activities, and perhaps the speech, of that group. It does so, however, because of the group's past actions in the context of a specific dispute between real parties. The parties seeking the injunction assert a violation of their rights; the court hearing the action is charged with fashioning a remedy for a specific deprivation, not with the drafting of a statute addressed to the general public.

The fact that the injunction in the present case did not prohibit activities of those demonstrating in favor of abortion is justly attributable to the lack of any similar demonstrations by those in favor of abortion, and of any consequent request that their demonstrations be regulated by injunction. There is no suggestion in this record that Florida law would not equally restrain similar conduct directed at a target having nothing to do with abortion; none of the restrictions imposed by the court were directed at the contents of petitioner's message.

Our principal inquiry in determining content neutrality is whether the government has adopted a regulation of speech "without reference to the content of the regulated speech." *Ward v. Rock Against Racism.* We thus look to the government's purpose as the threshold consideration. Here, the state court imposed restrictions on petitioners incidental to their antiabortion message because they repeatedly violated the court's original order. That petitioners all share the same viewpoint regarding abortion does not in itself demonstrate that some invidious content- or viewpoint-based purpose motivated the issuance of the order. It suggests only that those in the group whose conduct violated the court's order happen to share the same opinion regarding abortions being performed at the clinic. In short, the fact that the injunction covered people with a particular viewpoint does not itself render the injunction content or viewpoint based. Accordingly, the injunction issued in this case does not demand the level of heightened scrutiny set forth in *Perry Education Assn.* And we proceed to discuss the standard which does govern.

III

If this were a content-neutral, generally applicable statute, instead of an injunctive order, its constitutionality would be assessed under the standard set forth in *Ward v. Rock Against Racism*, and similar cases. Given that the forum around the clinic is a traditional public forum, we would determine whether the time, place, and manner regulations were "narrowly tailored to serve a significant governmental interest."

There are obvious differences, however, between an injunction and a generally applicable ordinance. Ordinances represent a legislative choice regarding the promotion of particular societal interests. Injunctions, by contrast, are remedies imposed for violations (or threatened violations) of a legislative or judicial decree. Injunctions also carry greater risks of censorship and discriminatory application than do general ordinances. "[T]here is no more effective practical guaranty against arbitrary and unreasonable government than to require that the principles of law which officials would impose upon a minority must be imposed generally." *Railway Express Agency, Inc. v. New York*, 336 U.S. 106, 112–113 (1949). Injunctions, of course, have some advantages over generally applicable statutes in that they can be tailored by a trial judge to afford more precise relief than a statute where a violation of the law has already occurred.

We believe that these differences require a somewhat more stringent application of general First Amendment principles in this context. In past cases evaluating injunctions restricting speech, we have relied upon such general principles while also seeking to ensure that the injunction was no broader than necessary to achieve its desired goals. . . . Accordingly, when evaluating a content-neutral injunction, we think that our standard time, place, and manner analysis is not sufficiently rigorous. We must ask instead whether the challenged provisions of the injunction burden no more speech than necessary to serve a significant government interest.

. . .

Justice SCALIA contends that precedent compels the application of strict scrutiny in this case. Under that standard, we ask whether a restriction is "'necessary to serve a compelling state interest and [is] narrowly drawn to achieve that end.'" Justice SCALIA fails to cite a single case, and we are aware of none, in which we have applied this standard to a content-neutral injunction. He cites a number of cases in which we have struck down, with little or no elaboration, prior restraints on free expression. . . . [W]e do not believe that this injunction constitutes a prior restraint, and we therefore believe that the "heavy presumption" against its constitutionality does not obtain here.

. . .

The Florida Supreme Court concluded that numerous significant government interests are protected by the injunction. It noted that the State has a strong interest in protecting a woman's freedom to seek lawful medical or counseling services in connection with her pregnancy. The State also has a strong interest in ensuring the public safety and order, in promoting the free flow of traffic on public streets and sidewalks, and in protecting the property rights of all its citizens. In addition, the court believed that the State's strong interest in residential privacy, acknowledged in *Frisby v. Schultz*, applied by analogy to medical privacy. The court observed that while targeted picketing of the home threatens the psychological well-being of the "captive" resident, targeted picketing of a hospital or clinic threatens not only the psychological, but the physical well-being of the patient held "captive" by medical circumstance. We agree with the Supreme Court of Florida that the combination of these governmental interests is quite sufficient to justify an appropriately tailored injunction to protect them. We now examine each contested provision of the injunction to see if it burdens more speech than necessary to accomplish its goal.

A

We begin with the 36-foot buffer zone. The state court prohibited petitioners from "congregating, picketing, patrolling, demonstrating or entering" any portion of the public right-of-way or private property within 36 feet of the property line of the clinic as a way of ensuring access to the clinic. This speech-free buffer zone requires that petitioners move to the other side of Dixie Way and away from the driveway of the clinic, where the state court found that they repeatedly had interfered with the free access of patients and staff. The buffer zone also applies to private property to the north and west of the clinic property. We examine each portion of the buffer zone separately.

We have noted a distinction between the type of focused picketing banned from the buffer zone and the type of generally disseminated communication that cannot be completely banned in public places, such as hand billing and solicitation. See *Frisby*. Here the picketing is directed primarily at patients and staff of the clinic.

The 36-foot buffer zone protecting the entrances to the clinic and the parking lot is a means of protecting unfettered ingress to and egress from the clinic, and ensuring that petitioners do not block traffic on Dixie Way. The state court seems to have had few other options to protect access given the narrow confines around the clinic. . . . The need for a complete buffer zone near the clinic entrances and driveway may be debatable, but some deference must be given to the state court's familiarity with the facts and the background of the dispute between the parties even under our heightened review. Moreover, . . . [p]rotesters standing across the narrow street from the clinic can still be seen and heard from the clinic parking lots. We also bear in mind the fact that the state court originally issued a much narrower injunction, providing no buffer zone, and that this order did not succeed in protecting access to the clinic. . . . On balance, we hold that the 36-foot buffer zone around the clinic entrances and driveway burdens no more speech than necessary to accomplish the governmental interest at stake.

. . .

B

. . .

In response to high noise levels outside the clinic, the state court restrained the petitioners from "singing, chanting, whistling, shouting, yelling, use of bullhorns, auto horns, sound amplification equipment or other sounds or images observable to or within earshot of the patients inside the [c]linic" during the hours of 7:30 a.m. through noon on Mondays through Saturdays. We must, of course, take account of the place to which the regulations apply in determining whether these restrictions burden more speech than necessary. We have upheld similar noise restrictions in the past, and as we noted in upholding a local noise ordinance around public schools, "the nature of a place, 'the pattern of its normal activities, dictate the kinds of regulations . . . that are reasonable.'" *Grayned v. City of Rockford*, 408 U.S. 104, 116 (1972). Noise control is particularly important around hospitals and medical facilities during surgery and recovery periods. . . .

We hold that the limited noise restrictions imposed by the state court order burden no more speech than necessary to ensure the health and well-being of the patients at the clinic. The First Amendment does not demand that patients at a medical facility undertake Herculean efforts to escape the cacophony of political protests. "If over amplified loudspeakers assault the citizenry, government may turn them down." *Grayned*. That is what the state court did here, and we hold that its action was proper.

C

The same, however, cannot be said for the "images observable" provision of the state court's order. Clearly, threats to patients or their families, however communicated, are proscribable under the First Amendment. But rather than prohibiting the display of signs that could be interpreted as threats or veiled threats, the state court issued a blanket ban on all "images observable." This broad prohibition on all "images observable" burdens more speech than necessary to achieve the purpose of limiting threats to clinic patients or their families. Similarly, if the blanket ban on "images observable" was intended to reduce the level of anxiety and hypertension suffered by the patients inside the clinic, it would still fail. The only plausible reason a patient would be bothered by "images observable" inside the clinic would be if the patient found the expression contained in such images disagreeable. But it is much easier for the clinic to pull its curtains than for a patient to stop up her ears, and no more is required to avoid seeing placards through the windows of the clinic. This provision of the injunction violates the First Amendment.

D

The state court ordered that petitioners refrain from physically approaching any person seeking services of the clinic "unless such person indicates a desire to communicate" in an area within 300 feet of the clinic. The state court was attempting to prevent clinic patients and staff from being "stalked" or "shadowed" by the petitioners as they approached the clinic.

But it is difficult, indeed, to justify a prohibition on all uninvited approaches of persons seeking the services of the clinic, regardless of how peaceful the contact may be, without burdening more speech than necessary to prevent intimidation and to ensure access to the clinic. Absent evidence that the protesters' speech is independently proscribable (i.e., "fighting words" or threats), or is so infused with violence as to be indistinguishable from a threat of physical harm, this provision cannot stand. . . . The "consent" requirement alone invalidates this provision; it burdens more speech than is necessary to prevent intimidation and to ensure access to the clinic.

E

The final substantive regulation challenged by petitioners relates to a prohibition against picketing, demonstrating, or using sound amplification equipment within 300 feet of the residences of clinic staff. The prohibition also covers impeding access to streets that provide the sole access to streets on which those residences are located. The same analysis applies to the use of sound amplification equipment here as that discussed above: the government may simply demand that petitioners turn down the volume if the protests overwhelm the neighborhood.

As for the picketing, our prior decision upholding a law banning targeted residential picketing remarked on the unique nature of the home, as "'the last citadel of the tired, the weary, and the sick.'" *Frisby*. . . . But the 300-foot zone around the residences in this case is much larger than the zone provided for in the ordinance which we approved in *Frisby*. The ordinance at issue there made it "unlawful for any person to engage in picketing before or about the residence or dwelling of any individual." The prohibition was limited to "focused picketing taking place solely in front of a particular residence." By contrast, the 300-foot zone would ban "[g]eneral marching through residential neighborhoods, or even walking a route in front of an entire block of houses." The record before us does not contain sufficient justification for this broad a ban on picketing; it appears that a limitation on the time, duration of picketing, and number of pickets outside a smaller zone could have accomplished the desired result.

. . .

[Justice SOUTER's concurring opinion is omitted].

Justice STEVENS, concurring in part and dissenting in part.

. . . The Court correctly and unequivocally rejects petitioners' argument that the injunction is a "content-based restriction on free speech." . . . I part company with the Court, however, on its treatment of the [consent requirement], including its enunciation of the applicable standard of review.

I

I agree with the Court that a different standard governs First Amendment challenges to generally applicable legislation than the standard that measures such challenges to judicial remedies for proven wrongdoing. Unlike the Court, however, I believe that injunctive relief should be judged by a more lenient standard than legislation. As the Court notes, legislation is imposed on an entire community, regardless of individual culpability. By contrast, injunctions apply solely to an individual or a limited group of individuals who, by engaging in illegal conduct, have been judicially deprived of some liberty—the normal consequence of illegal activity. Given this distinction, a statute prohibiting demonstrations within 36 feet of an abortion clinic would probably violate the First Amendment, but an injunction directed at a limited group of persons who have engaged in unlawful conduct in a similar zone might well be constitutional.

The standard governing injunctions has two obvious dimensions. On the one hand, the injunction should be no more burdensome than necessary to provide complete relief. In a First Amendment context, as in any other, the propriety of the remedy depends almost entirely on the character of the violation and the likelihood of its recurrence. For this reason, standards fashioned to determine the constitutionality of statutes should not be used to evaluate injunctions.

On the other hand, even when an injunction impinges on constitutional rights, more than "a simple proscription against the precise conduct previously pursued" may be required; the remedy must include appropriate restraints on "future activities both to avoid a recurrence of the violation and to eliminate its consequences." Moreover, "[t]he judicial remedy for a proven violation of law will often include commands that the law does not impose on the community at large." As such, repeated violations may justify sanctions that might be invalid if applied to a first offender or if enacted by the legislature.

In this case, the trial judge heard three days of testimony and found that petitioners not only had engaged in tortious conduct, but also had repeatedly violated an earlier injunction. The injunction is thus twice removed from a legislative proscription applicable to the general public and should be judged by a standard that gives appropriate deference to the judge's unique familiarity with the facts.

II

The second question presented by the certiorari petition asks whether the "consent requirement before speech is permitted" within a 300-foot buffer zone around the clinic unconstitutionally infringes on free speech. Petitioners contend that these restrictions create a "no speech" zone in which they cannot speak unless the listener indicates a positive interest in their speech. And, in Part III-D of its opinion, the Court seems to suggest that, even in a more narrowly defined zone, such a consent requirement is constitutionally impermissible. Petitioners' argument and the Court's conclusion, however, are based on a misreading of ¶(5) of the injunction.

That paragraph does not purport to prohibit speech; it prohibits a species of conduct. Specifically, it prohibits petitioners "from physically approaching any person seeking the services of the Clinic unless such person indicates a desire to communicate by approaching or by inquiring" of petitioners . . . As long as petitioners do not physically approach patients in this manner, they remain free not only to communicate with the public but also to offer verbal or written advice on an individual basis to the clinic's patients through their "sidewalk counseling."

Petitioners' "counseling" of the clinic's patients is a form of expression analogous to labor picketing. It is a mixture of conduct and communication. "In the labor context, it is the conduct element rather than the particular idea being expressed that often provides the most persuasive deterrant to third persons about to enter a business establishment." *NLRB v. Retail Store Employees*, 447 U.S. 607, 619 (1980) (STEVENS, J., concurring in part and concurring in result). As with picketing, the principal reason why handbills containing the same message are so much less effective than "counseling" is that "the former depend entirely on the persuasive force of the idea." Just as it protects picketing, the First Amendment protects the speakers' right to offer "sidewalk counseling" to all passerby. That protection, however, does not encompass attempts to abuse an unreceptive or captive audience, at least under the circumstances of this case. One may register a public protest by placing a vulgar message on his jacket and, in so doing, expose unwilling viewers, *Cohen v. California*. Nevertheless, that does not mean that he has an unqualified constitutional right to follow and harass an unwilling listener, especially one on her way to receive medical services.

The "physically approaching" prohibition entered by the trial court is no broader than the protection necessary to provide relief for the violations it found. The trial judge entered this portion of the injunction only after concluding that the injunction was necessary to protect the clinic's patients and staff from "uninvited contacts, shadowing and stalking" by petitioners. The protection is especially appropriate for the clinic patients given that the trial judge found that petitioners' prior conduct caused higher levels of "anxiety and hypertension" in the patients, increasing the risks associated with the procedures that the patients seek. Whatever the proper limits on a court's power to restrict a speaker's ability to physically approach or follow an unwilling listener, surely the First Amendment does not prevent a trial court from imposing such a restriction given the unchallenged findings in this case.

Justice SCALIA, with whom Justice KENNEDY and Justice THOMAS join, concurring in the judgment in part and dissenting in part.

The judgment in today's case has an appearance of moderation and Solomonic wisdom, upholding as it does some portions of the injunction while disallowing others. That appearance is deceptive. The entire injunction in this case departs so far from the established course of our jurisprudence that in any other context it would have been regarded as a candidate for summary reversal.

But the context here is abortion. A long time ago, in dissent from another abortion-related case, Justice O'CONNOR, joined by then-Justice REHNQUIST, wrote:

"This Court's abortion decisions have already worked a major distortion in the Court's constitutional jurisprudence. Today's decision goes further, and makes it painfully clear that no legal rule or doctrine is safe from Admissions Committee hoc nullification by this Court when an occasion for its application arises in a case involving state regulation of abortion. . . *Thornburgh v. American College of Obstetricians and Gynecologists.*

Today the Admission Committee hoc nullification machine claims it latest, greatest, and most surprising victim: the First Amendment.

Because I believe that the judicial creation of a 36-foot zone in which only a particular group, which had broken no law, cannot exercise its rights of speech, assembly, and association, and the judicial enactment of a noise prohibition, applicable to that group and that group alone, are profoundly at odds with our First Amendment precedents and traditions, I dissent.

I

The record of this case contains a videotape, with running caption of time and date, displaying what one must presume to be the worst of the activity justifying the injunction issued by Judge McGregor and partially approved today by this Court. The tape was shot by employees of, or volunteers at, the Aware Woman Clinic on three Saturdays in February and March 1993; the camera location, for the

first and third segments, appears to have been an upper floor of the clinic. . . .

Anyone seriously interested in what this case was about must view that tape. And anyone doing so who is familiar with run-of-the-mine labor picketing, not to mention some other social protests, will be aghast at what it shows we have today permitted an individual judge to do. I will do my best to describe it.

On Saturday, March 6, 1993, a group of antiabortion protesters is gathered in front of the clinic, arrayed from east (camera-left) to west (camera-right) on the clinic side of Dixie Way, a small, nonartery street. Men, women, and children are also visible across the street, on the south side of Dixie Way; some hold signs and appear to be protesters, others may be just interested onlookers.

. . .

Clinic supporters are more or less steadily chanting the following slogans: "Our right, our right, our right, to decide"; "Right to life is a lie, you don't care if women die." Then abortion opponents can be heard to sing: "Jesus loves the little children, all the children of the world, red and yellow, black and white, they are precious in His sight, Jesus loves the little children of the world." Clinic supporters respond with: Q: "What do we want?" A: "Choice." Q: "When do we want it?" A: "Now." ("Louder!") And that call and response is repeated. Later in the tape, clinic supporters chant "1-2-3-4, we won't take it anymore; 5-6-7-8, Separate the Church and State." On placards held by picketers and by stationary protestors on both sides of the line, the following slogans are visible: "Abortionists lie to women." "Choose Life: Abortion Kills." "N.O.W. Violence." "The God of Israel is Pro-Life." "RU 486 Now." "She Is a Child, Not a Choice." "Abortion Kills Children." "Keep Abortion Legal." "Abortion: God Calls It Murder." Some abortion opponents wear T-shirts bearing the phrase "Choose Life."

. . .

Later, at a point when the crowd appears to be larger and the picketers more numerous, a red car is delayed approximately 10 seconds as the picketers (and clinic supporters) move out of the driveway. Police are visible helping to clear a path for the vehicle to enter. As the car waits, two persons appearing to bear leaflets approach, respectively, the driver and front passenger doors. . . . At no time is there any apparent effort to prevent entry or exit, or even to delay it, except for the time needed for the picketers to get out of the way. There is no sitting down, packing en masse, linking of hands or any other effort to blockade the clinic property.

. . .

. . . The date-time register indicates that it is the morning of Saturday, February 20,

1993. A teenage girl faces the clinic and exclaims: "Please don't let them kill me, Mommy. Help me, Daddy, please." Clinic supporters chant, "We won't go back." A second woman, the one who spoke at greatest length in the first segment calls, "If you [inaudible], help her through it." Off camera, a group sings "Roe, Roe, Roe v. Wade, we will never quit, Freedom of choice is the law of the land, better get used to it." The woman from the first segment appears to address specific persons on clinic property: "Do you ever wonder what your baby would have looked like? Do you wonder how old it would have been? Because I did the same thing. . . ." Then a police officer is visible writing someone a citation. The videotape ends with a shot of an automobile moving eastbound on Dixie Way. As it slows to a stop at the intersection of U.S. 1, two leafletters approach the car and then pull back as it passes on.

The videotape and the rest of the record, including the trial court's findings, show that a great many forms of expression and conduct occurred in the vicinity of the clinic. These include singing, chanting, praying, shouting, the playing of music both from the clinic and from hand held boom boxes, speeches, peaceful picketing, communication of familiar political messages, hand billing, persuasive speech directed at opposing groups on the issue of abortion, efforts to persuade individuals not to have abortions, personal testimony, interviews with the press, and media efforts to report on the protest. What the videotape, the rest of the record, and the trial court's findings do not contain is any suggestion of violence near the clinic, nor do they establish any attempt to prevent entry or exit.

II

A

Under this Court's jurisprudence, there is no question that this public sidewalk area is a "public forum," where citizens generally have a First Amendment right to speak. . . . The Court . . . creates, brand-new for this abortion-related case, an additional standard that is (supposedly) "somewhat more stringent," than intermediate scrutiny, yet not as "rigorous," as strict scrutiny. The Court does not give this new standard a name, but perhaps we could call it intermediate-intermediate scrutiny. The difference between it and intermediate scrutiny (which the Court acknowledges is inappropriate for injunctive restrictions on speech) is frankly too subtle for me to describe, so I must simply recite it: whereas intermediate scrutiny requires that the restriction be "narrowly tailored to serve a significant government interest," the new standard requires that the restriction "burden no more speech than

necessary to serve a significant government interest."

. . . The real question in this case is not whether intermediate scrutiny, which the Court assumes to be some kind of default standard, should be supplemented because of the distinctive characteristics of injunctions; but rather whether those distinctive characteristics are not, for reasons of both policy and precedent, fully as good a reason as "content-basis" for demanding strict scrutiny. . . . [A] restriction upon speech imposed by injunction (whether nominally content based or nominally content neutral) is at least as deserving of strict scrutiny as a statutory, content-based restriction.

That is so for several reasons: The danger of content-based statutory restrictions upon speech is that they may be designed and used precisely to suppress the ideas in question rather than to achieve any other proper governmental aim. But that same danger exists with injunctions. Although a speech-restricting injunction may not attack content *as content* (in the present case, as I shall discuss, even that is not true), it lends itself just as readily to the targeted suppression of particular ideas. When a judge, on the motion of an employer, enjoins picketing at the site of a labor dispute, he enjoins (and he *knows* he is enjoining) the expression of pro-union views. Such targeting of one or the other side of an ideological dispute cannot readily be achieved in speech-restricting general legislation except by making content the basis of the restriction; it is achieved in speech-restricting injunctions almost invariably. The proceedings before us here illustrate well enough what I mean. The injunction was sought against a single-issue advocacy group by persons and organizations with a business or social interest in suppressing that group's point of view.

The second reason speech-restricting injunctions are at least as deserving of strict scrutiny is obvious enough: they are the product of individual judges rather than of legislatures—and often of judges who have been chagrined by prior disobedience of their orders. The right to free speech should not lightly be placed within the control of a single man or woman. And the third reason is that the injunction is a much more powerful weapon than a statute, and so should be subjected to greater safeguards. Normally, when injunctions are enforced through contempt proceedings, only the defense of factual innocence is available. . . .

. . .

Finally, though I believe speech-restricting injunctions are dangerous enough to warrant strict scrutiny even when they are not technically content based, I think the injunction in the present case was content based (indeed, viewpoint based) to boot. The Court claims that it was directed, not at those who spoke certain things (anti-abortion sentiments), but at those who did certain things (violated the earlier injunction). If that were true, then the injunction's residual coverage of "all persons acting in concert or participation with [the named individuals and organizations], or on their behalf" would not include those who merely entertained the same beliefs and wished to express the same views as the named defendants. But the construction given to the injunction by the issuing judge, which is entitled to great weight, is to the contrary: all those who wish to express the same views as the named defendants are deemed to be "acting in concert or participation." Following issuance of the amended injunction, a number of persons were arrested for walking within the 36-foot speech-free zone. At an April 12, 1993, hearing before the trial judge who issued the injunction, the following exchanges occurred:

> Mr. Lacy: "I was wondering how we can—why we were arrested and confined as being in concert with these people that we don't know, when other people weren't, that were in that same buffer zone, and it was kind of selective as to who was picked and who was arrested and who was obtained for the same buffer zone in the same public injunction."
>
> The Court: "Mr. Lacy, I understand that those on the other side of the issue [abortion-rights supporters] were also in the area. If you are referring to them, the Injunction did not pertain to those on the other side of the issue, *because the word in concert with means in concert with those who had taken a certain position in respect to the clinic, adverse to the clinic. If you are saying that is the selective basis that the pro-choice were not arrested when pro-life was arrested, that's the basis of the selection. . . ."*

. . .

[This] colloquy[ ] leave[s] no doubt that the revised injunction here is tailored to restrain persons distinguished, not by proscribable *conduct*, but by proscribable *views*.

. . .

III

. . .

I turn now to the Court's performance in the present case. I am content to evaluate it under the lax (intermediate-intermediate scrutiny) standard that the Court has adopted, because even by that distorted light it is inadequate.

The first step under the Court's standard would be, one should think, to identify the "sig-nificant government interest" that justifies the portions of the injunction it upheld. . . .

According to the Court, the state court imposed the later injunction's "restrictions on petitioner[s'] . . . antiabortion message because they repeatedly violated the court's original order." Surprisingly, the Court accepts this reason as valid, without asking whether the court's findings of fact support it—whether, that is, the acts of which the petitioners stood convicted were violations of the original injunction.

The Court simply takes this on faith—even though violation of the original injunction is an essential part of the reasoning whereby it approves portions of the amended injunction, even though petitioners denied any violation of the original injunction, even though the utter lack of proper basis for the other challenged portions of the injunction hardly inspires confidence that the lower courts knew what they were doing, and even though close examination of the factual basis for essential conclusions is the usual practice in First Amendment cases. . . .

. . . [T]he only findings and conclusions of the court that could conceivably be considered to relate to a violation of the original injunction . . . all concern behavior by the protestors causing traffic on the street in front of the abortion clinic to slow down, and causing vehicles crossing the pedestrian right-of-way, between the street and the clinic's parking lot, to slow down or even, occasionally, to stop momentarily while pedestrians got out of the way. As far as appears from the court's findings, all of these results were produced, not by anyone intentionally seeking to block oncoming traffic, but as the incidental effect of persons engaged in the activities of walking a picket line and leafletting on public property in front of the clinic. There is no factual finding that petitioners engaged in any intentional or purposeful obstruction.

. . .

If the original injunction is read as it must be, there is nothing in the trial court's findings to suggest that it was violated. The Court today speaks of "the failure of the first injunction to protect access." But the first injunction did not broadly "protect access." It forbade particular acts that impeded access, to-wit, intentionally "blocking, impeding or obstructing." The trial court's findings identify none of these acts, but only a mild interference with access that is the incidental by-product of leafletting and picketing. There was no sitting down, no linking of arms, no packing en masse in the driveway; the most that can be alleged (and the trial court did not even make this a finding) is that on one occasion protestors "took their time to get out of the way." If that is enough to support this one-man proscription of free speech, the First Amendment is in grave peril.

I almost forgot to address the facts showing prior violation of law (including judicial order) with respect to the other portion of the injunction the Court upholds: the no-noise-within-earshot-of-patients provision. That is perhaps because, amazingly, neither the Florida courts *nor this Court* makes the slightest attempt to link that provision to prior violations of law. The relevant portion of the Court's opinion, Part II-B, simply reasons that hospital patients should not have to be bothered with noise, from political protests or anything else (which is certainly true), and that therefore the noise restrictions could be imposed *by injunction* (which is certainly false). Since such a law is reasonable, in other words, it can be enacted by a single man to bind only a single class of social protesters. The pro-abortion demonstrators who were often making (if respondents' videotape is accurate) *more* noise than the petitioners, can continue to shout their chants at their opponents exiled across the street to their hearts' content. . . .

. . .

Finally, I turn to the Court's application of the second part of its test: whether the provisions of the injunction "burden no more speech than necessary" to serve the significant interest protected.

. . .

Assuming a "significant state interest" of the sort cognizable for injunction purposes (i.e., one protected by a law that has been or is threatened to be violated) in both (1) keeping pedestrians off the paved portion of Dixie Way, and (2) enabling cars to cross the public sidewalk at the clinic's driveways without having to slow down or come to even a "momentary" stop, there are surely a number of ways to protect those interests short of banishing the entire protest demonstration from the 36-foot zone. For starters, the Court could have (for the first time) ordered the demonstrators to stay out of the street (the original injunction did not remotely require that). It could have limited the number of demonstrators permitted on the clinic side of Dixie Way. And it could have forbidden the pickets to walk on the driveways. The Court's only response to these options is that "[t]he state court was convinced that [they would not work] in view of the failure of the first injunction to protect access." But must we accept that conclusion as valid—when the original injunction contained no command (or at the very least no *clear* command) that had been disobeyed, and contained nothing even *related* to staying out of the street? If the "burden no more speech than necessary" requirement can be avoided by merely opining that (for some reason) no lesser restriction than *this* one will be obeyed, it is not much of a requirement at all.

. . . In application, in other words, the "burden no more speech than is necessary" test has become an "arguably burden no more speech than is necessary" test. This renders the Court's intermediate-intermediate scrutiny not only no *more* stringent than plain old intermediate scrutiny, but considerably *less* stringent.

. . .

What we have decided seems to be, and will be reported by the media as, an abortion case. But it will go down in the lawbooks, it will be cited, as a free-speech injunction case—and the damage its novel principles produce will be considerable. The proposition that injunctions against speech are subject to a standard indistinguishable from (unless perhaps more lenient in its application than) the "intermediate scrutiny" standard we have used for "time, place, and manner" legislative restrictions; the notion that injunctions against speech need not be closely tied to any violation of law, but may simply implement sound social policy; and the practice of accepting trial-court conclusions permitting injunctions without considering whether those conclusions are supported by any findings of fact—these latest by-products of our abortion jurisprudence ought to give all friends of liberty great concern.

For these reasons, I dissent from that portion of the judgment upholding parts of the injunction.

5. Government-Supported Speech

Although the government generally is not required to subsidize expressive activities, there are many contexts in which the government "speaks" either by disseminating its own messages or by supporting in some way the speech of others. The government has the ability, for example, to insert its views in the expression of its employees, recipients of government benefits, and public school students. In the public forum cases, where the government is not itself a speaker, the Court has required that government restrictions on speech remain viewpoint neutral. At the same time, the government may provide access to "nonpublic" forums to some speakers while denying it to others.

Should neutrality be required in cases where the state plays an active role in the communications at issue? Government-supported speech may raise special concerns about abridgement of speech rights and official distortion of the public debate. On the other hand, there may reasons for permitting the government to express its viewpoint in these public contexts that do not apply to private ones.

a. Speech by Government Employees

At the turn of the century, government employees' freedom to speak was governed by the right-privilege distinction: the Court distinguished between individual "rights" grounded in the constitution and mere "privileges" granted conditionally by the government. According to this framework, public employees relinquished their right to speak freely when they agreed to work for the state upon the terms that the state prescribed. Justice Holmes explained this principle in the 1892 case *McAuliffe v. New Bedford*, which dismissed the appeal of a police officer who was fired for his criticism of police department management:

> The petitioner may have a constitutional right to talk politics, but he has no constitutional right to be a policeman. There are few employments for hire in which the servant does not agree to suspend his constitutional right of free speech, as well as of idleness, by the implied terms of his contract. The servant cannot complain, as he takes the employment on the terms which are offered him.[106]

The rights-privilege distinction no longer dictates the speech rights of government employees. The Court has replaced the government's absolute control over public employees' speech with a balancing approach. *Pickering v. Board of Education of Will County, Illinois*, for example, held that a public school teacher could not constitutionally be dismissed for writing a letter to the editor that contained erroneous statements attacking the School Board's handling of bond issue proposals and its allocation of school funds between educational and athletic programs.[107] The Court rejected the Illinois Supreme Court's suggestion that "teachers may constitutionally be compelled to relinquish the First Amendment rights they would otherwise enjoy as citizens to comment on matters of public interest in connection with the operation of the public schools in which they work." The Court nevertheless recognized that "the State has interests as an employer in regulating the speech of its employees that differ significantly from those it possesses in connection with regulation of the speech of the citizenry in general." The Court suggested that evaluating the discharge of a public employee for engaging in speech requires "a balance between the interests of the [employee], as a citizen, in commenting upon matters of public concern and the interest of the State, as employer, in promoting the efficiency of the public services it performs through its employees."

The Court has reconciled the government's interest as employer with the First Amendment rights of public employees by examining the nature of the speech at issue. In *Connick v. Myers*, a divided Court (5-4) held that the dismissal of an assistant district attorney for distributing a questionnaire to her co-workers did not violate the First Amendment because the questionnaire did not involve a matter of public concern.[108] Sheila Myers prepared the questionnaire when she was informed that she would be transferred to prosecute cases in a different section of the criminal court. The questionnaire solicited the views of her fellow staff members concerning office transfer policy,

---

[106] McAuliffe v. Mayor of New Bedford, 155 Mass. 216, 220, 29 N.E. 517, 518 (1892).

[107] Pickering v. Board of Education, 391 U.S. 563 (1968).

[108] Connick v. Myers, 461 U.S. 138 (1983).

office morale, the need for a grievance committee, and whether employees felt pressured to work in political campaigns. The majority granted broad deference to District Attorney Connick's judgment that Myers' questionnaire was "an act of insubordination which interfered with working relationships" that were essential to fulfilling the office's public responsibilities. On the other side of the balance, the majority concluded that Myers' questionnaire "touched upon matters of public concern in only a most limited sense":

> [H]er survey, in our view, is most accurately characterized as an employee grievance concerning internal office policy. The limited First Amendment interest involved here does not require that Connick tolerate action which he reasonably believed would disrupt the office, undermine his authority, and destroy close working relationships. Myers' discharge therefore did not offend the First Amendment.

In another closely divided decision, *Rankin v. McPherson*, the balance between state and employee interests weighed in favor of protecting the employee's speech rights. The Justices sharply disputed whether the statement at issue—commenting on the attempted assassination of President Reagan—addressed a matter of public concern, as well as disagreed about the government's interest in regulating such statements.

Rankin v. McPherson
483 U.S. 378 (1987)

JUSTICE MARSHALL delivered the opinion of the Court.

. . .

I

On January 12, 1981, respondent Ardith McPherson was appointed a deputy in the office of the Constable of Harris County, Texas. The Constable is an elected official who functions as a law enforcement officer. At the time of her appointment, McPherson, a black woman, was 19 years old and had attended college for a year, studying secretarial science. Her appointment was conditional for a 90-day probationary period.

Although McPherson's title was "deputy constable," this was the case only because all employees of the Constable's office, regardless of job function, were deputy constables. She was not a commissioned peace officer, did not wear a uniform, and was not authorized to make arrests or permitted to carry a gun. McPherson's duties were purely clerical. . . .

On March 30, 1981, McPherson and some fellow employees heard on an office radio that there had been an attempt to assassinate the President of the United States. Upon hearing that report, McPherson engaged a co-worker, Lawrence Jackson, who was apparently her boyfriend, in a brief conversation, which according to McPherson's uncontroverted testimony went as follows:

. . .

" . . . Well, we were talking—it's a wonder why they did that. I felt like it would be a black person that did that, because I feel like most of my kind is on welfare and CETA, and they use Medicaid, and at the time, I was thinking that's what it was.

"... But then after I said that, and then Lawrence said, yeah, he's cutting back Medicaid and food stamps. And I said, yeah, welfare and CETA. I said, shoot, if they go for him again, I hope they get him."

McPherson's last remark was overheard by another Deputy Constable, who, unbeknownst to McPherson, was in the room at the time. The remark was reported to Constable Rankin, who . . . fired McPherson.

. . .

II

It is clearly established that a State may not discharge an employee on a basis that infringes that employee's constitutionally protected interest in freedom of speech. Even though McPherson was merely a probationary employee, and even if she could have been discharged for any reason or for no reason at all, she may nonetheless be entitled to reinstatement if she was discharged for exercising her constitutional right to freedom of expression.

The determination whether a public employer has properly discharged an employee for engaging in speech requires "a balance between the interests of the [employee], as a citizen, in commenting upon matters of public concern and the interest of the State, as an employer, in promoting the efficiency of the public services it performs through its employees." *Pickering v. Board of Education; Connick v. Myers*. This balancing is necessary in order to accommodate the dual role of the public employer as a provider of public services and as a government entity operating under the constraints of the First Amendment. On the one hand, public employers are *employers*, concerned with the efficient function of their operations; review of every personnel decision made by a public employer could, in the long run, hamper the performance of public functions. On the other hand, "the threat of dismissal from public employment is . . . a potent means of inhibiting speech." *Pickering*. Vigilance is necessary to ensure that public employers do not use authority over employees to silence discourse, not because it hampers public functions but simply because superiors disagree with the content of employees' speech.

A

The threshold question in applying this balancing test is whether McPherson's speech may be "fairly characterized as constituting speech on a matter of public concern." *Connick*. "Whether an employee's speech addresses a matter of public concern must be determined by the content, form, and context of a given statement, as revealed by the whole record." The District Court apparently found that McPherson's speech did not address a matter of public concern. The Court of Appeals rejected this conclusion, finding that "the life and death of the President are obviously matters of public concern." Our view of these determinations of the courts below is limited in this context by our constitutional obligation to assure that the record supports this conclusion: "'[W]e are compelled to examine for ourselves the statements in issue and the circumstances under which they [were] made to see whether or not they . . . are of a character which the principles of the First Amendment, as adopted by the Due Process Clause of the Fourteenth Amendment, protect.'" *Connick*.

Considering the statement in context, as *Connick* requires, discloses that it plainly dealt with a matter of public concern. The statement was made in the course of a conversation addressing the policies of the President's administration. It came on the heels of a news bulletin regarding what is certainly a matter of heightened public attention: an attempt on the life of the President. While a statement that amounted to a threat to kill the President would not be protected by the First Amend-

ment, the District Court concluded, and we agree, that McPherson's statement did not amount to a threat punishable under 18 U.S.C. § 871(a) or 18 U.S.C. § 2385, or, indeed, that could properly be criminalized at all. The inappropriate or controversial character of a statement is irrelevant to the question whether it deals with a matter of public concern. "[D]ebate on public issues should be uninhibited, robust, and wide-open, and . . . may well include vehement, caustic, and sometimes unpleasantly sharp attacks on government and public officials." *New York Times Co. v. Sullivan.* . . .

B

Because McPherson's statement addressed a matter of public concern, *Pickering* next requires that we balance McPherson's interest in making her statement against "the interest of the State, as an employer, in promoting the efficiency of the public services it performs through its employees." The State bears a burden of justifying the discharge on legitimate grounds. *Connick*.

In performing the balancing, the statement will not be considered in a vacuum; the manner, time, and place of the employee's expression are relevant, as is the context in which the dispute arose. We have previously recognized as pertinent considerations whether the statement impairs discipline by superiors or harmony among co-workers, has a detrimental impact on close working relationships for which personal loyalty and confidence are necessary, or impedes the performance of the speaker's duties or interferes with the regular operation of the enterprise.

These considerations, and indeed the very nature of the balancing test, make apparent that the state interest element of the test focuses on the effective functioning of the public employer's enterprise. Interference with work, personnel relationships, or the speaker's job performance can detract from the public employer's function; avoiding such interference can be a strong state interest. From this perspective, however, petitioners fail to demonstrate a state interest that outweighs McPherson's First Amendment rights. While McPherson's statement was made at the workplace, there is no evidence that it interfered with the efficient functioning of the office. . . . In fact, Constable Rankin testified that the possibility of interference with the functions of the Constable's office had *not* been a consideration in his discharge of respondent and that he did not even inquire whether the remark had disrupted the work of the office.

Nor was there any danger that McPherson had discredited the office by making her statement in public. McPherson's speech took place in an area to which there was ordinarily no public access; her remark was evidently made in a private conversation with another employee. There is no suggestion that any member of the general public was present or heard McPherson's statement. Nor is there any evidence that employees other than Jackson who worked in the room even heard the remark. Not only was McPherson's discharge unrelated to the functioning of the office, it was not based on any assessment by the Constable that the remark demonstrated a character trait that made respondent unfit to perform her work.

While the facts underlying Rankin's discharge of McPherson are, despite extensive proceedings in the District Court, still somewhat unclear, it is undisputed that he fired McPherson based on the *content* of her speech. Evidently because McPherson had made the statement, and because the Constable believed that she "meant it," he decided that she was not a suitable employee to have in a law enforcement agency. But in weighing the State's interest in discharging an employee based on any claim that the content of a statement made by the employee somehow undermines the mission of the public employer, some attention must be paid to the responsibilities of the employee within the agency. The burden of caution employees bear with respect to the words they speak will vary with the extent of authority and public accountability the employee's role entails. Where, as here, an employee serves no confidential, policy making, or public contact role, the danger to the agency's successful functioning from that employee's private speech is minimal. We cannot believe that every employee in Constable Rankin's office, whether computer operator, electrician, or file clerk, is equally required, on pain of discharge, to avoid any statement susceptible of being interpreted by the Constable as an indication that the employee may be unworthy of employment in his law enforcement agency. At some point, such concerns are so removed from the effective functioning of the public employer that they cannot prevail over the free speech rights of the public employee.

This is such a case. McPherson's employment-related interaction with the Constable was apparently negligible. Her duties were purely clerical and were limited solely to the civil process function of the Constable's office. There is no indication that she would ever be in a position to further—or indeed to have any involvement with—the minimal law enforcement activity engaged in by the Constable's office. Given the function of the agency, McPherson's position in the office, and the nature of her statement, we are not persuaded that Rankin's interest in discharging her outweighed her rights under the First Amendment.

Because we agree with the Court of Appeals that McPherson's discharge was im-

proper, the judgment of the Court of Appeals is

Affirmed.

JUSTICE POWELL, concurring.

It is not easy to understand how this case has assumed constitutional dimensions and reached the Supreme Court of the United States. The fact that the case is here, however, illustrates the uniqueness of our Constitution and our system of judicial review: courts at all levels are available and receptive to claims of injustice, large and small, by any and every citizen of this country.

. . .

There is no dispute that McPherson's comment was made during a private conversation with a co-worker who happened also to be her boyfriend. She had no intention or expectation that it would be overheard or acted on by others. Given this, I think it is unnecessary to engage in the extensive analysis normally required by *Connick v. Myers* and *Pickering v. Board of Education.* If a statement is on a matter of public concern, as it was here, it will be an unusual case where the employer's legitimate interests will be so great as to justify punishing an employee for this type of private speech that routinely takes place at all levels in the workplace. The risk that a single, offhand comment directed to only one other worker will lower morale, disrupt the work force, or otherwise undermine the mission of the office borders on the fanciful. To the extent that the full constitutional analysis of the competing interests is required, I generally agree with the Court's opinion.

. . .

JUSTICE SCALIA, with whom THE CHIEF JUSTICE [REHNQUIST], JUSTICE WHITE, and JUSTICE O'CONNOR join, dissenting.

I agree with the proposition, felicitously put by Constable Rankin's counsel, that no law enforcement agency is required by the First Amendment to permit one of its employees to "ride with the cops and cheer for the robbers." The issue in this case is whether Constable Rankin, a law enforcement official, is prohibited by the First Amendment from preventing his employees from saying of the attempted assassination of President Reagan—on the job and within hearing of other employees—"If they go for him again, I hope they get him." . . . [T]he Court significantly and irrationally expands the definition of "public concern"; it also carves out a new and very large class of employees—i.e., those in "nonpolicymaking" positions—who, if today's decision is to be believed, can never be disciplined for statements that fall within the Court's expanded definition. . . .

I

To appreciate fully why the majority errs in reaching its first conclusion, it is necessary to recall the origins and purposes of Connick's "public concern" requirement. The Court long ago rejected Justice Holmes' approach to the free speech rights of public employees, that "[a policeman] may have a constitutional right to talk politics, but he has no constitutional right to be a policeman," *McAuliffe v. Mayor of New Bedford*. We have, however, recognized that the government's power as an employer to make hiring and firing decisions on the basis of what its employees and prospective employees say has a much greater scope than its power to regulate expression by the general public.

Specifically, we have held that the First Amendment's protection against adverse personnel decisions extends only to speech on matters of "public concern," *Connick*, which we have variously described as those matters dealing in some way with "the essence of self-government," matters as to which "free and open debate is vital to informed decisionmaking by the electorate," and matters as to which "'debate . . . [must] be uninhibited, robust, and wide-open.' "...

McPherson fails this threshold requirement. The statement for which she was fired—and the only statement reported to the Constable—was, "If they go for him again, I hope they get him." It is important to bear in mind the District Judge's finding that this was *not* hyperbole. . . . [H]e assuredly found that, whether McPherson later said she meant it or not, and whether she even meant it at the time or not, the idea she expressed was not just an exaggerated expression of her disapproval for the President's policies, but a voicing of the hope that, next time, the President would be killed. . . .

That McPherson's statement does not constitute speech on a matter of "public concern" is demonstrated by comparing it with statements that have been found to fit that description in prior decisions involving public employees. McPherson's statement is a far cry from the question by the Assistant District Attorney in *Connick* whether her co-workers "ever [felt] pressured to work in political campaigns," *Connick*; from the letter written by the public school teacher in *Pickering* criticizing the Board of Education's proposals for financing school construction, from the legislative testimony of a state college teacher in *Perry v. Sindermann*, 408 U.S. 593, 595 (1972), advocating that a particular college be elevated to 4-year status. . . .

McPherson's statement is indeed so different from those that it is only one step removed from statements that we have previously held entitled to no First Amendment protection even in the nonemployment context—including assassination threats against the President (which are illegal under 18 U.S.C. § 871);

"'fighting' words," epithets or personal abuse; and advocacy of force or violence. A statement lying so near the category of completely unprotected speech cannot fairly be viewed as lying within the "heart" of the First Amendment's protection; it lies within that category of speech that can neither be characterized as speech on matters of public concern nor properly subject to criminal penalties. Once McPherson stopped explicitly criticizing the President's policies and expressed a desire that he be assassinated, she crossed the line.

. . .

II

Even if I agreed that McPherson's statement was speech on a matter of "public concern," I would still find it unprotected. It is important to be clear on what the issue is in this part of the case. It is not, as the Court suggests, whether "Rankin's interest *in discharging* [McPherson] outweighed her rights under the First Amendment." Rather, it is whether his interest *in preventing the expression of such statements in his agency* outweighed her First Amendment interest in making the statement. We are not deliberating, in other words, (or at least should not be) about whether the sanction of dismissal was, as the concurrence puts it, "an . . . intemperat[e] employment decision." It may well have been—and personally I think it was. But we are not sitting as a panel to develop sound principles of proportionality for adverse actions in the state civil service. We are asked to determine whether, given the interests of this law enforcement office, McPherson had a *right* to say what she did—so that she could not only not be fired for it, but could not be formally reprimanded for it, or even prevented from repeating it endlessly into the future. It boggles the mind to think that she has such a right.

The Constable testified that he "was very concerned that this remark was made." Rightly so. As a law enforcement officer, the Constable obviously has a strong interest in preventing statements by any of his employees approving, or expressing a desire for, serious, violent crimes—regardless of whether the statements actually interfere with office operations at the time they are made or demonstrate character traits that make the speaker unsuitable for law enforcement work. . . .

. . .

The Court's sweeping assertion (and apparent holding) that where an employee "serves no confidential, policymaking, or public contact role, the danger to the agency's successful functioning from that employee's private speech is minimal," is simply contrary to reason and experience. Nonpolicymaking employees (the Assistant District Attorney in

Connick, for example) can hurt working relationships and undermine public confidence in an organization every bit as much as policymaking employees. I, for one, do not look forward to the new First Amendment world the Court creates, in which nonpolicymaking employees of the Equal Employment Opportunity Commission must be permitted to make remarks on the job approving of racial discrimination, nonpolicymaking employees of the Selective Service System to advocate noncompliance with the draft laws, and (since it is really quite difficult to contemplate anything more absurd than the present case itself), nonpolicymaking constable's deputies to express approval for the assassination of the President.

In sum, since Constable Rankin's interest in maintaining both an esprit de corps and a public image consistent with his office's law enforcement duties outweighs any interest his employees may have in expressing on the job a desire that the President be killed, even assuming that such an expression addresses a matter of public concern it is not protected by the First Amendment from suppression. . . .

b. Government Subsidies

Most First Amendment problems arise when the government abridges speech by exacting a penalty, such as a criminal conviction, a fee, or a damages judgment, upon the speaker. The government's capacity to disburse public funds also gives it the power to condition these benefits on recipients' surrender of their freedom of expression. The state's conditional spending may constitute as effective a restriction on speech as its direct punishment of speech. The unconstitutional conditions doctrine addresses this indirect power of government to abridge constitutional freedoms. This doctrine provides that the government may not condition the conferral of a benefit on the beneficiary's waiver of a constitutional right, although the government may choose not to provide the benefit altogether. In the First Amendment context, the doctrine recognizes the potential for government use of conditions on benefits to prefer one constitutionally protected viewpoint over another. Although the state has no obligation to subsidize citizens' speech, the doctrine goes, it should not be able to use its largesse to impose its viewpoint upon citizens. As the Court explained in *Speiser v. Randall*, "the denial of [funding] for engaging in certain speech necessarily will have the effect of coercing the claimants to refrain from the prescribed speech. The denial is 'frankly aimed at the suppression of dangerous ideas.'"[109] *Speiser* invalidated a California rule requiring anyone who sought to take advantage of a property tax exemption to sign a declaration stating that he did not advocate the forcible overthrow of the Government of the United States.

The results of unconstitutional conditions analysis are not always clear because the Court sometimes interprets a restriction on government funding as an unconstitutional condition that violates the First Amendment and other times as a legitimate government decision to subsidize one speech activity and not another. Scholars have noted the use of the doctrine to justify irreconcilable decisions. The Court applied the unconstitutional conditions doctrine in cases after *Speiser* to determine the constraints imposed by the First Amendment on government's discretion in supporting speech through taxation schemes. In *Regan v. Taxation with Representation of Washington*, the Court unanimously upheld an Internal Revenue Code provision that allowed veterans' organizations to engage in political lobbying with tax deductible contributions while denying this benefit to other charitable organizations.[110] The Court rejected the Court of Appeals' conclusion that Congress' special tax treatment for lobbying by veterans was subject to heightened scrutiny because it "facilitates the speech of one speaker over another." Rather, the Court interpreted the tax scheme as Congress' reasonable

---

[109] Speiser v. Randall, 357 U.S. 513, 519 (1958).
[110] Regan v. Taxation with Representation of Washington, 461 U.S. 540 (1983).

choice "not to subsidize lobbying as extensively as it chose to subsidize other activities that non profit organizations undertake to promote the public welfare." Distinguishing *Speiser*, the Court held that the strict scrutiny standard did not apply:

> [The] case would be different if Congress were to discriminate invidiously in its subsidies in such a way as to "'aim[ ] at the suppression of dangerous ideas.'" But the veterans' organizations that qualify under [the tax exemption] are entitled to receive tax-deductible contributions regardless of the content of any speech they may use, including lobbying. We find no indication that the statute was intended to suppress any ideas or any demonstration that it has had that effect. The sections of the Internal Revenue Code here at issue do not employ any suspect classification. The distinction between veterans' organizations and other charitable organizations is not at all like distinctions based on race or national origin.

> The Court of Appeals nonetheless held that "strict scrutiny" is required because the statute "*affect[s]* First Amendment rights on a discriminatory basis." Its opinion suggests that strict scrutiny applies whenever Congress subsidizes some speech, but not all speech. This is not the law. Congress could, for example, grant funds to an organization dedicated to combating teenage drug abuse, but condition the grant by providing that none of the money received from Congress should be used to lobby state legislatures. . . . Such a statute would be valid. Congress might also enact a statute providing public money for an organization dedicated to combating teenage alcohol abuse, and impose no condition against using funds obtained from Congress for lobbying. The existence of the second statute would not make the first statute subject to strict scrutiny.

Several years later, the Court invalidated a Minnesota sales tax scheme that taxed general interest magazines, but exempted newspapers and religious, professional, trade, and sports journals as "a discriminatory tax on the press [that] burdens rights protected by the First Amendment."[111] The majority in *Arkansas Writers' Project, Inc. v. Ragland* reasoned that the state's use of selective taxation was particularly repugnant to First Amendment principles because "a magazine's tax status depends entirely on its *content*." Justice Scalia, joined by Chief Justice Rehnquist, dissented on the ground that the denial of participation in a tax exemption or other subsidy scheme generally does not have any coercive effect. "It is implausible," Scalia argued, "that the 4% sales tax . . . was meant to inhibit, or had the effect of inhibiting, this appellant's publication." Scalia also cautioned that the majority's decision "casts doubt on a wide variety of tax preferences and subsidies that draw distinctions based upon subject matter."

In a controversial decision concerning abortion, the Court harked back to its distinction in *Regan v. TWR* between an unconstitutional condition on speech and the government's constitutional refusal to subsidize certain expressive activities. *Rust v. Sullivan* upheld regulations that prohibited employees of government-funded family planning clinics from discussing abortion with their patients. Despite the jurisprudential importance of the Court's decision, the regulations were never widely implemented. Reproductive rights organizations immediately challenged them in court and a District of Columbia federal judge enjoined the government from enforcing them. Newly elected President Clinton repealed the regulations on January 22, 1993—the twentieth anniversary of the *Roe v. Wade* decision.

---

[111] Arkansas Writers' Project, Inc. v. Ragland, 481 U.S. 221 (1987).

Rust v. Sullivan
500 U.S. 173 (1991)

CHIEF JUSTICE REHNQUIST delivered the opinion of the Court.

. . .

I

In 1970, Congress enacted Title X of the Public Health Service Act (Act), which provides federal funding for family-planning services. The Act authorizes the Secretary to "make grants to and enter into contracts with public or nonprofit private entities to assist in the establishment and operation of voluntary family planning projects which shall offer a broad range of acceptable and effective family planning methods and services." . . . Section 1008 of the Act, however, provides that "[n]one of the funds appropriated under this subchapter shall be used in programs where abortion is a method of family planning." . . .

In 1988, the Secretary promulgated new regulations designed to provide "'clear and operational guidance' to grantees about how to preserve the distinction between Title X programs and abortion as a method of family planning." . . . The regulations attach three principal conditions on the grant of federal funds for Title X projects. First, the regulations specify that a "Title X project may not provide counseling concerning the use of abortion as a method of family planning or provide referral for abortion as a method of family planning." . . . Title X projects must refer every pregnant client "for appropriate prenatal and/or social services by furnishing a list of available providers that promote the welfare of the mother and the unborn child." The list may not be used indirectly to encourage or promote abortion, "such as by weighing the list of referrals in favor of health care providers which perform abortions, by including on the list of referral providers health care providers whose principal business is the provision of abortions, by excluding available providers who do not provide abortions, or by 'steering' clients to providers who offer abortion as a method of family planning." The Title X project is expressly prohibited from referring a pregnant woman to an abortion provider, even upon specific request. One permissible response to such an inquiry is that "the project does not consider abortion an appropriate method of family planning and therefore does not counsel or refer for abortion."

Second, the regulations broadly prohibit a Title X project from engaging in activities that "encourage, promote or advocate abortion as a method of family planning." Forbidden activities include lobbying for legislation that would increase the availability of abortion as a method of family planning, developing or disseminating materials advocating abortion as a method of family planning, providing speakers to promote abortion as a method of family planning, using legal action to make abortion available in any way as a method of family planning, and paying dues to any group that advocates abortion as a method of family planning as a substantial part of its activities.

Third, the regulations require that Title X projects be organized so that they are "physically and financially separate" from prohibited abortion activities. To be deemed physically and financially separate, "a Title X project must have an objective integrity and independence from prohibited activities. Mere bookkeeping separation of Title X funds from other monies is not sufficient." . . .

. . .

Petitioners contend that the regulations violate the First Amendment by impermissibly discriminating based on viewpoint because they prohibit "all discussion about abortion as a lawful option—including counseling, referral, and the provision of neutral and accurate information about ending a pregnancy—while compelling the clinic or counselor to provide information that promotes continuing a pregnancy to term." They assert that the regulations violate the "free speech rights of private health care organizations that receive Title X funds, of their staff, and of their patients" by impermissibly imposing "viewpoint-discriminatory conditions on government subsidies" and thus penaliz[e] speech funded with non-Title X monies." Because "Title X continues to fund speech ancillary to pregnancy testing in a manner that is not evenhanded with respect to views and information about abortion, it invidiously discriminates on the basis of viewpoint." Relying on *Regan v. Taxation With Representation of Wash.*, and *Arkansas Writers Project, Inc. v. Ragland*, petitioners also assert that while the Government may place certain conditions on the receipt of federal subsidies, it may not "discriminate invidiously in its subsidies in such a way as to 'ai[m]' at the suppression of dangerous ideas.'"

There is no question but that the statutory prohibition contained in § 1008 is constitutional. In *Maher v. Roe*, we upheld a state welfare regulation under which Medicaid recipients received payments for services related to childbirth, but not for nontherapeutic abortions. The Court rejected the claim that this unequal subsidization worked a violation of the Constitution. We held that the government may "make a value judgment favoring childbirth over abortion, and ... implement that judgment by the allocation of public funds." Here the Government is exercising the authority it possesses under *Maher* and *Harris v. McRae* to subsidize family planning services which will lead to conception and childbirth, and declining to "promote or encourage abortion." The Government can, without violating the Constitution, selectively fund a program to encourage certain activities it believes to be in the public interest, without at the same time funding an alternate program which seeks to deal with the problem in another way. In so doing, the Government has not discriminated on the basis of viewpoint; it has merely chosen to fund one activity to the exclusion of the other. . . .

The challenged regulations implement the statutory prohibition by prohibiting counseling, referral, and the provision of information regarding abortion as a method of family planning. They are designed to ensure that the limits of the federal program are observed. The Title X program is designed not for prenatal care, but to encourage family planning. A doctor who wished to offer prenatal care to a project patient who became pregnant could properly be prohibited from doing so because such service is outside the scope of the federally funded program. The regulations prohibiting abortion counseling and referral are of the same ilk; "no funds appropriated for the project may be used in programs where abortion is a method of family planning," and a doctor employed by the project may be prohibited in the course of his project duties from counseling abortion or referring for abortion. This is not a case of the Government "suppressing a dangerous idea," but of a prohibition on a project grantee or its employees from engaging in activities outside of its scope.

To hold that the Government unconstitutionally discriminates on the basis of viewpoint when it chooses to fund a program dedicated to advance certain permissible goals, because the program in advancing those goals necessarily discourages alternate goals, would render numerous government programs constitutionally suspect. When Congress established a National Endowment for Democracy to encourage other countries to adopt democratic principles, it was not constitutionally required to fund a program to encourage competing lines of political philosophy such as Communism and Fascism. Petitioners' assertions ultimately boil down to the position that if the government chooses to subsidize one protected right, it must subsidize analogous counterpart rights. But the Court has soundly rejected that proposition. Within far broader limits than petitioners are willing to concede, when the government appropriates public funds to establish a program it is entitled to define the limits of that program.

We believe that petitioners' reliance upon our decision in *Arkansas Writers Project* is misplaced. That case involved a state sales tax which discriminated between magazines on the basis of their content. Relying on this fact, and on the fact that the tax "targets a small group within the press," . . . the Court held the tax invalid. But we have here not the case of a general law singling out a disfavored group on the basis of speech content, but a case of the Government refusing to fund activities, including speech, which are specifically excluded from the scope of the project funded.

. . .

Petitioners also contend that the restrictions on the subsidization of abortion-related speech contained in the regulations are impermissible because they condition the receipt of a benefit, in this case Title X funding, on the relinquishment of a constitutional right, the right to engage in abortion advocacy and counseling. Relying on *Perry v. Sindermann*, 408 U.S. 593, 597 (1972), and *FCC v. League of Women Voters of Cal.*, 468 U.S. 364 (1984), petitioners argue that "even though the government may deny [a] . . . benefit for any number of reasons, there are some reasons upon which the government may not rely. It may not deny a benefit to a person on a basis that infringes his constitutionally protected interests—especially, his interest in freedom of speech." *Perry*.

Petitioners' reliance on these cases is unavailing, however, because here the government is not denying a benefit to anyone, but is instead simply insisting that public funds be spent for the purposes for which they were authorized. The Secretary's regulations do not force the Title X grantee to give up abortion-related speech; they merely require that the grantee keep such activities separate and distinct from Title X activities. Title X expressly distinguishes between a Title X *grantee* and a Title X *project*. The grantee, which normally is a health care organization, may receive funds from a variety of sources for a variety of purposes. The grantee receives Title X funds, however, for the specific and limited purpose of establishing and operating a Title X project. The regulations govern the scope of the Title X *project's* activities, and leave the grantee unfettered in its other activities. The Title X *grantee* can continue to perform abortions, provide abortion-related services, and engage in abortion advocacy; it simply is required to conduct those activities through programs that are separate and independent from the project that receives Title X funds.

In contrast, our "unconstitutional conditions" cases involve situations in which the government has placed a condition on the *recipient* of the subsidy rather than on a particular program or service, thus effectively prohibiting the recipient from engaging in the protected conduct outside the scope of the federally funded program. In *FCC v. League of Women Voters of Cal.*, we invalidated a federal law providing that noncommercial television and radio stations that receive federal grants may not "engage in editorializing." Under that law, a recipient of federal funds was "barred absolutely from all editorializing" because it "is not able to segregate its activities according to the source of its funding" and thus "has no way of limiting the use of its federal funds to all noneditorializing activities." . . .

Similarly, in *Regan* we held that Congress could, in the exercise of its spending power, reasonably refuse to subsidize the lobbying activities of tax-exempt charitable organizations by prohibiting such organizations from using tax-deductible contributions to support their lobbying efforts. In so holding, we explained that such organizations remained free "to receive deductible contributions to support . . . nonlobbying activit[ies]." . . .

By requiring that the Title X grantee engage in abortion-related activity separately from activity receiving federal funding, Congress has, consistent with our teachings in *League of Women Voters* and *Regan*, not denied it the right to engage in abortion-related activities. Congress has merely refused to fund such activities out of the public fisc, and the Secretary has simply required a certain degree of separation from the Title X project in order to ensure the integrity of the federally funded program. . . .

This is not to suggest that funding by the Government, even when coupled with the freedom of the fund recipients to speak outside the scope of the Government-funded project, is invariably sufficient to justify government control over the content of expression. For example, this Court has recognized that the existence of a Government "subsidy," in the form of Government-owned property, does not justify the restriction of speech in areas that have "been traditionally open to the public for expressive activity," or have been "expressly dedicated to speech activity." Similarly, we have recognized that the university is a traditional sphere of free expression so fundamental to the functioning of our society that the Government's ability to control speech within that sphere by means of conditions attached to the expenditure of Government funds is restricted by the vagueness and overbreadth doctrines of the First Amendment. It could be argued by analogy that traditional relationships such as that between doctor and patient should enjoy protection under the First Amendment from

government regulation, even when subsidized by the Government. We need not resolve that question here, however, because the Title X program regulations do not significantly impinge upon the doctor-patient relationship. Nothing in them requires a doctor to represent as his own any opinion that he does not in fact hold. Nor is the doctor-patient relationship established by the Title X program sufficiently all-encompassing so as to justify an expectation on the part of the patient of comprehensive medical advice. The program does not provide post-conception medical care, and therefore a doctor's silence with regard to abortion cannot reasonably be thought to mislead a client into thinking that the doctor does not consider abortion an appropriate option for her. The doctor is always free to make clear that advice regarding abortion is simply beyond the scope of the program. In these circumstances, the general rule that the Government may choose not to subsidize speech applies with full force.

. . .

JUSTICE BLACKMUN, with whom JUSTICE MARSHALL joins, with whom JUSTICE STEVENS joins as to Part[ ] II . . . , dissenting.

. . .

II

. . .

Until today, the Court never has upheld viewpoint-based suppression of speech simply because that suppression was a condition upon the acceptance of public funds. Whatever may be the Government's power to condition the receipt of its largess upon the relinquishment of constitutional rights, it surely does not extend to a condition that suppresses the recipient's cherished freedom of speech based solely upon the content or viewpoint of that speech. . . .

It cannot seriously be disputed that the counseling and referral provisions at issue in the present cases constitute content-based regulation of speech. Title X grantees may provide counseling and referral regarding any of a wide range of family planning and other topics, save abortion.

The Regulations are also clearly viewpoint-based. While suppressing speech favorable to abortion with one hand, the Secretary compels anti-abortion speech with the other. For example, the Department of Health and Human Services' own description of the Regulations makes plain that "Title X projects are *required* to facilitate access to prenatal care and social services, including adoption services, that might be needed by the pregnant client to promote her well-being and that of her child, while making it abundantly clear that the project is not permitted to promote abortion by facilitating access to abortion through the referral process."

Moreover, the Regulations command that a project refer for prenatal care each woman diagnosed as pregnant, irrespective of the woman's expressed desire to continue or terminate her pregnancy. If a client asks directly about abortion, a Title X physician or counselor is required to say, in essence, that the project does not consider abortion to be an appropriate method of family planning. Both requirements are antithetical to the First Amendment.

The Regulations pertaining to "advocacy" are even more explicitly viewpoint-based. These provide: "A Title X project may not *encourage, promote or advocate* abortion as a method of family planning." They explain: "This requirement prohibits actions to assist women to obtain abortions or *increase* the availability or accessibility of abortion for family planning purposes." § 59.10(a) (emphasis added). The Regulations do not, however, proscribe or even regulate anti-abortion advocacy. These are clearly restrictions aimed at the suppression of "dangerous ideas."

Remarkably, the majority concludes that "the Government has not discriminated on the basis of viewpoint; it has merely chosen to fund one activity to the exclusion of another." But the majority's claim that the Regulations merely limit a Title X project's speech to preventive or preconceptional services rings hollow in light of the broad range of non-preventive services that the Regulations authorize Title X projects to provide. By refusing to fund those family-planning projects that advocate abortion *because* they advocate abortion, the Government plainly has targeted a particular viewpoint. The majority's reliance on the fact that the Regulations pertain solely to funding decisions simply begs the question. Clearly, there are some bases upon which government may not rest its decision to fund or not to fund. For example, the Members of the majority surely would agree that government may not base its decision to support an activity upon considerations of race. As demonstrated above, our cases make clear that ideological viewpoint is a similarly repugnant ground upon which to base funding decisions.

The majority's reliance upon *Regan* in this connection is . . . misplaced. That case stands for the proposition that government has no obligation to subsidize a private party's efforts to petition the legislature regarding its views. Thus, if the challenged Regulations were confined to non-ideological limitations upon the use of Title X funds for lobbying activities, there would exist no violation of the First Amendment. The advocacy Regulations at issue here, however, are not limited to lobbying but extend to all speech having the effect of encouraging, promoting, or advocating abortion as a method of family planning. Thus, in addition to their impermissible focus upon the viewpoint of regulated speech, the provisions intrude upon a wide range of communicative conduct, including the very words spoken to a woman by her physician. By manipulating the content of the doctor/patient dialogue, the Regulations upheld today force each of the petitioners "to be an instrument for fostering public adherence to an ideological point of view [he or she] finds unacceptable." This type of intrusive, ideologically based regulation of speech goes far beyond the narrow lobbying limitations approved in *Regan*, and cannot be justified simply because it is a condition upon the receipt of a governmental benefit.

. . .

Finally, it is of no small significance that the speech the Secretary would suppress is truthful information regarding constitutionally protected conduct of vital importance to the listener. One can imagine no legitimate governmental interest that might be served by suppressing such information. Concededly, the abortion debate is among the most divisive and contentious issues that our Nation has faced in recent years. "But freedom to differ is not limited to things that do not matter much. That would be a mere shadow of freedom. The test of its substance is the right to differ as to things that touch the heart of the existing order." *West Virginia Board of Education v. Barnette*.

. . .

[The dissenting opinions of JUSTICES STEVENS and O'CONNOR are omitted.]

DER: The reasoning of both the majority and the dissents in *Rust v. Sullivan* rests on the premise that the First Amendment guarantees primarily government neutrality in the marketplace of ideas. The two sides differed, however, in their delineation of the marketplace at issue. Petitioners presented the marketplace as the Title X project itself, which was monopolized entirely by the government. Respondents, on the other hand, described the government as a participant in a bigger social marketplace of diverse ideas. Framing the First Amendment problem in *Rust* as an unconstitutional condition is also a demand for government neutrality. The decision in *Rust* demonstrates several shortcomings of this singular focus on government neutrality. The logical extension of the neutrality requirement is that government must stay out of the marketplace of ideas altogether and fund no viewpoint, or it must fund each and every viewpoint equally. As the Court pointed out, this assertion would mean that, if government chooses to subsidize one protected view, it also must subsidize all counterpart views. But we *do* want the government to be somewhat selective in its funding decisions; state funding of messages promoting racial harmony, for example, should not require funding for hate speech. Nor do we want the government to remedy cases of viewpoint discrimination by eliminating funding altogether. The government's total retreat from the marketplace of reproductive information, for example, would have a devastating impact on the health of poor women. Moreover, the exclusive focus on neutrality obscures the inequalities in the power to communicate and receive information caused by social and economic disparities in American society. It mistakenly assumes that if the government remains neutral the marketplace of ideas will operate fairly.

An alternative approach would reject the exclusive focus on government neutrality with respect to ideas and consider the political implications of government speech. The regulation's First Amendment violation was not solely the government's distinction between two views on abortion; it was the denial of poor clients' interest in information about abortion because of their dependence on government assistance. The important First Amendment issue raised by the regulations is not whether the government should remain neutral about views on abortion, but whether poor patients are entitled to information critical to their health and reproductive decisionmaking.

DEL: The *Rust* decision denotes substantial hypocrisy on the part of a Court that, in cases such as *Maher* and *Harris* (upholding restrictions on public funding of abortions), stressed its disinterest in how relative power and opportunity to enjoy rights or liberties are distributed. In the abortion funding decisions, the Court concluded that government was not obligated to ensure meaningful access to or exercise of a right or liberty. The bottom line of *Rust*, however, is that government may interfere with supposedly protected freedoms—not only of those who disseminate information about a lawful activity, but those who receive it. The Court's analysis, so tilted in particular against the First Amendment interests at stake (not to mention the Fourteenth Amendment concern), allows the redistributive methods that *Maher* and *Roe* did not require. To the extent that case law reflects indifference to the relativities of power and opportunity, but endorses redistributive initiatives that enhance those disparities and their consequences, doctrinal priorities seem inverted and even perverse.

c. Speech in Public Schools

Concerns about government speech also arise in cases involving the clash between students' interest in speaking in public schools and the government's interest in instructing students, maintaining classroom discipline, and inculcating proper values. In *Tinker v. Des Moines School District*, the Court rejected the argument that students lose their right to free expression when they enter the school grounds.[112] *Tinker* held that school officials violated the First Amendment by imposing a ban on armbands after three students wore black armbands to school to protest American involvement in the Vietnam War. The school officials defended the ban and their suspension of the students for defying it on the ground that it was necessary in order to prevent a disturbance which the armbands might provoke. Noting that the passive wearing of armbands had not actually interfered with the school's work, the majority concluded that the state had not justified its infringement of the students' symbolic message:

---

[112] Tinker v. Des Moines School District, 393 U.S. 503 (1969).

In order for the State in the person of school officials to justify prohibition of a particular expression of opinion, it must be able to show that its action was caused by something more than a mere desire to avoid the discomfort and unpleasantness that always accompany an unpopular viewpoint. Certainly where there is no finding and no showing that the exercise of the forbidden right would "materially and substantially interfere with the requirements of appropriate discipline in the operation of the school," the prohibition cannot be sustained.

In the present case, the District Court made no such finding, and our independent examination of the record fails to yield evidence that the school authorities had reason to anticipate that the wearing of the armbands would substantially interfere with the work of the school or impinge upon the rights of other students. . . . On the contrary, the action of the school authorities appears to have been based upon an urgent wish to avoid the controversy which might result from the expression, even by the silent symbol of armbands, of opposition to this Nation's part in the conflagration in Vietnam. . . .

. . .

In our system, state-operated schools may not be enclaves of totalitarianism. School officials do not possess absolute authority over their students. Students in school as well as out of school are "persons" under our Constitution. They are possessed of fundamental rights which the State must respect, just as they themselves must respect their obligations to the State. In our system, students may not be regarded as closed-circuit recipients of only that which the State chooses to communicate. They may not be confined to the expression of those sentiments that are officially approved. In the absence of a specific showing of constitutionally valid reasons to regulate their speech, students are entitled to freedom of expression of their views.

The *Tinker* opinion offered a strong defense of the speech rights of public school students. Subsequent decisions, however, have emphasized the schools' institutional authority to teach students proper values, which may override students' interest in unfettered expression of their views. *Bethel School District v. Fraser* upheld the three-day suspension of a high school student who delivered a speech nominating a school mate for student elective office at a school assembly which referred repeatedly to his candidate "in terms of an elaborate, graphic, and explicit sexual metaphor."[113] The student began his speech, for example, with the statement, "I know a man who is firm—he's firm in his pants, he's firm in his shirt, his character is firm—but most . . . of all, his belief in you, the students of Bethel, is firm." The Court distinguished *Tinker* based on the "marked distinction between the political 'message' of the armbands in *Tinker* and the sexual content of respondent's speech," as well as the neutrality of the action taken by the Bethel School District officials, which was "unrelated to any political viewpoint." Unlike the armbands in *Tinker*, the student's sexual innuendo interfered with the school's educational mission:

Surely it is a highly appropriate function of public school education to prohibit the use of vulgar and offensive terms in public discourse. Indeed, the "fundamental values necessary to the maintenance of a democratic political system" disfavor the use of terms of debate highly offensive or highly threatening to others. Nothing in the Constitution prohibits the states from insisting that certain modes of expression are inappropriate and subject to sanctions.

---

[113] Bethel School Dist. No. 403 v. Fraser, 478 U.S. 675 (1986).

The inculcation of these values is truly the "work of the schools." *Tinker*. The determination of what manner of speech in the classroom or in school assembly is inappropriate properly rests with the school board.

The process of educating our youth for citizenship in public schools is not confined to books, the curriculum, and the civic class; schools must teach by example the shared values of a civilized social order. Consciously or otherwise, teachers—and indeed the older students—demonstrate the appropriate form of civil discourse and political expression by their conduct and deportment in and out of class. Inescapably, like parents, they are role models. The schools, as instruments of the state, may determine that the essential lessons of civil, mature conduct cannot be conveyed in a school that tolerates lewd, indecent, or offensive speech and conduct such as that indulged in by this confused boy. . . . Accordingly, it was perfectly appropriate for the school to disassociate itself to make the point to the pupils that vulgar speech and lewd conduct is wholly inconsistent with the "fundamental values" of public school education.

The Court next applied these considerations of the schools' educational objectives to the question of school officials' editorial control over school-sponsored expressive activities.

Hazelwood School District v. Kuhlmeier
484 U.S. 260 (1988)

JUSTICE WHITE delivered the opinion of the Court.

This case concerns the extent to which educators may exercise editorial control over the contents of a high school newspaper produced as part of the school's journalism curriculum.

I

Petitioners are the Hazelwood School District in St. Louis County, Missouri; various school officials; Robert Eugene Reynolds, the principal of Hazelwood East High School; and Howard Emerson, a teacher in the school district. Respondents are three former Hazelwood East students who were staff members of Spectrum, the school newspaper. They contend that school officials violated their First Amendment rights by deleting two pages of articles from the May 13, 1983, issue of Spectrum.

. . .

The practice at Hazelwood East during the spring 1983 semester was for the journalism teacher to submit page proofs of each Spectrum issue to Principal Reynolds for his review prior to publication. On May 10, Emerson delivered the proofs of the May 13 edition to Reynolds, who objected to two of the articles scheduled to appear in that edition. One of the stories described three Hazelwood East students' experiences with pregnancy; the other discussed the impact of divorce on students at the school.

Reynolds was concerned that, although the pregnancy story used false names "to keep the identity of these girls a secret," the pregnant students still might be identifiable from the text. He also believed that the article's references to sexual activity and birth control were inappropriate for some of the younger students at the school. In addition, Reynolds was concerned that a student identified by name in the divorce story had complained that her father "wasn't spending enough time with my mom, my sister and I" prior to the divorce, "was always out of town on business or out late playing cards with the guys," and "always argued about everything" with her mother. Reynolds believed that the student's parents should have been given an opportunity to respond to these remarks or to consent to their publication. He was unaware that Emerson had deleted the student's name from the final version of the article.

Reynolds believed that there was no time to make the necessary changes in the stories before the scheduled press run and that the newspaper would not appear before the end of the school year if printing were delayed to any significant extent. He concluded that his only options under the circumstances were to publish a four-page newspaper instead of the planned six-page newspaper, eliminating the two pages on which the offending stories appeared, or to publish no newspaper at all. Accordingly, he directed Emerson to withhold from publication the two pages containing the stories on pregnancy and divorce. He informed his superiors of the decision, and they concurred.

. . .

II

Students in the public schools do not "shed their constitutional rights to freedom of speech or expression at the schoolhouse gate." *Tinker*. They cannot be punished merely for expressing their personal views on the school premises—whether "in the cafeteria, or on the playing field, or on the campus during the authorized hours"—unless school authorities have reason to believe that such expression will "substantially interfere with the work of the school or impinge upon the rights of other students."

We have nonetheless recognized that the First Amendment rights of students in the public schools "are not automatically coextensive with the rights of adults in other settings," *Bethel School District No. 403 v. Fraser*, and must be "applied in light of the special characteristics of the school environment." *Tinker*. A school need not tolerate student speech that is inconsistent with its "basic educational mission," even though the government could not censor similar speech outside the school. Accordingly, we held in Fraser that a student could be disciplined for having delivered a speech that was "sexually explicit" but not legally obscene at an official school assembly, because the school was entitled to "disassociate itself" from the speech in a manner that would demonstrate to others that such vulgarity is "wholly inconsistent with the 'fundamental values' of public school education." We thus recognized that "[t]he determination of what manner of speech in the classroom or in school assembly is inappropriate properly rests with the school board," rather than with the federal courts. It is in this context that respondents' First Amendment claims must be considered.

. . .

The question whether the First Amendment requires a school to tolerate particular student speech—the question that we addressed in *Tinker*—is different from the question whether the First Amendment requires a school affirmatively to promote particular student speech. The former question addresses educators' ability to silence a student's personal expression that happens to occur on the school premises. The latter question concerns educators' authority over school-sponsored publications, theatrical productions, and other expressive activities that students, parents, and members of the public might reasonably perceive to bear the imprimatur of the school. These activities may fairly be characterized as part of the school curriculum, whether or not they occur in a traditional classroom setting, so long as they are supervised by faculty members and designed to impart particular knowledge or skills to student participants and audiences.

Educators are entitled to exercise greater control over this second form of student expression to assure that participants learn whatever lessons the activity is designed to teach, that readers or listeners are not exposed to material that may be inappropriate for their level of maturity, and that the views of the individual speaker are not erroneously attributed to the school. Hence, a school may in its capacity as publisher of a school newspaper or producer of a school play "disassociate itself," *Fraser*, not only from speech that would "substantially interfere with [its] work . . . or impinge upon the rights of other students," *Tinker*, but also from speech that is, for example, ungrammatical, poorly written, inadequately researched, biased or prejudiced, vulgar or profane, or unsuitable for immature audiences. A school must be able to set high standards for the student speech that is disseminated under its auspices—standards that may be higher than those demanded by some newspaper publishers or theatrical producers in the "real" world—and may refuse to disseminate student speech that does not meet those standards. In addition, a school must be able to take into account the emotional maturity of the intended audience in determining whether to disseminate student speech on potentially sensitive topics, which might range from the existence of Santa Claus in an elementary school setting to the particulars of teenage sexual activity in a high school setting. A school must also retain the authority to refuse to sponsor student speech that might reasonably be perceived to advocate drug or alcohol use, irresponsible sex, or conduct otherwise inconsistent with "the shared values of a civilized social order," *Fraser*, or to associate the school with any position other than neutrality on matters of political controversy. Otherwise, the schools would be unduly constrained from fulfilling their role as "a principal instrument in awakening the child to cultural values, in preparing him for later professional training, and in helping him to adjust normally to his environment." *Brown v. Board of Education*.

Accordingly, we conclude that the standard articulated in *Tinker* for determining when a school may punish student expression need not also be the standard for determining when a school may refuse to lend its name and resources to the dissemination of student expression. Instead, we hold that educators do not offend the First Amendment by exercising editorial control over the style and content of student speech in school-sponsored expressive activities so long as their actions are reasonably related to legitimate pedagogical concerns.

This standard is consistent with our oft-expressed view that the education of the Nation's youth is primarily the responsibility of parents, teachers, and state and local school officials, and not of federal judges. It is only when the decision to censor a school-sponsored publication, theatrical production, or other vehicle of student expression has no valid educational purpose that the First Amendment is so "directly and sharply implicate[d]," as to require judicial intervention to protect students' constitutional rights.

III

We also conclude that Principal Reynolds acted reasonably in requiring the deletion from the May 13 issue of Spectrum of the pregnancy article, the divorce article, and the remaining articles that were to appear on the same pages of the newspaper.

. . .

. . . Reynolds could reasonably have concluded that the students who had written and edited these articles had not sufficiently mastered those portions of the Journalism II curriculum that pertained to the treatment of controversial issues and personal attacks, the need to protect the privacy of individuals whose most intimate concerns are to be revealed in the newspaper, and "the legal, moral, and ethical restrictions imposed upon journalists within [a] school community" that includes adolescent subjects and readers. Finally, we conclude that the principal's decision to delete two pages of Spectrum, rather than to delete only the offending articles or to require that they be modified, was reasonable under the circumstances as he understood them. Accordingly, no violation of First Amendment rights occurred.

JUSTICE BRENNAN, with whom JUSTICE MARSHALL and JUSTICE BLACKMUN join, dissenting.

. . .

II

. . . I . . . reject the Court's rationale for abandoning *Tinker* in this case. The Court offers no more than an obscure tangle of three excuses to afford educators "greater control" over school-sponsored speech than the *Tinker* test would permit: the public educator's prerogative to control curriculum; the pedagogical interest in shielding the high school audience from objectionable viewpoints and sensitive topics; and the school's need to dissociate itself from student expression. None of the excuses, once disentangled, supports the distinction that the Court draws. *Tinker* fully addresses the first concern; the second is illegitimate; and the third is readily achievable through less oppressive means.

A

The Court is certainly correct that the First Amendment permits educators "to assure that participants learn whatever lessons the activity is designed to teach. . . . " That is, however, the essence of the *Tinker* test, not an excuse to abandon it. Under *Tinker*, school officials may censor only such student speech as would "materially disrup[t]" a legitimate curricular function. Manifestly, student speech is more likely to disrupt a curricular function when it arises in the context of a curricular activity—one that "is designed to teach" something—than when it arises in the context of a noncurricular activity. Thus, under *Tinker*, the school may constitutionally punish the budding political orator if he disrupts calculus class but not if he holds his tongue for the cafeteria. That is not because some more stringent standard applies in the curricular context. (After all, this Court applied the same standard whether the students in *Tinker* wore their armbands to the "classroom" or the "cafeteria." It is because student speech in the noncurricular context is less likely to disrupt materially any legitimate pedagogical purpose.

I fully agree with the Court that the First Amendment should afford an educator the prerogative not to sponsor the publication of a newspaper article that is "ungrammatical, poorly written, inadequately researched, biased or prejudiced," or that falls short of the "high standards for . . . student speech that is disseminated under [the school's] auspices. . . . " But we need not abandon *Tinker* to reach that conclusion; we need only apply it. The enumerated criteria reflect the skills that the curricular newspaper "is designed to teach." The educator may, under *Tinker*, constitutionally "censor" poor grammar, writing, or research because to reward such expression would "materially disrup[t]" the newspaper's curricular purpose.

The same cannot be said of official censorship designed to shield the *audience* or dissociate the *sponsor* from the expression. Censorship so motivated might well serve . . . some other school purpose. But it in no way furthers the curricular purposes of a student *newspaper*, unless one believes that the purpose of the school newspaper is to teach students that the press ought never report bad news, express unpopular views, or print a thought that might upset its sponsors. Unsurprisingly, Hazelwood East claims no such pedagogical purpose.

The Court relies on bits of testimony to portray the principal's conduct as a pedagogical lesson to Journalism II students who "had not sufficiently mastered those portions of the . . . curriculum that pertained to the treatment of controversial issues and personal attacks, the need to protect the privacy of individuals . . . , and 'the legal, moral, and ethical restrictions imposed upon journalists. . . . ' " ...

But the principal never consulted the students before censoring their work. . . . Further, he explained the deletions only in the broadest of generalities. In one meeting called at the behest of seven protesting Spectrum staff members (presumably a fraction of the full class), he characterized the articles as "'too sensitive' for 'our immature audience of readers,'" and in a later meeting he deemed them simply "inappropriate, personal, sensitive and unsuitable for the newspaper." The Court's supposition that the principal intended (or the protesters understood) those generalities as a lesson on the nuances of journalistic responsibility is utterly incredible. If he did, a fact that neither the District Court nor the Court of Appeals found, the lesson was lost on all but the psychic Spectrum staffer.

B

The Court's second excuse for deviating from precedent is the school's interest in shielding an impressionable high school audience from material whose substance is "unsuitable for immature audiences." Specifically, the majority decrees that we must afford educators authority to shield high school students from exposure to "potentially sensitive topics" (like "the particulars of teenage sexual activity") or unacceptable social viewpoints (like the advocacy of "irresponsible se[x] or conduct otherwise inconsistent with 'the shared values of a civilized social order' ") through school-sponsored student activities.

Tinker teaches us that the state educator's undeniable, and undeniably vital, mandate to inculcate moral and political values is not a general warrant to act as "thought police" stifling discussion of all but state-approved topics and advocacy of all but the official position. Otherwise educators could transform students into "closed-circuit recipients of only that which the State chooses to communicate," *Tinker*, and cast a perverse and impermissible "pall of orthodoxy over the classroom," *Keyishian v. Board of Regents*, 385 U.S. 589, 603 (1967). Thus, the State cannot constitutionally prohibit its high school students from recounting in the locker room "the particulars of [their] teen-age sexual activity," nor even from advocating "irresponsible se[x]" or other presumed abominations of "the shared values of a civilized social order." Even in its capacity as educator the State may not assume an Orwellian "guardianship of the public mind," *Thomas v. Collins*, 323 U.S. 516, 545 (1945) (Jackson, J., concurring).

The mere fact of school sponsorship does not, as the Court suggests, license such

thought control in the high school, whether through school suppression of disfavored viewpoints or through official assessment of topic sensitivity. The former would constitute unabashed and unconstitutional viewpoint discrimination, as well as an impermissible infringement of the students' "'right to receive information and ideas.'" Just as a school board may not purge its state-funded library of all books that " 'offen[d] [its] social, political and moral tastes,' " [*Board of Education v. Pico* 457 U.S. 853 (1982)], school officials may not, out of like motivation, discriminatorily excise objectionable ideas from a student publication. The State's prerogative to dissolve the student newspaper entirely (or to limit its subject matter) no more entitles it to dictate which viewpoints students may express on its pages, than the State's prerogative to close down the schoolhouse entitles it to prohibit the nondisruptive expression of antiwar sentiment within its gates.

Official censorship of student speech on the ground that it addresses "potentially sensitive topics" is, for related reasons, equally impermissible. I would not begrudge an educator the authority to limit the substantive scope of a school-sponsored publication to a certain, objectively definable topic, such as literary criticism, school sports, or an overview of the school year. Unlike those determinate limitations, "potential topic sensitivity" is a vaporous nonstandard—like "'public welfare, peace, safety, health, decency, good order, morals or convenience,'" *Shuttlesworth v. Birmingham*, or "'general welfare of citizens,'" *Staub v. Baxley*, 355 U.S. 313, 322 (1958)—that invites manipulation to achieve ends that cannot permissibly be achieved through blatant viewpoint discrimination and chills student speech to which school officials might not object. In part because of those dangers, this Court has consistently condemned any scheme allowing a state official boundless discretion in licensing speech from a particular forum. See, *e.g.*, *Shuttlesworth v. Birmingham*.

. . .

C

The sole concomitant of school sponsorship that might conceivably justify the distinction that the Court draws between sponsored and nonsponsored student expression is the risk "that the views of the individual speaker [might be] erroneously attributed to the school." Of course, the risk of erroneous attribution inheres in any student expression, including "personal expression" that, like the armbands in *Tinker*, "happens to occur on the school premises." Nevertheless, the majority is certainly correct that indicia of school sponsorship increase the likelihood of such attribution, and that state educators may therefore have a legitimate interest in dissociating themselves from student speech.

But "'[e]ven though the governmental purpose be legitimate and substantial, that purpose cannot be pursued by means that broadly stifle fundamental personal liberties when the end can be more narrowly achieved.'" *Keyishian v. Board of Regents* (quoting *Shelton v. Tucker*, 364 U.S. 479, 488 (1960)). Dissociative means short of censorship are available to the school. It could, for example, require the student activity to publish a disclaimer, such as the "Statement of Policy" that Spectrum published each school year announcing that "[a]ll ... editorials appearing in this newspaper reflect the opinions of the *Spectrum* staff, which are not necessarily shared by the administrators or faculty of Hazelwood East"; or it could simply issue its own response clarifying the official position on the matter and explaining why the student position is wrong. Yet, without so much as acknowledging the less oppressive alternatives, the Court approves of brutal censorship.

III

Since the censorship served no legitimate pedagogical purpose, it cannot by any stretch of the imagination have been designed to prevent "materia[l] disrup[tion of] classwork," *Tinker*. Nor did the censorship fall within the category that *Tinker* described as necessary to prevent student expression from "inva[ding] the rights of others." If that term is to have any content, it must be limited to rights that are protected by law....

...

IV

The Court opens its analysis in this case by purporting to reaffirm *Tinker*'s time-tested proposition that public school students "do not 'shed their constitutional rights to freedom of speech or expression at the schoolhouse gate.'" That is an ironic introduction to an opinion that denudes high school students of much of the First Amendment protection that *Tinker* itself prescribed. Instead of "teach[ing] children to respect the diversity of ideas that is fundamental to the American system," *Board of Education v. Pico* (BLACKMUN, J., concurring in part and concurring in judgment), and "that our Constitution is a living reality, not parchment preserved under glass," *Shanley v. Northeast Independent School Dist., Bexar Cty., Tex.*, 462 F.2d 960, 972 (CA5 1972), the Court today "teach[es] youth to discount important principles of our government as mere platitudes." *West Virginia Board of Education v. Barnette.* The young men and women of Hazelwood East expected a civics lesson, but not the one the Court teaches them today.

DER: Although the majority and dissenting Justices disputed whether the student articles interfered with the school's pedagogical purposes, they accepted the premise that inculcation of values is a proper pedagogical function of public schools. The Court's First Amendment inquiry focuses on the students' disruption of the school's educational mission rather than examining the mission itself. The Court grants school authorities broad discretion in determining the appropriate values to teach students. Its restrictions on schools' inculcation of values have been limited largely to religious issues. For example, the Court held that the non-sectarian invocation of God at a public school graduation ceremony violated the Establishment Clause and required a state to exempt Amish children from compulsory high school attendance rules because those rules violated the right to free exercise of religion.[114] But differences of opinion about the values taught in public schools are not restricted to religious viewpoints. Radical educators have theorized that schools function to reproduce biased social structures and ways of thinking. For example, schools tend to organize the curriculum in a hierarchy that obscures information about women, people of color, and the poor and working class. They uphold social values that may be more acceptable to powerful groups than to minorities. In a religion case, *Wisconsin v. Yoder*, the Court observed that the public schools' emphasis on "intellectual and scientific accomplishments, self-distinction, competitiveness, worldly success, and social life with other students" conflicted with the opposite values of Amish society.[115] The First Amendment's protection of dissident religious values in the public school context may apply to

---

[114] *See* Lee v. Weisman, 112 S. Ct. 2649 (1992); Wisconsin v. Yoder, 406 U.S. 205 (1972).
[115] Wisconsin v. Yoder, 406 U.S. at 211.

conflicts over secular values as well. The First Amendment may require the Court to ask not only whether student speech interferes with the schools' inculcation of values but to examine more critically this function of public education.

DEL: Having the Court inquire into whether student expression interferes with the educational process does not provide a logical departure point for widespread judicial interest in what values the schools inculcate. The *Yoder* Court provides a workable model, if extrapolated into the secular world, of proscribing doctrinal imposition that compels repudiation of a person's political or social beliefs. Insofar as schools reflect the values of what the dominant culture believes is essential and useful to individual self-development and achievement, however, it is utopian to expect curriculum or instruction to be neutral. For all of the cultural biases and blindness that may exist, it is hard to imagine that the judiciary would manage a better result. Given the judiciary's own record, that includes construction of a fundamental right to own slaves, maintenance of official segregation, espousal of contractual liberty and delimitation of desegregation and anti-discrimination principles, institutional competence to monitor or appraise comprehensively the inculcation of values in schools is to be doubted.

6. Procedural Safeguards

The First Amendment places not only substantive limits on the government's power to regulate speech, but also requirements that are more akin to special procedural or due process protections. Courts may invalidate a state restriction on speech because it constitutes a prior restraint or because it is vague or overbroad, without reaching the question whether or not the content of the speech at issue deserves First Amendment protection. Even if the government may constitutionally punish the particular speech involved, its regulation may be struck down for violating one of these technical safeguards. As Thomas Emerson explained about prior restraints, "[t]he issue is not whether the government may impose a particular restriction of substance in an area of public expression, such as forbidding obscenity in newspapers, but whether it may do so by a particular method, such as advance screening of newspaper copy."[116] The state may have the power to restrain the speaker's message, yet exercise its power in a manner that unconstitutionally infringes protected freedoms.

a. Prior Restraints and Permits

Despite the debate over the Framers' understanding of the freedom of expression, there is general agreement that the First Amendment was intended to prohibit prior restraints on the press—even if the publisher subsequently could be fined for an offending publication. The Framers probably had in mind administrative licensing schemes such as the onerous English licensing laws abolished in the late seventeenth century which required publishers to obtain a license before printing books and pamphlets. In its seminal decision in *Near v. Minnesota*, the Court seemed constrained to interpret a court injunction against publication of a newspaper as a prior restraint in order to justify invalidating it. The dissenting opinion disagreed that the injunction was similar enough to the administrative censorship that constituted the classic prior restraint.

---

[116] Thomas I. Emerson, *The Doctrine of Prior Restraint*, 20 L. & CONTEMP. PROB. 648 (1955).

Near v. Minnesota
283 U.S. 697 (1931)

MR. CHIEF JUSTICE HUGHES delivered the opinion of the Court.

Chapter 285 of the Session Laws of Minnesota for the year 1925 provides for the abatement, as a public nuisance, of a "malicious, scandalous and defamatory newspaper, magazine or other periodical." . . . Under this statute . . . the County Attorney of Hennepin county brought this action to enjoin the publication of what was described as a 'malicious, scandalous and defamatory newspaper, magazine or other periodical,' known as "The Saturday Press," published by the defendants in the city of Minneapolis. . . .

. . . [T]he articles charged, in substance, that a Jewish gangster was in control of gambling, bootlegging, and racketeering in Minneapolis, and that law enforcing officers and agencies were not energetically performing their duties. Most of the charges were directed against the chief of police; he was charged with gross neglect of duty, illicit relations with gangsters, and with participation in graft. The county attorney was charged with knowing the existing conditions and with failure to take adequate measures to remedy them. The mayor was accused of inefficiency and dereliction. One member of the grand jury was stated to be in sympathy with the gangsters. A special grand jury and a special prosecutor were demanded to deal with the situation in general, and, in particular, to investigate an attempt to assassinate one Guilford, one of the original defendants, who, it appears from the articles, was shot by gangsters after the first issue of the periodical had been published. There is no question but that the articles made serious accusations against the public officers named and others in connection with the prevalence of crimes and the failure to expose and punish them.

. . .

The district court made findings of fact, which followed the allegations of the complaint and found in general terms that the editions in question were "chiefly devoted to malicious, scandalous and defamatory articles" concerning the individuals named. The court further found that the defendants through these publications "did engage in the business of regularly and customarily producing, publishing and circulating a malicious, scandalous and defamatory newspaper," and that "the said publication" "under said name of The Saturday Press, or any other name, constitutes a public nuisance under the laws of the State." Judgment was thereupon entered adjudging that "the newspaper, magazine and periodical known as

The Saturday Press," as a public nuisance, "be and is hereby abated." The judgment perpetually enjoined the defendants "from producing, editing, publishing, circulating, having in their possession, selling or giving away any publication whatsoever which is a malicious, scandalous or defamatory newspaper, as defined by law," and also "from further conducting said nuisance under the name and title of said The Saturday Press or any other name or title."

The defendant Near appealed from this judgment to the Supreme Court of the State, again asserting his right under the Federal Constitution, and the judgment was affirmed upon the authority of the former decision. . . .

This statute, for the suppression as a public nuisance of a newspaper or periodical, is unusual, if not unique, and raises questions of grave importance transcending the local interests involved in the particular action. It is no longer open to doubt that the liberty of the press and of speech is within the liberty safeguarded by the due process clause of the Fourteenth Amendment from invasion by state action. . . . In maintaining this guaranty, the authority of the state to enact laws to promote the health, safety, morals, and general welfare of its people is necessarily administered. The limits of this sovereign power must always be determined with appropriate regard to the particular subject of its exercise. . . .

. . .

First. The statute is not aimed at the redress of individual or private wrongs. Remedies for libel remain available and unaffected. The statute, said the state court "is not directed at threatened libel but at an existing business which, generally speaking, involves more than libel." It is aimed at the distribution of scandalous matter as "detrimental to public morals and to the general welfare," tending "to disturb the peace of the community" and "to provoke assaults and the commission of crime." In order to obtain an injunction to suppress the future publication of the newspaper or periodical, it is not necessary to prove the falsity of the charges that have been made in the publication condemned. In the present action there was no allegation that the matter published was not true. . . . The court sharply defined the purpose of the statute, bringing out the precise point, in these words: "There is no constitutional right to publish a fact merely because it is true. It is a matter of common knowledge that prosecutions under the criminal libel statutes do not result in efficient repression or suppression of the evils of scandal. Men who are the victims of such assaults seldom resort to the courts.

This is especially true if their sins are exposed and the only question relates to whether it was done with good motive and for justifiable ends. This law is not for the protection of the person attacked nor to punish the wrongdoer. It is for the protection of the public welfare."

Second. The statute is directed not simply at the circulation of scandalous and defamatory statements with regard to private citizens, but at the continued publication by newspapers and periodicals of charges against public officers of corruption, malfeasance in office, or serious neglect of duty. Such charges by their very nature create a public scandal. They are scandalous and defamatory within the meaning of the statute, which has its normal operation in relation to publications dealing prominently and chiefly with the alleged derelictions of public officers.

Third. The object of the statute is not punishment, in the ordinary sense, but suppression of the offending newspaper or periodical. The reason for the enactment, as the state court has said, is that prosecutions to enforce penal statutes for libel do not result in "efficient repression or suppression of the evils of scandal." Describing the business of publication as a public nuisance does not obscure the substance of the proceeding which the statute authorizes. It is the continued publication of scandalous and defamatory matter that constitutes the business and the declared nuisance. In the case of public officers, it is the reiteration of charges of official misconduct, and the fact that the newspaper or periodical is principally devoted to that purpose, that exposes it to suppression. . . . In such a case, these officers are not left to their ordinary remedy in a suit for libel, or the authorities to a prosecution for criminal libel. Under this statute, a publisher of a newspaper or periodical, undertaking to conduct a campaign to expose and to censure official derelictions, and devoting his publication principally to that purpose, must face not simply the possibility of a verdict against him in a suit or prosecution for libel, but a determination that his newspaper or periodical is a public nuisance to be abated, and that this abatement and suppression will follow unless he is prepared with legal evidence to prove the truth of the charges and also to satisfy the court that, in addition to being true, the matter was published with good motives and for justifiable ends.

This suppression is accomplished by enjoining publication, and that restraint is the object and effect of the statute.

Fourth. The statute not only operates to suppress the offending newspaper or periodical, but to put the publisher under an effective censorship. When a newspaper or periodical is found to be "malicious, scandalous and defamatory," and is suppressed as such, resumption of publication is punishable as a contempt of court by fine or imprisonment. Thus, where a newspaper or periodical has been suppressed because of the circulation of charges against public officers of official misconduct, it would seem to be clear that the renewal of the publication of such charges would constitute a contempt, and that the judgment would lay a permanent restraint upon the publisher, to escape which he must satisfy the court as to the character of a new publication. Whether he would be permitted again to publish matter deemed to be derogatory to the same or other public officers would depend upon the court's ruling. . . .

If we cut through mere details of procedure, the operation and effect of the statute in substance is that public authorities may bring the owner or publisher of a newspaper or periodical before a judge upon a charge of conducting a business of publishing scandalous and defamatory matter—in particular that the matter consists of charges against public officers of official dereliction—and, unless the owner or publisher is able and disposed to bring competent evidence to satisfy the judge that the charges are true and are published with good motives and for justifiable ends, his newspaper or periodical is suppressed and further publication is made punishable as a contempt. This is of the essence of censorship.

The question is whether a statute authorizing such proceedings in restraint of publication is consistent with the conception of the liberty of the press as historically conceived and guaranteed. In determining the extent of the constitutional protection, it has been generally, if not universally, considered that it is the chief purpose of the guaranty to prevent previous restraints upon publication. The struggle in England, directed against the legislative power of the licenser, resulted in renunciation of the censorship of the press. The liberty deemed to be established was thus described by Blackstone: "The liberty of the press is indeed essential to the nature of a free state; but this consists in laying no *previous* restraints upon publications, and not in freedom from censure for criminal matter when published. Every freeman has an undoubted right to lay what sentiments he pleases before the public; to forbid this, is to destroy the freedom of the press; but if he publishes what is improper, mischievous or illegal, he must take the consequence of his own temerity." The distinction was early pointed out between the extent of the freedom with respect to censorship under our constitutional system and that enjoyed in England. Here, as Madison said, "the great and essential rights of the people are secured against legislative as well as against executive ambition.

They are secured, not by laws paramount to prerogative, but by constitutions paramount to laws. This security of the freedom of the press requires that it should be exempt not only from previous restraint by the Executive, as in Great Britain, but from legislative restraint also." Report on the Virginia Resolutions, Madison's Works, vol. IV, p. 543. . . .

. . .

The objection has . . . been made that the principle as to immunity from previous restraint is stated too broadly, if every such restraint is deemed to be prohibited. That is undoubtedly true; the protection even as to previous restraint is not absolutely unlimited. But the limitation has been recognized only in exceptional cases. "When a nation is at war many things that might be said in time of peace are such a hindrance to its error that their utterance will not be endured so long as men fight and that no Court could regard them as protected by any constitutional right." *Science v. United States*. No one would question but that a government might prevent actual obstruction to its recruiting service or the publication of the sailing dates of transports or the number and location of troops. On similar grounds, the primary requirements of decency may be enforced against obscene publications. The security of the community life may be protected against incitements to acts of violence and the overthrow by force of orderly government. The constitutional guaranty of free speech does not "protect a man from an injunction against uttering words that may have all the effect of force." *Science*. These limitations are not applicable here. . . .

The exceptional nature of its limitations places in a strong light the general conception that liberty of the press, historically considered and taken up by the Federal Constitution, has meant, principally although not exclusively, immunity from previous restraints or censorship. The conception of the liberty of the press in this country had broadened with the exigencies of the colonial period and with the efforts to secure freedom from oppressive administration. That liberty was especially cherished for the immunity it afforded from previous restraint of the publication of censure of public officers and charges of official misconduct. As was said by Chief Justice Parker, in *Commonwealth v. Blanding*, 3 Pick. 304, 313, with respect to the Constitution of Massachusetts: "Besides, it is well understood and received as a commentary on this provision for the liberty of the press, that it was intended to prevent all such *previous restraints* upon publications as had been practiced by other governments, and in early times here, to stifle the efforts of patriots towards enlightening their fellow subjects upon their rights and the duties of rulers.

The liberty of the press was to be unrestrained, but he who used it was to be responsible in case of its abuse." . . . Madison, who was the leading spirit in the preparation of the First Amendment of the Federal Constitution, thus described the practice and sentiment which led to the guaranties of liberty of the press in State Constitutions: . . . "Some degree of abuse is inseparable from the proper use of everything, and in no instance is this more true than in that of the press. It has accordingly been decided by the practice of the States, that it is better to leave a few of its noxious branches to their luxuriant growth, than, by pruning them away, to injure the vigour of those yielding the proper fruits. . . . Had 'Sedition Acts,' forbidding every publication that might bring the constituted agents into contempt or disrepute, or that might excite the hatred of the people against the authors of unjust or pernicious measures, been uniformly enforced against the press, might not the United States have been languishing at this day under the infirmities of a sickly Confederation? Might they not, possibly, be miserable colonies, groaning under a foreign yoke?"

The fact that for approximately one hundred and fifty years there has been almost an entire absence of attempts to impose previous restraints upon publications relating to the malfeasance of public officers is significant of the deep-seated conviction that such restraints would violate constitutional right. Public officers, whose character and conduct remain open to debate and free discussion in the press, find their remedies for false accusations in actions under libel laws providing for redress and punishment, and not in proceedings to restrain the publication of newspapers and periodicals. . . .

The importance of this immunity has not lessened. While reckless assaults upon public men, and efforts to bring obloquy upon those who are endeavoring faithfully to discharge official duties, exert a baleful influence and deserve the severest condemnation in public opinion, it cannot be said that this abuse is greater, and it is believed to be less, than that which characterized the period in which our institutions took shape. Meanwhile, the administration of government has become more complex, the opportunities for malfeasance and corruption have multiplied, crime has grown to most serious proportions, and the danger of its protection by unfaithful officials and of the impairment of the fundamental security of life and property by criminal alliances and official neglect, emphasizes the primary need of a vigilant and courageous press, especially in great cities. The fact that the liberty of the press may be abused by miscreant purveyors of scandal does not make any the less necessary the immunity of the press from previous restraint in dealing with official misconduct. . . .

. . .

The statute in question cannot be justified by reason of the fact that the publisher is permitted to show, before injunction issues, that the matter published is true and is published with good motives and for justifiable ends. If such a statute, authorizing suppression and injunction on such a basis, is constitutionally valid, it would be equally permissible for the Legislature to provide that at any time the publisher of any newspaper could be brought before a court, or even an administrative officer (as the constitutional protection may not be regarded as resting on mere procedural details), and required to produce proof of the truth of his publication, or of what he intended to publish and of his motives, or stand enjoined. If this can be done, the Legislature may provide machinery for determining in the complete exercise of its discretion what are justifiable ends and restrain publication accordingly. And it would be but a step to a complete system of censorship. The recognition of authority to impose previous restraint upon publication in order to protect the community against the circulation of charges of misconduct, and especially of official misconduct, necessarily would carry with it the admission of the authority of the censor against which the constitutional barrier was erected. The preliminary freedom, by virtue of the very reason for its existence, does not depend, as this court has said, on proof of truth.

Equally unavailing is the insistence that the statute is designed to prevent the circulation of scandal which tends to disturb the public peace and to provoke assaults and the commission of crime. Charges of reprehensible conduct, and in particular of official malfeasance, unquestionably create a public scandal, but the theory of the constitutional guaranty is that even a more serious public evil would be caused by authority to prevent publication. . . .

For these reasons we hold the statute, so far as it authorized the proceedings in this action . . . to be an infringement of the liberty of the press guaranteed by the Fourteenth Amendment. We should add that this decision rests upon the operation and effect of the statute, without regard to the question of the truth of the charges contained in the particular periodical. The fact that the public officers named in this case, and those associated with the charges of official dereliction, cannot be deemed to be impeccable, cannot affect the conclusion that the statute imposes an unconstitutional restraint upon publication.

Judgment reversed.

Mr. Justice Butler, dissenting.

The decision of the Court in this case declares Minnesota and every other state power-less to restrain by injunction the business of publishing and circulating among the people malicious, scandalous, and defamatory periodicals that in due course of judicial procedure has been adjudged to be a public nuisance. It gives to freedom of the press a meaning and a scope not heretofore recognized, and construes "liberty" in the due process clause of the Fourteenth Amendment to put upon the states a federal restriction that is without precedent.

. . .

The record shows, and it is conceded, that defendants' regular business was the publication of malicious, scandalous, and defamatory articles concerning the principal public officers, leading newspapers of the city, many private persons, and the Jewish race. It also shows that it was their purpose at all hazards to continue to carry on the business. In every edition slanderous and defamatory matter predominates to the practical exclusion of all else. Many of the statements are so highly improbable as to compel a finding that they are false. The articles themselves show malice.

. . .

The Court quotes Blackstone in support of its condemnation of the statute as imposing a previous restraint upon publication. But the *previous restraints* referred to by him subjected the press to the arbitrary will of an administrative officer. He describes the practice: "To subject the press to the restrictive power of a licenser, as was formerly done, both before and since the revolution [of 1688], is to subject all freedom of sentiment to the prejudices of one man, and make him the arbitrary and infallible judge of all controverted points in learning, religion, and government."

. . .

The Minnesota statute does not operate as a previous restraint on publication within the proper meaning of that phrase. It does not authorize administrative control in advance such as was formerly exercised by the licensers and censors, but prescribes a remedy to be enforced by a suit in equity. In this case there was previous publication made in the course of the business of regularly producing malicious, scandalous, and defamatory periodicals. The business and publications unquestionably constitute an abuse of the right of free press. The statute denounces the things done as a nuisance on the ground, as stated by the state Supreme Court, that they threaten morals, peace, and good order. There is no question of the power of the state to denounce such transgressions. The restraint authorized is only in respect of continuing to do what has been duly adjudged to constitute a nuisance. . . . It is fanciful to suggest similarity between the granting or enforcement of the decree authorized by this statute to prevent *further* publication of malicious, scandalous, and defamatory articles and the *previous restraint* upon the press by licensers as referred to by Blackstone and described in the history of the times to which he alludes.

. . .

It is well known, as found by the state Supreme Court, that existing libel laws are inadequate effectively to suppress evils resulting from the kind of business and publications that are shown in this case. The doctrine that measures such as the one before us are invalid because they operate as previous restraints to infringe freedom of press exposes the peace and good order of every community and the business and private affairs of every individual to the constant and protracted false and malicious assaults of any insolvent publisher who may have purpose and sufficient capacity to contrive and put into effect a scheme or program for oppression, blackmail or extortion.

The judgment should be affirmed.

MR. JUSTICE VAN DEVANTER, MR. JUSTICE McREYNOLDS, and MR. JUSTICE SUTHERLAND concur in this opinion.

More recently, the Court has balanced the First Amendment's protection of a free press and its heavy presumption against prior restraints on the one hand against the government's also weighty interest in preserving national security on the other.

New York Times Co. v. United States
403 U.S. 713 (1971)

PER CURIAM.

We granted certiorari in these cases in which the United States seeks to enjoin the New York Times and the Washington Post from publishing the contents of a classified study entitled "History of U.S. Decision-Making Process on Vietnam Policy."

"Any system of prior restraints of expression comes to this Court bearing a heavy presumption against its constitutional validity." *Bantam Books, Inc. v. Sullivan*, 372 U.S. 58, 70 (1963); see also *Near v. Minnesota*. The Government "thus carries a heavy burden of showing justification for the imposition of such a restraint." The District Court for the Southern District of New York in the *New York Times* case and the District Court for the District of Columbia and the Court of Appeals for the District of Columbia Circuit in the *Washington Post* case held that the Government had not met that burden. We agree.

The judgment of the Court of Appeals for the District of Columbia is therefore affirmed. The order of the Court of Appeals for the Second Circuit is reversed. . . .

MR. JUSTICE BLACK, with whom MR. JUSTICE DOUGLAS joins, concurring.

I adhere to the view that the Government's case against the Washington Post should have been dismissed and that the injunction against the New York Times should have been vacated without oral argument when the cases were first presented to this Court. I believe that every moment's continuance of the injunctions against these newspapers amounts to a flagrant, indefensible, and continuing violation of the First Amendment. . . .

. . .

In the First Amendment the Founding Fathers gave the free press the protection it must have to fulfill its essential role in our democracy. The press was to serve the governed, not the governors. The Government's power to censor the press was abolished so that the press would remain forever free to censure the Government. The press was protected so that it could bare the secrets of government and inform the people. Only a free and unrestrained press can effectively expose deception in government. And paramount among the responsibilities of a free press is the duty to prevent any part of the government from deceiving the people and sending them off to distant lands to die of foreign fevers and foreign shot and shell. In my view, far from deserving condemnation for their courageous reporting, the New York Times, the Washington Post, and other newspapers should be commended for serving the purpose that the Founding Fathers saw so clearly. In revealing the workings of government that led to the Vietnam war, the newspapers nobly did precisely that which the Founders hoped and trusted they would do.

The Government's case here is based on premises entirely different from those that guided the Framers of the First Amendment. The Solicitor General has carefully and emphatically stated:

"Now, Mr. Justice [BLACK], your construction of . . . [the First Amendment] is well known, and I certainly respect it. You say that no law means no law, and that should be obvious. I can only say, Mr. Justice, that to me it is equally obvious that 'no law' does not mean 'no law', and I would seek to persuade the Court that that is true.... [T]here are other parts of the Constitution that grant powers and responsibilities to the Executive, and . . . the First Amendment was not intended to make it impossible for the Executive to function or to protect the security of the United States."

And the Government argues in its brief that in spite of the First Amendment, "[t]he authority of the Executive Department to protect the nation against publication of information whose disclosure would endanger the national security stems from two interrelated sources: the constitutional power of the President over the conduct of foreign affairs and his authority as Commander-in-Chief."

In other words, we are asked to hold that despite the First Amendment's emphatic command, the Executive Branch, the Congress, and the Judiciary can make laws enjoining publication of current news and abridging freedom of the press in the name of "national security." The Government does not even attempt to rely on any act of Congress. Instead it makes the bold and dangerously far reaching contention that the courts should take it upon themselves to "make" a law abridging freedom of the press in the name of equity, presidential power and national security, even when the representatives of the people in Congress have adhered to the command of the First Amendment and refused to make such a law. To find that the President has "inherent power" to halt the publication of news by resort to the courts would wipe out the First Amendment and destroy the fundamental liberty and security of the very people the Government hopes to make "secure." No one can read the history of the adoption of the First Amendment without being convinced beyond any doubt that it was injunctions like those sought here that Madison and his collaborators intended to outlaw in this Nation for all time.

The word "security" is a broad, vague generality whose contours should not be invoked to abrogate the fundamental law embodied in the First Amendment. The guarding of military and diplomatic secrets at the expense of informed representative government provides no real security for our Republic. The Framers of the First Amendment, fully aware of both the need to defend a new nation and the abuses of the English and Colonial Governments, sought to give this new society strength and security by providing that freedom of speech, press, religion, and assembly should not be abridged....

MR. JUSTICE BRENNAN, concurring.

I

I write separately in these cases only to emphasize what should be apparent: that our judgments in the present cases may not be taken to indicate the propriety, in the future, of issuing temporary stays and restraining orders to block the publication of material sought to be suppressed by the Government. So far as I can determine, never before has the United States sought to enjoin a newspaper from publishing information in its possession. . . .

II

The error that has pervaded these cases from the outset was the granting of any injunctive relief whatsoever, interim or otherwise. The entire thrust of the Government's claim throughout these cases has been that publication of the material sought to be enjoined "could," or "might," or "may" prejudice the national interest in various ways. But the First Amendment tolerates absolutely no prior judicial restraints of the press predicated upon surmise or conjecture that untoward consequences may result. Our cases, it is true, have indicated that there is a single, extremely narrow class of cases in which the First Amendment's ban on prior judicial restraint may be overridden. Our cases have thus far indicated that such cases may arise only when the Nation "is at war," *Schenck v. United States*, during which times "[n]o one would question but that a government might prevent actual obstruction to its recruiting service or the publication of the sailing dates of transports or the number and location of troops." *Near v. Minnesota*. Even if the present world situation were assumed to be tantamount to a time of war, or if the power of presently available armaments would justify even in peacetime the suppression of information that would set in motion a nuclear holocaust, in neither of these actions has the Government presented or even alleged that publication of items from or based upon the material at issue would cause the happening of an event of that nature. . . .

MR. JUSTICE STEWART, with whom MR. JUSTICE WHITE joins, concurring.

In the governmental structure created by our Constitution, the Executive is endowed with enormous power in the two related areas of national defense and international relations. This power, largely unchecked by the Legislative and Judicial branches, has been pressed to the very hilt since the advent of the nuclear missile age. For better of for worse, the simple fact is that a President of the United States possesses vastly greater constitutional independence in these two vital areas of power than does, say, a prime minister of a country with a parliamentary form of government.

In the absence of the governmental checks and balances present in other areas of our national life, the only effective restraint upon executive policy and power in the areas of national defense and international affairs may lie in an enlightened citizenry—in an informed and critical public opinion which alone can here protect the values of democratic government. For this reason, it is perhaps here that a press that is alert, aware, and free most vitally serves the basic purpose of the First Amendment. For without an informed and free press there cannot be an enlightened people.

Yet it is elementary that the successful conduct of international diplomacy and the maintenance of an effective national defense require both confidentiality and secrecy. Other nations can hardly deal with this Nation in an atmosphere of mutual trust unless they can be assured that their confidences will be kept. And within our own executive departments, the development of considered and intelligent international policies would be impossible if those charged with their formulation could not communicate with each other freely, frankly, and in confidence. In the area of basic national defense the frequent need for absolute secrecy is, of course, self-evident.

I think there can be but one answer to this dilemma, if dilemma it be. The responsibility must be where the power is. If the Constitution gives the Executive a large degree of unshared power in the conduct of foreign affairs and the maintenance of our national defense, then under the Constitution the Executive must have the largely unshared duty to determine and preserve the degree of internal security necessary to exercise that power successfully. It is an awesome responsibility, requiring judgment and wisdom of a high order. I should suppose that moral, political, and practical considerations would dictate that a very first principle of that wisdom would be an insistence upon avoiding secrecy for its own sake. For when everything is classified, then nothing is classified, and the system becomes one to be disregarded by the cynical or the careless, and to be manipulated by those intent on self-protection or self-promotion. I should suppose, in short, that the hallmark of a truly effective internal security system would be the maximum possible disclosure, recognizing that secrecy can best be preserved only when credibility is truly maintained. But be that as it may, it is clear to me that it is the constitutional duty of the Executive—as a matter of sovereign prerogative and not as a matter of law as the courts know law—through the promulgation and enforcement of executive regulations, to protect the confidentiality necessary to carry out its responsibilities in the fields of international relations and national defense.

. . .

. . . [I]n the cases before us we are asked neither to construe specific regulations nor to apply specific laws. We are asked, instead, to perform a function that the Constitution gave to the Executive, not the Judiciary. We are asked, quite simply, to prevent the publication by two newspapers of material that the Executive Branch insists should not, in the national interest, be published. I am convinced that the Executive is correct with respect to some of the documents involved. But I cannot say that disclosure of any of them will surely result in direct, immediate, and irreparable damage to our Nation or its people. That being so, there can under the First Amendment be but one judicial resolution of the issues before us. I join the judgments of the Court.

MR. JUSTICE WHITE, with whom MR. JUSTICE STEWART joins, concurring.

I concur in today's judgments, but only because of the concededly extraordinary protection against prior restraints enjoyed by the press under our constitutional system. I do not say that in no circumstances would the First Amendment permit an injunction against publishing information about government plans or operations. Nor, after examining the materials the Government characterizes as the most sensitive and destructive, can I deny that revelation of these documents will do substantial damage to public interests. Indeed, I am confident that their disclosure will have that result. But I nevertheless agree that the United States has not satisfied the very heavy burden that it must meet to warrant an injunction against publication in these cases, at least in the absence of express and appropriately limited congressional authorization for prior restraints in circumstances such as these.

. . .

It is not easy to reject the proposition urged by the United States and to deny relief on its good-faith claims in these cases that publication will work serious damage to the country. But that discomfiture is considerably dispelled by the infrequency of prior-restraint cases. Normally, publication will occur and the damage be done before the Government has either opportunity or grounds for suppression. So here, publication has already begun and a substantial part of the threatened damage has already occurred. The fact of a massive breakdown in security is known, access to the documents by many unauthorized people is undeniable, and the efficacy of equitable relief against these or other newspapers to avert anticipated damage is doubtful at best.

What is more, terminating the ban on publication of the relatively few sensitive documents the Government now seeks to suppress does not mean that the law either requires or invites newspapers or others to publish them or that they will be immune from criminal action if they do. Prior restraints require an unusually heavy justification under the First

Amendment; but failure by the Government to justify prior restraints does not measure its constitutional entitlement to a conviction for criminal publication. That the Government mistakenly chose to proceed by injunction does not mean that it could not successfully proceed in another way.

. . .

[The concurring opinions of Justice Douglas and Justice Marshall are omitted].

MR. CHIEF JUSTICE BURGER, dissenting.

. . . In these cases, the imperative of a free and unfettered press comes into collision with another imperative, the effective functioning of a complex modern government and specifically the effective exercise of certain constitutional powers of the Executive. Only those who view the First Amendment as an absolute in all circumstances—a view I respect, but reject—can find such cases as these to be simple or easy.

These cases are not simple for another and more immediate reason. We do not know the facts of the cases. No District Judge knew all the facts. No Court of Appeals judge knew all of the facts. No member of this Court knows all the facts.

Why are we in this posture, in which only those judges to whom the First Amendment is absolute and permits of no restraint in any circumstances or for any reason, are really in a position to act?

I suggest we are in this posture because these cases have been conducted in unseemly haste. . . . The prompt settling of these cases reflects our universal abhorrence of prior restraint. But prompt judicial action does not mean unjudicial haste.

Here, moreover, the frenetic haste is due in large part to the manner in which the Times proceeded from the date it obtained the purloined documents. It seems reasonably clear now that the haste precluded reasonable and deliberate judicial treatment of these cases and was not warranted. The precipitate action of this Court aborting trials not yet completed is not the kind of judicial conduct that ought to attend the disposition of a great issue.

. . .

Would it have been unreasonable, since the newspaper could anticipate the Government's objections to release of secret material, to give the Government an opportunity to review the entire collection and determine whether agreement could be reached on publication? Stolen or not, if security was not in fact jeopardized, much of the material could no doubt have been declassified, since it spans a period ending in 1968. With such an approach—one that great newspapers have in the past practiced and stated editorially to be the duty of an honorable press—the newspapers and Government might well have nar-

rowed the area of disagreement as to what was and was not publishable, leaving the remainder to be resolved in orderly litigation, if necessary. To me it is hardly believable that a newspaper long regarded as a great institution in American life would fail to perform one of the basic and simple duties of every citizen with respect to the discovery or possession of stolen property or secret government documents. That duty, I had thought—perhaps naively—was to report forthwith, to responsible public officers. This duty rests on taxi drivers, Justices, and the New York Times. The course followed by the Times, whether so calculated or not, removed any possibility of orderly litigation of the issues. If the action of the judges up to now has been correct, that result is sheer happenstance.

. . .

I would affirm the Court of Appeals for the Second Circuit and allow the District Court to complete the trial aborted by our grant of certiorari, meanwhile preserving the status quo in the *Post* case. I would direct that the District Court on remand give priority to the *Times* case to the exclusion of all other business of that court but I would not set arbitrary deadlines.

. . .

MR. JUSTICE HARLAN, with whom THE CHIEF JUSTICE and MR. JUSTICE BLACKMUN join, dissenting.

. . . With all respect, I consider that the Court has been almost irresponsibly feverish in dealing with these cases.

Both the Court of Appeals for the Second Circuit and the Court of Appeals for the District of Columbia Circuit rendered judgment on June 23. The New York Times' petition for certiorari, its motion for accelerated consideration thereof, and its application for interim relief were filed in this Court on June 24 at about 11 a.m. The application of the United States for interim relief in the *Post* case was also filed here on June 24 at about 7:15 p.m. This Court's order setting a hearing before us on June 26 at 11 a.m., a course which I joined only to avoid the possibility of even more peremptory action by the Court, was issued less than 24 hours before. The record in the *Post* case was filed with the Clerk shortly before 1 p.m. on June 25; the record in the *Times* case did not arrive until 7 or 8 o'clock that same night. The briefs of the parties were received less than two hours before argument on June 26.

This frenzied train of events took place in the name of the presumption against prior restraints created by the First Amendment. Due regard for the extraordinarily important and difficult questions involved in these litigations should have led the Court to shun such a precipitate timetable. . . .

. . .

It is a sufficient basis for affirming the Court of Appeals for the Second Circuit in the *Times* litigation to observe that its order must rest on the conclusion that because of the time elements the Government had not been given an adequate opportunity to present its case to the District Court. At the least this conclusion was not an abuse of discretion.

In the *Post* litigation the Government had more time to prepare.... But I think there is another and more fundamental reason why this judgment cannot stand—a reason which also furnishes an additional ground for not reinstating the judgment of the District Court in the *Times* litigation, set aside by the Court of Appeals. It is plain to me that the scope of the judicial function in passing upon the activities of the Executive Branch of the Government in the field of foreign affairs is very narrowly restricted. This view is, I think, dictated by the concept of separation of powers upon which our constitutional system rests.

In a speech on the floor of the House of Representatives, Chief Justice John Marshall, then a member of that body, stated:

> "The President is the sole organ of the nation in its external relations, and its sole representative with foreign nations." 10 Annals of Cong. 613. (1800).

From that time, shortly after the founding of the Nation, to this, there has been no substantial challenge to this description of the scope of executive power.

...

The power to evaluate the "pernicious influence" of premature disclosure is not, however, lodged in the Executive alone. I agree that, in performance of its duty to protect the values of the First Amendment against political pressures, the judiciary must review the initial Executive determination to the point of satisfying itself that the subject matter of the dispute does lie within the proper compass of the President's foreign relations power.... Moreover, the judiciary may properly insist that the determination that disclosure of the subject matter would irreparably impair the national security be made by the head of the Executive Department concerned—here the Secretary of State or the Secretary of Defense—after actual personal consideration by that officer....

But in my judgment the judiciary may not properly go beyond these two inquiries and redetermine for itself the probable impact of disclosure on the national security....

Even if there is some room for the judiciary to override the executive determination, it is plain that the scope of review must be exceedingly narrow. I can see no indication in the opinions of either the District Court or the Court of Appeals in the *Post* litigation that the conclusions of the Executive were given even the deference owing to an administrative agency, much less that owing to a co-equal branch of the Government operating within the field of its constitutional prerogative.

...

MR. JUSTICE BLACKMUN, dissenting.

...

The New York Times clandestinely devoted a period of three months to examining the 47 volumes that came into its unauthorized possession. Once it had begun publication of material from those volumes, the New York case now before us emerged. It immediately assumed, and ever since has maintained, a frenetic pace and character. Seemingly once publication started, the material could not be made public fast enough. Seemingly, from then on, every deferral or delay, by restraint or otherwise, was abhorrent and was to be deemed violative of the First Amendment and of the public's "right immediately to know." Yet that newspaper stood before us at oral argument and professed criticism of the Government for not lodging its protest earlier than by a Monday telegram following the initial Sunday publication.

...

The First Amendment, after all, is only one part of an entire Constitution. Article II of the great document vests in the Executive Branch primary power over the conduct of foreign affairs and places in that branch the responsibility for the Nation's safety. Each provision of the Constitution is important, and I cannot subscribe to a doctrine of unlimited absolutism for the First Amendment at the cost of downgrading other provisions. First Amendment absolutism has never commanded a majority of this Court. What is needed here is a weighing, upon properly developed standards, of the broad right of the press to print and of the very narrow right of the Government to prevent. Such standards are not yet developed. The parties here are in disagreement as to what those standards should be. But even the newspapers concede that there are situations where restraint is in order and is constitutional....

I therefore would remand these cases to be developed expeditiously, of course, but on a schedule permitting the orderly presentation of evidence from both sides, with the use of discovery, if necessary, as authorized by the rules, and with the preparation of briefs, oral argument, and court opinions of a quality better than has been seen to this point....

... I hope that damage has not already been done. If, however, damage has been done, and if, with the Court's action today, these newspapers proceed to publish the critical documents and there results therefrom "the death of soldiers, the destruction of alliances, the greatly increased difficulty of negotiation with our enemies, the inability of our diplomats to negotiate," to which list I might add the factors of prolongation of the war and of further delay in the freeing of United States prisoners, then the Nation's people will know where the responsibility for these sad consequences rests.

The government may impose prior restraints on speech in public spaces by requiring speakers to obtain official permission in advance. The Court has considered in numerous cases whether or not such permit or licensing systems impose an unconstitutional prior restraint of speech. A city ordinance requiring a permit to pass out leaflets on a public sidewalk would violate the First Amendment because the government's interest in clean streets does not justify such an extreme prior restraint. (Recall the Court's decision in *Schneider v. State*.) Public marches and demonstrations, however, pose a greater threat to public safety and traffic control. The Supreme Court has held that permit systems that require citizens to obtain official permission for parades and demonstrations on public streets do not necessarily run afoul of the First Amendment. In *Cox v. New Hampshire*, for example, the Court upheld a parade permit statute that was narrowly drawn to prevent traffic congestion and to give officials sufficient notice to allow them to provide police protection.[117]

The close association between permit requirements and classic prior restraints, however, raises concerns about the standards authorities use to grant and deny permission to speakers. Permit systems give local officials unusual power to censor expression based on its content. The Court has responded to this danger by requiring that the wording of statutes precisely delineate the standards for granting permits in order to prevent excessive official discretion and discriminatory treatment.

The First Amendment questions raised by permit systems are complicated when speakers decide to defy a vague permit statute or a denial of permission to parade before a court has an opportunity to decide the constitutionality of the denial. May marchers violate a permit statute and subsequently challenge its constitutionality after they are arrested? Two Supreme Court cases concerning this issue arose from the Good Friday march in 1963 led by a group of Black ministers to protest racial injustice in Birmingham, Alabama. The infamous segregationist Commissioner Eugene "Bull" Connor had stated definitively that he would not issue a permit to march under the city's standardless ordinance. Two days before the march, Birmingham officials filed a complaint in a state circuit court asking for injunctive relief against the individuals and organizations planning to march, alleging that the march was "calculated to provoke breaches of the peach," "threaten[ed] the safety, peace and tranquility of the City," and placed "an undue burden and strain upon the manpower of the Police Department." The circuit judge enjoined the demonstrators from encouraging or participating in any parade without a permit as required by the Birmingham ordinance. When the ministers violated the injunction they were held in criminal contempt.

In *Walker v. Birmingham*, the Supreme Court, divided five to four, sustained the contempt convictions, refusing to consider the ministers' constitutional challenge of the Birmingham parade law.[118] The majority emphasized the importance of respect for judicial process, reasoning that "in the fair administration of justice no man can judge his own case, however exalted his station, however righteous his motives, and irrespective of his race, color, politics, or religion." The Court suggested, however, that it might have considered the statute's unconstitutionality as a defense to the contempt convic-

---

[117] Cox v. New Hampshire, 312 U.S. 569 (1941).
[118] Walker v. Birmingham, 388 U.S. 307 (1967).

tion if the ministers had unsuccessfully sought state appellate review of the injunction or could demonstrate that such review was unavailable: "This case would arise in quite a different posture if the petitioners, before disobeying the injunction, had challenged it in the Alabama courts, and had been met with delay or frustration of their constitutional claims. But there is no showing that such would have been the fate of a timely motion to modify or dissolve the injunction."

Two years after its decision in *Walker v. Birmingham*, the Court—this time faced with the marchers' convictions for parading without a permit—tested the constitutionality of the Birmingham permit law. Although under *Walker* the unconstitutionality of the underlying statute was not available as a defense to their convictions for contempt of a court injunction, the Court did allow it as a defense to their convictions for violating the statute itself.

Shuttlesworth v. City of Birmingham
394 U.S. 147 (1969)

MR. JUSTICE STEWART delivered the opinion of the Court.

. . .

On the afternoon of April 12, Good Friday, 1963, 52 people, all Negroes, were led out of a Birmingham church by three Negro ministers, one of whom was the petitioner, Fred L. Shuttlesworth. They walked in orderly fashion, two abreast for the most part, for four blocks. The purpose of their march was to protest the alleged denial of civil rights to Negroes in the city of Birmingham. The marchers stayed on the sidewalks except at street intersections, and they did not interfere with other pedestrians. No automobiles were obstructed, nor were traffic signals disobeyed. The petitioner was with the group for at least part of this time, walking alongside the others, and once moving from the front to the rear. As the marchers moved along, a crowd of spectators fell in behind them at a distance. The spectators at some points spilled out into the street, but the street was not blocked and vehicles were not obstructed.

At the end of four blocks the marchers were stopped by the Birmingham police, and were arrested for violating § 1159 of the General Code of Birmingham [which prohibited parading without a permit].

. . .

There can be no doubt that the Birmingham ordinance, as it was written, conferred upon the City Commission virtually unbridled and absolute power to prohibit any "parade," "procession," or "demonstration" on the city's streets or public ways. For in deciding whether or not to withhold a permit, the members of the Commission were to be guided only by their own ideas of "public welfare, peace, safety, health, decency, good order, morals or convenience." This ordinance as it was written,

therefore, fell squarely within the ambit of the many decisions of this Court over the last 30 years, holding that a law subjecting the exercise of First Amendment freedoms to the prior restraint of a license, without narrow, objective, and definite standards to guide the licensing authority, is unconstitutional. "It is settled by a long line of recent decisions of this Court that an ordinance which, like this one, makes the peaceful enjoyment of freedoms which the Constitution guarantees contingent upon the uncontrolled will of an official—as by requiring a permit or license which may be granted or withheld in the discretion of such official—is an unconstitutional censorship or prior restraint upon the enjoyment of those freedoms." *Staub v. City of Baxley*, 355 U.S. 313, 322. And our decisions have made clear that a person faced with such an unconstitutional licensing law may ignore it and engage with impunity in the exercise of the right of free expression for which the law purports to require a license. "The Constitution can hardly be thought to deny to one subjected to the restraints of such an ordinance the right to attack its constitutionality, because he has not yielded to its demands." *Jones v. City of Opelika*, 316 U.S. 584, 602 (Stone, C.J., dissenting), adopted *per curiam* on rehearing, 319 U.S. 103, 104.

It is argued, however, that what was involved here was not "pure speech," but the use of public streets and sidewalks, over which a municipality must rightfully exercise a great deal of control in the interest of traffic regulation and public safety. That, of course, is true. We have emphasized before this that "the First and Fourteenth Amendments [do not] afford the same kind of freedom to those who would communicate ideas by conduct such as patrolling, marching, and picketing on streets and highways, as these amendments afford to those who communicate ideas by pure speech." *Cox v. Louisiana*, 379 U.S. 536, 555. "Governmental authorities have the duty and responsibility to keep their streets open and available for movement." *Id.*, at 554–555.

But our decisions have also made clear that picketing and parading may nonetheless constitute methods of expression, entitled to First Amendment protection. . . .

. . .

Accordingly, "although this Court has recognized that a statute may be enacted which prevents serious interference with normal usage of streets and parks, . . . we have consistently condemned licensing systems which vest in an administrative official discretion to grant or withhold a permit upon broad criteria unrelated to proper regulation of public places." *Kunz v. New York*, 340 U.S. 290, 293–294. Even when the use of its public streets and sidewalks is involved, therefore, a municipality may not empower its licensing officials to roam essentially at will, dispensing or withholding permission to speak, assemble, picket, or parade according to their own opinions regarding the potential effect of the activity in question on the "welfare," "decency," or "morals" of the community.

Understandably, under these settled principles, the Alabama Court of Appeals was unable to reach any conclusion other than that § 1159 was unconstitutional. The terms of the Birmingham ordinance clearly gave the City Commission extensive authority to issue or refuse to issue parade permits on the basis of broad criteria entirely unrelated to legitimate municipal regulation of the public streets and sidewalks.

It is said, however, that no matter how constitutionally invalid the Birmingham ordinance may have been as it was written, nonetheless the authoritative construction that has now been given it by the Supreme Court of Alabama has so modified and narrowed its terms as to render it constitutionally acceptable. It is true that in affirming the petitioner's conviction in the present case, the Supreme Court of Alabama performed a remarkable job of plastic surgery upon the face of the ordinance. The court stated that when § 1159 provided that the City Commission could withhold a permit whenever "in its judgment the public welfare, peace, safety, health, decency, good order, morals or convenience require," the ordinance really meant something quite different:

"[We] do not construe this [language] as vesting in the Commission an unfettered discretion in granting or denying permits, but, in view of the purpose of the ordinance, one to be exercised in connection with the safety, comfort and convenience in the use of the streets by the general public. . . . The members of the Commission may not act as censors of what is to be said or displayed in any parade. . . .

. . .

". . . A systematic, consistent and just order of treatment with reference to the convenience of public use of the streets and sidewalks must be followed. Applications for permits to parade must be granted if, after an investigation it is found that the convenience of the public in the use of the streets or sidewalks would not thereby be unduly disturbed."

In transforming § 1159 into an ordinance authorizing no more than the objective and even-handed regulation of traffic on Birmingham's streets and public ways, the Supreme Court of Alabama made a commendable effort to give the legislation "a field of operation within constitutional limits." We may assume that this exercise was successful, and that the ordinance as now authoritatively construed would pass constitutional muster. It does not follow, however, that the severely narrowing construction put upon the ordinance by the Alabama Supreme Court in November of 1967 necessarily serves to restore constitutional validity to a conviction that occurred in 1963 under the ordinance as it was written.

. . . In April of 1963 the ordinance that was on the books in Birmingham contained language that affirmatively conferred upon the members of the Commission absolute power to refuse a parade permit whenever they thought "the public welfare, peace, safety, health, decency, good order, morals or convenience require that it be refused." It would have taken extraordinary clairvoyance for anyone to perceive that this language meant what the Supreme Court of Alabama was destined to find that it meant more than four years later; and, with First Amendment rights hanging in the balance, we would hesitate long before assuming that either the members of the Commission or the petitioner possessed any such clairvoyance at the time of the Good Friday march.

But we need not deal in assumptions. For, as the respondent in this case has reminded us, in assessing the constitutional claims of the petitioner, "[i]t is less than realistic to ignore the surrounding relevant circumstances. These include not only facts developed in the Record in this case, but also those shown in the opinions in the related case of *Walker v. City of Birmingham.* . . . " The petitioner here was one of the petitioners in the *Walker* case, in which, just two Terms ago, we had before us a record showing many of the "surrounding relevant circumstances" of the Good Friday march. As the respondent suggests, we may properly take judicial notice of the record in that litigation between the same parties who are now before us.

Uncontradicted testimony was offered in *Walker* to show that over a week before the Good Friday march petitioner Shuttlesworth sent a representative to apply for a parade permit. She went to the City Hall and asked "to see the person or persons in charge to issue permits, permits for parading, picketing, and demonstrating." She was directed to Commissioner Connor, who denied her request in no uncertain terms. "He said, 'No, you will not get a permit in Birmingham, Alabama to picket. I will picket you over to the City Jail,' and he repeated that twice."

Two days later petitioner Shuttlesworth himself sent a telegram to Commissioner Connor requesting, on behalf of his organization, a permit to picket "against the injustices of segregation and discrimination." His request specified the sidewalks where the picketing would take place, and stated that "the normal rules of picketing" would be obeyed. In reply, the Commissioner sent a wire stating that permits were the responsibility of the entire Commission rather than of a single Commissioner, and closing with the blunt admonition: "I insist that you and your people do not start any picketing on the streets in Birmingham, Alabama."[7]

These "surrounding relevant circumstances" make it indisputably clear, we think, that in April of 1963—at least with respect to this petitioner and his organization—the city authorities thought the ordinance meant exactly what it said. The petitioner was clearly given to understand that under no circumstances would he and his group be permitted to demonstrate in Birmingham, nor that a demonstration would be approved if a time and place were selected that would minimize traffic problems. There is no indication whatever that the authorities considered themselves obligated—as the Alabama Supreme Court more than four years later said that they were—to issue a permit "if, after an investigation [they] found that the convenience of the public in the

---

[7] The legal and constitutional issues involved in the *Walker* case were quite different from those involved here. The Court recently summarized the *Walker* decision as follows:

"In that case, the Court held that demonstrators who had proceeded with their protest march in face of the prohibition of an injunctive order against such a march, could not defend contempt charges by asserting the unconstitutionality of the injunction. The proper procedure, it was held, was to seek judicial review of the injunction and not to disobey it, no matter how well-founded their doubts might be as to its validity." Carroll v. President and Commissioners of Princess Anne, 393 U.S. 175, 179.

use of the streets or sidewalks would not thereby be unduly disturbed."

This case, therefore, is a far cry from *Cox v. New Hampshire* [312 U.S. 569 (1941)], where it could be said that there was nothing to show "that the statute has been administered otherwise than in the . . . manner which the state court has construed it to require." Here, by contrast, it is evident that the ordinance was administered so as, in the words of Chief Justice Hughes, "to deny or unwarrantedly abridge the right of assembly and the opportunities for the communication of thought . . . immemorially associated with resort to public places." The judgment is

Reversed.

MR. JUSTICE BLACK concurs in the result.

MR. JUSTICE MARSHALL took no part in the consideration or decision of this case.

MR. JUSTICE HARLAN, concurring.

The Alabama Supreme Court's opinion makes it clear that if petitioner Shuttlesworth had carried his efforts to obtain a parade permit to the highest state court, he could have required the city authorities to grant permission for his march, so long as his proposals were consistent with Birmingham's interest in traffic control. Thus, the difficult question this case presents is whether the Fourteenth Amendment ever bars a State from punishing a citizen for marching without a permit which could have been procured if all available remedies had been pursued.

The Court answers that a citizen is entitled to rely on the statutory construction adopted by the state officials who are on the front line, administering the permit scheme. If these officials construe a vague statute unconstitutionally, the citizen may take them at their word, and act on the assumption that the statute is void. The Court's holding seems to me to carry seeds of mischief that may impair the conceded ability of the authorities to regulate the use of public thoroughfares in the interests of all. The right to ignore a permit requirement should, in my view, be made to turn on something more substantial than a minor official's view of his authority under the governing statute.

. . . Situations do exist, however, in which there can be no effective review of the decision of an inferior state official. . . . Given the absence of speedy procedures, the Reverend Shuttlesworth and his associates were faced with a serious dilemma when they received their notice from Mr. Connor. If they attempted to exhaust the administrative and judicial remedies provided by Alabama law, it was almost certain that no effective relief could be obtained by Good Friday. Since the right to engage in peaceful and orderly political demonstrations is, under appropriate conditions, a fundamental aspect of the "liberty" protected by the Fourteenth Amendment, the petitioner was not obliged to invoke procedures which could not give him effective relief. With fundamental rights at stake, he was entitled to adopt the more probable meaning of the ordinance and act on his belief that the city's permit regulations were unconstitutional.

It may be suggested, however, that Shuttlesworth's dilemma was of his own making. He could have requested a permit months in advance of Good Friday, thereby allowing Alabama's administrative and judicial machinery the necessary time to operate fully before the date set for the march. But such a suggestion ignores the principle established in *Freedman v. Maryland*, 380 U.S. 51, 58–61, (1965), which prohibits the States from requiring persons to invoke unduly cumbersome and time-consuming procedures before they may exercise their constitutional right of expression. *Freedman* holds that if the State is to protect the public from obscene movies, it must afford exhibitors a speedy administrative or judicial right of review, lest "the victorious exhibitor might find the most propitious opportunity for exhibition [passed]." The *Freedman* principle is applicable here. The right to assemble peaceably to voice political protest is at least as basic as the right to exhibit a motion picture which may have some aesthetic value. Moreover, slow-moving procedures have a much more severe impact in the instant case than they had in

Freedman. Though a movie exhibitor might suffer some financial loss if he were obliged to wait for a year or two while the administrative and judicial mills ground out a result, it is nevertheless quite likely that the public would ultimately see the film. In contrast, timing is of the essence in politics. It is almost impossible to predict the political future; and when an event occurs, it is often necessary to have one's voice heard promptly, if it is to be considered at all. To require Shuttlesworth to submit his parade permit application months in advance would place a severe burden upon the exercise of his constitutionally protected rights.

I do not mean to suggest that a State or city may not reasonably require that parade permit applications be submitted early enough to allow the authorities and the judiciary to determine whether the parade proposal is consistent with the important interests respecting the use of the streets which local authority may legitimately protect. But such applications must be handled on an expedited basis so that rights of political expression will not be lost in a maze of cumbersome and slow-moving procedures.

. . .

. . . Since neither the city nor the State provided sufficiently expedited procedures for the consideration of parade permits, petitioner Shuttlesworth cannot be punished for the exercise of his constitutionally protected right of political expression.

In *Alexander v. United States*,[119] the Supreme Court rejected the argument that forfeiture of expressive materials under the Racketeer Influenced and Corrupt Organizations Act (RICO) constitutes a prior restraint on speech. The defendant was convicted of violating RICO and federal obscenity laws based on a finding that four magazines and three videotapes sold at his stores were obscene. In addition to imposing a prison term and fines, the trial court granted the government's request for forfeiture, pursuant to the RICO statute, of defendant's entire wholesale and retail businesses and all their assets acquired through racketeering activity—including books and films that had not been adjudicated obscene.

The Court, in an opinion by Chief Justice Rehnquist, held that the forfeiture was a permissible criminal punishment for past racketeering offenses and not a restraint on future speech. The government forfeited defendant's assets not because of their expressive content but because they were related to his prior criminal violations. Moreover the potential "chilling" effect of forfeiture on the speech of others was not greater than that created by the threat of imprisonment or fines. But Justice Kennedy, joined by Justices Blackmun and Stevens, and in part by Justice Souter, disagreed. Kennedy warned that the majority's "rule that would find no affront to the First Amendment in the Government's destruction of a book and film business and its entire inventory of legitimate expression as punishment for a single past offense" posed an "ominous,

---

[119] 509 U.S. ____, 113 S.Ct. 2766 (1993).

onerous threat [that] undermines free speech and press principles essential to our personal freedom."

b. Overbreadth and Vagueness

Like permit and licensing systems, vague and overbroad laws risk giving officials extraordinary discretion to abridge speech based on their disagreement with its message. Although these statutes may justifiably permit state authorities to punish speech that merits no protection, they also chill speech that the First Amendment protects. Citizens faced with a vague or overbroad law may refrain from engaging in protected expression for fear of being drawn into the law's wide net. Moreover, even the litigant whose speech is not protected has the right "to be judged in accordance with a constitutionally valid rule of law."[120]

One of the Court's earliest condemnations of vague speech-infringing laws was its 1937 decision in *Herndon v. Lowry*. This case was significant for several reasons: it marked the first time that the Court used the clear and present danger test to uphold a citizen's free speech claims against government censorship, as well as the first time the Court reviewed a political-crimes conviction that involved an African American defendant.[121] The case arose when Eugene Angelo Braxton Herndon, a 19-year-old Black organizer for the Communist Party, USA, was convicted in Atlanta of attempting to incite insurrection and sentenced to a lengthy prison term. Herndon was arrested in 1932 after he helped to lead a peaceful march to the Fulton County court building calling for hunger relief and unemployment insurance.

Section 56 of the Georgia Criminal Code—the provision at issue in *Herndon*—prohibited "any attempt, by persuasion or otherwise, to induce others to join in any combined resistance to the lawful authority of the State." The Code imposed the death penalty for this crime, unless the jury recommended mercy. The Georgia insurrection law was originally enacted in 1833 in response to slave rebellions and the increasingly militant abolitionist movement; it explicitly prohibited exciting insurrection by writing or speaking in an attempt to stop the circulation of abolitionist literature in the state.[122] In the 1941 edition of the classic *Free Speech in the United States*, Zechariah Chaffee noted that in *Herndon* "the Supreme Court was faced for the first time with the possibility that American citizens might be hanged or electrocuted for nothing except expressing objectionable opinions or owning objectionable books."[123]

In his dissent, Justice Van Devanter described the evidence against Herndon at length:

> Herndon is a negro and a member of the Communist Party of the U.S.A., which is a section of the Communist International. He was sent from Kentucky to Atlanta, Ga., as a paid organizer for the party. Atlanta is within an area where there is a large negro population, and the Communist Party has been endeavoring to extend its activities and membership to that population among others. Herndon's duties as an organizer were to call and conduct meetings, to disseminate information respecting the party, to distribute its literature, to educate prospects and secure members, to receive dues and contributions, and to work up a subordinate organization of the party. He called and conducted meetings which evidently were secret, solicited and secured members, and received dues and contributions. He and others, when becoming members, sub-

---

[120] Monaghan, *Overbreadth*, 1981 S. CT. REV. 1, 3.

[121] Kendall Thomas, *Rouge et Noir Reread: A Popular Constitutional History of the Angelo Herndon Case*, 65 S. CAL. L. REV. 2599 (1992).

[122] *Id.* at 2632.

[123] ZECHARIAH CHAFEE, JR., FREE SPEECH IN THE UNITED STATES 393 (1941).

scribed to an obligation saying "The undersigned declares his adherence to the program and statutes of the Communist International and the Communist Party of the U.S.A., and agrees to submit to the discipline of the party and to engage actively in its work."

When arrested, he had under his arm a box in which he was carrying membership and collection books which he had been using and various pamphlets, books and documents, all pertaining to the structure, purposes, and activities of the party. Two or three of the papers had been prepared by him and disclosed that he was an active spirit in the "Section Committee" and the "Unemployment Committee," both subordinate local agencies of the party.

. . .

. . . The literature which he had with him when arrested was produced in evidence and will now be described, chiefly by titles and extracts (italics supplied).

. . .

"LIFE AND STRUGGLES OF NEGRO TOILERS."

"In no other so-called civilized country in the world are human beings treated as badly as these 15 million negroes (in the United States). They live under a perpetual regime of white terror. . . . They are absolutely at the mercy of every fiendish mob incited by the white landlords and capitalists."

. . .

"COMMUNIST POSITION ON THE NEGRO QUESTION."

This is a booklet of several pages and bears on the front of its cover a map of the United States showing a dark belt stretching across considerable portions of Georgia and eight other southern states. Parts of the text are here copied.

"The slogan of the right of self-determination occupies the central place in the liberation struggle of the Negro population in the Black Belt against the yoke of American imperialism. But this slogan, as we see it, must be carried out only in connection with two other basic demands. Thus, there are three basic demands to be kept in mind in the Black Belt, namely, the following:

"(a) *Confiscation of the landed property of the white landowners and capitalists for the benefit of the negro farmers.* The land property in the hands of the white American exploiters constitutes the most important material basis of the entire system of national oppression and serfdom of the Negroes in the Black Belt. More than three-quarters of all Negro farmers here are bound in actual serfdom to the farms and plantations of the white exploiters by the feudal system of 'share cropping.'

. . .

"(b) Establishment of the State Unity of the Black Belt. At the present time this Negro zone—precisely for the purpose of facilitating national oppression—is artificially split up and divided into a number of various states which include distant localities having a majority of white population. If the right of self-determination of the Negroes is to be put into force, it is necessary wherever possible to bring together into one governmental unit all districts of the South where the majority of the settled population consists of negroes. Within the limits of this state there will of course remain a fairly significant white minority which must submit to the right of self-determination of the negro majority. . . .

"(c) Right of Self-Determination. This means complete and unlimited right of the negro majority to exercise governmental authority in the entire territory of the Black Belt, as well as to decide upon the relations *between their territory and other nations, particularly the United States.*"

. . .

"Hereby, every single fundamental demand of the liberation struggle of the negroes in the Black Belt is such that—if once thoroughly understood by the negro masses and adopted as their slogan—it will lead them into the struggle for the overthrow of the power of the ruling bourgeoisie, which is impossible without such revolutionary struggle. One cannot deny that it is just possible for the negro population of the Black Belt to win the right to self-determination during capitalism; but it is perfectly clear and indubitable that this is possible only through *successful revolutionary struggle* for power against the American bourgeoisie, through *wresting* the negroes' right of self-determination *from American imperialism.* Thus, the slogan of right to self-determination is a real slogan of *National Rebellion.* . . .

The prosecutor focused the trial on the perceived threat that Herndon posed to the local racial order.[124] For example, he cross-examined an expert witness called by the defense by asking him whether the pamphlet entitled *The Communist Position on the Negro Question* advocated "the right of a colored boy to marry your daughter, if you have one."[125] The prosecution's chief witness insisted on referring to Herndon as "this darkey," despite the objections of Herndon's attorney, a recent African American graduate of Harvard Law School. The Supreme Court twice refused to hear Herndon's appeal of his conviction. In its 1935 decisions in *Herndon v. Georgia*, the Court held that it lacked jurisdiction because "no federal question was seasonably raised in the court below" and denied Herndon's petition for rehearing without opinion.[126] Two years later, however, the Court considered Herndon's petition for a writ of *habeas corpus.*

---

[124] Thomas, *supra* note 121, at 2641.
[125] *Id.* at 2639.
[126] Herndon v. Georgia, 295 U.S. 441 (1935); Herndon v. Georgia, 296 U.S. 661 (1935).

Herndon v. Lowry
301 U.S. 242 (1937)

Mr. Justice Roberts delivered the opinion of the Court.

. . . The petition alleged the judgment and sentence were void and appellant's detention illegal because the statute under which he was convicted denies and illegally restrains his freedom of speech and of assembly and is too vague and indefinite to provide a sufficiently ascertainable standard of guilt. . . .

At the July term, 1932, of the superior court of Fulton county an indictment was returned charging against the appellant an attempt to induce others to join in combined resistance to the lawful authority of the state with intent to deny, to defeat, and to overthrow such authority by open force, violent means, and unlawful acts; alleging that insurrection was intended to be manifested and accomplished by unlawful and violent acts. The indictment specified that the attempt was made by calling and attending public assemblies and by making speeches for the purpose of organiz-

ing and establishing groups and combinations of white and colored persons under the name of the Communist Party of Atlanta for the purpose of uniting, combining, and conspiring to incite riots and to embarrass and impede the orderly processes of the courts and offering combined resistance to, and, by force and violence, overthrowing and defeating the authority of the state; that by speech and persuasion, the appellant solicited and attempted to solicit persons to join, confederate with, and become members of the Communist Party and the Young Communist League and introduced into the state and circulated, aided, and assisted in introducing and circulating, booklets, papers, and other writings with the same intent and purpose. . . .

. . .

There is no evidence the appellant distributed any writings or printed matter found in the box he carried when arrested, or any other advocating forcible subversion of governmental authority. There is no evidence the appellant advocated, by speech or written word, at meetings or elsewhere, any doctrine or action implying such forcible subversion. There is evidence tending to prove that the appellant held meetings for the purpose of recruiting members of the Communist Party and solicited contributions for the support of that party and there is proof of the doctrines which that party espouses. Appellant's intent to incite insurrection, if it is to be found, must rest upon his procuring members for the Communist Party and his possession of that party's literature when he was arrested.

> . . .

To ascertain how the Act is held to apply to the appellant's conduct we turn to the rulings of the state courts in his case. The trial court instructed the jury: "In order to convict the defendant, . . . it must appear clearly by the evidence that immediate serious violence against the State of Georgia was to be expected or advocated." The jury rendered a verdict of guilty. In the Supreme Court the appellant urged that the evidence was wholly insufficient to sustain the verdict under the law as thus construed. That court sustained the conviction by construing the statute thus:

> "Force must have been contemplated, but, as said above, the statute does not include either its occurrence or its imminence as an ingredient of the particular offense charged. . . . Nor would it be necessary to guilt that the alleged offender should have intended that an insurrection should follow instantly or at any given time, but it would be sufficient that he intended it to happen at any time, as a result of his influence, by those whom he sought to incite."

Upon application for rehearing the court further elaborated its views as to the meaning of the statute:

> "Force must have been contemplated, but the statute does not include either its occurrence or its imminence as an ingredient of the particular offense charged. Nor would it be necessary to guilt that the alleged offender should have intended that an insurrection should follow instantly or at any given time, but as to this element it would be sufficient if he intended that it should happen at any time within which he might reasonably expect his influence to continue to be directly operative in causing such action by those whom he sought to induce. . . . "

The affirmance of conviction upon the trial record necessarily gives section 56 the construction that one who seeks members for or attempts to organize a local unit of a party which has the purposes and objects disclosed by the documents in evidence may be found guilty of an attempt to incite insurrection.

The questions are whether this construction and application of the statute deprives the accused of the right of freedom of speech and of assembly guaranteed by the Fourteenth Amendment, and whether the statute so construed and applied furnishes a reasonably definite and ascertainable standard of guilt.

The appellant, while admitting that the people may protect themselves against abuses of the freedom of speech safeguarded by the Fourteenth Amendment by prohibiting incitement to violence and crime, insists that legislative regulation may not go beyond measures forefending against "clear and present danger" of the use of force against the state. For this position he relies upon our decisions under the Federal Espionage Acts and cognate state legislation. . . .

The legislation under review differs radically from the Espionage Acts in that it does not deal with a willful attempt to obstruct a described and defined activity of the government.

The State, on the other hand, insists that our decisions uphold state statute making criminal utterances which have a "dangerous tendency" towards the subversion of government. It relies particularly upon *Gitlow v. New York*. There, however, we dealt with a statute which, quite unlike § 56 of the Georgia Criminal Code, denounced as criminal certain acts carefully and adequately described. . . .

It is evident that the decision sustaining the New York statute furnishes no warrant for the appellee's contention that under a law general in its description of the mischief to be remedied and equally general in respect of the intent of the actor, the standard of guilt may be made the "dangerous tendency" of his words.

The power of a state to abridge freedom of speech and of assembly is the exception rather than the rule and the penalizing even of utterances of a defined character must find its justification in a reasonable apprehension of danger to organized government. The judgment of the Legislature is not unfettered. The limitation upon individual liberty must have appropriate relation to the safety of the state. Legislation which goes beyond this need violates the principle of the Constitution. If, therefore, a state statute penalize innocent participation in a meeting held with an innocent purpose merely because the meeting was held under the auspices of an organization membership in which, or the advocacy of whose principles, is also denounced as criminal, the law, so construed and applied, goes beyond the power to restrict abuses of freedom of speech and arbitrarily denies that freedom. And, where a statute is so vague and uncertain as to make criminal an utterance or an act which may be innocently said or done with no intent to induce resort to violence or on the other hand may be said or done with a purpose violently to subvert government, a conviction under such a law cannot be sustained. . . .

. . .

Thus, the crucial question is not the formal interpretation of the statute by the Supreme Court of Georgia but the application given it. In its application the offense made criminal is that of soliciting members for a political party and conducting meetings of a local unit of that party when one of the doctrines of the party, established by reference to a document not shown to have been exhibited to any one by the accused, may be said to be ultimate resort to violence at some indefinite future time against organized government. It is to be borne in mind that the Legislature of Georgia has not made membership in the Communist Party unlawful by reason of its supposed dangerous tendency even in the remote future. The question is not whether Georgia might, in analogy to what other states have done, so declare. The appellant induced others to become members of the Communist Party. Did he thus incite to insurrection by reason of the fact that they agreed to abide by the tenets of the party, some of them lawful, others, as may be assumed, unlawful, in the absence of proof that he brought the unlawful aims to their notice, that he approved them, or that the fantastic program they envisaged was conceived of by any one as more than an ultimate ideal? Doubtless circumstantial evidence might affect the answer to the question if appellant had been shown to have said that the Black Belt should be organized at once as a separate state and that that objective was one of his principal aims. But here circumstantial evidence is all to the opposite effect. The only objectives appellant is proved to have urged are those having to do with unemployment and emergency relief which are void of criminality. His membership in the Communist Party and his solicitation of a few members wholly fails to establish an attempt to incite others to insurrection. Indeed, so far as appears, he had but a single copy of the booklet the state claims to be objectionable; that copy he retained. The same may be said with respect to the other books and pamphlets, some of them of more innocent purport. In these circumstances, to make membership in the party and solicitation of members for that party a criminal offense, punishable by death, in the discretion of a jury, is an unwarranted invasion of the right of freedom of speech.

The statute, as construed and applied in the appellant's trial, does not furnish a sufficiently ascertainable standard of guilt. The Act does not prohibit incitement to violent interference with any given activity or operation of the state. By force of it, as construed, the judge and jury trying an alleged offender cannot appraise the circumstances and character of the defendant's utterances or activities as begetting a clear and present danger of forcible obstruction of a particular state function. Nor is any specified conduct or utterance of the accused made an offense.

The test of guilt is thus formulated by the Supreme Court of the state. Forcible action must have been contemplated, but it would be sufficient to sustain a conviction if the accused intended that an insurrection "should happen at any time within which he might reasonably expect his influence to continue to be directly operative in causing such action by those whom he sought to induce." If the jury conclude that the defendant should have contemplated that any act or utterance of his in opposition to the established order or advocating a change in that order, might, in the distant future, eventuate in a combination to offer forcible resistance to the state, or, as the state says, if the jury believe he should have known that his words would have "a dangerous tendency" then he may be convicted. To be guilty under the law, as construed, a defendant need not advocate resort to force. He need not teach any particular doctrine to come within its purview. Indeed, he need not be active in the formation of a combination or group if he agitate for a change in the frame of government, however peaceful his own intent. If, by the exercise of prophesy, he can forecast that, as a result of a chain of causation, following his proposed action a group may arise at some future date which will resort to force, he is bound to make the prophesy and abstain, under pain of punishment, possibly of execution. Every person who attacks existing conditions, who agitates for a change in the form of government, must take the risk that if a jury should be of opinion he ought to have foreseen that his utterances might contribute in any measure to some future forcible resistance to the existing government he may be convicted of the offense of inciting insurrection. Proof that the accused in fact believed that his effort would cause a violent assault upon the state would not be necessary to conviction. It would be sufficient if the jury thought he reasonably might foretell that those he persuaded to join the party might, at some time in the indefinite future, resort to forcible resistance of government. The question thus proposed to a jury involves pure speculation as to future trends of thought and action. Within what time might one reasonably expect that an attempted organization of the Communist Party in the United States would result in violent action by that party? If a jury returned a special verdict saying twenty years or even fifty years, the verdict could not be shown to be wrong. The law, as thus construed, licenses the jury to create its own standard in each case. . . .

The statute, as construed and applied, amounts merely to a dragnet which may enmesh any one who agitates for a change of government if a jury can be persuaded that he ought to have foreseen his words would have some effect in the future conduct of others. No reasonably ascertainable standard of guilt is prescribed. So vague and indeterminate are the boundaries thus set to the freedom of speech and assembly that the law necessarily violates the guarantees of liberty embodied in the Fourteenth Amendment.

The judgment is reversed and the cause is remanded for further proceedings not inconsistent with this opinion.

MR. JUSTICE VAN DEVANTER, dissenting.

I am of opinion that the Georgia statute, as construed and applied by the Supreme Court of the state of Herndon's Case, prescribes a reasonably definite and ascertainable standard by which to determine the guilt or innocence of the accused, and does not encroach on his right of freedom of speech or of assembly.

It plainly appears, I think, that the offense defined in the statute, and of which Herndon was convicted, was not that of advocating a change in the state government by lawful means, such as an orderly exertion of the elective franchise or of the power to amend the State Constitution, but was that of attempting to induce and incite others to join in combined forcible resistance to the lawful authority of the State.

. . .

By the indictment he was charged with attempting to induce others to join in combined resistance to the lawful authority of the State "by open force and by violent means, and by unlawful acts," the modes of attempted inducement being specified. Upon the trial the court instructed the jury that neither "possession of literature insurrectionary in its nature," nor "engaging in academic or philosophical discussion of abstract principles of economics or political or other subjects, however, radical or revolutionary in their nature," would warrant a conviction; and that a verdict of guilt could not be given unless it clearly appeared from the evidence that "immediate serious violence against the State" was expected or advocated by the accused.

. . .

It . . . is made quite plain that the case proceeded from beginning to end, and in both state courts, upon the theory that the offense denounced by the statute and charged in the indictment was that of attempting to induce and incite others to join in combined *forcible* resistance to the lawful authority of the State; that the jury returned a verdict of guilty upon that the theory; and that it was upon the same theory that the supreme court held the jury's verdict was supported by the evidence, and affirmed the conviction.

If it be assumed that on this appeal the evidence produced on the trial in the criminal case may be examined to ascertain how the statute was applied, I am of opinion, after such an examination, that the statute was applied as if the words "combined resistance" therein were in letter and meaning "combined forcible resistance."

. . .

There was no direct testimony that Herndon distributed the literature. . . . No member of the Communist Party came forward to tell what he did in their meetings or in inducing them to become members. Nor does this seem strange when regard is had to the obligation taken by members and to the discipline imposed. Nevertheless there was evidence from which distribution by him reasonably could be inferred. It was shown that he was an active member, was sent to Atlanta as a paid organizer, and was subject to party discipline; also that he received the literature for distribution in the course of his work and had copies of it, together with current membership and collection books, under his arm when he was arrested; and further that he had been soliciting and securing members, which was part of the work in which the literature was to be used. He had declared his "adherence to the program and statutes" of the party and had taken like declarations from those whom he secured as members; and this tended strongly to show not only that he understood the party program and statutes as outlined in the literature, but also that he brought them to the attention of others whom he secured as members. Besides, at the trial he made an extended statement to the court and jury in his defense, but did not refer in any wise to the literature or deny that he had been using or distributing it. Thus there was in the evidence not merely some but adequate and undisputed basis for inferring that he had been using the literature for the purposes for which he received it. Evidently, and with reason, the jury drew this inference.

It should not be overlooked that Herndon was a negro member and organizer in the Communist Party and was engaged actively in inducing others, chiefly southern negroes, to become members of the party and participate in effecting its purposes and program. The literature placed in his lands by the party for that purpose was particularly adapted to appeal to negroes in that section, for it pictured their condition as an unhappy one resulting from asserted wrongs on the part of white landlords and employers, and sought by alluring statements of resulting advantages to induce them to join in an effort to carry into effect the measures which the literature proposed. These measures included a revolutionary uprooting of the existing capitalist state, as it was termed; confiscation of the landed property of white landowners and capitalists for the benefit of negroes; establishment in the black belt of an independent State, possibly followed by secession from demonstrations, strikes, and tax boycotts in aid of this measure; adoption of a fighting alliance with the revolutionary white proletariat; revolutionary overthrow of capitalism and establishment of Communism through effective physical struggles against the class enemy. Proposing these measures was nothing short of advising a resort to force and violence, for all know that such measures could not be effected otherwise. Not only so, but the literature makes such repelling use of the terms "revolution," "national rebellion," "revolutionary struggle," "revolutionary overthrow," "effective physical struggle," "smash the National Guard," "mass strikes," and "violence," as to leave no doubt that the use of force in an unlawful sense is intended.

. . .

And so it is that examination and consideration of the evidence convince me that the Supreme Court of the state applied the statute, conformably to its opinion, as making criminal an attempt to induce and incite others to join in combined *forcible* resistance to the lawful authority of the state.

That the constitutional guaranty of freedom of speech and assembly does not shield or afford protection for acts of intentional incitement to forcible resistance to the lawful authority of a state is settled by repeated decisions of this Court. . . .

. . .

Believing that the statute under which the conviction was had is not subject to the objections leveled against it, I think the judgment of the Supreme Court of the State denying the petition for *habeas corpus* should be affirmed.

Mr. Justice McReynolds, Mr. Justice Sutherland, and Mr. Justice Butler join in this dissent.

Statutes that restrict or burden the exercise of First Amendment rights must be narrowly drawn in order to ensure "breathing space" for speech that remains protected. A statute is void on its face due to overbreadth if it "does not aim specifically at evils within the allowable area of [government] control but, . . . sweeps within its ambit other activities that constitute an exercise" of protected speech rights.[127] As a corollary to the rule against overbroad laws, the Court has modified the traditional requirement of standing to permit litigants to challenge overly broad statutes without showing that their own activities could not be regulated by a properly drawn statute. "Litigants, therefore, are permitted to challenge a statute not because their own rights of free expression are violated, but because of a judicial prediction or assumption that the statute's very existence may cause others not before the court to refrain from constitutionally protected speech or expression."[128]

While this rule against overbroad laws safeguards free expression from over-reaching censorial power, it also interferes with the state's ability to enforce its legitimate interests. In many cases, it might be sufficient to prohibit a statute's enforcement against constitutionally protected activity rather than invalidate the statute altogether. The Supreme Court has progressively become more reluctant to strike down entire statutes, making it harder for litigants to challenge statutes as facially overbroad. Overbreadth analysis turns on determining whether the challenged statute substantially concerns protected expression and whether it is possible to separate its constitutional components from its unconstitutional applications. This determination will depend on whether lower courts have offered a limiting construction of the statute that sufficiently removes its threat to constitutionally protected expression.

The turning point in the Court's approach was reflected in its divided decision

---

[127] Thornhill v. Alabama, 310 U.S. 88, 97 (1940).
[128] Broadrick v. Oklahoma, 413 U.S. 601, 612 (1973).

in *Gooding v. Wilson*, reversing a conviction for using "opprobrious words or abusive language." The defendant was among a group of anti-war demonstrators who blocked the entrance to an army headquarters building. When police officers attempted to remove them from the door, a scuffle ensued. The defendant was charged with using, without provocation, abusive language and opprobrious words to two police officers, tending to cause a breach of the peace. (The statements cited in the indictment were: "White son of a bitch, I'll kill you"; "You son of a bitch, I'll choke you to death"; and "You son of a bitch, if you ever put your hands on me again, I'll cut you all to pieces.")

Gooding v. Wilson
405 U.S. 518 (1972)

MR. JUSTICE BRENNAN delivered the opinion of the Court.

Appellee was convicted in Superior Court, Fulton County, Georgia, on two counts of using opprobrious words and abusive language in violation of Georgia Code Ann. § 26–6303, which provides: "Any person who shall, without provocation, use to or of another, and in his presence . . . opprobrious words or abusive language, tending to cause a breach of the peace . . . shall be guilty of a misdemeanor." Appellee appealed the conviction to the Supreme Court of Georgia on the ground, among others, that the statute violated the First and Fourteenth Amendments because vague and overbroad. The Georgia Supreme Court rejected that contention and sustained the conviction. [The District Court for the Northern District of Georgia set aside Wilson's conviction and the Court of Appeals for the Fifth Circuit affirmed.]

Section 26–6303 punishes only spoken words. It can therefore withstand appellee's attack upon its facial constitutionality only if, as authoritatively construed by the Georgia courts, it is not susceptible of application to speech, although vulgar or offensive, that is protected by the First and Fourteenth Amendments, *Cohen v. California*. Only the Georgia courts can supply the requisite construction, since of course "we lack jurisdiction authoritatively to construe state legislation." It matters not that the words appellee used might have been constitutionally prohibited under a narrowly and precisely drawn statute. At least when statutes regulate or proscribe speech and when "no readily apparent construction suggests itself as a vehicle for rehabilitating the statutes in a single prosecution," *Dombrowski v. Pfister*, 380 U.S. 479, 491 (1965), the transcendent value to all society of constitutionally protected expression is deemed to justify allowing "attacks on overly broad statutes with no requirement that the person making the attack demonstrate that his own conduct could not be regulated by a statute drawn with the requisite narrow specificity," *id.*, at 486. This is deemed necessary because persons whose expression is constitutionally protected may well refrain from exercising their rights for fear of criminal sanctions provided by a statute susceptible of application to protected expression.

"Although a statute may be neither vague, overbroad, nor otherwise invalid as applied to the conduct charged against a particular defendant, he is permitted to raise its vagueness or unconstitutional overbreadth as applied to others. And if the law is found deficient in one of these respects, it may not be applied to him either, until and unless a satisfactory limiting construction is placed on the statute. The statute, in effect, is stricken down on its face. This result is deemed justified since the otherwise continued existence of the statute in unnarrowed form would tend to suppress constitutionally protected rights." *Coates v. City of Cincinnati*, [402 U.S. 611, 619–20 (1971)] (opinion of WHITE, J.).

The constitutional guarantees of freedom of speech forbid the States to punish the use of words or language not within "narrowly limited classes of speech." *Chaplinsky v. New Hampshire*. Even as to such a class, however, because "the line between speech unconditionally guaranteed and speech which may legitimately be regulated, suppressed, or punished is finely drawn," *Speiser v. Randall*, "[i]n every case the power to regulate must be so exercised as not, in attaining a permissible end, unduly to infringe the protected freedom," *Cantwell v. Connecticut*. In other words, the statute must be carefully drawn or be authoritatively construed to punish only unprotected speech and not be susceptible of application to protected expression. "Because First Amendment freedoms need breathing space to survive, government may regulate in the area only with narrow specificity." *NAACP v. Button*.

Appellant does not challenge these principles but contends that the Georgia statute is narrowly drawn to apply only to a constitutionally unprotected class of words—"fighting" words—"those which by their very utterance inflict injury or tend to incite an immediate breach of the peace." *Chaplinsky v. New Hampshire*.... Chaplinsky challenged the constitutionality of the statute as inhibiting freedom of expression because it was vague and indefinite. The Supreme Court of New Hampshire, however, "long before the words for which Chaplinsky was convicted," sharply limited the statutory language "offensive, derisive or annoying word" to "fighting" words: "[N]o words were forbidden except such as have a direct tendency to cause acts of violence by the person to whom, individually, the remark is addressed...."

. . .

... Our decisions since *Chaplinsky* have continued to recognize state power constitutionally to punish "fighting" words under carefully drawn statutes not also susceptible of application to protected expression. We reaffirm that proposition today.

Appellant argues that the Georgia appellate courts have by construction limited the proscription of § 26–6303 to "fighting" words, as the New Hampshire Supreme Court limited the New Hampshire statute.... Neither the District Court nor the Court of Appeals so read the Georgia decisions. On the contrary, the District Court expressly stated, "Thus, in the decisions brought to this Court's attention, no meaningful attempt has been made to limit or properly define these terms."... We have, however, made our own examination of the Georgia cases, both those cited and others discovered in research. That examination brings us to the conclusion, in agreement with the courts below, that the Georgia appellate decisions have not construed § 26–6303 to be limited in application, as in *Chaplinsky*, to words that "have a direct tendency to cause acts of violence by the person to whom, individually, the remark is addressed."

The dictionary definitions of "opprobrious" and "abusive" give them greater reach than "fighting" words. Webster's Third New International Dictionary (1961) defined "opprobrious" as "conveying or intended to convey disgrace," and "abusive" as including "harsh insulting language." Georgia appellate decisions have construed § 26–6303 to apply to utterances that, although within these definitions, are not "fighting" words as Chaplinsky defines them. In *Lyons v. State*, 94 Ga. App. 570, 95 S.E.2d 478 (1956), a conviction under the statute was sustained for awakening 10 women scout leaders on a camp-out by shouting, "Boys, this is where we are going to spend the night."

"Get the G—- d—- bed rolls out . . . let's see how close we can come to the G—- d—- tents." Again, in *Fish v. State*, 124 Ga. 416, 52 S.E. 737 (1905), the Georgia Supreme Court held that a jury question was presented by the remark, "You swore a lie." Again, *Jackson v. State*, 14 Ga.App. 19, 80 S.E. 20 (1913), held that a jury question was presented by the words addressed to another, "God damn you, why don't you get out of the road?" Plainly, although "conveying . . . disgrace" or "harsh insulting language," these were not words "which by their very utterance . . . tend to incite an immediate breach of the peace." *Chaplinsky v. New Hampshire*.

. . .

...[W]e agree with the District Court that our decisions in *Ashton v. Kentucky*, 384 U.S. 195 (1966), and *Cox v. Louisiana*, 379 U.S. 536 (1965), compel the conclusion that § 26–6303, as construed, does not define the standard of responsibility with requisite narrow specificity. In *Ashton* we held that "to make an offense of conduct which is 'calculated to create disturbances of the peace' leaves wide open the standard of responsibility." In *Cox v. Louisiana* the statute struck down included as an element congregating with others "with intent to provoke a breach of the peace, or under circumstances such that a breach of the peace may be occasioned thereby." As the District Court observed, "[a]s construed by the Georgia courts, especially in the instant case, the Georgia provision as to breach of the peace is even broader than the Louisiana statute."

We conclude that "[t]he separation of legitimate from illegitimate speech calls for more sensitive tools than [Georgia] has supplied." *Speiser v. Randall*. The most recent decision of the Georgia Supreme Court, in rejecting appellee's attack on the constitutionality of § 26–6303, stated that the statute "conveys a definite meaning as to the conduct forbidden, measured by common understanding and practice." Because earlier appellate decisions applied § 26–6303 to utterances where there was no likelihood that the person addressed would make an immediate violent response, it is clear that the standard allowing juries to determine guilt "measured by common understanding and practice" does not limit the application of § 26–6303 to "fighting" words defined by *Chaplinsky*. Rather, that broad standard effectively "licenses the jury to create its own standard in each case." *Herndon v. Lowry*. Accordingly, we agree with the conclusion of the District Court, "[t]he fault of the statute is that it leaves wide open the standard of responsibility, so that it is easily susceptible to improper application." Unlike the construction of the New Hampshire statute by the New Hampshire Supreme Court, the Georgia appellate courts have not construed § 26–6303 "so as to avoid all constitutional difficulties."

Affirmed.

MR. JUSTICE POWELL and MR. JUSTICE REHNQUIST, took no part in the consideration or decision of this case.

MR. CHIEF JUSTICE BURGER, dissenting.

I fully join in MR. JUSTICE BLACKMUN'S dissent against the bizarre result reached by the Court. It is not merely odd, it is nothing less than remarkable that a court can find a state statute void on its face, not because of its language—which is the traditional test—but because of the way courts of that State have applied the statute in a few isolated cases, decided as long ago as 1905 and generally long before this Court's decision in *Chaplinsky v. New Hampshire*. Even if all of those cases had been decided yesterday, they do nothing to demonstrate that the narrow language of the Georgia statute has any significant potential for sweeping application to suppress or deter important protected speech.

In part the Court's decision appears to stem from its assumption that a statute should be regarded in the same light as its most vague clause, without regard to any of its other language. Thus, since the statute contains the words "tending to cause a breach of the peace" the Court finds its result "compelled" by such decisions as *Ashton v. Kentucky* and *Cox v. Louisiana*. The statute at bar, however, does not prohibit language "tending to cause a breach of the peace." Nor does it prohibit the use of "opprobrious words or abusive language" without more. Rather, it prohibits use "to or of another, and in his presence [of] opprobrious words or abusive language, tending to cause a breach of the peace." If words are to bear their common meaning, and are to be considered in context, rather than dissected with surgical precision using a semantic scalpel, this statute has little potential for application outside the realm of "fighting words" that this Court held beyond the protection of the First Amendment in *Chaplinsky*. Indeed, the language used by the *Chaplinsky* Court to describe words properly subject to regulation bears a striking resemblance to that of the Georgia statute, which was enacted many, many years before *Chaplinsky* was decided. And if the early Georgia cases cited by the majority establish any proposition, it is that the statute, as its language so clearly indicates, is aimed at preventing precisely that type of personal, face-to-face, abusive and insulting language likely to provoke a violent retaliation—self-help, as we euphemistically call it—that the *Chaplinsky* case recognized could be validly prohibited. The facts of the case now before the Court demonstrate that the Georgia statute is serving that valid and entirely proper purpose. There is no persuasive reason to wipe the statute from the books, unless we want to encourage victims of such verbal assaults to seek their own private redress.

The Court apparently acknowledges that the conduct of the defendant in this case is not protected by the First Amendment, and does not contend that the Georgia statute is so ambiguous that he did not have fair notice that his conduct was prohibited. Nor does the Court deny that under normal principles of constitutional adjudication, appellee would not be permitted to attack his own conviction on the ground that the statute in question might in some hypothetical situation be unconstitutionally applied to the conduct of some party not before the Court. Instead, the Court relies on certain sweeping language contained in a few opinions for the proposition that, without regard to the nature of appellee's conduct, the statute in question must be invalidated on its face unless "it is not susceptible of application to speech, . . . that is protected by the First and Fourteenth Amendments."

Such an expansive statement of the technique of invalidated state statutes on their face because of their *substantial* overbreach finds little in policy or the actual circumstances of the Court's past decisions to commend it. As the Court itself recognizes, if the First Amendment overbreadth doctrine serves any legitimate purpose, it is to allow the Court to invalidate statutes because their language demonstrates their potential for sweeping improper applications posing a significant likelihood of deterring important First Amendment speech—not because of some insubstantial or imagined potential for occasional and isolated applications that go beyond constitutional bounds. . . .

Consistent with this properly restrained approach, the overbreadth decisions of this Court, including most of those relied on by the majority, have up to now invalidated state statutes on their face only when their potential for sweeping and improper application in important areas of First Amendment concern was far more apparent—both from the language of the statute and the subject matter of its coverage—than in this case. Indeed, in many of the Court's leading cases, the statute's improper sweep and deterrent potential were amply documented by the very facts of the case before the Court. *Cox v. Louisiana*, heavily relied on by the majority, for example, involved a "breach of the peace" conviction of a leader of black students on the basis of his participation in a peaceful demonstration protesting racial discrimination and a speech urging a "sit in" at segregated lunch counters. Although the Court held, in the alternative, that a statutory prohibition against congregating with others on a public sidewalk "with intent to provoke a breach of the peace, or under circumstances such that a breach of the peace may be occasioned thereby" was unconstitutionally vague and overbroad, it is clear that its primary holding was that the statute had been unconstitutionally *applied* to appellant's conduct as revealed by the record before the Court. In contrast to today's opinion, which mentions the facts of the instant case only by way of passing in a footnote, the *Cox* opinion contained a careful recital and examination of the facts involved, and took care to observe that there was not in the record "any evidence . . . of 'fighting words.'" It was clear, therefore, that in *Cox* not only the language of the statute, but the facts of the very case before the Court, involving as it did protected political speech concerning a burning issue of great social concern, were cogent and persuasive evidence of the statute's potential for sweeping and improper applications. By way of contrast, there is nothing in the language of the Georgia statute, or even in the isolated and ancient Georgia decisions relied on by the Court today that indicates that the statute involved in this case has ever been applied to suppress speech even remotely comparable to that involved in *Cox.*

. . .

MR. JUSTICE BLACKMUN, with whom THE CHIEF JUSTICE joins, dissenting.

It seems strange, indeed, that in this day a man may say to a police officer, who is attempting to restore access to a public building, "White son of a bitch, I'll kill you" and "You son of a bitch, I'll choke you to death," and say to an accompanying officer, "You son of a bitch, if you ever put your hands on me again, I'll cut you all to pieces," and yet constitutionally cannot be prosecuted and convicted under a state statute that makes it a misdemeanor to "use to or of another, and in his presence . . . opprobrious words or abusive language, tending to cause a breach of the peace. . . . " This, however, is precisely what the Court pronounces as the law today.

The Supreme Court of Georgia, when the conviction was appealed, unanimously held the other way. Surely any adult who can read—and I do not exclude this appellee-defendant from that category—should reasonably expect no other conclusion. The words of Georgia Code § 26–6303 are clear. They are also concise. They are not, in my view, overbroad or incapable of being understood. Except perhaps for the "big" word "opprobrious"—and no point

is made of its bigness—any Georgia schoolboy would expect that this defendant's fighting and provocative words to the officers were covered by § 26–6303. Common sense permits no other conclusion. This is demonstrated by the fact that the appellee, and this Court, attack the statute, not as it applies to the appellee, but as it conceivably might apply to others who might utter other words.

The Court reaches its result by saying that the Georgia statute has been interpreted by the State's courts so as to be applicable in practice to otherwise constitutionally protected speech. It follows, says the Court, that the statute is overbroad and therefore is facially unconstitutional and to be struck down in its entirety. Thus Georgia apparently is to be left with no valid statute on its books to meet Wilson's bullying tactic. This result, achieved by what is indeed a very strict construction, will be totally incomprehensible to the State of Georgia, to its courts, and to its citizens.

. . .

This Court appears to have developed its overbreadth rationale in the years since these early Georgia cases. The State's statute, therefore, is condemned because the State's courts have not had an opportunity to adjust to this Court's modern theories of overbreadth.

I wonder, now that § 26–6303 is voided, just what Georgia can do if it seeks to proscribe what the Court says it still may constitutionally proscribe. The natural thing would be to enact a new statute reading just as § 26–6303 reads. But it, too, presumably would be overbroad unless the legislature would add words to the effect that it means only what this Court says it may mean and no more.

. . .

For me, *Chaplinsky v. New Hampshire* was good law when it was decided and deserves to remain as good law now. . . . But I feel that by decisions such as this one and, indeed, *Cohen v. California,* the Court, despite its protestations to the contrary, is merely paying lip service to *Chaplinsky.* As the appellee states in a footnote to his brief, "Although there is no doubt that the state can punish 'fighting words' this appears to be about all that is left of the decision in *Chaplinsky.*" If this is what the overbreadth doctrine means, and if this is what it produces, it urgently needs re-examination. The Court has painted itself into a corner from which it, and the States, can extricate themselves only with difficulty.

A year later, in *Broadrick v. Oklahoma,* the Court shifted its approach, adopting Justice Burger's dissenting view in *Gooding v. Wilson.*[129] Three state employees chal-

---

[129] Broadrick v, Oklahoma, 413 U.S. 601 (1973).

lenged provisions of Oklahoma's Merit System of Personnel Administration Act that restricted a wide range of political activities by state civil servants. The employees conceded that the restrictions served commendable goals and would be constitutional as applied to the partisan political activities they had engaged in, including the solicitation of money from coworkers. On the other hand, the statute's language seemed to reach such protected acts as wearing campaign buttons or displaying bumper stickers. Noting that facial overbreadth had not been invoked when a limiting construction could be placed on the challenged statute, the majority refused to discard the provisions *in toto*.

It remains a "matter of no little difficulty" to determine when a law may properly be held void on its face and when "such summary action" is inappropriate. But the plain import of our cases is, at the very least, that facial overbreadth adjudication is an exception to our traditional rules of practice and that its function, a limited one at the outset, attenuates as the otherwise unprotected behavior that it forbids the State to sanction moves from "pure speech" toward conduct and that conduct—even if expressive—falls within the scope of otherwise valid criminal laws that reflect legitimate state interests in maintaining comprehensive controls over harmful, constitutionally unprotected conduct. Although such laws, if too broadly worded, may deter protected speech to some unknown extent, there comes a point where that effect—at best a prediction—cannot, with confidence, justify invalidating a statute on its face and so prohibiting the State from enforcing the statute against conduct that is admittedly within its power to proscribe. To put the matter another way, particularly where conduct and not merely speech is involved, we believe that the overbreadth of a statute must not only be real, but substantial as well, judged in relation to the statute's plainly legitimate sweep. It is our view that [the restrictions are] not substantially overbroad and that whatever overbreadth may exist should be cured through case-by-case analysis of the fact situations to which its sanctions, assertedly, may not be applied.

In his dissenting opinion, Justice Brennan, joined by Justices Stewart and Marshall, noted that the Oklahoma Supreme Court had never attempted to construe the provisions or narrow their reach, and that, under *Gooding v. Wilson*, the Court could not undertake that task. According to the dissenting opinion, the provisions' susceptibility to improper applications required a finding that the statute was unconstitutional on its face.

The Court has continued to display its unwillingness to strike down statutes wholesale on overbreadth grounds, favoring partial, rather than facial, invalidation. In *Brockett v. Spokane Arcades, Inc.* the Court held that the Ninth Circuit erred in invalidating in its entirety a Washington statute that punished publication of obscene materials.[130] Four days after the effective date of the statute, sellers of sexually oriented books and movies sought a declaratory judgment that the statute's definition of "prurient" to include "that which incites . . . lust" was unconstitutionally overbroad because it reached material that aroused only a normal, healthy interest in sex. The Court distinguished overbreadth cases in which "an individual whose own speech or expressive conduct may validly be prohibited or sanctioned is permitted to challenge a statute on its face because it also threatens others not before the court—those who desire to engage in legally protected expression but who may refrain from doing so rather than risk prosecution or undertake to have the law declared partially invalid." Here, in

---

[130] Brockett v. Spokane Arcades, Inc., 472 U.S. 491 (1985).

contrast, the parties challenging the statute wished to publish protected as well as unprotected material. The Court therefore concluded, "[t]here is then no want of a proper party to challenge the statute, no concern that an attack on the statute will be unduly delayed or protected speech discouraged. The statute may forthwith be declared invalid to the extent that it reaches too far, but otherwise left intact." Moreover, the issue of severability posed no obstacle to partial invalidation since the statute itself had a severability clause and, once the offending interpretation was eliminated, the remainder of the statute retained its effectiveness as a regulation of obscenity. Although the Court had no need to decide whether the statute's overbreadth was substantial, it noted that *Broadrick*'s substantiality requirement extended to cases involving "pure speech," as well as conduct.

Despite its recent limits on the use of the overbreadth doctrine, the Court has struck down statutes on their face when the language contained no "core of easily identifiable and constitutionally proscribable conduct that the statute prohibits" that could be separated from the part that infringed protected expression.[131] The possibility of imagining some constitutional applications of a statute that sweeps broadly over protected activities is not enough to save it from a facial challenge.

---

[131] See Secretary of State of Maryland v. Joseph H. Munson Co., 467 U.S. 947, 965–66 (1984).

Board of Airport Commissioners
v.
Jews for Jesus, Inc.,
482 U.S. 569 (1987)

JUSTICE O'CONNOR delivered the opinion of the Court.

The issue presented in this case is whether a resolution banning all "First Amendment activities" at Los Angeles International Airport (LAX) violates the First Amendment.

I

On July 13, 1983, the Board of Airport Commissioners (Board) adopted Resolution No. 13787, which provides in pertinent part:

"NOW, THEREFORE, BE IT RESOLVED by the Board of Airport Commissioners that the Central Terminal Area at Los Angeles International Airport is not open for First Amendment activities by any individual and/or entity;

. . .

"BE IT FURTHER RESOLVED that after the effective date of this Resolution, if any individual and/or entity seeks to engage in First Amendment activities within the Central Terminal Area at Los Angeles International Airport, said individual and/or entity shall be deemed to be acting in contravention of the stated policy of the Board of Airport Commissioners in reference to the uses permitted within the Central Terminal Area at Los Angeles International Airport. . . .

Respondent Jews for Jesus, Inc., is a nonprofit religious corporation. On July 6, 1984, Alan Howard Snyder, a minister of the Gospel for Jews for Jesus, was stopped by a Department of Airports peace officer while distributing free religious literature on a pedestrian walkway in the Central Terminal Area at LAX. The officer showed Snyder a copy of the resolution, explained that Snyder's activities violated the resolution, and requested that Snyder leave LAX. The officer warned Snyder that the city would take legal action against him if he refused to leave as requested. Snyder stopped distributing the leaflets and left the airport terminal.

Jews for Jesus and Snyder then filed this action in the District Court for the Central District of California, challenging the constitutionality of the resolution under both the California and Federal Constitutions. . . . [T]he Court of Appeals concluded that "an airport complex is a traditional public forum" and held that the resolution was unconstitutional on its face under the Federal Constitution. We . . . now affirm, but on different grounds.

. . .

Under the First Amendment overbreadth doctrine, an individual whose own speech or conduct may be prohibited is permitted to challenge a statute on its face "because it also threatens others not before the court—those who desire to engage in legally protected expression but who may refrain from doing so rather than risk prosecution or undertake to have the law declared partially invalid." *Brockett v. Spokane Arcades, Inc.* A statute may be invalidated on its face, however, only if the overbreadth is "substantial." *Broadrick v. Oklahoma.* The requirement that the overbreadth be substantial arose from our recognition that application of the overbreadth doctrine is, "manifestly, strong medicine," *Broadrick v. Oklahoma*, and that "there must be a realistic danger that the statute itself will significantly compromise recognized First Amendment protections of parties not before the Court for it to be facially challenged on overbreadth grounds." *City Council of Los Angeles v. Taxpayers for Vincent.*

On its face, the resolution at issue in this case reaches the universe of expressive activity, and, by prohibiting *all* protected expression, purports to create a virtual "First Amendment Free Zone" at LAX. The resolution does not merely regulate expressive activity in the Central Terminal Area that might create problems such as congestion or the disruption of the activities of those who use LAX. Instead, the resolution expansively states that LAX "is not open for First Amendment activities by any individual and/or entity," and that "any individual and/or entity [who] seeks to engage in First Amendment activities within the Central Terminal Area . . . shall be deemed to be acting in contravention of the stated policy of the Board of Airport Commissioners." The resolution therefore does not merely reach the activity of respondents at LAX; it prohibits even talking and reading, or the wearing of campaign buttons or symbolic clothing. Under such a sweeping ban, virtually every individual who enters LAX may be found to violate the resolution by engaging in some "First Amendment activit[y]." We think it obvious that such a ban cannot be justified even if LAX were a nonpublic forum because no conceivable governmental interest would justify such an absolute prohibition of speech.

Additionally, we find no apparent saving construction of the resolution. The resolution expressly applies to all "First Amendment activities," and the words of the resolution simply leave no room for a narrowing construction. In the past the Court sometimes has used either abstention or certification when, as here, the state courts have not had the opportunity to give the statute under challenge a definite construction. Neither option, however, is appropriate in this case because California has no certification procedure, and the resolution is not "fairly subject to an interpretation which will render unnecessary or substantially modify the federal constitutional question." *Harmon v. Forssenius*, 380 U.S. 528, 535 (1965). The difficulties in adopting a limiting construction of the resolution are not unlike those found in *Baggett v. Bullitt*, 377 U.S. 360 (1964). At issue in *Baggett* was the constitutionality of several statutes requiring loyalty oaths. The *Baggett* Court concluded that abstention would serve no purpose given the lack of any limiting construction, and held the statutes unconstitutional on their face under the First Amendment overbreadth doctrine. We observed that the challenged loyalty oath was not "open to one or a few interpretations, but to an indefinite number," and concluded that "[i]t is fictional to believe that anything less than extensive adjudications, under the impact of a variety of factual situations, would bring the oath within the bounds of permissible constitutional certainty." Here too, it is difficult to imagine that the resolution could be limited by anything less than a series of adjudications, and the chilling effect of the resolution on protected speech in the meantime would make such a case-by-case adjudication intolerable.

The petitioners suggest that the resolution is not substantially overbroad because it is intended to reach only expressive activity unrelated to airport-related purposes. Such a limiting construction, however, is of little assistance in substantially reducing the overbreadth of the resolution. Much nondisruptive speech—such as the wearing of a T-shirt or button that contains a political message—may not be "airport related," but is still protected speech even in a nonpublic forum. See *Cohen v. California.* Moreover, the vagueness of this suggested construction itself presents serious constitutional difficulty. The line between airport-related speech and nonairport-related speech is, at best, murky. The petitioners, for example, suggest that an individual who reads a newspaper or converses with a neighbor at LAX is engaged in permitted "airport-related" activity because reading or conversing permits the traveling public to "pass the time." We presume, however, that petitioners would not so categorize the activities of a member of a religious or political organization who decides to "pass the time" by distributing leaflets to fellow travelers. In essence, the result of this vague limiting construction would be to give LAX officials alone the power to decide in the first instance whether a given activity is airport related. Such a law that "confers on police a virtually unrestrained power to arrest and charge persons with a violation" of the resolution is unconstitutional because "[t]he opportunity for abuse, especially where a statute has received a virtually open-ended interpretation, is self-evident." *Lewis v. City of New Orleans,*

415 U.S. 130, 135–136 (1974) (Powell, J., concurring).

We conclude that the resolution is substantially overbroad, and is not fairly subject to a limiting construction. Accordingly, we hold

that the resolution violates the First Amendment.

[The concurring opinion of Justice White, with whom Chief Justice Rehnquist joined, is omitted.]

7. Freedom of Association

Although "freedom of association" is not explicitly mentioned in the Constitution, the Court has recognized the importance of citizens' ability to join with others in pursuing First Amendment goals. The right to associate can be derived from the First Amendment's guarantees of speech, press, petition and assembly because it is necessary to enable citizens to exercise these enumerated freedoms effectively. The Court first articulated an constitutional right to freedom of association in *NAACP v. Alabama*. The case arose in 1956 when the Attorney General of Alabama brought an action against the NAACP in an attempt to oust the civil rights organization from the state. In the course of the action, Alabama moved for the production of a large number of the NAACP's records and papers, including bank statements, leases, deeds, and records containing the names and addresses of all its Alabama "members" and "agents." When the NAACP failed to comply with the court's production order, it was held in contempt and fined $100,000. The NAACP argued that the order compelling it to reveal the names and addresses of its members and agents to the Alabama Attorney General violated the Due Process Clause of the Fourteenth Amendment.

N.A.A.C.P. v. Alabama
357 U.S. 449 (1958)

Mr. Justice Harlan delivered the opinion of the Court.

. . .

. . . Petitioner argues that in view of the facts and circumstances shown in the record, the effect of compelled disclosure of the membership lists will be to abridge the rights of its rank-and-file members to engage in lawful association in support of their common beliefs. It contends that governmental action which, although not directly suppressing association, nevertheless carries this consequence, can be justified only upon some overriding valid interest of the State.

Effective advocacy of both public and private points of view, particularly controversial ones, is undeniably enhanced by group association, as this Court has more than once recognized by remarking upon the close nexus between the freedoms of speech and assembly. It is beyond debate that freedom to engage in association for the advancement of beliefs and ideas is an inseparable aspect of the "liberty" assured by the Due Process Clause of the Fourteenth Amendment, which embraces freedom of speech. Of course, it is immaterial whether the beliefs sought to be advanced by associa-

tion pertain to political, economic, religious or cultural matters, and state action which may have the effect of curtailing the freedom to associate is subject to the closest scrutiny.

The fact that Alabama, so far as is relevant to the validity of the contempt judgment presently under review, has taken no direct action to restrict the right of petitioner's members to associate freely, does not end inquiry into the effect of the production order. In the domain of these indispensable liberties, whether of speech, press, or association, the decisions of this Court recognize that abridgement of such rights, even though unintended, may inevitably follow from varied forms of governmental action. . . . The governmental action challenged may appear to be totally unrelated to protected liberties. . . .

It is hardly a novel perception that compelled disclosure of affiliation with groups engaged in advocacy may constitute [an] effective a restraint on freedom of association. . . . This Court has recognized the vital relationship between freedom to associate and privacy in one's associations. When referring to the varied forms of governmental action which might interfere with freedom of assembly, it said in

American Communications Ass'n v. Douds, [339 U.S. 382, 402 (1950)]: "A requirement that adherents of particular religious faiths or political parties wear identifying arm-bands, for example, is obviously of this nature." Compelled disclosure of membership in an organization engaged in advocacy of particular beliefs is of the same order. Inviolability of privacy in group association may in many circumstances be indispensable to preservation of freedom of association, particularly where a group espouses dissident beliefs.

We think that the production order, in the respects here drawn in question, must be regarded as entailing the likelihood of a substantial restraint upon the exercise by petitioner's members of their right to freedom of association. Petitioner has made an uncontroverted showing that on past occasions revelation of the identity of its rank-and-file members has exposed these members to economic reprisal, loss of employment, threat of physical coercion, and other manifestations of public hostility. Under these circumstances, we think it apparent that compelled disclosure of petitioner's Alabama membership is likely to affect adversely the ability of petitioner and its members to pursue their collective effort to foster beliefs which they admittedly have the right to advocate, in that it may induce members to withdraw from the Association and dissuade others from joining it because of fear of exposure of their beliefs shown through their associations and of the consequences of this exposure.

It is not sufficient to answer, as the State does here, that whatever repressive effect compulsory disclosure of names of petitioner's members may have upon participation by Alabama citizens in petitioner's activities follows not from *state* action but from *private* community pressures. The crucial factor is the interplay of governmental and private action, for it is only after the initial exertion of state power represented by the production order that private action takes hold.

We turn to the final question whether Alabama has demonstrated an interest in obtaining the disclosures it seeks from petitioner which is sufficient to justify the deterrent effect which we have concluded these disclosures may well have on the free exercise by petitioner's members of their constitutionally protected right of association. Such a " . . . subordinating interest of the State must be compelling," *Sweezy v. New Hampshire*, 354 U.S. 234, 265 (concurring opinion). . . .

It is important to bear in mind that petitioner asserts no right to absolute immunity from state investigation, and no right to disregard Alabama's laws. As shown by its substantial compliance with the production order, petitioner does not deny Alabama's right to obtain

from it such information as the State desires concerning the purposes of the Association and its activities within the State. Petitioner has not objected to divulging the identity of its members who are employed by or hold official positions with it. It has urged the rights solely of its ordinary rank-and-file members. This is therefore not analogous to a case involving the interest of a State in protecting its citizens in their dealings with paid solicitors or agents of foreign corporations by requiring identification.

Whether there was "justification" in this instance turns solely on the substantiality of Alabama's interest in obtaining the membership lists. During the course of a hearing before the Alabama Circuit Court on a motion of petitioner to set aside the production order, the State Attorney General presented at length, under examination by petitioner, the State's reason for requesting the membership lists. The exclusive purpose was to determine whether petitioner was conducting intrastate business in violation of the Alabama foreign corporation registration statute, and the membership lists were expected to help resolve this question. The issues in the litigation commenced by Alabama by its bill in equity were whether the character of petitioner and its activities in Alabama had been such as to make petitioner subject to the registration statute, and whether the extent of petitioner's activities without qualifying suggested its permanent ouster from the State. Without intimating the slightest view upon the merits of these issues, we are unable to perceive that the disclosure of the names of petitioner's rank-and-file members has a substantial bearing on either of them. . . .

From what has already been said, we think it apparent that *Bryant v. Zimmerman*, 278 U.S. 63, cannot be relied on in support of the State's position, for that case involved markedly different considerations in terms of the interest of the State in obtaining disclosure. There, this Court upheld as applied to a member of a local chapter of the Ku Klux Klan, a New York statute requiring any unincorporated association which demanded an oath as a condition to membership to file with state officials copies of its " . . . constitution, by-laws, rules, regulations and oath of membership, together with a roster of its membership and a list of its officers for the current year." In its opinion, the Court took care to emphasize the nature of the organization which New York sought to regulate. The decision was based on the particular character of the Klan's activities, involving acts of unlawful intimidation and violence, which the Court assumed was before the state legislature when it enacted the statute, and of which the Court itself took judicial notice. . . .

We hold that the immunity from state scrutiny of membership lists which the Association claims on behalf of its members is here so related to the right of the members to pursue their lawful private interests privately and to associate freely with others in so doing as to come within the protection of the Fourteenth Amendment. And we conclude that Alabama has fallen short of showing a controlling justification for the deterrent effect on the free enjoyment of the right to associate which disclosure of membership lists is likely to have. Accordingly, the judgment of civil contempt and the $100,000 fine which resulted from petitioner's refusal to comply with the production order in this respect must fall.

. . .

Reversed.

The Court more recently reiterated the significance of concerted action to achieve political objectives in another case involving the NAACP. In *NAACP v. Claiborne Hardware Co.*, the Court overturned a state antitrust judgment amounting to over $1 million against the NAACP and other Black citizens of Claiborne County, Mississippi, for business losses suffered by white stores as a result of an economic boycott against them.[132] Although the boycott, organized to pressure white merchants and officials to agree to civil rights demands, was largely peaceful, some boycotters engaged in acts of violence. A unanimous Court held that liability could not be imposed on individual boycotters simply because they belonged to a group that contained some violent members. Liability was only appropriate against those individuals who committed violent acts and for losses proximately caused by unlawful conduct. For liability to be based on group membership, "it is necessary to establish that the group itself possessed unlawful goals and that the individual held a specific intent to further those illegal aims." The Court stressed the importance of freedom of association to prolonged efforts to achieve political change: "In litigation of this kind the stakes are high. Concerted action is a powerful weapon. History teaches that special dangers are associated with conspiratorial activity. And yet one of the foundations of our society is the right of individuals to combine with other persons in pursuit of a common goal by lawful means."

Recently, the Court has addressed a conflict between the constitutional freedom of association and state civil rights statutes that enforce the government's interest in eliminating sex, race, and other forms of discrimination. An organization's freedom to associate includes its right to choose its own members. This freedom may entail, however, excluding people from membership based on invidious standards. The government's power to scrutinize the membership decisions of organizations may in some cases further legitimate egalitarian goals and in others constitute an egregious interference with First Amendment freedoms. The Court has upheld laws regulating the membership of large, business associations designed to ensure citizens equal access to public accommodations and to economic, social, and political opportunities.[133]

---

[132] NAACP v. Claiborne Hardware Co., 458 U.S. 886 (1982).

[133] See Roberts v. United States Jaycees, 468 U.S. 609 (1984); Board of Directors of Rotary International v. Rotary Club of Duarte, 481 U.S. 537 (1987); New York State Club Association, Inc. v. City of New York, 487 U.S. 1 (1988).

Roberts v. United States
468 U.S. 609 (1984)

JUSTICE BRENNAN delivered the opinion of the Court.

This case requires us to address a conflict between a State's efforts to eliminate gender-based discrimination against its citizens and the constitutional freedom of association asserted by members of a private organization. In the decision under review, the Court of Appeals for the Eighth Circuit concluded that, by requiring the United States Jaycees to admit women as full voting members, the Minnesota Human Rights Act violates the First and Fourteenth Amendment rights of the organization's members. We ... reverse.

I

The United States Jaycees (Jaycees), founded in 1920 as the Junior Chamber of Commerce, is a nonprofit membership corporation, incorporated in Missouri with national headquarters in Tulsa, Oklahoma. The objective of the Jaycees, as set out in its bylaws, is to pursue

> "such educational and charitable purposes as will promote and foster the growth and development of young men's civic organizations in the United States, designed to inculcate in the individual membership of such organization a spirit of genuine Americanism and civic interest, and as a supplementary education institution to provide them with opportunity for personal development and achievement and an avenue for intelligent participation by young men in the affairs of their community, state and nation, and to develop true friendship and understanding among young men of all nations."

The organization's bylaws establish seven classes of membership, including individual or regular members, associate individual members, and local chapters. Regular membership is limited to young men between the ages of 18 and 35, while associate membership is available to individuals or groups ineligible for regular membership, principally women and older men. An associate member, whose dues are somewhat lower than those charged regular members, may not vote, hold local or national office, or participate in certain leadership training and awards programs. ... At the time of trial in August 1981, the Jaycees had approximately 295,000 members in 7,400 local chapters affiliated with 51 state organizations. There were at that time about 11,915 associate members. The national organization's Executive Vice President estimated at trial that women associate members make up about two percent of the Jaycees' total membership.

. . .

In 1974 and 1975, respectively, the Minneapolis and St. Paul chapters of the Jaycees began admitting women as regular members. Currently, the memberships and boards of directors of both chapters include a substantial proportion of women. As a result, the two chapters have been in violation of the national orga-

nization's bylaws for about 10 years. The national organization has imposed a number of sanctions on the Minneapolis and St. Paul chapters for violating the bylaws, including denying their members eligibility for state or national office or awards programs, and refusing to count their membership in computing votes at national conventions.

In December 1978, the president of the national organization advised both chapters that a motion to revoke their charters would be considered at a forthcoming meeting of the national board of directors in Tulsa. Shortly after receiving this notification, members of both chapters filed charges of discrimination with the Minnesota Department of Human Rights. The complaints alleged that the exclusion of women from full membership required by the national organization's bylaws violated the Minnesota Human Rights Act (Act), which provides in part:

> "It is an unfair discriminatory practice:
>
> > "To deny any person the full and equal enjoyment of the goods, services, facilities, privileges, advantages, and accommodations of a place of public accommodation because of race, color, creed, religion, disability, national origin or sex."

. . .

II

Our decisions have referred to constitutionally protected "freedom of association" in two distinct senses. In one line of decisions, the Court has concluded that choices to enter into and maintain certain intimate human relationships must be secured against undue intrusion by the State because of the role of such relationships in safeguarding the individual freedom that is central to our constitutional scheme. In this respect, freedom of association receives protection as a fundamental element of personal liberty. In another set of decisions, the Court has recognized a right to associate for the purpose of engaging in those activities protected by the First Amendment—speech, assembly, petition for the redress of grievances, and the exercise of religion. The Constitution guarantees freedom of association of this kind as an indispensable means of preserving other individual liberties.

The intrinsic and instrumental features of constitutionally protected association may, of course, coincide. In particular, when the State interferes with individuals' selection of those with whom they wish to join in a common endeavor, freedom of association in both of its forms may be implicated. The Jaycees contend that this is such a case. Still, the nature and degree of constitutional protection afforded freedom of association may vary depending on the extent to which one or the other aspect of the constitutionally protected liberty is at stake in a given case. We therefore find it useful to consider separately the effect of applying the Minnesota statute to the Jaycees on what could be called its members' freedom of intimate association and their freedom of expressive association.

A

The Court has long recognized that, because the Bill of Rights is designed to secure individual liberty, it must afford the formation and preservation of certain kinds of highly personal relationships a substantial measure of sanctuary from unjustified interference by the State. Without precisely identifying every consideration that may underlie this type of constitutional protection, we have noted that certain kinds of personal bonds have played a critical role in the culture and traditions of the Nation by cultivating and transmitting shared ideals and beliefs; they thereby foster diversity and act as critical buffers between the individual and the power of the State. Moreover, the constitutional shelter afforded such relationships reflects the realization that individuals draw much of their emotional enrichment from close ties with others. Protecting these relationships from unwarranted state interference therefore safeguards the ability independently to define one's identity that is central to any concept of liberty.

The personal affiliations that exemplify these considerations, and that therefore suggest some relevant limitations on the relationships that might be entitled to this sort of constitutional protection, are those that attend the creation and sustenance of a family—marriage; childbirth; the raising and education of children; and cohabitation with one's relatives. Family relationships, by their nature, involve deep attachments and commitments to the necessarily few other individuals with whom one shares not only a special community of thoughts, experiences, and beliefs but also distinctively personal aspects of one's life. Among other things, therefore, they are distinguished by such attributes as relative smallness, a high degree of selectivity in decisions to begin and maintain the affiliation, and seclusion from others in critical aspects of the relationship. As a general matter, only relationships with these sorts of qualities are likely to reflect the considerations that have led to an understanding of freedom of association as an intrinsic element of personal liberty. Conversely, an association lacking these qualities—such as a large business enterprise—seems remote from the concerns giving rise to this constitutional protection. Accordingly, the Constitution undoubtedly imposes constraints on the State's power to control the selection of one's spouse that would not apply to regulations affecting the choice of one's fellow employees.

Between these poles, of course, lies a broad range of human relationships that may make greater or lesser claims to constitutional protection from particular incursions by the State. Determining the limits of state authority over an individual's freedom to enter into a particular association therefore unavoidably entails a careful assessment of where that relationship's objective characteristics locate it on a spectrum from the most intimate to the most attenuated of personal attachments. We need not mark the potentially significant points on this terrain with any precision. We note only that factors that may be relevant include size, purpose, policies, selectivity, congeniality, and other characteristics that in a particular case may be pertinent. In this case, however, several features of the Jaycees clearly place the organization outside of the category of relationships worthy of this kind of constitutional protection.

The undisputed facts reveal that the local chapters of the Jaycees are large and basically unselective groups. At the time of the state administrative hearing, the Minneapolis chapter had approximately 430 members, while the St. Paul chapter had about 400. Apart from age and sex, neither the national organization nor the local chapters employs any criteria for judging applicants for membership, and new members are routinely recruited and admitted with no inquiry into their backgrounds. In fact, a local officer testified that he could recall no instance in which an applicant had been denied membership on any basis other than age or sex. Furthermore, despite their inability to vote, hold office, or receive certain awards, women affiliated with the Jaycees attend various meetings, participate in selected projects, and engage in many of the organization's social functions. Indeed, numerous non-members of both genders regularly participate in a substantial portion of activities central to the decision of many members to associate with one another, including many of the organization's various community programs, awards ceremonies, and recruitment meetings.

In short, the local chapters of the Jaycees are neither small nor selective. Moreover, much of the activity central to the formation and maintenance of the association involves the participation of strangers to that relationship. Accordingly, we conclude that the Jaycees chapters lack the distinctive characteristics that might afford constitutional protection to the decision of its members to exclude women. We turn therefore to consider the extent to which application of the Minnesota statute to compel the Jaycees to accept women infringes the group's freedom of expressive association.

B

An individual's freedom to speak, to worship, and to petition the Government for the redress of grievances could not be vigorously protected from interference by the State unless a correlative freedom to engage in group effort toward those ends were not also guaranteed. According protection to collective effort on behalf of shared goals is especially important in preserving political and cultural diversity and in shielding dissident expression from suppression by the majority. Consequently, we have long understood as implicit in the right to engage in activities protected by the First Amendment a corresponding right to associate with others in pursuit of a wide variety of political, social, economic, educational, religious, and cultural ends. In view of the various protected activities in which the Jaycees engage, that right is plainly implicated in this case.

Government actions that may unconstitutionally infringe upon this freedom can take a number of forms. Among other things, government may seek to impose penalties or withhold benefits from individuals because of their membership in a disfavored group; it may attempt to require disclosure of the fact of membership in a group seeking anonymity; and it may try to interfere with the internal organization or affairs of the group. By requiring the Jaycees to admit women as full voting members, the Minnesota Act works an infringement of the last type. There can be no clearer example of an intrusion into the internal structure or affairs of an association than a regulation that forces the group to accept members it does not desire. Such a regulation may impair the ability of the original members to express only those views that brought them together. Freedom of association therefore plainly presupposes a freedom not to associate.

The right to associate for expressive purposes is not, however, absolute. Infringements on that right may be justified by regulations adopted to serve compelling state interests, unrelated to the suppression of ideas, that cannot be achieved through means significantly less restrictive of associational freedoms. We are persuaded that Minnesota's compelling interest in eradicating discrimination against its female citizens justifies the impact that application of the statute to the Jaycees may have on the male members' associational freedoms.

On its face, the Minnesota Act does not aim at the suppression of speech, does not distinguish between prohibited and permitted activity on the basis of viewpoint, and does not license enforcement authorities to administer the statute on the basis of such constitutionally impermissible criteria. Nor do the Jaycees contend that the Act has been applied in this case

for the purpose of hampering the organization's ability to express its views. Instead, as the Minnesota Supreme Court explained, the Act reflects the State's strong historical commitment to eliminating discrimination and assuring its citizens equal access to publicly available goods and services. That goal, which is unrelated to the suppression of expression, plainly serves compelling state interests of the highest order.

The Minnesota Human Rights Act at issue here is an example of public accommodations laws that were adopted by some States beginning a decade before enactment of their federal counterpart, the Civil Rights Act of 1875. Indeed, when this Court invalidated that federal statute in the *Civil Rights Cases*, 109 U.S. 3 (1883), it emphasized the fact that state laws imposed a variety of equal access obligations on public accommodations. In response to that decision, many more States, including Minnesota, adopted statutes prohibiting racial discrimination in public accommodations. These laws provided the primary means for protecting the civil rights of historically disadvantaged groups until the Federal Government reentered the field in 1957. Like many other States, Minnesota has progressively broadened the scope of its public accommodations law in the years since it was first enacted, both with respect to the number and type of covered facilities and with respect to the groups against whom discrimination is forbidden. In 1973, the Minnesota legislature added discrimination on the basis of sex to the types of conduct prohibited by the statute.

By prohibiting gender discrimination in places of public accommodation, the Minnesota Act protects the State's citizenry from a number of serious social and personal harms. In the context of reviewing state actions under the Equal Protection Clause, this Court has frequently noted that discrimination based on archaic and overbroad assumptions about the relative needs and capacities of the sexes forces individuals to labor under stereotypical notions that often bear no relationship to their actual abilities. It thereby both deprives persons of their individual dignity and denies society the benefits of wide participation in political, economic, and cultural life. These concerns are strongly implicated with respect to gender discrimination in the allocation of publicly available goods and services. Thus, in upholding Title II of the Civil Rights Act of 1964, which forbids race discrimination in public accommodations, we emphasized that its "fundamental object . . . was to vindicate 'the deprivation of personal dignity that surely accompanies denials of equal access to public establishments.'" *Heart of Atlanta Motel v. United States*, 379 U.S. 241, 250 (1964). That stigmatizing injury, and the denial of equal opportunities that accompanies it, is surely felt as strongly by persons suffering discrimination on the basis of their sex as by those treated differently because of their race.

Nor is the state interest in assuring equal access limited to the provision of purely tangible goods and services. A State enjoys broad authority to create rights of public access on behalf of its citizens. Like many States and municipalities, Minnesota has adopted a functional definition of public accommodations that reaches various forms of public, quasi-commercial conduct. This expansive definition reflects a recognition of the changing nature of the American economy and of the importance, both to the individual and to society, of removing the barriers to economic advancement and political and social integration that have historically plagued certain disadvantaged groups, including women. . . . Assuring women equal access to such goods, privileges, and advantages clearly furthers compelling state interests.

In applying the Act to the Jaycees, the State has advanced those interests through the least restrictive means of achieving its ends. Indeed, the Jaycees have failed to demonstrate that the Act imposes any serious burdens on the male members' freedom of expressive association. To be sure, as the Court of Appeals noted, a "not insubstantial part" of the Jaycees' activities constitutes protected expression on political, economic, cultural, and social affairs. Over the years, the national and local levels of the organization have taken public positions on a number of diverse issues, and members of the Jaycees regularly engage in a variety of civic, charitable, lobbying, fundraising and other activities worthy of constitutional protection under the First Amendment. There is, however, no basis in the record for concluding that admission of women as full voting members will impede the organization's ability to engage in these protected activities or to disseminate its preferred views. The Act requires no change in the Jaycees' creed of promoting the interests of young men, and it imposes no restrictions on the organization's ability to exclude individuals with ideologies or philosophies different from those of its existing members. Moreover, the Jaycees already invite women to share the group's views and philosophy and to participate in much of its training and community activities. Accordingly, any claim that admission of women as full voting members will impair a symbolic message conveyed by the very fact that women are not permitted to vote is attenuated at best.

While acknowledging that "the specific content of most of the resolutions adopted over the years by the Jaycees has nothing to do with sex," the Court of Appeals nonetheless entertained the hypothesis that women members might have a different view or agenda with respect to these matters so that, if they are allowed to vote, "some change in the Jaycees' philosophical cast can reasonably be expected." It is similarly arguable that, insofar as the Jaycees is organized to promote the views of young men whatever those views happen to be, admission of women as voting members will change the message communicated by the group's speech because of the gender-based assumptions of the audience. Neither supposition, however, is supported by the record. In claiming that women might have a different attitude about such issues as the federal budget, school prayer, voting rights, and foreign relations, or that the organization's public positions would have a different effect if the group were not "a purely young men's association," the Jaycees rely solely on unsupported generalizations about the relative interests and perspectives of men and women. Although such generalizations may or may not have a statistical basis in fact with respect to particular positions adopted by the Jaycees, we have repeatedly condemned legal decisionmaking that relies uncritically on such assumptions. In the absence of a showing far more substantial than that attempted by the Jaycees, we decline to indulge in the sexual stereotyping that underlies appellee's contention that, by allowing women to vote, application of the Minnesota Act will change the content or impact of the organization's speech.

In any event, even if enforcement of the Act causes some incidental abridgement of the Jaycees' protected speech, that effect is no greater than is necessary to accomplish the State's legitimate purposes. As we have explained, acts of invidious discrimination in the distribution of publicly available goods, services, and other advantages cause unique evils that government has a compelling interest to prevent—wholly apart from the point of view such conduct may transmit. Accordingly, like violence or other types of potentially expressive activities that produce special harms distinct from their communicative impact, such practices are entitled to no constitutional protection. In prohibiting such practices, the Minnesota Act therefore "responds precisely to the substantive problem which legitimately concerns" the State and abridges no more speech or associational freedom than is necessary to accomplish that purpose.

. . .

The judgment of the Court of Appeals is
Reversed.

JUSTICE REHNQUIST concurs in the judgment.

THE CHIEF JUSTICE and JUSTICE BLACKMUN took no part in the decision of this case.

JUSTICE O'CONNOR, concurring in part and concurring in the judgment.

. . . With respect to Part II-A of the Court's opinion, I agree with the Court that the Jaycees cannot claim a right of association deriving from this Court's cases concerning "marriage, procreation, contraception, family relationships, and child rearing and education." Those cases, "while defying categorical description," identify certain zones of privacy in which certain personal relationships or decisions are protected from government interference. Whatever the precise scope of the rights recognized in such cases, they do not encompass associational rights of a 295,000-member organization whose activities are not "private" in any meaningful sense of that term.

I part company with the Court over its First Amendment analysis in Part II-B of its opinion. I agree with the Court that application of the Minnesota law to the Jaycees does not contravene the First Amendment, but I reach that conclusion for reasons distinct from those offered by the Court. I believe the Court has adopted a test that unadvisedly casts doubt on the power of States to pursue the profoundly important goal of ensuring nondiscriminatory access to commercial opportunities in our society. At the same time, the Court has adopted an approach to the general problem presented by this case that accords insufficient protection to expressive associations and places inappropriate burdens on groups claiming the protection of the First Amendment.

I

The Court analyzes Minnesota's attempt to regulate the Jaycees' membership using a test that I find both over-protective of activities undeserving of constitutional shelter and under-protective of important First Amendment concerns. The Court declares that the Jaycees' right of association depends on the organization's making a "substantial" showing that the admission of unwelcome members "will change the message communicated by the group's speech." I am not sure what showing the Court thinks would satisfy its requirement of proof of a membership-message connection, but whatever it means, the focus on such a connection is objectionable.

Imposing such a requirement, especially in the context of the balancing-of-interests test articulated by the Court, raises the possibility that certain commercial associations, by engaging occasionally in certain kinds of expressive activities, might improperly gain protection for discrimination. The Court's focus raises other problems as well. How are we to analyze the First Amendment associational claims of an organization that invokes its right, settled by the Court in *NAACP v. Alabama* to protect the privacy of its membership? And would the Court's analysis of this case be differ-

ent if, for example, the Jaycees membership had a steady history of opposing public issues thought (by the Court) to be favored by women? It might seem easy to conclude, in the latter case, that the admission of women to the Jaycees' ranks would affect the content of the organization's message, but I do not believe that should change the outcome of this case. Whether an association is or is not constitutionally protected in the selection of its membership should not depend on what the association says or why its members say it.

The Court's readiness to inquire into the connection between membership and message reveals a more fundamental flaw in its analysis. The Court pursues this inquiry as part of its mechanical application of a "compelling interest" test, under which the Court weighs the interests of the State of Minnesota in ending gender discrimination against the Jaycees' First Amendment right of association. The Court entirely neglects to establish at the threshold that the Jaycees is an association whose activities or purposes should engage the strong protections that the First Amendment extends to expressive associations.

On the one hand, an association engaged exclusively in protected expression enjoys First Amendment protection of both the content of its message and the choice of its members. Protection of the message itself is judged by the same standards as protection of speech by an individual. Protection of the association's right to define its membership derives from the recognition that the formation of an expressive association is the creation of a voice, and the selection of members is the definition of that voice. "In the realm of protected speech, the legislature is constitutionally disqualified from dictating . . . the speakers who may address a public issue." *First National Bank of Boston v. Bellotti*. A ban on specific group voices on public affairs violates the most basic guarantee of the First Amendment—that citizens, not the government, control the content of public discussion.

On the other hand, there is only minimal constitutional protection of the freedom of *commercial* association. There are, of course, some constitutional protections of commercial speech—speech intended and used to promote a commercial transaction with the speaker. But the State is free to impose any rational regulation on the commercial transaction itself. The Constitution does not guarantee a right to choose employees, customers, suppliers, or those with whom one engages in simple commercial transactions, without restraint from the State. A shopkeeper has no constitutional right to deal only with persons of one sex.

. . .

Many associations cannot readily be described as purely expressive or purely commercial. No association is likely ever to be exclusively engaged in expressive activities, if only because it will collect dues from its members or purchase printing materials or rent lecture halls or serve coffee and cakes at its meetings. And innumerable commercial associations also engage in some incidental protected speech or advocacy. The standard for deciding just how much of an association's involvement in commercial activity is enough to suspend the association's First Amendment right to control its membership cannot, therefore, be articulated with simple precision. Clearly the standard must accept the reality that even the most expressive of associations is likely to touch, in some way or other, matters of commerce. The standard must nevertheless give substance to the ideal of complete protection for purely expressive association, even while it readily permits state regulation of commercial affairs.

In my view, an association should be characterized as commercial, and therefore subject to rationally related state regulation of its membership and other associational activities, when, and only when, the association's activities are not predominantly of the type protected by the First Amendment. It is only when the association is predominantly engaged in protected expression that state regulation of its membership will necessarily affect, change, dilute, or silence one collective voice that would otherwise be heard. An association must choose its market. Once it enters the marketplace of commerce in any substantial degree it loses the complete control over its membership that it would otherwise enjoy if it confined its affairs to the marketplace of ideas.

Determining whether an association's activity is predominantly protected expression will often be difficult, if only because a broad range of activities can be expressive. It is easy enough to identify expressive words or conduct that are strident, contentious, or divisive, but protected expression may also take the form of quiet persuasion, inculcation of traditional values, instruction of the young, and community service. The purposes of an association, and the purposes of its members in adhering to it, are doubtless relevant in determining whether the association is primarily engaged in protected expression. Lawyering to advance social goals may be speech, but ordinary commercial law practice is not. A group boycott or refusal to deal for political purposes may be speech, though a similar boycott for purposes of maintaining a cartel is not. Even the training of outdoor survival skills or participation in community service might become expressive when the activity is intended to develop good morals, reverence, patriotism, and a desire for self-improvement.

. . .

In summary, this Court's case law recognizes radically different constitutional protections for expressive and non-expressive associations. The First Amendment is offended by direct state control of the membership of a private organization engaged exclusively in protected expressive activity, but no First Amendment interest stands in the way of a State's rational regulation of economic transactions by or within a commercial association. The proper approach to analysis of First Amendment claims of associational freedom is, therefore, to distinguish non-expressive from expressive associations and to recognize that the former lack the full constitutional protections possessed by the latter.

II

Minnesota's attempt to regulate the membership of the Jaycees chapters operating in that State presents a relatively easy case for application of the expressive-commercial dichotomy. . . . Notwithstanding its protected expressive activities, the Jaycees—otherwise known as the Junior Chamber of Commerce—is, first and foremost, an organization that, at both the national and local levels, promotes and practices the art of solicitation and management. The organization claims that the training it offers its members gives them an advantage in business, and business firms do indeed sometimes pay the dues of individual memberships for their employees. Jaycees members hone their solicitation and management skills, under the direction and supervision of the organization, primarily through their active recruitment of new members. "One of the major activities of the Jaycees is the sale of memberships in the organization. It encourages continuous recruitment of members with the expressed goal of increasing membership. . . . The Jaycees itself refers to its members as customers and membership as a product it is selling. More than 80 percent of the national officers' time is dedicated to recruitment, and more than half of the available achievement awards are in part conditioned on achievement in recruitment." . . .

Recruitment and selling are commercial activities, even when conducted for training rather than for profit. The "not insubstantial" volume of protected Jaycees activity found by the Court of Appeals is simply not enough to preclude state regulation of the Jaycees' commercial activities. The State of Minnesota has a legitimate interest in ensuring nondiscriminatory access to the commercial opportunity presented by membership in the Jaycees. The members of the Jaycees may not claim constitutional immunity from Minnesota's antidiscrimination law by seeking to exercise their First Amendment rights through this commercial organization.

. . .

DER: The *Jaycees* Court properly decided that the state's interest in combating gender discrimination outweighed the Jaycees' interest in freely choosing its members. The basis for this decision, however, is troubling. The majority gives too little attention to the importance of membership selection to the associational freedoms of groups that are dedicated to pursuing expressive goals. Its reasoning depends on a dangerous judicial examination of the organization's purposes and determination of whether or not a change in membership will affect those ends. The formation of an advocacy group is the creation of a particular voice, expressed partly by its membership. The selection of members, like the wording of its political platform, helps to define its message. The First Amendment does not allow state scrutiny of a private advocacy group's membership any more than it does scrutiny of the content of its message. On the other hand, commercial entities that distribute important economic goods, services, and other advantages should not be allowed to cloak their discriminatory practices in the guise of First Amendment freedoms. The Jaycees should be compelled to admit women whether or not their inclusion would change its policies. Justice O'Connor is correct that the majority's analysis allows too much interference with the membership decisions of protected groups and too much protection for commercial organizations.

DEL: Distinguishing advocacy groups from commercial organizations seems as treacherous an exercise as distinguishing commercial speech from political expression or news from entertainment. Responding to concern that the distinction between commercial and other forms of expression may be difficult to establish, the Court observed that: "The line . . . will not always be easy to draw, . . . but that is no reason for avoiding the undertaking."[134] A similar attitude seems to inspire the Court to plunge ahead in distinguishing advocacy groups from commercial societies. It should not be surprising, therefore, when analysis leads to procrustean results. To the extent unanimity is not achieved, with respect to whether an environmental group's solicitation of donations is political or commercial,[135] dissension can be expected over how to characterize the organization itself. An alternative inquiry may be to ask simply, without classifying a group as advocacy or commercial, whether a compelling or important justification exists for curtailing associational freedom. To the extent that exclusionary policies affect a group whose equal protection interests are constitutionally significant, as measured by whether a state-imposed burden would justify a stricter standard of review, a compelling justification may exist for subordinating associational freedom regardless of how the organization is denominated. If associational freedom undermines compelling constitutional values such as nondiscrimination, it may not be unreasonable to prioritize the state interest regardless of a group's nature. To the extent that the Court is willing to balance such interests, within or beyond the confines of its advocacy-commercial distinction, associational freedom is a weakened defense against state management of priorities that otherwise would be ordered by the individual. If a racially exclusive organization committed itself to improving the material condition of traditionally disadvantaged minorities, and focused primarily upon fund-raising and distribution of monetary resources, it may not be unreasonable to argue that the organization was commercially driven. Notwithstanding the group's mission, and sense that a minorities-only policy was essential to progress, its ability to function as an agent of social change might be determined by a diluted version of associational freedom balanced against the value of color-blindness. Justice O'Connor suggests that the Court's analytical criteria understate the value of associational freedom and overstate the importance of commercial organizations. Given the various permutations of advocacy and commercial interests that may exist, and the concerns that may weigh against them, the real problem

---

[134] In re Primus, 436 U.S. 412, 438 n.32 (1978).
[135] Citizens for a Better Environment v. Schaumberg, 444 U.S. 620 (1980).

with the Court's standards is that they are a blunt instrument in circumstances when sensitivity and delicacy are imperative.

In *Hurley v. Irish-American Gay, Lesbian and Bisexual Group of Boston*,[136] a unanimous Court upheld the First Amendment right of parade organizers to exclude a group of gay, lesbian, and bisexual activists from their St. Patrick's Day parade. The South Boston Allied Veterans Council, an association of representatives of various veterans groups, was authorized by the City of Boston to organize the St. Patrick's Day-Evacuation Day Parade. GLIB filed an action alleging that the Council's refusal to allow GLIB to participate in the 1993 parade violated state law prohibiting discrimination in public accommodations on account of sexual orientation. The Council argued that its exclusion of groups with sexual themes reflected the parade's expression of traditional religious and social values.

The trial court ordered the Council to include GLIB in the St. Patrick's Day parade, finding that the parade had no common theme other than the public involvement of the participants. Given the Council's lack of selectivity in choosing parade participants (including the Ku Klux Klan and an antibusing group), the court reasoned, the parade lacked any expressive purpose. The Massachusetts Supreme Judicial Court affirmed.

The Supreme Court held that the state court's application of the state public accommodations law to require private citizens to include in their parade a group imparting a message the organizers opposed violated the First Amendment. In an opinion written by Justice Souter, the Court conducted its own examination of the Council's activity to determine whether it consititited expressive conduct. The Court noted that parades are a form of protected expression because they include marchers who are making a collective point through symbolic acts, as well as banners and songs. The Constitution's protection of this expressive activity was not forfeited by the organizers' inclusion of multifarious voices. GLIB's desired participation was equally expressive, since the organization was formed to celebrate its members' sexual identities and to express solidarity with like individuals who sought to march in New York's St. Patrick's Day parade. The Council had disclaimed any intent to exclude homosexuals or bisexuals from parading as members of any of the approved groups.

The Court concluded:

> Since every participating unit affects the message conveyed, by the private organizers, the state courts' application of the [Massachusetts public accommodations] statute produced an order essentially requiring petitioners to alter the expressive content of their parade. Although the state courts spoke of the parade as a place of public accommodation, once the expressive character of both the parade and the marching GLIB contingent is understood, it becomes apparent that the state courts' application of the statue had the effect of declaring the sponsors' speech itself to be the public accommodation. Under this approach, any contingent of protected individuals with a message would have the right to participate in petitioners' speech, so that the communicaiton produced by the private organizers would be shaped by all those protected by law who wished to join in with some expressive demonstration of their own. But this use of the State's power violated the fundamental rule of protection under the First Amendment that a speaker has autonomy to choose the content of his own message. . . .

---

[136] _____ U.S._____, 115 S. Ct. 2338 (1995).

Petitioners' claim to the benefit of this principle of autonomy to control one's own speech is as sound as the South Boston parade is expressive. Rather like a composer, the Council selects the expressive units of the parade from potential participants and though the score may not produce a particularized message, each contingent's expression in the Council's eyes comports with what merits celebration on that day.

The Court distinguished *New York State Club Association* and *Roberts* on the ground that, in those cases, compelled access to the organization's benefits, which was upheld, did not trespass on the organization's message itself: "Assuming the parade to be large enough and a source of benefits (apart from its expression) that would generally justify a mandated access provision, GLIB could nonetheless be refused admission as an expressive contingent with its own message just as readily as a private club could exclude an applicant whose manifest views were at odds with a position taken by the club's existing members."

B. Freedom of the Press

As a formal guarantee of editorial freedom, the press clause emerged against a backdrop of suppressive methodologies dating back to the advent of print technology in the sixteenth century. Unlike the unamplified spoken word, publication introduced new dimensions to communication including the potential for reaching and influencing a broader audience and the permanent recording of thoughts and ideas. Initial official reaction to methods of mass dissemination of information reflected a concern with their potentially destabilizing consequences for authoritarian regimes premised upon notions of divine revelation. Control in England was achieved by licensing requirements, which enabled the Crown to hand-pick and limit the number of printers.[137] Even after licensing's abandonment in 1694, publication was subject to criminal sanctions pursuant to the law of seditious libel. Merely upon proof of publication, and regardless of truth, criticism of government was subject to criminal sanction.[138]

Although systems of prior restraint were not a significant aspect of the colonial American culture, the law of seditious libel was a prominent method of control prior to and even after ratification of the First Amendment. Popular resentment of Crown policies toward the colonies was a significant factor in the evolution of press liberty.[139] A notable waystation in the march toward broader press freedom was the trial of John Peter Zenger.[140] As the printer of tracts criticizing the royal governor of New York, Zenger was charged with seditious libel. The trial court's rejection of arguments, that truth should be a defense to libel, preordained a finding of guilt based simply upon publication. Notwithstanding the absence of a legal defense, the jury ignored formal law and acquitted Zenger. Even if emblemizing values central to the First Amendment's eventual inspiration, the Zenger verdict was rendered against a contextual norm of suppression. Abridgment of press liberty persisted not only as a function of Crown policies but of colonial legislatures which responded to published criticism with such methods as contempt.[141]

Colonial circumstances begetting the American Revolution enhanced political in-

---

[137] Leonard W. Levy, Legacy of Suppression 8–17 (1960).

[138] *Id.* at 9–13.

[139] *Id.* at 18–175.

[140] IV William Blackstone, Commentaries on the Laws of England 151–52 (1765–69).

[141] Leonard W. Levy, Legacy of Suppression at 3.

terest in a system of press freedom. The revolutionary press performed a critical function in propagandizing and galvanizing anti-colonialist fervor.[142] The revolution, however, also previewed cultural perils to press liberty. Publishers with Tory sympathies, during the war itself, became victims of mobs who smashed printing presses or engaged in other acts of intimidation.[143] The First Amendment textually enshrined press freedom as a constitutional liberty but did not extinguish intolerance. Less than a decade after ratification, the Sedition Act was enacted as a means for President Adams and a Federalist-dominated Congress to silence their Jeffersonian rivals. The law prohibited "publishing any false, scandalous and malicious writing or writings against the government of the United States, or either house of Congress . . . or the President . . . with intent to defame . . . or to bring them . . . into contempt or disrepute."[144] Although the Sedition Act was repealed after the election of President Jefferson, who pardoned those who had been convicted under the law, it never was challenged in court. As the Supreme Court eventually observed, "the attack upon its validity has carried the day in the court of history, . . . [and its unconstitutionality] has also been assumed by Justices of this Court."[145]

Notwithstanding a "broad consensus that the [Sedition] Act, because of the restraint it imposed upon criticism of government and public officials, was inconsistent with the First Amendment,"[146] history discloses a persisting tradition of political suppression. Jeffersonians who were the target of a suppressive regime themselves proved selective in their fidelity to editorial liberty.[147] During the 1830s, the abolitionist movement effectively was put out of business in southern states that enacted laws prohibiting distribution of anti-slavery literature.[148] In the twentieth century, publications critical of American participation in World War I or advocating radical political change generated prosecutions under federal espionage and state sedition laws.[149] The evolution of free speech principles, including clear and present danger criteria for inciteful speech[150] and the actual malice standard for defamation actions by public officials and figures,[151] have enhanced the press's security in criticizing government. The constitutional legacy of the press clause, beyond its textual existence, comprehends only several decades. Not until 1931 was the press clause incorporated through the Fourteenth Amendment.[152] Since then, case law has expanded at a seemingly exponential rate.

1. Defining the Press

On its face, the freedom of the press clause presents two key terms needing definition. The "freedom" of the press has been the subject of interpretation that has begotten

---

[142] The Zenger trial and its consequences are recounted in JONATHAN W. EMORD, FREEDOM, TECHNOLOGY AND THE FIRST AMENDMENT 55–62 (1991); JETHRO LIEBERMAN, FREE SPEECH, FREE PRESS 62–88 (1985).

[143] Harold L. Nelson, *Seditious Libel in Colonial America*, 3 AM. J. LEG. HIST. 160, 164 (1959).

[144] 2 Stat. at Large 596 (1798).

[145] New York Times Co. v. Sullivan, 376 U.S. 254, 276 (1964).

[146] *Id.*

[147] LEONARD W. LEVY, JEFFERSON AND CIVIL LIBERTIES: THE DARKER SIDE 58–66 (1963).

[148] DONALD E. LIVELY, THE CONSTITUTION AND RACE 13 (1992).

[149] *E.g.*, Whitney v. California, 274 U.S. 357 (1927) (upholding conviction under state criminal syndicalism law against First Amendment challenge); Schenck v. United States, 249 U.S. 47 (1919) (upholding conviction under Espionage Act against First Amendment challenge).

[150] Brandenburg v. Ohio, 395 U.S. 444 (1969).

[151] Gertz v. Robert Welch, Inc., 418 U.S. 323 (1974) (adopting actual malice standard for defamation claims of public figures); New York Times Co. v. Sullivan, 376 U.S. 254 (1965) (adopting actual malice standard for defamation claims of public officials).

[152] Near v. Minnesota, 283 U.S. 697 (1931).

an extensive body of law delineating the contours and conditions of liberty. Although an understanding of what "the press" comprehends may be crucial for purposes of determining who may claim protection under the press clause, the term remains largely unclarified. How the press is characterized has significance for purposes of determining whether it has a special role distinct from speech. In propounding an institutional definition of the press, Justice Stewart suggested that the speech and press clauses were not redundancies, but have a special role distinct from speech.

Potter Stewart, *"Or of the Press"*
26 Hastings Law Journal 631 (1975)

. . .

It seems to me that the Court's approach to all these cases has uniformly reflected its understanding that the Free Press guarantee is, in essence, a *structural* provision of the Constitution. Most of the other provisions in the Bill of Rights protect specific liberties or specific rights of individuals: freedom of speech, freedom of worship, the right to counsel, the privilege against compulsory self-incrimination, to name a few. In contrast, the Free Press Clause extends protection to an institution. The publishing business is, in short, the only organized private business that is given explicit constitutional protection.

This basic understanding is essential, I think, to avoid an elementary error of constitutional law. It is tempting to suggest that freedom of the press means only that newspaper publishers are guaranteed that freedom, to be sure, but so are we all, because of the Free Speech Clause. If the Free Press guarantee meant no more than freedom of expression, it would be a constitutional redundancy. Between 1776 and the drafting of our constitution, many of the state constitutions contained clauses protecting freedom of the press while at the same time recognizing no general freedom of speech. By including both guarantees in the First Amendment, the Founders quite clearly recognized the distinction between the two.

. . .

Competing against Stewart's emphasis upon structure is a functional definition of the press advanced by Chief Justice Burger.

First National Bank of Boston v. Bellotti
435 U.S. 765 (1978)

Mr. Chief Justice Burger, concurring.

. . .

[T]hose who view the Press Clause as somehow conferring special and extraordinary privileges or status on the "institutional press"—which are not extended to those who wish to express ideas other than by publishing a newspaper—might perceive no danger to institutional media corporations flowing from [such an understanding]. Under this narrow reading of the Press Clause, government could perhaps impose on nonmedia corporations restrictions not permissible with respect to "media" enterprises. The Court has not yet squarely resolved whether the Press Clause confers upon the "institutional press" any freedom from government restraint not enjoyed by all others.

I perceive two fundamental difficulties with a narrow reading of the Press Clause. First, although certainty on this point is not possible, the history of the Clause does not suggest that the authors contemplated a "special" or "institutional" privilege. The common 18th century understanding of freedom of the press is suggested by Andrew Bradford, a colonial American newspaperman. In defining the nature of the liberty, he did not limit it to a particular group:

"But, by the *Freedom of the Press*, I mean a Liberty, within the Bounds of Law, for any Man to communicate to the Public, his Sentiments on the Important Points of *Religion and Government;* of proposing any

Laws, which he apprehends may be for the Good of his Country, and of applying for the Repeal of such, as he Judges pernicious. . . .

"This is the *Liberty of the Press*, the great *Palladium* of all our other *Liberties*, which I hope the good People of this Province, will forever enjoy. . . ."

Indeed most pre-First Amendment commentators "who employed the term 'freedom of speech' with great frequency, used it synonymously with freedom of the press."

Those interpreting the Press Clause as extending protection only to, or creating a special role for, the "institutional press" must either (a) assert such an intention on the part of the Framers for which no supporting evidence is available; (b) argue that events after 1791 somehow operated to "constitutionalize" this interpretation; or (c) candidly acknowledging the absence of historical support, suggest that the intent of the Framers is not important today.

To conclude that the Framers did not intend to limit the freedom of the press to one select group is not necessarily to suggest that the Press Clause is redundant. The Speech Clause standing alone may be viewed as a protection of the liberty to express ideas and beliefs, while the Press Clause focuses specifically on the liberty to disseminate expression broadly and "comprehends every sort of publication which affords a vehicle of information and opinion." Yet there is no fundamental distinction between expression and dissemination. The liberty encompassed by the Press Clause, although complementary to and a natural extension of Speech Clause liberty, merited special mention simply because it had been more often the object of official restraints. Soon after the invention of the printing press, English and continental monarchs, fearful of the power implicit in its use and the threat to Establishment thought and order—political and religious—devised restraints, such as licensing, censors, indices of prohibited books, and prosecutions for seditious libel, which generally were unknown in the pre-printing press era. Official restrictions were the official response to the new, disquieting idea that this invention would provide a means for mass communication.

The second fundamental difficulty with interpreting the Press Clause as conferring special status on a limited group is one of definition. The very task of including some entities within the "institutional press" while excluding others, whether undertaken by legislature, court, or administrative agency, is reminiscent of the abhorred licensing system of Tudor and Stuart England—a system the First Amendment was intended to ban from this country. Further, the officials undertaking that task would be required to distinguish the protected from the unprotected on the basis of such variables as content of expression, frequency or fervor of expression, or ownership of the technological means of dissemination. Yet nothing in this Court's opinions supports such a confining approach to the scope of Press Clause protection. Indeed, the Court has plainly intimated the contrary view:

"Freedom of the press is a 'fundamental personal right' which 'is not confined to newspapers and periodicals. It necessarily embraces pamphlets and leaflets. . . . The press in its historic connotation comprehends every sort of publication which affords a vehicle of information and opinion.' . . . The informative function asserted by representatives of the organized press . . . is also performed by lecturers, political pollsters, novelists, academic researchers, and dramatists. Almost any author may quite accurately assert that he is contributing to the flow of information to the public. . . . "

Because the First Amendment was meant to guarantee freedom to express and communicate ideas, I can see no difference between the right of those who seek to disseminate ideas by way of a newspaper and those who give lectures or speeches and seek to enlarge the audience by publication and wide dissemination. "[T]he purpose of the Constitution was not to erect the press into a privileged institution but to protect all persons in their right to print what they will as well as to utter it. ' . . . [T]he liberty of the press is no greater and no less . . .' than the liberty of every citizen of the Republic."

In short, the First Amendment does not "belong" to any definable category of persons or entities: It belongs to all who exercise its freedoms.

Instead of choosing between structural and functional definitions, some have suggested that both models are relevant depending upon circumstance. When the press is engaged in mere expression, Justice Brennan has suggested that traditional freedom of speech principles should operate. To the extent it is performing tasks, such as gathering or disseminating information, he has urged an institutional understanding.

William J. Brennan, Jr., *Address*
32 Rutgers Law Review 173 (1979)[153]

. . .

Under one model—which I call the "speech" model—the press requires and is accorded the absolute protection of the First Amendment. In the other model—I call it the "structural" model—the press interests may conflict with other societal interests and adjustment of the conflict on occasion favors the competing claim.

The "speech" model is familiar. It is as comfortable as a pair of old shoes, and the press, in its present conflict with the Court, most often slips into the language and rhetorical stance with which this model is associated even when only the "structural" model is at issue. According to this traditional "speech" model, the primary purpose of the First Amendment is more of less absolutely to prohibit any interference with freedom of expression. The press is seen as the public spokesman *par excellence*. Indeed, this model sometimes depicts the press as simply a collection of individuals who wish to speak out and broadly disseminate their views. This model draws its considerable power—I emphasize—from the abiding commitment we all feel to the right of self-expression, and, so far as it goes, this model commands the widest consensus. In the past two years, for example, the Court has twice unanimously struck down state statutes which prohibited the press from speaking out on certain subjects, and the Court has firmly rejected judicial attempts to muzzle press publication through prior restraints. The "speech" model thus readily lends itself to the heady rhetoric of absolutism.

The "speech" model, however, has its limitations. It is a mistake to suppose that the First Amendment protects *only* self-expression, only the right to speak out. I believe that the First Amendment in addition fosters the values of democratic self-government. In the words of Professor Zechariah Chafee, "[t]he First Amendment protects . . . a social interest in the attainment of truth, so that the country may not only adopt the wisest course of action but carry it out in the wisest way." The Amendment therefore also forbids the government from interfering with the communicative processes through which we citizens exercise and prepare to exercise our rights of self-government. The individual right to speak out, even millions of such rights aggregated together, will not sufficiently protect these social interests. It is in recognition of this fact that the Court has referred to "the circulation of information to which *the public is entitled* in virtue of the constitutional guaranties."

Another way of saying this is that the First Amendment protects the structure of communications necessary for the existence of our democracy. This insight suggest the second model to describe the role of the press in our society. This second model is structural in nature. It focuses on the relationship of the press to the communicative functions required by our democratic beliefs. To the extent the press makes these functions possible, this model requires that it receive the protection of the First Amendment. A good example is the press' role in providing and circulating the information necessary for informed public discussion. To the extent the press, or, for that matter, to the extent that any institution uniquely performs this role, it should receive unique First Amendment protection.

---

[153] Reprinted with permission of Rutgers Law Review.

Regardless of how the press is defined, exclusion from its ambit has profound consequences for a medium. Common carriers, such as telephone and telegraph companies, historically have been denied First Amendment status and thus subjected to nondiscriminatory access requirements.[154] Motion pictures, until the middle of the twentieth century, were regarded as "a business, pure and simple . . . not to be regarded . . . as part of the press."[155] Without constitutional status for the medium, government had a free hand to regulate. Censorship boards functioned minus the First Amendment's

---

[154] Federal Communications Commission v. Midwest Video Corp., 440 U.S. 689, 700–02 (1979).

[155] Mutual Film Corp. v. State Industrial Commission of Ohio, 236 U.S. 230, 244 (1915), overruled, Joseph Burstyn, Inc. v. Wilson, 343 U.S. 495 (1951).

instruction and routinely subjected motion pictures to a panoply of restraints and conditions.

United Artists Corp. v. Board of Censors of City of Memphis
225 S.W.2d 550 (Tenn. 1949)

. . .

NEIL, CHIEF JUSTICE.

This case involves the validity of the Private Acts creating the Board of Censors of the City of Memphis, and also of Shelby County. For a clear understanding of the questions raised in the numerous assignments of error, it is necessary that we give a summary of the facts which gave rise to the proceedings in the circuit court in which petitioners sought a review of the official acts of the Board of Censors in writing a letter to one of the petitioners (United Artists Corporation) "that it was unable to approve" a certain motion-talking picture for exhibition in the City of Memphis. For convenience we will refer to the parties as they appeared in the trial court. The picture which is the subject of the present controversy, entitled "Curley," was produced by Hal Roach Studios,, Inc. in the State of California and supposed to be distributed exclusively by United Artists Corporation to exhibitors in Tennessee. Both petitioners are foreign corporations.

. . .

The Board of Censors, following a private exhibition of the picture, wrote the following letter to the United Artists:

> "Commission Government
> "Memphis, Tenn.
> "August 9 1947
> "United Artists Corporation
> "St. Louis, Missouri
> "Gentlemen:
> "The Memphis Board of Censors passes 'The Maurauders' and the Beebe Daniels Picture, but I am sorry to have to inform you that it is unable to approve your 'Curley' picture with the little Negroes as the south does not permit Negroes in white school nor recognize social equality between the races even in children.
> "Yours truly
> "/s/Lloyd T. Binford Chairman"

Upon the receipt of this letter the petitioners filed a joint petition in the circuit court seeking a review of the action of the Board of Censors. The petition alleged that the Board had banned the picture without legal authority, (1) that the Private Acts under which it acted were unconstitutional in that they denied to petitioner the right of freedom of speech and due process, (2) that it acted "solely on the ground that members of the colored race appear therein," (3) that in refusing to approve the picture for exhibition it was not supported by any fact and was "illegal, capricious and arbitrary," and "contravenes any authority purportedly delegated to or vested in said Boards," and hence was in derogation of the "due process," and "equal protection of the laws," as guaranteed by the constitution of Tennessee and of the United States.

. . .

. . . It clearly appears from the averments of the petition that before any contract is made between the distributor and any picture that it is first shown to the Board of Censors for their approval or disapproval. This was done in the instant case.

. . .

Able counsel for the appellants have cited many cases in which the courts have dealt with the propositions relating to freedom of speech and of the press. We are in no wise in disagreement with the appellants as to the fundamental principles announced in these decisions, and especially with the insistence that there is no authority in the law "To use race or color as the sole legal basis for censorship of talking-motion pictures." The trial judge pretermitted consideration of the constitutional guarantee of free speech because in his opinion the statutes and ordinances assailed by the appellants did not apply to them in that they were not exhibitors, and furthermore the letter of the Board to United Artists was only advisory and was coram non judice.

We think the constitutionality of these statutes and ordinances cannot be questioned on the grounds of their abridgement of the right of "freedom of speech" except by someone who has the right to speak and is denied the privilege of speaking. The gist of the present action is that the statutes and ordinances herein assailed constitute an abridgement not of their right to speak but of the right of third persons to speak and who are not parties to this cause. In the instant case no exhibitors of moving pictures in Memphis, to whom these ordinances and statutes apply are claiming that they are denied "freedom of speech" or the right to contract with the petitioners.

. . .

How the press is conceptualized also determines whether its constitutional protection will be coextensive with or more extensive than First Amendment guarantees for speech. An institutional definition is friendlier toward development of special rights and immunities in deference to and accommodation of the press' newsgathering function, at least to the extent that role is essential to informing the public. Insofar as a functional definition is subscribed to, the press clause is unlikely to provide protection beyond what accrues to individuals under the speech clause. Although the Court has never formally defined what constitutes the press, case law largely has rejected the premise that media have a higher order of First Amendment liberty or rights. It has acknowledged that the newsgathering process merits constitutional protection, but generally declined the invitation to establish a discrete set of rights or freedoms that would enable the press to immunize itself from demands of the criminal justice system or to have special access to government information, proceedings or facilities. An early casualty of doctrine that has rejected a privileged press status was the proposition that the First Amendment shields reporters from disclosing their sources to grand juries.

2. A First Amendment Privilege?

Branzburg v. Hayes
408 U.S. 665 (1972)

Opinion of the Court by MR. JUSTICE WHITE, announced by the CHIEF JUSTICE.

. . .

The sole issue before us is the obligation of reporters to respond to grand jury subpoenas as other citizens do and to answer questions relevant to an investigation into the commission of crime. Citizens generally are not constitutionally immune from grand jury subpoenas; and neither the First Amendment nor any other constitutional provision protects the average citizen from disclosing to a grand jury information that he has received in confidence. The claim is, however, that reporters are exempt from these obligations because if forced to respond to subpoenas and identify their sources or disclose other confidences, their informants will refuse to be reluctant to furnish newsworthy information in the future. This asserted burden on news gathering is said to make compelled testimony from newsmen constitutionally suspect and to require a privileged position for them. . . .

. . .

. . . Until now the only testimonial privilege for unofficial witnesses that is rooted in the Federal Constitution is the Fifth Amendment privilege against compelled self-incrimination. We are asked to create another by interpreting the First Amendment to grant newsmen a testimonial privilege that other citizens do not

enjoy. This we decline to do. Fair and effective law enforcement aimed at providing security for the person and property of the individual is a fundamental function of government, and the grand jury plays an important, constitutionally mandated role in this process. On the records now before us, we perceived no basis for holding that the public interest in law enforcement and in ensuring effective grand jury proceedings is insufficient to override the consequential, but uncertain, burden on news gathering that is said to result from insisting that reporters, like other citizens, respond to relevant questions put to them in the course of a valid grand jury investigation or criminal trial.

This conclusion itself involves no restraint on what newspapers may publish or on the type or quality of information reporters may seek to acquire, nor does it threaten the vast bulk of confidential relationships between reporters and their sources. Grand juries address themselves to the issues of whether crimes have been committed and who committed them. Only where news sources themselves are implicated in crime or possess information relevant to the grand jury's task need they or the reporter be concerned about grand jury subpoenas. Nothing before us indicates that a large number or percentage of *all* confidential news sources falls into either category and would in any way be deterred by our holding that the Constitution does not, as it never has, exempt the newsman from performing the citizen's normal duty of appearing and furnishing information relevant to the grand jury's task.

. . .

. . . [W]e cannot seriously entertain the notion that the First Amendment protects a newsman's agreement to conceal the criminal conduct of his source, or evidence thereof, on the theory that it is better to write about crime than to do something about it. Insofar as any reporter in these cases undertook not to reveal or testify about the crime he witnessed, his claim of privilege under the First Amendment presents no substantial question. The crimes of news sources are no less reprehensible and threatening to the public interest when witnessed by a reporter than when they are not.

There remain those situations where a source is not engaged in criminal conduct but has information suggesting illegal conduct by others. Newsmen frequently receive information from such sources pursuant to a tacit or express agreement to withhold the source's name and suppress any information that the source wishes not published. Such informants presumably desire anonymity in order to avoid being entangled as a witness in a criminal trial or grand jury investigation. They may fear that disclosure will threaten their job security or personal safety or that it will simply result in dishonor or embarrassment.

The argument that the flow of news will be diminished by compelling reporters to aid the grand jury in a criminal investigation is not irrational, nor are the records before us silent on the matter. But we remain unclear how often and to what extent informers are actually deterred from furnishing information when newsmen are forced to testify before a grand jury. The available data indicate that some newsmen rely a great deal on confidential sources and that some informants are particularly sensitive to the threat of exposure and may be silenced if it is held by this Court that, ordinarily, newsmen must testify pursuant to subpoenas, but the evidence fails to demonstrate that there would be a significant constriction of the flow of news to the public if this Court reaffirms the prior common-law and constitutional rule regarding the testimonial obligations of newsmen. Estimates of the inhibiting effect of such subpoenas on the willingness of informants to make disclosures to newsmen are widely divergent and to a great extent speculative. It would be difficult to canvass the views of the informants themselves; surveys of reporters on this topic are chiefly opinions of predicted informant behavior and must be viewed in the light of the professional self-interest of the interviewees. Reliance by the press on confidential informants does not mean that all such sources will in fact dry up because of the later possible appearance of the newsman before a grand jury. The reporter may never be called and if he objects to testifying, the prosecution may not insist. Also, the relationship of many informants to the press is a symbiotic one which is unlikely to be greatly inhibited by the threat of subpoena: quite often, such informants are members of a minority political or cultural group that relies heavily on the media to propagate its views, publicize its aims, and magnify its exposure to the public. Moreover, grand juries characteristically conduct secret proceedings, and law enforcement officers are themselves experienced in dealing with informers, and have their own methods for protecting them without interference with the effective administration of justice. There is little before us indicating that informants whose interest in avoiding exposure is that it may threaten job security, personal safety, or peace of mind, would in fact be in a worse position, or would think they would be, if they risked placing their trust in public officials as well as reporters. We doubt if the informer who prefers anonymity but is sincerely interested in furnishing evidence of crime will always or very often be deterred by the prospect of dealing with these public authorities characteristically charged with the duty to protect the public interest as well as his.

Accepting the fact, however, that an undetermined number of informants not themselves implicated in crime will nevertheless, for whatever reason, refuse to talk to newsmen if they fear identification by a reporter in an official investigation, we cannot accept the argument that the public interest in possible future news about crime from undisclosed, unverified sources must take precedence over the public interest in pursuing and prosecuting those crimes reported to the press by informants and in thus deterring the commission of such crimes in the future. . . .

We are admonished that refusal to provide a First Amendment reporter's privilege will undermine the freedom of the press to collect and disseminate news. But this is not the lesson history teaches us. As noted previously, the common law recognized no such privilege, and the constitutional argument was not even asserted until 1958. From the beginning of our country the press has operated without constitutional protection for press informants, and the press has flourished. The existing constitutional rules have not been a serious obstacle to either the development or retention of confidential news sources by the press.

. . .

At the federal level, Congress has freedom to determine whether a statutory newsman's privilege is necessary and desirable and to fashion standards and rules as narrow or broad as deemed necessary to deal with the evil discerned and, equally important, to refashion those rules as experience from time to time may dictate. There is also merit in leaving state legislatures free, within First Amendment limits, to fashion their own standards in light of the conditions and problems with respect to the relations between law enforcement officials and press in their own areas. It does without saying, of course, that we are powerless to bar state courts from responding in their own way and construing their own constitutions so as to recognize a newsman's privilege, either qualified or absolute.

In addition, there is much force in the pragmatic view that the press has at its disposal powerful mechanisms of communication and is far from helpless to protect itself from harassment or substantial harm. Furthermore, if what the newsmen urged in these cases is true—that law enforcement cannot hope to gain and may suffer from subpoenaing newsmen before grand juries—prosecutors will be loath to risk so much for so little. . . .

Finally, as we have earlier indicated, news gathering is not without its First Amendment protections, and grand jury investigations if instituted or conducted other than in good faith, would pose wholly different issues for resolution under the First Amendment. Official harassment of the press undertaken not for purposes of law enforcement but to disrupt a reporter's relationship with his news sources would have no justification. Grand juries are subject to judicial control and subpoenas to motions to quash. We do not expect courts will forget that grand juries must operate within the limits of the First Amendment as well as the Fifth.

. . .

Mr. Justice Powell, concurring.

I add this brief statement to emphasize what seems to me to be the limited nature of the Court's holding. The Court does not hold that newsmen, subpoenaed to testify before a grand jury, are without constitutional rights with respect to the gathering of news or in safeguarding their sources. Certainly, we do not hold, as suggested in Mr. Justice Stewart's dissenting opinion, that state and federal authorities are free to "annex" the news media as "an investigative arm of government." The solicitude repeatedly shown by this Court for First Amendment freedoms should be sufficient assurance against any such effort, even if one seriously believed that the media—properly free and untrammeled in the fullest sense of these terms—were not able to protect themselves.

As indicated in the concluding portion of the opinion, the Court states that no harassment of newsmen will be tolerated. If a newsman believe that the grand jury investigation is not being conducted in good faith he is not without remedy. Indeed, if the newsman is called upon to give information bearing only a remote and tenuous relationship to the subject of the investigation, or if he has some other reason to believe that his testimony implicates confidential source relationships without a legitimate need of law enforcement, he will have access to the court on a motion to quash and an appropriate protective order may be entered. The asserted claim to privilege should be judged on its facts by the striking of a proper balance between freedom of the press and the obligation of all citizens to give relevant testimony with respect to criminal conduct. The balance of these vital constitutional and societal interests on a case-by-case basis accords with the tried and traditional way of adjudicating such questions.

In short, the courts will be available to newsmen under circumstances where legitimate First Amendment interests require protection. Mr. Justice Douglas, dissenting in No. 70–57, *United States v. Caldwell.*

Today's decision will impede the wide-open and robust dissemination of ideas and counter-thought which a free press both fosters and protects and which is essential to the success of intelligent self-government. Forcing a reporter before a grand jury will have two retarding effects upon the ear and the pen of the press. Fear of exposure will cause dissidents to communicate less openly to trusted reporters. And, fear of accountability will cause editors and critics to write with more restrained pens.

. . .

I see no way of making mandatory the disclosure of a reporter's confidential source of the information on which he bases his news story.

The press has a preferred position in our constitutional scheme, not to enable it to make money, not to set newsmen apart as a favored class, but to bring fulfillment to the public's right to know. The right to know is crucial to the governing powers of the people, to paraphrase Alexander Meiklejohn. Knowledge is essential to informed decisions.

. . .

A reporter is not better than his source of information. Unless he has a privilege to withhold the identity of his source, he will be the victim of governmental intrigue or aggression. If he can be summoned to testify in secret before a grand jury, his sources will dry up and the attempted exposure, the effort to enlighten the public, will be ended. If what the Court sanctions today becomes settled law, then the reporter's main function in American society will be to pass on to the public the press releases which the various departments of government issue.

. . .

The intrusion of government into this domain is symptomatic of the disease of this society. As the years pass the power of government becomes more and more pervasive. It is a power to suffocate both people and causes. Those in power, whatever their politics, want only to perpetuate it. Now that the fences of the law and the tradition that has protected the press are broken down, the people are the victims. The First Amendment, as I read it, was designed precisely to prevent that tragedy.

MR. JUSTICE STEWART, with whom MR. JUSTICE BRENNAN and MR. JUSTICE MARSHALL join, dissenting.

The Court's crabbed view of the First Amendment reflects a disturbing insensitivity to the critical role of an independent press in our society. The question whether a reporter has a constitutional right to a confidential relationship with his source is of first impression here, but the principles that should guide our decision are as basic as any to be found in the Constitution. While Mr. Justice Powell's enigmatic concurring opinion gives some hope of a more flexible view in the future, the Court in these cases holds that a newsman has no First Amendment right to protect his sources when called before a grand jury. The Court thus invites state and federal authorities to undermine the historic independence of the press by attempting to annex the journalistic profession as an investigative arm of government. Not only will this decision impair performance of the press' constitutionally protected functions, but it will, I am convinced, in the long run harm rather than help the administration of justice.

I respectfully dissent. . . .

A corollary to the right to publish must be the right to gather news. . . .

The right to gather news implies, in turn, a right to a confidential relationship between a reporter and his source. This proposition follows as a matter of simple logic once three factual predicates are recognized: (1) newsmen require informants to gather news; (2) confidentiality—the promise or understanding that

names or certain aspects of communications will be kept off the record—is essential to the creation and maintenance of a news-gathering relationship with informants; and (3) an unbridled subpoena power—the absence of a constitutional right protecting, in *any* way, a confidential relationship from compulsory process—will either deter sources from divulging information or deter reporters from gathering and publishing information.

It is obvious that informants are necessary to the news-gathering process as we know it today. If it is to perform its constitutional mission, the press must do far more than merely print public statements or publish prepared handouts. Familiarity with the people and circumstances involved in the myriad background activities that result in the final product called "news" is vital to complete and responsible journalism, unless the press is to be a captive mouthpiece of "newsmakers."

It is equally obvious that the promise of confidentiality may be a necessary prerequisite to a productive relationship between a newsman and his informants. An officeholder may fear his superior; a member of the bureaucracy, his associates; a dissenter, the scorn of majority opinion. All may have information valuable to the public discourse, yet each may be willing to relate that information only in confidence to a reporter whom he trusts, either because of excessive caution or because of a reasonable fear of reprisals or censure for unorthodox views. The First Amendment concern must not be with the motives of any particular news source, but rather with the conditions in which informants of all shades of the spectrum may make information available through the press to the public.

Finally, and most important, when governmental officials possess an unchecked power to compel newsmen to disclose information received in confidence, sources will clearly be deterred from giving information, and reporters will clearly be deterred from publishing it, because uncertainty about exercise of the power will lead to "self-censorship." The uncertainty arises, of course, because the judiciary has traditionally imposed virtually no limitations on the grand jury's broad investigatory powers.

The *Branzburg* decision is a source of mixed constitutional signals. Justice Powell's assertion that a grand jury subpoena should be assessed against standards of good faith, relevance and need—when combined with the position of the four dissenters—provides the basis for an argument that a qualified privilege exists. Some courts have used such arithmetic in determining that the First Amendment protects reporters from compelled disclosure of sources.[156] In the civil context, discovery against media parties has been conditioned upon showings of relevance and need pursuant to the sense that less weighty interests are at stake.[157]

3.   First Amendment Immunity from Searches and Seizures?

Arguments referenced to the media's function as a proxy for the public and the potential chilling of sources fared no better in the context of searches and seizures than it did with respect to the grand jury process. Apart from noting that search warrant standards must be especially exacting when First Amendment interests at stake, the Court in *Zurcher v. Standard Daily* determined that the press was not to receive special immunity from police searches and seizures.

---

[156] *E.g.,* Silkwood v. Kerr-McGee Corp., 563 F.2d 433, 437 (10th Cir. 1977).

[157] *E.g.*, Baker v. F&F Investment, 470 F.2d 778 (2d Cir. 1972), cert. denied, 411 U.S. 966 (1973).

Zurcher v. Stanford Daily
436 U.S. 547 (1979)

MR. JUSTICE WHITE delivered the opinion of the Court.

Late in the day of Friday, April 9, 1971, officers of the Palo Alto Police Department and of the Santa Clara County Sheriff's Department responded to a call from the director of the Stanford University Hospital requesting the removal of a large group of demonstrators who had seized the hospital's administrative offices and occupied them since the previous afternoon. After several futile efforts to persuade the demonstrators to leave peacefully, more drastic measures were employed. The demonstrators had barricaded the doors at both ends of a hall adjacent to the administrative offices. The police chose to force their way in at the west end of the corridor. As they did so, a group of demonstrators emerged through the doors at the east end and, armed with sticks and clubs, attacked the group of nine police officers stationed there. One officer was knocked to the floor and struck repeatedly on the head; another suffered a broken shoulder. All nine were injured. There were no police photographers at the east doors, and many bystanders and reporters were on the west side. The officers themselves were able to identify only two of their assailants, but one of them did see at least one person photographing the assault at the east doors.

On Sunday, April 11, a special edition of the Stanford Daily (Daily), a student newspaper published at Stanford University, carried articles and photographs devoted to the hospital protest and the violent clash between demonstrators and police. The photographs carried the byline of a Daily staff member and indicated that he had been at the east end of the hospital hallway where he could have photographed the assault on the nine officers. The next day, the Santa Clara County District Attorney's Office secured a warrant from the Municipal Court for an immediate search of the Daily's offices for negatives, film, and pictures showing the events and occurrences at the hospital on the evening of April 9. The warrant issued on a finding of "just, probable and reasonable cause for believing that: Negatives and photographs and films, evidence material and relevant to the identity of the perpetrators of felonies, to wit, Battery on a Peace Officer, and Assault with Deadly Weapon, will be located [on the premises of the Daily]." The warrant affidavit contained no allegation or indication that members of the Daily staff were in any way involved in unlawful acts at the hospital.

The search pursuant to the warrant was conducted later that day by four police officers and took palace in the presence of some members of the Daily staff. The Daily's photographic laboratories, filing cabinets, desks, and wastepaper baskets were searched. Locked drawers and rooms were opened. The officers apparently had opportunity to read notes and correspondence during the search; but, contrary to claims of the staff, the officers denied that they had exceeded the limits of the warrant. They had not been advised by the staff that the areas they were searching contained confidential materials. The search revealed only the photographs that had already been published on April 11, and no materials were removed from the Daily's office.

. . .

The District Court held, and respondents assert here, that whatever may be true of third-party searches generally, where the third party is a newspaper, there are additional factors derived from the First Amendment that justify a nearly *per se* rule forbidding the search warrant and permitting only the subpoena *duces tecum*. The general submission is that searches of newspaper offices for evidence of crime reasonably believed to be on the premises will seriously threaten the ability of the press to gather, analyze, and disseminate news. This is true for several reasons: First, searches will be physically disruptive to such an extent that timely publication will be impeded. Second, confidential sources of information will dry up, and the press will also lose opportunities to cover various events because of fears of the participants that press files will be readily available to the authorities. Third, reporters will be deterred from recording and preserving their recollections for future use if such information is subject to seizure. Fourth, the processing of news and its dissemination will be chilled by the prospects that searches will disclose internal editorial deliberations. Fifth, the press will resort to self-censorship to conceal its possession of information of potential interest to the police.

It is true that the struggle from which the Fourth Amendment emerged "is largely a history of conflict between the Crown and the press," and that in issuing warrants and determining the reasonableness of a search, state and federal magistrates should be aware that "unrestricted power of search and seizure could also be an instrument for stifling liberty of expression." Where the material sought to be seized may be protected by the First Amendment, the requirements of the Fourth Amendment must be applied with "scrupulous exactitude." "A seizure reasonable as to one type of material in one setting may be unreasonable in a different setting or with respect to another kind of material." Hence, the Court invalidated a warrant authorizing the search of a private home for all books, records, and other materials relating to the Communist Party, on the ground that whether or not the warrant would have been sufficient in other contexts, it authorized the searchers to rummage among and make judgments about books and papers and was the functional equivalent of a general warrant, one of the principal targets of the Fourth Amendment. Where presumptively protected materials are sought to be seized, the warrant requirement should be administered to leave as little as possible to the discretion or whim of the officer in the field.

Similarly, where seizure is sought of allegedly obscene materials, the judgment of the arresting officer alone is insufficient to justify issuance of a search warrant or a seizure without a warrant incident to arrest. The procedure for determining probable cause must afford an opportunity for the judicial officer to "focus searchingly on the question of obscenity."

Neither the Fourth Amendment nor the cases requiring consideration of First Amendment values in issuing search warrants, however, call for imposing the regime ordered by the District Court. Aware of the long struggle between Crown and press and desiring to curb unjustified official intrusions, the Framers took the enormously important step of subjecting searches to the test of reasonableness and to the general rule requiring search warrants to be issued by neutral magistrates. They nevertheless did not forbid warrants where the press must be shown to be implicated in the offense being investigated. Further, the prior cases do no more than insist that the courts apply the warrant requirements with particular exactitude when First Amendment interests would be endangered by the search. As we see it, no more than this is required where the warrant requested is for the seizure of criminal evidence reasonably believed to be on the premises occupied by a newspaper. Properly administered, the preconditions for a warrant—probable cause, specificity with respect to the place to be searched and the things to be seized, and overall reasonableness—should afford sufficient protection against the harms that are assertedly threatened by warrants for searching newspaper offices.

There is no reason to believe, for example, that magistrates cannot guard against searches of the type, scope, and intrusiveness that would actually interfere with the timely publication of a newspaper. Nor, if the requirements of specificity and reasonableness are properly applied, policed, and observed, will there be any occasion or opportunity for officers to rummage at large in newspaper files or to intrude into or to deter normal editorial and publication decisions. The warrant issued in this case authorized nothing of this sort. Nor are we convinced, any more than we were in *Branzburg v. Hayes*, that confidential sources will disappear and that the press will suppress news because of fears of warranted searches. Whatever incremental effect there may be in this regard if search warrants, as well as subpoenas, are permissible in proper circumstances, it does not make a constitutional difference in our judgment.

The fact is that respondents and *amici* have pointed to only a very few instances in the entire United States since 1971 involving the issuance of warrants for searching newspaper premises. This reality hardly suggests abuse; and if abuse occurs, there will be time enough to deal with it. Furthermore, the press is not only an important, critical, and valuable asset to society, but it is not easily intimidated—nor should it be.

. . .

MR. JUSTICE POWELL, concurring.

I join the opinion of the Court, and I write simply to emphasize what I take to be the fundamental error of MR. JUSTICE STEWART'S dissenting opinion. As I understand that opinion, it would read into the Fourth Amendment, a new and *per se* exception, the rule that any search of an entity protected by the Press Clause of the First Amendment is unreasonable so long as a subpoena could be used as a substitute procedure. Even aside from the difficulties involved in deciding on a case-by-case basis whether a subpoena can serve as an adequate substitute, I agree with the Court that there is no constitutional basis for such a reading.

If the Framers had believed that the press was entitled to a special procedure, not available to others, when government authorities required evidence in its possession, one would have expected the terms of the Fourth Amendment to reflect that belief. . . .

This is not to say that a warrant which would be sufficient to support the search of an apartment or an automobile necessarily would be reasonable in supporting the search of a newspaper office. As the Court's opinion makes clear, the magistrate must judge the reasonableness of every warrant in light of the circumstances of the particular case, carefully considering the description of the evidence sought, the situation of the premises, and the position and interests of the owner or occupant. While there is no justification for the establishment of a separate Fourth Amendment procedure for the press, a magistrate asked to issue a warrant for the search of press offices can and should take cognizance of the independent values protected by the First Amendment—such as those highlighted by MR. JUSTICE STEWART—when he weighs such factors. If the reasonableness and particularity requirements are thus applied, the dangers are likely to be minimal.

In any event, considerations such as these are the province of the Fourth Amendment. There is no authority either in history or in the Constitution itself exempting certain classes of person or entities from its reach.

MR. JUSTICE STEWART, with whom MR. JUSTICE MARSHALL joins, dissenting.

Believing that the search by the police of the offices of the Stanford Daily infringed the First and Fourteenth Amendments' guarantee of a free press, I respectfully dissent.

It seems to me self-evident that police searches of newspaper offices burden the freedom of the press. The most immediate and obvious First Amendment injury caused by such a visitation by the police is physical disruption of the operation of the newspaper. Policemen occupying a newsroom and searching it thoroughly for what may be an extended period of time will inevitably interrupt its normal operations, and thus impair or even temporarily prevent the processes of newsgathering, writing, editing, and publishing. By contrast, a subpoena would afford the newspaper itself an opportunity to locate whatever material might be requested and produce it.

But there is another and more serous burden on a free press imposed by an unannounced police search of a newspaper office: the possibility of disclosure of information received from confidential sources, or of the identity of the sources themselves. Protection of those sources is necessary to ensure that the press can fulfill its constitutionally designed function of informing the public, because important information can often be obtained only by an assurance that the source will not be revealed. . . .

A search warrant allows police officers to ransack the files of a newspaper, reading each and every document until they have found the one named in the warrant, while a subpoena would permit the newspaper itself to produce only the specific documents requested. A search, unlike a subpoena, will therefore lead to the needless exposure of confidential information completely unrelated to the purpose of the investigation. The knowledge that police officers can make an unannounced raid on a newsroom is thus bound to have a deterrent effect on the availability of confidential news sources. The end result, wholly inimical to the First Amendment, will be a diminishing flow of potentially important information to the public.

. . .

It is well to recall the actual circumstances of this litigation. The application for a warrant showed only that there was reason to believe that photographic evidence of assaults on the police would be found in the offices of the Stanford Daily. There was no emergency need to protect life or property by an immediate search. The evidence sought was not contraband, but material obtained by the Daily in the normal exercise of its journalistic function. Neither the Daily nor any member of its staff was suspected of criminal activity. And there was no showing that the Daily would not respond to a subpoena commanding production of the photographs, or that for any other reason a sub-poena could not be obtained. Surely, then, a subpoena *duces tecum* would have been just as effective as a police raid in obtaining the pro-duction of the material sought by the Santa Clara County District Attorney.

Perhaps as a matter of abstract policy a newspaper office should receive no more pro-tection from unannounced police searches than, say, the office of a doctor or the office of a bank. But we are here to uphold a Constitution. And our Constitution does not explicitly pro-tect the practice of medicine or the business of banking from all abridgement by government. It does not explicitly protect the freedom of the press.

From a practical standpoint, Justice Stewart's concerns with the ransacking of editorial operations and chilling of sources have been alleviated by federal legislation prohibiting newsroom searches unless probable cause exists that the person possessing the desired materials has committed a crime or the need to prevent death or serious bodily injury exists.[158] Immunity is a function of legislative action, however, rather than First Amendment principle.

4. First Amendment Access

The Court has not been entirely unresponsive to the press' role in informing the public. Acknowledgment that the press and a free flow of information are crucial to informed self-government has generated constitutional attention to the newsgathering process itself. As the Court has stressed, however, the press' role does not provide an access right "to information not available to the public generally."[159]

a. Prisons

---

[158] Privacy Protection Act of 1980, 42 U.S.C. § 2000a et seq.
[159] Branzburg v. Hayes, 408 U.S. 665, 684 (1972).

Pell v. Procunier
417 U.S. 817 (1974)

MR. JUSTICE STEWART delivered the opin-ion of the Court.

. . .

The facts are undisputed. [Reporters] Pell, Segal, and Jacobs each requested permission from the appropriate corrections officials to in-terview inmates, Spain, Bly, and Guile, respec-tively. In addition, the editors of a certain peri-odical requested permission to visit inmate Hillery to discuss the possibility of publishing certain of his writings and to interview him concerning conditions at the prison. Pursuant to § 415.071, these requests were all denied. The plaintiffs thereupon sued to enjoin the con-tinued enforcement of this regulation. The in-mate plaintiffs contended that § 415.071 vio-lates their rights of free speech under the First and Fourteenth Amendments. Similarly, the media plaintiffs asserted that the limitation that this regulation places on their newsgath-ering activity unconstitutionally infringes the freedom of the press guaranteed by the First and Fourteenth Amendments.

The District Court granted the inmate plaintiffs' motion for summary judgment, hold-ing that § 415.071, insofar as it prohibited in-mates from having face-to-face communication with journalists, unconstitutionally infringed their First and Fourteenth Amendment free-doms. With respect to the claims of the media plaintiffs, the court granted the defendants' motion to dismiss. The court noted that "[e]ven under § 415.071 as it stood before today's ruling [that inmates' constitutional rights were vio-lated by § 415.071] the press was given the free-dom to enter the California institutions and in-terview at random," and concluded "that the even broader access afforded prisoners by to-day's ruling sufficiently protects whatever rights the press may have with respect to inter-views with inmates."

. . .

[Before assessing the media's freedom of the press arguments, the Court rejected inmate claims that their speech freedom had been wrongly abridged].

. . . [T]he media plaintiffs ask us to hold that the limitation on press interviews imposed by § 415.071 violates the freedom of the press guaranteed by the First and Fourteenth Amendments. They contend that, irrespective of what First Amendment liberties may or may not be retained by prison inmates, members of the press have a constitutional right to interview any inmate who is willing to speak with them, in the absence of an individualized determination that the particular interview might create a clear and present danger to prison security or to some other substantial interest served by the corrections system. In this regard, the media plaintiffs do not claim any impairment of their freedom to publish, for California imposes no restrictions on what may be published about its prisons, the prison inmates, or the officers who administer the prisons. Instead, they rely on their right to gather news without governmental interference, which the media plaintiffs assert includes a right of access to the sources of what is regarded as newsworthy information.

We note at the outset that this regulation is not part of an attempt by the State to conceal the conditions in its prisons or to frustrate the press' investigation and reporting of those conditions. Indeed, the record demonstrates that, under current corrections policy, both the press and the general public are accorded full opportunities to observe prison conditions. The Department of Corrections regularly conducts public tours through the prisons for the benefit of interested citizens. In addition, newsmen are permitted to visit both the maximum security and minimum security sections of the institutions and to stop and speak about any subject to any inmates whom they might encounter. If security considerations permit, corrections personnel will step aside to permit such interviews to be confidential. Apart from general access to all parts of the institutions, newsmen are also permitted to enter the prisons to interview inmates selected at random by the corrections officials. By the same token, if a newsman wishes to write a story on a particular prison program, he is permitted to sit in on group meetings and to interview the inmate participants. In short, members of the press enjoy access to California prisons that is not available to other members of the public.

The sole limitation of newsgathering in California prisons is the prohibition in § 415.071 of interviews with individual inmates specifically designated by representatives of the press. This restriction is of recent vintage, having been imposed in 1971 in response to a violent episode that the Department of Correc-

tions felt was at least partially attributable to the former policy with respect to face-to-face prisoner-press interviews. Prior to the promulgation of § 415.071, every journalist had virtually free access to interview any individual inmate whom he might wish. Only members of the press were accorded this privilege; other members of the general public did not have the benefit of such an unrestricted visitation policy. Thus, the promulgation of § 415.071 did not impose a discrimination against press access, but merely eliminated a special privilege formerly given to representatives of the press *vis-à-vis* members of the public generally.

In practice, it was found that the policy in effect prior to the promulgation of § 415.071 had resulted in press attention being concentrated on a relatively small number of inmates who, as a result, became virtual "public figures" within the prison society and gained a disproportionate degree of notoriety and influence among their fellow inmates. Because of this notoriety and influence, these inmates often became the source of severe disciplinary problems. For example, extensive press attention to an inmate who espoused a practice of noncooperation with prison regulations encouraged other inmates to follow suit, thus eroding the institutions' ability to deal effectively with the inmates generally. Finally, in the words of the District Court, on August 21, 1971, "[d]uring an escape attempt at San Quentin three staff members and two inmates were killed. This was viewed by the officials as the climax of mounting disciplinary problems caused, in part, by its liberal posture with regard to press interviews, and on August 23, § 415.071 was adopted to mitigate the problem." It is against this background that we consider the media plaintiffs' claims under the First and Fourteenth Amendments.

The constitutional guarantee of a free press "assures the maintenance of our political system, and an open society," and secures "the paramount public interest in a free flow of information to the people concerning public officials." By the same token, "'[a]ny system of prior restraints of expression comes to this Court bearing a heavy presumption against its constitutional validity.'" Correlatively, the First and Fourteenth Amendments also protect the right of the public to receive such information and ideas as are published.

In *Branzburg v. Hayes*, the Court went further and acknowledged that "news gathering is not without its First Amendment protections," for "without some protection for seeking out the news, freedom of the press could be eviscerated." In *Branzburg* the Court held that the First and Fourteenth Amendments were not abridged by requiring reporters to disclose the identity of their confidential sources to a grand jury when that information was needed in the course of a good-faith criminal investigation. The Court there could "perceive no basis for holding that the public interest in law enforcement and in ensuring effective grand jury proceedings [was] insufficient to override the consequential, but uncertain, burden on news gathering that is said to result from insisting that reporters, like other citizens, respond to relevant questions put to them in the course of a valid grand jury investigation or criminal trial."

In this case, the media plaintiffs contend that § 415.071 constitutes governmental interference with their news-gathering activities that is neither consequential nor uncertain, and that no substantial governmental interest can be shown to justify the denial of press access to specially designated prison inmates. More particularly, the media plaintiffs assert that, despite the substantial access to California prisons and their inmates accorded representatives of the press—access broader than is accorded members of the public generally—face-to-face interviews with specifically designated inmates is such an effective and superior method of newsgathering that its curtailment amounts to unconstitutional state interference with a free press. We do not agree.

"It has generally been held that the First Amendment does not guarantee the press a constitutional right of special access to information not available to the public generally.... Despite the fact that news gathering may be hampered, the press is regularly excluded from grand jury proceedings, our own conferences, the meetings of other official bodies gathering in executive session, and the meetings of private organizations. Newsmen have no constitutional right of access to the scenes of crime or disaster when the general public is excluded." Similarly, newsmen have no constitutional right of access to prisons or their inmates beyond that afforded the general public.

The First and Fourteenth Amendments bar government from interfering in any way with a free press. The Constitution does not, however, require government to accord the press special access to information not shared by members of the public generally. It is one thing to say that a journalist is free to seek out sources of information not available to members of the general public, that he is entitled to some constitutional protection of the confidentiality of such sources, and that government cannot restrain the publication of news emanating from such sources. It is quite another thing to suggest that the Constitution imposes upon government the affirmative duty to make available to journalists sources of information not available to members of the public generally. That proposition finds no support in the words of the Constitution or in any decision of this Court. Accordingly, since § 415.071 does not deny the press access to sources of information available to members of the general public, we hold that it does not abridge the protections that the First and Fourteenth Amendments guarantee.

. . .

MR. JUSTICE DOUGLAS, with whom MR. JUSTICE BRENNAN and MR. JUSTICE MARSHALL join, dissenting.

. . .

... [T]he media claim that the state and federal prison regulations here, by flatly prohibiting interviews with inmates selected by the press, impinge upon the First Amendment's free press guarantee, directly protected against federal infringement and protected against state infringement and by the Fourteenth Amendment. In rejecting the claim, the Court notes that the ban on access to prisoners applies as well to the general public, and it holds that "newsmen have no constitutional right of access to prisons or their inmates beyond that afforded the general public."

In dealing with the free press guarantee, it is important to note that the interest it protects is not possessed by the media themselves.... but rather the right of the people, the true sovereign under our constitutional scheme, to govern in an informed manner. "The press has preferred position in our constitutional scheme, not to enable it to make money, not to set newsmen apart as a favored class, but to bring fulfillment to the public's right to know. The right to know is crucial to the governing powers of the people."

Prisons, like all other public institutions, are ultimately the responsibility of the populace. Crime, like the economy, health, education, defense, and the like, is a matter of grave concern in our society and people have the right and the necessity to know not only of the incidence of crime but of the effectiveness of the system designed to control it. "On any given day, approximately 1,500,000 people are under the authority of [federal, state and local prison] systems. The cost to taxpayers is over one billion dollars annually. Of those individuals sentenced to prison, 98% will return to society." The public's interest in being informed about prisons is thus paramount.

As with the prisoners' free speech claim, no one asserts that the free press right is such that the authorities are powerless to impose reasonable regulations as to the time, place, and manner of interviews to effectuate prison discipline and order. The only issue here is whether the complete ban on interviews with inmates selected by the press goes beyond what is necessary for the protection of these interests and infringes upon our cherished right of a free press. . . .

It is thus not enough to note that the press—the institution which "[t]he Constitution specifically selected to play an important role in the discussion of public affairs"—is denied no more access to the prisons than is denied the public generally. The prohibition of visits by the public has no practical effect upon their right to know beyond that achieved by the exclusion of the press. The average citizen is most unlikely to inform himself about the operation of the prison system by requesting an interview with a particular inmate with whom he has no prior relationship. He is likely instead, in a society which values a free press, to rely upon the media for information.

It is indeed ironic for the Court to justify the exclusion of the press by noting that the government has gone beyond the press and expanded the exclusion to include the public. Could the government deny the press access to all public institutions and prohibit interviews with all governmental employees? Could it find constitutional footing by expanding the ban to deny such access to everyone?

. . . [T]he absolute ban on press interviews with specifically designated federal inmates is far broader than is necessary to protect any legitimate governmental interests and is an unconstitutional infringement on the public's right to know protected by the free press guarantee of the First Amendment. . . .

A few years after the *Pell* decision, the Court examined another set of restrictions on prison access. In *Houchins v. KQED, Inc.*, a plurality opinion reiterated that the First Amendment provides no more access to the press than it does to the public. Justice Stewart, who concurred in the judgment, agreed that the press and public's access rights were coextensive but maintained that terms of access reasonable for the public may be unreasonable for the press if they impede journalistic functions. The dissent objected to a result that allowed the state to foreclose access both to the press and the public.

Houchins v. KQED, Inc.
438 U.S. 1 (1978)

MR. CHIEF JUSTICE BURGER announced the judgment of the Court and delivered an opinion, in which MR. JUSTICE WHITE and MR. JUSTICE REHNQUIST joined.

The question presented is whether the news media have a constitutional right of access to a county jail, over and above that of other persons, to interview inmates and make sound recordings, films, and photographs for publication and broadcasting by newspapers, radio and television.

Petitioner Houchins, as Sheriff of Alameda County, Cal., controls all access to the Alameda County Jail at Santa Rita. Respondent KQED operates licensed television and radio broadcasting stations which have frequently reported newsworthy events relating to penal institutions in the San Francisco Bay Area. On March 31, 1975, KQED reported the suicide of a prisoner in the Greystone portion of the Santa Rita jail. The report included a statement by a psychiatrist that the conditions at the Greystone facility were responsible for the illnesses of his patient-prisoners there, and a statement from petitioner denying that prison conditions were responsible for the prisoners' illnesses.

KQED requested permission to inspect and take pictures within the Greystone facility. After permission was refused, KQED and the Alameda and Oakland branches of the National Association for the Advancement of Colored People (NAACP) filed suit under 42 U.S.C. § 1983. They alleged that petitioner had violated the First Amendment by refusing to permit media access and failing to provide any effective means by which the public could be informed of conditions prevailing in the Greystone facility or learn of the prisoners' grievances. Public access to such information was essential, they asserted, in order for NAACP members to participate in the public debate on jail conditions in Alameda County. They further asserted that television coverage of the conditions in the cells and facilities was the most effective way of informing the public of prison conditions.

The complaint requested a preliminary and permanent injunction to prevent petitioner from "excluding KQED news personnel from the Greystone cells and Santa Rita facilities and generally preventing full and accurate news coverage of the conditions prevailing therein." On June 17, 1975, when the complaint was filed, there appears to have been no formal policy regarding public access to the Santa Rita jail. However, according to petitioner, he had been in the process of planning a program of regular monthly tours since he took office six months earlier. On July 8, 1975, he announced the program and invited all interested persons to make arrangements for the regular tours. News media were given notice in advance of the public and presumably could have made early reservations.

. . .

In support of the request for a preliminary injunction, respondents presented testimony and affidavits stating that other penal complexes had permitted media interviews of inmates and substantial media access without experiencing significant security or administrative problems. They contended that the monthly public tours at Santa Rita failed to provide adequate access to the jail for two reasons: (a) once the scheduled tours had been filled, media representatives who had not signed up for them had no access and were unable to cover newsworthy events at the jail; (b) the prohibition on photography and tape recordings, the exclusion of portions of the jail from the tours, and the practice of keeping inmates generally removed from view substantially reduced the usefulness of the tours to the media.

In response, petitioner admitted that Santa Rita had never experimented with permitting media access beyond that already allowed; he did not claim that disruption had been caused by media access to other institutions. He asserted, however, that unregulated access by the media would infringe inmate privacy, and tend to create "jail celebrities," who in turn tend to generate internal problems and undermine jail security. He also contended that unscheduled media tours would disrupt jail operations.

. . .

Petitioner filed an affidavit noting the various means by which information concerning the jail could reach the public. Attached to the affidavit were the current prison mail, visitation, and phone call regulations. The regulations allowed inmates to send an unlimited number of letters to judges, attorneys, elected officials, the Attorney General, petitioner, jail officials, or probation officers, all of which could be sealed prior to mailing. Other letters were subject to inspection for contraband but the regulations provided that no inmate mail would be read.

With few exceptions, all persons, including representatives of the media, who knew a prisoner could visit him. Media reporters could interview inmates awaiting trial with the consent of the inmate, his attorney, the district attorney, and the court. Social services officers were permitted to contact "relatives, community agencies, employers, etc.," by phone to assist in counseling inmates with vocational, educational, or personal problems. Maximum-security inmates were free to make unmonitored collect telephone calls from designated areas of the jail without limit.

. . .

Notwithstanding our holding in *Pell v. Procunier,* respondents assert that the right recognized by the Court of Appeals flows logically from our decisions construing the First Amendment. They argue that there is a constitutionally guaranteed right to gather news under *Pell v. Procunier* and *Branzburg v. Hayes.* From the right to gather news and the right to receive information, they argue for an implied special right of access to government-controlled sources of information. This right, they contend, compels access as a *constitutional* matter. First Amendment right in the language of *Grosjean v. American Press Co.,* 197 U.S. 233, 250 (1936), and *Mills v. Alabama,* 384 U.S. 214, 219 (1966), which notes the importance of an informed public as a safeguard against "misgovernment" and the crucial role of the media in providing information. Respondents contend that public access to penal institutions is necessary to prevent officials from concealing prison conditions from the voters and impairing the public's right to discuss and criticize the prison system and its administration.

The public importance of conditions in penal facilities and the media's role of providing information afford no basis for reading into the Constitution a right of the public or the media to enter these institutions, with camera equipment, and take moving and still pictures of inmates for broadcast purposes. This Court has never intimated a First Amendment guarantee of a right of access to all sources of information within government control. Nor does the rationale of the decisions upon which respondents rely lead to the implication of such a right.

Grosjean v. American Press Co., and *Mills v. Alabama,* emphasized the importance of informed public opinion and the traditional role of a free press as a source of public information. But an analysis of those cases reveals that the Court was concerned with the freedom of the media to *communicate* information once it is obtained; neither case intimated that the Constitution *compels* the government to provide the media with information or access to it on demand. *Grosjean* involved a challenge to a state tax on advertising revenues of newspapers, the "plain purpose" of which was to penalize the publishers and curtail the publication of a selected group of newspapers. The Court summarized the familiar but important history of the attempts to prevent criticism of the Crown in England by the infamous licensing requirements and special taxes on the press, and concluded that the First Amendment had been designed to prevent similar restrictions or any other "form of previous restraint upon printed publications, or their circulation."

Branzburg v. Hayes, offers even less support for the respondents' position. Its observation, in dictum, that "news gathering is not without its First Amendment protections," in no sense implied a constitutional right of access to news sources. That observation must be read in context; it was in response to the contention that forcing a reporter to disclose to a grand jury information received in confidence would violate the First Amendment by deterring news sources from communicating information. There is an undoubted right to gather news "from any source by means within the law," but that affords no basis for the claim that the First Amendment compels others—private persons or governments—to supply information.

. . .

Pell v. Procunier and *Saxbe v. Washington Post Co.* also assumed that there is no constitutional right of access such as the Court of Appeals conceived. In those cases the Court declared, explicitly and without reservation, that the media have "no constitutional right of access to prisons or their inmates beyond that afforded the general public," and on that premise the Court sustained prison regulations that prevented media interviews with inmates.

. . .

The respondents' argument is flawed, not only because it lacks precedential support and is contrary to statements in this Court's opinions, but also because it invites the Court to involve itself in what is clearly a legislative task which the Constitution has left to the political processes. Whether the government should open penal institutions in the manner sought by respondents is a question of policy which a legislative body might appropriately resolve one way or the other.

A number of alternatives are available to prevent problems in penal facilities from escaping public attention. The early penal reform movements in this country and England gained impetus as a result of reports from citizens and visiting committees who volunteered or received commissions to visit penal institutions and make reports. Citizen task forces and prison visitation committees continue to play an important role in keeping the public informed on deficiencies of prison systems and need for reforms. Grand juries, with the potent subpoena power—not available to the media—traditionally concern themselves with

conditions in public institutions; a prosecutor or judge may initiate similar inquiries, and the legislative power embraces an arsenal of weapons for inquiry relating to tax-supported institutions. In each case, these public bodies are generally compelled to publish their findings and, if they default, the power of the media is always available to generate public pressure for disclosure. But the choice as to the most effective and appropriate method is a policy decision to be resolved by legislative decision. We must not confuse what is "good," "desirable," or "expedient" with what is constitutionally commanded by the First Amendment. To do so is to trivialize constitutional adjudication.

Unarticulated but implicit in the assertion that media access to the jail is essential for informed public debate on jail conditions is the assumption that media personnel are the best qualified persons for the task of discovering malfeasance in public institutions. But that assumption finds no support in the decisions of this Court or the First Amendment. Editors and newsmen who inspect a jail may decide to publish or not to publish what information they acquire. Public bodies and public officers, on the other hand, may be coerced by public opinion to disclose what they might prefer to conceal. No comparable pressures are available to anyone to compel publication by the media of what they might prefer not to make known.

There is no discernible basis for a constitutional duty to disclose, or for standards governing disclosure of or access to information. Because the Constitution affords no guidelines, absent statutory standards, hundreds of judges would, under the Court of Appeals' approach, be at large to fashion ad hoc standards, in individual cases, according to their own ideas of what seems "desirable" or "expedient." We, therefore, reject the Court of Appeals' conclusory assertion that the public and the media have a First Amendment right to government information regarding the conditions of jails and their inmates and presumably all other public facilities such as hospitals and mental institutions.

. . .

Petitioner cannot prevent respondents from learning about jail conditions in a variety of ways, albeit not as conveniently as they might prefer. Respondents have a First Amendment right to receive letters from inmates criticizing jail officials and reporting on conditions. Respondents are free to interview those who render the legal assistance to which inmates are entitled. They are also free to seek out former inmates, visitors to the prison, public officials, and institutional personnel, as they sought out the complaining psychiatrist here.

Moreover, California statutes currently

provide for a prison Board of Corrections that has the authority to inspect jails and prisons and *must* provide a public report at regular intervals. . . .

Neither the First Amendment nor the Fourteenth Amendment mandates a right of access to government information or sources of information within the government's control. Under our holdings in *Pell v. Procunier*, and *Saxbe v. Washington Post Co.*, until the political branches decree otherwise, as they are free to do, the media have no special right of access to the Alameda County Jail different from or greater than that accorded the public generally.

. . .

MR. JUSTICE MARSHALL and MR. JUSTICE BLACKMUN took no part in the consideration or decision of this case.

MR. JUSTICE STEWART, concurring in the judgment.

. . .

When on assignment, a journalist does not tour a jail simply for his own edification. He is there to gather information to be passed on to others, and his mission is protected by the Constitution for very specific reasons. "Enlightened choice by an informed citizenry is the basic ideal upon which an open society is premised. . . . " Our society depends heavily on the press for that enlightenment. Though not without its lapses, the press "has been a mighty catalyst in awakening public interest in governmental affairs, exposing corruption among public officers and employees and generally informing the citizenry of public events and occurrences. . . . "

That the First Amendment speaks separately of freedom of speech and freedom of the press is no constitutional accident, but an acknowledgment of the critical role played by the press in American society. The Constitution requires sensitivity to that role, and to the special needs of the press in performing it effectively. A person touring Santa Rita jail can grasp its reality with his own eyes and ears. But if a television reporter is to convey the jail's sights and sounds to those who cannot personally visit the place, he must use cameras and sound equipment. In short, terms of access that are reasonably imposed on individual members of the public may, if they impede effective reporting without sufficient justification, be unreasonable as applied to journalists who are there to convey to the general public what the visitors see.

Under these principles, KQED was clearly entitled to some form of preliminary injunctive relief. At the time of the District Court's decision, members of the public were permitted to visit most parts of the Santa Rita jail, and the First and Fourteenth Amendments required the Sheriff to give members of the press *effective* access to the same areas. The Sheriff evidently assumed that he could fulfill this obligation simply by allowing reporters to sign up for tours on the same terms as the public. I think he was mistaken in this assumption, as a matter of constitutional law.

. . .

MR. JUSTICE STEVENS, with whom MR. JUSTICE BRENNAN and MR. JUSTICE POWELL join, dissenting.

The Court holds that the scope of press access to the Santa Rita jail required by the preliminary injunction issued against petitioner is inconsistent with the holding in *Pell v. Procunier*, that "newsmen have no constitutional right of access to prisons or their inmates beyond that afforded the general public" and therefore the injunction was an abuse of the District Court's discretion. I respectfully disagree.

Respondent KQED, Inc., has televised a number of programs about prison conditions and prison inmates, and its reporters have been granted access to various correctional facilities in the San Francisco Bay area, including San Quentin State Prison, Soledad Prison, and the San Francisco County Jails at San Bruno and San Francisco, to prepare program material. They have taken their cameras and recording equipment inside the walls of those institutions and interviewed inmates. No disturbances or other problems have occurred on those occasions.

KQED has also reported newsworthy events involving the Alameda County Jail in Santa Rita, including a 1972 newscast reporting a decision of the United States District Court finding that the "shocking and debasing conditions which prevailed [at Santa Rita] constituted cruel and unusual punishment for man or beast as a matter of law." On March 31, 1975, KQED reported the suicide of a prisoner in the Greystone portion of the Santa Rita jail. That program also carried a statement by a psychiatrist assigned to Santa Rita to the effect that conditions in the Greystone facility were responsible for illnesses of inmates. Petitioner's disagreement with that conclusion was reported on the same newscast.

KQED requested permission to visit and photograph the area of the jail where the suicide occurred. Petitioner refused, advising KQED that it was his policy not to permit any access to the jail by the news media. This policy was also invoked by petitioner to deny subsequent requests for access to the jail in order to cover news stories about conditions and alleged incidents within the facility. Except for a carefully supervised tour in 1972, the news media were completely excluded from the inner portions of the Santa Rita jail until after this action was commenced. Moreover, the prison rules provided that all outgoing mail, except letters to judges and lawyers, would be inspected; the rules also prohibited any mention in outgoing correspondence of the names or actions of any correctional officers.

. . .

In a letter to the County Board of Supervisors dated two days after this suit was instituted, petitioner proposed a pilot public tour program. He suggested monthly tours for 25 persons, with the first tentatively scheduled for July 14. The tours, however, would not include the cell portions of Greystone and would not allow any use of cameras or communication with inmates. . . .

An evidentiary hearing on the motion for a preliminary injunction was held after the first four guided tours had taken place. The evidence revealed the inadequacy of the tours as a means of obtaining information about the inmates and their conditions of confinement for transmission to the public. They afforded no opportunity to photograph conditions within the facility, and the photographs which the county offered for sale to tour visitors omitted certain jail characteristics, such as catwalks above the cells from which guards can observe the inmates. The tours provided no opportunity to question randomly encountered inmates about jail conditions. Indeed, to the extent possible, inmates were kept out of sight during the tour, preventing the tour visitors from obtaining a realistic picture of the conditions of confinement within the jail. In addition, the fixed scheduling of the tours prevented coverage of newsworthy events at the jail.

For two reasons, which will be discussed separately, the decisions in *Pell* and *Saxbe* do not control the propriety of the District Court's preliminary injunction. First, the unconstitutionality of petitioner's policies which gave rise to this litigation does not rest on the premise that the press has a greater right of access to information regarding prison conditions than do other members of the public. Second, relief tailored to the needs of the press may properly be awarded to a representative of the press which is successful in proving that it has been harmed by a constitutional violation and need not await the grant of relief to members of the general public who may also have been injured by petitioner's unconstitutional access policy but have not yet sought to vindicate their rights.

. . .

The decision in *Pell* . . . does not imply that a state policy of concealing prison conditions from the press, or a policy denying the press any opportunity to observe those conditions, could have been justified simply by pointing to like concealment from, and denial to, the general public. If that were not true, there would have been no need to emphasize the substantial press and public access reflected in the record of that case. What *Pell* does indicate is that the question whether respondents established a probability of prevailing on their constitutional claim is inseparable from the question whether petitioner's policies unduly restricted the opportunities of the general public to learn about the conditions of confinement in Santa Rita jail. As in *Pell*, in assessing its adequacy, the total access of the public and the press must be considered.

Here, the broad restraints on access to information regarding operation of the jail that prevailed on the date this suit was instituted are plainly disclosed by the record. The public and the press had consistently been denied any access to those portions of the Santa Rita facility where inmates were confined and there had been excessive censorship of inmate correspondence. Petitioner's no-access policy, modified only in the wake of respondents' resort to the courts, could survive constitutional scrutiny only if the Constitution affords no protection to the public's right to be informed about conditions within those public institutions where some of its members are confined because they have been charged with or found guilty of criminal offenses.

The preservation of a full and free flow of information to the general public has long been recognized as a core objective of the First Amendment to the Constitution. It is for this reason that the First Amendment protects not only the dissemination but also the receipt of information and ideas. . . .

In addition to safeguarding the right of one individual to receive what another elects to communicate, the First Amendment serves an essential societal function. Our system of self-government assumes the existence of an informed citizenry. As Madison wrote:

> "A popular Government, without popular information, or the means of acquiring it, is but a Prologue to a Farce or a Tragedy; or, perhaps both. Knowledge will forever govern ignorance: And a people who mean to be their own Governors, must arm themselves with the power which knowledge gives."

It is not sufficient, therefore, that the channels of communication be free of governmental restraints. Without some protection for the acquisition of information about the operation of public institutions such as prisons by the public at large, the process of self-governance contemplated by the Framers would be stripped of its substance.

For that reason information gathering is

entitled to some measure of constitutional protection. As this Court's decisions clearly indicate, however, this protection is not for the private benefit of those who might qualify as representatives of the "press" but to insure that the citizens are fully informed regarding matters of public interest and importance.

. . .

A recognition that the "underlying right is the right of the public generally" is also implicit in the doctrine that "newsmen have no constitutional right of access to prisons or their inmates beyond that afforded the general public." In *Pell* it was unnecessary to consider the extent of the public's right of access to information regarding the prison and its inmates in order to adjudicate the press claim to a particular form of access, since the record demonstrated that the flow of information to the public, both directly and through the press, was adequate to survive constitutional challenge; institutional considerations justified denying the single, additional mode of access sought by the press in that case.

Here, in contrast, the restrictions on access to the inner portions of the Santa Rita jail that existed on the date this litigation commenced concealed from the general public the conditions of confinement within the facility. The question is whether petitioner's policies, which cut off the flow of information at its source, abridged the public's right to be informed about those conditions.

The answer to that question does not depend upon the degree of public disclosure which should attend the operation of most governmental activity. Such matters involve questions of policy which generally must be resolved by the political branches of government. Moreover, there are unquestionably occasions when governmental activity may properly be carried on in complete secrecy. For example, the public and the press are commonly excluded from "grand jury proceedings, our own conferences, [and] the meetings of other official bodies gathered in executive session. . . . " In addition, some functions of government—essential to the protection of the public and indeed our country's vital interests—necessarily require a large measure of secrecy, subject to appropriate legislative oversight. In such situations the reasons for withholding information from the public are both apparent and legitimate.

In this case, however "[r]espondents do not assert a right to force disclosure of confidential information or to invade in any way the deci-sionmaking processes of governmental officials." They simply seek an end to petitioner's policy of concealing prison conditions from the public. Those conditions are wholly without claim to confidentiality. While prison officials have an interest in the time and manner of public acquisition of information about the institutions they administer, there is no legitimate pedological justification for concealing from citizens the conditions in which their fellow citizens are being confined.

The reasons which militate in favor of providing special protection to the flow of information to the public about prisons relate to the unique function they perform in a democratic society. Not only are they public institutions, financed with public funds and administered by public servants, they are an integral component of the criminal justice system. The citizens confined therein are temporarily, and sometimes permanently, deprived of their liberty as a result of a trial which must conform to the dictates of the Constitution. By express command of the Sixth Amendment the proceeding must be a "public trial." It is important not only that the trial itself be fair, but also that the community at large have confidence in the integrity of the proceeding. That public interest survives the judgment of conviction and appropriately carries over to an interest in how the convicted person is treated during his period of punishment and hoped-for rehabilitation. While a ward of the State and subject to its stern discipline, he retains constitutional protections against cruel and unusual punishment, a protection which may derive more practical support from access to information about prisons by the public than by occasional litigation in a busy court.

Some inmates—in Santa Rita, a substantial number—are pretrial detainees. Though confined pending trial, they have not been convicted of an offense against society and are entitled to the presumption of innocence. Certain pedological objectives, *i.e.*, punishment, deterrence, and rehabilitation, which are legitimate in regard to convicted prisoners, are inapplicable to pretrial detainees. Society has a special interest in ensuring that unconvicted citizens are treated in accord with their status.

. . .

. . . An official prison policy of concealing such knowledge from the public by arbitrarily cutting off the flow of information at its source abridges the freedom of speech and of the press protected by the First and Fourteenth Amendments to the Constitution.

b. Judicial Proceedings

Even when the press has prevailed on grounds that newsgathering interests have been compromised, its First Amendment rights have been defined coextensively with those of the public. The contours of access rights have been most extensively litigated in the context of the judicial process. At stake in the coverage of criminal proceedings are the risk of prejudice to defendants from prejudicial publicity and the public's interest in being informed. The access question has been analyzed on both Sixth Amendment and First Amendment grounds. In *Gannett, Inc. v. DePasquale*, the Court upheld a district court order closing pretrial proceedings to the press and public.[160] It did so on grounds the Sixth Amendment right to a public trial was personal to the defendant and could not be asserted by the press or public.[161] The *Gannett* decision, which concerned a suppression hearing, discounted the consequences of closure insofar as a transcript of the hearing was available when the risk of prejudice abated.[162]

A year after *Gannett*, in the context of an actual trial, a majority of the Court determined that the First Amendment secured access to trials. Primary themes of the various opinions prioritizing First Amendment values, in *Richmond Newspapers, Inc. v. Virginia*, were that trials traditionally had been open to the public, openness was a critical check upon the risks of collusion and official misconduct, and access to the judicial process was essential for an educated and informed public.[163] In *Globe Newspaper Co. v. Superior Court*, the Court identified a right of access to trials that could not be compromised minus proof of a compelling state interest and narrowly tailored order.

---

[160] Gannett, Inc. v. DePasquale, 443 U.S. 363 (1979).

[161] *Id.*

[162] *Id.*

[163] Richmond Newspapers, Inc. v. Virginia, 448 U.S. 555 (1980).

Globe Newspaper Co. v. Superior Court
457 U.S. 596 (1982)

JUSTICE BRENNAN delivered the opinion of the Court.

Section 16A of Chapter 278 of the Massachusetts General Laws, as construed by the Massachusetts Supreme Judicial Court, requires trial judges, at trials for specific sexual offenses involving a victim under the age of 18, to exclude the press and general public from the courtroom during the testimony of that victim. The question presented is whether the statute thus construed violates the First Amendment as applied to the States through the Fourteenth Amendment.

The Court's recent decision in *Richmond Newspapers* firmly established for the first time that the press and general public have a constitutional right of access to criminal trials. . . .

Of course, this right of access to criminal trials is not explicitly mentioned in terms in the First Amendment. But we have long eschewed any "narrow, literal conception" of the Amendment's terms, for the Framers were concerned with broad principles, and wrote against a background of shared values and practices. The First Amendment is thus broad enough to encompass those rights that, while not unambiguously enumerated in the very terms of the Amendment, are nonetheless necessary to the enjoyment of other First Amendment rights. . . .

. . . Thus to the extent that the First Amendment embraces a right of access to criminal trials, it is to ensure that this constitutionally protected "discussion of governmental affairs" is an informed one.

Two features of the criminal justice system, emphasized in the various opinions in *Richmond Newspapers*, together serve to explain why a right of access to *criminal trials* in particular is properly afforded protection by the First Amendment. First, the criminal trial historically has been open to the press and general public. "[A]t the time when our organic laws were adopted, criminal trials both here and in England had long been presumptively open." *Richmond Newspapers, Inc. v. Virginia*, (plurality opinion). And since that time, the presumption of openness has remained secure. Indeed, at the time of this Court's decision *In re Oliver*, the presumption was so solidly grounded that the Court was "unable to find a single instance of a criminal trial conducted in camera in any federal, state, or municipal court during the history of this country. This uniform rule of openness has been viewed as significant in constitutional terms not only "because the Constitution carries the gloss of history," but also because "a tradition of accessibility implies the favorable judgment of experience." *Richmond Newspapers, Inc., v. Virginia* (Brennan, J., concurring in judgment).

Second, the right of access to criminal trials plays a particularly significant role in the functioning of the judicial process and the government as a whole. Public scrutiny of a criminal trial enhances the quality and safeguards the integrity of the factfinding process, with benefits to both the defendant and to society as a whole. Moreover, public access to the criminal trial fosters an appearance of fairness, thereby heightening public respect for the judicial process. And in the broadest terms, public access to criminal trials permits the public to participate in and serve as a check upon the judicial process—an essential component in our structure of self-government. In sum, the institutional value of the open criminal trial is recognized in both logic and experience.

Although the right of access to criminal trials is of constitutional stature, it is not absolute. But the circumstances under which the press and public can be barred from a criminal trial are limited; the State's justification in denying access must be a weighty one. Where, as in the present case, the State attempts to deny the right of access in order to inhibit the disclosure of sensitive information, it must be shown that the denial is necessitated by a compelling governmental interest, and is narrowly tailored to serve that interest. . . .

The state interests asserted to support § 16A, though articulated in various ways, are reducible to two: the protection of minor victims of sex crimes from further trauma and embarrassment; and the encouragement of such victims to come forward and testify in a truthful and credible manner. We consider these interests in turn.

We agree with appellee that the first interest—safeguarding the physical and psychological well-being of a minor—is a compelling one. But as compelling as that interest is, it does not justify a *mandatory* closure rule, for it is clear that the circumstances of the particular case may affect the significance of the interest. A trial court can determine on a case-by-case basis whether closure is necessary to protect the welfare of a minor victim. Among the factors to be weighed are the minor victim's age,

psychological maturity and understanding, the nature of the crime, the desires of the victim, and the interests of parents and relatives. Section 16A, in contrast, requires closure even if the victim does not seek the exclusion of the press and general public and would not suffer injury by their presence. . . .

Nor can § 16A be justified on the basis of the Commonwealth's second asserted interest—the encouragement of minor victims of sex crimes to come forward and provide accurate testimony. The Commonwealth has offered no empirical support for the claim that the rule of automatic closure contained in § 16A will lead to an increase in the number of minor sex victims coming forward and cooperating with state authorities. Not only is the claim speculative in empirical terms, but it is also open to serious questions as a matter of logic and common sense. Although § 16A bars the press and general public from the courtroom during the testimony of minor sex victims, the press is not denied access to the transcript, court personnel, or another possible source that could provide an account of the minor victim's testimony. Thus § 16A cannot prevent the press from publicizing the substance of a minor victim's testimony, as well as his or her identity. If the commonwealth's interest in encouraging minor victims to come forward depends on keeping such matters secret, § 16A hardly advances that interest in an effective manner. And even if § 16A effectively advanced the State's interest, it is doubtful that the interest would be sufficient to overcome the constitutional attack, for that same interest could be relied on to support an array of mandatory closure rules designed to encourage victims to come forward. Surely it cannot be suggested that minor victims of sex crimes are the *only* crime victims who, because of publicity attendant to criminal trials, are reluctant to come forward and testify. The State's argument based on this interest therefore proves too much, and runs contrary to the very foundation of the right of access recognized in *Richmond Newspapers*: namely, "that a presumption of openness inheres in the very nature of a criminal trial under our system of justice." (plurality opinion).

For the foregoing reasons, we hold that § 16A, as construed by the Massachusetts Supreme Judicial Court, violates the First Amendment to the Constitution. Accordingly, the judgment of the Massachusetts Supreme Judicial Court is

Reversed.

CHIEF JUSTICE BURGER, with whom JUSTICE REHNQUIST joins, dissenting.

Historically our society has gone to great lengths to protect minors *charged* with crime, particularly by prohibiting the release of the names of offenders, barring the press and public from juvenile proceedings, and sealing the records of those proceedings. Yet today the Court holds unconstitutional a state statute designed to protect not the *accused*, but the minor *victims* of sex crimes. In doing so, it advances a disturbing paradox. Although states are permitted, for example, to mandate the closure of all proceedings in order to protect a 17-year-old charged with rape, they are not permitted to require the closing of part of criminal proceedings in order to protect an innocent child who has been raped or otherwise sexually abused.

The Court has tried to make its holding a narrow one by not disturbing the authority of state legislatures to enact more narrowly drawn statutes giving trial judges the discretion to exclude the public and the press from the courtroom during the minor victim's testimony.

I also do not read the Court's opinion as foreclosing a state statute which mandates closure except in cases where the victim agrees to testify in open court. But the Court's decision is nevertheless a gross invasion of state authority and a state's duty to protect its citizens—in this case minor victims of crime. I cannot agree with the Court's expansive interpretation of our decision in *Richmond Newspapers, Inc. v. Virginia*, or its cavalier rejection of the serious interests supporting Massachusetts' mandatory closure rule. Accordingly, I dissent.

Given the *Gannett* Court's emphasis upon a defendant's Sixth Amendment interests, in the context of preliminary hearings, the scope of access to the judicial process remained somewhat confused. Uncertainty was significantly resolved by a series of decisions stressing the value of openness beyond just a trial itself. In extending access rights to voir dire, the Court stressed the linkage of open proceedings to the public interest and concluded that jury selection in criminal trials is presumptively open and closure impermissible absent an overriding justification, narrow tailoring and consideration of alternatives.[164] In *Waller v. Georgia*, the Court determined that a First Amendment access right extended to suppression hearings.[165] The result, which was further supported by Sixth Amendment concerns insofar as the defendant not had objected to closure, reflected an understanding of pretrial proceedings as a critical aspect of the criminal justice process. Because the vast majority of cases are disposed of by plea bargaining, a preliminary hearing "is often the final and most important step in the criminal proceeding."[166]

A First Amendment right of access to proceedings other than trials hinges upon considerations of tradition and exigencies. Determinative factors are whether a given jurisdiction's proceedings historically have been open or closed, particularized findings have been made that the defendant's right to a fair trial would be prejudiced and reasonable alternatives to closure exist.

---

[164] Press Enterprise Co. v. Superior Court, 464 U.S. 501 (1984).

[165] Waller v. Georgia, 467 U.S. 39 (1984).

[166] *Id.* at 46–47.

Press-Enterprise Co. v. Superior Court
478 U.S. 1 (1986)

CHIEF JUSTICE BURGER delivered the opinion of the Court.

. . .

The right to an open public trial is a shared right of the accused and the public, the common concern being the assurance of fairness. Only recently, in *Waller v. Georgia*, 467 U.S. 39 (1984), for example, we considered whether the defendant's Sixth Amendment right of the accused is no less protective of a public trial than the implicit First Amendment right of the press and public." When the defendant objects to the closure of a suppression hearing, therefore, the hearing must be open unless the party seeking to close the hearing advances an overriding interest that is likely to be prejudiced.

Here, unlike *Waller*, the right asserted is not the defendant's Sixth Amendment right to a public trial since the defendant requested a *closed* preliminary hearing. Instead, the right asserted here is that of the public under the First Amendment. The California Supreme Court concluded that the First Amendment was not a criminal trial, but a preliminary hearing. However, the First Amendment question cannot be resolved solely on the label we give the event, i.e. "trial" or otherwise, particularly where the preliminary hearing functions much like a full-scale trial. . . . [P]ublic access to criminal trials and the selection of jurors is essential to the proper functioning of the criminal justice system. California preliminary hearings are sufficiently like a trial to justify the same conclusion.

In California, to bring a felon to trial, the prosecutor has a choice of securing a grand jury indictment or a finding of probable cause following a preliminary hearing. Even when the accused has been indicted by a grand jury, however, he has an absolute right to an elaborate preliminary hearing before a neutral magistrate. The accused has the right to personally appear at the hearing, to be represented by counsel, to cross-examine hostile witnesses, to present exculpatory evidence, and to exclude illegally obtained evidence. If the magistrate determines that probable cause exists, the accused is bound over for trial; such a finding leads to a guilty plea in the majority of cases.

It is true that unlike a criminal trial, the California preliminary hearing cannot result in the conviction of the accused and the adjudication is before a magistrate or other judicial officer without a jury. But these features, standing alone, do not make public access any less essential to the proper functioning of the proceedings in the overall criminal justice process. Because of its extensive scope, the preliminary hearing is often the final and most impor-

tant step in the criminal proceeding. As the California Supreme Court [has] stated, . . . the preliminary hearing in many cases provides "the sole occasion for public observation of the criminal justice system."

Similarly, the absence of a jury, long recognized as "an inestimable safeguard against the corrupt or overzealous prosecutor and against the compliant, biased, or eccentric judge," makes the importance of public access to a preliminary hearing even more significant. "People in an open society do not demand infallibility from their institutions, but it is difficult for them to accept what they are prohibited from observing."

Denying the transcript of a 41-day preliminary hearing would frustrate what we have characterized as the "community therapeutic value" of openness. Criminal acts, especially certain violent crimes, provoke public concern, outrage, and hostility. "When the public is aware that the law is being enforced and the criminal justice system is functioning, an outlet is provided for these understandable reactions and emotions." In sum:

> The value of openness lies in the fact that people not actually attending trials can have confidence that standards of fairness are being observed; the sure knowledge that *anyone* is free to attend gives assurance that established procedures are being followed and that deviations will become known. Openness thus enhances both the basic fairness of the criminal trial and the appearance of fairness so essential to public confidence in the system. *Press-Enterprise [Co. v. Superior Court]*, 464 U.S. 501, 508 (1984).

We therefore conclude that the qualified First Amendment right of access to criminal proceedings applies to preliminary hearings as they are conducted in California.

Even if grounds exist for closure, First Amendment interests are not extinguished. As the Court itself noted in upholding a closed proceeding in *Gannett*, a transcript must be made available when the risk of prejudicial publicity subsides.[167]

---

[167] Gannett Co. v. DePasquale, 443 U.S. 368, 393 (1979).

DEL: Case law with respect to the press' status and function, insofar as pertinent to the delineation of press rights and freedom, is characterized by incongruity and illogic. At the most general level, the pertinent jurisprudence seems at odds with basic values assigned to a system of expressive freedom. The Court, for instance, has prioritized speech that is essential to informed self-government. It also has recognized that the newsgathering process is not without First Amendment protection. Yet it has concluded that the press' interest in access, or any privilege or immunity, is coextensive with the public's. The practical distinction between interests in speech and press are evident in everyday reality. When the White House holds a news conference, for example, its doors are open to the press rather than the public. Controlled access in significant part is a function of a logical understanding that the press has an agency relationship with the public. As that proxy role has grown, consistent with evolution over the course of the twentieth century toward a mass media culture, the rationale for special attention and dispensation has become more compelling.

To the extent it is uncertain whether sources would be chilled if reporters must disclose their sources to grand juries, as the Court asserted in *Branzburg*, doubt should cut in favor of protecting the clear and profound First Amendment interests at stake. Allowance otherwise, absent a showing of relevance and need, subordinates a free flow of information to bureaucratic shortcuts. When the Court denies the press access to prison facilities because they are not open to the public, as in *Houchins*, coextensive rights become the ally of government secrecy. Notwithstanding the acknowledged interest in an informed public, and the press' role in facilitating that objective, case law affords no meaningful advantage to the press as the press. Especially in the context of a mass media society, wherein institutionalized rather than individual time and resources are crucial to accessing information, a refusal to account meaningfully for the press' unique function seems misconceived. If even dedicated textualists and originalists such as Justice Black can infer a right to associate from the freedom of speech, it is hard to avoid special attention to the news media's interest in accessing information and facilities or protecting its sources. As the right to associate is crucial to effectuating the core guarantee of freedom of speech, special privileges and immunities for the press enable it to perform its crucial function of informing the public.

DER: The Court's conclusion that the First Amendment does not give the press access "to information not available to the public generally" begs the question of the public's First Amendment right of access to information. The Court's limits on the press's right of access stems not only from its undervaluation of the press's role in informing the public, but also from its undervaluation of the public's need for information. Some constitutional scholars have argued that the First Amendment confers a "right to know," as well as a right to speak.[168] Although the Court has recognized that the First Amendment "prohibit[s] government from limiting the stock of information from which members of the public may draw,"[169] the Court has not interpreted this restriction as a positive right of citizens to compel the government to provide information. But access to information within the government's control is critical to citizens' ability to participate in political activities and to scrutinize government action. The First Amendment's structural functions of ensuring well-informed citizens and government accountability support an affirmative right to government information. The news media's access to government institutions such as prisons and courtrooms is the only practical way to guarantee citizens' First Amendment right to know. Recognizing this role served by the press does not really give it a special advantage over ordinary citizens. Rather, it fulfills the First Amendment's guarantees to ordinary citizens.

---

[168] *See, e.g.,* Thomas I. Emerson, *Legal Foundations of the Right to Know,* 1976 WASH. U.L.Q 1; Note, *The Rights of the Public and the Press To Gather Information,* 87 HARV. L. REV. 1505 (1974). *See also* Daniel A. Farber, *Free Speech Without Romance: Public Choice and the First Amendment,* 105 HARV. L. REV. 554 (1991) (showing that public choice theory, which views information as a public good, suggests a government duty to promote speech).

[169] Griswold v. Connecticut, 381 U.S. 479, 482 (1965).

C. The Press and Due Process

Among the various perils to a fair trial is the very function or presence of media. Reporting that precedes a trial and the presence of video and sound equipment in the courtroom under certain circumstances may implicate the imperatives of due process. Prejudicial publicity and disruptive media behavior at trial merged in *Sheppard v. Maxwell* to a point that the Court discerned a fair trial violation. It responded by setting forth standards, reflecting a balance between competing constitutional concerns.

Sheppard v. Maxwell
384 U.S. 333 (1966)

MR. JUSTICE CLARK delivered the opinion of the Court.

Petitioner's wife was bludgeoned to death July 4, 1954. From the outset officials focused suspicion on petitioner, who was arrested on a murder charge July 30 and indicted August 17. His trial began October 18 and terminated with his conviction December 21, 1954. During the entire pretrial period virulent and incriminating publicity about petitioner and the murder made the case notorious, and the news media frequently aired charges and countercharges besides those for which petitioner was tried. Three months before trial he was examined for more than five hours without counsel in a televised three-day inquest conducted before an audience of several hundred spectators in a gymnasium. Over three weeks before trial the newspapers published the names and addresses of prospective jurors causing them to receive letters and telephone calls about the case. The trial began two weeks before a hotly contested election at which the chief prosecutor and the trial judge were candidates for judgeships. Newsmen were allowed to take over almost the entire small courtroom, hounding petitioner, and most of the participants. Twenty reporters were assigned seats by the court within the bar and in close proximity to the jury and counsel, precluding privacy between petitioner and his counsel. The movement of the reporters in the courtroom caused frequent confusion and disrupted the trial; and in the corridors and elsewhere in and around the courthouse they were allowed free rein by the trial judge. A broadcasting station was assigned space next to the jury room. Before the jurors began deliberations they were not sequestered and had access to all news media though the court made "suggestions" and "requests" that the jurors not expose themselves to comment about the case. Though they were sequestered during the five days and four nights of their deliberations, the jurors were allowed to make inadequately supervised telephone calls during that period. Pervasive publicity was given to the case throughout the trial, much of it involving incriminating matter not introduced at the trial, and the jurors were thrust into the role of celebrities. At least some of the publicity deluge reached the jurors. At the very inception of the proceedings and later, the trial judge announced that neither he nor anyone else could restrict the prejudicial news accounts. Despite his awareness of the excessive pretrial publicity, the trial judge failed to take effective measures against the massive publicity which continued throughout the trial or to take adequate steps to control the conduct of the trial. The petitioner filed a habeas corpus petition contending that he did not receive a fair trial. The District Court granted the writ. The Court of Appeals reversed.

The principle that justice cannot survive behind walls of silence has long been reflected in the "Anglo-American distrust for secret trials." In re Oliver, 333 U.S. 257, 268 (1948). A responsible press has always been regarded as the handmaiden of effective judicial administration, especially in the criminal field. Its function in this regard is documented by an impressive record of service over several centuries. The press does not simply publish information about trials but guards against the miscarriage of justice by subjecting the police, prosecutors, and judicial processes to extensive public scrutiny and criticism. This Court has, therefore, been unwilling to place any direct limitations on the freedom traditionally exercised by the news media for "what transpires in the court room is public property." . . .

But the Court has also pointed out that "legal trials are not like elections, to be won through the use of the meeting-hall, the radio, and the newspaper." And the Court has insisted that no one be punished for a crime without "a charge fairly made and fairly tried in a public tribunal free of prejudice, passion, excitement, and tyrannical power." "Freedom of discussion should be given the widest range compatible with the essential requirement of the fair and orderly administration of justice." . . .

. . .

The undeviating rule of this Court was expressed by Mr. Justice Holmes over half a century ago in *Patterson v. Colorado*, 205 U.S. 454, 462 (1907):

> The theory of our system is that the conclusions to be reached in a case will be induced only by evidence and argument in open court, and not by any outside influence, whether of private talk or public print.

Moreover, "the burden of showing essential unfairness . . . as a demonstrable reality," need not be undertaken when television has exposed the community "repeatedly and in depth to the spectacle of [the accused] personally confessing in detail to the crimes with which he was later to be charged." *Rideau v. Louisiana*, 373 U.S. 723, 726 (1963). . . .

[W]e cited with approval the language of MR. JUSTICE BLACK for the Court in In re Murchison, 349 U.S. 133, 136 (1955), that "our system of law has always endeavored to prevent even the probability of unfairness."

It is clear that the totality of circumstances in this case also warrants such an approach. . . . Sheppard was not granted a change of venue to a locale away from where the publicity originated; nor was his jury sequestered. The Estes jury saw none of the television broadcasts from the courtroom. . . . [T]he Sheppard jurors were subjected to newspaper, radio and television coverage of the trial while not taking part in the proceedings. They were allowed to go their separate ways outside of the courtroom, without adequate directions not to read or listen to anything concerning the case. The judge's "admonitions" at the beginning of the trial are representative:

> I would suggest to you and caution you that you do not read any newspapers during the progress of this trial, that you do not listen to radio comments nor watch or listen to television comments, insofar as this case is concerned. You will feel very much better as the trial proceeds. . . . I am sure that we shall all feel very much better if we do not indulge in any newspaper reading or listening to any comments whatever about the matter while the case is in progress. After it is all over, you can read it all to your heart's content. . . .

At intervals during the trial, the judge simply repeated his "suggestions" and "requests" that the jurors not expose themselves to comment upon the case. Moreover, the jurors were thrust into the role of celebrities by the judge's failure to insulate them from reporters and photographers. The numerous pictures of the jurors, with their addresses, which appeared in the newspapers before and during the trial itself exposed them to expressions of opinion from both cranks and friends. The fact that anonymous letters had been received by prospective jurors should have made the judge aware that this publicity seriously threatened the jurors' privacy.

. . . Sheppard stood indicted for the murder of his wife; the State was demanding the death penalty. For months the virulent publicity about Sheppard and the murder had made the case notorious. Charges and countercharges were aired in the news media besides those for which Sheppard was called to trial. In addition, only three months before trial, Sheppard was examined for more than five hours without counsel during a three-day inquest which ended in a public brawl. The inquest was televised live from a high school gymnasium seating hundreds of people. Furthermore, the trial began two weeks before a hotly contested election at which both Chief Prosecutor Mahon and Judge Blythin were candidates for judgeships.

While we cannot say that Sheppard was denied due process by the judge's refusal to take precautions against the influence of pretrial publicity alone, the court's later rulings must be considered against the setting in which the trial was held. In light of this background, we believe that the arrangements made by the judge with the news media caused Sheppard to be deprived of that "judicial serenity and calm to which [he] was entitled." *Estes v. Texas*, supra, at 536. The fact is that bedlam reigned at the courthouse during the trial and newsmen took over practically the entire courtroom, hounding most of the participants in the trial, especially Sheppard. At a temporary table within a few feet of the jury box and counsel table sat some 20 reporters staring at Sheppard and taking notes. The erection of a press table for reporters inside the bar is unprecedented. The bar of the court is reserved for counsel, providing them a safe place in which to keep papers and exhibits, and to confer privately with client and co-counsel. It is designed to protect the witness and the jury from any distractions, intrusions or influences, and to permit bench discussions of the judge's rulings away from the hearing of the public and the jury. Having assigned almost all of the available seats in the courtroom to the news media the judge lost his ability to supervise that environment. The movement of the reporters in and out of the courtroom caused frequent confusion and disruption of the trial. And the record reveals constant commotion within the bar. Moreover, the judge gave the throng of newsmen gathered in the corridors of the courthouse absolute free rein. Participants in the trial, including the jury, were forced to run a gauntlet of reporters and photographers each time they entered or left the courtroom. The total lack of consideration for the privacy of the jury was demonstrated by the assignment to a broadcasting station of space next to the jury room on the floor above the courtroom, as well as the fact that jurors were allowed to make telephone calls during their five-day deliberation.

There can be no question about the nature of the publicity which surrounded Sheppard's trial. We agree, as did the Court of Appeals, with the findings in Judge Bell's opinion for the Ohio Supreme Court:

> Murder and mystery, society, sex and suspense were combined in this case in such a manner as to intrigue and captivate the public fancy to a degree perhaps unparalleled in recent annals. Throughout the preindictment investigation, the subsequent legal skirmishes and the nine-week trial, circulation-conscious editors catered to the insatiable interest of the American public in the bizarre. . . . In this atmosphere of a 'Roman holiday' for the news media, Sam Sheppard stood trial for his life.

Indeed, every court that has considered this case, save the court that tried it, has deplored the manner in which the news media inflamed and prejudiced the public.

Much of the material printed or broadcast during the trial was never heard from the witness stand, such as the charges that Sheppard had purposely impeded the murder investigation and must be guilty since he had hired a prominent criminal lawyer; that Sheppard was a perjurer; that he had sexual relations with numerous women; that his slain wife had characterized him as a "Jekyll-Hyde"; that he was "a bare-faced liar" because of his testimony as to police treatment; and, finally, that a woman convict claimed Sheppard to be the father of her illegitimate child. As the trial progressed, the newspapers summarized and interpreted the evidence, devoting particular attention to the material that incriminated Sheppard, and often drew unwarranted inferences from testimony. At one point, a front-page picture of Mrs. Sheppard's blood-stained pillow was published after being "doctored" to show more clearly an alleged imprint of a surgical instrument.

Nor is there doubt that this deluge of publicity reached at least some of the jury. On the only occasion that the jury was queried, two jurors admitted in open court to hearing the highly inflammatory charge that a prison inmate claimed Sheppard as the father of her illegitimate child. Despite the extent and nature of the publicity to which the jury was exposed during trial, the judge refused defense counsel's other requests that the jurors be asked whether they had read or heard specific prejudicial comment about the case, including the incidents we have previously summarized. In these circumstances, we can assume that some of this material reached members of the jury.

The court's fundamental error is compounded by the holding that it lacked power to control the publicity about the trial. From the very inception of the proceedings the judge announced that neither he nor anyone else could restrict prejudicial news accounts. And he reiterated this view on numerous occasions. Since he viewed the news media as his target, the judge never considered other means that are often utilized to reduce the appearance of prejudicial material and to protect the jury from outside influence. We conclude that these procedures would have been sufficient to guarantee Sheppard a fair trial and so do not consider what sanctions might be available against a recalcitrant press nor the charges of bias now made against the state trial judge.

The carnival atmosphere at trial could easily have been avoided since the courtroom and courthouse premises are subject to the control of the court. As we stressed in Estes, the presence of the press at judicial proceedings must be limited when it is apparent that the accused might otherwise be prejudiced or disadvantaged. Bearing in mind the massive pretrial publicity, the judge should have adopted stricter rules governing the use of the courtroom by newsmen, as Sheppard's counsel requested. The number of reporters in the courtroom itself could have been limited at the first sign that their presence would disrupt the trial. They certainly should not have been placed inside the bar. Furthermore, the judge should have more closely regulated the conduct of newsmen in the courtroom. For instance, the judge belatedly asked them not to handle and photograph trial exhibits lying on the counsel table during recess.

Secondly, the court should have insulated the witnesses. All of the newspapers and radio stations apparently interviewed prospective witnesses at will, and in many instances disclosed their testimony. A typical example was the publication of numerous statements by Susan Hayes, before her appearance in court, regarding her love affair with Sheppard. Although the witnesses were barred from the courtroom during the trial the full verbatim testimony was available to them in the press. This completely nullified the judge's imposition of the rule.

Thirdly, the court should have made some effort to control the release of leads, information, and gossip to the press by police officers, witnesses, and the counsel for both sides. Much of the information thus disclosed was inaccurate, leading to groundless rumors and confusion. . . .

The fact that many of the prejudicial news items can be traced to the prosecution, as well as the defense, aggravates the judge's failure to take any action. Effective control of these sources—concededly within the court's power—might well have prevented the divulgence of inaccurate information, rumors, and accusations that made up much of the inflammatory publicity, at least after Sheppard's indictment.

More specifically, the trial court might well have proscribed extrajudicial statements by any lawyer, party, witness, or court official which divulged prejudicial matters, such as the refusal of Sheppard to submit to interrogation or take any lie detector tests; any statement made by Sheppard to officials; the identity of prospective witnesses or their probable testimony; any belief in guilt or innocence; or like statements concerning the merits of the case. . . . Being advised of the great public interest in the case, the mass coverage of the press, and the potential prejudicial impact of publicity, the court could also have requested the appropriate city and county officials to promulgate a regulation with respect to dissemination of information about the case by their employees. In addition, reporters who wrote or broadcast prejudicial stories, could have been warned as to the impropriety of publishing material not introduced in the proceedings. The judge was put on notice of such events by defense counsel's complaint about the WHK broadcast on the second day of trial. In this manner, Sheppard's right to a trial free from outside interference would have been given added protection without corresponding curtailment of the news media. Had the judge, the other officers of the court, and the police placed the interest of justice first, the news media would have soon learned to be content with the task of reporting the case as it unfolded in the courtroom—not pieced together from extrajudicial statements.

From the cases coming here we note that unfair and prejudicial news comment on pending trials has become increasingly prevalent. Due process requires that the accused receive a trial by an impartial jury free from outside influences. Given the pervasiveness of modern communications and the difficulty of effacing prejudicial publicity from the minds of the jurors, the trial courts must take strong measures to ensure that the balance is never weighed against the accused. And appellate tribunals have the duty to make an independent evaluation of the circumstances. Of course, there is nothing that proscribes the press from reporting events that transpire in the courtroom. But where there is a reasonable likelihood that prejudicial news prior to trial will prevent a fair trial, the judge should continue the case until the threat abates, or transfer it to another county not so permeated with publicity. In addition, sequestration of the jury was something the judge should have raised sua sponte with counsel. If publicity during the proceedings threatens the fairness of the trial, a new trial should be ordered. But we must remember that reversals are but palliatives; the cure lies in those remedial measures that will prevent the prejudice at its inception. The courts must take such steps by rule and regulation that will protect their processes from prejudicial outside interferences. Neither prosecutors, counsel for defense, the accused, witnesses, court staff nor enforcement officers coming under the jurisdiction of the court should be permitted to frustrate its function. Collaboration between counsel and the press as to information affecting the fairness of a criminal trial is not only subject to regulation, but is highly censurable and worthy of disciplinary measures.

Since the state trial judge did not fulfill his duty to protect Sheppard from the inherently prejudicial publicity which saturated the community and to control disruptive influences in the courtroom, we must reverse the denial of the habeas petition. The case is remanded to the District Court with instructions to issue the writ and order that Sheppard be released from custody unless the State puts him to its charges again within a reasonable time.

Constitutional principles of openness governing trials and related proceedings have yet to protect usage of electronic equipment necessary for broadcasting or cablecasting. Case law and legislation until recently have indicated significant wariness about the impact of televised proceedings upon fair trial rights. Responding to the emergence of electronic media, the American Bar Association Canons of Judicial Ethics were amended in 1937 to require exclusion of cameras from courtrooms on grounds they undermined the dignity of proceedings. The canon eventually was replaced in 1982 with a new provision to the effect that judges could allow an unintrusive electronic presence in the courtroom. The change responded to a movement among states to permit broadcast coverage of court proceedings—a trend accelerated by technology that has miniaturized and muted the electronic media's presence. Allowance of cameras in the courtroom is a pervasive phenomenon at the state court level and has been experimented with (but rejected) in federal courts. Electronic coverage of court proceedings remains a function, however, not of federal constitutional principle of statute or rule. To the extent constitutional interests are a factor in analysis, the concern historically has been with the risk to fair trial interests.

Seminal case law was quick to assume a due process violation when the criminal justice process was touched by broadcast coverage. In *Irwin v. Dowd*, the Court determined that a jury verdict was influenced by prejudicial publicity and thus reversed a murder conviction.[170] Two years later, in *Rideau v. Louisiana*, it found that the broadcast of a defendant's confession before trial amounted to a denial of due process.[171] Given extensive public exposure to the confession as a consequence of television, the Court assumed rather than required actual proof of prejudice.[172] In *Estes v. Texas*, the Court almost endorsed the proposition that the mere presence of electronic media in the courtroom created such a high probability of prejudice that due process was inherently denied. The understanding fell short of a majority position due largely to Justice Harlan's sense that, despite the risks of cameras in the courtroom, technological progress might minimize their disruptive capacity.

---

[170] Irvin v. Dowd, 366 U.S. 717 (1961).
[171] Rideau v. Louisiana, 373 U.S. 723 (1963).
[172] *Id.*

Estes v. Texas
381 U.S. 532 (1965)

. . .

Mr. Justice Harlan, concurring.

I concur in the opinion of the Court, subject, however, to the reservations and only to the extent indicated in this opinion.

The constitutional issue presented by this case is far-reaching in its implications for the administration of justice in this country. The precise question is whether the Fourteenth Amendment prohibits a State, over the objection of a defendant, from employing television in the courtroom to televise contemporaneously, or subsequently by means of videotape, the courtroom proceedings of a criminal trial of widespread public interest. The issue is no narrower than this because petitioner has not asserted any isolatable prejudice resulting from the presence of television apparatus within the courtroom or from the contemporaneous or subsequent broadcasting of the trial proceedings. On the other hand, the issue is no broader, for we are concerned here only with a criminal trial of great notoriety, and not with criminal proceedings of a more or less routine nature.

The question is fraught with unusual difficulties. Permitting television in the courtroom undeniably has mischievous potentialities for intruding upon the detached atmosphere which should always surround the Judicial process. Forbidding this innovation, however, would doubtless impinge upon one of the valued attributes of our federalism by preventing the States from pursuing a novel course of procedural experimentation. My conclusion is that there is no constitutional requirement that television be allowed in the courtroom, and, at least as to a notorious criminal trial such as this one, the considerations against allowing television in the courtroom so far outweigh the countervailing factors advanced in its support as to require a holding that what was done in this case infringed the fundamental right to a fair trial assured by the Due Process Clause of the Fourteenth Amendment.

Some preliminary observations are in order: All would agree, I am sure, that at its worst, television is capable of distorting the trial process so as to deprive it of fundamental fairness. Cables, klieg lights, interviews with the principal participants, commentary on their performances, "commercials" at frequent intervals, special wearing apparel and makeup for the trial participants—certainly such things would not conduce to the sound administration of justice by any acceptable standard. But that is not the case before us. We must judge television as we find it in this trial—relatively unobtrusive, with the cameras contained in a booth at the back of the courtroom.

The free speech and press guarantees of the First and Fourteenth Amendments are . . . asserted as embodying a positive right to televise trials, but the argument is greatly overdrawn. Unquestionably, television has become a very effective medium for transmitting news. Many trials are newsworthy, and televising them might well provide the most accurate and comprehensive means of conveying their content to the public. Furthermore, television is capable of performing an educational function by acquainting the public with the judicial process in action. Albeit these are credible policy arguments in favor of television, they are not arguments of constitutional proportions. The rights to print and speak, over television as elsewhere, do not embody an independent right to bring the mechanical facilities of the broadcasting and printing industries into the courtroom. Once beyond the confines of the courthouse, a news-gathering agency may publicize, within wide limits, what its representatives have heard and seen in the courtroom. But the line is drawn at the courthouse door; and within, a reporter's constitutional rights are not greater than those of any other member of the public. Within the courthouse the only relevant constitutional consideration is that the accused be accorded a fair trial. If the presence of television substantially detracts from that goal, due process requires that its use be forbidden.

I see no force in the argument that to exclude television apparatus from the courtroom, while at the same time permitting newspaper reporters to bring in their pencils and notebooks, would discriminate in favor of the press as against the broadcasting services. The distinctions to be drawn between the accouterments of the press and the television media turn not on differences of size and shape but of function and effect. The presence of the press at trials may have a distorting effect, but it is not caused by their pencils and notebooks. If it were, I would not hesitate to say that such physical paraphernalia should be barred.

I do not deem the constitutional inquiry in this case ended by the finding, in effect conceded by petitioner's counsel, that no isolatable prejudice was occasioned by the manner in which television was employed in this case. Courtroom television introduces into the conduct of a criminal trial the element of professional "showmanship," an extraneous influence whose subtle capacities for serious mischief in a case of this sort will not be underestimated by any lawyer experienced in the elusive imponderables of the trial arena. In the context of a trial of intense public interest, there is certainly a strong possibility that the timid or reluctant witness, for whom a court appearance even at its traditional best is a har-rowing affair, will become more timid or reluctant when he finds that he will also be appearing before a "hidden audience" of unknown but large dimensions. There is certainly a strong possibility that the "cocky" witness having a thirst for the limelight will become more "cocky' under the influence of television. And who can say that the juror who is gratified by having been chosen for a front-line case, an ambitious prosecutor, a publicity-minded defense counsel, and even a conscientious judge will not stray, albeit unconsciously, from doing what "comes naturally" into pluming themselves for a satisfactory television "performance"?

Surely possibilities of this kind carry grave potentialities for distorting the integrity of the judicial process bearing on the determination of the guilt or innocence of the accused, and, more particularly, for casting doubt on the reliability of the fact-finding process carried on under such conditions. To be sure, such distortions may produce no telltale signs, but in a highly publicized trial the danger of their presence is substantial, and their effects may be far more pervasive and deleterious than the physical disruptions which all concede would vitiate a conviction. A lively public interest could increase the size of the viewing audience immensely, and the masses of spectators to whom the trial is telecast would have become emotionally involved with the case through the dissemination of pretrial publicity, the usual concomitant of such a case. The presence of television would certainly emphasize to the trial participants that the case is something "special." Particularly treacherous situations are presented in cases where pretrial publicity has been massive even when jurors positively state they will not be influenced by it[.] To increase the possibility of influence and the danger of a "popular verdict" by subjecting the jurors to the view of a mass audience whose approach to the case has been conditioned by pretrial publicity can only make a bad situation worse. The entire thrust of rules of evidence and the other protections attendant upon the modern trial is to keep extraneous influences out of the courtroom. As we recently observed, "Mr. Justice Holmes stated no more than a truism when he observed that 'Any judge who has sat with juries knows that in spite of forms they are extremely likely to be impregnated by the environing atmosphere.' The knowledge on the part of the jury and other trial participants that they are being televised to an emotionally involved audience can only aggravate the atmosphere created by pretrial publicity.

The State argues that specific prejudice must be shown for the Due Process Clause to apply. I do not believe that the Fourteenth Amendment is so impotent when the trial practices in question are instinct with dangers to constitutional guarantees. I am at a loss to understand how the Fourteenth Amendment can be thought not to encompass protecting of a state criminal trial from the dangers created by the intrusion of collateral and wholly irrelevant influences into the courtroom. The Court has not hesitated in the past to condemn such practices even without any positive showing of isolatable prejudice. . . .

. . .

The arguments advanced against the constitutional banning of televised trials seem to me peculiarly unpersuasive. It is said that the pictorial broadcasting of trials will serve to educate the public as to the nature of the judicial process. Whatever force such arguments might have in run-of-the-mill cases, they carry little weight in cases of the sort before us, where the public's interest in viewing the trial is likely to be engendered more by curiosity about the personality of the well-known figure who is the defendant (as here), or about famous witnesses or lawyers who will appear on the television screen, or about the details of the particular crime involved, than by innate curiosity to learn about the workings of the judicial process itself. Indeed it would be naive not to suppose that it would be largely such factors that would qualify a trial for commercial television "billing," and it is precisely that kind of case where the risks of permitting television coverage of the proceedings are at their greatest.

It is also asserted that televised trials will cause witnesses to be more truthful, and jurors, judges, and lawyers more diligent. To say the least this argument is sophistic, for it is impossible to believe that the reliability of a trial as a method of finding facts and determining guilt or innocence increases in relation to the size of the crowd which is watching it. Attendance by interested spectators in the courtroom will fully satisfy the safeguards of "public trial." Once openness is thus assured, the addition of masses of spectators would, I venture to say, detract rather than add to the realizability of the process. A trial in Yankee Stadium, even if the crowd sat in stony silence, would be a substantially different affair from a trial in a traditional courtroom under traditional conditions, and the difference would not, I think, be that the witnesses, lawyers, judges, and jurors in the stadium would be more truthful, diligent, and capable of reliably finding facts and determining guilt or innocence. There will be no disagreement, I am sure, among those competent to judge that precisely the opposite would likely be the case.

Finally, we should not be deterred from making the constitutional judgment which this case demands by the prospect that the day may come when television will have become so commonplace an affair in the daily life of the average person as to dissipate all reasonable likelihood that its use in courtrooms may disparage the judicial process. If and when that day arrives the constitutional judgment called for now would of course be subject to re-examination in accordance with the traditional workings of the Due Process Clause. At the present juncture I can only conclude that televised trials, at least in cases like this one, possess such capabilities for interfering with the even course of the judicial process that they are constitutionally banned. On these premises I concur in the opinion of the Court.

Harlan's grasp of technological potential ultimately was prescient. As television in particular acquired the capability to function portably, less intrusively and in low light conditions, states began to relax their prohibitions against broadcast coverage of court proceedings. The trend toward allowing cameras in the courtroom was facilitated by the Court's decision, in *Chandler v. Florida*, requiring a particularized showing of prejudice to support the claim of a due process deprivation.

Chandler v. Florida
449 U.S. 560 (1981)

CHIEF JUSTICE BURGER delivered the opinion of the Court.

The question presented on this appeal is whether, consistent with constitutional guarantees, a state may provide for radio, television, and still photographic coverage of a criminal trial for public broadcast, notwithstanding the objection of the accused.

. . .

Since we are satisfied that *Estes* did not announce a constitutional rule that all photographic or broadcast coverage of criminal trials is inherently a denial of due process, we turn to consideration, as a matter of first impression, of the appellants' suggestion that we now promulgate such a *per se* rule. . . .

Not unimportant to the position asserted by Florida and other states is the change in television technology since 1962, when *Estes* was tried. It is urged, and some empirical data are presented, that many of the negative factors found in *Estes*—cumbersome equipment, cables, distracting lighting, numerous camera technicians—are less substantial factors today than they were at that time.

It is also significant that safeguards have been built into the experimental programs in state courts, and into the Florida program, to avoid some of the most egregious problems envisioned by the six opinions in the *Estes* case. Florida admonishes its courts to take special pains to protect certain witnesses—for example, children, victims of sex crimes, some informants, and even the very timid witness or party—from the glare of publicity and the tensions of being "on camera."

The Florida guidelines place on trial judges positive obligations to be on guard to protect the fundamental right of the accused to a fair trial. The Florida Canon, being one of the few permitting broadcast coverage of criminal trials over the objection of the accused, raises problems not present in the rules of other states. Inherent in electronic coverage of trial is the risk that the very awareness by the accused of the coverage and the contemplated broadcast may adversely affect the conduct of the participants and the fairness of the trial, yet leave no evidence of how the conduct or the trials' fairness was affected. Given this danger, it is significant that Florida requires that objections of the accused to coverage be heard and considered on the record by the trial court. In addition to providing a record for appellate review, a pretrial hearing enables a defendant to advance the basis of his objection to broadcast coverage and allows the trial court to define the steps necessary to minimize or eliminate the risks of prejudice to the accused. Experiments such as the one presented here may well increase the number of appeals by adding a new basis for claims to reverse, but this is a risk Florida has chosen to take after preliminary experimentation. Here, the record does not in-

dicate that appellants requested an evidentiary hearing to show adverse impact or injury. Nor does the record reveal anything more than generalized allegations of prejudice. . . .

To say that the appellants have not demonstrated that broadcast coverage is inherently a denial of due process is not to say that the appellants were in fact accorded all of the protections of due process in their trial. As noted earlier, a defendant has the right on review to show that the media's coverage of his case—printed or broadcast—compromised the ability of the jury to judge him fairly. Alternatively, a defendant might show that broadcast coverage of his particular case had an adverse impact on the trial participants sufficient to constitute a denial of due process. Neither showing was made in this case.

To demonstrate prejudice in a specific case a defendant must show something more than juror awareness that the trial is such as to attract the attention of broadcasters. No doubt the very presence of a camera in the courtroom made the jurors aware that the trial was thought to be of sufficient interest to the public to warrant coverage. Jurors, forbidden to watch all broadcasts, would have had no way of knowing that only fleeting seconds of the proceeding would be reproduced. But the appellants have not attempted to show with any specificity that the presence of cameras impaired the ability of the jurors to decide the case on only the evidence before them or that their trial was affected adversely by the impact on any of the participants of the presence of cameras and the prospect of broadcast.

Although not essential to our holding, we note that at *voir dire*, the jurors were asked if the presence of the camera would in any way compromise their ability to consider the case. Each answered that the camera would not prevent him or her from considering the case solely on the merits. The trial court instructed the jurors not to watch television accounts of the trial, and the appellants do not contend that any juror violated this instruction. The appellants have offered no evidence that any participant in this case was affected by the presence of cameras. In short, there is no showing that the trial was compromised by television coverage, as was the case in *Estes*.

DEL: Despite advancing the law to a more logical state, given modern technological realities, the *Chandler* decision could have gone further. Instead of a due process focus, the Court logically might have opened courtrooms to broadcast coverage pursuant to First Amendment principle. Such a result rationally would have extended Justice Stewart's argument that terms of access, failing to distinguish between press and public, are unreasonable. It also would comport with the Court's own understanding, in the courtroom access cases, of the educational function of open proceedings. Insofar as video cameras have become a pervasive instrumentality of both press and public, it is increasingly difficult to take seriously arguments that they disrupt or distract. Even if accepted that the presence of recording devices enhances self-consciousness, and alters thinking and behavior, the reality is that the spotlight radiated upon trial participants by a court's own processes and surroundings historically and without controversy have had the same if not an even greater effect. To the extent pockets of resistance to live or recorded proceedings persist, as they do in the Supreme Court itself, policy seems at odds with constitutionally recognized interests in informed self-rule. Especially at the appellate level, where jurors and defendants are not a factor in the proceedings, prohibition of broadcast or cable technology seems hypocritically inimical to imperatives of governmental openness and accountability.

DER: The news media's presence in the courtroom has complicated the process of selecting and sustaining an impartial jury. It is practically impossible in notorious cases to find a juror who has not already begun to form an opinion about the evidence based on newspaper and television news reports and commentaries. Keeping the jurors ignorant of ongoing press coverage of the trial may require sequestering them for months at a time. These difficulties in producing an unbiased jury have led some commentators to look more favorably upon regimes even more restrictive of press access to trials than our own. Canadian and British judges, for example, often severely limit the information about court proceedings that the press may make public in order to ensure that defendants receive a fair trial. Defendants' rights are jeopardized more, however, by trials held in secrecy than by public knowledge and discussion about trials. The tension between open trials and open-minded juries requires re-examining our expectations about jurors' deliberations and the meaning of impartiality.

D.   Medium-Specific First Amendment Standards

In contrast with its analysis rejecting a preferred status for the press and insisting upon constitutional parity between the press and public, the Court has developed First Amendment standards that uniquely diminish much of its interest in expressive freedom. Speech that may be protected in its own right sometimes may be regulated when propagated by the press. Differentiation of First Amendment principle also may be a function of a medium's particular nature. Freedom of the press as it has evolved over the past half century in particular comprehends not a single set of standards or a universal doctrine for all media but a multiplicity of premises and principles that depend upon the editorial source itself. Medium specific analysis is the central feature of case law that has evolved a hierarchy of press freedom. Within that constitutional order, print media have received the highest level of protection and broadcasting the least.[173]

Medium specific analysis responds to the emergence over the past century of new communication methodologies that have expanded the press universe beyond the traditional print model. As the press evolved from small business in the late eighteenth century to a modern economically concentrated industry with diverse capabilities, concern has grown over its role and influence. To the extent such attention inspires regula-

---

[173] Federal Communications Commission v. Pacifica Foundation, 438 U.S. 726, 748 (1978) ("of all forms of communication, it is broadcasting that has received the most limited First Amendment protection"); Miami Herald Publishing Co. v. Tornillo, 418 U.S. 241, 258 (1974) (right of reply provision comparable to regulation upheld in broadcasting not "consistent with First Amendment guarantees of a free press as they have evolved to this time").

tory initiative, First Amendment tension is inevitable. The conflict between editorial freedom and regulatory interest was previewed toward the end of the nineteenth century when Samuel D. Warren and Louis D. Brandeis warned of the press' expanding capabilities and influence. With newspapers having acquired photojournalistic capability and publishers having calculated that sensationalism turned profits, Warren and Brandeis argued that interests of privacy and decency were being compromised.

Samuel D. Warren & Louis D. Brandeis
The Right to Privacy
4 Harvard Law Review 193 (1890)

THAT the individual shall have full protection in person and in property is a principle as old as the common law; but it has been found necessary from time to time to define anew the exact nature and extent of such protection. Political, social, and economic changes entail the recognition of new rights, and the common law, in its eternal youth, grows to meet the demands of society. Thus, in very early times, the law gave a remedy only for physical interference with life and property, for trespasses *vi et armis.* Then the "right to life" served only to protect the subject from battery in its various forms; liberty meant freedom from actual restraint; and the right to property secured to the individual his lands and his cattle. Later, there came a recognition of man's spiritual nature, of his feelings and his intellect. Gradually the scope of these legal rights broadened; and now the right to life has come to mean the right to enjoy life—the right to be let alone; the right to liberty secures the exercise of extensive civil privileges; and the term "property" has grown to comprise every form of possession—intangible, as well as tangible. . . .

This development of the law was inevitable. The intense intellectual and emotional life, and the heightening of sensations which came with the advance of civilization, made it clear to men that only a part of the pain, pleasure, and profit of life lay in physical things. Thoughts, emotions, and sensations demanded legal recognition, and the beautiful capacity for growth which characterizes the common law enabled the judges to afford the requisite protection, without the interposition of the legislature.

Recent inventions and business methods call attention to the next step which must be taken for the protection of the person, and for securing to the individual what Judge Cooley calls the right "to be let alone." Instantaneous photographs, and newspaper's enterprise have invaded the sacred precincts of private and domestic life; and numerous mechanical devices threaten to make good the prediction that "what is whispered in the closet shall be proclaimed from the house-tops." For years there has been a feeling that the law must afford some remedy for the unauthorized circulation of portraits of private persons and the evil of the invasion of privacy by the newspapers, long keenly felt, has been but recently discussed by an able writer. The alleged facts of a somewhat notorious case brought before an inferior tribunal in New York a few months ago, directly involved the consideration of the right of circulating portraits; and the question whether our law will recognize and protect the right to privacy in this and in other respects must soon come before our courts for consideration.

Of the desirability—indeed of the necessity—of some such protection, there can, it is believed, be no doubt. The press is overstepping in every direction the obvious bounds of propriety and of decency. Gossip is no longer the resource of the idle and of the vicious, but has become a trade, which is pursued with industry as well as effrontery. To satisfy a prurient taste the details of sexual relations are spread broadcast in the columns of the daily papers. To occupy the indolent, column upon column is filled with idle gossip, which can only be procured by intrusion upon the domestic circle. The intensity and complexity of life, attendant upon advancing civilization, have rendered necessary some retreat from the world, and man, under the refining influence of culture, has become more sensitive to publicity, so that solitude and privacy have become more essential to the individual; but modern enterprise and invention have, through invasions upon his privacy, subjected him to mental pain and distress, far greater than could be inflicted by mere bodily injury. Nor is the harm wrought by such invasions confined to the suffering of those who may be made the subjects of journalistic or other enterprise. In this, as in other branches of commerce, the supply creates the demand. Each crop of unseemly gossip, thus harvested, becomes the seed of more, and, in direct proportion to its circulation, results in a lowering of social standards and of morality. Even gossip apparently harmless, when widely and persistently circulated, is potent for evil. It both belittles and perverts. It belittles by inverting the relative importance of things, thus dwarfing the thoughts and aspirations of a people. When personal gossip attains the dignity of print, and crowds the space available for matters of real interest to the community, what wonder that the ignorant and thoughtless mistake its relative importance. Easy of comprehension, appealing to that weak side of human nature which is never wholly cast down by the misfortunes and frailties of our neighbors, no one can be surprised that it usurps the place of interest in brains capable of other things. Triviality destroys at once robustness of thought and delicacy of feeling. No enthusiasm can flourish, no generous impulse can survive under its blighting influence. . . .

As new electronic media became dominant over the course of the twentieth century, the concern with quality of editorial output originally articulated by Warren and Brandeis heightened. Pursuant to his sense that radio had defaulted in its "First Amendment . . . purpose [of ensuring] that all the citizens of our self-governing society shall be 'equally' educated," Alexander Meiklejohn argued that the medium had forfeited its constitutional status.[174]

---

[174] ALEXANDER MEIKLEJOHN, FREE SPEECH AND ITS RELATION TO SELF-GOVERNMENT 104–06 (1948).

Alexander Meiklejohn
Free Speech and Its Relation to Self-Government (1948)

. . .

When this new form of communication became available, there opened up before us the possibility that, as a people living a common life under a common agreement, we might communicate with one another freely with regard to the values, the opportunities, the difficulties, the joys and sorrows, the hopes and fears, the plans and purposes, of that common life. It seemed possible that, amid all our differences, we might become a community of mutual understanding and of shared interests. It was that hope which justified our making the radio "free," our giving it the protection of the First Amendment.

But never was a human hope more bitterly disappointed. The radio as it now operates among us is not free. Nor is it entitled to the protection of the First Amendment. It is not engaged in the task of enlarging and enriching human communication. It is engaged in making money. And the First Amendment does not intend to guarantee men freedom to say what some private interest pays them to say what, as citizens, they think, what they believe, about the general welfare.

. . . [T]he total effect, as judged in terms of education value, is one of terrible destruction. The radio, as we now have it, is not cultivating those qualities of taste, of reasoned judgment, of integrity, of loyalty, of mutual understanding upon which the enterprise of self-government depends. On the contrary, it is a mighty force for breaking them down. It corrupts both our morals and our intelligence. And that catastrophe is significant for our inquiry, because it reveals how hollow may be the victories of the freedom of speech when our acceptance of the principle is merely formalistic. Misguided by that formalism we Americans have given to the doctrine merely its negative meaning. We have used it for the protection of private, possessive interests with which it has no concern. It is misinterpretations such as this which, in our use of the radio, the moving picture, the newspaper and other forms of publication, are giving the name "freedoms" to the most flagrant enslavements of our minds and wills. . . .

Such sentiment echoed in the statement of the Chair of the Federal Communications Commission who, in the early 1960s, described television as "a vast wasteland" and stressed that broadcasters should promote the "character, citizenship and intellectual capacity of the people."[175] Contemporary case law enables the FCC to regulate broadcast programming that the Court has equated with "a pig in the parlor."[176] Such concern with the quality of editorial output is not a permissible basis for regulating print media. For publishing, the traditional First Amendment understanding is that "the State has no right to cleanse public debate to the point where it is grammatically palatable to the most squeamish of us."[177] Different constitutional results for newer media are a function of medium specific analysis which, as described by Justice Jackson, is based upon the understanding that "[t]he moving picture screen, the radio, the newspaper, the handbill, the sound truck and the street orator have differing natures, values, abuses, and dangers. Each . . . is a law unto itself."[178]

Medium specific criteria not only have become the basis for divergent sets of press freedom but for determining whether a communications methodology is part of the press. In eventually determining that motion pictures had First Amendment status, despite its earlier determination that they did not qualify as the press,[179] the Court nonetheless observed that the scope of the medium's protection was to be referenced to the idiosyncratic problems it presented.

---

[175] Remarks of Newton Minow to the National Association of Broadcasters, May 9, 1961.
[176] Federal Communications Commission v. Pacifica Foundation, 438 U.S. at 750.
[177] Cohen v. California, 403 U.S. 15, 25 (1971).
[178] Kovacs v. Cooper, 336 U.S. 77, 97 (1949) (Jackson, J., concurring).
[179] Mutual Film Corp. v. Industrial Commission of Ohio, 236 U.S. 230 (1915).

Joseph Bursytyn, Inc. v. Wilson
343 U.S. 495 (1952)

Mr. Justice Clark delivered the opinion of the Court.

The issue here is the constitutionality, under the First and Fourteenth Amendments, of a New York statute which permits the banning of motion picture films on the ground that they are "sacrilegious."

. . .

It cannot be doubted that motion pictures are a significant medium for the communication of ideas. They may affect public attitudes and behavior in a variety of ways, ranging from direct espousal of a political or social doctrine to the subtle shaping of thought which characterizes all artistic expression. The importance of motion pictures as an organ of public opinion is not lessened by the fact that they are designed to entertain as well as to inform. As was said in *Winters v. People of State of New York*, 1948, 333 U.S. 507, 510:

"The line between the informing and the entertaining is too elusive for the protection of that basic right [a free press]. Everyone is familiar with instances of propaganda through fiction. What is one man's amusement, teaches another's doctrine."

It is urged that motion pictures do not fall within the First Amendment's aegis because their production, distribution, and exhibition is a large-scale business conducted for private profit. We cannot agree. That books, newspapers, and magazines are published and sold for profit does not prevent them from being a form of expression whose liberty is safeguarded by the First Amendment. We fail to see why operation for profit should have any different effect in the case of motion pictures.

It is further urged that motion pictures possess a greater capacity for evil, particularly among the youth of a community, than other modes of expression. Even if one were to accept this hypothesis, it does not follow that motion pictures should be disqualified from First Amendment protection. If there be capacity for evil it may be relevant in determining the permissible scope of community control, but it does not authorize substantially unbridled censorship such as we have here.

For the foregoing reasons, we conclude that expression by means of motion pictures is included within the free speech and free press guaranty of the First and Fourteenth Amendments. To the extent that language in the opinion in *Mutual Film Corp. v. Industrial Comm.*, is out of harmony with the views here set forth, we no longer adhere to it.

To hold that liberty of expression by means

of motion pictures is guaranteed by the First and Fourteenth Amendments, however, is not the end of our problem. It does not follow that the Constitution requires absolute freedom to exhibit every motion picture of every kind at all times and all places. That much is evident from the series of decisions of this Court with respect to other media of communication of ideas. Nor does it follow that motion pictures are necessarily subject to the precise rules governing any other particular method of express. Each method tends to present its own peculiar problems. But the basic principles of freedom of speech and the press, like the First Amendment's command, do not vary. Those principles, as they have frequently been enunciated by this Court, make freedom of expression the rule. There is no justification in this case for making an exception to that rule.

. . .

The Court's allowance of regulatory attention to risks attributed to motion pictures enabled censorship boards to survive despite the conferral of First Amendment status upon the medium. The demise of film review boards does not obscure the option states still have to maintain censorship boards if they choose. Key to the constitutionality of a system for officially reviewing motion pictures would be a system of prompt administrative procedures, speedy judicial review of any decision to censor and a burden upon the censor to prove a film is constitutionally unprotected.[180]

Broadcasting has become subject to special forms of regulation pursuant to the sense that it is a scarce, pervasive and invasive medium that is readily accessible to children. The scarcity premise has been the basis for content diversification regimes that reckon with the problem that "there are substantially more individuals who want to broadcast than there are frequencies to allocate."[181] An understanding of broadcasting as a pervasive medium, which intrudes upon the privacy of homeowners and is easily accessed by children, has generated restrictions on programming that trades in indecent or offensive language.[182]

As newer media have evolved, inquiries with respect to their First Amendment status have commenced with attention to whether they are more like print or broadcast methodology. In initially considering the constitutional status of cable, the Supreme Court acknowledged that cable "plainly implicate[s] First Amendment interests" but has attributes of both publishing and broadcasting.[183] Lower courts thereafter divided over what medium cable is most akin to, although most tend to analogize cable to newspapers rather than broadcasting. In *Quincy Cable TV, Inc. v. Federal Communications Commission*, the Court of Appeals for the District of Columbia Circuit concluded that cable more logically fit the model of publishing.

---

[180] Freedman v. Maryland, 380 U.S. 51, 58–60 (1965).

[181] Red Lion Broadcasting Co. v. Federal Communications Commission, 395 U.S. 367, 388 (1969).

[182] Federal Communications Commission v. Pacifica Foundation, 438 U.S. 726, 749–50 (1978).

[183] City of Los Angeles v. Preferred Communications, Inc., 476 U.S. 488, 494 (1984).

Quincy Cable TV, Inc. v. Federal Communications Commission
768 F.2d 1434 (D.C. Cir. 1985), *cert. denied*
476 U.S. 1169 (1986)

J. SKELLY WRIGHT, Circuit Judge.

. . . It has become something of a truism to observe that "differences in the characteristics of news media justify differences in the First Amendment standards applied to them." The suggestion is not that traditional First Amendment doctrine falls by the wayside when evaluating the protection due novel modes of communication. For the core values of the First Amendment clearly transcend the particular details of the various vehicles through which messages are conveyed. Rather, the objective is to recognize that those values are best served by paying close attention to the distinctive features that differentiate the increasingly diverse mechanisms through which a speaker may express his view.

This sensitivity to the uniqueness of each medium precludes facile adoption of the First Amendment jurisprudence that has developed around challenges to FCC regulation of broadcast television and radio, From the perspective of the viewer, no doubt, cable and broadcast television appear virtually indistinguishable. For purposes of First Amendment analysis, however, they differ in at least one critical respect. Unlike ordinary broadcast television, which transmits the video image over airwaves capable of bearing only a limited number of signals, cable reaches the home over a coaxial cable with the technological capacity to carry 200 or more channels.

The distinction is of fundamental significance in light of the Supreme Court's oft-repeated suggestion that the First Amendment tolerates far more intrusive regulation of broadcasters than of other media precisely because of the inescapable physical limitations on the number of voices that can simultaneously be carried over the electromagnetic spectrum. These limitations, the Supreme Court observed early on, engender a peculiar irony of the broadcast medium: limited regulation, by converting aural and visual chaos into channels of effective communication, furthers rather than impedes the First Amendment's mission. "With everybody on the air," wrote Justice Frankfurter, "nobody could be heard. . . . [T]he radio spectrum is simply not large enough to accommodate everybody." Without the imposition of some governmental control, "the cacophony of competing voices" would drown each other out. Moreover, quite independent of the objective of bringing communicative order to the otherwise chaotic airwaves, the First Amendment tolerates a modest degree of government oversight of broadcast radio and television because such regulation assures that broadcasters, privileged occupants of a physically scare resource, act in a manner consistent with their status as fiduciaries of the public's interest in responsible use of the spectrum.

As this and other courts have recognized, the "scarcity rationale" has no place in evaluating government regulation of cable television.

The First Amendment theory [governing broadcasting] cannot be directly applied to cable television since an essential precondition of that theory—physical interference and scarcity requiring an umpiring role for govern-

ment—is absent. . . .

Nor do we discern other attributes of cable television that would justify a standard of review analogous to the more forgiving First Amendment analysis traditionally applied to the broadcast media. We cannot agree, for example, that the mere fact that cable operators require use of a public right of way—typically utility poles—somehow justifies lesser First Amendment scrutiny. The potential for disruption inherent in stringing coaxial cables above city streets may well warrant some governmental regulation of the process of installing and maintaining the cable system. But hardly does it follow that such regulation could extend to controlling the nature of the programming that is conveyed over that system. No doubt a municipality has some power to control the placement of newspaper vending machines. But any effort to use that power as the basis for dictating what must be placed in such machines would surely be invalid.

Nor, on this record, can we concur in the suggestion that the "natural monopoly characteristics" of cable create economic constraints on competition comparable to the physical constraints imposed by the limited size of the electromagnetic spectrum. At the outset, the "economic scarcity" argument rests on the entirely unproven—and indeed doubtful—assumption that cable operators are in a position to exact monopolistic charges. Moreover, the tendency toward monopoly, if present at all, may well be attributable more to governmental action—particularly the municipal franchising process—than to any "natural" economic phenomenon. In any case, whatever the outcome of the debate over the monopolistic characteristics of cable, the Supreme Court has categorically rejected the suggestion that purely economic constraints on the number of voices available in a given community justify otherwise unwarranted intrusions into First Amendment rights. *Miami Herald Publishing Co. v. Tornillo*, 418 U.S. 241, 247–256 (1974). While *Miami Herald* involved the conventional press, as this court has had prior occasion to observe, there is no meaningful "distinction between cable television and newspapers on this point."

Indeed, once one has cleared the conceptual hurdle of recognizing that all forms of television need not be treated as a generic unity for purposes of the First Amendment, the analogy to more traditional media is compelling. Two influential commissions have in fact reached precisely that conclusion. In the words of the Cabinet Committee on Cable Communications, "[C]able development has the potential of creating an electronic medium of communications more diverse, more pluralistic and more open, more like the print and film media than like our present broadcast system."

In sum, beyond the obvious parallel that both cable and broadcast television impinge on the senses via a video receiver, the two media differ in constitutionally significant ways. In light of cable's virtually unlimited channel capacity, the standard of First Amendment review reserved for occupants of the physically scarce airwaves is plainly inapplicable. Accordingly, we must look elsewhere to determine the appropriate yardstick against which to measure the constitutionality of the must-carry rules.

Competing against the *Quincy TV Court's* perspective on cable's nature is the view, expressed in *Berkshire Cablevision of Rhode Island, Inc.*, that the medium is more like broadcasting.

Berkshire Cablevision of Rhode Island, Inc. v. Burke
571 F.Supp. 976 (D.R.I. 1983) *vacated as moot*
773 F.2d 382 (1st Cir. 1985)

PETTINE, SENIOR DISTRICT JUDGE.

. . .

. . . Newspapers and cable television cannot be equated. More to the point, the two media are constitutionally distinguishable. Although a cable operator's selection of its programming is similar to the editorial function of a newspaper publisher or a television broadcaster, this similarity does not mean that each medium is entitled to the same measure of First Amendment protection. "Each method of communicating ideas is a 'law unto itself' and that law must reflect the 'differing natures, values, abuses and dangers of each method.'"

CATV and newspapers first differ in that only the latter have historically operated virtually free from any form of government control over their content. As Justice White noted in his concurrence in *Miami Herald Publishing Co. v. Tornillo*: "According to our accepted jurisprudence, the First Amendment erects a virtually insurmountable barrier between government and the print media so far as government tampering, in advance of publication, with news and editorial content is concerned." It was in this historical setting that the *Tornillo* court struck down the Florida right-of-access law.

Cable television does not have a similar history of freedom from government regulation over either its operations or the content of its programming. Indeed, government franchising of the cable television industry is virtually indispensable. For example, since constructing a cable television system requires use of the public streets or telephone poles, the government has a substantial interest in limiting the number of cable operators who build cable systems.

Of course, the flip side to government franchising is that it insulates cable operators from unnecessary competition. The award of a franchise serves as a rational way of choosing which cable operator will provide cable television service within a particular service area. Cable operators often compete for a cable franchise but very rarely develop competing cable systems, for the same service area. Such a franchising system recognizes the economic realities of the cable industry, which, as a practical matter, create a "natural monopoly" for the first cable operator to construct a cable system, in a given service area. Testimony in this case established that to construct the Newport County cable system would cost approximately seven million dollars. Because of these start-up costs and the nature of the cable television market, cable systems have operated largely free from competition.

. . .

Clearly, then, one basic issue in the instant case is whether or not economic "scarcity" is a constitutionally sufficient rationale for the regulation of cable television. . . . While it is true that the Supreme Court has rejected economic scarcity as a basis for the regulation of newspapers, the lack of any access requirement for newspapers simply does not prevent a member of the general public from expressing his opinions *in that same medium*, which in such a case is print, of course. Any person may distribute a written message in the form of a leaflet, pamphlet, or other relatively inexpensive form of "publication." In contrast, a resident of Newport County who does not have seven million dollars to develop his own cable system is shut out of that medium with no way to express his ideas with the widely acknowledged power of the small screen. Quite frankly, I am unwilling to say that the Supreme Court would ignore this distinction were the issue to come before it.

. . .

How a medium is characterized in relationship to other media is critical for First Amendment purposes. As the communications universe increasingly is characterized by convergence of capabilities, and the union of televisions, telephones and computers into single networks with multidimensional capabilities for processing and transferring voice, data and video, the traditional analytical model has been challenged on grounds it is obsolete and risky.

Ithiel de Sola Pool
Technologies of Freedom (1983)

Comment re: medium specific standards

1. A Shadow Darkens

Civil liberty functions today in a changing technological context. For five hundred years a struggle was fought, and in a few countries won, for the right of people to speak and print freely, unlicensed, uncensored, and uncontrolled. But new technologies of electronic communication may now relegate old and freed media such as pamphlets, platforms, and periodicals to a corner of the public forum. Electronic modes of communication that enjoy lesser rights are moving to center stage. The new communication technologies have not inherited all the legal immunities that were won for the old. When wires, radio waves, satellites, and computers became major vehicles of discourse, regulation seemed to be a technical necessity. And so, as speech increasingly flows over those electronic media, the five-century growth of an unabridged right of citizens to speak without controls may be endangered. . . .

Although the first principle of communications law in the United States is the guarantee of freedom in the First Amendment, in fact this country has a trifurcated communications system. In three domains of communication—print, common carriage, and broadcasting—the law has evolved separately, and in each domain with but modest relation to the others.

In the domain of print and other means of communication that existed in the formative days of the nation, such as pulpits, periodicals, and public meetings, the First Amendment truly governs. In well over one hundred cases dealing with publishing, canvassing, public speeches, and associations, the Supreme Court has applied the First Amendment to the media that existed in the eighteenth century.

In the domain of common carriers, which includes the telephone, the telegraph, the postal system, and now some computer networks, a different set of policies has been applied, designed above all to ensure universal service and fair access by the public to the facilities of the carrier. That right of access is what

defines a common carrier: it is obligated to serve all on equal terms without discrimination.

Finally, in the domain of broadcasting, Congress and the courts have established a highly regulated regime, very different from that of print. On the grounds of a supposed scarcity of usable frequencies in the radio spectrum, broadcasters are selected by the government for merit in its eyes, assigned a slice each of the spectrum of frequencies, and required to use that assignment fairly and for community welfare as defined by state authorities. The principles of common carriage and of the First Amendment have been applied to broadcasting in only atrophied form. For broadcasting, a politically managed system has been invented.

The electronic modes of twentieth century communication, whether they be carriers or broadcasters, have lost a large part of the eighteenth and nineteenth century constitutional protections of no prior restraint, no licenses, no special taxes, no regulations, and no laws. Every radio spectrum user, for example, must be licensed. This requirement started in 1912, almost a decade before the beginning of broadcasting, at a time when radio was used mainly for maritime communications. Because the United States Navy's communications were suffering interference, Congress, in an effort at remedy, imposed licensing on transmitters, thereby breaching a tradition that went back to John Milton against requiring licenses for communicating.

Regulation as a response to perceived technical problems has now reached the point where transmissions enclosed in wires or cables, and therefore causing no over-the-air interference, are also licensed and regulated. . . .

The mystery is how the clear intent of the Constitution, so well and strictly enforced in the domain of print, has been so neglected in the electronic revolution. The answer lies partly in changes in the prevailing concerns and historical circumstances from the time of the founding fathers to the world of today; but it lies at least as much in the failure of Congress and the courts to understand the character of the new technologies. Judges and legislators have tried to fit technological innovations under conventional legal concepts. The errors of understanding by these scientific laymen, though honest, have been mammoth. They have sought to guide toward good purposes technologies they did not comprehend.

"It would seem," wrote Alexis Dean Tocqueville, "that if despotism were to be established among the democratic nations of our days . . . it would be more extensive and more mild; it would degrade men without tormenting them." This is the kind of mild but degrading erosion of freedom that our system of communication faces today, not a rise of dictators or totalitarian movements. The threat in America, as Tocqueville perceived, is from well-intentioned policies, with results that are poorly foreseen. The danger is "tutelary power," which aims at the happiness of the people but also seeks to be the "arbiter of that happiness." . . .

The erosion of traditional freedoms that has occurred as government has striven to cope with problems of new communications media would not have surprised Tocqueville, for it is a story of how, in pursuit of the public good, a growing structure of controls has been imposed. But one part of the story would have surprised him, for it tells how a legal institution that he overlooked, namely the First Amendment, has up to now maintained the freedom and individualism that he saw as endangered.

A hundred and fifty years from now, today's fears about the future of free expression may prove as alarmist as Tocqueville's did. But there is reason to suspect that our situation is more ominous. What has changed in twentieth century communications is its technological base. Tocqueville wrote in a pluralistic society of small enterprises where the then new mass media consisted entirely of the printed press which the First Amendment protected. In the period since his day, new and mostly electronic media have proliferated in the form of great oligopolistic networks of common carriers and broadcasters. Regulation was a natural response. Fortunately and strangely, as electronics advances further, another reversal is now taking place, toward growing decentralization and toward fragmentation of the audience of the newest media. The transitional era of giant media may nonetheless leave a permanent set of regulatory practices implanted on a system that is coming to have technical characteristics that would otherwise be conducive to freedom.

The interaction over the past two centuries between the changing technologies of communication and the practice of free speech, I would argue, fits a pattern that is sometimes described as "soft technological determinism." Freedom is fostered when the means of communication are dispersed, decentralized, and easily available, as are printing presses or microcomputers. Central control is more likely when the means of communication are concentrated, monopolized, and scarce, as are great networks. But the relationship between technology and institutions is not simple or unidirectional, nor are the effects immediate. Institutions that evolve in response to one technological environment persist and to some degree are later imposed on what may be a changed technology. The First Amendment came out of a pluralistic world of small communicators, but it shaped the present treatment of great national networks. Later on, systems of regulation that emerged for national common carriers and for the use of "scarce" spectrum for broadcasting tended to be imposed on more recent generations of electronic technologies that no longer require them. . . .

Today, in an era of advanced (and still advancing) electronic theory, it has become possible to build virtually any kind of communications device that one might wish, though at a price. The market, not technology, sets most limits. For example technology no longer imposes licensing and government regulation. That pattern was established for electronic media half-century ago, when there seemed to be no alternative, but the institutions of control then adopted persist. That is why today's alarms could turn out to be more portentous than Tocqueville's.

The key technological change, at the root of the social changes, is that communication, other than conversation face to face, is becoming overwhelmingly electronic. Not only is electronic communication growing faster than traditional media of publishing, but also the convergence of modes of delivery is bringing the press, journals, and books into the electronic world. One question raised by these changes is whether some social features are inherent in the electronic character of the emerging media. Is television the model of the future? Are electromagnetic pulses simply an alternative conduit to deliver whatever is wanted, or are there aspects of electronic technology that make it different from print—more centralized or more decentralized, more banal or more profound, more private or more government dependent?

The electronic transformation of media occurs not in a vacuum but in a specific historical and legal context. Freedom for publishing has been one of America's proudest traditions. But just what is it that the courts have protected, and how does this differ from how the courts acted later when the media through which ideas flowed came to the telegraph, telephone, television, or computers? What images did policy makers have of how each of these media works; how far were their images valid; and what happened to their images when the facts changed?

In each of the three parts of the American communications system—print, common carriers, and broadcasting—the law has rested on a perception of technology that is sometimes accurate, often inaccurate, and which changes slowly as technology changes fast. Each new advance in the technology of communications disturbs a status quo. It meets resistance from those whose dominance it threatens, but if useful, it begins to be adopted. Initially, because it is new and a full scientific mastery of the options is not yet at hand, the invention comes into use in a rather clumsy form. Technical laymen, such as judges, perceive the new technology in that early, clumsy form, which then becomes their image of its nature, possibilities, and use. This perception is an incubus on later understanding.

The courts and regulatory agencies in the American system (or other authorities elsewhere) enter as arbiters of the conflicts among entrepreneurs, interest groups, and political organizations battling for control of the new technology. The arbiters, applying familiar analogies from the past to their lay image of the new technology, create a partly old, partly new structure of rights and obligations. The telegraph was analogized to railroads, the telephone to the telegraph, and cable television to broadcasting. The legal system thus invented for each new technology may in some instances, like the First Amendment, be a *tour de force* of political creativity, but in other instances it may be less worthy. The system created can turn out to be inappropriate to more habile forms of the technology which gradually emerge as the technology progresses. This is when problems arise, as they are arising so acutely today.

Historically, the various media that are now converging have been differently organized and differently treated under the law. The outcome to be feared is that communications in the future may be unnecessarily regulated under the unfree tradition of law that has been applied so far to the electronic media. The clash between the print, common carrier, and broadcast models is likely to be a vehement communications policy issue in the next decades. Convergence of modes is upsetting the trifurcated system developed over the past two hundred years, and questions that had seemed to be settled centuries ago are being reopened, unfortunately sometimes not in a libertarian way . . . .

The American case is unique only in the specific feature of the First Amendment and in the role of the courts in upholding it. The First Amendment, as interpreted by the courts, provides an anchor for freedom of the press and thus accentuates the difference between publishing and the electronic domain. Because of the unique power of the American courts, the issue in the United States unfolds largely in judicial decisions. But the same dilemmas and trends could be illustrated by citing declarations of policy and institutional structures in each advanced country.

If the boundaries between publishing, broadcasting, cable television, and the telephone network are indeed broken in the coming decades, then communications policies in all advanced countries must address the issue of which of the three models will dominate public policy regarding them. Public interest regulation could begin to extend over the print media as those media increasingly use regulated electronic channels. Conversely, concern for the traditional notion of a free press could lead to finding ways to free the electronic media from regulation. The policies adopted, even among free nations, will differ, though with much in common. The problems in all of them are very much the same.

The phrase "combinations policy" rings oddly in a discussion of freedom from government. But freedom is also a policy. The question it poses is how to reduce the public control of communications in an electronic era. A policy of freedom aims at pluralism of expression rather than at dissemination of preferred ideas. . . .

. . . The specific question to be answered is whether the electronic resources for communication can be as free of public regulation in the future as the platform and printing press have been in the past. Not a decade goes by in free counties, and not a day in the world, without grim oppressions that bring protesters once more to picket lines and demonstrations. Vigilance that must be so eternal becomes routine, and citizens grow callous.

The issue of the handling of the electronic media is the salient free speech problem for this decade, at least as important for this moment as were the last generation's issues for them, and as the next generation's will be for them too. But perhaps it is more than that. The move to electronic communication may be a turning point that history will remember. Just as in seventeenth- and eighteenth-century Great Britain and America a few tracts and acts set precedents for print by which we live today, so what we think and do today may frame the information system for a substantial period in the future.

In that future society the norms that govern information and communication will be even more crucial than in the past. Those who read, wrote, and published in the seventeenth and eighteenth centuries, and who shaped whatever heritage of art, literature, science, and history continues to matter today, were part of a small minority, well under one-tenth of the work force. Information activities now occupy the lives of much of the population. In advanced societies about half the work force are "information processors." It would be dire if the laws we make today governing the dominant mode of information handling in such an information society were subversive of its freedom. The onus is on us to determine whether free societies in the twenty-first century will conduct electronic communication under the conditions of freedom established for the domain of print through centuries of struggle, or whether that great achievement will become lost in a confusion about new technologies.

Notwithstanding the debatable future utility of medium specific analysis, modern case law with respect to press freedom is largely structured upon the premise that media have significant differences which must be accounted for in defining the scope of editorial liberty. Although the First Amendment never has been understood as an absolute,[184] freedom of the press is least subject to qualification when print media are implicated. Doctrinal fallout of medium specific analysis includes the reality that regulation prevailing over the First Amendment interests of one medium may be barred by the First Amendment when applied to the print media. A state law enabling political candidates to obtain space in a newspaper to reply to published criticism thus was struck down despite validation of a similar regulation in the context of broadcasting.

---

[184] Konigsberg v. State Bar of California, 366 U.S. 36, 49–51 (1961).

Miami Herald Publishing Co. v. Tornillo
418 U.S. 241 (1974)

MR. CHIEF JUSTICE BURGER delivered the opinion of the Court.

The issue in this case is whether a state statute granting a political candidate a right to equal space to reply to criticism and attacks on his record by a newspaper violates the guarantees of a free press.

The elimination of competing newspapers in most of our large cities, and the concentration of control of media that results from the only newspaper's being owned by the same interests which own a television station and a radio station, are important components of [a] trend toward concentration of control of outlets to inform the public.

The result of these vast changes has been to place in a few hands the power to inform the American people and shape public opinion. Much of the editorial opinion and commentary that is printed is that of syndicated columnists distributed nationwide and, as a result, we are told, on national and world issues there tends to be a homogeneity of editorial opinion, commentary, and interpretive analysis. The abuses of bias and manipulative reportage are, likewise, said to be the result of the vast accumulations of unreviewable power in the modern media empires. In effect, it is claimed, the public has lost any ability to respond or to contribute in a meaningful way to the debate on issues. . . .

The obvious solution, which was available to dissidents at an earlier time when entry into publishing was relatively inexpensive, today would be to have additional newspapers. But the same economic factors which have caused the disappearance of vast numbers of metropolitan newspapers, have made entry into the marketplace of ideas served by the print media almost impossible. It is urged that the claim of newspapers to be "surrogates for the public" carries with it a concomitant fiduciary obligation to account for that stewardship. From this premise it is reasoned that the only effective way to insure fairness and accuracy and to provide for some accountability is for government to take affirmative action. The First Amendment interest of the public in being informed is said to be in peril because the "marketplace of ideas" is today a monopoly controlled by the owners of the market.

　　. . .

The Court foresaw the problems relating to government-enforced access as early as its decision in *Associated Press v. United States*. There it carefully contrasted the private "compulsion to print" called for by the Association's bylaws with the provisions of the District Court decree against appellants which "does not compel appointment of its members to permit publication of anything which their 'reason' tells them should not be published." . . .

We see that beginning with *Associated Press*, the Court has expressed sensitivity as to whether a restriction or requirement constituted the compulsion exerted by government on a newspaper to print that which it would not otherwise print. The clear implication has been that any such compulsion to publish that which "'reason' tells them should not be published" is unconstitutional. A responsible press is an undoubtedly desirable goal, but press responsibility is not mandated by the Constitution and like many other virtues it cannot be legislated.

Appellee's argument that the Florida statute does not amount to a restriction of appellant's right to speak because "the statute in question here has not prevented the *Miami Herald* from saying anything it wished" begs the core question. Compelling editors or publishers to publish that which "'reason' tells them should not be published" is what is at issue in this case. The Florida statute operates as a command in the same sense as a statute or regulation forbidding appellant to publish specified matter. Governmental restraint on publishing need not fall into familiar or traditional patterns to be subject to constitutional limitations on governmental powers. The Florida statute exacts a penalty on the basis of the content of a newspaper. The first phase of the penalty resulting from the compelled printing of a reply is exacted in terms of the cost in printing and composing time and materials and in taking up space that could be devoted to other material the newspaper may have preferred to

print. It is correct, as appellee contends, that a newspaper is not subject to the finite technological limitations of time that confront a broadcaster but it is not correct to say that, as an economic reality, a newspaper can proceed to infinite expansion of its column space to accommodate the replies that a government agency determines or a statute commands the readers should have available.

Faced with the penalties that would accrue to any newspaper that published news or commentary arguably within the reach of the right-of-access statute, editors might well conclude that the safe course is to avoid controversy. Therefore, under the operation of the Florida statute, political and electoral coverage would be blunted or reduced. Government-enforced right of access inescapably "dampens the vigor and limits the variety of public debate," *New York Times Co. v. Sullivan*, 376 U.S., at 279. The Court, in *Mills v. Alabama*, 384 U.S. 214, 218 (1966), stated:

> [T]here is practically universal agreement that a major purpose of [the First] Amendment was to protect the free discussion of governmental affairs. This of course includes discussions of candidates.

Even if a newspaper would face no additional costs to comply with a compulsory access law and would not be forced to forgo publication of news or opinion by the inclusion of a reply, the Florida statute fails to clear the barriers of the First Amendment because of its intrusion into the function of editors. A newspaper is more than a passive receptacle or conduit for news, comment, and advertising. The choice of material to go into a newspaper, and the decision made as to limitations on the size and content of the paper, and treatment of public issues and public officials—whether fair or unfair—constitute the exercise of editorial control and judgment. It has yet to be demonstrated how governmental regulation of this crucial process can be exercised consistent with First Amendment guarantees of a free press as they have evolved to this time. Accordingly, the judgment of the Supreme Court of Florida is reversed.

The argument in *Tornillo*, that a right of reply was justified by the economics of a newspaper industry characterized by concentrated ownership and declining competition, attempted to extend the scarcity premise that has supported content diversification schemes in broadcasting. An understanding of the broadcast spectrum as a scarce resource underlies much radio and television regulation. Broadcasting is an object of a comprehensive regulatory scheme in the form of the Communications Act of 1934[185]

---

[185] 47 U.S.C. § 301 *et seq.*

and rules promulgated thereunder by the Federal Communications Commission ("FCC"). Even before the FCC's creation by the 1934 Act,[186] broadcast regulation was inspired by the sense that "for every school of thought, religious, political, social, and economic, ... a well-founded complaint will receive ... careful consideration ... with reference to the station complained of."[187] Such official interest in significant part was based upon historical experience. Prior to the advent of federal regulation, the broadcast industry was characterized by chaos and confusion as radio operators battled over frequencies, attempted to overpower each other and generated much static and interference. Interest in a comprehensive national scheme of governance emerged against a backdrop of stations using any frequencies they desired, regardless of the interference thereby caused to others. Existing stations changed to other frequencies and increased their power and hours of operation at will. The result was confusion and chaos. With everybody on the air nobody could be heard. The situation became so intolerable that the President, in his message of December 7, 1926, appealed to Congress to enact a comprehensive radio law:

> Due to the decisions of the courts, the authority of the department [of Commerce] under the law of 1912 has broken down; many more stations have been operating than can be accommodated within the limited number of wave lengths available; further stations are in course of construction; many stations have departed from the scheme of allocations set down by the department, and the whole service of this most important public function has drifted into such chaos as seems likely, if not remedied, to destroy its great value. I most urgently recommend that this legislation should be speedily enacted.

> The plight into which radio fell prior to 1927 was attributable to certain basic facts about radio as a means of communication—its facilities are limited; they are not available to all who may wish to use them; the radio spectrum simply is not large enough to accommodate everybody. There is a fixed natural limitation upon the number of stations that can operate without interfering with one another. Regulation of radio was therefore as vital to its development as traffic control was to the development of the automobile. In enacting the Radio Act of 1927, the first comprehensive scheme of control over radio communication, Congress acted upon the knowledge that if the potentialities of radio were not to be wasted, regulation was essential.[188]

> . . .

Central to federal regulation of broadcasting is a system of licensing. Applicants for a broadcast license are judged on a variety of grounds, including character, citizenship, financial and technical qualifications.[189] Federal regulation imposes limits upon the number of stations a licensee may own.[190] The touchstone consideration for licensure is whether "public interest, convenience, and necessity would be served by the granting thereof."[191] Despite investment in a system that is reminiscent in form if not purpose to the now discredited English licensing of publishers, abandoned in the late seventeenth century, licensing has become a generally accepted linchpin of broadcast regulation. It is a method that responds to the perceived problem of scarcity, insofar as it creates a structure for rational use of the spectrum.

---

[186] *Id.*, § 151.

[187] Great Lakes Broadcasting Co., 3 F.R.C. Ann. Representative. 32 (1929), aff'd in part, rev'd in part, 37 F.2d 993 (D.C. Cir.), cert. denied, 281 U.S. 706 (1930).

[188] National Broadcasting Co. v. United States, 319 U.S. 190, 212–13 (1943).

[189] 47 U.S.C. § 308(b).

[190] *E.g.*, Radio Multiple Ownership Rules, 7 F.C.C. Rcd. 6387 (1992).

[191] 47 U.S.C. § 309(a).

The need to license does not by itself support an interest in content regulation. Within a decade of Congress' creation of a licensing process under the 1934 Act, however, the Supreme Court indicated that the FCC had a regulatory interest that transcended mere technical concerns. As the Court put it, in *National Broadcasting Co. v. United States*, the agency was more than a "traffic officer, policing the engineering and technical aspects of broadcasting."[192] With authorization to account for more, and an abiding concern with the consequences of spectrum scarcity, the FCC acquired an enhanced interest in content. Responding to what it perceived as risks to content diversity in broadcasting, because of spectrum scarcity, it imposed upon licensees requirements of editorial fairness and balance. Central to such regulatory obligations was the fairness doctrine, which required broadcasters to provide reasonable amounts of time for coverage of public issues and an opportunity for contrasting views.[193] Related regulation affords personal access to air time for individuals whose honesty, character or integrity is attacked in the course of coverage of a controversial public issue,[194] an opportunity for political candidates to respond to a broadcaster's endorsement of an opponent,[195] equal time for a political candidate in the event a broadcaster provides air time to a rival candidate[196] and reasonable access to broadcast time for candidates for federal office.[197] In *Red Lion Broadcasting Co. v. Federal Communications Commission*, the Court referenced the scarcity premise in rejecting arguments that the fairness doctrine and personal attack rule abridged freedom of the press.

---

[192] National Broadcasting Co. v. United States, 319 U.S. at 217–18.

[193] The Handling of Public Issues under the Fairness Doctrine and the Public Interest Standards of the Communications Act, 48 F.C.C. 2d 1, 8 (1974).

[194] 47 C.F.R. § 73.1920.

[195] *Id.*, § 73.1930.

[196] 47 U.S.C. § 315.

[197] *Id.*, § 312 (a)(7).

Red Lion Broadcasting Co. v. Federal Communications Commission
395 U.S. 367 (1969)

MR. JUSTICE WHITE delivered the opinion of the Court.

. . .

The broadcasters challenge the fairness doctrine and its specific manifestations in the personal attack and political editorial rules on conventional First Amendment grounds, alleging that the rules abridge their freedom of speech and press. Their contention is that the First Amendment protects their desire to use their allotted frequencies continuously to broadcast whatever they choose, and to exclude whomever they choose from ever using that frequency. No man may be prevented from saying or publishing what he thinks, or from refusing in his speech or other utterances to give equal weight to the views of his opponents. This right, they say, applies equally to broadcasters.

Although broadcasting is clearly a medium affected by a First Amendment interest, differences in the characteristics of new media justify differences in the First Amendment standards applied to them. For example, the ability of new technology to produce sounds more raucous than those of the human voice justifies restrictions on the sound trucks so long as the restrictions are reasonable and applied without discrimination.

Just as the Government may limit the use of sound-amplifying equipment potentially so noisy that it drowns out civilized private speech, so may the Government limit the use of broadcast equipment. The right of free speech of a broadcaster, the user of a sound truck, or any other individual does not embrace a right to snuff out the free speech of others.

When two people converse face to face, both should not speak at once if either is to be clearly understood. But the range of the human voice is so limited that there could be meaningful communications if half the people in the United States were talking and the other half listening. Just as clearly, half the people might publish and the other half read. But the reach of radio signals is incomparably greater than the range of the human voice and the problem of interferences is a massive reality. The lack of know-how and equipment may keep many from the air, but only a tiny fraction of those with resources and intelligence can hope to communicate by radio at the same time if intelligible communication is to be had, even if the entire radio spectrum is utilized in the present state of commercially acceptable technology.

It was this fact, and the chaos which ensued from permitting anyone to use any frequency at whatever power level he wished, which made necessary the enactment of the Radio Act of 1927 and the Communications Act of 1934, as the Court has noted at length before. It was this reality which at the very least necessitated first the division of the radio spectrum into portions reserved respectively for public broadcasting and for other important radio uses such as amateur operation, aircraft, police, defense, and navigation; and then the subdivision of each portion, and assignment of specific frequencies to individual users or groups of users. Beyond this, however, because the frequencies reserved for public broadcasting were limited in number, it was essential for the Government to tell some applicants that they could not broadcast at all because there was room for only a few.

Where there are substantially more individuals who want to broadcast than there are frequencies to allocate, it is idle to posit an unbridgeable First Amendment right to broadcast comparable to the right of every individual to speak, write, or publish. If 100 persons want broadcast licenses but there are only 10 frequencies to allocate, all of them may have the same "right" to a license; but if there is to be any effective communication by radio, only a few can be licensed and the rest must be barred from the airwaves. It would be strange if the First Amendment, aimed at protecting and furthering communications, prevented the Government from making radio communication possible by requiring licenses to broadcast and by limiting the number of licenses so as not to overcrowd the spectrum.

. . .

. . . [A]s far as the First Amendment is concerned those who are licensed stand no better than those to whom licenses are refused. A license permits broadcasting, but the licensee has no constitutional right to be the one who holds the license or to monopolize a radio frequency to the exclusion of his fellow citizens. There is nothing in the First Amendment which prevents the Government from requiring a licensee to share his frequency with others and to conduct himself as a proxy or fiduciary with obligations to present those views and voices which are representative of his community and which would otherwise, by necessity, be barred from the airwaves.

This is not to say that the First Amendment is irrelevant to public broadcasting. . . . Because of the scarcity of radio frequencies, [however], the Government is permitted to put restraints on licensees in favor of others whose views should be expressed on this unique medium. But the people as a whole retain their interest in free speech by radio and their collective right to have the medium function consistently with the ends and purposes of the First Amendment. It is the right of the viewers and listeners, not the right of the broadcasters, which is paramount. It is the purpose of the First Amendment to preserve an uninhibited marketplace of ideas in which truth will ultimately prevail, rather than to countenance monopolization of that market, whether it be by the Government itself or a private licensee. "[S]peech concerning public affairs is more than self-expression; it is the essence of self-government." It is the right of the public to receive suitable access to social, political, esthetic, moral, and other ideas and experiences which is crucial here. That right may not constitutionally be abridged either by Congress or by the FCC.

. . .

It is strenuously argued, however, that if political editorials or personal attacks will trigger an obligation in broadcasters to afford the opportunity for expression to speakers who need not pay for time and whose views are unpalatable to the licensees, then broadcasters will be irresistibly forced to self-censorship and their coverage of controversial public issues will be eliminated or at least rendered wholly ineffective. Such a result would indeed be a serious matter, for should licensees actually eliminate their coverage of controversial issues, the purposes of the doctrine would be stifled. . . . The fairness doctrine in the past has had no such overall effect.

That this will occur now seems unlikely, however, since if present licensees should suddenly prove timorous, the Commission is not powerless to insist that they give adequate and fair attention to public issues. It does not violate the First Amendment to treat licensees given the privilege of using scarce radio frequencies as proxies for the entire community, obligated to give suitable time and attention to matters of great public concern. To condition the granting or renewal of licenses on a willingness to present representative community views on controversial issues is consistent with the ends and purposes of those constitutional provisions forbidding the abridgment of freedom of speech and freedom of the press. Congress need not stand idly by and permit those with licenses to ignore the problems which beset the people or to exclude from the airways anything but their own views of fundamental questions. The statute, long administrative practice, and cases are to this effect.

The *Red Lion* decision endorsed a redistribution of First Amendment interests. The public's viewing and listening interests not only were identified as a First Amendment right but were prioritized over the First Amendment freedom of broadcasters. The public's "paramount" First Amendment rights, however, did not extinguish the editorial liberty interest of broadcasters. Without refuting the scarcity rationale, the Court in *Columbia Broadcasting, Inc. v. Democratic National Committee* spurned the notion that the First Amendment created a right of direct public access to the nation's airwaves. The diverging opinions in *Columbia Broadcasting* cover a broad spectrum of perspective upon broadcasting's First Amendment status.

Columbia Broadcasting System, Inc. v. Democratic National Committee
412 U.S. 94 (1973)

MR. CHIEF JUSTICE BURGER delivered the opinion of the Court (Parts I, II, and IV) together with an opinion (Part III), in which MR. JUSTICE STEWART and MR. JUSTICE REHNQUIST joined.

We granted the writs of certiorari in these cases to consider whether a broadcast licensee's general policy of not selling advertising time to individuals or groups wishing to speak out on issues they consider important violates the . . . First Amendment.

The complainants in these actions are the Democratic National Committee (DNC) and the Business Executives' Move for Vietnam Peace (BEM), a national organization of businessmen opposed to United States involvement in the Vietnam conflict. In January 1970, BEM filed a complaint with the Commission charging that radio station WTOP in Washington, D.C., had refused to sell it time to broadcast a series of one-minute spot announcements expressing BEM views on Vietnam. WTOP, in common with many, but not all, broadcasters, followed a policy of refusing to sell time for spot announcements to individuals and groups who wished to expound their views on controversial issues. WTOP took the position that since it presented full and fair coverage of important public questions, including the Vietnam conflict, it was justified in refusing to accept editorial advertisements. WTOP also submitted evidence showing that the station had aired the views of critics of our Vietnam policy on numerous occasions. BEM challenged the fairness of WTOP's coverage of criticism of that policy, but it presented no evidence in support of that claim. . . .

I

. . .

Because the broadcast media utilize a valuable and limited public resource, there is . . . present an unusual order of First Amendment values. *Red Lion* discussed at length the appli-

cation of the First Amendment to the broadcast media. . . .

Balancing the various First Amendment interests involved in the broadcast media and determining what best serves the public's right to be informed is a task of a great delicacy and difficulty. The process must necessarily be undertaken within the framework of the regulatory scheme that has evolved over the course of the past half century. For, during that time, Congress and its chosen regulatory agency have established a delicately balanced system of regulation intended to serve the interests of all concerned. The problems of regulation are rendered more difficult because the broadcast industry is dynamic in terms of technological change; solutions adequate a decade ago are not necessarily so now, and those acceptable today may well be outmoded 10 years hence.

Thus, in evaluating the First Amendment claims of respondents, we must afford great weight to the decisions of Congress and the experience of the Commission. . . .

. . .

II

[After examining the history of broadcast regulation and legislative emphasis upon public obligations for licensees, the Court found it] clear that Congress intended to permit private broadcasting to develop with the widest journalistic freedom consistent with its public obligations. Only when the interests of the public are found to outweigh the private journalistic interests of the broadcasters will government power be asserted within the framework of the Act. License renewal proceedings, in which the listening public can be heard, are a principal means of such regulation.

. . .

IV

. . .

The Commission was justified in concluding that the public interest in providing access to the marketplace of "ideas and experiences" would scarcely be served by a system so heavily weighted in favor of the financially affluent, or those with access to wealth. Even under a first-come-first-served system, proposed by the dissenting Commissioner in these cases, the views of the affluent could well prevail over those of others, since they would have it within their power to purchase time more frequently. Moreover, there is the substantial danger, . . . that the time allotted for editorial advertising could be monopolized by those of one political persuasion.

These problems would not necessarily be solved by applying the Fairness Doctrine . . . to editorial advertising. If broadcasters were required to provide time, free when necessary, for the discussion of the various shades of opinion on the issue discussed in the advertisement, the affluent could still determine in large part the issues to be discussed. Thus, the very premise of the Court of Appeals' holding—that a right of access is necessary to allow individuals and groups the opportunity for self-initiated speech—would have little meaning to those who could not afford to purchase time in the first instance.

If the Fairness Doctrine were applied to editorial advertising, there is also the substantial danger that the effective operation of that doctrine would be jeopardized. To minimize financial hardship and to comply fully with its public responsibilities a broadcaster might well be forced to make regular programming time available to those holding a view different from that expressed in an editorial advertisement; indeed, BEM has suggested as much in its brief. The result would be a further erosion of the journalistic discretion of broadcasters in the coverage of public issues from the licensees who are accountable for broadcast performance to private individuals who are not. The public interest would no longer be "paramount" but, rather, subordinate to private whim especially since, under the Court of Appeals' decision, a broadcaster would be largely precluded from rejecting editorial advertisements that dealt with matters trivial or insignificant or already fairly covered by the broadcasters. If the Fairness Doctrine and the *Cullman* doctrine were suspended to alleviate these problems, as respondents suggest might be appropriate, the question arises whether we would have abandoned more than we have gained. Under such a regime the congressional objective of balanced coverage of public issues would be seriously threatened.

Nor can we accept the Court of Appeals' view that every potential speaker is "the best judge" of what the listening public ought to hear or indeed the best judge of the merits of his or her views. All journalistic tradition and experience is to the contrary. For better or worse, editing is what editors are for; and editing is selection and choice of material. That editors—newspaper or broadcast—can and do abuse this power is beyond doubt, but that is not reason to deny the discretion Congress provided. Calculated risks of abuse are taken in order to preserve higher values. The presence of these risks is nothing new; the authors of the Bill of Rights accepted the reality that these risks were evils for which there was no acceptable remedy other than a spirit of moderation and a sense of responsibility—and civility—on the part of those who exercise the guaranteed freedoms of expression.

. . .

MR. JUSTICE DOUGLAS, concurring in the judgment.

While I join the Court in reversing the judgment below, I do so for quite different reasons.

My conclusion is that TV and radio stand in the same protected position under the First Amendment as do newspapers and magazines. The philosophy of the First Amendment requires that result, for the fear that Madison and Jefferson had of government intrusion is perhaps even more relevant to TV and radio than it is to newspapers and other like publications. That fear was founded not only on the spectre of a lawless government but of government under the control of a faction that desired to foist its views of the common good on the people.

. . .

The sturdy people who fashioned the First Amendment would be shocked at that intrusion of Government into a field which in this Nation has been reserved for individuals, whatever part of the spectrum of opinion they represent. Benjamin Franklin, one of the Founders who was in the newspaper business, wrote in simple and graphic form what I had always assumed was the basic American newspaper tradition that became implicit in the First Amendment. In our early history one view was that the publisher must open his columns

> to any and all controversialists, especially if paid for it. Franklin disagreed, declaring that his newspaper was not a stagecoach, with seats for everyone; he offered to print pamphlets for private distribution, but refused to fill his paper with private altercations.

It is said that TV and radio have become so powerful and exert such an influence on the public mind that they must be controlled by Government. Some newspapers in our history have exerted a powerful—and some have thought—a harmful interest on the public mind. But even Thomas Jefferson, who knew how base and obnoxious the press could be, never dreamed of interfering. For he thought that government control of newspapers would be the greater of two evils. . . .

Of course there is private censorship in the newspaper field. But for one publisher who may suppress a fact, there are many who will print it. But if the Government is the censor, administrative *fiat*, not freedom of choice, carries the day. . . .

Red Lion, in a carefully written opinion that was built upon predecessor cases, put TV and radio under a different regime. I did not participate in that decision and, with all respect, would not support it. The Fairness Doctrine has no place in our First Amendment regime. It puts the head of the camel inside the tent and enables administration after administration to toy with TV and radio in order to serve its sordid or its benevolent ends. In 1973, as in other years—there is clamoring to make TV and radio emit the messages that console certain groups. There are charges that these mass media are too slanted, too partisan, too hostile in their approach to candidates and the issues.

Both TV and radio news broadcasts frequently tip the news one direction or another and even try to turn a public figure into a character of disrepute. Yet so do the newspapers and the magazines and other segments of the press. The standards of TV, radio, newspapers, or magazines—whether of excellence or mediocrity—are beyond the reach of Government. Government—acting through courts—disciplines lawyers. Government makes criminal some acts of doctors and engineers. But the First Amendment puts beyond the reach of Government federal regulation of news agencies save only business or financial practices which do not involve First Amendment rights. . . .

We have . . . witnessed a slow encroachment by Government over that segment of the press that is represented by TV and radio licensees. Licensing is necessary for engineering reasons; the spectrum is limited and wavelengths must be assigned to avoid stations interfering with each other. The Commission has a duty to encourage a multitude of voices but only in a limited way, *viz.*, by preventing monopolistic practices and by promoting technological developments that will open up new channels. But censorship or editing or the screening by Government of what licensees may broadcast goes against the grain of the First Amendment.

The Court in *National Broadcasting Co. v. United States*, 329 U.S. 190, 226, said, "Unlike other modes of expression, radio inherently is not available to all. This is its unique characteristic, and that is why, unlike other modes of expression, it is subject to governmental regulation."

That uniqueness is due to engineering and technical problems. But the press in a realistic sense is likewise not available to all. Small or "underground" papers appear and disappear; and the weekly is an established institution. But the daily papers now established are unique in the sense that it would be virtually impossible for a competitor to enter the field due to the financial exigencies of this era. The result is that in practical terms the newspapers and magazines, like TV and radio, are available only to a select few. Who at this time would have the folly to think he could combat the *New York Times* or *Denver Post* by building a new plant and becoming a competitor? That may argue for a redefinition of the responsibilities of the press in First Amendment terms. But I do not think it gives us carte blanche to design systems of supervision and control or empower Congress to read the mandate in the First Amendment that "Congress shall make no law . . . abridging the freedom . . . of the press" to mean that Congress may, acting directly or through any of its agencies such as the FCC make "some" laws "abridging" freedom of the press.

. . .

What kind of First Amendment would best serve our needs as we approach the 21st century may be an open question. But the old-fashioned First Amendment that we have is the Court's only guideline; and one hard and fast principle which it announces is that Government shall keep its hands off the press. That principle has served us through days of calm and eras of strife and I would abide by it until a new First Amendment is adopted. That means, as I view it, that TV and radio, as well as the more conventional methods for disseminating news, are all included in the concept of "press" as used in the First Amendment and therefore are entitled to live under the laissez-faire regime which the First Amendment sanctions.

It is said, of course, that Government can control the broadcasters because their channels are in the public domain in the sense that they use the airspace that is the common heritage of all the people. But parks are also in the public domain. Yet people who speak there do not come under Government censorship. It is the tradition of Hyde Park, not the tradition of the censor, that is reflected in the First Amendment. TV and radio broadcasters are a vital part of the press; and since the First Amendment allows no Government control over it, I would leave this segment of the press to its devices.

. . .

(T)he regime of federal supervision under the Fairness Doctrine is contrary to our constitutional mandate and makes the broadcast licensee an easy victim of political pressures and reduces him to a timid and submissive segment of the press whose measure of the public interest will now be echoes of the dominant political voice that emerges after every election. The affair with freedom of which we have been proud will now bear only a faint likeness of our former robust days. I said that it would come as a surprise to the public as well as to the publishers and editors of newspapers to learn that they were under a newly created federal bureau. Perhaps I should have said that such an event *should* come as a surprise. In fact it might not in view of the retrogressive steps we have witnessed.

BRENNAN, J., dissenting.

. . .

As a practical matter, the Court's reliance on the Fairness Doctrine as an "adequate" alternative to editorial advertising seriously overestimates the ability—or willingness—of broadcasters to expose the public to the "widest possible dissemination of information from diverse and antagonistic sources." As Professor Jaffe has noted, "there is considerable possibility the broadcaster will exercise a large amount of self-censorship and try to avoid as much controversy as he safely can." Indeed, in light of the strong interest of broadcasters in maximizing their audience, and therefore their profits, it seems almost naive to expect the majority of broadcasters to produce the variety and controversiality of material necessary to reflect a full spectrum of viewpoints. Stated simply, angry customers are not good customers and, in the commercial world of mass communications, it is simply "bad business" to espouse—or even to allow others to espouse—the heterodox or the controversial. As a result, even under the Fairness Doctrine, broadcasters generally tend to permit only established—or at least moderated—views to enter the broadcast world's "marketplace of ideas."

Moreover, the Court's reliance on the Fairness Doctrine as the *sole* means of informing the public seriously misconceives and underestimates the public's interest in receiving ideas and information directly from the advocates of those ideas without the interposition of journalistic middlemen. Under the Fairness Doctrine, broadcasters decide what issues are "important," how "fully" to cover them, and what format, time, and style of coverage are "appropriate." The retention of such *absolute* control in the hands of a few Government licensees is inimical to the First Amendment, for vigorous, free debate can be attained only when members of the public have at least *some* opportunity to take the initiative and editorial control into their own hands.

Our legal system reflects a belief that truth is best illuminated by a collision of genu-

ine advocates. Under the Fairness Doctrine, however, accompanied by an absolute ban on editorial advertising, the public is compelled to rely *exclusively* on the "journalistic discretion" of broadcasters, who serve in theory as surrogate spokesmen for all sides of all issues. This separation of the advocate from the expression of his views can serve only to diminish the effectiveness of that expression. . . . Thus, if the public is to be honestly and forthrightly apprised of opposing views on controversial issues, it is imperative that citizens be permitted at least *some* opportunity to speak directly for themselves as genuine advocates on issues that concern them.

Moreover, to the extent that broadcasters actually permit citizens to appear on "their" airwaves under the Fairness Doctrine, such appearances are subject to extensive editorial control. Yet it is clear that the effectiveness of an individual's expression of his views is as dependent on the style and format of presentation as it is on the content itself. And the relegation of an individual's views to such tightly controlled formats as the news, documentaries, edited interviews, or panel discussions may tend to minimize, rather than maximize the effectiveness of speech. Under a limited scheme of editorial advertising, however, the crucial editorial controls are in the speaker's own hands.

Nor are these cases concerned solely with the adequacy of coverage of those views and issues which generally are recognized as "newsworthy." For also at stake is the right of the public to receive suitable access to new and generally unperceived ideas and opinions. Under the Fairness Doctrine, the broadcaster is required to present only "*representative* community views and voices on controversial issues" of public importance. Thus, by definition, the Fairness Doctrine tends to perpetuate coverage of those "views and voices" that are already established, while failing to provide for exposure of the public to those "views and voices" that are novel, unorthodox, or unrepresentative of prevailing opinion. . . .

. . . [I]t is . . . clear that, with the assistance of the Federal Government, the broadcast industry has become what is potentially the most efficient and effective "marketplace of ideas" ever devised. Indeed, the electronic media are today "the public's prime source of information," and we have ourselves recognized that broadcast "technology . . . supplants atomized, relatively informal communication with mass media as a prime source of national cohesion and news. . . . " *Red Lion.* Thus, although "full and free discussion" of ideas may have been a reality in the heyday of political pamphleteering, modern technological developments in the field of communications have made the soapbox orator and the leafleteer virtually obsolete. And, in light of the current dominance of the electronic media as the most effective means of reaching the public, any policy that *absolutely* denies citizens access to the airwaves necessarily renders even the concept of "full free discussion" practically meaningless.

. . .

The First Amendment values of individual self-fulfillment through expression and individual participation in public debate are central to our concept of liberty. If these values are to survive in the age of technology, it is essential that individuals be permitted at least *some* opportunity to express their views on public issues over the electronic media. Balancing those interests against the limited interest of broadcasters in exercising "journalistic supervision" over the mere allocation of *advertising* time that is already made available to some members of the public, I simply cannot conclude that the interest of broadcasters must prevail.

The scarcity principle, which generated what the Court in *Columbia Broadcasting System, Inc.* characterized as an "unusual order" of First Amendment interests, remains a subject of much controversy. Fairness regulation itself, as an extension of scarcity concerns, has been criticized on grounds it stunts rather than facilitates diversity. Because broadcasters are profit-oriented, and thus concerned with antagonizing viewers or listeners, an incentive exists to shy away from controversy. Even though the FCC traditionally deferred to licensee discretion when fairness violations were alleged,[198] critics have stressed significant risks that enforcement power presents to First Amendment interests.

---

[198] Public Issues under the Fairness Doctrine and the Public Interest Standards of the Communications Act, 56 F.C.C.2d 691, 706 (1976) (C'mr. Robinson dissenting) (citing statistics indicating vast majority of fairness complaints resolves in licensees' favor).

Bazelon, FCC Regulation of the Telecommunications Press
1975 Duke L.J. 213

The main, main thing is The Post is going to have damnable, damnable problems out of this one. They have a television station. . . . And they're going to have to get it renewed.

Taped Statement of Richard Nixon
to H.R. Haldeman and John Dean,
September 15, 1972.

This statement is indicative, albeit an unusual example, of the First Amendment problems raised by a comprehensive system for the licensing of speakers. Individuals who must obtain permission to engage in activity protected by the First Amendment are vulnerable to the various substantive silentio pressures that prior approval permits and which Richard Nixon threatens in the statement quoted above. They may, therefore, find it easier to tailor their views to the wishes of the licensor rather than risk its displeasure. The manner in which the licensor conveys its wishes or exercises pressure on the speaker under a comprehensive licensing scheme often is disguised in an apparently noncoerceive action, which might seem innocuous to others not subject to the licensing scheme. Control of these pressures is thus particular difficult. The motivation for communicating pressure may involve the rather crass political concerns voiced by Richard Nixon in the statement quoted above. The motivation may range from racial discrimination to a laudable desire to upgrade the quality of the particular speech involved. But under the First Amendment, the licensor's motivation should be irrelevant: the exercise of power over speech leads the government knee-deep into regulation of expression. And that, we have always assumed, is forbidden by the First Amendment. The Supreme Court has so held, time and again.

But traditional assumptions do not apply to the regulation of telecommunications speech. The licensing scheme mandated by the Federal Communications Act permits a wide-ranging and largely uncontrolled administrative discretion in the review of telecommunications programming. That discretion has been used, as we might expect and as traditional First Amendment doctrine presumes, to apply substantive silentio pressure against broadcast of song lyrics that allegedly promote the use of drugs, to halt radio talk shows that deal explicitly with sex, to discourage specialized or highly opinionated programming, to force networks to schedule "adult" programming after 9:00 p.m., and to restrict, through Executive Office pressure, adverse commentary on presidential speeches. The methods of communicating these pressures are by now familiar to FCC practitioners: the prominent speech by a Commissioner, the issuance of a notice of inquiry, an official statement of licensee responsibility couched in general terms but directed against specific programming, setting the licensee down for a hearing on "misrepresentations," forwarding listener complaints with requests for a formal response to the FCC, calling network executives to "meetings" in the office of the Chairman of the FCC or some other Executive Branch officials, compelled disclosure of future programming on forms with already delineated categories and imposing specific regulatory action on a particularly visible offender against this background. All these actions assume their *in terrorem* effect because of the FCC power to deny renewal of broadcast licenses or to order a hearing on the renewal application. Recently, there have been indications

that the threat of antitrust or Internal Revenue Service actions has served to buttress certain "raised eyebrow" suggestions. I do not mean by recitation of these examples to alert you to a great danger or to engage in any sort of journalistic effort to inform the public. This has been fully accomplished by persons more able than myself. My only concern is with the legal implications of these examples in the context of our traditional constitutional order.

. . .

. . . [T]he Federal Communications Act permits . . . overt forms of speech regulation: these include the Fairness Doctrine (encompassing also the equal time and editorial reply rules) and review of programming at license renewal and at assignment to determine whether past and proposed future programming meets the FCC's criteria of balance.

I think it is beyond cavil that we would not tolerate this sort of regulation in any context other than telecommunications; the First Amendment would forbid it. But somehow telecommunications speech is different and permits, many think, a different First Amendment regime.

Not only the fairness doctrine but the scarcity rationale itself has been a subject of sharp criticism. If scarcity is a function of raw numbers, the problem is worse in the field of publishing where the number of commercial broadcast outlets far exceeds that of daily newspapers.[199] As understood by the Court, however, scarcity is more than a problem of arithmetic. Unique to scarcity in the broadcast medium is a resource (the spectrum) that is finite, contrasted with the economically induced scarcity of the newspaper industry. Critics have challenged the distinction, noting among other things that all resources are scarce.

---

[199] At the time of the *Red Lion* decision, a total of 6,519 commercial radio stations, 862 commercial television stations and 1,838 daily newspapers existed. U.S. DEPT. OF COMMERCE, STATISTICAL ABSTRACT OF THE UNITED STATES 1991, No. 932, at 560.

Fowler and Brenner, A Marketplace Approach to Broadcast Regulation
60 Tex. L.Rev. 207 (1982)

. . .

D. THE FLAWED RATIONALES SUPPORTING THE MODEL

1. *Defects of the Scarcity Rationale*—Spectrum scarcity always has been the cornerstone of the justification for abandoning the marketplace approach and reducing first amendment protection for broadcasters. The Supreme

Court pointed to spectrum scarcity in its ratification of the trusteeship model in *NBC*, and the Court has cited scarcity in some of its other, although not in all, pronouncements supporting Commission content regulation. But the use of spectrum scarcity to justify "public interest" determination over licensees is fraught with serious logical and empirical infirmities.

First, virtually all goods in society are

scarce. In most sectors of the economy, the interplay of supply and demand regulates the distribution of goods. If a good becomes especially scarce, its price is bid up. Ideally the highest bidder will make the best use of the resource. The application of the trusteeship model to broadcasting is a substantial deviation from the ordinary allocation of scarce goods and services in society.

One might argue, however, that deviations from the market should occur with regard to communications media. For instance, in wartime the government might be justified in regulating the amount of newsprint any one paper received. The supply of newsprint could be reduced for other purely entertainment features. But no factors remotely comparable exist in broadcasting today. Yet the trusteeship model results in broadcast regulation that resembles this hypothetical.

Apart from this basic misunderstanding of scarcity, other factors should lead to a rejection of the belief that a condition of true scarcity prevails in broadcasting. Scarcity is a relative concept even when applied to the limited spectrum earmarked for broadcast use. Additional channels can be added, without increasing the portion reserved for broadcast, by decreasing the band width of each channel. Technology is an independent variable that makes scarcity a relative concept. At some point, quality becomes so reduced or costs so great that new channels should not be added. But until that point is reached, saturation of the spectrum has not occurred. The continued evolution of spectrum efficiency techniques makes it difficult to say with certainty that saturation of channels will ever be permanent in any market.

. . .

The scarcity rationale focuses on the wrong scarce resource, [frequencies], instead of advertising dollars. Even in the indirect marketplace of over-the-air commercial broadcasting, the number of stations depends on the amount of advertising dollars or on other funding sources in the community. Except in the largest cities, where the Commission's allocation policies have limited the number of outlets, advertising support or subscriber dollars restrict broadcast opportunities more than does the number of channels.

In addition, scarcity is not the only reason behind the present limited number of VHF television stations (channels 2-13), which are the most profitable outlets. The Commission's allocation of only three VHF commercial outlets in most communities is hardly an unavoidable product of the limited ether; rather, it derives from the Commission's landmark allocation scheme for television. . . . At the very least, one can hardly explain the availability of only the three VHF television outlets carrying the three commercial networks as a force of nature caused by a limited spectrum. It should serve instead as a basis for authorizing more outlets, not for regulating those that already exist.

The scarcity upon which the trusteeship model relies exists only in some, not all, markets. Even under the current allocation scheme, which assigns fewer channels than could be accommodated on the available spectrum, channels outside larger cities go wanting for lack of a taker. This situation is especially true for allocations in the UHF band, where some channels have remained unclaimed for decades. It is capricious to justify regulation of broadcasters in nonsaturated markets by claiming that their operation employs a scarce resource unavailable to potential entrants in other markets.

Scarcity does not exist in the sense that there is no more room for additional full-power VHF stations in the largest markets under current levels of permitted interference. Yet one can always buy an existing station, just as one may be likelier to consider buying to launch a new one. Furthermore, the current complement of VHF stations exceeds the number of daily newspapers in large cities, and the total number of broadcast outlets far exceeds the number of daily circulated newspapers. So a relatively low number of outlets in one medium should not lead to content-based rules in another.

Finally, the scarcity notion also fails to recognize the substitutes for over-the-air distribution. In audio service, cassette and phono disc recordings vie with AM and FM channels and their subcarrier services like Muzak. Cable television, low power television, multipoint distribution service, cassette and disc, and, in the future, direct broadcast satellites provide substitutes for over-the-air video service in many markets. A five-meter backyard satellite dish can, for those who can afford them, bring in more channels "off the air" than a television antenna picks up in a city with the greatest number of stations on the air.

Nonspectrum-utilizing distribution modes like cable and video cassette provide virtually limitless diversity of scheduling and content. Where new high-capacity cable systems are in place, no scarcity exits with respect to the television spectrum. What may inhibit the number of cable channels is, again, a scarcity of dollars to support advertiser based or subscription channels. Similarly, choice in video cassette programming is completely determined by what the consumer is willing to spend for software. Thus, the scarcity rationale, as used to justify the regulation of broadcasting in a different manner than other media, misperceives what scarcity is in a free economy. Moreover, it ignores the practical realities that go a long way toward explaining the limited number of channels in some markets.

Even if one assumes that the absence of more television channel space in the largest markets justifies a licensing policy in those markets, this assumption establishes nothing about the form the regulations should take.

The trusteeship model endorsed the giant leap from scarcity to the current panoply of federal regulation over all broadcasters, not just those in saturated markets. Logic, however, does not support the assumption that the trusteeship scheme is more likely to maximize consumer welfare, even in markets without available outlets, than would a system relying on the judgment of marketplace players.

As the critical assault upon scarcity persisted, both the FCC and the courts began to rethink doctrinal logic. In *Federal Communications Commission v. League of Women Voters*, the Supreme Court indicated that it was prepared to reexamine both the utility of fairness regulation and the validity of the scarcity premise. Writing for a majority, Justice Brennan noted that

> [T]he prevailing rationale for broadcast regulation based on spectrum scarcity has come under increasing criticism in recent years. Critics, including the incumbent Chairman of the FCC, charge that with the advent of cable and satellite television technology, communities now have access to such a wide variety of stations that the scarcity doctrine is obsolete. We are not prepared, however, to reconsider our longstanding approach without some signal from Congress or the FCC that technological developments have advanced so far that some revision of the system of broadcast regulation may be required.[200]

> The Court also stressed that were it to be shown by the Commission that the fairness doctrine "[has] the net effect of reducing rather than enhancing" speech, we would then be forced to reconsider the constitutional basis of our decision in that case.

> [A]lthough the broadcasting industry plainly operates under restraints not imposed upon other media, the thrust of these restrictions has generally been to secure the public's First Amendment interest in receiving a balanced presentation of views on diverse matters of public concern. As a result of these restrictions, of course, the absolute freedom to advocate one's own positions without also presenting opposing viewpoints—a freedom, enjoyed, for example, by newspaper publishers and soapbox orators—is denied to broadcasters. But, as our cases attest, these restrictions have been upheld only when we were satisfied that the restriction is narrowly tailored to further a substantial governmental interest, such as ensuring adequate and balanced coverage of public issues. Making that judgment requires a critical examination of the interests of the public and broadcasters in light of the particular circumstances of each case.[201]

As the FCC formally reassessed the sensibility of the fairness doctrine and underlying scarcity rationale,[202] a federal appeals court raised significant questions about regulatory assumptions. In upholding a Commission decision not to extend the fairness doctrine to teletext service, the court challenged the wisdom of the scarcity premise itself.

---

[200] Federal Communications Commission v. League of Women Voters, 468 U.S. 364, 376–77 n.11 (1984).

[201] *Id.* at 378–79 n.12.

[202] Inquiry into Section 73.1910 of the Commission's Rules and Regulations Concerning the General Fairness Obligation of Broadcast Licensees, 102 F.C.C. 2d 145 (1985).

Telecommunications Research and Action Center v. Federal Communications Commission
801 F.2d 501 (D.C. Cir. 1986),
cert. denied, 428 U.S. 919 (1987)

BORK, CIRCUIT JUDGE:

Petitioners challenge the Federal Communications Commission's decision not to apply three forms of political broadcast regulation to a new technology, teletext. Teletext provides a means of transmitting textual and graphic material to the television screens of home viewers.

. . .

The case before us presents the question whether the Commission erred in determining that these three political broadcast provisions do not apply to teletext. . . .

. . .

The Commission believes . . . that the regulation of teletext falls not within the permissive approach of *Red Lion*, but rather within the strict first amendment rule applied to content regulation of the print media. . . .

The Commission has offered two grounds for its view that *Tornillo* rather than *Red Lion* is pertinent. Both reasons relate to the textual nature of teletext services. First the Commission read an "immediacy" component into the scarcity doctrine:

> Implicit in the "scarcity" rational . . . is an assumption that broadcasters, through their access to the radio spectrum, possess a power to communicate ideas through sound and visual images in a manner that is significantly different from traditional avenues of communication because of the immediacy of the medium.

Second, the Commission held that the print nature of teletext "more closely resembles, and will largely compete with, other print communication media such as newspapers and magazines." *Id*. Under this analysis, scarcity of alternative first amendment resources does not exist with respect to teletext. We address these points in turn.

With respect to the first argument, the deficiencies of the scarcity rationale as a basis for depriving broadcasting of full first amendment protection, have led some to think that it is the immediacy and the power of broadcasting that causes it differential treatment. Whether or not that is true, we are unwilling to endorse an argument that makes the very effectiveness of speech the justification for according it less first amendment protection. More important, the Supreme Court's articulation of the scarcity doctrine contains no hint of any immediacy rationale. The Court based its reasoning entirely on the physical scarcity of broadcasting frequencies, which, it thought, permitted attaching fiduciary duties to the receipt of a license to use a frequency. This "immediacy" distinction cannot, therefore, be employed to affect the ability of the Commission to regulate public affairs broadcasting on teletext to ensure "the right of the public to receive suitable access to social, political, esthetic, moral, and other ideas and experiences."

The Commission's second distinction—that a textual medium is not scarce insofar as it competes with other "print media"—also fails to dislodge the holding of *Red Lion*. The dispositive fact is that teletext is transmitted over broadcast frequencies that the Supreme Court has ruled scarce and this makes teletext's content regulable. We can understand, however, why the Commission thought it could reason in this fashion. The basic difficulty in this entire area is that the line drawn between the print media and the broadcast media, resting as it does on the physical scarcity of the latter, is a distinction without a difference. Employing the scarcity concept as an analytic tool, particularly with respect to new and unforeseen technologies, inevitably leads to strained reasoning and artificial results.

It is certainly true that broadcast frequencies are scarce but it is unclear why that fact justifies content regulation of broadcasting in a way that would be intolerable if applied to the editorial process of the print media. All economic goods are scarce, not least the newsprint, ink, delivery trucks, computers, and other resources that go into the production and dissemination of print journalism. Not everyone who wishes to publish a newspaper, or even a pamphlet, may do so. Since scarcity is a universal fact as a distinguishing principle necessarily leads to analytical confusion.

Neither is content regulation explained by the fact that broadcasters face the problem of interference, so that the government must define useable frequencies and protect those frequencies from encroachment. This governmental definition of frequencies is another instance of a universal fact that does not offer an explanatory principle for differing treatment. A publisher can deliver his newspapers only because government provides streets and regulates traffic on the streets by allocating rights of way. Yet no one would contend that the necessity for these governmental functions, which are certainly analogous to the government's function in allocating broadcast frequencies, could justify regulation of the content of a newspaper to ensure that it serves the needs of the citizens.

There may be ways to reconcile *Red Lion* and *Tornillo* but the "scarcity" of broadcast frequencies does not appear capable of doing so. Perhaps the Supreme Court will one day revisit this area of the law and either eliminate the distinction between print and broadcast media, surely by pronouncing *Tornillo* applicable to both, or announce a constitutional distinction

that is more usable than the present one. In the meantime, neither we nor the commission are free to seek new rationales to remedy the inadequacy of the doctrine in this area. The attempt to do that has led the Commission to find "implicit" considerations in the law that are not really there. The Supreme Court has drawn a first amendment distinction between broadcast and print media on a premise of the physical scarcity of broadcast frequencies. Teletext, whatever its similarities to print media, uses broadcast frequencies, and that, given *Red Lion*, would seem to be that.

. . .

The influence of critical ferment eventually eroded the FCC's own faith in and support of the fairness doctrine. In 1985, it asserted that "the multiplicity of voices in the marketplace today" had erased the problem of spectrum scarcity, so the regulation no longer was a "necessary . . . or appropriate means by which to effectuate this interest." Despite evidence it cited in support of the fairness doctrine's deficiencies, and articulated judicial misgivings about the principle, the FCC deferred steps that would negate the principle pending legislative action. Although Congress voted to incorporate the fairness doctrine into statute, the president vetoed it. In the meantime, the FCC was under increasing pressure to correlate policies and actions with its new sense that the fairness doctrine subverted First Amendment interests. A direct constitutional challenge to the doctrine's constitutionality was dismissed on jurisdictional grounds, although a companion claim regarding the Commission's failure to commence a rule-making to eliminate or modify it was found reviewable. The matter subsequently was vacated following the resolution of *Meredith Corp. v. Federal Communications Commission*. 809 F.2d 863 (D.C. Cir. 1987). The court of appeals ordered the FCC, which had found a fairness violation, to consider the licensee's contention that the fairness doctrine was unconstitutional. Consistent with an approving cue from the *Telecommunication Research and Action Committee* decision, to the effect that the fairness doctrine had not been implicitly codified by congressional action, the Commission abandoned the fairness doctrine for many of the reasons sounded over the years by critics.

Without reaching the constitutional issues, the court of appeals upheld the FCC's decision in *Syracuse Peace Council v. Federal Communications Commission* as a legitimate rendition under the "public interest" standard. Finding that the fairness doctrine was not absolutely compelled by the constitution or by statute, the appeals court deferred to the FCC's determination that it chilled coverage of important issues, subjected the editorial process to official second guessing and potential abuse, and no longer was necessary owing to the expanded availability of broadcasting outlets.

Nearly two decades after the fairness doctrine was upheld in *Red Lion*, pursuant to scarcity concerns, the FCC abandoned the regulation and its rationale. Its changed position reflected the sense that such editorial control undermined rather than facilitated program diversity and unduly diminished the First Amendment interests of broadcasters. The FCC also concluded that scarcity was a universal condition and thus inapt as a medium specific reference point.

Syracuse Peace Council
2 F.C.C. Rcd. 5043 (1987)

. . .

47. The Commission demonstrated in the *1985 Fairness Report* that broadcasters—from network television anchors to those in the smallest radio stations—recounted that the fear of governmental sanction resulting from the doctrine creates a climate of timidity and fear, which deters the coverage of controversial issue programming. The record contained numerous instances in which the broadcasters decided that it was "safer" to avoid broadcasting specific controversial issue programming, such as series prepared for local news programs, than to incur the potentially burdensome administrative, legal, personnel, and reputational costs of either complying with the doctrine or defending their editorial decisions to governmental authorities.

. . .

61. In sum, the fairness doctrine in operation disserves both the public's right to diverse sources of information and the broadcaster's interest in free expression. Its chilling effect thwarts its intended purpose, and it results in excessive and unnecessary government intervention into the editorial processes of broadcast journalists. We hold, therefore, that under the constitutional standard established by *Red Lion* and its progeny, the fairness doctrine contravenes the First Amendment and its enforcement is no longer in the public interest.

. . .

75. Because there is no longer a scarcity in the number of broadcast outlets, proponents of a scarcity rationale for the justification of diminished First Amendment rights applicable to the broadcast medium must rely on the concept of spectrum (or allocational) scarcity. This concept is based upon the physical limitations of the electromagnetic spectrum. Because only a limited number of persons can utilize broadcast frequencies at any particular point in time, spectrum scarcity is said to be present when the number of persons desiring to disseminate information on broadcast frequencies exceeds the number of available frequencies. Consequently, these frequencies, like all scarce resources, must be allocated among those who wish to use them.

. . .

78. Nevertheless, we recognize that technological advancements and the transformation of the telecommunications market described above have not eliminated spectrum scarcity. All goods, however, are ultimately scarce, and there must be a system through which to allocate their use. Although a free enterprise system relies heavily on a system of property rights and voluntary exchange to allo-

cate most of these goods, other methods of allocation, including first-come-first-served, administrative hearings, lotteries, and auctions, are or have been relied on for certain other goods. Whatever the method of allocation, there is not any logical connection between the method of allocation for a particular good and the level of constitutional protection afforded to the uses of that good.

. . .

80. Additionally, there is nothing inherent in the utilization of the licensing method of allocation that justifies the government acting in a manner that would be proscribed under a traditional First Amendment analysis. . . .

83. We believe that the articulation of lesser First Amendment rights for broadcasters on the basis of the existence of scarcity, the licensing of broadcasters, and the paramount rights of listeners departs from traditional First Amendment jurisprudence in a number of respects. Specifically, the Court's decision that the listeners' rights justifies government intrusion appears to conflict with several fundamental principles underlying the constitutional guarantee of free speech.

. . . (A) cardinal tenet of the First Amendment is that governmental intervention in the marketplace of ideas of the sort involved in enforcement of the fairness doctrine is not acceptable and should not be tolerated. . . .

86. The fairness doctrine is at odds with this fundamental constitutional precept. While the objective underlying the fairness doctrine is that of the First Amendment itself—the promotion of debate on important controversial issues—the means employed to achieve this objective, government coercion, is the very one which the First Amendment is designed to prevent. . . .

. . .

90. Further, the *Red Lion* decision cannot be reconciled with well-established constitutional precedent that governmental regulations directly affecting the content of speech are subjected to particularly strict scrutiny. . . .

93. . . . The problem is not with the goal of the fairness doctrine, it is with the use of government intrusion as the means to achieve that goal. With the existence of a fairness doctrine, broadcasters who intend to, and who do in fact, present contrasting viewpoints on controversial issues of public importance are nevertheless exposed to potential entanglement with the government over the exercise of their editorial discretion. Consequently, these broadcasters may shy away from extensive coverage of these issues. We believe that, in the

absence of the doctrine, broadcasters will more readily cover controversial issues, which, when combined with sound journalistic practices, will result in more coverage and more diversity of viewpoint in the electronic media; that is, the goals of the First Amendment will be enhanced by employing the very means of the First Amendment: government restraint.

94. Finally, we believe that under the First Amendment, the right of viewers and listeners to receive diverse viewpoints is achieved by guaranteeing them the right to receive speech unencumbered by government intervention....

. . .

97. We believe that the role of the electronic press in our society is the same as that of the printed press. Both are sources of information and viewpoint. Accordingly, the reasons for proscribing government intrusion into the editorial discretion of print journalists provide the same basis for proscribing such interference into the editorial discretion of broadcast journalists. The First Amendment was adopted to protect the people *not from journalists, but from government*. It gives the people the right to receive ideas that are unfettered by government interference. We fail to see how that right changes when individuals choose to receive ideas from the electronic media instead

of the print media. There is no doubt that the electronic media is powerful and that broadcasters can abuse their freedom of speech. But the framers of the Constitution believed that the potential for abuse of private freedoms posed far less a threat to democracy than the potential for abuse by a government given the power to control the press. We concur. We therefore believe that full First Amendment protections against content regulation should apply equally to the electronic and the printed press. . . .

99. We further believe, as the Supreme Court indicated in *FCC v. League of Women Voters of California*, that the dramatic transformation in the telecommunications marketplace provides a basis for the Court to reconsider its application of diminished First Amendment protection to the electronic media. Despite the physical differences between the electronic and print media, their roles in our society are identical, and we believe that the same First Amendment principles should be equally applicable to both. This is the method set forth in our Constitution for maximizing the public interest; and furthering the public interest is likewise our mandate under the Communications Act. It is, therefore, to advance the public interest that we advocate these rights for broadcasters.

Within months of the *Syracuse Peace Council* decision, Congress passed a law resurrecting the fairness doctrine only to have it vetoed by the president. Since then efforts to resurrect it have become virtually an annual exercise. Despite the FCC's own rejection of scarcity as a unique condition of broadcasting, and the Court's expressed readiness to rethink it, subsequent case law uncritically has subscribed to it. In *Metro Broadcasting, Inc. v. Federal Communications Commission*, the Court upheld minority preferences in the broadcast licensing process on grounds that they were an apt regulatory response to a scarce medium.

Metro Broadcasting, Inc. v. Federal Communications Commission
497 U.S. 547 (1990)

MR. JUSTICE BRENNAN delivered the opinion of the Court.

The issue in these cases . . . is whether certain minority preference policies of the Federal Communications Commission violate the equal protection component of the Fifth Amendment. The policies in question are (1) a program awarding an enhancement for minority ownership in comparative proceedings for new licenses, and (2) the minority "distress sale" program, which permits a limited category of existing radio and television broadcast

stations to be transferred only to minority-controlled firms. We hold that these policies do not violate equal protection principles.

. . .

We hold that the FCC minority ownership policies pass muster under the test we announce today. First, . . . they serve the important governmental objective of broadcast diversity. Second, . . . they are substantially related to the achievement of that objective.

Congress found that "the effects of past inequities stemming from racial and ethnic discrimination have resulted in a severe under-representation of minorities in the media of mass communications." Congress and the Commission do not justify the minority ownership policies strictly as remedies for victims of this discrimination, however. Rather, Congress and the FCC have selected the minority ownership policies primarily to promote programming diversity, and they urge that such diversity is an important governmental objective that can serve as a constitutional basis for the preference policies. We agree.

... [I]t is axiomatic that broadcast diversity is, at the very least, an important governmental objective.... Just as a "diverse student body" contributing to a "'robust exchange of ideas'" is a "constitutionally permissible goal" on which a race-conscious university admissions program may be predicted, the diversity of views and information on the airwaves serves important First Amendment values. The benefits of such diversity are not limited to the members of minority groups who gain access to the broadcasting industry by virtue of the ownership policies; rather, the benefits redound to all members of the viewing and listening audience. As Congress found, "the American public will benefit by having access to a wider diversity of information sources." ...

Like any other new medium, cable during its early years struggled to have its First Amendment status acknowledged. Although not specifically vested with power to regulate the cable industry until 1984,[203] the FCC adopted numerous regulations in reaction to the cable industry's emergence and impact upon broadcasting. Responding to arguments that rules prohibiting cablecasters from importing distant signals would destabilize the market for local broadcasters, the Supreme Court determined that the FCC's authority was "restricted to that reasonably ancillary to the effective performance of the Commission's various responsibilities for the regulation of television broadcasting" and thus could generate regulation as the "public convenience, interest, or necessity requires" with respect to broadcasting.[204] Pursuant to the reasonably ancillary standard, the FCC imposed upon cable operators a series of requirements including the obligation to originate programming and provide public access. In upholding the origination requirement, the Court nonetheless stressed that the FCC had "strain[ed] the outer limits of . . . [its] jurisdiction."[205] Striking down public access provisions several years later, the Court determined that the FCC had exceeded its ancillary authority to facilitate its regulatory obligations in broadcasting.[206] Although both regulations had burdened the editorial freedom of cablecasters, neither decision was referenced to the First Amendment. Invalidation of access rules was based upon the Court's sense that the FCC had exceeded its regulatory power by treating cable operators as common carriers.[207]

Extensive deregulation of the cable industry by the FCC and subsequent enactment of cable legislation has reduced the aforementioned cases to a background status. Collectively, they demonstrate the cable industry's efforts to have its First Amendment claims taken seriously. Not until the mid-1980s, however, did the Court explicitly acknowledge that cable operators possess a First Amendment interest.[208] Another decade elapsed before the Court meaningfully explored the nature and scope of that liberty. During the 1980s, the Court of Appeals for the District of Columbia Circuit twice struck

---

[203] The Cable Communications Act of 1984 augmented the Communications Act of 1934 so as to authorize specifically a division of regulatory responsibilities between federal and state government. 47 U.S.C. §§ 521 *et seq.*

[204] United States v. Southwestern Cable Co., 392 U.S. 156, 176–77 (1968).

[205] United States v. Midwest Video Corp., 406 U.S. 649, 676 (1972).

[206] Federal Communications Commission v. Midwest Video Corp., 440 U.S. 689, 709 (1979).

[207] *Id.* at 700–01.

[208] City of Los Angeles v. Preferred Communications, Inc., 476 U.S. 488, 494 (1984).

down rules requiring cable operators to carry the signals of local broadcasters.[209] Following congressional enactment of cable legislation in 1992, that included yet another set of must carry requirements, the Court discoursed upon the nature and extent of cable's First Amendment stake.

---

[209] Century Communications Corp. v. Federal Communications Commission, 835 F.2d 292 (D.C. Cir. 1987), cert. denied, 486 U.S. 1032 (1988); Quincy Cable TV, Inc. v. Federal Communications Commission, 768 F.2d 1434 (D.C. Cir. 1985), cert. denied, 476 U.S. 1169 (1986).

Turner Broadcasting System, Inc. v. Federal Communications Commission
114 S. Ct. 2445 (1994)

. . .

JUSTICE KENNEDY announced the judgement of the Court and delivered the opinion of the Court, except as to Part III-B.

Sections 4 and 5 of the Cable Television Consumer Protection and Competition Act of 1992 require cable television to devote a portion of their channels to the transmission of local broadcast stations. This case presents the question whether provisions abridge the freedom of speech or of the press, in violation of the First Amendment.

The United States District Court for the District of Columbia granted summary judgment for the United States, holding that the challenged provisions are consistent with the First Amendment. Because issues of material fact remain unresolved in the record as developed thus far, we vacate the District Court's judgment and remand the case for further proceedings.

I
A

The role of cable television in the Nation's communications system has undergone dramatic change over the past 45 years. Given the pace of technological advancement and the increasing convergence between cable and other electronic media, the cable industry today stands at the center of an ongoing telecommunications revolution with still undefined potential to affect the way we communicate and develop our intellectual resources.

The earliest cable systems were built in the late 1940's to bring clear broadcast television signals to remote or mountainous communities. The purpose was not to replace broadcast television but to enhance it. Modern cable systems do much more than enhance the reception of nearby broadcast television stations. With the capacity to carry dozens of channels and import distant programming signals via satellite or microwave relay, today's cable systems are in direct competition with over-the-air broadcasters as an independent source of television programming.

Broadcast and cable television are distinguished by the different technologies through which they reach viewers. Broadcast stations radiate electromagnetic signals from a central transmitting antenna. These signals can be captured, in turn, by any television set within the antenna's range. Cable systems, by contrast, rely upon a physical, point-to-point connection between a transmission facility and the television sets of individual subscribers. Cable systems make this connection much like telephone companies, using cable or optical fibers strung aboveground or buried in ducts to reach the homes or businesses of subscribers. The construction of this physical infrastructure entails the use of public rights-of-way and easements and often results in the disruption of traffic on streets and other public property. As a result, the cable medium may depend for its very existence upon express permission from local governing authorities.

Cable technology affords two principal benefits over broadcast. First, it eliminates the signal interference sometimes encountered in over-the-air broadcasting and thus gives viewers undistorted reception of broadcast stations. Second, it is capable of transmitting many more channels than are available through broadcasting, giving subscribers access to far greater programming variety. More than half of the cable systems in operation today have a capacity to carry between 30 and 53 channels. And about 40 percent of cable subscribers are served by systems with a capacity of more than 53 channels. Newer systems can carry hundreds of channels, and many older systems are being upgraded with fiber optic rebuilds and digital compression technology to increase channel capacity.

The cable television industry includes both cable operators (those who own the physical cable network and transmit the cable signal to the viewer) and cable programmers (those who produce television programs and sell or license them to cable operators). In some cases, cable operators have acquired ownership of cable programmers, and vice versa. Although cable operators may create some of their own programming, most of their programming is drawn from outside sources. These outside sources include not only local or distant broadcast stations, but also the many national and regional cable programming networks that have emerged in recent years. . . . Once the cable operator has selected the programming sources, the cable system functions in essence as a conduit for the speech of others, transmitting it on a continuous and unedited basis to subscribers.

In contrast to commercial broadcast stations, which transmit signals at no charge to viewers and generate revenues by selling time to advertisers, cable systems charge subscribers a monthly fee for the right to receive cable programming and rely to a lesser extent on advertising. In most instances, cable subscribers choose the stations they will receive by selecting among various plans, or "tiers," of cable service. . . .

B

On October 5, 1992, Congress overrode a Presidential veto to enact the Cable Television Consumer Protection and Competition Act of 1992, (1992 Cable Act or Act). . . . At issue in this case is the constitutionality of the so-called must-carry provisions, contained in §§4 and 5 of the Act, which require cable operators to carry the signals of a specified number of local broadcast television stations.

Section 4 requires carriage of "local commercial television stations," defined to include all full power television broadcasters other than those qualifying as "noncommercial educational" stations under §5, that operate within the same television market as the cable system. Cable systems with more than 12 active channels, and more than 300 subscribers, are required to set aside up to one-third of their channels for commercial broadcast stations that request carriage. Cable systems with more than 300 subscribers, but only 12 or fewer active channels, must carry the signals of three commercial broadcast stations.

If there are fewer broadcasters requesting carriage than slots made available under the Act, the cable operator is obligated to carry only those broadcasters who make the request. If, however, there are more requesting broadcast stations than slots available, the cable operator is permitted to choose which of these stations it will carry. The broadcast signals carried under this provision must be transmitted on a continuous, uninterrupted basis, and must be placed in the same numerical channel position as when broadcast over the air. Further, subject to a few exceptions, a cable operator may not charge a fee for carrying broadcast signals in fulfillment of its must-carry obligations.

Section 5 of the Act imposes similar requirements regarding the carriage of local public broadcast television stations, referred to in the Act as local "noncommercial educational television stations." . . .

Taken together, therefore, §§ 4 and 5 subject all but the smallest cable systems nationwide to must-carry obligations, and confer must-carry privileges on all full power broadcasters operating within the same television market as a qualified system.

C

Congress enacted the 1992 Cable Act after conducting three years of hearings on the structure and operation of the cable television industry. The conclusions Congress drew from its factfinding process are recited in the text of the Act itself. In brief, Congress found that the physical characteristics of cable transmission, compounded by the increasing concentration of economic power in the cable industry, are endangering the ability of over-the-air broadcast television stations to compete for a viewing audience and thus for necessary operating revenues. Congress determined that regulation of the market for video programming was necessary to correct this competitive imbalance.

In particular, Congress found that over 60 percent of the households with television sets subscribe to cable, and for these households cable has replaced over-the-air broadcast television as the primary provider of video programming. This is so, Congress found, because "[m]ost subscribers to cable television systems do not or cannot maintain antennas to receive broadcast television services, do not have input selector switches to convert from a cable to antenna reception system, or cannot otherwise receive broadcast television services." In addition, Congress concluded that due to "local franchising requirements and the extraordinary expense of constructing more than one cable television system to serve a particular geographic area," the overwhelming majority of cable operators exercise a monopoly over cable service. "The result," Congress determined, "is undue market power for the cable operator as compared to that of consumers and video programmers."

According to Congress, this market position gives cable operators the power and the incentive to harm broadcast competitors. The power derives from the cable operator's ability as owner of the transmission facility, to "terminate the retransmission of the broadcast signal, refuse to carry new signals, or reposition a broadcast signal to a disadvantageous challenge position." The incentive derives from the economic reality that "[c]able television systems and broadcast television stations increasingly compete for television advertising revenues." By refusing carriage of broadcasters' signals, cable operators, as a practical matter, can reduce the number of households that have access to the broadcasters' programming, and thereby capture advertising dollars that would otherwise go to broadcast stations. Congress found, in addition, that increased vertical integration in the cable industry is making it even harder for broadcasters to secure carriage on cable systems, because cable operators have a financial incentive to favor their affiliated programmers. Congress also determined that the cable industry is characterized by horizontal concentration, with many cable operators sharing common ownership. This has resulted in greater "barriers to entry for new programmers and a reduction in the number of media voices available to consumers."

In light of these technological and economic conditions, Congress concluded that unless cable operators are required to carry local broadcast stations, "[t]here is a substantial likelihood that . . . additional local broadcast signals will be deleted, repositioned, or not carried," §2(a)(15); the "marked shift in market share" from broadcast to cable will continue to erode the advertising revenue base which sustains free local broadcast television, and that, as a consequence, "the economic viability of free local broadcast television and its ability to originate quality local programming will be seriously jeopardized."

D

Soon after the Act became law, appellants filed these five consolidated actions in the United States District Court for the District of Columbia against the United States and the Federal Communications Commission (hereinafter referred to collectively as the Government), challenging the constitutionality of the must-carry provisions. Appellants, plaintiffs below, are numerous cable programmers and cable operators. After additional parties intervened, a three-judge District court convened . . . to hear the actions. Each of the plaintiffs filed a motion for summary judgment; several intervenor-defendants filed cross-motions for summary judgment; and the Government filed a cross-motion to dismiss. Although the Government had not asked for summary

judgment, the District Court, in a divided opinion, granted summary judgment in favor of the Government and their other intervenor-defendants, ruling that the must-carry provisions are consistent with the First Amendment.

. . .

II

There can be no disagreement on an initial premise: Cable programmers and cable operators engage in and transmit speech, and they are entitled to the protection of the speech and press provisions of the First Amendment. *Leathers v. Medlock*, 499 U.S. 439, 444 (1991). Through "original programming or by exercising editorial discretion over which stations or programs to include in its repertoire," cable programmers and operators "see[k] to communicate messages on a wide variety of topics and in a wide variety of formats." *Los Angeles v. Preferred Communications, Inc.*, 476 U.S. 488, 494 (1986). By requiring cable systems to set aside a portion of their channels for local broadcasters, the must-carry rules regulate cable speech in two respects: The rules reduce the number of channels over which cable operators exercise unfettered control, and they render it more difficult for cable programmers to compete for carriage on the limited channels remaining. Nevertheless, because not every interference with speech triggers the same degree of scrutiny under the First Amendment, we must decide at the outset the level of scrutiny applicable to the must-carry provisions.

A

We address first the Government's contention that regulation of cable television should be analyzed under the same First Amendment standard that applies to regulation of broadcast television. It is true that our cases have permitted more extrusive regulation of broadcast speakers than of speakers in other media. But the rationale for applying a less rigorous standard of First Amendment scrutiny to broadcast regulation, whatever its validity in the cases elaborating it, does not apply in the context of cable regulation.

The justification for our distinct approach to broadcast regulation rests upon the unique physical limitations of the broadcast medium. As a general matter, there are more would-be broadcasters than frequencies available in the electromagnetic spectrum. And if two broadcasters were to attempt to transmit over the same frequency in the same locale, they would interfere with one another's signals, so that neither could be heard at all. The scarcity of broadcast frequencies thus required the establishment of some regulatory mechanism to divide the electromagnetic spectrum and assign specific frequencies to particular broadcasters.

In addition, the inherent physical limitation on the number of speakers who may use the broadcast medium has been thought to require some adjustment in traditional First Amendment analysis to permit the Government to place limited content restraints, and impose certain affirmative obligations, on broadcast licensees. As we said in *Red Lion*, "[w]here there are substantially more individuals who want to broadcast than there are frequencies to allocate, it is idle to posit an unbridgeable First Amendment right to broadcast comparable to the right of every individual to speak, write, or publish."

Although courts and commentators have criticized the scarcity rationale since its inception, we have declined to question its continuing validity as support for our broadcast jurisprudence, and see no reason to do so here. The broadcast cases are inapposite in the present context because cable television does not suffer from the inherent limitations that characterize the broadcast medium. Indeed, given the rapid advances in fiber optics and digital compression technology, soon there may be no practical interference between two cable speakers attempting to share the same channel. In light of these fundamental technological differences between broadcast and cable transmission, application of the more relaxed standard of scrutiny adopted in *Red Lion* and the other broadcast cases is inapt when determining the First Amendment validity of cable regulation.

This is not to say that the unique physical characteristics of cable transmission should be ignored when determining the constitutionality of regulations affecting cable speech. They should not. But whatever relevance these physical characteristics may have in the evaluation of particular cable regulations, they do not require the alteration of settled principles of our First Amendment jurisprudence.

Although the Government acknowledges the substantial technological differences between broadcast and cable, it advances a second argument for application of the *Red Lion* framework to cable regulation. It asserts that the foundation of our broadcast jurisprudence is not the physical limitations of the electromagnetic spectrum, but rather the "market dysfunction" that characterizes the broadcast market. Because the cable market is beset by a similar dysfunction, the government maintains, the *Red Lion* standard of review should also apply to cable. While we agree that the cable market suffers certain structural impediments, the Government's argument is flawed in two respects. First, as discussed above, the special physical characteristics of broadcast transmission, not the economic characteristics of the broadcast market, are what underlies our broadcast jurisprudence. Second, the mere assertion of dysfunction or failure in a speech market, without more, is not sufficient to shield a speech regulation from the First Amendment standards applicable to nonbroadcast media.

By a related course of reasoning, the Government and some appellees maintain that the must-carry provisions are nothing more than industry-specific antitrust legislation, and thus warrant rational basis scrutiny under this Court's "precedents governing legislative efforts to correct market failure in a market whose commodity is speech." . . . But while the enforcement of a generally applicable law may or may not be subject to heightened scrutiny under the First Amendment, laws that single out the press, or certain elements thereof, for special treatment "pose a particular danger of abuse by the State," and so are always subject to at least some degree of heightened First Amendment scrutiny. . . . Because the must-carry provisions impose special obligations upon cable operators and special burdens upon cable programmers, some measure of heightened First Amendment scrutiny is demanded.

B

At the heart of the First Amendment lies the principle that each person should decide for him or herself the ideas and beliefs deserving of expression, consideration, and adherence. Our political system and cultural life rest upon this ideal. Government action that stifles speech on account of its message, or that requires the utterance of a particular message favored by the Government, contravenes this essential right. . . .

. . . In contrast, regulations that are unrelated to the content of speech are subject to an intermediate level of scrutiny, because in most cases they pose a less substantial risk of excising certain ideas or viewpoints from the public dialogue.

Deciding whether a particular regulation is content-based or content-neutral is not always a simple task. We have said that the "principle inquiry in determining content-neutrality . . . is whether the government has adopted a regulation of speech because of [agreement or] disagreement with the message it conveys." . . .

As a general rule, laws that by their terms distinguish favored speech from disfavored speech on the basis of the ideas or views expressed are content-based. . . . By contrast, laws that confer benefits or impose burdens on speech without reference to the ideas or views expressed are in most instances content-neutral. . . .

C

Insofar as they pertain to the carriage of full power broadcasters, the must-carry rules, on their face, impose burdens and confer benefits without reference to the content of speech. Although the provisions interfere with cable operators' editorial discretion by compelling them to offer carriage to a certain minimum number of broadcast stations, the extent of the interference does not depend upon the content of the cable operators' programming....

The must-carry provisions also burden cable programmers by reducing the number of channels for which they can compete. But, again, this burden is unrelated to content, for it extends to all cable programmers irrespective of the programming they choose to offer viewers....

It is true that the must-carry provisions distinguish between speakers in the television programming market. But they do so based only upon the manner in which speakers transmit their messages to viewers, and not upon the messages they carry: Broadcasters, which transmit over the airwaves, are favored, while cable programmers, which do not, are disfavored. Cable operators, too, are burdened by the carriage obligations, but only because they control access to the cable conduit. So long as they are not a subtle means of exercising a content preference, speaker distinctions of this nature are not presumed invalid under the First Amendment.

That the must-carry provisions, on their face, do not burden or benefit speech of a particular content does not end the inquiry. Our cases have recognized that even a regulation neutral on its face may be content-based if its manifest purpose is to regulate speech because of the message it conveys....

Appellants contend, in this regard, that the must-carry regulations are content-based because Congress' purpose in enacting them was to promote speech of a favored content. We do not agree. Our review of the Act and its various findings persuades us that Congress' overriding objective in enacting must-carry was not to favor programming of a particular subject matter, viewpoint, or format, but rather to preserve access to free television programming for the 40 percent of Americans without cable.

. . .

By preventing cable operators from refusing carriage to broadcast television stations, the must-carry rules ensure that broadcast television stations will retain a large enough potential audience to earn necessary advertising—revenue—or, in the case of noncommercial broadcasters, sufficient viewer contributions—to maintain their continued operation. In so doing, the provisions are designed to guarantee the survival of a medium that has become a vital part of the Nation's communication system, and to ensure that every individual with a television set can obtain access to free television programming.

This overriding congressional purpose is unrelated to the content of expression disseminated by cable and broadcast speakers....

The design and operation of the challenged provisions confirm that the purposes underlying the enactment of the must-carry scheme are unrelated to the content of speech. The rules, as mentioned, confer must-carry rights on all full power broadcasters, irrespective of the content of their programming. They do not require or prohibit the carriage of particular ideas or points of view. The do not penalize cable operators or programmers because of the content of their programming. They do not compel cable operators to affirm points of view with which they disagree. They do not produce any net decrease in the amount of available speech. And they leave cable operators free to carry whatever programming they wish on all channels not subject to must-carry requirements.

Appellants and the dissent make much of the fact that, in the course of describing the purposes behind the Act, Congress referred to the value of broadcast programming. In particular, congress noted that broadcast television is "an important source of local news[,] public affairs programming and other local broadcast services critical to an informed electorate," §2(a)(11); see also §2(a)(10), and that noncommercial television "provides educational and informational programming to the Nation's citizens." §2(a)(8). We do not think, however, that such references cast any material doubt on the content-neutral character of must-carry. That Congress acknowledged the local orientation of broadcast programming and the role that noncommercial stations have played in educating the public does not indicate that Congress regarded broadcast programming as *more* valuable than cable programming. Rather, it reflects nothing more than the recognition that the services provided by broadcast television have some intrinsic value and, thus, are worth preserving against the threats posed by cable....

In short, the must-carry provisions are not designed to favor or disadvantage speech of any particular content. Rather, they are meant to protect broadcast television from what Congress determined to be unfair competition by cable systems. In enacting the provisions, Congress sought to preserve the existing structure of the Nation's broadcast television medium while permitting the concomitant expansion and development of cable television, and, in particular, to ensure that broadcast television remains available as a source of video programming for those without cable. Appellants' ability to hypothesize a content-based purpose for these provisions rests on little more than speculation and does not cast doubt upon the content-neutral character of must-carry. Indeed, "[i]t is a familiar principle of constitutional law that this Court will not strike down an otherwise constitutional statute on the basis of an alleged illicit legislative motive."

D

Appellants advance three additional arguments to support their view that the must-carry provisions warrant strict scrutiny. In brief, appellants contend that the provisions (1) compel speech by cable operators, (2) favor broadcast programmers over cable programmers, and (3) single out certain members of the press for disfavored treatment. None of these arguments suffices to require strict scrutiny in the present case.

1

Appellants maintain that the must-carry provisions trigger strict scrutiny because they compel cable operators to transmit speech not of their choosing. Relying principally on *Miami Herald Publishing Co. v. Tornillo*, appellants say this intrusion on the editorial control of cable operators amounts to forced speech which, if not *per se* invalid, can be justified only if narrowly tailored to a compelling government interest.

Tornillo affirmed an essential proposition: The First Amendment protects the editorial independence of the press. The right-of-reply statute at issue in *Tornillo* required any newspaper that assailed a political candidate's character to print, upon request by the candidate and without cost, the candidate's reply in equal space and prominence. Although the statute did not censor speech in the traditional sense—it only required newspapers to grant access to the messages of others—we found that it imposed an impermissible content-based burden on newspaper speech. Because the right of access at issue in *Tornillo* was triggered only when a newspaper elected to print matter critical of political candidates, it "exact[ed] a penalty on the basis of . . . content." We found, and continue to recognize, that right-of-reply statutes of this sort are an impermissible intrusion on newspapers' "editorial control and judgment."

. . .

Tornillo . . . do[es] not control this case for the following reasons. First, unlike the access rules struck down in those cases, the must-carry rules are content-neutral in application. They are not activated by any particular message spoken by cable operators and thus exact no content-based penalty. Likewise, they do not grant access to broadcasters on the ground that the content of broadcast programming will counterbalance the messages of cable operators. Instead, they confer benefits upon all full power, local broadcasters, whatever the content of their programming.

Second, appellants do not suggest, nor do we think it the case, that must-carry will force cable operators to alter their own messages to respond to the broadcast programming they are required to carry. Given cable's long history of serving as a conduit for broadcast signals, there appears little risk that cable viewers would assume that the broadcast stations carried on a cable system convey ideas or messages endorsed by the cable operator. . . . Moreover, in contrast to the statute at issue in *Tornillo*, no aspect of the must-carry provisions would cause a cable operator or cable programmer to conclude that "the safe course is to avoid controversy," and by so doing diminish the free flow of information and ideas.

Finally, the asserted analogy to *Tornillo* ignores an important technological difference between newspapers and cable television. Although a daily newspaper and a cable operator both may enjoy monopoly status in a given locale, the cable operator exercises far greater control over access to the relevant medium. A daily newspaper, no matter how secure its local monopoly, does not possess the power to obstruct readers' access to other competing publications—whether they be weekly local newspapers, or daily newspapers published in other cities. Thus, when a newspaper asserts exclusive control over its own news copy, it does not thereby prevent other newspapers from being distributed to willing recipients in the same locale.

The same is not true of cable. When an individual subscribes to cable, the physical connection between the television set and the cable network gives the cable operator bottleneck, or gatekeeper, control over most (if not all) of the television programming that is channeled into the subscriber's home. Hence, simply by virtue of its ownership of the essential pathway for cable speech, a cable operator can prevent its subscribers from obtaining access to programming it chooses to exclude. A cable operator, unlike speakers in other media, can thus silence the voice of competing speakers with a mere flick of the switch.

The potential for abuse of this private power over a central avenue of communication cannot be overlooked. ("Each medium of expression . . . must be assessed for First Amendment purposes by standards suited to it, for each may present its own problems"). The First Amendment's command that government not impede the freedom of speech does not disable the government from taking steps to ensure that private interests not restrict, through physical control of a critical pathway of communication, the free flow of information and ideas. We thus reject appellants' contention that *Tornillo* require[s] strict scrutiny of the access rules in question here.

2

Second, appellants urge us to apply strict scrutiny because the must-carry provisions favor one set of speakers (broadcast programmers) over another (cable programmers). Appellants maintain that as a consequence of this speaker preference, some cable programmers who would have secured carriage in the absence of must-carry may now be dropped. Relying on language in *Buckley v. Valeo*, 424 U.S. 1 (1976), appellants contend that such a regulation is presumed invalid under the First Amendment because the government may not "restrict the speech of some elements of our society in order to enhance the relative voice of others."

. . .

Our holding in *Buckley* does not support appellant's broad assertion that all speaker-partial laws are presumed invalid. Rather, it stands for the proposition that speaker-based laws demand strict scrutiny when they reflect the Government's preference for the substance of what the favored speakers have to say (or aversion to what the disfavored speakers have to say). . . .

The question here is whether Congress preferred broadcasters over cable programmers based on the content of programming each group offers. The answer, as we explained above is no. . . .

3

Finally, appellants maintain that strict scrutiny applies because the must-carry provisions single out certain members of the press—here, cable operators—for disfavored treatment. In support, appellants point out that Congress has required cable operators to provide carriage to broadcast stations, but has not imposed like burdens on analogous video delivery systems, such as multichannel multipoint distribution (MMDS) systems and satellite master antenna television (SMATV) systems. Relying upon our precedents invalidating discriminatory taxation of the press, appellants contend that this sort of differential treatment poses a particular danger of abuse by the government and should be presumed invalid.

Regulations that discriminate among media, or among different speakers with a single medium, often present serious First Amendment concerns. *Minneapolis Star*, for example, considered a use tax imposed on the paper and ink used in the production of newspapers. We subjected the tax to strict scrutiny for two reasons: first, because it applied only to the press; and, second, because in practical application it fell upon only a small number of newspapers. The sales tax at issue in *Arkansas*

Writers Project, which applied to general interest magazines but exempted religious, professional, trade, and sports magazines, along with all newspapers, suffered the second of these infirmities. In operation, the tax was levied upon a limited number of publishers and also discriminated on the basis of subject matter. Relying in part on *Minneapolis Star*, we held that this selective taxation of the press warranted strict scrutiny.

It would be error to conclude, however, that the First Amendment mandates strict scrutiny for any speech regulation that applies to one medium (or a subset thereof) but not others. In *Leathers v. Medlock*, 499 U.S. 439 (1991), for example, we upheld against First Amendment challenge the application of a general state tax to cable television services, even though the point media and scrambled satellite broadcast television services were exempted from taxation. As *Leathers* illustrates, the fact that a law singles out a certain medium, or even the press as a whole, "is insufficient by itself to raise First Amendment concerns." Rather, laws of this nature are "constitutionally suspect only in certain circumstances." The taxes invalidated in *Minneapolis Star* and *Arkansas Writers' Project*, for example, targeted a small number of speakers and thus threatened to "distort the market for ideas." Although there was no evidence that an illicit governmental motive was behind either of the taxes, both were structured in a manner that raises suspicion that their objective was, in fact, the suppression of ideas. But such heightened scrutiny is unwarranted when the differential treatment is "justified by some special characteristic of" the particular medium being regulated.

The must-carry provisions, as we have explained above, are justified by special characteristics of the cable medium: the bottleneck monopoly power exercised by cable operators and the dangers this power poses to the viability of broadcast television. Appellants do not argue, nor does it appear, that other media—in particular, media that transmit video programming such as MMDS and SMATV—subject to bottleneck monopoly control, or pose a demonstrable threat to the survival of broadcast television. It should come as no surprise, then, that Congress decided to impose the must-carry obligations upon cable operators only.

In addition, the must-carry provisions are not structured in a manner that carries the inherent risk of undermining First Amendment interests. The regulations are broad-based, applying to almost all cable systems in the country, rather than just a select few. As a result, the provisions do not pose the same dangers of suppression and manipulation that were posed by the more narrowly targeted regulations in *Minneapolis Star* and *Arkansas Writers' Project*. For these reasons, the must-carry rules do not call for strict scrutiny.

III

A

In sum, the must-carry provisions do not pose such inherent dangers to free expression, or present such potential for censorship or manipulation, as to justify application of the most exacting level of First Amendment scrutiny. We agree with the District Court that the appropriate standard by which to evaluate the constitutionality of must-carry is the intermediate level of scrutiny applicable to content-neutral restrictions that impose an incidental burden on speech.

Under *O'Brien*, a content-neutral regulation will be sustained if

> "it furthers an important or substantial governmental interest; if the governmental interest is unrelated to the suppression of free expression; and if the incidental restriction on alleged First Amendment freedoms is no greater than is essential to the furtherance of that interest."

To satisfy this standard, a regulation need not be the least speech-restrictive means of advancing the Government's interests. "Rather, the requirement of narrow tailoring is satisfied 'so long as the . . . regulation promotes a substantial government interest that would be achieved less effectively absent the regulation.'" Narrow tailoring in this context requires, in other words, that the means chosen do not "burden substantially more speech than is necessary to further the government's legitimate interests."

Congress declared that the must-carry provisions serve three interrelated interests: (1) preserving the benefits of free, over-the-air local broadcast television, (2) promoting the widespread dissemination of information from a multiplicity of sources, and (3) promoting fair competition in the market for television programming. None of these interests is related to the "suppression of free expression," or to the content of any speakers' messages. And viewed in the abstract, we have no difficulty concluding that each of them is an important governmental interest.

In the Communications Act of 1934, Congress created a system of free broadcast service and directed that communications facilities be licensed across the country in a "fair, efficient, and equitable" manner. Congress designed this system of allocation to afford each community of appreciable size an over-the-air source of information and an outlet for exchange on matters of local concern. As we recognized in *Southwestern Cable*, the importance of local broadcasting outlets "can scarcely be exaggerated, for broadcasting is demonstrably a principal source of information and entertainment for a great part of the Nation's population." The interest in maintaining the local broadcasting structure does not evaporate simply because cable has come upon the scene. Although cable and other technologies have ushered in alternatives to broadcast television, nearly 40 percent of American households still rely on broadcast stations as their exclusive source of television programming. And as we said in *Capital Cities Cable, Inc. v. Crisp*, "protecting noncable households from loss of regular television broadcasting service due to competition from cable systems" is an important federal interest. 467 U.S., at 714.

Likewise, assuring that the public has access to a multiplicity of information sources is a governmental purpose of the highest order, for it promotes values central to the First Amendment. Indeed, "it has long been a basic tenet of national communications policy that "the widest possible dissemination of information from diverse and antagonistic sources is essential to the welfare of the public." Finally, the Government's interest in eliminating restraints on fair competition is always substantial, even when the individuals or entities subject to a particular regulations are engaged in expressive activity protected by the First Amendment.

B

That the Government's asserted interests are important in the abstract does not mean, however, that the must-carry rules will in fact advance those interests. When the Government defends a regulation on speech as a means to redress past harms or prevent anticipated harms, it must do more than simply "posit the existence of the disease sought to be cured." It must demonstrate that the recited harms are real, not merely conjectural, and that the regulation will in fact alleviate these harms in a direct material way.

Thus, in applying *O'Brien* scrutiny we must ask first whether the Government has adequately shown that the economic health of local broadcasting is in genuine jeopardy and in need of the protection afforded by must-carry. Assuming an affirmative answer to the foregoing question, the Government still bears the burden of showing that the remedy it has adopted does not "burden substantially more speech than is necessary to further the government's legitimate interests." On the state of the record developed thus far, and in the absence of findings of fact from the District Court, we are unable to conclude that the Government has satisfied either inquiry.

. . .

The Government's assertion that the must-carry rules are necessary to protect the viability of broadcast television rests on two essential propositions: (1) that unless cable operators are compelled to carry broadcast stations, significant numbers of broadcast stations will be refused carriage on cable systems; and (2) that the broadcast stations denied carriage will either deteriorate to a substantial degree or fail altogether.

As support for the first proposition, the Government relies upon a 1988 FCC study showing, at a time when no must-carry rules were in effect, that approximately 20 percent of cable systems reported dropping or refusing carriage to one or more local broadcast stations on at least one occasion. The record does not indicate, however, the time frame within which these drops occurred, or how many of these stations were dropped for only a temporary period and then restored to carriage. The same FCC study indicates that about 23 percent of the cable operators reported shifting the channel positions of one or more local broadcast stations, and that, in most cases, the repositioning was done for "marketing" rather than "technical" reasons.

The parties disagree about the significance of these statistics. But even if one accepts them as evidence that a large number of broadcast stations would be dropped or repositioned in the absence of must-carry, the Government must further demonstrate that broadcasters so affected would suffer financial difficulties as a result. Without a more substantial elaboration in the District Court of the predictive or historical evidence upon which Congress relied, or the introduction of some additional evidence to establish that the dropped or repositioned broadcasters would be at serious risk of financial difficulty, we cannot determine whether the threat to broadcast television is real enough to overcome the challenge to the provisions made by these appellants. We think it significant, for instance, that the parties have not presented any evidence that local broadcast stations have fallen into bankruptcy, turned in their broadcast licenses, curtailed their broadcast operations, or suffered a serious reduction in operating revenues as a result of their being dropped from, or otherwise disadvantaged by, cable systems.

The paucity of evidence indicating that broadcast television is in jeopardy is not the only deficiency in this record. Also lacking are any findings concerning the actual effects of must-carry on the speech of cable operators and cable programmers—*i.e.*, the extent to which cable operators will, in fact, be forced to make changes in their current or anticipated programming selections; the degree to which cable programmers will be dropped from cable systems to make room for local broadcasters; and the extent to which cable operators can satisfy their must-carry obligations by devoting previously unused channel capacity to the carriage of local broadcasters. The answers to these and perhaps other questions are critical to the narrow tailoring step of the *O'Brien* analysis, for unless we know the extent to which the must-carry provisions in fact interfere with protected speech, we cannot say whether they suppress "substantially more speech than . . . necessary" to ensure the viability of broadcast television. Finally, the record fails to provide any judicial findings concerning the availability and efficacy of constitutionally acceptable "less restrictive means" of achieving the Government's asserted interests.

In sum, because there are genuine issues of material fact still to be resolved on this record, we hold that the District Court erred in granting summary judgment in favor of the Government. Because of the unresolved factual questions, the importance of the issues to the broadcast and cable industries, and the conflicting conclusions that the parties contend are to be drawn from the statistics and other evidence presented, we think it necessary to permit the parties to develop a more thorough factual record, and to allow the District Court to resolve any factual disputes remaining, before passing upon the constitutional validity of the challenged provisions.

The judgment below is vacated, and the case is remanded for further proceedings consistent with this opinion.

. . .

JUSTICE BLACKMUN, concurring.

I join JUSTICE KENNEDY'S opinion, which aptly identifies and analyzes the First Amendment concerns and principles that should guide consideration of free speech issues in the expanding cable industry. I write to emphasize the paramount importance of according substantial deference to the predictive judgments of Congress, particularly where, as here, that legislative body has compiled an extensive record in the course of reaching its judgment. . . .

. . .

JUSTICE O'CONNOR, with whom JUSTICE SCALIA and JUSTICE GINSBURG, join, and with whom JUSTICE THOMAS joins as to Parts I and III, concurring in part and dissenting in part.

There are only so many channels that any cable system can carry. If there are fewer channels than programmers who want to use the system, some programmers will have to be dropped. In the must-carry provisions of the Cable Television Consumer Protection and Competition Act of 1992, Congress made a choice: By reserving a little over one-third of the channels on a cable system for broadcasters, it ensured that in most cases it will be a cable programmer who is dropped and a broadcaster who is retained. The question presented in this case is whether this choice comports with the commands of the First Amendment.

I

A

The 1992 Cable Act implicates the First Amendment rights of two classes of speakers. First, it tells cable operators which programmers they must carry, and keeps cable operators from carrying others that they might prefer. Though cable operators do not actually originate most of the programming they show, the Court correctly holds that they are, for First Amendment purposes, speakers. Selecting which speech to retransmit is, as we know from the example of publishing houses, movie theaters, bookstores, and Reader's Digest, no less communication than is creating the speech in the first place.

Second, the Act deprives a certain class of video programmers—those who operate cable channels rather than broadcast stations—of access to over one-third of an entire medium. Cable programmers may compete only for those channels that are not set aside by the must-carry provisions. A cable programmer that might otherwise have been carried may well be denied access in favor of a broadcaster that is less appealing to the viewers but is favored by the must-carry rules. It is as if the government ordered all movie theaters to reserve at least one-third of their screening for films made by American production companies, or required all bookstores to devote one-third of their shelf space to nonprofit publishers. As the Court explains in Parts I, II-A and II-B of its opinion, which I join, cable programmers and operators stand in the same position under the First Amendment as do the more traditional media.

. . .

I agree with the Court that some speaker-based restrictions--those genuinely justified without reference to content—need not be subject to strict scrutiny. But looking at the statute at issue, I cannot avoid the conclusion that its preference for broadcasters over cable programmers is justified with reference to content. The findings, enacted by Congress as §2 of the Act, and which I must assume state the justifications for the law, make this clear. "There is a substantial governmental and First Amendment interest in promoting a diversity of views provided through multiple technology media." "[P]ublic television provides educational and informational programming to the Nation's citizens, thereby advancing the Gov-

ernment's compelling interest in educating its citizens." "A primary objective and benefit of our Nation's system of regulation of television broadcasting is the local origination of programming. There is a substantial governmental interest in ensuring its continuation." "Broadcast television stations continue to be an important source of local news and public affairs programming and other local broadcast services critical to an informed electorate."

. . .

Preferences for diversity of viewpoints, for localism, for educational programming, and for news and public affairs all make reference to content. They may not reflect hostility to particular points of view, or a desire to suppress certain subjects because they are controversial or offensive. They may be quite benignly motivated. But benign motivation, we have consistently held, is not enough to avoid the need for strict scrutiny of content-based justifications. The First Amendment does more than just bar government from intentionally suppressing speech of which it disapproves. It also generally prohibits the government from regulation because it thinks the speech is especially valuable.

This is why the Court is mistaken in concluding that the interest in diversify—in "access to a multiplicity" of "diverse and antagonistic sources,"—is content neutral. Indeed, the interest is not "related to the *suppression* of free expression," (emphasis added and internal quotation marks omitted), but that is not enough for content neutrality. The interest in giving a tax break to religious, sports, or professional magazines, see *Arkansas Writers' Project*, is not related to the suppression of speech; the interest in giving labor picketers an exemption from a general picketing ban, see *Carey* and *Mosley*, is not related to the suppression of speech. But they are both related to *content* of speech—to its communicative impact. The interest in ensuring access to a multiplicity of diverse and antagonistic sources of information, no matter how praiseworthy, is directly tied to the content of what the speakers will likely say.

B

. . .

. . . The controversial judgment at the heart of the statute is not that broadcast television has some value—obviously it does—but that broadcasters should be preferred over cable programmers. The best explanation for the findings, it seems to me, is that they represent Congress' reasons for adopting this preference; and, according to the findings, these reasons rest in part on the content of broadcasters' speech. To say in the face of the findings that the must-carry rules "impose burdens and confer benefits without reference to the content of speech," cannot be correct, especially in light of the care with which we must normally approach speaker-based restrictions.

It may well be that Congress also had other, content-neutral, purposes in mind when enacting the statute. But we have never held that the presence of a permissible justification lessens the impropriety of relying in part on an impermissible justification. . . .

C

Content-based speech restrictions are generally unconstitutional unless they are narrowly tailored to a compelling state interest. This is an exacting test. It is not enough that the goals of the law be legitimate, or reasonable, or even praiseworthy. There must be some pressing public necessity, some essential value that has to be preserved; and even then the law must restrict as little speech as possible to serve the goal.

The interest in localism, either in the dissemination of opinions held by the listeners' neighbors or in the reporting of events that have to do with the local community cannot be described as "compelling" for the purposes of the compelling state interest test. It is a legitimate interest, perhaps even an important one—certainly the government can foster it by, for instance, providing subsidies from the public fisc—but it does not rise to the level necessary to justify content-based speech restrictions. It is for private speakers and listeners, not for the government, to decide what fraction of their news and entertainment ought to be of a local character and what fraction ought to be of a national (or international) one. And the same is true of the interest in diversity of viewpoints. While the government may subsidize speakers that it thinks provide novel points of view, it may not restrict other speakers on the theory that what they say is more conventional.

The interests in public affairs programming and educational programming seem somewhat weightier, though it is a difficult question whether they are compelling enough to justify restricting other sorts of speech. We have never held that the Government could impose educational content requirements on, say, newsstands, bookstores, or movie theaters; and it is not clear that such requirements would in any event appreciably further the goals of public education.

But even assuming arguendo that the Government could set some channels aside for educational or news programming, the Act is insufficiently tailored to this goal. To benefit the educational broadcasters, the Act burdens more than just the cable entertainment programmers. It equally burdens CNN, C-SPAN, the Discovery Channel, the New Inspirational Network, and other channels, with as much claim as PBS to being educational or related to public affairs.

Even if the Government can restrict entertainment in order to benefit supposedly more valuable speech, I do not think the restriction can extend to other speech that is as valuable as the speech being benefited. In the rare circumstances where the government may draw content-based distinctions to serve its goals, the restrictions must serve the goals a good deal more precisely than this.

Finally, my conclusion that the must-carry rules are content-based leads me to conclude that they are an impermissible restraint on the cable operators' editorial discretion as well as on the cable programmers' speech. For reasons related to the content of speech, the rules restrict the ability of cable operators to put on the programming they prefer, and require them to include programming they would rather avoid. . . .

II

Even if I am mistaken about the must-carry provisions being content based, however, in my view they fail content-neutral scrutiny as well. Assuming arguendo that the provisions are justified with reference to the content-neutral interests in fair competition and preservation of free television, they nonetheless restrict too much speech that does not implicate these interests.

Sometimes, a cable system's choice to carry a cable programmer rather than a broadcaster may be motivated by anticompetitive impulses, or might lead to the broadcaster going out of business. That some speech within a broad category causes harm, however, does not justify restricting the whole category. If Congress wants to protect those stations that are in danger of going out of business, or bar cable operators from preferring programmers in which the operators have an ownership stake, it may do that. But it may not, in the course of advancing these interests, restrict cable operators and programmers in circumstances where neither of these interests is threatened.

. . .

The must-carry provisions are fatally overbroad, even under a content-neutral analysis: They disadvantage cable programmers even if the operator has no anticompetitive motives, and even if the broadcaster that would have to be dropped to make room for the cable programmer would survive without cable access. None of the factfinding that the District Court is asked to do on remand will change this. The Court does not suggest that either the antitrust interest or the loss of free television interest are implicated in all, or even most, of the situations in which must-carry makes a difference. Perhaps on remand the District Court will find out just how many broadcasters will be jeopardized, but the remedy for this jeopardy will remain the same: Protect those broadcasters that are put in danger of bankruptcy, without unnecessarily restricting cable programmers in markets where free broadcasting will thrive in any event.

III

Having said all this, it is important to acknowledge one basic fact: The question is not whether there will be control over who gets to speak over cable—the question is who will have this control. Under the FCC's view, the answer is Congress, acting within relatively broad limits. Under my view, the answer is the cable operator. Most of the time, the cable operator's decision will be largely dictated by the preferences of the viewers; but because many cable operators are indeed monopolists, the viewers' preferences will not always prevail. Our recognition that cable operators are speakers is bottomed in large part on the very fact that the cable operator has editorial discretion.

I have no doubt that there is danger in having a single cable operator decide what millions of subscribers can or cannot watch. And I have no doubt that Congress can act to relieve this danger. In other provisions of the Act, Congress has already taken steps to foster competition among cable systems. Congress can encourage the creation of new media, such as inexpensive satellite broadcasting, or fiber-optic networks with virtually unlimited channels, or even simple devices that would let people easily switch from cable to over-the-air broadcasting. And of course Congress can subsidize broadcasters that it thinks provide especially valuable programming.

An industry need not be in its death throes before Congress may act to protect it from economic harm threatened by a monopoly. The mandatory access mechanism that Congress fashioned . . . is a simple and direct means of delaying with the dangers posed by cable operators' exclusive control of what is fast becoming the preeminent means of transferring video signals to homes. The must-carry mechanism is analogous to the relief that might be appropriate for a threatened violation of the antitrust laws; one need only refer to undisputed facts concerning the structure of the cable and broadcast industries to agree that threat is at least plausible. Moreover, Congress did not have to find that all broadcasters were at risk before acting to protect vulnerable ones, for the interest in preserving access to free television is valid throughout the Nation. Indeed, the Act is well tailored to assist those broadcasters who are most in jeopardy. Because thriving commercial broadcasters will likely avail themselves of the remunerative "retransmission consent" procedure . . . those broadcasters who gain access via the §4 must-carry route are apt to be the most economically vulnerable ones. . . .

It is thus my view that we should affirm the judgment of the District Court. Were I to vote to affirm, however, no disposition of this appeal would command the support of a majority of the Court. An accommodation is therefore necessary. Accordingly, because I am in substantial agreement with JUSTICE KENNEDY's analysis of the case, I concur in judgment vacating and remanding for further proceedings.

. . .

JUSTICE GINSBURG, concurring in part and dissenting in part.

. . . I conclude that Congress' "must-carry" regime, which requires cable operators to set aside just over one-third of their channels for local broadcast stations, reflects an unwarranted content-based preference and hypothesizes a risk to local stations that remains imaginary. I therefore concur in Parts I, II-A, and II-B of the Court's opinion, and join JUSTICE O'CONNOR's opinion concurring in part and dissenting in part.

The "must-carry" rules Congress has ordered do not differentiate on the basis of "viewpoint," and therefore do not fall in the category of speech regulation that Government must avoid most assiduously. The rules, however, do reflect a content preference and on that account demand close scrutiny.

The Court has identified as Congress' "overriding objective in enacting must-carry," the preservation of over-the-air television service for those unwilling or unable to subscribe to cable, and has remanded the case for further airing centered on that allegedly overriding, content-neutral purpose. But an intertwined or even discrete content-neutral justification does not render speculative, or reduce to harmless surplus, Congress' evident plan to advance local programming.

. . .

DEL: The notion of scarcity at best has outlived its utility and at worst has been an artificial construct that undermines rather than facilitates both regulatory and constitutional interests. Spectrum scarcity may provide a credible basis for a rational allocation scheme, but it strains the premise when used to support content regulation such as the fairness doctrine. History demonstrates a tendency for broadcasters to avoid controversy, rather than incur fairness responsibilities and the burdens of compliance, review or litigation. As recent courts and commentators have pointed out, scarcity is a phenomenon that characterizes resource use by all media. Attempting to draw distinctions that are based upon a universal fact inherently is problematic. Critical attention to resource scarcity, however, is somewhat misdirected. If barriers to the opportunity to compete as a broadcaster or publisher are what count, as the relevant jurisprudence suggests, the primary preclusive factor is the same for all media. Notwithstanding the special licensing requirements for broadcasters, or franchising conditions for cablecasters, the reality is that capital requirements rather than limited resources or regulation are the most significant impediment to entry into the media business. If the understanding of *Tornillo* is accurate, that economic scarcity is not grounds for a redistribution of First Amendment rights, editorial freedom in broadcasting or any other medium should not be compromised minus development of a more compelling rationale.

DER: Scarcity may no longer be a compelling reason for distinguishing between electronic and print media or for overriding editorial freedom. There certainly is far more diversity in programming than when Congress instituted the fairness doctrine in 1949. Nevertheless, the influence that broadcasters wield over public discussion of social issues raises serious First Amendment concerns. This power is presently concentrated in the hands of a very limited group of huge communications companies that control numerous media organs. Capital Cities, for example, owns not only the major television network ABC, but also several cable networks, newspapers and magazines. The colossal power that media giants have over information available to the public has led some commentators to call the media a fourth branch of government. Just as the media helps to hold government accountable to citizens, the media's power may justify government holding media accountable to citizens. It is true that tested remedies such as the fairness doctrine provide a very limited solution to the problem of unequal access to the media. Since the government dictates which issues are important and what constitutes fair coverage, it is unlikely that the doctrine will give the most radical dissenters an opportunity to air their views. But the First Amendment's goals of political participation and expressive diversity are frustrated by leaving access to media and the messages they disseminate purely to market forces. A laissez-faire market inevitably will produce an exchange of ideas dominated by those with the most economic and social power. Most citizens, especially the poor, must depend on the government to express or subsidize their views. Government involvement is therefore necessary to counterbalance the overwhelming communications power wielded by corporate and wealthy interests. Although the fairness doctrine may not have been the most effective means, government efforts to broaden the spectrum of views expressed by broadcasters further rather than infringe First Amendment freedoms.

In abandoning the fairness doctrine, the FCC concluded that the roles of the electronic and printed medial are identical and thus the "full First Amendment protections against content regulation should apply equally to the electronic and the printed press."[210] Constitutional parity has yet to be established by relevant jurisprudence which continues to be inspired by medium specific analysis. To the extent that broadcasters are prohibited from trading in content that is perceived as indecent or offensive, moreover, it is debatable whether regulatory actions match up with regulatory rhetoric.

---

[210] Syracuse Peace Council, 2 F.C.C. Rcd. at 5058.

When initially confronted with a complaint that programming was "patently offensive" and thus at odds with the public interest, the FCC accommodated licensee judgment. Responding to the objections of some listeners to a radio broadcast of poetry and literature reflecting a gay and lesbian perspective, the FCC determined that "those offended [had no] right, through the Commission's licensing power, to rule such programming off the airwaves."[211] Had it penalized the broadcaster, the FCC was concerned that "only the wholly offensive, the bland [would] gain access to the radio microphone or TV camera."[212] It thus determined that an accounting for what some perceived as indecent expression would have compromised "diversity of programming."[213]

Diversification enhancement and restriction concerns eventually collided when the FCC responded to radio talk shows that traded in sexually explicit language or innuendo. In finding that a particular call-in show was obscene, the agency stressed its concern with children who might access such programming and with radio's "pervasive, intrusive nature."[214] The FCC's determination was upheld by an appeals court which, in *Illinois Citizens Committee for Broadcasting v. Federal Communications Commission*, concluded that

> where a radio call-in show during daytime hours broadcasts explicit discussions of ultimate sexual acts in a titillating context, the Commission does not unconstitutionally infringe upon the public's right to listening alternatives when it determines that the broadcast is obscene.[215]

Two years after the *Illinois Citizens Committee* decision, the Supreme Court entered the broadcast indecency controversy. Although rejecting the notion that obscenity was a standard which varied from one medium to another, as intimated in the *Illinois Citizens Committee* ruling, the Court in *Federal Communications Commission v. Pacifica Foundation* upheld the FCC's power to regulate indecent albeit constitutionally protected expression. At issue in the *Pacifica* case was the following monologue by George Carlin, whom the broadcaster described as a prominent "social satirist . . . who 'like Twain and Sahl before him' examines the language of ordinary people."

---

[211] Pacifica Foundation, 36 F.C.C. 147, 149 (1964).

[212] *Id.* at 151.

[213] *Id.*

[214] Illinois Citizens for Broadcasting v. Federal Communications Commission, 515 F.2d 397, 401 (7th Cir. 1974).

[215] *Id.*

Appendix to Opinion of the Court in *Federal Communications Commission v. Pacifica Foundation*

The following is a verbatim transcript of "Filthy Words" prepared by the Federal Communications Commission.

Aruba-du, ruba-tu, ruba-tu. I was thinking about the curse words and the swear words, the cuss words and the words that you can't say, that you're not supposed to say all the time, [']cause words or people into words want to hear your words. Some guys like to record your words and sell them back to you if they can, (laughter) listen in on the telephone, write down what words you say. A guy who used to be in Washington knew that his phone was tapped, used to answer, Fuck Hoover, yes, go ahead.(laughter) Okay, I was thinking one night about the words you couldn't say on the public, ah, airwaves, um, the ones you definitely wouldn't say, ever, [']cause I heard a lady say bitch one night on television, and it was cool like she was talking about, you know, ah, well, the bitch is the first one to notice that in the litter Johnnie right (murmur) Right. And, uh, bastard you can say, and hell and damn so I have to figure out which ones you couldn't and ever and it came down to seven but the list is open to amendment, and in fact, has been changed, uh, by now, ha, a lot of people pointed things out to me, and I noticed some myself. The original seven words were, shit, piss, fuck, cunt, cocksucker, motherfucker, and tits. Those are the ones that will curve your spine, grow hair on your hands and (laughter) maybe, even bring us, God help us, peace without honor (laughter) um, and a bourbon. (laughter). And now the first thing that we noticed was that word fuck was really repeated in there because the word motherfucker is a compound word and it's another form of the word fuck. (laughter) You want to be a purist it doesn't really—it can't be on the list of basic words. Also, cocksucker is a compound word and neither half of that is really dirty. The word—the half sucker that's merely suggestive (laughter) and the word cock is a half-way dirty word, 50% dirty—dirty half the time, depending on what you mean by it. (laughter) Uh, remember when you first heard it, like in 6th grade, you used to giggle. And the cock crowed three times, heh (laughter) the cock—three times. It's in the Bible, cock in the Bible. (laughter) And the first time you heard about a cock-fight, remember—What? Huh? naw. It ain't that, are you stupid? man. (laughter, clapping) It's chickens, you know, (laughter) Then you have the four letter words from the old Anglo-Saxon fame. Uh, shit and fuck. The word shit, uh, is an interesting kind of word in that the middle class has never really accepted it and approved it. They use it like, crazy but it's not really okay. It's still a rude, dirty, old kind of gushy word. (laughter) They don't like that, but they say it, like, they say it like, a lady now in a middle-class home, you'll hear most of the time she says it as an expletive, you know, it's out of her mouth before she knows. She says, Oh shit oh shit, (laughter) oh shit. If she drops something, Oh, the shit hurt the broccoli. Shit. Thank you.- (footsteps fading away) (papers shuffling)

Read it! (from audience)

Shit! (laughter) I won the Grammy, man, for the comedy album. Isn't that groovy? (clapping, whistling) (murmur) That's true. Thank you. Thank you man. Yeah. (murmur) (continuous clapping) Thank you man. Thank you. Thank you very much, man. Thank, no (end of continuous clapping) for that and for the Grammy, man, [']cause (laughter) that's based on people liking it man, yeh, that's ah, that's okay man. (laugher) Let's let that go, man. I got my Grammy. I can let my hair hang down now, shit. (laughter) Ha! So! Now the word shit is okay for the man. At work you can say it like crazy. Mostly figuratively, Get that shit out of here, will ya? I don't want to see that shit anymore. I can't *cut* that shit, buddy. I've had that shit up to here. I think you're full of shit myself.

(laughter) He don't know shit from Shinola. (laughter) you know that? (laughter) Always wondered how the Shinola people felt about that (laugher) Hi, how are ya? Nice to see ya. (laughter) How are ya? (laughter) Boy, I don't know whether to shit or wind my watch. (laughter) Guess, I'll shit on my watch. (laughter) Oh, *the* shit is going to hit the fan. (laughter) Built like a brick shit-house. (laughter) Up, he's up shit's creek. (laughter) He's had it. (laughter) He hit me, I'm sorry. (laughter) Hot shit, holy shit, tough shit, eat shit, (laughter) shit-eating grin. Uh, whoever thought of that was ill. (murmur laughter) He had a shit-eating grin! He had a what? (laughter) Shit on a stick. (laughter) Shit in a handbag. I always like that. He ain't worth shit in a handbag. (laughter) Shitty. He acted real shitty. (laughter) You know what I mean? (laughter) I got the money back, but a real shitty attitude. Heh, he had a shit-fit. (laughter) Wow! Shit-fit. Whew! Glad I wasn't there. (murmur, laughter) All the animals—Bull shit, horse shit, cow shit, rat shit, bat shit. (laughter) First time I heard bat shit, I really came apart. A guy in Oklahoma, Boggs, said it, man. Aw! Bat shit. (laughter) Vera reminded me of that last night, ah (murmur). Snake shit, slicker than owl shit. (laughter) Get your shit together. Shit or get off the pot. (laughter) I got a shit-load full of them. (laughter) I got a ship-pot full, all right. Shit-head, shit-heel, shit in your heart, shit for brains, (laughter) shit-face, heh (laughter) I always try to think how that could have originated; the first guy that said that. Somebody got drunk and fell in some shit, you know. (laughter) Hey, I'm shit-face. (laughter) Shit-face, *today*. (laughter) Anyway, enough of that shit. (laughter) The big one, the word fuck that's the one that hangs them up the most. [']Cause in a lot of cases that's the very act that hangs them up the most. So, it's natural that the word would, uh, have the same effect. It's a great word, fuck, nice word, easy word, cute word, kind of. Easy word to say. One syllable, short Universal. (laughter) Fuck. (Murmur) You know, it's easy. Starts with a nice soft sound fuh ends with a *kuh*. Right? (laughter) A little something for everyone. Fuck (laughter) Good word. Kind of a proud word, too. Who are you? I am FUCK. (laughter) FUCK OF THE MOUNTAIN. (laughter) Tune in again next week to FUCK OF THE MOUNTAIN. (laughter) It's an interesting word too, [']cause it's got a double kind of life—personality—dual, you know, whatever the right phrase is. It leads a double life, the word fuck. First of all, it means, sometimes, most of the time, fuck. What does it mean? It means to make love. Right? We're going to make love, yeh, we're going to fuck, yeh, we're going to fuck, yeh, we're going to make love, (laughter) we're really going to fuck, yeh, we're going to make love. Right? And it also means the beginning of life, it's the act that begins life, so there's the word hanging around with words like love, and life, and yet on the other hand, it's also a word that we really use to hurt each other with, man. It's a heavy. It's one that you have toward the end of the argument. (laughter) Right? (laughter) You finally can't make out. Oh, fuck you man. I said, fuck you. (laughter, murmur) Stupid fuck. (laugher) Fuck you and everybody that looks like you, (laughter) man. It would be nice to change the movies that we already have and substitute the word fuck for the word kill, wherever we could, and some of those movies clichés would change a little bit. Mad fuckers still on the loose. Stop me before I fuck again. Fuck the ump, fuck the ump, fuck the ump, fuck the ump, fuck the ump. Easy on the clutch Bill, you'll fuck that engine again. (laughter) The other shit one was, I don't give a shit. Like it's worth something, you know? (laugher) I don't give a shit. Hey, well, I don't take no shit, (laughter) you know what I mean? You know why I don't take no shit? (laughter) [']Cause I don't give a shit. (laugher) If I give a shit, I would have to pack shit. (laughter) But I don't pack no shit cause I don't give a shit. (laughter) You wouldn't shit me, would you? (laughter) That's a joke when you're a kid with a worm looking out the bird's ass. You wouldn't shit me, would you? (laughter) It's an eight-year-old

joke but a good one. (laughter) The additions to the list. I found three more words that had to be put on the list of words you could never say on television, and they were fart, turd and twat, those three. (laughter) Fart, we talked about, it's harmless. It's like tits, it's a cutie word, no problem. Turd, you can't say but who wants to, you know? (laughter) The subject never comes up on the panel so I'm not worried about that one. Now the word twat is an interesting word. Twat! Yeh, right in the twat. (laughter) Twat is an interesting word because it's the only one I know of, the only slang word applying to the, a part of the sexual anatomy that doesn't have another meaning to it. Like, ah, snatch, box and pussy all have other meanings, man. Even in a Walt Disney movie, you can say, We're going to snatch that pussy and put him in a box and bring him on the airplane. (murmur, laughter) Everybody loves it. The twat stands alone, man, as it should. And two-way words. Ah, ass is okay providing you're riding into town on a religious feast day. (laughter) You can't say, up your *ass*. (laughter) You can say, stuff it! (murmur) There are certain things you can say its weird but you can just come so close. Before I cut, I, uh, want to, ah, thank your for listening to my words, man, fellow, uh space travelers. Thank you man for tonight and thank you also. (clapping, whistling)

The monologue, presented by a radio station with a programming strategy calculated to target a particular audience, elicited a formal complaint to the FCC. Described by the Court as a father who ran across the program in the middle of the afternoon while driving in the company of his son, the complainant also was associated with political movements to eliminate indecency from the airwaves.[216] Although determining that the programming was neither obscene nor constitutionally unprotected, the Court employed medium specific analysis and concluded that patently offensive material could be regulated in the broadcast arena even if it did not appeal to prurient interests. In so doing, the *Pacifica* Court advanced as important state regulatory interests the broadcast medium's pervasive and intrusive nature and ready accessibility to children.

---

[216] Nat Hentoff, *How the FCC Saves You from Indecency*, THE VILLAGE VOICE, May 25, 1993, at 28–29.

Federal Communications Commission v. Pacifica Foundation
438 U.S. 726 (1978)

MR. JUSTICE STEVENS delivered the opinion of the Court (Parts I, II, III, and IV-C) and an opinion in which the CHIEF JUSTICE and MR. JUSTICE REHNQUIST joined (Parts IV-A and IV-B).

This case requires that we decide whether the Federal Communications Commission has any power to regulate a radio broadcast that is indecent but not obscene.

. . .

At about 2 o'clock in the afternoon on Tuesday, October 30, 1973, a New York radio station, owned by respondent Pacifica Foundation, broadcast the "Filthy Words" monologue. A few weeks later a man, who stated that he had heard the broadcast while driving with his young son, wrote a letter complaining to the Commission. He stated that, although he could perhaps understand the "record's being sold for private use, I certainly cannot understand the broadcast of same over the air that, supposedly, you control."

The complaint was forwarded to the station for comment. In its response, Pacifica explained that the monologue had been played during a program about contemporary society's attitude toward language and that, immediately before its broadcast, listeners had been advised that it included "sensitive language which might be regarded as offensive to some." Pacifica characterized George Carlin as "a significant social satirist" who "like Twain and Sahl before him, examines the language of ordinary people.... Carlin is not mouthing obscenities, he is merely using words to satirize as harmless and essentially silly our attitudes towards those words." Pacifica stated that it was not aware of any other complaints about the broadcast.

On February 21, 1975, the Commission issued a declaratory order granting the complaint and holding that Pacifica "could have been the subject of administrative sanctions." 56 F.C.C. 2d 94, 99. The Commission did not impose formal sanctions, but it did state that the order would be "associated with the station's license file, and in the event that subsequent complaints are received, the Commission will then decide whether it should utilize any of the available sanctions it has been granted by Congress."

...

IV

...

B

...

The question in this case is whether a broadcast of patently offensive words dealing with sex and excretion may be regulated because of its content. Obscene materials have been denied the protection of the First Amendment because their content is so offensive to contemporary moral standards. But the fact that society may find speech offensive is not a sufficient reason for suppressing it. Indeed, if it is the speaker's opinion that gives offense, that consequence is a reason for according it constitutional protection. For it is a central tenet of the First Amendment that the government must remain neutral in the marketplace of ideas. If there were any reason to believe that the Commission's characterization of the Carlin monologue as offensive could be traced to its political content—or even to the fact that it satirized contemporary attitudes about four-letter words—First Amendment protection might be required. But that is simply not this case. These words offend for the same reasons that obscenity offends. Their place in the hierarchy of First Amendment values was aptly sketched by Mr. Justice Murphy when he said: "[S]uch utterances are no essential part of any exposition of ideas, and are of such slight social value as a step to truth that any benefit that may be derived from them is clearly outweighed by the social interest in order and morality."

Although these words ordinarily lack literary, political, or scientific value, they are not entirely outside the protection of the First Amendment. Some uses of even the most offensive words are unquestionably protected. Indeed, we may assume, *arguendo*, that this monologue would be protected in other contexts. Nonetheless, the constitutional protection accorded to a communication containing such patently offensive sexual and excretory language need not be the same in every context. It is a characteristic of speech such as this that both its capacity to offend and its "social value," to use Mr. Justice Murphy's term, vary with the circumstances. Words that are commonplace in one setting are shocking in another. To paraphrase Mr. Justice Harlan, one occasion's lyric is another's vulgarity.

In this case it is undisputed that the content of Pacifica's broadcast was "vulgar," "offensive," and "shocking." Because content of that character is not entitled to absolute constitutional protection under all circumstances, we must consider its context in order to determine whether the Commission's action was constitutionally permissible.

C

We have long recognized that each medium of expression presents special First Amendment problems. And of all forms of communication, it is broadcasting that has received the most limited First Amendment protection. Thus, although other speakers cannot be licensed except under laws that carefully define and narrow official discretion, a broadcaster may be deprived of his license and his forum if the Commission decides that such an action would serve "the public interest, convenience, and necessity." Similarly, although the First Amendment protects newspaper publishers from being required to print the replies of those whom they criticize, it affords no such protection to broadcasters; on the contrary, they must give free time to the victims of their criticism.

The reasons for these distinctions are complex, but two have relevance to the present case. First, the broadcast media have established a uniquely pervasive presence in the lives of all Americans. Patently offensive, indecent material presented over the airwaves confronts the citizen, not only in public, but also in the privacy of the home, where the individual's right to be left alone plainly outweighs the First Amendment rights of an intruder. Because the broadcast audience is constantly tuning in and out, prior warnings cannot completely protect the listener or viewer from unexpected program content. To say that one may avoid further offense by turning off the radio when he hears indecent language is like saying that the remedy for an assault is to turn away after the first blow. One may hang up on an indecent phone call, but that option does not give the caller a constitutional immunity or avoid a harm that has already taken place.

Second, broadcasting is uniquely accessible to children, even those too young to read. Although Cohen's written message might have been incomprehensible to a first grader, Pacifica's broadcast could have enlarged a child's vocabulary in an instant. Other forms of offensive expression may be withheld from the young without restricting the expression at its source. Bookstores and motion picture theaters, for example, may be prohibited from making indecent material available to children. We held in *Ginsberg v. New York*, that the government's interest in the "well-being of its young" and in supporting "parents' claim to authority in their household" justified the regulation of otherwise protected expression. The ease with which children may obtain access to broadcast material, coupled with the concerns recognized in *Ginsberg*, amply justify special treatment of indecent broadcasting.

It is appropriate, in conclusion, to emphasize the narrowness of our holding. This case does not involve a two-way radio conversation between a cab driver and a dispatcher, or a telecast of an Elizabethan comedy. We have not decided that an occasional expletive in either setting would justify any sanction or, indeed, that this broadcast would justify a criminal prosecution. The Commission's decision rested entirely on a nuisance rationale under which context is all-important. The concept requires consideration of a host of variables. The time of day was emphasized by the Commission. The content of the program in which the language is used will also affect the composition of the audience, and differences between radio, television, and perhaps closed-circuit transmission, may also be relevant. As Mr. Justice Sutherland wrote, a "nuisance may be merely a right thing in the wrong place,—like a pig in the parlor instead of the barnyard." We simply hold that when the Commission finds that a pig has entered the parlor, the exercise of its regulatory power does not depend on proof that the pig is obscene.

The judgment of the Court of Appeals is reversed.

MR. JUSTICE POWELL, with whom MR. JUSTICE BLACKMUN joins, concurring in part and concurring in the judgment.

I join Parts, I, II, III, and IV-C of MR. JUSTICE STEVENS' opinion. . . .

It is conceded that the monologue at issue here is not obscene in the constitutional sense. Nor, in this context, does its language constitute "fighting words." Some of the words used have been held protected by the First Amendment in other cases and contexts. I do not think Carlin, consistently with the First Amendment, could be punished for delivering the same monologue to a live audience composed of adults who, knowing what to expect, chose to attend his performance. And I would assume that an adult could not constitutionally be prohibited from purchasing a recording or transcript of the monologue and playing or reading it in the privacy of his own home.

In most instances, the dissemination of this kind of speech to children may be limited without also limiting willing adults' access to it. Sellers of printed and recorded matter and exhibitors of motion pictures and live performances may be required to shut their doors to children, but such a requirement has not effect of adults' access. The difficulty is that such a physical separation of the audience cannot be accomplished in the broadcast media. During most of the broadcast hours, both adults and unsupervised children are likely to be in the broadcast audience, and the broadcaster cannot reach willing adults without also reaching children. This, as the Court emphasizes, is one of the distinctions between the broadcast and other media to which we often have adverted as justifying a different treatment of the broadcast media for First Amendment purposes. In my view, the Commission was entitled to give substantial weight to this difference in reaching its decision in this case.

A second difference, not without relevance, is that broadcasting—unlike most other forms of communication—comes directly into the home, the one place where people ordinarily have the right not to be assaulted by uninvited and offensive sights and sounds. Although the First Amendment may require unwilling adults to absorb the first blow of offensive but protected speech when they are in public before they turn away, a different order of values obtains in the home. . . .

The Commission's holding does not prevent willing adults from purchasing Carlin's record, from attending his performances, or, indeed, from reading the transcript reprinted as an appendix to the Court's opinion. On its face, it does not prevent respondent Pacifica Foundation from broadcasting the monologue during late evening hours when fewer children are likely to be in the audience, nor from broadcasting discussions of the contemporary use of language at any time during the day. The Commission's holding, and certainly the Court's holding today, does not speak to cases involving the isolated use of a potentially offensive word in the course of a radio broadcast, as distinguished from the verbal shock treatment administered by respondent here. In short, I agree that on the facts of this case, the Commission's order did not violate respondent's First Amendment rights.

II

As the foregoing demonstrates, my views are generally in accord with what is said in Part IV-C of Mr. Justice Stevens' opinion. I therefore join that portion of his opinion. I do not join Part IV-B, however, because I do not subscribe to the theory that the Justices of this Court are free generally to decide on the basis of its content which speech protected by the First Amendment is not "valuable" and hence deserving of the most protection, and which is less "valuable" and hence deserving of less protection.

. . .

The result turns instead on the unique characteristics of the broadcast media, combined with society's right to protect its children from speech generally agreed to be inappropriate for their years, and with the interests of unwilling adults in not being assaulted by such offensive speech in their homes. . . .

MR. JUSTICE BRENNAN, with whom MR. JUSTICE MARSHALL joins, dissenting.

For the second time in two years, see *Young v. American Mini Theatres, Inc.*, 427 U.S. 50 (1976), the Court refuses to embrace the notion, completely antithetical to basic First Amendment values, that the degree of protection the First Amendment affords protected speech varies with the social value ascribed to that speech by five Members of this Court. . . .

A

Without question, the privacy interests of an individual in his home are substantial and deserving of significant protection. In finding these interests sufficient to justify the content regulation of protected speech, however, the Court commits two errors. First, it misconceives the nature of the privacy interests involved where an individual voluntarily chooses to admit radio communications into his home. Second, it ignores the constitutionally protected interests of both those who wish to transmit and those who desire to receive broadcasts that many—including the FCC and this Court—might find offensive.

. . .

. . . I believe that an individual's actions in switching on and listening to communications transmitted over the public airways and directed to the public at large do not implicate fundamental privacy interests, even when engaged in within the home. Instead, because the radio is undeniably a public medium, these actions are more properly viewed as a decision to take part, if only as a listener, in an ongoing public discourse. Although an individual's decision to allow public radio communications into his home undoubtedly does not abrogate all of his privacy interests, the residual privacy interests he retains vis-a-vis the communication he voluntarily admits into his home are surely no greater than those of the people present in the corridor of the Los Angeles courthouse in *Cohen* who bore witness to the words "Fuck the Draft" emblazoned across Cohen's jacket. Their privacy interests were held insufficient to justify punishing Cohen for his offensive communication.

. . .

The Court's balance, of necessity, fails to accord proper weight to the interests of listeners who wish to hear broadcasts the FCC deems offensive. It permits majoritarian tastes completely to preclude a protected message from entering the homes of a receptive, unoffended minority. No decision of this Court supports such a result. Where the individuals constituting the offended majority may freely choose to reject the material being offered, we have never found their privacy interests of such moment to warrant the suppression of speech on privacy grounds.

Most parents will undoubtedly find understandable as well as commendable the Court's sympathy with the FCC's desire to prevent offensive broadcasts from reaching the ears of unsupervised children. Unfortunately, the facial appeal of this justification for radio censorship masks its constitutional insufficiency. . . .

Because the Carlin monologue is obviously not an erotic appeal to the prurient interests of children, the Court, for the first time, allows the government to prevent minors from gaining access to materials that are not obscene, and are therefore protected, as to them. It thus ignores our recent admonition that "[s]peech that is neither obscene as to youths nor subject to some other legitimate proscription cannot be suppressed solely to protect the young from ideas or images that a legislative body thinks unsuitable for them." The Court's refusal to follow its own pronouncements is especially lamentable since it has the anomalous subsidiary effect, at least in the radio context at issue here, of making completely unavailable to adults material which may not constitutionally be kept even from children. This result violates in spades the principle of *Butler v. Michigan....* Speaking for the Court, Mr. Justice Frankfurter reasoned:

> The incidence of this enactment is to reduce the adult population of Michigan to reading only what is fit for children. It thereby arbitrarily curtails one of those liberties of the individual, now enshrined in the Due Process Clause of the Fourteenth Amendment, that history has attested as the indispensable conditions for the maintenance and progress of a free society.

. . .

In concluding that the presence of children in the listening audience provides an adequate basis for the FCC to impose sanctions for Pacifica's broadcast of the Carlin monologue, the opinions of my Brother Powell, and my Brother Stevens, both stress the time-honored right of a parent to raise his child as he sees fit—a right this Court has consistently been vigilant to protect. See *Wisconsin v. Yoder,* 406 U.S. 205 (1972); *Pierce v. Society of Sisters,* 268 U.S. 510 (1925). Yet this principle supports a result directly contrary to that reached by the Court. *Yoder* and *Pierce* hold that parents, *not* the government, have the right to make certain decisions regarding the upbringing of their children. As surprising as it may be to individual Members of this Court, some parents may actually find Mr. Carlin's unabashed attitude towards the seven "dirty words" healthy, and deem it desirable to expose their children to the manner in which Mr. Carlin defuses the taboo surrounding the words. Such parents may constitute a minority of the American public, but the absence of great numbers willing to exercise the right to raise their children in this fashion does not alter the right's nature or its existence. Only the Court's regrettable decision does that.

II

The absence of any hesitancy in the opinions of my Brothers Powell and Stevens to approve the FCC's censorship of the Carlin monologue on the basis of two demonstrably inadequate grounds is a function of their perception that the decision will result in little, if any, curtailment of communicative exchanges protected by the First Amendment....

My Brother Stevens, in reaching a result apologetically described as narrow, takes comfort in his observation that "[a] requirement that indecent language be avoided will have its primary effect on the form, rather than the content, of serious communication," and finds solace in his conviction that "[t]here are few, if any, thoughts that cannot be expressed by the

use of less offensive language." The idea that the content of a message and its potential impact on any who might receive it can be divorced from the words that are the vehicle for its expression is transparently fallacious. A given word may have a unique capacity to capsule an idea, evoke an emotion, or conjure up an image. Indeed, for those of us who place an appropriate high value on our cherished First Amendment rights, the word, "censor" is such a word....

My Brother Stevens also finds relevant to his First Amendment analysis the fact that "[a]dults who feel the need may purchase tapes and records or go to theaters and nightclubs to hear [the tabooed] words." My Brother Powell agrees: "The Commission's holding does not prevent willing adults from purchasing Carlin's record, from attending his performances, or, indeed, from reading the transcript reprinted as an appendix to the Court's opinion." The opinions of my Brethren display both a sad insensitivity to the fact that these alternatives involve the expenditure of money, time, and effort that many of those wishing to hear Mr. Carlin's message may not be able to afford, and a naive innocence of the reality that in many cases, the medium may well be the message....

III

It is quite evident that I find the Court's attempt to unstitch the warp and woof of First Amendment law in an effort to reshape its fabric to cover the patently wrong result the Court reaches in this case dangerous as well as lamentable. Yet there runs throughout the opinions of my Brother Powell and Stevens another view I find equally disturbing: a depressing inability to appreciate that in our land of cultural pluralism, there are many who think, act, and talk differently from the Members of this Court, and who do not share their fragile sensibilities. It is only an acute ethnocentric myopia that enables the Court to approve the censorship of the words they contain.

"A word is not a crystal, transparent and unchanged, it is the skin of a living thought and may vary greatly in color and content according to the circumstances and the time in which it is used." The words that the Court and the Commission find so unpalatable may be the stuff of everyday conversations in some, if not many, of the innumerable subcultures that compose this Nation. Academic research indicates that this is indeed the case. As one researcher concluded, "[w]ords generally considered obscene like 'bullshit' and 'fuck' are considered neither obscene nor derogatory in the [black] vernacular except in particular contextual situations and when used with certain intonations."

Today's decision will thus have its greatest

impact on broadcasters desiring to reach, and listening audiences composed of, persons who do not share the Court's view as to which words or expressions are acceptable and who, for a variety of reasons, including a conscious desire to flout majoritarian conventions, express themselves using words that may be regarded as offensive by those from different socio-economic backgrounds. In this context, the Court's decision may be seen for what, in the broader perspective, it really is: another of the dominant culture's inevitable efforts to force those groups who do not share its mores to conform to its way of thinking, acting, and speaking.

Pacifica, in response to an FCC inquiry about its broadcast of Carlin's satire on "'the words you couldn't say on the public . . . airways.'" explained that Carlin is not mouthing obscenities, he is merely using words to satirize as harmless and essentially silly our attitudes towards those words." . . . In confirming Carlin's prescience as a social commentator by the result it reaches today, the Court evinces an attitude toward the "seven dirty words" that many others besides Mr. Carlin and Pacifica might describe as "silly." Whether today's decision will similarly prove "harmless" remains to be seen. One can only hope that it will.

The aftermath of the *Pacifica* decision has included enhanced attention by the FCC to indecent programming. In a series of administrative decisions and a recitation of indecency enforcement standards, the Commission asserted that its concern was not confined to the *Pacifica* circumstances of "repetitive use of specific sexual or excretory words or phrases."[217] It thus notified broadcasters that it would look not only at sexually explicit expression but "innuendo or double entendre."[218] Moreover, it would factor "context to determine whether its meaning can reasonably be considered to contain patently offensive references to sexual or excretory activities and organs."[219] The central regulatory concern was with programming at times "when there was a reasonable risk that children may be in the audience.[220] Initially, therefore, it constructed a safe harbor enabling broadcasters to air such programming after midnight.[221] Because the FCC's time channeling decision was found too burdensome to "broadcaster freedom and adult listener choice," the Court of Appeals for the District of Columbia Circuit remanded the rule for development of more precise and accommodating standards.[222]

Pursuant to congressional mandate, the FCC in 1988 adopted a 24-hour ban on indecent programming. Concluding that children are part of the broadcast audience at all hours, the FCC reasoned that it was impossible to find a time of day or night when the risk of their presence was nonexistent.[223] Cited in support of its comprehensive ban was the Supreme Court's decision, in *Sable Communications of California, Inc. v. Federal Communications Commission*, overturning a congressional prohibition of dial-a-porn services. Unlike access blocking methods available to telephone customers, broadcast technology, as the FCC argued, did not afford comparable protection against children.[224] Again, the court of appeals vacated the regulation and ordered the FCC to formulate a time channeling scheme that accommodated adult listening interests and

---

[217] New Indecency Enforcement Standards to be Applied to All Broadcast and Amateur Radio Licensees, 2 F.C.C. Rcd. 2726, 2726 (1987); Infinity Broadcasting Corp. of Pennsylvania, 2 F.C.C. Rcd. 2705, 2706 (1987).

[218] Infinity, 2 F.C.C. Rcd. at 2705–06.

[219] *Id*. at 2706.

[220] *Id*.

[221] Infinity Broadcasting Corp. of Pennsylvania, 3 F.C.C. Rcd. 930, 934 n.47 (1989).

[222] Action for Children's Television v. Federal Communications Commission, 852 F.2d 1332, 1341 (D.C. Cir. 1988).

[223] Enforcement of Prohibitions Against Broadcast Indecency in 18 U.S.C. § 1464, 5 F.C.C. Rcd. 5297, 5306 (1990).

[224] *Id.,* citing Sable Communication of California, Inc. v. Federal Communications Commission, 492 U.S. 115 (1990).

regulatory concern with protecting children from exposure to such programming.[225] Noting that nothing "had reduced the precedential force of" its earlier decision, the court of appeals stressed that

> [I]ndeed, the Supreme Court's decision in Sable, striking down a total ban on indecent commercial telephone messages, affirmed the protected status of indecent speech and reiterated the strict constitutional standard that government efforts to regulate the content of speech must satisfy. Even the Commission, prior to congressional enactment of the appropriations rider, shared this view.
>
> Thus, neither the Commission's action prohibiting the broadcast of indecent material, nor the congressional mandate that prompted it, can pass constitutional muster under the law of this circuit.
>
> We appreciate the Commission's constraints in responding to the appropriations rider. It would be unseemly for a regulatory agency to throw down the gauntlet, even a gauntlet grounded on the Constitution, to Congress. But just as the FCC may not ignore the dictates of the legislative branch, neither may the judiciary ignore its independent duty to check the constitutional excesses of Congress. We hold that Congress' action here cannot preclude the Commission from creating a safe harbor exception to its regulation of indecent broadcasts.
>
> . . . We direct he Commission, in "redetermin[ing], after a full and fair hearing, . . . the times at which indecent material may be broadcast," to carefully review and address the specific concerns we raised in ACT I: among them, the appropriate definitions of "children" and "reasonable risk" for channeling purposes, the paucity of station-or program-specific audience data expressed as a percentage of the relevant age group population, and the scope of the government's interest in regulating indecent broadcasts.[226]

Following the court of appeals' determination that a 24-hour ban on indecent programming could not be mandated by federal law, Congress directed the FCC to prohibit such broadcasts from 6 am to 10 pm on public radio and television stations that went off the air at midnight and from 6 am to midnight on all other stations.[227] Finding that the time channeling had not been shown to be the least restrictive means of protection children, the appeals court vacated the FCC's order.

---

[225] Action for Children's Television v. Federal Communications Commission, 932 F.2d 1504, 1510 (D.C. Cir. 1991), cert. denied, 112 S.Ct. 1282 (1992).

[226] 932 F.2d at 1509–10.

[227] Enforcement of Prohibitions Against Broadcast Indecency in 18 U.S.C. § 1464, 8 F.C.C. Rcd. 704, 711 (1993).

Action for Children's Television v. Federal Communications Commission
11 F.3d 170 (D.C. Cir. 1993)

WALD, Circuit Judge:

Petitioners, a group of broadcasters, authors, program suppliers, listeners and viewers challenge the constitutionality of a Federal Communications Commission ("FCC" or "Commission") order, issued at the direction of Congress, banning "indecent" material from broadcasting during the hours from 6 a.m. to midnight. While we break some new ground, our decision that the ban violates the First Amendment relies principally upon two prior decisions of this court in which we addressed similar challenges to FCC orders restricting the broadcasting of "indecent" material, as defined by the FCC.

. . .

The Commission . . . [has identified] the government's interests as (I) "ensuring that parents have an opportunity to supervise their children's listening and viewing of over-the-air broadcasts," (ii) "ensuring the well being of minors" regardless of parental supervision, and (iii) protecting "the right of all members of the public to be free of indecent material in the privacy of their homes." . . .

II.

PROTECTION OF ADULTS

Relying mainly on *FCC v. Pacifica Foundation*, the government maintains that the 6 a.m.-to-midnight ban promotes its compelling interest in protecting the privacy of every American's home. It argues that *Pacifica* and *Sable* acknowledge the "'uniquely pervasive presence'" of broadcasting which invades residential privacy where "'the individual's right to be left alone plainly outweighs the First Amendment rights of an intruder.'" This inherently intrusive nature of broadcasting, the government contends, permits it to ban indecent material from the airwaves during all but the hours when most people are asleep.

. . .

We . . . are reluctant to recognize any generalized government interest in protecting adults from indecent speech, primarily because the official suppression of constitutionally protected speech runs counter to the fundamental principle of the First Amendment "that debate on public issues should be uninhibited, robust, and wide-open." While we recognize that in broadcasting the First Amendment primarily protects "the right of the viewers and listeners, not the right of the broadcasters," *Red Lion,* we note that by the same token, the First Amendment protects the rights of all listeners and viewers—not just of that part of the audience whose listening and viewing habits meet with government approval. Therefore, "'at least where obscenity is not involved, [the Supreme Court] has consistently held that the fact that protected speech may be offensive to some does not justify its suppression.'" . . .

We refrain . . . from extending the captive audience rationale to the context of scheduled broadcast programming. Cf. *Columbia Broadcasting Sys., Inc. v. Democratic Nat'l Comm.*, 412 U.S. 94, 127–28 (1973) (noting that broadcast audience is captive with respect to advertisements that interrupt scheduled programs). Viewers and listeners of scheduled programs do retain options that the resident who is involuntarily picketed, or the commuter who must use public transportation in order to earn her livelihood does not. Viewers and listeners re-

tain the option of using program guides to select with care the programs they wish to view or hear. Occasional exposure to offensive material in scheduled programming is of roughly the same order that confronts the reader browsing in a bookstore. And as a last resort, unlike residential picketing or public transportation advertising "the radio [and television] can be turned off."

. . .

III.

PROTECTION OF CHILDREN

. . .

A. The Government's Interests in the Protection of Children

The government's interest in helping parents supervise their children has been repeatedly recognized as sufficiently important to justify restrictions on First Amendment activities. But where constitutionally protected speech is restricted, the government must demonstrate that the restriction is narrowly tailored to advance the asserted compelling interest. . . .

. . .

B. Least Restrictive Means

The government has, however, failed to demonstrate that its 6 a.m.-to-midnight ban on indecent material is the least restrictive means to advance its interests in the protection of children. Upon a thorough examination of the legislative and administrative record, we conclude that the government did not properly weigh viewers' and listeners' First Amendment rights when balancing the competing interests in determining the widest safe harbor period consistent with the protection of children. More broadly, we are at a loss to detect any reasoned analysis supporting the particular safe harbor mandated by Congress.

1. Parental Supervision

To begin with, the particular safe harbor chosen by Congress and the FCC is not satisfactorily explained as an attempt to prohibit the broadcasting of indecent material at times when parental supervision is apt to be least effective. Indeed, one could intuitively assume that as the evening hours wear on, parents would be better situated to keep track of their children's viewing and listening habits. The FCC, on the other hand, argues broadly that "parents can effectively supervise their children only by co-viewing or co-listening, or, at a minimum, by remaining actively aware of what their children are watching and listening at all times.'" Because "it is not practical for parents to exercise this type of control," the FCC's argument continues, "parents who seek to avoid exposing their children to indecency face a nearly impossible task if such material is broadcast." The Commission's argument appears to assume that, regardless of the time of day or night, parents cannot effectively supervise their children's television or radio habits. Accordingly, the government has not adduced any evidence suggesting that the effectiveness of parental supervision varies by time of day or night, or that the particular safe harbor of midnight-to-6-a.m. was crafted to assist parents at specific times when they especially require the government's help to supervise their children. The inevitable logic of the government's line of argument is that indecent material can never be broadcast, or, at most, can be broadcast during times when children are surely asleep; it could as well support a limited 3:00 a.m.-to-3:30 a.m. safe harbor as one from midnight-to-6 a.m.

2. Shielding Minors from Indecent Material

Alternatively, the government has justified its safe harbor as an effort to shield all minors regardless of age from exposure to indecent material. The government undoubtedly has a compelling interest in preventing exposure to indecent material of children "both old enough to understand and young enough to be adversely affected" by the indecent material. *Pacifica*, 438 U.S. at 750. Yet, while the interest in preventing children's exposure to indecent material is compelling, the grounds for restricting a minor's First Amendment rights (here as listener or viewer) fade as the minor matures.

. . .

In addition, even assuming that the government's interest in protecting older minors persistently outweighs the First Amendment interests of the minors themselves, the government's weaker interest in shielding older minors from indecent speech may not suffice to outweigh the adults' First Amendment interests that are sacrificed along the way. Therefore, where First Amendment rights of adults are involved, the government may not be heard to argue globally that "there is a reasonable risk that significant numbers of children ages 17 and under" are in the listening and viewing audience "at all times of the day and night." The government must adduce data which permits a more finely tuned trade-off between adults' First Amendment rights and the government's interest in protecting children from indecent material as that interest varies in importance with their age.

Candidly, we can locate no evidence in the record that the government has taken the First Amendment interests of adults into account in advancing its compelling interests in the protection of children. . . . As the government frankly admits, the sole operating principle by which Congress determined this particular safe harbor was to find a time when "the risk

of children in the broadcast audience would . . . be lessened." This exclusive focus on the number of children in the audience indicates that the government wholly failed to balance its child-oriented compelling interests against the countervailing First Amendment rights of adult listeners and viewers. What it should have been aiming at was a time when the risk of child viewing was low and yet adult viewers could exercise a meaningful choice to view the material while still awake.

IV.

CONCLUSION

In *ACT I*, we held that the FCC had not adequately justified its administrative decision to impose a 6 a.m.-to-midnight ban on the broadcasting of "indecent" material. Congress subsequently ordered a 24-hour ban on "indecent" material. In *ACT II*, we held the 24-hour ban unconstitutional and remanded the case to the FCC with the same directions as in *ACT I*, to redetermine the proper safe harbor after a full and fair hearing. Once again Congress intervened, now enacting into law the original FCC-imposed 6 a.m.-to-midnight ban, in order to (i) protect the privacy of every American's home, (ii) help parents supervise their children's listening and viewing, and (iii) independently shield minors from "indecent" material. The government has not demonstrated to this court the compelling nature of any interest in suppressing constitutionally protected material in order to protect an abstract privacy of the home at the expense of First Amendment rights of its inhabitants. We do recognize, however, the compelling nature of the government's interest in helping parents supervise their children and in independently protecting the well-being of its youth. "A democratic society rests, for its continuance, upon the healthy, well-rounded growth of young people into full maturity as citizens, with all that implies." Nevertheless, restrictions on First Amendment rights, even when imposed in the best interest of children, must still be narrowly tailored and no more burdensome than necessary to advance the protective goal. The boundaries of the 6 a.m.-to-midnight ban were arrived at solely on the basis of a judgment that fewer children are in the broadcast audience between the hours of midnight and 6 a.m. than at other times. That might even more assuredly have been said for a 1:00 a.m. to 5:00 a.m. or 3:00 a.m. to 4:00 a.m. safe harbor; no such one-dimensional analysis takes account of the First Amendment interests of older minors and adult viewers in receiving constitutionally protected material. Our system of government demands more precision when rights protected by the First Amendment are curtailed.

We conclude that the government has not tailored its 6 a.m.-to-midnight ban on constitutionally protected speech narrowly so as to advance the interests asserted without unnecessary abridgment of First Amendment rights. Accordingly we vacate the FCC's 1993 Order, and hold section 16(a) of the Public Telecommunications Act of 1992 unconstitutional.

Once again the curtain falls and the FCC finds itself in the same position that it occupied at the close of *ACT I*. The FCC's 1987 Reconsideration Order was neither vacated by this court in *ACT I*, nor retracted by the Commission. Thus, the Commission's declared intention to broaden enforcement beyond situations like the mid-day "Filthy Words" scenario approved by the Supreme Court in *Pacifica* still remains.... Therefore, should the Commission maintain its intention to broaden the enforcement of § 1464, we must, once again, direct the Commission to take up its administrative task to "'redetermin[e], after a full and fair hearing, ... the times at which indecent material may be broadcast,' [and] to carefully review and address the specific concerns we raised in *ACT I*: among them, the appropriate definitions of 'children' and 'reasonable risk' [of exposure of children to indecent material] for channeling purposes, the paucity of station- or program-specific audience data expressed as a percentage of the relevant age group population, and the scope of the government's interest in regulating indecent broadcasts."

HARRY T. EDWARDS, Circuit Judge, concurring specifically in the reversal.

. . .

The instant regulation, ... seems to rest on vague notions that too many parents are either unavailable to supervise their children or inept at the task of parenting, at least insofar as the Government sees it. There are two problems with these views.

First, in effectively setting itself up as the final arbiter of what American children may see and hear, the Government tramples heedlessly on parents' rights to rear their children as they see fit and to inculcate in them moral values of the parents' choosing. This countervailing interest is not grounded solely in the First Amendment. As at least one scholar has persuasively posited, this parental interest also derives from our constitutional vision of liberty and the role of the individual in a true democracy. "Free people require 'private realms' in which they can develop differently. The child must not be the creature of the state, but must be 'conceived in liberty' and nurtured in contexts sheltered from homogenizing control."

Second, in acting to limit children's exposure to indecent material, the Government's stated purposes rest on inconsistent, confused and possibly false premises. Many persons in society (and I am such a person) suppose that

there must be ill effects from exposing children (especially young ones) to "indecent" material; but the truth of the matter is that we have yet to unearth those ill effects with any precision, and we have yet to understand whether the effects are measurably different when parents are available and willing to "supervise" their children. Indeed, "parental supervision" itself is a vague notion, for we surely cannot assume that all parents will act in some uniform way in "supervising" their children. When acting consciously, some parents might prohibit their children from any exposure to indecent material; some might modify a prohibition depending upon the nature of the material and the age of the child; still others might view or listen to indecent material with their children, either to criticize, endorse or remain neutral about what they see or hear (and these responses might vary depending upon the age of the child and family values). Thus, if facilitation of "parental supervision" is the principal interest to be served, then a good argument can be made that ensuring the availability of "blocking" devices—to permit parents to block their children from seeing and hearing indecent material in their absence—is the most that Government ought to do. For the interest of facilitating parental control assumes that parents are entitled to do as they prefer.

If, however, the interest to be served is the protection of children, without regard to their parents' preferences, then it seems to me that the issue is quite complicated. A principal problem is that we do not appear to know how the exposure to indecent (as opposed to violent) material affects children, either with respect to their senses of self-worth, their senses of respect for members of the opposite sex, or their behavior patterns as functioning members of society. Thus, to highlight the issue, suppose that we knew for sure that most parents would prefer to retain the right to decide whether and on what terms to allow their children to be exposed to indecent material: could Congress still ban the showing of indecent material? If so, on what terms? Would it be prompted by a "moral judgment" that indecent material is bad for all children of all ages? And, if so, how can that be squared with the Supreme Court's rulings that distinguish between unprotected "obscene" and protected "indecent" materials, and suggest that the ages of minors must be considered in assessing the vulnerability of children? Or, rather, would it be premised on a purpose to save children from harm? If so, what is the nature of the harm, how does it manifest itself, and are children of all ages affected in the same say? Alternatively, would the action be designed to protect society from harm that can come from children who have been exposed to indecent material (or from adults who were exposed when they were minors)? If so, what is the nature of that harm and how pervasive is it?

In short, it seems to me that the strength of the Government's interest in shielding children from exposure to indecent programming is tied directly to the magnitude of the harms sought to be prevented. On the record before us, however, I have difficulty discerning precisely what those harms are. . . . [T]he FCC asserts only that "harm to children from exposure to [indecent] material may be presumed as a matter of law" and adverts to the existence of studies demonstrating certain undefined "negative effects of television on young viewers' sexual development and behavior." This does not provide a very secure basis on which to anchor significant First Amendment intrusions. The apparent lack of specific evidence of harms from indecent programming stands in direct contrast, for example, to the evidence of harm caused by violent programming—a genre that, as yet, has gone virtually unregulated.

. . .

In a subsequent decision, the court of appeals directed the FCC to establish a safe harbor for broadcasting indecent programming between the hours of 10 p.m. and 6 a.m. *Action for Children's Television v. FCC*, 56 F.3d 105 (D.C. Cir. 1995).

Given regulatory concern with broadcasting's accessibility to children, and what is perceived as the medium's pervasive or intrusive nature, the availability of access restrictive technology may be a critical analytical factor. In responding to concerns with violent television programming, Congress has required television set manufacturers to include a special chip that facilitates blockage of such fare. In the indecency context, the Court affirmed without opinion a lower court decision that indecent cable programming was distinguishable from like broadcast material.[228] Technology also was central to the Court's decision, in *Sable Communications of California, Inc. v. Federal Communications Commission*, that congressional prohibition of dial-a-porn services could not stand to the extent it reached indecent expression.

---

[228] Community Television of Utah, Inc. v. Wilkinson, 611 F.Supp. 1099 (D.Utah), *aff'd*, 800 F.2d 989 (10th Cir. 1986), *aff'd*, 480 U.S. 926 (1987).

Sable Communications of California, Inc. v. Federal Communications Commission
492 U.S. 115 (1989)

JUSTICE WHITE delivered the opinion of the Court.

The issue before us is the constitutionality of § 223(b) of the Communications Act of 1934, 47 U.S.C. § 223(b), [which] imposes an outright ban on indecent as well as obscene interstate commercial telephone messages. The Disctrict Court upheld the prohibition against obscene interstate telephone communications for commercial purposes, but enjoined the enforcement of the statute insofar as it applied to indecent messages. We affirm the District Court in both respects.

I

In 1983, Sable Communications, Inc., a Los Angeles-based affiliate of Carlin Communications, Inc., began offering sexually-oriented prerecorded telephone messages (popularly known as "dial-a-porn") through the Pacific Bell telephone network. In order to provide the messages, Sable arranged with Pacific Bell to use special telephone lines, designed to handle large volumes of calls simultaneously. Those who called the adult message number were charged a special fee. The fee was collected by Pacific Bell and divided between the phone company and the message provider. Callers outside the Los Angeles metropolitan area could reach the number by means of a long-distance toll call to the Los Angeles area code.

. . .

IV

. . .

Sexual expression which is indecent but not obscene is protected by the First Amendment; and the government does not submit that the sale of such materials to adults could be criminalized solely because they are indecent. The government may, however, regulate the content of constitutionally protected speech in order to promote a compelling interest if it chooses the least restrictive means to further the articulated interest. We have recognized that there is a compelling interest in protecting the physical and psychological well-being of minors. This interest extends to shielding minors from the influence of literature that is not obscene by adult standards. The government may serve this legitimate interest, but to withstand constitutional scrutiny, "it must do so by narrowly drawn regulations designed to serve those interests without unnecessarily interfering with First Amendment freedoms. It is not enough to show that the government's ends are compelling; the means must be carefully tailored to achieve those ends.

In *Butler v. Michigan*, 352 U.S. 380 (1957), a unanimous Court reversed a conviction under a statute which made it an offense to make available to the general public materials found to have a potentially harmful influence on minors. The Court found the law to be insufficiently tailored since it denied adults their free speech rights by allowing them to read only what was acceptable for children. As Justice Frankfurter said in that case, "Surely this is to burn the house to roast the pig." In our judgment, this case, like *Butler*, presents us with "legislation not reasonably restricted to the evil with which it is said to deal."

Pacifica is readily distinguished from this case, most obviously because it did not involve a total ban on broadcasting indecent material. The FCC rule was not "'intended to place an absolute prohibition on the broadcast of this type of language, but rather sought to channel it to times of day when children most likely would not be exposed to it.'" The issue of a total ban was not before the Court.

The *Pacifica* opinion also relied on the "unique" attributes of broadcasting, noting that broadcasting is "uniquely pervasive," can intrude on the privacy of the home without prior warning as to program content, and is "uniquely accessible to children, even those too young to read." The private commercial telephone communications at issue here are substantially different from the public radio broadcast at issue in *Pacifica*. In contrast to public displays, unsolicited mailings and other means of expression which the recipient has no meaningful opportunity to avoid, the dial-it medium requires the listener to take affirmative steps to receive the communication. There is no "captive audience" problem here; callers will generally not be unwilling listeners. The context of dial-in services, where a caller seeks and is willing to pay for the communication, is manifestly different from a situation in which a listener does not want the received message. Placing a telephone call is not the same as turning on a radio and being taken by surprise by an indecent message. Unlike the unexpected outburst on a radio broadcast, the message received by one who places a call to a dial-a-porn service is not so invasive or surprising that it prevents an unwilling listener form avoiding exposure to it.

The Court in *Pacifica* was careful "to emphasize the narrowness of [its] holding." . . . [W]e distinguish *Pacifica* from the case before us and reiterate that "the government may not 'reduce the adult population . . . to . . . only what is fit for children.'"

The Government nevertheless argues that the total ban on indecent commercial telephone communications is justified because nothing less could prevent children from gaining access to such messages. We find the argument quite unpersuasive. The FCC, after lengthy proceedings, determined that its credit card, access code, and scrambling rules were a satisfactory solution to the problem of keeping indecent dial-a-porn messages out of the reach of minors. The Court of Appeals, after careful consideration, agreed that these rules represented a "feasible and effective" way to serve the Government's compelling interest in protecting children.

The Government now insists that the rules would not be effective enough—that enterprising youngsters could and would evade the rules and gain access to communications from which they should be shielded. There is no evidence in the record before us to that effect, nor could there be since the FCC's implementation of § 223(b) prior to its 1988 amendment has never been tested over time. In this respect, the Government asserts that in amending § 223(b) in 1988, Congress expressed its view that there was not a sufficiently effective way to protect minors short of the total ban that it enacted. The Government claims that we must give deference to that judgment.

. . .

There is no doubt Congress enacted a total ban on both obscene and indecent telephone communications. But aside from conclusory statements during the debates by proponents of the bill, as well as similar assertions in hearings on a substantially identical bill the year before, H.R. 1786, that under the FCC regulations minors could still have access to dial-a-porn messages, the Congressional record presented to us contains no evidence as to *how* effective or ineffective the FCC's most recent regulations were or might prove to be. . . .

For all we know from this record, the FCC's technological approach to restricting dial-a-porn messages to adults who seek them would be extremely effective, and only a few of the most enterprising and disobedient young people will manage to secure access to such messages. If this is the case, it seems to us that § 223(b) is not a narrowly tailored effort to serve the compelling interest of preventing minors from being exposed to indecent telephone messages. Under our precedents, § 223(b), in its present form, has the invalid effect of limiting the content of adult telephone conversations to that which is suitable for children to hear. It is another case of "burn[ing] up the house to road the pig."

Because the statute's denial of adult access to telephone messages which are indecent but not obscene far exceeds that which is necessary to limit the access of minors to such messages, we hold that the ban does not survive constitutional scrutiny.

JUSTICE SCALIA, concurring.

I note that while we hold the Constitution prevents Congress from banning indecent speech in this fashion, we do not hold that the Constitution requires public utilities to carry it.

JUSTICE BRENNAN, with whom JUSTICE MARSHALL and JUSTICE STEVENS join, concurring in part and dissenting in part.

I agree that a statute imposing criminal penalties for making, or for allowing others to use a telephone under one's control to make, any indecent telephone communication for a commercial purpose is patently unconstitutional. I therefore join Parts I, II, and IV of the Court's opinion.

DEL: Regulation of indecent expression, especially since the mid-1980s, has become a primary fetish of the FCC that collides with its historically expressed interests in content diversification. To prohibit the airing of a monologue by George Carlin, that is the essence of satire, reflects a disregard of First Amendment values and an exercise in elitism. Such a ruling is consistent with Warren and Brandeis' concern with the civility of public discourse. It is inimical, however, to the imperatives of expressive diversity and cultural pluralism. The *Pacifica* decision itself, which was quick to emphasize its willingness to accept offensive terminology if appearing in an "Elizabethan comedy," demonstrates an anti-pluralistic bent when it equates the Carlin monologue with "a pig enter[ing] the parlor." By publishing as an appendix to its own opinion what would be punished if aired by a broadcaster, the Court discloses its continuing commitment to medium specific analysis. What the Court and the FCC offer in support of their work are dubious rationales. If privacy is at stake, a strong argument exists that the interest is profoundly compromised by rules that deny viewers and listeners the opportunity to exercise their autonomous judgment with respect to the programming they will be exposed to. With respect to concern with broadcasting's intrusive nature, the reality is that televisions and radios are not present in a household minus a decision by the occupant to put them there. Insofar as the viewer or listener retains control, pursuant to on-off switches and channel selection devices, it strains logic to indicate that the medium's presence is not equivalent to an invited guest who may be disinvited pursuant to reason or whim. Even if accessibility to children may be greater with respect to broadcasting, than to cable or telephone systems affording blocking technology, the reality is that children are as readily exposed to indecent language in a variety of contexts as they are by watching television or listening to the radio. Regulation characterizing indecency regulation as mere time channeling, akin to zoning regulation of adult bookstores or theaters, ignores the reality that access to the Carlin monologue is unrestricted except in the broadcast media. Especially to the extent that sexually-oriented programming generates impressive ratings, it is arguable that indecency controls are at odds with the "public interest" unless the standard is to be defined in an elitist or paternalistic fashion. To the extent that regulators and the Court favor the decency concerns of an organized few, moreover, they create another "unusual order" in which expression is taxed at the expense of diversity.

As media technology has evolved beyond print capability, medium specific analysis has been established as a primary constitutional stock in trade. The modern trend of media, however, is toward common rather than divergent natures and effects. As newspapers use satellites to distribute their editorial output from newsrooms to printing plants, or generate their product upon video terminals, and all media acquire interactive capability, a fundamental constitutional choice looms. Given an evolution toward media convergence, it eventually must be determined whether the long-term meaning of press liberty will be defined by reference to a print model that prioritizes editorial freedom or standards for newer media that elevate competing concerns.

DER: In protecting the interests of unwilling listeners and children, the *Pacifica* court grossly discounted the countervailing interests of two other groups of citizens—listeners who wanted to hear Carlin's monologue and parents who wanted to regulate their children's listening themselves. In terms of sheer numbers, it is likely that there were far more people who purposely tuned in to the program than those who accidently happened upon it. Indeed, the lone complaint, from a Florida member of the national planning board of Morality in the Media, appeared to be concocted. More important, the Court seriously miscalculated the balance of interests by concluding that the momentary offense outweighed the value of Carlin's satirical message. The Court allowed the government to overstep its role in protecting children from language it deems unsuitable for them to hear, as well. Although the FCC should help parents to supervise their children's listening, it should not supersede parental prerogatives. The FCC's policy, for example, made it difficult for parents who approved of the monologue to expose their children to Carlin's way of defusing the taboos surrounding "dirty words." While the government may have a compelling interest in protecting unwilling listeners and children from harmful speech, it should not be able to ban speech from the airwaves because some listeners find it offensive.

DEL: Medium specific analysis essentially is an anachronism. Given the overarching function of all media to disseminate information and data to the public, it at least is debatable whether attention to difference was a logical departure point for the construction of First Amendment standards. Response to the profound changes in the media industry, wherein newspapers, broadcasters, cablecasters, wireless cable operators and even telephone companies possess identical capabilities including those of choice and interactivity, will determine whether freedom of the press survives as a vital or vestigial concept.

E. Freedom of Religion

The Constitution's attention to religious freedom is not surprising, given the relevant history that preceded framing and ratification of the Bill of Rights. American colonization was driven in significant part by persons seeking to escape religious persecution. As the Supreme Court has noted

> [t]he centuries immediately before and contemporaneous with the colonization of America had been filled with turmoil, civil strife, and persecutions generated in large part by established sects determined to maintain their absolute political and religious supremacy. . . . [As the] practices of the old world were transplanted . . . [to] the soil of the new America, . . . [they] became so commonplace as to shock the freedom-loving colonials into a feeling of abhorrence. . . . It was these feelings which found expression in the First Amendment.[229]

Constitutional guarantees of religious freedom reflect a complex attitude toward religion that has contributed to a body of jurisprudence that at times is confounding and even inscrutable. A primary interpretative problem is presented by the terms of the First Amendment itself which create an inherent tension. The establishment clause prohibits enactments "respecting an establishment of religion."[230] The exercise clause

---

[229] Everson v. Board of Education, 330 U.S. 1 (1947).
[230] U.S. Const. amend. I.

bars laws "prohibiting the free exercise thereof."[231] As the Supreme Court put it in *Cantwell v. Connecticut,*

> [T]he constitutional inhibition of legislation on the subject of religion has a double aspect. On the one hand, it forestalls compulsion by law of the acceptance of any creed or the practice of any form of worship. Freedom of conscience and freedom to adhere to such religious organization or form of worship as the individual may choose cannot be restricted by law. On the other hand, it safeguards the free exercise of the chosen form of religion. Thus the Amendment embraces two concepts,—freedom to believe and freedom to act. The first is absolute but, in the nature of things, the second cannot be. Conduct remains subject to regulation for the protection of society. The freedom to act must have appropriate definition to preserve the enforcement of that protection. In every case the power to regulate must be so exercised as not, in attaining a permissible end, unduly to infringe the protected freedom.[232]

Although the establishment and exercise clauses both speak to the general ideal of religious freedom, it often is difficult to account for one interest without compromising the other. State financial support to parochial schools, for instance, may be challenged on grounds it offends the establishment clause. Such aid may be defended, however, on the basis that denying it would interfere with the free exercise of religion. Recognition of the religion clauses' differing gravitational pulls dates back to the earliest cases on religious freedom. In upholding treaty obligations for funding the education of Native Americans, including support for parochial schooling, the Court in *Reuben Quick Bear v. Leupp* dismissed an establishment clause argument in part because of the risk it presented to free exercise values.

---

[231] *Id.*

[232] Cantwell v. Connecticut, 310 U.S. 296, 303–04 (1940).

Reuben Quick Bear v. Leupp
210 U.S. 50 (1908)

Mr. Chief Justice Fuller, after making the foregoing statement, delivered the opinion of the court.

. . .

Some reference is made to the Constitution, in respect to this contract with the Bureau of Catholic Indian Missions. It is not contended that it is unconstitutional, and it could not be. But it is contended that the spirit of the Constitution requires that the declaration of policy that the Government "shall make no appropriation whatever for education in any sectarian schools" should be treated as applicable, on the ground that the actions of the United States were to always be undenominational, and that, therefore, the Government can never act in a sectarian capacity, either in the use of its own funds or in that of the funds of others, in respect of which it is a trustee; hence that even the Sioux trust fund cannot be applied for edu-

cation in Catholic schools, even though the owners of the fund so desire it. But we cannot concede the proposition that Indians cannot be allowed to use their own money to educate their children in the schools of their own choice because the Government is necessarily undenominational, as it cannot make any law respecting an establishment of religion or prohibiting the free exercise thereof. The Court of Appeals well said:

"The 'Treaty' and 'Trust' moneys are the only moneys that the Indians can lay claim to as matter of right; the only sums on which they are entitled to rely as theirs for education; and while these moneys are not delivered to them in hand, yet the money must not only be provided, but be expended, for their benefit and in part for their education; it seems inconceivable that Congress should have intended to prohibit them from receiving religious education at their own cost if they so desired it; such an intent would be one 'to prohibit the free exercise of religion' amongst the Indians, and such would be the effect of the construction for which the complainants contend."

. . .

To avoid the analytical quagmire characterizing interpretation of the religion clauses, one theorist has suggested that they should be read together as supporting the transcendent principle of neutrality. Read thusly, the First Amendment provisions would preclude government from using "religion as a standard for action or inaction because these clauses prohibit classification in terms of religion to confer a benefit or to impose a burden."[233] Such a unifying theory might result in a brighter line between permissible and impermissible government action. Aid to parochial education would be allowable, for instance, to the extent that it was part of a broader program for assistance to private education generally. A state-supported nativity scene on public property, however, might be less likely to survive constitutional review.

Regardless of its appeal, the Supreme Court has not invested in such a merger of doctrine. Rather it has evolved separate standards of review for establishment and free exercise problems. Establishment clause analysis is characterized by attention to government purpose, the effect of the challenged action and the risks of entangling government and religion.[234] Attention also is devoted to concern with accommodating religion.[235] Exercise clause analysis focuses upon whether the regulatory interest is compelling enough to outweigh the constitutional freedom.[236]

1. Defining Religion

Like the First Amendment's speech and press clauses, the religion clauses present basic definitional problems. For the most part, the Court generally has avoided inquiry into or judgment upon the nature or validity of a given religion. Although allowing evaluation of the sincerity of religious belief, the Court generally has declined the opportunity to assess doctrinal legitimacy.

---

[233] Philip Kurland, *Of Church, State, and the Supreme Court*, 29 University. Chi. L. Rev. 1, 2–6 (1961).

[234] Lemon v. Kurtzman, 403 U.S. 602, 612–13 (1971).

[235] *E.g.*, Marsh v. Chambers, 463 U.S. 783, 792 (1983).

[236] *E.g.*, Bob Jones University v. United States, 461 U.S. 574, 604 (1983).

United States v. Ballard
322 U.S. 78 (1944)

Mr. Justice Douglas delivered the opinion of the Court.

Respondents were indicted and convicted for using, and conspiring to use, the mails to defraud.... The indictment ... charged a scheme to defraud by organizing and promoting the I Am movement through the use of the mails. The false representations [included]

that Guy W. Ballard, now deceased, alias Saint Germain, Jesus, George Washington, and Godfre Ray King, had been selected and thereby designated by the alleged "ascertained masters," Saint Germain, as a divine messenger; and that the words of "ascended masters" and the words of the alleged divine entity, Saint Germain, would be transmitted to mankind through the medium of the said Guy W. Ballard; that Guy W. Ballard, during his lifetime, and Edna W. Ballard, and Donald Ballard, by reason of their alleged high spiritual attainments and righteous conduct, had been selected as divine messengers through which the words of the alleged "ascended masters," including the alleged Saint Germain, would be communicated to mankind under the teachings commonly known as the "I Am" movement; that Guy W. Ballard, during his lifetime, and Edna W. Ballard and Donald Ballard had, by reason of supernatural attainments, the power to heal persons of ailments and diseases and to make well persons afflicted with any diseases, injuries, or ailments, and did falsely represent to persons intended to be defrauded that the three designated persons had the ability and power to cure persons of those diseases normally classified as curable and also of diseases which are ordinarily classified by the medical profession as being incurable diseases; and did further represent that the three designated persons had in fact cured either by the activity of one, either, or all of said persons, hundreds of persons afflicted with diseases and ailments;

Each of the representations enumerated in the indictment was followed by the charge that respondents "well knew" it was false. After enumerating the eighteen misrepresentations the indictment also alleged:

At the time of making all of the afore-alleged representations by the defendants, and each of them, the defendants, and each of them, well knew that all of said aforementioned representations were false and untrue and were made with the intention on the part of the defendants, and each of them, to cheat, wrong, and defraud persons intended to be defrauded, and to obtain from persons intended to be defrauded by the defendants, money, property, and other things of value and to convert the same to the use and the benefit of the defendants, and each of them. . . .

[In charging the jury, the District Court instructed that]

The question of the defendants' good faith is the cardinal question in this case. You are not to be concerned with the religious belief of the defendants, or any of them. The jury will be called upon to pass on the question of whether or not the defendants honestly and in good faith believed the representations which are set forth in the indictment, and honestly and in good faith believed that the benefits which they represented would flow from their belief to those who embraced and followed their teachings, or whether these representations were mere pretenses without honest belief on the part of the defendants or any of them, and, were the representations made for the purpose of procuring money, and were the mails used for this purpose.

. . .

The Circuit Court of Appeals reversed the judgment of conviction and granted a new trial, one judge dissenting. In its view the restriction of the issue in question to that of good faith was error. . . .

. . .

. . . Freedom of thought, which includes freedom of religious belief, is basic in a society of free men. It embraces the right to maintain theories of life and of death and of the hereafter which are rank heresy to followers of the orthodox faiths. Heresy trials are foreign to our Constitution. Men may believe what they cannot prove. They may not be put to the proof of their religious doctrines or beliefs. Religious experiences which are as real as life to some may be incomprehensible to others. Yet the fact that they may be beyond the ken of mortals does not mean that they can be made suspect before the law. Many take their gospel from the New Testament. But it would hardly be supposed that they could be tried before a jury charged with the duty of determining whether those teachings contained false representations. The miracles of the New Testament, the Divinity of Christ, life after death, the power of prayer are deep in the religious convictions of many. If one could be sent to jail because a jury in a hostile environment found those teachings false, little indeed would be left of religious freedom. The Fathers of the Constitution were not unaware of the varied and extreme views of religious sects, of the violence of disagreement among them, and of the lack of any one religious creed on which all men would agree. They fashioned a charter of government which envisaged the widest possible toleration of conflicting views. Man's relation to his God was made no concern of the state. He was granted the right to worship as he pleased and to answer to no man for the verity of his religious views. The religious views espoused by respondents might seem incredible, if not preposterous, to most people. But if those doctrines are subject to trial before a jury charged with finding their truth or falsity, then the same can be done with the religious beliefs of any sect. When the triers of fact undertake that task, they enter a forbidden domain. The First Amendment does not select any one group or any one type of religion for preferred treatment. It puts them all in that position. "With man's relations to his Maker and the obligations he may think they impose, and the manner in which an expression shall be made by him of his belief on those subjects, no interference can be permitted, provided always the laws of society, designed to secure its peace and prosperity, and the morals of its people, are not interfered with." So we conclude that the District Court ruled properly when it withheld from the jury all questions concerning the truth or falsity of the religious beliefs or doctrines of respondents.

. . .

MR. CHIEF JUSTICE STONE, dissenting:

. . .

The indictment charges respondents' use of the mails to defraud and a conspiracy to commit that offense by false statements of their religious experiences which had not in fact occurred. But it also charged that the representations were "falsely and fraudulently" made, that respondents "well knew" that these representations were untrue, and that they were made by respondents with the intent to cheat and defraud those to whom they were made. With the assent of the prosecution and the defense the trial judge withdrew from the consideration of the jury the question whether the alleged religious experiences had in fact occurred, but submitted to the jury the single issue whether petitioners honestly believed that they had occurred, with the instruction that if the jury did not so find, then it should return a verdict of guilty. On this issue the jury, on ample evidence that respondents were without belief in the statements which they had made to their victims, found a verdict of guilty. The state of one's mind is a fact as capable of fraudulent misrepresentation as is one's physical condition or the state of his bodily health. There are no exceptions to the charge and no contention that the trial court rejected any relevant evidence which petitioners sought to offer. Since the indictment and the evidence support the conviction, it is irrelevant whether the religious experiences alleged did or did not in fact occur or whether that issue could or could not, for constitutional reasons, have been rightly submitted to the jury. Certainly none of respondents' constitutional rights are violated if they are prosecuted for the fraudulent procurement of money by false representations as to their beliefs, religious or otherwise.

. . .

MR. JUSTICE ROBERTS and MR. JUSTICE FRANKFURTER join in this opinion.

MR. JUSTICE JACKSON, dissenting:

I should say the defendants have done just that for which they are indicted. If I might agree to their conviction without creating a precedent, I cheerfully would do so. I can see in their teachings nothing but humbug, untainted by any trace of truth. But that does not dispose of the constitutional question whether misrepresentation of religious experience or belief is prosecutable; it rather emphasizes the danger of such prosecutions.

The Ballard family claimed miraculous communication with the spirit world and supernatural power to heal the sick. They were brought to trial for mail fraud on an indictment which charged that their representations were false and that they "well knew" they were false. The trial judge, obviously troubled, ruled that the court could not try whether the statements were untrue, but could inquire whether the defendants knew them to be untrue; and, if so, they could be convicted.

I find it difficult to reconcile this conclusion with our traditional religious freedoms.

In the first place, as a matter of either practice or philosophy I do not see how we can separate an issue as to what is believed from considerations as to what is believable. The most convincing proof that one believes his statements is to show that they have been true in his experience. Likewise, that one knowingly falsified is best proved by showing that what he said happened never did happen. How can the Government prove these persons knew something to be false which it cannot prove to be false? If we try religious sincerity severed from religious verity, we isolate the dispute from the very considerations which in common experience provide its most reliable answer.

In the second place, any inquiry into intellectual honesty in religion raises profound psychological problems. William James, who wrote on these matters as a scientist, reminds us that it is not theology and ceremonies which keep religion going. Its vitality is in the religious experiences of many people. "If you ask what these experiences are, they are conversations with the unseen, voices and visions, responses to prayer, changes of heart, deliverances from fear, inflowings of help, assurances of support, whenever certain persons set their own internal attitude in certain appropriate ways." If religious liberty includes, as it must, the right to communicate such experiences to others, it seems to me an impossible task for juries to separate fancied ones from real ones, dreams from happenings, and hallucinations from true clairvoyance. Such experiences, like some tones and colors, have existence for one, but none at all for another. They cannot be verified to the minds of those whose field of consciousness does not include religious insight. When one comes to trial which turns on any aspect of religious belief or representation, unbelievers among his judges are likely not to understand and are almost certain not to believe him.

And then I do not know what degree of skepticism or disbelief in a religious representation amounts to actionable fraud. James points out that "Faith means belief in something concerning which doubt is still theoretically possible." Belief in what one may demonstrate to the senses is not faith. All schools of religious thought make enormous assumptions, generally on the basis of revelations authenticated by some sign or miracle. The appeal in such matters is to a very different plane of credulity than is invoked by representations of secular fact in commerce. Some who profess belief in the Bible read literally what others read as allegory or metaphor, as they read Aesop's fables. Religious symbolism is even used by some with the same mental reservations one has in teaching of Santa Claus or Uncle Sam or Easter bunnies or dispassionate judges. It is hard in matters so mystical to say how literally one is bound to believe the doctrine he teaches and even more difficult to say how far it is reliance upon a teacher's literal belief which induces followers to give him money.

There appear to be persons—let us hope not many—who find refreshment and courage in the teachings of the "I Am" cult. If the members of the sect get comfort from the celestial guidance of their "Saint Germain," however doubtful it seems to me, it is hard to say that they do not get what they pay for. Scores of sects flourish in this country by teaching what to me are queer notions. It is plain that there is wide variety in American religious taste. The Ballards are not alone in catering to it with a pretty dubious product.

The chief wrong which false prophets do to their following is not financial. The collections aggregate a tempting total, but individual payments are not ruinous. I doubt if the vigilance of the law is equal to making money stick by over-credulous people. But the real harm is on the mental and spiritual plane. There are those who hunger and thirst after higher values which they feel wanting in their humdrum lives. They live in mental confusion or moral anarchy and seek vaguely for truth and beauty and moral support. When they are deluded and then disillusioned, cynicism and confusion follow. The wrong of these things, as I see it, is not in the money the victims part with half so much as in the mental and spiritual poison they get. But that is precisely the thing the Constitution put beyond the reach of the prosecutor, for the price of freedom of religion or of speech or of the press is that we must put up with, and even pay for, a good deal of rubbish.

Prosecutions of this character easily could degenerate into religious persecution. I do not doubt that religious leaders may be convicted of fraud for making false representations on matters other than faith or experience, as for example if one represents that funds are being used to construct a church when in fact they are being used for personal purposes. But that is not this case, which reaches into wholly dangerous ground. When does less than full belief in a professed credo become actionable fraud if one is soliciting gifts or legacies? Such inquiries may discomfort orthodox as well as unconventional religious teachers, for even the most regular of them are sometimes accused of taking their orthodoxy with a grain of salt.

I would dismiss the indictment and have done with this business of judicially examining other people's faiths.

Official standards to determine what constitutes a religion in themselves might abrogate the establishment clause, insofar as decisions of inclusion and exclusion were made. They also might cross the exercise clause, to the extent their operation interfered with religious freedom.[237] The Court nonetheless has made some intellectual forays into the nature of religion. In *Torcaso v. Watkins*, it struck down a state law requiring a profession of belief in the existence of God as a condition for holding public office.[238] The Court, in an opinion by Justice Black, found that

[t]here is, and can be, no dispute about the purpose or effect of the . . . requirement before us—it sets up a religious test which was designed to and, if valid, does bar every person who refuses to declare a belief in God from holding a public "office of profit or trust" in Maryland. The power and authority of the State of Maryland thus is put on the side of one particular sort of believers—those who are willing to say they believe in "the existence of God." . . .

We repeat and again reaffirm that neither a State nor the Federal Government can constitutionally force a person "to profess a belief or disbelief in any religion." Neither can constitutionally pass laws or impose requirements which aid all religions as against non-believers, and neither can aid those religions

---

[237] Jonathan Weiss, *Privilege, Posture and Protection—"Religion" in the Law*, 73 YALE L.J. 593, 604 (1964).
[238] Torcaso v. Watkins, 367 U.S. 488, 489 (1961).

based on a belief in the existence of God as against those religions founded on different beliefs.[239]

. . .

The meaning of religion became a critical question in cases concerning conscientious objection to service in the military. In *United States v. Seeger*, the Court reviewed federal law exempting "from combat any person 'who, by reason of religious training and belief, is conscientiously opposed to participation in war in any form.' "[240] The key qualifying standard was "an individual's belief in a relation to a Supreme Being involving duties superior to those arising from any human relation."[241] Specifically excluded were individuals objecting pursuant to "essentially political, sociological or philosophical views or a merely personal moral code."[242]

---

[239] *Id.* at 490, 495.
[240] United States v. Seeger, 380 U.S. 163, 164–65 (1965).
[241] *Id.* at 165.
[242] *Id.*

United States v. Seeger
380 U.S. 163 (1965)

MR. JUSTICE CLARK delivered the opinion of the Court.

These cases involve claims of conscientious objectors under . . . the Universal Military Training and Service Act, which exempts from combatant training and service in the armed forces of the United States those persons who by reason of their religious training and belief are conscientiously opposed to participation in war in any form. The cases were consolidated for argument and we consider them together although each involves different facts and circumstances. The parties raise the basic question of the constitutionality of the section which defines the term "religious training and belief," as used in the Act, as "an individual's belief in a relation to a Supreme Being involving duties superior to those arising from any human relation, but [not including] essentially political, sociological, or philosophical views or a merely personal moral code." . . .

We have concluded that Congress, in using the expression "Supreme Being" rather than the designation "God," was merely clarifying the meaning of religious training and belief so as to embrace all religions and to exclude essentially political, sociological, or philosophical views. We believe that under this construction, the test of belief "in a relation to a Supreme Being" is whether a given belief that is sincere and meaningful occupies a place in the life of its possessor parallel to that filled by the orthodox belief in God of one who clearly qualifies for the exemption. Where such beliefs have parallel positions in the lives of their respective hold-

ers we cannot say that one is "in a relation to a Supreme Being" and the other is not. . . .

INTERPRETATION OF § 6 (j).

1. The crux of the problem lies in the phrase "religious training and belief" which Congress has defined as "belief in a relation to a Supreme Being involving duties superior to those arising from any human relation." In assigning meaning to this statutory language we may narrow the inquiry by noting briefly those scruples expressly excepted from the definition. The section excludes those persons who, disavowing religious belief, decide on the basis of essentially political, sociological or economic considerations that war is wrong and that they will have no part of it. These judgments have historically been reserved for the Government, and in matters which can be said to fall within these areas the conviction of the individual has never been permitted to override that of the state. . . . We also pause to take note of what is not involved in this litigation. No party claims to be an atheist or attacks the statute on this ground. The question is not, therefore, one between theistic and atheistic beliefs. We do not deal with or intimate any decision on that situation in these cases. Nor do the parties claim the monotheistic belief that there is but one God; what they claim (with the possible exception of Seeger who bases his position here not on factual but on purely constitutional grounds) is that they adhere to theism, which is the "Belief in the existence of a god or gods; . . . Belief in superhuman powers or spiritual

agencies in one or many gods," as opposed to atheism. Our question, therefore, is the narrow one: Does the term "Supreme Being" as used mean the orthodox God or the broader concept of a power or being, or a faith, "to which all else is subordinate or upon which all else is ultimately dependent"? In considering this question we resolve it solely in relation to the language of § 6 (j) and not otherwise.

2. Few would quarrel, we think, with the proposition that in no field of human endeavor has the tool of language proved so inadequate in the communication of ideas as it has in dealing with the fundamental questions of man's predicament in life, in death or in final judgment and retribution. This fact makes the task of discerning the intent of Congress in using the phrase "Supreme Being" a complex one. Nor is it made the easier by the richness and variety of spiritual life in our country. Over 250 sects inhabit our land. Some believe in a purely personal God, some in a supernatural deity; others think of religion as a way of life envisioning as its ultimate goal the day when all men can live together in perfect understanding and peace. There are those who think of God as the depth of our being; others, such as the Buddhists, strive for a state of lasting rest through self-denial and inner purification; in Hindu philosophy, the Supreme Being is the transcendental reality which is truth, knowledge and bliss. . . . This vast panoply of beliefs reveals the magnitude of the problem which faced the Congress when it set about providing an exemption from armed service. It also emphasizes the care that Congress realized was necessary in the fashioning of an exemption which would be in keeping with its long-established policy of not picking and choosing among religious beliefs. In spite of the elusive nature of the inquiry, we are not without certain guidelines. In amending the 1940 Act, Congress adopted almost intact the language of Chief Justice Hughes in *United States v. Macintosh,*

> "The essence of religion is belief in a relation to God involving duties superior to those arising from any human relation."

By comparing the statutory definition with those words, however, it becomes readily apparent that the Congress deliberately broadened them by substituting the phrase "Supreme Being" for the appellation "God." And in so doing it is also significant that Congress did not elaborate on the form or nature of this higher authority which it chose to designate as "Supreme Being." By so refraining it must have had in mind the admonitions of the Chief Justice when he said in the same opinion that even the word "God" had myriad meanings for men of faith:

> "[P]utting aside dogmas with their particular conceptions of deity, freedom of con-

science itself implies respect for an innate conviction of paramount duty. The battle for religious liberty has been fought and won with respect to religious beliefs and practices, which are not in conflict with good order, upon the very ground of the supremacy of conscience within its proper field."

. . .

[The challenged law] continues the congressional policy of providing exemption from military service for those whose opposition is based on grounds that can fairly be said to be "religious." To hold otherwise would not only fly in the face of Congress' entire action in the past; it would ignore the historic position of our country on this issue since its founding.

. . .

. . . [I]t must be remembered that in resolving these exemption problems one deals with the beliefs of different individuals who will articulate them in a multitude of ways. In such an intensely personal area, of course, the claim of the registrant that his belief is an essential part of a religious faith must be given great weight. . . .

The validity of what he believes cannot be questioned. Some theologians, and indeed some examiners, might be tempted to question the existence of the registrant's "Supreme Being" or the truth of his concepts. But these are inquiries foreclosed to Government. . . . Local boards and courts in this sense are not free to reject beliefs because they consider them "incomprehensible." Their task is to decide whether the beliefs professed by a registrant are sincerely held and whether they are, in his own scheme of things, religious.

But we hasten to emphasize that while the "truth" of a belief is not open to question, there remains the significant question whether it is "truly held." This is the threshold question of sincerity which must be resolved in every case. It is, of course, a question of fact—a prime consideration to the validity of every claim for exemption as a conscientious objector. . . .

As we noted earlier, the statutory definition excepts those registrants whose beliefs are based on a "merely personal moral code." . . .

MR. JUSTICE DOUGLAS, concurring.

. . .

. . . When the Congress spoke in the vague general terms of a Supreme Being I cannot, therefore, assume that it was so parochial as to use the words in the narrow sense urged on us. I would attribute tolerance and sophistication to the Congress, commensurate with the religious complexion of our communities. In sum, I agree with the Court that any person opposed to war on the basis of a sincere belief, which in his life fills the same place as a belief in God fills in the life of an orthodox religionist, is entitled to exemption under the statute. . . .

The *Seeger* decision primarily was concerned with whether belief in "a Supreme Being" was coextensive with an "orthodox belief in God." In *Welsh v. United States*, the Court considered whether strongly held ethical or moral beliefs might constitute the functional equivalent of religion.

Welsh v. United States
398 U.S. 353 (1970)

MR. JUSTICE BLACK, announced the judgment of the Court and delivered an opinion which MR. JUSTICE DOUGLAS, MR. JUSTICE BRENNAN, and MR. JUSTICE MARSHALL join.

The petitioner, Elliott Ashton Welsh II, was convicted by a United States District Judge of refusing to submit to induction into the Armed Forces in violation of 50 U.S. C. App. § 462 (a), and was on June 1, 1966, sentenced to imprisonment for three years. One of petitioner's defenses to the prosecution was that § 6 (j) of the Universal Military Training and Service Act exempted him from combat and noncombat service because he was "by reason of religious training and belief . . . conscientiously opposed to participation in war in any form." After finding that there was no religious basis for petitioner's conscientious objector claim, the Court of Appeals . . . affirmed the conviction. We granted certiorari chiefly to review the contention that Welsh's conviction should be set aside on the basis of this Court's decision in *United States v. Seeger*, 380 U.S. 163 (1965). . . .

The controlling facts in this case are strikingly similar to those in *Seeger*. . . .

In filling out their exemption applications both Seeger and Welsh were unable to sign the statement that, as printed in the Selective Service form, stated "I am, by reason of my religious training and belief, conscientiously opposed to participation in war in any form." Seeger could sign only after striking the words "training and" and putting quotation marks around the word "religious." Welsh could sign only after striking the words "my religious training and." On those same applications, neither could definitely affirm or deny that he believed in a "Supreme Being," both stating that they preferred to leave the question open. But both Seeger and Welsh affirmed on those applications that they held deep conscientious scruples against taking part in wars where people were killed. Both strongly believed that killing in war was wrong, unethical, and immoral, and their consciences forbade them to take part in such an evil practice. Their objection to participating in war in any form could not be said to come from a "still, small voice of conscience"; rather, for them that voice was so loud and insistent that both men preferred to go to jail rather than serve in the Armed Forces. There was never any question about the sincerity and depth of Seeger's convictions as a conscientious objector, and the same is true of Welsh. . . . But in both cases the Selective Service System concluded that the beliefs of these men were in some sense insufficiently "religious" to qualify them for conscientious objector exemptions under the terms of § 6 (j). Seeger's conscientious objector claim was denied "solely because it was not based upon a 'belief in a relation to a Supreme Being' as required by § 6 (j) of the Act," while Welsh was denied the exemption because his Appeal Board and the Department of Justice hearing officer "could find no religious basis for the registrant's beliefs, opinions and convictions." Both Seeger and Welsh subsequently refused to submit to induction into the military and both were convicted of that offense.

. . .

. . . What is necessary under *Seeger* for a registrant's conscientious objection to all war to be "religious" within the meaning of [the selective service law] is that this opposition to war stem from the registrant's moral, ethical, or religious beliefs about what is right and wrong and that these beliefs be held with the strength of traditional religious convictions. Most of the great religions of today and of the past have embodied the idea of a Supreme Being or a Supreme Reality—a God—who communicates to man in some way a consciousness of what is right and should be done, of what is wrong and therefore should be shunned. If an individual deeply and sincerely holds beliefs that are purely ethical or moral in source and content but that nevertheless impose upon him a duty of conscience to refrain from participating in any war at any time, those beliefs certainly occupy in the life of that individual "a place parallel to that filled by . . . God" in traditionally religious persons. Because his beliefs function as a religion in his life, such an individual is as much entitled to a "religious" conscientious objector exemption . . . as is someone who derives his conscientious opposition to war from traditional religious convictions.

The Government . . . seeks to distinguish *Seeger* on the ground that Welsh's views, unlike Seeger's, were "essentially political, sociological, or philosophical views or a merely personal moral code." As previously noted, the Government made the same argument about Seeger, and not without reason, for Seeger's views had a substantial political dimension. In this case, Welsh's conscientious objection to war was undeniably based in part on his perception of world politics. . . .

We certainly do not think that . . . exclusion of those persons with "essentially political, sociological, or philosophical views or a merely personal moral code" should be read to exclude those who hold strong beliefs about our domestic and foreign affairs or even those whose conscientious objection to participation in all wars is founded to a substantial extent upon considerations of public policy. The two groups of registrants that obviously do fall within these exclusions from the exemption are those whose beliefs are not deeply held and those whose objection to war does not rest at all upon moral, ethical, or religious principle but instead rests solely upon considerations of policy, pragmatism, or expediency. . . .

. . . On the basis of [his] beliefs and the conclusion of the Court of Appeals that he held them "with the strength of more traditional religious convictions," we think Welsh was clearly entitled to a conscientious objector exemption. Section 6 (j) requires no more. That section exempts from military service all those whose consciences, spurred by deeply held moral, ethical, or religious beliefs, would give them no rest or peace if they allowed themselves to become a part of an instrument of war.

The judgment is

Reversed.

Mr. Justice Blackmun took no part in the consideration or decision of this case.

Mr. Justice Harlan, concurring in the result.

Candor requires me to say that I joined the Court's opinion in *United States v. Seeger*, 380 U.S. 163 (1965), only with the gravest misgivings as to whether it was a legitimate exercise in statutory construction, and today's decision convinces me that in doing so I made a mistake which I should now acknowledge.

In *Seeger* the Court construed § 6 (j) of the Universal Military Training and Service Act so as to sustain a conscientious objector claim not founded on a theistic belief. . . . Today the prevailing opinion makes explicit its total elimination of the statutorily required religious content for a conscientious objector exemption. The prevailing opinion now says: "If an individual deeply and sincerely holds beliefs that are purely ethical or moral in source and content but that nevertheless impose upon him a duty

of conscience to refrain from participating in any war at any time" he qualifies for a[n] exemption.

The natural reading of [the provision], which quite evidently draws a distinction between theistic and nontheistic religions, is the only one that is consistent with the legislative history. . . .

Against this legislative history it is a remarkable feat of judicial surgery to remove, as did *Seeger*, the theistic requirement. . . . The prevailing opinion today, however, in the name of interpreting the will of Congress, has performed a lobotomy and completely transformed the statute by reading out of it any distinction between religiously acquired beliefs and those deriving from "essentially political, sociological, or philosophical views or a merely personal moral code."

. . .

. . . That it is difficult to plot the semantic penumbra of the word "religion" does not render this term so plastic in meaning that the Court is entitled, as matter of statutory construction, to conclude that any asserted and strongly held belief satisfies its requirements. It must be recognized that the permissible shadow of connotation is limited by the context in which words are used. . . .

For me this dichotomy reveals that Congress was not embracing that definition of religion that alone speaks in terms of "devotion or fidelity" to individual principles acquired on an individualized basis but was adopting, at least, those meanings that associate religion with formal, organized worship or shared beliefs by a recognizable and cohesive group. . . .

Unless we are to assume an Alice-in-Wonderland world where words have no meaning, I think it fair to say that Congress' choice of language cannot fail to convey to the discerning reader the very policy choice that the prevailing opinion today completely obliterates: that between conventional religions that usually have an organized and formal structure and dogma and a cohesive group identity, even when nontheistic, and cults that represent schools of thought and in the usual case are without formal structure or are, at most, loose and informal associations of individuals who share common ethical, moral, or intellectual views.

. . .

The constitutional question that must be faced in this case is whether a statute that defers to the individual's conscience only when his views emanate from adherence to theistic religious beliefs is within the power of Congress. Congress, of course, could, entirely consistently with the requirements of the Constitution, eliminate all exemptions for conscientious objectors. Such a course would be wholly "neutral" and, in my view, would not offend the Free Exercise Clause. . . . However, having chosen to exempt, it cannot draw the line between theistic or nontheistic religious beliefs on the one hand and secular beliefs on the other. Any such distinctions are not, in my view, compatible with the Establishment Clause of the First Amendment. . . .

The policy of exempting religious conscientious objectors is one of longstanding tradition in this country and accords recognition to what is, in a diverse and "open" society, the important value of reconciling individuality of belief with practical exigencies whenever possible. That it has been phrased in religious terms reflects, I assume, the fact that ethics and morals, while the concern of secular philosophy, have traditionally been matters taught by organized religion and that for most individuals spiritual and ethical nourishment is derived from that source. It further reflects, I would suppose, the assumption that beliefs emanating from a religious source are probably held with great intensity.

When a policy has roots so deeply embedded in history, there is a compelling reason for a court to hazard the necessary statutory repairs if they can be made within the administrative framework of the statute and without impairing other legislative goals, even though they entail, not simply eliminating an offending section, but rather building upon it. Thus I am prepared to accept the prevailing opinion's conscientious objector test, not as a reflection of congressional statutory intent but as patchwork of judicial making that cures the defect of underinclusion . . . and can be administered by local boards in the usual course of business. Like the prevailing opinion, I also conclude that petitioner's beliefs are held with the required intensity and consequently vote to reverse the judgment of conviction.

MR. JUSTICE WHITE, with whom THE CHIEF JUSTICE and MR. JUSTICE STEWART join, dissenting.

Whether or not *United States v. Seeger*, 380 U.S. 163 (1965), accurately reflected the intent of Congress in providing draft exemptions for religious conscientious objectors to war, I cannot join today's construction . . . extending draft exemption to those who disclaim religious objections to war and whose views about war represent a purely personal code arising not from religious training and belief as the statute requires but from readings in philosophy, history, and sociology. . . .

. . . If it is contrary to the express will of Congress to exempt Welsh, as I think it is, then there is no warrant for saving the religious exemption and the statute by redrafting it in this Court to include Welsh and all others like him.

The *Seeger* and *Welsh* cases focused upon the meaning of religion for statutory purposes. Any potential carryover of the Court's conceptualization in those cases seems to have been delimited significantly by it's definitional inquiry in *Wisconsin v. Yoder*. The Court in *Yoder* determined that the refusal of Amish parents to send their children to public school after the eighth grade was a function of their religious belief.[243] Preliminary to finding a constitutional violation, the Court noted that personal or philosophical objections to compulsory education laws would not implicate the exercise clause.[244] It then identified some factors it considered relevant for purposes of determining whether lifestyle and belief implicated religion.

---

[243] Wisconsin v. Yoder, 406 U.S. 205, 210–11, 216–17 (1972).
[244] *Id.* at 25.

Wisconsin v. Yoder
406 U.S. 205 (1972)

We come then to the quality of the claims of the respondents concerning the alleged encroachment of Wisconsin's compulsory school-attendance statute on their rights and the rights of their children to the free exercise of the religious beliefs they and their forebears have adhered to for almost three centuries. In evaluating those claims we must be careful to determine whether the Amish religious faith and their mode of life are, as they claim, inseparable and interdependent. A way of life, however virtuous and admirable, may not be interposed as a barrier to reasonable state regulation of education if it is based on purely secular considerations; to have the protection of the Religion Clauses, the claims must be rooted in religious belief. Although a determination of what is a "religious" belief or practice entitled to constitutional protection may present a most delicate question, the very concept of ordered liberty precludes allowing every person to make his own standards on matters of conduct in which society as a whole has important interests. Thus, if the Amish asserted their claims because of their subjective evaluation and rejection of the contemporary secular values accepted by the majority, much as Thoreau rejected the social values of his time and isolated himself at Walden Pond, their claims would not rest on a religious basis. Thoreau's choice was philosophical and personal rather than religious, and such belief does not rise to the demands of the Religion Clauses.

Giving no weight to such secular considerations, however, we see that the record in this case abundantly supports the claim that the traditional way of life of the Amish is not merely a matter of personal preference, but one of deep religious conviction, shared by an organized group, and intimately related to daily living. . . . Moreover, for the Old Order Amish, religion is not simply a matter of theocratic be-lief. As the expert witnesses explained, the Old Order Amish religion pervades and determines virtually their entire way of life, regulating it with the detail of the Talmudic diet through the strictly enforced rules of the church community.

The record shows that the respondents' religious beliefs and attitude toward life, family, and home have remained constant—perhaps some would say static—in a period of unparalleled progress in human knowledge generally and great changes in education. The respondents freely concede, and indeed assert as an article of faith, that their religious beliefs and what we would today call "life style" have not altered in fundamentals for centuries. Their way of life in a church-oriented community, separated from the outside world and "worldly" influences, their attachment to nature and the soil, is a way inherently simple and uncomplicated, albeit difficult to preserve against the pressure to conform. Their rejection of telephones, automobiles, radios, and television, their mode of dress, of speech, their habits of manual work do indeed set them apart from much of contemporary society; these customs are both symbolic and practical.

Resistance to development of standards for defining religion has reflected abiding concern with compromising constitutional interests in a society defined by religious pluralism. Insofar as the First Amendment "by its terms, gives special protection to the exercise of religion,"[245] as the Supreme Court itself has noted, the need for some attention to definition may be implicit. To the extent even a highly generalized definition "excludes some philosophies," it has been argued "that . . . is exactly what the Constitution intended."[246] Even so, the Court seems inclined to stand by the principle that probing inquiry into religious belief itself is constitutionally offensive.

---

[245] Thomas v. Review Board, 450 U.S. 707, 713 (1981).

[246] John H. Mansfield, *The Religion Clauses of the First Amendment and the Philosophy of the Constitution*, 72 CAL. L. REV. 847, 851 (1984).

Thomas v. Review Board, Indiana Employment Security Division
450 U.S. 707 (1981)

CHIEF JUSTICE BURGER delivered the opinion of the Court.

We granted certiorari to consider whether the State's denial of unemployment compensation benefits to the petitioner, a Jehovah's Witness who terminated his job because his religious beliefs forbade participation in the production of armaments, constituted a viola-tion of his First Amendment right to free exercise of religion.

Thomas terminated his employment in the Blaw-Knox Foundry & Machinery Co. when he was transferred from the roll foundry to a department that produced turrets for military tanks. He claimed his religious beliefs prevented him from participating in the production of war materials. The respondent Review Board denied him unemployment compensation benefits by applying disqualifying provisions of the Indiana Employment Security Act

Thomas, a Jehovah's Witness, was hired initially to work in the roll foundry at Blaw-Knox. The function of that department was to fabricate sheet steel for a variety of industrial uses. On his application form, he listed his membership in the Jehovah's Witnesses, and noted that his hobbies were Bible study and Bible reading. However, he placed no conditions on his employment; and he did not describe his religious tenets in any detail on the form.

Approximately a year later, the roll foundry closed, and Blaw-Knox transferred Thomas to a department that fabricated turrets for military tanks. On his first day at this new job, Thomas realized that the work he was doing was weapons related. He checked the bulletin board where in-plant openings were listed, and discovered that all of the remaining departments at Blaw-Knox were engaged directly in the production of weapons. Since no transfer to another department would resolve his problem, he asked for a layoff. When that request was denied, he quit, asserting that he could not work on weapons without violating the principles of his religion. . . .

Upon leaving Blaw-Knox, Thomas applied for unemployment compensation benefits under the Indiana Employment Security Act. At an administrative hearing . . . , he testified that he believed that contributing to the production of arms violated his religion. . . .

When asked at the hearing to explain what kind of work his religious convictions would permit, Thomas said that he would have no difficulty doing the type of work that he had done at the roll foundry. He testified that he could, in good conscience, engage indirectly in the production of materials that might be used ultimately to fabricate arms—for example, as an employee of a raw material supplier or of a roll foundry.

The hearing referee found that Thomas' religious beliefs specifically precluded him from producing or directly aiding in the manufacture of items used in warfare. He also found that Thomas had terminated his employment because of these religious convictions. . . .

The [State Supreme] court found the basis and the precise nature of Thomas' belief unclear—but it concluded that the belief was more "personal philosophical choice" than religious belief.

Only beliefs rooted in religion are protected by the Free Exercise Clause, which, by its terms, gives special protection to the exercise of religion. The determination of what is a "religious" belief or practice is more often

than not a difficult and delicate task, as the division in the Indiana Supreme Court attests. However, the resolution of that question is not to turn upon a judicial perception of the particular belief or practice in question; religious beliefs need not be acceptable, logical, consistent, or comprehensible to others in order to merit First Amendment protection.

In support of his claim for benefits, Thomas testified:

> "Q. And then when it comes to actually producing the tank itself, hammering it out; that you will not do. . . .
> "A. That's right, that's right when . . . I'm daily faced with the knowledge that these are tanks. . . .
>
> . . .
>
> "A. I really could not, you know, conscientiously continue to work with armaments. It would be against all of the . . . religious principles that . . . I have come to learn. . . ."

Based upon this and other testimony, the referee held that Thomas "quit due to his religious convictions." The Review Board adopted that finding, and the finding is not challenged in this Court.

The Indiana Supreme Court apparently took a different view of the record. It concluded that "although the claimant's reasons for quitting were described as religious, it was unclear what his belief was, and what the religious basis of his belief was." In that court's view, Thomas had made a merely "personal philosophical choice rather than a religious choice."

In reaching its conclusion, the Indiana court seems to have placed considerable reliance on the facts that Thomas was "struggling" with his beliefs and that he was not able to "articulate" his belief precisely. It noted, for example, that Thomas admitted before the referee that he would not object to

> "working for United States Steel or Inland Steel . . . [producing] the raw product necessary for the production of any kind of tank . . . [because I] would not be a direct party to whoever they shipped it to [and] would not be . . . chargeable in . . . conscience.

The court found this position inconsistent with Thomas' stated opposition to participation in the production of armaments. But Thomas' statements reveal no more than that he found work in the roll foundry sufficiently insulated from producing weapons of war. We see, therefore, that Thomas drew a line, and it is not for us to say that the line he drew was an unreasonable one. Courts should not undertake to dissect religious beliefs because the believer admits that he is "struggling" with his position or because his beliefs are not articulated with the clarity and precision that a more sophisticated person might employ.

The Indiana court also appears to have given significant weight to the fact that another Jehovah's Witness had no scruples about working on tank turrets; for that other Witness, at least, such work was "scripturally" acceptable. Intrafaith differences of that kind are not uncommon among followers of a particular creed, and the judicial process is singularly ill equipped to resolve such differences in relation to the Religion Clauses. One can, of course, imagine an asserted claim so bizarre, so clearly nonreligious in motivation, as not to be entitled to protection under the Free Exercise Clause; but that is not the case here, and the guarantee of free exercise is not limited to beliefs which are shared by all of the members of a religious sect. Particularly in this sensitive area, it is not within the judicial function and judicial competence to inquire whether the petitioner or his fellow worker more correctly perceived the commands of their common faith.

Courts are not arbiters of scriptural interpretation.

. . .

2. The Establishment Clause

a. Historical Understandings

Formulation of establishment clause doctrine has been a highly competitive exercise among theorists. History has been a primary reference point in the formulation of principles that have defined the meaning of the establishment clause. Much establishment clause jurisprudence has been driven by metaphor, specifically the notion of a wall between church and state. A primary wellspring of such analysis is the Court's decision in *Everson v. Board of Education.* Although doctrinally investing in the premise of a wall between church and state, the Court upheld a tuition reimbursement plan for parents sending their children to nonpublic schools—including those providing parochial education.

Everson v. Board of Education, Township of Ewing
300 U.S. 1 (1947)

MR. JUSTICE BLACK delivered the opinion of the Court.

A New Jersey statute authorizes its local school districts to make rules and contracts for the transportation of children to and from schools. The appellee, a township board of education, acting pursuant to this statute, authorized reimbursement to parents of money expended by them for the business transportation of their children on regular busses operated by the public transportation system. Part of this money was for the payment of transportation of some children in the community to Catholic parochial schools. These church schools give their students, in addition to secular education, regular religious instruction conforming to the religious tenets and modes of worship of the Catholic Faith. The superintendent of these schools is a Catholic priest.

The appellant, in his capacity as a district taxpayer, filed suit in a state court challenging the right of the Board to reimburse parents of parochial school students. He contended that the statute and the resolution passed pursuant to it violated both the State and the Federal Constitutions. That court held that the legislature was without power to authorize such payment under the state constitution. . . .

The only contention here is that the state statute and the resolution, insofar as they authorized reimbursement to parents of children attending parochial schools, violate the Federal Constitution in these two respects, which to some extent overlap. First. They authorize the State to take by taxation the private property of some and bestow it upon others, to be used for their own private purposes. This, it is alleged, violates the due process clause of the Fourteenth Amendment. Second. The statute and the resolution forced inhabitants to pay taxes to help support and maintain schools which are dedicated to, and which regularly teach, the Catholic Faith. This is alleged to be a use of state power to support church schools contrary to the prohibition of the First Amendment which the Fourteenth Amendment made applicable to the states.

. . .

It is much too late to argue that legislation intended to facilitate the opportunity of children to get a secular education serves no public purpose. The same thing is no less true of legislation to reimburse needy parents, or all parents, for payment of the fares of their children so that they can ride in public busses to and from schools rather than run the risk of traffic and other hazards incident to walking or "hitchhiking." Nor does it follow that a law has a private rather than a public purpose because it provides that tax-raised funds will be paid to reimburse individuals on account of money spent by them in a way which furthers a public program. Subsidies and loans to individuals such as farmers and home-owners, and to privately owned transportation systems, as well as many other kinds of businesses, have been commonplace practices in our state and national history.

. . . The New Jersey statute is challenged as a "law respecting an establishment of religion." The First Amendment, as made applicable to the states by the Fourteenth, commands that a state "shall make no law respecting an establishment of religion, or prohibiting the free exercise thereof. . . . " These words of the First Amendment reflected in the minds of early Americans a vivid mental picture of conditions and practices which they fervently wished to stamp out in order to preserve liberty for themselves and for their posterity. Doubtless their goal has not been entirely reached; but so far has the Nation moved toward it that the expression "law respecting an establishment of religion," probably does not so vividly remind present-day Americans of the evils, fears, and political problems that caused that expression to be written into our Bill of Rights. Whether this New Jersey law is one respecting an "establishment of religion" requires an understanding of the meaning of that language, particularly with respect to the imposition of taxes. Once again, therefore, it is not inappropriate briefly to review the background and environment of the period in which that constitutional language was fashioned and adopted.

A large proportion of the early settlers of this country came here from Europe to escape the bondage of laws which compelled them to support and attend government-favored churches. The centuries immediately before and contemporaneous with the colonization of America had been filled with turmoil, civil strife, and persecutions, generated in large part by established sects determined to maintain their absolute political and religious supremacy. With the power of government supporting them, at various times and places, Catholics had persecuted Protestants, Protestants had persecuted Catholics, Protestant sects had persecuted other Protestant sects, Catholics of one shade of belief had persecuted Catholics of another shade of belief, and all of these had from time to time persecuted Jews. In efforts to force loyalty to whatever religious group happened to be on top and in league with the government of a particular time and place, men and women had been fined, cast in jail, cruelly tortured, and killed. Among the offenses for which these punishments had been inflicted were such things as speaking disrespectfully of the views of ministers of government-established churches, non-attendance at those churches, expressions of nonbelief in their doctrines, and failure to pay taxes and tithes to support them.

These practices of the old world were transplanted to and began to thrive in the soil of the new America. The very charters granted by the English Crown to the individuals and companies designated to make the laws which would control the destinies of the colonials authorized these individuals and companies to erect religious establishments which all, whether believers or non-believers, would be required to support and attend. An exercise of this authority was accompanied by a repetition of many of the old-world practices and persecutions. . . .

These practices became so commonplace as to shock the freedom-loving colonials into a feeling of abhorrence. The imposition of taxes to pay ministers' salaries and to build and maintain churches and church property aroused their indignation. It was these feelings which found expression in the First Amendment. No one locality and no one group throughout the Colonies can rightly be given entire credit for having aroused the sentiment that culminated in adoption of the Bill of Rights' provisions embracing religious liberty. But Virginia, where the established church had achieved a dominant influence in political affairs and where many excesses attracted wide public attention, provided a great stimulus and able leadership for the movement. The people there, as elsewhere, reached the conviction that individual religious liberty could be achieved best under a government which was stripped of all power to tax, to support, or otherwise to assist any or all religions, or to interfere with the beliefs of any religious individual or group.

The movement toward this end reached its dramatic climax in Virginia in 1785–86 when the Virginia legislative body was about to renew Virginia's tax levy for the support of the established church. Thomas Jefferson and James Madison led the fight against this tax. Madison wrote his great Memorial and Remonstrance against the law. In it, he eloquently argued that a true religion did not need the support of law; that no person, either believer or non-believer, should be taxed to support a religious institution of any kind; that the best interest of a society required that the minds of men always be wholly free; and that cruel persecutions were the inevitable result of government-established religions. Madison's Remonstrance received strong support throughout Virginia, and the Assembly postponed consideration of the proposed tax measure until its next session. When the proposal came up for consideration at that session, it not only died in committee, but the Assembly enacted the famous "Virginia Bill for Religious Liberty" originally written by Thomas Jefferson. . . .

[T]he statute itself enacted

"That no man shall be compelled to frequent or support any religious worship, place, or ministry whatsoever, nor shall be enforced, restrained, molested, or burthened in his body or goods, nor shall otherwise suffer on account of his religious opinions or belief. . . ."

This Court has previously recognized that the provisions of the First Amendment, in the drafting and adoption of which Madison and Jefferson played such leading roles, had the same objective and were intended to provide the same protection against governmental intrusion on religious liberty as the Virginia statute. . . .

The "establishment of religion" clause of the First Amendment means at least this: Neither a state nor the Federal Government can set up a church. Neither can pass laws which aid one religion, aid all religions, or prefer one religion over another. Neither can force nor influence a person to go to or to remain away from church against his will or force him to profess a belief or disbelief in any religion. No person can be punished for entertaining or professing religious beliefs or disbeliefs, for church attendance or non-attendance. No tax in any amount, large or small, can be levied to support any religious activities or institutions, whatever they may be called, or whatever form they may adopt to teach or practice religion. Neither a state nor the Federal Government can, openly or secretly, participate in the affairs of any religious organizations or groups and vice versa. In the words of Jefferson, the clause against establishment of religion by law was intended to erect "a wall of separation between church and State." . . .

Measured by these standards, we cannot say that the First Amendment prohibits New Jersey from spending tax-raised funds to pay the business fares of parochial school pupils as a part of a general program under which it pays the fares of pupils attending public and other schools. It is undoubtedly true that children are helped to get to church schools. There is even a possibility that some of the children might not be sent to the church schools if the parents were compelled to pay their children's business fares out of their own pockets when transportation to a public school would have been paid for by the State. The same possibility exists where the state requires a local transit company to provide reduced fares to school children including those attending parochial schools, or where a municipally owned transportation system undertakes to carry all school children free of charge. Moreover, state-paid policemen, detailed to protect children going to and from church schools from the very real hazards of traffic, would serve much the same purpose and accomplish much the same result as state provisions intended to guarantee free transportation of a kind which the state deems to be best for the school children's welfare. And parents might refuse to risk their children to the serious danger of traffic accidents going to and from parochial schools, the approaches to which were not protected by policemen. Similarly, parents might be reluctant to permit their children to attend schools which the state had cut off from such general government services as ordinary police and fire protection, connections for sewage disposal, public highways and sidewalks. Of course, cutting off church schools from these services, so separate and so indisputably marked off from the religious function, would make it far more difficult for the schools to operate. But such is obviously not the purpose of the First Amendment. That Amendment requires the state to be a neutral in its relations with groups of religious believers and non-believers; it does not require the state to be their adversary. State power is no more to be used so as to handicap religions than it is to favor them.

This Court has said that parents may, in the discharge of their duty under state compulsory education laws, send their children to a religious rather than a public school if the school meets the secular educational requirements which the state has power to impose. It appears that these parochial schools meet New Jersey's requirements. The State contributes no money to the schools. It does not support them. Its legislation, as applied, does no more than provide a general program to help parents get their children, regardless of their religion, safely and expeditiously to and from accredited schools.

The First Amendment has erected a wall between church and state. That wall must be kept high and impregnable. We could not approve the slightest breach. New Jersey has not breached it here.

Affirmed.

MR. JUSTICE JACKSON, dissenting.

I find myself, contrary to first impressions, unable to join in this decision. I have a sympathy, though it is not ideological, with Catholic citizens who are compelled by law to pay taxes for public schools, and also feel constrained by conscience and discipline to support other schools for their own children. Such relief to them as this case involves is not in itself a serious burden to taxpayers and I had assumed it to be as little serious in principle. Study of this case convinces me otherwise. The Court's opinion marshals every argument in favor of state aid and puts the case in its most favorable light, but much of its reasoning confirms my conclusions that there are no good grounds upon which to support the present legislation. In fact, the undertones of the opinion, advocating complete and uncompromising separation of Church from State, seem utterly discordant with its conclusion yielding support to their commingling in educational matters. The case which irresistibly comes to mind as the most fitting precedent is that of Julia who, according to Byron's reports, "whispering 'I will ne'er consent,'—consented."

. . .

It seems to me that the basic fallacy in the Court's reasoning, which accounts for its failure to apply the principles it avows, is in ignoring the essentially religious test by which beneficiaries of this expenditure are selected. A policeman protects a Catholic, of course—but not because he is a Catholic; it is because he is a man and a member of our society. The fireman protects the Church school—but not because it is a Church school; it is because it is property, part of the assets of our society. Neither the fireman nor the policeman has to ask before he renders aid "Is this man or building identified with the Catholic Church?" But before these school authorities draw a check to reimburse for a student's fare they must ask just that question, and if the school is a Catholic one they may render aid because it is such, while if it is of any other faith or is run for profit, the help must be withheld. To consider the converse of the Court's reasoning will best disclose its fallacy. That there is no parallel between police and fire protection and this plan of reimbursement is apparent from the incongruity of the limitation of this Act if applied to police and fire service. Could we sustain an Act that said the police shall protect pupils on the way to or from public schools and Catholic schools but not while going to and coming from other schools, and firemen shall extinguish a blaze in public or Catholic school buildings but shall not put out a blaze in Protestant Church schools or private schools operated for profit? That is the true analogy to the case we have

before us and I should think it pretty plain that such a scheme would not be valid.

The Court's holding is that this taxpayer has no grievance because the state has decided to make the reimbursement a public purpose and therefore we are bound to regard it as such. I agree that this Court has left, and always should leave to each state, great latitude in deciding for itself, in the light of its own conditions, what shall be public purposes in its scheme of things. It may socialize utilities and economic enterprises and make taxpayers' business out of what conventionally had been private business. It may make public business of individual welfare, health, education, entertainment or security. But it cannot make public business of religious worship or instruction, or of attendance at religious institutions of any character. There is no answer to the proposition, more fully expounded by MR. JUSTICE RUTLEDGE, that the effect of the religious freedom Amendment to our Constitution was to take every form of propagation of religion out of the realm of things which could directly or indirectly be made public business and thereby be supported in whole or in part at taxpayers' expense. That is a difference which the Constitution sets up between religion and almost every other subject matter of legislation, a difference which goes to the very root of religious freedom and which the Court is overlooking today. This freedom was first in the Bill of Rights because it was first in the forefathers' minds; it was set forth in absolute terms, and its strength is its rigidity. It was intended not only to keep the states' hands out of religion, but to keep religion's hands off the state, and, above all, to keep bitter religious controversy out of public life by denying to every denomination any advantage from getting control of public policy or the public purse. Those great ends I cannot but think are immeasurably compromised by today's decision.

. . .

. . . [W]e cannot have it both ways. Religious teaching cannot be a private affair when the state seeks to impose regulations which infringe on it indirectly, and a public affair when it comes to taxing citizens of one faith to aid another, or those of no faith to aid all. If these principles seem harsh in prohibiting aid to Catholic education, it must not be forgotten that it is the same Constitution that alone assures Catholics the right to maintain these schools at all when predominant local sentiment would forbid them. Nor should I think that those who have done so well without this aid would want to see this separation between Church and State broken down. If the state may aid these religious schools, it may therefore regulate them. Many groups have sought aid from tax funds only to find that it carried political controls with it. Indeed this Court has declared that "It is hardly lack of due process for the Government to regulate that which it subsidizes."

But in any event, the great purposes of the Constitution do not depend on the approval or convenience of those they restrain. I cannot read the history of the struggle to separate political from ecclesiastical affairs, . . . without a conviction that the Court today is unconsciously giving the clock's hands a backward turn.

MR. JUSTICE FRANKFURTER joins in this opinion.

MR. JUSTICE RUTLEDGE, with whom MR. JUSTICE FRANKFURTER, MR. JUSTICE JACKSON and MR. JUSTICE BURTON agree, dissenting.

. . .

Not simply an established church, but any law respecting an establishment of religion is forbidden. The Amendment was broadly but not loosely phrased. It is the compact and exact summation of its author's views formed during his long struggle for religious freedom. In Madison's own words characterizing Jefferson's Bill for Establishing Religious Freedom, the guaranty he put in our national charter, like the bill he piloted through the Virginia Assembly, was "a Model of technical precision, and perspicuous brevity." Madison could not have confused "church" and "religion," or "an established church" and "an establishment of religion."

The Amendment's purpose was not to strike merely at the official establishment of a single sect, creed or religion, outlawing only a formal relation such as had prevailed in England and some of the colonies. Necessarily it was to uproot all such relationships. But the object was broader than separating church and state in this narrow sense. It was to create a complete and permanent separation of the spheres of religious activity and civil authority by comprehensively forbidding every form of public aid or support for religion. In proof the Amendment's wording and history unite with this Court's consistent utterances whenever attention has been fixed directly upon the question.

. . .

Compulsory attendance upon religious exercises went out early in the process of separating church and state, together with forced observance of religious forms and ceremonies. Test oaths and religious qualification for office followed later. These things none devoted to our great tradition of religious liberty would think of bringing back. Hence today, apart from efforts to inject religious training or exercises and sectarian issues into the public schools, the only serious surviving threat to maintaining that complete and permanent separation of religion and civil power which the First Amendment commands is through use of the taxing power to support religion, religious establishments, or establishments having a religious foundation whatever their form or special religious function.

Does New Jersey's action furnish support for religion by use of the taxing power? Certainly it does, if the test remains undiluted as Jefferson and Madison made it, that money taken by taxation from one is not to be used or given to support another's religious training or belief, or indeed one's own. Today as then the furnishing of "contributions of money for the propagation of opinions which he disbelieves" is the forbidden exaction; and the prohibition is absolute for whatever measure brings that consequence and whatever amount may be sought or given to that end.

The funds used here were raised by taxation. The Court does not dispute, nor could it, that their use does in fact give aid and encouragement to religious instruction. It only concludes that this aid is not "support" in law. But Madison and Jefferson were concerned with aid and support in fact, not as a legal conclusion "entangled in precedents." Here parents pay money to send their children to parochial schools and funds raised by taxation are used to reimburse them. This not only helps the children to get to school and the parents to send them. It aids them in a substantial way to get the very thing which they are sent to the particular school to secure, namely, religious training and teaching.

Believers of all faiths, and others who do not express their feeling toward ultimate issues of existence in any creedal form, pay the New Jersey tax. When the money so raised is used to pay for transportation to religious schools, the Catholic taxpayer to the extent of his proportionate share pays for the transportation of Lutheran, Jewish and otherwise religiously affiliated children to receive their non-Catholic religious instruction. Their parents likewise pay proportionately for the transportation of Catholic children to receive Catholic instruction. Each thus contributes to "the propagation of opinions which he disbelieves" in so far as their religions differ, as do others who accept no creed without regard to those differences. Each thus pays taxes also to support the teaching of his own religion, an exaction equally forbidden since it denies "the comfortable liberty" of giving one's contribution to the particular agency of instruction he approves.

New Jersey's action therefore exactly fits the type of exaction and the kind of evil at which Madison and Jefferson struck. Under the test they framed it cannot be said that the cost of transportation is no part of the cost of education or of the religious instruction given.

That it is a substantial and a necessary element is shown most plainly by the continuing and increasing demand for the state to assume it. Nor is there pretense that it relates only to the secular instruction given in religious schools or that any attempt is or could be made toward allocating proportional shares as between the secular and the religious instruction. It is precisely because the instruction is religious and relates to a particular faith, whether one or another, that parents send their children to religious schools . . . And the very purpose of the state's contribution is to defray the cost of conveying the pupil to the place where he will receive not simply secular, but also and primarily religious, teaching and guidance.

For me, therefore, the feat is impossible to select so indispensable an item from the composite of total costs, and characterize it as not aiding, contributing to, promoting or sustaining the propagation of beliefs which it is the very end of all to bring about. Unless this can be maintained, and the Court does not maintain it, the aid thus given is outlawed. Payment of transportation is no more, nor is it any the less essential to education, whether religious or secular, than payment for tuitions, for teachers' salaries, for buildings, equipment and necessary materials. Nor is it any the less directly related, in a school giving religious instruction, to the primary religious objective all those essential items of cost are intended to achieve. No rational line can be drawn between payment for such larger, but not more necessary, items and payment for transportation. The only line that can be so drawn is one between more dollars and less. Certainly in this realm such a line can be no valid constitutional measure. Now, as in Madison's time, not the amount but the principle of assessment is wrong.

. . .

The reasons underlying the Amendment's policy have not vanished with time or diminished in force. Now as when it was adopted the price of religious freedom is double. It is that the church and religion shall live both within and upon that freedom. There cannot be freedom of religion, safeguarded by the state, and intervention by the church or its agencies in the state's domain or dependency on its largesse. The great condition of religious liberty is that it be maintained free from sustenance, as also from other interferences, by the state. For when it comes to rest upon that secular foundation it vanishes with the resting. Public money devoted to payment of religious costs, educational or other, brings the quest for more. It brings too the struggle of sect against sect for the larger share or for any. Here one by

numbers alone will benefit most, there another. That is precisely the history of societies which have had an established religion and dissident groups. It is the very thing Jefferson and Madison experienced and sought to guard against, whether in its blunt or in its more screened forms. The end of such strife cannot be other than to destroy the cherished liberty. The dominating group will achieve the dominant benefit; or all will embroil the state in their dissensions.

. . .

No one conscious of religious values can be unsympathetic toward the burden which our constitutional separation puts on parents who desire religious instruction mixed with secular for their children. They pay taxes for others' children's education, at the same time the added cost of instruction for their own. Nor can one happily see benefits denied to children which others receive, because in conscience they or their parents for them desire a different kind of training others do not demand.

But if those feelings should prevail, there would be an end to our historic constitutional policy and command. No more unjust or discriminatory in fact is it to deny attendants at religious schools the cost of their transportation than it is to deny them tuitions, sustenance for their teachers, or any other educational expense which others receive at public cost. Hardship in fact there is which none can blink. But, for assuring to those who undergo it the greater, the most comprehensive freedom, it is one written by design and firm intent into our basic law.

. . .

Two great drives are constantly in motion to abridge, in the name of education, the complete division of religion and civil authority which our forefathers made. One is to introduce religious education and observances into the public schools. The other, to obtain public funds for the aid and support of various private religious schools. In my opinion both avenues were closed by the Constitution. Neither should be opened by this Court. The matter is not one of quantity, to be measured by the amount of money expended. Now as in Madison's day it is one of principle, to keep separate the separate spheres as the First Amendment drew them; to prevent the first experiment upon our liberties; and to keep the question from becoming entangled in corrosive precedents. We should not be less strict to keep strong and untarnished the one side of the shield of religious freedom than we have been of the other.

The judgment should be reversed.

Despite the Court's doctrinal unanimity in *Everson*, subsequent case law challenged the wall of separation premise on grounds it was historically misplaced. Justice Rehnquist in particular has characterized it as a "metaphor based on bad history."[247] In *Wallace v. Jaffree*, he argued that the original purpose of the establishment clause was only to prohibit creation of a national religion and possibly prevent discrimination among sects.

---

[247] Wallace v. Jaffree, 472 U.S. 38, 107 (1985) (Rehnquist, J., dissenting).

Wallace v. Jaffree
472 U.S. 38 (1985)

JUSTICE REHNQUIST, dissenting.

Thirty-eight years ago this Court, in *Everson v. Board of Education*, 330 U.S. 1, 16 (1947), summarized its exegesis of Establishment Clause doctrine thus:

> "In the words of Jefferson, the clause against establishment of religion by law was intended to erect 'a wall of separation between church and State.' *Reynolds v. United States*, [98 U.S. 145, 164 (1879)]."

This language . . . quoted from Thomas Jefferson's letter to the Danbury Baptist Association the phrase "I contemplate with sovereign reverence that act of the whole American people which declared that their legislature should 'make no law respecting an establishment of religion, or prohibiting the free exercise thereof,' thus building a wall of separation between church and State."

It is impossible to build sound constitutional doctrine upon a mistaken understanding of constitutional history, but unfortunately the Establishment Clause has been expressly freighted with Jefferson's misleading metaphor for nearly 40 years. Thomas Jefferson was of course in France at the time the constitutional Amendments known as the Bill of Rights were passed by Congress and ratified by the States. His letter to the Danbury Baptist Association was a short note of courtesy, written 14 years after the Amendments were passed by Congress. He would seem to any detached observer as a less than ideal source of contemporary history as to the meaning of the Religion Clauses of the First Amendment.

Jefferson's fellow Virginian, James Madison, with whom he was joined in the battle for the enactment of the Virginia Statute of Religious Liberty of 1786, did play as large a part as anyone in the drafting of the Bill of Rights. He had two advantages over Jefferson in this regard: he was present in the United States, and he was a leading Member of the First Congress. But when we turn to the record of the proceedings in the First Congress leading up to the adoption of the Establishment Clause of the Constitution, including Madison's significant contributions thereto, we see a far different picture of its purpose than the highly simplified "wall of separation between church and State."

. . .

On June 8, 1789, James Madison rose in the House of Representatives and "reminded the House that this was the day that he had heretofore named for bringing forward amendments to the Constitution." Madison's subsequent remarks in urging the House to adopt his drafts of the proposed amendments were less those of a dedicated advocate of the wisdom of such measures than those of a prudent statesman seeking the enactment of measures sought by a number of his fellow citizens which could surely do no harm and might do a great deal of good. . . .

On the basis of the record of these proceedings in the House of Representatives, James Madison was undoubtedly the most important architect among the Members of the House of the Amendments which became the Bill of Rights, but it was James Madison speaking as an advocate of sensible legislative compromise, not as an advocate of incorporating the Virginia Statute of Religious Liberty into the United States Constitution. During the ratification debate in the Virginia Convention, Madison had actually opposed the idea of any Bill of Rights. His sponsorship of the Amendments in the House was obviously not that of a zealous believer in the necessity of the Religion Clauses, but of one who felt it might do some good, could do no harm, and would satisfy those who had ratified the Constitution on the condition that Congress propose a Bill of Rights. His original language "nor shall any national religion be established" obviously does not conform to the "wall of separation" between church and State idea which latter-day commentators have ascribed to him. His explanation on the floor of the meaning of his language—that Congress should not establish a religion, and enforce the legal observation of it by law"—is of the same ilk. When he replied . . . in the debate over the proposal which came from the Select Committee of the House, he urged that the language "no religion shall be established by law" should be amended by inserting the word "national" in front of the word "religion."

It seems indisputable from these glimpses of Madison's thinking, as reflected by actions on the floor of the House in 1789, that he saw the Amendment as designed to prohibit the establishment of a national religion, and perhaps to prevent discrimination among sects. He did not see it as requiring neutrality on the part of government between religion and irreligion. Thus the Court's opinion in *Everson*—while correct in bracketing Madison and Jefferson together in their exertions in their home State leading to the enactment of the Virginia Statute of Religious Liberty—is totally incorrect in suggesting that Madison carried these views onto the floor of the United States House of Representatives when he proposed the language which would ultimately become the Bill of Rights.

. . .

None of the other Members of Congress who spoke during the August 15th debate expressed the slightest indication that they thought the language before them from the Select Committee, or the evil to be aimed at, would require that the Government be absolutely neutral as between religion and irreligion. The evil to be aimed at, so far as those who spoke were concerned, appears to have been the establishment of a national church, and perhaps the preference of one religious sect over another; but it was definitely not concerned about whether the Government might aid all religions evenhandedly. . . .

The actions of the First Congress, which reenacted the Northwest Ordinance for the governance of the Northwest Territory in 1789, confirm the view that Congress did not mean that the Government should be neutral between religion and irreligion. The House of Representatives took up the Northwest Ordinance on the same day as Madison introduced his proposed amendments which became the Bill of Rights; while at that time the Federal Government was of course not bound by draft amendments to the Constitution which had not yet been proposed by Congress, say nothing of ratified by the States, it seems highly unlikely that the House of Representatives would simultaneously consider proposed amendments to the Constitution and enact an important piece of territorial legislation which conflicted with the intent of those proposals. The Northwest Ordinance, 1 Stat. 50, reenacted the

Northwest Ordinance of 1787 and provided that "[religion], morality, and knowledge, being necessary to good government and the happiness of mankind, schools and the means of education shall forever be encouraged." . . .

On the day after the House of Representatives voted to adopt the form of the First Amendment Religion Clauses which was ultimately proposed and ratified, Representative Elias Boudinot proposed a resolution asking President George Washington to issue a Thanksgiving Day proclamation. Boudinot said he "could not think of letting the session pass over without offering an opportunity to all the citizens of the United States of joining with one voice, in returning to Almighty God their sincere thanks for the many blessings he had poured down upon them." . . .

Boudinot's resolution was carried in the affirmative on September 25, 1789. . . .

Within two weeks of this action by the House, George Washington responded to the Joint Resolution which by now had been changed to include the language that the President "recommend to the people of the United States a day of public thanksgiving and prayer, to be observed by acknowledging with grateful hearts the many and signal favors of Almighty God, especially by affording them an opportunity peaceably to establish a form of government for their safety and happiness." . . .

As the United States moved from the 18th into the 19th century, Congress appropriated time and again public moneys in support of sectarian Indian education carried on by religious organizations. . . .

Joseph Story, a Member of this Court from 1811 to 1845, and during much of that time a professor at the Harvard Law School, published by far the most comprehensive treatise on the United States Constitution that had then appeared. Volume 2 of Story's Commentaries on the Constitution of the United States 630–632 (5th ed. 1891) discussed the meaning of the Establishment Clause of the First Amendment this way:

> "Probably at the time of the adoption of the Constitution, and of the amendment to it now under consideration [First Amendment], the general if not the universal sentiment in America was, that Christianity ought to receive encouragement from the State so far as was not incompatible with the private rights of conscience and the freedom of religious worship. An attempt to level all religions, and to make it a matter of state policy to hold all in utter indifference, would have created universal disapproval, if not universal indignation.
>
> . . .

"The real object of the [First] [Amendment] was not to countenance, much less to advance, Mahometanism, or Judaism, or infidelity, by prostrating Christianity; but to exclude all rivalry among Christian sects, and to prevent any national ecclesiastical establishment which should give to a hierarchy the exclusive patronage of the national government. It thus cut off the means of religious persecution (the vice and pest of former ages), and of the subversion of the rights of conscience in matters of religion, which had been trampled upon almost from the days of the Apostles to the present age. . . ."

Thomas Cooley's eminence as a legal authority rivaled that of Story. Cooley stated in his treatise entitled Constitutional Limitations that aid to a particular religious sect was prohibited by the United States Constitution, but he went on to say:

But while thus careful to establish, protect, and defend religious freedom and equality, the American constitutions contain no provisions which prohibit the authorities from such solemn recognition of a superintending Providence in public transactions and exercises as the general religious sentiment of mankind inspires, and as seems meet and proper in finite and dependent beings. . . . Undoubtedly the spirit of the Constitution will require, in all these cases, that care be taken to avoid discrimination in favor of or against any one religious denomination or sect; but the power to do any of these things does not become unconstitutional simply because of its susceptibility to abuse. . . ."

Cooley added that

"[this] public recognition of religious worship, however, is not based entirely, perhaps not even mainly, upon a sense of what is due to the Supreme Being himself as the author of all good and of all law; but the same reasons of state policy which induce the government to aid institutions of charity and seminaries of instruction will incline it also to foster religious worship and religious institutions, as conservators of the public morals and valuable, if not indispensable, assistants to the preservation of the public order."

It would seem from this evidence that the Establishment Clause of the First Amendment had acquired a well-accepted meaning: it forbade establishment of a national religion, and forbade preference among religious sects or denominations. Indeed, the first American dictionary defined the word "establishment" as "the act of establishing, founding, ratifying or ordaining," such as in "[the] episcopal form of religion, so called, in England." The Establishment Clause did not require government neutrality between religion and irreligion nor did it prohibit the Federal Government from providing nondiscriminatory aid to religion. There is simply no historical foundation for the proposition that the Framers intended to build the "wall of separation" that was constitutionalized in *Everson*.

. . .

. . . [T]he greatest injury of the "wall" notion is its mischievous diversion of judges from the actual intentions of the drafters of the Bill of Rights. The "crucible of litigation," is well adapted to adjudicating factual disputes on the basis of testimony presented in court, but no amount of repetition of historical errors in judicial opinions can make the errors true. The "wall of separation between church and State" is a metaphor based on bad history, a metaphor which has proved useless as a guide to judging. It should be frankly and explicitly abandoned.

. . . We have done much straining since 1947, but still we admit that we can only "dimly perceive" the *Everson* wall. Our perception has been clouded not by the Constitution but by the mists of an unnecessary metaphor.

The true meaning of the Establishment Clause can only be seen in its history. As drafters of our Bill of Rights, the Framers inscribed the principles that control today. Any deviation from their intentions frustrates the permanence of that Charter and will only lead to the type of unprincipled decisionmaking that has plagued our Establishment Clause cases since *Everson*.

The Framers intended the Establishment Clause to prohibit the designation of any church as a "national" one. The Clause was also designed to stop the Federal Government from asserting a preference for one religious denomination or sect over others. Given the "incorporation" of the Establishment Clause as against the States via the Fourteenth Amendment in *Everson*, States are prohibited as well from establishing a religion or discriminating between sects. As its history abundantly shows, however, nothing in the Establishment Clause requires government to be strictly neutral between religion and irreligion, nor does that Clause prohibit Congress or the States from pursuing legitimate secular ends through nondiscriminatory sectarian means.

. . .

Rehnquist's reading of history diverges from other readings of the same events. Dissenting from the Court's decision in *Everson*, Justice Rutledge argued that the framers meant to distance church and state even at the cost of some real societal hardship:

> No provision of the Constitution is more closely tied to or given content by its generating history than the religious clause of the First Amendment. It is at once the refined product and the terse summation of that history. The history includes not only Madison's authorship and the proceedings before the First Congress, but also the long and intensive struggle for religious freedom in America, more especially in Virginia, of which the Amendment was the direct culmination. In the documents of the times, particularly of Madison, who was leader in the Virginia struggle before he became the Amendment's sponsor, but also in the writings of Jefferson and others and in the issues which engendered them is to be found irrefutable confirmation of the Amendment's sweeping content.
>
> For Madison, as also for Jefferson, religious freedom was the crux of the struggle for freedom in general. Madison was coauthor with George Mason of the religious clause in Virginia's great Declaration of Rights of 1776. He is credited with changing it from a mere statement of the principle of tolerance to the first official legislative pronouncement that freedom of conscience and religion are inherent rights of the individual. He sought also to have the Declaration expressly condemn the existing Virginia establishment. But the forces supporting it were then too strong.
>
> Accordingly Madison yielded on this phase but not for long. At once he resumed the fight, continuing it before succeeding legislative sessions. As a member of the General Assembly in 1779 he threw his full weight behind Jefferson's historic Bill for Establishing Religious Freedom. That bill was a prime phase of Jefferson's broad program of democratic reform undertaken on his return from the Continental Congress in 1776 and submitted for the General Assembly's consideration in 1779 as his proposed revised Virginia code. With Jefferson's departure for Europe in 1784, Madison became the Bill's prime sponsor. Enactment failed in successive legislatures from its introduction in June, 1779, until its adoption in January, 1786. But during all this time the fight for religious freedom moved forward in Virginia on various fronts with growing intensity. Madison led throughout, against Patrick Henry's powerful opposing leadership, until Henry was elected governor in November, 1784.
>
> The climax came in the legislative struggle of 1784–1785 over the Assessment Bill. See Supplemental Appendix hereto. This was nothing more nor less than a taxing measure for the support of religion, designed to revive the payment of tithes suspended since 1777. So long as it singled out a particular sect for preference it incurred the active and general hostility of dissentient groups. It was broadened to include them, with the result that some subsided temporarily in their opposition. As altered, the bill gave to each taxpayer the privilege of designating which church should receive his share of the tax. In default of designation the legislature applied it to pious uses. But what is of the utmost significance here, "in its final form the bill left the taxpayer the option of giving his tax to education."
>
> Madison was unyielding at all times, opposing with all his vigor the general and nondiscriminatory as he had the earlier particular and discriminatory assessments proposed. The modified Assessment Bill passed second reading in December, 1784, and was all but enacted. Madison and his followers, however,

maneuvered deferment of final consideration until November, 1785. And before the Assembly reconvened in the fall he issued his historic Memorial and Remonstrance.

This is Madison's complete, though not his only, interpretation of religious liberty. It is a broadside attack upon all forms of "establishment" of religion, both general and particular, nondiscriminatory or selective. Reflecting not only the many legislative conflicts over the Assessment Bill and the Bill for Establishing Religious Freedom but also, for example, the struggles for religious incorporations and the continued maintenance of the glebes, the Remonstrance is at once the most concise and the most accurate statement of the views of the First Amendment's author concerning what is "an establishment of religion." Because it behooves us in the dimming distance of time not to lose sight of what he and his coworkers had in mind when, by a single sweeping stroke of the pen, they forbade an establishment of religion and secured its free exercise, the text of the Remonstrance is appended at the end of this opinion for its wider current reference, together with a copy of the bill against which it was directed.

The Remonstrance, stirring up a storm of popular protest, killed the Assessment Bill. It collapsed in committee shortly before Christmas, 1785. With this, the way was cleared at last for enactment of Jefferson's Bill for Establishing Religious Freedom. Madison promptly drove it through in January of 1786, seven years from the time it was first introduced. This dual victory substantially ended the fight over establishments, settling the issue against them.

The next year Madison became a member of the Constitutional Convention. Its work done, he fought valiantly to secure the ratification of its great product in Virginia as elsewhere, and nowhere else more effectively. Madison was certain in his own mind that under the Constitution "there is not a shadow of right in the general government to intermeddle with religion" and that "this subject is, for the honor of America, perfectly free and unshackled. The government has no jurisdiction over it. . . ." Nevertheless he pledged that he would work for a Bill of Rights, including a specific guaranty of religious freedom, and Virginia, with other states, ratified the Constitution on this assurance.

Ratification thus accomplished, Madison was sent to the first Congress. There he went at once about performing his pledge to establish freedom for the nation as he had done in Virginia. Within a little more than three years from his legislative victory at home he had proposed and secured the submission and ratification of the First Amendment as the first article of our Bill of Rights.

All the great instruments of the Virginia struggle for religious liberty thus became warp and woof of our constitutional tradition, not simply by the course of history, but by the common unifying force of Madison's life, thought and sponsorship. He epitomized the whole of that tradition in the Amendment's compact, but nonetheless comprehensive, phrasing.

As the Remonstrance discloses throughout, Madison opposed every form and degree of official relation between religion and civil authority. For him religion was a wholly private matter beyond the scope of civil power either to restrain or to support. Denial or abridgment of religious freedom was a violation of rights both of conscience and of natural equality. State aid was no less obnoxious or destructive to freedom and to religion itself than other forms of state interference. "Establishment" and "free exercise" were correlative and coextensive ideas, representing only different facets of the single great and fundamental freedom. The Remonstrance, following the Virginia statute's example, referred to the history of religious conflicts and the effects of all sorts of establishments, current and historical, to suppress religion's free exercise. With Jefferson, Madison believed that to tolerate any fragment of establishment would be by so much to perpetuate restraint upon that freedom. Hence he sought to tear out the institution not partially but root and branch, and to bar its return forever.

In no phase was he more unrelentingly absolute than in opposing state support or aid by taxation. Not even "three pence" contribution was thus to be exacted from any citizen for such a purpose. Tithes had been the lifeblood of establishment before and after other compulsions disappeared. Madison and his coworkers made no exceptions or abridgments to the complete separation they created. Their objection was not to small tithes. It was to any tithes whatsoever. "If it were lawful to impose a small tax for religion, the admission would pave the way for oppressive levies." Not the amount but "the principle of assessment was wrong." And the principle was as much to prevent "the interference of law in religion" as to restrain religious intervention in political matters. In this field the authors of our freedom would not tolerate "the first experiment on our liberties" or "wait till usurped power had strengthened itself by exercise, and entangled the question in precedents." Nor should we.

In view of this history no further proof is needed that the Amendment forbids any appropriation, large or small, from public funds to aid or support any and all religious exercises. But if more were called for, the debates in the First Congress and this Court's consistent expressions, whenever it has touched on the matter directly, supply it.

By contrast with the Virginia history, the congressional debates on consideration of the Amendment reveal only sparse discussion, reflecting the fact that the essential issues had been settled. Indeed the matter had become so well understood as to have been taken for granted in all but formal phrasing. Hence, the only enlightening reference shows concern, not to preserve any power to use public funds in aid of religion, but to prevent the Amendment from outlawing private gifts inadvertently by virtue of the breadth of its wording.[34] In the margin are noted also the principal decisions in which expressions of this Court confirm the Amendment's broad prohibition.[248]

Revisionist understanding of historical reality, especially Madison's role and influence, has begotten further inquiry into the framers' establishment clause expectations. In *Lee v. Weisman*, Justice Souter revisited the historical evidence and found the metaphorical wall to have been well-constructed.

---

[34] At one point the wording was proposed: "No religion shall be established by law, nor shall the equal rights of conscience be infringed." Representative Huntington of Connecticut feared this might be construed to prevent judicial enforcement of private pledges. He stated "that he feared . . . that the words might be taken in such latitude as to be extremely hurtful to the cause of religion. He understood the amendment to mean what had been expressed by the gentleman from Virginia; but others might find it convenient to put another construction upon it. The ministers of their congregations to the Eastward were maintained by the contributions of those who belonged to their society; the expense of building meeting-houses was contributed in the same manner. These things were regulated by by-laws. If an action was brought before a Federal Court on any of these cases, the person who had neglected to perform his engagements could not be compelled to do it; for a support of ministers or building of places of worship might be construed into a religious establishment."

To avoid any such possibility, Madison suggested inserting the word "national" before "religion," thereby not only again disclaiming intent to bring about the result Huntington feared but also showing unmistakably that "establishment" meant public "support" of religion in the financial sense.

[248] Everson v. Board of Education, 300 U.S. 1, 33–43 (1947) (Rutledge, J., dissenting).

Lee v. Weisman
112 S.Ct. 2649 (1992)

MR. JUSTICE SOUTER, concurring.

Some have challenged this precedent by reading the Establishment Clause to permit "nonpreferential" state promotion of religion. The challengers argue that, as originally understood by the Framers, "the Establishment Clause did not require government neutrality between religion and irreligion nor did it prohibit the Federal Government from providing nondiscriminatory aid to religion." *Wallace* (REHNQUIST, J., dissenting). While a case has been made for this position, it is not so convincing as to warrant reconsideration of our settled law; indeed, I find in the history of the Clause's textual development a more powerful argument supporting the Court's jurisprudence following *Everson.*

When James Madison arrived at the First Congress with a series of proposals to amend the National Constitution, one of the provisions read that "the civil rights of none shall be abridged on account of religious belief or worship, nor shall any national religion be established, nor shall the full and equal rights of conscience be in any manner, or on any pretext, infringed." Madison's language did not last long. It was sent to a Select Committee of the House, which, without explanation, changed it to read that "no religion shall be established by law, nor shall the equal rights of conscience be infringed." Thence the proposal went to the Committee of the Whole, which was in turn dissatisfied with the Select Committee's language and adopted an alternative proposed by Samuel Livermore of New Hampshire: "Congress shall make no laws touching religion, or infringing the rights of conscience." Livermore's proposal would have forbidden laws having anything to do with religion and was thus not only far broader than Madison's version, but broader even than the scope of the Establishment Clause as we now understand it.

The House rewrote the amendment once more before sending it to the Senate, this time adopting, without recorded debate, language derived from a proposal by Fisher Ames of Massachusetts: "Congress shall make no law establishing Religion, or prohibiting the free exercise thereof, nor shall the rights of conscience be infringed." . . .

The sequence of the Senate's treatment of this House proposal, and the House's response to the Senate, confirm that the Framers meant the Establishment Clause's prohibition to encompass nonpreferential aid to religion. In September 1789, the Senate considered a number of provisions that would have permitted such aid, and ultimately it adopted one of them. First, it briefly entertained this language: "Congress shall make no law establishing One Religious Sect or Society in preference to others, nor shall the rights of conscience be infringed." After rejecting two minor amendments to that proposal, the Senate dropped it altogether and chose a provision identical to the House's proposal, but without the clause protecting the "rights of conscience." With no record of the Senate debates, we cannot know what prompted these changes, but the record does tell us that, six days later, the Senate went half circle and adopted its narrowest language yet: "Congress shall make no law establishing articles of faith or a mode of worship, or prohibiting the free exercise of religion." The Senate sent this proposal to the House along with its versions of the other constitutional amendments proposed.

Though it accepted much of the Senate's work on the Bill of Rights, the House rejected the Senate's version of the Establishment Clause and called for a joint conference committee, to which the Senate agreed. The House conferees ultimately won out, persuading the Senate to accept this as the final text of the Religion Clauses: "Congress shall make no law respecting an establishment of religion, or prohibiting the free exercise thereof." What is remarkable is that, unlike the earliest House drafts or the final Senate proposal, the prevailing language is not limited to laws respecting an establishment of "a religion," "a national religion," "one religious sect," or specific "articles of faith." The Framers repeatedly considered and deliberately rejected such narrow language and instead extended their prohibition to state support for "religion" in general.

Implicit in their choice is the distinction between preferential and nonpreferential establishments, which the weight of evidence suggests the Framers appreciated. Of particular note, the Framers were vividly familiar with efforts in the colonies and, later, the States to impose general, nondenominational assessments and other incidents of ostensibly ecumenical establishments. The Virginia Statute for Religious Freedom, written by Jefferson and sponsored by Madison, captured the separationist response to such measures. Condemning all establishments, however nonpreferentialist, the Statute broadly Guaranteed that "no man shall be compelled to frequent or support any religious worship, place, or ministry whatsoever," including his own. Forcing a citizen to support even his own church would, among other things, deny "the ministry those temporary rewards, which proceeding from an approbation of their personal conduct, are an additional incitement to earnest and unremitting labours for the instruction of mankind." In general, Madison later added, "religion & Govt. will both exist in greater purity, the less they are mixed together."

What we thus know of the Framers' experience underscores the observation of one prominent commentator, that confining the Establishment Clause to a prohibition on preferential aid "requires a premise that the Framers were extraordinarily bad drafters—that they believed one thing but adopted language that said something substantially different, and that they did so after repeatedly attending to the choice of language." We must presume, since there is no conclusive evidence to the contrary, that the Framers embraced the significance of their textual judgment. Thus, on bal-

ance, history neither contradicts nor warrants reconsideration of the settled principle that the Establishment Clause forbids support for religion in general no less than support for one religion or some.

While these considerations are, for me, sufficient to reject the nonpreferentialist position, one further concern animates my judgment. In many contexts, including this one, nonpreferentialism requires some distinction between "sectarian" religious practices and those that would be, by some measure, ecumenical enough to pass Establishment Clause muster. Simply by requiring the enquiry, nonpreferentialists invite the courts to engage in comparative theology. I can hardly imagine a subject less amenable to the competence of the federal judiciary, or more deliberately to be avoided where possible.

. . .

DEL: History is a logical reference point in attempting to understand and develop the establishment clause's meaning. Searching for the historically correct meaning of the provision, however, has largely been an elusive quest. Reality is that the establishment clause was framed and ratified as a function of different and even competing agendas. As William Van Alstyne has noted, the religion clauses were the product of diverse concerns of voluntarism, separatism and federalism. The first, voluntarism was derived largely from the moderate spirit of religious toleration associated with the Quaker tradition of Pennsylvania. The second, separatism, was derived principally from the successful efforts of Madison and Jefferson in Virginia to disentangle the affairs of government from religious establishments, especially in respect to taxes and levies for religious assistance. The third, federalism, was derived from the preferences of other states that—in contrast with Virginia—maintained particular religious establishments, which they were concerned to keep free from the interference of the national government. It was quite consistent with all three concerns that they would converge on a single proposition: Congress should be disabled from legislating on religion.[249]

The history that one stresses is outcome-determinative for virtually any establishment clause controversy. If the reference point is federalism, questions of public aid to religious institutions, school prayer or bible readings and religious displays on public property tend to be resolved with deference toward the state. Just the opposite result is reached if analysis proceeds from the premise of a wall separating church and government. Inquiries into original purpose are inherently problematic. In "nam[ing] just a few" of the difficulties with motive-referenced standards, in the dormant commerce clause area, Justice Rehnquist noted the faulty assumption that "individual legislators are motivated by one discernible 'actual' purpose, and . . . that different legislators may vote for a single piece of legislation for widely different reasons."[250] Rehnquist's argument against inquiry into original purpose thus makes a particularly effective statement against his case for it. To the extent

---

[249] William Van Alstyne, *Trends in the Supreme Court: Mr. Jefferson's Crumbling Wall—A Comment on Lynch v. Donnelly*, 1984 Duke L. J. 770, 773–74 (1984).

[250] Kassel v. Consolidated Freightways Corp., 450 U.S. 662, 702–03 (1981) (Rehnquist, J., dissenting).

that constitutional principle reflects a selective reading of history, it follows that case law will be vulnerable to allegations that it is inspired by political convenience.

Translating the command against making any "law respecting a religion" into actual standards of review has proved to be a nettlesome and for many, including a significant segment of the Court itself, an unsatisfactory exercise. With at least the assumption that a wall had been erected between church and state, analytical attention focused initially upon whether state action had a religious purpose or effect.[251] Thereafter, standards were glossed by consideration of whether a relationship between church and state fostered excessive entanglement.[252] Further factored into analysis, as case law evolved, was an imperative of accommodating religion.[253] Because entanglement and accommodation considerations are especially subjective, results have been confusing and unpredictable. Outcome may be a function of which analytical factor is prioritized. Although legislative prayer and nativity scenes on public property might be perceived as a problem, when analyzed pursuant to purpose, effect and entanglement criteria, accommodation may function as a superseding consideration.[254]

---

[251] Board of Education v. Allen, 392 U.S. 236, 243 (1968).

[252] Walz v. Tax Commission, 397 U.S. 664, 674 (1970).

[253] Lynch v. Donnelly, 465 U.S. 668, 676–78, 686 (1984).

[254] *Id.* (nativity scenes); Marsh v. Chambers, 463 U.S. 783, 792 (1983) (legislative prayer).

Primary areas of establishment clause controversy have included religious exercises and instruction in public schools and other venues, public aid to parochial schools and religious ceremonies in public settings. With respect to the presentation or facilitation of religious values in public schools, the Court has upheld release time programs to the extent that religious education is provided off campus[255] but invalidated them insofar as religious instruction was offered on campus.[256] It has prohibited school prayer,[257] bible readings[258] and classroom religious displays[259] but at least intimated that a secular moment of silence which a student voluntarily may devote to prayer is permissible.[260] The Court has struck down laws that prohibit the teaching of evolution[261] or require the balancing of such instruction with teaching of creationism.[262] Legislative prayer directed by chaplains[263] and Sunday blue laws have survived establishment clause review.

In the area of aid to parochial education, the Court has upheld transportation reimbursement plans,[264] textbook loans,[265] tax deductions for educational costs,[266] government funding of standardized testing,[267] subsidization of physical and psychological

---

[255] Zorach v. Clauson, 343 U.S. 306, 315 (1952).

[256] McCollum v. Board of Education, 333 U.S. 203, 212 (1948).

[257] Engel v. Vitale, 370 U.S. 421, 433 (1962).

[258] Abington School District v. Schempp, 373 U.S. 203, 223 (1963).

[259] Stone v. Graham, 449 U.S. 39, 42–43 (1980).

[260] Wallace v. Jaffree, 472 U.S. 38, 59 (1985).

[261] Epperson v. Arkansas, 393 U.S. 97, 109 (1968).

[262] Edwards v. Aguillard, 482 U.S. 578, 596–97 (1987).

[263] Marsh v. Chambers, 463 U.S. 783, 793 (1983).

[264] Everson v. Board of Education, 330 U.S. 1, 18 (1947).

[265] Board of Education v. Allen, 392 U.S. 236, 245–48 (1968).

[266] Mueller v. Allen, 463 U.S. 388, 403 (1983).

[267] Committee for Public Education and Religious Liberty v. Regan, 444 U.S. 646, 662 (1980).

diagnostic services[268] and funding of construction at sectarian colleges.[269] It has identified establishment clause violations, however, in the form of loans of instructional materials to parochial schools,[270] field trip transportation,[271] tax credits for educational costs,[272] teacher salary supplements,[273] reimbursement for non-standardized testing[274] and special educational programs for students and adults.[275]

With respect to religious ceremony, the Court has upheld the display of religiously significant symbols on public property to the extent they have a substantial secular dimension.[276] It has struck down such exhibitions to the effect they are perceived as endorsing a religious message.[277]

Not surprisingly, such fine line-drawing between the constitutionally permissible and impermissible has become a source of considerable vexation and uncertainty. Although standards referenced to purpose, effect, entanglement and accommodation have been touted for their "flexibility,"[278] critics have characterized such terminology as "a euphemism . . . for . . . the absence of any principled rationale"[279] and urged the sacrifice of "some 'flexibility' for 'clarity and predictability.'"[280]

b. Evolving Standards

i. *Purpose and Effect*

Formal attention to the purpose and effect of governmental action arose initially in the context of prayer and other religious-oriented exercises and instruction in public schools. In *Engel v. Vitale*, the Court struck down a state law providing for voluntary student recitation of a non-denominational prayer at the start of each school day.[281] In finding an establishment clause violation, the *Engel* Court referenced general underlying policy. It thus noted that the establishment clause's "most immediate purpose rested on the belief that a union of government and religion tends to destroy government and to degrade religion."[282] The Court also stressed that the clause reflected "an awareness of the historical fact that governmentally established religions and religious persecutions go hand in hand."[283]

Purpose and effect emerged as primary focal points a year after *Engel* in a like controversy. Reviewing a state law requiring bible readings and recitation of the Lord's prayer at the commencement of the school day, the Court in *Abington School District v. Schempp* determined that "to withstand the strictures of the Establishment Clause there must be a secular legislative purpose and a primary effect that neither advances

---

[268] Wolman v. Walter, 433 U.S. 229, 244, 248 (1977).

[269] Roemer v. Board of Public Works of Maryland, 426 U.S. 736, 766–67 (1976).

[270] Wolman, 433 U.S. at 251.

[271] *Id.* at 254–55.

[272] Committee for Public Education v. Nyquist, 413 U.S. 756, 797–98 (1973).

[273] Lemon v. Kurtzman, 403 U.S. 602, 625 (1971).

[274] Levitt v. Committee for Public Education, 413 U.S. 472, 482 (1980).

[275] Grand Rapids School District v. Ball, 473 U.S. 373, 397–98 (1985).

[276] Lynch v. Donnelly, 465 U.S. 668, 685–86 (1984).

[277] County of Allegheny v. American Civil Liberties Union Greater Pittsburgh Chapter, 492 U.S. 573, 601–02 (1989).

[278] Committee for Public Education and Religious Liberty v. Regan, 444 U.S. 646, 662 (1980).

[279] Jesse H. Choper, *The Religion Clauses of the First Amendment: Reconciling the Conflict*, 41. Pitt. L. Rev. 673, 680–81 (1980).

[280] Edwards v. Aguillard, 482 U.S. 578, 640 (1987) (Scalia, J., dissenting).

[281] Engel v. Vitale, 370 U.S. 421, 422 (1962).

[282] *Id.* at 431.

[283] *Id.* at 432.

nor inhibits religion."[284] Although noting that study of the Bible or religion as part of an objective secular program of education was permissible, the *Schempp* Court determined that the exercises under review violated the Establishment Clause.[285] Notwithstanding a state's avowal of a secular purpose for posting copies of the Ten Commandments in public school classrooms, the Court in *Stone v. Graham* discerned in the Commandments' very content a "plainly religious" purpose.[286] A similar result was reached in *Epperson v. Arkansas*, when the Court identified an unmistakable religious purpose behind a state law prohibiting the teaching of evolution in public schools.

---

[284] Abington School District v. Schempp, 374 U.S. 203, 222 (1963).
[285] *Id*. at 223.
[286] Stone v. Graham, 449 U.S. 39, 41 (1980).

Epperson v. Arkansas
393 U.S. 97 (1968)

MR. JUSTICE FORTAS delivered the opinion of the Court.

I.

This appeal challenges the constitutionality of the "anti-evolution" statute which the State of Arkansas adopted in 1928 to prohibit the teaching in its public schools and universities of the theory that man evolved from other species of life. The statute was a product of the upsurge of "fundamentalist" religious fervor of the twenties. The Arkansas statute was an adaptation of the famous Tennessee "monkey law" which that State adopted in 1925. The constitutionality of the Tennessee law was upheld by the Tennessee Supreme Court in the celebrated Scopes case in 1927.

The Arkansas law makes it unlawful for a teacher in any state-supported school or university "to teach the theory or doctrine that mankind ascended or descended from a lower order of animals," or "to adopt or use in any such institution a textbook that teaches" this theory. Violation is a misdemeanor and subjects the violator to dismissal from his position.

. . .

In the present case, there can be no doubt that Arkansas has sought to prevent its teachers from discussing the theory of evolution because it is contrary to the belief of some that the Book of Genesis must be the exclusive source of doctrine as to the origin of man. No suggestion has been made that Arkansas' law may be justified by considerations of state policy other than the religious views of some of its citizens. It is clear that fundamentalist sectarian conviction was and is the law's reason for existence. Its antecedent, Tennessee's "monkey law," candidly stated its purpose: to make it unlawful "to teach any theory that denies the story of the Divine Creation of man as taught in the Bible, and to teach instead that man has descended from a lower order of animals." Perhaps the sensational publicity attendant upon the Scopes trial induced Arkansas to adopt less explicit language. It eliminated Tennessee's reference to "the story of the Divine Creation of man" as taught in the Bible, but there is no doubt that the motivation for the law was the same: to suppress the teaching of a theory which, it was thought, "denied" the divine creation of man.

Arkansas' law cannot be defended as an act of religious neutrality. Arkansas did not seek to excise from the curricula of its schools and universities all discussion of the origin of man. The law's effort was confined to an attempt to blot out a particular theory because of its supposed conflict with the Biblical account, literally read. Plainly, the law is contrary to the mandate of the First, and in violation of the Fourteenth, Amendment to the Constitution.

The judgment of the Supreme Court of Arkansas is

Reversed.

MR. JUSTICE BLACK, concurring.

. . .

A . . . question that arises for me is whether this Court's decision forbidding a State to exclude the subject of evolution from its schools infringes the religious freedom of those who consider evolution an anti-religious doctrine. If the theory is considered anti-religious, as the Court indicates, how can the State be bound by the Federal Constitution to permit its teachers to advocate such an "anti-religious" doctrine to schoolchildren? The very cases cited by the Court as supporting its conclusion hold that the State must be neutral, not favoring one religious or anti-religious view over another. The Darwinian theory is said to challenge the Bible's story of creation; so too have some of those who believe in the Bible, along with many others, challenged the Darwinian theory. Since there is no indication that the literal Biblical doctrine of the origin of man is included in the curriculum of Arkansas schools, does not the removal of the subject of evolution leave the State in a neutral position toward these supposedly competing religious and anti-religious doctrines? Unless this Court is prepared simply to write off as pure nonsense the views of those who consider evolution an anti-religious doctrine, then this issue presents problems under the Establishment Clause far more troublesome than are discussed in the Court's opinion.

. . .

Certainly the Darwinian theory, precisely like the Genesis story of the creation of man, is not above challenge. In fact the Darwinian theory has not merely been criticized by religionists but by scientists, and perhaps no scientist would be willing to take an oath and swear that everything announced in the Darwinian theory is unquestionably true. The Court, it seems to me, makes a serious mistake in bypassing the plain, unconstitutional vagueness of this statute in order to reach out and decide this troublesome, to me, First Amendment question. However wise this Court may be or may become hereafter, it is doubtful that, sitting in Washington, it can successfully supervise and censor the curriculum of every public school in every hamlet and city in the United States. I doubt that our wisdom is so nearly infallible.

I would either strike down the Arkansas Act as too vague to enforce, or remand to the State Supreme Court for clarification of its holding and opinion.

MR. JUSTICE HARLAN, concurring.

. . .

I concur in so much of the Court's opinion as holds that the Arkansas statute constitutes an "establishment of religion" forbidden to the States by the Fourteenth Amendment. . . .

MR. JUSTICE STEWART, concurring in the result.

. . .

Discernment of a religious purpose has undone state provisions for a moment of silence at the start of the school day. In *Wallace v. Jaffree*, the Court indicated that such a dedication of time may be constitutionally permissible to the extent it did not favor prayer.[287] With respect to the particular law being challenged, however, the Court found it was inspired by a clearly religious purpose.

---

[287] Wallace v. Jaffree, 472 U.S. 38, 59 (1985).

Wallace v. Jaffree
472 U.S. 38 (1983)

JUSTICE STEVENS delivered the opinion of the Court.

At [issue in] this litigation [are] three Alabama statutes. . . . (1) § 16–1-20, enacted in 1978, which authorized a 1-minute period of silence in all public schools "for meditation"; (2) § 16–1-20.1, enacted in 1981, which authorized a period of silence "for meditation or voluntary prayer"; and (3) § 16–1-20.2, enacted in 1982, which authorized teachers to lead "willing students" in a prescribed prayer to "Almighty God . . . the Creator and Supreme Judge of the world."

. . .

Just as the right to speak and the right to refrain from speaking are complementary components of a broader concept of individual freedom of mind, so also the individual's freedom to choose his own creed is the counterpart of his right to refrain from accepting the creed established by the majority. At one time it was thought that this right merely proscribed the preference of one Christian sect over another, but would not require equal respect for the conscience of the infidel, the atheist, or the adherent of a non-Christian faith such as Islam or Judaism. But when the underlying principle has been examined in the crucible of litigation, the Court has unambiguously concluded that the individual freedom of conscience protected by the First Amendment embraces the right to select any religious faith or none at all. This conclusion derives support not only from the interest in respecting the individual's freedom of conscience, but also from the conviction that religious beliefs worthy of respect are the product of free and voluntary choice by the faithful, and from recognition of the fact that the political interest in forestalling intolerance extends beyond intolerance among Christian sects—or even intolerance among "religions"—to encompass intolerance of the disbeliever and the uncertain. . . .

> "If there is any fixed star in our constitutional constellation, it is that no official, high or petty, can prescribe what shall be orthodox in politics, nationalism, relation, or other matters of opinion or force citizens to confess by word or act their faith therein."

The State of Alabama, no less than the Congress of the United States, must respect that basic truth.

When the Court has been called upon to construe the breadth of the Establishment Clause, it has examined the criteria developed over a period of many years. Thus, in *Lemon v. Kurtzman*, we wrote:

> "Every analysis in this area must begin with consideration of the cumulative criteria developed by the Court over many years. Three such tests may be gleaned from our cases. First, the statute must have a secular legislative purpose; second, its principal or primary effect must be one that neither advances nor inhibits religion; finally, the statute must not foster 'an excessive government entanglement with religion.'"

It is the first of these three criteria that is most plainly implicated by this case. As the District Court correctly recognized, no consideration of the second or third criteria is necessary if a statute does not have a clearly secular purpose. For even though a statute that is motivated in part by a religious purpose may satisfy the first criterion, the First Amendment requires that a statute must be invalidated if it is entirely motivated by a purpose to advance religion.

In applying the purpose test, it is appropriate to ask "whether government's actual purpose is to endorse or disapprove of religion." In this case, the answer to that question is dispositive. For the record not only provides us with an unambiguous affirmative answer, but it also reveals that the enactment of § 16–1-20.1 was not motivated by any clearly secular purpose—indeed, the statute had no secular purpose.

The sponsor of the bill that became § 16–1-20.1, . . . inserted into the legislative record—apparently without dissent—a statement indicating that the legislation was an "effort to return voluntary prayer" to the public schools. Later [he] confirmed this purpose before the District Court. In response to the question whether he had any purpose for the legislation other than returning voluntary prayer to pub-

lic schools, he stated: "No, I did not have no other purpose in mind." The State did not present evidence of any secular purpose.

. . .

The legislative intent to return prayer to the public schools is, of course, quite different from merely protecting every student's right to engage in voluntary prayer during an appropriate moment of silence during the schoolday. The 1978 statute already protected that right, containing nothing that prevented any student from engaging in voluntary prayer during a silent minute of meditation. Appellants have not identified any secular purpose that was not fully served by § 16–1-20 before the enactment of § 16–1-20.1. Thus, only two conclusions are consistent with the text of § 16–1-20.1: (1) the statute was enacted to convey a message of state endorsement and promotion of prayer; or (2) the statute was enacted for no purpose. No one suggests that the statute was nothing but a meaningless or irrational act.

The importance of that principle does not permit us to treat this as an inconsequential case involving nothing more than a few words of symbolic speech on behalf of the political majority. For whenever the State itself speaks on a religious subject, one of the questions that we must ask is "whether the government intends to convey a message of endorsement or disapproval of religion." The well-supported concurrent findings of the District Court and the Court of Appeals—that § 16–1-20.1 was intended to convey a message of state approval of prayer activities in the public schools—make it unnecessary, and indeed inappropriate, to evaluate the practical significance of the addition of the words "or voluntary prayer" to the statute. Keeping in mind, as we must, "both the fundamental place held by the Establishment Clause in our constitutional scheme and the myriad, subtle ways in which Establishment Clause values can be eroded," we conclude that § 16–1-20.1 violates the First Amendment.

. . .

The judgment of the Court of Appeals is affirmed.

JUSTICE POWELL, concurring.

. . . My concurrence is prompted by Alabama's persistence in attempting to institute state-sponsored prayer in the public schools by enacting three successive statutes.

I write separately to express additional views and to respond to criticism of the three-pronged *Lemon* test. *Lemon v. Kurtzman* identifies standards that have proved useful in analyzing case after case both in our decisions and in those of other courts. It is the only coherent test a majority of the Court has ever adopted. Only once since our decision in *Lemon*, have we addressed an Establishment Clause issue without resort to its three-pronged test. See

Marsh v. Chambers. Lemon has not been overruled or its test modified. Yet, continued criticism of it could encourage other courts to feel free to decide Establishment Clause cases on an Admissions Committee hoc basis.

. . .

I would vote to uphold the Alabama statute if it also had a clear secular purpose. Nothing in the record before us, however, identifies a clear secular purpose, and the State also has failed to identify any nonreligious reason for the statute's enactment. Under these circumstances, the Court is required by our precedents to hold that the statute fails the first prong of the *Lemon* test and therefore violates the Establishment Clause.

Although we do not reach the other two prongs of the *Lemon* test, I note that the "effect" of a straightforward moment-of-silence statute is unlikely to "[advance] or [inhibit] religion." Nor would such a statute "foster 'an excessive government entanglement with religion.'"

JUSTICE O'CONNOR, concurring in the judgment.

Nothing in the United States Constitution as interpreted by this Court or in the laws of the State of Alabama prohibits public school students from voluntarily praying at any time before, during, or after the schoolday. Alabama has facilitated voluntary silent prayers of students who are so inclined by enacting Ala. Code § 16-1-20, which provides a moment of silence in appellees' schools each day. The parties to these proceedings concede the validity of this enactment. . . . I write separately to identify the peculiar features of the Alabama law that render it invalid, and to explain why moment of silence laws in other States do not necessarily manifest the same infirmity. I also write to explain why neither history nor the Free Exercise Clause of the First Amendment validates the Alabama law struck down by the Court today.

. . .

As these cases once again demonstrate, . . . "it is far easier to agree on the purpose that underlies the First Amendment's Establishment and Free Exercise Clauses than to obtain agreement on the standards that should govern their application." It once appeared that the Court had developed a workable standard by which to identify impermissible government establishments of religion. See *Lemon v. Kurtzman.* Under the now familiar *Lemon* test, statutes must have both a secular legislative purpose and a principal or primary effect that neither advances nor inhibits religion, and in addition they must not foster excessive government entanglement with religion. Despite its initial promise, the *Lemon* test has proved problematic. The required inquiry into "entanglement" has been modified and questioned,

and in one case we have upheld state action against an Establishment Clause challenge without applying the *Lemon* test at all. *Marsh v. Chambers.* The author of *Lemon* himself apparently questions the test's general applicability. See *Lynch v. Donnelly.* JUSTICE REHNQUIST today suggests that we abandon *Lemon* entirely, and in the process limit the reach of the Establishment Clause to state discrimination between sects and government designation of a particular church as a "state" or "national" one.

Perhaps because I am new to the struggle, I am not ready to abandon all aspects of the *Lemon* test. I do believe, however, that the standards announced in *Lemon* should be reexamined and refined in order to make them more useful in achieving the underlying purpose of the First Amendment. We must strive to do more than erect a constitutional "signpost," to be followed or ignored in a particular case as our predilections may dictate. Instead, our goal should be "to frame a principle for constitutional adjudication that is not only grounded in the history and language of the first amendment, but one that is also capable of consistent application to the relevant problems." . . .

The *Lynch* concurrence suggested that the religious liberty protected by the Establishment Clause is infringed when the government makes adherence to religion relevant to a person's standing in the political community. Direct government action endorsing religion or a particular religious practice is invalid under this approach because it "sends a message to nonadherents that they are outsiders, not full members of the political community, and an accompanying message to adherents that they are insiders, favored members of the political community." Under this view, *Lemon's* inquiry as to the purpose and effect of a statute requires courts to examine whether government's purpose is to endorse religion and whether the statute actually conveys a message of endorsement.

The endorsement test is useful because of the analytic content it gives to the *Lemon*-mandated inquiry into legislative purpose and effect. In this country, church and state must necessarily operate within the same community. Because of this coexistence, it is inevitable that the secular interests of government and the religious interests of various sects and their adherents will frequently intersect, conflict, and combine. A statute that ostensibly promotes a secular interest often has an incidental or even a primary effect of helping or hindering a sectarian belief. Chaos would ensue if every such statute were invalid under the Establishment Clause. For example, the State could not criminalize murder for fear that it would thereby promote the Biblical command against killing. The task for the Court is to sort out those statutes and government practices whose purpose and effect go against the grain of religious liberty protected by the First Amendment.

The endorsement test does not preclude government from acknowledging religion or from taking religion into account in making law and policy. It does preclude government from conveying or attempting to convey a message that religion or a particular religious belief is favored or preferred. Such an endorsement infringes the religious liberty of the nonadherent, for "[when] the power, prestige and financial support of government is placed behind a particular religious belief, the indirect coercive pressure upon religious minorities to conform to the prevailing officially approved religion is plain." At issue today is whether state moment of silence statutes in general, and Alabama's moment of silence statute in particular, embody an impermissible endorsement of prayer in public schools.

. . .

The *Engel* and *Abington* decisions are not dispositive on the constitutionality of moment of silence laws. In those cases, public school teachers and students led their classes in devotional exercises. In *Engel*, a New York statute required teachers to lead their classes in a vocal prayer. The Court concluded that "it is no part of the business of government to compose official prayers for any group of the American people to recite as part of a religious program carried on by the government." In *Abington*, the Court addressed Pennsylvania and Maryland statutes that authorized morning Bible readings in public schools. The Court reviewed the purpose and effect of the statutes, concluded that they required religious exercises, and therefore found them to violate the Establishment Clause. Under all of these statutes, a student who did not share the religious beliefs expressed in the course of the exercise was left with the choice of participating, thereby compromising the nonadherent's beliefs, or withdrawing, thereby calling attention to his or her nonconformity. The decisions acknowledged the coercion implicit under the statutory schemes, but they expressly turned only on the fact that the government was sponsoring a manifestly religious exercise.

A state-sponsored moment of silence in the public schools is different from state-sponsored vocal prayer or Bible reading. First, a moment of silence is not inherently religious. Silence, unlike prayer or Bible reading, need not be associated with a religious exercise. Second, a pupil who participates in a moment of silence need not compromise his or her beliefs. During a moment of silence, a student who objects to prayer is left to his or her own thoughts, and is not compelled to listen to the prayers or thoughts of others. For these simple reasons, a moment of silence statute does not stand or fall under the Establishment Clause according to how the Court regards vocal prayer or Bible reading. Scholars and at least one Member of this Court have recognized the distinction and suggested that a moment of silence in public schools would be constitutional. As a general matter, I agree. It is difficult to discern a serious threat to religious liberty from a room of silent, thoughtful schoolchildren.

By mandating a moment of silence, a State does not necessarily endorse any activity that might occur during the period. Even if a statute specifies that a student may choose to pray silently during a quiet moment, the State has not thereby encouraged prayer over other specified alternatives. Nonetheless, it is also possible that a moment of silence statute, either as drafted or as actually implemented, could effectively favor the child who prays over the child who does not. For example, the message of endorsement would seem inescapable if the teacher exhorts children to use the designated time to pray. Similarly, the face of the statute or its legislative history may clearly establish that it seeks to encourage or promote voluntary prayer over other alternatives, rather than merely provide a quiet moment that may be dedicated to prayer by those so inclined. The crucial question is whether the State has conveyed or attempted to convey the message that children should use the moment of silence for prayer. This question cannot be answered in the abstract, but instead requires courts to examine the history, language, and administration of a particular statute to determine whether it operates as an endorsement of religion.

Before reviewing Alabama's moment of silence law to determine whether it endorses prayer, some general observations on the proper scope of the inquiry are in order. First, the inquiry into the purpose of the legislature in enacting a moment of silence law should be deferential and limited. In determining whether the government intends a moment of silence statute to convey a message of endorsement or disapproval of religion, a court has no license to psychoanalyze the legislators. If a legislature expresses a plausible secular purpose for a moment of silence statute in either the text or the legislative history, or if the statute disclaims an intent to encourage prayer over alternatives during a moment of silence, then courts should generally defer to that stated intent. It is particularly troublesome to denigrate an expressed secular purpose due to postenactment testimony by particular legislators or by interested persons who witnessed the drafting of the statute. Even if the text and official history of a statute express no secular purpose, the statute should be held to have an improper purpose only if it is beyond purview that endorsement of religion or a religious belief "was and is the law's reason for existence." Since there is arguably a secular pedagogical value to a moment of silence in public schools, courts should find an improper purpose behind such a statute only if the statute on its face, in its official legislative history, or in its interpretation by a responsible administrative agency suggests it has the primary purpose of endorsing prayer.

JUSTICE REHNQUIST suggests that this sort of deferential inquiry into legislative purpose "means little," because "it only requires the legislature to express any secular purpose and omit all sectarian references." It is not a trivial matter, however, to require that the legislature manifest a secular purpose and omit all sectarian endorsements from its laws. That requirement is precisely tailored to the Establishment Clause's purpose of assuring that government not intentionally endorse religion or a religious practice. It is of course possible that a legislature will enunciate a sham secular purpose for a statute. I have little doubt that our courts are capable of distinguishing a sham secular purpose from a sincere one, or that the *Lemon* inquiry into the effect of an enactment would help decide those close cases where the validity of an expressed secular purpose is in doubt. While the secular purpose requirement alone may rarely be determinative in striking down a statute, it nevertheless serves an important function. It reminds government that when it acts it should do so without endorsing a particular religious belief or practice that all citizens do not share. In this sense the secular purpose requirement is squarely based in the text of the Establishment Clause it helps to enforce.

Second, the *Lynch* concurrence suggested that the effect of a moment of silence law is not entirely a question of fact. . . .

Although evidentiary submissions may help answer it, the question is, like the question whether racial or sex-based classifications communicate an invidious message, "in large part a legal question to be answered on the basis of judicial interpretation of social facts." The relevant issue is whether an objective observer, acquainted with the text, legislative history, and implementation of the statute, would perceive it as a state endorsement of prayer in public schools. A moment of silence law that is clearly drafted and implemented so as to permit prayer, meditation, and reflection within the prescribed period, without endorsing one alternative over the others, should pass this test.

The analysis above suggests that moment of silence laws in many States should pass Establishment Clause scrutiny because they do not favor the child who chooses to pray during a moment of silence over the child who chooses to meditate or reflect. Alabama Code § 16–1–20.1 (Supp. 1984) does not stand on the same footing. However deferentially one examines its text and legislative history, however objectively one views the message attempted to be conveyed to the public, the conclusion is unavoidable that the purpose of the statute is to endorse prayer in public schools. . . . . . .

CHIEF JUSTICE BURGER, dissenting.

Some who trouble to read the opinions in these cases will find it ironic—perhaps even bizarre—that on the very day we heard arguments in the cases, the Court's session opened with an invocation for Divine protection. Across the park a few hundred yards away, the House of Representatives and the Senate regularly open each session with a prayer. These legislative prayers are not just one minute in duration, but are extended, thoughtful invocations and prayers for Divine guidance. They are given, as they have been since 1789, by clergy appointed as official chaplains and paid from the Treasury of the United States. Congress has also provided chapels in the Capitol, at public expense, where Members and others may pause for prayer, meditation—or a moment of silence.

Inevitably some wag is bound to say that the Court's holding today reflects a belief that the historic practice of the Congress and this Court is justified because members of the Judiciary and Congress are more in need of Divine guidance than are schoolchildren. Still others will say that all this controversy is "much ado about nothing," since no power on earth—including this Court and Congress—can stop any teacher from opening the schoolday with a moment of silence for pupils to meditate, to plan their day—or to pray if they voluntarily elect to do so.

. . .

. . . To suggest that a moment-of-silence statute that includes the word "prayer" unconstitutionally endorses religion, while one that simply provides for a moment of silence does not, manifests not neutrality but hostility toward religion. For decades our opinions have stated that hostility toward any religion or toward all religions is as much forbidden by the Constitution as is an official establishment of religion. The Alabama Legislature has no more "endorsed" religion than a state or the Congress does when it provides for legislative chaplains, or than this Court does when it opens each session with an invocation to God. Today's decision recalls the observations of Justice Goldberg:

"[Untutored] devotion to the concept of neutrality can lead to invocation or approval of results which partake not simply of that noninterference and noninvolvement with the religious which the Constitution commands, but of a brooding and pervasive dedication to the secular and a passive, or even active, hostility to the religious. Such results are not only not compelled by the Constitution, but, it seems to me, are prohibited by it."

. . .

Curiously, the opinions do not mention that all of the sponsor's statements relied upon—including the statement "inserted" into the Senate Journal—were made after the legislature had passed the statute; indeed, the testimony that the Court finds critical was given well over a year after the statute was enacted. As even the appellees concede, there is not a shred of evidence that the legislature as a whole shared the sponsor's motive or that a majority in either house was even aware of the sponsor's view of the bill when it was passed. The sole relevance of the sponsor's statements, therefore, is that they reflect the personal, subjective motives of a single legislator. No case in the 195-year history of this Court supports the disconcerting idea that postenactment statements by individual legislators are relevant in determining the constitutionality of legislation.

Even if an individual legislator's after-the-fact statements could rationally be considered relevant, all of the opinions fail to mention that the sponsor also testified that one of his purposes in drafting and sponsoring the moment-of-silence bill was to clear up a widespread misunderstanding that a schoolchild is legally prohibited from engaging in silent, individual prayer once he steps inside a public school building. That testimony is at least as important as the statements the Court relies upon, and surely that testimony manifests a permissible purpose.

. . .

The several preceding opinions conclude that the principal difference between § 16–1-20.1 and its predecessor statute proves that the sole purpose behind the inclusion of the phrase "or voluntary prayer" in § 16-1-20.1 was to endorse and promote prayer. This reasoning is simply a subtle way of focusing exclusively on the religious component of the statute rather than examining the statute as a whole. Such logic—if it can be called that—would lead the Court to hold, for example, that a state may enact a statute that provides reimbursement for bus transportation to the parents of all schoolchildren, but may not add parents of parochial school students to an existing program providing reimbursement for parents of public school students. Congress amended the statu-

tory Pledge of Allegiance 31 years ago to add the words "under God." Act of June 14, 1954, Pub. L. 396, 68 Stat. 249. Do the several opinions in support of the judgment today render the Pledge unconstitutional? That would be the consequence of their method of focusing on the difference between § 16-1-20.1 and its predecessor statute rather than examining § 16–1-20.1 as a whole. Any such holding would of course make a mockery of our decisionmaking in Establishment Clause cases. And even were the Court's method correct, the inclusion of the words "or voluntary prayer" in § 16-1-20.1 is wholly consistent with the clearly permissible purpose of clarifying that silent, voluntary prayer is not forbidden in the public school building.

. . .

The Court's extended treatment of the "test" of *Lemon v. Kurtzman* suggests a naive preoccupation with an easy, bright-line approach for addressing constitutional issues. We have repeatedly cautioned that *Lemon* did not establish a rigid caliper capable of resolving every Establishment Clause issue, but that it sought only to provide "signposts." "In each [Establishment Clause] case, the inquiry calls for line-drawing; no fixed, per se rule can be framed." *Lynch v. Donnelly.* In any event, our responsibility is not to apply tidy formulas by rote; our duty is to determine whether the statute or practice at issue is a step toward establishing a state religion. Given today's decision, however, perhaps it is understandable that the opinions in support of the judgment all but ignore the Establishment Clause itself and the concerns that underlie it.

The notion that the Alabama statute is a step toward creating an established church borders on, if it does not trespass into, the ridiculous. The statute does not remotely threaten religious liberty; it affirmatively furthers the values of religious freedom and tolerance that the Establishment Clause was designed to protect. Without pressuring those who do not wish to pray, the statute simply creates an opportunity to think, to plan, or to pray if one wishes—as Congress does by providing chaplains and chapels. It accommodates the purely private, voluntary religious choices of the individual pupils who wish to pray while at the same time creating a time for nonreligious reflection for those who do not choose to pray. The statute also provides a meaningful opportunity for schoolchildren to appreciate the absolute constitutional right of each individual to worship and believe as the individual wishes. The statute "endorses" only the view that the religious observances of others should be tolerated and, where possible, accommodated. If the government may not accommodate religious needs when it does so in a wholly neutral and noncoercive manner, the "benevolent neutrality" that we have long considered the correct constitutional standard will quickly translate into the "callous indifference" that the Court has consistently held the Establishment Clause does not require.

. . .

The mountains have labored and brought forth a mouse.

JUSTICE WHITE, dissenting.

For the most part agreeing with the opinion of THE CHIEF JUSTICE, I dissent from the Court's judgment invalidating Ala. Code § 16-1-20.1. . . .

I appreciate JUSTICE REHNQUIST'S explication of the history of the Religion Clauses of the First Amendment. Against that history, it would be quite understandable if we undertook to reassess our cases dealing with these Clauses, particularly those dealing with the Establishment Clause. Of course, I have been out of step with many of the Court's decisions dealing with this subject matter, and it is thus not surprising that I would support a basic reconsideration of our precedents.

For Justice Rehnquist's dissenting opinion, *see supra.*

Motive-based criteria have been a source of concern and controversy in a variety of constitutional settings. In the context of freedom of speech, the Court has resisted inquiry into legislative motive on grounds that it is largely an exercise in guesswork, essentially futile and a peril to constitutional interests.[288] Although utilized in equal protection[289] and dormant commerce clause analysis,[290] such standards have been criticized extensively.[291] In *Edwards v. Aguillard*, the Court revisited the evolution controversy and determined that a state law requiring instruction in "creation science" as an accompaniment to any teaching of evolution theory had no secular purpose. Dissenting from the Court's opinion, Justice Scalia scorned the use of motive-based inquiry.

---

[288] United States v. O'Brien, 391 U.S. 367, 383–84 (1968).

[289] *E.g.,* Washington v. Davis, 426 U.S. 229, 240 (1976).

[290] Kassel v. Consolidated Freightways Corp., 450 U.S. 662, 677–78 (1981).

[291] *E.g., Kassel*, 450 U.S. at 702–03 (Rehnquist, J., dissenting) (criticizing motive-based inquiry in dormant commerce clause analysis); Keyes v. School District No. 1, 413 U.S. 189, 219 (1973) (Powell, J., concurring and dissenting) (criticizing motive-based inquiry in equal protection context).

Edwards v. Aguillard
482 U.S. 578 (1987)

JUSTICE BRENNAN delivered the opinion of the Court.

JUSTICE O'CONNOR joins all but Part II of this opinion.

The question for decision is whether Louisiana's "Balanced Treatment for Creation-Science and Evolution-Science in Public School Instruction" Act is violative of the Establishment Clause of the First Amendment.

I

The Creationism Act forbids the teaching of the theory of evolution in public schools unless accompanied by instruction in "creation science." No school is required to teach evolution or creation science. If either is taught, however, the other must also be taught. The theories of evolution and creation science are statutorily defined as "the scientific evidences

for [creation or evolution] and inferences from those scientific evidences."

. . .

II

The Establishment Clause forbids the enactment of any law "respecting an establishment of religion." The Court has applied a three-pronged test to determine whether legislation comports with the Establishment Clause. First, the legislature must have adopted the law with a secular purpose. Second, the statute's principal or primary effect must be one that neither advances nor inhibits religion. Third, the statute must not result in an excessive entanglement of government with religion. State action violates the Establishment Clause if it fails to satisfy any of these prongs.

III

... If the law was enacted for the purpose of endorsing religion, "no consideration of the second or third criteria [of Lemon] is necessary." In this case, appellants have identified no clear secular purpose for the Louisiana Act.

True, the Act's stated purpose is to protect academic freedom. This phrase might, in common parlance, be understood as referring to enhancing the freedom of teachers to teach what they will. The Court of Appeals, however, correctly concluded that the Act was not designed to further that goal. We find no merit in the State's argument that the "legislature may not [have] used the terms 'academic freedom' in the correct legal sense. They might have [had] in mind, instead, a basic concept of fairness; teaching all of the evidence." Even if "academic freedom" is read to mean "teaching all of the evidence" with respect to the origin of human beings, the Act does not further this purpose. The goal of providing a more comprehensive science curriculum is not furthered either by outlawing the teaching of evolution or by requiring the teaching of creation science.

. . .

It is clear from the legislative history that the purpose of the legislative sponsor was to narrow the science curriculum. During the legislative hearings, [he] stated: "My preference would be that neither [creationism nor evolution] be taught." Such a ban on teaching does not promote—indeed, it undermines—the provision of a comprehensive scientific education.

It is equally clear that requiring schools to teach creation science with evolution does not advance academic freedom. The Act does not grant teachers a flexibility that they did not already possess to supplant the present science curriculum with the presentation of theories, besides evolution, about the origin of life. Indeed, the Court of Appeals found that no law prohibited Louisiana public school teachers from teaching any scientific theory. As the president of the Louisiana Science Teachers Association testified, "any scientific concept that's based on established fact can be included in our curriculum already, and no legislation allowing this is necessary." The Act provides Louisiana schoolteachers with no new authority. Thus the stated purpose is not furthered by it.

. . .

Furthermore, the goal of basic "fairness" is hardly furthered by the Act's discriminatory preference for the teaching of creation science and against the teaching of evolution. While requiring that curriculum guides be developed for creation science, the Act says nothing of comparable guides for evolution. Similarly, resource services are supplied for creation science but not for evolution. Only "creation scientists" can serve on the panel that supplies the resource services. The Act forbids school boards to discriminate against anyone who "chooses to be a creation-scientist" or to teach "creationism," but fails to protect those who choose to teach evolution or any other noncreation science theory, or who refuse to teach creation science.

If the Louisiana Legislature's purpose was solely to maximize the comprehensiveness and effectiveness of science instruction, it would have encouraged the teaching of all scientific theories about the origins of humankind. But under the Act's requirements, teachers who were once free to teach any and all facets of this subject are now unable to do so. Moreover, the Act fails even to ensure that creation science will be taught, but instead requires the teaching of this theory only when the theory of evolution is taught. Thus we agree with the Court of Appeals' conclusion that the Act does not serve to protect academic freedom, but has the distinctly different purpose of discrediting "evolution by counterbalancing its teaching at every turn with the teaching of creationism. . . . "

. . .

In this case, the purpose of the Creationism Act was to restructure the science curriculum to conform with a particular religious viewpoint. Out of many possible science subjects taught in the public schools, the legislature chose to affect the teaching of the one scientific theory that historically has been opposed by certain religious sects. As in Epperson, the legislature passed the Act to give preference to those religious groups which have as one of their tenets the creation of humankind by a divine creator. . . . [T]he Creationism Act is designed either to promote the theory of creation science which embodies a particular religious tenet by requiring that creation science be taught whenever evolution is taught or to prohibit the teaching of a scientific theory disfavored by certain religious sects by forbidding the teaching of evolution when creation science is not also taught. The Establishment Clause, however, "forbids alike the preference of a religious doctrine or the prohibition of theory which is deemed antagonistic to a particular dogma." Because the primary purpose of the Creationism Act is to advance a particular religious belief, the Act endorses religion in violation of the First Amendment.

. . .

V

The Louisiana Creationism Act advances a religious doctrine by requiring either the banishment of the theory of evolution from public school classrooms or the presentation of a religious viewpoint that rejects evolution in its entirety. The Act violates the Establishment Clause of the First Amendment because it seeks to employ the symbolic and financial support of government to achieve a religious purpose. The judgment of the Court of Appeals therefore is

Affirmed.

JUSTICE POWELL, with whom JUSTICE O'CONNOR joins, concurring.

I write separately to note certain aspects of the legislative history, and to emphasize that nothing in the Court's opinion diminishes the traditionally broad discretion accorded state and local school officials in the selection of the public school curriculum.

. . .

Even though I find Louisiana's Balanced Treatment Act unconstitutional, I adhere to the view "that the States and locally elected school boards should have the responsibility for determining the educational policy of the public schools." A decision respecting the subject matter to be taught in public schools does not violate the Establishment Clause simply because the material to be taught "'happens to coincide or harmonize with the tenets of some or all religions.'" In the context of a challenge under the Establishment Clause, interference with the decisions of these authorities is warranted only when the purpose for their decisions is clearly religious.

. . .

As a matter of history, schoolchildren can and should properly be informed of all aspects of this Nation's religious heritage. I would see no constitutional problem if schoolchildren were taught the nature of the Founding Father's religious beliefs and how these beliefs affected the attitudes of the times and the structure of our government. Courses in comparative religion of course are customary and constitutionally appropriate. In fact, since religion permeates our history, a familiarity with the nature of religious beliefs is necessary to understand many historical as well as contemporary events. In addition, it is worth noting that the Establishment Clause does not prohibit per se the educational use of religious documents in public school education. Although this Court has recognized that the Bible is "an instrument of religion," it also has made clear that the Bible "may constitutionally be used in an appropriate study of history, civilization, ethics, comparative religion, or the like." The book is, in fact, "the world's all-time best seller" with undoubted literary and historic value apart from its religious content. The Establishment Clause is properly understood to prohibit the use of the Bible and other religious documents in public school education only when the purpose of the use is to advance a particular religious belief.

In sum, I find that the language and the legislative history of the Balanced Treatment Act unquestionably demonstrate that its purpose is to advance a particular religious belief. Although the discretion of state and local authorities over public school curricula is broad, "the First Amendment does not permit the State to require that teaching and learning must be tailored to the principles or prohibitions of any religious sect or dogma." Accordingly, I concur in the opinion of the Court and its judgment that the Balanced Treatment Act violates the Establishment Clause of the Constitution.

JUSTICE WHITE, concurring in the judgment.

. . .

JUSTICE SCALIA, with whom THE CHIEF JUSTICE joins, dissenting.

Even if I agreed with the questionable premise that legislation can be invalidated under the Establishment Clause on the basis of its motivation alone, without regard to its effects, I would still find no justification for today's decision. The Louisiana legislators who passed the "Balanced Treatment for Creation-Science and Evolution-Science Act" each of whom had sworn to support the Constitution, were well aware of the potential Establishment Clause problems and considered that aspect of the legislation with great care. After seven hearings and several months of study, resulting in substantial revision of the original proposal, they approved the Act overwhelmingly and specifically articulated the secular purpose they meant it to serve. Although the record contains abundant evidence of the sincerity of that purpose (the only issue pertinent to this case), the Court today holds, essentially on the basis of "its visceral knowledge regarding what must have motivated the legislators," that the members of the Louisiana Legislature knowingly violated their oaths and then lied about it. I dissent. Had requirements of the Balanced Treatment Act that are not apparent on its face been clarified by an interpretation of the Louisiana Supreme Court, or by the manner of its implementation, the Act might well be found unconstitutional; but the question of its constitutionality cannot rightly be disposed of on the gallop, by impugning the motives of its supporters.

. . .

In sum, even if one concedes, for the sake of argument, that a majority of the Louisiana Legislature voted for the Balanced Treatment Act partly in order to foster (rather than merely eliminate discrimination against) Christian fundamentalist beliefs, our cases establish that that alone would not suffice to invalidate the Act, so long as there was a genuine secular purpose as well. We have, moreover, no adequate basis for disbelieving the secular purpose set forth in the Act itself, or for concluding that it is a sham enacted to conceal the legislators' violation of their oaths of office. I am astonished by the Court's unprecedented readiness to reach such a conclusion, which I can only attribute to an intellectual predisposition created by the facts and the legend of *Scopes v. State*, an instinctive reaction that any governmentally imposed requirements bearing upon the teaching of evolution must be a manifestation of Christian fundamentalist repression. In this case, however, it seems to me the Court's position is the repressive one. The people of Louisiana, including those who are Christian fundamentalists, are quite entitled, as a secular matter, to have whatever scientific evidence there may be against evolution presented in their schools, just as Mr. Scopes was entitled to present whatever scientific evidence there was for it. Perhaps what the Louisiana Legislature has done is unconstitutional because there is no such evidence, and the scheme they have established will amount to no more than a presentation of the Book of Genesis. But we cannot say that on the evidence before us in this summary judgment context, which includes ample uncontradicted testimony that "creation science" is a body of scientific knowledge rather than revealed belief. Infinitely less can we say (or should we say) that the scientific evidence for evolution is so conclusive that no one could be gullible enough to believe that there is any real scientific evidence to the contrary, so that the legislation's stated purpose must be a lie. Yet that illiberal judgment, that Scopes-in-reverse, is ultimately the basis on which the Court's facile rejection of the Louisiana Legislature's purpose must rest.

Since the existence of secular purpose is so entirely clear, and thus dispositive, I will not go on to discuss the fact that, even if the Louisiana Legislature's purpose were exclusively to advance religion, some of the well-established exceptions to the impermissibility of that purpose might be applicable—the validating intent to eliminate a perceived discrimination against a particular religion, to facilitate its free exercise, or to accommodate it. I am not in any case enamored of those amorphous exceptions, since I think them no more than unpredictable correctives to what is (as the next Part of this opinion will discuss) a fundamentally unsound rule. It is surprising, however, that the Court does not address these exceptions, since the context of the legislature's

action gives some reason to believe they may be applicable.

I have to this point assumed the validity of the *Lemon* "purpose" test. In fact, however, I think the pessimistic evaluation that THE CHIEF JUSTICE made of the totality of *Lemon* is particularly applicable to the "purpose" prong: it is "a constitutional theory [that] has no basis in the history of the amendment it seeks to interpret, is difficult to apply and yields unprincipled results. . . . "

Putting that problem aside, however, where ought we to look for the individual legislator's purpose? We cannot of course assume that every member present (if, as is unlikely, we know who or even how many they were) agreed with the motivation expressed in a particular legislator's preenactment floor or committee statement. Quite obviously, "what motivates one legislator to make a speech about a statute is not necessarily what motivates scores of others to enact it." Can we assume, then, that they all agree with the motivation expressed in the staff-prepared committee reports they might have read—even though we are unwilling to assume that they agreed with the motivation expressed in the very statute that they voted for? Should we consider postenactment floor statements? Or postenactment testimony from legislators, obtained expressly for the lawsuit? Should we consider media reports on the realities of the legislative bargaining? All of these sources, of course, are eminently manipulable. Legislative histories can be contrived and sanitized, favorable media coverage orchestrated, and postenactment recollections conveniently distorted. Perhaps most valuable of all would be more objective indications—for example, evidence regarding the individual legislators' religious affiliations. And if that, why not evidence regarding the fervor or tepidity of their beliefs?

Because there are no good answers to these questions, this Court has recognized from Chief Justice Marshall, to Chief Justice Warren, that determining the subjective intent of legislators is a perilous enterprise. It is perilous, I might note, not just for the judges who will very likely reach the wrong result, but also for the legislators who find that they must assess the validity of proposed legislation—and risk the condemnation of having voted for an unconstitutional measure—not on the basis of what the legislation contains, nor even on the basis of what they themselves intend, but on the basis of what others have in mind.

In the past we have attempted to justify our embarrassing Establishment Clause jurisprudence on the ground that it "sacrifices clarity and predictability for flexibility." One commentator has aptly characterized this as "a euphemism . . . for . . . the absence of any principled rationale." I think it time that we sacrifice some "flexibility" for "clarity and predictability." Abandoning *Lemon's* purpose test—a test which exacerbates the tension between the Free Exercise and Establishment Clauses, has no basis in the language or history of the Amendment, and, as today's decision shows, has wonderfully flexible consequences—would be a good place to start.

ii. Entanglement

During the 1970s, establishment clause analysis expanded beyond a focus upon purpose and primary effect to include attention to excessive entanglement of government and religion. The three dimensions of establishment clause review—purpose, effect and excessive entanglement—coalesced into a general standard in *Lemon v. Kurtzman*. At issue in *Lemon* were state funded salary supplements for teachers in nonpublic schools and state programs for reimbursing nonpublic schools for teacher salaries, textbooks and instructional materials.

Lemon v. Kurtzman
403 U.S. 602 (1971)

MR. CHIEF JUSTICE BURGER delivered the opinion of the Court.

These two appeals raise questions as to Pennsylvania and Rhode Island statutes providing state aid to church-related elementary and secondary schools. Both statutes are challenged as violative of the Establishment and Free Exercise Clauses of the First Amendment and the Due Process Clause of the Fourteenth Amendment.

Pennsylvania has adopted a statutory program that provides financial support to nonpublic elementary and secondary schools by way of reimbursement for the cost of teachers' salaries, textbooks, and instructional materials in specified secular subjects. Rhode Island has adopted a statute under which the State pays directly to teachers in nonpublic elementary schools a supplement of 15% of their annual salary. Under each statute state aid has been given to church-related educational institutions. We hold that both statutes are unconstitutional.

. . .

. . . Candor compels acknowledgment . . . that we can only dimly perceive the lines of demarcation in this extraordinarily sensitive area of constitutional law.

The language of the Religion Clauses of the First Amendment is at best opaque, particularly when compared with other portions of the Amendment. Its authors did not simply prohibit the establishment of a state church or a state religion, an area history shows they regarded as very important and fraught with great dangers. Instead they commanded that there should be "no law respecting an establishment of religion." A law may be one "respecting" the forbidden objective while falling short of its total realization. A law "respecting" the proscribed result, that is, the establishment of religion, is not always easily identifiable as one violative of the Clause. A given law might not establish a state religion but nevertheless be one "respecting" that end in the sense of being a step that could lead to such establishment and hence offend the First Amendment.

In the absence of precisely stated constitutional prohibitions, we must draw lines with reference to the three main evils against which the Establishment Clause was intended to afford protection: "sponsorship, financial support, and active involvement of the sovereign in religious activity."

Every analysis in this area must begin with consideration of the cumulative criteria developed by the Court over many years. Three such tests may be gleaned from our cases. First, the statute must have a secular legislative purpose; second, its principal or primary effect must be one that neither advances nor inhibits religion; finally, the statute must not foster "an excessive government entanglement with religion."

Inquiry into the legislative purposes of the Pennsylvania and Rhode Island statutes affords no basis for a conclusion that the legislative intent was to advance religion. On the contrary, the statutes themselves clearly state that they are intended to enhance the quality of the secular education in all schools covered by the compulsory attendance laws. There is no reason to believe the legislatures meant anything else. A State always has a legitimate concern for maintaining minimum standards in all schools it allows to operate. As in *Allen*, we find nothing here that undermines the stated legislative intent; it must therefore be accorded appropriate deference.

Our prior holdings do not call for total separation between church and state; total separation is not possible in an absolute sense. Some relationship between government and religious organizations is inevitable. Fire inspections, building and zoning regulations, and state requirements under compulsory school-attendance laws are examples of necessary and permissible contacts. Indeed, under the statutory exemption before us in *Walz*, the State had a continuing burden to ascertain that the exempt property was in fact being used for religious worship. Judicial caveats against entanglement must recognize that the line of separation, far from being a "wall," is a blurred, indistinct, and variable barrier depending on all the circumstances of a particular relationship.

. . .

In order to determine whether the government entanglement with religion is excessive, we must examine the character and purposes of the institutions that are benefited, the nature of the aid that the State provides, and the resulting relationship between the government and the religious authority. . . . Here we find that both statutes foster an impermissible degree of entanglement.

Rhode Island program

. . .

The church schools involved in the program are located close to parish churches. This understandably permits convenient access for religious exercises since instruction in faith and morals is part of the total educational process. The school buildings contain identifying religious symbols such as crosses on the exterior and crucifixes, and religious paintings and statues either in the classrooms or hallways. Although only approximately 30 minutes a day are devoted to direct religious instruction, there are religiously oriented extracurricular activities. Approximately two-thirds of the teachers in these schools are nuns of various religious orders. Their dedicated efforts provide an atmosphere in which religious instruction and religious vocations are natural and proper parts of life in such schools. Indeed, as the District Court found, the role of teaching nuns in enhancing the religious atmosphere has led the parochial school authorities to attempt to maintain a one-to-one ratio between nuns and lay teachers in all schools rather than to permit some to be staffed almost entirely by lay teachers.

. . .

We need not and do not assume that teachers in parochial schools will be guilty of bad faith or any conscious design to evade the limitations imposed by the statute and the First Amendment. We simply recognize that a dedicated religious person, teaching in a school affiliated with his or her faith and operated to inculcate its tenets, will inevitably experience great difficulty in remaining religiously neutral. Doctrines and faith are not inculcated or advanced by neutrals. With the best of intentions such a teacher would find it hard to make a total separation between secular teaching and religious doctrine. What would appear to some to be essential to good citizenship might well for others border on or constitute instruction in religion. Further difficulties are inherent in the combination of religious discipline and the possibility of disagreement between teacher and religious authorities over the meaning of the statutory restrictions.

We do not assume, however, that parochial school teachers will be unsuccessful in their attempts to segregate their religious beliefs from their secular educational responsibilities. But the potential for impermissible fostering of religion is present. The Rhode Island Legislature has not, and could not, provide state aid on the basis of a mere assumption that secular teachers under religious discipline can avoid conflicts. The State must be certain, given the Religion Clauses, that subsidized teachers do not inculcate religion—indeed the State here has undertaken to do so. To ensure that no trespass occurs, the State has therefore carefully conditioned its aid with pervasive restrictions. An eligible recipient must teach only those courses that are offered in the public schools and use only those texts and materials that are found in the public schools. In addition the teacher must not engage in teaching any course in religion.

A comprehensive, discriminating, and continuing state surveillance will inevitably be required to ensure that these restrictions are obeyed and the First Amendment otherwise respected. Unlike a book, a teacher cannot be inspected once so as to determine the extent and intent of his or her personal beliefs and subjective acceptance of the limitations imposed by the First Amendment. These prophylactic contacts will involve excessive and enduring entanglement between state and church.

There is another area of entanglement in the Rhode Island program that gives concern. The statute excludes teachers employed by nonpublic schools whose average per-pupil expenditures on secular education equal or exceed the comparable figures for public schools. In the event that the total expenditures of an otherwise eligible school exceed this norm, the program requires the government to examine the school's records in order to determine how much of the total expenditures is attributable to secular education and how much to religious activity. This kind of state inspection and evaluation of the religious content of a religious organization is fraught with the sort of entanglement that the Constitution forbids. It is a relationship pregnant with dangers of excessive government direction of church schools and hence of churches. . . .

Pennsylvania program

The Pennsylvania statute also provides state aid to church- related schools for teachers' salaries. The complaint describes an educational system that is very similar to the one existing in Rhode Island. According to the allegations, the church-related elementary and secondary schools are controlled by religious organizations, have the purpose of propagating and promoting a particular religious faith, and conduct their operations to fulfill that purpose. . . .

As we noted earlier, the very restrictions and surveillance necessary to ensure that teachers play a strictly nonideological role give rise to entanglements between church and state. The Pennsylvania statute, like that of Rhode Island, fosters this kind of relationship. . . .

The Pennsylvania statute, moreover, has the further defect of providing state financial aid directly to the church-related school. This factor distinguishes both Everson and Allen, for in both those cases the Court was careful to point out that state aid was provided to the student and his parents—not to the church-related school. . . .

The history of government grants of a continuing cash subsidy indicates that such programs have almost always been accompanied by varying measures of control and surveillance. The government cash grants before us now provide no basis for predicting that comprehensive measures of surveillance and controls will not follow. In particular the government's post-audit power to inspect and evaluate a church-related school's financial records and to determine which expenditures are religious and which are secular creates an intimate and continuing relationship between church and state.

A broader base of entanglement of yet a different character is presented by the divisive political potential of these state programs. In a community where such a large number of pupils are served by church-related schools, it can be assumed that state assistance will entail considerable political activity. Partisans of parochial schools, understandably concerned with rising costs and sincerely dedicated to both the religious and secular educational missions of their schools, will inevitably champion this cause and promote political action to achieve their goals. Those who oppose state aid, whether for constitutional, religious, or fiscal reasons, will inevitably respond and employ all of the usual political campaign techniques to prevail. Candidates will be forced to declare and voters to choose. It would be unrealistic to ignore the fact that many people confronted with issues of this kind will find their votes aligned with their faith.

Ordinarily political debate and division, however vigorous or even partisan, are normal and healthy manifestations of our democratic system of government, but political division along religious lines was one of the principal evils against which the First Amendment was intended to protect. The potential divisiveness of such conflict is a threat to the normal political process. To have States or communities divide on the issues presented by state aid to parochial schools would tend to confuse and obscure other issues of great urgency. We have an expanding array of vexing issues, local and national, domestic and international, to debate and divide on. It conflicts with our whole history and tradition to permit questions of the Religion Clauses to assume such importance in our legislatures and in our elections that they could divert attention from the myriad issues and problems that confront every level of government. The highways of church and state relationships are not likely to be one-way streets, and the Constitution's authors sought to protect religious worship from the pervasive power of government. The history of many countries attests to the hazards of religion's intruding into the political arena or of political power intruding into the legitimate and free exercise of religious belief.

. . .

Finally, nothing we have said can be construed to disparage the role of church-related elementary and secondary schools in our national life. Their contribution has been and is enormous. Nor do we ignore their economic plight in a period of rising costs and expanding need. Taxpayers generally have been spared vast sums by the maintenance of these educational institutions by religious organizations, largely by the gifts of faithful adherents.

The merit and benefits of these schools, however, are not the issue before us in these cases. The sole question is whether state aid to these schools can be squared with the dictates of the Religion Clauses. Under our system the choice has been made that government is to be entirely excluded from the area of religious instruction and churches excluded from the affairs of government. The Constitution decrees that religion must be a private matter for the individual, the family, and the institutions of private choice, and that while some involvement and entanglement are inevitable, lines must be drawn.

. . .

MR. JUSTICE DOUGLAS, whom MR. JUSTICE BLACK joins, concurring.

. . .

The analysis of the constitutional objections to these two state systems of grants to parochial or sectarian schools must start with the admitted and obvious fact that the raison d'etre of parochial schools is the propagation of a religious faith. They also teach secular subjects; but they came into existence in this country because Protestant groups were perverting the public schools by using them to propagate their faith. The Catholics naturally rebelled. If schools were to be used to propagate a particular creed or religion, then Catholic ideals should also be served. Hence the advent of parochial schools.

. . .

. . . (T)he major force in shaping the pattern of education in this country was the conflict between Protestants and Catholics. The Catholics logically argued that a public school was sectarian when it taught the King James version of the Bible. They therefore wanted it removed from the public schools; and in time they tried to get public funds for their own parochial schools.

. . .

The story of conflict and dissension is long and well known. The result was a state of so-called equilibrium where religious instruction was eliminated from public schools and the use of public funds to support religious schools was deemed to be banned.

But the hydraulic pressures created by political forces and by economic stress were great and they began to change the situation. Laws were passed—state and federal—that dispensed public funds to sustain religious schools and the plea was always in the educational frame of reference: education in all sectors was needed, from languages to calculus to nuclear physics. And it was forcefully argued that a linguist or mathematician or physicist trained in religious schools was just as competent as one trained in secular schools.

And so we have gradually edged into a situation where vast amounts of public funds are supplied each year to sectarian schools.

And the argument is made that the private parochial school system takes about $9 billion a year off the back of government—as if that were enough to justify violating the Establishment Clause.

While the evolution of the public school system in this country marked an escape from denominational control and was therefore admirable as seen through the eyes of those who think like Madison and Jefferson, it has disadvantages. The main one is that a state system may attempt to mold all students alike according to the views of the dominant group and to discourage the emergence of individual idiosyncrasies.

Sectarian education, however, does not remedy that condition. The advantages of sectarian education relate solely to religious or doctrinal matters. They give the church the opportunity to indoctrinate its creed delicately and indirectly, or massively through doctrinal courses.

Many nations follow that course: Moslem nations teach the Koran in their schools; Sweden vests its elementary education in the parish; Newfoundland puts its school system under three superintendents—one from the Church of England, one from the Catholic church, one from the United Church. In Ireland the public schools are under denominational managership—Catholic, Episcopalian, Presbyterian, and Hebrew.

England puts sectarian schools under the umbrella of its school system. It finances sectarian education; it exerts control by prescribing standards; it requires some free scholarships; it provides nondenominational membership on the board of directors.

The British system is, in other words, one of surveillance over sectarian schools. We too have surveillance over sectarian schools but only to the extent of making sure that minimum educational standards are met, viz., competent teachers, accreditation of the school for diplomas, the number of hours of work and credits allowed, and so on.

But we have never faced, until recently, the problem of policing sectarian schools. Any surveillance to date has been minor and has related only to the consistently unchallenged matters of accreditation of the sectarian school in the State's school system.

. . .

If the government closed its eyes to the manner in which these grants are actually used it would be allowing public funds to promote sectarian education. If it did not close its eyes but undertook the surveillance needed, it would, I fear, intermeddle in parochial affairs in a way that would breed only rancor and dissension.

. . .

[T]here are those who have the courage to announce that a State may nonetheless finance the secular part of a sectarian school's educational program. That, however, makes a grave constitutional decision turn merely on cost accounting and bookkeeping entries. A history class, a literature class, or a science class in a parochial school is not a separate institute; it is part of the organic whole which the State subsidizes. The funds are used in these cases to pay or help pay the salaries of teachers in parochial schools; and the presence of teachers is critical to the essential purpose of the parochial school, viz., to advance the religious endeavors of the particular church. It matters not that the teacher receiving taxpayers' money only teaches religion a fraction of the time. Nor does it matter that he or she teaches no religion. The school is an organism living on one budget. What the taxpayers give for salaries of those who teach only the humanities or science without any trace of proselytizing enables the school to use all of its own funds for religious training. [W]e would be blind to realities if we let "sophisticated bookkeeping" sanction "almost total subsidy of a religious institution by assigning the bulk of the institution's expenses to 'secular' activities." And sophisticated attempts to avoid the Constitution are just as invalid as simple-minded ones.

In my view the taxpayers' forced contribution to the parochial schools in the present cases violates the First Amendment.

[I]t is argued . . . in these cases that sectarian schools and universities perform two separable functions. First, they provide secular education, and second, they teach the tenets of a particular sect. Since the State has determined that the secular education provided in sectarian schools serves the legitimate state interest in the education of its citizens, it is contended that state aid solely to the secular education function does not involve the State in aid to religion. *Pierce v. Society of Sisters*, 268 U.S. 510 (1925), and *Board of Education v. Allen*, are relied on as support for the argument.

Our opinion in Allen recognized that sectarian schools provide both a secular and a sectarian education. But I do not read Pierce or Allen as supporting the proposition that public subsidy of a sectarian institution's secular training is permissible state involvement. I read them as supporting the proposition that

as an identifiable set of skills and an identifiable quantum of knowledge, secular education may be effectively provided either in the religious context of parochial schools, or outside the context of religion in public schools. The State's interest in secular education may be defined broadly as an interest in ensuring that all children within its boundaries acquire a minimum level of competency in certain skills, such as reading, writing, and arithmetic, as well as a minimum amount of information and knowledge in certain subjects such as history, geography, science, literature, and law. Without such skills and knowledge, an individual will be at a severe disadvantage both in participating in democratic self-government and in earning a living in a modern industrial economy. But the State has no proper interest in prescribing the precise forum in which such skills and knowledge are learned since acquisition of this secular education is neither incompatible with religious learning, nor is it inconsistent with or inimical to religious precepts.

When the same secular educational process occurs in both public and sectarian schools, *Allen* held that the State could provide secular textbooks for use in that process to students in both public and sectarian schools. Of course, the State could not provide textbooks giving religious instruction. But since the textbooks involved in *Allen* would, at least in theory, be limited to secular education, no aid to sectarian instruction was involved.

. . .

Allen, in my view, simply sustained a statute in which the State was "neutral in its relations with groups of religious believers and non-believers." . . .

Mr. Justice White. . . dissenting.

. . .

It is enough for me that the States and the Federal Government are financing a separable secular function of overriding importance in order to sustain the legislation here challenged. That religion and private interests other than education may substantially benefit does not convert these laws into impermissible establishments of religion.

. . .

The unpredictability of and consequent dissatisfaction with the three-part *Lemon* test was immediate. Referring to the Court's first post-*Lemon* decision in *Tilton v. Richardson*,[292] Justice White decried "[j]udicial caveats against entanglement" as a "blurred, indistinct and variable barrier."[293] The Court itself acknowledged that it could "only dimly perceive the boundaries of permissible governmental activity in this sensi-

---

[292] 403 U.S. 672 (1971).
[293] *Lemon*, 403 U.S. at 671 (White, J., dissenting).

tive area of constitutional adjudication."[294] At issue in *Tilton* were federal construction grants to parochial colleges and universities to be used for facilities dedicated to secular educational purposes.[295] Even if such direct financial support would be constitutionally dubious if provided to primary or secondary parochial education, the Court in *Tilton* emphasized "significant differences between the religious aspects of church-related institutions of higher learning and parochial elementary schools."[296] Specifically, as the Court put it, "college students are less impressionable and susceptible to religious indoctrination, . . . by their very nature, college and postgraduate courses tend to limit the opportunities for sectarian influence by virtue of their own internal disciplines, . . . [and] religious indoctrination is not a substantial purpose" of denominational institutions of higher learning.[297] Although concurring, Justice White warned of a bind that the Court's reasoning and conclusion created.

> The Court creates an insoluble paradox for the State and the parochial schools. The State cannot finance secular instruction if it permits religion to be taught in the same classroom; but if it exacts a promise that religion not be so taught—a promise the school and its teachers are quite willing and . . . able to give—and enforces it, it is then entangled in the 'no entanglement' aspect of the Court's Establishment Clause.
>
> Why the federal program in the *Tilton* case is not embroiled in the same difficulties is never adequately explained. Surely the notion that college students are more mature and resistant to indoctrination is a makeweight, for in *Tilton* there is careful note of the federal condition on funding and the enforcement mechanism available. Nor can I imagine the basis for finding college clerics more reliable in keeping their promises than their counterparts in elementary schools—particularly those in the Rhode Island case, since within five years the majority of teachers in Rhode Island parochial schools will be lay persons, many of them Catholic.[298]

iii.   Accommodation

Further exacerbating the difficulties of review referenced to purpose, effect and entanglement has been an interest in accommodating religion. Although reflecting an awareness of free exercise values, accommodationist inclinations have heightened the unpredictability factor in establishment clause cases. Rigid application of the purpose, effect and entanglement test, as Justice Brennan noted in *Marsh v. Chambers*, would have required invalidation of a state legislature's practice of opening its sessions with prayer led by a chaplain who was paid by the state.[299] Stressing accommodationist values, however, the Court determined that such invocations were "simply a tolerable acknowledgment of beliefs widely held among the people of this country."[300]

Striking a balance between the imperatives of avoiding sectarian purpose, effects that are primarily religious and entanglement between church and state on the one hand, and accommodation on the other, has proved to be especially confounding when public property is used for religious displays. A divided Court, in *Lynch v. Donnelly*, upheld a Christmas season display of a nativity scene paid for by the city and erected

---

[294] Tilton, 403 U.S. at 678.

[295] *Id.* at 674–75.

[296] *Id.* at 685.

[297] *Id.* at 686.

[298] Lemon, 403 U.S. at 668 (1971)(White, J., dissenting).

[299] Marsh v. Chambers, 463 U.S. 783, 796 (1983)(Brennan, J., dissenting).

[300] *Id.* at 792 (majority opinion).

on municipal property.[301] Writing for the Court, Chief Justice Burger found that the concept of a wall between church and state was a useful metaphor but not an entirely accurate description of a relationship requiring accommodation. Justice Brennan, joined by Justices Marshall, Blackmun and Stevens, dissented on grounds that the Court had discounted too heavily the requirements of *Lemon*.

---

[301] Lynch v. Donnelly, 465 U.S. 668, 671 (1984).

Lynch v. Donnelly
465 U.S. 668 (1984)

CHIEF JUSTICE BURGER delivered the opinion of the Court.

We granted certiorari to decide whether the Establishment Clause of the First Amendment prohibits a municipality from including a creche, or Nativity scene, in its annual Christmas display.

I

Each year, in cooperation with the downtown retail merchants' association, the city of Pawtucket, R. I., erects a Christmas display as part of its observance of the Christmas holiday season. The display is situated in a park owned by a nonprofit organization and located in the heart of the shopping district. The display is essentially like those to be found in hundreds of towns or cities across the Nation—often on public grounds—during the Christmas season. The Pawtucket display comprises many of the figures and decorations traditionally associated with Christmas, including, among other things, a Santa Claus house, reindeer pulling Santa's sleigh, candy-striped poles, a Christmas tree, carolers, cutout figures representing such characters as a clown, an elephant, and a teddy bear, hundreds of colored lights, a large banner that reads "SEASONS GREETINGS," and the creche at issue here. All components of this display are owned by the city.

The creche, which has been included in the display for 40 or more years, consists of the traditional figures, including the Infant Jesus, Mary and Joseph, angels, shepherds, kings, and animals, all ranging in height from 5" to 5'. In 1973, when the present creche was acquired, it cost the city $1,365; it now is valued at $200. The erection and dismantling of the creche costs the city about $20 per year; nominal expenses are incurred in lighting the creche. No money has been expended on its maintenance for the past 10 years.

. . .

In every Establishment Clause case, we must reconcile the inescapable tension between the objective of preventing unnecessary intrusion of either the church or the state upon the other, and the reality that, as the Court has so often noted, total separation of the two is not possible.

The Court has sometimes described the Religion Clauses as erecting a "wall" between church and state, The concept of a "wall" of separation is a useful figure of speech probably deriving from views of Thomas Jefferson. The metaphor has served as a reminder that the Establishment Clause forbids an established church or anything approaching it. But the metaphor itself is not a wholly accurate description of the practical aspects of the relationship that in fact exists between church and state.

No significant segment of our society and no institution within it can exist in a vacuum or in total or absolute isolation from all the other parts, much less from government. "It has never been thought either possible or desirable to enforce a regime of total separation. . . ." Nor does the Constitution require complete separation of church and state; it affirmatively mandates accommodation, not merely tolerance, of all religions, and forbids hostility toward any. Anything less would require the "callous indifference" we have said was never intended by the Establishment Clause. Indeed, we have observed, such hostility would bring us into "war with our national tradition as embodied in the First Amendment's guaranty of the free exercise of religion."

B

The Court's interpretation of the Establishment Clause has comported with what history reveals was the contemporaneous understanding of its guarantees. A significant example of the contemporaneous understanding of that Clause is found in the events of the first week of the First Session of the First Congress in 1789. In the very week that Congress approved the Establishment Clause as part of the Bill of Rights for submission to the states, it enacted legislation providing for paid Chaplains for the House and Senate. In *Marsh v. Chambers*, we noted that 17 Members of that First Congress had been Delegates to the Constitutional Convention where freedom of speech, press, and religion and antagonism toward an established church were subjects of frequent discussion. We saw no conflict with the Establishment Clause when Nebraska employed members of the clergy as official legislative Chaplains to give opening prayers at sessions of the state legislature.

The interpretation of the Establishment Clause by Congress in 1789 takes on special significance in light of the Court's emphasis that the First Congress

"was a Congress whose constitutional decisions have always been regarded, as they should be regarded, as of the greatest weight in the interpretation of that fundamental instrument."

It is clear that neither the 17 draftsmen of the Constitution who were Members of the First Congress, nor the Congress of 1789, saw any establishment problem in the employment of congressional Chaplains to offer daily prayers in the Congress, a practice that has continued for nearly two centuries. It would be difficult to identify a more striking example of the accommodation of religious belief intended by the Framers.

C

There is an unbroken history of official acknowledgment by all three branches of government of the role of religion in American life from at least 1789. . . .

Our history is replete with official references to the value and invocation of Divine guidance in deliberations and pronouncements of the Founding Fathers and contemporary leaders. Beginning in the early colonial period long before Independence, a day of Thanksgiving was celebrated as a religious holiday to give thanks for the bounties of Nature as gifts from God. President Washington and his successors proclaimed Thanksgiving, with all its religious overtones, a day of national celebration and Congress made it a National Holiday more than a century ago. That holiday has not lost its theme of expressing thanks for Divine aid any more than has Christmas lost its religious significance.

"To the end that we may bear more earnest witness to our gratitude to Almighty God, I suggest a nationwide reading of the Holy Scriptures during the period from Thanksgiving Day to Christmas." Presidental Proclamation No. 2629, 58 Stat. 1160. President Reagan and his immediate predecessors have issued similar Proclamations.

Executive Orders and other official announcements of Presidents and of the Congress have proclaimed both Christmas and Thanksgiving National Holidays in religious terms. And, by Acts of Congress, it has long been the practice that federal employees are released from duties on these National Holidays, while being paid from the same public revenues that provide the compensation of the Chaplains of the Senate and the House and the military services. Thus, it is clear that Government has long recognized—indeed it has subsidized—holidays with religious significance.

Other examples of reference to our religious heritage are found in the statutorily prescribed national motto "In God We Trust," which Congress and the President mandated for our currency, and in the language "One nation under God," as part of the Pledge of Allegiance to the American flag. That pledge is recited by many thousands of public school children—and adults—every year.

Art galleries supported by public revenues display religious paintings of the 15th and 16th centuries, predominantly inspired by one religious faith. The National Gallery in Washington, maintained with Government support, for example, has long exhibited masterpieces with religious messages, notably the Last Supper, and paintings depicting the Birth of Christ, the Crucifixion, and the Resurrection, among many others with explicit Christian themes and messages. The very chamber in which oral arguments on this case were heard is decorated with a notable and permanent—not seasonal—symbol of religion: Moses with the Ten Commandments. Congress has long provided chapels in the Capitol for religious worship and meditation.

There are countless other illustrations of the Government's acknowledgment of our religious heritage and governmental sponsorship of graphic manifestations of that heritage. Congress has directed the President to proclaim a National Day of Prayer each year "on which [day] the people of the United States may turn to God in prayer and meditation at churches, in groups, and as individuals." Our Presidents have repeatedly issued such Proclamations. Presidential Proclamations and messages have also issued to commemorate Jewish Heritage Week, Presidential and the Jewish High Holy Days. One cannot look at even this brief resume without finding that our history is pervaded by expressions of religious beliefs. . . . Equally pervasive is the evidence of accommodation of all faiths and all forms of religious expression, and hostility toward none. . . .

This history may help explain why the Court consistently has declined to take a rigid, absolutist view of the Establishment Clause. We have refused "to construe the Religion Clauses with a literalness that would undermine the ultimate constitutional objective as illuminated by history." In our modern, complex society, whose traditions and constitutional underpinnings rest on and encourage diversity and pluralism in all areas, an absolutist approach in applying the Establishment Clause is simplistic and has been uniformly rejected by the Court.

Rather than mechanically invalidating all governmental conduct or statutes that confer benefits or give special recognition to religion in general or to one faith—as an absolutist approach would dictate—the Court has scrutinized challenged legislation or official conduct to determine whether, in reality, it establishes a religion or religious faith, or tends to do so. . . .

In each case, the inquiry calls for line-drawing; no fixed, per se rule can be framed. The Establishment Clause like the Due Process Clauses is not a precise, detailed provision in a legal code capable of ready application. The purpose of the Establishment Clause "was to state an objective, not to write a statute." The line between permissible relationships and those barred by the Clause can no more be straight and unwavering than due process can be defined in a single stroke or phrase or test. The Clause erects a "blurred, indistinct, and variable barrier depending on all the circumstances of a particular relationship."

In the line-drawing process we have often found it useful to inquire whether the challenged law or conduct has a secular purpose, whether its principal or primary effect is to advance or inhibit religion, and whether it creates an excessive entanglement of government with religion. *Lemon*. But, we have repeatedly emphasized our unwillingness to be confined to any single test or criterion in this sensitive area. In two cases, the Court did not even apply the *Lemon* "test." We did not, for example, consider that analysis relevant in *Marsh v. Chambers.* Nor did we find *Lemon* useful in *Larson v. Valente*, 456 U.S. 228, where there was substantial evidence of overt discrimination against a particular church.

In this case, the focus of our inquiry must be on the creche in the context of the Christmas season. . . .

. . . When viewed in the proper context of the Christmas Holiday season, it is apparent that, on this record, there is insufficient evidence to establish that the inclusion of the creche is a purposeful or surreptitious effort to express some kind of subtle governmental advocacy of a particular religious message. In a pluralistic society a variety of motives and purposes are implicated. The city, like the Congresses and Presidents, however, has principally taken note of a significant historical religious event long celebrated in the Western World. The creche in the display depicts the historical origins of this traditional event long recognized as a National Holiday.

The narrow question is whether there is a secular purpose for Pawtucket's display of the creche. The display is sponsored by the city to celebrate the Holiday and to depict the origins of that Holiday. These are legitimate secular purposes. The District Court's inference, drawn from the religious nature of the creche, that the city has no secular purpose was, on this record, clearly erroneous.

The District Court found that the primary effect of including the creche is to confer a substantial and impermissible benefit on religion in general and on the Christian faith in particular. Comparisons of the relative benefits to religion of different forms of governmental support are elusive and difficult to make. But to conclude that the primary effect of including the creche is to advance religion in violation of the Establishment Clause would require that we view it as more beneficial to and more an endorsement of religion, for example, than expenditure of large sums of public money for textbooks supplied throughout the country to students attending church-sponsored schools, *Board of Education v. Allen*, expenditure of public funds for transportation of students to church-sponsored schools, *Everson v. Board of Education*, federal grants for college buildings of church-sponsored institutions of higher education combining secular and religious education, *Tilton* noncategorical grants to church-sponsored colleges and universities, and the tax exemptions for church properties sanctioned in *Walz*. It would also require that we view it as more of an endorsement of religion than the Sunday Closing Laws upheld in *McGowan v. Maryland*, the release time program for religious training in *Zorach,* and the legislative prayers upheld in *Marsh*.

We are unable to discern a greater aid to religion deriving from inclusion of the creche than from these benefits and endorsements previously held not violative of the Establishment Clause. What was said about the legislative prayers in *Marsh*, and implied about the Sunday Closing Laws in *McGowan* is true of the city's inclusion of the creche: its "reason or effect merely happens to coincide or harmonize with the tenets of some . . . religions."

. . .

The dissent asserts some observers may perceive that the city has aligned itself with the Christian faith by including a Christian symbol in its display and that this serves to advance religion. We can assume, arguendo, that the display advances religion in a sense; but our precedents plainly contemplate that on occasion some advancement of religion will result from governmental action. The Court has made it abundantly clear, however, that "not every law that confers an 'indirect,' 'remote,' or 'incidental' benefit upon [religion] is, for that reason alone, constitutionally invalid." Here, whatever benefit there is to one faith or religion or to all religions, is indirect, remote, and incidental; display of the creche is no more an advancement or endorsement of religion than the Congressional and Executive recognition of the origins of the Holiday itself as "Christ's Mass," or the exhibition of literally hundreds of religious paintings in governmentally supported museums.

Entanglement is a question of kind and degree. In this case, however, there is no reason to disturb the District Court's finding on the absence of administrative entanglement. There is no evidence of contact with church authorities concerning the content or design of the exhibit prior to or since Pawtucket's purchase of the creche. No expenditures for maintenance of the creche have been necessary; and since the city owns the creche, now valued at $200, the tangible material it contributes is de minimis. In many respects the display requires far less ongoing, day-to-day interaction between church and state than religious paintings in public galleries. There is nothing here, of course, like the "comprehensive, discriminating, and continuing state surveillance" or the "enduring entanglement" present in *Lemon*.

. . .

We are satisfied that the city has a secular purpose for including the creche, that the city has not impermissibly advanced religion, and that including the creche does not create excessive entanglement between religion and government.

IV

JUSTICE BRENNAN describes the creche as a "re-creation of an event that lies at the heart of Christian faith." The creche, like a painting, is passive; admittedly it is a reminder of the origins of Christmas. Even the traditional, purely secular displays extant at Christmas, with or without a creche, would inevitably recall the religious nature of the Holiday. The display engenders a friendly community spirit of goodwill in keeping with the season. The creche may well have special meaning to those whose faith includes the celebration of religious Masses, but none who sense the origins of the Christmas celebration would fail to be aware of its religious implications. That the display brings people into the central city, and serves commercial interests and benefits merchants and their employees, does not, as the dissent points out, determine the character of the display. That a prayer invoking Divine guidance in Congress is preceded and followed by debate and partisan conflict over taxes,

budgets, national defense, and myriad mundane subjects, for example, has never been thought to demean or taint the sacredness of the invocation.

Of course the creche is identified with one religious faith but no more so than the examples we have set out from prior cases in which we found no conflict with the Establishment Clause. It would be ironic, however, if the inclusion of a single symbol of a particular historic religious event, as part of a celebration acknowledged in the Western World for 20 centuries, and in this country by the people, by the Executive Branch, by the Congress, and by the courts for 2 centuries, would so "taint" the city's exhibit as to render it violative of the Establishment Clause. To forbid the use of this one passive symbol—the creche—at the very time people are taking note of the season with Christmas hymns and carols in public schools and other public places, and while the Congress and legislatures open sessions with prayers by paid chaplains, would be a stilted overreaction contrary to our history and to our holdings. If the presence of the creche in this display violates the Establishment Clause, a host of other forms of taking official note of Christmas, and of our religious heritage, are equally offensive to the Constitution.

The Court has acknowledged that the "fears and political problems" that gave rise to the Religion Clauses in the 18th century are of far less concern today. We are unable to perceive the Archbishop of Canterbury, the Bishop of Rome, or other powerful religious leaders behind every public acknowledgment of the religious heritage long officially recognized by the three constitutional branches of government. Any notion that these symbols pose a real danger of establishment of a state church is far-fetched indeed.

. . .

We hold that, notwithstanding the religious significance of the creche, the city of Pawtucket has not violated the Establishment Clause of the First Amendment. . . .

The *Lynch* decision was important not only for its prioritization of accommodationist values but for questions that were raised about the viability of the three dimensional *Lemon* test. In a concurring opinion, Justice O'Connor suggested that an inquiry into purpose, effect and excessive entanglement had no clear relationship to establishment clause principle.

JUSTICE O'CONNOR, concurring.

I concur in the opinion of the Court. I write separately to suggest a clarification of our Establishment Clause doctrine. The suggested approach leads to the same result in this case as that taken by the Court, and the Court's opinion, as I read it, is consistent with my analysis.

I

The Establishment Clause prohibits government from making adherence to a religion relevant in any way to a person's standing in the political community. Government can run afoul of that prohibition in two principal ways. One is excessive entanglement with religious institutions, which may interfere with the independence of the institutions, give the institutions access to government or governmental powers not fully shared by nonadherents of the religion, and foster the creation of political constituencies defined along religious lines. The second and more direct infringement is government endorsement or disapproval of religion. Endorsement sends a message to nonadherents that they are outsiders, not full members of the political community, and an accompanying message to adherents that they are insiders, favored members of the political community. Disapproval sends the opposite message.

Our prior cases have used the three-part test articulated in *Lemon v. Kurtzman*, as a guide to detecting these two forms of unconstitutional government action. It has never been entirely clear, however, how the three parts of the test relate to the principles enshrined in the Establishment Clause. Focusing on institutional entanglement and on endorsement or disapproval of religion clarifies the *Lemon* test as an analytical device.

. . .

The central issue in this case is whether Pawtucket has endorsed Christianity by its display of the creche. To answer that question, we must examine both what Pawtucket intended to communicate in displaying the creche and what message the city's display actually conveyed. The purpose and effect prongs of the *Lemon* test represent these two aspects of the meaning of the city's action.

The meaning of a statement to its audience depends both on the intention of the speaker and on the "objective" meaning of the statement in the community. Some listeners need not rely solely on the words themselves in discerning the speaker's intent: they can judge the intent by, for example, examining the context of the statement or asking questions of the speaker. Other listeners do not have or will not seek access to such evidence of intent. They will rely instead on the words themselves; for them the message actually conveyed may be something not actually intended. If the audience is large, as it always is when government "speaks" by word or deed, some portion of the audience will inevitably receive a message determined by the "objective" content of the statement, and some portion will inevitably receive the intended message. Examination of both the subjective and the objective components of the message communicated by a government action is therefore necessary to determine whether the action carries a forbidden meaning.

The purpose prong of the *Lemon* test asks whether government's actual purpose is to endorse or disapprove of religion. The effect prong asks whether, irrespective of government's actual purpose, the practice under review in fact conveys a message of endorsement or disapproval. An affirmative answer to either question should render the challenged practice invalid.

A

The purpose prong of the *Lemon* test requires that a government activity have a secular purpose. That requirement is not satisfied, however, by the mere existence of some secular purpose, however dominated by religious purposes. In *Stone v. Graham*, for example, the Court held that posting copies of the Ten Commandments in schools violated the purpose prong of the *Lemon* test, yet the State plainly had some secular objectives, such as instilling most of the values of the Ten Commandments and illustrating their connection to our legal system. The proper inquiry under the purpose prong of *Lemon*, I submit, is whether the government intends to convey a message of endorsement or disapproval of religion.

Applying that formulation to this case, I would find that Pawtucket did not intend to convey any message of endorsement of Christianity or disapproval of non-Christian religions. The evident purpose of including the creche in the larger display was not promotion of the religious content of the creche but celebration of the public holiday through its traditional symbols. Celebration of public holidays, which have cultural significance even if they also have religious aspects, is a legitimate secular purpose.

B

Focusing on the evil of government endorsement or disapproval of religion makes clear that the effect prong of the *Lemon* test is properly interpreted not to require invalidation of a government practice merely because it in fact causes, even as a primary effect, advancement or inhibition of religion. . . . What is crucial is that a government practice not have the effect of communicating a message of government endorsement or disapproval of religion. It is only practices having that effect, whether intentionally or unintentionally, that make religion relevant, in reality or public perception, to status in the political community.

Pawtucket's display of its creche, I believe, does not communicate a message that the government intends to endorse the Christian beliefs represented by the creche. Although the religious and indeed sectarian significance of the creche, as the District Court found, is not neutralized by the setting, the overall holiday setting changes what viewers may fairly understand to be the purpose of the display—as a typical museum setting, though not neutralizing the religious content of a religious painting, negates any message of endorsement of that content. The display celebrates a public holiday, and no one contends that declaration of that holiday is understood to be an endorsement of religion. The holiday itself has very strong secular components and traditions. Government celebration of the holiday, which is extremely common, generally is not understood to endorse the religious content of the holiday, just as government celebration of Thanksgiving is not so understood. The creche is a traditional symbol of the holiday that is very commonly displayed along with purely secular symbols, as it was in Pawtucket.

These features combine to make the government's display of the creche in this particular physical setting no more an endorsement of religion than such governmental "acknowledgments" of religion as legislative prayers of the type approved in *Marsh,* government declaration of Thanksgiving as a public holiday, printing of "In God We Trust" on coins, and opening court sessions with "God save the United States and this honorable court." Those government acknowledgments of religion serve, in the only ways reasonably possible in our culture, the legitimate secular purposes of solemnizing public occasions, expressing confidence in the future, and encouraging the recognition of what is worthy of appreciation in society. For that reason, and because of their history and ubiquity, those practices are not understood as conveying government approval of particular religious beliefs. The display of the creche likewise serves a secular purpose—celebration of a public holiday with traditional symbols. It cannot fairly be understood to convey a message of government endorsement of religion. It is significant in this regard that the creche display apparently caused no political divisiveness prior to the filing of this lawsuit, although Pawtucket had incorporated the creche in its annual Christmas display for some years. For these reasons, I conclude that Pawtucket's display of the creche does not have the effect of communicating endorsement of Christianity.

Justice Brennan, with whom Justice Marshall, Justice Blackmun, and Justice Stevens join, dissenting.

The principles announced in the compact phrases of the Religion Clauses have, as the Court today reminds us, ante, at 678–679, proved difficult to apply. Faced with that un-

certainty, the Court properly looks for guidance to the settled test announced in *Lemon,* for assessing whether a challenged governmental practice involves an impermissible step toward the establishment of religion. Applying that test to this case, the Court reaches an essentially narrow result which turns largely upon the particular holiday context in which the city of Pawtucket's nativity scene appeared. The Court's decision implicitly leaves open questions concerning the constitutionality of the public display on public property of a creche standing alone, or the public display of other distinctively religious symbols such as a cross. Despite the narrow contours of the Court's opinion, our precedents in my view compel the holding that Pawtucket's inclusion of a life-sized display depicting the biblical description of the birth of Christ as part of its annual Christmas celebration is unconstitutional. Nothing in the history of such practices or the setting in which the city's creche is presented obscures or diminishes the plain fact that Pawtucket's action amounts to an impermissible governmental endorsement of a particular faith.

I

Last term, I expressed the hope that the Court's decision in *Marsh,* would prove to be only a single, aberrant departure from our settled method of analyzing Establishment Clause cases. That the Court today returns to the settled analysis of our prior cases gratifies that hope. At the same time, the Court's less-than-vigorous application of the *Lemon* test suggests that its commitment to those standards may only be superficial. After reviewing the Court's opinion, I am convinced that this case appears hard not because the principles of decision are obscure, but because the Christmas holiday seems so familiar and agreeable. Although the Court's reluctance to disturb a community's chosen method of celebrating such an agreeable holiday is understandable, that cannot justify the Court's departure from controlling precedent. In my view, Pawtucket's maintenance and display at public expense of a symbol as distinctively sectarian as a creche simply cannot be squared with our prior cases. And it is plainly contrary to the purposes and values of the Establishment Clause to pretend, as the Court does, that the otherwise secular setting of Pawtucket's nativity scene dilutes in some fashion the creche's singular religiosity, or that the city's annual display reflects nothing more than an "acknowledgment" of our shared national heritage. Neither the character of the Christmas holiday itself, nor our heritage of religious expression supports this result. Indeed, our remarkable and precious religious diversity as a Nation, which the Establishment Clause seeks to protect, runs directly counter to today's decision.

A

As we have sought to meet new problems arising under the Establishment Clause, our decisions, with few exceptions, have demanded that a challenged governmental practice satisfy the following criteria:

"First, the [practice] must have a secular legislative purpose; second, its principal or primary effect must be one that neither advances nor inhibits religion; finally, [it] must not foster 'an excessive government entanglement with religion.'" *Lemon.*

This well-defined three-part test expresses the essential concerns animating the Establishment Clause. Thus, the test is designed to ensure that the organs of government remain strictly separate and apart from religious affairs, for "a union of government and religion tends to destroy government and degrade religion." And it seeks to guarantee that government maintains a position of neutrality with respect to religion and neither advances nor inhibits the promulgation and practice of religious beliefs. In this regard, we must be alert in our examination of any challenged practice not only for an official establishment of religion, but also for those other evils at which the Clause was aimed—" 'sponsorship, financial support, and active involvement of the sovereign in religious activity.'"

Applying the three-part test to Pawtucket's creche, I am persuaded that the city's inclusion of the creche in its Christmas display simply does not reflect a "clearly secular . . . purpose." Unlike the typical case in which the record reveals some contemporaneous expression of a clear purpose to advance religion, or, conversely, a clear secular purpose, here we have no explicit statement of purpose by Pawtucket's municipal government accompanying its decision to purchase, display, and maintain the creche. Governmental purpose may nevertheless be inferred. For instance, in *Stone v. Graham*, this Court found, despite the State's avowed purpose of reminding schoolchildren of the secular application of the commands of the Decalogue, that the "pre-eminent purpose for posting the Ten Commandments on schoolroom walls is plainly religious in nature." In the present case, the city claims that its purposes were exclusively secular. Pawtucket sought, according to this view, only to participate in the celebration of a national holiday and to attract people to the downtown area in order to promote pre-Christmas retail sales and to help engender the spirit of goodwill and neighborliness commonly associated with the Christmas season.

. . .

The "primary effect" of including a nativity scene in the city's display is, as the District Court found, to place the government's imprimatur of approval on the particular religious beliefs exemplified by the creche. Those who believe in the message of the nativity receive the unique and exclusive benefit of public recognition and approval of their views. For many, the city's decision to include the creche as part of its extensive and costly efforts to celebrate Christmas can only mean that the prestige of the government has been conferred on the beliefs associated with the creche, thereby providing "a significant symbolic benefit to religion. . . ." The effect on minority religious groups, as well as on those who may reject all religion, is to convey the message that their views are not similarly worthy of public recognition nor entitled to public support. It was precisely this sort of religious chauvinism that the Establishment Clause was intended forever to prohibit. In this case, as in *Engel v. Vitale*, "[when] the power, prestige and financial support of government is placed behind a particular religious belief, the indirect coercive pressure upon religious minorities to conform to the prevailing officially approved religion is plain." Our decision in *Widmar v. Vincent*, 454 U.S. 263, rests upon the same principle. There the Court noted that a state university policy of "equal access" for both secular and religious groups would "not confer any imprimatur of state approval" on the religious groups permitted to use the facilities because "a broad spectrum of groups" would be served and there was no evidence that religious groups would dominate the forum. Here, by contrast, Pawtucket itself owns the creche and instead of extending similar attention to a "broad spectrum" of religious and secular groups, it has singled out Christianity for special treatment.

. . .

Finally, it is evident that Pawtucket's inclusion of a creche as part of its annual Christmas display does pose a significant threat of fostering "excessive entanglement." As the Court notes, ante, the District Court found no administrative entanglement in this case, primarily because the city had been able to administer the annual display without extensive consultation with religious officials. Of course, there is no reason to disturb that finding, but it is worth noting that after today's decision, administrative entanglements may well develop. Jews and other non-Christian groups, prompted perhaps by the Mayor's remark that he will include a Menorah in future displays, can be expected to press government for inclusion of their symbols, and faced with such requests, government will have to become involved in accommodating the various demands. More importantly, although no political divisiveness was apparent in Pawtucket prior to the filing of respondents' lawsuit, that act, as the District Court found, unleashed powerful emotional reactions which divided the city along religious lines. The fact that calm had prevailed prior to this suit does not immediately suggest the absence of any division on the point for, as the District Court observed, the quiescence of those opposed to the creche may have reflected nothing more than their sense of futility in opposing the majority. Of course, the Court is correct to note that we have never held that the potential for divisiveness alone is sufficient to invalidate a challenged governmental practice; we have, nevertheless, repeatedly emphasized that "too close a proximity" between religious and civil authorities, may represent a "warning signal" that the values embodied in the Establishment Clause are at risk. Furthermore, the Court should not blind itself to the fact that because communities differ in religious composition, the controversy over whether local governments may adopt religious symbols will continue to fester. In many communities, non-Christian groups can be expected to combat practices similar to Pawtucket's; this will be so especially in areas where there are substantial non-Christian minorities.

. . .

The Court advances two principal arguments to support its conclusion that the Pawtucket creche satisfies the *Lemon* test. Neither is persuasive.

First. The Court, by focusing on the holiday "context" in which the nativity scene appeared, seeks to explain away the clear religious import of the creche and the findings of the District Court that most observers understood the creche as both a symbol of Christian beliefs and a symbol of the city's support for those beliefs. Thus, although the Court concedes that the city's inclusion of the nativity scene plainly serves "to depict the origins" of Christmas as a "significant historical religious event," and that the creche "is identified with one religious faith," we are nevertheless expected to believe that Pawtucket's use of the creche does not signal the city's support for the sectarian symbolism that the nativity scene evokes. The effect of the creche, of course, must be gauged not only by its inherent religious significance but also by the overall setting in which it appears. But it blinks reality to claim, as the Court does, that by including such a distinctively religious object as the creche in its Christmas display, Pawtucket has done no more than make use of a "traditional" symbol of the holiday, and has thereby purged the creche of its religious content and conferred only an "incidental and indirect" benefit on religion.

. . .

Finally, and most importantly, even in the context of Pawtucket's seasonal celebration, the creche retains a specifically Christian religious meaning. I refuse to accept the notion implicit in today's decision that non-Christians would find that the religious content of the creche is eliminated by the fact that it appears as part of the city's otherwise secular celebration of the Christmas holiday. The nativity scene is clearly distinct in its purpose and effect from the rest of the Hodgson Park display for the simple reason that it is the only one rooted in a biblical account of Christ's birth. It is the chief symbol of the characteristically Christian belief that a divine Savior was brought into the world and that the purpose of this miraculous birth was to illuminate a path toward salvation and redemption. For Christians, that path is exclusive, precious, and holy. But for those who do not share these beliefs, the symbolic reenactment of the birth of a divine being who has been miraculously incarnated as a man stands as a dramatic reminder of their differences with Christian faith. When government appears to sponsor such religiously inspired views, we cannot say that the practice is "'so separate and so indisputably marked off from the religious function,' . . . that [it] may fairly be viewed as [reflecting] a neutral posture toward religious institutions." To be so excluded on religious grounds by one's elected government is an insult and an injury that, until today, could not be countenanced by the Establishment Clause.

Second. The Court also attempts to justify the creche by entertaining a beguilingly simple, yet faulty syllogism. The Court begins by noting that government may recognize Christmas Day as a public holiday; the Court then asserts that the creche is nothing more than a traditional element of Christmas celebrations; and it concludes that the inclusion of a creche as part of a government's annual Christmas celebration is constitutionally permissible. The Court apparently believes that once it finds that the designation of Christmas as a public holiday is constitutionally acceptable, it is then free to conclude that virtually every form of governmental association with the celebration of the holiday is also constitutional. The vice of this dangerously superficial argument is that it overlooks the fact that the Christmas holiday in our national culture contains both secular and sectarian elements. To say that government may recognize the holiday's traditional, secular elements of gift-giving, public festivities, and community spirit, does not mean that government may indiscriminately embrace the distinctively sectarian aspects of the holiday. Indeed, in its eagerness to approve the creche, the Court has advanced a rationale so simplistic that it would appear to allow the

Mayor of Pawtucket to participate in the celebration of a Christmas Mass, since this would be just another unobjectionable way for the city to "celebrate the holiday." As is demonstrated below, the Court's logic is fundamentally flawed both because it obscures the reason why public designation of Christmas Day as a holiday is constitutionally acceptable, and blurs the distinction between the secular aspects of Christmas and its distinctively religious character, as exemplified by the creche.

When government decides to recognize Christmas Day as a public holiday, it does no more than accommodate the calendar of public activities to the plain fact that many Americans will expect on that day to spend time visiting with their families, attending religious services, and perhaps enjoying some respite from preholiday activities. The Free Exercise Clause, of course, does not necessarily compel the government to provide this accommodation, but neither is the Establishment Clause offended by such a step. Because it is clear that the celebration of Christmas has both secular and sectarian elements, it may well be that by taking note of the holiday, the government is simply seeking to serve the same kinds of wholly secular goals—for instance, promoting goodwill and a common day of rest—that were found to justify Sunday Closing Laws in *McGowan*. If public officials go further and participate in the secular celebration of Christmas—by, for example, decorating public places with such secular images as wreaths, garlands, or Santa Claus figures—they move closer to the limits of their constitutional power but nevertheless remain within the boundaries set by the Establishment Clause. But when those officials participate in or appear to endorse the distinctively religious elements of this otherwise secular event, they encroach upon First Amendment freedoms. For it is at that point that the government brings to the forefront the theological content of the holiday, and places the prestige, power, and financial support of a civil authority in the service of a particular faith.

The inclusion of a creche in Pawtucket's otherwise secular celebration of Christmas clearly violates these principles. Unlike such secular figures as Santa Claus, reindeer, and carolers, a nativity scene represents far more than a mere "traditional" symbol of Christmas. The essence of the creche's symbolic purpose and effect is to prompt the observer to experience a sense of simple awe and wonder appropriate to the contemplation of one of the central elements of Christian dogma—that God sent His Son into the world to be a Messiah. Contrary to the Court's suggestion, the creche is far from a mere representation of a "particular historic religious event." It is, instead, best understood as a mystical re-creation of an event that lies at the heart of Christian faith. To suggest, as the Court does, that such a symbol is merely "traditional" and therefore no different from Santa's house or reindeer is not only offensive to those for whom the creche has profound significance, but insulting to those who insist for religious or personal reasons that the story of Christ is in no sense a part of "history" nor an unavoidable element of our national "heritage."

. . .

II

Although the Court's relaxed application of the *Lemon* test to Pawtucket's creche is regrettable, it is at least understandable and properly limited to the particular facts of this case. The Court's opinion, however, also sounds a broader and more troubling theme. Invoking the celebration of Thanksgiving as a public holiday, the legend "In God We Trust" on our coins, and the proclamation "God save the United States and this Honorable Court" at the opening of judicial sessions, the Court asserts, without explanation, that Pawtucket's inclusion of a creche in its annual Christmas display poses no more of a threat to Establishment Clause values than these other official "acknowledgments" of religion.

Intuition tells us that some official "acknowledgment" is inevitable in a religious society if government is not to adopt a stilted indifference to the religious life of the people. It is equally true, however, that if government is to remain scrupulously neutral in matters of religious conscience, as our Constitution requires, then it must avoid those overly broad acknowledgments of religious practices that may imply governmental favoritism toward one set of religious beliefs. This does not mean, of course, that public officials may not take account, when necessary, of the separate existence and significance of the religious institutions and practices in the society they govern. Should government choose to incorporate some arguably religious element into its public ceremonies, that acknowledgment must be impartial; it must not tend to promote one faith or handicap another; and it should not sponsor religion generally over nonreligion. Thus, in a series of decisions concerned with such acknowledgments, we have repeatedly held that any active form of public acknowledgment of religion indicating sponsorship or endorsement is forbidden.

. . . [T]he Court has never comprehensively addressed the extent to which government may acknowledge religion by, for example, incorporating religious references into public ceremonies and proclamations, and I do not presume to offer a comprehensive approach. Nevertheless, it appears from our prior decisions that at least three principles—tracing the narrow channels which government acknowledgments must follow to satisfy the Establishment Clause—may be identified. First, although the government may not be compelled to do so by the Free Exercise Clause, it may, consistently with the Establishment Clause, act to accommodate to some extent the opportunities of individuals to practice their religion. That is the essential meaning, I submit, of this Court's decision in *Zorach*, finding that government does not violate the Establishment Clause when it simply chooses to "close its doors or suspend its operations as to those who want to repair to their religious sanctuary for worship or instruction." And for me that principle would justify government's decision to declare December 25th a public holiday.

Second, our cases recognize that while a particular governmental practice may have derived from religious motivations and retain certain religious connotations, it is nonetheless permissible for the government to pursue the practice when it is continued today solely for secular reasons. As this Court noted with reference to Sunday Closing Laws in *McGowan v. Maryland*, the mere fact that a governmental practice coincides to some extent with certain religious beliefs does not render it unconstitutional. Thanksgiving Day, in my view, fits easily within this principle, for despite its religious antecedents, the current practice of celebrating Thanksgiving is unquestionably secular and patriotic. We all may gather with our families on that day to give thanks both for personal and national good fortune, but we are free, given the secular character of the holiday, to address that gratitude either to a divine beneficence or to such mundane sources as good luck or the country's abundant natural wealth.

Finally, we have noted that government cannot be completely prohibited from recognizing in its public actions the religious beliefs and practices of the American people as an aspect of our national history and culture. While I remain uncertain about these questions, I would suggest that such practices as the designation of "In God We Trust" as our national motto, or the references to God contained in the Pledge of Allegiance to the flag can best be understood, in Dean Rostow's apt phrase, as a form a "ceremonial deism," protected from Establishment Clause scrutiny chiefly because they have lost through rote repetition any significant religious content. Moreover, these references are uniquely suited to serve such wholly secular purposes as solemnizing public occasions, or inspiring commitment to meet some national challenge in a manner that simply could not be fully served in our culture if government were limited to purely nonreligious phrases.

The practices by which the government has long acknowledged religion are therefore probably necessary to serve certain secular functions, and that necessity, coupled with their long history, gives those practices an essentially secular meaning.

The creche fits none of these categories. Inclusion of the creche is not necessary to accommodate individual religious expression. . . .

By insisting that such a distinctively sectarian message is merely an unobjectionable part of our "religious heritage," the Court takes a long step backwards to the days when Justice Brewer could arrogantly declare for the Court that "this is a Christian nation." *Church of Holy Trinity v. United States*, 143 U.S. 457, 471. Those days, I had thought, were forever put behind us by the Court's decision in *Engel*, in which we rejected a similar argument advanced by the State of New York that its Regent's Prayer was simply an acceptable part of our "spiritual heritage."

III

The American historical experience concerning the public celebration of Christmas, if carefully examined, provides no support for the Court's decision. The opening sections of the Court's opinion, while seeking to rely on historical evidence, do no more than recognize the obvious: because of the strong religious currents that run through our history, an inflexible or absolutistic enforcement of the Establishment Clause would be both imprudent and impossible. This observation is at once uncontroversial and unilluminating. Simply enumerating the various ways in which the Federal Government has recognized the vital role religion plays in our society does nothing to help decide the question presented in this case.

Indeed, the Court's approach suggests a fundamental misapprehension of the proper uses of history in constitutional interpretation. Certainly, our decisions reflect the fact that an awareness of historical practice often can provide a useful guide in interpreting the abstract language of the Establishment Clause. But historical acceptance of a particular practice alone is never sufficient to justify a challenged governmental action, since, as the Court has rightly observed, "no one acquires a vested or protected right in violation of the Constitution by long use, even when that span of time covers our entire national existence and indeed predates it." Attention to the details of history should not blind us to the cardinal purposes of the Establishment Clause, nor limit our central inquiry in these cases—whether the challenged practices "threaten those consequences which the Framers deeply feared." In recognition of this fact, the Court has, until today, consistently limited its historical inquiry to the particular practice under review.

. . .

. . . The Court . . . simply asserts, without any historical analysis or support whatsoever, that the now familiar celebration of Christmas springs from an unbroken history of acknowledgment "by the people, by the Executive Branch, by the Congress, and the courts for 2 centuries. . . . " The Court's complete failure to offer any explanation of its assertion is perhaps understandable, however, because the historical record points in precisely the opposite direction. Two features of this history are worth noting. First, at the time of the adoption of the Constitution and the Bill of Rights, there was no settled pattern of celebrating Christmas, either as a purely religious holiday or as a public event. Second, the historical evidence, such as it is, offers no uniform pattern of widespread acceptance of the holiday and indeed suggests that the development of Christmas as a public holiday is a comparatively recent phenomenon.

The intent of the Framers with respect to the public display of nativity scenes is virtually impossible to discern primarily because the widespread celebration of Christmas did not emerge in its present form until well into the 19th century. . . .

In sum, there is no evidence whatsoever that the Framers would have expressly approved a federal celebration of the Christmas holiday including public displays of a nativity scene; accordingly, the Court's repeated invocation of the decision in *Marsh*, is not only baffling, it is utterly irrelevant. Nor is there any suggestion that publicly financed and supported displays of Christmas creches are supported by a record of widespread, undeviating acceptance that extends throughout our history. Therefore, our prior decisions which relied upon concrete, specific historical evidence to support a particular practice simply have no bearing on the question presented in this case. Contrary to today's careless decision, those prior cases have all recognized that the "illumination" provided by history must always be focused on the particular practice at issue in a given case. Without that guiding principle and the intellectual discipline it imposes, the Court

is at sea, free to select random elements of America's varied history solely to suit the views of five Members of this Court.

IV

Under our constitutional scheme, the role of safeguarding our "religious heritage" and of promoting religious beliefs is reserved as the exclusive prerogative of our Nation's churches, religious institutions, and spiritual leaders. Because the Framers of the Establishment Clause understood that "religion is too personal, too sacred, too holy to permit its 'unhallowed perversion' by civil [authorities]," the Clause demands that government play no role in this effort. The Court today brushes aside these concerns by insisting that Pawtucket has done nothing more than include a "traditional" symbol of Christmas in its celebration of this national holiday, thereby muting the religious content of the creche. But the city's action should be recognized for what it is: a coercive, though perhaps small, step toward establishing the sectarian preferences of the majority at the expense of the minority, accomplished by placing public facilities and funds in support of the religious symbolism and theological tidings that the creche conveys. . . .

I dissent.

JUSTICE BLACKMUN, with whom JUSTICE STEVENS joins, dissenting.

As JUSTICE BRENNAN points out, the logic of the Court's decision in *Lemon* compels an affirmance here. If that case and its guidelines mean anything, the presence of Pawtucket's creche in a municipally sponsored display must be held to be a violation of the First Amendment.

. . .

The import of the Court's decision is to encourage use of the creche in a municipally sponsored display, a setting where Christians feel constrained in acknowledging its symbolic meaning and non-Christians feel alienated by its presence. Surely, this is a misuse of a sacred symbol. Because I cannot join the Court in denying either the force of our precedents or the sacred message that is at the core of the creche, I dissent and join JUSTICE BRENNAN's opinion.

iv. Endorsement

Drawing a line between government actions that accommodate religion and that endorse it has proved to be a treacherous and confusing exercise. Uncertainty in the area has been evidenced in part by post-*Lynch* persistence of controversy over seasonal religious displays on government property. So too did debate over establishment clause standards of review. In *County of Allegheny v. American Civil Liberties Union Greater Pittsburgh Chapter*, a fragmented Court determined that display of a menorah next to a Christmas tree at a county courthouse was permissible but a nativity scene on the main staircase of the building was not. Attention to whether the display represented governmental endorsement made placement and context of the exhibit especially crucial factors.

County of Allegheny v. American Civil Liberties Union Greater Pittsburgh Chapter
492 U.S. 573 (1989)

JUSTICE BLACKMUN announced the judgment of the Court and delivered the opinion of the Court with respect to Parts III-A, IV, and V, an opinion with respect to Parts I and II, in which JUSTICE STEVENS and JUSTICE O'CONNOR join, an opinion with respect to Part III-B, in which JUSTICE STEVENS joins, an opinion with respect to Part VII, in which JUSTICE O'CONNOR joins, and an opinion with respect to Part VI.

This litigation concerns the constitutionality of two recurring holiday displays located on public property in downtown Pittsburgh. The first is a creche placed on the Grand Staircase of the Allegheny County Courthouse. The second is a Chanukah menorah placed just outside the City-County Building, next to a Christmas tree and a sign saluting liberty. The Court of Appeals for the Third Circuit ruled that each display violates the Establishment Clause of the First Amendment because each has the impermissible effect of endorsing religion. We agree that the creche display has that unconstitutional effect but reverse the Court of Appeals' judgment regarding the menorah display.

I

A

The county courthouse is owned by Allegheny County and is its seat of government. It houses the offices of the county commissioners, controller, treasurer, sheriff, and clerk of court. Civil and criminal trials are held there. The "main," "most beautiful," and "most public" part of the courthouse is its Grand Staircase, set into one arch and surrounded by others, with arched windows serving as a backdrop.

. . .

The creche in the county courthouse, like other creches, is a visual representation of the scene in the manger in Bethlehem shortly after the birth of Jesus, as described in the Gospels of Luke and Matthew. The creche includes figures of the infant Jesus, Mary, Joseph, farm animals, shepherds, and wise men, all placed in or before a wooden representation of a manger, which has at its crest an angel bearing a banner that proclaims "Gloria in Excelsis Deo!"

. . .

III

A

. . .

In the course of adjudicating specific cases, this Court has come to understand the Establishment Clause to mean that government may not promote or affiliate itself with any religious doctrine or organization, may not discriminate among persons on the basis of their religious beliefs and practices, may not delegate a governmental power to a religious institution, and may not involve itself too deeply in such an institution's affairs. Although "the myriad, subtle ways in which Establishment Clause values can be eroded," are not susceptible to a single verbal formulation, this Court has attempted to encapsulate the essential precepts of the Establishment Clause. . . .

In *Lemon v. Kurtzman*, the Court sought to refine these principles by focusing on three "tests" for determining whether a government practice violates the Establishment Clause. . . .

Our subsequent decisions further have refined the definition of governmental action that unconstitutionally advances religion. In recent years, we have paid particularly close attention to whether the challenged governmental practice either has the purpose or effect of "endorsing" religion, a concern that has long had a place in our Establishment Clause jurisprudence. . . .

Of course, the word "endorsement" is not self-defining. Rather, it derives its meaning from other words that this Court has found useful over the years in interpreting the Establishment Clause. . . .

Whether the key word is "endorsement," "favoritism," or "promotion," the essential principle remains the same. The Establishment Clause, at the very least, prohibits government from appearing to take a position on questions of religious belief or from "making adherence to a religion relevant in any way to a person's standing in the political community."

. . .

The rationale of the majority opinion in *Lynch* is none too clear: the opinion contains two strands, neither of which provides guidance for decision in subsequent cases. First, the opinion states that the inclusion of the creche in the display was "no more an advancement or endorsement of religion" than other "endorsements" this Court has approved in the past, but the opinion offers no discernible measure for distinguishing between permissible and impermissible endorsements. Second, the opinion observes that any benefit the government's display of the creche gave to religion was no more than "indirect, remote, and incidental,"—without saying how or why.

Although Justice O'Connor joined the majority opinion in *Lynch*, she wrote a concurrence that differs in significant respects from the majority opinion. The main difference is that the concurrence provides a sound analytical framework for evaluating governmental use of religious symbols.

First and foremost, the concurrence squarely rejects any notion that this Court will tolerate some government endorsement of religion. Rather, the concurrence recognizes any endorsement of religion as "invalid, "because it "sends a message to nonadherents that they are outsiders, not full members of the political community, and an accompanying message to adherents that they are insiders, favored members of the political community."

Second, the concurrence articulates a method for determining whether the government's use of an object with religious meaning has the effect of endorsing religion. The effect of the display depends upon the message that the government's practice communicates: the question is "what viewers may fairly understand to be the purpose of the display." That inquiry, of necessity, turns upon the context in which the contested object appears: "[A] typical museum setting, though not neutralizing the religious content of a religious painting, negates any message of endorsement of that content." . . .

The concurrence applied this mode of analysis to the Pawtucket creche, seen in the context of that city's holiday celebration as a whole. In addition to the creche, the city's display contained: a Santa Claus house with a live Santa distributing candy; reindeer pulling Santa's sleigh; a live 40-foot Christmas tree strung with lights; statues of carolers in old-fashioned dress; candy-striped poles; a "talking" wishing well; a large banner proclaiming "SEASONS GREETINGS"; a miniature "village" with several houses and a church; and various "cut-out" figures, including those of a clown, a dancing elephant, a robot, and a teddy bear. The concurrence concluded that both because the creche is "a traditional symbol" of Christmas, a holiday with strong secular elements, and because the creche was "displayed along with purely secular symbols," the creche's setting "changes what viewers may fairly understand to be the purpose of the display" and "negates any message of endorsement" of "the Christian beliefs represented by the creche."

The four *Lynch* dissenters agreed with the concurrence that the controlling question was "whether Pawtucket ha[d] run afoul of the Establishment Clause by endorsing religion through its display of the creche." The dissenters also agreed with the general proposition that the context in which the government uses a religious symbol is relevant for determining the answer to that question. They simply reached a different answer: the dissenters concluded that the other elements of the Pawtucket display did not negate the endorsement of Christian faith caused by the presence of the creche. They viewed the inclusion of the creche in the city's overall display as placing "the government's imprimatur of approval on the particular religious beliefs exemplified by the creche." Thus, they stated: "The effect on minority religious groups, as well as on those who may reject all religion, is to convey the message that their views are not similarly worthy of public recognition nor entitled to public support."

Thus, despite divergence at the bottom line, the five Justices in concurrence and dissent in *Lynch* agreed upon the relevant constitutional principles: the government's use of religious symbolism is unconstitutional if it has the effect of endorsing religious beliefs, and the effect of the government's use of religious symbolism depends upon its context. These general principles are sound, and have been adopted by the Court in subsequent cases. . . .

We turn first to the county's creche display. There is no doubt, of course, that the creche itself is capable of communicating a religious message. Indeed, the creche in this lawsuit uses words, as well as the picture of the Nativity scene, to make its religious meaning unmistakably clear. "Glory to God in the Highest!" says the angel in the creche—Glory to God because of the birth of Jesus. This praise to God in Christian terms is indisputably religious—indeed sectarian—just as it is when said in the Gospel or in a church service.

Under the Court's holding in *Lynch*, the effect of a creche display turns on its setting. Here, unlike in *Lynch*, nothing in the context of the display detracts from the creche's religious message. The *Lynch* display comprised a series of figures and objects, each group of which had its own focal point. Santa's house and his reindeer were objects of attention separate from the creche, and had their specific visual story to tell. Similarly, whatever a "talking" wishing well may be, it obviously was a center of attention separate from the creche. Here, in contrast, the creche stands alone: it is the single element of the display on the Grand Staircase.

The floral decoration surrounding the creche cannot be viewed as somehow equivalent to the secular symbols in the overall *Lynch* display. The floral frame, like all good frames, serves only to draw one's attention to the message inside the frame. The floral decoration surrounding the creche contributes to, rather than detracts from, the endorsement of religion conveyed by the creche. It is as if the county had allowed the Holy Name Society to display a cross on the Grand Staircase at Easter, and the county had surrounded the cross with Easter lilies. The county could not say that surrounding the cross with traditional flowers of the season would negate the endorsement of Christianity conveyed by the cross on the Grand Staircase. Its contention that the traditional Christmas greens negate the endorsement effect of the creche fares no better.

Furthermore, the creche sits on the Grand Staircase, the "main" and "most beautiful part" of the building that is the seat of county government. No viewer could reasonably think that it occupies this location without the support and approval of the government. Thus, by permitting the "display of the creche in this particular physical setting," *Lynch*, the county sends an unmistakable message that it supports and promotes the Christian praise to God that is the creche's religious message.

. . .

In sum, *Lynch* teaches that government may celebrate Christmas in some manner and form, but not in a way that endorses Christian doctrine. Here, Allegheny County has transgressed this line. It has chosen to celebrate Christmas in a way that has the effect of endorsing a patently Christian message: Glory to God for the birth of Jesus Christ. Under *Lynch*, and the rest of our cases, nothing more is required to demonstrate a violation of the Establishment Clause. The display of the creche in this context, therefore, must be permanently enjoined.

V

Justice Kennedy and the three Justices who join him would find the display of the creche consistent with the Establishment Clause. He argues that this conclusion necessarily follows from the Court's decision in *Marsh v. Chambers*, which sustained the constitutionality of legislative prayer. He also asserts that the creche, even in this setting, poses "no realistic risk" of "represent[ing] an effort to proselytize," having repudiated the Court's endorsement inquiry in favor of a "proselytization" approach. The Court's analysis of the creche, he contends, "reflects an unjustified hostility toward religion."

Justice Kennedy's reasons for permitting the creche on the Grand Staircase and his condemnation of the Court's reasons for deciding otherwise are so far reaching in their implications that they require a response in some depth.

In *Marsh*, the Court relied specifically on the fact that Congress authorized legislative prayer at the same time that it produced the Bill of Rights. Justice Kennedy, however, argues that *Marsh* legitimates all "practices with no greater potential for an establishment of religion" than those "accepted traditions dating back to the Founding." Otherwise, the Justice asserts, such practices as our national motto ("In God We Trust") and our Pledge of Allegiance (with the phrase "under God," added in 1954, are in danger of invalidity.

Our previous opinions have considered in dicta the motto and the pledge, characterizing them as consistent with the proposition that government may not communicate an endorsement of religious belief. We need not return to the subject of "ceremonial deism," because there is an obvious distinction between creche displays and references to God in the motto and the pledge. However history may affect the constitutionality of nonsectarian references to religion by the government, history cannot legitimate practices that demonstrate the government's allegiance to a particular sect or creed.

. . .

Justice Kennedy's reading of *Marsh* would gut the core of the Establishment Clause, as this Court understands it. The history of this Nation, it is perhaps sad to say, contains numerous examples of official acts that endorsed Christianity specifically. Some of these examples date back to the Founding of the Republic, but this heritage of official discrimination against non-Christians has no place in the jurisprudence of the Establishment Clause. Whatever else the Establishment Clause may mean (and we have held it to mean no official preference even for religion over nonreligion, it certainly means at the very least that government may not demonstrate a preference for one particular sect or creed (including a preference for Christianity over other religions). "The clearest command of the Establishment Clause is that one religious denomination cannot be officially preferred over another." There have been breaches of this command throughout this Nation's history, but they cannot diminish in any way the force of the command.

Although Justice Kennedy's misreading of *Marsh* is predicated on a failure to recognize the bedrock Establishment Clause principle that, regardless of history, government may not demonstrate a preference for a particular faith, even he is forced to acknowledge that some instances of such favoritism are constitutionally intolerable. He concedes also that the term "endorsement" long has been another way of defining a forbidden "preference" for a particular sect, but he would repudiate the Court's endorsement inquiry as a "jurisprudence of minutiae," because it examines the particular contexts in which the government employs religious symbols.

. . .

This label, of course, could be tagged on many areas of constitutional adjudication. . . .

Indeed, perhaps the only real distinction between Justice Kennedy's "proselytization" test and the Court's "endorsement" inquiry is a burden of "unmistakable" clarity that Justice Kennedy apparently would require of government favoritism for specific sects in order to hold the favoritism in violation of the Establishment Clause. The question whether a particular practice "would place the government's weight behind an obvious effort to proselytize for a particular religion," is much the same as whether the practice demonstrates the government's support, promotion, or "endorsement" of the particular creed of a particular sect—except to the extent that it requires an "obvious" allegiance between the government and the sect.

Our cases, however, impose no such burden on demonstrating that the government has favored a particular sect or creed. On the contrary, we have expressly required "strict scrutiny" of practices suggesting "a denominational preference," *Larson v. Valente*. Thus, when all is said and done, Justice Kennedy's effort to abandon the "endorsement" inquiry in favor of his "proselytization" test seems nothing more than an attempt to lower considerably the level of scrutiny in Establishment Clause cases. We choose, however, to adhere to the vigilance the Court has managed to maintain thus far, and to the endorsement inquiry that reflects our vigilance.

Although Justice Kennedy repeatedly accuses the Court of harboring a "latent hostility" or "callous indifference" toward religion, nothing could be further from the truth, and the accusations could be said to be as offensive as they are absurd. Justice Kennedy apparently has misperceived a respect for religious pluralism, a respect commanded by the Constitution, as hostility or indifference to religion. No misperception could be more antithetical to the values embodied in the Establishment Clause.

Justice Kennedy's accusations are shot from a weapon triggered by the following proposition: if government may celebrate the secular aspects of Christmas, then it must be allowed to celebrate the religious aspects as well because, otherwise, the government would be discriminating against citizens who celebrate Christmas as a religious, and not just a secular, holiday. This proposition, however, is flawed at its foundation. The government does not discriminate against any citizen on the basis of the citizen's religious faith if the government is secular in its functions and operations. On the contrary, the Constitution mandates that the government remain secular, rather than affiliate itself with religious beliefs or institutions, precisely in order to avoid discriminating among citizens on the basis of their religious faiths.

A secular state, it must be remembered, is not the same as an atheistic or antireligious state. A secular state establishes neither atheism nor religion as its official creed. Justice Kennedy thus has it exactly backwards when he says that enforcing the Constitution's requirement that government remain secular is a prescription of orthodoxy. It follows directly from the Constitution's proscription against government affiliation with religious beliefs or institutions that there is no orthodoxy on religious matters in the secular state. Although Justice Kennedy accuses the Court of "an Orwellian rewriting of history," perhaps it is Justice Kennedy himself who has slipped into a form of Orwellian newspeak when he equates the constitutional command of secular government with a prescribed orthodoxy.

. . .

VI

The display of the Chanukah menorah in front of the City-County Building may well present a closer constitutional question. The menorah, one must recognize, is a religious symbol: it serves to commemorate the miracle of the oil as described in the Talmud. But the menorah's message is not exclusively religious. The menorah is the primary visual symbol for a holiday that, like Christmas, has both religious and secular dimensions.

. . .

Accordingly, the relevant question for Establishment Clause purposes is whether the combined display of the tree, the sign, and the menorah has the effect of endorsing both Christian and Jewish faiths, or rather simply recognizes that both Christmas and Chanukah are part of the same winter-holiday season, which has attained a secular status in our society. Of the two interpretations of this particular display, the latter seems far more plausible and is also in line with *Lynch*.

The Christmas tree, unlike the menorah, is not itself a religious symbol. Although Christmas trees once carried religious connotations, today they typify the secular celebration of Christmas. Numerous Americans place Christmas trees in their homes without subscribing to Christian religious beliefs, and when the city's tree stands alone in front of the City-County Building, it is not considered an endorsement of Christian faith. Indeed, a 40-foot Christmas tree was one of the objects that validated the creche in *Lynch*. The widely accepted view of the Christmas tree as the preeminent secular symbol of the Christmas holiday season serves to emphasize the secular component of the message communicated by other elements of an accompanying holiday display, including the Chanukah menorah.

The tree, moreover, is clearly the predominant element in the city's display. The 45-foot tree occupies the central position beneath the middle archway in front of the Grant Street entrance to the City-County Building; the 18-foot menorah is positioned to one side. Given this configuration, it is much more sensible to interpret the meaning of the menorah in light of the tree, rather than vice versa. In the shadow of the tree, the menorah is readily understood as simply a recognition that Christmas is not the only traditional way of observing the winter-holiday season. In these circumstances, then, the combination of the tree and the menorah communicates, not a simultaneous endorsement of both the Christian and Jewish faiths, but instead, a secular celebration of Christmas coupled with an acknowledgment of Chanukah as a contemporaneous alternative tradition.

Although the city has used a symbol with religious meaning as its representation of Chanukah, this is not a case in which the city has reasonable alternatives that are less religious in nature. It is difficult to imagine a predominantly secular symbol of Chanukah that the city could place next to its Christmas tree. An 18-foot dreidel would look out of place and might be interpreted by some as mocking the celebration of Chanukah. The absence of a more secular alternative symbol is itself part of the context in which the city's actions must be judged in determining the likely effect of its use of the menorah. Where the government's secular message can be conveyed by two symbols, only one of which carries religious meaning, an observer reasonably might infer from the fact that the government has chosen to use the religious symbol that the government means to promote religious faith. But where, as here, no such choice has been made, this inference of endorsement is not present.

The mayor's sign further diminishes the possibility that the tree and the menorah will be interpreted as a dual endorsement of Christianity and Judaism. The sign states that during the holiday season the city salutes liberty. Moreover, the sign draws upon the theme of light, common to both Chanukah and Christmas as winter festivals, and links that theme with this Nation's legacy of freedom, which allows an American to celebrate the holiday season in whatever way he wishes, religiously or otherwise. While no sign can disclaim an overwhelming message of endorsement, an "explanatory plaque" may confirm that in particular contexts the government's association with a religious symbol does not represent the government's sponsorship of religious beliefs. Here, the mayor's sign serves to confirm what the context already reveals: that the display of the menorah is not an endorsement of religious faith but simply a recognition of cultural diversity.

Given all these considerations, it is not "sufficiently likely" that residents of Pittsburgh will perceive the combined display of the tree, the sign, and the menorah as an "endorsement" or "disapproval . . . of their individual religious choices." While an adjudication of the display's effect must take into account the perspective of one who is neither Christian nor Jewish, as well as of those who adhere to either of these religions, the constitutionality of its effect must also be judged according to the standard of a "reasonable observer," When measured against this standard, the menorah need not be excluded from this particular display. The Christmas tree alone in the Pittsburgh location does not endorse Christian belief; and, on the facts before us, the addition of the menorah "cannot fairly be understood to" result in the simultaneous endorsement of Christian and Jewish faiths. *Lynch*, On the contrary, for purposes of the Establishment Clause, the city's overall display must be understood as conveying the city's secular recognition of different traditions for celebrating the winter-holiday season.

The conclusion here that, in this particular context, the menorah's display does not have an effect of endorsing religious faith does not foreclose the possibility that the display of the menorah might violate either the "purpose" or "entanglement" prong of the *Lemon* analysis. These issues were not addressed by the Court of Appeals and may be considered by that court on remand.

Lynch v. Donnelly confirms, and in no way repudiates, the longstanding constitutional principle that government may not engage in a practice that has the effect of promoting or endorsing religious beliefs. The display of the creche in the county courthouse has this unconstitutional effect. The display of the menorah in front of the City-County Building, however, does not have this effect, given its "particular physical setting."

. . .

JUSTICE O'CONNOR, with whom JUSTICE BRENNAN and JUSTICE STEVENS join as to Part II, concurring in part and concurring in the judgment.

I

Judicial review of government action under the Establishment Clause is a delicate task. The Court has avoided drawing lines which entirely sweep away all government recognition and acknowledgment of the role of religion in the lives of our citizens for to do so would exhibit not neutrality but hostility to religion. Instead the courts have made case-specific examinations of the challenged government action and have attempted to do so with the aid of the standards described by Justice Blackmun in Part III-A of the Court's opinion. Unfortunately, even the development of articulable standards and guidelines has not always resulted in agreement among the Members of this Court on the results in individual cases. And so it is again today.

. . .

II

In his separate opinion, Justice Kennedy asserts that the endorsement test "is flawed in its fundamentals and unworkable in practice." In my view, neither criticism is persuasive. . . .

An Establishment Clause standard that prohibits only "coercive" practices or overt efforts at government proselytization, but fails to take account of the numerous more subtle ways that government can show favoritism to particular beliefs or convey a message of disapproval to others, would not, in my view, adequately protect the religious liberty or respect the religious diversity of the members of our pluralistic political community. Thus, this Court has never relied on coercion alone as the touchstone of Establishment Clause analysis. To require a showing of coercion, even indirect coercion, as an essential element of an Establishment Clause violation would make the Free Exercise Clause a redundancy. Moreover, as even Justice Kennedy recognizes, any Establishment Clause test limited to "direct coercion" clearly would fail to account for forms of "[s]ymbolic recognition or accommodation of religious faith" that may violate the Establishment Clause.

. . . To be sure, the endorsement test depends on a sensitivity to the unique circumstances and context of a particular challenged practice and, like any test that is sensitive to context, it may not always yield results with unanimous agreement at the margins. But that is true of many standards in constitutional law, and even the modified coercion test offered by Justice Kennedy involves judgment and hard choices at the margin. He admits as much by acknowledging that the permanent display of a Latin cross at city hall would violate the Establishment Clause, as would the display of symbols of Christian holidays alone. Would the display of a Latin cross for six months have such an unconstitutional effect, or the display of the symbols of most Christian holidays and one Jewish holiday? Would the Christmastime display of a creche inside a courtroom be "coercive" if subpoenaed witnesses had no opportunity to "turn their backs" and walk away? Would displaying a creche in front of a public school violate the Establishment Clause under Justice Kennedy's test? We cannot avoid the obligation to draw lines, often close and difficult lines, in deciding Establishment Clause cases, and that is not a problem unique to the endorsement test.

Justice Kennedy submits that the endorsement test is inconsistent with our precedents and traditions because, in his words, if it were "applied without artificial exceptions for historical practice," it would invalidate many traditional practices recognizing the role of religion in our society. This criticism shortchanges both the endorsement test itself and my explanation of the reason why certain longstanding government acknowledgments of religion do not, under that test, convey a message of endorsement. Practices such as legislative prayers or opening Court sessions with "God save the United States and this honorable Court" serve the secular purposes of "solemnizing public occasions" and "expressing confidence in the future," *Lynch*. These examples of ceremonial deism do not survive Establishment Clause scrutiny simply by virtue of their historical longevity alone. Historical acceptance of a practice does not in itself validate that practice under the Establishment Clause if the practice violates the values protected by that Clause, just as historical acceptance of racial or gender based discrimination does not immunize such practices from scrutiny under the Fourteenth Amendment. . . .

III

For reasons which differ somewhat from those set forth in Part VI of Justice Blackmun's opinion, I also conclude that the city of Pittsburgh's combined holiday display of a Chanukah menorah, a Christmas tree, and a sign saluting liberty does not have the effect of conveying an endorsement of religion. . . .

The message of pluralism conveyed by the city's combined holiday display is not a message that endorses religion over nonreligion. . . . Here, by displaying a secular symbol of the Christmas holiday season rather than a religious one, the city acknowledged a public holiday celebrated by both religious and nonreligious citizens alike, and it did so without endorsing Christian beliefs. A reasonable observer would, in my view, appreciate that the combined display is an effort to acknowledge the cultural diversity of our country and to convey tolerance of different choices in matters of religious belief or nonbelief by recognizing that the winter holiday season is celebrated in diverse ways by our citizens. In short, in the holiday context, this combined display in its particular physical setting conveys neither an endorsement of Judaism or Christianity nor disapproval of alternative beliefs, and thus does not have the impermissible effect of "mak-[ing] religion relevant, in reality or public perception, to status in the political community."

My conclusion does not depend on whether or not the city had "a more secular alternative symbol" of Chanukah, just as the Court's decision in *Lynch* clearly did not turn on whether the city of Pawtucket could have conveyed its tribute to the Christmas holiday season by using a "less religious" alternative to the creche symbol in its display of traditional holiday symbols. ("Justice Brennan argues that the city's objectives could have been achieved without including the creche in the display. True or not, that is irrelevant. The question is whether the display of the creche violates the Establishment Clause.") In my view, Justice Blackmun's new rule, that an inference of endorsement arises every time government uses a symbol with religious meaning if a "more secular alternative" is available is too blunt an instrument for Establishment Clause analysis, which depends on sensitivity to the context and circumstances presented by each case. Indeed, the opinion appears to recognize the importance of this contextual sensitivity by creating an exception to its new rule in the very case announcing it: the opinion acknowledges that "a purely secular symbol" of Chanukah is available, namely, a dreidel or foursided top, but rejects the use of such a symbol because it "might be interpreted by some as mocking the celebration of Chanukah." This recognition that the more religious alternative may, depending on the circumstances, convey a message that is least likely to implicate Establishment Clause concerns is an excellent example of the need to focus on the specific practice in question in its particular physical setting and context in determining whether government has conveyed or attempted to convey a message that religion or a particular religious belief is favored or preferred.

In sum, I conclude that the city of Pittsburgh's combined holiday display had neither the purpose nor the effect of endorsing religion, but that Allegheny County's creche display had such an effect. Accordingly, I join Parts I, II, III-A, IV, V, and VII of the Court's opinion and concur in the judgment.

. . . I continue to believe that the display of an object that "retains a specifically Christian [or other] religious meaning," is incompatible with the separation of church and state demanded by our Constitution. I therefore agree with the Court that Allegheny County's display of a creche at the county courthouse signals an endorsement of the Christian faith in violation of the Establishment Clause, and join Parts III-A, IV, and V of the Court's opinion. I cannot agree, however, that the city's display of a 45-foot Christmas tree and an 18-foot Chanukah menorah at the entrance to the building housing the mayor's office shows no favoritism towards Christianity, Judaism, or both. Indeed, I should have thought that the answer as to the first display supplied the answer to the second.

. . .

Positioned as it was, the Christmas tree's religious significance was bound to come to the fore. Situated next to the menorah—which, Justice Blackmun acknowledges, is "a symbol with religious meaning," and indeed, is "the central religious symbol and ritual object of" Chanukah,—the Christmas tree's religious dimension could not be overlooked by observers of the display. Even though the tree alone may be deemed predominantly secular, it can hardly be so characterized when placed next to such a forthrightly religious symbol. Consider a poster featuring a star of David, a statue of Buddha, a Christmas tree, a mosque, and a drawing of Krishna. There can be no doubt that, when found in such company, the tree serves as an unabashedly religious symbol.

. . .

II

. . . It is no surprise and no anomaly that Chanukah has historical and societal roots that range beyond the purely religious. I would venture that most, if not all, major religious holidays have beginnings and enjoy histories studded with figures, events, and practices that are not strictly religious. It does not seem to me that the mere fact that Chanukah shares this kind of background makes it a secular holiday in any meaningful sense. The menorah is indisputably a religious symbol, used ritually in a celebration that has deep religious significance. That, in my view, is all that need be said. Whatever secular practices the holiday of Chanukah has taken on in its contemporary observance are beside the point.

Indeed, at the very outset of his discussion of the menorah display, Justice Blackmun recognizes that the menorah is a religious symbol. That should have been the end of the case. But, as did the Court in *Lynch*, Justice Blackmun, "by focusing on the holiday 'context' in which the [menorah] appeared, seeks to explain away the clear religious import of the [menorah]. . . ." By the end of the opinion, the menorah has become but a coequal symbol, with the Christmas tree, of "the winter-holiday season." Pittsburgh's secularization of an inherently religious symbol, aided and abetted here by Justice Blackmun's opinion, recalls the effort in

Lynch to render the creche a secular symbol. As I said then: "To suggest, as the Court does, that such a symbol is merely 'traditional' and therefore no different from Santa's house or reindeer is not only offensive to those for whom the creche has profound significance, but insulting to those who insist for religious or personal reasons that the story of Christ is in no sense a part of 'history' nor an unavoidable element of our national 'heritage.'" As Justice O'Connor rightly observes, Justice Blackmun "obscures the religious nature of the menorah and the holiday of Chanukah."

I cannot, in short, accept the effort to transform an emblem of religious faith into the innocuous "symbol for a holiday that . . . has both religious and secular dimensions."

JUSTICE BRENNAN, with whom JUSTICE MARSHALL and JUSTICE STEVENS join, concurring in part and dissenting in part.

. . .

III

Justice Blackmun, in his acceptance of the city's message of "diversity," and, even more so, Justice O'Connor, in her approval of the "message of pluralism and freedom to choose one's own beliefs," appear to believe that, where seasonal displays are concerned, more is better. Whereas a display might be constitutionally problematic if it showcased the holiday of just one religion, those problems vaporize as soon as more than one religion is included. I know of no principle under the Establishment Clause, however, that permits us to conclude that governmental promotion of religion is acceptable so long as one religion is not favored. We have, on the contrary, interpreted that Clause to require neutrality, not just among religions, but between religion and nonreligion.

Nor do I discern the theory under which the government is permitted to appropriate particular holidays and religious objects to its own use in celebrating "pluralism." The message of the sign announcing a "Salute to Liberty" is not religious, but patriotic; the government's use of religion to promote its own cause is undoubtedly offensive to those whose religious beliefs are not bound up with their attitude toward the Nation.

The uncritical acceptance of a message of religious pluralism also ignores the extent to which even that message may offend. Many religious faiths are hostile to each other, and indeed, refuse even to participate in ecumenical services designed to demonstrate the very pluralism Justices Blackmun and O'Connor extol. To lump the ritual objects and holidays of religions together without regard to their attitudes toward such inclusiveness, or to decide which religions should be excluded because of

the possibility of offense, is not a benign or beneficent celebration of pluralism: it is instead an interference in religious matters precluded by the Establishment Clause.

. . .

JUSTICE STEVENS, with whom JUSTICE BRENNAN and JUSTICE MARSHALL join, concurring in part and dissenting in part.

. . .

Treatment of a symbol of a particular tradition demonstrates one's attitude toward that tradition. Thus the prominent display of religious symbols on government property falls within the compass of the First Amendment, even though interference with personal choices about supporting a church, by means of governmental tithing, was the primary concern in 1791. Whether the vice in such a display is characterized as "coercion," or "endorsement," or merely as state action with the purpose and effect of providing support for specific faiths, it is common ground that this symbolic governmental speech "respecting an establishment of religion" may violate the Constitution.

In my opinion the Establishment Clause should be construed to create a strong presumption against the display of religious symbols on public property. There is always a risk that such symbols will offend nonmembers of the faith being advertised as well as adherents who consider the particular advertisement disrespectful. Some devout Christians believe that the creche should be placed only in reverential settings, such as a church or perhaps a private home; they do not countenance its use as an aid to commercialization of Christ's birthday. In this very suit, members of the Jewish faith firmly opposed the use to which the menorah was put by the particular sect that sponsored the display at Pittsburgh's City-County Building. Even though "[p]assersby who disagree with the message conveyed by these displays are free to ignore them, or even to turn their backs," displays of this kind inevitably have a greater tendency to emphasize sincere and deeply felt differences among individuals than to achieve an ecumenical goal. The Establishment Clause does not allow public bodies to foment such disagreement.

Application of a strong presumption against the public use of religious symbols scarcely will "require a relentless extirpation of all contact between government and religion," for it will prohibit a display only when its message, evaluated in the context in which it is presented, is nonsecular. For example, a carving of Moses holding the Ten Commandments, if that is the only adornment on a courtroom wall, conveys an equivocal message, perhaps of respect for Judaism, for religion in general, or for law. The addition of carvings depicting Confucius and Mohammed may honor religion, or particular religions, to an extent that the First Amendment does not tolerate any more than it does "the permanent erection of a large Latin cross on the roof of city hall." Placement of secular figures such as Caesar Augustus, William Blackstone, Napoleon Bonaparte, and John Marshall alongside these three religious leaders, however, signals respect not for great proselytizers but for great lawgivers. It would be absurd to exclude such a fitting message from a courtroom, as it would to exclude religious paintings by Italian Renaissance masters from a public museum. Far from "border[ing] on latent hostility toward religion," this careful consideration of context gives due regard to religious and nonreligious members of our society.

I cannot agree with the Court's conclusion that the display at Pittsburgh's City-County Building was constitutional. Standing alone in front of a governmental headquarters, a lighted, 45-foot evergreen tree might convey holiday greetings linked too tenuously to Christianity to have constitutional moment. Juxtaposition of this tree with an 18-foot menorah does not make the latter secular, as Justice Blackmun contends. Rather, the presence of the Chanukah menorah, unquestionably a religious symbol, gives religious significance to the Christmas tree. The overall display thus manifests governmental approval of the Jewish and Christian religions. Although it conceivably might be interpreted as sending "a message of pluralism and freedom to choose one's own beliefs," the message is not sufficiently clear to overcome the strong presumption that the display, respecting two religions to the exclusion of all others, is the very kind of double establishment that the First Amendment was designed to outlaw. . . .

JUSTICE KENNEDY, with whom THE CHIEF JUSTICE, JUSTICE WHITE and JUSTICE SCALIA join, concurring in the judgment in part and dissenting in part.

. . .

I

In keeping with the usual fashion of recent years, the majority applies the *Lemon* test to judge the constitutionality of the holiday displays here in question. I am content for present purposes to remain within the *Lemon* framework, but do not wish to be seen as advocating, let alone adopting, that test as our primary guide in this difficult area. Persuasive criticism of *Lemon* has emerged. Substantial revision of our Establishment Clause doctrine may be in order; but it is unnecessary to undertake that task today, for even the *Lemon* test, when applied with proper sensitivity to our traditions and our case law, supports the conclusion that both the creche and the menorah are permissible displays in the context of the holiday season.

The only *Lemon* factor implicated in these cases directs us to inquire whether the "principal or primary effect" of the challenged govern-

ment practice is "one that neither advances nor inhibits religion." The requirement of neutrality inherent in that formulation has sometimes been stated in categorical terms. For example, in *Everson* the first case in our modern Establishment Clause jurisprudence, Justice Black wrote that the Clause forbids laws "which aid one religion, aid all religions, or prefer one religion over another." We have stated that government "must be neutral in matters of religious theory, doctrine, and practice" and "may not aid, foster, or promote one religion or religious theory against another or even against the militant opposite." And we have spoken of a prohibition against conferring an "'imprimatur of state approval'" on religion.

These statements must not give the impression of a formalism that does not exist. Taken to its logical extreme, some of the language quoted above would require a relentless extirpation of all contact between government and religion. But that is not the history or the purpose of the Establishment Clause. Government policies of accommodation, acknowledgment, and support for religion are an accepted part of our political and cultural heritage. As Chief Justice Burger wrote for the Court in *Walz v. Tax Comm'n of New York City*, we must be careful to avoid "[t]he hazards of placing too much weight on a few words or phrases of the Court," and so we have "declined to construe the Religion Clauses with a literalness that would undermine the ultimate constitutional objective as illuminated by history."

Rather than requiring government to avoid any action that acknowledges or aids religion, the Establishment Clause permits government some latitude in recognizing and accommodating the central role religion plays in our society. Any approach less sensitive to our heritage would border on latent hostility toward religion, as it would require government in all its multifaceted roles to acknowledge only the secular, to the exclusion and so to the detriment of the religious. A categorical approach would install federal courts as jealous guardians of an absolute "wall of separation," sending a clear message of disapproval. In this century, as the modern administrative state expands to touch the lives of its citizens in such diverse ways and redirects their financial choices through programs of its own, it is difficult to maintain the fiction that requiring government to avoid all assistance to religion can in fairness be viewed as serving the goal of neutrality.

. . .

The ability of the organized community to recognize and accommodate religion in a society with a pervasive public sector requires diligent observance of the border between accommodation and establishment. Our cases disclose two limiting principles: government may not coerce anyone to support or participate in any religion or its exercise; and it may not, in the guise of avoiding hostility or callous indifference, give direct benefits to religion in such a degree that it in fact "establishes a [state] religion or religious faith, or tends to do so." These two principles, while distinct, are not unrelated, for it would be difficult indeed to establish a religion without some measure of more or less subtle coercion, be it in the form of taxation to supply the substantial benefits that would sustain a state-established faith, direct compulsion to observance, or governmental exhortation to religiosity that amounts in fact to proselytizing.

It is no surprise that without exception we have invalidated actions that further the interests of religion through the coercive power of government. . . . The freedom to worship as one pleases without government interference or oppression is the great object of both the Establishment and the Free Exercise Clauses. Barring all attempts to aid religion through government coercion goes far toward attainment of this object. . . .

As Justice Blackmun observes, some of our recent cases reject the view that coercion is the sole touchstone of an Establishment Clause violation. That may be true if by "coercion" is meant direct coercion in the classic sense of an establishment of religion that the Framers knew. But coercion need not be a direct tax in aid of religion or a test oath. Symbolic recognition or accommodation of religious faith may violate the Clause in an extreme case. I doubt not, for example, that the Clause forbids a city to permit the permanent erection of a large Latin cross on the roof of city hall. This is not because government speech about religion is per se suspect, as the majority would have it, but because such an obtrusive year-round religious display would place the government's weight behind an obvious effort to proselytize on behalf of a particular religion. Speech may coerce in some circumstances, but this does not justify a ban on all government recognition of religion.

. . .

In determining whether there exists an establishment, or a tendency toward one, we refer to the other types of church state contacts that have existed unchallenged throughout our history, or that have been found permissible in our case law. . . .

II

These principles are not difficult to apply to the facts of the cases before us. In permitting the displays on government property of the menorah and the creche, the city and county sought to do no more than "celebrate the season," and to acknowledge, along with many of their citizens, the historical background and the religious, as well as secular, nature of the Chanukah and Christmas holidays. This interest falls well within the tradition of government accommodation and acknowledgment of religion that has marked our history from the beginning. . . .

If government is to participate in its citizens' celebration of a holiday that contains both a secular and a religious component, enforced recognition of only the secular aspect would signify the callous indifference toward religious faith that our cases and traditions do not require; for by commemorating the holiday only as it is celebrated by nonadherents, the government would be refusing to acknowledge the plain fact, and the historical reality, that many of its citizens celebrate its religious aspects as well. Judicial invalidation of government's attempts to recognize the religious underpinnings of the holiday would signal not neutrality but a pervasive intent to insulate government from all things religious. The Religion Clauses do not require government to acknowledge these holidays or their religious component; but our strong tradition of government accommodation and acknowledgment permits government to do so.

There is no suggestion here that the government's power to coerce has been used to further the interests of Christianity or Judaism in any way. No one was compelled to observe or participate in any religious ceremony or activity. Neither the city nor the county contributed significant amounts of tax money to serve the cause of one religious faith. The creche and the menorah are purely passive symbols of religious holidays. Passersby who disagree with the message conveyed by these displays are free to ignore them, or even to turn their backs, just as they are free to do when they disagree with any other form of government speech.

There is no realistic risk that the creche and the menorah represent an effort to proselytize or are otherwise the first step down the road to an establishment of religion. *Lynch* is dispositive of this claim with respect to the creche, and I find no reason for reaching a different result with respect to the menorah. Both are the traditional symbols of religious holidays that over time have acquired a secular component. Without ambiguity, *Lynch* instructs that "the focus of our inquiry must be on the [religious symbol] in the context of the [holiday] season." In that context, religious displays that serve "to celebrate the Holiday and to depict the origins of that Holiday" give rise to no Establishment Clause concern. If Congress and the state legislatures do not run afoul of the Establishment Clause when they begin each day with a state-sponsored prayer for divine guidance offered by a chaplain whose salary is paid at government expense, I cannot comprehend how a menorah or a creche, displayed in the limited context of the holiday season, can be invalid.

... Crucial to the Court's conclusion was not the number, prominence, or type of secular items contained in the holiday display but the simple fact that, when displayed by government during the Christmas season, a creche presents no realistic danger of moving government down the forbidden road toward an establishment of religion. Whether the creche be surrounded by poinsettias, talking wishing wells, or carolers, the conclusion remains the same, for the relevant context is not the items in the display itself but the season as a whole.

The fact that the creche and menorah are both located on government property, even at the very seat of government, is likewise inconsequential. . . .

Nor can I comprehend why is should be that placement of a government-owned creche on private land is lawful while placement of a privately owned creche on public land is not. If anything, I should have thought government ownership of a religious symbol presented the more difficult question under the Establishment Clause, but as *Lynch* resolved that question to sustain the government action, the sponsorship here ought to be all the easier to sustain. In short, nothing about the religious displays here distinguishes them in any meaningful way from the creche we permitted in *Lynch*.

If *Lynch* is still good law—and until today it was—the judgment below cannot stand. I accept and indeed approve both the holding and the reasoning of Chief Justice Burger's opinion in *Lynch*, and so I must dissent from the judgment that the creche display is unconstitutional. On the same reasoning, I agree that the menorah display is constitutional.

. . .

Even if *Lynch* did not control, I would not commit this Court to the test applied by the majority today. The notion that cases arising under the Establishment Clause should be decided by an inquiry into whether a "'reasonable observer'" may "'fairly understand'" government action to "'sen[d] a message to nonadherents that they are outsiders, not full members of the political community,'" is a recent, and in my view most unwelcome, addition to our tangled Establishment Clause jurisprudence. . . . For the reasons expressed below, I submit that the endorsement test is flawed in its fundamentals and unworkable in practice. The uncritical adoption of this standard is every bit as troubling as the bizarre result it produces in the cases before us.

A

. . .

. . . Whatever test we choose to apply must permit not only legitimate practices two centuries old but also any other practices with no greater potential for an establishment of religion. The First Amendment is a rule, not a digest or compendium. A test for implementing the protections of the Establishment Clause that, if applied with consistency, would invalidate longstanding traditions cannot be a proper reading of the Clause.

If the endorsement test, applied without artificial exceptions for historical practice, reached results consistent with history, my objections to it would have less force. But, as I understand that test, the touchstone of an Establishment Clause violation is whether nonadherents would be made to feel like "outsiders" by government recognition or accommodation of religion. Few of our traditional practices recognizing the part religion plays in our society can withstand scrutiny under a faithful application of this formula.

Some examples suffice to make plain my concerns. Since the Founding of our Republic, American Presidents have issued Thanksgiving Proclamations establishing a national day of celebration and prayer. The first such proclamation was issued by President Washington at the request of the First Congress, and "recommend[ed] and assign[ed]" a day "to be devoted by the people of these States to the service of that great and glorious Being who is the beneficent author of all the good that was, that is, or that will be," so that "we may then unite in most humbly offering our prayers and supplications to the great Lord and Ruler of Nations, and beseech Him to . . . promote the knowledge and practice of true religion and virtue. . . . " Most of President Washington's successors have followed suit, and the forthrightly religious nature of these proclamations has not waned with the years. President Franklin D. Roosevelt went so far as to "suggest a nationwide reading of the Holy Scriptures during the period from Thanksgiving Day to Christmas" so that "we may bear more earnest witness to our gratitude to Almighty God." It requires little imagination to conclude that these proclamations would cause nonadherents to feel excluded, yet they have been a part of our national heritage from the beginning.

The Executive has not been the only Branch of our Government to recognize the central role of religion in our society. The fact that this Court opens its sessions with the request that "God save the United States and this honorable Court" has been noted elsewhere. The Legislature has gone much further, not only employing legislative chaplains, but also setting aside a special prayer room in the Capitol for use by Members of the House and Senate. The room is decorated with a large stained glass panel that depicts President Washington kneeling in prayer; around him is etched the first verse of the 16th Psalm: "Preserve me, O God, for in Thee do I put my trust." Beneath the panel is a rostrum on which a Bible is placed; next to the rostrum is an American Flag.

The United States Code itself contains religious references that would be suspect under the endorsement test. Congress has directed the President to "set aside and proclaim a suitable day each year . . . as a National Day of Prayer, on which the people of the United States may turn to God in prayer and meditation at churches, in groups, and as individuals." This statute does not require anyone to pray, of course, but it is a straightforward endorsement of the concept of "turn[ing] to God in prayer." Also by statute, the Pledge of Allegiance to the Flag describes the United States as "one Nation under God." To be sure, no one is obligated to recite this phrase, but it borders on sophistry to suggest that the "'reasonable'" atheist would not feel less than a "'full membe[r] of the political community'" every time his fellow Americans recited, as part of their expression of patriotism and love for country, a phrase he believed to be false. Likewise, our national motto, "In God we trust," which is prominently engraved in the wall above the Speaker's dias in the Chamber of the House of Representatives and is reproduced on every coin minted and every dollar printed by the Federal Government, must have the same effect.

If the intent of the Establishment Clause is to protect individuals from mere feelings of exclusion, then legislative prayer cannot escape invalidation. It has been argued that "[these] government acknowledgments of religion serve, in the only ways reasonably possible in our culture, the legitimate secular purposes of solemnizing public occasions, expressing confidence in the future, and encouraging the recognition of what is worthy of appreciation in society." I fail to see why prayer is the only way to convey these messages; appeals to patriotism, moments of silence, and any number of other approaches would be as effective, were the only purposes at issue the ones described by the *Lynch* concurrence. Nor is it clear to me why "encouraging the recognition of what is worthy of appreciation in society" can be characterized as a purely secular purpose, if it can be achieved only through religious prayer. No doubt prayer is "worthy of appreciation," but that is most assuredly not because it is secular. Even accepting the secular-solemnization explanation at face value,

moreover, it seems incredible to suggest that the average observer of legislative prayer who either believes in no religion or whose faith rejects the concept of God would not receive the clear message that his faith is out of step with the political norm. Either the endorsement test must invalidate scores of traditional practices recognizing the place religion holds in our culture, or it must be twisted and stretched to avoid inconsistency with practices we know to have been permitted in the past, while condemning similar practices with no greater endorsement effect simply by reason of their lack of historical antecedent. Neither result is acceptable.

. . .

The result the Court reaches in these cases is perhaps the clearest illustration of the unwisdom of the endorsement test. Although Justice O'Connor disavows Justice Blackmun's suggestion that the minority or majority status of a religion is relevant to the question whether government recognition constitutes a forbidden endorsement, the very nature of the endorsement test, with its emphasis on the feelings of the objective observer, easily lends itself to this type of inquiry. If there be such a person as the "reasonable observer," I am quite certain that he or she will take away a salient message from our holding in these cases: the Supreme Court of the United States has concluded that the First Amendment creates classes of religions based on the relative numbers of their adherents. Those religions enjoying the largest following must be consigned to the status of least favored faiths so as to avoid any possible risk of offending members of minority religions. I would be the first to admit that many questions arising under the Establishment Clause do not admit of easy answers, but whatever the Clause requires, it is not the result reached by the Court today.

IV

The approach adopted by the majority contradicts important values embodied in the Clause. Obsessive, implacable resistance to all but the most carefully scripted and secularized forms of accommodation requires this Court to act as a censor, issuing national decrees as to what is orthodox and what is not. What is orthodox, in this context, means what is secular; the only Christmas the State can acknowledge is one in which references to religion have been held to a minimum. The Court thus lends its assistance to an Orwellian rewriting of history as many understand it. I can conceive of no judicial function more antithetical to the First Amendment.

. . .

The suit before us is admittedly a troubling one. It must be conceded that, however neutral the purpose of the city and county, the eager proselytizer may seek to use these symbols for his own ends. The urge to use them to teach or to taunt is always present. It is also true that some devout adherents of Judaism or Christianity may be as offended by the holiday display as are nonbelievers, if not more so. To place these religious symbols in a common hallway or sidewalk, where they may be ignored or even insulted, must be distasteful to many who cherish their meaning.

For these reasons, I might have voted against installation of these particular displays were I a local legislative official. But we have no jurisdiction over matters of taste within the realm of constitutionally permissible discretion. Our role is enforcement of a written Constitution. In my view, the principles of the Establishment Clause and our Nation's historic traditions of diversity and pluralism allow communities to make reasonable judgments respecting the accommodation or acknowledgment of holidays with both cultural and religious aspects. No constitutional violation occurs when they do so by displaying a symbol of the holiday's religious origins.

c. Doctrinal Challenge and Turmoil

Dissatisfaction with establishment clause standards has been widely expressed by critics and by much of the Court. Chief Justice Rehnquist[302] and Justices Kennedy,[303] O'Connor[304], Scalia[305] and Thomas[306] at various times have articulated unhappiness with the *Lemon* test and suggested that principled decision-making would be better facilitated by revamped criteria. In a dissenting opinion joined by Chief Justice Rehnquist and Justices White and Thomas, Justice Scalia in *Lee v. Weisman* inferred from the Court's disregard of the *Lemon* test in that case its "internment."[307] Notwithstanding the *Lee* dissenters' advocacy of doctrine that would be more accommodating of religion, Justice Souter in an opinion joined by Justices Stevens and O'Connor urged attention to shoring up the wall between church and state.[308] Despite a majority of justices having expressed exasperation with the doctrinal status quo, the three-part *Lemon* test has yet to be formally abandoned. In *Lee* itself, the Court specifically declined "the invitation . . . to reconsider our decision in *Lemon.*"[309]

---

[302] *E.g.*, Wallace v. Jaffree, 472 U.S. 38, 108–12 (1985) (Rehnquist, J., dissenting).

[303] *E.g.*, County of Allegheny v. American Civil Liberties Union Greater Pittsburgh Chapter, 492 U.S. 573, 655–56 (1989) (opinion of Kennedy, J.).

[304] *E.g.*, Lynch v. Donnelly, 465 U.S. 668, 688–89 (1984) (O'Connor, J., concurring).

[305] *E.g.*, Lee v. Weisman, 112 S.Ct. 2649, 2685–86 (1992) (Scalia, J., dissenting).

[306] *E.g., id.*

[307] *Id.* at 2685.

[308] *Id.* at 2667–78.

[309] *Id.* at 2655.

Lee v. Weisman
112 S.Ct. 2649 (1992)

JUSTICE KENNEDY delivered the opinion of the Court.

School principals in the public school system of the city of Providence, Rhode Island, are permitted to invite members of the clergy to offer invocation and benediction prayers as part of the formal graduation ceremonies for middle schools and for high schools. The question before us is whether including clerical members who offer prayers as part of the official school graduation ceremony is consistent with the Religion Clauses of the First Amendment, provisions the Fourteenth Amendment makes applicable with full force to the States and their school districts.

I

A

Deborah Weisman graduated from Nathan Bishop Middle School, a public school in

Providence, at a formal ceremony in June 1989. She was about 14 years old. For many years it has been the policy of the Providence School Committee and the Superintendent of Schools to permit principals to invite members of the clergy to give invocations and benedictions at middle school and high school graduations. Many, but not all, of the principals elected to include prayers as part of the graduation ceremonies. Acting for himself and his daughter, Deborah's father, Daniel Weisman, objected to any prayers at Deborah's middle school graduation, but to no avail. The school principal, petitioner Robert E. Lee, invited a rabbi to deliver prayers at the graduation exercises for Deborah's class. . . .

It has been the custom of Providence school officials to provide invited clergy with a pamphlet entitled Guidelines for Civic Occasions," prepared by the National Conference of Christians and Jews. The Guidelines recommend that public prayers at nonsectarian civic ceremonies be composed with inclusiveness and sensitivity," though they acknowledge that prayer of any kind may be inappropriate on some civic occasions." The principal gave Rabbi Gutterman the pamphlet before the graduation and advised him the invocation and benediction should be nonsectarian.

. . .

II

These dominant facts mark and control the confines of our decision: State officials direct the performance of a formal religious exercise at promotional and graduation ceremonies for secondary schools. Even for those students who object to the religious exercise, their attendance and participation in the state-sponsored religious activity are in a fair and real sense obligatory, though the school district does not require attendance as a condition for receipt of the diploma.

This case does not require us to revisit the difficult questions dividing us in recent cases, questions of the definition and full scope of the principles governing the extent of permitted accommodation by the State for the religious beliefs and practices of many of its citizens. For without reference to those principles in other contexts, the controlling precedents as they relate to prayer and religious exercise in primary and secondary public schools compel the holding here that the policy of the city of Providence is an unconstitutional one. We can decide the case without reconsidering the general constitutional framework by which public schools' efforts to accommodate religion are measured. Thus we do not accept the invitation of petitioners and amicus the United States to reconsider our decision in *Lemon v. Kurtzman*. The government involvement with religious activity in

this case is pervasive, to the point of creating a state-sponsored and state-directed religious exercise in a public school. Conducting this formal religious observance conflicts with settled rules pertaining to prayer exercises for students, and that suffices to determine the question before us.

The principle that government may accommodate the free exercise of religion does not supersede the fundamental limitations imposed by the Establishment Clause. It is beyond dispute that, at a minimum, the Constitution guarantees that government may not coerce anyone to support or participate in religion or its exercise, or otherwise act in a way which establishes a [state] religion or religious faith, or tends to do so." The State's involvement in the school prayers challenged today violates these central principles.

That involvement is as troubling as it is undenied. A school official, the principal, decided that an invocation and a benediction should be given; this is a choice attributable to the State, and from a constitutional perspective it is as if a state statute decreed that the prayers must occur. The principal chose the religious participant, here a rabbi, and that choice is also attributable to the State. The reason for the choice of a rabbi is not disclosed by the record, but the potential for divisiveness over the choice of a particular member of the clergy to conduct the ceremony is apparent.

Divisiveness, of course, can attend any state decision respecting religions, and neither its existence nor its potential necessarily invalidates the State's attempts to accommodate religion in all cases. The potential for divisiveness is of particular relevance here though, because it centers around an overt religious exercise in a secondary school environment where, as we discuss below, subtle coercive pressures exist and where the student had no real alternative which would have allowed her to avoid the fact or appearance of participation.

. . .

We are asked to recognize the existence of a practice of nonsectarian prayer, prayer within the embrace of what is known as the Judeo-Christian tradition, prayer which is more acceptable than one which, for example, makes explicit references to the God of Israel, or to Jesus Christ, or to a patron saint. There may be some support, as an empirical observation, to the statement of the Court of Appeals for the Sixth Circuit, picked up by Judge Campbell's dissent in the Court of Appeals in this case, that there has emerged in this country a civic religion, one which is tolerated when sectarian exercises are not. If common ground can be defined which permits once conflicting faiths to express the shared conviction that there is an ethic and a morality which transcend human invention, the sense of community and purpose sought by all decent societies might be advanced. But though the First Amendment does not allow the government to stifle prayers which aspire to these ends, neither does it permit the government to undertake that task for itself.

The First Amendment's Religion Clauses mean that religious beliefs and religious expression are too precious to be either proscribed or prescribed by the State. The design of the Constitution is that preservation and transmission of religious beliefs and worship is a responsibility and a choice committed to the private sphere, which itself is promised freedom to pursue that mission. It must not be forgotten then, that while concern must be given to define the protection granted to an objector or a dissenting non-believer, these same Clauses exist to protect religion from government interference. James Madison, the principal author of the Bill of Rights, did not rest his opposition to a religious establishment on the sole ground of its effect on the minority. A principal ground for his view was: Experience witnesseth that ecclesiastical establishments, instead of maintaining the purity and efficacy of Religion, have had a contrary operation."

These concerns have particular application in the case of school officials, whose effort to monitor prayer will be perceived by the students as inducing a participation they might otherwise reject. Though the efforts of the school officials in this case to find common ground appear to have been a good-faith attempt to recognize the common aspects of religions and not the divisive ones, our precedents do not permit school officials to assist in composing prayers as an incident to a formal exercise for their students. And these same precedents caution us to measure the idea of a civic religion against the central meaning of the Religion Clauses of the First Amendment, which is that all creeds must be tolerated and none favored. The suggestion that government may establish an official or civic religion as a means of avoiding the establishment of a religion with more specific creeds strikes us as a contradiction that cannot be accepted.

. . .

The lessons of the First Amendment are as urgent in the modern world as in the 18th Century when it was written. One timeless lesson is that if citizens are subjected to state-sponsored religious exercises, the State disavows its own duty to guard and respect that sphere of inviolable conscience and belief which is the mark of a free people. To compromise that principle today would be to deny our own tradition and forfeit our standing to urge others to secure the protections of that tradition for themselves.

As we have observed before, there are heightened concerns with protecting freedom of conscience from subtle coercive pressure in the elementary and secondary public schools. Our decisions in *Engel v. Vitale*, and *Abington School District*, recognize, among other things, that prayer exercises in public schools carry a particular risk of indirect coercion. The concern may not be limited to the context of schools, but it is most pronounced there. What to most believers may seem nothing more than a reasonable request that the nonbeliever respect their religious practices, in a school context may appear to the nonbeliever or dissenter to be an attempt to employ the machinery of the State to enforce a religious orthodoxy.

We need not look beyond the circumstances of this case to see the phenomenon at work. The undeniable fact is that the school district's supervision and control of a high school graduation ceremony places public pressure, as well as peer pressure, on attending students to stand as a group or, at least, maintain respectful silence during the Invocation and Benediction. This pressure, though subtle and indirect, can be as real as any overt compulsion. Of course, in our culture standing or remaining silent can signify adherence to a view or simple respect for the views of others. And no doubt some persons who have no desire to join a prayer have little objection to standing as a sign of respect for those who do. But for the dissenter of high school age, who has a reasonable perception that she is being forced by the State to pray in a manner her conscience will not allow, the injury is no less real. There can be no doubt that for many, if not most, of the students at the graduation, the act of standing or remaining silent was an expression of participation in the Rabbi's prayer. That was the very point of the religious exercise. It is of little comfort to a dissenter, then, to be told that for her the act of standing or remaining in silence signifies mere respect, rather than participation. What matters is that, given our social conventions, a reasonable dissenter in this milieu could believe that the group exercise signified her own participation or approval of it.

Finding no violation under these circumstances would place objectors in the dilemma of participating, with all that implies, or protesting. We do not address whether that choice is acceptable if the affected citizens are mature adults, but we think the State may not, consistent with the Establishment Clause, place primary and secondary school children in this position. Research in psychology supports the common assumption that adolescents are often susceptible to pressure from their peers towards conformity, and that the influence is strongest in matters of social convention. To recognize that the choice imposed by the State constitutes an unacceptable constraint only acknowledges that the government may no more use social pressure to enforce orthodoxy than it may use more direct means.

. . .

There was a stipulation in the District Court that attendance at graduation and promotional ceremonies is voluntary. Petitioners and the United States, as amicus, made this a center point of the case, arguing that the option of not attending the graduation excuses any inducement or coercion in the ceremony itself. The argument lacks all persuasion. Law reaches past formalism. And to say a teenage student has a real choice not to attend her high school graduation is formalistic in the extreme. True, Deborah could elect not to attend commencement without renouncing her diploma; but we shall not allow the case to turn on this point. Everyone knows that in our society and in our culture high school graduation is one of life's most significant occasions. A school rule which excuses attendance is beside the point. Attendance may not be required by official decree, yet it is apparent that a student is not free to absent herself from the graduation exercise in any real sense of the term voluntary," for absence would require forfeiture of those intangible benefits which have motivated the student through youth and all her high school years. Graduation is a time for family and those closest to the student to celebrate success and express mutual wishes of gratitude and respect, all to the end of impressing upon the young person the role that it is his or her right and duty to assume in the community and all of its diverse parts.

The importance of the event is the point the school district and the United States rely upon to argue that a formal prayer ought to be permitted, but it becomes one of the principal reasons why their argument must fail. Their contention, one of considerable force were it not for the constitutional constraints applied to state action, is that the prayers are an essential part of these ceremonies because for many persons an occasion of this significance lacks meaning if there is no recognition, however brief, that human achievements cannot be understood apart from their spiritual essence. We think the Government's position that this interest suffices to force students to choose between compliance or forfeiture demonstrates fundamental inconsistency in its argumentation. It fails to acknowledge that what for many of Deborah's classmates and their parents was a spiritual imperative was for Daniel and Deborah Weisman religious conformance compelled by the State. While in some societies the wishes of the majority might prevail, the Establishment Clause of the First Amendment is addressed to this contingency and rejects the balance urged upon us. The Constitution forbids the State to exact religious conformity from a student as the price of attending her own high school graduation. This is the calculus the Constitution commands.

. . .

Our society would be less than true to its heritage if it lacked abiding concern for the values of its young people, and we acknowledge the profound belief of adherents to many faiths that there must be a place in the student's life for precepts of a morality higher even than the law we today enforce. We express no hostility to those aspirations, nor would our oath permit us to do so. A relentless and all-pervasive attempt to exclude religion from every aspect of public life could itself become inconsistent with the Constitution. We recognize that, at graduation time and throughout the course of the educational process, there will be instances when religious values, religious practices, and religious persons will have some interaction with the public schools and their students. But these matters, often questions of accommodation of religion, are not before us. The sole question presented is whether a religious exercise may be conducted at a graduation ceremony in circumstances where, as we have found, young graduates who object are induced to conform. No holding by this Court suggests that a school can persuade or compel a student to participate in a religious exercise. That is being done here, and it is forbidden by the Establishment Clause of the First Amendment.

. . .

Justice Blackmun, with whom Justice Stevens and Justice O'Connor join, concurring.

Nearly half a century of review and refinement of Establishment Clause jurisprudence has distilled one clear understanding: Government may neither promote nor affiliate itself with any religious doctrine or organization, nor may it obtrude itself in the internal affairs of any religious institution. The application of these principles to the present case mandates the decision reached today by the Court.

. . .

II

I join the Court's opinion today because I find nothing in it inconsistent with the essential precepts of the Establishment Clause developed in our precedents. The Court holds that the graduation prayer is unconstitutional because the State "in effect required participation in a religious exercise." Although our precedents make clear that proof of government coercion is not necessary to prove an Establishment Clause violation, it is sufficient. Government pressure to participate in a religious ac-

1094   Part V: The First Amendment

tivity is an obvious indication that the government is endorsing or promoting religion.

But it is not enough that the government restrain from compelling religious practices: it must not engage in them either. . . .

. . .

The mixing of government and religion can be a threat to free government, even if no one is forced to participate. When the government puts its imprimatur on a particular religion, it conveys a message of exclusion to all those who do not adhere to the favored beliefs. A government cannot be premised on the belief that all persons are created equal when it asserts that God prefers some. Only "anguish, hardship and bitter strife" result "when zealous religious groups struggle with one another to obtain the Government's stamp of approval." . . .

When the government arrogates to itself a role in religious affairs, it abandons its obligation as guarantor of democracy. Democracy requires the nourishment of dialogue and dissent, while religious faith puts its trust in an ultimate divine authority above all human deliberation. When the government appropriates religious truth, it "transforms rational debate into theological decree." Those who disagree no longer are questioning the policy judgment of the elected but the rules of a higher authority who is beyond reproach.

. . .

It is these understandings and fears that underlie our Establishment Clause jurisprudence. We have believed that religious freedom cannot exist in the absence of a free democratic government, and that such a government cannot endure when there is fusion between religion and the political regime. We have believed that religious freedom cannot thrive in the absence of a vibrant religious community and that such a community cannot prosper when it is bound to the secular. And we have believed that these were the animating principles behind the adoption of the Establishment Clause. To that end, our cases have prohibited government endorsement of religion, its sponsorship, and active involvement in religion, whether or not citizens were coerced to conform.

I remain convinced that our jurisprudence is not misguided, and that it requires the decision reached by the Court today. Accordingly, I join the Court in affirming the judgment of the Court of Appeals.

JUSTICE SOUTER, with whom JUSTICE STEVENS and JUSTICE O'CONNOR join, concurring.

I join the whole of the Court's opinion, and fully agree that prayers at public school graduation ceremonies indirectly coerce religious observance. I write separately nonetheless on two issues of Establishment Clause analysis that underlie my independent resolution of this case: whether the Clause applies to govern-

mental practices that do not favor one religion or denomination over others, and whether state coercion of religious conformity, over and above state endorsement of religious exercise or belief, is a necessary element of an Establishment Clause violation.

. . .

II

Petitioners rest most of their argument on a theory that, whether or not the Establishment Clause permits extensive nonsectarian support for religion, it does not forbid the state to sponsor affirmations of religious belief that coerce neither support for religion nor participation in religious observance. I appreciate the force of some of the arguments supporting a "coercion" analysis of the Clause. But we could not adopt that reading without abandoning our settled law, a course that, in my view, the text of the Clause would not readily permit. Nor does the extratextual evidence of original meaning stand so unequivocally at odds with the textual premise inherent in existing precedent that we should fundamentally reconsider our course.

A

Over the years, this Court has declared the invalidity of many noncoercive state laws and practices conveying a message of religious endorsement. . . .

C

. . .

Petitioners contend that because the early Presidents included religious messages in their inaugural and Thanksgiving Day addresses, the Framers could not have meant the Establishment Clause to forbid noncoercive state endorsement of religion. The argument ignores the fact, however, that Americans today find such proclamations less controversial than did the founding generation, whose published thoughts on the matter belie petitioners' claim. . . .

Madison's failure to keep pace with his principles in the face of congressional pressure cannot erase the principles. He admitted to backsliding, and explained that he had made the content of his wartime proclamations inconsequential enough to mitigate much of their impropriety. While his writings suggest mild variations in his interpretation of the Establishment Clause, Madison was no different in that respect from the rest of his political generation. That he expressed so much doubt about the constitutionality of religious proclamations, however, suggests a brand of separationism stronger even than that embodied in our traditional jurisprudence. So too does his characterization of public subsidies for legislative and military chaplains as unconstitutional "establishments," and for the federal courts, however expansive their general view of the Establishment Clause, have upheld both practices.

To be sure, the leaders of the young Republic engaged in some of the practices that separationists like Jefferson and Madison criticized. The First Congress did hire institutional chaplains, and Presidents Washington and Adams unapologetically marked days of public thanksgiving and prayer." Yet in the face of the separationist dissent, those practices prove, at best, that the Framers simply did not share a common understanding of the Establishment Clause, and, at worst, that they, like other politicians, could raise constitutional ideals one day and turn their backs on them the next. . . . Ten years after proposing the First Amendment, Congress passed the Alien and Sedition Acts, measures patently unconstitutional by modern standards. If the early Congress's political actions were determinative, and not merely relevant, evidence of constitutional meaning, we would have to gut our current First Amendment doctrine to make room for political censorship.

While we may be unable to know for certain what the Framers meant by the Clause, we do know that, around the time of its ratification, a respectable body of opinion supported a considerably broader reading than petitioners urge upon us. This consistency with the textual considerations is enough to preclude fundamentally reexamining our settled law, and I am accordingly left with the task of considering whether the state practice at issue here violates our traditional understanding of the Clause's proscriptions.

While the Establishment Clause's concept of neutrality is not self-revealing, our recent cases have invested it with specific content: the state may not favor or endorse either religion generally over nonreligion or one religion over others. . . .

That government must remain neutral in matters of religion does not foreclose it from ever taking religion into account. The State may "accommodate" the free exercise of religion by relieving people from generally applicable rules that interfere with their religious callings. Contrary to the views of some, such accommodation does not necessarily signify an official endorsement of religious observance over disbelief.

In everyday life, we routinely accommodate religious beliefs that we do not share. A Christian inviting an Orthodox Jew to lunch might take pains to choose a kosher restaurant; an atheist in a hurry might yield the right of way to an Amish man steering a horse-drawn carriage. In so acting, we express respect for, but not endorsement of, the fundamental values of others. We act without expressing a position on the theological merit of those values or of religious belief in general, and no one perceives us to have taken such a position.

The government may act likewise. Most religions encourage devotional practices that are at once crucial to the lives of believers and idiosyncratic in the eyes of nonadherents. By definition, secular rules of general application are drawn from the nonadherent's vantage and, consequently, fail to take such practices into account. Yet when enforcement of such rules cuts across religious sensibilities, as it often does, it puts those affected to the choice of taking sides between God and government. In such circumstances, accommodating religion reveals nothing beyond a recognition that general rules can unnecessarily offend the religious conscience when they offend the conscience of secular society not at all. . . .

Whatever else may define the scope of accommodation permissible under the Establishment Clause, one requirement is clear: accommodation must lift a discernible burden on the free exercise of religion. Concern for the position of religious individuals in the modern regulatory state cannot justify official solicitude for a religious practice unburdened by general rules; such gratuitous largesse would effectively favor religion over disbelief. By these lights one easily sees that, in sponsoring the graduation prayers at issue here, the State has crossed the line from permissible accommodation to unconstitutional establishment.

Religious students cannot complain that omitting prayers from their graduation ceremony would, in any realistic sense, "burden" their spiritual callings. To be sure, many of them invest this rite of passage with spiritual significance, but they may express their religious feelings about it before and after the ceremony. They may even organize a privately sponsored baccalaureate if they desire the company of like-minded students. Because they accordingly have no need for the machinery of the State to affirm their beliefs, the government's sponsorship of prayer at the graduation ceremony is most reasonably understood as an official endorsement of religion and, in this instance, of Theistic religion. One may fairly say, as one commentator has suggested, that the government brought prayer into the ceremony "precisely because some people want a symbolic affirmation that government approves and endorses their religion, and because many of the people who want this affirmation place little or no value on the costs to religious minorities."

Petitioners would deflect this conclusion by arguing that graduation prayers are no different from presidential religious proclamations and similar official "acknowledgments" of religion in public life. But religious invocations in Thanksgiving Day addresses and the like, rarely noticed, ignored without effort, conveyed over an impersonal medium, and directed at no one in particular, inhabit a pallid zone worlds apart from official prayers delivered to a captive audience of public school students and their families. Madison himself respected the difference between the trivial and the serious in constitutional practice. Realizing that his contemporaries were unlikely to take the Establishment Clause seriously enough to forgo a legislative chaplainship, he suggested that "rather than let this step beyond the landmarks of power have the effect of a legitimate precedent, it will be better to apply to it the legal aphorism de minimis non curat lex. . . ." But that logic permits no winking at the practice in question here. When public school officials, armed with the State's authority, convey an endorsement of religion to their students, they strike near the core of the Establishment Clause. However "ceremonial" their messages may be, they are flatly unconstitutional.

JUSTICE SCALIA, with whom THE CHIEF JUSTICE, JUSTICE WHITE, and JUSTICE THOMAS join, dissenting.

. . .

The history and tradition of our Nation are replete with public ceremonies featuring prayers of thanksgiving and petition. Illustrations of this point have been amply provided in our prior opinions, but since the Court is so oblivious to our history as to suggest that the Constitution restricts "preservation and transmission of religious beliefs . . . to the private sphere," it appears necessary to provide another brief account.

From our Nation's origin, prayer has been a prominent part of governmental ceremonies and proclamations. . . .

. . .

The Court presumably would separate graduation invocations and benedictions from other instances of public "preservation and transmission of religious beliefs" on the ground that they involve "psychological coercion." I find it a sufficient embarrassment that our Establishment Clause jurisprudence regarding holiday displays, has come to "require scrutiny more commonly associated with interior decorators than with the judiciary." *American Jewish Congress v. Chicago*, 827 F. 2d 120, 129 (Easterbrook, J., dissenting). But interior decorating is a rock-hard science compared to psychology practiced by amateurs. A few citations of "research in psychology" that have no particular bearing upon the precise issue here, cannot disguise the fact that the Court has gone beyond the realm where judges know what

they are doing. The Court's argument that state officials have "coerced" students to take part in the invocation and benediction at graduation ceremonies is, not to put too fine a point on it, incoherent.

The Court identifies two "dominant facts" that it says dictate its ruling that invocations and benedictions at public-school graduation ceremonies violate the Establishment Clause. Neither of them is in any relevant sense true.

The Court declares that students' "attendance and participation in the [invocation and benediction] are in a fair and real sense obligatory." But what exactly is this "fair and real sense"? According to the Court, students at graduation who want "to avoid the fact or appearance of participation," in the invocation and benediction are psychologically obligated by "public pressure, as well as peer pressure, . . . to stand as a group or, at least, maintain respectful silence" during those prayers. This assertion—the very linchpin of the Court's opinion—is almost as intriguing for what it does not say as for what it says. It does not say, for example, that students are psychologically coerced to bow their heads, place their hands in a Drer-like prayer position, pay attention to the prayers, utter "Amen," or in fact pray. (Perhaps further intensive psychological research remains to be done on these matters.) It claims only that students are psychologically coerced "to stand . . . or, at least, maintain respectful silence." Both halves of this disjunctive (both of which must amount to the fact or appearance of participation in prayer if the Court's analysis is to survive on its own terms) merit particular attention.

To begin with the latter: The Court's notion that a student who simply sits in "respectful silence" during the invocation and benediction (when all others are standing) has somehow joined—or would somehow be perceived as having joined—in the prayers is nothing short of ludicrous. We indeed live in a vulgar age. But surely "our social conventions," have not coarsened to the point that anyone who does not stand on his chair and shout obscenities can reasonably be deemed to have assented to everything said in his presence. . . .

But let us assume the very worst, that the nonparticipating graduate is "subtly coerced". . . to stand! Even that half of the disjunctive does not remotely establish a "participation" (or an "appearance of participation") in a religious exercise. The Court acknowledges that "in our culture standing . . . can signify adherence to a view or simple respect for the views of others." (Much more often the latter than the former, I think, except perhaps in the proverbial town meeting, where one votes by standing.) But if it is a permissible inference that one who is standing is doing so simply out of respect for the prayers of others that are in progress, then how can it possibly be said that a "reasonable dissenter . . . could believe that the group exercise signified her own participation or approval"? Quite obviously, it cannot. . . .

The opinion manifests that the Court itself has not given careful consideration to its test of psychological coercion. For if it had, how could it observe, with no hint of concern or disapproval, that students stood for the Pledge of Allegiance, which immediately preceded Rabbi Gutterman's invocation? The government can, of course, no more coerce political orthodoxy than religious orthodoxy. *West Virginia Board of Education v. Barnette*. Moreover, since the Pledge of Allegiance has been revised since *Barnette* to include the phrase "under God," recital of the Pledge would appear to raise the same Establishment Clause issue as the invocation and benediction. If students were psychologically coerced to remain standing during the invocation, they must also have been psychologically coerced, moments before, to stand for (and thereby, in the Court's view, take part in or appear to take part in) the Pledge. Must the Pledge therefore be barred from the public schools (both from graduation ceremonies and from the classroom)? In *Barnette* we held that a public-school student could not be compelled to recite the Pledge; we did not even hint that she could not be compelled to observe respectful silence—indeed, even to stand in respectful silence—when those who wished to recite it did so. Logically, that ought to be the next project for the Court's bulldozer.

The other "dominant fact" identified by the Court is that "state officials direct the performance of a formal religious exercise" at school graduation ceremonies. "Directing the performance of a formal religious exercise" has a sound of liturgy to it, summoning up images of the principal directing acolytes where to carry the cross, or showing the rabbi where to unroll the Torah. A Court professing to be engaged in a "delicate and fact-sensitive" line-drawing, would better describe what it means as "prescribing the content of an invocation and benediction." But even that would be false. All the record shows is that principals of the Providence public schools, acting within their delegated authority, have invited clergy to deliver invocations and benedictions at graduations. . . .

The deeper flaw in the Court's opinion does not lie in its wrong answer to the question whether there was state-induced "peer-pressure" coercion; it lies, rather, in the Court's making violation of the Establishment Clause hinge on such a precious question. The coercion that was a hallmark of historical establishments of religion was coercion of religious orthodoxy and of financial support by force of law and threat of penalty. Typically, attendance at the state church was required; only clergy of the official church could lawfully perform sacraments; and dissenters, if tolerated, faced an array of civil disabilities. Thus, for example, in the colony of Virginia, where the Church of England had been established, ministers were required by law to conform to the doctrine and rites of the Church of England; and all persons were required to attend church and observe the Sabbath, were tithed for the public support of Anglican ministers, and were taxed for the costs of building and repairing churches.

The Establishment Clause was adopted to prohibit such an establishment of religion at the federal level (and to protect state establishments of religion from federal interference). I will further acknowledge for the sake of argument that, as some scholars have argued, by 1790 the term "establishment" had acquired an additional meaning—"financial support of religion generally, by public taxation"—that reflected the development of "general or multiple" establishments, not limited to a single church. But that would still be an establishment coerced by force of law. And I will further concede that our constitutional tradition, from the Declaration of Independence and the first inaugural address of Washington, quoted earlier, down to the present day, has, with a few aberrations, ruled out of order government-sponsored endorsement of religion—even when no legal coercion is present, and indeed even when no ersatz, "peer-pressure" psycho-coercion is present—where the endorsement is sectarian, in the sense of specifying details upon which men and women who believe in a benevolent, omnipotent Creator and Ruler of the world, are known to differ (for example, the divinity of Christ). But there is simply no support for the proposition that the officially sponsored nondenominational invocation and benediction read by Rabbi Gutterman—with no one legally coerced to recite them—violated the Constitution of the United States. To the contrary, they are so characteristically American they could have come from the pen of George Washington or Abraham Lincoln himself.

Thus, while I have no quarrel with the Court's general proposition that the Establishment Clause "guarantees that government may not coerce anyone to support or participate in religion or its exercise," I see no warrant for expanding the concept of coercion beyond acts backed by threat of penalty—a brand of coercion that, happily, is readily discernible to those of us who have made a career of reading the disciples of Blackstone rather than of Freud. The Framers were indeed opposed to coercion of religious worship by the National Government; but, as their own sponsorship of nonsectarian prayer in public events demonstrates, they understood that "speech is not coercive; the listener may do as he likes."

This historical discussion places in revealing perspective the Court's extravagant claim that the State has "for all practical purposes," and "in every practical sense," compelled students to participate in prayers at graduation. Beyond the fact, stipulated to by the parties, that attendance at graduation is voluntary, there is nothing in the record to indicate that failure of attending students to take part in the invocation or benediction was subject to any penalty or discipline. . . .

The Court relies on our "school prayer" cases. But whatever the merit of those cases, they do not support, much less compel, the Court's psycho-journey. In the first place, *Engel* and *Schempp* do not constitute an exception to the rule, distilled from historical practice, that public ceremonies may include prayer; rather, they simply do not fall within the scope of the rule (for the obvious reason that school instruction is not a public ceremony). Second, we have made clear our understanding that school prayer occurs within a framework in which legal coercion to attend school (i. e., coercion under threat of penalty) provides the ultimate backdrop. In *Schempp*, for example, we emphasized that the prayers were "prescribed as part of the curricular activities of students who are required by law to attend school." *Engel*'s suggestion that the school-prayer program at issue there—which permitted students "to remain silent or be excused from the room,"—involved "indirect coercive pressure," should be understood against this backdrop of legal coercion. The question whether the opt-out procedure in *Engel* sufficed to dispel the coercion resulting from the mandatory attendance requirement is quite different from the question whether forbidden coercion exists in an environment *utterly devoid of legal compulsion*. And finally, our school-prayer cases turn in part on the fact that the classroom is inherently an instructional setting, and daily prayer there—where parents are not present to counter "the students' emulation of teachers as role models and the children's susceptibility to peer pressure," —might be thought to raise special concerns regarding state interference with the liberty of parents to direct the religious upbringing of their children: "Families entrust public schools with the education of their children, but condition their trust on the understanding that the classroom will not purposely be used to advance religious views that may conflict with the private beliefs of the student and his or her family." Voluntary prayer at graduation—a one-time ceremony at which parents, friends and relatives are present—can hardly be thought to raise the same concerns.

Our religion-clause jurisprudence has become bedeviled (so to speak) by reliance on formulaic abstractions that are not derived from, but positively conflict with, our long-accepted constitutional traditions. Foremost among these has been the so-called *Lemon* test, which has received well-earned criticism from many members of this Court. The Court today demonstrates the irrelevance of *Lemon* by essentially ignoring it, and the interment of that case may be the one happy byproduct of the Court's otherwise lamentable decision. Unfortunately, however, the Court has replaced *Lemon* with its psycho-coercion test, which suffers the double disability of having no roots whatever in our people's historic practice, and being as infinitely expandable as the reasons for psychotherapy itself.

Another happy aspect of the case is that it is only a jurisprudential disaster and not a practical one. Given the odd basis for the Court's decision, invocations and benedictions will be able to be given at public-school graduations next June, as they have for the past century and a half, so long as school authorities make clear that anyone who abstains from screaming in protest does not necessarily participate in the prayers. All that is seemingly needed is an announcement, or perhaps a written insertion at the beginning of the graduation Program, to the effect that, while all are asked to rise for the invocation and benediction, none is compelled to join in them, nor will be assumed, by rising, to have done so. That obvious fact recited, the graduates and their parents may proceed to thank God, as Americans have always done, for the blessings He has generously bestowed on them and on their country.

* * *

The reader has been told much in this case about the personal interest of Mr. Weisman and his daughter, and very little about the personal interests on the other side. They are not inconsequential. Church and state would not be such a difficult subject if religion were, as the Court apparently thinks it to be, some purely personal avocation that can be indulged entirely in secret, like pornography, in the privacy of one's room. For most believers it is not that, and has never been. Religious men and women of almost all denominations have felt it necessary to acknowledge and beseech the blessing of God as a people, and not just as individuals, because they believe in the "protection of divine Providence," as the Declaration of Independence put it, not just for individuals but for societies; because they believe God to be, as Washington's first Thanksgiving Proclamation put it, the "Great Lord and Ruler of Nations." One can believe in the effectiveness of such public worship, or one can deprecate and deride it. But the longstanding American tradition of prayer at official ceremonies displays with unmistakable clarity that the Establishment Clause does not forbid the government to accommodate it.

The narrow context of the present case involves a community's celebration of one of the milestones in its young citizens' lives, and it is a bold step for this Court to seek to banish from that occasion, and from thousands of similar celebrations throughout this land, the expression of gratitude to God that a majority of the community wishes to make. The issue before us today is not the abstract philosophical question whether the alternative of frustrating this desire of a religious majority is to be preferred over the alternative of imposing "psychological coercion," or a feeling of exclusion, upon nonbelievers. Rather, the question is whether a mandatory choice in favor of the former has been imposed by the United States Constitution. As the age-old practices of our people show, the answer to that question is not at all in doubt.

I must add one final observation: The founders of our Republic knew the fearsome potential of sectarian religious belief to generate civil dissension and civil strife. And they also knew that nothing, absolutely nothing, is so inclined to foster among religious believers of various faiths a toleration—no, an affection—for one another than voluntarily joining in prayer together, to the God whom they all worship and seek. Needless to say, no one should be compelled to do that, but it is a shame to deprive our public culture of the opportunity, and indeed the encouragement, for people to do it voluntarily. The Baptist or Catholic who heard and joined in the simple and inspiring prayers of Rabbi Gutterman on this official and patriotic occasion was inoculated from religious bigotry and prejudice in a manner that can not be replicated. To deprive our society of that important unifying mechanism, in order to spare the nonbeliever what seems to me the minimal inconvenience of standing or even sitting in respectful nonparticipation, is as senseless in policy as it is unsupported in law.

For the foregoing reasons, I dissent.

The dissenters' trumpeting of the *Lemon* test's demise in *Lee* sounded a death knell that proved premature. In *Lamb's Chapel v. Center Moriches Union Free School District*, the Court seemed to go out of its way to demonstrate the standard's continuing vitality. Finding that the freedom of speech clause prohibited a school district from denying churches access to school premises, when they were open to other groups, the Court stressed that such an exclusion did not offend the establishment clause.[310] The reference elicited a dissent from Justice Scalia, joined by Justice Thomas, who chastised the Court for holding onto the *Lemon* formula as a tool of convenience and pledged not to participate in its future use.[311]

---

[310] Lamb's Chapel v. Center Moriches Union Free School District, 113 S.Ct. 2141, 2148 (1993).

[311] *Id.* at 2050 (Scalia, J., concurring).

Lamb's Chapel v. Center Moriches Union Free School District
113 S.Ct. 2141 (1993)

JUSTICE WHITE delivered the opinion of the Court.

(New York) authorizes local school boards to adopt reasonable regulations for the use of school property for 10 specified purposes when the property is not in use for school purposes. Among the permitted uses is the holding of "social, civic and recreational meetings and entertainments, and other uses pertaining to the welfare of the community; but such meetings, entertainment and uses shall be non-exclusive and open to the general public." The list of per-mitted uses does not include meetings for religious purposes, and a New York . . . court ruled that local boards could not allow student bible clubs to meet on school property because "religious purposes are not included in the enumerated purposes for which a school may be used. . . .

The District . . . as a respondent, would save its judgment below on the ground that to permit its property to be used for religious purposes would be an establishment of religion forbidden by the First Amendment. This Court suggested in *Widmar v. Vincent*, 454 U.S. 263, 271, 70 L. Ed. 2d 440, 102 S. Ct. 269 (1981), that the interest of the State in avoiding an Establishment Clause violation "may be [a] compelling" one justifying an abridgment of free speech otherwise protected by the First Amendment; but the Court went on to hold that permitting use of University property for religious purposes under the open access policy involved there would not be incompatible with the Court's Establishment Clause cases.

We have no more trouble than did the Widmar Court in disposing of the claimed defense on the ground that the posited fears of an Establishment Clause violation are unfounded. The showing of this film would not have been during school hours, would not have been sponsored by the school, and would have been open to the public, not just to church members. The District property had repeatedly been used by a wide variety of private organizations. Under these circumstances, as in *Widmar*, there would have been no realistic danger that the community would think that the District was endorsing religion or any particular creed, and any benefit to religion or to the Church would have been no more than incidental. As in *Widmar*, permitting District property to be used to exhibit the film involved in this case would not have been an establishment of religion under the three-part test articulated in *Lemon v. Kurtzman*: The challenged governmental action has a secular purpose, does not have the principal or primary effect of advancing or inhibiting religion, and does not foster an excessive entanglement with religion.[7]

. . .

JUSTICE KENNEDY, concurring in part and concurring in the judgment.

Given the issues presented as well as the apparent unanimity of our conclusion that this overt, viewpoint-based discrimination contradicts the Speech Clause of the First Amendment and that there has been no substantial showing of a potential Establishment Clause violation, I agree with JUSTICE SCALIA that the Court's citation of *Lemon v. Kurtzman*, is unsettling and unnecessary. The same can be said of the Court's use of the phrase "endorsing religion," which I have indicated elsewhere, cannot suffice as a rule of decision consistent with our precedents and our traditions in this part of our jurisprudence. . . .

---

[7] While we are somewhat diverted by JUSTICE SCALIA'S evening at the cinema, post, at 1–3, we return to the reality that there is a proper way to inter an established decision and Lemon, however frightening it might be to some, has not been overruled. . . .

JUSTICE SCALIA, with whom JUSTICE THOMAS joins, concurring in the judgment.

. . . I also agree with the Court that allowing Lamb's Chapel to use school facilities poses "no realistic danger" of a violation of the Establishment Clause, but I cannot accept most of its reasoning in this regard. . . .

As to the Court's invocation of the *Lemon* test: Like some ghoul in a late-night horror movie that repeatedly sits up in its grave and shuffles abroad, after being repeatedly killed and buried, *Lemon* stalks our Establishment Clause jurisprudence once again, frightening the little children and school attorneys of Center Moriches Union Free School District. Its most recent burial, only last Term, was, to be sure, not fully six-feet under: our decision in *Lee v. Weisman*, conspicuously avoided using the supposed "test" but also declined the invitation to repudiate it. Over the years, however, no fewer than five of the currently sitting Justices have, in their own opinions, personally driven pencils through the creature's heart (the author of today's opinion repeatedly), and a sixth has joined an opinion doing so.

The secret of the *Lemon* test's survival, I think, is that it is so easy to kill. It is there to scare us (and our audience) when we wish it to do so, but we can command it to return to the tomb at will. When we wish to strike down a practice it forbids, we invoke it, when we wish to uphold a practice it forbids, we ignore it entirely, see *Marsh v. Chambers*. Sometimes, we take a middle course, calling its three prongs "no more than helpful signposts," Such a docile and useful monster is worth keeping around, at least in a somnolent state; one never knows when one might need him.

For my part, I agree with the long list of constitutional scholars who have criticized *Lemon* and bemoaned the strange Establishment Clause geometry of crooked lines and wavering shapes its intermittent use has produced. I will decline to apply *Lemon*—whether it validates or invalidates the government action in question—and therefore cannot join the opinion of the Court today.

I cannot join for yet another reason: the Court's statement that the proposed use of the school's facilities is constitutional because (among other things) it would not signal endorsement of religion in general. What a strange notion, that a Constitution which itself gives "religion in general" preferential treatment (I refer to the Free Exercise Clause) forbids endorsement of religion in general. The Attorney General of New York not only agrees with that strange notion, he has an explanation for it: "Religious advocacy," he writes, "serves the community only in the eyes of its adherents and yields a benefit only to those who already believe." That was not the view of those who adopted our Constitution, who believed that the public virtues inculcated by religion are a public good. It suffices to point out that during the summer of 1789, when it was in the process of drafting the First Amendment, Congress enacted the famous Northwest Territory Ordinance of 1789, Article III of which provides, "Religion, morality, and knowledge, being necessary to good government and the happiness of mankind, schools and the means f education shall forever be encouraged." Unsurprisingly, then, indifference to "religion in general" is not what our cases, both old and recent, demand.

* * *

. . . As for the asserted Establishment Clause justification, I would hold, simply and clearly, that giving Lamb's Chapel nondiscriminatory access to school facilities cannot violate that provision because it does not signify state or local embrace of a particular religious sect.

Despite the Court's show of support for the *Lemon* test in *Lamb's Chapel*, it made no reference to it in its next decision. In *Zobrest v. Catalina Foothills School District*, the Court considered whether a public school district could provide an interpreter for a deaf student in a parochial school. Although comparable issues had been resolved in the past with reference to *Lemon*, the Court in *Zobrest* stressed principles of neutrality in allowing the State to provide such support.

Zobrest v. Catalina Foothills District
113 S.Ct. 2462 (1993)

CHIEF JUSTICE REHNQUIST delivered the opinion of the Court.

Petitioner James Zobrest, who has been deaf since birth, asked respondent school district to provide a sign-language interpreter to accompany him to classes at a Roman Catholic high school in Tucson, Arizona, pursuant to the Individuals with Disabilities Education Act. The United States Court of Appeals for the Ninth Circuit decided, however, that provision of such a publicly employed interpreter would violate the Establishment Clause of the First Amendment. We hold that the Establishment Clause does not bar the school district from providing the requested interpreter.

. . .

We have never said that "religious institutions are disabled by the First Amendment from participating in publicly sponsored social welfare programs." For if the Establishment Clause did bar religious groups from receiving general government benefits, then "a church could not be protected by the police and fire departments, or have its public sidewalk kept in repair." Given that a contrary rule would lead to such absurd results, we have consistently held that government programs that neutrally provide benefits to a broad class of citizens defined without reference to religion are not readily subject to an Establishment Clause challenge just because sectarian institutions may also receive an attenuated financial benefit. . . .

. . .

. . . The service at issue in this case is part of a general government program that distrib-utes benefits neutrally to any child qualifying as "handicapped" under the IDEA, without regard to the "sectarian-nonsectarian, or public-nonpublic nature" of the school the child attends. By according parents freedom to select a school of their choice, the statute ensures that a government-paid interpreter will be present in a sectarian school only as a result of the private decision of individual parents. In other words, because the IDEA creates no financial incentive for parents to choose a sectarian school, an interpreter's presence there cannot be attributed to state decisionmaking. . . . When the government offers a neutral service on the premises of a sectarian school as part of a general program that "is in no way skewed towards religion," it follows under our prior decisions that provision of that service does not offend the Establishment Clause. . . . The only indirect economic benefit a sectarian school might receive by dint of the IDEA is the handicapped child's tuition—and that is, of course, assuming that the school makes a profit on each student; that, without an IDEA interpreter, the child would have gone to school elsewhere; and that the school, then, would have been unable to fill that child's spot.

. . .

. . . (R)espondent argues that this case more closely resembles *Meek v. Pittenger*, and *School Dist. of Grand Rapids v. Ball*. In *Meek*, we struck down a statute that, inter alia, provided "massive aid" to private schools—more than 75% of which were church related—through a direct loan of teaching material and equipment. The material and equipment covered by the statute included maps, charts, and tape recorders. According to respondent, if the government could not place a tape recorder in a sectarian school in *Meek*, then it surely cannot place an interpreter in Salpointe. The statute in *Meek* also authorized state-paid personnel to furnish "auxiliary services"—which included remedial and accelerated instruction and guidance counseling—on the premises of religious schools. We determined that this part of the statute offended the First Amendment as well. *Ball* similarly involved two public programs that provided services on private school premises; there, public employees taught classes to students in private school classrooms. We found that those programs likewise violated the Constitution, relying largely on *Meek*. According to respondent, if the government could not provide educational services on the premises of sectarian schools in *Meek* and *Ball*, then it surely cannot provide James with an interpreter on the premises of Salpointe.

Respondent's reliance on *Meek* and *Ball* is misplaced for two reasons. First, the programs in *Meek* and Ball—through direct grants of government aid—relieved sectarian schools of costs they otherwise would have borne in educating their students. For example, the religious schools in *Meek* received teaching material and equipment from the State, relieving them of an otherwise necessary cost of performing their educational function. Substantial aid to the educational function of such schools," we explained, "necessarily results in aid to the sectarian school enterprise as a whole," and therefore brings about "the direct and substantial advancement of religious activity." So, too, was the case in Ball: The programs challenged there, which provided teachers in addition to instructional equipment and material, "in effect subsidized the religious functions of the parochial schools by taking over a substantial portion of their responsibility for teaching secular subjects." "This kind of direct aid," we determined, "is indistinguishable from the provision of a direct cash subsidy to the religious school." The extension of aid to petitioners, however, does not amount to "an impermissible 'direct subsidy'" of Salpointe. For Salpointe is not relieved of an expense that it otherwise would have assumed in educating its students. And, as we noted above, any attenuated financial benefit that parochial schools do ultimately receive from the IDEA is attributable to "the private choices of individual parents." Handicapped children, not sectarian schools, are the primary beneficiaries of the IDEA; to the extent sectarian schools benefit at all from the IDEA, they are only incidental beneficiaries. Thus, the function of the IDEA is hardly

"'to provide desired financial support for nonpublic, sectarian institutions.'"

Second, the task of a sign-language interpreter seems to us quite different from that of a teacher or guidance counselor. Notwithstanding the Court of Appeals' intimations to the contrary, the Establishment Clause lays down no absolute bar to the placing of a public employee in a sectarian school. Such a flat rule, smacking of antiquated notions of "taint," would indeed exalt form over substance. Nothing in this record suggests that a sign-language interpreter would do more than accurately interpret whatever material is presented to the class as a whole. In fact, ethical guidelines require interpreters to "transmit everything that is said in exactly the same way it was intended." James' parents have chosen of their own free will to place him in a pervasively sectarian environment. The sign-language interpreter they have requested will neither add to nor subtract from that environment, and hence the provision of such assistance is not barred by the Establishment Clause.

The IDEA creates a neutral government program dispensing aid not to schools but to individual handicapped children. If a handicapped child chooses to enroll in a sectarian school, we hold that the Establishment Clause does not prevent the school district from furnishing him with a sign-language interpreter there in order to facilitate his education. The judgment of the Court of Appeals is therefore Reversed.

JUSTICE BLACKMUN, with whom JUSTICE SOUTER joins . . . dissenting.

The majority attempts to elude the impact of the record by offering three reasons why this sort of aid to petitioners survives Establishment Clause scrutiny. First, the majority observes that provision of a sign-language interpreter occurs as "part of a general government program that distributes benefits neutrally to any child qualifying as 'handicapped' under the IDEA, without regard to the 'sectarian-nonsectarian, or public-nonpublic' nature of the school the child attends." Second, the majority finds significant the fact that aid is provided to pupils and their parents, rather than directly to sectarian schools. As a result,'" any aid . . . that ultimately flows to religious institutions does so only as a result of the genuinely independent and private choices of aid recipients.'" And, finally, the majority opines that "the task of a sign-language interpreter seems to us quite different from that of a teacher or guidance counselor."

But the majority's arguments are unavailing. As to the first two, even a general welfare program may have specific applications that are constitutionally forbidden under the Establishment Clause. For example, a general program granting remedial assistance to disadvantaged schoolchildren attending public and private, secular and sectarian schools alike would clearly offend the Establishment Clause insofar as it authorized the provision of teachers. Such a program would not be saved simply because it supplied teachers to secular as well as sectarian schools. Nor would the fact that teachers were furnished to pupils and their parents, rather than directly to sectarian schools, immunize such a program from Establishment Clause scrutiny.

"Although Establishment Clause jurisprudence is characterized by few absolutes," at a minimum "the Clause does absolutely prohibit government-financed or government-sponsored indoctrination into the beliefs of a particular religious faith." In keeping with this restriction, our cases consistently have rejected the provision by government of any resource capable of advancing a school's religious mission. Although the Court generally has permitted the provision of "secular and nonideological services unrelated to the primary, religion-oriented educational function of the sectarian school," it has always proscribed the provision of benefits that afford even "the opportunity for the transmission of sectarian views."

Thus, the Court has upheld the use of public school buses to transport children to and from school, while striking down the employment of publicly funded buses for field trips controlled by parochial school teachers, *Wolman.* Similarly, the Court has permitted the provision of secular textbooks whose content is immutable and can be ascertained in advance, while prohibiting the provision of any instructional materials or equipment that could be used to convey a religious message, such as slide projectors, tape recorders, record players, and the like, *Wolman.* State-paid speech and hearing therapists have been allowed to administer diagnostic testing on the premises of parochial schools, whereas state-paid remedial teachers and counselors have not been authorized to offer their services because of the risk that they may inculcate religious beliefs.

These distinctions perhaps are somewhat fine, but "'lines must be drawn.'" And our cases make clear that government crosses the boundary when it furnishes the medium for communication of a religious message. If petitioners receive the relief they seek, it is beyond question that a state-employed sign-language interpreter would serve as the conduit for petitioner's religious education, thereby assisting Salpointe in its mission of religious indoctrination. But the Establishment Clause is violated when a sectarian school enlists "the machinery of the State to enforce a religious orthodoxy."

. . .

Questions about the vitality of *Lemon* were raised again by the Court's decision in *Board of Education of Kiryas Joel Village School District v. Grumet.* Emphasizing again principles of neutrality, Justice Souter's majority decision invalidated a special school district created to include only members of a particular religious sect. Responsive to the obvious questions raised by the ruling and its rationale, Justice Blackmun authored a concurring opinion to "note my disagreement with any suggestion that today's decision signals a departure from the principles described in *Lemon.*"[312]

---

[312] Board of Education of Kiryas Joel Village School District v. Grumet, 114 S.Ct. 2481, 2495 (1994)(Blackmun, J., concurring).

Board of Education, Kiryas Joel Village School District v. Grumet
114 S.Ct. 2481 (1994)

JUSTICE SOUTER delivered the opinion of the Court.

The Village of Kiryas Joel in Orange County, New York, is a religious enclave of Satmar Hasidim, practitioners of a strict form of Judaism. The village fell within the Monroe-Woodbury Central School District until a special state statute passed in 1989 carved out a separate district, following village lines, to serve this distinctive population. The question is whether the Act creating the separate school district violates the Establishment Clause of the First Amendment, binding on the States through the Fourteenth Amendment. Because this unusual act is tantamount to an allocation of political power on a religious criterion and neither presupposes nor requires governmental impartiality toward religion, we hold that it violates the prohibition against establishment.

I

The Satmar Hasidic sect takes its name from the town near the Hungarian and Romanian border where, in the early years of this century, Grand Rabbi Joel Teitelbaum molded the group into a distinct community. After World War II and the destruction of much of European Jewry, the Grand Rabbi and most of his surviving followers moved to the Williamsburg section of Brooklyn, New York. Then, 20 years ago, the Satmars purchased an approved but undeveloped subdivision in the town of Monroe and began assembling the community that has since become the Village of Kiryas Joel. When a zoning dispute arose in the course of settlement, the Satmars presented the Town Board of Monroe with a petition to form a new village within the town, a right that New York's Village Law gives almost any group of residents who satisfy certain procedural niceties. Neighbors who did not wish to secede with the Satmars objected strenuously, and after arduous negotiations the proposed boundaries of the Village of Kiryas Joel were drawn to include just the 320 acres owned and inhabited entirely by Satmars. The village, incorporated in 1977, has a population of about 8,500 today. Rabbi Aaron Teitelbaum, eldest son of the current Grand Rabbi, serves as the village rov (chief rabbi) and rosh yeshivah (chief authority in the parochial schools).

The residents of Kiryas Joel are vigorously religious people who make few concessions to the modern world and go to great lengths to avoid assimilation into it. They interpret the Torah strictly; segregate the sexes outside the home; speak Yiddish as their primary language; eschew television, radio, and English-language publications; and dress in distinctive ways that include headcoverings and special garments for boys and modest dresses for girls. Children are educated in private religious schools, most boys at the United Talmudic Academy where they receive a thorough grounding in the Torah and limited exposure to secular subjects, and most girls at Bais Rochel, an affiliated school with a curriculum designed to prepare girls for their roles as wives and mothers.

These schools do not, however, offer any distinctive services to handicapped children, who are entitled under state and federal law to special education services even when enrolled in private schools. Starting in 1984 the Monroe-Woodbury Central School District provided such services for the children of Kiryas Joel at an annex to Bais Rochel, but a year later ended that arrangement in response to our decisions ... Children from Kiryas Joel who needed special education (including the deaf, the mentally retarded, and others suffering from a range of physical, mental, or emotional disorders) were then forced to attend public schools outside the village, which their families found highly unsatisfactory. Parents of most of these children withdrew them from the Monroe-Woodbury secular schools, citing "the panic, fear and trauma [the children] suffered in leaving their own community and being with people whose ways were so different," and some sought administrative review of the public-school placements.

By 1989, only one child from Kiryas Joel was attending Monroe-Woodbury's public schools; the village's other handicapped children received privately funded special services or went without. It was then that the New York Legislature passed the statute at issue in this litigation, which provided that the Village of Kiryas Joel "is constituted a separate school district, . . . and shall have and enjoy all the powers and duties of a union free school district. . . ." The statute thus empowered a locally elected board of education to take such action as opening schools and closing them, hiring teachers, prescribing textbooks, establishing disciplinary rules, and raising property taxes to fund operations. In signing the bill into law, Governor Cuomo recognized that the residents of the new school district were "all members of the same religious sect," but said that the bill was "a good faith effort to solve the unique problem" associated with providing special education services to handicapped children in the village.

Although it enjoys plenary legal authority over the elementary and secondary education of all school-aged children in the village, the Kiryas Joel Village School District currently runs only a special education program for handicapped children. The other village children have stayed in their parochial schools, relying on the new school district only for transportation, remedial education, and health and welfare services. If any child without handicap in Kiryas Joel were to seek a public-school education, the district would pay tuition to send the child into Monroe-Woodbury or another school district nearby. Under like arrangements, several of the neighboring districts send their handicapped Hasidic children into Kiryas Joel, so that two thirds of the full-time students in the village's public school come from outside. In all, the new district serves just over 40 full-time students, and two or three times that many parochial school students on a part-time basis.

. . .

"A proper respect for both the Free Exercise and the Establishment Clauses compels the State to pursue a course of 'neutrality' toward religion," favoring neither one religion over others nor religious adherents collectively over nonadherents. Chapter 748, the statute creating the Kiryas Joel Village School District, departs from this constitutional command by delegating the State's discretionary authority over public schools to a group defined by its character as a religious community, in a legal and historical context that gives no assurance that governmental power has been or will be exercised neutrally.

. . .

It is, first, not dispositive that the recipients of state power in this case are a group of religious individuals united by common doctrine, not the group's leaders or officers. Although some school district franchise is common to all voters, the State's manipulation of the franchise for this district limited it to Satmars, giving the sect exclusive control of the political subdivision. In the circumstances of this case, the difference between thus vesting state power in the members of a religious group as such instead of the officers of its sectarian organization is one of form, not substance. . . .

Of course, Chapter 748 delegates power not by express reference to the religious belief of the Satmar community, but to residents of the "territory of the village of Kiryas Joel." . . . (T)he context here persuades us that Chapter 748 effectively identifies these recipients of governmental authority by reference to doctrinal adherence, even though it does not do so expressly. We find this to be the better view of the facts because of the way the boundary lines of the school district divide residents according to religious affiliation, under the terms of an unusual and special legislative act.

It is undisputed that those who negotiated the village boundaries when applying the general village incorporation statute drew them so as to exclude all but Satmars, and that the New York Legislature was well aware that the village remained exclusively Satmar in 1989 when it adopted Chapter 748. The significance of this fact to the state legislature is indicated by the further fact that carving out the village school district ran counter to customary districting practices in the State. Indeed, the trend in New York is not toward dividing school districts but toward consolidating them. . . . The object of the State's practice of consolidation is the creation of districts large enough to provide a comprehensive education at affordable cost, which is thought to require at least 500 pupils for a combined junior-senior high school. The Kiryas Joel Village School District, in contrast, has only 13 local, full-time students in all (even including out-of-area and part-time students leaves the number under 200), and in offering only special education and remedial programs it makes no pretense to be a full-service district.

The origin of the district in a special act of the legislature, rather than the State's general laws governing school district reorganization, is likewise anomalous. . . .

Because the district's creation ran uniquely counter to state practice, following the lines of a religious community where the customary and neutral principles would not have dictated the same result, we have good reasons to treat this district as the reflection of a religious criterion for identifying the recipients of civil authority. Not even the special needs of the children in this community can explain the legislature's unusual Act, for the State could have responded to the concerns of the Satmar parents without implicating the Establishment Clause, as we explain in some detail further on. We therefore find the legislature's Act to be substantially equivalent to defining a political subdivision and hence the qualification for its franchise by a religious test, resulting in a purposeful and forbidden "fusion of governmental and religious functions."

The fact that this school district was created by a special and unusual Act of the legislature also gives reason for concern whether the benefit received by the Satmar community is one that the legislature will provide equally to other religious (and nonreligious) groups. . . .

The fundamental source of constitutional concern here is that the legislature itself may fail to exercise governmental authority in a religiously neutral way. The anomalously case-specific nature of the legislature's exercise of state authority in creating this district for a religious community leaves the Court without any direct way to review such state action for the purpose of safeguarding a principle at the heart of the Establishment Clause, that government should not prefer one religion to another, or religion to irreligion. . . .

. . . Here the benefit flows only to a single sect, but aiding this single, small religious group causes no less a constitutional problem than would follow from aiding a sect with more members or religion as a whole, and we are forced to conclude that the State of New York has violated the Establishment Clause.

In finding that Chapter 748 violates the requirement of governmental neutrality by extending the benefit of a special franchise, we do not deny that the Constitution allows the state to accommodate religious needs by alleviating special burdens. Our cases leave no doubt that in commanding neutrality the Religion Clauses do not require the government to be oblivious to impositions that legitimate exercises of state power may place on religious belief and practice. Rather, there is "ample room under the Establishment Clause for 'benevolent neutrality which will permit religious exercise to exist without sponsorship and without interference; "government may (and sometimes must) accommodate religious practices and . . . may do so without violating the Establishment Clause." The fact that Chapter 748 facilitates the practice of religion is not what renders it an unconstitutional establishment.

But accommodation is not a principle without limits, and what petitioners seek is an adjustment to the Satmars' religiously grounded preferences that our cases do not countenance. . . . Petitioners' proposed accommodation singles out a particular religious sect for special treatment, and whatever the limits of permissible legislative accommodations may be, it is clear that neutrality as among religions must be honored.

This conclusion does not, however, bring the Satmar parents, the Monroe-Woodbury school district, or the State of New York to the end of the road in seeking ways to respond to the parents' concerns. (T)here are several alternatives here for providing bilingual and bicultural special education to Satmar children. Such services can perfectly well be offered to village children through the Monroe-Woodbury Central School District. Since the Satmars do not claim that separatism is religiously mandated, their children may receive bilingual and bicultural instruction at a public school already run by the Monroe-Woodbury district. Or if the educationally appropriate offering by Monroe-Woodbury should turn out to be a separate program of bilingual and bicultural education at a neutral site near one of the village's parochial schools, this Court has already made it clear that no Establishment Clause difficulty would inhere in such a scheme, administered in accordance with neutral principles that would not necessarily confine special treatment to Satmars.

III

Justice Cardozo once cast the dissenter as "the gladiator making a last stand against the lions." JUSTICE SCALIA'S dissent is certainly the work of a gladiator, but he thrusts at lions of his own imagining. We do not disable a religiously homogeneous group from exercising political power conferred on it without regard to religion. Unlike the states of Utah and New Mexico (which were laid out according to traditional political methodologies taking account of lines of latitude and longitude and topographical features, the reference line chosen for the Kiryas Joel Village School District was one purposely drawn to separate Satmars from non-Satmars. Nor do we impugn the motives of the New York Legislature, which no doubt intended to accommodate the Satmar community without violating the Establishment Clause; we simply refuse to ignore that the method it chose is one that aids a particular religious community, as such, rather than all groups similarly interested in separate schooling. The dissent protests it is novel to insist "up front" that a statute not tailor its benefits

to apply only to one religious group, post. . . . Indeed, under the dissent's theory, if New York were to pass a law providing school buses only for children attending Christian day schools, we would be constrained to uphold the statute against Establishment Clause attack until faced by a request from a non-Christian family for equal treatment under the patently unequal law. And to end on the point with which JUSTICE SCALIA begins, the license he takes in suggesting that the Court holds the Satmar sect to be New York's established church, is only one symptom of his inability to accept the fact that this Court has long held that the First Amendment reaches more than classic, 18th century establishments.

Our job, of course would be easier if the dissent's position had prevailed with the Framers and with this Court over the years. An Establishment Clause diminished to the dimensions acceptable to JUSTICE SCALIA could be enforced by a few simple rules, and our docket would never see cases requiring the application of a principle like neutrality toward religion as well as among religious sects. But that would be as blind to history as to precedent, and the difference between JUSTICE SCALIA and the Court accordingly turns on the Court's recognition that the Establishment Clause does comprehend such a principle and obligates courts to exercise the judgment necessary to apply it.

In this case we are clearly constrained to conclude that the statute before us fails the test of neutrality. It delegates a power this Court has said "ranks at the very apex of the function of a State," to an electorate defined by common religious belief and practice, in a manner that fails to foreclose religious favoritism. It therefore crosses the line from permissible accommodation to impermissible establishment. The judgment of the Court of Appeals of the State of New York is accordingly

Affirmed.

JUSTICE BLACKMUN, concurring.

. . . I write separately only to note my disagreement with any suggestion that today's decision signals a departure from the principles described in *Lemon v. Kurtzman*, relies upon several decisions, that explicitly rested on the criteria set forth in *Lemon*. Indeed, the two principles on which the opinion bases its conclusion that the legislative act is constitutionally invalid essentially are the second and third *Lemon* criteria.

I have no quarrel with the observation of JUSTICE O'CONNOR, that the application of constitutional principles, including those articulated in *Lemon*, must be sensitive to particular contexts. But I remain convinced of the general validity of the basic principles stated in *Lemon*, which have guided this Court's Establishment Clause decisions in over 30 cases.

JUSTICE STEVENS, with whom JUSTICE BLACKMUN and JUSTICE GINSBURG join, concurring.

New York created a special school district for the members of the Satmar religious sect in response to parental concern that children suffered "panic, fear and trauma" when "leaving their own community and being with people whose ways were so different." Ante, at 3. To meet those concerns, the State could have taken steps to alleviate the children's fear by teaching their schoolmates to be tolerant and respectful of Satmar customs. Action of that kind would raise no constitutional concerns and would further the strong public interest in promoting diversity and understanding in the public schools.

. . .

Affirmative state action in aid of segregation of this character is unlike the evenhanded distribution of a public benefit or service, a "release time" program for public school students involving no public premises or funds, or a decision to grant an exemption from a burdensome general rule. It is, I believe, fairly characterized as establishing, rather than merely accommodating, religion. For this reason, as well as the reasons set out in JUSTICE SOUTER'S opinion, I am persuaded that the New York law at issue in these cases violates the Establishment Clause of the First Amendment.

JUSTICE O'CONNOR, concurring in part and concurring in the judgment.

. . .

. . . In my view, the Religion Clauses . . . and the Equal Protection Clause as applied to religion—all speak with one voice on this point: Absent the most unusual circumstances, one's religion ought not affect one's legal rights or duties or benefits. As I have previously noted, "the Establishment Clause is infringed when the government makes adherence to religion relevant to a person's standing in the political community."

That the government is acting to accommodate religion should generally not change this analysis. What makes accommodation permissible, even praiseworthy, is not that the government is making life easier for some particular religious group as such. Rather, it is that the government is accommodating a deeply held belief. Accommodations may thus justify treating those who share this belief differently from those who do not; but they do not justify discriminations based on sect. A state law prohibiting the consumption of alcohol may exempt sacramental wines, but it may not exempt sacramental wine use by Catholics but not by Jews. A draft law may exempt conscientious objectors, but it may not exempt conscientious objectors whose objections are based on theistic belief (such as Quakers) as opposed to nontheistic belief (such as Buddhists) or atheistic belief. The Constitution permits "nondiscriminatory religious-practice exemptions," not sectarian ones.

III

I join Parts I, II-B, II-C, and III of the Court's opinion because I think this law, rather than being a general accommodation, singles out a particular religious group for favorable treatment. The Court's analysis of the history of this law and of the surrounding statutory scheme, persuades me of this.

IV

One aspect of the Court's opinion in this case is worth noting: Like the opinions in two recent cases, the Court's opinion does not focus on the Establishment Clause test we set forth in *Lemon v. Kurtzman.*

It is always appealing to look for a single test, a Grand Unified Theory that would resolve all the cases that may arise under a particular clause. There is, after all, only one Establishment Clause, one Free Speech Clause, one Fourth Amendment, one Equal Protection Clause.

But the same constitutional principle may operate very differently in different contexts. We have, for instance, no one Free Speech Clause test. We have different tests for content-based speech restrictions, for content-neutral speech restrictions, for restrictions imposed by the government acting as employer, for restrictions in nonpublic fora, and so on. This simply reflects the necessary recognition that the interests relevant to the Free Speech Clause inquiry—personal liberty, an informed citizenry, government efficiency, public order, and so on—are present in different degrees in each context.

And setting forth a unitary test for a broad set of cases may sometimes do more harm than good. Any test that must deal with widely disparate situations risks being so vague as to be useless. I suppose one can say that the general test for all free speech cases is "a regulation is valid if the interests asserted by the government are stronger than the interests of the speaker and the listeners," but this would hardly be a serviceable formulation. Similarly, *Lemon* has, with some justification, been criticized on this score.

Moreover, shoehorning new problems into a test that does not reflect the special concerns raised by those problems tends to deform the language of the test. Relatively simple phrases like "primary effect . . . that neither advances nor inhibits religion" and "entanglement," acquire more and more complicated definitions which stray ever further from their literal meaning. . . .

Finally, another danger to keep in mind is that the bad test may drive out the good. Rather than taking the opportunity to derive narrower, more precise tests from the case law, courts tend to continually try to patch up the broad test, making it more and more amorphous and distorted. This, I am afraid, has happened with *Lemon*.

Experience proves that the Establishment Clause, like the Free Speech Clause, cannot easily be reduced to a single test. There are different categories of Establishment Clause cases, which may call for different approaches. Some cases, like this one, involve government actions targeted at particular individuals or groups, imposing special duties or giving special benefits. Cases involving government speech on religious topics, seem to me to fall into a different category and to require an analysis focusing on whether the speech endorses or disapproves of religion, rather than on whether the government action is neutral with regard to religion.

Another category encompasses cases in which the government must make decisions about matters of religious doctrine and religious law. These cases, which often arise in the application of otherwise neutral property or contract principles to religious institutions, involve complicated questions not present in other situations. Government delegations of power to religious bodies may make up yet another category. (G)overnment impartiality towards religion may not be enough in such situations.

As the Court's opinion today shows, the slide away from *Lemon*'s unitary approach is well under way. A return to *Lemon*, even if possible, would likely be futile, regardless of where one stands on the substantive Establishment Clause questions. I think a less unitary approach provides a better structure for analysis. If each test covers a narrower and more homogeneous area, the tests may be more precise and therefore easier to apply. There may be more opportunity to pay attention to the specific nuances of each area. There might also be, I hope, more consensus on each of the narrow tests than there has been on a broad test. And abandoning the *Lemon* framework need not mean abandoning some of the insights that the test reflected, nor the insights of the cases that applied it.

Perhaps eventually under this structure we may indeed distill a unified, or at least a more unified, Establishment Clause test from the cases. But it seems to me that the case law will better be able to evolve towards this if it is freed from the *Lemon* test's rigid influence. The hard questions would, of course, still have to be asked; but they will be asked within a more carefully tailored and less distorted framework.

. . .

JUSTICE KENNEDY, concurring in the judgment.

The Court's ruling that the Kiryas Joel Village School District violates the Establishment Clause is in my view correct, but my reservations about what the Court's reasoning implies for religious accommodations in general are sufficient to require a separate writing. As the Court recognizes, a legislative accommodation that discriminates among religions may become an establishment of religion. But the Court's opinion can be interpreted to say that an accommodation for a particular religious group is invalid because of the risk that the legislature will not grant the same accommodation to another religious group suffering some similar burden. This rationale seems to me without grounding in our precedents and a needless restriction upon the legislature's ability to respond to the unique problems of a particular religious group. The real vice of the school district, in my estimation, is that New York created it by drawing political boundaries on the basis of religion. I would decide the issue we confront upon this narrower theory, though in accord with many of the Court's general observations about the State's actions in this case.

. . .

JUSTICE SCALIA, with whom THE CHIEF JUSTICE and JUSTICE THOMAS join, dissenting.

The Court today finds that the Powers That Be, up in Albany, have conspired to effect an establishment of the Satmar Hasidim. I do not know who would be more surprised at this discovery: the Founders of our Nation or Grand Rebbe Joel Teitelbaum, founder of the Satmar. The Grand Rebbe would be astounded to learn that after escaping brutal persecution and coming to America with the modest hope of religious toleration for their ascetic form of Judaism, the Satmar had become so powerful, so closely allied with Mammon, as to have become an "establishment" of the Empire State. And the Founding Fathers would be astonished to find that the Establishment Clause—which they designed "to insure that no one powerful sect or combination of sects could use political or governmental power to punish dissenters,"—has been employed to prohibit characteristically and admirably American accommodation of the religious practices (or more precisely, cultural peculiarities) of a tiny minority sect. I, however, am not surprised. Once this Court has abandoned text and history as guides, nothing prevents it from calling religious toleration the establishment of religion.

. . .

JUSTICE SOUTER'S steam rolling of the difference between civil authority held by a church, and civil authority held by members of a church, is breathtaking. To accept it, one must believe that large portions of the civil authority exercised during most of our history were unconstitutional, and that much more of it than merely the Kiryas Joel School District is unconstitutional today. The history of the populating of North America is in no small measure the story of groups of people sharing a common religious and cultural heritage striking out to form their own communities. It is preposterous to suggest that the civil institutions of these communities, separate from their churches, were constitutionally suspect. And if they were, surely JUSTICE SOUTER cannot mean that the inclusion of one or two nonbelievers in the community would have been enough to eliminate the constitutional vice. If the conferral of governmental power upon a religious institution as such (rather than upon American citizens who belong to the religious institution) is not the test . . . there is no reason why giving power to a body that is overwhelmingly dominated by the members of one sect would not suffice to invoke the Establishment Clause. That might have made the entire States of Utah and New Mexico unconstitutional at the time of their admission to the Union, and would undoubtedly make many units of local government unconstitutional today.

JUSTICE SOUTER'S position boils down to the quite novel proposition that any group of citizens (say, the residents of Kiryas Joel) can be invested with political power, but not if they all belong to the same religion. Of course such disfavoring of religion is positively antagonistic to the purposes of the Religion Clauses, and we have rejected it before. . . .

Perhaps appreciating the startling implications for our constitutional jurisprudence of collapsing the distinction between religious institutions and their members, JUSTICE SOUTER tries to limit his "unconstitutional conferral of civil authority" holding by pointing out several features supposedly unique to the present case: that the "boundary lines of the school district divide residents according to religious affiliation," that the school district was created by "a special act of the legislature," and that the formation of the school district ran counter to the legislature's trend of consolidating districts in recent years. Assuming all these points to be true (and they are not), they would certainly bear upon whether the legislature had an impermissible religious motivation in creating the district (which is JUSTICE SOUTER'S next point, in the discussion of which I shall reply to these arguments). But they have nothing to do with whether conferral of power upon a group of citizens can be the conferral of power upon a religious institution. It can not. Or if it can, our Establishment Clause jurisprudence has been transformed.

I turn, next, to JUSTICE SOUTER'S second justification for finding an establishment of religion: his facile conclusion that the New York Legislature's creation of the Kiryas Joel School District was religiously motivated. But in the Land of the Free, democratically adopted laws are not so easily impeached by unelected judges. To establish the unconstitutionality of a facially neutral law on the mere basis of its asserted religiously preferential (or discriminatory) effects—or at least to establish it in conformity with our precedents—JUSTICE SOUTER "must be able to show the absence of a neutral, secular basis" for the law. . . .

There is of course no possible doubt of a secular basis here. The New York Legislature faced a unique problem in Kiryas Joel: a community in which all the non-handicapped children attend private schools, and the physically and mentally disabled children who attend public school suffer the additional handicap of cultural distinctiveness. It would be troublesome enough if these peculiarly dressed, handicapped students were sent to the next town, accompanied by their similarly clad but unimpaired classmates. But all the unimpaired children of Kiryas Joel attend private school. The handicapped children suffered sufficient emotional trauma from their predicament that their parents kept them home from school. Surely the legislature could target this problem, and provide a public education for these students, in the same way it addressed, *by a similar law*, the unique needs of children institutionalized in a hospital.

Since the obvious presence of a neutral, secular basis renders the asserted preferential effect of this law inadequate to invalidate it, JUSTICE SOUTER is required to come forward with direct evidence that religious preference was the objective. His case could scarcely be weaker. It consists, briefly, of this: The People of New York created the Kiryas Joel Village School District in order to further the Satmar religion, rather than for any proper secular purpose, because (1) they created the district in an extraordinary manner—by special Act of the legislature, rather than under the State's general laws governing school-district reorganization; (2) the creation of the district ran counter to a State trend towards consolidation of school districts; and (3) the District includes only adherents of the Satmar religion. On this indictment, no jury would convict.

One difficulty with the first point is that it is not true. There was really nothing so "special" about the formation of a school district by an Act of the New York Legislature. . . . But in any event all that the first point proves, and the second point as well (countering the trend toward consolidation), is that New York regarded Kiryas Joel as a special case, requiring special measures. I should think it *obvious* that it did, and obvious that it *should have*. But even if the New York Legislature had never before created a school district by special statute (which is not true), and even if it had done nothing but consolidate school districts for over a century (which is not true), how could the departure from those past practices possibly demonstrate that the legislature had religious favoritism in mind? It could not. To be sure, when there is no special treatment there is no possibility of religious favoritism; but it is not logical to suggest that when there is special treatment there is proof of religious favoritism.

JUSTICE SOUTER'S case against the statute comes down to nothing more, therefore, than his third point: the fact that all the residents of the Kiryas Joel Village School District are Satmars. But all its residents also wear unusual dress, have unusual civic customs, and have not much to do with people who are culturally different from them. (The Court recognizes that "the Satmars prefer to live together 'to facilitate individual religious observance and maintain social, cultural and religious values,' but that it is not 'against their religion' to interact with others." On what basis does JUSTICE SOUTER conclude that it is the theological distinctiveness rather than the cultural distinctiveness that was the basis for New York State's decision? The normal assumption would be that it was the latter, since it was not theology but dress, language, and cultural alienation that posed the educational problem for the children. JUSTICE SOUTER not only does not adopt the logical assumption, he does not even give the New York Legislature the benefit of the doubt. . . .

I have little doubt that JUSTICE SOUTER would laud this humanitarian legislation if all of the distinctiveness of the students of Kiryas Joel were attributable to the fact that their parents were nonreligious commune-dwellers, or American Indians, or gypsies. The creation of a special, one-culture school district for the benefit of those children would pose no problem. The neutrality demanded by the Religion Clauses requires the same indulgence towards cultural characteristics that are accompanied by religious belief.

. . .

But even if Chapter 748 were intended to create a special arrangement for the Satmars because of their religion (not including, as I have shown in Part I, any conferral of governmental power upon a religious entity), it would be a permissible accommodation.

. . .

In today's opinion, however, the Court seems uncomfortable with this aspect of our constitutional tradition. Although it acknowledges the concept of accommodation, it quickly points out that it is "not a principle without limits," and then gives reasons why the present case exceeds those limits, reasons which simply do not hold water. "We have never hinted," the Court says, "that an otherwise unconstitutional delegation of political power to a religious group could be saved as a religious accommodation." Putting aside the circularity inherent in referring to a delegation as "otherwise unconstitutional" when its constitutionality turns on whether there is an accommodation, if this statement is true, it is only because we have never hinted that delegation of politi-

cal power to citizens who share a particular religion could be unconstitutional. . . .

At bottom, the Court's "no guarantee of neutrality" argument is an assertion of this Court's inability to control the New York Legislature's future denial of comparable accommodation. We have "no assurance," the Court says, "that the next similarly situated group seeking a school district of its own will receive one," since "a legislature's failure to enact a special law is . . . unreviewable." That is true only in the technical (and irrelevant) sense that the later group denied an accommodation may need to challenge the grant of the first accommodation in light of the later denial, rather than challenging the denial directly. But one way or another, "even if [an administrative agency is] not empowered or obliged to act, [a litigant] would be entitled to a judicial audience. Ultimately the courts cannot escape the obligation to address [a] plea that the exemption [sought] is mandated by the first amendment's religion clauses."

The Court's demand for "up front" assurances of a neutral system is at war with both traditional accommodation doctrine and the judicial role. As we have described, Congress's earliest accommodations exempted duties paid by specific churches on particular items. Moreover, most efforts at accommodation seek to solve a problem that applies to members of only one or a few religions. Not every religion uses wine in its sacraments, but that does not make an exemption from Prohibition for sacramental wine-use impermissible, accord, nor does it require the State granting such an exemption to explain in advance how it will treat every other claim for dispensation from its controlled-substances laws. Likewise, not every religion uses peyote in its services, but we have suggested that legislation which exempts the sacramental use of peyote from generally applicable drug laws is not only permissible, but desirable, without any suggestion that some "up front" legislative guarantee of equal treatment for sacramental substances used by other sects must be provided. The record is clear that the necessary guarantee can and will be provided, after the fact, *by the courts.*

Contrary to the Court's suggestion, I do not think that the Establishment Clause prohibits formally established "state" churches and nothing more. I have always believed, and all my opinions are consistent with the view, that the Establishment Clause prohibits the favoring of one religion over others. In this respect, it is the Court that attacks lions of straw. What I attack is the Court's imposition of novel "up front" procedural requirements on state legislatures. Making law (and making exceptions) one case at a time, whether through adjudication or through highly particularized rulemaking or legislation, violates, ex ante, no principle of fairness, equal protection, or neutrality, simply because it does not announce in advance how all future cases (and all future exceptions) will be disposed of. If it did, the manner of proceeding of this Court itself would be unconstitutional. It is presumptuous for this Court to impose—*out of nowhere*—an unheard-of prohibition against proceeding in this manner upon the Legislature of New York State. I never heard of such a principle, nor has anyone else, nor will it ever be heard of again. Unlike what the New York Legislature has done, this *is* a special rule to govern only the Satmar Hasidim.

. . .

Finally, JUSTICE O'CONNOR observes that the Court's opinion does not focus on the so-called *Lemon* test, and she urges that that test be abandoned, at least as a "unitary approach" to all Establishment Clause claims, I have previously documented the Court's convenient relationship with *Lemon*, which it cites only when useful, and I no longer take any comfort in the Court's failure to rely on it in any particular case, as I once mistakenly did. But the Court's snub of *Lemon* today (it receives only two "see also" citations . . .) is particularly noteworthy because all three courts below (who are not free to ignore Supreme Court precedent at will) relied on it, and the parties (also bound by our case law) dedicated over 80 pages of briefing to the application and continued vitality of the *Lemon* test. In addition to the other sound reasons for abandoning *Lemon*, it seems quite inefficient for this Court, which in reaching its decisions relies heavily on the briefing of the parties and, to a lesser extent, the opinions of lower courts, to mislead lower courts and parties about the relevance of the *Lemon* test.

Unlike JUSTICE O'CONNOR, however, I would not replace *Lemon* with nothing, and let the case law "evolve" into a series of situation-specific rules (government speech on religious topics, government benefits to particular groups, etc.) unconstrained by any "rigid influence." The problem with (and the allure of) *Lemon* has not been that it is "rigid," but rather that in many applications it has been utterly meaningless, validating whatever result the Court would desire. To replace *Lemon* with nothing is simply to announce that we are now so bold that we no longer feel the need even to pretend that our haphazard course of Establishment Clause decisions is governed by any principle. The foremost principle I would apply is fidelity to the longstanding traditions of our people, which surely provide the diversity of treatment that JUSTICE O'CONNOR seeks, but do not leave us to our own devices.

* * *

The Court's decision today is astounding. Chapter 748 involves no public aid to private schools and does not mention religion. In order to invalidate it, the Court casts aside, on the flimsiest of evidence, the strong presumption of validity that attaches to facially neutral laws, and invalidates the present accommodation because it does not trust New York to be as accommodating toward other religions (presumably those less powerful than the Satmar Hasidim) in the future. This is unprecedented—except that it continues, and takes to new extremes, a recent tendency in the opinions of this Court to turn the Establishment Clause into a repealer of our Nation's tradition of religious toleration. I dissent.

DEL: Establishment clause review has evolved from a state of analytical equivocation to chaos. In initially investing in the notion of separation between church and state, the Court demonstrated an uncertainty of commitment that has infected its general body of establishment clause jurisprudence. Its rhetorical flourishes on behalf of the metaphorical wall in *Everson* set up in the same case a deviation from principle that was the prelude to modern unpredictability of result. For all the savaging of and dissatisfaction with the *Lemon* formula, it hangs on as Justice Scalia puts it "[l]ike some ghoul in a late-night horror movie that repeatedly sits up in its grave and shuffles abroad, after being repeatedly killed and buried."[313] Its many lives in part attest to unhappiness with alternative analytical regimes. Chief Justice Rehnquist's notion that the establishment clause merely prohibits establishment of a national religion and sectarian discrimination represents a selective reading of history. Scalia's understanding, that the establishment clause read together with the exercise clause does not forbid government endorsement of religion, would seem to resolve the tension between those provisions by effectively demolishing one of them. Principles of accommodation have compounded the reality of inconsistency and introduced new problems of judicial micromanagement evidenced in the Pittsburgh creche case. In sum, modern establishment clause problems are a result of the Court's reluctance to take the Jeffersonian metaphor seriously, reliance upon a three-part test that has no clear relevance to the constitutional provision it has been tied to, and failure to evolve a standard that is defined and applied with a sense of integrity.

Insofar as the establishment clause, by itself and together with the exercise clause, responds to problems of official favoritism and politically divisive consequences, it may be useful to factor those two concerns as primary analytical reference points. Although attention to divisive potential generally has been bypassed, reasons for avoiding it have not been especially well-developed. Arguments that such an inquiry would be essentially speculative[314] ignore the reality, noted by Justice Scalia, that determinations of purpose presently required by *Lemon* are highly conjectural.[315] In significant part, such analysis would be coextensive with Chief Justice Rehnquist's concern with sectarian discrimination. Attention to political dissonance would be more responsive to the imperatives of cultural pluralism, however, insofar as it responded also to favoritism or religion at the expense of irreligion. A final argument against a focus on potential divisiveness is that the remedy may be worse than the cure. The point has been made that a principle which precludes state assistance to parochial schools, for instance, actually may enhance division insofar as a group that desires benefits is denied access to them. The response to that argument seems fairly simple. Political divisiveness resulting from the mixing of religion and politics is a result that the Constitution aims to avoid. To the extent that the establishment clause generates political discord, the consequence is a reality that the Constitution accepts.

RLW: I agree. The Court should place greater emphasis on the potential for political divisiveness. In Louisville, the Catholic Archdiocese frequently seeks subsidies for parochial schools. The churches efforts have resulted in discord and litigation.

DER: Religious involvement in politics is protected, not prohibited, by the First Amendment. In seeking to avoid political divisiveness based on religious difference, the state risks unduly restricting the political participation of religious groups. Using political divisiveness as the test also heightens the tension between the establishment clause and the free exercise clause. Government accommodation of minority religious groups, for example, may cause political discord because of objections to these groups' dissident views. Denying government support to unpopular religions when support is extended to other political groups may infringe upon the rights of citizens freely to exercise their religion. The establishment clause does not compel government to discriminate against people whose political involvement stems from religious conviction. The establishment clause prohibits the government from justifying its actions based on a particular religious view. But it does not require the government to ban religious views from political debate in the name of religious harmony.

---

[313] *Id.* at 2149 (Scalia, J., concurring).

[314] *E.g.,* Lynch v. Donnelly, 465 U.S. 668, 689 (1984) (O'Connor, J., concurring).

[315] Edwards v. Aguillard, 482 U.S. 578, 636–37 (1987)(Scalia, J., dissenting).

d.   Purpose, Effect and Enganglement

Religious speech in public forums has implicated not only establishment clause but free speech values. The seminal case on the subject, *Widmar v. Vincent*, concerned a state university policy restricting facilities usage to secular student organizations.[316] Student religious groups challenged the policy as a denial of their freedom of speech. The Court found that by opening its facilities to some student organizations, the university had created a public forum. Although acknowledging that the university had a

---

[316] Widmar v. Vincent, 454 U.S. 263 (1981).

compelling interest in content discrimination, if necessary to comply with the establishment clause, the Court determined that an equal access policy would not be odds with that constitutional mandate. Using the *Lemon* test, it concluded that an equal access policy would have a secular purpose, would not have the primary effect of promoting religion (insofar as it mainly benefited open and diverse discourse) and would not excessively entangle government and religion.

Similar analysis guided the Court in the *Lamb's Chapel*, decision discussed at pp. 1099–1101, and *Capitol Square Review Board v. Pinette*, 115 S.Ct. 2440 (1995). In the latter decision, the Court determined that a statehouse plaza was a traditional public forum and thus private religious expression could not be excluded from it. The ruling vindicated the Ku Klux Klan's right to erect a cross as one of the religious symbols by various groups displayed on a statehouse plaza during the Christmas season. In a dissenting opinion, Justice Ginsburg argued that the display did not have sufficient disclaimers to indicate nonendorsement by the state and thus violated the Establishment Clause. An even more controversial extension of *Widmar's* logic was made in *Rosenberger v. University of Virginia*, when the Court ruled that free speech imperatives obligated a state university to subsidize printing cost for religious student organizations to the extent it underwrote those expenses for other student groups.

Rosenberger v. University of Virginia
115 S.Ct. 2510 (1995)

Respondent University of Virginia, a state instrumentality, authorizes payments from its Student Activities Fund (SAF) to outside contractors for the printing costs of a variety of publications issued by student groups called "Contracted Independent Organizations" (CIOs). The SAF receives its money from mandatory student fees and is designed to support a broad range of extracurricular student activities related to the University's educational purpose. CIOs must include in their dealings with third parties and in all written materials a disclaimer stating that they are independent of the University and that the University is not responsible for them. The University withheld authorization for payments to a printer on behalf of petitioners' CIO, Wide Awake Productions (WAP), solely because its student newspaper, Wide Awake: A Christian Perspective at the University of Virginia, "primarily promotes or manifests a particular belief in or about a deity or an ultimate reality," as prohibited by the University's SAF Guidelines. Petitioners filed this suit under 42 U.S.C. § 1983, alleging, inter alia, that the refusal to authorize payment violated their First Amendment right to freedom of speech. After the District Court granted summary judgment for the University, the Fourth Circuit affirmed, holding that the University's invocation of viewpoint discrimination to deny third-party payment violated the Speech Clause, but concluding that the discrimination was justified by the necessity of complying with the Establishment Clause.

JUSTICE KENNEDY delivered the opinion of the Court.

. . .

The SAF is a forum more in a metaphysical than in a spatial or geographic sense, but the same principles are applicable. The most recent and most apposite case is our decision in *Lamb's Chapel*. . . .

The University's denial of WAP's request for third-party payments in the present case is based upon viewpoint discrimination not unlike the discrimination the school district relied upon in *Lamb's Chapel* and that we found invalid. The church group in *Lamb's Chapel* would have been qualified as a social or civic organization, save for its religious purposes. Furthermore, just as the school district in *Lamb's Chapel* pointed to nothing but the religious views of the group as the rationale for excluding its message, so in this case the University justifies its denial of SAF participation to WAP on the ground that the contents of Wide Awake reveal an avowed religious perspective. It bears only passing mention that the dissent's attempt to distinguish *Lamb's Chapel* is entirely without support in the law. Relying on the transcript of oral argument, the dissent seems to argue that we found viewpoint discrimination in that case because the government excluded Christian, but not atheistic, viewpoints from being expressed in the forum there. The Court relied on no such distinction in holding that discriminating against religious speech was discriminating on the basis of viewpoint. There is no indication in the opinion of the Court (which, unlike an advocate's statements at oral argument, is the law) that exclusion or inclusion of other religious or anti-religious voices from that forum had any bearing on its decision.

The University tries to escape the consequences of our holding in *Lamb's Chapel* by urging that this case involves the provision of funds rather than access to facilities. The University begins with the unremarkable proposition that the State must have substantial discretion in determining how to allocate scarce resources to accomplish its educational mission. . . . (T)he University argues that content-based funding decisions are both inevitable and lawful. Were the reasoning of *Lamb's Chapel* to apply to funding decisions as well as to those involving access to facilities, it is urged, its holding "would become a judicial juggernaut, constitutionalizing the ubiquitous content-based decisions that schools, colleges, and other government entities routinely make in the allocation of public funds."

To this end the University relies on our assurance in *Widmar v. Vincent*. There, in the course of striking down a public university's exclusion of religious groups from use of school facilities made available to all other student groups, we stated: "Nor do we question the right of the University to make academic judgments as to how best to allocate scarce resources." The quoted language in *Widmar* was but a proper recognition of the principle that when the State is the speaker, it may make content-based choices. When the University determines the content of the education it provides, it is the University speaking, and we have permitted the government to regulate the content of what is or is not expressed when it is the speaker or when it enlists private entities to convey its own message. . . .

It does not follow, however, and we did not suggest in *Widmar*, that viewpoint-based restrictions are proper when the University does not itself speak or subsidize transmittal of a message it favors but instead expends funds to encourage a diversity of views from private speakers. A holding that the University may not discriminate based on the viewpoint of private persons whose speech it facilitates does not restrict the University's own speech, which is controlled by different principles. . . .

The distinction between the University's own favored message and the private speech of students is evident in the case before us. The University itself has taken steps to ensure the distinction in the agreement each CIO must sign. The University declares that the student groups eligible for SAF support are not the University's agents, are not subject to its control,

and are not its responsibility. Having offered to pay the third-party contractors on behalf of private speakers who convey their own messages, the University may not silence the expression of selected viewpoints.

The University urges that, from a constitutional standpoint, funding of speech differs from provision of access to facilities because money is scarce and physical facilities are not. Beyond the fact that in any given case this proposition might not be true as an empirical matter, the underlying premise that the University could discriminate based on viewpoint if demand for space exceeded its availability is wrong as well. The government cannot justify viewpoint discrimination among private speakers on the economic fact of scarcity. Had the meeting rooms in *Lamb's Chapel* been scarce, had the demand been greater than the supply, our decision would have been no different. It would have been incumbent on the State, of course, to ration or allocate the scarce resources on some acceptable neutral principle; but nothing in our decision indicated that scarcity would give the State the right to exercise viewpoint discrimination that is otherwise impermissible.

Vital First Amendment speech principles are at stake here. The first danger to liberty lies in granting the State the power to examine publications to determine whether or not they are based on some ultimate idea and if so for the State to classify them. The second, and corollary, danger is to speech from the chilling of individual thought and expression. That danger is especially real in the University setting, where the State acts against a background and tradition of thought and experiment that is at the center of our intellectual and philosophic tradition. In ancient Athens, and, as Europe entered into a new period of intellectual awakening, in places like Bologna, Oxford, and Paris, universities began as voluntary and spontaneous assemblages or concourses for students to speak and to write and to learn. The quality and creative power of student intellectual life to this day remains a vital measure of a school's influence and attainment. For the University, by regulation, to cast disapproval on particular viewpoints of its students risks the suppression of free speech and creative inquiry in one of the vital centers for the nation's intellectual life, its college and university campuses.

The Guideline invoked by the University to deny third-party contractor payments on behalf of WAP effects a sweeping restriction on student thought and student inquiry in the context of University sponsored publications. The prohibition on funding on behalf of publications that "primarily promote or manifest a particular belief in or about a deity or an ultimate reality," in its ordinary and common sense meaning, has a vast potential reach. The

term "promotes" as used here would comprehend any writing advocating a philosophic position that rests upon a belief in a deity or ultimate reality. And the term "manifests" would
bring within the scope of the prohibition any
writing that is explicable as resting upon a
premise which presupposes the existence of a
deity or ultimate reality. Were the prohibition
applied with much vigor at all, it would bar
funding of essays by hypothetical student contributors named Plato, Spinoza, and Descartes.
And if the regulation covers, as the University
says it does, those student journalistic efforts
which primarily manifest or promote a belief
that there is no deity and no ultimate reality,
then undergraduates named Karl Marx, Ber-
trand Russell, and Jean-Paul Sartre would
likewise have some of their major essays excluded from student publications. If any manifestation of beliefs in first principles disqualifies the writing, as seems to be the case, it is
indeed difficult to name renowned thinkers
whose writings would be accepted, save perhaps for articles disclaiming all connection to
their ultimate philosophy. Plato could contrive
perhaps to submit an acceptable essay on making pasta or peanut butter cookies, provided he
did not point out their (necessary) imperfections.

Based on the principles we have discussed,
we hold that the regulation invoked to deny
SAF support, both in its terms and in its application to these petitioners, is a denial of their
right of free speech guaranteed by the First
Amendment. It remains to be considered
whether the violation following from the University's action is excused by the necessity of
complying with the Constitution's prohibition
against state establishment of religion. We
turn to that question.

· · ·

A central lesson of our decisions is that a
significant factor in upholding governmental
programs in the face of Establishment Clause
attack is their neutrality towards religion. . . .
We have held that the guarantee of neutrality
is respected, not offended, when the government, following neutral criteria and evenhanded policies, extends benefits to recipients
whose ideologies and viewpoints, including religious ones, are broad and diverse. More than
once have we rejected the position that the Establishment Clause even justifies, much less
requires, a refusal to extend free speech rights
to religious speakers who participate in broad-
reaching government programs neutral in design.

The governmental program here is neutral
toward religion. There is no suggestion that the
University created it to advance religion or
adopted some ingenious device with the purpose of aiding a religious cause. The object of
the SAF is to open a forum for speech and to
support various student enterprises, including

the publication of newspapers, in recognition
of the diversity and creativity of student life.
The University's SAF Guidelines have a separate classification for, and do not make third-
party payments on behalf of, "religious organizations," which are those "whose purpose is to
practice a devotion to an acknowledged ultimate reality or deity." The category of support
here is for "student news, information, opinion,
entertainment, or academic communications
media groups," of which Wide Awake was 1 of
15 in the 1990 school year. WAP did not seek
a subsidy because of its Christian editorial
viewpoint; it sought funding as a student journal, which it was.

The neutrality of the program distinguishes the student fees from a tax levied for
the direct support of a church or group of
churches. A tax of that sort, of course, would
run contrary to Establishment Clause concerns
dating from the earliest days of the Republic. . . .

Government neutrality is apparent in the
State's overall scheme in a further meaningful
respect. The program respects the critical difference "between government speech endorsing religion, which the Establishment Clause
forbids, and private speech endorsing religion,
which the Free Speech and Free Exercise
Clauses protect." In this case, "the government
has not willfully fostered or encouraged" any
mistaken impression that the student newspapers speak for the University. The University
has taken pains to disassociate itself from the
private speech involved in this case. . . .

The Court of Appeals (and the dissent) are
correct to extract from our decisions the principle that we have recognized special Establishment Clause dangers where the government
makes direct money payments to sectarian institutions. The error is not in identifying the
principle but in believing that it controls this
case. Even assuming that WAP is no different
from a church and that its speech is the same
as the religious exercises conducted in *Widmar*
(two points much in doubt), the Court of Appeals decided a case that was, in essence, not
before it, and the dissent would have us do the
same. We do not confront a case where, even
under a neutral program that includes nonsectarian recipients, the government is making direct money payments to an institution or group
that is engaged in religious activity. Neither
the Court of Appeals nor the dissent, we believe, takes sufficient cognizance of the undisputed fact that no public funds flow directly to
WAP's coffers.

. . . There is no difference in logic or principle, and no difference of constitutional significance, between a school using its funds to operate a facility to which students have access,
and a school paying a third-party contractor
to operate the facility on its behalf. The latter
occurs here. The University provides printing

services to a broad spectrum of student newspapers qualified as CIOs by reason of their officers and membership. Any benefit to religion is incidental to the government's provision of secular services for secular purposes on a religion-neutral basis. Printing is a routine, secular, and recurring attribute of student life.

By paying outside printers, the University in fact attains a further degree of separation from the student publication, for it avoids the duties of supervision, escapes the costs of upkeep, repair, and replacement attributable to student use, and has a clear record of costs. As a result, and as in *Widmar*, the University can charge the SAF, and not the taxpayers as a whole, for the discrete activity in question. It would be formalistic for us to say that the University must forfeit these advantages and provide the services itself in order to comply with the Establishment Clause. It is, of course, true that if the State pays a church's bills it is subsidizing it, and we must guard against this abuse. That is not a danger here, based on the considerations we have advanced and for the additional reason that the student publication is not a religious institution, at least in the usual sense of that term as used in our case law, and it is not a religious organization as used in the University's own regulations. It is instead a publication involved in a pure forum for the expression of ideas, ideas that would be both incomplete and chilled were the Constitution to be interpreted to require that state officials and courts scan the publication to ferret out views that principally manifest a belief in a divine being.

Were the dissent's view to become law, it would require the University, in order to avoid a constitutional violation, to scrutinize the content of student speech, lest the expression in question—speech otherwise protected by the Constitution—contain too great a religious content. The dissent, in fact, anticipates such censorship as "crucial" in distinguishing between "works characterized by the evangelism of Wide Awake and writing that merely happens to express views that a given religion might approve." That eventuality raises the specter of governmental censorship, to ensure that all student writings and publications meet some baseline standard of secular orthodoxy. To impose that standard on student speech at a university is to imperil the very sources of free speech and expression. As we recognized in *Widmar*, official censorship would be far more inconsistent with the Establishment Clause's dictates than would governmental provision of secular printing services on a religion-blind basis.

. . .

To obey the Establishment Clause, it was not necessary for the University to deny eligibility to student publications because of their viewpoint. The neutrality commanded of the State by the separate Clauses of the First Amendment was compromised by the University's course of action. The viewpoint discrimination inherent in the University's regulation required public officials to scan and interpret student publications to discern their underlying philosophic assumptions respecting religious theory and belief. That course of action was a denial of the right of free speech and would risk fostering a pervasive bias or hostility to religion, which could undermine the very neutrality the Establishment Clause requires. There is no Establishment Clause violation in the University's honoring its duties under the Free Speech Clause.

The judgment of the Court of Appeals must be, and is, reversed.

. . .

JUSTICE O'CONNOR, concurring.

"We have time and again held that the government generally may not treat people differently based on the God or gods they worship, or don't worship." This insistence on government neutrality toward religion explains why we have held that schools may not discriminate against religious groups by denying them equal access to facilities that the schools make available to all. Withholding access would leave an impermissible perception that religious activities are disfavored: "the message is one of neutrality rather than endorsement; if a State refused to let religious groups use facilities open to others, then it would demonstrate not neutrality but hostility toward religion." "The Religion Clauses prohibit the government from favoring religion, but they provide no warrant for discriminating against religion." Neutrality, in both form and effect, is one hallmark of the Establishment Clause.

As Justice Souter demonstrates, however, there exists another axiom in the history and precedent of the Establishment Clause. "Public funds may not be used to endorse the religious message." Our cases have permitted some government funding of secular functions performed by sectarian organizations. These decisions, however, provide no precedent for the use of public funds to finance religious activities.

This case lies at the intersection of the principle of government neutrality and the prohibition on state funding of religious activities. It is clear that the University has established a generally applicable program to encourage the free exchange of ideas by its students, an expressive marketplace that includes some 15 student publications with predictably divergent viewpoints. It is equally clear that petitioners' viewpoint is religious and that publication of Wide Awake is a religious activity, under both the University's regulation and a fair reading of our precedents. Not to finance

Wide Awake, according to petitioners, violates the principle of neutrality by sending a message of hostility toward religion. To finance Wide Awake, argues the University, violates the prohibition on direct state funding of religious activities.

When two bedrock principles so conflict, understandably neither can provide the definitive answer. Reliance on categorical platitudes is unavailing. Resolution instead depends on the hard task of judging—sifting through the details and determining whether the challenged program offends the Establishment Clause. Such judgment requires courts to draw lines, sometimes quite fine, based on the particular facts of each case. . . .

So it is in this case. The nature of the dispute does not admit of categorical answers, nor should any be inferred from the Court's decision today. Instead, certain considerations specific to the program at issue lead me to conclude that by providing the same assistance to Wide Awake that it does to other publications, the University would not be endorsing the magazine's religious perspective.

. . .

The Court's decision today . . . neither trumpets the supremacy of the neutrality principle nor signals the demise of the funding prohibition in Establishment Clause jurisprudence. As I observed last Term, "experience proves that the Establishment Clause, like the Free Speech Clause, cannot easily be reduced to a single test." When bedrock principles collide, they test the limits of categorical obstinacy and expose the flaws and dangers of a Grand Unified Theory that may turn out to be neither grand nor unified. The Court today does only what courts must do in many Establishment Clause cases—focus on specific features of a particular government action to ensure that it does not violate the Constitution. By withholding from Wide Awake assistance that the University provides generally to all other student publications, the University has discriminated on the basis of the magazine's religious viewpoint in violation of the Free Speech Clause. And particular features of the University's program—such as the explicit disclaimer, the disbursement of funds directly to third-party vendors, the vigorous nature of the forum at issue, and the possibility for objecting students to opt out—convince me that providing such assistance in this case would not carry the danger of impermissible use of public funds to endorse Wide Awake's religious message.

Subject to these comments, I join the opinion of the Court.

JUSTICE THOMAS, concurring.

I agree with the Court's opinion and join it in full, but I write separately to express my disagreement with the historical analysis put forward by the dissent. Although the dissent starts down the right path in consulting the original meaning of the Establishment Clause, its misleading application of history yields a principle that is inconsistent with our Nation's long tradition of allowing religious adherents to participate on equal terms in neutral government programs.

. . .

Though our Establishment Clause jurisprudence is in hopeless disarray, this case provides an opportunity to reaffirm one basic principle that has enjoyed an uncharacteristic degree of consensus: The Clause does not compel the exclusion of religious groups from government benefits programs that are generally available to a broad class of participants. Under the dissent's view, however, the University of Virginia may provide neutral access to the University's own printing press, but it may not provide the same service when the press is owned by a third party. Not surprisingly, the dissent offers no logical justification for this conclusion, and none is evident in the text or original meaning of the First Amendment.

If the Establishment Clause is offended when religious adherents benefit from neutral programs such as the University of Virginia's Student Activities Fund, it must also be offended when they receive the same benefits in the form of in-kind subsidies. The constitutional demands of the Establishment Clause may be judged against either a baseline of "neutrality" or a baseline of "no aid to religion," but the appropriate baseline surely cannot depend on the fortuitous circumstances surrounding the form of aid. The contrary rule would lead to absurd results that would jettison centuries of practice respecting the right of religious adherents to participate on neutral terms in a wide variety of government-funded programs.

Our Nation's tradition of allowing religious adherents to participate in evenhanded government programs is hardly limited to the class of "essential public benefits" identified by the dissent. A broader tradition can be traced at least as far back as the First Congress, which ratified the Northwest Ordinance of 1787. Article III of that famous enactment of the Confederation Congress had provided: "Religion, morality, and knowledge . . . being necessary to good government and the happiness of mankind, schools and the means of learning shall forever be encouraged." Congress subsequently set aside federal lands in the Northwest Territory and other territories for the use of schools. Many of the schools that enjoyed the benefits of these land grants undoubtedly were church-affiliated sectarian institutions as there was no requirement that the schools be "public." Nevertheless, early Congresses found no problem with the provision of such neutral benefits.

Numerous other government benefits traditionally have been available to religious adherents on neutral terms. Several examples may be found in the work of early Congresses, including copyright protection for "the author and authors of any map, chart, book or books," and a privilege allowing "every printer of newspapers [to] send one paper to each and every other printer of newspapers within the United States, free of postage." Neither of these laws made any exclusion for the numerous authors or printers who manifested a belief in or about a deity. Thus, history provides an answer for the constitutional question posed by this case, but it is not the one given by the dissent. The dissent identifies no evidence that the Framers intended to disable religious entities from participating on neutral terms in evenhanded government programs. The evidence that does exist points in the opposite direction and provides ample support for today's decision.

JUSTICE SOUTER, with whom JUSTICE STEVENS, JUSTICE GINSBURG and JUSTICE BREYER join, dissenting.

The Court today, for the first time, approves direct funding of core religious activities by an arm of the State. It does so, however, only after erroneous treatment of some familiar principles of law implementing the First Amendment's Establishment and Speech Clauses, and by viewing the very funds in question as beyond the reach of the Establishment Clause's funding restrictions as such. Because there is no warrant for distinguishing among public funding sources for purposes of applying the First Amendment's prohibition of religious establishment, I would hold that the University's refusal to support petitioners' religious activities is compelled by the Establishment Clause. I would therefore affirm.

The central question in this case is whether a grant from the Student Activities Fund to pay Wide Awake's printing expenses would violate the Establishment Clause. Although the Court does not dwell on the details of Wide Awake's message, it recognizes something sufficiently religious in the publication to demand Establishment Clause scrutiny. Although the Court places great stress on the eligibility of secular as well as religious activities for grants from the Student Activities Fund, it recognizes that such evenhanded availability is not by itself enough to satisfy constitutional requirements for any aid scheme that results in a benefit to religion. Something more is necessary to justify any religious aid. Some members of the Court, at least, may think the funding permissible on a view that it is indirect, since the money goes to Wide Awake's printer, not through Wide Awake's own checking account. The Court's principal reliance, however, is on an argument that providing religion with economically valuable services is permissible on the theory that services are economically indistinguishable from religious access to governmental speech forums, which sometimes is permissible. But this reasoning would commit the Court to approving direct religious aid beyond anything justifiable for the sake of access to speaking forums. The Court implicitly recognizes this in its further attempt to circumvent the clear bar to direct governmental aid to religion. Different members of the Court seek to avoid this bar in different ways. The opinion of the Court makes the novel assumption that only direct aid financed with tax revenue is barred, and draws the erroneous conclusion that the involuntary Student Activities Fee is not a tax. . . . The resulting decision is in unmistakable tension with the accepted law that the Court continues to avow.

The Court's difficulties will be all the more clear after a closer look at Wide Awake than the majority opinion affords. . . .

This writing is no merely descriptive examination of religious doctrine or even of ideal Christian practice in confronting life's social and personal problems. Nor is it merely the expression of editorial opinion that incidentally coincides with Christian ethics and reflects a Christian view of human obligation. It is straightforward exhortation to enter into a relationship with God as revealed in Jesus Christ, and to satisfy a series of moral obligations derived from the teachings of Jesus Christ. These are not the words of "student news, information, opinion, entertainment, or academic communication . . ." but the words of "challenge [to] Christians to live, in word and deed, according to the faith they proclaim and . . . to consider what a personal relationship with Jesus Christ means." The subject is not the discourse of the scholar's study or the seminar room, but of the evangelist's mission station and the pulpit. It is nothing other than the preaching of the word, which (along with the sacraments) is what most branches of Christianity offer those called to the religious life.

Using public funds for the direct subsidization of preaching the word is categorically forbidden under the Establishment Clause, and if the Clause was meant to accomplish nothing else, it was meant to bar this use of public money. Evidence on the subject antedates even the Bill of Rights itself, as may be seen in the writings of Madison, whose authority on questions about the meaning of the Establishment Clause is well settled. Four years before the First Congress proposed the First Amendment, Madison gave his opinion on the legitimacy of using public funds for religious purposes, in the

Memorial and Remonstrance Against Religious Assessments, which played the central role in ensuring the defeat of the Virginia tax assessment bill in 1786 and framed the debate upon which the Religion Clauses stand: "Who does not see that . . . the same authority which can force a citizen to contribute three pence only of his property for the support of any one establishment, may force him to conform to any other establishment in all cases whatsoever?"

. . .

The principle against direct funding with public money is patently violated by the contested use of today's student activity fee. Like today's taxes generally, the fee is Madison's threepence. The University exercises the power of the State to compel a student to pay it, and the use of any part of it for the direct support of religious activity thus strikes at what we have repeatedly held to be the heart of the prohibition on establishment. . . .

The Court, accordingly, has never before upheld direct state funding of the sort of proselytizing published in Wide Awake and, in fact, has categorically condemned state programs directly aiding religious activity. . . .

Even when the Court has upheld aid to an institution performing both secular and sectarian functions, it has always made a searching enquiry to ensure that the institution kept the secular activities separate from its sectarian ones, with any direct aid flowing only to the former and never the latter.

Reasonable minds may differ over whether the Court reached the correct result [past] cases, but their common principle has never been questioned or repudiated. "Although Establishment Clause jurisprudence is characterized by few absolutes, the Clause does absolutely prohibit government-financed . . . indoctrination into the beliefs of a particular religious faith."

Why does the Court not apply this clear law to these clear facts and conclude, as I do, that the funding scheme here is a clear constitutional violation? The answer must be in part that the Court fails to confront the evidence set out in the preceding section. . . .

Nevertheless, even without the encumbrance of detail from Wide Awake's actual pages, the Court finds something sufficiently religious about the magazine to require examination under the Establishment Clause, and one may therefore ask why the unequivocal prohibition on direct funding does not lead the Court to conclude that funding would be unconstitutional. The answer is that the Court focuses on a subsidiary body of law, which it correctly states but ultimately misapplies. That subsidiary body of law accounts for the Court's substantial attention to the fact that the University's funding scheme is "neutral," in the formal sense that it makes funds available on an evenhanded basis to secular and sectarian applicants alike. While this is indeed true and relevant under our cases, it does not alone satisfy the requirements of the Establishment Clause, as the Court recognizes when it says that evenhandedness is only a "significant factor" in certain Establishment Clause analysis, not a dispositive one. This recognition reflects the Court's appreciation of two general rules: that whenever affirmative government aid ultimately benefits religion, the Establishment Clause requires some justification beyond evenhandedness on the government's part; and that direct public funding of core sectarian activities, even if accomplished pursuant to an evenhanded program, would be entirely inconsistent with the Establishment Clause and would strike at the very heart of the Clause's protection.

In order to understand how the Court thus begins with sound rules but ends with an unsound result, it is necessary to explore those rules in greater detail than the Court does. (T)he relationship between the prohibition on direct aid and the requirement of evenhandedness when affirmative government aid does result in some benefit to religion reflects the relationship between basic rule and marginal criterion. At the heart of the Establishment Clause stands the prohibition against direct public funding, but that prohibition does not answer the questions that occur at the margins of the Clause's application. Is any government activity that provides any incidental benefit to religion likewise unconstitutional? Would it be wrong to put out fires in burning churches, wrong to pay the bus fares of students on the way to parochial schools, wrong to allow a grantee of special education funds to spend them at a religious college? These are the questions that call for drawing lines, and it is in drawing them that evenhandedness becomes important. However the Court may in the past have phrased its line-drawing test, the question whether such benefits are provided on an evenhanded basis has been relevant, for the question addresses one aspect of the issue whether a law is truly neutral with respect to religion. In *Widmar v. Vincent*, for example, we noted that "the provision of benefits to [a] broad . . . spectrum of [religious and nonreligious] groups is an important index of secular effect." In the doubtful cases (those not involving direct public funding), where there is initially room for argument about a law's effect, evenhandedness serves to weed out those laws that impermissibly advance religion by channeling aid to it exclusively. Evenhandedness is therefore a prerequisite to further enquiry into the constitutionality of a doubtful law, but evenhandedness goes no further. It does not guarantee success under Establishment Clause scrutiny.

. . .

Evenhandedness as one element of a permissibly attenuated benefit is, of course, a far cry from evenhandedness as a sufficient condition of constitutionality for direct financial support of religious proselytization, and our cases have unsurprisingly repudiated any such attempt to cut the Establishment Clause down to a mere prohibition against unequal direct aid. . . .

Since conformity with the marginal or limiting principle of evenhandedness is insufficient of itself to demonstrate the constitutionality of providing a government benefit that reaches religion, the Court must identify some further element in the funding scheme that does demonstrate its permissibility. For one reason or another, the Court's chosen element appears to be the fact that under the University's Guidelines, funds are sent to the printer chosen by Wide Awake, rather than to Wide Awake itself.

. . . The formalism of distinguishing between payment to Wide Awake so it can pay an approved bill and payment of the approved bill itself cannot be the basis of a decision of Constitutional law. If this indeed were a critical distinction, the Constitution would permit a State to pay all the bills of any religious institution; in fact, despite the Court's purported adherence to the no-direct-funding principle, the State could simply hand out credit cards to religious institutions and honor the monthly statements (so long as someone could devise an evenhanded umbrella to cover the whole scheme). . . .

It is more probable, however, that the Court's reference to the printer goes to a different attempt to justify the payment. On this purported justification, the payment to the printer is significant only as the last step in an argument resting on the assumption that a public university may give a religious group the use of any of its equipment or facilities so long as secular groups are likewise eligible. . . . The Court reasons that the availability of a forum has economic value (the government built and maintained the building, while the speakers saved the rent for a hall); and that economically there is no difference between the University's provision of the value of the room and the value, say, of the University's printing equipment; and that therefore the University must be able to provide the use of the latter. Since it may do that, the argument goes, it would be unduly formalistic to draw the line at paying for an outside printer, who simply does what the magazine's publishers could have done with the University's own printing equipment.

The argument is as unsound as it is simple, and the first of its troubles emerges from an examination of the cases relied upon to support it. The common factual thread running through *Widmar,* . . . and *Lamb's Chapel,* is that a governmental institution created a limited forum for the use of students in a school or college, or for the public at large, but sought to exclude speakers with religious messages. In each case the restriction was struck down either as an impermissible attempt to regulate the content of speech in an open forum or to suppress a particular religious viewpoint. In each case, to be sure, the religious speaker's use of the room passed muster as an incident of a plan to facilitate speech generally for a secular purpose, entailing neither secular entanglement with religion nor risk that the religious speech would be taken to be the speech of the government or that the government's endorsement of a religious message would be inferred. But each case drew ultimately on unexceptionable Speech Clause doctrine treating the evangelist, the Salvation Army, the millennia list or the Hare Krishna like any other speaker in a public forum. It was the preservation of free speech on the model of the street corner that supplied the justification going beyond the requirement of evenhandedness.

The Court's claim of support from these forum-access cases is ruled out by the very scope of their holdings. While they do indeed allow a limited benefit to religious speakers, they rest on the recognition that all speakers are entitled to use the street corner (even though the State paves the roads and provides police protection to everyone on the street) and on the analogy between the public street corner and open classroom space. Thus, the Court found it significant that the classroom speakers would engage in traditional speech activities in these forums, too, even though the rooms (like street corners) require some incidental state spending to maintain them. The analogy breaks down entirely, however, if the cases are read more broadly than the Court wrote them, to cover more than forums for literal speaking. There is no traditional street corner printing provided by the government on equal terms to all comers, and the forum cases cannot be lifted to a higher plane of generalization without admitting that new economic benefits are being extended directly to religion in clear violation of the principle barring direct aid. The argument from economic equivalence thus breaks down on recognizing that the direct state aid it would support is not mitigated by the street corner analogy in the service of free speech. Absent that, the rule against direct aid stands as a bar to printing services as well as printers.

. . . The novelty of the assumption that the direct aid bar only extends to aid derived from taxation, however, requires some response.

. . .

Allowing non-tax funds to be spent on religion would, in fact, fly in the face of clear principle. Leaving entirely aside the question whether public non-tax revenues could ever be used to finance religion without violating the endorsement test, any such use of them would ignore one of the dual objectives of the Establishment Clause, which was meant not only to protect individuals and their republics from the destructive consequences of mixing government and religion, but to protect religion from a corrupting dependence on support from the Government. Since the corrupting effect of government support does not turn on whether the Government's own money comes from taxation or gift or the sale of public lands, the Establishment Clause could hardly relax its vigilance simply because tax revenue was not implicated. Accordingly, in the absence of a forthright disavowal, one can only assume that the

Court does not mean to eliminate one half of the Establishment Clause's justification.

Nothing in the Court's opinion would lead me to end this enquiry into the application of the Establishment Clause any differently from the way I began it. The Court is ordering an instrumentality of the State to support religious evangelism with direct funding. This is a flat violation of the Establishment Clause.

. . .

Since I cannot see the future I cannot tell whether today's decision portends much more than making a shambles out of student activity fees in public colleges. Still, my apprehension is whetted by Chief Justice Burger's warning in *Lemon v. Kurtzman*, "in constitutional adjudication some steps, which when taken were thought to approach 'the verge,' have become the platform for yet further steps. A certain momentum develops in constitutional theory and it can be a 'downhill thrust' easily set in motion but difficult to retard or stop."

I respectfully dissent.

DEL: The speech vs. establishment clause decisions are deficient in clarity and coherence. If viewed as making a constitutional choice, they reflect a prioritization process that is invariable when constitutional guarantees are in conflict. The Court maintains that compliance with the establishment clause is a compelling state interest. Still, at least formalistically in *Widmar* and its progeny, the Court has avoided a real First Amendment collision by finding that the Establishment Clause interests are not significantly implicated by speech neutral policies. Creation of a "metaphysical" public forum, however, fits into a category of judicial inventiveness seldom seen since the now largely discredited fabrication of penumbras a generation ago. For all the free speech rhetoric used to discount consequences that the dissenters view as Establishment Clause problems, it may be excusable to suspect that if First Amendment tables were turned Establishment Clause values might not be so quickly or loudly trumpeted.[317]

---

[317] *Cf.* Rust v. Sullivan, 500 U.S. 173 (1991)(freedom of speech not implicated by conditioning federal aid to health clinics upon refraining from providing information on abortions): Harris v. McRae, 448 U.S. 297 (1980)(Establishment Clause not implicated by congressional restrictions upon funding of abortions).

---

3. The Exercise Clause

By its terms, the exercise clause appears structurally and terminologically more congruent with the speech clause. Unlike the establishment clause that forbids government from affirmative initiatives to promote religion, the exercise clause like the speech clause precludes official acts of impairment.[318] The exercise clause was inspired, as

---

[318] Especially given case law that forbids official content and viewpoint discrimination with respect to speech, an analogy between the exercise and speech clauses ultimately breaks down. To the extent nondiscrimination is a concern, common ground also exists between the establishment and speech clauses.

the Supreme Court has noted, by "historical instances of religious persecution and intolerance."[319] Consistent with such concerns, and "(a)t a minimum, the protections of the Free Exercise Clause pertain if the law at issue discriminates against some or all religious beliefs or regulates or prohibits conduct because it is undertaken for religious reasons."[320]

a. Seminal Criteria: Belief and Action

Initial attention to exercise questions worked toward distinguishing belief and action. In *Reynolds v. United States*, the Court reviewed a federal anti-polygamy law challenged by a Mormon who claimed that it interfered with his religious obligations.

---

[319] Church of Lukumi Babalu Aye, Inc. v. City of Hialeah, 113 S.Ct. 2217, 2226 (1993)(quoting Bowen v. Roy, 476 U.S. 693, 703 (1986)(opinion of Burger, C.J.).
[320] *Lukumi Babalu Aye*, 113 S.Ct. at 2226.

Reynolds v. United States
98 U.S. 145 (1878)

MR. CHIEF JUSTICE WAITE delivered the opinion of the Court.

. . .

The assignments of error, when grouped, [include] the following questions:

. . .

5. Should the accused have been acquitted if he married the second time, because he believed it to be his religious duty?

. . .

On the trial, the plaintiff in error, the accused, proved that at the time of his alleged second marriage he was, and for many years before he had been, a member of the Church of Jesus Christ of Latter-Day Saints, commonly called the Mormon Church, and a believer in its doctrines; that it was the duty of male members of said church, circumstances permitting, to practice polygamy; . . . that this duty was enjoined by different books which the members of said church believed that the practice of polygamy was directly enjoined upon the male members thereof by the Almighty God, in a revelation to Joseph Smith, the founder and prophet of said church; that the failing or refusing to practice of polygamy by such male members of said church, when circumstances would admit, would be punished, and that the penalty for such failure and refusal would be damnation in the life to come." He also proved "that he received permission from the recognized authorities in said church to enter into polygamous marriage. . . .

Congress cannot pass a law for the government of the Territories which shall prohibit the free exercise of religion. The first amendment to the Constitution expressly forbids such legislation. Religious freedom is guaranteed everywhere throughout the United States, so far as congressional interference is concerned. The question to be determined is, whether the law now under consideration comes within this prohibition.

. . .

In our opinion, the statute immediately under consideration is within the legislative power of Congress. It is constitutional and valid as prescribing a rule of action for all those residing in the Territories, and in places over which the United States have exclusive control. This being so, the only question which remains is, whether those who make polygamy a part of their religion are excepted from the operation of the statute. If they are, then those who do not make polygamy a part of their religious belief may be found guilty and punished, while those who do, must be acquitted and go free. This would be introducing a new element into criminal law. Laws are made for the government of actions, and while they cannot interfere with mere religious belief and opinions, they may with practices. Suppose one believed that human sacrifices were a necessary part of religious worship, would it be seriously contended that the civil government under which he lived could not interfere to prevent a sacrifice? Or if a wife religiously believed it was her duty to burn herself upon the funeral pile of her dead husband, would it be beyond the power of the civil government to prevent her carrying her belief into practice?

So here, as a law of the organization of society under the exclusive dominion of the United States, it is provided that plural marriages shall not be allowed. Can a man excuse his practices to the contrary because of his religious belief? To permit this would be to make the professed doctrines of religious belief superior to the law of the land, and in effect to permit every citizen to become a law unto himself. Government could exist only name under such circumstances.

. . .

Although the *Reynolds* decision has never been overruled, the distinction between belief and action no longer is the focal point of exercise clause analysis. Investment in such line-drawing would result in a rather hollow constitutional guarantee. Pursuant to such a differentiation, government could interfere with and burden religion freely so long as it did not formally proscribe belief.

b. Modern Analysis
i. *Balancing Constitutional and Regulatory Interests*

Contemporary case law analysis was previewed in significant part by Chief Justice Warren's plurality opinion in *Braunfeld v. Brown*. At issue were Sunday closing laws challenged by Orthodox Jews who, because they observed another day as the Sabbath, claimed they were economically burdened as a consequence of their beliefs.[321] Although the constitutional claims were rejected, analysis was referenced to imperatives of balancing rather than distinctions between belief and action. In an opinion joined by three other justices, Warren stressed that laws impeding observance of a religion, or invidiously discriminating among religions, would be constitutionally invalid.[322] General regulation advancing a secular goal, however, would be "valid despite its indirect burden on religious observance unless the State may accomplish its purpose by means which do not impose such a burden."[323] With respect to the circumstances at hand, however, Warren conceded the profundity of the State's interest in providing a uniform day of rest and concluded that no less restrictive methodologies existed.[324]

Doctrinal evolution toward the balancing of exercise and regulatory concerns continues in *Sherbert v. Verner*.[325] The question in *Sherbert* was whether state unemployment benefits could be denied to a Seventh Day Adventist who claimed that religious beliefs precluded her from working on Saturdays.[326] In assessing the constitutionality of the denial of benefits, the Court considered whether the exercise of religion had been burdened and, if so, whether such an imposition was supported by "a compelling state interest."[327] It determined that the state's action had a significant coercive effect in forcing a choice between belief and benefits and was not supported by a compelling regulatory justification.[328] The state's avowed antifraud interests were unimpressive to the Court, which noted the absence of proof that alternative methods would not work[329]

Exercise clause analysis hardened further into a balancing exercise in subsequent case law. In *Wisconsin v. Yoder*, a state law requiring children to attend school until age 16 was challenged by Amish parents. Pursuant to standards of review consistent with *Sherbert*, the Court concluded that the law at least as applied to the Amish was unconstitutional.

---

[321] Braunfeld v. Brown, 366 U.S. 599, 607 (1961).

[322] *Id.* at 607 (opinion of Warren, C.J.).

[323] *Id.*

[324] *Id.*

[325] 374 U.S. 398 (1965).

[326] *Id.* at 399–403.

[327] *Id.* at 403, 406.

[328] *Id.* at 410.

[329] *Id.* at 407.

Wisconsin v. Yoder

406 U.S. 205 (1972)

MR. CHIEF JUSTICE BURGER delivered the opinion of the Court.

On petition of the State of Wisconsin, we granted the writ of certiorari in this case to review a decision of the Wisconsin Supreme Court holding that respondents' convictions of violating the State's compulsory school-attendance law were invalid under the Free Exercise Clause of the First Amendment to the United States Constitution made applicable to the States by the Fourteenth Amendment. For the reasons hereafter stated we affirm the judgment of the Supreme Court of Wisconsin.

Respondents Jonas Yoder and Wallace Miller are members of the Old Order Amish religion, and respondent Adin Yutzy is a member of the Conservative Amish Mennonite Church. They and their families are residents of Green County, Wisconsin. Wisconsin's compulsory school-attendance law required them to cause their children to attend public or private school until reaching age 16 but the respondents declined to send their children, ages 14 and 15, to public school after they completed the eighth grade. The children were not enrolled in any private school, or within any recognized exception to the compulsory-attendance law, and they are conceded to be subject to the Wisconsin statute.

. . .

On complaint of the school district administrator for the public schools, respondents were charged, tried, and convicted of violating the compulsory-attendance law in Green County Court and were fined the sum of $5 each. Respondents defended on the ground that the application of the compulsory-attendance law violated their rights under the First and Fourteenth Amendments. The trial testimony showed that respondents believed, in accordance with the tenets of Old Order Amish communities generally, that their children's attendance at high school, public or private, was contrary to the Amish religion and way of life. They believed that by sending their children to high school, they would not only expose themselves to the danger of the censure of the church community, but, as found by the county court, also endanger their own salvation and that of their children. The State stipulated that respondents' religious beliefs were sincere.

. . .

[I]n order for Wisconsin to compel school attendance beyond the eighth grade against a claim that such attendance interferes with the practice of a legitimate religious belief, it must appear either that the State does not deny the free exercise of religious belief by its require-ment, or that there is a state interest of sufficient magnitude to override the interest claiming protection under the Free Exercise Clause. . . .

. . . We can accept it as settled, . . . that, however strong the State's interest in universal compulsory education, it is by no means absolute to the exclusion or subordination of all other interests.

As the society around the Amish has become more populous, urban, industrialized, and complex, particularly in this century, government regulation of human affairs has correspondingly become more detailed and pervasive. The Amish mode of life has thus come into conflict increasingly with requirements of contemporary society exerting a hydraulic insistence on conformity to majoritarian standards. So long as compulsory education laws were confined to eight grades of elementary basic education imparted in a nearby rural schoolhouse, with a large proportion of students of the Amish faith, the Old Order Amish had little basis to fear that school attendance would expose their children to the worldly influence they reject. But modern compulsory secondary education in rural areas is now largely carried on in a consolidated school, often remote from the student's home and alien to his daily home life. As the record so strongly shows, the values and programs of the modern secondary school are in sharp conflict with the fundamental mode of life mandated by the Amish religion; modern laws requiring compulsory secondary education have accordingly engendered great concern and conflict. The conclusion is inescapable that secondary schooling, by exposing Amish children to worldly influences in terms of attitudes, goals, and values contrary to beliefs, and by substantially interfering with the religious development of the Amish child and his integration into the way of life of the Amish faith community at the crucial adolescent stage of development, contravenes the basic religious tenets and practice of the Amish faith, both as to the parent and the child.

The impact of the compulsory-attendance law on respondents' practice of the Amish religion is not only severe, but inescapable, for the Wisconsin law affirmatively compels them, under threat of criminal sanction, to perform acts undeniably at odds with fundamental tenets of their religious beliefs. . . .

In sum, the unchallenged testimony of acknowledged experts in education and religious history, almost 300 years of consistent practice, and strong evidence of a sustained faith pervading and regulating respondents' entire mode of life support the claim that enforcement of the State's requirement of compulsory formal education after the eighth grade would gravely endanger if not destroy the free exercise of respondents' religious beliefs.

. . .

Wisconsin concedes that under the Religion Clauses religious beliefs are absolutely free from the State's control, but it argues that "actions," even though religiously grounded, are outside the protection of the First Amendment. But our decisions have rejected the idea that religiously grounded conduct is always outside the protection of the Free Exercise Clause. It is true that activities of individuals, even when religiously based, are often subject to regulation by the States in the exercise of their undoubted power to promote the health, safety, and general welfare, or the Federal Government in the exercise of its delegated powers. But to agree that religiously grounded conduct must often be subject to the broad police power of the State is not to deny that there are areas of conduct protected by the Free Exercise Clause of the First Amendment and thus beyond the power of the State to control, even under regulations of general applicability. . . .

Nor can this case be disposed of on the grounds that Wisconsin's requirement for school attendance to age 16 applies uniformly to all citizens of the State and does not, on its face, discriminate against religions or a particular religion, or that it is motivated by legitimate secular concerns. A regulation neutral on its face may, in its application, nonetheless offend the constitutional requirement for governmental neutrality if it unduly burdens the free exercise of religion. The Court must not ignore the danger that an exception from a general obligation of citizenship on religious grounds may run afoul of the Establishment Clause, but that danger cannot be allowed to prevent any exception no matter how vital it may be to the protection of values promoted by the right of free exercise. . . .

We turn, then, to the State's broader contention that its interest in its system of compulsory education is so compelling that even the established religious practices of the Amish must give way. Where fundamental claims of religious freedom are at stake, however, we cannot accept such a sweeping claim; despite its admitted validity in the generality of cases, we must searchingly examine the interests that the State seeks to promote by its requirement for compulsory education to age 16, and the impediment to those objectives that would flow from recognizing the claimed Amish exemption.

The State advances two primary arguments in support of its system of compulsory education. It notes, as Thomas Jefferson pointed out early in our history, that some degree of education is necessary to prepare citizens to participate effectively and intelligently in our open political system if we are to preserve freedom and independence. Further, education prepares individuals to be self-reliant and self-sufficient participants in society. We accept these propositions.

However, the evidence adduced by the Amish in this case is persuasively to the effect that an additional one or two years of formal high school for Amish children in place of their long-established program of informal vocational education would do little to serve those interests. Respondents' experts testified at trial, without challenge, that the value of all education must be assessed in terms of its capacity to prepare the child for life. It is one thing to say that compulsory education for a year or two beyond the eighth grade may be necessary when its goal is the preparation of the child for life in modern society as the majority live, but it is quite another if the goal of education be viewed as the preparation of the child for life in the separated agrarian community that is the keystone of the Amish faith.

The State attacks respondents' position as one fostering "ignorance" from which the child must be protected by the State. No one can question the State's duty to protect children from ignorance but this argument does not square with the facts disclosed in the record. Whatever their idiosyncrasies as seen by the majority, this record strongly shows that the Amish community has been a highly successful social unit within our society, even if apart from the conventional "mainstream." Its members are productive and very law-abiding members of society; they reject public welfare in any of its usual modern forms. The Congress itself recognized their self-sufficiency by authorizing exemption of such groups as the Amish from the obligation to pay social security taxes.

It is neither fair nor correct to suggest that the Amish are opposed to education beyond the eighth grade level. What this record shows is that they are opposed to conventional formal education of the type provided by a certified high school because it comes at the child's crucial adolescent period of religious development. Dr. Donald Erickson, for example, testified that their system of learning-by-doing was an "ideal system" of education in terms of preparing Amish children for life as adults in the Amish community, and that "I would be inclined to say they do a better job in this than most of the rest of us do." As he put it, "These people aren't purporting to be learned people, and it seems to me the self-sufficiency of the community is the best evidence I can point to—whatever is being done seems to function well."

We must not forget that in the Middle Ages important values of the civilization of the Western World were preserved by members of religious orders who isolated themselves from all worldly influences against great obstacles. There can be no assumption that today's majority is "right" and the Amish and others like them are "wrong." A way of life that is odd or even erratic but interferes with no rights or interests of others is not to be condemned because it is different.

. . .

The requirement for compulsory education beyond the eighth grade is a relatively recent development in our history. Less than 60 years ago, the educational requirements of almost all of the States were satisfied by completion of the elementary grades, at least where the child was regularly and lawfully employed. The independence and successful social functioning of the Amish community for a period approaching almost three centuries and more than 200 years in this country are strong evidence that there is at best a speculative gain, in terms of meeting the duties of citizenship, from an additional one or two years of compulsory formal education. Against this background it would require a more particularized showing from the State on this point to justify the severe interference with religious freedom such additional compulsory attendance would entail.

Finally, the State, argues that a decision exempting Amish children from the State's requirement fails to recognize the substantive right of the Amish child to a secondary education, and fails to give due regard to the power of the State as parens patriae to extend the benefit of secondary education to children regardless of the wishes of their parents. . . .

This case, of course, is not one in which any harm to the physical or mental health of the child or to the public safety, peace, order, or welfare has been demonstrated or may be properly inferred. The record is to the contrary, and any reliance on that theory would find no support in the evidence.

Contrary to the suggestion of the dissenting opinion of MR. JUSTICE DOUGLAS, our holding today in no degree depends on the assertion of the religious interest of the child as contrasted with that of the parents. It is the parents who are subject to prosecution here for failing to cause their children to attend school, and it is their right of free exercise, not that of their children, that must determine Wisconsin's power to impose criminal penalties on the parent. The dissent argues that a child who expresses a desire to attend public high school in conflict with the wishes of his parents should not be prevented from doing so. There is no reason for the Court to consider that point since it is not an issue in the case. The children

are not parties to this litigation. The State has at no point tried this case on the theory that respondents were preventing their children from attending school against their expressed desires, and indeed the record is to the contrary. The State's position from the outset has been that it is empowered to apply its compulsory-attendance law to Amish parents in the same manner as to other parents—that is, without regard to the wishes of the child. That is the claim we reject today.

Our holding in no way determines the proper resolution of possible competing interests of parents, children, and the State in an appropriate state court proceeding in which the power of the State is asserted on the theory that Amish parents are preventing their minor children from attending high school despite their expressed desires to the contrary. Recognition of the claim of the State in such a proceeding would, of course, call into question traditional concepts of parental control over the religious upbringing and education of their minor children recognized in this Court's past decisions. It is clear that such an intrusion by a State into family decisions in the area of religious training would give rise to grave questions of religious freedom comparable to those raised here and those presented in *Pierce v. Society of Sisters*, 268 U.S. 510 (1925). On this record we neither reach nor decide those issues.

. . .

Indeed it seems clear that if the State is empowered, as parens patriae, to "save" a child from himself or his Amish parents by requiring an additional two years of compulsory formal high school education, the State will in large measure influence, if not determine, the religious future of the child. Even more markedly than in Prince, therefore, this case involves the fundamental interest of parents, as contrasted with that of the State, to guide the religious future and education of their children. The history and culture of Western civilization reflect a strong tradition of parental concern for the nurture and upbringing of their children. This primary role of the parents in the upbringing of their children is now established beyond debate as an enduring American tradition. . . .

However read, the Court's holding in Pierce stands as a charter of the rights of parents to direct the religious upbringing of their children. And, when the interests of parenthood are combined with a free exercise claim of the nature revealed by this record, more than merely a "reasonable relation to some purpose within the competency of the State" is required to sustain the validity of the State's requirement under the First Amendment. To be sure, the power of the parent, even when linked to a free exercise claim, may be subject to limitation under Prince if it appears that parental decisions will jeopardize the health or safety of the child, or have a potential for significant social burdens. But in this case, the Amish have introduced persuasive evidence undermining the arguments the State has advanced to support its claims in terms of the welfare of the child and society as a whole. The record strongly indicates that accommodating the religious objections of the Amish by forgoing one, or at most two, additional years of compulsory education will not impair the physical or mental health of the child, or result in an inability to be self-supporting or to discharge the duties and responsibilities of citizenship, or in any other way materially detract from the welfare of society.

In the face of our consistent emphasis on the central values underlying the Religion Clauses in our constitutional scheme of government, we cannot accept a parens patriae claim of such all-encompassing scope and with such sweeping potential for broad and unforeseeable application as that urged by the State.

. . .

MR. JUSTICE POWELL and MR. JUSTICE REHNQUIST took no part in the consideration or decision of this case.

MR. JUSTICE STEWART, with whom MR. JUSTICE BRENNAN joins, concurring.

. . .

This case in no way involves any questions regarding the right of the children of Amish parents to attend public high schools, or any other institutions of learning, if they wish to do so. As the Court points out, there is no suggestion whatever in the record that the religious beliefs of the children here concerned differ in any way from those of their parents. . . .

MR. JUSTICE WHITE, with whom MR. JUSTICE BRENNAN and MR. JUSTICE STEWART join, concurring.

Cases such as this one inevitably call for a delicate balancing of important but conflicting interests. I join the opinion and judgment of the Court because I cannot say that the State's interest in requiring two more years of compulsory education in the ninth and tenth grades outweighs the importance of the concededly sincere Amish religious practice to the survival of that sect.

This would be a very different case for me if respondents' claim were that their religion forbade their children from attending any school at any time and from complying in any way with the educational standards set by the State. Since the Amish children are permitted to acquire the basic tools of literacy to survive in modern society by attending grades one through eight and since the deviation from the State's compulsory-education law is relatively slight, I conclude that respondents' claim must prevail, largely because "religious freedom—the freedom to believe and to practice strange and, it may be, foreign creeds—has classically been one of the highest values of our society."

The importance of the state interest asserted here cannot be denigrated, however. . . .
. . . In the present case, the State is not concerned with the maintenance of an educational system as an end in itself, it is rather attempting to nurture and develop the human potential of its children, whether Amish or non-Amish: to expand their knowledge, broaden their sensibilities, kindle their imagination, foster a spirit of free inquiry, and increase their human understanding and tolerance. It is possible that most Amish children will wish to continue living the rural life of their parents, in which case their training at home will adequately equip them for their future role. Others, however, may wish to become nuclear physicists, ballet dancers, computer programmers, or historians, and for these occupations, formal training will be necessary. There is evidence in the record that many children desert the Amish faith when they come of age. A State has a legitimate interest not only in seeking to develop the latent talents of its children but also in seeking to prepare them for the life style that they may later choose, or at least to provide them with an option other than the life they have led in the past. In the circumstances of this case, although the question is close, I am unable to say that the State has demonstrated that Amish children who leave school in the eighth grade will be intellectually stultified or unable to acquire new academic skills later. The statutory minimum school attendance age set by the State is, after all, only 16.

Decision in cases such as this and the administration of an exemption for Old Order Amish from the State's compulsory school-attendance laws will inevitably involve the kind of close and perhaps repeated scrutiny of religious practices, as is exemplified in today's opinion, which the Court has heretofore been anxious to avoid. But such entanglement does not create a forbidden establishment of religion where it is essential to implement free exercise values threatened by an otherwise neutral program instituted to foster some permissible, nonreligious state objective. I join the Court because the sincerity of the Amish religious policy here is uncontested, because the potentially adverse impact of the state requirement is great, and because the State's valid interest in education has already been largely satisfied by the eight years the children have already spent in school.

MR. JUSTICE DOUGLAS, dissenting in part.

I agree with the Court that the religious scruples of the Amish are opposed to the education of their children beyond the grade schools, yet I disagree with the Court's conclusion that the matter is within the dispensation of parents alone. The Court's analysis assumes that the only interests at stake in the case are those of the Amish parents on the one hand, and those of the State on the other. The difficulty with this approach is that, despite the Court's claim, the parents are seeking to vindicate not only their own free exercise claims, but also those of their high-school-age children.

. . .

On this important and vital matter of education, I think the children should be entitled to be heard. While the parents, absent dissent, normally speak for the entire family, the education of the child is a matter on which the child will often have decided views. He may want to be a pianist or an astronaut or an oceanographer. To do so he will have to break from the Amish tradition.

It is the future of the student, not the future of the parents, that is imperiled by today's decision. If a parent keeps his child out of school beyond the grade school, then the child will be forever barred from entry into the new and amazing world of diversity that we have today. The child may decide that is the preferred course, or he may rebel. It is the student's judgment, not his parents', that is essential if we are to give full meaning to what we

have said about the Bill of Rights and of the right of students to be masters of their own destiny. If he is harnessed to the Amish way of life by those in authority over him and if his education is truncated, his entire life may be stunted and deformed. The child, therefore, should be given an opportunity to be heard before the State gives the exemption which we honor today.

. . .

The Court rightly rejects the notion that actions, even though religiously grounded, are always outside the protection of the Free Exercise Clause of the First Amendment. In so ruling, the Court departs from the teaching of *Reynolds v. United States*, where it was said concerning the reach of the Free Exercise Clause of the First Amendment, "Congress was deprived of all legislative power over mere opinion, but was left free to reach actions which were in violation of social duties or subversive of good order." . . .

Action, which the Court deemed to be antisocial, could be punished even though it was grounded on deeply held and sincere religious convictions. What we do today, at least in this respect, opens the way to give organized religion a broader base than it has ever enjoyed; and it even promises that in time Reynolds will be overruled.

Notwithstanding the prioritization of exercise interests in *Yoder,* the Court a decade later found other regulatory concerns more significant than the impositions they imposed upon Amish beliefs. In *United States v. Lee,* the Court upheld application of the social security tax law to an Amish employer who challenged it because his religion mandated provision "for their fellow members."[330] The *Lee* Court distinguished *Yoder* on grounds that the governmental interest with respect to social security was more compelling.[331] Chief Justice Burger's majority opinion reflected concern that, if Amish interests were accommodated, the social security system would be subject to "myriad exceptions flowing from a wide variety of religious beliefs."[332] Seeing no basis for distinguishing social security and other taxes, the Court also seemed inspired by perceived peril to the tax system generally "if denominations were allowed to challenge the tax system because tax payments were spent in a manner that violates their religious belief."[333]

The identification of an "overriding" governmental interest was crucial to the Court's determination, in *Bob Jones University v. United States,* that the Internal Revenue Service properly denied tax exempt status to religious universities with ra-

---

[330] United States v. Lee, 455 U.S. 252, 257 (1982).

[331] *Id.* at 259–60.

[332] *Id.* at 260.

[333] *Id.*

[334] Bob Jones University v. United States, 461 U.S. 574, 602–05 (1983).

cially discriminatory admissions policies.[334] Notwithstanding the burdening of religious beliefs, the Court found that government's "overriding interest in eradicating racial discrimination in education" should prevail.[335]

As in other contexts where constitutional claims implicate military interests, exercise clause review under such circumstances is less rigorous. In *Goldman v. Weinberger*, the Court abandoned strict scrutiny in upholding military regulations that precluded the wearing of hats indoors. The rule was challenged by an Air Force officer who, in wearing a yarmulke consistent with his Orthodox Jewish faith, was disciplined.[336] Insofar as armed forces' policy was contested, the Court's review was "far more deferential" than if the issue had arisen in "civilian society."[337] As Justice Rehnquist put it for the majority, "courts must give great deference to the professional judgment of military authorities concerning the relative importance of a particular military interest" even when the result is a "restriction on religiously motivated conduct."[338] The Court thus deferred to the military's interest in subordinating "personal preferences and identities in favor of the overall group mission."[339] Justice Brennan, in a dissent joined by Justice Marshall, protested the majority's deference. From their perspective, "a *credible* explanation of how the contested practice is likely to interfere with the preferred military interest" was missing and "*ipse dixit* cannot outweigh a constitutional right."[340] The dissent urged a standard of review at least capable of determining whether "the reasons a service branch offers for prohibiting personnel from wearing [religiously significant apparel] while in uniform . . . have a *reasoned* basis in, for example, functional utility, health and safety considerations, and the goal of a polished professional appearance."[341]

ii. Toward More Restrictive Conditions for Strict Scrutiny

After nearly a quarter of a century of relatively simple balancing exercises, the Court has evolved somewhat more complex analytical regimes for the review of exercise claims. Although not dispensing with balancing, it has limited the operation of strict scrutiny. The trend toward relaxed review of certain free exercise claims was foreshadowed in *Bowen v. Roy*.[342] At issue in *Bowen* was a federal law requiring welfare applicants to provide their social security numbers.[343] The law was challenged on free exercise grounds by parents who argued that the condition would "rob the spirit" of their daughter.[344] Although a majority found that the exercise clause did not compel government "to behave in ways that the individual believes will further his or her spiritual development,"[345] it did not rule specifically on whether the applicants had to provide their social security number.[346] In an opinion joined by Justices Powell and Rehnquist, Chief Justice Burger suggested a diminished standard of review when government conditions rather than compels. To the extent that regulation is "facially neutral and

---

[335] *Id.* at 604.

[336] Goldman v. Weinberger, 475 U.S. 503, 505 (1986).

[337] *Id.* at 507.

[338] *Id.*

[339] *Id.* at 508.

[340] *Id.* at 516 (Brennan, J., dissenting).

[341] *Id.* at 519.

[342] 476 U.S. 693 (1986).

[343] *Id. at 695.*

[344] *Id.* at 696.

[345] *Id.* at 699.

[346] Taken together, the dissents of Justices White, O'Connor, Brennan and Marshall and the concurrence of Justice Blackmun suggest a majority position in favor of not having to furnish a social security number.

uniformly applicable," even though "indirectly and incidentally call[ing] for a choice between securing a government benefit and adherence to religious beliefs," the Burger plurality maintained that strict scrutiny was inapt.[347] Unless official action discriminated against religion generally or a particular religious belief, therefore, Burger would have found it sufficient that government had "demonstrate[d] that a challenged requirement . . . is a reasonable means of promoting legitimate public interest."[348]

Notwithstanding any uncertainty about standards of review, as a consequence of *Bowen*, the Court subsequently employed strict scrutiny in reviewing a state's denial of unemployment compensation benefits to a woman who refused to work Saturdays because of her Seventh-day Adventist beliefs. A majority saw no difference in the issue presented by *Hobbie v. Unemployment Appeals Commission of Florida* and what was decided in *Sherbert* and *Thomas*.

---

[347] *Id.* at 706 (opinion of Burger, C.J.).
[348] *Id.* at 708.

Hobbie v. Unemployment Appeals Commission of Florida
480 U.S. 136 (1987)

JUSTICE BRENNAN delivered the opinion of the Court.

Appellant's employer discharged her when she refused to work certain scheduled hours because of sincerely held religious convictions adopted after beginning employment. The question to be decided is whether Florida's denial of unemployment compensation benefits to appellant violates the Free Exercise Clause of the First Amendment of the Constitution, as applied to the States through the Fourteenth Amendment.

Under our precedents, the Appeals Commission's disqualification of appellant from receipt of benefits violates the Free Exercise Clause of the First Amendment, applicable to the States through the Fourteenth Amendment. . . .

We see no meaningful distinction among the situations of Sherbert, Thomas, and Hobbie. We again affirm, as stated in Thomas:

"Where the state conditions receipt of an important benefit upon conduct proscribed by a religious faith, or where it denies such a benefit because of conduct mandated by religious belief, thereby putting substantial pressure on an adherent to modify his behavior and to violate his beliefs, a burden upon religion exists. While the compulsion may be indirect, the infringement upon free exercise is nonetheless substantial."

Both *Sherbert* and *Thomas* held that such infringements must be subjected to strict scrutiny and could be justified only by proof by the State of a compelling interest. The Appeals Commission does not seriously contend that its denial of benefits can withstand strict scrutiny; rather it urges that we hold that its justification should be determined under the less rigorous standard articulated in Chief Justice Burger's opinion in *Bowen v. Roy*, "[The] Government meets its burden when it demonstrates that a challenged requirement for governmental benefits, neutral and uniform in its application, is a reasonable means of promoting a legitimate public interest." Five Justices expressly rejected this argument in *Roy*. We reject the argument again today. As JUSTICE O'CONNOR pointed out in Roy, "[such] a test has no basis in precedent and relegates a serious First Amendment value to the barest level of minimal scrutiny that the Equal Protection Clause already provides." ("[Only] those interests of the highest order and those not otherwise served can overbalance legitimate claims to the free exercise of religion").

The Appeals Commission also suggests two grounds upon which we might distinguish *Sherbert* and *Thomas* from the present case. First, the Appeals Commission points out that in *Sherbert* the employee was deemed completely ineligible for benefits under South Carolina's unemployment insurance scheme because she would not accept work that conflicted with her Sabbath. The Appeals Commission contends that, under Florida law, Hobbie faces only a limited disqualification from receipt of benefits, and that once this fixed term has been served, she will again "be on an equal footing with all other workers, provided she avoids employment that conflicts with her religious beliefs." The Appeals Commission argues that such a disqualification provision is less coercive than the ineligibility determination in *Sherbert*, and that the burden it imposes on free exercise is therefore permissible.

This distinction is without substance. The immediate effects of ineligibility and disqualification are identical, and the disqualification penalty is substantial. Moreover, *Sherbert* was given controlling weight in *Thomas*, which involved a disqualification provision similar in all relevant respects to the statutory section implicated here.

The Appeals Commission also attempts to distinguish this case by arguing that, unlike the employees in *Sherbert* and *Thomas*, Hobbie was the "agent of change" and is therefore responsible for the consequences of the conflict between her job and her religious beliefs. In *Sherbert* and *Thomas*, the employees held their respective religious beliefs at the time of hire; subsequent changes in the conditions of employment made by the employer caused the conflict between work and belief. In this case, Hobbie's beliefs changed during the course of her employment, creating a conflict between job and faith that had not previously existed. The Appeals Commission contends that "it is . . . unfair for an employee to adopt religious beliefs that conflict with existing Employment and expect to continue the employment without compromising those beliefs" and that this "intentional disregard of the employer's interests . . . constitutes misconduct."

In effect, the Appeals Commission asks us to single out the religious convert for different,

less favorable treatment than that given an individual whose adherence to his or her faith precedes employment. We decline to do so. The First Amendment protects the free exercise rights of employees who adopt religious beliefs or convert from one faith to another after they are hired. The timing of Hobbie's conversion is immaterial to our determination that her free exercise rights have been burdened; the salient inquiry under the Free Exercise Clause is the burden involved. . . .

Finally, we reject the Appeals Commission's argument that the awarding of benefits to Hobbie would violate the Establishment Clause. This Court has long recognized that the government may (and sometimes must) accommodate religious practices and that it may do so without violating the Establishment Clause.

. . .

We conclude that Florida's refusal to award unemployment compensation benefits to appellant violated the Free Exercise Clause of the First Amendment. . . .

CHIEF JUSTICE REHNQUIST, dissenting.

I adhere to the views I stated in dissent in *Thomas v. Review Bd. of Indiana Employment Security Div.* Accordingly, I would affirm.

JUSTICE POWELL, concurring in the judgment.

. . .

JUSTICE STEVENS, concurring in the judgment.

. . .

The scope of strict scrutiny was narrowed in *Lyng v. Northwest Indian Cemetery Protection Association.* Under review in *Lyng* were national forest timber and road construction policies challenged by Native Americans on grounds they interfered with sacred areas reserved for religious rituals. For a majority, the critical factor in determining the standard of review was the magnitude of the burden.

Lyng v. Northwest Indian Cemetery Protection Association
485 U.S. 439 (1988)

JUSTICE O'CONNOR delivered the opinion of the Court.

This case requires us to consider whether the First Amendment's Free Exercise Clause forbids the Government from permitting timber harvesting in, or constructing a road through, a portion of a National Forest that has traditionally been used for religious purposes by members of three American Indian tribes in northwestern California. We conclude that it does not.

. . .

The Free Exercise Clause of the First Amendment provides that "Congress shall make no law ..prohibiting the free exercise [of religion]." University. S. Const., Amdt. 1. It is undisputed that the Indian respondents' beliefs are sincere and that the Government's proposed actions will have severe adverse effects on the practice of their religion. Respondents contend that the burden on their religious practices is heavy enough to violate the Free Exercise Clause unless the Government can demonstrate a compelling need to complete the G-O road or to engage in timber harvesting in the Chimney Rock area. We disagree.

In *Bowen v. Roy*, we considered a challenge to a federal statute that required the States to use Social Security numbers in administering certain welfare programs. Two applicants for benefits under these programs contended that their religious beliefs prevented them from acceding to the use of a Social Security number for their two-year-old daughter because the use of a numerical identifier would " rob the spirit' of [their] daughter and prevent her from attaining greater spiritual power." Similarly, in this case, it is said that disruption of the natural environment caused by the G-O road will diminish the sacredness of the area in question and create distractions that will interfere with" training and ongoing religious experience of individuals using [sites within] the area for personal medicine and growth ... and as integrated parts of a system of religious belief and practice which correlates ascending degrees of personal power with a geographic hierarchy of power." The Court rejected this kind of challenge in Roy:

> "The Free Exercise Clause simply cannot be understood to require the Government to conduct its own internal affairs in ways that comport with the religious beliefs of particular citizens. Just as the Government may not insist that [the Roys] engage in any set form of religious observance, so [they] may not demand that the Government join in their chosen religious practices by refraining from using a number to identify their daughter....
>
> "... The Free Exercise Clause affords an individual protection from certain forms of governmental compulsion; it does not afford an individual a right to dictate the conduct of the Government's internal procedures."

The building of a road or the harvesting of timber on publicly owned land cannot meaningfully be distinguished from the use of a Social Security number in *Roy*. In both cases, the challenged government action would interfere significantly with private persons' ability to pursue spiritual fulfillment according to their own religious beliefs. In neither case, however, would the affected individuals be coerced by the Government's action into violating their religious beliefs; nor would either governmental action penalize religious activity by denying any person an equal share of the rights, benefits, and privileges enjoyed by other citizens.

. . .

Whatever may be the exact line between unconstitutional prohibitions on the free exercise of religion and the legitimate conduct by government of its own affairs, the location of the line cannot depend on measuring the effects of a governmental action on a religious objector's spiritual development. The Government does not dispute, and we have no reason to doubt, that the logging and road-building projects at issue in this case could have devastating effects on traditional Indian religious practices. . . .

Even if we assume that we should accept the Ninth Circuit's prediction, according to which the G-O road will "virtually destroy the Indians' ability to practice their religion," the Constitution simply does not provide a principle that could justify upholding respondents' legal claims. However much we might wish that it were otherwise, government simply could not operate if it were required to satisfy every citizen's religious needs and desires. A broad range of government activities—from social welfare programs to foreign aid to conservation projects—will always be considered essential to the spiritual well-being of some citizens, often on the basis of sincerely held religious beliefs. Others will find the very same activities deeply offensive, and perhaps incompatible with their own search for spiritual fulfillment and with the tenets of their religion. The First Amendment must apply to all citizens alike, and it can give to none of them a veto over public programs that do not prohibit the free exercise of religion. The Constitution does not, and courts cannot, offer to reconcile the various competing demands on government, many of them rooted in sincere religious belief, that inevitably arise in so diverse a society as ours. That task, to the extent that it is feasible, is for the legislatures and other institutions.

. . .

Justice KENNEDY took no part in the consideration or decision of this case.

JUSTICE BRENNAN, with whom JUSTICE MARSHALL and JUSTICE BLACKMUN join, dissenting.

" 'The Free Exercise Clause,' " the Court explains today, " 'is written in terms of what the government cannot do to the individual, not in terms of what the individual can exact from the government.' " Pledging fidelity to this unremarkable constitutional principle, the Court nevertheless concludes that even where the Government uses federal land in a manner that threatens the very existence of a Native American religion, the Government is simply not "doing" anything to the practitioners of that faith. Instead, the Court believes that Native Americans who request that the Government refrain from destroying their religion effectively seek to exact from the Government Dean facto beneficial ownership of federal property. These two astonishing conclusions follow naturally from the Court's determination that federal land-use decisions that render the practice of a given religion impossible do not burden that religion in a manner cognizable under the Free Exercise Clause, because such decisions neither coerce conduct inconsistent with religious belief nor penalize religious activity. The constitutional guarantee we interpret today, however, draws no such fine distinctions between types of restraints on religious exercise, but rather is directed against any form of governmental action that frustrates or inhibits religious practice. Because the Court today refuses even to acknowledge the constitutional injury respondents will suffer, and because this refusal essentially leaves Native Americans with absolutely no constitutional protection against perhaps the gravest threat to their religious practices, I dissent.

The Court does not for a moment suggest that the interests served by the G-O road are in any way compelling, or that they outweigh the destructive effect construction of the road will have on respondents' religious practices. Instead, the Court embraces the Government's contention that its prerogative as landowner should always take precedence over a claim that a particular use of federal property infringes religious practices. Attempting to justify this rule, the Court argues that the First Amendment bars only outright prohibitions, indirect coercion, and penalties on the free exercise of religion. All other "incidental effects of government programs," it concludes, even those "which may make it more difficult to practice certain religions but which have no tendency to coerce individuals into acting contrary to their religious beliefs," simply do not give rise to constitutional concerns. Since our recognition nearly half a century ago that restraints on religious conduct implicate the concerns of the Free Exercise Clause, we have never suggested that the protections of the guarantee are limited to so narrow a range of governmental burdens. The land-use decision challenged here will restrain respondents from practicing their religion as surely and as completely as any of the governmental actions we have struck down in the past, and the Court's efforts simply to define away respondents' injury as nonconstitutional is both unjustified and ultimately unpersuasive.

The Court ostensibly finds support for its narrow formulation of religious burdens in our decisions in *Hobbie* and *Sherbert*. In those cases, the laws at issue forced individuals to choose between adhering to specific religious tenets and forfeiting unemployment benefits on the one hand, and accepting work repugnant to their religious beliefs on the other. The religions involved, therefore, lent themselves to the coercion analysis the Court espouses today, for they proscribed certain conduct such as munitions work (*Thomas*) or working on Saturdays (*Sherbert*, *Hobbie*) that the unemployment benefits laws effectively compelled. In sustaining the challenges to these laws, however, we nowhere suggested that such coercive compulsion exhausted the range of religious burdens recognized under the Free Exercise Clause.

. . .

I thus cannot accept the Court's premise that the form of the Government's restraint on religious practice, rather than its effect, controls our constitutional analysis. . . .

In the final analysis, the Court's refusal to recognize the constitutional dimension of respondents' injuries stems from its concern that acceptance of respondents' claim could potentially strip the Government of its ability to manage and use vast tracts of federal property. In addition, the nature of respondents' site-specific religious practices raises the specter of future suits in which Native Americans seek to exclude all human activity from such areas. These concededly legitimate concerns lie at the very heart of this case, which represents yet another stress point in the longstanding conflict between two disparate cultures—the dominant western culture, which views land in terms of ownership and use, and that of Native Americans, in which concepts of private property are not only alien, but contrary to a belief system that holds land sacred. Rather than address this conflict in any meaningful fashion, however, the Court disclaims all responsibility for balancing these competing and potentially irreconcilable interests, choosing instead to turn this difficult task over to the federal legislature. Such an abdication is more than merely indefensible as an institutional matter: by defining respondents' injury as "non-constitutional," the Court has effectively bestowed on one party to this conflict the unilateral authority to resolve all future disputes in its favor, subject only to the Court's toothless exhortation to be "sensitive" to affected religions. In my view, however, Native Americans deserve—and the Constitution demands—more than this.

. . .

Today, the Court holds that a federal land-use decision that promises to destroy an entire religion does not burden the practice of that faith in a manner recognized by the Free Exercise Clause. Having thus stripped respondents and all other Native Americans of any constitutional protection against perhaps the most serious threat to their age-old religious practices, and indeed to their entire way of life, the Court assures us that nothing in its decision "should be read to encourage governmental insensitivity to the religious needs of any citizen," I find it difficult, however, to imagine conduct more insensitive to religious needs than the Government's determination to build a marginally useful road in the face of uncontradicted evidence that the road will render the practice of respondents' religion impossible. Nor do I believe that respondents will derive any solace from the knowledge that although the practice of their religion will become "more difficult" as a result of the Government's actions, they remain free to maintain their religious beliefs.

Given today's ruling, that freedom amounts to nothing more than the right to believe that their religion will be destroyed. The safeguarding of such a hollow freedom not only makes a mockery of the "'policy of the United States to protect and preserve for American Indians their inherent right of freedom to believe, express, and exercise their traditional religions,'" it fails utterly to accord with the dictates of the First Amendment.

I dissent.

Employment of strict scrutiny in exercise clause cases was further delimited in *Employment Division, Oregon Department of Human Resources v. Smith*. Reflecting concern with the wisdom of heightened review for all exercise claims, the Court exempted from strict scrutiny regulation that was generally applicable and religiously neutral.

Employment Division, Department of Human Resources of Oregon v. Smith
494 U.S. 872 (1990)

JUSTICE SCALIA delivered the opinion of the Court.

This case requires us to decide whether the Free Exercise Clause of the First Amendment permits the State of Oregon to include religiously inspired peyote use within the reach of its general criminal prohibition on use of that drug, and thus permits the State to deny unemployment benefits to persons dismissed from their jobs because of such religiously inspired use.

I

Respondents Alfred Smith and Galen Black (hereinafter respondents) were fired from their jobs with a private drug rehabilitation organization because they ingested peyote for sacramental purposes at a ceremony of the Native American Church, of which both are members. When respondents applied to petitioner Employment Division (hereinafter petitioner) for unemployment compensation, they were determined to be ineligible for benefits because they had been discharged for work-related "misconduct." The Oregon Court of Appeals reversed that determination, holding that the denial of benefits violated respondents' free exercise rights under the First Amendment.

. . .

Before this Court in 1987, petitioner . . . maintained that the illegality of respondents' peyote consumption was relevant to their constitutional claim. We agreed. . . . We noted, however, that the Oregon Supreme Court had not decided whether respondents' sacramental use of peyote was in fact proscribed by Oregon's controlled substance law, and that this issue was a matter of dispute between the parties. . . .

On remand, the Oregon Supreme Court held that respondents' religiously inspired use of peyote fell within the prohibition of the Oregon statute, which "makes no exception for the sacramental use" of the drug. It then considered whether that prohibition was valid under the Free Exercise Clause, and concluded that it was not. The court therefore reaffirmed its previous ruling that the State could not deny unemployment benefits to respondents for having engaged in that practice.

. . .

II

Respondents' claim for relief rests on our decisions in *Sherbert v. Verner, Thomas v. Review Bd. of Indiana Employment Security Div.*, and *Hobbie v. Unemployment Appeals Comm'n of Florida*, in which we held that a State could not condition the availability of unemployment insurance on an individual's willingness to forgo conduct required by his religion. As we observed in Smith I, however, the conduct at issue in those cases was not prohibited by law. We held that distinction to be critical. . . .

. . . We have never held that an individual's religious beliefs excuse him from compliance with an otherwise valid law prohibiting conduct that the State is free to regulate. On the contrary, the record of more than a century of our free exercise jurisprudence contradicts that proposition. . . .

The only decisions in which we have held that the First Amendment bars application of a neutral, generally applicable law to religiously motivated action have involved not the Free Exercise Clause alone, but the Free Exercise Clause in conjunction with other constitutional protections, such as freedom of speech and of the press. . . .

. . .

Respondents argue that even though exemption from generally applicable criminal laws need not automatically be extended to religiously motivated actors, at least the claim for a religious exemption must be evaluated under the balancing test set forth in *Sherbert*. Under the *Sherbert* test, governmental actions that substantially burden a religious practice must be justified by a compelling governmental interest. Applying that test we have, on three occasions, invalidated state unemployment compensation rules that conditioned the availability of benefits upon an applicant's willingness to work under conditions forbidden by his religion. See *Sherbert; Thomas; Hobbie*. We have never invalidated any governmental action on the basis of the Sherbert test except the denial of unemployment compensation. . . .

Even if we were inclined to breathe into *Sherbert* some life beyond the unemployment compensation field, we would not apply it to require exemptions from a generally applicable criminal law. The *Sherbert* test, it must be recalled, was developed in a context that lent itself to individualized governmental assessment of the reasons for the relevant conduct. As a plurality of the Court noted in *Roy*, a distinctive feature of unemployment compensation programs is that their eligibility criteria invite consideration of the particular circumstances behind an applicant's unemployment: "The statutory conditions [in *Sherbert* and *Thomas*] provided that a person was not eligible for unemployment compensation benefits if, 'without good cause,' he had quit work or refused available work. The 'good cause' standard created a mechanism for individualized exemptions." As the plurality pointed out in *Roy*, our decisions in the unemployment cases stand for the proposition that where the State has in place a system of individual exemptions, it may not refuse to extend that system to cases of "religious hardship" without compelling reason.

Whether or not the decisions are that limited, they at least have nothing to do with an across-the-board criminal prohibition on a particular form of conduct. Although, as noted earlier, we have sometimes used the *Sherbert* test to analyze free exercise challenges to such laws, we have never applied the test to invalidate one. We conclude today that the sounder approach, and the approach in accord with the vast majority of our precedents, is to hold the test inapplicable to such challenges. The government's ability to enforce generally applicable prohibitions of socially harmful conduct, like its ability to carry out other aspects of public policy, "cannot depend on measuring the effects of a governmental action on a religious objector's spiritual development." To make an individual's obligation to obey such a law contingent upon the law's coincidence with his religious beliefs, except where the State's interest is "compelling"—permitting him, by virtue of his beliefs, "to become a law unto himself," —contradicts both constitutional tradition and common sense.

The "compelling government interest" requirement seems benign, because it is familiar from other fields. But using it as the standard that must be met before the government may accord different treatment on the basis of race, or before the government may regulate the content of speech, is not remotely comparable to using it for the purpose asserted here. What it produces in those other fields—equality of treatment and an unrestricted flow of contending speech—are constitutional norms; what it would produce here—a private right to ignore generally applicable laws—is a constitutional anomaly.

Nor is it possible to limit the impact of respondents' proposal by requiring a "compelling state interest" only when the conduct prohibited is "central" to the individual's religion. It is no more appropriate for judges to determine the "centrality" of religious beliefs before applying a "compelling interest" test in the free exercise field, than it would be for them to determine the "importance" of ideas before applying the "compelling interest" test in the free speech field. What principle of law or logic can be brought to bear to contradict a believer's assertion that a particular act is "central" to his personal faith? Judging the centrality of different religious practices is akin to the unacceptable "business of evaluating the relative merits of differing religious claims." As we reaffirmed only last Term, "[i]t is not within the judicial ken to question the centrality of particular beliefs or practices to a faith, or the validity of particular litigants' interpretations of those creeds." Repeatedly and in many different contexts, we have warned that courts must not presume to determine the place of a particular belief in a religion or the plausibility of a religious claim.

If the "compelling interest" test is to be applied at all, then, it must be applied across the board, to all actions thought to be religiously commanded. Moreover, if "compelling interest" really means what it says (and watering it down here would subvert its rigor in the other fields where it is applied), many laws will not meet the test. Any society adopting such a system would be courting anarchy, but that danger increases in direct proportion to the society's diversity of religious beliefs, and its determination to coerce or suppress none of them. Precisely because "we are a cosmopolitan nation made up of people of almost every conceivable religious preference," and precisely because we value and protect that religious divergence, we cannot afford the luxury of deeming presumptively invalid, as applied to the religious objector, every regulation of conduct that does not protect an interest of the highest order. The rule respondents favor would open the prospect of constitutionally required religious exemptions from civic obligations of almost every conceivable kind—ranging from compulsory military service, to the payment of taxes, to health and safety regulation such as manslaughter and child neglect laws, compulsory vaccination laws, and traffic laws, to social welfare legislation such as minimum wage laws, child labor laws, animal cruelty laws, environmental protection laws, and laws providing for equality of opportunity for the races. The First Amendment's protection of religious liberty does not require this.

Values that are protected against government interference through enshrinement in the Bill of Rights are not thereby banished from the political process. Just as a society that believes in the negative protection accorded to the press by the First Amendment is likely to enact laws that affirmatively foster the dissemination of the printed word, so also a society that believes in the negative protection accorded to religious belief can be expected to be solicitous of that value in its legislation as well. It is therefore not surprising that a number of States have made an exception to their drug laws for sacramental peyote use. But to say that a nondiscriminatory religious-practice exemption is permitted, or even that it is desirable, is not to say that it is constitutionally required, and that the appropriate occasions for its creation can be discerned by the courts. It may fairly be said that leaving accommodation to the political process will place at a relative disadvantage those religious practices that are not widely engaged in; but that unavoidable consequence of democratic government must be preferred to a system in which each conscience is a law unto itself or in which judges weigh the social importance of all laws against the centrality of all religious beliefs.

* * *

Because respondents' ingestion of peyote was prohibited under Oregon law, and because that prohibition is constitutional, Oregon may, consistent with the Free Exercise Clause, deny respondents unemployment compensation when their dismissal results from use of the drug. The decision of the Oregon Supreme Court is accordingly reversed.

It is so ordered.

JUSTICE O'CONNOR, with whom JUSTICE BRENNAN, JUSTICE MARSHALL, and JUSTICE BLACKMUN join as to Parts I and II, concurring in the judgment.

Although I agree with the result the Court reaches in this case, I cannot join its opinion. In my view, today's holding dramatically departs from well-settled First Amendment jurisprudence, appears unnecessary to resolve the question presented, and is incompatible with our Nation's fundamental commitment to individual religious liberty.

. . .

I

. . .

II

. . .

The Court today gives no convincing reason to depart from settled First Amendment jurisprudence. There is nothing talismanic about neutral laws of general applicability or general criminal prohibitions, for laws neutral toward religion can coerce a person to violate his religious conscience or intrude upon his religious duties just as effectively as laws aimed at religion. Although the Court suggests that the compelling interest test, as applied to generally applicable laws, would result in a "constitutional anomaly," the First Amendment unequivocally makes freedom of religion, like freedom from race discrimination and freedom of speech, a "constitutional nor[m]," not an "anomaly." Nor would application of our established free exercise doctrine to this case necessarily be incompatible with our equal protection cases. We have in any event recognized that the Free Exercise Clause protects values distinct from those protected by the Equal Protection Clause. As the language of the Clause itself makes clear, an individual's free exercise of religion is a preferred constitutional activity. A law that makes criminal such an activity therefore triggers constitutional concern—and heightened judicial scrutiny—even if it does not target the particular religious conduct at issue. Our free speech cases similarly recognize that neutral regulations that affect free speech values are subject to a balancing, rather than categorical, approach. The Court's parade of horribles, not only fails as a reason for discarding the compelling interest test, it instead demonstrates just the opposite: that courts have been quite capable of applying our free exercise jurisprudence to strike sensible balances between religious liberty and competing state interests.

Finally, the Court today suggests that the disfavoring of minority religions is an "unavoidable consequence" under our system of government and that accommodation of such religions must be left to the political process. In my view, however, the First Amendment was enacted precisely to protect the rights of those whose religious practices are not shared by the majority and may be viewed with hostility. The history of our free exercise doctrine amply demonstrates the harsh impact majoritarian rule has had on unpopular or emerging religious groups such as the Jehovah's Witnesses and the Amish. . . .

III

The Court's holding today not only misreads settled First Amendment precedent; it appears to be unnecessary to this case. I would reach the same result applying our established free exercise jurisprudence.

There is no dispute that Oregon's criminal prohibition of peyote places a severe burden on the ability of respondents to freely exercise their religion. Peyote is a sacrament of the Native American Church and is regarded as vital to respondents' ability to practice their religion. . . . Under Oregon law, as construed by that State's highest court, members of the Native American Church must choose between carrying out the ritual embodying their religious beliefs and avoidance of criminal prosecution. That choice is, in my view, more than sufficient to trigger First Amendment scrutiny.

There is also no dispute that Oregon has a significant interest in enforcing laws that control the possession and use of controlled substances by its citizens. As we recently noted, drug abuse is "one of the greatest problems affecting the health and welfare of our population" and thus "one of the most serious problems confronting our society today." Indeed, under federal law (incorporated by Oregon law in relevant part, peyote is specifically regulated as a Schedule I controlled substance, which means that Congress has found that it has a high potential for abuse, that there is no currently accepted medical use, and that there is a lack of accepted safety for use of the drug under medical supervision. . . . In light of our recent decisions holding that the governmental interests. (R)espondents do not seriously dispute that Oregon has a compelling interest in prohibiting the possession of peyote by its citizens.

Thus, the critical question in this case is whether exempting respondents from the State's general criminal prohibition "will unduly interfere with fulfillment of the govern-

mental interest." Although the question is close, I would conclude that uniform application of Oregon's criminal prohibition is "essential to accomplish," its overriding interest in preventing the physical harm caused by the use of a Schedule I controlled substance. Oregon's criminal prohibition represents that State's judgment that the possession and use of controlled substances, even by only one person, is inherently harmful and dangerous. Because the health effects caused by the use of controlled substances exist regardless of the motivation of the user, the use of such substances, even for religious purposes, violates the very purpose of the laws that prohibit them. Moreover, in view of the societal interest in preventing trafficking in controlled substances, uniform application of the criminal prohibition at issue is essential to the effectiveness of Oregon's stated interest in preventing any possession of peyote.

. . .

JUSTICE BLACKMUN, with whom JUSTICE BRENNAN and JUSTICE MARSHALL join, dissenting.

This Court over the years painstakingly has developed a consistent and exacting standard to test the constitutionality of a state statute that burdens the free exercise of religion. Such a statute may stand only if the law in general, and the State's refusal to allow a religious exemption in particular, are justified by a compelling interest that cannot be served by less restrictive means.

Until today, I thought this was a settled and inviolate principle of this Court's First Amendment jurisprudence. The majority, however, perfunctorily dismisses it as a "constitutional anomaly." As carefully detailed in JUSTICE O'CONNOR'S concurring opinion, the majority is able to arrive at this view only by mischaracterizing this Court's precedents. . . .

This distorted view of our precedents leads the majority to conclude that strict scrutiny of a state law burdening the free exercise of religion is a "luxury" that a well-ordered society cannot afford, and that the repression of minority religions is an "unavoidable consequence of democratic government." I do not believe the Founders thought their dearly bought freedom from religious persecution a "luxury," but an essential element of liberty—and they could not have thought religious intolerance "unavoidable," for they drafted the Religion Clauses precisely in order to avoid that intolerance.

For these reasons, I agree with JUSTICE O'CONNOR'S analysis of the applicable free exercise doctrine, and I join parts I and II of her opinion. As she points out, "the critical question in this case is whether exempting respondents from the State's general criminal prohibition 'will unduly interfere with fulfillment of the governmental interest.'" I do disagree, however, with her specific answer to that question.

I

In weighing the clear interest of respondents Smith and Black (hereinafter respondents) in the free exercise of their religion against Oregon's asserted interest in enforcing its drug laws, it is important to articulate in precise terms the state interest involved. It is not the State's broad interest in fighting the critical "war on drugs" that must be weighed against respondents' claim, but the State's narrow interest in refusing to make an exception for the religious, ceremonial use of peyote. . . . Failure to reduce the competing interests to the same plane of generality tends to distort the weighing process in the State's favor.

The State's interest in enforcing its prohibition, in order to be sufficiently compelling to outweigh a free exercise claim, cannot be merely abstract or symbolic. The State cannot plausibly assert that unbending application of a criminal prohibition is essential to fulfill any compelling interest, if it does not, in fact, attempt to enforce that prohibition. In this case, the State actually has not evinced any concrete interest in enforcing its drug laws against religious users of peyote. Oregon has never sought to prosecute respondents, and does not claim that it has made significant enforcement efforts against other religious users of peyote. The State's asserted interest thus amounts only to the symbolic preservation of an unenforced prohibition. But a government interest in "symbolism, even symbolism for so worthy a cause as the abolition of unlawful drugs," cannot suffice to abrogate the constitutional rights of individuals.

Similarly, this Court's prior decisions have not allowed a government to rely on mere speculation about potential harms, but have demanded evidentiary support for a refusal to allow a religious exception. . . .

The State proclaims an interest in protecting the health and safety of its citizens from the dangers of unlawful drugs. It offers, however, no evidence that the religious use of peyote has ever harmed anyone. The factual findings of other courts cast doubt on the State's assumption that religious use of peyote is harmful. . . .

The fact that peyote is classified as a Schedule I controlled substance does not, by itself, show that any and all uses of peyote, in any circumstance, are inherently harmful and dangerous. . . .

The carefully circumscribed ritual context in which respondents used peyote is far removed from the irresponsible and unrestricted recreational use of unlawful drugs. . . .

The State also seeks to support its refusal to make an exception for religious use of peyote by invoking its interest in abolishing drug trafficking. There is, however, practically no illegal traffic in peyote. . . .

Finally, the State argues that granting an exception for religious peyote use would erode its interest in the uniform, fair, and certain enforcement of its drug laws. The State fears that, if it grants an exemption for religious peyote use, a flood of other claims to religious exemptions will follow. It would then be placed in a dilemma, it says, between allowing a patchwork of exemptions that would hinder its law enforcement efforts, and risking a violation of the Establishment Clause by arbitrarily limiting its religious exemptions. This argument, however, could be made in almost any free exercise case. . . .

The State's apprehension of a flood of other religious claims is purely speculative. Almost half the States, and the Federal Government, have maintained an exemption for religious peyote use for many years, and apparently have not found themselves overwhelmed by claims to other religious exemptions. . . .

III

Finally, although I agree with Justice O'Connor that courts should refrain from delving into questions whether, as a matter of religious doctrine, a particular practice is "central" to the religion, I do not think this means that the courts must turn a blind eye to the severe impact of a State's restrictions on the adherents of a minority religion. . . .

Respondents believe, and their sincerity has never been at issue, that the peyote plant embodies their deity, and eating it is an act of worship and communion. Without peyote, they could not enact the essential ritual of their religion. . . .

If Oregon can constitutionally prosecute them for this act of worship, they, like the Amish, may be "forced to migrate to some other and more tolerant region." This potentially devastating impact must be viewed in light of the federal policy—reached in reaction to many years of religious persecution and intolerance—of protecting the religious freedom of Native Americans. . . . Congress recognized that certain substances, such as peyote, "have religious significance because they are sacred, they have power, they heal, they are necessary to the exercise of the rites of the religion, they are necessary to the cultural integrity of the tribe, and, therefore, religious survival."

The American Indian Religious Freedom Act, in itself, may not create rights enforceable against government action restricting religious freedom, but this Court must scrupulously apply its free exercise analysis to the religious claims of Native Americans, however unorthodox they may be. Otherwise, both the First Amendment and the stated policy of Congress will offer to Native Americans merely an unfulfilled and hollow promise.

Despite the narrowing of circumstances warranting strict scrutiny, the Court in *Church of the Lukumi Babalu Aye v. City of Hialeah* discerned a violation of the exercise clause. Finding that a city ordinance prohibiting ritual animal sacrifice was directed toward a particular religion, the Court found a failure to satisfy *Smith's* neutrality requirements. Support for the result was qualified by dissatisfaction on the part of some justices with the analytical standards.

Church of the Lukumi Babalu Aye, Inc. v. Hialeah
113 S.Ct. 2217 (1993)

JUSTICE KENNEDY delivered the opinion of the Court, except as to Part II-A-2.*

. . .

I

A

This case involves practices of the Santeria religion, which originated in the nineteenth century. When hundreds of thousands of members of the Yoruba people were brought as slaves from eastern Africa to Cuba, their traditional African religion absorbed significant elements of Roman Catholicism. The resulting syncretion, or fusion, is Santeria, "the way of the saints." The Cuban Yoruba express their devotion to spirits, called orishas, through the iconography of Catholic saints, Catholic symbols are often present at Santeria rites, and Santeria devotees attend the Catholic sacraments.

The Santeria faith teaches that every individual has a destiny from God, a destiny fulfilled with the aid and energy of the orishas. The basis of the Santeria religion is the nurture of a personal relation with the orishas, and one of the principal forms of devotion is an animal sacrifice. The sacrifice of animals as part of religious rituals has ancient roots. Animal sacrifice is mentioned throughout the Old Testament and it played an important role in the practice of Judaism before destruction of the second Temple in Jerusalem. In modern Islam, there is an annual sacrifice commemorating Abraham's sacrifice of a ram in the stead of his son.

According to Santeria teaching, the orishas are powerful but not immortal. They depend for survival on the sacrifice. Sacrifices are performed at birth, marriage, and death rites, for the cure of the sick, for the initiation of new members and priests, and during an annual celebration. Animals sacrificed in Santeria rituals include chickens, pigeons, doves, ducks, guinea pigs, goats, sheep, and turtles. The animals are killed by the cutting of the carotid arteries in the neck. The sacrificed animal is cooked and eaten, except after healing and death rituals.

Santeria adherents faced widespread persecution in Cuba, so the religion and its rituals were practiced in secret. The open practice of Santeria and its rites remains infrequent. The religion was brought to this Nation most often by exiles from the Cuban revolution. The District Court estimated that there are at least 50,000 practitioners in South Florida today.

. . .

B

In September 1987, the city council adopted three substantive ordinances addressing the issue of religious animal sacrifice. . . . Declaring, moreover, that the city council "has determined that the sacrificing of animals within the city limits is contrary to the public health, safety, welfare and morals of the community," the city council adopted Ordinance 87–71. That ordinance defined sacrifice as had Ordinance 87–52, and then provided that "it shall be unlawful for any person, persons, corporations or associations to sacrifice any animal within the corporate limits of the City of Hialeah, Florida." The final Ordinance, 87–72, defined "slaughter" as "the killing of animals for food" and prohibited slaughter outside of areas zoned for slaughterhouse use. The ordinance provided an exemption, however, for the slaughter or processing for sale of "small numbers of hogs and/or cattle per week in accordance with an exemption provided by state law." All ordinances and resolutions passed the city council by unanimous vote. Violations of each of the four ordinances were punishable by fines not exceeding $500 or imprisonment not exceeding 60 days, or both.

. . .

---

* THE CHIEF JUSTICE, JUSTICE SCALIA,and JUSTICE THOMAS join all but Part II-A-2 of this opinion. JUSTICE WHITE joins all but Part II-A of this opinion. JUSTICE SOUTER joins only Parts I, III, and IV of this opinion.

II

. . .

In addressing the constitutional protection for free exercise of religion, our cases establish the general proposition that a law that is neutral and of general applicability need not be justified by a compelling governmental interest even if the law has the incidental effect of burdening a particular religious practice. *Employment Div., Dept. of Human Resources of Oregon v. Smith.* Neutrality and general applicability are interrelated, and, as becomes apparent in this case, failure to satisfy one requirement is a likely indication that the other has not been satisfied. A law failing to satisfy these requirements must be justified by a compelling governmental interest and must be narrowly tailored to advance that interest. These ordinances fail to satisfy the *Smith* requirements. We begin by discussing neutrality.

A

. . .

At a minimum, the protections of the Free Exercise Clause pertain if the law at issue discriminates against some or all religious beliefs or regulates or prohibits conduct because it is undertaken for religious reasons. Indeed, it was "historical instances of religious persecution and intolerance that gave concern to those who drafted the Free Exercise Clause." . . . These principles, though not often at issue in our Free Exercise Clause cases, have played a role in some. In *McDaniel v. Paty*, 435 U.S. 618, for example, we invalidated a State law that disqualified members of the clergy from holding certain public offices, because it "imposed special disabilities on the basis of . . . religious status." . . .

1

Although a law targeting religious beliefs as such is never permissible, if the object of a law is to infringe upon or restrict practices because of their religious motivation, the law is not neutral, and it is invalid unless it is justified by a compelling interest and is narrowly tailored to advance that interest. There are, of course, many ways of demonstrating that the object or purpose of a law is the suppression of religion or religious conduct. To determine the object of a law, we must begin with its text, for the minimum requirement of neutrality is that a law not discriminate on its face. A law lacks facial neutrality if it refers to a religious practice without a secular meaning discernable from the language or context. Petitioners contend that three of the ordinances fail this test of facial neutrality because they use the words "sacrifice" and "ritual," words with strong religious connotations. We agree that these words are consistent with the claim of facial discrimination, but the argument is not conclusive. The words "sacrifice" and "ritual" have a religious origin, but current use admits also of secular meanings. The ordinances, furthermore, define "sacrifice" in secular terms, without referring to religious practices.

. . . Official action that targets religious conduct for distinctive treatment cannot be shielded by mere compliance with the requirement of facial neutrality. The Free Exercise Clause protects against governmental hostility which is masked, as well as overt. . . .

The record in this case compels the conclusion that suppression of the central element of the Santeria worship service was the object of the ordinances. First, though use of the words "sacrifice" and "ritual" does not compel a finding of improper targeting of the Santeria religion, the choice of these words is support for our conclusion. There are further respects in which the text of the city council's enactments discloses the improper attempt to target Santeria. Resolution 87–66, adopted June 9, 1987, recited that "residents and citizens of the City of Hialeah have expressed their concern that certain religions may propose to engage in practices which are inconsistent with public morals, peace or safety," and "reiterated" the city's commitment to prohibit "any and all [such] acts of any and all religious groups." No one suggests, and on this record it cannot be maintained, that city officials had in mind a religion other than Santeria.

. . .

It is a necessary conclusion that almost the only conduct subject to Ordinances 87–40, 87–52, and 87–71 is the religious exercise of Santeria church members. The texts show that they were drafted in tandem to achieve this result. We begin with Ordinance 87–71. It prohibits the sacrifice of animals but defines sacrifice as "to unnecessarily kill . . . an animal in a public or private ritual or ceremony not for the primary purpose of food consumption." The definition excludes almost all killings of animals except for religious sacrifice, and the primary purpose requirement narrows the proscribed category even further, in particular by exempting Kosher slaughter. We need not discuss whether this differential treatment of two religions is itself an independent constitutional violation. It suffices to recite this feature of the law as support for our conclusion that Santeria alone was the exclusive legislative concern. The net result of the gerrymander is that few if any killings of animals are prohibited other than Santeria sacrifice, which is proscribed because it occurs during a ritual or ceremony and its primary purpose is to make an offering to the orishas, not food consumption. Indeed, careful drafting ensured that, although Santeria sacrifice is prohibited, killings that are no more necessary or humane in almost all other circumstances are unpunished.

Operating in similar fashion is Ordinance

87–52, which prohibits the "possession, sacrifice, or slaughter" of an animal with the "intent to use such animal for food purposes." This prohibition, extending to the keeping of an animal as well as the killing itself, applies if the animal is killed in "any type of ritual" and there is an intent to use the animal for food, whether or not it is in fact consumed for food. The ordinance exempts, however, "any licensed [food] establishment" with regard to "any animals which are specifically raised for food purposes," if the activity is permitted by zoning and other laws. This exception, too, seems intended to cover Kosher slaughter. Again, the burden of the ordinance, in practical terms, falls on Santeria adherents but almost no others: If the killing is—unlike most Santeria sacrifices—unaccompanied by the intent to use the animal for food, then it is not prohibited by Ordinance 87–52; if the killing is specifically for food but does not occur during the course of "any type of ritual," it again falls outside the prohibition; and if the killing is for food and occurs during the course of a ritual, it is still exempted if it occurs in a properly zoned and licensed establishment and involves animals "specifically raised for food purposes." A pattern of exemptions parallels the pattern of narrow prohibitions. Each contributes to the gerrymander.

Ordinance 87–40 incorporates the Florida animal cruelty statute. Its prohibition is broad on its face, punishing "whoever . . . unnecessarily . . . kills any animal." The city claims that this ordinance is the epitome of a neutral prohibition. The problem, however, is the interpretation given to the ordinance by respondent and the Florida attorney general. Killings for religious reasons are deemed unnecessary, whereas most other killings fall outside the prohibition. The city, on what seems to be a per se basis, deems hunting, slaughter of animals for food, eradication of insects and pests, and euthanasia as necessary. There is no indication in the record that respondent has concluded that hunting or fishing for sport is unnecessary. Indeed, one of the few reported Florida cases decided under § 828.12 concludes that the use of live rabbits to train greyhounds is not unnecessary. Further, because it requires an evaluation of the particular justification for the killing, this ordinance represents a system of "individualized governmental assessment of the reasons for the relevant conduct," As we noted in Smith, in circumstances in which individualized exemptions from a general requirement are available, the government "may not refuse to extend that system to cases of 'religious hardship' without compelling reason." Respondent's application of the ordinance's test of necessity devalues religious reasons for killing by judging them to be of lesser import than nonreligious reasons. Thus, religious practice is being singled out for discriminatory treatment.

The legitimate governmental interests in protecting the public health and preventing cruelty to animals could be addressed by restrictions stopping far short of a flat prohibition of all Santeria sacrificial practice.' If improper disposal, not the sacrifice itself, is the harm to be prevented, the city could have imposed a general regulation on the disposal of organic garbage. It did not do so. Indeed, counsel for the city conceded at oral argument that, under the ordinances, Santeria sacrifices would be illegal even if they occurred in licensed, inspected, and zoned slaughterhouses. Thus, these broad ordinances prohibit Santeria sacrifice even when it does not threaten the city's interest in the public health. The District Court accepted the argument that narrower regulation would be unenforceable because of the secrecy in the Santeria rituals and the lack of any central religious authority to require compliance with secular disposal regulations. It is difficult to understand, however, how a prohibition of the sacrifices themselves, which occur in private, is enforceable if a ban on improper disposal, which occurs in public, is not. The neutrality of a law is suspect if First Amendment freedoms are curtailed to prevent isolated collateral harms not themselves prohibited by direct regulation.

Under similar analysis, narrower regulation would achieve the city's interest in preventing cruelty to animals. With regard to the city's interest in ensuring the adequate care of animals, regulation of conditions and treatment, regardless of why an animal is kept, is the logical response to the city's concern, not a prohibition on possession for the purpose of sacrifice. The same is true for the city's interest in prohibiting cruel methods of killing. Under federal and Florida law and Ordinance 87–40, which incorporates Florida law in this regard, killing an animal by the "simultaneous and instantaneous severance of the carotid arteries with a sharp instrument"—the method used in Kosher slaughter—is approved as humane. Ordinance 87–40, § 1. The District Court found that, though Santeria sacrifice also results in severance of the carotid arteries, the method used during sacrifice is less reliable and therefore not humane. If the city has a real concern that other methods are less humane, however, the subject of the regulation should be the method of slaughter itself, not a religious classification that is said to bear some general relation to it.

. . .

2

That the ordinances were enacted "'because of,' not merely 'in spite of,'" their suppression of Santeria religious practice, is revealed by the events preceding enactment of the ordinances. Although respondent claimed at oral argument that it had experienced significant problems resulting from the sacrifice of animals within the city before the announced opening of the Church, the city council made no attempt to address the supposed problem before its meeting in June 1987, just weeks after the Church announced plans to open. The minutes and taped excerpts of the June 9 session, both of which are in the record, evidence significant hostility exhibited by residents, members of the city council, and other city officials toward the Santeria religion and its practice of animal sacrifice. The public crowd that attended the June 9 meetings interrupted statements by council members critical of Santeria with cheers and the brief comments of Pichardo with taunts. When Councilman Martinez, a supporter of the ordinances, stated that in prerevolution Cuba "people were put in jail for practicing this religion," the audience applauded.

Other statements by members of the city council were in a similar vein. . . .

Various Hialeah city officials made comparable comments. . . . The city attorney commented that . . . "This community will not tolerate religious practices which are abhorrent to its citizens. . . . " Similar comments were made by the deputy city attorney. This history discloses the object of the ordinances to target animal sacrifice by Santeria worshippers because of its religious motivation.

3

In sum, the neutrality inquiry leads to one conclusion: The ordinances had as their object the suppression of religion. The pattern we have recited discloses animosity to Santeria adherents and their religious practices; the ordinances by their own terms target this religious exercise; the texts of the ordinances were gerrymandered with care to proscribe religious killings of animals but to exclude almost all secular killings; and the ordinances suppress much more religious conduct than is necessary in order to achieve the legitimate ends asserted in their defense. These ordinances are not neutral, and the court below committed clear error in failing to reach this conclusion.

B

We turn next to a second requirement of the Free Exercise Clause, the rule that laws burdening religious practice must be of general applicability. . . .

The principle that government, in pursuit of legitimate interests, cannot in a selective manner impose burdens only on conduct motivated by religious belief is essential to the protection of the rights guaranteed by the Free Exercise Clause. . . .

Respondent claims that Ordinances 87–40, 87–52, and 87–71 advance two interests: protecting the public health and preventing cruelty to animals. The ordinances are un-

derinclusive for those ends. They fail to prohibit non-religious conduct that endangers these interests in a similar or greater degree than Santeria sacrifice does. The underinclusion is substantial, not inconsequential. Despite the city's proffered interest in preventing cruelty to animals, the ordinances are drafted with care to forbid few killings but those occasioned by religious sacrifice. Many types of animal deaths or kills for nonreligious reasons are either not prohibited or approved by express provision. For example, fishing—which occurs in Hialeah,—is legal. Extermination of mice and rats within a home is also permitted. Florida law incorporated by Ordinance 87–40 sanctions euthanasia of "stray, neglected, abandoned, or unwanted animals," destruction of animals judicially removed from their owners "for humanitarian reasons" or when the animal "is of no commercial value;" the infliction of pain or suffering "in the interest of medical science;" the placing of poison in one's yard or enclosure and the use of a live animal "to pursue or take wildlife or to participate in any hunting," and "to hunt wild hogs."

The city concedes that "neither the State of Florida nor the City has enacted a generally applicable ban on the killing of animals." It asserts, however, that animal sacrifice is "different" from the animal killings that are permitted by law. According to the city, it is "self-evident" that killing animals for food is "important"; the eradication of insects and pests is "obviously justified"; and the euthanasia of excess animals "makes sense." These ipse dixits do not explain why religion alone must bear the burden of the ordinances, when many of these secular killings fall within the city's interest in preventing the cruel treatment of animals.

The ordinances are also underinclusive with regard to the city's interest in public health, which is threatened by the disposal of animal carcasses in open public places and the consumption of uninspected meat. Neither interest is pursued by respondent with regard to conduct that is not motivated by religious conviction. The health risks posed by the improper disposal of animal carcasses are the same whether Santeria sacrifice or some nonreligious killing preceded it. The city does not, however, prohibit hunters from bringing their kill to their houses, nor does it regulate disposal after their activity. Despite substantial testimony at trial that the same public health hazards result from improper disposal of garbage by restaurants, restaurants are outside the scope of the ordinances. Improper disposal is a general problem that causes substantial health risks, but which respondent addresses only when it results from religious exercise.

The ordinances are underinclusive as well with regard to the health risk posed by consumption of uninspected meat. Under the city's ordinances, hunters may eat their kill and fisherman may eat their catch without undergoing governmental inspection. Likewise, state law requires inspection of meat that is sold but exempts meat from animals raised for the use of the owner and "members of his household and nonpaying guests and employees." The asserted interest in inspected meat is not pursued in contexts similar to that of religious animal sacrifice.

Ordinance 87–72, which prohibits the slaughter of animals outside of areas zoned for slaughterhouses, is underinclusive on its face. The ordinance includes an exemption for "any person, group, or organization" that "slaughters or processes for sale, small numbers of hogs and/or cattle per week in accordance with an exemption provided by state law." Respondent has not explained why commercial operations that slaughter "small numbers" of hogs and cattle do not implicate its professed desire to prevent cruelty to animals and preserve the public health. Although the city has classified Santeria sacrifice as slaughter, subjecting it to this ordinance, it does not regulate other killings for food in like manner.

We conclude, in sum, that each of Hialeah's ordinances pursues the city's governmental interests only against conduct motivated by religious belief. The ordinances "have every appearance of a prohibition that society is prepared to impose upon [Santeria worshippers] but not upon itself." This precise evil is what the requirement of general applicability is designed to prevent.

III

A law burdening religious practice that is not neutral or not of general application must undergo the most rigorous of scrutiny. To satisfy the commands of the First Amendment, a law restrictive of religious practice must advance "'interests of the highest order'" and must be narrowly tailored in pursuit of those interests. . . . A law that targets religious conduct for distinctive treatment or advances legitimate governmental interests only against conduct with a religious motivation will survive strict scrutiny only in rare cases. It follows from what we have already said that these ordinances cannot withstand this scrutiny.

First, even were the governmental interests compelling, the ordinances are not drawn in narrow terms to accomplish those interests. . . .

Respondent has not demonstrated, moreover, that, in the context of these ordinances, its governmental interests are compelling. Where government restricts only conduct protected by the First Amendment and fails to enact feasible measures to restrict other conduct producing substantial harm or alleged harm of the same sort, the interest given in justification of the restriction is not compelling. . . .

The Free Exercise Clause commits government itself to religious tolerance, and upon even slight suspicion that proposals for state intervention stem from animosity to religion or distrust of its practices, all officials must pause to remember their own high duty to the Constitution and to the rights it secures. Those in office must be resolute in resisting importunate demands and must ensure that the sole reasons for imposing the burdens of law and regulation are secular. Legislators may not devise mechanisms, overt or disguised, designed to persecute or oppress a religion or its practices. The laws here in question were enacted contrary to these constitutional principles, and they are void.

Reversed.

JUSTICE SCALIA, with whom THE CHIEF JUSTICE joins, concurring in part and concurring in the judgment.

. . .

The terms "neutrality" and "general applicability" are not to be found within the First Amendment itself, of course, but are used . . . to describe those characteristics which cause a law that prohibits an activity a particular individual wishes to engage in for religious reasons nonetheless not to constitute a "law . . . prohibiting the free exercise" of religion within the meaning of the First Amendment. In my view, the defect of lack of neutrality applies primarily to those laws that by their terms impose disabilities on the basis of religion (e. g., a law excluding members of a certain sect from public benefits,); whereas the defect of lack of general applicability applies primarily to those laws which, though neutral in their terms, through their design, construction, or enforcement target the practices of a particular religion for discriminatory treatment, But certainly a law that is not of general applicability (in the sense I have described) can be considered "nonneutral"; and certainly no law that is nonneutral (in the relevant sense) can be thought to be of general applicability. Because I agree with most of the invalidating factors set forth in Part II of the Court's opinion, and because it seems to me a matter of no consequence under which rubric ("neutrality," Part II-A, or "general applicability," Part II-B) each invalidating factor is discussed, I join the judgment of the Court and all of its opinion except section 2 of Part II-A.

I do not join that section because it departs from the opinion's general focus on the object of the laws at issue to consider the subjective motivation of the lawmakers, i.e., whether the Hialeah City Council actually intended to disfavor the religion of Santeria. As I have noted elsewhere, it is virtually impossible to determine the singular "motive" of a collective legislative body, see, e. g., *Edwards v. Aguillard*, and this Court has a long tradition of refraining from such inquiries.

Perhaps there are contexts in which determination of legislative motive must be undertaken. But I do not think that is true of analysis under the First Amendment (or the Fourteenth, to the extent it incorporates the First). The First Amendment does not refer to the purposes for which legislators enact laws, but to the effects of the laws enacted: "Congress shall make no law . . . prohibiting the free exercise [of religion]. . . ." This does not put us in the business of invalidating laws by reason of the evil motives of their authors. Had the Hialeah City Council set out resolutely to suppress the practices of Santeria, but ineptly adopted ordinances that failed to do so, I do not see how those laws could be said to "prohibit the free exercise" of religion. Nor, in my view, does it matter that a legislature consists entirely of the pure-hearted, if the law it enacts in fact singles out a religious practice for special burdens. Had the ordinances here been passed with no motive on the part of any councilman except the ardent desire to prevent cruelty to animals (as might in fact have been the case), they would nonetheless be invalid.

JUSTICE SOUTER, concurring in part and concurring in the judgment.

This case turns on a principle about which there is no disagreement, that the Free Exercise Clause bars government action aimed at suppressing religious belief or practice. The Court holds that Hialeah's animal-sacrifice laws violate that principle, and I concur in that holding without reservation.

. . . I write separately to explain why the *Smith* rule is not germane to this case and to express my view that, in a case presenting the issue, the Court should re-examine the rule Smith declared.

· · ·

II

· · ·

B

The *Smith* rule, in my view, may be reexamined consistently with principles of stare decisis. To begin with, the *Smith* rule was not subject to "full-dress argument" prior to its announcement. The State of Oregon in *Smith* contended that its refusal to exempt religious peyote use survived the strict scrutiny required by "settled free exercise principles," inasmuch as the State had "a compelling interest in regulating" the practice of peyote use and could not "accommodate the religious practice without compromising its interest." Respondents joined issue on the outcome of strict scrutiny on the facts before the Court, and neither party squarely addressed the proposition the Court was to embrace, that the Free Exercise Clause was irrelevant to the dispute. Sound judicial decisionmaking requires "both a vigorous prosecution and a vigorous defense" of the issues in dispute.

The *Smith* rule's vitality as precedent is limited further by the seeming want of any need of it in resolving the question presented in that case. JUSTICE O'CONNOR reached the same result as the majority by applying, as the parties had requested, "our established free exercise jurisprudence," and the majority never determined that the case could not be resolved on the narrower ground, going instead straight to the broader constitutional rule. But the Court's better practice, one supported by the same principles of restraint that underlie the rule of stare decisis, is not to " 'formulate a rule of constitutional law broader than is required by the precise facts to which it is to be applied.' " While I am not suggesting that the *Smith* Court lacked the power to announce its rule, I think a rule of law unnecessary to the outcome of a case, especially one not put into play by the parties, approaches without more the sort of "dicta . . . which may be followed if sufficiently persuasive but which are not controlling."

I do not, of course, mean to imply that a broad constitutional rule announced without full briefing and argument necessarily lacks precedential weight. Over time, such a decision may become "part of the tissue of the law," and may be subject to reliance in a way that new and unexpected decisions are not. *Smith*, however, is not such a case. By the same token, by pointing out *Smith*'s recent vintage I do not mean to suggest that novelty alone is enough to justify reconsideration. "Stare decisis," as Justice Frankfurter wrote, "is a principle of policy and not a mechanical formula," and the decision whether to adhere to a prior decision, particularly a constitutional decision, is a complex and difficult one that does not lend itself to resolution by application of simple, categorical rules, but that must account for a variety of often competing considerations.

The considerations of full-briefing, necessity, and novelty thus do not exhaust the legitimate reasons for reexamining prior decisions, or even for reexamining the *Smith* rule. One important further consideration warrants mention here, however, because it demands the reexamination I have in mind. *Smith* presents not the usual question of whether to follow a constitutional rule, but the question of which constitutional rule to follow, for *Smith* refrained from overruling prior free-exercise cases that contain a free-exercise rule fundamentally at odds with the rule *Smith* declared. *Smith*, indeed, announced its rule by relying squarely upon the precedent of prior cases. Since that precedent is nonetheless at odds with the *Smith* rule, as I have discussed above, the result is an intolerable tension in free-exercise law which may be resolved, consistently with principles of stare decisis, in a case in which the tension is presented and its resolution pivotal.

While the tension on which I rely exists within the body of our extant case law, a re-reading of that case law will not, of course, mark the limits of any enquiry directed to reexamining the *Smith* rule, which should be reviewed in light not only of the precedent on which it was rested but also of the text of the Free Exercise Clause and its origins. As for text, *Smith* did not assert that the plain language of the Free Exercise Clause compelled its rule, but only that the rule was "a permissible reading" of the Clause. Suffice it to say that a respectable argument may be made that the pre-*Smith* law comes closer to fulfilling the language of the Free Exercise Clause than the rule *Smith* announced. "The Free Exercise Clause . . . , by its terms, gives special protection to the exercise of religion," specifying an activity and then flatly protecting it against government prohibition. The Clause draws no distinction between laws whose object is to prohibit religious exercise and laws with that effect, on its face seemingly applying to both.

Nor did *Smith* consider the original meaning of the Free Exercise Clause, though overlooking the opportunity was no unique transgression. Save in a handful of passing remarks, the Court has not explored the history of the Clause since its early attempts in 1879 and 1890, attempts that recent scholarship makes clear were incomplete. The curious absence of history from our free-exercise decisions creates a stark contrast with our cases under the Establishment Clause, where historical analysis has been so prominent.

This is not the place to explore the history that a century of free-exercise opinions have overlooked, and it is enough to note that, when the opportunity to reexamine *Smith* presents itself, we may consider recent scholarship raising serious questions about the *Smith* rule's consonance with the original understanding and purpose of the Free Exercise Clause. There appears to be a strong argument from the Clause's development in the First Congress, from its origins in the post-Revolution state constitutions and pre-Revolution colonial charters, and from the philosophy of rights to which the Framers adhered, that the Clause was originally understood to preserve a right to engage in activities necessary to fulfill one's duty to one's God, unless those activities threatened the rights of others or the serious needs of the State. If, as this scholarship suggests, the Free Exercise Clause's original "purpose [was] to secure religious liberty in the individual by prohibiting any invasions thereof by civil authority," then there would be powerful reason to interpret the Clause to accord with its natural reading, as applying to all laws prohibiting religious exercise in fact, not just those aimed at its prohibition, and to hold the neutrality needed to implement such a purpose

to be the substantive neutrality of our pre-*Smith* cases, not the formal neutrality sufficient for constitutionality under Smith.

The scholarship on the original understanding of the Free Exercise Clause is, to be sure, not uniform. And there are differences of opinion as to the weight appropriately accorded original meaning. But whether or not one considers the original designs of the Clause binding, the interpretive significance of those designs surely ranks in the hierarchy of issues to be explored in resolving the tension inherent in free-exercise law as it stands today.

. . .

JUSTICE BLACKMUN, with whom JUSTICE O'CONNOR joins, concurring in the judgment.

The Court holds today that the city of Hialeah violated the First and Fourteenth Amendments when it passed a set of restrictive ordinances explicitly directed at petitioners' religious practice. With this holding I agree. I write separately to emphasize that the First Amendment's protection of religion extends beyond those rare occasions on which the government explicitly targets religion (or a particular religion) for disfavored treatment, as is done in this case. In my view, a statute that burdens the free exercise of religion "may stand only if the law in general, and the State's refusal to allow a religious exemption in particular, are justified by a compelling interest that cannot be served by less restrictive means." . . . I continue to believe that Smith was wrongly decided, because it ignored the value of religious freedom as an affirmative individual liberty and treated the Free Exercise Clause as no more than an antidiscrimination principle. Thus, while I agree with the result the Court reaches in this case, I arrive at that result by a different route.

. . .

In this case, the ordinances at issue are both overinclusive and underinclusive in relation to the state interests they purportedly serve. They are overinclusive, as the majority correctly explains, because the "legitimate governmental interests in protecting the public health and preventing cruelty to animals could be addressed by restrictions stopping far short of a flat prohibition of all Santeria sacrificial practice." They are underinclusive as well, because "despite the city's proffered interest in preventing cruelty to animals, the ordinances are drafted with care to forbid few killings but those occasioned by religious sacrifice." Moreover, the "ordinances are also underinclusive with regard to the city's interest in public health. . . . "

When a law discriminates against religion as such, as do the ordinances in this case, it automatically will fail strict scrutiny under *Sherbert v. Verner*. This is true because a law that targets religious practice for disfavored treatment both burdens the free exercise of religion and, by definition, is not precisely tailored to a compelling governmental interest.

Thus, unlike the majority, I do not believe that "[a] law burdening religious practice that is not neutral or not of general application must undergo the most rigorous of scrutiny." In my view, regulation that targets religion in this way, ipso facto, fails strict scrutiny. It is for this reason that a statute that explicitly restricts religious practices violates the First Amendment. Otherwise, however, "the First Amendment . . . does not distinguish between laws that are generally applicable and laws that target particular religious practices."

It is only in the rare case that a state or local legislature will enact a law directly burdening religious practice as such. Because the respondent here does single out religion in this way, the present case is an easy one to decide.

A harder case would be presented if petitioners were requesting an exemption from a generally applicable anticruelty law. The result in the case before the Court today, and the fact that every Member of the Court concurs in that result, does not necessarily reflect this Court's views of the strength of a State's interest in prohibiting cruelty to animals. This case does not present, and I therefore decline to reach, the question whether the Free Exercise Clause would require a religious exemption from a law that sincerely pursued the goal of protecting animals from cruel treatment. The number of organizations that have filed amicus briefs on behalf of this interest, however, demonstrates that it is not a concern to be treated lightly.

DEL: Although much less convoluted than establishment clause analysis, the Court's recent exercise clause efforts are a source of confoundment. Its abandonment of strict scrutiny across a significant spectrum of exercise clause claims is mystifying. Responding to the realities of cultural pluralism, the Court concludes that the society cannot "afford the luxury" of presuming the invalidity of every regulation that does not promote a compelling interest.[349] Confronted with the phenomenon of diversity, the Court's reaction seems to be a somewhat paranoid demand for conformity. It thus warns of a parade of horribles that strict scrutiny would license—notwithstanding an absence of any overwhelming demand for exemption from "civil obligations of almost every conceivable kind"[350] over the history of such review. To the contrary, the analytical pains which the Court suffered in stressing the legitimacy of Amish religion and concerns in *Yoder* (and its rejection of the same group's interests in *Lee*) suggests an institution unlikely to put itself in the role of presiding over floodgates. Avoidance of such risk without derogating constitutional interests, however, must be achieved by strict scrutiny that honestly factors competing concerns rather than by wholesale riddance of much state action from meaningful review.

RLW: The Court has placed much less emphasis on the exercise clause than the establishment clause. Despite decisions like *Yoder*, the Court has generally been unsympathetic to exercise claims. *Smith* is typical of the Court's attitude.

DER: The Court's free exercise analysis suffers from the same malady that plagues its recent equal protection and free expression decisions—an unwillingness to unsettle the status quo in order to protect the interests of minority groups and viewpoints. By deferring to states' assertion of an interest in uniform enforcement of statutes, the Court gives little weight to the expressive and political value of religious practices. While the Court generally has failed to *require* states to grant exemptions to religious observers, it has carved out a "zone of permissible accommodation."[351] Thus, in a number of cases the Court has noted that the establishment clause does not forbid Congress and state legislatures from facilitating certain religious practices, although the free exercise clause does not mandate special treatment.

---

[349] Employment Division, Department of Human Resources of Oregon, 494 U.S., 872, 888 (1990).

[350] *Id.*

[351] Laurence Tribe, American Constitutional Law 1194 (2d ed. 1988).

PART VI

LITIGATIVE PREREQUISITES

In *Marbury v. Madison*, Chief Justice Marshall boldly characterized the judiciary's authority: "it is emphatically the province and duty of the judicial department to say what the law is." Despite Marshall's sweeping declaration, the judicial power has always been subject to limitations. Some of these limitations are constitutionally imposed. Others are imposed by the court itself. In this chapter, we explore jurisdictional prerequisites to judicial intervention.

A. Congressional Control of Judicial Power

Article III of the Constitution establishes the judiciary, and imposes limitations on the scope of judicial authority. Article III, § 2, Cl. 2 gives the Supreme Court original jurisdiction over cases involving "Ambassadors, other Public Ministers and Consuls, and those in which a State shall be a Party," and also gives the Court appellate jurisdiction "with such Exceptions, and under such Regulations as the Congress shall make." Given that most cases arrive at the Court by appeal, Congress' control over the Court's appellate jurisdiction creates the potential for abuse.

Ex Parte McCardle
74 U.S. 506 (1868)

[McCardle was charged with libel, and various other offenses, for publishing newspaper articles about the post-Civil War military government in Mississippi. McCardle sought a writ of habeas corpus from a federal court, but the writ was denied. McCardle appealed to the U.S. Supreme Court. While the case was pending, Congress passed an act repealing the Court's jurisdiction over the case.]

The CHIEF JUSTICE delivered the opinion of the court.

The first question necessarily is that of jurisdiction; for, if the act of March, 1868, takes away the jurisdiction defined by the act of February, 1867, it is useless, if not improper, to enter into any discussion of other questions.

It is quite true, as was argued by the counsel for the petitioner, that the appellate jurisdiction of this court is not derived from acts of Congress. It is, strictly speaking, conferred by the Constitution. But it is conferred "with such exceptions and under such regulations as Congress shall make."

It is unnecessary to consider whether, if Congress had made no exceptions and no regulations, this court might not have exercised general appellate jurisdiction under rules prescribed by itself. For among the earliest acts of the first Congress, at its first session, was the act of September 24th, 1789, to establish the judicial courts of the United States. That act provided for the organization of this court, and prescribed regulations for the exercise of its jurisdiction.

The source of that jurisdiction, and the limitations of it by the Constitution and by statute, have been on several occasions subjects of consideration here. In the case of *Durousseau v. The United States** particularly, the whole matter was carefully examined, and the court held, that while "the appellate powers of this court are not given by the judicial act, but are given by the Constitution," they are, nevertheless, "limited and regulated by that act, and by such other acts as have been passed on the subject." The court said, further, that the judicial act was an exercise of the power given by the Constitution to Congress "of making exceptions to the appellate jurisdiction of the Supreme Court." "They have described affirmatively," said the court, "its jurisdiction, and this affirmative description has been understood to imply a negation of the exercise of such appellate power as is not comprehended within it."

---

* Cranch, 312; Wiscart v. Dauchy, 3 Dallas, 321.

The principle that the affirmation of appellate jurisdiction implies the negation of all such jurisdiction not affirmed having been thus established, it was an almost necessary consequence that acts of Congress, providing for the exercise of jurisdiction, should come to be spoken of as acts granting jurisdiction, and not as acts making exceptions to the constitutional grant of it.

The exception to appellate jurisdiction in the case before us, however, is not an inference from the affirmation of other appellate jurisdiction. It is made in terms. The provision of the act of 1867, affirming the appellate jurisdiction of this court in cases of habeas corpus is expressly repealed. It is hardly possible to imagine a plainer instance of positive exception.

We are not at liberty to inquire into the motives of the legislature. We can only examine into its power under the Constitution; and the power to make exceptions to the appellate jurisdiction of this court is given by express words.

What, then, is the effect of the repealing act upon the case before us? We cannot doubt as to this. Without jurisdiction the court cannot proceed at all in any cause. Jurisdiction is power to declare the law, and when it ceases to exist, the only function remaining to the court is that of announcing the fact and dismissing the cause. And this is not less clear upon authority than upon principle.

. . .

It is quite clear, therefore, that this court cannot proceed to pronounce judgment in this case, for it has no longer jurisdiction of the appeal; and judicial duty is not less fitly performed by declining ungranted jurisdiction than in exercising firmly that which the Constitution and the laws confer.

Counsel seem to have supposed, if effect be given to the repealing act in question, that the whole appellate power of the court, in cases of habeas corpus, is denied. But this is an error. The act of 1868 does not except from that jurisdiction any cases but appeals from Circuit Courts under the act of 1867. It does not affect the jurisdiction which was previously exercised.

The appeal of the petitioner in this case must be

DISMISSED FOR WANT OF JURISDICTION.

RLW: *McCardle* seems to give Congress plenary authority over the Supreme Court's appellate jurisdiction. During the 1970s and 1980s, some congressmen tried to remove the Court's authority over controversial issues like school prayer, abortion and school busing. Whether these bills would have been constitutional is debatable. One commentator argued that, even though Congress has the authority to make "exceptions" to the Supreme Court's jurisdiction, as well as to "regulate" that jurisdiction, Congress cannot "destroy the essential role of the Supreme Court in the constitutional plan."[1] A second commentator agrees: "It is not reasonable to conclude that the Constitution gave Congress the power to destroy that role. Reasonably interpreted the clause means 'With such exceptions and under such regulations as Congress may make,' not inconsistent with the essential functions of the Supreme Court under this Constitution."[2]

At least one commentator disagrees with these assessments:

> [The] courts do not pass on constitutional questions because there is a special function vested in them to enforce the Constitution or police the other agencies of government. They do so rather for the reason that they must decide a litigated case that is otherwise within their jurisdiction and in doing so must give effect to the supreme law of the land.[3]

Which of these views is more consistent with *Marbury*? Does *Marbury* really make it "the province and duty of the judicial department to say what the law is," or does the judiciary share this authority with other branches?

---

[1] Hart, *The Power of Congress to Limit the Jurisdiction of Federal Courts*, 66 Harv. L. Rev. 1362, 1365 (1953).

[2] Ratner, *Congressional Power over the Appellate Jurisdiction of the Supreme Court*, 109 U. Pa. L. Rev. 157 (1960).

[3] Wechsler, *The Courts and the Constitution*, 65 Colum. L. Rev. 1001, 1005–06 (1965).

If the Court has an "essential role," there is disagreement regarding the scope of that role. Consider the statements of one commentator:

> The supremacy clause of article VI mandates one supreme federal law throughout the land, and Article III establishes the Supreme Court as the constitutional instrument for implementing that clause. [I]ts essential functions under the Constitution are: 1) ultimately to resolve inconsistent or conflicting interpretations of federal law, and particularly of the Constitution, by state and federal courts; 2) to maintain the supremacy of federal law, and particularly the Constitution, when it conflicts with state law or is challenged by state authority.[4]

DEL: All theory aside, it is notable that the most significant challenges to the Court's authority by the political branches have occurred when the judiciary was perceived as steering too far on one side or the other from the mainstream. Relatively contemporary threats to rein in the Court, because of controversial rulings in the areas of school prayer, abortion and busing, extend that legacy. They are reminiscent of President Roosevelt's strategy to rough up the Court for failing to play along with his New Deal initiatives and the Republican response to *Dred Scott* that effectively marginalized the Court until it regained its stature. Such clashes periodically remind the judiciary that it exists within rather than apart from the political order. Two centuries of jurisprudential output indicate that, despite some notable exceptions, the Court generally has avoided adventurism and even developed significant prudential limitations upon itself to minimize the risk of political conflict.

DER: The Supreme Court's "essential role" includes protecting the constitutional rights of dissidents and minorities whose interests are most likely to be sacrificed in state majoritarian politics. This role would be thwarted if Congress could impose state authority by stripping the Court's jurisdiction over specific controversial issues. Such might be the result if, for example, Congress passed a law depriving the Supreme Court of appellate jurisdiction in school desegregation cases. Often the Court will be seen as diverging from the mainstream if it aggressively upholds the demands of minorities for political equality against the perceived interests of dominant groups. On the other hand, if the Court itself has relinquished this role, congressional action may be required to enforce minority groups' constitutional challenges to state and private power. Ironically, the Fourteenth Amendment overruled a Supreme Court decision—*Dred Scott*—in order to extend equal protection of the laws to Black citizens. Some scholars have advocated a progressive and redistributive interpretation of the constitutional guarantees of liberty and equality as "political ideals to guide legislation, rather than as legal restraints on legislation."[5] Congressional control of judicial authority has served to override conservative Court decisions, as well as to make the Court more reluctant to enter political controversies.

---

[4] Ratner, *supra.*

[5] Robin West, *Progressive and Conservative Constitutionalism*, 88 Mich. L. Rev. 641, 715 (1990).

Just three years after the Court decided *McCardle*, the Court decided *United States v. Klein.*[6] That case involved a law authorizing the government to seize abandoned or captured property from those who had aided, countenanced and abetted the Confederacy during the war. Pursuant to this law, the U.S. Treasury Department took possession of the late V. F. Wilson's cotton, sold it, and placed the proceeds in the U.S. Treasury.

---

[6] 80 U.S. 128 (1871).

Prior to his death, Wilson had taken advantage of a presidential proclamation offering a "full pardon" with restoration of all rights to those who agreed to "take and keep inviolate a prescribed oath" to support the Constitution of the United States and the union of the States thereunder. After Wilson's death, Klein, the administrator of Wilson's estate, sued to recover proceeds from the sale of the cotton claiming that the pardon had restored Wilson's rights and property. Klein won in the Court of Claims, and the government appealed to the U.S. Supreme Court. While the appeal was pending, Congress passed a statute altering the effect of a pardon. The statute declared a presidential pardon shall not be admissible in the Court of Claims to support a claim for recovery. The statute also provided that, to the extent that the Court of Claims had ruled in favor of a claimant based on a presidential pardon:

> [T]he Supreme Court, on appeal, shall have no further jurisdiction of the cause, and shall dismiss the same for want of jurisdiction. It is further provided that whenever any pardon, granted to any suitor in the Court of Claims, for the proceeds of captured and abandoned property, shall recite in substance that the person pardoned took part in the late rebellion, or was guilty of any act of rebellion or disloyalty, and shall have been accepted in writing without express disclaimer and protestation against the fact so recited, such pardon or acceptance shall be taken as conclusive evidence in the Court of Claims, and on appeal, that the claimant did give aid to the rebellion; and on proof of such pardon, or acceptance, which proof may be made summarily on motion or otherwise, the jurisdiction of the court shall cease, and the suit shall be forthwith dismissed.

Based on this statute, the government moved to dismiss the appeal. The Supreme Court ruled the act unconstitutional, and refused to apply it:

> [T]he language of the proviso shows plainly that it does not intend to withhold appellate jurisdiction except as a means to an end. Its great and controlling purpose is to deny to pardons granted by the President the effect which this court had adjudged them to have. The proviso declares that pardons shall not be considered by this court on appeal. We had already decided that it was our duty to consider them and give them effect, in cases like the present, as equivalent to proof of loyalty. . . .
>
> . . .
>
> It seems to us that this is not an exercise of the acknowledged power of Congress to make exceptions and prescribe regulations to the appellate power.
>
> The court is required to ascertain the existence of certain facts and thereupon to declare that its jurisdiction on appeal has ceased, by dismissing the bill. What is this but to prescribe a rule for the decision of a cause in a particular way? In the case before us, the Court of Claims has rendered judgment for the claimant and an appeal has been taken to this court. We are directed to dismiss the appeal, if we find that the judgment must be affirmed, because of a pardon granted to the intestate of the claimants. Can we do so without allowing one party to the controversy to decide it in its own favor? Can we do so without allowing that the legislature may prescribe rules of decision to the Judicial Department of the government in cases pending before it? We think not. . . .
>
> We must think that Congress has inadvertently passed the limit which separates the legislative from the judicial power.
>
> It is of vital importance that these powers be kept distinct. The Constitution provides that the judicial power of the United States shall be vested in one Supreme Court and such inferior courts as the Congress shall from time to

time ordain and establish. The same instrument, in the last clause of the same article, provides that in all cases other than those of original jurisdiction, "the Supreme Court shall have appellate jurisdiction both as to law and fact, with such exceptions and under such regulations as the Congress shall make."

Congress has already provided that the Supreme Court shall have jurisdiction of the judgments of the Court of Claims on appeal. Can it prescribe a rule in conformity with which the court must deny to itself the jurisdiction thus conferred, because and only because its decision, in accordance with settled law, must be adverse to the government and favorable to the suitor? This question seems to us to answer itself.

See also Ex Parte Yerger.[7]

---

[7] 75 U.S. (8 Wall.) 75 (1869).

RLW: In light of *Klein*, many question whether *McCardle* retains vitality. Consider *Glidden v. Zdanok*: "There is serious question whether the *McCardle* case could command a majority view today."[8] Consider also Robert Bork's comments: *"McCardle* is a rather enigmatic precedent. If it stands for the proposition that Congress may take away any category of the Supreme Court's jurisdiction, it obviously is capable of destroying the entire institution of judicial review since *Marbury v. Madison*. So read, there is good reason to doubt McCardle's vitality as a precedent today."[9]

Another limitation on the judiciary's power is contained in Article III, § 1, which authorizes creation of the lower federal courts: "The judicial Power of the United States, shall be vested in one supreme Court, and in such inferior Courts as the Congress may from time to time ordain and establish." Since Congress has the power to "ordain and establish" inferior federal courts, it also has the power to abolish them as well as to limit their jurisdiction.[10]

May Congress strip the lower federal courts of their jurisdiction over an issue (*e.g.*, school prayer), and simultaneously strip the Supreme Court of its appellate jurisdiction over that issue? Senator Jesse Helms of North Carolina introduced the following bill in 1985:

> The Supreme Court shall not have jurisdiction to review, by appeal, writ of certiorari, or otherwise, any case arising out of any State statute, ordinance, rule, regulation, practice, or any part thereof, which relates to voluntary prayer, Bible reading, or religious meetings in public schools or public buildings.
>
> Notwithstanding any other provision of law, the district courts shall not have jurisdiction of any case or question which the Supreme Court does not have jurisdiction to review [under this law].

If this bill had passed, would it have been constitutional? Consider the views of one commentator: "To remove or permit the removal from the entire federal judiciary, including the Supreme Court, of the constitutional review of state conduct would be to alter the balance of federal authority fundamentally and dangerously."[11]

---

[8] 370 U.S. 530, 605 n.11 (1962) (Douglas, J., dissenting).

[9] ROBERT BORK, CONSTITUTIONALITY OF THE PRESIDENT'S BUSING PROPOSALS 7 (1972).

[10] *See Yakus v. United States*, 321 U.S. 414 (1944); *Lockerty v. Phillips*, 319 U.S. 182 (1943); *Sheldon v. Sill*, 49 U.S. (8 How.) 441 (1850).

[11] Sager, *Foreword: Constitutional Limitations on Congress' Authority to Regulate the Jurisdiction of the Federal Courts*, 95 HARV. L. REV. 17, 55 (1981).

DEL: The perils of judicial overreaching tend to reflect a concern that is more academic than real. With a few notable exceptions over the course of two centuries, constitutional jurisprudence is notable for its deference to rather than challenges of the established order. When the political branches have perceived the Court as too far ahead or behind the general culture, as with the New Deal in the 1930s or desegregation in the 1970s, the Court eventually receives the message as a function of new personnel or realization that its role otherwise will be marginalized. The possibility that Congress actually might move to disable the Court has been avoided in large part by the judiciary's inherent conservatism and normative disinclination to cross lines that the political branches have drawn in the sand. The relatively few exceptions to the rule, such as the desegregation mandate in 1954 and economic rights doctrine earlier this century, prove the point.

DER: The danger raised by congressional control of federal court jurisdiction often is not judicial overreaching but congressional overreaching. Despite the federal courts' conservative tendencies, we should be concerned about the power of an even more conservative Congress to undo the Court's rare attempts to dismantle unjust social arrangements. At the same time, the exceptional nature of these attempts reminds us that social change is more likely to be accomplished through political battles and social movements than by litigation before the courts.

B. Political Question Doctrine

Even though a case fits ostensibly within the Court's original or appellate jurisdiction, the Court might refuse to hear the case if it presents a "political" question. The Court has had difficulty determining what constitutes a political question.

Baker v. Carr
369 U.S. 186 (1962)

[Tennessee's General Assembly failed to reapportion its legislative districts between 1901 and 1961 even though the population of some districts changed dramatically during this period.

Because of this failure, the state's electoral districts became so badly malapportioned that a single vote in Moore County, Tennessee, was worth 19 votes in Hamilton County, and one vote in Stewart or Chester County was worth nearly eight votes in Shelby or Knox County. Although reapportionment measures were introduced in the legislature during the intervening years, they were always defeated.]

Mr. Justice BRENNAN delivered the opinion of the Court.

. . .

In holding that the subject matter of this suit was not justiciable, the District Court relied on *Colegrove v. Green, supra,* and subsequent per curiam cases [holding that] the federal courts . . . will not intervene . . . to compel legislative reapportionment. We understand the District Court to have read the cited cases as compelling the conclusion that since the ap-

pellants sought to have a legislative apportionment held unconstitutional, their suit presented a "political question" and was therefore nonjusticiable. We hold that this challenge to an apportionment presents no nonjusticiable "political question." The cited cases do not hold the contrary.

Of course the mere fact that the suit seeks protection of a political right does not mean it presents a political question. Such an objection "is little more than a play upon words." *Nixon v. Herndon,* 273 U.S. 536, 540. Rather, it is argued that apportionment cases, whatever the actual wording of the complaint, can involve no federal constitutional right except one resting on the guaranty of a republican form of government,[30] and that complaints based on that

---

[30] "The United States shall guarantee to every State in this Union a Republican Form of Government, and shall protect each of them against Invasion; and on Application of the Legislature, or of the Executive (when the Legislature cannot be convened) against domestic Violence." U.S. CONST. art. IV, § 4.

clause have been held to present political questions which are nonjusticiable.

We hold that the claim pleaded here neither rests upon nor implicates the Guaranty Clause and that its justiciability is therefore not foreclosed by our decisions of cases involving that clause. The District Court misinterpreted *Colegrove v. Green* and other decisions of this Court on which it relied. Appellants' claim that they are being denied equal protection is justiciable, and if "discrimination is sufficiently shown, the right to relief under the equal protection clause is not diminished by the fact that the discrimination relates to political rights." *Snowden v. Hughes*, 321 U.S. 1, 11. To show why we reject the argument based on the Guaranty Clause, we must examine the authorities under it. But because there appears to be some uncertainty as to why those cases did present political questions, and specifically as to whether this apportionment case is like those cases, we deem it necessary first to consider the contours of the "political question" doctrine.

Our discussion, even at the price of extending this opinion, requires review of a number of political question cases, in order to expose the attributes of the doctrine—attributes which, in various settings, diverge, combine, appear, and disappear in seeming disorderliness. Since that review is undertaken solely to demonstrate that neither singly nor collectively do these cases support a conclusion that this apportionment case is nonjusticiable, we of course do not explore their implications in other contexts. That review reveals that in the Guaranty Clause cases and in the other "political question" cases, it is the relationship between the judiciary and the coordinate branches of the Federal Government, and not the federal judiciary's relationship to the States, which gives rise to the "political question."

We have said that "In determining whether a question falls within (the political question) category, the appropriateness under our system of government of attributing finality to the action of the political departments and also the lack of satisfactory criteria for a judicial determination are dominant considerations." *Coleman v. Miller*, 307 U.S. 433, 454–455. The nonjusticiability of a political question is primarily a function of the separation of powers. Much confusion results from the capacity of the "political question" label to obscure the need for case-by-case inquiry. Deciding whether a matter has in any measure been committed by the Constitution to another branch of government, or whether the action of that branch exceeds whatever authority has been committed, is itself a delicate exercise in constitutional interpretation, and is a responsibility of this Court as ultimate interpreter of the Constitution. To demonstrate this requires

no less than to analyze representative cases and to infer from them the analytical threads that make up the political question doctrine. We shall then show that none of those threads catches this case.

Foreign relations: There are sweeping statements to the effect that all questions touching foreign relations are political questions.[31] Not only does resolution of such issues frequently turn on standards that defy judicial application, or involve the exercise of a discretion demonstrably committed to the executive or legislature; but many such questions uniquely demand single-voiced statement of the Government's views. Yet it is error to suppose that every case or controversy which touches foreign relations lies beyond judicial cognizance. Our cases in this field seem invariably to show a discriminating analysis of the particular question posed, in terms of the history of its management by the political branches, of its susceptibility to judicial handling in the light of its nature and posture in the specific case, and of the possible consequences of judicial action. For example, though a court will not ordinarily inquire whether a treaty has been terminated, since on that question "governmental action * * * must be regarded as of controlling importance," if there has been no conclusive "governmental action" then a court can construe a treaty and may find it provides the answer. Though a court will not undertake to construe a treaty in a manner inconsistent with a subsequent federal statute, no similar hesitancy obtains if the asserted clash is with state law.

While recognition of foreign governments so strongly defies judicial treatment that without executive recognition a foreign state has been called "a republic of whose existence we know nothing," and the judiciary ordinarily follows the executive as to which nation has sovereignty over disputed territory, once sovereignty over an area is politically determined and declared, courts may examine the resulting status and decide independently whether a statute applies to that area. Similarly, recognition of belligerency abroad is an executive responsibility, but if the executive proclamations fall short of an explicit answer, a court may construe them seeking, for example, to determine whether the situation is such that statutes designed to assure American neutrality have become operative. *The Three Friends*,

---

[31] *E.g.*, "The conduct of the foreign relations of our government is committed by the Constitution to the executive and legislative—'the political'—departments of the government, and the propriety of what may be done in the exercise of this political power is not subject to judicial inquiry or decision." Oetjen v. Central Leather Co., 246 U.S. 297, 302.

166 U.S. 1, 63, 66. Still again, though it is the executive that determines a person's status as representative of a foreign government, the executive's statements will be construed where necessary to determine the court's jurisdiction, *In re Baiz*, 135 U.S. 403. Similar judicial action in the absence of a recognizably authoritative executive declaration occurs in cases involving the immunity from seizure of vessels owned by friendly foreign governments.

Dates of duration of hostilities: Though it has been stated broadly that "the power which declared the necessity is the power to declare its cessation, and what the cessation requires," *Commercial Trust Co. v. Miller*, 262 U.S. 51, 57, here too analysis reveals isolatable reasons for the presence of political questions, underlying this Court's refusal to review the political departments' determination of when or whether a war has ended. Dominant is the need for finality in the political determination, for emergency's nature demands "A prompt and unhesitating obedience," *Martin v. Mott*, 12 Wheat. 19, 30 (calling up of militia). Moreover, "the cessation of hostilities does not necessarily end the war power. It was stated in *Hamilton v. Kentucky Distilleries & W. Co.*, 251 U.S. 146, 161, that the war power includes the power 'to remedy the evils which have arisen from its rise and progress' and continues during that emergency. *Stewart v. Kahn*, 11 Wall. 493, 507." *Fleming v. Mohawk Wrecking Co.*, 331 U.S. 111, 116. But deference rests on reason, not habit. The question in a particular case may not seriously implicate considerations of finality—e.g., a public program of importance (rent control) yet not central to the emergency effort. Further, clearly definable criteria for decision may be available. In such case the political question barrier falls away: "(A) Court is not at liberty to shut its eyes to an obvious mistake, when the validity of the law depends upon the truth of what is declared. * * * (It can) inquire whether the exigency still existed upon which the continued operation of the law depended." *Chastleton Corp. v. Sinclair*, 264 U.S. 543, 547–548. On the other hand, even in private litigation which directly implicates no feature of separation of powers, lack of judicially discoverable standards and the drive for evenhanded application may impel reference to the political departments' determination of dates of hostilities' beginning and ending. The Protector, 12 Wall. 700.

Validity of enactments: In *Coleman v. Miller*, *supra*, this Court held that the questions of how long a proposed amendment to the Federal Constitution remained open to ratification, and what effect a prior rejection had on a subsequent ratification, were committed to congressional resolution and involved criteria of decision that necessarily escaped the judicial grasp. Similar considerations apply to the enacting process: "The respect due to coequal and independent departments," and the need for finality and certainty about the status of a statute contribute to judicial reluctance to inquire whether, as passed, it complied with all requisite formalities. *Field v. Clark*, 143 U.S. 649, 672, 676–677. But it is not true that courts will never delve into a legislature's records upon such a quest. If the enrolled statute lacks an effective date, a court will not hesitate to seek it in the legislative journals in order to preserve the enactment. *Gardner v. Collector*, 6 Wall. 499. The political question doctrine, a tool for maintenance of governmental order, will not be so applied as to promote only disorder.

The status of Indian tribes: This Court's deference to the political departments in determining whether Indians are recognized as a tribe, while it reflects familiar attributes of political questions, *United States v. Holliday*, 3 Wall. 407, 419, also has a unique element in that "the relation of the Indians to the United States is marked by peculiar and cardinal distinctions which exist no where else. * * * (The Indians are) domestic dependent nations * * * in a state of pupilage. Their relation to the United States resembles that of a ward to his guardian." *Cherokee Nation v. Georgia*, 5 Pet. 1, 16, 17. Yet, here too, there is no blanket rule.

While "It is for (Congress) . . . , and not for the courts, to determine when the true interests of the Indian require his release from (the) condition of tutelage . . . , it is not meant by this that Congress may bring a community or body of people within the range of this power by arbitrarily calling them an Indian tribe. . . ." *United States v. Sandoval*, 231 U.S. 28, 46. Able to discern what is "distinctly Indian," the courts will strike down any heedless extension of that label. They will not stand impotent before an obvious instance of a manifestly unauthorized exercise of power.

It is apparent that several formulations which vary slightly according to the settings in which the questions arise may describe a political question, although each has one or more elements which identify it as essentially a function of the separation of powers. Prominent on the surface of any case held to involve a political question is found a textually demonstrable constitutional commitment of the issue to a coordinate political department; or a lack of judicially discoverable and manageable standards for resolving it; or the impossibility of deciding without an initial policy determination of a kind clearly for nonjudicial discretion; or the impossibility of a court's undertaking independent resolution without expressing lack of the respect due coordinate branches of government; or an unusual need for unquestioning adherence to a political decision already made; or the potentiality of embarrassment from multifarious pronouncements by various departments on one question.

Unless one of these formulations is inextricable from the case at bar, there should be no dismissal for non-justiciability on the ground of a political question's presence. The doctrine of which we treat is one of "political questions," not one of "political cases." The courts cannot reject as "no law suit" a bona fide controversy as to whether some action denominated "political" exceeds constitutional authority. The cases we have reviewed show the necessity for discriminating inquiry into the precise facts and posture of the particular case, and the impossibility of resolution by any semantic cataloguing.

But it is argued that this case shares the characteristics of decisions that constitute a category not yet considered, cases concerning the Constitution's guaranty, in Art. IV, § 4, of a republican form of government. A conclusion as to whether the case at bar does present a political question cannot be confidently reached until we have considered those cases with special care. We shall discover that Guaranty Clause claims involve those elements which define a "political question," and for that reason and no other, they are nonjusticiable. In particular, we shall discover that the nonjusticiability of such claims has nothing to do with their touching upon matters of state governmental organization.

Republican form of government: Luther v. Borden, 7 How. 1, though in form simply an action for damages for trespass was, as Daniel Webster said in opening the argument for the defense, "an unusual case." The defendants, admitting an otherwise tortious breaking and entering, sought to justify their action on the ground that they were agents of the established lawful government of Rhode Island, which State was then under martial law to defend itself from active insurrection; that the plaintiff was engaged in that insurrection; and that they entered under orders to arrest the plaintiff. The case arose "out of the unfortunate political differences which agitated the people of Rhode Island in 1841 and 1842," 7 How., at 34, and which had resulted in a situation wherein two groups laid competing claims to recognition as the lawful government. The plaintiff's right to recover depended upon which of the two groups was entitled to such recognition; but the lower court's refusal to receive evidence or hear argument on that issue, its charge to the jury that the earlier established or "charter" government was lawful, and the verdict for the defendants, were affirmed upon appeal to this Court.

Chief Justice Taney's opinion for the Court reasoned as follows: (1) If a court were to hold the defendants' acts unjustified because the charter government had no legal existence during the period in question, it would follow that all of that government's actions—laws enacted, taxes collected, salaries paid, accounts settled, sentences passed—were of no effect; and that "the officers who carried their decisions into operation (were) answerable as trespassers, if not in some cases as criminals." There was, of course, no room for application of any doctrine of de facto status to uphold prior acts of an officer not authorized de jure, for such would have defeated the plaintiff's very action. A decision for the plaintiff would inevitably have produced some significant measure of chaos, a consequence to be avoided if it could be done without abnegation of the judicial duty to uphold the Constitution.

(2) No state court had recognized as a judicial responsibility settlement of the issue of the locus of state governmental authority. Indeed, the courts of Rhode Island had in several cases held that "it rested with the political power to decide whether the charter government had been displaced or not," and that that department had acknowledged no change.

(3) Since "(t)he question relates, altogether, to the constitution and laws of (the) . . . State," the courts of the United States had to follow the state courts' decisions unless there was a federal constitutional ground for overturning them.

(4) No provision of the Constitution could be or had been invoked for this purpose except Art. IV, § 4, the Guaranty Clause. Having already noted the absence of standards whereby the choice between governments could be made by a court acting independently, Chief Justice Taney now found further textual and practical reasons for concluding that, if any department of the United States was empowered by the Guaranty Clause to resolve the issue, it was not the judiciary: "Under this article of the Constitution it rests with Congress to decide what government is the established one in a State. For as the United States guarantees to each State a republican government, Congress must necessarily decide what government is established in the State before it can determine whether it is republican or not. And when the senators and representatives of a State are admitted into the councils of the Union, the authority of the government under which they are appointed, as well as its republican character, is recognized by the proper constitutional authority. And its decision is binding on every other department of the government, and could not be questioned in a judicial tribunal. It is true that the contest in this case did not last long enough to bring the matter to this issue; and . . . Congress was not called upon to decide the controversy. Yet the right to decide is placed there, and not in the courts. "So, too, as relates to the clause in the above-mentioned article of the Constitution, providing for cases of domestic violence. It rested with Congress,

adopted to fulfill this guarantee.... (B)y the act of February 28, 1795, (Congress) provided, that, 'in case of an insurrection in any State against the government thereof, it shall be lawful for the President of the United States, on application of the legislature of such State or of the executive (when the legislature cannot be convened) to call forth such number of the militia of any other State or States, as may be applied for, as he may judge sufficient to suppress such insurrection." "By this act, the power of deciding whether the exigency had arisen upon which the government of the United States is bound to interfere, is given to the President.... " After the President has acted and called out the militia, is a Circuit Court of the United States authorized to inquire whether his decision was right? ... If the judicial power extends so far, the guarantee contained in the Constitution of the United States is a guarantee of anarchy, and not of order.... It is true that in this case the militia were not called out by the President. But upon the application of the governor under the charter government, the President recognized him as the executive power of the State, and took measures to call out the militia to support his authority if it should be found necessary for the general government to interfere.... (C)ertainly no court of the United States, with a knowledge of this decision, would have been justified in recognizing the opposing party as the lawful government.... In the case of foreign nations, the government acknowledged by the President is always recognized in the courts of justice.... 7 How., at 42–44.

Clearly, several factors were thought by the Court in Luther to make the question there "political": the commitment to the other branches of the decision as to which is the lawful state government; the unambiguous action by the President, in recognizing the charter government as the lawful authority; the need for finality in the executive's decision; and the lack of criteria by which a court could determine which form of government was republican.[48]

---

[48] [T]he Court plainly implied that the political question barrier was no absolute: "Unquestionably a military government, established as the permanent government of the State, would not be a republican government, and it would be the duty of Congress to overthrow it." 7 How., at 45. Of course, it does not necessarily follow that if Congress did not act, the Court would. For while the judiciary might be able to decide the limits of the meaning of "republican form," and thus the factor of lack of criteria might fall away, there would remain other possible barriers to decision because of primary commitment to another branch, which would have to be considered in the particular fact setting presented....

But the only significance that Luther could have for our immediate purposes is in its holding that the Guaranty Clause is not a repository of judicially manageable standards which a court could utilize independently in order to identify a State's lawful government. The Court has since refused to resort to the Guaranty Clause—which alone had been invoked for the purpose—as the source of a constitutional standard for invalidating state action....

Just as the Court has consistently held that a challenge to state action based on the Guaranty Clause presents no justiciable question so has it held, and for the same reasons, that challenges to congressional action on the ground of inconsistency with that clause present no justiciable question. In *Georgia v. Stanton*, 6 Wall. 50, the State sought by an original bill to enjoin execution of the Reconstruction Acts, claiming that it already possessed "A republican State, in every political, legal, constitutional, and juridical sense," and that enforcement of the new Acts "Instead of keeping the guaranty against a forcible overthrow of its government by foreign invaders or domestic insurgents, ... is destroying that very government by force." Congress had clearly refused to recognize the republican character of the government of the suing State. It seemed to the Court that the only constitutional claim that could be presented was under the Guaranty Clause, and Congress having determined that the effects of the recent hostilities required extraordinary measures to restore governments of a republican form, this Court refused to interfere with Congress' action at the behest of a claimant relying on that very guaranty.

In only a few other cases has the Court considered Art. IV, § 4, in relation to congressional action. It has refused to pass on a claim relying on the Guaranty Clause to establish that Congress lacked power to allow the States to employ the referendum in passing on legislation redistricting for congressional seats. Ohio ex rel. *Davis v. Hildebrant, supra*. And it has pointed out that Congress is not required to establish republican government in the territories before they become States, and before they have attained a sufficient population to warrant a popularly elected legislature. *Downes v. Bidwell*, 182 U.S. 244, 278–279 (dictum).

We come, finally, to the ultimate inquiry whether our precedents as to what constitutes a nonjusticiable "political question" bring the case before us under the umbrella of that doctrine. A natural beginning is to note whether any of the common characteristics which we have been able to identify and label descriptively are present. We find none: The question here is the consistency of state action with the Federal Constitution. We have no question decided, or to be decided, by a political branch of government coequal with this Court. Nor do we risk embarrassment of our government abroad, or grave disturbance at home if we take issue with Tennessee as to the constitutionality of her action here challenged. Nor need the appellants, in order to succeed in this action, ask the Court to enter upon policy determinations for which judicially manageable standards are lacking. Judicial standards under the Equal Protection Clause are well developed and familiar, and it has been open to courts since the enactment of the Fourteenth Amendment to determine, if on the particular facts they must, that a discrimination reflects no policy, but simply arbitrary and capricious action.

This case does, in one sense, involve the allocation of political power within a State, and the appellants might conceivably have added a claim under the Guaranty Clause. Of course, as we have seen, any reliance on that clause would be futile. But because any reliance on the Guaranty Clause could not have succeeded it does not follow that appellants may not be heard on the equal protection claim which in fact they tender. True, it must be clear that the Fourteenth Amendment claim is not so enmeshed with those political question elements which render Guaranty Clause claims nonjusticiable as actually to present a political question itself. But we have found that not to be the case here.

. . .

We conclude then that the nonjusticiability of claims resting on the Guaranty Clause which arises from their embodiment of questions that were thought "political," can have no bearing upon the justiciability of the equal protection claim presented in this case. Finally, we emphasize that it is the involvement in Guaranty Clause claims of the elements thought to define "political questions," and no other feature, which could render them nonjusticiable. Specifically, we have said that such claims are not held nonjusticiable because they touch matters of state governmental organization. . . .

. . .

Since, as has been established, the equal protection claim tendered in this case does not require decision of any political question, and since the presence of a matter affecting state government does not render the case nonjusticiable, it seems appropriate to examine again the reasoning by which the District Court reached its conclusion that the case was nonjusticiable.

. . .

[C]omplainant's allegations of a denial of equal protection present a justiciable constitutional cause of action upon which appellants are entitled to a trial and a decision. The right

asserted is within the reach of judicial protection under the Fourteenth Amendment.

Mr. Justice CLARK, concurring.

. . .

Although I find the Tennessee apportionment statute offends the Equal Protection Clause, I would not consider intervention by this Court into so delicate a field if there were any other relief available to the people of Tennessee. But the majority of the people of Tennessee have no "practical opportunities for exerting their political weight at the polls" to correct the existing "invidious discrimination." Tennessee has no initiative and referendum. I have searched diligently for other "practical opportunities" present under the law. I find none other than through the federal courts. The majority of the voters have been caught up in a legislative strait jacket. Tennessee has an "informed, civically militant electorate" and "an aroused popular conscience," but it does not sear "the conscience of the people's representatives." This is because the legislative policy has riveted the present seats in the Assembly to their respective constituencies, and by the votes of their incumbents a reapportionment of any kind is prevented. The people have been rebuffed at the hands of the Assembly; they have tried the constitutional convention route, but since the call must originate in the Assembly it, too, has been fruitless. They have tried Tennessee courts with the same result, and Governors have fought the tide only to flounder. It is said that there is recourse in Congress and perhaps that may be, but from a practical standpoint this is without substance. To date Congress has never undertaken such a task in any State. We therefore must conclude that the people of Tennessee are stymied and without judicial intervention will be saddled with the present discrimination in the affairs of their state government

. . .

Finally, we must consider if there are any appropriate modes of effective judicial relief. The federal courts are of course not forums for political debate, nor should they resolve themselves into state constitutional conventions or legislative assemblies. Nor should their jurisdiction be exercised in the hope that such a declaration as is made today may have the direct effect of bringing on legislative action and relieving the courts of the problem of fashioning relief. To my mind this would be nothing less than blackjacking the Assembly into reapportioning the State. If judicial competence were lacking to fashion an effective decree, I would dismiss this appeal. However, like the Solicitor General of the United States, I see no such difficulty in the position of this case. One plan might be to start with the existing assembly districts, consolidate some of them, and award the seats thus released to those counties suffering the most egregious discrimination. Other possibilities are present and might be more effective. But the plan here suggested would at least release the stranglehold now on the Assembly and permit it to redistrict itself.

. . .

Mr. Justice FRANKFURTER, whom Mr. Justice HARLAN joins, dissenting.

. . .

In sustaining appellants' claim, based on the Fourteenth Amendment, . . . this Court's uniform course of decision over the years is overruled or disregarded. . . .

. . .

The present case involves all of the elements that have made the Guarantee Clause cases non-justiciable. It is, in effect, a Guarantee Clause claim masquerading under a different label. But it cannot make the case more fit for judicial action that appellants invoke the Fourteenth Amendment rather than Art. IV, § 4, where, in fact, the gist of their complaint is the same—unless it can be found that the Fourteenth Amendment speaks with greater particularity to their situation. We have been admonished to avoid "the tyranny of labels." *Snyder v. Massachusetts*, 291 U.S. 97, 114, Art. IV, § 4, is not committed by express constitutional terms to Congress. It is the nature of the controversies arising under it, nothing else, which has made it judicially unenforceable. Of course, if a controversy falls within judicial power, it depends "on how he (the plaintiff) casts his action," *Pan American Petroleum Corp. v. Superior Court*, 366 U.S. 656, 662, whether he brings himself within a jurisdictional statute. But where judicial competence is wanting, it cannot be created by invoking one clause of the Constitution rather than another. When what was essentially a Guarantee Clause claim was sought to be laid, as well, under the Equal Protection Clause in *Pacific States Telephone & Telegraph Co. v. Oregon, supra*, the Court had no difficulty in "dispelling any mere confusion resulting from forms of expression, and considering the substance of things . . ." 223 U.S., at 140.

. . . Accepting appellants' own formulation of the issue, one can know this handsaw from a hawk. Such a claim would be non-justiciable not merely under Art. IV, § 4, but under any clause of the Constitution, by virtue of the very fact that a federal court is not a forum for political debate. *Massachusetts v. Mellon, supra.*

But appellants, of course, do not rest on this claim simpliciter. In invoking the Equal Protection Clause, they assert that the distortion of representative government complained of is produced by systematic discrimination against them, by way of "a debasement of their votes. . . ." Does this characterization, with due regard for the facts from which it is derived, add anything to appellants' case?

. . .

Manifestly, the Equal Protection Clause supplies no clearer guide for judicial examination of apportionment methods than would the Guarantee Clause itself. Apportionment, by its character, is a subject of extraordinary complexity, involving—even after the fundamental theoretical issues concerning what is to be represented in a representative legislature have been fought out or compromised—considerations of geography, demography, electoral convenience, economic and social cohesions or divergences among particular local groups, communications, the practical effects of political institutions like the lobby and the city machine, ancient traditions and ties of settled usage, respect for proven incumbents of long experience and senior status, mathematical mechanics, censuses compiling relevant data, and a host of others. Legislative responses throughout the country to the reapportionment demands of the 1960 Census have glaringly confirmed that these are not factors that lend themselves to evaluations of a nature that are the staple of judicial determinations or for which judges are equipped to adjudicate by legal training or experience or native wit. And this is the more so true because in every strand of this complicated, intricate web of values meet the contending forces of partisan politics. The practical significance of apportionment is that the next election results may differ because of it. Apportionment battles are overwhelmingly party or intra-party contests. It will add a virulent source of friction and tension in federal-state relations to embroil the federal judiciary in them.

. . .

Appellants, however, contend that the federal courts may provide the standard which the Fourteenth Amendment lacks by reference to the provisions of the constitution of Tennessee. The argument is that although the same or greater disparities of electoral strength may be suffered to exist immune from federal judicial review in States where they result from apportionment legislation consistent with state constitutions, the Tennessee Legislature may not abridge the rights which, on its face, its own constitution appears to give, without by that act denying equal protection of the laws. It is said that the law of Tennessee, as expressed by the words of its written constitution, has made the basic choice among policies in favor of representation proportioned to population, and that it is no longer open to the State to allot its voting power on other principles.

This reasoning does not bear analysis. Like claims invoking state constitutional requirement have been rejected here and for good reason. . . .

In . . . all of the apportionment cases which have come before the Court, a consideration which has been weighty in determining their non-justiciability has been the difficulty or impossibility of devising effective judicial remedies in this class of case. An injunction restraining a general election unless the legislature reapportions would paralyze the critical centers of a State's political system and threaten political dislocation whose consequences are not foreseeable. A declaration devoid of implied compulsion of injunctive or other relief would be an idle threat. Surely a Federal District Court could not itself remap the State: the same complexities which impede effective judicial review of apportionment a fortiori make impossible a court's consideration of these imponderables as an original matter. And the choice of elections at large as opposed to elections by district, however unequal the districts, is a matter of sweeping political judgment having enormous political implications, the nature and reach of which are certainly beyond the informed understanding of, and capacity for appraisal by, courts.

. . .

Dissenting opinion of Mr. Justice HARLAN, whom Mr. Justice FRANKFURTER joins.

. . .

[W]hat lies at the core of this controversy is a difference of opinion as to the function of representative government. It is surely beyond argument that those who have the responsibility for devising a system of representation may permissibly consider that factors other than bare numbers should be taken into account. The existence of the United States Senate is proof enough of that. To consider that we may ignore the Tennessee Legislature's judgment in this instance because that body was the product of an asymmetrical electoral apportionment would in effect be to assume the very conclusion here disputed. Hence we must accept the present form of the Tennessee Legislature as the embodiment of the State's choice, or, more realistically, its compromise, between competing political philosophies. The federal courts have not been empowered by the Equal Protection Clause to judge whether this resolution of the State's internal political conflict is desirable or undesirable, wise or unwise.

. . .

The suggestion of my Brother FRANKFURTER that courts lack standards by which to decide such cases as this, is relevant not only to the question of "justiciability," but also, and perhaps more fundamentally, to the determination whether any cognizable constitutional claim has been asserted in this case. Courts are unable to decide when it is that an apportionment originally valid becomes void because the factors entering into such a decision are basically matters appropriate only for legislative judgment. And so long as there exists a possible rational legislative policy for retaining an existing apportionment, such a legislative decision cannot be said to breach the bulwark against arbitrariness and caprice that the Fourteenth Amendment affords. Certainly, with all due respect, the facile arithmetical argument contained in Part II of my Brother CLARK's separate opinion (369 U.S., pp. 253–258) provides no tenable basis for considering that there has been such a breach in this instance.

. . .

In conclusion, it is appropriate to say that one need not agree, as a citizen, with what Tennessee has done or failed to do, in order to deprecate, as a judge, what the majority is doing today. Those observers of the Court who see it primarily as the last refuge for the correction of all inequality or injustice, no matter what its nature or source, will no doubt applaud this decision and its break with the past. Those who consider that continuing national respect for the Court's authority depends in large measure upon its wise exercise of self-restraint and discipline in constitutional adjudication, will view the decision with deep concern.

I would affirm.

Does the majority clearly explain why, on these facts, the guaranty clause claim presents a political question, but the equal protection claim does not? Why are the equal protection standards more ascertainable than the guaranty clause standards?

Goldwater v. Carter[12] involved a challenge to President Carter's termination of a treaty with Taiwan and his recognition of the People's Republic of China. Justice Rehnquist, joined by three other justices, concluded that the case involved a political question:

[This] case is a nonjusticiable political dispute that should be left for resolution by the Executive and Legislative Branches of the Government. [W]hile the

---

[12] 444 U.S. 996 (1979).

Constitution is express as to the manner in which the Senate shall participate in the ratification of a treaty, it is silent as to that body's participation in the abrogation of a treaty. In this respect the case is directly analogous to *Coleman, supra*. As stated in *Dyer v. Blair*, 390 F.Supp. 1291, 1302 (N.D.Ill.1975) (three-judge court): "A question that might be answered in different ways for different amendments must surely be controlled by political standards rather than standards easily characterized as judicially manageable." In light of the absence of any constitutional provision governing the termination of a treaty, and the fact that different termination procedures may be appropriate for different treaties, the instant case in my view also "must surely be controlled by political standards."

. . .

[T]he justifications for concluding that the question here is political in nature are even more compelling than in Coleman because it involves foreign relations—specifically a treaty commitment to use military force in the defense of a foreign government if attacked.

Mr. Justice Brennan disagreed: "The issue of decisionmaking authority must be resolved as a matter of constitutional law, not political discretion; accordingly, it falls within the competence of the courts."

Powell v. McCormack[13] involved Adam Clayton Powell, Jr., who was duly elected to the United States House of Representatives, but who the House refused to seat because he had engaged in misconduct. When Powell sued, the House claimed that the case should be dismissed on "political question" grounds. In the House's view, Art. I, § 5 of the Constitution, which provides that "[e]ach House shall be the Judge of the Elections, Returns, and Qualifications of its own Members . . . ," contained a "textually demonstrable commitment of the issue to the House. As a result, the House argued that "the House, and the House alone, has power to determine who is qualified to be a member." The Supreme Court disagreed:

[A]nalysis of the "textual commitment" under Art. I, § 5, has demonstrated that in judging the qualifications of its members Congress is limited to the standing qualifications prescribed in the Constitution. Respondents concede that Powell met these. Thus, there is no need to remand this case to determine whether he was entitled to be seated in the 90th Congress. Therefore, we hold that, since Adam Clayton Powell, Jr., was duly elected by the voters of the 18th Congressional District of New York and was not ineligible to serve under any provision of the Constitution, the House was without power to exclude him from its membership. The Court concluded that it could decide the case without producing a "potentially embarrassing confrontation between coordinate branches of the Federal Government" or resulting in "multifarious pronouncements by various departments on one question."

C. Case or Controversy Requirement

Article III, § 2, contains perhaps the most important limitation on the judicial power: the "case" or "controversy" requirement. This limitation has spawned multiple restrictions on the scope of judicial authority including the prohibition against advisory opinions, the ripeness and mootness doctrines, and the standing requirement.

1. Advisory Opinions

---

[13] 395 U.S. 486 (1969).

Muskrat v. United States
219 U.S. 346 (1911)

[In 1902, Congress passed legislation setting aside certain lands for the use of Cherokee Indians. In 1904 and 1906, Congress passed laws allowing other Indians to share in the lands. By expanding the number of participants, the 1904 and 1906 laws diminished the quantity of land allocated to those who benefitted from the 1902 statute. In 1907, Congress passed a law authorizing four named individuals, including Muskrat (one of the Indians who benefitted by the 1902 statute), to bring suit challenging the 1904 and 1906 statutes.]

Mr. JUSTICE DAY delivered the opinion of the court:

. . .

The first question in these cases, as in others, involves the jurisdiction of the court to entertain the proceeding, and that depends upon whether the jurisdiction conferred is within the power of Congress, having in view the limitations of the judicial power, as established by the Constitution of the United States.

. . .

In 1793, by direction of the President, Secretary of State Jefferson addressed to the justices of the Supreme Court a communication soliciting their views upon the question whether their advice to the Executive would be available in the solution of important questions of the construction of treaties, laws of nations and laws of the land, which the Secretary said were often presented under circumstances which "do not give a cognizance of them to the tribunals of the country." The answer to the question was postponed until the subsequent sitting of the Supreme Court, when Chief Justice Jay and his associates answered to President Washington that, in consideration of the lines of separation drawn by the Constitution between the three departments of government, and being judges of a court of last resort, afforded strong arguments against the propriety of extrajudicially deciding the questions alluded to, and expressing the view that the power given by the Constitution to the President, of calling on heads of departments for opinions, "seems to have been purposely, as well as expressly, united to the executive departments." Correspondence & Public Papers of John Jay, vol. 3, p. 486.

[B]y the express terms of the Constitution, the exercise of the judicial power is limited to "cases" and "controversies." Beyond this it does not extend, and unless it is asserted in a case or controversy within the meaning of the Constitution, the power to exercise it is nowhere conferred.

What, then, does the Constitution mean in conferring this judicial power with the right to determine "cases" and "controversies." A "case" was defined by Mr. Chief Justice Marshall as early as the leading case of *Marbury v. Madison*, 1 Cranch, 137, to be a suit instituted according to the regular course of judicial procedure. And what more, if anything, is meant in the use of the term "controversy?" That question was dealt with by Mr. Justice Field, at the circuit, in the case of *Re Pacific R. Commission*, 32 Fed. 241, 255. Of these terms that learned justice said:

> By cases and controversies are intended the claims of litigants brought before the courts for determination by such regular proceedings as are established by law or custom for the protection or enforcement of rights, or the prevention, redress, or punishment of wrongs. Whenever the claim of a party under the Constitution, laws, or treaties of the United States takes such a form that the judicial power is capable of acting upon it, then it has become a case. The term implies the existence of present or possible adverse parties, whose contentions are submitted to the court for adjudication."

. . .

Applying the principles thus long settled by the decisions of this court to the act of Congress undertaking to confer jurisdiction in this case, . . . the object and purpose of the suit is wholly comprised in the determination of the constitutional validity of certain acts of Congress; and furthermore, in the last paragraph of the section, should a judgment be rendered in the court of claims or this court, denying the constitutional validity of such acts, then the amount of compensation to be paid to attorneys employed for the purpose of testing the constitutionality of the law is to be paid out of funds in the Treasury of the United States belonging to the beneficiaries, the act having previously provided that the United States should be made a party, and the Attorney General be charged with the defense of the suits.

It is therefore evident that there is neither more nor less in this procedure than an attempt to provide for a judicial determination, final in this court, of the constitutional validity of an act of Congress. Is such a determination within the judicial power conferred by the Constitution, as the same has been interpreted and defined in the authoritative decisions to which we have referred? We think it is not. That judicial power, as we have seen, is the right to determine actual controversies arising between adverse litigants, duly instituted in courts of proper jurisdiction. The right to declare a law unconstitutional arises because an act of Congress relied upon by one or the other of such parties in determining their rights is in conflict with the fundamental law. The exercise of this, the most important and delicate duty of this court, is not given to it as a body with revisory power over the action of Congress, but because the rights of the litigants in justiciable controversies require the court to choose between the fundamental law and a law purporting to be enacted within constitutional authority, but in fact beyond the power delegated to the legislative branch of the government. This attempt to obtain a judicial declaration of the validity of the act of Congress is not presented in a "case" or "controversy," to which, under the Constitution of the United States, the judicial power alone extends. It is true the United States is made a defendant to this action, but it has no interest adverse to the claimants. The object is not to assert a property right as against the government, or to demand compensation for alleged wrongs because of action upon its part. The whole purpose of the law is to determine the constitutional validity of this class of legislation, in a suit not arising between parties concerning a property right necessarily involved in the decision in question, but in a proceeding against the government in its sovereign capacity, and concerning which the only judgment required is to settle the doubtful character of the legislation in question. Such judgment will not conclude private parties, when actual litigation brings to the court the question of the constitutionality of such legislation. In a legal sense the judgment could not

be executed, and amounts in fact to no more than an expression of opinion upon the validity of the acts in question. Confining the jurisdiction of this court within the limitations conferred by the Constitution, which the court has hitherto been careful to observe, and whose boundaries it has refused to transcend, we think the Congress, in the act of March 1, 1907, exceeded the limitations of legislative authority, so far as it required of this court action not judicial in its nature within the meaning of the Constitution.

. . .

The questions involved in this proceeding as to the validity of the legislation may arise in suits between individuals, and when they do and are properly brought before this court for consideration they, of course, must be determined in the exercise of its judicial functions. For the reasons we have stated, we are constrained to hold that these actions present no justiciable controversy within the authority of the court, acting within the limitations of the Constitution under which it was created. As Congress, in passing this act, as a part of the plan involved, evidently intended to provide a review of the judgment of the court of claims in this court, as the constitutionality of important legislation is concerned, we think the act cannot be held to intend to confer jurisdiction on that court separately considered. *Connolly v. Union Sewer Pipe Co.* 184 U.S. 540, 565; *Employers' Liability Cases (Howard v. Illinois C.R. Co.)* 207 U.S. 463.

The judgments will be reversed and the cases remanded to the Court of Claims, with directions to dismiss the petitions for want of jurisdiction.

In *Muskrat*, the Court concludes that Article III prohibits the federal courts from issuing advisory opinions. Why should courts refrain from hearing cases that do not present cases or controversies? Is judicial abstention consistent with *Marbury's* conception of the judicial function?

Muskrat's prohibition against advisory opinions is well established. *United States v. Johnson*,[14] involved a suit by a tenant against his landlord claiming violations of the Emergency Price Control Act of 1942. That Act limited the amount of rent the landlord could charge. The evidence revealed that the lawsuit was collusively brought to challenge the Act:

The affidavit of the plaintiff, submitted by the Government on its motion to dismiss the suit as collusive, shows without contradiction that he brought the present proceeding in a fictitious name; that it was instituted as a "friendly suit" at appellee's request; that the plaintiff did not employ, pay, or even meet, the attorney who appeared of record in his behalf; that he had no knowledge who paid the $15 filing fee in the district court, but was assured by appellee

---

[14] 319 U.S. 302 (1943).

that as plaintiff he would incur no expense in bringing the suit; that he did not read the complaint which was filed in his name as plaintiff; that in his conferences with the appellee and appellee's attorney of record, nothing was said concerning treble damages and he had no knowledge of the amount of the judgment prayed until he read of it in a local newspaper.

The Court held that the case should have been dismissed:

> Here an important public interest is at stake—the validity of an Act of Congress having far-reaching effects on the public welfare in one of the most critical periods in the history of the country. That interest has been adjudicated in a proceeding in which the plaintiff has had no active participation, over which he has exercised no control, and the expense of which he has not borne. He has been only nominally represented by counsel who was selected by appellee's counsel and whom he has never seen. Such a suit is collusive because it is not in any real sense adversary. It does not assume the "honest and actual antagonistic assertion of rights" to be adjudicated—a safeguard essential to the integrity of the judicial process, and one which we have held to be indispensable to adjudication of constitutional questions by this Court. *Chicago & G.T. Ry. Co. v. Wellman,* 143 U.S. 339, 345. Whenever in the course of litigation such a defect in the proceedings is brought to the court's attention, it may set aside any adjudication thus procured and dismiss the cause without entering judgment on the merits. It is the court's duty to do so where, as here, the public interest has been placed at hazard by the amenities of parties to a suit conducted under the domination of only one of them. . . .

RLW: Is it really clear that *Muskrat* did not present a "case" or "controversy?" Secretary Jefferson's 1793 request for advice constituted an advisory opinion because no "case" or "controversy" was then before the Court. But was there really no "controversy" in *Muskrat*? Muskrat sued to strike down the 1904 and 1906 statutes. Had he prevailed, he would have obtained a benefit.

DER: One justification for the case or controversy requirement is that it maintains the constitutional separation of powers, preventing the judiciary from performing legislative or executive functions. The prohibition of advisory opinions also reflects our reliance on an adversarial system to adjudicate legal matters. The rule is based on the belief that judges can properly determine legal questions only through a process that places in dispute parties who have a genuine and conflicting stake in the outcome. Presumably only this adversarial process will present the legal questions concretely enough and generate sufficiently zealous arguments to enable judges to render sound decisions. But justiciability requirements have often worked against people who are harmed by laws but face financial, knowledge, or other barriers to bringing their challenges to court. It has also provided the Court with a technical device for avoiding controversial issues. For example, the Court relied on the case-or-controversy doctrine for decades in order to avoid ruling on the constitutionality of state laws banning contraceptives—despite the laws' practical effect of closing down public birth control clinics that served poor women. Questioning the necessity of an adversarial approach to justice might raise doubts about the meaning of the case-or-controversy requirement.

2. Ripeness

The "case or controversy" requirement also includes the ripeness doctrine. This doctrine prohibits the federal courts from prematurely considering or resolving cases.

United Public Workers v. Mitchell
330 U.S. 75 (1947)

Mr. Justice REED delivered the opinion of the Court.

The Hatch Act, enacted in 1940, declares unlawful certain specified political activities of federal employees. Section 9 forbids officers and employees in the executive branch of the Federal Government, with exceptions, from taking "any active part in political management or in political campaigns." Section 15 declares that the activities theretofore determined by the United States Civil Service Commission to be prohibited to employees in the classified civil service of the United States by the civil service rules shall be deemed to be prohibited to federal employees covered by the Hatch Act. These sections of the Act cover all federal officers and employees whether in the classified civil service or not and a penalty of dismissal from employment is imposed for violation. There is no designation of a single governmental agency for its enforcement.

. . .

The present appellants sought an injunction before a statutory three judge district court of the District of Columbia against appellees, members of the United States Civil Service Commission to prohibit them from enforcing against petitioners the provisions of the second sentence of § 9(a) of the Hatch Act. . . . A declaratory judgment of the unconstitutionality of the sentence was also sought. The sentence referred to reads, "No officer or employee in the executive branch of the Federal Government . . . shall take any active part in political management or in political campaigns."

Various individual employees of the federal executive civil service and the United Public Workers of America, a labor union with these and other executive employees as members, as a representative of all its members, joined in the suit. It is alleged that the individuals desire to engage in acts of political management and in political campaigns. . . . From the affidavits it is plain, and we so assume, that these activities will be carried on completely outside of the hours of employment. . . .

None of the appellants, except George P. Poole, has violated the provisions of the Hatch Act. They wish to act contrary to its provisions and those of § 1 of the Civil Service Rules and desire a declaration of the legally permissible limits of regulation. Defendants moved to dismiss the complaint for lack of a justiciable case or controversy. . . .

. . .

At the threshold of consideration, we are called upon to decide whether the complaint states a controversy cognizable in this Court.

We defer consideration of the cause of action of Mr. Poole until section Three of this opinion. The other individual employees . . . declare a desire to act contrary to the rule against political activity but not that the rule has been violated. . . .

As is well known the federal courts established pursuant to Article III of the Constitution do not render advisory opinions. For adjudication of constitutional issues "concrete legal issues, presented in actual cases, not abstractions" are requisite. This is as true of declaratory judgments as any other field. These appellants seem clearly to seek advisory opinions upon broad claims of rights protected by the First, Fifth, Ninth and Tenth Amendments to the Constitution. As these appellants are classified employees, they have a right superior to the generality of citizens, but the facts of their personal interest in their civil rights, of the general threat of possible interference with those rights by the Civil Service Commission under its rules, if specified things are done by appellants, does not make a justiciable case or controversy. Appellants want to engage in "political management and political campaigns," to persuade others to follow appellants' views by discussion, speeches, articles and other acts reasonably designed to secure the selection of appellants' political choices. Such generality of objection is really an attack on the political expediency of the Hatch Act, not the presentation of legal issues. It is beyond the competence of courts to render such a decision.

The power of courts, and ultimately of this Court to pass upon the constitutionality of acts of Congress arises only when the interests of litigants require the use of this judicial authority for their protection against actual interference. A hypothetical threat is not enough. We can only speculate as to the kinds of political activity the appellants desire to engage in or as to the contents of their proposed public statements or the circumstances of their publication. It would not accord with judicial responsibility to adjudge, in a matter involving constitutionality, between the freedom of the individual and the requirements of public order except when definite rights appear upon the one side and definite prejudicial interferences upon the other.

The Constitution allots the nation's judicial power to the federal courts. Unless these courts respect the limits of that unique authority, they intrude upon powers vested in the legislative or executive branches. Judicial adherence to the doctrine of the separation of powers preserves the courts for the decision of issues, between litigants, capable of effective determination. Judicial exposition upon political proposals is permissible only when necessary to decide definite issues between litigants. When the courts act continually within these constitutionally imposed boundaries of their power, their ability to perform their function as a balance for the people's protection against abuse of power by other branches of government remains unimpaired. Should the courts seek to expand their power so as to bring under their jurisdiction ill defined controversies over constitutional issues, they would become the organ of political theories. Such abuse of judicial power would properly meet rebuke and restriction from other branches. By these mutual checks and balances by and between the branches of government, democracy undertakes to preserve the liberties of the people from excessive concentrations of authority. No threat of interference by the Commission with rights of these appellants appears beyond that implied by the existence of the law and the regulations. We should not take judicial cognizance of the situation presented on the part of the appellants considered in this subdivision of the opinion. These reasons lead us to conclude that the determination of the trial court, that the individual appellants, other than Poole, could maintain this action, was erroneous.

The appellant Poole does present by the complaint and affidavit matters appropriate for judicial determination. The affidavits filed by appellees confirm that Poole has been charged by the Commission with political activity and a proposed order for his removal from his position adopted subject to his right under Commission procedure to reply to the charges and to present further evidence in refutation.[24] We proceed to consider the controversy over constitutional power at issue between Poole and the Commission as defined by the charge and preliminary finding upon one side and the admissions of Poole's affidavit upon the other. Our determination is limited to those facts. This proceeding so limited meets the requirements of defined rights and a defi-

nite threat to interfere with a possessor of the menaced rights by a penalty for an act done in violation of the claimed restraint.

Because we conclude hereinafter that the prohibition of § 9 of the Hatch Act and Civil Service Rule 1 are valid, it is unnecessary to consider, as this is a declaratory judgment action, whether or not this appellant sufficiently alleges that an irreparable injury to him would result from his removal from his position. Nor need we inquire whether or not a court of equity would enforce by injunction any judgment declaring rights. Since Poole admits that he violated the rule against political activity and that removal from office is therefore mandatory under the act, there is no question as to the exhaustion of administrative remedies. The act provides no administrative or statutory review for the order of the Civil Service Commission. As no prior proceeding, offering an effective remedy or otherwise, is pending in the courts, there is no problem of judicial discretion as to whether to take cognizance of this case. Under such circumstances, we see no reason why a declaratory judgment action, even though constitutional issues are involved, does not lie. . . .

. . .

The judgment of the District Court is accordingly affirmed.

Affirmed.

Mr. Justice DOUGLAS, dissenting in part.

. . .

What these appellants propose to do is plain enough. If they do what they propose to do, it is clear that they will be discharged from their positions. . . .

On a discharge these employees would lose their jobs, their seniority, and other civil service benefits. They could, of course, sue in the Court of Claims. But the remedy there is a money judgment, not a restoration to the office formerly held. Of course, there might be other remedies available in these situations to determine their rights to the offices from which they are discharged. But to require these employees first to suffer the hardship of a discharge is not only to make them incur a penalty; it makes inadequate, if not wholly illusory, any legal remedy which they may have. Men who must sacrifice their means of livelihood in order to test their rights to their jobs must either pursue prolonged and expensive litigation as unemployed persons or pull up their roots, change their life careers, and seek employment in other fields. At least to the average person in the lower income groups the burden of taking that course is irreparable injury, no matter how exact the required showing.

. . .

The declaratory judgment procedure is designed "to declare rights and other legal relations of any interested party . . . whether or not

---

[24] The tentative change and finding reads: "I. It is charged: That * * * 'The said George P. Poole held the political party office of Democratic Ward Executive Committeeman in the City of Philadelphia, Pennsylvania. 'The said George P. Poole was politically active by aiding and assisting the Democratic Party in the capacity of worker at the polls on general election day, November 5, 1940, and assisted in the distribution of funds in paying party workers for their services on general election day, November 5, 1940." 'III. The above described activity constitutes taking an active part in political management and in a political campaign in contravention of Section 1, Civil Service Rule I, and the regulations adopted by the Commissioners thereunder."

further relief is or could be prayed." 28 U.S.C. § 400. The right to hold an office or public position against such threats is a common example of its use. Declaratory relief is the singular remedy available here to preserve the status quo while the constitutional rights of these appellants to make these utterances and to engage in these activities are determined. The

threat against them is real not fanciful, immediate not remote. The case is therefore an actual not a hypothetical one. And the present case seems to me to be a good example of a situation where uncertainty, peril, and insecurity result from imminent and immediate threats to asserted rights.

. . .

Abbott Laboratories v. Gardner
387 U.S. 136 (1967)

Mr. Justice HARLAN delivered the opinion of the Court.

In 1962 Congress amended the Federal Food, Drug, and Cosmetic Act . . . to require manufacturers of prescription drugs to print the "established name" of the drug "prominently and in type at least half as large as that used thereon for any proprietary name or designation for such drug," on labels and other printed material, § 502(e)(1)(B), 21 U.S.C. § 352(e)(1)(B). The "established name" is one designated by the Secretary of Health, Education, and Welfare pursuant to § 502(e)(2) of the Act; the "proprietary name" is usually a trade name under which a particular drug is marketed. The underlying purpose of the 1962 amendment was to bring to the attention of doctors and patients the fact that many of the drugs sold under familiar trade names are actually identical to drugs sold under their "established" or less familiar trade names at significantly lower prices. The Commissioner of Food and Drugs, exercising authority delegated to him by the Secretary, published proposed regulations designed to implement the statute. After inviting and considering comments submitted by interested parties the Commissioner promulgated the following regulation for the "efficient enforcement" of the Act, § 701(a): "If the label or labeling of a prescription drug bears a proprietary name or designation for the drug or any ingredient thereof, the established name, if such there be, corresponding to such proprietary name or designation, shall accompany each appearance of such proprietary name or designation." The rule was made applicable to advertisements for prescription drugs.

The present action was brought by a group of 37 individual drug manufacturers and by the Pharmaceutical Manufacturers Association, of which all the petitioner companies are members, and which includes manufacturers of more than 90% of the Nation's supply of prescription drugs. They challenged the regulations on the ground that the Commissioner exceeded his authority under the statute by promulgating an order requiring labels, advertisements, and other printed matter relating to prescription drugs to designate the established name of the particular drug involved every time its trade name is used anywhere in such material.

. . .

[I]njunctive and declaratory judgment remedies are discretionary, and courts traditionally have been reluctant to apply them to administrative determinations unless these arise in the context of a controversy "ripe" for judicial resolution. Without undertaking to survey the intricacies of the ripeness doctrine it is fair to say that its basic rationale is to prevent the courts, through avoidance of premature adjudication, from entangling themselves in abstract disagreements over administrative policies, and also to protect the agencies from judicial interference until an administrative decision has been formalized and its effects felt in a concrete way by the challenging parties. The problem is best seen in a twofold aspect, requiring us to evaluate both the fitness of the issues for judicial decision and the hardship to the parties of withholding court consideration.

As to the former factor, we believe the issues presented are appropriate for judicial resolution at this time. First, all parties agree that the issue tendered is a purely legal one: whether the statute was properly construed by the Commissioner to require the established name of the drug to be used every time the proprietary name is employed. Both sides moved for summary judgment in the District Court, and no claim is made here that further administrative proceedings are contemplated. It is suggested that the justification for this rule might vary with different circumstances, and that the expertise of the Commissioner is relevant to passing upon the validity of the regulation. This of course is true, but the suggestion overlooks the fact that both sides have approached this case as one purely of congressional intent, and that the Government made no effort to justify the regulation in factual terms.

. . .

This is also a case in which the impact of the regulations upon the petitioners is sufficiently direct and immediate as to render the issue appropriate for judicial review at this stage. These regulations purport to give an authoritative interpretation of a statutory provision that has a direct effect on the day-to-day business of all prescription drug companies; its promulgation puts petitioners in a dilemma that it was the very purpose of the Declaratory Judgment Act to ameliorate. As the District Court found on the basis of uncontested allegations, "Either they must comply with the every time requirement and incur the costs of changing over their promotional material and labeling or they must follow their present course and risk prosecution." 228 F.Supp. 855, 861. The regulations are clear-cut, and were made effective immediately upon publication; as noted earlier the agency's counsel represented to the District Court that immediate compliance with their terms was expected. If petitioners wish to comply they must change all their labels, advertisements, and promotional materials; they must destroy stocks of printed matter; and they must invest heavily in new printing type and new supplies. The alternative to compliance—continued use of material which they believe in good faith meets the statutory requirements, but which clearly does not meet the regulation of the Commissioner—may be even more costly. That course would risk serious criminal and civil penalties for the unlawful distribution of "misbranded" drugs.

It is relevant at this juncture to recognize that petitioners deal in a sensitive industry, in which public confidence in their drug products is especially important. To require them to challenge these regulations only as a defense to an action brought by the Government might harm them severely and unnecessarily. Where the legal issue presented is fit for judicial resolution, and where a regulation requires an immediate and significant change in the plaintiffs' conduct of their affairs with serious penalties attached to noncompliance, access to the courts under the Administrative Procedure Act and the Declaratory Judgment Act must be permitted, absent a statutory bar or some other unusual circumstance, neither of which appears here.

The Government does not dispute the very real dilemma in which petitioners are placed by the regulation, but contends that "mere financial expense" is not a justification for pre-enforcement judicial review. It is of course true that cases in this Court dealing with the standing particular parties to bring an action have held that a possible financial loss is not by itself a sufficient interest to sustain a judicial challenge to governmental action. *Frothingham v. Mellon*, 262 U.S. 447; *Perkins v. Lukens Steel Co.*, 310 U.S. 113. But there is no question in the present case that petitioners have sufficient standing as plaintiffs: the regulation is directed at them in particular; it requires them to make significant changes in their everyday business practices; if they fail to observe the Commissioner's rule they are quite clearly exposed to the imposition of strong sanctions. This case is, therefore, remote from the Mellon and Perkins cases.

The Government further contends that the threat of criminal sanctions for noncompliance with a judicially untested regulation is unrealistic; the Solicitor General has represented that if court enforcement becomes necessary, "the Department of Justice will proceed only civilly for an injunction * * * or by condemnation." We cannot accept this argument as a sufficient answer to petitioners' petition. This action at its inception was properly brought and this subsequent representation of the Department of Justice should not suffice to defeat it.

. . .

Poe v. Ullman[15] involved a challenge to a Connecticut statute prohibiting the use of contraceptive devices and the giving of medical advice regarding the use of such devices. Two of the plaintiffs, the Poes, were husband and wife. Mrs. Poe had suffered three consecutive pregnancies that had terminated in infants with multiple congenital abnormalities. Each child died shortly after birth. Plaintiffs had consulted Dr. Buxton, an obstetrician and gynecologist of eminence, and it was Dr. Buxton's opinion that the cause of the infants' abnormalities was genetic. Plaintiffs had suffered great emotional stress, and feared that an additional pregnancy would be damaging to plaintiff's physical and mental health. Dr. Buxton testified that Mrs. Poe should use methods designed to prevent conception as the best and safest way to protect her health. Mrs. Poe claimed

---

[15] 367 U.S. 497 (1961).

that she was unable to obtain contraceptive information "for the sole reason that its delivery and use may or will be claimed by the defendant State's Attorney to constitute offenses against Connecticut law." Plaintiffs argued that the statutes deprived them of "life and liberty without due process of law."

Two other plaintiffs joined the suit. One was a woman who had recently undergone a pregnancy which induced in her a critical physical illness—two weeks' unconsciousness and a total of nine weeks' acute sickness which left her with partial paralysis, marked impairment of speech, and emotional instability. She, too, feared another pregnancy and made claims similar to those advanced by the Poes. The final plaintiff was Dr. Buxton who claimed that the statutes prohibited him from giving contraceptive advice thereby depriving him of liberty and property without due process.

Referencing the principle of ripeness, the Court refused to hear any of the claims:

> The Connecticut law prohibiting the use of contraceptives has been on the State's books since 1879. Conn.Acts 1879, c. 78. During the more than three-quarters of a century since its enactment, a prosecution for its violation seems never to have been initiated, save in *State v. Nelson*, 126 Conn. 412. The circumstances of that case, decided in 1940, only prove the abstract character of what is before us. There, a test case was brought to determine the constitutionality of the Act as applied against two doctors and a nurse who had allegedly disseminated contraceptive information. After the Supreme Court of Errors sustained the legislation on appeal from a demurrer to the information, the State moved to dismiss the information. Neither counsel nor our own researches have discovered any other attempt to enforce the prohibition of distribution or use of contraceptive devices by criminal process. The unreality of these law suits is illumined by another circumstance. We were advised by counsel for appellants that contraceptives are commonly and notoriously sold in Connecticut drug stores. Yet no prosecutions are recorded; and certainly such ubiquitous, open, public sales would more quickly invite the attention of enforcement officials than the conduct in which the present appellants wish to engage—the giving of private medical advice by a doctor to his individual patients, and their private use of the devices prescribed. The undeviating policy of nullification by Connecticut of its anti-contraceptive laws throughout all the long years that they have been on the statute books bespeaks more than prosecutorial paralysis. . . .
>
> . . .
>
> [I]t is clear that the mere existence of a state penal statute would constitute insufficient grounds to support a federal court's adjudication of its constitutionality in proceedings brought against the State's prosecuting officials if real threat of enforcement is wanting. If the prosecutor expressly agrees not to prosecute, a suit against him for declaratory and injunctive relief is not such an adversary case as will be reviewed here. Eighty years of Connecticut history demonstrate a similar, albeit tacit agreement. The fact that Connecticut has not chosen to press the enforcement of this statute deprives these controversies of the immediacy which is an indispensable condition of constitutional adjudication. This Court cannot be umpire to debates concerning harmless, empty shadows. To find it necessary to pass on these statutes now, in order to protect appellants from the hazards of prosecution, would be to close our eyes to reality.
>
> Nor does the allegation by the Poes and Doe that they are unable to obtain information concerning contraceptive devices from Dr. Buxton, "for the sole reason that the delivery and use of such information and advice may or will be claimed by the defendant State's Attorney to constitute offenses," disclose a necessity for present constitutional decision. . . . [W]e cannot accept, as the basis of constitutional adjudication, other than as chimerical the fear of enforce-

ment of provisions that have during so many years gone uniformly and without exception unenforced.

Mr. Justice Douglas dissented:

When the Court goes outside the record to determine that Connecticut has adopted "The undeviating policy of nullification . . . of its anti-contraceptive laws," it selects a particularly poor case in which to exercise such a novel power. This is not a law which is a dead letter. Twice since 1940, Connecticut has reenacted these laws as part of general statutory revisions. Consistently, bills to remove the statutes from the books have been rejected by the legislature. In short, the statutes—far from being the accidental left-overs of another era—are the center of a continuing controversy in the State.

Again, the Court relies on the inability of counsel to show any attempts, other than the Nelson case, "to enforce the prohibition of distribution or use of contraceptive devices by criminal process." Yet, on oral argument, counsel for the appellee stated on his own knowledge that several proprietors had been prosecuted in the "minor police courts of Connecticut" after they had been "picked up" for selling contraceptives. . . .

What are these people—doctor and patients—to do? Flout the law and go to prison? Violate the law surreptitiously and hope they will not get caught? By today's decision we leave them no other alternatives. It is not the choice they need have under the regime of the declaratory judgment and our constitutional system. It is not the choice worthy of a civilized society. A sick wife, a concerned husband, a conscientious doctor seek a dignified, discrete, orderly answer to the critical problem confronting them. We should not turn them away and make them flout the law and get arrested to have their constitutional rights determined. *See Railway Mail Ass'n v. Corsi*, 326 U.S. 88. They are entitled to an answer to their predicament here and now.

. . .

[T]he most substantial claim which these married persons press is their right to enjoy the privacy of their marital relations free of the enquiry of the criminal law, whether it be in a prosecution of them or of a doctor whom they have consulted. And I cannot agree that their enjoyment of this privacy is not substantially impinged upon, when they are told that if they use contraceptives, indeed whether they do so or not, the only thing which stands between them and being forced to render criminal account of their marital privacy is the whim of the prosecutor.

Socialist Labor Party v. Gilligan[16] involved a challenge to an Ohio law restricting the ability of minority party candidates to place themselves on the ballot. After the law was struck down, the Ohio Legislature enacted a new law containing a loyalty oath. The Socialist Party challenged the revised law:

Appellants did not in their action that came here in 1968 challenge the loyalty oath. Their 1970 complaint respecting the loyalty oath is singularly sparse in its factual allegations. There is no suggestion in it that the Socialist Labor Party has ever refused in the past, or will now refuse, to sign the required oath. There is no allegation of injury that the party has suffered or will suffer because of the existence of the oath requirement.

It is fairly inferable that the absence of such allegations is not merely an oversight in the drafting of a pleading. The requirement of the affidavit under

---

[16] 406 U.S. 583 (1972).

oath was enacted in 1941, 119 Ohio Laws 586, and has remained continuously in force since that date. The Socialist Labor Party has appeared on the state ballot since the law's passage, and, unless the state officials have ignored what appear to be mandatory oath provisions, it is reasonable to conclude that the party has in the past executed the required affidavit.

. . .

. . . Nothing in the record shows that appellants have suffered any injury thus far, and the law's future effect remains wholly speculative. Notwithstanding the indications that appellants have in the past executed the required affidavit without injury, it is, of course, possible that at some future time they may be able to demonstrate some injury as a result of the application of the provision challenged here. Our adjudication of the merits of such a challenge will await that time. This appeal must be dismissed.

Anderson v. Green,[17] involved a challenge to California's attempt to change its Aid to Families With Dependent Children (AFDC) program by limiting new residents, for the first year they live in California, to the benefits paid in the State from which they came. Green and other new residents who receive AFDC benefits sought to challenge the constitutionality of California's change on the basis that the payment differential between new and long-term residents burdens interstate migration and thus violates the right to travel recognized in *Shapiro v. Thompson*,[18] and its progeny. The Court concluded that the case was not ripe for review:

> The California statute provides that the payment differential shall not take effect absent receipt by the State of an HHS waiver. See Cal.Welf. & Inst.Code Ann. § 11450.03(b) (West Supp.1994). HHS originally granted a waiver, which was in effect when the District Court and Court of Appeals ruled. But "ripeness is peculiarly a question of timing," and "it is the situation now rather than the situation at the time of the [decision under review] that must govern." Regional Rail Reorganization Act Cases, 419 U.S. 102, 140 (1974). After the Court of Appeals ruled in this case, it vacated the HHS waiver in a separate proceeding, concluding that the Secretary had not adequately considered objections to California's program. *Beno v. Shalala*, 30 F.3d 1057, 1073–1076 (CA9 1994). The Secretary did not seek this Court's review of the *Beno* decision. California acknowledges that even if it prevails here, the payment differential will not take effect. Absent favorable action by HHS on a renewed application for a waiver, California will continue to treat Green and others similarly situated the same way it treats long-term California residents. The parties have no live dispute now, and whether one will arise in the future is conjectural. *See Hall v. Beals*, 396 U.S. 45 (1969) (per curiam) (after this Court noted probable jurisdiction, Colorado legislature reduced to two months challenged six-month residency requirement for voting in presidential elections; revival of controversy consequently became too speculative to warrant Court's passing on substantive issues).

. . .

3. Mootness

The mootness doctrine also involves a question of timing. But, when this doctrine applies, the claim is that a case was presented too late. Even though the claim may have been ripe at one point, subsequent events have rendered it "moot."

---

[17] 115 S. Ct. 1059 (1995).
[18] 349 U.S. 618 (1969).

DeFunis v. Odegaard
416 U.S. 312 (1974)

PER CURIAM.

m 1971 the petitioner Marco DeFunis, Jr., applied for admission as a first-year student at the University of Washington Law School, a state-operated institution. The size of the incoming first-year class was to be limited to 150 persons, and the Law School received some 1,600 applications for these 150 places. DeFunis was eventually notified that he had been denied admission. He thereupon commenced this suit in a Washington trial court, contending that the procedures and criteria employed by the Law School Admissions Committee invidiously discriminated against him on account of his race in violation of the Equal Protection Clause of the Fourteenth Amendment to the United States Constitution.

DeFunis . . . asked the trial court to issue a mandatory injunction commanding the respondents to admit him as a member of the first-year class entering in September 1971, on the ground that the Law School admissions policy had resulted in the unconstitutional denial of his application for admission. The trial court agreed with his claim and granted the requested relief. DeFunis was, accordingly, admitted to the Law School and began his legal studies there in the fall of 1971. On appeal, the Washington Supreme Court reversed the judgment of the trial court and held that the Law School admissions policy did not violate the Constitution. By this time DeFunis was in his second year at the Law School.

He then petitioned this Court for a writ of certiorari, and Mr. Justice Douglas, as Circuit Justice, stayed the judgment of the Washington Supreme Court pending the "final disposition of the case by this Court." By virtue of this stay, DeFunis has remained in law school, and was in the first term of his third and final year when this Court first considered his certiorari petition in the fall of 1973. Because of our concern that DeFunis' third-year standing in the Law School might have rendered this case moot, we requested the parties to brief the question of mootness before we acted on the petition. In response, both sides contended that the case was not moot. The respondents indicated that, if the decision of the Washington Supreme Court were permitted to stand, the petitioner could complete the term for which he was then enrolled but would have to apply to the faculty for permission to continue in the school before he could register for another term.[2]

· · ·

In response to questions raised from the bench during the oral argument, counsel for the petitioner has informed the Court that DeFunis has now registered "for his final quarter in law school." Counsel for the respondents have made clear that the Law School will not in any way seek to abrogate this registration. In light of DeFunis' recent registration for the last quarter of his final law school year, and the Law School's assurance that his registration is fully effective, the insistent question again arises whether this case is not moot, and to that question we now turn.

The starting point for analysis is the familiar proposition that "federal courts are without power to decide questions that cannot affect the rights of litigants in the case before them." *North Carolina v. Rice*, 404 U.S. 244, 246 (1971). The inability of the federal judiciary "to review moot cases derives from the requirement of Art. III of the Constitution under which the exercise of judicial power depends upon the existence of a case or controversy." *Liner v. Jafco, Inc.*, 375 U.S. 301, 306 n.3 (1964). Although as a matter of Washington state law it appears that this case would be saved from mootness by "the great public interest in the continuing issues raised by this appeal," 507 P.2d 1169, 1177 n.6 (1973), the fact remains that under Art. III "(e)ven in cases arising in the state courts, the question of mootness is a federal one which a federal court must resolve before it assumes jurisdiction." *North Carolina v. Rice, supra*, 404 U.S., at 246.

The respondents have represented that, without regard to the ultimate resolution of the issues in this case, DeFunis will remain a student in the Law School for the duration of any term in which he has already enrolled. Since he has now registered for his final term, it is evident that he will be given an opportunity to complete all academic and other requirements for graduation, and, if he does so, will receive his diploma regardless of any decision this Court might reach on the merits of this case. In short, all parties agree that DeFunis is now entitled to complete his legal studies at the University of Washington and to receive his degree from that institution. A determination by this Court of the legal issues tendered by the parties is no longer necessary to compel that result, and could not serve to prevent it. DeFunis did not cast his suit as a class action,

---

[2] By contrast, in their response to the petition for certiorari, the respondents had stated that De-

Funis "will complete his third year (of law school) and be awarded his J.D. degree at the end of the 1973—74 academic year regardless of the outcome of this appeal."

and the only remedy he requested was an injunction commanding his admission to the Law School. He was not only accorded that remedy, but he now has also been irrevocably admitted to the final term of the final year of the Law School course. The controversy between the parties has thus clearly ceased to be "definite and concrete" and no longer "touch(es) the legal relations of parties having adverse legal interests." *Aetna Life Ins. Co. v. Haworth*, 300 U.S. 227, 240–241 (1937).

It matters not that these circumstances partially stem from a policy decision on the part of the respondent Law School authorities. The respondents, through their counsel, the Attorney General of the State, have professionally represented that in no event will the status of DeFunis now be affected by any view this Court might express on the merits of this controversy. And it has been the settled practice of the Court, in contexts no less significant, fully to accept representations such as these as parameters for decision.

There is a line of decisions in this Court standing for the proposition that the "voluntary cessation of allegedly illegal conduct does not deprive the tribunal of power to hear and determine the case, i.e., does not make the case moot." *United States v. W.T. Grant Co.*, 345 U.S. 629, 632 (1953). These decisions and the doctrine they reflect would be quite relevant if the question of mootness here had arisen by reason of a unilateral change in the admissions procedures of the Law School. For it was the admissions procedures that were the target of this litigation, and a voluntary cessation of the admissions practices complained of could make this case moot only if it could be said with assurance "that there is no reasonable expectation that the wrong will be repeated." *United States v. W.T. Grant Co., supra*, 345 U.S., at 633. Otherwise, "(t)he defendant is free to return to his old ways," *id.*, at 632, and this fact would be enough to prevent mootness because of the "public interest in having the legality of the practices settled." Ibid. But mootness in the present case depends not at all upon a "voluntary cessation" of the admissions practices that were the subject of this litigation. It depends, instead, upon the simple fact that DeFunis is now in the final quarter of the final year of his course of study, and the settled and unchallenged policy of the Law School to permit him to complete the term for which he is now enrolled.

It might also be suggested that this case presents a question that is "capable of repetition, yet evading review," *Southern Pacific Terminal Co. v. ICC*, 219 U.S. 498, 515 (1911), and is thus amenable to federal adjudication even though it might otherwise be considered moot. But DeFunis will never again be required to run the gauntlet of the Law School's admission

process, and so the question is certainly not "capable of repetition" so far as he is concerned. Moreover, just because this particular case did not reach the Court until the eve of the petitioner's graduation from Law School, it hardly follows that the issue he raises will in the future evade review. If the admissions procedures of the Law School remain unchanged, there is no reason to suppose that a subsequent case attacking those procedures will not come with relative speed to this Court, now that the Supreme Court of Washington has spoken. This case, therefore, in no way presents the exceptional situation in which the Southern Pacific Terminal doctrine might permit a departure from "(t)he usual rule in federal cases . . . that an actual controversy must exist at stages of appellate or certiorari review, and not simply at the date the action is initiated." *Roe v. Wade, supra*, at 125.

Because the petitioner will complete his law school studies at the end of the term for which he has now registered regardless of any decision this Court might reach on the merits of this litigation, we conclude that the Court cannot, consistently with the limitations of Art. III of the Constitution, consider the substantive constitutional issues tendered by the parties.[5] Accordingly, the judgment of the Supreme Court of Washington is vacated, and the cause is remanded for such proceedings as by that court may be deemed appropriate.

It is so ordered.

Vacated and remanded.

Mr. Justice BRENNAN, with whom Mr. Justice DOUGLAS, Mr. Justice WHITE, and Mr. Justice MARSHALL concur, dissenting.

I respectfully dissent. Many weeks of the school term remain, and petitioner may not receive his degree despite respondents' assurances that petitioner will be allowed to complete this term's schooling regardless of our decision. Any number of unexpected events—illness, economic necessity, even academic failure—might prevent his graduation at the end of the term. Were that misfortune to befall, and were petitioner required to register for yet another term, the prospect that he would again face the hurdle of the admissions policy is real, not fanciful; for respondents warn that "Mr. DeFunis would have to take some appropriate action to request continued

---

[5] It is suggested in dissent that "(a)ny number of unexpected events—illness, economic necessity, even academic failure—might prevent his graduation at the end of the term." Post, at 1721. "But such speculative contingencies afford no basis for our passing on the substantive issues (the petitioner) would have us decide," *Hall v. Beals*, 396 U.S. 45, 49 (1969), in the absence of "evidence that this is a prospect of 'immediacy and reality.'" *Golden v. Zwickler*, 394 U.S. 103, 109 (1969).

admission for the remainder of his law school education, and some discretionary action by the University on such request would have to be taken." Respondents' Memorandum on the Question of Mootness 3–4 (emphasis supplied). Thus, respondents' assurances have not dissipated the possibility that petitioner might once again have to run the gauntlet of the University's allegedly unlawful admissions policy. The Court therefore proceeds on an erroneous premise in resting its mootness holding on a supposed inability to render any judgment that may affect one way or the other petitioner's completion of his law studies. For surely if we were to reverse the Washington Supreme Court, we could insure that, if for some reason petitioner did not graduate this spring, he would be entitled to re-enrollment at a later time on the same basis as others who have not faced the hurdle of the University's allegedly unlawful admissions policy.

In these circumstances, and because the University's position implies no concession that its admissions policy is unlawful, this controversy falls squarely within the Court's long line of decisions holding that the "(m)ere voluntary cessation of allegedly illegal conduct does not moot a case." *United States v. Concentrated Phosphate Export Assn.*, 393 U.S. 199, 203 (1968). Since respondents' voluntary representation to this Court is only that they will permit petitioner to complete this term's studies, respondents have not borne the "heavy burden," *United States v. Concentrated Phosphate Export Assn., supra*, 393 U.S., at 203, of demonstrating that there was not even a "mere possibility" that petitioner would once again be subject to the challenged admissions policy. *United States v. W.T. Grant Co., supra*, 345 U.S., at 633. On the contrary, respondents have positioned themselves so as to be "free to return to (their) old ways." *Id.*, at 632.

I can thus find no justification for the Court's straining to rid itself of this dispute. While we must be vigilant to require that litigants maintain a personal stake in the outcome of a controversy to assure that "the questions will be framed with the necessary specificity, that the issues will be contested with the necessity adverseness and that the litigation will be pursued with the necessary vigor to assure that the constitutional challenge will be made in a form traditionally thought to be capable of judicial resolution," *Flast v. Cohen*, 392 U.S. 83, 106 (1968), there is no want of an adversary contest in this case. Indeed, the Court concedes that, if petitioner has lost his stake in this controversy, he did so only when he registered for the spring term. But appellant took that action only after the case had been fully litigated in the state courts, briefs had been filed in this Court, and oral argument had been heard. The case is thus ripe for decision on a fully developed factual record with sharply defined and fully canvassed legal issues.

Moreover, in endeavoring to dispose of this case as moot, the Court clearly disserves the public interest. The constitutional issues which are avoided today concern vast numbers of people, organizations, and colleges and universities, as evidenced by the filing of twenty-six amicus curiae briefs. Few constitutional questions in recent history have stirred as much debate, and they will not disappear. They must inevitably return to the federal courts and ultimately again to this Court. Because avoidance of repetitious litigation serves the public interest, that inevitability counsels against mootness determinations, as here, not compelled by the record. *Cf. United States v. W.T. Grant Co., supra*, 345 U.S., at 632; *Parker v. Ellis*, 362 U.S. 574, 594 (1960) (dissenting opinion). Although the Court should, of course, avoid unnecessary decisions of constitutional questions, we should not transform principles of avoidance of constitutional decisions into devices for sidestepping resolution of difficult cases.

On what appears in this case, I would find that there is an extant controversy and decide the merits of the very important constitutional questions presented.

Roe v. Wade[19] involved a Texas statute criminalizing abortion. Jane Roe, a single unmarried woman who was pregnant, sought to challenge the statute. Roe claimed that she wished to terminate her pregnancy by an abortion "performed by a competent, licensed physician, under safe, clinical conditions;" that she was unable to get a "legal" abortion in Texas because her life did not appear to be threatened by the continuation of her pregnancy; and that she could not afford to travel to another jurisdiction in order to secure a legal abortion under safe conditions." By the time the case was heard by the Court, Roe was no longer pregnant. Accordingly, the state moved to dismiss her appeal on mootness grounds. The Court held that the case was not moot:

---

[19] 410 U.S. 113 (1973).

The usual rule in federal cases is that an actual controversy must exist at stages of appellate or certiorari review, and not simply at the date the action is initiated.

But when, as here, pregnancy is a significant fact in the litigation, the normal 266-day human gestation period is so short that the pregnancy will come to term before the usual appellate process is complete. If that termination makes a case moot, pregnancy litigation seldom will survive much beyond the trial stage, and appellate review will be effectively denied. Our law should not be that rigid. Pregnancy often comes more than once to the same woman, and in the general population, if man is to survive, it will always be with us. Pregnancy provides a classic justification for a conclusion of nonmootness. It truly could be "capable of repetition, yet evading review."

We, therefore, agree with the District Court that Jane Roe had standing to undertake this litigation, that she presented a justiciable controversy, and that the termination of her 1970 pregnancy has not rendered her case moot.

4. Standing

The final aspect of the case or controversy requirement is the element of standing. Unlike ripeness and mootness cases, which focus on the timing of adjudication, standing cases focus on whether plaintiff has a sufficient interest in the litigation. Although standing is related to ripeness and mootness, because plaintiff may lack sufficient interest when a case is not yet ripe or has become moot, standing cases do not always involve questions of timing.

The following cases involve suits by individuals who seek to challenge governmental action. Some have based their standing claims on their status as citizens or taxpayers. Others rely on a federal statute authorizing those "adversely affected" by agency action to sue.

a. Taxpayer and Citizen Standing

Can individuals base standing on their status as citizens or taxpayers?

Frothingham v. Mellon
262 U.S. 447 (1923)

Mr. Justice SUTHERLAND delivered the opinion of the Court.

These cases . . . challenge the constitutionality of the . . . Maternity Act. Briefly, it provides for an initial appropriation and thereafter annual appropriations for a period of five years, to be apportioned among such of the several states as shall accept and comply with its provisions, for the purpose of co-operating with them to reduce maternal and infant mortality and protect the health of mothers and infants. It creates a bureau to administer the act in co-operation with state agencies, which are required to make such reports concerning their operations and expenditures as may be prescribed by the federal bureau. Whenever that bureau shall determine that funds have not been properly expended in respect of any state, payments may be withheld.

[In the] . . . Massachusetts Case it is alleged that the plaintiff's rights and powers as a sovereign state and the rights of its citizens have been invaded and usurped by these expenditures and acts, and that, although the state has not accepted the act, its constitutional rights are infringed by the passage thereof and the imposition upon the state of an illegal and unconstitutional option either to yield to the federal government a part of its reserved rights or lose the share which it would otherwise be entitled to receive of the moneys appropriated. In the Frothingham Case plaintiff alleges that the effect of the statute will be to take her property, under the guise of taxation, without due process of law.

We have reached the conclusion that the cases must be disposed of for want of jurisdiction, without considering the merits of the constitutional questions.

. . .

First, the state of Massachusetts in its own behalf, in effect, complains that the act in question invades the local concerns of the state, and is a usurpation of power, viz. the power of local self-government, reserved to the states.

Probably it would be sufficient to point out that the powers of the state are not invaded, since the statute imposes no obligation but simply extends an option which the state is free to accept or reject. . . . [It] is plain that question, as it is thus presented, is political, and not judicial in character, and therefore is not a matter which admits of the exercise of the judicial power.

. . .

We come next to consider whether the suit may be maintained by the state as the representative of its citizens. To this the answer is not doubtful. We need not go so far as to say that a state may never intervene by suit to protect its citizens against any form of enforcement of unconstitutional acts of Congress. . . . But the citizens of Massachusetts are also citizens of the United States. It cannot be conceded that a state, as parens patriae, may institute judicial proceedings to protect citizens of the United States from the operation of the statutes thereof. While the state, under some circumstances, may sue in that capacity for the protection of its citizens . . . , it is no part of its duty or power to enforce their rights in respect of their relations with the federal government. In that field it is the United States, and not the state, which represents them as parens patriae, when such representation becomes appropriate; and to the former, and not to the latter, they must look for such protective measures as flow from that status.

Second. The attack upon the statute in the Frothingham Case is, generally, the same, but this plaintiff alleges, in addition that she is a taxpayer of the United States; and her contention, though not clear, seems to be that the effect of the appropriations complained of will be to increase the burden of future taxation and thereby take her property without due process of law. The right of a taxpayer to enjoin the execution of a federal appropriation act, on the ground that it is invalid and will result in taxation for illegal purposes, has never been passed upon by this court. In cases where it was presented, the question has either been allowed to pass sub silentio or the determination of it expressly withheld. . . . [*Bradfield v. Roberts*, 175 U.S. 291 articulated the] rule, frequently stated by this court, that resident taxpayers may sue to enjoin an illegal use of the moneys of a municipal corporation. . . . The interest of a taxpayer of a municipality in the application of its moneys is direct and immediate and the remedy by injunction to prevent their misuse is not inappropriate. It is upheld by a large number of state cases and is the rule of this court. . . . The reasons which support the extension of the equitable remedy to a single taxpayer in such cases are based upon the peculiar relation of the corporate taxpayer to the corporation, which is not without some resemblance to that subsisting between stockholder and private corporation. 4 Dillon, Municipal Corporations (5th Ed.) § 1580 et seq. But the relation of a taxpayer of the United States to the federal government is very different. His interest in the moneys of the treasury—partly realized from taxation and partly from other sources—is shared with millions of others, is comparatively minute and indeterminable, and the effect upon future taxation, of any payment out of the funds, so remote, fluctuating and uncertain, that no basis is afforded for an appeal to the preventive powers of a court of equity.

The administration of any statute, likely to produce additional taxation to be imposed upon a vast number of taxpayers, the extent of whose several liability is indefinite and constantly changing, is essentially a matter of public and not of individual concern. If one taxpayer may champion and litigate such a cause, then every other taxpayer may do the same, not only in respect of the statute here under review, but also in respect of every other appropriation act and statute whose administration requires the outlay of public money, and whose validity may be questioned. The bare suggestion of such a result, with its attendant inconveniences, goes far to sustain the conclusion which we have reached, that a suit of this character cannot be maintained. It is of much significance that no precedent sustaining the right to maintain suits like this has been called to our attention, although, since the formation of the government, as an examination of the acts of Congress will disclose, a large number of statutes appropriating or involving the expenditure of moneys for nonfederal purposes have been enacted and carried into effect.

The functions of government under our system are apportioned. To the legislative department has been committed the duty of making laws, to the executive the duty of executing them, and to the judiciary the duty of interpreting and applying them in cases properly brought before the courts. The general rule is that neither department may invade the province of the other and neither may control, direct, or restrain the action of the other. We are not now speaking of the merely ministerial duties of officials. *Gaines v. Thompson*, 7 Wall. 347. We have no power per se to review and annul acts of Congress on the ground that they are unconstitutional. That question may be considered only when the justification for some direct injury suffered or threatened, presenting a justiciable issue, is made to rest upon such an act. Then the power exercised is that of ascertaining and declaring the law applicable to the controversy. It amounts to little more than the negative power to disregard an unconstitutional enactment, which otherwise would stand in the way of the enforcement of a legal right. The party who invokes the power must be able to show, not only that the statute is invalid, but that he has sustained or is immediately in danger of sustaining some direct injury as the result of its enforcement, and not merely that he suffers in some indefinite way in common with people generally. If a case for preventive relief be presented, the court enjoins, in effect, not the execution of the statute, but the acts of the official, the statute notwithstanding. Here the parties plaintiff have no such case. Looking through forms of words to the substance of their complaint, it is merely that officials of the executive department of the government are executing and will execute an act of Congress asserted to be unconstitutional; and this we are asked to prevent. To do so would be, not to decide a judicial controversy, but to assume a position of authority over the governmental acts of another and coequal department, an authority which plainly we do not possess.

Doremus v. Board of Education[20] involved an establishment clause challenge to Bible reading in the New Jersey public schools. One plaintiff was the parent of a child subjected to the Bible readings, and both plaintiffs claimed that they were taxpayers burdened by the requirement. The Court dismissed the case on standing grounds. The child had graduated so the issue was moot as to him. The Court concluded that the taxpayers lacked standing: "There is no allegation that this activity is supported by any separate tax or paid for from any particular appropriation or that it adds any sum whatever to the cost of conducting the school." "It is apparent that the grievance which it is sought to litigate here is not a direct dollars-and-cents injury but is a religious difference."

Mr. Justice Douglas dissented:

I think this case deserves a decision on the merits. There is no group more interested in the operation and management of the public schools than the taxpayers who support them and the parents whose children attend them. Certainly a suit by all the taxpayers to enjoin a practice authorized by the school board would be a suit by vital parties in interest. They would not be able to show, any more than the two present taxpayers have done, that the reading of the Bible adds to the taxes they pay. But if they were right in their contentions on the merits, they would establish that their public schools were being deflected from the educational program for which the taxes were raised. That seems to me to be an adequate interest for the maintenance of this suit by all the taxpayers. . . .

---

[20] 342 U.S. 429 (1952).

RLW: Taxpayers always have standing to challenge a tax that they are required to pay. Thus, if Congress had levied a tax on hospitals to finance the Maternity Act, the hospitals would have had standing to challenge the tax. But, as the holding in *Frothingham* suggests, taxpayers find it more difficult to challenge spending programs.

DEL: In fact, case law has evolved to the point that the only decision recognizing taxpayer standing to challenge a federal spending program, *Flast v. Cohen*, has been narrowed to the point that it seems to apply only to circumstances identical to those presented in the case.

Flast v. Cohen
392 U.S. 83 (1968)

Mr. Chief Justice WARREN delivered the opinion of the Court.

In *Frothingham v. Mellon*, 262 U.S. 447 (1923), this Court ruled that a federal taxpayer is without standing to challenge the constitutionality of a federal statute. That ruling has stood for 45 years as an impenetrable barrier to suits against Acts of Congress brought by individuals who can assert only the interest of federal taxpayers. In this case, we must decide whether the Frothingham barrier should be lowered when a taxpayer attacks a federal statute on the ground that it violates the Establishment and Free Exercise Clauses of the First Amendment.

Appellants filed suit in the United States District Court for the Southern District of New York to enjoin the allegedly unconstitutional expenditure of federal funds under Titles I and II of the Elementary and Secondary Education Act of 1965. The complaint alleged that the seven appellants had as a common attribute that "each pay(s) income taxes of the United States," and it is clear from the complaint that the appellants were resting their standing to maintain the action solely on their status as federal taxpayers. The appellees, who are charged by Congress with administering the Elementary and Secondary Education Act of 1965, were sued in their official capacities.

The gravamen of the appellants' complaint was that federal funds appropriated under the Act were being used to finance instruction in reading, arithmetic, and other subjects in religious schools, and to purchase textbooks and other instructional materials for use in such schools. Such expenditures were alleged to be in contravention of the Establishment and Free Exercise Clauses of the First Amendment.... The complaint asked for a declaration that appellees' actions in approving the expenditure of federal funds for the alleged purposes were not authorized by the Act or, in the alternative, that if appellees' actions are deemed within the authority and intent of the Act, "the Act is to that extent unconstitutional and void." The complaint also prayed for an injunction to enjoin appellees from approving any expenditure of federal funds for the allegedly unconstitutional purposes....

. . .

Although the barrier Frothingham erected against federal taxpayer suits has never been breached, the decision has been the source of some confusion and the object of considerable criticism. The confusion has developed as commentators have tried to determine whether Frothingham establishes a constitutional bar to taxpayer suits or whether the Court was simply imposing a rule of self-restraint which was not constitutionally compelled.... The opinion delivered in Frothingham can be read to support either position....

To the extent that Frothingham has been viewed as resting on policy considerations, it has been criticized as depending on assumptions not consistent with modern conditions. For example, some commentators have pointed out that a number of corporate taxpayers today have a federal tax liability running into hundreds of millions of dollars, and such taxpayers have a far greater monetary stake in the Federal Treasury than they do in any municipal treasury. To some degree, the fear expressed in Frothingham that allowing one taxpayer to sue would inundate the federal courts with countless similar suits has been mitigated by the ready availability of the devices of class actions and joinder under the Federal Rules of Civil Procedure, adopted subsequent to the decision in Frothingham. Whatever the merits of the current debate over Frothingham, its very existence suggests that we should undertake a fresh examination of the limitations upon standing to sue in a federal court and the application of those limitations to taxpayer suits.

. . .

The jurisdiction of federal courts is defined and limited by Article III of the Constitution. In terms relevant to the question for decision in this case, the judicial power of federal courts is constitutionally restricted to "cases" and "controversies." As is so often the situation in constitutional adjudication, those two words have an iceberg quality, containing beneath their surface simplicity submerged complexities which go to the very heart of our constitutional form of government. Embodied in the words "cases" and "controversies" are two complementary but somewhat different limitations. In part those words limit the business of federal courts to questions presented in an adversary context and in a form historically viewed as capable of resolution through the judicial process. And in part those words define the role assigned to the judiciary in a tripartite allocation of power to assure that the federal courts will not intrude into areas committed to the other branches of government. Justiciability is the term of art employed to give expression to this dual limitation placed upon federal courts by the case-and-controversy doctrine.

. . .

Additional uncertainty exists in the doctrine of justiciability because that doctrine has become a blend of constitutional requirements and policy considerations. And a policy limitation is "not always clearly distinguished from the constitutional limitation." *Barrows v. Jackson*, 346 U.S. 249, 255 (1953). . . .

It is in this context that the standing question presented by this case must be viewed and that the Government's argument on that question must be evaluated. As we understand it, the Government's position is that the constitutional scheme of separation of powers, and the deference owed by the federal judiciary to the other two branches of government within that scheme, present an absolute bar to taxpayer suits challenging the validity of federal spending programs. The Government views such suits as involving no more than the mere disagreement by the taxpayer "with the uses to which tax money is put." According to the Government, the resolution of such disagreements is committed to other branches of the Federal Government and not to the judiciary. Consequently, the Government contends that, under no circumstances, should standing be conferred on federal taxpayers to challenge a federal taxing or spending program. An analysis of the function served by standing limitations compels a rejection of the Government's position.

Standing is an aspect of justiciability and, as such, the problem of standing is surrounded by the same complexities and vagaries that inhere in justiciability. Standing has been called one of "the must amorphous (concepts) in the entire domain of public law." . . .

Despite the complexities and uncertainties, some meaningful form can be given to the jurisdictional limitations placed on federal court power by the concept of standing. The fundamental aspect of standing is that it focuses on the party seeking to get his complaint before a federal court and not on the issues he wishes to have adjudicated. The "gist of the question of standing" is whether the party seeking relief has "alleged such a personal stake in the outcome of the controversy as to assure that concrete adverseness which sharpens the presentation of issues upon which the court so largely depends for illumination of difficult constitutional questions." *Baker v. Carr*, 369 U.S. 186, 204 (1962). In other words, when standing is placed in issue in a case, the question is whether the person whose standing is challenged is a proper party to request an adjudication of a particular issue and not whether the issue itself is justiciable. Thus, a party may have standing in a particular case, but the federal court may nevertheless decline to pass on the merits of the case because, for example, it presents a political question. A proper party is demanded so that federal courts will not be asked to decide "ill-defined controversies over constitutional issues," *United Public Workers of America v. Mitchell*, 330 U.S. 75, 90 (1947), or a case which is of "a hypothetical or abstract character." *Aetna Life Insurance Co. of Hartford, Conn. v. Haworth*, 300 U.S. 27, 240 (1937). So stated, the standing requirement is closely related to, although more general than, the rule that federal courts will not entertain friendly suits, or those which are feigned or collusive in nature.

When the emphasis in the standing problem is placed on whether the person invoking a federal court's jurisdiction is a proper party to maintain the action, the weakness of the Government's argument in this case becomes apparent. The question whether a particular person is a proper party to maintain the action does not, by its own force, raise separation of powers problems related to improper judicial interference in areas committed to other branches of the Federal Government. Such problems arise, if at all, only from the substantive issues the individual seeks to have adjudicated. Thus, in terms of Article III limitations on federal court jurisdiction, the question of standing is related only to whether the dispute sought to be adjudicated will be presented in an adversary context and in a form historically viewed as capable of judicial resolution. It is for that reason that the emphasis in standing problems is on whether the party invoking federal court jurisdiction has "a personal stake in the outcome of the controversy," *Baker v. Carr, supra*, 369 U.S. at 204, and whether the dispute touches upon "the legal relations of parties having adverse legal interests." *Aetna Life Insurance Co. v. Haworth, supra*, 300 U.S. at 240–241. A taxpayer may or may not have the requisite personal stake in the outcome, depending upon the circumstances of the particular case. Therefore, we find no absolute bar in Article III to suits by federal taxpayers challenging allegedly unconstitutional federal taxing and spending programs. There remains, however, the problem of determining the circumstances under which a federal taxpayer will be deemed to have the personal stake and interest that impart the necessary concrete adverseness to such litigation so that standing can be conferred on the taxpayer qua taxpayer consistent with the constitutional limitations of Article III.

. . .

The various rules of standing applied by federal courts have not been developed in the abstract. Rather, they have been fashioned with specific reference to the status asserted by the party whose standing is challenged and to the type of question he wishes to have adjudicated. We have noted that, in deciding the question of standing, it is not relevant that the substantive issues in the litigation might be nonjusticiable. However, our decisions establish that, in ruling on standing, it is both appropriate and necessary to look to the substantive issues for another purpose, namely, to determine whether there is a logical nexus between the status asserted and the claim sought to be adjudicated. For example, standing requirements will vary in First Amendment religion cases depending upon whether the party raises an Establishment Clause claim or a claim under the Free Exercise Clause. *See* MᶜGᴏᴡᴀɴ v. State of Maryland, 366 U.S. 420, 429–430 (1961). Such inquiries into the nexus between the status asserted by the litigant and the claim he presents are essential to assure that he is a proper and appropriate party to invoke federal judicial power. Thus, our point of reference in this case is the standing of individuals who assert only the status of federal taxpayers and who challenge the constitutionality of a federal spending program. Whether such individuals have standing to maintain that form of action turns on whether they can demonstrate the necessary stake as taxpayers in the outcome of the litigation to satisfy Article III requirements.

The nexus demanded of federal taxpayers has two aspects to it. First, the taxpayer must establish a logical link between that status and the type of legislative enactment attacked. Thus, a taxpayer will be a proper party to allege the unconstitutionality only of exercises of congressional power under the taxing and spending clause of Art. I, § 8, of the Constitution. It will not be sufficient to allege an incidental expenditure of tax funds in the administration of an essentially regulatory statute. This requirement is consistent with the limitation imposed upon state-taxpayer standing in federal courts in *Doremus v. Board of Education*, 342 U.S. 429 (1952). Secondly, the taxpayer must establish a nexus between that status and the precise nature of the constitutional infringement alleged. Under this requirement, the taxpayer must show that the challenged enactment exceeds specific constitutional limitations imposed upon the exercise of the congressional taxing and spending power and not simply that the enactment is generally beyond the powers delegated to Congress by Art. I, § 8. When both nexuses are established, the litigant will have shown a taxpayer's stake in the outcome of the controversy and will be a proper and appropriate party to invoke a federal court's jurisdiction.

The taxpayer-appellants in this case have satisfied both nexuses to support their claim of standing under the test we announce today. Their constitutional challenge is made to an exercise by Congress of its power under Art. I, § 8, to spend for the general welfare, and the challenged program involves a substantial expenditure of federal tax funds.[23] In addition, appellants have alleged that the challenged expenditures violate the Establishment and Free Exercise Clauses of the First Amendment. Our history vividly illustrates that one of the specific evils feared by those who drafted the Establishment Clause and fought for its adoption was that the taxing and spending power would be used to favor one religion over another or to support religion in general. James Madison, who is generally recognized as the leading architect of the religion clauses of the First Amendment, observed in his famous Memorial and Remonstrance Against Religious Assessments that "the same authority which can force a citizen to contribute three pence only of his property for the support of any one establishment, may force him to conform to any other establishment in all cases whatsoever." 2 Writings of James Madison 183, 186 (Hunt ed. 1901). The concern of Madison and his supporters was quite clearly that religious liberty ultimately would be the victim if government could employ its taxing and spending powers to aid one religion over another or to aid religion in general. The Establishment Clause was designed as a specific bulwark against such potential abuses of governmental power, and that clause of the First Amendment operates as a specific constitutional limitation upon the exercise by Congress of the taxing and spending power conferred by Art. I, § 8.

The allegations of the taxpayer in *Frothingham v. Mellon, supra*, were quite different from those made in this case, and the result in Frothingham is consistent with the test of taxpayer standing announced today. The taxpayer in Frothingham attacked a federal spending program and she, therefore, established the first nexus required. However, she lacked standing because her constitutional attack was not based on an allegation that Congress, in enacting the Maternity Act of 1921, had breached a specific limitation upon its taxing and spending power. The taxpayer in Frothingham alleged essentially that Congress, by enacting the challenged statute, had exceeded the general powers delegated to it by Art. I, § 8, and that Congress had thereby invaded the legislative province reserved to the States by the Tenth Amendment. To be sure, Mrs. Frothingham made the additional allegation that her tax liability would be increased as a result of the allegedly unconstitutional enactment, and she framed that allegation in terms of a deprivation of property without due process of law. However, the Due Process Clause of the

---

[23] Almost $1,000,000,000 was appropriated to implement the Elementary and Secondary Education Act in 1965. 79 Stat. 832.

Fifth Amendment does not protect taxpayers against increases in tax liability, and the taxpayer in Frothingham failed to make any additional claim that the harm she alleged resulted from a breach by Congress of the specific constitutional limitations imposed upon an exercise of the taxing and spending power. In essence, Mrs. Frothingham was attempting to assert the States' interest in their legislative prerogatives and not a federal taxpayer's interest in being free of taxing and spending in contravention of specific constitutional limitations imposed upon Congress' taxing and spending power.

We have noted that the Establishment Clause of the First Amendment does specifically limit the taxing and spending power conferred by Art. I, § 8. Whether the Constitution contains other specific limitations can be determined only in the context of future cases. However, whenever such specific limitations are found, we believe a taxpayer will have a clear stake as a taxpayer in assuring that they are not breached by Congress. Consequently, we hold that a taxpayer will have standing consistent with Article III to invoke federal judicial power when he alleges that congressional action under the taxing and spending clause is in derogation of those constitutional provisions which operate to restrict the exercise of the taxing and spending power. The taxpayer's allegation in such cases would be that his tax money is being extracted and spent in violation of specific constitutional protections against such abuses of legislative power. Such an injury is appropriate for judicial redress, and the taxpayer has established the necessary nexus between his status and the nature of the allegedly unconstitutional action to support his claim of standing to secure judicial review. Under such circumstances, we feel confident that the questions will be framed with the necessary specificity, that the issues will be contested with the necessary adverseness and that the litigation will be pursued with the necessary vigor to assure that the constitutional challenge will be made in a form traditionally thought to be capable of judicial resolution. We lack that confidence in cases such as Frothingham where a taxpayer seeks to employ a federal court as a forum in which to air his generalized grievances about the conduct of government or the allocation of power in the Federal System.

While we express no view at all on the merits of appellants' claims in this case, their complaint contains sufficient allegations under the criteria we have outlined to give them standing to invoke a federal court's jurisdiction for an adjudication on the merits.

Reversed.

Mr. Justice DOUGLAS, concurring.

. . .

Taxpayers can be vigilant private attorneys general. Their stake in the outcome of litigation may be de minimis by financial standards, yet very great when measured by a particular constitutional mandate. . . .

. . .

The judiciary is an indispensable part of the operation of our federal system. With the growing complexities of government it is often the one and only place where effective relief can be obtained. If the judiciary were to become a super-legislative group sitting in judgment on the affairs of people, the situation would be intolerable. But where wrongs to individuals are done by violation of specific guarantees, it is abdication for courts to close their doors.

. . .

We have a Constitution designed to keep government out of private domains. But the fences have often been broken down; and Frothingham denied effective machinery to restore them. The Constitution even with the judicial gloss it has acquired plainly is not adequate to protect the individual against the growing bureaucracy in the Legislative and Executive Branches. He faces a formidable opponent in government, even when he is endowed with funds and with courage. The individual is almost certain to be plowed under, unless he has a well-organized active political group to speak for him. The church is one. The press is another. The union is a third. But if a powerful sponsor is lacking, individual liberty withers—in spite of glowing opinions and resounding constitutional phrases.

. . .

There need be no inundation of the federal courts if taxpayers' suits are allowed. There is a wise judicial discretion that usually can distinguish between the frivolous question and the substantial question, between cases ripe for decision and cases that need prior administrative processing, and the like. . . .

. . .

Mr. Justice FORTAS, concurring.

I would confine the ruling in this case to the proposition that a taxpayer may maintain a suit to challenge the validity of a federal expenditure on the ground that the expenditure violates the Establishment Clause. As the Court's opinion recites, there is enough in the constitutional history of the Establishment Clause to support the thesis that this Clause includes a specific prohibition upon the use of the power to tax to support an establishment of religion. There is no reason to suggest, and no basis in the logic of this decision for implying, that there may be other types of congressional expenditures which may be attacked by a litigant solely on the basis of his status as a taxpayer.

. . .

Mr. Justice HARLAN, dissenting.

. . .

The complaint in this case, unlike that in Frothingham, contains no allegation that the contested expenditures will in any fashion affect the amount of these taxpayers' own existing or foreseeable tax obligations. Even in cases in which such an allegation is made, the suit cannot result in an adjudication either of the plaintiff's tax liabilities or of the propriety of any particular level of taxation. The relief available to such a plaintiff consists entirely of the vindication of rights held in common by all citizens. . . .

Nor are taxpayers' interests in the expenditure of public funds differentiated from those of the general public by any special rights retained by them in their tax payments. The simple fact is that no such rights can sensibly be said to exist. Taxes are ordinarily levied by the United States without limitations of purpose; absent such a limitation, payments received by the Treasury in satisfaction of tax obligations lawfully created become part of the Government's general funds. . . .

. . .

[The Court declares] that taxpayers will be "deemed" to have the necessary personal interest if their suits satisfy two criteria. . . . The difficulties with these criteria are many and severe, but it is enough for the moment to emphasize that they are not in any sense a measurement of any plaintiff's interest in the outcome of any suit. . . .

. . .

The Court's position is equally precarious if it is assumed that its premise is that the Establishment Clause is in some uncertain fashion a more "specific" limitation upon Congress' powers than are the various other constitutional commands. It is obvious, first, that only in some Pickwickian sense are any of the provisions with which the Court is concerned "specific(ally)" limitations upon spending, for they contain nothing that is expressly directed at the expenditure of public funds. . . .

Even if it is assumed that such distinctions may properly be drawn, it does not follow that federal taxpayers hold any "personal constitu-

tional right" such that they may each contest the validity under the Establishment Clause of all federal expenditures. The difficulty, with which the Court never comes to grips, is that taxpayers' suits under the Establishment Clause are not in these circumstances meaningfully different from other public actions. If this case involved a tax specifically designed for the support of religion, as was the Virginia tax opposed by Madison in his Memorial and Remonstrance, I would agree that taxpayers have rights under the religious clauses of the First Amendment that would permit them standing to challenge the tax's validity in the federal courts. But this is not such a case, and appellants challenge an expenditure, not a tax. Where no such tax is involved, a taxpayer's complaint can consist only of an allegation that public funds have been, or shortly will be, expended for purposes inconsistent with the Constitution. The taxpayer cannot ask the return of any portion of his previous tax payments, cannot prevent the collection of any existing tax debt, and cannot demand an adjudication of the propriety of any particular level of taxation. His tax payments are received for the general purposes of the United States, and are, upon proper receipt, lost in the general revenues. . . . The interests he represents, and the rights he espouses, are, as they are in all public actions, those held in common by all citizens. To describe those rights and interests as personal, and to intimate that they are in some unspecified fashion to be differentiated from those of the general public, reduces constitutional standing to a word game played by secret rules.

. . .

This does not mean that we would, under such a rule, be enabled to avoid our constitutional responsibilities, or that we would confine to limbo the First Amendment or any other constitutional command. . . . The recent history of this Court [shows] . . . that questions involving the religious clauses will not, if federal taxpayers are prevented from contesting federal expenditures, be left "unacknowledged, unresolved, and undecided."

Schlesinger v. Reservists Committee to Stop the War[21] involved Article I, § 6, Club. 2 of the U.S. Constitution which provides: "No Senator or Representative shall, during the Time for which he was elected, be appointed to any civil Office under the Authority of the United States, which shall have been created, or the Emoluments whereof shall have been increased during such time; and no Person holding any Office under the United States, shall be a Member of either House during his Continuance in Office." Respondents, the Reservists Committee to Stop the War and certain named individ-

---

[21] 418 U.S. 208 (1974).

uals who were taxpayers and reservists, challenged the Reserve membership of Members of Congress[22] as being in violation of the Incompatibility Clause. Respondents claimed that, as reservists, members of Congress were subject to the possibility of undue influence from the Executive Branch given the President's power to call reservists to active duty without their consent, and his power to discharge commissioned reservists who serve only at his pleasure. Respondents also claimed that reserve membership "deprives or may deprive the individual named plaintiffs and all other citizens and taxpayers of the United States of the faithful discharge by members of Congress who are members of the Reserves of their duties as members of Congress, to which all citizens and taxpayers are entitled."

Mr. Chief Justice Burger, writing for the majority, concluded that respondents could not establish "citizen" standing:

> The only interest all citizens share in the claim advanced by respondents is one which presents injury in the abstract. Respondents seek to have the Judicial Branch compel the Executive Branch to act in conformity with the Incompatibility Clause, an interest shared by all citizens. The very language of respondents' complaint, reveals that it is nothing more than a matter of speculation whether the claimed nonobservance of that Clause deprives citizens of the faithful discharge of the legislative duties of reservist Members of Congress. And that claimed nonobservance, standing alone, would adversely affect only the generalized interest of all citizens in constitutional governance, and that is an abstract injury.[23] The Court has previously declined to treat "generalized grievances" about the conduct of Government as a basis for taxpayer standing. . . .

> . . . All citizens, of course, share equally an interest in the independence of each branch of Government. In some fashion, every provision of the Constitution was meant to serve the interests of all. Such a generalized interest, however, is too abstract to constitute a "case or controversy" appropriate for judicial resolution.[24] The proposition that all constitutional provisions are enforceable by any citizen simply because citizens are the ultimate beneficiaries of those provisions has no boundaries.

Closely linked to the idea that generalized citizen interest is a sufficient basis for standing was the District Court's observation that it was not irrelevant that if respondents could not obtain judicial review of petitioners' action, "then as a practical matter no one can." Our system of government leaves many crucial decisions to the political processes. The assumption that if respondents have no standing to sue, no one would have standing, is not a reason to find standing. The Court also held that

---

[22] At the time suit was filed, 130 Members of the 91st Congress were also members of the Reserves, which are divided into Ready, Standby, and Retired components. By the end of the 92d Congress, 119 Members were reservists. . . .

[23] The generalized nature of respondents' claim is revealed by the scope of relief sought, i.e., removal of all reservist Members of Congress from Reserve status rather than the removal of only those reservist Members who manifested by their actions that they were influenced by their Reserve status to act adversely to respondents' interest.

[24] Satisfaction of the Data Processing "zone of interest" requirement seemingly relied upon to find citizen standing does not support such standing for two reasons: first, that case involved judicial review under the Administrative Procedure Act of regulatory agency action alleged to have caused private competitive injury; second, Data Processing required a showing of injury in fact, in addition to the "zone of interest" requirement. Until a judicially cognizable injury is shown no other inquiry is relevant to consideration of citizen standing.

respondents could not establish taxpayer standing because they "did not challenge an enactment under Art. I, § 8, but rather the action of the Executive Branch in permitting Members of Congress to maintain their Reserve status."

Mr. Justice Stewart, concurring, concluded that "respondents seek only to air what we described in Flast as 'generalized grievances about the conduct of government.'[25] Our prior cases make clear that such abstract allegations cannot suffice to confer Art. III standing. . . ."

Mr. Justice Douglas dissented:

The . . . complaint alleges injuries to the ability of the average citizen to make his political advocacy effective whenever it touches on the vested interests of the Pentagon. It is said that all who oppose the expansion of military influence in our national affairs find they are met with a powerful lobby—the Reserve Officers Association—which has strong congressional allies.

Whether that is true or not we do not know. So far as the Incompatibility Clause of the Constitution is concerned that contention is immaterial. It is as immaterial to the function of Art. I, § 6, Club. 2, of the Constitution as would be a suggestion that the establishment of a religion under the First Amendment is benign in a given case. What the Framers did in each case was to set up constitutional fences barring certain affiliations, certain kinds of appropriations. Their judgment was that the potential for evil was so great that no appropriations of that character should be made.

The interest of citizens in guarantees written in the Constitution seems obvious. Who other than citizens has a better right to have the Incompatibility Clause enforced? It is their interests that the Incompatibility Clause was designed to protect. The Executive Branch under our regime is not a fiefdom or principality competing with the Legislative as another center of power. It operates within a constitutional framework, and it is that constitutional framework that these citizens want to keep intact. That is, in my view, their rightful concern. . . . The "personal stake" in the present case is keeping the Incompatibility Clause an operative force in the Government by freeing the entanglement of the federal bureaucracy with the Legislative Branch.

. . .

The interest of the citizen in this constitutional question is of course, common to all citizens. But as we said in *United States v. SCRAP*, "standing is not to be denied simply because many people suffer the same injury. . . . To deny standing to persons who are in fact injured simply because many others are also injured, would mean that the most injurious and widespread Government actions could be questioned by nobody."

Mr. Justice Marshall, dissenting, contended that the "specific interest" which respondents asserted is not "'general interest common to all members of the public.' Not all citizens desired to have the Congress take all steps necessary to terminate American involvement in Vietnam, and not all citizens who so desired sought to persuade members of Congress to that end."

United States v. Richardson[26] involved a taxpayer's challenge to the Central Intelligence Agency Act of 1949 which allowed the government to conceal CIA expenditures from the general public. Respondent, suing as a citizen and a taxpayer, sought a detailed statement of CIA expenditures after unsuccessfully attempting to obtain such

---

[25] 392 U.S., at 106.
[26] 418 U.S. 166 (1974).

information from various governmental agencies. Respondent claimed that he was entitled to such statement by virtue of Art. I, § 9, Club. 7, of the Constitution which provides:

No Money shall be drawn from the Treasury, but in Consequence of Appropriations made by Law; and a regular Statement and Account of the Receipts and Expenditures of all public Money shall be published from time to time.

In an opinion written by Mr. Justice Burger, the Court dismissed the complaint on standing grounds:

Respondent makes no claim that appropriated funds are being spent in violation of a "specific constitutional limitation upon the . . . taxing and spending power. . . . " 392 U.S., at 104. Rather, he asks the courts to compel the Government to give him information on precisely how the CIA spends its funds. Thus there is no "logical nexus" between the asserted status of taxpayer and the claimed failure of the Congress to require the Executive to supply a more detailed report of the expenditures of that agency.

The question presented thus is simply and narrowly whether these claims meet the standards for taxpayer standing set forth in Flast; we hold they do not. Respondent is seeking "to employ a federal court as a forum in which to air his generalized grievances about the conduct of government." 392 U.S., at 106. Both *Frothingham and Flast, supra,* reject that basis for standing.

. . .

The respondent's claim is that without detailed information on CIA expenditures—and hence its activities—he cannot intelligently follow the actions of Congress or the Executive, nor can he properly fulfill his obligations as a member of the electorate in voting for candidates seeking national office.

This is surely the kind of a generalized grievance described in both Frothingham and Flast since the impact on him is plainly undifferentiated and "common to all members of the public." *Ex parte Levitt,* 302 U.S. 633, 634 (1937). . . .

. . .

It can be argued that if respondent is not permitted to litigate this issue, no one can do so. In a very real sense, the absence of any particular individual or class to litigate these claims gives support to the argument that the subject matter is committed to the surveillance of Congress, and ultimately to the political process. . . . The Constitution created a representative Government with the representatives directly responsible to their constituents at stated periods of two, four, and six years. . . .

Mr. Justice Powell concurred:

[I] would lay to rest the approach undertaken in Flast. I would not overrule Flast on its facts, because it is now settled that federal taxpayer standing exists in Establishment Clause cases. I would not, however, perpetuate the doctrinal confusion inherent in the Flast two-part "nexus" test. That test is not a reliable indicator of when a federal taxpayer has standing, and it has no sound relationship to the question whether such a plaintiff, with no other interest at stake, should be allowed to bring suit against one of the branches of the Federal Government. In my opinion, it should be abandoned.

Mr. Justice Douglas dissented:

. . . Flast recognizes "standing" of a taxpayer to challenge appropriations made in the face of a constitutional prohibition, and it logically asks, "how can

a taxpayer make that challenge unless he knows how the money is being spent?"
465 F.2d 844, 853.

History shows that the curse of government is not always venality; secrecy
is one of the most tempting coverups to save regimes from criticism. As the
Court of Appeals said: "The Framers of the Constitution deemed fiscal information essential if the electorate was to exercise any control over its representatives and meet their new responsibilities as citizens of the Republic; and they
mandated publication, although stated in general terms, of the Government's
receipts and expenditures. Whatever the ultimate scope and extent of that
obligation, its elimination generates a sufficient, adverse interest in a taxpayer." Ibid.

Whatever may be the merits of the underlying claim, it seems clear that
the taxpayer in the present case is not making a generalized complaint about
the operation of Government. He does not even challenge the constitutionality
of the Central Intelligence Agency Act. He only wants to know the amount
of tax money exacted from him that goes into CIA activities. Secrecy of the
Government acquires new sanctity when his claim is denied. . . .

. . .

From the history of the clause it is apparent that the Framers inserted it
in the Constitution to give the public knowledge of the way public funds are
expended. No one has a greater "personal stake" in policing this protective
measure than a taxpayer. . . .

Mr. Justice Stewart, joined by Mr. Justice Marshall, also dissented:

Seeking a determination that the Government owes him a duty to supply
the information he has requested, the respondent is in the position of a traditional Hohfeldian plaintiff.[27] He contends that the Statement and Account
Clause gives him a right to receive the information and burdens the Government with a correlative duty to supply it. Courts of law exist for the resolution
of such right-duty disputes.

. . .

On the merits, I presume that the Government's position would be that
the Statement and Account Clause of the Constitution does not impose an
affirmative duty upon it; that any such duty does not in any event run to
Richardson; that any such duty is subject to legislative qualifications, one of
which is applicable here; and that the question involved is political and thus
not justiciable. Richardson might ultimately be thrown out of court on any one
of these grounds, or some other. But to say that he might ultimately lose his
lawsuit certainly does not mean that he had no standing to bring it.

Laird v. Tatum[28] involved a claim that the Department of the Army had engaged
in "surveillance of lawful and peaceful civilian political activity." Respondents alleged
that the surveillance had a "chilling" effect on the exercise of their First Amendment
rights. In an opinion written by Mr. Justice Burger, the Court concluded that respondents lacked standing:

[R]espondents . . . claim, simply stated, is that they disagree with the judgments made by the Executive Branch with respect to the type and amount of

---

[27] Jaffe, *The Citizen as Litigant in Public Actions: The Non-Hohfeldian or Ideological Plaintiff*, 116 U. Pa. L. Rev. 1033 (1968). *See* Hohfeld, *Some Fundamental Legal Conceptions as
Applied in Judicial Reasoning*, 23 Yale L.J. 16 (1913).

[28] 408 U.S. 1 (1972).

information the Army needs and that the very existence of the Army's data-gathering system produces a constitutionally impermissible chilling effect upon the exercise of their First Amendment rights. That alleged "chilling" effect may perhaps be seen as arising from respondents' very perception of the system as inappropriate to the Army's role under our form of government, or as arising from respondents' beliefs that it is inherently dangerous for the military to be concerned with activities in the civilian sector, or as arising from respondents' less generalized yet speculative apprehensiveness that the Army may at some future date misuse the information in some way that would cause direct harm to respondents. Allegations of a subjective "chill" are not an adequate substitute for a claim of specific present objective harm or a threat of specific future harm; "the federal courts established pursuant to Article III of the Constitution do not render advisory opinions." *United Public Workers of America (C.I.O.) v. Mitchell*, 330 U.S. 75, 89 (1947).

Stripped to its essentials, what respondents appear to be seeking is a broad-scale investigation, conducted by themselves as private parties armed with the subpoena power of a federal district court and the power of cross-examination, to probe into the Army's intelligence-gathering activities, with the district court determining at the conclusion of that investigation the extent to which those activities may or may not be appropriate to the Army's mission. . . .

Carried to its logical end, this approach would have the federal courts as virtually continuing monitors of the wisdom and soundness of Executive action; such a role is appropriate for the Congress acting through its committees and the "power of the purse"; it is not the role of the judiciary, absent actual present or immediately threatened injury resulting from unlawful governmental action.

Mr. Justice Brennan, joined by two other justices, dissented:

[I] agree with Judge Wilkey, writing for the Court of Appeals, that . . . "[t]o the extent that the Army's argument against justiciability here includes the claim that (respondents) lack standing to bring this action, we cannot agree. If the Army's system does indeed derogate First Amendment values, the (respondents) are persons who are sufficiently affected to permit their complaint to be heard. The record shows that most if not all of the (respondents) and/or the organizations of which they are members have been the subject of Army surveillance reports and their names have appeared in the Army's records. Since this is precisely the injury of which (respondents) complain, they have standing to seek redress for that alleged injury in court and will provide the necessary adversary interest that is required by the standing doctrine, on the issue of whether the actions complained of do in fact inhibit the exercise of First Amendment rights. Nor should the fact that these particular persons are sufficiently uninhibited to bring this suit be any ground for objecting to their standing." *Id.*, at 79 n.17.

Valley Forge Christian College v. Americans United
454 U.S. 464 (1982)

Justice REHNQUIST delivered the opinion of the Court.

. . .

The property which spawned this litigation was acquired by the Department of the Army in 1942, as part of a larger tract of approximately

181 acres of land northwest of Philadelphia. The Army built on that land the Valley Forge General Hospital, and for 30 years thereafter, that hospital provided medical care for members of the Armed Forces. In April 1973, as part of a plan to reduce the number of military installations in the United States, the Secretary of Defense proposed to close the hospital, and the General Services Administration declared it to be "surplus property."

The Department of Health, Education, and Welfare (HEW) eventually assumed responsibility for disposing of portions of the property, and in August 1976, it conveyed a 77-acre tract to petitioner, the Valley Forge Christian College. The appraised value of the property at the time of conveyance was $577,500. This appraised value was discounted, however, by the Secretary's computation of a 100% public benefit allowance, which permitted petitioner to acquire the property without making any financial payment for it. The deed from HEW conveyed the land in fee simple with certain conditions subsequent, which required petitioner to use the property for 30 years solely for the educational purposes described in petitioner's application. . . .

. . .

Petitioner is a nonprofit educational institution operating under the supervision of a religious order known as the Assemblies of God. By its own description, petitioner's purpose is "to offer systematic training on the collegiate level to men and women for Christian service as either ministers or laymen." Its degree programs reflect this orientation by providing courses of study "to train leaders for church related ministries." Faculty members must "have been baptized in the Holy Spirit and be living consistent Christian lives," and all members of the college administration must be affiliated with the Assemblies of God. In its application for the 77-acre tract, petitioner represented that, if it obtained the property, it would make "additions to its offerings in the arts and humanities," and would strengthen its "psychology" and "counselling" courses to provide services in inner-city areas.

[R]espondents Americans United for Separation of Church and State, Inc. (Americans United), and four of its employees, . . . [sought] to challenge the conveyance on the ground that it violated the Establishment Clause of the First Amendment. In its amended complaint, Americans United described itself as a nonprofit organization composed of 90,000 "taxpayer members." The complaint asserted that each member "would be deprived of the fair and constitutional use of his (her) tax dollar for constitutional purposes in violation of his (her) rights under the First Amendment of the United States Constitution." Respondents sought a declaration that the conveyance was

null and void, and an order compelling petitioner to transfer the property back to the United States.

. . .

Unlike the plaintiffs in Flast, respondents fail the first prong of the test for taxpayer standing. Their claim is deficient in two respects. First, the source of their complaint is not a congressional action, but a decision by HEW to transfer a parcel of federal property.[15] Flast limited taxpayer standing to challenges directed "only [at] exercises of congressional power."

Second, and perhaps redundantly, the property transfer about which respondents complain was not an exercise of authority conferred by the Taxing and Spending Clause of Art. I, § 8. The authorizing legislation, the Federal Property and Administrative Services Act of 1949, was an evident exercise of Congress' power under the Property Clause, Art. IV, § 3, Club. 2. Respondents do not dispute this conclusion, and it is decisive of any claim of taxpayer standing under the Flast precedent.[17]

. . .

Although the Court of Appeals properly doubted respondents' ability to establish

---

[15] Respondents do not challenge the constitutionality of the Federal Property and Administrative Services Act itself, but rather a particular Executive Branch action arguably authorized by the Act.

[17] Although not necessary to our decision, we note that any connection between the challenged property transfer and respondents' tax burden is at best speculative and at worst nonexistent. Although public funds were expended to establish the Valley Forge General Hospital, the land was acquired and the facilities constructed 30 years prior to the challenged transfer. Respondents do not challenge this expenditure, and we do not immediately perceive how such a challenge might now be raised. Nor do respondents dispute the Government's conclusion that the property has become useless for federal purposes and ought to be disposed of in some productive manner. In fact, respondents' only objection is that the Government did not receive adequate consideration for the transfer, because petitioner's use of the property will not confer a public benefit. Assuming, arguendo, that this proposition is true, an assumption by no means clear, there is no basis for believing that a transfer to a different purchaser would have added to Government receipts. As the Government argues, "the ultimate purchaser would, in all likelihood, have been another non-profit institution or local school district rather than a purchaser for cash." Moreover, each year of delay in disposing of the property depleted the Treasury by the amounts necessary to maintain a facility that had lost its value to the Government. Even if respondents had brought their claim within the outer limits of Flast, therefore, they still would have encountered serious difficulty in establishing that they "personally would benefit in a tangible way from the court's intervention." *Warth v. Seldin*, 422 U.S., at 508.

standing solely on the basis of their taxpayer status, it considered their allegations of taxpayer injury to be "essentially an assumed role." "Plaintiffs have no reason to expect, nor perhaps do they care about, any personal tax saving that might result should they prevail. The crux of the interest at stake, the plaintiffs argue, is found in the Establishment Clause, not in the supposed loss of money as such. As a matter of primary identity, therefore, the plaintiffs are not so much taxpayers as separationists. . . . " In the court's view, respondents had established standing by virtue of an "'injury in fact' to their shared individuated right to a government that 'shall make no law respecting the establishment of religion.'" The court distinguished this "injury" from "the question of 'citizen standing' as such." Although citizens generally could not establish standing simply by claiming an interest in governmental observance of the Constitution, respondents had "set forth instead a particular and concrete injury" to a "personal constitutional right."

. . .

In finding that respondents had alleged something more than "the generalized interest of all citizens in constitutional governance," *Schlesinger, supra,* 418 U.S., at 217, the Court of Appeals relied on factual differences which we do not think amount to legal distinctions. The court decided that respondents' claim differed from those in Schlesinger and Richardson, which were predicated, respectively, on the Incompatibility and Accounts Clauses, because "it is at the very least arguable that the Establishment Clause creates in each citizen a 'personal constitutional right' to a government that does not establish religion." The court found it unnecessary to determine whether this "arguable" proposition was correct, since it judged the mere allegation of a legal right sufficient to confer standing.

This reasoning process merely disguises, we think with a rather thin veil, the inconsistency of the court's results with our decisions in Schlesinger and Richardson. The plaintiffs in those cases plainly asserted a "personal right" to have the Government act in accordance with their views of the Constitution; indeed, we see no barrier to the assertion of such claims with respect to any constitutional provision. But assertion of a right to a particular kind of Government conduct, which the Government has violated by acting differently, cannot alone satisfy the requirements of Art. III without draining those requirements of meaning.

Nor can Schlesinger and Richardson be distinguished on the ground that the Incompatibility and Accounts Clauses are in some way less "fundamental" than the Establishment Clause. Each establishes a norm of conduct which the Federal Government is bound to honor—to no greater or lesser extent than any other inscribed in the Constitution. To the extent the Court of Appeals relied on a view of standing under which the Art. III burdens diminish as the "importance" of the claim on the merits increases, we reject that notion. The requirement of standing "focuses on the party seeking to get his complaint before a federal court and not on the issues he wishes to have adjudicated." *Flast v. Cohen, supra,* 392 U.S., at 99. Moreover, we know of no principled basis on which to create a hierarchy of constitutional values or a complementary "sliding scale" of standing which might permit respondents to invoke the judicial power of the United States. "The proposition that all constitutional provisions are enforceable by any citizen simply because citizens are the ultimate beneficiaries of those provisions has no boundaries." *Schlesinger v. Reservists Committee to Stop the War, supra,* 418 U.S., at 227.

The complaint in this case shares a common deficiency with those in Schlesinger and Richardson. Although respondents claim that the Constitution has been violated, they claim nothing else. They fail to identify any personal injury suffered by them as a consequence of the alleged constitutional error, other than the psychological consequence presumably produced by observation of conduct with which one disagrees. That is not an injury sufficient to confer standing under Art. III, even though the disagreement is phrased in constitutional terms. It is evident that respondents are firmly committed to the constitutional principle of separation of church and State, but standing is not measured by the intensity of the litigant's interest or the fervor of his advocacy. "[T]hat concrete adverseness which sharpens the presentation of issues," *Baker v. Carr,* 369 U.S., at 204, is the anticipated consequence of proceedings commenced by one who has been injured in fact; it is not a permissible substitute for the showing of injury itself.

In reaching this conclusion, we do not retreat from our earlier holdings that standing may be predicated on noneconomic injury. *See, e.g., United States v.* SCRAP, 412 U.S., at 686–688; *Association of Data Processing Service Orgs. v. Camp,* 397 U.S., at 153–154. We simply cannot see that respondents have alleged an injury of any kind, economic or otherwise, sufficient to confer standing.[22] Respond-

---

[22] Respondents rely on our statement in *Association of Data Processing Service Orgs. v. Camp,* 397 U.S., at 154, that "[a] person or family may have a spiritual stake in First Amendment values sufficient to give standing to raise issues concerning the Establishment Clause and the Free Exercise Clause. Abington School District v. Schempp, 374 U.S. 203."

ents complain of a transfer of property located in Chester County, Pa. The named plaintiffs reside in Maryland and Virginia;[23] their organizational headquarters are located in Washington, D.C. They learned of the transfer through a news release. Their claim that the Government has violated the Establishment Clause does not provide a special license to roam the country in search of governmental wrongdoing and to reveal their discoveries in federal court.[24] The federal courts were simply not constituted as ombudsmen of the general welfare.

The Court of Appeals in this case ignored unambiguous limitations on taxpayer and citizen standing. It appears to have done so out of the conviction that enforcement of the Establishment Clause demands special exceptions from the requirement that a plaintiff allege "'distinct and palpable injury to himself,' . . . that is likely to be redressed if the requested relief is granted." . . .

Implicit in the foregoing is the philosophy that the business of the federal courts is correcting constitutional errors, and that "cases and controversies" are at best merely convenient vehicles for doing so and at worst nuisances that may be dispensed with when they become obstacles to that transcendent endeavor. This philosophy has no place in our constitutional scheme. It does not become more palatable when the underlying merits concern the Establishment Clause. Respondents' claim of standing implicitly rests on the presumption that violations of the Establishment Clause typically will not cause injury sufficient to confer standing under the "traditional" view of Art. III. But "[t]he assumption that if respondents have no standing to sue, no one would

have standing, is not a reason to find standing." *Schlesinger v. Reservists Committee to Stop the War*, 418 U.S., at 227. This view would convert standing into a requirement that must be observed only when satisfied. Moreover, we are unwilling to assume that injured parties are nonexistent simply because they have not joined respondents in their suit. The law of averages is not a substitute for standing.

Were we to accept respondents' claim of standing in this case, there would be no principled basis for confining our exception to litigants relying on the Establishment Clause. Ultimately, that exception derives from the idea that the judicial power requires nothing more for its invocation than important issues and able litigants.[26] The existence of injured parties who might not wish to bring suit becomes irrelevant. Because we are unwilling to countenance such a departure from the limits on judicial power contained in Art. III, the judgment of the Court of Appeals is reversed.

It is so ordered.

Justice BRENNAN, with whom Justice MARSHALL and Justice BLACKMUN join, dissenting.

. . .

The opinion of the Court is a stark example of this unfortunate trend of resolving cases at the "threshold" while obscuring the nature of the underlying rights and interests at stake. . . .

. . .

The "case and controversy" limitation of Art. III overrides no other provision of the Constitution. To construe that Article to deny standing "'to the class for whose sake [a] constitutional protection is given,'" *Jones v. United States*, 362 U.S. 257, 261 (1960), simply turns the Constitution on its head. . . . The Framers . . . surely intended that the particular beneficiaries of their legacy should enjoy rights legally enforceable in courts of law. . . .

. . .

[T]he general rule of Frothingham displays sound judgment: Courts must be circumspect in dealing with the taxing power in order to avoid unnecessary intrusion into the functions of the Legislative and Executive Branches. . . . But in *Flast* the Court faced a

---

[23] Respondent Americans United claims that it has certain unidentified members who reside in Pennsylvania. It does not explain, however, how this fact establishes a cognizable injury where none existed before. Respondent is still obligated to allege facts sufficient to establish that one or more of its members has suffered, or is threatened with, an injury other than their belief that the transfer violated the Constitution.

[24] Respondents also claim standing by reference to the Administrative Procedure Act, 5 U.S.C. § 702, which authorizes judicial review at the instance of any person who has been "adversely affected or aggrieved by agency action within the meaning of a relevant statute." Neither the Administrative Procedure Act, nor any other congressional enactment, can lower the threshold requirements of standing under Art. III. Respondents do not allege that the Act creates a legal right, "the invasion of which creates standing," Linda R.S. v. Richard D., 410 U.S., at 617, n.3, and there is no other basis for arguing that its existence alters the rules of standing otherwise applicable to this case.

[26] Were we to recognize standing premised on an "injury" consisting solely of an alleged violation of a "'personal constitutional right' to a government that does not establish religion," a principled consistency would dictate recognition of respondents' standing to challenge execution of every capital sentence on the basis of a personal right to a government that does not impose cruel and unusual punishment, or standing to challenge every affirmative-action program on the basis of a personal right to a government that does not deny equal protection of the laws, to choose but two among as many possible examples as there are commands in the Constitution.

different sort of constitutional claim, and found itself compelled to retreat from the general assertion in *Frothingham* that taxpayers have no interest in the disposition of their tax payments....

. . .

"One of our basic rights is to be free of taxation to support a transgression of the constitutional command that the authorities 'shall make no law respecting an establishment of religion, or prohibiting the free exercise thereof.'" "[A]part from efforts to inject religious training or exercises and sectarian issues into the public schools, the only serious threat to maintaining that complete and permanent separation of religion and civil power which the First Amendment commands is through the use of the taxing power to support religion, religious establishments, or establishments having a religious foundation whatever their form or special religious function.... [M]oney taken by taxation from one is not to be used or given to support another's religious training or belief, or indeed one's own."

. . .

It may be that Congress can tax for almost any reason, or for no reason at all. There is, so far as I have been able to discern, but one constitutionally imposed limit on that authority. Congress cannot use tax money to support a church, or to encourage religion. That is "the forbidden exaction." *Everson v. Board of Education*, 330 U.S., at 45 (Rutledge, J., dissenting) (emphasis added).... In absolute terms the history of the Establishment Clause of the First Amendment makes this clear. History also makes it clear that the federal taxpayer is a singularly "proper and appropriate party to invoke a federal court's jurisdiction" to challenge a federal bestowal of largesse as a violation of the Establishment Clause. Each, and indeed every, federal taxpayer suffers precisely the injury that the Establishment Clause guards against when the Federal Government directs that funds be taken from the pocketbooks of the citizenry and placed into the coffers of the ministry.

A taxpayer cannot be asked to raise his objection to such use of his funds at the time he pays his tax. Apart from the unlikely circumstance in which the Government announced in advance that a particular levy would be used for religious subsidies, taxpayers could hardly assert that they were being injured until the Government actually lent its support to a religious venture. Nor would it be reasonable to require him to address his claim to those officials charged with the collection of federal taxes. Those officials would be without the means to provide appropriate redress....

. . .

[The] Court finds this case different from *Flast* because here the "source of [plaintiffs'] complaint is not a congressional action, but a decision by HEW to transfer a parcel of federal property." This attempt at distinction cannot withstand scrutiny. *Flast* involved a challenge to the actions of the Commissioner of Education, and other officials of HEW, in disbursing funds under the Elementary and Secondary Education Act of 1965 to "religious and sectarian" schools. Plaintiffs disclaimed "any intent[ion] to challenge ... all programs under ... the Act." Rather, they claimed that defendant-administrators' approval of such expenditures was not authorized by the Act, or alternatively, to the extent the expenditures were authorized, the Act was "unconstitutional and void." In the present case, respondents challenge HEW's grant of property pursuant to the Federal Property and Administrative Services Act of 1949, seeking to enjoin HEW "from making a grant of this and other property to the [defendant] so long as such a grant will violate the Establishment Clause." It may be that the Court is concerned with the adequacy of respondents' pleading; respondents have not, in so many words, asked for a declaration that the "Federal Property and Administrative Services Act is unconstitutional and void to the extent that it authorizes HEW's actions." I would not construe their complaint so narrowly.

More fundamentally, no clear division can be drawn in this context between actions of the Legislative Branch and those of the Executive Branch. To be sure, the First Amendment is phrased as a restriction on Congress' legislative authority; this is only natural since the Constitution assigns the authority to legislate and appropriate only to the Congress. But it is difficult to conceive of an expenditure for which the last governmental actor, either implementing directly the legislative will, or acting within the scope of legislatively delegated authority, is not an Executive Branch official. The First Amendment binds the Government as a whole, regardless of which branch is at work in a particular instance.

. . .

It can make no constitutional difference in the case before us whether the donation to the petitioner here was in the form of a cash grant to build a facility, or in the nature of a gift of property including a facility already built.... The complaint here is precisely that, although the property at issue is actually being used for a sectarian purpose, the Government has not received, nor demanded, full value payment. Whether undertaken pursuant to the Property Clause or the Spending Clause, the breach of the Establishment Clause, and the relationship of the taxpayer to that breach, is precisely the same.

. . .

Justice STEVENS, dissenting.

. . .

[A] taxpayer has a special claim to status as a litigant in a case raising the "establishment" issue. This special claim is enough, I think, to permit us to allow the suit, coupled, as it is, with the interest which the taxpayer and all other citizens have in the church-state issue. In terms of the structure and basic philosophy of our constitutional government, it would be difficult to point to any issue that has a more intimate, pervasive, and fundamental impact upon the life of the taxpayer—and upon the life of all citizens. . . . I believe we must recognize that our principle of judicial scrutiny of legislative acts which raise important constitutional questions requires that the issue here presented—the separation of state and church—which the Founding Fathers regarded as fundamental to our constitutional system—should be subjected to judicial testing. . . . [The Court's] decision rests on the premise that the difference between a disposition of funds pursuant to the Spending Clause and a disposition of realty pursuant to the Property Clause is of fundamental jurisprudential significance. With all due respect, I am persuaded that the essential holding of *Flast v. Cohen* attaches special importance to the Establishment Clause and does not permit the drawing of a tenuous distinction between the Spending Clause and the Property Clause.

RLW: *Valley Forge* holds only that these plaintiffs cannot establish standing. A non-sectarian college that also wanted the building would have standing, especially if it could show competitive injury.

Legislator Standing. *Coleman v. Miller*[29] involved the proposed Child Labor Act amendment to the U.S. Constitution. Kansas' Secretary of State endorsed a resolution with the notation that it had been passed by the legislature. Thereafter, twenty-one members of the Kansas Senate sued to force the Secretary of State to change his endorsement to "not passed" on the basis that the Lieutenant Governor had, without authority, cast the deciding vote. Plaintiffs also claimed that the amendment was not ratified within a reasonable period of time. Mr. Chief Justice Hughes, writing for the Court, concluded that the senators had standing to challenge the endorsement:

> [P]laintiffs include twenty senators, whose votes against ratification have been overridden and virtually held for naught although if they are right in their contentions their votes would have been sufficient to defeat ratification. We think that these senators have a plain, direct and adequate interest in maintaining the effectiveness of their votes. Petitioners come directly within the provisions of the statute governing our appellate jurisdiction. They have set up and claimed a right and privilege under the Constitution of the United States to have their votes given effect and the state court has denied that right and privilege. . . .

Mr. Justice Frankfurter, joined by three other justices, dissented:

> . . .

> Indeed the claim that the Amendment was dead or that it was no longer open to Kansas to ratify, is not only not an interest which belongs uniquely to these Kansas legislators; it is not even an interest special to Kansas. For it is the common concern of every citizen of the United States whether the Amendment is still alive, or whether Kansas could be included among the necessary "three-fourths of the several States."

b. Congressionally Authorized Standing

Can Congress authorize plaintiffs to bring suit when standing would not otherwise exist? As the foregoing cases suggest, there is a constitutional aspect to the standing

---

[29] 307 U.S. 433 (1939).

doctrine, as well as a prudential aspect. The constitutional aspect stems from Article III's case and controversy requirement, and cannot be waived by Congress. The prudential aspect is a limitation imposed by the Court on itself. In some instances, even though a case or controversy may exist, the Court refuses to hear the case in deference to a coordinate branch of government. If Congress has invited the Court to hear a particular type of case, prudential restraints are minimized or disappear.

Association of Data Processing Service Organizations, Inc. v. Camp
397 U.S. 150 (1970)

Mr. Justice DOUGLAS delivered the opinion of the Court.

Petitioners sell data processing services to businesses generally. In this suit they seek to challenge a ruling by respondent Comptroller of the Currency that, as an incident to their banking services, national banks, including respondent American National Bank & Trust Company, may make data processing services available to other banks and to bank customers. The District Court dismissed the complaint for lack of standing of petitioners to bring the suit. . . .

Generalizations about standing to sue are largely worthless as such. One generalization is, however, necessary and that is that the question of standing in the federal courts is to be considered in the framework of Article III which restricts judicial power to "cases" and "controversies." As we recently stated in *Flast v. Cohen*, 392 U.S. 83, 101 "(I)n terms of Article III limitations on federal court jurisdiction, the question of standing is related only to whether the dispute sought to be adjudicated will be presented in an adversary context and in a form historically viewed as capable of judicial resolution." *Flast* was a taxpayer's suit. The present is a competitor's suit. And while the two have the same Article III starting point, they do not necessarily track one another.

The first question is whether the plaintiff alleges that the challenged action has caused him injury in fact, economic or otherwise. There can be no doubt but that petitioners have satisfied this test. The petitioners not only allege that competition by national banks in the business of providing data processing services might entail some future loss of profits for the petitioners, they also allege that respondent American National Bank & Trust Company was performing or preparing to perform such services for two customers for whom petitioner Data Systems, Inc., had previously agreed or negotiated to perform such services. The petitioners' suit was brought not only against the American National Bank & Trust Company,

but also against the Comptroller of the Currency. The Comptroller was alleged to have caused petitioners injury in fact by his 1966 ruling which stated: "Incidental to its banking services, a national bank may make available its data processing equipment or perform data processing services on such equipment for other banks and bank customers." Comptroller's Manual for National Banks 3500 (October 15, 1966).

. . .

The . . . question of standing is different. It concerns, apart from the "case" or "controversy" test, the question whether the interest sought to be protected by the complainant is arguably within the zone of interests to be protected or regulated by the statute or constitutional guarantee in question. Thus the Administrative Procedure Act grants standing to a person "aggrieved by agency action within the meaning of a relevant statute." 5 U.S.C. § 702 (1964 ed., Supp. IV). That interest, at times, may reflect "aesthetic, conservational, and recreational" as well as economic values. A person or a family may have a spiritual stake in First Amendment values sufficient to give standing to raise issues concerning the Establishment Clause and the Free Exercise Clause. We mention these noneconomic values to emphasize that standing may stem from them as well as from the economic injury in which petitioners rely here. Certainly he who is "likely to be financially" injured, *FCC v. Sanders Bros. Radio Station*, 309 U.S. 470, at 477, may be a reliable private attorney general to litigate the issues of the public interest in the present case.

Apart from Article III jurisdictional questions, problems of standing, as resolved by this Court for its own governance, have involved a "rule of self-restraint." *Barrows v. Jackson*, 346 U.S. 249, 255. Congress can, of course, resolve the question one way or another, save as the requirements of Article III dictate otherwise. *Muskrat v. United States*, 219 U.S. 346.

Where statutes are concerned, the trend is toward enlargement of the class of people who may protest administrative action. The whole drive for enlarging the category of aggrieved "persons" is symptomatic of that trend. In a closely analogous case we held that an existing entrepreneur had standing to challenge the legality of the entrance of a newcomer into the business, because the established business was allegedly protected by a valid city ordinance that protected it from unlawful competition. *Chicago v. Atchison, T. & S.F.R. Co.*, 357 U.S. 77, 83—84. In that tradition was *Hardin v. Kentucky Utilities Co.*, 390 U.S. 1, which involved a section of the TVA Act designed primarily to protect, through area limitations, private utilities against TVA competition. We held that no explicit statutory provision was necessary to confer standing, since the private utility bringing suit was within the class of persons that the statutory provision was designed to protect.

It is argued that the *Chicago* case and the *Hardin* case are relevant here because of § 4 of the Bank Service Corporation Act of 1962, 76 Stat. 1132, 12 U.S.C. § 1864, which provides: "No bank service corporation may engage in any activity other than the performance of bank services for banks."

The Court of Appeals for the First Circuit held in *Arnold Tours, Inc. v. Camp*, 408 F.2d

1147, 1153, that by reason of § 4 a data processing company has standing to contest the legality of a national bank performing data processing services for other banks and bank customers: "Section 4 had a broader purpose than regulating only the service corporations. It was also a response to the fears expressed by a few senators, that without such a prohibition, the bill would have enabled 'banks to engage in a nonbanking activity,' S.Rep.No.2105, (87th Cong., 2d Sess., 7–12) (Supplemental views of Senators Proxmire, Douglas, and Neuberger), and thus constitute 'a serious exception to the accepted public policy which strictly limits banks to banking.' (Supplemental views of Senators Muskie and Clark). We think Congress has provided the sufficient statutory aid to standing even though the competition may not be the precise kind Congress legislated against." We do not put the issue in those words, for they implicate the merits. We do think, however, that § 4 arguably brings a competitor within the zone of interests protected by it.

. . .

We hold that petitioners have standing to sue and that the case should be remanded for a hearing on the merits.

Reversed and remanded.

Sierra Club v. Morton[30] involved the Sierra Club's challenge to the United States Forest Service's (USFS) decision to build a 20 mile road in the Mineral King Valley of the Sierra Nevada Mountains in California. The Court described the area as a "quasi-wilderness" area of "great natural beauty." But the area's "relative inaccessibility and lack of development" limited the number of tourists who could visit it. In order to increase usage, the USFS, authorized construction of a $35 million resort and a 20 mile road designed to give access to the resort.

The Sierra Club, which wanted to maintain Mineral King as it was, sought a declaratory judgment that various aspects of the proposed development contravened federal laws and regulations governing the preservation of national parks, forests, and game refuges, and also sought preliminary and permanent injunctions restraining federal officials from granting their approval or issuing permits in connection with the Mineral King project. The petitioner Sierra Club sued as a membership corporation with "a special interest in the conservation and the sound maintenance of the national parks, game refuges and forests of the country," and invoked the judicial-review provisions of the Administrative Procedure Act, 5 U.S.C. § 701 et seq. The Court concluded that the Club lacked standing:

> The injury alleged by the Sierra Club will be incurred entirely by reason of the change in the uses to which Mineral King will be put, and the attendant change in the aesthetics and ecology of the area. Thus, in referring to the road to be built through Sequoia National Park, the complaint alleged that the development "would destroy or otherwise adversely affect the scenery, natural and his-

[30] 405 U.S. 727 (1972).

toric objects and wildlife of the park and would impair the enjoyment of the park for future generations." We do not question that this type of harm may amount to an "injury in fact" sufficient to lay the basis for standing under § 10 of the APA. Aesthetic and environmental well-being, like economic well-being, are important ingredients of the quality of life in our society, and the fact that particular environmental interests are shared by the many rather than the few does not make them less deserving of legal protection through the judicial process. But the "injury in fact" test requires more than an injury to a cognizable interest. It requires that the party seeking review be himself among the injured.

The impact of the proposed changes in the environment of Mineral King will not fall indiscriminately upon every citizen. The alleged injury will be felt directly only by those who use Mineral King and Sequoia National Park, and for whom the aesthetic and recreational values of the area will be lessened by the highway and ski resort. The Sierra Club failed to allege that it or its members would be affected in any of their activities or pastimes by the Disney development. . . .

The Club apparently [believed that its] longstanding concern with and expertise in such matters were sufficient to give it standing as a "representative of the public." . . .

[I]f a "special interest" in this subject were enough to entitle the Sierra Club to commence this litigation, there would appear to be no objective basis upon which to disallow a suit by any other bona fide "special interest" organization however small or short-lived. And if any group with a bona fide "special interest" could initiate such litigation, it is difficult to perceive why any individual citizen with the same bona fide special interest would not also be entitled to do so.

Mr. Justice Blackmun dissented:

I would permit an imaginative expansion of our traditional concepts of standing in order to enable an organization such as the Sierra Club, possessed, as it is, of pertinent, bona fide, and well-recognized attributes and purposes in the area of environment, to litigate environmental issues. This incursion upon tradition need not be very extensive. Certainly, it should be no cause for alarm. It is no more progressive than was the decision in *Data Processing* itself. It need only recognize the interest of one who has a provable, sincere, dedicated, and established status. We need not fear that Pandora's box will be opened or that there will be no limit to the number of those who desire to participate in environmental litigation. The courts will exercise appropriate restraints just as they have exercised them in the past. Who would have suspected 20 years ago that the concepts of standing enunciated in *Data Processing* and *Barlow* would be the measure for today? And Mr. Justice Douglas, in his eloquent opinion, has imaginatively suggested another means and one, in its own way, with obvious, appropriate, and self-imposed limitations as to standing. As I read what he has written, he makes only one addition to the customary criteria (the existence of a genuine dispute; the assurance of adversariness; and a conviction that the party whose standing is challenged will adequately represent the interests he asserts), that is, that the litigant be one who speaks knowingly for the environmental values he asserts.

United States v. SCRAP[31] involved a challenge to the ICC's failure to suspend a surcharge of 2.5% which various railroads proposed to impose on the shipment of

---

[31] 412 U.S. 669 (1973).

freight. The railroads claimed that the surcharge was needed to combat increasing costs and inadequate resources.

The suit was brought by various groups including Students Challenging Regulatory Agency Procedures (SCRAP), an unincorporated group of five law students, and the Environmental Defense Fund (EDF). They challenged the ICC's failure to suspend the surcharge claiming that it "economic, recreational and aesthetic harm":

> [T]hey claimed that the rate structure would discourage the use of "recyclable" materials, and promote the use of new raw materials that compete with scrap, thereby adversely affecting the environment by encouraging unwarranted mining, lumbering, and other extractive activities. The members of these environmental groups were allegedly forced to pay more for finished products, and their use of forests and streams was allegedly impaired because of unnecessary destruction of timber and extraction of raw materials, and the accumulation of otherwise recyclable solid and liquid waste materials. The railroads replied that since this was a general rate increase, recyclable materials would not be made any less competitive relative to other commodities, and that in the past general rate increases had not discouraged the movement of scrap materials.

The Court concluded that SCRAP had standing to challenge the ICC's failure to suspend:

> [A]ppellees respond that unlike the petitioner in *Sierra Club*, their pleadings sufficiently alleged that they were "adversely affected" or "aggrieved" within the meaning of § 10 of the Administrative Procedure Act (APA), and they point specifically to the allegations that their members used the forests, streams, mountains, and other resources in the Washington metropolitan area for camping, hiking, fishing, and sightseeing, and that this use was disturbed by the adverse environmental impact caused by the nonuse of recyclable goods brought about by a rate increase on those commodities. The District Court found these allegations sufficient to withstand a motion to dismiss. We agree.
>
> . . .
>
> In interpreting "injury in fact" we made it clear that standing was not confined to those who could show "economic harm," although both *Data Processing* and *Barlow* had involved that kind of injury. Nor, we said, could the fact that many persons shared the same injury be sufficient reason to disqualify from seeking review of an agency's action any person who had in fact suffered injury. Rather, we explained: "Aesthetic and environmental well-being, like economic well-being, are important ingredients of the quality of life in our society, and the fact that particular environmental interests are shared by the many rather than the few does not make them less deserving of legal protection through the judicial process." *Id.*, at 734. Consequently, neither the fact that the appellees here claimed only a harm to their use and enjoyment of the natural resources of the Washington area, nor the fact that all those who use those resources suffered the same harm, deprives them of standing.
>
> [This case is different than the *Sierra Club* case. In this case,] appellees claimed that the specific and allegedly illegal action of the Commission would directly harm them in their use of the natural resources of the Washington Metropolitan Area.
>
> Unlike the specific and geographically limited federal action of which the petitioner complained in *Sierra Club*, the challenged agency action in this case is applicable to substantially all of the Nation's railroads, and thus allegedly has an adverse environmental impact on all the natural resources of the coun-

try. Rather than a limited group of persons who used a picturesque valley in California, all persons who utilize the scenic resources of the country, and indeed all who breathe its air, could claim harm similar to that alleged by the environmental groups here. But we have already made it clear that standing is not to be denied simply because many people suffer the same injury. Indeed some of the cases on which we relied in *Sierra Club* demonstrated the patent fact that persons across the Nation could be adversely affected by major governmental actions. To deny standing to persons who are in fact injured simply because many others are also injured, would mean that the most injurious and widespread Government actions could be questioned by nobody. We cannot accept that conclusion.

But the injury alleged here is also very different from that at issue in Sierra Club because here the alleged injury to the environment is far less direct and perceptible. The petitioner there complained about the construction of a specific project that would directly affect the Mineral King Valley. Here, the Court was asked to follow a far more attenuated line of causation to the eventual injury of which the appellees complained—a general rate increase would allegedly cause increased use of nonrecyclable commodities as compared to recyclable goods, thus resulting in the need to use more natural resources to produce such goods, some of which resources might be taken from the Washington area, and resulting in more refuse that might be discarded in national parks in the Washington area. The railroads protest that the appellees could never prove that a general increase in rates would have this effect, and they contend that these allegations were a ploy to avoid the need to show some injury in fact.

Of course, pleadings must be something more than an ingenious academic exercise in the conceivable. A plaintiff must allege that he has been or will in fact be perceptibly harmed by the challenged agency action, not that he can imagine circumstances in which he could be affected by the agency's action. And it is equally clear that the allegations must be true and capable of proof at trial. But we deal here simply with the pleadings in which the appellees alleged a specific and perceptible harm that distinguished them from other citizens who had not used the natural resources that were claimed to be affected. If, as the railroads now assert, these allegations were in fact untrue, then the appellants should have moved for summary judgment on the standing issue and demonstrated to the District Court that the allegations were sham and raised no genuine issue of fact. We cannot say on these pleadings that the appellees could not prove their allegations which, if proved, would place them squarely among those persons injured in fact by the Commission's action, and entitled under the clear import of *Sierra Club* to seek review. The District Court was correct in denying the appellants' motion to dismiss the complaint for failure to allege sufficient standing to bring this lawsuit.

Mr. Justice Blackmun, joined by Mr. Justice Brennan, concurred:

. . . I would not require that the appellees, in their individual capacities, prove that they in fact were injured. Rather, I would require only that appellees, as responsible and sincere representatives of environmental interests, show that the environment would be injured in fact and that such injury would be irreparable and substantial.

Mr. Justice Douglas dissented in part:

[A]ny resident of an area whose paths are strewn with litter, whose parks, or picnic grounds are defaced by it has standing to tender his complaint to the court. *Sierra Club v. Morton* would seem to cover this case, for littering abetted by the failure to recycle would clearly seem to implicate residents to whom "the aesthetic and recreational values of the area" are important. For the reasons stated in my opinion in *Sierra Club v. Morton, supra*, I agree with the Court that appellees have standing, but like Mr. Justice BLACKMUN, I would not require appellees, in their individual capacity, to prove injury in fact. . . .

c. Third Party Standing

To what extent do litigants have standing to raise the rights of other parties not before the Court?

Singleton v. Wulff
428 U.S. 106 (1976)

Mr. Justice BLACKMUN delivered the opinion of the Court (Parts I, II-A, and III) together with an opinion (Part II-B), in which Mr. Justice BRENNAN, Mr. Justice WHITE, and Mr. Justice MARSHALL joined.

[This] . . . case involves a claim of a State's unconstitutional interference with the decision to terminate pregnancy. The particular object of the challenge is a Missouri statute excluding abortions that are not "medically indicated" from the purposes for which Medicaid benefits are available to needy persons. In its present posture, however, the case presents two issues not going to the merits of this dispute. The first is whether the plaintiff-appellees, as physicians who perform nonmedically indicated abortions, have standing to maintain the suit, to which we answer that they do. . . .

. . .

[T]here is no doubt now that the respondent-physicians suffer concrete injury from the operation of the challenged statute. Their complaint and affidavits, described above, allege that they have performed and will continue to perform operations for which they would be reimbursed under the Medicaid program, were it not for the limitation of reimbursable abortions to those that are "medically indicated." If the physicians prevail in their suit to remove this limitation, they will benefit, for they will then receive payment for the abortions. The State (and Federal Government) will be out of pocket by the amount of the payments. The relationship between the parties is classically adverse, and there clearly exists between them a case or controversy. . . .

B. The question of what rights the doctors may assert in seeking to resolve that controversy is more difficult. The Court of Appeals adverted to what it perceived to be the doctor's own "constitutional rights to practice medicine." 508 F.2d, at 1213. We have no occasion to decide whether such rights exist. Assuming

that they do, the doctors, of course, can assert them. It appears, however, that the Court of Appeals also accorded the doctors standing to assert, and indeed granted them relief based partly upon, the rights of their patients. We must decide whether this assertion of *jus tertii* was a proper one.

Federal courts must hesitate before resolving a controversy, even one within their constitutional power to resolve, on the basis of the rights of third persons not parties to the litigation. The reasons are two. First, the courts should not adjudicate such rights unnecessarily, and it may be that in fact the holders of those rights either do not wish to assert them, or will be able to enjoy them regardless of whether the in-court litigant is successful or not. . . . Second, third parties themselves usually will be the best proponents of their own rights. The courts depend on effective advocacy, and therefore should prefer to construe legal rights only when the most effective advocates of those rights are before them. The holders of the rights may have a like preference, to the extent they will be bound by the courts' decisions under the doctrine of Stare decisis. . . . These two considerations underlie the Court's general rule: "Ordinarily, one may not claim standing in this Court to vindicate the constitutional rights of some third party." *Barrows v. Jackson*, 346 U.S. at 255.

Like any general rule, however, this one should not be applied where its underlying justifications are absent. With this in mind, the Court has looked primarily to two factual elements to determine whether the rule should apply in a particular case. The first is the relationship of the litigant to the person whose right he seeks to assert. . . . [T]he relationship between the litigant and the third party may be such that the former is fully, or very nearly, as effective a proponent of the right as the latter. Thus in *Griswold v. Connecticut*, 381 U.S.

479 (1965), where two persons had been convicted of giving advice on contraception, the Court permitted the defendants, one of whom was a licensed physician, to assert the privacy rights of the married persons whom they advised. . . . A doctor-patient relationship similar to that in *Griswold* existed in *Doe v. Bolton*, where the Court also permitted physicians to assert the rights of their patients. Indeed, since that right was the right to an abortion, *Doe* would flatly control the instant case were it not for the fact that there the physicians were seeking protection from possible criminal prosecution.

The other factual element to which the Court has looked is the ability of the third party to assert his own right. Even where the relationship is close, the reasons for requiring persons to assert their own rights will generally still apply. If there is some genuine obstacle to such assertion, however, the third party's absence from court loses its tendency to suggest that his right is not truly at stake, or truly important to him, and the party who is in court becomes by default the right's best available proponent. . . .

Application of these principles to the present case quickly yields its proper result. The closeness of the relationship is patent, as it was in *Griswold* and in *Doe*. A woman cannot safely secure an abortion without the aid of a physician, and an impecunious woman cannot easily secure an abortion without the physician's being paid by the State. The woman's exercise of her right to an abortion, whatever its dimension, is therefore necessarily at stake here. Moreover, the constitutionally protected abortion decision is one in which the physician is intimately involved. Aside from the woman herself, therefore, the physician is uniquely qualified to litigate the constitutionality of the State's interference with, or discrimination against, that decision.

As to the woman's assertion of her own rights, there are several obstacles. For one thing, she may be chilled from such assertion by a desire to protect the very privacy of her decision from the publicity of a court suit. A second obstacle is the imminent mootness, at least in the technical sense, of any individual woman's claim. Only a few months, at the most, after the maturing of the decision to undergo an abortion, her right thereto will have been irrevocably lost, assuming, as it seems fair to assume, that unless the impecunious woman can establish Medicaid eligibility she must forgo abortion. It is true that these obstacles are not insurmountable. Suit may be brought under a pseudonym, as so frequently has been done. A woman who is no longer pregnant may nonetheless retain the right to litigate the

point because it is "'capable of repetition yet evading review.'" *Roe v. Wade*, 410 U.S., at 124–125. And it may be that a class could be assembled, whose fluid membership always included some women with live claims. But if the assertion of the right is to be "representative" to such an extent anyway, there seems little loss in terms of effective advocacy from allowing its assertion by a physician.

For these reasons, we conclude that it generally is appropriate to allow a physician to assert the rights of women patients as against governmental interference with the abortion decision, and we decline to restrict our holding to that effect in *Doe* to its purely criminal context. In this respect, the judgment of the Court of Appeals is affirmed.

. . .

Mr. Justice POWELL, with whom THE CHIEF JUSTICE, Mr. Justice STEWART, and Mr. Justice REHNQUIST join, concurring in part and dissenting in part.

. . .

[Prior precedent holds] that a party may assert another's rights . . ., not when there is merely some "obstacle" to the rightholder's own litigation, but when such litigation is in all practicable terms impossible. Thus, in its framing of this principle, the plurality has gone far beyond our major precedents.

[T]he litigation of third-party rights cannot be justified in this case. The plurality virtually concedes, as it must, that the two alleged "obstacles" to the women's assertion of their rights are chimerical. Our docket regularly contains cases in which women, using pseudonyms, challenge statutes that allegedly infringe their right to exercise the abortion decision. Nor is there basis for the "obstacle" of incipient mootness when the plurality itself quotes from the portion of *Roe v. Wade*, 410 U.S. 113, 124–125 (1973), that shows no such obstacle exists. . . .

. . .

The plurality places primary reliance on a second element, the existence of a "confidential relationship" between the rightholder and the party seeking to assert her rights. Focusing on the professional relationships present in *Griswold*, *Doe* and *Planned Parenthood of Missouri v. Danforth*, *ante*, 428 U.S. 52, the plurality suggests that allowing the physicians in this case to assert their patients' rights flows naturally from those three. . . .

. . .

The physicians have offered no special reason for allowing them to assert their patients' rights in an attack on this welfare statute, and I can think of none. Moreover, there are persuasive reasons not to permit them to do so. It seems wholly inappropriate, as a matter of judicial self-governance, for a court to reach unnecessarily to decide a difficult constitutional issue in a case in which nothing more is at stake than remuneration for professional services. And second, this case may well set a precedent that will prove difficult to cabin. No reason immediately comes to mind, after today's holding, why any provider of services should be denied standing to assert his client's or customer's constitutional rights, if any, in an attack on a welfare statute that excludes from coverage his particular transaction.

NAACP v. Alabama[32] involved an Alabama statute which required foreign corporations to report the names and addresses of its members to Alabama's Attorney General. The NAACP refused to comply with the reporting requirement, and the State of Alabama filed suit to prohibit the NAACP from conducting further activities within the state. The NAACP responded by challenging the reporting requirements as a violation of First Amendment speech and assembly provisions. It sued on its own behalf as well as on behalf of its members. The Court concluded that the NAACP had standing to assert the constitutional rights of its members:

> If petitioner's rank-and-file members are constitutionally entitled to withhold their connection with the Association despite the production order, it is manifest that this right is properly assertable by the Association. To require that it be claimed by the members themselves would result in nullification of the right at the very moment of its assertion. Petitioner is the appropriate party to assert that rights, because it and its members are in every practical sense identical. The Association, which provides in its constitution that "(a)ny person who is in accordance with (its) principles and policies * * *" may become a member, is but the medium through which its individual members seek to make more effective the expression of their own views. The reasonable likelihood that the Association itself through diminished financial support and membership may be adversely affected if production is compelled is a further factor pointing towards our holding that petitioner has standing to complain of the production order on behalf of its members. . . .

Griswold v. Connecticut[33] involved a Connecticut law prohibiting the use of contraceptive devices for the purpose of preventing conception. Appellants, Executive Director of the Planned Parenthood Association and a professor at the Yale Medical School, gave "information, instruction and medical advice" to married persons as the means of preventing conception. Both were found guilty as accessories and fined $100 each. They sought to challenge the law as violative of the Fourteenth Amendment. The Court held that they could establish standing:

> We think that appellants have standing to raise the constitutional rights of the married people with whom they had a professional relationship. *Tileston v. Ullman*, 318 U.S. 44, is different, for there the plaintiff seeking to represent others asked for a declaratory judgment. In that situation we thought that the requirements of standing should be strict, lest the standards of "case or controversy" in Article III of the Constitution become blurred. Here those doubts are removed by reason of a criminal conviction for serving married couples in violation of an aiding-and-abetting statute. Certainly the accessory should have standing to assert that the offense which he is charged with assisting is not, or cannot constitutionally be a crime.

---

[32] 357 U.S. 449 (1958).
[33] 381 U.S. 479 (1965).

Eisenstadt v. Baird[34] involved a Massachusetts statute which made it a crime to give "away . . . any drug, medicine, instrument or article whatever for the prevention of conception."[35] Baird was convicted of "exhibiting contraceptive articles in the course of delivering a lecture on contraception to a group of students at Boston University and, second, for giving a young woman a package of Emko vaginal foam at the close of his address." The Court rejected the state's contention that Baird lacked standing to raise the rights of unmarried persons denied access to contraceptives because he was neither an authorized distributor under § 21A nor a single person unable to obtain contraceptives:

> [We think] that our self-imposed rule against the assertion of third-party rights must be relaxed in this case. . . . [T]he doctor-patient and accessory-principal relationships are not the only circumstances in which one person has been found to have standing to assert the rights of another. [H]ere the relationship between Baird and those whose rights he seeks to assert is not simply that between a distributor and potential distributees, but that between an advocate of the rights of persons to obtain contraceptives and those desirous of doing so. The very point of Baird's giving away the vaginal foam was to challenge the Massachusetts statute that limited access to contraceptives.
>
> In any event, more important than the nature of the relationship between the litigant and those whose rights he seeks to assert is the impact of the litigation on the third-party interests. [T]he case for according standing to assert third-party rights is stronger in this regard here than in *Griswold* because unmarried persons denied access to contraceptives in Massachusetts, unlike the users of contraceptives in Connecticut, are not themselves subject to prosecution and, to that extent, are denied a forum in which to assert their own rights. The Massachusetts statute, unlike the Connecticut law considered in *Griswold*, prohibits, not use, but distribution.

Chief Justice Burger dissented:

> It is undisputed that appellee is not a physician or pharmacist and was prohibited under Massachusetts law from dispensing contraceptives to anyone, regardless of marital status. To my mind the validity of this restriction on dispensing medicinal substances is the only issue before the Court, and appellee has no standing to challenge that part of the statute restricting the persons to whom contraceptives are available. . . .

d. Causation

In recent years, the Court has begun to restrict standing. One way it has done so is through the imposition of a "causation" requirement.

---

[34] 405 U.S. 438 (1972).

[35] The statute distinguished between married persons (who were allowed to obtain contraceptives to prevent pregnancy, but only from doctors or druggists on prescription), single persons (who were not allowed to obtain contraceptives from anyone for the purpose of preventing pregnancy) & both married or single persons (who could obtain contraceptives from anyone for the purpose of preventing the spread of disease).

Warth v. Seldin
422 U.S. 490 (1975)

Mr. Justice Powell delivered the opinion of the Court.

Petitioners, various organizations and individuals resident in the Rochester, N.Y., metropolitan area, brought this action in the District Court for the Western District of New York against the town of Penfield, an incorporated municipality adjacent to Rochester, and against members of Penfield's Zoning, Planning and Town Boards. Petitioners claimed that the town's zoning ordinance, by its terms and as enforced by the defendant board members, respondents here, effectively excluded persons of low and moderate income from living in the town, in contravention of petitioners' First, Ninth, and Fourteenth Amendment rights and in violation of 42 U.S.C. §§ 1981, 1982, and 1983. . . .

I

Petitioners Metro-Act of Rochester, Inc., and eight individual plaintiffs, on behalf of themselves and all persons similarly situated,[1] filed this action. . . . The complaint identified Metro-Act as a not-for-profit New York corporation, the purposes of which are "to alert ordinary citizens to problems of social concern; . . . to inquire into the reasons for the critical housing shortage for low and moderate income persons in the Rochester area and to urge action on the part of citizens to alleviate the general housing shortage for low and moderate income persons." Plaintiffs Vinkey, Reichert, Warth, and Harris were described as residents of the city of Rochester, all of whom owned real property in and paid property taxes to that city.[3] Plaintiff Ortiz, "a citizen of Spanish/Puerto Rican extraction," also owned real property in and paid taxes to Rochester. Ortiz, however, resided in Wayland, N.Y., some 42 miles from

Penfield where he was employed.[4] The complaint described plaintiffs Broadnax, Reyes, and Sinkler as residents of Rochester and "persons fitting within the classification of low and moderate income as hereinafter defined. . . ."[5] Although the complaint does not expressly so state, the record shows that Broadnax, Reyes, and Sinkler are members of ethnic or racial minority groups: Reyes is of Puerto Rican ancestry; Broadnax and Sinkler are Negroes.

Petitioners' complaint alleged that Penfield's zoning ordinance, adopted in 1962, has the purpose and effect of excluding person of low and moderate income from residing in the town. In particular, the ordinance allocates 98% of the town's vacant land to single-family detached housing, and allegedly by imposing unreasonable requirements relating to lot size, setback, floor area, and habitable space, the ordinance increases the cost of single-family detached housing beyond the means of persons of low and moderate income. Moreover, according to petitioners, only 0.3% of the land available for residential construction is allocated to multifamily structures (apartments, townhouses, and the like), and even on this limited space, housing for low and moderate income persons is not economically feasible because of low density and other requirements. Petitioners also alleged that "in furtherance of a policy of exclusionary zoning," the defendant members of Penfield's Town, Zoning, and Planning Boards had acted in an arbitrary and discriminatory manner: they had delayed action on proposals for low- and moderate-cost housing for inordinate periods of time; denied such proposals for arbitrary and insubstantial reasons; refused to grant necessary variances and permits, or to allow tax abatements; failed to provide necessary support services for low- and moderate-cost housing projects; and had amended the ordinance to make approval of such projects virtually impossible.

In sum, petitioners alleged that, in violation of their "rights, privileges and immunities secured by the Constitution and laws of the United States," the town and its officials had

---

[1] Plaintiffs claimed to represent, pursuant to Fed.Rule Civ.Proc. 23(b)(2), classes constituting "all taxpayers of the City of Rochester, all low and moderate income persons residing in the City of Rochester, all black and/or Puerto Rican/Spanish citizens residing in the City of Rochester and all persons employed but excluded from living in the Town of Penfield who are affected or may in the future be affected by the defendants' policies and practices. . . ." App. 9.

[3] Plaintiff Harris further described in the complaint as "a negro person who is denied certain rights by virtue of her race. . . ." App. 5. We find no indication in the record that Harris had either the desire or intent to live in Penfield was suitable housing to become available. Indeed, petitioners now appear to claim standing for Harris only on the ground that she is a taxpayer of Rochester.

[4] According to Ortiz' affidavit, submitted in answer to respondents' motion to dismiss, he was employed in Penfield from 1966 to May 1972.

[5] In fact, however, the complaint nowhere defines the term "low and moderate income" beyond the parenthetical phrase "without the capital requirements to purchase real estate." In addition to the inadequacy of this definition, the record discloses wide variations in the income, housing needs, and money available for housing among the various "low and moderate income" plaintiffs.

made "practically and economically impossible the construction of sufficient numbers of low and moderate income . . . housing in the Town of Penfield to satisfy the minimum housing requirements of both the Town of Penfield and the metropolitan Rochester area. . . . " Petitioners alleged, moreover, that by precluding low- and moderate-cost housing, the town's zoning practices also had the effect of excluding persons of minority racial and ethnic groups, since most such persons have only low or moderate incomes.

Petitioners further alleged certain harm to themselves. The Rochester property owners and taxpayers—Vinkey, Reichert, Warth, Harris, and Ortiz—claimed that because of Penfield's exclusionary practices, the city of Rochester had been forced to impose higher tax rates on them and other similarly situated than would otherwise have been necessary. The low- and moderate-income, minority plaintiffs—Ortiz, Broadnax, Reyes, and Sinkler—claimed that Penfield's zoning practices had prevented them from acquiring, by lease or purchase, residential property in the town, and thus had forced them and their families to reside in less attractive environments. To relieve these various harms, petitioners asked the District Court to declare the Penfield ordinance unconstitutional, to enjoin the defendants from enforcing the ordinance, to order the defendants to enact and administer a new ordinance designed to alleviate the effects of their past actions, and to award $750,000 in actual and exemplary damages.

On May 2, 1972, petitioner Rochester Home Builders Association, an association of firms engaged in residential construction in the Rochester metropolitan area, moved the District Court for leave to intervene as a party-plaintiff. In essence, Home Builders' intervenor complaint repeated the allegations of exclusionary zoning practices made by the original plaintiffs. It claimed that these practices arbitrarily and capriciously had prevented its member firms from building low- and moderate-cost housing in Penfield, and thereby had deprived them of potential profits. Home Builders prayed for equitable relief identical in substance to that requested by the original plaintiffs, and also for $750,000 in damages. On June 7, 1972, Metro-Act and the other original plaintiffs moved to join petitioner Housing Council in the Monroe County Area, Inc., as a party plaintiff. Housing Council is a not-for-profit New York corporation, its membership comprising some 71 public and private organizations interested in housing problems. An affidavit accompanying the motion stated that 17 of Housing Council's member groups were or hoped to be involved in the development of low- and moderate-cost housing, and that one of its members—the Penfield Better Homes Corp.—"is and has been actively attempting to develop moderate income housing" in Penfield, "but has been stymied by its inability to secure the necessary approvals. . . . "

. . .

III

[W]e turn first to the claims of petitioners Ortiz, Reyes, Sinkler, and Broadnax, each of whom asserts standing as a person of low or moderate income and, coincidentally, as a member of a minority racial or ethnic group. We must assume, taking the allegations of the complaint as true, that Penfield's zoning ordinance and the pattern of enforcement by respondent officials have had the purpose and effect of excluding persons of low and moderate income, many of whom are members of racial or ethnic minority groups. We also assume, for purposes here, that such intentional exclusionary practices, if proved in a proper case, would be adjudged violative of the constitutional and statutory rights of the persons excluded.

But the fact that these petitioners share attributes common to persons who may have been excluded from residence in the town is an insufficient predicate for the conclusion that petitioners themselves have been excluded, or that the respondents' assertedly illegal actions have violated their rights. Petitioners must allege and show that they personally have been injured, not that injury has been suffered by other, unidentified members of the class to which they belong and which they purport to represent. Unless these petitioners can thus demonstrate the requisite case or controversy between themselves personally and respondents, "none may seek relief on behalf of himself or any other member of the class." *O'Shea v. Littleton*, 414 U.S. 488, 494 (1974).

In their complaint, petitioners Ortiz, Reyes, Sinkler, and Broadnax alleged in conclusory terms that they are among the persons excluded by respondents' actions.[13] None of them has ever resided in Penfield; each claims at least implicitly that he desires, or has desired, to do so. Each asserts, moreover, that he made some effort, at some time, to locate housing in Penfield that was at once within his means and adequate for his family's needs. Each claims that

---

[13] Petitioner Ortiz also alleged that as a result of such exclusion he had to incur substantial commuting expenses between his residence and his former place of employment in Penfield; and, in supporting affidavits, each petitioner recites at some length the disadvantages of his or her present housing situation and how that situation might be improved were residence in Penfield possible. For purposes of standing, however, it is the exclusion itself that is of critical importance, since exclusion alone would violate the asserted rights quite apart from any objective or subjective disadvantage that may flow from it.

his efforts proved fruitless. We may assume, as petitioners allege, that respondents' actions have contributed, perhaps substantially, to the cost of housing in Penfield. But there remains the question whether petitioners' inability to locate suitable housing in Penfield reasonably can be said to have resulted, in any concretely demonstrable way, from respondents' alleged constitutional and statutory infractions. Petitioners must allege facts from which it reasonably could be inferred that, absent the respondents' restrictive zoning practices, there is a substantial probability that they would have been able to purchase or lease in Penfield and that, if the court affords the relief requested, the asserted inability of petitioners will be removed. *Linda R.S. v. Richard D., supra.*

We find the record devoid of the necessary allegations. As the Court of Appeals noted, none of these petitioners has a present interest in any Penfield property; none is himself subject to the ordinance's strictures; and none has even been denied a variance or permit by respondent officials. Instead, petitioners claim that respondents' enforcement of the ordinance against third parties—developers, builders, and the like—has had the consequence of precluding the construction of housing suitable to their needs at prices they might be able to afford. The fact that the harm to petitioners may have resulted indirectly does not in itself preclude standing. When a governmental prohibition or restriction imposed on one party causes specific harm to a third party, harm that a constitutional provision or statute was intended to prevent, the indirectness of the injury does not necessarily deprive the person harmed of standing to vindicate his rights. But it may make it substantially more difficult to meet the minimum requirement of Art. III: to establish that, in fact, the asserted injury was the consequence of the defendants' actions, or that prospective relief will remove the harm.

Here, by their own admission, realization of petitioners' desire to live in Penfield always has depended on the efforts and willingness of third parties to build low- and moderate-cost housing. The record specifically refers to only two such efforts: that of Penfield Better Homes Corp., in late 1969, to obtain the rezoning of certain land in Penfield to allow the construction of subsidized cooperative townhouses that could be purchased by persons of moderate income; and a similar effort by O'Brien Homes, Inc., in late 1971.[15] But the record is devoid of

any indication that these projects, or other like projects, would have satisfied petitioners' needs at prices they could afford, or that, were the court to remove the obstructions attributable to respondents, such relief would benefit petitioners. Indeed, petitioners' descriptions of their individual financial situations and housing needs suggest precisely the contrary—that their inability to reside in Penfield is the consequence of the economics of the area housing market, rather than of respondents' assertedly illegal acts.[16] In short, the facts alleged fail to

---

[15] Penfield Better Homes contemplated a series of one-to three-bedroom units and hoped to sell them—at that time—to persons who earned from $5,000 to $8,000 per year. The Penfield Planning Board denied the necessary variance on September 9, 1969, because of incompatibility with the sur-

rounding neighborhood, projected traffic congestion, and problems of severe soil erosion during construction. O'Brien Homes, Inc., projected 51 buildings, each containing four family units, designed for single people and small families, and capable of being purchased by persons "of low income and accumulated funds" and "of moderate income with limited funds for down payment . . . ." The variance for this project was denied by the Planning Board on October 12, 1971; a revision of the proposal was reconsidered by the Planning Board in April 1972, and, from all indications of record, apparently remains under consideration. The record also indicates the existence of several proposals for "planned unit developments"; but we are not told whether these projects would allow sale at prices that persons of low or moderate income are likely to be able to afford. There is, more importantly, not the slightest suggestion that they would be adequate, and of sufficiently low cost, to meet these petitioners' needs.

[16] Ortiz states in his affidavit that he is now purchasing and resides in a six-bedroom dwelling in Wayland, N.Y.; and that he owns and receives rental income from a house in Rochester. He is concerned with finding a house or apartment large enough for himself, his wife, and seven children, but states that he can afford to spend a maximum of $120 per month for housing. Broadnax seeks a four-bedroom house or apartment for herself and six children, and can spend a maximum of about $120 per month for housing. Sinkler also states that she can spend $120 per month for housing for herself and two children. Thus, at least in the cases of Ortiz and Broadnax, it is doubtful that their stated needs could have been satisfied by the small housing units contemplated in the only moderate-cost projects specifically described in the record. Moreover, there is no indication that any of the petitioners had the resources necessary to acquire the housing available in the projects. . . . The vague description of the proposed O'Brien development strongly suggests that the units, even if adequate for their needs, would have been beyond the means at least of Sinkler and Broadnax. The Penfield Better Homes projected price figures were for 1969, and must be assumed—even if subsidies might still be available—to have increased substantially by 1972, when the complaint was filed. Petitioner Reyes presents a special case: she states that her family has an income of over $14,000 per year, that she can afford $231 per month for housing, and that, in the past and apparently now, she wants to purchase a residence. As noted above, the term "low and moderate income" is nowhere defined in the complaint; but Penfield Better Homes defined the term as between

support an actionable causal relationship between Penfield's zoning practices and petitioners' asserted injury.

In support of their position, petitioners refer to several decisions in the District Courts and Courts of Appeals, acknowledging standing in low-income, minority-group plaintiffs to challenge exclusionary zoning practices. In those cases, however, the plaintiffs challenged zoning restrictions as applied to particular projects that would supply housing within their means, and of which they were intended residents. The plaintiffs thus were able to demonstrate that unless relief from assertedly illegal actions was forthcoming, their immediate and personal interests would be harmed. Petitioners here assert no like circumstances. Instead, they rely on little more than the remote possibility, unsubstantiated by allegations of fact, that their situation might have been better had respondents acted otherwise, and might improve were the court to afford relief.

We hold only that a plaintiff who seeks to challenge exclusionary zoning practices must allege specific, concrete facts demonstrating that the challenged practices harm him, and that he personally would benefit in a tangible way from the court's intervention.[18] Absent the necessary allegations of demonstrable, particularized injury, there can be no confidence of "a real need to exercise the power of judicial review" or that relief can be framed "no (broader) than required by the precise facts to which the court's ruling would be applied." *Schlesinger v. Reservists to Stop the War*, 418 U.S., at 221–222.

IV

The petitioners who assert standing on the basis of their status as taxpayers of the city of Rochester present a different set of problems.

$5,000 and $8,000 per year. Since that project was to be subsidized, presumably petitioner Reyes would have been ineligible. There is no indication that in nonsubsidized projects, removal of the challenged zoning restrictions—in 1972—would have reduced the price on new single-family residences to a level that petitioner Reyes thought she could afford.

[18] This is not to say that the plaintiff who challenges a zoning ordinance or zoning practices must have a present contractual interest in a particular project. A particularized personal interest may be shown in various ways, which we need not undertake to identify in the abstract. But usually the initial focus should be on a particular project. We also note that zoning laws and their provisions, long considered essential to effective urban planning, are peculiarly within the province of state and local legislative authorities. They are, of course, subject to judicial review in a proper case. But citizens dissatisfied with provisions of such laws need not overlook the availability of the normal democratic process.

These "taxpayer-petitioners" claim that they are suffering economic injury consequent to Penfield's allegedly discriminatory and exclusionary zoning practices. Their argument, in brief, is that Penfield's persistent refusal to allow or to facilitate construction of low- and moderate-cost housing forces the city of Rochester to provide more such housing than it otherwise would do; that to provide such housing, Rochester must allow certain tax abatements; and that as the amount of tax-abated property increases, Rochester taxpayers are forced to assume an increased tax burden in order to finance essential public services.

"Of course, pleadings must be something more than an ingenious academic exercise in the conceivable." We think the complaint of the taxpayer-petitioners is little more than such an exercise. Apart from the conjectural nature of the asserted injury, the line of causation between Penfield's actions and such injury is not apparent from the complaint. Whatever may occur in Penfield, the injury complained of—increases in taxation—results only from decisions made by the appropriate Rochester authorities, who are not parties to this case.

But even if we assume that the taxpayer-petitioners could establish that Penfield's zoning practices harm them, their complaint nonetheless was properly dismissed. Petitioners do not, even if they could, assert any personal right under the Constitution or any statute to be free of action by a neighboring municipality that may have some incidental adverse effect on Rochester. On the contrary, the only basis of the taxpayer-petitioners' claim is that Penfield's zoning ordinance and practices violate the constitutional and statutory rights of third parties, namely, persons of low and moderate income who are said to be excluded from Penfield. In short the claim of these petitioners falls squarely within the prudential standing rule that normally bars litigants from asserting the rights or legal interests of others in order to obtain relief from injury to themselves. As we have observed above, this rule of judicial self-governance is subject to exceptions, the most prominent of which is that Congress may remove it by statute. Here, however, no statute expressly or by clear implication grants a right of action, and thus standing to seek relief, to persons in petitioners' position. In several cases, this Court has allowed standing to litigate the rights of third parties when enforcement of the challenged restriction against the litigant would result indirectly in the violation of third parties' rights. But the taxpayer-petitioners are not themselves subject to Penfield's zoning practices. Nor do they allege that the challenged zoning ordinance and practices preclude or otherwise adversely affect a relationship existing between them and the persons whose rights assertedly are violated.

V

We turn next to the standing problems presented by the petitioner associations—Metro-Act of Rochester, Inc., one of the original plaintiffs; Housing Council in the Monroe County Area, Inc., which the original plaintiffs sought to join as a party-plaintiff; and Rochester Home Builders Association, Inc., which moved in the District Court for leave to intervene as plaintiff. There is no question that an association may have standing in its own right to seek judicial relief from injury to itself and to vindicate whatever rights and immunities the association itself may enjoy. Moreover, in attempting to secure relief from injury to itself the association may assert the rights of its members, at least so long as the challenged infractions adversely affect its members' associational ties. With the limited exception of Metro-Act, however, none of the associational petitioners here has asserted injury to itself.

Even in the absence of injury to itself, an association may have standing solely as the representative of its members. . . .

. . .

Metro-Act also alleges, however, that 9% of its membership is composed of present residents of Penfield. It claims that, as a result of the persistent pattern of exclusionary zoning practiced by respondents and the consequent exclusion of persons of low and moderate income, those of its members who are Penfield residents are deprived of the benefits of living in a racially and ethnically integrated community. Referring to our decision in *Trafficante v. Metropolitan Life Ins. Co.*, 409 U.S. 205 (1972), Metro-Act argues that such deprivation is a sufficiently palpable injury to satisfy the Art. III case-or-controversy requirement, and that it has standing as the representative of its members to seek redress.

We agree with the Court of Appeals that Trafficante is not controlling here. In that case, two residents of an apartment complex alleged that the owner had discriminated against rental applicants on the basis of race, in violation of § 804 of the Civil Rights Act of 1968. They claimed that, as a result of such discrimination, "they had been injured in that (1) they had lost the social benefits of living in an integrated community; (2) they had missed business and professional advantages which would have accrued if they had lived with members of minority groups; (3) they had suffered embarrassment and economic damage in social, business, and professional activities from being 'stigmatized' as residents of a 'white ghetto.'" 409 U.S., at 208. In light of the clear congressional purpose in enacting the 1968 Act, and the broad definition of "person aggrieved" in § 810(a), we held that petitioners, as "person(s) who claim(ed) to have been injured by a discriminatory housing practice," had standing to litigate violations of the Act. We concluded that Congress had given residents of housing facilities covered by the statute an actionable right to be free from the adverse consequences to them of racially discriminatory practices directed at and immediately harmful to others.

Metro-Act does not assert on behalf of its members any right of action under the 1968 Civil Rights Act, nor can the complaint fairly be read to make out any such claim. In this, we think, lies the critical distinction between Trafficante and the situation here. As we have observed above, Congress may create a statutory right or entitlement the alleged deprivation of which can confer standing to sue even where the plaintiff would have suffered no judicially cognizable injury in the absence of statute. No such statute is applicable here.

Even if we assume, arguendo, that apart from any statutorily created right the asserted harm to Metro-Act's Penfield members is sufficiently direct and personal to satisfy the case-or-controversy requirement of Art. III, prudential considerations strongly counsel against according them or Metro-Act standing to prosecute this action. We do not understand Metro-Act to argue that Penfield residents themselves have been denied any constitutional rights, affording them a cause of action under 42 U.S.C. § 1983. Instead, their complaint is that they have been harmed indirectly by the exclusion of others. This is an attempt to raise putative rights of third parties, and none of the exceptions that allow such claims is present here.[22] In these circumstances, we conclude that it is inappropriate to allow Metro-Act to invoke the judicial process.

. . .

Petitioner Home Builders, in its intervenor-complaint, asserted standing to represent its member firms engaged in the development and construction of residential housing in the Rochester area, including Penfield. Home Builders alleged that the Penfield zoning restrictions, together with refusals by the town officials to grant variances and permits for the construction of low- and moderate-cost housing, had deprived some of its members of "substantial business opportunities and profits." App. 156. Home Builders claimed damages of $750,000 and also joined in the original plain-

---

[22] Metro-Act does not allege that a contractual or other relationship protected under §§ 1981 and 1982 existed between its Penfield members and any particular person excluded from residing in the town, nor that any such relationship was either punished or disrupted by respondents.

tiffs' prayer for declaratory and injunctive relief.

As noted above, to justify any relief the association must show that it has suffered harm, or that one or more of its members are injured. . . .

[H]ere an association seeks relief in damages for alleged injuries to its members. Home Builders alleges no monetary injury to itself, nor any assignment of the damages claims of its members. No award therefore can be made to the association as such. Moreover, in the circumstances of this case, the damages claims are not common to the entire membership, nor shared by all in equal degree. To the contrary, whatever injury may have been suffered is peculiar to the individual member concerned, and both the fact and extent of injury would require individualized proof. Thus, to obtain relief in damages, each member of Home Builders who claims injury as a result of respondents' practices must be a party to the suit, and Home Builders has no standing to claim damages on his behalf.

Home Builders' prayer for prospective relief fails for a different reason. It can have standing as the representative of its members only if it has alleged facts sufficient to make out a case or controversy had the members themselves brought suit. No such allegations were made. The complaint refers to no specific project of any of its members that is currently precluded either by the ordinance or by respondents' action in enforcing it. There is no averment that any member has applied to respondents for a building permit or a variance with respect to any current project. Indeed, there is no indication that respondents have delayed or thwarted any project currently proposed by Home Builders' members, or that any of its members has taken advantage of the remedial processes available under the ordinance. In short, insofar as the complaint seeks prospective relief, Home Builders has failed to show the existence of any injury to its members of sufficient immediacy and ripeness to warrant judicial intervention.

A like problem is presented with respect to petitioner Housing Council. The affidavit accompanying the motion to join it as plaintiff states that the Council includes in its membership "at lease seventeen" groups that have been, are, or will be involved in the development of low- and moderate-cost housing. But with one exception, the complaint does not suggest that any of these groups has focused its efforts on Penfield or has any specific plan to do so. Again with the same exception, neither the complaint nor any materials of record indicate that any member of Housing Council has taken any step toward building housing in Penfield, or has had dealings of any nature with

respondents. The exception is the Penfield Better Homes Corp. As we have observed above, it applied to respondents in late 1969 for a zoning variance to allow construction of a housing project designed for persons of moderate income. The affidavit in support of the motion to join Housing Council refers specifically to this effort, the supporting materials detail at some length the circumstances surrounding the rejection of Better Homes' application. It is therefore possible that in 1969, or within a reasonable time thereafter, Better Homes itself and possibly Housing Council as its representative would have had standing to seek review of respondents' action. The complaint, however, does not allege that the Penfield Better Homes project remained viable in 1972 when this complaint was filed, or that respondents' actions continued to block a then-current construction project.[23] In short, neither the complaint nor the record supplies any basis from which to infer that the controversy between respondents and Better Homes, however vigorous it may once have been, remained a live, concrete dispute when this complaint was filed.

VI

The rules of standing, whether as aspects of the Art. III case-or-controversy requirement or as reflections of prudential considerations defining and limiting the role of the courts, are threshold determinants of the propriety of judicial intervention. It is the responsibility of the complainant clearly to allege facts demonstrating that he is a proper party to invoke judicial resolution of the dispute and the exercise of the court's remedial powers. We agree with the District Court and the Court of Appeals that none of the petitioners here has met this threshold requirement. Accordingly, the judgment of the Court of Appeals is

Affirmed.

Mr. Justice DOUGLAS, dissenting.

With all respect, I think that the Court reads the complaint and the record with antagonistic eyes. There are in the background of this case continuing strong tides of opinion touching on very sensitive matters, some of which involve race, some class distinctions based on wealth.

A clean, safe, and well-heated home is not enough for some people. Some want to live where the neighbors are congenial and have social and political outlooks similar to their

---

[23] If it had been averred that the zoning ordinance or respondents were unlawfully blocking a pending construction project, there would be a further question as to whether Penfield Better Homes had employed available administrative remedies, and whether it should be required to do so before a federal court can intervene.

own. This problem of sharing areas of the community is akin to that when one wants to control the kind of person who shares his own abode. Metro-Act of Rochester, Inc., and the Housing Council in the Monroe County Area, Inc.—two of the associations which bring this suit—do in my opinion represent the communal feeling of the actual residents and have standing.

The associations here are in a position not unlike that confronted by the Court in *NAACP v. Alabama*, 357 U.S. 449 (1958). Their protest against the creation of this segregated community expresses the desire of their members to live in a desegregated community—a desire which gives standing to sue under the Civil Rights Act of 1968 as we held in *Trafficante v. Metropolitan Life Ins. Co.*, 409 U.S. 205 (1972). Those who voice these views here seek to rely on other Civil Rights Acts and on the Constitution, but they too should have standing, by virtue of the dignity of their claim, to have the case decided on the merits.

Standing has become a barrier to access to the federal courts, much as "the political question" was in earlier decades. The mounting caseload of federal courts is well known. But cases such as this one reflect festering sores in our society; and the American dream teaches that if one reaches high enough and persists there is a forum where justice is dispensed. I would lower the technical barriers and let the courts serve that ancient need. They can in time be curbed by legislative or constitutional restraints if an emergency arises.

We are today far from facing an emergency. For in all frankness, no Justice of this Court need work more than four days a week to carry his burden. I have found it a comfortable burden carried even in my months of hospitalization.

As Mr. Justice BRENNAN makes clear in his dissent, the alleged purpose of the ordinance under attack was to preclude low- and moderate-income people and nonwhites from living in Penfield. The zoning power is claimed to have been used here to foist an un-American community model on the people of this area. I would let the case go to trial and have all the facts brought out. Indeed, it would be better practice to decide the question of standing only when the merits have been developed.

I would reverse the Court of Appeals.

Mr. Justice BRENNAN, with whom Mr. Justice WHITE and Mr. Justice MARSHALL join, dissenting.

In this case, a wide range of plaintiffs, alleging various kinds of injuries, claimed to have been affected by the Penfield zoning ordinance, on its face and as applied, and by other practices of the defendant officials of Penfield. Alleging that as a result of these laws and practices low- and moderate-income and minority

people have been excluded from Penfield, and that this exclusion is unconstitutional, plaintiffs sought injunctive, declaratory, and monetary relief. The Court today, in an opinion that purports to be a "standing" opinion but that actually, I believe, has overtones of outmoded notions of pleading and of justiciability, refuses to find that any of the variously situated plaintiffs can clear numerous hurdles, some constructed here for the first time, necessary to establish "standing." While the Court gives lip service to the principle, oft repeated in recent years, that "standing in no way depends on the merits of the plaintiff's contention that particular conduct is illegal," in fact the opinion, which tosses out of court almost every conceivable kind of plaintiff who could be injured by the activity claimed to be unconstitutional, can be explained only by an indefensible hostility to the claim on the merits. I can appreciate the Court's reluctance to adjudicate the complex and difficult legal questions involved in determining the constitutionality of practices which assertedly limit residence in a particular municipality to those who are white and relatively well off, and I also understand that the merits of this case could involve grave sociological and political ramifications. But courts cannot refuse to hear a case on the merits merely because they would prefer not to, and it is quite clear, when the record is viewed with dispassion, that at least three of the groups of plaintiffs have made allegations, and supported them with affidavits and documentary evidence, sufficient to survive a motion to dismiss for lack of standing.

I

Before considering the three groups I believe clearly to have standing—the low-income, minority plaintiffs, Rochester Home Builders Association, Inc., and the Housing Council in the Monroe County Area, Inc.—it will be helpful to review the picture painted by the allegations as a whole, in order better to comprehend the interwoven interests of the various plaintiffs. Indeed, one glaring defect of the Court's opinion is that it views each set of plaintiffs as if it were prosecuting a separate lawsuit, refusing to recognize that the interests are intertwined, and that the standing of any one group must take into account its position vis-a-vis the others. For example, the Court says that the low-income minority plaintiffs have not alleged facts sufficient to show that but for the exclusionary practices claimed, they would be able to reside in Penfield. The Court then intimates that such a causal relationship could be shown only if "the initial focus (is) on a particular project." Later, the Court objects to the ability of the Housing Council to prosecute the suit on behalf of its member, Penfield Better Homes Corp., despite the fact that Better Homes had displayed an interest in a particular project, because that project was no longer live. Thus, we must suppose that even if the low-income plaintiffs had alleged a desire to live in the Better Homes project, that allegation would be insufficient because it appears that that particular project might never be built. The rights of low-income minority plaintiffs who desire to live in a locality, then, seem to turn on the willingness of a third party to litigate the legality of preclusion of a particular project, despite the fact that the third party may have no economic incentive to incur the costs of litigation with regard to one project, and despite the fact that the low-income minority plaintiffs' interest is not to live in a particular project but to live somewhere in the town in a dwelling they can afford.

Accepting, as we must, the various allegations and affidavits as true, the following picture emerges: The Penfield zoning ordinance, by virtue of regulations concerning "lot area, set backs, . . . population density, density of use, units per acre, floor area, sewer requirements, traffic flow, ingress and egress (, and) street location," makes "practically and economically impossible the construction of sufficient numbers of low and moderate income" housing. App. 25. The purpose of this ordinance was to preclude low-and moderate-income people and nonwhites from living in Penfield, *id.*, at 15, and, particularly because of refusals to grant zoning variances and building permits and by using special permit procedures and other devices, *id.*, at 17, the defendants succeeded in keeping "low and moderate income persons . . . and non-white persons . . . from residing within . . . Penfield." *Id.*, at 18.

As a result of these practices, various of the plaintiffs were affected in different ways.

For example, plaintiffs Ortiz, Reyes, Sinkler, and Broadnax, persons of low or moderate income and members of minority groups, alleged that "as a result" of respondents' exclusionary scheme, they could not live in Penfield, although they desired and attempted to do so, and consequently incurred greater commuting costs, lived in substandard housing, and had fewer services for their families and poorer schools for their children than if they had lived in Penfield. Members of the Rochester Home Builders Association were prevented from constructing homes for low- and moderate-income people in Penfield, harming them economically. And Penfield Better Homes, a member of the Housing Council, was frustrated in its attempt to build moderate-income housing.

Thus, the portrait which emerges from the allegations and affidavits is one of total, purposeful, intransigent exclusion of certain classes of people from the town, pursuant to a conscious scheme never deviated from. Because of this scheme, those interested in building homes for the excluded groups were faced with insurmountable difficulties, and those of the excluded groups seeking homes in the locality quickly learned that their attempts were futile. Yet, the Court turns the very success of the allegedly unconstitutional scheme into a barrier to a lawsuit seeking its invalidation. In effect, the Court tells the low income minority and building company plaintiffs they will not be permitted to prove what they have alleged—that they could and would build and live in the town if changes were made in the zoning ordinance and its application—because they have not succeeded in breaching, before the suit was filed, the very barriers which are the subject of the suit.

. . .

Simon v. Eastern Kentucky Welfare Rights Organization[36] involved a challenge to an Internal Revenue Service (IRS) Revenue Ruling allowing favorable tax treatment to a nonprofit hospital that offered only emergency-room services to indigents. Plaintiffs were an unincorporated association and several nonprofit corporations each of which included low-income persons among its members and represented the interests of all such persons in obtaining hospital care and services. The named plaintiffs included twelve people who described themselves as "subsisting below the poverty income levels established by the Federal Government and suffering from medical conditions requiring hospital services." Plaintiffs offered proof that they had been discriminated against in obtaining medical care on the basis of their indigency by hospitals. The complaint alleged that:

[B]y extending tax benefits to such hospitals despite their refusals fully to serve the indigent, the defendants were "encouraging" the hospitals to deny

[36] 426 U.S. 26 (1976).

services to the individual plaintiffs and to the members and clients of the plaintiff organizations. Those persons were alleged to be suffering "injury in their opportunity and ability to receive hospital services in nonprofit hospitals which receive . . . benefits . . . as 'charitable' organizations" under the Code. They also were alleged to be among the intended beneficiaries of the Code sections that grant favorable tax treatment to "charitable" organizations.

The Court concluded that plaintiffs lacked standing:

> We note at the outset that the five respondent organizations, which described themselves as dedicated to promoting access of the poor to health services, could not establish [standing]. . . . Our decisions make clear that an organization's abstract concern with a subject that could be affected by an adjudication does not substitute for the concrete injury required by Art. III. . . .

Adarand Constructors, Inc. v. Pena,[37] involved Adarand's challenge to the Federal Government's practice of giving general contractors on government projects a financial incentive to hire subcontractors controlled by "socially and economically disadvantaged individuals," and in particular, that the Government's use of race-based presumptions in identifying such individuals violates the equal protection component of the Fifth Amendment's Due Process Clause. The court found that Adarand had standing to challenge the practice:

> In 1989, the Central Federal Lands Highway Division (CFLHD), which is part of the United States Department of Transportation (DOT), awarded the prime contract for a highway construction project in Colorado to Mountain Gravel & Construction Company. Mountain Gravel then solicited bids from subcontractors for the guardrail portion of the contract. Adarand, a Colorado-based highway construction company specializing in guardrail work, submitted the low bid. Gonzales Construction Company also submitted a bid.
>
> The prime contract's terms provide that Mountain Gravel would receive additional compensation if it hired subcontractors certified as small businesses controlled by "socially and economically disadvantaged individuals," App. 24. Gonzales is certified as such a business; Adarand is not. Mountain Gravel awarded the subcontract to Gonzales, despite Adarand's low bid, and Mountain Gravel's Chief Estimator has submitted an affidavit stating that Mountain Gravel would have accepted Adarand's bid, had it not been for the additional payment it received by hiring Gonzales instead. *Id.,* at 28–31. Federal law requires that a subcontracting clause similar to the one used here must appear in most federal agency contracts, and it also requires the clause to state that "[t]he contractor shall presume that socially and economically disadvantaged individuals include Black Americans, Hispanic Americans, Native Americans, Asian Pacific Americans, and other minorities, or any other individual found to be disadvantaged by the [Small Business] Administration pursuant to section 8(a) of the Small Business Act." 15 U.S.C. §§ 637(d)(2), (3). Adarand claims that the presumption set forth in that statute discriminates on the basis of race in violation of the Federal Government's Fifth Amendment obligation not to deny anyone equal protection of the laws.
>
> . . .
>
> Adarand, in addition to its general prayer for "such other and further relief as to the Court seems just and equitable," specifically seeks declaratory and injunctive relief against any future use of subcontractor compensation clauses.

[37] 115 S. Ct. 2097 (1995).

Before reaching the merits of Adarand's challenge, we must consider whether Adarand has standing to seek forward-looking relief. Adarand's allegation that it has lost a contract in the past because of a subcontractor compensation clause of course entitles it to seek damages for the loss of that contract. [As] we explained in *Los Angeles v. Lyons*, 461 U.S. 95 (1983), the fact of past injury, "while presumably affording [the plaintiff] standing to claim damages . . . , does nothing to establish a real and immediate threat that he would again" suffer similar injury in the future. *Id.*, at 105.

If Adarand is to maintain its claim for forward-looking relief, our cases require it to allege that the use of subcontractor compensation clauses in the future constitutes "an invasion of a legally protected interest which is (a) concrete and particularized, and (b) actual or imminent, not conjectural or hypothetical." *Lujan v. Defenders of Wildlife*, 504 U.S. 555, 560 (1992). Adarand's claim that the Government's use of subcontractor compensation clauses denies it equal protection of the laws of course alleges an invasion of a legally protected interest, and it does so in a manner that is "particularized" as to Adarand. We note that, contrary to the respondents' suggestion, Adarand need not demonstrate that it has been, or will be, the low bidder on a government contract. The injury in cases of this kind is that a "discriminatory classification prevent[s] the plaintiff from competing on an equal footing." *General Contractors v. Jacksonville*, 113 S.Ct. 2297, 2304 (1993). The aggrieved party "need not allege that he would have obtained the benefit but for the barrier in order to establish standing." *Id.*, at 2303.

It is less clear, however, that the future use of subcontractor compensation clauses will cause Adarand "imminent" injury. We said in *Lujan* that "[al]though 'imminence' is concededly a somewhat elastic concept, it cannot be stretched beyond its purpose, which is to insure that the alleged injury is not too speculative for Article III purposes—that the injury is 'certainly impending.'" *Lujan, supra*, at 565, n. 2. We therefore must ask whether Adarand has made an adequate showing that sometime in the relatively near future it will bid on another government contract that offers financial incentives to a prime contractor for hiring disadvantaged subcontractors.

We conclude that Adarand has satisfied this requirement. Adarand's general manager said in a deposition that his company bids on every guardrail project in Colorado. According to documents produced in discovery, the CFLHD let fourteen prime contracts in Colorado that included guardrail work between 1983 and 1990. [S]tatistics from the years 1983 through 1990 indicate that the CFLHD lets on average one and one half contracts per year that could injure Adarand in the manner it alleges here. Nothing in the record suggests that the CFLHD has altered the frequency with which it lets contracts that include guardrail work. And the record indicates that Adarand often must compete for contracts against companies certified as small disadvantaged businesses. Because the evidence in this case indicates that the CFLHD is likely to let contracts involving guardrail work that contain a subcontractor compensation clause at least once per year in Colorado, that Adarand is very likely to bid on each such contract, and that Adarand often must compete for such contracts against small disadvantaged businesses, we are satisfied that Adarand has standing to bring this lawsuit.

In two other cases decided in 1995, the Court further defined the standing requirement. *Miller v. Johnson*,[38] involved a challenge to Georgia's congressional redistricting

---

[38] 115 S. Ct. 2475 (1995).

plan. Under the prodding of the Justice Department, the Georgia Assembly created three majority-black districts. Five white voters who resided in a majority-black district sought to challenge the district. The Court concluded that the plaintiffs had standing. Justice Stevens dissented:

. . . Neither in *Shaw* [*v. Reno*] itself nor in the cases decided today has the Court coherently articulated what injury this cause of action is designed to redress. Because respondents have alleged no legally cognizable injury, they lack standing, and these cases should be dismissed.

Even assuming the validity of *Shaw*, I cannot see how respondents in these cases could assert the injury the Court attributes to them. Respondents, plaintiffs below, are white voters in Georgia's Eleventh Congressional District. The Court's conclusion that they have standing to maintain a *Shaw* claim appears to rest on a theory that their placement in the Eleventh District caused them "'representational harms.'" The *Shaw* Court explained the concept of "representational harms" as follows: "When a district obviously is created solely to effectuate the perceived common interests of one racial group, elected officials are more likely to believe that their primary obligation is to represent only the members of that group, rather than their constituency as a whole." Although the *Shaw* Court attributed representational harms solely to a message sent by the legislature's action, those harms can only come about if the message is received—that is, first, if all or most black voters support the same candidate, and, second, if the successful candidate ignores the interests of her white constituents. Respondents' standing, in other words, ultimately depends on the very premise the Court purports to abhor: that voters of a particular race "'think alike, share the same political interests, and will prefer the same candidates at the polls.'" This generalization, as the Court recognizes, is "offensive and demeaning."

In particular instances, of course, members of one race may vote by an overwhelming margin for one candidate, and in some cases that candidate will be of the same race. "Racially polarized voting" is one of the circumstances plaintiffs must prove to advance a vote dilution claim. *Thornburg v. Gingles*, 478 U.S. 30, 56–58 (1986). Such a claim allows voters to allege that gerrymandered district lines have impaired their ability to elect a candidate of their own race. The Court emphasizes, however, that a so-called *Shaw* claim is "'analytically distinct' from a vote dilution claim." Neither in *Shaw*, nor in *Hays*, nor in the instant cases has the Court answered the question its analytic distinction raises: If the *Shaw* injury does not flow from an increased probability that white candidates will lose, then how can the increased probability that black candidates will win cause white voters, such as respondents, cognizable harm?

The Court attempts an explanation in these cases by equating the injury it imagines respondents have suffered with the injuries African Americans suffered under segregation. The heart of respondents' claim, by the Court's account, is that "a State's assignment of voters on the basis of race," violates the Equal Protection Clause for the same reason a State may not "segregate citizens on the basis of race in its public parks, buses, golf courses, beaches, and schools. This equation, however, fails to elucidate the elusive *Shaw* injury. Our desegregation cases redressed the exclusion of black citizens from public facilities reserved for whites. In this case, in contrast, any voter, black or white, may live in the Eleventh District. What respondents contest is the inclusion of too many black voters in the District as drawn. In my view, if respondents allege no vote dilution, that inclusion can cause them no conceivable injury.

The Court's equation of *Shaw* claims with our desegregation decisions is inappropriate for another reason. In each of those cases, legal segregation frustrated the public interest in diversity and tolerance by barring African Americans from joining whites in the activities at issue. The districting plan here, in contrast, serves the interest in diversity and tolerance by increasing the likelihood that a meaningful number of black representatives will add their voices to legislative debates. "There is no moral or constitutional equivalence between a policy that is designed to perpetuate a caste system and one that seeks to eradicate racial subordination." *Adarand Constructors, Inc. v. Pena.* That racial integration of the sort attempted by Georgia now appears more vulnerable to judicial challenge than some policies alleged to perpetuate racial bias is anomalous, to say the least.

The Court also decided *United States v. Hays*,[39] involving a challenge to majority-black districts in Louisiana. In *Hays*, the Court concluded that white voters who did not live in the challenged districts could not establish standing:

> The rule against generalized grievances applies with as much force in the equal protection context as in any other. *Allen v. Wright* made clear that even if a governmental actor is discriminating on the basis of race, the resulting injury "accords a basis for standing only to 'those persons who are personally denied equal treatment' by the challenged discriminatory conduct.".

> [W]here a plaintiff does not live in [a racially-gerrymandered] district, he or she does not suffer those special harms, and any inference that the plaintiff has personally been subjected to a racial classification would not be justified absent specific evidence tending to support that inference. Unless such evidence is present, that plaintiff would be asserting only a generalized grievance against governmental conduct of which he or she does not approve.

> In this case, appellees have not produced evidence sufficient to carry the burden our standing doctrine imposes upon them. [A]ppellees have pointed to no evidence tending to show that they have suffered that injury, and our review of the record has revealed none. [Nothing] in the record indicates that appellees, or any other residents of Lincoln Parish, have been subjected to racially discriminatory treatment. The record does contain evidence tending to show that the legislature was aware of the racial composition of District 5, and of Lincoln Parish. We recognized in Shaw, however, that "the legislature always is aware of race when it draws district lines, just as it is aware of age, economic status, religious and political persuasion, and a variety of other demographic actors. That sort of race consciousness does not lead inevitably to impermissible race discrimination." It follows that proof of "[t]hat sort of race consciousness" in the redistricting process is inadequate to establish injury in fact.

> Appellees urge that District 5 is a "segregated" voting district, and thus that their position is no different from that of a student in a segregated school district. But even assuming arguendo that the evidence in this case

---

[39] 115 S. Ct. 2431 (1995).

is enough to state a *Shaw* claim with respect to District 4, that does not prove anything about the legislature's intentions with respect to District 5, nor does the record appear to reflect that the legislature intended District 5 to have any particular racial composition. Of course, it may be true that the racial composition of District 5 would have been different if the legislature had drawn District 4 in another way. But an allegation to that effect does not allege a cognizable injury under the Fourteenth Amendment. We have never held that the racial composition of a particular voting district, without more, can violate the Constitution.

Appellees insist that they challenged Act 1 in its entirety, not District 4 in isolation. That is true. It is also irrelevant. The fact that Act 1 affects all Louisiana voters by classifying each of them as a member of a particular congressional district does not mean—even if Act 1 inflicts race-based injury on some Louisiana voters—that every Louisiana voter has standing to challenge Act 1 as a racial classification. Only those citizens able to allege injury "as a direct result of having personally been denied equal treatment," *Allen*, 468 U.S., at 755, may bring such a challenge, and citizens who do so carry the burden of proving their standing, as well as their case on the merits.

Appellees' reliance on *Powers v. Ohio*, 499 U.S. 400 (1991), is unavailing. *Powers* held that "[a]n individual juror does not have a right to sit on any particular petit jury, but he or she does possess the right not to be excluded from one on account of race." *Id.*, at 409. But of course, where an individual juror is excluded from a jury because of race, that juror has personally suffered the race-based harm recognized in *Powers*, and it is the fact of personal injury that appellees have failed to establish here. Thus, appellees' argument that "they do have a right not to be placed into or excluded from a district because of the color of their skin," Brief for Appellees 16, cannot help them, because they have not established that they have suffered such treatment in this case.

[We] conclude that appellees have failed to show that they have suffered the injury our standing doctrine requires. Appellees point us to no authority for the proposition that an equal protection challenge may go forward in federal court absent that showing of individualized harm, and we decline appellees' invitation to approve that proposition in this case. Accordingly, the judgment of the District Court is vacated, and the case is remanded with instructions to dismiss the complaint.

Justice Stevens concurred:

The term "gerrymander" has long been understood to mean "any set of districts which gives some advantage to the party which draws the electoral map." P. Musgrove, The General Theory of Gerrymandering 6 (1977). As Justice Powell noted, "a colorable claim of discriminatory gerrymandering presents a justiciable controversy under the Equal Protection Clause." *Davis v. Bandemer*, 478 U.S. 109 (1986) (Powell, J., dissenting). The complaint in this case, however, did not allege a discriminatory gerrymander. Respondents made no claim that any political or racial majority had drawn district lines to disadvantage a weaker segment of the community. Indeed, the complaint did not even identify the race or the political affiliation of any of the respondents. It simply alleged that every voter in Louisiana was injured by being deprived of the right "to participate in a process for electing members of the House of Representatives which is color-blind and wherein the right to vote is not limited or abridged on account of the designated race or color of the majority of the voters placed in the designated districts."

Because the Court does not recognize standing to enforce "'a personal right to a government that does not deny equal protection of the laws,'" it holds that the mere fact of respondents' Louisiana residency does not give them standing. I agree with that conclusion. . . .

D. State Action

Most provisions of the Bill of Rights, as well as the fourteenth and fifteenth amendments, are designed to protect individuals against governmental action. They do not apply to actions by private individuals.

The Civil Rights Cases
109 U.S. 3 (1883)

[The Civil Rights Act of 1875 prohibited racial discrimination in public accommodations. The Act was challenged on the basis that Congress exceeded its authority in passing the Act.]

BRADLEY, J.

. . .

The essence of the law is . . . to declare that, in the enjoyment of the accommodations and privileges of inns, public conveyances, theaters, and other places of public amusement, no distinction shall be made between citizens of different race or color, or between those who have, and those who have not, been slaves. Its effect is to declare that in all inns, public conveyances, and places of amusement, colored citizens, whether formerly slaves or not, and citizens of other races, shall have the same accommodations and privileges in all inns, public conveyances, and places of amusement, as are enjoyed by white citizens; and vice versa. . . .

Has congress constitutional power to make such a law? . . .

The first section of the fourteenth amendment,—which is the one relied on,—after declaring who shall be citizens of the United States, and of the several states, is prohibitory in its character, and prohibitory upon the states. It declares that "no state shall make or enforce any law which shall abridge the privileges or immunities of citizens of the United States; nor shall any state deprive any person of life, liberty, or property without due process of law; nor deny to any person within its jurisdiction the equal protection of the laws." It is state action of a particular character that is prohibited. Individual invasion of individual rights is not the subject-matter of the amend-

ment. It has a deeper and broader scope. It nullifies and makes void all state legislation, and state action of every kind, which impairs the privileges and immunities of citizens of the United States, or which injures them in life, liberty, or property without due process of law, or which denies to any of them the equal protection of the laws. It not only does this, but, in order that the national will, thus declared, may not be a mere brutum fulmen, the last section of the amendment invests congress with power to enforce it by appropriate legislation. To enforce what? To enforce the prohibition. To adopt appropriate legislation for correcting the effects of such prohibited state law and state acts, and thus to render them effectually null, void, and innocuous. This is the legislative power conferred upon congress, and this is the whole of it. . . . It does not authorize congress to create a code of municipal law for the regulation of private rights; but to provide modes of redress against the operation of state laws, and the action of state officers, executive or judicial, when these are subversive of the fundamental rights specified in the amendment. . . .

. . .

An inspection of the law shows that it makes no reference whatever to any supposed or apprehended violation of the fourteenth amendment on the part of the states. It is not predicated on any such view. It proceeds ex directo to declare that certain acts committed by individuals shall be deemed offenses, and shall be prosecuted and punished by proceedings in the courts of the United States. It does not profess to be corrective of any constitutional wrong committed by the states; it does not make its operation to depend upon any such wrong committed. It applies equally to cases arising in states which have the justest laws respecting the personal rights of citizens, and whose authorities are ever ready to enforce such laws as to those which arise in states that may have violated the prohibition of the amendment. In other words, it steps into the domain of local jurisprudence, and lays down rules for the conduct of individuals is society towards each other, and imposes sanctions for the enforcement of those rules, without referring in any manner to any supposed action of the state or its authorities.

If this legislation is appropriate for enforcing the prohibitions of the amendment, it is difficult to see where it is to stop. Why may not congress, with equal show of authority, enact a code of laws for the enforcement and vindication of all rights of life, liberty, and property? If it is supposable that the states may deprive persons of life, liberty, and property without due process of law, (and the amendment itself does suppose this,) why should not congress proceed at once to prescribe due process of law for the protection of every one of these fundamental rights, in every possible case, as well as to prescribe equal privileges in inns, public conveyances, and theaters. The truth is that the implication of a power to legislate in this manner is based upon the assumption that if the states are forbidden to legislate or act in a particular way on a particular subject, and power is conferred upon congress to enforce the prohibition, this gives congress power to legislate generally upon that subject, and not merely power to provide modes of redress against such state legislation or action. The assumption is certainly unsound. It is repugnant to the tenth amendment of the constitution, which declares that powers not delegated to the United States by the constitution, nor prohibited by it to the states, are reserved to the states respectively or to the people.

. . .

[C]ivil rights, such as are guarantied by the constitution against state aggression, cannot be impaired by the wrongful acts of individuals, unsupported by state authority in the shape of laws, customs, or judicial or executive proceedings. The wrongful act of an individual, unsupported by any such authority, is simply a private wrong, or a crime of that individual; an invasion of the rights of the injured party, it is true, whether they affect his person, his property, or his reputation; but if not sanctioned in some way by the state, or not done under state authority, his rights remain in full force, and may presumably be vindicated by resort to the laws of the state for redress. . . .

Of course, these remarks do not apply to those cases in which congress is clothed with direct and plenary powers of legislation over the whole subject, accompanied with an express or implied denial of such power to the states, as in the regulation of commerce with foreign nations, among the several states, and with the Indian tribes, the coining of money, the establishment of post-offices and post-roads, the declaring of war, etc. In these cases congress has power to pass laws for regulating the subjects specified, in every detail, and the conduct and transactions of individuals respect thereof. But where a subject is not submitted to the general legislative power of congress, but is only submitted thereto for the purpose of rendering effective some prohibition against particular state legislation or state action in reference to that subject, the power given is limited by its object, and any legislation by congress in the matter must necessarily be corrective in its character, adapted to counteract and redress the operation of such prohibited state laws or proceedings of state officers.

If the principles of interpretation which we have laid down are correct, . . . it is clear that the law in question cannot be sustained by any grant of legislative power made to congress by the fourteenth amendment. . . .

. . .

But the power of congress to adopt direct and primary, as distinguished from corrective, legislation on the subject in hand, is sought, in the second place, from the thirteenth amendment, which abolishes slavery. This amendment declares "that neither slavery, nor involuntary servitude, except as a punishment for crime, whereof the party shall have been duly convicted, shall exist within the United States, or any place subject to their jurisdiction;" and it gives congress power to enforce the amendment by appropriate legislation.

. . .

[I]t is assumed that the power vested in congress to enforce the article by appropriate legislation, clothes congress with power to pass all laws necessary and proper for abolishing all badges and incidents of slavery in the United Stated; and upon this assumption it is claimed that this is sufficient authority for declaring by law that all persons shall have equal accommodations and privileges in all inns, public conveyances, and places of public amusement; the argument being that the denial of such equal accommodations and privileges is in itself a subjection to a species of servitude within the meaning of the amendment. . . .

. . .

The only question under the present head, therefore, is, whether the refusal to any persons of the accommodations of an inn, or a public conveyance, or a place of public amusement, by an individual, and without any sanction or support from any state law or regulation, does inflict upon such persons any manner of servitude, or form of slavery, as those terms are understood in this country? Many wrongs may be obnoxious to the prohibitions of the fourteenth amendment which are not, in any just sense, incidents or elements of slavery. . . .

. . .

After giving to these questions all the consideration which their importance demands, we are forced to the conclusion that such an act of refusal has nothing to do with slavery or involuntary servitude, and that if it is violative of any right of the party, his redress is to be sought under the laws of the state; or, if those laws are adverse to his rights and do not protect him, his remedy will be found in the corrective legislation which congress has adopted, or may adopt, for counteracting the effect of state laws, or state action, prohibited by the fourteenth amendment. It would be running the slavery argument into the ground to make it apply to every act of discrimination which a person may see fit to make as to the guests he will entertain, or as to the people he will take into his coach or cab or car, or admit to his concert or theater, or deal with in other matters of intercourse or business. . . .

. . .

[W]e are of opinion that no countenance of authority for the passage of the law in question can be found in either the thirteenth or fourteenth amendment of the constitution; and no other ground of authority for its passage being suggested, it must necessarily be declared void, at least so far as its operation in the several states is concerned.

HARLAN, J., dissenting.

. . .

[T]he power of congress is not restricted to the enforcement of prohibitions upon state laws or state action. It is, in terms distinct and positive, to enforce "the provisions of this article" of amendment; not simply those of a prohibitive character, but the provisions,—all of the provisions,—affirmative and prohibitive, of the amendment. It is, therefore, a grave misconception to suppose that the fifth section of the amendment has reference exclusively to express prohibitions upon state laws or state action. If any right was created by that amendment, the grant of power, through appropriate legislation, to enforce its provisions authorizes congress, by means of legislation operating throughout the entire Union, to guard, secure, and protect that right.

. . .

In most cases, when a citizen complains about a violation of the Bill of Rights or the fourteenth amendment, state involvement is obvious. Congress or a state legislature has passed a law infringing the citizen's rights, or a governmental agency or government official has taken action against the citizen. More difficult questions arise when the violation seems to be the result of private action, but the government is involved or implicated in the private action in some way. As we shall see, government is involved in virtually all private conduct. Thus, the question is whether the government is sufficiently involved so that the ostensibly private action effectively becomes "state action." Questions about state action have vexed the courts.

1. Government Function

One situation in which the Court has found state action is when a private entity performs a governmental function. There are a number of "governmental function" cases.

a. Company Towns

Marsh v. Alabama
326 U.S. 501 (1946)

Mr. Justice BLACK delivered the opinion of the Court.

In this case we are asked to decide whether a State, consistently with the First and Fourteenth Amendments, can impose criminal punishment on a person who undertakes to distrib-

ute religious literature on the premises of a company-owned town contrary to the wishes of the town's management. The town, a suburb of Mobile, Alabama, known as Chickasaw, is owned by the Gulf Shipbuilding Corporation. Except for that it has all the characteristics of any other American town. The property consists of residential buildings, streets, a system of sewers, a sewage disposal plant and a "business block" on which business places are situated. A deputy of the Mobile County Sheriff, paid by the company, serves as the town's policeman. Merchants and service establishments have rented the stores and business places on the business block and the United States uses one of the places as a post office from which six carriers deliver mail to the people of Chickasaw and the adjacent area. The town and the surrounding neighborhood, which can not be distinguished from the Gulf property by anyone not familiar with the property lines, are thickly settled, and according to all indications the residents use the business block as their regular shopping center. To do so, they now, as they have for many years, make use of a company-owned paved street and sidewalk located alongside the store fronts in order to enter and leave the stores and the post office. Intersecting company-owned roads at each end of the business block lead into a four-lane public highway which runs parallel to the business block at a distance of thirty feet. There is nothing to stop highway traffic from coming onto the business block and upon arrival a traveler may make free use of the facilities available there. In short the town and its shopping district are accessible to and freely used by the public in general and there is nothing to distinguish them from any other town and shopping center except the fact that the title to the property belongs to a private corporation.

Appellant, a Jehovah's Witness, came onto the sidewalk we have just described, stood near the post-office and undertook to distribute religious literature. In the stores the corporation had posted a notice which read as follows: "This Is Private Property, and Without Written Permission, No Street, or House Vendor, Agent or Solicitation of Any Kind Will Be Permitted." Appellant was warned that she could not distribute the literature without a permit and told that no permit would be issued to her. She protested that the company rule could not be constitutionally applied so as to prohibit her from distributing religious writings. When she was asked to leave the sidewalk and Chickasaw she declined. The deputy sheriff arrested her and she was charged in the state court with violating Title 14, Section 426 of the 1940 Alabama Code which makes it a crime to enter or remain on the premises of another after having been warned not to do so. Appellant contended that to construe the state statute as applicable to her activities would abridge her right to freedom of press and religion contrary to the First and Fourteenth Amendments to the Constitution. This contention was rejected and she was convicted. . . .

Had the title to Chickasaw belonged not to a private but to a municipal corporation and had appellant been arrested for violating a municipal ordinance rather than a ruling by those appointed by the corporation to manage a company-town it would have been clear that appellant's conviction must be reversed. Under our decision in *Lovell v. Griffin*, 303 U.S. 444, and others which have followed that case, neither a state nor a municipality can completely bar the distribution of literature containing religious or political ideas on its streets, sidewalks and public places or make the right to distribute dependent on a flat license tax or permit to be issued by an official who could deny it at will. We have also held that an ordinance completely prohibiting the dissemination of ideas on the city streets can not be justified on the ground that the municipality holds legal title to them. . . .

We do not agree that the corporation's property interests settle the question. The State urges in effect that the corporation's right to control the inhabitants of Chickasaw is coextensive with the right of a homeowner to regulate the conduct of his guests. We can not accept that contention. Ownership does not always mean absolute dominion. The more an owner, for his advantage, opens up his property for use by the public in general, the more do his rights become circumscribed by the statutory and constitutional rights of those who use it. . . .

We do not think it makes any significant constitutional difference as to the relationship between the rights of the owner and those of the public that here the State, instead of permitting the corporation to operate a highway, permitted it to use its property as a town, operate a "business block" in the town and a street and sidewalk on that business block. Whether a corporation or a municipality owns or possesses the town the public in either case has an identical interest in the functioning of the community in such manner that the channels of communication remain free. As we have heretofore stated, the town of Chickasaw does not function differently from any other town. The "business block" serves as the community shopping center and is freely accessible and open to the people in the area and those passing through. The managers appointed by the corporation cannot curtail the liberty of press and religion of these people consistently with the purposes of the Constitutional guarantees, and a state statute, as the one here involved, which enforces such action by criminally punishing those who attempt to distribute religious literature clearly violates the First and Fourteenth Amendments to the Constitution.

. . .

When we balance the Constitutional rights of owners of property against those of the people to enjoy freedom of press and religion, as we must here, we remain mindful of the fact that the latter occupy a preferred position. As we have stated before, the right to exercise the liberties safeguarded by the First Amendment "lies at the foundation of free government by free men" and we must in all cases "weigh the circumstances and appraise * * * the reasons * * * in support of the regulation of (those) rights." *Schneider v. State*, 308 U.S. 147, 161. In our view the circumstance that the property rights to the premises where the deprivation of liberty, here involved, took place, were held by others than the public, is not sufficient to justify the State's permitting a corporation to govern a community of citizens so as to restrict their fundamental liberties and the enforcement of such restraint by the application of a State statute. Insofar as the State has attempted to impose criminal punishment on appellant for undertaking to distribute religious literature in a company town, its action cannot stand. The case is reversed and the cause remanded for further proceedings not inconsistent with this opinion.

Reversed and remanded.

Mr. Justice REED, dissenting.

Former decisions of this Court have interpreted generously the Constitutional rights of people in this Land to exercise freedom of religion, of speech and of the press. . . . [But] [t]his is the first case to extend by law the privilege of religious exercises beyond public places or to private places without the assent of the owner. . . .

[W]e find nothing in the principles of the First Amendment, adopted now into the Fourteenth, which justifies their application to the facts of this case.

. . .

b. Shopping Centers

Are shopping centers the modern equivalent of company towns? In a series of decisions issued in the 1960s and 1970s, the Court struggled with this issue. In *Amalgamated Food Employees Union v. Logan Valley Plaza, Inc.*,[40] union members peacefully picketed a business located in a private shopping center. When the owners of the center sought to enjoin the picketing as a trespass, the picketers defended on First Amendment grounds. The Court held that the shopping center's actions constituted state action so that the First Amendment applied:

[It] is clear that if the shopping center premises were not privately owned but instead constituted the business area of a municipality, which they to a large extent resemble, petitioners could not be barred from exercising their First Amendment rights there on the sole ground that title to the property was in the municipality. *Lovell v. City of Griffin*, 303 U.S. 444 (1938). . . .

. . .

The similarities between the business block in Marsh and the shopping center in the present case are striking. The perimeter of Logan Valley Mall is a little less than 1.1 miles. Inside the mall were situated, at the time of trial, two substantial commercial enterprises with numerous others soon to follow. Immediately adjacent to the mall are two roads, one of which is a heavily traveled state highway and from both of which lead entrances directly into the mall. Adjoining the buildings in the middle of the mall are sidewalks for the use of pedestrians going to and from their cars and from building to building. In the parking areas, roadways for the use of vehicular traffic entering and leaving the mall are clearly marked out. The general public has unrestricted access to the mall property. The shopping center here is clearly the functional equivalent of the business district of Chickasaw involved in Marsh.

. . .

We see no reason why access to a business district in a company town for the purpose of exercising First Amendment rights should be constitutionally

---

[40] 391 U.S. 308 (1968).

required, while access for the same purpose to property functioning as a business district should be limited simply because the property surrounding the "business district" is not under the same ownership. . . .

Logan Valley was followed by the holding in *Lloyd Corp., Ltd. v. Tanner.*[41] *Lloyd Corp.* involved a shopping center that covered nearly 50 acres of ground. All stores in the Center were located within a single large, multi-level, building complex that contained interior promenades with large sidewalks. The center was generally open to the public, and various civic groups were allowed to hold events on the premises. The center was "policed" by private security guards hired by the Center. Litigation arose when the Center's security guards told several individuals, who were distributing handbills in the shopping center, to leave or they would be arrested. The handbills stated opposition to the Vietnam War and the draft. The handbillers left, but then sought declaratory relief and injunctive relief on First Amendment grounds. The Supreme Court concluded that the center's conduct constituted private action distinguishing *Marsh* and *Logan Valley*:

> Marsh was never intended to apply to this kind of situation. Marsh dealt with the very special situation of a company-owned town, complete with streets, alleys, sewers, stores, residences, and everything else that goes to make a town. [T]he basis on which the Marsh decision rested was that the property involved encompassed an area that for all practical purposes had been turned into a town; the area had all the attributes of a town and was exactly like any other town in Alabama. 391 U.S., at 330—331.
>
> The holding in Logan Valley was not dependent upon the suggestion that the privately owned streets and sidewalks of a business district or a shopping center are the equivalent, for First Amendment purposes, of municipally owned streets and sidewalks. No such expansive reading of the opinion of the Court is necessary or appropriate. The opinion was carefully phrased to limit its holding to the picketing involved, where the picketing was "directly related in its purpose to the use to which the shopping center property was being put," 391 U.S., at 320 n.9, and where the store was located in the center of a large private enclave with the consequence that no other reasonable opportunities for the pickets to convey their message to their intended audience were available.
>
> Neither of these elements is present in the case now before the Court.

Finally, in *Hudgens v. NLRB*,[42] the Court overruled *Logan Valley* completely. *Hudgens* involved union members who engaged in peaceful protesting inside a privately owned shopping center. When they were threatened with arrest by an agent of the owner, they sought declaratory and injunctive relief. The question was whether the threat constituted an unfair labor practice within the meaning of the National Labor Relations Act. The NLRB issued a cease and desist order concluding that the picketers had a First Amendment right to picket Hudgens' mall. The Court disagreed:

> [I]f the respondents in the Lloyd case did not have a First Amendment right to enter that shopping center to distribute handbills concerning Vietnam, then the pickets in the present case did not have a First Amendment right to enter this shopping center for the purpose of advertising their strike against the Butler Shoe Co.

---

[41] 407 U.S. 551 (1972).
[42] 424 U.S. 507 (1976).

We conclude [that] the constitutional guarantee of free expression has no part to play in a case such as this.

c. Party Primaries

In a series of cases decided during the first half of this century, the Court was confronted by claims that the Texas Democratic Party was precluding Negroes from participating in party primaries. In theory, political parties are nothing more than voluntary associations of private individuals. Hence, their primaries might be regarded as private action. In a series of cases decided between 1927 and 1953, the Court concluded otherwise.

Nixon v. Herndon[43] was the first of these cases. It involved a state statute that explicitly prohibited Negroes from voting in the Democratic primary. In *Nixon*, the Court struck down the Texas law concluding that its mandated discrimination constituted state action. Following *Nixon*, the Texas Legislature passed a new law giving the Democratic Party's Executive Committee power to decide who could vote in party primaries. When the Executive Committee passed a resolution providing that only white Democrats would be allowed to vote or participate, the Court again struck the law down. The Court found "state action" on the basis that the "Committee operated as representative of the State in the discharge of the State's authority."[44] The question of the inherent power of a political party in Texas "without restraint by any law to determine its own membership" was left open.

That issue was presented in *Smith v. Allwright*.[45] After the previously-discussed laws were struck down, the Texas Democratic Party passed a resolution limiting membership to white citizens of the State of Texas. Since only party members could vote in the Democratic primary, this resolution effectively precluded Negroes from participating. This resolution had been adopted by the party on its own without statutory authorization. In *Grovey v. Townsend*,[46] the Court concluded that no state action was involved. *Smith* reversed *Grovey* and held that state action existed: the "statutory system for the selection of party nominees for inclusion on the general election ballot makes the party which is required to follow these legislative directions an agency of the state in so far as it determines the participants in a primary election." "The privilege of membership in a party may be . . . no concern of a state. But when, as here, that privilege is also the essential qualification for voting in a primary to select nominees for a general election, the state makes the action of the party the action of the state. . . ." Following *Smith*, the following case came before the Court.

---

[43] 273 U.S. 536 (1927).
[44] Nixon v. Condon, 286 U.S. 73 (1932).
[45] 321 U.S. 649 (1944).
[46] 295 U.S. 45 (1935).

Terry v. Adams
345 U.S. 461 (1953)

Mr. Justice BLACK announced the judgment of the Court and an opinion in which Mr. Justice DOUGLAS and Mr. Justice BURTON join. . . . This case raises questions concerning the constitutional power of a Texas county political organization called the Jaybird Democratic Association or Jaybird Party to exclude Negroes from its primaries on racial grounds. The Jaybirds deny that their racial exclusions violate the Fifteenth Amendment. They contend that the Amendment applies only to elections or primaries held under state regulation, that their association is not regulated by the state at all, and that it is not a political party but a self-governing voluntary club. . . .

There was evidence that:

The Jaybird Association or Party was organized in 1889. Its membership was then and always has been limited to white people; they are automatically members if their names appear on the official list of county voters. It has been run like other political parties with an executive committee named from the county's voting precincts. Expenses of the party are paid by the assessment of candidates for office in its primaries. Candidates for county offices submit their names to the Jaybird Committee in accordance with the normal practice followed by regular political parties all over the country. Advertisements and posters proclaim that these candidates are running subject to the action of the Jaybird primary. While there is no legal compulsion on successful Jaybird candidates to enter Democratic primaries they have nearly always done so and with few exceptions since 1889 have run and won without opposition in the Democratic primaries and the general elections that followed. Thus the party has been the dominant political group in the county since organization, having endorsed every county-wide official elected since 1889.

It is apparent that Jaybird activities follow a plan purposefully designed to exclude Negroes from voting and at the same time to escape the Fifteenth Amendment's command that the right of citizens to vote shall neither be denied nor abridged on account of race. . . .

. . .

It is significant that precisely the same qualifications as those prescribed by Texas entitling electors to vote at county-operated primaries are adopted as the sole qualifications entitling electors to vote at the county-wide Jaybird primaries with a single proviso—Negroes are excluded. Everyone concedes that such a proviso in the county-operated primaries would be unconstitutional. The Jaybird Party thus brings into being and holds precisely the kind of election that the Fifteenth Amendment seeks to prevent. When it produces the equivalent of the prohibited election, the damage has been done.

For a state to permit such a duplication of its election processes is to permit a flagrant abuse of those processes to defeat the purposes of the Fifteenth Amendment. The use of the county-operated primary to ratify the result of the prohibited election merely compounds the offense. It violates the Fifteenth Amendment for a state, by such circumvention, to permit within its borders the use of any device that produces an equivalent of the prohibited election.

The only election that has counted in this Texas county for more than fifty years has been that held by the Jaybirds from which Negroes were excluded. The Democratic primary and the general election have become no more than the perfunctory ratifiers of the choice that has already been made in Jaybird elections from which Negroes have been excluded. It is immaterial that the state does not control that part of this elective process which it leaves for the Jaybirds to manage. The Jaybird primary has become an integral part, indeed the only effective part, of the elective process that determines who shall rule and govern in the county. The effect of the whole procedure, Jaybird primary plus Democratic primary plus general election, is to do precisely that which the Fifteenth Amendment forbids—strip Negroes of every vestige of influence in selecting the officials who control the local county matters that intimately touch the daily lives of citizens.

We . . . affirm the District Court's holding that the combined Jaybird-Democratic-general election machinery has deprived these petitioners of their right to vote on account of their race and color. . . .

Reversed and remanded.

Mr. Justice FRANKFURTER.

. . .

[T]he Jaybird primary is as a practical matter the instrument of those few in this small county who are politically active—the officials of the local Democratic party and, we may assume, the elected officials of the county. As a matter of practical politics, those charged by State law with the duty of assuring all eligible voters an opportunity to participate in the selection of candidates at the primary . . . participate by voting in the Jaybird primary. They join the white voting community in proceeding with elaborate formality, in almost all respects parallel to the procedures dictated by Texas law for the primary itself, to express their preferences in a wholly successful effort to withdraw significance from the State-prescribed primary, to subvert the operation of what is formally the law of the State for primaries in this county.

Mr. Justice CLARK, with whom the CHIEF JUSTICE, Mr. Justice REED, and Mr. Justice JACKSON join, concurring.

. . .

An old pattern in new guise is revealed by the record. . . . Not every private club, association or league organized to influence public candidacies or political action must conform to the Constitution's restrictions on political parties. Certainly a large area of freedom permits peaceable assembly and concerted private action for political purposes to be exercised separately by white and colored citizens alike. More, however, is involved here.

. . .

Quite evidently the Jaybird Democratic Association operates as an auxiliary of the local Democratic Party organization, selecting its nominees and using its machinery for carrying out an admitted design of destroying the weight and effect of Negro ballots in Fort Bend County. To be sure, the Democratic primary and the general election are nominally open to the colored elector. But his must be an empty vote case after the real decisions are made. And because the Jaybird-indorsed nominee meets no opposition in the Democratic primary, the Negro minority's vote is nullified at the sole stage of the local political process where the bargaining and interplay of rival political forces would make it count.

Mr. Justice MINTON, dissenting.

I am not concerned in the least as to what happens to the Jaybirds or their unworthy scheme. I am concerned about what this Court says is state action within the meaning of the Fifteenth Amendment to the Constitution. For, after all, this Court has power to redress a wrong under that Amendment only if the wrong is done by the State. That has been the holding of this Court since the earliest cases. . . . That Amendment erects no shield against merely private conduct, however discriminatory or wrongful.

. . .

Mr. Justice FRANKFURTER . . . seems to think it is enough to constitute state action if a state official participates in the Jaybird primary. That I cannot follow. For it seems clear to me that everything done by a person who is an official is not done officially and as a representative of the State. However, I find nothing in this record that shows the state or county officials participating in the Jaybird primary.

Mr. Justice CLARK seems to recognize that state action must be shown. He finds state action in assumption, not in facts. This record will be searched in vain for one iota of state action sufficient to support an anemic inference that the Jaybird Association is in any way associated with or forms a part of or cooperates in any manner with the Democratic Party of the County or State, or with the State. It calls itself the Jaybird Democratic Association because its interest is only in the candidates of the Democratic Party in the county, a position understandable in Texas. It is a gratuitous assumption on the part of Mr. Justice CLARK that: "Quite evidently the Jaybird Democratic Association operates as an auxiliary of the local Democratic Party organization, selecting its nominees and using its machinery for carrying out an admitted design of destroying the weight and effect of Negro ballots in Fort Bend County." . . .

Neither is there any more evidence that the Jaybird Association avails itself of or conforms in any manner to any law of the State of Texas. . . . Even if it be said to be a political organization, the Jaybird Association avails itself of no state law open to political organizations, such as Art. 3163.

However, its action is not forbidden by the law of the State of Texas. Does such failure of the State to act to prevent individuals from doing what they have the right as individuals to do amount to state action? I venture the opinion it does not.

Mr. Justice CLARK'S opinion agrees with District Judge Kennerly that this Jaybird Democratic Association is a political party whose activities fall within the Fifteenth Amendment's self-executing ban. In the same paragraph, he admits that not all meetings for political action come under the constitutional ban. Surely white or colored members of any political faith or economic belief may hold caucuses. It is only when the State by action of its legislative bodies or action of some of its officials in their official capacity cooperates with such political party or gives it direction in its activities that the Federal Constitution may come into play. A political organization not using state machinery or depending upon state law to authorize what it does could not be within the ban of the Fifteenth Amendment. As the stipulation quoted shows, the Jaybird Association did not attempt to conform or in any way to comply with the statutes of Texas covering primaries. No action of any legislative or quasi-legislative body or of any state official or agency ever in any manner denied the vote to Negroes, even in the Jaybird primaries.

So it seems to me clear there is no state action, and the Jaybird Democratic Association is in no sense a part of the Democratic Party. If it is a political organization, it has made no attempt to use the State, or the State to use it, to carry on its poll.

. . .

I do not understand that concerted action of individuals which is successful somehow becomes state action. However, the candidates endorsed by the Jaybird Association have several times been defeated in primaries and elections. Usually but not always since 1938, only the Jaybird-endorsed candidate has been on the Democratic official ballot in the County.

In the instant case, the State of Texas has provided for elections and primaries. This is separate and apart and wholly unrelated to the Jaybird Association's activities. Its activities are confined to one County where a group of citizens have appointed themselves the censors of those who would run for public offices. Apparently so far they have succeeded in convincing the voters of this County in most instances that their supported candidates should win. This seems to differ very little from situations common in many other places far north of the Mason-Dixon line, such as areas where a candidate must obtain the approval of a religious group. In other localities, candidates are carefully selected by both parties to give proper weight to Jew, Protestant and Catholic, and certain posts are considered the sole possession of certain ethnic groups. The propriety of these practices is something the courts sensibly have left to the good or bad judgment of the electorate. It must be recognized that elections and other public business are influenced by all sorts of pressures from carefully organized groups. We have pressure from labor unions, from the National Association of Manufacturers, from the Silver Shirts, from the National Association for the Advancement of Colored People, from the Ku Klux Klan and others. Far from the activities of these groups being properly labeled as state action, under either the Fourteenth or the Fifteenth Amendment, they are to be considered as attempts to influence or obtain state action.

The courts do not normally pass upon these pressure groups, whether their causes are good or bad, highly successful or only so-so. It is difficult for me to see how this Jaybird Association is anything but such a pressure group. Apparently it is believed in by enough people in Fort Bend County to obtain a majority of the votes for its approved candidates. This differs little from the situation in many parts of the "Bible Belt" where a church stamp of approval or that of the Anti-Saloon League must be put on any candidate who does not want to lose the election.

. . .

In this case the majority have found that this pressure group's work does constitute state action. The basis of this conclusion is rather difficult to ascertain. Apparently it derives mainly from a dislike of the goals of the Jaybird Association. I share that dislike. I fail to see how it makes state action. I would affirm.

Consider also *Peterson v. City of Greenville*.[47] In that case, petitioners were convicted of trespass for their refusal to leave a lunch counter when asked to do so "because integrated service was "contrary to local customs" of segregation at lunch counters" as well as in violation of a Greenville City ordinance requiring separation of the races in restaurants." Petitioners argued that South Carolina had deprived them of equal protection under the Fourteenth Amendment. The Court agreed finding that the restaurant's action constituted state action:

> It cannot be denied that here the City of Greenville, an agency of the State, has provided by its ordinance that the decision as to whether a restaurant facility is to be operated on a desegregated basis is to be reserved to it. When the State has commanded a particular result, it has saved to itself the power to determine that result and thereby "to a significant extent" has "become involved" in it, and, in fact, has removed that decision from the sphere of private choice. . . .

> [T]hese convictions cannot stand, even assuming, as respondent contends, that the manager would have acted as he did independently of the existence of the ordinance. The State will not be heard to make this contention in support of the convictions. For the convictions had the effect, which the State cannot deny, of enforcing the ordinance passed by the City of Greenville, the agency of the State. When a state agency passes a law compelling persons to discriminate against other persons because of race, and the State's criminal processes are employed in a way which enforces the discrimination mandated by that law, such a palpable violation of the Fourteenth Amendment cannot be saved by attempting to separate the mental urges of the discriminators.

d. Utility Service

Marsh, Nixon and *Herndon* were decided during the first half of the century. The following case deals with whether a utility company is engaged in private action. Has the Court's attitude regarding state action and the governmental function exception changed?

---

[47] 373 U.S. 244 (1963).

Jackson v. Metropolitan Edison Company
419 U.S. 345 (1974)

Mr. Justice REHNQUIST delivered the opinion of the Court.

Respondent Metropolitan Edison Co. is a privately owned and operated Pennsylvania corporation which holds a certificate of public convenience issued by the Pennsylvania Public Utility Commission empowering it to deliver electricity to a service area which includes the city of York, Pa. As a condition of holding its certificate, it is subject to extensive regulation by the Commission. Under a provision of its general tariff filed with the Commission, it has the right to discontinue service to any customer on reasonable notice of nonpayment of bills.

Petitioner Catherine Jackson is a resident of York, who has received electricity in the past from respondent. [When petitioner failed to pay her bills, Metropolitan terminated her service.] Petitioner then filed suit against Metropolitan in the United States District Court for the Middle District of Pennsylvania under the Civil Rights Act of 1871, 42 U.S.C. § 1983, seeking damages for the termination and an injunction requiring Metropolitan to continue providing power to her residence until she had been afforded notice, a hearing, and an opportunity to pay any amounts found due. She urged that under state law she had an entitlement to reasonably continuous electrical service to her home and that Metropolitan's termination of her service for alleged nonpayment, action allowed by a provision of its general tariff filed with the Commission, constituted "state action" depriving her of property in violation of the Fourteenth Amendment's guarantee of due process of law.

. . .

The Due Process Clause of the Fourteenth Amendment provides: "(N)or shall any State deprive any person of life, liberty, or property, without due process of law." In 1883, this Court in the Civil Rights Cases, 109 U.S. 3, affirmed the essential dichotomy set forth in that Amendment between deprivation by the State, subject to scrutiny under its provisions, and private conduct, "however discriminatory or wrongful," against which the Fourteenth Amendment offers no shield. *Shelley v. Kraemer*, 335 U.S. 1 (1948).

We have reiterated that distinction on more than one occasion since then. While the principle that private action is immune from the restrictions of the Fourteenth Amendment is well established and easily stated, the question whether particular conduct is "private," on the one hand, or "state action," on the other, frequently admits of no easy answer.

Here the action complained of was taken by a utility company which is privately owned and operated, but which in many particulars of its business is subject to extensive state regulation. The mere fact that a business is subject to state regulation does not by itself convert its action into that of the State for purposes of the Fourteenth Amendment. Nor does the fact that the regulation is extensive and detailed, as in the case of most public utilities, do so. *Public Utilities Comm'n v. Pollak*, 343 U.S. 451, 462 (1952). It may well be that acts of a heavily regulated utility with at least something of a governmentally protected monopoly will more readily be found to be "state" acts than will the acts of an entity lacking these characteristics. But the inquiry must be whether there is a sufficiently close nexus between the State and the challenged action of the regulated entity so that the action of the latter may be fairly treated as that of the State itself. The true nature of the State's involvement may not be immediately obvious, and detailed inquiry may be required in order to determine whether the test is met.

. . .

Petitioner first argues that "state action" is present because of the monopoly status allegedly conferred upon Metropolitan by the State of Pennsylvania. As a factual matter, it may well be doubted that the State ever granted or guaranteed Metropolitan a monopoly. But assuming that it had, this fact is not determinative in considering whether Metropolitan's termination of service to petitioner was "state action" for purposes of the Fourteenth Amendment. In Pollak, where the Court dealt with the activities of the District of Columbia Transit Co., a congressionally established monopoly, we expressly disclaimed reliance on the monopoly status of the transit authority. 343 U.S., at 462. Similarly, although certain monopoly aspects were presented in Moose Lodge No. 107, we found that the Lodge's action was not subject to the provisions of the Fourteenth Amendment. In each of those cases, there was insufficient relationship between the challenged actions of the entities involved and their monopoly status. There is no indication of any greater connection here.

Petitioner next urges that state action is present because respondent provides an essential public service required to be supplied on a reasonably continuous basis by Pa.Stat.Ann., Tit. 66, § 1171 (1959), and hence performs a "public function." We have, of course, found state action present in the exercise by a private entity of powers traditionally exclusively reserved to the State. If we were dealing with the exercise by Metropolitan of some power delegated to it by the State which is traditionally associated with sovereignty, such as eminent domain, our case would be quite a different one. But while the Pennsylvania statute imposes an obligation to furnish service on regulated utilities, it imposes no such obligation on the State. The Pennsylvania courts have rejected the contention that the furnishing of utility services is either a state function or a municipal duty.

Perhaps in recognition of the fact that the supplying of utility service is not traditionally the exclusive prerogative of the State, petitioner invites the expansion of the doctrine of this limited line of cases into a broad principle that all businesses "affected with the public interest" are state actors in all their actions. We decline the invitation for reasons stated long ago in *Nebbia v. New York*, 291 U.S. 502 (1934), in the course of rejecting a substantive due process attack on state legislation: "It is clear that there is no closed class or category of businesses affected with a public interest.... The phrase 'affected with a public interest' can, in the nature of things, mean no more than that an industry, for adequate reason, is subject to control for the public good. In several of the decisions of this court wherein the expressions 'affected with a public interest,' and 'clothed with a public use,' have been brought forward as the criteria ... it has been admitted that they are not susceptible of definition and form an unsatisfactory test...." *Id.*, at 536.

Doctors, optometrists, lawyers, Metropolitan, and Nebbia's upstate New York grocery selling a quart of milk are all in regulated businesses, providing arguably essential goods and services, "affected with a public interest." We do not believe that such a status converts their every action, absent more, into that of the State.

We also reject the notion that Metropolitan's termination is state action because the State "has specifically authorized and approved" the termination practice. In the instant case, Metropolitan filed with the Public Utility Commission a general tariff—a provision of which states Metropolitan's right to terminate service for nonpayment. This provision has appeared in Metropolitan's previously filed tariffs for many years and has never been the subject of a hearing or other scrutiny by the Commission.[11] Although the Commission did hold hearings on portions of Metropolitan's general tariff relating to a general rate increase, it never even considered the reinsertion of this provision in the newly filed general tariff. The provision became effective 60 days after filing when not disapproved by the Commission.

As a threshold matter, it is less than clear under state law that Metropolitan was even required to file this provision as part of its tariff or that the Commission would have had the power to disapprove it. The District Court observed that the sole connection of the Commission with this regulation was Metropolitan's simple notice filing with the Commission and the lack of any Commission action to prohibit it.

. . .

Metropolitan is a privately owned corporation, and it does not lease its facilities from the State of Pennsylvania. It alone is responsible for the provision of power to its customers. In common with all corporations of the State it pays taxes to the State, and it is subject to a form of extensive regulation by the State in a way that most other business enterprises are not. But this was likewise true of the appellant club in *Moose Lodge No. 107 v. Irvis, supra*, where we said: "However detailed this type of regulation may be in some particulars, it cannot be said to in any way foster or encourage racial discrimination. Nor can it be said to make the State in any realistic sense a partner or even a joint venturer in the club's enterprise." 407 U.S., at 176—177.

All of petitioner's arguments taken together show no more than that Metropolitan was a heavily regulated, privately owned utility, enjoying at least a partial monopoly in the providing of electrical service within its territory, and that it elected to terminate service to petitioner in a manner which the Pennsylvania Public Utility Commission found permissible under state law. Under our decision this is not sufficient to connect the State of Pennsylvania with respondent's action so as to make the latter's conduct attributable to the State for purposes of the Fourteenth Amendment.

We conclude that the State of Pennsylvania is not sufficiently connected with respondent's action in terminating petitioner's service so as to make respondent's conduct in so doing attributable to the State for purposes of the Fourteenth Amendment. We therefore have no occasion to decide whether petitioner's claim to continued service was "property" for purposes of that Amendment, or whether "due process of law" would require a State taking similar action to accord petitioner the procedural rights for which she contends. The judgment of the Court of Appeals for the Third Circuit is therefore

Affirmed.

Mr. Justice DOUGLAS, dissenting.

. . .

. . . May a State allow a utility—which in this case has no competitor—to exploit its monopoly in violation of its own tariff? May a utility have complete immunity under federal law

---

[11] Petitioner does not contest the fact that Metropolitan had this right at common law before the advent of regulation.

when the State allows its regulatory agency to become the prisoner of the utility or, by a listless attitude of no concern, to permit the utility to use its monopoly power in a lawless way?

. . .

. . . I agree that doctors, lawyers, and grocers are not transformed into state actors simply because they provide arguably essential goods and services and are regulated by the State. In the present case, however, respondent is not just one person among many; it is the only public utility furnishing electric power to the city. When power is denied a householder, the home, under modern conditions, is likely to become unlivable.

[I]n the present case the State is heavily involved in respondent's termination procedures, getting into the approved tariff a requirement of "reasonable notice." Pennsylvania has undertaken to regulate numerous aspects of respondent's operations in some detail, and a "hands-off" attitude of permissiveness or neutrality toward the operations in this case is at war with the state agency's functions of supervision over respondent's conduct in the area of servicing householders, particularly where (as here) the State would presumably lend its weight and authority to facilitate the enforcement of respondent's published procedures. . . .

In the aggregate, these factors depict a monopolist providing essential public services as a licensee of the State and within a framework of extensive state supervision and control. The particular regulations at issue, promulgated by the monopolist, were authorized by state law and were made enforceable by the weight and authority of the State. Moreover, the State retains the power of oversight to review and amend the regulations if the public interest so requires. Respondent's actions are sufficiently intertwined with those of the State, and its termination-of-service provisions are sufficiently buttressed by state law to warrant a holding that respondent's actions in terminating this householder's service were "state action" for the purpose of giving federal jurisdiction over respondent under 42 U.S.C. § 1983. Though the Court pays lip service to the need for assessing the totality of the State's involvement in this enterprise, its underlying analysis is fundamentally sequential rather than cumulative. In that perspective, what the Court does today is to make a significant departure from our previous treatment of state-action issues.

. . .

Mr. Justice MARSHALL, dissenting.

. . .

The Metropolitan Edison Co. provides an essential public service to the people of York, Pa. It is the only entity public or private, that is authorized to supply electric service to most of the community. As a part of its charter to the company, the State imposes extensive regulations, and it cooperates with the company in myriad ways. Additionally, the State has granted its approval to the company's mode of service termination—the very conduct that is challenged here. Taking these factors together, I have no difficulty finding state action in this case. As the Court concluded in *Burton v. Wilmington Parking Authority*, 365 U.S. 715, 725 (1961), the State has sufficiently "insinuated itself into a position of interdependence with (the company) that it must be recognized as a joint participant in the challenged activity."

Our state-action cases have repeatedly relied on several factors clearly presented by this case: a state-sanctioned monopoly; an extensive pattern of cooperation between the "private" entity and the State; and a service uniquely public in nature. Today the Court takes a major step in repudiating this line of authority and adopts a stance that is bound to lead to mischief when applied to problems beyond the narrow sphere of due process objections to utility terminations.

. . .

2. State Involvement or Encouragement

State action may also be found to exist when the government is involved with, or encourages, private action.

Burton v. Wilmington Parking Authority
365 U.S. 715 (1961)

Mr. Justice CLARK delivered the opinion of the Court.

[T]he Eagle Coffee Shoppe, Inc., a restaurant located within an off-street automobile parking building in Wilmington, Delaware, . . . refused to serve appellant food or drink solely because he is a Negro. The parking building is owned and operated by the Wilmington Parking Authority, an agency of the State of Delaware, and the restaurant is the Authority's lessee. Appellant claims that such refusal abridges his rights under the Equal Protection Clause of the Fourteenth Amendment to the United States Constitution. The Supreme Court of Delaware has held that Eagle was acting in "a purely private capacity" (157 A.2d 902) under its lease; that its action was not that of the Authority and was not, therefore, state action within the contemplation of the prohibitions contained in that Amendment. . . . [W]e have concluded that the exclusion of appellant under the circumstances shown to be present here was discriminatory state action in violation of the Equal Protection Clause of the Fourteenth Amendment.

The Authority was created by the City of Wilmington pursuant to 22 Del.Code, §§ 501—515. It is "a public body corporate and politic, exercising public powers of the State as an agency thereof." § 504. Its statutory purpose is to provide adequate parking facilities for the convenience of the public and thereby relieve the "parking crisis, which threatens the welfare of the community * * *." § 501(7), (8) and (9). . . .

Before it began actual construction of the facility, the Authority was advised by its retained experts that the anticipated revenue from the parking of cars and proceeds from sale of its bonds would not be sufficient to finance the construction costs of the facility. Moreover, the bonds were not expected to be marketable if payable solely out of parking revenues. To secure additional capital needed for its "debt-service" requirements, and thereby to make bond financing practicable, the Authority decided it was necessary to enter long-term leases with responsible tenants for commercial use of some of the space available in the projected "garage building." The public was invited to bid for these leases.

In April 1957 such a private lease, for 20 years and renewable for another 10 years, was made with Eagle Coffee Shoppe, Inc., for use as a "restaurant, dining room, banquet hall, cocktail lounge and bar and for no other use and purpose." The multi-level space of the building which was let to Eagle, although "within the exterior walls of the structure, has no marked public entrance leading from the parking portion of the facility into the restaurant proper * * * (whose main entrance) is located on Ninth Street." 157 A.2d at page 899. In its lease the Authority covenanted to complete construction expeditiously, including completion of "the decorative finishing of the leased premises and utilities therefor, without cost to Lessee," including necessary utility con-

nections, toilets, hung acoustical tile and plaster ceilings; vinyl asbestos, ceramic tile and concrete floors; connecting stairs and wrought iron railings; and wood-floored show windows. Eagle spent some $220,000 to make the space suitable for its operation and, to the extent such improvements were so attached to realty as to become part thereof, Eagle to the same extent enjoys the Authority's tax exemption. The Authority further agreed to furnish heat for Eagle's premises, gas service for the boiler room, and to make, at its own expense, all necessary structural repairs, all repairs to exterior surfaces except store fronts and any repairs caused by lessee's own act or neglect. The Authority retained the right to place any directional signs on the exterior to the let space which would not interfere with or obscure Eagle's display signs. Agreeing to pay an annual rental of $28,700, Eagle covenanted to "occupy and use the leased premises in accordance with all applicable laws, statutes, ordinances and rules and regulations of any federal, state or municipal authority." Its lease, however, contains no requirement that its restaurant services be made available to the general public on a nondiscriminatory basis, in spite of the fact that the Authority has power to adopt rules and regulations respecting the use of its facilities except any as would impair the security of its bondholders. § 511.

Other portions of the structure were leased to other tenants, including a bookstore, a retail jeweler, and a food store. Upon completion of the building, the Authority located at appropriate places thereon official signs indicating the public character of the building, and flew from mastheads on the roof both the state and national flags.

. . .

[Only] by sifting facts and weighing circumstances can the nonobvious involvement of the State in private conduct be attributed its true significance.

The trial court's disposal of the issues on summary judgment has resulted in a rather incomplete record, but the opinion of the Supreme Court as well as that of the Chancellor presents the facts in sufficient detail for us to determine the degree of state participation in Eagle's refusal to serve petitioner. In this connection the Delaware Supreme Court seems to have placed controlling emphasis on its conclusion, as to the accuracy of which there is doubt, that only some 15% of the total cost of the facility was "advanced" from public funds; that the cost of the entire facility was allocated three-fifths to the space for commercial leasing and two-fifths to parking space; that anticipated revenue from parking was only some 30.5% of the total income, the balance of which was expected to be earned by the leasing; that the

Authority had no original intent to place a restaurant in the building, it being only a happenstance resulting from the bidding; that Eagle expended considerable moneys on furnishings; that the restaurant's main and marked public entrance is on Ninth Street without any public entrance direct from the parking area; and that "the only connection Eagle has with the public facility * * * is the furnishing of the sum of $28,700 annually in the form of rent which is used by the Authority to defray a portion of the operating expense of an otherwise unprofitable enterprise." 157 A.2d 894, 901. While these factual considerations are indeed validly accountable aspects of the enterprise upon which the State has embarked, we cannot say that they lead inescapably to the conclusion that state action is not present. Their persuasiveness is diminished when evaluated in the context of other factors which must be acknowledged.

The land and building were publicly owned. As an entity, the building was dedicated to "public uses" in performance of the Authority's "essential governmental functions." 22 Del.Code, §§ 501, 514. The costs of land acquisition, construction, and maintenance are defrayed entirely from donations by the City of Wilmington, from loans and revenue bonds and from the proceeds of rentals and parking services out of which the loans and bonds were payable. Assuming that the distinction would be significant, the commercially leased areas were not surplus state property, but constituted a physically and financially integral and, indeed, indispensable part of the State's plan to operate its project as a self-sustaining unit. Upkeep and maintenance of the building, including necessary repairs, were responsibilities of the Authority and were payable out of public funds. It cannot be doubted that the peculiar relationship of the restaurant to the parking facility in which it is located confers on each an incidental variety of mutual benefits. Guests of the restaurant are afforded a convenient place to park their automobiles, even if they cannot enter the restaurant directly from the parking area. Similarly, its convenience for diners may well provide additional demand for the Authority's parking facilities. Should any improvements effected in the leasehold by Eagle become part of the realty, there is no possibility of increased taxes being passed on to it since the fee is held by a tax-exempt government agency. Neither can it be ignored, especially in view of Eagle's affirmative allegation that for it to serve Negroes would injure its business, that profits earned by discrimination not only contribute to, but also are indispensable elements in, the financial success of a governmental agency.

Addition of all these activities, obligations and responsibilities of the Authority, the benefits mutually conferred, together with the obvious fact that the restaurant is operated as an integral part of a public building devoted to a public parking service, indicates that degree of state participation and involvement in discriminatory action which it was the design of the Fourteenth Amendment to condemn. It is irony amounting to grave injustice that in one part of a single building, erected and maintained with public funds by an agency of the State to serve a public purpose, all persons have equal rights, while in another portion, also serving the public, a Negro is a second-class citizen, offensive because of his race, without rights and unentitled to service, but at the same time fully enjoys equal access to nearby restaurants in wholly privately owned buildings. As the Chancellor pointed out, in its lease with Eagle the Authority could have affirmatively required Eagle to discharge the responsibilities under the Fourteenth Amendment imposed upon the private enterprise as a consequence of state participation. But no State may effectively abdicate its responsibilities by either ignoring them or by merely failing to discharge them whatever the motive may be. It is of no consolation to an individual denied the equal protection of the laws that it was done in good faith. Certainly the conclusions drawn in similar cases by the various Courts of Appeals do not depend upon such a distinction. By its inaction, the Authority, and through it the State, has not only made itself a party to the refusal of service, but has elected to place its power, property and prestige behind the admitted discrimination. The State has so far insinuated itself into a position of interdependence with Eagle that it must be recognized as a joint participant in the challenged activity, which, on that account, cannot be considered to have been so "purely private" as to fall without the scope of the Fourteenth Amendment.

Because readily applicable formulae may not be fashioned, the conclusions drawn from the facts and circumstances of this record are by no means declared as universal truths on the basis of which every state leasing agreement is to be tested. . . . [W]hat we hold today is that when a State leases public property in the manner and for the purpose shown to have been the case here, the proscriptions of the Fourteenth Amendment must be complied with by the lessee as certainly as though they were binding covenants written into the agreement itself.

The judgment of the Supreme Court of Delaware is reversed and the cause remanded for further proceedings consistent with this opinion.

Reversed and remanded.

Mr. Justice STEWART, concurring.

I agree that the judgment must be reversed, but I reach that conclusion by a route much more direct than the one traveled by the

Court. . . . The highest court of Delaware has thus construed this legislative enactment as authorizing discriminatory classification based exclusively on color. Such a law seems to me clearly violative of the Fourteenth Amendment. I think, therefore, that the appeal was properly taken, and that the statute, as authoritatively construed by the Supreme Court of Delaware, is constitutionally invalid.

Mr. Justice FRANKFURTER, dissenting.

I certainly do not find the clarity that my brother STEWART finds in the views expressed by the Supreme Court of Delaware regarding 24 Del.Code, § 1501. If I were forced to construe that court's construction, I should find the balance of considerations leading to the opposite conclusion from his, namely, that it was merely declaratory of the common law and did not give state sanction to refusing service to a person merely because he is colored. . . .

Gilmore v. City of Montgomery[48] involved the City of Montgomery, Alabama's decision to allow racially segregated schools, and other nonschool groups that allegedly discriminate on the basis of race, to use public park recreational facilities. Petitioners claimed that Montgomery officials were under an affirmative duty to bring about and to maintain a desegregated public school system, and argued that the City's decision to allow the schools and groups to use the parks involved the state in the private discrimination. The Court agreed:

[T]he city's policy of allocating facilities to segregated private schools, in the context of the 1959 parks desegregation order and subsequent history, created, in effect, "enclaves of segregation" and deprived petitioners of equal access to parks and recreational facilities. The city was under an affirmative constitutional duty to eliminate every "custom, practice, policy or usage" reflecting an "impermissible obeisance to the now thoroughly discredited doctrine of 'separate but equal.'" *Watson v. Memphis*, 373 U.S. 526, 538 (1963). This obviously meant that discriminatory practices in Montgomery parks and recreational facilities were to be eliminated "root and branch," to use the phrase employed in *Green v. County School Board of New Kent County*, 391 U.S. 430, 438 (1968).

. . .

Here, the city's actions significantly enhanced the attractiveness of segregated private schools, formed in reaction against the federal court school order, by enabling them to offer complete athletic programs. The city's provision of stadiums and recreational fields resulted in capital savings for those schools and enabled them to divert their own funds to other educational programs. It also provided the opportunity for the schools to operate concessions that generated revenue. [T]his assistance significantly tended to undermine the federal court order mandating the establishment and maintenance of a unitary school system in Montgomery. It therefore was wholly proper for the city to be enjoined from permitting exclusive access to public recreational facilities by segregated private schools and by groups affiliated with such schools.

Mr. Justice White, joined by Mr. Justice Douglas, concurred:

I [would also] bar the use of city-owned recreation facilities by students from segregated schools for events or occasions that are part of the school curriculum or organized and arranged by the school as part of its own program. I see no difference of substance between this type of use and the exclusive use that the majority agrees may not be permitted consistent with the Equal Protection Clause.

---

[48] 417 U.S. 556 (1974).

Shelly v. Kraemer
334 U.S. 1 (1948)

Mr. Chief Justice VINSON delivered the opinion of the Court.

These cases present for our consideration questions relating to the validity of court enforcement of private agreements, generally described as restrictive covenants, which have as their purpose the exclusion of persons of designated race or color from the Basic constitutional issues of obvious importance have been raised.

The first of these cases comes to this Court on certiorari to the Supreme Court of Missouri. On February 16, 1911, thirty out of a total of thirty-nine owners of property fronting both sides of Labadie Avenue between Taylor Avenue and Cora Avenue in the city of St. Louis, signed an agreement, which was subsequently recorded, providing in part:

'* * * the said property is hereby restricted to the use and occupancy for the term of Fifty (50) years from this date, so that it shall be a condition all the time and whether recited and referred to as (sic) not in subsequent conveyances and shall attach to the land, as a condition precedent to the sale of the same, that hereafter no part of said property or any portion thereof shall be, for said term of Fifty-years, occupied by any person not of the Caucasian race, it being intended hereby to restrict the use of said property for said period of time against the occupancy as owners or tenants of any portion of said property for resident or other purpose by people of the Negro or Mongolian Race.'

The entire district described in the agreement included fifty-seven parcels of land. The thirty owners who signed the agreement held title to forty-seven parcels, including the particular parcel involved in this case. At the time the agreement was signed, five of the parcels in the district were owned by Negroes. One of those had been occupied by Negro families since 1882, nearly thirty years before the restrictive agreement was executed. The trial court found that owners of seven out of nine homes on the south side of Labadie Avenue, within the restricted district and "in the immediate vicinity" of the premises in question, had failed to sign the restrictive agreement in 1911. At the time this action was brought, four of the premises were occupied by Negroes, and had been so occupied for periods ranging from twenty-three to sixty-three years. A fifth parcel had been occupied by Negroes until a year before this suit was instituted.

On August 11, 1945, pursuant to a contract of sale, petitioners Shelley, who are Negroes, for valuable consideration received from one Fitzgerald a warranty deed to the parcel in question.[1] The trial court found that petitioners had no actual knowledge of the restrictive agreement at the time of the purchase.

On October 9, 1945, respondents, as owners of other property subject to the terms of the restrictive covenant, brought suit in Circuit Court of the city of St. Louis praying that petitioners Shelley be restrained from taking possession of the property and that judgment be entered divesting title out of petitioners Shelley and reverting title in the immediate grantor or in such other person as the court should direct. The trial court denied the requested relief. . . .

. . .

Petitioners have placed primary reliance on their contentions, first raised in the state courts, that judicial enforcement of the restrictive agreements in these cases has violated rights guaranteed to petitioners by the Fourteenth Amendment of the Federal Constitution and Acts of Congress passed pursuant to that Amendment. Specifically, petitioners urge that they have been denied the equal protection of the laws, deprived of property without due process of law, and have been denied privileges and immunities of citizens of the United States. We pass to a consideration of those issues.

I.

Whether the equal protection clause of the Fourteenth Amendment inhibits judicial enforcement by state courts of restrictive covenants based on race or color is a question which this Court has not heretofore been called upon to consider. . . .

It is well, at the outset, to scrutinize the terms of the restrictive agreements involved in these cases. In the Missouri case, the covenant declares that no part of the affected property shall be [355 Monopolistic. 814, 198 S.W.2d 681] "occupied by any person not of the Caucasian race, it being intended hereby to restrict the use of said property * * * against the occupancy as owners or tenants of any portion of said property for resident or other purpose by people of the Negro or Mongolian Race." Not

---

[1] The trial court found that title to the property which petitioners Shelley sought to purchase was held by one Bishop, a real estate dealer, who placed the property in the name of Josephine Fitzgerald. Bishop, who acted as agent for petitioners in the purchase, concealed the fact of his ownership.

only does the restriction seek to proscribe use and occupancy of the affected properties by members of the excluded class, but as construed by the Missouri courts, the agreement requires that title of any person who uses his property in violation of the restriction shall be divested. . . .

It should be observed that these covenants do not seek to proscribe any particular use of the affected properties. Use of the properties for residential occupancy, as such, is not forbidden. The restrictions of these agreements, rather, are directed toward a designated class of persons and seek to determine who may and who may not own or make use of the properties for residential purposes. The excluded class is defined wholly in terms of race or color; "simply that and nothing more."

. . .

But the present cases . . . do not involve action by state legislatures or city councils. Here the particular patterns of discrimination and the areas in which the restrictions are to operate, are determined, in the first instance, by the terms of agreements among private individuals. Participation of the State consists in the enforcement of the restrictions so defined. The crucial issue with which we are here confronted is whether this distinction removes these cases from the operation of the prohibitory provisions of the Fourteenth Amendment.

Since the decision of this Court in the Civil Rights Cases, 1883, 109 U.S. 3, the principle has become firmly embedded in our constitutional law that the action inhibited by the first section of the Fourteenth Amendment is only such action as may fairly be said to be that of the States. That Amendment erects no shield against merely private conduct, however discriminatory or wrongful.

We conclude, therefore, that the restrictive agreements standing alone cannot be regarded as a violation of any rights guaranteed to petitioners by the Fourteenth Amendment. So long as the purposes of those agreements are effectuated by voluntary adherence to their terms, it would appear clear that there has been no action by the State and the provisions of the Amendment have not been violated.

But here there was more. These are cases in which the purposes of the agreements were secured only by judicial enforcement by state courts of the restrictive terms of the agreements. The respondents urge that judicial enforcement of private agreements does not amount to state action; or, in any event, the participation of the State is so attenuated in character as not to amount to state action within the meaning of the Fourteenth Amendment. . . .

. . .

That the action of state courts and of judicial officers in their official capacities is to be regarded as action of the State within the meaning of the Fourteenth Amendment, is a proposition which has long been established by decisions of this Court. That principle was given expression in the earliest cases involving the construction of the terms of the Fourteenth Amendment. Thus, in Commonwealth of *Virginia v. Rives*, 1880, 100 U.S. 313, 318, this Court stated: "It is doubtless true that a State may act through different agencies,—either by its legislative, its executive, or its judicial authorities; and the prohibitions of the amendment extend to all action of the State denying equal protection of the laws, whether it be action by one of these agencies or by another." In Ex parte Commonwealth of Virginia, 1880, 100 U.S. 339, 347, the Court observed: "A State acts by its legislative, its executive, or its judicial authorities. It can act in no other way." In the Civil Rights Cases, 1883, 109 U.S. 3, 11, 17, this Court pointed out that the Amendment makes void "state action of every kind" which is inconsistent with the guaranties therein contained, and extends to manifestations of "state authority in the shape of laws, customs, or judicial or executive proceedings." Language to like effect is employed no less than eighteen times during the course of that opinion.

Similar expressions, giving specific recognition to the fact that judicial action is to be regarded as action on the State for the purposes of the Fourteenth Amendment, are to be found in numerous cases which have been more recently decided. In *Twining v. New Jersey*, 1908, 211 U.S. 78, 90, 91, the Court said: "The judicial act of the highest court of the state, in authoritatively construing and enforcing its laws, is the act of the state." In *Brinkerhoff—Faris Trust & Savings Co. v. Hill*, 1930, 281 U.S. 673, the Court, through Mr. Justice Brandeis, stated: "The federal guaranty of due process extends to state action through its judicial as well as through its legislative, executive, or administrative branch of government." Further examples of such declarations in the opinions of this Court are not lacking.

One of the earliest applications of the prohibitions contained in the Fourteenth Amendment to action of state judicial officials occurred in cases in which Negroes had been excluded from jury service in criminal prosecutions by reason of their race or color. These cases demonstrate, also, the early recognition by this Court that state action in violation of the Amendment's provisions is equally repugnant to the constitutional commands whether directed by state statute or taken by a judicial official in the absence of statute. Thus, in *Strauder v. West Virginia*, 1880, 100 U.S. 303, this Court declared invalid a state statute restricting jury service to white persons as amounting to a denial of the equal protection of the laws to the colored defendant in that case. In the notice and opportunity to defend, has, *Ex parte Virginia, supra*, held that a similar discrimination imposed by the action of a state judge denied rights protected by the Amendment, despite the fact that the language of the state statute relating to jury service contained no such restrictions.

The action of state courts in imposing penalties or depriving parties of other substantive rights without providing adequate notice and opportunity to defend, has, of course, long been regarded as a denial of the due process of law guaranteed by the Fourteenth Amendment.

In numerous cases, this Court has reversed criminal convictions in state courts for failure of those courts to provide the essential ingredients of a fair hearing. Thus it has been held that convictions obtained in state courts under the domination of a mob are void. *Moore v. Dempsey*, 1923, 261 U.S. 86. Convictions obtained by coerced confessions, by the use of perjured testimony known by the prosecution to be such, or without the effective assistance of counsel, have also been held to be exertions of state authority in conflict with the fundamental rights protected by the Fourteenth Amendment.

But the examples of state judicial action which have been held by this Court to violate the Amendment's commands are not restricted to situations in which the judicial proceedings were found in some manner to be procedurally unfair. It has been recognized that the action of state courts in enforcing a substantive common-law rule formulated by those courts, may result in the denial of rights guaranteed by the Fourteenth Amendment, even though the judicial proceedings in such cases may have been in complete accord with the most rigorous conceptions of procedural due process. Thus, in *American Federation of Labor v. Swing*, 1941, 312 U.S. 321, enforcement by state courts of the common-law policy of the State, which resulted in the restraining of peaceful picketing, was held to be state action of the sort prohibited by the Amendment's guaranties of freedom of discussion. In *Cantwell v. Connecticut*, 1940, 310 U.S. 296, a conviction in a state court of the common-law crime of breach of the peace was, under the circumstances of the case, found to be a violation of the Amendment's commands relating to freedom of religion. In *Bridges v. California*, 1941, 314 U.S. 252, enforcement of the state's common-law rule relating to contempts by publication was held to be state action inconsistent with the prohibitions of the Fourteenth Amendment.

The short of the matter is that from the time of the adoption of the Fourteenth Amendment until the present, it has been the consistent ruling of this Court that the action of the States to which the Amendment has reference, includes action of state courts and state judicial officials. Although, in construing the terms of the Fourteenth Amendment, differences have from time to time been expressed as to whether particular types of state action may be said to offend the Amendment's prohibitory provisions, it has never been suggested that state court action is immunized from the operation of those provisions simply because the act is that of the judicial branch of the state government.

. . .

Against this background of judicial construction, extending over a period of some three-quarters of a century, we are called upon to consider whether enforcement by state courts of the restrictive agreements in these cases may be deemed to be the acts of those States; and, if so, whether that action has denied these petitioners the equal protection of the laws which the Amendment was intended to insure.

We have no doubt that there has been state action in these cases in the full and complete sense of the phrase. The undisputed facts disclose that petitioners were willing purchasers of properties upon which they desired to establish homes. The owners of the properties were willing sellers; and contracts of sale were accordingly consummated. It is clear that but for the active intervention of the state courts, supported by the full panoply of state power, petitioners would have been free to occupy the properties in question without restraint.

These are not cases, as has been suggested, in which the States have merely abstained from action, leaving private individuals free to impose such discriminations as they see fit. Rather, these are cases in which the States have made available to such individuals the full coercive power of government to deny to petitioners, on the grounds of race or color, the enjoyment of property rights in premises which petitioners are willing and financially able to acquire and which the grantors are willing to sell. The difference between judicial enforcement and nonenforcement of the restrictive covenants is the difference to petitioners between being denied rights of property available to other members of the community and being accorded full enjoyment of those rights on an equal footing. The enforcement of the restrictive agreements by the state courts in these cases was directed pursuant to the common-law policy of the States as formulated by those courts in earlier decisions. In the Missouri case, enforcement of the covenant was directed in the first instance by the highest court of the State after the trial court had determined the agreement to be invalid for want of the requisite number of signatures. In the Michigan case, the order of enforcement by the trial court was affirmed by the highest state court. The judicial action in each case bears the clear and unmistakable imprimatur of the State. We have noted that previous decisions of this Court have established the proposition that judicial action is not immunized from the operation of the Fourteenth Amendment simply because it is taken pursuant to the state's common-law policy. Nor is the Amendment ineffective simply because the particular pattern of discrimination, which the State has enforced, was defined initially by the terms of a private agreement. State action, as that phrase is understood for the purposes of the Fourteenth Amendment, refers to exertions of state power in all forms. And when the effect of that action is to deny rights subject to the protection of the Fourteenth Amendment, it is the obligation of this Court to enforce the constitutional commands.

We hold that in granting judicial enforcement of the restrictive agreements in these cases, the States have denied petitioners the equal protection of the laws and that, therefore, the action of the state courts cannot stand. . . .

. . .

For the reasons stated, the judgment of the Supreme Court of Missouri and the judgment of the Supreme Court of Michigan must be reversed.

Reversed.

RLW: Indisputably, the actions of judicial officials in their official capacities constitute governmental action. But, if judicial enforcement of private rights constitutes state action, is any distinction left between private action and state action? All private rights come from the state in the sense that state law grants the right, or fails to forbid it. Moreover, rights are generally enforceable in state courts. Otherwise, they do not constitute rights.

How far can *Shelley's* reasoning be pushed? Suppose, for example, a racist couple plans a dinner party and they issue invitations on a racially discriminatory basis. Someone of a different race, who was not invited to the dinner party, decides to crash it. The racists call the police and seek to press charges against the trespassers. Does judicial enforcement of state trespass laws, which necessarily involves state support for the discrimination, transform the private discrimination into state sanctioned discrimination?

DEL: State action is a variable concept that vexes the interests of bright line-drawing. Whether the result in *Shelley* represents an exercise in judicial overreaching depends upon one's understanding of the values and reference points that may be factored into state action analysis. If only pure state action, unadulterated by any relationship with private action was the condition for constitutional relevance, *Shelley* and many other decisions would be misconceived. When state involvement exists but is not the exclusive force begetting a constitutional claim, the challenge is to identify the point at which the merger of public and private conduct becomes significant. Logically considered would be not only the extent of state participation but the nature of the interest allegedly burdened. But for judicial enforcement, racially restrictive covenants would be essentially precatory. The judicial function thus is not only significant but determinative of whether a federally protected interest is undermined. Identification of such an interest not only warrants concern with judicial facilitation of its compromise but establishes a significant check upon the possibility that a court would find state action in other circumstances. The focus upon not just any right or liberty, but those protected by the Fourteenth Amendment, allows for invalidation of a restrictive covenant as a function of state action but permits the bigoted party host to exclude unwanted guests for any reason. Although enforcement of a racially restrictive covenant undermines rights and freedoms secured by the Fourteenth Amendment, enforcement of a trespassing law does not. It thus overreacts to suggest that the *Shelley* decision imperils the distinction between state action and private conduct. To the extent that the initial purpose of the Fourteenth Amendment reflects an accounting for rights and freedoms that the Reconstruction Congress regarded as essential for individual self-development (i.e., contractual liberty and property rights), *Shelley* even might be understood as an exercise in originalist interpretation.

DER: Some constitutional scholars have argued that the Fourteenth Amendment commands government affirmatively to ensure the rights and freedoms essential for equality and self-determination, as well as to refrain from infringing them. Achieving the Civil War Amendments' goals may require state protection against private exercises of power that deny citizens equal membership in society. This view of the prerequisites for equal citizenship blurs even further the distinction between state versus private action and between government action versus its failure to act.

Also important is the baseline from which government action and inaction are measured. Courts tend to use a baseline of the current arrangements of wealth and privilege, seeing state action only when these arrangements are threatened. As one commentator noted, "[d]ecisions that upset existing distributions are treated as 'action'; decisions that do not are thought to stay close to nature and thus to amount to no action at all."[49] State enforcement of a restrictive covenant can be deemed state "action" only if we are willing to question the settled norm in *Shelley*'s day of officially-sanctioned segregation.

The Court would do well to revive some of the insights of *Shelley* about the power of private action to deny equal citizenship and the importance of questioning the baseline for determining state action. Instead, the Court tends to deny any affirmative government obligation either to ensure the social conditions and resources necessary for equality or to protect the individual from degradation inflicted by social forces other than the state. It often fails to recognize, as well, the ways in which the government uses its authority to fortify private relationships of power.

---

[49] Cass R. Sunstein, *Neutrality in Constitutional Law (With Special Reference to Pornography, Abortion, and Surrogacy)*, 92 COLUM. L. REV. 1, 2 (1992).

Evans v. Newton[50] involved a will, executed by U.S. Senator Augustus O. Bacon executed devising land to the City of Macon on the condition that the land be used as "a park and pleasure ground" for white people only. The Senator stated in his will that while he had only the kindest feeling for the Negroes he was of the opinion that "in their social relations the two races (white and Negro) should be forever separate." The City kept the park segregated for some years but began to violate the restriction. The City contended that, as a public facility, the park could not be constitutionally managed and maintained on a segregated basis. At that point, individual members of the Board of Managers of the park brought suit in state court to remove the City as trustee and force the appointment of new trustees to whom title to the park would be transferred. The Court concluded that, whether or not the transfer occurred, the park could not be segregated:

> If a testator wanted to leave a school or center for the use of one race only and in no way implicated the State in the supervision, control, or management of that facility, we assume arguendo that no constitutional difficulty would be encountered. This park, however, is in a different posture. For years it was an integral part of the City of Macon's activities. From the pleadings we assume it was swept, manicured, watered, patrolled, and maintained by the city as a public facility for whites only, as well as granted tax exemption under Ga.Code Ann. § 92—201. The momentum it acquired as a public facility is certainly not dissipated ipso facto by the appointment of "private" trustees. So far as this record shows, there has been no change in municipal maintenance and concern

---

[50] 382 U.S. 296 (1966).

over this facility. . . . [W]here the tradition of municipal control had become firmly established, we cannot take judicial notice that the mere substitution of trustees instantly transferred this park from the public to the private sector.

[A park] is more like a fire department or police department that traditionally serves the community. Mass recreation through the use of parks is plainly in the public domain, *Watson v. Memphis*, 373 U.S. 526; and state courts that aid private parties to perform that public function on a segregated basis implicate the State in conduct proscribed by the Fourteenth Amendment. Like the streets of the company town in *Marsh v. State of Alabama, supra,* the elective process of *Terry v. Adams, supra,* and the transit system of *Public Utilities Commission of District of Columbia v. Pollak, supra,* the predominant character and purpose of this park are municipal.

. . .

Under the circumstances of this case, we cannot but conclude that the public character of this park requires that it be treated as a public institution subject to the command of the Fourteenth Amendment, regardless of who now has title under state law. . . .

Mr. Justice Black dissented:

I find nothing in the United States Constitution that compels any city or other state subdivision to hold title to property it does not want or to act as trustee under a will when it chooses not to do so. And I had supposed until now that the narrow question of whether a city could resign such a trusteeship and whether a state court could appoint successor trustees depended entirely on state law. . . .

Mr. Justice Harlan, joined by Mr. Justice Stewart, also dissented:

This decision, in my opinion, is more the product of human impulses, which I fully share, than of solid constitutional thinking. It is made at the sacrifice of long-established and still wise procedural and substantive constitutional principle. I must respectfully dissent.

. . .

On the merits, which I reach only because the Court has done so, I do not think that the Fourteenth Amendment permits this Court in effect to frustrate the terms of Senator Bacon's will, now that the City of Macon is no longer connected, so far as the record shows, with the administration of Baconsfield. If the majority is in doubt that such is the case, it should remand for findings on that issue and not reverse.

The Equal Protection Clause reaches only discriminations that are the product of capricious state action; it does not touch discriminations whose origins and effectuation arise solely out of individual predilections, prejudices, and acts. . . .

Evans v. Abney[51] also involved the will of Senator Bacon. After the decision in *Abney,* Macon could not continue to operate the park on a racially discriminatory basis. Thereafter, Senator Bacon's heirs sued to recover the property claiming that Senator Bacon's intention to provide a park for whites only could not be fulfilled and therefore that the trust had failed and the parkland and other trust property had reverted by operation of Georgia law to the heirs of the Senator. Petitioners, the same Negro citizens of Macon who sought to integrate the park, sued claiming that the termination violated

---

[51] 396 U.S. 435 (1970).

their rights to equal protection and due process under the Fourteenth Amendment. The Court concluded that judicial enforcement of the reversion provision did not constitute state action:

> When a city park is destroyed because the Constitution requires it to be integrated, there is reason for everyone to be disheartened. We agree with petitioners that in such a case it is not enough to find that the state court's result was reached through the application of established principles of state law. No state law or act can prevail in the face of contrary federal law, and the federal courts must search out the fact and truth of any proceeding or transaction to determine if the Constitution has been violated. Here, however, the action of the Georgia Supreme Court declaring the Baconsfield trust terminated presents no violation of constitutionally protected rights, and any harshness that may have resulted from the state court's decision can be attributed solely to its intention to effectuate as nearly as possible the explicit terms of Senator Bacon's will.

> [P]etitioners now want to extend [*Evans v. Newton*] to forbid the Georgia courts from closing Baconsfield on the ground that such a closing would penalize the city and its citizens for complying with the Constitution. We think, however, that the will of Senator Bacon and Georgia law provide all the justification necessary for imposing such a "penalty." The construction of wills is essentially a state-law question, *Lyeth v. Hoey*, 305 U.S. 188 (1938), and in this case the Georgia Supreme Court, as we read its opinion, interpreted Senator Bacon's will as embodying a preference for termination of the park rather than its integration. Given this, the Georgia court had no alternative under its relevant trust laws, which are long standing and neutral with regard to race, but to end the Baconsfield trust and return the property to the Senator's heirs.

> [P]etitioners stress the similarities between this case and the case in which a city holds and absolute fee simple title to a public park and then closes that park of its own accord solely to avoid the effect of a prior court order directing that the park be integrated as the Fourteenth Amendment commands. Yet, assuming arguendo that the closing of the park would in those circumstances violate the Equal Protection Clause, that case would be clearly distinguishable from the case at bar because there it is the State and not a private party which is injecting the racially discriminatory motivation. In the case at bar there is not the slightest indication that any of the Georgia judges involved were motivated by racial animus or discriminatory intent of any sort in construing and enforcing Senator Bacon's will. Nor is there any indication that Senator Bacon in drawing up his will was persuaded or induced to include racial restrictions by the fact that such restrictions were permitted by the Georgia trust statutes. On the contrary, the language of the Senator's will shows that the racial restrictions were solely the product of the testator's own full-blown social philosophy. Similarly, the situation presented in this case is also easily distinguishable from that presented in *Shelley v. Kraemer*, 334 U.S. 1 (1948), where we held unconstitutional state judicial action which had affirmatively enforced a private scheme of discrimination against Negroes. Here the effect of the Georgia decision eliminated all discrimination against Negroes in the park by eliminating the park itself, and the termination of the park was a loss shared equally by the white and Negro citizens of Macon since both races would have enjoyed a constitutional right of equal access to the park's facilities had it continued.

Mr. Justice Brennan dissented:

> The . . . exculpation of the State and city from responsibility for the closing of the park is simply indefensible on this record. This discriminatory closing

is permeated with state action: at the time Senator Bacon wrote his will Georgia statutes expressly authorized and supported the precise kind of discrimination provided for by him; in accepting title to the park, public officials of the City of Macon entered into an arrangement vesting in private persons the power to enforce a reversion if the city should ever incur a constitutional obligation to desegregate the park; it is a public park that is being closed for a discriminatory reason after having been operated for nearly half a century as a segregated public facility; and it is a state court that is enforcing the racial restriction that keeps apparently willing parties of different races from coming together in the park. That is state action in overwhelming abundance. I need emphasize only three elements of the state action present here.

First, there is state action whenever a State enters into an arrangement that creates a private right to compel or enforce the reversion of a public facility. . . . Where, as in this case, the State's enforcement role conflicts with its obligation to comply with the constitutional command against racial segregation the attempted enforcement must be declared repugnant to the Fourteenth Amendment.

. . .

A finding of discriminatory state action is required here on a second ground. *Shelley v. Kraemer*, 334 U.S. 1 (1948), stands at least for the proposition that where parties of different races are willing to deal with one another a state court cannot keep them from doing so by enforcing a privately devised racial restriction. [S]o far as the record shows, this is a case of a state court's enforcement of a racial restriction to prevent willing parties from dealing with one another. The decision of the Georgia courts thus, under *Shelley v. Kraemer*, constitutes state action denying equal protection.

Finally, a finding of discriminatory state action is required on a third ground. In *Reitman v. Mulkey*, 387 U.S. 369 (1967), this Court announced the basic principle that a State acts in violation of the Equal Protection Clause when it singles out racial discrimination for particular encouragement, and thereby gives it a special preferred status in the law, even though the State does not itself impose or compel segregation. . . . [Georgia law expressly permitted the] dedication of land to the public for use as a park open to one race only. Thereby Georgia undertook to facilitate racial restrictions as distinguished from all other kinds of restriction on access to a public park. Reitman compels the conclusion that in doing so Georgia violated the Equal Protection Clause.

. . .

This, then, is not a case of private discrimination. It is rather discrimination in which the State of Georgia is "significantly involved," and enforcement of the reverter is therefore unconstitutional.

Barrows v. Jackson[52] involved a suit for damages by one party to a restrictive covenant against another. The covenant prohibited the sale or realty to non-Caucasians. The covenant was allegedly violated by selling the property without incorporating the covenant in deed restrictions as well as by permitting non-Caucasians to move in and occupy the premises. Applying *Shelley*, the Court concluded that, if the trial court awarded damages, the court would deprive the non-Caucasians of equal protection:

[V]oluntary adherence [to the covenant] would constitute individual action only. When, however, the parties cease to rely upon voluntary action to carry

---

[52] 346 U.S. 249 (1953).

out the covenant and the State is asked to step in and give its sanction to the enforcement of the covenant, the first question that arises is whether a court's awarding damages constitutes state action under the Fourteenth Amendment. To compel respondent to respond in damages would be for the State to punish her for her failure to perform her covenant to continue to discriminate against non-Caucasians in the use of her property. The result of that sanction by the State would be to encourage the use of restrictive covenants. To that extent, the State would act to put its sanction behind the covenants. If the State may thus punish respondent for her failure to carry out her covenant, she is coerced to continue to use her property in a discriminatory manner, which in essence is the purpose of the covenant. Thus, it becomes not respondent's voluntary choice but the State's choice that she observe her covenant or suffer damages. The action of a state court at law to sanction the validity of the restrictive covenant here involved would constitute state action as surely as it was state action to enforce such covenants in equity, as in *Shelley, supra*.

Reitman v. Mulkey[53] involved Art. I, § 26, of the California Constitution, an initiated measure submitted to the people as Proposition 14 in a statewide ballot in 1964, which provided:

> Neither the State nor any subdivision or agency thereof shall deny, limit or abridge, directly or indirectly, the right of any person, who is willing or desires to sell, lease or rent any part or all of his real property, to decline to sell, lease or rent such property to such person or persons as he, in his absolute discretion, chooses.

The real property covered by § 26 was limited to residential property and contained an exception for state-owned real estate. Justice White wrote an opinion striking down the law:

> [T]he adoption of Proposition 14 "generally nullifies both the Rumford and Unruh Acts as they apply to the housing market," and establishes "a purported constitutional right to privately discriminate on grounds which admittedly would be unavailable under the Fourteenth Amendment should state action be involved."
>
> [The California Supreme Court] conceded that the State was permitted a neutral position with respect to private racial discriminations and that the State was not bound by the Federal Constitution to forbid them. But, because a significant state involvement in private discriminations could amount to unconstitutional state action, *Burton v. Wilmington Parking Authority*, 365 U.S. 715, the court deemed it necessary to determine whether Proposition 14 invalidly involved the State in racial discriminations in the housing market. Its conclusion was that it did.
>
> [To] the California court "(t)he instant case presents an undeniably analogous situation" wherein the State had taken affirmative action designed to make private discriminations legally possible. Section 26 was said to have changed the situation from one in which discrimination was restricted "to one wherein it is encouraged, within the meaning of the cited decisions"; § 26 was legislative action "which authorized private discrimination" and made the State "at least a partner in the instant act of discrimination * * *." The court could "conceive of no other purpose for an application of section 26 aside from authorizing the perpetration of a purported private discrimination * * *." The

---

[53] 387 U.S. 369 (1967).

judgment of the California court was that § 26 unconstitutionally involves the State in racial discriminations and is therefore invalid under the Fourteenth Amendment.

. . .

The California court could very reasonably conclude that § 26 would and did have wider impact than a mere repeal of existing statutes. Section 26 mentioned neither the Unruh nor Rumford Act in so many words. Instead, it announced the constitutional right of any person to decline to sell or lease his real property to anyone to whom he did not desire to sell or lease. . . . Private discriminations in housing were now not only free from Rumford and Unruh but they also enjoyed a far different status than was true before the passage of those statutes. The right to discriminate, including the right to discriminate on racial grounds, was now embodied in the State's basic charter, immune from legislative, executive, or judicial regulation at any level of the state government. Those practicing racial discriminations need no longer rely solely on their personal choice. They could now invoke express constitutional authority, free from censure or interference of any kind from official sources.

Mr. Justice Douglas concurred:

Since the real estate brokerage business is one that can be and is state-regulated and since it is state-licensed, it must be dedicated, like the telephone companies and the carriers and the hotels and motels to the requirements of service to all without discrimination—a standard that in its modern setting is conditioned by the demands of the Equal Protection Clause of the Fourteenth Amendment.

Mr. Justice HARLAN, whom Mr. Justice BLACK, Mr. Justice CLARK, and Mr. Justice STEWART join, dissenting.

. . .

In the case at hand California, acting through the initiative and referendum, has decided to remain "neutral" in the realm of private discrimination affecting the sale or rental of private residential property; in such transactions private owners are now free to act in a discriminatory manner previously forbidden to them. In short, all that has happened is that California has effected a pro tanto repeal of its prior statutes forbidding private discrimination. This runs no more afoul of the Fourteenth Amendment than would have California's failure to pass any such antidiscrimination statutes in the first instance. The fact that such repeal was also accompanied by a constitutional prohibition against future enactment of such laws by the California Legislature cannot well be thought to affect, from a federal constitutional standpoint, the validity of what California has done. The Fourteenth Amendment does not reach such state constitutional action any more than it does a simple legislative repeal of legislation forbidding private discrimination.

. . .

I think that this decision is not only constitutionally unsound, but in its practical potentialities short-sighted. Opponents of state antidiscrimination statutes are now in a position to argue that such legislation should be defeated because, if enacted, it may be unrepealable. More fundamentally, the doctrine underlying this decision may hamper, if not preclude, attempts to deal with the delicate and troublesome problems of race relations through the legislative process. The lines that have been and must be drawn in this area, fraught as it is with human sensibilities and frailties of whatever race or creed, are difficult ones. The drawing of them requires understanding, patience, and compromise, and is best done by legislatures rather than by courts. When legislation in this field is unsuccessful there should be wide opportunities for legislative amendment, as well as for change through such processes as the popular initiative and referendum. This decision, I fear, may inhibit such flexibility. Here the electorate itself overwhelmingly wished to overrule and check its own legislature on a matter left open by the Federal Constitution. By refusing to accept the decision of the people of California, and by contriving a new and ill-defined constitutional concept to allow federal judicial interference, I think the Court has taken to itself powers and responsibilities left elsewhere by the Constitution.

Moose Lodge v. Irvis
407 U.S. 163 (1972)

Mr. Justice REHNQUIST delivered the opinion of the Court.

Appellee Irvis, a Negro (hereafter appellee), was refused service by appellant Moose Lodge, a local branch of the national fraternal organization located in Harrisburg, Pennsylvania. Appellee then brought this action under 42 U.S.C. § 1983 for injunctive relief in the United States District Court for the Middle District of Pennsylvania. He claimed that because the Pennsylvania liquor board had issued appellant Moose Lodge a private club license that authorized the sale of alcoholic beverages on its premises, the refusal of service to him was "state action" for the purposes of the Equal Protection Clause of the Fourteenth Amendment. He named both Moose Lodge and the Pennsylvania Liquor Authority as defendants, seeking injunctive relief that would have required the defendant liquor board to revoke Moose Lodge's license so long as it continued its discriminatory practices. Appellee sought no damages.

. . .

Appellee, while conceding the right of private clubs to choose members upon a discriminatory basis, asserts that the licensing of Moose Lodge to serve liquor by the Pennsylvania Liquor Control Board amounts to such state involvement with the club's activities as to make its discriminatory practices forbidden by the Equal Protection Clause of the Fourteenth Amendment. The relief sought and obtained by appellee in the District Court was an injunction forbidding the licensing by the liquor authority of Moose Lodge until it ceased its discriminatory practices. We conclude that Moose Lodge's refusal to serve food and beverages to a guest by reason of the fact that he was a Negro does not, under the circumstances here presented, violate the Fourteenth Amendment.

. . .

The Court has never held, of course, that discrimination by an otherwise private entity would be violative of the Equal Protection Clause if the private entity receives any sort of benefit or service at all from the State, or if it is subject to state regulation in any degree whatever. Since state-furnished services include such necessities of life as electricity, water, and police and fire protection, such a holding would utterly emasculate the distinction between private as distinguished from state conduct set forth in *The Civil Rights Cases, supra,* and adhered to in subsequent decisions. Our holdings indicate that where the impetus for the discrimination is private, the State must have "significantly involved itself with invidious discriminations," *Reitman v. Mulkey,* 387 U.S. 369, 380 (1967), in order for the discriminatory action to fall within the ambit of the constitutional prohibition.

Our prior decisions dealing with discriminatory refusal of service in public eating places are significantly different factually from the case now before us. *Peterson v. City of Greenville,* 373 U.S. 244 (1963), dealt with the trespass prosecution of persons who "sat in" at a restaurant to protest its refusal of service to Negroes. There the Court held that although the ostensible initiative for the trespass prosecution came from the proprietor, the existence of a local ordinance requiring segregation of races in such places was tantamount to the State having "commanded a particular result," 373 U.S., at 248. With one exception, there is no suggestion in this record that the Pennsylvania statutes and regulations governing the sale of liquor are intended either overtly or covertly to encourage discrimination.

. . .

Here there is nothing approaching the symbiotic relationship between lessor and lessee that was present in Burton, where the private lessee obtained the benefit of locating in a building owned by the state-created parking authority, and the parking authority was enabled to carry out its primary public purpose of furnishing parking space by advantageously leasing portions of the building constructed for that purpose to commercial lessees such as the owner of the Eagle Restaurant. Unlike *Burton*, the Moose Lodge building is located on land owned by it, not by any public authority. Far from apparently holding itself out as a place of public accommodation, Moose Lodge quite ostentatiously proclaims the fact that it is not open to the public at large. Nor is it located and operated in such surroundings that although private in name, it discharges a function or performs a service that would otherwise in all likelihood be performed by the State. In short, while Eagle was a public restaurant in a public building, Moose Lodge is a private social club in a private building.

With the exception hereafter noted, the Pennsylvania Liquor Control Board plays absolutely no part in establishing or enforcing the membership or guest policies of the club that it licenses to serve liquor. There is no suggestion in this record that Pennsylvania law, either as written or as applied, discriminates against minority groups either in their right to apply for club licenses themselves or in their right to purchase and be served liquor in places of public accommodation. The only effect that the state licensing of Moose Lodge to serve liquor can be said to have on the right of any other Pennsylvanian to buy or be served liquor on premises other than those of Moose Lodge is that for some purposes club licenses are counted in the maximum number of licenses that may be issued in a given municipality. Basically each municipality has a quota of one retail license for each 1,500 inhabitants. Licenses issued to hotels, municipal golf courses, and airport restaurants are not counted in this quota, nor are club licenses until the maximum number of retail licenses is reached. Beyond that point, neither additional retail licenses nor additional club licenses may be issued so long as the number of issued and outstanding retail licenses remains at or above the statutory maximum.

The District Court was at pains to point out in its opinion what it considered to be the "pervasive" nature of the regulation of private clubs by the Pennsylvania Liquor Control Board. As that court noted, an applicant for a club license must make such physical alterations in its premises as the board may require, must file a list of the names and addresses of its members and employees, and must keep extensive financial records. The board is granted the right to inspect the licensed premises at any time when patrons, guests, or members are present.

However detailed this type of regulation may be in some particulars, it cannot be said to in any way foster or encourage racial discrimination. Nor can it be said to make the State in any realistic sense a partner or even a joint venturer in the club's enterprise. The limited effect of the prohibition against obtaining additional club licenses when the maximum number of retail licenses allotted to a municipality has been issued, when considered together with the availability of liquor from hotel, restaurant, and retail licensees, falls far short of conferring upon club licensees a monopoly in the dispensing of liquor in any given municipality or in the State as a whole. We therefore hold that, with the exception hereafter noted, the operation of the regulatory scheme enforced by the Pennsylvania Liquor Control Board does not sufficiently implicate the State in the discriminatory guest policies of Moose Lodge to make the latter "state action" within the ambit of the Equal Protection Clause of the Fourteenth Amendment. The District Court found that the regulations of the Liquor Control Board adopted pursuant to statute affirmatively require that "(e)very club licensee shall adhere to all of the provisions of its Constitution and By-Laws." Appellant argues that the purpose of this provision "is purely and simply and plainly the prevention of subterfuge," pointing out that the bona fides of a private club, as opposed to a place of public accommodation masquerading as a private club, is a matter with which the State Liquor Control Board may legitimately concern itself. Appellee concedes this to be the case. . . .

. . .

Even though the Liquor Control Board regulation in question is neutral in its terms, the result of its application in a case where the constitution and bylaws of a club required racial discrimination would be to invoke the sanctions of the State to enforce a concededly discriminatory private rule. State action, for purposes of the Equal Protection Clause, may emanate from rulings of administrative and regulatory agencies as well as from legislative or judicial action. *Shelley v. Kraemer*, 334 U.S. 1 (1948), makes it clear that the application of state sanctions to enforce such a rule would violate the Fourteenth Amendment. Although the record before us is not as clear as one would like, appellant has not persuaded us that the District Court should have denied any and all relief.

Appellee was entitled to a decree enjoining the enforcement of § 113.09 of the regulations promulgated by the Pennsylvania Liquor Control Board insofar as that regulation requires compliance by Moose Lodge with provisions of its constitution and bylaws containing racially discriminatory provisions. He was entitled to no more. The judgment of the District Court is reversed, and the cause remanded with instructions to enter a decree in conformity with this opinion.

Reversed and remanded.

Mr. Justice DOUGLAS, with whom Mr. Justice MARSHALL joins, dissenting.

... Liquor licenses in Pennsylvania, unlike driver's licenses, or marriage licenses, are not freely available to those who meet racially neutral qualifications. There is a complex quota system, which the majority accurately describes. What the majority neglects to say is that the quota for Harrisburg, where Moose Lodge No. 107 is located, has been full for many years. No more club licenses may be issued in that city.

This state-enforced scarcity of licenses restricts the ability of blacks to obtain liquor, for liquor is commercially available only at private clubs for a significant portion of each week. Access by blacks to places that serve liquor is further limited by the fact that the state quota is filled. A group desiring to form a nondiscriminatory club which would serve blacks must purchase a license held by an existing club, which can exact a monopoly price for the transfer. The availability of such a license is speculative at best, however, for, as Moose Lodge itself concedes, without a liquor license a fraternal organization would be hard pressed to survive.

Thus, the State of Pennsylvania is putting the weight of its liquor license, concededly a valued and important adjunct to a private club, behind racial discrimination.

. . .

Mr. Justice BRENNAN, with whom Mr. Justice MARSHALL joins, dissenting.

When Moose Lodge obtained its liquor license, the State of Pennsylvania became an active participant in the operation of the Lodge bar. Liquor licensing laws are only incidentally revenue measures; they are primarily pervasive regulatory schemes under which the State dictates and continually supervises virtually every detail of the operation of the licensee's business. Very few, if any, other licensed businesses experience such complete state involvement. . . .

. . .

CBS, Inc. v. Democratic National Committee[54] involved the Democratic National Committee (DNC) and the Business Executives' Move for Vietnam Peace (BEM), a national organization of businessmen opposed to United States involvement in the Vietnam conflict. In January 1970, BEM filed a complaint with the Federal Communications Commission charging that radio station WTOP in Washington, D.C., had refused to sell it time to broadcast a series of one-minute spot announcements expressing BEM views on Vietnam. WTOP, in common with many, but not all, broadcasters, followed a policy of refusing to sell time for spot announcements to individuals and groups who wished to expound their views on controversial issues. WTOP took the position that since it presented full and fair coverage of important public questions, including the Vietnam conflict, it was justified in refusing to accept editorial advertisements. WTOP submitted evidence showing that the station had aired the views of critics of our Vietnam policy on numerous occasions. BEM challenged the fairness of WTOP's coverage of criticism of that policy, but it presented no evidence in support of that claim. DNC and BEM challenged WTOP's action on First Amendment grounds. The Court concluded that WTOP's actions did not constitute state action:

[I]t must be kept in mind that [the] electronic media have swiftly become a major factor in the dissemination of ideas and information. More than 7,000 licensed broadcast stations undertake to perform this important function. . . .

. . . Congress was faced with a fundamental choice between total Government ownership and control of the new medium—the choice of most other countries—or some other alternative. Long before the impact and potential of the medium was realized, Congress opted for a system of private broadcasters licensed and regulated by Government. . . .

The regulatory scheme evolved slowly, but very early the licensee's role

[54] 412 U.S. 94 (1973).

developed in terms of a "public trustee" charged with the duty of fairly and impartially informing the public audience. In this structure the Commission acts in essence as an "overseer," but the initial and primary responsibility for fairness, balance, and objectivity rests with the licensee. This role of the Government as an "overseer" and ultimate arbiter and guardian of the public interest and the role of the licensee as a journalistic "free agent" call for a delicate balancing of competing interests. . . .

. . .

The licensee policy challenged in this case is intimately related to the journalistic role of a licensee for which it has been given initial and primary responsibility by Congress. The licensee's policy against accepting editorial advertising cannot be examined as an abstract proposition, but must be viewed in the context of its journalistic role. It does not help to press on us the idea that editorial ads are "like" commercial ads, for the licensee's policy against editorial spot ads is expressly based on a journalistic judgment that 10-to 60-second spot announcements are ill-suited to intelligible and intelligent treatment of public issues; the broadcaster has chosen to provide a balanced treatment of controversial questions in a more comprehensive form. Obviously the licensee's evaluation is based on its own journalistic judgment of priorities and newsworthiness.

Moreover, the Commission has not fostered the licensee policy challenged here; it has simply declined to command particular action because it fell within the area of journalistic discretion. The Commission explicitly emphasized that "there is of course no Commission policy thwarting the sale of time to comment on public issues." 25 F.C.C.2d, at 226. The Commission's reasoning, consistent with nearly 40 years of precedent, is that so long as a licensee meets its "public trustee" obligation to provide balanced coverage of issues and events, it has broad discretion to decide how that obligation will be met. . . .

Thus, it cannot be said that the Government is a "partner" to the action of the broadcast licensee complained of here, nor is it engaged in a "symbiotic relationship" with the licensee, profiting from the invidious discrimination of its proxy. The First Amendment does not reach acts of private parties in every instance where the Congress or the Commission has merely permitted or failed to prohibit such acts.

. . .

Were we to read the First Amendment to spell out governmental action in the circumstances presented here, few licensee decisions on the content of broadcasts or the processes of editorial evaluation would escape constitutional scrutiny. In this sensitive area so sweeping a concept of governmental action would go far in practical effect to undermine nearly a half century of unmistakable congressional purpose to maintain—no matter how difficult the task—essentially private broadcast journalism held only broadly accountable to public interest standards. . . .

Mr. Justice Stewart concurred:

[T]he Court of Appeals held, and the dissenters today agree, that the First Amendment requires the Government to impose controls upon private broadcasters—in order to preserve First Amendment "values." The appellate court accomplished this strange convolution by the simple device of holding that private broadcasters are Government. This is a step along a path that could eventually lead to the proposition that private newspapers "are" Government. Freedom of the press would then be gone. In its place we would have such governmental controls upon the press as a majority of this Court at any particular moment might consider First Amendment "values" to require. It is a frightening specter.

. . .

[W]hen examined as a whole, the Federal Communications Act establishes a system of privately owned broadcast licensees. These licensees, though regulated by the Commission under a fairly broad "public interest" standard, have, quite apart from whatever additional protections the First Amendment may provide, important statutory freedoms in conducting their programming.

Mr. Justice Brennan, joined by Mr. Justice Marshall, dissented:

[G]iven the confluence of these various indicia of "governmental action"—including the public nature of the airwaves, the governmentally created preferred status of broadcasters, the extensive Government regulation of broadcast programming, and the specific governmental approval of the challenged policy—I can only conclude that the Government "has so far, insinuated itself into a position" of participation in this policy that the absolute refusal of broadcast licensees to sell air time to groups or individuals wishing to speak out on controversial issues of public importance must be subjected to the restraints of the First Amendment.

3. Recent Developments

Has the Court taken a more restrictive attitude towards state action issues in recent years? Consider the following cases.

Rendell-Baker v. Kohn
457 U.S. 830 (1982)

Chief Justice BURGER delivered the opinion of the Court.

We granted certiorari to decide whether a private school, whose income is derived primarily from public sources and which is regulated by public authorities, acted under color of state law when it discharged certain employees.

. . .

Respondent Kohn is the director of the New Perspectives School, a nonprofit institution located on privately owned property in Brookline, Massachusetts. The school was founded as a private institution and is operated by a board of directors, none of whom are public officials or are chosen by public officials. The school specializes in dealing with students who have experienced difficulty completing public high schools; many have drug, alcohol, or behavioral problems, or other special needs. In recent years, nearly all of the students at the school have been referred to it by the Brookline or Boston School Committees, or by the Drug Rehabilitation Division of the Massachusetts Department of Mental Health. The school issues high school diplomas certified by the Brookline School Committee.

When students are referred to the school by Brookline or Boston under Chapter 766 of the Massachusetts Acts of 1972, the School Committees in those cities pay for the students' education. The school also receives funds from a number of other state and federal agencies. In recent years, public funds have accounted for at least 90%, and in one year 99%, of respondent school's operating budget. There were approximately 50 students at the school in those years and none paid tuition.

To be eligible for tuition funding under Chapter 766, the school must comply with a variety of regulations, many of which are common to all schools. The State has issued detailed regulations concerning matters ranging from recordkeeping to student-teacher ratios. Concerning personnel policies, the Chapter 766 regulations require the school to maintain written job descriptions and written statements describing personnel standards and procedures, but they impose few specific requirements.

The school is also regulated by Boston and Brookline as a result of its Chapter 766 funding. By its contract with the Boston School Committee, which refers to the school as a "contractor," the school must agree to carry out the individualized plan developed for each student referred to the school by the Committee. See n. 1, *supra*. The contract specifies that school employees are not city employees.

The school also has a contract with the State Drug Rehabilitation Division. Like the contract with the Boston School Committee, that agreement refers to the school as a "contractor." It provides for reimbursement for services provided for students referred to the school by the Drug Rehabilitation Division, and includes requirements concerning the services to be provided. Except for general requirements, such as an equal employment opportunity requirement, the agreement does not cover personnel policies.

While five of the six petitioners were teachers at the school, petitioner Rendell-Baker was a vocational counselor hired under a grant from the federal Law Enforcement Assistance Administration, whose funds are distributed in Massachusetts through the State Committee on Criminal Justice. As a condition of the grant, the Committee on Criminal Justice must approve the school's initial hiring decisions. The purpose of this requirement is to insure that the school hires vocational counselors who meet the qualifications described in the school's grant proposal to the Committee; the Committee does not interview applicants for counselor positions.

. . .

Rendell-Baker was discharged by the school in January 1977, and the five other petitioners were discharged in June 1978. Rendell-Baker's discharge resulted from a dispute over the role of a student-staff council in making hiring decisions. A dispute arose when some students presented a petition to the school's board of directors in December 1976, seeking greater responsibilities for the student-staff council. Director Kohn opposed the proposal, but Rendell-Baker supported it and so advised the board. On December 13, Kohn notified the State Committee on Criminal Justice, which funded Rendell-Baker's position, that she intended to dismiss Rendell-Baker and employ someone else. Kohn notified Rendell-Baker of her dismissal in January 1977. Rendell-Baker then advised the board of directors that she had been discharged without due process because she exercised her First Amendment rights. She demanded reinstatement or a hearing. The school agreed to apply a new policy, calling for appointment of a grievance committee, to consider her claims. Rendell-Baker also complained to the State Committee on Criminal Justice, which asked the school to provide a written explanation for her discharge. After the school complied, the Committee responded that it was satisfied with the explanation, but notified the school that it would not pay any backpay or other damages award Rendell-Baker might obtain from it as a result of her discharge. The Committee told Rendell-Baker that it had no authority to order a hearing, although it would refuse to approve the hiring of another counselor if the school disregarded its agreement to apply its new grievance procedure in her case. At this point Rendell-Baker objected to the composition of the grievance committee, and its proceedings apparently never went forward. Rendell-Baker filed this suit in July 1977 under 42 U.S.C. § 1983, alleging that she had been discharged in violation of her rights under the First, Fifth, and Fourteenth Amendments.

In the spring of 1978, students and staff voiced objections to Kohn's policies. The five petitioners other than Rendell-Baker, who were all teachers at the school, wrote a letter to the board of directors urging Kohn's dismissal. When the board affirmed its confidence in Kohn, students from the school picketed the home of the president of the board. The students were threatened with suspension; a local newspaper then ran a story about the controversy at the school. In response to the story, the five petitioners wrote a letter to the editor in which they stated that they thought the prohibition of picketing was unconstitutional. On the day the letter to the editor appeared, the five teachers told the president of the board that they were forming a union. Kohn discharged the teachers the next day. They brought suit against the school and its directors in December 1978. Like Rendell-Baker, they sought relief under § 1983, alleging that their rights under the First, Fifth, and Fourteenth Amendments had been violated.

. . .

[The] core issue presented in this case is not whether petitioners were discharged because of their speech or without adequate procedural protections, but whether the school's action in discharging them can fairly be seen as state action. If the action of the respondent school is not state action, our inquiry ends.

. . .

In *Blum v. Yaretsky*, 457 U.S. 991, the Court analyzed the state action requirement of the Fourteenth Amendment. The Court considered whether certain nursing homes were state actors for the purpose of determining whether decisions regarding transfers of patients could be fairly attributed to the State, and hence be subjected to Fourteenth Amendment due process requirements. The challenged transfers primarily involved decisions, made by physicians and nursing home administrators, to move patients from "skilled nursing facilities" to less expensive "health related facilities." . . . Like the New Perspectives School, the nursing homes were privately owned and operated. . . . [This] Court held that, "a State normally can be held responsible for a private decision only when it has exercised coercive power or has provided such significant encouragement, either overt or covert, that the choice must in law be deemed to be that of the State." 457 U.S. at 1004. In determining that the transfer decisions were not actions of the State, the Court considered each of the factors alleged by petitioners here to make the discharge decisions of the New Perspectives School fairly attributable to the State.

First, the nursing homes, like the school, depended on the State for funds; the State subsidized the operating and capital costs of the nursing homes, and paid the medical expenses of more than 90% of the patients. 457 U.S., at 1011. Here the Court of Appeals concluded that the fact that virtually all of the school's income was derived from government funding was the strongest factor to support a claim of state action. 641 F.2d, at 24. But in *Blum v. Yaretsky*, we held that the similar dependence of the nursing homes did not make the acts of the physicians and nursing home administrators acts of the State, and we conclude that the school's receipt of public funds does not make the discharge decisions acts of the State.

The school, like the nursing homes, is not fundamentally different from many private corporations whose business depends primarily on contracts to build roads, bridges, dams, ships, or submarines for the government. Acts of such private contractors do not become acts of the government by reason of their significant or even total engagement in performing public contracts.

. . .

A second factor considered in *Blum v. Yaretsky* was the extensive regulation of the nursing homes by the State. There the State was indirectly involved in the transfer decisions challenged in that case because a primary goal of the State in regulating nursing homes was to keep costs down by transferring patients from intensive treatment centers to less expensive facilities when possible. Both state and federal regulations encouraged the nursing homes to transfer patients to less expensive facilities when appropriate. 457 U.S., at 1007–1008, 1009–1110. The nursing homes were extensively regulated in many other ways as well. The Court relied on *Jackson*, where we held that state regulation, even if "extensive and detailed," 419 U.S., at 350, did not make a utility's actions state action.

Here the decisions to discharge the petitioners were not compelled or even influenced by any state regulation. Indeed, in contrast to the extensive regulation of the school generally, the various regulators showed relatively little interest in the school's personnel matters. The most intrusive personnel regulation promulgated by the various government agencies was the requirement that the Committee on Criminal Justice had the power to approve persons hired as vocational counselors. Such a regulation is not sufficient to make a decision to discharge, made by private management, state action.

The third factor asserted to show that the school is a state actor is that it performs a "public function." However, our holdings have made clear that the relevant question is not simply whether a private group is serving a "public function." We have held that the question is whether the function performed has been "traditionally the exclusive prerogative of the State." *Jackson, supra*, at 353; quoted in *Blum v. Yaretsky*, 457 U.S., at 1011. There can be no doubt that the education of maladjusted high school students is a public function, but that is only the beginning of the inquiry. Chapter 766 of the Massachusetts Acts of 1972 demonstrates that the State intends to provide services for such students at public expense. That legislative policy choice in no way makes these services the exclusive province of the State. Indeed, the Court of Appeals noted that until recently the State had not undertaken to provide education for students who could not be served by traditional public schools. That a private entity performs a function which serves the public does not make its acts state action.

Fourth, petitioners argue that there is a "symbiotic relationship" between the school and the State similar to the relationship involved in *Burton v. Wilmington Parking Authority*, 365 U.S. 715 (1961). Such a claim is rejected in *Blum v. Yaretsky*, and we reject it here. In *Burton*, the Court held that the refusal of a restaurant located in a public parking garage to serve Negroes constituted state action. The Court stressed that the restaurant was located on public property and that the rent from the restaurant contributed to the support of the garage. 365 U.S., at 723. In response to the argument that the restaurant's profits, and hence the State's financial position, would suffer if it did not discriminate, the Court concluded that this showed that the State profited from the restaurant's discriminatory conduct. The Court viewed this as support for the conclusion that the State should be charged with the discriminatory actions. Here the school's fiscal relationship with the State is not different from that of many contractors performing services for the government. No symbiotic relationship such as existed in *Burton* exists here.

C

We hold that petitioners have not stated a claim for relief under 42 U.S.C. § 1983; accordingly, the judgment of the Court of Appeals for the First Circuit is

Affirmed.

Justice WHITE, concurring in the judgments.

. . .

... In this case, the question of state action focuses on an employment decision made by a private school that receives most of its funding from public sources and is subject to state regulation in certain respects. For me, the critical factor is the absence of any allegation that the employment decision was itself based upon some rule of conduct or policy put forth by the State. As the majority states, "in contrast to the extensive regulation of the school generally, the various regulators showed relatively little interest in the school's personnel matters." *Ante*, at 2772. The employment decision remains, therefore, a private decision not fairly attributable to the State.

Justice MARSHALL, with whom Justice BRENNAN joins, dissenting.

. . .

The decisions of this Court clearly establish that where there is a symbiotic relationship between the State and a privately owned enterprise, so that the State and a privately owned enterprise are participants in a joint venture, the actions of the private enterprise may be attributable to the State. "Conduct that is formally "private" may become so entwined with governmental policies or so impregnated with a governmental character" that it can be regarded as governmental action. . . . The question whether such a relationship exists "can be determined only in the framework of the peculiar facts or circumstances present." *Burton, supra*, at 726. Here, an examination of the facts and circumstances leads inexorably to the conclusion that the actions of the New Perspectives School should be attributed to the State; it is difficult to imagine a closer relationship between a government and a private enterprise.

The New Perspectives School receives virtually all of its funds from state sources. This financial dependence on the State is an important indicium of governmental involvement. The school's very survival depends on the State. If the State chooses, it may exercise complete control over the school's operations simply by threatening to withdraw financial support if the school takes action that it considers objectionable.

The school is heavily regulated and closely supervised by the State. This fact provides further support for the conclusion that its actions should be attributed to the State. The school's freedom of decisionmaking is substantially circumscribed by the Massachusetts Department of Education's guidelines and the various contracts with state agencies. For example, the school is required to develop and comply with written rules for hiring and dismissal of personnel. Almost every decision the school makes is substantially affected in some way by the State's regulations.

The fact that the school is providing a substitute for public education is also an important indicium of state action. The provision of education is one of the most important tasks performed by government: it ranks at the very apex of the function of a State. *Ambach v. Norwick*, 441 U.S. 68, 77 (1979). Of course, as the majority emphasizes, performance of a public function is by itself sufficient to justify treating a private entity as a state actor only where the function has been "traditionally the exclusive prerogative of the State." *Jackson, supra*, at 353. But the fact that a private entity is performing a vital public function, when coupled with other factors demonstrating a close connection with the State, may justify a finding of state action.

The school's provision of a substitute for public education deserves particular emphasis because of the role of Chapter 766. Under this statute, the State is required to provide a free education to all children, including those with special needs. Clearly, if the State had decided to provide the service itself, its conduct would be measured against constitutional standards. The State should not be permitted to avoid constitutional requirements simply by delegating its statutory duty to a private entity. In my view, such a delegation does not convert the performance of the duty from public to private action when the duty is specific and the private institution's decisionmaking authority is significantly curtailed.

National Collegiate Athletic Ass'n v. Tarkanian[55] involved a suit by a basketball coach against the University of Nevada-Las Vegas (UNLV) and the National Collegiate Athletic Association (NCAA). The coach was investigated by the NCAA who found that he had engaged in rules violations. Based on the NCAA findings, UNLV took action to remove the coach from his job. The coach claimed that he was denied due process.

The NCAA defended on the basis that no state action was involved. The NCAA was, and is, an unincorporated association composed of public and private universities

---

[55] 488 U.S. 179 (1988).

and 4-year colleges conducting major athletic programs in the United States. Its policies are determined by the members at annual conventions. Between conventions, the Association is governed by its Council, which appoints various committees to implement specific programs.

The Supreme Court agreed that state action was not involved in the dismissal:

> This case uniquely mirrors the traditional state-action case. Here the final act challenged by Tarkanian—his suspension—was committed by UNLV. A state university without question is a state actor. When it decides to impose a serious disciplinary sanction upon one of its tenured employees, it must comply with the terms of the Due Process Clause of the Fourteenth Amendment to the Federal Constitution. Thus when UNLV notified Tarkanian that he was being separated from all relations with the university's basketball program, it acted under color of state law within the meaning of 42 U.S.C. § 1983.

> The mirror image presented in this case requires us to step through an analytical looking glass to resolve the case. Clearly UNLV's conduct was influenced by the rules and recommendations of the NCAA, the private party. But it was UNLV, the state entity, that actually suspended Tarkanian. Thus the question is not whether UNLV participated to a critical extent in the NCAA's activities, but whether UNLV's actions in compliance with the NCAA rules and recommendations turned the NCAA's conduct into state action.

> We examine first the relationship between UNLV and the NCAA regarding the NCAA's rulemaking. UNLV is among the NCAA's members and participated in promulgating the Association's rules; it must be assumed, therefore, that Nevada had some impact on the NCAA's policy determinations. Yet the NCAA's several hundred other public and private member institutions each similarly affected those policies. Those institutions, the vast majority of which were located in States other than Nevada, did not act under color of Nevada law. It necessarily follows that the source of the legislation adopted by the NCAA is not Nevada but the collective membership, speaking through an organization that is independent of any particular State.

> . . .

> The NCAA enjoyed no governmental powers to facilitate its investigation. It had no power to subpoena witnesses, to impose contempt sanctions, or to assert sovereign authority over any individual. Its greatest authority was to threaten sanctions against UNLV, with the ultimate sanction being expulsion of the university from membership. Contrary to the premise of the Nevada Supreme Court's opinion, the NCAA did not—indeed, could not—directly discipline Tarkanian or any other state university employee. The express terms of the Confidential Report did not demand the suspension unconditionally; rather, it requested "the University . . . to show cause" why the NCAA should not impose additional penalties if UNLV declines to suspend Tarkanian. Even the university's vice president acknowledged that the Report gave the university options other than suspension: UNLV could have retained Tarkanian and risked additional sanctions, perhaps even expulsion from the NCAA, or it could have withdrawn voluntarily from the Association.

> . . .

> [It] would be ironic indeed to conclude that the NCAA's imposition of sanctions against UNLV—sanctions that UNLV and its counsel, including the Attorney General of Nevada, steadfastly opposed during protracted adversary

proceedings—is fairly attributable to the State of Nevada. It would be more appropriate to conclude that UNLV has conducted its athletic program under color of the policies adopted by the NCAA, rather than that those policies were developed and enforced under color of Nevada law.

Mr. Justice White, joined by three other justices, dissented:

. . .

[T]he NCAA acted jointly with UNLV in suspending Tarkanian. First, Tarkanian was suspended for violations of NCAA rules, which UNLV embraced in its agreement with the NCAA. As the Nevada Supreme Court found in its first opinion in this case, *University of Nevada v. Tarkanian*, 594 P.2d 1159, 1160 (1979), "[a]s a member of the NCAA, UNLV contractually agrees to administer its athletic program in accordance with NCAA legislation." Indeed, NCAA rules provide that NCAA "enforcement procedures are an essential part of the intercollegiate athletic program of each member institution."

Second, the NCAA and UNLV also agreed that the NCAA would conduct the hearings concerning violations of its rules. Although UNLV conducted its own investigation into the recruiting violations alleged by the NCAA, the NCAA procedures provide that it is the NCAA Committee on Infractions that "determine[s] facts related to alleged violations," subject to an appeal to the NCAA Council. *Id.*, at 98, 101. As a result of this agreement, the NCAA conducted the very hearings the Nevada Supreme Court held to have violated Tarkanian's right to procedural due process.

Third, the NCAA and UNLV agreed that the findings of fact made by the NCAA at the hearings it conducted would be binding on UNLV. By becoming a member of the NCAA, UNLV did more than merely "promise to cooperate in the NCAA enforcement proceedings." It agreed, as the university hearing officer appointed to rule on Tarkanian's suspension expressly found, to accept the NCAA's "findings of fact as in some way superior to [its] own." By the terms of UNLV's membership in the NCAA, the NCAA's findings were final and not subject to further review by any other body, and it was for that reason that UNLV suspended Tarkanian, despite concluding that many of those findings were wrong, *id.*, at 76.

. . .

[T]he majority relies extensively on the fact that the NCAA and UNLV were adversaries throughout the proceedings before the NCAA. . . . But this opportunity for opposition, provided for by the terms of the membership agreement between UNLV and the NCAA, does not undercut the agreement itself. . . .

[Had] UNLV refused to suspend Tarkanian, and the NCAA responded by imposing sanctions against UNLV, it would be hard indeed to find any state action that harmed Tarkanian. But that is not this case. Here, UNLV did suspend Tarkanian, and it did so because it embraced the NCAA rules governing conduct of its athletic program and adopted the results of the hearings conducted by the NCAA concerning Tarkanian, as it had agreed that it would. Under these facts, I would find that the NCAA acted jointly with UNLV and therefore is a state actor.

Flagg Brothers, Inc. v. Brooks
436 U.S. 149 (1978)

Mr. Justice REHNQUIST delivered the opinion of the Court.

The question presented by this litigation is whether a warehouseman's proposed sale of goods entrusted to him for storage, as permitted by New York Uniform Commercial Code § 7–210 (McKinney 1964), is an action properly attributable to the State of New York. . . .

I

According to her complaint, the allegations of which we must accept as true, respondent Shirley Brooks and her family were evicted from their apartment in Mount Vernon, N.Y., on June 13, 1973. The city marshal arranged for Brooks' possessions to be stored by petitioner Flagg Brothers, Inc., in its warehouse. Brooks was informed of the cost of moving and storage, and she instructed the workmen to proceed, although she found the price too high. On August 25, 1973, after a series of disputes over the validity of the charges being claimed by petitioner Flagg Brothers, Brooks received a letter demanding that her account be brought up to date within 10 days "or your furniture will be sold." A series of subsequent letters from respondent and her attorneys produced no satisfaction.

Brooks thereupon initiated this class action in the District Court under 42 U.S.C. § 1983, seeking damages, an injunction against the threatened sale of her belongings, and the declaration that such a sale pursuant to § 7–210 would violate the Due Process and Equal Protection Clauses of the Fourteenth Amendment. She was later joined in her action by Gloria Jones, another resident of Mount Vernon whose goods had been stored by Flagg Brothers following her eviction. . . .

. . .

We granted certiorari to resolve the conflict over this provision of the Uniform Commercial Code, in effect in 49 States and the District of Columbia, and to address the important question it presents concerning the meaning of "state action" as that term is associated with the Fourteenth Amendment.

II

A claim upon which relief may be granted to respondents against Flagg Brothers under § 1983 must embody at least two elements. Respondents are first bound to show that they have been deprived of a right "secured by the Constitution and the laws" of the United States. They must secondly show that Flagg Brothers deprived them of this right acting "under color of any statute" of the State of New York. It is clear that these two elements denote two separate areas of inquiry. *Adickes v. S.H. Kress & Co.*, 398 U.S. 144, 150 (1970).

Respondents allege in their complaints that "the threatened sale of the goods pursuant to New York Uniform Commercial Code § 7–210" is an action under color of state law. We have previously noted, with respect to a private individual, that "[w]hatever else may also be necessary to show that a person has acted "under color of [a] statute" for purposes of § 1983, . . . we think it essential that he act with the knowledge of and pursuant to that statute." *Adickes, supra*, at 162 n.23. Certainly, the complaints can be fairly read to allege such knowledge on the part of Flagg Brothers. However, we need not determine whether any further showing is necessary, since it is apparent that neither respondent has alleged facts which constitute a deprivation of any right "secured by the Constitution and laws" of the United States.

A moment's reflection will clarify the essential distinction between the two elements of a § 1983 action. Some rights established either by the Constitution or by federal law are protected from both governmental and private deprivation. Although a private person may cause a deprivation of such a right, he may be subjected to liability under § 1983 only when he does so under color of law. However, most rights secured by the Constitution are protected only against infringement by governments. Here, respondents allege that Flagg Brothers has deprived them of their right, secured by the Fourteenth Amendment, to be free from state deprivations of property without due process of law. Thus, they must establish not only that Flagg Brothers acted under color of the challenged statute, but also that its actions are properly attributable to the State of New York.

It must be noted that respondents have named no public officials as defendants in this action. The City Marshal, who supervised their evictions, was dismissed from the case by the consent of all the parties. This total absence of overt official involvement plainly distinguishes this case from earlier decisions imposing procedural restrictions on creditors' remedies such as *North Georgia Finishing, Inc. v. Di-Chem, Inc.*, 419 U.S. 601 (1975); *Fuentes v. Shevin*, 407 U.S. 67 (1972); *Sniadach v. Family Finance Corp.*, 395 U.S. 337 (1969). In those cases, the Court was careful to point out that the dictates of the Due Process Clause "attac[h] only to the deprivation of an interest encompassed within the Fourteenth Amendment's protection." *Fuentes, supra*, 407 U.S. at 84. While as a factual matter any person with sufficient physical power may deprive a person of his property, only a State or a private person whose action "may be fairly treated as that of the State itself," *Jackson, supra*, 419 U.S. at 351, may deprive him of "an interest encompassed within the Fourteenth Amendment's protection," *Fuentes, supra*, 407 U.S. at 84. Thus, the only issue presented by this case is whether Flagg Brothers' action may fairly be attributed to the State of New York. We conclude that it may not.

III

Respondents' primary contention is that New York has delegated to Flagg Brothers a power "traditionally exclusively reserved to the State." *Jackson, supra*, 419 U.S. at 352. They argue that the resolution of private disputes is a traditional function of civil government, and that the State in § 7–210 has delegated this function to Flagg Brothers. Respondents, however, have read too much into the language of our previous cases. While many functions have been traditionally performed by governments, very few have been "exclusively reserved to the State."

One such area has been elections. While the Constitution protects private rights of association and advocacy with regard to the election of public officials, our cases make it clear that the conduct of the elections themselves is an exclusively public function. Although the rationale of these cases may be subject to some dispute, their scope is carefully defined. The doctrine does not reach to all forms of private political activity, but encompasses only state-regulated elections or elections conducted by organizations which in practice produce "the uncontested choice of public officials." *Terry, supra*, 345 U.S. at 484 (Clark, J., concurring).

A second line of cases under the public-function doctrine originated with *Marsh v. Alabama*, 326 U.S. 501 (1946). Just as the Texas Democratic Party in *Smith* and the Jaybird Democratic Association in *Terry* effectively performed the entire public function of selecting public officials, so too the Gulf Shipbuilding Corp. performed all the necessary municipal functions in the town of Chickasaw, Ala., which it owned. . . .

These two branches of the public-function doctrine have in common the feature of exclusivity. Although the elections held by the Democratic Party and its affiliates were the only meaningful elections in Texas, and the streets owned by the Gulf Shipbuilding Corp. were the only streets in Chickasaw, the proposed sale by Flagg Brothers under § 7–210 is not the only means of resolving this purely private dispute. Respondent Brooks has never alleged that

state law barred her from seeking a waiver of Flagg Brothers' right to sell her goods at the time she authorized their storage. Presumably, respondent Jones, who alleges that she never authorized the storage of her goods, could have sought to replevy her goods at any time under state law. See N.Y. Civ. Prac. Law § 7101 et seq. (McKinney 1963). The challenged statute itself provides a damages remedy against the warehouseman for violations of its provisions. N.Y.U.C.C. § 7–210(9) (McKinney 1964). This system of rights and remedies, recognizing the traditional place of private arrangements in ordering relationships in the commercial world, can hardly be said to have delegated to Flagg Brothers an exclusive prerogative of the sovereign.[10]

Whatever the particular remedies available under New York law, we do not consider a more detailed description of them necessary to our conclusion that the settlement of disputes between debtors and creditors is not traditionally an exclusive public function.[11] Creditors and debtors have had available to them historically a far wider number of choices than has one who would be an elected public official, or a member of Jehovah's Witnesses who wished to distribute literature in Chickasaw,

---

[10] [This case] is clearly distinguishable from cases such as *North Georgia Finishing, Inc. v. Di-Chem, Inc.*, 419 U.S. 601 (1975); *Fuentes v. Shevin*, 407 U.S. 67 (1972); and *Sniadach v. Family Finance Corp.*, 395 U.S. 337 (1969). In each of those cases a government official participated in the physical deprivation of what had concededly been the constitutional plaintiff's property under state law before the deprivation occurred. The constitutional protection attaches not because, as in North Georgia Finishing, a clerk issued a ministerial writ out of the court, but because as a result of that writ the property of the debtor was seized and impounded by the affirmative command of the law of Georgia.

[11] [Here] New York, unlike Florida in *Fuentes*, Georgia in *North Georgia Finishing*, and Wisconsin in *Sniadach*, has not ordered respondents to surrender any property whatever. It has merely enacted a statute which provides that a warehouseman conforming to the provisions of the statute may convert his traditional lien in good title. There is no reason whatever to believe that either Flagg Brothers or respondents could not, if they wished, seek resort to the New York courts in order to either compel or prevent the "surrenders of property" to which that dissent refers, and that the compliance of Flagg Brothers with applicable New York property law would be reviewed after customary notice and hearing in such a proceeding. The fact that such a judicial review of a self-help remedy is seldom encountered bears witness to the important part that such remedies have played in our system of property rights. The conduct of private actors in relying on the rights established under these liens to resort to self-help remedies does not permit their conduct to be ascribed to the State.

Ala., at the time Marsh was decided. Our analysis requires no parsing of the difference between various commercial liens and other remedies to support the conclusion that this entire field of activity is outside the scope of Terry and Marsh. This is true whether these commercial rights and remedies are created by statute or decisional law. To rely upon the historical antecedents of a particular practice would result in the constitutional condemnation in one State of a remedy found perfectly permissible in another.

Thus, even if we were inclined to extend the sovereign-function doctrine outside of its present carefully confined bounds, the field of private commercial transactions would be a particularly inappropriate area into which to expand it. We conclude that our sovereign-function cases do not support a finding of state action here.

Our holding today impairs in no way the precedential value of such cases as *Norwood v. Harrison*, 413 U.S. 455 (1973), or *Gilmore v. City of Montgomery*, 417 U.S. 556 (1974), which arose in the context of state and municipal programs which benefited private schools engaging in racially discriminatory admissions practices following judicial decrees desegregating public school systems. And we would be remiss if we did not note that there are a number of state and municipal functions not covered by our election cases or governed by the reasoning of Marsh which have been administered with a greater degree of exclusivity by States and municipalities than has the function of so-called "dispute resolution." Among these are such functions as education, fire and police protection, and tax collection. We express no view as to the extent, if any, to which a city or State might be free to delegate to private parties the performance of such functions and thereby avoid the strictures of the Fourteenth Amendment. The mere recitation of these possible permutations and combinations of factual situations suffices to caution us that their resolution should abide the necessity of deciding them.

IV

Respondents further urge that Flagg Brothers' proposed action is properly attributable to the State because the State has authorized and encouraged it in enacting § 7–210. Our cases state "that a State is responsible for the . . . act of a private party when the State, by its law, has compelled the act." Adickes, 398 U.S., at 170. This Court, however, has never held that a State's mere acquiescence in a private action converts that action into that of the State. The Court rejected a similar argument in *Jackson*, 419 U.S., at 357: "Approval by a state utility commission of such a request from a regulated utility, where the commission has

not put its own weight on the side of the proposed practice by ordering it, does not transmute a practice initiated by the utility and approved by the commission into 'state action.'" (Emphasis added.) The clearest demonstration of this distinction appears in *Moose Lodge No. 107 v. Irvis*, 407 U.S. 163 (1972), which held that the Commonwealth of Pennsylvania, although not responsible for racial discrimination voluntarily practiced by a private club, could not by law require the club to comply with its own discriminatory rules. These cases clearly rejected the notion that our prior cases permitted the imposition of Fourteenth Amendment restraints on private action by the simple device of characterizing the State's inaction as "authorization" or "encouragement." See *id.*, at 190 (Brennan, J., dissenting).

It is quite immaterial that the State has embodied its decision not to act in statutory form. If New York had no commercial statutes at all, its courts would still be faced with the decision whether to prohibit or to permit the sort of sale threatened here the first time an aggrieved bailor came before them for relief. A judicial decision to deny relief would be no less an "authorization" or "encouragement" of that sale than the legislature's decision embodied in this statute. It was recognized in the earliest interpretations of the Fourteenth Amendment "that a State may act through different agencies,—either by its legislative, its executive, or its judicial authorities; and the prohibitions of the amendment extend to all action of the State" infringing rights protected thereby. *Virginia v. Rives*, 100 U.S. 313, 318 (1880). If the mere denial of judicial relief is considered sufficient encouragement to make the State responsible for those private acts, all private deprivations of property would be converted into public acts whenever the State, for whatever reason, denies relief sought by the putative property owner.

Not only is this notion completely contrary to that "essential dichotomy," *Jackson, supra*, 419 U.S. at 349, between public and private acts, but it has been previously rejected by this Court. In *Evans v. Abney*, 396 U.S. 435, 458 (1970), our Brother BRENNAN in dissent contended that a Georgia statutory provision authorizing the establishment of trusts for racially restricted parks conferred a "special power" on testators taking advantage of the provision. The Court nevertheless concluded that the State of Georgia was in no way responsible for the purely private choice involved in that case. By the same token, the State of New York is in no way responsible for Flagg Brothers' decision, a decision which the State in § 7–210 permits but does not compel, to threaten to sell these respondents' belongings. Here, the State of New York has not compelled the sale of a bailor's goods, but has merely announced the circumstances under which its courts will not interfere with a private sale. Indeed, the crux of respondents' complaint is not that the State has acted, but that it has refused to act. This statutory refusal to act is no different in principle from an ordinary statute of limitations whereby the State declines to provide a remedy for private deprivations of property after the passage of a given period of time.

We conclude that the allegations of these complaints do not establish a violation of these respondents' Fourteenth Amendment rights by either petitioner Flagg Brothers or the State of New York. The District Court properly concluded that their complaints failed to state a claim for relief under 42 U.S.C. § 1983. The judgment of the Court of Appeals holding otherwise is

Reversed.

Mr. Justice MARSHALL, dissenting.

. . .

By ignoring . . . history, the Court approaches the question before us as if it can be decided without reference to the role that the State has always played in lien execution by forced sale. In so doing, the Court treats the State as if it were, to use the Court's words, "a monolithic, abstract concept hovering in the legal stratosphere." *Ante,* at 1735 n.10. The state-action doctrine, as developed in our past cases, requires that we come down to earth and decide the issue here with careful attention to the State's traditional role. I dissent.

Mr. Justice STEVENS, with whom Mr. Justice WHITE and Mr. Justice MARSHALL join, dissenting.

. . .

[W]hatever power of sale the warehouseman has, it does not derive from the consent of the respondents. The claimed power derives solely from the State, and specifically from § 7–210 of the New York Uniform Commercial Code. The question is whether a state statute which authorizes a private party to deprive a person of his property without his consent must meet the requirements of the Due Process Clause of the Fourteenth Amendment. This question must be answered in the affirmative unless the State has virtually unlimited power to transfer interests in private property without any procedural protections.

In determining that New York's statute cannot be scrutinized under the Due Process Clause, the Court reasons that the warehouseman's proposed sale is solely private action because the state statute "permits but does not compel" the sale, and because the warehouseman has not been delegated a power "exclusively reserved to the State." Under this approach a State could enact laws authorizing private citizens to use self-help in countless situations without any possibility of federal challenge. A state statute could authorize the warehouseman to retain all proceeds of the lien sale, even if they far exceeded the amount of the alleged debt; it could authorize finance companies to enter private homes to repossess merchandise; or indeed, it could authorize "any person with sufficient physical power," to acquire and sell the property of his weaker neighbor. An attempt to challenge the validity of any such outrageous statute would be defeated by the reasoning the Court uses today: The Court's rationale would characterize action pursuant to such a statute as purely private action, which the State permits but does not compel, in an area not exclusively reserved to the State.

As these examples suggest, the distinctions between "permission" and "compulsion" on the one hand, and "exclusive" and "nonexclusive," on the other, cannot be determinative factors in state-action analysis. There is no great chasm between "permission" and "compulsion" requiring particular state action to fall within one or the other definitional camp. Even *Moose Lodge No. 107 v. Irvis,* 407 U.S. 163, upon which the Court relies for its distinction between "permission" and "compulsion," recognizes that there are many intervening levels of state involvement in private conduct that may support a finding of state action. In this case, the State of New York, by enacting § 7–210 of the Uniform Commercial Code, has acted in the most effective and unambiguous way a State can act. This section specifically authorizes petitioner Flagg Brothers to sell respondents' possessions; it details the procedures that petitioner must follow; and it grants petitioner the power to convey good title to goods that are now owned by respondents to a third party.

While Members of this Court have suggested that statutory authorization alone may be sufficient to establish state action, it is not necessary to rely on those suggestions in this case because New York has authorized the warehouseman to perform what is clearly a state function. The test of what is a state function for purposes of the Due Process Clause has been variously phrased. Most frequently the issue is presented in terms of whether the State has delegated a function traditionally and historically associated with sovereignty. In this Court, petitioners have attempted to argue that the nonconsensual transfer of property rights is not a traditional function of the sovereign. The overwhelming historical evidence is to the contrary, however,[7] and the Court wisely

---

[7] The New York State courts have recognized that the execution of a lien is a traditional function of the State. . . .

does not adopt this position. Instead, the Court reasons that state action cannot be found because the State has not delegated to the warehouseman an exclusive sovereign function. This distinction, however, is not consistent with our prior decisions on state action; is not even adhered to by the Court in this case; and, most importantly, is inconsistent with the line of cases beginning with *Sniadach v. Family Finance Corp.*, 395 U.S. 337.

Since *Sniadach* this Court has scrutinized various state statutes regulating the debtor-creditor relationship for compliance with the Due Process Clause. *See also North Georgia Finishing, Inc. v. Di-Chem, Inc.*, 419 U.S. 601; *Mitchell v. W.T. Grant Co.*, 416 U.S. 600; *Fuentes v. Shevin*, 407 U.S. 67. In each of these cases a finding of state action was a prerequisite to the Court's decision. The Court today seeks to explain these findings on the ground that in each case there was some element of "overt official involvement." *Ante*, at 1734. Given the facts of those cases, this explanation is baffling. In *North Georgia Finishing*, for instance, the official involvement of the State of Georgia consisted of a court clerk who issued a writ of garnishment based solely on the affidavit of the creditor. 419 U.S., at 607. The clerk's actions were purely ministerial, and, until today, this court had never held that purely ministerial acts of "minor governmental functionaries" were sufficient to establish state action. The suggestion that this was the basis for due process review in *Sniadach*, *Shevin*, and *North Georgia Finishing* marks a major and, in my judgment, unwise expansion of the state-action doctrine. The number of private actions in which a governmental functionary plays some ministerial role is legion;[12] to base due process review on the fortuity of such governmental intervention would demean the majestic purposes of the Due Process Clause.

Instead, cases such as *North Georgia Finishing*, must be viewed as reflecting this Court's recognition of the significance of the State's role in defining and controlling the debtor-creditor relationship. The Court's language to this effect in the various debtor-creditor cases has been unequivocal. In *Fuentes v. Shevin* the Court stressed that the statutes in question "abdicate[d] effective state control over state power." 407 U.S., at 93. And it is clear that what was of concern in *Shevin* was the private use of state power to achieve a nonconsensual resolution of a commercial dispute.

The state statutes placed the state power to repossess property in the hands of an interested private party, just as the state statute in this case places the state power to conduct judicially binding sales in satisfaction of a lien in the hands of the warehouseman. "Private parties, serving their own private advantage, may unilaterally invoke state power to replevy goods from another. No state official participates in the decision to seek a writ; no state official reviews the basis for the claim to repossession; and no state official evaluates the need for immediate seizure. There is not even a requirement that the plaintiff provide any information to the court on these matters." Ibid.

This same point was made, equally emphatically, in *Mitchell v. W.T. Grant Co., supra*, 416 U.S., at 614–616, and *North Georgia Finishing, supra*, 419 U.S., at 607. Yet the very defect that made the statutes in *Shevin* and *North Georgia Finishing* unconstitutional—lack of state control—is, under today's decision, the factor that precludes constitutional review of the state statute. The Due Process Clause cannot command such incongruous results. If it is unconstitutional for a State to allow a private party to exercise a traditional state power because the state supervision of that power is purely mechanical, the State surely cannot immunize its actions from constitutional scrutiny by removing even the mechanical supervision.

Not only has the State removed its nominal supervision in this case, it has also authorized a private party to exercise a governmental power that is equally, if not more, significant than the power exercised in *Shevin* or *North Georgia Finishing*. In *Shevin*, the Florida statute allowed the debtor's property to be seized and held pending the outcome of the creditor's action for repossession. The property would not be finally disposed of until there was an adjudication of the underlying claim. Similarly, in *North Georgia Finishing*, the state statute provided for a garnishment procedure which deprived the debtor of the use of property in the garnishee's hands pending the outcome of litigation. The warehouseman's power under § 7–210 is far broader, as the Court of Appeals pointed out: "After giving the bailor specified notice, . . . the warehouseman is entitled to sell the stored goods in satisfaction of whatever he determines the storage charges to be. The warehouseman, unquestionably an interested party, is thus authorized by law to resolve any disputes over storage charges finally and unilaterally." 553 F.2d 764, 771.

Whether termed "traditional," "exclusive," or "significant," the state power to order binding, nonconsensual resolution of a conflict be-

---

[12] For instance, state officials often perform ministerial acts in the transferring of ownership in motor vehicles or real estate. It is difficult to believe that the Court would hold that all car sales are invested with state action. *See* Parks v. "Mr. Ford," *supra*, 556 F.2d, at 141.

tween debtor and creditor is exactly the sort of power with which the Due Process Clause is concerned. And the State's delegation of that power to a private party is, accordingly, subject to due process scrutiny. This, at the very least, is the teaching of *Sniadach, Shevin,* and *North Georgia Finishing.*

It is important to emphasize that, contrary to the Court's apparent fears, this conclusion does not even remotely suggest that "all private deprivations of property [will] be converted into public acts whenever the State, for whatever reason, denies relief sought by the putative property owner." *Ante,* at 1738. The focus is not on the private deprivation but on the state authorization. "[W]hat is always vital to remember is that it is the state's conduct, whether action or inaction, not the private conduct, that gives rise to constitutional attack." Friendly, The Dartmouth College Case and The Public-Private Penumbra, 12 Texas Quarterly, No. 2, p. 17 (1969) (Supp.) (emphasis in original). The State's conduct in this case takes the concrete form of a statutory enactment, and it is that statute that may be challenged.

. . .

Finally, it is obviously true that the overwhelming majority of disputes in our society are resolved in the private sphere. But it is no longer possible, if it ever was, to believe that a sharp line can be drawn between private and public actions. The Court today holds that our examination of state delegations of power should be limited to those rare instances where the State has ceded one of its "exclusive" powers. As indicated, I believe that this limitation is neither logical nor practical. More troubling, this description of what is state action does not even attempt to reflect the concerns of the Due Process Clause, for the state-action doctrine is, after all, merely one aspect of this broad constitutional protection.

In the broadest sense, we expect govern-ment "to provide a reasonable and fair framework of rules which facilitate commercial transactions . . . ." *Mitchell v. W.T. Grant Co.,* 416 U.S., at 624. (Powell, J., concurring). This "framework of rules" is premised on the assumption that the State will control nonconsensual deprivations of property and that the State's control will, in turn, be subject to the restrictions of the Due Process Clause.[17] The power to order legally binding surrenders of property and the constitutional restrictions on that power are necessary correlatives in our system. In effect, today's decision allows the State to divorce these two elements by the simple expedient of transferring the implementation of its policy to private parties. Because the Fourteenth Amendment does not countenance such a division of power and responsibility, I respectfully dissent.

---

[17] Mr. Justice Harlan explained this principle as follows: "American society, of course, bottoms its systematic definition of individual rights and duties, as well as its machinery for dispute settlement, not on custom or the will of strategically placed individuals, but on the common-law model. It is to courts, or other quasi-judicial official bodies, that we ultimately look for the implementation of a regularized, orderly process of dispute settlement. Within this framework, those who wrote our original Constitution, in the Fifth Amendment, and later those who drafted the Fourteenth Amendment, recognized the centrality of the concept of due process in the operation of this system. Without this guarantee that one may not be deprived of his rights, neither liberty nor property, without due process of law, the State's monopoly over techniques for binding conflict resolution could hardly be said to be acceptable under our scheme of things. Only by providing that the social enforcement mechanism must function strictly within these bounds can we hope to maintain an ordered society that is also just. It is upon this premise that this Court has through years of adjudication put flesh upon the due process principle." *Boddie v. Connecticut,* 401 U.S. 371, 375.

In *Lugar v. Edmondson Oil Co., Inc.,*[56] a creditor obtained prejudgment attachment of petitioner's property pursuant to state law. The statute required only that the creditor allege, in an ex parte petition, that petitioner was disposing of or might dispose of his property in order to defeat his creditors. The debtor sought to challenge the attachment on due process grounds. The Court of Appeals, applying *Flagg Brothers,* dismissed the case. The Supreme Court reversed:

> Beginning with *Sniadach v. Family Finance Corp.,* 395 U.S. 337 (1969), the Court has consistently held that constitutional requirements of due process apply to garnishment and prejudgment attachment procedures whenever officers of the State act jointly with a creditor in securing the property in dispute. *Sniadach* and *North Georgia Finishing, Inc. v. Di-Chem, Inc.,* 419 U.S. 601

---

[56] 457 U.S. 922 (1982).

(1975), involved state-created garnishment procedures; *Mitchell v. W.T. Grant Co.*, 416 U.S. 600 (1974), involved execution of a vendor's lien to secure disputed property. In each of these cases state agents aided the creditor in securing the disputed property; but in each case the federal issue arose in litigation between creditor and debtor in the state courts and no state official was named as a party. Nevertheless, in each case the Court entertained and adjudicated the defendant-debtor's claim that the procedure under which the private creditor secured the disputed property violated federal constitutional standards of due process. Necessary to that conclusion is the holding that private use of the challenged state procedures with the help of state officials constitutes state action for purposes of the Fourteenth Amendment.

. . .

While private misuse of a state statute does not describe conduct that can be attributed to the State, the procedural scheme created by the statute obviously is the product of state action. This is subject to constitutional restraints and properly may be addressed in a § 1983 action, if the second element of the state-action requirement is met as well.

[W]e have consistently held that a private party's joint participation with state officials in the seizure of disputed property is sufficient to characterize that party as a "state actor" for purposes of the Fourteenth Amendment. The rule in these cases is the same as that articulated in *Adickes v. S.H. Kress & Co., supra*, 398 U.S., at 152, in the context of an equal protection deprivation: "Private persons, jointly engaged with state officials in the prohibited action, are acting "under color" of law for purposes of the statute. To act "under color" of law does not require that the accused be an officer of the State. It is enough that he is a willful participant in joint activity with the State or its agents,'" quoting *United States v. Price*, 383 U.S., at 794. The Court of Appeals erred in holding that in this context "joint participation" required something more than invoking the aid of state officials to take advantage of state-created attachment procedures. That holding is contrary to the conclusions we have reached as to the applicability of due process standards to such procedures. Whatever may be true in other contexts, this is sufficient when the State has created a system whereby state officials will attach property on the ex parte application of one party to a private dispute.

Chief Justice Burger dissented:

[I]t cannot be said that the actions of the named respondents are fairly attributable to the State. Respondents did no more than invoke a presumptively valid state prejudgment attachment procedure available to all. Relying on a dubious "but for" analysis, the Court erroneously concludes that the subsequent procedural steps taken by the State in attaching a putative debtor's property in some way transforms respondents' acts into actions of the State. This case is no different from the situation in which a private party commences a lawsuit and secures injunctive relief which, even if temporary, may cause significant injury to the defendant. Invoking a judicial process, of course, implicates the State and its officers but does not transform essentially private conduct into actions of the State. *Dennis v. Sparks*, 449 U.S. 24 (1980). Similarly, one who practices a trade or profession, drives an automobile, or builds a house under a state license is not engaging in acts fairly attributable to the state. In both Dennis and the instant case petitioner's remedy lies in private suits for damages such as malicious prosecution. The Court's opinion expands the reach of the statute beyond anything intended by Congress. It may well be a consequence of too casually falling into a semantical trap because of the figurative use of the term "color of state law."

Justice Powell, joined by two other justices, also dissented:

[Here] it is not disputed that the Virginia Sheriff and Clerk of Court, the state officials who sequestered petitioner's property in the manner provided by Virginia law, engaged in state action. Yet the petitioner, while alleging constitutional injury from this action by state officials, did not sue the State or its agents. In these circumstances the Court of Appeals correctly stated that the relevant inquiry was the second identified in Flagg Bros.: whether the respondent, a private citizen whose only action was to invoke a presumptively valid state attachment process, had acted under color of state law in "causing" the State to deprive petitioner of alleged constitutional rights. Consistently with past decisions of this Court, the Court of Appeals concluded that respondent's private conduct had not occurred under color of law.

Rejecting the reasoning of the Court of Appeals, the Court opinion inexplicably conflates the two inquiries mandated by Flagg Bros. Ignoring that this case involves two sets of actions—one by respondent, who merely filed a suit and accompanying sequestration petition; another by the state officials, who issued the writ and executed the lien—it wrongly frames the question before the Court, not as whether the private respondent acted under color of law in filing the petition, but as "whether . . . respondents, who are private parties, may be appropriately characterized as 'state actors.'" It then concludes that they may, on the theory that a private party who invokes "the aid of state officials to take advantage of state-created attachment procedures" is a "joint participant" with the State and therefore a "state actor." "The rule," the Court asserts, "is as follows: "Private persons, jointly engaged with state officials in the prohibited action, are acting "under color" of law for purposes of the statute. To act "under color" of law does not require that the accused be an officer of the State. It is enough that he is a willful participant in a joint activity with the State or its agents." *Ante*, at 2756, quoting *Adickes v. S.H. Kress & Co., supra*, at 152, in turn quoting *United States v. Price*, 383 U.S. 787, 794 (1966).

Of the cases cited by the Court, *Sniadach, Mitchell*, and *Di-Chem* all involved attacks on the validity of state attachment or garnishment statutes. None of the cases alleged that the private creditor was a joint actor with the State, and none involved a claim for damages against the creditor. Each case involved a state suit, not a federal action under § 1983. It therefore was unnecessary in any of these cases for this Court to consider whether the creditor, by virtue of instituting the attachment or garnishment, became a state actor or acted under color of state law. There is not one word in any of these cases that so characterizes the private creditor. In *Fuentes v. Shevin*, the Court did consider a § 1983 action against a private creditor as well as the State Attorney General. Again, however, the only question before this Court was the validity of a state statute. No claim was made that the creditor was a joint actor with the State or had acted under color of law. No damages were sought from the creditor. Again, there was no occasion for this Court to consider the status under § 1983 of the private party, and there is not a word in the opinion that discusses this. As with *Sniadach, Mitchell,* and *Di-Chem, Fuentes* thus fails to establish that a private party's mere invocation of state attachment or garnishment procedures represents action under color of law—even in a case in which those procedures are subsequently held to be unconstitutional.

DeShaney v. Winnebago County[57] involved a boy who was beaten and permanently injured by his father. Petitioner sued respondents who were social workers and other local officials who received complaints that petitioner was being abused by his father and had reason to believe that this was the case, but nonetheless did not act to remove petitioner from his father's custody. Petitioner claimed that their failure to act deprived him of his liberty in violation of the Due Process Clause of the Fourteenth Amendment to the United States Constitution. The Supreme Court, in an opinion written by Mr. Justice Rehnquist, concluded that there was no state action:

> [N]othing in the language of the Due Process Clause itself requires the State to protect the life, liberty, and property of its citizens against invasion by private actors. The Clause is phrased as a limitation on the State's power to act, not as a guarantee of certain minimal levels of safety and security. It forbids the State itself to deprive individuals of life, liberty, or property without "due process of law," but its language cannot fairly be extended to impose an affirmative obligation on the State to ensure that those interests do not come to harm through other means. Nor does history support such an expansive reading of the constitutional text. Like its counterpart in the Fifth Amendment, the Due Process Clause of the Fourteenth Amendment was intended to prevent government "from abusing [its] power, or employing it as an instrument of oppression," *Davidson v. Cannon, supra*, 474 U.S., at 348. Its purpose was to protect the people from the State, not to ensure that the State protected them from each other. The Framers were content to leave the extent of governmental obligation in the latter area to the democratic political processes.
>
> . . .
>
> Petitioners contend, however, that even if the Due Process Clause imposes no affirmative obligation on the State to provide the general public with adequate protective services, such a duty may arise out of certain "special relationships" created or assumed by the State with respect to particular individuals. Petitioners argue that such a "special relationship" existed here because the State knew that Joshua faced a special danger of abuse at his father's hands, and specifically proclaimed, by word and by deed, its intention to protect him against that danger. Having actually undertaken to protect Joshua from this danger—which petitioners concede the State played no part in creating—the State acquired an affirmative "duty," enforceable through the Due Process Clause, to do so in a reasonably competent fashion. . . .
>
> We reject this argument. It is true that in certain limited circumstances the Constitution imposes upon the State affirmative duties of care and protection with respect to particular individuals. In *Estelle v. Gamble*, 429 U.S. 97 (1976), we recognized that the Eighth Amendment's prohibition against cruel and unusual punishment, made applicable to the States through the Fourteenth Amendment's Due Process Clause, requires the State to provide adequate medical care to incarcerated prisoners. We reasoned that because the prisoner is unable "'by reason of the deprivation of his liberty [to] care for himself,'" it is only' 'just' "that the State be required to care for him.
>
> In *Youngberg v. Romeo*, 457 U.S. 307 (1982), we extended this analysis beyond the Eighth Amendment setting, holding that the substantive component of the Fourteenth Amendment's Due Process Clause requires the State to provide involuntarily committed mental patients with such services as are

---

[57] 489 U.S. 189 (1989).

necessary to ensure their "reasonable safety" from themselves and others. *Id.*, at 314–325. . . .

. . .

The Estelle-Youngberg analysis simply has no applicability in the present case. Petitioners concede that the harms Joshua suffered occurred not while he was in the State's custody, but while he was in the custody of his natural father, who was in no sense a state actor. While the State may have been aware of the dangers that Joshua faced in the free world, it played no part in their creation, nor did it do anything to render him any more vulnerable to them. That the State once took temporary custody of Joshua does not alter the analysis, for when it returned him to his father's custody, it placed him in no worse position than that in which he would have been had it not acted at all; the State does not become the permanent guarantor of an individual's safety by having once offered him shelter. Under these circumstances, the State had no constitutional duty to protect Joshua.

. . .

Mr. Justice Blackmun dissented:

. . .

The Court fails to recognize this duty [to aid] because it attempts to draw a sharp and rigid line between action and inaction. But such formalistic reasoning has no place in the interpretation of the broad and stirring Clauses of the Fourteenth Amendment. . . .

. . .

Poor Joshua! Victim of repeated attacks by an irresponsible, bullying, cowardly, and intemperate father, and abandoned by respondents who placed him in a dangerous predicament and who knew or learned what was going on, and yet did essentially nothing except, as the Court revealingly observes, "dutifully recorded these incidents in [their] files." It is a sad commentary upon American life, and constitutional principles—so full of late of patriotic fervor and proud proclamations about "liberty and justice for all"—that this child, Joshua DeShaney, now is assigned to live out the remainder of his life profoundly retarded. Joshua and his mother, as petitioners here, deserve—but now are denied by this Court—the opportunity to have the facts of their case considered in the light of the constitutional protection that 42 U.S.C. § 1983 is meant to provide.

DER: The tragedy of Joshua DeShaney powerfully demonstrates the power of private actors to deprive citizens of their liberty and the emptiness, in many cases, of constitutional protections without the government's affirmative duty to act on behalf of disempowered citizens. Akhil R. Amar and Daniel Widawsky take advantage of the Thirteenth Amendment's affirmative mandate abolishing slavery to argue that *DeShaney* was wrongly decided.[58] They contend that child abuse becomes a form of slavery when parents fail to treat their children as free persons with interests of their own: "Like the antebellum slave, an abused child is subject to near domination and degradation by another person, and is treated more as a possession than as a person."[59] Thus, they argue, the Thirteenth Amendment's prohibition of slavery imposes a government duty to protect children from abuse.

---

[58] *See* Akhil R. Amar & Daniel Widawsky, *Child Abuse as Slavery: A Thirteenth Amendment Response to DeShaney*, 105 HARV. L. REV. 1359 (1992).

[59] *Id.* at 1364.

Lebron v. National Railroad Passenger Corporation
115 S.Ct. 961 (1995)

Justice SCALIA delivered the opinion of the Court.

In this case we consider whether actions of the National Railroad Passenger Corporation, commonly known as Amtrak, are subject to the constraints of the Constitution.

I

Petitioner, Michael A. Lebron, creates billboard displays that involve commentary on public issues, and that seemingly propel him into litigation. In August 1991, he contacted Transportation Displays, Incorporated (TDI), which manages the leasing of the billboards in Amtrak's Pennsylvania Station in New York City, seeking to display an advertisement on a billboard of colossal proportions, known to New Yorkers (or at least to the more Damon Runyonesque among them) as "the Spectacular." The Spectacular is a curved, illuminated billboard, approximately 103 feet long and 10 feet high, which dominates the main entrance to Penn Station's waiting room and ticket area.

On November 30, 1992, Lebron signed a contract with TDI to display an advertisement on the Spectacular for two months beginning in January 1993. The contract provided that "[a]ll advertising copy is subject to approval of TDI and [Amtrak] as to character, text, illustration, design and operation." Lebron declined to disclose the specific content of his advertisement throughout his negotiations with TDI, although he did explain to TDI that it was generally political. On December 2 he submitted to TDI (and TDI later forwarded to Amtrak) an advertisement described by the District Court as follows: "The work is a photomontage, accompanied by considerable text. Taking off on a widely circulated Coors beer advertisement which proclaims Coors to be the 'Right Beer,' Lebron's piece is captioned 'Is it the Right's Beer Now?' It includes photographic images of convivial drinkers of Coors beer, juxtaposed with a Nicaraguan village scene in which peasants are menaced by a can of Coors that hurtles towards them, leaving behind a trial of fire, as if it were a missile. The accompanying text, appearing on either end of the montage, criticizes the Coors family for its support of right-wing causes, particularly the contras in Nicaragua. Again taking off on Coors' advertising which uses the slogan of 'Silver Bullet' for its beer cans, the text proclaims that Coors is 'The Silver Bullet that aims The Far Right's political agenda at the heart of America.'" Amtrak's vice president disapproved the advertisement, invoking Amtrak's policy, inherited from its predecessor as landlord of Penn Station, the Pennsylvania Railroad Company, "that it will not allow political advertising on the [S]pectacular advertising sign."

Lebron then filed suit against Amtrak and TDI, claiming, inter alia, that the refusal to place his advertisement on the Spectacular had violated his First and Fifth Amendment rights. . . .

II

We have held once, *Burton v. Wilmington Parking Authority*, 365 U.S. 715 (1961), and said many times, that actions of private entities can sometimes be regarded as governmental action for constitutional purposes. *See, e.g., San Francisco Arts & Athletics, Inc. v. United States Olympic Committee*, 483 U.S. 522, 546 (1987). . . .

III

[Congress] established Amtrak in order to avert the threatened extinction of passenger trains in the United States. The statute that created it begins with the congressional finding, redolent of provisions of the Interstate Commerce Act, that "the public convenience and necessity require the continuance and improvement" of railroad passenger service. Rail Passenger Service Act of 1970 (RPSA), § 101, 84 Stat. 1328. . . .

Amtrak is incorporated under the District of Columbia Business Corporation Act, D.C.Code § 29–301 et seq. (1981 and Supp.1994), but is subject to the provisions of that Act only insofar as the RPSA does not provide to the contrary, see § 541. It does provide to the contrary with respect to many matters of structure and power, including the manner of selecting the company's board of directors. The RPSA provides for a board of nine members, six of whom are appointed directly by the President of the United States. The Secretary of Transportation, or his designee, sits ex officio. § 543(a)(1)(A). The President appoints three more directors with the advice and consent of the Senate, § 543(a)(1)(C), selecting one from a list of individuals recommended by the Railway Labor Executives Association, § 543(a)(1)(C)(I), one "from among the Governors of States with an interest in rail transportation," § 543(a)(1)(C)(ii), and one as a "representative of business with an interest in rail transportation," § 543(a)(1)(C)(iii). These directors serve 4-year terms. § 543(a)(2)(A). The President appoints two additional directors without the involvement of the Senate, choosing them from a list of names submitted by various commuter rail authorities. § 543(a)(1)(D). These directors serve 2-year terms. § 543(a)(2)(B). The holders of Amtrak's preferred stock select two more directors, who serve 1-year terms. § 543(a)(1)(E). Since the United States presently holds all of Amtrak's preferred stock, which it received (and still receives) in exchange for its subsidization of Amtrak's perennial losses, see § 544(c), the Secretary of Transportation selects these two directors. The ninth member of the board is Amtrak's president, § 543(a)(1)(B), who serves as the chairman of the board, § 543(a)(4), is selected by the other eight directors, and serves at their pleasure, § 543(d). Amtrak's four private shareholders have not been entitled to vote in selecting the board of directors since 1981.

By § 548 of the RPSA, Amtrak is required to submit three different annual reports to the President and Congress. One of these, a "report on the effectiveness of this chapter in meeting the requirements for a balanced national transportation system, together with any legislative recommendations," is made part of the Department of Transportation's annual report to Congress. § 548(c).

[Amtrak's] authorizing statute declares that it "will not be an agency or establishment of the United States Government." 84 Stat., at 1330. [Its] board of directors is controlled by Government appointees. And unlike all three of those "private" corporations, it has been added to the list of corporations covered by the GCCA. As one perceptive observer has concluded with regard to the post-Comsat Government-sponsored "private" enterprises: "There is no valid basis for distinguishing between many government-sponsored enterprises and other types of government activities, except for the fact that they are designed [designated?] by law as 'not an agency and instrumentality of the United States Government.' Comparable powers and immunities could be granted to such agencies without characterizing them as non-government." Seidman, *supra*, at 93.

IV

Amtrak claims that, whatever its relationship with the Federal Government, its charter's disclaimer of agency status prevents it from being considered a Government entity in the present case. This reliance on the statute is misplaced. Section 541 is assuredly dispositive of Amtrak's status as a Government entity for purposes of matters that are within Congress' control—for example, whether it is subject to statutes that impose obligations or confer powers upon Government entities, such as the Administrative Procedure Act, 5 U.S.C. § 551 et seq. (1988 ed. and Supp. V), the Federal Advisory Committee Act, 5 U.S.C.App. § 1 et seq., and the laws governing Government procurement, see 41 U.S.C. § 5 et seq. (1988 ed.

and Supp. V). And even beyond that, we think § 541 can suffice to deprive Amtrak of all those inherent powers and immunities of Government agencies that it is within the power of Congress to eliminate. We have no doubt, for example, that the statutory disavowal of Amtrak's agency status deprives Amtrak of sovereign immunity from suit, and of the ordinarily presumed power of Government agencies authorized to incur obligations to pledge the credit of the United States. But it is not for Congress to make the final determination of Amtrak's status as a government entity for purposes of determining the constitutional rights of citizens affected by its actions. If Amtrak is, by its very nature, what the Constitution regards as the Government, congressional pronouncement that it is not such can no more relieve it of its First Amendment restrictions than a similar pronouncement could exempt the Federal Bureau of Investigation from the Fourth Amendment. The Constitution constrains governmental action "by whatever instruments or in whatever modes that action may be taken." *Ex parte Virginia*, 100 U.S. 339, 346–347 (1880). And under whatever congressional label. As we said of the Reconstruction Finance Corporation in deciding whether debts owed it were owed the United States Government: "That the Congress chose to call it a corporation does not alter its characteristics so as to make it something other than what it actually is. . . ." *Cherry Cotton Mills, Inc. v. United States*, 327 U.S. 536, 539 (1946).

. . .

V

The question before us today is unanswered, therefore, by governing statutory text or by binding precedent of this Court. Facing the question of Amtrak's status for the first time, we conclude that it is an agency or instrumentality of the United States for the purpose of individual rights guaranteed against the Government by the Constitution.

This conclusion seems to us in accord with public and judicial understanding of the nature of Government-created and -controlled corporations over the years. A remarkable feature of the heyday of those corporations, in the 1930's and 1940's, was that, even while they were praised for their status "as agencies separate and distinct, administratively and financially and legally, from the government itself, [which] has facilitated their adoption of commercial methods of accounting and financing, avoidance of political controls, and utilization of regular procedures of business management," it was fully acknowledged that they were a "device" of "government," and constituted "federal corporate agencies" apart from "regular government departments." Pritchett,

40 Am.Pol.Sci.Rev., at 495. The Reference Manual of Government Corporations, prepared in 1945 by the Comptroller General, contains as one of its Tables "Corporations arranged according to supervising or interested Government department or agency," see GAO Corporation Manual x-xi. This lists the 58 then-extant Government corporations under the various departments and agencies, from the Agriculture Department to the War Department, and then concludes the list with five "Independent corporations"—analogous, one supposes, to the "independent agencies" of the Executive Branch proper. The whole tenor of the Manual is that these corporations are part of the Government.

This Court has shared that view. For example, in *Reconstruction Finance Corp. v. J.G. Menihan Corp.*, 312 U.S. 81 (1941), Chief Justice Hughes, writing for the Court, described the RFC, whose organic statute did not state it to be a Government instrumentality, as, nonetheless, "a corporate agency of the government," and said that "it acts as a governmental agency in performing its functions." *Id.*, at 83. In *Cherry Cotton Mills, Inc. v. United States*, 327 U.S. 536 (1946), we had little difficulty finding that the RFC was "an agency selected by Government to accomplish purely governmental purposes," *id.*, at 539, and was thus entitled to the benefit of a statute giving the Court of Claims jurisdiction over "counterclaims . . . on the part of the Government of the United States," 28 U.S.C. § 250(2) (1940 ed.). . . .

Even Congress itself appeared to acknowledge, at least until recent years, that Government-created and -controlled corporations were part of the Government. The Government Corporation Control Act of 1945, discussed above, which brought to an end the era of uncontrolled growth of Government corporations, provided that, without explicit congressional authorization, no corporation should be acquired or created by "any officer or agency of the Federal Government or by any Government corporation for the purpose of acting as an agency or instrumentality of the United States. . . ." § 304(a), 59 Stat., at 602. That was evidently intended to restrict the creation of all Government-controlled policy-implementing corporations, and not just some of them. And the companion provision that swept away many of the extant corporations said that no wholly owned government corporation created under state law could continue "as an agency or instrumentality of the United States," § 304(b), 59 Stat., at 602. . . . From the 1930's onward, many of the statutes creating Government-controlled corporations said explicitly that they were agencies or instrumentalities of the United States. . . .

That Government-created and -controlled corporations are (for many purposes at least) part of the Government itself has a strong basis, not merely in past practice and understanding, but in reason itself. It surely cannot be that government, state or federal, is able to evade the most solemn obligations imposed in the Constitution by simply resorting to the corporate form. On that thesis, *Plessy v. Ferguson*, 163 U.S. 537 (1896), can be resurrected by the simple device of having the State of Louisiana operate segregated trains through a state-owned Amtrak. In *Pennsylvania v. Board of Directors of City Trusts of Philadelphia*, 353 U.S. 230 (1957) (per curiam), we held that Girard College, which had been built and maintained pursuant to a privately erected trust, was nevertheless a governmental actor for constitutional purposes because it was operated and controlled by a board of state appointees, which was itself a state agency. *Id.*, at 231. Amtrak seems to us an a fortiori case.

Amtrak was created by a special statute, explicitly for the furtherance of federal governmental goals. As we have described, six of the corporation's eight externally named directors (the ninth is named by a majority of the board itself) are appointed directly by the President of the United States—four of them (including the Secretary of Transportation) with the advice and consent of the Senate. See §§ 543(a)(1)(A), (C)-(D). Although the statute restricts most of the President's choices to persons suggested by certain organizations or persons having certain qualifications, those restrictions have been tailor-made by Congress for this entity alone. They do not in our view establish an absence of control by the Government as a whole, but rather constitute a restriction imposed by one of the political branches upon the other. Moreover, Amtrak is not merely in the temporary control of the Government (as a private corporation whose stock comes into federal ownership might be); it is established and organized under federal law for the very purpose of pursuing federal governmental objectives, under the direction and control of federal governmental appointees. It is in that respect no different from the so-called independent regulatory agencies such as the Federal Communications Commission or the Securities Exchange Commission, which are run by Presidential appointees with fixed terms. It is true that the directors of Amtrak, unlike commissioners of independent regulatory agencies, are not, by the explicit terms of the statute, removable by the President for cause, and are not impeachable by Congress. But any reduction in the immediacy of accountability for Amtrak directors vis-a-vis regulatory commissioners seems to us of minor consequence for present purposes—especially since, by the very terms of the chartering Act, Congress's "right to repeal, alter, or amend this chapter at any time is expressly reserved." 45 U.S.C. § 541.

[We] hold that where, as here, the Government creates a corporation by special law, for the furtherance of governmental objectives, and retains for itself permanent authority to appoint a majority of the directors of that corporation, the corporation is part of the Government for purposes of the First Amendment. We express no opinion as to whether Amtrak's refusal to display Lebron's advertisement violated that Amendment, but leave it to the Court of Appeals to decide that. The judgment of the Court of Appeals is reversed, and the case is remanded for further proceedings consistent with this opinion.

It is so ordered.

Justice O'CONNOR, dissenting.

* * *

[I] remain of the view that the conduct of a private actor is not subject to constitutional challenge if such conduct is "fundamentally a matter of private choice and not state action." *Edmonson v. Leesville Concrete Co.*, 500 U.S. 614, 632 (1991) (O'CONNOR, J., dissenting).

[U]nless the Government affirmatively influenced or coerced the private party to undertake the challenged action, such conduct is not state action for constitutional purposes. . . .

[A] more refined inquiry is that established by *Jackson, Rendell-Baker, Blum*, and *San Francisco Arts & Athletics*: The conduct of a private entity is not subject to constitutional scrutiny if the challenged action results from the exercise of private choice and not from state influence or coercion.

Applying this principle to the facts before us, I see no basis to impute to the Government Amtrak's decision to disapprove Lebron's advertisement. Although a number of factors indicate the Government's pervasive influence in Amtrak's management and operation, none suggest that the Government had any effect on Amtrak's decision to turn down Lebron's proposal. The advertising policy that allegedly violates the First Amendment originated with a predecessor to Amtrak, the wholly private Pennsylvania Railroad Company. A 1967 lease

by that company, for example, prohibited "any advertisement which in the judgement of Licensor is or might be deemed to be slanderous, libelous, unlawful, immoral, [or] offensive to good taste. . . . " App. 326, P 19. Amtrak simply continued this policy after it took over. The specific decision to disapprove Lebron's advertising was made by Amtrak's Vice President of Real Estate and Operations Development, who, as a corporate officer, was neither appointed by the President nor directed by the President-appointed board to disapprove Lebron's proposal.

Lebron nevertheless contends that the board, through its approval of the advertising policy, controlled the adverse action against him. This contention rests on the faulty premise that Amtrak's directors are state actors simply because they were appointed by the President; it assumes that the board members sit as public officials and not as business directors, thus begging the question whether Amtrak is a Government agency or a private entity. In any event, even accepting Lebron's premise that the board's approval has constitutional significance, the factual record belies his contention. The particular lease which permitted Amtrak to disallow Lebron's billboard was neither reviewed nor approved directly by the board. In fact, minutes of meetings dating back to 1985 showed that the board approved only one contract between Amtrak and Transportation Displays, Incorporated, the billboard leasing company that served as Amtrak's agent, and even then it is not clear whether the board approved the contract or merely delegated authority to execute the licensing agreement. In short, nothing in this case suggests that the Government controlled, coerced, or even influenced Amtrak's decision, made pursuant to corporate policy and private business judgment, to disapprove the advertisement proposed by Lebron.

Presented with this question, the Court of Appeals properly applied our precedents and did not impute Amtrak's decision to the Government. I would affirm on this basis and not reverse the Court of Appeals based on a theory that is foreign to this case. Respectfully, I dissent.

INDEX